THE READER'S DIGEST OF BOOKS

THE MACMILLAN COMPANY
NEW YORK · BOSTON · CHICAGO · DALLAS
ATLANTA · SAN FRANCISCO

MACMILLAN AND CO., Limited
LONDON · BOMBAY · CALCUTTA · MADRAS
MELBOURNE

THE MACMILLAN COMPANY
OF CANADA, Limited
TORONTO

THE
READER'S DIGEST
OF BOOKS

BY

HELEN REX KELLER

NEW AND GREATLY
ENLARGED EDITION

New York
THE MACMILLAN COMPANY
1944

THE READER'S DIGEST OF BOOKS

PUBLISHER'S NOTE

This book was first published in 1896-97 as a volume of the " Library of the World's Best Literature," edited by Charles Dudley Warner, recast in 1917 under the editorship of John W. Cunliffe and Ashley H. Thorndike in the " University Edition." References are given in the text of this book to articles in this " Library."

THE READER'S DIGEST OF BOOKS

ABBÉ CONSTANTIN, THE, by Ludovic Halévy. The great estate of Longueval, consisting of the castle and its dependencies, two splendid farms and a forest, is advertised for sale by auction. The Abbé Constantin, a generous, genial, self-sacrificing priest, who has been thirty years the curé of the little villge, is disconsolate at the thought that all his associations must be broken up. His distress is increased when he learns that the whole property has been bought by an American millionaire. He is about to sit down to his frugal dinner in company with his godson Lieutenant Jean Renaud, the orphaned son of the good village doctor, when his vicarage is invaded by two ladies who have just arrived by train from Paris. On their arrival the plot hinges; simple as it is, it has a great charm, and the style is delightful. It sparkles with light and graceful epigrams: "The Frenchman has only one real luxury — his revolutions." "In order to make money the first thing is to have no need of it." "It is only the kings of France who no longer live in France." "The heart is very little, but it is also very large." "Love and tranquillity seldom dwell at peace in the same heart." First published in 1882, it has had more than one hundred and fifty editions and still enjoys uninterrupted popularity both in France and in English-speaking countries.

ABBÉ MOURET'S TRANSGRESSION, THE, see **ROUGON-MACQUART.**

ABBOT, THE, by Sir Walter Scott (1820). A sequel to 'The Monastery,' but dealing with more stirring and elevated situations and scenes. The time of the action is 1567-68, when Shakespeare was a boy of three, and Elizabeth was newly established on the throne of England. While the action goes on partly at Avenel Castle, and Halbert Glendinning of 'The Monastery,' as well as his brother Edward (now an abbot), figure prominently in the story, the reader finds that he has exchanged the humble events of the little border vale by Melrose for thrilling and romantic adventures at Lochleven Castle on its island in the lake, north of Edinburgh, where Mary Queen of Scots is imprisoned; and in place of the braw and bonny Scotch of Tibb and Dame Elspeth, we have the hearty English of Adam Woodcock the falconer, — as masterly a portrait in Scott's gallery as Gurth, Hal o' the Wynd, or Dandie Dinmont. The chief interest centres around the unfortunate queen; and the framework of the tale is historically true. The masterpiece of description in 'The Abbot' is the signing of the abdication by Mary at the stern insistence of the commissioners Lindsay and Ruthven, — a scene made famous by more than one great painting and by more than one historian.

ABSALOM AND ACHITOPHEL, a satirical poem in heroic couplets by John Dryden, published in November, 1681; a second part by Dryden and Nahum Tate (1652-1715) was published a year later. The poem was undertaken by Dryden at the request of Charles II. in support of the royal party against the machinations of the

Whigs. Under the leadership of Anthony Ashley Cooper, Earl of Shaftesbury (1621–1683), they were attempting to exclude the king's brother James, Duke of York, from the throne on the ground of his Roman Catholicism and to transfer the succession to the king's illegitimate son, James, Duke of Monmouth. Their cause was advanced by a skillful use of the discovery of an alleged 'Popish Plot' to murder the king, enthrone his brother, and suppress Protestantism (1678). For a time they were in control of the government and nearly succeeded in excluding James and making Monmouth the king's heir. But a reaction set in, Charles dismissed Shaftesbury, recalled James, and rallied the Tories about him, driving Monmouth and Shaftesbury into an attitude of rebellion. At this point Dryden wrote his 'Absalom and Achitophel,' skillfully adapting the Biblical narrative of Absalom's rebellion against King David to the political situation. Under the guise of the crafty Achitophel, Shaftesbury plies Monmouth, who appears as the handsome and popular Absalom, with arguments for claiming the throne. He yields to the temptation and begins a progress through the kingdom, corresponding to an actual progress made by Monmouth in defiance of the king's orders in 1680. An enumeration of the chief supporters of Monmouth and of the king under the thin disguise of appropriate Hebrew names emphasizes the gravity of the contest, gives new opportunity of stating the principles involved, and illustrates Dryden's skill in portraiture and in verse-argument. Especially vigorous are the descriptions of Achitophel (the Earl of Shaftesbury), Zimri (the Duke of Buckingham), and Corah (Titus Oates). The poem ends with a dignified and manly speech by David (Charles II.) asserting his prerogative but promising forgiveness if Absalom will repent. Dryden's known contributions of the second part are confined to lines 310–509, in which he satirizes two poets of the opposite party, Doeg (Elkanah Settle, 1648–1724) and Og (Thomas Shadwell, 1642–1692, already pilloried in Dryden's 'Mac Flecknoc,' October 4, 1682). As a writer of brilliant satire or panegyric and as a vigorous controversialist Dryden is unsurpassed, and this poem is a fine instance of his power.

ACROSS THE CONTINENT: 'A Summer's Journey to the Rocky Mountains, the Mormons, and the Pacific States' (May–September, 1865), by Samuel Bowles (1865). A volume of newspaper letters and supplementary papers, by an exceptionally able journalist, designed to give to Eastern American readers an account of the nature, the material resources, and the social and industrial development of the vast region between the Mississippi River and the Pacific Ocean; and with this to make revelations and raise discussion on such themes as the Pacific Railroad, the Mormons, and the mines. Bowles spent another summer vacation, 1869, in travel and exploration among the mountains of Colorado, and made a second book of newspaper letters on Colorado as 'The Switzerland of America.' He then incorporated the two sketches of far west journeyings in what was designed to be a new and permanent work. The papers were carefully revised, amplified, and illustrated, and a work made with the title 'Our New West,' 1869, in which the author attempted to convey some true idea of the condition and promise of the western half of the continent. Thoroughly well executed, Bowles's narrative of natural resources and of industrial developments remains full of interest. His vigorous style, keen insight, unfailing sense of humor, and judicial mind made him an almost unrivaled observer and reporter.

ACTS OF THE APOSTLES ('Actes des Apôtres') (9 vols. 1789–91), a series of satirical pamphlets directed against the French Revolutionists, by Peltier, who was assisted by several royalist writers. It is full of witty attacks on the leaders of the Revolution, and especially on the framers of the constitution of '89, who are represented as rope-dancers performing their feats on a very thin wire. It attacks all new ideas, ridicules reforms of every kind, and boldly defends the principles of the aristocracy.

ADAM is a dramatic work of the twelfth century by an unknown author. It is written in French, with the exception of the responses and canticles, which are in Latin; and it derives its chief importance from the fact that it is the oldest drama in the language. It gives the history of the fall of Adam and the murder of Abel, followed by a procession of all the prophets who foretold the coming of the Messiah. The piece was played on the public square in front of the church. The platform upon which it was represented must have been backed against the portal; for in the stage directions, the actor who takes the part of God is told to return at once to the church, whenever he leaves the stage. Some of the scenes are managed with considerable skill; and there is a good deal of clever character-drawing and vigorous dialogue. The scene where the serpent tempts Eve is especially noteworthy for its simplicity and animation.

ADAM BEDE, the earliest of George Eliot's novels, was published in 1859, as "by the author of 'Scenes of Clerical Life.'" The story was at once pronounced by the critics to be not more remarkable for its grace, its unaffected Saxon style, and its charm of naturalness, than for its perception of those universal springs of action that control society, and for that patient development of character and destiny that inferior novelists slight or ignore. The chief scene is the Poyser farm in the Midlands, a delightful place of shining kitchens, sweet-smelling dairy-houses, cool green porches, wide barns, and spreading woods. Here Mrs. Poyser, a kind-hearted woman with an incorrigibly sharp tongue, has taken her husband's niece, Hester Sorrel,— an ambitious, vain, empty-headed little beauty, — to bring up. Adam Bede, the village carpenter, an admirable young fellow, is her slave.

A skeleton of the plot would convey no impression of the strength and charm of the story. It seems to have been, in the author's mind, a recognition of the heroism of commonplace natures in commonplace surroundings, of the nobility of noble character wherever found. But Adam Bede, intelligent, excellent, satisfactory though he is, is quite subordinated in interest to the figure of poor Hetty, made tragic through suffering and injustice. Her beauty, her vanity, her very silliness, endear her. Dinah Morris, the woman preacher, is a study from life, serene and lovely. Mr. Irwine, the easy-going old parson, is a typical English clergyman of the early nineteenth century; Bartle Massey, the schoolmaster, is one of those humble folk, full of character, foibles, absurdities, and homely wisdom, whom George Eliot draws with loving touches; while Mrs. Poyser, with her epigrammatic shrewdness, her untiring energy, her fine pride of respectability, her acerbity of speech, and her charity of heart, belongs to the company of the Immortals.

ADAM BLAIR, by John Gibson Lockhart, Scott's son-in-law, who wrote the famous Life of Sir Walter, is a Scotch story of rural life in the last century. It gives intimate descriptions of native manners, and has tragic power in the portrayal of the human heart. This novel, the best of the three written by Lockhart, was published in 1822, the full title being 'Some Passages in the Life of Mr. Adam Blair, Minister of the Gospel at Cross-Meikle.'

ADMIRABLE CRICHTON, THE, by Sir J. M. Barrie (1902). The Earl of Loam, a widower and a believer in the equality of man, gives practical shape to his ideas by insisting that his daughters should receive the servants at monthly teas, an arrangement heartily disliked by both the young ladies and the servants. In a monthly address to the servants Lord Loam expresses a wish that the artificial barriers of society could be swept away and announces that in less than forty-eight hours he and his daughters will start on a voyage to distant parts of the world, and in order to show active opposition to the prevailing luxury of the day, he has decided to allow the three daughters only one maid among them. Crichton, the butler, whose ideal is a haughty, aristocratic English house, with everyone kept in his place, and who says that servants like disdain from their superiors, at first refuses to go, but is afterwards persuaded to go in the capacity of valet to Lord Loam. After a voyage of two months the yacht is wrecked on a desert island, where there is an opportunity of putting theories of equality to the test. In a short space of time Crichton, who thinks there must always be "one to command and others to obey," becomes virtually the master. Lady Mary, the least docile of the Earl's three daughters, becomes his fiancée. A ship comes to the island, and all leave Crichton except Lady Mary, who says she will never give him up. On the return to England to their former set, Crichton informs Lady Brocklehurst, whose son is engaged to Lady Mary, that on the island there was as little equality as elsewhere, that all the social distinctions were preserved, and the servants had to keep their place.

ADOLESCENCE, 'its psychology, and its relations to physiology, anthropology, sociology, sex, crime, religion, and education,' a monumental psychological and sociological treatise by G. Stanley Hall, was published in 1904. The first three chapters are devoted to the general physical changes of adolescence, chapters four and five to its diseases and crimes, chapters six and seven to sexual changes and perils, and the eighth to the records of adolescence in literature and autobiography. The remaining chapters, which constitute the second volume, are occupied with the genetic psychology of adolescence, "beginning with sensation and proceeding to feelings, will, and intellect." The new susceptibility of the senses, the development of love, and of the sentiment of nature, the psychology of conversion, the rise of social instincts, and the characteristics of adolescent intellect form the principal topics discussed in this volume. Abundant illustrative detail, thorough grasp of physiological, psychological, and sociological principles, sympathetic entrance into the troubles and enthusiasms of youth, and wise suggestions for its direction and education are some of the merits of this valuable book.

ADOLPHE, a romance by Benjamin Constant (1816). The story has very little incident or action. The whole plot may be summed up in a few words: Adolphe loves Eléonore, and can be happy neither with her nor without her. The beauty of the author's style and the keenness and delicacy with which he analyzes certain morbid moods of the soul have placed this work among the masterpieces of French literature. The romance is almost universally believed to be an autobiography, in which Constant narrates a portion of the adventures of his own youth.

ADRIENNE LECOUVREUR, a play by Scribe and Légouvé, which first appeared in 1849, possesses witty dialogue and strong dramatic situations. The scene is laid in Paris, in March, 1730. Maurice, Count de Saxe, a former admirer of the Princess de Bouillon, now loves and is loved by Adrienne Lecouvreur, a beautiful actress of the Comédie Française; who, not knowing his real name and rank, believes him a poor soldier of fortune. Though the action resulting from this mistake occupies the space of two days only, it is very complicated; yet the unity of the play is vividly clear, and the strongly contrasted characters stand out with great distinctness, while the dialogue is epigrammatic and full of power.

ADVANCEMENT OF LEARNING, THE, by Francis Bacon (1605), the original title being 'Of the Proficience and Advancement of Learning, Divine and Human.' This book, received with great favor by the court and by scholars, was afterwards enlarged and published in Latin with the title 'De Augmentis Scientiarum,' as the first part of a monumental labor, 'The Instauration of the Sciences,' of which the second part was the still famous 'Novum Organum,' on which Bacon's fame as a philosopher rests. The 'Advancement of Learning' considers first the excellence of knowledge and the best way of spreading it, what has been already done to scatter it, and what left undone. The author then proceeds to divide all knowledge into three kingdoms or inclosures, — history, poetry, and philosophy; which appeal directly to the three manifestations of human understanding, memory, imagination, and reason. The smaller third of the book relates to revealed religion.

ADVENTURES IN CRITICISM, by Sir A. T. Quiller-Couch (1896), is a collection of brief critical essays, including a handful of graceful commentaries on some of the Elizabethans, two or three eighteenth-century studies, an examination of Zola, some excellent appreciations of Ibsen, Björnson, and the Scandinavian cult, and twenty or more estimates of modern English writers from Scott to Caine. The critic has a large view of literature, entire sincerity, a charming style, simple and direct as Thackeray's, fine scholarship, and absolute independence of judgment. His book, therefore, surrounds old subjects with a new atmosphere, and gives the reader the agreeable sense of being made a co-discoverer of profitable places in well-known territory; so that his essays have become almost as much liked as his stirring romances.

ADVENTURES OF A GUINEA, see **CHRYSAL.**

ADVENTURES OF CALEB WILLIAMS, see **CALEB WILLIAMS.**

ADVENTURES OF FRANÇOIS, see **FRANÇOIS.**

ADVENTURES OF GIL BLAS, see **GIL BLAS.**

ADVENTURES OF HAJJI BABA, see **HAJJI BABA.**

ADVENTURES OF HUCKLEBERRY FINN, see **HUCKLEBERRY FINN.**

ADVENTURES OF MR. OBADIAH OLDBUCK, see **OBADIAH OLDBUCK.**

ADVENTURES OF MR. VERDANT GREEN, see **VERDANT GREEN.**

ADVENTURES OF SHERLOCK HOLMES, see **SHERLOCK HOLMES.**

ÆNEID, THE, the golden branch on the ilex-tree of Latin literature, was the work of Publius Virgilius Maro, who was born October 15th, 70 B.C., and died September 22d, 19 B.C.

The poem is interwoven with pre-Christian civilization, with mediæval and modern thought, as is no other poem of the ancient world. It is the Bible of the later classical literature, as the Iliad is of the earlier, linked by its very nature to the visionary Middle Ages. For in the Æneid, conflict has become spiritualized; and the warrior Æneas bears always about him the remoteness of the priest, or of one mindful ever of the place of souls. It is the detachment of the hero from the passion of love, from the passion of war, which made him appeal so powerfully to the mediæval mind, preoccupied with the Unseen. Only the creator of Æneas could be Dante's guide among the shades. Of him Tennyson writes:

" Light among the vanished ages; star that gildest yet this phantom shore;
  Golden branch among the shadows, kings and realms that set to rise no more."

The Æneid is in twelve books: the first six in imitation of the Odyssey; the last six, of the Iliad. The Trojan hero is led to Italy, where he is to be the father of a race and of an empire supreme among nations. On his way thither he tarries at Carthage, whose queen, Dido, loves him as with the first love of a virgin. To her he tells the story of Troy. For love of him she slays herself when the gods lead him from her shores. Arrived in Italy he seeks the underworld, under the protection of the Sibyl of Cumæ. He emerges thence to overcome his enemies. The Æneid was not perfected at the time of Virgil's death, and his friends Varius and Tucca edited it at the request of the emperor Augustus. It has since become the heritage of the world.

ÆNEID, THE, TRANSLATIONS AND ADAPTATIONS OF. Gawain Douglas translated the Æneid into the Scottish dialect in 1513. This vigorous adaptation probably suggested to the Earl of Surrey the idea of turning the second and fourth books into blank verse, the earliest example of blank verse in the language. Douglas takes some strange liberties with his author. He changes the sibyl into a nun, and makes her admonish Æneas to be sure to say his prayers and tell his beads. The English translations are numerous; Dryden's, Conington's, Sir Charles Bowen's, William Morris's, J. W. Mackail's are among the best, while in America the versions of C. P. Cranch and of Geo. H. Palmer are examples of good scholarship and good taste. The epic has been often travestied. The first travesty, entitled 'Eneide de Virgilio Travestida,' appeared at Rome in 1633. It was very popular among the frivolous; but scholars, to whom everything written by the Mantuan was sacred, were scandalized. The 'Eneide Travestie' of Scarron is a French classic.

ÆSTHETIC AS SCIENCE OF EXPRESSION AND GENERAL LINGUISTIC, 'Estetica come scienza d' espressione e linguistica generale,' a philosophic treatise by Benedetto Croce, was published in 1902, and in an English translation by Douglas Ainslie in 1910. A revised edition appeared in 1912. The work consists of two parts, the first theoretic, the second historical. The general theory is that beauty is the successful expression of an intuition, an expression quite independent of intellectual and moral standards, complete and self-sufficient. The only difference between the artist and the man of taste is that one produces the beautiful and the other recognizes it; the function in each case is an intuition differing only in circumstances from the other. In the second part the author traces the history of the science from the Greek thinkers to the present day, refuting the hedonistic, the moralistic, and the mystical theory of æsthetics. A fuller exposition and estimate of the book will be found in the introductory essay on Croce in the LIBRARY.

ÆTHIOPICA, by Heliodorus, bishop of Tricca in Thessaly. This romance was written in his youth towards the close of the fourth century, or according to some, in the second century; and was the occasion of reproach to him in his manhood, though without reason. It is divided into ten books, and relates the adventures of the Ethiopian princess Chariclea; who, having as an infant been exposed to death by her mother, is discovered by some humane people and carried to Delphi, where she meets the beautiful Theagenes, and after innumerable adventures, marries him. The pair live happily for a while, and then encounter dangers of the most varied character. They are about to be killed, when Chariclea is recognized and restored to her proper station. This interminable romance enjoyed a great reputation from the Renaissance down to the close of the eighteenth century.

AFFECTED LADIES, THE, see **PRÉCIEUSES RIDICULES.**

AFTER THE PARDON ('Dopo il Perdone'), by Mathilde Serao (1906). In this romance, Donna Maria, who has left her husband for her lover, returns home after three years' absence. Her husband, realizing that the fault was his in part, desires her return, and offers her his pardon. The great passion of her life, "beyond all laws and duties," is over, and she wishes only to atone to her husband for his suffering by devoting herself to his happiness. She advises her lover, Count Marco, to marry the betrothed he had deserted for her sake. The second part of the book is the story of their failure to escape from the past. Count Marco fails to make his young bride happy, because she is jealous of his past, and refuses to be content with the fond affection he offers her. Donna Maria's husband, also, is unwilling to accept less than his wife has given to another. His love is jealousy and suspicion, and the pardon becomes a tragic farce of daily accusation and condemnation. He wishes Donna Maria had never returned. Traveling alone in Switzerland, Donna Maria meets Count Marco, whose wife's coldness has driven him from her. They have learned that they can never bring happiness to the two they have wronged, who desire the impossible. United by the memory of their dead love, they are still dear to each other, and decide it is their destiny to spend the rest of their lives together since their only happiness is the remembrance of the happiness they have lost.

AFTERMATH, see **KENTUCKY CARDINAL.**

AGAMEMNON, a tragedy by Æschylus, setting forth the theme of retribution with a dramatic power, a depth of religious insight, and a splendor of diction unequaled in Greek literature. The play is the first of a trilogy, which includes 'The Choëphoræ' and ' The Suppliants ' and which is concerned with the purging of the ancestral guilt of the house of Atreus. Because of the crime of that king in feeding his brother, Thyestes, with the flesh of his own children, destiny has involved Agamemnon, the son of Atreus, in another crime. He has sacrificed his daughter, Iphigenia, in order to obtain favorable winds for the Greek expedition to Troy. As a vengeance upon her husband for this cruelty, his wife, Clytæmnestra, becomes the paramour of Ægistheus, the son of Thyestes, and plans to murder Agamemnon upon his return.

The situations in this play are exceptionally striking. The lonely figure of the watchman on the palace roof in the opening scene, waiting for the beacon light that shall announce the fall of Troy, and muttering that all is not well at home, creates expectancy and suggests trouble. Clytæmnestra's jubilant description of the fires that carried the news from height to height until it reached the palace at Argos is one of the most stirring speeches in literature, and is significant of her forceful, dominating character. She is magnificent in the calm assumption of wifely fidelity with which she welcomes home Agamemnon and the conquering blandishments by which she induces him to commit the irreverence of walking into the palace on purple embroideries sacred to the gods in order that he may be in their eyes a fitter subject for her vengeance. Greatest of all, however, is the scene in which Cassandra, Agamemnon's captive, left in the courtyard with the chorus, recognizes by her prophetic gift the divine vengeance that broods upon the palace, and in shuddering outbursts of horror foretells Agamemnon's murder and her own sacrifice to the jealousy of Cly-tæmnestra. Then immediately follows the deep groan of Agamemnon, smitten by Clytæmnestra in his bath behind the scene.

The chorus in this play, consisting of old counselors of Argos, is of unusual importance. Not only are the choric odes weighted with thoughts, rich in poetic expression, and intensely significant in their references to divine retribution, but in the more purely dramatic scenes, especially at the close, the chorus, through its leader, takes a resolute part in the action, denouncing the crime of Clytæmnestra, and the compliance of Ægistheus, who now accepts the kingship, and prophesying that vengeance will be taken by Agamemnon's absent son, Orestes, whose name points the way to the other plays of the trilogy.

AGE OF CHIVALRY, THE, or, THE LEGENDS OF KING ARTHUR, by Thomas Bulfinch, was published in 1858. More than twenty years after, an enlarged edition appeared under the editorship of Edward Everett Hale. In Part First, the legends of King Arthur and his knights are considered. Part Second deals with the Mabinogion, or ancient prose tales of the Welsh; Part Third with the knights of English history, King Richard, Robin Hood, and the Black Prince. From the time of its first publication the popularity of the book has been great. No more sympathetic and fitting introduction could be found to the legends of chivalry. The book is written in a youthful spirit that commends it to the young.

AGE OF FABLE, THE, or, THE BEAUTIES OF MYTHOLOGY, by Thomas Bulfinch, was published in 1855, and republished in 1882 under the editorship of Edward Everett Hale. It has become a standard work upon mythology, by reason of its full and extensive yet delicate treatment of the Greek and Roman myths. While especially adapted for young people, it possesses qualities which commend it alike to the scholar and to the general reader.

AGE OF REASON, THE, by Thomas Paine, was first published in a complete edition on October 25th, 1795. In 1793 the First Part appeared, but no copy bearing that date can be found. When it went to press the author was in prison, in France, having been arrested almost at the hour of its completion. Referring to this in the preface to the Second Part, he writes: "Conceiving . . . that I had but a few days of liberty, I sat down and brought the work to a close as speedily as possible; and I had not finished it more than six hours, in the state it has since appeared, before a guard came there about three in the morning, with an order signed by the two committees of Public Safety and Surety General for putting me in arrestation as a foreigner, and conveying me to the prison of the Luxembourg. I contrived on my way there to call on Joel Barlow, and I put the manuscript of the work into his hands, as more safe than in my possession in prison; and not knowing what might be the fate in France either of the writer or the work, I addressed it to the protection of the citizens of the United States." His motive in writing the book is thus set forth in the first chapter: "It has been my intention, for several years past, to publish my thoughts upon religion; . . . the circumstance that has now taken place in France of the total abolition of the whole national order of priesthood, and of everything appertaining to compulsive systems of religion, and compulsive articles of faith, has not only precipitated my intention, but rendered a work of this kind exceedingly necessary, lest, in the general wreck of superstition, of false systems of government and false theology, we lose sight of morality, of humanity, and of the theology that is true." He goes on to state his creed, his belief in one God, in the future life, in the equality of man, and in the duty of benevolence. Part First consists of an inquiry into the bases of Christianity, its theology, its miracles, its claims of revelation. The process is destructive and revolutionary. In Part Second, the author makes critical examination of the Old and New Testament, to support the conclusions and inferences of Part First. Yet the work is not wholly negative. "The Word of God is the creation we behold." Lanthenas's French rendering of Part First contains this remarkable reference to Jesus, found presumably in the lost original version: "Trop peu imité, trop oublié, trop méconnu."

AGNES GREY, Anne Brontë's first novel, was published in December, 1847, a year and a half before her death, when she was twenty-seven years old. Her talents were of the moonlight order. The book is but a pale reflection of the brilliant Brontë genius.

The heroine, Agnes Grey, the daughter of a clergyman in the North of England, becomes, through reverses of fortune, a governess. Her experiences are those of Anne Brontë herself, the unpleasant side of such a position being set forth. The book, however, ends happily in the marriage of Agnes to a clergyman. Although well written, it lacks the elements of strength and warmth. It lives by the name of the author rather than by its intrinsic merit.

AGNES OF SORRENTO, a romance by Harriet Beecher Stowe (1862). The scene is laid in central Italy during the time of the infamous Pope Alexander VI. (from 1492 to 1503). Agnes is the daughter of a Roman prince who secretly marries, and then deserts, a girl of humble parentage. The young mother dies of grief, and Elsie, the grandmother, takes Agnes to Sorrento, where she lives by selling oranges in the streets. Her beauty and her purity attract to her many lovers, worthy and unworthy, and involve her in many romantic and dramatic incidents. The story is delightfully told, the Italian atmosphere is well suggested, and the book, though not Mrs. Stowe's best, takes good literary rank.

AGRICULTURE ('De Re Rustica'), by Columella in the first century. It consists of twelve books, of which the tenth is in verse and devoted to gardens. The work is preceded by an introduction, in which the author deplores the contempt into which agriculture has fallen. He sees on all sides schools open to teach rhetoric, dancing, and music. Even mountebanks, cooks, and barbers are fashionable, and infamous houses in which gambling and all sorts of vices that ruin youth are patronized; while for the art of fertilizing the earth there are neither masters nor pupils, neither justice nor protection. The author begins with general views on agriculture and rural economy, and concludes with a sort of agricultural calendar, in which he points out the labors to be performed according to the order of the seasons. The work is much consulted by scholars, who find in it many valuable details on important points of Roman civilization. The style has all the purity of the Augustan age.

AGRICULTURE ('L'Agriculture'), a French translation by Clément Mullet of the Book of Ibn-el-Awam, written in Arabic, in the twelfth century. Besides preserving a multitude of quotations from lost Latin and Greek authors, it gives very interesting details of the life and domestic economy of the Arabs in Spain. It enters fully into the administration of rural property, the interior life of the household, the treatment of workmen, and the position of the wife. The author discusses everything connected with agriculture; but is especially instructive on aromatic plants, and the different methods of distilling perfumes from them. We have also an account of the superstitions that prevailed among the Moors of the period in the rural districts.

AGRICULTURE ('L'Agriculture'), a didactic poem by Rosset (1774–82). It is remarkable as being the first georgic poem in the French language. The subjects dwelt on are fields, vineyards, woods, meadows, plants, kitchen-gardens, ponds, and English gardens. While it contains some very fine descriptive passages, the work on the whole is cold and monotonous.

AGRICULTURE ('Agricultura'), by Terentius Varro (116–27 B.C.). The best work on this subject that has come down from the ancients. It is divided into three books, preceded by a long preface addressed to Fundania, the author's wife. The first book contains sixty-nine chapters, and treats of agriculture in general: the nature of soils; the places most suitable for a farm; the attention that ought to be given to sheepfolds, stables, and cattle-sheds; the right kind of casks for wine, oil, etc.; the necessary domestic animals, including the watch-dogs. The author then turns his attention to the cultivation of the vine, of the olive, and of gardens. He designates the work of each season, and tells when and how seed should be sown, and crops gathered in and preserved. In the eleven chapters of the second book, Varro speaks of the care and training of beasts, and their profitableness. The third book, consisting of seventeen chapters, is devoted to the *villaticæ pastiones*, — that is, to the care of the poultry-yard, and to hunting, fishing, the keeping of bees, and the propagation and care of fish. The book, once a great favorite, now belongs among the curiosities of literature.

AGRICULTURE AND PRICES, 'A History of, in England from the year after the Oxford Parliament (1259) to the commencement of the Continental War,' (1793). By James E. Thorold Rogers (8 vols., 1866–98). This work opened up a field of immense research and monumental significance, undertaking to recover aspects of the history of the people of England which contemporary records of prices of every kind give the means of knowing. Through this and subsequent researches, it has become possible to study almost every particular of the lives of the occupants of the soil of England; particulars as to the land, as to farms and farming, and as to every fact of the daily life of the landlord, the farmer, and the laborer. There is thus recovered for history no small portion of the bygone life of the English people; and with this, much light is thrown on principles of political and social economy which must be taken account of, not only by the philanthropist, but in all wise governmental administration.

AIDS TO REFLECTION, by S. T. Coleridge, which appeared in 1825, is a collection of moral and religious aphorisms, with commentaries. While these are not sequentially connected, they are yet so arranged as to illustrate the author's purpose, to address his thought to the unspiritual but reflecting mind of the supposed pilgrim, who is led from worldly-mindedness to the acceptance of spiritual religion. Coleridge takes up the argument on the pilgrim's (imputed) principles of worldly calculation. Beginning with religion as Prudence, resultant from the sense and sensuous understanding, he ascends to the ground of morality, as inspired by the heart and conscience, and finally to Spiritual Religion, as presented by reason and the will.

This argument is by no means patent to the casual reader, for the author addresses himself to the heart rather than to the reasoning faculties. The doctrines of the book are held to be those of the Church of England, broadly interpreted. The language is choice; and notwithstanding the philosophical and somewhat sentious nature of the treatment, the book is eminently readable, exhibiting, in several passages, Coleridge's prose at its best

L'AIGLON, a play by Edmond Rostand (1900). After Napoleon's downfall, his son, the Duke of Reichstadt, is virtually a prisoner at the court of his grandfather, the emperor of Austria. Metternich tries to keep him in ignorance of his father's triumphs, lest he dream of greatness and trouble the peace of Europe. Bonapartists from Paris succeed in escaping the vigilant Metternich, and disguised as servants, a tailor, a milliner, and a dancer, watch over the little "eaglet," teach him to fight Wagram and Marengo over again with painted wooden soldiers, and encourage him to take the leadership of a conspiracy to seize the throne of France. He contrives to win over his grandfather to his plans, but is checkmated by Metternich. Metternich ruthlessly forces the Duke of Reichstadt to the mirror, and shows him he has, not the features of Napoleon, but the pale face of a descendant of the Hapsburgs, whose weakness and impotence he inherits. This dramatic scene is given in the LIBRARY. The pathetic little shadow of the mighty Napoleon reaches the field of Wagram on the flight to France, but in anxiety over the peril of his cousin, the Countess Camarata, who is impersonating him at a masked ball, he hesitates and delays and is overtaken by Austrian soldiers. Left alone in the night on the battlefield, he has a vision of the battle. He hears the moans and groans of the wounded and dying, and is overcome with the realization of the cost of his father's imperial ambition. He begs heaven to forgive his attempt to raise again the standard of war, and offers his own life in expiation. The captive "eaglet" dies amid the trivialities and dullness of the court, in the prime of his young manhood, heartbroken at his failure to imitate and avenge his great father.

AINO FOLK-TALES, by Basil H. Chamberlain (1888). Twelve hundred years ago a Chinese historian wrote that "on the eastern frontier of Japan there exists a barrier of great mountains, beyond which is the land of the Hairy Men." These were the Aino, so called from the word in their language signifying "man." In the dawn of history they appear living far to the south and west of their present haunts, century by century retreating eastward and northward, as steadily as the American Indian has retreated westward. In this collection of stories Professor Chamberlain has sought to preserve those strange folk-tales which were told in the huts of this untutored people ages ago, and retold to each succeeding generation. The interest in these stories consists in their pictures of Aino ideas, morals, and customs. The stories of 'The Salmon-King,' 'The Island of Women,' and others, are based on episodes of Japanese tales, sometimes belonging to world-wide cycles of myth, as in the theme of the mortal who eats the deadly food of the underworld. On the other hand there is much genuine Aino matter in the collection.

AIRY FAIRY LILIAN, by Mrs. Hungerford ("The Duchess") (1879), needs no elaborate plot to make it interesting. Its slender thread of story traces the willful though winsome actions of Lilian Chesney. An orphaned heiress — piquant, airy, changeful, lovable — she lives, after the death of her parents, with Lady Chetwoode. Sir Guy Chetwoode, her rather young guardian; Cyril, his brother, and Florence Beauchamp, his cousin, complete the household. Sir Guy, staid, earnest, and manly, alternately quarrels with and pays sincere court to his ward, winning her after she has led him a weary chase, the details of which form the chief charm of the story. Cyril, twenty-six, pleasant but headstrong, finds his love in a fair young widow, Mrs. Arlington, about whose character an unfortunate haze of doubt has been cast — to be dissipated, however, in the end. The ambitious Florence, as vapid as she is designing, fails to impress Sir Guy, and contents herself with a Mr. Boer, appropriately named. Two of Lilian's cousins, Arthur Chesney (a vain suitor for her hand), and Taffy Musgrave (a young British red-coat whom everybody likes), add no little interest to the group, who are of a marrying mind generally. Wholesome, pretty, not too serious, the story maintains its interest to the last without introducing any startling episodes. It paints a pleasant picture of English country life at that time with sufficient fidelity to detail and an agreeable variety of light and shadow.

AJAX, a tragedy by Sophocles (495–406 B.C.). After the death of Achilles, the Greek leaders decide to give his arms to Ulysses, as the most worthy to bear them. The neglected Ajax is furious, and goes forth in the night to avenge the affront. Minerva deprives him of reason, and he attacks the flocks of sheep in the Greek camp, mistaking them for his enemies. When exhausted with slaughter, he leads the surviving sheep, chained as prisoners, to his tent. When he recovers his senses he sees into what abysses the wrath of the gods has plunged him. He must become the jest of the army if he remains before Troy; he will shame his old father if he returns to Salamis: he resolves to end his dishonored life. The prayers of Tecmessa, his captive mistress, and of his Salaminian comrades, are unavailing. Yet it is with regret that he quits this beautiful world. The monologue in which he bids it farewell, and which is the most remarkable passage in the drama, contains entrancing pictures of the life he is about to abandon. He takes leave of his country, his father's hearth, the companions of his childhood, and of glorious Athens. He has tears even for Troy, a land he lately called his foe, but become for him now a second country, by reason of so many years of combats and of glory. The names of his beloved parents are his last words on earth; the next will be uttered in Hades. Then follow the attempt to prevent his burial, which, if successful, would doom him to wander forever, an unhappy and restless ghost, through the infernal regions; the despair of his brother Teucer, Teucer's vehement invectives against the enemies of the hero, and the noble generosity of Ulysses, who undertakes the defense of the dead.

AKBAR-NAHMAH, by Abū-al-Fazl (1605). A history in Persian of the nearly fifty years' reign of Akbar, Mogul emperor of India (a contemporary of Queen Elizabeth); the greatest Asiatic monarch of modern times, and in genius and character one of the most remarkable men that ever lived. A modern 'Life' has appeared in the English 'Rulers of India' series, edited by Sir W. W. Hunter. According to this history, Akbar was the grandson of Baber, the first of the Great Moguls in India. He succeeded his father, Baber's eldest son Humayun, when barely fourteen. At Akbar's birth, October 14th, 1542, Humayun had lost his dominions, and had only begun after twelve years of exile to recover them, when his death in 1556 left Akbar the throne of Delhi, with an able but despotic Turkoman noble acting as regent. Akbar at seventeen took the government into his own hands; and by his vigilance, energy, and wisdom, with a magnanimity, toleration, and generosity rarely seen in powerful rulers, extended and consolidated his empire on a scale of territory and strength, and to a degree of order, peace, and prosperity, wholly unexampled. In addition to economic and social reforms of the most enlightened and equitable character, Akbar rose far above his age, and above his own creed as a Moslem, in establishing absolute toleration. He gave the Hindus freedom of worship, only prohibiting inhuman barbarities. He had Christian teachers expound their faith at his court, and made Hindu, Moslem, and Christian meet in a parliament of religions, to study the sympathy of faiths. He even founded a new-departure faith for uniting all believers in God. He promoted schools for Hindus as well as Moslems, and was a munificent patron of literature.

ALASKA, OUR NEW, see **OUR NEW ALASKA.**

ALBERT NYANZA, THE 'Great Basin of the Nile and Explorations of the Nile Sources,' by Sir Samuel White Baker (1866). The record of over four years explorations in Africa, from March, 1861, to August, 1865, by which the geographical knowledge of the sources of the Nile was completed. Bruce, ninety years before, had found the source of the Blue Nile, and Speke and Grant were about to report finding in the Victoria Nyanza the remotest eastern source of the White Nile. Baker's explorations made known the immense lake, named by him Albert Nyanza, into the northeast corner of which the outlet stream from the Victoria empties, and out from the northern point of which the White Nile issues to flow through thirty degrees of latitude to the Mediterranean. The equatorial lake system, by which the Nile is fed for ten months in the year, became fully known when Baker had supplemented the discoveries of Speke and Grant. In a second work of great interest, 'The Nile Tributaries of Abyssinia' (1867), Baker completed the true story of the Nile, showing that the annual flood by which the special agriculture of the Nile valley is created, would not take place at all but for the Blue Nile and other Abyssinian branches of the main Nile. Baker spent twelve months in exploring all the Abyssinian tributaries of the Nile; and he was thus able to give an accurate account of all the sources through which nature gives to Egypt, not only a great river all the year round, but an immense fertilizing midsummer flood.

ALBION'S ENGLAND, by William Warner (1586): a collection of poetical narratives or ballads, many of them legendary rather than authoritative, relating to the history of England "from the originals of the first inhabitants thereof unto the Raigne of Queen Elizabeth." So runs the sub-title. In reality the narrative begins with the Deluge. The poem was promptly suppressed by the Star Chamber, presumably on the score of indelicacy; but it has been repeatedly reprinted, the last edition being Crawford's in 1854. During the sixteenth and seventeenth centuries it enjoyed great popularity. Though Meres tells us that he has heard Warner termed "by ye best wits of both our universities 'our English Homer,'" his master work is tedious and turgid at best, and frequently lapses into doggerel. The episode of Argentile and Curan is the most famous in the book. The princess Argentile succeeds to the throne of Northumberland, on the death of her father Adelbright, under the wardship of Edel. The latter seeks to win her hand. But she has another lover in a servant of her household, who is in reality the Danish Prince Curan. He has adopted this subterfuge to woo her. Edel, discovering the mutual love of the young people, forces Curan to quit her service; and he becomes a neatherd. Argentile, to escape her guardian's importunities, flees from the palace and becomes a neatherd's maid. Curan wooes and wins her, and leads a revolt against the wicked Edel, who is vanquished and put to death. Curan and Argentile then become king and queen of Northumberland.

ALCESTIS, a tragedy by Euripides (480–406 B.C.). Admetus is doomed to die, but the Fates consent to spare him if he can find someone willing to die in his stead; and he is unmanly enough to beseech his aged parents, who refuse. His wife Alcestis, however, offers herself, and the unheroic Admetus accepts. Hercules passes that way, is entertained by Admetus, and becomes scandalously merry and roystering, till he discovers the cause of the wailings and the signs of sorrow in the house, upon which he undertakes to rescue Alcestis from her fate. The chorus of old men bewail the lot of their mistress. Admetus reproaches his father bitterly for not saving her by the sacrifice of his life; and the old man hurls back his insults, and taunts him with his cowardice in consenting to accept the offer of Alcestis. In the midst of this, Hercules once more stands on the threshold, this time with the veiled form of Alcestis beside him. 'Alceste, ou, Triomphe d'Hercule,' was acted with great success at Paris in 1674. The music was by Lulli. The libretto of the 'Alcestis' of Gluck, the most admired opera of the great master, was written by Calzabigi; and unlike most librettos, is a dramatic poem of a high order, full of strong situations and instinct with fervid passion. Browning deals with the same subject in 'Balaustion's Adventure.'

ALEXANDRA, a poem by Lycophron of Chalcis, who lived in the third century before Christ. Alexandra is the name which the author gives Cassandra. The poem is in part a prophecy of the downfall of Troy, and is related, not by Cassandra, but by a soldier, who tells Priam that the princess is kept a prisoner by Apollo, and that he now rehearses to the king what he has heard from her lips. The work contains 1,474 verses, and is a confused medley of mythology, history, and geography, with here and there a few traces of real poetry. Some of Lycophron's inventions are of a very grotesque character. Among other marvels, he makes Hercules live a considerable time in the belly of a whale, and chop up the entrails of the monster for food.

ALEXIAD, a life of the Emperor Alexis Comnenus (1081–1118) by the Princess Anna Comnena, his daughter. This work, which is one of the most important authorities for the history of the closing years of the eleventh century, is written in modern Greek, and divided into fifteen books. It gives a vivid picture of the First Crusade, which the author had seen, and of the antagonistic interests of the Greeks and Crusaders, united indeed against the Infidels, but in a state of constant hostility to each other. Her father is her hero; she defends all his acts, and attempts especially to prove that the charge of perfidy brought against him by the Franks was baseless. She shows him to have been an active and energetic prince, a good captain, a thorough tactician, an intrepid soldier, and a consummate statesman. She reproaches the Crusaders with all sorts of crime, particularly Bohemund, the son of Robert Guiscard and the personal enemy of her father. The work is crowded with useless details, which Byzantine etiquette rendered important; but Anna Comnena has preserved the knowledge of a multitude of curious incidents, which but for her would have been lost to history. She has been criticized for relating marvels as if they were real facts, a habit which simply proves that the Greeks were as superstitious as the Latins. The old Greek and the new Frank civilization contrast strongly in her pages.

ALHAMBRA, THE, by Washington Irving (1832. Revised, enlarged, and rearranged, 1852). This Spanish Sketch-Book grew out of the experiences and studies of Irving, while an actual resident in the old royal palace of the Moors at Granada. Many of the forty sketches have their foundation only in the author's fancy, but others are veritable history. It was his object, he says, in describing scenes then almost unknown, to present a faithful and living picture of that singular little world in which he found himself, and to depict its half-Spanish, half-Oriental character, its mixture of the heroic, the poetic, and the grotesque. The sketches revive in the colors of life itself the splendid Moorish civilization of the Middle Ages, its industries, festivities, traditions, and catastrophes. The author is steeped in the atmosphere of Moorish Spain; and his book has hardly a rival in its appreciation of the pathetic grotesque, cruel, tender, and wholly fascinating past of Cordova, Seville, and Granada,

ALICE, OR, THE MYSTERIES, see **ERNEST MALTRAVERS.**

ALICE-FOR-SHORT, by William De Morgan (1907). The scene of this story is laid in London, where Alicia Kavanagh, called Alice-for-short, is introduced as a neglected child overwhelmed with grief at the breaking of a beer-jug with which she is returning to her drunken mother. The child is befriended by Charles Heath, a young artist whose studio proves to be in the same house in which the Kavanagh family occupy the cellar. A drunken brawl ensues in which Kavanagh first kills his wife and then takes poison, after which the frightened child is conveyed by the artist to his own London home where his family adopt her. His sister Peggy devotes herself to the sick and exhausted Alice and later falls in love with Rupert Johnson, the young doctor who comes to tend the child. Eventually the doctor risks his life to rescue Alice from a perilous fall over a cliff, and Peggy, who has frowned upon his suit, relents, owns that she loves him, and their marriage takes place. Charles is entrapped by a scheming model, whom he marries, and who elopes with another man after having led the artist a wretched existence. News of the death of the erring wife is soon followed by the illness of their only son Pierre, who is stricken with small-pox. Alice, now a lovely young woman, has studied nursing and at once takes her place by the boy's bedside; she nurses him back to health and then succumbs to the disease. Charles who has loved Alice from childhood, is frantic at the catastrophe and devotes himself to furthering her welfare, but refrains from making love to her thinking she must prefer some younger man. In the end, he discovers that she prefers him to any of the others and they are joyfully united. Throughout the tale runs a ghost-story connected with the house in which Charles has his studio, and interwoven with the history of Alice's forebears. The tenants see visions of a lovely lady of long ago who has been murdered in the house. At last her skeleton is found in the cellar and the mystery is cleared up which is connected with a curious ring found on the premises by Alice's mother and left to the little girl. Documents are introduced which make it clear that Alice is the descendant of the titled family that once lived in this house, and her possession of the ring entitles her to a valuable property, for which, however, she has no desire to enter a claim.

ALICE IN WONDERLAND (1865), and **THROUGH THE LOOKING-GLASS** (1871), by Lewis Carroll (Charles L. Dodgson). ALICE'S ADVENTURES IN WONDERLAND. — Alice, a bright well-behaved little girl, quite normal in every way, is the heroine of this fantastic tale, the great charm of which consists in the perfect plausibility of all its impossibilities. By following an extraordinary rabbit down into a rabbit hole, she finds herself in a land where unreal things seem real. But however absurd the doings of the inhabitants of Wonderland, she is never surprised at them. Her mistakes at first barely save her from drowning in her own tears; but afterwards she meets many queer animal friends besides a crusty old Duchess, a mad Hatter, a sleepy Dormouse, and a March Hare with whom she has strange experiences, and finally they take her to play croquet with the Queen of Hearts. During a trial by jury at the court of the Queen, Alice becomes excited and calls everyone there nothing but a pack of cards. As they rise into the air and come flying down upon her, she awakes and finds herself beside her sister on a bank where she had fallen asleep. THROUGH THE LOOKING-GLASS. — The next time Alice dreams, she steps through the looking-glass; in this land the people are all chessmen, and the country is divided up like a chessboard, with little brooks and hedges marking the squares. She travels extensively as she moves in the game, and is crowned queen at the end. This dream also comes to a climax by the violence of her resentment against so much nonsense, and she wakes suddenly. Besides kings, knights, pawns, and the other pieces of the game, there are more eccentric animals and people who have something to say. The careless White Queen and the fiery-tempered Red Queen are very amusing, and Tweedledum and Tweedledee are responsible for the song of 'The Walrus and the Carpenter'; where, to quote the Duchess, one has to "take care of the sense, and the sounds will take care of themselves."

ALICE OF OLD VINCENNES, by Maurice Thompson, was published in 1900. The scene of the story is laid in old Vincennes on the Wabash, in 1778, and describes the life of the northwest during the Revolutionary period. The heroine, Alice Roussillon, by birth a Tarleton, and therefore a member of one of the "first" Colonial families, has been stolen in her infancy and educated as a creole girl amid the hardships of pioneer life and the uncertainty of Indian warfare. Her adopted father is Gaspard Roussillon, a successful French trader with the Indians, and Alice grows up strong and beautiful and an expert with gun and sword. Lieutenant Beverly, Alice's lover, is a man of aristocratic birth whose affection for one he considers a simple creole girl portends a hard struggle between his patrician feelings and his love. However, this obstacle is removed by the discovery of Alice's true lineage, and, after many exciting adventures, she and Beverly are at length united. There are many thrilling episodes described in the story, among which may be mentioned the rescue of the settlement by the young American Colonel George Rogers Clark, who puts the British soldiers to route after one of the most trying marches ever described in fiction. Among the conspicuous characters in the tale is good old Père Beret, who is a mountain of strength in more ways than one, and his duel with Colonel Hamilton over the supposed dead body of Alice is powerfully described. The Indians are most graphically pictured and "Long Hair," with his craft and cruelty, savage nobility and meanness, and splendid but hideous physique, is one of the most picturesque figures in the book. Old frontier life in all its rudeness and simplicity is vividly portrayed, and the stirring times when men went about with scalps hanging at their belts are brought forcibly before the reader.

ALKAHEST, or, THE HOUSE OF CLAËS ('La Recherche de l'Absolu'—The Search for the Absolute), is a striking novel by Honoré de Balzac. The scene is laid in the Flemish town of Douai early in the last century; and the tale gives, with all the author's care and richness of detail, a charming representation of Flemish family life. The central character, Balthazar Claës, is a wealthy chemist, whose ancestral name is the most respected and important in the place. His aim, the dream of his life, is to solve the mystery of matter. He would by chemical analysis discover the secret of the absolute. Hence he toils early and late in his private laboratory: everything is given up to the god of science. Gradually the quest becomes a fixed idea, for which money, family, health, sanity, are sacrificed. Claës dies heart-broken and defeated; — a tragic figure, touching in its pathos, having dignity even in its downfall. As foils to him stand his devoted wife and his eldest daughter Marguerite, noble women, the latter one of the finest creations of Balzac's genius. They sympathize sorrowfully yet tenderly with his ideal, and bear with true heroism the misery to which his mad course subjects them. Simple in its plot, the story displays some of the deepest human passions, and is a powerful romance. It belongs to that series of the Human Comedy known as 'Philosophical Studies,' and appeared in 1834.

ALL FOOLS, by George Chapman. 'All Fools,' the original name of which was 'The World Runs on Wheels,' was completed at least as early as 1599, though not printed until 1605. The later title suggests the nature of the plot, which plays off one set of characters against another. Fortunio, elder son of Marc Antonio, "an honest knight, but much too much indulgent to his presuming children" loves Bellonora, daughter of Gostanzo, "the wretched Machiavellian, the covetous knight," whose son Valerio has secretly married Gratiana. Gostanzo thinks that Valerio is "the most tame and thrifty groom in Europe," though he is really devoted to dice, cards, tennis, and even more questionable activities. Rinaldo, a younger son of Marc Antonio, a woman hater who is by way of being a scholar, persuades Gostanzo that Fortunio and Gratiana are secretly wedded. Gostanzo informs Marc Antonio, at the same time offering to take them to his house that Fortunio may be reformed by his precepts and by the example of the chaste Valerio. During their stay at his house Gostanzo seeing the intimacy between Valerio and Gratiana resolves to send her away, but is persuaded by the scheming Rinaldo to send her to Marc Antonio, on the plea that she is wife of Valerio, married without his knowledge. In the end Rinaldo himself, whose "fortune is to win renown by gulling" the others, is "gulled" by his own greed.

ALL FOR LOVE, or, THE WORLD WELL LOST, by John Dryden (1678). In the preface to this, which most critics would agree is Dryden's finest play, the author claims that "the unities of time, place, and action are more exactly observed than perhaps the English theatre requires." While endeavoring to follow the practice of the ancients, he thinks that their models are too little for English tragedy which requires larger compass. On the other hand he thinks that the French poets, while strict observers of the punctilios of manners, lacked the genius which animated the English stage. In style he professes "to imitate the divine Shakespeare, and in order to "perform more freely" disencumbers himself from rhyme. The play is to some extent based on Shakespeare's 'Antony and Cleopatra,' and enters into competition with it. In accordance with the suggestion of the title, 'All for Love,' he represents Antony and Cleopatra as being more under the sway of passion than in Shakespeare's play. In the older drama Antony in the mid-tide of his passion has thoughts of other and higher ties of duty and country. In Dryden he is completely enslaved and reacts to no other impulse. Cleopatra is also so completely enslaved that she has no wit left over to devise the meretricious arts by which the Shakespearean heroine tried to draw her lover to herself. Another great difference in the treatment of the theme is that Dryden confines the action to Alexandria and to a period of a few days, whereas Shakespeare allows several years and a great variety of scene for the development of the dénouement. The play of passion is therefore much more circumscribed in Dryden than in Shakespeare.

ALL SORTS AND CONDITIONS OF MEN, by Sir Walter Besant (1882). The famous People's Palace of East London had its origin in this story; and because of it mainly the author, Walter Besant, was knighted. The story concerns chiefly two characters, — the very wealthy orphan Angela Messenger, and Harry Goslett, ward of Lord Joscelyn. Miss Messenger, after graduating with honors at Newnham, resolves to examine into the condition of the people of Stepney Green, Whitechapel region, where she owns great possessions (including the famed Messenger Brewery). To indicate to the workingwomen of East London a way of escape from the meanness, misery, and poverty of their lives, she sets up among them a co-operative dress-

2

making establishment, she herself living with her work-girls. Her goodness and wealth bring happiness to many, whose quaint stories of poverty and struggle form a considerable portion of the novel. The book ends with the opening of the People's Palace, and with the heroine's marriage to Harry Goslett, whose dramatic story is clearly interwoven with the main plot.

ALLAN QUATERMAIN, by H. Rider Haggard (1888), rehearses the adventures of the old hunter and traveler who tells the story, and whose name gives the title to the book. He is accompanied from England on an African expedition by Sir Henry Curtis — huge, fair, and brave — and Captain Good, a retired seaman. They take with them Umslopogaas, a trusty and gigantic Zulu, who has served before under Quartermain. At a mission station the party leads an expedition to rescue the daughter of the missionary, Flossie Mackenzie, who had been captured by hostile blacks. The interest of the book is found in the swift movement of the narrative, and the excitement of incessant adventure.

ALL'S WELL THAT ENDS WELL, by Shakespeare (1602) is a play, the story of which came to the poet from Boccaccio, through Paynter's 'Palace of Pleasure,' although he introduces variations. It tells how Helen de Narbon, a physician's daughter, and orphaned, forced her love on a handsome and birth-proud young French nobleman, Bertram de Rousillon, with whom she had been brought up from childhood. It is a tale of husband-catching by a curious kind of trick. Helena heals the king with her father's receipt, asks for and accepts Bertram as her reward, and is married. But the proud boy flies to the Florentine wars on his wedding-day, leaving his marriage unconsummated. Helen returns sorrowfully to Rousillon; and finds there a letter from her husband, to the effect that when she gets his ring upon her finger and shows him a child begotten of his body, then he will acknowledge her as his wife. She undertakes to outwit him and reclaim him. Leaving Rousillon on pretense of a pilgrimage to the shrine of Saint Jacques le Grand, she presently contrives to have it thought she is dead. In reality she goes to Italy, and becomes Bertram's wife in fact and not mere name, by the secret substitution of herself for the pretty Diana, with whom he has an assignation arranged. There is an entanglement of petty accidents and incidents connected with an exchange of rings, etc. But, finally, Helen makes good before the King her claim of having fulfilled Bertram's conditions; and she having vowed obedience, he takes her to his heart, and we may suppose they live happily together "till there comes to them the destroyer of delights and the sunderer of societies." One's heart warms to the noble old Countess of Rousillon, who loves Helen as her own daughter. She is wise and ware in worldly matters, and yet full of sympathy, remembering her own youth. Parolles is a cross between Thersites and Pistol, — a volte-faced scoundrel who has to pull the devil by the tail for a living. His pretense of fetching off his drum, and his trial blindfolded before the soldiers, raises a laugh; but the humor is much inferior to that of 'Henry IV.'

ALMAGEST, THE, by Ptolemy of Alexandria, about 150 A.D. This great astronomi cal and mathematical work established the "Ptolemaic System" as astronomical science for 1400 years, until the Copernican overthrew it, and gave to celestial calculations the permanent basis of trigonometrical methematics. Hipparchus, nearly three hundred years before, had made those advances in astronomy and mathematics of which Ptolemy's work is the only existing report. It was mainly as a systematic expounder, correcting and improving earlier work, that Ptolemy became so great a representative figure in the literature of science. The system which bears his name was implicitly held by earlier philosophers, but his statement became the authority to which it was referred. His work, entitled 'The Great Composition,' was called by the Arabs *magistē*, "greatest," and with *al*, "the," the name 'Almagest' came into use. — The Geography of Ptolemy, in which he was more original than in his other great work, was the geographical authority in science even longer than the 'Almagest' was in astronomy. The materials of the work were derived in great part from Marinus of Tyre, who lived shortly before him, but the skill with which Ptolemy used them gave his work its high authoritative character. A series of twenty-six maps, and a general map of the world, illustrated the 'Geography.' See also "Geography" of Ptolemy.

ALMAYER'S FOLLY, by Joseph Conrad (1895), is a novel of Eastern life, whose scene is laid on a little-known river of Borneo, and whose personages are fierce Malays, cunning Arabs, stolid Dutch traders, slaves, half-breeds, pirates, and white renegades. Almayer, the son of a Dutch official in Java, has been adopted in a sort of way by one Captain Lingard, a disreputable English adventurer, who persuades him to marry a Malay girl, whom also he has adopted, the sole survivor of a crew of Malay pirates sent by Lingard to their last account. The story is crowded with adventure, and the characters stand out, living creatures, against a gorgeous tropical background. But its merit lies in its careful rendering of race traits, and in its study of that dry-rot of character, indecision, irresolution, procrastination. It is quite plain that the sins Mr. Conrad imputes to his "frustrate ghosts" are "the unlit lamp and the ungirt loin."

ALONE, by Mrs. Mary Virginia Terhune (who is better known by her pen-name, "Marian Harland"), was her first novel, and appeared in 1854, when she was twenty-four. The scene is laid in Richmond, Virginia, where Ida Ross, an orphan of fifteen, goes to live with her guardian Mr. Read, and his daughter Josephine, a girl of her own age. With the Reads, who are cold, worldly, and reserved, the impulsive and affectionate Ida is extremely unhappy. Fortunately her life is changed by friendship with a schoolmate, Carry Carleton. In the well-bred and kindly households of the Carletons and their relatives, Ida finds friends and lovers. When the girls enter society, Josephine becomes jealous of Ida's greater attractiveness, chiefly because a certain Mr. Lacy falls in love with her. Misunderstandings ensue. Ida gives up her lover, and returns to the home of her childhood to devote her life to philanthropy. But the misunderstandings are explained, and the well-disciplined recluse is married to Mr. Lacy. The book had a very great vogue, and made a reputation for the author. It is simple in plot, contains a transcript of every-day life, and is deeply religious in tone, but belongs to a fashion in fiction which no longer prevails.

ALTON LOCKE, by Charles Kingsley, was published in 1850, when the author was thirty-one. It was his first novel, and like 'Yeast,' which closely followed it, showed Kingsley's broad humanitarianism, unconventionality, interest in and sympathy for the wrongs of the English working classes. It made a great stir, and did much in England to turn the thoughts of the upper ranks to their responsibility for the lower. Its hero is a poet-tailor of a mystic turn — 'Alton Locke, Tailor and Poet,' is the full title; he feels deep in his soul the horrors of the sweating system and other abuses which grind the poor, and devotes himself to their amelioration. "I am," he says of himself, "a Cockney among Cockneys": he is sketched from his boyhood in a mean, suburban quarter of the city, through his struggle for education and maintenance, which brings him into contact with the case of the toiling city masses, to his leadership of their cause, his advocacy of Chartism, and final failure to realize his dreams. The purity, ideality, and altruism of Locke and his friends Crossthwaite, MacKaye, Lady Ellerton, and Eleanor, make them inspiring prophets of the war of the Emancipation of Labor. The story is full of vigorous, earnest, eloquent preaching, and would now be called "problem fiction" of the frankest sort; and it is also often dramatic and thrilling.

ALZIRE, a well-known tragedy by Voltaire (1736). The time is the sixteenth century. Montèze, the native king of a part of Potosi, has, with his daughter Alzire and a large number of American Indians, fallen into the power of Guzman, the Spanish governor of Peru. The Spaniard falls in love with Alzire, who has become a Christian. Having been betrothed to an Indian chief now believed to be dead, she hesitates to marry the governor, but is persuaded by her father, and by Alvares the father of Guzman. After the marriage, Zamore, her first lover, reappears among a crowd of prisoners. His fury becomes uncontrollable when he learns that Guzman, who has already wrested from him everything else he valued, — power, wealth, and liberty, — has now deprived him of his betrothed. In vain does Alzire contrive the captive's escape. He will not fly without her. In disguise he penetrates to the chamber of his enemy, and mortally wounds him. Both Alzire and Alvares seek to save him, but cannot unless he adopts Christianity. He refuses; but when his rival Guzman says, "Your God has enjoined on you vengeance and murder: mine commands me to pity and forgive my murderer," he is overcome, and makes a profession of faith. Dying, Guzman unites the lovers. This play is often rated as Voltaire's dramatic masterpiece. In elegance of diction, in picturesqueness and vigor of conception, it leaves little to be desired. The dramatist's intention was to contrast the noble but imperfect virtues of the natural man with those of the man trained under the influences of Christianity and civilization.

AMADIS OF GAUL, formerly attributed to Vasco Lobeira. Robert Southey, in the introduction to his English version of this romance, says: "'Amadis of Gaul' is among prose what 'Orlando Furioso' is among metrical romances, not the oldest of its kind but the best." It is however so old as to have belonged to the age of the fairest bloom of chivalry, the days of the Black Prince and the glorious reign of Edward III. in the two realms of England and France. It is a tale of the knightly career of Amadis and his two brothers, Galaor and Florestan, the sons of King Perion of Gaul. The name of the knight's mistress is Oriana; but many are the damsels, ladies, and queens, whom he rescues in peril, not without wounding their hearts, but remaining loyal to the last to his liege lady — his marriage with whom terminates, in Southey's opinion, the narration of the original author. The remaining adventures after the Fourth Book are, as he thinks, added by the Spanish translator Garcia Ordonez de Montalvo, and exhibit a much lower type both of literary style and of morals. The author is a Portuguese who was born at Porto; fought at Aljubarrota, where he was knighted by King João; and died at Elvas, 1403. The oldest version extant is that of Montalvo in Spanish, and the oldest edition is supposed to be that of Seville, 1526. But the romance was familiar to the Spanish discoverers of America, and must have enjoyed a wide popularity since the time when, in the reign of João I., the Infante Dom Pedro wrote a sonnet in praise of Vasco Lobeira, "the inventor of the Books of Chivalry." Cervantes, whose own romance was the death-knell of these unnatural and preternatural extravaganzas, names this as one of the three romances spared in the burning of Don Quixote's library, "because it was the first of the kind and the best." It depicts a time "not many years after the passion of our Redeemer," when Garinter, a Christian, was King of lesser Britain, Languines King of Scotland, Perion King of Gaul, and Lesuarte King of Great Britain. The scene is laid in such mystic parts of the earth as the island of Windsor, the forest of Angaduza, and "Sobradisa which borders upon Serolis." The manly love of tho three brother knights, their honor, fidelity, and bravery, are noble types of the ideal of the chivalric romance. It is to the interpolations and additions of the Spanish and French translators through whom the romance has come down to us, that we owe the gross and offensive passages which mar the otherwise pure and charming narrative.

AMATEUR POACHER, THE, by Richard Jefferies, was published in 1889. Like the other works by this author, "The Gamekeeper at Home,' 'Wild Life in a Southern Country,' etc., it displays a genius for the observation of nature, yet its scope is narrow and simple. "The following pages," says the author, "are arranged somewhat in the order of time, beginning with the first gun and attempts at shooting. Then come the fields, the first hills and woods explored, often without a gun or any thought of destruction; and next the poachers and other odd characters observed at their work."

The book opens with a tempting sentence: — "They burned the old gun that used to stand in the dark corner up in the garret, close to the stuffed fox that always grinned so fiercely." The narrative goes on in the same familiar, brisk, hunting-morning style, carrying the reader far afield, into damp woods, and over sweet, rich pastures. In conclusion the author writes: "Let us go out of these indoor, narrow, modern days, whose twelve hours somehow have become shortened, into the sunlight and pure wind. A something that the ancients called divine can be found and felt there still." The book is cheerful and wholesome, possessing the charm of nature itself.

AMBASSADORS, THE, a novel by Henry James (1902-03). Lambert Strether comes from Woolett, Massachusetts, on an embassy from the wealthy Mrs. Newsome to bring back her son Chad from Paris to the business he has inherited, and to discover, if possible, what is the sinister influence which has prevented him from returning heretofore. It is inferred that Strether has been selected to marry Mrs. Newsome and her fortune. He finds Chad greatly changed for the better by his intimacy with the Countess de Vinnoet, a woman of inexpressible charm, and becomes converted to their relations as beyond the comprehension and standards of Woolett, Massachusetts. It is long before he learns their secret, and his reaction is to be ashamed of his mission, and to urge Chad not to return. The second embassy is composed of Mrs. Pocock, Chad's sister, her husband, and young sister-in-law, who come to find out what is keeping Strether in Paris, and call him to account for his failure as ambassador. Chad tries to divert his sister by attentions and entertainments, but Europe has no effect on her New England conscience. She convinces Strether of his own delinquency, and he returns to Woolett; but Chad remains faithful to the ties he has formed in Paris.

AMBER GODS, THE, a novel in miniature, by Harriet Prescott Spofford, was published in 1863. It is remarkable neither for plot nor for character-drawing, but for a magnificent depth and richness of color, like a painting by Titian. An amber amulet or rosary, possessing mysterious influences, gives the title to the story.

AMBITIOUS WOMAN, AN, a novel by Edgar Fawcett, appeared in 1883. It is a keen yet sympathetic analysis of an American female type whose dominant trait is social ambition. Claire Twining is reared in the ugly poverty of a Brooklyn suburb. She is clever, capable, with a great desire for the luxuries of life. Through the good offices of a schoolmate she gains a social foothold. If Claire's transformation seems a little sudden, there is yet much genuine strength in the story and much truthful observation of city life in New York.

AMBROSIO, see **MONK.**

AMELIA, by Henry Fielding, was published in 1751, and was the last of that novelist's works of fiction, as well as one of the most famous novels of the eighteenth century. He was forty-four when it appeared, and in impaired health. It has, perhaps for this reason, less of the exuberant vitality which characterized 'Tom Jones,' a novel preceding it by two years. The plot is more serious; but in a rich, quiet fund of humor it is not far behind that masterpiece. In 'Amelia,' Fielding drew the portrait of a virtuous and lovely wife; his own, it is believed, furnishing the model. It is a story of married life. Mr. Booth, the husband of the heroine, an impoverished gentleman, is introduced to the reader in prison, where he has been taken for participation in a street quarrel. His companion there, Miss Matthews, is a handsome young woman of easy virtue, who has murdered her betrayer. The relations of Booth and this woman are improper; but the husband is saved from this, as from other faults of conduct, by the purity, goodness, and devotion of Amelia, whom he devotedly loves. Eventually she brings him a fortune, he is released from prison, and happiness reigns. In contrasting Booth's poorer nature with the noble character of his wife, Fielding is supposed to have had himself in mind. It is noteworthy that the novelist, in depicting her, emphasized her beauty of mind and heart by stating that her bodily beauty was marred through the disfigurement of her nose in a carriage accident. The story is strong in portraiture of character, in sincerity, in analysis of motive, and in wit.

AMENITIES OF LITERATURE, by Isaac Disraeli, father of Lord Beaconsfield, was published in 1841, when the author was seventy-five years old. The title was adopted to connect it with two preceding volumes, 'Curiosities of Literature' and 'Miscellanies of Literature.' As the author relates in the preface, it forms a portion of a great work projected, but never accomplished. "A history of our vernacular literature has occupied my studies for many years. It was my design, not to furnish an arid narrative of books or of authors, but following the steps of the human mind through the wide track of time, to trace from their beginning the rise, progress, and decline of public opinions. . . . In the progress of these researches many topics presented themselves, some of which from their novelty and curiosity courted investigation. Literary history, in this enlarged circuit, becomes not merely a philological history of critical erudition, but ascends into a philosophy of books." In the midst of his studies toward the working-out of this design, Disraeli was arrested by loss of sight. The papers in 'Amenities of Literature' form a portion of the projected history. The first volume consists of thirty-eight chapters on subjects connected with early English life and literature; among them The Druidical Institution; Cædmon and Milton; Dialects; Early Libraries; The Ship of Fools; and Roger Ascham. The second volume, possessing less unity of design, has thirty-two chapters on subjects strange, familiar, and quaint: Rhyming Dictionaries are treated of; Allegories and the Rosicrucian Fludd are discussed. There are chapters on Sir Philip Sidney, on Spenser,

Hooker, and Drayton, and a dissertation on Pamphlets. The book as a whole is a pleasant guide into the half-hidden by-paths of English literary history. It is a repository of much curious book-gossip and of authors' lore.

AMERICA, DISCOVERY OF, see **DISCOVERY OF AMERICA.**

AMERICA, NARRATIVE AND CRITICAL HISTORY OF, see **NARRATIVE, ETC.**

AMERICAN, THE, by Henry James, was published in 1877. It was the novelist's third book of fiction, a volume of short tales and a novel preceding it. The central character, Christopher Newman, is a typical product of the United States: cool, self-confident, and able, impressing, by the force and directness of his nature, all who come in contact with him. Having made his fortune, he is traveling in Europe for pleasure. He falls in love with a Parisian lady of noble birth, who is half English, — Madame de Cintré, a widow; and she comes to care for him enough to engage herself to him. The obstacles in the way of their marriage give rise to many dramatic incidents.

AMERICAN COMMONWEALTH, THE (1888. New ed., rev. 2 vols. 1913), by Viscount James Bryce (the eminent historian of the Holy Roman Empire), is a study of the political, social, and economic features of what its author calls "the nation of the future"; and the most important study since De Tocqueville's 'Democracy.' Lord Bryce deals with his subject in six grand divisions: Part i. treats of the federal government, — its executive, legislative, and judiciary departments, with a survey of their powers and limitations; the relation existing between the federal government and the State governments; constitutional development and its results. Part ii. considers the State governments (including rural and city governments), their departments, constitutions, merits, and defects. Part iii. is devoted to the political machinery and the party system, giving a history of the origin and growth of political parties; their composition; their leaders, past and present; and their existing conditions and influences. Part iv. is concerned with public opinion, — its nature and tendencies; the means and causes for its control of all important issues in the various sections of the Union. Part v. gives concrete illustrations of the matters in the foregoing chapters, together with a discussion of the "strength and weakness of democratic government as it exists in the United States." Part vi. is confined to non-political institutions: the aspects of society, the intellectual and spiritual forces upon which depend the personal and political welfare of unborn generations of American citizens; and upon whose success or failure rests the promulgation of American democratic ideals and principles among the nations. The work is lucidly written, free from technicalities, and fluent in style, so that it is as easy for the laity to comprehend, as for those initiated by practical experience into the workings of our government. The chapters dealing with the professional and social sides of American life, and especially those devoted to the American universities, have been enthusiastically received by Americans, — some American universities accepting the work as a text-book in their schools of law, economics, and sociology.

AMERICAN CONFLICT, THE, by Horace Greeley (1864-66). This history is not restricted to the period of armed conflict between the North and South in the sixties; but purports to give, in two large volumes, an account of the drift of public opinion in the United States regarding human slavery from 1776 to the close of the year 1865. The most valuable feature of this history is the incorporation into it of letters, speeches, political platforms, and other documents, which show authentically and beyond controversy the opinions and dogmas accepted by political parties and their chiefs, and approved by public opinion North and South; as the author justly remarks, nothing could so clearly show the influences of slavery in molding the opinions of the people and in shaping the destinies of the country. Thus the work is a great magazine of materials for the political history of the United States with regard to slavery; and whatever judgment may be passed on its author's philosophy of the great conflict, the trustworthiness of his volumes, simply as a record of facts and authentic declarations of sectional and partisan opinion, is unquestionable.

AMERICAN CONTRIBUTIONS TO CIVILIZATION, and Other Essays and Addresses, by Charles W. Eliot (1897). A collection of miscellaneous addresses and magazine articles, written during the previous twenty-five years by the president of Harvard; not, however, including any educational papers. The 'American Contributions' is the subject of the first only, out of about twenty papers. There are included also the remarkable set of inscriptions prepared by Mr. Eliot for the Water Gate of the World's Fair at Chicago, 1893; that for the Soldiers' Monument on Boston Common; and those for the Robert Gould Shaw monument, commemorating the 54th Regiment Massachusetts Infantry. Through the entire volume there appear a grasp of conception, a strength and refinement of thought, and a clearness and vigor of style, very rarely found in writers on themes not involving imagination or making appeal to feeling.

AMERICAN CRISIS, THE, is the general name given to a series of political articles by Thomas Paine. These articles are thirteen in number, exclusive of a 'Crisis Extraordinary' and a 'Supernumerary Crisis.' The first and most famous, published in the Pennsylvania Journal, December 19th, 1776, began with the famous sentence, "These are the times that try men's souls." "It was written during the retreat of Washington across the Delaware, and by order of the commander was read to groups of his dispirited and suffering soldiers. Its opening sentence was adopted as the watchword of the movement on Trenton, a few days after its publication, and is believed to have inspired much of the courage which won that victory." The second 'Crisis' is addressed to Lord Howe on the occasion of his proclamations to the American people, in the interests of Great Britain. The third 'Crisis' is dated April 19th, 1777, two days after the appointment of Paine to the secretaryship of the Committee of Foreign Affairs. The fourth appeared shortly after the battle of Brandywine, in the fall of 1777. The fifth was addressed to General William Howe, and was written when Paine was employed by the Pennsylvania Assembly and Council to obtain intelligence of the movements of Washington's army. The sixth was addressed to the British Commissioners appointed to "treat, consult, and agree, upon the means of quieting the Disorders" in the colonies. The seventh and eighth addressed the people of England; and the ninth, no particular person or body of persons. The tenth was on the King of England's speech at the opening of Parliament, November 27th, 1781. The eleventh considered the Present State of News. The twelfth was addressed to the Earl of Shelburne. The thirteenth and last, published April 19th, 1783, bears the title, 'Thoughts on the Peace, and the Probable Advantages thereof.' It opens with the words, "The times that tried men's souls are over." The pamphlets throughout exhibit political acumen and the common-sense for which Paine was remarkable. As historical evidence of the underlying forces in a unique struggle, and as a monument to patriotism, they possess great and lasting value.

AMERICAN LAW, see COMMENTARIES ON.

AMERICAN MUNICIPAL PROGRESS, by Charles Zueblin (latest ed. 1915). A revised edition of this book, first published in 1902, was needed, as it is just in the years since 1900 that the municipal idea has been most extensively developed both in Europe and America. What steps have been taken in the direction of municipalization in the western world may be seen from a concise statement in the preface. "Already this century has witnessed the first municipalized street railways and telephone in American cities; a national epidemic of street paving and cleaning; the quadrupling of electric lighting service and the national appropriation of display lighting; a successful crusade against dirt of all kinds — smoke, flies, germs — and the diffusion of constructive provisions for health like baths, laundries, comfort stations, milk stations, school-nurses, and open air schools; fire prevention; the humanizing of the police and the advent of the policewoman; the transforming of some municipal courts into institutions for the prevention of crime and the cure of offenders; the elaboration of the school curriculum to give every child a complete education from the kindergarten to the vocational course in school or university or shop; municipal reference libraries; the completion of park systems in most large cities and the acceptance of the principle that the smallest city without a park and playground is not quite civilized; the modern playground movement giving organized and directed play to young and old; the social centre; the democratic art museum; municipal theatres; the commission form of government; the city manager; home rule for cities; direct legislation — a greater advance than the whole nineteenth century compassed." The book is a mine of information for civil and social workers, municipal officials, and intelligent citizens generally, and its value is enhanced by a full bibliography.

AMERICAN PAINTING, THE HISTORY OF, by Samuel Isham (1915). The plan of the editor and author of this book is to present the history of a particular art in a given area from the artist's point of view. As the United States is the youngest of the great nations, the student must not expect to find in the history of its art either organic growth or logical development, but rather the continual desertion of one set of models for another, with the retention at each change of hardly any tradition of former ideals. American painting, however, may roughly be classified in three periods — the Colonial, during which the inspiration was mainly English; the Provincial, when English influence waned and painters looked for guidance to Düsseldorf, Rome, or Paris; the Cosmopolitan, immediately succeeding the Civil War, when American painting took its place in rivalry with the rest of the world. The present tendency, which is proceeding with extraordinary rapidity, is the attempt to develop an indigenous painting adapted to native needs and tastes. The aim of the author has been to trace the development of painting and of the appreciation of painting. Particular artists and their works are mentioned at such length as will record the growth of the country in intelligence and culture, and show how the painter has been inspired or at least influenced by his environment and how later he has reacted upon it. The evolution of the art in the United States from Copley and Benjamin West, the latter of whom got his first colors from the painted savages of the forest, to the superb craftsmanship of Whistler and Sargent is skillfully traced with proportion, candor, and clarity.

AMERICAN PROSE MASTERS, by William Crary Brownell (1909). A series of critical essays on Cooper, Hawthorne, Emerson, Poe, Lowell, and Henry James.

With great acuteness the author applies to these authors a rigid critical standard, considering in turn their substance, philosophy, culture, and style. Cooper he places unusually high, but depreciates Hawthorne as lacking in substance. Emerson he praises as an apostle of refinement to an age of democracy. Poe is a consummate artist but without intellectual content and "therefore valueless." Lowell's criticism he condemns as dilettante because, though based on sound scholarship, it was impressionistic and pictorial rather than intellectual. Henry James he values for his penetrative analysis of the complicated relations of modern life. This critic is somewhat over-fastidious, but his conscientiousness, perspicuity, precision, and impartiality are valuable contributions to American criticism, relieving it from the suspicion of provincial partiality and holding favorite authors up to the highest standards.

AMERICAN REVOLUTION, THE, by John Fiske (1891). This volume, originally intended for beginners in history, owes its vogue to the author's terse and flexible vernacular; his sense of harmonious and proportionate literary treatment; and that clear perception of the relative importance of details, and firm yet easy grasp of principles and significant facts, resulting from the trained exercise of his philosophic powers. 'The American Revolution' was first published in 1891; but the edition of 1896 is "illustrated with portraits, maps, facsimiles, contemporary views, prints, and other historic materials." This work exhibits a delightful vivacity and dramatic skill in the portraiture of Washington as the central figure of the American revolt against the arbitrary government of George the Third. A full treatment of the earlier tyranny of the Lords of Trade, leading up to the crisis, is followed by Washington's entrance on the scene, at Cambridge, as commander-in-chief of the American forces. The military gains of Washington in spite of the enemy's large resources, and the varying fortunes of the patriot army, leading down through the discouragements of Valley Forge and up again, through the campaigns of the South and of Virginia, to final success, are shown by Mr. Fiske with remarkable clearness and skill. Finally he points out the broad results to all future civilization of the triumph of the Colonial cause, in the surrender of Cornwallis. His point of view is one with that of John Morley, who says: "The War of Independence was virtually a second English Civil War. The ruin of the American cause would have been also the ruin of the Constitutional cause in England; and a patriotic Englishman may revere the memory of Patrick Henry and George Washington, not less justly than the patriotic American."

AMERICAN REVOLUTION, LITERARY HISTORY OF THE, see **LITERARY, ETC.**

AMERICANS AND OTHERS, 'a collection of essays on contemporary manners' by Agnes Repplier (1912). The point of view is that of an educated gentlewoman, witty, satirical, gracious, and refined, a valiant upholder of sane and wholesome ideals. Her essays ridicule the defects and strive to encourage the merits of American social life. 'A Question of Politeness' attacks the common delusion that rudeness is a mark of sincerity. In 'The Mission of Humor' she criticizes the cheap wit of the comic supplements and the lack of intellectual content in American humor. 'Goodness and Gayety' pleads for the union of wit and sanctity. 'The Nervous Strain' attempts to check the American habit of rush and worry by an appeal to commonsense and to the sayings of Marcus Aurelius. 'The Greatest of these is Charity' is a satire on the charitable enterprises of wealthy American women. Other essays are

The Girl Graduate,' 'The Estranging Sea,' 'The Customary Correspondent,' and 'The Condescension of Borrowers.' The style is finished, and refined, and attractively combines gayety and seriousness.

AMIEL'S JOURNAL, a selection of daily meditations from the diary of Henri Frédéric Amiel, who was a professor of aesthetics and later of philosophy at the University of Geneva, but published little, putting his best work into this 'Journal Intime,' which extends from 1848 to 1881, the year of his death, and appeared in 1882. A good English translation by Mrs. Humphry Ward was published in 1889. The work consists of detached meditations of a philosophic, religious, descriptive, and personal character written in a lucid, aphoristic style. Amiel was a man of reflective temperament and had the habit of introspection, fostered by a skeptical and analyzing age. Four years of philosophical studies in Germany had intensified this tendency, and directed his contemplations too exclusively to the infinite, paralyzing his will and his power of seeking positive truth. Some of the entries in the journal express a yearning for Nirvana, for absorption in the universe; in others he attempts to fuse into one the most diverse systems of thought. Others are nicely discriminating appreciations of literature and art, or penetrating criticisms of society and national life. Concerning religion Amiel disbelieves in the permanency of dogma but holds that an element of faith is essential if religion is to retain its power over the masses. He maintains the unity of the religious aspirations beneath diverse creeds. His descriptions of Genevan landscape show genuine power of suggesting the spiritual presence immanent in nature.

AMOS JUDD, by J. A. Mitchell (1895). On the outbreak of civil war in a province of Northern India, the seven-year-old rajah is smuggled away to save his life, by three faithful followers, two Hindoos and an American; and for absolute safety is taken to the Connecticut farmhouse of the American's brother. Under the name of Amos Judd he is brought up in ignorance of his origin. The most dramatic incidents of his life hinge upon his wonderful faculty of foreseeing events. In this story the atmosphere of a world invisible seems to surround and control that of the visible world; and the shrewd and unimaginative Yankee type is skillfully and dramatically set against the mystical Hindu character, to whom the unseen is more real than the actual. The story is well told.

L'AMOUR, by the noted French historian Michelet, was published in 1859, when he was sixty-one years old. In the Introduction he writes: — "The title which would fully express the design of this book, its signification, and its import, would be 'Moral Enfranchisement Effected by True Love.'" Judged by the standards of the present day, 'L'Amour' seems old-fashioned; its ideals of women obvious. At the time of its publication, however, it appeared revolutionary and daring. Yet it was merely an attempt to establish reverence for the physical life of woman. Her intellectual life was considered only as a kind of appendage to the physical. Michelet apparently had no other conception of woman and her destiny than as maiden, wife, mother, housekeeper. Of the end-of-the-century woman he had no foreknowledge. The conception of his work rested on a sentimental basis. It was the fruit of a philanthropic motive. He saw about him not a nation of families, but of individuals. He wished to hold before his countrymen an ideal of family life. This ideal was noble but narrow. Woman was to him a fragile plant to be cared for and cherished by man. One muscular girl playing golf would have destroyed his pretty conception, but the athletic college woman did not belong to the fifties. The work however served its purpose. As far as it went it was good. Its conception of love, though one-sided, was sufficiently in advance of contemporary thought on the subject to render the book remarkable.

ANABASIS, THE ('Retreat of the Ten Thousand,' 401–399 B. C.), by Xenophon. The word means the *going up* or expedition,—*i. e.*, to Babylon, the capital of the Persian Empire; but most of the narrative is occupied with the retreat. The occasion of the famous expedition was the attempt of Cyrus the Younger to unseat his elder brother Artaxerxes from the throne of Persia by aid of a Greek army, which he gathered in or near his satrapy in Asia Minor, and then moved swiftly across Persia against the miscellaneous barbarian hordes of his brother with their small centre of disciplined Persian guards. The plan succeeded, and Cyrus was about to win the great battle of Cunaxa, when he was killed in the fray, and the Ten Thousand were left leaderless and objectless in the heart of a hostile empire a thousand miles from their kin. To complete their ruin, all the head officers were decoyed into a mock negotiation by Artaxerxes and murdered to a man. In their despair, Xenophon, a volunteer without command, came forward, heartened them into holding together and fighting their way back to the Euxine, and was made leader of the retreat; which was conducted with such success, through Persia and across the snow-clad Armenian mountains, against both Persian forces and Kurdish savages, that the troops reached Trapezus (Trebizond) with very little loss. Even then their dangers were not over: Xenophon had now to turn diplomatist; to gain the good graces of the Greek cities on the Black Sea, and to negotiate with Seuthes the Thracian king who tried to assassinate him, and with the governors of the different cities subject to Sparta. At last the adventure was over. Many of the survivors went back to Greece; but the larger number took service under Spartan harmosts, and were subsequently instrumental in freeing several Greek cities in Asia Minor.

Merely as a travel sketch the tale is highly interesting. The country traversed in Persia was almost utterly unknown to the Greeks: and Xenophon makes memoranda in which he enumerates the distances from one halting-place to another; notes the cities inhabited or cities deserted; gives a brief but vivid description of a beautiful plain, a mountain pass, a manœuvre skillfully executed, or any amusing episode that falls under his eye. And we find that camp gossip and scandal were as rife, as rank, and as reliable as in other ages. He is especially delightful in his portraits, sketched in a few sentences, but vigorous and lifelike: Cyrus, a man at once refined and barbarous, an impressive picture of a Persian prince brought in contact with Greek civilization; Clearchus, the type of an excellent general, upright but harsh: Proxenus, a fine gentleman, but too soft and weak; the unscrupulous Menon, a natural product of civil dissension. Xenophon tells the story in the third person, after the fashion in the classic times; and if he makes himself out a most eloquent, courageous, resourceful, and self-sacrificing leader, his other work makes one willing to accredit him cheerfully.

ANACHARSIS, THE YOUNGER, see **PILGRIMAGE OF.**

ANALOGY OF RELIGION, THE, by Bishop Joseph Butler, first appeared in 1736, and has ever since been held in high esteem by orthodox Christians. The full title is 'The Analogy of Religion, Natural and Revealed, to the Constitution and Course of Nature.' The argument, which is orderly and concise, is briefly this: The author lays down three premises, — the existence of God; the known course of nature; and the necessary limitations of our knowledge. These premises enable him to take common ground with those whom he seeks to convince — the exponents of a "loose kind of deism." He then argues that he who denies the Divine authorship of the Scriptures, on account of difficulties found in them, may, for the same reason, deny the world to have been created by God: for inexplicable difficulties are found in the course of nature; therefore no sound deist should be surprised to find similar difficulties in the Christian religion. Further, if both proceed from the same author, the wonder would rather be, that there should not be found on both the mark of the same hand of authorship. If man can follow the works of God but a little way, and if his world also greatly transcends the efforts of unassisted reason, why should not His word likewise be beyond man's perfect comprehension? In no sense a philosophy of religion, but an attempt rather to remove common objections thereto, the work is necessarily narrow in scope: but within its self-imposed limitations the discussion is exhaustive, dealing with such problems as a future life; God's moral government; man's probation; the doctrine of necessity; and most largely, the question of revelation. To the 'Analogy' there are generally subjoined two dissertations: one on Personal Identity, and one on The Nature of Virtue.

ANALYSIS OF BEAUTY, THE, an essay on certain artistic principles, by William Hogarth, was published in 1753. In 1745 he had painted the famous picture of himself and his pug dog Trump, now in the National Gallery. In a corner of this picture appeared a palette bearing a serpentine line under which was inscribed: "The Line of Beauty and Grace." This inscription provoked so much inquiry and comment that Hogarth wrote 'The Analysis of Beauty' in explanation of it. In the introduction he says: "I now offer to the public a short essay accompanied with two explanatory prints, in which I shall endeavor to show what the principles are in nature, by which we are directed to call the forms of some bodies beautiful, others ugly; some graceful and others the reverse." The first chapters of the book deal with Variety, Uniformity, Simplicity, Intricacy, Quantity, etc. Lines and the composition of lines are then discussed, followed by chapters on Light and Shade, on Proportion, and on Action. The 'Analysis of Beauty' subjected Hogarth to extravagant praise from his friends and to ridicule from his detractors. Unfortunately he had himself judged his work on the title-page, in the words "written with a view of fixing the fluctuating ideas of taste." This ambition it was not possible for Hogarth to realize. The essay contains, however, much that is pertinent and suggestive.

ANASTASIUS or, MEMOIRS OF A MODERN GREEK, WRITTEN AT THE CLOSE OF THE EIGHTEENTH CENTURY, by Thomas Hope (1819). The author of this romance, a rich retired merchant, woke one morning, like Byron, to find himself famous. He was known to have written some learned books on furnishing and costume; but 'Anastasius' gave him rank as an accomplished painter of scenery and delineator of manners. The hero, a young Greek ruined by injudicious indulgence, is an apostate, a robber, and a murderer. To avoid the consequences of a disgraceful love affair, he runs away from Chios, his birthplace, and seeks safety on a Venetian ship. This is captured by the Turks, and Anastasius is haled before a Turkish magistrate. Discharged, he fights on the side of the Crescent, and goes to Constantinople, where he resorts to all sorts of shifts for a livelihood, — jugglery, peddling, nostrum-making; becomes a Mussulman, visits Egypt, Arabia, Sicily, and Italy. His adventures "dizzy the arithmetic of memory": he goes through plague and famine, battle and accident, and finally dies young, a worn-out and worthless adventurer. He is a man of the world, and through his eyes the reader is made to see the world that he lives in. The book has passages of great power, often of brilliancy and wit; but it belongs to the fashion of a more leisurely day, and is now seldom read.

ANATHEMA, a drama by Leonid Andreyev (1909). Anathema is the Devil, the tempter of man. In the prologue he stands outside the gates of eternity, and calls on the silent Guardian to open them for an instant that he may have a glimpse of the mysteries to illumine the way for the Devil and for man, alike groping in darkness. The Guardian bars the way, and in anger Anathema swears to return to earth and ruin the soul of David Leizer. David Leizer is not a Faust or a Job, but an insignificant Jewish shopkeeper dying of poverty in a Russian town. Anathema appears to him as a lawyer to announce that he has inherited a fortune. David divides his wealth among the poor and outcast. His attempt to help his fellow-man results in strife and bloodshed. His millions are not sufficient, and the mob stones him to death because he does not work miracles to clothe and feed them and bring back the dead to life. Anathema in an epilogue again approaches the eternal gates and challenges the Guardian to answer him. Did not David manifest in his life and death the powerlessness of love and create a great evil? The Guardian replies that David has attained immortality, but that Anathema will never know the secret of life.

ANATOL: A SEQUENCE OF DIALOGUES, by Arthur Schnitzler (1893). A cycle of seven different love affairs of a young Viennese man of fashion, ending with his marriage. He flirts from heart to heart, and such is his incurable sentimentality that anticipations and retrospects are often more to him than the sweetheart of the moment. Suffering agonies of doubt as to whether his mistress is true to him or not, he proposes to hypnotize the lady and ask the fatal question; but when the opportunity comes, he lacks courage to put his happiness to the test. A most amusing episode is "The Farewell Dinner." While waiting for Mimi to come from the ballet, he confides to his friend Max that he is on with a new love before he is off with the old, and finds it too inconvenient to have two suppers every evening, so intends to break the news to Mimi that all is over. His amazement and pique are delightful when Mimi anticipates his announcement with her own farewell and her new love affair. Another episode, at once amusing and pathetic, is given in the LIBRARY. A last lapse on the eve of his wedding almost prevents him from meeting his bride in time for the ceremony.

ANATOMIE OF ABUSES, by Philip Stubbes, was entered upon the Stationers' Register in 1582–83; republished by the New Shakspere Society in 1877–79 under the editorship of Frederick J. Furnivall.

This most curious work — without the aid of which, in the opinion of the editor, "no one can pretend to know Shakspere's England" — is an exposure of the abuses and corruptions existing in all classes of Elizabethan society. Written from the Puritan standpoint, it is yet not over-prejudiced nor bigoted.

Little is known of Philip Stubbes. Thomas Nash makes a savage attack on the 'Anatomie' and its author, in a tract published in 1589. Stubbes himself throws some light upon his life, in his memorial account of his young wife, whose "right virtuous life and Christian death" are circumstantially set forth. The editor believes him to have been a gentleman — "either by birth, profession, or both"; to have written, from 1581 to 1610, pamphlets and books strongly on the Puritan side; before 1583 to have spent "seven winters and more, traveling from place to place, even all the land over indifferently." It is supposed that in 1586 he married a girl of fourteen. Her death occurred four years and a half afterwards, following not many weeks the birth of a "goodly man childe." Stubbes's own death is supposed to have taken place not long after 1610.

'The Anatomie of Abuses' was published in two parts. These are in the form of a dialogue between Spudens and Philoponus (Stubbes), concerning the wickedness of the people of Ailgna (England). Part First deals with the abuses of Pride, of Men's and Women's Apparel; of the vices of whoredom, gluttony, drunkenness, covetousness, usury, swearing, Sabbath-breaking, stage-plays; of the evils of the Lords of Misrule, of May-games, church-ales, wakes, feasts, of "pestiferous dancing," of music, cards, dice-tables, tennis, bowls, bear-baiting; of cock-fighting, hawking, and hunting, on the Sabbath; of markets, fairs, and foot-ball playing, also on the Sabbath; and finally of the reading of wicked books; the whole being followed by a chapter on the remedy for these evils.

Part Second deals with corruptions in the Temporalty and the Spiritualty. Under temporal corruptions the author considers abuses in law, in education, in trade, in the manufacture of apparel, in the relief of the poor, in husbandry and farming. He also considers abuses among doctors, chandlers, barbers, apothecaries, astronomers, astrologers, and prognosticators.

Under matters spiritual the author sets forth the Church's sins of omission rather than of commission; but he treats of wrong preferment, of simony, and of the evils of substitution.

The entire work is most valuable, as throwing vivid light upon the manners and customs of the time, especially in the matter of dress. An entire Elizabethan wardrobe of fashion might be reproduced from Stubbes's circumstantial descriptions. Concerning hose he writes:

"The Gally-hosen are made very large and wide, reaching downe to their knees onely, with three or four guardes a peece laid down along either hose. And the Venetian hosen, they reach beneath the knee to the gartering place to the Leg, where they are tyed finely with silk points, or some such like, and laied on also with reeves of lace, or gardes as the other before. And yet notwithstanding all this is not sufficient, except they be made of silk, velvet, saten damask, and other such precious things beside."

ANATOMY OF MELANCHOLY, by Robert Burton (1621), is a curious miscellany, covering so wide a range of subjects as to render classification impossible. This torrent of erudition flows in channels scientifically exact. Melancholy is treated as a malady, first in general, then in particular. Its nature, seat, varieties, causes, symptoms, and prognosis are considered in an orderly manner, with a great number of differentiations. Its cure is next examined, and the various means discussed which may be adopted to accomplish this. Permissible means, forbidden means, moral means, and pharmaceutical means are each analyzed. After disposing of the scholastic method, the author descends from the general to the particular, and treats of emotions and ideas minutely, endeavoring to classify them. In early editions of the book, there appear at the head of each part, synoptical and analytical tables, with divisions and subdivisions, — each subdivision in sections and each section in subsections, after the manner of an important scientific treatise. While the general framework is orderly, the author has filled in the details with most heterogeneous material. Every conceivable subject is made to illustrate his theme: quotations, brief and extended, from many authors; stories and oddities from obscure sources; literary descriptions of passions and follies; recipes and advices; experiences and biographies.

ANCIENT LAW, by Henry Sumner Maine (1861). In his remarkable work on 'Ancient Law: Its Connection with the Early History of Society, and Its Relation to Modern Ideas,' Sir Henry Maine attempted to indicate some of the earliest ideas of mankind, as reflected in ancient law, and to point out the relation of those ideas to modern thought. To a large extent the illustrations were drawn from Roman law, because it bears in its earliest portions traces of the most remote antiquity, and at the same time it supplies many elements of modern culture. A principal contention of Maine was that patriarchal or fatherly authority was the earliest germ of social order. The distinction given the author by this work led to his having a seven years' period of service in India as legal member of the Council; and on his return to England and appointment to a professorship of jurisprudence at Oxford, his first course of lectures was published as 'Village Communities' (1871). It was another course of Oxford lectures which gave the substance of his 'History of Early Institutions' (1875); in which, as in 'Village Communities,' he drew from knowledge gained in India to throw light upon ancient social and political forms. Not only were these works among the first examples of thorough historical research into the origins of social order and political organization, but the skill in exposition and admirable style in which they are executed make them of permanent interest as models of investigation. The work of Maine on the origin and growth of legal and social institutions was completed by a volume in 1883 on 'Early Law and Custom.' His effort is still to reconcile the growth of jurisprudence with the results obtained by modern anthropology, while each study is made to explain and illuminate the other. Beginning with the primitive religion and law, as disclosed in the earliest written monuments preserved in the sacred Hindoo laws, the rise of the kingly power and prerogative and the meaning of ancestor-worship are discussed. The book closes with a study of the feudal theory of property, and its effect upon modern systems of rental and landholding.

ANCIENT MARINER, see **RIME OF THE**.

ANCIENT POTTERY, HISTORY OF, GREEK, ETRUSCAN, AND ROMAN, by H. B. Walters (1905). The importance of ceramics to the historic student is obvious. "Among the simplest yet most necessary adjuncts of a developing civilization," says Mr. Walters, "Pottery may be recognized as one of the most universal. The very earliest and rudest remains of any people generally take the form of coarse and common pots, in which they cooked their food or consumed their beverages." Moreover the evidence supplied by ceramics is contemporary, and from this study we not only learn what were the common everyday lives of a people, but see the first beginnings and the gradual evolution of such artistic instinct as they may have possessed. The scope of the book is to trace the history of the art of working in clay from its use among the oldest nations of antiquity to the period of the decline of the Roman Empire. The importance of Greek ceramics is twofold. In grace of artistic form the Greeks excelled all nations, either past or present. So rapid and successful in recent years has been the progress of investigation that no branch of classical archæology has become so firmly established or so fertile in results as the study of fictile art among the Greeks. Moreover to the Greek art was the language by which he expressed his ideas of the gods. The pottery of the Etruscan epoch, that is the period previous to the Roman domination of Italy, was characterized by a development of geometrical decoration, probably under Eastern influence. The work of the Roman period, from the second century onwards and including the remains of similar pottery from Gaul, Britain, and other countries over which Roman sway extended, was in nearly all respects inferior to Greek. It had less artistic skill, and, generally speaking, bore the same relation to Greek ceramic products as all Roman art did to Greek art. It was, in other words, more mechanical and less imaginative and inspired. Mr. Walters has enriched his history with a large number of valuable illustrations which really elucidate the text.

ANCIENT RÉGIME, THE, by H. A. Taine (1875). A study of the France which, after twelve hundred years of development, existed in 1789; the part which clergy, nobles, and king played in it; the organization of politics, society, religion, and the church; the state of industry, education, science, and letters; and the condition of the people: with reference especially to the causes which produced the French Revolution, and through that catastrophic upheaval created a new France. Not only the more general facts are brought to view, but the particulars of industrial, domestic, and social life are abundantly revealed. First the structure of society is examined; then the habits and manifestations of character which were most notably French; then the elements of a dawning revolution, the representative figures of a new departure, master minds devoted to new knowledge; philosophers, scientists, economists, seeking a remedy for existing evils; then the working of the new ideas in the public mind; and finally the state of suffering and struggle in which the mass of the people were. A masterly study of great value for the history of France and for judgment of the future of the French Republic. Taine's phenomenal brilliancy of style and picturesqueness of manner, his philosophical contemplation of data, and his keen reasoning, have never been more strikingly exhibited than in these volumes, which are as absorbing as fiction.

ANCIENT ROME IN THE LIGHT OF RECENT DISCOVERIES, by Rodolfo Lanciani, Professor of Archæology in the University of Rome, and Director of Excavations for the National Government and the Municipality of Rome (1888). In his character of official investigator, Professor Lanciani has grouped, in this volume, various illustrations of the life of ancient Rome as shown in its recovered antiquities, — columns, capitals, inscriptions, lamps, vases; busts or ornaments in terra-cotta, marble, alabaster, or bronze; gems, intaglios, cameos, bas-reliefs, pictures in mosaic, objects of art in gold, silver, and bronze; coins, relics in bone, glass, enamel, lead, ivory, iron, copper, and stucco: most of these newly found treasures being genuine masterpieces. From these possessions he reads the story of the wealth, taste, habits of life, ambitions, and ideals of a vanished people. The book does not attempt to be systematic or exhaustive, but it is better. It is full of a fine historic imagination, with great charm of language, and perennial richness of incident and anecdote which make it not only delightful reading, but the source of a wide new knowledge. With the true spirit of the story-teller, Professor Lanciani possesses an unusual knowledge of out-of-the-way literature which enriches his power of comparison and illustration. 'Pagan and Christian Rome' (1892) made up in part of magazine articles, and intentionally discursive, attempts to measure in some degree the debt of Christian art, science, and ceremonial to their Pagan predecessors. 'Ruins and Excavations of Ancient Rome, a Companion Book for Students and Travelers' (1897) is, on the other hand, a systematic treatise on modern discovery, supplied with maps, diagrams, tables, lists, and a bibliography. The descriptions begin with the primitive palisades, and come down to the present time, treating prehistoric, republican, imperial, mediæval, and modern Rome; and the book, though more formal, is hardly less entertaining than its predecessors.

3

ANCIENT STONE IMPLEMENTS, WEAPONS, AND ORNAMENTS OF GREAT BRITAIN, THE, by Sir John Evans (1872). The various forms, probable uses, methods of manufacture and in some instances the circumstances of discovery of these relics of the Stone Age are the theme of this volume. Stone instruments found in ossiferous caves and ancient alluvial deposits and associated with the remains of a fauna now largely extinct are said to belong to the palæolithic as distinguished from the neolithic period, the remains of which are usually found on or near the surface of the soil. The discoveries of Dr. Schmerling in the caves of Belgium, first published in 1833 and confirmed by later investigators, showed that human bones, worked flints, and bone instruments were often found close to the remains of extinct animals. Sir John Evans describes in detail a number of stone implements of the earlier and later periods, which had been manufactured for use as flints, hatchets, arrowheads, grinding utensils, or for other purposes of war, the chase, or peace. Stone celts, which at first were universally believed to have been thunderbolts and therefore to possess medical or preservative virtues, were in the early stages of their evolution chipped or rough hewn, then ground at the edge only, then polished, then hafted. Axes and hammers were first employed as weapons and only later served as tools. Knives, occasionally perhaps used as lanceheads, were sometimes oval, sometimes circular or triangular. Javelin and arrowheads, supposed to have fallen from heaven, and therefore worn as amulets, sling-stones, roughly chipped from flint, or the ornamented balls which prehistoric Scotland used as missiles; the implements of war, the chase, and domestic use are described with a wealth of historic evidence and a large number of admirable illustrations.

ANDES AND THE AMAZON, THE, or, Across the Continent of South America, by James Orton (1870). In 1868, under the auspices of the Smithsonian Institution, Mr. Orton, who for many years was professor of natural history in Vassar College, led an exploring expedition to the equatorial Andes and the river Amazon; the experiences of the party being vivaciously set forth in this popular book. Before this exploration, as Mr. Orton explains, even central Africa had been more fully explored than that region of equatorial America which lies in the midst of the western Andes, and upon the slopes of those mountain monarchs which look toward the Atlantic. A Spanish knight, Orellana, during Pizarro's search for the fabled city of El Dorado in 1541, had descended this King of Waters (as the aborigines called it); and with the eyes of romance, thought he discovered on its banks the women warriors for whom he then newly named the stream the "Amazon," — a name still used by the Spaniards and the Portuguese in the plural form, Amazonas. Except for one Spanish exploration up the river in 1637, the results of which were published in a quaint and curious volume, and one French exploration from coast to coast eastward in 1745, and the indefatigable missionary pilgrimages of Catholic priests and friars, the great valley remained but vaguely known. National jealousies had kept the river closed to foreign navigation, until, by a larger policy, it was made free to the flags of all nations in 1867. 'The Andes and the Amazon' is not intended to be a scientific record of newly discovered data. Whatever biological or archæological contributions it offers are sufficiently intelligible and accurate, and there is scattered through the three hundred and fifty pages of the book a large amount of general information, such as a trained observer would instinctively gather, and an intelligent audience delight to share.

ANDROMACHE, a tragedy by Euripides. The heroine (Hector's widow) is part of the spoil of Pyrrhus, the son of Achilles, in the sack of Troy. She has of course undergone the usual fate of feminine captives, and has borne her master a son named Molossus. Hermione, the daughter of Menelaus and lawful wife of Pyrrhus, is furiously jealous of this Trojan slave; and with the aid of her father, resolves to kill Andromache and the child during the absence of her husband. Fortunately the aged Peleus, the grandfather of Pyrrhus, arrives just in time to prevent the murder. Orestes, a cousin of Hermione, to whom she had formerly been betrothed, stops at her house on his way to Dodona. Hermione, fearing the resentment of her spouse, flies with him. Then they lay an ambuscade for Pyrrhus at Delphi and slay him. Peleus is heart-broken when he learns the tidings of his grandson's fate; but he is visited by his wife, the sea-goddess Thetis, who bids him have done with sorrow, and send Andromache and her child to Molossia. There she is to wed Helenus, the son of Priam, and for the rest of her life enjoy unclouded happiness. Thetis orders the burial of Pyrrhus in Delphi. Peleus himself will be released from human griefs, and live with his divine spouse forever in the palace of Nereus beneath the sea, in the company of his son Achilles.

ANDROMACHE ('Andromaque'), a tragedy by Racine (1667), suggested to him by some lines in the Æneid of Virgil. The play owes very little to the 'Andromache' of Euripides except the title. In Euripides, everything is simple and true; in Racine, everything is noble, profound, and impassioned. The Andromache of the French poet is a modern Andromache, not the real Andromache of antiquity; but the drama is one of his greatest works, and wrought a revolution in French dramatic art by proving that the delicate shades and almost imperceptible movements of the passion of love could be an inexhaustible source of interest on the stage. The drama was parodied by Subligny in his 'Folle Querelle.' Racine suspected that the parody was written by Molière, and the affair was the occasion of a serious breach between them.

ANGEL IN THE HOUSE, THE, Coventry Patmore's most noted poem, was published in four parts between 1854 and 1862. 'The Betrothal' appeared in 1854, 'The Espousals' in 1856, 'Faithful Forever' in 1860, and 'The Victories of Love' in 1862. The entire poem is idyllic in form. It is a glorification of domestic life, of love sheltered in the home, and guarded by the gentle and tender wife. In consequence it has been extremely popular in British families of the class it describes, — highbred gentlefolk, to whom the household is the centre of refining affection.

ANIMAL SYMBOLISM IN ECCLESIASTICAL ARCHITECTURE, by E. P. Evans (1896). A work of curious interest, designed to trace the very wide use of animal symbols in religious relations. The famous work of an Alexandrian Greek, known as the 'Physiologus' or The Naturalist, became at a very early date a compendium of current opinions and ancient traditions touching the characteristics of animals and of plants, viewed as affording moral or religious suggestion. The mystical meaning of the various beasts grew to be a universally popular study, and the 'Physiologus' was translated into every language used by readers. "Perhaps no book," says Mr. Evans, "except the Bible, has ever been so widely diffused among so many peoples and for so many centuries as the 'Physiologus.'" The story of this symbolism in its application, with modifications, in architecture, is told by Mr. Evans with fullness of knowledge and sound judgment of significance of facts. It is a very curious and a singularly interesting history.

ANNA KARÉNINA, a famous novel of contemporary life, by Count Lyof Tolstoy (1873-76), was first published as a serial in the Russian Contemporary, an English translation appearing in 1886. The remarkable character of the book places it in the category of world-novels. Its theme — the simple one of the wife, the husband, and the lover — is treated with a marvelous perception of the laws of morality and of passion. The author depicts the effect upon a high-bred sensitive woman of the violation of the moral code, through her abandonment to passion. The character of Anna Karénina is the subject of a subtle psychological study. A Russian noble-woman, young, beautiful, and impressionable, she is married to a man much older than herself. While visiting in Moscow, in the household of her brother Prince Stepan Oblonsky, she meets Count Vronsky, a brilliant young officer. He loves her, and exercises a fascination over her which she cannot resist. The construction of the novel is intricate, involving the fortunes of many other characters; fortunes which present other aspects of the problems of love and marriage. The interest is centred, however, in Anna Karénina. No criticism can convey the powerful impression of her personality, a personality colored by the mental states through which she passes, — dawning love, blind passion, maternal tenderness, doubt, apprehension, defiance, sorrow, and finally despair. The whole of a woman's heart is laid bare. The realism of Anna Karénina is supreme and merciless. Its fidelity to the life it depicts, its strong delineation of character, above all its masterly treatment of a theme of world-wide interest, place it among the first novels of the nineteenth century.

ANNALS OF A FORTRESS, by E. Viollet-le-Duc: translated by Benjamin Bucknall (1876). A work of highly practical fiction, telling the story through successive ages of an ideal fortress, supposed to have been situated at a point on a branch of the Saône River which is now of special importance in view of the present eastern fron-tier of France. The story follows the successive ages of military history from early times down to the present, and shows what changes were made in the fortress to meet the changes in successive times in the art of war. The eminence of the author, both as an architect and military engineer, enabled him to design plans for an ideal fortress, and to give these in pictorial illustrations. The work is as entertaining to the reader as it is instructive to the student of architecture, and the student of war for whom it is especially designed.

ANNALS OF A PUBLISHING HOUSE, see **BLACKWOOD, WILLIAM.**

ANNALS OF A QUIET NEIGHBORHOOD, by George Macdonald (1866), records a young vicar's effort to be a brother as well as a priest to his parishioners; and tells incidentally how he became more than a brother to Ethelwyn Oldcastle, whose aristocratic, overbearing mother, and madcap niece Judy, have leading rôles in the story. At first Judy's pertness repels the reader; but like the bad boy who was not so very bad either, she wins increasing respect, and is able, without forfeiting it, to defy her grandmother, the unlovely Mrs. Oldcastle, whose doting indulgence has come so near ruining her disposition. Anyone wishing to grasp the true inwardness, as well as the external features, of the life of an English clergyman trying to get on to some footing with his flock, has it all here in his own words, with some sensational elements intermingled, for which he makes ample apology. But the book on the whole is free from puritanical self-arraignment. The constant moralizing never becomes tiresome, as in some of the author's later work. "If I can put one touch of rosy sunset into the life of any man or woman of my cure, I shall feel that I have worked with God," mutters the young vicar on overhearing a lad exclaim that he should like to be a painter, because then he could help God paint the sky; and this hope, the first the clergyman dares form, is equally carried out in the case of rich and poor. With regard to both these divisions of society there is much wholesome plain-speaking, as where it seems to the vicar "as if the rich had not quite fair play; . . . as if they were sent into the world chiefly for the sake of the cultivation of the virtues of the poor, and without much chance for the cultivation of their own." From this acute but pleasant preamble to his heart-warming "God be with you" at the end, this mellow character, capable of innocent diplomacy and of sudden firmness upon occasion, only loses his temper once, and that is when the intolerable Mrs. Oldcastle makes a sneering reference to the "cloth."

ANNALS OF A SPORTSMAN, by Ivan Turgéneff, consists of a number of sketches of Russian peasant life, which appeared in book form in 1852, and established the author's reputation as a writer of realistic fiction. Turgéneff represents himself with gun on shoulder tramping the country districts in quest of game and, in passing, noting the local life and social conditions, and giving closely observed, truthful studies of the state of the serfs before their liberation by Alexander II.; his book, it is believed, being one of the agencies that brought about that reform. Twenty-two short sketches, sometimes only half a dozen pages long, make up the volume. Peasant life is depicted, and the humble Russian toiler is put before the reader in his habit as he lived in the earlier years of the nineteenth century; contrast being furnished by sketches of the overseer, the landed proprietor, and representatives of other intermediate classes. The general impression is sombre: the facts are simply stated, leaving the inference of oppression, cruelty, and unenlightened misery to be drawn. There is no preaching. The best of the studies 'The Burgomaster,' 'Lgove,' 'The Prairie,' 'The Singers,' 'Kor and Kalmitch,' 'The District Doctor' — are little masterpieces of analysis and concise portrayal, and a gentle poetic melancholy runs through all. Especially does the poetry come out in the beautiful descriptions of nature, which are a relief to the poignant pathos of some of the human scenes.

ANNALS OF RURAL BENGAL (1868, 5th ed. 1872), and its sequel **ORISSA** (2 vols., 1872), by Sir William Wilson Hunter. In these volumes one of the most admirable civilians that England ever sent to India displays his finest qualities: not alone his immense scholarship and his literary charm, but his practical ability, his broad humanity and interest in the "dim common populations sunk in labor and pain," and his sympathy with religious aspiration. The first volume is a series of essays on the life of the peasant cultivator in Bengal after the English ascendency: his troubles over the land, the currency, the courts, the village and general governments, the religious customs, and the other institutions, all bearing directly on his prosperity. A valuable chapter is on the rebellion of the Santal tribes and its causes. It is interesting to know that he ranks Warren Hastings very high as a sagacious and disinterested statesman, and says that no other name is so cherished by the masses in India as their benefactor. 'Orissa' is a detailed account of all elements of life and of history in a selected Indian province; a study in small of what the government has to do, not on great theatrical occasions but as the beneficial routine of its daily work. Incidentally, it contains the best account anywhere to be found of the pilgrimages of "Juggernaut" (Jaganath); and an excellent summary of the origins of Indian history and religions.

ANNALS OF THE PARISH, by John Galt,— a native of Ayrshire, Scotland, — was published in 1821. In the spirit, if not in the letter, this work is the direct ancestor of the tales of Maclaren and Barrie. Although it cannot properly be called a novel. it is rich in dramatic material. It purports to be written by Mr. Balwhidder, a Scottish clergyman, who recounts the events in the parish of Dalmailing where he ministered. He carries the narrative on from year to year, sometimes recording an occurrence of national importance, sometimes a homely happening, as that William Byres's cow had twin calves "in the third year of my ministery." There was no other thing of note this year, "saving only that I planted in the garden the big pear-tree, which had two great branches that we call the Adam and Eve." Concerning a new-comer in the parish he writes: "But the most remarkable thing about her coming into the parish was the change that took place in the Christian names among us. Old Mr. Hooky, her father, had, from the time he read his Virgil, maintained a sort of intromission with the nine Muses by which he was led to baptize her Sabrina, after a name mentioned by John Milton in one of his works. Miss Sabrina began by calling our Jennies Jessies, and our Nannies Nancies. . . . She had also a taste in the mantua-making line, which she had learnt in Glasgow; and I could date from the very Sabbath of her first appearance in the Kirk, a change growing in the garb of the younger lassies, who from that day began to lay aside the silken plaidie over the head, the which had been the pride and bravery of their grandmothers."

The 'Annals' are written in a good homely style, full of Scotch words and Scotch turns of expression. The book holds a permanent place among classics of that country.

ANNE, a novel, by Constance Fenimore Woolson, appeared serially in 1882. It immediately took, and has since maintained, high rank among American novels. The story traces the fortunes, often sad and always varied, of Anne Douglas, a young orphan of strong impulses, fine character, and high devotion to duty. The plot centres in Ward Heathcote's ardent and abiding love for Anne, and her equally constant affection for him. It is managed with much ingenuity, the study of character is close and convincing, and the interest never flags. Like all Miss Woolson's work it is admirably written.

ANNE OF GEIERSTEIN, by Sir Walter Scott (1829). This romance finds its material in the wild times of the late fifteenth century, when the factions of York and Lancaster were convulsing England, and France was constantly at odds with the powerful fief of Burgundy. When the story opens, the exiled Earl of Oxford and his son, under the name of Philipson, are hiding their identity under the guise of merchants traveling in Switzerland. Arthur, the son, is rescued from death by Anne, the young countess of Geierstein, who takes him for shelter to the home of her uncle, Arnold Biedermann, where his father joins him. On their departure they are accompanied by the four Biedermanns, who are sent as a deputation to remonstrate with Charles the Bold, concerning the oppression of Count de Hagenbach, his steward. When the supposed merchants reach the castle, they are seized, despoiled, and cast into separate dungeons by order of Hagenbach. The Black Priest of St. Paul's, a mysterious but powerful personage, now appears on the scene; and Charles, Margaret of Anjou, Henry of Richmond, and other great historic personages, are met with — all living and realizable personages, not mere names.

The story is filled with wild adventure, and the reader follows the varying fortunes of its chief characters with eager interest. It presents vivid pictures of the still-lingering life — lawless and picturesque — of the Middle Ages.

ANNEAU D'AMÉTHYSTE, see L'HISTOIRE CONTEMPORAINE.

ANNIE KILBURN, a novel of New England life, by W. D. Howells, was published in 1888. Its heroine, a woman in her later youth, returns to her native New England village after a prolonged sojourn in Rome, terminated by the death of her father. Her foreign environment has unfitted her for sympathetic residence with the friends of her girlhood, yet it has not diminished the insistency of her Puritan conscience. She does good with malice prepense, and labors to be a power for well-being in the community. Her acquaintance with a fervid young minister increases her moral intensity. She makes many mistakes, however, and grieves over them with feminine uselessness of emotion. At last she finds her balance-wheel in Dr. Morrell, a healthy-minded man. Annie is an excellent portrait of a certain type of woman. Her environment, the fussy "good society" of a progressing New England village, is drawn with admirable realism; while the disintegrating effect of the new industrial order upon the older and simpler life of narrow ambitions and static energy is skill-fully suggested.

ANTARCTIC, THE HEART OF THE, see **HEART OF THE ANTARCTIC.**

ANTE-NICENE LIBRARY, THE. 'Writings of the Apostolic Fathers Prior to 325 A.D.,' by Drs. A. Roberts and J. Donaldson (24 vols., 1867–72). A work giving in English translation the writings of the leading Christian authors for three centuries after Christ. It includes apocryphal gospels, liturgies, apologies, or defenses, homilies, commentaries, and a variety of theological treatises; and is of great value for learning what Christian life and thought and custom were, from the time of the Apostles to the Council of Nicæa. To supplement the 'Ante-Nicene Library,' Dr. Philip Schaff edited a 'Select Library of Nicene and Post-Nicene Fathers,' 14 vols. (1890–1908), beginning with Augustine and ending with Chrysostom. This covers some of the most important, and is of great value. A second series of 14 vols. (1890–1903) begins with the historians Eusebius and Socrates, and ends with Ephraem Syrus.

ANTHIA AND HABROCOMUS, or, THE EPHESIACA, a Greek romance, by Xenophon of Ephesus, written during the fourth century of the Christian era. It was lost until the eighteenth century, and then found in the Florentine library by Bernard de Montfaucon. It was at once translated into most modern languages. The subject of the story is the lot of two lovers united by marriage, but separated by destiny, and coming together again only after a long series of misfortunes. Their beauty is the cause of all their afflictions, lighting the fires of passion, jealousy, and revenge, and constantly endangering the fidelity they have sworn to each other. But, by marvelous stratagems, they triumph over all the attempts made to compel them to break their vows, and escape unharmed from the most difficult situations. At length, after many wanderings over land and sea, they meet once more. Anthia declares that she is as faithful as when she first left Tyre for Syria. She has escaped unscathed from the menaces of brigands, the assaults of pirates, the outrages of debauchees, and many a threat of death. Habrocomus assures her, in reply, that no other young girl has seemed to him beautiful, no woman has pleased him, and he is now as devotedly hers as when she left him a prisoner in a Tyrian dungeon. The faults of the story are the grotesque improbability of many of its inventions and its want of proportion; its merits are pithiness, clearness, and elegance of style.

ANTHROPOLOGY, 'An Introduction to the Study of Man and Civilization,' by E. B. Tylor (1881). A work designed to give so much of the story of man as can be made interesting to the general reader.   It tells what is known of the earliest appearance of man on the globe; of the races of mankind; of languages and writing; of the various arts of life and arts of pleasure, as they were developed; of the beginnings of science; of the earliest stages of religion, mythology, and literature; and of the first customs of human society.   The work is a valuable contribution to popular knowledge of the origins of human culture.   Like all Professor Tylor's books, it is eminently readable, though now somewhat out of date.

ANTIDOSIS, or, EXCHANGE OF PROPERTIES.   An oration by Isocrates (436–338 B. C.).   Three hundred of the richest citizens of Athens were obliged by law to build and equip a fleet at their own expense, whenever it was needed.   If one of the three hundred was able to show that a citizen, not included in the list, was wealthier than he, he could compel him to take his place or else make an exchange of property. Megacleides, a personal enemy of Isocrates, being ordered to furnish a war vessel, insisted that it was the duty of the latter to do so, adding that he was a man of bad character.   In the trial that ensued, Isocrates was condemned to deliver the trireme, or else exchange his property for that of Megacleides.

The defense, written after the trial, has the form of a forensic oration spoken before an imaginary jury, but is really an open letter addressed to the public.   Isocrates not only shows why he should not be condemned, but vindicates his whole career; he describes what a true "sophist" ought to be, and gives his ideas of the conduct of life.   Megacleides (called Lysimachus in the discourse) is termed a "miserable informer," who, by an appeal to the vulgar prejudice against the Sophists, would relieve himself from a just obligation at the expense of others.   Isocrates goes into a detailed account of his conduct as statesman, orator, and teacher.   "My discourse shall be a real image of my mind and life."   He enters minutely into his views on philosophy and education.   The object he has always set before himself has been to impart a general culture suitable for the needs of practical life.   He despises the people who "teach justice, virtue, and all such things at three minæ a head."   By philosophy he understands culture, simply; and the chief elements of culture are the art of speaking, and whatever trains the citizen for social and political success.   He attaches the utmost importance to the art of expression, for it is absolutely essential to any scheme of general culture.   To instruct his pupils how to act in unforeseen emergencies should be the great aim of the teacher.   "As we cannot have an absolute knowledge of what will happen, whereby we might know how to act and speak in all circumstances, we ought to train ourselves and others how we should act, supposing such or such a thing occurred.   The true philosophers are those who are successful in this.   Absolute knowledge of what may happen being impossible, absolute rules for guidance are absurd."   To prove the success of his system, he calls attention to the number of illustrious Greeks he has taught.

ANTIGONE, a tragedy by Sophocles (495–406 B.C.).   Thebes has been besieged by Polynices, the dethroned and banished brother of Eteocles, who rules in his stead.   The two brothers kill each other in single combat, and Creon, their kinsman, becomes king.   The play opens on the morning of the retreat of the Argives, who supported Polynices.   Creon has decreed that the funeral rites shall not be performed over a prince who has made war upon his country, and that all who contravene this decree shall be punished with death.   Antigone declares to her sister Ismene that she herself will fulfill the sacred ceremonies over her brother's corpse in spite of the royal proclamation. The tragedy turns on the inexorable execution of the law by Creon, and the obedience of Antigone to the higher law of love. Apart from its beauty and grandeur as a picture of the woman-hero, the 'Antigone' has a political value. It contains noble maxims on the duties of a citizen, and on the obligation imposed on the head of a State to be always ready to sacrifice his private feelings to the public good. While the poet attacks anarchy and frowns on any attempt to disobey the laws or the magistracy, he sees as clearly the danger of mistaken tyrannical zeal. There have been several imitations of this great drama. In Alfieri's, all the minor personages who add so much to the excellence of Sophocles's play disappear, and only Creon, Hæmon, and Antigone are left on the stage; it has many beauties and the dialogue is forceful and impassioned. Rotrou imitates the 'Thebaid' of Seneca and 'The Phœnicians' of Euripides in the second part of his 'Antigone,' and Sophocles in the first.

ANTIQUARY, THE, by Sir Walter Scott (1816). 'The Antiquary' is not one of Scott's most popular novels, but it nevertheless ranks high. If it is weak in its supernatural machinery, it is strong in its dialogue and humor. The plot centres about the fortunes and misfortunes of the Wardour and Glenallan families. The chief character is Mr. Jonathan Oldbuck, the Antiquary, whose odd sayings and garrulous knowledge are inimitably reported. Sir Arthur Wardour, the Antiquary's pompous friend, and his beautiful daughter Isabella, suffer reverses of fortune brought about mainly by the machinations of Herman Dousterswivel, a pretended adept in the black arts. Taking advantage of Sir Arthur's superstition and antiquarian vanity, he dupes that credulous gentleman into making loans, until the hero of the tale (Mr. William Lovel) comes to his rescue. He has already lost his heart to Miss Wardour, but has not put his fate to the test. His friend, and host, the Antiquary, has a nephew, the fiery Captain Hector M'Intyre, who also loves Miss Wardour. Their rivalry, the machinations and exposure of Dousterswivel, a good old-fashioned wicked mother-in-law, and other properties, make up a plot with abundance of incidents and a whole series of cross-purposes to complicate it. The best-remembered character in the book is the daft Edie Ochiltree.

ANTIQUITIES OF THE JEWS, see JEWS, HISTORY OF THE.

ANTONINA, by Wilkie Collins (1850). A romance of the fifth century, in which many of the scenes described in the 'Decline and Fall of the Roman Empire' are reset to suit the purpose of the author. Only two historical personages are introduced into the story, — the Emperor Honorius, and Alaric the Goth; and these attain only a secondary importance. Among the historical incidents used are the arrival of the Goths at the gates of Rome, the Famine, the last efforts of the besieged, the Treaty of Peace, the introduction of the Dragon of Brass, and the collection of the ransom, — most of these accounts being founded on the chronicles of Zosimus. The principal characters are Antonina, the Roman daughter of Numarian; Hermanric, a Gothic chieftain in love with Antonina; Goisvintha, sister to Hermanric; Vetranio, a Roman poet; Ulpius, a pagan priest; Numarian, a Roman Christian, father of Antonina and a fanatic; and Guillamillo, a priest. This book does not show the intricacy of plot and clever construction of the author's modern society stories: but it is full of action, vivid in color, and sufficiently close to history to convey a dramatic sense of the Rome of Honorius and the closing-in of the barbarians.

ANTONIO AND MELLIDA, History of, The First Part, and Antonio's Revenge, The Second Part, by John Marston (1602). Both parts of this play appear to have been acted as early as 1600, though not printed till 1602. In 1601 they were ridiculed in "Poetaster" by Ben Jonson, who satirized the pomposity which abounds in them. Lamb speaks with approval of the "passionate earnestness" of some passages, and later critics, while agreeing that the style and matter are unequal, accord to Marston's work the power of moving the reader by scenes of tragedy and mystery. Antonio, son of Andrugio, Duke of Genoa, and Mellida, daughter of Piero, the Duke of Venice, are in love. Andrugio is defeated by Piero, and compelled to fly for refuge to the marshes with an old nobleman, Lucio, and a page. The Duke of Venice offered a reward for the capture of Andrugio and Antonio and the latter "to apprehend the sight of Mellida," daughter of Piero, with whom he is in love, appears in the guise of an Amazon at Piero's court. Mellida flees but is captured again by her father. Andrugio, seeing his son fall dead to all appearance, offers himself to Piero, who pretends to be appeased and gives the gold, which he had promised as a reward for the heads of Andrugio and Antonio, to solemnize the unity of the two houses. Thus "the comic crosses of true love" seem to meet with a happy ending. In the second part the prologue sounds "a tragic note of preparation" for an orgy of crime. Piero poisons Andrugio, murders Antonio's friend Feliche, and places the corpse by the side of Mellida, that she may be supposed guilty of unfaithfulness to Antonio. He then plots to compass the death of Antonio and to win the hand of Antonio's mother, Maria. Mellida dies of grief, and Antonio with the help of Pandulfo (father of Feliche) and Alberto (friend of Feliche) plans revenge. They appear as maskers at a banquet given by Piero on the evening before his wedding, and, having by a ruse got the hall cleared of the guests and servants, they bind the tyrant in his chair, taunt him, and finally cut him to pieces with their swords. The avengers are invited by a grateful people to accept high offices, but they prefer "to live enclosed in holy verge of some religious order."

ANTONY AND CLEOPATRA, written about 1607, is the second of Shakespeare's Roman plays, 'Julius Cæsar' being the first. For breadth of treatment and richness of canvas it excels the latter. There is a splendid audacity and self-conscious strength, almost diablerie, in it all. In Cleopatra, the gipsy sorceress queen, the gorgeous Oriental voluptuousness is embodied; in the strong-thewed Antony, the stern soldier-power of Rome weakened by indulgence in lust. There is no more affecting scene in Shakespeare than the death, from remorse, of Enobarbus. In the whole play the poet follows North's 'Plutarch' for his facts. The three rulers of the Roman world are Mark Antony, Octavius Cæsar, and their weak tool, Lepidus. While Antony is idling away the days in Alexandria with Cleopatra, and giving audience to Eastern kings, in Italy things are all askew. His wife Fulvia has died. Pompey is in revolt with a strong force on the high seas. At last Antony is shamed home to Rome. Lepidus and other friends patch up a truce between him and Cæsar, and it is cemented by Antony marrying Cæsar's sister Octavia, to the boundless vexation of Cleopatra. What a contrast between the imperial Circe, self-willed, wanton, spell-weaving, and the sweet, gentle Octavia, wifely and loyal! From the time when Antony first met his "serpent of old Nile," in that rich Venetian barge of beaten gold, wafted by purple sails along the banks of the Cydnus, up to the fatal day of Actium, when in her great trireme she fled from Cæsar's ships, and he shamefully fled after her, he was infatuated over her, and she led him to his death. After the great defeat at Actium, Enobarbus and other intimate followers deserted the waning fortunes of Antony. Yet once more he tried the fortune of battle, and on the first day was victorious, but on the second was defeated by sea and land. Being falsely told that Cleopatra is dead, Antony falls on his sword. Cleopatra has taken refuge in her monument, and she and her women draw up the dying lover to its top. But the monument is forced by Cæsar's men, and the queen put under a guard. She has poisonous asps smuggled in a basket of figs, and applies one to her breast and another to her arm, and so dies, looking in death "like sleep," and

> "As she would catch another Antony
> In her strong toil of grace."

ANTS, BEES, AND WASPS, 'a record of observations on the habits of the social hymenoptera,' by Sir John Lubbock (Baron Avebury), was published in 1882. Based on painstaking research and a thorough acquaintance with previous investigations and written in a clear and attractive style with an abundance of interesting anecdotes and curious information, this is a book which appeals both to the scientist and to the general reader. The author had kept numerous colonies of ants under continuous observation and made some important experiments which are carefully recorded in the appendix. He is impressed by the keen instincts of ants, their social organization, and their constructive ability. Numerous experiments prove their power to distinguish colors and scents, to find their way, and to recognize and communicate with members of their own colony. They are organized in elaborate social groups, including queens, sterile female workers, and males. Among the workers a division of labor prevails, some caring for the young ants or larvæ, and the pupæ which will later turn into full-grown ants, others capturing and milking the aphides, which serve the ants as cattle and are domesticated by them, some caring for the beetles which are kept as pets, others guarding the queen or going out to make war on other ants and bringing them back as slaves. Among the numerous species of ants the author distinguishes three stages of organization, corresponding to three periods in man's social development. There are the ants which live in small communities and subsist mainly by preying upon insects, like man in the savage state, who lives in the woods and supports life by hunting; there are the ants which have developed large social groups, constructed elaborate dwellings, and domesticated the "aphides" whom they "milk." These are like man in the pastoral age, who lived on his flocks. Lastly there are ants which cultivate rice about their dwellings and store up grain. These correspond to the agricultural stage of man's progress. The worker-ants, being wingless, are of less value than bees in securing cross-fertilization of flowers, since in crawling from one flower to another they often take pollen from one blossom to another on the same plant. On the other hand, by devouring harmful insects ants render growing things an extremely beneficial service. The book is completed by two chapters recording some experiments with bees and wasps. Both can distinguish color and recognize members of their own hive or colony, but there is no evidence of family affection. A book of facts so remarkable and so reliably and pleasantly stated is deservedly the most popular of the author's productions.

APOCRYPHAL GOSPELS, and other Documents relating to the History of Christ. Translated from the originals in Greek, Syriac, Latin, etc., by B. H. Cowper. A trustworthy, scholarly, and complete collection of the writings, not included in the New Testament, which sprang up in various quarters as attempts to recover the story of Christ. They form a singular body of curious stories, mostly legendary fictions without historical value, but very interesting and significant as showing how legends could arise, what form they could take, and what ideas they embodied.

APOLLO, 'an Illustrated Manual of the History of Art throughout the Ages,' by Salomon Reinach (1904, new ed. 1913). This illustrated record of the evolution of art is a reproduction of twenty-five lectures delivered at the École du Louvre. Professor Reinach assumes that art is a social phenomenon and not merely the efflorescence of individual genius. He therefore traces the growth of the artistic faculty from the stone and bronze ages, the civilizations of Egypt, Chaldea, and Persia, and the later products of Greece and Rome to the masterpieces of Romanesque and Gothic, the architecture of the renaissance and modern times, the painting of the Netherlands, Italy, France, and Germany, and the varied products of the eighteenth and nineteenth centuries. The work is written by a master and an expert for students and learners. The variety of subjects upon which it touches is amazing and no less astonishing is its unfailing sure-footedness and sense of proportion. M. Reinach concludes with a prophecy that the social mission of art is far from coming to an end, that in the twentieth century greater importance than ever will be attached to the study of art as a branch of education. "The art of the twentieth century," he says, "will be idealistic and poetical, as well as popular; it will translate the eternal aspiration of man, of all men, towards that which is lacking in daily life, and that which completes it, those elements of superfluity and luxury which our sensibility craves and which no mere utilitarian progress can supplant." There are nearly six hundred clear and appropriate illustrations.

APOLOGIA PRO VITA SUA, Cardinal Newman's famous justification of his religious career, was published in 1865. The occasion of his writing it was the accusation by Charles Kingsley that he had been, in all but the letter, a Romanist while preaching from the Anglican pulpit at Oxford. This accusation was incorporated in an article by Kingsley upon Queen Elizabeth, published in January, 1864, in a magazine of wide circulation. In Newman's preface to his 'Apology' he quotes from this article a pivotal paragraph: — "Truth, for its own sake, has never been a virtue with the Roman clergy. Father Newman informs us that it need not and on the whole ought not to be; that cunning is the weapon which heaven has given to the saints wherewith to withstand the brute male force of the wicked world, which marries and is given in marriage. Whether his notion be doctrinally correct or not, it is at least historically so." A correspondence ensued between Kingsley and Newman, which appeared later in the shape of a pamphlet. Kingsley replied in another pamphlet. Newman then deemed the time ripe for a full and searching justification of his position, and of the position of his brother clergy. The 'Apologia' appeared the next year. In it Newman endeavors to show that from his childhood his development was a natural, logical, instinctive progress toward the Catholic Church; that the laws of his nature, and not intellectual trickery or sophistry, led him to Rome. His reason was one with his heart, his heart with his reason. Yet he does not neglect the recital of the external influences which marked the changes in his religious life. For this reason the 'Apologia' casts remarkable light upon the religious England of the first half of the nineteenth century; and especially upon its concentrated expression, the Oxford movement. Its supreme value, however, is its intimate revelation of a luminous spirituality, of a personality of lofty refinement and beauty.

APOLOGY FOR HIS LIFE. Colley Cibber's autobiography was published in 1740, when the author, poet-laureate, actor, and man-about-town was in his seventieth year. In the annals of the stage this curious volume holds an important place, as throwing light upon dramatic conditions in London after the Restoration, when the theatre began to assume its modern aspect. Cibber, born in 1671, had become a member of a London company when only eighteen years of age.

Cibber gives a very full account of famous contemporary actors and actresses: Mrs. Oldfield, Mrs. Barry, Mrs. Bracegirdle, Betterton, Kynaston, Mountford, and others. His record is valuable also as revealing the relations between the stage and the State, indicated by the various laws and restrictions in regard to the drama.

The 'Apology' is brimful of personal gossip. Cibber talks a great deal about himself, his friends, his enemies, his plays, his acting, but in a good-humored, nonchalant way. The ill-nature of Pope, who had placed him in the Dunciad, only moves him to an airy protest. Altogether his autobiography reveals an interesting eighteenth-century type of character, witty, worldly, without a gleam of spirituality, almost non-moral, yet withal kindly and companionable. Such, by his own confession, was the man who became poet-laureate to George II.

APOSTOLIC FATHERS, THE: Revised Texts, with English Translations (2 pts., 2d ed. 1889–90), by J. B. Lightfoot. A collection of about twelve of the earliest Christian writings, directly following those of the Apostles, made with great care and learning by the ablest of recent English Biblical scholars. The writings gathered into the volume represent those teachers of Christian doctrine who stand in the history nearest to the New Testament writers, and the account of them given by Dr. Lightfoot is not only the best for students, but it is of great interest to the general reader.

APRIL HOPES, a novel of two young people, by W. D. Howells, was published in 1887. In the heroine, Alice Pasmer, he has portrayed the high-bred New England girl with the Puritan conscience. The hero, Dan Mavering, a Harvard graduate of good family, has this conscience to contend with in his wooing of Alice and during his engagement with her. Their most serious misunderstandings arise from the girl's iron-clad code, which "makes no allowance for human nature." The book is well written, exhibiting the author's characteristic realism of style and treatment.

ARABIA, Central and Eastern: A Personal Narrative of a Year's Journey through (1862–63), by William Gifford Palgrave: 2 vols., 1865. One of the best reports of travel ever made. The author was a brilliant Englishman, who, after graduating at Oxford with great distinction, and a very short connection with military service in India, became a priest in the Society of Jesus, and was sent as a missionary to Syria. Here he perfectly mastered the Arabic language, and the Syrian and Arab customs. Napoleon III. called him to France in 1860 to report on the Syrian massacres; and upon this he undertook to make, at the Emperor's expense, an expedition through Arabia, where no Christian could safely risk his life. He assumed the guise of a Syrian physician and a Mohammedan, and succeeded in going through the kingdom under fanatical Wahabee rule, making observations of the greatest value.

ARABIAN NIGHTS, or, THE THOUSAND AND ONE NIGHTS, a collection of about two hundred and fifty stories, romantic and realistic, enclosed in a frame-story of a cruel king who postpones, night after night, the execution of his queen through interest in her narratives, which she takes care to leave unfinished, when the hour of execution arrives. The idea of the frame comes from India and many of the stories also, though other oriental countries have also contributed. The fourteenth or fifteenth century was the approximate date of the collection as we know it. For fuller information see the essay on 'The Arabian Nights' in the LIBRARY.

D'ARBLAY, MADAME, DIARY AND LETTERS OF. The diary and letters of Madame d'Arblay, the gifted Fanny Burney, surpass in modern estimation the rest of her writings. The record begins with 'Evelina.' The success of her first effort, the dinings, winings, and compliments that followed, are recorded with a naïve garrulousness perfectly consistent with simplicity and sincerity. The three periods of the authoress's life — her home life, her service as maid of honor to Queen Charlotte, and her subsequent travels and residence abroad with General D'Arblay — are described. She draws portraits of her friends: Johnson, Burke, Sir Joshua Reynolds, Thrale, Boswell, and her "Dear Daddy Crisp." Outside their talk of literary celebrities, these memoirs describe court etiquette under the coarse Madame Schwellenberg, the trial of Warren Hastings, the king's insanity during 1788–89, and many other incidents which were the talk of the town. In later life, after her husband had regained his command, the stay of the D'Arblays in Waterloo just before the day of the battle furnishes a passage upon great events. From this source, Thackeray, when describing the departure and death of George Osborne in 'Vanity Fair,' probably drew his material. Lively, talkative, gossipy, full of prejudices, the book is as interesting as little Frances Burney herself must have been.

ARCADIA, a rpastoral romance by Sir Philip Sidney, was begun in 1580, while he was in retirement at the seat of his brother-in-law, the Earl of Pembroke; and published in 1590, four years after his death. Composed with no thought of publication, but as an offering to a beloved sister, the Countess of Pembroke, the 'Arcadia' bears the character of a work intended for no harsher judgment than that of love and intimacy. It seems to have been written in a dreamy leisure, filling the idle spaces of long summer days, sheet after sheet passing from the poet's hand without revision, sometimes without completion. It is a pastoral of the artificial order: Arcadia is in Greece; its inhabitants are half-gods in mediæval dress, knights and shepherds, princes and helots; fair maidens who worship Christ and Apollo and other people of the same order, who never lived save in the fair and bright imagination of a poet-soldier. That the 'Arcadia' is formless and without plot constitutes much of its charm. In fairy-land there are no direct roads; and no destinations, since it is all enchanted country. There the shepherd-boy pipes "as though he should never be old," in meadows "enameled with all sorts of eye-pleasing flowers"; there the "humble valleys" are comforted with the "refreshing of silver rivers"; there, there are "pretty lambs" and "well-tuned birds."

Such was the popularity of the 'Arcadia,' that, previous to the middle of the seventeenth century, upwards of ten editions were published; a French translation appeared in 1624.

ARCHITECTURE, A HISTORY OF, in all Countries, from the Earliest Times to the Present Day, by James Fergusson (1st ed. 1867–76; 3d ed., 5 vcls., 1891–99). The method of treatment in these volumes is historical, and the aim is to trace every form from its origin and note the influence one style has had upon another. Architecture thus becomes "one of the most important adjuncts of history, filling up many gaps in the written record and giving life and reality to much that without its presence could with difficulty be realized." Still more important is its ethnographic use, for if studied in this way it may be made a more trustworthy and intelligible guide even than language to discriminate between different races of mankind. A valuable section of the book, "Ethnography as Applied to Architectural Art," shows how the religion, government, morals, literature, arts, and sciences are reflected in the architectural remains of the Turanian, Semitic, Celtic, and Aryan races. Following the historical method, Dr. Fergusson then proceeds to deal with the architecture of ancient times, under the headings (1) Egyptian, (2) Assyrian, (3) Grecian, (4) Etruscan, Roman, and Sassanian. Christian architecture is discussed topographically and the great masterpieces of France, Flanders, Germany, Scandinavia, England, Spain and Portugal, Italy, and Byzantine countries are described and criticized. Saracenic and ancient American buildings are also included in a work of vast scope and immense learning. The author thus replies to the charge that he has criticized Gothic architecture with undue severity: "My faith in the exclusive pre-eminence of mediæval art was first shaken when I became familiar with the splendid remains of the Mogul and Pathan emperors of Agra and Delhi, and saw how many beauties of even the pointed style had been missed in Europe in the Middle Ages. My confidence was still further weakened when I saw what richness and variety the Hindu had elaborated not only without pointed arches, but indeed without any arches at all. And I was cured when, after a personal inspection of the ruins of Thebes and Athens, I perceived that at least equal beauty could be obtained by processes diametrically opposed to those employed by the mediæval architects."

ARCTIC BOAT JOURNEY, AN, in the autumn of 1854, by Isaac Israel Hayes, M.D. (1860. Enlarged edition, 1867). The record of a boat journey of nearly four months, amid perils of ice and storm and extreme cold, the object of which was to carry intelligence to Upernavik, in North Greenland, of the peril in which Dr. Kane's second Grinnell expedition found itself, with their vessel hopelessly fast in the ice. The simple story of adventures is a thrilling one, and with it Dr. Hayes gives, in his final edition, information in regard to the Open Polar Sea discovered in 1854; the great Mer de Glace of Northern Greenland, of which he was one of the discoverers in 1853; and Grinnell Land, the most northern known land of the globe, his own discovery in 1854.

ARCTIC EXPLORATIONS, the Second Grinnell Expedition in search of Sir John Franklin, 1853–55, by Elisha Kent Kane (2 vols., 1856). Dr. Kane's first Grinnell Expedition voyage, which he made as a surgeon under E. J. DeHaven, 1850–51, was described in his 'U. S. Grinnell Expedition' (1854). It was by the second expedition, under his own command, that his fame as an Arctic explorer was made. The incidents of the voyage along the coast of Smith Sound to a latitude never before attained, 78° 43' N.; the winter spent in that far region; the discovery of the Humboldt glacier of Greenland, and the attempt the next spring to follow its course northward; and the series of adventures following, until the frozen-in ship had to be abandoned, and the party escaped perishing only through Kane's indefatigable exertions, supplied rich materials for the book in which Kane told the story of the more than two years' voyage. In the additions made to geographical knowledge also, and in many accurate and valuable scientific observations, Kane's work was exceptionally interesting and valuable. It brought him both popular applause from delighted readers, and honors from societies, English and French, representing the scholars of the time.

ARCTIC SERVICE, see **THREE YEARS OF.**

L'ARGENT, see **ROUGON-MACQUART.**

ARGONAUTICA, an epic poem in four cantos, by Apollonius of Rhodes, a contemporary of Ptolemy Philadelphus. Apollonius found all the elements of his poem in the legendary traditions of the Greeks; the expedition of the Argonauts being, next to the siege of Troy, the most famous event of the heroic ages, and the most celebrated poets having sung some one or other of its heroes. The first two cantos contain an explanation of the motives of the expedition, the election of Jason as commander-in-chief, the preparations for departure, and a narrative of the incidents that marked the voyage from Chalcis. The third describes the conquest of the Golden Fleece, and the beginning of Medea's love for Jason, the development of which forms the finest portion of the poem. Her hesitations and interior struggles supplied Virgil with some of his best material for the fourth book of the Æneid. In the fourth canto Medea leaves her father to follow Jason. This book is full of incident. The Argonauts go through the most surprising adventures, and encounter perils of every description, before they are able to reach the port from which they started. These various events have allowed the poet to introduce brilliant mythological pictures, such as his account of the Garden of the Hesperides. The work has been frequently translated into almost every modern language, and is admittedly the masterpiece of Alexandrian literature. The 'Argonautica' of Valerius Flaccus is an imitation of that of Apollonius, while the style is that of Virgil. Quintilian and other contemporaries of the author considered the imitation superior to the original. Most modern scholars, however, regard it as without originality or invention, and as a mere tasteless display of erudition.

ARISTOTLE'S WORKS. An English translation of the works of Aristotle is now being published by the Oxford University Press with funds, left by Professor Jowett, "to promote the study of Greek literature, especially by the publication of new translations and editions of Greek authors" (Pref.). The series was begun in 1907 under the general editorship of Professors J. A. Smith and W. D. Ross of Oxford university, with the co-operation of various scholars. The editors hope to include translations of all extant works of Aristotle. Those which have appeared are — The 'Parva naturalia,' translated by J. I. Beare and G. R. T. Ross; 'De mundo,' translated by E. S. Forster; 'De spiritu,' translated by J. F. Dobson; 'Historia animalium,' translated by D. W. Thompson; 'De partibus animalium' translated by William Ogle; 'De motu animalium,' 'De incessu animalium,' translated by A. S. L. Farquharson; 'De generatione animalium,' translated by A. Platt; 'Opuscula,' 'De coloribus,' 'De audibilibus,' 'Physiognomonica,' 'De Melisso,' 'Xenophane,' 'Georgia,' translated by T. Loveday and E. S. Forster; 'De plantis,' 'Mechanica,' 'Ventorum situs et cognomina,' translated by E. S. Forster; 'De mirabilibus auscultationibus,' translated by L. D. Dowdall; 'De lineis insecabilibus,' translated by H. H. Joachim; 'Metaphysica,' translated by W. D. Ross; 'Magna moralia,' translated by St. George Stock; 'Ethica eudemia,' 'De virtutibus et vitiis,' translated by J. Solomon. Among books of chief importance are the following:

'The Parts of Animals,' translated, with Introduction and Notes, by W. Ogle 1882, opens for the reader a special field of interest. One of the subjects of Aristotle's interest and research was animal life, the phenomena of which he carefully observed, and a theory of which he endeavored to form. In his work on the parts of animals, following that on their history, he undertook to find the causes of biological phenomena, and set forth his physiological conclusions. He showed profound scientific insight in recognizing the importance of comparative anatomy as the foundation of biology, and was one of the first to look for the laws of life in all organic beings. Although making but little approach to the exact knowledge of to-day, Aristotle's study of animals is of great interest from its anticipation of the best modern method, and to some extent from the material which it furnishes. The whole work is carefully translated and explained in Mr. Ogle's volume.

Aristotle's 'History of Animals,' in ten books, is counted one of his greatest achievements. It shows an acquaintance with about 500 species, and enumerates observations very remarkable for the time at which they were made. A translation in two volumes is given in Bohn's Library.

'On Youth and Old Age; Life and Death and Respiration,' translated, with Introduction and Notes, by W. Ogle, 1897, is the latest of the treatises devoted by Aristotle to the phenomena of animal life; and a specially important one as containing ideas of vitality, of the soul, of youth compared with age, of the contrast of life and death, and of respiration or the breath of life, and its function in the animal system. Even the errors of Aristotle are curiously interesting, and in some of his ideas there are remarkable suggestions of truth as modern research has established it. Not a little of Aristotle's reference of the phenomena of life to fire would prove sound science if a doctrine of electricity as the cause of vitality should be adopted. The translator of the work devotes an elaborate introduction to a careful review of all the points made by Aristotle, and he further appends full notes to his translation of Aristotle's text. It is easy now to correct the errors of Aristotle, but even as wrong guesses at truth they are interesting. In his conception of the animal system the play of the heart causes heat; heat causes the lungs and chest to expand; and cold air rushing in checks this expansion by neutralizing the heat.

'The Metaphysics' is one of Aristotle's most famous works and enjoyed a particular popularity in the Mediæval Universities. The title would have mystified Aristotle for it means merely "a supplement to the 'Physics,'" and was given to the work by an editor in Roman times. It deals with being as being; its properties and causes, and with God, the first mover of all things. The earlier portions contain an important review of previous Greek thought. It is not a finished work but a rather confused and repetitious compilation from various essays and discourses in which the author was grasping toward a coherent metaphysical theory. By far the best translation is that by Ross, in the Oxford edition.

'On the Soul,' the 'De Anima,' as it was called in the Middle Ages, is a species of psychology, dealing with the vital principle in men, animals, and even plants. After a review of the objections to the prevailing conception of the soul and a historical retrospect of earlier theories the author deals with the five powers of the soul, nutrition, desire, perception, movement from place to place, and, finally, thinking. Much attention is given to the nature and organs of sensation and to the deep philosophic problems involved in thought. There are many obscure and dislocated passages which have left readers in doubt as to whether Aristotle believed in the immortality of the soul; and, if he did, in what sense and to what extent. Translated by R. D. Hicks in 1907.

Aristotle's 'Politics,' G. Bekker's Greek Text of Books i., iii., iv. (vii.), with an English translation by W. E. Bolland, and short Introductory Essays by A. Lang, gives a good introduction to this part of Aristotle's writings. The essays by Lang, extending to 105 pages, give an excellent view of Greek political ideas represented by Aristotle. The fine two-volume edition of Jowett's 'Politics' of Aristotle, translated into English with an elaborate Introduction, a whole volume of critical notes, and a very full Index, puts the reader in complete possession of the means of thoroughly knowing what Aristotle taught on politics. In every respect the work is one of the most admirable presentations ever made of a masterpiece of Greek antiquity. A second work of great value is the elaborate 'Politics of Aristotle,' by W. L. Newman, who devotes an introductory volume of 580 pages to a very careful study of the political theories of Aristotle, in comparison with other Greek political teaching, and in his second and third volumes gives the Greek text of the 'Politics' with very elaborate and valuable notes. A less expensive work than Jowett's, for a good English translation of the 'Politics,' is J. E. C. Welldon's; a complete English version, with an analysis in 96 pages, and some critical footnotes. To scholars a work of elaborate learning will be found in 'The Politics of Aristotle: A Revised [Greek] Text, with Introduction, Analysis, and Commentary,' by Franz Susemihl and R. D. Hicks, of which the first volume, of 700 pages, was published in 1894.

Aristotle's 'Constitution of Athens' — Translation, Introduction, and Notes, by F. G. Kenyon, 1891; also an edition, translated, by E. Poste — is an important recent addition to our knowledge of Greek politics.

'The Nicomachean Ethics of Aristotle,' newly translated into English, by Robert Williams, 1869–91, is the most important to the modern reader of all that Aristotle has left us. The work is a brief and methodical system of moral philosophy, with much in it of connection with modern thought. The translation here given is de signed to reproduce the original in an intelligible and connected form for the benefit of the general reader. J. A. Stewart's 'Notes on the Nicomachean Ethics of Aristotle' is a two-volume work of more than a thousand pages, devoted to notes discussing and explaining, from the Greek text, the thoughts of Aristotle and the exact meaning of the Greek terms employed by him. It can be used by the English reader, without reference to knowledge of Greek.

The 'Rhetoric of Aristotle,' with a Commentary; by Edward Meredith Cope: Revised by John Edwin Sandys: (3 vols., 1877), gives Aristotle's work in the original Greek, with very full and valuable notes. Mr. Cope published in 1867 an 'Introduction to Aristotle's Rhetoric,' in which he gives a general outline of the contents of the treatise and paraphrases of the more difficult portions. With the four volumes the English reader can readily find the points and arguments of Aristotle's treatment of the art of rhetoric.

'Aristotle's Theory of Poetry and Fine Art,' with a Critical [Greek] Text and a Translation of the 'Poetics,' by S. H. Butcher (1895), is an excellent treatment of Aristotle's theory of poetry in connection with other aspects of his comprehensive thought. The insight of Aristotle in his conception of the essential character of poetry, his penetrating analysis of the imaginative creations of Greece, and his views of tragedy, limited by the theatre of his time, give a special interest to Dr. Butcher's volume.

ARMADALE, by Wilkie Collins (1866). The plot of this, like that of 'The New Magdalen,' and other of its author's later novels, is a gauntlet of defiance to the critics who had asserted that all the interest of his stories lay in the suspension of knowledge as to the dénouement. The machinery is in full view, yet in spite of this disclosure, the reader's attention is held until he knows whether the villain or her victims will come out victorious. This villain is one Lydia Gwilt, who, as a girl of twelve, has forged a letter to deceive a father into letting his daughter throw herself away. Hateful and hideous as is her character, Lydia is so drawn as to exact a certain pity from the reader, by reason of her lonely childhood and her strong qualities. The few minor characters of the book, though distinct enough, do not detain the reader, eager to know the fate of poor Ozias, the hero, who is a lovable fellow. Among the few minor characters in this novel are Mrs. Oldershaw, Mr. Felix Bashwood, and Mr. Pedgift the lawyer.

ARMOREL OF LYONESSE, by Sir Walter Besant, published in 1884. The scene is the Scilly (or Lyonesse) Isles (twenty-five miles south of England). Alone on one of these (Samson) lives an old woman of nearly a hundred, Ursula Rosevean, with her great-great-great-granddaughter Armorel and the Tryeth family of four. To them come Dick Stephenson and Roland Lee, the latter an artist saved from shipwreck by Armorel. Roland finds a strong attraction in Armorel, and remains at the islands three weeks. He returns to London, where, later, Armorel is instrumental in extricating him from a network of evil in which he has become involved through one false step. The intricacy of the plot is worthy of Wilkie Collins.

ARMY LIFE IN A BLACK REGIMENT, by Thomas Wentworth Higginson (1870). The First South Carolina Volunteers was the first slave regiment mustered into the service of the United States during the late Civil War. It was viewed in the beginning more in the light of an experiment than as an actual factor in the war, and Colonel Higginson, who left a company of his own raising to take command, tells the story of this experiment in the form of a diary, the first entry being dated Camp Saxton, Beaufort, South Carolina, November 24th, 1862; the last, February 29th, 1864. While the regiment did not engage in any great battles, it made many minor expeditions, was on picket duty, engaged in constructing forts, etc., all these duties being described in detail. The diary is valuable, in the first place, for the account of camp life, its privations and pleasures, work and recreation; secondly, for the description of the colored man as a soldier, and the amusing accounts of his peculiarities before freedom had made him "more like white men, less naïve, less grotesque." Many quaint negro songs are given, and stories told in dialect. The diary displays great moderation and good taste, — merits never absent from Colonel Higginson's work; and had it no other merit, it would be delightful reading, from its vivid description of Southern scenes and its atmosphere of Southern life.

ARNE, by Björnstjerne Björnson, was published in 1858, when the author was twenty-six. It was the second of the delightful idyllic tales of Norwegian country life with which Björnson began his literary career. It is a simple, beautiful story of the native life among the fiords and fells, with a charming love interest running through it. There is no intricacy of plot, and the charm and power come from the sympathetic insight into peasant character and the poetical way it is handled. Arne is a typical son of the region, sketched from his days of boyhood to his happy marriage. The portrayal of Margit, Arne's mother, is a pathetic and truthful one; and many of the domestic scenes have an exquisite naturalness.

ARNOLD, THOMAS, LIFE AND CORRESPONDENCE OF, by A. P. Stanley (1844). Dean Stanley's vivid and fascinating personality will perhaps best be remembered as a magnetic influence rather than as a figure in literature. His first work of importance, and by common consent his best and the one most likely to live, is his Life of the famous head-master of Rugby School. Arnold's greatness as a schoolmaster consisted in his recognizing, to use Stanley's words, "in the peculiar vices of boys the same evils which, when full grown, become the source of so much social mischief"; "he governed the school precisely on the same principles as he would have governed a great empire"; "constantly, to his own mind or to his scholars, he exemplified the highest truths of theology and philosophy in the simplest relations of the boys towards each other, or towards him." "The business of a schoolmaster," he used to say, "no less than that of a parish minister, is the cure of souls." The lads were treated as schoolboys, but as schoolboys who must grow up to be Christian men. The aim of the teacher was to foster, first, religious and moral principles; second, gentlemanly conduct; third, intellectual ability. As a scholar Arnold was one of the first to introduce into England the historic methods of men of the school of Niebuhr, the historian of Rome. In his view the aim of education should be to attain to Christianity without sectarianism. Similarly, Church and State should be coterminous and the aim of the Church should be "to Christianize the nation, to introduce the principles of Christianity into men's social and civic relations, and expose the wickedness of that spirit which maintains the game laws, and in agriculture and trade seems to think that there is no such sin as covetousness, and that if a man is not dishonest, he has nothing to do but to make all the profit of his capital that he can." Stanley has adopted the unfortunate method of appending Arnold's letters at the end of each chapter, instead of weaving them into the narrative.

AROUND A SPRING ('Autour d'une Source'), by Gustave Droz, is a French idyl of country life in the last century, charming in its truthful presentation of a village community. It was published in 1869. The hero is the Abbé Roche, a middle-aged priest in a mountain town. He is a man of noble, vigorous nature, and fine presence, with no experience of the outside world. To the long-untenanted château of Manteigney comes its count, with his pretty young wife, a rather light fashionable Parisian, whose money has enabled her husband to rehabilitate his ancestral possessions. She is a strange, alluring apparition to the priest, and he loves her, to his sorrow. She is a somewhat cynical study of a social butterfly. The attraction of the tale lies in the romantic nobility of the Abbé, the poetry with which the country scenes are depicted, — the fact that Droz was originally a painter comes out in his picturesque descriptions, — and the light touch with which the frivolous folk of the château are portrayed. The title of the story refers to a medicinal spring that is discovered on the Manteigney estate.

AROUND THE WORLD IN EIGHTY DAYS, by Jules Verne (1873). Phileas Fogg, a respectable English gentleman of phlegmatic temperament and methodical habits, maintains, during a discussion at his club in London, that a man can travel around the world in eighty days; and to prove it, he makes a wager of half his fortune that he can do it himself in that time. The bet is accepted, and he starts the same night, taking his French servant Passepartout with him. He wins his wager, after a series of adventures in which nature, man, accident, and the novelist combine to defeat him, but are all baffled by his unfailing resource, iron will, invincible coolness.

and Napoleonic readiness to sacrifice everything else to the one essential point; — everything except humanity, in whose behalf he twice risks defeat, first to save from suttee the beautiful young Hindoo widow Aouda, and second to save Passepartout from murder by a Chinese mob. His virtue is rewarded by success and Aouda.

ART, LECTURES ON, by H. A. Taine (1865). M. Taine in this volume applies to art the same theory as to literature in his 'Histoire de la Littérature Anglaise.' A work of art is not an isolated creative act but is the product of (1) the sum total of the author's artistic tendencies; (2) the school to which he belongs; (3) the society amid which he lives. Hence we speak of Greek tragedy, or Gothic architecture, or Flemish painting, or French tragedy. M. Taine divides art into two groups, (1) painting, sculpture, poetry, and (2) architecture, music. "The end of a work of art," he says, "is to manifest some essential or salient character, consequently some important idea, clearer and more completely than is attainable from real objects. Art accomplishes this end by employing a group of connected parts, the relationships of which it systematically modifies. In the three imitative arts of sculpture, painting, and poetry, these groups correspond to real objects." The remainder of the lectures are devoted to an exposition of the philosophy of art in Italy, the Netherlands, and Greece. In Italy the special object of classic art was to express the ideal human form. In the Netherlands art was intimately associated with the national life and rooted in the national character itself. Greek art was marked by a sensitiveness to delicate relationships, propriety and clearness of perception, and love of beauty.

ART IN ANCIENT EGYPT, A HISTORY OF, from the French of Georges Perrot and Charles Chipiez; translated and edited by Walter Armstrong. 2 vols., 1883. — Art in Chaldea and Assyria. 2 vols., 1884. — Art in Phœnicia and its Dependencies. 2 vols., 1885. — Art in Sardinia, Judæa, and Asia Minor. 2 vols., 1890. — Art in Persia. 1 vol., 1892. — Art in Phrygia, Lydia, Caria, and Lycia. 1 vol., 1892. — Art in Primitive Greece. 3 vols., 1894.

This entire series not only constitutes a monumental contribution to the history of art in its earlier and more remote fields, but serves most admirably the purpose of a realistic recovery of the almost lost histories of the eastern originators of human culture. Perrot as author of all the narratives, and Chipiez as the maker of all the drawings and designs, have together put upon the printed and pictured page a conscientious and minutely accurate history, fully abreast of the most recent research, — French, English, German, and American, — and supplying revelations of the life, the worship, the beliefs, the industries, and the social customs of the whole eastern group of lands, from Egypt and Babylonia to Greece.

ART OF JAPAN, THE ('L'Art Japonais'), by Louis Gonse. This standard work, published in 1886, treats successively of painting, architecture, sculpture, decorative work in metal, lacquer, weaving, embroidery, porcelain, pottery, and engraving. It points out the unity and harmony of all artistic production in a country where no distinction is made between the minor and the fine arts, where even handwriting — done with the most delicate of implements, the brush — is an art within an art, and where perfect equipment implies a universality of aptitudes. But painting is the key to the entire art, and the book dwells upon all that is indigenous or not due to Chinese influence. It traces the development of the parallel schools of painting: the Tosa, dependent on the fortunes of the imperial family, and the Kano, following Chinese tradition and supported by the shogunate. The shrines of Nikko are regarded as the culminating point of architecture and painting: there is nothing in the modern Tokio to compare with them. Many pages are devoted to Hokusai; long disdained by his countrymen, but now become so important that a painting with his signature is the white blackbird of European and Japanese curiosity. Kiosai, who was fifty-two at the time of writing, is commended for his resistance to European influence. Among the abundant illustrations, several examples of colored prints are given, as well as reproductions of bronzes and lacquer. Still more interesting is the reproduction — a bronze nine feet in height, now in Paris — of the colossal Buddha of Nara, the largest statue ever cast in bronze. Throughout the book all materials and processes are clearly explained. The method of casting is the same as in Europe, the perfection of the workmanship constituting the only difference. The best ivory is of a milky transparency, — the reader is warned against *netzkes* that have been treated with tea to make them look old. Cherry-wood lends itself to the most minute requirements of the engraver. A Japanese connoisseur could judge the æsthetic value of a piece of lacquer by the quality of the materials alone. The etiquette, significance, and wonderful temper of the Japanese blade are discussed, and the deterioration of art since the revolution of 1868 lamented.

ART OF PHEIDIAS, ESSAYS ON THE, see **PHEIDIAS.**

ART OF POETRY, THE ('L'Art Poétique'), a didactic poem, by Boileau (1674). The work is divided into four cantos. In the first, the author intermingles his precepts with an account of French versification since Villon, now taking up and now dropping the subject, with apparent carelessness but with real art. The second canto treats of the different classes of poetry, beginning with the least important: eclogue, elegy, ode, epigram, sonnet, etc. The third deals with tragedy, comedy, and the epic. In the fourth, Boileau returns to more general questions. He gives, not rules for writing verse, but precepts addressed to the poet; and points out the limits within which he must move, if he wishes to become perfect in his art. Although his work is recognized as one of the masterpieces of the age of Louis XIV., Boileau has prejudices that have long been out of date. He ridicules the choice of modern or national subjects by a poet, and would have him confine himself exclusively to the history or mythology of Greece and Rome.

ART OF POETRY, OF THE ('Ars Poetica'), by Horace (65–8 B.C.). The name by which this famous work is known is not the name given it by its author, who called it simply a 'Letter to the Pisos.' It does not pretend to be a didactic treatise and is rather in the nature of a friendly talk by a man of exquisite taste and discernment. It has become the type of all works of a similar character. In the first part Horace treats of the unity that is essential to every composition, and the harmonious combination of the several parts, without which there can be no lasting success. The metre and style must also be in unison with the particular kind of poetry in question: the form of verse suited to tragedy not being suited to comedy, although it is allowable for a tragic hero to use occasionally the speech of ordinary life. The language must be adapted to the situation and passions of the character, and must be consistent throughout with the disposition assigned him by history or fable and with the age in which he lived. In the second part, the poet confines himself to the form of the drama, the principles he has already established being so general that they apply to every class of composition. This form is the representation of the action itself, and he points out the limits beyond which the dramatic writer may not go. In the third part Horace shows how a young poet will find ample material for his works in the writings of the philosophers, and above all in a careful observation of life and society. He then traces the character of a perfect poem. But perfection is not to be expected. Faults are excusable if they are rare and unimportant. What neither gods nor publishers will excuse is mediocrity. Yet mediocrity is the order of the day. One of the causes of this is that poets do not take their art seriously. But poetry is of more importance than many think. Horace concludes by counseling the author not to be in a hurry to publish, and to seek the advice of some sate guide and critic.

ARTEVELDE, see PHILIP VAN.

ARTHUR, see MORTE D'ARTHUR.

ARTIST'S LETTERS FROM JAPAN, AN, by John La Farge (1887). "The pale purple even melts around my flight," ran the author's telegram at the moment of turning his face toward those islands where, as he afterwards wrote from Nikko, "everything exists for the painter's delight." And the telegram struck the keynote of the journey; for it is *atmosphere* even more than varied information, that renders these letters remarkable. The wonderful whiteness, the "silvery milkiness," of the atmosphere was the first "absorbingly new thing" that struck the painter when he landed at Yokohama. He erects a series of brilliant *toriis* or gateways (literally *bird-perches* of the gods), the reader getting the most exquisite glimpses of life and art in the "land of inversion," where "art is a common possession." Like the shrines to which they lead, the letters are enriched with elaborate carving and delicate designs. But unlike the actual toriis, they do not of necessity point out any place, pleased rather with some tone "of meditation slipping in between the beauty coming and the beauty gone." Or they serve as a frame to a "torrent rushing down in a groove of granite" between "two rows of dark cryptomeria," or a garden or a sunset: "a rosy bloom, pink as the clouds themselves, filled the entire air, near and far, toward the light." The idealist easily passes to the effect of the moral atmosphere. The whole drift of the book is toward a purer art; but it contains much lively matter, — accounts of the butterfly dance in the temple of the Green Lotus, and of fishing with trained cormorants. A thread runs through the letters, tracing the character and progress of the usurping Tokugawa family, from the cradle of their fisherman ancestors to the graves of the great shogun and his grandson in the Holy Mountain of Nikko. In Nikko the interest culminates: there was written the chapter on *Tao*, serene as the peculiar philosophy it diffuses, and perhaps the best part of the book, which sets forth the most serious convictions on universal as well as Japanese art. Yet the letters were written without thought of publication or final gathering into this unique volume, with its various addenda and the "grass characters" of its dedicatory remarks peeping out irregularly, like the "lichens and mosses and small things of the forest" that "grow up to the very edges of the carvings and lacquers."

ARYAS, SACRED LAWS OF THE, see SACRED BOOKS OF THE EAST.

AS IT WAS WRITTEN, 'a Jewish Musician's Story,' by Sidney Luska (Henry Harland). This story is as fatalistic as the Rubáiyát, though the scene is laid in modern New York. Ernest Neumann, a young violinist of great promise, but of painfully sensitive temperament, falls in love with a beautiful girl of his own race, Veronika Pathzuol, living with her uncle Tibulski, a kindly old dreamer and an unsuccessful musician, whom she supports by singing and teaching. Ernest and Veronika are shortly to be married, when she, in the absence of her uncle, is murdered in her bed. The mystery of this murder is the motive of the ensuing plot. Sombre and tragic though it is, the romance shows unusual vigor of conception and execution, and extraordinary intuitive knowledge of the psychology of an alien race.

AS YOU LIKE IT (1600). In this happiest of his middle-period comedies, Shake-speare is at no pains to avoid a tinge of the fantastical and ideal. Its realism lies in its gay riant feeling, the fresh woodland sentiment, the exhilaration of spirits that attend the escape from the artificialities of urban society. For one reason or another all the characters get exiled, and all meet in the Forest of Arden, where "as you like it" is the order of the day. There is the manly young Orlando, his villainous elder brother Oliver, and their servant Adam. At court is the reigning duke, his daughter Celia, her cousin Rosalind, and Touchstone the clown. In the forest, the banished elder duke (father of Rosalind) and the melancholy Jacques, and other lords who are blowzed with sun and wind a-chasing the dappled deer under the greenwood tree; the pealing bugle, the leaping arrow, the *al fresco* table loaded with the juicy roast of venison, and long idle summer hours of leisurely converse. On the outskirts of the forest are shepherd swains and lasses, — old Corin, Silvius (in love with Phebe), and the wench Audrey. Orlando has had to fly from his murderous brother. Rosa-lind has been banished the court by her uncle, and she and Celia disguised as shepherd men have slipped away with Touchstone. Now Rosalind has been deeply smitten with Orlando since she saw him overcome the duke's wrestler, and he is equally in love with her. We may imagine her as "a nut-brown maid, tall, strong, rustically clad in rough forest garments," and possessing a perennial flow of cheerful spirits, a humor of the freshest and kindliest. Touchstone is a fellow of twinkling eye and dry and caustic wit, his face as solemn as a churchyard while his hearers are all agrin. He and Jacques look at life with a cynical squint. Jacques is a blasé libertine, who is pleased when things run counter and athwart with people, but is after all not so bad as he feigns to be. Like a series of dissolving views, scene after scene is glimpsed through the forest glades — here the forester lords singing, and bearing the antlers of the stag; there lovesick Orlando carving verses on the bark of trees, or rescuing his brother from the lion. The youth Ganymede (really Rosalind) pretends she can cure Orlando of his lovesickness by teaching him to woo him as if he were Rosalind, all of which makes a pretty pastoral picture. Anon Touchstone passes by, leading by the hand the captive of his spear, Audrey, who has never heard of poetry; or in another part of the woodland he is busy mystifying and guying the shepherd Corin. Ganymede gets the heartless coquette Phebe to promise that if she ever refuses to wed him (with whom she is smitten) she will wed her scorned and despairing admirer Silvius, and makes her father promise to give Rosalind to Orlando; then retires and comes back in her own garments as Rosalind. The play ends with a fourfold marriage and a dance under the trees.

ASLAUGA'S KNIGHT, 'a tale of mediæval chivalry,' by Friedrich Fouqué, Baron de la Motte (1814). Aslauga was a Danish queen, whose memory was preserved in an illuminated volume that told of her good and beautiful life. The fair knight Froda read in this book, and made a vow that Aslauga should be his lady, the object of his love and worship. She thereupon appears to him, an entrancing visionary form. From that day forth he often sees her, in the dimness of the forest, or mingling with the glory of the sunset, or gliding in rosy light over the winter sea. She protects him in a great tournament, where the bravest knights of Germany fight for the hand of the Princess Hildegardis. Only Froda contends for glory, not for love, and wins.

Froda's dear friend Edwald desires to win the princess; but as he is second, not first, the scorns him. Froda is to wed the princess; but on the day of their nuptials, Froda's skyey bride, Aslauga, again appears in her golden beauty to claim her faithful knight; he dies that Edwald and Hildegardis may be one.

ASMODEUS, The Lame Devil ('Le Diable Boiteux'). A novel by Alain Réne Le Sage, first published in 1707, and republished by the author, with many changes and additions, in 1725. It is sometimes known in English as 'Asmodeus,' and sometimes as 'The Devil on Two Sticks,' under which title the first English translation appeared, and was dramatized by Henry Fielding in 1768.

The title and some of the incidents are borrowed from 'El Diablo Cojuelo' (1641) of the Spanish Luiz Veloz de Guevara. But after the first few chapters Le Sage departs widely from his predecessor. The very plan is abandoned, and the new episodes and characters introduced are entirely original with Le Sage. Guevara ends his story with awkward abruptness; while the French romancer winds up with a graceful romance, dismissing Don Cleofas to happiness with his beloved Seraphina. In short, where the two diverge the advantage is wholly with the later comer in style, wit, and ingenuity of invention. Nevertheless the conception is Guevara's. Don Cleofas, a young Spanish profligate of high lineage, proud and revengeful but brave and generous, delivers from his imprisonment in a bottle the demon Asmodeus; who in gratitude assists him in his pranks, and carries him triumphantly through a series of amusing adventures. Especially does the demon bestow on his deliverer the power of sailing through the air, and seeing through the roofs what is going on within the houses of Madrid. Le Sage introduced into his story, under Spanish names, many anecdotes and portraits of Parisian celebrities. These were all immediately recognized, and contributed greatly to the contemporary vogue of the novel, which was greater even than that of 'Gil Blas.' It is one of the famous traditions of the book trade that two young French noblemen actually fought a duel in a book-store for the possession of the only remaining copy.

ASPECTS OF FICTION, AND OTHER VENTURES IN CRITICISM (1896), by Brander Matthews, is a collection of crisp articles relating largely to novelists and novel-writing. A clever practitioner in the art of short-story writing, the author speaks here as of and to the brothers of his own craft, with an eye especially for good technique, that artistic sense of proportion and presentation so dear to his own half-Gallicized taste. 'The Gift of Story-Telling,' 'Cervantes, Zola, Kipling & Co.,' are brilliant analyses, fresh, original, pregnant, and spiced with a just measure of sparkling wit; by means of his close study of the history of fiction, he often brings the traits and practices of older authors to illuminate by a felicitous application those of contemporary novelists, discovering permanent canons of art in fresh, elusive guises. A lighter vein of humor and observation renders the paper in 'Pen and Ink' upon the 'Antiquity of Jests' an interesting and amusing bypath of research. 'Studies of the Stage' is the fruit of many years' intimacy with the history of the stage and stage conventions, aided, enriched, and deepened by an experience with such present methods of stagecraft behind the footlights as falls to the lot of a practical playwright. Mr. Matthews writes of 'The Old Comedies' and 'The American Stage' in a happy tone of reminiscence and sympathetic observation. 'The French Dramatists of the Nineteenth Century,' the best work accessible on the subject in English, is a scholarly contribution to the history of the French stage from the Romantic movement to the present day. A lifelong familiarity with French people and literature gives the judgments of Professor Matthews an especial convincingness. His 'Americanisms and Briticisms' contains a series of telling strokes at the provincialism that still characterizes some aspects of our literature.

L'ASSOMMOIR, see ROUGON-MACQUART.

ASTORIA, OR, ANECDOTES OF AN ENTERPRISE BEYOND THE ROCKY MOUNTAINS, by Washington Irving (1836; revised ed. 1849). An early work, of a somewhat rambling and disjointed nature, comprising stories of expeditions by land and sea, but presenting the history of a grand scheme, devised and conducted by a master mind, the national character and importance of which fully justified the interest which Irving was led to take in it. The characters, the catastrophe of the story, and the incidents of travel and wild life, were easily made by Irving to have the interest of a novel; and in that light, not less than as a chapter of Far West history, the work does not lose its value by the lapse of time.

ASTREA ('L'Astrée'), by Honoré d'Urfé, a famous French novel, is in five volumes. The first volume appeared in 1609, the second was published in 1616, the third in 1619, and in 1627 his posthumous notes and manuscripts were compiled into the fourth and fifth volumes, and published by his secretary Baro. Probably no other novel was ever so successful, all cultivated Europe being enthusiastic over it for many years. The period is the fourth century. Céladon, a shepherd, lover of the beautiful shepherdess Astrea, lives in the enchanted land of Foreste. While their marriage awaits parental sanction, a jealous shepherd persuades Astrea that Céladon loves Aminthe. She therefore angrily repulses him. Céladon throws himself into the river Lignon, and Astrea faints on the bank. Her parents sorrow so bitterly over her grief that both soon die. Astrea may now weep unreservedly without being suspected of mourning for Céladon. But Céladon lives. He has been succored by the Princess Galatea and her attendant nymphs, taken to court, and tenderly cared for. Thence he escapes to a gloomy cavern, where he spends his time bewailing Astrea. Meeting a friendly shepherd, he sends a letter to "the most beautiful shepherdess in the world." Astrea at once sets out to find him. Thus the story rambles on, a long, inconsequent sequence of descriptions, adventures, and moral reflections. War breaks out in Foreste. Céladon, who, disguised as a druidess, has become Astrea's friend, is with her taken prisoner, but both escape. At last he reveals himself, but is repulsed. Once more he resolves to die; all the characters accompanying him to the Fountain of Truth, whose guardian lions devour hypocrites and defend the virtuous. They spare him; and Astrea, looking into the truth-revealing water, is at last convinced of his fidelity. Everybody is a model of virtue, and the story ends with a general marriage fête. Whether 'L'Astrée' requires a key is not important. Euric may have been Henri IV., Céladon and Astrea other names for D'Urfé and his wife Diane; but probably the story is fanciful. Its charm lies in its pastoral setting, and its loftily romantic conception of love. It is a day-dream, which solaced the soldier-author himself. The story is written in straightforward, fluent French, and is full of sentiment and ingenuity; but like so many other immortal works of fiction, it lives only in the limbo of the forgotten.

ASTRONOMY, THE DAWN OF, see DAWN etc.

AT THE RED GLOVE, by Katharine S. Macquoid (1885). The scene of this slight but pleasant story is laid among the bourgeois of Berne. Madame Robineau, a mean and miserly glove-dealer, takes her pretty orphan cousin, Marie Peyrolles, to serve in her shop. The girl finds two admirers among her cousin's lodgers, — one Captain Loigerot, an elderly retired French officer, the very genius of rollicking fun and kindness; the other a handsome young bank clerk, Rudolph Engemann. The chief interest in the story follows the clever character-study of Madame Carouge and the simple life of the homely Bernese.

ATALA, a romance of the American wilderness, by Chateaubriand, was published in 1801. In a letter in the Journal des Débats, the preceding year, the author makes this reference to it: — "In my work upon the 'Genius of Christianity, or the Beauties of the Christian Religion,' a certain portion is devoted exclusively to the poesy of Christianity; . . . the work is terminated by a story extracted from my 'Travels in America,' and written beneath the very huts of the savages. It is entitled 'Atala.'" 'Atala' is an extravagant and artificial but beautiful romance of two lovers, — a young Indian brave, Chactas (i.e., Choctaw), and an Indian maiden, Atala. Chateaubriand drew his conception of Chactas — a savage, half civilized by contact with European culture — from the tradition of an Indian chief, who, having been a galley-slave at Marseilles, was afterwards liberated and presented to Louis XIV. The pivot of the romance is the power of Christianity to subdue the wildest passions of man. Atala, a Christian, has taken the vow of virginity by the death-bed of her mother. Afterwards she finds herself in love with Chactas, who has been taken prisoner by her tribe. She aids him to escape, and together they roam through the pathless forests of the New World surrounded by luxuriant nature, haunted by the genius of the wilderness, the genius of productive life. Chactas would fain be one with nature in his abandonment to instinct; but Atala, although she is consumed with love for him, is obedient to what she believes to be a higher law. In a great tempest of lightning and rain they lose their way, being found and sheltered by a pious hermit, Father Aubrey, who takes them to his cave. Atala tells him the story of her vow, and of her temptation. He replies that she may be released, but his assurance comes too late. She has taken a poison, that she may become death's bride ere she has given herself to another. The hermit fills her last hours with the comfort of his ministrations, and she departs reconciled and soothed. Chactas carries her in his arms to the grave prepared by the hermit, the wind blowing her long hair back against his face. Together they leave her to her sleep in the wilderness. 'Atala,' despite its artificiality, retains its charm to this day. Chateaubriand's savages are Europeans, his forests are in Arcadia; nevertheless the narrative has a fascination which gives it a place among the fairy-tales of fiction, — due not only to its charm of style but its noble elevation of thought.

ATALANTA IN CALYDON, by Algernon Charles Swinburne (1865), is a tragedy dealing with a Greek theme, and employing the Greek chorus and semichorus in its amplification. To this chorus are given several songs, which exemplify the highest charms of Swinburne's verse, — his inexhaustible wealth of imagery, and his flawless musical sense. The story is as follows: Althæa, the daughter of Thestius and Eurythemis, and wife to Œneus, dreams that she has brought forth a burning brand. At the birth of her son Meleager come the three Fates to spin his thread of life, prophesying three things: that he should be powerful among men; that he should be most fortunate; and that his life should end when the brand, then burning in the fire, should be consumed. His mother plucks the burning brand from the hearth and keeps it; the child grows apace and becomes in due time a great warrior. But Artemis, whose altars Œneus, King of Calydon, has neglected, grows wroth with him, and sends a wild boar to devastate his land, a beast which the mightiest hunters cannot slay. Finally all the warriors of Greece gather to rid Œneus of this plague. Among them comes the Arcadian Atalanta, a virgin priestess of Artemis, who for his love of her lets Meleager slay the boar; and he presents her the horns and hide. But his uncles, Toxeus and Plexippus, desire to keep the spoil in Calydon, and attempt to wrest it from Atalanta. In defending her, Meleager slays the two men. When Althæa hears that Meleager has slain her brothers for love of Atalanta, she throws the half-burned brand upon the fire, where it burns out, and with it his life. The feast becomes a funeral. Althæa dies of sorrow, but Meleager has preceded her; his last look being for the beautiful Atalanta, whose kiss he craves at parting, ere the night sets in, the night in which "shall no man gather fruit."

ATHALIE, a tragedy, by Racine (1691). The drama is founded on one of the most tragic events in sacred history, described in 2 Kings xi., and in 2 Chronicles xxii. and xxiii. Athaliah is alarmed by a dream in which she is stabbed by a child clad in priestly vestments. Going to the Temple, she recognizes this child in Joash, the only one of the seed royal saved from destruction at her hands. From that moment she bends all her efforts to get possession of him or have him killed. The interests and passions of all the characters in the play are now concentrated on the boy, whose restoration to the throne of his fathers is finally effected through the devotion of his followers. The drama is lofty and impressive in character, and well adapted to the subject with which it deals.

ATLANTIS, a novel by Gerhart Hauptmann (1912). A German physician, Frederick von Kammacher, is the victim of a morbid passion for a depraved young girl, Ingigerd, who has made a sensation on the stage in a dance which portrays the struggle and surrender of a spider's victim. He has recently placed his wife in an insane asylum; a scientific monograph he has written has been ridiculed by other scientists; and in the psycho-pathological state induced by depression, he is obsessed by Ingigerd's fascination. He takes passage on the ship with her to America where she is to appear in vaudeville. The action takes place almost entirely on shipboard. It is a stormy passage, and they are shipwrecked in mid-ocean, possibly on a mountain peak of the lost Atlantis. The narration of events leading up to the wreck, the description of the wreck itself, and the struggle for the lifeboats is vivid realism. He saves Ingigerd and becomes her lover. In New York they meet theatre managers, and artists, and Ingigerd begins her professional career. Frederick escapes from her to a log cabin in the country, recovering from his obsession after an attack of brain fever. His wife dies, and he marries an artist whose sane, normal comradeship had helped him to free himself from Ingigerd's toils; together the newly married pair return to Europe. The description of American personalities attracted attention because some of them seemed to be taken from the life during Hauptmann's visit to this country in 1892, and the account of the shipwreck was notable as a kind of prophetic version of the loss of the Titanic, which followed in 1912.

ATTIC PHILOSOPHER, AN ('Un Philosophe sous les Toits'), appeared in 1850. The author, Émile Souvestre, then forty-four, was already well known as a writer of stories; but this book was less a story than a collection of sympathetic moralizings upon life, "the commonplace adventures of an unknown thinker in those twelve hostelries of time called months." He shows us one year in the life of a poor working-man who, watching brilliant Paris from his garret window, knows moments of envy, ambition, and loneliness. For these moods he finds a cure in kindness to others, in a recognition of his own limitations, and in a resolve to make the best of things. The voice is that of Souvestre himself, deducing from his own experience lessons of contentment, brotherly love, and simplicity. His character sketches include the frail and deformed Uncle Maurice, learning self-abnegation; the drunken Michael Arout, regenerated through love and care for his child; the kind and ever-youthful Frances and Madeleine, middle-aged workwomen, cheerful under all hardships; and many more vivid personalities. He excels in presenting the nobility hidden under commonplace exteriors, and the pathos involved in commonplace conditions. In 1851 the French Academy crowned the 'Attic Philosopher'; and in 1854, after the death of Souvestre, it awarded his widow the Lambert prize, which is always bestowed upon the most useful author of the year.

AUCASSIN AND NICOLETTE, a twelfth-century *cante-fable*, or tale in alternating prose and verse, composed by an unknown minstrel probably of the borders of Champagne and Picardy. Its subject, the idyllic love of a youthful pair separated by religion, birth, and romantic vicissitudes, bears a general resemblance to that of the lay of *Floire et Blanchefor*. The narrative medium, a simple prose giving way at intervals to seven-syllable verses with refrain, though unique in Old-French literature, is well known to students of the popular ballad and tale in various countries. The style has an apparently artless grace and a freshness suitable to the portrayal of young love; and there is a whole-souled almost pagan devotion to worldly beauty which anticipates the Italian Renaissance. Aucassin, son of the Count de Biaucaire, falls in love with Nicolette, a Saracen maiden, brought up a Christian in the home of his father's captain. On learning of Aucassin's passion the Count orders the captain to remove her, and the latter shuts her up in his own house. Aucassin's efforts to find Nicolette are frustrated by the captain, who warns the youth that a liaison with her would conduct him to Hell. At this Aucassin bursts out that Hell, the abode of fine knights and ladies and minstrels, would be preferable to Paradise, the home of beggars, priests, and monks. Later he does valiant service against his father's enemy, Count Bougars de Valence, on the promise of a short interview with Nicolette; and when the promise is broken, he releases the Count, whom he has made prisoner. For this act Aucassin is imprisoned in a tower. Through a crevice in the wall he is addressed by Nicolette, who has escaped by letting herself down from her window. As she is telling him of her resolution to flee the country and he is begging her to be true, they are interrupted by the arrival of the city guards. Nicolette manages to cross the wall and ditch and to escape to the neighboring woods. With some shepherd boys, who take her for a fay, she leaves a message for Aucassin and then constructs a bower of boughs and leaves, where she lives in hiding. Meanwhile her escape becomes known and Aucassin is released from prison. Riding through the forest he meets the shepherd boys, who inform him of Nicolette's presence there; and after a long search, and a meeting with a gigantic swain to whom he gives money to replace a lost ox, Aucassin reaches the bower. The meeting of the lovers is described in a strain of simple, idyllic beauty and is followed by an account of their journey to the land of Torelore, a topsy-turvy realm, where the king lies in child-bed and the queen goes out to a battle in which apples, eggs, and cheeses are used for missiles. Carried off in separate vessels by Saracens the lovers are brought to their respective countries. Aucassin finds his parents dead and rules in their place; Nicolette is restored to her father, the King of Carthage. When, however, he arranges a marriage for her she steals away disguised as a jongleur, reaches the palace of Aucassin, relates to him her own story in the form of a lay, and at last reveals herself. Their happy marriage ends the tale. 'Aucassin and Nicolette' was charmingly translated by Andrew Lang in 1887.

AUDREY, by Mary Johnston, published in 1902, has taken its place with the other successful historical novels of that day. The scene is laid in Virginia in the early part of the eighteenth century, where Marmaduke Haward, a wealthy young man, rescues a little orphan girl Audrey, whose parents have been killed by the Indians, and makes her his ward. He puts her in the care of the minister Darden, and his wife Deborah, who take charge of her during Haward's absence of ten years in England. Darden proves himself dissolute and Audrey receives but scant kindness from her guardians. Haward returns to his country estate, Fairview, and, upon finding Audrey grown into a girl of wondrous beauty, begins to take a deep interest in her. At this time he is paying his addresses to Mistress Evelyn Bird, a charming woman of wealth and position who really loves him, but hesitates about accepting his advances, fearing they may not be sincere. Hugon, a half-breed trader, whose attentions to Audrey are most distasteful to her, feels he has a rival in Haward and his plot to kill him is only prevented by the prompt action of Audrey and McLean, the storekeeper of Fairview. Haward and Audrey are much together and gossip is already rife, when the former, piqued by Evelyn's refusal to dance with him at the Governor's ball, in a fit of feverish bravado determines to make Audrey his partner at the Palace. In doing this he draws upon himself and upon her the anger of the guests, especially of Evelyn, and Audrey is publicly rebuked in the church the following Sunday. She is completely crushed when she realizes the position in which she has been placed by Haward and her faith in him is destroyed. He has a long illness and upon his recovery endeavors to persuade Audrey that he loves her and wishes her to become his wife, but she eludes him and repulses him on every occasion. Audrey becomes an actress and her beauty and talents bring the world to her feet. Haward is unceasing in his efforts to win back her love and has just succeeded in doing so, when the blow of the assassin Hugon, which was intended for him, is intercepted by Audrey, who sacrifices her life for his.

AULD LICHT IDYLLS, by Sir James M. Barrie (1888), is a series of twelve sketches of life in Glen Quharity and Thrums. In all of them the same characters appear, not a few being reintroduced in the author's later books, — notably Tammas Haggart, Gavin Ogilvy, and the Rev. Gavin Dishart, "the little minister," who figures in the novel of that name. The titles of the sketches suggest the nature of their contents: The School-House; Thrums; The Auld Licht Kirk; Lads and Lasses; The Auld Lichts in Arms; The Old Dominie; Cree Queery and Mysy Drolly; The Courting of T'nowhead's Bell (reprinted in this LIBRARY); Davit Lunan's Political Reminiscences; A Very Old Family; Little Rathie's "Bural"; and A Literary Club. Humor and pathos mingle, and the characters are vividly real. The charm of the sketches — the author's earliest important work — lies in their delineation of rural Scottish character. Barrie's peculiar characteristics are well illustrated in the 'Idylls.'

AULULARIA (from *Aulula*, a pot), a comedy by Plautus (254–184 B. C.). Although an old miser is the principal character in the play, the real hero, or heroine, is the pot. The favor of his Lar, or household god, enables Euclion to dig up a pot of gold, buried beneath the hearth by his grandfather. No sooner has he become rich than avarice takes hold of him. With trembling hands he buries the pot deeper still: he has found it, others may; the very thought makes his hair stand on end. The dramatic situations of the play turn on this dread of Euclion's that someone will rob him of his new-found treasure. The fifth act is supposed to have been written by Antonius Urceus Codrus, a professor in the University of Bologna, sometime during the fifteenth century. Molière's 'L'Avare' is an imitation of the 'Aulularia.' It has been imitated also, at least in the principal character, by Le Mercier in his 'Comédie Latine.' See also 'L'Avare.'

AURELIAN, a historical novel by William Ware, an American author born in 1797, was first published in 1838 under the title 'Probus.' It was a sequel to 'Letters of Lucius M. Piso,' published the year before; and like that novel, it is written in the form of letters. The full title reads 'Aurelian; or, Rome in the third century. In Letters of Lucius M. Piso, from Rome, to Fausta, the daughter of Gracchus, at Palmyra.' The novel presents a singularly faithful picture of the Rome of the second half of the third century, and of the intellectual and spiritual life of the time as expressed in both Christians and pagans. The Emperor Aurelian figures prominently in the story, which closes with the scene of his assassination. The style of 'Aurelian' is dignified and graceful, with enough of the classical spirit to meet the requirements of the narrative.

AURORA LEIGH, a poem by Elizabeth Barrett Browning, which appeared in 1857. She called it the "most mature" of her works, the one in which "the highest convictions upon life and art are entered." It is in reality a novel in blank verse. The principal characters are Aurora Leigh, who is supposed to write the story; Romney Leigh, her cousin; Marian Earle, the offspring of tramps; and a fashionable young widow, Lady Waldemar. The book discusses various theories for the regeneration of society. The chief theme is the final reconcilement of Aurora's ideals with Romney's practical plans for the improvement of the masses. Bits of scenery, hints of philosophy, and many of Mrs. Browning's own emotions and reflections regarding art are interspersed through the narrative. Aurora Leigh, the child of a cultivated and wealthy Englishman, is at his death sent from Tuscany to England, and put into the care of a prim maiden aunt. She devotes herself to study; refuses the hand of her rich cousin Romney, who has become a socialist; and goes to London to gain a livelihood by literary work. Romney Leigh wishes to afford society a moral lesson by a marriage with Marian Earle, a woman of the slums, who becomes involved in a tragedy which renders the marriage impossible, when Romney retires to Leigh Hall. Through an accident he becomes blind, and these misfortunes reveal to Aurora her love for him; and the poem closes with a mutual exchange of vows and aspirations. It is filled with passages of great beauty, and ethical utterances of a lofty nature.

AUSTRALASIA. Vol. i.: Australia and New Zealand, by A. R. Wallace (1893); with 14 Maps and 91 Illustrations. Vol. ii.: Malaysia and the Pacific Archipelagoes, by F. H. H. Guillemard; with 16 Maps and 47 Illustrations. The first of these volumes, by an eminent English naturalist and traveler, describes from full information the remote southern regions in which the expansion of England is going on upon a scale very inadequately understood in America. These regions, moreover, are of extreme interest, from their natural features, and from the part which they have played in the history of mankind. It would be difficult to have their story from a hand more competent than that of A. R. Wallace. The second volume supplies by far the most interesting and accurate account extant of the tropical portion of the great eastern Archipelago, the northern part of which is really a portion of Asia.

AUTOBIOGRAPHY OF A SLANDER, THE, by Edna Lyall (1887). The slander is born in a small dull English country town, called Muddleton, in the summer of 1886. It is introduced to the world by an old lady, Mrs. O'Reilly, a pleasant, talkative woman, who imagines it and puts it into words over the teacups to her young friend Lena Houghton. "I assure you, my dear," she says, "Mr. Zaluski is nothing less than a Nihilist." Sigismund Zaluski, a young Polish merchant of irreproachable character, has recently come to Muddleton, achieved an instant popularity in its society, and won the affections and promised hand of Gertrude Morley, one of the village belles. Miss Houghton repeats this slander to the young curate, who, jealous of the Pole's success, tells it to Mrs. Milton Cleave, his gossipy hostess, who writes it to a friend in London. It makes its next appearance at a dinner party, where, with the additions it has gained, it is related to a popular novelist. Struck with its dramatic possibilities, he repeats it to a friend at the Club, where it is overheard by an uncle of Gertrude, who writes to St. Petersburg to find out the truth. By this time, in addition to being a Nihilist, the young Pole is an atheist, an unprincipled man, besides being instrumental in the assassination of the Czar. The letter is found by the police; and Zaluski, returning to St. Petersburg on business, is arrested, and dies in a dungeon. The story is strongly told, its probabilities seeming often actual facts. It needs no commentary; its truth is epitomized in the apt quotation of the author: "Of thy words unspoken thou art master: thy spoken word is master of thee."

AUTOCRAT OF THE BREAKFAST TABLE, THE, by Oliver Wendell Holmes (1858),— a series of essays appearing first in the Atlantic Monthly, — consists of imaginary conversations around a boarding-house table, and contains also many of his most famous poems: 'The Deacon's Masterpiece, or the Wonderful One-Hoss Shay'; 'The Chambered Nautilus'; 'The Old Man Dreams'; 'Contentment'; 'Æstivation'; the bacchanalian ode with the teetotal committee's matchless alterations; and others. The characters are introduced to the reader as the Autocrat, the Schoolmistress, the Old Gentleman Opposite, the Young Man Called John, The Landlady, the Landlady's Daughter, the Poor Relation, and the Divinity Student; but Holmes is far too good an artist to make them talk always the "patter" of their situations or functions, like automata. Many subjects — art, science, theology, philosophy, travel, etc. — are touched on in a delightfully rambling way; ideas widely dissimilar following each other, with anecdotes, witticisms, flowers of fact and fancy plentifully interwoven. This is the most popular of Dr. Holmes's books; and in none of them are his ease of style, his wit, his humor, his kindly sympathy and love of humanity more clearly shown. While there is no attempt to weave these essays into a romance, there is a suggestion of sentimental interest between the Autocrat and the Schoolmistress, which affords an opportunity for a graceful ending to the conversations, when, having taken the "long walk" across Boston Common,— a little journey typical of their life's long walk, — they announce their approaching marriage to the circle around the immortal boarding-house table.

L'AVARE ('The Miser'), one of the most famous of Molière's prose comedies, first produced September 9th, 1668. It is founded on the 'Aulularia' of Plautus (which see above), and was paraphrased by Fielding in his comedy of 'The Miser.' Harpagon, a sexagenarian miser who incarnates the spirit of avarice, has determined to marry a young woman named Mariane, who lives in obscure poverty with her invalid mother. He has likewise determined to bestow the hand of his own daughter

Elise upon Anselme, a friend and companion of his own age, who has consented to take her without a *dot* or marriage portion. But the young women prefer to choose their own lovers. Harpagon's son, Cléante, is the favored suitor of Marianc. Valère is desperately smitten with Elise, and for the purpose of wooing her has introduced himself into the Harpagon household under the guise of the house steward. Harpagon's dearest possession is a casket containing ten thousand francs, which he has buried in his garden, and with which his thoughts are ever occupied. La Flêche, a valet, discovers the chest. Harpagon's despair and fury, the complications ensuing, and the disentanglement necessary to a successful stage ending, are given with all Molière's inexhaustible *verve* and humor. See also 'Aulularia.'

AVE, see **HAIL AND FAREWELL,** by George Moore.

AVERAGE MAN, AN, by Robert Grant (1883), is a New York society story; a novel of manners rather than plot, concerning itself more with types than with individuals. Two young men, both clever and of good family, educated at Harvard with an after-year of Europe, settle down in New York to practice law. One of them, Arthur Remington, is content to win a fair income by hard work at his profession, and finally marries a poor but charming girl, who has always represented his ideal, and who refuses a millionaire for his sake. His friend, Woodbury Stoughton, eager for money and fame, dabbles in stocks and loses most of his small fortune. He marries for her money the beautiful uncultivated daughter of a railway king, who loves him devotedly, and to whom he is indifferent. He is elected to the Assembly as a leader of the "better element" in politics; but his ambition to get into Congress leads him into such double-dealing that the Independents desert him, and he is overwhelmingly defeated. On the eve of election, also, his young wife learns of his infidelity to her, and leaves him. The story is slight, but the portraiture of a certain phase of New York fashionable society is vivid, and the study of the inevitable deterioration of life without principle is searching and dramatic.

AVESTA, THE ZEND-, see **SACRED BOOKS OF THE EAST.**

AWAKENING OF HELENA RICHIE, THE, by Margaret Deland (1906). The scene of this story is laid in Old Chester and depicts many of the same characters that have appeared in previous tales by the author. Helena Richie is an attractive and fascinating woman who is something of a mystery to her neighbors. She has recently moved to the town and settled herself in a comfortable home, where she lives alone with her servants and holds herself aloof from the residents of Old Chester. She is known as a widow and her only visitor is Lloyd Pryor, who passes as her brother. This, however, is not the truth, as he is in reality Helena's lover and she in her desire for happiness blinds herself to her wrongdoing. She has been separated for thirteen years from her husband whom she despises, and expects in the event of his death to marry Pryor. He, however, is selfish and cruel and in spite of her intense love for him his affection for her has cooled. Helena adopts a small boy named David, who is brought to her notice by her two friends Dr. William King and Dr. Lavendar, and becomes passionately attached to him. She has an unsought admirer in Sam Wright, a village youth of artistic temperament, who shoots himself when he learns her secret. This tragedy makes a deep impression on Helena and she decides to marry Pryor at once, as her husband has died at last, and she feels this act will restore her womanhood. However, Pryor is not at all anxious for this step, partly on account of his daughter Alice, a girl of nineteen, who is in complete ignorance of her father's past, and partly because his feelings for Helena have undergone a change. He consents with rather bad grace to the plan, stipulating, however, that she part with David. This Helena refuses to do, and when called upon to choose between them takes David. Her plan is frustrated by Dr. King, who convinces her she is not qualified to bring up a child. She confesses everything to Dr. Lavendar, renounces David, and becomes so chastened that he restores the child to her care.

AWAKENING OF SPRING ('Frühlings Erwachen'), by Frank Wedekind (1891). This "children's tragedy" is "one of the documents in a paper war which has resulted . . . in having the physiology of sex taught in many of the German schools" (Translator's preface). The play is a frank but withal artistic presentañon of the necessity of enlightening the child with regard to the problems of sex. In the story, two boys, the sensitive Moritz and the more assertive Melchior, speculate about sex, and Melchior promises to write out the physiological facts with drawings for his friend. Wendla, one of the group of school-children, questions her mother about her sister's new baby, but her mother evades the question, and seems interested only in the flounces to lengthen her growing daughter's dress. Later Wendla and Melchoir take refuge from a thundershower in the hayloft, and being, in the author's view, as innocent as mating birds and spring flowers are exposed to the dangers of their ignorance at this critical period. The play is also an indictment of the cramming system of education. Moritz fails in his examinations and commits suicide. The paper Melchior had written for Moritz is judged by his parents and teachers to be a contributing cause to his suicide. One of the few touches of humor is the scene in which the faculty of the Gymnasium pass judgment on Melchior and spend the time quarreling over the opening and closing of a window. Melchior is not allowed to defend himself. In vain he says he has written nothing obscene. He is sent to a reformatory by his unintelligent parents. Wendla dies at fourteen in giving birth to a child, from the abortives given her to avoid a scandal. She says reproachfully, "Oh mother, why didn't you tell me everything?" and her mother replies: "My mother told me no more." In the last scene, Melchior, escaping from the reformatory, discovers Wendla's tombstone in the graveyard. Moritz appears carrying his head under his arm, and tries to induce Melchior to kill himself. A masked man, typifying the spirit of Life as Moritz symbolizes Death, urges Melchior to trust to him. The contest in the soul of Melchior is externalized in this duel between Life and Death, and Life wins him.

AZTEC TREASURE-HOUSE, THE, by Thomas A. Janvier (1890), is a narration of the thrilling adventures of a certain Professor Thomas Palgrave, Ph.D.; an archæologist who goes to Mexico to discover, if possible, remains of the early Aztec civilization. The reader is hurried with breathless interest from incident to incident; and the mingling of intense pathos and real humor is characteristic of the author of 'The Uncle of an Angel' and other charming books. Professor Palgrave, in company with Fray Antonio, a saintly Franciscan priest; Pablo, an Indian boy; and two Americans, — Young, a freight agent, and Rayburn, an engineer, — starts in search of the treasure-house of the early Aztecs. The professor goes to advance science; Fray Antonio to spread his faith; Pablo because he loves his master; and the rest for gold. What befell them in the search must be learned from the story. This volume, considered either as a piece of English or as a tale of adventure, deserves a high place.

BABYLONIAN INFLUENCE ON THE BIBLE AND POPULAR BELIEFS, by A. Smythe Palmer, D.D. (1897). A small volume specially devoted to showing how the Hebrew Mosaic books evince "familiarity with the great religious epics of Babylonia, which go back to the twenty-third century B.C., — to a date, that is, about 800 years earlier than the reputed time of Moses"; and how, in consequence of this familiarity, "Babylonian ideas were worked into these early Hebrew documents, and were thus insured persistence and obtained a world-wide currency." That "Babylon still survives in our culture," is Dr. Palmer's general conclusion. He especially devotes his work to showing how the Babylonian conception of *Tiamat* was reproduced in the Hebrew conception of *Tehom*, "the Deep"; how the Babylonian idea of the Deep, suggesting the Dragon of the Deep, gave the Hebrew mind its idea of Satan; and how again the idea of the Deep became, first to the Babylonians, and then to the Hebrews, the idea of a Hades, or Tartaros, or Hell. Dr. Palmer makes prominent these points: (1) that "the Hebrew record of the creation is based on the more ancient accounts which have been preserved in the Babylonian tablets"; (2) that "religious conceptions of the Babylonians, suggested by phenomenal aspects of nature, especially the Sun, lay at the base of the Hebrews' early faith"; (3) that "the Great Deep was constituted a symbol of lawlessness," "was personified as a dragon or great serpent," and "became a symbol of moral evil"; (4) that "among the Hebrews this serpent or dragon introduces sin"; and (5) that "this Chaos-Dragon contributed shape to later conceptions of the Devil." He further says, with reference to "the mediatorial god, Merodach" of Babylonian belief: "It has often been remarked that Merodach, as mediator, healer, and redeemer, as forgiving sin, defeating the Tempter, and raising the dead, in many of his features foreshadowed the Hebrew Messiah"; and also: "The Babylonians themselves seem to have considered their Merodach (or Bel) and the Hebrew Ya (Jah — Jehovah) to be one and the same." In such suggestions of study as these, Dr. Palmer's pages are very rich.

BABYLONIAN TALMUD, see **TALMUD.**

BALAUSTION'S ADVENTURE, by Robert Browning, see **ALCESTIS.**

BALLADES AND VERSES VAIN, by Andrew Lang (1884). Mr. Lang's light and graceful touch is well illustrated in this little volume, containing some of his prettiest lyrics. He is fond of the old French verse forms, and the sentiments which belong to them. The gay verses are wholly gay; the serious ones are pervaded with a pensive sadness — that of old memories and legends. Mr. Lang's sober muse is devoted to Scotland, and after that to old France and older Greece; but whether grave or gay, his exquisite workmanship never fails him.

BALLADS, English and Scottish Popular, by Francis J. Child (Ten Parts, or Five Volumes, Imperial Quarto. 1897.) A complete collection of all known English and Scottish popular ballads; every one entire and according to the best procurable text, including also every accessible independent version; and with an introduction to each, illustrated by parallels from every European language. In its recovery and permanent preservation of songs which date far back of modern civilization, — songs which show the thought and feeling of the child-life of humanity, and the seed from which the old epics sprang, — the collection is of the highest value to the student of primitive history. It is a storehouse of language, of poetry, of fiction, and of folklore, so many times the richest ever made, so complete, learned, and accurate, as to occupy a final position. It is a monument of research, scholarship, and laborious service to literature, — and of the essential unity of all races and peoples in their popular poetry, — to have raised which was the work of a noble life.

BALLADS AND BARRACK-ROOM BALLADS, by Rudyard Kipling (1892). This volume is about evenly divided between poems written in English and those written in cockney dialect. The first half is serious; and most of its themes are found in Hindoo legends and wild sea-tales. The last half deals with the joys and woes of Tommy Atkins, and the various experiences of the British private, from the "arf-made recruity" to the old pensioner on a shilling a day. No such vivid portraiture of the common soldier, with his dullness, his obedience, and his matter-of-course heroism, has ever been drawn by any other artist. The book contains, among other favorites, 'Danny Deever,' 'Fuzzy Wuzzy,' and 'The Road to Mandalay,' besides the grim story of Tomlinson, too ineffective either in virtue or sin to find place in heaven or hell.

BANQUET, THE, a dialogue by Plato (427–347 B.C.). 'The Banquet' is usually considered the finest of Plato's dialogues, because of its infinite variety, its vivid and truthful discrimination of character, and the ease with which the author rises naturally from the comic, and even the grotesque, to the loftiest heights of sublimity. A number of guests assemble at the house of Agathon. The subject of love is introduced; they proceed to discuss, praise, and define it, each according to his ideas, disposition, and character. Socrates, summoned to give his opinion, relates a conversation he once had with a woman of Mantinea named Diotime. This artifice enables Plato to make Socrates responsible for ideas that are really his own. In the opinion of the Mantinean lady, the only way to reach love is to begin with the cultivation of beauty here below, and then rise gradually, by steps of the ladder, to supreme beauty. Thus we should proceed from the contemplation of one beautiful body to two, from two to several; then from beautiful functions and occupations to beautiful sciences. Thus we come at last to the perfect science, which is nothing else but the science of supreme beauty. A man absorbed in the contemplation of pure, simple, elementary beauty — beauty devoid of flesh, color, and all other perishable vanities; in a word, divine beauty, one and absolute — could never endure to have his ideas distressed by the consideration of ephemeral things. Such a man will perceive beauty by means of the organ by which beauty is perceptible; and will engender here below, not phantoms of virtue, because he does not embrace phantoms, but true virtues, because he embraces truth. Now, he who engenders and fosters true virtue is loved by God; and if anyone deserves to be immortal, surely it is he. The end of the dialogue is almost entirely devoted to the praise of Socrates, and to a picture of his life as a man, a soldier, and an instructor of youth. It is Alcibiades who draws the portrait of his master. He has just entered the banquet hall with some of his boon companions, and is himself tipsy. His potations, however, serve to add fire and energy to his description of the philosopher, whom he says he knows thoroughly, and of whom he has also a good many personal reasons to complain. Socrates, he continues, is not unlike those Silenuses you find in the studios of the sculptors, with reed-pipes or flutes between their fingers. Separate the two pieces composing a Silenus, and lo! the sacred figure of some god or other, which was hidden by the outer covering, is revealed to your eyes. As far as outward appearance goes, then, Socrates resembles a Silenus or satyr. Indeed, anyone who looks closely can perceive clearly that he is the very image of the satyr Marsyas, morally as well as physically. Can he deny that he is an unblushing scoffer? If he does, witnesses are within call ready to prove the contrary. Is he not also a flute-player, and a far better one than Marsyas, too? It was by the potency of the sounds which the satyr's lips drew from his instruments that he charmed men. The only difference between him and Socrates is that the latter, without instruments and by his discourses simply, produces the same effects. Alcibiades next dwells on the oracles that predicted the advent of his divine teacher, and their mutual relations at Athens during the military expedition to Potidæa and in the defeat at Delium. He then returns to his comparison between Socrates and a Silenus, and declares that his discourses also are Silenuses. With all his admiration for the philosopher, he must acknowledge that at first his language seemed to him as grotesque as his person. The words and expressions forming the exterior garb of his thought are quite as rugged and uncouth as the hide of some repulsive satyr. And then he is always talking of such downright asses as black-smiths, cobblers, curriers, and so forth, and he is always saying the same thing in the same terms. But a person has only to open his discourses and take a peep inside, and he will discover, first, that there is some meaning in them after all; and after closer observation, that they are altogether divine, and enshrine the sacred images of every virtue and almost of every principle that must guide anyone ambitious to become a good man.

BANQUET, THE, a dialogue by Xenophon (430–357 B.C.), is the third work directly inspired by the author's recollections of Socrates, and was probably written with the view of giving a correcter idea of his master's doctrines than is presented in 'The Banquet' of Plato. The scene takes place at the home of the wealthy Callias during the Panathenaic festival. Callias has invited a large party to a banquet arranged in honor of young Autolycos. Socrates and a number of his friends are among the guests. The extraordinary beauty of Autolycos has such an effect on the assembly that everyone is struck dumb with admiration. The buffoon Philippos makes vain efforts to dispel this universal gravity; but he has only poor success, and complains with mock solemnity of his failure. When the tables are removed, three comedians, a harper, a flute-player, and a dancer enter, and with them their manager. The artists play, sing, and dance; while the guests exchange casual remarks, which, on account of the distraction caused by the entertainment, become more and more disconnected. Socrates proposes that conversation take the place of music entirely, and that each describe the art he cultivates, and speak in praise of it. Then several discourses follow. The most important of them are two by Socrates, in one of which he eulogizes the dignity of the trade he himself has adopted. In the other, he speaks of love. The love, however, which he celebrates, is the pure love that has the heavenly Aphrodite for its source, and has no connection with the popular Aphrodite. After these discourses an imitative dance is given by the artists, in which the loves of Bacchus and Ariadne are portrayed.

BARABBAS: 'A Dream of the World's Tragedy,' by Marie Corelli (1893), is briefly the story of the last days of Christ, his betrayal, crucifixion, and resurrection. The scene opens in a Syrian prison where Barabbas, a convicted murderer and thief, is awaiting sentence. It being the feast of the Passover, according to the Law the Jews can demand the release of a prisoner. Fearful that Christ will be given up, they ask the freedom of Barabbas. Leaving his cell, he joins the crowd in the Hall of Judgment, is present on the journey to Calvary, at the crucifixion, and at its tragic ending. The crimes of Barabbas had been instigated by the wiles of Judith Iscariot, a beautiful wanton, who also prompts her brother to the betrayal of his Lord. Judas Iscariot is described as a weak-minded youth, a willing tool in his sister's hands. His self-destruction and her ruin by Caiaphas unite in driving her insane. During her madness she attempts to kill the High Priest; who however escapes, and hating Barabbas for his rivalry in Judith's affections, has him imprisoned on the false charges of attempted murder and the theft of Christ's body from the tomb. Barabbas dies in prison, after being converted to Christianity. He is depicted as a "type of Human Doubt aspiring unto Truth."

The story is dramatically told, but gives the author's imaginary conception of persons and events rather than historic portraits. It shows, however, a certain amount of study of Jewish manners and customs. The style is florid and meretricious.

BARBARA'S HISTORY, by Amelia Blandford Edwards, appeared in 1864. It is the romance of a pretty girl, clever and capable, who, passing through some vexations and serious troubles, settles down to an unclouded future. Barbara Churchill is the youngest daughter of a selfish widower, who neglects his children. When ten years old, she visits her rich country aunt, Mrs. Sandyshaft, with whom she is far happier than in her London home. Here she meets Hugh Farquhar, owner of the neighboring estate of Broomhill; a man of twenty-seven, who has sowed wild oats in many lands and reaped an abundant harvest of troubles. He makes a great pet of Barbara, who loves him devotedly. The story thenceforth is of their marriage, her jealousy in regard to an Italian girl whom her husband has protected, and an explanation and reconciliation. It is well told, the characterization is good, and Barbara is made an extremely attractive little heroine.

BARBER OF SEVILLE, THE, by Pierre Augustin Caron (who later assumed the *nom de guerre* "Beaumarchais"), appeared in 1775 as a five-act French comedy. It is the first of the Figaro trilogy, the later plays being the 'Marriage of Figaro' and the 'Guilty Mother.' The whole drift of the 'Barbier,' as of the 'Mariage,' is to satirize the privileged classes, from the political and "rights-of-man" point of view rather than from that of the social moralist. The plays proved to be formidable political engines.

Full of sparkling, incisive, and direct dialogue, eminently artistic as a piece of dramatic construction, yet lacking the high literary merit which characterizes some of the author's other work, the 'Barbier,' the embodiment of Beaumarchais's vivacious genius, lives to the world in its leading character, Figaro the inimitable. The simple plot follows the efforts and "useless precautions" of Bartholo, tutor and guardian of Rosine, — a coquettish beauty loved by Count Almaviva, — to prevent his pupil-ward from marrying, for he himself loves her. But Bartholo is outwitted, though with difficulty, by younger and more adroit gallants, whose schemes form the episodes of the comedy. Don Basilio, an organist and Rosine's teacher of singing, is the typical calumniator, operating by covert insinuation rather than by open disparagement. Figaro is, as the title indicates, a barber of Seville, where the action is laid, though the play has an air unmistakably French. He is presented as a master in cunning, dexterity, and intrigue, never happier than when he has several audacious plots on hand. "Perpetually witty, inexhaustibly ingenious, perennially gay," says Austin Dobson, "he is pre-eminently the man of his country, the irrepressible mouthpiece of the popular voice, the cynical and incorrigible laugher . . . who opposes to rank, prescription, and prerogative, nothing but his indomitable audacity or his sublime indifference."

BARCHESTER TOWERS, by Anthony Trollope (1857), is the second of the eight volumes comprised in his 'Chronicles of Barsetshire.' The noteworthy success of 'The Warden' led him to continue his studies of social life in the clerical circle centring at the episcopal palace of Barchester. He gives us a pleasant love story evolved from an environment of clerical squabblings, schemes of preferment, and heart-burnings over church government and forms of service. The notable characters are Bishop Proudie, his arrogant and sharp-tongued wife Mrs. Proudie, and Eleanor Bold, a typical, spirited, loving English girl. Trollope excels in showing the actuating motives, good and bad, of ordinary men and women. In a book as thoroughly "English as roast beef," he tells a story of every-day life, and gives us the interest of intimate acquaintance with every character. A capital sense of the "Establishment" pervades the book like an atmosphere.

BARFÜSSELE, see **LITTLE BAREFOOT.**

BARLAAM AND JOSAPHAT, one of the most popular of early mediæval romances, is supposed to have been written by St. John of Damascus, — or Damascenus, as he is sometimes called, — a Syrian monk born about the end of the seventh century. The name of Barlaam and Josaphat appear in both the Greek and Roman lists of saints. According to the narrative of Damascenus, Josaphat was the son of a king of India brought up in magnificent seclusion, to the end that he might know nothing of human misery. Despite his father's care, the knowledge of sickness, poverty, and death cannot be hidden from him: he is oppressed by the mystery of existence. A Christian hermit, Barlaam, finds his way to him at the risk of life, and succeeds in converting him to Christianity. The prince uses his influence to promote the new faith among his people. When he has raised his kingdom to high prosperity, he leaves it to spend the remainder of his days as a holy hermit.

Professor Max Müller traces a very close connection between the legend of Barlaam and Josaphat, and the Indian legends of the Buddha as related in the Sanskrit of the Lalita Vistara. This connection was first noticed, according to Professor Müller, by M. Laboulaye in the Journal des Débats (July, 1859). A year later, Dr Felix Liebrecht made an elaborate treatment of the subject.

The episodes and apologues of the romance furnished poetic material to Boccaccio, to Gower, to the compiler of the 'Gesta Romanorum,' and to Shakespeare; who is indebted to this source, through Wynkyn de Worde's English translation, for the casket incident in the 'Merchant of Venice.' The entire story is found in the 'Speculum Historiale' of Vincent of Beauvais, and in a briefer form in the 'Golden Legend' of Jacobus de Voragine. It has been translated into several European tongues, "including Bohemian, Polish, and Icelandic. A version in the last, executed by a Norwegian king, dates from 1204; in the East there were versions in Arabic, Ethiopic, Armenian, and Hebrew, at least; whilst a translation into the Tagala language of the Philippines was printed at Manila in 1712."

BARNABY RUDGE was Dickens's fifth novel, and was published in 1841. The plot is extremely intricate. Barnaby is a poor half-witted lad, living in London toward the close of the eighteenth century, with his mother and his raven Grip. His father had been the steward of a country gentleman named Haredale, who was found murdered in his bed, while both his steward and his gardener had disappeared. The body of the steward, recognizable only by the clothes, is presently found in a pond. Barnaby is born the day after the double murder. Affectionate and usually docile, credulous and full of fantastic imaginings, a simpleton but faithful, he grows up to be liked and trusted. His mother having fled to London to escape a mysterious blackmailer, he becomes involved in the famous "No Popery" riots of Lord George Gordon in 1780, and is within an ace of perishing on the scaffold. The blackmailer, Mr. Haredale the brother and Emma the daughter of the murdered man, Emma's lover Edward Chester, and his father, are the chief figures of the nominal plot; but the real interest is not with them but with the side characters and the episodes. Some of the most whimsical and amusing of Dickens's character-studies appear in the pages of the novel; while the whole episode of the gathering and march of the mob, and the storming of Newgate (quoted in the LIBRARY), is surpassed in dramatic intensity by no passage in modern fiction, unless it is by Dickens's own treatment of the French Revolution in the 'Tale of Two Cities.' Among the important characters, many of whom are the authors of sayings now proverbial, are Gabriel Varden, the cheerful and incorruptible old locksmith, father of the charming flirt Dolly Varden; Mrs. Varden, a type of the narrow-minded zealot; Miss Miggs, their servant, mean, treacherous, and self-seeking; Sim Tappertit, an apprentice, an admirable portrait of the half-fool, half-knave, so often found in the English servile classes about a century ago; Hugh the hostler and Dennis the hangman; and Grip the raven, who fills an important part in the story, and for whom Dickens himself named a favorite raven.

BARNAVAUX ET QUELQUES FEMMES, see **UNDER THE TRICOLOUR.**

BARNEVELD, JOHN OF, THE LIFE AND DEATH OF, by John Lothrop Motley (1874). In this brilliant biography, the author shows that as William the Silent is called the author of the independence of the Dutch Provinces, so John of Barneveld deserves the title of the "Founder of the Dutch Republic." The Advocate and Keeper of the Great Seal of the Province of Holland, the most powerful of the seven provinces of the Netherlands, was virtually "prime minister, president, attorney-general, finance minister, and minister of foreign affairs, of the whole re-.public." Standing in the background and veiled from public view behind "Their High Mightinesses, the States-General," the Advocate was really their spokesman, or practically the States-General themselves, in all important measures at home and abroad, during those years which intervened between the truce with Spain in 1609 and the outbreak of the Thirty Years' War in 1618.

Born in Amersfoort in 1547, of the ancient and knightly house of Oldenbarneveld, he received his education in the universities of Holland, France, Italy, and Germany, and became one of the first civilians of his time, the friend and trusted councilor of William the Silent, and the chief negotiator of the peace with Spain. The tragedy with which his life ended owes itself, as Motley points out, to the opposition between the principle of States-rights and religious freedom advocated by Barneveld, and that of the national and church supremacy maintained by Prince Maurice the Stadt-holder, whose desire to be recognized as king had met with Barneveld's prompt opposition. The Arminian doctrine of free-will, as over against the Calvinists' principle of predestination, had led to religious divisions among the provinces; and Barneveld's bold defense of the freedom of individual belief resulted at length in his arrest and that of his companion and former pupil, Hugo Grotius, both of whom were condemned to execution. His son, engaging later in a conspiracy of revenge against the Stadtholder, was also with the other conspirators arrested and put to death.

The historian obtained his materials largely from the Advocate's letters and other MS. archives of the Dutch government, and experienced no little difficulty in deciphering those papers "covered now with the satirical dust of centuries, written in the small, crabbed, exasperating characters which make Barneveld's handwriting almost cryptographic; but which were once, "sealed with the Great Seal of the haughty burgher aristocracy, documents which occupied the close attention of the cabinets of Christendom."

Of Barneveld's place in history the author says: — "He was a public man in the fullest sense of the word; and without his presence and influence the record of Holland, France, Britain, and Germany might have been essentially modified. The Republic was so integral a part of that system which divided Europe into two great hostile camps, according to creeds rather than frontiers, that the history of its foremost citizen touches at every point the general history of Christendom."

BARRACK-ROOM BALLADS, see **BALLADS, ETC.**

BARRIERS BURNED AWAY, by Edward Payson Roe, after appearing as a serial story in the New York Evangelist, was published in book form in 1872. Of a cheap edition, issued ten years later, 87,500 copies were sold. It was the author's first novel, and its great popularity led him to adopt story-writing as a profession. The plot of this book is very simple. Dennis Fleet finds the support of his mother and the younger children devolving upon him, after the death of his father. Seeking work in Chicago, he finds it impossible to secure a position suited to his social rank and education. After many hard experiences, he is hired to shovel snow in front of a fine-arts shop where he afterward becomes a porter. Though he cheerfully performs the humblest duties, his superiority to them is evident. His employer, Mr. Ludolph, a rich and money-loving German, finds him valuable enough to be made a salesman. Mr. Ludolph is a widower, having an only daughter, Christine, with whom Dennis falls in love. She treats him contemptuously at first, but soon discovers his trained talent for music and knowledge of art. He rises above the slights he receives, and makes the impression of a nobleman in disguise. Then follow an estrangement and a reconciliation. The most noteworthy feature of the novel is the striking description of the Chicago fire.

BARRY LYNDON, the best of Thackeray's shorter novels, originally written as a serial for Fraser's Magazine, was published in book form in 1844. It is cast in the form of an autobiography. The hero is an Irish gambler and fortune-hunter, a braggart and a blackleg, but of audacious courage and of picturesque versatility. He tells his story in a plain matter-of-fact way, without concealment or sophistication, glorying in episodes which would seem shameful to the most rudimentary conscience, and holding himself to be the best and greatest but most ill-used of men. The irony is as fine as that of Fielding in 'Jonathan Wild the Great,' a prototype obviously in Thackeray's mind.

BASHKIRTSEFF, MARIE, THE JOURNAL OF ('Le Journal'), which appeared in Paris in 1885, and was abridged and translated into English in 1889, was called by Gladstone "a book without a parallel." Like Rousseau's 'Confessions,' it claims to be an absolutely candid expression of individual experience. But the 'Journal' was written avowedly to win posthumous fame; and the reader wonders if the gifted Russian girl who wrote it had not too thoroughly artistic a temperament for matter-of-fact statement. The child she portrays is always interpreted by a maturer mind. Marie is genuinely unhappy, and oppressed with modern unrest; but she studies her troubles as if they belonged to someone else, and is interested rather than absorbed by them.   After a preface, summarizing her birth in Russia of noble family and her early years with an adoring mother, grandmother, and aunt, she begins the 'Journal' at the age of twelve, when she is passionately in love with Count H —— whom she knows only by sight.   A few years later a handsome Italian engages her vanity rather than her heart.   But, as she herself vaguely felt, her struggle for self-expression unfits her for marriage.   From the age of three years she cherished inordinate ambition, and felt herself destined to become great either as singer, or writer, or artist, or queen of society.   Admiration was essential to her, and she records compliments to her beauty or her erudition with equal pleasure.   Her life was a curious mixture of the interests of an attractive society girl with those of a serious student.   The twenty-four years that the diary covers were crowded with ambitions and partial successes. Her chronic discontent was due to the disproportion between her aspirations and her achievements.   In spite of the encouragement which her brilliant work received in the Julian studio, she suspected herself of mediocrity.   "The canvas is there, everything is ready, I alone am wanting," she exclaims despairingly, shortly before her death, — when, although far advanced in consumption, she is planning a chef-d'œuvre.   She was never unselfconscious, and her book reveals her longings, her petty vanities, and her childish crudities, as well as her versatile and brilliant talents.

BATRACHOMYOMACHIA, see BATTLE OF THE FROGS AND MICE.

BATTLE OF DORKING, THE, by Charles Cornwallis Chesney.   This little skit appeared first in Blackwood's Magazine in 1871, and has since been reprinted under the title 'The Fall of England.'   After the ignominious defeat of the French at Sedan, Colonel Chesney, professor of military history at Sandhurst, foresaw a similar fate for his own country unless it should reorganize its army.   He urged vigorous measures of reform; and as the necessity for these was not perceived by the country at large he contributed to the press various articles, both technical and popular. Among the latter was this realistic and matter-of-fact account of an imaginary invasion of England by a foreign power.   The fleet and army are scattered when war is declared, but the government has a sublime confidence that British luck and pluck will save the country now as hitherto.   To universal surprise and consternation, the hostile fleet annihilates the available British squadron and the enemy lands on the south coast.   Volunteers are called out and respond readily; but ammunition is lacking, the commissariat is unorganized, and the men, though brave, have neither discipline nor endurance.   The decisive battle is fought at Dorking, and the British are routed in confusion.   Woolwich and London are in the hands of the enemy, and England is compelled to submit to the humiliating terms of the conqueror.   She is stripped of her colonies, and pays a heavy war indemnity, all because power has come into the hands of the rabble, who have neither foresight nor patriotism to preserve the liberties of their country.   The book was widely read and quoted in its day, then forgotten, and recalled at the beginning of the Great War.

BATTLE OF THE BOOKS, THE, by Jonathan Swift, was written in 1697, but remained in manuscript until 1704.   It was a travesty on the endless controversy over the relative merits of the ancients and moderns, first raised in France by Perrault.   Its immediate cause, however, was the position of Swift's patron, Sir William Temple, as to the genuineness of the 'Letters of Phalaris.'

In the satire, the Bee, representing the ancients who go direct to nature, and the Spider, representing the moderns weaving their webs from within, have a sharp dispute in a library, where the books have mutinied and taken sides, preparatory to battle. In the description of this battle, Swift's arrows of wit fly thick and fast, Dryden and Bentley coming in for a goodly share of their destructive force. Nothing is left of the poor moderns when he has finished with them. The work, despite its vast cleverness, was not taken with entire seriousness by Swift's contemporaries. He was not then the great Dean; and besides, he was dealing with subjects he was not competent to treat. It remains, however, a brilliant monument to his satirical powers, and to the spirit of destruction which impelled him even as a youth to audacious attacks on great names.

BATTLE OF THE FROGS AND MICE, THE ('Batrachomyomachia'), a mock-heroic poem written in imitation of the Iliad. The authorship has been attributed to Homer, and to Pigres the brother of Queen Artemisia, but without any foundation in either case. It is really a parody on the style of Homer. The mouse Prigcheese, who has just escaped the tooth of a hideous monster (a weasel perhaps, or it may be a cat), stops on the border of a marsh to slake his thirst; for he has been running fast and long. Chubbycheek, Queen of the Frogs, enters into conversation with him. She invites him to come to her palace, and politely offers her back as a mode of conveyance. The novelty of the journey enchants Prigcheese, but his joy is not of long duration. A water-snake rears its awful head above the waters. Chubbycheek, wild with terror, plunges to the bottom; and Prigcheese, after heroic struggles, perishes in the waves, but not before he has devoted Chubbycheek to the wrath of the avenging gods. A mouse who happens to be sauntering along the shore hastens to announce to the mouse nation the sad fate of their fellow-citizen. A general assembly is convoked; and on the motion of Nibbleloaf, the father of the victim, war is declared against the frogs, and the herald Lickthepot is charged with the duty of entering the enemy's territories and proclaiming hostilities. Chubbycheek asserts her perfect innocence, nay her ignorance, of the death of Prigcheese. The frogs, fired by her eloquence, prepare to make a vigorous resistance. Meanwhile the gods, from their Olympian thrones, view with anxiety and fear the agitations that are disturbing the earth. But Minerva is of opinion that for the present it would be rash to interfere, and the lords of heaven decide to remain simply spectators of the direful event that is drawing near. Soon the conflict rages, furious, terrible, the chances leaning now to the one side, now to the other. At length the mice are victorious, and Greedyguts, their leader, announces his determination to wipe out the entire vile race of their enemies from the face of the earth. Jupiter is alarmed, and resolves to prevent such a disaster. He will send Pallas or Mars to assuage the wrath of the ferocious Greedyguts. Mars recoils in terror from the rough task. Then the King of Heaven seizes his thunderbolt, and hurls it among the conquerors; even the thunderbolt is powerless. They are frightened for a moment, and then renew the work of destruction with more fury than ever. Jupiter thereupon enrolls another army, and sends it against these haughty victors: it is composed of warriors supplied by nature with arms defensive and offensive, who in the twinkling of an eye change the issue of the battle. These new antagonists are crabs. The mice fly in confusion, and the conflict ends at sunset.

BAVIAD, THE, and **THE MÆVIAD,** by William Gifford. It was through these two satires that the author, who later was the first editor of the Quarterly Review, first became known. 'The Baviad,' which first appeared in 1792, is an attack on a band of English writers living in Florence, Italy, among them being Mrs. Piozzi, Mr. Greathead, Mr. Murray, Mr. Parsons, and others, who had formed themselves into a kind of mutual admiration society. It is an imitation of the first satire of Perseus, and in it the author not only attacks the "Della Cruscans" but all who sympathize with them: "Boswell, of a song and supper vain," "Colman's flippant trash," "Morton's catch-word," and "Holcroft's Shug-lane cant," receive his attention; while the satire ends with the line, "the hoarse croak of Kemble's foggy throat." The 'Mæviad,' which appeared in 1795, is an imitation of the tenth satire of Horace, and was called forth, the author says, "by the reappearance of some of the scattered enemy." He also avails himself of the opportunity briefly to notice "the present wretched state of dramatic poetry." It was generally considered that the author was engaged in a task of breaking butterflies on wheels, but he says, "There was a time (when 'The Baviad' first appeared) that these butterflies were eagles and their obscure and desultory flights the object of universal envy and admiration."

BEACONSFIELD, LORD, see **DISRAELI, BENJAMIN, EARL OF BEACONSFIELD, THE LIFE OF.**

BEAUCHAMP'S CAREER, one of George Meredith's novels (1876). This story presents a complex network of social and political problems, in which the chief figures are enmeshed. Nevil Beauchamp, the hero, is a young English naval officer, of distinguished lineage and aristocratic environment and traditions. But he takes little pride in these accidents of fortune. With the temper and ambition of a martyr, he is prepared to sacrifice himself or his caste to the interests of his country. In Venice he meets a French girl, Renée de Croisnel, whose father has betrothed her to the middle-aged Marquis de Rouaillat. Nevil and Renée fall in love. Beauchamp, with characteristic impetuosity and lack of humor, urges that the larger interests of humanity condemn the proposed marriage as a sin against nature, and that it is her sacred duty to accept him. Renée remains unmoved in the conviction that her duty to her father is paramount. The disappointed lover plunges again into politics. On his return to England he falls under the influence of the radical, Dr. Shrapnel (an enthusiastic advocate of the rights of the democracy), and of his adopted daughter, Jenny Denham. He has many sharp and bitter conflicts with his own people. They are ultra-conservative, he is a radical and a republican. Always ready for sacrifice and indifferent to ridicule, often blundering, he yet succeeds in preserving a certain dash and distinction even in the midst of his failures. Renée presently leaves her husband to come to England and throw herself into his arms; but is foiled by the ready wit of Rosamund Culling, the housekeeper of Beauchamp's uncle. Eventually the young radical makes a loveless marriage with Jenny Denham. Shortly after, he is drowned in saving the life of a nameless little urchin in the harbor of Southampton. The novel is a remarkable study of youthful radicalism.

BEAUTY AND THE BEAST, see **FAIRY TALES.**

BEAUX' STRATAGEM, THE, by George Farquhar (1707). "The rules of English comedy," says Farquhar, "don't lie in the compass of Aristotle or his followers, but in the pit, box, and galleries. . . . Comedy is no more at present than a well-framed tale handsomely told as an agreeable vehicle for counsel or reproof." Farquhar's dramatic work is marked by rollicking spirits, good humor, manliness, and spontaneity. His last and best play, 'The Beaux' Strategem,' was written in six weeks during a "settled illness." Before he had finished the second act he knew that his malady was mortal, but he persevered and tried to be "consumedly lively to the end." Archer and Aimwell, two gentlemen of broken fortunes, disguised as master and servant, are a source of perpetual amusement. The innkeeper Boniface is an original creation which met with immediate success on the stage. Scrub, servant to the stupid and brutal Squire Sullen, is not only the ornament of the kitchen but a reliable repository for the secrets of the young ladies. Lady Bountiful, the "old civil country gentlewoman that cures all her neighbors of all distempers and is foolishly fond of her son, Squire Sullen," and who besides is the gullible benefactress of the whole parish, has passed into a proverb.

BEE, see LIFE OF THE.

BEES, BRAMBLE AND OTHERS, see MASON-BEES.

BEES, THE MASON, see MASON-BEES.

BEGGAR'S OPERA, THE, by John Gay, was first played in 1728, exciting "a tempest of laughter." Dean Swift, upon whose suggestion this "Newgate pastoral" was written, declared that "'The Beggar's Opera' hath knocked down Gulliver." The object of the play was to satirize the predatory habits of "polite" society in thief-infested London, and incidentally to hold up to ridicule Italian opera. The chief characters are thieves and bandits. Captain Macheath, the hero, is the leader of a gang of highwaymen. A handsome, bold-faced ruffian, "game" to the last, he is loved by the ladies and feared by all but his friends — with whom he shares his booty. Peachum is the "respectable" patron of the gang, and the receiver of stolen goods. Though eloquently indignant when his honor is impeached, he betrays his confederates from self-interest. Macheath is married to Polly Peachum, a pretty girl, who really loves her husband. She remains constant under many vicissitudes, despite the influence of her mother, whose recommendation to Polly to be "somewhat nice in her deviations from virtue" will sufficiently indicate her character. Having one wife does not deter Macheath from engaging to marry others, but his laxity causes him much trouble. Being betrayed, he is lodged in Newgate gaol. His escape, recapture, trial, condemnation to death, and reprieve, form the leading episodes in his dashing career. After his reprieve he makes tardy acknowledgment of Polly as his wife, and promises to remain constant to her for the future. Polly is one of the most interesting of dramatic characters, at least three actresses having attained matrimonial peerages through artistic interpretation of the part. Gay's language often conforms to the coarse taste and low standards of his time; and the opera, still occasionally sung, now appears in expurgated form. Its best-known piece is Macheath's famous song when two of his inamoratas beset him at once —

> "How happy could I be with either
> Were t'other dear charmer away!"

BEGINNERS OF A NATION, THE. 'A history of the source and rise of the earliest English settlements in America, with special reference to the life and character of the people.' By Edward Eggleston (1896). This is the first volume of a proposed History of the United States, on the lines set forth by Mr. Eggleston in the sub-title quoted above. The volume is fully and carefully treated in the LIBRARY, under 'Eggleston.'

BEGINNINGS OF NEW ENGLAND, THE, by John Fiske (1889). The occasion and manner of this book, in the author's series of American History volumes, are indicated in a few sentences of the preface: —

"In this sketch of the circumstances which attended the settlement of New

England, I have purposely omitted many details which in a formal history of that period would need to be included. It has been my aim to give the outline of such a narrative as to indicate the principles at work in the history of New England down to the Revolution of 1689. . . . In forming historical judgments, a great deal depends upon our perspective. Out of the very imperfect human nature which is so slowly and painfully casting off the original sin of its inheritance from primeval savagery, it is scarcely possible in any age to get a result which will look quite satisfactory to the man of a riper and more enlightened age. Fortunately we can learn something from the stumblings of our forefathers; and a good many things seem quite clear to us to-day, which two centuries ago were only beginning to be dimly discerned by a few of the keenest and boldest spirits. The faults of the Puritan theocracy, which found its most complete development in Massachusetts, are so glaring that it is idle to seek to palliate them or to explain them away. But if we would really understand what was going on in the Puritan world of the seventeenth century, and how a better state of things has grown out of it, we must endeavor to distinguish and define the elements of wholesome strength in that theocracy, no less than its elements of crudity and weakness."

In the scientific spirit, which seeks the truth only and never the buttressing of any theory, yet with the largest liberality of judgment, the historian illustrates the upward trend of mankind from its earlier low estate. His philosophic bent appears most lucidly expressed in the first chapter, where the Roman idea of nation-making is contrasted with the English idea; the Roman conquest, with incorporation but without representation, with the English conquest, which always meant incorporation with representation. Then follow a description of the Puritan exodus, and the planting of New England, with comments on its larger meanings, a picture of the New England confederacy; the scenes of King Philip's lurid war, and the story of the tyranny of Andros, — James the Second's despotic viceroy, — which began the political troubles between the New England and the Old, that ended only with American independence. This volume, as will be inferred, is among the most interesting and suggestive of Mr. Fiske's many monographs.

BEGUM'S DAUGHTER, THE, by Edwin Lassetter Bynner (1890), is a tale of Dutch New York when Sir Edmund Andros was royal governor of New England.

The chief figures are Jacob Leisler and his family; the Van Cortlandts; and Dr. Staats, with his wife and daughter. This daughter, Catalina, child of a Dutch physician and an East-Indian mother (the Begum), combines the characteristics of both parents. She is the best friend of Hester Leisler, who is betrothed — against her father's will — to Steenie Van Cortlandt. When Leisler succeeds in overthrowing the royal governor, he forbids Hester's intercourse with Steenie, whose father is of the governor's party. Hester is defiant; but her sister Mary is forced by her father to marry Milborne, one of his supporters, though her heart is with Abram Gouverneur, a young Huguenot. Leisler tries to marry Hester to Barent Rhynders, a junker from Albany, whose people are of use to him, but she refuses; and before her father can press the point, matters of graver importance claim his entire attention, — he is sentenced to death as a traitor. After his execution, Hester still refuses to marry the patient Steenie, until she has cleared her father's reputation; and she finally dismisses him and becomes betrothed to Barent Rhynders, after her widowed sister Mary has wedded her first love, Gouverneur. Steenie lays his heart at the feet of the capricious Catalina, who refuses him because she thinks him in love with Hester. She presently accepts him, however: and when he reminds her of their former meeting, saying,

"But you told me — " she interrupts, blushing, "A wicked lie!" This scene closes one of the quaintest stories in the large number of tales that depict colonial New York. The student finds in it nothing with which to quarrel; and the lover of fiction enjoys it all.

BELINDA, by Maria Edgeworth (1801). Belinda Portman, the charming niece of Mrs. Stanhope, goes to spend the winter in London with Lady Delacour, a brilliant and fashionable woman; at her house she meets Clarence Hervey for the first time. He admires Belinda and she likes him, but mutual distrust serves to keep them apart. Belinda is greatly beloved in the household; and her influence almost succeeds in bringing about a reconciliation between Lady Delacour and her dissipated husband, when her Ladyship becomes most unreasonably jealous, and Belinda is forced to seek refuge with her friends the Percivals. While there, Mr. Vincent, a young Creole, falls violently in love with her; but the old friendship with Lady Delacour is re-established, and Belinda returns without having bound herself to him. Believing that Clarence Hervey's affections are already engaged, she would have married Mr. Vincent had she not discovered his taste for gaming. Clarence is deeply in love with Belinda, but feels obliged to marry Virginia St. Pierre, whom he had educated to be his wife. Fortunately she loves another. The story ends happily with the reconciliation of the Delacours, and the marriage of Clarence Hervey and Belinda.

BELL OF ST. PAUL'S, THE, by Sir Walter Besant (1889), is a romance covering in actual development only three months, but going back twenty years or more for a beginning. Lawrence Waller, a typical hero of romance, a young, handsome, rich Australian, comes to London and takes up his residence at Bank Side, in the house of Lucius Cottle. Although they are not aware of the fact, Cottle and his family are cousins to Lawrence's mother; whose husband, an unsuccessful London boatbuilder, having emigrated to Australia, has become after thirty years premier of that colony. On the night of his arrival the young Australian sees two lovely girls rowing out of the sunset, — Althea Indagine, and Cottle's younger daughter Cassie. Althea is the daughter of an unsuccessful and embittered poet, with whom the girl leads a hermit life, seeing no one but the Cottle family and an adopted cousin, Oliver, — whom twenty years before, her uncle Dr. Luttrell had bought from his grandmother for £5, intending to see how far education, kindness, and refined association could eradicate the brutish tendencies in a gipsy child of the worst type. The boy, having become an eminent chemist, displays when opportunity offers the worst characteristics of his race. Lawrence falls in love with Althea; and Oliver Luttrell appears as his rival, having already, unknown to Althea, trifled with the affections of her friend Cassie. In the end Oliver is exposed as a forger, a discovery which deeply pains his foster-father. Like a fairy prince Lawrence comes to the assistance of all his relatives, revealing himself at the most dramatic moment, and shipping most of them to Australia, where there is room for all. The unhappy poet, too, decides to emigrate.

BELOVED VAGABOND, THE, by William J. Locke (1906). This is the story of Paragot, the Beloved Vagabond, told by his adopted son, whom he had picked up from among the unwashed urchins of London and transplanted to his Bohemian quarters which were as Paradise to the neglected boy. Amid untidy surroundings Paragot reigns a king of philosophers instructing his pupil, whom he christens Anti-cot, in art, literature, and the humanities, and enlightening the frequenters of "The Lotus Club" with his droll wit and philosophic lore. Later, the pair set out for a tour of Europe and travel from place to place picking up general information and performing odd jobs. They fall in with Blanquette, a friendless country girl, and a stray dog, who are by Paragot annexed to his wandering household. Paragot for a time exercises his skill as a violinist and they practice the rôles of traveling musicians, the girl playing the zither and the boy the tamborine. Chance brings together the "Beloved Vagabond" and his early love Joanna, who has become Countess de Verneuil, and from whom he was separated by the treachery of the man she later married. She recognizes her old lover and during her husband's illness summons him to her aid. After the Count's death the truth regarding his treachery is revealed to the Countess who recalls the still adoring Paragot and renews their previous engagement believing that they can resume the old relations at the point where they were broken off thirteen years before. But the result is an absolute failure. Paragot gives up his Bohemian habits and tries to adapt himself to the conventional standard sweetly set by his adored Joanna; he dresses in prescribed garb and meekly endeavors to become as are the others in a placid English country town. Gradually the couple begin to realize that they have changed irrevocably in the intervening years. Paragot, unable longer to endure the strain, rushes off without a word and turns up in a state of blissful hilarity at a Bohemian resort in Paris, where he is captured and brought home to his old lodgings by his adopted son and the faithful Blanquette, who worships the ground he walks on. Paragot returns with rejoicing to his free and easy methods of existence and realizing the futility of restoring his old ideal world turns to that of commonplace reality; he marries the devoted Blanquette and goes to live on a small farm. Here the reader takes final leave of him as he is visited by his protégé who has become a successful artist, thanks to his adopted father's training. Paragot has at last attained the happiness he sought for, in cultivating the soil and resting content in the ministrations of his cheerful wife while he views with pride the growth of his infant son.

BEN HUR: A TALE OF THE CHRIST, by Lew Wallace (1880).   The scene of this extremely popular story is laid in the East, principally in Jerusalem, just after the Christian era.   The first part is introductory, and details the coming of the three wise men, Melchior, Kaspar, and Balthasar, to worship the Babe born in the manger at Bethlehem. Some fifteen years later the hero of the tale, Judah Ben Hur, a young lad, the head of a rich and noble family, is living in Jerusalem, with his widowed mother and little sister to whom he is devotedly attached. When Valerius Gratus, the new Roman governor, arrives in state, and the brother and sister go up on the roof to see the great procession pass, Judah accidentally dislodges a tile which fells the governor to the ground. Judah is accused of intended murder; his (till then) lifelong friend Messala, a Roman noble, accuses him of treasonable sentiments; his property is confiscated, and he is sent to the galleys for life. In the course of the narrative, which involves many exciting adventures of the hero, John the Baptist and Jesus of Nazareth are introduced, and Ben Hur is converted to the Christian faith through the miracles of our Lord.

This book is one of the most successful examples of modern romantic fiction. It displays great familiarity with Oriental customs and habits of mind, good constructive ability, and vivid powers of description. The story of the Sea Fight, for example, and of the Chariot Race (quoted in the LIBRARY), are admirably vivid and exciting episodes.

BEOWULF, an old English epic poem of unknown author and uncertain date, probably composed from earlier heroic lays, about 650 A.D., by a Christian poet, familiar with court life. As the scene and characters of the poem are entirely Scandinavian it is inferred that the material was brought over by the Angles when they settled in Britain or that the author obtained it by a visit to Scandinavia. Beowulf gives a representative picture of the courts of Germanic kings at a stage of society not dissimilar to the heroic age of Greece; and in its dignity, warlike ideals, and literary form is not incomparable to the Homeric poems. Each represents the point of development at which the rudely improvised lay of the bard is passing into the finished epic — though in Beowulf the transition is less complete. Popular superstition is the basis of the story. Heorot, the palace of Hrothgar, King of the Danes, is visited nightly by a monster named Grendel, who devours the king's thanes as they sleep. Beowulf, the nephew of Hygelac, King of the Geats, a tribe in Southern Sweden (or, according to some scholars, the Jutes), comes across the sea with fourteen followers to free the Danes from this scourge. After a cordial welcome by Hrothgar and his court the visitors are left alone in the hall for the night. As they sleep, the monster Grendel enters, and devours one of the Geats. Though invulnerable to weapons Grendel is seized by Beowulf and held in a mighty grip from which he breaks away only with the loss of his arm, and flees to his cavern beneath a lake to die. Great are the rejoicings in Heorot. The minstrels sing heroic lays to honor Beowulf and the king loads him with gifts. But another monster, Grendel's mother, still lives and comes to the hall that night to avenge her son's death. The followers of Hrothgar are now sleeping there, and one of them, Æschere, she carries off and devours. Beowulf pursues her to the depths of the gloomy lake, where she grapples with him and drags him into the cavern beneath the water. A desperate struggle ensues, in which after Beowulf's sword has failed and he has been flung to the ground and almost killed by her dagger, he slays the monster with an enchanted sword, found in the cavern. He then decapitates the lifeless Grendel and returns with his head to the shore. He is again thanked by Hrothgar, and after many ceremonious speeches returns to the palace of Hygelac, where his narration of his exploits gives occasion for another picture of court life. A long interval ensues, in the course of which Hygelac and his son Heardred are successively killed in battle, leaving the kingdom to Beowulf, who rules well for fifty years. Then a dragon with fiery breath devastates the kingdom. Beowulf with twelve followers goes out to kill it. Sorely wounded and deserted by all his comrades but one, he finally slays the dragon, but at the cost of his own life. His body is burned by the Geats on a funeral pure and the ashes are enclosed in a barrow.

The poem contains many references to other Scandinavian saga heroes, and at least one historical personage, Hygelac, who has been conclusively identified with a chieftain, Chochilaicus, who was slain during a raid upon the Franks and Frisians, about 515 A.D. Beowulf may also have been an actual person but has affiliations with the heroes of popular story and with certain Scandinavian deities.

BERRY, MISS, EXTRACTS OF THE JOURNALS AND CORRESPONDENCE OF. Edited by Lady Theresa Lewis. These interesting records cover the long period, 1783–1852,—say from the American Revolution to the Crimean War. They were edited by Lady Lewis at Miss Berry's request, and were published in three volumes in 1865.

Miss Mary Berry was born in 1763, and was brought up with her younger sister Agnes. Neither of the two was robust, and a large part of their lives was spent

ε

traveling on the Continent in search of health. While young girls the Misses Berry became acquainted with Horace Walpole, afterwards Lord Orford, and the friend-ship then begun ended only with his death in 1797. The lonely old man was charmed with their good sense and simplicity, and his intercourse and correspondence with them comforted his declining years. He bequeathed his papers to Miss Berry, who edited and published them, as well as the letters of his friend Madame du Deffand. She also wrote some original works, the most important being 'A Comparative View of Social Life in England and in France,' in which she strongly advocated a better understanding between the two countries. She devoted herself to the serious study of events and character, and lived with her sister in modest retirement. They were long the centre of a little coterie of choice spirits, and both died in 1852, beloved and lamented by the children and grandchildren of their early friends.

The extracts from the journals are chiefly descriptive of Miss Berry's travels, and are valuable as pictures of manners and customs that have changed, and of modes of travel long obsolete. But the main interest attaches to her account of the people she met, among whom were Scott, Byron, Louis Philippe, and the Duke of Wellington. She was an intimate friend of Princess Charlotte; and one of the most important papers in the collection is Lady Lindsay's journal of the trial of Queen Caroline, written expressly for Miss Berry.

The correspondence is even more interesting than the journals, and contains many of Horace Walpole's letters hitherto unpublished. They touch lightly on political and social topics, and show his genial nature and brilliant style, as well as his unaffected devotion to the young ladies. We find several letters from Joanna Baillie and from Madame de Staël, who were both warm personal friends of Miss Berry. There are also cordial letters from Canova, Lord Jeffrey, Sydney Smith, and other celebrities. The reader owes a debt of gratitude to Miss Berry for preserving these interesting and valuable papers, and to Lady Lewis for her careful and sympathetic editorship.

BESIDE THE BONNIE BRIAR BUSH (1894), by Ian Maclaren (the Rev. Dr. John Watson), delineates Scottish character and life among the lowly. It consists of short sketches with no attempt at plot, but interest attaches to the well-drawn characters. Domsie, the schoolmaster, bent on having Drumtochty fitly represented by "a lad o' pairts" in the University; Drumsheugh, with a tender love-sorrow, and a fine passion for concealing from his left hand the generous deeds of his right: the Rev. Dr. Davidson, long the beloved minister at Drumtochty; Burnbræ, with apt comments upon men and events; Marget Howe, whose mother heart still beats warm even after her Geordie's death; "Posty," the mail carrier; and Dr. Weelum Maclure, going through field and flood at the call of duty, — these with many others are drawn with a quaint intermingling of pathos and humor. The church life of rural Scotland affords a rich field for the powers of the author.

BÊTE HUMAINE, LA, see **ROUGON-MACQUART.**

BETROTHED, THE, ('I Promessi Sposi') by Alessandro Manzoni. 'A Milanese story of the 17th century. Discovered and Retold by Alessandro Manzoni. Milan, 1825-26. Paris, 1827,' is the title of a book which, the author's only romance, sufficed to give him a European reputation. The purity and nobility of his life and the spiritual tone of his writing make him the fit companion of his compatriot Mazzini in morals and politics. He wrote little, but all was from his heart and bespoke the real man. Skeptical in early life, and marrying a Protestant woman, she in restoring him to the Christian church herself became Roman Catholic, and their union was one of both heart and faith. It was under these influences, and amid the religious and political reaction which followed the death of Napoleon I., that Manzoni — who had already become famous through his 'Sacred Hymns,' and his tragedies the 'Adelchi' and 'Carmagnola,' both relating to remote periods of the past — now produced a colossal romance which combined in one narrative a complete picture of Italian life. The scene of the story is laid within the country around Milan, and the plot concerns only the troubled and impeded but at last happily liberated course of true love between the humble peasant Renzo and his already betrothed Lucia, the village maiden, for whom Don Rodrigo, the chief of a band of outlaws, has laid his snares. On this simple scheme the author manages to introduce a graphic picture of the Italian robber-baron life, as represented by the outlawed but law-defying Don Rodrigo and his retainers; of various phases of the clerical and monastic life, as represented by the craven village curate Abbondio, the heroic priest Cristoforo, and the gentle and magnanimous Cardinal Borromeo; of a devastating plague in all its terrors and demoralizing power, as witnessed by the lover in searching the great city and the lazaretto for his beloved; of the "monatti," the horrible band of buriers of the dead; of the calming and restoring influence of the Church in bringing order out of tumult, the wicked to punishment, and virtue to its reward. The story is like a heritage of Boccaccio, Defoe, and Walter Scott, in a single superb panorama of which Salvator Rosa might have been the painter. The religious motive of the book is sincere but not exaggerated, and never runs to fanaticism. Its original publication was in three volumes, and occupied two years, 1825-26, during which time it awakened a wide interest in European circles; and having been soon translated into all modern languages, it has become probably the best known of all Italian romances to foreign readers.

BETTY ALDEN, by Jane G. Austin. When 'Betty Alden' appeared in 1891, it was at once received as among the best of Mrs. Austin's historical novels. Betty was the daughter of John Alden and Priscilla; and from the fact that she was the first girl born among the Plymouth Pilgrims, her career has an especial interest for readers of history. Yet although Betty gives her name to the book, she is not the heroine. The story opens when she is about four years old, and continues until after her marriage with William Pabodie, — critical years in the history of the Plymouth colony, whose events are skillfully woven into the narrative, and whose great men — Winslow, and Bradford, and the doughty Miles Standish, with Dr. Fuller, and the Howlands, and John Alden himself — appear and reappear, with Barbara Bradford and Priscilla, and the pure, fragile Lora Standish, whose early death causes her father such sorrow. In sharp contrast with the upright Pilgrims stand out Sir Christopher Gardiner, the *soi-disant* knight of the Holy Sepulchre, with his fine clothes and light morals; Oldham and Lyford, with their treacherous reports to the Adventurers; and other outsiders, who were thorns in the flesh of the Pilgrims. Mrs. Austin is accurate as well as picturesque in her descriptions of the merrymakings and feasts of the time, and of the everyday life of these first settlers.

BEVERLY OF GRAUSTARK, by George Barr McCutcheon (1904). This is a sequel to the story entitled Graustark, and gives the reader a further glimpse of the romantic adventurer Grenfall Lorry and his lovely wife, the Princess Yetive. When the story opens they are living in Washington but are called suddenly back to Graustark by the news that political troubles have broken out there. Prince Gabriel, who was the villain of the previous volume, has escaped from prison where he has been confined and has wrested the throne of Dansbergen from his step-brother, Prince Dantan. In consequence war is eminent and Graustark is likely to be involved. While in Washington the Princess Yetive has become greatly attached to a charming American girl named Beverly Calhoun and invites her to visit her at the royal palace. Beverly, who is ready for adventure, starts from St. Petersburg in the company of a negro maid-servant to make the journey by coach to Graustark. She is provided with an escort as she is to pass through a rough and dangerous country, but is deserted by her false protector who mistakes her for the Princess Yetive, and is left in a most dangerous position. She is rescued from this predicament by a band of goat-hunters, headed by a chief named Baldos, who also takes her for the princess but who protects her until she reaches her destination. Baldos, who has been seriously injured in saving Beverly from the attack of a wild beast, is put into a hospital by her, and while he is convalescing she persuades the princess to make him one of the palace guards. Beverly and Yetive conspire to keep up the illusion that the former is the princess of Graustark, but though they lay their plans very cleverly, Baldos sees through their deception. He does not let them know, however, that he has discovered the conspiracy and plays his part without committing himself. His manners and bearing, which are so far above his position, baffle the princess and her household and they endeavor to solve the mystery. Beverly finds herself becoming deeply in love with her unknown hero and after having tried in vain to conquer her feelings agrees to marry him and share his humble lot. After a series of thrilling adventures Gabriel is captured and the real identity of Baldos is revealed, as he acknowledges himself to be the dethroned Prince Dantan.

BEWICK, THOMAS, AND HIS PUPILS, by Austin Dobson (1884). This informal biography, in the poet's charmingly familiar style, is further enlivened by extracts from the great engraver's autobiography, prepared for his daughter, and in its descriptions of nature almost striking the note of English poetry. Born in 1753, when the art of wood-engraving was at its lowest ebb, Bewick falsified the saying of Horace Walpole that the world would "scarcely be persuaded to return to wooden cuts." It would be easy to draw a parallel between this son of a Northumberland farmer and his contemporary the Japanese Hokusai. Both were pioneers, indefatigable workers, lovers of nature from early childhood, acute observers of all objects, and artists whose best work is unrivaled, though their field lay in the prints displayed in the homes of the people. Both the efforts and the escapades of the English lad are spicy reading. He had never heard of the word *drawing*, and knew no other paintings than the King's Arms in Ovingham Church, and a few public signs. Without patterns, and for coloring having recourse to brambleberry juice, he went directly to the birds and beasts of the fields for his subjects. He covered the margins of his books, then the gravestones of Ovingham Church and the floor of its porch; then the flags and hearth of Cherryburn, the farm-house where he was born. Soon the neighbors' walls were ornamented with his rude productions, at a cheap rate. He was always angling, and knew the history and character of wild and domestic animals; but did not become so absorbed in them as to ignore the villagers, their Christmas festivities and other features of their life. After serving his apprenticeship to an engraver in Newcastle, he went to London; but pined for the country, and though he abhorred war, said that he would rather enlist than remain. He opened a shop in Newcastle, where for nearly fifty years he carried on his work. His serious work begins with his illustrations to a work called 'Select Fables.' His cut for 'Poor Honest Puss' is worthy of a Landseer in little. Bewick considered his Chillingham Bull, drawn with difficulty from the living model, his masterpiece; and its rarity, owing to the accidental destruction of the original block, enhances its value. But he reached his high-water mark in birds. We see them as he saw them, — alive; for he had an eye-memory like that of Hogarth. One of the last things he ever did was to prepare a picture and a biography, in some seven hundred words, of a broken-down horse, dedicating the work to the Society for the Prevention of Cruelty to Animals. This forerunner of 'Black Beauty' was entitled 'Waiting for Death.' His own death occurred in 1828, before the head of the old horse had been entirely engraved. Among many delightful passages, this life contains an interesting account of the visit that the naturalist Audubon paid him in 1827. Although Bewick was responsible for the revival of wood engraving, he had no "school" in the conventional sense. Mr. Dobson explains the marked differences between Bewick's method and that of Dürer and Holbein, and credits him with several inventions.

BEYOND THE PALE, by B. M. Croker (1897). The scene of this story is laid in Munster, Ireland. The heroine is Geraldine O'Bierne, better known as Galloping Jerry, the last representative of an old and ruined race. At her father's death, the great estate of Carrig is seized by the mortgage holders; and her mother, a penniless and silly beauty, marries Matt Scully, a neighboring horse-dealer, — a match so far beneath her that the indignant county cuts her altogether. Scully despises his stepdaughter till he discovers that she can ride with judgment and dauntless courage; whereupon he takes her from school, and sets her to breaking his horses. Her mother being dead, she is bullied and abused by him and his niece Tilly, a vulgar slattern; pursued by Casey Walsh, jockey and blackleg; cut by the county, and adored by the peasantry. The Irish pride of race is the main element of interest. The story is bright, original, and very well told; while two or three character-studies of Irish peasants are portraitures that deserve to live with Miss Edgeworth's.

BHAGAVADGITA, see **SACRED BOOKS OF THE EAST.**

BIBLE, THE; 'that is the holy Scripture of the Olde and Newe Testament, faithfully & truly translated out of Douche and Latyn into Englishe (1535).' The first complete English Bible, being the earliest translation of the whole Bible into English. The Psalms of this translation are still used in the Book of Common Prayer and much of the rare quality of our most familiar version is due to Coverdale. Born in Yorkshire in 1488, and educated at Cambridge, Miles Coverdale was able to contribute to English popular literature a version of the Bible "translated out of Dutch and Latin," before a translation from the original tongues had been attempted. He superintended also the bringing out in 1539 of the first 'Great Bible'; and the next year edited the second 'Great Bible,' known also as 'Crammer's Bible.' He is supposed to have assisted in the preparation of the 'Geneva Bible' (1560), which was the favorite Puritan Bible, both in England and in New England.

BIBLE, see also **THE INDIAN BIBLE:** also **APOCRYPHAL GOSPELS** and articles on the **OLD TESTAMENT** and **NEW TESTAMENT** in the LIBRARY.

BIBLE, THE POLYCHROME. A new translation of the Scriptures from a re-vised text, by eminent Biblical scholars of Europe and America; Professor Paul Haupt, Johns Hopkins University, editor, with the assistance in America of Dr. Horace Howard Furness. The special scheme of this great work is its use of color backgrounds upon which to print the various passages by different writers which have been made up into one work, as Isaiah or the Psalms. It is based on the general conviction of Biblical scholars that only good can come from making perfectly clear to the public the full results of modern critical research. The Revised Version is considered by the projectors of the Polychrome an unsatisfactory compromise, in that it fails to show the results of modern research, either in its text of the original or in its translation. In particular it does not show the exact facts of the Hebrew originals; where in many cases a book is made up by fitting together parts of two or three writings, differing in character, authorship, and date. The Poly-chrome device to show these facts is that of printing what is of one writer on the white paper, what is of a second writer on a color impressed on the page over just space enough for the passage, and so with a third, or more. Each has his color, and the reader easily follows the respective writers. In the translation a marked change is effected by the use of modern literary English, in place of Biblical English, which does not faithfully show the true meaning. In the texts followed and the translation adopted, the general agreement of Biblical scholars is represented. In the preparations made for its execution, and the plans for a collaboration of eminent specialists throughout the world, the work is perhaps the greatest yet attempted in the field of Biblical scholarship. Its translators especially represent the best scholarship of America, England, and Continental Europe. A corresponding Polychrome edition of the Hebrew text, edited by eminent Hebraists under Profes-sor Haupt's direction, was issued in advance of the English version.

BIBLE IN SPAIN, THE, by George Borrow, was published in 1843. It is an account of the author's five-years' residence in Spain as an agent of the English Bible Society. In the preface he thus explains his book: —

"Many things, it is true, will be found in the following volumes, which have lit-tle connection with religion or religious enterprise; I offer, however, no apology for introducing them. I was, as I may say, from first to last adrift in Spain, the land of old renown, the land of wonder and mystery, with better opportunities of becoming acquainted with its strange secrets and peculiarities than perhaps ever yet were afforded to any individual, certainly to a foreigner; and if in many in-stances I have introduced scenes and characters perhaps unprecedented in a work of this description, I have only to observe that during my sojourn in Spain I was so unavoidably mixed up with such, that I could scarcely have given a faithful nar-rative of what befell me had I not brought them forward in the manner I have done."

'The Bible in Spain' is therefore a fascinating story of adventure and pictur-esque life in a land where, to the writer at least, the unusual predominates. As a reviewer wrote of the book at the time of its publication, 'We are frequently re-minded of Gil Blas in the narratives of this pious, single-hearted man.' Borrow's work is unique in the annals of missionary literature.

BIBLE LANDS, Recent Research in: Its Progress and Results. Edited by Her-mann V. Hilprecht (1897). A work of definitive and comprehensive excellence presenting in eight chapters, by as many writers of high authority, the best new knowledge of the fruits of Oriental exploration throwing light on the Bible. It grew out of a series of articles prepared by leading American and European specialists for the Sunday-School Times; and it thus carries an attestation which will commend it to readers who desire a trustworthy account of the recent most remarkable expansion of knowledge concerning Palestine, Babylonia, Egypt, and Arabia, in respect of their history previous to and during the "Mosaic" period. As some of the art objects pictured in the illustrations are of date 4000 B.C., it will be seen that the recovery of a time long before Abraham's opens to view pages of the story of mankind of extreme interest and significance. The new light thus thrown upon the ancient East shows how "Ur of the Chaldees" was, to older cities near the head of the Persian Gulf, a new mart of trade and seat of culture, such as Chicago is to New York; and how Abraham in going to Palestine went to the Far West of that Oriental world, where the east coast of the Mediterranean was to the world of culture what the American Pacific coast is to-day. It was Abraham who thus first acted on the advice, "Young man, Go West." The date of his defensive expedition related in Genesis xiv. is now definitely fixed by Babylonian inscriptions at about 2250 B.C.; and the invasion he repelled is found to have been in pursuance of aims on which the kings of Babylonia are known to have acted as early as 3800 B.C., or fully 1500 years before Abraham.

BIGLOW PAPERS, THE, by James Russell Lowell, a series of political satire, in alternating prose and verse. The first series, relating to the war between the United States and Mexico, appeared in various journals from 1846 to 1848 and was published in the latter year in book form. Lowell believed the Mexican war a device of the Southern states to increase the extent of slave-holding territory and vehemently opposed it. For the expression of his views he created three typical Yankee characters: the Reverend Homer Wilbur, a New England country parson, scholar, and antiquarian, whose stilted and pedantic introductions to the verses serve as a medium for conveying Lowell's more serious moods; Hosea Biglow, a downeast farmer, whose shrewdness, common sense, and zeal for liberty find congenial expression in racy Yankee dialect, both prose and verse; and Birdofredum Sawin, a rascally fellow-villager of Biglow's, who enlists for the Mexican war, becomes a convert to slavery and later to secession, and writes from the South epistles full of uproarious adventure and absurd arguments in favor of the cause he has adopted. This first series voices Lowell's hatred of a war which he considered un-Christian and of those Northern Whigs who supported it in order to gain political power. Few political invectives are more withering than Hosea Biglow's first poem, attacking the recruiting agents and the editorial supporters of the war; and the famous third poem, 'What Mr. Robinson Thinks,' with its stinging sarcasm and catchy metre, is not easily matched in the annals of satire. 'The Pious Editor's Creed' is worthy of Burns as an ironical presentation of hypocrisy. 'I du believe in Freedom's cause. . . . But libbaty's a kind of thing that don't agree with niggers.'

The second series of Biglow papers appeared in the Atlantic Monthly from 1862 to 1866 and was published in book form in 1867. The Civil War had induced Lowell to revive the literary figures created in an earlier crisis, and he handles these characters with the old brilliance and power. Of particular interest are the comments of Wilbur and Biglow on the Trent Affair which constitute the second paper, entitled 'Mason and Slidell: a Yankee Idyll.' In a dignified prose introduction, a vernacular dialogue in heroic couplets between Concord Bridge and Bunker Hill Monument (suggested by Burns's 'Brigs o' Ayr'), and a homely epistle from Jonathan to John, Lowell expresses his indignation at England's sympathy for the Confederacy, her supercilious attitude toward the North, and her resentment at an act of seizure similar to that which she had herself defended in 1812; he approves, however, the action of Lincoln in giving up the captured Confederate commissioners, and prophesies a future understanding between Great Britain and the Union. Birdofredum Sawin excites ridicule by his long epistles descriptive of his settlement and marriage in the South and his conversion to slavery and separation from the Union. Biglow's imaginary message to the Confederate Congress by Jefferson Davis illustrates the growing encouragement of the North at the weakening of Southern credit and morale. In the closing papers there are some attractive pictures of New England scenery and some fine prophecies of peace and reconstruction. The book is a brilliant and witty embodiment of the best abolitionist and unionist sentiment. The often ponderous but genuine and earnest zeal of the Reverend Homer Wilbur, the vigorous native wit and humor of Hosea Biglow, whose dialect, a spontaneous development of the race and soil, was deliberately chosen by Lowell as a source of life and freshness in diction, and the characteristically American exaggeration and caricature of Birdofredum Sawin are merely different phases of Lowell's attitude and temper. Many of the political allusions are obscure to the modern reader but the general drift of the satire is easy to follow and its effectiveness is unquestionable.

BIMBI: STORIES FOR CHILDREN (1882). Ouida has done nothing so perfectly as her stories of child-life. In 'Bimbi' we see her at her best. The stories are simply but charmingly told, and show a wonderfully intimate sympathy with children. The characters are mostly little peasants, sweet, natural, and thoughtful, filled with a love of beauty and of old legends, and touched with the simple spontaneous heroism that is possible only to a child.

'Hirschvogel,' which opens the volume, is the story of a German boy's romantic attachment for a beautiful porcelain stove, made by the great master Hirschvogel. August's father having sold the stove, the child secretes himself in it, and after a terrible journey of three days is found inside by the young king who has bought it; and who, pleased with the child's devotion, allows him to stay with his beloved Hirschvogel and receive an artist's education.

'Moufflou' takes its name from a clever poodle, which Lolo, his little lame master, had taught to do many tricks. Lolo's mother having sold the dog while he was away, the child takes the loss so much to heart that he becomes ill, and is saved from death only by the opportune arrival of Moufflou, who has escaped and walked many miles to find his little master.

Findelkind is a boy whose whole life is saddened because some twin lambs from his flock stray, and are frozen to death, while he is away upon a quest for money with which to found a monastery.

The Little Earl who gives his name to the last story in the book learns early the lesson that "It is the title they give me and the money I have got that make people so good to me. When I am only *me* you see what it is."

'In the Apple Country' relates how a young Englishman receives into his home Gemma, a hot-tempered, warm-hearted little Italian girl, with her grandfather and brother, who have been arrested for strolling. And when Gemma has grown into a beautiful girl, impulsive still, but sweet and gentle, she consents to give up forever the grapes and oranges of Italy to live in the "Apple Country," as Philip Corey's wife.

Perhaps the most charming of the stories is 'The Child of Urbino.' Two friends of the child Rafaelle — Luca, a noble youth, and his sweetheart Pacifica, a gentle maiden — are in great trouble. Pacifica's father, a great artist, has promised his daughter's hand to the painter winning in a contest to be decided by the duke, and Luca could paint but ill. On the day of the decision the duke and all present gaze in wonder upon one piece, which is found to be the work of the seven-year-old child Rafaelle. Modestly and quietly the child claims Pacifica, takes her hand and places it in Luca's. They tell Luca that an angel has come down for him. "But Luca heard not: he was still kneeling at the feet of Rafaelle, where the world has knelt ever since."

BIOGRAPHIA LITERARIA, a loosely-knit series of chapters, autobiographical, philosophical, and critical, by Samuel Taylor Coleridge, published in 1817. In the more philosophical chapters Coleridge explains his distinction between fancy and imagination and shows its relation to the views of Kant and other idealists. In chapters xiv. to xxii. he presents an extremely valuable examination and criticism of the poetical theories of Wordsworth as expressed in his Preface to the 'Lyrical Ballads' (1800). To the first edition of this famous collection Coleridge had contributed 'The Ancient Mariner.' He had been in close association with Wordsworth at the time when the book was planned and had discussed that plan with him. While warmly praising Wordsworth's power of investing common objects and scenes with an atmosphere of wonder he took exception to his dicta that the language of poetry should as far as possible be identical with that of common life and that there is no essential difference between the language of prose and that of poetry. He points out that poetry, being idealistic in its aims, must express concepts for which there are no words in ordinary conversation, that Wordsworth himself frequently uses in his poetry language utterly removed from that of humble, uneducated people, and that metre, by its emotional effect, differentiates poetry from prose. This admirable critique forms a salutary corrective to the excesses of Wordsworth's theory and brings out with sympathetic and appreciative insight the poetic beauties of his practice. It also enriched English criticism by some very important principles and judgments.

BIRCH DENE, by William Westall (1891). The scene of this sombre story is laid in London and the North of England, the England of George IV. and the landed proprietor. A young gentlewoman, wife of an officer, comes up to London with her child, to meet her husband, on his return from extended foreign service. He does not arrive, and she can hear no news of him. Friendless and alone, she falls into dire want; and finally, one stormy day, snatches a little cloak hanging outside a shop, for her shivering boy. She is immediately seized and brought to trial. In the criminal code of that day, stealing an article valued at five shillings or more was one among one hundred and fifty capital crimes; and the poor woman is sentenced to be hanged, a fate she escapes by dropping dead in the dock. Stricken with brain fever after the trial, the poor little lad, Robin, cannot remember his father's name, which his mother had carefully concealed, nor where he was born. He is sheltered and brought up by a kindly old bookseller; but on the death of his benefactor, when no will is found, the little property passes to a nephew, a miserly undertaker. To get rid of Robin, now aged nineteen, he apprentices him to a cotton-spinner in the Lancashire village of Birch Dene. The interest of the story lies in its graphic portraiture of the English industrial life of the early part of the century, in its study of artisan character, its clever invention of incident and plot, and its humane spirit.

BIRD, THE ('L'Oiseau'), by Jules Michelet. In the year 1855 the eminent historian took up the study of natural science, as a relief from the too great strain of continued observation of the course of human events; and in three volumes, of which 'L'Oiseau' is one, he treated of non-human nature in a manner sympathetic and stimulating, but thoroughly imbued with his peculiar ethical and scientific theories. These works partook of the exceeding popularity which had met his studies in human history; and naturally, for they had all the charm of style, the grace and color and poetic feeling, which belonged to Michelet, together with the interest of an entirely novel attitude toward the subject presented.

'L'Oiseau' is less a treatise on ornithology than a biography of the bird and, as a translator says, "an exposition of the attractiveness of natural history." It tells the story of bird-life in a delightful, somewhat discursive fashion, as the story of a being like ourselves. A hint of Pantheism, a suggestion of metempsychosis, a faint foreshadowing of Darwin, infuse the story of the birds as told by Michelet. Through it breathes a tender love for nature, a love which strove rather to establish a sympathy between man and his environment than to inform him concerning it. The author says that he shall try "to reveal the bird as soul, to show that it is a person. The bird, then, a single bird, — that is all my book, but the bird in all the variations of its destiny, as it accommodates itself to the thousand vocations of winged life. . . . What are these? They are your brothers, embryo souls, — souls especially set apart for certain functions of existence, candidates for the more widely harmonic life to which the human soul has attained." This conception colors the whole treatment of the subject. A translation, with illustrations by Giacomelli, was published in London and New York, 1869, three years after it first appeared in Paris.

BIRDS, THE ('Aves'), by the Greek dramatist Aristophanes, is a comedy that appeared in 414 B.C. It belongs with the writer's earlier plays, in which farcical situations, exuberant imagination, and a linguistic revel are to be noted. The comedy is a burlesque on the national mythology: the author creates a cloudland for his fancy to sport in without restraint. A couple of old Athenians, Euelpides and Peisthetairos, sick of the quarrels and corruptions of the capital, decide to quit the country. They seek Epops, now called Tereus, who has become King of the Birds. He tells them so much about the bird kingdom that they are interested; and after a council of the birds, — who, at first hostile, finally give the strangers a friendly reception, — propose to build a walled city (Cloud-Cuckoo-Land) to shut out the gods and enhance bird power. This is done under Peisthetairos's supervision. Various messengers come from Athens and are summarily treated; a deputation from the gods also comes, offering peace, which is accepted on condition that the birds are reinstated in all their old-time rights. The comedy closes with the marriage hymn for Peisthetairos and Basileia, the beautiful daughter of Zeus. Throughout, the bird chorus sings lofty poetry, and the comedy parts are full of rollicking audacity of wit, — much of it, however, so dependent upon local allusion or verbal play as to make it obscure for the English reader.

BIRDS OF AMERICA, THE, the monumental work of John James Audubon, the great American naturalist, was published first in England between the years 1827 and 1830. It contained colored illustrations of 1065 species of birds. The text of this remarkable book is descriptive of the habits and manners of the birds observed by Audubon himself in his long wanderings over the North-American continent. Aside from its scientific value, it is most interesting because written throughout with the same enthusiasm which prompted the original investigations of the author.

BISMARCK, SOME SECRET PAGES OF HIS HISTORY, by J. H. M. Busch (1898). From 1870 Busch had been employed by Bismarck as one of his press agents, and in this capacity was with the Chancellor during the whole of the Franco-Prussian War. His work is a priceless record, not only as a moving picture of Bismarck's daily life, but as a revelation of the means which the Chancellor used to manipulate opinion in Germany, in England and other neutral countries, and even in France. The most illuminating side-lights are thrown upon the great events which led up to the formation of the German Confederation and the war of 1870-1. Speaking of Moltke, for example, Bismarck said (October 4, 1870): " I have not seen him looking so well for a long time past. That is the result of the war. It is his trade. I remember, when the Spanish question became acute, he looked ten years younger. Afterwards, when I told him that the Hohenzollern had withdrawn, he suddenly looked quite old and infirm. And when the French showed their teeth again, 'Molk' was once more fresh and young. The matter finally ended in a *diner à trois* — Molk, Roon, and I — which resulted (here the Chancellor smiled a cunning smile) in the Ems telegram."

BITTER-SWEET, by J. G. Holland, is a narrative didactic poem, of about three thousand five hundred lines, which appeared in 1858 and won great popularity. Israel, a good old Puritan farmer, dwells in his ancestral New England home.

> " His daughter Ruth orders the ancient house,
> And fills her mother's place beside the board."

On Thanksgiving eve the patriarch's children, with their families, gather for the festival. Round the hearth God's justice and providence and the mystery of evil are discussed. Israel stands for faith. Ruth expresses her doubts, having looked in vain for justice in the world. David, a poet, husband to Ruth's sister Grace, undertakes to teach Ruth that there is no incongruity in the existence of evil in a world created by beneficent design. His first illustration is drawn from nature, as David and Ruth seek the cellar to bring cider and apples for the company, and is epitomized in the couplet: —

> " Hearts, like apples, are hard and sour,
> Till crushed by Pain's resistless power,"

Grace, and Mary, a foster-daughter of the house, exchange the stories of their domestic sorrows, while each finds in the other consolation and sympathy. Grace tells of her husband's apparent interest in some unknown woman; but admits her griefs to be trivial beside those of Mary, whose dissolute husband has deserted her and their child. The question is next illustrated by story. Joseph, one of Israel's sons, tells to the children the old story of Bluebeard. The older folk find in it serious lessons in line with the main theme of the poem. Finally there is heard the cry of a man perishing in the storm which rages without. Brought to the fireside and revived, he proves to be the weak but now repentant Edward, husband to Mary. The injured wife forgives all, and discloses that the friend who has been comforting her is the poet David. The revelation shows Grace that her jealousies have been groundless. Edward dies peacefully, and all see more clearly that God has not forgotten the world, and that there is

> "In every evil a kind instrument
> To chasten, elevate, correct, subdue."

BLACK BEAUTY, HIS GROOMS AND COMPANIONS, by Anna Sewall (1877). This story, written in the form of a horse's autobiography, is really a tract on the proper treatment of horses. Black Beauty, a high-bred gentle creature, accustomed to kind treatment in a gentleman's stables, has his knees broken by a drunken groom, and is so much disfigured that he is sold to the keeper of a livery stable. In turn he becomes a cab-horse, a cart-horse, then a cab-horse again, and finally, when he is utterly broken down by overwork and hard treatment, he is bought by a farmer who recognizes his good blood, and nurses him patiently into health again. He is then sold to a family of ladies, whose coachman is an old friend, and in whose stable he passes the rest of his days happily. The story, told with simplicity and restraint, and without a word of preaching, is the best of sermons. Its vogue was great, and it remains a favorite with young readers.

BLACK DIAMONDS, by Maurice Jokai, the famous Hungarian novelist, is a strong story of industrial and aristocratic life in Hungary, with a complicated plot, and dramatic — even sensational — features. It was published in 1870. Its interest centres around the coal-mining business; the black diamonds are coal — also, by a metaphor, the humble folk who work in the mines and exhibit the finest human virtues. The hero is Ivan Behrends, owner of the Bondavara coal mine; a man of great energy and ability, with a genius for mechanics. He does a small conservative business, and a syndicate of capitalists try to crush him by starting an enormous colliery near by; only to make a gigantic failure, after floating the company by tricky stock-exchange methods. Ivan outwits them by sticking to honest ways and steady work. Edila, the pretty little colliery girl whom Ivan loves, goes to the city as the wife of a rich banker, and has a checkered career there, becoming the protégée of a prince and a conspicuous actress; but eventually she prefers to come back to the mine, don her old working clothes to show her humility, and marry Ivan. Very graphic scenes in the stock exchange, in the underground world of the miner, and in the fashionable society life of Vienna and Pesth, are given; the author being thoroughly familiar with Hungary, high and low, and crowding his book with lively incidents, and varied clearly drawn characters.

BLACK SHEEP, THE. A novel by Edmund Yates (1867). George Dallas is the black sheep of his family. His mother, a widow, has married Capel Carruthers, a wealthy, pompous, narrow-minded bit of starched propriety. Carruthers refuses to make a home for the youth on his splendid estates, and casts him adrift on the world. George becomes wild and reckless, and moves in a set of "black sheep": men and women mostly of gentle birth like himself, who have fallen into evil ways. Chief among these are George Routh and his wife Harriet, professional sharpers, who deem it to their interest to get him into their power. Routh is a scamp by nature. His wife, an innocent girl, falls to his level through her overwhelming love for him. Routh lends Dallas the money to pay a gambling debt to a mysterious American named Deane. The style of the story is energetic, and its rapid complications make it interesting.

BLACKWOOD, WILLIAM, AND HIS SONS, their Magazine and Friends; Annals of a publishing house, by Mrs. M. O. W. Oliphant (1897). This book, projected in three volumes, — the last of which, unhappily, the author did not live to complete, — is in effect an outline sketch of English letters for the greater part of the eighteenth century. In the form of a biography of the great Scotch publishing-house, the relations of its partners to the writing world of their time are detailed with infinite humor and enjoyment. William Blackwood, first of the name, began as a dealer in second-hand books in Edinburgh; his first publication being a catalogue of his own stock, done with so much knowledge and so excellent a classification that it still remains in use. The great London house of Murray wanting a Scotch agency, the enterprising and determined Blackwood secured it, — the first "ten-strike" in his game of life. His next good fortune was the honor of publishing 'The Tales of My Landlord,' which, though anonymous, Blackwood confidently ascribed to Scott. Unluckily, he ventured afterward to find some fault with 'The Black Dwarf'; and the indignant author of Waverley repudiated him and all his works in a sharp letter, closing "I'll be cursed but this is the most impudent proposal that ever was made." Blackwood therefore lost the opportunity of becoming Scott's publisher; but poor Scott doubtless lost the assurance of a comfortable and tranquil age. Miss Susan Ferrier, the author of 'Marriage,' 'Destiny,' etc., was one of Blackwood's protégées, as were so many of the successful writers of the early century. But all his other débuts and successes were eclipsed, Mrs. Oliphant considers, by the association of Wilson, Lockhart, and Blackwood in the founding and editing of Blackwood's Magazine. 'Maga,' the Blackwood venture, on the other hand, was a Tory rival to the well-established Edinburgh Review. For those were days when politics colored opinion to a degree which is now almost incredible. "When the reviewer sits down to criticize," wrote Lockhart, "his first question is not, 'Is the book good or bad?' but 'Is the writer a Ministerialist or an Oppositionist?'" Mrs. Oliphant confesses freely the blunders of 'Maga': its mean attack on Coleridge in the first number, its foolish and baseless onslaught on the "Cockney school" represented by Leigh Hunt, and its promise of judgment to come on "the Shelleys, the Keatses, and the Webbes." On the other hand, she shows the friendly connection of George Eliot and of Lord Lytton with the house, and its pleasant relations with many less famous persons whom Blackwood introduced to the world. Full of the most agreeable gossip as they are, the real value of these volumes lies perhaps not more in the history of the time which they present, than in the impression they give of the kindly and helpful influence of the Blackwoods themselves upon the lives and work of their many clients.

BLEAK HOUSE. A novel by Charles Dickens (1853). One theme of this story is the monstrous injustice and even ruin that could be wrought by the delays in the old Court of Chancery, which defeated all the purposes of a court of justice; but the romance proper is unconnected with this. The scene is laid in England about the middle of last century. Lady Dedlock, a beautiful society woman, successfully hides a disgraceful secret. She has been engaged to a Captain Hawdon; but through circumstances beyond their control, they were unable to marry, and her infant she believes to have died at birth. Her sister, however, has brought up the child under the name of Esther Summerson. Esther becomes the ward of Mr. Jarndyce, of the famous chancery law case of Jarndyce *vs.* Jarndyce, and lives with him at Bleak House. Her unknown father, the Captain, dies poor and neglected in London. A veiled lady visits his grave at night; and this confirms a suspicion of Mr. Tulkinghorn, Sir Leicester Dedlock's lawyer, already roused by an act of Lady Dedlock. With the aid of a French maid he succeeds in unraveling the mystery, and determines to inform his friend and client Sir Leicester of his wife's youthful misconduct. On the night before this revelation is to be made, Mr. Tulkinghorn is murdered. Lady Dedlock is suspected of the crime, disappears, and after long search is found by Esther and a detective, lying dead at the gates of the graveyard where her lover is buried. The story is told partly in the third person, and partly as autobiography by Esther. Among the other characters are the irresponsible and impecunious Mr. Skimpole; Mrs. Jellyby, devoted to foreign missions; crazy Miss Flite; Grandfather Smallweed; Krook, the rag-and-bottle dealer; Mr. Guppy, who explains all his actions by the statement that "There *are* chords in the human mind"; the odiously benevolent Mrs. Pardiggle; Mr. Turvey-drop, the model of deportment; Mr. Chadband, whose name has become prover-bial for a certain kind of loose-jointed pulpit exhortation; Caddy Jellyby, with inky fingers and spoiled temper, — all of whom Dickens portrays in his most humorous manner; and, among the most touching of his children of the slums, the pathetic figure of poor Jo, the crossing-sweeper, who "don't know nothink." The story is long and complicated; but its clever satire, its delightful humor, and its ingrained pathos, make it one of Dickens's most popular novels.

BLIND, THE ('Les Aveugles') (1890), by Maurice Maeterlinck, the Belgian poet-dramatist, is a play of symbolism, which, like the earlier 'The Intruder,' is one of the writer's best-known and most striking works. It is an eerie kind of alle-gory. On an island, in a mystic norland wood, under the night stars, sit a company of blind folk, men and women, under the guidance of an old priest returned from the dead. They grope about in a maze and query as to their location and destiny, — a strange, striking effect being produced by the grewsome setting of the scene and the implication of the words, through which the reader gathers that this is a sym-bolic picture of life, in which mankind wanders without faith or sight in the forest of ignorance and unfaith, depending upon a priestcraft that is defunct, and knowing naught of the hereafter. The poetry and humanity of this picture-play are very strong. Good English translations of this and other dramatic pieces by Maeter-linck have been made by Richard Hovey, Alexander Teixeira de Mattos, and Alfred Sutro.

BLITHEDALE ROMANCE, THE, the third of Nathaniel Hawthorne's romances, published in 1852, was the outcome of an intimate acquaintance with the members of the Brook Farm Community; and immortalized the brief attempt of that little group of transcendentalists to realize equality and fraternity in labor. It is more objective and realistic than Hawthorne's other works, and therefore in a sense more ordinary. Its central figure is Zenobia, a beautiful, intellectual, passionate woman; drawn as to some outlines from Margaret Fuller. At the time it opens, she has taken up her abode at Blithedale Farm, the counterpart of Brook Farm. The other members of the community are Hollingsworth, a self-centred philanthropist; a Yankee farmer, Silas Forster, and his wife; Miles Coverdale, the relater of the story; and Priscilla, who is Zenobia's half-sister, though of this fact Zenobia is ignorant. 'The Blithedale Romance' is a brilliant instance of Hawthorne's power as a story-teller. No scene in the whole range of fiction is more realistic than the finding of Zenobia's body in the dead of night; drawn from the dank stream, a crooked, stiff shape. and carried to the farm-house where old women in nightcaps jabber over it. Nothing could be more in the manner of Hawthorne than his comment that if Zenobia could have foreseen her appearance after drowning, she would never have committed the act.

BLOT IN THE 'SCUTCHEON, A, a tragedy by Robert Browning, published in 1843 and acted in the same year. Mildred Tresham, only sister of Thorold, Earl Tresham, has been seduced by Henry, Earl Mertoun, whose lands adjoin those of her brother. Anxious to repair this wrong he formally requests her in marriage. Thorold, who knows nothing of his sister's fall, readily consents. But a retainer sees Mertoun climb to Mildred's chamber and informs his master, without being able to identify the intruder. Questioned by her brother, Mildred admits the truth of the story, but refuses to divulge her lover's name or to dismiss Earl Mertoun. Deeply wounded in his family pride, which is morbidly intense, Thorold is too emotionally stirred to infer that Mertoun and the lover are the same. Denouncing Mildred as a shameless woman he rushes into the park, where he wanders until midnight. Meanwhile, Mildred's cousin, Gwendolen, in a talk with Mildred, has divined the identity of Mertoun and the offender, and with her fiancé and the earl's brother, Austin Tresham, goes out to find Thorold and to persuade him to forgiveness. They are too late, however. At midnight Thorold encounters Mertoun on his way to an interview with Mildred, and in his anger compelled him to fight a duel in which Mertoun, refusing to defend himself, is mortally wounded. Realizing at length his own harshness and injustice towards a boy who was penitent and eager to atone for his fault, Thorold exchanges forgiveness with Mertoun, and on his death, takes poison. He then goes to beg forgiveness of his sister who grants it and dies of a broken heart, closely followed by her brother. In dying he says that he leaves to Austin and Gwendolen an unblotted 'scutcheon. The catastrophe has been criticized as not inevitable and the speeches as too analytical for the stage, but there can be no doubt of the pathos and tragic power of this drama.

BLUE BIRD, THE ('L'Oiseau bleu'), by Maurice Maeterlinck (1908). In the opening scene of this charming play the children of a woodcutter dream on Christmas eve that a fairy sends them on a quest for the blue bird of happiness for her little girl. Tyltyl, the boy, wears a green hat with a magic diamond in the cockade, which enables human beings to see like the fairies. At a turn of the diamond, the hours come dancing from the clock, and the souls of Light, Bread, Milk, the Dog, and the Cat awaken to accompany the children on their journey. They first visit their grandparents in the Land of Memory, where the dead return to life whenever we remember them. Then they search the caverns of the Palace of the Night for the blue bird, and see wonderful things. In the Kingdom of the Future, under the guardianship of Father Time, they see the unborn babies, with all sorts of things they are to bring to earth, crimes, inventions, and blessings for mankind. In the forest, the Cat warns the trees that the children of the woodcutter, their enemy, are in their power. The ivy binds the paws of the Dog, but he bursts his bonds to defend his master. At a turn of the magic diamond they find themselves back in the cottage, and the blue bird in their own cage at home. They give the bird to a neighbor to please her little girl who is sick, and it flies away. This fantasy paints the moral that happiness, though sought far away, and in the past or the future, can best be found close by in acts of unselfishness. The final flight of the blue bird out of the little girl's hand implies that happiness lies in the quest, not the possession.

BLUEBEARD, see **FAIRY TALES.**

BOB, SON OF BATTLE, by Alfred Ollivant (1898). It is the author's mission to be the inventor of the novelistic dog, for though horses have often figured in fiction, this is the first fully fledged novel with a dog for the central figure. The scene of the story is laid in the Cumberland fells and much of the interest turns on the trials of the sheep dog of the North. Bob or "Owd Bob," as he is called, is the last of the renowned "gray dogs of Kennion," a wonderfully fine and sagacious breed of shepherd dogs, in which the dalesmen took great pride. The deeds of this splendid creature and those of his rival, "Red Wull," the "Tailless Tyke," are set forth in a powerful manner. The dogs' contest for the "Champion Challenge Dale Cup" is described in a most spirited way, and the contrast in the characteristics of the two rivals is as great as that between their respective owners. Bob's master, James Moore, the farmer of Kenmuir, calm, firm, and gentle-hearted, one of a race of gallant "statesmen," is as widely distinguished from the blasphemous little Adam McAdams as is the noble gray dog from his sanguinary foe. McAdams's attachment to his dog, which is so much stronger than that which he feels for his own son, whom he treats with much cruelty, is set forth with remarkable strength. The search for the mysterious sheep slayer, and the capture of "Red Wullie," red-fanged and caught in the commission of the one capital crime of the sheep-dog, causes the breakdown of the culprit's master and reveals a bit of tenderness yet left in his hardened nature. Many of the episodes are eminently pathetic, especially so is the action of the "gray dog of Kenmuir" upon the tragic occasion of the downfall of his rival.

BOCCACCIO, GIOVANNI, 'As Man and Author,' by John Addington Symonds (1895). A monograph in a hundred pages of fine learning and rare criticism, on one of "the three founders of modern literature." Dante, first of the three, stood within the shadow of mediæval theology; Petrarch, coming next, initiated the Revival of Learning, — humanism, scholarship, the modern intellectual ideal. Boccaccio was the founder of Greek studies, and Petrarch's ablest lieutenant in the pioneering work of the Revival of Learning. He created the novel; and though a second only to Petrarch, as Petrarch was a second only to Dante, in force of character and quality of genius, he ruled the course of Italian literature, and its far-reaching influences, for three centuries. Such in outline is the story to which Symonds devotes his monograph.

BOHEMIANS OF THE LATIN QUARTER, THE, 'Scènes de la Vie de Bohème,' by Henri Murger (1848). Murger knew intimately the life of the penniless Parisian artists, musicians, and literary men who congregated in the Latin Quarter, and in this story has faithfully depicted it. Not possessed of genius or not yet recognized at their true worth they were unwilling to devote themselves to mere money-making tasks and therefore continued to strive for success in painting, the drama, poetry, or music. They endured cold and hunger, spent money freely and generously when they had it, and when it was gone were not above evading their tailors or landlords, upon whom as on the industrious *bourgeoisie* they looked down as Philistines. In this story we are introduced to a poet, Rodolphe; a painter, Marcel; a musician, Schaunard; and a philosopher, Colette. All have the same high artistic ambitions joined with impecuniosity; all employ the same tricks to deceive the bill-collector and the waiter. The story of Rodolphe's connection with Mimi and Marcel's with Musette, and of the delights, jealousies, separations, and reconciliations that ensued gives a certain unity to the book, which is, however, mainly episodic. The pathetic death of Mimi closes the story, as it also forms the crisis of the drama, 'La Vie de Bohème,' which Murger and Théodore Barrière staged in 1849. This play is the source of the libretto of Puccini's opera, 'La Bohème' (1898). Murger's tale and drama will live as a vivid record of a noted phase of literary life in the nineteenth century.

BOHN'S LIBRARIES. A uniform 'Publication Series' of standard works of English and European literature, of which Thomas Carlyle said: "I may say in regard to all manner of books, Bohn's Publication Series is the usefulest thing I know." It covers the whole ground of history, biography, topography, archæology, theology, antiquities, science, philosophy, natural history, poetry, art, and fiction, with dictionaries and other books of reference; and comprises translations from French, German, Italian, Spanish, Scandinavian, Anglo-Saxon, Latin, and Greek. The originator of the enterprise, Henry George Bohn, a London bookseller, who startled the English trade by issuing in 1841 a guinea catalogue of some 25,000 important and valuable old books, began in 1846 with the Standard Library. His design was to promote the sale of good books by a cheap uniform issue of works of a solid and instructive kind. The choice of type, paper, and binding was most judicious, and for cheap books nothing equal to it had ever been done. The Standard soon numbered 371 vols. The other libraries added later were the Historical Library, 26 vols.; the Philosophical, 23 vols.; Ecclesiastical and Theological, 19 vols.; Antiquarian, 24 vols.; Illustrated, 61 vols.; Sports and Games, 6 vols.; Classical, 104 vols.; Collegiate, 9 vols.; Scientific, 30 vols.; Economics and Finance, 5 vols.; Reference, 24 vols.; Novelists, 17 vols.; and Artists, 9 vols.; making 721 volumes classified under 14 heads. The great success of Mr. Bohn's scheme initiated a period of inexpensive production and wide distribution of books of real value, which cannot but have done much for the spread of real culture throughout the English-speaking world.

BONDMAN, THE (1890), one of Hall Caine's best-known romances, abounds in action and variety. Stephen Orry, a dissolute seaman, marries Rachael, the daughter of Iceland's Governor-General, and deserts her before their boy Jason is born. Twenty years later, at his mother's death-bed, Jason vows vengeance upon his father and his father's house. Orry, drifting to the Isle of Man, has married a low woman, and sunk to the depths of squalid shame. Finally the needs of their neglected boy, Sunlocks, arouse Orry to play the man; he reforms and saves some money. Sunlocks grows up like a son in the home of the Manx Governor, and wins the love of his daughter Greeba. The youth is sent to Iceland to school, and is commissioned by Orry to find Jason and give him his father's money — a mission he is unable to fulfill. In trying to wreck, and then to save, an incoming vessel (which, unknown to Orry, is bearing the avenging Jason from Iceland to Man) Orry is fatally hurt; but is saved from drowning by Jason, who learns from the dying man's delirium that he has rescued the father and missed the brother whom he has sworn to kill. Throughout the story, his blind attempts at doing new wrongs to revenge the old are overruled by Providence for good; and at the last, no longer against his will but by the development of his own nature, he fulfills his destiny of blessing those he has sworn to undo.

BONHEUR DES DAMES, AU, see **ROUGON-MACQUART.**

7

BOOK OF DAYS, THE, edited by Robert Chambers. These two large volumes (which have for their sub-title 'A Miscellany of Popular Antiquities in connection with the Calendar') contain a curious and interesting collection of what its editor calls "old fireside ideas." This encyclopedic work was published in Edinburgh in 1863; and in bringing it out, the editor expressed a desire to preserve interest in what is "poetical, elevated, honest, and of good report, in the old national life," — recognizing the historical, and even the ethical, importance of keeping this active and progressive age in touch with obsolescent customs, manners, and traditions. Beginning with January first, each day of the year has its own curious or appropriate selection, and its allowance of matters connected with the Church Calendar, — including the popular festivals, saints' days, and holidays, — with illustrations of Christian antiquities in general. There is also much folk-lore of the United Kingdom, embracing popular notions and observances connected with times and seasons and notable events, biographies, anecdotes, historical sketches, and oddities of human life and character, as well as articles on popular archæology tending to illustrate the progress of civilization, manners, and literature, besides many fugitive bits and odd incidents.

BOOK OF MARTYRS, THE, by John Foxe, sometimes known as the 'History of the Acts and Monuments of the Church,' was first published in Latin in 1554, when the author was in exile in Holland. The first English edition appeared in 1563. By order of the Anglican Convocation meeting in 1571, the book was placed in the hall of every episcopal palace in England. Before Foxe's death in 1587 it had gone through four editions.

This strange work kept its popularity for many years. The children of succeeding generations found it a fascinating story-book. Older persons read it for its noble English, and its quaint and interesting narrative.

The scope of the 'Book of Martyrs' is extensive. The author calls the roll of the noble army from St. Stephen to John Rogers. From the persecutions of the early Church, he passes to those of the Waldenses and Albigenses, from these to the Inquisition, and from the Inquisition to the persecutions under English Mary. Foxe, as a low-churchman, was strongly prejudiced against everything that savored of Catholicism. His accounts are at times overdrawn and false. The value of the work, however, does not lie in its historical accuracy, nor in its scholarship; but rather in the fervent spirit which inspired its composition.

He writes, in conclusion, of the unknown martyrs: "Ah, ye unknown band, your tears, your sighs, your faith, your agonies, your blood, your deaths, have helped to consecrate this sinful earth, and to add to its solemn originality as the battle-field of good and evil of Christ and Belial."

BOOK OF MORMON, see **MORMON.**

BOOK OF NONSENSE, by Edward Lear (1846). This nursery classic, as much cherished by many adults as by hosts of children, is made up from four minor collections published at intervals during a long life. The author began as an artist; colored drawings for serious purposes were supplemented by others for the amusement of the groups of little ones he loved to gather around him; and the text added to them has proved able to endure the test of time without the aid of drawing, and much of it has become part of the recognized humorous literature of the language. Of pure illustration, save for an amusing title to each, his nonsense flora, fauna, and — shall we say, in his own manner

— deadthingsia, are full of wit; — for pictures can be witty as well as words, and the drawings of the "nastikreechia krorluppia," the "armchairia comfortabilis," and many other scientific curiosities, never pall. A grade beyond this in verbal accompaniment are the five-line stanzas after the manner of the "Old Man of Tobago," in 'Mother Goose': a few of these — as that of the "young lady of Lucca, Whose lovers had all forsook her," and of the "old man who said, 'How shall I manage this terrible cow?'" — rank as familiar quotations, but he has been so greatly surpassed by others in this line that they can hardly be thought his best. The "Nonsense Cookery," in one recipe of which we are told to "serve up in a clean table-cloth or dinner napkin, and throw the whole mess out of window as fast as possible"; and the voyage around the world of the four children, who are looked on by their elders with "affection mingled with contempt," add each their quota of good things. But unquestionably his highest level is reached in the famous ballads, such as 'The Jumblies,' who "went to sea in a sieve," and reached "the lakes, and the Torrible Zone, and the hills of the Chankly Bore"; the Pelican Song, with some really lovely poetry in it, and its inimitable nonsense refrain; 'The Owl and the Pussy Cat'; 'The Pobble who Has No Toes'; 'The Yonghy Bonghy Bo'; 'The Quangle Wangle Quee'; 'The Old Man from the Kingdom of Tess'; 'The Two Old Bachelors'; and others, — all together making up a melange of buoyant fun which entitles the author to the gratitude of everybody.

BOOK OF SNOBS, THE, a series of sketches by William Makepeace Thackeray, appeared first in Punch, and was published in book form in 1848. The idea of the work may have been suggested to Thackeray when, as an undergraduate at Cambridge in 1829, he contributed to a little weekly periodical called The Snob. In any case, the genus Snob could not long have escaped the satirical notice of the author of 'Vanity Fair.' He was in close contact with a social system that was the very nursery of snobbishness. In his delightful category, he omits no type of the English-bred Snob of the university, of the court, of the town, of the country, of the Church; he even includes himself, when on one occasion he severed his friendship for a man who ate peas with a knife, — an exhibition of snobbery he repented of later, when the offender had discovered the genteel uses of the fork. The half-careless, half-cynical humor of it all becomes serious in the last paragraph of the last paper: —

"I am sick of court circulars. I loathe *haut-ton* intelligence. I believe such words as Fashionable, Exclusive, Aristocratic, and the like, to be wicked unchristian epithets that ought to be banished from honest vocabularies. A court system that sends men of genius to the second table, I hold to be a Snobbish System. A society that sets up to be polite, and ignores Art and Letters, I hold to be a Snobbish Society. You who despise your neighbor are a Snob; you who forget your friends, meanly to follow after those of a higher degree, are a Snob; you who are ashamed of your poverty and blush for your calling, are a Snob; as are you who boast of your pedigree or are proud of your wealth."

BOOK OF THE COURTIER, THE, by the Count Baldassare Castiglione, a treatise in the form of a dialogue on the qualities and ideals of a gentleman, was published in 1528. The author, a distinguished courtier and diplomatist, was in the service of the Duke of Urbino from 1503 to 1516, and his book records the elegance and literary culture of that court, the most brilliant of the Italian Renaissance. Under the leadership of the gracious and accomplished duchess, Elisabetta Gonzaga,

a group of ladies and gentlemen, including Giuliano de' Medici, Bembo, and Bib-
biera, resolve to spend several evenings in discussing the nature of the perfect courtier.   That the courtier should be skilled in arms and manly exercises, socially gifted,
a good musician, well-read, a prudent and high-principled counsellor, and that his
accomplishments should be manifested with a careless ease and grace free from all
indication of labored study are the central conceptions of the company.   There is
an interesting digression on the ideal court lady and an eloquent panegyric by Bembo
on Platonic love.   A skill akin to Plato's is shown in the management of the dialogue,
the graceful play of repartee, and the invention of natural and picturesque incidents to add life and variety to the record.   An English translation by Thomas
Hoby (published 1561, reprinted 1900) is an important monument of Tudor prose
and had a marked influence on Elizabethan literature and ideals.

BOOKS AND BOOKMEN, by Andrew Lang (1886), is, as the author states in
the preface, "the swan-song of a book-hunter. The author does not book-hunt
any more: he leaves the sport to others, and with catalogues he lights a humble
cigarette."   Thus humorously he ushers in a little volume of rare vintage; the
mellow reflections of one whose scholarship in the subjects he treats is only equaled
by his geniality.   He writes with pleasant nonchalance of 'Literary Forgeries';
of 'Parish Registers'; of 'Bookmen at Rome'; of 'Bibliomania in France'; of
'Book-Bindings'; of 'Elzevirs'; of 'Japanese Bogie-Books,' — a feast indeed for
an epicurean!   The volume ends with a prayer that it may be somehow made legitimate "to steal the books that never can be mine."

BOOKS AND CULTURE, see **ESSAYS** of Hamilton Wright Mabie.

BOOKS AND THEIR MAKERS, A.D. 476–1709; by George Haven Putnam,
A.M. (2 vols., 1896).   A history of the production and distribution of the books
that constitute literature, from the fall of the Roman Empire to the close of the
seventeenth century, when copyright law, in an English statute of 1710, first recognized the writings of an author as property to be protected.   In an earlier work,
'Authors and their Public in Ancient Times,' Mr. Putnam covers the whole ground
of the making and circulation of books down to the fall of the Roman Empire.
The three volumes admirably tell the story of books, from their beginnings in Babylonia, Egypt, India, Persia, China, Greece, and Rome, to the age of the printed
in place of the manuscript book; and then the immensely expanded story from
Gutenberg's production of a working printing-press to the "Act of Queen Anne."
It would be hard to find a more entertaining or a more delightfully instructive story
than that here drawn from wide resources of scholarly research, critical discernment,
and broadly sympathetic appreciation of every phase of a great theme, and handled
with happy literary skill.   The history of the making of manuscript books in the
monasteries, and later in the universities, and of some libraries of such books; and
the further history of the great printer-publishers after the revival of learning, and
of some of the greatest authors, such as Erasmus and Luther, is a record of that
pathway through twelve centuries which has more of light and life than any other
we can follow.   By readers who value literature as bread of life and source of light
to mankind, Mr. Putnam's volumes will be given an important place.

BOOTS AND SADDLES; or, LIFE IN DAKOTA WITH GENERAL CUSTER, by Elizabeth B. Custer (1885).   The author says that her object in writing this book,
which records her experiences in garrison and camp with her husband, was to give

civilians a glimpse of the real existence of soldiers in the field. Her married life was not serene: she was left in 1864 in a lonely Virginia farmhouse to finish her honeymoon alone, her husband being summoned to the front; and at scarcely any time during the next twelve years was she free from fear of immediate or threatened peril. General Custer was ordered to Dakota in the spring of 1873. Mrs. Custer's book gives a lively and detailed account of their life there from 1873 to 1876, the time of the general's death. All those little details — the household habits and changes, the packings and movings, the servants' remarks, the costumes, the weather, the frolics and the feasts — that are so much to women, and the absence of which makes the picture so dim, here appear. The regimental balls, the pack of hounds, her husband's habits and looks and horsemanship, the coyotes, the sleigh-rides, the carrying of the mail, the burning of the officers' quarters, the curious characters and excursionists, the perplexities and pleasures of army domestic life, the Indians, the gossip, the ins and outs of army etiquette, the deserters, the practical jokes, are duly described. Her sketch of thirty-six hours spent in a cabin during a Dakota blizzard, with no fire, the general sick in bed and requiring her attention, the wind shrieking outside and at times bursting in the door, the air outdoors almost solid with snow that penetrated the smallest cracks and collected on the counterpane, and (to help matters) a party of bewildered soldiers, some of them partially frozen, claiming her hospitality and care, — is very graphic.

There is an interesting chapter on General Custer's literary habits, and an appendix containing extracts from his letters. Captain King has described army life in the West from the masculine side; such a book as this paints it from the feminine.

BORIS GODOUNOFF, an historical drama, mainly in blank verse, written by Alexander Sergyéevitch Pushkin, in 1826 and first acted in 1831. Inspired by the chronicle-histories of Shakespeare, Pushkin chose for his theme the troubled period of Russian history that followed the death of Czar Theodore, the son of Ivan the Terrible, in 1598. The play begins at Moscow, where conversations of the nobles and the people show the dangerous condition of the realm. Theodore has died without an heir, his younger brother, Dimitry, having been assassinated in 1591. Although suspected of having ordered the death of Dimitry, the late czar's brother-in-law, Boris Godounoff, is felt to be the strongest man in Russia and is urged by nobles and people to accept the crown. After some show of resistance he complies. The scenes now shift to the year 1603. In the monastery of Tchudoff is a young monk, Gregory Otrepieff, of a noble Galician family. Restless and ambitious he listens with delight to the stories of an old monk who tells him of the exploits of Ivan and Theodore and the murder of Dimitry, which he knows to have been ordered by Boris. Learning that he and the murdered prince would have been of the same age, Gregory resolves to pass himself off as Dimitry, saved from death. He escapes from the monastery, by cleverness and address evades the guards who have overtaken him at a tavern, and gets across the border into Lithuania. News soon comes that he has proclaimed himself as Dimitry and that the Polish king and people have accepted him and are preparing an invasion to seat him on the throne. The Russians are profoundly stirred by the intelligence, though restrained by the stern measures of Czar Boris. Meanwhile Gregory, the false Dimitry, delays his attack, while he makes love to the beautiful Marina, daughter of the Polish voyevod, Mnichek. In a powerful scene with her he admits that he is an impostor, not enduring to receive her love in another's name. At first she overwhelms him with scorn and contempt; but when he says defiantly that he *is* the czarevitch in spirit, that whether the Poles believe him to be the true or false Dimitry they will follow him as a pretext of war, and that he will prove himself worthy in spite of her scorn, she admires his manliness and promises that if he conquers Boris and makes himself czar she will marry him. We are then shown a number of battle and counsel scenes as the invaders enter Russia and Boris takes measures against them. A preliminary victory for the false Dimitry is followed by his defeat by superior numbers. He retires, however, and raises a new army, stirred up by the belief that he is Dimitry. At this juncture Czar Boris suddenly dies, giving to his son advice which resembles that of Henry IV. to Prince Hal. The young Theodore has no opportunity to follow it, however. An ambassador from Dimitry soon urges the people to an uprising; and the new czar with his sister Xenia is killed in prison. The play is a mere succession of historical tableaux without division into acts and without any well-marked structure. The style has the simple directness of the old chronicles from which the story is drawn. The incidents are represented with historic faithfulness and dramatic force. The opera by Moussorgsky founded on this drama was given in St. Petersburg in 1874, and in a first performance in New York in 1913.

BORIS LENSKY, a German novel by Ossip Schubin, was published in an English translation in 1891. The story is centred in the career of a famous musician, whose name gives the title to the book. A violinist of world-wide reputation, a man to whom life has brought golden gifts, he is yet unhappy, as forever possessed with a craving for the unattainable. The most unselfish love of his barren life is for his beautiful daughter Mascha. Her downfall, when little more than a child, becomes a means of testing this love. Nita von Sankjévich, a woman whom Lensky had once sought to ruin, comes to his rescue in Mascha's trouble, and procures the girl's marriage to her false lover. The book closes with Lensky's death; when his son Nikolai, who had cherished a hopeless love for Nita, begins a new life of calm renunciation, free from the selfishness of passion.

BOSTONIANS, THE, by Henry James, was published in 1886. Written in a satirical vein, it presents with unpleasant fidelity a strong-minded Boston woman possessed by a "mission." Olive Chancellor, a pale, nervous, intense Bostonian, "who takes life hard," is never so happy as when struggling, striving, suffering in a cause. The cause to which she is devoted throughout the novel is the emancipation of women. Living in a one-sex universe of her own creation, she takes no account of men, or regards them as monsters and tyrants. When the book opens she discovers, or believes she discovers, a kindred soul, — Verena Tarrant, the daughter of a mesmeric healer, a beautiful red-haired impressionable girl; a singularly attractive prey for the monster man, but possessed nevertheless of gifts invaluable to the cause of women's rights, if properly utilized. Certain phases of Boston life — as women's club meetings, intellectual séances, and lectures — are depicted with great cleverness; and the characters are delineated with James's wonted shrewdness and humor. The novel abounds in epigrammatic sentences. Olive's smile is likened to "a thin ray of moonlight resting upon the wall of a prison." The smile of Miss Birdseye, a worn philanthropist, was "a mere sketch of a smile, — a kind of installment, or payment on account; it seemed to say that she would smile more if she had time." Miss Chancellor "was not old — she was sharply young."

BOSWELL'S LIFE OF JOHNSON, see **JOHNSON.**

BOTANIC GARDEN, THE, by Erasmus Darwin.   The first part of this long poem appeared in 1781; and received so warm a welcome that the second part, containing the 'Loves of the Plants,' was published in 1789.   It was intended "to describe, adorn, and allegorize the Linnæan system of botany."   After the classic fashion of his day, the poet adopts a galaxy of gnomes, fays, sylphs, nymphs, and salamanders; affording, as he says, "a proper machinery for a botanic poem, as it is probable they were originally the names of hieroglyphic figures representing the elements."   And concerning the 'Loves of the Plants,' he remarks that as Ovid transmuted men and women, and even gods and goddesses, into trees and flowers, it is only fair that some of them should be re-transmuted into their original shapes.

> "From giant oaks, that wave their branches dark,
> To the dwarf moss that clings upon their bark,
> What beaux and beauties crowd the gaudy groves,
> And woo and win their vegetable loves!"

The whole poem, of many hundreds of lines, is written in this glittering heroic verse; some of which is poetical, but the greater part labored, prosaic, and uninteresting.   The book might have been forgotten but for the parody upon it, 'The Loves of the Triangles,' which appeared in the Anti-Jacobin; much to the amusement, it is said, of the caricatured poet.   As the grandfather of Charles Darwin, and as an early observer of some of the natural phenomena upon which the Darwinian system rests, Erasmus Darwin has of late years become once more an interesting figure.

BRAMBLE-BEES, see **MASON-BEES.**

BRAVO, THE, by James Fenimore Cooper (1831), is a tale of Venice in the sixteenth century, full of mystery and intrigue, and the high-sounding language which fifty years ago was thought the natural utterance of romance.   Don Camillo Monforte, a Paduan noble, has a right by inheritance to a place in the Venetian Senate. He becomes obnoxious to the Council, and a bravo is set on his track to kill him. He has fallen in love with Violetta, a young orphan heiress designed for the son of an important senator; and she consents to elope with him.   A priest marries them; but by a trick she is separated from him and carried off.   The Bravo, sick of his horrible trade, has refused to take a hand in the kidnapping of Violetta; and confesses to Don Camillo all he knows of it, promising to help him recover his bride. Jacopo, the Bravo, finds her in prison, and contrives her escape to her husband; but is himself denounced to the Council of Three, and pays for his treachery to them with his head.   The romance is of an antiquated fashion; and has not the genuineness and personal force of Cooper's sea stories and 'Leatherstocking Tales,' which grew out of an honest love for his subjects.

BREAD-WINNERS, THE, by John Hay, appeared anonymously in 1883.   It is a social study of modern life.   Alfred Farnham, a retired army officer, takes a kindly interest in Maud Matchin, the handsome but vulgar daughter of a master carpenter in a Western city.   Maud's head is turned by Farnham's kindness, and she boldly confesses her love to him — which is not reciprocated.   Maud's rejected lover, Sam Sleeny, an honest but ignorant journeyman in Matchin's employ, is jealous of Farnham.   He is dominated by Offitt, a vicious demagogue, and joins a labor-reform organization.   Farnham loves his beautiful neighbor Alice Belding.   She refuses his addresses, but soon discovers that her heart is really his.   During a riotous labor strike (described at length), Farnham organizes a band of volunteer patrolmen for the protection of life and property. His own house is attacked by the mob, and Sleeny assaults its owner with a hammer; but failing to kill him, threatens future vengeance. Offitt now pays his addresses to Maud, who intimates that she desires to see Farnham suffer for his affront to her. Offitt stealthily enters Farnham's home, strikes him with a hammer borrowed from Sleeny, and makes off with a large sum of money — just as Alice and Mrs. Belding arrive in time to care for Farnham's serious hurts. Offitt dexterously directs suspicion to Sleeny, who is arrested. The real culprit hastens to Maud, and urges her to fly with him. Suspecting the truth, she refuses, and wheedles from Offitt his secret, which she at once reveals. In the meanwhile, Sleeny breaks jail and flies to Maud's home. Here he meets Offitt, and kills him for his perfidy. Sleeny is at once cleared of the charge of assaulting Farnham, but is tried for the killing of Offitt and acquitted upon the ground of temporary insanity. The novel is brilliantly written, and its presentation of the conditions of labor is very graphic.

BRIDE FROM THE BUSH, A, by Ernest William Hornung (1890), is a simple tale, directly told. There is little descriptive work in it, the characters are few and distinct, and the story is developed naturally.

Sir James and Lady Bligh, at home in England, are startled by the news from their elder son, Alfred, that he is bringing home a "bride from the bush," to his father's house. The bride arrives, and drives to distraction her husband's conventional family, by her outrages upon conventional propriety. Gladys tries hard to improve; but after an outbreak more flagrant than usual, she runs away home to Australia, because she has overheard a conversation which implies that her husband's prospects will be brighter without her, and that he has ceased to love her. Alfred, broken-hearted at her disappearance, and apprehensive for a time that she has drowned herself, breaks down completely; and as soon as he is partially recovered, he goes out to Australia to find her. On the way to her father's "run," he takes shelter from a sand-storm in the hut of the "boundary rider," finds a picture of himself on the pillow, and surmises the truth, of which he is assured a few moments later, when Gladys, the "boundary rider," comes galloping in. Explanations follow; and the reunited couple decide to remain in Australia, and never to return "home" except for an occasional visit. The book is full of a spirit of adventure, and a keen sense of humor, which give value to a somewhat slight performance.

BRIDE OF LAMMERMOOR, THE, by Sir Walter Scott (1819), is included in the group of 'Waverley Novels' called 'Tales of my Landlord.' The plot was suggested by an incident in the family history of the earls of Stair. The scene is laid on the east coast of Scotland, in the year 1700. The hero is Edgar, Master of Ravenswood, a young man of noble family, penniless and proud. He has vowed vengeance against the present owner of the Ravenswood estates, Sir William Ashton, Lord Keeper, whom he considers guilty of fraud; but foregoes his plans on falling in love with Lucy, Sir William's daughter. There is a secret betrothal; the ambitious Lady Ashton endeavors to force her daughter to marry another suitor; and in the struggle Lucy goes mad, and Ravenswood, thinking himself rejected, comes to an untimely end. The most famous character in the book is the amusing Caleb Balderstone, the devoted old steward of Ravenswood, who endeavors constantly to save the family honor and to conceal his master's poverty by ingenious devices and lies, and whose name has become the symbol of "the constant service of the antique world." Though sombre and depressing, the 'Bride of Lammermoor' is very popular; and the plot has been used by Donizetti in the opera 'Lucia.'

BRIDGEWATER TREATISES, THE, were the result of a singular contest in compliance with the terms of the will of the Earl of Bridgewater, who died in 1829. He left £8000 to be paid to the author of the best treatise on 'The Power, Wisdom, and Goodness of God, as manifested in the Creation.' The judges decided to divide the money among the authors of the eight following treatises: — 'The Adaptation of External Nature to the Moral and Intellectual Constitution of Man,' by Dr. Thomas Chalmers, 1833; 'Chemistry, Meteorology, and the Function of Digestion,' by William Prout, 1834; 'History, Habits, and Instincts of Animals,' by William Kirby, 1835; 'Geology and Mineralogy,' by Dean (William) Buckland, 1836; 'The Hand . . . as Evincing Design,' by Sir Charles Bell, 1833; 'The Adaptation of External Nature to the Physical Condition of Man,' by John Kidd, M.D., 1833; 'Astronomy and General Physics,' by William Whewell, 1833; 'Animal and Vegetable Physiology,' by Peter Mark Roget, 1834. All these essays were published as Tracts for the Times; they had a large circulation, and no small influence in their own period.

BRIGHT, JOHN, THE LIFE OF, by G. M. Trevelyan (1913). Bright's biographer has the supreme qualifications of sympathy for the subject, interest in the material which he has to handle, and consummate literary skill. Besides supplying a detailed account of Bright's early days, entrance into public life, and public activities, he paints an intimate and life-like portrait of the man which enables the reader to realize Bright's unique power as an orator. "Bright," he says, "was first and foremost a preacher of broad principles in their moral and poetic force, a speaker less instructive, but even more moving than Gladstone." He has himself described the difference between them thus: "When I speak I strike across from headland to headland. Mr. Gladstone follows the coastline; and when he comes to a navigable river he is unable to resist the temptation of tracing it to its source." On another occasion Bright said, quoting Milton, "'True Eloquence I find to be none but the serious and hearty love of truth.' And I have endeavored, as far as I have had the opportunities of speaking in public, to abide by that wise and weighty saying. So far as I am able to examine myself, during the thirty years that I have been permitted to speak at meetings of my countrymen, I am not conscious that I have ever used an argument which I did not believe to be sound, or have stated anything as a fact which I did not believe to be true." Hence the man who at the beginning of his career was so hated by some people that they used to say "they would go twenty miles to see John Bright hanged" became a national institution.

BRITAIN, see **HISTORIA BRITONUM.**

BRITAIN, ECCLESIASTICAL HISTORY OF, see **ECCLESIASTICAL.**

BRITISH INDUSTRY AND COMMERCE, THE GROWTH OF, see **GROWTH.**

BROAD HIGHWAY, THE, by Jefferey Farnol (1911). The scene of this story is laid in England in the early part of the eighteenth century. It gives the adventures and experiences of Peter Vibart, related in a graphic and picturesque manner by himself. An orphan, he has been brought up by a rich and eccentric uncle who dies leaving him his fortune if he marries Lady Sophia Sefton within the year, otherwise he is cut off with a legacy of ten guineas. Peter, being independent in spirit, declines to marry a person whom he does not know and taking his ten guineas starts out on

"The Broad Highway" to seek his fortune. He meets with all sorts of thrilling adventures, is soon robbed of his money and left penniless. Being skilled in wrestling, Peter is victorious on many occasions when he is called upon to show his prowess, and bearing a striking resemblance to his dissolute cousin Maurice Vibart, who is a famous fighter, he is frequently taken for him. A great lover of nature, as well as a scholar, Peter thoroughly enjoys his wandering existence and decides to try his hand at the trade of blacksmith, meanwhile, taking up his habitation in a deserted hut in a hollow in the woods. One night he is awakened by the bursting in of his door and the sudden entrance of a beautiful woman who is fleeing from a pursuer. Peter at once comes to the rescue and after a fierce fight downs his adversary, who proves to be his cousin Maurice. The lady gives her name as Charmian Brown and explains that she has started to elope with Maurice Vibart but repenting her rash act has sought Peter's hut as refuge. Finding Peter much injured by his encounter, Charmian binds up his wounds and ministers to his comfort. Wishing to hide herself and finding Peter a thorough gentleman, Charmian remains at the hut, cooks his meals, and makes an ideal home for him. Peter, of course, falls in love with his charming companion and they decide to go to the minister's house to be married. On their return Peter is called to the bedside of a dying friend and during his absence Maurice Vibart is mysteriously shot outside of his house. Peter suspects Charmian, who tells him she only shot her pistol in the air, and lets himself be arrested for the murder. He escapes from prison and runs across the real murderer who is an old enemy of Maurice's and who confesses to the crime. Peter overjoyed, hastens to his wife, who proves to be Lady Sophia Sefton, who has disguised herself as Charmian Brown.

BRONTË, CHARLOTTE, LIFE OF, by Mrs. Gaskell, was published in 1857, two years after the death of the author of 'Jane Eyre.' It has taken rank as a classic in biographical literature, though not without inaccuracies. Its charm and enduring quality are the result of its ideal worth. It is a strong, human, intimate record of a unique personality, all the more valuable because biased by friendship. A biography written by the heart as well as the head, it remains for that reason the most vital of all lives of Charlotte Brontë. A mere scrap-book of facts goes very little way toward explaining a genius of such intensity. A new edition, ed. by Clement K. Shorter was published in 1900.

BRONTË, CHARLOTTE, AND HER CIRCLE, by Clement K. Shorter, was published in 1896. It is not a biography, but a new illumination of a rare personality, through an exhaustive collection of letters written by, or relating to, the novelist of Haworth. In the preface the editor writes: "It is claimed for the following book of some five hundred pages that the larger part of it is an addition of entirely new material to the romantic story of the Brontës." This material was furnished partly by the Rev. Arthur Bell Nicholls, Charlotte's husband, and partly by her lifelong friend Miss Ellen Nussey.

The arrangement of the book is calculated to assist the reader to a clearer understanding of Charlotte Brontë's life. A chapter is given to each person or group of persons in any way closely related to her. Even the curates of Haworth are not overlooked. Yet the editor's discrimination is justified in every instance by letters relating directly to the person or persons under consideration. The entire work is an interesting contribution to the ever-growing body of Brontë literature.

BROOK KERITH, THE, by George Moore (1915). The author's theory of the "Christ myth" is the theme of an historical novel, the life of Jesus. The first part of the book is the story of Joseph of Arimathea, the son of the rich merchant. The setting is the little Galilean village on the lake, the picture of the period, and the customs of Jewish family life, and primitive sects like the Essenes. Joseph becomes interested in Jesus, the shepherd, who has left his flocks to foretell the end of the world. Peter, James, and John, fishermen in his father's employ, become disciples of Jesus, and Joseph would also follow him but for his father's illness and his promise not to leave him. He does not see Jesus again until he finds him crucified on the cross in Jerusalem. Joseph asks his friend Pilate for permission to remove the body for burial, and takes Jesus to his own tomb. After the holy women, Mary and Martha, have left the tomb, Joseph discovers that Jesus is still living, and carries him home in the night and hides him in the empty gardener's cottage. Joseph listens to the tales of the resurrection without comment. As soon as Jesus recovers from his wounds, Joseph goes with him to the Essenes by the Brook Kerith, where Jesus had lived before his ministry, as the humble shepherd of the community. For thirty years Jesus tends the flocks. He comes to admit to himself that he committed a great sin of blasphemy against God when he believed he was the Messiah prophesied by the Book of Daniel. He repents the violence of his teachings in Jerusalem. Paul, persecuted for preaching Christianity, takes refuge one night with the brethren. Jesus asks him, "And who are these Christians?" Paul tells him the story of the resurrection and the mediation of the Son, dying on the cross for the sins of the world. Jesus is horrified at the supernatural Christianity of Paul's imagination, and resolves to go to Jerusalem and tell the truth. Paul considers him a mad man and impostor, and Jesus is forced to see that his story will not be believed. In accordance with one of the old legends it is suggested that Jesus goes to preach in India. Moore's conception of Jesus is two-fold, the spiritual leader of the Sermon on the Mount, the fanatic, misled by pride of the scourging in the Temple, and always one of the great men of the ages.

BROTHERS KARAMAZOV, THE, a novel by Fedor Dostoevsky (1879–1880). The three brothers are the sons of a depraved, debauched father, for whom the two older sons, Dmitri and Ivan, feel hatred and contempt. The youngest son, Alyosha, is a character like Prince Myshkin, the "Idiot," a friend to all humanity, loved and trusted by his father and brothers. Ivan is the intellectual member of the family, a materialist and sceptic, whose restless mind finally tortures itself to its own destruction. Dmitri, the eldest, is a man of violent undisciplined passions. He quarrels with his father over his inheritance and is his rival for the love of Grushenka, a woman who had been seduced and abandoned when a very young girl, and is now the mistress of a rich old merchant. The father's passion is entirely base, but Dmitri loves her and wants to marry her. The frenzied jealousy of the two is known by everyone, and Dmitri threatens to kill his father. When the old man is found murdered and robbed, all the circumstances point to Dmitri's guilt. There is a fourth son, Smerdyakov, the illegitimate child of an innocent imbecile girl. Smerdyakov is a servant in the house, but is not suspected because he is an epileptic and is found in convulsions when the crime is discovered. He confesses to Ivan that he killed the father, following to their logical conclusion Ivan's idea that "all is permissible"; Ivan who desired his father's death, realizes that he unknowingly has instigated the murder. Ivan's evidence at the trial does not save his brother Dmitri, because he is almost delirious with brain fever, and mixes fact and hallucination. Smerdyakov commits suicide before the trial. In drunken anger Dmitri had written a letter to a young girl, Katerina Ivanovna, to whom he was betrothed, in which he threatens to kill his father to get money. She produces the letter to save Ivan whom she really loves. Dmitri is thus condemned through his own folly, which prejudices the peasant jury against him.

BROWNING, ELIZABETH BARRETT, LETTERS OF. Edited by Frederic G. Kenyon. (2 vols., 1897.) This definitive presentation of Mrs. Browning's character and career is a selection from a very large mass of letters collected by Mr. Browning, and now used with the consent of R. Barrett Browning. It is made a chronicle, and practically a life, by the character of the letters and the addition of connecting links of narrative. The letters give an unusually full and interesting revelation of Mrs. Browning's character, and of the course of her life. The absence of controversy, of personal ill-feeling of any kind, and of bitterness except on certain political topics, is noted by the editor as not the result of any excision of passages, but as illustrating Mrs. Browning's sweetness of temperament. The interest of the work as a chapter of life and poetry in the nineteenth century is very great.

BRUT, THE, a metrical chronicle of early British history, both fabulous and authentic, and the chief monument of Transitional Old English, first appeared not long after the year 1200. Its author Layamon, the son of Leovenath, was a priest, residing at Ernley on the banks of the Severn in Worcestershire. His work is the first MS. record of a poem written after the Conquest in the tongue of the people. The Norman-French influences had scarcely penetrated to the region where he lived. On the other hand, the inhabitants were in close proximity to the Welsh. The additions that Layamon made to the 'Brut' show how deeply the Arthurian legends had sunk into the minds of the people.

The 'Brut' is a translation, with many additions, of the French 'Brut d'Angleterre' of Wace, which in its turn is a translation of Geoffrey of Monmouth's 'Historia Britonum.' Layamon's version begins thus: —

"There was a priest in the land Who was named Layamon. He was son of Leovenath, — May the Lord be gracious to him! — He dwelt at Ernley, at a noble church Upon Severn's bank. Good it seemed to him, Near Radstone, Where he read book. It came to him in mind, And in his chief thought That he would of England Tell the noble deeds. What the men were named, and whence they came, Who English land First had, After the flood That came from the Lord That destroyed all here That is found alive Except Noah and Sem Japhet and Cane And their four wives That were with them in the Ark. Layamon began the Journey Wide over this land, And procured the noble books Which he took for pattern. He took the English book that Saint Bede made, Another he took, in Latin, That Saint Albin made, And the fair Austin Who brought baptism in hither; the third book he took, Laid there in the midst, That a French clerk made, Who was named Wace, Who well could write, and he gave it to the noble Eleanor that was Henry's Queen, the high King's. Layamon laid down these books and turned the leaves. He beheld them lovingly."

The 'Brut' contains, however, few traces of Bede's chronicle. It follows Wace closely, but amplifies his work and adds to it. Some of the additions are concerned with the legendary Arthur. Layamon's most poetical work is found in them. The beautiful legends of the great king seem to have appealed powerfully to his imagination and to his sympathies as a poet. He makes Arthur say in his dying speech: —

"I will fare to Avalun, to the fairest of all maidens, to Argante the Queen, an elf most fair, and She shall make my wounds all sound; make me all whole with healing draughts. And afterwards I will come again to my kingdom, and dwell with the Britons with Mickle Joy."

BRUT, ROMAN DE. A poem in eight-syllable verse, composed by Robert Wace, but indirectly modeled upon a legendary chronicle of Brittany entitled 'Brut y Brenhined' (Brutus of Brittany), which it seems was discovered in Armorica by Walter, archdeacon of Oxford, and translated into Latin by Geoffrey of Monmouth. This translation is declared to have been the source from which Wace drew his materials. He presented his poem to Eleonore of Guyenne in 1155, and it was translated into Anglo-Saxon by Layamon.

The 'Roman de Brut' relates that after the capture of Troy by the Greeks, Æneas came to Italy with his son Ascanius, and espoused Lavinia, daughter of King Latinus; she duly presented a son to him. This son, as well as Ascanius, succeeded to the kingly power; and the throne devolved at last upon Silvius, son of Ascanius. Silvius fell in love with a damsel who died upon giving birth to Brutus, from whom the 'Roman de Brut' takes its name. Brutus was a mighty hunter. One day he had the misfortune to slay his father with a misdirected arrow aimed at a stag, and forthwith he fled. First he went to Greece, where he delivered the Trojan captives; and next he gained the Armorican Isles, which he conquered, giving them the name of Britain. Afterward he made war upon the king of Poitou, founding the city of Tours, which he named in honor of his son. From Poitou he returned to the Armorican Isles, overcoming the giants in possession of that region, and once more naming it Britain. He immediately founded the city of London, and reigned long and gloriously there.

The narrative now concerns itself with the descendants of Brutus. The adventures of Lear, of Belin, of Brennus who voyaged to Italy, of Cassivellaunus who so bravely resisted Cæsar, of all the bellicose chiefs who opposed the dominion of the Roman emperors, are minutely related. But not until King Arthur is introduced do we meet the real hero of the 'Roman de Brut.' Arthur performs prodigies of valor, is the ideal knight of his order of the Round Table, and finally departs for some unknown region, where it is implied he becomes immortal, and never desists from the performance of deeds of valor. In this portion of the narrative figure the enchanter Merlin, bard to King Arthur; the Holy Grail, or chalice in which were caught the last drops of the Savior's blood as he was taken from the cross; Lancelot of the Lake, so styled from the place in which he was trained to arms; Tristan and his unhallowed love; Perceval and his quest of the Holy Grail. These and other features of the 'Roman de Brut' made it unprecedentedly popular. It was publicly read at the court of the Norman kings, that the young knights might be filled with emulation; while fair ladies recited it at the bedside of wounded cavaliers, in order that their pain might be assuaged.

BRUTUS, or, DIALOGUE CONCERNING ILLUSTRIOUS ORATORS, by Cicero (106–143 B. C.). The work takes its title from Brutus, who was one of the persons engaged in the discussion. The author begins by expressing his sorrow for the death of Hortensius, and the high esteem in which he held him as a speaker. Still he feels rather inclined to congratulate him on dying when he did, since he has thus escaped the calamities that ravage the republic. Then he explains the occasion and the object of this dialogue, which is a complete history of Latin eloquence. He relates the origin of the art of oratory among the Romans, its progress, and its aspect at different epochs; enters into an elaborate criticism of the orators that have successively appeared; and gives, in an informal sort of way, rules for those who seek tü excel in the oratorical art, and lays down the conditions without which success is impossible. The work is at once historical and didactic, and embraces every variety of style: being at one time simple and almost familiar, at another almost sublime; but always pure, sweet, and elegant.

BUDDHA FIELDS, see **GLEANINGS IN.**

BUDDHIST MAHÀYANA TEXTS, see **SACRED BOOKS OF THE EAST.**

BUDDHIST SUTTAS, see **SACRED BOOKS OF THE EAST.**

BURNS, LIFE OF, by J. G. Lockhart (1828).   Lockhart possessed in full measure the two indispensable qualifications for a biographer, love of the subject, and a discriminating candor. Both these characteristics are displayed in the 'Life of Burns,' which originally appeared unambitiously in Constable's Miscellany in 1828, and which has never been excelled by any of the numerous later biographers of the poet, though these have had the advantage of access to abundance of fresh material, especially in the form of correspondence. The picture which he has painted is unforgettable. The poet's father, immortalized as the saint, the father, and the husband of "The Cotter's Saturday Night"; his mother, whose inexhaustible store of ballads and tales stirred the imagination of the future poet; the mean cottage of his early years in which, as Murdoch, his teacher, said, "there dwelt a larger portion of content than in any palace in Europe"; the books and people that influenced his youth and first touched the chords of poetry within him; his numerous loves and the exquisite lyrics inspired by them; the strivings of genius held down by grinding poverty; the success of his first published book of poems and his manly independence when he became the lion of literary Edinburgh; his heresies in theology and politics; his letters, amongst the finest in English literature; his life at Dumfries; and his ostracism on account of his revolutionary opinions, — all these Lockhart describes with exquisite sympathy, fine literary skill, and sense of proportion. "Burns," he says, "short and painful as were his years, has left behind him a volume in which there is inspiration for every fancy, and music for every mood. . . . Already, in the language of Childe Harold, has,

> "' Glory without end
> Scattered the clouds away; and on that name attend
> The tears and praises of all time.' "

BURTON, CAPTAIN SIR RICHARD F., LIFE OF, by his wife. One of the most romantic figures of the nineteenth century was Sir Richard Burton. He was of mixed Irish, Scotch, English, French, and possibly Arabian and Gipsy blood; he claimed his descent direct from Louis XIV. of France; he published upwards of eighty bulky volumes, including translations of the 'Arabian Nights' and the 'Lusiad' of Camoens; he began the study of Latin when he was three, and Greek when he was four, and knew twenty-nine languages; he was the pioneer discoverer of Darkest Africa, and his adventures took him into all parts of the world. Out of such lives myths are made. In 1887, Francis Hitchman, aided by Isabel, Lady Burton, of whose character and ability he speaks in the highest terms, published an account of Burton's private and public life, including his travels and explorations in Asia, Africa, and both North and South America. After Sir Richard's death, his wife published in 1893, in two octavo volumes, with many portraits and other illustrations, a voluminous 'Life.'

in which she argues with passionate insistance that she, and she alone, is fitted to give a truthful and complete account of his wonderful career and his unique person-ality. "There are three people in the world," she says, "who might possibly be able to write sections of his life. Most of his intimate friends are dead, but still there are a few left." She insists that she was the one person who for more than thirty years knew him best. Daily, for all that time, she "cheered him in hunger and toil, attended to his comforts, watched his going out and coming in, had his slippers, dressing-gown, and pipe ready for him every evening, copied and worked for him, rode and walked at his side, through hunger, thirst, cold, and burning heat, with hardships and privations and danger. Why," she adds, "I was wife and mother, and comrade and secretary, and aide-de-camp and agent for him; and I was proud, happy, and glad to do it all, and never tired, day or night, for thirty years. . . . At the moment of his death, I had done all I could for the body, and then I tried to follow his soul. I am following, and I shall reach it before long." Lady Isabel belonged to a Roman Catholic family, and her relatives, like his, were opposed to the marriage, which took place by special dispensation in 1861. At the time of his death, Lady Burton startled society by declaring that he had joined "the true Church." She says: "One would describe him as a deist, one as an agnostic, and one as an atheist and freethinker, but I can only describe the Richard that I knew. I, his wife, who lived with him day and night for thirty years, believed him to be half-Sufi, half Catholic, or I prefer to say, as nearer the truth, alternately Sufi and Catholic." A little later she aroused much indignant criticism by burning Sir Richard's translation of 'The Scented Garden, Men's Hearts to Gladden,' by the Arabic poet, the Shaykh al Nafzâwi. She justifies her action with elaborate argu-ment, and declares that two projected volumes, to be entitled 'The Labors and Wisdom of Richard Burton,' will be a better monument to his fame than the unchaste and improper work that she destroyed.

Her alleged misrepresentations are corrected in a small volume entitled 'The True Life of Captain Sir Richard F. Burton,' by his niece, Georgiana M. Stisted, who uses the severest terms in her portrayal of the character of the woman whom her uncle married, as she declares, in haste and secrecy, and with effects so disastrous to his happiness and advantage.

Still another contribution to the topic is found in two thick volumes called 'The Romance of Isabel, Lady Burton,' which is the story of her life, told in part by herself and in part by W. H. Wilkins, whose special mission it is to correct the slanderous misrepresentations of the author of 'The True Life.' Whether as romance or reality, the story of this gifted couple, with all their faults, is an extraordinary contribution to the literature of biography.

BUSINESS OF BEING A WOMAN, THE, by Ida M. Tarbell (1913). The book is an appeal to the modern woman who is discontented with woman's rôle of child-bearing and home-making and desires to complete her emancipation by de-voting herself to some supposedly higher activity, usually by attempting to do the work of men. This type Miss Tarbell calls 'The Uneasy Woman' because of its restlessness, dissatisfaction, and unsettled state. Miss Tarbell is no enemy to the extension of woman's opportunities for education and employment but she is con-servative enough to hold that the main business of being a woman is still that of motherhood and the making of the home. She proceeds to show that these tasks, far from being narrow, tedious, and unworthy of an emancipated being, are of the noblest, the most absorbing, and the most rewarding kind, requiring all the added culture and power which woman's freedom has bestowed. The mere efficient management of the household requires an economic knowledge and a practical ability equal to that of the business man. The moral training of the children is a problem worthy of the highest energies. The proper training of domestic servants, usually foreigners, would do much to make them useful citizens, and thus promote democracy in the most practical way. Above all, the woman's business is noble because it is not merely material and mechanical but consists in the creation of a spirit that makes home a happy social centre. By these and other shrewd and practical arguments the author successfully combats the view that "celibacy is the aristocracy of the future" and makes her work a material contribution to the subject of her last chapter, "the ennobling of the woman's business."

BUSSY D'AMBOIS, by George Chapman. This, the most popular of Chapman's tragedies, first appeared in 1607 and was republished in 1608, 1616, 1641, 1657. The scene is set in the Court of Henry III. of France, who with his brother, Monsieur the Duke of Alençon, and the Duke of Guise, the head of the Spanish party in the French Wars of Religion, takes part in the action of the play. Bussy d'Ambois, of noble birth, but a child of fortune who has to depend on his valor and his character, is introduced to the Court by Monsieur whose purpose it is to use him as a tool to smooth his own path to the throne. But Bussy raises himself to a position of power and independence, and Monsieur and Guise, whom he has flaunted, combine to compass his destruction. This they attempt to accomplish by revealing to the Count of Mountsurry Bussy's passion for the Countess Tamyra, whom he used to visit by a subterranean passage known only to himself and a friar who had acted as his guide. The friar is killed and his ghost warns the lovers of his fate and their danger. Bussy is deceived by a letter which the Countess had been compelled by her husband to write in her blood, and going to meet her for the last time is confronted by the Count in the habit of the friar. Although he defeats his immediate adversary, he is shot by the hireling assassins of his other foes. The character of Bussy is powerfully drawn, but the other figures are bloodless and the style often degenerates into bombast.

BUT YET A WOMAN, by Arthur Sherburne Hardy (1883), is a romance of real life, its scene laid mainly in Paris during the time of the Second Empire. Renée Michael, a fair young girl destined to be a *réligieuse*, shares the home and adorns the salon of her elderly bachelor uncle, M. Michael. They enjoy the friendship of M. Lande, and his son, Dr. Roger Lande. The four, together with Father Le Blanc, a kindly old curé, and Madame Stephanie Milevski, make up a congenial house party at M. Michael's summer home on Mt. St. Jean. Stephanie, the half-sister of her host, is the young widow of a Russian nobleman who has died in exile. She was associated with the eminent journalist M. De Marzac in the Bourbon restoration plot, and became the object of his ardent though unrequited love. Her affection is for Dr. Roger Lande; but he loves Renée, and not in vain. Stephanie induces M. Michael to allow her to take Renée on a journey to Spain. Upon the eve of their departure, De Marzac, angered by Stephanie's continued denial of his suit, accuses her of taking Renée to Spain in order to prevent Roger from wooing her until the time set to begin her novitiate shall have arrived. The unraveling of this situation makes an excellent story. The book is written with charming delicacy of treatment, and conceived entirely in the French spirit.

CABOT, JOHN, The Discoverer of North America, and **SEBASTIAN,** his Son, 'a Chapter of the Maritime History of England under the Tudors,' (1496–1557) by Henry Harrisse (1895). A work of authority for the earliest history of America; especially valuable for its complete recovery of the true Cabot history, and exposure of the false tradition of things done and honors won by Sebastian, the son, who is proved to have grossly falsified the course of events to make himself a far more important figure than he ever was. He did indeed play no small part in the story after his father; but it not only gave no ground for the claims made by him in connection with the work of the father, but left him discredited by notable want of success. The entire history is admirably dealt with by Harrisse, and the story is one of great interest.

CÆDMON, SAINT, a Northumbrian poet of the seventh century and reputed author of the Anglo-Saxon metrical paraphrases of the Old Testament, is known to us chiefly through the account in Bede's 'Ecclesiastical History.' Cædmon is there described as an unlearned man who was often abashed when in company he in his turn was called upon to sing a song to the harp. On one of these occasions after he had left the company in shame at his inability, he dreamt that he heard a voice commanding, "Cædmon, sing something to me." He protested his ignorance but the voice repeated its command, and he asked: "What shall I sing." "Sing the beginning of created things," was the response. Then Cædmon sang verses which Bede renders as follows: "Now ought we to praise the founder of the heavenly Kingdom, the power of the Creator. His wise design, and the deeds of the Father in glory: how He, eternal God, was the Author of all things wonderful, who first created for the children of men the heaven for a roof and afterwards the earth — He, almighty guardian of mankind." On awakening Cædmon remembered his verses and added others. He was taken to Hild, abbess of the monastery at Whitby, who at once recognized that the unlearned herdsman had received the miraculous gift of inspiration. He became a monk and reproduced portions of the Bible in verse so beautiful that soon "his teachers were glad to become his hearers." The Anglo-Saxon poems 'Genesis,' 'Exodus,' and 'Daniel,' in a manuscript of the tenth century, edited by Junius in 1655, were ascribed by him to Cædmon, but they were not in the Northumbrian dialect. These and other poems are, however, usually known as 'Cædmonic,' and may have been based on his originals. Special interest attaches itself to a fragment on the "Fall of Man" interpolated in the 'Genesis' because of its resemblances to Milton's 'Paradise Lost.' It is possible that Milton may have become acquainted with the Cædmonic poem through Junius. See "Anglo-Saxon Literature" in the LIBRARY.

CÆSAR: A SKETCH, by James Anthony Froude (1880). A life of the great soldier, consul, and dictator of Rome, — a general and statesman of unequaled abilities, and an orator second only to Cicero. Mr. Froude calls his book a sketch only, because materials for a complete history do not exist. Cæsar's career of distinction began in 74 B.C., later than Cicero's, and ended March 15th, 44 B.C., nearly two years before the death of Cicero. The fascinations of style in Mr. Froude's brilliant picture of Cæsar are not equally accompanied with sober historical judgment. As in his other works, he exaggerates in drawing the figure of his hero. He is to be listened to, not for a verdict but a plea.

CÆSAR AND CLEOPATRA, by Bernard Shaw (1899). In an amusing preface to 'Three Plays for Puritans' the author claims that the Cæsar of Shakespeare is an

"admitted failure" and asks to be allowed to "set forth Cæsar in modern light."
In his theory of history the world in 48 B.C. was exactly like the world in 1907 A.D.,
and the comic satire of the play is the utterance of modern thoughts, allusions, and
slang of our own times by historic personages of this remote age.   His middle-aged
Cæsar is master of war but satiated with it.   Made pacific by the sight of nations
drenched in blood, he values clemency above all things.   Efficiency and a genius for
hard work are the qualities by which he has conquered the world.   The serpent of
the Nile is a charming young barbarian, by turns spitfire, petulant, and kittenish.
Terrified at the approach of the Roman legions and by rumors of the ferocity of
Cæsar, she has fled from the palace, seeking the protection of a baby sphinx in the
nearby desert.   Cæsar, alone, musing upon the vanities of life and the littleness of
man, finds her cuddled up asleep between the paws of the sphinx.   She invites the
"kind old gentleman" to come up and take the other paw, and warns him that
Cæsar will probably eat him.   This scene is quoted in the LIBRARY.   Cæsar insists
that Cleopatra return to the palace and act the queen without fear, and as the
Roman soldiers salute her companion, she falls into his arms sobbing with relief.
Ptolemy, king of Egypt, who disputes his sister's reign, is a boy of ten.   Brittanicus,
Cæsar's secretary, the exponent of respectability from the British Isles, is shocked to
learn that the custom of Egypt makes the brother and sister man and wife.   Cleopatra longs for power to cut off her brother's head, and poison her slaves to see them
wriggle.   During the siege by the Egyptians, while Cæsar waits for reinforcements,
Cleopatra is a prisoner in the palace.   She passes the Roman guards by rolling herself
in a rug which she sends to Cæsar.   Cæsar is most noble when he rebukes Cleopatra,
drunk with her newly-discovered power, for procuring the assassination of an enemy.
Cæsar departs for Rome with the promise that he will send Mark Antony back as a
present.   The curtain falls with the Queen in tears, but expressing the hope, nevertheless, that Cæsar will never return.

CÆSARS, THE LIVES OF THE FIRST TWELVE, by Caius Suetonius, 130–135
A.D.   A book of biographies of the Roman emperors from Julius Cæsar to Domitian;
and largely a book of anecdotes, mere personal facts, and, to no small extent, scandal,
much of which may have been fiction.   It throws hardly any light on the society of
the time, the character and tendencies of the period; but gives the twelve personal
stories with a care in regard to facts and a brevity which makes every page interesting.   The first six are much fuller than the last six.   In none of them is there any
attempt at historical judgment of the characters whose picture is drawn.   We get
the superficial view only, and to no small extent the view current in the gossip of the
time.   A fair English translation is given in the Bohn Classical Library.   A recent
English translation is by J. C. Rolfe in the Loeb Classical Library.

CÆSAR'S COMMENTARIES.   This great work contains the narrative of Cæsar's
military operations in Gaul, Germany, and Britain.   It was given to the world in
the year 51 B.C.   Every victory won by Cæsar had only served to increase the alarm
and hostility of his enemies at Rome, and doubt and suspicion were beginning to
spread among the plebeians, on whom he chiefly relied for help in carrying out his
designs.   When public opinion was evidently taking the side of the Gauls and
Germans, the time had come for Cæsar to act on public opinion.   Hence the 'Commentaries,' a hasty compilation made from notes jotted down in his tent or during a
journey.   "They form," says Mommsen, "a sort of military memoir, addressed by a
democratic general to the people from whom he derived his power."   To prove in an

indirect way, he himself keeping in the background, that he has done his best for the honor and advantage of Rome, is his main object.   He proceeds, then, to demonstrate the following propositions: A Germanic invasion threatened Gaul.   With Gaul in the hands of the Germans, the Romans knew from experience that Italy herself was not safe from invasion.   Cæsar's first achievement was to drive the Germans back across the Rhine.   Every event that followed was the necessary consequence of this victory.   The Belgæ, sympathizers with their Teutonic kinsmen, revolted after the defeat of Ariovistus.   To convince them that west of the Rhine, Rome was supreme, was the reason of Cæsar's campaigns in the north and east.   But how long would the Belgæ, Nervii, and other warlike tribes continue submissive, if the clans in the west remained independent?   It must be plain, therefore, to any patriotic Roman, that the naval and military operations of Cæsar and his lieutenants against the Veneti, the Armoricans, and the Aquitanians, were inevitable.   Perhaps, too, the patriotic Roman will conclude, although Cæsar is silent on the matter, that these brilliant campaigns redound as much to the glory of the Roman name as to that of Cæsar.   Although Gaul, protected by Rome, was now invincible, it was very desirable that the Germans and Britons should have tangible evidence of the fact, and so Cæsar crossed the Rhine and the Channel.   But unfortunately, the Gauls were not wise enough to accept the situation.   They revolted.   Cæsar suppressed the insurrection with a vigor and sternness they were never likely to forget; and at Alesia, a year before these Military Memoirs were to be circulated, the finest conquest that Rome ever made was forever completed.   The quality that especially gives distinction to the work is its simplicity.   "It is as unadorned," says Cicero, "as an ancient statue; and it owes its beauty and its grace to its nudity."   As to its truthfulness, we cannot decide absolutely, the Gauls not having written *their* Commentaries. But if Cæsar sinned in this respect, it was probably by omission, not by commission. Things the Romans might not like he does not mention: the sole aim of the book is to gain their suffrages.   There is no allusion to the enormous fortune Cæsar acquired by plunder.   On the other hand, he speaks of his cruelties — for instance, the killing in cold blood of 20,000 or 100,000 prisoners — with a calmness that to us is horrible, but which the Romans would deem natural and proper.

CALEB WILLIAMS, ADVENTURES OF, by William Godwin (1794), a curious, rambling, half sensational and half psychological story, met with immediate popularity, and furnished the suggestion of the well-known play 'The Iron Chest.'   Caleb, a sentimental youth, who tells his own story, is the secretary of a Mr. Falkland, a gentleman of fortune, cold, proud, and an absolute recluse.   Caleb learns that his patron had once been a favorite in society; his retiring habits dating from his trial some years earlier for the murder of one Tyrrel, a man of bad character, who had publicly insulted him.   Falkland having been acquitted, two laborers, men of excellent reputation, both of whom had reason to hate the knavish Tyrrel, have been hanged on circumstantial evidence.   Caleb, a sort of religious Paul Pry, is convinced that Falkland is the murderer, and taxes him with the crime.   Falkland confesses it, but threatens Caleb with death should he betray his suspicions.   The frightened secretary runs away in the night; is seized, and charged with the theft of Mr. Falkland's jewels, which are found hidden among his belongings.   He escapes from jail only to fall among thieves, is re-arrested, and makes a statement to a magistrate of Falkland's guilt, a statement which is not believed.   The trial comes on; Falkland declines to prosecute, and the victim is set at liberty.   Falkland, whose one idea in life is to keep his name unspotted, then offers to forgive Caleb and assist him if he will recant.   When he refuses, his enemy has him shadowed, and manages to hound him out of every corner of refuge by branding him as a thief.   Caleb, driven to bay, makes a formal accusation before the judge of assizes and many witnesses. Falkland, in despair, acknowledges his guilt, and shortly after dies, leaving Caleb — who, most curiously, has passionately loved him all this time — the victim of an undying remorse.

CALIPH VATHEK, see **VATHEK.**

CALL OF THE BLOOD, THE, by Robert Hichens (1906).   This is the story of an Englishwoman named Hermione Lester who marries a man named Maurice Delarey, ten years her junior.   At the time of her marriage Hermione is thirty-four and while having a striking personality is very plain in form and feature.   Her husband on the contrary is very handsome and has the coloring of the south, which shows his Sicilian blood that he has inherited from his grandmother.   Hermione has a warm friend in Emile Artois, an author and a man of genius, and between them a strong platonic friendship has existed for some years.   Before her marriage Hermione brings about a meeting between the two men and though Artois is impressed with Delarey's beauty and charm of manner he cannot help a feeling of distrust.   Hermione and Maurice go to Sicily on their honeymoon as the latter has never been there, and Hermione, who loves it, feels sure he will share her enthusiasm.   Her anticipations are realized as Maurice enters at once into the spirit of the place and is actually boyish in his enjoyment of everything.   After a couple of months of happiness Hermione is called to the bedside of Artois in Africa, where he is thought to be dying.   Hermione, however, nurses him back to health and after several weeks of convalescence is able to bring him back with her to Sicily.   During her absence Maurice, who is lonely and somewhat piqued that she should leave him, amuses himself with the friendship of a pretty Sicilian girl named Maddelena.   The acquaintance which begins innocently ends however in wrong doing, as "the call of the blood" is strong in Maurice and he cannot withstand the impulses of his nature. He is overwhelmed with shame at the thought of Hermione's learning of his falseness, and upon her return both she and Artois notice the change that has taken place in him.   Hermione ascribes it to jealousy of Artois, but the latter interprets it differently.   Maurice goes to bathe and is murdered by Salvatore, Maddelena's father, and his body is found in the water.   The truth is known by Artois and a faithful servant named Gaspare, but they hide everything from Hermione and she mourns truly for her husband whose character remains for her unblemished.

CALL OF THE WILD, by Jack London (1903).   The hero of this story, Buck, the offspring of a St. Bernard sire and a Scotch shepherd dog, is a pampered house dog on a large estate.   It is the time of the rush for gold in the Klondike, and he is stolen and shipped north to be brutally broken and trained to be a sledge dog.   He learns the primitive law of club and fang and wins the leadership of the dog team from the old leader, Spitz, in a terrible battle for survival.   There are many journeys in the ice and snow and much hardship until he finds in John Thornton the real master to whom he gives his heart and allegiance.   His master, proud of his dog, recklessly accepts a wager that Buck can break from the ice and walk away with a thousand pound load on a sledge, a task for ten dogs, and Buck wins for him.   Thornton is murdered by the Indians and Buck responds to the call of the wild, harking back to the life of his remote forbears as leader of a pack of wolves.   A vivid picture of the wild life of dog and man in the Alaska gold fields.

CALLED BACK, by "Hugh Conway" (Frederick John Fargus) (1884). Gilbert Vaughn, the hero of this story of mystery, is a young Englishman of fortune, totally blind from cataract. By a curious accident, he strays one midnight into a strange house, mistaking it for his own, and walks in upon a murder. He hears a scuffle and a woman's shrieks, and bursting into the room, stumbles over the body of a man. His keen sense of hearing informs him that there are three other men in the room, and a moaning woman. As he cannot identify them, the men spare his life, and drug him. Found by the police in a suburb, he is identified and taken home. On recovery, he finds no one to believe in his story. Two years later, the cataract is operated upon and he recovers his sight, when he falls in love with and marries a young girl of extraordinary beauty, Pauline March. She is half English, half Italian; her only living relative being an uncle, Dr. Ceneri, an Italian physician. After his marriage Vaughn discovers that his bride is mentally weak; that she has no memory, and scarcely any comprehension of what passes. The story then becomes complicated, and full of adventures in Italy and Siberia. Extremely sensational in character, and with little literary merit, the graphic force of this story, the rapidity of its movement, its directness, and its skillful suspension of interest, gave it for a season so extraordinary a vogue that it outsold every other work of fiction of its year.

CALLISTA, 'a Sketch of the Third Century', by John Henry Newman. Cardinal Newman tells us that this is an attempt to imagine, from a Catholic point of view, the feelings and mutual relations of Christians and heathen at the period described. The first few chapters were written in 1848, the rest not until 1855. The events here related occur in Proconsular Africa; giving opportunity for description of the luxurious mode of life, the customs and ceremonies, then and there prevailing. Agellius, a Christian, loves Callista, a beautiful Greek girl, who sings like a Muse, dances like a Grace, and recites like Minerva, besides being a rare sculptor. Jucundus, uncle to Agellius, hopes she may lead him from Christianity; but she wishes to learn more concerning that faith. Agellius, falling ill, is nursed by Cyprian, bishop of Carthage, who is in hiding. A plague of locusts comes. Frenzied by their devastations and the consequent famine, the mob rises against the Christians. Agellius is summoned to his uncle for safety. Callista, going to his hut to warn him, meets Cyprian, who gives her the Gospel of St. Luke. While they discourse, the mob approaches and they are captured. Cyprian and Agellius, however, are helped to escape. Callista studies St. Luke and embraces Christianity. She refuses to abjure her religion, is put to death by torture, is canonized, and still works miracles. Her body is rescued by Agellius and given Christian burial. Her death proves the resurrection of the church at Sicca where she died: the heathen said that her history affected them with constraining force. Agellius becomes a bishop, and is likewise martyred and sainted.

CAMBRIDGE DESCRIBED AND ILLUSTRATED: 'Being a Short History of the Town and University.' By Thomas Dinham Atkinson. With introduction by John Willis Clark (1897). A very complete, interesting, and richly illustrated account of the English town and university, which has been in some respects even more than Oxford a seat of literature, as well as education, in England. To American readers especially, the work is of importance because of the extent to which Cambridge University graduates were leaders in the planting of New England. The story of the old town opens many a picture of early English life and that of the great group of famous colleges which constitute the university; and supplies chapters in the history of English culture peculiarly rich in interest, from the fact that Cambridge has so largely stood for broad and progressive views, while Oxford has until recently represented narrow conservatism.

CAMILLE ('La Dame Aux Camélias'), a novel by Alexandre Dumas the younger, was published in 1848, the celebrated play founded upon it appearing in 1852 at the Vaudeville Theatre in Paris. The popularity of both the novel and the play is owing, perhaps, to the fact that the incidents of the story admit of many interpretations of the character of the heroine. Like other women of her class, she is linked to, is indeed a representative of, the most inexplicable yet most powerful force in human nature. Camille is the portrait of a woman who actually lived in Paris. Dumas had seen her, and relates a love story of which she was the central figure. Like Aspasia, she has a strange immortality. Each reader of the book, like each spectator of the play, gains an impression of Camille that is largely subjective. The elusiveness of the personality, the young ardor that forced Dumas to tell the story straight from the heart, straight to the heart, give to 'Camille' its fascination.

CAMP, MAJOR HENRY WARD, see **THE KNIGHTLY SOLDIER.**

CANDIDA, by Bernard Shaw (1897). Candida, the heroine of this successful comedy, is the engaging wife of a clergyman who is fond of preaching in the pulpit and out of it. When Eugene Marchbanks, a youthful poet, tells him he is in love with Candida, the Rev. James Morell first laughs with condescending superiority but is finally goaded into dropping his rhetoric to shake Eugene. Though Eugene screams with fright, he has the courage of his ideas and succeeds in terrifying the clergyman out of his complacent attitude of model husband. The Rev. James, however, is a likeable, sincere person, not simply the "moralist and windbag" Eugene calls him. Eugene is an extraordinary character, reminiscent of Shelley, with the range of vision of a seer, beyond the comprehension of the conventional preacher. He is too sensitive for the everyday world, in which the clergyman deals out spiritual gruel, suitable for "cheap earthenware souls," and his domestic wife soils her beautiful hands to fill the lamps and slice the onions for supper. The two men agree that Candida shall choose between them. This scene of the "choice" is quoted in the LIBRARY. Candida calmly asks for bids since she is up at auction. Her husband offers her his strength, and Eugene, his weakness. She says she will choose the weaker of the two, and to his surprise it is her husband who holds her because of his need and dependence on her loving care. One of the most audacious speeches in the play is Candida's reply to her husband, when he tells her he relies on her goodness and purity. She says, "I would give them both to Eugene as willingly as I would give my shawl to a beggar dying of cold, if there were nothing else to restrain me. Put your trust in my love for you, James, for if that went I should care very little for your sermons — mere phrases that you cheat yourself and others with every day." Candida's frankness wounds her big boy of a husband at first, but her love convinces his pride. Eugene rejects this idea of love, and departs cured of his infatuation.

CANDIDE, ou, L'Optimisme, a satirical novel by Voltaire, was published anonymously in 1759, with the fictitious statement appended that it had been translated from the German by "M. le Docteur Ralph." Voltaire's aim was to ridicule the facile optimism so current in the eighteenth century, particularly as expressed in Pope's "Whatever is is right," and the dictum of Leibnitz that "All is for the best in this, the best of all possible worlds." The Lisbon earthquake of 1755 and the sufferings caused by the Seven Years' War had done something to shake this creed. Vol-taire determined to complete the overthrow by a burlesque narrative in which optimism should be reduced to absurdity. The hero, Candide, is the illegitimate scion of a noble German family. He is brought up at the Castle of Thunder-ten-tronckh, where he learns from the philosopher, Pangloss, that every effect has a cause, that every cause has a sufficient reason, and that all is for the best in this, the best of all possible worlds. Caught by the baron in making love to his daughter, Cunégonde, Candide is kicked out of the castle, forced into military service, beaten for desertion, forced into a great battle, and made a witness of the atrocities com-mitted in neighboring villages. Escaping from the army he falls in with a humane Anabaptist, Jacques, and later with Pangloss who tells him that the baron's castle has been destroyed by the soldiers and Cunégonde outraged and killed. Pangloss, who is suffering from the most abhorred of maladies, is cured by the kindly Jacques, and the three set out on a business voyage to Lisbon. They are shipwrecked in a dreadful tempest and the Anabaptist is drowned. Candide and Pangloss on arrival find the city destroyed by the famous earthquake of 1755 and thirty thousand people killed. Pangloss, attempting to console the survivors by his usual formula, is arrested for heresy and is hanged by the Inquisition, while Candide is flogged. He is, however, rescued by Cunégonde, who had not been killed but had been sold to a Portuguese Jew, who with the Grand Inquisitor, kept her as mistress. Candide manages to kill both these personages, and he and his lady love make their escape to Cadiz, where Candide obtains a captain's commission in an expedition against the Jesuit rebellion in Paraguay. During the journey an old attendant of Cunégonde, who has made her escape with them, relates her adventures, which are much more distressing than those of the young people. On arrival at Buenos Ayres Cunégonde is seized by the gover-nor and Candide is forced to fly to the rebels by the advent of Spanish officials who are pursuing the murderer of the Inquisitor. Among the rebels he finds the brother of Cunégonde, a priest and military commandant, who at first welcomes him, but whose insults when he hears of Candide's aspirations to the hand of his sister lead to a fight in which Candide severely wounds him. Accompanied by a half-breed servant, Cacambo, Candide traverses the forests of South America, visits the country of El Dorado, where the people are virtuous, brings away great treasures, despatches his servant to win back Cunégonde from Buenos Ayres, and sails for Venice, with a pessimistic philosopher, Martin, who believes the world ruled by evil. They visit France, where they meet with frivolity and dishonesty, touch the English coast, where they witness the execution of Admiral Byng "pour encourager les autres," and sojourn in Venice, where they make the acquaintance of the cultured and fastidious Pococurante, a nobleman who is weary of all the pleasures that the world can give. At length Candide gets word from Cacambo that Cunégonde is a slave in Con-stantinople. Cacambo had faithfully ransomed her and started for Venice, but they had been seized by a pirate and sold as slaves in Turkey. Candide, Cacambo, and Martin immediately go to Constantinople. On a galley they find two slaves who turn out to be Cunégonde's brother and Pangloss. Their lives have been miracu-lously saved, and by a series of adventures they have come to be rowers in the same galley. Candide now finds and ransoms Cunégonde, who has unfortunately become very ugly; but regard for his promise and anger at her brother, who still refuses his consent and is finally sent back to the galley, confirms Candide in his purpose of marrying her. The whole group now settles on a little farm beside the Bosphorus, where, on the advice of an old peasant, they find a measure of content in hard work. Pangloss is still an optimist; Martin says that work without thought is the only means of rendering life supportable; and Candide's unfailing motto is "il faut cultiv?t notre jardin." Voltaire never wrote a more brilliant polemic than this, and in spite of its cynicism the book has a core of sound sense, vehement hatred of oppression, and wise practical philosophy.

CANTERBURY PILGRIMS, THE, by Percy Mackaye (1903). This is a modern treatment in verse of the famous pilgrimage on which Geoffrey Chaucer, poet at King Richard's court, travels incognito with the pilgrims in order to come nearer their hearts and their lives to put them into verse. Alisoun, the jovial Wife of Bath, survivor of five husbands, has vowed to find a sixth spouse among the pilgrims, and in spite of the devotion of the miller and a dozen swains who aspire to her hand, her roving eye lights on Chaucer. He has already fallen under the spell of the gentle prioress, Madame Eglantine, charmed with her sweet simplicity and her French of "Stratford-atte-Bowe." She appeals to his chivalry for the needs of her little dog, "one ounce of wastel-bread, toasted a pleasant brown; one little cup of fresh milk." She confides to him that she expects to meet her brother, the Knight returning from the Holy Land. She has not seen him for many years, but will know him by his ring, marked with the letter "A" like the brooch she wears, with the motto "Amor vincit omnia." The jealous Alisoun overhears the conversation, and plots to win Geoffrey by guile. She insinuates that the prioress is on her way to meet a lover. A bet is made that if the prioress gives her brooch to any man except her brother, Chaucer must marry Alisoun at Canterbury. To secure the brooch Alisoun and her sweethearts kidnap the Knight; Alisoun dons his clothes, deceives the gentle prioress, and wins the bet. From the Man of Law, however, Geoffrey learns that no woman in England can be married more than five times. In the last act in front of Canterbury cathedral, King Richard and his court welcome the poet, and the king extricates him from his predicament, by allowing the suspension of the marriage law only in case of a miller, and the enamored miller relieves him of his ale-drinking sweetheart. A scene from the Tabard Inn is quoted in the LIBRARY.

CANTERBURY TALES, a collection of twenty-four stories, all but two of which are in verse, written by Geoffrey Chaucer mainly between 1386 and his death in 1400. The stories are supposed to be related by members of a company of thirty-one pilgrims (including the poet himself) who are on their way to the shrine of St. Thomas at Canterbury. The prologue which tells of their assembly at the Tabard Inn in Southwark and their arrangement that each shall tell two stories on the way to Canterbury and two on the return journey, is a remarkable picture of English social life in the fourteenth century, inasmuch as every class is represented from the gentle-folks to the peasantry. The transitional narratives between the stories, exhibiting the incidents of the journey, the effect of the tales on the company, the outbreaks of personal or professional jealousy among the pilgrims, and the other by-play incidental to a large and diverse group of fellow-travelers, are extremely entertaining and dramatic, the host, who presides over the proceedings, being an especially lifelike figure. The narrative is not continuous. Gaps have been left between certain stages of the journey for Chaucer did not live to fill out the vast scheme he had outlined, and instead of the one hundred and twenty-four tales which it would require has left but twenty-four. Some of these, like the Knight's Tale, and the Second Nun's Tale, were earlier works, others, like the Miller's Tale, the Reeve's Tale, the Nun's Priest's Tale, and the Pardoner's Tale, were written expressly for this collection and with its dramatic background in mind. The Canon's Yeoman's Tale was introduced as an afterthought and involved the bringing in of two additional members of the company. Practically all the tales, old and new, are skillfully adapted to their tellers. The tales represent almost every type of mediæval literature: the *fabliau*, the *märchen*, the pious tale, the saints' legend, the sermon, the *exemplum*, the lay, the metrical romance, and the romantic epic. They are masterpieces of narrative art, revealing the author's close observation of men and women, his delight in the process, his ready human sympathy, and his elusive humor. For fuller comments see the critical essay in the LIBRARY under 'Chaucer.'

CAPE COD, by Henry D. Thoreau (1865). Until Thoreau arrived to make acquaintance with its hard yet fascinating personality, Cape Cod remained unknown and almost unseen, though often visited and written about by tourists and students of nature. Something in the asceticism, or the directness, or the amazing keenness, or Thoreau's mind brought him into sympathetic understanding of the thing he saw, and he interpreted the level stretches of shore with absolute fidelity. In these pages the melancholy land looks as "long, lank, and brown" as it looks lying under the gray autumn sky. Nor does he spare any prosaic detail. The salt wholesomeness of his sea breeze does not wholly overcome the offensive flotsam and jetsam drifted up on the sand; but on the other hand, with the simplest means, he communicates what he feels so fully, — the savage grandeur of the sea, and its evanescent and ever-changing loveliness. In this, as in all his other books, Thoreau rises from the observation of the most familiar and commonplace facts, the comparison of the driest bones of observed data, to the loftiest spiritual speculation, the most poetic interpretation of nature. His accuracy almost convinces the reader that his true field was history or science, until some aerial flight of his fancy seems to show him as a poet lost to the Muse. But whatever his gifts, he was above all, as he shows himself in 'Cape Cod,' Nature's dearest observer, to whom she had given the microscopic eye, the weighing mind, and the interpretative voice.

CAPITAL, by Karl Marx (1867), English translation edited by Fred Engels, 1889. A book of the first importance, by the founder of international socialism; written with marvelous knowledge of economic literature and of the economic development of modern Europe, and not less with masterly skill in the handling of his extraordinary knowledge; a book of which a conservative authority has said: "Since the beginning of literature, few books have been written like the first volume of Marx's 'Capital.' It is premature to offer any definitive judgment on his work as a revolutionary thinker and agitator, because that is still very far from completion. There need, however, be no hesitation in saying that he, incomparably more than any other man, has influenced the labor movement all over the civilized world." The conservative aspect of Marx's teaching is in the fact that he honestly seeks to understand what, apart from any man's opinion or theory, the historical development actually is; and that he does not think out and urge his own ideal programme of social reform, but strives to understand and to make understood what must inevitably take place.

CAPTAIN FRACASSE, by Théophile Gautier. The scene is laid in France during the reign of Louis XIII.; the manners, morals, and language of that age being carefully depicted. The Château de la Misère, situated in Gascony, is the home of the young Baron de Sicognac, where he lives alone in poverty, with his faithful Pierre, and his four-footed friends Bayard, Miraut, and Beëlzebub. To a troop of strolling players he offers shelter, they in turn sharing with him their supper. Falling under the charms of Isabella, the pretty *ingénue* of the troop, he accepts their kindly offer to continue with them to Paris, where good fortune may await him. Martamoro, one of the actors, perishes in the snow; and Sicognac, ashamed of being a burden to his companions, takes his place, assuming the name of Captain Fracasse, and passing through many adventures on the road. Isabella returns the love of Captain Fracasse, but will not allow him to commit a mésalliance by making her his wife.

'Captain Fracasse,' although announced in 1840, was not published until 1863, when it met with most brilliant success. Much of the story is borrowed from the 'Roman Comique' of Scarron.

CAPTAIN VENENO, by Pedro Antonio de Alarcón (1881). The opening scene of this clever and amusing story is laid in Madrid, in the month of March, 1848. In a skirmish between the royal troops and a handful of Republicans, Don Jorge de Córdoba, called Captain Veneno (poison) on account of his brusque, pugnacious manner, is wounded before the house of Doña Teresa Barbastro, who shelters him. A professed hater of women and marriage, he laments his prolonged imprisonment in terms which anger the mother and amuse the daughter; but his kind heart is so apparent that his foibles are humored. When Doña Teresa dies she confides to him that she has spent her fortune in trying to secure the confirmation of the title of Count de Santurce, conferred on her husband by Don Carlos. He hides the truth from the daughter, Angustias, for a few days; but when she learns that he is paying the household expenses, she insists upon his leaving, now that he can walk. He tries to induce her to let him pension her, or provide for her in any honorable way except by marrying her, although he professes to adore her. His offers being rejected, he proposes marriage with one inexorable condition, — that if there should be children, they shall be sent to the foundling asylum; to which she laughingly agrees. The story is written with a breezy freshness; and the evolution of the Captain's character is delightfully done, from his first appearance to his last, where he is discovered on all-fours with an imp of three on his back, and a younger one pulling him by the hair, and shouting "Go lang, mule!" After 'The Child of the Ball,' this is the most popular of Alarcón's stories, as it deserves to be.

CAPTAINS ALL, by W. W. Jacobs (1905). Humorous stories of the escapades and wooings of sailors on shore. The night-watchman at the docks spins yarns reminiscent of the doings of Sam Small, Ginger Dick, and Peter Russett. Sam tries to elude his mates to pay court to a widow, the proprietress of a prosperous tobacco shop. They find him out, and for a time two more "captains" are his rivals, until they are disenchanted by the arrival of the widow's nine children who have been away on a visit. Sam signs up for a voyage to China instead of settling down on land, as he planned. The boatswain, hoping to win the landlady of an inn, hires another man to pretend to break into the inn one night to give him a chance to rescue his lady love from burglars. The lady unexpectedly locks the burglar in the closet, and the plot collapses. The boatswain hears a pistol shot and the widow rushes out to tell him she has killed a man. While he digs a grave in the yard to hide the body, the lady and the burglar become better acquainted as they are watching his efforts from the window. 'The Temptation' is the farcical tale of a converted burglar, a preacher in the sect of the Seventh Day Primitive Apostles, billeted on a brother apostle, who is a jeweler. Both he and the jeweler fear he may be tempted to relapse into sin. The jeweler spends a nervous night, hearing brother Burge in terrific conflict with the Devil, who apparently urges him to rifle the shop. The two men meet on the stairs, and the jeweler makes the excuse that he thought he heard burglars below, whereat the ex-burglar rushes terrified to his room, and shouts out the window for the police The officer arrests him, and in later explanations, it comes out that lurid allusions to a guilty past are covered in fact by a sentence of fourteen days for stealing milk cans Another story relates the confounding of a stingy sailor by a girl's wit. The old gaffer at the Cauliflower Inn relates anecdotes of the successful roguery of Bob Pretty-man, the poacher, and there is a gruesome tale of death on board ship at sea.

CAPTAINS COURAGEOUS, by Rudyard Kipling (1897), is a study in the evolution of character. The hero is an American boy, Harvey Cheyne, the son of a millionaire, a spoiled little puppy, but with latent possibilities of manliness smothered by his pampered life. A happy accident to the boy opens the way for the development of his better nature. In a fit of seasickness he falls from the deck of a big Atlantic liner, and is picked up by a dory from the Gloucester fishing schooner We're Here, commanded by Disko Troop, a man of strong moral character and purpose. This skipper is unmoved by Harvey's tales of his father's wealth and importance, nor will he consent to take him back to New York until the fishing season is over; but proposes instead to put the boy to work on the schooner at ten dollars a month. This enforced captivity is Harvey's regeneration. He learns to know the value of work, of obedience, of good-will. He is sent back to his father as a boy really worth the expense of bringing up. Mr. Cheyne returns good office with good office by securing Troop's son, Dan, a chance to rise as a seaman.

The simple story is told with a directness and clarity characteristic of Kipling, who appears so little in the pages of the book that they might be leaves from life itself. The strength and charm of the story lies in its rare detachment from the shackles of the author's personality, and in its intrinsic morality.

CAPTAIN'S DAUGHTER, THE, by Alexander Pushkin. This story, published in 1832, narrates the adventures of a young officer and his sweetheart, during Puga-chéf's rebellion, in the reign of Catherine II. Piotr Andreyevich Grinef, son of a wealthy Russian noble, joins the army, and is sent to the small fortress of Byélogorsk. Savelich, an old family servant, accompanies him thither, and with wonderful love and devotion acts the part of guardian angel. Captain Mironof, the commandant, a kindly old soldier, receives him with much affection and offers him the hospitality of his house; where Vasilisa his wife, good-hearted but inquisitive, oversees the affairs of the whole fortress. Piotr and the sweet-faced daughter Maria soon fall in love; but Schvabrin, the girl's rejected lover, causes the devoted pair to undergo many trials. In time, Emilian Pugachéf, a Cossack, assuming the title Peter III., arrives at the fortress with a band of insurgents, among them the traitor Schvabrin; and overpowering the garrison, captures the town. Captain Mironof and his wife are murdered, and Schvabrin, the traitor and deserter, is left in charge. Pugachéf, with unexpected gratitude, remembering a former kindness of Piotr, pardons him and permits him to leave the town, although Piotr will not swear allegiance. He goes to Orenburg with his servant; and while there receives a letter from Maria, who prays for help from Schvabrin's persecutions. Piotr rescues her, and she goes to his parents, who gladly welcome her, while Piotr joins a detachment of the army under Jurin. Here Schvabrin gives information that leads to his arrest as a spy and his sentence as an exile to Siberia. From this fate he is saved by Maria, who obtains his pardon from the Empress, and he is released in time to see Pugachéf hanged as a traitor. The author, who also wrote a serious history of the Pugachéf rebellion, gives in this delightful romance a very true account of that remarkable uprising.

CARACTÈRES, ou, MŒURS DE CE SIÈCLE, by La Bruyere. The first edition appeared in 1688. The eight editions that followed during the author's lifetime contained so many additional portraits, maxims, and paragraphs, that they were really new works. Each 'Caractère' is the portrait of some individual type studied by La Bruyère in the world around him. His position in the family of Condé, and consequent opportunities for character-study, afforded him all the materials he needed; and so he has given us a whole gallery of dukes, marquises, court prelates, court chamberlains, court ladies, pedants, financiers, and in fact representatives of every department of court, professional, literary, or civic life. He gets at them in the different situations in which they are most likely to reveal their personal and mental characteristics, and then makes them tell him their several secrets. Unlike Montaigne and La Rochefoucauld, he does not much care to meddle with the man and woman of all times and places. His victim is this or that man or woman belonging to the second half of the seventeenth century. Naturally, a mind-reader of this sort, who was also a master of the most polished sarcasm, clothed in the most classical French ever written save that of Racine and Massillon, would make many enemies; for under the disguise of Elmire, Clitiphon, and other names borrowed from the plays and romances of the age, many great personages of the literary and fashionable world recognized themselves. La Bruyère protested his innocence, and no doubt in most cases several individuals sat for a single portrait; but it is also pretty certain that he painted the great Condé in 'Émile,' and Fontenelle in 'Cydias,' and that many others had cause for complaint. While it is admitted that the picture he presents of the society of his time is almost complete, it does not appear that the 'Caractères' were composed after any particular plan. Still, although there may not be a very close connection between the chapters, there is a certain order in their succession. The first, which paints society in its general features, is a sort of introduction to the nine following, which paint it in its different castes. Universal ethics are the subject of the eleventh and twelfth, while the eccentricities and abuses of the age are dealt with in the thirteenth and fourteenth, and in the fifteenth we have the Christian solution. Some critics hold La Bruyère a democrat and a precursor of the French Revolution. The Caractères, however, teem with passages that prove he accepted all the essential ideas of his time in politics and religion. A large number of manuscript "keys" to the 'Caractères' appeared after their publication. Quite a literature has grown up around these keys. The 'Comédie de La Bruyère' of Édouard Fournier deals with the key question, both exhaustively and amusingly. The 'Édition Servois' (1867) of the 'Caractères' is considered by French critics unrivaled; but English readers will find that of Chassary (1876) more useful, as it contains everything of interest that had appeared in the preceding editions.

CARICATURE AND OTHER COMIC ART, 'in All Times and Many Lands,' by James Parton. This elaborate work, first published in 1877, is full of information to the student of caricature, giving over 300 illustrations of the progress of the art from its origin to modern times. Beginning with the caricature of India, Egypt, Greece, and Rome, as preserved in ceramics, frescoes, mosaics, and other mural decoration, Mr. Parton points out that the caricature of the Middle Ages is chiefly to be found in the grotesque ornamentations of Gothic architecture; in the ornamentation of castles, the gargoyles and other decorative exterior stonework of cathedrals, and the wonderful wood-carvings of choir and stalls. Since that time, printing has preserved for us abundant examples. The great mass of pictorial caricature is political; the earliest prints satirizing the Reformation, then the issues of the English

Revolution, the French Revolution, our own Civil War, the policies and blunders of the Second Empire, and many other lesser causes and questions. Social caricature is represented by its great apostle, Hogarth, and by Gillray, Cruikshank, and many lesser men in France, Spain, and Italy, England and America; and in all times and all countries, women and matrimony, dress and servants, chiefly occupy the artist's pencil. When this volume was published, the delightful Du Maurier had not reached a prominent place on Punch, and the American comic papers, Life, Puck, and the rest, were not born; but English caricature of the past century is treated at great length. The book opens with a picture of two 'Pigmy Pugilists' from a wall in Pompeii, and closes with a sentimental street Arab of Woolf exactly like those which for twenty years after he continued to draw. The volume is not only amusing, but most instructive as a compendium of social history.

CARISSIMA, THE, by the lady who chooses the pen-name of "Lucas Malet" (1896),—and who is a daughter of Charles Kingsley, — is a character-study of a most subtle description. The heroine, Charlotte Perry, affectionately called Carissima, is a "modern" young woman, very pretty and charming, apparently full of imagination and sympathy, and a lover of all things true and beautiful. She is engaged to Constantine Leversedge, a manly, straightforward, honest Englishman, who has made a large fortune by hard work in South Africa, and who adores his beautiful fiancée. At the Swiss hotel, where Leversedge and the Perrys are staying, she meets an old friend, Anthony Hammond, who tells the story. Hammond finds out that Leversedge is suffering from an extraordinary obsession or incubus; he is haunted by a dog, which he had once killed. He never sees it except at night, and then he sees only its horrible eyes; but he can feel it as it jumps on his knees or lies against his breast in bed. Hammond advises him to tell Charlotte of this apparition, and she accepts the revelation with great courage, professing her willingness to help her lover to drive the horror from his mind. She declares her only fear to be that instead of conquering the hallucination, she may, after her marriage, come to share it. Leversedge offers to give her up; but she bravely sticks to her promise, Leversedge telling her that if the grisly thing finds her out, he will free her by taking his own life. On the night after the wedding, she cries out in terror that she sees the dog. Her husband, horror-stricken that what he dreaded has happened, yet implores his wife to stay by him, to help him fight the spectre; certain that together they may lay the ghost. Then she tells him that she will not remain; that she does not love him; that she has lied about the dog, playing a trick to get rid of him. The trick is successful, for the next morning Leversedge's body is found in the lake. The Carissima assumes the properly becoming attitude of despair, but it is plain that she will marry another lover. The book displays a skillful intricacy of subordinate causes and effects, but its chief interest lies in the study of the Carissima, who seems an angel but who is "top-full of direst cruelty."

CARLINGFORD, see CHRONICLES OF.

CARLYLE, THOMAS, LIFE OF, by J. A. Froude (1882). The historian Froude was not only the pupil but the devoted friend of Thomas Carlyle. Fortunately for the reader he has gone to his master for ideas, but not for style, and in this biography his love for the vivid and picturesque is seen at its best. A great deal of the material, particularly correspondence upon which the book is based had been put into his hands by Carlyle himself with permission to use it at his discretion. He has produced one of the most fascinating, but one of the most misleading of biographies, which nevertheless holds the attention of the reader by its consummate literary art. He has made the sage of Ecclefechan less generous, less considerate, and less lovable than he was, but he has left an extraordinarily vivid picture of the grim, gruff (though, at bottom, kindly-natured) philosopher. "His function was sacred to him, and he had laid down as a fixed rule that he would never write merely to please, never for money, that he would never write anything save when specially moved to write by an impulse from within; above all, never to set down a sentence which he did not in his heart believe to be true, and to spare no labor till his work to the last fibre was as good as he could possibly make it." Hardly less fascinating is the picture of Jane Welsh, the delicately-nurtured, highly-gifted woman who had been passionately devoted to Edward Irving, later the founder of the Catholic Apostolic Church, but who had married Carlyle, whom she merely esteemed. "She had the companionship of an extraordinary man. Her character was braced by the contact with him, and through the incessant self-denial which the determination that he should do his very best inevitably exacted of her. But she was not happy. Long years after, in the late evening of her laborious life, she said: 'I married for ambition. Carlyle has exceeded all that my wildest hopes ever imagined of him — and I am miserable.'"

CARMEN, by Prosper Mérimée (1847). Don José Lizzarrabengoa, Navarrese and corporal in a cavalry regiment, meets at Seville a gipsy known as Carmen. While taking her to prison for a murderous assault on another woman, he is induced to connive at her escape, and is reduced to the ranks therefor. Jealously infatuated with her, he kills his lieutenant, and becomes a member of a band of smugglers of which she is the leading spirit. In a duel with Garcia, her *rom* or husband, he kills Garcia also, and becomes in his turn the *rom* of the fascinating Carmen. Jealous of every man who sees her, he offers to forget everything if she will go with him to America. She refuses — for the sake of another lover as he believes; and he declares that he will kill her if she persists. A thorough fatalist, she answers that it is so written and that she has long known it, but that "free Carmen has been and free she will always be." Don José kills her, buries her body in the woods, and riding to Cordova, delivers himself to the authorities. In this story, the author, turning away from an artificial society, has returned to the passion and ferocity of primitive nature. The romance is best known in its operatic version.

CASA BRACCIO, by F. Marion Crawford, was published in 1896, and is one of the author's stories of Italian life. Angus Dalrymple, a young Scotch physician, falls in love with a beautiful nun, Sister Maria Addolorata, who is of the distinguished Roman house of Braccio. She is in a convent in Subiaco, near Tivoli. Dalrymple persuades her to run off with him, and they fly, pursued by the curses of Stefanone, the peasant father of a girl whose hopeless love for Angus leads to her suicide. The scene then shifts to Rome, seventeen years having elapsed. Dalrymple appears with his daughter Gloria, the mother having died. Gloria is very beautiful and sings superbly. She is loved by two men: Reanda, a gifted Italian artist, and Paul Griggs, an American journalist. She marries the former; but after a while leaves him and lives with Griggs, gives birth to a child by him, and kills herself. Before her death she writes to Reanda, confessing to him that she deplores having left him and has always loved him. The letters containing the admission are sent by Reanda to Griggs, out of revenge, and break his heart, for he has idolized Gloria. Meanwhile the father, Dalrymple, is at last tracked down and murdered by Stefanone, the peasant of Subiaco, in a church where the Scotchman was musing on his wife's memory. The first half of the novel is much the best.

CASTLE DALY, by Annie Keary. 'Castle Daly,' the most popular of Annie Keary's stories, was published in 1875. It relates the fortunes of an English and an Irish family. The scene is laid in Connemara, Ireland, during the famine of 1846 and the formation and insurrection of the party of "Young Irelanders" in 1846–49. The impartial delineation of the strong and weak points of Celtic character, the combination of acute observation and deep feeling, and the exciting history of the rebellion led by O'Brien, make it very interesting. The Irish nature is typified in the golden-haired heroine, Ellen, daughter of Squire Daly; in Connor, her brother, who joins the "Young Irelanders"; and in Cousin Anne of "Good People's Hollow," who, heedless of the precepts of political economy, rules her tenants with lavish kindness. On the other hand, the careful foresight of the Saxon race is well portrayed in John Thornely, and in Pelham, the eldest son of Squire Daly, who inherits English characteristics from his mother.

CASTILIAN DAYS, by John Hay, has gone through many editions since its publication in 1871; a prosperity at which no reader of the book can wonder. Its seventeen essays present a vivid picture of the life of Spain. Joining a graceful and brilliant style with the happiest perception of the significance of things seen, the author finds a subject worthy of his interpretation in that mediæval civilization of the Iberian peninsula which has lasted over into the nineteenth century — a civilization where the Church holds sway as it did in the Middle Ages: where the upper classes believe in devils, and the peasants dare not yawn without crossing themselves, lest an imp find lodgment within them; where duels are fought in all deadliness whenever a caballero's delicate honor is offended; where alone the Carnival survives as an unforced, naïve, popular fête; where rich and poor play together, and enjoy themselves like children. Madrid, Segovia, Toledo, Alcalá, Seville, are so described that we see the people abroad, at home, at church, at the bull-fights, at the miracle-play, in the brilliant light of their sub-tropical skies. The whole history of Spain — of its Moors, its Goths, its Castilians — is written in its streets and its customs; and Mr. Hay has translated it for Western eyes to read. His book is the work at once of the shrewd social observer and the imaginative poet.

CASTING AWAY OF MRS. LECKS AND MRS. ALESHINE, THE (1886), by Frank R. Stockton. This chronicle sets forth the curious experiences of Mrs. Lecks and Mrs. Aleshine; two middle-aged widows, from a little New England village, who, having "means," decide to see the world and pay a visit to the son of one of them, who has gone into business in Japan. On the steamer crossing the Pacific they meet a young Mr. Craig, who tells the story. The two ladies and Mr. Craig are cast away in most preposterous circumstances, on a lonely isle in mid-ocean. Many of the scenes, like the escape from drowning of the two widows, are of the very essence of true humor, of a grotesque form; and the story-teller's invention and humor never once flag. It is a good example of Stockton's unique method of story-telling — the matter extremely absurd and the manner extremely grave, the narrative becoming more and more matter-of-fact and minutely realistic, as the events themselves grow more and more incredible.

CASTLE OF OTRANTO, THE, by Horace Walpole. It is curious that a man with no purpose in life beyond drinking tea with Lady Suffolk, or filling quarto note-books with court gossip, should produce an epoch-making book; — for the 'Castle of Otranto,' with its natural personages actuated by supernatural agencies, is the prototype of that extraordinary series of romantic fictions which began with Anne Radcliffe, and was superseded only by the Waverley novels.

The reader's interest is aroused with the first page of the romance, and never flags. Conrad, son of Manfred, Prince of Otranto, about to marry Isabella, daughter of the Marquis of Vicenza, is found in the castle court, dashed to pieces under an enormous helmet. Now deprived of an heir, Manfred declares to Isabella his intention of marrying her himself; when, to his horror, his grandfather's portrait descends from the wall, and signs to Manfred to follow him. Isabella meanwhile, by the assistance of a peasant, Theodore, escapes to Friar Jerome. For this intervention, Manfred, now returned from his tête-à-tête with his grandfather's phantom, leads the youth into the court to be executed, when he is found to be Jerome's son, and is spared. At this moment a herald appears demanding of Manfred, in the name of Prince Frederick, his daughter Isabella and the resignation of the principality of Otranto usurped from Frederick; who follows the proclamation, is admitted to the castle and informed of Manfred's desire to marry Isabella, when word comes that she has escaped from Jerome's protection. A series of ludicrous portents hastens the dénouement: drops of blood flow from the nose of the statue of Alphonso, the prince from whose heirs the dukedom has been wrested; unrelated arms and legs appear in various parts of the castle; and finally, in the midst of the rocking of earth, and the rattling of "more than mortal armor," the walls of the castle are thrown down, the inmates having presumably escaped. From the ruins the statue of Alphonso, raised to gigantic proportions, cries, "Behold in Theodore the true heir of Alphonso." Isabella, having been rescued at the critical moment, is of course married to Theodore.

This wildly romantic tale, published in 1764, was enthusiastically received by the public; who, as Sir Leslie Stephen so well says, "rejoiced to be reminded that men once lived in castles, believed in the Devil, and did not take snuff or wear powdered wigs."

CASTLE RACKRENT, by Maria Edgeworth. This, as the author announces, is "an Hibernian tale taken from facts and from the manners of the Irish squire before the year 1782." The memoirs of the Rackrent family are recounted by Thady Quirk, an old steward, who has been from childhood devotedly attached to the house of Rackrent. The old retainer's descriptions of the several masters under whom he has served, vividly portray various types of the "fine old Irish gentleman"; foremost among them all being Sir Patrick Rackrent, "who lived and died a monument of old Irish hospitality," and whose "funeral was such a one as was never known before or since in the county." Then comes Sir Murtagh Rackrent, whose famous legal knowledge brought the poor tenants little consolation; and his wife, of the Skinflint family, who "had a charity school for poor children, where they were taught to read and write gratis, and where they were kept spinning gratis for my lady in return." Next follows Sir Kit, "God bless him! He valued a guinea as little as any man, money was no more to him than dirt, and his gentleman and groom and all belonging to him the same." Also his Jewish wife, whom he imprisons in her room for seven years because she refuses to give up her diamonds. In the words of Thady, "it was a shame for her not to have shown more duty, when he condescended to ask so often for such a bit of a trifle in his distresses, especially when he all along made it no secret that he married her for money." The memoirs close with the history of Sir Condy Rackrent, who dies from quaffing on a wager a great horn of punch, after having squandered the remainder of the family fortune. 'Castle Rackrent' was issued in 1801, and was the first of a series of successful novels produced by the author, whose descriptions of Irish character, whether grave or gay, are unsurpassed. Sir Walter Scott has acknowledged that his original idea, when he began his career as a novelist, was to be to Scotland what Miss Edgeworth was to Ireland.

CATHARINE, by Jules Sandau (Paris: 1846). The scene of the story is laid in the little village of Saint-Sylvain, in the ancient province of La Marche. The curé, a priest patterned after the Vicar of Wakefield, who spends most of his income of 800 francs in relieving his poor, discovers that there is no money left to buy a soutane for himself and a surplice for his assistant; while the festival of the patron of the parish is close at hand, and their old vestments are in rags. There is consternation in the presbytery, especially when the news arrives that the bishop of Limoges himself is to be present. Catharine, the priest's little niece, determines to make a collection, and goes to the neighboring château, although warned that the Count de Sougères is a wicked and dangerous man. But Catharine, in her innocence, does not understand the warning; and besides, Claude, her uncle's choir-leader and her friend from childhood, will protect her. When she reaches the château she meets, not the count, but his son Roger, who gives a liberal donation to the fair collector, and afterward sends hampers of fowl, silver plate, etc., to the presbytery, so that Monseigneur of Limoges and his suite are received with all due honor. Universal joy pervades the parish, which Claude does not share. He is jealous; and with reason, for Catharine and Roger quickly fall in love with each other. 'Catharine' ranks as one of the best, if not the best, of Sandeau's works. While some of the scenes show intense dramatic power, and others are of the most pathetic interest, a spirit of delicious humor pervades the whole story, an unforced and kindly humor that springs from the situations, and is of a class seldom found in French literature.

CATHARINE FURZE, "by Mark Rutherford; edited by his friend Reuben Shapcott." Published in 1893, this book opens with a description of Easthorpe, the market town of the English Eastern Midlands, in 1840. The two inns are patronized by landlords, farmers, tenants, and commercial travelers; especially on election days. The story centres about the life of Mr. and Mrs. Furze, and their daughter Catharine, aged about nineteen. Mike Catchpole, by an accident in the factory of Mr. Furze, loses his eyesight. Catharine, with a sense of justice, insists that he shall be made an apprentice in the business. The girl is sent to school to the Misses Ponsonby, who are very strict in their religious habits and manner of instruction, and whose pupils are questioned upon the weekly sermon by the preacher, Mr. Cardew. He has not learned the art of being happy with his wife; and when he meets Catharine they discuss Milton, Satan, and the divine eternal plan. Cardew's presence is inspiriting to her. Tom Catchpole, a clerk in her father's store, worships Catharine from afar. At last he confesses his love and she refuses him. After her return from school she finds life utterly uninteresting, having no scope for her powers. When she falls ill and fades away, Cardew is sent for: she tells him that he has saved her. "By their love for each other they were both saved." She takes up her life once more, and the book ends without a climax — almost without incident. Written with an almost heartless impersonality, it is a striking portraiture of that English lower middle-class life which Matthew Arnold pronounced so deadly for mind and soul. It might be called a tragedy of the unfulfilled.

CATO OF UTICA, by Joseph Addison. A tragedy in five acts and in blank verse. It was first represented in 1713. The scene is laid in a hall of the governor's palace at Utica. The subject is Cato's last desperate struggle against Cæsar, and his determination to die rather than survive his country's freedom. All the "unities" are strictly observed: there is no change of place, the action occurs on the same day, and all the incidents centre around Cato and conduce to his death. 'Cato' owed its extraordinary success to the deadly hatred that raged between the Whigs and Tories at the time: the Whigs cheered when an actor mentioned the word "liberty"; and the Tories, resenting the implied innuendo, cheered louder than they. To the Whigs Marlborough was a Cato, to the Tories he was a Cæsar. Bolingbroke, immediately after the performance, gave Booth, the Cato of the tragedy, fifty guineas "for having so well defended liberty against the assaults of a would-be dictator" (Marlborough). Every poet of the time wrote verses in honor of 'Cato,' the best being Pope's prologue; and it was translated into French, German, and Italian. The German adaptation of Gottsched was almost as great a success as the original.

CAUSERIES DU LUNDI, by Sainte-Beuve. Every prominent name in French literature, from Villehardouin and Joinville to Baudelaire and Halévy, is exhaustively discussed in the 'Causeries' of Sainte-Beuve, in his own day the greatest critic of the nineteenth century. The author sometimes discusses foreign literature; his articles on Dante, Goethe, Gibbon, and Franklin being excellent. What is most original in Sainte-Beuve is his point of view. Before his time, critics considered only the work of an author. Sainte-Beuve widened the scope of criticism by inventing what has been called "biographical criticism." In the most skillful and delicate manner, he dissects the writer to find the man. He endeavors to explain the work by the character of the author, his early training, his health, his idiosyncrasies, and above all, by his environment. The 'Causeries' were first published as *feuilletons* in the papers. They may be divided into two distinct classes: those written before, and those written after, the Restoration. In the former there is more fondness for polemics than pure literary purpose; but they represent the most brilliant period in Sainte-Beuve's literary career. After the Restoration, his method changes: there are no polemics; however little sympathy the critic may have with the works of such writers as De Maistre, Lamartine, or Béranger, he analyzes their lives solely for the purpose of finding the source of their ideas. The most curious portion of the 'Causeries' is that in which he discusses his contemporaries. He seems in his latter period to be desirous of refuting his earlier positions. Where he had been indulgent to excess, he is now extremely severe. Châteaubriand, Lamartine, and Béranger, who were once his idols, are relegated to a very inferior place in literature. Perhaps there is nothing more characteristic of Sainte-Beuve than the sweetness and delicacy with which he slays an obnoxious brother craftsman. In the tender regretfulness which he displays in assassinating Gautier or Hugo, he follows the direction of Izaak Walton with regard to the gentle treatment of the worm. Many lists of the most valuable of the 'Causeries' have been made; but as they all differ, it is safe to say that none of Sainte-Beuve's criticisms is without a high value.

CAVALIER, THE, by George W. Cable (1901). This is a lively story of love and adventure in the days of the Civil War, and details the experiences of Richard Thorndyke Smith, a young soldier in the Southern army, who gives the reader his personal reminiscences. At the age of nineteen he becomes a scout under Lieutenant Ferry; figures in many thrilling adventures and performs many valorous deeds. Ferry, whose rightful name is Edgard Ferry Durand, is a brilliant and fascinating character whose noble and fearless nature makes him loved by men and women alike. He has fallen victim to the charms of Charlotte Oliver, a beautiful and daring Confederate spy, but, owing to the fact that she is already married, he feels the hopelessness of his love. Charlotte, who also goes by the name of Coralie Rothvelt, is wife in name only of a miserable rascal who deceived her into marrying him, but whose real character she discovered immediately after the ceremony, and who has done everything he could to make her life wretched. Charlotte is devoted to the Confederate cause and undertakes perilous risks without thought of danger, and is at the front in time of battle, caring for the wounded and dying. Although she reciprocates Ferry's affection, she will not encourage him until she is absolutely convinced of the death of her husband, who finally dies as a traitor, after having attempted her life and seriously wounded her. At last, her courage and fidelity are rewarded and she becomes the wife of the man she loves. Smith, who has been the faithful ally of both Charlotte and Ferry, wins the love of Camille Harper, the Major's daughter, and the curtain falls on the closing of the war, with strife and discord at an end. This story exhibits the author's simple and unaffected manner of writing, and the plot runs with unusual swiftness and ease.

CAVALLERIA RUSTICANA ('Rustic Chivalry'), a short story by the Sicilian Giovanni Verga, published in a collection entitled 'Novelle rusticane' in 1883 and presented in dramatic form at Turin in 1884. Pietro Mascagni made this prose play the basis of the verse-libretto of his one-act opera, 'Cavalleria Rusticana' (1890). The scene is a Sicilian village and the time Easter Day at the hour of mass. Turiddù Macca, a young peasant, son of a widowed mother, was in love with the coquette, Lola. On his return from military service he found her married to Alfio, a carter. Out of pique he paid his addresses to Santuzza, who fell desperately in love with him and on receiving his promise of marriage admitted him to her chamber. Lola, annoyed that Turiddù should love anyone else, ensnares him again, and her husband's frequent absences enable them to meet at her house. Meanwhile Santuzza finds herself about to become a mother. During the time of mass on Easter morning she rebukes Turiddù for his infidelity and begs him to return to her; but he refuses roughly, and Santuzza then reveals to Alfio, who has just returned from a journey, the relations of his wife, Lola, and Turiddù. Alfio finds Turiddù drinking in the village square after church and challenges him to a duel — a challenge which is sealed by the peasants' custom of embracing and biting the ear. They go out quietly and word comes almost immediately that Turiddù is slain. The story both in its narrative and its dramatic form presents in lively colors the fierce passions and primitive customs of the Sicilian peasantry.

CAVOUR, a short biography, by the Countess Evelyn Martinengo-Cesaresco, was published in 1904, as one of the 'Foreign Statesmen Series,' edited by Professor Bury. In a succinct yet clear and complete manner the writer tells the remarkable story of Cavour's achievement of the unification of Italy. Born in 1810, the younger son of a noble Piedmontese house, Camillo Benso, Count Cavour, early manifested tendencies strangely out of harmony with his rank and surroundings in a petty Italian principality. He was supremely interested in scientific farming and in political life, a pronounced Liberal, and an opponent of clerical influence in secular government. Travel in France and Italy strengthened these views. Just prior to the Revolutionary year of 1848, he started at Turin a newspaper entitled 'Il Risorgimento,' a name which has since been applied to the movement which it inaugurated for the unification of Italy. Through this paper he was able to influence the King of Piedmont, Charles Albert, to declare war on Austria, in order to drive her out of Italy. After the failure of the Piedmontese at Novara and the abdication of the king, Cavour, now called to the government, induced the new King, Victor Emmanuel, to join England and France in the Crimean war, hoping thus to gain the support of these powers for a renewed attempt to liberate Italy from Austria. As a consequence, Cavour, representing Piedmont, was given a place at the peace conference in 1856. Finally in 1859 he succeeded in committing Napoleon III. to an alliance, and with his aid, drove Austria from Lombardy. Insurrections then broke out in the other Italian states, particularly in the kingdom of Naples, which was conquered by Garibaldi and his thousand volunteers (1860). By the close of the year Austria had agreed to make peace and the whole of Italy except Rome was declared an independent kingdom in February, 1861. In the same year Cavour died of fatigue brought on by overwork (June 6, 1861). His career, dominated as it was by the determination to set Italy free, is an inspiring one and the writer has risen to the height of her subject—the unification of Italy. She tells how he gradually prepared the way for war against Austria, by strengthening the army, by diplomacy, and by co-operating with Garibaldi up to a certain point. "Possibly," she says, "he was the only continental statesman who ever saw liberty in an Anglo-Saxon light." At first he had to work against distrust, but his extraordinary powers as a diplomatist enabled him to succeed where Mazzini and Garibaldi would have failed. None will question his unwavering devotion to the cause of the emancipation of Italy. His extraordinary political acumen may be seen in his anticipation of the advance of Prussia. "In 1848," says the Countess Cesaresco, "he prophesied that Germanism would disturb the European equilibrium, and that the future German Empire would aim at becoming a naval power in order to combat and rival England on the seas. But he saw that the rise of Prussia meant the decline of Austria, and this was all that, as an Italian statesman, with Venetia still in chains, he was bound to consider."

CAVOUR, THE LIFE AND TIMES OF, by William Roscoe Thayer (2 vols., 1911). This is a more elaborate and detailed critical study than the biography of Countess Martinengo-Cesaresco, giving the history of Italy's deliverance from the yoke of a divided rule, great detail of movements and events in "the life of the great man whose daring genius conceived and carried out his country's emancipation." The book is a masterpiece of historical biography, and ranks with the scholarly and well constructed histories of the present time. He has studied apparently all available printed sources, including the new material of the last decade.

CAXTONS, THE, by Edward Bulwer, Lord Lytton. 'The Caxtons' was not only instantly popular in England, but 35,000 copies were sold in America within three years after its publication in 1850. The Caxtons are Austin Caxton, a scholar engaged on a great work, 'The History of Human Error'; his wife Kitty, much his junior; his brother Roland, the Captain, who has served in the Napoleonic campaigns:

the two children of the latter, Herbert and Blanche; and Austin's son, Pisistratus, who tells the story. The quiet country life of the family of Austin Caxton is interrupted by a visit to London. There Pisistratus, who has had a good school education, though he has not yet entered the university, is offered the position of secretary to Mr. Trevanion, a leader in Parliament. Lady Ellinor, Mr. Trevanion's wife, was loved as a girl by Roland and Austin Caxton; but she had passed them both by to make a marriage better suited to an ambitions woman. By a freak of fate Pisistratus now falls in love with her daughter Fannie, and when he finds that his suit is hopeless, he gives up his position under Mr. Trevanion, and enters Cambridge University, where his college course is soon closed by the financial troubles of his father. A further outline of this story would give no idea of its charm. The mutual affection of the Caxtons is finely indicated, and the gradations of light and shade make a beautiful picture. Never before had Bulwer written with so light a touch and so gentle a humor, and this novel has been called the most brilliant and attractive of his productions. His gentle satire of certain phases of political life was founded, doubtless, on actual experience.

CECIL DREEME, by Theodore Winthrop (1862), by its brilliancy of style, crisp dialogue, sharp characterization, and ingenuity of structure, won an immediate popularity. Robert Byng, the hero, returning from ten years of study in Europe, meets on shipboard a remarkably accomplished and brilliant man, Densdeth, to whom he is much attracted, while conscious at the same time of an unacknowledged but powerful repulsion. Byng settles himself in rooms in Chrysalis College, a pseudo-mediæval building which houses an unsuccessful university and receives lodgers in its unused chambers. On the floor above Byng is Cecil Dreeme, a mysterious young artist, who is evidently in hiding for some unknown reason. Densdeth takes Byng to renew an old acquaintance and friendship with the Denmans, a rich and important family. Mr. Denman and his only living child, the beautiful Emma, are in deep mourning for the younger daughter Clara; who some months before, when about to be married to Densdeth, — a marriage believed to be most distasteful to her, — is believed to have wandered from home while delirious from fever, and to have been drowned. These are the characters, who, with John Churm, — an old friend of Byng's father, and a fellow-lodger in Chrysalis, and to whom the Denman girls have been like adopted children, — carry on the story. A definite plot is worked out with adequate skill, but the strength of the story lies in its fine insight and spiritual significance. As Densdeth stands for evil, so Byng stands for manliness rather than for conscience, and Clara for incarnate good.

CECILIA, by Frances Burney. 'Cecilia; or Memoirs of an Heiress,' is a typical English novel of the eighteenth century. The plot is simple, the story long drawn out, the style stilted, and the characters alone constitute the interest of the book, and justify Dr. Johnson's praise of Miss Burney as "a little character-monger." The charming heroine, Cecilia Beverley, has no restriction on her fortune but that her future husband must take her name. She goes to London to stay with Mr. Harrel, one of her guardians, and is introduced into society by his wife. Mr. Harrel contrives to influence her for his own advantage, and succeeds in keeping about her only those admirers who serve him personally. She and the hero, Mortimer Delvile, have therefore little intercourse. After borrowing money from Cecilia and gambling it all away, Mr. Harrel in despair commits suicide. Cecilia then visits her other guardian, Mr. Delvile, at his castle, where she is constantly thrown with Mortimer.

his son. Family pride keeps him from proposing to Cecilia, whose birth does not equal his own; but her beauty and gentleness overcome his resolves, and he persuades her to a secret marriage. Mr. Monckton, who wishes to secure Cecilia's fortune, discovers her plans, and with the help of an accomplice prevents the marriage at the very church. Cecilia returns to the country, and after a harrowing family scene gives up Mortimer. But the heroine has her reward at the end. It is hard, in our day, to understand the overpowering family pride and prejudice, the effects of which constitute largely the story of the heroine. 'Cecilia' was published in 1782, four years after the issue of 'Evelina,' and met with public favor almost as great as that which welcomed the earlier romance. Sentimental, artificial, and unliterary though they are, Miss Burney's stories present a vivid picture of the society of her time, and are likely to remain among the English classics.

CELLINI, BENVENUTO, THE LIFE OF, — one of the few world-famous autobiographies, and itself the Italian Renaissance as expressed in personality, — was written between the years 1558 and 1562. It circulated in MS. and was copied frequently, until its publication in 1730. The original and authoritative MS. belongs to the Laurentian Collection in Florence. It was written "for the most part by Michele di Goro Vestri, the youth whom Cellini employed as his amanuensis. Perhaps we owe its abrupt and infelicitous conclusion to the fact that Benvenuto disliked the trouble of writing with his own hand. From notes upon the codex it appears that this was the MS. submitted to Benedetto Varchi in 1559. It once belonged to Andrea, the son of Lorenzo Cavalcanti. His son, Lorenzo Cavalcanti gave it to the poet Redi, who used it as a *testo di lingua* for the Della Cruscan vocabulary. Subsequently it passed into the hands of the booksellers, and was bought by L. Poirot, who bequeathed it, on his death in 1825, to the Laurentian Library."

Cellini's autobiography has been translated into German by Goethe, into English by Nugent, Roscoe, and Symonds, and into French by Leopold Leclauché. Symonds's translation is pre-eminent for its truthfulness and sympathy. It is fitting that Cellini's record of himself should be translated into the foremost modern tongues, since he stood for a civilization unapproached in cosmopolitan character since the age of Sophocles. Judged by his own presentment, he was an epitome of that world which sprang from the marriage of Faust with Helen. He, like his contemporaries, was a "natural" son of Greece; witnessing to his wayward birth in his adoration of beauty, in his violent passions, in his magnificent bombast, in his turbulent, highly colored life, in his absence of spirituality, in his close clinging to the sure earth. He was most mediæval in that whatever feeling he had, of joy in the tangible or fear of the intangible, was intensely alive. "This is no book: who touches this touches a man."

CENCI, THE, a tragedy in blank verse, by Percy Bysshe Shelley, written and printed in Italy in 1819 and published in England in 1820. Though designed for the stage it was not acted in Shelley's lifetime, but a special performance was arranged by the Shelley Society in 1886. The play is based on an early manuscript account of the murder of the Roman Count Francesco Cenci, September 9, 1598, and the execution of his wife, Lucretia, his daughter, Beatrice, and his son Giacomo, as instigators of the murder, on May 11, 1599. The dramatist, who follows closely the statements of the manuscript, presents in the opening scene Count Cenci, a monster of lust and cruelty, who buys immunity for his crimes by heavy contributions to the Pope Clement VIII. Two of his sons he has sent to the University of

Salamanca where he refuses to support them until compelled by the Pope. Another,
Giacomo, he has robbed of his wife's dowry (II. ii.); his eldest daughter has escaped
his household by marriage; a younger daughter, Beatrice, and a son, Bernardo,
with their step-mother Lucretia, live in the Cenci palace where they are starved,
imprisoned, beaten, and generally ill-treated, while Cenci fills Rome with tales of
his debauchery and cruelty.   But Cenci's wealth, influence, and ruthlessness, and
the Roman idea of the *patria potestas*, which the Pope warmly upholds, make interference difficult for friends of the family.   Orsino, a former suitor of Beatrice, now
a priest, offers to carry to the Pope a petition for her release from her father's house;
but fearing lest Clement should marry her to someone else he does not deliver the
petition, hoping thus to further his own selfish ends and win her love (Act I., sc. ii.).
The devilish glee with which Cenci announces at a feast of his friends and relatives
the death of his two sons at Salamanca stirs Beatrice to make an impassioned appeal
to the guests.   But they do not dare to interfere.   Beatrice's conduct incites Count
Cenci to a crowning infamy, already half-planned.   To satisfy his malignant hate
he will ruin his own daughter and corrupt her mind until she consents to the crime.
On the night of the feast he drops to her a hint of his purpose; and after she has
suffered for a day the torments of apprehension, he outrages her.   Realizing his
further purpose of utterly debasing her, she resolves on killing him as her only hope;
and in consultation with her step-mother and with Orsino, who from her distracted
words and bearing have partly guessed what she has suffered, they arrange that
Count Cenci shall be killed by assassins on the morrow, as he is transporting his
wife and daughter to the lonely castle of Petrella, in the Apulian Apennines.   Giacomo, coming in to kill his father for further persecution of him and his family,
becomes an accessory to the plan (Act III., sc. i.).   In the next scene Orsino
brings word to Giacomo that Count Cenci has escaped the ambush by arriving too
early; but a new attempt is to be made, through the instrumentality of Olimpio
and Marzio, two dismissed and aggrieved servants of Cenci.   In Act IV., sc. i., Lucretia
who has given Cenci an opiate strives to induce him to confess his sins on the ground
that Beatrice has seen a vision warning him of death.   His only reply is a threat
of new outrage.   In scene ii. the murderers arrive and in scene iii., though awed at
first by the innocent appearance of the old man as he sleeps, they are goaded on by
Beatrice to put him to death.   No sooner has he been strangled and thrown from
a window than the papal legate, Savella, comes to summon him to answer his wicked
deeds.   Lucretia shows great agitation, but Beatrice is perfectly composed even
when they are arrested and taken to Rome to be examined on suspicion of being
concerned in the crime.   Orsino now reveals his baseness by betraying Giacomo
to justice and making his escape in disguise (Act V., sc. v.).   In the trial scene which
follows, Marzio admits, under torture, that he did the murder, instigated by Giacomo, Orsino, and the ladies.   But Beatrice, confronting him in the presence of the
court, forces him by the strength of her personality and the power of her essential
innocence to withdraw his accusation and declare himself alone guilty.   He is removed for further torture and dies on the rack.   But Giacomo and Lucrezia prove
less resolute, and they with Beatrice are condemned to death.   The Pope, jealous
of his own *patria potestas* and alarmed by another case of parricide, refuses a pardon;
and after one outburst of natural terror of death, Beatrice goes calmly to the scaffold.
This drama shows the influence of Shakespeare in its diction and of Ford and Webster in its horror.   The theme is treated with restraint and its repulsiveness is
tempered and well-nigh obliterated by the emphasis placed on the mental sufferings
and emotions of Beatrice and the masterly way in which she and her father are

characterized. The Italian atmosphere and temper is realistically preserved and the dignity and pathos of tragedy are never forgotten.

CENT NOUVELLES NOUVELLES. This collection of facetious tales was first published at Paris in 1486. They were told at the table of the dauphin, afterwards Louis XI., in the Castle of Genappe during his exile. Their arrangement in their present form has been attributed to the Count of Croi, to Louis himself, and to Antoine de La Salle. The latter, however, seems to have been the editor. In spite of the difference in character and position of the narrators, the 'Nouvelles' are uniform in tone and style, and have the same elegance and clearness of diction that distinguished La Salle's 'Quinze Joyes de Mariage.' Besides, the number actually related was far in excess of a hundred. A practiced writer therefore must have selected and revised the best. The work is one of the most curious monuments of a kind of literature distinctively French, and which, since its revival by Voltaire in the eighteenth century, has always been successfully cultivated: the literature that considers elegant mockery and perfection of form adequate compensation for the lack of morality and lofty ideals. Although several of the stories are traceable to Boccaccio, Poggio, and other Italian *novellieri*, most of them are original. The historical importance of the collection arises from its giving details regarding the manners and customs of the fifteenth century that can be found nowhere else. Its very licentiousness is commentary enough on the private life of the men and women of the time. In spite of its title, however, there is nothing novel in the incidents upon which the 'Nouvelles' are based. Their novelty consists in their high-bred brightness and vivacity, their delicately shaded and refined but cruel sarcasm. With a slight modernization of the language, they might have been told at one of the Regent's suppers, and they are far superior of those related in the Heptameron of the Queen of Navarre. The 'Nouvelles' also show us that the Middle Ages are past. Instead of gallant knights performing impossible feats to win a smile from romantic châtelaines, we have a crowd of princes and peasants, nobles and tradesmen; all, with their wives and mistresses, jostling and duping one another on a footing of perfect equality. Another sign that a new era has come is the mixed social condition of the thirty-two story-tellers; for among them obscure and untitled men, probably domestics of the Duke of Burgundy, figure side by side with some of the greatest names in French history.

CENTRAL AMERICA, Incidents of Travel in Chiapas and Yucatan, by John Lloyd Stephens (2 vols., 1841). The story of a journey of nearly 3000 miles, including visits to eight ruined cities, monuments of a marvelously interesting lost civilization; that of the Maya land, the many cities of which, of great size, splendor, and culture, rivaled those of the Incas and the Montezumas. Ten editions of this book were published within three months. Two years later, Mr. Stephens supplemented this first adequate report of the character of Central American antiquities by a second work, his 'Travel in Yucatan,' in which he reported further explorations extended to forty-four ruined cities.

CENTRAL AMERICA, Notes on, by Ephraim George Squier: 1854. The States of: 1857. Two works by an American archæologist of distinction, who, after a special experience in similar researches in New York, Ohio, and other States, entered on a wide and protracted research in Central America in 1849; published a work on Nicaragua in 1852; and later gave, in the two works named above, a report of observations on both the antiquities and the political condition of Central America, the value of which has been widely recognized. The 'Serpent Symbols' (1852) of Mr. Squier attracted attention as a study of great value in the baffling science of primitive religion and speculation on nature; and his 'Peru: Incidents and Explorations in the Land of the Incas' (1877), was the result of exhaustive investigations of Inca remains, and a most valuable contribution to knowledge of ancient Peru.

CERAMIC INDUSTRIES, TREATISE ON, by Émile Bourry (1897), translated by W. P. Rix (1901) and by Alfred B. Searle (1911). The publication of a translation of M. Bourry's classic work is justified because at the date when it was issued (1901) there was no adequate textbook on ceramics in English. Its value both for the student and the manufacturer consists in the fact that it treats with equal fullness the manipulation of every class of ceramics from the common brick to the finest porcelain and supplies a description of a judicious selection of the best known machines and appliances in use in various countries. The translator appropriately calls attention to the fact that the governments of continental Europe have stimulated the industry by giving either direct or indirect assistance to students or factories engaged in research, and suggests that manufacturers should combine to engage in such technical research as relates to subjects and methods common to all pottery manufacture, and leave to individual manufacturers the opportunity to specialize in details peculiar to their own section. The volume opens with a classification and definitions of ceramic products and a useful historic summary of ceramic art. These are followed by discussions of raw materials and the means of trying them; of the properties, composition, and preparation of plastic bodies; of the processes of molding, drying, glazing, firing, and decorating. The second half of the book is devoted to special pottery methods, whether terra cotta, fireclay, faïence, stoneware, or porcelain. There are three hundred and twenty-three well chosen illustrations of machines and processes.

CESAR BIROTTEAU, The Greatness and Decline of, by Honoré de Balzac (1838). This novel pictures in a striking and accurate manner the bourgeois life of Paris at the time of the Restoration. César Birotteau, a native of the provinces, comes to the city in his youth, works his way up until he becomes the proprietor of a perfumery establishment, and amasses a considerable fortune. He is decorated with the Cross of the Legion of Honor, in consequence of having been an ardent Loyalist; and this mark of distinction, coupled with his financial success, causes him to become more and more ambitious. He grows extravagant, indulges in speculation, and loses everything. This stroke of misfortune brings out the strength of character which, during his prosperity, had remained concealed beneath many petty foibles. In this story the life of the French shopkeeper who values his credit as his dearest possession, and his failure as practically death, is faithfully portrayed. The other characters in the book are lifelike portraits. Constance, the faithful and sensible wife of Birotteau, and his gentle daughter Césarine, are in pleasing contrast to many of the women Balzac has painted. Du Tillet, the unscrupulous clerk, who repays his master's kindness by hatred and dishonesty; Roquin the notary; Vauquelin the great chemist; and Pillerault, uncle of Constance, — are all striking individualities. The book is free from any objectionable atmosphere, and is exceedingly realistic as to manners and customs. It has been admirably translated into English by Katharine Prescott Wormeley.

CHALDEE MS., THE (1817). This production, in its day pronounced one of the most extraordinary satires in the language, is now almost forgotten save by students of literature. It was a skit at the expense of the publisher Constable, and of the Edinburgh notables specially interested in the Whig Edinburgh Review; prepared by the editors for the seventh number of the new Tory Blackwood's Magazine, October, 1817. In form it was a Biblical narrative in four chapters, attacking Constable, and describing many of the Constable clientage with more or less felicitous phrases. Scott was "that great magician which hath his dwelling in the old fastness." Constable was "the man which is crafty," who "shook the dust from his feet, and said, 'Beloved, I have given this magician much money, yet see, now, he hath utterly deserted me.'" Francis Jeffrey was "a familiar spirit unto whom the man which was crafty had sold himself, and the spirit was a wicked and a cruel." Many of the characterizations cannot be identified at this day, but they were all scathing and many of them mean. The joke was perpetrated by James Hogg, the "Ettrick Shepherd," whose original paper was greatly enlarged and modified by Wilson and Lockhart, and who himself declared that "the young lions in Edinboro' interlarded it with a good deal of devilry of their own." To escape detection, the Blackwood men described themselves as well as their rivals: Wilson was "the beautiful leopard from the valley of the palm-trees, whose going forth was comely as the greyhound and his eyes like the lighting of fiery flame. And he called from a far country the scorpion [Lockhart] which delighteth to sting the faces of men." Hogg was "the great wild boar from the forests of Lebanon, who roused up his spirit, and whetted his dreadful tusks for the battle." The satire which now seems so harmless shook the old city to its foundations, and produced not only the bitterest exasperation in the Constable set, but a plentiful crop of lawsuits; one of these being brought by an advocate who had figured as a "beast." As it originally appeared, the satire was headed 'Translation from an Ancient Chaldee Manuscript,' and pretended to be derived by an eminent Orientalist from an original preserved in the great Library of Paris. In after years both Wilson and Lockhart repented the cruelty of this early prank.

CHANCE ACQUAINTANCE, A, by William Dean Howells (1873). This agreeable and entertaining sketch is one of Mr. Howells's earlier stories. It relates the experience of a pretty Western girl, Kitty Ellison, who, while traveling on the St. Lawrence with her cousins Colonel and Mrs. Ellison, has an "affaire du cœur" with Mr. Miles Arbuton, of Boston. The latter, an aristocrat of the most conventional type, is thrown much with Kitty on the steamer, and finally falls in love with her. Mrs. Ellison, a rather commonplace but kind-hearted woman, sprains her ankle, and this misfortune delays their party in Quebec. During this interval Mr. Arbuton and Kitty explore the city, — an occupation affording ample time for the maturing of their friendship. Arbuton at length declares himself, and Kitty asks for time to consider his proposal. She feels the unsuitability of the match; he being of distinguished family, rich and cultivated, while she is a poor girl, with little to boast of but her own natural charms. She finally accepts him, however, when some of his aristocratic friends appear on the scene. He ignores Kitty for the time being and leaves her by herself, while he does the honors for the newcomers. She realizes that he is ashamed of her, and decides to give him up. On his return she tells him of her decision, and resists his entreaties to overlook his conduct. The story ends with the departure of the Ellisons from Quebec, and the reader is left in ignorance of the fate of Mr. Miles Arbuton. The book contains many charming descriptions of the picturesque scenery and places about Quebec, and the story is told with delightful airiness and charm.

CHANSON DE ROLAND. This is the culmination of a cycle of 'Chansons de Geste' or Songs of Valor, celebrating the heroic achievements of Charlemagne, and inspired especially by the joy and pride of the triumph of Christian arms over the Mohammedan invasion, which, through the gate opened by the Moors of Spain, threatened to subdue all Europe. The Song of Roland or of Roncesvalles celebrates the valor of Roland, a Count Paladin of Charlemagne, who, on the retreat of the King from an expedition against the Moors in Spain, is cut off with the rear-guard of the army in the pass of Roncevaux; and, fatally wounded in the last desperate struggle, crawls away to die beneath the shelter of a rock, against which he strikes in vain his sword Durandal, in the effort to break it so that it may not fall into the hands of his enemy: —

> "Be no man your master who shall know the fear of man:
> Long were you in the hands of a captain
> Whose like shall not be seen in France set free!"

The French text of the 'Chanson' was first published in Paris by M. Francisque Michel in 1837, and afterward in many editions. The original form of the lines above quoted is as follows: —

> "Ne vos ait hume ki pur altre feiet!
> Mult bon vassal vos ad lung tens tenue:
> Jamais n'ert tel in France la solue."

Around this incident have grown a multitude of heroic and romantic tales which have taken form in all the mediæval literature of Europe; but especially in Italy, — where however the hero appears with little more than the name to identify him, — in the 'Orlando Furioso' of Ariosto, and the 'Orlando Innamorato' of Boiardo. Tyrwhitt, in his edition of Chaucer, was the first to call the attention of English readers to the 'Chanson'; but English tradition has it that the song was sung by the Norman Taillefer just before the battle of Hastings. The best and oldest French MS., called the "Digby," is preserved in the Bodleian library at Oxford. The French poem contains 6,000 lines. A Fragment of 1,049 lines, translated in Middle English from what is known as the Lansdowne MS., is published by the Early English Text Society.

CHANTECLER, by Edmond Rostand (1910). The scene of this romantic French drama is a farmyard, the hero, a cock, and the dramatis personæ, hens, guinea hens, ducks, turkeys, a blackbird, a dog, and a cat. Chantecler believes that his cock-a-doodle-doo each morning brings the day, that the sun rises at his call. He confides this secret of his song to a lovely hen-pheasant who has flown into the barnyard to escape a hunting dog. She falls in love with the splendid self-assertion of the Gallic cock. His enemies the owls, who hate the day, and the cat, conspire against the cock. At the guinea hen's five o'clock tea he is driven to fight and is nearly killed by a gamecock, armed with a steel spur. The fickle crowd of hens applaud the gamecock until a hawk appears and Chantecler asserts his real supremacy. He leaves them and goes to the forest with the pheasant. She is jealous of the Dawn, wishing to rule alone in his heart. One morning she covers his eyes with her wings, and he discovers that the ungrateful Dawn has come without his help. Disillusioned, he suffers, but regains his faith in himself and leaves her to return to the barnyard, to cheer his fellows with his call to the sun.

> "For in gray mornings when poor beasts awake,
> Not daring to believe that night is done,
> My ringing clarion will replace the sun."

The pheasant sees the hunter and fearing for Chantecler, flies up, forgetting the snare of the net, in which she is caught. The symbolism of the play is obvious. The chattering hens, the turkey, a solemn pretentious philosopher, the tuft-hunting guinea hen and her troupe of celebrities, the blackbird, cynical and modern, are a delightful satire on human society. Chantecler's hymn to the sun is quoted in the LIBRARY.

CHAPLAIN OF THE FLEET, THE, by Sir Walter Besant and James Rice (1881). This story opens on the last day of the year 1750, and gives a detailed account of the famous Liberties or Rules of the old Fleet prison in London, and of the Fleet marriages. These "Rules" were houses in certain streets near the Fleet Market, where prisoners for debt were allowed to live, outside the prison, on payment of fees. Among these prisoners were clergymen, who performed clandestine marriages. A regular trade sprang up, touters were employed to bring clients, and every species of enormity was practiced. Gregory Shovel was one of these clergy, and so plumed himself on his success in this iniquitous traffic that he took the name of "Chaplain of the Fleet," which gives the book its title, — the whole plot turning upon one of these Fleet marriages. This novel is considered one of the best of those written under the firm-name of Besant and Rice.

CHARACTERISTICS, by Anthony Ashley Cooper, Earl of Shaftesbury. The three volumes of Shaftesbury's 'Characteristics' appeared anonymously in 1713, two years before the death of the author at the age of forty-two. These, with a volume of letters, and a certain preface to a sermon, constitute the whole of his published works. The 'Characteristics' immediately attracted wide attention; and in twenty years had passed through five editions, at that time a large circulation for a book of this kind. The first volume contains three rather desultory and discursive essays: 'A Letter concerning Enthusiasm'; 'On Freedom of Wit and Humor'; 'Soliloquy; or, Advice to an Author.' The second volume, with its 'Inquiry concerning Virtue and Merit,' and the dialogue 'The Moralists: A Philosophical Rhapsody,' forms his most valuable contribution to the science of ethics. In the third volume he advances various 'Miscellaneous Reflections,' including certain defenses of his philosophical theories, together with some essays on artistic and literary subjects.

From the first appearance of the 'Characteristics,' it was seen that its philosophical theories were to have an important part in the whole science of ethics. De Mandeville in later years attacked him, Hutcheson defended him, and Butler and Berkeley discussed him, — not always with a perfect comprehension of his system. Its leading ideas are of the relation of parts to a whole. As the beauty of an external object consists in a certain proportion between its parts, or a certain harmony of coloring, so the beauty of a virtuous act lies in its relation to the virtuous character as a whole. Yet morality cannot be adequately studied in the individual man. Man must be considered in his relation to our earth, and this again in its relation to the universe.

The faculty which approves of right and disapproves of wrong is by Shaftesbury called the moral sense and this is perhaps the distinctive feature of his system. Between this sense and good taste in art he draws a strong analogy. In its recognition of a rational as well as an emotional element, Shaftesbury's "moral sense" is much like the "conscience" described later by Butler. While the "moral sense" and the love and reverence of God are, with Shaftesbury, the proper sanctions of right conduct, a tone of banter which he assumed toward religious questions, and his leaning toward Deism, drew on him more or less criticism from the strongly orthodox. By his 'Characteristics' Shaftesbury became the founder of what has been called the "benevolent" system of ethics; in which subsequently Hutcheson closely followed him.

CHARICLES, by W. A. Becker. The first idea of 'Charicles; or Scenes from the Private Life of Ancient Greece,' as well as of his preceding work 'Gallus' (Leipsic: 1840), was probably suggested to the author by Böttiger's 'Sabina; or, Scenes from the Morning Toilette of a Great Roman Lady.' The story, which in itself is of much interest, serves but as a framework for pictures of the everyday pursuits and lighter occupations of the Greeks. A young Athenian, the son of an exile, on his return home passes through Corinth, and meets with many adventures among the hetæræ and swindlers of that gay city. When he reaches Athens, he is agreeably surprised by the news that his father's property has not been sold. A large sum of money remains to his credit in the hands of an honest banker, and he compels a dishonest one who tries to cheat him out of three talents, to disgorge. Then follow wrestling-matches at the gymnasia, banquets in his honor given by his school-boy friends, shipwrecks, revelries at the Dionysia, etc; the whole ending in a marriage with the wealthy and charming young widow of an old friend of his father. 'Charicles' is the first work devoted to the private life of the Greeks; and without entering into its darker details, it gives an instructive and suggestive portraiture of all its aspects. But the most valuable portions of the work are the notes and excursuses, which compose a complete manual of antique usages and customs, and are commentaries on each of the twelve scenes into which the story is divided. Thus, after the first Scene, 'Youthful Friends,' we have an excursus on education, and so on. The English translation, in one volume, by the Rev. F. Metcalfe, is admirable, and in form superior to the original; the excursuses being thrown together at the end of the volume, so as not to interfere with the tenor of the narrative.

CHARLES AUCHESTER, a musical novel by Elizabeth Sara Sheppard, an Englishwoman, was written when she was sixteen, and published a few years later, in 1853. The manuscript was first submitted to Disraeli, who prophesied that the book would become a classic. His enthusiasm may have been owing in part to the fact that the hero is of Jewish extraction, and that the author pays the highest tributes to the genius and glory of the Hebrew race. The novel records the development of one Charles Auchester, who from earliest childhood has his very being in the world of harmony. His story, told by himself, is a blending of his outer and inner life in one beautiful web of experience. He introduces himself as a child in an old English town, living a quiet sequestered life with his mother and sister. Afterwards he goes to the Cæcilia School in Germany to carry on his musical education. The guiding star of his life there is Seraphael, a marvelous young genius, whose very presence is an inspiration. By Seraphael is meant Mendelssohn, whose career is followed closely throughout. Jenny Lind is supposed to be the original of another of Auchester's friends, Clara Bennette, a famous singer. Many musical events are described with remarkable fidelity to the spirit as well as to the letter of such occurrences. The entire book, fanciful and extravagant though it is in parts, is steeped in an indescribable golden atmosphere of music, and of the spiritual exaltation which musicians know. As the record of spiritual experiences whose source is harmonious sound, 'Charles Auchester' is perhaps unique in the whole range of fiction.

CHARLES THE BOLD, Duke of Burgundy, History of. By John Foster Kirk (3 vols., 1863–68). An excellent special book on a most interesting and significant figure in the history of France and of Europe (1433–77). He was the last in the long line of princes who for centuries, almost since Charlemagne's time, had endeavored to build up a "middle" or "buffer" kingdom along the Rhine and the Rhone, between the exclusively French and the exclusively German powers: the old kingdom of Lotharingia, later Lorraine, the mediæval kingdom of Arles, the ever-varying duchy of Burgundy, all represented this most promising, most determined, and most futile of political efforts. With the crushing defeat and death of Charles, — in his prime the most powerful potentate of the age, his dominion stretching like a gigantic bow almost from Savoy to the German Ocean, around the entire east and north of France, — the unnatural ribbon-State of unrelated parts without common interests went to pieces, and with it the dream of a buffer kingdom perished forever. The Burgundian duchy and Picardy were seized by Louis XI. of France, the Netherlands went by marriage to Austria and ultimately to Spain, — Charles's daughter Mary being the ancestress of Charles V. and Philip II. The career of Charles the Bold is therefore one of the chief landmarks of European history, the direct precursor of the Franco-German War; Granson, Morat, and Nancy are the forerunners of Sedan. Charles is most familiarly known through Scott's 'Quentin Durward'; but Mr. Kirk's history gives the real man, as well as his great rival Louis XI., and much of great interest and instruction besides.

CHARLES XII., HISTORY OF, by Voltaire. This history was published in 1731. It is divided into eight books, of which the first sketches briefly the history of Sweden before the accession of Charles. The last seven deal with his expedition into Poland, its consequences, his invasion of Russia and pursuit of Peter the Great, his defeat at Pultowa and retreat into Turkey, his sojourn at Bender and its results, his departure thence, his return home, his death at the siege of Frederickshall in Norway. Intermingled with the narrative of battles, marches, and sieges, we have vivid descriptions of the manners, customs, and physical features of the countries in which they took place. It resembles the 'Commentaries' of Cæsar in the absence of idle details, declamation, and ornament. There is no attempt to explain mutable and contingent facts by constant underlying principles. Men act, and the narrative accounts for their actions. Of course, Voltaire is not an archivist with a document ready at hand to witness for the truth of every statement; and many of his contemporaries treated his history as little better than a romance. But apart from some inaccuracies, natural to a writer dealing with events in distant countries at the time, the 'History of Charles XII.' is a true history. According to Condorcet, it was based on memoirs furnished Voltaire by witnesses of the events he describes; and King Stanislas, the victim as well as the friend and companion of Charles, declared that every incident mentioned in the work actually occurred. This book is considered the historical masterpiece of Voltaire.

CHARLOTTE TEMPLE, by Susanna Haswell Rowson. This 'Tale of Truth' was written about 1790. It was, if not the first, one of the first works of fiction written in America; 25,000 copies were sold within a few years; and it has been republished again and again. It was written by an Englishwoman who came to America with her husband, the leader of the band attached to a British regiment. She was for some years favorably known as an actress, and then opened a boarding-school which for twenty-five years ranked first among such institutions in New

England. Her other writings were numerous, but were soon forgotten, while 'Charlotte Temple' still sells. It is a true story, the heroine's real name being Stanley. She was granddaughter to the Earl of Derby; and her betrayer, Col. John Montressor of the English army, was a relative of Mrs. Rowson herself. Charlotte's grave in Trinity Churchyard, New York, but a few feet away from Broadway, is marked by a stone sunk in the grass. Mrs. Dall, in her 'Romance of the Association,' tells us that Charlotte's daughter was adopted by a rich man, and in after years met the son of her true father, Montressor, or Montrevale as the book has it. They fell in love, and the young man showed his dying father a miniature of his sweetheart's mother (the wretched Charlotte), to whom she bore a striking likeness, and thus the truth was made known. The story in brief is this: Charlotte Temple, a girl of fifteen elopes from school with Montrevale, an army officer; they come to America, where he deserts her and marries an heiress. She gives birth to a daughter and dies of want. The style and language are strangely old-fashioned, hysterics and fainting fits occur on every page; yet a romantic interest will always attach to it.

CHASTELARD, by Algernon Charles Swinburne (1869). The scene of this tragedy is laid at Holyrood Castle, during the reign of Mary Queen of Scots. Mary Beaton, one of the "four Maries," promises Chastelard to arrange a meeting between him and the Queen. When he comes to the audience-room, however, he finds only Mary Beaton herself, who, in shame, confesses her love for him. While he is assuring her of his pardon, they are discovered by the other Maries. The Queen, angry at what she has heard, tries to make Chastelard confess his desertion of her; and declares her intention of marrying Darnley. Chastelard, by the agency of Mary Beaton, gains access to the Queen's chamber, discloses himself when she is alone, and after having convinced her of his love for her, submits to the guards, who take him to prison. Mary, fickle and heartless, in her desire to avoid both the shame of letting him live and the shame of putting her lover to death, tries to shift the responsibility to Murray, signs his death-warrant, and orders a reprieve, in quick succession. Then, going in person to the prison, she asks Chastelard to return the reprieve. He has already destroyed it; and after one short, happy hour with her, he goes bravely to his death. From an upper window in the palace, Mary Beaton watches the execution and curses the Queen just as Mary enters — with Bothwell.

In 'Chastelard' Swinburne has portrayed a fickle, heartless, vain, and beautiful queen; and in the few touches given to a character of secondary importance, has delicately and distinctly drawn Mary Beaton. The male characters are less sympathetic.

The tragedy is conspicuously one to be read, not acted. It is too long, too much lacking in action, and of too sustained an intensity for the stage. The style is essentially lyric, full of exquisite lines and phrases; and as a whole, the play presents an intense passion in a form of adequate beauty. It contains a number of charming French songs, and is dedicated to Victor Hugo. It was published in 1869.

CHAUCER, STUDIES IN: 'His Life and Writings,' by Thomas R. Lounsbury, LL.D. (3 vols., 1892). One of the most interesting and valuable books, both in matter and treatment, which recent research in letters has produced; alike admirable in learning and singularly sagacious and lucid in criticism. The first design of the work was that of a compendious and easily accessible account of the results of recent investigation; but examination showed that many of these were questionable or worthless, and that the field of Chaucer interest presented a range of problems not half of which had been treated adequately, and many of which had not been touched at all. The exact scope and design of the work were therefore changed, not only from what was at first contemplated, but to attempt a task far larger and more thorough than anything yet undertaken.

Dr. Lounsbury modestly describes his work, in three volumes and sixteen hundred pages, as "eight chapters bearing upon the life and writings of Chaucer; eight distinct essays, or rather monographs"; but the Chaucer unity and the unity of masterly treatment hardly permit any such distinction of parts. The life of Chaucer, the Chaucer legend, the text of Chaucer, and what exactly are the true writings of Chaucer, are the topics of Vol. i., and of a third of Vol. ii. The two double chapters which follow, to the end of Vol. ii., are on the learning of Chaucer, first in works still known, and second in works and authors now hardly known at all; and on Chaucer's relations to, first the English language, and second the religion of his time. The succeeding chapters, which fill the third volume, on Chaucer in Literary History and Chaucer as a Literary Artist, even increase our grateful and delighted estimate of the author's wealth of knowledge and mastery of exposition; not to speak of a refinement of style and felicity of wit rarely found in English prose.

CHERRY ORCHARD, THE, by Anton Chekhov (1904). The play is historical and symbolic, a picture of the passing of the old order of Russian aristocracy. Madame Ranievskaia, her seventeen year old daughter, and her brother return from Paris to their country estate after an absence of five years. Their affairs are in confusion and the estate is about to be sold for debt. A wealthy neighbor, Lopachin, whose grandfather was a serf on the estate, makes the practical suggestion that the famous cherry orchard be sold in lots for suburban villas to restore the family fortune. To cut down the cherry trees and remove the old house with its associations of childhood is sacrilege not to be considered by these aristocrats. Each member of the family has some plan to get money, but no plan is practical or practised. The day of the sale approaches, and they talk interminably, but are incapable of action. See scene in the LIBRARY. The practical neighbor buys the property, after trying in vain to help these sentimental, amiable, ineffectual people to save themselves. They arrive in the first scene in May when the cherry orchard is in bloom. In the last scene it is autumn; the charming old house is dismantled; the family are leaving forever; and we hear the stroke of the axe cutting down the cherry trees to make room for the suburban villas and for the new class in Russian society, which is not gentleman or peasant, but the energetic rich self-made men, the sons of the peasants.

CHESTERFIELD, LORD, see **LETTERS TO HIS SON.**

CHIEN D'OR, LE, see **THE GOLDEN DOG.**

CHILD OF THE BALL, THE ('El Niño de la Bola'), by Pedro Antonio de Alarcón (1880). The scene of this powerful and tragic novel is Andalusia. Don Rodrigo Venegas mortgages his hacienda to Don Elias Perez, and his whole estate is eaten up by usury. When Perez's house burns, no one tries to save it; and he proclaims that it is the work of an incendiary trying to destroy all evidence of his debt. Rodrigo rushes into the flames and saves the papers, dying as he delivers them. Rodrigo's estate is put at auction, and bid in by Perez for one million reals less than his claims. Rodrigo leaves a young son, Manuel, who is adopted by the curate, Don Trinidad. For three years after, Manuel speaks not a word; till one day, standing before the

image of the infant Christ with a ball in its hand (called the "Child of the Ball")
he says, "Child Jesus, why don't *you* speak either?" Meeting Perez's daughter
Soledad when a young man, he falls in love with her. He fights this passion; living
for months at a time on the mountains, and with no weapon but his hands, battling
with the wild beasts. To bring him back to civilization, Don Trinidad tells him
that Soledad reciprocates his love. At the feast day of the "Child of the Ball,"
it is customary to bid for the privilege of dancing with any lady; the money going
to the cult of the Child. Manuel bids for a dance with Soledad; but her father
outbids him and he is obliged to desist. Perez accuses him of his debt of one million reals; and Manuel, to pay it, determines to leave Spain. He promises to return
on the anniversary of this day and claim Soledad; and woe to him who in the meantime dares to come between them. Eight years after he returns and finds Soledad
married to Antonio Arregui. All efforts of Don Trinidad to dissuade him from
killing Arregui are in vain; but he is left alone with the "Child of the Ball," and
finally decorates it with the jewels he had brought for his bride, and lays at its feet
the dagger he had concealed. The next morning he leaves, but is overtaken by a
letter from Soledad. He returns, bids a sum which Arregui cannot equal, and Soledad
flies to his arms. Arregui takes the dagger from the feet of the image and stabs
Manuel, and the lovers fall to the ground dead. The story is told with dramatic
force; and tender, idyllic passages lighten its tragic gloom.

CHILD OF THE JAGO, A, by Arthur Morrison (1896), is a sadly realistic
sketch of life among the slums of London. The Jago is a name given to certain
streets in the neighborhood of Shoreditch, East City. The author knows the
district from residence there, while he was in the employment of a humanitarian society. The "child" is Dicky Perott, whose father, Josh Perott, is a thief,
bruiser, and murderer, who ends on the gallows. The lad is bred to vice as the
sparks fly upward, and what few feeble efforts he makes towards a better life are
nipped in the bud. Yet he has his own queer, warped code of ethics; and when he
is stricken down by a knife in a street row, dies with a lie on his lips to shield the
culprit. Dicky feels that on the whole, death is an easy way out of a sorry tangle.
The Jago scenes are given with photographic distinctness, the dialect is caught,
the life both external and internal — sordid, brutal, incredibly vicious, yet relieved
with gleams and hints of higher things — is depicted with truth and sympathy.
The study of Father Sturt, the self-sacrificing clergyman is a very suggestive setting-
forth of the difficulty of helping these demoralized human beings. The story is one
of great power, very sombre and painful, but valuable as a statement of the real
conditions among the lowest class of London poor.

CHILDE HAROLD'S PILGRIMAGE, a narrative-descriptive poem in the Spenserian stanza, by George Gordon, Lord Byron. The first and second cantos were
published together in 1812, the third and fourth in 1816 and 1818 respectively.
The first two cantos describe the poet's journey through Portugal, Spain, the Mediterranean, and Greece. Autobiographic references are thinly disguised under
the pseudonym 'Childe Harold' and an archaic diction which the poet soon lays
aside. Representing himself as hardened and world-weary from youthful dissipation but sentimentally fond of brooding on his lost affections and present misery
he conducts the reader through the famous scenes of the Peninsula and Hellas,
pausing to give word-pictures of landscape, historical and political reflections, and
accounts of characteristic amusements and occupations of the people visited. An

10

account of an Albanian chieftain and the war-song of his robber band is particularly striking. The third canto, written shortly after Byron's separation from his wife and retirement to Switzerland, strikes a deeper note in its now frankly personal references to his lost daughter, his rebellious attitude against society, and his attempts to fathom the mystery of his own emotions. Some of Byron's best known lines — descriptive and reflective — occur in this and the succeeding canto in which he portrays the field of Waterloo, the journey up the Rhine, the glories of sunset and storm in the Alps, and the historic, artistic, and literary associations of Geneva, Venice, Florence, and Rome. In addition to the sentimental and pictorial passages of the poem, Byron has a critical power of estimating great men and movements which is responsible for some often-quoted lines, like those on Voltaire, Gibbon, Napoleon, the Italian poets, and the French Revolution. The whole poem is a gallery of pictures — landscapes and historical pieces — commented on by a powerful but self-centred mind, over-dominated by sentiment and by the spirit of revolt.

CHILDREN OF GIBEON (1886). Walter Besant's 'Children of Gibeon,' like his 'All Sorts and Conditions of Men,' deals with society in both the West and East Ends of London, and their relations to each other. A rich widow, Lady Mildred Eldredge, adopts the two-year-old daughter of a former servant, to be brought up with her own daughter. The children are of the same age, and look so much alike that Lady Mildred conceives the idea of calling them Valentine and Violet, and keeping them and the world in ignorance as to which is Beatrice Eldredge, the heiress, and which Polly Monument, the washerwoman's daughter, a secret which is to be revealed when they are of age. At twenty they are introduced to Polly's family; her mother being then in an almshouse, her brother Joe a plumber, Sam a board-school teacher, Milenda a sewing-girl, and Claude a young lawyer and university man whom Lady Mildred has educated. Violet is filled with the fear that she shall turn out to be the sister of these dreadful people; but Valentine, who is sure that she herself is the real Polly, wishes to go to live with her sister Milenda, and to work among her own people. With Lady Mildred's consent she takes up her abode in Hoxton, and on the first day of her sojourn there finds accidental proof of the fact that she is Beatrice Eldredge. Nevertheless, as Polly she goes on with her work, in order to help Milenda and two young sewing-girls, who live with her, and with whom she spends the summer. Meantime Claude, having also found out the truth, falls deeply in love with her, and finally marries her. The plot is so ingeniously managed that it seems entirely plausible; the studies of London wage-earners and London slums are faithful, without being too repulsive; and the tone of the book is cheerful, while many social problems are touched in the course of an entertaining story. The 'Children of Gibeon' has proved one of the most popular of Besant's novels.

CHILDREN OF THE ABBEY, THE, by Regina Maria Roche (1796). The Earl of Dunreath, marrying a second time, is induced by the machinations of his wife to cast aside her stepdaughter, for a luckless marriage. It is with the children of this marriage that the story deals. The motherless Amanda is the heroine; and she encounters all the vicissitudes befitting the heroine of the three-volume novel. These include the necessity of living under an assumed name, of becoming the innocent victim of slander, of losing a will, refusing the hands of dukes and earls, and finally, with her brother, overcoming her enemies, and living happy in the highest society forever after. The six hundred pages, with the high-flown gallantry, the emotional excesses, and the reasonless catastrophes of the eighteenth-century novel, fainting heroines, love-lorn heroes, oppressed innocence, and abortive schemes of black-hearted villainy, form a fitting accompaniment to the powdered hair, muslin gowns, stage-coaches, postilions, and other picturesque accessories.

CHILDREN OF THE GHETTO, by I. Zangwill.   This book was published in 1892, and is, as the author says, "intended as a study, through typical figures, of a race whose persistence is the most remarkable fact in the history of the world."   It is divided into two parts, the first of which gives the title to the whole, and describes life in the London Ghetto, its sordid squalor and rigid ritualism, combined with genuine religious faith and enthusiasm.   The wretched inhabitants, huddled together in misery, and constrained to keep many fasts not prescribed in the calendar, are still scrupulous about all the detailed observances of their religion, and bound by a remarkable loyalty among themselves.   A good example of their subjection to form is shown in the rigid but kindly Reb Shemuel, who would give the coat off his back to help a needy Jew, and yet could ruin his daughter's whole life on account of an un-important text in the Torah.   The second part, 'Grandchildren of the Ghetto,' develops some of the characters who are children in the earlier portion, and also introduces us to the Jew who has acquired wealth and culture, while retaining his race characteristics.   This division of the book deals rather with the problems of Judaism, both of the race and of individuals.   It shows the effects of culture on differ-ent types of mind, and gives us the noble aspiration of Raphael Leon, the profound discontent of Esther, the fanatical zeal and revolt of Strelitski, and the formalism of the Goldsmiths, serving merely as a cloak for their ambition.   There are many touches of the author's characteristic wit and irony.   He tells of the woman "who wrote domestic novels to prove that she had no sense of humor"; and makes certain wealthy Jews say with apparent unconsciousness, that they are obliged to abandon a favorite resort "because so many Jews go there."   The book raises problems that it does not solve; but the masterly and sympathetic exposition of the Jewish tempera-ment invites a better comprehension of that wonderful race.

CHILDREN OF THE SOIL, a novel of modern Polish life, by Henryk Sienkiewicz (1894).   The plot centres itself in the career of Pan Stanislas Polanyetski, a man of wealth and education, who at the age of thirty "wanted to marry, and was convinced that he ought to marry."   The story opens with his business visit to the estate of Kremen, — on which he has a claim, — the home of a relative, Pan Plaritski, and his daughter Maryina.   He falls in love with Maryina; but the refusal of her father to pay his debt to Polanyetski causes misunderstanding between the latter and the young girl, and they are alienated for the time being.   Their reconcilia-tion and marriage are brought about by a little invalid girl, Litka, who loves them both, and who wishes to see them happy.   After his marriage, Polanyetski conceives an unworthy attachment for the wife of his friend Mashko, but finally overcomes temptation.   The book closes upon his happiness with his wife and child.   There are interesting side issues to the story, involving questions of property, of the social order, of marriage.   The work as a whole, although realistic, is sane in spirit, genial and broad in its conception of life and character.   Maryina is one of the most finished of Sienkiewicz's types of noble women.

CHILDREN OF THE WORLD, by Paul Heyse (1873), obtained immediate popularity, and caused great controversy over the fearless treatment of the theme. The children of the world are represented by a young doctor of philosophy, a strong, well-balanced character; his younger brother, an almost Christlike idealist; and their circle of friends and fellow-students, who, in spite of mistakes and eccentricities, bear the stamp of true nobility of soul. They are all either on the road to, or have already reached, what the children of God are pleased to call unbelief. In the portraiture of the differing camps there are no sharp contrasts, no unfair caricaturing, but an impartiality, a blending of one into the other, that makes one of the strongest claims of the book to attention.

CHINA, SACRED BOOKS OF, see **SACRED BOOKS OF THE EAST.**

CHINESE, see **SOCIAL LIFE OF THE.**

CHINESE LETTERS, see **CITIZEN OF THE WORLD.**

CHIPS FROM A GERMAN WORKSHOP. By F. Max Müller (5 vols. 1867–75. New ed. 1895). A collection of special studies incidental to the author's editing of a library of the 'Sacred Books of the East.' The several volumes cover various fields, as follows: (1) the Science of Religion; (2) Mythology, Traditions, and Customs; (3) Literature, Biography, and Antiquities; (4) chiefly the Science of Language; (5) Miscellaneous and later topics. Although they are "occasional" work, their wealth of material and thoroughness of treatment, and the importance of the views presented, give them not only interest but permanent value. On many of the points treated, discussion is still open, and some of the views advanced by Professor Müller may come into doubt; but his contributions to a great study will not soon lose their value.

CHOICE OF BOOKS, THE, and other Literary Pieces, by Frederic Harrison (1886). The title essay of this volume is a discourse on Reading, its benefits and its perils. In the first section, 'How to Read,' an eloquent plea is made for the right of rejection; for the avoidance of books that one "comes across," and even of the habit of one-sided reading. The essayist pleads that the choice of books "is really a choice of education, of a moral and intellectual ideal, of the whole duty of man." He warns readers that pleasure in the reading of great books is a faculty to be acquired, not a natural gift, — at least not to those who are spoiled by our current education and habits of life. And he offers as a touchstone of taste and energy of mind, the names of certain immortal books, which if one have no stomach for, he should fall on his knees and pray for a cleaner and quieter spirit. The second division is given to the 'Poets of the Old World,' the third to the 'Poets of the Modern World,' and the last to the 'Misuse of Books.' The essay is full of instruction and of warning, most agreeably offered; and the penitent reader concludes with the writer, that the art of printing has not been a gift wholly unmixed with evil, and may easily be made a clog on the progress of the human mind. An extract is given in the LIBRARY, under Mr. Harrison's name; and the other side of the shield is shown in Mr. Arthur J. Balfour's answer, also given under his name. Fourteen other essays, partly critical, partly historical, partly æsthetic, fill the volume; the ablest and one of the most delightful among them being perhaps the famous paper, 'A Few Words about the Eighteenth Century.'

CHOIR INVISIBLE, THE, by James Lane Allen, appeared in 1897, and is one of his most popular and pleasing stories. It was enlarged from an earlier story called 'John Gray.' Its scene is the Kentucky of a hundred years ago. The hero is John Gray, a schoolmaster and idealist, who, disappointed in his love for Amy Falconer, a pert, pretty, shallow flirt, gradually comes to care for Mrs. Falconer, her aunt, a noble woman in reduced circumstances, who with her husband has left a former stately home in Virginia and come to live in the Kentucky wilderness. She loves him in return with a deep, tender passion that has in it something of the motherly instinct of protection; but, her husband being alive, she conceals her feeling from Gray until after he has departed from Lexington and settled in another State. She then writes him to say she is free — and he replies that he is married. But he tells her in a final letter that she has remained his ideal and guiding star to noble action. The romantic atmosphere and the ideal cast of these two leading characters make the fiction very attractive; and the fresh picturesque descriptions of pioneer life in Kentucky give the tale historical value.

CHOUANS, THE, by Balzac. This was the novelist's first important work. The title, when it appeared in 1829, was 'The Last Chouan: or, Bretagne in 1800.' In 1846 it was rearranged in its present form. It is the story of a young girl, Marie de Verneuil, sent by Fouché to entrap the leader of the royalists in Bretagne, the Marquis de Montauran. She falls in love with him, reveals her disgraceful mission, and devotes all her energies to save him, until a trick of his enemies leads her to believe him false. Then she plots his ruin, is undeceived too late; and both die together. Marie is an exquisite creation, revealing that deep and intuitive knowledge of the soul of woman of which Balzac was to give so many proofs afterward. Montauran also is an original character, vigorously and delicately drawn. In Hulot, the rough republican commandant sprung from the ranks, and in Marche-à-Terre, the ferocious but honest fanatic, we have two of Balzac's "types," designed and classified truthfully and convincingly. Many of the scenes are of tragic intensity. Nothing could be more terrible than that of the massacre of the Blues at Vivetière, that of the unmasking of the spy among her enemies, or that of the roasting of the old miser by the Chouans to compel him to reveal his treasure. The description of a mass said by a priest in rags, in the midst of the forest, before a granite altar, while the insurgents, kneeling near their guns, beat their breasts and repeat the responses, is singularly grand and imposing. The author made a profound study of the scenery of Bretagne, and the manners of its people, before he wrote his romance; and his pictures of both scenery and people have the stamp of reality and truth.

CHRISTIAN, THE, by Hall Caine (1897), is a popular romance. For the most part the scene is laid in London. The main characters are Glory Quayle, the granddaughter of a Manx clergyman, and John Storm, the son of a nobleman and nephew of the prime minister. Glory has actor's blood in her veins; John is a religious enthusiast whom his father, disappointed in his choice of life, disinherits. The girl goes to London as a hospital nurse; the man, as assistant clergyman of a fashionable church. But she is soon tired of a life she is unfitted for, and longs for pleasure, change, excitement; while he is sickened at the worldliness, fraud, and pretense of West End piety, and resigns his position to join a monastic brotherhood, — finding, however, after a year of trial, that the ascetic retirement from the world is not the true religious ideal for him. The thought, too, of Glory mingles ever subtly with the thought of God. Meanwhile, she has had some hard knocks in the struggle to get on the stage and show her unusual powers. She becomes a music-hall singer, to John's great distress, and for a long while he keeps away from her and her fashionable friends. But his desire to save Glory's soul — and to win the girl herself — leads him to a declaration, and he finds he is loved in return; but she is unwilling to give up her profession and associate herself with him in his work. She makes a brilliant début as a star on the regular stage. Father Storm breaks down as a hermit and a crusading Christian, and ends in failure. The details of London life are spectacular, and the object of the book seems to be to show the inadequacy of London churches to save the city.

CHRISTIAN WOMAN, A ('Una Cristiana'), by Emilia Pardo-Bazán (1890). In this interesting novel, the author presents a very realistic picture of modern Spanish life, into which are introduced many current social and political questions. The story is an autobiography of Salustio Unceta, a student in the School of Engineers in Madrid, and a liberal in politics and religion. His tuition is paid by his uncle Felipe, who invites Salustio to be present at his marriage to Carmen Aldoa. There is in the Unceta family a trace of Hebrew blood, which has declared itself both in the personal appearance and the power of acquisition of Felipe, and which excites a feeling of loathing in Salustio. He cannot understand why Carmen should marry Felipe, but overhears her secret when she is telling it to Father Moreno: she marries to escape sanctioning by her presence in the house a scandalous flirtation of her father. After the marriage, Felipe, to save expenses, takes Salustio into his house; and the results are very unfortunate.

CHRISTIANITY, THE GENIUS OF, see **GENIUS OF CHRISTIANITY.**

CHRISTIANITY IN CHINA, TARTARY, AND THIBET, by the Abbé Huc. A curiously interesting and elaborate history of the presence in the Chinese Empire of Christian missions from the time of the Apostles to the end of the seventeenth century. The author was a Roman Catholic missionary in China, 1840–52. By shaving his head and dyeing his skin yellow, and wearing a queue and Chinese costume, and by a thorough command of the Chinese language, he was able to travel not only in China proper, but in Thibet and Tartary. He published in 1850 an exceedingly interesting account of his travels during 1844–46, and in 1854 a work on the Chinese Empire. His first work related marvels of travel which aroused incredulity; but later researches have amply shown that this was unjust. The final work, connecting the history of the Chinese Empire with the maintenance through centuries of Christian missions, is a work of great value for the history of the far East. Huc wrote in French; but all the works here mentioned were brought out in English, and met with wide popular acceptance. The 'Travels in the Chinese Empire' came out in a cheap edition, 1859; the 'Chinese Empire, Tartary, and Thibet,' was in 5 vols., 1855–58; and the 'Christianity,' etc., 3 vols.,1857–58.

CHRISTIE JOHNSTONE, by Charles Reade, was published in 1855, three years after 'Peg Woffington' had given the author his reputation. It is one of the best and most charming of modern stories. It depicts a young viscount, rich and blasé, who loves his cousin Lady Barbara, but is rejected because of his lack of energy and his aimlessness in life. He grows pale and listless; a doctor is called in, and prescribes yachting and taking daily interest in the "lower classes." The story, by turns pathetic and humorous, abounds in vivid and dramatic scenes of Scotch life by the sea; and Christie, with her superb physique, her broad dialect, her shrewd sense, and her noble heart, is a heroine worth while. Reade's wit and humor permeate the book, and his vigorous ethics make it a moral tonic.

CHRISTOPHER, by Richard Pryce (1911). This is the story of an English boy named Christopher Herrick, and is a detailed account of his career from the time of his birth till he reaches manhood. He is born on an ocean steamer, which is bringing his widowed and heart-broken young mother back from India to her home in England. Christopher's early years are carefully watched over by his devoted mother, his faithful nurse Trimmer, his grandmother and his two unmarried aunts. He early develops an observing nature and a receptive mind and is a most lovable and thoughtful child. His quaint sayings and his original way of looking at things make interesting pages for the reader. While Christopher is still a child his mother marries again and becomes the wife of John Hemming, one of her early admirers. Previous to his marriage Hemming had had an affair with a fascinating divorcée, Mrs. St. Jemison, whose beauty had made a deep impression upon Christopher and later he finds in her daughter Cora his ideal. Christopher has finished his second year at Oxford and is off for a foreign trip with a friend when he sees at a railroad station an unusually pretty girl who later proves to be Cora St. Jemison. Christopher's impressionable nature is immediately touched and he journeys from place to place in search of his paragon, whom he finally meets in London in the drawing-room of a friend. From this moment Christopher's every thought is of Cora, and though he does not see her again for two years she is constantly in his mind. He finishes college and adopts writing for his vocation. At last he and Cora come together again but after a period of earnest devotion on Christopher's part rewarded by a shallow affection which is all that the frivolous Cora can offer, she finally tells him they can not be happy together and marries another man. Christopher is crushed with disappointment and grief, but the reader takes leave of him at this crisis filled with the assurance that better things are in store for him.

CHRONICLES OF CARLINGFORD. The general title of 'Chronicles of Carlingford' covers a number of tales and novels by Mrs. Margaret Oliphant, which have no direct sequence or continuous plot, but which have more or less connection through the reappearance of some of the same characters. These novels — which can hardly be called a series, but rather a group — include 'Salem Chapel,' 'The Rector,' 'The Doctor's Family,' 'The Perpetual Curate,' 'Miss Marjoribanks,' and 'Phœbe Junior.' The earliest to appear was 'Salem Chapel,' which was published anonymously in 1863, but was readily attributed to Mrs. Oliphant, who had then been for fourteen years before the public as a writer, and whose style was recognizable. 'Salem Chapel' holds perhaps the foremost place among the Chronicles, having a strong dramatic interest in addition to that which it possesses as a tale of English middle-class life. Carlingford is a country town; and its chronicles are for the most part those of ordinary persons, set apart by no unusual qualities or circumstances. The portraits of these people are vividly drawn, with humor and delicacy as well as strength. The vicissitudes in the ministry of Arthur Vincent, preacher in the Dissenting Salem Chapel, form the framework of the tale. The hopeless infatuation of Vincent for Lady Western, and the temptation of Mildmay, Lady Western's brother, constitute the romance and tragedy of the story. Mr. Tozer, the rich dealer in butter, who is the financial pillar of the Dissenting chapel; his pretty but vulgar daughter Phœbe, who is more than half in love with the handsome young minister; Dr. Marjoribanks, the old country doctor; Dr. Rider, his younger successor, and in some sense his rival; Mr. Wentworth, the curate of St. Roques; the Wodehouse family, — all the many dwellers in Carlingford who appear and reappear through these tales, — become familiar acquaintances of the reader. A great charm of these novels is the distinctness with which each character is portrayed, and the individuality which is preserved for each among the large number introduced in the action.

CHRONICLES OF CLOVERNOOK, THE, by Douglas Jerrold. Clovernook is a "hamlet wherein fancy has loitered away a truant hour," "the work of some sprite that in an idle and extravagant mood made it a choice country-seat." Into this land of fantasy the author rides in the twilight; the sagacity of his ass, whose name is Bottom, bringing him through unknown paths to the house of the Hermit of Belly-fulle — "the very pope of Hermits," as Dickens styled him in one of his letters. In the companionship of the Hermit, and under his guidance, the adventurer explores Clovernook, and discourses of it. He learns of the Kingdom of As-you-like, whither the dwellers in Clovernook repair yearly; the Land of Turveytop, where men are purged of their worldliness; the Isle of Jacks; Honey-Bee Bay; and at the pleasant inn called "Gratis" he meets the Twenty-five Club and other gentle philosophers, in whose tales and conversation the realities of the crude world outside are refined into the dreams of this realm of fancy. 'Clovernook' charms by its quiet humor, the grace of its fancies, and the benevolence which characterizes even its satire. It is the work to which Mr. Jerrold referred as, in certain parts, best expressing himself as he wished the world to understand him. It was written in the prime of his literary career at the age of forty years, while he was the leading contributor to Punch, with his position well established as one of the popular writers of the day. Appearing serially in that paper, 'The Chronicles of Clovernook' was published separately in 1846, and has since had its place in the collected works of its author.

CHRONICLES OF FROISSART, THE. The Chronicles of the French poet and historian Jean Froissart embrace the events occurring from 1325 to 1400 in England, Scotland, France, Spain, Brittany, and the Low Countries. They are of great value in illustrating the manners and character of the fourteenth century. Froissart began his work on them when but twenty years old, in 1357; they were not completed until 1400. They present a vivid and interesting picture of the long-continued wars of the times, setting forth in detail not only the fighting, but the feasts, spectacles, and all the pageantry of feudal times; and they are enlivened throughout by Froissart's shrewd comments and observations. Among the many interesting historic personages are King Edward III. of England, Queen Philippa, Robert Bruce of Scotland, and Lord James Douglas who fought so valiantly for the heart of Bruce. Froissart depicts the invasion of France by the English, the battle of Crécy, the great siege of Calais, and the famous battle of Poitiers; describes the brilliant court of the great Béarnese, Lord Gaston Phœbus, Count de Foix, whom he used to visit; and portrays among other events the coronation of Charles VI. of France, the heroic struggle of Philip van Artevelde to recover the rights of Flanders, and the insurrection of Wat Tyler. There is also a valuable description of the Crusade of 1390. Froissart obtained his material by journeying about and plying with questions the knights and squires whom he met, lodging at the castles of the great, and jotting down all that he learned of stirring events and brave deeds. He was much in England, being at different times attached to the households of Edward III. of England and of King John of France, and becoming an especial favorite with Queen Philippa, who made him clerk of her chamber. The 'Chronicles' first appeared in Paris about the end of the fifteenth century. In the Library at Breslau is a beautiful MS. of them, executed in 1468.

CHRONICLES OF THE SCHÖNBERG-COTTA FAMILY, by Mrs. Elizabeth Charles (1863). These chronicles, dealing with the period of the Reformation in Germany, are written chiefly by Friedrich and Else, the eldest children of the Schönberg-

Cotta family. Their father is an improvident printer with eight children to provide for. Martin Luther, adopted by their aunt Ursula Cotta, is prominent throughout. The chronicles open with the efforts of Friedrich and Else to understand the Romanist religious life, and their brave efforts to hold the family together. The family, which is very religious, sends the eldest son, Friedrich, to the University of Erfurt, where Luther has already shown great promise. In fulfillment of vows, Luther and Friedrich next enter an Augustinian monastery, where they struggle hard to destroy their worldly ties, Friedrich being especially beset on account of his love for a young girl named Eva. Rising rapidly, the two friends are intrusted with a mission to Rome. The lives of the easy-going monks distress them; finally the selling of indulgences brings Luther to outspoken denunciation of the abuses of the Church. In this Friedrich supports him, and both are excommunicated and thrown into prison. Luther escapes, and appeals to the people with his new doctrine that personal responsibility to God is direct, without mediation of priests. This teaching is proclaimed broadcast, and Luther becomes an object of fear to Rome; but he lives to the age of sixty-three, and dies a happy father and husband, having espoused Catherine von Bora, a former nun. Friedrich, after many hindrances, marries Eva. The book is written with an effort after the archaic style, and has much of the simplicity and directness of the old chronicles. Its point of view is that of evangelical Protestantism, and it lacks the judicial spirit that would have presented a true picture of the time. It is interesting, however, and has proved a very great favorite, though accurate scholarship finds fault with its history.

CHRYSAL, or, THE ADVENTURES OF A GUINEA, "containing curious and interesting anecdotes of the most noted persons in every rank of life whose hands it passed through, in America, England, Holland, Germany, and Portugal." This satirical novel, by Charles Johnstone, an Irishman, was published in 1760. In 'Davis's Olio of Bibliographical and Literary Anecdote,' a key to the characters is presented. The first two volumes of the work were written for the author's amusement. Its popularity induced him to extend it to four volumes.

Chrysal, signifying gold or golden, is the spirit inhabiting a guinea, which passes through many hands, from the prince's to the beggar's. It tells its own story, which is chiefly the adventures of those in whose possession it is for the time being. This curious and now rare work is written in an old-fashioned, ponderous style; and judged by modern standards of melodramatic fiction, is not very readable.

CHURCH OF ENGLAND, see **REFORMATION OF THE.**

CHURCHILL, LORD RANDOLPH, by Winston Churchill (1906). The life of Lord Randolph Churchill by his son is one of the foremost of English political biographies. With the exception of the first two chapters and the last, the events which it describes are included within the stormy period between 1880 and 1890. Lord Randolph had no long years of office to his credit, no great legislation called by his name, no easily tabulated list of achievements, yet his forceful and magnetic personality exercised an extraordinary influence upon the Conservative party when it was in danger of being overwhelmed by Gladstone. He was a leader of that progressive variety of English Conservatism which came to be known as Tory Democracy, urging the Conservatives to adopt popular reforms and to dispute the claim of Liberals to be the only true champions of the working classes. Although he had much sympathy with Ireland, he was a bitter opponent of Gladstone's Home Rule proposals of 1885. The great force which he was just beginning to exercise on British politics was broken by his death at the comparatively early age of forty-six, yet he has a secure place in English political history, for, in the words with which his biographer closes, "there is an England which stretches far beyond the well-drilled masses who are assembled by party machinery to salute with appropriate acclamation the utterances of their recognized fuglemen; an England of wise men who gaze without self-deception at the failings and follies of both political parties; of brave and earnest men who find in neither faction fair scope for the effort that is in them; of 'poor men' who increasingly doubt the sincerity of party philanthropy. It was to that England that Lord Randolph Churchill appealed; it was that England he so nearly won; it is by that England he will be justly judged."

CICERO, MARCUS TULLIUS, LIFE OF. By William Forsyth (2 vols., 1863) A chapter of personal history, and of the story of classical culture, in the first half of the last century before Christ, of great interest and value. It deals not only with the orator and statesman, and the public affairs in which he played so great a part, but with Cicero as a man, a father, husband, friend, and gentleman, and with the culture of the time, of which Cicero was so conspicuous a representative. The picture serves particularly to show along what lines moral and religious development had taken place before the time of Christ. Cicero's public career covered the years 80-43 B.C., and within these years fell the career of Cæsar.

CICERO AND HIS FRIENDS, by Gaston Boissier (1892). There is probably no man of ancient times of whose public and private life we know so much as we do of Cicero's: the sixteen extant books of his 'Letters to Various Persons,' or as they are usually styled, his 'Letters to Friends,' and those to his friend Atticus, reveal the man in his littleness and vanity no less than in his greatness. He was a great man and a great patriot; but with his incontestable virtues he combined almost incredible weaknesses of character, — his wheedling letters to one Lucius Lucellus, a writer of histories, whom he asks to write an account of his consulship, is sufficient proof of this. From these letters of Cicero, and also from his forensic orations and his philosophical and rhetorical writings, the author of this book draws the material for a singularly interesting account of the great orator's public and private life. It has been the fashion of scholars of late to belittle Cicero; to write him down an egotist, a shallow, time-serving politician, a mere phrase-maker. M. Boissier admits that Cicero was timid, hesitating, irresolute; he was by nature a man of letters rather than a statesman. But the mind of the man of letters is often broader, more comprehensive than that of the practical statesman; and "it is precisely this breadth that cramps and thwarts him when he undertakes the direction of public affairs." He redeemed the vacillations and timidities of his political career by meeting death at the hand of the hired assassin with stoic fortitude. In a chapter on Cicero's private life, the question comes up as to the ways in which he acquired his very considerable wealth. In accounting for it, the author cites numerous instances of the orator's clients making him their heir for large sums: the law forbade payment of money to advocates, and the method of making payment by legacies was invented as a means of circumventing the statute. Another way was "borrowing" money from rich clients; and many instances are cited of large sums being loaned to Cicero by wealthy men whom he had defended in the courts. Besides wealthy clients in private life, there were towns and provinces whose interests he had defended in the Senate; and above all, there were the rich corporations of the farmers of the public revenues whom he had served: these interests found a means of recompensing the advocate liberally.

The domestic life of Cicero was embittered by the unhappy marital experiences of his daughter Tulliola, the extravagances of his first wife Terentia, and the dissolute character of his son Marcus. But in his household was one faithful servitor, his slave and amanuensis Tiro, whom he loved with parental affection. In one of his letters to Tiro he writes: "You have rendered me numberless services at home, in the forum, at Rome, in my province, in my public and private affairs, in my studies and my literary work." Tiro survived his master many years; but to the day of his death he labored to perpetuate the fame of Cicero by writing his life and preparing editions of his works. The Friends of Cicero, of whom notices are given in the volume, are Atticus, Cælius, Julius Cæsar, Brutus, and Octavius.

CID, THE ('Poema del Cid,' 'Cantares del Cid,' or 'Gesta de myo Cid'), a popular epic poem of the twelfth century, narrating in long assonant couplets, events real and legendary from the life of a Castilian noble, Rodrigo Diaz de Bivar (d. 1099), who was exiled by the king of Leon-Castile and thenceforward lived as an independent chieftain, in alliance now with Christian and now with Moorish princes. The name Cid, or Lord, was given to him by the Arabs. The poem describes the Cid's exile, his campaign against the Moors, his capture of Valencia (1094), and the marriage of his daughters, first to the Infantes of Carrion, who insult them, and then to the Infantes of Navarre and Arragon. A second poem, the 'Cronaca Rimada del Cid,' 'Cantar de Rodrigo,' or 'Leyenda de las Mocedades de Rodrigo' relates his *enfances* or first exploits — his slaying of his father's enemy, Count Gomez, and his marriage to Jimena, daughter of Gomez. The exploits of the Cid are also celebrated in the later *Romances* or ballads (c. 1500). As a specimen of the epic of the people, as a direct, vigorous narrative, and as a revelation of mediæval Spain, this poetry has great importance. For a full account, see the LIBRARY under 'The Cid.'

CID, THE, a drama by Pierre Corneille, first performed in 1636. It is closely modeled on a Spanish play by Guillem de Castro (1569–1631) 'Las Mocedades del Cid' *i.e.*, 'The Youth of the Cid,' a romantic treatment of the mediæval poem on that subject. The play presents Corneille's favorite theme of the strong character faced by conflicting duties. Don Rodrigue loves Chimène but is bound by filial duty to kill her father, Don Gomès, for insulting his father, Don Diègue. Chimène, who reciprocates the love of Don Rodrigue, is now equally bound to enmity against him. She refuses to take his life when he gives her the opportunity; but although he rescues the city of Seville from the Moors she feels obliged to demand of the king a champion against him. Nevertheless her distress at the supposed victory of this champion Don Sanche, a rival suitor, reveals her true feelings; and by the command of the king she weds the real victor, Don Rodrigue. The character of the Infanta, who also loves the hero, but suppresses this emotion in deference to her duty to Chimène and to the king, is another example of the strong-willed personages so typical of Corneille. Though romantic in theme the play, by its observance of the unities and of stage decorum, initiated the reign of classicism in the French drama.

CINDERELLA, see **FAIRY TALES.**

CINQ-MARS, by Alfred de Vigny (1826). The subject of this historical romance is the conspiracy of Cinq-Mars and De Thou against Richelieu, its detection, and the execution of the offenders at Lyons in 1642. The work is modeled after the Waverley novels. All the action centres around the great figure of Richelieu. The aristocratic prejudices of the author prevent him from doing full justice, perhaps, to the statesman who curbed the power of the French noblesse; and many critics think that Bulwer depicts him more truly. The Richelieu of De Vigny is Richelieu as he appeared to the courtiers of the time: the organizer of assassination and espionage, in conjunction with Father Joseph and Laubardemont, — Richelieu in his days of hatred and murder. The author is more just to the Cardinal when he shows him making successful efforts to place France at the head of Europe, preparing and winning victories, and sending his king to fight like an obscure captain. The character of Louis XIII. is finely drawn, and we have a lifelike and admirably colored portrait of that strange and gloomy monarch, who is the master of France and the slave of Richelieu, and who sends his most devoted friends to the scaffold at the bidding of the man he hates. Indeed, the contrast between the obedient monarch and his imperious servant is the most striking feature in the romance. There are many scenes of great historic value; as for instance, that in which Richelieu retires on the King's refusal to sign a death-warrant, and abandons Louis to himself. The presentation of Cinq-Mars is also very vivid: we have a Cinq-Mars, who, if not true to history, is at least true to human nature. The outline of De Thou is perhaps just a little shadowy.

CITIES OF NORTHERN AND CENTRAL ITALY, by Augustus J. C. Hare (1876). In this work, consisting of three volumes, not only the cities but the towns and even the villages of Northern and Central Italy receive the careful and comprehensive attention of the writer. Entering Italy by the Cornice Road at Mentone, the reader is plunged at once into the land of the citron and myrtle. The district described embraces the whole country from the Alps to the environs of Rome: Genoa, Turin, Milan, Venice, Bologna, Verona, Padua, and Florence are treated at length. Nothing of interest has been omitted: cathedrals, palaces, homes and haunts of great men, the Old Masters and their works, all have place, while well-known names of history and legend have been studied with painstaking care. The volumes contain hotel and pension rates, omnibus and railway fares, and catalogues of the exhibits in the various galleries, — that of the Pitti Palace being particularly noteworthy. Yet they are not "guides" merely; for they offer the reader not only the excellent comments of Mr. Hare, but whole pages of quotations from famous art critics and historical authorities, such as Ruskin, Goethe, Gautier, Dickens, Symonds, Freeman, Perkins, Story, and others. The writer's love for his subject produced a delightful work.

CITIZEN OF THE WORLD, by Oliver Goldsmith. Published under this title in the Public Ledger, a weekly journal of London, they ran through the year 1760, and were published in book form in 1762 as 'The Citizen of the World; or Letters from a Chinese Philosopher Residing in London to his Friends in the East.' Their charm lies in their delicate satire rather than in any foreign air which the author may have tried to lend them. They amused the town, they still divert and instruct us, and they will delight future generations. Lien Chi Altangi became real, and lives. He detects and exposes not merely the follies and foibles lying on the surface, but the greater evils rankling at the heart, of English society. He warns England of her insecure tenure of the American colonies, her exaggerated social pretenses, and the evil system of the magistracy. He ridicules English thought and the fashions which make beauty hideous, and avows his contempt for the cant of professed connoisseurs. The abuses of church patronage did not escape him; and he comments on the incidents of the day. As we read these 'Chinese Letters' all London of the eighteenth century rises before us. "Beau Tibbs," and t̶ ̶ "Man in Black" who accompanies the philosopher to the theatre are immortal; and 'The White Mouse and Prince Bonbennin' is founded on an actual experience of Goldsmith.

CITOYENNE JACQUELINE, by Sarah Tytler (1865). The scene opens in the early months of the French Revolution, 1792, in Faye-aux-Jonquilles, a village near Paris; the home of Jacqueline de Faye, only child of "Monsieur" and "Madame," nobles of the old régime.   Jacqueline has inherited the traditional ideas of her aristocratic ancestry, and is trained in the fantastic etiquette of her age; but displays disquieting symptoms of independence, a character sure to lead its possessor into strange paths. She is in love with her cousin, the Chevalier de Faye, to whom she is betrothed; but owing to the changes brought about by the Revolution, he transfers his attentions to another cousin, a wealthy and vivacious widow, Petronille de Croï.   In her anger and despair, Jacqueline takes a step that separates her from her order: she marries a handsome young peasant proprietor.   The wild days of '93 arrive, and she and her family are deeply involved in the turmoils of the time.   After they have suffered together, and he has sheltered her mother, she comes to love her plebeian husband. The story moves swiftly through scenes of conspiracy and bloodshed, to close among the green fields of Jonquilles.   It presents a vivid picture of the days of the Terror; a realistic portrayal of the inhumanities and self-sacrifices of that lurid period.   The meetings of Citoyenne Jacqueline with Charlotte Corday, and with Lydia, daughter of Laurence Sterne, are interesting episodes of her Paris life.

CITY OF GOD, THE, by St. Augustine.   This work, the most important of all his writings, was begun in 413, three years after the capture and pillage of Rome by the Visigoths under Alaric.   The pagans had endeavored to show that this calamity was the natural consequence of the spread of the Christian religion, and the main purpose of Augustine is to refute them.   The work, which was finished about 426, is divided into twenty-two books.   The first five deal with the arguments of those who seek to prove that the worship of the gods is necessary to the welfare of the world and that the recent catastrophe was caused by its abolition; the five following are addressed to those who claim that the worship of the divinities of paganism is useful for the attainment of happiness in the next life; and in the last twelve we have an elaborate discussion of the subject that gives its title to the whole work, — the contrast to be drawn between two cities, the City of God and the city of the world, and their progress and respective ends.   It would obviously be impossible to give in this space anything like a satisfactory résumé of this vast monument of genius, piety, and erudition. Notwithstanding its learning, profound philosophy, and subtle reasoning, it can be still read with ease and pleasure, owing to the variety, multiplicity, and interest of its details.   Augustine bases many of his arguments on the opinions held by profane authors; and his numerous and extensive quotations, some of them of the greatest value, from writers whose works have been long since lost, would alone suffice to entitle the author to the gratitude of modern scholars.   Few books contain so many curious particulars with regard to ancient manners and philosophical systems.   In the 'City of God' a vivid comparison is instituted between the two civilizations that preceded the Middle Ages; and the untiring efforts of ambition and the vain achievements of conquerors are judged according to the maxims of Christian humility and self-denial.   The 'City of God' is the death-warrant of ancient society; and in spite of its occasional mystic extravagance and excessive subtlety of argument, the ardent conviction that animates it throughout will make it one of the lasting possessions of humanity.

CIVIL WAR IN AMERICA, A HISTORY OF THE, by Philippe, Comte de Paris. In the summer of 1861, Philippe, Comte de Paris, joined the Northern army, rather as a spectator than as an active participant in affairs. He was appointed to McClellan's staff, and for a year followed the fortunes of the North. He returned to France with much valuable material concerning the history of that first year, to which he added, between 1862 and 1874, an equal amount of important information bearing upon the remaining years of the war. In 1875 the first volume of the translation was issued. Three other volumes appeared, in 1876, 1883, and 1888, respectively. The banishment of the Comte de Paris from France cut short the work, which has never been finished, but ends with the close of the account of the Red River Expedition under General Banks.

The historian writes from the point of view of an unprejudiced spectator. His object was not to uphold one side or the other, but to present to Europe a clear and impartial account of one of the most momentous struggles in history. As his work was addressed primarily to a European audience, much space is devoted to the conditions which brought about the conflict, to the formation and history of the United States army, and to the character of the country which was the scene of action. His is an essentially military history: marches and countermarches are described with an amount of detail which, but for the admirable clearness of style, would sadly confuse the lay mind. In his judgments, both of men and of events, the Comte de Paris is very impartial; though a slightly apologetic tone is often adopted in regard to the Administration, and a certain lack of enthusiasm appears towards many officers of Volunteers, notably in the later years of the war. This attitude of mind was doubtless due to his natural prepossession in favor of a regular army and an unchanging form of government.

CIVILIZATION IN ENGLAND, HISTORY OF, a philosophical history by Henry Thomas Buckle, the first volume published in 1857 and the second in 1861. In his introduction Buckle asserts that the actions of men, both individually and collectively, are determined solely by their antecedents and are therefore subject to scientific laws like any other natural phenomena. He accordingly proposes to write a history of civilization in which every stage of progress shall be accounted for by scientific laws. The principal external agents which determine the course of history are climate, food, soil, and the general aspect of nature; according to the abundance or scarcity of these material things man·is dominated by nature or dominates her. Moral forces and conservative tendencies as exhibited in respect for old beliefs, opinions, and institutions have been a retarding influence in human development, which has been forwarded by the growth of intellect, by the spirit of independent investigation, and by the principle of skepticism. Buckle then proceeds to apply these principles to the history of civilization in England, France, and Spain from the sixteenth to the eighteenth centuries. He did not live to extend his survey to other times and countries.

Appearing when the theory of evolution was in the air and naturalistic views were gaining converts, Buckle's work made a great sensation. The boldness and vigor of its position gained it enthusiastic adherents and bitter enemies. It showed men the implications of the new scientific doctrines and forced them to take sides. The book is made extremely readable by the broad powerful sweep of its generalizations and the incisiveness of its style.

CIVILIZATION IN EUROPE, History of. By François P. G. Guizot (new edition with critical and supplementary notes by George W. Knight, 1896). A standard work of great value, much improved by Professor Knight's critical and supplementary notes. The general summary of the progress of culture in Europe is admirably done, with all the new light to date. In a larger work, the 'History of Civilization,' Guizot surveyed a wider field, and dealt more thoroughly with some of the great problems of human progress. President C. K. Adams has said of this larger work that "perhaps no historical book is capable of stirring more earnest and fruitful thought in the student."

In his 'Civilization in Europe' Guizot begins with the fall of the Roman Empire, and ends with the opening of the French Revolution. Although he analyzes all the important facts of history between the great landmark of 476 and the convocation of the States-General in 1789, he is far more anxious to grasp their import than to give a vivid relation of them; and therefore, facts in themselves play but a small part in his exposition. They are simply a help in his effort to discover the great laws that direct the evolution of humanity, and to show its development in the individual and in society. "Civilization," he says, "consists of two facts, the development of the social state and the development of the intellectual state; the development of the exterior and general condition, and of the interior nature of man, — in a word, the perfection of society and humanity." It was impossible for the author to examine every aspect of the problem in a single volume. His investigations are therefore limited to purely social development, and he does not touch upon the intellectual side of the question. But the precision with which he notes the origin, meaning, and bearing of all accomplished events renders his work of great value.

CLARA VAUGHAN, by Richard Doddridge Blackmore (1864). This rather sensational story comes fairly under the head of pathological novels. The heroine, Clara Vaughan, inheriting an abnormal nervous susceptibility, has the misfortune at ten years of age to see her father murdered. Henceforth she devotes her life to the identification and punishment of his murderer. She suspects her uncle, Edgar Vaughan, and so insults and torments him that he turns her out of doors at seventeen. She goes to South Devon for a while, thence to London, where she meets Professor Ross (whose real name is De la Croce) and his children Isola and Conrad. With Conrad she falls in love, but impediments hinder their marriage. Her uncle becoming dangerously ill, she nurses him back to life. They are reconciled; and it is discovered that Isola and Conrad are his long-lost children, and that Clara's father has been killed in mistake, for his brother Edgar, by De la Croce, his Corsican wife's brother. Crowded with remarkable incidents and hair-breadth escapes, this is the most fantastic, as it was the earliest and least mature, of Blackmore's novels. Not the least attractive character is Giudice, the bloodhound, who plays an active part in the development of the plot.

CLARISSA FURIOSA, by W. E. Norris. This story, which may be regarded in the light of a satire on the "New Woman," is perhaps the least successful of the clever author's novels. Clarissa Dent, an orphan, rich, petted, and pretty, after a brief courtship marries Guy Luttrell, a soldier. Clarissa goes with the regiment to Ceylon, where Guy flirts, and she concludes that incompatibility of views must separate them; she returns to England, and most of the story is taken up with the semi-public life to which she devotes herself. The book is amusing, like all of Norris's, and the workmanship is of course good. But the note is forced, and the reader feels the writer's want of genuine interest in his characters. It was first published in the Cornhill Magazine, in 1896.

CLARISSA HARLOWE, by Samuel Richardson, was published in 1751, ten years after 'Pamela,' when Richardson was over sixty years old. In 'Pamela' he tried to draw the portrait of a girl of humble class in distress; in 'Clarissa' he essayed to do the same thing for a young woman of gentility. She is of a good country family (the scene being laid in rural England of the first half of the eighteenth century, Richardson's time), and is wooed by Lovelace, a well-known but profligate gentleman. The match is opposed by the Harlowes because of his dubious reputation. Clarissa for some time declines his advances; but as she is secretly taken by his dashing ways, he succeeds in abducting her, and so compromising her good name that she dies of shame, — her betrayer being killed in a duel by her cousin, Colonel Morden. Lovelace's name has become a synonym for the fine-gentleman profligate. He is drawn as by no means without his good side, and as sincerely loving Clarissa, who stands as a sympathetic study of a noble-minded young woman in misfortune. The story is largely told by letters exchanged between Clarissa and her confidante Miss Howe, and between Lovelace and his friend Belford. Its affecting incidents moved the heart of the eighteenth century, and ladies of quality knelt at Richardson's feet imploring him to spare his heroine. To the present-day reader, the tale seems slow and prolix; but it was able to enchain the attention of a man like Macaulay, and has much merit of plot and character. It is, moreover, a truthful picture of the conventions and ideals of its period, while it possesses a perennial life because it deals with some of the elemental interests and passions.

CLARK'S FIELD, by Robert Herrick (1914). Left an orphan at an early age, Ardelle Clark lives with her uncle and his wife and assists the latter in keeping lodgers. The financial hopes of the family are based on a large tract of land called "Clark's Field," in the centre of a manufacturing town, adjacent to the city of B. (presumably Boston), which they have owned for several generations but have been unable to realize upon. When Ardelle is fourteen the property is sold, and her uncle and aunt having died, she becomes sole heir to a fortune which amounts later to several million dollars. Being a minor, Ardelle becomes a ward of the Washington Trust Co. and is sent to a fashionable school and later to Paris. Here she meets an impecunious and worthless young art-student from California named Archie Davis, and marries him much to the disapproval of her guardians. Ardelle and her husband drift aimlessly about leading an idle, useless existence until the former attains her majority, when they return to America and take possession of the five million dollars awaiting them. This they proceed to waste in every conceivable way, settling eventually in California where they build a palatial residence. Ardelle has a son on whom she lavishes the affection she once felt for Archie, who, now, through weakness and dissipation, has alienated her love. Among the workmen on the place is a young mason named Tom Clark who proves to be a long-lost cousin of Ardelle and presumably an equal heir to the property. Ardelle decides not to acquaint Tom with this knowledge but the moment arrives when he makes a heroic attempt to save her child from a burning house, and though the child is dead, Ardelle insists he shall share her fortune. She parts finally with Archie and returns East to inform the Trust Co. of her decision. She finds complications awaiting her as the property so long unclaimed by the lost heirs stands irrevocably in her name. Nevertheless she is able to compensate Tom according to her desire, and decides with his assistance to use her money for the welfare and uplift of the poor people who live in the tenements built upon Clark's Field.

CLASSICAL GREEK POETRY, THE GROWTH AND INFLUENCE OF, by Professor R. C. Jebb (1893). Delivered originally as lectures at Johns Hopkins University, these chapters compose a brilliant sketch of the history and character of Greek poetry, epic, lyric, and dramatic. The introductory analysis of the Greek temperament is followed by an account of the rise of the lyric in Ionia, — as a partial outgrowth of the earlier epic, — and of the newer form, the drama, which came to supersede it in popularity. One of the most interesting chapters is occupied with the discussion of Pindar, in some respects the most interesting individuality in Greek literature, — "the most wonderful, perhaps, in lofty power, that the lyric poetry of any age can show." In the last chapter, on 'The Permanent Power of Greek Poetry,' Professor Jebb sums up the great elements in our present civilization directly traceable to the force and genius of the Greeks. In this work he unites rare literary skill with the ripest scholarship. To the student who seeks to know what Greece and her literature means to the present age, but who has no time for superfluous dates or facts, or disquisitions, this work is indispensable; for the author, a true Greek in a modern age, stands among the leading interpreters of her greatness.

CLAVERINGS, THE, by Anthony Trollope (1867), is a novel of contemporary English life, as shown in the fortunes of a country family. The story treats of the inconstant affections of Harry Clavering, the rector's son and cousin of the head of the family. The fickle lover is so agreeable and kind-hearted a young fellow that the tale of his fickleness wins the reader to friendship. All the characters are so typical of the commonplace respectable life that Trollope describes, as to seem like personal acquaintances. The reader is certain of meeting again Lady Ongar, Florence Burton, Lady Clavering, and the rest, and is pleased with the prospect. The book was a great favorite.

CLAYHANGER (1910), by Arnold Bennett. At the opening of the novel Edwin Clayhanger, of Bursley, is a fifteen-year-old lad just leaving school. His ambition to become an architect is overridden by his stern father, Darius Clayhanger, who insists on his going into the family printing business. Though Edwin proves invaluable, Darius refuses to pay him more than a pittance. Edwin's love for art and literature is stimulated through Mr. Orgreave, a Bursley architect, and he finds a congenial companion in Mr. Orgreave's charming daughter, Janet, through whom he comes to know Hilda Lessways, an odd girl who comes down from Brighton on a visit. Edwin and Hilda are mutually attracted, because she has an interesting mind which runs parallel to his, but when he informs his father of his intention to marry her, Darius refuses to pay his son more than a pound a week. But Edwin is saved the embarrassment of trying to establish a home on that amount by the startling news that Hilda has married a Mr. Cannon. Edwin is heartbroken. He cannot return Janet's affection because he is still devoted to the faithless Hilda. When Hilda sends her little son, George Edwin, down to visit "aunt" Janet, Edwin and the boy become inseparable companions, and when Edwin finally succeeds in getting Hilda's address he hurries to Brighton to see his old love. He arrives just in time to save Hilda's furniture from being attached for debt, and he gives her enough money to tide her over; he learns from her that the marriage with Cannon was forced upon her; that Cannon is now in prison for bigamy and that her marriage to him is void. Edwin returns to Bursley, considerably comforted. Little George's illness in Bursley brings Hilda down from Brighton in hot haste. Edwin stays with Hilda until the child is well out of danger. Then he goes home to trouble of his own. Darius Clayhanger suffers a shock, and softening of the brain follows. Always hard to manage, Darius becomes exceedingly difficult in his last illness. The dictatorial old man suffers keenly when he has to give over entire charge of the business to Edwin, including the keys, and the power of signing checks. The illness and death of Darius are described in Bennett's most masterly style, and the reader is left to look forward to the marriage of Hilda and Edwin.

The sequel, 'Hilda Lessways,' tells the story again from Hilda's point of view, clearing up the mystery of her marriage to Cannon, in which she was the victim partly of circumstances, partly of her own ardent and erratic temperament. 'These Twain,' which completes the trilogy, recounts Edwin's success in the printing business and his married life with Hilda and her son George. Some of the minor characters are admirable studies in Bennett's realistic manner.

CLEANNESS, see PEARL.

CLÉLIE, a romance in ten volumes by Mademoiselle de Scudéry (1654–60). The name of her brother figured on the title-pages of the first volumes; but the secret of the authorship having been discovered, her name replaced it. It would be difficult to summarize the incidents of this once famous production. The subject is the siege of Rome after the expulsion of Tarquin the Proud. The heroine is the young Roman girl who was a hostage of Porsena, and swam across the Tiber under a shower of arrows from the Etruscan army. Lucretia, Horatius, Mucius Scævola, Brutus, and all the heroes of the young republic are actors in the drama; and all are desperately in love, and spend most of their time in asking questions and solving riddles that have a serious connection with love, and especially with a very mysterious species of gallantry, according to the taste of the time in which it was written. They draw maps of love on the noted country of Tendre. We see the river of Inclination, on its right bank the villages of Jolis-Vers and Épîtres Galantes, and on its left those of Complaisance, Petits-Soins, and Assiduities. Further on are the hamlets of Abandon and Perfidie. By following the natural twists and turns of the river, the lover will have a pretty fair chance of arriving at the city of Tendre-sur-Estime; and should he be successful, it will then be his own fault if he do not reach the city of Tendre-sur-Inclination. The French critics of the present century do not accept Boileau's sweeping condemnation of Clélie; they consider that the work which excited the admiration of Madame de Sévigné and Madame de La Fayette has merits that fully justify their admiration. The manners and language assigned the Roman characters in the romance are utterly ridiculous and grotesque; but if we consider the Romans as masks behind which the great lords and ladies of the time simper and babble, its pictures of life are as true to nature as anything in literature. The fashionable people who recognized themselves under their Roman disguises were charmed with Mademoiselle de Scudéry's skill as a portrait-painter. The work marks the transition from the era of Montaigne to that of Corneille; and as such may, to some extent, be considered epoch-making.

CLEOPATRA, by H. Rider Haggard (1889). This, the most ambitious of Haggard's romances, presents a vigorous picture of Egypt under the rule of the wonderful Queen. Harmachis, priest and magician, descendant of the Pharaohs, tells his own story. Certain nobles, hating the Greek Cleopatra and her dealings with Rome, plot to overthrow her, and seat Harmachis on her throne. He enters her service to kill her when the revolt is ripe, but falls in love with her and cannot strike. Following this complication come plot and counterplot, treason and detection, — private griefs and hates that overthrow empires, and the later tragedy of Cleopatra's stormy life; more than one historic figure adding dignity and verisimilitude to the tale. The plot is well managed, and the interest maintained. The book is written in a curiously artificial manner, carefully studied. It contains many dramatic passages, with now and then an unexpected reminiscence of the manner of 'King Solomon's Mines' and 'She'; while its pages are crowded with gorgeous pictures of the splendid material civilization of Egypt.

CLIFF-DWELLERS, THE, by Henry B. Fuller (1893), is a story of Chicago at the end of the nineteenth century; a sober arraignment of the sin and greed of a purely material civilization. The protagonists of the drama take their title of "cliff-dwellers" from their occupation of various strata of an enormous office building, owned by the millionaire Ingles, whose beautiful wife is in reality the central character of the story, though she is not presented to the reader till the very last page. A young Easterner, George Ogden, a well-bred, average man of good intentions, is perhaps the hero; as the villain may be identified with Erastus Brainerd, a self-made man, utterly selfish and hard, who has ridden rough-shod over every obstacle, to the goal of a large fortune. Into the life whose standards are set chiefly by the unscrupulous successes of Brainerd, and the æsthetic luxury of the beautiful Mrs. Ingles, all the characters of the story are brought. The motives of the play are envy, ambition, love of ostentation, a thorough worship of the material, as these characteristics manifest themselves in a commercial community. There is a distinct and well-ordered plot, and the characters develop consistently from within. This clever story is too sincere to be called a satire, and too artistic to be called a photograph; but it is executed with a merciless faithfulness that has often elicited both characterizations.

CLOCKMAKER, THE: OR, THE SAYINGS AND DOINGS OF SAMUEL SLICK OF SLICK-VILLE, by Thomas Chandler Haliburton. It would be hard to prove that the conventional Yankee, as he is commonly understood, did not exist before Judge Haliburton published his account of that impossible person; yet no other book has so widely spread before the world the supposed characteristics of the typical New-Englander. Sam Slick, first presented to the public in a series of letters in the Nova-Scotian, in 1835, appeared two years later in a volume. The author was then but forty-three, although for eight years he had been chief justice of the court of Common Pleas. Having the interests of his province greatly at heart, he invented the clever clockmaker less to satirize the Yankees than to goad the Nova-Scotians to a higher sense of what they might accomplish politically and economically. To carry out his plan, he imagined a Nova-Scotian riding across country on a fast horse, and meeting Slick, the peddler, bound on a clock-selling expedition. The Yankee horse proves the faster, while his owner, in spite of an unattractive exterior, shows himself a man of wit. The peddler, with his knowledge of human nature and his liberal use of "soft sawder," is more than a match for the natives he has dealings with. Thus two birds are hit by Judge Haliburton with one stone. The average Yankee is satirized in the grotesque personality of the peddler, and the Nova-Scotians are lashed for their short-sightedness and lack of energy. The fund of anecdote and keen wit displayed in this book won it many admirers on both sides of the line. Either the Nova-Scotians as a whole did not feel hurt by its hits at themselves, or they found consolation in the picture presented of the sharp-bargaining, boastful Yankee. The Yankee enjoyed its humor without being bored by its local politics, and most readers made allowance for its intentional caricature. The later chronicles of Sam Slick, including 'The Attaché; or Sam Slick in England,' met with less success than the first.

CLOISTER AND THE HEARTH, THE, by Charles Reade (1861). The masterpiece of this vigorous novelist recreates the fifteenth century, and presents to modern eyes the Holland, Germany, France, and Italy of the Middle Ages, as they appeared to mediæval people. The hero of the story is Gerard, son of a Tergouw mercer; a studious sweet-natured lad, strongly artistic in bent, but designed for the Church, where a good benefice is promised him. He falls in love with Margaret Brandt, the daughter of a poor scholar, and giving up the Church career, betroths himself to her; and is on the eve of marriage when his irate father imprisons him in the stadthuys for disobedience, as a mediæval parent has power to do. From this point the story ceases to be a simple domestic tale, and becomes a record of swift adventure in Holland, Germany, and Italy. Then follows a most touching tale of betrayed affection, of noble womanly patience and heroism; and through all, a vivid and thrilling portrayal of the awful power of the mediæval Church. Scene crowds on scene, and incident on incident, aflame with the imagination of the romancer. The dramatic quality of the story, its vivid descriptive passages, the force and individuality impressed on its dialogue, its virile conception of the picturesque brutality and the lofty spirituality of the age it deals with, the unfailing brilliancy of the novelist's treatment of his theme, and its humorous quaintness, place 'The Cloister and the Hearth' among the half-dozen great historical romances of the world.

CLOUDS, THE ('Nubes'), a comedy by Aristophanes; acted in 423 B. C. Though one of the most interesting and poetic of the author's plays, the people refused to hear it a second time. But its literary popularity counterbalanced its failure on the stage; most unfortunately for Socrates, whose enemies, twenty-five years afterward, found in it abundant material for their accusations. Strepsiades, an unscrupulous old rascal almost ruined by his spendthrift son Pheidippides, requests the philosopher to teach him how to cheat his creditors. The Clouds, personifying the high-flown ideas in vogue, enter and speak in a pompous style, which is all lost on Strepsiades. He asks mockingly, "Are these divinities?" "No," answers Socrates, "they are the clouds of heaven: still they are goddesses for idle people, — it is to them we owe our thoughts, words, cant, insincerity, and all our skill in twaddle and palaver." Then he explains the causes of thunder, etc., substituting natural phenomena for the personal intervention of the gods; to the great scandal of Strepsiades, who has not come to listen to such blasphemy, but to learn how to get rid of his debts. The Clouds tell him that Socrates is his man. "Have you any memoranda about you?" asks the latter. "Of my debts, not one; but of what is due me, any number." Socrates tries to teach his new disciple grammar, rhythms, etc.; but Strepsiades laughs at him. Here two new characters are introduced, the Just and the Unjust. The former represents old times and manners; the latter the new principles taught by the Sophists. When the Just taught the young, they did not gad about in the forum or lounge in the bath-rooms. They were respectful to their elders, modest and manly. It was the Just who "formed the warriors of Marathon." The Unjust scoffs at such training. If the young may not have their fling, their lives are not worth living. "You tell me," he adds, "that this is profligacy. Well, are not our tragic poets, orators, demagogues, and most of their auditors profligate?" The Just has to admit this. Strepsiades, discovering that the lessons of Socrates are too much for him, sends his clever son to take his place.

Pheidippides becomes an accomplished Sophist, mystifies the creditors, and beats his father, all the time proving to him that he is acting logically. The old man, at length undeceived, summons his slaves and neighbors, and sets fire to the house and school of Socrates.

CLOVERNOOK, see CHRONICLES OF.

CODEX ARGENTEUS, a Gothic translation of parts of the Bible, attributed to Ulfilas, bishop of the Dacian Goths in the fourth century. It is written on vellum, the leaves of which are stained with a violet color; and on this ground, the letters, all uncials or capitals, are painted in silver, except the initials, which are gold. The book, however, gets its name from its elaborately wrought silver cover, and not from its lettering. Ulfilas may in a certain sense be considered the founder of all Teutonic literature, as he was the first to raise a barbarous Teutonic dialect to the dignity of a literary language. Although the language of the 'Codex' is very different from that of later Teutonic nations, it serves as a standard by which subsequent variations may be estimated, and throws much light on the kindred languages of Germany. The Gothic version contains a number of words borrowed from Finnish, Burgundian, Slavic, Dacian, and other barbarous languages; but those taken from the Greek far exceed all others. The translator uses the Greek orthography. He employs the double gamma, *gg*, to express the nasal *n* followed by *g:* thus, we have *tuggo* for *tungo*, the tongue; *figgr* for *fingor;* *dragg* for *drunk*, and so on. The similarity of most of the characters to Greek letters, and the exact conformity of the Gothic Scriptures to the original Greek text, prove that the version must have been made under Greek influence. Strabo, the author of an ecclesiastical history in the early part of the ninth century, says that the Goths on the borders of the Greek empire had an old translation of the Scriptures. The language of the 'Codex' differs importantly from mediæval and modern German. Thus the verb *haben* is never used to express past time, while it is employed to denote future time; and the passive voice is represented by inflected forms, forms utterly foreign to other Teutonic dialects. The 'Codex' does not contain the entire Bible, but only fragments of the Gospels and Epistles of St. Paul, some Psalms, and several passages from Esdras and Nehemiah. It was discovered by some Swedish soldiers in the monastery of Werden in Westphalia in 1648; then deposited in Prague; afterward presented to Queen Christina, who placed it in the library of Upsala; next carried off by Vossius; and finally restored to the University of Upsala which regards it as its most precious possession.

CŒLEBS IN SEARCH OF A WIFE, by Hannah More. This is the best-known work of fiction by that prolific moralist of a past era. It was written after she had passed her sixtieth year, and was intended as an antidote to what she considered the deleterious influence of the romantic tales of that day. In 'Cœlebs' she sought to convey precepts of religion, morals, and manners, in the form of a novel. Cœlebs, a young gentleman of fortune and estate in the north of England, sets out to find a woman who shall meet the somewhat exacting requirements of his departed mother. This estimable matron held that "the education of the present race of females is not very favorable to domestic happiness." His dying father had also enjoined Cœlebs to take the advice of an old friend, Mr. Stanley, before marrying. Cœlebs goes to Stanley Grove in Hampshire, taking London on his way, and meeting at the house of Sir John Bedfield several fashionable women who fail to reach his standard of eligibility. At Stanley Grove he finds his ideal in one of the six daughters of the house, Lucilla, with whom he dutifully falls in love, to be at once accepted. In the month of his probation he meets Dr. Barlow, rector of the parish; Lady Ashton, a gloomy religionist; the Carltons, — a dissolute and unbelieving husband who is converted by a saintly wife; and Tyrril, holding the Antinomian doctrine of faith without works, whose foil is Flam, a Tory squire, simple in faith and practicing good works. The conversation of these and other personages supplies the didactic features of the novel. 'Cœlebs' was published in London in 1808, and had an instant and great popularity. The first edition was sold in a fortnight; the book went through three more within three months, and eleven within a year. Its republication in the United States was also highly successful.

CŒUR D'ALENE, by Mary Hallock Foote (1894). Like her 'Led Horse Claim' and 'The Cup of Trembling,' this is a story of the Colorado mining camps, full of realistic details. Its situations turn upon the labor strife between Union and non-Union miners in 1892, which forms the sombre background of a bright lovers' comedy. There is a thread of serious purpose running through it, — an attempt to show in dramatic fashion what wrongs to personal liberty are often wrought in the name of liberty by labor organizations. The best-drawn character in the book is Mike McGowan, the hero's rough comrade, a Hibernian Mark Tapley. If the love passages seem at times over-emphasized, the author's general dialogue and descriptive writing have the easy strength of finished art; and her evident familiarity through actual acquaintance with the scenes described, gives to her work much permanent value of reality aside from its artistic merits.

COLERIDGE, SAMUEL TAYLOR: 'a Narrative of the Events of his Life,' by James Dyke Campbell (1894). A thoroughly independent and original narrative of the events of Coleridge's life, carefully sifting the familiar material and supplementing it by fresh researches, but studiously avoiding critical or moralizing comment; a definitive biography of the poet and the man. A briefer biography based on this standard work is now prefixed to the Globe edition of Coleridge's poems.

COLIN CLOUT (or **COLYN CLOUTE**), by John Skelton. This satire of the early British poet (1460?-1529) was a vigorous pre-Reformation protest against the clergy's lack of learning and piety, disregard for the flock,—

> "How they take no hede
> Theyre sely shepe to fede,"—

and gross self-indulgence. It was written in from four to six syllable rhymes and even double rhymes, whose liquid though brief measures served their eccentric author's purpose: a form since designated as Skeltonical or Skeltonian verse. The poet employed various other verse forms: often the easily flowing seven-line stanzas of his true parent in the poet's art, Chaucer, dead less than a hundred years. Like Chaucer, he helped to establish and make flexible the vernacular English tongue. Under Henry VII. Skelton had been tutor to his second son, Henry, who succeeded to the throne; and though his satires, published in both reigns, often hit the sins and follies of the court, he was not seriously molested by these monarchs. But in 'Colin Clout' he sped more than one clothyard shaft of wit at Wolsey; and at last in 'Speke, Parrot,' and 'Why Come Ye Not to Court,' so assailed the prelate's arrogant abuse of power that he found it prudent to take sanctuary with Bishop Islip in Westminster Abbey; and there he died and was buried "in the chancel of the neighboring church of St.

THE READER'S DIGEST OF BOOKS 167

Margaret's," says Dyce. His most famous poem gets its title from the rustic personage supposed to be speaking through it: —

> "And if ye stand in doubte
> Who brought this ryme aboute,
> My name is Colyn Cloute."

The surname is clearly suited to the ostensibly dull-witted clown of the satire; and the Colin is modified from Colas, short for Nicolas or Nicholas, a typical proper name. This dramatic cognomen was copied by several poets of the following reign, Elizabeth's, — her favorite Edmund Spenser using it to designate himself in pastoral poems, and rendering it once more famous as a poem-title in 'Colin Clout's Come Home Again.'

COLLEGIANS, THE, by Gerald Griffin. As a teller of Irish stories, Griffin takes his place with Carleton, Banim, and Miss Edgeworth. Boucicault's famous play 'The Colleen Bawn' was based on this tale, which was published in 1828. Not many years later the broken-hearted writer entered a convent, where he died at the early age of thirty-seven, under the name of Brother Joseph. The incidents of the book are founded on fact, having occurred near Limerick, Ireland. The story is one of disappointed love, of successful treachery, broken hearts, and "evil fame deserved"; but in the end virtue is rewarded. Like most other novels of its period, it is diffuse and over-sentimental; but it is likely to live for its faithful delineation of Irish character at its best — and worst.

COLLOQUIES OF ERASMUS, THE. This work, a collection of dialogues in Latin, was first published in 1521, and over 24,000 copies were sold in a short time. No book of the sixteenth and seventeenth centuries has had so many editions, and it has been frequently reprinted and retranslated down to the present day, — though it is now perhaps more quoted than read. The 'Colloquies' generally ridicule some new folly of the age, or discuss some point of theology; or inflict some innocent little vengeance on an opponent, who is made to play the part of a buffoon in the drama, while the sentiments of Erasmus are put in the mouth of a personage with a fine Greek name and with any amount of wisdom and sarcasm. Few works have exercised a greater and more fruitful influence on their age than these little dialogues. They developed and reduced to form the principles of free thought that owed their birth to the contentions of religious parties; for those who read nothing else of the author's were sure to read the 'Colloquies.' Their very moderation, however, gave offense in all quarters: to the followers of Luther as well as to those of the ancient Church. They manifest the utmost contempt for excess of every sort, and their moderation and prudent self-restraint were alien to the spirit of the time. Erasmus shows himself much more concerned about the fate of Greek letters than he does about religious changes. He has been styled 'The Voltaire of the Renaissance'; and certainly his caustic vivacity, and his delicate, artistic irony and mockery, entitle him to the distinction. The Latin of the 'Colloquies' is not always strictly Ciceronian, but it is something better, — it has all the naturalness of a spoken language; and this it is that made them so popular in their day — to the great regret of Erasmus, who complains of the "freak of fortune" that leads the public to believe "a book full of nonsense, bad Latin, and solecisms" to be his best work.

COLOMBA, a romance by Prosper Mérimée (1853), is the story of a Corsican vendetta, followed up to the end by the heroine, with a wild ferocity tempered with a queer sort of piety.   The story has an ethical significance of a rather unfortunate kind, for the author's belief in the dogma of fatalism underlies the whole of it, — that circumstances control the human will, and whether a man is a brigand or a philanthropist depends purely on chance, crime and virtue being mere accidents.

COLONEL ENDERBY'S WIFE, by "Lucas Malet" (Charles Kingsley's daughter, now Mrs. Harrison).   The scene of this story, published in 1886, is laid in England and Italy during the seventies.   Colonel Enderby is a disinherited Englishman of middle age, whose life has been shadowed by his father's neglect and injury.   At the age of forty-eight he marries in Italy a glittering young creature of wonderful beauty. The tragedy which follows is that which always comes when a crass and brutal selfishness arrays itself against the generosity of a higher nature, if two people are so bound together that they cannot escape each other.   The ending, though sad, is that which the logic of the situation makes inevitable.   The book has been very widely read and praised.

COLONEL'S DAUGHTER, THE, — an early novel of Captain Charles King's, and one of his best, — was published in 1883.   The author disclaims all charms of rhetoric and literary finish in the conversations of his characters.   They "talk like soldiers," in a brief plain speech.   For that very reason, perhaps, they are natural and human. The author has depicted army life in the West with the sure touch of one who knows whereof he writes.   'The Colonel's Daughter' is pre-eminently a soldier's story, admirably fitted in style and character to its subject-matter.

COLUMBUS, CHRISTOPHER, The Life and Voyages of, by Washington Irving. This history, published in three volumes, was written by Irving in 1828, during his residence in Madrid.   He was at the time an attaché of the United States legation, having been summoned there by Alexander H. Everett, then minister to Spain, who desired him to translate Navarrete's 'Voyages of Columbus,' which were then in course of publication.   Irving entered upon this work with much interest, but soon came to the conclusion that he had before him rather a mass of rich materials for history than a history itself; and being inspired by the picturesque aspect of the subject and the great facilities at hand, he at once gave up the work of translation and set about writing a 'Life of Columbus' of his own.   Having access to the archives of the Spanish government, to the royal library of Madrid, to that of the Jesuits' college of San Isidoro, and to many valuable private collections, he found numberless historic documents and manuscripts to further his work.   He was aided by Don Martin de Navarrete, and by the Duke of Veraguas, the descendant of Columbus, who submitted the family archives and treasures to his inspection.   In this way he was enabled to obtain many interesting and previously unknown facts concerning Columbus.   He was less than a year in completing his work, which has been called "the noblest monument to the memory of Columbus."   This history, a permanent contribution to English and American literature, is clear and animated in narrative, graphic in its descriptive episodes, and finished in style.   Recent historians have differed from Irving with regard to the character and merits of Columbus, and have produced some evidence calculated to shatter a too exalted ideal of the great discoverer; but despite this, his valuable work still fills an honored place in all historic libraries.

COMEDY OF ERRORS, THE, by William Shakespeare (1593), is the shortest of the plays, and one of the very earliest written.   The main story is from the 'Menæchmi' of Plautus. The Syracusans and the men of Ephesus have mutually decreed death to a citizen of one city caught in the other, unless he can pay a heavy ransom. Ægeon of Syracuse is doomed to death by the Duke of Ephesus. He tells the duke his story, — how at Epidamnum many years ago his wife had borne male twins, and at the same hour a humbler woman near by had also twin boys; how he had bought and brought up the latter; and how he and his wife had become separated by shipwreck, she with one of each pair of twins and he with one of each; and how five years ago his boy and servant had set out in search of their twin brothers, and he himself was now searching for them and his wife. Of these twins, one Antipholus and one Dromio live in Ephesus as master and servant respectively, the former being married to Adriana, whose sister Luciana dwells with her. By chance the Syracusan Antipholus and his Dromio are at this time in Ephesus. The mother Æmilia is abbess of a priory in the town. Through a labyrinth of errors they all finally discover each other. Antipholus of Syracuse sends his Dromio to the inn with a bag of gold, and presently meets Dromio of Ephesus, who mistaking him, urges him to come at once to dinner: his wife and sister are waiting. In no mood for joking, he beats his supposed servant. The other Dromio also gets a beating for denying that he had just talked about dinner and wife. In the meantime, Adriana and her sister meet the Syracusans on the street, and amaze them by their reproaches. As in a dream the men follow them home, and Dromio of Syracuse is bid keep the door. Now comes home the rightful owner with guests, and knocks in vain for admittance. So he goes off in a rage to an inn to dine. At his home the coil thickens. There Antipholus of Syracuse makes love to Luciana, and downstairs the amazed Dromio of Syracuse flies from the greasy kitchen wench who claims him as her own. Master and man finally resolve to set sail at once from this place of enchantment. After a great many more laughable puzzles and *contretemps*, comes Adriana, with an exorciser—Doctor Pinch—and others, who bind her husband and servant as madmen and send them away. Presently enter the bewildered Syracusans with drawn swords, and away flies Adriana, crying, "They are loose again!" The Syracusans take refuge in the abbey. Along comes the duke leading Ægeon to execution. Meantime the real husband and slave have really broken loose, bound Doctor Pinch, singed off his beard, and nicked his hair with scissors. At last both pairs of twins meet face to face, and Ægeon and Æmilia solve all puzzles.

COMING RACE, THE, by Edward Bulwer-Lytton. This is a race of imaginary beings, called Vrilya or Ana, who inhabit an imaginary world placed in a mysterious subterranean region. They have outstripped us by many centuries in scientific acquirements; making the great discovery of a force, "vril," of which all other forces are but modifications. They possess perpetual light; they can fly; and produce all the phenomena of personal magnetism. They have no laboring class, which has been superseded by machinery; there is absolute social equality; the ruler merely looks after a few necessary details. Intelligence supersedes force. Women are superior to men, their greater power over the force "vril" giving them greater physical and intellectual ability; still the more emotional and affectionate sex, in courtship they take the initiative; they are second to men only in practical science. In philosophy and religion there is unanimity: all believe in God and immortality. The discoverer of this kingdom is a New-Yorker, who tries to entertain his hosts with a eulogy on the American democracy; but this form of government, he learns, is called Koom-Bosh (Government of the Ignorant) in the Vrilya language. The finding of this new world gives rise to many speculations on human destiny. The entire devotion of these wonderful beings to science means the disappearance of all the arts. There are no great novels or poems or musical compositions. There are no criminals and no heroes. Life has lost its evils, and with them all that is worth struggling for. Everything is reduced to a dead level; everywhere ennui seems to reign supreme. This story, published in 1871, was a skit on certain assumptions of science; but its cleverness of invention and brilliancy of treatment, added to the craving wonder of humanity as to what its evolution is to be toward, gave it a large popularity.

COMMENTARIES, by Pius II. (Æneas Sylvius). The great humanist Pope devoted all his spare moments to the composition of this work, which is a mine of information on the literature, history, and politics of his age. Part of it was written by his own hand, the rest dictated. He was not only in the habit of taking notes on every subject, important or trivial, but, even during the stormiest periods of a life that was full of variety, he was always eager to glean information from the distinguished men of every country, with whom he was constantly brought into contact, so that the 'Commentaries' are both an autobiography and the history of a momentous and fruitful epoch. The disproportion between the length of the chapters, and their occasional want of connection, are accounted for by the interruptions in his literary labors which his absorption in public affairs rendered inevitable. When he could snatch only an hour from his duties as pope, he wrote a short chapter. When he had more leisure, he wrote a long one. The first book, which treats of his early career and his elevation to the pontificate, was evidently composed with more care and attention to style than those which succeed. In general, he wrote or dictated on a given day the facts that had come to his knowledge on the day before. Sometimes an incident is preceded by a historical or geographical notice, or is an apology for introducing an episode in the author's life. The book has thus some of the intimate and confidential qualities of a diary. It wants precision, is not always impartial, and in a word, has the defects common to all the historians of the time. But it is full of color and exuberant life, and its value as a historic source is inestimable. It gives a vivid idea not only of the Pope's extraordinary and almost universal erudition and exalted intelligence, but of the charm exercised by his affability, gentleness, and simple manners on everyone who came within reach. The classical, the Christian, and the modern spirit are intermingled in the 'Commentaries.' No earlier writer has so sympathetically described scenes that have a classical suggestiveness: the grotto of Diana on the opal waters of Lake Nemi; the villa of Virgil; the palace of Adrian near Tivoli, "where serpents have made their lair in the apartments of queens." But he avoids anything that might hint of too great fondness for paganism. If the name of a god drops from his pen, he at once adds that he was an idol or a demon; if he quotes an idea from a pagan philosopher, he immediately rectifies it in a Christian sense. Shortly before his death in 1464, Pius II. charged his poet-friend Campano to correct its faults, — which of course Campano did not do.

COMMENTARIES ON AMERICAN LAW, by James Kent (4 vols., 1826–30). Edition Annotated by C. M. Barnes, 1884. The celebrated 'Kent's Commentaries,' ranking in the literature of law with the English Blackstone. The work of one of the most conspicuous and remarkable scholars in law and founders of legal practice in American history. A professor of law in Columbia College in 1796; judge of the Supreme Court of the State in 1798; Chief Justice in 1804; Chancellor in 1814–23. On retiring from the bench in 1823, Kent resumed the work of a Columbia professor, and gave lectures which grew into the 'Commentaries'; the wide and accurate learning of which, with their clearness of exposition, have given him a high and permanent place among the greatest teachers of law. His decisions as Chancellor, published 1816–24, almost created American chancery law: and he added to his great work a 'Commentary on International Law,' 1866; Abdy's Edition, 1877. A notable edition of the 'Commentaries' is that edited by O. W. Holmes, Jr., 1873.

COMMENTARIES ON THE LAWS OF ENGLAND, appearing from 1765 to 1768, is the title of the celebrated law-book composed at forty-two by Sir William Blackstone, successively professor of law at Oxford and justice of the Court of Common Pleas in London. Unique among law treatises, it passed through eight editions in the author's lifetime, and has been annotated numberless times since, for the use of students and practitioners. It comprises a general discussion of the legal constitution of England, its laws, their origin, development, and present state; viewed as if the author were at work enthusiastically detailing the plans and structure of a stately edifice, complete, organic, an almost perfect human creation, with such shortcomings only as attend all human endeavor. The complacent, often naïve, tone of fervent admiration betrays the attitude of an urbane, typical Tory gentleman of the eighteenth century, speaking to others of equal temper and station concerning their glorious common inheritance, — the splendid instrument for promoting and regulating justice that had been wrought out from the remnants of the Roman jurisprudence through slow, laborious centuries, by dint of indomitable British common-sense, energy, and intellect. The insularity and concordant air of tolerance with the established order of things gives piquancy to the limpid, easy style, dignified and graceful, with which a mass of legal facts is ordered, arranged, and presented, with abundant pertinent illustration. Especially characteristic is the account of the rise and status of equity practice, and of the various courts of the realm. Thoroughly a man of his complacent time, untroubled by any forecast of the intellectual and social ferment at the close of his century, Blackstone has yet written for the generations since his day the most fascinating and comprehensive introduction to legal study in English; and has the distinction of having written the sole law-book that by its literary quality holds an unquestioned position in English literature.

COMMERCE OF NATIONS, THE, by C. F. Bastable (1892). "One of the most striking features of modern times is the growth of international relations of ever-increasing complexity and influence . . . it is in the sphere of material relations that the increase in international solidarity has been most decisively marked, and can be best followed and appreciated." Professor Bastable describes the leading features of international commerce; the overthrow of "the mercantile system" and the transition to protection; the English customs system from 1815 to 1860; the United States tariff and commercial policy; the European tariffs of the last generation of the nineteenth century. Later chapters constitute an examination, from the point of view of a free trader, of modern protectionist theory and the political, social, and economic arguments for protection. To many the most interesting section of the book is the concluding, which deals with reciprocity, retaliation, and commercial federation. The student who is endeavoring to discover permanent principles should, however, remember these words of Professor Bastable: "One lesson that the study of commercial policy from the historical point of view teaches with the utmost plainness is the dependence of the particular trade regulations adopted by any community rather on the existing social conditions and the interest of the strongest classes, than on any precise theoretical doctrines."

COMMODORE'S DAUGHTERS, THE ('Kommandorens Dottre') by the Norwegian novelist Jonas Lie (1889), is a story of family life in Norway, characterized by unerring analysis and a convincing truthfulness. The novel, though somewhat pessimistic and sad in its drift, is relieved by satiric humor and charm of description. The Commodore is elderly, amiable, henpecked; his wife ambitious and ill-tempered, with a foolish fondness for her son Karsten, a lazy young naval officer who marries for money to find himself duped. The daughters Cicely and Martha, girls of high spirits, good looks, and fresh, unspoiled natures, suffer in their love affairs through the narrow conventionality which surrounds them, and the marplot interferences of mother and brother. Cicely is parted from a fine young officer who is deeply in love with her; and poor Martha dies broken-hearted because through an intrigue of her ambitious mother, her devoted boy lover is sent off to sea to get rid of him, and is drowned on the eve of her intended marriage. The plot is a mere thread; but the fretful social atmosphere of the household, with its jarring personalities constantly misunderstanding each other to their mutual harm, is delineated with fine, subtle strokes of character-drawing: it would seem to be the author's intention to give an idea of the petty, stifling social bonds in a small Norwegian town of to-day.

COMPLETE ANGLER, THE, or, CONTEMPLATIVE MAN'S RECREATION: being 'A Discourse on Rivers, Fish-Ponds, Fish, and Fishing'; by Izaak Walton and Charles Cotton. The 'Complete Angler,' which was first published in England in 1653, was designed primarily by its author to teach the art of angling, of which long experience with hook and line had made him master. The book is written in dialogue form, and is filled with conversations touching the theme in question, which are carried on by an angler, a hunter, a falconer, a milkmaid, and others. In this way observations are made regarding the various kinds of fish, their habits, whereabouts, and the best methods of securing them, with endless details and minute descriptions of the ways and means necessary to the success of this sport. The book is distinguished by a pastoral simplicity, is admirable in style, and is filled with fine descriptions of rural scenery. It is moreover interspersed with many charming lyrics, old songs and ballads, among them the 'Song of the Milkmaid.' It is attributed to Christopher Marlowe, and begins:—

"Come live with me, and be my love,
And we will all the pleasures prove,
That valleys, groves, or hills, or field,
Or woods and steepy mountains yield."

The 'Angler' is not alone devoted to sport, but is filled with precepts which recommend the practice of religion and the exercise of patience, humility, contentment, and other virtues. Before the publication of this book, rules and directions for angling had been handed down from age to age chiefly by tradition, having only in a few instances been set down in writing. Whether considered as a treatise on the art of angling, or as a delightful pastoral filled with charming descriptions of rural scenery, 'The Complete Angler' ranks among English classics. In 1676, when Walton was eighty-two and was preparing a fifth edition for the press, Charles Cotton, also a famous angler, and an adopted son of Walton's, wrote a second part for the book, which is a valuable supplement. It is written in imitation of the style and discourses of the original, upon "angling for trout or grayling in a clear stream." Walton, though an expert angler, knew but little of fly-fishing, and so welcomed Cotton's supplement, which has since that time been received as a part of his book. Walton is called the "Father of all Anglers"; indeed, there has been hardly a writer upon the subject since his time who has not made use of his rules and practice.

COMPROMISE, ON, by John Morley (1874). The problem of this book is stated by its author. The right of thinking freely and acting independently, of using our minds without excessive awe of authority, and shaping our lives without unquestioning obedience to custom, is now a finally accepted principle in some sense or other with every school of thought that has the smallest chance of commanding the future. Under what circumstances does the exercise and vindication of the right, thus conceded in theory, become a positive duty in practice? It is his opinion that the general mental climate, outside the domain of physical science, has ceased to be invigorating and encourages an already existing tendency "to acquiesce in a lazy accommodation with error, an ignoble economy of truth, and a vicious compromise of the permanent gains of adhering to a sound general principle, for the sake of the temporary gains of departing from it." He discusses, therefore, the causes of this tendency, the influence of French examples, the increase in the power of the press, the growth of material prosperity, the sway exercised by a State Church. In later chapters he deals at large with individual intellectual responsibility in the sphere of politics and religion and concludes with an examination of the means by which opinion may be realized. What is most needed is a firm faith in the self-protecting quality and stability of society which will not be shattered by the firmness and sincerity of lovers of truth. "It is better to wait and to defer the realization of our ideas until we can realize them fully, than to defraud the future by truncating them, if truncate them we must in order to secure a partial triumph for them in the immediate present."

CONCERNING ISABEL CARNABY, by Ellen Thorneycroft Fowler, was published in 1898. This is the story of Isabel Carnaby, a brilliant and spoiled child of fortune, who fascinates Paul Seaton, the ambitious and distinguished son of a Methodist minister. Paul, after being tutor to a baronet's son, gravitates into journalism, where his literary ability is soon recognized. His character being both serious and sensitive, his patience is exhausted by Isabel's exacting ways and her fondness for testing his affection, and their engagement is broken off. Isabel, shortly afterwards, writes an anonymous novel full of caricatures of society personages with herself as the central figure. The book achieves notoriety and there is much curiosity as to its author. Paul, on being taxed with its authorship by a member of Isabel's set who never suspects her, assumes the responsibility, causing much disapproval among his Methodist friends. Isabel subsequently becomes engaged to Lord Wrexham, a very chivalrous nobleman who releases her when he learns that her heart is given to another. Paul goes into politics, where he is most successful, and eventually he and Isabel, who deeply regrets her indiscreet literary production, are happily re-united. The book is full of clever epigrams, bright dialogue, and apt quotations and its character-drawing is strong and original.

CONCILIATION; WITH THE AMERICAN COLONIES, SPEECH ON, by Edmund Burke, was delivered March 22, 1775, in submitting a set of resolutions affirming the principle of autonomy for the American colonies with the view of preventing their defection. Emphasizing the gravity of the crisis and the desirability of a peace based on a restoration of confidence and not on conquest, Burke inquires first into the desirability of concession to the colonies and then into the nature of the proposed concession. Taking up the first question and following his usual method of going to the heart of a subject, he makes a brilliant analysis of the American point of view. Owing to their growing population, their expanding commerce, agriculture, and fisheries, the wise neglect by which England has left them to develop these resources, their English descent, the Puritanism of the New Englanders and the slaveholding of the Southerners, the prevalence of lawyers and litigation, and their distance from the mother country, the American people are filled with a fierce spirit of liberty. Should this state of mind be changed as inconvenient, prosecuted as criminal, or complied with as necessary? It cannot be changed, because the causes just enumerated are inalterable: population and wealth cannot be checked or the national temper broken. To prosecute it as criminal is impossible; one cannot indict a whole people, and force only begets further resistance. It remains to comply with it as necessary, in other words to make concessions. As to the nature of these concessions, they should meet the Americans' desire by giving them an interest in the constitution. To obtain a people's good-will is more prudent than to insist on abstract rights over them. As Ireland and Wales were contented by the granting of representative government, so will America be contented if allowed to raise all taxes by free grant and not by imposition. After denouncing the principle of coercion and of barter in colonial relations, Burke ends by exalting the ties of common descent, common institutions, and common sentiment as the strongest links of empire. Though the cogency of Burke's arguments and the depth of his political wisdom were as usual ignored by the House of Commons and his resolutions were defeated 270 to 78, his speech remains a final pronouncement of the true principles of colonial government.

CONFESSION OF A FOOL, THE, by August Strindberg. An autobiographical novel of which no authorized Swedish edition has ever appeared. Written in French, it appeared first in German in 1893. The suffering and the torture which one personality can inflict upon another awakens the sympathy of the reader, and explains the author's attitude toward women in his writings. The hero's friendship with the pretty Baroness Marie began in her husband's home, where he was a welcome guest. He comes to adore her, and decides to flee from temptation. He actually embarks on a steamer for France, but, unable to endure the loneliness of the voyage and the thought of the separation, he returns on the pilot-boat. The baroness wishes to go on the stage, and makes this the public excuse for the divorce from her husband. After they are married he alternately loves and hates her. He makes several vain attempts to escape from the physical obsession she has for him. It is a frank, almost pathological description of the struggle which the intellectual man makes to free himself from the slavery of passionate love for this worthless woman, who finally drives him to madness. The most painful details are given concerning the relation of husband and wife. It is not a book which can be recommended to young readers or indeed to any whose nerves and intellectual digestion are not unusually strong.

CONFESSIONS, by Jean Jacques Rousseau. The 'Confessions' of Rousseau were written during the six most agitated years of his life, from 1765 to 1770; and his state of health at this time, both mental and bodily, may account for some of the peculiarities of this famous work. The first six books were not published until 1781, and the second six not until 1788. According to more than one critic, the 'Confessions,' however charming as literature, are to be taken as documentary evidence with great reserve. They form practically a complete life of Rousseau from his earliest years, in which he discloses not only all his own weaknesses, but the faults of those who had been his friends and intimates. In the matter of his many love affairs he is unnecessarily frank, and his giving not only details but names has been severely condemned. The case is all the worse, if, as has been supposed, these love affairs are largely imaginary. As the first half of the 'Confessions' is, in the main, a romance with picturesque embellishments, the second half has little more foundation in fact, with its undue melancholy and its stories of imaginary spies and enemies. In the matter of style, the 'Confessions' leaves little to be desired, in this respect surpassing many of Rousseau's earlier works. It abounds in fine descriptions of nature, in pleasing accounts of rural life, and in interesting anecdotes of the peasantry. The influence of the 'Confessions,' unlike that of Rousseau's earlier works, was not political nor moral, but literary. He may be called from this work the father of French *Romantisme*. Among those who acknowledged his influence were Bernardin de St. Pierre, Châteaubriand, George Sand, and the various authors who themselves indulged in confessions of their own, — like De Musset, Vigny, Hugo, Lamartine, and Madame de Staël, as well as many in Germany, England, and other countries.

CONFESSIONS OF AN ENGLISH OPIUM-EATER, by Thomas De Quincey. These Confessions, first published in the London Magazine during 1821, start with the plain narrative of how his approach to starvation when a runaway schoolboy, wandering about in Wales and afterwards in London, brought on the chronic ailment whose relief De Quincey found in opium-eating; and how he at times indulged in the drug for its pleasurable effects, "but struggled against this fascinating enthrallment with a religious zeal   and untwisted, almost to its final links, the accursed chain." Then follow nightmare experiences, with a certain Malay who reappeared to trouble him from time to time, in the opium dreams; and also with a young woman, Ann, whom he had known in his London life. But the story's chief fascination lies in its gorgeous and ecstatic visions or experiences of some transcendental sort, while under the influence of the drug; the record of Titanic struggles to get free from it, and the pathetic details of sufferings that counterbalanced its delights.

The 'Confessions of an English Opium-Eater' is one of the most brilliant books in literature. As an English critic has said, "It is not opium in De Quincey, but De Quincey in opium, that wrote the 'Suspiria' and the 'Confessions.'" All the essays are filled with the most unexpected inventions, the most gorgeous imagery, and, strange to say, with a certain insistent good sense. As a rhetorician De Quincey stands unrivaled.

CONFESSIONS OF SAINT AUGUSTINE, THE. This famous work, written in 397, is divided into thirteen books. The first ten contain an account of his life down to his mother's death, and give a thrilling picture of the career of a profligate and an idolater who was to become a Father of the Church. We have in them the story of his childhood, and the evil bent of his nature even then; of his youth and its uncontrollable passions and vices; of his first fall at the age of sixteen, his subsequent struggle and relapses, and the untiring efforts of his mother, Saint Monica, to save him. Side by side with the pictures he paints of his childhood (the little frivolities of which he regards as crimes), and of his wayward youth and manhood, we have his variations of belief and his attempts to find an anchor for his faith among the Manichæans and Neo-Platonists, and in other systems that at first fascinated and then repelled him, until the supreme moment of his life arrived, — his conversion at the age of thirty-two. There are many noble but painful pictures of these inward wrestlings, in the eighth and ninth books. The narrative is intermingled with prayers (for the Confessions are addressed to God), with meditations and instructions, several of which have entered into the liturgies of every section of the Christian Church. The last three books treat of questions that have little connection with the life of the author: of the opening chapters of Genesis, of prime matter, and the mysteries of the First Trinity. They are, in fact, an allegorical explanation of the Mosaic account of the Creation. According to St. Augustine, the establishment of his Church, and the sanctification of man, is the aim and end God has proposed to himself in the creation.

CONGRESS, TWENTY YEARS OF, see **TWENTY YEARS, ETC.**

CONINGSBY, by Benjamin Disraeli, Lord Beaconsfield, published in 1844, when Disraeli was thirty-nine years old, was his sixth and most successful novel. In three months it had gone through three editions, and 50,000 copies had been sold in England and the United States. It was a novel with a purpose: the author himself explained that his aim was to elevate the tone of public life, to ascertain the true character of political parties, and especially to vindicate the claims of the Tories. Incidentally he wished to emphasize the importance of the church in the development of England, and he tried to do some justice to the Jews. The story opens in the spring of 1832, on the very day of the resignation of Lord Grey's ministry. This gives Disraeli a good opportunity for a dissertation on the politics of the time, including the call of the Duke of Wellington to the ministry. The hero, Coningsby, at this time a lad of ten, is visiting his grandfather, the rich and powerful Marquis of Monmouth. The latter had disinherited the father of Coningsby for marrying an amiable girl of less exalted station than his own. Their orphan son is now entirely dependent on his grandfather. Lord Monmouth, though showing little affection for the boy, is generous to him. He sends him to Eton and to Cambridge, and has him often visit him at his town-house or his Castle. These visits bring the boy in contact with many interesting persons, such as the fascinating Sidonia, in whom Disraeli paints his ideal Jew; the Princess Colonna, and her stepdaughter Lucretia, whom the Marquis marries: the Duke (who has been identified as the Duke of Rutland); the subservient Rigby (in whom John Wilson Croker is supposed to be portrayed), and a host of personages of high degree with imposing titles. There are more than threescore characters in the book, and part of its popularity came from people's interest in identifying them with men and women prominent in English social and political life. Sidonia, the brilliant Jew, is said to be either Disraeli himself or Baron Alfred de Rothschild. Lucian Gay is Theodore Hook, and Oswald Millbank is W. E. Gladstone. The Marquis of Monmouth is the Marquis of Hertford, and Coningsby himself has been variously regarded as a picture of Lord Littleton, Lord Lincoln, or George Smythe.

Some of the charm of Coningsby has passed away with the waning interest in the political events which it describes. Its satire, however, is still keen, particularly that directed against the Peers.

CONISTON, by Winston Churchill (1906). The scene of this story is laid in a country town in Vermont called Coniston, at the time of President Jackson's administration. The central figure in the book is Jethro Bass, whose political career is described in a most detailed and picturesque manner. When a youth, Jethro is rough and uncouth, but in spite of his eccentricities there is a hidden strength that forces people to respect him. He becomes enamored of a lovely girl named Cynthia Ware, the belle of the village, and in spite of his peculiarities she is strongly drawn towards him. Jethro becomes interested in politics and places all his influence upon an issue to which Cynthia is greatly opposed. She goes to him and tells him that he must choose between her and the issue he has at stake, but he tells her he cannot give up his plans, and they part forever. Cynthia marries a man named Wetherell and has one child, a daughter, who is named for her. Although Cynthia is fond of her husband she has never felt the intense love she had for Jethro and she confesses this to him before her death, which occurs a few years after her marriage. Wetherell, poor and broken in health, returns to Coniston with little Cynthia. Jethro, who has become the big man of the town and "boss" of the political machine, recognizes Cynthia's child and becomes greatly attached to her. He assists Wetherell financially, and after the latter's death takes Cynthia to live with him. Cynthia loves him blindly and trusts him implicitly, never imagining that his dealings are anything but the most honorable. At last her eyes are opened and she is grief stricken to find her idolized "Uncle Jethro" has gained his power by foul means as well as fair. Although she still loves him she leaves his home and goes away to teach school. In course of time Cynthia marries Bob Worthington, the son of a wealthy magnate, one of her mother's old admirers, and a bitter enemy of Jethro Bass. Mr. Worthington is at first bitterly opposed to his son's marriage but is won over by Jethro, who forces a compromise through sacrificing a measure for which he has worked untiringly.

CONNECTICUT YANKEE IN KING ARTHUR'S COURT, A, by "Mark Twain" (1889). This humorous tale purports to be that of an American encountered by the author when "doing" Warwick Castle. The two meet again in the evening at the Warwick inn; then over pipes and Scotch whisky, the stranger explains that he is from Hartford, Connecticut, where he used to be superintendent of an arms factory; that one day, in a quarrel with one of his men, he lost consciousness from a blow on the head with a crowbar; that when he awoke he found himself in England at the time of King Arthur, where he was taken captive by a knight, and conveyed to Camelot. Here sleep overpowers the narrator, and he goes to bed; first, however, committing to the author's hands a manuscript, wherein sitting down by the fire again, he reads the rest of the stranger's adventures. The contact of Connecticut Yankeedom with Arthurian chivalry gives rise to strange results. England at the time of Arthur was a society in which the church "took it out" of the king, the king of the noble, and the noble of the freeman; in which "anybody could kill somebody, except the commoner and the slave, — these had no privileges"; and in which departure from custom was the one crime that the nation could not commit. Sir Lancelot of the Lake, Galahad, Bedivere, Merlin, Guinevere, Arthur himself, etc., duly appear; and amidst all the fun and pathos, the courtliness, the sincerity, and the stern virtues — as well as what seems to us the ridiculousness — of the age.

CONQUEROR, THE; being the true and romantic story of Alexander Hamilton, by Gertrude Atherton (1902). The recorded facts of Hamilton's career find their historical place in this "dramatized biography." His early life in the West Indies is based on family tradition as well as documentary evidence. The description of the hurricane which devastated the beautiful island is a dramatic word picture. At seventeen Hamilton's remarkable mind made him a leader among the young patriots at King's College who demanded the independence of the American colonies. Washington recognized his ability and appealed to his patriotism to give up a military career and become his aide and secretary. He married Elizabeth, the charming, vivacious daughter of General Schuyler. After the war he studied law, passing his bar examination with only three months' preparation, a phenomenal achievement.

As secretary of the treasury and organizer of the new government his ideas were opposed by Jefferson, who in this book is shown in most unfavorable light. The unscrupulous Aaron Burr became his enemy, jealous of his success and great charm of personality. Mme. Croix, a clever, beautiful Egeria, with a talent for politics, drew Hamilton into the circle of public men about her. She loved him and the romance was an inspiration which he gave up at his wife's request, thus incurring Mme. Croix's tigerish hatred. Challenged by Burr to secret duel, he was wounded mortally. Eliza Croix, now Mme. Jumel, came to him the night before the duel to tell him that Burr was her deputy, and that neither her hate nor her love had ceased. At his death, the bells were tolled until sundown. The city and the people wore mourning for a month, the bar for six weeks. A monument erected to him by leading citizens bore the inscription, "The patriot of incorruptible integrity, the soldier of approved valor, the statesman of consummate wisdom."

CONQUEST OF CANAAN, THE, by Booth Tarkington (1905). The scene of this story is laid in an Indiana town called Canaan, where intolerance and narrow-mindedness hold full sway among the inhabitants. The central figure is Joe Louden, who begins life under adverse circumstances. His father marries a second wife with a son of her own, named Eugene Bantry, whom she idolizes, and in consequence she prejudices her husband against his own son and causes him to treat him most unfairly. Joe is not even decently clothed and is allowed to run wild, while his stepbrother is sent to college and dressed in the latest fashion. Joe falls in with low companions and is avoided and disliked by the townspeople, who see only the bad in him. His one champion is a girl about his own age named Ariel Tabor, who is poor like himself and snubbed by her companions. Ariel's rich uncle dies, making her an heiress, and she and her old grandfather depart for several years' stay in Paris. Just at this time Joe gets himself into trouble and runs away from home. He works his way through college and the law school, and becoming a successful lawyer, returns after some years to his native town to practise. He is treated rudely and ignored by everybody but determines to stay and live down his past. He has always admired Mamie Pike, the daughter of Judge Pike, the leading man of the town, but she becomes engaged to his stepbrother Eugene, who is a poor specimen of manhood. Ariel returns from Paris a dazzling vision of elegance and beauty and takes the town by storm. She discovers how shamefully Joe has been treated and begins at once to try to mend matters. She gives Joe charge of her affairs, taking her property out of the hands of Judge Pike, who has administered her uncle's estate. Joe finds that the Judge has been dishonest, but deals with him leniently in spite of the outrageous treatment he has received from him in the past. After Ariel's return Joe appreciates that she is the girl he really loves and he not only wins her for his wife, but, re-instated in the opinion of his townspeople, is elected mayor of Canaan.

CONQUEST OF PERU, HISTORY OF THE, by William Hickling Prescott (.847). Of the five books into which this admirable work is divided, the first treats of the wonderful civilization of the Incas; the second of the discovery of Peru; the third of its conquest; the fourth of the civil wars of the conquerors; and the fifth of the settle-ment of the country. The first book hardly yields in interest to any of the others, describing as it does, on the whole, an unparalleled state of society. In it some of the votaries of modern socialism have seen confirmation of the practicability and success-ful working of their own theory; but Prescott's verdict of the system is that it was "the most oppressive, though the mildest, of despotisms." At least it was more lenient, more refined, and based more upon reason as contrasted with force, than was that of the Aztecs. He describes it very fully: the orders of society, the divisions of the kingdom, the administration of justice, the revenues, religion, education, agriculture, manners, manufactures, architecture, etc. From the necessities of its material, the work is more scattered in construction than is the 'History of the Conquest of Mexico,' which is usually regarded as the author's most brilliant production. Of the opportunities this afforded, Prescott himself remarks: "The natural development of the story . . . is precisely what would be prescribed by the severest rules of art." The portrait drawn of Pizarro, who is the principal figure in the drama, is that of a man brave, energetic, temperate, and though avaricious, extravagant; bold in action, yet slow, and at the same time inflexible of resolution; ambitious; exceptionally perfidious. An effort is made to counterbalance the tendency to hero-worship and picturesque coloring by the occasional insertion of passages of an opposite character.

CONQUÊTE DE PLASSANS, LA, see **ROUGON-MACQUART.**

CONSCRIPT, THE ('Histoire d'un Conscrit de 1813'), by Erckmann-Chatrian, was published at Paris in four volumes (1868–70). Joseph Bertha, a watchmaker's apprentice, aged 20, is in despair when he learns that in spite of his lameness, he must shoulder a gun and march against the allies. Hitherto his own little affairs have had much more concern for him than the quarrels of kings and powers, and he has an instinctive dislike to the spirit of conquest. Still his is a loyal heart, and he resists the temptation to desert. After an affecting farewell to his betrothed, he marches to join his regiment, resolved to do his duty. Of the terrific battles of the period Joseph relates only what he saw. He does not pretend to be a hero, but he is always true to his nature and to human nature in his alternate fits of faint-heartedness and warlike fury. He obeys his leaders when they bid him rush to death or glory; but he cannot help turning his eyes back, at the same time, to the poor little cottage where he has left all his happiness. His artless soul is a battle-field whereon the feelings natural to him are in constant conflict with those of his new condition: the former prevailing when the miseries of the soldier's life are brought home to him; the latter, when he is inflamed by martial ardor. All the narrative, up to the time he returns wounded to his family, turns on the contrast between the perpetual mourning that is going on in families and the perpetual Te Deums for disastrous victories. This is the dominant note; and in the mouth of this obscure victim of war, this thesis, interpreted by scenes of daily carnage, is more eloquent and persuasive than if it borrowed arguments from history or philosophy. The style is simple, familiar; perhaps at times even vulgar; but it is never trivial or commonplace, and is always in harmony with the speaker. As the work was hostile to the Napoleonic legend, numerous obstacles were put in the way of its circulation at the time of publication. But, notwithstanding, it was scattered in profusion throughout France by means of cheap illustrated editions.

CONSIDERATIONS ON REPRESENTATIVE GOVERNMENT, see **REPRESENTATIVE GOVERNMENT.**

CONSIDERATIONS ON THE GREATNESS AND DECAY OF THE ROMANS, see **GREATNESS AND DECAY, ETC.**

CONSOLATIONS OF PHILOSOPHY, THE, by Boëthius. This work — called in Latin 'De Consolatione Philosophica' — was written in prison just before the author was put to death in 525 by Theodoric, whose favorite minister he had been before his incarceration. It is divided into five books; and has for its object to prove from reason the existence of Providence. A woman of lofty mien appears to the prisoner, and tells him she is his guardian, Philosophy, come to console him in his misfortunes and point out their remedy. Then ensues a dialogue in which are discussed all the questions that have troubled humanity: the origin of evil, God's omniscience, man's free will, etc. The 'Consolations' are alternately in prose and verse; a method afterwards adopted by many authors in imitation of Boëthius, who was himself influenced by a work of Martianus Capella entitled 'De Nuptiis Philologiæ et Mercurii.' Most of the verses are suggested by passages in Seneca, then the greatest moral authority in the West, outside of Christianity. The success of the work was as immense as it was lasting; and it was translated into Greek, Hebrew, German, French, and Anglo-Saxon, at an early period. The Anglo-Saxon version was by Alfred the Great; and is the oldest monument of importance in Anglo-Saxon prose. It has been imitated by Chaucer in the 'Testament of Love,' by James I. of Scotland in the 'Kinges Quhair,' and by many other distinguished writers. In some sort, it connects the period of classic literature with that of the Middle Ages, of which Boëthius was one of the favorite authors; and in classic purity of style and elevation of thought, is fully equal to the works of the philosophers of Greece and Rome, while, at the same time, it shows the influence of Christian ideals. "It is," says Gibbon, "a golden volume, not unworthy of the leisure of Plato or Tully."

CONSTABLE, ARCHIBALD, AND HIS LITERARY CORRESPONDENTS, by Thomas Constable (1873). The story of the great Edinburgh publishing house which established the Edinburgh Review; became the chief of Scott's publishers; issued, with valuable supplementary Dissertations by Dugald Stewart, the fifth edition of the 'Encyclopædia Britannica'; initiated the publication of cheap popular volumes of literature, art, and science; and by a bold liberality in payment of authors, with remarkable sagacity in judging what would succeed with the public, virtually transformed the business of publishing. An apprenticeship of six years with Peter Hill, Burns's friend, enabled Constable to start as a bookseller, January, 1795. He began by publishing theological and political pamphlets for authors, but in 1798 made some ventures on his own account. In 1800 he started the Farmer's Magazine as a quarterly. The next year he became proprietor of the Scots Magazine, and in October, 1802, the first number of the Edinburgh Review appeared. The generous scale of payment soon adopted, — twenty-five guineas a sheet, — startled the trade, and greatly contributed to make Constable the foremost among publishers of his day. He began with Scott in 1802, a part interest only, but secured entire interest in 1807 by paying Scott a thousand guineas in advance for 'Marmion,' and the next year one thousand five hundred pounds for his edition of Swift's 'Life and Works.' Differences arising now separated Scott and Constable until 1813, but in 1814 'Waverley' appeared with Constable's imprint. The financial breakdown of various parties in 1826 not only overthrew Constable, but involved Scott to the extent of £120,000. Constable died July 21, 1827.

CONSTABLE, JOHN, THE MEMOIR OF, by C. R. Leslie (1845). Leslie, himself an artist of note, was qualified to write the biography of John Constable (1776–1837) by an intense affection for his subject, qualified by never-failing good taste and discrimination. He has so skillfully chosen and arranged the letters of Constable that the story becomes almost an autobiographical record. The work of Constable as revealed in these pages was his combination of the art of portrait-painting with the power of reproducing the color of nature. He was the first to seek inspiration in the soft, rich colors of ordinary English scenery, "the first," says a writer in the 'Dictionary of National Biography,' "to suggest so fully not only the sights, but the sounds of nature, the gurgle of the water, the rustle of the trees. Other painters have made us see nature at a distance or through a window; he alone has planted our feet in her midst." His principles of art, formed in early manhood, and faithfully followed throughout life, appear in a letter dated May 29, 1802, which Leslie quotes. "There is room enough for a natural painter. The great vice of the present day is bravura, an attempt to do something beyond the truth. Fashion always had, and will have, its day; but truth in all things only will last, and can only have just claims on posterity." The character of the man who thus took truth, and truth only, as his standard was simple, noble, lovable, and blameless. His originality was happily described by Blake, who said on seeing one of his sketches, "Why, this is not drawing, but inspiration."

CONSTANCE TRESCOT, by S. Weir Mitchell (1905). In this story the author has pictured a woman who could love and hate with equal intensity. Constance Hood is a Northern girl who marries a Union officer, named George Trescot, a few years after the war, and goes with him to live in the South. Trescot is a fine man, of sterling character and high principles, and Constance loves him passionately, though she differs from him in many vital points. George is deeply religious while Constance, who has been brought up by a rich and skeptical uncle, has never been to church or known the comfort of a faith. The removal of the newly married couple to the South is something that Trescot objects to at first but he was overruled by Constance whose uncle has offered him the opportunity of being his land agent in a Missouri town, called St. Ann. This position, as George has surmised, proves to be a difficult one and he soon finds himself surrounded by enemies and those who will injure him if possible. An important law-suit comes up for trial, the opposing attorney being a man of violent nature named John Greyhurst. Trescot wins the suit and his opponent filled with rage shoots him as he is leaving the Court House. Constance is crushed and heartbroken at the death of her husband but as she recovers her strength she is filled with a desire for revenge. After an absence of a year abroad she returns to St. Ann prepared to ruin the happiness of her husband's murderer if she can do so, as he has been acquitted of the charge of manslaughter and is leading an apparently comfortable existence. Constance sends Greyhurst letters showing her husband's nobility of character, haunts him by her presence, and interferes with his financial schemes. Finally she writes to the girl he is hoping to marry and, stating the facts of her husband's death, causes the girl to reject Greyhurst's suit. The latter, whose peace of mind has been gradually shattered by Constance's course is driven to frenzy by this last act, and seeking her presence, he shoots himself and falls dead at her feet. Constance leaves St. Ann never to return, wrecked in health and happiness, and without hope for the future.

CONSTITUTIONAL HISTORY OF ENGLAND, see **ENGLAND.**

CONSUELO, by Amandine Lucile Aurore Dudevant (George Sand), published in 1842, and its sequel 'The Countess of Rudolstadt,' issued the following year, form a continuous romantic narrative, of which the first book is the more famous. While not the most characteristic novel, perhaps, of the great French authoress, 'Consuelo' is the best known to general readers. It is a magnificent romance, kept always within the bounds of the possible yet exhibiting a wealth of imagination and idyllic fancy not always found in conjunction with such restraint. Consuelo, like her creator, has in her veins the blood of the people; she has no dowry but a wonderful voice, and a noble natural purity that is her defense in all trials and temptations. Her childhood is spent in the Venice of the eighteenth century; a golden childhood of love and music, and a poverty which means freedom. After a bitter experience of deception, she leaves Venice to live in the Castle of Rudolstadt in Bohemia, as companion to the Baroness Amelia. One of the household is Count Albert, a melancholy, half-distraught man of noble character, over whom Consuelo establishes a mysterious influence of calmness and benignity.

The interest of the story is now held by certain psychic experiments and experiences, and it closes as the reader hopes to have it. 'Consuelo' abounds in picturesque and dramatic scenes and incidents, in glowing romance, in the poetry of music and the musical life. It retains its place as one of the most fascinating novels of its century.

CONSULATE AND THE EMPIRE OF FRANCE, UNDER NAPOLEON, HISTORY OF THE (1799–1815), by Louis Adolphe Thiers. The 'History of the Consulate and Empire' fills twenty octavo volumes, and was published in installments between 1845 and 1862. Written from an imperialistic point of view, it met with unusual success in France. It was crowned by the Academy, and Thiers was given the title of "national historian." The French found in it their own enthusiastic admiration for success, and their own prejudices. Thiers has little regard for the morality of actions: "You have failed, therefore you are wrong," seems to be his maxim. He rejoices in the establishment of absolutism and the suppression of liberty; nor does he see, beyond the glory of a victorious campaign, the excesses of warfare.

Literature, philosophy, and art do not attract him; in the twenty volumes, he devotes but a scant half-dozen pages to such subjects. He imagines that the Consulate realized the ideal of a perfect government, and that the misfortunes of the Empire would have been avoided had Napoleon continued the tradition of the earlier time. It is evident, however, that the later policy was but the development of the earlier. Though admiring every act of unrestrained ambition on the part of his hero, Thiers deplores its consequences. At first the Continental system is Napoleon's gigantic plan to conquer England on the sea; later Thiers recognizes that Napoleon's own ports were the chief victims of the designed conquest. His inaccuracy as a historian is shown in his treatment of English affairs. He consulted no authentic document in the English language; and in his chapter on the Continental System, he says that England's violation of international law by "paper" blockades in 1806 furnished Napoleon with just pretext for issuing the Berlin and Milan Decrees, — the exact opposite of the facts in the case. Thiers is proud of his knowledge of military tactics, and likes to explain how defeat might have been avoided; but even his descriptions of battles are inexact, as Charras in his 'History of the Campaign of 1815' points out. His style is easy; its prolixity, however, frequently deprives it of clearness and force, by requiring a whole volume to describe a military action which might have been more vividly presented in a few pages.

CONTEMPORARY AMERICAN OPINION OF THE FRENCH REVOLUTION, by Charles Downer Hazen (1897). An extra volume in the Johns Hopkins University Studies in Historical and Political Science, — a volume of three hundred pages, rich in interest to the student of American history. The first part of the work is devoted to the opinion of the French Revolution formed by Americans who were in France at the time. These were Thomas Jefferson, Gouverneur Morris, and James Monroe. Jefferson and Morris were eye-witnesses, who held themselves aloof from the conflict about them, and reported upon it as judicial and clear sighted spectators. These two tell a continuous story from 1784 to 1794, with a change from Jefferson to Morris in 1789. Then comes Monroe, from August, 1794 to October, 1795.

The second part of the work gathers from a variety of sources the opinions of the Revolution which Americans at home formed, the Republicans on one side and the Federalists on the other. These opinions had much to do with American politics for a considerable time, and altogether they form an interesting chapter in our national life.

CONVENTIONAL LIES OF OUR CIVILIZATION, by Max Nordau. Max Nordau was twenty-nine years old, when in 1878 he began to publish the results of his extensive travels and his observations of life. 'Conventional Lies,' his first real study of social pathology, was issued in 1883, and in ten years passed through fifteen editions, in spite of the fact that by imperial mandate it was suppressed in Austria on its first appearance, and later in Prussia. The author, in his preface to the sixth edition, warns people not to buy his book in the belief that from its suppression it contains scandalous things. "I do not attack persons, either high or low, but ideas." The book, he had asserted in an earlier edition, is a faithful presentation of the views of the majority of educated, cultivated people of the present day Cowardice, he thinks, prevents them from bringing their outward lives into harmony with their inward convictions, and they believe it to be worldly policy to cling to relics of former ages when at heart they are completely severed from them. The Lie of Religion, of Monarchy and Aristocracy, the Political, Economic, and Matrimonial Lies, are those which Nordau chiefly attacks.

It is form, however, not substance, which he usually criticizes; as in the case of religion, where he says that by religion he does not mean the belief in supernatural abstract powers, which is usually sincere, but the slavery to forms, which is a physical relic of the childhood of the human race.

"Very seldom," he says, in discussing monarchy, "do we find a prince who is what would be called in every-day life a capable man; and only once in centuries does a dynasty produce a man of commanding genius." In the case of matrimony his plea is directed not against the institution, but in favor of love in marriage, as distinguished from the marriage of convenience. Nordau's judgments are often based on insufficient foundation; and he is inclined to be too dogmatic. Yet he is not wholly an iconoclast; and he believes that out of the existing egotism and insincerity, humanity will develop an altruism built on perpetual good-fellowship.

COOK, CAPTAIN, see **VOYAGES OF.**

CO-OPERATIVE WHOLESALE SOCIETY, see **STORY OF THE C. W. S.**

CORINNE; or, ITALY, by Madame de Staël. Corinne's story is quite secondary, in the author's intention, to her characterization of Italy, but it runs thus: Oswald, Lord Nelvil, an Englishman, while traveling in Italy, meets Corinne, artist, poet, and musician, with a mysterious past. Their friendship ripens into love; but Oswald tells Corinne that his dying father desired him to marry Lucile, the daughter of Lord Edgermond. Corinne then discloses that her mother, an Italian, was the first wife of Lord Edgermond: and that after her mother's death and her father's second marriage, her life had been made so unhappy by her stepmother that she had returned to Italy, where she had been for eight years when Oswald arrived. He goes back to England, with the intention of restoring to Corinne her fortune and title; and there meets Lucile, and learns that his father had really wished him to marry Lord Edgermond's elder daughter, but had distrusted Corinne because of her religion and Italian training. And now the too facile Oswald falls in love with Lucile. Corinne, who has secretly followed him, sends him his ring and his release. Believing that Corinne knows nothing of his change of feelings, but has set him free of her own desire, he marries Lucile. Five years later, Oswald and Lucile visit Florence, where Corinne is still living, but in the last stages of a decline which began when Oswald broke her heart by marrying. The sisters are reconciled, but Oswald sees Corinne only as she is dying.

In Corinne and Lucile, the author has endeavored to represent the ideal women of two nations; the qualities which make Corinne the idol of Italians, however, repel the unemotional Englishman. But besides its romantic and sentimental interest, in its treatment of literature and art it has always been considered authoritative. It served indeed for many years as a guide-book for travelers in Italy, though modern discoveries have somewhat impugned its sufficiency. When it first appeared in 1807, its success was instantaneous: and Napoleon, who detested the author, was so much chagrined that he himself wrote an unfavorable criticism which appeared in the Moniteur.

CORIOLANUS, a powerful drama of Shakespeare's later years (written about 1609), retells from North's 'Plutarch,' in terse sinewy English, the fate that overtook the too haughty pride of a Roman patrician, — generous, brave, filial, but a mere boy in discretion, his soul a dynamo always overcharged with a voltage current of scorn and rage, and playing out its live lightnings on the least provocation. See his fierce temper reflected in his little boy, grinding his teeth as he tears a butterfly to pieces: "Oh, I warrant how he mammocked it!" Mark his strength: "Death, that dark spirit, in's nervy arm doth lie." "What an arm he has! he turned me about with his finger and thumb as one would set up a top." In battle "he was a thing of blood, whose every motion was timed with dying cries." In the Volscian war, at the gates of Corioli, this Caius Marcius performed such deeds of derring-do that he was nigh worshiped; and there he got his addition of 'Coriolanus.' His scorn of the rabble, their cowardice, vacillation, dirty faces, and uncleaned teeth, was boundless. The patricians were with him: if the plebeians rose in riot, accusing the senatorial party of "still cupboarding the viand," but never bearing labor like the rest, Menenius could put them down with the apologue of the belly and the members, — the belly, like the Senate, indeed receiving all, but only to distribute it to the rest. Coriolanus goes further, and angers the tribunes by roundly denying the right of the cowardly plebs to a distribution of grain in time of scarcity. The tribunes stir up the people against him; and when he returns from the war, wearing the oaken garland and covered with wounds, and seeks the consulship, they successfully tempt his temper by taunts, accuse him of treason, and get him banished by decree. In a towering rage he cries, "You common cry of curs, I banish you!" and taking an affecting farewell of his wife, and of Volumnia his mother (type of the stern and proud Roman matron), he goes disguised to Antium and offers his services against Rome to his hitherto mortal foe and rival, Tullus Aufidius. The scene with the servants forms the sole piece of humor in the play. But his success leads to his ruin; his old stiff-necked arrogance of manner again appears. The eyes of all the admiring Volscians are on him. Aufidius, now bitterly jealous, regrets his sharing of the command; and when, softened by the entreaties of weeping wife and mother, Coriolanus spares Rome and returns with the Volscians to Antium, his rival and a band of conspirators "stain all their edges" in his blood, and he falls, like the great Julius, the victim of his own willful spirit.

CORLEONE, by F. Marion Crawford, published in 1897, is the fourth in the 'Saracinesca' series of modern Italian stories. The scene is mainly in Sicily. The leading character is Don Orsino, son of Giovanni Saracinesca and hero of 'Sant' Ilario.' The novel takes its title from the fact that Vittoria, the Sicilian hero, is of the Corleone race. The spirited scenes in which the Sicilian peasantry and bandits are leagued against the intruding Romans; the handling of the passions of love, hate, jealousy and revenge; and the subsidiary scenes of Roman society life in which the Saracinesca move and have their being, afford Mr. Crawford opportunity for characteristic work. As a study of Sicilian character the book is also valuable.

CORTES, HERNANDO, LIFE OF, by Sir Arthur Helps, English historian and essayist, was published in 1871, being dedicated to Thomas Carlyle. It is a clear, simple, scholarly account of the picturesque conquest of Mexico — a conquest by a gallant gentleman and warrior, who was no better than his age. The author seeks neither to extenuate nor to conceal the doubtful qualities in the character of Cortez, but accepts him in the impersonal spirit of the historian.

COSMIC PHILOSOPHY, OUTLINES OF, by John Fiske (1875). In these two small volumes, one of the most eminent of modern thinkers presents the philosophic and scientific doctrines of Herbert Spencer, developed into a complete theory of the universe. Added to the outline of the evolutionary philosophy, as represented by Spencer, is a body of original speculation and criticism set forth with immense learning and ingenuity, and in a style which is a model of clearness and force. Most of Fiske's first volume is taken up with the Prolegomena, in which are expounded the fundamental principles of Cosmism. The second volume comprises the Synthesis, containing the laws of life, of mind, and of society. Life of every kind is shown to consist in a process of change within meeting change without; and this process applies alike to the lowest rudimentary organism struggling against a hostile environment, and to the highest creature making use of those slowly evolved adaptations which enable it to overcome opposing conditions. Mind is an immaterial process similar in character, but more complex and more efficient. No true Cosmist will affect to know at what precise point the process becomes so complex as to deserve the name of mind. Though the extremes seem to have nothing in common, the chain of means has no break, and the real difference is of degree and not of kind. A like process is seen in the growth of society, from the homogeneousness of the primitive family to the heterogeneousness of the nation. Thus it appears that the method and the significance of all changes may be defined in the one word *adaptation*. Organic existence begins at some indefinitely remote point in inorganic existence; life must somewhere be foreshadowed in simple chemical activity. In short, the essayist's definition of the Cosmic theory is as follows: "Life — including also intelligence as the highest known manifestation of life — is the continuous establishment of relations within the organism in correspondence with relations existing or arising in the environment"; and his statement of the Cosmic law of social progress is this: —

"The evolution of society is a continuous establishment of psychical relations within the community, in conformity to physical and psychical relations arising in the environment; during which both the community and the environment pass from a state of relatively indefinite incoherent homogeneity, to a state of relatively definite coherent heterogeneity; and during which the constituent units of the community become ever more distinctly individuated."

Fiske obtains his generalizations by means of broad historical researches, and his great knowledge and aptness of illustration constantly enrich his pages. In the final chapters he sets forth the Cosmic religion, which, as he interprets it, seems to be an attitude of awe and submission to the Unknowable.

COSMOPOLIS, by Paul Bourget (1892). This novel is written to demonstrate the influence of heredity. The scene is at Rome, but a glance at the principal characters shows the fitness of the title.

Countess Steno is a descendant of the Doges. Bolislas Gorka shows the nervous irritability and facile conscience of the Slav; his wife is English. Lincoln Maitland is an American artist, whose wife has a drop of African blood. The clever Dorsenne is French. From the alien ambitions and the selfish intrigues of these persons the story arises. It is most disagreeable in essence, but subtle in analysis, dramatic in quality, and brilliant in execution.

COSSACK FAIRY TALES. This collection of folk-lore was selected, edited, and translated from the Ruthenian by R. Nisbet Bain, and published in 1894. The Ruthenian or Cossack language, though proscribed by the Russian government, is spoken by more than twenty million people. There are in the original three important collections of folk-tales, from which Mr. Bain has made a representative selection for translation. There are, Slavonic scholars maintain, certain elements in these stories found in the folklore of no other European people. Among these may be mentioned the magic handkerchief, which causes a bridge across the sea to appear before a fugitive, or a forest to spring up in his rear delaying his pursuer. There is the magic egg, which produces a herd of cattle when broken; and the magic whip, which can expel evil spirits. Many elements and episodes common to other mythologies are found, however. There are, for example, Cossack versions of Cinderella and the woman who took her pig to market. One tale of a Tsar expelled by an angel is an almost literal rendering of King Robert of Sicily, with Cossack coloring. There is a Samson-like hero, who reveals the secret of his strength; and an episode of a man in a fish's belly, which resembles Hiawatha and the sturgeon rather than Jonah and the whale.

The serpent figures prominently in these stories; and is generally, though by no means invariably, malign, and always represents superior intellectual power. The women are frequently treacherous, especially when beguiled by the serpent; but it is interesting to notice the number of men who cannot keep a secret. The lower animals are always friendly to man, and frequently assist him in performing difficult tasks. The whole tenor of the stories is charmingly naïve and inconsequent; among the vampires and magic fires it is somewhat startling to encounter guns and passports. The style is simple and poetic, especially in 'The Little Tsar Novishny,' perhaps the prettiest and most characteristic story of all.

COSSACKS, THE, by Tolstoy (1852). This Russian romance is a series of picturesque studies on the life of the Cossacks of the Terek, rather than a romance. The slight love story that runs through it simply serves as an excuse for the author's graphic descriptions of strange scenes and strange peoples. The hero, Olenin, is a ruined young noble, who, to escape his creditors and begin a new life, enters a sotnia of Cossacks as ensign. One fine night he leaves Moscow; and at the first station on his way, he begins already to dream of battles, glory, and of some divinely beautiful out half-savage maiden, whom he will tame and polish. His arrival at the camp of his regiment on the Terek gives occasion for a fascinating and most realistic picture of the wild races he meets so suddenly. The young ensign falls in at once with his half-savage maiden, a tall, statuesque girl, with red lips, a rose-colored undergarment, and a blue jacket, who looks back at him with a frightened air as she runs after the buffalo she is trying to milk. As he is lodging with her parents, he sets about taming her immediately. But he has a rival, young Lukashka, whose threadbare kaftan and bearskin shako had long before captivated the fair Marianka. The love affairs of the rivals, whom she treats impartially, although she has already made up her mind, go on in the midst of hunting, ambuscade, and battle, which are the real subjects of the book. At last Olenin discovers that he is too civilized for Marianka. "Ah!" he says to himself, "if I were a Cossack like Lukashka, got drunk, stole horses, assassinated now and then for a little change, she would understand me, and I should be happy. But the cruelty and the sweetness of it is that I understand her and she will never understand me." The young Cossack is wounded in battle; and the ensign, not displaying much emotion at this calamity, receives a look from Marianka that tells him his company is no longer desirable: so he decides to exchange into another sotnia. Tolstoy's pictures of the rough life of the Cossacks have a wonderful charm. The story is particularly interesting as showing the first germs of the altruistic philosophy which Tolstoy later developed into a cult of self-renunciation.

COTTON KINGDOM, THE, by Frederick Law Olmsted. These two volumes of "a traveler's observations on cotton and slavery" were published in 1861, being compiled from three previous works on the same subject, which had originally appeared as letters to the New York Times, between 1856 and 1860. The book, written with especial reference to English readers, was dedicated to John Stuart Mill. It is intended for the class of persons that would consider 'Uncle Tom's Cabin' overdrawn and hysterical, and deals exclusively with facts. Authorities are cited, government reports quoted, names and places specified; everything is done to make the work convincing.

Though the author began his observations in a fair and judicial spirit, he was everywhere impressed with the disadvantages of slavery. Even in States like Virginia, where slaves were generally well treated, the economic evils were great, while farther south things were much worse. The slaveholding proprietors experienced so much difficulty in managing their estates that they had no energy for public affairs. There were no good roads, and no community life existed. Though the railroad and steamboat had been introduced, they were operated in a primitive and desultory fashion, mails were irregular, and intercommunication was uncertain and precarious. Slave labor, of course, made free labor unremunerative and despised, and the poor white lived from hand to mouth on the brink of pauperism. In the cotton States the large plantations were worked with profit, but the small ones frequently failed to pay expenses. In every instance the cost of maintaining and managing the negroes was so great, and their labor so forced and reluctant, that much better results could have been obtained from free labor. In fact, had there been no other question involved, its monstrous wastefulness would have condemned slavery. But the moral evils were incalculably great. The slave was reduced, virtually, to the level of the brute, and all efforts to raise him morally and intellectually were regarded as unsafe and revolutionary He lost the good qualities of barbarism, and gained the vices of civilization, and was deliberately made as helpless as possible. The degradation of the master was even more deplorable. His sensibilities were blunted by the daily spectacle of brutality, his moral fibre was loosened, and there was no incentive to self-control, since he was subject to no law save his own capricious will.

Not only was this book of value at the time of its publication, but it is useful at the present day. It explains how the curse of slavery retarded the industrial development of the South; and by showing the condition of master and negro before the emancipation, it affords a better comprehension of the grave problems that confront America to-day.

COUNT FRONTENAC AND NEW FRANCE UNDER LOUIS XIV., see **FRANCE AND ENGLAND IN NORTH AMERICA.**

COUNT OF MONTE CRISTO, THE, by Alexandre Dumas (1844), is the only novel of modern times which the great romancer has written; and it is so widely known that "the treasure of Monte Cristo" has passed into a proverb. The story opens in Marseilles, in the year 1815, just before the "Hundred Days." Young Edward Dantès, the hero, mate of the merchant ship Pharaon, is about to be made her captain and marry his sweetheart, the lovely Catalan Mercedes, when his disappointed rivals, one of whom wants the ship and the other the girl, conspire against him, and lodge information with the "Procurateur du Roi" that Dantès is a dangerous Bonapartist, and is carrying letters from the Emperor, exiled in Elba, to his supporters. Although there is circumstantial evidence against him, the magistrate knows Dantès to be innocent; but he has reasons of his own for wanting him out of the way. He sends him to the gloomy Château of If, a fortress built on a rocky ledge in the sea, where he suffers an unmerited captivity of nearly twenty years. He escapes at length in a miraculous manner, with the knowledge, confided to him by a supposed madman, a fellow prisoner, of an enormous treasure hidden on the barren Island of Monte Cristo, off the Italian coast. Dantès discovers the treasure, and starts out anew in life, to dazzle the world as the mysterious Count of Monte Cristo, with the one fixed purpose of avenging himself on his persecutors, all of whom have risen high in the world to wealth and honors. He becomes a private Nemesis for the destruction of the rich banker, the honored general, and the distinguished magistrate, each of whom his tireless, relentless hand brings low. The first half of the book is a story of romantic and exciting adventure; the second is in a different key, sombre and unlovely, and not likely to convince anyone that revenge is sweet. But the splendid imagination of Dumas transfigures the whole, its intensity persuades the reader that the impossible is the actual, and its rush and impetuosity sweep him breathless to the end.

COUNT ROBERT OF PARIS, by Sir Walter Scott. The scene is laid in Constantinople during the reign of Alexius Comnenus (1080–1118). The hero is a French nobleman who with his wife, Brenhilda, has gone on the first Crusade (1096–99). While dining at the palace they are separated by the Emperor's treachery, and the Count is thrown into prison, from which he releases himself with the assistance of the Varangian Hereward the Saxon. Brenhilda, in the meanwhile, is exposed to the unwelcome attentions of the Emperor's son-in-law, Nicephorus Briennius, whom she challenges to combat. When the time for the duel comes, Count Robert appears himself; in the absence of Briennius Hereward engages him and is overcome, but his life is spared in return for his past services. While the interest is centred in the fortunes of the hero and Hereward, these are closely connected with the conspiracy of the false philosopher Agelastes, Briennius, and Achilles Tatius, the commander of the Varangian Guard, to dethrone the Emperor. The plot is exposed by Hereward, who refuses all rewards, and joins Count Robert and Brenhilda, in whose maid he has discovered his old Saxon love Bertha. Other characters introduced are Anna Comnena, daughter of Alexius and author of the Alexiad; the Patriarch of the Greek Church; Ursel, a former conspirator; Godfrey of Bouillon, and other leaders of the Crusade. Many historical facts are altered for artistic effect. At the time of the story Anna was only fourteen instead of over thirty, and was not the heiress to the throne. The conspiracy anticipates her later attempt to overthrow her brother John, and substitute her husband. The most striking scene is the swearing allegiance by the Crusaders to the Emperor as overlord, in which Count Robert defiantly seats himself on the throne with his dog at his feet. The story was, with 'Castle Dangerous,' the last of the Waverley novels, having appeared in 1831, the year before the author's death.

COUNTESS JULIE, see **MISS JULIA.**

COUNTESS OF RUDOLSTADT, THE, see **CONSUELO.**

COUNTRY DOCTOR, THE ('Le Médecin de Campagne'), by Honoré de Balzac, belongs to the series known as 'Scenes from Country Life'; a part of his great cycle of fiction, 'The Comedy of Human Life.' It appeared in French in 1833, and in the standard English translation by Miss Wormeley in 1887. It is one of Balzac's noblest pieces of fiction, presenting beautiful traits of human nature with sympathy and power. The scene is laid in a village near Grenoble in France, and the story begins with the year 1829. To this village comes Genestas, a noble old soldier who adores Napoleon, and believes in the certainty of his return to save France. Under the assumed name of Captain Bluteau, he rests from his wounds, and is cared for by Dr. Benassis, the country doctor, the central character, and a remarkable study of the true physician. He is a sort of Father Bountiful in Grenoble. He treats the poor peasants without pay, and dislikes taking money except from the rich. He teaches the peasantry how to improve their land, introduces methods of work which make for prosperity, suggests new industries, and effects a great change for the better in the neighborhood; so that in ten years the population is tripled, and comfort and happiness are substituted for poverty and misery. The Doctor lives in an attractive old house with two servants, one of whom, Jacquotte, the cook, a scolding, faithful, executive, and skillful woman, proud of her culinary ability and devoted to Benassis's interest, is one of the most enjoyable personages in the story. The incidents of the plot have their explanation in the events of a preceding generation. The novel as a whole is one of the simplest of Balzac's, free from over-analysis of character and motive.

COUNTRY HOUSE, THE, by John Galsworthy (1907). On a visit to the paternal seat of Worsted Skeynes, young George Pendyce falls in love with Helen Bellew, a pretty woman who is separated from her husband, but not divorced. When George returns to London he spends most of his time with the fascinating Mrs. Bellew. Unexpected complications arise from the love affair. Mr. Gregory Vigil, Mrs. Bellew's guardian and fond admirer, pitying her for her uncomfortable position in society, and knowing nothing of her affair with George, decides that she must secure a divorce from Captain Bellew. Vigil is much discouraged to hear from a lawyer that until Captain Bellew gives his wife cause, there can be no divorce. Finally he decides to hire detectives and waits news of Captain Bellew's misdemeanors. Rumor of the intended suit reaches Captain Bellew. Knowing his wife's close acquaintance with young Pendyce, he writes to George's father. Squire Pendyce, that unless his son George breaks with Mrs. Bellew, he will be named as corespondent in the divorce suit, Bellew vs. Bellew and Pendyce. George absolutely refuses to give up Mrs. Bellew. The Squire is so angry that he revises his will, leaving George only the estate. While her husband the Squire is working off his feelings in bluster, quiet Mrs. Pendyce suffers keenly because of her son's entanglement. Unable to stay away from her boy, she defies the Squire and goes up to London to comfort George, whom she pictures as bowed to the earth by his parent's anger. To her dismay she finds George annoyed at her visit and in deep trouble over racing debts. What troubles him most, however, is that Helen Bellew has thrown him over. Mrs. Pendyce stays with George through the first desperate stage of disappointed love in which he threatens to kill himself and then returns to Worsted Skeynes. With deep humiliation she goes to tell Captain Bellew that his wife has tired of her poor boy. Dressed in her best frock of dove-gray, she crosses the fields to the Bellew place. Captain Bellew shelters her from a thunderstorm, and touched by her distress, agrees to withdraw the divorce suit and save George's reputation. Mrs. Pendyce comes home very happy, her ambition for George's career kindled afresh, and something like forgiveness in her heart for Mrs. Bellew

COUNTRY LIVING AND COUNTRY THINKING (1862), by Gail Hamilton (Mary Abigail Dodge, born in Hamilton, Massachusetts), contains a dozen or more essays on all sorts of subjects, from flower-beds to marriage. They are written in an easy conversational style, full of fun and pungent humor, though earnest and even fiery at times. The author, always witty and whimsical, talks laughingly of the sorrows of gardening, the trials of moving, or whatever other occupation is engaging her for the moment, but with such brilliancy and originality that the topic takes on a new aspect. A keen vision for sham and pretense of any sort, however venerable, distinguishes her, and she is not afraid to fire a shot at any enthroned humbug. Her brightness conceals great earnestness of purpose, and it is impossible not to admire the sound and wholesome quality of her discourse.

COUNTRY OF THE POINTED FIRS, THE, by Sarah Orne Jewett (1896).   Like her other works, it is a study of New England character, subtle, delicate, temperate, a revelation of an artist's mind as well as of people and things.

The homely heroine is Mrs. Todd, living at Dunnet Landing, on the eastern sea-coast of Maine, a dispenser to the village-folk of herb medicines made from herbs in her little garden. "The sea-breezes blew into the low end-window of the house, laden with not only sweet-brier and sweet-mary, but balm and sage and borage and mint, wormwood and southernwood." Mrs. Todd's summer-boarder (Miss Jewett herself, no doubt) tells the story of her sojourn in the sweet, wholesome house, of her many excursions with her hostess, now to a family reunion, now to visit Mrs. Todd's mother on Green Island, now far afield to gather rare herbs. The fisher folk, the farm folk, and the village folk are depicted with the author's unique skill, living and warm through her sympathetic intuition. The book is fresh and clean with sea-air and the scent of herbs. Its charm is that of nature itself.

COURTIER, see BOOK OF THE COURTIER.

COUSIN PONS, by Honoré de Balzac. 'Cousin Pons,' written in 1847, belongs to Balzac's series of 'Scenes from Parisian Life.' In it he intended to portray "a poor and simple-minded man, an old man, crushed by humiliations and insults, forgiving all and revenging himself only by benefits." The hero is Sylvain Pons, a simple-hearted old musician who has seen his best days professionally, whom his purse-proud cousins the Marvilles, wearying of his visits, slight and insult. The vicissitudes of the poor fellow make the story. Greed and cunning, in all grades of society, receive their due celebration. The Marvilles, the titled Popinots, the theatre director Gaud-issard, the various lawyers, the Jewish picture dealers, down to the very lodging-house keepers, all are leagued against the one simple-hearted man and triumph at last. It is interesting to know that Cousin Pons's great collection, as described in the story, was actually Balzac's own, which M. Champfleury visited in 1848, and which, al-though seen for the first time, seemed strangely familiar to him until "the truth flashed upon me. I was in the gallery of Cousin Pons. Here were Cousin Pons's pictures, Cousin Pons's curios. I knew them now." The American translation is by Katherine Prescott Wormeley.

COUSINE BETTE, by Honoré de Balzac (1846). This powerful story is a vivid picture of the tastes and vices of Parisian life in the middle of last century. Lisbeth Fischer, commonly called Cousin Bette, is an eccentric poor relation, a worker in gold and silver lace. The keynote of her character is jealousy, the special object of it her beautiful and noble-minded cousin Adeline, wife of Baron Hector Hulot. The chief interest of the story lies in the development of her character, of that of the unscrupulous beauty Madame Marneffe, and of the base and empty voluptuary Hulot. 'Les Parentes Pauvres,' including both 'Cousine Bette' and 'Cousin Pons,' are the last volumes of 'Scènes de la Vie Parisienne.' Gloomy and despairing, they are yet terribly powerful.

COVENTRY PLAYS, THE. Four complete sets of ancient English Mysteries, or Miracle Plays, have descended to modern times: the "Chester," the "Towneley," the "York," and the "Coventry" from these we derive nearly all our knowledge of the early English drama. Coventry was formerly famous for the performance of its Corpus Christi plays by the Gray Friars. These plays contained the story of the New Testament, composed in Old English rhythm. The earliest record of their performance is in 1392, the latest in 1589. There are 42 of these Coventry plays, published in a volume by the Shakspere Society in 1841, under such titles as 'The Creation,' 'The Fall of Man,' 'Noah's Flood,' 'The Birth of Christ,' 'Adoration of the Magi,' 'Last Supper,' 'The Pilgrim of Emmaüs,' 'The Resurrection,' 'The Ascension,' 'Doomsday.' The modern reader will require a glossary for the proper understanding of these queer old plays, written in early English.

CRANFORD, by Mrs. Gaskell. Cranford is a village in England (identified as Knuts-ford); and the story of the quaint old ladies there—who scorned the "vulgarity of wealth" and practiced "elegant economy"—is told by Mary Smith, a sympathetic and discerning young person from the neighboring town of Drumble. During her first visits in the village stately Miss Deborah Jenkyns is alive; but afterwards she dies, leaving her gentle sister Miss Matty to battle with life and its problems alone. Miss Matty lives comfortably, and is able to entertain her friends in a genteel way, until the bank fails, and then she is obliged to keep a little shop and sell tea. In the end her long-lost brother Peter comes home from India with money enough to enable her to live as becomes a rector's daughter. The other characters are great-hearted

Captain Brown, who is killed by the train while saving a child's life; Mr. Holbrook, Miss Matty's old lover; the Honorable Mrs. Jamieson and her sister-in-law Lady Glenmire, who afterwards marries Mr. Hoggins the doctor; Miss Betty Barker and her cow, famous for its suit of gray flannel; Miss Pole and Mrs. Forrester. Some of the chapters in 'Cranford' tell of old love affairs and old letters, and others of the society and various incidents of village life. It holds its place as one of the best stories of its kind. Mrs. Gaskell was born in 1810; and 'Cranford' was first published in 1853.

CREATION, HISTORY OF (Natürliche Schöpfungs-Geschichte), by Ernst Heinrich Haeckel (1868). A brilliantly written exposition of evolution theories in their most extreme form, of which Darwin said, "If this work had appeared before my essay had been written, I should probably never have completed it." The acceptance of the work is shown by eight editions of the German original within ten years, and translation into twelve languages. Haeckel's 'Evolution of Man,' the English translation of his 'Anthropogenie' (1874), is another widely popular exposition of his extreme tendencies in science. The immense labor which Haeckel performed in his monumental five-volume contribution to the Challenger Reports, and his lucid and brilliant 'Generale Morphologie,' have placed him in the highest rank of living naturalists. He is especially unsurpassed among naturalists in his mastery of artistic execution. See Critical Essay in LIBRARY.

CREATION, THE STORY OF: 'A Plain Account of Evolution,' by Edward Clodd (1888–89). An instructive study of what evolution means, and how it is supposed to have operated in the upward development from the lowest level of the two kingdoms of living things, animals and plants. The book is especially adapted to popular reading. In another work of the same general character, 'The Childhood of the World: A Simple Account of Man in Early Times' (1873), Mr. Clodd has in a most interesting manner dealt with the latest stage of the evolutionary creation, showing how the theory is supposed to explain the origin and early history of the human species. A third volume, on the same plan of popular exposition, 'The Childhood of Religions,' (1875), covers the ground of the earliest development of man in a spiritual direction, and especially explains the first origin and the growth of myths and legends.

CREATIVE EVOLUTION ('L'Évolution créatrice'), a philosophical treatise by Henri Bergson, published in 1907 and in an English translation by Arthur Mitchell in 1911. Rejecting monism both idealistic and materialistic, the writer conceives of the universe as neither all spirit nor all matter but as an eternal process, a *becoming*, which preserves the past and creates the future. The world is not fixed but eternally moving, creating, evolving. Time as we ordinarily conceive it is a mere figment of our minds, borrowed from the idea of juxtaposition in space. Actual time is eternally present time. This conception solves the antinomies of instinct and intelligence, matter and spirit, freedom and determinism. Instead of being bound in iron fetters of necessity, the universe is ever moving forward, ever evolving in free, creative activity. A full summary and criticism of these views will be found in the introductory essay to the extracts from Bergson in the LIBRARY. Bergson's admirable expository gifts, his success as a lecturer not only in France but in England and in America, and the agreement of his philosophy with strong tendencies in modern thought both practical and metaphysical, as expressed for example by William James, have won his philosophy an extraordinary popularity.

CRETAN INSURRECTION OF 1866-8, THE, by William J. Stillman, United States consul to Greece during the period of which the book treats, was published in 1874, making a valuable contribution to the literature of the Eastern Question. Recounting the incidents of those years, the author does not attempt to conceal his sympathies with the Cretans. "I feel," he writes in the Preface, "that the Hellenes are less responsible for the vices of their body politic than are their guardian Powers, who interfere to misguide, control to pervert, and protect to enfeeble, every good impulse and quality of the race; while they foster the spirit of intrigue, themselves enter into the domestic politics of Greece in order to be able to control her foreign, and each in turn, lest Greece should some day be an aid to some other of the contestants about the bed of the sick man, does all it can to prevent her from being able to help herself."

CRIME AND PUNISHMENT, a Russian realistic novel by Féodor M. Dostoévsky, 1866, is a subtle and powerful psychological study, revolving about one incident, — the murder of an old woman, a money-lender, and her sister, by a student in St. Petersburg, Raskolnikoff. The circumstances leading to the murder are extreme poverty, and the resultant physical and mental depletion. Raskolnikoff is by nature generous, warm-hearted, and high-spirited; but when his body is weakened and his mind depressed, the morbid desire takes possession of him to kill the greasy and repellent old woman, whose wealth seems as lawfully his as hers. From this desire he cannot escape. It terrifies yet fascinates him. His state of mind in this crisis is depicted with admirable skill. The murder accomplished, he gains nothing by it: in the sudden awful confusion of mind that immediately follows the committal of the deed, he can form no definite idea of robbery, and escapes with no booty but the memory of one terrific scene which throws him into a delirious fever. At this juncture his mother and sister come to the city. His excited state is perceptible, but they can make nothing of it. By a singular chain of incidents he makes the acquaintance of a girl, Sonia, who has been driven to an evil life that she may save her family from starvation. Believing that her nature is intrinsically noble, Raskolnikoff compels her to read aloud to him the story of the raising of Lazarus. This she does in a manner which confirms his belief in her. His regeneration then begins. As he was impelled to murder, he is now impelled to confess the murder. His sentence is seven years' exile to Siberia; but he accepts it with joy, for at its expiration he will begin with Sonia, the woman he loves, a life of purity and nobility. They will progress together, out of the old order into the new.

CRIME OF HENRY VANE, THE: 'A Study with a Moral,' by J. S. of Dale (F. J. Stimson) (1884). Henry Vane is a man whose youthful enthusiasm has been paralyzed by successive misfortunes. He is a cynic before he is out of his teens. Disappointed and disillusioned, he never regains his natural poise. The moral of his life is, that he who swims continuously against the current will in time be overcome, and he who daily antagonizes the world will find his only peace in death. The events of the story might occur in any American city, and in any good social setting. It is vividly told, interesting, and good in craftsmanship; while the author's pictures of the crudities of American society and the unrestraint of American girls are well if pitilessly drawn.

CRIME OF SYLVESTRE BONNARD, THE, by Anatole France (1881). This charming story, by a distinguished critic and academician, not only paints the literary life of Paris, but depicts the nobler human emotions with delicate humor and pathos. In a short prelude entitled 'The Log,' the kindliness and simplicity of nature of the learned archæologist Sylvestre Bonnard, member of the Institute, are revealed. It relates how he sends a Christmas log to a poor young mother, in the attic above him, on the birth of her boy; how, like a fairy gift, the log comes back to him on a later Christmas, hollowed out, and containing a precious manuscript of the 'Golden Legend,' for which he has journeyed to Sicily in vain; and how the Princess Trépof, who is the gracious donor, turns out to be the poor attic-neighbor, whom he had befriended years before. When the story opens, we find Sylvestre Bonnard at the château of a Monsieur de Gabry, for whom he is cataloguing old manuscripts. Here he meets a charming young girl named Jeanne, and discovers her to be the portionless daughter of his first and only love. He resolves to provide for and dower her; but she has already a guardian in a crafty notary, Maître Mouche, who has placed her in a third-rate school near Paris. Here the good Bonnard visits her and gradually wins her filial affection; but unluckily at the same time arouses in the pretentious schoolmistress, Mademoiselle Préfère, the ambition of becoming the wife of a member of the Institute who is reputed wealthy. The defenseless savant, upon receiving a scarcely veiled offer of wedlock from the lady, cannot conceal his horror; upon which she turns him out of the house, and denies him all further intercourse with Jeanne. On the discovery that his protégée is immured and cruelly treated, he is driven to commit his great crime, the abduction of a minor. This deed is effected by bribing the portress of the school and carrying away the willing victim in a cab to the shelter of Madame de Gabry's house. Here he finds that he has committed a penal offense; but escapes prosecution owing to Jeanne's unworthy guardian's having decamped a week previous with the money of all his clients. Jeanne thus becomes the ward of her good old friend, who later sells his treasured library to secure her a marriage portion, and retires to a cottage in the country, where his declining days are brightened by the caresses of Jeanne and her child.

CRIME OF THE BOULEVARD, THE, a novel, by Jules Claretie (1897), is the history of a crime which occurred in Paris, on the Boulevard de Clichy, in 1896. Pierre de Rovère is found murdered in his apartment. Bernadet, the police agent, who has a passion for photography, takes a picture of the retina of the dead man's eyes, and finds the image of a man whom he recognizes at the funeral. He arrests this person, who proves to be Rovère's dearest friend, Jacques Dantin. He is, however, not the real murderer. The mixture of pseudo-science and sensational detail in this novel is thoroughly French.

CRIPPS THE CARRIER, by R. D. Blackmore (1876). With one exception, this is the most sensational and the least probable of Blackmore's stories. The scene is laid in Kent, and the plot hinges on the disappearance of a young heiress, and her very strange experiences. Through an agreeable way of telling it, the book is much less startling and more attractive than a bare synopsis of the plan would make it sound. The interest is sustained, and the situations are ingeniously planned.

CRISIS, THE, by Winston Churchill, was published in 1901, and, like its predecessor 'Richard Carvel,' met with overwhelming popularity.
The story is of keen dramatic interest and has for its background the incidents of the Civil War. Its hero Stephen Brice, a young New England lawyer seeking his fortune in the Southern States, is naturally opposed to slavery and from his small capital purchases a young slave for the sole purpose of freeing her and restoring her to her mother. This episode brings him to the notice of Virginia Carvel, the heroine of the tale, an aristocratic beauty and descendant of Richard Carvel, whose heart is all with

the South and whose attitude toward the abolitionists is most unrelenting. Stephen falls deeply in love with her, but she stifles her love for him on account of her prejudices, and becomes engaged to her cousin Clarence Colfax, who joins the Southern army. Brice fights for the North and the reader is given many graphic pictures of his experiences, through all of which he shows great nobleness and courage, and, when he has the opportunity, saves the life of his rival. After many trials and tribulations Stephen and Virginia are at length united, at the moment when she is suing President Lincoln for the pardon of her cousin, who has been sentenced to death. The book has many dramatic situations and its characters are strongly drawn. Among the latter may be mentioned Eliphalit Hopper, who figures prominently in the book as an unscrupulous carpetbagger; Judge Whipple, an ardent abolitionist, who, in spite of his eccentricities, would sacrifice everything to his convictions; Colonel Carvel, a true Southern gentleman; and Mrs. Brice, whose charm and strength of character are felt by all who come in contact with her. The love-story is well told and the historical flavor is enhanced by the introduction of Lincoln and Grant.

CRITIC, THE; or, A Tragedy Rehearsed, by R. B. Sheridan (1779). In 'The Critic' Sheridan dexterously pokes fun at the ridiculous foibles of patrons, authors, actors, critics, and audience—all who make or support the stage. Sir Fretful Plagiary, who is "never so well pleased as when a judicious critic points out any defect" to him, but who is very irritable when anyone takes the hint, is the most diverting of butts. Dangle, "at the head [as he fancies] of a band of critics, who take upon them to decide for the whole town, whose opinion and patronage all writers solicit, and whose recommendation no manager dare refuse," finds his own keenest critic in his wife, who thinks that the public is the only tribunal that matters. Puff, who makes no secret of the trade he follows—to advertise himself *viva voce* and to act as "a Practitioner in Panegyric or a Professor of the Art of Puffing," at anybody's service—is an inimitable creation. The tragedy of "The Spanish Armada" inserted in the play is a roaring farce from first to last. "The Spanish Fleet thou *canst* not see"—says the Governor to his daughter Tilburina—"because—it is not yet in sight!" Don Ferolo Whiskerandos, in love with Tilburina whom he persuades to convey his proposal to her father, the governor, finds that "the Father softens, but the Governor's resolved."

CRITICAL AND MISCELLANEOUS ESSAYS, see **ESSAYS.**

CRITICAL PERIOD OF AMERICAN HISTORY, THE, 1783-1789, by John Fiske (1888). In this volume Mr. Fiske's powers are especially tested, and his success in a great task conspicuously shown. The study which he makes of the characters of the two contrasted originators of policies, Washington and Jefferson, of the economic problems of the time, of the way in which the Tories or Loyalists were dealt with at the close of the war, and of the course of events in Great Britain upon the close of the Revolution, conspicuously illustrates his method, and his mastery of the materials of a story second to none in our whole national history in both interest and importance.

CRITIQUE OF PURE REASON, a philosophical treatise by Immanuel Kant, published in 1781, revised edition in 1787; with the 'Critique of Practical Reason' (1788) and the 'Critique of Judgment' (1790) it constitutes a complete statement of Kant's transcendental philosophy. This philosophy consists in the critical examination of the activities of human reason, which, it finds, transcend the materials furnished by sensation. The 'Critique of Pure Reason' is devoted to an analysis of knowledge or thought. The judgments of which knowledge consists are the result of intuition and understanding. Intuitions present us with perceptions of objects in space and time;

these ideas of space and time are not realities but modes of perceiving objects, they are instinctive habits of our minds. Hence our intuitions give us not things in themselves but the appearances of things, "phenomena." Understanding is subdivided into *Verstand*, the faculty of connecting our intuitions to form judgments, and *Vernunft*, the combination of these judgments into universal ideas. The study of the first is called by Kant *Transcendental Analytic*, that of the second *Transcendental Dialectic*. In the former he reduces the categories or modes of judgment to four— quantity, quality, relation, and modality, from which he deduces the laws of continuity and of causality. All these categories and principles, he says, are inherent in the mind itself and not derived from the external world. The connecting link between them and the phenomena conveyed by our intuition is the idea of time which interprets between the intuitions and the judgment. Thus our judgments of the external world are the products of our own mind and reveal to us phenomena not noumena or realities. *Transcendental Dialectic* is the analysis of those general ideas, such as the thing-in-itself, the absolute, the universe, the soul, and God, which result from the combination of our various concepts, judgments, and scientific propositions. These ideas, however, like space and time, and the categories, are not realities but the methods in which our minds operate. In other words, all knowledge is relative and limited by our minds. This leads to absolute scepticism as to the reality corresponding to these general ideas. It leads also to the demonstration of the *antinomies* or theories which, though contradicting one another, are equally capable of proof. It may be proved or disproved with equal cogency that the universe is limited or infinite, that matter is composed of atoms or infinitely divisible, that free will is possible or impossible, and that there is and is not a great first cause. We know only phenomena and the corresponding realities are unattainable by our minds, which are limited by their own modes of thinking. But in the 'Critique of Practical Reason,' in which he turns from knowledge to volition, Kant maintains that the sense of obligation, with its direct appeal to the will, brings a certitude in regard to the ultimate realities of the universe which pure reason cannot give. The reality of God, of free will, and of individual immortality are postulates of the practical reason, *i. e.* convictions incapable of logical proof but deriving their certainty from their appeal to the will. The fact that they cannot be proved but must be accepted by an act of will strengthens their appeal. Finally, in the 'Critique of Judgment,' Kant passes from the realms of knowledge and of will to that of feeling, and considers the origin of the æsthetic and the teleological senses. These also he finds to be modes of operation of the human mind. The beautiful is that which pleases universally by a sense of harmony between the understanding and the imagination; the sublime is that which disturbs us by a sense of conflict between our imagination and our inability to understand infinity. The teleological sense is the feeling that certain things in nature are a result of adaptation. This feeling, an illusion to pure reason, is due to our conception of time, which considers as successive phenomena which are really co-existent.

The three Critiques form the most important and influential work of modern philosophy. They demolished the old dogmatic spiritualism and the old dogmatic materialism and set up foundations for a new idealism. Their conceptions have contributed to the development of all subsequent systems.

'The Critique of Pure Reason' was translated into English by John P. Mahaffy and John H. Bernard, and also by F. Max Müller. 'The Critique of Practical Reason' was translated by T. K. Abbott; 'The Critique of Judgment' was translated by John H. Bernard. Another book of value for the English reader is 'The Critical Philosophy of Kant,' by Dr. Edward Caird.

CROMWELL'S LETTERS AND SPEECHES: With Elucidations by Thomas Carlyle. These elucidations amount to an *ex-parte* favorable rearrangement of Oliver Cromwell's case before the world, supported by the documentary evidence of the Protector's public speeches and his correspondence of every sort, from communications on formal State affairs to private and familiar letters to his family. For almost two hundred years, till Carlyle's work came out in 1845, the memory of Cromwell had suffered under defamation cast upon it through the influence of Charles the Second's court. When the truncheon of the "Constable for the people of England"—as Cromwell (deprecating the title of king) called himself—proved too heavy for his son Richard after Oliver's death, and the Stuarts reascended the throne and assumed the old power, all means were used to destroy the good name of Cromwell. While to the present day opinion widely differs concerning Cromwell's actual conduct, and his character and motives, the prophetic zeal and enthusiasm of Carlyle has done much to reverse the judgment that had long been practically unanimous against him.

CROMWELL'S PLACE IN HISTORY. Founded on Lectures delivered at Oxford. By Samuel Rawson Gardiner (1897). Among scholarly estimates of Cromwell's true rank as a statesman and stature as a man, Mr. Gardiner's may perhaps take the first place. It interprets him as the greatest of Englishmen, in respect especially of both the powers of his mind and the grandeur of his character: "in the world of action what Shakespeare was in the world of thought, the greatest because the most typical Englishman of all time," yet not "the masterful saint" of Carlyle's "peculiar Valhalla." It explains, but does not deny, "the errors of Cromwell in dealing with Ireland"; admits that "Ireland's evils were enormously increased by his drastic treatment," and consents to a verdict of "guilty of the slaughters of Drogheda and Wexford." But it refers the errors and the crime to "his profound ignorance of Irish social history prior to 1641," "his hopeless ignorance of the past and the present" of Ireland. In this, and in every respect, the volume, though small, is of great weight for the study of a period of English history second in interest to no other.

CROTCHET CASTLE, by Thomas Love Peacock (1831). Richard Garnett, in his recent edition of the book, says of it that it "displays Peacock at his zenith. Standing halfway between 'Headlong Hall' and 'Gryll Grange,' it is equally free from the errors of immaturity and the infirmities of senescence." Like the author's other works, 'Crotchet Castle' is less a novel than a cabinet of human curios which may be examined through the glass of Peacock's clear, cool intellect. It is the collection of a dilettante with a taste for the odd. Yet among these curios are one or two flesh-and-blood characters: Dr. Folliott, a delightful Church-of-England clergyman of the old school, and Miss Susannah Touchandgo, who is very much alive. They are all the guests of Mr. Crotchet of Crotchet Castle. Their doings make only the ghost of a plot. Their sayings are for the delight of Epicureans in literature.

CRUSADES, THE HISTORY AND LITERATURE OF THE. From the German of Von Sybel, by Lady Duff-Gordon (1861). A concise but thoroughly learned and judicious study of the Crusades, — by far the best historical sketch in English. Michaud's 'History of the Crusades' is badly translated, but it is the best comprehensive book on the subject. Cox's 'The Crusades,' in the 'Epochs of Modern History,' is an excellent summary. Sybel devotes the second part of his work to an account of the original and later authorities. An excellent history will be found in 'The Age of the Crusades,' by James M. Ludlow (1896); a work which inquires into the conditions of life and thought which made the Crusades possible, — conditions peculiar to the eleventh century, — and then tells the story of eight Crusades, during the period from March, 1096, to August, 1270, together with the results of the period. The most recent work in English, 'The Crusaders in the East,' by W. B. Stevenson, is excellent.

CUDJO'S CAVE, by J. T. Trowbridge, an anti-slavery novel, first published in 1863, was, like its predecessor 'Neighbor Jackwood,' very widely read. The scene of the story is eastern Tennessee, at the outbreak of the rebellion. The State, though seceding, contained many Unionists; and their struggles against the persecution of their Confederate neighbors, slave-holders, and poor whites, form the plot of the book. The ostensible hero is Penn Hapgood, a young Quaker school-teacher, whose abolitionist doctrines get him into constant trouble; but the really heroic figure of the book is a gigantic full-blooded negro, Pomp, a runaway slave, living in the woods in a great cave with another runaway, Cudjo. Cudjo is dwarfish and utterly ignorant, a mixture of stupidity and craft; but Pomp is one of nature's noblemen. Cudjo's cave becomes a refuge for the persecuted abolitionists of the neighborhood, a basis of operations for the Union sympathizers, and finally the seat of war in the region. The novel, though written with a strong ethical purpose, is interesting and effective simply as a story, containing much incident and some capital character-studies.

CULTURE AND ANARCHY, an essay in social criticism by Matthew Arnold, first published in 1869. Its purpose is to define true culture and to show how it may overcome the unintelligent and anti-social tendencies of English life of the author's day. Culture he defines as a study of perfection, that is the harmonious expansion of all the powers of human nature. It is attained by a knowledge of the best that has been said and thought in the world, by the free play of the mind over the facts of life, and by a sympathetic attitude towards all that is beautiful. For a further definition of culture Arnold borrows a phrase from Swift, "Sweetness and light," the first word indicating the sense of beauty and the second the active intelligence. Against this ideal are arrayed all the undisciplined forces of the age — prejudice, narrowness, the worship of liberty for liberty's sake, faith in machinery whether governmental, economic, or religious — in short an unthinking individualism that leads to anarchy. English society may be divided into three classes—Barbarians, Philistines, and Populace. The Barbarians or aristocracy have a superficial sweetness and light but are too much concerned with the maintenance and enjoyment of their privileges to attain a true sense of beauty and a free mental activity. The Philistines or middle classes are devoted to money-making and a narrow form of religion and are indifferent or hostile to beauty. The Populace are violent in their prejudices and brutal in their pleasures. All are agreed that "doing as one likes" is the chief end of man and all are self-satisfied. In a further analysis of this English preference of doing to thinking Arnold distinguishes two forces which he names Hebraism and Hellenism. Hebraism is concerned with resolute action and strict obedience to conscience; Hellenism with clear thinking and spontaneity of consciousness. Harmoniously combined they lead to that perfect balance of our nature which is the end of culture. The excessive development of one of them results in imperfection. Hebraism with its insistence on conduct is the more essential and it triumphed in the form of Christianity; but the reaction from the pagan revival of the sixteenth century led to its over-development into Puritanism, a discipline intolerant of beauty and free intelligence. The English middle class is still dominated by Puritanism, despising art and mental cultivation as an end in itself and adhering to a narrow and unenlightened religious and ethical standard as "the one thing needful." By a revival of the best in Hellenism Arnold would bring sweetness and light into the English middle classes; and he would overcome the unthinking individualism of all classes by developing the idea of right reason embodied in the State. By its power of telling phraseology and its pleasing expository method the book stimulated English society to thought and self-criticism. The evils it attacks and the remedies it proposes are by no means out of date.

CULTURE DEMANDED BY MODERN LIFE. A Series of Addresses and Arguments on the Claims of Scientific Education. Edited by E. L. Youmans (1867). A book of importance as a landmark indicating the expansion of education to embrace science with literature, as both knowledge of highest value and a means of mental discipline not second to any other. Dr. Youmans, to whose service in this direction American culture owes a deep debt, supplied an Introduction to the volume, on mental discipline in education, and also an essay on the scientific study of human nature. Other essays on studies in science are: Tyndall on physics, Huxley on zoölogy, Dr. James Paget on physiology, Herbert Spencer on political education, Faraday on education of the judgment, Henfrey on botany, Dr. Barnard on early mental training, Whewell on science in educational history, and Hodgson on economic science. The wealth of suggestion, stimulus to study, and guidance of interest in these chapters, give the volume a permanent value both to the educator and to studious readers generally. It is a book, moreover, the counsels of which have been accepted; and its prophecies, of advantage to follow from giving science an equal place with literature as a means of culture, have been abundantly fulfilled.

CUORE, by Edmondo de Amicis (15th ed. English translation, 1894). A series of delightfully written sketches, describing the school life of a boy of twelve, in the year 1882, in the third grade of the public schools of Turin. They are said to be the genuine impressions of a boy, written each day of the eight months of actual school life; the father, in editing them, not altering the thought, and preserving as far as possible the words of the son. Interspersed are the monthly stories told by the schoolmaster, and letters from the father, mother, and sister, to the boy. The stories of the lives of the national heroes are given, as well as essays on The School, The Poor, Gratitude, Hope, etc.; all inculcating the love of country, of one's fellow-beings, of honor, honesty, and generosity. The title, 'Cuore' (heart), well expresses the contents of the book — actions caused by the best impulses of a noble heart. Although it is dedicated to children, older persons cannot read the book without pleasure and profit.

CURÉE, LA, see **ROUGON-MACQUART.**

CURIOSITIES OF LITERATURE, by Isaac D'Israeli. This work of "some literary researches," as the author calls it, comprises three volumes, of which the first was published anonymously in 1791, the second two years later, while the third did not appear until 1817. Repeated editions were called for, and it was translated into various languages. A sentence from the preface explains the style and object of the book. "The design of this work is to stimulate the literary curiosity of those, who, with a taste for its tranquil pursuits, are impeded in their acquirement."

From every field the author has gathered interesting and recondite facts and anecdotes on diverse literary and historical topics, and has grouped them under headings totally without sequence. The subjects vary from Cicero's puns to Queen Elizabeth's lovers, and from metempsychosis to waxwork figures. For example, it is asserted that in the reign of Charles II. the prototype of the steam-engine and the telegraph had been invented. We learn the source of the extraordinary legends of the saints, the true story of the printer Faust, and the Venetian origin of newspapers. In short, the work is a library of the little known, and is as entertaining as it is instructive.

CURIOSITIES OF NATURAL HISTORY, by Francis Trevelyan Buckland, a series of descriptive essays published from 1857 to 1872. They embody the results of minute observation of common creatures like frogs, snakes, rats, fishes, and monkeys, written for the general reader and not for the specialist, in a lively and entertaining style. The author was an enthusiastic collector of live animals and a life-long fisherman. He has many novel anecdotes to relate, which he does with the skill of a born *raconteur.*

CUSTOM AND MYTH, by Andrew Lang (1886). This book of fifteen sketches, ranging in subject from the Method of Folk-lore and Star Myths to the Art of Savages, illustrates the author's conception of the inadequacy of the generally accepted methods of comparative mythology. He does not believe that "myths are the result of a disease of language, as the pearl is the result of a disease of the oyster." The notion that proper names in the old myths hold the key to their explanation, as Max Müller, Kuhn, Bréal, and many other eminent philologists maintain, Mr. Lang denies; declaring that the analysis of names, on which the whole edifice of philological "comparative mythology" rests, is a foundation of sifting sand. Stories are usually anonymous at first, he believes, names being added later, and adventures naturally grouping themselves around any famous personage, divine, heroic, or human. Thus what is called a Greek myth or a Hindu legend may be found current among a people who never heard of Greece or India. The story of Jason, for example, is told in Samoa, Finland, North America, Madagascar. Each of the myths presented here is made to serve a controversial purpose in so far as it supports the essayist's theory that explanations of comparative mythology do not explain. He believes that folk-lore contains the survivals of primitive ideas common to many peoples, as similar physical and social conditions tend to breed the same ideas. The hypothesis of a myth common to several races rests on the assumption of a common intellectual condition among them. We may push back a god from Greece to Phœnicia, from Phœnicia to Accadià, but at the end of the end, we reach a legend full of myths like those which Bushmen tell by the camp fire, Eskimo in their dark huts, and Australians in the shade of the "gunweh," — myths cruel, puerile, obscure, like the fancies of the savage myth-makers from which they sprang. The book shows on every page the wide reading, the brilliant faculty of generalization, and the delightful popularity and the unfailing entertainingness of this literary "Universal Provider," who modestly says that these essays are "only flint-like flakes from a neolithic workshop."

CYCLE OF CATHAY, A, by W. A. P. Martin (1896). A Chinese cycle, explains the author of this volume, is sixty years, the period covered in the sketches of China here included. Dr. Martin, whom forty-five years of residence qualify to speak with knowledge of that mysterious empire, describes the face of the country, the villages and cities, productions, commerce, language, institutions, beliefs, but above all, the every-day life of the people, and its significance in the general progress of mankind. History is made to explain the present, and the present to throw its light on the future. The tone is, indeed, that of the foreign observer, but an observer who honestly tries to disabuse his mind of Occidental prejudice, and to give an uncolored report. 'A Cycle of Cathay' ranks among the most interesting and valuable of modern books on China.

CYMBELINE was written by Shakespeare late in his life, probably about 1609. A few facts about Cymbeline and his sons he took from Holinshed; but the story of Imogen forms the ninth novel of the second day of Boccaccio's 'Decameron.' These two stories Shakespeare has interwoven; and the atmosphere of the two is not dissimilar: there is a tonic moral quality in Imogen's unassailable virtue like the bracing mountain air in which the royal youths have been brought up. The beautiful song 'Fear No More the Heat o' the Sun' was a great favorite with Tennyson. Cymbeline wanted his daughter Imogen to marry his stepson Cloten, a boorish lout and cruel villain, but she has secretly married a brave and loyal private gentleman, Posthumus Leonatus, and he is banished for it. In Italy one Iachimo wagers him ten thousand ducats to his diamond ring that he can seduce the honor of Imogen. He miserably fails, even by the aid of lies as to the disloyalty of Posthumus, and then pretends he was but testing her virtue for her husband's sake. She pardons him, and receives into her chamber, for safe-keeping, a trunk, supposed to contain costly plate and jewels, but which really contains Iachimo himself, who emerges from it in the dead of night; slips the bracelet from her arm; observes the mole, cinque-spotted with crimson on her breast; and notes down in his book the furniture and ornaments of the room. He returns to Italy. Posthumus despairingly yields himself beaten, and writes to his servant Pisanio to kill Imogen; to facilitate the deed, he sends her word to meet him at Milford Haven. Thither she flies with Pisanio, who discloses all, gets her to disguise herself in men's clothes and seek to enter the service of Lucius, the Roman ambassador. She loses her way, and arrives at the mountain cave in Wales where dwell, unknown to her, her two brothers, Guiderius and Arviragus, stolen in infancy. Imogen is hospitably received by them under the name of Fidele. While they are at the chase she partakes of a box of drugged medicine which the wicked queen had prepared, and sinks into a trance resembling death. Her brothers sing her requiem. In the end Cloten is killed, the paternity of the youths revealed, Iachimo confesses his crime, and Imogen recovers both her husband and her brothers.

CYRANO DE BERGERAC, by Edmond Rostand (1897). Cyrano de Bergerac, the hero of this popular romantic drama, was a poet, prince among wits, brave soldier and duellist of the time of Louis XIII. and Richelieu. The play opens in 1640 at a Parisian playhouse, where a performance is about to be given by a troupe of the King's players. Cyrano has forbidden one of the actors to appear. He drives him from the stage, and entertains the audience, including his cousin, Roxanne, whom he adores, by fighting a duel with a titled young fop who resents the interruption of the play and provokes a quarrel by mocking Cyrano's immense nose, which none may mention with impunity. Cyrano fights the duel with his pointed wit as well as his sword, improvising a brilliant ballade on his nose and marking each thrust at his opponent with a verse. This scene is quoted in the LIBRARY. Cyrano despairs of winning Roxanne because of his grotesque ugliness, but hopes she may love him for his valor when she seeks an interview with him after the duel. In his exuberance, he singlehanded puts to flight a hundred men, who are waiting in ambush to attack his friend. The meeting of Cyrano and Roxanne is at the shop of the poetical pastry cook, who sells tarts for sonnets, and is finally reduced to the horrid necessity of wrapping up patties in a poem to Phyllis.

Roxanne confesses that she loves one who loves her from afar, but it turns out to be not Cyrano but Christian, a stupid handsome youth about to become a member of Cyrano's company, the Gascon Cadets. Cyrano hides his heartbreak, promises his protection to Christian, and from that moment sacrifices himself to the lovers.

The ugly Cyrano teaches gallantry to the dull Christian, writes the impassioned poetic letters which win his lady-love, and even impersonates him in the darkness, while Roxanne leans from her balcony.

The Gascons go to the war, and Christian is killed. Roxanne retires to a convent where for fifteen years the faithful Cyrano pays her a weekly visit. As he is leaving his house some enemy lets fall a large piece of wood, which strikes his head and wounds him mortally. He goes on to the convent and in this last scene of his death, Roxanne, who had loved her hero first for his beauty and then for his soul, as shown in his letters, discovers the secret of the double wooing and laments, "I loved but once, yet twice I lose my love."

DAISY MILLER, by Henry James, a novelette published in 1878, is one of his most famous stories. Its heroine is a young girl from Schenectady, "admirably pretty," who is traveling about Europe with her placid mother, and her dreadful little brother Randolph. Mrs. Miller never thinks of interfering with her children, and allows her daughter to go for moonlight drives with young men, and her son of ten to sit up eating candies in hotel parlors till one o'clock, — with an occasional qualm, indeed, but with no consciousness of countenancing a social lapse, her code of etiquette being that of a rural American town, with no authority of long descent. From the constant incongruity between the Miller social standards and the Draconian code of behavior of the older European communities, come both the motive and the plot of the story, which is one of the most skillful and convincing of the very clever artist who wrote it. Upon its publication, however, American society at home and abroad was mightily indignant over what it pronounced Mr. James's base libel on the American young girl, and American social training. But when it came to be read more soberly, the reader perceived that the subtle painter of manners had really delineated a charming type of innocence and self-respect, a type so confident of its own rectitude as to be careless of external standards. It was seen to be the environment only that distorted and misrepresented this type, and that in the more primitive civilization which produced it, it would have been without flaw. In a word, the thoughtful reader discovered that Mr. James's sketch, so far as it had a bias at all, was a plea for justice to a new manifestation of character, the product of new conditions, that can never hope to be understood when measured by standards wholly outside its experience. The book is one of the most brilliant, as it is one of the most subtle and artistic, of this author's productions.

DAME CARE ('Frau Sorge'), a novel by Hermann Sudermann, was issued in 1888. The story follows the life of Paul Meyerhofer, a boy at whose cradle Care seemed to preside. He was born on the day his father's estate was sold at auction. His childhood was spent in poverty, his boyhood and youth in hard work. He had always before him the spectacle of a cowed, suffering mother; of an overbearing, shiftless father, whose schemes for making money only plunged his family in deeper misfortune. His younger sisters, when they grow up, bring disgrace upon him. To save their honor he makes enormous sacrifices; in short, his whole career is one of misfortune. The one brightness of his life is his love for Elsbeth Douglas, the daughter of his godmother. At the close of the novel it is intimated that he will marry her, and that "Dame Care," his foster-mother, will not trouble him again. The story, written with much pathos and beauty, is a peculiar blending of realism and romanticism.

DAMNATION OF THERON WARE, THE, by Harold Frederic, appeared in 1896, and is a brilliant realistic study of modern American life. Theron Ware, a handsome and eloquent young preacher, is placed in charge of the Methodist church at Octavius, New York State. Needing money, thirsting for fame, and quite ignorant of his own limitations, he plans to write an epoch-making book upon Abraham. His damnation comes to him in the form of self-knowledge, through his acquaintance with a beautiful woman. The book belongs in the ranks of realism, but of the true realism that is interpreted through the imagination.

DANIEL DERONDA (1876), George Eliot's last novel, considered by some critics her greatest work, has repelled others by its careful analysis of Jewish character. It really has two separate parts, and two chief figures, each very unlike the other. Gwendolen Harleth, the heroine, and Daniel Deronda, the hero, first see each other at Baden, where Gwendolen tries her luck at the gaming-table. When they next meet, Gwendolen is the fiancée of Henleigh Grandcourt, nephew of young Deronda's guardian, Sir Hugh Mallinger. Grandcourt is a finished type of the selfish man of the world. He marries the beautiful, penniless Gwendolen, less for love than in a fit of obstinacy, as his confidant Mr. Lush puts it. Gwendolen, as selfish as he, consents to marry him because only thus can she save her mother, her stepsisters, and herself, from the poverty which the sudden loss of their property is likely to bring them. The tragedy of her married life is told with dramatic force and profound insight. Deronda has been brought up by Sir Hugh in ignorance of his parentage. His fine education and great talents he is always ready to place at the service of others. By befriending a Jewish girl, Mirah Lapidoth, he comes in close contact with several Jewish families, grows deeply interested in Jewish history and religion, and when the secret of his birth is revealed to him is glad to cast in his lot with theirs. The influence of Deronda on Gwendolen is very marked, and the story closes with the prophecy of a lessening selfishness and egotism on her part. Gwendolen's mother, Mrs. Davilow; her uncle and aunt, Mr. and Mrs. Gascoigne, and their children; the wealthy Mr. and Mrs. Arrowsmith, whose daughter has the courage to marry the man she loves, a poor music teacher, one Herr Klesmer, — are the chief minor characters. Other people appear, like Lord Brackenshaw and Mrs. Gadsby; but less care is given to the portrayal of these than to the noble Mordecai, the garrulous Cohens, and the other Jewish types, or even to Deronda's friend Mrs. Merrick, and her artist son Hans.

In 'Daniel Deronda' George Eliot had three objects in view: 1. To show the influence of heredity; 2. To show that ideals and sentiments lie at the basis of religion; 3. To contrast a social life founded on tradition (that of the Jews) with mere individualism. As a plea for the Jews this book not only met the approval of the thoughtful men of that race, but also gave the world in general a just idea of this complex people.

DANIELE CORTISS, see **THE POLITICIAN.**

DANTE, A SHADOW OF: 'Being an Essay towards Studying Himself, his World, and his Pilgrimage'; by Maria Francesca Rossetti (4th ed. 1884). A volume of criticism and selections, designed to enable the reader to comprehend the poet and his great poem. The study begins with Dante's conception of the universe, and what autobiography and history show his life experience to have been. It then proceeds to expound the physical and moral theories on which the poet constructed his three worlds, and narrates the course of his pilgrimage through them. In this narration the main object is to read Dante's autobiography in the poem, to make out his character as self-revealed, and to enter into his inspiration or spiritual life. The extracts, of which there are many, are made with this view, many of the episodes being passed over.

DANVERS JEWELS, THE, and **SIR CHARLES DANVERS** (1889), by Mary Cholmondeley. These stories, first published anonymously, were so cleverly told that they excited much interest in the unknown author. In 'The Danvers Jewels' Colonel Middleton relates the adventures of a bag of priceless jewels, which he is commissioned to carry from India to England, to Sir John Danvers's heir, Ralph Danvers. A professional thief named Carr attempts to rob him, but Colonel Middleton delivers the jewels safely at Stoke Moreton, the Danvers's country-seat. Private theatricals are in progress there, and another actor being necessary, the Colonel sends for Carr, whom unsuspectingly he considers his friend. Shortly after Carr's arrival the jewels disappear; suspicion falls on Sir Charles Danvers, Ralph's charming but unpopular brother. Sir Charles suspects Carr to be the thief; who, however, proves to be the beautiful and fascinating girl to whom Ralph is engaged. This young woman is really Carr's wife. On her way to London to sell the jewels a railroad accident occurs, and Sir Charles and Ralph find her dead, with the jewels concealed about her. Ralph marries his cousin Evelyn; and the Colonel's story comes to an end. 'Sir Charles Danvers' is written in the third person; Ruth Deyncourt is the heroine; a clever, attractive girl, who fancies that her duty lies in helping Alfred Dare, a poor foreigner to whom she becomes secretly engaged. Sir Charles wooes her, but although she loves him she remains true to Dare until a woman arrives who claims to be Dare's wife. Through Reymond Deyncourt, Ruth's good-for-nothing brother, Sir Charles discovers that the woman's claim is false, and generously tells Dare. Ruth realizes her mistaken self-sacrifice at last, and ends by marrying Sir Charles. Lady Mary, a worldly old woman, is a delightful character; while Molly Danvers, a queer little girl who alone would make the fortune of any story, is one of the most fascinating children in fiction. Sir Charles Danvers, with his gentleness and strength, his reserved but sympathetic nature, and his delightful sense of humor, is, however, rightly entitled to the place of hero. In 'The Danvers Jewels' the interest centres in a well-told plot; and in 'Sir Charles Danvers' the charm lies in the character studies, and in the descriptions of English country life.

DAPHNIS AND CHLOE, by Longus. This charming pastoral romance was written in Greek during the fourth century of our era. It was first translated into a modern language by Amyot, who published a French version in 1559. Other renderings were soon made, and had great influence on European literature. Many English, French, and Italian pastorals were suggested by this work; but the one derived most directly from this source is Saint-Pierre's 'Paul and Virginia,' which is almost a parallel story, with Christian instead of pagan ethics. On the island of Lesbos, a goatherd named Lamon finds one of his goats suckling a fine baby boy, evidently exposed by his parents. The good man adopts him as his own child, calling him Daphnis, and brings him up to herd his goats. The year after he was found, a neighbor, Dryas, discovers a baby girl nourished by a ewe in the grotto of the nymphs. She is adopted under the name of Chloe, and trained to tend the sheep. The two young people pasture their herds in common, and are bound by an innocent and childlike affection. Eventually, this feeling ripens on both sides to something deeper; but in their innocence they know not the meaning of love, even when they learn that the little god has them in his especial keeping. After a winter of forced separation, which only inflames their passion, Daphnis sues for the hand of Chloe. In spite of his humble station, he is accepted by her foster-parents; but the marriage is deferred till after the vintage, when Lamon's master is coming. On his arrival the goatherd describes the finding of the child, and exhibits the tokens found with him. Hereupon he is recognized as the son of the master of the estate, and restored to his real position. By the aid of Daphnis's parents, Chloe is soon identified as the daughter of a wealthy Lesbian, who in a time of poverty had intrusted her to the nymphs. The young people are married with great pomp, but return to their pastoral life, in which they find idyllic happiness.

DARK FLOWER, THE, by John Galsworthy (1913), is the story of one man's love-affairs. We first see the hero, Mark Lennan, when he is a student at Oxford. During the Easter holidays, he goes to the Tyrol with his tutor, Harold Stormer. There he falls in love with Stormer's Austrian wife, Anna. When Mark is called home suddenly to attend the wedding of his sister in Derbyshire, he makes Anna promise that she and her husband will come to visit him before the Oxford term begins. When he goes, Anna gives him a clove pink, the "dark flower" of passion which gives the book its title. The Stormers come down to Derbyshire. Anna notices something of which Mark himself is as yet unaware—that he loves Sylvia, the pretty cousin who had been his sister's bridesmaid. Unable to remain and see the romance blossom, Anna hurries her husband back to Oxford. Mark's guardian has guessed Anna's secret, and arranges for Mark to go to Italy instead of to Oxford to study. Thus Mark's first flame passes out of his life. When the reader meets him eight years later Mark is in Rome. He is already a sculptor to be reckoned with. He is in love with Olive Cramier, a beautiful poetic creature yoked to an adoring but materialistic husband. When she returns to England, Mark follows. Cramier feels that his wife sees too much of the young sculptor and sends her to the country, to a pretty cottage on the river. There Olive struggles in vain against her passion. Finally she telegraphs Mark to come down, feigns a headache to deceive her kindly old aunt and uncle, meets Mark at the bank, and goes away with him in a canoe. When they return, hours after, they have formulated plans for an elopement. As they are getting out of the canoe, Olive's husband, who had come down from London to watch his wife, comes from behind a bush. He pushes the woman into the deep water, and though Mark struggles to save her, she is drowned. The truth about Olive's death is never known; there is report of "an accident." When we meet Lennan again, he is forty-six, married to the charming Sylvia, childless, and embarked upon another passion. This time he falls in love with a young girl, Nell Dromore, the natural daughter of an Oxford classmate. Unschooled in control, Nell finds it impossible to hide her passion from Mark. Unable to repulse a young girl who is devoted to him, although at first he has no more than a fatherly affection for her, Mark makes flimsy excuses to Sylvia, and visits the Dromores frequently. When he once realizes the true state of his feelings, Lennan confesses to his wife, secures her forgiveness, and goes with her to Italy, leaving Nell behind with her father and the adoring young cousin whom one assumes she will finally marry.

DARK FOREST, THE, by Hugh Walpole (1916). The story opens with the departure of a Red Cross unit from Petrograd. All are Russians except two Englishmen, Durward, of analytic temperament, who tells the story, and Trenchard, timid, blunder-

ing, inefficient, who is the chief character. Trenchard is seeking the sympathy and
affection he has not found at home. Sister Marie, a young Russian girl, eager for
life, becomes engaged to Trenchard in the excitement and exaltation of the last days
of preparation. On the journey Trenchard is the butt of the party and especially
of the efficient dominating male, Dr. Semyonov, who finally wins Marie from him.
The narrative is the struggle of these two men for complete possession of Marie, since
she has given something different of herself to each lover. She is killed by an Austrian bullet in the Dark Forest, but the duel between the two men continues, as each
believes that the one who meets death first will find her. The war is the background
and atmosphere for the story. The Forest is present as vividly as the War, perhaps
typifying the War. It is uncanny with its thick bright foliage which seems to give no
shade. The Dark Forest covers dead Austrians, villages of starving old people,
cholera villages, trenches, and Red Cross shelters, where "the wounded were brought
in without pause." Again the Forest, always green and glittering, is lovely in an
early summer morning with the singing of birds. At night "the Forest was deep
black," the soldiers' fires gleaming here and there like beasts' eyes." The stress and
strain of the Red Cross service is continuous. Trenchard goes out with wagons to
the "screaming Forest" and is "overwhelmed by the blind indifference of the place,
listening still to the incredible birds." He is exhausted with "endless bandaging,
cleaning of filthy wounds, paring away the ragged ends of flesh, smelling, breathing,
drinking blood and dust and dirt." Death, which is as close as life, has a glamor and
fascination. Trenchard and Dr. Semyonov covet death, because of their obsession of
its reward of union with Marie. In his last diary, death to Trenchard has ceased to
be the terror of his childhood; he had laughed at death under fire; he had cursed it
when Marie died; face to face with it, he feels "one is simply face to face with one's
self." A shell breaks overhead, and of the four it is Trenchard who is killed and the
stronger character, Semyonov the realist, who is left.

DARKEST ENGLAND, see IN DARKEST ENGLAND.

DARLING AND OTHER STORIES, THE, by Anton Chekhov (1916). These short
stories describe a variety of types of women. The title story, 'The Darling' is a
study of a woman, who lives only in her affections, and takes her opinions from others.
Olinka is equally devoted to two husbands and a lover in succession. Losing her
lover, she adopts his son, a schoolboy, whose world she lives in, perfectly satisfied.
The transference of her affections is as automatic as the reflection of a chamelion to its
surroundings. 'Ariadne' is a type of parasite, caring for nothing but attention and
luxury. She travels about Europe with one lover until his money is exhausted, then
calls another to her, and leaves him to marry a wealthy old prince. 'The Helpmate'
is also an ironical study of sex. In 'The Two Volodyas' the neurotic Sofya thinks
she is in love with her elderly husband one day, and abandons herself to the other
'Volodya,' his young friend, the next. Still another type is Polinka, a deluded little
dressmaker who loses her head over a student, and is bewitched away from the
young salesman who loves her. 'Three Years' begins with the passionate love of
Laptev for the indifferent Yulia. After three years she comes to love him, and his
only feeling is that he is hungry for his lunch. 'The Princess' is another satire on a
woman who believes herself an angel beloved by everyone, but is shown to be a selfish
egotist justly hated by those for whom she poses as benefactress. An exquisite old
mother in 'The Trousseau,' spends her life making a wonderful trousseau for a
daughter who never marries, and dies when they are two old women together. This

story is reprinted in the LIBRARY. Destiny plays with the happiness of all these people as a cat with mice, and they accept life, Russian fashion, as a thing to be patiently endured.

DAUGHTER OF HETH, A, a novel, by William Black, was published in 1871. It is the story of a child of sunny France, transplanted into the bleak uncongenial atmosphere of Scotland. Catherine Cassilis, familiarly called Coquette, is the daughter of a Scotch father and French mother. On the death of her parents she is intrusted to her uncle, the minister of Airlie. There her unselfishness and eagerness to harmonize herself with her new surroundings win her universal love. Her story has, however, a tragic ending. From beginning to end the "dour" atmosphere of a Scotch hamlet is seen to darken the sunshine of Coquette's sunny disposition, and to prophesy a future of shadow.

DAUGHTER OF JORIO ('La Figlia di Iorio'), by Gabriele d'Annunzio (1904). The scene of this poetic drama is laid in the mountain land of the Abruzzi, primitive Italian people. Mila, the daughter of Jorio, a sorcerer, pursued by the brutal reapers who are crazed with heat and drunk with red wine, seeks sanctuary at the hearth of Aligi, a shepherd about to celebrate his espousal feast with the bride his mother has chosen for him. His mother and the women kindred, interrupted in the ceremony of the scattering the grain on the heads of the bridal pair, urge him to give up the woman, who brings sorrow and dark omen. Already Lazaro, his father, has fallen under her spell, and has been wounded in a fight for her. As the reapers tear down the iron-barred door to get their prey, Aligi lays the crucifix across the threshold, knowing that none dare pass the sacred emblem.

In the second act Aligi and Mila are living together in innocence in his shepherd's cave in the mountains. See Scene quoted in the LIBRARY. Aligi hopes to join a band of pilgrims to go to Rome for permission to annul his marriage, never consummated, so that he may take Mila to his father's house.

Ornella, the youngest sister of Aligi, comes to the cave to seek Mila's promise to give up Aligi and restore him to his home. She has hardly left when Lazaro, the father, comes in search of Mila. He has a rope on his arm like an ox driver to tie up his beast. The terrified girl calls for help and Aligi comes to her. He appeals in vain to the bestial Lazaro and finally in a terrible scene strikes his father dead.

The third act is the funeral rites, half Pagan, half Catholic. Aligi has been given to the crude social justice of his tribe, and is to be barbarously killed, when Mila appears inspired with the noble lie with which her great love is to save him. Aligi, she asserts, is innocent; she Mila, killed Lazaro and blinded Aligi to her guilt with the secret herbs that her father, the sorcerer, taught her.

The crowd turn on her and take her away in triumph of blood lust to be burned alive. Even Aligi, delirious with the "cup of forgetfulness" his mother has given him, calls down curses upon her. As she is carried to the flames only Ornella the youngest sister recognizes the sacrifice.

DAVID BALFOUR; 'Being Memoirs of His Adventures at Home and Abroad,' by Robert Louis Stevenson (1893). A sequel to 'Kidnapped,' this novel follows the further fortunes of David Balfour. When the story opens David is about to attempt the escape of his friend, Alan Breck Stewart, from Scotland; and to aid Stewart's brother, unjustly imprisoned on a charge of murder. At this critical juncture he falls in love with Catriona Drummond, whose father, James More Drummond, is a plausible scoundrel. David's efforts to help Alan and his brother bring about his own imprisonment, but not until he has seen Alan safely into France. After his release he goes to Holland, where he lives with Catriona without marriage. Her father interfering, the two are separated; but by the intervention of Alan Stewart they meet again in Paris, where they are married.

The novel throughout is in Stevenson's romantic vein, but written with simplicity and clearness, and artistic in construction.

DAVID BLAIZE, a story of school-life, by E. F. Benson (1916). David Blaize, a pupil at Holmsworth Preparatory School, is with the other boys writing letters home on a Sunday afternoon. Mr. Dutton is the master in charge of this arduous task, to which twenty minutes is the time allotted. The Head of the School, Mr. Anscam, a man of rare qualities, who inspires his pupils with both terror and admiration, suddenly appears and detects Dutton reading under cover of his Bible and Prayer-book a yellow-covered volume of stories by de Maupassant. The Head tears the book apart, and excuses his assistant from the lessons to follow, taking charge himself, and finding a sad lack of knowledge on the part of the pupils. David is a genuine boy, full of spirit, love of mischief and of sport, with a lovable disposition which makes him a favorite with the best of his schoolmates. Everything that is beautiful, especially in poetry, attracts him, and he is so impressed by the Headmaster's reading of Keats that he longs to possess a volume of his poems. The great event of the year is the cricket-match with Eagles school. Although David belongs to the eleven he feels "beastly" on the day of the match because his father, an archdeacon, comes to see the game. The boys make fun of the archdeacon's peculiarities in dress and manner, and this causes the son to feel so uncomfortable that he fails to do himself justice and loses the match, although he does some fine playing later in the day, after his staunch friend Bags has lured his father out of the way. The following week David goes to Marchester to take his examinations for a scholarship, and there he meets Frank Maddox, a fellow three years his senior, who becomes a great hero in his eyes. David's last days at Holmsworth pass in triumph, for although he loses the scholarship he wins the final cricket-match for the school. During the vacation at Baxminster, where his father and sister live, he meets Frank Maddox again and his admiration for him increases. When he goes to Marchester in the autumn he becomes Maddox's fag and devoted slave. David still keeps up his interest in cricket and distinguishes himself in many matches which are described with great detail. When David has reached the sixth form, Maddox is at Cambridge. Just before the end of the summer term David is seriously injured in trying to stop a runaway horse. His life is despaired of. Maddox, who happens to have come at this juncture, succeeds in soothing his restlessness, so that he falls into a long sleep at the critical moment and his life is saved.

DAVID COPPERFIELD. "Of all my books," says Charles Dickens in his preface to this immortal novel, "I like this the best. . . . Like many fond parents, I have in my heart of hearts a favorite child. And his name is David Copperfield." When 'David Copperfield' appeared in 1850, after 'Dombey and Son' and before 'Bleak House,' it became so popular that its only rival was 'Pickwick.' Beneath the fiction lies much of the author's personal life, yet it is not an autobiography. The story treats of David's sad experiences as a child, his youth at school, and his struggles for a livelihood, and leaves him in early manhood, prosperous and happily married. Pathos, humor, and skill in delineation give vitality to this remarkable work: and nowhere has Dickens filled his canvas with more vivid and diversified characters. Forster says that the author's favorites were the Peggotty family, composed of David's nurse Peggotty, who was married to Barkis, the carrier; Dan'el Peggotty, her brother, a Yarmouth fisherman; Ham Peggotty, his nephew; the doleful Mrs. Gummidge; and Little Em'ly, ruined by David's schoolmate, Steerforth. "It has been their fate," says Forster, "as with all the leading figures of his invention, to pass their names into the language and become types; and he has nowhere given happier embodiment to that purity of homely goodness, which, by the kindly and all-reconciling influences of humor, may exalt into comeliness and even grandeur the clumsiest forms of humanity."

Miss Betsy Trotwood, David's aunt; the half-mad but mild Mr. Dick; Mrs. Copperfield, David's mother; Murdstone, his brutal stepfather; Miss Murdstone, that stepfather's sister; Mr. Spenlow and his daughter Dora, — David's "child-wife"; — Steerforth, Rosa Dartle, Mrs. Steerforth, Mr. Wickfield, his daughter Agnes (David's second wife), and the Micawber family, are the persons around whom the interest revolves. A host of minor characters, such as the comical little dwarf hair-dresser, Miss Mowcher, Mr. Mell, Mr. Creakle, Tommy Traddles, Uriah Heep, Dr. Strong, Mrs. Markleham, and others, are portrayed with the same vivid strokes.

DAVID GRIEVE, THE HISTORY OF, a novel by Mrs. Humphry Ward (1892). Like 'Robert Elsmere,' it takes greatly into account social and educational forces of contemporary life. It was written apparently under the influence of 'Amiel's Journal,' as it embodies the same cheerless and somewhat negative philosophy.

The hero, David Grieve, and his sister Louie, are the children of Sandy Grieve, a Scotch workingman, and of a Frenchwoman, a grisette, of depraved tendencies. The girl inherits the mother's nature, the boy the father's. David begins life as a country boy in Derbyshire, tending his uncle's sheep. His leisure moments are devoted to reading and study. As a boy of sixteen he leaves the home that had become intolerable, and goes to Manchester, where he learns the bookseller's trade and educates himself further, becoming finally the head of a publishing-house well known for its publications of economic and political works. His life, however, is far from happy. His sister goes to the bad in Paris. He marries a woman unworthy of him. Throughout, he clings to a high ethical ideal as the only hope, the only faith open to a nineteenth century man. Conduct is for him the whole of life. On right-doing his soul rests and depends, in the stress of the tempest of passion and sin about him.

The novel is well written, abounding in striking and dramatic scenes, and rich in delineation of character.

DAVID HARUM, by Edward N. Westcott, was published in 1899 and met with a great success, which, however, its author did not live to see, as he died before its publication. The scene of the story is laid in central New York, where in a town called Homeville, lives David Harum, a country banker, dry, quaint, and somewhat illiterate, but possessing an amazing amount of knowledge not to be found in books. His quaint and original sayings have become household words and his cheerful belief that there is nothing wholly bad or useless in the world carries with it a strong lesson. The love story which is told in the book concerns John Lenox, a young man of education and refinement, brought up among conditions of wealth and luxury, who suddenly finds himself thrown upon his own resources and decides to accept a position under David Harum in his country bank. At first he is somewhat puzzled by the latter's bluff ways and the apparent hardness which he affects in order to try his new clerk, but he soon discovers that underneath the rough exterior are sterling qualities

and a warm heart.   Before going to Homeville, Lenox has had a delightful acquaintance with Mary Blake a charming New York girl, and has been on the point of
declaring himself when a missent letter causes a misunderstanding which is not
cleared away until the closing chapters of the story, when they meet in Europe five
years later.   Here Lenox at first labors under the delusion that she is married but
when he discovers his mistake he loses no time in winning her for his wife.   David
Harum who has become much attached to Lenox takes him into partnership and
when he dies makes him his heir.   The many amusing anecdotes related in David's
quaint and original vernacular afford most entertaining reading and his horse trading,
which is his favorite pastime is described in an inimitable manner.

DAVID PENSTEPHEN, a novel by Richard Pryce (1915), begins when the boy is
seven years old and covers a little more than ten years of his life; it deals with the
affairs of grown-people from the angle of a boy's vision.   David's father is a brilliant
young writer of unorthodox convictions, and he and David's mother have never been
married.   The family live a wandering life on the Continent.   Penstephen is a well-
known name among the English aristocracy and unpleasant situations continually
arise, which prey upon the mind of David's mother and eventually make her very ill.
Finally, Betsy, the nurse, takes it upon herself to inform her master of her mistresses's
feelings which he has failed to realize; he hastens to atone for the wrong he has done,
and the marriage takes place.   Almost immediately a message comes from England
telling of the drowning of two relatives who have stood between John Penstephen
and a baronetcy.   The family return to England, but Mary's happiness is clouded
by the knowledge that her two children have no legal status.   The birth of a son, a
year later, who is made much of by the relatives who ignore the other children, does
not lessen the mother's anxiety concerning her two eldest, though they grow up in
blissful ignorance of the situation, David frequently wondering at things he cannot
understand.   During his school-days David's liking for the theatre crystallizes into
the determination to become an actor.   When an opportunity comes for him to take
an important part in a play, he invites his mother to witness the performance; she is
prepared to do so when she learns that Lady Harbington, who has already caused her
much humiliation, is now in the neighborhood where David is visiting and she regrets
not having enlightened David regarding his legal status.   The disclosure, which is the
climax of the story, comes in a highly dramatic fashion before the entire cast assembled
for rehearsal.   The result of this dénouement is but to increase David's popularity,
while his knowledge of his own position gives him an added impetus in seeking the
stage as a permanent field, where he now resolves to "make a name for himself."

DAWN OF ASTRONOMY, THE, by Sir J. Norman Lockyer (1897).   A popular
study of the temple worship and mythology of the ancient Egyptians, designed to
show that in the construction of their magnificent temples the Egyptians had an eye
to astronomical facts, such as the rising or setting of the sun at a particular time in
the year, or to the rising of certain stars; and so planned the long axis of a great
temple as to permit a beam of light to pass at a particular moment the whole length
of the central aisle into the Holy Place, and there illuminate the image of the deity, —
giving at once an exact note of time, and a manifestation of the god by the illumination, which the people supposed to be miraculous.   Mr. Lockyer's clear discovery of
these astronomical facts explains very interestingly the nature of the gods and
goddesses, many of whom are found to be different aspects of the same object in
nature.   For both the science and the religion of Egypt the work is of great value.

DAWN OF CIVILIZATION, THE; EGYPT AND CHALDÆA, by G. Maspero. Revised edition (1897). Translated by M. L. McClure. Introduction by A. H. Sayce. With map and over 470 illustrations. A work devoted to the earlier history of Egypt and Babylonia; especially full and valuable for the early history of Egypt, which Maspero puts before that of Babylonia. "Chaldæa" is a comparatively late name for Babylonia; and since Maspero wrote, new discoveries have carried the "dawn" very far back in Babylonia, to a date much earlier than that of the earliest known records of origins in Egypt.

In a later volume, 'Egypt, Syria, and Assyria: The Struggle of the Nations,' M. Maspero has carried on the story of the early Oriental world, its remarkable civilization, its religious developments, and its wars of conquest and empire, down to a time in the last half of the ninth century B.C., when Ahab was the King of Israel in northern Palestine. Babylon had risen and extended her influence westward as early as 2250 B.C.; and even this was 1500 years later than Sargon I., who had carried his arms from the Euphrates to the peninsula of Sinai on the confines of Egypt. As early at least as this, Asiatic conquerors had founded a "Hyksos" dominion in Egypt, which lasted more than six and a half centuries (661 years, to about 1600 B. C.). At this last date a remarkable civilization filled the region between the Euphrates and the Mediterranean; and to this, M. Maspero devotes an elaborate chapter, including a most interesting account of the Canaanites and their kindred the Phœnicians, whose commerce westward to Cyprus and North Africa and Greece was a notable fact of the time. The conquest of the region by Egypt from the southwest, and again by the Hittites from the north, prepared the way for Israelite invasion and settlement; upon which followed the rise and domination of Assyria, under which Israel was destined to be blotted out. The story of all this, including the earliest rise, and the development for many centuries, of Hebrew power and culture, gives M. Maspero's pages very great interest. The wealth of illustration, all of it strictly instructive, showing scenes in nature and ancient objects from photographs, adds very much to the reader's interest and to the value of the work. The two superb volumes are virtually the story of the ancient Eastern world for 3000 years, or from 3850 B. C. to 850 B. C. And the latest discoveries indicate that a record may be made out going back through an earlier 3000 years to about 7000 B. C.

DAWN OF THE XIXTH CENTURY IN ENGLAND, THE: 'A Social Sketch of the Times,' by John Ashton (1890. 5th ed. 1906). With 116 illustrations, drawn by the author from contemporary engravings. Never in the history of the world has there been such a change in things social as since the beginning of the nineteenth century; and to those who are watching its close, already at the dawn of the twentieth, this work is one of invaluable reference and comparison. The arts, sciences, manufactures, customs, and manners, were then so widely divergent from those of to-day, that it seems hardly possible that they belong to the same era, or could have existed less than one hundred years ago. Steam was then in its infancy; locomotives and steamships just beginning to be heard of; gas a novel experiment; electricity a scientific plaything. Beginning with a slight retrospect of the eighteenth century, the author briefly outlines the influence of Bonaparte in matters political; follows with a description of the food riots in London; the union with Ireland; death of Lord Nelson; abolition of the slave trade; amusing photographs of the streets with their beggars, chimney-sweeps, dealers of small wares and great cries; then the postal drawbacks and stage-coach infelicities; the famous prisons, notably the Fleet; museums and museum gardens, theatres and operas; Tattersall's and Gretna Green marriages; with innumerable extracts relating to people and places of note; — all taken from original and authentic sources, newspapers being an authority of constant reference. The quaint illustrations add much to the interest of the work which extends a little over a decade.

DAY OF DOOM, THE, by Michael Wigglesworth. When this poem was published in 1662, Michael Wigglesworth was only thirty-one, — young enough to have had greater compassion on the unbaptized infants and others whom he condemned to eternal punishment. 'The Day of Doom: or, A Poetical Description of the Great and Last Judgment, with a short Discourse about Eternity,' was the full title of this grim poem. The taste of our ancestors was strangely shown by their quickly buying up nine editions of this work in America, and two in England. Its narrow theology and severity of style gave it a charm for those inflexible Puritans, to find which, we of to-day look in vain. It is said to have been the most widely read book in America before the Revolution. The modern reader finds the verse mere sing-song, the metaphors forced, and the general tone decidedly unpleasant. Some of the passages meant to be most impressive have become merely ludicrous, and it seems incredible that it could ever have been taken seriously. It is merely a rhymed catalogue of the punishments to be visited on those whose ways of life, or whose theology, differed from the theology or ways of life of the bard.

DAYS NEAR ROME, by Augustus J. C. Hare (1875). A very pleasant and instructive record of excursions into the country around Rome. The book is supplementary to the author's 'Walks in Rome,' which supplies an excellent handbook of the city and environs of Rome. As that work treated, more fully and carefully than the usual guide-book, the most interesting aspects of the ancient city, and especially the latest discoveries of the recent explorers, so the 'Days' gives an interesting story of what can be seen in a variety of journeys away from the city. It is to a large extent a story of regions unknown to travel, and not reported upon in any of the guide-books. It is so written, moreover, as to serve the purpose of those who must travel only as readers. The author added to his 'Days' a third work of like character and interest, on 'Cities of Northern and Central Italy,' designed to be a companion to all those parts of Italy which lie between the Alps and the districts, described in the 'Days.' The three works tell the present story of the city and of Italy, whether for the traveler or for the reader.

DE JURE BELLI AC PACIS, see RIGHTS OF WAR AND PEACE.

DEAD SOULS, by N. V. Gogol (1846). This panorama of Russian national life is the greatest humorous novel in the Russian language. In the days of serfdom, "serfs" were referred to as "souls," and the value of a man's estate was reckoned by the number of "souls" he owned. The government, to induce colonization in southern Russia, offered tracts of land to anyone who would go there with enough serfs to till the soil. The hero, Chichikov, conceives the plan of buying up on paper serfs who have died since the last decennial census and are therefore officially alive in the records. With his hundreds of "dead souls" he will obtain the land, and then raise money by mortgaging serfs and land. While engaged in the acquisition of this strange property, he travels through Russia, and has many ludicrous adventures. In one community it is rumored that he is Napoleon, escaped from St. Helena, traveling in disguise. The reader is introduced to every kind of Russian of every grade of society, officials, landed proprietors, Russians drunk and sober. The general ignorance, dullness, and stupidity of the small town society is reflected in a comic mirror. At last he comes to grief through a scheme to forge a will. His former history of smuggling goods through the custom house, and his present transactions in dead souls are brought to light in the examination before the judge, and he is thrown into prison, just as he had acquired an estate, and repenting his crooked ways is about to turn his energies to living a respectable life. He escapes by spiriting away the witnesses, bribing the officials and involving prominent people in his scandalous affairs. He starts on his travels again, this time to find a wife and settle down, and after some misadventures he succeeds in his quest. After ten years of the life of a model country gentleman he is elected marshall for his district, in spite of rumors that he had once speculated in corpses to utilize their bones for commerce. He lives to a green old age with his wife and nine children, generally esteemed and respected. Gogol wrote a second part, but destroyed the manuscript. See the Library.

DEATH AND THE FOOL (' Der Tor und der Tod),' by Hugo von Hofmannsthal (1893). In this type of symbolic drama, mood and sensation are represented rather than character or event. Claudio, alone at the window of his luxurious study, watching the sunset, broods over the melancholy thought that he has never been more than a spectator of life, that though he has had everything, nothing has brought him happiness or sorrow. The music of a violin enchants him and seems to stir his sluggish soul. He looks for the musician and sees it is Death come to claim his life. Claudio in terror makes the plea that he is not ready to die, because he has not yet really lived. Death summons his lost opportunities to teach him the lesson he has not learned in mortal life. First his mother appears to tell of the love he had not appreciated; then the woman he threw aside "unthinking, cruel, as a child, of playing wearied, drops his flowers"; last the man whose friendship he betrayed. Claudio sinks at Death's feet, asking death as a boon, since Death has given him in one little hour more of life than he has ever known. He reflects that at last he has lived — "passed out of life's dreaming into death's awakening."

DEATH OF IVAN ILYITCH, THE, AND OTHER STORIES, by Count Lyof N. Tolstoy (1886), contains a series of short stories which represent the latest phase in the evolution of the author's peculiar views. With the exception of 'The Death of Ivan Ilyitch,' a sombre and powerful study of the insidious progress of fatal disease, and a vehicle of religious philosophy, these tales were written as tracts for the people, illustrated in many cases with quaint wood-cuts; aiming to bring a word of cheer and comfort to the poorer classes oppressed by Russian despotism. The second story, 'If You Neglect the Fire, You Don't Put It Out,' describes a trivial neighborhood quarrel resulting in ruin. 'Where Love Is, there God Is Also' is the study of a humble shoemaker who blames God for the death of his child, but reaches peace through the New Testament. 'A Candle' and 'Two Old Men,' told in a few pages, point a wide moral. 'Six Texts for Wood-Cuts,' the titles of which suggest the subject of each cut, follow. Under the heading of 'Popular Legends' are the subjects 'How the Little Devil Earned a Crust of Bread'; 'The Repentant Sinner'; 'A Seed as Big as a Hen's Egg'; and 'Does a Man Need Much Land?'

DÉBÂCLE, LA, see **ROUGON-MACQUART.**

DEBIT AND CREDIT ('Soll und Haben'), by Gustav Freytag (1855). In this story are portrayed with rare keenness and fidelity the characteristics of German nationality in its various classes. The honorable independence, patriotism, commercial

sagacity, and cultured commonsense of the middle industrial class, which forms the
solid substratum of society, are well contrasted with the impassible exclusiveness and
pecuniary irresponsibility of the nobility on the one hand, and the stolid ignorance
of the peasantry and the scheming of the Jews on the other. Written in the troublous
times after '48, its avowed purpose was to arouse the German youth to a sense of their
opportunities and responsibilities, — a purpose in which it succeeded. Its truthfulness to life, its delightful diction and variety of incident, assured its immediate
popularity; and to-day it is regarded as the best German novel of the age. Most of
the action is influenced by counting-house ethics; and it is emphatically the story of
the old commercial house of Schröter. Yet with what an inferior artist would have
found prosaic material, Freytag produces an intensely dramatic tale, its realism
transfused and illuminated by a glowing imagination. The plot is intricate and
exciting, but the value of the story lies in its strong studies of character, and the sense
it conveys of inevitability, in its logical deduction of event from cause. An excellent
English translation was published in 1874.

DECAMERON, THE, written by Giovanni Boccaccio about 1349, is a collection of
one hundred prose tales, enclosed in a clever and attractive framework. During the
pestilence of 1348 seven ladies and three gentlemen of Florence take refuge in the
country, traveling from one country-house to another and passing the time in games,
reading, conversation, love-making, and the telling of stories. One of the number is
appointed king or queen for each day, and under his or her direction each member of
the company contributes one narrative each day, for ten days; after which they
return to their homes. The various stories are adapted to their narrators, and are
told in a natural sequence, one suggesting another; moreover the descriptions of the
surroundings and occupations of the company and of the by-play between them make
an effective and dramatic background. The stories taken as a whole cover almost
every phase of human life, the pathetic, the humorous, the base, and the noble.
Many are satirical tales of clerical misconduct or of feminine guile; others are humorous but indecent anecdotes of the French *fabliau* type. These classes spring from
the revolt against asceticism. Other groups are elaborated from popular tales or
romances like the story of Gilletta of Narbonne, the source of Shakespeare's 'All's
Well that Ends Well.' Among the tragic love stories are those of Tancred and
Ghismonda and Isabella and the Pot of Basil. Famous tales of an idealistic and
moral character are the Jew's story of the three rings, used by Lessing in 'Nathan
der Weise'; the story of the Knight and the Falcon, retold by Tennyson and Longfellow; and an analogue of Chaucer's 'Franklin's Tale' of the rash promise; and the
original of his story of Griselda. Boccaccio was supremely interested in humanity,
was a consummate narrator, and, though overfond of involved classical periods, is
the father of modern Italian prose style.

DECLINE AND FALL OF THE ROMAN EMPIRE, THE, by Edward Gibbon.
"It was at Rome, on the 15th of October, 1764, as I sat musing amidst the ruins of
the capitol, while the barefooted friars were singing vespers in the temple of Jupiter,
that the idea of writing the decline and fall of the city first entered my mind," wrote
Gibbon in his autobiography. In 1776 the first volume of the great work was
finished. Its success was tremendous; and the reputation of the author was firmly
established before the religious world could prepare itself for an attack on its famous
15th and 16th chapters. The last volume was finished on the 27th of June, 1787, at
Lausanne, whither he had retired for quiet and economy. In his 'Memoirs' he

tells the hour of his release from those protracted labors — between eleven o'clock and midnight; and records his first emotions of joy on the recovery of his freedom, and then the sober melancholy that succeeded it when he realized that his life's work was done.

'The Decline and Fall' has been pronounced by many the greatest achievement of human thought and erudition in the department of history. The tremendous scope of the work is best explained by a brief citation from the author's preface to the first volume: "The memorable series of revolutions which, in the course of thirteen centuries, gradually undermined, and at length destroyed, the solid fabric of human greatness, may, with some propriety, be divided into the three following periods: I. The first of these periods may be traced from the age of Trajan and the Antonines, when the Roman monarchy, having attained its full strength and maturity, began to verge toward its decline. . . . II. The second may be supposed to begin with the reign of Justinian, who by his laws as well as his victories restored a transient splendor to the Eastern Empire. . . . III. The third from the revival of the Western Empire to the taking of Constantinople by the Turks It is, then, a history of the civilized world for thirteen centuries, during which paganism was breaking down, and Christianity was superseding it; and so bridges over the chasm between the old world and the new.

The great criticism of the work has always been upon the point of Gibbon's estimate of the nature and influence of Christianity.

Aside from this, it can safely be said that modern scholarship finds very little that is essential to be changed in Gibbon's wonderful studies; while his noble dignity of style and his picturesqueness of narration make this still the most fascinating of histories.

DEEMSTER, THE, by Hall Caine (1877). 'The Deemster' is a sensational novel, setting forth the righteousness of just retribution. The author calls it the story of the Prodigal Son. The scene is laid in the Isle of Man, in the latter part of the seventeenth century and the early part of the eighteenth.

The Deemster is Thorkell Mylrea, whose brother Gilchrist is bishop of the island. These two brothers, with Ewan and Mona, the son and daughter of the Deemster, and Daniel, the son of the Bishop, are the chief actors in the story. Ewan is a young clergyman, but Dan is the prodigal who wastes his father's substance. He loves his cousin Mona deeply, but her brother considers this love dishonorable to her. The cousins engage in a duel, which results in the death of Ewan. Dan surrenders himself to justice, is declared guilty, and receives a sentence worse than death. He is declared cut off forever from his people. None shall speak to him or look upon him or give him aid. He shall live and die among the beasts in a remote corner of the island.

At length a strange plague comes upon the people. Daniel obtains the privilege of taking the place of Father Dalby, the Irish priest. He effects many cures, and at last dies of the pestilence, after the office of deemster made vacant by his uncle's death has been offered to him as a reward for his services. Like all of Hall Caine's work, it is sombre and oppressive, but its delineation of Manx character is striking and convincing. A dramatization has been produced by Wilson Barrett under the title 'Ben-Ma-Chree.'

DEEPHAVEN, by Sarah Orne Jewett. Deephaven is an imaginary seaport town, famous for its shipping in the old days, — like so many towns along the northern coast of New England, — and now a sleepy, picturesque old place in which to dream away a summer.   Kate Lancaster and Helen Denis, two bright, sympathetic girls, go to live in the Brandon house there; and the story tells of the glimpses they get into New England life, and the friendships they make, during that summer.   Mrs. Kew, of the lighthouse, is the most delightful character in the book, although Mrs. Dockum and the alert "Widow Jim" prove to be interesting neighbors.   Mr. Lorimer the minister, his sister Miss Honora Carew and the members of her household, represent the gentlefolk of the town, and visionary Captain Sands, Isaac Horn, and kind-hearted Danny, the seafaring ones, — not without Jacob Lunt "condemned as unseaworthy."   Old Mrs. Bonny lives in the woods beyond the town; and Miss Chauncey, a pathetic old lady who has lost her mind, lives alone in the village of East Parish.   When the leaves have fallen and the sea looks rough and cold, the two heroines close the old house and return to their homes in the city, — the inevitable end.   This was one of the first books on New England life Miss Jewett wrote; and it was published in 1877, when she was only twenty years old.   The book has done for the region it describes something of what Irving's writing did for the Hudson River.

DEERSLAYER, THE, a novel of frontier life, one of the 'Leatherstocking Tales' by James Fenimore Cooper, published in 1841.   The hero, Natty Bumppo, called Deerslayer in this novel, is represented as a young hunter brought up among the Delawares and engaged in guerilla warfare with the Hurons in the wilderness of northern New York State between the years 1740 and 1745.   With a gigantic trapper, Henry March, nicknamed "Hurry Harry" he defends the family of a settler, Tom Hutter, who has built a wooden fortress in the midst of a lonely lake, which he also navigates in a kind of house-boat.   After a series of exciting adventures in which a band of invading Hurons, a Delaware chief, Chingachgook, and a Delaware maiden, Wah-ta-wah, are involved, and in the course of which the hero is imprisoned by the redskins, the Hurons are driven off with the aid of the British troops.   The love of Judith Hutter for Deerslayer is not reciprocated, and they part.   The other sister, Hetty Hutter, who loves Hurry Harry is slain by a chance bullet in the assault by the soldiers.   Although lacking humor, psychological subtlety, and delicacy of characterization this story is of absorbing narrative interest and preserves some excellent types of pioneer days.   See also 'Leatherstocking Tales.'

DEGENERATION, by Max Nordau (1895).   A work which attracted great attention, and provoked a storm of opposition and of argument.   A product in equal parts of German profundity of learning and one-sidedness of outlook, it is an attempt at "scientific criticism" of those "degenerates" not upon the acknowledged lists of the criminal classes.   The author in his dedication says: "Degenerates are not always criminals, prostitutes, anarchists, and pronounced lunatics; they are often authors and artists.   These, however, manifest the same mental characteristics, and for the most part the same somatic features, as the members of the above-mentioned anthropological family, who satisfy their unhealthy impulses with the knife of the assassin or the bomb of the dynamiter, instead of with pen and pencil.   Some among these degenerates in literature, music, and painting, have in recent years come into extraordinary prominence. . . .   Now I have undertaken the work of investigating the tendencies of the fashions in art and literature; of proving that they have their source in the degeneracy of their authors, and that the enthusiasm of their admirers is for manifestations of more or less pronounced moral insanity and dementia."

The author undertakes this large task with cheerfulness and assurance.   In five subdivisions of his tonic — 'Fin-de-Siècle,' 'Mysticism,' 'Ego-Mania,' 'Realism,' and 'The Twentieth Century' — he discusses those manifestations of modern thought and feeling in art and literature which he is pleased to term "degenerate." Scarcely a man of note in these departments escapes. Zola, Wagner, Tolstoy, Ibsen, Nietzsche, Rossetti, and the other pre-Raphaelites, are, so to speak, placed in strait-jackets and confined in padded cells.

The book is an extraordinary manifestation of the philistine spirit of the close of the 19th century. For a time it had an enormous vogue; the calm judgment of science, however, tends to deny many of its propositions.

DELECTABLE DUCHY, THE, by "Q" (Sir A. T. Quiller-Couch). A book of stories, studies, and sketches, some gay and some tragic, but all brief, concise, and dramatic. The scene of all is laid in Cornwall (the Delectable Duchy); they are full of folk-lore, local superstitions and expressions. Among the best are 'The Spinster's Maying,' where the old maid induces the twin brother of her dead lover to court her every year on May Day; 'When the Sap Rose,' full of the joy of springtime; 'The Plumpers'; 'Egg-Stealing'; 'The Regent's Wager,' a mistake which lost one man his life and another his reason; and 'The Conspiracy aboard the Midas,' to make a dying child's last days happy. These stories were published in 1893, and are the high-water mark of the writer's work, though he has won reputation as a critic and journalist as well as a story-teller. See the LIBRARY.

DELIVERANCE, THE, by Ellen Glasgow (1904). This is a romance of the Virginia tobacco fields and has for its central figure Christopher Blake. He is the descendant of a rich and aristocratic family, and through reduced fortunes is obliged to work as a laborer on the estate which for generations had been owned by his forbears. Upon the death of his father, when he is only ten years old, he suddenly finds home and fortune snatched from him, and with a blind mother and two sisters to support he begins a life of toil. He foregoes education and drudges unceasingly that his mother may be kept in ignorance of her change of fortune and that his twin sister may not have to work. After fifteen years of this existence his nature becomes hardened and his heart is filled with hatred for Mr. Fletcher, the past manager of the estate, who is now its possessor. Fletcher, who is a vulgar and ugly tempered man, has gained his possessions by cheating and dishonesty, and Christopher's one thought from childhood has been a desire for revenge. He finds his opportunity in leading to ruin Fletcher's grandson, Will, a weak young fellow, who is idolized by his grandfather. Christopher leads him into dissipation and teaches him to despise his grandfather till finally in a moment of drunken frenzy he kills him. Then Christopher realizes the enormity of his sin, aids Will to escape, himself confesses to the crime, and takes the punishment. He goes to prison to serve out a five years' sentence, but after three years have passed is pardoned out through the efforts of Maria Wyndham, Fletcher's granddaughter, whom he has loved for years. Maria, who has returned his affection and is now the heir to the estate, is only too glad to restore it to its rightful owner, and the lovers, after their many years of unhappiness, are at last united.

DELPHINE, by Madame de Staël, was her first romance; it was published in 1802. The heroine is an ideal creation. Madame d'Albemar (Delphine), a young widow, devotedly attached to her husband's memory, falls promptly in love with Léonce as soon as she meets him. The feeling is reciprocated, and Léonce bitterly repents his engagement to Delphine's cousin Mathilde. But Delphine's mother, Madame de

Vernon, a treacherous, intriguing woman, determines to separate the lovers; and the story relates the progress of her machinations.

Its bold imagery, keenness of observation, and power of impassioned description, perhaps justify 'Delphine's' position among the masterpieces of French literature. But neither situations nor characters are true to nature. The only real person in the book is Madame de Vernon, a mixture of pride, duplicity, ostentation, avarice, polished wickedness, and false good-nature. But the romance had a special interest for Madame de Staël's contemporaries, for several of the great men and women of the time appear in it under the thinnest of disguises. M. de Lebensée, the noble Protestant, is Benjamin Constant; the virtuous and accomplished Madame de Cerlèbe is Madame de Staël's mother; Delphine is of course Madame de Staël herself; and Madame de Vernon is Talleyrand: "So we are both," said he to her, "in your last book, I hear; I disguised as an old woman, and you as a young one." The liberal ideas scattered through the story drew down on the author the anger of Napoleon, who ordered her to leave France.

DELUGE, THE, by David Graham Phillips (1905). This is the story, given in his own words, of Matthew Blacklock, a hero of finance and a self-made man. He is endowed with brains, a powerful will, and striking personality and has worked his way from the foot of the ladder until he has become a conspicuous figure in Wall Street. While still young, he has amassed a fortune and has surrounded himself with all the luxuries of life, but is not admitted to the inner circles of society where he aspires to be. Blacklock, or Black Matt as he is familiarly called has men friends belonging to this exclusive class who have not scrupled to accept his business "tips" but who never entertain him socially. This is a source of great dissatisfaction to Matt who does not realize his lack of social training and feels his success in life has made him eligible for any company. He meets Anita Ellersly, the sister of one of his aristocratic friends, and in spite of her evident repugnance for him makes up his mind to win her for his wife. He secures his entrée into their family circle by assisting Anita's father, who is financially involved, and when he proposes marriage is accepted by Anita who tells him she can never care for him as she loves someone else. The latter proves to be Mowray Langdon, an old lover of Anita's, who is unhappily married and who has had business dealings with Matt. After the engagement is made public Langdon does everything in his power to ruin Matt financially and almost succeeds. Mr. and Mrs. Ellersly hearing that Matt is ruined cast him off, but Anita disgusted at her parents' actions decides to marry him and does so immediately. Matt extricates himself from his financial embarrassment by a series of successful business coups which are graphically described in the story, and tries to win the affection of his wife who holds herself aloof from him. Finally Matt, who has never known the meaning of the word fail, succeeds in gaining Anita's love and she confesses that she has cared for him almost from the first but has been too proud to acknowledge it.

DELUGE, by Henryk Sienkiewicz, see **WITH FIRE AND SWORD.**

DEMOCRACY AND EDUCATION, a sociological and philosophical treatise by John Dewey, was published in 1916. It affords the clearest statement of the author's psychological, ethical, and educational views, which are here applied to the solution of educational problems in the modern democratic state. The book falls into four parts. Chapters I. to VII. outline the general nature of education and its function in society. Education is defined as "that reconstruction or reorganizati   of experience which adds to the meaning of experience, and which increases ability to direct the course of subsequent experience." This result is obtained by a process of transmission, partly spontaneous, partly deliberate, of the acquirements of society, with the aim of preserving social continuity. Democratic societies are those which afford equal opportunity for development and equal social privileges to all their members. To be adapted to a democratic society, education must give all individuals a personal interest in social relationships, and the power of effecting social changes without disorder. It must not trust merely to the force of custom, operating under the control of a superior class.

In the second part of the book (Chapters VIII.–XVII.), coming down to particular questions of subject-matter and method, the author shows that education aims at natural development, social efficiency, and mental enrichment; that discipline, or the presentation of a lesson to be learned as a task, must be united with interest, or the realization by the pupil of the relation of this task to his own activities and — personal concerns; that thinking must be preceded by experience, mental instruction by physical experiment; that the pupil must be encouraged to think for himself and to work out his own mental conclusions; and that the subject-matter of education must not be mere information, but information which he can apply in some way to some situation of his own. Occupational training, in order to be truly educative, must require the pupil's judgment and admit the possibility of mistakes. Play is distinguished from work in that its aim is continued activity and not a definite result. Being a necessity of our nature, it must be provided for in every scheme of education. Geography and history enlarge the significance of the pupil's experience of nature and man; science broadens his horizon and cultivates the power of generalized thinking.

The third part (Chapters XVIII.–XXIII.) examines the hindrances to ideal democratic education which spring from the notion "that experience consists of a variety of segregated domains or interests, each having its own independent value, material, and method, each checking every other." This theory, which results from the division of society into rigidly-marked classes and groups, issues in certain dualisms or antitheses between culture and utility, leisure and labor, intellectual and practical studies, social and physical subjects, the individual and society, liberal and vocational training. All these contradictions Dewey would remove by rejecting the dualism which prompted them. All pupils are to have the opportunity of enjoying both types of training, in preparation for serving the state as a whole.

In conclusion (Chapters XXIV.–XXVI.) the author states his philosophy of education in connection with the theory of knowledge and of conduct. As regards knowledge he is a pragmatist, or, as he prefers to call himself, an experimentalist, believing that truth is determined by the practical test of experience. In ethics he believes that the moral life of the individual is one, not separated into provinces of inner and outer, duty and interest, intelligence and character.

The book abounds in helpful definitions, clear distinctions, and genuine reconciliations of opposite ideas. The expository method is clear, and made even more lucid by the summaries appended to each chapter and by the plain, sometimes even colloquial diction. A reviewer has called this the most important educational treatise since Plato and Rousseau.

DEMOCRACY AND LIBERTY, by W. E. H. Lecky (2 vols., 1896). A strong book "dealing with the present aspects and tendencies of the political world in many different countries," and with special reference to the fact that "the most remarkable political characteristic of the latter part of the nineteenth century has unquestionably been the complete displacement of the centre of power in free governments, — a profound and far-reaching revolution, over a great part of the civilized world." The work is not one of history, but one of "discussion of contemporary questions, some of them lying in the very centre of party controversies," and one "expressing strong opinions on many much-contested party questions." Besides dealing with England, Ireland, America, and much of Europe, it also discusses socialism, Sunday and drink legislation, woman questions and labor questions, marriage and divorce, religious liberty, and Catholicism. It is a book of able discussion and strong convictions, by a writer who has many doubts about modern democratic developments, but too competent and too just to be scouted.

DEMOCRACY AND THE ORGANIZATION OF POLITICAL PARTIES, by M. Ostrogorski with a preface by Bryce (1902). As Lord Bryce well points out in the preface to this book there is room for a treatise which shall take Party Organization and Party Machinery for its specific subject, and shall endeavor to treat these phenomena of modern politics with a fulness commensurate to the importance of the part which they play to-day in popular governments. The author, a Frenchman of extraordinarily thorough and penetrating intellect, who has at the same time the clarity and impartiality of the best writers of his race, spares neither the Republicans nor the Democrats of the United States, neither the Tories nor the Liberals of England. He perhaps allows too much influence to the caucus in England and to the social pressure which has undoubtedly been exercised by landlords or other interested parties. After a most careful examination of the facts in both countries he reaches the conclusion that party organization in England is on the highway to becoming what it already is in the United States. "The democratization of the party system," he says, "was nothing but a change of form and could not cure the original defect, either of its principle, or of the methods by which it was carried out. Thenceforth the system could only produce effects which were the negation of democracy. Incapable of realizing its essence, the system reduced political relations to an external conformity, which warped their moral spring and ended by enslaving the mind of the citizens and opening the door to corruption. To the low types which the human race has produced, from Cain down to Tartuffe, the age of democracy has added a new one — the politician . . . the motley soul of the politician is made up of innumerable pettinesses, with but one trait to give them unity — cowardice." The remedy for these evils, in the opinion of M. Ostrogorski is, on the practical side, to discard the use of permanent parties whose aim is political power, and to establish a system of proportional representation. But obviously the victory over machine politics must first be won in the mind of the elector. "Men must be taught to use their judgment, and to act independently. It is on the accomplishment of this work of liberation that the whole future of democracy depends. Hitherto the victorious struggle which democracy has carried on in the world has been mainly, and necessarily, a struggle for material liberty; moral liberty, which consists in thinking and acting as free reason dictates, has yet to be achieved by it. It has carried the habeas corpus by force, but the decisive battle of democracy will be fought on the habeas animum."

DEMOCRACY IN AMERICA, an account of the government and institutions of the United States by Alexis de Tocqueville, published in 1835. For a summary and estimate of this work see the introductory essay on De Tocqueville in the LIBRARY.

DEMOCRACY IN EUROPE: 'A History,' by T. Erskine May (2 vols., 1877). A thoroughly learned and judicious study of popular power and political liberty throughout the history of Europe. Starting from an introduction on the causes of freedom, especially its close connection with civilization, the research deals with the marked absence of freedom in Oriental history, and then reviews the developments of popular power in Greece and Rome, and the vicissitudes of progress in the Dark Ages to the Revival of Learning. It then traces the new progress in the Italian republics, Switzerland, the Netherlands, France, and England. The work shows careful study of the inner life of republics, ancient and modern; of the most memorable revolutions, and the greatest national struggles for civil and religious liberty; and of the various degrees and conditions of democracy, considered as the sovereignty of the whole body of the people. The author regards popular power as an essential condition of the social advancement of nations, and writes as an ardent admirer of rational and enlightened political liberty.

DEMONOLOGY AND DEVIL-LORE, by Moncure D. Conway (1879). In this scholarly history of a superstition, the author has set before himself the task of finding "the reason of unreason, the being and substance of unreality, the law of folly, and the logic of lunacy." His business is not alone to record certain dark vagaries of human intelligence, but to explain them; to show them as the inevitable expression of a mental necessity, and as the index to some spiritual facts with large inclusions. He sees that primitive man has always personified his own thoughts in external personal forms; and that these personifications survive as traditions long after a more educated intelligence surrenders them as facts. He sets himself, therefore, to seek in these immature and grotesque imaginings the soul of truth and reality that once inspired them. From anthropology, history, tradition, comparative mythology and philology; from every quarter of the globe; from periods which trail off into prehistoric time, and from periods almost within our own remembrance; from savage and from cultivated races; from extinct peoples and those now existing; from learned sources and the traditions of the unlearned, he has sought his material. This vast accumulation of facts he has so analyzed and synthesized as to make it yield its fine ore of truth concerning spiritual progress. Related beliefs he has grouped either in natural or historical association; migrations of beliefs he has followed, with a keen sense for their half-obliterated trail; through diversities his trained eye discovers likenesses. He finds that devils have always stood for the type of pure malignity; while demons are creatures driven by fate to prey upon mankind for the satisfaction of their needs, but not of necessity malevolent. The demon is an inference from the physical experience of mankind; the devil is a product of his moral consciousness. The dragon is a creature midway between the two.

DESCENT OF MAN AND SELECTION IN RELATION TO SEX, THE, by Charles Darwin. The 'Descent of Man' was given to the world in 1871, eleven years after the appearance of the 'Origin of Species,' when Darwin was sixty-two years old. In spite of the opposition which the theories of the earlier work had met in some quarters, it had already given him a place as a leader of scientific thought, not only in England but in the whole world. "Darwinism" had in fact become a definite term, and the new book was received with interest. The evidences of the descent of man from some earlier, less-developed form, collected and marshaled by Darwin, consist of minute inferential proofs of similarity of structure; at certain stages of development, between man and the lower animals. This similarity is especially marked in the embryonic stages; and taken with the existence in man of various rudimentary organs, seems to imply that he and the lower animals come from a common ancestor. From the evidences thus collected, Darwin reasons that the early ancestors of man must have been more or less monkey-like animals of the great anthropoid group, and related to the progenitors of the orang-outang, the chimpanzee, and the gorilla. They must have been hairy, with pointed, movable ears, and a movable tail. They probably lived in trees, and had a thumb-like great toe, ate fruit chiefly, and made their home in a warm forest land. Going back still farther, Darwin shows that the remotest ancestor of humanity must have been aquatic. As a partial proof of this, human lungs are said to be modified swim-bladders. The general descent is given by Darwin some- what in this fashion: From the jelly-like larva to the early fishes, such as the lancelet, then to the ganoids (as the mudfish), to the newt and other amphibians, then to the platypus and other mammals such as the kangaroo, and to the insectivorous animals such as the shrews and hedgehogs; after this by well-marked stages to the lemurs of Madagascar, and then to the monkeys, which branch into those of the Old and the New World, — from the latter of which man is descended. Without entering here into the question as to whether all the steps were proved, it is enough to say that the 'Descent of Man' was received with enthusiasm by scientific men, and that its immediate influence was even greater than that of the 'Origin of Species.' It had an effect not merely on physical and biological science, but it led to many new con- ceptions in ethics and religion. In the volumes containing the 'Descent of Man' Darwin placed his elaborate treatise on 'Sexual Selection,' which indeed may be regarded as a part of the theory of man's descent. The theory of a common origin of man and the other vertebrates was not new; but he was the first to develop a tenable theory as to the process.

DESTINY, by Susan Edmonston Ferrier. This story, published in 1831, is the last and best of the three novels by the Scotch authoress. The scene of action is the Highlands, and fashionable London society in the first part of the nineteenth century. Written in a clear, bright style, in spite of its length it is interesting throughout. Its tone is serious, but the gravity is brightened by a delightful humor, which reveals both the ludicrous and the sad side of a narrow-minded and conventional society. The reader laughs at the arrogant and haughty chief Glenroy, growing more child- ishly obstinate and bigoted as he grows older, and at his echo and retainer Benbowie, at the self-sufficient and uncouth pastor M'Dow; and at the supercilious Lady Elizabeth, who thinks herself always *recherchée*.

The plot involves constant changes in the lot of the characters, the moral being that no man can escape his destiny. Somewhat old-fashioned, and much too long the book is still agreeable reading.

DESTINY OF MAN, THE, 'Viewed in the Light of his Origin,' by John Fiske. (1884. 9th ed. 1886). This argument, originally an address delivered before the Concord School of Philosophy, gives the simplest possible statement of the general theory — not the particular processes — of evolution, and openly endeavors to reconcile the spirit and teachings of modern science with those of the New Testament. While declaring that the brain of an Australian savage is many times further removed from Shakespeare's than from an orang-outang's, he yet shows that evolution, far from degrading man to the level of the beast, makes it evident that man is the chief object of the Divine care. Man *is*, after all, the center of the universe — though not in the sense that the oppressors of Bruno and Galileo supposed. And before man's reinstatement in his central and dominant position became possible, the limited and distorted hypothesis of theologians and poets had to be overthrown. Much stress is laid on the insignificance of physical in comparison with psychical phenomena: more amazing than the change from a fin to a fore-limb are the psychical variations that set in (almost to the exclusion of physical variations) after the beginnings of intelligence in the human species. The superiority of man lies not in perfection but in *improvableness*. The body is becoming a mere vehicle for that soul which for a long time was only an appendage to it. On scientific grounds there is no argument for immortality and none against it; but if the work of evolution does not culminate in immortality, then the universe is indeed reduced to a meaningless riddle.

DEVIL ON TWO STICKS, THE, see **ASMODEUS.**

DHAMMAPADA, see **SACRED BOOKS OF THE EAST.**

DIALOGUES OF PLATO, a series of philosophical treatises in dramatic form, in which problems metaphysical, ethical, and political are discussed by Socrates, his friends and pupils. They were written between the death of Socrates in 399 B. C. and that of Plato in 347 B. C., mainly at the Academy, which Plato established just outside of Athens in 387 B. C. Thirty-five extant dialogues are attributed to Plato, of which seven are now regarded as spurious. Of these the most noted are. the 'Laches,' 'Charmides,' and 'Lysis' in which Socrates attempts to elicit by questions the definition of courage, temperance, and friendship respectively; 'Protagoras' and 'Meno' discussing the question whether virtue can be taught and attacking the Sophists; 'Ion,' relating to poetical inspiration; 'Euthyphro,' 'Apologia,' 'Crito,' and 'Phædo' all concerned with the trial and death of Socrates; the 'Symposium,' 'Phædrus' and 'Cratylus,' which develop fully the Platonic doctrine of ideas; the 'Gorgias,' a discussion of justice; the 'Republic,' a description of an ideal state; the 'Euthydemus,' 'Parmenides,' 'Theætetus,' 'Sophist,' 'Statesman,' 'Philebus,' all dealing with the theory of knowledge; the 'Timæus,' an account of the origin and nature of the external world; and the 'Laws,' a suggested code for a Greek state. For a statement of Plato's distinctive doctrines and an estimate of their worth and influence see Professor Shorey's article under 'Plato' in the 'LIBRARY.' The best English translation of Plato is that by Benjamin Jowett (1871–1892).

DIALOGUES OF THE DEAD, by Lucian. These dialogues, written at Athens during the latter half of the second century, are among the author's most popular and familiar works. They have been translated by many hands, from the days of Erasmus to the present; an excellent modern translation being that by Howard Williams in Bohn's Classical Library. They are filled with satire, bitter or delicate according to the subject, and illustrate admirably Lucian's ready wit, and light, skillful touch.

The scene is laid in Hades; and the only persons appearing to advantage are the Cynics Menippus and Diogenes, who are distinguished by their scorn of falsehood and pretense. The Sophists are mercilessly treated; and even Aristotle is accused of corrupting the youthful Alexander by his flatteries. Socrates is well spoken of, but is said to have dreaded death, the Cynics being the only ones to seek it willingly. The decadent Olympian religion and the old Homeric heroes are exposed to ridicule, and it is twice demonstrated that the conception of Destiny logically destroys moral responsibility. There are several dialogues that hold up to scorn the parasites and legacy-hunters so abundant at Athens and Rome; and Alexander and Crœsus make themselves ridiculous by boasting of their former prowess and wealth. The futility of riches and fame is shown in the dialogue of the boat-load of people who have to discard all their cherished belongings and attributes before Charon will give them passage; only sterling moral qualities avail in the shadowy land of Hades, and only the Cynics are happy, for they have nothing left behind to regret, but have brought their treasure with them in an upright and fearless character.

DIALOGUES OF THE DEAD, by George, Lord Lyttelton. Lord Lyttelton is a writer with whom only students of the English language and literature are likely to be familiar. In fact, his only claims to recognition as a littérateur rest upon his 'Observations on the Conversion and Apostleship of St. Paul,' and the 'Dialogues' here presented, which first appeared in 1760. The conversation of the 'Dialogues' shows how thoroughly versed the writer must have been in the history of all times. The ruthless Cortez sneers at the humanitarian efforts of William Penn; Cardinal Ximenes haughtily pulls to pieces the reputation of his rival Wolsey; Boileau and Pope, the satirists, hold a highly instructive conversation upon the merits of their respective literatures; and then comes Charles XII. of Sweden in hot haste to Alexander the Great, with a proposition that they two "turn all these insolent scribblers out of Elysium, and throw them down headlong to the bottom of Tartarus in spite of Pluto and all his guards," because "an English poet, one Pope, has called us 'two madmen.'" Alexander demurs at this Draconic measure, and by a few leading questions, which he answers himself, soon shows the royal Swede that he was only a fool. In connection with this work, it is interesting to note the 'Dialogues des Morts,' by the French free-thinker Fontenelle, and the 'Imaginary Conversations,' by Walter Savage Landor. The first complete edition of Lord Lyttelton's works was published in London in 1776.

DIAMOND LENS, THE, a short story by Fitz-James O'Brien, which appeared originally in the Atlantic Monthly in 1858 and in a volume of his stories and essays collected and edited by William Winter in 1881. The narrator, Linley, becoming fascinated with microscopic study, determines to devote his life to its pursuit. His parents object, but being financially independent he goes to New York on the pretense of studying medicine, and buying the most expensive apparatus succeeds in one year in making himself an accomplished microscopist. Dissatisfied, however, with the revealing power of the best instruments he seeks the aid of a spiritualist medium, Madame Vulpes, who puts him into communication with the spirit of Leeuwenhoek, the father of microscopy. The great scientist informs him that the universal lens may be formed of a diamond of one hundred and forty carats, which must be subjected to electro-magnetic currents and pierced through its axis. On returning to the house on Fourth Avenue in which he has his rooms, an impulse leads Linley to visit a fellow-lodger, a French Jew named Jules Simon, who hastily conceals something on his friend's entrance and is greatly agitated when he learns of Lindley's desire for a diamond. The latter, by making Simon drunk, finds out that the Jew has a diamond of exactly one hundred and forty carats which he has stolen from a mine in Brazil and is unable to dispose of. Lindley promptly administers laudanum to the Frenchman and then stabs him to the heart, so arranging the room that every evidence points to suicide, and that this explanation is adopted in the inquiry which follows. Possessed of the diamond, Lindley now constructs the lens and on its completion tests it with a drop of water. A marvelous world of richly colored vegetation and pure etherial radiance is revealed to his delighted gaze; and from the depths of these enchanted forests emerges a beautiful woman's form. With this being whom he christens Animula, the microscopist falls passionately in love; but as she inhabits a drop of water he can only spend hours in gazing at her beauty and in longing that he might enter her world. At length the water dries up, forests and lovely form wither and die, and Lindley goes mad and wrecks his microscope. For the rest of his life he is an object of derision or pity as "Lindley the mad microscopist." This exceedingly clever tale is told with an artistry and technical skill worthy of high honor in the annals of the American short story.

DIANA OF THE CROSSWAYS, a remarkable novel by George Meredith, appeared in 1885. It displays his power of drawing a living vibrant woman, in whom beauty and intellect and noble character are united. Diana is the centre of the book. In her light the other men and women live and move, and by her light they are judged. She is an Irishwoman of good family. As a girl she makes an unfortunate marriage with a Mr. Warwick, who so little knows her true character that he suspects her of an intrigue with a Lord Dannisburg, and begins proceedings against her. Diana's separation from her husband is the beginning of her picturesque but always honorable career, and the true initial point of the story. She is one of the most charming of Meredith's women. The famous incident of her betrayal of a political secret, as well as some traits of her character, was drawn from Lady Caroline Norton, Sheridan's granddaughter, famous for her beauty, her wit, and her independence of conventional opinion. It was later proved, however, that Lady Norton did not betray the secret; and this act remains to many readers an incomprehensible act on the part of Diana.

DIANA TEMPEST, by Mary Cholmondeley (1893). The clever author of 'Sir Charles Danvers' here attempts a more elaborate novel. It is a story of good society, wherein the motives potent in bad society — greed, envy, malice, and all unchari- tableness—have "room and verge enough." The plot deals with many sensational incidents, but the novel is really not sensational but an interesting study of the history of a family through several generations. The children in the book are drawn with a loving hand, the characterization is as good as in 'Sir Charles Danvers,' the dialogue is clever, the general treatment brilliant, and in its charming refinement the story has a place apart.

DIARY OF TWO PARLIAMENTS, by Sir H. W. Lucy (2 vols., 1885-86). A very graphic narrative of events as they passed in the Disraeli Parliament, 1874-80, and in the Gladstone Parliament, 1880-85. Mr. Lucy was the House of Commons reporter for the London Daily News, and as "Toby, M. P.," he supplied the Par- liamentary report published in Punch. His diary especially undertakes descriptions of the more remarkable scenes of the successive sessions of Parliament, and to give in skeleton form the story of Parliaments which are universally recognized as having been momentous and distinctive in recent English history. It includes full and minute descriptions of memorable episodes and notable men.

DICKENS, THE LIFE OF CHARLES, by John Forster (3 vols., 1872-74). This book of many defects has the excellence of being entertaining. It follows the life of its subject from his birth in poverty and obscurity in 1812, to his death in riches and fame in 1870. It extenuates nothing, because the biographer was incapable of seeing a foible, much more a fault, in the character and conduct of the friend whom he admired even more than he loved him. The poverty and sensitiveness of the lad, his menial work and his sense of responsibility for his elders, his thirst for knowledge and for the graces of life, his training to be a reporter, his experience on a newspaper, his early sketches, his first success in 'Pickwick,' his sudden reputation and prosperity, his first visit to America and his disillusionment, the history of his novels, of his readings, of his friendships, of his home life, of his second triumphant journey in the United States, — this time to read from his own books, — his whimsical and fun-loving nature, his agreeableness as a father, a comrade, and a host, his generosity, his respect for his profession, the sum of the qualities that made him both by temperament and performance a great actor, — all these things are fully set forth in the elaborate tribute which the biographer pays to his friend.   The books are interesting because the mass of material is interesting.   But it must be admitted that they give an exaggerated impression of one side of the character of Dickens, — his energetic, restless, insatiable activity, — and fail to do justice to his less self-conscious and more lovable qualities.   They are, however, to be reckoned among the important biographies of the time.   There are later studies of Dickens by George Gissing and by G. K. Chesterton, but these are literary interpretations rather than biographies.

DICTATOR, THE, by Justin McCarthy.   When Justin McCarthy published 'The Dictator,' in 1893, he had been known to the novel-reading public for twenty-six years, and had written a score of books.   'The Dictator,' a story of contemporary life in England, gives scope to its author for the display of his knowledge of politics.

The Dictator of the story, Ericson, when first introduced to the reader, has just been ejected by a revolution from his position as chief of the South American Republic, Gloria.   Of mixed English and Spanish blood, he has a fearless and honest soul.   The novel comes to a climax in a plot made against him by his enemies in Gloria.   Besides the hero, 'The Dictator' introduces two or three other characters of especial interest: Captain Sarrasin, who has traveled and fought in many countries, and whose wife on occasion can don men's garments and handle a gun; Dolores Paulo; and the Duchess of Deptford, of American birth, a caricature rather than a true type.   The plot involves the use of dynamite, and much mining and countermining; in spite of which the book remains an entertaining domestic story.

DICTIONARY, HISTORICAL AND CRITICAL, by Pierre Bayle (1697.   Second edition in 1702).   A work of the boldest "new-departure" character, by one of the master spirits of new knowledge and free thought two hundred years since.   Its author had filled various university positions from 1675 to 1693, and had been ejected at the latter date from the chair of philosophy and history at Rotterdam on account of his bold dealing with Maimbourg's 'History of Calvinism.'   From 1684 for several years he had published with great success a kind of journal of literary criticism, entitled 'Nouvelles de la République des Lettres.'   It was the first thoroughly successful attempt to popularize literature.   Bayle was essentially a modern journalist, whose extensive and curious information, fluent style, and literary breadth made him, and still make him, very interesting reading.   He was a skeptic on many subjects, not so much from any skeptical system as from his large knowledge and his broadly modern spirit.   His Dictionary is a masterpiece of fresh criticism, of inquiry conducted with great literary skill, and of emancipation of the human mind from the bonds of authority.   Its influence on the thought of the eighteenth century was profound, and the student of culture may still profitably consult its stores of information.

DICTUNG UND WAHRHEIT, see **GOETHE, AUTOBIOGRAPHY OF.**

DIDEROT AND THE ENCYCLOPEDISTS, by Viscount John Morley (1878). This examination of the life, the work, and the influence of "the most encyclopædic head that ever existed" (as Grimm termed Diderot), and his fellow-workers, is an admirable monograph. Of all the literary preparation for the French Revolution the 'Encyclopédie' was the symbol: it spread through the world a set of ideas that entered into vigorous conflict with the ancient scheme of authority. Diderot, as the head of the movement, D'Alembert his coadjutor, Voltaire, J. J. Rousseau, Buffon, Helvétius, Holbach, Raynal, etc., with other famous persons of the day, as Goethe, Garrick, the Empress Catherine II., — are here vividly depicted, with wide knowledge of books and of life, great skill in reading character, facility in disentangling causes and results, and broad philosophical perception of the historic position of the age. Anglo-Saxon readers find this work less one-sided than Taine's on the same subject. Appended to the book is a translation of the greater part of 'Rameau's Nephew,' Diderot's famous dialogue.

DIEUX ONT SOIF, LES, see **GODS ARE ATHIRST.**

DISCIPLE, THE ('Le Disciple') by Paul Bourget (1889), in its eloquent preface, which is the best part of the book, calls upon the young men of the present to shake off the apathy that overcame the author's own generation after the disheartening siege of 1870. Without this preface, the reader would be likely to set the book down as unwholesome, and not grasp the idea that the character of the disciple is intended as a warning against the habit of analyzing and experimenting with the emotions. The boy's imagination, drawn out by the brilliant but often enervating literature that comes in the way of all university students, is further stimulated by the works of an agnostic philosopher, who treats exhaustively of the passions. The young man becomes his devoted follower, and makes a practical application of his teachings. In a family where he becomes a tutor he experiments with the affection he inspires in a young girl, and is the direct cause of her death. The philosopher, recognizing the logical outcome of his theory that the scientific spirit demands impartial investigation, even in the things of the mind and heart, feels no small remorse. His disciple escapes the vengeance of the law, only to fall in a duel with the dead girl's brother. The recluse, who according to the journals was the original of the character of the philosopher, died in Paris in 1896. Unlike the philosopher, he was a lifelong botanist, devoting all his energies to that science, so that the points of resemblance between the real and the fictitious professor are mostly external. Both lived near the Jardin des Plantes, their sole recreation consisting in looking at the animals. Both held aloof from society, never marrying, and practicing the severest economy. When an officer of the Legion of Honor sought the botanist to confer the red ribbon upon him, he found that member of the Institute on the point of cooking his dinner, and unwilling to admit him to his garret. In the story, the mice that overrun the garret, the caprices of Ferdinand, and a pet rooster kept by the *concierge*, are the only enlivening elements. But the holes and corners in the region of the Jardin des Plantes, and the exquisite vistas of the Observatory and Luxembourg Garden, have never been better described.

DISCOURSES DELIVERED IN THE ROYAL ACADEMY (1769–1791), by Sir Joshua Reynolds. These, among the most famous of all discourses on art, are not so much based on the results of reading as on the author's own wide experience. They contain advice to students, to use the words of the 'Dictionary of National Biography,' "which is of permanent value, expressed in language which could scarcely be improved. His ideas and criticism were generally sound, and for the most part were accepted by later ages. 'Study the works of the great masters forever,' he tells his students. 'Study as nearly as you can, in the order, in the manner, and on the principles, on which they studied. Study nature attentively, but always with those masters in your company; consider them as models which you are to imitate, and at the same time as rivals with whom you are to contend.' 'As our art is not a divine *gift*, so neither is it a mechanical *trade*. Its foundations are laid in solid science: and practice, though essential to perfection, can never attain that to which it aims, unless it works under the direction of principle.'" (Discourses VI. and VII.)

The most frequent burden of the Discourses is that the only worthy motive in art is the attempt to attain ideal beauty of form. He never admitted that elegance and the pursuit of color could in themselves constitute a defensible motive. Nevertheless his own studies in Italy had brought him under the sway of the colorists whom he denounced so vigorously in his addresses. Ruskin ranks him among the seven supreme colorists, and for a generation the works which he poured forth in such profusion owed their charm and attractiveness to the sense of color, against which year by year in his addresses to the Academy he was to warn his students. Notwithstanding this inconsistency between theory and practice, the Discourses have been frequently reprinted and even at the present day cannot be neglected by any serious student of art criticism.

DISCOURSES OF EPICTETUS, see MORALS.

DISCOVERIES OF AMERICA to the year 1525, by Arthur James Weise (1884). A work of importance for its careful review and comparison of the various statements of historical writers concerning the voyages of the persons whom they believed to have been the discoverers of certain parts of the coast of America between Baffin's Bay and Terra del Fuego. The full statements are given, as well as a judgment upon them. "It appears," says Mr. Weise, "that Columbus was not the discoverer of the continent, for it was seen in 1497 not only by Giovanni Caboto [or John Cabot, his English name], but by the commander of the Spanish fleet with whom Amerigo Vespucci sailed to the New World." The entire story of the discoveries of the continental coasts, north and south, apart from the islands to which Columbus almost wholly confined his attention, is of very great interest. John Cabot was first, about June, 1497. Columbus saw continental coast land for the first time fourteen months later, August, 1498. It was wholly in relation to continental lands that the names New World and America were originally given; and at the time it was not considered as disturbing in any way the claims of Columbus, whose whole ambition was to have the credit of having reached "the isles of India beyond the Ganges" — isles which were still 7000 miles distant, but which to the last he claimed to have found. The names "West Indies" and "Indians" (for native Americans) are monuments to Columbus, who did not at the time think it worth while to pay attention to the continents. It was by paying this attention, and by a remarkably opportune report, which had the fortune of being printed, that Vespucius came to the front in a way to suggest to the editor and publisher of his report the use of the word "America" as a general New World name not including Columbus's "West Indies." That inclusion came later; and from first to last Vespucius had no more to do with it than Columbus himself.

DISCOVERY OF AMERICA, THE, by John Fiske (2 vols., 1892). The initial work of Mr. Fiske, designed to serve as the first section of a complete History of

America. It very fully and carefully covers the ground of aboriginal America in the light of recent research; and of the long and slow process through which the New World became fully known to the Old. The story of voyages before Columbus by the Portuguese, and of what Cabot accomplished, is given at length; the part also which Vespucius played, and the questions about it which have been so much discussed. Mr. Fiske's estimate of Columbus does not depart very much from the popular view. He gives an account of ancient Mexico and Central America, and a full sketch of the conquest of Mexico and Peru. The work thus makes a complete Introduction to American history as most known to English readers: the history of the planting of North America in Virginia, New England, New York, Delaware, Pennsylvania, Maryland, and the Carolinas.

DISRAELI, BENJAMIN, EARL OF BEACONSFIELD, THE LIFE OF, is an exhaustive biography based on the letters and papers of Lord Beaconsfield. The first volume, narrating his ancestry, education, youthful authorship, political ventures, and entry into Parliament in 1837, is the work of William Flavelle Monypenny and was published in 1910; volume two, also by Monypenny, includes his early parliamentary career, marriage, success as a novelist, and contribution to the defeat of Peel in 1846. On the death of Monypenny in 1912 the work was continued by George Earle Buckle, who brought out the third volume in 1914 and the fourth in 1916. These two volumes bring the story of Disraeli's public career down to 1855 and 1868 respectively, the latter volume concluding with his attainment of the premiership. Abundantly illustrated by portraits and by frequent extracts from the letters of Disraeli, and fully discussing and presenting the extraordinary and romantic events of his brilliant and meteoric progress to the highest position a subject could occupy, this is one of the most fascinating of biographies.

DIVERSIONS OF PURLEY, THE, by John Horne (Tooke) (1786–1805). The author, a political writer and grammarian, was a supporter of Wilkes, whom he aided in founding a Society for supporting the Bill of Rights, 1769. Starting a subscription for the widows and orphans of the Americans "murdered by the king's troops at Lexington and Concord," he was tried and found guilty of libel and sentenced to a year's imprisonment. While in prison he began to write 'The Diversions of Purley,' — so called from the country-seat of William Tooke, who made the author his heir, and whose name Horne added to his own.

The work is a treatise on etymology: the author contending that in all languages there are but two sorts of words necessary for the communication of thought, viz., nouns and verbs; that all the other so-called parts of speech are but abbreviations of these, and are "the wheels of the vehicle language."

He asserts also that there are no indefinable words, but that every word, in all languages, has a meaning of its own. To prove this, he traces many conjunctions, prepositions, adverbs, etc., back to their source as comparisons or contractions; accounting for their present form by the assertion that "abbreviation and corruption are always busiest with the words most frequently in use; letters, like soldiers, being very apt to desert and drop off in a long march."

Throughout the work, the author constantly refers to his imprisonment and trial, introducing sentences for dissection which express his political opinions, and words to be treated etymologically which describe the moral or physical defects of his enemies. The book had an immense popularity in its own day.

DIVERSITY OF CREATURES, A, by Rudyard Kipling (1917). Fourteen stories, each followed by a poem on the theme of the story. 'As Easy as A. B. C.' is a strange tale of the future, A.D. 2065, when the planet is under the benevolent rule of an Aërial Board of Control. The disease of crowds and democracy has ceased, and a small outbreak of democratic agitation makes it necessary to deal with the American district of Illinois through aërial artillery of sound vibrations and withering rays of light. Stalky and Beetle reappear in the 'Honors of War' hazing a priggish cad who is converted from the error of his ways. 'Regulus' is a schoolboy comedy having to do with the teaching of Latin, the connection of classic learning and everyday boy life. There are three psychical stories. The phantom dog who haunts a man is the real dog "Harvey," owned by the woman he subconsciously loves. 'Swept and Garnished' is a grim war story, in which the ghosts of murdered children appear to a complacent German woman making it impossible for her to disbelieve comfortably. 'Mary Postgate' deals with the effect of resentment for the slaughter of the innocents in the European war on one woman in England. She has an unexpected opportunity to be judge and executioner. 'The Edge of the Evening' tells of an encounter with spies who descend from an aeroplane on the lawn of a country house just before dinner. There are stories of the British peasant in real possession of the land whether its nominal ownership is Roman or English. 'The Village that Voted the Earth was Flat' is a comic extravaganza, the revenge of a party of motorists upon the magistrate who fines them unjustly for speeding. One of the group is a producer of opera, one a member of parliament, one a journalist, and all are brilliantly equipped in different ways for the confounding of their enemy.

DIVINE COMEDY, THE, by Dante Alighieri, was written between his exile in 1302 and his death in 1321, although the events of the poem are supposed to occur in 1300, Dante's thirty-fifth year. The Divine Comedy is at once a vision of the other world, an allegory of the Christian life, a spiritual autobiography, and a cyclopædic embodiment of all the knowledge of its day. Dante sets forth as though from personal experience the Catholic beliefs as to the nature of Hell, Purgatory, and Paradise; he makes his imaginary journey through these realms a symbol of the Christian's struggle through repentance and purification towards the beatific vision; he introduces also his own redemption from sensuality through the influence of his ideal devotion to Beatrice, who became for him the medium of divine grace; and in adequately explaining and adorning these great conceptions he employs all the learning, all the science, and all the literary devices, mythological figures, and poetic machinery which could be furnished by the best learning of the time. Of this learning the figure of Virgil, his guide through Hell and Purgatory, is the representative. Noteworthy is the symmetry of the poem and the exact correspondence of its arrangement to the scientific preciseness with which the other world is conceived and depicted. There are three divisions, Hell, Purgatory, and Paradise, the first including thirty-four cantos, and the two last, thirty-three cantos each, making one hundred in all. Each canto is of approximately the same length; and the three realms are described in symmetrical order and proportion. The metre is the *terza rima*, consisting of 10-syllabled or 11-syllabled lines which fall into groups of three with interlacing rhymes — the first and third lines rhyming, and the second rhyming with the first and third of the next group, thus: aba, bcb, cdc, etc. The sustained music of this measure, the concentration and intensity of the style, its wealth of brief and pointed allusion, its pictorial vividness, and its austere beauty are the distinctive marks of the Divine Comedy as poetry.

DIVINE FANCIES, see **EMBLEMS.**

DIVINE FIRE, THE, by May Sinclair (1905). This novel is the record of the career of Keith Rickman, a Cockney poet, and son of a sordid London bookseller, in whose soul dwells "the divine fire." Rickman finds his feminine ideal in the aristocratic and high-minded Lucia Harden, whose library he has been sent to catalogue. Lucia is on the point of becoming betrothed to her cousin Horace Jewdwine, the deterioration of whose character is outlined in contrast to the development of that of Rickman, who triumphs over his disadvantages of birth and breeding and over the temptations which arise in connection with his business and journalistic life. Jewdwine, the priggish and refined Oxford don, comes to London to edit the Museion, a progressive literary journal, with idealistic aims; through his association with the embryo poet the latter becomes acquainted with Lucia Harden; she, while repelled by the young poet's crudeness and lack of breeding, nevertheless discerns his genius and is gradually more and more strongly drawn towards him. Lucia's cousin, for whom she feels no genuine sentiment, finds it to his advantage to defer any immediate matrimonial project and in the meantime she learns to love Rickman, who adores her at a distance. Many complications spring from the disposition of the Harden library, which contains priceless volumes and falls a prey to sharpers. Rickman passes through many vicissitudes, social, financial, and literary, and his connection with editors and magazines gives the writer of the book an ample opportunity, which she improves, to discourse upon the varying types of editors and reviewers.

DIVINE POEMS, see **EMBLEMS.**

DMITRI ROUDIN, a story by Turgeneff. This great novel was first published in 1860. The action passes in the country, some distance from Moscow, at the country-seat of Daria Mikhailovna, a great lady who protects literature and art and is determined to have a salon. She has one in embryo already, made up of an old French governess, a young Circassian secretary, and a Cossack. The advent of Dmitri, a vainglorious creature who thinks himself a great man, completes it. He has retained a few scraps from the books he has read, some ideas borrowed from the German transcendentalists, and a number of keen aphorisms; and so he imagines he is able to pull down and set up everything. He dazzles and fascinates the women by his expressive looks and serene self-confidence; and being treated as a genius, he naturally believes himself one. He speaks of his immense labors; but all his literary baggage consists of newspaper and magazine articles which he *intends* to write. He is soon found out, however; and from Daria's salon passes into that of an affected old lady, a bluestocking also, who takes him even more seriously than Daria did at first. She believes she can understand Hegel's metaphysics when he explains them; so she lodges and boards him, lends him money, and insists that all her visitors shall acknowledge his superiority. Unfortunately, her daughter, a proud beauty, hears so much of this superiority that she believes in it, becomes smitten with the great man, and wishes to marry him. This is too much for the old lady, and Dmitri is shown the door. He is at last forced to quit Russia, and dies defending a barricade at Paris. In the character of Dmitri, Turgeneff satirizes a class common enough in every country as well as Russia, especially among the young, — the class of people who mistake words, in which they abound, for ideas, in which they are lacking. And yet, such is Turgeneff's fine and delicate skill in the analysis of feeling that he interests us in this poor boaster: he excites our pity for him, — and it is a singular fact that the lower Dmitri falls, the more interesting he becomes. He is a mixture of pride and weakness; and his good faith and harmlessness somewhat palliate his faults.

DOCTEUR PASCAL, LE, see **ROUGON-MACQUART.**

DOCTOR, THE, a ponderous romance by Robert Southey, appeared anonymously in 1834, though Vols. vi. and vii. were not published until after his death in 1847. It records the observations, philosophizing, and experiences of a quaint physician, "Dr. Love, of Doncaster," who, with his faithful horse "Nobbs," travels the country over and ministers to the needs of men. While little read in present days, it has generally received the moderate praise of scholars. In form it is a peculiar medley of essay, colloquy, and criticism, lacking coherence; a vast accumulation of curious erudition, meditative wisdom, and somewhat labored humor. Southey manifested much pride in the book, from whose pure English, freshness of innovation, and brilliant though mechanical diorama of thought, he expected a larger meed of praise than has ever been accorded it, by either critics or the public.

DOCTOR, THE, a tale of the Rockies, by Ralph Connor (1906). This narrative deals with the lives of two brothers, Barney and Richard Boyle, who are of Scotch-Irish parentage, but are Canadian born. The father is a respectable miller, but the sons, who are endowed with good intellect and strong characters, are ambitious to make something of themselves. The younger boy, Dick, is sent to college to study for the ministry and this is the first separation that has come between the two brothers, who are absolutely devoted to each other. Barney fits himself for his chosen profession of medicine, and later on works his way through the medical school, there being only enough money for the education of one son. Before leaving home Barney has won the affection of an attractive young girl named Iola Lane, who has taught school in his native town and who has a beautiful voice. Iola goes to the city to study music as she is anxious for a career. This ambition causes a break between herself and Barney and he goes to a distant city to teach in a university. During his absence Dick and Iola are much together though Dick has been for years in love with Margaret Robertson, a childhood's friend and neighbor. Margaret however loves Barney and rejects his brother's advances. Dick when finishing his theological course is refused his degree on account of opinions which the Presbytery consider heretical. He goes into journalism and becomes reckless in many ways. He is tempted on one occasion to kiss Iola and Barney suddenly appearing at the crucial moment casts him off forever. Later Dick goes west as a missionary and works among men in the mountain camps. Barney also practices his profession among these same people, but avoids meeting his brother who is ignorant of his proximity. Margaret, who has become a nurse, is made matron of a hospital in connection with Dick's work. Barney saves Dick's life and the brothers are re-united, and then learning that Iola is sick in Scotland Barney goes to her, reaching her just before her death. Heart-broken he returns to his work and dies a sacrifice to his profession. Margaret and Dick, sharing a common loss, are brought together and happiness comes after sorrow.

DOCTOR ANTONIO, by Giovanni Ruffini (1856), is a novel of modern life, the scene of which is laid mainly in Italy, the political troubles there being made the source of the story's action. The chief characters are Sir John Davenne, an Englishman traveling in Italy, his daughter Lucy, and Doctor Antonio, a Sicilian exile.

The personality of the Doctor is one of singular charm, and holds interest throughout the book. When published this novel became a universal favorite, and it is still read with pleasure.

DR. CLAUDIUS, by F. Marion Crawford (1883), was the second of Mr. Crawford's novels, following a year after its predecessor 'Mr. Isaacs.' Unlike the latter, it contains no element of the supernatural, and is merely a love story of contemporary life. Dr. Claudius, himself, when first introduced, is a privatdocent at Heidelberg, living simply, in a state of philosophical content. He plans no change in his life when the news comes to him that he has inherited more than a million dollars by the death of his uncle Gustavus Lindstrand, who had made a fortune in New York. The son of his partner, Silas B. Barker, soon arrives in Heidelberg to see what manner of man Dr. Claudius may be, and persuades the blond, stalwart Scandinavian to go with him to America; securing an invitation for the two on the private yacht of an English duke, whom he knows well. Before leaving Heidelberg, Claudius has fallen in love with a beautiful woman met by chance in the ruins of the Schloss. Since she is also a friend of the Duke, Barker is able to introduce Claudius to her. This Countess Margaret, with her companion, Miss Skeat, is asked to cross the Atlantic with the Duke, his sister Lady Victoria, Barker, and Claudius, Margaret, though an American, is the widow of a Russian count. Claudius is not wholly disheartened, when, on the yacht, she refuses to marry him. But in America, she succumbs to the romantic surroundings of the Cliff Walk at Newport, and admits that she loves the philosophical millionaire. Claudius then starts off on a hasty journey to St. Petersburg, where he obtains from the government the return of Margaret's estates confiscated on account of her brother-in-law's republicanism. Just what the secret is of Dr. Claudius's power with Russia, we are not told; but Mr. Crawford lets us infer that he is the posthumous son of some European potentate. The Duke and the courteous Horace Bellingham know who he is, but the reader's curiosity is not gratified.

DOCTOR FAUSTUS, by Christopher Marlowe. This play, written about the year 1589, is remarkable both as the chief work of the founder of English tragedy, and as the first play based on the Faust legend. At the time of the Reformation, when chemistry was in its infancy, any skill in this science was attributed to a compact with the Evil One. Hence wandering scholars who performed tricks and wonders were considered magicians, their achievements were grossly exaggerated, and they were supposed to have surrendered their souls to the Devil. The last of these traveling magicians to gain notoriety was John Faustus, whose public career lasted from 1510 to 1540; and to him were ascribed all the feats of his predecessors. In 1587 the 'Faustbuch' was printed, giving the story of his life and exploits. An English translation, made soon after, was doubtless the source of Marlowe's plot. The theme was afterwards variously elaborated in Germany, and there were many puppet plays on the subject; but it remained for Goethe's master-hand to ennoble the popular legend, and make it symbolic of the struggles and aspirations of the whole human race. Marlowe's 'Doctor Faustus' is rather a tragic poem than a drama, consisting of only fourteen scenes without any grouping into acts. It is remarkable for singleness of aim and simplicity of construction, though there is plenty of variety and incident. The passionate and solemn scenes are very impressive, and the final tremendous monologue before Lucifer seizes Faustus's soul is unsurpassed in all the range of tragedy. Faustus, dissatisfied with philosophy, resolves to enlarge his sphere by

cultivating magic. He conjures up Mephistopheles and bids him be his servant.
The spirit, however, replies that Lucifer's permission must first be gained. Faustus
then voluntarily offers to surrender his soul after four-and-twenty years, if during
that time Mephistopheles shall be his slave. Lucifer agrees, and demands a promise
written in Faustus's blood. Then Faustus sets out in search of knowledge and
pleasure, traveling about invisible. He provides grapes in midwinter, and calls up
the spirits of Alexander and Thais to please the emperor. At the request of his
scholars he summons Helen of Troy, and impressed by her beauty, exclaims: —

> " Was this the face that launched a thousand ships,
> And burnt the topless towers of Ilium?
> Sweet Helen, make me immortal with a kiss!"

At times the desire for repentance seizes him; but the exhilaration of pleasure is too
great, and the powers of evil are too strong. Finally the time expires, and Faustus in
agony awaits the coming of Lucifer. He appeals to God and Christ, but has forfeited
the right to pray; and at the stroke of twelve Lucifer bears him away to everlasting
doom.

DR. JEKYLL AND MR. HYDE, by Robert Louis Stevenson (1886), is a psychologic
romance illustrating the complex quality of man's nature. The scene is London.
Dr. Jekyll is a physician of position and good character, a portly, kindly man. In
his youth, however, he showed that he had strong capacities for evil, which he
succeeded in suppressing for years. His professional tastes lead him to experiment
in drugs, and he hits on one whereby he is changed physically so that his lower nature
receives external dress. He becomes Mr. Hyde, a pale, misshapen, repulsive creature
of evil and violent passions. Again and again Dr. Jekyll effects this change, and gives
his bad side more and more power. His friend Utterson, a lawyer, is puzzled by
Jekyll's will in favor of Hyde, and seeks to unravel the mystery. The brutal murder
of Sir Danvers Carew, which is traced to Hyde, who of course disappears, adds to the
mystery and horror. At last, by the aid of letters left by Dr. Lanyon, another of
Dr. Jekyll's lawyer friends, to whom he has revealed the secret and who is killed by
the shock of the discovery, the strange facts are exposed. Utterson breaks into
Jekyll's laboratory, only to find Hyde, who has just taken his own life; and Jekyll is
gone forever.

DR. LATIMER, by Clara Louise Burnham (1893). This is called "A Story of
Casco Bay"; and it contains many charming pictures of that beautiful Maine coast
and its fascinating islands. Dr. Latimer, a man of fine character and position,
beloved by all who know him, becomes interested in three orphan girls, Josephine,
Helen, and Vernon Ivison, who come to Boston to support themselves by teaching
and music. He falls in love with Josephine, the eldest, who returns his affection;
and he invites the three girls to his island home for the summer. He has hesitated to
avow his love for Josephine on account of the difference of age between them, and
also on account of a former unhappy marriage made in early youth with a woman
who had first disgraced and then deserted him, and whom he has long supposed
dead. Her sudden reappearance destroys his newly found happiness; he leaves the
island, bidding Josephine a final farewell. Recalled by the news that his wife has
drowned herself and that he is at last free, he marries Josephine. Helen and Vernon
are mated to the men of their choice: the former to Mr. Brush, a German teacher;
the latter to Olin Randolph, a society youth of much charm and character, whose

aunts, Miss Charlotte and Miss Agnes Norman, are characters of interest, as is also Persis Applebee, the doctor's old-fashioned housekeeper.

DR. SEVIER, by George W. Cable (1882), is one of the author's group of stories of life in New Orleans. The time of the action is just before the war, when the city was at the height of its prosperity. Dr. Sevier, the brusque, laconic, skillful, kind-hearted physician, is less the central figure than his young beneficiary, John Richling, the son of a rich planter, who having estranged his family by marrying a Northern girl, has come to the metropolis of the South to earn his living. The struggle of the Richlings, unequipped for the battle of life, against poverty and sickness, forms the plot of the story, which is glowing with local color and filled with personages peculiar to the place and time. There is no plot in the sense of a complicated play of forces, or labyrinth of events; but the interest lies in the development of character under conditions supplied by an untried environment. The scope of the book is wide and the detail extremely minute.

DR. SYNTAX, THE THREE TOURS OF, by William Combe. This famous book, or rather series of three books, was first devised by its author at the suggestion of the publisher, Mr. Ackermann, who desired some amusing text to accompany a series of caricatures which he had engaged from the celebrated Rowlandson.

William Combe, then past sixty-five years of age, had already produced a large number of volumes, of which all had appeared anonymously. The first part of 'Dr. Syntax,' which was published in 1809, describes the adventures of a certain Dr. Syntax, clergyman and teacher, who, on his horse Grizzle, deliberately sets out in search of adventures which he might make material for a book. His plan, as he gives it to his wife Dolly, is as follows: —

> "You well know what my pen can do,
> And I'll employ my pencil too;—
> I'll ride and write and sketch and print,
> And thus create a real mint;
> I'll prose it here and verse it there,
> And picturesque it everywhere."

In this long series of eight-foot iambic couplets with the real Hudibras swing, Combe tells the story of the travels of the clerical Don Quixote. The author endows him with much of his own sense of humor and Horatian philosophy; and even though the adventures are not always thrilling, the account of them, and the accompanying reflections, are extremely entertaining. Pleasure, Wealth, Content, Ambition, Riches, are among the abstractions of which the author or his hero discourses; and many of the passages are undoubtedly intended by Combe as autobiographic.

In the course of his travels Dr. Syntax meets various persons whom the author makes food for his mild satire, — the merchant, the critic, the bookseller, the country squire, the Oxford don, and other well-marked types. The descriptions of rural scenery and of the cities visited by Dr. Syntax are often clever, and even today are agreeable to read. The very great popularity of the first tour of Dr. Syntax "in search of the picturesque" encouraged author and publisher to follow it with a second and a third series.

DOCTOR THORNE, by Anthony Trollope (1858). 'Doctor Thorne' is a story of quiet country life; and the interest of the book lies in the character studies rather than in the plot. The scene is laid in the west of England about 1854. The heroine,

Mary Thorne, is a sweet, modest girl, living with her kind uncle Doctor Thorne, in the village of Greshambury, where Frank Gresham, the young heir of Greshambury Park, falls in love with her. The estate is incumbered; and as it is necessary that Frank should marry for money, his mother, Lady Arabella, banishes Mary from the society of her daughters, and sends Frank to Courcy Castle, where he is expected to win the affections of Miss Dunstable, a wealthy heiress. He remains true to Mary, however; and after a year of enforced absence abroad, he returns and claims her for his wife in the face of every opposition. Roger Scatcherd, the brother of Mary's unfortunate mother, is creditor to Mr. Gresham for a sum of money amounting to the value of the entire estate. After his death his entire fortune falls to Mary Thorne; and the story concludes with the marriage of Frank and Mary, and a return of prosperity to Greshambury Park.

The character of Doctor Thorne stands out vividly in the book as an independent, honest Englishman, offering a pleasing contrast to Lady Arabella with her conventionality and worldliness and the coarse vulgarity of Roger Scatcherd and his son.

DOLL'S HOUSE, A, one of the best-known plays of Henrik Ibsen, was published in 1879. It is the drama of the Woman, the product of man's fostering care through centuries, — his doll, from whom nature has kindly removed the unused faculties which produce clear thinking and business-like action. Nora, the particular doll in question, adorns a little home with her pretty dresses, her pretty manner, her sweet, childish ignorance. She must bring up her babies, love her husband, and have well-cooked dinners. For the sake of this husband, she ventures once beyond the limit of the nest. He is ill, and she forges her rich father's name to obtain money to send him abroad. The disclosure of her guilt, the guilt of a baby, a doll who did not know better, brings her face to face with the realities of the world and of life. The puppet becomes vitalized, changed into a suffering woman who realizes that there is "something wrong" in the state of women as wives. She leaves her husband's house, "a moth flying towards a star." She will not return until she is different, or marriage is different, or — she knows not what. 'A Doll's House' is the most striking embodiment in the range of modern drama, of the new awakening of Eve. The last scene of the play is given in the LIBRARY.

DOMBEY AND SON, by Charles Dickens. The story opens with the death of Mrs. Dombey, who has left her husband the proud possessor of a baby son and heir. He neglects his daughter Florence and loves Paul, in whom all his ambitions and worldly hopes are centred; but the boy dies. Mr. Dombey marries a beautiful woman, who is as cold and proud as he, and who has sold herself to him to escape from a designing mother. She grows fond of Florence, and this friendship is so displeasing to Mr. Dombey that he tries to humble her by remonstrating through Mr. Carker, his business manager and friend. This crafty villain, realizing his power, goads her beyond endurance, and she demands a separation from Mr. Dombey, but is refused. After an angry interview, she determines upon a bold stroke and disgraces her husband by pretending to elope with Carker to France, where she meets him once, shames and defies him and escapes. Mr. Dombey, after spurning Florence, whom he considers the cause of his trouble, follows Carker in hot haste. They encounter each other without warning at a railway station, and as Carker is crossing the tracks he falls and is instantly killed by an express train. Florence seeks refuge with an old sea-captain whom her little brother, Paul, has been fond of, marries Walter Gay, the friend of her childhood, and they go to sea. After the failure of Dombey and

Son, when Mr. Dombey's pride is humbled and he is left desolate, Florence returns and takes care of him.   The characters in the book not immediately concerned in the plot, but famous for their peculiar qualities, are Captain Cuttle, Florence's kind protector, who has a nautical manner of expression; Sol Gills, Walter's uncle; Mr. Toots, who suffers from shyness and love; and Joe Bagstock, the major.   The scene is laid in England at the time the novel was published, in 1848.

DON JOHN, a novel by Jean Ingelow, was published in 1881.   The story turns on the well-worn incident of the changing of two children in their cradles.   The plot follows their development, the gradual manifestation through character of their true origin.   'Don John' is admirably written, bearing about it the same atmosphere of simplicity and nobility that surrounds this author's poems.   Though a mere mention of the chief incident implies a poverty of invention, the book is really one of unusual freshness of imagination.   The delineation of character is delightfully delicate and exact; and the skill with which the puzzle of identity is treated leaves the reader in the desired mood of doubt to the end of the excellent story.

DON JUAN, a narrative and satirical poem in eight-line stanzas by George Gordon, Lord Byron.   Cantos I and II were published in 1819, III to V in 1821, VI–XIV at different times in 1823, and XV and XVI in 1824.   The poem is unfinished.   Its theme is the Spanish legend of Don Juan, a libertine who killed the father of a girl he had seduced and while on a mocking visit to his victim's tomb was swallowed up in Hell along with the statue of the man he had killed.   Byron's Juan is also a libertine; but the poet is more interested in the varied amors of his hero and the opportunity afforded by them for pictures and reflections — cynical, sentimental, and realistic — of life and human nature, particularly the numerous aspects of love and passion — than in drawing an edifying moral or providing for the punishment of the culprit.   He had not decided, he said, whether to make him end in Hell or in an unhappy marriage.   Don Juan a Spanish grandee of Seville is forced into exile at the age of sixteen through being detected in an intrigue with Donna Julia, the beautiful young wife of the elderly Don Alfonso.   Embarking from Cadiz for Leghorn he is shipwrecked, and after enduring dreadful privations in an open boat is cast, the sole survivor, upon an island in the Ægean.   Here he is secretly nursed back to life by Haidee, the lovely seventeen-year-old daughter of the pirate-chieftain, Lambro, and they become lovers.   On a report that her father has died while absent on a piratical expedition, Haidee with Juan assumes the sovereignty of the island.   But Lambro returns during a feast, surprises the lovers, disarms Juan, and sells him for a slave.   While Haidee dies of a broken heart, Juan is taken to Constantinople, where he is purchased by the Sultana, Guyalbez, who has fallen in love with him and introduces him, disguised as a woman, into the seraglio.   Enraged at his rejection of her, and at a subsequent escapade with one of the women of the seraglio she orders Juan to be drowned.   But he makes his escape to the Russian army, then fighting the Turks, distinguishes himself at a siege under General Souwaroff, and is sent as a special messenger to the notorious Empress Catherine at St. Petersburg.   He becomes the reigning favorite and is then sent to England on a special diplomatic mission.   Here Byron introduces the reader to a group of English aristocrats at a country house, where Juan is a guest; and ends in the midst of another amatory adventure, in which the Duchess of Fitz-Fulke, masquerading as the ghost of a friar, seeks a midnight interview with the hero.   The poem exhibits Byron's full power as a creative poet and a satirist.   Perhaps the finest part is the account of the shipwreck, many details of which are taken from the autobiography of his grandfather, Admiral John Byron, and the ensuing episode of the love of Haidee and Juan.

DON ORSINO, by F. Marion Crawford (1892). This book gives a good idea of Rome after the unification of Italy, as the author's purpose is to describe a young man of the transition period. It will probably never attain the popularity of the two earlier Saracinesca stories, because many readers find the plot unpleasant and the ending unsatisfactory. In analysis and development of character, however, and in sparkling dialogue, it far surpasses its predecessors.

Orsino Saracinesca longs for a career, and being rebuffed at home, is attracted by the sympathetic womanliness of Madame Maria Consuelo d'Aranjuez, whose antecedents are mysterious. With the aid of Del Ferice he undertakes some building operations, mortgaging his house in advance. One day he makes love to Madame d'Aranjuez, but soon realizes the shallowness of his emotions. Subsequently constant intercourse renews his affection on a firmer basis, and he wishes to marry her. Though she loves him she leaves Rome, soon writing that a stain on her birth prevents her marrying him. On the day of her refusal he learns that his business is ruined; but Del Ferice renews the contract in terms to which Orsino submits, only to avoid an appeal to his father. Thus he gets more and more into Del Ferice's power, until the united fortunes of the Saracinesca could hardly save him. At this crisis he receives from Maria Consuelo a friendly letter, asking merely that he tell her about himself. This he gladly does, writing freely of his business difficulties. Finally the bank releases him from his obligations, an action inexplicable until the announcement of Consuelo's marriage to Del Ferice. Then Orsino guesses, what he afterwards learns, that she has sold herself to save him. The story moves rapidly, the atmosphere is strikingly Italian, and the various complications are well managed and interesting.

DON QUIXOTE DE LA MANCHA, THE HISTORY OF, a satirical romance by Miguel Cervantes, the first part of which appeared in 1605 and the second in 1615. A kindly and simple-minded country gentleman has read the romances of chivalry until they have turned his brain. Clad in a suit of old armor and mounted on a broken-down hack which he christens Rozinante, he sets out on a career of knight-errantry, assuming the name of Don Quixote de la Mancha. For the object of his devotion he chooses a village girl, whom he names Dulcinea del Toboso and as squire he takes an ignorant but faithful peasant, Sancho Panza. The ordinary wayfarers of the Spanish roads of the seventeenth century are transformed by the knight's disordered imagination into warriors, distressed damsels, giants, and monsters. For instance, he tilts on one occasion, at the sails of a group of wind-mills, thinking them living creatures, and his attempts to right fictitious wrongs and win chivalric honor among them lead him and his squire into ludicrous and painful situations. Yet amidst their discomfitures Don Quixote retains a dignity, a certain nobility, and a pathetic idealism, and Sancho a natural shrewdness and popular humor which endear them to the reader. In the second part the interest is fully sustained, and variety is introduced by the sojourn of the pair with a duke and duchess and Sancho's appointment as governor of the imaginary island of Baratoria. At the end, Don Quixote, as the result of a dangerous illness, recovers his senses, renounces all books of chivalry, and dies penitent. The book was begun as an attack on the absurdities of the late chivalric romances, not on the essential chivalric ideals. As the work progresses it becomes a picture of human nature, its absurdities and its aspirations, its coarse materialism and lofty enthusiasm. The best English translations are

Shelton's (1612–1620) reprinted with an introduction by J. Fitzmaurice-Kelly in the 'Tudor Translations,' 4 vols., 1896, and that by John Ormsby, 1885, reprinted with critical introduction and notes by J. Fitzmaurice-Kelly in 1901.

DOÑA LUZ, by Juan Valera. The scene of this brilliant emotional story is laid in Spain, during the seventies. Doña Luz, at the death of her father, the dissipated Marquis of Villafria, takes up her abode with his old steward Don Ascisclo, into whose hands a large part of the estate of the marquis has fallen. High-strung and sensitive, with a rare beauty of mind and person, and entertaining no hope of marrying according to her inclinations, she gently repulses all admirers. Among her friends she counts Don Miguel, the parish priest; Don Anselmo, a skillful physician but a fierce materialist; and his daughter Doña Manolita, a charming brunette, capricious and merry, loyal and affectionate. Into this circle comes the missionary, Father Enrique, nephew of Don Ascisclo, a man of great wisdom and elevation of thought; and last of all, the hero, Don Jaime Pimental. Around this group the movement of the story takes place. The dominant motives spring from avarice and ambition; and the action is complicated by religious animosities. 'Doña Luz' was published in Madrid in 1891, and its English translation by Mrs. Serrano came out in 1894.

DOÑA PERFECTA, by Benito Pérez Galdós. This exquisite romance, the translation of which was published in 1880, is a vivid description of life in a Spanish provincial town, just before the Carlist war. Doña Perfecta Rey de Polentinos is a wealthy widow, just in all her dealings, kind and charitable, but a perfect type of the narrow-minded and even cruel spirit of old Spain. The Spanish hate the national government, but have a peculiar local patriotism, which in this case turns an apparently kind and honorable woman against her own nephew, because he dislikes the customs of her beloved town.

This nephew, Don José Rey, handsome, generous, and rich, is the hero of the story, whose incidents are the outgrowth of old prejudice — religious and political.

The author endeavors to show that the offenses of Doña Perfecta are the result of her position and surroundings rather than inherent in her character. In this book he begins to exploit the modern Spain and its clashing interests. He brings "the new and the old face to face," to use the words of Professor Marsh: "the new in the form of a highly-trained, clear-thinking, frank-speaking modern man; the old in the guise of a whole community so remote from the current of things that its religious intolerance, its social jealousy, its undisturbed confidence and pride in itself, must of necessity declare instant war upon that which comes from without, unsympathetic and critical. The inevitable result is ruin for the party whose physical force is less, the single individual; yet hardly less complete ruin for those whom intolerance and hate have driven to the annihilation of their adversary." The story was published in 1876, and reached its ninth edition in 1896.

DONAL GRANT, a novel by George Macdonald, was published in 1883, when he was fifty-nine. It is a modern story; the hero, Donal Grant, being one of the muscular and intellectual young Scotchmen whom Macdonald loves to describe. Introduced as a poor student seeking a situation, he reaches the town of Auchars, where he meets a spiritually minded cobbler and his wife with whom he lodges. In Auchars he finds a field of work, and the story deals with the effect produced on careless and selfish characters by contact with an upright and generous nature. The plot involves a forced marriage, and other well-known incidents; but the book shows all Macdonald's familiar qualities, though it is less eventful and more didactic than many of his stories.

DONOVAN, a novel of modern English life, by Edna Lyall (1882), has for its sub-ject a man's spiritual struggles from doubt to faith. The hero, Donovan Farrant, is well drawn, if somewhat conventional in character. The book obtained great popu-larity and still enjoys it, especially in England. 'We Two' is a sequel to 'Donovan.'

DOSIA, by Henri Gréville (Madame Durand) (1877), is a vivacious story of Russian life. The heroine, Léodocia Zaptine, is a frolicsome young madcap, with the kindest heart, who is always getting into scrapes. Grief-stricken because of well-deserved scoldings, she decides to elope with her cousin Pierre Mourief, a young lieutenant staying in the house; but thinks better of it when they are but a mile or two from home, and returns to the paternal roof. After this escapade, Dosia is taken in hand by the young widow Princess Sophie Koutsky, the sister of Pierre's comrade in arms Count Platon Sourof. Dosia and Pierre make the mutual discovery that they are not in the least in love with each other; and the headlong, generous Pierre wins the Princess Sophie, while her grave brother Platon loves and marries the naughty Dosia. The story is agreeably told, and is a good specimen of the best type of domestic novel.

DOSTOÉVSKY, LETTERS OF, see **LETTERS.**

DOUBTING HEART, A, by Annie Keary. The scene of the story is laid in England, although there are some charming and picturesque descriptions of the Riviera, where the author passed the last months of her life. Published in 1879, it was left unfinished, the last chapters being written by Mrs. Macquoid. The story principally concerns itself with the love affairs of two cousins, Emmie West and Alma Rivers; and the moral of it is that tribulation worketh patience, and patience godliness. Lady Rivers, Sir Francis, and charming Madame de Florimel, are cleverly sketched characters. The story, which is very simple, is so natural and homely, and its psychology is so faithful, that it became at once a favorite, and is still one of the most popular domestic novels.

DOWNFALL, THE, see **ROUGON-MACQUART.**

DRAM SHOP, THE, see **ROUGON-MACQUART.**

DRAPIER LETTERS, THE, by Jonathan Swift. These famous letters took their name from their signature, "M. B. Drapier." They were written to protest against an unjust aggression of the Crown, which, at a time of great scarcity of copper coin in Ireland, had granted a patent to furnish this to one William Wood, who was to share his profits with the Duchess of Kendal, the king's mistress, through whose influence the patent had been obtained. These profits were to be derived from the difference between the real and the nominal value of the halfpence, which was forty per cent. The Irish were bitterly enraged, became turbulent, and every effort was made to conciliate them. A report sustaining Wood, which had been drawn up by Sir Robert Walpole, was answered by Swift in these letters. Swift, who viewed Wood's patent as a death-blow to Irish independence, asserts that the English Parliament cannot, without usurpation, maintain the power of binding Ireland by laws to which it does not consent. This assertion led to the arrest of the printer of the letters; but the grand jury refused to find a true bill. Swift triumphed, and Wood's patent was revoked. The 'Letters' were published in 1724; the sub-title being, "very proper to be kept in every family."

DREAM, THE, see **ROUGON-MACQUART.**

DREAM CHILDREN, by Horace E. Scudder (1863), is a collection of "Once-Upon-a-Time" stories, in which memory and imagination combine to preserve the fleeting fancies of childhood; some of them merely fantastic; others with a lesson of life hidden under a semblance of adventure — as in 'The Pot of Gold,' where Chief is always seeking, always unsuccessful, because just at the moment of capture of the coveted treasure, his attention is distracted by the vision of his adoring and forsaken Rhoda; or in the last charming sketch entitled 'The Prince's Visit,' where weak Job loses the sight of a grand procession while he is succoring the lame boy, — a sacrifice rewarded by the vision of a "pageant such as poor mortals may but whisper of." The offspring of dreams, the 'Dream Children,' pass before the mind's eye, a charming company of unrealities, with ordinary attributes, but invested with supernatural excellence. Who can tell when the realities begin and the dreams end? Who can separate, in the cyclorama of existence, the painted canvas from the real objects in the foreground? It is into this borderland of doubt the author takes us, with the children who hear the birds and beasts talk: where inanimate objects borrow attributes of humanity; where fact masquerades as fancy and fancy as fact; where the young and old meet together in a childish unconsciousness of awakenings.

DREAMTHORPE: 'a Book of Essays Written in the Country,' by Alexander Smith. A collection of twelve essays, which appeared in 1863, the first prose work of their author. The title is that of the first essay, and is the name of the imaginary village in which they were written: — "An inland English village where everything around one is unhurried, quiet, moss-grown and orderly. On Dreamthorpe centuries have fallen, and have left no more trace than last winter's snowflakes. Battles have been fought, kings have died, history has transacted itself, but all unheeding and untouched, Dreamthorpe has watched apple-trees redden, and wheat ripen, and smoked its pipe, and rejoiced over its newborn children, and with proper solemnity carried its dead to the church-yard.

"The library is a kind of Greenwich Hospital for disabled novels and romances. Each of the books has been in the wars. The heroes and heroines are of another generation. Lovers, warriors, and villains — as dead to the present generation as Cambyses — are weeping, fighting, and intriguing. It is with a certain feeling of tenderness that I look upon these books: I think of the dead fingers that have turned over the leaves, of the dead eyes that have traveled along the lines.

"Here I can live as I please, here I can throw the reins on the neck of my whim. Here I play with my own thoughts; here I ripen for the grave."

Perhaps no better idea can be given of the rest of the essays than by these quotations. Dreamthorpe — the village of dreams — casts its spell over all of them. The love of quiet, of old books, and reverence for the past, finds its place in them, and if they be dreams, the reader does not care to be awakened.

The titles of the other essays are: 'On the Writing of Essays'; 'Of Death and the Fear of Dying'; 'William Dunbar'; 'A Lark's Flight'; 'Christmas'; 'Men of Letters'; 'On the Importance of Man to Himself'; 'A Shelf in my Bookcase'; 'Geoffrey Chaucer'; 'Books and Gardens'; 'On Vagabonds.'

D'RI AND I, by Irving Bacheller, was published in 1901, and like the author's first book, 'Eben Holden,' met with popular favor. Darius Olin, nicknamed "D'ri," is a brawny, raw-boned Northwoodsman, who goes out to fight the soldiers of King George in the War of 1812, accompanying Ramon Bell, the son of his employer. The opening of the tale shows Mr. Bell and his family leaving their Vermont home and working their way over rough trails to the valley of the St. Lawrence. Ramon, then a sturdy boy of ten, and D'ri, the hired man, are the central figures of the story. They settle in their new home in the North, and the years pass quickly till Ramon becomes a man and the second war with Great Britain breaks out. D'ri and Ramon enlist and enter the service of Commodore Perry, where they get more than their share of the blows and have many perilous adventures and hairbreadth escapes. Young Bell becomes a frequent visitor at the house of a French nobleman, a refugee from the Reign of Terror, and falls in love with his two lovely daughters, Louise and Louison de Lambert. This is quite a predicament, but he finally extricates himself and with unerring judgment chooses the sister who has the finer character of the two. An interesting scene is the rescue of Ramon, on the night before his execution, by Lord Rowley, whom Mlle. Lambert has promised to marry, but she is subsequently released from him, and her romantic roadside marriage with Ramon follows. The loyal and brave D'ri is always ready to lend his strong arm for Ramon's aid or protection, and his surprise at receiving the medal for bravery in the terrible sea-fight on board the Lawrence on Lake Erie is characteristic of his simple and unassuming nature. His quaint sayings enliven the pages and add to the interest of the tale.

DUCHESS OF MALFI, THE, by John Webster (acted 1616, published, 1623). "The Duchess of Malfi," says Mr. Edmund Gosse "has finer elements of tragedy than exist elsewhere outside the works of Shakespeare." The Duchess of Malfi, a widow, falls in love with and marries Antonio Bologna, steward of her household. Her brothers, the Cardinal and Ferdinand, Duke of Calabria, incensed at her for thus dishonoring the family, pursue her with every form of vindictiveness. They cause her to be banished from Ancona, where she and her husband and children had taken sanctuary at the shrine of our Lady of Loretto. Daniel de Bosola, the Duchess's own gentleman of the horse, who is used as a spy and tool by her brothers, is sent to tell her that she must be parted from her husband. The fourth act is a crescendo of horrors. Ferdinand gives to the Duchess the hand of her dead husband, wearing the ring she gave him. Eight madmen are let loose to dance round her without shaking her resolution. "I am Duchess of Malfi still," she proudly says to the tool Bosola. Preparations for her own violent death are made in her presence, her coffin brought in and a dirge sung before she is strangled. Her children, and Cariola, her faithful servant and confidante, suffer a like fate. Even Ferdinand, who with diabolic cruelty had ordered her death is seized with penitent horror. "Cover her face: mine eyes dazzle: she died young," he cries. Ferdinand goes mad, Bosola stabs the Cardinal, and Bosola receives his death wound from Ferdinand, but kills his assailant. The last words of Ferdinand were:

> " Whether we fall by ambition, blood, or lust
> Like diamonds we are cut with our own dust."

DUCHESS OF WREXE, THE; HER DECLINE AND DEATH: a romantic commentary by Hugh Walpole (1914). This novel pictures the social system of the Victorian era, which ended with the South African war. The duchess and her class believed England's greatness depended on government by a few blue-blooded autocrats, the clear-headed despots managing the muddle-headed majority. As head of the Beaminster clan, the last of the autocrats, she ruled by the power of tradition, and by continual ceremony, pomp, and circumstance. For thirty years the duchess had not left her room; invisible to the world, she sat in magnificence in her Oriental chair, flanked by two Chinese dragons, and tyrannized over her family and friends, the Beaminster clan. The enemies within her gates were the rising generation, her two grandchildren, both children of misalliances, in whom the Beaminster tradition is at war with a freer spirit. Rachel, her hated granddaughter, feels the terrible old lady's power and fears her, but still refuses to be dominated and insists on thinking for herself. To gain freedom she marries her friend Sir Roderick, one of the Beaminster circle, and a favorite of her grandmother's. Soon after their marriage his flirtation with one of her guests brings about their estrangement. The fascination of her forbidden friendship with her cousin, Francis, the outcast grandson, almost brings her to disaster. She is about to leave her husband to go to him, when Sir Roderick is thrown from his horse and laid on his back for life. It has been a marriage of convenience on both sides, but Sir Roderick has fallen in love with his wife, and his illness and the expectation of a child awakes her love for him. As Rachel's happiness is assured, and the grandson, Francis Beaminster, is recognized by the family without the knowledge of the duchess, the guns of the South African war mark the beginning of democracy, and the duchess dies as her world slips from her dominion.

DUCHESSE DE LANGEAIS, THE, by Balzac (1834), analyzes carefully the Faubourg Saint-Germain, or the aristocracy of Paris under the Restoration. In a most logical and impartial way, Balzac explains how the patrician class loses its natural ascendency when it does not produce the results its advantage of birth and training warrant. After learning that the "Great Lady" had no influence on the morals of the time, that she was hypocritical and artificially educated, it is not to be expected that the heroine of the story, the Duchesse de Langeais, will prove an anomaly of virtue. Parisian to the core, the young duchess lives in the luxury of the boudoir and the fickle gayety of the ball-room. She is characterized as "supremely a woman and supremely a coquette." Unhampered by her husband, who lives his military life apart, the duchess feels free to attach to her suite numberless young men, whom she encourages and repulses by turns. In Armand de Montriveau, however, she finds at last a man of pride and strong will, as well as an ardent lover. He no sooner discovers that Madame is trifling with his affection than he resolves to have his revenge. He arranges an interview, brings the duchess face to face with herself, and denounces her as a murderer, on the ground that she has slain his happiness and his faith — and bids her farewell. The duchess immediately falls in love with him, sends him repentant letters which receive no response, and after a desperate attempt to see him in his own house, leaves Paris just as Monsieur is hastening to call upon her. Armand de Montriveau searches five years for his lady, finding her at last immured in a convent in Spain. Determined to rescue her from such an imprisonment, he succeeds in penetrating to the cell of her who was called by the nuns "Sister Thérèse," only to find the dead body of the Duchesse de Langeais. This is one of the most famous of Balzac's novels. The story is told with all his vigor and minuteness, and the characters impress themselves on the memory as persons actually known.

DUEL, THE, by A. Kuprin (1905). The novel is a depressing revelation of the degradation and misery of garrison life in a frontier town. The officers are brutal, drunken beasts, unmercifully cruel to the soldiers, who live in a slavish state of abject terror. The central character, sub-lieutenant Romashov, is the typical Russian hero of the Russian novel, a talker, a sentimental dreamer with high ideals, but without will-power. In day-dreams he sees himself performing glorious deeds of valor before an admiring world. At the review, the great official event of the year, while he loses himself in romantic visions of promotion, his company is thrown into hopeless confusion by his absent-minded blunders, and he is subjected to a public reprimand.   Nasanki, a drunken officer who is the mouthpiece of the author, bitterly arraigns militarism which makes men low-minded debauchees, "ready for every villainy and cruelty."   Romashov longs to escape from this dreary society with its petty intrigue, petty jealousy, and petty social ambition.   He had a liaison with a vulgar married woman, but eventually falls genuinely in love with the beautiful, heartless Shurochka, married to a stupid husband whose advancement through the staff examinations is her great ambition.   She is willing to amuse herself with the boyish sub-lieutenant's chivalrous devotion, but the time comes when she must choose and she sacrifices him to her ambition.   The woman whom he has left for Shurochka's sake spreads scandal about them until there is open enemity between Shurochka's husband and Romashov, and a duel is arranged.   Shurochka tells Romashov that the duel must be without risk to either of them.   He assents, and is killed by her husband as she planned, in order that the affair may not be a stumbling-block in the way of her husband's future, which is her own hope of escape from the odious provincial town.   The story was translated in an abridged version in 1907 with the title 'In Honor's Name,' and newly translated in 1916.

DUFF-GORDON, LADY, see **LETTERS FROM.**

DUKE'S CHILDREN, THE, see **PARLIAMENTARY NOVELS.**

DUNCIAD, THE, by Alexander Pope.   This mock-heroic poem, the Iliad of the Dunces, was written in 1727, to gratify the spite of the author against the enemies his success and his malice had aroused.   It contains some of the bitterest satire in the language, and as Pope foresaw, has rescued from oblivion the very names that he vituperates.   The poem is divided into four books, in the first of which Dulness, daughter of chaos and eternal night, chooses a favorite to reign over her kingdom. In the early editions this prominence is assigned to Theobald, but in 1743 Pope substituted Colley Cibber.   In the second book, which contains passages as virulent and as nauseating as anything of Swift, the goddess institutes a series of games in honor of the new monarch.   First the booksellers race for a phantom poet, and then the poets contend in tickling and in braying, and end by diving into the mud of Fleet Ditch.   Lastly there is a trial of patience, in which all have to listen to the works of two voluminous writers, and are overcome by slumber.   In the third book the goddess transports the sleeping king to the Elysian shades, where he beholds the past, present, and future triumphs of Dulness, and especially her coming conquest of Great Britain. The fourth book represents the goddess coming with majesty to establish her universal dominion.   Arts and sciences are led captive, and the youth drinks of the cup of Magus, which causes oblivion of all moral or intellectual obligations.   Finally the goddess gives a mighty yawn, which paralyzes mental activity everywhere, and restores the reign of night and chaos over all the earth.   The poem underwent various revisions and its dates of publication of its different editions extend from 1728 to 1742.   Lewis Theobald, the Shakespearian scholar, was originally the hero, but he was deposed by Pope and Colley Cibber substituted in his stead.

DURABLE SATISFACTIONS OF LIFE, THE, a volume of essays and addresses by Charles William Eliot, sometime president of Harvard University.   The book, which was published in 1910, includes besides the title-essay, 'The Happy Life,' 'John Gilley,' 'Great Riches,' and 'The Religion of the Future.'   The purpose of the book is to show that the happy life, being dependent on simple and wholesome

pleasures within the reach of everyone, is a readily attainable ideal. The satisfactions of sense, of intellect, of the domestic affections and social sympathies and of
moral effort are reviewed; and a plea is made for a normal enjoyment of all of these
pleasures, the lower being duly subordinated to the higher. The point of view is an
enlightened hedonism, a sane optimism which is convinced of the preponderance of
good over evil, and a belief in the essential goodness of human nature. President
Eliot prophesies that the religion of the future will be free from dogmatism, other-
worldliness, asceticism, vindictiveness, and emphasis on the salvation of the
individual through propitiatory sacrifice, but characterized by a belief in the
immanence of God, His love for man, and the duty of man to love and serve his
fellows. An interesting illustration of the view of life here set forth is the essay
on 'John Gilley,' an extremely interesting biography of a humble Maine fisherman, who through industry, intelligence, a wholesome outdoor occupation, family
affection, and resolute adherence to duty lived a truly happy life.

DUTCH REPUBLIC, see RISE OF THE.

EARLY HISTORY OF INSTITUTIONS, LECTURES ON THE, by H. S. Maine, see ANCIENT LAW.

**EARLY HISTORY OF MANKIND, RESEARCHES INTO THE, by Edward B.
Tylor (1865).** A volume of investigation into the earliest origins of culture, which
at the time gave the author distinction as an authority in anthropology. The same
author's 'Primitive Culture: Researches into the Development of Mythology,
Philosophy, Religion, Language, Art and Custom,' 1871, carried on the investigation
into other branches of thought and belief, art and custom. The problems discussed
are those of animism or spiritism, as a universal development in early culture; the
origin of rites and ceremonies; the extent to which myths play a part in the early
history of mankind; the early use of numerals and of directly expressive language;
and survivals in culture which bring old ideas far down into later periods.

EARLY INSTITUTIONS, see ANCIENT LAW.

EARLY LAW AND CUSTOM, see ANCIENT LAW.

EARTH AND MAN, THE, by Arnold Guyot (1849). This fascinating book was
the first word upon its subject, — comparative physical geography and its relation to
mankind, — which had ever been addressed to a popular American audience. The
substance of these pages was first given in the form of lectures before the Lowell
Institute of Boston. Professor Guyot contends that geography means not a mere
description of the earth's surface, but an interpretation of the phenomena which it
describes; an endeavor to seize the incessant mutual action of the different portions
of physical nature upon each other, of inorganic nature upon organized beings —
upon man in particular — and upon the successive development of human societies.
In a word, says the author, it must explain the perpetual play of forces that constitutes what might be called the life of the globe, its physiology. Understood otherwise, geography loses its vital principle, and becomes a mere collection of partial,
unmeaning facts. He then goes on to explain how the contours of mountains, their
position, their direction, their height, the length and direction of rivers, the configura-
tion of coasts, the slope of plateaus, the neighborhood of islands, and in a word, all
physical conditions, have modified profoundly the life of man. He explains in detail
the relief of the continents. the characteristics of the oceans. the gradual formation of

the continents, the effects of winds, rains, and marine currents on vegetable and animal life, the causes of likenesses and of differences, and finally, the people and the life of the future. Foretold by their physical condition, the long waiting of the southern continents for their evolution has been inevitable; but the scientist foresees for them a full development when the industrious and skillful men of the northern continents shall join with the men of the tropics to establish a movement of universal progress and improvement.

EARTH AS MODIFIED BY HUMAN ACTION, THE, see **MAN AND NATURE.**

EARTHLY PARADISE, THE (1868–79), a poem by William Morris. One of the most beautiful of nineteenth-century romances, it was written, as the author says to furnish a doorway into the world of enchantment, that land beyond the "utmost purple rim" of earth, for which many are homesick. Yet 'The Earthly Paradise has about it the melancholy which pervades the pre-Raphaelite literature, and seems the fruit of unfulfilled desire, — of the state of those who must create their romance in an age unproductive of such food of the soul. The poem is a collection of the tales of Golden Greece, and of the dim, rich, mediæval time. Certain gentlemen and mariners of Norway having considered all that they had heard of the Earthly Paradise set sail to find it. They come at last, world-weary old men, to a strange Western land, and to a "strange people," descendants of the Greeks, the elders among whom receive them graciously. They agree to feast together twice a month, and to exchange stories: the Norwegians telling tales of "the altered world" of the Middle Ages; the Greeks, of their own bright time when men were young in heart. For a year they tell their tales: in March, Atalanta's Race, and The Man born to be King in April, The Doom of King Acrisius, and The Proud King; in May, The Story of Cupid and Psyche, and The Writing on the Image; in June, The Love of Alcestis and The Lady of the Land; in July, The Son of Crœsus, and The Watching of the Falcon; in August, Pygmalion and the Image, and Ogier the Dane; in September, The Death of Paris, and The Land East of the Sun and West of the Moon; in October, The Story of Accontius and Cydippe, and The Man who Never Laughed Again; in November, The Story of Rhodope, and The Lovers of Gudrun; in December, The Golden Apples, and The Fostering of Aslaug; in January, Bellerophon at Argos, and The Ring Given to Venus; in February, Bellerophon in Lycia, and The Hill of Venus

In these tales the author draws upon Greek mythology, upon the 'Gesta Romanorum,' the Nibelungenlied, the Eddas; indeed, upon the greatest story-books of the world. He has woven them all together in one beautiful Gothic tapestry of verse, in which the colors are dimmed a little. From "his master," Geoffrey Chaucer, the poet has borrowed the three styles of his metre, the heroic, sestina, and octosyllabic The music of the verse is low and sweet, well adapted to tales of "old, unhappy, far-off things, and battles long ago." His Prologue and Epilogue are especially beautiful.

EAST ANGELS, a novel, by Constance Fenimore Woolson (1888). Its setting is "Gracias-à-Dios, a little town lying half asleep on the southern coast of the United States, under a sky of almost changeless blue." The heroine, Edgarda Thorne, the child of a New England mother, but with Spanish blood in her veins, who has lived all her life in the South, is just ripening into womanhood when the story opens. The plot is concerned chiefly with her love-affairs, men of totally different types being thus brought into juxtaposition. Like the author's other novels, 'East Angels' lacks the romantic and ideal elements, but it is strong in the delineation of everyday character and incident.

AST LYNNE, by Mrs. Henry Wood, appeared in 1861. Its scene is laid in con-emporary England. Lady Isabel Vane, early orphaned by the death of a bankrupt ather, who has been compelled to sell East Lynne, his ancestral home, is loved by oth Archibald Carlyle and Francis Levison; the former as noble as the latter is base. he marries Carlyle, but is persuaded by Levison that her husband is unfaithful to er. His insidious slanders so work upon her mind that she presently elopes with im; but being at heart a good woman, she leaves him, and after a few years obtains n engagement as nurse to her own children. She returns disguised to her old home, vhere her husband has married again, and where she becomes the devoted attendant f the young Carlyles. The dénouement clears up her husband's apparent infidelity, eveals Levison to be a murderer, and discloses to Carlyle the identity of Isabel, vhom he has thought dead. Her sufferings break her heart, and upon her death-bed he receives his full forgiveness. The plot, though impossible, is well managed and 1ade to seem credible, and there are several strong and touching situations. The ominant tone of the book is distinctly minor. Although it has little literary merit, it ecured immediate popularity, has been through many editions on two continents, and roved extremely successful as an emotional drama.

BEN HOLDEN, by Irving Bacheller, published in 1900, was the author's first book nd met with great success. It is a simple and homely tale of the life and sayings of Eben Holden," a "hired man," whose affectionate and honest nature endears him o all who know him. In the opening chapters a description is given of his long and ard journey on foot carrying the orphaned boy of his late employer to some place vhere he can find a home for them both. At last a shelter is found at the farm of)avid Brower in the "northern country," where they obtain a permanent abiding-lace. David and his wife Elizabeth, who are good and kindly people, become greatly ttached to the orphan boy; they eventually adopt him and he is called William 3rower. He grows up with Hope Brower, the daughter of the house, a charming irl who is his early sweetheart and later his wife. William goes to college, works for Iorace Greeley on the Tribune, and fights in the Civil War, where he is severely vounded and wins commendation for his bravery. Through all his experiences Eben Iolden is his staunch friend and does everything in his power to bring about his appiness and prosperity, his unselfishness and kindliness being shown on every ccasion. Eben is also instrumental in bringing about the union of David Brower nd his son Nehemiah, who had left his home in his youth and had been mourned as lead for many years; he returns to his parents a rich man, able to make them com-ortable in their declining years. The quaint and original stories and sayings of ben Holden make up a large part of the book, and the creation of his character is a listinct contribution to American fiction.

CCE HOMO, by John Robert Seeley (1865), was a consideration of the life of Christ s a human being. In the preface the author writes: —

"Those who feel dissatisfied with the current conception of Christ, if they cannot est content without a definite opinion, may find it necessary to do what to persons iot so dissatisfied it seems audacious and perilous to do. They may be obliged to econsider the whole subject from the beginning, and placing themselves in imagina-ion at the time when he whom we call Christ bore no such name, to trace his biog-aphy from point to point, and accept those conclusions about him, not which church loctors, or even apostles, have sealed with their authority, but which the facts them-elves, critically weighed, appear to warrant. This is what the present writer under-ook to do "

The result of this undertaking was a portrait of Christ as a man, which, whethe accurate or not, is singularly luminous and suggestive. The author brought to hi task scholarship, historical acumen, above all the power to trace the original diversi ties and irregularities in a surface long since worn smooth. He takes into account th *Zeitgeist* of the age in which Christ lived; the thousand and one political and socia forces by which he was surrounded; and the national inheritances that were his on hi human side, with special reference to his office of Messiah. Thereby he throws ligh upon a character "so little comprehended" as a man. He makes many astute obser vations, such as this on the source of the Jews' antagonism to Christ: "They lai information against him before the Roman government as a dangerous character their real complaint against him was precisely this, that he was *not* dangerous Pilate executed him on the ground that his kingdom was of this world; the Jew procured his execution precisely because it was not. In other words, they could no forgive him for claiming royalty, and at the same time rejecting the use of physica force. . . . They did not object to the king, they did not object to the philosopher but they objected to the king in the garb of the philosopher." The 'Ecce Homo produced a great sensation in England and America. Its boldness, its scientifi character, combined with its spirituality and reverence for the life of Christ, made o it a work which could not be overlooked. Newman, Dean Stanley, Gladstone, an others high in authority, hastened to reply to it. The vitality of the work still remains

ECCLESIASTICAL HISTORY OF BRITAIN, by Bæda or Bede. A work doubl monumental (1) in the extent, faithfulness, care in statement, love of truth, an pleasant style, of its report from all trustworthy sources of the history (not merel ecclesiastical) of Britain, and especially of England, down to the eighth century; an (2) in its being the only authority for important church and other origins and de velopments through the whole period. Bæda was by far the most learned Englishma of his time; one of the greatest writers known to English literature; in a very hig sense "the Father of English History"; an extensive compiler for English use fror the writings of the Fathers of the Church; an author of treatises representing th existing knowledge of science; and a famous English translator of Scripture. In hig qualities of genius and rare graces of character, he was in the line of Shakespeare From one of his young scholars, Cuthbert, we have a singularly beautiful story of th venerable master's death, which befell about 735 A. D., when he was putting the las touches to his translation of the Fourth Gospel. From his seventh year, 680, to th day of his death, May 26, 735, he passed his life in the Benedictine abbey, first a Wearmouth and then at Jarrow; but it was a life of immense scholarly and educationa activity. Green's 'History' says of him: "First among English scholars, first amon English theologians, first among English historians, it is in the monk of Jarrow tha English literature strikes its roots. In the six hundred scholars who gathered roun him for instruction, he is the father of our national education." It was in point o view and name only that Bæda's great work was an ecclesiastical history. It covere all the facts drawn from Roman writers, from native chronicles and biographies from records and public documents, and from oral and written accounts by his con temporaries. It was written in Latin; first printed at Strasburg about 1473; Kin Alfred translated it into Anglo-Saxon; and it has had several editions and Englis versions in recent times. The whole body of Bæda's writings, some forty in number show his unwearied industry in learning, teaching, and writing, his gentle and culti vated feelings, his kindly sympathies, and the singular freshness of mind which gav life and beauty to so many pages of his story of England's past.

ECCLESIASTICAL POLITY, see **LAWS OF.**

ECHO OF PASSION, AN, by George Parsons Lathrop (1882), is one of Lathrop's earliest works. The interest of the story revolves around an accomplished and fascinating Southern widow, Mrs. Eulow; a trusting wife, Ethel Fenn; and a husband, Benjamin Fenn, whose chemical information is more exact than his moral principles. There is nothing intangible or echo-like about the passion depicted, which attains its zenith during the idle days of a summer outing amid the Massachusetts hills. The theme is not new; but in his treatment of it the author presents some interesting ethical arguments, by which the husband seeks to blind himself to his own short-comings, and some touching examples of the young wife's self-control and abnegation. Interspersed are amusing semi-caricatures of the typical boarding-house "guest," the flotsam and jetsam of vacation life.

ÉCOLE DES FEMMES, L' ('The School for Wives'), by Molière, produced in 1662, is a companion piece to 'L'École des Maris' ('The School for Husbands'). They have essentially the same plot; treated, however, with great dramatic dexterity, to clothe a different idea in each. In this comedy, Arnolphe, a typical middle-aged jealous guardian of Agnes, has educated his ward for his future model wife by carefully excluding from her mind all knowledge of good or evil; her little world is circumscribed by the grilled windows and strong doors of Arnolphe's house. Returning from a journey, he finds her sweet and tranquil in her ignorance as before. But soon meeting Horace, a son of his old friend Oronte, he learns by the ingenuous confession of the young fellow that, madly in love with "a young creature in that house," he intends to use the money just borrowed from his father's friend to carry her off. Frantic at this disclosure, Arnolphe rushes to the imprisoned Agnes, from whom by ingenious questioning he extracts a candid avowal of her affection for her lover, and an account of a visit from him. By a clever series of intrigues, the guardian is made the willing, unwitting go-between of the two young people; until at last Agnes, having determined to run away from her hated suitor, braves his anger. Then it is that Arnolphe displays a depth of real passion and tenderness, tragic in its intensity, in pleading with her to revoke her decision; a scene that remains unrivaled among the many fine scenes in Molière. When fiercest in denunciation, the guardian yields to a gentle glance and word. "Little traitress," he cries, "I pardon you all. I give you back my love. That word, that look, disarms my wrath." A pair of conventional stage fathers now appear, who, by revealing the fact that their children, the lovers, have been betrothed from their cradles, unite the two with their blessings; and the desolate Arnolphe receives the penalty of a selfish meddler with youthful affection. Obdurate and rigid in his theories, Arnolphe yet wins esteem by the strength of his character that dominates, even in defeat, the close of the play. Agnes, a type of maiden innocence, far from being colorless or insipid, is a living, glowing portrait of a genuinely interesting *ingénue*, using artifice naturally foreign to her disposition at the service of love only. Outside of the real merit of the play, and the curious sidelight it throws on the dramatist's opinions (married at this time at forty years of age to a girl of seventeen), it opened an attack upon him for suspected religious latitude; contemporary criticism being leveled at the scene in the third act, where a treatise, 'The Maxims of Marriage,' is presented by the guardian-lover to his ward.

ÉCOLE DES MARIS, L', see **L'ÉCOLE DES FEMMES.**

ECONOMIC INTERPRETATION OF HISTORY, by J. E. Thorold Rogers (1888). A volume of Oxford lectures, covering a wide range of important topics, with the general aim of showing how economic questions have come up in English history, and have powerfully influenced its development. The questions of labor, money, protection, distribution of wealth, social effect of religious movements, pauperism and taxation, are among those which are carefully dealt with. In a posthumously published volume, 'The Industrial and Commercial History of England,' 1892, another series of Professor Rogers's Oxford lectures appeared, completing the author's view both of the historical facts and of method of study.

EDDA, ELDER: EDDA, YOUNGER, see **HEIMSKRINGLA.**

EDUCATION, by Herbert Spencer (1860). It is the highest praise that can be bestowed upon this treatise, that it seems now a book of obvious if not of commonplace philosophy, whereas, when it was published, it was recognized as revolutionary in the extreme. So rapidly has its wisdom become incarnated in methods if not in systems. The book opens with an examination of what knowledge is of most worth: it shows that in the mental world as in the bodily, the ornamental comes before the useful; that we do not seek to develop our own individual capacities to their utmost, but to learn what will enable us to make the most show, or accomplish the greatest material successes. But if the important thing in life is to know how to live, in the widest sense, then education should be made to afford us that knowledge; and the knowledge is hence of most value which informs and develops the whole man. Mathematics, Physics, Chemistry, Biology, the Science of Society,—all these are important; but an education which teaches youth how to become fit for parentage is indispensable. Too many fathers and mothers are totally unfit to develop either the bodies, the souls, or the minds of their children. From the duty of preparation on the part of the parent, it is a short step to the duty of preparation on the part of the citizen. And still another division of human life, that which includes the relaxations and pleasures of existence, should be made a matter of intelligent study; for this comprehends the whole field of the fine arts, the whole æsthetic organization of society. The essayist now considers in detail, Intellectual Education, Moral Education, and Physical Education. He shows not only an unreasoned and unreasonable existing state of things, but he discloses the true philosophy underlying the question, and points out the true methods of reasonableness and rightness. Each chapter is enriched with a wealth of illustration drawn from history, literature, or life; and the argument, although closely reasoned, is very entertaining from first to last. Few books of the age have had a more direct and permanent effect upon the general thought than this; many parents and teachers who know Herbert Spencer only as a name follow the suggestions which are now a part of the common intellectual air

EDUCATION, SOME THOUGHTS CONCERNING, see **THOUGHTS, ETC.**

EDUCATION, TRACTATE ON, see **TRACTATE, ETC.**

EDWARD II., an historical play, by Christopher Marlowe acted in 1592?, first published in 1594, is generally regarded as the author's masterpiece. The scene opens in London. Gaveston, Edward's favorite, is invited by the King to come and share his kingdom. Earl Lancaster and the elder and younger Mortimer are incensed at Edward's infatuation for his favorite. In spite of the displeasure of his nobles, Edward bestows upon Gaveston the castle and rents of the Bishop of Coventry, who had previously been the chief cause of Gaveston's being sent into exile. The Archbishop of Canterbury and the nobles, the counsellors of the King, force Edward to banish Gaveston. Edward in pique becomes estranged from his Queen, Isabella, whom he accuses of familiarity with Mortimer, but sends Gaveston to be governor of Ireland. The Queen, anxious to win back the favor of the King, induces the nobles to consent to the repeal of Gaveston's banishment; but when Gaveston returns, he is received with satirical greetings by the nobles, headed by Warwick and the younger Mortimer, who seize him and keep him under arrest. In the meantime the King of France had seized Normandy, and Isabella and her son, who were sent to France on a mission of appeasement, returned without having accomplished their ends. In their absence the Spencers had come to the aid of Edward, who captured certain of the nobles. Others joined the Queen on her return and Edward was forced to resign his crown. The growing horror and pathos of the closing scenes which describe the events leading up to the king's assassination won the enthusiastic eulogy of Charles Lamb. The young prince who comes to the throne orders the death of Mortimer and the imprisonment of the Queen.

EGOIST, THE, by George Meredith (1879), is a fine illustration of a complete novel without a plot. It is a study of egotism. The egoist is Sir Willoughby Patterne, of Patterne Hall, a consummate young gentleman of fortune and rank, whose disposition and breeding make him only too well aware of his perfections, and of his value in the matrimonial market. He determines to choose his wife prudently and deliberately, as befits the selection of the rare creature worthy to receive the gift of his incomparable self. In describing the successive courtships by which the egotism of the egoist is thrown into high light, Meredith presents a most natural group of fair women: the brilliant Constantia Durham, Clara Middleton the "dainty rogue in porcelain," and Lætitia Dale with "romances on her eyelashes." The curtain falls on the dreary deadness of Sir Willoughby's incurable self-satisfaction.

EGYPT, A HISTORY OF, from the Earliest Times to the Persian Conquest, by J. H. Breasted (1905). A history for the general reader based on the results of archæological research. Professor Breasted has published his historical material in four volumes 'Ancient Records of Egypt' (1906), texts and translations of the inscriptions on the monuments in the museums of Europe and Cairo, and in the valley of the Nile. The period covered is from 4241 B. C., "the earliest fixed date in the history of the world," to 525 B. C. The most interesting discoveries of recent years come within the scope of the first two books on the prehistoric period, the pyramid builders and their ancestors. Book 1 gives a preliminary survey of the chronology and the documentary sources, and the facts known about the predynastic Egyptians. Book 2 is a picture of the Old Kingdom, the first known civilization, its politics, religion, industry, art, and customs. This early kingdom of the North declined and Book 3 discusses the feudal age of the Middle Kingdom of internal struggle between king and nobles. In Book 4 comes the century of Hyksos invasion and expulsion. Book 5 deals with the rise of the Empire, and its dissolution with the fall of Ikhnaton, 'the first individual in human history," a dreamer and idealist, who lost his empire while he was composing hymns to the sun and establishing a new religion. Book 6 is the story of the triumph of Amon and the reorganization of the Empire, the wars of Rameses I. and II. and the final decline of the Empire with the reign of Rameses III. Book 7 is the fall of the Empire and the supremacy first of the Libyans, then the Ethiopians, and finally of Assyria. Book 8, "The Restoration and the End" traces the history of the final struggle with Babylon and Persia to the creation in the East of the great Empire of Persia.   The decline of Egypt was caused by the rise to power of the priests of Amon.   Professor Breasted has written a modern readable scholarly history instead of a lifeless chronicle of Pharaohs and dynasties, making the people of this remote age as real as the Greeks and Romans.

EGYPT, A HISTORY OF (New ed., 6 vols., 1905).   Vol. i., from the Earliest Times to the Sixteenth Dynasty. Vol. ii., During the Seventeenth and Eighteenth dynasties. Vol. iii., The Nineteenth to the Thirtieth Dynasty, by W. M. Flinders Petrie. Vol. iv., Ptolemaic Dynasty, by J. P. Mahaffy. Vol. v., Egypt under Roman rule, by J. G. Milne.   Vol. vi., Egypt in the Middle Ages, by Stanley Lane-Poole.   These volumes embrace the whole history of Egypt down to modern times. The design of the whole work is to supply a book of reference which shall suffice for all ordinary purposes, but with special attention to facts and illustrations which are new, and with the utmost care to throw as much light as possible upon Egyptian dates. There is no intention of including a history of art, civilization, or literature; the one purpose of the work is to get into as accurate shape as possible the history and chronology of the successive dynasties. The figures settled upon by Professor Petrie, in his first volume, show seventeen dynasties ruling from 4777 B. C. to 1587 B. C., and Dynasty XVIII. carrying on the history to 1327 B. C. It is thus the story of 3450 years which he tells in the two volumes.   The history of the seventeenth dynasty (1738–1587 B. C.), and of the eighteenth, told in Vol. ii., are especially important; and for these, no record or monument has been left unnoticed.

EGYPT AND CHALDÆA, see DAWN OF CIVILIZATION.

EGYPTIAN ARCHÆOLOGY, MANUAL OF, and Guide to the Study of Antiquities in Egypt, by Gaston Maspero.   Translated by Amelia B. Edwards (Fourth Revised Edition: 1895). One of the most picturesque, original, and readable volumes in the immense literature to which our vast new knowledge of the long-buried Egypt has given rise.   With its many new facts and new views and interpretations, gleaned by M. Maspero with his unrivaled facilities as director of the great Boulak Museum at Cairo, the volume is, for the general reader and the student, the most adequate of text-books and handbooks of its subject.

EGYPTIAN PRINCESS, AN, a German historical romance by Georg Ebers, was published in 1864. Its scenes are laid in Egypt and Persia, toward the close of the sixth century B. C.   The narrative follows the fates of the royal families of the two nations, tracing the career of the headstrong, passionate Cambyses, from the days of his marriage with the Egyptian princess Nitetis, whom he was deceived into accepting as the daughter of Amasis, King of Egypt, down to the times when his ill-fated bride taking poison, he himself humbles the arms of Egypt in punishment for their deception; and, dissipated, violent, capricious, the haughty monarch meets his death, Darius the Mede reigning in his stead. A figure of infinite pathos is the gentle Nitetis; with pitiful patience meeting the cruel suspicions of Cambyses, and content to kiss his hand in her death agonies, the result of his intemperate anger.

Another interesting character is Bartja, the handsome and chivalrous younger brother of Cambyses, of whom the King is so unjustly jealous. His love for Sappho, granddaughter of the far-famed Rhodopis, is one of the most genuine conceptions in literature.   Several historic characters are introduced and placed in natural settings, notably Crœsus, mentor of the unhappy Cambyses; and Darius, whose future great-ness is foreshadowed in an early youth of discretion and prowess.

EGYPTIANS, RELIGIONS OF THE ANCIENT, see **RELIGIONS, ETC.**

EIKON BASILIKE: 'The True Portraiture of his Sacred Majestie in his Soli-tudes and Sufferings,' by John Gauden, February 9th, 1649. One of the most worthless yet most effective and famous literary forgeries ever attempted. Its author was a Presbyterian divine, bishop of Exeter and Worcester under Charles II. "It got Parson Gauden a bishopric," Carlyle wrote November 26th, 1840. On Thursday, January 4th, 1649, the change of England from a monarchy to a republic, or commonwealth, had been made by the passage in the Commons House of Parlia-ment of three resolutions: (1) That the people are the original of all just power in the State; (2) That the Commons represent that power; and (3) That their enactments needed no consent of king or peers to have the force of law. On Tuesday, January 30th, between two and three P.M., the execution of Charles I. had taken place. Ten days later, February 9th, there was published with great secrecy, and in very mys-terious fashion, the small octavo volume of 269 pages, the title of which is given above. The frontispiece to the volume was an elaborate study in symbols and mottoes, in a picture of the king on his knees in his cell looking for a crown of glory. The twenty-eight chapters purporting to have been written by Charles, and to tell the spiritual side of the later story of his life, each began with a fragment of narrative, or of meditation on some fact of his life, and then gave a prayer suited to the supposed circumstances. Not only was the whole scheme of the book a grotesque fiction, but the execution was cheap, pointless, "vapid falsity and cant," Carlyle said, and a vulgar imitation of the liturgy; yet fifty editions in a year did not meet the demand for it; and it created almost a worship of the dead king. It remains a singular example of what a literary forgery can accomplish.

EKKEHARD, by Joseph Victor von Scheffel (1857) is a story told by one who believed in the "union of poetry and fiction." To him "the characters of the past arose from out the mist of years, and bade him clothe them anew in living form to please his own and succeeding generations." The time is the tenth century, the century of King Canute's conquest of England. The hero, Ekkehard, is a young Benedictine monk of the holy house of St. Gall, in Suabia, a house whose abbot is an old man named Cralo. The abbot is a distant cousin to Hadwig, countess of Suabia, whose deceased lord, Burkhard, had been a tyrannical old nobleman who in his dotage wedded Hadwig, a fair daughter of Bavaria, who had entered into the alliance to please her father. At Burkhard's death the emperor has declared that the countess shall hold her husband's fiefs so long as she does not marry again. But the countess, — young, beautiful, rich, and idle, — in a moment of recklessness decides to visit the monastery of St. Gall, which has a rule that woman's foot must never step across its threshold; and while the countess waits without, and Cralo and his monks discuss what should be done, the ready-witted young Ekkehard suggests that some one *carry* the countess across the portal. He is deputed to do so, and from the hour when he takes her into his arms, the poet-monk loves the Countess Hadwig. Later, when he is sent to be her tutor, despite his self-restraint he reveals his love to her. He is as "the moth fluttering around a candle." Fleeing love's temptations, Ekkehard goes far up into the mountains with his lyre, and amid the snow-capped peaks, sings his master-song. This he transcribes, and tying it to an arrow, he shoots it so that it falls at the countess's feet. It is his parting gift. He journeys into the world, his songs making a welcome for him everywhere; and in her halls the countess keeps his memory to fill her lonely hours. In 1885 the story had reached its eighty-sixth edition in the original German, while innumerable translations have been made into English. Though Scheffel gave the world other volumes of prose and poetry, none is so well known, or considered so good.

ELEANOR, by Mrs. Humphry Ward, was published in 1900. The real interest of this book is not so much in its plot as in the development of the character of its heroine Eleanor Burgoyne, a woman of rare charm and of supreme intellectual endowment, who comes to Rome for the benefit of her health. She has had a brief and unhappy married life which has ended with the death of husband and child, since when she has for eight years been absorbed in the world of books. In Rome, she is brought into close companionship with her cousin Edward Manisty, with whom she falls devotedly in love. He is thoroughly self-centred and egotistical, moody and taciturn, and possesses insufferable manners. Despite her frail health, Eleanor throws herself body and soul into the endeavor to aid Manisty in the production of a successful book; she spends long and exhausting hours discussing, copying, and advising, and acts as an intellectual stimulus for his powers and perceptions. The introduction of Lucy Foster upon the scene, and an adverse criticism upon his book, bring about a change in Manisty's attitude towards Eleanor; he falls in love with the pretty young American girl and his cousin realizes that he has not a thought for her. She at first attempts to separate the lovers, and Lucy, loyal to the older woman, and true to the promptings of her Puritan conscience, rejects the advances of Manisty, and leaves Rome with Eleanor, whose health, impaired by the emotional and physical strain she has experienced, is gradually failing. After much suffering and a violent mental struggle, Eleanor rises above her own feelings and exerts her influence to bring about the union of the lovers, whose marriage she survives but by a few months.

ELECTIVE AFFINITIES ('Wahlverwandschaften') by Goethe, was published in 1809. The novel has four principal characters: Edward, a wealthy nobleman, and his wife Charlotte; her niece Ottilie; and a friend of Edward, known as the Captain. These four being together at Edward's country-seat, Ottilie falls in love with Edward, Charlotte with the Captain. The wife, however, remains faithful to her husband; but Ottilie yields to her passion, expiating her sin only with her death. The tragedy of the book seems designed to show that "elective affinities" may be fraught with danger and sorrow; that duty may have even a higher claim than the claim of the soul. The novel is throughout of the highest interest in the delineation of character and of the effects of passion.

ELEGANTIÆ LATINÆ SERMONIS ('Elegancies of Latin Speech'), by Laurentius Valla (Lorenzo della Valla), 1444; 59th ed. 1536. A standard work on Latin style, written in the days of the earlier Italian Renaissance, when the Latin Middle Ages were coming to a close. It is notable as the latest example of Latin used as a living tongue. Valla was a thoroughly Pagan Humanist. His 'De Voluptate,' written at Rome about 1443, was a scholarly and philosophical apology for sensual pleasure; the first important word of the new paganism. The 'Elegancies' followed, and the two works gave their author the highest reputation as a brilliant writer and critic of Latin composition. At an earlier date (1440) Valla had published a work designed to show that the papal claim of a grant made to the papacy by Constantine had no valid historical foundation. This was the first effort of skepticism in that direction; yet the successor of Eugenius IV., Nicholas V., invited Valla, as one of the chief scholars ɔf the age, to take the post of apostolic secretary at Rome, and paid him munificently for a translation of Thucydides into Latin. Valla further did pre-Reformation work by his 'Adnotationes' on the New Testament, in which for the first time the Latin Vulgate version was subjected to comparison with the Greek original. Erasmus re-edited this work, and Ulrich von Hutten republished the attack on the papal claims. The permanent interest of Valla is that of an able initiator of criticism, linguistic, historical, and ethical.

ELIA, see **ESSAYS OF ELIA.**

ELINE VERE, see **FOOTSTEPS OF FATE.**

ELIZABETH; or, THE EXILES OF SIBERIA, by Sophie Cottin (1805), is regarded in the English-speaking world as her best work; though in France her 'Mathilde,' founded on incidents in the life of Richard Cœur-de-Lion's sister, is more highly esteemed. The picturesque story of Elizabeth was founded on fact; its theme — the successful attempt of a Polish maiden of high birth to obtain the pardon of her exiled parents from the Emperor Alexander, at his coronation in 1801 — is so exalted that one cannot help wishing it had been told with more simplicity and fewer comments. The descriptions of nature and of remote corners of Russia are done with much fidelity — not to mention Elizabeth's peasant costume: her short red petticoat, reindeer trousers, squirrel-skin boots, and fur bonnet. A less virile writer than Madame de Staël, Madame Cottin nevertheless helped to pave the way for the romantic school in France.

ELIZABETH AND HER GERMAN GARDEN, by Countess Von Arnim (later Countess Russell) appeared anonymously in 1898. Elizabeth, a young married woman, tired of city life, persuades her husband to move into the country where they have an old family estate, which is rapidly going to decay. The opening pages describe in a most breezy and delightful way her first experience in bringing order out of chaos. She goes in advance of her family to the old house, accompanied by a housekeeper and a servant, and oversees the workman and gardeners, who are making the place habitable. Elizabeth who is a true lover of nature, finds perfect enjoyment in her out-of-door life, and her ecstasy and delight over her garden forms the motive of the tale. After some weeks spent entirely in communing with nature, she is joined by her family, and her journal then depicts their idyllic home life in the country. Her husband, whom she laughingly calls the "Man of Wrath," and her three children, designated severally as the "April," "May," and "June" babies, figure frequently in the pages of her journal. The trials she endures from unwelcome guests, stupid servants, and a disagreeable governess, are amusingly described, as are the minute details of her experimental gardening. The author's enthusiasm for nature, and keen knowledge of humanity makes the book both entertaining and agreeable reading. It is delightful in style, and Elizabeth muses, laughs, and moralizes over her garden, her husband, her babies, and her acquaintances in a peculiarly feminine way in which is blended humor, simplicity, shrewdness, and philosophy.

ELLE ET LUI, by George Sand (1859). A novel based on the author's relations twenty-five years before, in 1834, with Alfred de Musset, whose death occurred in 1857. As the story was one to which there could be no reply by the person most concerned, an indignant brother, Paul de Musset, wrote 'Lui et Elle' to alter the lights on the picture. At the entrance of the woman known in literature as George Sand upon the bohemian freedom in Paris, she shared her life with Jules Sandeau,

and first used the pen-name Jules Sand, when he and she worked together and brought
out a novel entitled 'Rose et Blanche.' Enabled shortly after to get a publisher for
'Indiana,' which was wholly her own work, she changed her pen-name to George
Sand. But Sandeau and she did not continue together. Alfred de Musset and she
entered upon a relationship of life and literary labor which took them to Italy at the
end of 1833, gave them a short experience of harmony in 1834, but came to an end by
estrangement between them in 1835. Her side of this estrangement is reflected in
'Elle et Lui,' and his in Paul de Musset's 'Lui et Elle.'

ELM-TREE ON THE MALL, THE, see **L'HISTOIRE CONTEMPORAINE.**

ELSIE VENNER, by Oliver Wendell Holmes, was first published serially, in 1859–
60, under the name of 'The Professor's Story.' The romance is a study in heredity,
introducing a peculiar series of phenomena closely allied to such dualism of nature
as may best be described by the word "ophianthropy." Delineations of the characters, social functions, and religious peculiarities of a New England village, form a
setting for the story. Elsie Venner is a young girl whose physical and psychical
peculiarities occasion much grief and perplexity to her father, a widower of gentle
nature and exceptional culture. The victim of some pre-natal casualty, Elsie shows
from infancy unmistakable traces of a serpent-nature intermingling with her higher
self. This nature dies within her only when she yields to an absorbing love. Like all
the work of Dr. Holmes, the story is brilliantly written and full of epigrammatic
sayings; it is acute though harsh in dissection of New England life, and distinguished
by psychological insight and the richest humor.

EMANUEL QUINT, see **FOOL IN CHRIST.**

EMBLEMS, by Francis Quarles (1635). A book of grotesque engravings, borrowed
from Hermann Hugo's 'Pia Desideria,' and fitted with crudely fanciful, studiously
quaint, and sometimes happily dramatic, religious poems, such as Quarles had earlier
published as 'Divine Poems' (a collected volume, 1630, representing ten years), and
'Divine Fancies' (1632). They mingle something of the sublime with a great deal of
the commonplace; and only lend themselves to admiration if we are prepared to
make the best of conceits and oddities along with some elevated thoughts. They
have come into favor of late as antique and curious, rather than upon any original
merit in respect either of poetry or of picture. The engravings, however, were by
Marshall.

ÉMILE, by Jean Jacques Rousseau, the most famous of pedagogic romances, was
composed in 1762. Its immediate effect was to call down on his head the denunciations of the Archbishop of Paris, who found him animated "by a spirit of insubordination and revolt," and to exile him for some years from France. Its lasting effect
was to lay the foundation of modern pedagogy. Due to the suggestion of a mother
who asked advice as to the training of a child, it was the expansion of his opinions
and counsels; the framework of a story sustaining an elaborate system of elementary
education. Émile, its diminutive hero, is reared apart from other children under a
tutor, by a long series of experiments conducted by the child himself, often with
painful consequences. Little by little, his childish understanding comes to comprehend at first-hand the principles of physics, mechanics, gardening, property, and
morals. At last the loosely woven plot leads to the marriage of Émile with Sophie, a
girl who has been educated in a similar fashion. Arbitrary, but always ingenious
and stimulating, the experiments introduced are veritable steps of knowledge. As

object-lessons, the altercation with the gardener and the visit to the mountebank are unsurpassed in the simplicity with which the complex ideas of property and magnetism are presented to a developing intelligence. From the hints contained in 'Émile,' Basedow, Pestalozzi, and Froebel drew their inspiration and laid the broad foundations of modern elementary education. Unsystematic, sometimes impracticable, full of suggestion, it invests the revolutionary ideas of its author with his customary literary charm.

EMINENT AUTHORS OF THE NINETEENTH CENTURY, translated from the Danish of Brandes by Rasmus B. Anderson (1882), is a collection of nine critical essays, "literary portraits," from the German, Danish, English, French, Swedish, and Norwegian literatures. "In all of them," says the author, "the characteristics of the individual are so chosen as to bring out the most important features of the author's life and works." In a close and brilliant analysis, influenced by Taine's method of reference to race, environment, and moment, Brandes develops what was most individual in the production of each. His subjects are all men whose maturest productions appeared during the middle or earlier half of the century, and exercised a formative influence upon modern literature. He shows the German poet Heyse abandoning traditional methods of thought to follow "the voice of instinct," and thus inaugurating the reign of individuality.

Hans Christian Andersen is the discoverer of the child in Northern literature, the man with the rare gift of viewing nature with childlike eyes; John Stuart Mill is the strong yet insular Englishman with a "matter-of-fact mind" which made him intolerant of German mysticism, yet wearing an "invisible nimbus of exalted love of truth"; Renan is the patient philosopher, hater of the commonplace, lover of the unfindable ideal, "a spectator in the universe"; Tegnér is the humanistic lyrist of the North; Flaubert the painful seeker after perfection of form; the Danish Paludan-Müller, a poet, who with a satiric realization of earthly discords, clings to orthodox religious ideals; Björnson, the poet-novelist of Norway, is the cheerful practical patriot, loving and serving his people in daily life; while his fellow-countryman Henrik Ibsen is the literary pathologist of the North, who diagnoses social evils without attempting to offer a remedy. The fact that they were all modern in spirit, all longed to express what is vital or of universal application has made their work as valuable to foreign readers as to their own countrymen. Its local color and feeling endeared it at home, and heightened its charm abroad.

EMMA, by Jane Austen. The story of 'Emma' is perhaps one of the simplest in all fiction, but the genius of Miss Austen manifests itself throughout. All her books show keen insight into human nature; but in 'Emma' the characters are so true to life, and the descriptions so vivid, that for the time one positively lives in the village of Highbury, the scene of the tale. At the opening of the story, Emma Woodhouse, the heroine, "handsome, clever, and rich," and somewhat spoilt by a weak fussy father, lives alone with him. Her married sister's brother-in-law, Mr. Knightley, is a frequent visitor at their house; as is Mrs. Weston, Emma's former governess. Mr. Knightley is a quiet, sensible English gentleman, the only one who tells Emma her faults. Finding life dull, Emma makes friends with Harriet Smith, an amiable, weak-minded young girl, and tries to arrange a match between her and Mr. Elton, the clergyman, but fails. Frank Churchill — Mrs. Weston's stepson — arrives in the village, pays marked attention to Emma, and supplies the town with gayety and gossip. Shortly after his departure, a letter brings the news of his rich aunt's death and his own secret engagement to Jane Fairfax, a beautiful girl in Highbury. Emma suspects Harriet of being in love with Mr. Churchill, but discovers that she cherishes instead a hidden affection for Mr. Knightley. The disclosure fills Emma with alarm, and she realizes for the first time that no one but herself must marry him. Fortunately he has long loved her; and the story ends with her marriage to him, that of Harriet to Mr. Martin, her rejected lover, and of Jane to Frank Churchill.

The gradual evolution of her better self in Emma, and her unconscious admiration for Mr. Knightley's quiet strength of character, changing from admiration to love as she herself grows, is exceedingly interesting. Chief among the other characters are Mr. Woodhouse, a nervous invalid with a permanent fear of colds, and a taste for thin gruel; and talkative Miss Bates, who flits from one topic of conversation to another like a distracted butterfly. Less brilliant than 'Pride and Prejudice,' 'Emma' is equally rich in humor, in the vivid portraiture of character, and a never-ending delight in human absurdities, which the fascinated reader shares from chapter to chapter. It was published in 1816, when Jane Austen was forty-one.

EN MÉNAGE, by J. K. Huysman, see **EN ROUTE.**

EN ROUTE, a novel, by J. K. Huysman (1895), is translated by Kegan Paul. The author, whose literary career began in 1875, has devoted himself largely to what may be termed a kind of brutal mysticism. His works 'Marthe,' 'Les Sœurs Vatard,' and 'En Ménage,' deal largely with themes that are sordid and scarred with hatred and ugliness, as if his mission were mainly to portray "la bêtise de l'humanité." A morbid delight in what is corrupt leads to a corrupt mysticism. What is known as Satanism finds its extreme expression in his novel 'Là-Bas.' It is a "surfeit of supernaturalism producing a mental nausea." 'En Route' depicts the "religious" conversion of a young debauché of Paris, Dartal by name, — a character who first appears in 'Là-Bas.' He is blasé, empty of motives of capacity for pleasure or endeavor. He takes to visiting the churches; feels a certain spell produced by the ritual and music; and at length, drawn into the monastic retreat of La Trappe, he becomes a convert to religion, and dwells with delight and much fine analysis on his experience of a kind of ecstasy of restraints, a "frenzy of chastity." The story is autobiographic: "the history of a soul." It abounds in passages of great brilliancy and beauty; and in some of the meditations on the inner meaning of the ritual, and the effect of the music of the church, his interpretations will meet with a very sympathetic response from many readers. His description of the Breviary is a splendid piece of writing. The book may be called a faithful account of the "ritualistic disease," as it affects the French mind. "It was not so much himself advancing into the unknown, as the unknown surrounding, penetrating, possessing him little by little." He closes suddenly with his entering into the "night obscure" of the mystics. "It is inexpressible. Nothing can reveal the anguish necessary to pass through to enter this mystic knowledge." The soul of the writer seems to think aloud in the pages of his book; he frankly portrays his condition: "too much writer to become a monk; too much monk to remain a writer." The reader remains in doubt, after all, as to whither the hero of the book is *en route.* 'En Route' is a perfect guide-book to the churches of Paris, their exteriors and interiors, their clergy, and the daily life of each church.

ENCYCLOPÆDIA BRITANNICA, THE. The First Edition of the Encyclopædia Britannica was begun in 1768 and completed in 1771 in three volumes, containing

2670 pages. Colin Macfarquar, an Edinburgh printer, and Andrew Bell, the principal Scottish engraver of that day, were the proprietors. The work was edited and in great part written by William Smellie, another Edinburgh printer. This work, "by a society of gentlemen in Scotland," according to the title-page, was compiled on a new plan. Instead of dismembering the sciences by attempting to treat them under a multitude of technical terms, they digested the principles of every science in the form of distinct treatises, and explained the terms as they occurred in order of the alphabet. The merits and novelty of this plan consist first in keeping important related subjects together, and secondly in facilitating references by numerous separate articles arranged in alphabetical order.

The Second Edition, 10 volumes containing 8595 pages, was issued from 1777 to 1784. The plan of the work was enlarged by the addition of history and biography, which encyclopædias in general had hitherto omitted. It was henceforth "an encyclopædia not solely of arts and sciences but of the whole wide circle of general learning and miscellaneous information." (Quarterly Review, cxiii., 362.) These first two editions of the Encyclopædia Britannica were made chiefly by compilation. They were produced by two or three men who took the whole realm of human knowledge for their province. In the Third Edition, however, a plan was adopted of seeking contributions on special and technical subjects from specialists — a plan which has since been followed and has won for the Encyclopædia Britannica a unique reputation. The Third Edition, in eighteen volumes, containing 14,579 pages, was issued from 1788 to 1797.

In the Fourth Edition, which came out from 1801 to 1810, in twenty volumes containing 16,033 pages, the principle of specialist contributions was considerably extended. The copyright was purchased in 1812 by Archibald Constable, who brought out the Fifth and Sixth Editions, each in twenty volumes, from 1815 to 1817 and from 1823 to 1824, respectively. These editions were little more than reprints and corrections of the Fourth. But Constable lavished his money and energy on a six volume Supplement (to the Fourth, Fifth, and Sixth Editions) which appeared from 1816 to 1824.

The publication of the Ninth Edition was commenced by A. and C. Black, publishers of the Seventh and Eighth Editions, in 1875, under the editorship of Thomas Spencer Baynes until 1880 and subsequently of W. Robertson Smith, and was completed in 1889. It consisted of twenty-five volumes (one being an index) containing 21,572 pages. The preparation of this edition had been undertaken on a scale which Adam Black considered so hazardous that he refused to have any part in the enterprise, and accordingly retired from the firm; indeed over one million dollars was spent in the editorial preparation alone; but the ultimate sale showed that his fears were groundless. It was the great success of this edition that led to the publication by The Times (London) in 1902 of an elaborate supplement in eleven volumes to form the Tenth Edition.

After eight years of diligent preparation the Eleventh Edition was completed. It was published, 1910–1911, in twenty-nine volumes (one a separate index containing over 500,000 references) by the Cambridge University Press, to which the copyright and control of the Encyclopædia Britannica had passed in 1909. The Eleventh Edition is particularly rich in maps and illustrations. There are 569 maps, and over 7000 illustrations, including 450 full-page plates. The Encyclopædia Britannica in the Eleventh Edition is the most comprehensive reference work in the world, containing over 44,000,000 words.

ENCYCLOPÉDIE, THE. An Encyclopædia of Arts and Sciences, which, in its character, its significance, and its results, was the most startling and striking production of its time, — an outburst of ideas, of intellectual audacity, of freedom, and a great passion for knowledge and of the sympathy of humanity, labor, and progress. No encyclopædia ever made compares with it in respect of its political influence and its commanding place in the civil and literary history of its own century. It grew out of a plan for a French translation of an early 'Chambers's Cyclopædia.' Diderot, to whom the glory of the colossal enterprise belongs, took occasion from this plan to conceive and to secure the execution of a thorough work, summarizing human knowledge, putting the sciences into the place which tradition had given to religion, and aiming at the service of humanity instead of the service of the church. The Titans of intelligence and of literature, says M. Martin's graphic sketch, had developed an excess of energy and boldness. Voltaire, bringing Locke's ideas into France, had changed Christian deism into Epicureanism, and prepared the way for Condillac's pushing the philosophy of sensation to an extreme beyond Locke; and for Helvetius to press the moral consequences of the system, justifying all the vices and all the crimes. Buffon, magnificent in knowledge, and in a noble style, had made Nature take the place of God, and the love of humanity do duty as religion. In sequel to such moral skepticism or naturalist pantheism came Diderot, with audacious repugnance to any limitations upon liberty, and impetuous passion for knowledge, for human progress. With D'Alembert drawing together a society of men of science and of letters, he launched a Prospectus in November, 1750, for an Encyclopédie or Dictionary of Arts and Sciences, and in 1751 began with 2 volumes, to finish in 1765 with 17 volumes; then to add 11 volumes of plates (1762-72), and 5 volumes of supplements (1776-77); and thus make, with 2 volumes of Index (1780), 35 volumes (1751-80), with 23,135 pages and 3132 plates. Not only information was given in these volumes, but opinions of the most radical character, hostile to the church, subversive of religion, intensely antagonistic towards everything in the old order of things. The clergy and the court had fought the work, had even broken into it with alterations secretly made at the printers', and left no stone unturned to prevent its circulation. Yet Europe was filled with it, and shaken with the effects of it. It was an immense burst of everything which journalism to-day means; a fierce prophecy of changes which are still hanging; a wild proclamation of the problems of human aspiration and desire. Not only were the sciences pushed to the utmost by Diderot, but he made industry, labor, human toil in the shop, an interest unceasingly cherished. It was an explosion heralding the Revolution a quarter of a century later.

ENDYMION, by Benjamin Disraeli, later Earl of Beaconsfield (1835). This is one of a series of political portraits under the form of a novel, which for a time attained great popularity among the English people, but for obvious reasons was less interesting to foreigners. 'Coningsby' and 'Endymion' are hardly more than descriptions of the rival political parties in England at the opening of the Reform Bill agitation, and of the Poor Law and "Protection" controversies, — colored with the pale glimmer of a passion cooled by shrewdness, and of a romance carefully trimmed to suit the stiff conventionalisms of English society, — and spiced with revenge on the author's foes.

'Endymion' relates the fortunes of a youth so named, and his sister Myra; children of one William Ferrars, who from humble life has won his way to a candidacy for the Speakership of the House of Commons, when suddenly, by a change of political sentiment in the boroughs, the administration is overthrown, and the ambitious

and flattered leader finds himself both deserted and bankrupt. To retrieve their
social and political position is the steady ambition and never-yielding effort of the
son and daughter; and to Endymion's advancement Myra makes every sacrifice
that a sister's devotion can devise. Through personal influence as well as his own
fascinating personality and brilliant gifts, Endymion finds an entry with the winning
side; and being untroubled by any scrupulous motive of consistency to principle,
keeps himself at the front in popular favor. Myra marries the Prime Minister, and at
his death she takes for her husband the king of a small Continental State. Endymion crowns her aspirations by marrying a widow in high station, who has long been
his admirer, and whose husband dies at a convenient moment in the narrative. At
the close of the story he sees, by a happy combination of political influence, the door
opened to his own appointment as Premier of England. The story moves along in the
stately monotonous measure of English high life, with not even any pronounced
villainy to heighten the uniform color effect of the characters and incidents. There
is a noticeable absence of anything like high patriotic motive associated with that of
personal advancement: it is difficult to conceive of such personages living without
some political predilection. Over all is the subdued glow of an intensely selfish
culture and refinement. Nigel, Endymion's student friend at Oxford, is the easily
recognized type of the Puseyite of the Tractarian religious movement, if not a personal portraiture of Cardinal Newman. Other characters are doubtless drawn from
life more or less plainly, but none more vividly than Endymion himself, in whose
career the reader sees outlined very clearly the character and political fortunes of the
author.

ENGLAND, CONSTITUTIONAL HISTORY OF, in its Origin and Development, by
William Stubbs (1875–78). A work of the highest authority on, not merely the
recognized developments of fundamental law, but the whole state of things constituting the nation, and giving it life, character, and growth. The three volumes cover
the respective periods from the first Germanic origins to 1215, when King John was
forced to grant the Great Charter; from 1215 to the deposition of Richard II., 1399;
and from 1399 to the close of the mediæval period, marked by the fall of Richard III.
at Bosworth, August 22d, 1485, and the accession of Henry of Richmond. The full
and exact learning of the author, his judgment and insight, and his power of clear
exposition, have made the work at once very instructive to students and very interesting to readers. The fine spirit in which it discusses parties and relates the
story of bitter struggles, may be seen in the fact that its last word commends to the
reader "that highest justice which is found in the deepest sympathy with erring and
straying men."

An additional volume of great importance is Professor Stubbs's 'Select Charters and Other Illustrations of English Constitutional History, from the earliest
times to the Reign of Edward the First,' 1876. It is designed to serve as a
treasury of reference and an outline manual for teachers and scholars. It follows the
history for a sufficiently long period to bring into view all the origins of constitutional
principle or polity on which politics have since built.

ENGLAND, CONSTITUTIONAL HISTORY OF, since the accession of George III.;
1760–1871. By Sir Thomas Erskine May, Baron Farnborough (1861–63). The
history of the British Constitution for a hundred years, showing its progress and
development, and illustrating every material change, whether of legislation, custom,
or policy, by which institutions have been improved and abuses in the government

corrected. The work deals also with the history of party; of the press, and political agitation; of the church; and of civil and religious liberty. It concludes with a general review of the legislation of the hundred years, its policy and results.

ENGLAND IN THE EIGHTEENTH CENTURY, HISTORY OF, by W. E. H. Lecky (8 vols., 1878–90). A work of thorough research and great literary excellence, the object of which is to disengage from the great mass of facts those which are of significance for the life and progress of the nation, and which reveal enduring characteristics. It deals with the growth or decline of the monarchy, the aristocracy, and the democracy; of the Church and of Dissent; of the agricultural, the manufacturing, and the commercial interests; the increasing power of Parliament and of the press; the history of political ideas, of art, of manners, and of belief; the changes that have taken place in the social and economical condition of the people; the influences that have modified national character; the relations of the mother country to its dependencies; and the causes that have accelerated or retarded the advancement of the latter. In its earliest form the work dealt with Ireland in certain sections, as the general course of the history required. But on its completion, Mr. Lecky made a separation, so as to bring all the Irish sections into a continuous work on Ireland in the eighteenth century, and leave the other parts to stand as England in the eighteenth century. In a new edition of twelve volumes, seven were given to England and five to Ireland. Mr. Lecky writes as a Liberal, but as a Unionist rather than Home Ruler.

ENGLAND, ITS PEOPLE, POLITY, AND PURSUITS, by T. H. S. Escott (2 vols., 1879). A work designed to present a comprehensive and faithful picture of the social and political condition of the England of the nineteenth century, the England of to-day. No attempt at historical retrospect is made, except in so far as it is necessary for understanding things as they are now. The author spent much time in visiting different parts of England, conversing with and living amongst the many varieties of people, which variety is a remarkable fact of English society. He made also a large collection of materials, to have at his command exact knowledge of the entire world of English facts. His general conception is that certain central ideas, which he explains in his introductory chapter, and around which he attempts to group his facts and descriptions, will enable him closely and logically to connect his chapters, and show a pervading unity of purpose throughout the work. The land and its occupation, the cities and towns, commerce, industries and the working classes, pauperism, co-operation, crime, travel and hotels, education, society, politics, the Crown, the crowd, official personages, the Commons, the Lords, the law courts, the public services, religion, philosophy, literature, professions, amusements, and imperial expansion, are his special themes.

ENGLAND WITHOUT AND WITHIN, by Richard Grant White (1881). Most of the chapters of this book appeared in the Atlantic Monthly, but were intended from the first as a presentation in book form of the subject indicated by its title. The author has put England, its people and their ways, before his readers just as he saw them: their skies; their methods of daily life; their men and women, to the latter of whom he pays a charming tribute; their nobility and gentry; parks and palaces; national virtues and vices. He has told only what anyone might have seen, though without the power of explicit description and photographic language. It is, says he, "the commonplaces of life that show what a people, what a country is; what all the influences, political, moral, and telluric, that have been there for centuries, have produced"; and it is of these commonplaces he treats. He saw England in an informal, unbusiness-like, untourist-like way, not stopping every moment to take notes, but relying on his memory to preserve everything of importance. There is a noticeable lack of descriptions of literary people in England, — a lapse intentional, not accidental; he believing that it is an "altogether erroneous notion that similarity in occupation, or admiration on one side, must produce liking in personal intercourse": but this disappointment — if it be a disappointment to the reader — is more than atoned for by the review of journeyings to Oxford and Cambridge, Warwick, Stratford-upon-Avon, Kenilworth, where, as his acquaintance of a railway compartment says, "every American goes"; rural England; pilgrimage to Canterbury, etc. However severe his criticism of national faults and individual blunderings, however caustic the sarcasms directed against the foibles of the "British Philistines," one is conscious of the author's underlying admiration for the home of his kindred; and the sincerity of his dictum — "England is not perfect, for it is upon the earth, and it is peopled by human beings; but I do not envy the man who, being able to earn enough to get bread and cheese and beer, a whole coat and a tight roof over his head, cannot be happy there."

ENGLISH AND SCOTTISH POPULAR BALLADS, see BALLADS.

ENGLISH CONSTITUTION, THE, AND OTHER ESSAYS. By Walter Bagehot (1867, 1885). A very interesting discussion of the underlying principles of the English Constitution, by a thoroughly independent and suggestive thinker. The central feature of the work is its proof that the House of Commons stands supreme as the seat of English law and that the throne and the Lords are of use to balance and check the Commons not directly, but indirectly through their action on public opinion, of which the action of the Commons should be the expression. By means of the cabinet, the executive government and the legislative Commons are a very close unity, and are the governmental machine, to which the Crown and the Lords are related only as seats of influence through which the public mind can be formed and can operate. He also shows that the function of the monarchy is not now that of a governing power, as once, but to gain public confidence and support for the real government, that of Parliament. "It [the monarchy] raises the army, though it does not win the battle." The lower orders suppose they are being governed by their old kingship, and obey it loyally: if they knew that they were being ruled by men of their own sort and choice they might not. Bagehot's work is a text-book at Oxford, and is used as such in American universities. See also his ' Parliamentary Reform.'

ENGLISH CONSTITUTION, HISTORY OF THE, by Dr. Rudolf Gneist. Translated by Philip A. Ashworth (2 vols., 1886). A history covering a full thousand years from the Anglo-Saxon foundation to the present. Hallam's 'Constitutional History' only comes down to the last century, Stubbs's only to Henry VII.; and even for the periods they cover, or that of Sir Erskine May's supplement, Dr. Gneist's work, though primarily designed only for the German public, is eminently worthy of a high place beside them among authorities accessible to English students. The same author's 'Student's History of the English Parliament' is a specially valuable handbook.

ENGLISH HUMORISTS OF THE EIGHTEENTH CENTURY, THE, by William Makepeace Thackeray, is a collection of lectures, delivered in England in 1851, in America during 1852–53, and published in 1853. Studying these pages, the reader

finds himself living in the society of the poets, essayists, and novelists of the eighteenth
century, as a friend conversant with their faults and signal merits. As twelve authors
are packed into six lectures, a characteristic disproportion is manifest. Swift is
belittled in forty pages; a like space suffices to hit off in a rapid touch-and-go manner
the qualities of Prior, Gay, and Pope. A page and a half disposes of Smollett to make
room for Hogarth and Fielding; Addison, Steele, Sterne, Congreve, and Goldsmith
receive about equal attention. These papers are the record of impressions made
upon a mind exceptionally sensitive to literary values, and reacting invariably with
original force and suggestiveness. Written for popular presentation, they are conversational in tone, and lighted up with swift flashes of poignant wit and humor.
Some of their characterizations are very striking: as that of Gay, helplessly dependent
upon the good offices of the Duke and Duchess of Queensberry, to a pampered lap-
dog, fat and indolent; and that of Steele, whose happy-go-lucky ups and downs and
general lovableness constituted a temperament after Thackeray's own heart. His
admiration for Fielding, his acknowledged master in the art of fiction, is very interesting. 'The English Humorists' will long remain the most inviting sketch in
literature of the period and the writers considered.

ENGLISH JUDGES, by Sir Francis Galton, see **HEREDITARY GENIUS.**

ENGLISH LANGUAGE, HISTORY OF THE, by T. R. Lounsbury (1879). This brief
manual states in a broad and clear manner the important facts in the growth of
the language, as considered apart from literature, and explains its history with delightful easy-going common-sense. "No speech can do more," says Prof. Lounsbury,
"than express the ideas of those who employ it at the time. It cannot live upon
its past meanings, or upon the past conceptions of great men which have been
recorded in it, any more than the race which uses it can live upon its past glory
or its past achievements. Proud therefore as we may now well be of our tongue,
we may rest assured that if it ever attains to universal sovereignty, it will do so
only because the ideas of the men who speak it are fit to become the ruling ideas of
the world, and the men themselves are strong enough to carry them over the
world; and that, in the last analysis, depends, like everything else, upon the development of the individual, — depends not upon the territory we buy or steal, not
upon the gold we mine or the grain we grow, but upon the men we produce. If we
fail there, no national greatness, however splendid to outward view, can be anything
but temporary and illusory; and when once national greatness disappears, no past
achievements in literature, however glorious, will perpetuate our language as a living
speech, though they may help for a time to retard its decay."

ENGLISH LITERATURE, HISTORY OF, by Hippolyte Adolphe Taine. (French
original, 5 vols., 1863–64. English Translation by Henri Van Laun, 4 vols., 1872–
74.) An admirably written, sympathetic, and penetrating account of the aspects
of English culture and the English race as revealed in English literature. To no
small extent it misses exact knowledge of English genius and of the finer aspects of
English literary culture; but it is a masterly study to come from the pen of a foreigner,
and rich in interest and suggestion to the thoughtful reader. The strength of the
work is in its study of race and civilization; but this is also its weakness, as to some
extent the view taken of literary production is too much colored by the author's
theory of race, which wholly fails in any such case as that of Shakespeare. "Just
as astronomy is at bottom a problem in mechanics, and physiology a problem in
chemistry, so history at bottom is a problem in psychology": and he aims here to give

a view, more or less complete, of the English intellect, illustrated by literary examples, and not a history at all, if by history is meant a record of books produced or of facts gathered together. The defects of the book are many and obvious; but when all abatement is made, it remains to the English reader a most stimulating intellectual performance. "In its powerful, though arbitrary, unity of composition, in its sustained æsthetic temper, its brilliancy, variety, and sympathy, it is a really monumental accession to a literature, which, whatever its limitations in the range of its ideas, is a splendid series of masterly compositions."

ENGLISH NATION, see LETTERS CONCERNING THE.

ENGLISH NOTEBOOKS, by Nathaniel Hawthorne (1870), was published by his wife after his death. During his residence as consul at Liverpool, he kept a close record of all that struck him as novel and important in the United Kingdom. Much of this material he afterwards developed in a series of sketches entitled 'Our Old Home.' The remaining notes, given to the public in their original form of disconnected impressions, are interesting for their animation and vigorous bits of description. They are a striking revelation of Hawthorne's personality, and show the cheerful side of a man usually considered gloomy. In spite of the shyness which made after-dinner speeches a trial to him, he formed many delightful friendships. With his wife and children he roamed about Liverpool and London, visited many cathedral towns, and lingered at Oxford and among the lakes. He speaks of himself as not observant, but if he missed detail, he had the rare faculty of seizing the salient features of what he saw, and conveying them to others. His constant preoccupation was with the unusual or fantastic in human experience, and this led him to observe much that most spectators would have failed to see.

ENGLISH NOVEL, THE: 'A Study in the Development of Personality,' by Sidney Lanier (1883. Revised Edition, 1897). A volume of singularly rich criticism, based on a course of twelve lectures at Johns Hopkins University, 1881. It was almost the last work of a writer whose death was a heavy loss to American letters. The full title given by Lanier to his course was, 'From Æschylus to George Eliot: The Development of Personality.' The idea suggesting this title was that in Greek tragedy, represented by Æschylus, the expression of personality is faint and crude, while in George Eliot it reached the clearness and strength of high literary art. The earlier work of Lanier on 'The Science of English Verse,' and the later study of the novel, were designed to serve as parts of a comprehensive philosophy of the form and substance of beauty in literature; and the execution of the plan, as far as he had proceeded, was of a quality rarely found in literary criticism. In the second edition of the work, the last six of the twelve chapters are devoted to George Eliot. The earlier six range over a wide field, and show wealth of knowledge with remarkable insight and felicity of expression.

ENGLISH PEOPLE, A SHORT HISTORY OF THE, see SHORT HISTORY.

ENGLISH POETRY, HISTORY OF, by William John Courthope (6 vols., 1895–1909). The work which in their day both Pope and Gray contemplated writing on the history of English poetry, and which Warton began but never finished, was taken up anew but with a far different scope by the professor of poetry at Oxford. His plan embraces a history of the art of English poetry — epic, dramatic, lyrical, and didactic — from the time of Chaucer to that of Scott, as well as "an appreciation of the motives by which each individual poet seems to have been consciously inspired." He

also inquires into "those general causes which have unconsciously directed imagina
tion in England into the various channels of metrical composition." Courthope
believes that in spite of the different sources from which the English national consciousness is derived, there is an essential unity and consistency, so that both the
technic of poetical production and the national genius — the common thought,
imagination, and sentiment — may be traced in its evolution. He shows with great
fullness the "progressive stages in the formation of the mediæval stream of thought,
which feeds the literatures of England, France, and Italy," and tries to connect it
with the great system of Græco-Roman cultures so prominent before the death of
Boethius. He also explores the course of the national language, to show the changes
produced by Saxon and Norman influences on the art of metrical expression before
Chaucer. To Chaucer himself are devoted less than fifty octavo pages, and this
chapter does not appear in the first volume until it is more than half finished. The
history closes with a careful account of the rise of the drama. Dry as the subject in its
earlier stages threatens to be, Mr. Courthope's brilliant style and his wealth of
illustration make it absorbingly interesting to the student. The second volume,
after surveying the influence of European thought in the sixteenth century, and the
effects of the Renaissance and Reformation, goes into a careful study of the works of
Wyatt and Surrey, the court poets and the Euphuists, Spenser and the early dramatists with all the various types of versifiers who were famous in that period. The
third volume begins with the successors of Spenser, and takes up the intellectual
conflict of the seventeenth century, the decadent influence of the feudal monarch, the
various schools of poetical "wit," and the growth of the national genius, and discusses Milton and Dryden. The fourth volume surveys the development and decline
of the poetic drama, and the influence of the court and the people, Shakespeare,
Ben Jonson, and Dryden. The fifth volume deals with the classical renaissance, its
effect on modern European poetry, and the early romantic renaissance, and closes
with a survey of English poetry in the eighteenth century. The sixth volume describes the romantic movement in English poetry and the effects produced on the
English imagination by the French Revolution. It has been the design of the author,
"not to furnish an exhaustive list of the English poets as individuals, but rather to
describe the general movements of English poetry, as an art illustrating the evolution
of national taste." Courthope's broad and generous spirit, his keenness of analysis,
his wide learning, and his clearness of vision make his work one of standard reference
for the history of English poetry.

ENGLISH POETS, see **LIVES OF THE.**

ENGLISH THOUGHT IN THE EIGHTEENTH CENTURY, HISTORY OF, in
two volumes, by Sir Leslie Stephen (1876). The scope of this important book is
hardly so broad as the title would indicate, for the subject treated with the greatest
fullness is theology. The first volume, indeed, is given almost entirely to the famous
deist controversy with which the names of Hume, Warburton, Chubb, Sherlock,
Johnson, and the rest of the great disputants of the time — names only to the modern
reader — are associated. The ground covered extends from the milestones planted
by Descartes by means of his doctrine of innate ideas, to the removal of the boundaries of the fathers by the "constructive" infidelity of Thomas Paine. This review
weighs with care the philosophical significance of the gradual change of thought, a
knowledge of which is conveyed through an examination of the representative books
upon theology and metaphysics. The historian's criticism upon these is fair-minded,

illuminative, and always interesting, by means of its wide knowledge and wealth of illustration. So broad is it that it seems to bring up for judgment all the pressing social, moral, and religious questions of the present time. Leslie Stephen points out that the deist controversy was only one form of that appeal from tradition and authority to reason, which was the special characteristic of the eighteenth century. In his method of dealing with the "body of divinity," which he explains to the worldly modern reader, he shows himself both the philosophic historian and the philosophic critic. He belongs to the Spencerian school, which regards society as an organism, and history as the record of its growth and development. The stream of tendency is so vividly indicated, that the analysis of the movement of the last century might almost be a statement of certain phases of thought and morals of to-day. If the terms of the problems discussed are obsolete, their discussion has a constant reference to the most modern theories.

Leslie Stephen is never the detached observer. These questions mean a great deal to him; and therefore the reader also, whether he approve or disapprove the bias of his guide, is compelled to find them important. In studying such books as this, and the admirable discussions of Lecky on European morals, and Rationalism in Europe, it is difficult to escape from a certain sense of the inevitableness of the opinions held by mankind at every stage of their development; so that the question of the importance of the truth of these opinions is apt to seem secondary. But Leslie Stephen does not belittle the duty of arriving at true opinions, nor does he assume that his side — and he takes sides — is the right side, and the question closed.

Volume ii. discusses moral philosophy, political theories, social economics, and literary developments. It gives with great fullness and fairness the position of the intuitional school of morals, and of the latest utilitarians, who now declare that society must be regulated not by the welfare of the individual, but by the well-being of that organism which is called the human race. "To understand the laws of growth and equilibrium, both of the individual and the race, we must therefore acquire a conception of society as a complex organism, instead of a mere aggregate of individuals." To Leslie Stephen history witnesses that the world can be improved, and that it cannot be improved suddenly. Of the value of the theory that society is an organism, this book is a conspicuous illustration. Its candor, its learning, its honest partisanship, its impartiality, with its excellent art of stating things, and its brilliant criticism, make it a most stimulating as well as a most informing book, while it is always entertaining.

ENGLISH TRAITS, by Ralph Waldo Emerson (1856), comprises an account of his English visits in 1833 and 1847, and a series of general observations on national character. It is the note-book of a philosophic traveler. In the earlier chapters, the sketches of his visits to Coleridge, Carlyle, and Wordsworth, while personal in some degree, reveal Emerson's character and humor in a delightful way. The trend of his mind to generalization is evident in the titles given to the chapters. With the exception of 'Stonehenge' and 'The Times,' they are all abstract, — 'Race,' 'Ability,' 'Character,' 'Wealth,' or 'Religion.' Far removed from provincialism, the tone is that of a beholder, kindred in race, who, while paying due respect to the stock from which he sprang, feels his own eyes purged of certain illusions still cherished by the Old World. These playthings, as it were, of a full-grown people, — the court and church ceremonial, thrones, mitres, bewigged officials, Lord Mayor's shows, — amused the observer. "Every one of these islanders is an island himself, safe, tranquil, incommunicable." This work remains unique as a searching analysis, full of generous admiration, of a foreign nation's racial temperament, by a strongly original individuality.

ENGLISH VILLAGE COMMUNITY, THE, by F. Seebohm (1883). The question propounded in this book is whether English Economic History began with the freedom or the serfdom of the masses of the people, whether the village communities were free or lived in serfdom under a manorial lordship. The problem is of wider interest than might appear on the surface because (1) the English and German land systems were the same, and there are also fundamental analogies between the village communities of the Eastern and the Western worlds, and (2) because on the answer to the question may depend the attitude of modern statesmen to the solution of present-day problems of social and political freedom. After a careful examination of the available evidence Mr. Seebohm is of the opinion that "the manorial system grew up in Britain as it grew up in Gaul and Germany, as the compound product of barbarian and Roman institutions mixing together during the periods first of Roman provincial rule, and secondly of German conquest." Throughout the whole period from pre-Roman to modern times there were in Britain two parallel systems of rural economy, the village community in the east, the tribal in the west, each of which were distinguished by the characteristics of community and equality, though their systems of open or common fields were different. Neither the village nor the tribal community can have been introduced later than 2000 years ago. The village community lived in settled serfdom under a lordship, though this serfdom was to the masses of the people, not a degradation, but a step upward out of a once more general slavery. The tribal community was bound together by an equality of blood relationship, which involved an equal division of land amongst the sons of tribesmen. "The fundamental principle of the new economic order," says Mr. Seebohm, "seems to be opposed to the community and equality of the old order in both its forms. The freedom of the individual and growth of individual enterprise and property which mark the new order imply a rebellion against the bonds of the communism and forced equality, alike of the manorial and of the tribal system. It has triumphed by breaking up both the communism of serfdom and the communism of the free tribe." It would seem, however, that the Great War may annihilate, or for a time submerge, the individualist economic order.

EŌTHEN; or, TRACES OF TRAVEL BROUGHT HOME FROM THE EAST, by Alexander William Kinglake (1844). 'Eōthen' — a title meaning 'From the Dawn' — is a lively and acute narrative of travel in the East, at a time when that region was comparatively new ground to English tourists. The author, starting from Constantinople, visits the Troad, Cyprus, the Holy Land, Cairo, the Pyramids, and the Sphinx; thence by the way of Suez he proceeds to Gaza, and returns by the way of Nablous and Damascus. He apologizes for his frankness of style, and gives his impressions with refreshing directness, modified as little as possible by conventional opinion. For this reason he provoked some criticism from conservative reviewers, who regarded his comments on the manners and morals of Mohammedan countries as too liberal to be encouraged in Christian circles. He confesses his inability to overcome a very worldly mood even in Jerusalem, and his failure to see things always in that light of romance that the reader might prefer; and he is unwilling that his own moral judgment shall stand in the way of a perfectly truthful narrative. Instances of his engaging style are the interview with the Pasha through the dragoman at the start, and his description of the Ottoman lady, — "a coffin-shaped bundle of white linen."

The incident of Mariam, a Christian bride converted to Islam, is full of humor, and contains a dash of that liberalism which roused the fears of the Christian critics.

EPHESIACA, see **ANTHIA AND HABROCOMUS.**

EPICENE; or THE SILENT WOMAN, by Ben Jonson (1609). This work, which to many critics recalls the manner of Molière, was said by Coleridge to be "the most entertaining of Jonson's comedies." The plot turns upon an audacious trick which the author plays upon his hearers. The chief character, Morose, a misanthrope who hates every kind of noise, — "Cutbeard" (he says to his barber), "thank me not but with thy leg," — is subjected to a series of trials, each of which jars upon him more than the former. He marries someone whom he believes to be a silent woman, but who turns out to be a chatterbox and ultimately proves to be a boy in disguise. Sir John Daw, another character, criticizes great classic names with audacious freedom and pretense of literary taste. Aristotle is "a mere commonplace fellow"; Plato, "a discourser"; Homer, an "old tedious, prolix ass," who "talks of curriers and chines of beef." His own constantly repeated oath is, "As I hope to finish Tacitus." Another, Sir Amorous La Foole, boasts that he belongs to "as ancient a family as any is in Europe," but regretfully adds, "antiquity is not respected now." Truewit directs the intrigue and, to admiration, plays off the characters against one another. The vivacity of the fun and the interest of the plot increase from act to act, until the fifth comes with its completely unexpected dénouement.

EPISTLE TO POSTERITY, AN, by Mrs. M. E. W. Sherwood (1897), is a series of pleasant reminiscences of one who has found life "an enjoyable experiment," and who has had unusual facilities for meeting interesting people. The author explains that she greeted with joy "the first green books which emanated from Boz and the yellow-colored Thackerays." When she had finished her studies at Mr. Emerson's private school in Boston, her father took her with him upon a business trip across the Wisconsin prairies, during which she met Martin Van Buren. Among the interesting homes which she visited were Marshfield, where she paid girlish homage to her great host, Daniel Webster; and the home in Watertown, Massachusetts, where she learned to love Maria White, the gracious first wife of James Russell Lowell. She saw much of Boston society in the days of its greatest literary fame, and had a glimpse of the Brook Farm Community. When her father was sent to Congress, she made her début in Washington society; and was a frequent attendant at the levees of President Polk and President Taylor. In Washington she renewed her friendship with Webster, and met Henry Clay, and "many of the young heroes destined later on to be world-renowned," — Farragut, Lee, Zachary Taylor, "and a quiet little man who shrank out of sight," known later on as U. S. Grant. The conclusion of the volume, the narration of her wedding trip to the West Indies in the early fifties; of her different trips to Europe, including her presentation at the English and the Italian courts; and of contemporary New York society, is less interesting.

EPISTLES OF PHALARIS, DISSERTATION ON THE, see **PHALARIS.**

EPISTOLÆ OBSCURORUM VIRORUM ('Letters of Obscure Men'), 1516–17. A satirical production which had a great influence in aid of the Reformation. A first part appeared in 1516, at Hagenau (but professedly at Venice), and a second in 1517. One Crotus Rubeanus suggested the scheme, and probably executed the first part. The second part was from the pen of the humanist and poet Ulrich von Hutten, the same year in which the Emperor Maximilian made him poet-laureate of Germany.

The plan of the letters was that of representing certain German ecclesiastics and professors as writing merciless denunciations of the morals, manners, writings, teachings, and way of life generally, of the scholastics and monks. One of these had attacked the great Hebrew scholar Reuchlin for his leaning to the Reformation; and these 'Epistolæ' were the reply. Their circulation and influence were immense.

EQUALITY, see **LOOKING BACKWARD.**

EQUATORIAL AFRICA, see **EXPLORATIONS AND ADVENTURES IN.**

ERNEST MALTRAVERS (1837), and its sequel **ALICE**; or, THE MYSTERIES (1838), by Bulwer-Lytton. In the preface to the first-named novel, the author states that he is indebted for the leading idea of the work — that of a moral education or apprenticeship — to Goethe's 'Wilhelm Meister.' The apprenticeship of Ernest Maltravers is, however, less to art than to life. The hero of the book, he is introduced to the reader as a young man of wealth and education just returned to England from a German university. Belated by a storm, he seeks shelter in the hut of Darvil, a man of evil character. Darvil has a daughter Alice, young and beautiful, but of undeveloped moral and mental power. Her father having planned to rob and murder Maltravers, she aids the traveler to escape. Moved by her helplessness, her beauty, and her innocence, Maltravers has her educated, and constitutes himself her protector. He yields at last to his passion, and Alice's first knowledge of love comes to her as a revelation of the meaning of honor and purity. From that time she remains faithful to Maltravers. By a series of circumstances they are separated and lost to each other, and do not meet for twenty years. Maltravers in the meantime loves many women: Valerie; Madame de Ventadour, whom he meets in Italy; Lady Florence Lascelles, to whom he becomes engaged, and from whom he is separated by the machinations of an enemy; and lastly, Evelyn Cameron, a beautiful English girl. Fate, however, reserves him for the faithful Alice, the love of his youth.

'Ernest Maltravers' is written in the Byronic strain, and is a fair example of the English romantic and sentimental novel of the thirties.

ES LEBE DAS LEBEN see **JOY OF LIVING.**

ESOTERIC BUDDHISM, by A. P. Sinnett, was first published in England in 1883, and appeared in America in a revised form in 1884.

The author's claims are modest; the work purporting to be but a partial exposition, not a complete defense, of Buddhism from the standpoint of the esoteric. There are difficulties for the exoteric reader in the terminology employed, which seems as yet to have come to no widely accepted definitiveness; but much of the exposition may be readily grasped by the attentive lay mind. Great stress is naturally laid on the Buddhist theory of cosmogony, which is a form of evolution, both physical and psychic; on the doctrine of reincarnation, distinctly affirmed; on Nirvana, "a sublime state of conscious rest in omniscience"; and on Karma, the idea of ethical causation. The author gives also a survey of occult and theosophic doctrines in general, and the esoteric conception of Buddha; in a word, he discusses the origin of the world and of man, the ultimate destiny of our race, and the nature of other worlds and states of existence differing from those of our present life. The exposition is frankly made, and the language, occasionally obscure, is generally incisive and clear.

ESSAY CONCERNING HUMAN UNDERSTANDING, AN, by John Locke, a philosophical treatise published in 1690. The author attacks the doctrine of innate ideas and maintains that all our knowledge is derived from sensations. The mind of the infant is a *tabula rasa*, a white sheet of paper; from the impressions made upon it by the senses he arrives at certain concepts by reflection. By the combination and comparison of these concepts he forms ideas of similarity and dissimilarity of the general and the special, which constitute knowledge. General ideas have no existence apart from the individual concepts from which they are derived; our will is absolutely determined by our mind, which is guided by the desire for happiness. In this work Locke developed the theory of Hobbes (see on his 'Leviathan') of the naturalistic source of our knowledge, and exercised a highly important influence upon subsequent philosophic thought, English and Continental. The development may be readily traced down to the scepticism of Hume and the idealism of Kant.

ESSAYS, by Ralph Waldo Emerson. The First Series, published in 1841, included essays on History, Self-Reliance, Compensation, Spiritual Laws, Love, Friendship, Prudence, Heroism, The Over-Soul, Circles, Intellect, and Art. The essays of the Second Series (1844) are: The Poet, Experience, Character, Manners, Gifts, Nature, Politics, Nominalist and Realist, and New England Reformers. Many of the essays were first delivered in the form of addresses and have, partly on that account, mainly because of the writer's temperament, a desultoriness of method and a tendency to create attention by keen epigrams and suggestive aphorisms rather than to present a subject in coherent order. Moreover, Emerson preferred intuition to reasoning and cared little for logical presentation but was eager to stimulate thought by flashes of insight and to inspire resolution by arresting emotional appeals. His main ideas are the immanence of God and the supreme importance of the individual. Transcendental and idealistic in his entire outlook on life he has no patience with mechanistic or materialistic opinions, with pessimistic or Calvinistic views of human nature, with passive or cowardly submission to commonly accepted tenets or practices. That man may make his own happiness anywhere and everywhere by opening his eyes to the goodness and beauty around him and by being true to himself is the view of this practical philosopher, who unites a Yankee shrewdness with an almost oriental mysticism. The style of the essays is somewhat abrupt and disconnected, but plain, pure, and unaffected in diction, with a vein of sinewy strength running through its homely, straightforward sentences.

ESSAYS, a collection of discursive and intensely personal essays by Michel Eyquem, Sieur de Montaigne, appeared first in 1580 in two books; again in 1588 with a third book; and posthumously, with additions in 1595. An English translation by John Florio appeared in 1603, and by Charles Cotton in 1685–1686. The essays are made up partly of meditations suggested by the author's wide classical reading and his observation of the life around him, partly of revelations of his own whims, habits, peculiarities, and modes of thought. They are the first conspicuous examples of the personal essay in which the writer entertains us by painting a complete portrait of himself and also of the disquisition on general topics illustrated from experience and literature. Montaigne's essays are very voluminous and rambling, filled with classical quotations, and without formal organization. But they are made intensely interesting by the mind and temper of the man they reveal. Montaigne was indolent, fond of solitude, lacking in public spirit, garrulous, sceptical. He exhibits himself without reserve, with all his foibles, peccadilloes, lack of enthusiasm, and absence of religious or metaphysical conviction. His constant remark is "Que sçais-je?" (What do I know?) But he evidently believes in heroism, in fraternity, in the need of toleration, and in the underlying goodness of humanity. He is therefore the leading representative of the French spirit in the Renaissance.

ESSAYS AND REVIEWS is a collection of seven scholarly papers upon different aspects of theological thought, written by as many well-known English divines and Biblical students. It appeared in England in 1860, and made a sensation because its writers expressed views which were then deemed radical and dangerous. Inasmuch as the writers were in several instances associated with Oxford University, the book became known as the Oxford 'Essays and Reviews.' So great was the opposition it aroused that three of the contributors were tried and condemned by an ecclesiastical court; the decision being afterwards reversed. The influence of the volume was fruitful in drawing attention to a broader interpretation of religious truth and the methods of modern scholarship. The papers and their authors were: 'The Education of the World,' by Dr. Frederick Temple; Bunsen's 'Biblical Researches,' by Professor Rowland Williams; 'On the Study of the Evidences of Christianity,' by Professor Baden Powell; 'Séances Historiques de Genève,' 'The National Church,' by the Rev. Henry B. Wilson; 'On the Mosaic Cosmogony,' by C. W. Goodwin; 'Tendencies of Religious Thought in England, 1688–1750,' by the Rev. Mark Pattison; and 'On the Interpretation of Scripture,' by Professor Benjamin Jowett.

ESSAYS, CRITICAL AND MISCELLANEOUS, by Macaulay, were published originally in the Edinburgh Review; beginning with the essay on Milton, in the August number, 1825, and continuing for twenty years after, when the glittering series ended with the paper on the Earl of Chatham, in the October number, 1844. These essays, of which the glory is but a little tarnished, run the gamut of great historical and literary subjects. They include reviews of current literature, historical sketches and portraits, essays in criticism. They are distinguished by a certain magnificent cleverness but they are lacking in human warmth, and in the sympathy which rises from the heart to the brain. They remain however a monument of what might be called a soldierly English style, with all the trappings and appurtenances of military rank.

ESSAYS IN CRITICISM, by Matthew Arnold (First Series, 1865; Second Series 1888). These essays are characterized by all the vivacity to which the author alludes with mock-serious repentance, as having caused a wounding of solemn sensibilities. They illustrate his famous though not original term, — "sweetness and light." So delicate, though sure, was his artistic taste, that some of his phrases were incomprehensible to those whom he classed with the Philistines. But the essays were not so unpopular as he modestly and perhaps despondently declared. In collected form, the First Series includes: The Function of Criticism at the Present Time, — a dignified defense of literary criticism in its proper form and place; The Literary Influence of Academies — like that in France of the Forty Immortals — upon national literatures; an estimate, with translations from his posthumous journal, of the French poet Maurice de Guérin; a paper on Eugènie de Guérin, "one of the rarest and most beautiful of souls"; a paper on Heine, revealing him less as the poet of no special aim, than as Heine himself had wished to be remembered, — "a brilliant, a most effective soldier, in the Liberation War of humanity"; essays on Pagan and Mediæval Sentiment; a Persian Passion Play; Joubert, a too little known French genius, who published nothing in his lifetime, but was influential during the Reign of Terror and Napoleon's supremacy; an essay on Spinoza and the Bible; and last, a tribute to the 'Meditations' of Marcus Aurelius, pointing out that "the paramount virtue of religion is that it lights up morality; that it has supplied the emotion and inspiration needful for carrying the sage along the narrow way perfectly, for carrying the ordinary man along it at all"; that "that which gives to the moral writings of the Emperor Marcus Aurelius their peculiar character and charm is their being suffused and softened by this very sentiment whence Christian morality draws its best power." The Second Series opens with a Study of Poetry, which draws a clear though subtle line between what is genuine and simple, and what does not ring absolutely true in even the masters of English verse. The rest are studies of some of these masters in detail: Milton, Gray, Keats, Wordsworth, and Shelley; with an essay under the title 'Count Leo Tolstoy,' concerning the Russian novel and its vogue in Western Europe, particularly Tolstoy's 'Anna Karénina'; and last, a well-balanced estimate of Amiel's 'Journal,' showing its beauties and faults impartially, with that judicial fairness which, notwithstanding his native warmth of temperament, prevails through most of Matthew Arnold's critical writings.

ESSAYS, MODERN AND CLASSICAL, by F. W. H. Myers (Two volumes, 1883). These studies reveal a pure literary taste, refined and strengthened by sound scholarship. Every essay is enriched with resources of knowledge outside its own immediate scope. The spiritual in poetry or in art appeals strongly to the author. His essay on Virgil, full of acute observations as it is, dwells most fondly on the poet's supreme elegance, tenderness, and stateliness, and on the haunting music with which his verse is surcharged. "Much of Rossetti's art," he says, "in speech and color, spends itself in the effort to communicate the incommunicable," — and it is his own love for, and comprehension of, the incommunicable that leads the essayist to choose many of his subjects: Marcus Aurelius, The Greek Oracles, George Sand, Victor Hugo, The Religion of Beauty, George Eliot, and Renan — "that subtlest of seekers after God." Penetrative, luminous, and fascinating, these essays show also an exquisite appreciation of beauty and the balance of a rare scholar.

ESSAYS OF ELIA, THE, by Charles Lamb, began to appear in The London Magazine in 1820, and were collected under the above title in 1823. A second volume, including those subsequently written, and entitled 'Last Essays of Elia' was published in 1833. Reminiscences of persons and scenes of earlier years form the principal subject-matter of these essays. Lamb's delicate and sympathetic power of interpreting the spirit of a locality, a house, or a person was best exercised when the object was surrounded by the golden haze of happy recollection. The persons chosen for description are his friends, acquaintances, or relatives and the places are those that he has often frequented. As a thin veil for these autobiographic elements he adopts as a pseudonym the name of an Italian fellow-clerk, Elia, whom he knew slightly; but Elia's ways and thoughts are Lamb's own; and his brother and sister, James and Bridget Elia, are James and Mary Lamb. Almost every period of the essayist's life is represented in one passage or another. His birthplace, his father, and his father's employer are described in 'The Old Benchers of the Inner Temple'; his father's household in 'Poor Relations'; his school-days in 'Christ's Hospital Five and Thirty Years Ago'; childish experiences in 'Witches and Other Night Fears' and 'My First Play'; entrance into business in 'The South Sea House'; disappointment in love in 'Dream Children'; his devotion to his sister and life with her in 'My Relations,' 'Mackery End in Hertfordshire,' and 'Old China'; his love of the city in 'Chimney Sweepers' and 'On the Decay of Beggars'; his friends in 'Oxford in the Vacation'; 'The Two Races of Men,' 'Mrs. Battle's Opinions on Whist,' 'Modern Gallantry,' 'Captain Jackson,' 'Barbara S.,' 'Amicus Redivivus,' and hosts of incidental passages in other essays; his personal prejudices and peculiarities in 'A Chapter on Ears,'

'New Year's Eve,' 'Imperfect Sympathies,' and 'Preface to Last Essays,' his be-
setting sin (exaggerated for literary effect) in 'Confessions of a Drunkard'; his
release from office labors in 'The Superannuated Man,' and his breaking health in the
sketch of sickness entitled 'The Convalescent.' Of the formal essay on some general
topic there are relatively few examples, and these on novel themes or approaching an
old subject from a new angle: 'All Fools' Day,' 'Valentine's Day,' 'Grace before
Meat,' 'Sanity of True Genius,' and the series of essays on 'Popular Fallacies' come
under this head. The 'Dissertation upon Roast Pig' is a clever travesty on learned
pedantry unlike anything else in the two series. Dramatic and literary criticism of
the finest taste is represented by 'On Some of the Old Actors,' 'On the Artificial
Comedy of the Last Century,' 'Stage Illusion,' 'Detached Thoughts on Books and
Reading,' 'Some Sonnets of Sir Philip Sidney,' and a few others. In general, therefore,
Lamb, though an appreciative critic and an adroit literary craftsman is best known
and loved for his reflection of happy scenes from his own past, and for the tenderness,
strength, refinement, and humor of his personality.

ESSAYS OF HAMILTON WRIGHT MABIE.   Several volumes are comprised unde
this general title. They are all concerned with man and nature, the soul and literature, art and culture. Their several titles are: 'Essays in Literary Interpretation,'
1892, 'Essays on Nature and Culture,' 1904, 'Short Studies in Literature,' 1891,
'Books and Culture,' 1897, 'My Study Fire' (2 vols., 1890-94), and 'Under the Trees
and Elsewhere,' 1891. They all express the views of a book-man on man and his
surroundings; but of a book-man who has studied man no less than books, and has
studied books rather as a means than an end — as giving insight into the soul of
man. Great books are for him not feats of intellect, but the result of the contact
of mind and heart with the great and terrible facts of life: they originate not in the
individual mind but in the soil of common human hopes, loves, fears, aspirations,
sufferings. Shakespeare did not invent Hamlet, he found him in human histories
already acted out to the tragic end; Goethe did not create Faust, he summoned him
out of the dim mediæval world and confronted him with the problems of life as it is
now. There are in these 'Essays' innumerable epigrammatic passages easily detach-
able from the context; a few of these will serve to illustrate the author's points of
view. Writing of 'Personality in Literary Work,' he says that there is no such thing
as a universal literature in the sense which involves complete escape from the water-
marks of place and time: no man can study or interpret life save from the point of
view where he finds himself; no truth gets into human keeping by any other path than
the individual soul, nor into human speech by any other medium than the individual
mind. In another essay occurs this fine remark on wit: Wit reveals itself in sudden
flashes, not in continuous glow and illumination; it is distilled in sentences; it is
preserved in figures, illustrations, epigrams, epithets, phrases. Then follows a comparison of wits and humorists: the wits entertain and dazzle us, the humorists reveal
life to us. Aristophanes, Cervantes, Molière, and Shakespeare — the typical humorists — are among the greatest contributors to the capital of human achievement;
they give us not glimpses but views of life. In the essay, 'The Art of Arts' — i. e.,
the art of living — is this remark on the Old Testament writings: Whatever view one
may take of the authority of those books, it is certain that in the noble literature
which goes under that title, there is a deeper, clearer, and fuller disclosure of the
human spirit than in all the historical works that have been written; for the real
history of man on this earth is not the record of the deeds he has done with his hands,
the journeys he has made with his feet; . . . but the record of his thoughts, feelings,

inspirations, aspirations, and experience. This, on the conditions of a broad mental and moral development of the individual, draws the essential line of distinction between the man of culture and the Philistine: To secure the most complete development one must live in one's time and yet live above it, and one must live in one's home and yet live in the world. The life which is bounded in knowledge, interest, and activity by the invisible but real and limiting walls of a small community is often definite in aim, effective in action, and upright in intention; but it cannot be rich, varied, generous, and stimulating. The life, on the other hand, which is entirely detached from local associations and tasks is often interesting, liberalizing, and catholic in spirit; but it cannot be original or productive. A sound life — balanced, poised, and intelligently directed — must stand strongly in both local and universal relations; it must have the vitality and warmth of the first, and the breadth and range of the second.

ESTHER WATERS; a novel by George Moore (1894). An English servant girl, Esther Waters, a member of the narrow religious sect of the Plymouth Brethren, takes her first situation in a horse-racing household in the country. The master owns winning horses, and the servants quarrel over their sweepstakes. The mistress belongs to the Plymouth Brethren, and therefore takes a special interest in her new kitchenmaid. The dashing footman, William, makes love to Esther, and then deserts her to elope with a rich young cousin of the family. Esther is dismissed from the house when it is discovered that she will soon be a mother. Her drunken stepfather takes most of her money from her, and when she is turned out of the hospital before she is able to work, she has to leave her baby with a baby-farmer and go out as a wet-nurse. She finds that the woman is letting her baby die of neglect and gives up her place and goes to the workhouse to keep her baby. The book is the story of Esther's plucky devoted maternity. By hard struggle she manages to support her boy. A young man becomes her friend and brings her again to the Plymouth Brethren. Just as they are going to be married, William turns up again, a bookmaker and keeper of a public house. He wins her from the marriage, because he is able to provide for her child. She goes to live with him, and after his divorce, they are married and very happy. There is illegal betting in the bar parlor, and William is fined and loses his license. He becomes ill from exposure in bad weather at the races and dies leaving Esther with nothing. She almost has to go to the workhouse again. Her first mistress, who is a widow and alone, takes her back, and helps support Esther's son until he is a fine young soldier. This novel pictures the evil results of betting among the British working class, the language and habits of the lower sporting world, and the horrors of baby-farming and lying-in hospitals. Its method is severely realistic.

ETERNAL CITY, THE, by Hall Caine was published in 1901. The story opens in London, where Prince Volonna, who has been exiled for conspiracy against the Italian government, lives a life of charity under an assumed name, being known as Dr. Roselli. He rescues from the snow, a street waif, David Leone, who is one of the many who are brought to England yearly from the south to play and beg in the streets. This lad grows up in the household of the good doctor and his English wife and little daughter Roma, imbibing his foster father's theories and becoming his disciple. Prince Volonna is finally tricked back to Italy, where he is captured and transported to Elba, and David Leone is likewise condemned as a conspirator; the latter escapes, and as David Rossi enters Rome and preaches his principle of the brotherhood of man. After the death of her father, Roma is discovered by the Baron

Bonelli, Secretary of State, and a man of cunning and duplicity, who brings her to Rome where she becomes the reigning belle of the capital, but one whose name has not remained untarnished. The author recounts her meeting with David Rossi, her recognition of her foster brother, their love and the various obstacles which beset their path. In 'The Eternal City' Mr. Caine has presented a sociological study with a strong element of love-making in it. Through the efforts of a humanizing socialism, the principles of which are based upon the Lord's Prayer, the Pope resigns all temporal power and the young King is brought to abdicate his throne, and an ideal republic is born, whose creed is the brotherhood of God and the brotherhood of man.

ETHAN FROME, by Edith Wharton (1911). This tale of a New England village tragedy is told by a stranger, who wonders at Ethan Frome, the limping "ruin of a man," and gradually pieces together the story of his life. Zenia, Ethan's wife, is an invalid, whose imaginary ailments thrive on patent medicines. He makes a bare living from the stony soil of the little farm. His wife refuses to be transplanted to the town where there are "lectures and big libraries and 'fellows doing things'" and a chance for congenial work for Ethan. A girl cousin of his wife's, left destitute, comes to live with them, bringing brightness and cheer and inevitably, love of youth for youth. Zenia goes away on one of her "therapeutic excursions" and Ethan and Mattie have a happy time keeping house together. When Zenia returns she announces that the doctor had advised her to save her health by getting a strong hired girl to do the work and there is no room for Mattie any longer. Ethan is helpless. "There were no means by which he could compel her to keep the girl under her roof." The friendship of Mattie and Ethan has apparently aroused her jealousy, and from a "state of sullen self-absorption she is transformed into an active mysterious alien presence" holding him in her power through his honesty and sense of duty. Ethan and Mattie speak their love for each other in the despair of parting. Driving to the station they yield to the impulse to coast once more down the long hill to the village, a steep breathless rush with a great elm at the foot, to be avoided by quick steering at the last minute. The temptation comes to Ethan to run into the elm and end it all, rather than to live apart. The girl agrees, but the fates are against them. They live on, she helpless with a broken back, and he crippled, both tied beyond escape to Zenia and the slow starvation of the barren farm.

ETHICAL AND SOCIAL SUBJECTS, STUDIES NEW AND OLD IN, by Frances Power Cobbe (1865). The various essays here collected are developments of the views of morals presented in the author's earlier works, while she was greatly influenced, among other forces, by the mind of Theodore Parker, whose works she edited. A strong and original thinker, fearless, possessing a clear and simple style, Miss Cobbe makes all her work interesting. With the essay upon 'Christian Ethics and the Ethics of Christ' — which have to her view little in common — the series begins. In her paper on 'Self-Development and Self-Abnegation,' she maintains that self-development is the saner, nobler duty of man. Her titles, 'The Sacred Books of the Zoroastrians,' 'The Philosophy of the Poor-Laws,' 'The Morals of Literature,' 'Decemnovenarianism' (the spirit of the nineteenth century), 'Hades,' and 'The Hierarchy of Art,' indicate the range of her interests. The 'Rights of Man and the Claims of Brutes,' affords a vigorous and humane protest against vivisection. It should be remembered that an early essay of Miss Cobbe on 'Intuitive Morals' has been pronounced by the most philosophic critics the ablest brief discussion of the subject in English. Her breadth of view, ripe culture, profoundly religious though unsectarian spirit, and excellence of style, make her writings important and helpful.

EUGENE ARAM, by Sir Edward Bulwer-Lytton (1832), was founded on the career of an English scholar, Eugene Aram, born 1704, executed for the murder of one Clark in 1759. The character of the murderer and the circumstances of his life made the case one of the most interesting from a psychological point of view, in the criminal annals of England. Aram was a scholar of unusual ability, who, self-taught, had acquired a considerable knowledge of languages, and was even credited with certain original discoveries in the domain of philology. Of a mild and refined disposition, his act of murder seemed a complete contradiction of all his habits and ideals of life.

At the suggestion of Godwin, Bulwer made this singular case the basis of his novel 'Eugene Aram.' He so idealized the character as to make of the murderer a romantic hero, whose accomplice in the crime, Houseman, is the actual criminal. He represents Aram as forced, by extreme poverty, into consenting to the deed, but not performing it. From that hour he suffers horrible mental torture. He leaves the scene of the murder and settles in Grassdale, a beautiful pastoral village, where he meets and loves a noble woman, Madeline Lester. She returns his love. Their marriage approaches, when the reappearance of Houseman shatters Aram's hopes forever. By the treachery of this wretch, he is imprisoned, tried, and condemned to death.

'Eugene Aram' is an unusually successful study in fiction of a complex psychological case. At the time of its publication, it caused a great stir in England, many attacks being made upon it on the ground of its false morality.

EUGÉNIE GRANDET, by Honoré de Balzac, appeared in 1833, and is included among the 'Scenes of Provincial Life.' In it, the great French master of realism depicts with his accustomed brilliant precision the life of a country girl, the only child of a rich miser. Eugénie and her mother know little pleasure in the "cold, silent, pallid dwelling" at Saumur where they live. Father Grandet loves his wife and daughter, but loves his money better, and cannot spare enough of it to supply his family with suitable food and clothing. His rare gifts to his wife he usually begs back, and Eugénie is expected to hoard her birthday gold-pieces. Eugénie's charming handsome cousin Charles arrives one day for a visit, and Eugénie braves her father's anger to supply him with sugar for his coffee and a wax instead of a tallow candle. Charles has been brought up in wealth, but his father now loses all and commits suicide. Eugénie's pity for her unhappy cousin turns to love, which he seems to reciprocate. Engaged to marry her, with her savings he goes to the West Indies. The years wear on drearily to her, and she does not hear from him. Her mother dies, and she is an heiress, but is persuaded by her father to make over her property to him. The old man dies too, and Eugénie is very rich. At last she receives a letter from Charles, who is ignorant of her wealth, asking for his liberty, and telling her of his wish to marry a certain heiress whose family can aid him in his career. The reserved and self-controlled Eugénie releases him without complaint; and discovering that his match is jeopardized by his father's debts, she sends to Paris her old friend Monsieur de Bonfons, president of the civil courts of Saumur, to pay this debt, and thus clear Charles's name. As a reward for his services, she marries Monsieur de Bonfons without love. Early left a widow, and the solitary owner of wealth which she has never learned to enjoy, she devotes the rest of her life to philanthropy, thus completing her career of self-abnegation.

EULENSPIEGEL, see TILL EULENSPIEGEL.

EUPHUES, THE ANATOMY OF WIT, and EUPHUES AND HIS ENGLAND, by John Lyly, were published respectively in 1578 and 1580, when the author was a young courtier still under thirty. They constitute the first and second part of a work which can only loosely be called fiction in the modern sense. Perhaps the word "romance" best expresses its nature. For a dozen years it was fashionable in the polite circles of England; and the word "Euphuism" survives in the language to designate the stilted, far-fetched, ornate style of writing introduced and made popular by Lyly. Euphues, the hero, is a native of Athens, who goes to Naples and there wooes Lucilla, fickle daughter of the governor. She is already plighted to his friend Philautus; and when Euphues seeks to win her in spite of this, both mistress and friend forsake him. Later, he is reconciled with Philautus, and writes a cynical blast against all womankind. He then returns to his own city, and forswearing love forever, takes refuge in writing disquisitions upon education and religion, interspersed with letters to and from various friends. Incidentally, a fine eulogy on Queen Elizabeth is penned. The narrative is loosely constructed and inconsecutive; the chief interest in the work for Lyly's contemporaries was the philosophical dissertations upon topics of timely pertinence, couched, not in the heavy manner of the formal thinker, but in the light, elegant, finicky tone of the man-about-court. The literary diction of 'Euphues' has been well characterized by a German scholar, Dr. Landmann, who says it showed "a peculiar combination of antithesis with alliteration, assonance, rhyme, and play upon words, a love for the conformity and correspondence of parallel sentences, and a tendency to accumulate rhetorical figures, such as climax, the rhetorical question, objections and refutations, the repetition of the same thought in other forms, etc." Although Lyly's style had in it too much of the affected to give it long life, he undoubtedly did something towards making the sixteenth-century speech refined, musical, and choice. It is this rather than any attraction of story that makes the 'Euphues' interesting to the modern student of literature.

EUROPEAN CITIES AT WORK, by F. C. Howe (1913). This work by an American author who believes that the city is the hope of democracy is a result of a close first-hand study of the great progressive municipalities of the European continent written with a view to the elucidation of the things in which European cities differ from American. In addition, to an English or a German reader it is a sympathetic and impartial account of the municipal activities of their respective countries by a clearheaded investigator who is able to distinguish the good from the bad. The gist of the book may be seen in passages like the following which are a perfectly just and accurate estimate of the merits of European municipal enterprise. "The German city is an experiment station for all of us. It is a *flei-stadt*, a little republic, with power to do almost anything for the welfare of the people. The city is sovereign, and it uses its sovereignty to build in a conscious, intelligent way. It can mould its destiny as did the cities of ancient Greece. It controls property as well as people. It acts with a vision of the future; not alone of the city, but of the lives and comfort of the people as well. The German city is being built something as Pericles built Athens, as Louis XIV. planned Versailles, as the two Napoleons rebuilt Paris. . . . Already the cities of Germany, and to a considerable extent those of Great Britain and the Continent, have demonstrated that many of the sacrifices of the modern industrial city can be avoided. Poverty can be reduced, and the life of the people be enriched in countless ways not possible under rural conditions. Cities realize that many activities are so closely related to the life of the people that they cannot with safety be left in private hands. There must be provision for play, for leisure, as well as for education. The landowner and the housebuilder, the means of transportation, and the supply of gas, water, and electricity environ life in so many ways that they must be subordinate to the rights of the community. Docks and harbors, the railroads and waterways, the houses men live in, and the factories they work in, are all so related to the well-being of the city that they must be owned or controlled in the interest of all." To the average American the city is a mere political agency, to the progressive European it is "a business corporation organized to realize the maximum of returns to the community." A detailed account of the finance, town-planning, transport arrangements, housing, administrative methods and above all of the conscious aims and ideals of the great European cities is set out in clear and readable fashion, with a number of opposite photographic illustrations.

EUROPEAN MORALS, HISTORY OF, FROM AUGUSTUS TO CHARLEMAGNE, by W. E. H. Lecky (1869). An elaborate examination, first of the several theories of ethics; then of the moral history of Roman Paganism, under philosophies that successively flourished, Stoical, Eclectic, and Egyptian; next the changes in moral life introduced by Christianity; and finally the position of woman in Europe under the influence of Christianity. In tracing the action of external circumstances upon morals, and examining what moral types have been proposed in different ages, to what degree they have been realized in practice, and by what causes they have been modified, impaired, or destroyed, Lecky's discussion, with illustrations found in the period of history covered, is singularly instructive and not less interesting.

EUROPEANS, THE, an early novel of Henry James (1878), describes the sojourn of two Europeans, Felix Young and his sister the Baroness Münster, with American cousins near Boston. The dramatic effects of the story are produced by the contrasts between the reserved Boston family, and the easy-going cosmopolitans, with their complete ignorance of the New England temperament. To one of the cousins, Gertrude Wentworth, the advent of Felix Young, with his foreign nonchalance, is the hour of a great deliverance from the insufferable boredom of her suburban home. To marry Young, she rejects the husband her father has chosen for her, Mr. Brand, a Unitarian clergyman, who consoles himself with her conscientious sister Charlotte. The novel is written in the author's clean, precise manner, and bears about it a wonderfully realistic atmosphere of a certain type of American home where plain living and high thinking are in order. The dreariness which may accompany this swept and garnished kind of life is emphasized.

EVANGELINE, a narrative poem in hexameters by Henry Wadsworth Longfellow, published in 1847. Like Goethe's 'Hermann und Dorothea' it is an idyllic tale, in hexameters, of two lovers who are involved in the disasters of a time of war. When the Acadians are expelled from their homes in Grand Pré in 1755 for lending aid to the agitators against English rule, a betrothal has just been celebrated between Gabriel Lajeunesse and Evangeline Bellefontaine, son and daughter of the two wealthiest peasants of the village. In the confusion of embarkation the lovers sail on different ships and fail to rejoin one another. Gabriel, and his father, Basil, make their way down the Mississippi to Louisiana; where they again become prosperous by raising cattle. Evangeline, whose father has died of grief on the shore of Grand Pré, journeys to New England, vainly looking for Gabriel. Refusing all offers of marriage she continues to seek him, under the protection of the parish priest, Father Felician. After many inquiries they arrive at Basil's ranch, only to find that Gabriel has just quitted it for the western prairies, and that they have unwittingly passed him on their way down the Mississippi. Evangeline now follows him across the prairies to the Ozark Mountains, but again misses him. She now remains for several months at the Jesuit Mission, awaiting Gabriel's expected return, and when he does not come follows him to the woods of Michigan and finds his camp deserted. After years of fruitless wandering, during which she becomes a faded and prematurely old woman, she comes to Philadelphia, where, as a sister of mercy, she cares for the poor and sick. At length, during an epidemic, she finds her long-lost lover, Gabriel, dying in the alms-house, and the lovers are united at his last breath. Both are buried in the Catholic cemetery. Though Longfellow had seen none of the places mentioned in the poem except Philadelphia he drew his information from excellent historical sources (among them Haliburton's 'Historical and Statistical Account of Nova Scotia,' 1829, Frémont's 'Expedition to the Rocky Mountains,' 1845, and Wm. Darby's 'Geographical Description of the State of Louisiana,' 1816), and has made the poem an imperishable gallery of American scenery. Without complexity, the poem is a genuine and affecting record of human suffering relieved by human resolution and devotion. It is a charming idyll, and its hexameters, though criticized as too dactylic, have strength and movement.

EVELINA, by Frances Burney. In 'Evelina; or, the History of a Young Lady's Entrance into the World,' Miss Burney, describing the experiences of her charming little heroine in London, gives a vivid picture of the manners and customs of the eighteenth century.

Some years before the opening of the story, Sir John Belmont has deserted his wife. When she dies, their child Evelina is brought up in the seclusion of the country by her kind guardian, Mr. Villars. Sir John is followed to France by an ambitious woman, a nurse, who carries her child to him in place of his own, and he educates this child believing her to be his daughter. Evelina, meantime, grown to be a pretty, unaffected girl, goes to visit Mrs. Mirvan in London, and is introduced to society. She meets Lord Orville, the dignified and handsome hero, and falls in love with him. Later she is obliged to visit her vulgar grandmother, Madame Duval; and while with her ill-bred relatives she undergoes great mortification on meeting Lord Orville and Sir Clement Willoughby, a persistent lover. During this visit Evelina saves a poor young man, Mr. Macartney, from committing suicide. He proves to be the illegitimate son of Sir John Belmont, and in Paris he has fallen in love with the supposed daughter of that gentleman, who, he is afterwards told, is his own sister. He tells Evelina his story; but as no names are mentioned, they remain in ignorance of their relationship. At Bath, Evelina sees Lord Orville again, and in spite of many misunderstandings they at last come together. Sir John returns from France, is made to realize the mistake that had been made, and accepts Evelina as his rightful heir. All mysteries are cleared up, Mr. Macartney marries the nurse's child so long considered Sir John's daughter, and Lord Orville marries Evelina.

The characters are interesting contrasts: Orville, Lovel, Willoughby, and Merton standing for different types of fashionable men; while Captain Mirvan, Madame Duval, and the Branghtons are excellent illustrations of eighteenth-century vulgarity. The story is told by letters, principally those of Evelina to her guardian. 'Evelina' was published in 1778, and immediately brought fame to the authoress, then only twenty-five years old.

EVELYN, JOHN, DIARY (1818–19).   The best-known of the books by which Evelyn is remembered is not a diary in the strict sense of the term, but a record apparently copied by the writer from memoranda made at the time of the occurrences noted in it, with occasional alterations and additions made in the course of transcription. The quarto volume in which it is contained consists of seven hundred pages clearly written by Evelyn in a small close hand, the continuous records of sixty-five years (1641–1706) crowded with remarkable events, the great plague and great fire, the Civil War, the Commonwealth, the Protectorate, the Revolution of 1688.   But it contains also the impressions of a cultivated, traveled, and thoughtful man, who made frequent tours on the continent of Europe, and had access to all who were prominent in the Church, in literature, art, and science both at home and abroad. No other man who lived through those breathless days knew intimately so many grades and classes of his fellow-countrymen, or had so much right to speak on subjects that are still of living interest to thoughtful people.   The book is an invaluable chronicle of contemporary events from the standpoint of one who was strongly attached to monarchy and personally devoted to Charles II. and James II., but opposed to their arbitrary measures.   The writer is a devout adherent of the Church of England, yet shows a tolerance, remarkable in his day, for Catholics and others who were outside that communion.   He has none of Pepys's love of gossip and triviality, insatiable curiosity, nor frankness of self-revelation.   But besides the high affairs with which the diary mostly deals the reader will find many quaint and interesting details.   At Haarlem "they showed us a cottage, where they told us, dwelt a woman who had been married to her twenty-fifth husband, and being now a widow, was prohibited to marry in future: yet it could not be proved that she had ever made away with any of her husbands, though" (the chronicler gravely adds) "the suspicion had brought her divers times to trouble."   At Lincoln he "saw a tall woman six foot two inches high, comely, middle aged and well-proportioned, who kept a very neat and clean ale-house, and got most by people's coming to see her on account of her height."

EVELYN INNESS; a novel by George Moore (1898).   The daughter of an organist and a great singer, Evelyn has a beautiful voice, and dreams of studying music in Paris, but is likely to be sacrificed to her father's hobby, the music of Palestrina and the revival of liturgic chants in church music.   Sir Owen Asher, a wealthy amateur, interested in the father's theories of music, hears Evelyn sing at her father's concerts and is at once attracted by her voice and beauty.   He wants to take her away from the drudgery of music lessons and it gratifies his vanity to discover a prima donna. Tempted by her ambition and in love with Sir Owen, she consents to go to Paris with him in order to have the best musical training.   She tells her father of her purpose, and while he is conventionally shocked, he is enough of a musical genius himself to understand and appreciate her temptation.   Sir Owen provides an English lady of title for chaperon, in order that the external conventions may be observed, and Evelyn enters an enchanted world of pleasure and success.   Six years later she returns to England to appear in Wagnerian opera.   Sir Owen adores her, and she intends to marry him when she leaves the stage, though with her, love has changed to affection. She becomes interested in a young Irish mystic and composer, a friend of her father's, and takes him as her lover, though she cannot bring herself to break with Sir Owen. Always a Catholic, she comes under the influence of a priest who arouses her conscience and spiritual nature, and induces her to give up both men, and make a retreat in a convent.   The conflict between the spirit and the flesh, and the Church and the

world is the occasion for an absorbing analysis of an artistic temperament. Early
music, the art of Wagner, and its expression of the emotions, mysticism and convent
life are successive interests, but the setting is pre-eminently musical. A sequel
'Sister Theresa' (1901) tells about Evelyn's spiritual trials as postulant, novice, and
nun, and is a detailed description of convent life.

EVERY MAN IN HIS HUMOUR, by Ben Jonson (1598), one of the earliest and
happiest of the author's efforts, is the first important comedy of character (as distinguished from comedy of incident) produced on the English stage. The aim of the
author, as announced in the Prologue, was to depart from the license of romantic
comedy, mixed with tragedy and history, and to adhere to comedy proper, "to sport
with human follies not with crimes." By "humour" he meant peculiarities of conduct, and he has grouped together a number of characters with strongly marked
personalities which stand out in contrast with each other. The most famous of these
is Captain Bobadil, the military braggart, who has a place of his own on the English
stage, a part which Charles Dickens, one of the most successful of amateur actors,
filled to admiration. Kitely, a jealous usurer, whose house is the rendezvous of
riotous young gallants, and who places a spy over his wife to warn him of any approach
to unfaithfulness, is another skilfully contrived figure. Stephen the county-gull,
Matthew the town-gull, and Cob the water-carrier help to complete the picture of
London life. The female characters are correctly drawn, but do not occupy a very
prominent part on the stage.

EVOLUTION OF MODERN GERMANY, THE, by W. H. Dawson (1908). The
writer of this, by far the best and most exhaustive book in English about Germany
since 1870, has made a life-long study of that country. He examines the causes of
the unexampled expansion since 1870, the scientific and technical education, which in
many parts of the country had been thoroughly established by the time of the
Franco-Prussian War and has since spread over the whole empire: the policy of
nationalization and municipalization, carried further by Germany than by any other
country in the world; the stimulation of research by the State and the application of
science to industry and agriculture; the thoroughness, foresight, and patient application to detail which Germany has devoted to every department of her national life.
Of these by far the most important has been Germany's devotion to her universities,
colleges, and schools. "Germany" (says Mr. Dawson) "had no sooner begun its
career as an industrial export country than it felt at once the full benefit of the system of education which it had adopted long before most of its rivals had learned to
regard public instruction as an affair of the State . . . Germany more than any other
European country found itself fully equipped by education for entering upon a fierce
competitive struggle, under entirely new conditions, for the commercial mastery of
the world. Its technical colleges turned out, as by word of command, an army of
trained directors, engineers, and chemists, armed with the last discovered secret
of science, and with her last uttered word concerning the industrial processes and
methods which henceforth were to hold the field."

EXCURSION, THE, a narrative and reflective poem in blank verse by William
Wordsworth. A portion of the first book was written as early as 1795–1797; books
I. and II. were mainly completed in 1801 and 1802; the remaining seven books were
written between 1809 and 1813, and the whole work was published in 1814. 'The
Excursion' was planned as part of a larger whole, to be entitled 'The Recluse,' a

fragment of the first division of which was posthumously published under the latter title in 1888. 'The Prelude' was a preliminary study to this great projected work (see the digest of 'The Prelude'). In the first book of 'The Excursion,' entitled 'The Wanderer,' the author, after a walk across a moorland on a glaringly hot summer morning, meets by appointment at a ruined cottage a middle-aged Scottish pedlar (The Wanderer) with whom he plans a walking tour. The Wanderer's stern up-bringing and the influences of simple manners and austere landscape on his character are described, after which he tells the pathetic story of the poor woman who had lived in the cottage. Left by her weaver husband to support two children while he went to the Napoleonic wars, she had maintained a lonely existence for nine years, had apprenticed one child and lost the other, and had finally died of a chill, due to the ruinous state of her dwelling. When this tale is over, the travelers go to a neighbor-ing village for the night. Next day, ascending to a secluded little valley high in the mountains, they visit the Solitary, the subject of Book II. He is a Scottish Presby-terian minister who had been chaplain of a Highland regiment, had resigned and married happily, but lost his wife and children, and, after some years of dull apathy, was stirred to life by the French Revolution. He became an ardent revolutionary and then a sceptic, renouncing his ministry; but the transformation of the revolu-tionary spirit into the spirit of conquest disillusioned him. He is now living a secluded life in the cottage of a shepherd where he entertains the travelers with a luncheon of cheese, oat-cakes, and fruit, and as he shows them the vale recounts the death on the mountains of an old pensioner of the shepherd's family whose funeral the visitors had seen as they descended into the valley. The Solitary then sketches for them his own life and despondency (Book III.), for which the Wanderer strives to supply a remedy in Book IV. ('Despondency Corrected'). The Wanderer, whose opinions are those of the poet, urges man's need of admiration, hope, and love, shows that these naturally spring from the contemplation of nature and association with our fellowmen, and deduces from these sources a confident belief in God, Free Will, and Immortality. After spending the night in the cottage the travelers depart next morning, and accompanied by the Solitary walk in the cool of the day to a beautiful village beside a mere, and pause to examine the monuments of the parish church (Book V., 'The Pastor'). The baptismal font suggests to the Solitary the great gulf between men's professions and performance, the weakness of human nature, and the consequent illusion of the lofty aspirations mentioned in the Wanderer's dis-course. The parish priest, who happens to come up, is called upon to solve the difficulty, and replies that though reason is powerless an attitude of trust in God will lighten life's gloom and ensure true happiness. It is admitted by all that this trust comes easiest to the humble and retired; and at the request of the Solitary the Parson gives some illustrations of it from the families of his own parish. A miner and his wife living in a rude stone cottage on a hilltop are first described in all their simplicity of faith and honest toil; and in the next book (VI.) the Parson tells of various persons buried in 'The Churchyard among the Mountains.' Among these are a man who sought refuge from disappointed love in botanizing in the Lake district; a miner who after a life of fruitless search discovered valuable deposits and died of joy; a clever and profligate actor, native to the country, who returned thither to die repentant; a Jacobite and a Whig squire, opposed in principles yet such close friends that they had a single monument; a wilful, jealous woman, subdued to charity and resignation in her last illness; a girl, Ellen, betrayed by her lover, who after the birth of her child went to nurse another infant and died of grief at the loss of her own baby, attributing this to her neglect; a man, Wilfred Armathwaite,

who died of remorse for his unfaithfulness to his wife; a wife and mother who lived
on in the strength and industry of her daughters; a country clergyman and his family;
another clergyman renowned for piety; a deaf and a blind man both of whom maintained cheerfulness in their affliction; the infant granddaughter of an aged Dalesman;
a young volunteer for the Napoleonic wars cut off by premature death; and a knight
of Queen Elizabeth's time, who had settled in those solitudes. To vary the monotony of these obituary notices, a hardy wood-cutter is introduced, a man of "cheerful
yesterdays and confident to-morrows." In Book VIII. on the way to the Parson's
house the company discusses the Industrial Revolution and the social and economic
changes it has wrought in the north country — its promotion of foreign commerce
and its degradation of the working-man by the factory system. Arrived at the
pleasant vicarage the travelers are greeted by the pastor's hospitable wife and
daughter and enjoy a social meal, interrupted by the advent of his young son and a
school-boy friend from a fishing excursion. This leads the Wanderer in the beginning
of Book IX. to a discourse on the blessedness of childhood, its nearness to God, and
the need of preserving this youthful confidence and faith up to old age. This can be
done, however, only if man be regarded not as an economic machine but as a human
being, who needs to develop harmoniously all his powers, intellectual, emotional, and
social. To this end an adequate scheme of universal education should be instituted
by the state. The whole party then goes out for an evening row at the lake, and
supper is served beside a camp-fire on the shore of one of the islands. Afterwards
they row to the mainland, climb a lofty hill, and enjoy a magnificent sunset during
which time the pastor offers up a prayer to the God, of whose glory the golden and
crimson clouds are but a faint reflection. The poet and the Wanderer remain all
night at the Parson's, but the Solitary returns to his valley. Wordsworth intimates
at the close that in a subsequent work he hopes to tell of this unfortunate man's
reclamation. The work, however, was never completed. 'The Excursion' has its
tedious and dull passages but is full of delightful pictures of the Lake District and
of the sturdy Dalesmen who inhabit it. It also contains some powerful narratives
of peasant life. Those who have not read the poem are not adequately familiar with
Wordsworth's environment or his power of portraying it. Moreover, 'The Excursion' furnishes the maturest statement of Wordsworth's philosophy of God, Nature,
and Man.

EXILES OF SIBERIA, THE, see **ELIZABETH.**

EXPANSION OF ENGLAND, THE, by J. R. Seeley (1883). In this volume Professor Seeley attempts, in effect, to shift the point of view of his countrymen as to
the boundaries of the history of England. It is not a single island that they should
contemplate, but a world empire, which can be compared with, and measured by,
only the two great powers of the future, Russia and the United States. Part first
deals with the history of England with relation to its colonies and the United States.
The writer complains that an arbitrary arrangement of reigns is apt to confuse our
sense of the continuity of events. Let us, he says, get rid of such useless headings as
Reign of Queen Anne, Reign of George III., and make divisions founded on some real
stage of progress in the national life; looking onward, not from king to king, but from
great event to great event. If we study its causes, every event puts on the character
of a development; and this development is a chapter in the national history. From
1688 to 1815, Mr. Seeley finds the formative events to have been foreign wars, beneath whose stormy surface he looks for the quiet current of progress. He finds the

clue he wants in the fact that almost all these wars involved French interests; and that "The whole period stands out as an age of gigantic rivalry between England and France; the expansion of England in the New World and Asia is the formula which sums up for England the history of the eighteenth century, — the great decisive duel between the two nations for the possession of the New World." Her colonies having been planted at a tremendous sacrifice of money, energy, and life, he would have them held as a vital part of the parent State, not as "possessions." "We must cease to think that emigrants, when they go to colonies, leave England, or are lost to England. . . . When we have accustomed ourselves to contemplate the whole empire together, and call it all England, we shall see that here too is a United States; here too is a great homogeneous people . . . but dispersed over a boundless space. . . . If we are disposed to doubt whether any system can be devised capable of holding together communities so distant from each other, then is the time to recollect the history of the United States. They have solved this problem."

The second half of the book contains eight lectures, chiefly given to the Indian empire, explaining the necessity of the conquest; the manner of the English governance of that empire, — a study in which he affirms boldly that if ever a universal feeling of nationality arises there, England cannot and should not preserve her dominancy; the mutual influence of England and India; the succeeding phases in the conquest; the internal dangers that threaten the stability of British control in the East; and finally, the condition of public opinion concerning the modern British empire. In a delightful manner, and with large resources of scholarship, Professor Seeley shows the continuity of the development of England, the orderly sequence and significance of her failures as well as her successes, and the way in which the story of her past should be made instructive for her future. And in conclusion he has this admirable deliverance, which every reader may lay to heart: "I am often told by those who, like myself, study the question how history should be taught, 'Oh, you must, before all things, make it interesting.' . . . But the word 'interesting' does not properly mean romantic. That is interesting, in the proper sense, which affects our interests, which closely concerns us, and is deeply important to us. I have tried to show you that the history of modern England from the beginning of the eighteenth century is interesting in this sense, because it is pregnant with great results, which will affect the lives of ourselves and our children and the future greatness of our country. Make history interesting, indeed! I cannot make history more interesting than it is! . . . And therefore when I meet a person who does *not* find history interesting, it does not occur to me to alter history, — I try to alter *him*."

EXPERIMENTAL RESEARCHES IN ELECTRICITY, by Michael Faraday (3 vols., 1839–1855). A monumental work in the literature of science; not merely recording the results of experiment in what Tyndall called "a career of discovery unparalleled in the history of pure experimental science," but enriching the record with thoughts, and clothing it in many passages in a style worthy of exceptional recognition. In devising and executing experiments for passing beyond the limits of existing knowledge, in a field the most difficult ever attempted by research, Faraday showed a genius, and achieved a success, marking him as a thinker not less than an observer of the first order. In strength and sureness of imagination, penetrating the secrets of force in nature, and putting the finger of exact demonstration upon them, he was a Shakespeare of research, the story of whose work has a permanent interest. He made electricity, in one of its manifestations, explain magnetism. He showed to demonstration that chemical action is purely electrical, and that to electricity the atoms of matter owe those properties which constitute them elements in nature. In language of lofty prophetic conception he more than suggested that the physical secret of living things, the animal and the plant, is electrical. He particularly dwelt on the amount of electricity forming the charge carried by the oxygen of the air, which is the active agent in combustion and the supporter of life in both animals and plants, and only stopped short of definitely pronouncing vitality electrical. He urged very strongly as a belief, to which no test of experiment could be applied, that gravitation is by electrical agency, and that in fact the last word of discovery and demonstration in physics will show that electricity is the universal agency in nature. And among his far-reaching applications of thought guided by new knowledge, was his rejection of the idea of "action at a distance," in the manner of "attraction." If a body is moved, it is not by a mysterious pull, but by a push. The moving force carries it. These ideas outran the power of science to immediately understand and accept. But Maxwell, Hertz, and Helmholtz have led the way after Faraday, to the extent that his electrical explanation of light is now fully accepted. Fifteen years after his death, the greatest of his successors in physics, Helmholtz of Berlin, said in a "Faraday Lecture" in London, that the later advances in electrical science had more than confirmed Faraday's conclusions, and that English science had made a mistake in not accepting them as its point of departure for new research. To the same effect President Armstrong of the Chemical Society, to which Helmholtz spoke, has recently declared his conviction that Faraday's explanation of chemical action as electrically caused should have been accepted long since.

In delicacy of character as well as rugged strength, in warmth and purity of emotion, in grace, earnestness, and refinement of manner, in the magnetism of his presence, and in masterly clearness in explanation, especially to his Christmas audiences of children (annual courses of six lectures), Faraday was as remarkable as he was in intellectual power and in discoveries. He was connected with the Royal Institution for fifty-five years, first as Sir Humphry Davy's assistant, 1812–29, and then as his successor, 1829–67.

EXPLORATIONS AND ADVENTURES IN EQUATORIAL AFRICA, by Paul Belloni Du Chaillu (1861; revised edition, 1871). A story of African travels, 1855–59, from the coast of West Africa inland, over the region on the equator to two degrees on each side. The intrepid explorer traveled 8000 miles on foot and with no white companion. The observations which he made are important contributions to geographical, ethnological, and zoölogical science. The game which he shot numbered 2000 birds (of which 60 were new to science), and over 1000 quadrupeds. The new knowledge of the gorilla and of other remarkable apes was a story savoring almost of invention, and the first impression of some critics was one of skepticism; but Murchison and Owen, and other authorities of eminence, upheld Du Chaillu's credit, and the substantial accuracy of his statements was confirmed by a French expedition in 1862, and by Du Chaillu's second exploration of the same region, 1863–65, an account of which he gave in 'A Journey to Ashango-Land,' 1867. He was also the first to discover the "Pigmies," rediscovered by Stanley.

EYES LIKE THE SEA, by the celebrated Hungarian novelist Maurice Jókai, was crowned by the Hungarian Academy as the best Magyar novel of the year 1890. It takes high rank among the author's one hundred and fifty works of fiction. The peculiar title of the book has reference to the eyes of the heroine, Bessy, a girl of gentle parentage, yet of a perverse, adventurous disposition, which during the course of the story leads her five times into matrimony; the five husbands representing almost every class of society, from the peasant to the nobleman. She is, indeed, the pivot on which the narrative turns; is both hero and heroine, as she partakes of the subtler qualities of both sexes. The second though unacknowledged hero is Maurice Jókai himself; his story being generally, if not circumstantially, autobiographical. In his youth he had loved Bessy. She rejects his love, but ever afterwards cherishes the memory of it as the one noble ideal in her wayward life. Even this may be a form of perversity. Jókai leaves her to console himself with the pursuit of literary fame. Later he takes a patriot's part in the Hungarian revolution of 1848. In the thick of it he marries an actress, who is most devoted and faithful to him. From time to time, Bessy seeks his rather unwilling advice and protection in her love affairs. From the lady with "eyes like the sea" he cannot escape. Its strong local color makes the book a faithful picture of Hungarian social life, while throughout it is tremendously stimulating, fresh, and boisterous as a wind from the Carpathian Mountains.

FABLES BY LA FONTAINE, see **FABLES OF ÆSOP.**

FABLES OF ÆSOP, THE, a collection of brief stories mostly about animals who think and speak like men, each tale illustrating some practical truth. They are attributed to Æsop, said to have been a deformed Greek slave of the seventh century B. C., who won his liberty by his skill as a fabulist, was favored by Crœsus, King of Lydia, and slain at Delphi in a tumult. They were not collected, however, until 320 B. C., and survive only in later versions — e. g., that of Babrius in Greek and that of Phædrius in Latin. Whether Æsop ever existed or not, the fables attributed to him were not his own invention but were Oriental in origin. As a literary type they represent an early stage of culture when man still feels kinship with the animals but is sophisticated enough to use them as representatives of human nature in stories that enforce some shrewd maxim of homely wisdom. Of modern adaptations of Æsop's Fables the most important are the three books of versified Fables by Jean de la Fontaine, published in 1668, 1679, and 1693 respectively. A lover of the woods and fields La Fontaine entered with fresh sympathy into the adventures of the animals in Æsop, who become for him real beasts; but his clear perception and genial toleration of the foibles of his fellowmen enabled him at the same time to make these beasts the representatives of the French peasants, bourgeoisie, and nobles of his own day; and his thoroughly Gallic wit, humor, realism, and grace of expression have elevated his fables to the highest rank of French poetry.

FAERY QUEEN, THE, a metrical romance by Edmund Spenser, dedicated to Queen Elizabeth, was published in 1590. The poet was already known by his 'Shepherd's Calendar,' but the appearance of the first three books of the 'Faery Queen' brought him fame. The second three books appeared in 1595–96. The poem is an allegory, founded on the manners and customs of chivalry, with the aim of portraying a perfect knight. Spenser planned twelve books, treating of the twelve moral virtues; but only six are now in existence. These are: The Legend of the Red Cross Knight, typifying holiness; The Legend of Sir Guyon, temperance; The Legend of Britomartis, chastity; The Legend of Cambel and Friamond, friendship; The Legend of Artegall, justice; and The Legend of Sir Calidore, courtesy. To these is sometimes added a fragment on Mutability. "In the Faery Queen," Spenser says, "I mean Glory in my general intention; but, in my particular, I conceive the most excellent and glorious person of our Sovereign the Queen and her Kingdom in Faery Land." He supposes

that the Faery Queen held a superb feast, lasting twelve days, on each of which a
complaint was presented. To redress these twelve injuries twelve knights sally
forth; and during his adventures, each knight proves himself the hero of some particular virtue. Besides these twelve knights there is one general hero, Prince Arthur,
who represents magnificence. In every book he appears; and his aim is to discover
and win Gloriana, or glory. The characters are numerous, being drawn from classic
mythology, mediæval romance, and the poet's fancy. The scene is usually the wood
where dragons are killed, where knights wander and meet with adventures of all
kinds, where magicians attempt their evil spells, and where all wrongs are vanquished.
Each canto is filled with incidents and short narratives; among the most beautiful of
which are Una with the Lion; and Britomart's vision of the Mask of Cupid in the
enchanted castle. The 'Faery Queen' has always been admired by poets; and it was
on the advice of a poet, Sir Walter Raleigh, that Spenser published the great work.

FAIR BARBARIAN, A, by Frances Hodgson Burnett, appeared in 1881. Like
James's 'Daisy Miller,' it is a study of the American girl in foreign surroundings.
Miss Octavia Bassett, of Nevada, aged nineteen, arrives with six trunks full of finery,
to visit her aunt, Miss Belinda Bassett, in the English village of Slowbridge. The
beautiful American soon sets tongues wagging. All the village young ladies wear
gowns of one pattern obsolete elsewhere, and chill propriety reigns. Octavia's
diamonds and Paris gowns, her self-possession and frank independence, are frowned
upon by the horrified mammas, especially when all the young men gather eagerly
about her. Octavia, serenely indifferent to the impression she creates at the tea-
drinkings and croquet parties, refuses to be awed even by the autocrat of the place,
Lady Theobald. Her ladyship's meek granddaughter is spurred by admiration of
the American to unprecedented independence. She has been selected to be Captain
Barold's wife, but as he does not care for her, she ventures to accept Mr. Burmistone,
upon whom her grandmother frowns. Barold meantime is enslaved by the charming
Octavia. But he disapproves of her unconventional ways, and considering it a condescension on his part to ally himself with so obscure a family, he proposes with
great reluctance and is astonished to meet a point-blank refusal. In due time, Octavia's father and her handsome Western lover join her; and after a wedding the like
of which had never been witnessed at Slowbridge, she says good-by to her English
friends. The story is slight, but the character-sketches are amusing, the contrast of
national traits striking, and the whole book very entertaining.

FAIR GOD, THE, by Lew Wallace (1873), passed through twenty editions in ten
years. It is a historical romance of the conquest of Mexico by the Spaniards, its
scene laid upon Aztec soil, in the early part of the sixteenth century. The title is
derived from Quetzalcoatl, "the fair god," the Aztec deity of the air. Descriptions
of the religion and national customs are pleasantly interwoven with the plot. The
Emperor Montezuma is drawn as a noble but vacillating prince, whom the efforts of
nobles and people alike fail to arouse to a determined opposition to the invading
Cortez. At first thinking that the Spaniards are gods, he insists upon welcoming
them as guests, ignoring the protests of his subjects, and even permitting himself
to be craftily shut up, a voluntary prisoner, in the quarters of the Spaniards. Guatamozin, nephew and son-in-law to Montezuma, mighty in arms as wise in counsel,
organizes the Aztecs for the overthrow of the Spaniards. A fierce conflict rages for
many days. Toward its close the melancholy Montezuma appears upon the prison
wall. Before all the people Guatamozin sends a shaft home to the breast of his

monarch, who lives long enough to intrust the empire to his slayer, and also free him from blame for his death, explaining that the shaft had been aimed at his (Montezuma's) own request. The Aztec army now rallies, and the Spaniards, yielding at length to starvation, disease, and superior numbers, leave the empire. Too shattered to regain its former vigor, even under the wise rule of Guatamozin, the State gradually totters to its eventual fall, a catastrophe which the author indicates but does not picture.

FAIR MAID OF PERTH, THE, by Sir Walter Scott (1831), is historic in setting and thoroughly Scotch. The time is the reign of the weak but well-meaning King Robert III. of Scotland. whose scapegrace son David, the crown prince, is the connecting link in the story between the nobility and the burgher-folk of the city of Perth. Catharine, the beautiful daughter of Simon Glover, an honest burgher, is admired by the crown prince, who seeks her love but not her hand. Repulsed in his suit, the prince, through Sir John Ramorny, his servant, tries to abduct Catharine on the eve of St. Valentine's day; but by the timely intervention of Henry Wynd, the armorer, she is saved; and Henry becomes, according to custom, her valentine for the year to come. Then follows a series of complications, political, ecclesiastical, and social, through which the eager reader follows the fate of the fair Catharine, the prince, the Black Douglas, and the other chief characters. Like all Scott's novels, 'The Fair Maid of Perth' contains fine descriptions of scenery, and stirring accounts of battle; and unlike many of his plots, this one allows the "course of true love" to run comparatively smooth, there being only obstacles enough to prove the mettle of the honest armorer.

FAIRY TALES. The stories of Cinderella, Beauty and the Beast, Hop o' my Thumb, Sleeping Beauty, and others, so fascinating to children and to peasants, were looked on merely as amusing tales, until the efforts of Grimm and his successors drew back, as it were, a curtain, and disclosed another fairy region of almost limitless perspective, whose vanishing-point may be nearly identical with the origin of the human race. For by the study of comparative mythology, it was discovered that these tales are not restricted to Europe alone, but are to be found, in varying forms, among almost all nations. Comparative philology then showed the original union of the Teutonic, Celtic, Latin, Greek, Persian, and Hindu races in the primitive Aryan race, whose home has been variously fixed in Western Central Asia, in Europe, and even in Africa; from which they broke away in prehistoric dispersions. This was discovered by tracing words through the German, Latin, Greek, and Persian forms up to the Sanskrit, the oldest literary form of all; their identity proves their descent from a common stock. Thus most of our popular tales date from the days "when the primitive Aryan took his evening meal of *yava*, and sipped his fermented mead, while the Laplander was master of Europe, and the dark-skinned Sudra roamed through the Punjab." The survival of popular tales is due to their being unconscious growths, to the strict adherence to form shown by illiterate and savage people in recitals, proved also by a child's insistence on accuracy, and to the laws of the permanence of culture. All these make the science of folk-lore possible.

There are several theories in regard to the origin of folk-tales. The oldest is the Oriental theory, which traces all back to a common origin in the Vedas, the Sanskrit sacred books of Buddhism, dating probably from 2000 B. C. It is true that the germs of most tales are found in the Vedas, but proofs of the Indian origin of stories are lacking; the discovery of tales in Egypt which were written down in the period of the

19

early empire are objections to its acceptance, and the idea of diffusion will not account for similar tales found in Australia, New Zealand, and America. The Aryan theory, supported by Max Müller, Grimm, and others, gives as their origin the explanation of natural phenomena, as the sun's daily course, the change of day and night, dawn, winter, and summer. These nature-myths must not be regarded as originally metaphors; they were primitive man's philosophy of nature, in the days when he could not distinguish between it and his personality, when "there was no supernatural, because it was not yet discovered that there was such a thing as nature"; and so every object was endowed with a personal life. This view is supported by the proper names in myths having been originally names of natural phenomena. The savage myths of to-day explain the myth-making of old: instance the New Zealand tale of 'The Children of Heaven and Earth' in Grey's 'Polynesian Mythology,' connected with the Sanskrit Dyauspitar (Jupiter), Heaven-father, and Prithivì-mâtar, Earth-mother, in the Vedas. Folk-lore is "the débris brought down by the streams of tradition from the distant highlands of ancient mythology," and the survivals which are unintelligible singly must be explained by comparing them with others. The tales have enough likeness to show that they come from the same source, and enough difference to show they were not copied from each other. Müller says, "Nursery tales are generally the last things to be adopted by one nation from another." The danger is that too many may be assigned to nature-myths. Even the 'Song of Sixpence' has been claimed as one: the pie representing earth and sky; the birds, the twenty-four hours; the opened pie, the daybreak, with singing birds; the king, the sun, with his money, sunshine; the queen, the moon; the maid, dawn hanging out the clothes, clouds, is frightened away by the blackbird, sunrise. Another theory, supported by Tylor and Lang, traces the origin of folk-lore to a far earlier source than the Aryan, — the customs and practices of early man: such as totemism, descent from animals or things, which were at last worshiped; and curious taboos or prohibitions, which can be explained by similar savage customs of the present. Thus tales become valuable both for the anthropologist and the mythologist. But late authorities declare that it is useless to seek any common origin of folk-tales; since the incidents, which are few, and the persons, who are types, are based on ideas that might occur to uncivilized races anywhere.

Our popular fairy-tales, or *contes*, have been, in the main, handed down orally. However, some of their elements or variants at least have come down through literary collections in the following succession: The Vedas, the Sanskrit sacred books; the Persian Zend-Avesta; the Jâtakas of about the fifth century B. C.; from some lost Sanskrit books came the 'Panchatantra,' a book of fables earlier than 550 A. D., of which the Hitopadeça is a compilation; a Pahlavi version of the same period; an Arabic version before the tenth century; and a Persian of about 1100 A. D.; the 'Syntipas,' a Greek version, belongs to the eleventh century. Then followed translations into several European languages. The earliest collection of European tales was made by Straparola, who published at Venice in 1550 his 'Notti Piacevola,' which was translated into French, and was probably the origin of the 'Contes des Fées.' It contains the tale of 'Puss in Boots,' and elements of some others. The best early collection is Basile's, the 'Pentamerone,' published at Naples in 1637. In 1696 there appeared in the Recueil, a magazine published by Moetjens at The Hague, the story 'La Belle au Bois Dormant' (our 'Sleeping Beauty'), by Charles Perrault; and in 1697 appeared seven others: 'Little Red Riding Hood,' 'Bluebeard,' 'Puss in Boots,' 'The Fairy,' 'Cinderella,' 'Riquet of the Tuft,' and 'Hop o' My Thumb.' These were published together under the title 'Contes du Temps Passé,

Avec des Moralités,' by P. Darmancour, Perrault's son, for whom he wrote them down from a nurse's stories. These fairy-tales became part of the world's literature; and in England at least, where scarcely any tales existed in literary form except 'Jack the Giant-Killer,' they superseded all the national versions. The investigations of Jacob and William Grimm, and their successors in this field, have reduced to written form the tales of nearly all nations, revealing the same characters and incidents under countless names and shapes. The method used by them has been to take down the tales from the recitals of the common people — generally of the old women who have been the chief conservers of stories, — exactly as given, rough or uncouth as the narrative may be. For in some apparently absurd feature may be a survival of ancient custom or myth of great historic interest; and the germs of these universal stories, in becoming part of a nation's folk-lore, take a local form and so become valuable to the ethnologist. Thus the beautiful myths of the South in the Northern forms, where winter's rigor alters the conditions of life, have an entirely different setting. We must include in the comparison of stories the Greek myths; as the Odyssey is now conceded to be a mass of popular tales (Gerland's 'Altgriechische Märchen in der Odyssee,' — 'Old Greek Tales in the Odyssey'). To these we must add the tales of ancient Egypt; those narrated by Herodotus, and other travelers and historians; the beautiful story of 'Cupid and Psyche,' given by Apuleius in his 'Metamorphoses' of the second century A. D., which also was taken from a popular myth, as we shall see, very widely distributed. Spreading all these before us, with the wealth of Eastern lore, and that gathered recently from every European nation, and from the savage or barbarian tribes of Asia, Africa, America, and Polynesia, we shall find running through them all the same germ, either in varying form, or simply in detached features, to our astonishment and delight. We shall examine in detail the most familiar of the popular fairy-tales, noting the principal variants or recurring incidents, what survival of nature-myth they contain, what ancient custom or religious rite, and their possible links with Oriental literary collections; showing thus in a limited way the basis on which the before-mentioned theories of their origin rest. Taking Perrault's 'Tales' as the best versions, we shall find that actual fairies appear but seldom, as is the case generally in traditional fairy stories; in 'Cinderella' and 'The Sleeping Beauty' the fairies are of the genuine traditional type, but in other tales we find merely the magical key or the fairy 'Seven-League Boots.' Yet the fairies have so identified themselves with popular tales by giving them their titles, that we may find it interesting to look up their origin. The derivation of the word is given from *fatare*, to enchant, *faé* or *fé*, meaning enchanted, and running into the varying forms of feé, fata, hada, feen, fay, and fairy; or with more probability from *fatum*, what is spoken, and Fata, the Fates, who speak, Faunus or Fatuus, the god, and his sister or wife Fatua. This points to the primitive personification of natural phenomena: all localities and objects were believed to be inhabited by spirits. Similar beings are found in the legend-lore of all nations; as the Nereids of Greece, the Apsaras of India, the Slavonic Wilis, the Melanesian Bius, the Scotch fairies or Good Ladies — as they are termed, just as the daughter of Faunus was not known by her real name, but as the Good Goddess ("Bona Dea"). Their mediæval connection with the nether-world and the dead may possibly point to their origin as ancestral ghosts. We shall find that "the story of the heroes of Teutonic and Hindu folk-lore, the stories of 'Boots' and 'Cinderella,' of Logedas Rajah and Surya Bai, are the story also of Achilleus and Oidipous, of Perseus and Theseus, of Helen and Odysseus, of Baldur and Rustem and Sigurd. Everywhere there is the search for the bright maiden who has been stolen away, everywhere the long struggle to reclaim her." (Cox.)

SLEEPING BEAUTY. — This story is regarded by mythologists as a nature-myth, founded on nature's long sleep in winter. The Earth-goddess pricked by winter's dart falls into a deep sleep, from which she is aroused by the prince, the Sun, who searches far for her. We may find a slight parallel in Demeter's search for her lost daughter, Proserpine, in the Greek myth; but a much more evident resemblance is seen in the sleep of Brynhild, stung to her sleep by the sleep-thorn. 'The Two Brothers,' found in an Egyptian papyrus of the Nineteenth Dynasty, — the time of Seti II., — had several incidents similar to those of 'The Sleeping Beauty.' The Hathors who pronounce the fate of the prince correspond to the old fairy, and both tales show the impossibility of escaping fate. The spindle whose prick causes the long slumber is a counterpart of the arrow that wounds Achilles, the thorn that pricks Sigurd, and the mistletoe fatal to Baldur. In 'Surya Bai' (from 'Old Deccan Days') the mischief is done by the poisoned nail of a demon. In the Greek myth of Orpheus, Eurydice is stung by the serpent of darkness. The hedge that surrounds the palace appears in the flames encircling Brynhild on the Glittering Heath, and the seven coils of the dragon; also in the Hindu tale of 'Panch Phul Ranee,' in which the heroine is surrounded by seven ditches, surmounted by seven hedges of spears. In the northern form of the story an interesting feature is the presence of the ivy, the one plant that can endure the winter's numbing touch. In a Transylvanian variant a maiden spins her golden hair in a cavern, from which she is rescued by a man who undergoes an hour of torture for three nights. The awakening by a kiss corresponds to Sigurd's rousing Brynhild by his magic sword; but the kiss may be a survival of an ancient form of worship, thus suggesting that the princess in the earlier forms of the tradition may have been a local goddess, which would support the anthropological theory. The version most closely reesmbling Perrault's is Grimm's 'Little Briar Rose,' which is however without the other's ending about the cruel mother-in-law. A few incidents are found in the 'Pentamerone,' and a beautiful modern version is found in Tennyson's 'Day-Dream.'

LITTLE RED RIDING-HOOD. — In this story we may detect a myth of day and night. Red Riding-Hood, the Evening Sun, goes to see her grandmother, the Earth, who is the first to be swallowed by the wolf of Night or Darkness. The red cloak is the twilight glow. In the German versions the wolf is cut open by the hunter, and both set free; here the hunter may stand for the rising sun that rescues all from night. The Russian version in the tale of 'Vasihassa' hints at a nature-myth in the incident of the white, red, and black horses, representing the changing day. The German version contains a widely spread incident, — the restoration of persons from monsters who have swallowed them. We find parallels in the Aryan story of the dragon swallowing the sun, and killed by the sun-god Indra; here it is interesting to note that the Sanskrit word for evening means "mouth of night." The incident occurs in the myth of Kronos swallowing his children; in the Maori legend in which Ihani, the New Zealand cosmic hero, tries to creep through his ancestress, Great-Woman of Night; in a Zulu version a princess is swallowed by a monster which becomes in a Karen tale a snake. We find it also in the Algonkin legend repeated in 'Hiawatha'; among the Bushmen, Kaffirs, Zulus; and in Melanesia, where the monster is night, showing quite plainly a savage nature-myth. The story has been compared to the Sanskrit Vartika, rescued by the Açvins (the Vedic Dioscuri) from the wolf's throat. Vartika is the Quail, the bird that returns at evening; and the Greek word for quail is *ortyx*, allied possibly to Ortygia, the old name for Delos, birthplace of Apollo.

BLUEBEARD. — This tale had been regarded by some as partly historic, of which the original was Gilles de Laval, Baron de Retz, who was burned in 1440 for his cruelty to children.   It is, however, really a *märchen,* and the leading idea of curiosity punished is world-wide.   The forbidden chamber is a counterpart of the treasure-house of Ixion, on entering which the intruder was destroyed, or betrayed by the gold or blood that clung to him; also of Pandora's box, as well as of Proserpine's pyx that Psyche opened in spite of the prohibition.   There are several parallels among the German fairy-tales collected by Grimm; and one feature at least is found in the Kaffir tale of the Ox (Callaway's 'Nursery Tales of the Zulus').   Variants are found in Russia, and among Gaelic popular tales; and in the Sanskrit collection 'Katha Sarit Sagara,' the hero Saktideva breaks the taboo, and like Bluebeard's wife, is confronted with the horrible sight of dead women.   Possibly in the punishment following the breaking of the taboo may be a survival of some ancient religious prohibition: among the Australians, Greeks, and Labrador Indians, such an error was regarded as the means by which death came into the world.

PUSS IN BOOTS. — Perrault's version of this popular and wide-spread tale was probably taken from Straparola's 'Piacevoli Notti.'   The story is found in a Norse version in 'Lord Peter,' and in the Swedish 'Palace with Pillars of Gold,' in which the cat befriends a girl, whose adventures are similar to those of the Marquis of Carabas. In a Sicilian version is found the first hint of a moral which is lacking in the above-mentioned tales; that is, the ingratitude of the man.   This moral appears more plainly in a popular French version, where man's ingratitude is contrasted with the gratitude of a beast.   This occurs likewise in the versions of the Avars and the Russians.   Cosguin imagined from the moral that its origin was Buddhistic, for the story could only have arisen in a comparatively civilized community; but the only Hindu version, the Match-Making Jackal, which was not discovered until about 1884 in Bengal, has no moral at all.   The most complete moral is found in Zanzibar, in the Swahili tale of 'Sultan Darai,' in which the beneficent beast is a gazelle: the ingratitude of the man is punished by the loss of all that he had gained; the gazelle, which dies of neglect, is honored by a public funeral.   An Arab tribe honors all dead gazelles with public mourning; from which may be inferred a primitive idea that the tribal origin was from a gazelle stock, — a hint of totemism.   Variants of 'Puss in Boots' are found among the Finns, Bulgarians, Scotch, Siberians, and in modern Hindustani stories; and some features are found in Grimm, and in the adventures of the Zulu hero Uhlakanyana.

TOADS AND DIAMONDS. — This story of the good sister who was rewarded, and the bad who was punished, is found in many forms.   Several variants are met in Grimm's tales; it is found in the collection of Mademoiselle L'Heritier dating from 1696; and again is met among the Zulus, Kaffirs, Norse, and Scotch.   In many cases the story runs into the tale of the substituted bride, — an example of the curious combinations of the limited number of incidents in popular lore.

CINDERELLA. — This fairy-tale, in the majority of the variants, contains several incidents which may be perhaps the remains of totemism and of a very old social custom.   The position of Cinderella in most versions as a stepchild may without much difficulty be supposed to have been that of the youngest, who by "junior's right" would have been the heir; the myth of ill-treatment would be natural if it arose when the custom was slipping away.   By that older law of inheritance, the hearth-place was the share of the youngest; so that Cinderella's position by it, and her consequent blackened condition, would be quite in keeping with this theory. This right of the youngest is met in Hesiod, who makes Zeus the youngest child of Kronos; it is also found in Hungary, among Slavic communities, in Central Asia, in parts of China, in Germany and Celtic lands; and it is alluded to in the Edda.   A similar custom among the Zulus is shown in one of Callaway's 'Zulu Nursery Tales.' The fragment of totemism is shown in the cases when the agent is a friendly beast or tree, which has some mystic connection with the heroine's dead mother. The most striking instance occurs in the Russian tale of 'The Wonderful Birch,' in which the mother is changed by a witch into a sheep, killed and buried by the daughter, and becomes a tree, that confers the magical gifts. The two features of a beast and a tree are found in the old Egyptian tale 'Two Brothers'; and the beast alone is seen in Servian, Modern Greek, Gaelic, and Lowland Scotch variants. In two versions of barbarous tribes, 'The Wonderful Horns' of the Kaffirs, and a tale of the Santals, a hill-tribe of India, the girl's place is taken by a boy whose adventures are similar to Cinderella's, but the agents are an ox and a cow. In Perrault's tale, the more refined fairy godmother takes the place of these beasts, which are in every case domesticated animals. The slipper is a feature that is found in the whole cycle of tales. In the Greek myth of 'Rhodopê,' the slipper is carried off by an eagle, and dropped in the lap of the King of Egypt, who seeks and marries the owner. In the Hindu tale, the Rajah's daughter loses her slipper in a forest, where it is found by a prince, on whom it makes the usual impression. Here we find the false bride, which is usually a part of these tales but is omitted by Perrault; and in most cases the warning is given by a bird. In several instances the recognition is effected by a lock of hair, which acts the part of the glass slipper — which should be fur (*vair*) according to some authorities; this is found in the Egyptian tale of the 'Two Brothers,' and re-appears in the Santal version and in the popular tales of Bengal. It occurs likewise in an entirely different cycle, in the lock of Iseult's hair which a swallow carries to King Mark of Cornwall. We can also trace a slight resemblance in the search of Orpheus for Eurydice, and the Vedic myth of Mitra, the Sun-god, as well as the beautiful Deccan tale of 'Sodewa Bai.' If we search for indications of a nature-myth in the story of Cinderella, we shall find that it belongs to the myths of the Sun and the Dawn. The maiden is the Dawn, dull and gray, away from the brightness of the Sun; the sisters are the clouds, that screen and overshadow the Dawn, and the step-mother takes the part of Night. The Dawn fades away from the Sun, the prince, who after a long search finds her at last in her glorious robes of sunset. Max Müller gives the same meaning to the Vedic myth of 'Urvasî,' whose name ("great-desires") seems to imply a search for something lost.

HOP O' MY THUMB. — A mythic theory of this tale has been given, by which the forest represents the night; the pebbles, the stars; and the ogre, the devouring sun. The idea of cannibalism which it contains may possibly be a survival of an early savage state; and thus the story very obligingly supports two of the schools of mythic interpretation. It contains traces of very great antiquity, and the main features are frequently met with. We find them, for instance, in the Indian story of 'Surya Bai,' where a handful of grain is scattered; in the German counterpart, 'Hänsel and Gretel'; in the Kaffir tale, in which the girl drops ashes; and that is found again in a story in the 'Pentamerone.' The incident of the ogre's keen scent is found in a Namaqua tale, in which the elephant takes the part. In a Zulu story an ogress smells the hero Uzembeni, and the same feature is seen in Polynesian myths, and even among the Canadian Indians. In Perrault's tale Hop o' My Thumb makes the ogre kill his own children; but in many forms the captor is either cooked, or forced to eat some of his relatives, by means generally of some trick. The substitution of the ogre's daughters is suggested by the story of Athamas and Themisto, whose children are dressed by her orders in white, while those of her rival are clad in black; then by a reversal of the plan, she murders her own. In most variants the flight of the brothers is magically helped; but Perrault uses only the Seven-League Boots, which are no doubt identical with the sandals of Hermes and Loki's magic shoes.

BEAUTY AND THE BEAST. — This ancient story is very evidently a myth of the Sun and the Dawn. In all the variants the hero and the heroine cannot behold each other without misfortune. Generally the bride is forbidden to look upon her husband, who is enchanted under the form of a monster. The breaking of the taboo results in separation, but they are finally reunited after many adventures. The anthropological school of myth interpreters see in this feature a primitive marriage custom, which still exists among many savage races of the present day. One of the earliest forms of the story is the Vedic myth of 'Urvasî and Purûravas.' Another is the Sanskrit Bhekî, who marries on condition she shall never see water; thus typifying the dawn, vanishing in the clouds of sunset. Müller gives an interesting philological explanation of this myth. Bhekî means frog, and stands for the rising or setting sun, which like amphibious creatures appears to pass from clouds or water. But in its Greek form Bhekî means seaweed which is red, thus giving dark red; and the Latin for toad means "the red one," hence the term represents the dawn-glow or gloaming which is quenched in water. In Greek myths we find a resemblance in some features of 'Orpheus and Eurydice'; and the name of Orpheus in its Sanskrit form of Arbhu, meaning the sun, hints quite plainly at a solar origin of this cycle of tales. A more marked likeness exists in the myth of Eros and Psyche by Apuleius, and in the Scandinavian tale of the 'Land East of the Sun and West of the Moon.' More or less striking parallels are seen in the Celtic 'Battle of the Birds'; in the 'Soaring Lark,' by Grimm; in the Kaffir 'Story of Five Heads'; in Gaelic, Sicilian, and Bengal folk-lore; and even in as remote a quarter as Chili. The investigation of minor fairy-tales, nursery rhymes, and detached features running through many myths, will yield an abundance of interesting information. For instance, the swan-maidens and werewolves, the beanstalk (which is probably a form of the sacred ash of the Eddas, Yggdrasil, the heaven-tree of many myths), can be found in ever-varying combinations.

We can allude to only a portion of the voluminous literature on this subject. In the general works on mythology, the Aryan theory is maintained by Müller in his 'Essay on Comparative Mythology' (1856), and 'Chips from a German Workshop' (1867–75); by Grimm in his 'Teutonic Mythology' ('Deutsche Mythologie,' translated by Stallybrass, 1880–88); and by many others.

The most important works on the basis of the anthropological theory are E. B. Tylor's 'Primitive Culture' (1871); Andrew Lang's 'Custom and Myth' (1885); his 'Myth Ritual and Religion' (1887); John Fiske's 'Myths and Myth-Makers' (1872); and J. G. Frazer's 'Golden Bough' (1890). W. A. Clouston in 'Popular Tales and Fictions' (1887) supports the Indian theory. There are numerous works directly bearing on Fairy Tales and several collections of the folk-tales of individual nations which should be sought under the heading of the nation concerned.

FAITH GARTNEY'S GIRLHOOD, by Mrs. A. D. T. Whitney (1863), is a story for girls, containing a record of their thought and life between the ages of fourteen and twenty. In "Sortes," at a New-Year's party, Faith, who is a New England maiden, draws this oracle:—

> " Rouse to some high and holy work of love,
> And thou an angel's happiness shalt know."

The story tells how she fulfilled this condition, and what was her reward. Her haps and mishaps, her trials and tribulations, her sorrows and her joys (including two lovers who may be placed in either category, as the reader pleases), are duly recorded, together with the experiences of her immediate circle. The story is brightly told, and the desirable element of fun is not wanting. It is a good Sunday-school book, if Sunday-school books are meant to influence the behavior of the secular six days.

FALL OF ENGLAND, see **BATTLE OF DORKING.**

FAMILIAR STUDIES OF MEN AND BOOKS, by Robert Louis Stevenson (1882), is a collection of essays, remarkable for a certain youthful originality and freshness in the expression of opinion. "In truth," the author writes, "these are but the readings of a literary vagrant. One book led to another, one study to another. The first was published with trepidation. Since no bones were broken, the second was launched with greater confidence. So, by insensible degrees, a young man of our generation acquires in his own eyes a kind of roving judicial commission through the ages; . . . sets himself up to right the wrongs of universal history and criticism."

This he does with his usual charm and gentleness, but not without exercising sturdy criticism, even at the risk of running full tilt against conventional opinion. In the essay on Thoreau he boldly intimates that the plain-living, high-thinking code of life, of which the Walden recluse was an embodiment, may lead a man dangerously near to the borderland of priggishness. He challenges Walt Whitman's relations with the Muse of Poetry as illicit, but does full justice to the honest brain and the sweet heart back of the lumbering verse. For Villon, poet and scamp, he has no praise and little patience, — the scamp outweighing the poet.

The other essays treat, luminously and with much power of suggestion, of Victor Hugo's romances, of Robert Burns, of Yoshida-Tora Jiro, of Charles of Orleans, of Samuel Pepys, and of John Knox. The men he tries by the touchstone of his own manliness, the poets by the happy spirit of romance that was his. The book is altogether readable and pleasant.

FAR COUNTRY, A, by Winston Churchill (1913), is the story of a man who wanders far from the ideals of his youth. Hugh Paret, the son of an upright country lawyer, has such perseverance and such a keen eye for the legal loophole that he becomes a successful corporation lawyer while he is still a young man. He marries Maude Hutchinson and they settle down in a comfortable little house. For a while they are happy. Then, Paret's income grows, and he wants to live more pretentiously, but his wife insists on modest living, for the children's sake. Paret, who begins to think that Maude is over-domestic, becomes attracted to Nancy Durrett, the wife of a millionaire. He realizes that it is Nancy whom he ought to have married; for she loves spending money and admires the cleverness of sharp-dealing. When Maude hears of the intimacy between her husband and Mrs. Durrett, she takes the children away from the atmosphere of money-getting and shallow living and goes to Europe with them. Hugh is shocked, but he continues his visits to Mrs. Durrett, whose husband's illness brings her to a realization of her duty. She sends Paret away and he throws himself into politics, and accepts the nomination for Governor. Working against him is Hermann Krebs, a self-made man who had worked his way through Harvard while Paret was lounging through. Anxious to hear one of his opponent's speeches, Paret goes to one of the Krebs meetings and as he listens, he feels himself in the presence of something bigger than his mercenary ideals. Krebs rouses his secret envy. In the middle of the meeting, Krebs is taken ill, and is removed to a hospital where Paret visits him. There Krebs puts into words the idea which runs through the book: "In order to arrive at salvation, most of us have to take our journey into a far country; we have to leave what seem the safe things; we have to wander and suffer in order to realize that the only safety lies in development." Gradually it dawns upon Paret that his whole life has been a journey afar: in striving for money he has overlooked straight-dealing, and has warped laws to suit the needs of capital; in his search for fame and wealth, he has found only the husks of things. After relinquishing his practice he sails for Europe to be with his family.

FAR EAST, see **SOUL OF THE FAR EAST.**

FAR FROM THE MADDING CROWD, a pastoral novel by Thomas Hardy (1874), is perhaps the best example of his earlier manner, and of his achievements in the domain of comedy. The story is mainly concerned with the love affairs of Bathsheba Everdene, a country girl with enough cleverness in her composition to render her impatient of the rustic Darby-and-Joan conception of marriage. Her first wooer, honest Farmer Oak, promises her all the insignia of married rank if she will accept him. She is pleased with the prospect of possessing a piano, and a "ten-pound gig for market"; but when Oak adds, "and at home by the fire, whenever you look up, there I shall be, and whenever I look up, there will be you," the intolerable ennui of married life instantly weighs upon her imagination. She throws Oak over for a possible lover of more worldly pretensions. Only through an unfortunate marriage with a certain dashing Sergeant Troy does she learn to appreciate her first suitor's sterling worth. He for his part proves his devotion to her by serving her faithfully as her farm bailiff, after a change in her fortunes has placed her apparently out of his reach. 'Far from the Madding Crowd' is exceedingly rich in humor, in descriptions of rustic scenes, and of rustic character. The day laborers who gather at the malthouse to pass around the huge mug called "The God-Forgive-Me" ("probably because its size makes any given toper feel ashamed of himself") — these clowns are hardly surpassed in Shakespeare for their natural humor, their rustic talk, or their shrewd observation. Not less remarkable are certain rustic pictures, as that of the lambing on a windy St. Thomas's night, the starlight and the light from Oak's lantern making a picture worthy of Rembrandt. The novel takes rank as a classic in pastoral fiction.

FAR HORIZON, THE, by "Lucas Malet" (1906). This is a romance of modern times the scene of which is laid in London. The principal character in the story is Dominic Iglesias, a man of gentle nature and fine instincts. He is a bachelor in middle life, when the story opens, leading a quiet and secluded existence in comfortable lodgings, where he has been located since his mother's death eight years before. During her lifetime he was a devoted son and denied himself the pleasures of youth in order to minister to her during her years of failing health. Dominic's occupation has been that of clerk in a banking-house and after thirty-five years of faithful service, his health becoming impaired, he is summarily retired on a pension, to his astonishment and chagrin. During his first leisure hours he accidentally becomes acquainted with Poppy St. John, an actress, whose warmheartedness and unconventional ways strongly attract him. Dominic has a friend named George Loveland, whose spinster cousin Serena feels a deep attachment for him, but Dominic is in ignorance of this fact and she arouses no emotion in him. Poppy, who has led a struggling existence, has been married at an early age to de Courcy Smyth, an unsuccessful dramatist.

whom she did not love and who continually hounds her for money and causes her great unhappiness. Smyth is a fellow-lodger of Dominic's, who is in ignorance of his history, and he induces the latter to lend him large sums of money in order to finance a play which he hopes to bring out. Dominic and Poppy grow to love each other but do not allow their affection to exceed the limits of friendship. Smyth commits suicide after a failure of his hopes and rids the world of a miserable scoundrel. Poppy is rejoiced to be free and is also delighted at receiving a theatrical engagement where she makes a hit and receives a great ovation. Her happiness however is short-lived as Dominic who has been gradually failing in health dies suddenly of heart trouble while Poppy is at the theatre, and she returns to find his gentle spirit has departed from this earth.

FARADAY AS A DISCOVERER, by John Tyndall, appeared in 1868, less than a year after Faraday's death. The volume is not a "life" in the ordinary sense, but rather a calm estimate of the scientist's work, with incidental views of the spirit in which it was done, and introducing such personal traits as serve to complete the picture of the philosopher, if inadequate fully to present the idea of the man. The study, which reveals the author as at once a graceful writer and an accomplished savant, is approached from the point of view of an intimate coadjutor and friend. In Faraday's notable career, his achievements in magnetism and electricity are presented as being among the most remarkable; while his connection with the Royal Institution proved distinguished no less for the discoveries which he there made than for his lucid discussions of scientific questions. Of his own relation to Faraday, Tyndall says, with modesty, beauty, and feeling: "It was my wish to play the part of Schiller to this Goethe." And again: "You might not credit me were I to tell you how lightly I value the honor of being Faraday's successor compared with the honor of having been Faraday's friend. His friendship was energy and inspiration; his 'mantle' is a burden almost too heavy to be borne."

FARTHEST NORTH, a narrative of polar exploration by Dr. Fridtjof Nansen, was published in 1897. It is an account, put together from the explorer's journals, of his expedition in the schooner "Fram" ("Forward") in search of the North Pole. Nansen's plan was to construct an exceedingly strong vessel, to take her as far north as possible, and to let her drift in the ice of the polar sea. He believed that the currents would carry her near enough for a dash to the pole. He left Christiania June 24th, 1893, obtained a supply of dogs at the entrance to the Kara Sea early in August, followed the Siberian coast eastward, then turned north, and on September 25th allowed his vessel to be frozen in in latitude 78° 45', about 150 miles north of the Siberian Islands. Two winters were passed in the vessel, which drifted steadily northwestward till March, 1895, when Nansen, with a companion, Johansen, set out with dogs, kayaks, sledges, and provisions to reach the pole. They traveled from March 14th to April 8th over exceedingly rough ice. After attaining latitude 86° 13' 6", within 272 miles of the pole and 184 miles nearer to it than any previous explorer had attained, they decided that progress was too slow and difficult to make it wise to go on. After a perilous journey, during which they killed all their dogs for food and were often forced to take to the water in their kayaks, they reached one of the islands of the Franz-Josef Archipelago on August 15th. Here they wintered in a stone hut built by themselves. In the following spring they made their way south, and were finally picked up in Franz-Josef Land by Jackson of the Harmsworth Expedition. They returned to Norway August 7th, 1896. Meanwhile the "Fram" had drifted on.

reaching as high as latitude 85° 55′ 5″ until in August, 1896, she emerged into open water near Spitzbergen, and returned to Norway almost simultaneously with Nansen. This work is a popular and not a scientific account of the expedition. It is somewhat hastily written, but is extremely interesting and entertaining.

FATE OF MANSFIELD HUMPHREYS, THE, by Richard Grant White (1884) A few chapters of this work appeared in the Atlantic Monthly Magazine, and the first three were published in Edinburgh, with the title, 'Mr. Washington Adams in England.' There is the thread of a love-story involving Mansfield Humphreys, a young and successful American, and Margaret Duffield, a beautiful English girl with small expectations and large accumulations of titled relatives. It terminates in an international marriage, a residence in Boston, unfortunate business speculations, and the triumphant withdrawal of Margaret — who achieves greatness of income by the timely removal of an eccentric relative — with her husband in train, to reside in her beloved England, where, according to Mr. White, even the most cultured drop their final "g's." The story is one, if not with a moral, at least with a purpose, and certainly with a grievance. The lingual difficulties of our trans-oceanic cousins are exploited at length, as well as our own shortcomings in the matter of speech. The popular impression in England of the characteristic American traits is accentuated in a humorous scene, where Humphreys, masquerading as "Washington Adams,"—a "gee-hawking" American with "chin whiskers," "linen duster," "watch-chain which would have held a yacht to its moorings," and other equally attractive personal accessories, — appears at the garden party of Lord Toppingham's, and by his absurdities of speech and action presents an exaggerated caricature of a resident of "the States," which is placidly accepted by the English guests as the realization of their preconceived ideas. The book aroused so much diverse comment, public and private, that an explanation of its occasion and original purpose was given in a lengthy apology of some seventy pages, concerning which the author says: "Some apologies aggravate offense; always those which show the unjust their injustice, for they will be unjust still. This apology is one of that kind."

FATHERS AND SONS, a novel by Ivan S. Turgeneff, appeared first in 1861 in the Russian Messenger, a Moscow review. As the name implies, it is an embodiment in fiction of the conflicting old and new forces at work in modern society; forces peculiarly active and noticeable in Russia, where iron-bound authority exists side by side with intellectual license. This novel brought into general use the term "nihilist," applied by the author to the chief character of the story, Bazarof, a young man of iconoclastic temperament, whose code of life was rebellion against all authority. His short, vivid career is depicted with remarkable strength and realism. Another "son" is his friend Arcadi Kirsanof, at whose paternal estate he is a guest. Kirsanof's father and uncle, representing the older generation, are brought into sharp contact and contrast with Bazarof. It is difficult to determine whether "fathers" or "sons" suffer most in the delineation of their peculiarities. The novel divided reading Russia into two camps, — those who sided with the "fathers," and those who sided with the "sons." The government seized on the word "nihilist" as a designation of political reproach, — a sense in which it has ever since been employed. With its terrible sincerity, its atmosphere of menacing calm presaging a storm, the book remains one of the most noted in the category of Russian fiction.

FAUST, a dramatic poem in two parts by Johann Wolfgang von Goethe, is literally the work of a lifetime. The poem was projected and partly written in the stormy youthful years between 1773 and 1775. (A copy of the earliest portions has been preserved, usually referred to as the 'Urfaust'.) 'Faust, A Fragment' appeared in 1790; 'Faust, The First Part of the Tragedy' in 1808; and the Second Part was completed in 1831, the year before the poet's death. Goethe takes the theme of the Renaissance scholar who sold himself to the Devil in his eagerness to win the knowledge which is power; but instead of condemning him to a remorseful death followed by damnation as the reactionary authors of the tale had done, Goethe, the spokesman of a new Renaissance, represents the scholar's bold aspiration as laudable and destined in spite of error and disaster to lead him ultimately to happiness and peace with God and his fellowmen. After a beautiful dedication and a playful bit of self-criticism in the form of a prelude on the stage in which the stage-manager, the poet, and the clown discuss the coming entertainment, the drama begins, in the fashion of a mediæval mystery-play, with a prologue in Heaven. The archangels' hymn of the glories of creation is interrupted by Mephistopheles, the cynical spirit of negation, who ridicules the lofty aims and low performances of man, the crown of the world, and offers to wager that he can lure God's servant Faust into utter baseness. The Almighty gives him free permission to tempt Faust but prophesies that although Faust will fall he will ultimately attain a clearer vision and truer service, to which, indeed, strife and error are a necessary process. Faust is now depicted as a famous scholar and scientist, discontented with all that books and learning have brought him and longing for intellectual certainty and emotional release. He seeks inspiration by means of magical books but shrinks back in terror from the vision of the infinite, inscrutable mystery of the universe which they reveal to him. In despair he is about to kill himself when a surviving religious impulse, aroused by the Easter bells, restrains him. Next day he finds further alleviation in mingling with people who are enjoying the spring-festival. But the mood of human sympathy and faith is interrupted by Mephistopheles, who enters Faust's study in the form of a black poodle, suddenly changing to the appearance of a traveling scholar. He fills Faust's mind once again with dissatisfaction, and endeavors to entice him by promise of sensual delights to give up his soul in exchange for the devil's assistance. Faust, who has desperately renounced faith and hope, has no belief that Mephistopheles can please him but is ready to make a bargain that if the devil can make him perfectly contented for one moment he, Faust, will forfeit his soul. The bargain made and sealed in Faust's blood they prepare to go out and see the world — first the little world of desire and passion and then the great world of affairs. Faust is to test the pleasures of the senses and affections (Part I.) and then the pleasures of power exercised in public business and of art (Part II.). After Mephistopheles, disguised as Faust, has given some ironical advice to an incoming student, the pair see something of drink and debauchery at Auerbach's wine-cellar. Faust is disgusted, but Mephistopheles takes him to the Witches' Kitchen where he shows him in a magic mirror a female form of ideal beauty and gives him a love-potion which renews his youth. Soon afterwards Faust meets an innocent young girl, Margaret (Gretchen), on her way from church, is captivated by her beauty, and offers himself as her escort. Her refusal only stimulates his interest and he demands that Mephistopheles procure her as his love. They go unseen to her room, where the devil leaves a casket of jewels and Faust's passion through the atmosphere of sweetness and purity is ennobled and idealized. Later, however, Mephistopheles by a little flattery contrives to arrange a meeting between them at the house of a foolish neighbor. Faust is torn between a high ideal devotion and the cynical promptings of his companion; Gretchen falls deeply and devotedly in love with Faust but has an instinctive dislike of Mephistopheles. The lovers meet clandestinely and she gives herself to him. After some months her brother Valentine, returning from the wars, finds that she is about to become a mother. He makes an attack on Faust, who, through Mephistopheles's incitation, kills Valentine and hastily leaves the city. Distracted by her lover's departure, her brother's death, and that of her mother, through an overdose of the sleeping-draught which Faust had provided to facilitate their meetings, Margaret goes mad, drowns her child, and is condemned to be beheaded. Meanwhile Faust has been taken by Mephistopheles to the Witches' Sabbath on the Brocken where in wild pleasures he forgets his unfortunate love until recalled by a phantasm of Margaret with the thin red line of the headsman's axe about her neck. He insists that Mephistopheles rescue her at once; and they hasten on spectral chargers through the air past the place of execution to the prison, which they reach at midnight a few hours before Margaret is to suffer. She is in a demented condition, but recognizes Faust, and in a poignant scene recalls their past happiness and guilt. Seeing Mephistopheles, however, she refuses to be rescued and prays to Heaven for forgiveness. As Mephistopheles and Faust hurry away, she dies; and the sneer of the former "She is judged" is answered by a voice from above "She is saved."

In the Second Part Faust is introduced to the great world, to the outer world of public affairs and the inner world of æsthetic beauty in classic and romantic art. After an opening scene in which Faust is purged from the effects of former suffering by the healing influences of a delightful landscape he is conducted by Mephistopheles to the court of the Emperor, whom they entertain with marvelous pageantry and whose realms they save from bankruptcy by persuading the people of the existence of buried treasure. At the request of the Emperor, Faust then conjures up as a spectacle the phantoms of Paris and Helen of Troy; but becoming enamored of the ideal beauty of Helen he attempts to seize her, and the vision disappears. In the quest for a union with this ideal beauty, Faust and Mephistopheles are conducted by the Homunculus, a tiny being whom Wagner, Faust's old pupil, has manufactured in his laboratory, to the fields of Pharsalia. Here, in the scene called the Classical Walpurgis-Night because it corresponds to the romantic *diablerie* of the Brocken scene in Part One, the various figures of Greek mythology, beautiful and ugly, appear before the northern pilgrims. The general meaning is that Faust is approaching ideal beauty through the appreciation of classic art; and his quest is attained in Act III.— an act modeled on the Greek drama — when Helen comes to life before the palace of Menelaus in Sparta as though just brought back from Troy, and is rescued from her husband's vengeance by Faust and Mephistopheles, who bear her to a mediæval castle guarded by a troop of Gothic warriors. Here she is wooed and won by Faust; and they have a child, Euphorion, who represents the spirit of poetry that results from the union of the classic and the romantic. At length he soars into the air, and falls to the ground, his body vanishes and his soul ascends in light. Helen too disappears, but union with her has left Faust ennobled. He now desires to subdue nature to the service of man. An insurrection which he and Mephistopheles are able to quell for the Emperor in Act IV. puts them in possession of a great stretch of half-submerged seacoast, which Faust determines to reclaim and make the abode of a contented people. At the beginning of Act V. Faust, now in extreme old age, has nearly completed his task. His realm now supports a great population; but there still remains a noisome marsh to be reclaimed; and there is a little cottage which its owners, Philemon and Baucis, will not sell. He orders Mephistopheles to dispossess them and is punished by the infliction of blindness. Nevertheless he gives directions for the clearing of the marsh. As he contemplates this final work he realizes that neither in the satisfaction of passion, in intellectual development, nor in the cultivation of art does happiness exist, but in the unselfish service of others; and with this realization he declares himself perfectly contented and dies. Thus he apparently loses the wager made with Mephistopheles, who immediately summons the demons to carry off Faust's soul. But the happiness which Faust has attained is one which was beyond Mephistopheles's power to grant and the nobility of which releases Faust from the bargain. Through error and suffering, experience and aspiration he has attained to a true service of God; and the angels transport his soul to Heaven amid a triumphant chorus of angels, saints, and pardoned sinners (Margaret included), while they worship the Divine Love as revealed in the Virgin Mother — "das Ewigweibliche."

In cosmic range, multiformity of symbolism, integration of diverse ideas, systems, and types of character in dramatic insight, flexibility of style and versification, architectonic faculty, and wise interpretation of life Faust stands alone in the literature of its century. It touches every sphere of life and sums up all the tendencies of the age which succeeded the French Revolution.

FAUTE DE L'ABBÉ MOURET, LA, see **ROUGON-MACQUART.**

FEDERALIST, THE, a series of papers which appeared in The Independent Journal of New York between October 27, 1787, and April 2, 1788, and were published in book form in the latter year. There are eighty-five essays in the collection, of which eight were previously unpublished. Though the essays were signed 'Publius' they were the work of three men. Alexander Hamilton wrote probably fifty-one of them, James Madison twenty-nine, and John Jay five. Their purpose in writing was to recommend to the people of New York State the adoption of the Federal Constitution drawn up by the Constitutional Convention at Philadelphia in 1787. The essays both in newspaper and book form circulated widely, became the most authoritative and influential defense of the new Constitution, and had an important share in bringing about its acceptance by the State of New York. In a perspicuous and rational manner, without appeals to passion and prejudice but by the force of logic and sound principles, the authors point out the weaknesses of the old Confederation, show the necessity of a centralized government as a check to war from without and disorder within, explain in detail the functions of each division of the government under the new scheme, and rebut the accusation that the centralization of the Constitution will tend to arbitrariness and autocracy. As an exposition as well as a defense of the Constitution by men who were intimately acquainted with its intention the book has permanent value, particularly for students of Constitutional Law, and it is taken into account by the courts in their interpretations.

FELIX HOLT, THE RADICAL, by George Eliot (1866). As a picture of upper middle-class and industrial English life of the period of the Reform Bill agitation, this book is unsurpassed. If the critics who set George Eliot highest as a delineator of character find the story clogged with moralities, and hindered by its machinery, the critics who value her most for her pictures of life and nature rank 'Felix Holt' among her best achievements. It is bright in tone, it shows little of the underlying melancholy of George Eliot's nature, and its humor is rich and pervading. Its hero, Felix Holt, is a young workman whose capacity might attain anything, if his overpowering conscience would let him conform to the ways of a comfort-loving world. But he is as much compelled by his dæmon as Socrates. He throws away his chances, comes near to shipwrecking his happiness, and accepts his unpleasant position as a matter of course. Contrasted with roughness and noble intolerance, which are his most obtrusive characteristics, is the charming daintiness of the exquisite Esther Lyon, whom he loves, and who dreads above all things to be made ridiculous, till a sight grander than many women ever see — a man absolutely honest with man and God — stirs the depths of her moral nature. The character of Harold Transome, the fine gentleman of the book, is struck out by the same strong hand that drew Grandcourt in 'Daniel Deronda,' — a handsome, clever, frank, good-natured egoist. The minor characters stand out distinct and vivid. The covetous upstart, Jermyn; Esther's father, the rusty old Puritan preacher; Mrs. Transome, well-born, high-bred, splendid in her sumptuous, fading, anxious beauty, and carrying her tragical secret in a hand that scarcely trembles, but that may be made to drop the fragile thing by a rude touch; the shadowy squire, her husband; Mrs. Holt, the eulogist of the priceless infallible pills; Denner, the butler's hardheaded and faithful wife; the white-faced human monkey, Job; the aristocratic Debarrys; gipsy-eyed and irrepressible Harry; the sporting and port-drinking parson, John Lingon, not half a bad fellow, with his doctrine, "If the mob can't be turned back, a man of family must try to head the mob," — they all live and move. "One group succeeds another, and not a single figure appears in any of them, though it be ever so far in the background, which is not perfectly drawn and perfectly colored."

FELIX O'DAY, by F. Hopkinson Smith (1915). This was the last work of its author and was published after his death. The scene of the story is laid in New York at the present time; Felix O'Day, an Englishman of distinguished mien and bearing, is introduced in the act of trying to raise money on a costly traveling case in order to pay his board bill. He is recognized as a gentleman, by the curio dealer, who advances him money on his case and also offers him a position in his shop when he discovers his knowledge of antiques. O'Day finds a home in the neighborhood with an energetic and kindhearted woman named Kitty Cleary, who realizes he is passing through a great sorrow and does all in her power to cheer and help him. Through Kitty, O'Day meets Father Cruse, a noble and unselfish priest to whom he confides his past and tells him he is really Sir Felix O'Day, and is in New York searching for his wife Lady Barbara, who had run away with another man some months previously. Her desertion of her husband had been caused by her youth and wilfulness coupled with the loss of his property, which he had relinquished in order to pay his father's debts. The latter's financial ruin had been brought about by Guy Dalton, the plausible villain with whom Lady Barbara had eloped. Being obliged to flee the country, Dalton had brought Lady Barbara to New York, where after enduring poverty and abuse she finally leaves him and supports herself by sewing. Dalton discovers her hiding place, and when she refuses to return to him steals a valuable lace mantilla which she is mending for a business house. The proprietor has Lady Barbara arrested and taken to the stationhouse, but she is recognized by Father Cruse, who has seen her picture, and he rescues her from this terrible situation and restores her to her husband. O'Day meanwhile has received word from England that part of his property has been restored to him so the reader feels that brighter days are in store for him at last.

FENWICK'S CAREER, by Mrs. Humphry Ward (1906). This is the story of an artist named John Fenwick, who is endowed with talent, but also with an unfortunate temperament which is a great drawback to his success in life. He comes to London to seek his fortune, leaving behind him in the country his wife Phœbe and his little daughter Carrie. He has many discouragements and for a long time barely succeeds in keeping the wolf from the door. Finally, fortune smiles upon him in the shape of Eugenie de Pastourelles, a charming and cultivated Englishwoman of wealth, who appreciates his talent and becomes his benefactress. He paints her portrait and through her efforts in his behalf gets his first large commission. He is overjoyed at his good luck and making a shrine about the portrait of Eugenie, whom he calls his patron saint, he rushes out to purchase presents for his wife and child. During his absence, Phœbe, who has been growing jealous and unhappy on account of their separation, visits her husband's studio, having come to the city to see how he was situated. She sees the enshrined portrait and finding letters from Eugenie which she completely misinterprets she is seized with jealous rage and resolves never to see Fenwick again. She destroys the portrait and then enclosing her wedding ring in a letter tells her husband she has gone out of his life forever. Fenwick on his return is horrified when he discovers what has occurred and makes every effort to trace Phœbe and the child without avail. His history is not known to his friends and he is thought to be a bachelor. Twelve years go by, during which time he has met with both success and failure, and never having had news of Phœbe he feels she must be dead. Eugenie's uncongenial husband dies, and Fenwick, carried away by his love, tells her of it and she accepts him. He is then overwhelmed by the wrong he has done her and confesses everything. Eugenie, who is a beautiful character, immediately devotes herself to the discovery of Phœbe and through her efforts the husband and wife and child are at last happily reunited.

FERDINAND AND ISABELLA, see **REIGN OF.**

FESTUS, a dramatic poem, mainly in blank verse, by Philip James Bailey, was first published in 1839 and attracted wide attention by the beauties with which it was scattered and the heterodoxy of the theological views that it expressed. Like Goethe's 'Faust' the poem begins and ends in Heaven, and in the intervening scenes a mortal under the guidance of Lucifer is conducted through a variety of experiences both in this world and beyond it. Bailey's Lucifer, however, does not tempt the hero, but unfolds to him in long monologues a Universalist theology and a Hegelian philosophy. Among the episodes of the poem are the love-affairs of Festus with various women — Angela, Clara, Helen, and Elissa, the last of whom he wins from Lucifer himself, who is devoted to her and had hoped to be redeemed by her influence. Lucifer takes Festus among the stars and planets, and even brings him to Heaven, where he attempts to see God and is shown his own name written in the Book of Life. At length Festus is made ruler of the whole world; but as his reign is about to begin the world is destroyed, the Millennium succeeds, and the Judgment Day follows. The prophecies of universal salvation are fulfilled and the poem ends in unclouded happiness. In spite of its length and crudities of thought, imagery, and expression, 'Festus' has many single passages of originality and power. See LIBRARY.

FICTION, see **ASPECTS OF.**

FICTION, HISTORY OF, by John Dunlop (1814). This familiar work, the fruit of many years' accumulation of materials, broke ground in a new field. It was the first attempt made in England to trace the development of the novel from its earliest beginnings in Greece to the position it held early in the nineteenth century. Considering the difficulties of the pioneer, the work is remarkably comprehensive and exact. Though later writers have disproved certain of the author's theories, as for instance his idea of the rise of the Greek novel, or the connection of the Gesta Romanorum with subsequent outgrowths of popular tales, his book still remains a good introduction for the student of fiction. The sections upon Oriental and modern fiction are least satisfactory, as the best are sketches on the romances of chivalry and the Italian novelists. His facts are massed in a workmanlike manner, and presented in a clear style, devoid of ornament, but used with vigor and effectiveness.

FIFTEEN DECISIVE BATTLES OF THE WORLD, by Sir E. S. Creasy (1852), describes and discusses (in the words of Hallam) "those few battles of which a contrary event would have essentially varied the drama of the world in all its subsequent scenes." The obvious and important agencies, and not incidents of remote and trifling consequence, are brought out in the discussion of the events which led up to each battle, the elements which determined its issue, and the results following the victories or defeats. The volume treats, in order: The Battle of Marathon, 490 B. C.; Defeat of the Athenians at Syracuse, 413 B. C.; The Battle of Arbela, 331 B. C.; The Battle of the Metaurus, 207 B. C.; Victory of Arminius over the Roman Legions under Varus, A. D. 9; The Battle of Châlons, 451; The Battle of Tours, 732; The Battle of Hastings, 1066; Joan of Arc's Victory over the English at Orleans, 1429; The Defeat of the Spanish Armada, 1588; The Battle of Blenheim, 1704; The Battle of Pultowa, 1709; Victory of the Americans over Burgoyne at Saratoga, 1777; The Battle of Valmy, 1792; The Battle of Waterloo, 1815.

The author concludes: "We have not (and long may we want) the stern excitement of the struggles of war; and we see no captive standards of our European neighbors brought in triumph to our shrines. But we witness an infinitely prouder spectacle. We see the banners of every civilized nation waving over the arena of our competition with each other in the arts that minister to our race's support and happiness, and not to its suffering and destruction.

> " Peace hath her victories
> No less renowned than war."

FIGHTING CHANCE, THE, by Robert W. Chambers (1906). This is the story of a man who has a "fighting chance" to win the girl he loves and to conquer his inherited taste for drink. His name is Stephen Siward; he belongs to a prominent New York family and has an attractive and winning personality. He goes to visit at a friend's country house and there meets Sylvia Landis, a charming society girl, who captivates him utterly. Stephen is under a cloud as he has just been dropped from his club on account of an escapade in which he had taken part while in an intoxicated condition; Sylvia, however, overlooks his failings, and although engaged to another man, feels strongly drawn towards Siward. Sylvia's engagement to Howard Quarrier, who is a very rich man, is not an affair of the heart as she has decided to marry him simply for the worldly advantages to be derived from the match. Quarrier, who poses as a model of virtue, is really false and deceitful, and is to blame for the affair at the club for which Siward is bearing the consequences. Siward makes love boldly to Sylvia, who responds to his advances and confesses that she loves him but cannot marry him, as it is necessary to her happiness to have great riches. She tells him, however, that he has a fighting chance to win her and to go ahead and do it if he can. Siward returns to town but his mother's death makes him

20

despondent and he falls into the clutches of his old enemy. Sylvia finds existence without him a blank and longs for his presence though she continues in her plan to marry Quarrier. Finally Sylvia and Siward meet accidentally in the Park as the latter is convalescing from an illness and fighting hard to conquer his old enemy. Sylvia realizes at last that nothing counts but her love for Siward and gives herself unreservedly to him. Many other interesting characters are introduced into the story, and life among the ultra-fashionable set is graphically described.

FILE NO. 113 (Le Dossier no. 113), by Émile Gaboriau, a French novel, introducing the author's favorite detective, M. Lecoq, appeared in 1867. The scene is laid in the Paris of the day; and the title indicates the case file number in the records of the detective bureau.

The story opens with the public details of a daring robbery which has been committed in the banking-house of M. Fauvel. Suspicion points to Prosper Bertomy, the head cashier. The deep mysteries of the case are fathomed by Fanferlot, a shrewd detective, and Lecoq, his superior in both skill and position. Lecoq figures as a French Sherlock Holmes, though his methods are essentially different. He is pictured as possessing surpassing insight, intelligence, and patient determination; employing the most impenetrable disguises for the pursuit of his inquiries.

The dénouement, gradually unfolded toward the close of the story, shows Prosper to have been the innocent victim of a plot. Madame Fauvel has had, before her marriage to the banker, an illegitimate son by the Marquis de Clameran, an arrant rogue who poses throughout as the benefactor of the Fauvels. De Clameran has caused Raoul de Lagors to personate this son (who is really dead). Raoul is introduced in Fauvel's home as Madame's nephew, though she believes him to be her son.

After frightening her into revealing the secrets of the bank-safe, Raoul commits the robbery. Her lips are sealed by her fear that her early life will become known to her husband. De Clameran plays upon these fears to force Madame Fauvel to induce Madeleine, her niece, to marry him. Madeleine consents in order to save her aunt, though she is really in love with Prosper.

The plot is at last discovered; Raoul escapes, De Clameran becomes insane, Madame Fauvel is forgiven, and Prosper marries Madeleine.

FINGAL, by James Macpherson, is an 'Ancient Epic Poem, in Six Books,' which appeared in 1762. 'Fingal' had an immense sale, and ever since controversy has raged as to the degree of authenticity of the material upon which it was founded. The subject of the epic is the invasion of Ireland by Swaran, king of Lochlin, Denmark, during the reign of Cormac II., and its deliverance by the aid of the father of Ossian, King Fingal of Morven, on the northwest coast of Scotland. The poem opens with the overthrow of Cuthullin, general of the Irish forces, and concludes with the return of Swaran to his own land. It is cast in imitation of primitive manners, and is written in a style which, in contemporary opinion, comported with its theme. While manifesting sympathy with the gloomy Scottish landscape, the author has presented a warmly colored variety of scenes, and the book contributed in no small degree to fostering interest in Celtic literature and promoting more scholarly investigation.

FIRE AND SWORD IN THE SUDAN, by Rudolf C. Slatin (1896), is a record of the author's experiences, fighting and serving the Dervishes, from 1879 to 1895. Slatin Pasha held the rank of colonel in the Egyptian army, and also occupied the post of governor and military commandant in Darfur. Having been compelled to surrender to the Mahdi's vastly superior numbers, he remained a prisoner of that remarkable leader (of whose career an admirable account is given), and of the Mahdi's successor, the Khalifa Abdullahi, for more than ten years. Thus the Pasha was forced to join the Khalifa's bodyguard, and was constituted his trusted, though unwilling, adviser. This relation afforded him almost unmatched opportunities for obtaining an inside view of the "rise, progress, and decline of that great religious movement which wrenched the country from its conquerors, and dragged it back into an almost indescribable condition of religious and moral decadence." Valuable information is given regarding those military operations which occupied European diplomacy and arms for two decades; the siege and fall of Khartum, and the fate of "Chinese" Gordon, being of particular interest. The narrative is vigorous and full of detail, although the writer was not permitted to keep even a diary. At length, wearying of the dangerous favors of the Khalifa, Slatin Pasha made a dangerous escape, and rejoined his family in his native city of Vienna.

FIRING LINE, THE, by Robert W. Chambers (1908). This story opens at Palm Beach, Florida, where Garret Hamil, a young landscape gardener from New York, has arrived to lay out a park on the magnificent estate of a wealthy man named Cardross. Hamil immediately falls victim to the charms of Shiela Cardross, an unusually beautiful and fascinating girl, who is an adopted daughter of the financier. When he proposes she tells him that it is impossible to accept him as she is already married. Shiela then explains that two years prior to this time, when she was eighteen years of age, she made the discovery that she was not the real child of her beloved parents but had been a nameless foundling. Her anguish was such that she was almost beside herself and in a hasty moment she had married a young college friend of her brother's, who had offered her his name in this time of stress. He returned at once to college and she had hardly seen him since the event, which she had kept a secret from everyone. Realizing her terrible mistake and regretting her hasty act, she confesses her love for Hamil, but tells him she can never be his. Hamil, who sees the injustice of the situation to all concerned, begs her to get a divorce, but she tells him she will never do that as she will not bring disgrace on the kind parents who have done everything for her. Meanwhile, her husband, Louis Malcourt, has become interested in a wealthy society girl, named Virginia Suydam, and being an attractive, irresponsible young fellow has also an affair with a pretty actress named Dolly Wilming. Nevertheless, he is willing to acknowledge his marriage whenever Shiela wishes it, and finally, in a burst of remorse, she decides to do so. The result is disastrous for all concerned as Shiela treats Malcourt with utter coldness and is wife only in name, while Hamil and Miss Suydam are heart-broken. In a short time Malcourt, who is an eccentric chap, and inherits suicidal mania from his father, decides to relieve the situation by removing his presence from the world, and shoots himself. Shiela is shocked and prostrated by the tragedy, but eventually recovers, and she and Hamil are at last happily united.

FIRST VIOLIN, THE, a noteworthy musical novel by Jessie Fothergill (1877), describes the romantic experiences of an English girl, May Wedderburn, while she is studying music in Germany. Although the plot is somewhat conventional, a certain freshness or enthusiasm in the composition of the book endows it with vitality. The heroine leaves home to avoid marriage with a Sir Peter Le Marchant. She is enabled to do this through an elderly neighbor, Miss Hallam, whose sister had been the first wife of Sir Peter, and had been cruelly treated by him. As Miss Hallam's companion, May goes to Elberthal on the Rhine near Cologne, one of those little German towns given up to music. On the journey thither, Miss Wedderburn is separated by accident from her traveling companions. A good-looking stranger comes to her assistance. He proves to be Eugen Courvoisier, first violin in the orchestra, a man about whom is the fascination of mystery. Taking offense at a supposed discourtesy of the beautiful young English girl whom he had protected, he refuses to recognize her. She, for her part, is already in love with him. By the kindness of Miss Hallam, she remains in Elberthal to have her voice cultivated, and her lessons in music and in love go on until the happy ending of the story. Her love is put to the touch by the supposed dishonor of Courvoisier, but bears the test without failing. 'The First Violin' abounds in dramatic descriptions of musical life in a small Rhine city, and makes the reader pleasantly at home in middle-class German households, where he learns to respect, if he does not admire, middle-class German respectability and calm content. If the book has the sentimentality of youth, its romance is altogether innocent and pleasing.

FISHER MAIDEN, THE, by Björnstjerne Björnson, the Norwegian novelist, dramatist, poet, and statesman, appeared in 1868, and has been translated into many tongues. It is an early work, written in his first flush of power, and is a characteristic story of Norwegian life among the common people. Several of the poems in the novel express fervently the author's optimistic patriotism. The early part of the tale is laid in a fishing village on the coast, where lives the fisher maiden, a strong-natured, handsome, imaginative girl, whose mother keeps a sailors' inn. Her development is traced in her love affairs, by which she gains a bad reputation, so that her mother sends her away from her native place; in her experience in Bergen, with its self-revelation of her own artist-nature by her first sight of a play; in her life in the family of a priest, with its chance for cultivation and training of her dramatic powers; and in the final adoption of the stage as a profession: the novel closing, rather tantalizingly, just as the curtain rises on her début. Petra, the fisher maiden, has the instincts, gifts, and ambitions of the artist, and her earlier love episodes are but ebullitions of this chief motor-power. She is portrayed sympathetically; for as Björnson stated to a friend, she is, in many of her traits, an embodiment of himself. The story is full of accurate yet charmingly idealized studies of native types and scenes, and is regarded as among the novelist's freshest, finest creations.

FLAME OF LIFE, THE (Il Fuoco), by Gabriele d'Annunzio (1899). The heroine, La Foscarina, is a great tragic actress, exquisite in everything, except that she is at the end of her youth. She denies the gift of herself to her lover, a young poet, whose inspiration she is, but finally yields, tormented always with the consciousness that this great passion has come too late, that she cannot hope to hold her lover. The glamor of Venice in the autumn, its melancholy, its past glories is the background, symbolic of La Foscarina, "both deep and tempting, tired with having lived too much, and languid with too many loves." Her faith and confidence and praise stimulate Stelio's genius. "The lonely wandering woman seemed to carry in the folds of her dress the silenced frenzy of those far-off multitudes from whose pent-up brutality her cry of passion or burst of sorrow or enthralling pause had wrenched the sublime pulsation that art quickens." There is almost no contact of other relations or interests. The entire drama is their intense consciousness of each other, the suffering of the sensitive, artistic woman, the flowering of the poet's genius, and the magic of Italy. She divines his desire for Donatella, a young and beautiful singer, even in the certainty of his present love for herself. When the spring comes she takes up her art again and leaves him, promising to return to present his drama now finished. It is supposed to be the story of the author's own amour with Duse and achieved a *succès de scandale* on that account. Its real merit consists in its florid metaphorical style and magnificent descriptions of Venice.

FLORENCE, THE HISTORY OF, by Niccolò Machiavelli. This great work placed its author in the first rank of modern historians. He was hailed by Italian critics as the peer of Tacitus and Thucydides, while Hallam thought the book "enough to immortalize the name of Machiavelli." Its chief merit lies in its method, wholly unlike that of the usual mediæval dry chronicle of facts. Machiavelli's treatment is philosophical; seeking always after motives, causes, and results; the lesson to be drawn from the subject in hand being always something to be made use of for instruction in the present and the future. His principal generalizations are placed as introductions to the several books; and no part of Machiavelli's work is more valuable than are these prologues. The history marked a giant stride in the evolution of Italian literature, and established a standard of purity for the language. Vigorous in thought, the narrative is developed with great skill. The period begins with the earliest times, and extends to the death of Lorenzo the Magnificent. The work was done as a commission from Clement VII. (when still Cardinal Julius), being finished and presented to the Pope in 1525.

FOMÁ GORDYEEF, by Maxim Gorky (1899). This is a gloomy story of an imaginative, affectionate youth who goes steadily to ruin through his better impulses. The opening chapters are a portrait of his brutal father, a self-made millionaire of the prosperous merchant class of Russia, who works and carouses with equal fury and energy. They live in a city on the Volga, and the river is connected with every crisis of Fomá's life. There are descriptions of the river in the spring, of his trips on the river as a child with his father, the life on the barges, and the first time he goes in charge of his own steamer. The gentle serious child is happy with his Aunt Anfisa, who tells him fairy tales and tries to answer his questions. When he grows up he is still asking questions no one can answer about the why and wherefore of existence. Without knowledge of books or men, or any developing influence, his idealism makes ineffectual struggle against circumstances. His fortune has been made for him, and he tries in vain to induce his godfather to take his wealth and manage his affairs so that he may be free from responsibility, since he is not interested in the warfare of business waged by his father's friends without honor or honesty. The only outlet he finds for his energy is drink and debauchery of every description. He is baffled at every turn in his efforts to break the bonds of the only life open to a rich Russian youth of his class, to which he is condemned by birth, circumstance, and custom. One day when the wealthy merchants are assembled for a fête at the christening of a new boat on the Volga, he makes a scornful speech condemning their vices and attacking their business methods. They agree that he must be mad and he is confined in an asylum by his worldly cunning old godfather, the merchant, Malákin. He comes out after three years only to abandon himself to drink.

FOOL IN CHRIST, THE (Der Narr in Christo), by Gerhart Hauptmann (1910). The life of Emmanuel Quint, a peasant youth, the illegitimate son of a carpenter, parallels in modern times the life of Jesus in Palestine. Emmanuel starts preaching in the market-place, exhorting the world to repentance, and subsisting on alms.   For weeks he lives alone in the mountains fasting and praying.   A gentle, sweet-natured man, he has a quieting effect on the sick, whom he visits, and tales of his healing are grossly exaggerated, until he is acclaimed a miracle worker, and a group of men and women follow him as disciples.   These followers prepare for the end of the world and indulge in the fanaticism and excess common to unbalanced religious sects.   They are poverty-stricken Silesian weavers, ignorant and superstitious, driven by their misery to the expectation of better things at hand.   It is judged that his influence incites these poor people to discontent, and he is reviled and persecuted.   He goes to the city, and lives among the outcasts of society at an inn, where all conditions of people come to him.   He makes no claims for himself except that he is the Son of Man, but is rather ambiguous in statement when asked to explain his meaning. At the height of his notoriety he is accused of the murder of a young girl, daughter of a man who has befriended him.   His followers desert him.   He refuses to answer questions before his judges, but is proved innocent.   Driven from the city, he knocks at every door by the way, saying, "I am Christ; give me a night's lodging."   He wanders as far as the Alps, and later his body is found in the snow.

FOOL OF QUALITY, THE, a curious novel by Henry Brooke, published originally in five volumes (1760–77), was considered of such spiritual value by John Wesley, the founder of Methodism, that he prepared a special edition of it for the use of his followers.   Its author, an Irishman, had been a courtier and man of the world before he became a recluse.   He had known Pope and Sheridan and Swift, who had prophesied for him a brilliant career.   He had been a favorite of the Prince of Wales, and had mingled intimately with the statesmen of the day.   His life, extending from 1706 to 1783, coincided with what was most peculiarly of the essence of the eighteenth century.

'The Fool of Quality' is a novel without a plot, or rather with no definite scheme of action.   It is concerned in the main with the boyhood and youth of Harry, second son of the Earl of Moreland, dubbed by his parents the "fool," because he appeared to be of less promise than his elder brother.   He is brought up by a foster-mother. After some years his parents discover that so far from lacking intellect, he is a child of unusual precocity and promise.   The novel relates how this promise was fulfilled. There are, however, many digressions from the main line cf the tale.   The author moralizes, puts long moral anecdotes in the lips of his characters, and holds imaginary conversations with the reader.   These anecdotes and conversations are chiefly on the power and wisdom and goodness of the Creator.   Towards the close of the book its mysticism becomes exceedingly exalted and visionary, suggesting the author's acquaintance with the teachings of the German mystic, Jacob Boehme.   The work as a whole is hardly capable of holding a modern reader's interest.   It had, however, no mean place in the popular fiction of the eighteenth century, and Charles Kingsley contributed a laudatory preface to a new edition in 1859.

FOOL'S ERRAND, A, by Albion W. Tourgee (1879), purports to have been written by one of the fools.   It is the first of a series dealing mainly with events connected with the Civil War.   "The Fool" is Comfort Servosse, a Union colonel, who removes from Michigan to a Southern plantation after peace is declared.   The story of his reception there and the difficulties encountered, arising out of old prejudices upon the one hand and his own training and convictions upon the other, is told with great detail and strong local coloring.   The author with great fairness considers the questions of reconstruction, while some thrilling chapters deal with the outrages of the Ku-Klux. A love episode is introduced, which proceeds as a simple narrative with no complications of plot.

FOOTSTEPS OF FATE ('Noodlot') by Louis Marie Anne Couperus (1891). Translation from the Dutch by Clara Bell. This story, by one of the latest and youngest novelists of Holland, is powerfully told, and is of absorbing if somewhat strange and morbid interest. It opens in a villa of suburban London, where a wealthy and idle young Hollander is surprised in his bachelor apartments by a visit at midnight of a man in tramp's attire, who seeks shelter and food in the name of early friendship and companionship. "Bertie," the name of the returned prodigal, is taken in by his large-hearted friend Frank, washed, clothed, and fed into respectability, and introduced into the club and made his intimate companion and peer in society. Wearying at last of an endless round of pleasure, marred at times for Frank by certain survivals of low habits in his friend, they, at Bertie's suggestion, go off for a tour in Norway, where Frank meets the young lady who will henceforth absorb his affections. Bertie seeing this, and dismayed at the prospect of being again thrown upon the world, all the more unfitted for struggle after his unstinted enjoyment of his friend's wealth, is prompted by his "fate" to plot for the prevention of the marriage of the loving couple; and the story is occupied with the progress and results of his evil scheme. There is in it a strong savor of Ibsen and of the Karma cult, a subtle portrayal of character, and much fine interpretation of nature. The author was already favorably known through his longer novel 'Eline Vere.'

FOR FAITH AND FREEDOM, by Sir Walter Besant (1888), is a story of Monmouth's Rebellion. The greater part of it purports to be told by Grace Abounding Eykin, the lovely Puritan daughter of the Rev. Comfort Eykin, D. D., rector of Bradford Orcas, Somersetshire. Followed by his wife and daughter, he joins the rebel forces as chaplain. With the insurgents enlist also Barnaby Eykin, his son, who receives the command of a company; Robin Challis, grandson and heir of Sir Christopher Challis (the magnate of their neighborhood), Grace's accepted lover; and Humphrey Challis, his cousin, another fine fellow though in a different way, and a skilled physician — also in love with Grace, and beloved by her as a brother. With the collapse of the uprising they all come to grief. The chaplain and his wife die in jail. The three young men are taken, imprisoned, and as a result of influence brought to bear at court by the Rev. Philip Boscorel, Sir Christopher's son-in-law, allowed with many others to be transported by an inhuman Bristol sharper to Barbadoes, where they are sold as slaves. From this point the story moves rapidly through joy and sorrow, through deception and disgrace, among the most wretched surroundings and exciting incidents. The victims finally escape from Barbadoes, and at last return to England, in time for the three men to take part in the Prince of Orange's triumphal invasion. In the wake of peace comes personal happiness at last.

FOREGONE CONCLUSION, A, by W. D. Howells (1875), one of his earlier and simpler novels, relates the love story of Florida Vervain, a young girl sojourning in Venice with her mother, an amiable, weak-headed woman, of the type so frequently drawn by the author. The daughter is beloved by the United States consul, a Mr. Ferris, and by Don Ippolito, a priest. The latter is a strongly drawn, interesting study. He is a man whom circumstances rather than inclination led into the priesthood. From the hour of his ordination he finds the holy office an obstacle to his normal development. He has the genius of the inventor; has spent years in perfecting impossible models. Florida Vervain becomes his pupil in Italian. Her young enthusiasm leads her to believe that if Don Ippolito were only in America his inventions would receive fruitful recognition. She proposes that he accompany her and her mother to Providence. He, in the first joy of the prospect, declares his love for her. She is horror-stricken because "he is a priest"; and her refusal of him eventually brings about his death. These events open the eyes of Ferris, whose jealousy of the poor priest had led him into a sullen attitude towards the woman he loved.

The novel, despite a happy ending, is overshadowed by the tragic central figure of Don Ippolito. The priest and the girl are remarkably vivid, well-drawn characters. There is just enough of the background of Venice to give color to the story.

FOREST LOVERS, THE, by Maurice Hewlett (1898) deals with the early romance days of France and with the manifold experiences of Prosper le Gai in the mysterious forest of Morgraunt. Prosper, who rides singing on his way, intent only upon adventure, and without a thought of love, finds himself, before a week has passed, the husband of a pathetic little waif. He marries this poor servant-girl, apparently of low degree, from pity, in order to rescue her from being hanged as a witch, or handed over to a false monk. In the end his wife, Isoult la Desirée, proves to be the long-lost daughter of the Countess Isabel, Countess of Hauterive and Lady of Morgraunt. The motive of the story is the triumphant progress of Isoult's love for her knight and lord. She serves him and as protégée and slave undergoes blood-curdling experiences and intense humiliation for his sake, almost sacrificing her life to save his credit. Prosper's feeling for the waif he has rescued passes from pity to interest and at last reaches the plane of noble and ideal love, which alone is what Isoult desires to attain. A mutual and perfect understanding is reached in the end when Isoult's love has been tried, and Prosper's developed by all the stirring incidents which the story contains. The book is well named, as the mysterious enchantment of the forest plays an important part in this mediæval romance, and the author has succeeded in combining real human interest with his fantastic setting.

FORMOSA, Historical and Geographical Description of, by George Psalmanaazaar. The title-page of this curious book, published in French at Amsterdam, by Pierre Mortier & Co., in 1708, bears this description of its contents:

"Description of the Island of Formosa in Asia: of its Government and its Laws: its Manners and the Religion of the Inhabitants: prepared from the Memoirs of the Sieur George Psalmanaazaar, a Native of that Isle: with a full and Exact Account of his Voyages in Many Parts of Europe, of the Persecution which he has Suffered on the Part of the Jesuits of Avignon, and of the Reasons which have Induced Him to Abjure Paganism and to Embrace the Reformed Christian Religion. By the Sieur N. F. D. B. R. Enriched with Maps and Pictures."

The book was evidently inspired by the sectarian zeal of the Reformed Church in Holland, and looked to palliating in Christian eyes the offense of the Japanese in putting to death the Jesuit missionaries in that country. No suspicion or charge is too bad to be entertained against the Jesuits. In the preface the author illustrates their aspiration to universal dominion by a remark of the General of the Order, Aquaviva, to a cardinal visiting him in his little chamber at Rome: "Little as my bedroom looks, without leaving it I govern all the world." The preface is employed in denouncing the Jesuits, and in defending the character and the veracity of the alleged author of the memoirs. His statements are contrasted with the reports of Candidius in the 'Collection of Voyages,' published in London, 1703, to the effect that the island was wholly without law and government; a statement which he argues is absurd. The purpose that animates the book, and the author's style, may be judged of by the following quotation:

"The Adventures of Sr. George Psalmanaazaar, Japanese and Pagan by birth, the education he received at home from a Jesuit passing for a Japanese and Pagan like himself, the artifice used by the Jesuit in abducting him from the home of his father and bringing him to France, the firmness with which he resisted all solicitations of a powerful and formidable organization which has used every means to make him embrace a religion that seemed to him absurd in practice, however reasonable in origin, finally his conversion to the Protestant religion under no other constraint than that of the simple truth, — all this is accompanied by circumstances so extraordinary as to have excited the curiosity of judicious minds both in Holland and in England, and in all other places visited by him. People have crowded to see him, talk with him, and hear from his lips these remarkable experiences."

FORTY-FIVE GUARDSMEN, THE ('Les Quarante-Cinq'), by Alexandre Dumas (1894), the most celebrated of French romance writers, is in two volumes, and is the third of a series known as 'The Valois Romances.' The scenes are laid in and about Paris during the autumn and winter of 1585–86, when political events made all France excited and immoral. The vexations of Henri III. and the ambitions of the queen mother, Catherine de' Medici, are vividly set before the reader, so as to hold his unflagging attention. "The Forty-five" are guardsmen led by the brave and noble soldier Crillon. The story opens on the morning of October 26th, 1585, with a description of a vast assembly of people before the closed gates of Paris, clamoring for admission, to witness the execution of Salcède, a convict murderer. This miscreant is no vulgar assassin, but a captain of good birth, even distantly related to the queen. King Henri III., his queen, Anne, and the queen mother, Catherine de' Medici, have come to witness the execution of the sentence, which is drawing and quartering. Word reaches the King that Salcède, on promise of pardon, will reveal important State secrets. Henri agrees to the condition, and receives a document which, to his disappointment, exonerates the Guises from the charge of conspiracy. The perfidious King orders the execution to take place, and a horrible spectacle ensues. After this dramatic opening incidents and events crowd thick and fast; and the two volumes are taken up with the unraveling of the political plots suggested in the first chapter. The story is one of the most famous of historical romances.

FORTY-ONE YEARS IN INDIA, by Lord Roberts of Kandahar, was published in 1897, and became immediately popular; passing through sixteen editions within three months. The work is a voluminous autobiography, tracing the life of the author from his days as a subaltern until his promotion to the position of commander-in-chief of the British forces in India, and written with the candor of an observer whose experiences have trained him to make broad generalizations in varied fields. With no attempt at melodramatic presentation, the account of the highly colored life of India during the critical period covered is both vivid and striking. Valuable notes are given upon governmental policies, international complications, and the affairs with the many Indian peoples; while religious, educational, commercial, and sanitary matters are treated with sufficient fullness. Lord Roberts came into close touch with all the leading minds who shaped Indian affairs during the previous half-century, and perhaps the most valuable pages of his book are those which describe these great men.

FO-SHO-HING-TSAN-KING, see **SACRED BOOKS OF THE EAST.**

FOUNDATIONS OF BELIEF, THE, 'Being Notes Introductory to the Study of Theology,' by Arthur James Balfour (1895. New ed. 1900). A work answering to its title, as the author states, in only the narrowest sense of the word "theology"; the writer's purpose being, not immediate aid to theological study, but attention to certain preliminaries to be settled before coming to that study. "My object," says Mr. Balfour, "is to recommend a particular way of looking at the world-problems which we are all compelled to face." He also states that he has designed his work for the general reader. It is a study calculated to assist thoughtful inquirers to adjust the relations of belief to doubt, and to maintain a healthy balance of the mind in presence of general unsettlement of traditional beliefs. Its specific question addressed to the doubter is whether belief in "a living God" is not required even by science, and still more by ethics, æsthetics, and theology. Near the close of his book Mr. Balfour says: "What I have so far tried to establish is this, — that the great body of our beliefs, scientific, ethical, æsthetic, theological, form a more coherent and satisfactory whole if we consider them in a Theistic setting, than if we consider them in a Naturalistic setting." In a few concluding pages the further question is raised whether this Theistic setting is not found in its best form in Christianity as a Doctrine of Incarnation and Supernatural Revelation.

FOUNDING OF THE GERMAN EMPIRE, THE: Based chiefly upon Prussian State Documents; by Heinrich von Sybel (7 vols., 1890–98). An able authoritative treatment of Prussian history during the period 1850–70. Dr. Von Sybel had published a 'History of the Revolutionary Period from 1789 to 1800,' in which he pictured the downfall of the Holy Roman Empire among the Germans. In sequel to this he undertook the history of the Prussian founding of a German Empire. Bismarck gave permission, March 19th, 1881, for him to use the records in the government archives; and through five volumes, bringing the story as far as to 1866, this privilege was of avail to secure an accurate and comprehensive picture of Prussian aims and efforts down to the war with Austria. A few months after Bismarck's retirement, the permission to consult the documents of the Foreign Office was withdrawn; but for a correct completion of the essential course of events this proved not a serious matter. The place of the official records was very well supplied by the literature already in print, by the personal knowledge of Von Sybel himself from his own participation in important events, and the knowledge of many other participants in the history, and by an abundance of written records freely placed at his disposal. The entire work, therefore, in seven stout volumes, cannot fail to be a most valuable contemporary history. It is introduced by an elaborate retrospect of German history from the earliest times to the middle (1850) of the reign of Frederick William IV. (June 7th, 1840, to January 2d, 1861). This monarch, after ten years of dogged refusal, finally granted Prussia a written constitution and a representative parliament (January 31st, 1850). It is at this point that Dr. von Sybel takes up the history for full and exact treatment of the steps of change by which the king of Prussia was to become in 1871, January 18th, at the close of the Franco-Prussian War the German emperor. King Frederick William's shattered health (from paralysis and occasional insanity) led to the appointment of his brother William as regent

October 7th, 1858; and upon the former's death, January 2d, 1861, the latter succeeded to the Prussian throne as William I. The policy of the new king was military
rather than popular, to strengthen the army rather than to develop a free Prussia;
and this might have overthrown him had he not found in Bismarck a minister able to
unite the conflicting interests. Bismarck's "Blood and Iron," which has been commonly misunderstood, meant German Blood or Race, — German Unity, — and Iron
or arms to enable Prussia to develop it. Dr. Von Sybel takes up in his first volume
the first attempt at German unity; then relates the failure of the projects for securing
it and the achievement of Prussian union. In Vol. ii. he deals with the revival of
the Confederate Diet; Germany at the time of the Crimean War; the first years of the
reign of William I.; and the beginning of the ministry of Bismarck. He devotes Vol.
iii. to the war with Denmark, and Vols. iv. and v. to the relations of Prussia with
Austria, and the settlement of their difficulties in "the Bohemian War" in which
Prussian success laid the foundation of the new empire. The development of Prussian
power in North Germany and the Franco-Prussian War, ending with the making of
King William emperor, are the topics of the concluding volumes. The English
translation of this great work is an American enterprise.

FOUR FEATHERS, THE, by A. E. W. Mason (1902). The scene of this story is
laid in England and in the Soudan in war time. Harry Feversham, the son of General Feversham, a Crimean veteran, has grown up with the strong impression that
he would prove himself a coward in any great emergency, and, knowing he was
destined for the army, this thought has cast a shadow over his youth.

He becomes engaged to a beautiful Irish girl named Ethne Eustace and announces
the fact at a bachelor dinner given by him to his old friend Jack Durrance and two
officers of his regiment, Captain Trench and Lieutenant Willoughby. While the
dinner is in progress a telegram is brought to Feversham from Castleton, a brother
officer, informing him that their regiment has been ordered into action and telling
him to notify Trench. He destroys the dispatch without explaining the contents,
tells his friends that on account of his approaching marriage he is going to resign
from the army, and sends in his papers that night. His action is soon discovered by
Trench and Willoughby and they unite with Castleton in sending him a box containing three white feathers with their cards enclosed. Feversham receives the box while
dancing with his fiancée at a ball given at her house the following evening and when
she calls for an explanation he tells her the story unsparingly. Ethne, who is a high-
minded girl, is horrified at his avowal and, after telling him that all is over between
them, breaks a white feather from her fan and adds it to the other three. Feversham,
overwhelmed with misery, informs his father of his disgrace, then seeks his old friend
Lieutenant Sutch, a past admirer of his dead mother, and tells him of his purpose
to leave the country for the seat of war, and not return until he has redeemed each
feather by some act of bravery.

Durrance, who has never known of Feversham's trouble, returns to England to
find Ethne in reduced circumstances and still unmarried. Having always loved her,
he presses his suit, when he finds he can do so without disloyalty to his friend, but
she refuses him and he returns to the Soudan. There he is suddenly stricken with
blindness and Ethne upon hearing this writes that she will marry him. While
engaged to Durrance, Willoughby brings to her the first white feather which Feversham has redeemed at the risk of his life, and this is followed some time later by the
return of Trench with his, his rescue from prison having been accomplished by
Feversham after frightful sufferings and privation. After six years of penance

(Castleton being dead) Feversham feels his purpose has been accomplished and returns to his native land. He finds Ethne engaged and prepares to give her up, but Durrance, having discovered her feeling for Feversham, generously resigns in his favor.

FOUR GEORGES, THE, by William Makepeace Thackeray (1860). As the subtitle states, this work consists of sketches of manners, morals, court and town life during the reign of these Kings. The author shows us "people occupied with their every-day work or pleasure: my lord and lady hunting in the forest, or dancing in the court, or bowing to their Serene Highnesses, as they pass in to dinner." Of special interest to American readers is the frank but sympathetic account of the third George, ending with the famous description of the last days of the old King: "Low he lies to whom the proudest used to kneel once, and who was cast lower than the poorest; dead, whom millions prayed for in vain. Driven off his throne; buffeted by rude hands; with his children in revolt; the darling of his old age killed before him, untimely, — our Lear hangs over her breathless lips and cries, 'Cordelia, Cordelia, stay a little!'" These essays do not profess to be history in any sense: they express the thoughts of the kindly satirist, of the novelist who sees not too deeply, but whose gaze misses nothing in the field it scans. Written in much the manner of 'Esmond' or 'Vanity Fair,' and in the author's inimitable style, they give delight which their readers never afterward wholly lose.

FOUR GEORGES, A HISTORY OF THE, in four volumes, by Justin McCarthy (1884-1901). In this work Mr. McCarthy deals, in his own words, "with history in its old — and we suppose its everlasting — fashion: that of telling what happened in the way of actual fact, telling the story of the time." His manner of writing is the old-fashioned, time-honored one; but it is very entertaining of its kind. His pictures are clear in color, full, and vivid; the figures that move across the pages are lifelike and complete.

FOUR MILLION, THE, by O. Henry (1906). O. Henry is the knight of the shop girl and the waitress, the romantic biographer of East Side New York. The title 'The Four Million' is a protest against the social arbiter, who counts only the exclusive "four-hundred" of fashionable society, leaving out of his reckoning such interesting humanity as the hall-bedroom young man, and the tramp. In the 'Gift of the Magi' a young husband and wife sacrifice their greatest treasures to buy Christmas presents for each other. He pawns his gold watch to buy a set of real shell combs for her beautiful hair, unaware that she that day has cut off her long hair and sold it to get him a handsome fob for his watch. Another story has a tramp hero. With winter coming "Soapy" finds the bench in the park no longer comfortable even with three Sunday newspapers distributed over his person. He makes desperate efforts to get sent up to the workhouse for winter lodging, as his more fortunate fellow-citizens would make arrangements for Palm Beach and the Riviera. He breaks a window, steals an umbrella, assumes the rôle of "masher," tries drunk and disorderly conduct, but all in vain, the police refuse to arrest him. As, however, he lingers near a church listening to the anthem, resolved to lead a better life, a policeman arrests him for loitering. 'An Unfinished Story' is a stern arraignment of the employer who underpays his shop-girls. Dulcie is saved from going out with the man known as "Piggie" this one night by the look of "sorrowful reproach," in the eyes of General Kitchener looking down at her from his gilt frame on her dresser, but the end of the story will be later. "sometime when Piggie asks Dulcie again to

THE READER'S DIGEST OF BOOKS

dine with him, and she is feeling lonelier than usual, and General Kitchener happens to be looking the other way." 'The Furnished Room' is really a ghost story. The ghost is a whiff of mignonette which suggests his lost sweetheart to the boy who by pathetic coincidence has come to the same "furnished room" where she had just ended her life. He is convinced that she has been in the room, and hopes to find trace of her, but the landlady will not tell the story of her last lodger, for fear of not renting the room. With loss of hope he loses faith, puts out the light, and turns on the gas, as she had done before him. 'The Sisters of the Golden Circle' are two brides who recognize their sisterhood on the top of a "rubber-neck wagon." The more fortunate sister allows her own husband to be arrested as a burglar long enough to let the real "Pinky" escape to finish his honeymoon. The humor, pathos, and philosophy of O. Henry are at their best in these varied sketches with characteristic surprise endings.

FOURTH ESTATE, THE ('El Cuarto Poder'), by Armando Palacio Valdes (1888). A satirical description of the effect of the establishment of a newspaper in a Spanish provincial town. An opposition journal is started to make war on the clique who are trying to keep abreast of the times. Everything that happens is indirectly caused by the paragraphs of the rival journals. "A Friendly Argument in the Café de La Marina" where the leading citizens assemble daily to discuss the news is reprinted in the LIBRARY. The story is mainly about the love of two sisters for the same man, Gonzalo. He is engaged to the oldest sister, Cecilia, a noble lovely woman, but is enticed away from her by the heartless beautiful younger sister, Ventura. The scene when Ventura wins a declaration of love from Gonzalo is given in the LIBRARY. Cecilia bears her loss with dignity, allowing the household to believe her without heart. She is a devoted sister to the young couple. To save the young wife from discovery, and Gonzalo from sorrow, she lets Gonzalo believe her guilty of a liaison with her sister's lover. Ventura at last elopes with her lover, an elderly nobleman. Gonzalo learns of her flight from the Convent, in which the family have placed her, through the newspaper account, and commits suicide. Aside from the tragic love story, we have a series of entertaining episodes illustrating the jealousies and corrupt journalism of the provincial town. The proprietor of the newspaper, the rich codfish merchant, who spends his leisure time making wooden toothpicks and writing letters to the press, is an interesting type.

FOX, CHARLES JAMES, THE EARLY HISTORY OF, by Sir G. O. Trevelyan, appeared in 1880. Following the method of his admirable 'Life and Letters of Lord Macaulay,' the author makes a profound study of the social and political environment of the youthful Fox as he entered upon his brilliant career. The loose morals of the times, and the prevalent political corruption, are reviewed with dispassionate candor. With charm of language, and the fascination of a romance, are presented the great but too often venal minds which shaped the course of public action during the Georgian era; and a review of the Parliamentary measures which made or marred the careers of men, the success of cabinets, and the fate of issues of national moment.

Altogether, Fox is presented as a young man of remarkable astuteness and vigor of intellect, a born orator and leader, and, considering his corrupt environment, a force making for political probity.

FOX, GEORGE, JOURNAL OF (1694). The Journal of the founder of the Society of Friends takes rank with Wesley's as one of the most remarkable and revealing of religious autobiographies, notwithstanding Macaulay's dictum that Fox was "too much disordered for liberty and not sufficiently disordered for Bedlam." He who would understand the doctrine of the inner light must turn to the pages of Fox in which, as Huxley, an avowed agnostic, handsomely acknowledged, the student will be rewarded by passages of great beauty and power. The facts of Fox's life, his early religious experiences, his months and years of imprisonment under vile conditions for conscience' sake, his brave and dignified pleas before the courts, his missionary journeys in which he visited every corner of England and Wales, are all transcribed with artless sincerity, and even loftiness of language.

FRANCE AND ENGLAND IN NORTH AMERICA: 'A Series of Historical Narratives' (7, in 9 volumes), by Francis Parkman. A magnificent frontispiece to the history of the United States; in conception and execution a performance of the highest character, interest, and value; for genius and fidelity in research perhaps never surpassed; graphic narrative bringing back the continental stretches of untrodden forest, the stealthy savage, the scheming soldier, the mission planted in the wilderness, the pioneers of settlement and the heroes of conquest, colonies founded upon the ideas of opposed European powers, the struggles of policy or of arms to widen control and make possession more secure, and the movements of world-destiny which turned and overturned to decide under what flag and along what paths empire should take her westward course from sea to sea, or broaden down from the lakes to the gulf.

It had been the dream of the author's youth, and the inspiration of his genius, to spend himself effectually in recovering the almost lost history of New France in America; to found upon original documents a continuous narrative of French efforts to occupy and control the continent: and at the date of his last preface, March 26th, 1892, he was able to refer to a collection of manuscript materials begun forty-five years before, and carried to completion in seventy volumes.

Part First of the great work, dating from January 1st, 1865, was a story of "France in the New World; the attempt of Feudalism, Monarchy, and Rome to master a continent; a memorable but half-forgotten chapter in the book of human life." It included an account of 'The Huguenots in Florida,' and of 'Champlain and his Associates,' to the death of Champlain, December 25th, 1635. Part Second was occupied with 'The Jesuits in North America in the seventeenth century'; "their efforts to convert the Indians." Its date was March 1st, 1867. Part Third, 'The Discovery of the Great West,' the valleys of the Mississippi and the Lakes, "a series of daring enterprises very little known," came out dated September 16th, 1869. Part Fourth, dated July 1st, 1874, gave the story of 'The Old Régime in Canada'; "the political and social machine set up by Louis XIV." Part Fifth, January 1st, 1877, was 'Count Frontenac and New France under Louis XIV.,' the story of the battle for the continent. Part Sixth, vols. vi. and vii., dated March 29th, 1892, told the story of 'A Half-Century of Conflict, to the Peace of Aix-la-Chapelle,' of which the news reached America in July, 1748. Part Seventh, Vols. viii. and ix., which had appeared earlier than Part Sixth, dated September 16th, 1884, was the story of Montcalm and Wolfe, not the least thrilling passage of the whole history.

Not only had the author read and collated with extreme care every fragment of evidence, published or unpublished, to secure the utmost accuracy of statement, but he had visited and examined every spot where events of any importance had taken place, that his words might recover the very scenes of the story. On his finished task he could look with a satisfaction rarely granted to human achievement in any field. In those nine volumes, he had made one of the best books ever added to the libraries of the world.

In 1851 the young author gave to the world his first historical work, 'The Conspiracy of Pontiac'; in which, hardly less than in his latest pages, the genius of the writer for research and for fascinating story was made brilliantly manifest. A revised and much enlarged edition was published in 1870, and the volumes form a proper sequel to his 'France and England in North America.'

FRANCE, HISTORY OF, by Jules Michelet (final edition, 1867, 16 vols.). The author of this story of France, from the earliest period down to the nineteenth century, ranks among great historical writers for ardor of research into origins and original materials, for power of imagination in restoring the past, and for passionate zeal in humanitarian interest of every kind. He cannot be read for exact, judicious, comprehensive narrative of the facts of French history, but rather as a great advocate at the bar of letters and learning, telling in his own way the things which most enlist his sympathy or arouse his indignation; perhaps rash in generalization, too lyrical and fiery for sober truth, in matters ecclesiastical especially giving way to violent wrath, but always commanding, by his scholarship and his genius, the interest of the reader, and always rewarding that interest. His work exists, both in French and in an English one-volume translation, as a history of France down to the close of the reign of Louis XI. It was due to the fact that he broke off at this point in 1843, and devoted eight years (1845-53) to writing, almost in the form of an impassioned epic, the story of the French Revolution. Later he resumed the suspended work, and made the whole reach to the nineteenth century. The French people was the idol of his enthusiasm, and human rights the gospel eternally set in the nature of things. Humanity, revealing divine ideas, and history, an ever-broadening combat for freedom, were the principles to which he continually recurred. He is specially interesting moreover as the complete embodiment of one type of French characteristics.

FRANCE, see **TRAVELS IN,** by Arthur Young.

FRANCIS OF ASSISI, LIFE OF SAINT, by Paul Sabatier, was published in French in 1894 and translated by Louise Seymour Houghton in the same year. The author is a French Protestant theologian of the liberal school, but has an intense admiration for the character and teaching of St. Francis and believes in the reality of his inspiration and even in the actuality of such mystical experiences as the receiving of the stigmata, though he would not call such phenomena miraculous. Sabatier has made long sojourns at Assisi, has saturated himself with the literature and thought of the period at which St. Francis lived, and has here presented in a remarkably sympathetic spirit a picture of that time and of the man who exemplified its noblest tendencies. The work has that combination of scholarly exactitude in the use of historical information and imaginative recreation of a past age of faith that seems typical of the French rationalist school and is exemplified particularly by Renan.

FRANÇOIS, THE ADVENTURES OF: 'Foundling, Thief, Juggler, and Fencing Master' during the French Revolution.' By S. Weir Mitchell (1898). A romance of the French Revolution, of special interest and value for its picture of the lower life of Paris during the period known as that of the Terror. Its hero is not a creature of fiction, but a real personage, and Dr. Mitchell's pages tell a story based upon genuine historical information. In his earlier book 'A Madeira Party,' the fine tale, 'A Little More Burgundy,' should be read for the light that it throws upon the scene of François's adventures.

FRANKENSTEIN; or, THE MODERN PROMETHEUS, by Mary Wollstonecraft Shelley (daughter of Mary Wollstonecraft Godwin and wife of the poet Shelley), was published in 1817, and many subsequent editions have appeared. It is a sombre psychological romance, and has a morbid power which makes it one of the most remarkable books of its kind in English. The story begins with some letters written by Robert Walton, on a voyage to the North Pole, to a sister in England. He tells of falling in with a mysterious and attractive stranger, who has been rescued from peril in the Northern Seas, and over whose life appears to hang some mysterious cloud. This stranger, Frankenstein, tells to Walton the story of his life. He is a Genevese by birth, and from childhood has taken interest in natural science and the occult mysteries of psychology. The reading of such writers as Paracelsus and Albertus Magnus has fostered this tendency. He has a dear adopted sister, Elizabeth, and a close friend, Henry Clerval. At the age of seventeen he becomes a student at the University of Ingolstadt, and plunges into the investigation of the unusual branches which attract him. Gradually he conceives the idea of creating by mechanical means a living being, who, independent of the ills of the flesh, shall be immortal. Like Prometheus of old, he hopes to bring down a vital spark from heaven to animate the human frame. After a long series of laboratory experiments, in which he sees himself gradually approaching his goal, he succeeds. But his creation turns out to be not a blessing but a curse. He has made a soulless monster, who will implacably pursue Frankenstein, and all his loved ones to the dire end. It is in vain that the unhappy scientist flees from land to land, and from sea to sea. The fiend he has brought into existence is ever on his track, and is the evil genius of his whole family. He murders Clerval, brings Elizabeth to an untimely end, and so preys upon the fears and terrors of Frankenstein that the latter at last succumbs to despair. The wretched man accompanies Walton on his northern expedition, hoping that he may throw his pursuer off the scent; but finally, in an ice-bound sea, worn out by his hideous experiences, he dies, and over his dead body hovers the horrid shape of the man-machine. The monster then leaps over the ship's side, and disappears in the ice and mist. The story is one of unrelieved gloom, but both in its invention and conduct exhibits unquestioned genius. It is unique in English fiction.

FRANKLIN'S AUTOBIOGRAPHY, a narrative of Franklin's life from 1706 to 1757 written partly in England in 1771, partly in France in 1784, and partly in Philadelphia in 1788–1789. A French translation of the first part appeared in 1791, an altered and incomplete version edited by Franklin's grandson in 1817, and an accurate edition of the entire work by John Bigelow in 1867. In clear limpid English Franklin tells of his birth and upbringing as the youngest son of a large family in Boston, of his apprenticeship to his brother, a printer, of his running away from home and successful entrance into the printing business at Philadelphia when only seventeen years of age; of his journey to England and experiences there as a journeyman printer; of his return to Philadelphia, acquirement of the 'Pennsylvania Gazette' (1729), his marriage (1730), his literary and journalistic successes; of his promotion of civic welfare by the establishment of an efficient police, a fire brigade, a philosophic club, a university and other social organizations; of his growing participation in public affairs, as clerk of the General Assembly, Postmaster of Philadelphia, and agent for Pennsylvania in negotiations with the British government (1757). Various personal anecdotes scattered among the records of his public activities illustrate his good sense, shrewdness, humor, and rationalistic views of life. His frank confession of his foibles and wrong-doing which he calmly dismisses as *errata* is typical of the "age of reason" as are his statements of religious belief and his methods of self-improvement. His helpfulness to his fellow-men both individually and socially is also in accordance with eighteenth-century ideas of practical goodness. The autobiography presents an able man without external advantages succeeding by force of clear thinking, geniality, thrift, and industry; its pictures of Franklin and his acquaintances are vivid, often humorous, and always entertaining.

FRATERNITY, by John Galsworthy (1909). Sylvanus Stone, Professor of Natural Science, an old man of eccentric habits and somewhat vague philanthropic aspirations, when his mind begins to fail, has given up teaching and come to live with his daughter, Bianca, an artist married to Hilary Dallison. In their home he becomes absorbed in writing a beautiful, mad book called the Book of Brotherhood. This volume is to embody the great truth that all men are brothers — that the rich, clever, and independent people of this world have a "shadow" somewhere, no less a part of them for being poverty-stricken, stupid, and weak. Professor Stone gives Bianca's model a job in copying sections of his book daily. The little model comes gladly, not because she cares for Professor Stone or understands anything about the book, but because she has conceived a dog-like devotion for Bianca's husband, Hilary. Hilary is kindly but at first but mildly interested. Inevitably, however, Bianca becomes jealous. Her suspicions are not quieted by the discovery that her quixotic husband has bought clothes for the little model. Through her sister, Cecilia, Bianca learns that Ivy Barton, the model, has ensnared one Hughs, the respectable husband of a hard-working seamstress. Cecilia persuades Hilary to secure lodgings for Ivy far away from the passionate Hughs, and to ask her to discontinue work on the Book of Brotherhood. Dumbly the little model obeys Hilary's orders and keeps away from the house. Unable to stand the interruption in his writing, Professor Stone falls ill. Realizing that the little model's presence is necessary to her father, Bianca seeks out the girl at her new lodgings. Ivy returns gratefully, only to reopen attack on the hitherto impassive Hilary. Finally, she kindles his passion, but in the end disgust at the thought of "going out of his class" keeps Hilary from the scandal of an elopement. We see this class feeling, in Cecilia, who finds herself physically unable to minister to Mrs. Hughs in the squalor of Hound Street; in her daughter Thyme, who can stand only one day of life in the slums; and in Cecilia's husband, Stephen, who makes no secret of the folly of "getting too close to those people." In contrast to all these is Sylvanus Stone. To him the world represents one great fraternity. But all the people in the book, from the little model to his granddaughter Thyme, regard his great ideal as harmless insanity, and the general impression of the book is one of subtle irony as to any real "fraternity" among people separated by their upbringing, tastes, position, and social environment. See the LIBRARY.

FRAU SORGE, see DAME CARE.

FREDERICK THE GREAT, HISTORY OF, by Thomas Carlyle (1858-65). A work of grand proportions and masterly execution, a monument at once of the lofty genius of Carlyle and of the kingly greatness of Frederick II. of Prussia. It was founded on the most thorough examination of all available materials, and with Carlyle's ardent faith in kingship was made as laudatory as the most zealous of Prussians could desire. The graphic power and humor of the work occasioned Emerson's declaration that it was "the wittiest book ever written." The scenes of Frederick's battle-fields were visited by Carlyle; and from his fidelity and wonderful power of description, the military student can see the battles as they were fought almost as if he were an eye-witness. Both England and Germany recognized the extraordinary merits of Carlyle's work. On the first two volumes of the six the author received within a few months nearly $15,000.

FREEDOM OF THE WILL, ON THE, by Jonathan Edwards, D.D. (1754). A book of American origin, made famous by the closeness of its reasoning, the boldness of its doctrine of necessity, and its bearing upon the religious questions raised concerning Calvinism of the old type by the rise of more liberal ideas. Its author had been a preacher and pastor of intellectual distinction and of intense piety for twenty-four years at Northampton, Massachusetts, when his objection to permitting persons not full church-members to receive the communion and have their children baptized, led to his retirement, and acceptance of a missionary position at Stockbridge, Massachusetts. Near the middle of his seven years thus spent, he wrote his book 'On the Freedom of the Will,' not so much with reference to the philosophical question, as with reference to the question between Calvinism of the extreme type and more liberal views. The philosophical doctrine set forth in the book, that the law of causality extends to every action; that there is in the mind no power of willing without a motive; that the will always follows the greatest seeming good; that what this may be to any mind depends upon the character of the person, or, in the religious phraseology of the book, upon the state of the person's soul; and that liberty only extends to a power of doing not of willing, — had been the Greek doctrine in Aristotle and his predecessors. The book on human freedom reflected its author, both in its doctrine and in its thoroughly benevolent and pious intent.

FRENCH AND GERMAN SOCIALISM IN MODERN TIMES, by Richard T. Ely, associate professor of political economy in Johns Hopkins University and later professor in the University of Wisconsin (1883). The author says: "My aim is to give a perfectly fair, impartial presentation of modern communism and socialism in their two strongholds, France and Germany. I believe that in so doing I am rendering a service to the friends of law and order." He further says: "It is supposed that advocates of these systems are poor, worthless fellows, who adopt the arts of a demagogue for the promotion in some way of their own interests, perhaps in order to gain a livelihood by agitating laborers and preying upon them. It is thought that they are moved by envy of the wealthier classes, and, themselves unwilling to work, long for the products of diligence and ability. . . . This is certainly a false and unjust view. The leading communists and socialists from the time of Plato up to the present have been, for the most part, men of character, wealth, talent, and high social standing." The work begins with an examination of the accusations brought against our present social order. It acknowledges the existence of wrongs and abuses and it conveys the warning that the time is not far distant when, in this country, we shall be confronted with social problems of the most appalling and urgent nature. "It is a laboring class," the author says, "without hope of improvement for themselves or their children, which will first test our institutions." Without expressing any personal view as to how threatening evils may best be avoided, and holding that only a fool would pretend to picture the ultimate organization of society, he describes the principal French and German plans of reform that have been proposed. These include the systems of Babœuf, Cabet, Saint-Simon, Fourier, Louis Blanc, Proudhon, French socialism since Proudhon, Rodbertus, Karl Marx, the International Association, Lassalle, the Social Democracy, Socialism of the Chair (*i. e.*, the socialism held by professors, among whom he includes John Stuart Mill), and Christian Socialism. While endeavoring to do justice to Karl Marx, he thinks Lassalle the most interesting figure of the Social Democracy; speaks of the more or less socialistic nature of some of Bismarck's projects and measures; and rejoices that socialists and men of all shades of opinion are more and more turning to Christianity for help in the solution of social problems. The book is fair, uncontroversial, and full of information concerning the many different schools of French and German socialism.

FRENCH HUMORISTS, THE, by Walter Besant (1873). Succeeding the author's admirable work on early French poetry, the present volume is for that reason somewhat incomplete, omitting even Clément Marot; and Voltaire, for other reasons no less valid.

After introducing the trouvère and chanson of mediæval times, the author takes up representative humorists (the designation is a broad one) from each century from the twelfth to our own. The studies present admirable pictures of the authors' life-conditions and the literary atmosphere they breathed. Accompanying these discriminating and delightfully original studies are translations of pieces to show the character and genius of the authors treated. There are in all about twenty-five writers to whom large treatment is given, prominent among them Rabelais, Montaigne, Scarron, La Fontaine, Boileau, Molière, Beaumarchais, and Béranger. There follow a number of exhaustive and learned inquiries into such famous productions as the 'Romance of the Rose' and 'La Satyre Ménippée,' not to mention the historical, critical, and interpretative notices of the author's famous books. Rich in anecdote, historical allusion, and condensed learning, the volume becomes in some sense a history of the rise of literature in France, contributing the while to our own tongue a distinctly valuable treatise, — exhaustive but not tedious; erudite, but not heavy; sparkling, but not effervescent.

FRENCH LITERATURE, HISTORY OF, by Henri Van Laun. (First English Edition, 1876-77.) This work, in three octavo volumes, — beginning with the origin of French Literature and ending with the last years of Louis Philippe's reign, — is the most detailed and elaborate work on the subject in English. Where Hallam, in his 'Literature of the Middle Ages,' has traversed some of the same ground, it is very incomplete. Saintsbury's 'Short History of French Literature' is much more condensed. Van Laun's theory of literature is the same as Taine's; and in his view, literature can be enjoyed or understood only when the reader possesses a proper knowledge of the history of the people among whom it was written, the conditions of race, of climate, of nature, and of life, the writer's personality, etc. These points he aims to supply in his treatment of the various writers. His treatment is scholarly, philosophical, and discriminating. He has divided his subject into the following periods: Origin of the French Nation, Feudal Society, The Renaissance, The Classical Renaissance, The Age of Louis XIV., The Forerunners of the Revolution, The Revolution, The Empire and the Restoration, The Reign of Louis Philippe.

FRENCH LITERATURE, A SHORT HISTORY OF, by George Saintsbury (1897). Among Professor Saintsbury's works, which have been mostly on literature, few have been more serviceable than this handbook. It covers a broad field, and one especially attractive to English readers, as well as not too accessible to them. Accurate in its statements of fact, short, simply and directly written, and yet comprehensive, it considers all departments of literature, including history, theology, philosophy, and science. It starts with origins, and ends with writers of the present day; treating respectively of 'Mediæval Literature,' 'The Renaissance,' 'The Seventeenth Century' 'The Eighteenth Century,' 'The Nineteenth Century,' and offering a sufficient though necessarily brief description of the various men and works "whereof knowledge is desirable to enable the reader to perceive the main outlines of the course of French literature." In the interchapters, inserted at the ends of the books, are summed up the general phenomena of the periods as distinguished from particular accomplishment.

FRENCH REVOLUTION, THE, by Hippolyte Adolphe Taine (1878). This forms the second part of that elaborate work on 'The Origin of Contemporary France' on which Taine spent the last years of his life (from 1876 to 1893), and which obtained for him his seat in the French Academy. Taine's famous formula of "Race, time, and circumstance," as accounting for all things and everybody, which underlay all his other work, lies at the basis of this also. From the opening argument in favor of his theory of "spontaneous anarchy," through the chapters on the Assembly, the Application of the Constitution, the Jacobites, and those on the overthrow of the Revolutionists' government, the pages hold the reader with an irresistible fascination. The essay on the psychology of the Jacobin leaders, — which characterizes Marat as partially a maniac, Danton as "an original, spontaneous genius" possessing "political aptitudes to an eminent degree," but furthering social ferment for his own ends, Robespierre as both obtuse and a charlatan "on the last bench of the eighteenth century, the most abortive and driest offshoot of the classical spirit," — that on the government which succeeded the rule of the revolutionists, and that concerning the current forms of French thought, are among the most striking in the book. Of these habits of thought Taine says: "Never were finer barracks constructed, more symmetrical and more decorative in aspect, more satisfactory to superficial view, more acceptable to vulgar good-sense, more suited to narrow egoism, better kept and cleaner, better adapted to the discipline of the average and low elements of human nature, and better adapted to etiolating or perverting the superior elements of human nature. In this philosophical barracks we have lived for eighty years."

FRENCH REVOLUTION, THE: A History, by Thomas Carlyle (1837). One of the monumental books of all literature. On its appearance John Stuart Mill took pains to review it in the Westminster; and Carlyle's name was securely placed on the roll of great English authors. Mr. R. H. Hutton pronounced it quite possible that it will be "as the author of the 'French Revolution,' a unique book of the century, that Carlyle will be chiefly remembered." Carlyle himself said, "You have not had for a hundred years any book that comes more direct and flamingly from the heart of a living man." With almost unequaled power of picturing incidents and portraying characters and scenes, Carlyle flung upon his pages a series of pictures such as the pen has rarely executed. He deals less with causes and effects, but for the immediate scenes of the story his power is almost perfect; and his book can never lose its living interest for readers, or its value in many ways to students, though it is often called a prose poem rather than a history.

FRENCH REVOLUTION, A HISTORY OF THE, by H. Morse Stephens. (Vol. i., 1886; Vol. ii., 1891; Vol. iii., not yet published.) An important definitive work considerably in advance of previous works, either French or English, in consequence of the wealth of materials now available, and the spirit of impartial examination of all evidence which Mr. Stephens has used. Taine and Michelet displayed great genius in their treatment of the subject; but could not, from French predisposition, weigh impartially the characters of the story. Martin's "continuation" of his great history was a poor work of his old age. Thiers is often inaccurate and unfair; Louis Blanc and Quinet were alike influenced by their political opinions. Mignet stands almost alone for a work which is still a most useful manual, and which is certain to retain its position. Carlyle wrote with marvelous power indeed, and fidelity to his sources; but these were few compared with those now available. Stephens traces the story of these sources, from the contemporary histories, the memoirs of a following age, and the more complete histories from Mignet to Taine, and leaving all these behind, uses for his work the labors of a new school of specialists created since the influence of Ranke and of German methods began to be operative in France. This new school has produced a great number of provincial histories of extraordinary excellence; it has brought out many valuable biographies, a large number of works on the foreign relations of France, and a rich succession of special papers in the reviews and magazines. There are available, also, a variety of publications of proceedings, which bring many early records to light. The great story, with its terrible lights and not less terrible darkness, begins therefore to be clearly open to unprejudiced investigation, and Mr. Stephens's volumes are an attempt to give the results of such investigat on. He leaves upon his readers a clear impression of his success.

FRENCH REVOLUTION, THE, a Political History, 1789–1804, by A. Aulard (1901) translated from the French of the third edition, by Bernard Miall (4 vols. 1910). The author, professor in the University of Paris, has devoted over twenty years to research and writing on the subject, and is distinguished from most of his predecessors by his unrivalled knowledge and critical use of printed and manuscript document sources. The substance of his narrative is based upon the laws, and decrees of government of the Committee of Public Safety, the executive Directory, etc., taken from their official texts, registers, bulletins, and minutes, and from papers and unpublished procès-verbaux in the National Archives. A general knowledge of the course of events is presupposed, and he does not include the military, diplomatic, and financial history of the period. It is exclusively a history of ideas and movements, the development of democracy in France, and the origin and progress of the republican form of government. He studies public opinion and institutions in their mutual relation and in relation to the Declaration of Rights. The period divides into four epochs: 1. "From 1789 to 1792, the formation of the democratic and republican parties under a constitutional monarchy by a property-owners suffrage." 2. "From 1792 to 1795, the Democratic Republic." 3. "From 1795 to 1799, the Bourgeois Republic." 4. "From 1799 to 1809, the Plebiscitary Republic." The theme of the first volume is the growth of democratic and republican ideas forced upon a reluctant, monarchical France by the conduct of Louis XVI. and his advisers. The first half of the second volume takes up the actual establishment of the First Republic and the latter half of the second volume and part of the third volume are a study of the revolutionary government during the Reign of Terror. The worship of reason, the final separation of church and state in 1794, and the later reëstablishment of liberty of worship are discussed in impartial objective statement. The fourth volume begins with the articles of Babœuf, and ends with the establishment of the Empire, 1804. His conclusions are that (1) "it is a mistake to believe that the French Revolution was effected by a few distinguished individuals. It was the work of the French people, not as a multitude, but in effective groups." (2) "The Revolution was only partially completed and was suspended during the rule of Napoleon; for the education of the people was the aim of the republicans while it was a part of Napoleon's despotism to discourage the people from learning and reasoning." (3) "It is an illusion to regard the men of the First Republic as a generation of giants." (4) The term French Revolution has been used to denote "on the one hand the principles which underlay the Revolution and the acts conformable to them; on the other hand, the period during which the Revolution was taking place, and all the acts of the time whether they were in harmony with the spirit of the Revolution or opposed to it." Aulard is the champion of the Revolutionary Legend and the Jacobins against Taine, whom he accuses in another work of gross misrepresentation of the characters and careers of its leaders. The translation includes a chronological summary of events, and biographical notes for each volume.

FRENCH REVOLUTION, CONTEMPORARY AMERICAN OPINION OF, see CONTEMPORARY ETC.

FRENCH SOCIETY, THE HISTORY OF, during the Revolution and the Directory ('The History of French Society during the Directory,' 1879; and 'The History of French Society during the Revolution,' 1880), by Edmond and Jules de Goncourt, are curious as well as interesting compilations of historical material. They show the authors' constant preoccupation with visual impressions. The Goncourts were not philosophers, and they throw no new light upon the causes of events; but they were tireless in research, and they tell us all the curious incidental little facts ignored by greater historians. Theirs is probably the least gloomy study of the Revolution ever written. Under the guillotine they note the cake-vender. Believing that the revolution originated in aristocratic salons, they picture the social life which preceded it, and tell us how the lords and ladies dressed their hair, and what they wore, and how they talked. They show that in spite of fear and bloodshed, people feasted, danced, and went to the theatre as usual. In their study of the Directory they show the country plunged in torpor after its period of excess. The people are weary of struggle, of success, of failure, of all things, until awakened to new energy by a youth of twenty-eight. Napoleon reconstructs society; and in the reaction which follows, cynicism changes to an eager rush for wealth, pleasure, and position. The Goncourts touch lightly upon the great political events, and emphasize the gardens and ball-rooms of Paris, — all the places where well-dressed people gather. They are not interested in masses of society, but delight in portrait-painting. Their histories abound in pictures and picturesque effects. But in spite of their careful word-searching, they are always "more sensitive than intelligent." The result of their labor is finally an enumeration of noteworthy details, which they have been unable to synthesize. They are not successful in presenting as a logical whole the period of which they treat.

FRENCH TRAITS, by W. C. Brownell (1889), appeared first as a series of essays in Scribner's Magazine. These essays offer an unusually astute yet sympathetic study of the French nation in everything which makes its members French, and not German or Italian. The instinct of the author guides him unerringly to the selection of those qualities which are the most perfect medium of national characteristics. He considers first the most prominent endowment of the French people, — the social instinct. This explains their kind of morality of intelligence; their standards of sense and sentiment; the peculiarity of their manners. Above all it explains the French woman, destined from her cradle to be a woman and not a hybrid. She refuses to be separated or to separate herself from men. She lives in the family, as the family lives in the nation. Four remaining essays treat of the art instinct, of the provincial spirit, of democracy, and of New York after Paris.

The author has evidently studied his subject at close range. His treatment of it is brilliant, epigrammatic, and at the same time solid.

FRIEND FRITZ ('L'Ami Fritz'), by the collaborating French authors Erckmann-Chatrain, was published in 1876. It is a charming Alsatian story of the middle nineteenth century, in which the hero is Fritz, a comfortable burgher with money enough to indulge his liking for good eating and drinking, and a stout defender of bachelorhood. He is a kindly, jovial, simple-natured fellow, with a broad, merry face and a big laugh. His dear friend David, an old rabbi, is always urging him to marry; but the rich widows of the town set their caps for him in vain. At dinner one day Fritz wagers David his favorite vineyard that he will never take a wife. David wins, for the invulnerable bachelor succumbs to the charms of Suzel, the pretty sixteen-year-old daughter of his farm-manager. Fritz learns that "he that loveth not knoweth not God, for God is love." Old David deeds the vineyard he has won to Suzel for her dowry, and dances at her wedding. The tale is a sweet idyl of provincial and country life, full of pleasing folk and pleasant scenes, described with loving fidelity. 'Friend Fritz' was dramatized and was very successful as a play.

FRIEND OLIVIA, by Amelia E. Barr (1890). Mrs. Barr possesses the rare talent of producing in her stories that elusive quality called "atmosphere." Whether reading of Knickerbocker days, of the times of Border warfare, or, as in the present case, of Roundhead and Cavalier, of Charles Stuart in Paris and Cromwell at Hampton Court, one loses touch with the present, to become for the time thoroughly imbued with "the charm of ancient story." 'Friend Olivia' deals with the last months of the Protector's Commonwealth; with the oppression of the Quakers under the leadership of the eloquent George Fox; with the tragedies produced by unrest and suspicion when religious intolerance flourished, and political differences separated family and friend: a dark background for a charming love story — that of the modest Quakeress, Olivia Prideaux, and her chivalrous neighbor Nathaniel, only son of Baron and Lady Kelder, strong advocates of Cromwell, and bitter enemies of the "canting" Quakers with their so-called affectations of dress and manner. The story is laid in the coast village of Kelderby. In those quiet streets pass the participants in tragic scenes: the pirate and outlaw John de Burg, his beautiful sister Anastatia, and her hated husband; Roger Prideaux on his way to prison, and others no less noteworthy; and there, finally, as on a miniature stage, are witnessed all the scenes of humiliation, of hopes crushed and expectations realized, when Cromwell dies and King Charles returns to his own.

FRIENDS IN COUNCIL, by Sir Arthur Helps, comprises two series of readings and discourses, which were collected and the first volume published in England, in 1847; the second in 1859. They are cast in the form of a friendly dialogue, interspersed with essays and dissertations, by the "friends in council." They cover a wide range of topics, from 'Worry' to 'War,' and from 'Criticism' to 'Pleasantness.' In style they are charming, the few angularities of diction being easily forgiven by reason of the fascination of the wise utterances and the shrewd observations which pervade the whole. In thought they are carefully worked out and free from monotony. The author evinces a fine moral feeling and a discriminating taste.

FROGS, THE, a comedy by Aristophanes, acted at Athens, 405 B.C. Dionysus, the patron of the theatre, deploring the death of the great Athenian dramatists resolves to descend to the realm of Pluto to bring back Euripides. For this purpose he assumes the garb of Hercules, whose successful expedition to that region is well-known. Accompanied by his slave, Xanthias, he goes to Hercules for advice, and then proceeds to Charon's ferry, to be transported to Hades. In these scenes Dionysus appears as an amusing but cowardly braggart who pretends great heroism but manifests the utmost silliness and imbecility. The slave, Xanthias is the usual low-comic servant and Hercules treats them both with good-humored contempt. During the passage of the Stygian march, Dionysus, whom Charon forces to row, is greeted by a chorus of frogs whose raucous refrain, "Brekekekex, ko-ax, ko-ax," derisively welcomes him to the lower regions. Arrived at his destination Dionysus, with the utmost poltroonery, trembles with fright at every noise. He attempts to assume the rôle of Hercules but on the first threats of the porter, Æacus, he persuades Xanthias to change clothes with him and take his place. This plan, however, he quickly reverses when a feast and agreeable company are promised to the visitor by an attendant of Proserpine. Further omens of trouble, however, induce him to make the exchange; and there follows a farcical scene in which the servant attempts to turn the expected tortures upon the master and the master upon the servant until Æacus solves the difficulty by flogging them both. It now develops that Euripides, the object of their mission, has just created an uproar in Hades by claiming precedence over Æschylus as a dramatic poet. A public disputation between them has been ordained by Pluto, and Dionysus, as patron of the drama, is now appointed judge. The discussion that follows is marked by brilliant wit, apt allusion, and minute acquaintance with the works of both poets. Euripides, with many parodies of specific Æschylean passages, arraigns the master of tragedy for pomposity, cumbrousness, and turgidity, and Æschylus condemns Euripides as monotonous and mean in style, immoral in subject-matter, and corrupting in his influence. For an amusing extract from the debate see the LIBRARY under Aristophanes, pp. 786–787. Dionysus at length gives decision in favor of Æschylus. In reward for his services he is teasted by Pluto and sent back to announce to the Athenians that Æschylus will be allowed to revisit them. With the latter's prayer that Sophocles may hold his place during his absence the drama closes. In accordance with the usual practice of the old comedy a number of personal and political allusions are scattered through the work, referring especially to the proposed recall of Alcibiades.

FROISSART, see **CHRONICLES OF.**

FRUIT, FLOWER, AND THORN PIECES, by Richter (Jean Paul) appeared in 1796–97. It is a strange combination of humor, tenderness, and fine imagination, purporting to be the record of the "married life, death, and wedding of the lawyer of the poor, Siebenkäs." The dream-indulging, impractical poet of a lawyer represents Jean Paul himself; while Siebenkäs's wife. Lenette. the embodiment of the practical in life, stands for Richter's good old mother. Her devotion to every-day ideas is well illustrated when "Siebenkäs," in the midst of a grandiloquent harangue upon eternity is interrupted by her exclaiming: "Don't forget to leave off your left stocking to-morrow morning: there is a hole in it!" Of all Jean Paul's more prominent characters, Siebenkäs is one of the least extravagantly sentimental; and his history, though less ambitious than either "Titan" or "Hesperus," is more popular. It displays Richter's kaleidoscopic variety of thought, wild figures of style, and bewildering leaps from the spiritual to the earthly and grotesque — and thence again to ideal heights. In some passages the rapid sweep of thought seems too strong for coherent utterance, and again it calms down to a placid sweetness very ingenuous. His phrases, linked by hyphens, brackets, and dashes, almost defy the translator's art, and are sufficiently difficult for even the German scholar.

GABRIEL CONROY, by Bret Harte (1876). In this, the longest of Bret Harte's novels, the scene is laid in California during the forties and fifties, and affords vivid pictures of life at a mining camp. The story opens in the California Sierras, where Captain Conroy's party of immigrants, lost in the snow, are dying of starvation and cold. Among them are Grace Conroy, the heroine; her brother and sister, Gabriel and "Olly"; Arthur Poinsett, an adventurous young fellow of high social standing, who is traveling under the name of Philip Ashley, and who has fallen in love with Grace; Dr. Devarges, a famous scientist, who, before he dies, bestows upon Grace the title to a silver mine which he has discovered; and Mr. Peter Dumphy, who spies upon the dying scientist, and afterwards tries to profit by his eavesdropping. A few of the party are rescued, among them Grace and Philip. Complications arising out of her inheritance, and other mining claims, afford an intricate and interesting plot, which a number of vividly conceived characters develop. So exciting and rapid is the action that the book would be classed among sensational novels, but for its artistic treatment and high literary quality. A great many personages are introduced, among them Doña Sepulvida, who is one of the author's best female characters. In this novel, as in most of Bret Harte's works, are vivid imagination, strong local color, dramatic dialogue, daring humor, and much keenness of perception; but most readers have preferred the author's short stories.

GADFLY, THE, by E. L. Voynich (1898). This is a story of the revolutionary party in Italy, written with great power, and with extreme bitterness against the priesthood. The English hero, Arthur Burton, bred in Italy, is studying at the Catholic Seminary in Pisa, where the director, Montanelli, is his devoted friend. The sensitive and ardent Arthur is an orphan, who, unhappy in the family of a worldly uncle, has thrown himself into the plots of young Italy. He is betrayed by a priest, his confessor, to the Austrian police, and sent to prison with his comrades, who regard him as the traitor. On being released, he encounters a young English girl, Gemma Warren, whom he loves, and who taunts him with his treachery and strikes him on the cheek. The same night his uncle's wife, who hates him, makes the terrible revelation that although he is the reputed son of an English gentleman, his real father is a priest who has expiated the sin of his youth by exile as a missionary in China, and who is no other than his beloved teacher, Montanelli. In despair under these redoubled blows, Arthur flees in disguise to South America. Thirteen years later, a club of revolutionists in Florence elects a new member to write its incendiary pamphlets. This member is a South-American, called for his wit and power to sting, the Gadfly. Gemma, now the widow of a revolutionary leader, begins by detesting the

Gadfly for his vindictiveness, which is shown especially towards the good bishop Montanelli; but becomes interested in his cleverness and his underlying melancholy, and ends by loving him, without suspecting that he is the lost Arthur. They engage together in a dangerous insurrection in the Apennines, during which the Gadfly, in the disguise of a pilgrim, makes a pretended confession to the bishop, and overhears him in agonized prayer for his lost son. The Gadfly is taken prisoner at the moment when the bishop is striving to interpose between the combatants. Though treated with horrible cruelty in the Austrian prison, nothing can tame his fiery spirit. The bishop, who, while living a life of piety and good works, is a constant prey to remorse, intercedes with the governor for the unfortunate prisoner, who rewards him only by mockery and insults. Finally, in an interview in the Gadfly's cell, after he has been wounded in an attempt to escape, he reveals himself to the bishop, but refuses his love and intercessions on his behalf, except on condition that his father shall give up for him his allegiance to the hated church, and renounce the Crucified One. This the unhappy bishop cannot do; and the Gadfly, refusing on his side all concessions, is led out to be shot in the prison-yard. The wretched father becomes insane; and in a terrible scene at the altar during the high mass, pours forth his madness and despair, and falls dead of a broken heart.

GAINA-SUTRAS, see **SACRED BOOKS OF THE EAST.**

GALEN'S COMPLETE WORKS, 'Opera Omnia' (158–200 A.D.). (Best modern edition by C. G. Kühn, 20 vols. 1821–33.) Galen's position and influence in medicine date from exceptionally brilliant practice, largely at Rome, in the years 170–200 A. D. For the time in which he lived he was a great scientific physician. He practiced dissection (not of the human body, but of lower animals), and not only made observations with patient skill, but gave clear and accurate expositions. He brought into a well-studied system all the medical knowledge of the time, with a mastery of the foundation truths of medicine which made him the great authority for centuries. He made less advance upon the notions of Hippocrates in physiology and therapeutics than might have been expected, and his pathology was largely speculative; but his works ruled all medical study for centuries. The Arabs translated him in the ninth century; and when Avicenna supplied in his 'Canon' the text-book used in European universities from the twelfth to the seventeenth centuries, it was still Galen (and Hippocrates) whose doctrine was taught.

GALLEGHER AND OTHER STORIES (1891), by Richard Harding Davis. The other stories include: 'A Walk Up the Avenue'; 'My Disreputable Friend, Mr. Raegen'; 'The Other Woman'; 'There Were Ninety and Nine'; 'The Cynical Miss Catherwaight'; 'Van Bibber and the Swan Boat'; 'Van Bibber's Burglar'; and 'Van Bibber as Best Man.' The most noteworthy of the collection are 'Gallegher,' the story of the little newspaper boy who brings to the office late at night "copy" relating to a famous burglary, after many thrilling adventures; 'The Other Woman,' which presents an unusual ethical problem to an engaged couple; and the trio of Van Bibber sketches, the hero of which is a unique type of man, — one of fortune's favorites, but who, by some malicious freak of fate, is perpetually placed in peculiar circumstances, from which he extricates himself with ease and self-possession; his coolness under trying circumstances never failing him, and his fund of humor being inexhaustible. It is only between the covers of so well-written a book as the author's that one can meet the pariahs and the preferred of society hobnobbing at their ease, and be sure that the acquaintance so formed will bring with it no after-taste of regret.

GALLERY OF CELEBRATED WOMEN ('Galerie des Femmes Célèbres') (1844) by C. A. Sainte-Beuve. This compilation of essays is drawn from the 'Causeries du Lundi' (Monday Chats) by M. Sainte-Beuve, in his own day the greatest literary critic of the century. The range of subjects treated extends from Madame de Sévigné and Madame de Lafayette, of the classic age of French literature, through the violent periods of the Revolution and the Empire as illustrated by Madame Roland and Madame de Remusat, well into the time of the Second Empire in the person of Madame Guizot, wife of the historian. Thanks to the peculiar methods of criticism introduced by the Romantic movement, which, awakening a taste for what was ancient and exotic, necessitated a careful historical knowledge of time, place, and environment, M. Sainte-Beuve was enabled both accurately and minutely to depict the literary efforts, and consequent claims to future consideration, of each of the various types of woman which he has treated in this book. The pioneer critics of the new school — as Mesdames de Staël, de Barante, and even the capable Ville-main — had contented themselves with seeing in literature simply the expression of society; but Sainte-Beuve pushed farther on, regarding it also as the expression of the personality of its authors as determined by the influences of heredity, of physical constitution, of education, and especially of social and intellectual environment. This introduces one not only into an understanding of the motives of the public acts and writings of the authors he treats, but also into the quiet domesticity of their homes. It has fallen to the lot of but few men equitably and dispassionately to judge of feminine effort and achievement in letters, but the general favor accorded to Sainte-Beuve proves sufficiently that he is preëminent among those few. True, by some he has here been reproached for lack of enthusiasm; but this, it would seem, is but another way of congratulating him on having broken the old cut-and-dried method of supplementing analysis with a series of exclamation points. Analysis, then, and explanation and comment, rather than dogmatic praise or blame, are what may be found in the 'Gallery.'

GALLUS; or, Roman Scenes of the Time of Augustus, by W. A. Becker. This work, first published in two volumes, Leipsic, 1838, appeared in three volumes in 1863, revised and enlarged by Rein. The story is historical; the principal hero being the poet Gallus to whom Virgil inscribed his 10th Eclogue, the friend, confidant, and eventually the victim, of Augustus. Pomponius, whom Gallus has supplanted in the affections of Lycoris, conspires with Largus to ruin him in the favor of the emperor. A few rash words, uttered at the close of a carouse, alarm Augustus, and convince him that the man upon whom he has heaped favors is a traitor. He confiscates his property and banishes him. Gallus cannot endure his fall, and kills himself with his sword. The work is divided into twelve scenes, each scene bringing us into touch with some department of Roman life. Thus, in the first, the return of Gallus from a party at midnight gives the author an opportunity of describing the domestic econ-omy of a great Roman noble; the second, the morning reception of his clients and friends; the third, his library and the relations between authors and publishers. Perhaps the most successful scene is the seventh: 'A Day at Baiæ,' which, allowing for certain changes, is not so unlike a day at a fashionable watering-place of the present time. Each scene is followed by copious notes intended to verify the state-ments in the text. The most important portion of the work is embraced in the two last volumes, in which the private life of the Romans is treated exhaustively and in systematic order. Each chapter, or excursus, is a commentary on a scene in the story. The style is simple, pleasing, and slightly poetical. The fine English translation by Metcalfe may be considered almost an original work. He has compressed Becker's three volumes into one, and curtailed and altered them greatly for the better.

GAMMER GURTON'S NEEDLE, is one of the two or three earliest comedies in our language. Its authorship is uncertain. In 1575, some years after it was staged at Christ's College, Cambridge, it made its appearance in print. The plot is very simple. An old woman, Gammer Gurton, while mending the breeches of her servant Hodge, loses her needle. The loss of an article so valuable in those days not only worries her, but throws the whole household into confusion. Tib, her maid, and Cock, her servant boy, join in the search. Presently Diccon the Bedlam appears, — a kind of wandering buffoon, who persuades Gammer Gurton that her gossip, or friend, Dame Chat, has taken the needle. Out of this false accusation arise all kinds of complications, and the whole village shares in the excitement. Dame Chat, and her maid Doll, Master Baily and his servant Scapethrift, and Dr. Rat the curate are brought into the discussion. In the end, as Diccon is belaboring Hodge with his hand, the latter is made painfully aware of the fact that the needle has been left by Gammer Gurton sticking in the back of his breeches. Broad jokes, extravagant language, and situations depending for their fun on the discomfiture of one or another of the actors gave this play great popularity in its day. Readers of the present time who penetrate behind its quaint and uncouth language will find in it an interesting picture of sixteenth-century village life.

GARDEN OF ALLAH, THE, by Robert Hichens (1904). The scene of this story is laid in North Africa, and interest centers in the Sahara Desert, which is called the Garden of Allah. Domini Enfilden, a charming English girl, arrives at Beni-Mora, one of the resorts for travelers in the Desert. She is accompanied only by her maid, as having lost her parents and being an only child she is virtually alone in the world. In spite of possessing both wealth and beauty, Domini has reached the age of thirty-two years without being touched by love, but her strong nature has found its outlet in religion, as she is a devout Catholic. At the hotel where Domini is staying she finds the only other visitor besides herself to be an awkward and uncouth man who is a mystery to her. As time goes on, however, Domini realizes that her strange companion, whose name is Boris Androvsky, is not intentionally rude, but is shy, and evidently laboring under some heavy sorrow, and she begins to feel an interest in him which soon develops into love. They are alone together in the beautiful garden of Count Anteoni when Boris tries to take leave of Domini but cannot resist confessing his love and finds that it is reciprocated. The lovers are soon united in marriage and journey into the desert for their honeymoon. Here their perfect happiness is clouded by the secret which Boris is evidently hiding from his wife and which causes her much anxiety and himself great suffering. Finally Boris confesses to Domini that he is a Trappist monk who after twenty years of service in the Monastery of El Largani had tired of his fetters and broken his vows and fled. Since that time he had suffered deep remorse and even his great happiness could not bring him peace. Domini is heart-broken but decides that it is his duty to return to the Monastery, as in that way only can he make restitution for the sin he has committed. Boris and Domini journey at once to El Largani where the latter parts with her husband at the Monastery gate never to see him again, and returns to the Desert, where she begins a life of loneliness and sorrow brightened only by the advent of her child in whom she centers all her affection.

GARDEN OF EPICURUS, THE ('Le Jardin d'Epicure'), a series of detached meditations and essays by Anatole France (Jacques Anatole Thibault) published in 1894 and translated into English in 1908. The essays are concerned with the uncertainties of science and metaphysics, the varying shades of paganism and of religious sentiment in modern life, the portrayal of numerous types of human character, male and female, and the discussion of various æsthetic and literary problems, and of the means of making life pass most tolerably. In one of the longest of the essays a body of philosophers, ancient and modern, is introduced, discussing in the Elysian Fields the nature and immortality of the soul. All the essays have that perfect limpidity, effortless simplicity, and keenness in drawing distinctions which are so typical of this modern exemplar of the best characteristics of French prose. As the title implies, they reflect the views of an indulgent but ironic sceptic, who aims at an unimpassioned and detached but graceful acceptance of the beauties as well as the whimsicalities and imperfections of life.

GARGANTUA AND PANTAGRUEL, by François Rabelais. Towards 1532, at Lyons, Rabelais edited a series of almanacs, in which are found 'La Pantagrueline Pronostication' (The Forecastings of Pantagruel), and 'Les Chroniques Gargantines' (The Chronicles of Gargantua), under the immediate title of 'Pantagruel, roi des Dipsodes, restitué en son naturel, avec ses faits et prouesses espouvantables; composés pour M. Alcofribas, abstracteur de quintessence' (Pantagruel, king of the Drunkards, portrayed according to life, with his amazing deeds and feats of prowess; written by M. Alcofribas, distiller of the very quintessence). This forms the second book of the work as it now stands; for Rabelais, seeing the success of his efforts, revised his 'Chroniques Gargantines' and made of them the 'Vie tres horrifique du grand Gargantua, père de Pantagruel' (The very horrible life of the great Gargantua, father of Pantagruel), which is now the first book. Then came the 'Tiers livre des faits et dicts héroiques du bon Pantagruel' (Third book of the heroic sayings and doings of the good Pantagruel), to which Rabelais affixed his own name with the additions of "docteur en médecine et calloier des isle d'Hieres" (physician and monk of the island of Hyeres). In 1552 appeared the fourth book. The fifth book (1564) is posthumous and it is doubtful if Rabelais composed it. The five books form a sort of satirical epopee. The first book, which alone forms a complete whole, relates the birth, childhood, the journey to Paris, the education, and the farcical adventures of the giant Gargantua, son of Grandgosier; also the war which he waged against the invader Picrocole, the mighty deeds of his friend and ally Jean des Entommeurs, and the foundation of the abby of Thélème. This book also is probably the best known and most prized, as illustrating the serious ideas of its author upon war, the education of children, and the organization of monastery life. The myth of Gargantua was of Celtic origin, dating from the time of the importation of the Arthurian legends into France by the troubadours of William the Conqueror.

GARIBALDI AND THE THOUSAND, by George Macaulay Trevelyan (1909), is a highly interesting account of the liberation of Sicily from the Bourbon sovereigns of Naples. Garibaldi's early life and the condition of Italy previous to the Risorgimento are first discussed and an account is then given of the war of Piedmont against Austria in 1859, of Garibaldi's share in it, and of his landing in Sicily in 1860 with an army of a thousand volunteers and conquering the country. In a sequel entitled 'Garibaldi and the Making of Italy' (1911) the author goes on to relate the crossing of the victorious Garibaldi into Calabria, his defeat of the Neapolitan armies at the

Volturno, his relinquishment of his army and conquered territory to Victor Emmanuel of Sardinia, and the surrender of Francis II. of Naples on February 13th, 1861. At the close his share in the conquest of Venice and Rome, which completed the unification of Italy is briefly outlined. Both volumes are written in Trevelyan's graphic and entertaining style and present a splendid picture of this romantic episode in the liberation of Italy.

GARRISON, WILLIAM LLOYD, 'The Story of His Life, Told by His Children' (Wendell Phillips Garrison and Francis Jackson Garrison), was published in four volumes in 1885, the fiftieth anniversary of the "Boston Mob" which played so dramatic a part in their father's life.

The account given of the great abolitionist's family antecedents is quite full, and his whole career circumstantially presented; though not as a mere agglomeration of facts and incidents, for the threads of his development are as sedulously kept together as in a novel. The ample space of the work permits the reproduction of historic documents, addresses, articles from the Liberator, and other periodicals, and some very valuable portraits. No less interesting, as presenting a near view of a phase of national development, are the records of Garrison's missions abroad and efforts to secure legislative recognition of the cause for which he stood. The reformer's character, as here revealed, shows his great humanitarian schemes to have been the inevitable outcome of a sensitive conscience, a humane spirit, and an overpowering sense of justice. The work pretends to no ornate literary style, but recognizes its own value to be in historic fullness, accuracy, and sympathy with its subject.

GARTH, by Julian Hawthorne, appeared first as a serial in Harper's Magazine (1875). Garth Urmson, the hero, is a member of a New Hampshire family, upon which rests a hereditary curse. In the seventeenth century the founder of the family in America had violated a sacred Indian grave. From that time forth, the shadow of the crime rests upon his descendants. Garth, the last of the race, seems to carry the weight of all their cares and sorrows; but at the same time he feels the dignity which was theirs by right of many noble qualities. He is a dreamer, but a lofty dreamer. He cannot, however, escape misfortune. His love affairs with two women, Madge Danvers and Elinor Lenterden, are unhappy, in so far as they are controlled by the hereditary curse. The novel possesses a peculiar haziness of atmosphere. It is perhaps an imitation of the elder Hawthorne's 'House of the Seven Gables.'

GATHERING CLOUDS: 'A Tale of the Days of St. Chrysostom,' by Frederick W. Farrar (1896). This story depicts the strifes of the see of Constantinople, in somewhat the manner of Kingsley's 'Hypatia' as that deals with Alexandria. The period, end of the fourth and beginning of the fifth century, is that bewildering age when the clouds are gathering over Church and State. The hero is John Chrysostom, the preacher of Antioch, beloved by Christian and respected by heathen. The first chapter describes the riot that followed the attempt of the Emperor Theodosius to take the opulent city on the Orontes. Then follows the story of its threatened doom averted by the devotion of Flavian and "Presbyter John"; and the rescue of the boy Philip, whose thoughtless act has led to the destruction of the statues of the Emperor's wife and children. It follows Chrysostom to Constantinople, to the patriarchate of which the modest preacher has been appointed by the new Emperor Arcadius. It tells of the sturdy faithfulness of the new chief, the envy and plots against him, the rising of the Goths and their massacre, and the exile and subsequent death of Chrysostom. Many historic characters find their way into the story; but not all of the alleged saints merit their aureoles. The valiant John, however, is a bulwark of righteousness; and is portrayed, not as an abstraction, but a living, large-hearted man. The stories of the devoted youths Philip and Eutyche, of David and Miriam, with the Gothic youths Thorismund and Walamar, are given; and the story ends with the martyrdom of Eutyche, the death of Chrysostom, and the capture of Rome by Alaric.

GAVEROCKS, THE, by S. Baring-Gould (1889), is one of the tales of English rural life and studies of distorted development of character, mingled with a touch of the supernatural, in which the author excels. Hender Gaverock is an eccentric old Cornish squire, who has two sons, Garens and Constantine, whose natural spirits have been almost wholly crushed by his harsh and brutal rule. Garens philosophically submits, but Constantine rebels; and the book is chiefly occupied with the misdeeds, and their consequences, of the younger son, whose revolt against his father's tyranny rapidly degenerates into a career of vice and crime. He marries secretly, deserts his wife, allows himself to be thought drowned, commits bigamy, robs his father, and is finally murdered as he is about to flee the country. Exciting events come thick and fast, and the various complications of the plot gradually unravel themselves. The chief characters are boldly and forcibly drawn, and the scenes on both land and water are vividly portrayed; notably the storm in which Constantine and his father are wrecked, the "Goose Fair," and Garens's samphire gathering. The interest is sustained to the end, and the book as a whole is a powerful one, though it can hardly be called pleasant or agreeable.

GAWAIN, see **PEARL.**

GAY LORD QUEX, THE, by Arthur W. Pinero (1900). Lord Quex, a reformed Don Juan, is about to marry Muriel, a young English girl. Muriel's foster-sister, Sophie Fullgarney, a manicurist, has heard of Lord Quex's past, and is determined to save Muriel from the marriage. Sophie plots to entrap Lord Quex into showing his true character, and tries to tempt him into flirtation with herself. She has the opportunity to spend the night at the country house where Muriel and Lord Quex are guests and overhears Lord Quex make an appointment with the Duchess of Strood, an old love, who has insisted on a farewell meeting. On pretext of supplying the place of the Duchess's maid, she is able to listen at the keyhole of her boudoir. Lord Quex discovers her, and sending the Duchess to the room of a friend, rings for Sophie and locks her in the room. He offers her money and explanations, and appeals to her generosity in vain. Then he points out to her that her own reputation will be ruined, and in her excitement she promises to be silent and writes a compromising letter at his dictation. Suddenly she realizes that she is sacrificing Muriel to save herself, and rings the bell to arouse the household. He appreciates her courage and real devotion to Muriel, and sets her free, and she in her turn is converted from an enemy into an ally. Captain Bastling, the young man whom Muriel fancies she loves, falls into the trap of flirtation with Sophie which failed to catch his rival, and Lord Quex marries Muriel.

GENDRE DE M. POIRIER, LE ('Mr. Poirier's Son-in-Law'), by Émile Augier and Jules Sandeau. This charming little French comedy, sparkling with wit, has already become what Francisque Sarcey says it will always continue to be — a classic, but not a dry classic. It describes the old struggle between the "bourgeoisie" and the aristocracy, pointing out the weaknesses of each. Monsieur Poirier, a rich tradesman, with the ambition of ultimately entering the peerage, has bought a ruined Marquis for his daughter. The Marquis, Gaston de Presles, finds himself at first in a most comfortable position. He lives in great luxury at the expense of his father-in-law, whom he continually holds up to ridicule. At the same time he resumes his old way of life; pays scant attention to his wife, supposing that she must be uninteresting; and devotes himself to Madame de Montjoy, about whom he cares nothing. Things do not continue to go so pleasantly however. Monsieur Poirier tries to force him into a political career, which he flatly refuses. Antoinette, his wife, begins to appear in a new light. She twice saves his honor, once by signing herself for a debt of which her father refuses to pay the usurious interest, a second time by destroying a letter from Madame de Montjoy, of which her father had got possession. Gaston de Presles is astonished to find himself desperately in love with his own wife. She however, having discovered his intrigues with Madame de Montjoy, declares herself a widow, but relents when for her sake he promises to give up fighting a duel. The reconciliation is complete. Verdelet, an old friend of Poirier, and Hector de Montmeyran, are the other important characters.

GENERAL HISTORY OF THE INDIES, see INDIES.

GENIUS, THE, by Theodore Dreiser (1915). The story of the amorous adventures of an artist, Eugene Witla, beginning with Stella and ending with Suzanne at the end of the book. He is the son of a sewing machine agent in a small town in Illinois. He studies art in Chicago, and makes a name for himself in New York as an illustrator. His love affairs and unfaithfulness to one woman after another are described with the minuteness of detail of a dictograph. He marries Angela because after waiting years for him to fulfil his promise to her, she threatens to kill herself in order to escape from becoming a mother before she is a wife, and his artistic temperament shrinks from the catastrophe. Studio life and intrigues bring about a nervous collapse, but he recovers his health in hard manual labor. He takes up advertising art, and quickly becomes a director of the United Magazines Corporation at a salary of twenty-five thousand a year. His wife dies giving birth to a daughter. Ultimately Eugene returns to painting. The end of the story leaves him in search of a guiding plan of life in Christian Science, mysticism, cosmic philosophy and Herbert Spencer, and dallying with his paternal duties.

GENIUS OF CHRISTIANITY, THE ('La Génie du Christianisme'), by François Auguste de Châteaubriand (1802). This favorite book was begun by Châteaubriand during his period of exile in England; though it was first published in France at the moment when Bonaparte, then First Consul, was endeavoring to restore Catholicism as the official religion of the country. The object of the 'Genius' was to illustrate and prove the triumph of religious sentiment, or more exactly, of the Roman Catholic cult. The framework upon which all is constructed is a sentence found near the beginning of the work, to the effect that of all religions that have ever existed, the Christian religion is the most poetic, the most humane, the most favorable to liberty, to literature, and to the arts. The book is divided into four parts, the first of which treats of the mysteries, the moralities, the truth of the Scriptures, the existence of God, and the immortality of the soul. The second and third parts bear upon the poetics of Christianity, and upon the fine arts and letters. The fourth is devoted to a minute study of the "Christian cult." However pious the feeling which prompted the composition of the 'Genius,' it by no means entitles its author to a position among religious writers. Critics have shown us that, at most, he was devoted only to the rude Christianity of the Dark Ages, vague and almost inexplicable. It was but the external, the picturesque, the sensuous side of religion that impressed him. He loved the vast and gloomy cathedral, dimly lighted and sweet with incense, the low chanting of the priests, the silent movements of the acolytes, all the pomp, magnificence, and mystery of the holy rites. It was this only that gave him pleasure, and through his artistic sensibilities alone. In short, he regarded religion much as he did some old Gothic ruin by moonlight, — a something majestic, grand, romantic, a fit subject to be treated by a man of letters.

GENTLEMAN FROM INDIANA, THE, by Booth Tarkington, was published in 1899. It is the story of John Harkless, a young college graduate, the most promising man in his class, who, instead of doing at once the great things expected of him, settles down in a dull little Indiana town and becomes proprietor and editor of a country newspaper. He attacks with both bravery and vigor the hosts of evil which prevail about him, and thereby wins for himself both friends and enemies. His personal efforts toward bringing to justice a number of White Caps, whose outrages have previously gone unpunished, single him out for their vengeance. With absurd indifference to danger, young Harkless goes about unarmed and pays slight attention to the stray bullets which cross his path. The climax of the story is reached when, in the midst of a scene with the girl he loves, he dashes off into the darkness and is set upon by a band of cut-throats. The only trace of him to be found the following day is a bloody stain near the railroad track and he is given up as dead. The people of the community, aroused from their lethargy by this last outrage, start out to devastate the neighboring settlement from which the White Caps come. News is received that Harkless is alive, the hamlet is spared, and the men who have taken part in the attempted murder receive the penalty of the law. The hero finally returns in triumph and marries the girl of his choice, who has run his paper with great success during his absence, and has been able by this means to get her lover nominated as a member to Congress. There are many stirring incidents in the story and they are narrated with much strength and vigor.

GEOGRAPHY, THE, of Ptolemy; see ALMAGEST.

GENTLEMAN OF FRANCE, A (1893), by Stanley J. Weyman. This story is a romance of the troublous times in France immediately preceding the accession of Henry IV. to the throne. Gaston de Bonne, Sieur de Marsac, reduced almost to poverty by the death of his patron, is unexpectedly offered a dangerous and thankless commission by Henry of Navarre. Accepting it, he finds himself engaged to abduct Mademoiselle de la Vire, a beautiful young lady, the niece and ward of the Duke de Turenne. Marsac is warned that he cannot look to Henry for aid in case of the miscarriage of the enterprise, as the king must not appear to be implicated. The abduction is necessary for political reasons, as the lady possesses information vitally important to Navarre in his efforts to unite the Huguenots with the Catholic forces of King Henry III., and which she alone can impart to the king. Marsac accomplishes his task after many hairbreadth escapes and delivers his charge to the Duke de Rosny, Navarre's chief counselor, who notifies the king that he can now produce the testimony needed to bring about the desired reconciliation. Marsac conducts Mademoiselle de la Vire to the king at Blois; but after the interview she is recaptured and spirited away by emissaries of Turenne. Marsac follows, overtakes and rescues the lady. The plague is raging in the neighborhood, and Marsac is stricken with the disease, but is nursed back to health by Mademoiselle de la Vire, for whom he forms an ardent attachment, which she reciprocates. Upon the death of Henry III., Henry of Navarre, now Henry IV., rewards Marsac for his fidelity and courage, with an appointment to a governorship and the hand of Mademoiselle de la Vire.

GEOGRAPHY, A, by Strabo (c. 64 B. C.–19 A. D.). The author visited most of the countries he describes, having traveled extensively in Asia Minor, Europe, and Africa. He was forty-three or forty-four years old when he returned to his birthplace, Amasea in Cappadocia, where he spent several years in arranging his materials. The work appeared some time about the beginning of the Christian era. It is divided into seventeen books, of which we possess almost the whole; and is a real encyclopædia, full of interesting details and brief but luminous sketches of the history, religion, manners, and political institutions of ancient nations. The first two books form a sort of introduction, in which he treats of the character of the science and refutes the errors of Eratosthenes. Then he devotes eight books to Europe, six to Asia, and the last to Africa. Strabo is very modern in the standpoint from which he views geography. In his way of looking at it, it is not a mere dry nomenclature, but an integral picture, not only of the physical phenomena but of all the social and political peculiarities that diversify the surface of our globe. His work even contains discussions of literary criticism of considerable importance; and he has very clear notions of the value of ancient fables and folk-lore as evidence of the ideas and wisdom of primitive times. The 'Geography' is the production of a judicious and consummate scholar and clear and correct writer; and besides being an inexhaustible mine for historians, philologists, and literary men, is very pleasant reading. Yet it appears to have been forgotten soon after its publication. Neither Pliny nor Pausanias refers to it, and Plutarch mentions only the historical part. Strabo suspected the existence of a continent between western Europe and Asia. "It is very possible," says he, "that by following the parallel of Athens across the Atlantic, we may find in the temperate zone one or several worlds inhabited by races different from ours."

GEOGRAPHY, THE, of Ptolemy, see **ALMAGEST.**

GEORGICS, THE (Georgica), by Virgil. This great work, admittedly the masterpiece of didactic poetry, and considered by many superior to the Æneid in style, was begun, probably at the request of Mæcenas, in 717, and completed in 724 A. U. C. It is divided into four books. The first treats of agriculture; the second of trees; the third of the raising of cattle; and the fourth of bees. Virgil has utilized the writings of all the authorities on agriculture and kindred subjects in the Greek and Roman world. Thus, besides the 'Œconomica' of Xenophon, the works of the Carthaginian Mago, translated by order of the Senate, and those of Cato and Varro, he consulted the 'Phenomena' of Aratos for the signs of the weather, those of Erastothenes for the celestial zones, the writings of Democritus for the revolution of the moon; and so admirably are all his materials used with his own poetic inspiration, that precept and sentiment, imagination and reality, are merged in one complete and harmonious unity. No matter how exact or technical the nature of the teaching, it is never dry. An image introduced with apparent carelessness vivifies the coldest formula: he tells the plowman he must break up the clods of his field and harrow it again and again, and then at once shows him golden-haired Ceres, who looks down on him from the

Olympian heights with propitious eyes. Besides mythology, which the poet uses with great reserve, he finds in geography resources that quicken the reader's interest. Tmolus, India, the countries of the Sabæans and Chalybes, enable him to point out that every land, by a secret eternal law, has its own particular products; and to predict to the husbandman that if he follow good counsels, a harvest as bounteous as that which arouses the pride of Mysia or Gargarus shall reward his toil. The episodes and descriptions scattered through the poem are of surpassing beauty. Among them may be mentioned: the death of Cæsar, with the prodigies that accompanied it, at the end of the first book; in the second, the praise of Italy, its climate and its flocks and herds; the pride and greatness of Clitumnus, with her numerous cities, her fine lakes, as broad and as terrible in their fury as seas, with her robust population and great men who gave to Rome the empire of the world; and, as a pendant to this sublime picture, the fresh, idyllic delineation of country life and the happiness of rustic swains, if they only knew, *sua sic bona norint !* then, at the end of the third book, the splendid games and the magnificent temple of white marble he proposes to raise to Augustus; the description of the pest that devastated the pasture-lands of Noricum, unrivaled for elegance and pathos; and the touching story of the love of Orpheus and Eurydice with which the poem concludes.

GERMAN EMPIRE, see **FOUNDING OF THE.**

GERMANY ('De l'Allemagne') by the Baroness de Staël Holstein (Anne Louise Germaine Necker) (1813). One of the most remarkable examples in literature of the genius of woman opening new paths and executing efforts of advance with full masculine strength and energy. Napoleon had in 1803 driven Madame de Staël from Paris, and in December of that year she had visited Schiller and Goethe at Weimar, and Schlegel at Berlin. The death of her father, a visit to Italy, and the composition of 'Corinne' which greatly added to her fame in Europe, were followed by a second visit to Germany in the latter part of 1807. The book 'De l'Allemagne' was finished in 1810, and printed in an edition of 10,000 copies after submission to the regular censorship, when Napoleon caused the whole to be seized and destroyed, and herself ordered to leave France at once. By good luck her son had preserved the manuscript; and the author was able, after a long wandering through Europe, to reach England, and secure the publication of her book in 1813. In dealing, as she did, with manners, society, literature, art, philosophy, and religion, from the point of view of her observations in Germany, Madame de Staël gave to France a more complete and sympathetic knowledge of German thought and literature than it had ever had. It was a presentation of the German mind and German developments at once singularly penetrating and powerful. The defects of the work were French, and promoted rather than hindered its influence in France. In England an immense enthusiasm was aroused by the author and by her brilliant book, which easily took the highest rank among books of the time.

GERMANY ('Germania'), by Tacitus. The full title of the work is 'De Origine, Situ, Moribus, ac Populis Germaniæ.' It was written probably in 99, and is a geographical and political description of ancient Germany, or at least of the part of it known to the Romans, which did not extend far beyond the Elbe. It may be divided into three parts: Chapters i.–v. describe the situation of the country, the origin of its population and the nature of the soil; Chapters vi.–xxvii., the manners of the Germans in general and their method of waging war; and the remaining chapters deal with the several

tribes, and give a careful and precise account of the manners and customs that distinguish one from another.   This fine work is at once a treatise on geography, a
political study of the peoples most dreaded by Rome, a study of barbarous manners,
and, by the simple effect of contrast, a satire on Roman manners.   It is not only the
chief source of the ancient history of the tribes that were to form the northern and
western nations of Europe, but it contains an account of the germs of almost every
modern institution, — military, judicial, and feudal.   Notwithstanding occasional
errors in geography and some misconceptions as to the religion of the Germans, the
striking accuracy of his details, as well as the correctness and precision of his general
views, have led some scholars to believe that Tacitus spent the four years of his life
which are unaccounted for, from 89 to 93, in Germany.   But this is only conjecture;
and the means of information within his reach were as valuable as a personal visit
to the country he describes might have been.   Many of his friends, like Rufus, had
made campaigns beyond the Rhine, and their knowledge was at his disposal.   He must
have consulted the numerous hostages and captives that were always in the city.
Deserters, such as Marbod and Catuald, not to mention the merchants who trafficked
with the Teutons, may also have helped him to give his work the character of truthfulness and the local color that distinguish it.   He is supposed, in addition, to have
derived great assistance from the 'History of the Wars in Germany,' in twenty books,
by Pliny the Elder, a work now lost.   Tacitus has been accused of a tendency to
idealize the ancient Germans, in order to contrast their virtues with the vices of the
Romans.   But while he no doubt intends now and then to point a moral for the
benefit of his countrymen, he is not blind to the faults of the people he describes, and
has no love for them.   He speaks of their bestial drunkenness, their gluttony, their
indolence, and rejoices with a ferocious joy at the destruction of sixty thousand of the
Brusteri, slain in sight of the Roman soldiers by their own countrymen.

GERMANY AND THE NEXT WAR ('Deutschland und der nächste Krieg') by
General Friedrich von Bernhardi, published in 1911, translated into English in 1916,
is an argument in favor of war in general and an aggressive German national policy
of industrial and territorial acquisition backed up by military preparedness.   The
first two chapters defend war as an essential to healthy national life, as the fountain
of social virtues and as the privilege and duty of the vigorous and expanding state,
which can tolerate the control of no international sentiment or external control on
earth.   War is not inconsistent with Christian morality, which applies to the individual and not to the state.   In the next two chapters the author traces rapidly
the political and economic development of the German empire and the mission of the
German people to promote scientific research and efficient government.   The chapter
headed by the famous title 'World Power or Downfall' demonstrates the isolation of
Germany and Austria among the European powers, shows the motives for a coalition
against them, and maintains that national disaster is the alternative to a vigorous and
aggressive policy.   The following chapter pleads for ample provision for war, which
the socialist parties and pacifists are hindering by their constant opposition and
propaganda.   Then follow three chapters forecasting the probable course of such a
world-war, both by land and sea, and discussing the means of victory.   They contain
some successful predictions and some that have been falsified by the event.   Germany's strength as the head of a coalition of central powers fighting on interior lines,
and the limitations of France and Russia are accurately predicted, and the general
nature of England's naval campaign is outlined; but there is no anticipation of the
possibility that England and her colonies might raise a great army or of the German

submarine campaign. The remainder of the book deals with army and navy organization, the need of a more practical and scientific education with additional military training, and the necessity of financial, economic, and political preparedness. The book is a valuable presentation of the popular German worship of the state as the highest authority in existence, with a morality transcending individual morality, and of the ruthless German application to international policy of the biological doctrine of the struggle for existence and the survival of the fittest.

GERMINAL, see ROUGON-MACQUART.

GERTRUDE OF WYOMING, by Thomas Campbell, was written at Sydenham, in 1809, when the author was thirty-two, eleven years after the publication of 'The Pleasures of Hope.' It had every advertisement which rank, fashion, reputation, and the poet's own standing, could lend it. He chose the Spenserian stanza for his form of verse, and for his theme the devastation by the Indians, in 1778, of the quiet valley of Wyoming, in Pennsylvania, on the Susquehanna. The poem, which is in three parts, opens with a description of "Delightful Wyoming," which Campbell, who had never seen it, paints as a terrestrial paradise. One day, to the house of Gertrude's father comes the Oneida warrior Outalissi, bringing a boy whom he has saved from the slaughter of a British force. The orphan, Albert Waldegrave, the son of a dear family friend, lives with them three years, until his relatives send for him. Gertrude grows up into a lovely woman, roaming among the forest aisles and leafy bowers, and reposing with her volume of Shakespeare in sequestered nooks. Albert returns, splendid to behold. They enjoy three months of wedded bliss, and both are killed in the incursion of Brant and his warriors. The style and manner seem old-fashioned to-day, and the treatment is vague, unreal, and indefinite; but a certain sweetness and pathos, combined with the subject, has kept the poem alive.

GERUSALEMME LIBERATA, see JERUSALEM DELIVERED.

GESCHICHTE JESU VON NAZARA, by Theodor Keim, see **JESUS, LIFE OF.**

GHOSTS, a powerful play by Henrik Ibsen (1881), gives dramatic embodiment to the modern realization of heredity. Ibsen, treating this subject on its tragic side, considers the case of the darker passions as they are handed down from father to son. The fatalistic atmosphere of 'Ghosts' resembles that of a Greek drama. It is a Greek tragedy translated into the littleness and barrenness of modern life.

Oswald Alving, the son of a dissipated, worthless father, has been brought up by his mother in ignorance of his dead parent's shame. Yet he has within him the seeds of a transmitted disease, — the evil sown by a previous generation. He has gone into the world to make a name for himself, but he is forced to return to his mother's home. He drinks to excess, and he exhibits tendencies to other more dangerous vices. His wretched mother sees in him the ghost of his father; she sees the old hateful life clothed in the form of the boy she has reared so carefully. He himself feels the poison working in his veins. The play closes upon the first sign of his incipient madness. In this drama, the mother, Mrs. Alving, is the type of the new woman in revolt against the hideous lies of society, because she has suffered through them. She is learning to think for herself; to weigh social morality in the balances. Her adviser, Pastor Manders, has been called "the consummate flower of conventional morality." He is a type of the world's cautiousness and policy in matters ethical;

of that world's disposition to cover up or refuse to see the sins of society. He is of those who make of marriage a talisman to juggle away vice.

'Ghosts' is perhaps the most remarkable of Ibsen's dramas in its searching judgment, its recognition of terrible fact, its logical following of the merciless logic of nature.

GIBBON, EDWARD, THE AUTOBIOGRAPHY OF. What goes at present under this title is a compilation made by Lord Sheffield, Gibbon's literary executor, from six different sketches left by the author in an unfinished state. The first edition appeared in 1796, with the complete edition of his works. "In the fifty-second year of my age," he begins, "after the completion of an arduous work, I now propose to employ some moments of my leisure in reviewing the simple transactions of a private and literary life." This modest, unaffected tone characterizes the book. The sincerity of the revelations is full of real soberness and dignity. The author of the 'Decline and Fall of the Roman Empire' recounts the years of preparation that preceded his masterpiece, and the difficulties conquered. Macaulay's "schoolboy" doubtless knows the lines concerning the origin at Rome of his first conception of the history — when he was "musing amidst the ruins of the capitol, while the barefooted friars were singing vespers in the temple of Jupiter." And many other passages are hardly less familiar. Had he lived, Gibbon would doubtless have completed these memoirs; but as they are, the simple, straightforward records of a famous student's labors and aims, who by his manly character made many lasting friendships, they form one of the most interesting, brilliant, and suggestive autobiographies in the English language.

GIL BLAS OF SANTILLANE, THE ADVENTURES OF, the work by which Alain René Le Sage is best and most widely known, is a series of pictures of life among all classes and conditions of people in Spain two centuries ago. Gil Blas, an orphan of seventeen years, is dispatched by his uncle, with the gift of a mule and a few ducats, to seek the University of Salamanca, there to finish his education and find a lucrative post. He does not reach the university, but falls in with robbers, actors, courtiers, politicians, in a long chain of adventures. By turns he enters the service of a physician, a lady of fashion, and a prime minister, with equal confidence; accepting luxury or destitution, palace or prison, with equal philosophy. The narrative runs on, with excursions and interpolated histories, and the thread of the story is as inconsequential as that of a tale of the 'Arabian Nights.' The charm of the work is its absolute truth to human nature, and its boundless humor and satire. These qualities have made it a classic. Dr. Sangrado, the quack physician to whom Gil Blas apprenticed himself, the Archbishop of Granada, with other of the personages of these adventures, have been accepted as universal types. Le Sage was a Frenchman, who never saw Spain; but through his familiarity with its literature he produced a work so essentially Spanish in its tone and spirit as to provoke long controversy as to its originality. Padre Isla, who translated 'Gil Blas,' declares on his title-page that the tale was "stolen from the Spanish, and now restored to its country and native language." 'Gil Blas' is Le Sage's greatest and most brilliant work. Its writing occupied twenty years of his literary prime; the first two volumes appearing in 1715, and the last in 1735. It has been translated into many languages, the earliest in English; the one which has remained the standard being by Tobias Smollett.

GINX'S BABY, by John Edward Jenkins, is a satire on the English poor-laws and the administration of sectarian charitable associations. Ginx, a navvy, earning twenty shillings a week, with a wife and twelve children living in two rooms of a crowded tenement in a squalid district of London, despairs of finding enough to feed another mouth, and declares he will drown the thirteenth when it arrives. He is swerved from his purpose by the offer of the "Sisters of Misery" to take charge of the infant, and Ginx's baby becomes an inmate of a Catholic Home. The child is "rescued" from this Home through the efforts of a Protestant society; this society, through dissensions and lack of funds, turns him over to the parish; parochial law requires his return to the parents: and Ginx finally leaves his baby, then grown to boyhood, on the steps of the Reform Club, and flies the country. Ginx's baby grows up a thief, and ends his life by jumping off Vauxhall bridge, at the spot where his father set out to drown him on the day of his birth. 'Ginx's Baby' was published anonymously in London in 1871, speedily ran through many editions, was republished in the United States, and excited warm controversy in the press and even in Parliament. It was followed by satires on other phases of social economy, Mr. Jenkins preserving his anonymity for some time under the signature of "The Author of Ginx's Baby"; but none of the other works of this author attained such a vogue or exerted such an undoubted influence upon the direction of social reforms.

GIOCONDA, LA, a drama, by Gabriele d'Annunzio (1898). The gifted young sculptor, Lucio Settala, is hopelessly divided in his allegiance between his wife Silvia and his model Gioconda, the inspiration of his art. In despair he has tried to commit suicide. The tender devotion of his wife has saved his life, and he pledges his love to her anew. With convalescence thoughts of his art return, and he confesses to his friend Cosimo that he knows Gioconda is waiting for him every day in the studio. His wife is a "soul of inestimable price" before whom he kneels and worships, but he is not a "sculptor of souls" and the future of his art is inseparable from the fascinating Gioconda. Gioconda has refused to give up the key of the studio to any one except Lucio. Silvia decides to confront the model herself and defends her newly won happiness. Gioconda tells her that she is the intruder in the studio where household affections and domestic virtue have no sanctuary. Silvia, dismayed by the assurance of her rival, tells the falsehood that Lucio has sent her to say that he loves Gioconda no longer. Gioconda believing that she is turned out, rushes in anger to destroy the statue. The wife saves his masterpiece at the cost of her beautiful hands. Her sacrifice is in vain, as the vacillating Lucio enters the studio to meet Gioconda, and ultimately goes away with her. In the last act the maimed Silvia is alone at the shore with her child. The little Beata offers her mother flowers, and is bewildered and frightened because she cannot take them without hands.

GIRL IN THE CARPATHIANS, A, by Menie Muriel Dowie (Mrs. Henry Norman, now Mrs. E. A. Fitzgerald) (1891). Mrs. Norman's volume has been called "the very carpet-baggery of art." She herself says that her book "is a series of impressions, drawing any interest or value it may possess from two sources: First, the accuracy of reporting those impressions, which springs from rough-shod honesty of intention; second, the color of the individual medium through which these have been seen — this second interesting only to those who happen to like that color." It is distinctly not a book of travel, as the author covered at the outside only eighty miles. Arrayed in a tweed suit, skirt, coat, and knickerbockers, and possessing three shirts, she sets out for the Carpathians, spending a few weeks in one primitive town and then going to another; and in a free, careless, independent manner coming into close contact with Ruthenian peasant and native Jew, and learning to know the real people as tourists never do. Dirt and unpalatable food do not disturb her to the extent of spoiling her enjoyment or her humorous appreciation of what goes on around her. She chats intelligently about the salient characteristics of the people, — how they live, eat, drink, work, play, and dispense with washing themselves; about their dwellings, their inquisitiveness, their picturesque dress, the delights of Polish cookery, the skinny little donkeys and her rides upon them, and the glorious scenery. Miss Dowie was a young English girl who disregarded such conventions as she saw no reason to respect; and this book tells the story — quite in her own way — of her roamings and her thoughts during the summer. It is a story which has captivated many readers by its thoroughly charming manner.

GLADSTONE, WILLIAM EWART, by Viscount John Morley (1903) is the standard biography of the most conspicuous figure in English politics during the Victorian era. Based on a vast accumulation of original papers collected at Gladstone's residence at Hawarden, and upon thousands of others lent by their owners, the work is not the product of party feeling, but a great critic's estimate of a marvelously many-sided mind. Lord Morley traces the formative influences of Gladstone's boyhood at Liverpool and the school and university days at Eton and Oxford the first adventures in politics, when, to use Macaulay's phrase, he was the rising hope of the stern, unbending Tories, and defended the slave trade, protection and other ways of political thinking which he was afterwards to reject. As the story unfolds, Gladstone is seen to have become the great protagonist of liberty. As orator he was a mighty influence, whether in the House of Commons in his Titanic conflicts with Disraeli, on the platform when he swayed great meetings, or as the spokesman when ceremonial addresses had to be delivered. The secret of his power over his hearers was that before whatever audience he appeared, he always gave of his best whether his listeners were University men, members of Parliament, business leaders, or villagers and artisans. His opponent wrote him down as a timeserver and an opportunist, but as Lord Morley well points out, in every one of his greatest achievements he expressly formed or tried to create and mould the public opinion which in the long run was to give him his mandate. This was true of his Balkan policy, his Irish Land and Home Rule Acts, of his wish to submit the Alabama claims to arbitration, above all of his financial policy and his passion for public economy, precisely the sphere in which he was most strenuous, and, owing to the spendthrift habits of democracy, least likely to win popularity. Politics, however, was only one of many interests which were needed to absorb Gladstone's prodigious energy. Religion was the master passion, and the unfailing inspiration of his life. With all his might he resisted the cynical doctrine that morality has no place in international relations, or in the public affairs of nations. In his private life none will deny that he strove to live up to the spirit of his own dictum. "Be inspired with the belief that life is a great and noble calling; not a mean and grovelling thing that we are to shuffle through as we can, but an elevated and lofty destiny."

GLASSE OF TIME IN THE FIRST AGE, THE, 'Divinely Handled by Thomas Peyton, of Lincolnes Inne, Gent. Seene and Allowed, London: Printed by Bernard Alsop, for Lawrence Chapman, and are to be Sold at his Shop over against Staple Inne, 1620,' runs the title-page of this account, in sonorous heroic couplets, of the fall of man and the progress of humanity down to the time of Noah. Peyton died soon after its completion, at the age of thirty-one; and there is no record of him outside of this work, which was not itself known till eighty years ago. A copy, bound in vellum, ornamented with gold, illustrated with curious cuts and quaintly printed, was found in a chest; and there is a copy in the British Museum. In 1860 an article on it appeared in the North American Review, pointing out that it appeared forty years before 'Paradise Lost,' but that the similarity of its plan was not disparaging to Milton, as it merely gave him certain suggestions, and had individual but inferior merit. It was reprinted in 1886.

GLEANINGS IN BUDDHA FIELDS, by Lafcadio Hearn (1897), the sub-title being 'Studies of Hand and Soul in the Far East.' Of its eleven chapters, two are travel sketches, describing trips to Kyoto and Osaka, with additions of much versatile information. Japanese art and folk-song are treated with affectionate care, while a discussion of certain phases of Shintoism and Buddhism unfolds them from within, the chapter on Nirvana showing deep reflection, and marvelous beauty of phrase. The story of 'The Rebirth of Katsugoro' is of unusual value and interest as belonging to the native literature of Japan. A translation of a series of documents dating back to the early part of the nineteenth century, it reflects the feudal Japan which is now passed away, and illustrates the "common ideas of the people concerning pre-existence and rebirth" Hearn's knowledge of, and sympathy with, his subject seem inexhaustible.

GLITTERING GATE, THE, by Lord Dunsany (1909). A one-act play staged in "The Lonely Place" before the "Gate of Heaven." Jim and Bill, ex-burglars, meet outside the golden door. Bill has just come from earth and is still hopeful. Jim has been hanged, and seems doomed forever to open bottles in search of something to quench his thirst, only to find the bottles are empty. A chorus of distant laughter mocks his efforts. Bill has brought his burglar's jimmy with him, and starts to work on the gate, talking to his companion of the joys of the heaven beyond, the old saints with their halos flickering, angels "thick as swallows along a cottage roof," orchards full of apples and cities of gold, and best of all a man's old mother who will be sure to have a dish of tripe and onions for her son. There is a noise of falling bolts, and the gates swing open revealing nothing but a vast night of stars. There is no heaven for Jim and Bill. The mocking laughter in the distance grows louder.

GODS ARE ATHIRST, THE ('Les Dieux ont Soif') by Anatole France (1912). A story of the French Revolution which pictures the extraordinary Paris of the Terror. The hero, a young artist, Evariste Gamelin, is a stern young idealist, a fanatical disciple of Robespierre, who is the dominating figure of the book. Evariste attends the nightly meetings of the Jacobin Club and absorbs the lofty abstractions and inquisitorial casuistry of his idol. He is made a member of the Revolutionary Tribune and becomes a veritable priest of the guillotine, ministering to the blood-thirsty gods. Marie Antoinette is tried and condemned before him and a procession of defeated generals, emigrés, and suspects are brought to the Tribunal from the over-flowing prisons. His office gradually makes a monster of him, and he votes constantly for death. It is his sacred mission to destroy the enemies of France, and to be accused is to be condemned. Evariste loves Elodie, daughter of a wealthy dealer in prints and engravings, who also undertakes fraudulent contracts for the army. She is not a typical daughter of the Revolution, which she secretly abhors, but she is fascinated by her gloomy lover, though his ideas terrify her. He sends an innocent aristocrat to the guillotine because he believes him to be Elodie's former lover and betrayer. With the downfall of Robespierre, Evariste is condemned to the guillotine to which he has sent countless others. He rides in the fatal cart, insulted by the same hostile crowd who so recently had jeered at the aristocrats. He dies without remorse, regretting only that he has betrayed the Republic by being "oversparing of blood." Elodie takes his best friend for her new lover in the last chapter. She throws the ring engraved with Marat's head which Evariste had given her into the fire, and makes her tryst with the new lover with the same password she had used for Evariste. Brotteau, a noble reduced to making jumping-jacks in an attic, but always a philosopher, is a contrast to the fanatical Evariste. He shares his room with an ex-monk, with whom he argues the existence of God. They are arrested, with a little girl from the street whom he has befriended, and he goes calmly to the guillotine reading his Lucretius to the last.

GOD'S FOOL, by Maarten Maartens (1892), a story of Dutch middle-class life, has for its central figure Elias Lossell, "God's Fool," a man accidentally deprived in childhood of his eyesight, and in part, of his reason. Of great physical beauty, gentle in disposition, religious in spirit, he lives a kind of sacred, shut-apart life, while surrounded by the stormy passions, the greedy hates and loves, the envyings and jealousies of those in full possession of their faculties. His father, a rich merchant, has made two marriages. Elias, the child of the first, inherited vast wealth from his mother. Hendryk and Hubert Lossell, sons of the second marriage, find on their father's death that Elias is the richest of the family, and the head of the firm in which his money is vested. Taking advantage of Elias's helplessness, his half-brothers get his property into their hands, although apparently with his consent; but their greed brings upon them their own destruction. The most pleasing character of the book is the fool himself. His pure, noble, childlike nature perfumes the heavy worldly atmosphere that surrounds him; and he comes in as a kind of gracious interlude between the dramatic but sordid incidents of the plot. The story is well conceived, if slightly improbable; and like Maartens's other books, is told with vigor and grace.

GOETHE, AUTOBIOGRAPHY OF, with a sub-title, 'Truth and Poetry (Dichtung und Wahrheit) from My Own Life,' has appeared in various forms since its first publication (3 pts. 1811–14). To the translation of John Oxenford is subjoined Goethe's 'Annals,' or 'Day and Year Papers' (1749–1822), which supplement the 'Autobiography.' The 'Autobiography' begins with the author's birth, ends some time after his important Italian journey in 1786, and belongs in construction to the didactic period of his career, not having been completed as late as 1816. Indeed, it ends quite abruptly, as though the purpose to add the later chapters of his life had been formed but never realized. To characterize this human document would be to characterize Goethe, for into it he has poured his whole mind at its earliest and at its ripest. From his wealth of material he selects with boldness and insight. Not only does he record his estimates of men and places, but he lets the reader into the inner places of his being, disclosing his friendships, his methods of creation, and the operations of his regal mind. Poet, thinker, critic, and original observer — all appear.

Many important personages are introduced, and such matters are discussed as usually occupy the autobiographer. It is, however, because it reveals Goethe the man as do none of his other works, that the book is so profoundly interesting.

GOETHE, THE LIFE OF, by George Henry Lewes (1864). The first important biography in English of the greatest of German writers, this book still holds its place in the front rank of biographical literature. The volume is a large one, and the detail is infinitely minute, beginning with the ancestry of the poet, and ending with his death in 1832. His precocity, the school-life and college-life of the beautiful youth, his welcome in society, his flirtations, the bohemian years that seemed prodigally wasted, yet that were to bear rich intellectual fruit when the wild nature should have sobered to its tasks, his friendships, his travels, his love-affairs, his theories of life, his scientific investigations, his dramatic studies, criticisms, and productions, his momentary absorption in educational problems, his official distinctions, his intellectual dictatorship, his ever-recurring sentimental experiences, — all the changing phases of that many-sided life are made to pass before the reader with extraordinary vividness. Like almost all biographers of imagination and strong feeling, Mr. Lewes, who means to maintain a strict impartiality, becomes an advocate. He presents Goethe's wonderful mentality without exaggeration. He does no more than justice to the personal charm which seems to have been altogether irresistible. But it is in spite of his biographer's admissions, rather than because of them, that Goethe appears in his pages a man from whose vital machinery the heart was omitted. Perfect taste he had, exquisite sentiment, great appreciation, a certain power of approbation that assumed the form of affection, but no love, — such the Goethe whom his admiring disciple paints. The book presents the sentimental German society of the late eighteenth century with entire understanding, and is very rich in memorabilia of many sorts.

GOLD BUG, THE, a short story by Edgar Allan Poe, first published in The Dollar Newspaper, Philadelphia, June 21–28, 1843, and then in a volume of Poe's Tales in 1845. The theme is the discovery of buried treasure through the solution of a cryptogram. William Legrand, an impoverished Southern gentleman, is living with a negro servant, Jupiter, on Sullivan's Island, a low, sandy strip of land near Charleston, South Carolina. During a walk on the beach of the mainland he captures a curious beetle of the scarab family, distinguished by its brilliant golden color, its weight, and its markings, which somewhat resemble a death's-head. When the insect bites its captor and forces him to let it drop, the negro recovers it, protecting his hand by a piece of parchment which he happens to notice sticking out of the sand near the remnants of an old wrecked ship's long-boat. This parchment, having been used by Legrand to sketch for a friend the outline of the gold-bug, is accidentally held by the friend close to a fire. The heat brings out on the side opposite to the sketch, a drawing of a death's-head made in chemicals which become visible when warmed. Suspecting that the parchment may be a pirate's directions for the recovery of buried treasure Legrand re-examines it in private and succeeds in revealing the figure of a kid (indicating Captain Kidd) and a series of numbers and signs forming a message in cypher. This cypher he ingeniously solves and by the aid of the landmarks obscurely hinted at in the message discovers the location indicated on a high plateau some miles from the coast. His friend and the servant Jupiter are now enlisted in the enterprise of finding and removing the treasure. Legrand's eccentricity of manner, his present high excitement, and his deliberate mystification of his assistants fill them with concern for his sanity, especially when he pretends that the gold-bug is possessed of magical powers. However, they obey his directions, which though apparently irrational, are really in accordance with the pirate's message. Jupiter climbs an immense tulip-tree, finds a skull on one of the branches, and drops the gold-bug, suspended on a string, through the eye to the ground. A line drawn from the tree to this point and produced fifty feet, gives the locality of the treasure. This is at length dug up, not before the negro's dropping the bug through the wrong eye has led to an error in his master's calculations and to the necessity of digging another pit. Gold coins and jewels to the value of a million and a half dollars are found in a chest, beside the skeletons of the pirate's helpers in the concealment. With the money, Legrand restores his fortunes. The story is artfully related, the reader being at first as mystified as Legrand's friend as to the meaning of his operations and being gradually enlightened as the story proceeds. Poe's gift of exhibiting the solution of a mystery by the power of ratiocination is nowhere more effectively illustrated. The gold-bug, though not an essential element in the narrative, adds a touch of picturesqueness to several of the scenes and creates a suggestion of an occult and fatalistic connection between the events leading to the recovery of the treasure.

GOLDEN ASS, by Apuleius. A collection of stories divided into eleven books, and written in Carthage, not later than 197 A. D. It is usually described as an imitation of 'The Ass' of Lucian; the author himself tells us that it is a "tissue woven out of the tales of Miletus"; but probably both works are based on the same earlier originals. The plot is of the thinnest. A young man sees an old sorceress transform herself into a bird after drinking a philter. He wishes to undergo a similar metamorphosis, but mistakes the vial and is turned into an ass. To become a man again, he must eat a certain species of roses, and the pilgrimage of the donkey in search of them is the author's excuse for stringing together a number of romantic episodes and stories: stories of robbers, such as 'The Brigand for Love,' where a youth becomes a bandit to deliver his betrothed; 'The Three Brothers,' where the three sons of a wealthy peasant are massacred by a ferocious squire and his servants; and 'The Bear of Platæa,' where a heroic robber lets dogs devour him in the bearskin in which he has hidden himself. Then come ghost stories: 'The Spectre,' where the phantom of a girl penetrates in full noonday into a miller's yard, and carries off the miller to a room where he hangs himself; 'Telephron,' where a poor man falls asleep, and supposes himself to awaken dead; 'The Three Goat-Skins,' where the witch Pamphile inadvertently throws some goats' hair into her crucible, instead of the red hair of her fat Bœotian lover, thus bringing back to life in place of him the goats to whom the hairs belonged. But the prettiest and most finely chiseled of these tales are those that paint domestic life: 'The Sandals,' where a gallant devises a very ingenious stratagem to get out of an unpleasant predicament and regain possession of his sandals, forgotten one night at the house of a decurion; and several of the same kind. Many others are real dramas of village life. The most famous of all is 'The Loves of Psyche.' It occupies two entire books, and has inspired poets, painters, and sculptors, in all ages and countries; though perhaps the author would have been rather astonished to learn that the moderns had discovered in the sufferings of his heroine a profound metaphysical allegory, symbolizing the tortures of the soul in its pursuit of the ideal. Apuleius excels every other ancient writer in catching the changing aspects of nature and of human comedy; and with all his fantastic imaginative power, he is as realistic as Zola, and sometimes as offensive. He describes, for instance, the agony of a broken-down horse tortured by swarms of ants, with the same precision that he uses to relate the gayety of a rustic breakfast, or a battle between wolves and dogs. On the other hand, he puts in no claim to be a moralist, and is much more concerned about the exteriors of his characters than about their souls.

GOLDEN BOUGH, THE, a Study in Magic and Religion, by J. G. Frazer (2 vols. 1890. 3d ed. 12 vols. 1911–15). The original edition was an epoch-making work in folk-lore. In its enlarged and completed form, the book is a treasury of primitive customs and beliefs, epitomizing the available information in eminently readable form. The priest of Nemi is the central figure of the mystery of the mythology of vegetation, the death and resurrection of the corn and wine. In the sacred grove of Diana on the woodland lake of Nemi, the priest or king of the wood guarded the oak of the divinity. Servius, four hundred years after Virgil, commenting on the "golden bough" which admitted Æneas to the underworld, writes that the priest of Nemi must be a fugitive slave, that he must gain his office by slaying his predecessor, his divinity, by plucking a bough from the sacred tree in which the god is animate. The successor must in his turn be slain in full vigor of life to enact the mystery play by which the return of spring is not only illustrated but enforced. The rite cannot be explained by the ideas and beliefs of classical antiquity, and Dr. Frazer traces its origin to the customs of the primitive life it has survived. Religion always involves an appeal to a god, Dr. Frazer contends. Magic, opposed to religion, tries to control nature by would-be science based on the association of ideas by similarity or contact. "Homeopathic magic commits the mistake of assuming that things which resemble each other are the same. Contagious magic commits the mistake of assuming that things which have once been in contact with each other are always in contact." The tales of primitive superstition with which he illustrates his theories of the origin of kings and priests are the entire ancient mythology, the worship of trees, sacred bonfires, taboo, initiation, ritual of the scapegoat, totems, etc. In concluding volumes the Norse god, Baldur the Beautiful, represents the pantheon of dying and reviving gods symbolic of the return of spring. The mistletoe growing on the oak is the "golden bough" over which Baldur like Diana's priest kept watch and ward. Volume 12 is a detailed subject index and bibliography.

GOLDEN BOWL, THE, by Henry James (1905). An impoverished Italian prince marries Maggie Verver, the daughter of an American millionaire. The prince and princess, her father and her little son, the "principino," have an ideally happy life together in their English home, until the advent of Charlotte Stant, an American girl of brilliant social qualities, friend of Maggie's schooldays. Charlotte and the prince were once lovers and would have married but for their poverty. The prince has never told his wife of their intimacy. He considers Charlotte's visit a suitable time to retire with Maggie to Italy. Charlotte marries the millionaire, Mr. Verver, and is thus brought into permanent relations with the prince. An exquisite affection exists between Maggie and her father. With the American innocence and artlessness, which Mr. James has depicted often since the days of Daisy Miller, father and daughter give so many hours to each other that the other two meet constantly. Maggie gradually discovers the relations between her husband and her father's wife; instead of making a fuss she quietly gives herself to the task of shielding her father from the knowledge of it, and winning her husband's love, "which she vows must be as complete and perfect as the original crystal of the broken bowl" that property of the story which takes a unique part in the development of the plot. Her father had married Charlotte in devotion to his daughter, to free her from the thought that she had left him lonely. His love discovers what she tries to conceal, and he solves the situation by taking Charlotte back to America never to return. In the first half of the book we see the problem as reflected in the consciousness of the prince; in the second half, Maggie is the refracting medium for the author and reader. But for two minor characters, friends of the family, a Mrs. Assingham and her husband, and their knowledge and understanding, it would be difficult for the reader to follow the turn of affairs, since everyone is trying to conceal from everyone else knowledge of what is known. At the end of the story the princess has already won her prince for her own in truly royal conquest of fineness of conduct and greatness of love.

GOLDEN BUTTERFLY, THE, by Walter Besant and James Rice. The main events of this lively and amusing story occur at London in 1875. The Butterfly is Gilead P. Beck's talisman. With a burdensome revenue from oil-wells he arrives in London, where he meets Dunquerque, who has saved his life in California, and Colquhoun, the hero of a love entanglement with Victoria, now wife of Cassilis. Colquhoun succeeds to the guardianship of Phillis Fleming, brought up by Abraham Dyson after high eccentric methods. Dyson leaves money for educating other girls in a similar way; but defeats his own end by not teaching Phillis how to read, so that she innocently destroys an important paper and renders the will inoperative. While living with Agatha, Colquhoun's cousin, Phillis becomes intimate with Dunquerque in an unconventional, idyllic fashion. Victoria is led to think Colquhoun wants to marry Phillis, and in a jealous fit divulges the secret of a Scotch marriage between him and herself. The disclosure throws Cassilis into partial paralysis; he fails to sell certain stocks at the right moment, and loses all, as do Phillis, Colquhoun, and Beck whose fortunes he had invested. The Butterfly mysteriously falls apart; but is repaired and presented to Phillis, who is married to Dunquerque; having now discovered, in Dyson's words, that "the coping-stone of every woman's education is love."

GOLDEN CHERSONESE, THE, by Isabella Bird Bishop (1883), is a record of travel and adventure in the Malay peninsula. The author, a veteran traveler, has journeyed so widely as to have gained that sweep of view which lends charm and accuracy to comparison. An excellent observer, she groups her effects, giving great variety to her descriptions of tropical scenery, — which so often appears monotonous, — and adding a touch of humor which makes her frank notes interesting. If the style is sometimes redundant, the narrative is brimful of incident and adventure bravely encountered by an indefatigable spirit and proceeds with a natural and cheery grace.

GOLDEN DOG, THE ('Le Chien d'Or') by William Kirby, was published in 1877, and is a story of life in Quebec about 1748, at the time that war was raging between Old England and New France, as Canada was then called. The Chien d'Or is the name of the large trading-house of the Bourgeois Philibert, a man much beloved by the people, and one of the leaders of the "Honnêtes Gens," the party opposed to the corrupt government. This house was a formidable rival of the Grand Company, owned by the wealthy and dishonest government officers under the Intendant, François Bigot; who, clever but unscrupulous and unprincipled, spends his time carousing with his boon companions. Into this dissolute company he draws Le Gardeur de Repentigny, handsome and generous but easily entrapped. The author gives a vivid description of the corrupt and dissolute viceregal court of Louis XV. in New France.

GOLDEN FLEECE, see ARGONAUTICA.

GOLDEN TREASURY, THE, OF SONGS AND LYRICS, by Francis Turner Palgrave. A volume attempting to bring together all the best lyrics in the language, by singers not living. In his selection Mr. Palgrave was aided by the taste and judgment of Tennyson as to the period between 1520 and 1850. The book has four divisions, informally designated as the books of Shakespeare, Milton, Gray, and Wordsworth, though hardly less space is given to Herrick or Shelley. The preface and notes are of great value.

The Second Series of 'The Golden Treasury' appeared in 1897, soon after Mr. Palgrave's death. Perfection of form, one of the main tests of the first volume' holds a subordinate place in the second; and here the commonplace has encroached upon the simple. The chief value of this collection lies in its serving as a kind of shrine for masterpieces like Arnold's 'Scholar Gipsy,' Patmore's 'The Toys,' the 'Christmas Hymn' of Alfred Domett, and 'The Crimson Thread' of F. H. Doyle.

GOLDMAKERS' VILLAGE, THE or, A HISTORY OF THE MANNER IN WHICH TWO AND THIRTY MEN SOLD THEMSELVES TO THE DEVIL ('Das Goldmacher-Dorf') by Johann Heinrich Zschokke (1817). Like the other works of Zschokke, this is renowned for its graphic description of natural scenery, its precise delineation of society and exact portraiture of the class of which it treats, as well as for its moral, philanthropic, and beneficial tendency. Its English equivalent may be found in the charming tales of Mary Howitt. Oswald, the Swiss soldier, "returning from the wars," finds his native village of Goldenthal sunk into the depths of misery and degradation; its inhabitants lazy, shiftless, hampered with debt, frequenters of public houses, lost to all sense of moral responsibility. He devotes himself to the amelioration of their condition; in which, by the help of the lovely Elizabeth, the miller's daughter and then his wife, he is successful: so developing the various sources of comfort and improvement; so exemplifying by practical illustration the multiplied methods by which a patriot of philanthropy may serve the best interests of his fellow-citizens and country, that in the end he is rewarded by seeing the home of his youth on a par with the best organized, best conducted, and best credited villages of the community, and the "Goldenthalers," from being a synonym to their neighbors for all that is worthless, at length known and honored as the "Goldmakers," for the thrift which changes everything it touches into precious metal. Although the precise locality of the "Goldmakers' Village" cannot be found, yet it is to be feared that many an obscure locality can be discovered where, in many points, the picture can be matched, and where the benevolent enterprise of another Oswald is equally necessary.

GOOD-BYE, SWEETHEART, by Miss Rhoda Broughton (1872) is a bright, amusing love story in three parts, — 'Morning,' 'Noon,' and 'Night,' — told in the third person by the author, and in the first by Jemima Herrick, the heroine's plain elder sister. In Part i. the scene is laid in Brittany, where Jemima and Lenore are leading a bohemian life. Lenore, who is young and beautiful, finds an admirer in Frederick West; but she prefers his friend Paul Le Mesurier. A spoilt child, she is accustomed to have her own way; and now that she is in love for the first time, she determines to win Paul. He is an ugly man with a bad temper, eighteen years her senior, but the only person who can conquer her willfulness. Against his better judgment he finally yields to her attractions, and the day before he returns to England they become engaged.

In Part ii. the scene is laid in England, where, after an absence of six months, Paul and Lenore come together again in a country-house. He is jealous of Charles Scrope, a handsome youth, who has followed Lenore to England; and at a ball where Paul exacts too much, the lovers quarrel, and Paul, mad with jealousy, leaves Lenore forever. In her desperation she promises to marry Scrope, but on the day of the wedding she finds that she cannot bring herself to become his wife.

In Part iii. Lenore goes to Switzerland with her sister, to recover her health, meets Paul accidentally, is more in love with him than ever, but learns that he is engaged to his cousin. From this time she grows rapidly worse; Scrope devotes himself to her comfort, but nothing can save her. Her last desire is to see Paul once more; Scrope travels night and day to bring him, but arrives on Paul's wedding day, and returns alone to find Lenore dead.

The change that love brings in Lenore, the effect Paul has on her intense, passionate nature, and the clashing of his will against hers, make interesting character studies.

GOOD THOUGHTS IN BAD TIMES, by Thomas Fuller (1645) is the first of a trio of volumes whose titles were inspired by the troublous days of Charles and Cromwell, when Fuller was an ardent loyalist. 'Good Thoughts in Worse Times' (1649), and — after the restoration of Charles II. — 'Mixed Contemplations in Better Times,' followed, completing the trilogy. The present volume, like its two successors, is packed with wise and pithy aphorisms, often humorous, but never trivial; and is pervaded by that "sound, shrewd good sense, and freedom of intellect," which Coleridge found there. A moralist, rather than an exponent of spiritual religion, the cavalier chaplain devotes more attention to a well-fed philosophy than to the claims of the soul. Though read to-day mainly by students of the author's style and times, this sententious volume has attractions for all lovers of quaint and pleasing English.

GORDON KEITH, by Thomas Nelson Page (1903). This is a story of American life, the first scenes of which are laid in the South soon after the Civil War. Gordon Keith is the son of General Keith, an old-time gentleman, whose large fortune has been swept away during the war. The family estate, "Elphinestone," which has been owned by the Keiths for generations, has to be sold and passes into the hands of a rich New Yorker named Aaron Wickersham, whose son, a wicked and unprincipled young fellow, plays a prominent part in the story. Gordon, with the help of a friend, Norman Wentworth, the son of a rich New York banker, and some assistance from his neighbor, Squire Rawson, is enabled to go to college and acquires the education he has so much desired. He teaches a country school and while so doing meets a rich and beautiful city girl named Alice Yorke, who captures his heart. Her ambitious mother discourages his suit, but he vows that some day he will be rich and influential and with this goal in view works with tireless energy. Rich mining interests become located at "Elphinestone" and upon Squire Rawson's land, and Wickersham endeavors to secure the latter property, but is balked in his desire. Rawson puts Keith in control of his interests and in course of time he becomes a very rich man. His business takes him to the city and he again sees Alice Yorke, but before he has attained his success, she marries a rich and elderly man named Lancaster. He subsequently dies, leaving Alice a rich and fascinating widow and Keith is divided between the admiration he feels for her and the warm interest he feels in Lois Huntington, a charming young girl whom he has known from childhood. In the end he marries Lois after having repaired some of the wrongs that Wickersham has caused.

GORKY, MAXIM, AUTOBIOGRAPHY, see **MY CHILDHOOD: IN THE WORLD.**

GOTHIC ARCHITECTURE, AN INTRODUCTION TO THE STUDY OF, by J. H. Parker (1849). The gradual evolution of architecture from the Roman period to the Renaissance and Jacobean Gothic is carefully traced in this handy little volume. To the interval between the Roman period and the end of the tenth century belong basilicas, apses, and crypts. The new building era introduced by the eleventh century brought many churches and some of the early towers. In the early Norman period many monasteries were founded and some churches begun under William I and II. of England were completed under Henry I. Between 1120 and 1170 a large number of richly but crudely decorated Norman Churches were built. From 1175–1200 a more chaste and delicate style succeeded. The early English style of the years between 1189 and 1272 may be studied in the great cathedrals of Canterbury, Lincoln, Winchester, Ely, Salisbury, Westminster, York. The decorated style of the reigns of the first three Edwards (1272–1377) gradually gave place to the perpendicular style which flourished between 1377–1547. Examples of the Renaissance and Jacobean Gothic are the Elizabethan Houses, the Colleges and Chapels in Oxford, Lambeth Palace and the Middle Temple Hall. A concluding chapter discusses briefly the styles of France, Italy, Lombardy, Spain, Flanders, and Germany, and a glossarial index explains the chief technical terms for the benefit of beginners in the study of architecture.

GOVERNMENT IN SWITZERLAND, by J. M. Vincent (1900). The aim of the writer is to describe in outline the methods of government, federal, cantonal, municipal, in a country which might well be called the political laboratory of Europe. He discusses the remote origins of the commonwealth, the cantonal executive and judiciary, education, finance, and public service in the cantons, and the accepted ideas of community and citizenship. The second part of the book is devoted to the federal executive and judiciary, the army, finance, international relations, the respective spheres of the canton and federation, direct legislation, the nationalization of railways and industries. The whole evolution of the Swiss Republic has been a struggle to secure and maintain popular rights. "As a crown to the whole edifice of popular rights," says Mr. Vincent, "the confederation guarantees to all citizens, not only the liberties and privileges contained in the federal constitution, but also those included in the laws of the cantons." Useful appendices include the text of the first constitution of 1291 and of the latest ot 1874.

GOVERNMENTS AND PARTIES IN CONTINENTAL EUROPE, by A. L. Lowell (1896). This work, which has already become a classic, aims to supply the need of a thorough examination into the actual working of modern political institutions and the relation between the development of parties and the mechanism of government "The treatment of each country begins with a description of its chief institutions, or political organization; this is followed by a sketch of its recent history, in order to show how the parties actually work; and, finally, an attempt is made to find the causes of the condition of party life. The investigation is limited to the principal countries where a division into two great parties does not prevail, and where there usually exists in its place a division into a number of more or less sharply defined political groups. This department of the subject seemed to separate itself naturally from the rest, and was selected mainly because it had been far less studied than the growth and influence of the by-party system that prevails generally in Anglo-Saxon countries." The countries discussed are France, Italy, Germany (with separate treatment of its component states), Austria-Hungary, and Switzerland; and the constitutions of all those which have a written constitution are appended in the tongue of the original text.

GRACE ABOUNDING TO THE CHIEF OF SINNERS, an autobiographical narrative by John Bunyan, written in Bedford Jail and first published in 1666. For the benefit of fellow-Christians similarly tempted Bunyan here sets forth with great plainness, vividness, and sincerity the spiritual experiences which preceded and accompanied his conversion. He relates his humble birth and poor education, his early dread of Hell, his subsequent carelessness about religion, and the wickedness (no doubt exaggerated by Bunyan) of his youthful life. Marriage with a serious-minded woman led him to attend church and respect the external forms of religion; a sermon on Sabbath-breaking and a woman's rebuke of his swearing induced him to give up these and other practices such as dancing and bell-ringing, to study the Bible, and to lead a moral life. He was now inclined to be self-satisfied; but through the instruction of some poor women of Bedford he came for the first time to a conviction of sin, the impossibility of salvation through his own righteousness, and the necessity of a new birth. These convictions were strengthened by the influence of John Gifford, a converted royalist officer, now a Baptist minister at Bedford. A long period followed in which Bunyan sought for assurance of salvation. Believing firmly that suggestions, both divine and diabolical might enter his mind in the form of recollected texts or wandering thoughts, he records minutely the alternations of hope and despair which exalted and dejected him by turns. Intellectual doubts assailed him. For about a year he was in morbid terror of committing the unpardonable sin. Later he was assailed by an irrational suggestion to blaspheme Christ by selling him. Convinced that he had committed this sin he was at length rescued from black despair by an intuition of pardon. Thus oscillating between fear and hope he at length found peace. The book is an absolutely sincere record of a genuine spiritual crisis in a nature of singular strength, emotional force, and religious insight.

GRAMMAR OF GREEK ART, A, by Percy Gardner (1905). Greek art has not been so widely studied in Northern Europe, as Greek literature, and yet, as Professor Gardner points out, the principles of each are exactly similar. "The Greek drama and the Greek temple are constructed on parallel lines, and equally embody the æsthetic ideas of the race." The priceless monuments of Greek art are the results of mental processes which express the outward working of the Greek spirit on the world around it. The chief characteristics of this artistic spirit are extreme simplicity, and an unswerving devotion to the ideal. The idealism of Greece was not individual but social, and belonged to the nation, the city, or the school rather than to this or that artist. All ages must owe a debt to Greece for the simple beauty, the sanity, the healthfulness of the ideal element which she introduced into art making it for the first time in history a true exponent of the human spirit. This general exposition of the aim of Greek art is followed by a detailed discussion of the characteristics of Greek architecture: the material, space, and coloring of sculpture; the space, balance and perspective of pottery; and the historic value of coins which of all Greek remains supply the most precise, reliable and varied material for a study of the facts of history.

GRAMMONT, MEMOIRS OF COUNT, by Anthony Hamilton. These memoirs were first given to the public in 1713, though the collection was begun as early as 1704. Hamilton was possessed of rare literary ability; and being brother-in-law to Count Grammont, was chosen by him to introduce him historically to the public. The author asserts that he acts merely as Grammont's secretary, and holds the pen at his dictation; but although this may be partially true, the ease and grace of the text prove it to be Hamilton's own work. The memoirs relate chiefly to the court life at the time of Charles II., and describe the intrigues and love affairs of the King and many of the courtiers. Grammont's adventures and experiences in love and war are minutely and graphically set forth, and he is depicted as a brilliant and fascinating gentleman. Hamilton says of him, that he was "the admiration of his age, and the delight of every country wherein he displayed his engaging wit, dispensed his generosity and munificence, or practiced his inconstancy." Among the many who figure prominently at this period in the profligate court of Charles II., are the Duke of York, the Duke of Buckingham, the Earl of St. Albans, George Hamilton, Lady Shrewsbury, the Countess of Castlemaine, the Duchess of Richmond, and the various ladies in waiting on the Queen. A French critic has observed that if any book were to be selected as affording the truest specimen of perfect French gayety, the 'Memoirs of Grammont' would be chosen in preference to all others. Macaulay speaks of their author as "the artist to whom we owe the most highly finished and vividly colored picture of the English court in the days when the English court was gayest."

GRANDEE, THE ('El Maestrante'), by Armando Palacio Valdés. This story of a Spanish town and its society, very picturesque in setting, but holding within it the tumult of passion and sin, was published in 1895. The scene is laid in quaint old Lancia (which is supposed to mean Oviedo), and reflects the life of thirty or forty years ago. The story opens with a bitter northeast wind and drenching rain; the clack of wooden shoes; the well-wrapped ladies (there were no carriages) struggling on toward the light and warmth of the palace of Quinones de Leon, the Grandee. The party has passed in; a man cowering beneath the storm creeps along the wall, reaches the palace, takes a bundle from under his cloak, places it near the door, and enters upon the gay scene. This is Luis Conde de Onis, who, engaged to Fernanda, has been enticed into an intrigue with Amalia, the young wife of the Grandee. It is their child that he has left at the door. The child is found when the guests are departing, and cared for by the old Grandee and his wife, the child's mother. Around these personages gathers a group of quaint characters: Don Christobal and his four marriageable daughters; the Señoritas de Mêre, kindly old spinsters who always help forward the marriage projects of the young people; and Paco Gomez, the rough jester. Fernanda, at a rural fête, discovers the infidelity of her fiancé, and madly throws herself away upon a boorish colonial planter, on whose death she returns to Lancia, and sets herself to win Luis from Amalia. The time of their wedding is at last announced; and Amalia, always reckless and desperate, revenges herself upon the helpless child of Luis, who has grown up a beautiful little girl, the pet of the household. With fiendish craft she tortures the child, under the plea of discipline. The gossips of the town have heard of what has been going on; and Luis, to save the child from her mother, promises Amalia to give up Fernanda. Luis appears at the house of Don Pedro, the Grandee, who although infirm, rises to attack him, and falls back dead. The father escapes with the little Josefina, and attempts to take her to his own home. The book closes in a pathetic scene, where the hapless child dies on the journey, in her father's arms.

GRANDISSIMES, THE, a story of Creole life, by George W. Cable. The Grandissimes, whose fortunes are here told, are one of the leading families in Louisiana. The head of the family is Honoré, a banker. He has an older half-brother, a quad-roon, of the same name, to whom the father leaves the bulk of his property. For a long time there has been a feud between the Grandissimes and the De Grapions, heightened, eighteen years before, by the killing in a duel by Honoré's uncle, Agricola, of Nancanou, the husband of Aurora, the last of the De Grapions. The cause of the duel is a quarrel over a gambling debt, which involves the loss of Nancanou's whole estate. At the opening of the story, Aurora, and her only daughter, Clotilde, are living in carefully concealed poverty in New Orleans, in an apartment belonging to the elder Honoré. Joseph Frowenfeld is a young German-American, who, without his knowledge, has been nursed during a fever by the Nancanous. The story develops the friendship of Honoré the younger with Frowenfeld, their falling in love with mother and daughter, and the course of their wooing. Other characters prominently connected with the story are the former domestic slave, Palmyre; Philosophe; Dr. Keene, a friend of Frowenfeld's; and Raoul Innerarity, the clerk of Frowenfeld and a typical young Creole. The final reconciliation of the hostile families and the marriage of the young people are brought about by the intervention of the fiery old Agricola. The book is of special interest in showing the attitude of the Creole population toward this country at the time of the cession of the Louisiana Purchase to the United States. Its character-study is close, and the sub-tropical atmosphere of place and people well indicated. It was Cable's first novel, being published in 1880.

GRANIA: THE STORY OF AN ISLAND, by the Hon. Emily Lawless (1892). 'Grania' has awakened much interest as the story of a little-understood section of Ireland, the Arran Isles. The aim of its author was to produce a picture true in atmosphere and in detail to all the characteristics of Irish life; an aim fully achieved. Grania is first introduced as a child of twelve, sailing in Galway Bay with her father, Con O'Malley, in his "hooker" or fishing smack. Grania, with her dark skin and hair, shows the strain of Spanish blood coming to her from her mother, a Joice, from the "Continent," as the people of Arran call Ireland itself. Six years later when Con is dead, Grania, a handsome, high-spirited girl, takes sole care of her invalid sister Honor. Humble though their two-roomed, square cabin is, it is the most comfortable in the neighborhood; and owning it and the bit of land around it, Grania is the richest girl of the place. She is industrious and independent, gets in her own crops of potatoes and oats, and fattens her calves and pigs for the market. Murdough Blake, handsome, vain, and a great braggart, accepts Grania's affection as a matter of course, almost feeling that he is doing her a favor when he condescends to borrow money from her. There is no plot, and the incidents serve to show the noble character of the girl. 'Grania' contains many glimpses of the folk-lore and customs of the Irish peasants, and the gloom and sordidness of their life as it was thirty years ago is vividly presented. Besides the chief figures of the story, there are several other interesting types: Shan Daly, the vagabond, and his neglected family; Peggy O'Dowd and other gossips; red-haired Teige O'Shaughnessey, who adores Grania; and Pete Durane and his father, with their old-school manners.

GRANT, U. S., PERSONAL MEMOIRS OF, (1885), has had an enormous sale. It is one of the most simple and effective of the many memoirs by soldiers. Tracing his own career from childhood, throughout his student days, his business life, the Mexican War, and his civilian period in the West, and outlining his conduct of the Federal forces during the Civil War, he closes the account with the end of the strife. Among the most valuable features of a work which takes first rank as a military autobiography, are the author's estimates of the leaders who had to do with the affairs of the armies and nation during the period of his own service. The descriptions of battles are technical, not sensational; the effort being to give the facts, not to paint pictures, while the outlines of campaigns and policies afford valuable historical material. Maps and indices add to the usefulness of the work.

GRAUSTARK, by George Barr McCutcheon, was published in 1901. It is entitled "the story of a love behind the throne" and is a thrilling tale of romance and adventure. The hero Grenfall Lorry, a rich and attractive young American, while traveling becomes acquainted with a charming foreigner who afterwards proves to be the Princess of Graustark visiting America incognito. The acquaintance is begun in a unique manner as Lorry and Miss Guggenslocker are accidentally left behind at a small way-station and only succeed in overtaking their train after a rough and perilous drive during which she clings to him for protection. This is the beginning of friendship which ripens into passionate love, and after the departure of the lovely foreigner from the country, Lorry finds life unendurable and starts in search of her. In his quest for Graustark he is joined by his friend Harry Anguish, whom he meets in Paris and who becomes the companion of his adventures. On the night of their arrival in Graustark they frustrate the plan of the wicked Prince Gabriel to kidnap the Princess, and while rescuing her, Lorry discovers to his astonishment that she is the object of his search. The Princess cannot accept Lorry's advances owing to her high position and also to the fact that she is about to consent to marry a neighboring Prince named Lorenze, in order to save her country from financial ruin. On the day of the betrothal, however, Lorenze is found murdered, and Lorry who has had an altercation with him is accused of the crime. Lorry is saved from the vengeance of the murdered man's father through the intervention of the Princess, who declares her love for him, and the real assassin, Gabriel, the rival Prince, is convicted by the cleverness of Anguish. Lorry, who has become a popular hero, is allowed to marry the Princess in spite of his lack of royal blood, and Harry Anguish marries the Countess Dagmar, the Princess's lady-in-waiting, which brings the story to a happy conclusion.

GRAY, THOMAS, see **LETTERS OF.**

GREAT DIVIDE, THE, by William Vaughn Moody (1906). In a lonely ranch in Arizona, Ruth Jordan, a New England girl of nineteen, is left to guard the premises. She is unconcerned at her loneliness, as she is full of the joy of life and of dreams of the ideal lover. Suddenly three men appear at the window. They are partly intoxicated and threaten her with violence. She offers to be the wife of one of them, Ghent, if he will save her. Ghent proposes to one of his companions "a square standup shoot, the best man taking her." Ghent wins and he and Ruth make their way to a mining claim beyond the Cordilleras. Here she wiles away many hours weaving Navajo blankets and secretly selling them so that she may not need to take money from Ghent. The mine prospers and Ghent plans to build a magnificent house, but when Ruth hears of it, she tells him scornfully that her price has risen. Her brother, and a former lover, Winthrop Newbury, whom she had rejected succeed in tracing her. After an interview with Ghent, in which she asks to be allowed to go free, she asks her brother Philip to take her home. Ghent reappears sometime after the birth of their child at her home, and the period of reflection has shown them both that they had each been faithful to the other, and that they had loved each other. "You have taken the good of our life and grown strong, I have taken the evil and grown weak, weak unto death. Teach me to live as you do," she says to him, and they are once more united to make a home for their child and for each other.

GREAT EXPECTATIONS, Dickens's tenth novel, was published in 1861, nine years before his death. As in 'David Copperfield,' the hero tells his own story from boyhood. Yet in several essential points 'Great Expectations' is markedly different from 'David Copperfield,' and from Dickens's other novels. Owing to the simplicity of the plot, and to the small number of characters, it possesses greater unity of design. These characters, each drawn with marvelous distinctness of outline, are subordinated throughout to the central personage "Pip," whose great expectations form the pivot of the narrative.

But the element that most clearly distinguishes this novel from the others is the subtle study of the development of character through the influence of environment and circumstance. In the career of Pip, a more careful and natural presentation of personality is made than is usual with Dickens.

He is a village boy who longs to be a "gentleman." His dreams of wealth and opportunity suddenly come true. He is supplied with money, and sent to London to be educated and to prepare for his new station in life. Later he discovers that his unknown benefactor is a convict to whom he had once rendered a service. The convict, returning against the law to England, is recaptured and dies in prison, his fortune being forfeited to the Crown. Pip's great expectations vanish into thin air.

The changes in Pip's character under these varying fortunes are most skillfully depicted. He presents himself first as a small boy in the house of his dearly loved brother-in-law, Joe Gargery, the village blacksmith; having no greater ambition than to be Joe's apprentice. After a visit to the house of a Miss Havisham, the nature of his aspirations is completely changed. Miss Havisham is one of the strangest of Dickens's creations. Jilted by her lover on her wedding night, she resolves to wear her bridal gown as long as she lives, and to keep her house, as it was when the blow fell upon her. The candles are always burning, the moldering banquet is always spread. In the midst of this desolation she is bringing up a beautiful little girl, Estella, as an instrument of revenge, teaching the child to use beauty and her grace to torture men. Estella's first victim is Pip. She laughs at his rustic appearance, makes him dissatisfied with Joe and the life at the forge. When he finds himself heir to a fortune, it is the thought of Estella's scorn that keeps him from returning Joe's honest and faithful love. As a "gentleman" he plays tricks with his conscience, seeking always to excuse his false pride and flimsy ideals of position. The convict's return, and the consequent revelation of the identity of his benefactor, humbles Pip. He realizes at last the dignity of labor, and the worth of noble character. He gains a new and manly serenity after years of hard work. Estella's pride has also been humbled and her character purified by her experiences. The book closes upon their mutual love.

"I took her hand in mine, and we went out of the ruined place; and as the morning mists had risen long ago, when I first left the forge, so the evening mists were rising now, and in all the broad expanse of tranquil light they showed to me, I saw the shadow of no parting from her."

'Great Expectations' is a delightful novel, rich in humor and free from false pathos. The character of Joe Gargery, simple, tender, quaintly humorous, would alone give imperishable value to the book. Scarcely less well-drawn are Pip's termagant sister, "Mrs. Joe"; the sweet and wholesome village girl, Biddy, who becomes Joe's second wife; Uncle Pumblechook, obsequious or insolent as the person he addresses is rich or poor; Pip's friend and chum in London, the dear boy Herbert Pocket; the convict with his wistful love of Pip; bright, imperious Estella: these are of the immortals in fiction.

GREAT GALEOTO, THE ('El gran Galeoto') by José Echegaray. This was the most successful of the author's plays, running through more than twenty editions. It was first acted in March, 1881, and so greatly admired that a popular subscription was at once started to buy some work of art to remind the writer of his triumph. In its printed form it is dedicated to "everybody," — another name for the subject of the play. Dante tells us in his story of Paolo and Francesca that "'Galeoto' was the book they read; that day they read no more!" Galeoto was the messenger between Launcelot and Queen Guinevere; and in all loves the *third* may be truthfully nicknamed "Galeoto." Ernest, a talented youth, is the secretary and adopted son of Julian and his wife Teodora, many years younger than himself. Ernest looks up to her as a mother; but gossip arises, he overhears Nebreda calumniate Teodora, challenges him to fight, and leaves Julian's house. Julian, a noble character, refuses to heed the charges against his wife and adopted son, but is at last made suspicious. Teodora visits Ernest, and implores him not to fight, as it will give color to the rumors. Julian meantime is wounded by Nebreda, and taken to Ernest's room, where he finds his wife. Ernest rushes out, kills Nebreda, and returns to find Julian dying, in the belief that his wife is guilty. The plays ends with Ernest's cry: "This woman is mine. The world has so desired it, and its decision I accept. It has driven her to my arms. You cast her forth. We obey you. But should any ask you who was the famous intermediary in this business, say: 'Ourselves, all unawares, and with us the stupid chatter of busybodies.'"

GREAT SHADOW, THE, by Sir A. Conan Doyle (1892). When Jack Calder, of West Inch near Edinburgh, is eighteen years old, his orphan cousin, Edie, comes to make her home with his family. As a child she has been a strange, wild girl with captivating ways. Now, more beautiful, her conquest of the boy is a matter of days only, and they are engaged to be married. At this moment Jack's friend, Jim Horscroft, appears upon the scene, and young Calder finds himself jilted. But now, — shortly after the battle of Leipsic, — while Horscroft is at Edinburgh working for his doctor's degree, a Frenchman who calls himself De Lapp appears. A man of stern and moody manners, he has a fascinating personality, thanks to his mysterious past. Edie spends long hours listening to his tales of war and adventure in foreign lands. In short, Jim comes back to find his fiancée fled with the French officer, who is hastening to join the Emperor, now returned from Elba.

In the thick of the fight at Waterloo, Horscroft and his successful rival go down in a mutual death-lock; and Jack, hurrying on with the Allies to Paris, again sees Edie. She talks to him a moment in her old familiar way, and then leaves him. A month after, he learns that she has married a certain Count de Breton. The admirable strength and restraint of this story, its faithful study of character, and its constant suggestion of the terror and apprehension that for a score of years enveloped Europe like a black atmosphere, give 'The Great Shadow' a first place among Conan Doyle's stories.

GREAT TRADITION, THE, by Katharine Fullerton Gerould (1915). Clever analysis of situations in married life involving conflict with tradition or habit. The story which gives the book its title deals with the sacrifice of a woman's dream of happiness with another man than her unspeakable husband, when she learns that her daughter has eloped with a married man, and realizes that the right kind of mother, socially, will be needed to give her the chance to return sometime to society. In another story "Pearls" a poverty stricken artist receives a reward of fifteen thousand dollars for finding a valuable string of pearls. In sudden irresponsibility he deserts his wife and daughter to voyage in tropical seas. 'The Dominant Strain' tells a story which leads up to the moment when a financier who has been unable to forgive his son for a foolish marriage, recognizes his grandson in one of his own endowed orphan asylums. 'Wesendonck' depicts the sordid poverty of a young college professor, whose opportunity to entertain a distinguished colleague is not met by his wife; she finds out too late to help her husband that it is sometimes necessary to endure the intolerable. In 'The Weaker Vessel' a husband gives up his hope of a free happy life because his wife, who cares nothing for him, refuses to be deserted.

GREATEST THING IN THE WORLD, THE, by Henry Drummond (1890) takes both theme and title from 1 Cor. xiii., wherein (R. V.) Love is declared to be the greatest of the three Christian graces.

The author treats Love as the supreme good; and following St. Paul, contrasts it favorably with eloquence, prophecy, sacrifice, and martyrdom. Then follows the analysis: "It is like light. Paul passes this thing, Love, through the magnificent prism of his inspired intellect, and it comes out on the other side broken up into its elements."

"The Spectrum of Love has nine ingredients:

Patience — 'Love suffereth long.'
Kindness — 'And is kind.'
Generosity — 'Love envieth not.'
Humility — 'Love vaunteth not itself, is not puffed up.'
Courtesy — 'Doth not behave itself unseemly.'
Unselfishness — 'Seeketh not her own.'
Good Temper — 'Is not easily provoked.'
Guilelessness — 'Thinketh no evil.'
Sincerity — 'Rejoiceth not in iniquity, but rejoiceth in the truth.'"

The author then declares that Love comes by induction — by contact with God; that it is an effect, — "we love because He first loved us."

The closing chapter dwells upon the lasting character of Love (1 Cor. xiii: 8), and asserts its absolute supremacy — "What religion is, what God is, who Christ is, and where Christ is, is Love."

GREATNESS AND DECAY OF THE ROMANS, CONSIDERATIONS ON THE, by Montesquieu. This work, which is superior to the other writings of the author in unity of plan and of execution, was published at Amsterdam in 1734 without the author's name. It resembles the 'Universal History' of Bossuet, but with this important difference: while the latter refers the regulation of the course of history to the direct agency of Providence, Montesquieu sees a sufficient explanation of it in the power of ideas, the characters of men, and the action and reaction of causes and effects. Of the twenty-seven chapters, seven are devoted to the greatness of the Romans, and the others treat of their downfall. How has it come to pass, Montesquieu asks, that Rome, at first a sort of Tartar camp, an asylum of robbers, has grown, physically and intellectually, to be the capital of the world? The causes of Rome's aggrandizement were, according to him, the love of the Romans for liberty and country; their military discipline, exercised despotically in the camp, but ceasing once the soldier entered the city; the public discussions of the laws in the forum, which enlightened their minds, and made them love a country that gave them such freedom; their constancy under reverses, and firm resolve not to make peace except they were victorious; the triumphs and rewards granted their generals; their policy of supporting foreign peoples who rebelled against their rulers; their respect for the religion of conquered nations; and their avoidance of a conflict with two or more countries at the same time. The causes of Rome's decay are studied with equal care. They were the excessive enlargements of the empire; distant wars, necessitating the maintenance of standing armies; the intrusion into Rome of Asiatic luxury; the proscriptions, which resulted in the disappearance of the real Romans and their replacement by slaves and degraded Asiatics; the Oriental character assumed by the emperors, and the military character assumed by the empire; and finally, the transfer of the seat of empire to Constantinople. The work closes with a remarkable dialogue between Sylla and Eucrates, in which the ex-dictator explains his motives for abandoning power. The 'Considerations' did not become immediately popular in France. The seriousness of the style, so different from that of the 'Persian Letters,' disappointed the salons, which spoke of the latter as "the grandeur" and of the 'Considerations' as "the decadence" of M. de Montesquieu. But they at once attracted the attention of the thoughtful, and were eagerly read abroad. A copy, minutely and carefully annotated by Frederick the Great, still exists. The work has continued to hold its rank as a European classic, though deficient in the historical criticism of facts, — which however was hardly a characteristic of the author's age, — and its merits do not lie in its facts but in its views. The 'Considerations' will always be remarkable for their depth, originality, and the completeness with which their plan is carried out.

GREATNESS AND DECLINE OF ROME ('Grandezza e Decadenza di Roma'), a history in five volumes by Guglielmo Ferrero, published between 1902 and 1908 inclusive, comprises the following sections: 'The Empire-Builders,' an account of the events from the death of Sulla to the establishment of the first triumvirate; 'Julius Cæsar,' which brings the story down to Cæsar's assassination, 'The Fall of an Aristocracy,' extending to the Battle of Philippi; 'Rome and Egypt,' which includes the defeat of Antony and the establishment of the authority of Octavius; and 'The Republic of Augustus,' which describes the beginnings of the Roman empire. An English translation appeared in 1909. Ferrero is distinguished by the freshness of his point of view, which results from his illustration of Roman history by tendencies of modern social and political life and from the independence with which he revises traditional historical judgments.

GREECE, see RAMBLES AND STUDIES IN.

GREECE, see SOCIAL LIFE IN.

GREECE UNDER FOREIGN DOMINATION, 'from its Conquest by the Romans to the present Time: 146 B. C.–1864 A. D.,' By George Finlay. (Final revised ed. 7 vols., 1877). A thoroughly learned, accurate, and interesting history of Greece for two thousand and ten years, by a writer who qualified himself for his task by life-long residence in Greece: a soldier there in Byron's time, a statesman and economist of exceptional intelligence, and a great historian of the more judicious and practical type. The work was executed in parts in the years 1844–1861. It consists of (1) Greece under the Romans 146 B. C.–717 A. D.; (2) The Byzantine Empire, 717–1204; (3) Mediæval Greece and Trebizond, 1204–1566; (4) Greece under Ottoman and Venetian Dominion, 1453–1821; and (5) The Greek Revolution and Greek Affairs, 1843–1864. The whole was thoroughly revised by the author before his death at Athens in 1875, and was very carefully edited for the Clarendon Press by Rev. H. F. Tozer. In comparison with Gibbon, it deals far more with interesting social particulars, and comes much nearer than Gibbon did to adequate treatment of the ages which both have covered. The author's prolonged residence in Greece, with very great sympathetic attention to Greek affairs, peculiarly qualified him to deal intelligently with the problems of Greek character through the long course of ages, from the Roman conquest to the latest developments. Taken in connection with Grote's admirable volumes for the ages of Greek story before Alexander the Great, the two works, even with a gap of two centuries between them, form one of the most interesting courses in history for thirty centuries to which the attention of intelligent readers can be given.

GREEK ART, see **GRAMMAR OF.**

GREEK EDUCATION, OLD, see **OLD GREEK EDUCATION.**

GREEK PHILOSOPHY, OUTLINES OF THE HISTORY OF, by Dr. Eduard Zeller. (English Translation, 1885). An extremely useful sketch of the whole history of Greek philosophy, from Thales, a contemporary of Solon and Crœsus in the first half of the sixth century B. C., to the death of Boëthius in the first half of the sixth century of Christ (525 A. D.). The story told by Plato of 'Seven Wise Men' of early Greece is wholly unhistorical. Not less than twenty-two names appear in different versions of the story, and only four are found in all of them, — Thales, Bias, Pittacus, and Solon. To Thales the first place is given. In the succession of early Greek philosophers there follow Anaximander, Anaximenes, and Diogenes; Pythagoras and his disciples; Xenophanes, Parmenides, and Zeno; Heracleitus, Empedocles, Leucippus, Democritus, and Anazagoras; and then the greatest names of all, Socrates, Plato, and Aristotle. From these onward there is a further long development, which Dr. Zeller admirably sketches. This volume of 'Outlines' is an Introduction to Dr. Zeller's large special works, such as 'Socrates and the Socratic Schools,' 'Plato and the Older Academy,' 'The Stoics, Epicureans, and Sceptics,' and 'Aristotle and the Earlier Peripatetics.' These works together constitute a complete history of Greek philosophy for more than a thousand years.

GREEK POETS, STUDIES OF THE, by J. A. Symonds (2 vols., 1873–76). One of the most admirable expositions ever made for English readers of the finer elements of Greek culture, the thoughts and beauties of utterance of the Greek poets, from Homer and Hesiod, through the lyrics of various types, to the drama, Æschylus, Sophocles, Euripides, and Aristophanes. Not only has Mr. Symonds a quick sense of poetic beauties in verse and expression, but he gleans with rare insight the notes of thought, of faith, of sentiment and worship, which are the indications of culture in the grand story of Greek song. In Homer, Hesiod, Pindar, and the four great dramatists, especially, the field of study is very rich.

GREEK STUDIES, a series of essays by Walter Pater (1892), are concerned with some of the most beautiful and uncommon aspects of Greek thought and art. The first two essays on 'Dionysus the Spiritual Form of Fire and Dew,' and on 'The Bacchanals of Euripides,' treat of the mystical significance of the vine, of the religion of the grape as a cult, — subtle, far-reaching, and mysterious as Nature herself. The essay on the 'Myth of Demeter and Persephone' goes back likewise to the great natural source of the magnificent worship of earth and its revolving seasons. 'Hippolytus Veiled' is a study from Euripides. The remaining essays are devoted to Greek art, the heroic age, the age of graven images, to the marbles of Ægina, and to the age of athletic prizemen.

Pater's treatment of these subjects is remarkably subtle and sympathetic. His peculiar gift of insight into the spirit of a great dead age here finds full manifestation. In no other of his writings is the style more perfectly adapted to the subject-matter; polished, chastened, chiseled, it resembles in its symmetry and beauty a monument of Greek sculpture.

GREEN BOOK, THE, by Maurice Jókai (1879). The author of this novel of Russian life is a Hungarian, who has achieved prominence as a politician, success as a journalist, and wide repute as a novelist. Nearly all the action of 'The Green Book' passes in St. Petersburg. Pushkin, the poet, is deeply in love with Zeneida Ilmarinen, the favorite opera singer, and indeed the favorite subject, of both the Tsar Nicholas and the Tsaritsa. She is a splendid creature, the really great character of the book. The Princess Ghedimin, a former favorite of the Tsar, is depicted as a fiend. "The Green Book" is the name of a large volume in which are recorded the names and the doings of the chief band of conspirators against the life of the Tsar. This is kept in a secret room in Zeneida's palace, where the conspirators meet. By an ingenious mechanism, when anyone opens the outer door the table containing the book disappears, and a roulette-board in active operation takes its place. Thus the authorities are deceived into thinking that she is trying merely to conceal from the police the evidences of gambling. Zeneida's noble and self-sacrificing behavior during the flood of the Neva results in bringing together Pushkin, Sophie Narishkin, — the illegitimate daughter of the Tsar by the Princess Ghedimin, — and Bethsaba, a beautiful young girl. Sophie falls deeply in love with Pushkin, as her mother has already done, and the Tsar favors the marriage. But the child falls ill, and on her death-bed makes Bethsaba and Pushkin promise to be married before her funeral. The Tsar dies at the hands of The Man with the Green Eyes; Zeneida's affection keeps Pushkin out of a conspiracy which promises to free Russia, but ends in failure; the conspirators are put to death; and Zeneida and Prince Ghedimin flee to Tobolsk, where they spend the rest of their lives. There are many romantic episodes.

GREEN CARNATION, THE, by Robert S. Hichens (1894), is a satire on the extreme æsthetic movement in England, as illustrated in the lives of pale, exquisite youths of rank, with gilt hair, Burne-Jones features, and eyes of blue. Of this type is the hero, Lord Reginald Hastings, "impure and subtle," "too modern to be reticent," a boy blasé at twenty-five, living a life of exquisite sensuousness, fearing nothing so much as the philistinism of virtue, loving nothing so much as original vice. His dearest friend is Esmé Amarinth, who is most brilliantly epigrammatic when intoxicated, and who dreads nothing so much as being found dead sober at improper times.

A mutual friend, Mrs. Windsor, belonging to the "green carnation" set, strives to bring about a marriage between her wealthy and beautiful cousin, Lady Locke, and Lord Reggie. For this purpose she asks them with Esmé Amarinth to spend a week at her country-house. Lady Locke is, however, of too wholesome a nature to marry a man whose badge "is the arsenic flower of an exquisite life." She refuses him, and at the same time gives her opinion of him and of his artificial cult.

"Lord Reggie's face was scarlet. 'You talk very much like ordinary people,' he said, a little rude in his hurt self-love. 'I am ordinary,' she said. 'I am so glad of it. I think that after this week I shall try to be even more ordinary than I am.'" So does the silly artificiality of a certain clique receive its castigation.

GREEN MANSIONS, by W. H. Hudson (1916). This is a romance of the South American tropical forest, and is prefaced by John Galsworthy, who praises its author most highly as a great writer, "the most valuable our age possesses." The heroine of this fantastic tale is the beautiful "bird-girl," Rima, who understands and speaks the language of nature and whose home is the leafy "Green Mansions." The story is told in the first person by its hero, Mr. Abel, who in his last years confides it to a friend. It is a description of Abel's early life in Venezuela, where, having taken part in a political uprising, he is forced to fly for his life. He penetrates to the interior of Guayana and ascends the Orinoco, encounters dangerous savages, endures many hardships, and almost perishes from fever. Finally, in a forest which the natives declare "haunted," he hears the bird-notes of the lovely Rima, with whom he becomes acquainted. He falls desperately in love with her and after an illusive courtship she returns his affection. Abel is made welcome by her supposed grandfather, with whom she dwells in the heart of the woods; he learns that she is really of some different race and the child of a beautiful woman on whom the old man took pity when he found her deserted among the hills of Riolama, which name shortened to Rima the daughter bears. Abel's story of the outside world arouses the girl's desire to go back to her mother's country, where she feels her strange language will be understood; she starts, accompanied by her grandfather and lover, but a glimpse of the desolate region where no trace of her kinsfolk remains overwhelms her sensitive nature and she faints in her lover's arms.

Recovering, she promises to become the bride of Abel, and relinquish her dreams of being understood by her kind. Yet she tears herself from his embrace, and darts back alone through the forest to prepare for her bridal in her own way. Abel and the old man hasten back to join her, but find that she has fallen into the hands of the superstitious savages who have looked upon her as an evil spirit. She is trapped up among the branches of the trees, which are set on fire by her enemies, and is consumed to ashes, her bird-notes calling to her lover to the end. Overwhelmed with sorrow Abel returns to the world of men and affairs, but the remainder of his life is shadowed by the loss of his "bird" love.

GREEN PASTURES AND PICCADILLY, by William Black (1877). The story begins in England, and ends in America, the time being about the year 1875. Hugh Balfour, M. P., a young reformer, busies himself with politics to the neglect of his London business and his newly wedded wife (whom he really loves); until the latter, thinking their marriage has been a mistake, asks for a separation. "Your life is in your work," Sylvia says: "I am only an incumbrance to you." He is stunned at first by her unexpected demand, but finally proposes that the separation be only experimental and temporary. Accordingly she goes away to America for a tour with a party among which are the Van Rosens, friends of the Balfours, who have inherited a large property in Colorado. While traveling in the United States, Sylvia hears through the newspapers that her husband's business has gone to smash, and infers that his political prospects are blasted. All her love reasserts itself, and she cables asking if she may return to him. He replies with the announcement that he is coming to her, a happy reunion ensues, and the pair take up a new career in Colorado, where Balfour is offered the stewardship of the Van Rosen ranch. The action of the last half of the story is delayed by a description of the American tour, as is the first half from being largely given over to accounts of political wire-pulling. But the descriptions of nature are delightful, and few readers object to the leisurely pace of the story.

GREIFENSTEIN, by Francis Marion Crawford (1889). The duplicity of a woman who brings disgrace on a proud old family forms the mainspring of an exciting narrative, certain episodes of which are even startling. Baron von Greifenstein supposes himself to be legally married to Clara Kurtz. After twenty-five years, his half-brother Von Rieseneck, a disgraced and fugitive ex-officer, confesses that the woman is his wife, though he had long believed her dead. The realization that his dearly loved son Greif is nameless fills the baron with rage against Clara, who is hated not less by her lawful husband for her desertion of him. The two men, feeling themselves disgraced and degraded, write explanatory letters to their respective sons, kill the woman and then themselves. The news reaches Greif at his university, but his father's letter does not appear. His friend (in reality his half-brother) Rex, son of Rieseneck, learns all; but keeps the secret to himself, and goes with Greif to his home. Greif wishes to release his cousin, Hilda von Sigmundskron, from her betrothal vows to him; but she refuses to give him up, and finally he assumes the name of Sigmundskron and marries her. After a happy year the baron's letter turns up in an old coat, and Greif discovers the whole truth. He is plunged into the depths of despair but Hilda tears up the letter, thus destroying all evidence of the ugly secret, and by her love and devotion she finally brings him to a more cheerful state of mind. Meantime Rex discovers that he has fallen in love unwittingly with Hilda. In consequence he tries to shoot himself, but is prevented from doing so by Greif and Hilda, who have a deep affection for him, and who finally persuade him that life is still full of opportunity, and, in time, of happiness. The events of the story occur in Swabia; and the time is from 1888 onward. The incidental pictures of German university life, student duels, etc., will be found interesting.

GREY DAYS AND GOLD, by William Winter (1889) is a record of the author's wanderings in England and Scotland and of his impressions of beauty in those countries. In the preface he writes: "The supreme need of this age in America is a practical conviction that progress does not consist in material prosperity, but in spiritual advancement. Utility has long been exclusively worshiped. The welfare of the future lies in the worship of beauty. To that worship these pages are devoted." The book is written with the enthusiasm of one to whom a new world has opened. Because the author sees his England with undimmed eyes, what he says of it is fresh and vital and original. The classic shrines of England, the haunts of Moore, old York, Bath, and Worcester, Stratford, London, and Edinburgh, become new places and new cities seen for the first time. In this summer light of appreciation the entire volume is steeped. It is written in an intimate conversational style, with the warmth of one who must share his pleasant memories with others.

GRIFFITH GAUNT, or, JEALOUSY, by Charles Reade (1866). Griffith Gaunt, a gentleman without fortune, marries Catharine Peyton, a Cumberland heiress, who is a devout Roman Catholic. After living happily together for eight years, the couple — each of whom has a violent temper, in the husband combined with insane jealousy — are gradually estranged by Catharine's spiritual adviser, Father Leonard, an eloquent young priest. Griffith discovers his wife and Leonard under apparently suspicious circumstances; and after a violent scene he rides away, with the intention of never returning. He reaches an inn in an adjoining county, where he is nursed through a fever by the innkeeper's daughter, Mercy Vint. Assuming the name of his illegitimate brother, Thomas Leicester, to whom he bears a superficial resemblance, he marries Mercy. Returning to his old home to obtain a sum of money belonging to him, he is reconciled to Catharine by her earlier adviser, Father Francis. Under a false pretext he goes back to the inn to break with Mercy; but finding it more difficult than he had anticipated, he defers final action, and returns to Cumberland. Here he is received by Catharine with furious reproaches and threats against his life; his crime having been disclosed to her through the real Leicester, and her maid Caroline Ryder. Griffith disappears; a few days after, a body that is discovered in the mere near the house is identified as his. Mrs. Gaunt is indicted for his murder, and pleads her own cause. The trial is going against her, when Mercy appears and proves that Griffith is alive, and that the body is that of Leicester. Griffith and Catharine are again reconciled, and Mercy marries Catharine's former lover, Sir George Neville. The scene is laid in the middle of the eighteenth century. The book was harshly criticized, both in England and America, on account of its so-called immoral teachings; but a more sober judgment has given it a high place among Reade's novels. It was dramatized by Daly in 1866, and later under the title of 'Jealousy,' by the author himself.

GRIHYA-SÛTRAS, THE, 'see **SACRED BOOKS OF THE EAST.**

GROATS-WORTH OF WIT BOUGHT WITH A MILLION OF REPENTANCE, A, by Robert Greene. This piece was published after Greene's death in 1592; and is his last work. In it the author tells the story of his own life. Govinius, an old usurer, has two sons, Lucanio and Roberto. Dying, he leaves to Lucanio all his wealth, and to Roberto "an olde Groate (being the stock I first began with), wherewith I wish him to buy a groatsworth of wit: for he, in my life, hath reproved my manner of gaine." Lucanio follows in his father's footsteps, until Roberto introduces him to a beautiful harpy who first despoils him of his wealth, and then refuses to share with Roberto as had been planned. Roberto, meeting some actors, begins to write plays. His successes obtain for him the friendship of an old gentleman, whose daughter he marries, but whom he abuses shamefully. Not until he is dying does he cry out, looking at his father's present, "Oh, now it is too late" — "Here (gentlemen), breake I off Roberto's speech; whose life, in most parts agreeing with my own, found one selfe punishment as I have doone." Greene says that his object in writing is to persuade all young men to profit by his errors, and change their mode of life. This work is remembered only because it contains the earliest notice of Shakespeare in London. Greene, calling upon Marlowe, Nash, and Peele to leave off writing for the stage, speaks of "an upstart crow, beautified with our feathers," who "supposes he is as well able to bumbast out a blank verse as the best of you; and being an absolute Johannes factotum, is, in his own conceit, the only Shake-scene in the countrie."

GROUND ARMS ('Die Waffen Nieder'), by the Baroness Bertha Félicie Sofie von Suttner (2 vols., 1889). This novel has been often republished since its appearance and rendered into nearly all the European languages. The English translation was made in 1892 by F. Holmes, at the request of the committee of the "International Arbitration and Peace Association" — under the title 'Lay Down Your Arms.'

The story is told in the form of a journal kept by a German noblewoman, whose life covered the period of Germany's recent wars. This lady relates the emotional and spiritual life of a woman during that terrible experience, in such a way as to make her story an appeal for the cessation of war. Having lost her young husband in the war with Italy, she has lived only for her son and her grief. In her maturity she meets and marries Friedrich von Tilling, an Austrian officer, who, after years of close companionship, is forced to leave her and her unborn child, at the new call to arms. The Schleswig-Holstein difficulty, the Austro-Prussian war, and finally the war with France, tear the family apart. The wife endures the fear of her husband's death, the actual suffering of sympathy with his wound, the horrors of plague, famine, and the sickening sights of a besieged city; and at last, when Von Tilling has retired from active service, and is with her in Paris for the winter, the blind hatred of the French towards their conquerors overtakes their new dream of happiness. The Austrian is seized and shot as a Prussian spy. Not only has the author presented a convincing picture of the untold suffering, the far-reaching loss and retrogression involved in war, but she shows the pitiful inadequacy of the causes of war. Many a German woman recognizes in Martha Tilling's tragical journal the unwritten record of her own pain and despair.

GROWTH OF BRITISH INDUSTRY AND COMMERCE, THE, by William Cunningham (1882. 5th ed. 1912). The aim of the author of this work is twofold, to show how intimately the political and economic history of the English nation have been interconnected and to describe the actual course of the material progress of England. The first volume deals with early and mediæval times — the primitive English in Frisia, the Norman Conquest, the Danish invasion, the rise of feudalism, the beginnings of commercial policy, the craft gilds, the growth of a mercantile class, and of industry and internal trade, the age of discovery and the extension of English commerce under the Tudors. The second volume discusses the mercantile system; the patriotic spirit of the Elizabethans and the ambition for maritime power as a mainstay of national defense, as an instrument of attack on commercial rivals, and as a means of expansion; the landed and moneyed interests under Elizabeth; the trading companies under the Stuarts; the parliamentary regulation of commercial development after the Revolution. Volume iii. covers the laissez faire period, — the industrial revolution, the introduction of machinery in the textile trades, the movement for factory legislation. The author's view of laissez faire in commerce is that it might be wise to abandon the policy for the sake of securing the food supply and of obtaining an open door for manufactures. These volumes are indispensable to every serious student of the subject. They are fully indexed. The table of contents is practically a synopsis. The text of a number of the original sources is given in an appendix, and there is an ample bibliography.

GRYLL GRANGE, by Thomas Love Peacock. The plot of this, as of all of Peacock's novels, is very simple. The heroine is Morgana Gryll, niece and heiress of Squire Gryll, who has persistently refused all offers of marriage, of which she has had many. The hero, Algernon Falconer, is a youth of fortune, who lives in a lonely tower in

New Forest, attended by seven foster sisters, and with every intention of continuing his singular mode of life. Morgana and Algernon are brought together by the familiar device of an accident to the lady which compels her to spend several days at the tower. A sub-plot of equal simplicity is given in the love-affairs of Lord Curryfin and Alice Niphet. The most interesting character in the book is the Rev. Doctor Opimian, a lover of Greek and madeira, who serves as a mouthpiece for the author's reactionary views on modern inventions, reforms, education, and competitive examinations. The material side of his character is summed up in his own words, "Whatever happens in this world, never let it spoil your dinner." 'Gryll Grange' was Peacock's last novel, having been published in serial form in 1860.

GUARDIAN ANGEL, THE, by Oliver Wendell Holmes (1867). The author says in his preface: "I have attempted to show the successive evolution of some inherited qualities in the character of Myrtle Hazard." The story opens in 1859 in the New England village of Oxbow. Myrtle, a beautiful orphan of fifteen, born in tropical climes, descended from a line of ancestors of widely varying natures, lives with an austere and uncongenial aunt, who fails utterly to control her turbulent, glowing impulses. Disguised as a boy she runs away, is rescued from drowning by Clement Lindsay, a handsome young sculptor, and brought home by Professor Gridley. An illness follows which leaves her for a time hysterical, highly impressionable, prone to seeing visions, and taking strong fancies. Thanks to the watchful care of Professor Gridley (whom she afterward calls her "Guardian Angel") she emerges safe from this state, and is sent to a city school to complete her education. Among her suitors is Murray Bradshaw, a lawyer possessed of the secret that under an old will she is likely to come into a large fortune. He plots to win her, but is balked by Professor Gridley; and she gives her love to Clement Lindsay, who joins the army and rises to the rank of Colonel. During the war she goes with him to the front, and "In the offices of mercy which she performed . . . (in the hospital) . . . the dross of her nature seemed to be burned away. The conflict of mingled lives in her blood had ceased." Dr. Holmes's characteristic wit is shown in many of the shrewd sayings of the kindly old Professor and other characters, and his delightful enthusiasm makes the book more interesting than most more formally constructed novels.

GULISTAN; or, ROSE GARDEN, by Sa'di. (The Sheikh Muslih-ud-din was his real name.) He was born about 1193 at Shiraz; and after many years of travel (once captured by the Christian Crusaders he was fighting), and visiting all the chief countries and cities of Asia, he settled down in a hermitage at Shiraz, and wrote many works, including the 'Gulistan.' He has been called "The Nightingale of Shiraz," and his works "the salt-cellar of poets." Emerson so admired him that he frequently used his name as an alias in his poems. Sa'di's daughter married the poet Hafiz. The 'Gulistan' is a poetical work, and consists of fascinating stories or anecdotes, with a moral, like the parables of the Bible. They are replete with homely wisdom and life experience; the prose portions are interspersed with verses out of Sa'di's wide experience of the manners and customs of many men. Their great charm can only be known by reading them. Delicacy, simplicity, and bonhomie are the chief features of Sa'di's style.

GULLIVER'S TRAVELS, Jonathan Swift's most famous book, was published in 1727. It is one of the most brilliant and profound of satires, one of the most imaginative of stories, and one of the best models of style. 'Gulliver's Travels' was given to the world anonymously; though a few of Swift's friends, including Pope, Gay, Bolingbroke, and Arbuthnot, were in the secret. It became immediately popular, and has never lost its interest for both young and old. "'Gulliver's Travels,'" says Leslie Stephen, "belongs to a literary genus full of grotesque and anomalous forms. Its form is derived from some of the imaginary travels of which Lucian's 'True History' — itself a burlesque of some early travelers' tales — is the first example. But it has an affinity to such books as Bacon's 'Atlantis' and More's 'Utopia,' and again to later philosophical romances like 'Candide' and 'Rasselas.'" It begins with Gulliver's account of himself and his setting forth upon the travels. A violent storm off Van Diemen's Land drives him, the one survivor, to Lilliput, where he is examined with curiosity by the tiny folk. They call him the "man-mountain," and make rules for his conduct. With equal curiosity he learns their arts of civilization and warfare. His next voyage is to Brobdingnag, where he is a Lilliputian in comparison to the size of the gigantic inhabitants of this strange land, in which he becomes a court toy. In Brobdingnag, Scott says Swift looked through the other end of the telescope, wishing to show the grossness of mankind as he had shown their pettiness.

The next adventure is a voyage to Laputa, where the inhabitants are absorbed in intellectual and scientific pursuits, and "taken up with intense speculations," and their conduct is most eccentric; this is probably a satire upon pedantry. Gulliver next visits Balnibarbi, Luggnagg, and Japan, and gives an account of the Struldbrugs, a famous tribe of men who have gained physical immortality without immortal youth, and find it an awful curse. The last voyage takes the traveler into the country of the Houyhnhnms, where the horses under this name have an ideal government, — Swift's Utopia, — and are immensely superior to the Yahoos, the embodiment of bestial mankind. The irony and satire may be understood when one remembers that Swift said: "Upon the great foundation of misanthropy the whole building of my travels is erected"; and the remark that the King of Brobdingnag made to Gulliver — "The bulk of your natives appear to me to be the most pernicious race of little odious vermin that Nature ever suffered to crawl upon the face of the earth" — may be accepted as the opinion of the cynic himself regarding mankind. Hazlitt said that in 'Gulliver's Travels' Swift took a view of human nature such as might be taken by a being of another sphere. His description of Brobdingnagian literature has been applied to the masterly prose of his great book: "Their style is clear, masculine, and smooth, but not florid; for they avoid nothing more than multiplying unnecessary words, or using various expressions."

GUN-MAKER OF MOSCOW, THE, by Sylvanus Cobb, Jr. (1888), tells the story of Ruric Nevel, a Russian armorer, who lived in Moscow toward the close of the seventeenth century. It is a fair example of the stories of this prolific writer, very popular with a certain class.

The youth loves and is loved by a young duchess, Rosalind Valdai. Her guardian, the Duke of Tula, opposes Ruric because he wishes to repair his own shattered fortunes by marrying Rosalind and securing her riches; and he plots the death of another of Rosalind's suitors, Count Damonoff, in order to secure his estates.

Hoping to provoke a quarrel, he sends the Count to Ruric demanding that he renounce Rosalind. A quarrel ensues, and Damonoff challenges the young gunmaker, who in the meanwhile has secretly received Rosalind's pledges of constancy. In the duel Ruric repeatedly spares Damonoff's life, but the Count's frenzy compels him to inflict a wound in self-defense. The whole affair has been witnessed by the

Emperor, Peter the Great, in the guise of Valdimir, a Black Monk of St. Michael, who thereafter takes a secret interest in Ruric. The Duke of Tula hales the young gun-maker before the Emperor upon the double charge of murder and assault. To prove that skill had defeated the Count, Ruric engages in a friendly sword contest with Demetrius, the Emperor's sword-master, and vanquishes him. The Emperor ex-claims with pleasure: "Now, Ruric Nevel, if you leave Moscow without my consent, you do so at your peril. I would not lose sight of you. You are at liberty."

The baffled Duke now seeks to wed his ward Rosalind; but, repulsed, threatens to seize her by violence. He employs Savotano, a villainous priest, to poison Damonoff while pretending to nurse him; and pays him to make way with Ruric also. Ruric and the dying Count become reconciled, however, and Ruric saves the Count's life; but is himself lured by the Duke's men to an ambush, whence he is rescued from death by the Emperor (still disguised as Valdimir). The monk and Ruric now hasten to the castle, and arrive in time to prevent the Duke from forcing Rosalind to marry him. Valdimir discloses his identity, much to the terror of the plotters. The Duke is banished, Savotano executed, and Ruric, endowed with the Duke's lands and titles, marries Rosalind in the royal palace.

GUNNAR: 'A Tale of Norse Life,' by Hjalmar Hjorth Boyesen (1874). 'Gun-nar,' the one romance of Boyesen, is also the earliest of his works of fiction. The scene of the story is a small parish in Bergen Stift, where Gunnar Thorson lives in the little hamlet Henjumhei with his father, Thor Gunnarson, and his grandmother, old Gunhild. Gunnar's mother, Birgit, having died when he was a baby, his father and grandmother bring him up carefully; and the latter fills his mind with stories of Huldre and Necken, and other strange creations of Norse mythology. As his father Thor is only a houseman or rent-payer, a sharp distinction is drawn between him and the families of the neighboring gaardmen or landowners. One of the chief of these is Atle Larsson, Thor's landlord and the leading man in the parish. As Gunnar grows up, he falls in love with the beautiful Ragnhild, "a birch in the pine forest," niece of Atle, and daughter of his haughty sister, Ingeborg Rimul. It is the love affair of Gunnar and Ragnhild which forms the texture of the story, — its troubled course, the dangers encountered, the loyalty and patience of the lovers. 'Gunnar' carries the reader into an unfamiliar world of romance and poetry, where he comes in contact with the minds of the simple Norwegian peasants, with their beliefs in fairies and other mystical beings. Many of their customs are described: the games of St. John's Eve, the ski race, the wedding festivities at Peer Berg's, and some of the religious ceremonies, such as those attending confirmation.

GUY LIVINGSTONE, by George Alfred Lawrence. This novel, published in Eng-land in 1857, was the first of a class of stories which extol and glorify a hero endowed with great muscular strength and physical prowess; and while not representing any particular school of thought or feeling, it expressed an increasing demand for a literary model possessed of strength and sternness both of mind and body. Guy Livingstone is a young Englishman of wealth, who combines enormous physical strength with grimness and ferocity of disposition. His pugilistic prowess enables him to thrash prize-fighters and perform various remarkable exploits, which are admiringly chroni-cled by Livingstone's intimate friend Hammond, the raconteur of the story, who is entertained among other guests at the hero's ancestral hall, Kerton Manor in North-amptonshire. Here had dwelt Guy's ancestors, whose portraits were characterized by "the same expression of sternness and decision" as distinguished their powerful descendant. In this circle of friends are Mr. Forrester, a dandified life-guardsman; Miss Raymond, with whom Forrester is in love; and Flora Bellasys, a voluptuous beauty. Mr. John Bruce, a Scotchman, is introduced, who is engaged to Miss Raymond, and who is made uncomfortable by the other guests on account of his lack of suitable enthusiasm for field sports. Forrester and Miss Raymond afterwards elope, aided by Livingstone, whose engagement to Miss Constance Brandon, a beautiful young woman of refined tastes, soon takes place. In a thoughtless moment the hero flirts with Flora, and is discovered by Constance kissing her rival in a conservatory. Constance at once casts Livingstone off, and then pines away and dies, after summoning her lover to her bedside, which he reaches in time for a last interview, in which she foretells his early death. He is stricken with brain fever, and during his convalescence is visited by Flora, whom he refuses either to see or to forgive. He emerges from his sick-room changed and softened in nature. He goes to Italy; where he tracks down Bruce, who has barbarously murdered his rival Forrester, and wrings from him a confession of guilt. Returning to Kerton, Livingstone gets a fatal fall from his enormous horse Axeine, who rolls on him and crushes his spine. He dies after some weeks of torture. The book enjoyed a wide popularity, and is the best known of the author's works.

GUY MANNERING, by Sir Walter Scott. 'Guy Mannering,' the second of Scott's novels, appeared anonymously in 1815, seven months after 'Waverley.' It is said to have been the result of six weeks' work, and by some critics is thought to show the marks of haste. Its time is the middle of the eighteenth century, its scene chiefly Scotland. Guy Mannering himself is a young Englishman, at the opening of the story traveling through Scotland. Belated one night, he is hospitably received at New Place, the home of the Laird of Ellangowan. When the laird learns that the young man has studied astrology, he begs him to cast the horoscope of his son, born that very night.

The young man, carrying out his promise, is dismayed to find two possible catastrophes overhanging the boy: one at his fifth, the other at his twenty-first year. He tells the father, however, what he has discovered, in order that he may have due warning; and later proceeds on his way.

The fortunes of the Laird of Ellangowan, Godfrey Bertram, are now on the ebb, and he has hardly money to keep up the estate. His troubles are increased when his son Harry, at the age of five, is spirited away. No one can learn whether the child is dead or alive, and the shock at once kills Mrs. Bertram. After some years the father himself dies, leaving his penniless daughter Lucy to the care of Dominie Sampson, an old teacher and a devoted friend of the family. When things are at their worst for Lucy Bertram, Guy Mannering, returning to England after many years' military service in India, hears accidentally of the straits to which she is reduced. He at once invites her and Dominie Sampson to make their home with him and his daughter Julia. He has leased a fine estate, and Dominie Sampson rejoices in the great collection of books to which Colonel Mannering gives him free access. In India Julia had formed an attachment for Vanbeest Brown, a young officer, against whom her father feels a strong prejudice. Captain Brown has followed the Mannerings to England; and to make a long story short, is proved in the end to be the long-lost Harry Bertram, and Lucy's brother. The abduction had been accomplished with the connivance of Meg Merrilies, a gipsy of striking aspect and six feet tall; of Frank Kennedy, a smuggler; Dirk Hatteraick, a Dutch sea-captain, also concerned in smuggling; and of Gilbert Glossin, once agent for the Laird of Ellangowan. Glossin had aimed to get possession of the laird's property, and finally succeeded; but after the discovery of his crime, he dies a violent death in prison.

All told, there are fewer than twoscore characters in 'Guy Mannering,' and the plot is not very complicated. Meg Merrilies, and Dominie Sampson the uncouth, honest pedant, are the only great creations.

GUY OF WARWICK. This old metrical romance belongs to that Anglo-Danish cycle from which the Norman trouvères drew so much material. 'King Horn' is perhaps the most famous poem of this cycle, but 'Guy of Warwick' was one of the most popular of those which appeared in the thirteenth century. The earliest existing manuscripts of this romance are in French; though it is supposed to have been written by Walter of Exeter, a Cornish Franciscan. It consists of about 12,000 verses, iambic measure, arranged in rhymed couplets. Although the value of this poem is less as literature than as a picture of ancient English manners, the story has considerable interest as an example of the kind of fiction that pleased our ancestors. The hero, Guy, is represented as the son of a gentleman of Warwick, living in the reign of King Edgar. The youth becomes great, after the fashion of mediæval heroes, entirely through his own unaided efforts. He is spurred on by his love for Felicia, daughter of Earl Rohand, for at first she scorns his suit because he has not distinguished himself; but when he sets out in search of adventures, they come thick and fast. He wins in a fight with Philbertus, kills a monstrous dun cow, makes peace between the Duke of Lovain and the Emperor, slays a dragon and a boar, with the help of Herraud rescues Earl Terry's lady from sixteen villains, travels with Terry and saves his father's life, and finally returns home to claim his bride. Not long after, he leaves Felicia to go on a pilgrimage. On his return, finding England invaded by the Danes, he kills in single combat the Danish giant, Colbrond. After his victory, entirely weary of the world, he retires to a cave and lives a hermit's life; all this time he is supported by alms, and sees no more of Felicia except for one brief interview just before he dies. Though Guy is probably a fictitious character, definite dates are given for his life, and he is said to have died about 929. For those who can follow the quaintness of its middle English style, this poem is very attractive. The story has been told in an excellent modern prose rendering also.

GUZMAN D'ALFARACHE, LIFE AND ADVENTURES OF, THE, by Mateo Aleman. This romance, dealing with the lives and adventures of *picaros* or rogues, contains more varied and highly colored pictures of thieves, beggars, and outlaws than any other work in this peculiar department of Spanish literature. It is divided into two parts, of which the first was published in 1599, the second in 1605. Guzman relates his own life from his birth up to the moment when his crimes consign him to the galleys. When a mere boy, he runs away from his mother after his father's death; goes to Madrid, where he is by turns scullion, cook, and errand boy; escapes to Toledo with some money intrusted to him, and sets up as a fine gentleman. After wasting all his money in profligacy he enlists, is sent to Italy, and quickly becomes the associate of cutpurses and vagabonds of every description. He is a versatile rascal, and feels equally at home among beggars and in the palace of a Roman cardinal, who takes an interest in him and makes him his page. But his natural depravity does not allow him to hold this position long; and he returns to Spain, where he eventually becomes a lackey in the French ambassador's household. The adventures he meets with there form the closing chapters of the story. The work was immensely popular, ran through several editions, and was translated into French and English immediately after its appearance. The episodes and long philosophical digressions, which now seem tedious and foreign to the action, were then greatly admired. Ben Jonson, in his poem prefixed to Mabbe's translation, describes the hero as "The Spanish Proteus . . . formed with the world's wit." Though inferior to Mendoza's 'Lazarillo' in grace and vivacity, this romance enables us to get a clear idea of certain aspects of society in the Spain and Italy of the sixteenth century, notwithstanding the exaggeration and excess of color in its descriptions. The French translation by Le Sage omits the digressions and philosophical reflections of the original, to which it is far superior.

HAIL AND FAREWELL, by George Moore (1911–14, 3 vols.). George Moore's reminiscences about Ireland and himself and his friends give the effect of a novel in which the characters are real people, W. B. Yeats, Lady Gregory, Edward Martyn, and others. He returns to Ireland after many years absence impressed with the belief that he has a mission to restore the ancient glory of Ireland by reviving the Irish language. One reason for leaving England is his hatred for the Boer war. Incidentally the Westminster Trust Company, determined to make improvements in his London home, is an amusing factor in his flight. He sits astride his window sill in the early morning to keep the workmen away, and is only ousted by fear of pneumonia, which loses him half his sill before he can dress sufficiently to save it.

'Ave,' the first volume of this trilogy of confidences, tells of the beginnings of the Irish Literary Theatre with plays by Yeats and Edward Martyn. His friend, Martyn, he considers "as typical of Ireland as Sancho Panza is of Spain. In the book he seems to me to set forth not only the Irish attitude of mind towards religious problems, he seems to reflect the Irish landscape, the Catholic landscape." For Yeats "lank as a rook, a-dream in black silhouette on the flowered wall-paper," he has profound admiration, though he caricatures him as a "literary fop" and accentuates his personal eccentricities. Mr. Douglas Hyde and other members of the group are more or less sympathetically sketched. The hero of the second volume 'Salve' is the poet, "A. E.," George Edward Russell. "A. E." finds a house for Moore and his Manets and Monets about which Moore talks delightfully. They make a pilgrimage together to the ancient cromlechs of the Druids in search of the gods, who for one cause and another do not reveal themselves as expected.

After much reflection and discussion, Moore comes to the conviction that the Roman Catholic church is hostile to art, and that "dogma and literature are incompatible." Protestanism only can free Ireland by removing the shackles of the mind. The book closes with his denunciation of the Catholic church, and his reception into the Anglican communion.

The first part of volume iii, 'Vale,' is a frank description of his gay past as an art student in Paris. As in all his reminiscences he confesses for his friends as well as himself, and lives up to his favorite motto "to be ashamed of nothing but of being ashamed."

The character sketches, anecdotes, and conversations on art, music, and literature make an interesting personal picture of the author and his friends in the Irish literary group.

HAJJI BABA OF ISPAHAN, THE ADVENTURES OF, a picaresque novel or narrative of roguery by James Morier, published in 1824, and followed in 1828 by 'Hajji Baba in England.' The writer had spent some years in Persia in the English diplomatic service, and under the guise of Hajji Baba, an adventurer like Gil Blas, he gives in this book a first-hand picture of Persian society.   The hero is in succession a barber, a robber, a servant, a doctor's assistant, an executioner's assistant, a religious fanatic, and a tobacco dealer.   At length he marries a rich widow, becomes a government official, and accompanies the ambassador to England.   The book is witty, entertaining, and shows a marvelous adaptation to Oriental ways of thought and a thorough acquaintance with Oriental institutions.

HALF-CENTURY OF CONFLICT, A, see **FRANCE AND ENGLAND IN NORTH AMERICA.**

HAMLET is Shakespeare's longest and most famous play.   It draws when acted as full a house to-day as it ever did.   It is the drama of the intellect, of the soul, of man, of domestic tragedy.   Five quarto editions appeared during the poet's life, the first in 1603.   The story, Shakespeare probably found in 'The Historie of Hamblet,' translated from the French of Belleforest, who in turn translated it from the Danish History of Saxo Grammaticus.   It has been deduced that he drew some of the dramatic material from a lost 'Hamlet,' probably the work of Thomas Kyd, the author of the popular 'Spanish Tragedy.'   Shakespeare's play, like many contemporary tragedies, deals with revenge.   Some time in winter ("'tis bitter cold"), the scene opens on a terrace in front of the castle of Kronberg in Elsinore, Denmark.   The ghost of his father appears to Hamlet, moody and depressed over his mother's marriage with Claudius, her brother-in-law.   Hamlet learns from his father the fatal secret of his death at the hands of Claudius.   He devises the court-play as a trap in which to catch his uncle's conscience; breaks his engagement with Ophelia; kills the wary old counselor Polonius; and is sent off to England under the escort of the treacherous courtiers Rosencrantz and Guildenstern, to be put to death.   On the way he rises in the night, unseals their murderous commission, rewrites it, and seals it with his father's ring, having worded it so that they themselves shall be the victims when they reach England.   In a fight with pirates Hamlet boards their ship, and is conveyed by them back to Denmark, where he tells his adventures to his faithful friend Horatio. At Ophelia's grave he encounters Laertes, her brother; and presently, in a fencing bout with him, is killed by Laertes's poisoned sword, but not before he has stabbed his treacherous uncle and forced the fatal cup of poison down his throat.   His mother Gertrude has just died from accidentally drinking the same poison, prepared by the King for Hamlet.   The old threadbare question, "Was Hamlet insane?" is hardly an open question nowadays.   The verdict is that he was not.   The strain upon his nerves of discovering his father's murderer, yet in such a manner that he could not prove it (*i.e.*, by the agency of a ghost), was so great that he verges on insanity, and this suggests to him the feigning of it.   But if you deprive him wholly of reason, you destroy our interest in the play.

HAMMER AND ANVIL ('Hammer und Amboss'), by Friedrich Spielhagen (1869), is a novel grounded on a conception of the continual struggle between castes, arising largely from the character of the social institutions of Germany, — the nobility, the military organization, and the industrial conditions.   The leading idea is expressed by one of the characters, the humane director of a house of correction, who says: "Everywhere is the sorry choice whether we will be the hammer or the anvil" in life. And the same character is made to express Spielhagen's solution of the difficulty when he says: "It shall not be 'hammer *or* anvil' but 'hammer *and* anvil'; for everything and every human being is both at once, and every moment."

It is not, however, easy to trace the development of this idea as the motive of the book; for the novelist's power lies rather in his charm as a narrator than in constructive strength or analytical ability. In this, as in most of his stories, he obtains sympathy for the personalities he creates, and enchains attention by his gift of story-telling. Georg Hartwig, the hero of the novel, is brought into contact with a fallen nobleman, a smuggler, "Von Zehren the wild," with his beautiful and heartless daughter Constance, and with a contrasted group of honorable and generous persons who teach him much. Chief of these is another Von Zehren, the prison director, an ideal character. His daughter Paula exercises the influence which opposes that of Constance in Hartwig's life, and leads him to new effort and success. Georg himself is one of those who by nature tend to become "anvil" rather than "hammer." The story, though less famous than 'Problematic Characters' or 'Through Night to Light,' is a great favorite with German readers.

HANDY ANDY, a novel by Samuel Lover (1842–43). "Andy Rooney was a fellow who had the most singularly ingenious knack of doing everything the wrong way." Thus begins a broadly humorous tale of life among the Irish gentry and peasantry in the first half of the nineteenth century, by an accomplished author who not only could illustrate his own narrative, but could write songs for it and furnish music for them as well. The ironically nicknamed hero, by his inveterate blundering, furnishes cause for ire and mirth alternately to all with whom he comes in contact. He goes out to service, first with Squire Egan, then with his enemy, Squire O'Grady. He brings on a duel by exchanging a writ for a blister; incenses a young lady by substituting a case of razors for the fan sent as a gift by her admirer; complicates an election by meddling with the mail and driving one of O'Grady's political allies to the house of his rival Egan; cools champagne by emptying it into a tub of ice; gets himself matrimonially mixed up with two women at once, meantime loving a third; and — always with the best intentions — encounters mishaps and tribulations without end. Furthermore the author relates how Egan lost and regained his seat in the House; how Tom Durfy wed the widow Flanagan; how ran the course of true love with Edward O'Connor and Fanny Dawson; how old Mrs. O'Grady challenged and thrashed the fop Furlong; how everybody feasted and drank, told stories and sang songs, played practical jokes that were sometimes dangerous, and fought duels that usually were not; and finally how Andy, the "omadhaun," turned out to be Lord Scatterbrain, and after nearly drowning himself and a party of friends in Lake Killarney, got loose from his matrimonial entanglements and wedded his pretty cousin Oonah.

HANNAH, by Dinah Mulock (Craik) (1871). This story, the scene of which is laid in England, with a short episode in France, finds its motive in the vexed question of marriage with a deceased wife's sister. The Rev. Bernard Rivers, at the death of his young wife Rosa, invites her sister, Hannah Thelluson, to take charge of his home and baby daughter. Hannah, a sweet and gentle woman of thirty, with a passionate love for children, resigns her position as governess, and accepts the offer, that she may bring up her little niece. The Rivers family, as well as all the parish, strongly disapprove the new arrangement; but Hannah, recognizing the fact that, in the eyes of the law, she is Bernard's sister, sees no harm in it. Soon, however, she finds herself in love with Bernard, who returns her affection. After passing through much misery and unhappiness, as well as scandalous notoriety, the lovers separate and Hannah takes little Rosie to France, whither they are soon followed by Mr. Rivers. Here they decide to marry, even though they must henceforth live in exile. The story flows on with the limpid clearness of Miss Muloch's habitual method.   If not exciting, it is refined, vivid, and always interesting.   As a powerful purpose-novel, it aroused much propagandist spirit in England.

HANNAH THURSTON, by Bayard Taylor.   The scene is said to be central New York.   The preface especially informs us that an author does not necessarily represent himself: "I am neither Mr. Woodberry, Mr. Waldo, nor Seth Wattles."   Yet many of the hero's dreams and experiences are those of Bayard Taylor; and those who know, say that no one familiar with Pennsylvania could fail to recognize the life of Chester County where Taylor was born.

Maxwell Woodberry returns from years of travel to make a home in the village where he lived as a child.   There he meets Hannah Thurston, a lovely Quaker girl, and admires her, but is repelled by her advocacy of woman's rights.   Love finally triumphs, and they are happily married, each yielding some part of his or her prejudice.   All the fads and crotchets of a country village find a place in the chronicle: total abstinence, vegetarianism, spiritualism, and abolition.   In Mr. Dyce we have the villain who advocates free love, acts the part of medium, and belongs to a colony of Perfectionists.   There are the Whitlows, who wish their children to follow their own inclinations, regardless of others; Silas Wattles, the tailor; good Mr. Waldo, the minister, and his wife who loved all the world; honest Bute, the farmer; and the coquettish little seamstress, Carry Dilworthy, who makes him such a sweet wife. Woodberry's "poverty party" has had many imitations in later days; and we have also sewing societies, temperance conventions, and other of the usual phases of American country life.   Begun in America, the book was finished in 1863, in St. Petersburg, where Taylor had been sent as secretary of legation.   It was his first novel; and is a strangely peaceful book to be written during the early days of the Civil War, and in Russia.   It had a large sale, was translated into Russian and German, and published simultaneously in London and New York.

HARBOR, THE, by Ernest Poole (1915).   A small boy at church in Brooklyn hears Henry Ward Beecher speak of the harbor as a place to come home to rest.   He thinks the preacher is mistaken, because the back windows and the garden of his home on the Heights look down on the harbor, and he knows it is a noisy, strange place of wharves inhabited by brutal dockers, and tall ships going to heathen lands.   When he grows older the harbor still seems to him repellant and ugly.   He goes to Paris to escape from the harbor and the drudgery of his father's warehouse, but returns to write "glory stories" about the life, energy, and wealth of the harbor.   He marries the daughter of an engineer, Dillon, who shows him his vision of a harbor organized for efficiency, the terminal for the railroads, and he writes a series of articles on "The First Port of the World."   Another influence is his friend, Joe Kramer, ultra-modern socialist, who even in college days scorned the history of the past as "news from the graveyard."   Joe sees the harbor only as a vast capitalist engine for the crushing of human lives.   Out of sympathy for the downtrodden, the hero takes part in a strike with the dockers, and sees the harbor from their point of view.   This experience leaves him a syndicalist, declaring his allegiance to the crowd intelligence, which he believes greater than the sum of the individual intelligences which makes it, and capable of evolving a solution of the social problem.   One god after another proves inadequate in the turmoil of life, the "kind god" of his mother's church, the "smiling goddess in Paris," the divinity of art, the "clear-eyed god of efficiency."   He elects to follow the "awakening god of the crowd," the god of service.   The environment throughout is the harbor, in different aspects, seen from docks, tugs, barges, ferry boats, decks of ocean liners, and in barrooms and tenements. He says, "I have seen three harbors; my father's harbor, which is now dead, Dillon's harbor of big companies, which is very much alive, and Joe Kramer's harbor which is struggling to be born."

HARD CASH, by Charles Reade. This book, originally published in 1863, as 'Very Hard Cash' is an alleged "exposure" of the abuses of private insane asylums in England and of the statutes under which they were sheltered. The "Hard Cash" is the sum of £14,000, the earnings of years, of which Richard Hardie, a bankrupt banker, defrauds David Dodd, a sea-captain. Dodd has a cataleptic shock and goes insane on realizing his loss. Hardie's son Alfred loves Julia, Dodd's daughter. He detects his father's villainy, accuses him of it, and to insure his silence is consigned by his father to a private insane asylum. There he meets Dodd; a fire breaks out, and both escape. Dodd enlists and serves as a common seaman, appearing to be capable but half-witted, until a second cataleptic shock restores his reason, when he returns home. Alfred reaches his friends, and vindicates his sanity in a court of law. The receipt for the £14,000 is found, and the money recovered from the elder Hardie. The book properly divides itself into two parts. One embraces the maritime adventures of Dodd with pirates, storms, shipwreck, and highwaymen, while bringing his money home; and his subsequent service as a half-witted foremast-hand until his restoration to reason. The other covers Alfred's thrilling experiences as a sane man among the insane. The author's analysis of all kinds of insanity is very thorough: with Alfred are contrasted Captain Dodd and many asylum patients, introduced incidentally; also Maxley, a worthy man driven insane by the bank failure, and who kills Alfred's sister in a maniacal rage; Dr. Wycherley, the asylum manager, who has epileptic fits himself; Thomas Hardie, Alfred's uncle, who is weak-minded; and others. Dr. Sampson, the sturdy Scotch physician, who despises all regular practitioners, and comes to Alfred's rescue at the crisis of the book, is one of Reade's strongest and most original characters. The love scenes are tender and touching. 'Hard Cash' is in some sense a sequel to 'Love me Little, Love me Long,' which relates the early history and marriage of Captain and Mrs. Dodd. This book caused much lively public correspondence between the author and various asylum managers, who felt themselves aggrieved, but failed, according to Reade, to shake the facts and arguments put forward in this book.

HARD TIMES, by Charles Dickens. When 'Hard Times' appeared as a serial in Household Words in 1854, Dickens was about midway in his literary career. In the same year this novel appeared in an octavo volume with a dedication to Thomas Carlyle. Its purpose, according to Dickens himself, was to satirize "those who see figures and averages and nothing else — the representatives of the wickedest and most enormous vice of this time — the men who through long years to come will do more to damage the really useful facts of Political Economy than I could do (if 1 tried) in my whole life." The satire, however, like much that Dickens attempted in the same vein, was not very bitter.

The characters in 'Hard Times' are not numerous; and the plot itself is less intricate than others by the same author. The chief figures are Mr. Thomas Gradgrind, "a man of realities," with his unbounded faith in statistics; Louisa, his eldest daughter; and Josiah Bounderby, as practical as Mr. Gradgrind, but less kind-hearted Louisa, though many years younger than Mr. Bounderby, is persuaded by her father to marry him. She is also influenced in making this marriage by her desire to smooth the path of her brother Tom, a clerk in Mr. Bounderby's office. Though not happy, she resists the blandishments of James Harthouse, a professed friend of her husband's. To escape him she has to go home to her father; and this leads to a permanent estrangement between husband and wife. In the meantime Tom Gradgrind has stolen money from Bounderby, and to avoid punishment runs away from England. Thus Louisa's sacrifice of herself has been useless. Mr. Gradgrind's wife, and his other children, play an unimportant part in the story. Of more consequence is Sissy (Cecilia) Jupe, whom the elder Gradgrind has befriended in spite of her being the daughter of a circus clown; and Mrs. Sparsit, Bounderby's housekeeper, who has seen better days, and is overpowering with her relationship to Lady Scadgers. Then there are Mr. McChoakumchild, the statistical school-teacher; Bitzer, the satisfactory pupil; and Mr. Sleary and his daughter Josephine, as the most conspicuous of the minor characters. Mrs. Pegler, the mother of Josiah Bounderby, is a curious and amusing figure; while a touch of pathos is given by the love of Stephen Blackpool the weaver, for Rachel, whom he cannot marry because his erring wife still lives.

Mr. Gradgrind came to see the fallacy of mere statistics; but Josiah Bounderby, the self-made man, who loved to belittle his own origin, never admitted that he could be wrong. When he died, Louisa was still young enough to repair her early mistake by a second and happier marriage.

HAROLD, by Sir Edward Bulwer-Lytton (1848) is the dramatic recital of the last years of Edward the Confessor's reign, — light being thrown upon those events which shaped the fortunes of Earl Godwin's son Harold. As in all Lord Lytton's works, vivid pictures are presented, sharp contrasts are employed to heighten dramatic situations, and inexorable fate plays an important rôle.

Earl Harold loved Edith the Fair, grandchild of Hilda the Saxon prophetess, and goddaughter to Harold's sister, the English queen. Hilda prophesied the union of Harold and Edith, though it was forbidden by the Church, they being members of the same family through Githa, Harold's mother.

To remove all doubts Queen Edith desired her goddaughter to enter a nunnery, — but Harold had his betrothed's promise to the contrary.

Duke William of Normandy had spent some time in England visiting King Edward; and he coveted the English realm. He had demanded and received as hostages Earl Godwin's youngest son, and his grandson Haco also; and when, after the old Earl's death, Harold crossed the sea to Normandy to demand back his father's hostages, William surrounded him with snares, and finally extorted from him a pledge to help forward William's claims in England at Edward's death. Then Harold returned home.

The English theyns, in council assembled, having chosen Harold as Edward's successor, the dying king confirmed their choice, and Harold became king. Now for State reasons, Harold *had* to marry Aldyth, the widowed sister of two powerful allies, and Edith demanded that he do so for his country's good; and so they parted, — he to do his country's behest, she to enter a convent to pray for him.

Tostig, Harold's traitor brother, having stirred up strife against him, Harold defeated and slew both Tostig and his ally, Hadrad the sea-king. Then came William and his Norman array, whom Harold met at Hastings in the autumn of 1066. History tells us, as the novelist does, how Harold and all his army were slain; but the romancer does not stop here. Edith the Fair, he tells us, came in the night and sought among the slain until she found the king. Laying her head upon his breast, she died, united to him as Hilda had prophesied.

HARRY LORREQUER, THE CONFESSIONS OF, a novel by Charles Lever (1839–40). The story is made up of a series of ludicrous adventures, very loosely connected. Of some of these Lever was himself the hero; others he gathered from his personal friends. Harry Lorrequer has scarcely landed in Cork, after campaigning with Wellington on the Continent, before he is entangled in the most tragic-comic perplexities. His first adventure consists in telling an inoffensive stranger an elaborate falsehood, and then shooting him in a duel, without disclosing any reason why he should fight at all. The scandalous immorality of the affair is forgotten in the grotesque drollery of it. In fact, the most characteristic note of the tale is the irresponsibility of every one. Drinking, duelling, getting into love and debt, are represented as an Irish gentleman's conception of the whole duty of man. Harry is presently sent in disgrace to the dull town of Kilrush. But his banishment is enlivened by every kind of adventure. The scene shifts to Dublin, and we have more hoaxes, practical jokes, and blunders. The hero starts "in a yellow postchaise" after the Kilkenny Royal Mail, traveling a hundred and fifty miles or so, the coach being all the time quietly in the court-yard of the Dublin post-office. We find him next in Germany, where he unconsciously hoaxes the Bavarian king and all his court. Lever knew the little German towns well, and his descriptions of their ludicrous aspects are true. Harry then proceeds to Paris, finds himself in a gambling saloon, and of course, breaks the bank. Most of the great men of France are among the gamblers; and Talleyrand, Marshal Soult, Balzac, and others, must have been surprised to learn of the part they took in the Donnybrook scrimmage with which the affair winds up. Finally, Harry weds the girl he has always adored, although his adoration has not hindered him from falling in love with scores of other ladies, and proposing marriage to some of them.

HARUSPICES, ON THE REPLY OF THE ('De Haruspicium responsis') an oration by Cicero (106–43 B. C.). After Cicero's recall from exile, different prodigies alarmed the people of Rome. The haruspices (priests who inspected the entrails of birds, etc., to draw omens of the gods' will or temper from their appearance), being consulted, answered that the public ceremonies had been neglected, the holy places profaned, and frightful calamities decreed in consequence. Thereupon Clodius assembled the citizens and denounced Cicero as the cause of the misfortunes that menaced the city. On the following day the orator replied in the Senate to the attack. In the first part of the oration he exposes the mendacity of Clodius, and says that as to his accusation that he, Cicero, had profaned the ground upon which his house stood, that was impossible, for it had already been officially decided that this ground had never been consecrated, in the legal sense. In the second part of the speech, which is full of fire and vehemence, he discusses each point in the reply of the haruspices, and shows that every one of them applies directly to Clodius, who has incurred the anger of the gods by his profanations, his impieties, and his unspeakable outrages. Therefore, Cicero concludes, Clodius himself is far more the foe of the gods than any other Roman, and is the most dangerous enemy of the State as well. This speech takes rank among the greatest of Cicero's orations, though the orator had little time for preparation, and suffered under the disadvantage of addressing an audience at first openly unfriendly.

HARVESTER, THE, by Gene Stratton-Porter (1911). The central figure in this story is David Langston, called the Harvester of the Woods, whose wholesome and honest nature commands the admiration of all who come in contact with him. When David is twenty his mother dies and for the next six years he carries on alone the work they had done together, of raising medicinal plants and herbs, and selling them. By great industry and constant study David develops his business until he becomes very prosperous and he is beginning to consider the subject of matrimony, when the vision of a beautiful girl comes to him, and he is convinced that she is his future wife. He at once builds a new house, furnishes it with every comfort and keeps on the lookout for the lovely face he saw in his vision. At last David sees his "dream-girl" alighting from a train but loses her immediately. He searches for her unceasingly and finally discovers her living with a cruel uncle who treats her shamefully. After a few meetings David begs his "dream-girl," whose name is Ruth Jameson, to marry him at once for protection if for nothing more, and she agrees to do so. David takes his wife to her new home, provides her with everything she can desire, and tells her she shall remain his honored guest until he succeeds in winning her love. The devotion and goodness of her husband win Ruth's affection but do not kindle the love which David craves. Ruth has a severe illness and David sends for Dr. Harmon for whom she had previously cared and offers to relinquish her to him if it is for her happiness. Ruth, however, soon tires of Dr. Harmon and David saves her life with one of his herb remedies when the doctors have given her up. Finally David sends Ruth on a long visit to her grandparents whom she has never seen on account of their estrangement from her parents, and the separation from David causes the awakening of the deep love for her husband for which he has longed and labored so patiently.

HARZREISE, DIE, by Heinrich Heine, the first of a series of descriptive essays of travel, entitled 'Reisebilder,' 'Die Harzreise,' ('The Harz-Journey') is an account of a walking tour made by the poet, during his student days in Göttingen, to the Harz Mountains, a wooded and hilly district of Hanover crowned by the celebrated Brocken which commands an extensive view over North Germany. The narrative is written in a spirit of mingled cynicism, satire, sentiment, and liberal zeal, and its delightful word-pictures and snatches of poetry alternate with wild phantasmagoric dreams, uproarious accounts of practical joking, daring jests on subjects commonly held sacred, exquisite idyllic passages and keen attacks on stupidity and reactionary thinking. The poet leaves Göttingen on a May morning, bidding farewell to effete civilization and welcoming the free mountain-life in a charming lyric. He traverses several small villages, encountering many odd wayfarers and stopping at various picturesque inns. In Klausthal he visits the silver mines and at Goslar inspects the relics of ancient imperial days; sheltered for the night in a miner's cottage among the pines, he records in delightful verse his conversations with a fair-haired child, who tells him fairy-tales, questions him as to his religious belief, and is told that he is a "knight of the Holy Ghost" in the war of liberation of the spirit. With thoughts of Goethe's Faust he ascends the wooded slopes and massive rocks of the Brocken; witnesses the sunset at the top; joins in hilarious supper in the inn at the summit; composes a lyric of greeting to the maiden in the valley as he looks over the wide landscape at sunrise; describes the downward course of the Ilse through its wooded and rocky valley; and personifies the river in a final lyric. The narrative is concluded with a passionate dedication to his cousin, Amalie, with whom he was in love.

THE READER'S DIGEST OF BOOKS — 381

HAUNTED POOL, THE, by George Sand. The 'Haunted Pool' (La Mare au Diable) was the first in a series of rustic novels begun by George Sand at Nohant in 1846, of which 'Les Maîtres Sonneurs' was the last. These simple stories, which have been called the 'Georgics' of France, are quite unlike the earliest works of their author, 'Indiana,' 'Valentine,' and 'Lelia,' both in style and in matter; and mark a distinct epoch in French literature. In explaining her purpose in writing them, George Sand disclaimed any pretense of accomplishing a revolution in letters: "I have wished neither to make a new tongue, nor to try a new manner." She had grown tired of the city, and her glimpses of rural life had led her to an exalted view of the peasant character. The poetry which she believed to exist in their lives, she succeeded in infusing into the romances which she wove around them.

'The Haunted Pool' has for its central figure Germain, a widower of twenty-eight, handsome, honorable, and living and working on the farm of his father-in-law, Maurice by name. The latter urges his son-in-law to marry again, both for his own good and for that of his three children. Germain demurs, largely because he cherishes so fondly the memory of his wife. But at last he consents to go to the neighboring village of Fourche, to see the widow Catherine Guérin, daughter of Farmer Leonard, who is well off, and according to Maurice, of suitable age to marry Germain. Before he starts on his journey, a neighbor of Germain, the poor widow Guillette, asks him to take in his care her sixteen-year-old daughter Mary, who has engaged to go as a shepherdess to a farmer at Fourche. On the way, Pierre, the young son of Germain, insists that his father shall take him as well as little Mary to Fourche on his horse, La Grise. The trio lose their way, the horse runs off, and they are obliged to spend the night on the borders of the "haunted pool." The tact of little Mary, and her kindness to his child, so work on Germain that he falls in love with her. He goes on, however, to see the widow; but her coquetry, and the insincerity of her father, disgust him, and he does not make his offer of marriage. On the way home he overtakes little Mary, who has been insulted by her employer at The Elms. At first she refuses to marry Germain, calling him too old. But in the course of a year she changes her mind, and makes him perfectly happy.

HAVELOK THE DANE. This legend is connected with the founding of Grimsby in Lincolnshire; and was written in English and French verse about 1280 A. D. The English version was lost for many years, but at last found in a manuscript of 'Lives of the Saints.' The author is unknown; the time of the story probably about the sixth century. Havelok, prince of Denmark, is left to the care of Earl Godard, who hires a fisherman, Grim, to drown him; but he, perceiving a miraculous light about the child, dares not put him to death, and carries him to England. The boy grows up, and finds work with the cook of Godrich, an earl who has in his charge the late king's daughter, Goldborough, whom he has promised to marry to the strongest and fairest man he can find. In a trial of strength, Havelok "puts the stone" farther than any other; and Godrich, who wants the kingdom for his son, marries Goldborough to this kitchen scullion. The princess is dissatisfied with the union; but in the night sees the same miraculous light, and a cross on Havelok's shoulder. He awakes immediately afterwards, and tells her he has dreamed that all England and Denmark were his own. He goes therefore to Denmark; and after performing deeds of great valor, is proclaimed king. Returning with an army to England, he makes Godrich a prisoner; and with Goldborough is crowned at London, where they reign for sixty years.

HAY, JOHN, LIFE AND LETTERS OF, a biography by William Roscoe Thayer, was published in 1915. Illustrating his narrative by abundant quotations from John Hay's letters and journals the author narrates in an extremely graphic and interesting manner Hay's boyhood in the Middle West, his happy student days at Brown University, his unique experiences as private secretary to Lincoln, his literary successes as poet, essayist, and biographer, and his career as ambassador and cabinet minister. His diplomatic achievements in connection with the Boxer Rebellion, at the close of which he successfully defended the principle of the "Open Door" in China, and in the Alaskan Boundary Dispute are here fully discussed. The book is a thoroughly adequate presentation of a great American statesman and is particularly successful in depicting the humor, gayety, and charm of his personality.

HAZARD OF NEW FORTUNES, A, by W. D. Howells (1890) is perhaps the most realistic and the most modern of all his novels, in its grasp upon the conditions of metropolitan life, especially as these are illustrated in the extremes of poverty and wealth. The scope of the story is unusually large, embracing as it does representatives from almost every prominent class of society: the artist, the bohemian, the business man, the capitalist, the society woman, the socialist, the labor agitator, the man of letters. The plot is, however, centred in one family, as typical of a certain kind of Americanism as the Lapham family is of another. The head of this family is Dryfoos, a Pennsylvania German who has come to New York to spend his newly acquired fortune. He is the capitalist of a journal, Every Other Week, edited by Basil March, the hero of 'Their Wedding Journey,' and conducted by Fulkerson, a pushing Westerner. Dryfoos has two daughters, vulgar by nature and breeding, who are struggling to get "into society." His son, Conrad, is of a different stamp. He has no sympathy with the gross pride of his father in the wealth gained by speculation. His sympathies are with the laboring classes, — with the down-trodden and unfortunate of the city. This sympathy is put to the last proof during the strike of the street-car drivers and conductors. In endeavoring to stand by Lindau, an old German socialist who is openly siding with the strikers, Conrad is killed by a chance shot. His death seems a kind of vicarious atonement for the greed and pride of his race. There are many side issues in the story, which as a whole forms a most striking and picturesque series of metropolitan scenes. New York has seldom been used with more skill as a dramatic background. But the novel is something more than a clever drawing of places and people. Deep ethical and social questions are involved in it. It is a drama of human life in the fullest sense.

HEADLONG HALL, by Thomas Love Peacock. Written in 1815, 'Headlong Hall' is a study of typical English life put into the form of numerous detached conversations, discussions, and descriptions. At first it tells how invitations have been sent to a perfectibilian, a deteriorationist, a statu-quo-ite, and a reverend doctor who had won the squire's fancy by a learned dissertation on the art of stuffing a turkey. There is a graphic picture of the squire at breakfast. After the arrival of the guests they are taken over the grounds, dined, fêted, taken to walk, introduced to the tower, and given a ball. In the interim one of them discovers the skull of Cadwallader and begs possession of it from the old sexton, and being somewhat of a physiologist, follows his discovery with a learned dissertation on the animal man. The whole story is bright, witty, humorous, devoid of plot, and elaborate in its phrasing. It is engaging as a relic of old English life. Mr. Peacock was born in 1785, and died in 1866. The present is perhaps a little better known than any of his other seven books, though

'Gryll Grange,' 'Crotchet Castle,' and 'Nightmare Abbey' are also to be reckoned among standard, if not classical, English literature. The story is distinguished by a display of varied erudition, and is to some extent, like his other books, a satire on well-known characters and fads of the day.

HEAPS OF MONEY, by W. E. Norris (1877), was the earliest of that clever author's stories, and won instant favor from competent critics. The heroine, Linda Howard, an earl's granddaughter, spends her young life wandering about the Continent with her somewhat disreputable father, who ekes out a slender income by great skill at *écarte*. At nineteen she inherits a large fortune from an uncle, and the scene changes. The Howards return to their native land, where Linda is quickly launched into society, and sought after by the match-making mammas of penniless sons. In the social experiences that follow, she discovers that life when one has heaps of money is quite as difficult an affair as when one has to count every shilling. This early story reveals the qualities which have made Mr. Norris so successful a novelist. He sees life from the point of view of the man of the world, but without cynicism or super-ciliousness. His personages are lifelike, his dialogue is always good and often brilliant, his story comes from the natural evolution of his characters, his insight into human nature is keen, he is often witty and always humorous. In no sense an imitator, Mr. Norris's style and manner remind one of Thackeray, chiefly perhaps in the ease with which each artist handles his material.

HEART OF MIDLOTHIAN, THE, by Sir Walter Scott. 'The Heart of Midlothian,' by many called the finest of the Waverley novels, was published anonymously in 1818. It takes its name from the Tolbooth or old jail of Edinburgh (pulled down in 1815), where Scott imagined Effie Deans, his heroine, to have been imprisoned. The charge against her is child murder, from which she is unable to clear herself. Her half-sister Jeanie, though loving her devotedly, on the witness stand cannot tell the lie which might save Effie. But when sentence of death is pronounced on the unhappy girl, Jeanie shows the depth of her affection by going on foot to London to get a pardon from the King, through the influence of John, Duke of Argyle. The latter obtains an interview for her with Queen Caroline and Lady Suffolk, and though at first the case seems hopeless enough, she procures the pardon. Before Jeanie has reached home, Effie (whose pardon carried with it banishment from Scotland) has eloped with George Staunton, her lover. The sisters who had last met when Effie was sitting on the bench of the condemned, do not meet again for many years, when Effie reappears as Lady Staunton, a woman of fashion. Her husband has succeeded to a title, and no one but her sister knows her as the former Effie Deans. By a strange combination of circumstances, Jeanie, now married to a Presbyterian minister, learns that Effie's son is alive. He had been given by Meg Murdockson, who attended Effie in her illness, to an unscrupulous woman. Sir George Staunton, on learning these facts, anxious to discover his son, traces him to a certain troop of vagabonds, of which Black Donald is chief. In an affray growing out of the effort to arrest Black Donald, Sir George is shot by a young lad called "the Whistler," who later proved to be the lost son. Lady Staunton, overcome by the tragedy, after vain efforts to drown her grief in society retires to a convent in France. Although she takes no vows, she remains there until her death. Her influence at court accomplishes much for the children of her sister Jeanie. The husband of the latter, Reuben Butler, has been given a good parish by the Duke of Argyle, whom Jeanie Deans's heroism had made a friend for life.

'The Heart of Midlothian' is notable for having fewer characters than any other of Scott's novels. It has also a smaller variety of incidents, and less description of scenery. One of the most remarkable scenes in all fiction is the meeting of the two sisters in prison under the eyes of the jailer Ratcliffe.

The plot was suggested to Scott by the story of Helen Walker, who unable to tell a lie to save a sister's life, really walked barefoot to London, and secured a pardon by the help of John, Duke of Argyle.

HEART OF THE ANTARCTIC, THE, 'being the story of the British Antarctic Expedition, 1907–1909' by Sir Ernest Henry Shackleton, is a highly readable and sumptuously illustrated account in two large volumes of the polar expedition which attained 88° 23' south latitude, reached the South Magnetic Pole, and discovered and explored a great range of mountains in the interior of the Antarctic Continent. Shackleton's general account of the expedition and special narrative of the "Southern Party" which achieved a point at that time "farthest south" occupies the first volume and part of the second. It is rendered especially interesting by the spectacular character of the discoveries. The landing at the great ice-barrier, one hundred and fifty feet high and the ascent by the world's largest glacier through a corridor of lofty peaks then seen for the first time, to the plateau eleven thousand feet high which is the site of the South Pole, are adventures of thrilling novelty. The second volume is mainly occupied with an account of the party which discovered the South Magnetic Pole, written by Professor T. W. Edgeworth David, its commander, and there is a highly interesting and entertaining appendix on the scientific discoveries of the expedition. James Murray, the biologist of the company, describes the habits and peculiarities of penguins and seals. Professor David and Raymond Priestley, geologists, give full information as to the physical geography, glaciology, and geology of the region with especial reference to the mountains. Douglas Mawson and James Murray add notes on physics, chemistry, and mineralogy. Their remarks on snow-crystals and on the atmospherical and optical phenomena of the antarctic zone, particularly the *aurora australis*, are full of interest. All these scientific data, as well as the travel-narratives are made vivid by the splendid illustrations, both photographs and colored drawings, with which the book abounds. The reader can see the vast polar ocean and the towering ice-barrier, the snowy, smoke-capped summits of Erebus and Terror, and the yawning volcanic crater of the former. Seals suckling their young on the ice, solemn penguins ceremonially bowing to one another, ponies tethered beside the tents on the plateau, enliven the pictures. Most impressive are the naked rocky peaks that rise sheer above the Great Glacier, the glowing reds, greens, and blues of the antarctic sunrise and the ethereal green palpitations of the *aurora australis*. Few travel-books surpass this one in sustained interest and novelty.

HEART OF THE HILLS, THE, by John Fox, Jr. (1913). The scene of this story is laid in the hills of Kentucky and it deals for the most part with the lives of the mountaineers. The principal character is Jason Hawn, who, when first introduced to the reader, is a small boy living with his widowed mother in a cabin in the hills. His father having been mysteriously shot by an unknown assassin, had told Jason on his death-bed to hunt down his murderer and avenge his death. As a feud of long standing had existed between the Hawns and the Honeycutts, a member of the latter clan is supposed to have committed the deed. Jason grows up with a bitter hatred for the Honeycutts and looks forward to the time when he shall avenge his father's murder. He has a pretty cousin of about his own age named Mavis Hawn who is devoted to him and has in him a warm champion. Steve Hawn, Mavis's father, a tricky and shiftless fellow, after a period of widowerhood marries Jason's mother much to the son's disappointment and grief. Steve persuades his wife to sell land, upon which Jason had discovered coal, and though the latter had not divulged his secret he had exacted from his mother a promise not to sell without his knowledge. The purchaser of the land is Colonel Pendleton, who represents a large company, and he has a son named Gray, who is about the age of Jason. Gray and his pretty little cousin Marjorie are brought by the Colonel to the hills where they meet Jason and Mavis and are strangely attracted to these children who are so different in manners and speech. Later Jason and Mavis go to school and then to college where they find themselves fellow-students with Gray and Marjorie. Here the old attraction reasserts itself and Gray and Mavis, and Marjorie and Jason, find themselves drawn to each other. Eventually however, both couples realize the inappropriateness of their union, and the book closes with the readjustment of their love affairs and the marriage of Gray and Marjorie, followed by that of Jason and Mavis. Previous to this Jason had inadvertently avenged his father's death by shooting a prowler, who was robbing Colonel Pendleton's estate after having committed many other crimes and acts of lawlessness. The robber proved to be Steve Hawn, and after his death, Jason's mother tells him he was the man who shot his father. Jason becomes a civil engineer and the reader takes leave of him as superintendent of the coal mines which are being developed upon his old property.

HEAT CONSIDERED AS A MODE OF MOTION, LECTURES ON, a course of twelve lectures delivered at the Royal Institution of Great Britain in 1862 and published in 1863. Tyndall's aim was to expound to a popular audience the mechanical or dynamical theory of heat as distinguished from the old material theory that heat was a substance called "caloric," and to illustrate it first in connection with solid, liquid, and gaseous bodies, and secondly in an account of the transmission or radiation of heat by means of the waves of ether. By a series of experiments he shows that all mechanical force when expended produces heat; explains how the mechanical equivalent of heat has been determined; sets forth the conception of heat as molecular motion; and applies this conception to the various forms of matter, to expansion and combustion, to specific and latent heat, and to calorific conduction. He then explains the operation of radiant heat from the sun and other heavenly bodies, through the ether; shows that the sun is the source of all life on the earth; and rises from this fact to a contemplation of the universe as dominated by the principle of the conservation of energy. Tyndall had great clearness of exposition and an abundance of interesting experiments to prove and enforce his points. He can excite the attention by homely illustrations and rouse the imagination by striking glimpses into the deeper problems of science.

HEAVENLY TWINS, THE, by Madame Sarah Grand (1893), is the novel which brought the author into notice and aroused great discussion for and against the book. It is a study of the advanced modern woman. The heroine, Evadne, finds herself married to a man of social position whose past has been impure. She therefore leaves him, to the scandal of her friends. An episode called 'The Tenor and the Boy,' bearing little relation to the main story but pleasing in itself, is then interpolated: it narrates the love between a male churchsinger and a lad who turns out to be a girl, one of the twins in disguise. The character of these twins, a pair of precocious, forward youngsters, boy and girl, is sketched amusingly in the early portion of the story. After the separation from her husband, Evadne leads a life of protest against society as it exists, and her sorrow and disillusionment prey upon her health to such an extent that her complex nervous system suffers from hysteria. Dr. Galbraith, the physician who narrates this phase of her career, becomes her husband; and in his professional care and honest love Evadne bids fair to find both physical and moral peace. The novel is too long, has grave faults of construction, and contains material for three separate stories and a tract on women's rights. But it was at once recognized as a sympathetic presentation of some of the social wrongs of women.

HEDDA GABLER, a play by Henrik Ibsen (1890). A remarkable study of the character of a selfish, hard-hearted woman endowed with beauty, good taste, education, and culture, but spiritually a monster. She is kept from expressing her evil genius only by cowardly fear of public opinion. In the discord of a dull cramping environment she has not courage to free herself and is shipwrecked. The play begins as Hedda and her husband return from their wedding trip, and Hedda reveals her character immediately by her unkind treatment of her husband's old aunt, who comes to welcome her. The aristocrat, Hedda, daughter of General Gabler, has married a kindly but stupid Ph.D., chiefly because he promised to buy her a certain luxurious villa she coveted for her home. His pedantry bores her. She has miscalculated his professional future as well as his income; and she dreads the prospect of a child. Before her marriage she had enjoyed an intimate friendship with a drunken dissipated young genius, Lövberg. He had misinterpretated her morbid curiosity about the details of his dissipation and they parted in a theatrical scene in which Hedda repelled his advances with her father's pistol. Lövberg becomes tutor to the stepchildren of Thea Elsted, who reclaims the degenerate genius with her sympathy and interest, and inspires him to write the book which brings him fame. Thea defies the conventions to follow him to the city, knowing that without her influence he will relapse into drunkenness and dissipation. The heartless Hedda, jealous of his good angel, contrives to make him fall into his old evil ways, simply to demonstrate her power over him. He loses the manuscript of his second book, which by perverse chance comes into Hedda's possession. She conceals it and malignantly burns it, giving as excuse to her husband, that Lövberg is his rival for a professorship. Lövberg accuses a disreputable woman of stealing the manuscript and gets into a brawl with the police in her house. He confesses the loss of the manuscript and the scandal to Hedda, and she presents him with one of her father's brace of pistols, advising him "to die beautifully." Later he returns to the woman, and in a violent quarrel is fatally shot in the stomach with the pistol. Hedda had indulged in a dangerous friendship with Judge Brack, an elderly rake, who recognizes the pistol and threatens to expose Hedda to the scandal she dreads, in order to get her in his power. While Thea and Tessman are planning the reconstruction of Lövberg's book, Hedda goes to the back of the room and kills herself with a pistol shot — in the head.

HEIMSKRINGLA, THE, by Snorri Sturlason. This chronicle of the kings of Norway (from the earliest times down to 1177), sometimes known as the 'Younger Edda' or the 'Mythic Ring of the World,' was originally written in Icelandic, in the early part of the thirteenth century. It has always been a household word in the home of every peasant in Iceland, and is entertaining reading to those who read for mere amusement, as well as to the student of history; being full of incident and anecdote, told with racy simplicity, and giving an accurate picture of island life at that early day. Short pieces of scaldic poetry originally recited by bards are interspersed, being quoted by Snorri as his authorities for the facts he tells. The writer, born in Iceland in 1178, was educated by a grandson of Sæmund Sigfusson, author of the 'Elder Edda,' who doubtless turned his pupil's thoughts in the direction of this book. A descendant of the early kings, he would naturally like to study their history. He became chief magistrate of Iceland, took an active part in politics, and was murdered in 1241 by his two sons-in-law, at the instigation of King Hakon. His book was first printed in 1697, in a Latin translation, having been inculcated in manuscript, or by word of mouth, up to that time. It was afterwards translated into Danish and English, and may be regarded as a classic work.

HEIR OF REDCLYFFE, THE (1853), by Charlotte Mary Yonge, is a sad but interesting love story, and gives a picture of the home life of an English family in the country.

Sir Guy Morville, the attractive young hero, leaves Redclyffe after the death of his grandfather, and becomes a member of his guardian's large household. Many incidents are related of his life there with Laura, Amy, and Charlotte, their lame brother Charles, and his own sedate, antagonistic cousin, Philip Morville. At the end of three years he and Amy confess their love for each other; but as he is still a youth, no engagement is made, and at the advice of his guardian he leaves Hollywell. Philip wrongly suspects Guy of gambling, and tells his guardian his suspicions. Guy has paid his uncle's gaming debts, and when called upon for an explanation he is too generous to clear his character at his uncle's expense. He is banished from Hollywell, and returns to Redclyffe at the end of the Oxford term. At Redclyffe Guy bravely rescues some shipwrecked men after a storm at sea, and before long his reputation is restored by his uncle. He returns to Hollywell, finds that Amy has been true to him, and they are married. They go abroad for their wedding journey; and after a few weeks of mutual happiness, they learn that Philip is sick with a fever in Italy. Guy overlooks past injustice, they go to him, and Guy nurses him through a severe illness. He takes the fever himself and dies shortly afterwards, leaving Amy to mourn his loss for the rest of her life. The story ends with the marriage of Philip and Laura, who had long been secretly engaged; and as Guy's child is a girl, Philip inherits Redclyffe.

The two characters which stand out in the book are Guy Morville, generous, manly, bright, and of a lovable disposition; and Philip, stern, honorable, self-esteeming, and unrelentingly prejudiced against Guy — until Guy's unselfish nobility of conduct forces him to humble contrition.

HELDENBUCH, a name given successively to several versions of a collection of German legends from the thirteenth century. The first 'Heldenbuch' was printed in Strasburg, probably in the year 1470; the second in Dresden in 1472. The latter version was almost entirely divested of the quaint poetic charm of the original legends by the dry, pedantic style of one of the editors, by whose name the collection is known, — Kasper von der Roen. The older volume, however, preserved the spirit of the thirteenth century with admirable fidelity, both in its text and in the delightfully naïve illustrations which accompany it.

Among the heroic myths which appear in the original 'Heldenbuch' are the ancient Gothic legends of 'King Laurin' and 'The Rose Garden at Worms,' together with three from the Lombard cycle, 'Ornit,' 'Wolfdietrich,' and 'Hugdietrich.' These have been rendered into Modern High German in the present century by Karl Josef Simrock, whose scholarly and sympathetic translation makes his 'Kleines

Heldenbuch' as valuable a contribution to the history of German literature as was the original collection of the same name.

HELEN, by Maria Edgeworth.   This old-fashioned novel describes the social life of England in the early part of the nineteenth century; and draws a moral by showing how one deception leads to another, and finally envelops the whole life in deceit and wretchedness.   A mere statement of the plot is of no interest: the value of the story is in its humor and its knowledge of the human heart.

Among the characters are Cecilia; her mother, Lady Devenant, a spirited society woman, and a very kind friend to Helen (the heroine); Miss Clarendon, a blunt outspoken woman, and a modern type to find in an old novel; besides Lord Beltravers, a false friend of Granville Beauclerc, the hero.   'Helen' was published in 1834.   It was the last novel Miss Edgeworth wrote before her death fifteen years afterwards.

HELMET OF NAVARRE, THE, by Bertha Runkle, was published in 1901, and was one of the successful novels of the year.   The scene is laid in France at the time that Henry of Navarre is about to ascend the throne, and deals with the adventures of Felix Broux, a youth whose family had for centuries faithfully served the Dukes of St. Quentin.   At a time when his master, as an open enemy of the League, is in great danger, Broux goes to Paris to join him and immediately finds himself involved in all sorts of intrigues and difficulties.   The Duke of St. Quentin and his son, the Comte de Mar, have become estranged through the villainies of one Lucas, who is employed as the Duke's secretary, but, who in reality is a spy of the League.   Young Broux is the means of bringing about a reconciliation between father and son, and of exposing the evil machinations of Lucas, and afterwards serves De Mar with unfailing loyalty and ingenuity.   He proves to be an invaluable aid in the love affair of the Comte and Lorance de Montluc, the ward of Monsieur de Mayenne, and helps to bring the lovers together in spite of the many difficulties placed in their way.   Lucas, the evil genius of the story, weaves plot after plot to bring the St. Quentins to ruin, and time after time when on the very brink of destruction they are saved by chance or strategy.   The book is full of adventures and hairbreadth escapes, has snares and secret passages, mysterious inns and rascally landlords, and plenty of sword play. The action of the romance extends over only four days but it is most spirited, and includes many exciting incidents which the young author has woven into her charming whole with surprising ease and skill.

HELPMATE, THE, by May Sinclair (1907).   The title of this novel is ironic.   It is a sympathetic study of the married life of a sinner and a saint, in which one's sympathies are always with the sinner.   The theme is that sin is more often weakness than wickedness, and that goodness can as often be pride as holiness.   While Walter and Anne Majendie are on their honeymoon, rumors reach the wife that seven years before he knew her, her husband had had a liaison with an older married woman. He had reason to suppose that Anne had been exactly informed concerning this affair before her marriage.   In her eyes he is a moral leper.   Though a man of no great force he has unusual sweetness of temper, and waits patiently for his wife to respond to his devoted affection.   He is constitutionally incapable of sinking to the depths of abasement and perpetual expiation to which she condemns him.   The cold virtue of his wife finally drives him to seek consolation in clandestine relations with a little shop girl.   Their child dies while Walter is away from home.   His grief and strain and Anne's accusations and reproaches precipitate a paralytic stroke.   She nurses him back to health and in the end all is well, since Anne through suffering comes to realize her own shortcomings, after nine tragic years of misunderstanding.

HENRY IV. by Shakespeare. Part i., stands at the head of all Shakespeare's historical comedies, as Falstaff is by far his best humorous character. The two parts of the drama were first published in 1598 and 1600 respectively, the source-texts for both being Holinshed's 'Chronicles' and the old play, 'The famous Victories of Henry the Fifth.' The contrasted portraits of the impetuous Hotspur (Henry Percy) and the chivalric Prince Henry in Part i., are masterly done. King Henry, with the crime of Richard II.'s death on his conscience, was going on a crusade, to divert attention from himself; but Glendower and Hotspur give him his hands full at home. Hotspur has refused to deliver up certain prisoners taken on Holmedon field: "My liege, I did deny no prisoners," he says in the well-known speech painting to the life the perfumed dandy on the field of battle. However, the Percys revolt from the too haughty monarch; and at Shrewsbury the Hotspur faction, greatly outnumbered by the King's glittering host, is defeated, and Percy himself slain by Prince Harry. For the humorous portions we have first the broad talk of the carriers in the inn-yard at Rochester; then the night robbery at Gadshill, where old Jack frets like a gummed varlet, and lards the earth with perspiration as he seeks his horse hidden by Bardolph behind a hedge. Prince Hal and Poins rob the robbers. Falstaff and his men hack their swords, and tickle their noses with grass to make them bleed. Then after supper, at the Boar's Head, in slink the disappointed Falstaffians, and Jack regales the Prince and Poins with his amusing whoppers about the dozen or so of rogues in Kendal green that set upon them at Gadshill. Hal puts him down with a plain tale. Great hilarity all around. Hal and Jack are in the midst of a mutual mock-judicial examination when the sheriff knocks at the door. The fat knight falls asleep behind the arras, and has his pockets picked by the Prince. Next day the latter has the money paid back, and he and Falstaff set off for the seat of war, Jack marching by Coventry with his regiment of tattered prodigals. Attacked by Douglas in the battle, Falstaff falls, feigning death. He sees the Prince kill Hotspur, and afterwards rises, gives the corpse a fresh stab, lugs it off on his back, and swears he and Hotspur fought a good hour by Shrewsbury clock, and that he himself killed him. The prince magnanimously agrees to gild the lie with the happiest terms he has, if it will do his old friend any grace.

HENRY IV., Part ii., by Shakespeare (First known Edition, 1600), forms a dramatic whole with the preceding. The serious parts are more of the nature of dramatized chronicle; but the humorous scenes are fully as delightful and varied as in the first part. Hotspur is dead, and King Henry is afflicted with insomnia and nearing his end. "Uneasy lies the head that wears a crown," he says in the fine apostrophe to sleep. At Gaultree Forest his son Prince John tricks his enemies into surrender, and sends the leaders to execution. The death-bed speeches of the King and Prince Henry are deservedly famous. All the low-comedy characters reappear in this sequel. Dame Quickly appears, with officers Snare and Fang, to arrest Falstaff, who has put all her substance into that great belly of his. In Part i. we found him already in her debt: for one thing, she had bought him a dozen of shirts to his back. Further, sitting in the Dolphin chamber by a sea-coal fire, had he not sworn upon a parcel-gilt goblet to marry her? But the merry old villain deludes her still more, and she now pawns her plate and tapestry for him. Now enter Prince Hal and Poins from the wars, and ribald and coarse are the scenes unveiled. Dame

Quickly has deteriorated: in the last act of this play she is shown being dragged to prison with Doll Tearsheet, to answer the death of a man at her inn. The accounts of the trull Doll, and her billingsgate talk with Pistol, are too unsavory to be entirely pleasant reading; and one gladly turns from the atmosphere of the slums to the fresh country air of Gloucestershire, where, at Justice Shallow's manse, Falstaff is "pricking down" his new recruits, — Mouldy, Feeble, Wart, etc. Shallow is like a forked radish with a beard carved on it, or a man made out of a cheese-paring. He is given to telling big stories about what a wild rake he was at Clement's Inn in his youth. Sir John swindles the poor fellow out of a thousand pounds. But listen to Shallow: "Let me see, Davy; let me see, Davy; let me see." "Sow the headland with red wheat, Davy"; "Let the smith's note for shoeing and plough-irons be cast and paid." "Nay, Sir John, you shall see my orchard, where, in an arbor, we shall eat a last year's pippin of my own graffing, with a dish of caraways and so forth." Amid right merry chaffing and drinking enters Pistol with news of the crowning of Henry V. "Away, Bardolph! saddle my horse; we'll ride all night; boot, boot, Master Shallow, I know the King is sick for me," shouts old Jack. Alas for his hopes! he and his companions are banished the new King's presence, although provided with the means to live.

HENRY V. is the last of Shakespeare's ten great war dramas. It was written in 1599, printed in 1600, the materials being derived from the same sources as are given above. Henry IV. is dead, and bluff King Hal is showing himself to be every inch a king. His claim to the crown of France is solemnly sanctioned. The Dauphin has sent him his merry mock of tennis balls, and got his stern answer. The traitors — Cambridge, Scroop, and Grey — have been sent to their death. The choice youth of England (and some riff-raff, too, such as Bardolph, Nym, and Pistol) have embarked at Southampton, and the threaden sails have drawn the huge bottoms through the sea to France. The third act opens in the very heat of an attack upon the walls of the seaport of Harfleur, and King Harry is urging on his men in that impassioned speech — "Once more unto the breach, dear friends" — which thrills the heart like a slogan in battle. We also catch glimpses of the army in Picardy, and finally see it on the eve of Agincourt. The night is rainy and dark, the hostile camps are closely joined. King Henry, cheerful and strong, goes disguised through his camp, and finds that whatever the issue of the war may be, he is expected to bear all the responsibility. A private soldier — Williams — impeaches the King's good faith, and the disguised Henry accepts his glove as a gauge and challenge for the morrow. Day dawns, the fight is on, the dogged English win the day. Then, as a relief to his nerves, Henry has his bit of fun with Williams, who has sworn to box the ear of the man caught wearing the mate of his glove. The wooing by King Henry of Kate, the French King's daughter, ends the play. But all through the drama runs also a comic vein. The humorous characters are Pistol, — now married to Nell Quickly, — Bardolph, Nym, and Fluellen. Falstaff, his heart "fracted and corroborate" by the King's casting of him off, and babbling o' green fields, has "gone to Arthur's bosom." His followers are off for the wars. At Harfleur, Bardolph, of the purple and bubukled nose, cries, "On to the breach!" very valorously, but is soon hanged for robbing a church. Le grand Capitaine Pistol so awes a poor Johnny Crapaud of a prisoner that he offers him two hundred crowns in ransom. Pistol fires off some stinging bullets of wit at the Saint Tavy's day leek in the cap of Fluellen, who presently makes him eat a leek, giving him the cudgel over the head for sauce. The blackguard hies him home to London to swear he got his scalp wound in the wars.

HENRY VI., Parts i., ii., iii.   (First printed in 1623).   Of the eight closely linked Shakespeare historical plays, these three cover nearly all of the fifteenth century in this order: 'Richard II.'; 'Henry IV.,' Parts i. and ii.; 'Henry V.'; 'Henry VI.' (three parts); and 'Richard III.' — Henry IV. grasped the crown from Richard II., the rightful owner, and became the founder of the house of Lancaster.   About 1455 began the Wars of the Roses.   (The Lancastrians wore as a badge the white rose, the Yorkists the red; Shakespeare gives the origin of the custom in Henry VI., Part i.. Act ii., Scene 4, adherents of each party chancing in the Temple Garden, London, to pluck each a rose of this color or that as symbol of his adherency.)   In 1485 the Lancastrian Henry VII., the conqueror of Richard III., ended these disastrous wars, and reconciled the rival houses by marriage with Elizabeth of York.

The three parts of 'Henry VI.,' like 'Richard II.,' present a picture of a king too weak-willed to properly defend the dignity of the throne.   They are reeking with blood and echoing with the clash of arms.   They are sensationally and bombastically written, and such parts of them as are by Shakespeare are known to be his earliest work.   His work seems to have been that of a reviser; and the general plan of the plays and their successor 'Richard III.' is after Marlowe's manner.

In Part i. the scene lies chiefly in France, where the brave Talbot and Exeter and the savage York and Warwick are fighting the French.   Joan of Arc is here represented by the poet (who only followed English chronicle and tradition) as a charlatan, a witch, and a strumpet.   The picture is an absurd caricature of the truth.   In Part ii., the leading character is Margaret, whom the Duke of Suffolk has brought over from France and married to the weak and nerveless poltroon King Henry VI., but is himself her guilty lover.   He and Buckingham and Margaret conspire successfully against the life of the Protector, Duke Humphrey, and Suffolk is killed during the rebellion of Jack Cade, — an uprising of the people which the play merely burlesques.   Part iii. is taken up with the horrible murders done by fiendish Gloster (afterward Richard III.) the defeat and imprisonment of Henry VI. and his assassination in prison by Gloster, and the seating of Gloster's brother Edward (IV.) on the throne.   The brothers, including Clarence, stab Queen Margaret's son and imprison her.   She appears again as a subordinate character in 'Richard III.'   In 1476 she renounced her claim to the throne and returned to the Continent.

HENRY VIII., a historical drama by Shakespeare (first printed in 1623), based on Edward Hall's 'Union of the Families of Lancaster and York,' Holinshed's 'Chronicles,' and Fox's 'Acts and Monuments of the Church.'   The key-idea is the mutability of earthly grandeur, and by one or another turn of Fortune's wheel, the overthrow of the mighty — i.e., of the Duke of Buckingham, of Cardinal Wolsey, and of Queen Katharine.   The action covers a period of sixteen years, from the Field of the Cloth of Gold, in 1520, described in the opening pages, to the death of Queen Katharine in 1536.   It is the trial and divorce of this patient, queenly, and unfortunate woman, that forms the main subject of the drama.   She was the daughter of Ferdinand and Isabella of Castile, and born in 1485.   She had been married when seventeen to Arthur, eldest son of Henry VII.   Arthur lived only five months after his marriage, and when at seventeen years Henry VIII. came to the throne (that "most hateful ruffian and tyrant"), he married Katharine, then twenty-four.   She bore him children, and he never lost his respect for her and her unblemished life.   But twenty years after his marriage he met Anne Bullen at a merry ball at Cardinal Wolsey's palace, and fell in love with her, and immediately conceived conscientious scruples against the legality of his marriage.   Queen Katharine is brought to trial before a solemn council of nobles and churchmen. With fine dignity she appeals to the Pope and leaves the council, refusing then and ever after to attend "any of their courts." The speeches are masterpieces of pathetic and noble defense. In all his facts the poet follows history very faithfully. The Pope goes against her, and she is divorced and sequestered at Kimbolton, where presently she dies heart-broken, sending a dying message of love to Henry. Intertwined with the sad fortunes of the queen are the equally crushing calamities that overtake Cardinal Wolsey. His high-blown pride, his oppressive exactions in amassing wealth greater than the king's, his *ego et rex meus*, his double dealing with Henry in securing the Pope's sanction to the divorce, — these and other things are the means whereby his many enemies work his ruin. He is stripped of all his dignities and offices, and wanders away, an old man broken with the storms of State, to lay his bones in Leicester Abbey. The episode of the trial of Archbishop Cranmer is so pathetically handled as to excite tears. He is brought to trial for heresy by his enemy Gardiner, bishop of Winchester, but has previously been moved to tears of gratitude by Henry's secretly bidding him be of good cheer, and giving him his signet ring as a talisman to conjure with if too hard pressed by his enemies. Henry is so placed as to oversee (himself unseen) Cranmer's trial and the arrogant persecution of Gardiner. Cranmer produces the ring just as they are commanding him to be led away to the Tower; and Henry steps forth to first rebuke his enemies and then command them to be at peace. He does Cranmer the high honor of asking him to become a godfather to the daughter (Elizabeth) of Anne Bullen; and after Cranmer's eloquent prophecy at the christening, the curtain falls. The setting of this play is full of rich and magnificent scenery and spectacular pomp.

HENRY ESMOND. This splendid romance, published in 1852, is one of the most important of Thackeray's novels. It is a romance of the time of Queen Anne, and purports to be told by the hero in the years of rest after the storm and stress of a checkered life. It is written after the manner of the time, which gives it a pleasant flavor of quaintness.

The hero, a boy of noble character, is the true heir to the Castlewood estate, but is supposed to be illegitimate, and grows up as a dependent in the home of his second cousin, the titular viscount, where he is treated with kindness and affection. The family consists of the young and lovely Lady Castlewood; a son, Francis, and a beautiful daughter, Beatrix. Lord Castlewood neglects his wife, and exposes her to the unwelcome attentions of Lord Mohun, with whom he subsequently fights a duel, in which he is killed. Without justification, Lady Castlewood holds Esmond responsible for the duel. Having learned that he is legally heir to Castlewood, he is constrained by gratitude to conceal the knowledge, and goes off to the wars. Returning to England on furlough, he is received with great affection, and immediately falls in love with Beatrix, whom he wooes unavailingly for ten years. The brilliant beauty becomes engaged to the Duke of Hamilton, but he is killed in a duel. Esmond, a devoted Jacobite, brings the Pretender to England in readiness to succeed Queen Anne, who is dying; but the Prince lays siege to the fair Beatrix instead of the throne. This wrecks the project; and Henry, now discovering his purposes, crosses swords with him. The Pretender then returns to Paris, where Beatrix joins him.

Henry now discovers that his very long attachment for Beatrix has given place to a tender affection for her mother, notwithstanding her eight years of superior age. This is the weakest point in the novel, but the author manages it skillfully. The attachment being mutual, no obstacle appears to their marriage. Frank is left in possession of the estate, while Esmond and his bride emigrate to the family plantations in Virginia; where their subsequent fortunes form the theme of 'The Virginians.'

HENRY, PRINCE OF PORTUGAL, SURNAMED THE NAVIGATOR, The Life of, and its Results; Comprising the Discovery, within One Century, of Half the World. From Authentic Contemporary Documents. By Richard Henry Major (1868). The remarkable story of a half-English son of "the greatest king that ever sat on the throne of Portugal" by his mother, Queen Philippa; a grandson of "old John of Gaunt, time-honored Lancaster"; nephew of Henry IV. of England; and great-grandson of Edward III. His father, King João or John, who formed a close English connection by marrying Philippa of Lancaster, was the first king of the house of Aviz, under which Portugal, for two hundred years, rose to its highest prosperity and power. The career of Portugal in exploration and discovery, due to the genius and devotion of Prince Henry, Mr. Major characterizes as "a phenomenon without example in the world's history, resulting from the thought and perseverance of one man." We see, he says, "the small population of a narrow strip of the Spanish peninsula [Portugal], limited both in means and men, become, in an incredibly short space of time, a mighty maritime nation, not only conquering the islands and western coasts of Africa, and rounding its southern cape, but creating empires and founding capital cities at a distance of two thousand leagues from their own homesteads"; and such results "were the effects of the patience, wisdom, intellectual labor, and example of one man, backed by the pluck of a race of sailors, who, when we consider the means at their disposal, have been unsurpassed as adventurers in any country or in any age." It was these brave men, many years before Columbus, who "first penetrated the Sea of Darkness, as the Arabs called the Atlantic beyond the Canaries"; and they did this in the employment and under the inspiration of Prince Henry, whose "courageous conception and unflinching zeal during forty long years of limited success" prepared the way for complete success after his death.

Born March 4, 1394, Prince Henry had become one of the first soldiers of his age when, in 1420, he refused offers of military command, and undertook to direct, at Sagres (the extreme point of land of Europe looking southwest into the Atlantic Sea of Darkness), plans of exploration of the unknown seas of the world lying to the west and south. His idea was to overcome the difficulties of the worst part of that immense world of storms, that lying west of Africa, and thereby get round Africa to the south and sail to India, and China, and the isles beyond India. Every year he sent out two or three caravels; but his great thought and indomitable perseverance had yielded only "twelve years of costly failure and disheartening ridicule," when, in 1434, the first great success was achieved by Gil Eannes, that of sailing beyond Cape Boyador. Prince Henry made his seat at Sagres, one of the most desolate spots in the world, a school of navigation, a resort for explorers and navigators. His contemporary Azurara says of him: "Stout of heart and keen of intellect, he was extraordinarily ambitious of achieving great deeds. His self-discipline was unsurpassed: all his days were spent in hard work, and often he passed the night without sleep; so that by dint of unflagging industry he conquered what seemed to be impossibilities to other men. His household formed a training-school for the young nobility of the country. Foreigners of renown found a welcome in his house, and none left it without proof of his generosity." To more perfectly devote himself to his great task, he never married, but took for his bride "Knowledge of the Earth."

HER DEAREST FOE, by Mrs. Alexander (1876).   The scene of this story (perhaps the best by this prolific writer) is laid in and about London, at the beginning of the last century.   Mr. Richard Travers, a middle-aged merchant seeking rest, goes to the little town of Cullingford, and there stays with a Mrs. Aylmer, a widow with one daughter.   Mr. Travers is charmed with Cullingford, and revisits the place from time to time.   Eventually he falls in love with Kate Aylmer, and marries her after the death of her mother.   Subsequently he makes a will in favor of his wife, which also disinherits his cousin and former heir, Sir Hugh Galbraith.   After the death of Travers, his widow succeeds to his estate; but is not long left in undisturbed possession, as Mr. Ford, a clerk in the office of her late husband, produces another will in favor of Sir Hugh.   Mrs. Travers is obliged to give up her property and compelled to support herself.   She settles in the village of Pierstoffe, which is picturesquely described; where, assisted by her friend and companion Fanny Lee, she opens a small fancy-goods shop.   Sir Hugh, while hunting in the neighborhood, meets with an accident, and is taken to the house of Mrs. Travers, of whose identity he remains in ignorance, as he has never seen his hostess before, and as she had assumed the name of Temple upon leaving London.   Sir Hugh falls in love with his charming nurse, and upon regaining his health, proposes marriage to her; but is rejected, as she believes him to have had a hand in defrauding her of her property.   Not long after this, Mrs. Travers, or Mrs. Temple, is enabled to prove that the will in favor of Sir Hugh is a forgery, for which the clerk Ford is wholly answerable.   Sir Hugh again offers himself, and this time she accepts him; afterwards revealing her identity, and rejoicing that she has an opportunity of "heaping coals of fire on the head of her dearest foe."   The story flows easily and pleasantly, the pictures of town and country life are natural and entertaining, and the interest is sustained to the end.

HERBERT OF CHERBURY, EDWARD, LORD, AUTOBIOGRAPHY. (First printed in 1764 by Horace Walpole).   Lord Herbert of Cherbury (1583–1648), who had some claim to recognition as a philosopher and a poet, is best known by his autobiography.   The chief characteristic of this remarkable piece of self-revelation is a naïf conceit which lays claim to the most diverse accomplishments.   The author is, by his own showing, the admired of all admirers, the hero (or knave) of a thousand gallantries, the physician able to cure all complaints, the fencer able to vanquish all rivals.   One typical passage well indicates the style and method of the book, which for all its foibles is one of the best remembered autobiographies: "I had also and have still a pulse on the crown of my head.   It is well known to those that wait in my chamber, that the shirts, waistcoats, and other garments I wear next my body, are sweet beyond what either easily can be believed, or hath been observed in any else, which sweetness also was found to be in my breath above others, before I used to take tobacco, which towards my latter time I was forced to take against certain rheums and catarrhs that trouble me, which yet did not taint my breath for any long time; I scarce ever felt cold in my life, though yet so subject to catarrhs, that I think no man was ever more obnoxious to it; all which I do in a familiar way mention to my posterity, though otherwise they might be thought scarce worth the writing."   Hardly any mention is made of his serious studies, important as these were, or of the serious side of his character.

HEREDITARY GENIUS, by Sir Francis Galton (1874).   In this intelligent and interesting study an attempt is made to submit the laws of Heredity to a quantitative test, by means of statistics.   To the result desired Galton contributes many figures, many facts, and few generalizations. His pursuit is purposely confined to the evidence of the inheritance of the fine mental condition or quality called genius, — whether a man endowed with it is likely to have inherited it, or to be reasonably certain to pass it on to his sons and grandsons. The author began his researches with a work on 'English Judges' from 1660 to 1865. In these two centuries and a half he found that out of the 286 judges 112 had more or less distinguished kinsmen, a result favoring the theory of a transmission of qualities in the ratio of 1: 3. He goes on to study seven groups composed of statesmen, generals, men of letters, men of science, artists, poets, and divines, the number of families considered being about three hundred, and including nearly one thousand more or less remarkable men. His conclusion is, that the probability that an exceptionally able or distinguished man will have had an exceptionally able father is thirty-one per cent., that he will have exceptionally able brothers forty-one per cent., exceptionally able sons forty-eight per cent., etc. He does not find it to be true that the female line bequeaths better qualities than the male line; and he suggests the explanation that the aunts, sisters, and daughters of great men, having been accustomed to a higher standard of mental and perhaps of moral life than the average prevailing standard will not be satisfied with the average man, and are therefore less apt to marry, and so to transmit their exceptional qualities. He admits, however, that it is impossible, with our present knowledge of statistics, to put this theory to the proof. Galton groups his facts with great skill, but his direct object is to arrive rather at a law of averages than a law of heredity. That is, his method is purely statistical, and cannot therefore be applied with finality to moral facts. "Number is an instrument at once too coarse to unravel the delicate texture of moral and social phenomena, and too fragile to penetrate deeply into their complicated and multiple nature." Yet Galton, in producing his extremely interesting and suggestive books, 'Hereditary Genius,' 'English Men of Science,' and 'Inquiries into Human Faculty and its Development,' has helped to establish the truth of psychological heredity, and the objective reality of its still mysterious laws.

HERETICS, a volume of essays by Gilbert K. Chesterton, published in 1905. Although they deal with a varied assortment of writers and topics — Kipling, Bernard Shaw, H. G. Wells, George Moore, Lewes Dickinson, Omar and the Sacred Vine, Celts and Celtophiles, Science and the Savages — they are unified by the idea that however heretical the authors discussed may be "they do, each of them, have a constructive and affirmative view and they do take it seriously and ask us to take it seriously." Kipling is preaching imperialism, Shaw and Wells socialism. They are, in various degrees, heretics; but they consider themselves orthodox; that is they believe themselves in possession of the truth and wish to share it with others. But for the heretic who believes in nothing, who will form no general ideas, who thinks that "everything matters — except everything," Chesterton has only contempt. Against this modern disposition to renounce all seriousness of conviction, to consider everyone a heretic and to use orthodoxy as a term of reproach, the whole book is a protest; and in spite of its title it may therefore be called a plea for orthodoxy. Chesterton's characteristic fondness for established customs and institutions, for material comforts and luxuries, for faith and conviction, and for the paradoxical expression of conservative views appear on every page of this stimulating volume.

HEREWARD THE WAKE, 'Last of the English,' by the Rev. Charles Kingsley. Kingsley was Regius Professor of Modern History in the University of Cambridge.

on the very site of his story. The author's propaganda of the religion of rugged strength also made him quite at home in his theme.

The story, which is largely based on the old ballads and chronicles, opens near the end of the reign of Edward the Confessor, when Hereward is made a "wake" or outlaw; and the tales of his wanderings, his freaks, and feats of arms, in the North, in Cornwall, in Ireland, and Flanders, have their foundation in the old English records. The author tells in dramatic style how the hero returns from Flanders, and begins his daring resistance to the Normans; running the gauntlet of William's most skillful generals, and at last meeting and defeating the forces of the great master. Hereward's strategy and daring elicits the admiration of the stern Conqueror himself. The story of the defense of the Camp of Refuge at Ely, and the successes attending the arms of the little band of patriots in that fen country; the sacking of Peterborough by the Danes; the last stand made by Hereward in the forest, are all graphically described. Kingsley is liberal sometimes in his allowance of redeeming faults to his virtuous characters; yet, in the fall of Hereward, he forcibly impresses the lesson that loss of self-respect is fatal to noble effort.

There are fine passages in the book; and the mourning of the stricken Torfrida and the true-hearted Martin Lightfoot over the defeated Hereward is full of pathos. The genial abbot of Peterborough, Uncle Brand, and Earl Leofric, are agreeably sketched. Ivo Taillebois is true to life, or rather to the chronicles and ballads; and William himself is well drawn. The novel is a book for Englishmen, and helps to popularize their heroic traditions; but it is of interest to all those who cherish the ideals of manliness and heroism. The story was first published in Good Words in 1866.

HERMANN AND DOROTHEA, by Johann Wolfgang Goethe, is a German idyllic pastoral of about 2000 hexameter lines. The scene is the broad Rhineplain, and the time the poet's own. This poem, considered the finest specimen of Goethe's narrative verse, was published in 1797, during the period of the author's inspiring friendship with Schiller. The sweet bucolic narrative describes how the host of the Golden Lion and his "sensible wife" have sent their stalwart and dutiful son, Hermann, to minister to the wants of a band of exiles, who are journeying from their homes, burned by the ravages of war. Among the exiles Hermann meets, and immediately loves, Dorothea. How this buxom Teutonic maiden of excellent good sense is wooed and won, taking a daughter's place in the cheerful hostelry, is told with charming simplicity.

HERMETIC BOOKS. The Greeks designated the lunar god of the Egyptians, Thoth, by the name of Hermes Trismegistus; i. e., Hermes the Thrice Greatest. The Greeks, and after them the Neo-Platonists and Christians, regarded him as an ancient king of Egypt, who invented all the sciences, and concealed their secrets in certain mysterious books. These ancient books, to the number of 20,000 according to some, and of 36,000 according to others, bore his name. Clement of Alexandria has described the solemn procession in which they were carried in ceremony. The tradition in virtue of which all secret works on magic, astrology, and chemistry were attributed to Hermes, persisted for a long time. The Arabians composed several of them; and the fabrication of Hermetic writings in Latin lasted during the entire Middle Ages. Some of these writings have come down to us, either in the original Greek or in Latin and Arabic translations. From a philosophic point of view, the most interesting of them is the 'Poimandres' (ποιμήν ἀνδρῶν, the shepherd of men, symbolizing the Divine Intelligence). It has been divided into twenty books by Patricius. It is a dialogue composed some time in the fourth century of the Christian era, and discusses such questions as the nature of the Divinity, the human soul, the creation and fall of man, and the divine illumination that alone can save him. It is written in a Neo-Platonic spirit, but bears evidence of the influence of Jewish and Christian thought. It was translated into German by Tiedemann in 1781. There have been several editions of it. The first appeared at Paris in 1554, and the last, by Parthez, in Berlin, in 1854. The Λόγος τέλειος (Logos telcios, the perfect Word) is somewhat older; it is a refutation of the doctrines of Christianity under the form of a dialogue between Hermes and his disciple Asclepius. An 'Address to the Human Soul' was translated from the Arabic and published by Fleischer in 1870. It is, doubtless, itself a translation from a Greek original. The most interesting passages in the Hermetic books have been rendered into French by Louis Ménard (Paris, 1886). Baumgarten-Crusius in his 'De Librorum Hermeticorum Origine et Indole' (Jena, 1827), and Pietschmann in his 'Hermes Trismegistos' (Leipsic, 1875), have discussed this subject very fully.

HERO OF OUR TIMES, A, by Mikhail Lermontof (1839). The novel portrays the vices of the modern Russian of rank, fashion, and adventure, and his utter selfishness and want of principle and conscience. The story takes the form of a series of tales, of which the libertine Petchorin, and his unhappy victims, mostly confiding women, are the subjects. Lermontof was a great admirer of Byron; and the fascinating Petchorin, the rascal of the stories, with his mysterious attractiveness, strongly resembles Don Juan. The publication of the story excited much controversy; and was the cause of the duel in which the author was killed in 1841. Many people claimed that Petchorin was a portrait; but the author distinctly states that he is not the portrait of any person, but personifies the vices of the whole generation. The author does not set himself up as a reformer, his idea being simply to denounce evil.

HEROES, HERO-WORSHIP, AND THE HEROIC IN HISTORY, ON, by Thomas Carlyle. Carlyle's 'Hero-Worship' made its first appearance as a series of lectures delivered orally in 1840. They were well attended, and were so popular that in book form they had considerable success when published in 1841.

There are five lectures in all, each dealing with some one type of hero. In the first, it is the Hero as Divinity, and in this the heroic divinities of Norse mythology are especially considered. Carlyle finds this type earnest and sternly impressive.

The second considers the Hero as Prophet, with especial reference to Mahomet and Islam. He chose Mahomet, he himself says, because he was the prophet whom he felt the freest to speak of.

As types of the Poet Hero in his third lecture, he brings forward Dante and Shakespeare. "As in Homer we may still construe old Greece; so in Shakespeare and Dante, after thousands of years, what our modern Europe was in faith and in practice will still be legible."

In the fourth lecture he considered the Hero as Priest, singling out Luther and the Reformation and Knox and Puritanism. "These two men we will account our best priests, inasmuch as they were our best reformers."

The Hero as Man of Letters, with Johnson, Rousseau, and Burns as his types, forms the subject of Carlyle's fifth lecture. "I call them all three genuine Men, more or less; faithfully, for the most part unconsciously, struggling to be genuine, and plant themselves on the everlasting truth of things."

Finally, for the Hero as King he selects as the subject of his sixth lecture Cromwell and Napoleon, together with the modern Revolutionism which they typify.

"The commander over men — he is practically the summary for us of all the various figures of Heroism; Priest, Teacher, whatever of earthly or of spiritual dignity we can fancy to reside in a man, embodies itself here."

Carlyle eulogizes his heroes for the work that they have done in the world. His tone, however, is that of fraternizing with them rather than of adoring them. He holds up his typical heroes as patterns for other men of heroic mold to imitate, and he makes it clear that he expects the unheroic masses to adore them. The style of 'Hero-Worship' is clearer than that in most of the other masterpieces of Carlyle, and on this account is much more agreeable to the average reader. There is less exaggeration, less straining after epigram.

HIAWATHA, by Henry Wadsworth Longfellow, a narrative poem based on traditions of the North American Indians, was published in 1855. It deals with the exploits of a culture-hero of various names, Michabou, Chiabo, Manabozho, Tarenyawagon, Hiawatha — the last and most melodious of which was chosen by the poet. The traditions of his birth, childhood, marriage, prodigious feats, invention of agriculture and writing, and departure to the kingdom of the blest before the coming of the white men are drawn from the various collections of Indian anthropology and folk-lore by Henry Rowe Schoolcraft (particularly 'Algic Researches,' 1839), from George Catlin's 'Letters and Notes on the Manners, Customs, and Condition of the North American Indians' (1841), and from other works of travel and topography. The metre of the poem (unrhymed trochaic octosyllabic) and certain incidents, such as the building of Hiawatha's canoe, his fight with the magician, Pearl-Feather, the objections of Nokomis to the marriage with a stranger, and the marvellous music of Chibiabos, were taken from the Finnish popular epic, the Kalevala, which Longfellow knew in a German translation and which depicted a similar hero and a similar stage of national culture. Hiawatha comprises in a remarkable way practically all that was then known of the beliefs, songs, dances, stories, superstitions, manners, and customs of the North American Indians; and all this antiquarian matter is skillfully interwoven into a fascinating heroic story. The locality selected is the abode of the Ojibways on the north coast of Lake Superior. Here Hiawatha is reared by his grandmother, Nokomis, daughter of the moon, is made a brother to the birds and animals, and learns their language. Growing older he becomes a mighty hunter and secures magic mittens which will crush rocks and magic moccasins which enable him to take a stride a mile in length. His first exploit is to seek vengeance on his father, the West Wind, Mudjekeewis, for wrong committed against his mother, Wenonah. The fight ends in a reconciliation and Hiawatha returns to be a defender and civilizer of his people. Through fasting and vigil he has revealed to him the corn-spirit, Mondamin, with whom he wrestles, and from whose buried body springs the Indian corn or maize, the food of the people. Then follow, the making of Hiawatha's canoe, his marvellous contest with the sturgeon, Nahma, who swallows both canoe and warrior, his destruction of the baleful magician, Pearl-Feather, his marriage to Minnehaha of the Dacotahs, the songs and stories of the wedding-feast, the blessing of the cornfields by Minnehaha, the invention of picture-writing, the death of his three friends, Chibiabos the musician, Pau-Puk-Keewis, the ne'er-do-weel, and the strong man, Kwasind, the coming of the ghosts of the departed, the death of Minnehaha from famine and fever, the coming of the missionary priest, and the departure of Hiawatha for the distant islands of the blest in the kingdom of the

North-West wind, Keewaydin, over which he was to rule. 'Hiawatha' is a truly American poem, preserving in delightful poetic form the characteristics of the continent before its conquest by the whites. The rhythm has been charged with monotony and the narrative with prolixity; but the former is adapted to the primitive life depicted and the latter is constantly enlivened by striking incident and local color.

HIGH PRIESTESS, THE, by Robert Grant (1915). This is the story of the married life of Mary Arnold, a modern woman, who strives to show that she can "fulfil all the functions of a wife and mother and yet demonstrate her faculty in some independent field."

Having refused the wealthy Henry Thornton because she could not reciprocate his feelings, she marries Oliver Randall, a promising young lawyer, in whom she feels that she has found a true soul-mate. They start out with the hope that their marriage will be "richer and more ennobling to both and on a higher plane of service and companionship than the world has hitherto known."

Mary's housekeeping is perfection, according to the most modern methods, but she manages to find some leisure each day for her architectural design work. Two children are born, a boy and a girl. Although a model mother, Mary continues her work and after the birth of the second child wins a prize for her design for a fountain. This leads to requests for more designs until she has on hand more work than she can attend to and still look after her household. Her husband, who is greatly interested in politics, is inclined to make light of her work. Finally Mary is compelled to secure someone to assist her in her household duties in order to pursue her profession which often calls her away from home. She installs as housekeeper an intimate friend, Sybil Fielding, whose father's death has made it necessary for her to support herself.

Sybil, who is an attractive girl, carries out Mary's orders in the household and is beloved by the children.

All goes well for two years when Mary suddenly discovers her husband making love to her friend. A scene ensues and both women leave the house that very evening, after Sybil announces her engagement to Henry Thornton, Mary's former suitor. Mary declares that she can never again live with Oliver, takes refuge in a friend's house, and demands the children. In vain Oliver pleads for an interview with his wife, saying that the affair was only an accident, and that he really loves no one but Mary. She is obdurate, takes her children to another part of the city, where she lives for seven years, supporting herself and them by means of her architecture.

Meantime Oliver, patiently waiting for Mary's return, achieves success in his political career and becomes governor. The children visit their father each week, and try to persuade their mother to return to him, but she still refuses to forgive his transgression; nevertheless he is constantly in her thoughts, and she follows his progress with keen interest.

Sybil's husband dies, and Oliver becomes executor of his large estate. Sybil once more tries to win Oliver. He can endure the strain no longer, and writes to Mary that he must see her at once and must either have her or his liberty. The note reaches her just as Oliver arrives at her apartment where she is wondering if she has not judged him too harshly. They find that they love each other as much as ever and are finally reunited.

HILLTOP ON THE MARNE, A, by Mildred Aldrich (1915). This book, which evoked great public interest, is in the form of letters written by the author between

June 3, and Sept. 8, 1914, and describes the beginning of the great conflict between Germany and France. The writer, an American, who has lived many years in France and become much attached to the country, decides to lease a little house in a hamlet called Huiry, about thirty miles from Paris. The house is on a hilltop commanding an extensive view of the river Marne and the surrounding country for many miles. The first letter describes the writer's delight in her new home, which she occupies entirely by herself, enjoying the peace and quiet, which surrounds her. She is served by a farmer's wife named Amélie, who lives nearby, and comes in each day for the necessary duties. After two months of this pastoral existence all is changed, war is declared, and the little hilltop becomes a centre of activities. Aeroplanes pass constantly overhead, troops march by steadily, and the little house becomes a refuge for all sorts and conditions of men. Officers make their headquarters there, and men come for rest and refreshment; though the writer is urged by her friends to flee from the place of danger, she stays bravely by her post, and with the assistance of her faithful Amélie serves the soldiers untiringly, providing them with everything that her larder can offer. The battle comes almost to the door of the little house; then the tide turns and the enemy is repulsed. The writer is an actual witness of the crisis; she sees the conflict wage and wane from her position on the hilltop, and the experience which she so graphically and so modestly describes is one that will thrill every reader.

HIND AND THE PANTHER, THE, a controversial poem in heroic couplets, by John Dryden, published in the spring of 1687. The author had become a Roman Catholic in the previous year, shortly after the accession of James II., who was of that persuasion. In this poem he pleads the cause of his newly-adopted church against the Church of England (which he had defended in his poem 'Religio Laici,' 1682) and against the Dissenters. The argument is presented under the somewhat incongruous form of a beast-fable, in which the Roman Catholic Church is represented by "a milk-white hind, unspotted and unchanged," the Church of England by a spotted panther, the Presbyterians by a wolf, the Independents by a bear, the Baptists by a boar, the Socinians by a fox, and the Atheists by an ape. The relation of these sects to one another at the beginning of the reign of James II. is graphically set forth by the statement that the panther and the other beasts of prey, though hating one another, are united in hostility to the hind but prevented from injuring her by the interposition of the lion. The reference is to James II., who since his accession had on his own authority freed Roman Catholics from the operation of the penal laws against them. He hoped to win over the Church of England to approve this measure and even to re-unite with the Roman Catholic Church. Dryden gives utterance to these hopes in the dialogue between the hind and the panther which makes up the body of the poem. In this discussion the animal personification is practically forgotten and what we have is a theological debate conducted by the poet with his usual vigor, clear-headedness, relative fairness, and dialectic skill. The first book is occupied by a brilliant description of the different churches and sects, with digressions in which Dryden asserts his own newly-formed convictions. Especially interesting is his argument in favor of the Roman Catholic doctrine of transubstantiation, his arraignment of the Church of England as an unworkable compromise, his denunciation of the Dissenters, and the modification of it introduced into the poem just before publication, when James II., in order to grant further benefits to the Roman Catholics, issued the Declaration of Indulgence (April 4, 1687), granting freedom of worship to Dissenters and Roman Catholics alike. The second part is a closely-reasoned discussion of the question of infallibility and authority.   In the third the policy of the king towards the different churches and sects is minutely discussed, and two subordinate fables are introduced by way of illustration, the one told by the panther and satirizing the machinations of the English Roman Catholics, under a tale of the swallows preparing to migrate, the other related by the hind, and ridiculing the hostility of the Anglican to the Roman Catholic clergy under the guise of a tale of the pigeons and the buzzard (Bishop Burnet).   In spite of the awkwardness of a fable in which the animals represent new abstractions and new individuals and in which the fiction cannot be sustained as a cloak for the facts the poem is in invention, expression, insight, cogency, and intellectual power unsurpassed by anything that Dryden ever wrote.

HIPPOCRATES, THE GENUINE WORKS OF.   (English Translation, 1849. Best complete edition, with French Translation of Littré, 11 vols., 1839–61). The most celebrated physician of antiquity, known as the Father of Medicine, was born 460 B. C., of the family of Priest-physicians, claiming descent from Æsculapius. He has the great distinction of having been the first to put aside the traditions of early ignorance and superstition, and to base the practice of medicine on the study of nature. He maintained, against the universal religious view, that diseases must be treated as subject to natural laws; and his observations on the natural history of disease, as presented in the living subject, show him to have been a master of clinical research. His accounts of phenomena show great power of graphic description. In treating disease he gave chief attention to diet and regimen, expecting nature to do the larger part. His ideas of the very great influence of climate, both on the body and the mind, were a profound anticipation of modern knowledge. He reflected in medicine the enlightenment of the great age in Greece of the philosophers and dramatists.

HIS DAUGHTER FIRST, by Arthur Sherburne Hardy (1903). This is a story of modern social life, the scene of which is laid in New York and its environs. Mrs. Kensett, who before her marriage was Dolly Graham, is a rich and attractive widow with a beautiful country home outside of the city. She is in love with John Temple, a friend of her late husband's, who has charge of her affairs, but refuses his offer of marriage on account of the opposition of his daughter Mabel. The latter, who is a beautiful but selfish girl, has been indulged by her father who has lavished his wealth and affection upon her until she has become self-willed and imperious. In a letter to Mrs. Kensett, written after her return from a visit at her house, Mabel boldly declares her dislike of second marriages and voices her antagonism towards any one who might marry her father. This letter causes Dolly to reject the advances of John Temple, but she confides in her cousin, Paul Graham, who advises her not to wreck two lives for the whim of a capricious girl. Paul, who has returned home after years of travel abroad, accepts Dolly's invitation to stay at her house and falls in love with Margaret Frazer, his cousin's dearest friend, who is also visiting her. Mabel Temple has for a companion a very pretty girl named Helen Grant, and both become interested in a man named Reginald Heald. The latter is a handsome and fascinating man who, finding it hard to choose between the beautiful heiress and her lovely companion, makes fervent love to both of them. This complication causes a rupture of the friendship between the two girls and although Mabel is deeply in love with Heald she refuses him. Heald, who really loves Mabel and regrets his flirtation with Helen, is regarded with disfavor by Temple, who suspects the doubtful character of

26

some mining business in which Heald is engaged. This matter is cleared up later, but at the climax of his affairs Heald is shot by a man who is crazed by the loss of his money through him. Heald who is wounded but not seriously injured makes good the man's loss and pretends that he has shot himself. Mabel hearing of the shooting flies to the sufferer and acknowledges her love for him; then softened by her experience she withdraws her opposition to her father's marriage and he and Dolly are happily united.

HIS EXCELLENCY EUGÉNE ROUGON, see **ROUGON-MACQUART.**

HIS FAMILY, by Ernest Poole (1916). New York City is the background for this story of an elderly man with a family of three grown daughters. Roger Gale comes from the New Hampshire farm of his forefathers to "young New York" "a city of houses, separate homes" turbulent "thoroughfares of shouting drivers," of thrilling enterprise compared with the "old New York" he heard about from his elders. He had promised his wife to live on in his children's lives, but after her death he had fallen into a lethargy, and it is twenty years later, when he is nearly sixty, that he tries to fulfil his promise and awakens to the tremendous modern New York of his children's lives. Edith the oldest daughter is a too devoted mother to her five children; everyone is sacrificed to her little family. Deborah, who is her father's close friend, is principal of a high school in the tenement house district; her vision of maternity includes the thousands of pitiful, striving, aspiring children she is making into good citizens, and she postpones marriage with the man she loves because she fears a child of her own might force her to choose between her work and the narrow motherhood of which her sister Edith is such an awful example. Laura, the young worldly pleasure-loving member of the family, marries a wealthy young New Yorker, and does not intend to be bothered with any children. She is divorced while still in her twenties to marry another man of the same sort, and triumphantly lives her own gay luxurious life. Edith's husband dies and her father ultimately provides for her with the old New Hampshire home, where her domestic tyranny is more circumscribed than in New York. His great achievement is to clear the way for Deborah's happiness; she marries and has her son and her school family also. In each of his children, he has seen some phase of his own life repeated.

HIS FATHER'S SON, by Brander Matthews (1896), is a novel dealing with the latter-day aspects of Wall Street speculation, the social influences directly or indirectly traceable to the spirit of respectable gambling. A stern father of Puritan stock, uncompromisingly orthodox, even harshly just to himself and others, in all other matters but those associated with deals in futures and in the stock market generally, has a son who inherits from his mother a disposition facile, impressionable, morbidly sensitive to moral questions, and devoid of the iron strength of will that has produced his father's business success. The son, gradually discovering his father's inability to see or confess any moral lapse or dishonesty in business methods that trade upon uncertainty and just cleverly evade legal responsibility, gradually disintegrates throughout morally and goes to ruin. The stress and stir of a great city mirrors itself here, as in Mr. Matthews's other efforts in fiction, — 'The Story of a Story and Other Stories'; 'Vignettes of Manhattan'; and 'Tom Paulding,' an excellent boys' tale, full of interest for younger readers.

HIS LAST BOW, see **SHERLOCK HOLMES.**

HIS VANISHED STAR, by Charles Egbert Craddock (Miss Mary Noailles Murfree) (1894). Miss Murfree is one of the few American writers who have possessed themselves of a distinct field in literature. She has found in the uncouth and unique inhabitants of the Tennessee mountains, human nature enough to fill a dozen strong books. While the general characteristics are the same, her stories are all unlike. 'His Vanished Star' deals with mountain schemers and "moonshiners," and matches town knavery with rustic cunning. The plot rests upon the effort of one Kenneth Kenniston, who owns a tract in the mountain country, to build a summer hotel. He is indefatigable in his attempts; but as a hotel would kill the business of the "moonshiners," his tricks are met by equally unscrupulous tricks on their part. The entire story is given to the contest of wits between the whisky distillers,—who are "jes' so durned ignorant they don't know sin from salvation, nor law from lying,"—and the schemer from civilization with legal right on his side, who is powerless to remove the squatters from the land which is legally his. Two beautiful mountain girls play into the hand of fate; but they serve to temper the belligerent air. Miss Murfree's glowing descriptions of mountain fastnesses are rich in color, distinct, and individual, and afford a striking background for her psychological studies.

L'HISTOIRE CONTEMPORAINE, by Anatole France, includes the following four novels: 1. 'L'Orme du Mail,' 1897 (translated into English under the title 'The Elm-Tree on the Mall'); 2. 'Le Mannequin d'Osier' ('The Wicker-Work Woman'); 3. 'L'Anneau d'Amethyste,' 1899 ('The Amethyst Ring'); 4. 'M. Bergeret à Paris,' 1901. The first novel of the series introduces us to the provincial professor whose personality and opinions are largely identical with those of Anatole France himself, although he is placed in entirely different surroundings. His conversations with various people in his provincial world and his reflections upon the few incidents which take place in the course of the story are the backbone of the book, which is hardly a novel in the ordinarily understood meaning of the word. The next book deals with Bergeret's domestic infelicity and the means he adopts to get rid of an uncongenial wife. In the last two books we see him freed not only from his domestic bonds but from the limitations imposed upon his intellectual activity by a petty provincial society. Thanks to a single-hearted devotion to the cause of Dreyfus, he is unexpectedly promoted to a professorship at Paris, and continues his philosophical comments on life under more favorable conditions. There are few aspects of life in France at the turn of the century which are not presented in these novels with the irony and pity of which Anatole France is the leading modern exponent. The particular incidents and issues may cease to be of interest, but his detached point of view and the extraordinary lucidity of his style will give the series a place in the history of literature so long as the French language endures.

HISTORIA BRITONUM, by Geoffrey of Monmouth, Bishop of St. Asaph, is a translation from the Cymric into Latin, made about the middle of the twelfth century. Before this, Geoffrey, who was known as a learned man, had translated the prophecies of Merlin; and the story is that he was asked to translate the 'Historia Britonum,' by Walter Map (or Calenius), who had come upon the manuscript in Brittany.

There is no known manuscript of the original in existence, and we cannot now decide to what extent Geoffrey may have interpolated material of his own. The question is still a mooted one with scholars; though no one now, as in former times, professes to believe that the work is a true record of events

The 'Historia Britonum' occupies the border ground between poetry and history and from the beginning was read for the delight of the fancy. Students, even at tha⁺ day, were indignant with its lack of veracity; and good Welshmen scouted it as history. In that day works of imagination were not recognized as having a close connection with history. Yet this very chronicle is the source of one of the purest streams of English poetry, — that which flows from the story of King Arthur.

As finally arranged, the history is divided into twelve books. In the first, Brut, escaping from Troy, is made the founder of New Troy, or London. In the next two books, various persons are invented to account for the names of English rivers and mountains and places. The fourth, fifth, and sixth books give the history of the Romans and Saxons in Britain; the seventh gives Merlin's prophecy; the eighth tells about Arthur's father, Uther Pendragon; King Arthur is the hero of the ninth and tenth; and the last two give a list of the British kings, and an account of Arthur's victory over Mordred.

In the twelfth century, Alfred of Beverly made an abridgment of this history, but it was not until the eighteenth century that it was translated into English. Geoffrey Gaimar made an early translation into Anglo-Norman verse; and Wace or Eustace made a version in French verse which became very popular.

Although there is probably much truth mingled with the fiction in this chronicle, it is valued now chiefly for the influence which it has had on literature.

HISTORIC AMERICANS, by Theodore Parker (1878), contains four essays, on Franklin, Washington, Jefferson, and Adams, essays originally delivered as lectures, shortly before the author's death in 1860. They were written when the anti-slavery agitation was at its height; and the preacher's uncompromising opinions on the evils of slavery decide their point of view and influence their conclusions. Yet in spite of the obsoleteness of that issue, the vigorous style and wide knowledge displayed in the papers insure them a permanent interest. Franklin, the tallow-chandler's son, is in the author's opinion incomparably the greatest man America has produced. Inventor, statesman, and philosopher, he had wonderful imagination and vitality of intellect, and true originality. In Washington, on the other hand, Mr. Parker sees the steady-moving, imperturbable, unimaginative country gentleman, directing the affairs of the nation with the same thoroughness with which he managed his farm. Level-headed and practical, Washington had organizing genius; and it was that attribute, with his dauntless integrity, which lifted him to command. He had not the mental power of any one of his ministers. Yet he was the best administrator of all. John Adams possessed the qualities of a brilliant lawyer, and the large forecast of a statesman. At the same time he was extremely impetuous, outspoken, and high-tempered, and made many enemies. Jefferson, like Washington, and unlike Franklin and Adams, was a man of position and means; and was perhaps the most cultivated man in America. With these incitements to aristocratic views, he was yet the truest democrat of them all, and did more than any one of the others to destroy the inherited class distinctions which were still so strong in this nominally republican country for years after the separation from England.

HISTORY OF THE WORLD, A, by Sir Walter Raleigh. This work, which was done by the author during his twelve years' imprisonment in the Tower of London was first published in 1614. From the present point of view it is obsolete, historically: but it passed through eight editions, in less time than it took for the plays of Shakespeare to attain four. In 1615 King James ordered the whole impression called in, giving as his reason that it was "too saucy in censuring the acts of princes." The history is divided into five books: the first covering the time from the Creation to Abraham; the second from the Birth of Abraham to the destruction of the Temple of Solomon; the third from the Destruction of Jerusalem to the time of Philip of Macedon; the fourth from the Reign of Philip to the death of Pyrrhus; the fifth, from the Reign of Antigonus to the Conquest of Asia and Macedon by the Romans. There are many digressions: one, "wherein is maintained the liberty of using conjectures in history"; another, "Of the Several Commandments of the Decalogue"; and another on "Tyranny." In the preface the author speaks of a second and third volume "if the first receive grace and good acceptance." It was his ambition to relate the successive fortunes of the four great empires of the world, by way of a preface to the History of England; but his release from imprisonment in 1615, his expedition to Guiana, and his execution in 1618, prevented the accomplishment of his plan.

Little as it answers the requirements of its comprehensive title, Sir Walter Raleigh's 'History' is nevertheless a monument to the great learning of its author. It was written under vast disadvantages, even though it may not have been penned in the narrow cell which the Tower "Beef-Eaters" still point out. Many passages present a rare eloquence, and exemplify an admirable English style, with the Elizabethan dignity and sonorous music.

HOLY LIVING AND DYING, by Bishop Jeremy Taylor, was published about 1650, and is the work by which the author is most widely known to the Christian world. It was composed at the desire of Lady Carberry, his patron and friend, and is inscribed to the Earl her husband. The introductory chapters consider the 'General Instruments and Means Serving to a Holy Life'; emphasizing particularly care of time, purity of intention, and the practice of realizing the presence of God. The main topics, of Sobriety (which he subdivides into soberness, temperance, chastity, humility, modesty, and contentedness), Justice (in which he includes duties to superiors and inferiors, civil contracts, and restitution), and Religion (which he treats under ten subdivisions), are then taken up and discussed with great minuteness. For all conditions in life there are copious rubrics for prayer, which he describes as "the peace of our spirit, the stillness of our thoughts, the evenness of recollection, the seat of meditation, the rest of our cares, and the calm of our tempest."

The second section, 'Holy Dying,' considers all the phases of preparation for "a holy and blessed death," dwelling upon the vanity and brevity of life, visitation of the sick, and conduct during sickness. The sentences are usually long and involved — many containing upwards of one hundred and fifty words — and the style is heavily figurative; though there are many beautiful phrases. It is still read, and has furnished suggestions to many modern religious writers.

HOLY STATE, THE (1642). **PROFANE STATE, THE** (1648). By Thomas Fuller. These books by the famous "Old Fuller," author of many favorite works in practical divinity and history, appeared during the stormy days of the English Revolution, and at once attained wide popularity. Both contained many characters drawn with great force and freedom, held up as examples to be imitated or execrated — such as The Good Master, The Good Father, The Good Soldier, etc., etc. There is no story, and the works are noted for their admirable sayings rather than for their interest as a whole. In whatever he did, Fuller was full of a quaint humor; and his comparisons are as pointed and effective as those of Hudibras. Charles Lamb found his pages "deeply steeped in human feeling and passion"; and in all his books, these pages bear, thickly strewed over them, such familiar sayings as: "The Pyramids themselves, doting with age, have forgotten the names of their founders"; or "Our captain counts the image of God — nevertheless his image — cut in ebony, as done in ivory"; or, again, "To smell to a turf of fresh earth is wholesome for the body; no less are thoughts of mortality cordial to the soul"; or "Overburden not thy memory to make so faithful a servant a slave. Remember Atlas was a-weary. . . . Memory, like a purse, if it be over-full that it cannot shut, all will drop out of it."

HOMER, ART AND HUMANITY IN, by William Cranston Lawton (1896). A volume of essays designed to introduce readers earnestly desirous of culture to the chief masterpieces of ancient literature, the Iliad and Odyssey of Homer. It discusses intelligently and thoughtfully the art of Homer in the Iliad, that perfect mastery of epic song which so charmed the Greek ear; the picture which the Iliad gives of womanhood; the scenes of pathetic tragedy with which it closes; the story which gives the Odyssey its plot; the conceptions of the future life which the Homeric epics shadow forth, including all the important passages alluding to the condition of the dead; the episode of Nausicaa, in which, in a tale of perfect simplicity, Homeric painting touched with infinite charm the scenes, the figures, the events, of an escape of Odysseus from shipwreck; and the accretions to the Troy myth which befell after Homer. The volume includes a scheme of aids to the study of Homer; and it presents a considerable number of examples of admirably felicitous use of hexameters in the essayist's versions of the poet, looking to the finding of an ideal of Homeric translation.

HOMER AND THE HOMERIC AGE, STUDIES ON, by W. E. Gladstone (1858). A work of notable interest in its day, in which Gladstone endeavored to state the results, in regard to the authorship and age of Homer, which he thought justified by the text of the poems ascribed to Homer. In his 'Juventus Mundi: The Gods and Men of the Heroic Age' (1869), Gladstone went over the same ground again, and embodied his results of research under a new form, but with considerable modifications in the ethnological and mythological parts of the work. He especially gave new light on Phœnician influence in the formation of the Greek nation. To this report of his Homeric studies he added, in 1876, his 'Homeric Synchronism: An Enquiry into the Time and Place of Homer.'

HON. PETER STERLING, THE, by Paul Leicester Ford (1896), is a distinctly American novel. As a political story, it shows a grasp on municipal politics; and as a novel, insight into the human heart. It introduces its hero as a Harvard student in the early seventies. His father has been a mill overseer, and Peter does not belong to the fashionable New York set, to which he is admitted through a favor which he has done by chance for Watts d'Alloi, its leader and the handsomest man in his class. In spite of striking differences in character and circumstances, the two become firm friends. Soon after his graduation, Peter falls in love; but when he is refused, persuades himself to be the cheerful best man at the lady's wedding. He begins to practice law in New York, gains clients slowly, becomes a favorite with his neighbors, and enters politics, becoming in time a "boss." But Peter is a "boss" with clean hands and a pure heart, and the aim of the author is to show what might be accomplished in politics by men of this high stamp. Nor in his new employment does Peter neglect his profession. On the contrary, he rises to great dignity and a large income. The character of Peter Sterling is finely drawn and many of the minor actors in the story are true to life: Miss De Voe, Ray Rivington, Dorothy Ogden, Bohlman the brewer, Dummer his attorney, and the various politicians in whom many persons will recognize real portraits.

HOOSIER CHRONICLE, A, by Meredith Nicholson (1912). The scene of this story is laid in Indiana and opens in the town of Montgomery, the seat of Madison College. Here Professor Kelton, retired from active labor, lives a quiet and secluded life with his grand-daughter Sylvia Garrison. The latter, a girl of sixteen, has lived with her grandfather since the death of her mother, his only child, which occurred when she was but three years old. Her antecedents are mysterious and even the Professor does not know who her father was, as her mother made a runaway match while away from home and kept her husband's identity a secret for some unexplained reason. Her short married life was spent in the Adirondacks in seclusion and when illness overtook her, she started to take her child to her father, but died before reaching him. No clue could be found to the husband, who had evidently deserted his young wife, and so Sylvia was cared for by her grandfather. She was taught by him until fitted for college which she was enabled to attend through the generosity of an old friend of the professor's, Mrs. Owen. The latter's niece is the wife of Morton Bassett, a prominent politician, unscrupulous and ambitious. His private secretary is Daniel Harwood, a Yale graduate, sound mentally and morally. Harwood loves Sylvia who refuses him, and retains his association with Bassett until the latter in his race for the senatorship employs methods which Harwood cannot endorse. A political rival unearths an episode in Bassett's early life which has been carefully hidden, and which he intends to divulge at the convention to the detriment of Bassett. It relates to his connection with an unknown woman and child in the Adirondacks and these are proven to be Sylvia and her mother. When Sylvia discovers the identity of her father she goes to him for an explanation and he tells her that his marriage to her mother was legal and his desertion of her unintentional. Sylvia tells him that to make reparation to her mother he must give up the senatorship, and though it has been the ambition of his life he does so. Sylvia marries Harwood, whom she had previously refused because of the mystery surrounding her birth.

HOOSIER SCHOOL-MASTER, THE, by Edward Eggleston, first appeared serially in Hearth and Home in 1870. It narrates the experiences of Ralph Hartsook, an Indiana youth who in ante-bellum days taught a back-country district school in his native State.

There is no attempt at complicated plot, the interest centring in the provincial manners and speech of the rustic characters, who find in the young schoolmaster almost the only force making for progress and culture — crude though it is. Though inexperienced, Ralph is manly and plucky, proving himself possessed of qualities which command the respect of the difficult patrons of the primitive country school.

With a keen sense of humor, and fidelity to detail, the author describes the unsuccessful efforts of the hitherto incorrigible pupils to drive out the teacher; the spelling-school, and how the master was spelled down; the exhortations of the "Hardshell" preacher; the triumphant rebuttal of a charge of theft lodged against Ralph; the sturdy help which he continually gives to the distressed; and the final success of his love for Hannah, a down-trodden girl of fine spirit, who begins really to live under the new light of affection.

With its companion volume, 'The Hoosier School-Boy,' the novel occupies a unique field; describing the manners, customs, thoughts, and feelings of a type full of interesting and romantic suggestiveness, humorous, and grotesque.

HOP O' MY THUMB, see **FAIRY TALES.**

HOPE LESLIE, by Miss Catherine M. Sedgwick (1827), is a tale of early colonial days in Massachusetts. Hope, an orphan, is brought up by her uncle Mr. Fletcher, and loves her cousin Everett; but in a moment of misunderstanding he engages himself to Miss Downing, Governor Winthrop's niece. At length Miss Downing discovering that he loves his cousin, releases him to marry the impetuous Hope. Colonial dignitaries and noble women figure equally in the book, which makes a faithful attempt to present a picture of the life of the middle of the seventeenth century in and near Boston. The story is very diffuse, is told with the long stride of the high-heeled and stiff-petticoated Muse of Fiction as she appeared early in the nineteenth century, and is more sentimental than modern taste quite approves. But as a picture of manners it is faithful; and its spirit is wholesome and healthful. In its day it enjoyed a very great popularity.

HORSESHOE ROBINSON, by John P. Kennedy, is a tale of the Loyalist ascendency, during the American Revolution. The chief characters are: Marion; Tarleton; Cornwallis; Horseshoe Robinson himself, so called because he was originally a blacksmith; Mary Musgrove and her lover John Ramsay; Henry and Mildred Lyndsay, ardent patriots; Mildred's lover, Arthur Butler, whom she secretly marries; Habershaw and his band of ruffians and brutal Indians. The scene is laid in Virginia and North Carolina; and we read of battles and hair-breadth captures, treachery and murder. Tyrrel, the British spy, is Butler's rival, favored by Mildred's father; he does Butler much harm, but is finally hanged as a traitor, while Mildred and her husband live happily after the war is ended. Horseshoe Robinson is a "character": huge in size, of Herculean strength and endless craft and cunning. His adventures by flood and field are well worth reading. The story was written in 1835. Though not his first novel, it is perhaps the most famous work of the author.

HOUR AND THE MAN, THE (1840), the most important work of fiction among the multitude of Harriet Martineau's writings, is a historical novel based on the career of Toussaint L'Ouverture. It opens with the uprising of the slaves in St. Domingo in August, 1791; at which time Toussaint, a negro slave on the Breda estate, remained faithful to the whites, and entered the service of the allies of the French king as against the Convention. The struggle between loyalty to the royalist cause and duty to his race, when he learns of the decree of the Convention proclaiming the liberty of the negroes, ends by his taking the leadership of the blacks; and from this point the story follows the course of history through dramatic successes to the pathetic ending of this remarkable life. The novel is a vivid page of history.

HOUR GLASS, THE, by W. B. Yeats (1903). The actors in this short but exquisite morality are a wise man, a fool, some pupils, an angel, and the wise man's wife and two children. The wise man is to explain to his pupils a passage in the book before him which says: "There are two living countries, the one visible and the one invisible . . . the learned in old times forgot the visible country." He thinks he has taught his pupils better than that. The fool asks for pennies and says he has seen that priests and people on account of the wise man's teaching have given up their old religious observances. The fool says that he often sees angels, the wise man that he has shut people's ears to "the imaginary harpings and speech of the angels." While he is yet speaking, an angel appears to him and tells him that he will die within the hour, because no souls have passed over the threshold of heaven since he came to the country. He pleads without avail for mercy from the angel, but is told that if before the last sands have run from the hour glass he can find one who believes, he shall come to heaven after years of purgatory. His pupils and the fool enter. None of his pupils believe. His wife says that a good wife only believes what her husband tells her. His own children repeat what he had formerly taught them "there is no heaven: there is no hell: there is nothing we cannot see." Teigne the fool says he believes in "the Fire that punishes, the Fire that purifies, and the Fire wherein the soul rejoices for ever." The wise man asks the fool to pray that a sign may be given to his pupils that they may be saved, and bows his head and dies.

HOURS IN A LIBRARY, by Sir Leslie Stephen (3 vols. 1874–79. New ed. 1892). These agreeable volumes are made up almost entirely of papers on writers and books of the eighteenth and nineteenth centuries: Defoe's Novels, Richardson's Novels, Balzac's Novels, Fielding's and Disraeli's Novels, Pope as a Moralist, Hawthorne, De Quincey, George Eliot, Charlotte Brontë, Dr. Johnson, Landor, — these, and three times as many equally illustrious names, show the range of Mr. Stephen's reflections. He has no theory of the growth of literature to support, — like Taine, for example; and so he enjoys what the Yankee calls a "good time," as he moves with careless but assured step whither he will through the field of letters. He is very sensible and clear-headed; he knows why one should dislike or admire any given book; and he gives his reason in simple, direct, and easy speech, as if he were seated in his library arm-chair after a comfortable dinner, an amiable Rhadamanthus, discoursing with a true urbanity upon the merits of his friends. He is unflaggingly agreeable, often extremely clever, not seldom witty, and always well-bred and sensible. He admires Pope, and sets him among the great poets, affirming that he is "the incarnation of the literary spirit," with his wit, his satirical keenness, his intellectual curiosity and his brilliant art of putting things. In the paper on Hawthorne, the essayist makes the subtle suggestion that it was better that that delicate genius should have been reared in America, because the more affluent and romantic environment of Europe might have dominated his gift. The essay on De Quincey has been called the best estimate of that extraordinary personality ever made. But the papers on Macaulay and on George Eliot are hardly less admirable, a judgment which might fairly include most of the papers.

HOUSE BY THE MEDLAR TREE, THE ('I Malavoglia') by Giovanni Verga (1890), is a realistic and touching story of lower-class life in an Italian fishing village. The fortunes of the Malavoglia, a title of ill luck which seems to have attached itself by heredity to the family so called, are connected with the old homestead, the house under the medlar tree; and these fortunes are affected by the changes in the anchovy trade, the coming of steam packets and railroads, increased taxes, and the general breaking-up of old ways in the decade before 1870. The good-hearted and thrifty grandfather, Padron 'Ntoni, sees his big family of grandchildren grow up to disappoint, one after another, all his brave wishes and hopes for the prosperity be th of his sturdy little fishing-sloop, the Provvidenza, and his ample old house. The story is full of action and of unsophisticated human feeling. To read its pages is to live in the little village of Aci Trezza and know personally every one of its forty or more

vividly drawn characters.   Nothing is concealed, nothing is indoors.   It is all in the
full glare of the southern sun, and the forms of light and shade stand out with pitiless
distinctness.

HOUSE OF CLAES, THE, see **ALKAHEST.**

HOUSE OF MIRTH, THE, by Edith Wharton (1905).   This story depicts life
among New York's "Four Hundred."   The central figure is Lily Bart, a girl in her
late twenties, well connected, possessed of great beauty and little money.   Being an
orphan she is given a home and an allowance by her aunt Mrs. Peniston, with whom
she lives, but having expensive tastes, her limited resources and dependence make
her very dissatisfied with her lot.   Her ambition and desire has been to make a
successful marriage, having been reared by a selfish and worldly mother with that
end in view, but so far, her aim has not been accomplished.   She visits her rich
friends the Gus Trenors and loses heavily at bridge thereby involving herself in debt
from which she allows her host to extricate her.   He offers to invest her small capital
in a way to bring in large returns and Lily being ignorant of business methods does
not realize the large checks he hands her are out of his own pocket.   Trenor endeavors
to force his attentions upon her and when she repulses him he taunts her with having
taken his money.   Lily is terrified and says she will repay every cent.   Meantime
she has several suitors; among these is Lawrence Selden, an attractive man without
money for whom she really cares, and a rich Jew named Simon Rosedale, who is
personally repulsive to her.   The former, she feels she cannot consider on account of
his limited income, and although the latter would bring her the wealth she craves
she cannot bring herself to accept him.   Lily goes on a yachting-trip with her friends
the Dorsets and through no fault of her own becomes involved in a scandal which
causes all of her fashionable friends to drop her.   Just at this time her aunt dies and
cuts her off with a small legacy.   Without money, or friends, Lily finds her way most
difficult and finally brings up in a cheap boarding-house while learning the trade of
milliner.   During her declining fortunes she has reconsidered her decision regarding
Rosedale but finds to her chagrin that he no longer cares to marry her.   Broken in
health and completely discouraged Lily finally takes an overdose of chloral which
ends her unhappy existence.   Just before this tragic event she visits Selden and tells
him how much he has been to her, and he is on his way to ask her to marry him when
he learns of her death.   Lily's last act is the paying over to Trenor of her aunt's
legacy which has just come to her and is sufficient to cancel her debt to him.

HOUSE OF PENARVAN, THE ('La Maison de Pénarvan') by Jules Sandeau (1858).
The scene of this semi-historical romance is laid in Brittany, and the story opens in
the year VI. of the Republic.   Mademoiselle René de Pénarvan is living in an old
château near Nantes, her only companion being the Abbé Pyrmil.   They are both
devoted to the glories of the ancient house; and Pyrmil is writing its history, the
chapters of which René illuminates with Gothic tracery and emblazonment.   She is
the last of her race and will not marry.   But an unexpected incident alters her resolve.
The Abbé has discovered that a male heir exists, — a plain, simple-hearted youth
living on the produce of his farm and about to marry a miller's daughter.   To prevent
such a horrible disgrace René marries him herself, somewhat against his will.   She
then puts a sword into his reluctant hand and sends him to La Vendeé to fight for
his legitimate king.   He returns wounded, and she is prouder of him than ever.   But
he dies, not without telling her that he no longer loves her, for she does not really

love him. She is a heroine, not a woman. She was in love with a hero, a paladin, not with the artless country boy, who only desired to live at peace. Their child, whom René cannot forgive for being a girl, grows up. Her timidity, gentleness, and simple tastes, are hateful to the proud châtelaine; and when she falls in love with a bourgeois, the mother's anger is terrible. But the daughter conceals a firm will under her modest exterior, and ultimately marries the man of her choice. René is forced to yield, and finally admits that she has not fulfilled her duties as a wife and a mother. This is the best known of Sandeau's works outside France. It contains one of his most skillfully constructed plots. The contrasted characters of René, her husband, and her daughter, show great psychological knowledge and skill. The portrait of the Abbé Pyrmil is not unworthy to rank beside that of Dominie Sampson.

HOUSE OF THE SEVEN GABLES, THE (1851), the second of Nathaniel Hawthorne's romances, follows the fortunes of a decayed New England family, consisting of four members, — Hephzibah Pyncheon, her brother Clifford, their cousin Judge Pyncheon, and another cousin, Phœbe, a country girl. At the time the story opens Hephzibah is living in great poverty at the old homestead, the House of the Seven Gables. With her is Clifford, just released from prison, where he had served a term of thirty years for the supposed murder of a rich uncle. Judge Pyncheon, who was influential in obtaining the innocent Clifford's arrest, that he might hide his own wrong-doing, now seeks to confine him in an asylum on the charge of insanity. Hephzibah's pitiful efforts to shield this brother, to support him and herself by keeping a centshop, to circumvent the machinations of the judge, are described through the greater portion of the novel. The sudden death of the malevolent cousin frees them and makes them possessors of his wealth. A lighter episode of the story is the wooing of little Phœbe by Holgrave, a lodger in the old house. 'The House of the Seven Gables' has about it the same dreamy atmosphere that envelops Hawthorne's other novels. The usual background of mystery is supplied in the hereditary curse resting upon the Pyncheon family. Hephzibah, the type of ineffectual, decayed aristocracy, the sensitive feeble Clifford, the bright little flower Phœbe, are prominent portraits in the author's strange gallery of New England types.

HOUSE OF THE WOLF, THE (1889), the first of Stanley J. Weyman's historical romances, deals with the adventures of three young brothers (the eldest of whom, Anne, Vicomte de Caylus, tells the story) in Paris, during the Massacre of St. Bartholomew. Catharine, the beautiful cousin of these young men, is sought in marriage by the most powerful noble of the province, the dreaded Vidame de Bezers, known from his armorial bearings as the "Wolf." She prefers the Huguenot Louis de Pavannes, and Bezers swears to have his life. To warn him, the country lads Anne, Marie, and St. Croix journey to Paris, only to fall into the power of the terrible Vidame. The plots of the Vidame, the struggle of the boys, and the dangers of M. de Pavannes, are woven with thrilling effect into the bloody drama of the Massacre; and the sinister figure of the proud, revengeful "Wolf," with his burst of haughty magnanimity, lingers long in the memory.

HOUSE OF THE WOLFINGS, THE, by William Morris (1889). "The tale tells that in times long past, there was a dwelling of men beside a great wood." Thus does the first sentence of the book take us into the atmosphere — half real, half mystical, and wholly poetic — which pervades the entire story. These "men" belonged to one of the Germanic tribes of Central Europe. Round about this "great

wood" were three settlements or "Marks," each mark containing many Houses; and
.t is with the House of the Wolfings of Mid-mark that the tale chiefly deals.

The chief of the Wolfings was Thiodolf, the wisest man, and of heart most dauntless. Hall-Sun, his daughter, exceeding fair and with the gift of prophecy, was first
among the women.

The leading theme of the story is the war between the Romans and the Markmen;
how it fared with Thiodolf, and how the Hall-Sun advises the Stay-at-Homes by
means of her wonderful insight. Thiodolf is chosen War-Duke. He meets the Wood-
Sun, his beloved, a woman descended from the gods. She gives him a hauberk to
wear in battle; but owing to a charm that caused who so wore this armor to weaken
in war, Thiodolf does not acquit himself bravely in their first skirmishes with the
foe. The Markmen become somewhat disheartened, and the Romans advance even
to the Hall of the Wolfings. Then Thiodolf is led by the Hall-Sun, who personifies
courage and duty, to the throne of the Wood-Sun, who confesses that, fearing his
death and the end of their love on earth, she had fastened the hauberk upon him.
Thereupon Thiodolf casts it away, and subordinating love to duty, he goes forth
to meet a hero's death on the morrow's battlefield. The sight of the War-Duke, in
his old strength and cheer, incites the "stark men and doughty warriors" to the
complete undoing of the Romans. The day is given up to the chanting of dirges for
the dead; and the night wears away in feasting. All the kindred hallow with song
the return of the warriors "with victory in their hands." And thereafter the Wolfings "throve in field and fold."

This fascinating story is pervaded with the charm of a primitive people, who live
a picturesque life both in agriculture and on the battlefield.

The style of the author, the quaint and simple English, molded frequently into a
beautiful chant or song, makes 'The House of the Wolfings' a most artistic and
attractive tale.

HOUSEHOLD OF SIR THOMAS MORE, THE, by Anne Manning (1869), is
written in the form of the diary of the Chancellor's daughter, Margaret. The story,
beginning when More is merely a private gentleman, a great lawyer, and friend of
Erasmus, afterward introduces the reader to his life at court, and the prosperous
days when he stood first in bluff King Hal's favor, and pathetically describes his
downfall and tragic death. The record of the high-minded and cultivated Margaret
presents a delightful picture of a lovely home life, and of the noble and accomplished
gentleman who was its head and its inspiration. Her devotion to her father never
wanes, even in the terrible hour when, after his execution, she "clasped in her last
trance her murdered father's head." The simplicity and sincerity of the author's
treatment give the book an air of reality, while its faithfulness to the tone of the period
makes it more historical than history.

HOW THE OTHER HALF LIVES, see **MAKING OF AN AMERICAN.**

HUCKLEBERRY FINN, THE ADVENTURES OF, by Samuel L. Clemens ("Mark
Twain"), was published in 1884. It is a sequel to, and follows the fortunes of, the
leading characters of the same author's 'Tom Sawyer,' from which it differs in tone
and construction, touching now and again upon vital social questions with an under-
tone of evidently serious interest. Like its predecessor, it is a story of boyhood for
boys; but it is also a vital study of American life, the Odyssey of Adventure on the
Mississippi. Many critics consider it Mark Twain's masterpiece.

The story traces the wanderings of "Huck" and Tom, who have run away from home; and tells how, with their old friend the negro Jim, they proceed down the Mississippi, mainly on a raft.

The boys pass through a series of experiences, now thrilling, now humorous; falling in with two ignorant but presumptuously clever sharpers, whose buffoonery, and efforts to escape justice and line their own pockets at the expense of the boys and the kindly but gullible folk whom they meet, form a series of the funniest episodes of the story. Tom's and Huck's return up the river puts an end to the anxiety of their friends, and to a remarkable series of adventures.

The author draws from his intimate knowledge of the great river and the Southern country along its banks; and not only preserves to us a valuable record of a rapidly disappearing social order, but throws light upon some questions of moment to the student of history.

HUDIBRAS, by Samuel Butler, a satirical poem in eight-syllable couplets. The first part appeared in 1662, the second in 1664, and the third in 1678. Under the guise of a burlesque tale of knight-errantry the author heaps ridicule upon the Puritan party. Hudibras, the hero, a knight and justice of the peace who rides out in quest of adventure, represents the Presbyterians, and perhaps also Butler's former employer, Sir Samuel Luke, a colonel in Cromwell's army; Ralpho, the squire of Hudibras, typifies the Independents. After a long description of the two men, with emphasis on the militancy, metaphysical subtlety, and hypocrisy of the Presbyterians and the mysticism and fanaticism of the Independents, the poet tells of the attempt of Hudibras and Ralpho to break up a bear-baiting. Successful at first in placing one of the revellers, Crowdero, a fiddler, in the stocks, they are overcome by a counterattack, led by Trulla, an Amazonian warrior, and themselves imprisoned. From this disgrace Hudibras is released by a wealthy widow, to whom he has paid his addresses, and who promises not only to loose him but also to marry him if he will promise to give himself a whipping. Having made the pledge and having been set at liberty Hudibras now attempts to evade it by having the whipping done by proxy in the person of his squire. In a clever imitation of contemporary theological discussion he and Ralpho dispute on the legitimacy of this subterfuge, until they are interrupted by a second rustic gathering, occupied in punishing a scold and her henpecked husband. Attempting again to interfere Hudibras and his squire are pelted with filth and seek refuge in a horse-pond. Unwilling to endure anything further, even voluntarily inflicted, the knight now goes to an astrologer, Sidrophel, to inquire whether he is destined to win the widow or not. They fall to dispute, and the astrologer with his man, Wachum, are beaten by the knight. The poem is now brought to an end by three epistles, one from Hudibras to Sidrophel, one from Hudibras to the Widow, and the third giving the widow's reply. The story is of less importance than the brilliant and still-quoted epigrams with which it abounds and the clever travesties on the theological hair-splitting and hypocritical austerity of the Puritans in their prosperous days.

HUGH WYNNE, FREE QUAKER, by Dr. S. Weir Mitchell (1897). This story is written in the form of an autobiography, and is told by Hugh Wynne, who later becomes Brevet Lieutenant-Colonel on the staff of his excellency, General Washington. The scene is laid in Philadelphia during the time of the Revolution, and a very truthful and striking picture is given of the social life and customs of the Quaker City. The hero, Hugh Wynne, is the son of a rigid old Philadelphia merchant intolerant of youth and pleasure, as well as of armed resistance to authority, who in his youth had married a gay and loving French woman, the direct opposite of her stiff-necked husband. Hugh endures the austerities of his grim father as long as his ardent and strong-willed nature will allow, and when the moment arrives that he can be spared from a business which has never been congenial to him, he follows the leading of his heart to the camp of Washington and takes service with the patriotic forces. Being a good shot and an admirable swordsman he soon gets a commission, and from that time shares the hardships and successes of the campaign. At one time a prisoner in Philadelphia, at another a spy seeking out weak spots in the enemy's defence, and again on the staff of Lafayette, he participates in the most important scenes of the long and wavering struggle. Darthea Peniston, the love of Hugh's life, is a fascinating and lovely girl whose coquetry and charm wins for her the love of Jack Warder, Hugh's faithful and constant friend, and also that of Arthur Wynne, Hugh's cousin, the plausible villain of the story. Darthea, however, remains true to Hugh, and Warder nobly stifles his affection and proves himself the loyal and unselfish friend. The story is full of charm and interest and pictures the life of the old régime of Philadelphia with all the variety and grace, elegance and refinement which then belonged to it.

HULL HOUSE, see **TWENTY YEARS AT.**

HUMAN INTERCOURSE, by Philip Gilbert Hamerton (1884), is a collection of essays on social relationships, opening with a short treatise on the difficulty of discovering fixed laws in this domain which all inhabit, which so few understand. The remaining essays treat of passionate love, of friendship, of filial duties and affections, of priests and women, of differences of rank and wealth; in short, they cover nearly all divisions of the subject. The author brings to the consideration of his theme reasonableness and sympathy. In his essays on marriage and on love, especially, he shows a keen knowledge of human nature, and of the hidden springs of passion. It is his comprehension of passion, indeed, which makes possible his intelligence on other subjects related to human intercourse. The essays are well supplied with concrete examples from life, in illustration of the points in question. They are written in everyday forcible English, well fitted to the subject-matter.

HUMAN MARRIAGE, THE HISTORY OF, by E. A. Westermarck (1891). Prof. Westermarck's definition of marriage is "a more or less durable connection between male and female, lasting till after the birth of the offspring." At the outset he enters a caveat against the custom of inferring, without sufficient reasons, from the prevalence of a custom or institution among some savage peoples that this custom or institution is the relic of a stage of development through which the whole human race has passed. His method is to endeavor to find out from a great variety of material the causes of social phenomena, and then from the prevalence of the causes to infer the prevalence of the phenomena themselves. This quest is extremely difficult because of the unsatisfactory nature of much of the evidence which sometimes comes from travelers and missionaries who on account of ignorance of native languages and customs have occasionally quite misrepresented native customs about marriage. Prof. Westermarck is of opinion that the promiscuity alleged to exist among primitive peoples is, in so far as it exists at all, frequently due to contact with "civilization," and that "there is not a shred of genuine evidence for the notion that promiscuity ever formed a general stage in the social history of mankind." There are chapters on celibacy, sexual selection, the prohibition of marriage between kindred, marriage by capture and marriage by purchase, the forms and duration of human marriage. He justifies his fearless treatment of a subject which sometimes involves the discussion of unpleasant details by a doctrine that has almost become a proverb. "The concealment of truth is the only indecorum known to science."

HUMAN UNDERSTANDING, AN ESSAY CONCERNING, see **ESSAY.**

HUMPHRY CLINKER, a novel in epistolary form by Tobias George Smollett was published in 1771. It records in a series of letters the adventures of a family party traveling in England and Scotland. The household consists of Matthew Bramble of Brambleton Hall in Wales, an eccentric and valetudinarian bachelor; his sister, Tabitha, a foolish old maid; their nephew, Jerry Melford, a Cambridge student; their niece, Lydia Melford, just out of boarding-school; Winifred Jenkins, the maid, whose spelling is fearful and wonderful; and Humphry Clinker the coachman, a poor, ragged ostler picked up *en route*, and taken into service by the benevolent Mr. Bramble in place of another man, Thomas, who has been dismissed. The journey begins at Gloucester, where Lydia has been at boarding-school and where her brother discovers that she is corresponding with a good-looking young actor who calls himself Wilson. A duel between the two men having been averted the party proceeds to Bath. A lively and interesting picture of the frivolities and absurdities of this famous watering-place and health-resort is presented from various points of view in the different letters written from here. A visit to London introduces us to Ranelagh and Vauxhall, the wits and the politicians. Humphry Clinker turns Methodist preacher, and is imprisoned for a time on a false charge of robbery. The route then turns northward through Yorkshire. At Durham the party is joined by an odd-looking Scottish soldier Lieutenant Obadiah Lismahago, who entertains them with a blood-curdling story of the cruelties he suffered as a captive of the Indians, and wins the favor of Tabitha Bramble. The most interesting description, however, is that of Scotland, the peculiarities of which country are vividly set forth. In the end Lydia's suitor, who has appeared on various disguises at different stages of the journey, proves to be one George Dennison, a gentleman of rank and wealth, who was masquerading as an actor to avoid an unwelcome marriage forced on him by his parents. He marries Lydia Melford. Tabitha is united to Lismahago. Humphry Clinker turns out to be a natural son of Matthew Bramble, and is happily married to Winifred Jenkins. In spite of its occasional coarseness of expression and its brutal realism the book is a highly entertaining picture of British society in the eighteenth century. It contains some definitely characterized personages, and the plot is sufficiently marked to arouse the reader's interest. The epistolary form is not tedious, for each letter sets the facts in a new light by reflecting them through a different personality.

HURRISH: A Study, by Emily Lawless. This is a picture of life on the west coast of Ireland, wild and sad as is that barren iron land itself. Horatio, or Hurrish O'Brien, the big, kindly, simple farmer, gives poor, pretty Ally a home, and is a father to weak vain Maurice Brady; but he becomes the victim of fate. His fierce old mother is an ardent patriot. They live in the midst of Fenians, but he will not strike a blow for rebellion. Maurice Brady's brutish brother Mat, hated by all, shoots at Hurrish from his hiding-place; Hurrish strikes one blow in self-defense, kills him, and is betrayed to the police by Maurice. Hurrish is tried and acquitted, but Maurice murders him in spite of Ally's warnings. Ally, though betrothed to Maurice, loves Hurrish without knowing it. Hurrish, in his devotion to Maurice, acquits him on his death-bed. Ally becomes a nun; Maurice goes to America, where he makes a fortune, but is shunned by his countrymen as an informer and a traitor. Hurrish's memory is cherished in his native village. This capital picture of Irish character, with all its weaknesses, inconsistencies, and superstitions, was published in 1886, — the writer's first book, and giving her high rank among Irish novelists.

HUTCHINSON, MEMOIRS OF COLONEL, by Mrs. Hutchinson (1701). Shortly after the death of her husband, who during the Great Rebellion in England had taken the side of the Parliament, and, as a governor of Nottingham Castle, defended his charge until the Parliamentary cause was victorious, Mrs. Hutchinson wrote this biography to preserve his memory and instruct his children. It is a unique picture of the life and character of a Puritan gentleman. "The figure of Colonel Hutchinson," says J. R. Green, "stands out from his wife's canvas with the grace and tenderness of a portrait by Van Dyck." The work is valuable as a record of the time in which Colonel Hutchinson lived, as an accurate account of the Civil War in Nottinghamshire, and, from the literary standpoint, for the simple beauty of the author's style and the unaffected frankness with which she details her opinions and the incidents of her private life. The personal description of her husband is a very good example of the manner of the book. "To sum up, therefore, all that can be said of his outward frame and disposition, we must truly conclude, that it was a very handsome and well-furnished lodging prepared for the reception of that prince, who in the administration of all excellent virtues reigned there a while, till he was called back to the palace of the universal emperor." Written between 1664 and 1671.

HYPATIA, by Charles Kingsley (1838). This famous romance presents a stirring picture of the fifth century of the Christian era, against the background of the learned city of Alexandria in Egypt. A young Christian monk, Philammon, a denizen of the rock monasteries on the Upper Nile, moved by a burning desire to save his fellowmen from sin and destruction, makes his abode in Alexandria. There his sleeping senses are aroused by the magnificent pageant of the decaying Roman world. His mystical visions vanish in the garish light of a too brilliant intellectuality. Greek culture, Roman order, the splendid certainties of the pagan world, fascinate a mind "half sick of shadows." Yet he is drawn to what is best in the old order. Its noble philosophy, its sane ideals, its fine temperance, seem embodied in Hypatia, a beautiful woman over whom ancient Greece exercises an all-potent fascination. In her lecture-room she expounds principles of religious philosophy, the fruit of a younger, purer, and brighter civilization. To Philammon she makes her appeal, as a woman and as a guiding intellect. Jealousy of her influence is however rife in Alexandria among the followers of the bishop Cyril, one of the arch-fanatics of history. Greek intelligence is brought face to face with mediæval blindness. The temper of the proselytizer conquers, because the zeitgeist is in its favor, while the Greek philosophy belongs to a dead age. The infuriated Christians fall upon Hypatia in her lecture-room, and tear her limb from limb. The book closes upon the conquerors each "going to his own place," and upon world-weary Alexandria settling down to its everlasting sleep.

'Hypatia' abounds in brilliant descriptions of the strange life of the period, with its opalescent colors of decay. It does full justice to the Christians of the fifth century to whom the urbanity of the earlier church was foreign. Its most beautiful picture is of the woman Hypatia, seeking the white light of old Greece through the intervening mists stained with the thought and passion of well-nigh a thousand years.

HYPERION, by H. W. Longfellow (1839). 'Hyperion' — The Wanderer on High — is a fitting title for this, the most romantic of Longfellow's works. It frankly declares itself 'A Romance,' on the title-page.

It is the tale of a young man in deepest sorrow, wandering from land to land in search of occupation for his mind, and forgetfulness of grief. This motive forms the thread of story which connects a series of philosophical discourses, and romantic legends and poems. Many of these last are Longfellow's translations of German poems; and they have found a place in his collected poems. The adventures and wanderings of the hero portray the experiences and travels of the author on his second trip through Germany and Switzerland after the death of his wife. Immediately after its publication, 'Hyperion' had a wide circulation.

This book more than any other brought on Longfellow the reproach of being more foreign than American in his sympathies. Yet it had great value in creating in this country a more extensive acquaintance with the German romantic poets, especially Heine and Uhland.

'Hyperion' also has historic interest in marking the transition in Longfellow's work. It stands between his translations and sketches of historical persons and places, and his original poems.

ICELAND FISHERMAN, AN ('Pêcheur d'Islande'), by Louis Marie Julien Viaud ("Pierre Loti") (1886), sometimes reckoned his strongest story, obtained the Vitet prize of the French Academy, and the honor of being translated into German by "Carmen Sylva," Queen of Roumania. It was written after the war between France and China, and for a moment the narrative is drawn into the current of that campaign, in which the author took part as a naval officer. The characters are not inhabitants of Iceland, but of the coast of Brittany, calling themselves Iceland fishermen because every year, leaving their wives and children, they are obliged to make the voyage to that island, remaining in its neighborhood till the fishing season is over. The book breathes a saner atmosphere than others by the same author, that impart all the languor as well as glamour of the tropics. Nothing could be simpler than its motive; yet even in this record of humble life, telling only of the gains and losses of fisher folk, the lad Sylvestre is pressed into the marine service and transported to a green meadow in China, where he gets his death-wound. He lives long enough to receive the medal of honor, but dies on the home voyage, and is buried at Singapore, — an episode whose equatorial pictures contrast with the cold scenery, the grays and greens of the rugged Icelandic coast. But the chief actor in the story is the ocean, that makes violent protest under the eaves of the stone dwelling, built into the cliff and reached by a flight of granite steps. Outside of 'Childe Harold' and 'The Flying Dutchman,' it would be difficult to find such intimate comprehension and contemplation of sea and sky, in so many moods and latitudes.

ICONOCLASTS; 'A Book of Dramatists,' by James Huneker, is a series of dramatic essays which first appeared in the New York Sun and were collected in this volume in 1905. The authors discussed are Ibsen (who occupies nearly a third of the book), Strindberg, Becque, Hauptmann, Sudermann, Hervieu, Gorky, D'Annunzio, Maeterlinck, Villiers de l'Isle Adam, Princess Mathilde, and George Bernard Shaw. The general resemblance between these modern dramatists is, first, that they have broken the standards of formal art and given their creative instincts an outlet in accordance with their own æsthetic impulses; and secondly, that they are dominated by symbolism. The author has an intimate acquaintance with modern tendencies in art, and a brilliant and facile pen. His constant application of musical terms to literary exposition is sometimes suggestive but often irritating; and in the attempt to be epigrammatic he occasionally becomes affected. His analysis of modern dramatic thought and form is, however, of value to the student of present-day literature.

IDIOT, THE, by F. M. Dostoévsky (1868). Prince Myshkin, the hero, is an epileptic, whose secluded invalid life has apparently destroyed the faults of the mind, the sins of egotism, ambition, pride, and deceit, and left him,the wise fool of lovely simple childlike character who wins all hearts. He returns to St. Petersburg to a mad chaotic world of villains and egoists, a corrupt and frivolous society, which laughs at his sincerity and innocence, but cannot escape his gentle influence. The reckless beautiful Nastasia loves him, and Aglaia, a young society girl, becomes engaged to him. The jealousy of the two women is incomprehensible to his simple nature. He radiates love and goodwill to both, and finally breaks his engagement to Aglaia to save Nastasia from the passionate violent merchant Rogozhin. On the wedding day, the impulsive Nastasia leaves him knowing his love is only pity and goes to Rogozhin, whom she hates. The jealous Rogozhin marries her and kills her. Prince Myshkin's exquisitely sensitive spirit cannot survive the horror of the night with the murderer in the room where she is lying dead, and he becomes in fact what he has often been called an "idiot." The character of Prince Myshkin is revealed in conversations in which he expresses the sweetness of his nature, his sympathy with the unfortunate and his understanding and love for children. He says, "What has always surprised me is the false idea that grown-up people have of children. They are not even understood by their fathers and mothers. We ought to conceal nothing from children under the pretext that they are little and that at their age they should remain ignorant of certain things. What a sad and unfortunate idea! And how clearly the children themselves perceive that their parents take them for babies who can't understand anything, when really they understand everything." His kindness to those who try to exploit him and his humility enrages Aglaia. She exclaims: "There isn't a person who deserves such words from you! here not one of them is worth your little finger, not one who has your intelligence or your heart! You are more honest than all of us, more noble than all, better than all, more clever than all! There isn't one of these people who is fit to pick up the handkerchief you let fall, so why then do you humiliate yourself and place yourself below everybody! Why have you crushed yourself, why haven't you any pride?" In the "idiot" Dostoévsky has drawn his own ideal of a Christlike character. He was himself subject to epilepsy.

IDYLLS OF THE KING, THE, by Alfred Tennyson, a series of twelve narrative episodes in the epic manner (completed 1885), the whole forming a unified epic of King Arthur, though without the structural continuity of the formal epic and therefore called by the author 'Idylls' that is pictures or scenes. Tennyson's principal sources were Malory's 'Morte D'Arthur,' Layamon's 'Brut,' Geoffrey of Monmouth's 'Chronicle,' and Lady Guest's translation of the Welsh 'Mabinogion.' These he handled freely, in accordance with the more finished and concentrated effect that he wished to produce and the ideas that he wished allegorically to embody. The poem sets forth the reign of King Arthur, from his supernatural coming, through his conquests and beneficent reign, to his fall and supernatural departure. Under the whole story is an allegorical meaning. Arthur is the soul struggling with the flesh or the temptations of the world, which are represented by his enemies and later by the worldly and corrupt among his knights. He is also the ideal knight and king contrasted with the less perfect though more human types, Lancelot, Gawain, and the rest. The poem developed gradually, and the twelve idylls were not written according to the chronological sequence of the story. 'The Passing of Arthur' which concludes the Idylls, was in part the first written, its principal episode having appeared under this title in the volume of Tennyson's poems published in 1842. The next idylls to be published were 'Enid' (afterwards divided into 'The Marriage of Geraint' and 'Geraint and Enid'), 'Vivien' (later 'Merlin and Vivien'), 'Elaine' (later 'Lancelot and Elaine'), and 'Guinevere' (1859). 'The Coming of Arthur,' 'The Holy Grail,' 'Pelleas and Etarre' and the completed 'Passing of Arthur' appeared in 1869; and the three additional phases of the story were furnished by 'The Last Tournament' (1871); 'Gareth and Lynette' (1872), and 'Balin and Balan' (1885). To summarize briefly the completed poem, 'The Coming of Arthur' narrates Arthur's mysterious origin, his winning of the kingdom of Britain by Merlin's assistance, his achievement of Guinevere as his bride, and his twelve great victories over the Saxons. This Idyll and the ensuing, 'Gareth and Lynette,' an attractive tale of a youthful knight winning a lady through humility towards her and valor against gigantic opponents, are characterized by a spirit of hope and confidence born of the high ideals and practical resolutions of a loyal and united court. 'The Marriage of Geraint' and 'Geraint and Enid' based on the Welsh Mabinogion, tell a romantic tale of a brave young knight rescuing and wedding a youthful beauty and of the wifely heroism and devotion of this same beauty when her husband put her to an undeserved test. In these two Idylls we first hear the rumor of guilty love between Lancelot and Queen Guinevere — a disloyalty destined to corrupt and disunite the whole realm. 'Balin and Balan' shows the first disastrous effects of this poison. The rumor of Guinevere's guilt, skilfully fanned by the malignant Vivien, mistress of Arthur's rival, Mark of Cornwall, so maddens Balin the Savage, who worships the queen, that he insults her colors and fights with his brother, Balan, a duel in which both are slain. In 'Merlin and Vivien,' the woman responsible for the brother's death comes to Arthur's court, blackens its reputation by spreading the foulest scandal, and at length captivates by her flatteries the mage, Merlin, whom she imprisons in a hollow oak by a charm that he has taught her. In 'Lancelot and Elaine' the relations of Guinevere and Lancelot are becoming more widely known and their sense of sin is manifested in their bickerings with one another. Yet Lancelot puts aside the pure love of Elaine, the lily maid of Astolat, and remains "falsely true" to the queen. In 'The Holy Grail,' to quote the note by Hallam, Lord Tennyson "In some, as faith declines, religion turns from practical goodness and holiness to superstition." The knights ride out in quest of the vision of the Holy Grail, which a few of their number have the spiritual gift to see. Three of these, Galahad, Percival, and Bors, attain the vision and retire from the world to the life of contemplation. The remainder, having no vocation, abandon the quest and many perish of misadventure. Lancelot fails to see the Grail because he will not abandon his love of Guinevere. 'Pelleas and Etarre' and 'The Last Tournament' show the gradual disintegration of the Table Round. The court is growing more cynical; the relations of Lancelot and Guinevere are known to all but the King; Etarre shamelessly flings aside the devotion of young Pelleas for the light-of-love, Gawain; Tristram, lover of Isote, King Mark's wife, openly proclaims infidelity to her and scoffs at all bonds of loyalty and affection ('The Last Tournament'). In 'Guinevere' the love of Lancelot and the Queen is reported to King Arthur by his nephew, Modred, and Vivien. The lovers flee and part, Lancelot for his realms overseas, Guinevere to the convent of Almesbury. Here Arthur, on his way to fight with Modred, now in rebellion, rebukes her, forgives her, and bids her farewell. 'The Passing of Arthur' describes his last battle, his mortal wound at the hands of Modred, and his departure to the supernatural world from whence he came. Although the character of Arthur is too blameless to win perfect sympathy the poem is not obtrusively didactic and the allegorical meaning is so subordinated and softened as to avoid inartistic prominence. The love-story of Lancelot and Guinevere is told with dramatic insight and human sympathy which is never sentimentalized into approval; the subordinate characters and the mediæval incidents and backgrounds are depicted in soft, brilliant colors; and the blank verse and lyrics mingle smoothness and strength. The poem is a thoroughly adequate handling of a great epic theme which had long awaited modern poetical treatment.

ILIAD, THE, an epic poem in Greek hexameters, existent as early as 1100–900 B. C. handed down by the rhapsodes or public reciters and reduced to writing about the time of Pisistratus. The poem was for ages attributed to Homer, said to have been a blind singer of one of the Greek cities of Asia Minor or one of the islands of the Ægean. At the close of the eighteenth century the theory was promulgated that Homer was either a myth or a figure of slight importance and that the Iliad was simply a compilation of various heroic lays of the siege of Troy. Most modern scholars, realizing the unity of the poem both in structure and in spirit, reject this hypothesis and hold that the Iliad is the creation of one directing intellect; but it is admitted that we have no certain knowledge about the author and that earlier lays, more or less modified, must have been incorporated by him into the structure of his great work. The theme of the poem is the wrath of Achilles against Agamemnon and its results. Indignant at Agamemnon, leader of the expedition against Troy, because he has seized Briseis, a captive maiden awarded to Achilles, the latter refuses to take part in the siege of Troy. As a result of his withdrawal the war goes badly for the Greeks. At their urgent request Achilles allows his friend, Patroclus, to put on his armor and fight in his place. Patroclus, however, is killed by Hector, the bravest of the Trojans. Maddened by his loss, Achilles obtains new armor from his goddess-mother, Thetis, executes great slaughter upon the Trojans, and kills Hector. To prolong his vengeance he drags the body around the walls of Troy at the wheels of his chariot; but through the intercession of Hector's father, Priam, the King of Troy, he yields up the body to the old man. This simple story is elaborated by full and particular accounts of the various battles, embassies, and feasts; by the intervention of the gods at numerous points in the story; and by such episodes as the exploits of Diomedes, and the funeral games of Patroclus. The unity of this great and diversified poem, the passionate intensity of its central theme, the marvellous ease, flexibility, and dignified simplicity of its style, and its vivid portrayal of the heroic age of Greece are some of the reasons of its greatness. The most famous English translations are Chapman's (1598–1611) in the long "fourteener" couplet, Pope's (1715–1725) in heroic couplets, Cowper's (1791) in blank verse, Lord Derby's (1867) in blank verse, William Cullen Bryant's (1870) in blank verse, Andrew Lang, Walter Leaf, and Ernest Myer's translation into archaic prose (1882), F. W. Newman's translation (1856) in unrhymed "fourteener's" — famous because it elicited Matthew Arnold's 'On Translating Homer' — A. S. Way's translation (1886), Samuel Butler's prose version (1916).

ILLUSTRIOUS PRINCE, THE, by E. Phillips Oppenheim (1910). This story opens with the mysterious murder of an American named Hamilton Tynes; the deed is perpetrated on a special train which he has chartered to convey him from Liverpool to London and as he is the only passenger, and his identity unknown, the tragedy is inexplicable. The following night Richard Vanderpool, a young American attaché of the Legation, is murdered in a taxi which is taking him to the theatre to join a party of friends. Subsequent events show that both murdered men were carrying important papers, which were being conveyed from the American to the English Government, and which contained confidential information relating to affairs in Japan. Suspicion centers on a charming Japanese prince, Maiyo by name, who is living temporarily in London in great magnificence and who is much sought after socially. No clues to the murderer can be found except the slender Japanese dagger with which Tynes was stabbed and the silken cord with which Vanderpool had been strangled. Prince Maiyo, who is most courtly in manner and attractive in every way is a great favorite with the ladies and among these Penelope Morse, a beautiful American girl, is especially attracted to him. Although suspecting the Prince of the crime, his charm is so great that when she is in his presence his strong personality conquers her distrust. The Prince invites his friends to visit his house and inspect his art treasures and Penelope noticing a curiously wrought casket asks the Prince to unlock it for her. He does so and Penelope putting her hand into its hidden recesses draws out a dagger and a silken cord identical with those used by the murderer. A glance into the Prince's face tells her the truth and she is filled with horror at her discovery. Feeling it her duty to make her discovery known, she informs the American minister, who is a personal friend, and he notifies the inspectors who have already secured other evidence. The prince, whose crime has been committed for the good of his country and not for any advantage to himself, is arrested and is about to give himself into the hands of the law when his devoted servant Soto, who bears a strong resemblance to Maiyo, rushes in and declaring himself the murderer takes poison and dies, thereby saving the life of his beloved master. The Prince's work being accomplished he returns to his own country and Penelope marries a young English lord, named Sir Charles Somerby.

IMAGINARY CONVERSATIONS, by Walter Savage Landor, a series of over one hundred prose dialogues, published from 1824 to 1829 with a few additions in 1846. The speakers are distinguished persons historical or contemporary, representing every quarter of the world and all history from the age of Pericles to modern times. Some of the dialogues are represented as preceding or following some great historical crisis like the execution of Charles I. or some interesting personal event like the meeting of Milton and Galileo; others are mere calm discourses without dramatic interest, such as the dialogues between Porson and Southey in which Wordsworth's poetry is discussed or those between Southey and Landor, which are occupied by a criticism of Milton. Owing to Landor's classical studies and sympathies the Greek and Roman conversations are particularly fitting and beautiful; but his Tudor and Stuart episodes, his French, Italian, and Russian scenes, his eighteenth century and contemporary colloquies, whether scholarly or arising from public affairs, all illustrate his versatility, wide reading, historic imagination, and gift for the management of dialogue. He is not thoroughly a dramatist, however, for the stately dignity and classic finish of the style is practically the same in all the characters and his own personality is traceable in them all.

IMITATION OF CHRIST, THE, attributed to Thomas à Kempis, a book of religious meditations originally written in Latin between 1417 and 1421, and subsequently translated into various languages. Next to the Bible it is the most widely-read

Christian book of devotion. The author was probably Thomas Hämmerken, a native of Kempen in Rhenish Prussia, afterwards priest and monk of the monastery of Agnetenberg near Zwolle in Holland. In a series of aphorisms, grouped under related headings into chapters and books, he inculcates submission to the divine will the subduing of the lower instincts and of the impulse to self-gratification, and the endeavor to conform ourselves to the model of Christ's goodness. Though ascetic and other-worldly in point of view, the author puts strong emphasis on the need of practical goodness, and lays down sound rules for moral cultivation. He is shrewd, clear-sighted, and discriminating in his analysis of faults and his indication of remedies; and he invests the spiritual life with a charm and an appeal which remind us of the Gospel discourses themselves. The fourth and last book is a manual for the instruction and guidance of those preparing for the Communion; the fervor and devotional insight of its prayers and counsels are of high religious value. Matthew Arnold calls the 'Imitation' "the most exquisite document after those of the New Testament, of all that the Christian spirit has ever inspired.'

IMMENSEE ('Bee Lake'), by Theodor Storm, a charming and idyllic *Novelle* or short story published in 1850. In a series of slightly-connected word-pictures the author tells a pathetic story of thwarted love and life-long regret. Reinhardt and Elizabeth live on two neighboring estates in a delightful country region near the beautiful wooded Immensee or Lake of Bees. They have the same tutor, spend their playtime together, and are entirely congenial playmates. Reinhardt has a gift for telling stories and often entertains Elizabeth with fairy-tales and later with verses. One day when the children are in their teens they lose their way in the woods beside the Immensee while hunting for strawberries for a picnic meal. As they sit resting in the woods (the charm of which is exquisitely described) Reinhardt seeing Elizabeth in the midst of this beauty comes half-consciously to realize that for him she is the center of it all. Soon afterwards we find him at the university, recalled from a student *kneipe* and the fascinations of a gypsy dancer by news of a Christmas package from home which he goes off to open. He finds a letter from Elizabeth, the freshened recollection of whom turns his thoughts to purer and simpler channels. On his vacation he finds Elizabeth on the threshold of womanhood, and the relations between them pass from those of boy and girl to those of potential lovers. They botanize together, and he presents her with some of his verses, all of which center in her; but he does not venture as yet to tell her of his love, although he speaks of a secret which he will reveal when he returns from the University two years hence. After his departure Elizabeth is persistently wooed by a friend of Reinhardt's, Erich, a young man of wealth, decision, and practicality. In the absence of the dreamier Reinhardt he at length succeeds, with the aid of her mother, in persuading Elizabeth to marry him. The news reaches Reinhardt at the University. Some years later he visits Erich and his wife at their fine new estate on the banks of Immensee, where in reading his poetry and revisiting the scenes of their past happiness he gives an unobtrusive expression to his regret, in which Elizabeth evidently shares. After a short visit Reinhardt bids Elizabeth farewell and leaves in the night. At the end as at the beginning of the story he is an old man, dreaming of this lost love of his youth. The artistic brevity and restraint of the book and its truthfulness and sincerity redeem it from every trace of sentimentality. It is an attractive study of the dreamy side of the German character, and is filled with beauty of landscape endeared by human associations and habitation.

IMMORTAL, THE, by Alphonse Daudet (1888). "L'Immortel' is the last noted work of the late distinguished French critic, dramatist, and novelist, Alphonse Daudet. It professes to be a description of *mœurs parisiennes*, but is really a satire on the pretensions of the French Academy; its title, 'The Immortal,' being the epithet popularly applied to the forty members of that exclusive and self-perpetuating body. Daudet himself, although his novel 'Fromont Jeune et Risler Aîné' was crowned by the Academy with the Jouy prize, was never elected to its membership and with the brothers Goncourt, Zola, and others, he formed a rival literary clique. The satirical thrusts in 'The Immortal' were keenly felt and resented by the Academicians. Apart from this personal connection, 'L'Immortel' cannot be said to vie in interest or merit with the celebrated tales of the 'Tartarins,' or with 'Numa Roumestan,' 'Kings in Exile,' or 'Sappho.' The hero of the story is a bookworm, an Academician whose works have been successively "crowned by the Academy" until its crowns were exhausted, and nothing remained but to elect him to membership. Meanwhile he has been employed by the government as Archivist of Foreign Affairs; but an unhappy expression introduced in the history of the house of Orleans — "Then as to-day, France, submerged under the wave of demagogism" — gave such offense to the government that it cost him his position, his salary, and his livelihood. He now devotes himself to the editing of certain MSS. of untold value, which have come into his possession, and his hopes and ambitions hang upon the delight with which the world will welcome these treasures. Treated by his ambitious wife and spendthrift son with ironical contempt and heartless neglect, his misfortunes are crowned by the revelation that his prized archæological documents are forgeries; and that the Academy, indignant at the disgrace thus brought upon it, is discussing his degradation among the "mortals." Ridiculed by all Paris, and berated at home by his angry and disappointed wife, "the perpetual secretary of the Academy," finding neither solace nor protection in its shelter in this hour of his dire need, ends his troubles by throwing himself into the Seine.

IMMORTALITY, see **INDIVIDUALITY AND IMMORTALITY.**

IMPRESSIONS OF LONDON SOCIAL LIFE, WITH OTHER PAPERS, by E. S. Nadal (1875), is a collection of short essays suggested to the author by his residence in London as a secretary of legation. From the standpoint of a loyal American, he notes in kindly, not too critical fashion the differences between life in England and at home. "London society is far the most perfect thing of the kind in the world"; and in NewYork, with its lack of social tradition and its constantly changing elements, Mr. Nadal thinks there can never be anything at all like it. He would admire it still more if it were not for the rigid canons of propriety, which forbid all public expression of individuality. The sturdy Englishman, so fond of asserting his independence, is after all curiously sensitive to public opinion; and hence his conservatism and apparent snobbishness. There is a pleasant description of life at Oxford, which makes that college seem like a great genial club; and one where the undergraduate is a person of far less importance than at Harvard or Cambridge.

Mr. Nadal touches lightly upon the social life at court; the Queen's drawing-room at Buckingham Palace, and the Prince of Wales's less grand but pleasanter levees at St. James's Palace. In its genial, homely, cultivated charm, he finds English scenery very different from American: for "there [England] man is scarcely conscious of the presence of nature; while here nature is scarcely conscious of the presence of man."

IMPROVISATORE, THE, by Hans Christian Andersen (1834). This romance is probably the best known to English readers of all the works of Danish literature, and its translation by Mary Howitt has become itself a classic. The work possesses the threefold interest of an autobiography of the author, a graphic description of Italy, and a romance of extremely emotional and passionate type. To those English and American tourists who knew Rome in the time when the beggar Beppo still saluted them with his *bon giorno* on the Piazza de Spagna steps, the story will serve almost as a narrative of their impressions of the ruins, the galleries and churches of Italy. It is to be classed with its great Italian contemporary 'I Promessi Sposi' of Manzoni, and the 'Corinne' of Madame de Staël, the national type of genius of the several authors presenting in these three works a very interesting contrast. All three are intensely romantic, — 'Corinne,' with the classic reserve of the Latin race; 'I Promessi Sposi,' with the frank naturalness of the Italian; the 'Improvisatore,' with the suppressed warmth of the Teuton.

The story of the 'Improvisatore' is related by one Antonio, a poor chorister boy in Rome, whose voice and quickness in improvisation are at once his fortune in bringing him into the favor and patronage of the aristocracy of Rome, Naples, and Venice, and the cause of many heart-breaking alliances and disengagements with the charming women of various types who come under the spell of his genius and personal attractions. The events of the story bring to the reader a vivid sense of participation in the successive scenes of the Roman church festivals: the Pifferari at Christmas, the Ara Cœli Bambino, and the boy orators at Epiphany, the Corso races and the Senza Moccolo of the Carnival, the Miserere of the Holy Week, and the illuminations at Easter. The chief romantic interest lies in the rival loves of Antonio and of his patrician friend Bernado for a famous Spanish singer, Annunziata, who makes her début in Rome and captivates both their hearts. The scene of the last chapters is placed in Venice; and here it is that Annunziata, a broken-down singer on a low-class stage, dies in poverty, leaving her blessing for her early lover and his bride. A visit to the Blue Grotto closes the brilliant narrative.

IN DARKEST ENGLAND AND THE WAY OUT, by William Booth (1890), general of the Salvation Army. This book, whose title was evidently suggested by Stanley's 'Darkest Africa,' treats of the want, misery, and vice, which cling like barnacles to the base of English society, as they do the base of all old civilizations, and which it is so much easier to shut one's eyes upon than to analyze, explain, and remedy. General Booth's opportunities for knowing whereof he speaks were exceptionally good. The statements he makes are appalling, but they are supported by figures and facts. The subject of his book is the temporal and spiritual rescue of "a population about equal to that of Scotland. Three million men, women, and children . . . nominally free, but really enslaved" — what he calls "the submerged tenth." The plan he proposes seems practical and practicable, — one indeed in the execution of which he has made some progress since the appearance of his book. The plan contemplates the establishment in the great centres of population of "city colonies" (establishments at which the destitute may be provided for, the temporarily unemployed given work, etc.); those for whom such a course seems best being passed on to the self-supporting "farm colony," which in turn contributes to English or other colonies or to the "colony over sea" (yet to be founded). The result would be a segregation of the needy into localities where they could be handled, with a draining off to unreaped fields, as this process became desirable, of a part of the great army of occupation. This book is the work of a man in deadly earnest, who feels himself to be an instrument in the hands of God for the rescue of the lost.

IN HIS NAME, by Edward Everett Hale (1873), is a story of the Waldenses, that radical religious body, which, seven hundred years ago, believed that every man should be free to read the Scriptures and to seek a personal interpretation of them. The story deals with the grievous punishments for heresy that were decreed against them by the Archbishop of Lyons. Pierre Waldo, the leader of the sect, is forced to flee the country; and his cousin Jean, a rich weaver, denies his kinship and despises his followers. But when Jean's only daughter, the apple of his eye, Félice, falls ill, it is found that only Father John of Lugio, one of the proscribed Waldenses, in hiding among the hills, has the medical skill which may save her. Jean Waldo's prejudices melt away, and he sends to entreat Father John, "for the love of Christ," to come to his stricken house. This phrase is the password of the secretly wide-spread sect, in answer to which gates fly open, and aid comes from all sides. Félice is saved, through the ardent service of those who labor "in His name." Round this slight framework are grouped the touching and often dramatic incidents of the story. The tone of the time is sympathetically caught, and the book is steeped in a tender and helpful religious feeling. All Mr. Hale's charm of narration characterizes it; and without didacticism, he never forgets present problems.

IN HONOR'S NAME, see **THE DUEL.**

IN MEMORIAM, an elegiac and reflective poem by Alfred Tennyson, published in 1850. In addition to the Prologue and the Epilogue, it is made up of one hundred and thirty-one brief lyrical pieces each forming a whole and written on a distinct occasion, but all connected by a thread of association or logical sequence so as to contribute to the development of one conception. The theme is the death of Tennyson's friend, Arthur Henry Hallam, and the poet's varying moods of grief and consolation arising from this bereavement. Hallam was the son of Henry Hallam, the historian, and was Tennyson's junior by a year and a half. When they met at Trinity College, Cambridge, in 1829, Hallam had already impressed his schoolfellows and all who knew him as a man of unusual promise, both in literary work and in debate. Three years of intimate friendship followed. Tennyson and Hallam were members of the same discussion club ("The Apostles") in Cambridge, took a walking tour together through the Pyrenees, and visited each other's homes in Lincolnshire and 67 Wimpole Street, London, respectively. Hallam became engaged to Tennyson's sister, Emily, and began the study of law in the Inner Temple, London. But in the summer of 1833, while on a vacation tour with his father, he died suddenly of apoplexy in Vienna, September 15th, 1833. The body was brought to England by sea from Trieste and buried in Clevedon Church, Somersetshire, January 3d, 1834. To relieve the profound depression of these days of bereavement Tennyson began about this time to express his sorrowful moods in brief poems:—

> " Short, swallow-flights of song that dip
> Their wings in tears and skim away."

These lyrics were all written in uniform metre — a stanza of four iambic tetrameter lines, with external and internal rhyme — which Tennyson believed he had invented, although it has since been found in the works of Lord Herbert of Cherbury, George

Herbert, and other seventeenth century poets.   Various occasions—the shifting seasons, the recurrent anniversaries of his association with the dead man, changes in the family life and circumstances of the poet, and moods of religious doubt or of confident reassurance — gave rise to a large number of these lyrics. Finding that he had done so many Tennyson resolved to make them the basis of a complete poem which should be a tribute to his friend.   The poems were therefore re-grouped and new ones written in accordance with a general scheme.   Tennyson was engaged upon this work for a period of seventeen years, although the bulk of it was probably completed by about 1842.   It was at length published in 1850.

Analysis of 'In Memoriam' shows that the poems form a cycle, representing a period of three years, during which the poet gradually passes from despairing grief, through alternating moods of calm recollection, agonizing doubt, and confident reassurance, to a serene faith in immortality.   The Prologue, written in 1849, when the remainder of the work was complete, is an acknowledgment of faith in immortality through the 'Strong Son of God, Immortal Love' whom the poet prays to forgive the grief and doubts expressed in the body of the poem.   Sections i–viii reflect the poet's depression and anguish when the news was still fresh; in ix–xix he finds some relief in his concern for the safe return of Hallam's body and in picturing the ship which conveys it, and the chapel wherein it is buried; a review of their friendship now leads to the conclusion. "'Tis better to have loved and lost than never to have loved at all" (xxii–xxvii).   More positive comfort is furnished by the intuition of immortality that comes during the celebration of the first Christmas since Hallam's death (xxviii–xxx).   This spiritual experience is strengthened by a consideration of the arguments, religious and intellectual, in favor of a future life (xxxi–xxxvii).   But with the coming of the *first spring-time* (xxxviii, xxxix), new doubts arise as to the possibility of recognition of and association with our friends in the future life (xl–xlix).   These are succeeded by more difficult and painful questionings whether we are justified, in view of the pain, suffering, and evil of the world and the apparent indifference of nature to man's sorrow and aspiration, in believing in immortality (l–lviii).   More hopeful thoughts succeed; by a number of analogies the poet gains conviction of the possibility that our friends in the other world take an interest in us (lix–lxvi).   A series of dreams, reflecting the hopes and fears of the poet with regard to his friend in the other world (lxvii–lxxi) leads to the *first anniversary of his friend's death* (lxxii) — a gloomy day expressive of the sorrow which still weighs the poet down. There follow reflections on Hallam's lost fame, on the transitory fame which a poem can bestow, and on the fame which survives in the other world (lxxiii–lxxvii).   On the *second Christmas* (lxxviii) there is no outward expression of sorrow though it is still mingled with the poet's whole being; but from now on the poems are more cheerful.   The poet endeavors to turn his loss to good by emulating Hallam's character (lxxx).   This means that he must not withdraw from his fellowmen; so he assures his brother (Frederick Tennyson-Turner) of his fraternal regard (lxxix); and without disloyalty of Hallam's memory he seeks a new friendship (lxxxv).   Moreover he meditates on what Hallam was and might have been; here we get some charming pictures of their former association at college and in vacation (lxxxiv, lxxxvii, lxxxix).   The poet's growing peace and healthfulness of mind find utterance in the *second spring-time poem* (lxxxiii) and two exquisite pictures of natural beauty (lxxxvi and lxxxviii).   Concentration on Hallam's character now leads to the question whether, if he is yet living, he cannot communicate with his friend; and on a calm summer night Tennyson at length has a mystical experience in which, he is convinced, he communes with his living soul (xc–xcv).

N THE CLOUDS, by "Charles Egbert Craddock" (Miss Murfree) (1887). The clouds" rest upon the Tennessee Mountains, where the strange class of people, the poor whites," whom the author has immortalized in this and other works, have heir homes. It is a story of mountaineering life: illicit distilling, lawlessness of outh, and retribution for sins, made impressive by a background of majestic silence. n a drunken jest, Reuben Lorey (called Mink for obvious reasons) destroys an old imble-down mill; and the idiot boy, "Tad," who disappears at that time, is supposed ɔ have been drowned in consequence of this act. "Mink" is indicted for man-aughter; and on the witness stand Alethea Sayles, one of his sweethearts, who emains faithful through all his troubles, discloses the whereabouts of the "moon-niners," a grave betrayal in that district. It is this trial and its results, Alethea's ɔve, Mink's final escape from jail, and death by the rifle-ball of a friend, who, with ie superstition of the average mountaineer, mistakes him for a "harnt" or ghost, ⁻ith which the story deals. Miss Murfree's character-drawing of these people with heir pathetic lives of isolation, of ignorance, and of superstition, is very strong. nterspersed are delicate word-paintings of sunsets and sunrises, those mysterious ɔlor effects of the Big Smoky Mountains; and underlying all is that conscious note f melancholy which dominates the thoughts and actions of the dwellers on the eights.

N THE PALACE OF THE KING, see **PALACE, ETC.**

N THE WORLD, by Maxim Gorky, see **MY CHILDHOOD.**

N THE YEAR OF JUBILEE, by George Gissing (1895). Gissing's realism is ɛlentless; and his tale of middle-class philistinism would be unbearable were it not lso the story of the growth of a soul through suffering. Nancy Lord, the heroine, aughter of a piano-dealer in a small way, has in her the elements of strength which nder other circumstances would have made her silent and rigid father great. Her ɔuth is full of mistakes, the tests of life are all too severe for her, and she seems to ave met total defeat before her "fighting soul" sets itself to win. Perhaps it is not very great victory to turn a foolish and compulsory marriage into a calm and ɔmfortable *modus vivendi*. But it is great to her. Besides the vivid and headlong Jancy, and her faithful friend and servant Mary Woodruffe, there is hardly a per-ɔnage in the book whose acquaintance the reader would voluntarily make. Even ie hero, a gentleman by birth and tradition, seems rather a plated article than "the ɛal thing," though he shows signs of grace as the story ends. All the women are ordid, mean, half-educated under a process which is mentally superficial and morally ɔn-existent. The men are petty, or vulgar, or both. Apparently both men and ⁻omen, typical as they are, and carefully studied, are meant to show the mischief hat may be done by imposing on the commonest mentality a system of instruction t only for brains with inherited tendencies towards culture. Yet the book is not a ⁻roblem work. It is a picture of the cheaper commercial London and the race it evelops; and it is so interesting a human document that the expostulating reader s forced to go on to the end.

N THE YEAR 13, 'Ut de Franzosentid' (1860), is a translation from the Low Dutch f Fritz Reuter, by Charles Lee Lewis (1867). It is one of a series to which Reuter gave he general name 'Old Camomile Flowers,' signifying "old tales useful as homely emedies." The delightfully homely narration of life in a Dutch village — the prim orderly ways of the women, the petty issues brought before the patriarcha' Amtshauptmann, and the general confusion resulting from the side issues of war — is both pathetic and humorous. The scene is laid in Reuter's native town of Stavenhagen; and the characters are real people, whose real names are preserved. The story is an animated presentation of the state of feeling prevailing among a people who detested yet feared Napoleon, and were forced to treat the French as allies while regarding them as bitterest enemies. A party of "rascally French" chasseurs throw the town into tumult, and finally ride off with several captives unjustly accused of theft. Before these are released come many adventures, quarrels, and a fierce pursuit of unlawful booty, through which runs an idyllic love story, that of Miller Voss's beautiful daughter Fieka. Back of all the somewhat slow and simple-minded Dutch folk looms the invisible yet dominant presence of Napoleon, as a force which they are always conscious of and always dreading.

INCIDENTS OF TRAVEL IN CENTRAL AMERICA, see **CENTRAL AMERICA.**

INDIAN BIBLE, THE, by John Eliot, "The Apostle to the North-American Indians." This first Indian translation of the Bible was in the dialect of the Naticks, a Massachusetts tribe of the Algonkins, and was made under the auspices of the Corporation for the Propagation of the Gospels among the Indians of New England, Eliot sending the sheets to England for approval as they came from the printing-press in Cambridge, Massachusetts.

The New Testament appeared first, in 1661; and two years after, the entire Bible, with the following title:

MAMUSSEE

WUNNEETUPANATAMWE
UP-BIBLUM GOD

NANEESIVE

NUKKONE TESTAMENT

KAH WONK

WUSKU TESTAMENT

NE QUOSHKINNUMUK NASHPE

WUTTINNENMOK CHRIST

JOHN ELIOT

CAMBRIDGE: PRINTENOOP NASHPE

SAMUEL GREEN KAH MARMADUK JOHNSON 1663

The English of which is: "The Entire — His Holy — Bible God — containing — the Old Testament — and the — New Testament — translated by — the Servant of Christ — [called] — John Eliot — Cambridge: printed by — Samuel Green and Marmaduke Johnson 1663."

The English title also adds: "Translated into the Indian Language and Ordered to be printed by the Commissioners of the United Colonies in New England at the charge and with the Consent of the Corporation in England for the Propagation of the Gospels among the Indians of New England."

Some of the Indian words used by Eliot are so extremely long that Cotton Mather thought they must have been stretching themselves ever since the confusion of tongues at Babel. A second revised and corrected edition was printed in 1685, only twelve copies of which are known to exist. An edition with notes by P. S. Du Poneau, and an introduction by J. Pickering, was published in Boston in 1822. When the original edition was issued, twenty copies were ordered to be sent to the Corporation, with the Epistle Dedicatory addressed — "To the High and Mighty Prince Charles the Second by the Grace of God, King of Great Britain, France, and Ireland, Defender of the Faith, etc. The Commissioners of the United Colonies in New England with all Happiness: Most Dread Sovereign, etc.!"

The commercial as well as the religious rivalry of England with Spain creeps out in the Epistle which compares the fruits of the Spanish Conquests in America, brought home in gold and silver, with "these fruits of the colder northern clime as much better than gold as the souls of men are more worth than the whole world!"

Henry the Seventh's failure to become the sole discoverer and owner of America finds its compensation in "the discovery unto the poor Americans of the True and saving knowledge of the Gospel," and "the honor of erecting the Kingdom of Jesus Christ among them was reserved for and does redound unto Your Majesty and the English Nation. After ages will not reckon this inferior to the other — May this nursling still suck the breast of Kings and be fostered by Your Majesty!"

A copy of the edition of 1663, with the Epistle Dedicatory, was sold in 1882 for 2900.

INDIANA, by "George Sand" (Madame Dudevant). A romantic tale published in 1832, which is of interest chiefly as being the first which brought the distinguished author into note, and also as portraying something of the author's own experience in married life. The scene is alternately in the Castle de Brie, the estate of the aged Colonel Delmare, a retired officer of Napoleon's army, where he lives with his youthful Creole wife Indiana; and in Paris, where the wife visits her aristocratic aunt, and where lives Raymond de Ramière, the heartless and reckless lover first of her foster-sister and maid Noun, and then of herself. Estranged from her ill-matched husband, the young wife is drawn into the fascinations of Raymond, whose artfulness succeeds in deceiving the Colonel, the wife, and all save the faithful English cousin, Sir Ralph, who secretly loves Indiana, but shields Raymond from discovery for fear of the pain that would result to her. Desperate situations and dire conflicts of emotions follow, with much discourse on love and marital duty, and frequent discussions of the social and political questions of the day; the Colonel representing the Napoleonic idea of empire, Raymond the conservative legitimist, and Sir Ralph the modern republican. The descriptions of nature are vivid, and the characters are skillfully drawn, however untrue they may seem to actual life.

INDIES, GENERAL HISTORY OF THE (Historia de las Indias, por Fr. Bartolomé de las Casas). The Spanish original in manuscript, 1527–61; only printed edition, vols., 1875–76. It is one of the most notable of books, not only in its contents, — is a history of Spanish discoveries from 1492 to 1520, and a contemporary Spanish Catholic criticism as well as story of Columbus, — but in the circumstances which prevented its publication for more than three hundred years, and which still leave it inaccessible except to readers of Spanish. Its author's entire life and all his writings

were devoted to urging the duty of humane treatment of the Indians; and after publishing in his lifetime appeals and protests which stirred the Catholic conscience
throughout Europe, he left at his death the great 'History' which Spanish feeling
refused the honors of the press until 1875. The whole matter is dealt with by a
writer of the highest authority, Mr. George Ticknor, in his 'History of Spanish
Literature.' Speaking of Oviedo, — whose 'General and Natural History of the
Indies,' an immense work in fifty-one books, of which the first twenty-one were
published in 1535, served as an authoritative account of the discoveries, treatment of
the natives, etc., — Mr. Ticknor says: —

"But, both during his life and after his death (1557), Oviedo had a formidable
adversary, who, pursuing nearly the same course of inquiries respecting the New
World, came almost constantly to conclusions quite opposite. This was no less a
person than Bartolomé de las Casas, the apostle and defender of the American
Indians, — a man who would have been remarkable in any age of the world, and who
does not seem yet to have gathered in the full harvest of his honors. He was born in
1474; and in 1502, having gone through a course of studies at [the university of
Salamanca, embarked for the Indies, where his father, who had been there with
Columbus nine years earlier, had already accumulated a decent fortune. The
attention of the young man was early drawn to the condition of the natives, from the
circumstance that one of them, given to his father by Columbus, had been attached
to his own person as a slave while he was still at the University; and he was not slow
to learn, on his arrival in Hispaniola [Hayti: 1502], that their gentle natures and slight
frames had already been subjected, in the mines and in other forms of toil, to a
servitude so harsh that the original inhabitants of the island were beginning to waste
away under the severity of their labors. From this moment he devoted his life to their
emancipation. In 1510 he took holy orders, and continued, as a priest, and for a
short time as bishop of Chiapa, nearly forty years, to teach, strengthen, and console
the suffering flock committed to his charge. Six times at least he crossed the Atlantic
in order to persuade the government of Charles the Fifth to ameliorate their condition, and always with more or less success. At last, but not until 1547, when he was
above seventy years old, he established himself at Valladolid in Spain, where he
passed the remainder of his serene old age, giving it freely to the great cause to which
he had devoted the freshness of his youth. He died in 1566, at ninety-two. Among
the principal opponents of his benevolence were Sepúlveda, — one of the leading men
of letters and casuists of the time in Spain, — and Oviedo, who, from his connection
with the mines and his share in the government of the newly discovered countries,
had an interest directly opposite to the one Las Casas defended. These two persons,
with large means and a wide influence to sustain them, intrigued, wrote, and toiled
against him, in every way in their power. But his was not a spirit to be daunted by
opposition or deluded by sophistry and intrigue. . . . The earliest of his works,
called 'A Very Short Account of the Ruin of the Indies,' was written in 1542, — a
tract in which, no doubt, the sufferings and wrongs of the Indians are much overstated by the indignant zeal of its author, but still one whose expositions are founded
in truth, and by their fervor awakened all Europe to a sense of the injustice they set
forth. Other short treatises followed, written with similar spirit and power; but none
was so often reprinted as the first, and none ever produced so deep and solemn an
effect on the world. They were all collected and published in 1522; and an edition, in
Spanish with a French version, appeared at Paris in 1822, prepared by Llorente.

"The great work of Las Casas, however, still remains inedited, — a 'General
History of the Indies from 1492 to 1520,' begun by him in 1527 and finished in 1561

ut of which he ordered that no portion should be published within forty years of
is death. Like his other works, it shows marks of haste and carelessness, and is
written in a rambling style; but its value, notwithstanding his too fervent zeal for
he Indians, is great. He had been personally acquainted with many of the early
iscoverers and conquerors, and at one time possessed the papers of Columbus, and a
arge mass of other important documents, which are now lost. He knew Gomara
'the oldest of the regular historians of the New World"], and Oviedo, and gives at
arge his reasons for differing from them. In short, his book, divided into three
arts, is a great repository, to which Herrera, and through him all the historians of the
ndies since, have resorted for materials; and without which the history of the earliest
eriod of the Spanish settlements in America cannot, even now, be properly written."

NDIVIDUALITY AND IMMORTALITY, a lecture delivered by Wilhelm Ostwald
t Harvard University in 1906 and published the same year. It is one of the series
f Ingersoll Lectures on 'The Immortality of Man' given annually at Harvard by
ectures chosen without restriction as to profession or religious belief. Professor
Ostwald's attitude towards personal immortality is that of a sceptic if not a material-
st. He can find nowhere in the universe any assurance of immortality. It is true
hat the living cell, in that it lives on in its offspring, enjoys a kind of immortality;
ut there is no guarantee that all cells may not some day be destroyed. Nor are
natter and energy certainly immortal, for the laws of the eternity of matter and the
onservation of energy are merely based on experience and therefore not absolute;
nd recent experiments have shown that elements are not immortal but may change,
nd that energy may develop where none previously existed. There is no permanence
f individuality either in matter or in force but a constant diffusion. Man's in-
ividuality also changes from youth to age; if he survives after death there is either a
ontinuance of change or a transcendent state without any relation to our life here.
he former alternative seems unlikely because up to death it was the body that
onditioned all changes and with its decay there seems no further reason for them.
)n the latter alternative there can be no evidence for immortality even if it exists.
here is a relative immortality of man's works, but these must in turn pass away.
3ut if we abandon the hope of immortality we still have left the ethical inspiration of
ove for our fellow-man and sacrifice for his welfare. This essay has the limitations
f the materialistic position, but it is free from dogmatism, arrogance, and prejudice
nd is inspired by a love of truth and an honest and serious attempt to discover it.

NDUCTIVE SCIENCES, HISTORY OF THE, by William Whewell (1837. Final
dition, 1857). The story of the progress of the physical sciences, from the earliest
3reek beginnings, and from the groping physical science of the Middle Ages, down to
he time of Darwin. Although the book is out of date, through the immense progress
hich science has made since 1837, and the greater accuracy and thoroughness with
which parts of the history are known, yet the ample learning and great ability of
Whewell, and the conception which he had of the progress of science, gives his work
permanent interest and value. His general ideas of science led him to supplement
is 'History' with a second work on 'The Philosophy of the Inductive Sciences,
'ounded upon their History' (1840). This second volume Dr. Whewell described as
an application of the plan of Bacon's 'Novum Organum' to the present condition
f physical science," and as an attempt "to extract from the actual past progress of
cience the elements of a more effectual and substantial method of discovery" than
3acon's.

INDUSTRIAL AND COMMERCIAL HISTORY OF ENGLAND, see **ECONOMIC INTERPRETATION OF HISTORY.**

INDUSTRIAL EFFICIENCY, by Arthur Shadwell (1905). This comparative study of industrial life in England, Germany, and America, important at its first appearance in 1905, has acquired additional significance owing to the outbreak of the Great War and the prospect of fierce industrial competition in the years succeeding the declaration of peace. It is written with the purely objective aim of presenting an impartial statement of facts and not with the desire to please or displease political or industrial combinations of any kind whatsoever. Dr. Shadwell deals out praise and blame with even-handed justice to Americans, Germans, and English, the English, for example he says are "less methodical than Germans, less alert than Americans." He discusses with great fulness of detail the industrial districts of the three countries, the standards of hours and wages, the general social conditions, the educational systems, and the benevolent institutions of Germany, the United States, and England. In the main, the picture which Dr. Shadwell draws is still sound, and his criticisms should be taken to heart by every reader in the three countries described, who really cares for the genuine progress of the nation to which he belongs and is not a mere chauvinist or egomaniac.

INDUSTRIAL SYSTEM, THE; 'An Inquiry into Earned and Unearned Income' by J. A. Hobson (1909). Failing to find in current economic writings any satisfactory exposition of the methods by which wealth is distributed among the owners of the several factors of production, the author attempts to give "a true outline picture of the industrial system of the present day as a single organic whole, continuously engaged in converting raw materials into commodities, and apportioning them by a continuous series of payments as incomes to the owners of the factors of production in the different processes." He finds that industry creates a product larger than is needed for the cost of maintenance, and that this surplus is taken by the owners of the several factors of production in accordance with the economic "pull" they are respectively able to exercise and passes in innumerable fragments to the owners of a scarce factor of production wherever it is found. The "unproductive surplus" includes the whole of the economic rent of land, and such payments made to capital, ability, or labor, in the shape of high interests, profits, salaries or wages, as do not tend to evoke a fuller or better productivity of these factors. "This unproductive surplus," says the author "is the principal source not merely of waste but of economic malady. . . ." As unearned income "it acts upon its recipients as a premium on idleness and inefficiency; spent capriciously on luxuries, it imparts irregularity of employment to the trades which furnish these; saved excessively, it upsets the right balance between the volume of production and consumption in the industrial system." As in the author's view, this surplus represents the failure of the competitive system to compete, it is the only properly taxable body. The volume as a whole, especially the last chapter, 'The Human Interpretation of Industry,' is one of the most stimulating and suggestive of modern books on economics.

INFLUENCE OF SEA-POWER UPON HISTORY, THE, an historical study by Captain A. T. Mahan, U.S.N. (1890). The influence of sea-power on defeat and victory had been neglected by historians, and Captain Mahan wrote this book in order to point out its high importance. After showing conclusively that the Roman defeat of Carthage in the second Punic war was in large part due to Roma

periority in the Mediterranean and after analyzing the elements of sea-power
proceeds to trace the naval history of Europe from 1660 to 1812, giving a delight-
ully clear and accurate account of the principal naval battles and campaigns and
troducing discussions of strategical and tactical problems involved, for which he
raws on his own experience of active service. In this narrative he never loses sight
f his thesis that the command of the sea spells success, and is quick to find illustra-
ons of it. A cruiser-war on the enemy's commerce by a nation of inferior naval
ower will not bring victory, though many instances are pointed out in which it was
ried. A leading practical aim of the book was to rouse the United States to the need
f a powerful navy as a defense against possible aggression from a European power
nd as a protection to the mercantile marine, which he believed she was destined to
evelop. This history is scholarly, just, entertaining in style, original in its ideas,
nd persuasive in their presentation.

NGOLDSBY LEGENDS, a collection of verse tales with a few in prose, first pub-
shed in 'Bentley's Miscellany,' 1837-1840, under the pseudonym of Thomas In-
oldsby, and afterwards collected in three series, published respectively in 1840,
842, and 1847. The real author was Richard Harris Barham, a beneficed clergyman
nd Dean of St. Paul's, whose comfortable circumstances, antiquarian tastes,
viality of temper, and gifts of humor and improvisation were happily reflected
these permanently entertaining narratives. The greater number are tales
superstition and diablerie, touched with uproarious humor like the Lays of
. Dunstan and St. Cuthbert, modern ghost stories like 'The Legend
Hamilton Tighe' (a narrative powerful in its tragic simplicity), clever tra-
esties on mediæval legends, like 'The Jackdaw of Rheims,' and satirical stories
the *fabliau* type like 'The Knight and the Lady,' which illustrates feminine
constancy.

NHERITANCE, THE, by Susan Edmonstone Ferrier (1824). The scenes of this
teresting novel are laid in Scotland and England, and the story deals with the
ntry of both. Some years before the opening of the story, Mrs. St. Clair, an
mbitious woman, has taken the child of a servant to bring up as her own. After
e death of her husband, Mrs. St. Clair and her supposed daughter Gertrude, a
arming girl, go to his brother's castle in Scotland, of whose estates Gertrude is to
come the heiress. Her two cousins, Edward Lyndsay and Colonel Delmour, visit
eir uncle, as well as Mr. Delmour, the Colonel's sedate brother. Lord Rossville
ishes his niece Gertrude to marry Mr. Delmour, but she loves his handsome brother
d refuses. Upon this the Earl sends Gertrude and her mother from the castle,
d the Colonel shows his true character by withdrawing his addresses. A reconcilia-
on is brought about, and a short time after Gertrude's return to the castle the Earl
es and she is made rich. Colonel Delmour then renews his love-making, and
comes her accepted lover in London. After their return to Scotland, a vulgar man,
ho has previously had secret interviews with Mrs. St. Clair to obtain money, comes
ldly forward and claims to be Gertrude's father. From this point the interest of
e story lies in the development of character in Gertrude and her lovers, and the way
which they face what seems an irremediable misfortune. The characters are
awn with humor, the descriptions are true to nature, and there are several original
uations in the book; as for instance the arrival at the castle of Miss Pratt, a gossip-
g old spinster, in a hearse drawn by eight horses, in which she has sought shelter
om a snow-storm.

28

INNER LAW, THE, by Will N. Harben (1916). This story is a study of the powe of heredity. Carter Crofton is a young Southerner, rich, aristocratic, and gifted as poet. He has graduated from Harvard, and is the favorite child of Gilbert Crofton who dies of paresis soon after the story opens. The father before his death is visite by his brother Thomas, a melancholy man who warns Carter of the curse in the blood and begs him to refrain from wrong-doing if he wishes happiness. Carte Crofton receives the bulk of his father's property, although he is the younger son, a his brother Henry, who has succumbed to the family tendency, is plunged in dissipa tion; Henry and his sister Millicent are, however, amply provided for. Carter, wh has high ideals, is strongly impressed by his uncle's warning and earnestly resolve to profit by it, but is carried away by the charms of a young country-girl name Lydia Romley, while visiting his uncle in his quiet home, and in a moment of passio betrays her. His anguish and horror when he realizes what he has done are grea and he is on the point of marrying the girl, as his uncle begs him to do, when he influenced by his friend Charles Farnham, who persuades him instead to go abroa and enjoy his acquired wealth. Carter spends more than twenty years in Europ trying to amuse himself and forget his past, but fails utterly. He returns to his nativ land bored with existence and broken in health and spirits. He finds Henry dying miserable death and foresees a similar fate in store for himself. He goes to New Yorl where finding life becoming unbearable he decides to commit suicide and end it al He is saved by coming in contact with a fine young fellow named Joe Allen, whos noble qualities make the elder man keenly realize his own short-comings. Meanwhi he has by chance met Lydia Romley, whom he finds he still loves; she has develope into a beautiful woman and is supporting herself as a trained nurse. She refuse however, to listen to his protestations. Carter's interest now centres in young Alle whose talent as a poet recalls his own ruined career, and whose high ideals and relig ous beliefs enter into his own life and change it completely. Finally he discovers tha Allen is Lydia Romley's child and his own son, and when at last Lydia consents t marry him his happiness is unbounded.

INNER SHRINE, THE, by Basil King (1908). At the opening of this story Dian Eveleth returns alone from a round of social festivities in Paris to find her mother-i law, who fears some impending tragedy, awaiting her in the palatial Paris residenc A telephone message shortly announces that George Eveleth has been killed in a due fought with the Marquis de Bienville in order to avenge the false accusations mad by the latter against his wife. Diane, who has been merely a reckless coquette, h led her husband into great extravagance and at his death finds herself face to fa with poverty, as well as the reproaches of Mrs. Eveleth senior. The repentant wido secretly transfers her remaining patrimony to her mother-in-law and the two wom sail for New York, where the elder woman has relatives. Here Diane encounte Derek Pruyn, a widower, whom she has known and admired in early years, and offered the situation of chaperone for his daughter Dorothea, a headstrong you woman in need of feminine guidance. After a year in Pruyn's household, during whi time Diane holds aloof from Pruyn's increasing devotion, he makes her an offer marriage; she withholds her answer until his return from a voyage to South Americ when she is prepared to accept him, but on his home-coming she finds his attitu towards her completely changed. Pruyn has encountered de Bienville on his voya and has heard from him a recital of the charge that Diane was unfaithful to h husband. Pruyn denounces Diane's perfidy and she being too proud to defend hers at once takes leave of him. Subsequently Pruyn's highhanded methods cause Do thea to plan an elopement which is successfully frustrated by Diane to whom the grateful father now turns again in love and gratitude; he renews his suit begging her to marry him no matter what her past may have been, but she indignantly refuses to wed one who could want her while believing in her previous guilt. In the end de Bienville confesses the falseness of his charges and clears Diane's reputation of the blot that has rested upon it, after which she gladly enters the "Inner Shrine" of the love that has been awaiting her.

INNOCENTS ABROAD, THE, by Samuel L. Clemens ("Mark Twain"). In a vein of highly original humor this world-read book records a pleasure excursion on the Quaker City to Europe, the Holy Land, and Egypt, in the sixties. Descriptions of real events and the peoples and lands visited are enlivened by more or less fictitious dialogue and adventures. These, while absurdly amusing, always suggest the truth, stripped of hypocrisy and cant, as to how the reader "would be likely to see Europe and the East if he looked at them sincerely with his own eyes and without reverence for the past." The side-wheel steamer Quaker City carried the now famous excursionists across from New York — touching at the Azores, described in a few rapid but wonderfully vivid strokes — and from important port to port on the other side; and waited for them during several of their inland journeys. Returning, they touched at Gibraltar, Madeira, and the Bermudas. As to the advertised "select" quality of the voyagers, a characteristic paragraph states: "Henry Ward Beecher was to have accompanied the expedition, but urgent duties obliged him to give up the idea. There were other passengers who might have been spared better, and would have been spared more willingly. Lieutenant-General Sherman was to have been one of the party also, but the Indian war compelled his presence on the plains. A popular actress had entered her name on the ship's books, but something interfered, and *she* couldn't go. The 'Drummer Boy of the Potomac' deserted; and lo, we had never a celebrity left!"

INQUISITION OF THE MIDDLE AGES, A HISTORY OF THE, by Henry Charles Lea (3 vols., 1888). A work at once comprehensive in scope, complete in learning, and judicious in thought. It tells the story of the organized effort against heresy made by the Christian Church of the Middle Ages, or for about three centuries previous to the Reformation (1215–1515 A. D.). For the entire history of this effort Lea makes two periods, that of the old or mediæval Inquisition, before the Reformation, and that of the new or reorganized Inquisition coming after the Reformation, except in Spain, where Ferdinand and Isabella "founded the New Inquisition."

This famous institution is not viewed by Lea as an organization arbitrarily devised and imposed upon the judicial system of Christendom by any ambition of the Church of that age or any special fanaticism. It was a natural development, an almost inevitable expression of the forces universally at work in the thirteenth and following centuries. To clearly understand it and judge it fairly, Lea carefully examines the whole field of intellectual and spiritual developments, and the condition of the jurisprudence of the period, as a means of ascertaining the origin and development of the inquisitorial process: some of the worst features of which would have been a blot upon the history none the less if there had never been any quest for heresy; while the idea of heresy was one of the deepest seated, not only of the period, but of later generations, and as relentlessly applied under Protestantism, in some special instances as under Catholicism.

An entire volume is devoted to 'The Origin and Organization of the Inquisition,' the sad story of how the giving way in jurisprudence of the old barbarisms was arrested by the use of those made by the Church; and how the worst of these barbarisms were given a consecration which kept them in force five hundred years after they might have passed away; and in force without the restraints which Roman law had imposed. The darkest curse brought by the Inquisition, in Lea's view, was the application of its unjust and cruel processes to all criminals, down to the closing years of the eighteenth century; and not to criminals only, but to all accused persons.

In his second volume Lea follows the story of the Inquisition in the several lands of Christendom. The third he devotes to special fields of Inquisitorial activity. It is a story, not only of how those whose motives, by the standard of their age, were only good, inflicted the worst wrong and cruelty upon their fellow-creatures under a false idea of the service of God, but how ambition and avarice took advantage of the system. At the best it was a monstrous application of mistaken zeal to keep men from following their honest thoughts into paths of desirable progress. Lea's masterly treatment of the whole history makes his work an authority second to none, and one of the great triumphs of American scholarship.

INSIDE OF THE CUP, THE, by Winston Churchill (1913). The rich men who control a fashionable city church call John Hodder to the pulpit from a small New England parish, because he is orthodox and not affected by the dangerous modern liberal ideas. The residence section of the city has moved farther up town, and the neighborhood of St. John's church is the home of poverty and vice. Modern problems are thrust upon the young rector, and he realizes the inadequacy of his mediæval theology and the shortcomings of his church and creed. He spends the summer vacation in the city slum, and learns a great deal about the life of the poor in his parish and the unsocial business methods of his parishioners. He also reads the books of higher criticism which he has neglected. When his congregation assemble again in the fall, he preaches a sermon in which he enlightens his parishioners as to his change of views and admonishes them from the text, "For ye make clean the outside of the cup and of the platter, but within they are full of extortion and excess." Eldon Parr, the magnate who is head of the vestry, demands his resignation, but he claims his right to remain rector, and his bishop and some of his old parishioners and many new ones from the neighborhood stand by him. Eldon Parr's daughter chooses between him and her father, and marries the rector. It is a remarkable discussion of religious problems in fiction, and a powerful presentation of the author's convictions.

INSTITUTES OF QUINTILIAN ('Institutionis Oratoriæ XII Libri'). 'Twelve Books concerning the Education of an Orator' is a treatise on pedagogy and rhetoric written at Rome by Marcus Fabius Quintilianus in the reigns of Vespasian, Titus and Domitian. For a summary and comment see the LIBRARY under Quintilian.

INSTITUTES OF THE CHRISTIAN RELIGION, by John Calvin (1536). The first great theological work after the Reformation, undertaking to establish, against Roman Catholic belief and usage, a Protestant system of doctrine and communion and through its service as such, and its masterly grasp of system and argument widely accepted as the standard of reformed theology. The original design of the author was to make a small work for popular instruction; and his first edition conformed to this design, except as he changed his plan in order to lay before the King of France, Francis I., a defense of the Reformed Confession. By enlargement in successive editions, the work reached the form in which it is now known.

INSTITUTES OF VISHNU, see **SACRED BOOKS OF THE EAST.**

INTEREST OF AMERICA IN SEA POWER, PRESENT AND FUTURE, by Captain A. T. Mahan (1897). A work of significance because of the author's idea of "an approaching change in the thoughts and policy of Americans as to their relations with the world outside their own borders." The age of "home markets for home products" has about closed, in Captain Mahan's view, and the United States must consider interests reaching to all parts of the world. Although, therefore, his volume consists only of a collection of detached papers, and he makes no attempt to recast them into a continuous work, he yet puts over them a broadly significant title, and offers them to the reader as studies of a great theme. They are in that view of particular interest.

INTRODUCTION TO THE STUDY OF GOTHIC ARCHITECTURE, AN, see **GOTHIC.**

INTRUDER, THE ('L'Intruse'), by Maurice Maeterlinck (1890), is a play by which the writer achieved an international reputation. It is a one-act piece of few characters and little action, simple in construction, rich in suggestion, potent in its realism. A family sit in the gloomy room of an old château and talk in the most natural, matter-of-fact way, while one member, a young wife, lies very ill in childbirth in the adjacent room. Through the commonplace speech one can feel the tension of their nerves; the effect is heightened by the skillful use of details by the dramatist. All is indirect, symbolic, pregnant with innuendo. It is as if Death, the Intruder, were knocking at each door and window. At length a sister of charity enters, and by the sign of the cross makes known that the wife is no more.

ION, a drama, by Euripides (423 B. C.). The story, wrought into a drama of high patriotic and of profound human interest by Euripides, was that of Ion as the ancestor of the Ionians, or Athenian Greeks, reputed to be the son of Xuthus and his wife Creusa, but in reality a son of Apollo and Creusa. The god had caused the infant to be taken by Mercury from the cave where his mother had left him, and to be carried to his temple at Delphi, and brought up as a youthful attendant. Ion's character, and the part he plays as a child devotee at the time of the play, offer a singularly beautiful parallel to the story of the child Samuel in the Hebrew Scripture. The situation in this play, which circumstances had created, is that of Creusa, the mother, in a distracted state, seeking unwittingly the death of her own son. One of the finest passages is a dialogue of splendid power and beauty between Ion and Creusa. For freshness, purity, and charm, Ion is a character unmatched in all Greek drama. The whole play is often pronounced the finest left by Euripides. Its melodramatic richness in ingenious surprises was a new feature of Greek drama, which was especially characteristic of the new comedy of the next century. Mr. Paley says that "none of the plays of Euripides so clearly show his fine mind, or impress us with a more favorable idea of his virtuous and humane character." The revelation of domestic emotions in the play, the singular beauty of the scenes which it presents, and the complexity and rapid transitions of its action, suggest a modern romantic drama rather than one strictly Greek. In its general design to represent Apollo, the god of music, poetry, medicine, and prophecy, as the head, through Ion, of the Ionians, the play was of great religious and patriotic interest to its Athenian audience. It can never fail, with its revelations of Greek "sweetness and light," to be of the deepest human interest.

The 'Ion' of Talfourd bears no relation beyond that of a borrowed name to the play of Euripides. Its Ion figures as king of Argos, and the dramatic interest centres in his readiness to give his life to appease the Divine anger shown by a pestilence raging at Argos. The king's character is finely brought out, and the impression given of the relentless working of destiny is in the Greek spirit.

IPHIGENIA, a drama, by Euripides (407 B.C.). The third and latest, and altogether the most modern, of the great masters of Greek drama, twice used the Iphigenia story, — once in the fine masterpiece which was represented during his life, and again in a drama brought out after his death. The latter represented the time and scene of the bringing of the heroine to the altar of sacrifice, and the climax of the play was her readiness to accept a divine behest by giving up her life. The other and the finer play represented a time twenty years later. It told how she was snatched from under the knife of sacrifice by Divine intervention, and carried away to the land of the Tauri (where is now the Crimea), to live in honor as a priestess of Artemis, a feature of whose Taurian worship was the sacrificial immolation of any luckless strangers cast on shore by shipwreck. Twenty years had passed, and the Greek passion of Iphigenia to return to her own land, to at least hear of her people, was at its height, when two strangers from a wreck were taken, and it was her duty to preside at their sacrifice. They were Orestes and Pylades, the former her own brother. The climax of the play is in her recognition of Orestes, and in the means employed by her for her own and their escape. A singularly fine soliloquy of Iphigenia, upon hearing of the capture of two strangers, is followed by a dialogue between her and Orestes, unsurpassed, if not unequaled, by anything in Greek dramatic poetry. Her proposal to spare one to be the bearer of a letter to her Greek home, brings on a contest of self-devotion between Orestes and Pylades of wonderful dramatic power. The whole play shows Euripides at his best in ingenuity of construction and depth of feeling; and all the odes of the play are marked by extreme lyrical beauty. A notable one among them is the final one on the establishment of the worship of Apollo at Delphi.

A celebrated parallel to the 'Iphigenia' of Euripides was conceived and executed by Goethe. It is not properly an imitation. Although using scenery and characters nominally Greek, it is a thoroughly modern play, on lines of thought and sentiment quite other than Greek, and with a diction very unlike Greek. Of this modern kind it is a drama of the highest merit, a splendid example of modern psychological dramatic composition.

IRON WOMAN, THE, by Margaret Deland (1911). This is a sequel to the 'Awakening of Helena Ritchie' and continues the narrative of her life. The story opens when her adopted son David is ten years old and she is living with him in the manufacturing town of Mercer, situated but a short distance from Old Chester. David has three playmates of his own age: Elizabeth Ferguson, a fascinating and passionate child, who lives with her bachelor uncle, and Blair and Nannie Maitland, whose mother is known as the "Iron Woman." Sarah Maitland is a woman of eccentric habits and masculine style. She manages the Maitland Iron Works which she has inherited from her husband, who only survived his marriage to her by a few months and who died before the birth of Blair. Nannie, the child by a previous marriage, is a gentle and timid girl devoted to her stepbrother. The children grow up and Elizabeth after having a youthful affair with Blair, becomes engaged to David who is studying to be a doctor. A misunderstanding arises between them and Elizabeth in a burst of wild passion, marries Blair who is so much in love with her that he is willing to be false to his old friend. Mrs. Maitland, whose rough exterior hides an honest and affectionate nature, is overwhelmed by the dishonorable action of her son, whom she has idolized, and at once disinherits him. Blair whose artistic nature has been so shocked and repulsed by his mother's eccentricities that he has no real affection for her, is furious, and severs all connection with her. An explosion occurs at the works, and Sarah Maitland is fatally hurt. Before her death she writes the name of Blair upon a check for a large sum of money which she had planned to give David for building a hospital. She is unable to sign the check and Nannie who is the only one present, anxious that Blair shall have the money, forges her mother's name after her death. Blair is gratified with the bequest and is preparing to invest it when the truth becomes known. Elizabeth, who has always loved David, asks Blair to give him the money and when he declines to do so, leaves him and goes to David. David, who has continued to love Elizabeth passionately, urges her to flee with him, and she is ready to do so when Helena Ritchie appears upon the scene and prevents the action by confessing to them her own experience. Elizabeth returns to Blair. But after futile ·efforts to win her love he finally agrees to free her and allows her to get a divorce and marry David. Helena, who has been ardently sought in marriage by Robert Ferguson, Elizabeth's uncle, at last gives in and acknowledges her love for him.

IRONMASTER, THE ('Le Maître de Forges'), by Georges Ohnet (1882), has both as novel and play, in English as well as French, been persistently popular; and in all the history of French fiction, few books have sold better. Ohnet wrote the story as a play; but no manager would accept it until, after its success as a novel, he redramatized it. It is a dramatic love story, whose characters are: Claire de Beaulieu; Madame de Beaulieu; Gaston, Duke de Bligny, a mercenary lover who breaks faith with Claire for the sake of a fortune, and engages himself to Athenais, the daughter of a rich but vulgar manufacturer; and a rich young ironmaster, Philippe Derblay, of plebeian birth but excellent character. Around this small group of actors moves an energetic drama of baffled hopes, disappointed ambitions, tribulations that purify, and final happiness. The book has little literary merit; but the rapidity of its movement and its strong situations have given it a secure, if temporary, place in French and English approval.

ISRAEL AMONG THE NATIONS: 'A Study of the Jews and Anti-Semitism,' by Anatole Leroy-Beaulieu, Translated by Frances Hellman (1896). A specially careful, thoughtful, philosophical study of the facts bearing upon the character of the Jew in history and his place in modern life. It is not so much a defense of the Jews against complaint and prejudice, as it is an impartial examination of the Jewish situation, and a summary of interesting facts in regard to the seven or eight millions of Jews scattered amongst five or six hundred millions of Christians in Europe and America, or Mohammedans in Asia. The author is a Frenchman and a Christian, who specially desires to see France maintain the ground taken in the emancipation of the Jews by the French Revolution. He is familiar with the Jewish situation in Russia, Poland, Roumania, and Hungary, where Jewish concentration is greatest, where "Israel's centre of gravity" is found, "a vast reservoir of Jews in the centre of Europe, whose overflow tends towards the West," and in view of whose movements it appears not unlikely that "the old European and especially the young American states will be swept by a long tidal wave of Jewish emigration." The reader of the story, with its episodes of discussion, will get a clear view of many interesting points touching Jewish origins and developments, and will find himself in a position to fairly judge the Jewish problem. There is no lack of sympathy in the writer, yet he frankly says that "modern Israel would seem to be morally, as well as physically, a dying race." Conscience, he says, "has become contracted and obscured"; and "as to honor, where could the Jew possibly have learnt its meaning?—beaten, reviled, scorned, abused by everybody."

ISRAEL, HISTORY OF THE PEOPLE OF, by Ernest Renan (5 vols.). The 'Vie de Jésus,' or Life of Jesus, of the most accomplished of recent authors, the charm of which has carried its sale in France alone to over 300,000 copies, came out in 1863; and was the first of a series of seven volumes devoted to a review of the origins and early development of Christianity, down to the date in Roman history marked by the death of the Emperor Marcus Aurelius. Upon the completion of this work M. Renan set himself the task of adding, by way of introduction to his history of Christian origins, a history of the Jews; and on October 24th, 1891, he was able to write, at the close of a fifth volume, that the task was finished. There are two "books" in each of his five volumes, and the successive stages of the history are these: (1) the Israelites in their nomad state, until their establishment in the land of Canaan; (2) the Israelites as settled tribes, until the establishment of the Kingdom of David; (3) the Single Kingdom; (4) the two kingdoms; (5) the Kingdom of Judah alone; (6) the Captivity in Babylon; (7) Judæa under Persian Domination; (8) the Jews under Greek Domination; (9) Jewish Autonomy; (10) the Jewish People under Greek Domination.

Asa philologist of distinction, an expert in the whole field of Semitic studies, a traveler and archæologist familar with the scenes and the surviving monuments of Palestine, Renan brought exceptional knowledge to the work of restoring the past of the Israelite race. The freedom of his opinions led him away from traditional paths while the warmth of his sentiment, often ardently Jewish, and the richness of his imagination, gave to the more significant pages of Hebrew story an illumination rarely found in sober history.

ITALIAN JOURNEYS, by W. D. Howells (1867), is the record of leisurely excursion up and down the land,—to Padua, Ferrara, Genoa, Pompeii, Naples, Rome, and many other towns of picturesque buildings and melodious names, from Capri to Trieste Mr. Howells knows his Italy so well that though he writes as a foreigner he is in perfect sympathy with his subject. He knows the innkeepers, guides, and railway men to be dead to truth and honesty, but he likes them; and he knows that Tasso's prison never held Tasso, and that the history of most of the historic places is purely legendary but he delights to believe in them all. He sees in the broken columns and fragmentary walls of Pompeii all the splendor of the first century, that time of gorgeous wealth and in an old house of Arquá, he has a vision of Petrarch writing at his curious carved table. In crumbling Herculaneum his spirit is touched to wistful sympathy by a garden of wild flowers: "Here — where so long ago the flowers had bloomed, and perished in the terrible blossoming of the mountain that sent up its awful fires in the awful similitude of Nature's harmless and lovely forms, and showered its destroying petals all abroad — was it not tragic to find again the soft tints, the graceful shape the sweet perfumes, of the earth's immortal life? Of them that planted and tende and plucked and bore in their bosoms and twined in their hair these fragile childre of the summer, what witness in the world? Only the crouching skeletons under th tables— Alas and alas!" His love of the beautiful is tempered by a keen sense of humor; and the combination makes his volume a delightful record, with the sunshine of Italy shut between its covers.

ITALIAN REPUBLICS: 'The Origin, Progress, and Fall of Italian Freedom,' by J. C. L. de Sismondi (1832). An extremely useful story of Italy from the beginning of the twelfth century to 1814 A.D., with an introductory sketch of the history from 476 A.D. to 1138. The work was prepared for Lardner's Cabinet 'Cyclopædia,' after its author had told the larger story in an elaborate work extending to sixteen volumes.

ITALY. see RENAISSANCE IN.

ITALY OF TO-DAY, by Bolton King and Thomas Okey (1901). The authors limit themselves to an attempt to describe the outer manifestations of the life of Italy, as they shape themselves in politics, in social movements, in literature. Approaching the subject without prepossessions they have endeavored to understand and describe the point of view of each section of the national life as described by its own advocates, whether Catholic, Liberal, Socialist, or Conservative. To the student who desires to understand the special characteristics of Northern and Southern Italy, the activities of trade and manufacture, the lives of the peasants and the remarkable agricultural revival, the education, finance, and local government of Italy, the existing relations between Church and State, the present volume will be most informing. A concluding chapter deals with the great names in the literature of the present generation, Carducci, Fogazzaro, Verga, Gabriele d'Annunzio. The conclusion to which the authors' careful and sympathetic investigation has led them is that "the divisions in Italian life are neither as deep nor as permanent as they are often thought to be; next, that underneath the slough of misgovernment and corruption and political apathy there is a rejuvenated nation, instinct with the qualities that make a great people."

IVANHOE, one of Sir Walter Scott's most famous novels, was written and published in 1819, a year of great domestic sorrow to its author. The manuscript is now at Abbotsford; and, according to Lockhart, is a remarkable and characteristic specimen of his penmanship. Immediately after its appearance, 'Ivanhoe' became a favorite, and now ranks among the most brilliant and stirring of romantic tales. Sir Wilfred, Knight of Ivanhoe, a young Saxon knight, brave, loyal, and handsome, is disinherited by his father, Cedric of Rotherwood, on account of his love for Rowena, a Saxon heiress and ward of Cedric's. Ivanhoe is a favorite with Richard I., Cœur-de-Lion, has won renown in Palestine, and now returns in the disguise of a palmer to see Rowena at Rotherwood. Under the name of Desdichado (The Disinherited), he enters the lists of the Ashby Tournament; and having won the victory, is crowned by the Lady Rowena. He is wounded, however, and returns to the care of his friends, Isaac of York, a wealthy Jew, and his daughter Rebecca. The latter tends him, and loses her heart to this chivalrous knight. On returning from the Tournament, Rowena is captured by the enamored De Bracy and confined in the Tower of Torquilstone. After her release she is united in marriage to Ivanhoe, through the effort of King Richard. While the Lady Rowena is a model of beauty, dignity, and gentleness, she is somewhat overshadowed by Rebecca, who was Scott's favorite of all his characters. She is as generous as her father is avaricious; and although loving Ivanhoe with intense devotion, realizes that her union with him is impossible. She nobly offers to the Templar Bois-Guilbert any sum that he may demand for the release of the imprisoned Rowena. A strong scene occurs when she defies this infatuated Crusader, and threatens to throw herself from the turret into the court yard. Bois-Guilbert carries her to the Preceptory of Templestowe, where she is convicted of sorcery on account of her religion, her skill in medicine, and her attractiveness. Condemned to the stake, she is permitted a trial by combat, and selects Ivanhoe for her champion. Rebecca is pronounced guiltless and free.

Another important character is Richard the Lion-Hearted, who returns to England from Palestine at the moment when his brother's conspiracy against him is most rank. Disguised as the Black Sluggard and the Knight of the Fetterlock, he performs feats of valor at the Ashby Tournament and as the Black Knight, wanders through Sherwood Forest and holds high revel with the Hermit of Copmanhurst, the jovial Friar Tuck. Through Robin Hood he escapes assassination, and conducts the successful siege against Torquilstone Castle. Maurice de Bracy, a conspirator against King Richard, is a suitor for the hand of Rowena; Front de Bœuf is a brutal baron in league with Prince John; Cedric the Saxon, Ivanhoe's father, supports Athelstane's suit for Rowena, desiring to see the Saxons reinstated; and Isaac of York, the wealthy Jew, is a well-drawn character. Gurth, Cedric's swineherd, who is generally accompanied by his faithful dog Fangs, is a typical feudal retainer; Wamba, Cedric's jester, is another; and Ulrica, a vindictive old Saxon hag, who perishes in the flames of Torquilstone Castle to which she sets fire, is one of those strange, half prophetic, half weird women whom Scott loves to introduce into his stories.

In the scenes in Sherwood Forest, Robin Hood's men perform feats of archery and deeds of valor, drawn from the Robin Hood ballads and legends.

Retainers, lords and ladies, knights, Templars, monks, priests, prisoners, jailors and men-at-arms are introduced; and the book is full of brilliantly colored pictures of the period which abounds in contrast between the Saxons and the Normans.

JACK, by Alphonse Daudet (1876), is a story of experience and emotion. Less skillful treatment would have made so tragical a tale revolting. But Daudet does not content himself with cold psychological analysis or brilliant exposition of character. His dominant quality is a passionate sympathy, which communicates itself to his readers, and forces them to share his pity or anger or admiration. Jack, introduced to us as a pretty boy, beautifully dressed, might have lived an adequate life but for his light and selfish mother. He is sacrificed to her moral weakness, and to the bitter selfishness of his stepfather D'Argenton. The latter, a noble idealist in theory while petty and base in practice, is jealous of this inconvenient, superfluous Jack, and thrusts him outside the home. Jack's life is a long martyrdom, from his home-sick days with the little black King of Dahomey, in a nondescript school somewhat like the Dotheboys Hall made famous by Dickens, until his final "release" from bed in the charity hospital. He becomes dull, sickly, inert; but his finer qualities die hard, and are perhaps only latent even during his worst days of labor in an iron foundry, and of fevered exhaustion as stoker on an ocean steamer. But life never becomes quite hopeless; for love and sympathy reach even to Jack, and offer him partial compensation. After the publication of 'Jack,' Daudet wrote a sketch of the original of the hero; for in its main outline the story is a true one. Here, as usual, he took a framework of fact, upon which his poetic instinct and sympathetic imagination reared a memorable work of art.

JACK OF THE MILL, THE LIFE AND ADVENTURES OF. Jack of the Mill, commonly called Lord Othmill, created for his eminent services Baron Waldeck and Knight of Kitcottie. A fireside story, by William Howitt (1844). The scenes of these adventures lie partly in England during the reign of Henry V., partly in Bohemia and Germany. They are a succession of bloodthirsty and thrilling conflicts, in which Jack, the hero, with scarcely an effort, overcomes robbers and gipsies, fights the opponents of the Lollards and the Hussites with equal vigor, and obtains honors, preferment, and a lovely wife. From the moment when, a runaway boy, he fills his pockets with fish-hooks to trap the hands of thieving companions, to the time when, with a single companion, he overcomes the robber-baron Hans von Stein, with his train, — a semi-historical character whose castle, honeycombed with dungeons, is still visited by tourists in Germany, — his wit and success never fail; and as valor as well as virtue has its due reward, Jack, the vagrant frequenter of the old mill, becomes in turn John Othmill, respected and feared by society, and finally the great Lord Waldeck. The author allows himself considerable latitude of imagination and plot, and the result is aptly named in the quaint term of apology he uses in the preface, a "hatch-up."

JACOB FAITHFUL; OR, THE ADVENTURES OF A WATERMAN, a novel, by Captain Marryat (1834), describes the career of a young man who is born on a Thames "lighter," and up to the age of eleven has never set foot on land. The "lighter" is manned by his father, his mother, and himself. His father is a round-bellied, phlegmatic little man, addicted to his pipe, and indulging in but few words: three apothegms, "It's no use crying—what's done can't be helped"; "Take it coolly"· "Better luck next time," serving him on every occasion. These Jacob inherits, and makes frequent use of in after life. His mother indulges in strong drink and comes to a terrible end. One of his first acts on beginning a life on shore is to sell his mother's asses for twenty pounds, — the earliest bargain he ever made. After spending several years at school, where his adventures are interesting, and some of them laughable, he is bound apprentice, at the age of fourteen, to a waterman. Now fairly launched in life, his real adventures begin. Some of the curious experiences that may befall a waterman form the staple of the book. It is written in a lively style, and is thought to be one of Marryat's best books.

JAN VEDDER'S WIFE, by Mrs. Amelia Barr (1885), is a story of life in the Shetland Islands seventy years ago. It is highly dramatic, with a delightful breeziness of atmosphere. The personages feel and think with the simple directness that seems a result of close contact with nature. Jan Vedder, a handsome young sailor, "often at the dance, seldom at the kirk," marries Margaret, the daughter of rich Peter Fae. He is clever but self-indulgent, and fettered by inertia; while Margaret is exacting, selfish, self-satisfied, and thrifty to meanness. He needs money, and when she refuses to help him, draws her savings from the bank without her knowledge. Then Margaret returns to her father's house, and refuses to see him. From this point a double thread of interest attracts the reader, who follows the separated fortunes of Jan and Margaret through years of unhappiness, poverty, and distrust. The moral of the story is the danger of the sin of selfishness; and when the "offending Adam is whipped out" of two struggling souls, the reader shares their happiness. The local color is vivid, and the story delightfully simple.

JANE EYRE (1847), the novel which established Charlotte Brontë's reputation as a writer of fiction, is in a large degree the record of her own development. In the character of Jane Eyre, the young authoress first found an outlet for the storm and stress of her own nature. The book is therefore autobiographical in the truest sense.

The heroine, Jane Eyre, is an orphan. As a child she is misunderstood and disliked by her protectors. She is sent early to Lowood School, an institution charitable in the coldest sense of the term. Its original was Cowan Bridge, the school attended by four of the Brontë sisters; from which Maria and Elizabeth were removed in a dying condition. The description of Jane Eyre's school days forms one of the most vivid, and in a sense dramatic, portions of the novel. After leaving Lowood, she becomes governess to the ward of a certain Mr. Rochester, an eccentric man of the world, whose eccentricity is largely the fruit of misfortune. He is tied to an insane wife, her insanity being the result of vicious living. She is confined at Thornwood, the house of Rochester; but the heroine does not know of her existence. Rochester falls in love with Jane Eyre, attracted by her nobility of nature, her strength, and her unconventionality; and finally asks her to marry him. His force and his love for her win her consent. They are separated at the altar, however, by the revelation of the existence of Rochester's first wife. The two are reunited at last only by a tragedy.

Charlotte Brontë invested the character of Rochester with a fascination that made him the hero in fiction of half the women in England. Jane Eyre herself is no ordinary heroine. Her creator had the boldness to reject the pink-and-white Amelia type of woman, that had reigned in the novel since Richardson, and to substitute one whose mind, not her face, was her fortune. Rochester himself is destitute of gallantry, of all those qualities belonging to the ideal lover in fiction. This new departure made the book famous at once. Its literary originality was not less striking than the choice of types.

JANICE MEREDITH, by Paul Leicester Ford (1899). This book presents with realistic accuracy the most dramatic episodes of the American Revolution. It gives a fair-minded picture of events and conditions and is most amusing in its old-time flavor, being faithful to the spirit of the times, and offering the reader a striking sketch of George Washington. The opening scene is laid near Brunswick in the province of New Jersey in the year 1774, and a view is presented of the Tory household of the Merediths, whose tea-drinking habits are protested against by the Sons of Liberty. Janice, the heroine, is a vivacious maid of fifteen at the time the story opens, and a natural coquette. This sprightly heroine is made the centre around which the most thrilling episodes of the Revolution revolve. She subdues the British hearts at Philadelphia, is the life of the captives in Virginia, and conquers both friend and foe in the trenches of Yorktown. The story of her varying fortunes is capitally told, and the reader follows Janice and her fiery lover, Col. John Brereton, through manifold wild adventures and hairbreadth escapes. Brereton fulfils perilous missions for the patriotic cause, undergoes the most trying ordeals and narrowly escapes being hanged as a spy. He exerts himself to the utmost to rescue the Meredith family from impending misfortunes and is misrepresented and unjustly accused of cruelty towards them. He becomes the trusted friend of Washington, and in the end wins the hand and heart of the impulsive and capricious Janice, whose fair face has wrought such havoc among her countrymen and their opponents. After endless misunderstandings, separations, and the unraveling of many complicated circumstances, Janice and Brereton are united and receive the blessing of General and Mrs. Washington.

JAPAN, AN ATTEMPT AT INTERPRETATION, by Lafcadio Hearn (1904), is an account of that country by one who had identified himself as closely as a

European possibly could with the life of Japan and who was moreover a master of English style. After a graceful introduction, emphasizing the unfamiliarity and charm of Japan for the foreigner, he proceeds to an exposition of the religion and the social institutions of the country, laying great importance on the former as the spring of all Japanese art, ethics, and government. In Shintoism, an indigenous type of ancestor-worship, modified by Chinese culture and by Buddhism, he finds the essence of the Japanese religion. The principle of loyalty, whether to the family dead, or to the great men of the nation as represented in the government, is the fundamental in all Japanese conduct. Its elaboration by Buddhism both popular and philosophic, its modification in feudal times, its return to an earlier simplicity in the present cult of the Emperor are all pointed out. The crushing of Roman Catholicism in the seventeenth century is described as a process regrettable for its cruelty but necessary to the happy and successful development of the nation. The writer also looks with disfavor on such modern missionary effort as shows no tolerance for the principle of ancestor-worship, which, he maintains, in an essential factor in the social continuity of Japan. There are some interesting speculations on the future development, political, social, and religious, of the nation which had just discomfited Russia and entered the ranks of the modern military powers and industrial states. In general Hearn believed that the way of safety for Japan lay in conservatism as to the relinquishing of her old beliefs and institutions.

JEAN CHRISTOPHE, by Romain Rolland (1904–12). A biographical psychological novel in ten volumes. The hero, Jean Christophe, is a musical genius of heroic character. He rebels against sham and hypocrisy and seeks sincerely for truth in literature, politics, and society as well as music. The book is a discussion of the intellectual movements and activities of modern times. "Nothing that has ever been said or thought of life is accepted without being brought to the test of Jean Christophe's own life." He is born into sordid poverty in a small German town near the French frontier. His drunken father trains him to appear as a musical prodigy before he is seven years old, and at fourteen he is the breadwinner for the family. He offends the musicians of his native town by his original ideas in music and the independence of his thought. A brawl with the soldiers is the occasion for a discussion of militarism, and forces Jean Christophe to leave Germany when he is twenty, and escape to Paris. Here in direst poverty he fights for recognition for his music and his uncompromising ideals, and French morals, manners, and music are passed in review. The true France is revealed to him through his rich friendship with Oliver. A volume is given to the story of Antoinette, the lovely devoted sister of Oliver, her struggle with poverty to educate her brother, and keep a home for him, and her death when she attains success. Oliver marries Jacqueline, and their love, marriage, and estrangement is an exquisite study. Jean Christophe becomes interested in syndicalism. In a first of May street fight Oliver is killed and Jean Christophe made a fugitive again. He crosses the frontier into Switzerland. There is a passionate episode with Anna, the wife of his friend and host. Jean Christophe falls desperately in love many times both spiritually and grossly. He suffers disillusion and recovers and then falls in love again. He finds happiness at last in a platonic friendship with Grazia, an Italian countess, whom he had known in Paris. In her salon in Rome he meets the young party of truth seekers of Italy whose motto is "Think with courage." His genius is recognized, and he returns to Paris, and dies unaffected by his success, and happy to have brought together Oliver's son and Grazia's daughter. The discussions of modern music and the conditions of musical success take up a large part of the series, one or two volumes being almost entirely devoted to these subjects. A description of the first appearance of the hero as an infant prodigy will be found in the LIBRARY under Romain Rolland.

JEAN TETEROL'S IDEA ('L'Idée de Jean Teterol'), by Charles Victor Cherbuliez (1878). A clever narrator rather than a keen psychologist, Cherbuliez can tell a good story in a picturesque style, with an accompaniment of interesting philosophic reflections. Jean Teterol, a young peasant abused by his master, the Baron Saligneux, shakes the dust of Saligneux from his shoes, and departs, vowing vengeance. The idea which comes to him then, and which thenceforth dominates his life, is a determination to become a rich proprietor of land instead of a serf. He goes to Paris, and there by hard work and by shrewdness amasses a fortune. At fifty-five, many times a millionaire, he is a widower with one son, Lionel, to whom he looks for the fruition of all his ambitions. This boy, his "Prince of Wales," has had every sort of advantage. He may marry an aristocrat and become one himself. His father regards him with a tyrannical pride and affection, somewhat galling to Lionel's more refined nature. Jean Teterol returns to the village of Saligneux and there learns that his old master is dead; that his son, the present Baron, has a beautiful daughter, Claire; and that the estate is embarrassed and the Baron in debt. Jean craftily manages to become his chief creditor, and then demands Claire's hand for Lionel. From this point the complications of the story multiply rapidly Claire is made an interesting heroine; Lionel rises in the esteem of the reader: and the fortunes of the two, and of the old estate, offer to Cherbuliez the material of an agreeable domestic tale. The manner of it is graceful, and its touch delightfully free.

JEFFERSON, JOSEPH, THE AUTOBIOGRAPHY OF (1890). The story of the third Joseph Jefferson, grandson of the great comedian of that name, runs from February 20, 1829, through more than sixty years to 1890; and it is little to say that there is not a dull page in it. In clearness and charm of manner, humor, and wealth of anecdote, Mr. Jefferson commands his readers in his story precisely as he has so long commanded his hearers on the stage.

The narrative begins at the beginning, — toddling infancy in Washington, and childhood in New York, Philadelphia, and Baltimore, — wherever the father, Joseph Jefferson, manager of a theatre, might be. The young actor is in Chicago in 1839, where James Wallack, Sr., the elder Booth, and Macready came into view; he goes to Mississippi and to Mexico; and returns to Philadelphia and New York. His reminiscences are of Mr. and Mrs. James Wallack, Jr., John E. Owens, William Burton, Charles Burke, Julia Dean, James E. Murdock, and Edwin Forrest. Then the scene shifts to London and Paris. Once more at home, we make acquaintance with Rip Van Winkle, and the climax of the master's creative power. Again he ranges the world as far as Australia, Van Diemen's Land, and New Zealand, coming home by way of London. Of so wide a life the scenes were many and varied, and a great number of the chief masters and notable ladies of the stage for half a century come up for mention; and always, in report of scenes or portrayal of character, a refinement both of thought and of style gives the narrative a peculiar charm.

JEROME; 'A Poor Man,' by Mary E. Wilkins (1897). Jerome is the vignette of a New England youth, relieved against a background of provincial types. When hardly out of his teens, he is called upon by the sudden disappearance of his father to take upon his shoulders the burden of the family. His course is a pathway of misfortune, sacrifice, and hardship, leading by rugged steps to a summit of well-earned prosperity. A great sacrifice to a high ideal is the turning-point of the story. Like Miss Wilkins's other works, 'Jerome' is a careful and truthful study of New England village character.

JERUSALEM, by Selma Lagerlöf (1901). Part 1 of this story is a series of quaint pictures of Swedish village life, centering around the fortunes of an ancient peasant family, the Ingmars of Ingmarson. The young owner of the Ingmar estate courted Brita and brought her home, but his thrift postponed the wedding too long, and the unhappy Brita did away with her child and is now serving a term in prison. Ingmar and his conscience debate as to whether he shall accept her family's offer to send her to America, or right the wrong he has done by bringing her home. He meets Brita at the prison, wins her love, and finds to his surprise that he has earned the respect of the community and his father's title of "Great Ingmar." Karin, Ingmar's daughter, takes the management of the estate at his death, and little Ingmar goes to live with the schoolmaster to escape his drunken brother-in-law, who fortunately dies before the inheritance is wasted. Karin marries her first love, joins a religious sect led by a revivalist from America, and puts up the farm at auction to get the money to join a pilgrimage to Jerusalem. Young Ingmar, penniless, stands watching the possessions of generations of Ingmars dispersed by the auctioneer, and finally yields to his devotion to the land, agreeing to give up his betrothed Gertrude, the schoolmaster's daughter, to marry a rich wife to save the farm. Gertrude joins the pilgrimo. Part 2 is the community life of the peasants in Jerusalem. The story ends in Sweden at the Ingmar farm, with the reconciliation and the love story of Ingmar and his wife after Ingmar has made a pilgrimage to Jerusalem to bring back Gertrude. This part of the story is founded on a religious pilgrimage made by the peasants of Dalecarlia, Switzerland, to the Holy Land, an enterprise in which the author took part.

JERUSALEM, THE CITY OF HEROD AND SALADIN, by Sir Walter Besant and Professor E. H. Palmer (1871, 1888). A history published under the auspices of the society known as "The Palestine Exploration Fund." It covers a period and is compiled from materials not included in any other work. It begins with the siege by Titus, 70 A.D., and continues to the fourteenth century; including the early Christian period, the Moslem invasion, the mediæval pilgrimages, the pilgrimages by Mohammedans, the Crusades, the Latin Kingdom from 1099 A.D. to 1291, the victorious career of Saladin, the Crusade of the Children, and other episodes in the history of the city and of the country. The use of Crusading and Arabic sources for the preparation of the work, and the auspices under which it has been published, give this history a value universally recognized.

JERUSALEM DELIVERED ('Gerusalemme Liberata'), an epic poem on the First Crusade by Torquato Tasso, completed in 1575 and published in a pirated edition in 1580 and with Tasso's authorization in 1581. The poem consists of twenty cantos written in ottava rima or eight-lined stanzas. The best known translation is that by Edward Fairfax (1600). A revision of the poem, 'Jerusalem Conquered' ('Gerusalemme Conquistata'), was published by Tasso in 1593, but has been universally judged inferior to the original. A general summary and estimate of the poem will be found in the biographical essay on Tasso in the LIBRARY, pp. 14473–14475.

THE JESUIT RELATIONS AND ALLIED DOCUMENTS: 'TRAVELS AND EXPLORATIONS OF THE JESUIT MISSIONARIES IN NEW FRANCE' (1610–1791). The original

French, Latin, and Italian texts, with English translations and notes; illustrated by portraits, maps, and fac-similes. Edited by Reuben Gold Thwaites. A republication of great magnitude and importance; the entire work consists, as to 'The Jesuit Relations,' in forty volumes of Jesuit annual reports in French, which began to appear in Paris in 1632, and came out year by year to 1673. The very great value of the work is that of original materials of the most interesting character for the history of North America from 1611, the date of the first landing of Jesuit missionaries on the shores of Nova Scotia.

JESUITS IN NORTH AMERICA IN THE SEVENTEENTH CENTURY, see FRANCE AND ENGLAND IN NORTH AMERICA.

JESUS, THE LIFE OF. The rationalistic movement of the eighteenth and nineteenth centuries is responsible for a large number of lives of Jesus in which an attempt is made to account for Jesus and for the rise of Christianity by modern critical and historical methods. Other biographies are then written with the aim of re-establishing the orthodox view. 'Das Leben Jesu' by David Friedrich Strauss was first published in 1835, and was translated into English by George Eliot in 1846; a second Life of Jesus from his pen appeared in 1864. Strauss agreed neither with those who accept the Gospels as literally true nor with those who explain them as a record of actual facts, distorted by popular delusion into miracles. In his opinion, the Gospel stories are almost pure myth, unintentionally created by the early Christian writers, and expressing the Hegelian doctrine of the unity of man with God. 'La vie de Jésus' by Ernest Renan was published in 1863. In preparation for writing it the author had journeyed through Palestine, and he endeavors to paint the landscapes, the costumes, and the manners of the time, with a richness of color which is somewhat touched with sentimentality. His general position is one of rationalistic interpretation of the miraculous which he explains as the unconscious distortion of natural incident. Frederick W. Farrar's 'Life of Christ' (1874) is an attractively-written biography and commentary with an orthodox point of view. German Liberal theology is represented by Theodor Keim's 'Geschichte Jesu von Nazara' (1867–1872), and by Bernhard Weiss's 'Das Leben Jesu' (1882). Alfred Edersheim's 'Life and Times of Jesus the Messiah' (1883) illustrates the subject with a wealth of rabbinical learning and is conservative in its attitude. A recent liberal treatment is Oskar Holzmann's 'Leben Jesu,' published in Germany in 1901 and in English translation in 1904. The literature of the subject is immense and shows no sign of diminution after more than a century of investigation. The attempt to rationalize the Gospel story has largely given place to a serious endeavor to appreciate it as a great fact of human experience. See also 'Ecce Homo.'

JEW, THE, by Joseph Ignatius Kraszewski (1865), is a story of the soil, simply told by one of Poland's best-known writers. When Jean Huba, a Polish exile, enters a tavern and swoons at the feet of the guests, Signor Firpo the landlord wishes to send him elsewhere to die; but the stranger regains consciousness, and finds himself surrounded by a motley society of Russians, Italians, Poles, Jews, Danes, and Tsigane (Gipsies), gathered at little tables enjoying themselves. A strange friendship is set on foot between Jacob Harmon, an educated Jew, and the exile Jean Huba, familiarly known as Ivas. Their conversation serves to put the reader in possession of many facts in Jewish history. Jacob undertakes to convert Ivas to Judaism; and argues well, using politics and philosophy as well as religion for illustrations. They agree to return to Poland to improve the intellectual condition of the Jews, become involved in political intrigues there, and are forced to quit the country. One or two love affairs give a slight tinge of romance to the story. The book is powerful, but possesses little interest for those readers who do not care for the ethical and ethnical questions it discusses.

JEWS, HISTORY OF THE ('Antiquitates Judaicæ'), by Flavius Josephus. This work was concluded in the thirteenth year of the reign of Domitian. It was addressed especially to the Greeks and the Gentiles; and for this purpose the author had condescended to acquire the Greek language, and to adopt the "smooth periods" of the pagan writers, held generally in contempt by a people who believed their language sacred and their law the repository of all wisdom. The well-known events of Josephus's life go to account for the singular largeness of view, liberal culture, and tolerant judgment which everywhere characterize his historic writings, and give them a liveliness of style not often found in lengthy national annals.

The 'Antiquities,' so far as they relate to events covered by the Bible, are hardly more than a free version of and running commentary on the books of the Old Testament, including the Apocrypha. After that the Persian, Macedonian, and Roman invasions, and the Herodian reigns, are told with varying degrees of thoroughness down to Nero's twelfth year, when the uprising occurred which gave rise to the Jewish War in which Josephus bore so conspicuous a part, and which he relates in the book so named. To Christians the most interesting passage in his writing, notwithstanding its disputed authenticity, is that containing his description of Jesus, Chapter iii., Book xviii.

"Now there was about this time Jesus, a wise man, if it be lawful to call him a man; for he was a doer of wonderful works, a teacher of such men as receive the truth with pleasure. He drew over to him both many of the Jews, and many of the Gentiles. He was [the] Christ. And when Pilate, at the suggestion of the principal men among us, had condemned him to the cross, those that loved him at the first did not forsake him: for he appeared to them alive again the third day, as the divine prophets had foretold these and ten thousand other wonderful things concerning him. And the tribe of Christians, so named from him, are not extinct at this day."

This passage is twice quoted by Eusebius, and is found in all the MSS.

JEWS OF ANGEVIN ENGLAND, THE, by Joseph Jacobs (1893). A most interesting volume of "Documents and Records from Latin and Hebrew sources, printed and manuscript, for the first time collected and translated," with notes and narrative forming an exhaustive history of the Jews in England, from the Norman Conquest to the year 1206. Mr. Jacobs finds no evidence that the Jews, as a class, were known in England until they were brought in by the Norman kings. It was not until the accession of Henry II., 1154 A.D., that they began to have a specially English history. It is substantially a history of their position as usurers in the service of the Royal Treasury. The whole story of the Jews in England goes on to their expulsion in 1290; and Mr. Jacobs estimates that a score of volumes would be required to complete their history on the scale of the volume which he has executed. It is thus a beginning only which he has made; but it is a very valuable beginning, as it enables him to indicate clearly what were the notable aspects of English Jewish life.

JOAN OF ARC, PERSONAL RECOLLECTIONS OF, by "Mark Twain" (S. L. Clemens) (1896). This story, founded on the history of Joan of Arc, professes to be a translation by Jean François Alden from the ancient French of the original un-published MSS. in the national archives of France, written by the Sieur Louis de Conte, her page and secretary. De Conte, who tells the story in the first person, has been reared in the same village with its subject, has been her daily playmate there, and has followed her fortunes in later life, serving her to the end, his being the friendly hand that she touches last. After her death, he comes to understand her greatness; he calls hers "the most noble life that was ever born into this world save only One." Beginning with a scene in her childhood that shows her innate sense of justice, good-ness of heart, and unselfishness, the story follows her throughout her stormy career. We have her audiences with the king; her marches with her army; her entry into Orleans; her fighting; her trial; her execution: all simply and naturally and yet vividly told. The historical facts are closely followed, while the fictitious form and simple style adopted bring the strange drama within the reader's understanding and sympathies. In the person of the Paladin, a boastful peasant of her native village who becomes her standard-bearer, is interwoven a humorous element in the author's own unmistakable vein, a humor essentially of the late nineteenth century. He crowds his stage with figures, most of them sufficiently individualized; and the energy and romantic atmosphere of his drama carry it to a successful conclusion.

JOCELYN, by Alphonse de Lamartine. A romantic and sentimental poem pub-lished in Paris in 1836, intervening between the author's 'Eastern Travels' and his 'Fall of an Angel,' and succeeded ten years after by his great prose work, the 'History of the Girondins.' 'Jocelyn' was widely read in England, and was the outcome of the extreme romanticism that held sway at the time in Europe. Suspected of containing a concealed attack on the celibacy of the priesthood, the author defends his poem as being purely a poetic creation, constituting a fragment of a great 'Epic of Humanity' which he had aspired to write. The poem expresses the conservative religious feeling of the country as opposed to the military and democratic spirit. There are in it echoes of Châteaubriand, St. Pierre, and Wordsworth; and despite its wordiness and long-drawn-out descriptions, which have called forth the comment of a reviewer that the author "will not allow even the sun to rise and set in peace," the piece often reaches a very high mark of poetic fervor and beauty. Jocelyn is a priest who leaves behind him certain records describing his suffering and temptations, which are after-wards discovered by his neighbor, a botanist, — the supposed writer of the poem, — who after the pastor's decease visits his dwelling. The story begins with a picture of Jocelyn at sixteen, a village youth of humble but respectable parentage. Morning and evening scenes of village life are graphically depicted, and the episodes of youth-ful love among the lads and maidens, in which Jocelyn, destined as he is for the priest-hood, feels that he has no rightful share. To provide for a suitable dowry in marriage for his sister, he has vowed himself to the Church. War breaking out, and the lives of the clergy being threatened, Jocelyn finds refuge among the solitudes of the Alps. There he meets an old man accompanied by a boy who as refugees are passing near his cave, pursued by soldiers. In the attack which follows, the old man is killed, and Jocelyn takes the boy into his cave. They enjoy a delightful companionship as brothers under the pure and sublime influences of the Alpine home. At length an accident reveals to Jocelyn that his orphan protégé and friend is a maiden, who had disguised herself in flight in male attire, and since had maintained the deception out of reverence for the priestly vows of her protector. The friendship of the two com-panions becoming now an avowed love, Jocelyn seeks his bishop for advice as to his duty, and is directed to renounce his passion as unlawful, and to be separated from

aurence, the object of his love. Laurence goes to Paris, where years afterwards
ocelyn finds her married, but unworthily, and leading a gay but miserable life
e returns to his mountain home to find solace in his severe round of duty. Called
ter to minister to a dying traveler on the pass to Italy, he discovers her to be his
aurence, who in breathing her last tells of her never-dying love for him, and be-
ueathes to him all her fortune, and the prayer that her body may be buried near the
ene of their mountain-home refuge. With the execution of this wish the story closes.
here are passages of tender emotion and deep piety in the poem that recall 'St.
ugustine' and the 'Imitation'; and a pure and lofty moral atmosphere pervades
e whole narrative.

OHN HALIFAX, GENTLEMAN, by Dinah Maria Mulock Craik (1856). The be-

OHN BRENT, by Theodore Winthrop, was published in 1862, after the death of
e author in one of the earliest engagements of the American Civil War, — that at
ig Bethel, Virginia. It is his best-known and most striking story. Richard Wade
n unsuccessful California miner, has been summoned East by family news and
ecides to travel across the plains on horseback. He exchanges his mine for a superb
ack stallion which is supposed to be unmanageable. In Wade's hands it becomes
ocile and kind, and he names it Don Fulano. An old friend, John Brent, a roving
enius of noble character, agrees to ride with him, Brent having a fine iron-gray horse.
n the way they are joined by a couple of low scoundrels, giving the names of Smith
nd Robinson; and near Salt Lake City they meet a cavalcade of Mormons under the
adership of a sleek rascal named Sizzum. In the company is an English gentleman,
r. Clitheroe, with his beautiful daughter Ellen; Clitheroe has become a Mormon
alf against his will, and is under the influence and in the power of Sizzum, who has
red him to America and who admires Ellen. In the Rockies she is abducted by
mith and Robinson, whose real names are Murker and Larrap. Wade and Brent,
ined by one Armstrong, whose brother has been murdered by the abductors, give
ase on their horses. This ride of the three avengers, side by side, over the plains, is
escribed with great vividness and dramatic power. There is something epic in its
tensity, largeness of sweep, and nobility of motive. Brent's horse, Pumps, breaks
wn; but Wade takes his friend on Don Fulano, and they finally ride the villains
wn in a mountain defile. Brent is wounded, but not dangerously. The tale then
ntinues the account of the eastward trip and the heroic exploits of Fulano, who is a
aragon of horses, Winthrop's warm love for these animals making the sketch very
mpathetic. Don Fulano is shot by Murker's brother, who thus avenges the death
his kin. Brent loves Ellen and she returns his love, but her faithfulness to her
ther leads her to return to London with him, and the friends lose track of them.
ade goes to find them, and by the aid of some paintings of their wild experiences in
e West, which he recognizes as the work of Miss Clitheroe, he is able to track down
ther and daughter, and the lovers are reunited. In spite of the pleasant love element
at runs through the story, the reader feels that Fulano, the noble brute, shares with
ohn Brent the honors of hero.

OHN BULL AND HIS ISLAND was translated from the French of "Max O'Rell"
Paul Blouet) in 1884. It is a humorous exposition of his view of English life and
aracter, which by its paradoxes attracted much attention when it appeared. The
een-visioned author was too fond of exercising his wit to be impartial. Some of his
onclusions, drawn from sensational articles in the daily newspapers, are based upon
sufficient premises. He presents a caricature rather than a portrait, but draws it so
everly that even its subject is forced to recognize his own faults and foibles. His

mockery of the conceited, domineering type of Englishman, always sure that he
right and others wrong, quibbling to preserve the letter of truth while disregarding i
spirit, and referring all values to a money standard, is sharp but without bitternes
He hits off the national character in startling paradox; for example, he says th
every year "a sum of money is spent in Bibles and alcoholic liquors alone, sufficies
to abolish pauperism and allow every freeborn Briton to live like a gentleman
But he recognizes fairly, too, the physical, mental, and moral qualities whic
make the English strong; and he finds much to admire in their home life and soci
institutions.

JOHN HALIFAX, GENTLEMAN, by Dinah Maria Muloch Craik (1856). The hes
of this story, John Halifax, is one of "nature's noblemen," who, beginning life as
poor boy, works his way up to prosperity and happiness, by means of his high pris
ciples, undaunted courage, and nobility of character. Orphaned at the age of eleve
years, from that time he is dependent on his own resources. He willingly undertak
any kind of honest work, and for three years gains a livelihood by working for farmes
but at the end of that time is taken into the employ of a Mr. Fletcher, a wealth
tanner. This is the beginning of his better fortune; for Phineas Fletcher, his master
invalid son, takes a great fancy to him and aids him with his education. The heroi
is Ursula March; and the simple domestic story includes few minor characters. Tl
interest lies in the development of character; and the author's assertion is that tr
nobility is of the soul, and does not inhere in wealth, in learning, or in position; as
that integrity and loftiness of purpose form the character of a true gentleman. Tl
story is fresh, healthful, and full of interest, and gives an ideal picture of home li
in England in the nineteenth century.

JOHN INGLESANT, a notable historical romance by J. H. Shorthouse, was pu
lished in 1881, when he was forty-seven years old. It depicts with a wonderful a
mosphere of reality the England of Charles I.'s time, and the Italy of the seventeen
century, when the tarnished glories of the Renaissance were concealed by exagger
tions of art and life and manners. In 'John Inglesant,' the hero, is drawn one of t
most complete portraits of a gentleman to be found in the whole range of fictic
Like a Vandyke courtier, he is an aristocrat of the soul, sustaining the obligations
his rank with a kind of gracious melancholy. Of a sensitive, dreamy temperames
possessing consummate tact, he has been trained from childhood by a Jesuit Fathe
St. Clare, for the office of court diplomat, and of mediator between the Catholics as
Protestants in England. His introduction to the court of Charles I. is the beginni
of a most picturesque and dramatic career in England, and afterwards in Italy, whe
he goes to seek the murderer of his twin-brother Eustace. He enters into the sum
tuous life of the Renaissance; but in his worldly environment he never blunts his fr
sense of honor, nor loses his ethereal atmosphere of purity. When he at last finds l
brother's murderer in his power, he delivers him over in a spirit of divine chivalry
the vengeance of Christ. The novel as a whole is like an old-world romance,
seventeenth-century Quest of the Holy Grail. It abounds in rich descriptions of t
highly colored spectacular existence of the time, and follows with sympathy as
comprehension the trend of its complex religious life.

JOHN WARD, PREACHER, a novel by Margaret Deland (1888). The Presb
terian minister whose name gives its title to the story has married Hel
Jeffrey. Mr. Ward is a logical Calvinist, who is assured that belief in election as

eprobation, eternal punishment, and kindred doctrines, is necessary to salvation; and
o preaches them with force and conviction. While his congregation agrees with
im, his wife, who is the niece of a liberal, easy going Episcopal rector, entertains
ecidedly broad theological views in general. The couple love each other with that
ingleness of devotion without which the course of the story would be manifestly
nprobable; for it depends upon the question whether love will be able to hold together
vhat conscientious habits of thought and ethical convictions tend to drive apart.
'he comments of the congregation of course have their part in promoting the difficul-
ies that follow. The story is well told, and extremely interesting, although it con-
sses itself a problem-novel on the very first page.

OHNSON, LIFE OF, by James Boswell, was published in 1791; Johnson's own
Journal of a Tour to the Hebrides' (1786) is usually included in editions of
he 'Life.'

The result of the association of Boswell, the born reporter, and Dr. Johnson, the
ighteenth-century great man, was a biography unsurpassed in literature. It has
one through many editions; it has been revised by many editors. It became at once
classic. Why this is so is not easy of explanation, since the man who wrote it was
nly Boswell. But in him hero-worship took on the proportions of genius. He merged
imself in Johnson. The Doctor looms large in every sentence of this singular work,
ritten in the very hypnotism of admiration. Every word is remembered; no detail
speech or manner is forgotten. Boswell begins with Johnson's first breath (drawn
seems, with difficulty), and will not let him draw a later breath without full
ommentary.

"We dined at Elgin, and saw the noble ruins of the Cathedral. Though it rained,
Or. Johnson examined them with the most patient attention." "Mr. Grant having
rayed, Dr. Johnson said his prayer was a very good one." "Next Sunday, July
st, I told him I had been at a meeting of the people called Quakers, where I had
eard a woman preach. *Johnson:* 'Sir, a woman's preaching is like a dog's walking
n his hind legs. It is not done well, but you are surprised to find it done at all.'"
he best-known edition is Croker's, upon which Macaulay poured out the vials of his
rath; but the new edition of Mr. George Birkbeck Hill is likely to supersede all
thers, for its admirable taste and scholarship.

OHNSONIAN MISCELLANIES, arranged and edited by George Birkbeck Hill
: vols., 1897). A work supplementing Mr. Hill's six volumes of the 'Life,' and two
olumes of the 'Letters,' of the famous Dr. Johnson. The first volume includes:
:) A collection of prayers and meditations; (2) Annals of his life to his eleventh year,
ritten by himself; (3) The Piozzi collection of anecdotes of the last twenty years of
s life; and (4) An essay on the life and genius of Johnson, by Arthur Murphy,
riginally published as an introduction to the twelve-volume edition of the complete
orks brought out in 1792. The second volume is largely concerned with anecdotes,
collections, studies by Sir Joshua Reynolds of Johnson's character and influence,
d a considerable variety of Johnson's letters. The work abounds in strikingly
teresting revelations of Johnson's character, habits, learning, wit, sincere piety,
nderness of sympathy, unaffected goodness, and endlessly active intellect. Equally
ch in literary and in human interest, in many of its pages delightfully picturesque, it
orthily completes Dr. Birkbeck Hill's monument to the great master.

OIE DE VIVRE, LA, see **ROUGON-MACQUART.**

JOLLY BEGGARS, THE, a cantata by Robert Burns, was first published in a poetica
miscellany in 1799. It consists of a series of recitatives and arias, the latter adapte
to well-known Scottish tunes, dramatically representing an assembly of vagrants a
the ale-house of Agnes Gibson — "Poosie Nansie" in Burns's native place, Mauc
line. A wounded veteran of Quebec and Gibraltar and his mistress, a camp-followe
recount their adventures and pledge their love; a traveling mountebank rails at ki
and state as he drinks with a tinker-wench; a female pickpocket laments the death
her John Highlandman, hanged for theft. She is wooed by a little fiddler, who i
however, scared off by a rival suitor, a sturdy tinker. The fiddler gets consolation i
the embraces of another dame, magnanimously yielded to him by a ballad-singe
"a wight of Homer's craft," who has two doxies still left. Amid deeper potatior
and thunderous applause he defies law and decorum in a rollicking ballad accom
panied by a roaring chorus. 'The Jolly Beggars' is a masterly picture of the outcas
of society. Its frank realism is saved from grossness by the poet's sympathet
presentation of the humanity of these vagabonds, by his incomparable humor, an
by the literary deftness of his narration. The poem illustrates Burns's command
the various Scottish staves and his gifts as a writer of convivial lyrics.

JONATHAN WILD THE GREAT, THE HISTORY OF, by Henry Fielding.
satirical portraiture, written by the author at the time of his retirement from pla
writing, 1742, owing to the prohibition of his plays by the Lord Chamberlain becaus
of satirical allusions to persons of quality. At this time the writer, who was of nob
descent and had been raised in affluence, was reduced to the hardships of povert
and the persecutions of many literary and social enemies; to actual suffering was adde
that of the extreme illness of his wife. His resentment at the disordered social cond
tions of the time, when merit was allowed to suffer and be laughed at, while dullne
and vulgarity were worshiped in the highest circles, found vent in the three volume
of 'Miscellanies' published in 1743, the last of which contained the 'History
Jonathan Wild the Great.' Thus the work has its place between 'Joseph Andrews
published in 1742, and the group of 'Tom Jones' (1749), and 'Amelia' (1751).
'Jonathan Wild' portrays the life of a dissolute rake, and of his low-lived con
panions, male and female, in unrestrained and often revolting frankness. The her
the embodiment of the "greatness" that is measured by success in crime and wicke
ness, is of descent more ancient than the Conqueror, his ancestor having come
with Hengist himself. Brought to London a youth, he is thrown in with a Fren
Count La Ruse, of whom he learns the gambler's art so skillfully that the cou
himself soon falls victim to it. Conspiring with Bagshot and a gang of scoundrels ar
villains, he persecutes the innocent Heartfree and his family even to having the
committed to prison. During the imprisonment Mrs. Heartfree tells the long tale
her adventures at sea, whither she had been allured by Wild after having her husba
lodged in prison. Wild is married to Letitia Snap, a match with himself in deceit ar
vileness. They all are brought up at last in prison, and most of the characters con
to the gallows. The visit of the ordinary of the prison to Wild, and their intervie
on the night before Wild s execution, is a sharp satire on the "consolations of r
ligion" as afforded in that day. Between the chapters there are discourses on "grea
ness" as exhibited in its successive stages in the progress of Wild's villainy.

JÖRN UHL, a novel by Gustav Frenssen (1901). "This book has appealed
modern Germany in somewhat the same way as Dickens appealed to the England
his day." (Preface.) It is a story of country life in Schleswig-Holstein. Jör

oungest son of a brutal farmer, tries by his own hard work to save the farm, which is
oing to waste while his father and brothers are carousing. He leaves school, giving
p his ambition to be a scholar to see "that the land and the cattle on the Uhl get
air treatment." The Franco-Prussian war takes him away from the farm for active
ervice. The description of the battle of Gravelotte is a powerful picture of war as
xperienced by the peasant soldiers who do the fighting. On his return home he
nds the farm bankrupt and settles down to fight debt and bad harvests. He is as
npressive as a figure in a Millet picture. Finally the old house is struck by lightning
nd burned and Jörn gives up his long struggle to save the family acres by hard toil.
Ie finds himself free to study again and make a new life for himself. His first mar-
age had been a charming rustic peasant idyll, ending with the death of his wife. The
ory ends with his happy marriage to the minister's daughter whom he has known
om childhood. He suggests to the friend who is to write about him that he shall
ıy "Although his path led through gloom and tribulation, he was still a happy man,
ecause he was humble and had faith."

OSEPH ANDREWS, by Henry Fielding, was the first novel by that master. It
ppeared in 1742, its full title being 'The Adventures of Joseph Andrews and his
riend Abraham Adams.' Fielding was thirty-five years old when it was published.
is intention in writing it was to satirize Richardson's 'Pamela.' This novel, given
 the world two years before, had depicted the struggle of an honest serving-maid
 escape from the snares laid for her by her master. Andrews, the hero of Fielding's
ory, is a brother of Pamela, like her in service; and the narrative details the trials he
idures in the performance of his duty. This story was begun satirically, with an
rident intention of burlesquing the high-flown virtue of Richardson's heroine by the
presentation of a man under similar temptation. But as the tale developed,
ielding grew serious, warming to his work so that it became in many respects a
enuine picture of life, and contained a number of his most enjoyable creations,
ıtably Parson Adams, a fine study of the old-style country clergyman, simple-
iinded, good-hearted, with a relish for meat and drink and a wholesome disdain of
ypocrisy and meanness. Andrews and Adams have numerous amusing adventures
igether, many of these being too coarse to please modern taste. In the end it falls
it that Andrews is really of good birth, while his sweetheart Fanny, a handsome girl
 humble rank, is the daughter of the parents who had adopted him; and the pair
e wedded amidst general jubilation. The confusion arising from the exchange of
ıildren at birth — a device since much used in English fiction — is cleverly managed.
he chief charm of the story, however, lies in its lively episodes, high spirits, and
elightful humor.

OSEPH VANCE; 'An Ill-Written Autobiography,' by William De Morgan (1906).
n elderly Englishman tells the story of his life, beginning with his inimitable
ther, a workman out of work, who becomes a wealthy contractor in a few years,
ırough the accident of acquiring from a peddler an old signboard, "C. Dance. Builder"
ısily changed to C. Vance. The magic board brings him a job, and a helper who is
ıle to do the work, while Vance stands by and looks wise. Without knowledge of
ıilding or any capital, he succeeds as an employer of labor. For an amusing picture
 Joseph Vance at the beginning of his career, see chapters quoted in the LIBRARY.
is father's first patron, Dr. Thorpe, takes an interest in the vulgar little boy, Joey,
ecause he shows a genius for mathematics, and arranges to send him to school.
Iiss Lossie Thorpe, the daughter, makes a pet of the child, and adopts him as a

small brother.   From the first day when he "glues" his eyes upon her, and devotedly
trots after her, she is the guiding influence of his life.   While he is at Oxford, she i
happily married, and he wakes up to realize his love for her and his loss.   Later he
marries a woman he sincerely loves, who knows she is his second choice.   After hi
mother's death his father takes to drink again, burns up his factory, and is ruined
because he has neglected the insurance.   In a shipwreck, Joseph's wife slips away
from him in the water and is lost.   Lossie's brother borrows his name along with his
trunk, and goes through a mock marriage in Italy.   Joseph adopts the child of thi
Italian marriage, who bears his name.   For Lossie's sake, he makes the sacrifice o
accepting the paternity of this child, to save her memory of the brother she loved
Years afterward, Lossie learns the truth, and finds him lonely and under a cloud
and they are married.   The story is leisurely told in the fashion of early Victorian
fiction, and is reminiscent of Dickens.

JOSHUA DAVIDSON, CHRISTIAN AND COMMUNIST, THE TRUE HISTORY OF
by E. Lynn Linton.   (Final edition [6th], 1874).   The name of the hero of thi
story is meant to be read "Jesus David's Son"; the word "Jesus" being the ol
Hebrew word "Joshua," changed by Greek usage.   The idea of the writer was t
picture a man of to-day, a man of the people, repeating under altered circumstance
the life of Jesus, and setting the world a Christ-example.   The work was planned o
the theory that "pure Christianity, as taught by Christ himself, leads us inevitably t
communism"; and with this view the hero of the story, who begins as a Cornis
carpenter, is carried to Paris, to lose his life in the Communard insurrection.   He i
represented as "a man working on the Christ plan, and that alone; dealing wit
humanity by pity and love and intolerance," living the life of "the crucified Com
munist of Galilee."   The question raised by the author is, "Which is true: moder
society, earnest for the dogma of Christianity, and rabid against its acted doctrines
or the brotherhood and communism taught by the Jewish carpenter of Nazareth?

JOURNEY IN THE SEABOARD SLAVE STATES, A, by Frederick Law Olmste
(1856), first appeared as a series of sketches in the New York Times.   It is the record o
a trip made by Mr. Olmsted at that period, through Virginia, North Carolina, Sout
Carolina, Georgia, Alabama, and Louisiana, for the purpose of noting the genera
aspects of those States; and particularly of studying the labor and agricultural condi
tions in comparison with those of the North.   His personal observations, enlivene
with humorous and anecdotal touches, are supplemented with statistics.   Thi
"honest growler" found much to criticize.   He detested slavery as an unmixed evi
and made it largely responsible for the prevailing ills.   Everywhere he finds plenty o
servants and no service.   He is astonished at the familiar intercourse between black
and whites, which however appears to be only tolerable to the latter as long as the
mastership is recognized.   He finds that the South has advanced far less in civiliza
tion than the North since the Revolution.   Shiftlessness prevails everywhere.   Th
slave system seems to enervate the whites, while rendering the blacks childish an
irresponsible.   It takes more of the latter than of Northern workmen to do a give
piece of work.   In spite of the abundance of labor, buildings remain out of repai
estates are neglected.   The farming is unintelligent.   There is a surprising quantit
of uncultivated land, and of land needlessly impoverished by repeated plantings o
the same crop.   The Southern economic conditions need revolutionizing; and alread
Mr. Olmsted notes their instability, and anticipates the storm of civil war soon t
break

OURNEYS THROUGH FRANCE ('Un Séjour en France de 1792 à 1795') by H. Taine (1897). This book is one of the French critic's earlier works, written in the orm of a diary. In the sixties, M. Taine, then an official examiner in the government schools, traveled about, up and down France, taking notes as he went, upon all the eatures of life in the provinces: agriculture and landscape, market-places and shops, astles and town-halls, professors and officers, peasants and bourgeois, as these existed in the years preceding the downfall of the Empire. He constantly accompanies his entertaining descriptions by social or economic inferences, and neat generalizations of French life and habits of thinking. Brilliantly written, and full of nsight as to the relation of the institution or the custom examined to the idea which t incarnates, the whole volume is one more illustration of Taine's formula of the effects of heredity and environment.

OWETT, BENJAMIN, 'Master of Balliol College, Oxford,' by Evelyn Abbott and Lewis Campbell (2 vols., 1897). A work exceptionally rich in personal nterest and in Oxford interest during nearly sixty years (1836-93). Born April 15th, 1817, and a student at St. Paul's School 1829-36, young Jowett won a scholarship in Balliol College, Oxford, in 1835; and from 1836 to the close of his career remained at Oxford. While yet an undergraduate he won a Balliol Fellowship, 1838, achieving his early rare distinction as a scholar. In 1842 he became a Balliol tutor, and also an ordained clergyman. He was an Examiner of Classical Schools in 1849, and again n 1853. In 1854 the death of the Master of Balliol gave him a chance to be elected o the position, as beyond question the ablest of Balliol tutors, and an eminent university man; but the more conservative party among the Fellows defeated him by a single vote. He served the same year as a member of the Commission on Examinations for the Indian civil service, and wrote their elaborate report. He published, in June, 1855, his remarkably bold and thoughtful commentary on Thessalonians, Galaians, and Romans, with special dissertations which greatly stirred public interest. The same year Lord Palmerston's government appointed him Regius Professor of Greek, with, however, only the nominal salary of £40. He was obliged to add his new duties to those of tutorship, and to figure as the most eminent scholar of his college, and an educator second to none at Oxford, not given a decent support. Jowett accepted his Greek chair as more to his mind than any other "except one of heology." But influences adverse to him on account of the broad views expressed n his 'Commentary' were at work. A favorable review of the book was stopped in the Times office by these influences after it had been put in type, and even the beggarly Greek position would have met the same fate if it had come on a little later. An accusation of heresy against Jowett was brought before the Vice-Chancellor, and the indignity put upon him of being summoned to appear and anew sign the Thirtynine Articles. It was assumed that he would not, but he did it, and taking up the duties of his Greek chair began lectures on Plato's 'Republic,' which he called "the greatest uninspired writing." Though practically unpaid, he made the lectures free, and for many years made them a great success. "I often think," he said, "that I have to deal with the greatest of all literatures." The sharp attacks made upon him caused a rapid sale of his book, and he gave great labor to its revision for a second edition, and it came out in the summer of 1859, much enlarged and in great part rewritten. The Times now published his friend Arthur P. Stanley's review of it. But the period of disfavor with conservatism upon which he had entered, and which specially found expression in the repeated defeats until February 17th, 1865, of all effort to provide pay for his brilliant labor in the Greek professorship, was made greatly darker in 1860-65 by the storm which arose over the publication of 'Essay and Reviews.' In 1863 a prosecution of Jowett on account both of his 'Commentary and of his 'Essay' was set on foot, but only to collapse upon being pressed. Two years later, the scandal of a great scholar at Oxford brilliantly discharging the duties of a professorship of Greek for ten years with hardly any salary came to an end. The next three years, 1865-68, saw liberal measures carried in Balliol councils, and great advances made. In 1869 Jowett was appointed preacher to the college. The next year, June, 1870, brought a vacancy in the Balliol Mastership. A plan for a second 'Essays and Reviews' volume was earnestly pressed by Jowett in 1869 and 1870, but not finally executed. In February, 1871, the earliest four-volume edition of Jowett' 'Plato' appeared. The second edition, with very great improvement of the translation and large additions to the introductions, came out in 1875. The final edition constituting Jowett's *magnum opus*, was published in 1892, with the perfected work in notes and dissertations, the matter and style of which are the author's lasting claim upon a high place in the literature of the century. From Plato, Jowett in 1871-72 went on to the translation of Thucydides, which appeared in 1881, and to a translation of Aristotle's 'Politics,' which was published in 1882. A work on the life of Christ had a place in his plans almost to the end of his life, but he did nothing toward it. His idea was that the life of Christ should be written "as a history of truths, to bring the mind and thoughts of Christ a little nearer to the human heart, in the spirit not in the letter"; and this he thought might be the work of another generation in theology. In 1882 Jowett became Vice-Chancellor of the university, and held the office four years. It was his final recognition as the foremost of Oxford educators His 'Life' is exceedingly rich in indications of character, in penetrating thoughts on a great variety of themes, in sagacious independent criticisms, and in reminiscences of Oxford and of English culture during sixty years, which will long give it a high place among books of the century.

JOY OF LIVING, THE ('Es lebe das Leben'), by Hermann Sudermann (1902) Fifteen years before the opening of the play, the Countess Beata and Baron Richard were lovers. Richard becomes her husband's intimate friend, and though their love does not cease the liaison is broken off. Beata's influence inspires Richard's ambition and as the play opens she has induced her husband, a man of mediocre intelligence, to resign his seat in the Reichstag in favor of the brilliant Count Richard. During the political campaign, Richard's opponent, a former secretary, brings to light the secret of their past. Duty to their party forbids the public scandal of the divorce court or the duel for the outraged husband; the men ask Richard's young son what should be done in such a case, and he, not knowing he is judging his father, replies that "a man of honor would be more eager to give his life than the husband could possibly be to take it." It is understood by the two men, and guessed by Beata, that Richard will commit suicide. The party leaders call on Richard to make a speech against divorce upon the sanctity of the marriage bond. Beata makes him promise to attend political luncheon she and her husband give the day following the speech for the sake of appearances. At the luncheon Beata proposes a toast to the joy of living Taking an overdose of her heart medicine which she has dropped unobserved into her glass she asks "which of us really dares to live?" and answers "the only living soul among you, I drink to the joy of living." The guests believe that she has succumbed to heart disease, but she has left a letter of explanation for her husband "I see that someone must pay the penalty — better I than he. He has his work before him — I have lived my life. . . . He cannot die without causing the scandal you have been so anxious to avert. I have always loved happiness, and I find happiness in doing this for his sake and the children's and yours."

JUDAISM AND CHRISTIANITY, by Crawford Howell Toy, professor in Harvard University (1890). The sub-title of this valuable book modestly describes it as a sketch of the progress of thought from Old Testament to New Testament. The history opens with an introduction of less than fifty pages, as clear as it is condensed, on the general laws of the advance from national to universal religions. The rise of Christianity out of Judaism Professor Toy treats as a logical and natural instance of progress. He points out the social basis of religion, and analyzes and describes the growth of society, with its laws of advance, retrogression, and decay; the internal development of ideas, and the relation between religion and ethics. He then treats of the influence of great men; of the external conditions that must modify a religion; of the general lines of progress; of the extra-national extension of a conquering religion; and of the universal religions, which he limits to three: Brahmanism, which has grown into Buddhism; Judaism, which has grown into Christianity; and the old Arabian faith, whose product is Islam. And the outlook is that as the great civilized and civilizing nations of the world, in whose hands are science and philosophy, literature and art, political and social progress, hold also to the tenets of Christianity, they will carry that faith with them and plant it wherever they go, but in a higher form than it now assumes.

In following the subject proper, Professor Toy begins with the period represented by the name of Ezra, examines the prophetic writings, and follows the literary development of the time as represented in the ceremonial and uncanonical books. The progress and variations of the doctrine of God and of subordinate supernatural intelligences, both good and evil; the Jewish and Christian ideas of the nature of man, his attitude towards God, his hopes of perfection, the nature of sin and righteousness; the inclusions of the ethical code of both Jew and Christian; the two conceptions of the kingdom of God; the beliefs respecting immortality, resurrection, and the new dispensation; and finally, an examination of the relation of Jesus to Christianity, — these occupy the remainder of the volume.

Mr. Toy concludes that both the Catholic and Protestant branches of Christianity have followed the currents of modern thought; that there is not a phase of science, philosophy, or literature, but has left its impress on the body of beliefs that control Christendom, yet that the person of Jesus has maintained its place as the centre of religious life. The tone of the book is undogmatic; and its fine scholarship, clearness of statement, and delightful narrative style, make it agreeable and instructive reading for the laic.

JUDE THE OBSCURE, a novel by Thomas Hardy (1896). The bar sinister which crosses many of his books is most prominent in 'Jude.'

It is the story of a young man of the people, ambitious to go to Oxford and to become a scholar. He is prevented from rising in the social scale by himself, by his environment, by a vulgar natural woman who loves him, and by a refined morbid woman whom he loves. Arabella first drags him in the mud; Sue then seeks to soar with him to the stars. Between Arabella's earthiness and Sue's heavenly code of love, poor Jude has not a shred of morals left.

He is pushed farther and farther from Oxford as the story goes on. The novel becomes at last a hopeless jumble of illegitimate children, other men's wives, misery, more misery, revolt, and death. It is a remarkable work, but not a cheerful or pleasant one.

JUDGMENT HOUSE, THE, by Gilbert Parker (1913). This is a powerful story dealing with social and political life in England. It opens at the opera in London, when Rudyard Byng, a young multi-millionaire, who has made his fortune in South Africa by his own efforts, meets for the first time Jasmine Grenfel. The latter, a beautiful but ambitious girl, is the same as engaged to Ian Stafford, a brilliant young diplomat, who has been devoted to her for some time and who is responsible for the introduction of Byng. At the close of the opera the clothing of the Prima Donna, who is named Almah, accidently catches fire, but the prompt action of Byng, who rushes to her rescue prevents a catastrophe. Jasmine, who is impressed by Byng's strong character, as well as by his great wealth, throws over Stafford and accepts Byng's offer of marriage, though she is not really in love with him. Three years elapse and Stafford, who has spent the time in foreign service, returns to England, where he and Jasmine meet again. Stafford treats Jasmine with indifference and in pique she makes up her mind to win him back to her. She succeeds in doing this and by political intriguing gets him an appointment for which he is working. At the same time she finds herself deeply in love with him and realizes that she has always cared for him. Jasmine has other admirers, one of whom is Adrian Fellowes who has had a long standing affair with Almah. A love-letter, written by Fellowes to Jasmine, falls into her husband's hands and he is horrified at the knowledge of her disloyalty. He denounces Fellowes and orders him to leave the country but before his departure Fellowes is mysteriously murdered. No clue is found to the murderer, and Stafford suspects Jasmine, and Jasmine and her husband suspect each other. The Boer War is declared and Byng and Stafford join the army, while Jasmine, who has separated from her husband, gives most of her money for a hospital ship and goes with it to South Africa, as a nurse. Almah also is there in the same capacity and confesses to the murder of Fellowes who had deceived her. Stafford is finally killed in battle, and Rudyard and Jasmine are again united, the latter realizing at last that she is deeply in love with her husband.

JULIA FRANCE AND HER TIMES; a novel by Gertrude Atherton (1912). The beautiful Julia, just eighteen, at her first ball attracts a dissolute English officer, whose ship is at anchor at St. Kitts, in the West Indies. Her worldly, ambitious mother forces her innocent daughter to marry Capt. France, because he is heir presumptive to a dukedom. Julia, trained to obedience and to her mother's belief in her horoscope, predicting a great destiny, sails away to England to discover the wickedness of the world in general and of her husband in particular. She makes two friends, Bridgit and Ishbel, who give her aid and comfort and finally rescue her from her husband, who is rapidly becoming a paranoic. Ishbel, one of fourteen beautiful daughters of an impoverished Irish peer, tired of society life and her dull millionaire husband, sets up a flourishing millinery business. Julia joins her, but her plans are foiled by her husband, and she has to go back to him. Armed with five pistols she is able to protect herself, but is a prisoner waiting for his inevitable mental breakdown. Before he becomes dangerous, she escapes again, this time to be secretary to Bridgit, who is an ardent suffrage leader. France tries to assassinate the duke and is sent to an asylum. Julia, after a trip to the East, devotes her freedom to the cause, becoming a militant leader and speaker, getting herself maltreated by the police and imprisoned. An American boy, Daniel Tay, whom she had met in the first years of her married life, had sworn to come back for her in ten years. He finds her at the height of her fame as suffrage leader, falls in love with her again, and wins her, an unwilling victim to the "splendid disease" of love, "induced by nature to further

her one end." She decides to visit her old home in the West Indies to take time to make her decision. Her mother, still clinging to the great destiny of Julia's horoscope again tries to dominate her life. She must remain a leader of women if she is not to be a duchess. The old lady throws her grandchild, Fanny, a young beauty, in Tay's way, while Julia is in retirement. A cablegram comes announcing the death of France, and Julia gives up her career and the comradeship of the women she admires, to be Tay's wife.

JULIUS CÆSAR. (First printed in 1623.) The material for this stately drama, the noblest of Shakespeare's historical plays, was taken from Plutarch. The action covers nearly two years, — 44 to 42 B. C. The dramatic treatment, and all the splendid portraiture and ornamentation, cluster around two points or nodes, — the passing of Cæsar to the Capitol and his assassination there, and the battle of Philippi. Of the three chief conspirators, — Brutus, Cassius, and Casca, — Brutus had the purest motives: "all the conspirators, save only he, did that they did in envy of great Cæsar"; but Brutus, while loving him, slew him for his ambition and to serve his country. His very virtues wrought Brutus's ruin: he was too generous and un-suspecting. The lean-faced Cassius gave him good practical advice: — first, to take off Antony too; and second, not to allow him to make an oration over Cæsar's body. Brutus overruled him: he spoke to the fickle populace first, and told them that Antony spoke only by permission of the patriots. The eloquent and subtle Antony seized the advantage of the last word, and swayed all hearts to his will. There lay the body of the world-conqueror and winner of hearts, now a mere piece of bleeding earth, with none so poor to do him reverence. Antony had but to hold up the toga with its dagger-rents and show the pitiful spectacle of the hacked body, and read the will of Cæsar, — giving each citizen a neat sum of money, and to all a beautiful park for their recreations, — to excite them to a frenzy of rage against the patriots. These fly from Rome, and, drawing their forces to a head at Philippi, are beaten by Octavius Cæsar and Antony. Both Brutus and Cassius fall upon their swords. The great "show" passages of the play are the speech of the tribune Marullus ("O you hard hearts, you cruel men of Rome"); the speeches of Antony by Pompey's statue ("O mighty Cæsar! dost thou lie so low?" — "Here wast thou bayed, brave hart." — "Over thy wounds now do I prophesy"); and of Brutus and Antony in the rostrum ("Not that I loved Cæsar less, but that I loved Rome more"; and "I come to bury Cæsar, not to praise him"), — these together with the quarrel and reconciliation of Brutus and Cassius in the tent at Philippi. Certain episodes, too, are deservedly famous: such as the description by blunt-speaking, superstitious Casca of the night-storm of thunder and lightning and rain (the ghosts, the surly-glaring lion, and other portents); the dispute at Brutus's house about the points of the compass ("Yon grey lines that fret the clouds are messengers of day"); the scenes in which that type of loyal wifeliness, Portia, appears (the wound she gave herself to prove her fortitude, and her sad death by swallowing fire); and finally the pretty scene in the last act, of the little page falling asleep over his musical instrument, in the tent in the dead silence of the small hours of morning, when by the waning taper as he read, Brutus saw the ghost of murdered Cæsar glide before him, a premonition of his death on the morrow at Philippi.

JUNGLE, THE, by Upton Sinclair (1906). In this book the author has vividly portrayed life in the Chicago stockyards and his revelations are so shocking and revolting that one cannot read them without being filled with horror. In fact after the book's publication the indignation of the general public was aroused and an investigation into the prevailing conditions of the stockyards was instituted by the United States government. The central figure in the story is Jurgis Rudkus, a poor Slav immigrant, who comes to the new world to make his fortune. He is accompanied on his venture by his father, Ona Lukoszaite the girl to whom he is engaged, and her family consisting of a stepmother and half a dozen brothers and sisters. Their experiences are harrowing in the extreme; they are cheated, abused, and oppressed on every hand, suffer privations of every kind and find death a blessed release when it finally ends their sufferings. In the beginning of the story Jurgis is young and strong, and fortified by undaunted courage and hope, but after struggling against the terrible conditions which surround him without avail, he becomes wrecked physically and morally. The first year of existence in the new country is hard for the newcomers, but they manage to get work in the yards and keep their heads above water, and Jurgis and Ona are married. Soon after, however, their troubles begin to increase and misfortunes of every kind overtake them. Ill treatment from those who employ them, unhealthy conditions where they are forced to work, and other evils, undermine their health and happiness. One by one the members of this unfortunate household sicken and die, working to the last in order to do their part in the great struggle. The death of Ona is particularly tragic as she dies in giving birth to her second child surrounded by the most frightful conditions of poverty and want that can be imagined. Jurgis takes to drink and finding it impossible to gain a living in an honest way gives way to the temptations that surround him and becomes utterly debased. In conclusion Jurgis becomes a socialist hoping thereby to improve his condition. Throughout the story the dominating influence of the trades' unions is strikingly illustrated and the futility of a workingman's struggle against them.

JUNGLE BOOKS, THE, by Rudyard Kipling. The central figure in these books is the boy Mowgli, who, straying from his village home when an infant, had been lost in the forest, and there sheltered and nursed with her own cubs by a mother-wolf, and the hairy Orson. Joined to this element of human interest, and with the coloring of high romance, these stories picture the personal characteristics and social and political life of the gaunt wolf-family in their cave and the free republic of wolves, assembled in the Pack; the snarling Bengal tiger, Shere Khan, who, though fearful, like the other beasts, of man's superior wit, roams boastfully for prey, attended by his obsequious but mischief-making jackal servant, Tabaqui, the Dish-Licker; they tell about Baloo, "the sleepy brown bear who teaches the wolf-cubs the Law of the Jungle, which is the reproof of human codes in its comprehensive justice"; the black panther, Bagheera; Kaa, the big rock python; and many others, including the monkey people, filthy chatterers despised by all the rest. They describe also how Mowgli's coming disturbed these forest creatures; how his human will proved more powerful than Shere Khan's jaws and claws; and how the brown bear and other friends rescued him with some trouble when he had been carried off through the tree-tops by the monkey people; and how he finally went back to live among men, but with a better knowledge of beasts. Unlike the talking beasts in Æsop's fables, those of the 'Jungle Books' are not men in hides and on all fours discussing human problems. Kipling's genius represents them thinking and behaving, each according to his own peculiar beastly habit and experience, with such dramatic skill that one is almost forced to believe that he has intimately dwelt among them as Mowgli did. The stories were published in St. Nicholas, and collected into two volumes in 1894 and 1895.

JUNIUS LETTERS, THE. During the period between November 21st, 1768, and January 21st, 1772, there appeared in the London Daily Advertiser a series of mysterious letters aimed at the British ministry of that day, and signed by various pen-names — the most remarkable of them by that of one "Junius." During the century ensuing, the authorship of these epistles has been assigned with some degree of probability. Yet enough of uncertainty, of mystery, still remains to make the genesis of the 'Junius Letters' one of the most interesting of literary puzzles. A bibliography has developed, and new light is still shed from time to time upon the problem. Meanwhile the merits of the 'Letters' have been sufficient to give them a life all the more vigorous, perhaps, because they have been conjecturally assigned to Sir Philip Francis.

The author was a man thoroughly cognizant of British politics; a vehement opponent of the government, and of the ministerial leaders, Sir William Draper, the Duke of Grafton, and the Duke of Bedford; a supporter of Wilkes, the opposition chief; and a fiery pleader for popular liberty. The dominant message is sounded in these words from the first letter of the series: "The admission of a free people to the executive authority of government is no more than compliance with laws which they themselves have enacted." Much constitutional knowledge is shown in these trenchant attacks, which continually refer to the British Constitution as the bulwark of the people's rights. In manner. the letters are vigorous, bold, and among the finest specimens of impassioned invective and irony in English literature. To read them now is to understand readily the stir they made on their appearance before an already excited public.

For years their authorship was not assigned to Francis. Burke, Lord Temple, Hamilton, Dr. Butler, Wilkes, and several others were suspected, and many ingenious arguments proved the validity of this claim or that, no less than thirty-five names having been considered by students of the subject. In 1813, forty years after their publication, John Taylor published his 'Discovery of the Author of the Letters of Junius,' in which they were attributed to Sir Philip Francis and his father; the first of whom was still living when the volume appeared, and did not deny them.

Sir Philip Francis, son of an Irish clergyman and schoolmaster of repute, a man of culture and travel, holding important governmental positions and having intimate knowledge of the political machine, was, at the time the 'Letters' appeared, in the War Office. Taylor points out that Junius shows remarkable familiarity with that department, many of the letters having been written upon war-office paper. It is known, too, that Francis kept elaborate note-books on the English constitutional questions so ably discussed in the 'Letters.' Woodfall, the publisher of the Daily Advertiser, in which the 'Junius Letters' were printed, was a schoolmate of Francis at Eton. Expert examination of the disguised handwriting in which the letters were penned, identified it with the hand of Francis. W. R. Francis, Sir Philip's grandson, in his 'Junius Revealed,' strengthens the case. He discovered a poem known to be written by Francis, yet copied out in the feigned hand of Junius. He found also that several of the seals used on the 'Junius Letters' were used on private letters by Francis. To these significant facts the grandson adds that Sir Philip's character, as revealed in his official work, was of the same arrogant, sarcastic strain which comes out in the Advertiser communications.

This testimony, some of it very significant, more of it cumulative in effect, makes altogether a good case for the Franciscan theory. Judging the 'Letters' as literature, however, the whole question of the personality of Junius becomes a secondary one. Enough that they represent one of the most powerful examples of political polemics in English literature, which even now, when the events that begot them seem but the shadow of a shade, stir the blood and compel admiration.   The letter which made the deepest sensation at the moment is the famous one addressed to the King. The edition of 1812, upon which the many later ones are based, is that of Woodfall, the publisher, who was arraigned for trial because of printing the Junius screeds.

JUST DAVID, by Eleanor H. Porter (1916), is the story of a little boy who is a musical genius and who by his loving and unworldly nature wins the hearts of all about him.   The death of David's father, a once celebrated musician, who has brought the motherless boy up in a lonely cabin on a mountain-top, teaching him to love nature and his music, leaves the orphan of ten years, a wanderer with only his violin for company.   The boy is taken into the household of a farmer, named Holley, who with his wife, takes pity upon the waif.   At first David finds his new home almost unbearable as Mr. and Mrs. Holley are plain, hard-working people with little sympathy for the artistic and spiritual side of life to which the boy has been accustomed in his intercourse with his father.   David's past is a mystery, as a letter left by his father, which contains certain suggestions for his future, has a signature which none of the village-folk can decipher.   David makes many friends among both rich and poor; he brightens the life of a blind boy, Joe Glaspell, to whom he lends his father's violin, and becomes devotedly attached to a rich and beautiful young woman named Barbara Holbrook, whom he calls his "Lady of Roses."   He acquires a warm friend in Jack Guernsey, a young man who is in love with Barbara Holbrook, but who does not approach her on account of her great wealth and his own poverty. Guernsey's little sister Jill becomes David's playmate and they spend happy hours together.   When at last David becomes dangerously ill his many friends realize his worth in the community and lavish attentions upon him.   By his bedside Jack Guernsey and Barbara Holbrook meet and are reunited through the boy's efforts. Mr. and Mrs. Holley, who are softened by the boy's influence, become reconciled to their son John, from whom they have been estranged for years.   John returns and discovers that David's father was a world-famous musician and that wealthy relatives are awaiting the coming of the gifted child, who is from this time to have the long-dreamed-of opportunity to develop his art.

JUSTICE; a tragedy by John Galsworthy (1910).   William Falder, a young clerk in a solicitor's office is in love with a woman, who is being cruelly treated by her husband.   In an ill-balanced moment he commits forgery in order to find money to rescue her from her husband's brutality.   He is discovered as he is on the point of sailing with her to South America.   At his trial his counsel pleads guilty for him, but asks the jury to believe that the prisoner acted under great emotional stress, and adds, "men like the prisoner are daily destroyed under our law for want of that human insight, which sees them as they are, patients, and not criminals."   The judge sums up against this plea, and the prisoner is sentenced to three years' penal servitude.   On his release, he is unable to keep employment that had been found for him, as his fellow-employees learned about his past.   "He seems (he tells someone who knew him) to be struggling against a thing that is all around him."   His old employers offer to take him back again on condition that he gives up the company of the woman for love of whom he had committed forgery.   He refuses, and his employers relent, but at that moment a detective enters to arrest him because for four weeks he has failed to report himself.   He throws himself out of a window and is killed.   This play made so great an impression on the public mind that certain important reforms in prison administration in England are directly to be traced to its influence.

"**K**," a novel by Mary Roberts Rinehart (1915), depicts a brilliant young surgeon who because of a fatal error in his work drops his chosen profession and takes an assumed name. He first appears in the narrative as K. Le Moyne, known familiarly as "K"; he has taken the position of bookkeeper in a gas-office and boards quietly with a family named Page. He falls in love with Sidney Page, a charming and attractive girl, but she does not suspect his feelings towards her and regards him only as a dear friend. Sidney enters a hospital to become a trained nurse and wins the love of the head surgeon Dr. Max Wilson who is handsome and fascinating but of doubtful reputation where women are concerned. Sidney becomes engaged to Max and although "K" has been associated with him in his old professional days and knows his character, he does not feel at liberty to interfere. Carlotta Harrison, an attractive young nurse, who had previously received the head surgeon's attentions, is violently jealous of Sidney and does everything possible to break up the match. She finally traps Dr. Wilson into a compromising situation with her at a disreputable road-house, and there he is shot by a jealous boy who loves Sidney and thinks she is Wilson's companion on this occasion. Wilson is thought to be fatally injured, but his old friend "K" saves his life by coming forward and performing the operation for which he was once famous. Subsequently Carlotta, who had also been associated with "K" in the past, confesses that while assisting at the fatal operation she had caused him to make the blunder which had shattered his career. "K" resumes his chosen profession, and Sidney, whose eyes have been opened to Wilson's failings, realizes that she does not love him, but does care for "K" the devoted and faithful friend who has been her protector and guide through all her trials.

KANT, IMMANUEL, HIS LIFE AND DOCTRINE, by F. Paulsen, translated by J. E. Creighton and A. Lefevre (1902). The recluse philosopher of Königsberg led such a routine and retired existence, that it is almost difficult to realize that he lived a human life at all. Born in the East Prussian town in 1724, he spent his days within a narrow circle. "He was a German professor of the old style: to work, to teach, to write books, was the sum and substance of his life. Important external events, exciting crises, other than intellectual, in his history there are none. His birthplace Königsberg, with its university, is the scene of his life and activity. He spent only a few years, as tutor in a country family, outside its walls, and never passed the boundaries of his native province." Sprung from parents of the poorest class, he nevertheless had the luck to get good schooling and to be entered at the University. His biographer traces the evolution of his thought and the development in his mind of the firm belief in immortality, the freedom of the human will, the existence of God, the "categorical imperative" or law of duty. Over his grave in the Cathedral are inscribed the well-known words from his Critique of Practical Reason,

> " The starry heavens above me
> The moral law within."

It is remarkable that to a philosopher whose influence upon thought has been incalculably great, the outer world was known only through books. Though he was the first academic teacher of physical geography, he had never seen a mountain, and had never visited the sea, though it was not more than forty miles away. While grateful to Frederick the Great for his firm administration, he was not one of that monarch's unqualified admirers. "He so often," says Dr. Paulsen, "and so emphatically expressed his abhorrence of war, this scourge of mankind, this destroyer of all that is good, expecially of war undertaken without necessity for political reasons, that one cannot refrain from including the wars of Frederick the Great in this judgment." His political sympathies were not with an absolute and monarchical form of government, but with a democracy of the kind that had recently been established in North America, and seemed likely to be set up in France. His philosophy brought him into contact with the ruling powers, especially on publication of his work 'Religion within the Bounds of Pure Reason.' In October, 1794, he received an order of the cabinet in these terms. "Our highest person has been greatly displeased to observe how you misuse your philosophy to undermine and destroy many of the most important and fundamental doctrines of the Holy Scriptures and of Christianity. We demand of you immediately an exact account, and expect that in the future you will give no such cause of offence, but rather that, in accordance with your duty, you will employ your talents and authority so that our paternal purpose may be more and more attained. If you continue to oppose this order, you may certainly expect unpleasant consequences to yourself." Kant in reply maintained the right of the scholar to form independent judgments on religious matters and to make his opinions known, but nevertheless agreed to refrain in future from all public address on religion, both natural and revealed, either in lectures or in writings.

KEMBLE, FRANCES ANNE, see **RECORDS OF A GIRLHOOD: RECORDS OF LATER LIFE.**

KENELM CHILLINGLY, 'His Adventures and Opinions,' by Edward Bulwer Lytton (Lord Lytton) (1873). This, one of Bulwer's artistic novels of English life, is considered by many a masterpiece, and is certainly one of his most popular works. Kenelm Chillingly is the long-desired heir of an old family, who develops symptoms of remarkable precocity, to the anxiety of his parents and teachers. After leaving school, he is given an insight into London society, and enters Cambridge with matured opinions and judgment, graduating with honors. Coming of age in the early part of the nineteenth century, — a time of unwonted progress, of unsettlement of beliefs, and of dissatisfaction with the existing state of affairs, — he adds to the general unrest of his generation an individual melancholy of temperament, a phenomenal clearness of vision which detects and despises shams, and an inability to fit himself into commonplace grooves and the ruts of inherited habit. In various phrases throughout his biography he is described, or describes himself — "A mere dreamer"; "He had woven a solitude round him out of his own heart"; "I do not stand in this world: like a ghost I glide beside it and look on." With the temperament of the idealist, Kenelm possesses an attractive face and figure, a fondness for athletic exercise, and a perfect physical development. He leaves home in search of adventures, an unknown pedestrian with a few pounds in his pocket (and unlimited credit at his bankers'), unincumbered by letters of introduction or social fetters. His adventures, which are in keeping with his personality, extend over a few years, varied by periodical returns to his family and reappearances in society; where he is courted for his wealth, his gentle birth, and his eccentricities. The culmination of his fortunes is reached in an unfortunate love affair with Lily Mordaunt, a spirituelle creature, half child, half woman, a "human poem," who dies broken-hearted when a cruel fate separates her from her lover.

'Kenelm Chillingly' is less the life of a man than the prelude to a life; a preface of dreams, of disappointments, of disillusionments, before the realities begin. He himself epitomizes his future and his past, when he says to his father, in their last recorded interview, "We must — at whatever cost to ourselves — we must go through the romance of life before we clearly detect what is grand in its possibilities"; and again, "My choice is made: not that of deserter, but that of soldier in the ranks."

Round him are grouped many interesting characters, — Sir Peter and Lady Caroline, his father and mother ; his cousin, Gordon Chillingly, the ambitious politician; Chillingly Mivers, the caustic editor of The Londoner; the reformed bully, Tom Bowles; the pretty village belle, Jessie Somers, and her crippled husband; Cecilia Travers, who remains faithful to her unreciprocated attachment for Kenelm; Mr. Welby, the polished man of society; Walter Melville, the celebrated artist and "Wandering Minstrel"; and several others.

KENILWORTH, by Sir Walter Scott, appeared in 1819, when its author was fifty and had long been distinguished both as poet and novelist. 'Kenilworth' was the second of his great romances drawn from English history. The central figure is that of Elizabeth, the haughty queen. She is surrounded by the brilliant and famous characters of the period — Burleigh, Edmund Spenser, Sir Walter Raleigh; and also by a host of petty sycophants. The Earl of Surrey and the Earl of Leicester are rivals, each high in her favor, each thought to be cherishing a hope of winning her hand. But beguiled by the charms of Amy Robsart, the daughter of a country gentleman, Leicester has secretly married her, and established her at Cumnor Place, a lonely manor-house where she lives with surly Tony Foster as guardian, and his honest young daughter, Janet, as attendant. Amy had formerly been engaged to Tressilian, a worthy protégé of her father. Tressilian discovers her hiding-place; and not believing her married, vainly tries to induce her to return home. He then appeals to the queen before the whole court. A disclosure of the truth means Leicester's ruin, but seems inevitable, when his confidential follower, the unscrupulous Richard Varney, saves the situation. He affirms Amy to be his own wife, and is ordered to appear with her at the approaching revels at Kenilworth, Leicester's castle, which the queen is to visit. Amy scornfully refuses to appear as Varney's wife, and Varney attempts to drug her. In fear of her life, she escapes and makes her way to Kenilworth. The magnificent pageant prepared there for Elizabeth, and the motley crowds flocking to witness it, are brilliantly described. Amy cannot gain access to her husband, but is discovered and misjudged by Tressilian. The Queen finds her half-fainting in a grotto, and again Varney keeps her from learning the truth. He persuades Elizabeth that Amy is mad. He persuades Leicester that she is false and loves Tressilian, and obtains the earl's signet ring and authority to act for him. Amy is hurried back to Cumnor Place. There, decoyed from her room by her husband's signal, she steps on a trap-door prepared by Varney and Foster, and is plunged to death, just before Tressilian and Sir Walter Raleigh arrive to take her back to Kenilworth. They have been sent by Elizabeth to whom Leicester, discovering the injustice of his suspicions, has confessed all. He falls into the deepest disgrace; and Elizabeth, feeling herself insulted both as queen and as woman, treats him with scorn and contempt. 'Kenilworth' is regarded as one of the most delightful of English historical romances.

KENNEDY SQUARE, by F. Hopkinson Smith (1911). This is a story of life in the South in the Ante-Bellum days. Kennedy Square is an aristocratic spot in one of

Maryland's principal cities, and here abides St. George Temple, in the ancestral mansion which his family has occupied for generations. He is a genial bachelor of middle age, who dispenses hospitality in a generous and courtly fashion, and is beloved by all, especially by the young people to whom he is "Uncle George." His particular favorites in this circle are Harry Rutter and Kate Seymour, both endowed with wealth, social position and personal charm, and who are in love with each other. Their engagement is to be announced at a large ball given by Harry's parents, but while it is in progress, and before the good news has been made public, Langdon Willetts, one of Harry's rivals, being excited by liquor, insults Kate. Harry's hot blood is aroused and he challenges Willetts to a duel, which takes place immediately, and Willetts is seriously wounded. This unhappy occurrence causes Harry's proud and autocratic father to disown him on the spot, as he considers his son has disgraced his blood by shooting a guest under his own roof. Kate also heart-broken over the affair, tells Harry all is over between them. St. George then slips into the breach and exonerating Harry from blame says he shall henceforth be as his own son. Harry stays with St. George until business reverses come to him and then rather than be a burden on his kind friend he books as a common seaman on a ship sailing for South America and is gone for three years. On his return he finds his kind Uncle George in poor health, reduced to absolute poverty, and living in the wretched home of one of his faithful negro servants. Harry makes immediate plans to restore to his old friend his home and his beloved possessions and is successful in his efforts. He and his father become reconciled and he is re-united to Kate who has never ceased to love him. The story closes with the return of St. George to his ancestral home, which Harry and Kate have restored and put in perfect order for his coming.

KENTUCKIANS, THE, by John Fox, Jr. (1898) is a study of the two races that inhabit the State of Kentucky: the prosperous and cultured dwellers of the "blue-grass" region, and the rough, savage, ignorant mountaineers, whose civilization to-day is exactly that of their ancestors, the early settlers. Hallard, the mountain leader, and Marshall, the brilliant townsman, are rivals in the legislature, and rivals for the love of Anne Bruce, the governor's daughter; and the struggle between them forms the story of the book, which is a remarkably brilliant picture of some interesting phases of American life, as well as a sober statement of certain social problems which insist on a settlement. Fox's pages bear their own assurance of authenticity, not less in their vividness of portraiture than in their reserve. Nothing is overstated.

KENTUCKY CARDINAL, A, and **AFTERMATH,** by James Lane Allen (1895–96). The 'Kentucky Cardinal' is a fresh and dainty tale, which may be called an "idyl of the woods." The story tells of the wooing of Adam Moss, a recluse who devotes himself to nature, and who dwells in a garden, which his loving touch converts almost into fairyland, where all the fruits and flowers blossom and ripen to perfection, and where all the birds have learned to rest on their migratory journeys. Adam knows all the birds and loves them best of all living creatures, until he meets Georgianna, his beautiful next-door neighbor. She is a lovely, tormenting, bewildering creature, who eludes him one day, encourages him the next, and scorns him on a third. Despite her endless resources for tormenting Adam, she is undeniably charming and alluring. She is, however, possessed by a vague fear that her lover's fondness for nature and for his birds is something that must prevent his entire allegiance to her. She tests his affection by demanding that he cage for her the splendid "Kentucky cardinal"; and Adam wages a bitter warfare with himself before allowing his love for Georgiann to triumph over his lifelong principle and conscientious attitude towards his feathery friends. The caging of the bird, which beats its life out in the prison, is converted by the author's skill into a veritable tragedy, wherein the reader keenly shares Adam's remorse and Georgianna's grief. The lovers quarrel; and then follows a reconciliation which reveals each more clearly to the other, and unites them finally. The conversations of Georgianna from her window to Adam in his strawberry bed below are a delightful feature of the story, which is enlivened by his dry humor and her witty repartee. 'Aftermath,' the second part of 'A Kentucky Cardinal,' follows the lovers through the days of their engagement and their brief wedded life, which is one of ideal happiness while it lasts. Georgianna strives to win her husband from his overmastering fondness for nature; and he, to please her, enters into social life and seeks to interest himself more in the "study of mankind." At the birth of a son Georgianna passes away, leaving her husband to seek consolation where he can best obtain it, — from his beloved "nature." Mr. Allen has a delicate touch and a charm of style; and his descriptions of nature and of bird life possess a really poetic beauty, while they are characterized by a ring of truthfulness which convinces the reader that the author's heart is in his words. There is a blending of pathos and humor in the work which makes it delightful reading.

KIDNAPPED, by Robert Louis Stevenson, was published in 1886, when the author was thirty-six, and was his seventh work of fiction. In his own opinion, it was his best novel; and it is generally regarded as one of his finest performances in romantic story-telling. The full title reads: 'Kidnapped: Being Memoirs of the Adventures of David Balfour in the Year 1751', and the contents of the tale are further indicated on the title-page, thus: "How he was Kidnapped and Cast away; his Sufferings in a Desert Isle; his Journey in the Wild Highlands; his Acquaintance with Alan Breck Stewart and other notorious Highland Jacobites; with all that he Suffered at the hands of his Uncle, Ebenezer Balfour of Shaws, falsely so called." David, on his father's death, visits his uncle near Edinburgh, and finds him a miser and villain, who, to get rid of his nephew, packs him off on the brig Covenant, intending to have him sold in America. On shipboard he falls in with Alan, the dare-devil Jacobite, one of the most spirited and vivid characterizations of Stevenson. David espouses the Stuart cause, and in company with Alan has a series of lively experiences narrated with great swing and color. The fight in the roundhouse of the brig, the flight in the heather from the red-coats of King George, and other scenes, are conceived and carried out in the finest vein of romance. After these wanderings, David, circumventing his rascally uncle, comes into his own.

KIM, by Rudyard Kipling (1901). In this brilliant piece of work the author offers a new example of his remarkable versatility. It exhibits his extraordinary power of characterization as well as his probably unsurpassed knowledge of Indian modes and customs. Kimball O'Hara, known as Kim, is a little vagabond of Irish parentage, orphaned when a baby, and left to shift for himself in the depths of the native quarter of Lahore. He meets an aged lama from Thibet, who is seeking the all-healing River of the Arrows, or stream of Immortality, and roams through India in his company. The two are lodged and fed by the pious people of the country and as they tramp about undergoing manifold experiences, a deep affection springs up between them. Kim is presently recognized, reclaimed and adopted by the Irish regiment, to which his father belonged, and is given an education in a Catholic college. He endures the thraldom of St. Xavier's in Lucknow, only upon the condition of being allowed to tramp the continent in the long vacation with his beloved Buddhist priest. Col. Creighton discovers Kim's remarkable fitness for employment in the Secret Service of the English government and he receives tuition from proficient natives. The result is that he distinguishes himself while yet a stripling by capturing in the high Himalayas, the credentials and dispatches of a formidable Russian spy. The author takes leave of Kim in the flush of his first victory. The book contains a marvelous picture of India with its wealth and poverty, and its crowded cities teeming with human life, where, with Kim, one may enter the bazaars of the natives and become intimately acquainted with the "brown" men and women who live and move in an atmosphere of their own. One may view the forgotten temples and holy rivers and terrible stretches of burning plain, and learn to appreciate the grandeur of the magnificent mountain barrier of the North. In 'Kim,' Kipling seems to have embodied not only the wonderful material and physical aspect, but the human soul of the Orient.

KING JOHN, a drama by Shakespeare, the source of which is an older play published in 1591. The date of the action is 1200 A. D. John is on the throne of England, but without right; his brother, Richard the Lion-Hearted, had made his nephew Arthur of Bretagne his heir. Arthur is a pure and amiable lad of fourteen, the pride and hope of his mother Constance. The maternal affection and the sorrows of this lady form a central feature of the drama. Arthur's father Geoffrey has long been dead, but his mother has enlisted in his behalf the kings of Austria and of France. Their forces engage King John's army under the walls of Angiers. While the day is still undecided, peace is made, and a match formed between Lewis, dauphin of France, and John's niece Blanche. The young couple are scarcely married when the pope's legate causes the league to be broken. The armies again clash in arms, and John is victorious, and carries off Prince Arthur to England, where he is confined in a castle and confided to one Hubert. John secretly gives a written warrant to Hubert to put him to death. The scene in which the executioners appear with red-hot irons to put out the boy's eyes, and his innocent and affectionate prattle with Hubert, reminding him how he had watched by him when ill, is one of the most famous and pathetic in all the Shakespearian historical dramas. Hubert relents; but the frightened boy disguises himself as a sailor lad, and leaping down from the walls of the castle, is killed. Many of the powerful lords of England are so infuriated by this pitiful event (virtually a murder, and really thought to be such by them), that they join the Dauphin, who has landed to claim England's crown in the name of his wife. King John meets him on the battle-field, but is taken ill, and forced to retire to Swinstead Abbey. He has been poisoned by a monk, and dies in the orchard of the abbey in great agony. His right-hand man in his wars and in counsel has been a bastard son of Richard I., by Lady Faulconbridge. The bastard figures conspicuously in the play as braggart and ranter; yet he is withal brave and patriotic to the last. Lewis, the dauphin, it should be said, makes peace and retires to France.

KING LEAR. Shakespeare's great drama, 'King Lear,' was written between 1603 and 1606. The bare historical outline of the story of the King he got probably from Holinshed or from an old play, the 'Chronicle History of Leir'; the sad story of Gloster was found in Sir Philip Sidney's 'Arcadia.' The motifs of the drama are the wronging of children by parents and of parents by children. With the fortunes of the King are interwoven those of Gloster. Lear has she-devils for daughters

(Goneril and Regan), and one ministering angel, Cordelia; Gloster has a he-devil for son (Edmund), and one faithful son, Edgar. The lustre of goodness in Cordelia, Edgar, Albany, loyal Kent, and the faithful Fool, redeems human nature, redresses the balance. At the time the play opens, Lear is magnanimously dividing his kingdom between his sons-in-law Cornwall and Albany. But he has already a predisposition to madness, shown by his furious wrath over trifles, his childish bids for affection, and his dowering of his favorite daughter Cordelia with poverty and a perpetual curse, simply for a little willful reserve in expressing her really profound love for him. Blind impulse alone sways him; his passions are like inflammable gas; for a mere whim he banishes his best friend, Kent. Coming into the palace of Goneril, after a day's hunt with his retinue of a hundred knights, his daughter (a fortnight after her father's abdication) calls his men riotous and asks him to dismiss half of them. Exasperated to the point of fury, he rushes out tired and supperless into a wild night storm; he is cut to the heart by her ingratitude. And there before the hovel, in the presence of Kent, the disguised Edgar, and the Fool, insanity sets in and never leaves him until he dies at Dover by the dead body of Cordelia. In a hurricane of fearful events the action now rushes on: Gloster's eyes are plucked out, and he wanders away to Dover, where Cordelia, now Queen of France, has landed with an army to restore her father to his rights. Thither, too, the stricken Lear is borne at night. The joint queens, most delicate friends, lust after Edmund. Regan, made a widow by the death of Cornwall, is poisoned by Goneril. Cordelia and Lear are taken prisoner, and Cordelia is hanged by Edmund's order. Edmund is slain in the trial by combat. Lear dies; Gloster and Kent are brokenhearted and dying· Regan has stabbed herself; Edgar and Albany alone survive. The Fool in 'Lear' is a man of tender feeling, and clings to his old comrade, the King, as to a brother. His jests are like smiles seen through tears; they relieve the terrible strain on our feelings. Edmund is a shade better than Iago; his bastardy, with its rankling humiliations, is an assignable cause, though hardly a palliation of his guilt.

KING MILINDA, QUESTIONS OF THE, see **SACRED BOOKS OF THE EAST.**

KING NOANETT, by F. J. Stimson ("J. S. of Dale" 1897). This novel is based upon the history of old New England and of England during the Protectorate. Bampfylde Moore Carew tells the story of his life. As a lad of twenty he is living with his grandfather, Farmer Slocombe. While wandering over his favorite moors of Devonshire, Carew first meets Mistress St. Aubyn, with whom he falls desperately in love. This love is henceforth to be the leading influence of his life; its first effect being, however, to bring him to arrest and exile. Having drawn his sword in defense of her grandfather, Lord Penruddock, he is taken under arms by Cromwell's soldiers, and is sentenced to the Colonies. Among his fellow-prisoners on the ship he meets Miles Courtenay, an Irishman and cavalier, and Jennifer, a young girl whom they take under their protection. Her gratitude to Courtenay expresses itself in a great and self-sacrificing love. Though themselves in ignorance of the fact, Carew and Courtenay both love the same woman, Mistress St. Aubyn. The desire of each is to find her. In Virginia they work as slaves on the tobacco plantations, then escape to join the army. While warring with a tribe of Indians, they capture the mighty chief King Noanett. The mystery surrounding this strange personage is at once penetrated by the two young men, and a romantic episode closes the story. The book contains beautiful descriptions of Devonshire, and most interesting sketches of old

Dedham and its laws. It is said that the dashing and warm-hearted Irishman was modeled on the character of the late John Boyle O'Reilly, with whom the author often talked over the plan of the book.

KING OF THE MOUNTAINS, THE ('Le Roi des Montagnes'), by Edmond About, appeared in 1856, when he was twenty-eight. The scene is laid in and near contemporary Athens. The story is an animated and delightfully humorous account of the adventures befalling two English ladies and a young German scientist, who are captured and held for ransom by the redoubtable Hadgi-Stavros, king of the brigands. Mrs. Simons is an amusing caricature of British arrogance. "I am an Englishwoman," is her constant refrain; and she cannot comprehend how any one dare interfere with the rights of herself and her daughter Mary Ann. The Simons family is rich. Hermann Schultze, the young German, is attracted by pretty Mary Ann, and with the thrift of his nation, wants to make his fortune by marrying her. He tries to ingratiate himself by proposing plans of escape which Mrs. Simons rejects. Hadgi-Stavros dictates his private correspondence in the presence of his captives. Thus Schultze learns that the king has a large sum of money in a London banking house to which Mrs. Simons's brother belongs. She writes to have the amount of her ransom paid; and the king is persuaded to give a receipt by which he can be tricked out of the amount. Mother and daughter are released. Schultze tries to escape, but fails, and is severely punished. He attacks the king, and nearly succeeds in poisoning him. A friend in Athens, John Harris, a typical American full of resources, rescues Hermann. The king is devoted to his one child Photini, a schoolgirl in Athens. Harris persuades Photini aboard his barge, keeps her prisoner, and threatens to treat her as Schultze is treated. Thereupon Schultze is released. He afterward narrates the whole story to a friend, between whiffs of his long porcelain pipe. This story is one of the most brilliant and delightful of About's telling.

KING RENÉ'S DAUGHTER: A Danish lyrical drama, by Henrik Hertz. (Translation by Theodore Martin: 1849.) The seven scenes of this drama are located in Provence, in the valley of Vaucluse, in the middle of the fifteenth century. The chief characters are King René of Provence, and his daughter Iolanthe, rendered blind by an accident in early infancy, but raised in ignorance of this deficiency to her sixteenth year, when by the skill of her Moorish physician she is to be restored to sight. Plighted in marriage by her father to Count Tristan of Vaudemont, for state reasons, without love, the two destined partners have never met; and the count on arriving at manhood repudiates the forced contract. Wandering with his fellow troubadours through the valley of Vaucluse, he comes by accident upon the secluded garden and villa where King René had kept his daughter in confinement under the care of the faithful Bertrand and Martha. The count, entering while Iolanthe is sleeping under the spell of the Moorish physician, and ignorant that she is the king's daughter, is ravished by her beauty, and lifts the amulet from her breast, at which she awakes. He first reveals to her the secret of her blindness, and declares his love. Surprised by the arrival of the king, he renounces his engagement with his daughter, and thereby his inheritance of a kingdom, that he may marry this beautiful stranger. The Moor appears, declaring the time and the conditions fulfilled for Iolanthe's restoration. Iolanthe comes forth seeing, and is owned by the king as his daughter, and the count as his bride. The whole transaction is between noonday and sunset, and takes place in the rose garden of Iolanthe's villa. The deep psychological motive of the play lies in the fact of the soul's vision independent of the physical sight, and

of the inflowing of the soul's vision into the sense rather than the reverse, as the
principle of seeing. Ebn Jahia, the Moor, teaches thus: —

> "You deem, belike, our sense of vision rests
> Within the eye; yet it is but a means.
> From the soul's depths the power of vision flows. . . .
> Iolanthe must be conscious of her state,
> Her inward eye must first be opened ere
> The light can pour upon the outward sense.
> A want must be developed in her soul:
> A feeling that anticipates the light."

The coming of the count, and the love inspired in Iolanthe by the sound of his voice
and the touch of his hand, creates the necessary discontent: —

> "Deep in the soul a yearning must arise
> For a contentment which it strives to win."

The interview between Iolanthe and the count and his companion is partly in inter-
changed songs after the Minnesingers's manner. The construction of the drama is
highly artistic, and the work is of rare and unique beauty. The play was performed
with success at the Strand Theatre, London, in 1849.

KLAUS HINRICH BAAS; the story of a Self-Made Man, by Gustav Frenssen (1909).
The life story of an energetic peasant boy from his childhood until he is a successful
merchant in a commercial German city, a typical self-made man. His father's death
makes it necessary for him to leave school and go to work. A kind old woman, an
artist, hires him to clean her studio, and introduces him to a merchant who gives him
employment. He is a faithful clerk, and is chosen to go with the son of the head of
the firm to India to examine a mine. He gains business experience, which helps him
to get a better position when he returns to Hamburg after two years. When he is
twenty-six he marries a frail flower of a girl whose nature is too different from his for
companionship. This ill-assorted marriage ends in a separation. His genius for
finance enables him to save from failure the aristocratic firm of Eschen, which had
sent him to India, and he becomes a partner. He marries Sanna Eschen and is happy
with her. Always he remains the primitive natural peasant secretly amazed at his
comfortable surroundings, his self-possessed fine looking wife and dainty children.
The book leaves him at middle-age, with his character formed through hardship,
labor, and passion to self-knowledge and self-mastery. A great variety of characters
appear in the story. The LIBRARY reprints chapters in the hero's early life which
picture his father and mother. His mother is a stern hard woman, from whom Klaus
inherits his masterful disposition. She works day and night to keep a home for her
children, and spends her life in the effort to stamp out the weakness and vanity which
comes to him from his handsome, lively father. Klaus is less arrogant in his success
in the closing chapters. He says to his wife, "Nature blindly endows people with a
collection of gifts which their ancestors had. They may be useful or useless, good or
bad. It is not possible to break or to reform the original character; nor is it right to
blame or despise it. The only thing that can be done is to improve it. You can
strengthen the weak somewhat, and soften the obstinate, and turn the mischievous
toward good; and you can humble the arrogant and presumptuous a little. I've found
that out."

KNICKERBOCKER'S HISTORY OF NEW YORK. In a later preface to this work,
first published in 1809, Washington Irving says: "Nothing more was contemplated

than a *jeu d'ésprit*, written in a serio-comic vein, and treating local errors, follies, and abuses with good-humored satire." Diedrich Knickerbocker is the imaginary historian who records the traditions of New Amsterdam. The book begins with the creation of the world, the discovery of America by the Dutch, and the settlement of the New Netherlands. Hendrick Hudson appears, with other navigators; there are descriptions of the "Bouwerie," Bowling Green, the Battery, and Fort Amsterdam, with the quaint Dutch houses, tiled roofs, and weathercocks, all complete. Dutchmen in wide trousers, big hats, feathers, and large boots, continually puffing long pipes, are seen with their wives and daughters in voluminous petticoats, shoes with silver buckles, girdles, and neat head-dresses. Along the Hudson sail high-pooped Dutch ships. Legends of the island of Manhattan and its surrounding shores are interwoven with the humorous chronicle. The history treats of Oloffe Van Kortlandt, the valiant Kip, the Ten Broecks, Hans Reiner Oothout, the renowned Wouter Van Twiller, descendant of a long line of burgomasters, the patroon Killian Van Rensselaer, Stoffel Brinkerhoff, William Kieft called "William the Testy," Antony Van Corlear the trumpeter, Peter Stuyvesant with his silver leg, and a complement of Indians, Dutch, and Yankee settlers. "Before the appearance of my work," says Irving, "the popular traditions of our city were unrecorded; the peculiar and racy customs and usages derived from our Dutch progenitors were unnoticed or regarded with indifference, or adverted to with a sneer."

KNIGHT OF THE BURNING PESTLE, THE, by Beaumont and Fletcher (1607). This mock-heroic drama owed in large part its influence to Don Quixote; the aim of the authors was to ridicule the military enthusiasm of the city of London and the romantic dramas by which it was stimulated in the same way as Cervantes had satirized the antiquated chivalry of Spain. Naturally, therefore, it did not meet with a favorable reception at first, though it began to have a reputation a generation later. The play opens with an entertainment performed before a citizen-grocer and his wife who keep up a running fire of comments on the progress of the piece. They are specially interested in the acting of Ralph, an apprentice of their own, for whom they have managed to secure a place in the cast in order that he may play the part of the hero. The pompous dialogues in the Quixotic manner between the Knight and his Squire, and between the Knight and the landlord of the Bell Inn are perhaps the most diverting parts in a diverting play.

KNIGHTLY SOLDIER, THE, by H. Clay Trumbull (1865) is a biography of Major Henry Ward Camp of the Tenth Connecticut Volunteers, who fell in one of the battles before Richmond in 1864. It was written while the War was still in progress; while the author, who was chaplain in the army and an attached friend of the subject of the memoir, was still amid the stress of the great conflict; and he writes with the warmth of personal affection and comradeship of the career of a young American soldier. It is a noble monument to the memory of the author's friend; at the same time it is a graphic chronicle of a soldier's life in the field. The letters of Major Camp interwoven with the narrative reveal the man's study of himself in the experiences of battle, prison, flight, recapture, liberation; and show him to be indeed a "knightly soldier."

KNITTERS IN THE SUN, by "Octave Thanet" (Miss Alice French, 1887) is a collection of nine short stories, all but one illustrating the life of the South or West. They are tales of every-day life and more or less every-day people; notable for simplicity and honesty, excellent as character-studies, and without striking incident, while a sunny wholesome philosophy pervades them all.

KORAN, see SACRED BOOKS OF THE EAST.

LADDER OF SWORDS, A, by Gilbert Parker (1904). The scene of this romance is laid in the Isle of Jersey during the reign of Queen Elizabeth. The principal characters in the story are a pair of Huguenot lovers named Michel de la Foret and Angele Aubert who have been forced to flee from France. Angele with her family precedes her lover to the Island of Jersey and there awaits his coming. Before his arrival she is sought in marriage by the Seigneur of Rozel, a big and blustering, but kind-hearted man, and when she declines the honor he has done her he tells her he will remain her true friend. The ship which is bringing Michel to his expectant betrothed is overtaken by a storm and wrecked within sight of land and those waiting to welcome him. Michel and his companion, a pirate named Buonespoir, are thrown into the sea where they would have perished had not the Seigneur of Rozel manned a boat and brought about their rescue. The re-united lovers have but a short time to enjoy their happiness as their intercourse is rudely interrupted by the arrest of Michel by the order of Queen Elizabeth. The cause of this edict is that Michel, who was an officer in the army of Comte Gabriel de Montgomery, who was slain by the Medici, is an innocent victim of the latter's rage. Catherine de Medici requests Elizabeth to render him into their hands and she in order to keep on good terms with France accedes to the other's request. Michel is taken to London where he is on trial for his life and is finally pardoned by Elizabeth. His two friends, the Seigneur of Rozel and Buonespoir, follow him to London and work faithfully for his release. Angele also intercedes with the Queen and does everything in her power to save her lover's life. After his acquittal Michel and Angele are married and return to the Isle of Jersey. After seven years of happiness Angele and her baby die of the plague and Michel, who prefers death to life, is killed in combat a year later.

LADY BALTIMORE, by Owen Wister (1906). The scene of this story is laid at the present time in a southern city called Kings Port, which has retained all the conservatism and old-fashioned customs which existed before the Civil War. It is visited by a young man from the North who makes quite a sojourn within its sacred limits, and has brought letters which admit him to the inner circles of society. The title of the story is derived from a certain kind of cake which is described as being most delectable and goes by the name of "Lady Baltimore." The visitor has his first introduction to it when he is taking luncheon at the Woman's Exchange, which is presided over by a very charming young woman whom he afterwards learns is Miss Eliza La Heu, a member of one of the oldest families but who is financially reduced. On this occasion, the visitor becomes interested in a young man who comes to the Exchange to order a Lady Baltimore cake for his wedding the following week. The visitor's curiosity being aroused he makes inquiries and finds that the young man is named John Mayrant and that he is also a member of an aristocratic family and is making a match which is highly disapproved of by his relations. The young lady in question who possesses beauty and much worldly wisdom is Hortense Rieppe, the daughter of an indigent General. She arrives upon the scene with a party of fashionable friends in the automobile of a rich admirer known to the reader as "Charley," and the visitor is puzzled to find out how John Mayrant fits into her scheme of life. He surmises that John has changed in his feelings towards Hortense but is too honorable to withdraw. The dénouement comes when Hortense jumps overboard from Charley's steam yacht to try her lovers and on being rescued by John, the latter feels that he can honorably release himself from his engagement and does so on the spot. John then marries Eliza who was to have made the wedding cake for Hortense and makes it instead for her own wedding, and Hortense marries Charley who will be able to supply her with all the worldly goods she requires.

LADY OF FORT ST. JOHN, THE, by Mary Hartwell Catherwood (1892). This weird and highly imaginative little story is a romance based on the history of Acadia in 1645, and describing how Marie de la Tour, in the absence of her lord, defends Fort St. John against the besieging forces of D'Aulnay de Charnisay. La Tour, as a Protestant, is out of favor with the king of France; D'Aulnay, with full permission from Louis XIII., is driving him from his hereditary estates. Marie sustains the siege with great courage, until news comes from her husband that their cause is definitely lost; then she capitulates. The end is tragic. There are several well-drawn subordinate characters. The story takes good rank among the hosts of historic romances of the time.

LADY OF QUALITY, A, by Mrs. Frances Hodgson Burnett (1896). The scene of this story is laid in England, during the reign of Queen Anne. Clorinda, the unwelcome daughter of a dissolute, poverty-stricken baronet, Sir Geoffrey Wildairs, loses her mother at birth, and with her little sister grows up neglected and alone, fleeing from the sound of her father's footsteps. At the age of six she wins his heart by belaboring him with blows and kicks; and from that day, dressed as a boy, she is the champion and plaything of his dissolute friends. Her child-life is pathetic in its lawlessness, and prophesies a future of wretchedness if not of degradation. But at fifteen she suddenly blossoms into a beautiful, fascinating, and — strange to say — refined young lady. Her adventures, from the time of this metempsychosis defy the potency of heredity and environment, and hold the reader in amazed attention till the curtain falls upon an unexpected conclusion. This story achieved so great a popular success that it has been followed by a sequel called 'His Grace of Osmonde,' wherein the same characters reappear, but the story is told from the point of view of the hero instead of that of the heroine. 'A Lady of Quality,' in spite of the severe strictures of many critics, has been dramatized by the author and performed with much success.

LADY OF ROME, A, by F. Marion Crawford (1906). This is a story of Maria, Countess of Montalto, a beautiful woman with a past. In the opening of the narrative she is twenty-seven years of age and has been separated for seven years from her husband Count of Montalto, whom she had married at the age of eighteen. This marriage, which was a brilliant one, brought about by parental persuasion, was contrary to the dictates of Maria's heart as she was deeply in love with Baldassare del Castiglione, a penniless young officer. After the marriage, a flirtation which at first seems harmless, is indulged in by the young wife and her old lover but before they realize their danger their passion has carried them beyond the limits of virtue. In course of time Maria's husband discovers the truth and being an honorable and generous man, avoids a public scandal and leaving his wife quietly goes to live with his mother in Spain. Maria continues to live in Rome with unsullied reputation and devotes herself to her son Leone, whose unlikeness to the Count cannot fail to be noticed. After seven years of absence Castiglione returns to Rome and Maria realizes that she still adores the man she has tried so hard to despise. Castiglione, who has bitterly repented of his sin and has since led a blameless life, sues for Maria's forgiveness and they agree to a platonic friendship. Soon after this the Count's mother dies and he writes to Maria begging for a reconciliation, as he still loves her passionately and she acquiesces to his proposal though she has no affection for him and is actually repelled by his presence. The Count returns and he and Maria take up life again, she promising to put Castiglione from her forever. This is a difficult proceeding and she goes frequently to the confessional for help. Finally some old love-letters of Castiglione's are stolen from her desk and are used for the purpose of blackmail. The matter is straightened out by Castiglione through the intervention of Maria's confessor, but her husband convinced that Maria has deceived him again becomes violently angry. He appreciates his mistake and is filled with remorse but is stricken with apoplexy and dies, leaving a letter telling Maria to marry Castiglione, which it is assumed she will do, after a proper period has elapsed.

LADY OF THE AROOSTOOK, THE, a novel of the present day, by W. D. Howells, was published in 1879. In its heroine, Lydia Blood, is drawn the portrait of a lady of nature's own making. She is a New England school-teacher, young, beautiful, and fragile. For the benefit of the sea voyage she leaves her grandparents on a remote New England farm, to visit an aunt and an uncle in Venice. Two of her fellow-passengers on the Aroostook are a Mr. Dunham and a Mr. Staniford, young gentlemen not at first attracted by a girl who says "I want to know." Before the voyage is over, however, Mr. Staniford falls in love with Lydia, whose high-bred nature cannot be concealed by her village rusticity. In Venice, among fashionable sophisticated people, she shows in little nameless ways that she is a lady in the true sense. The book closes with her marriage to Staniford.

'The Lady of the Aroostook' is in Howells's earlier manner, its genial realism imparting to it an atmosphere of delicate comedy.

LADY OR THE TIGER, THE, the first of a brief collection of short stories published under this title in 1884. A semi-barbaric king of olden times had decreed that every person accused of crime should be placed in a vast amphitheatre, where, in the presence of the king, the court, and the assembled multitude he was compelled to open one of two doors which were exactly alike and side by side. He might open which ever door he pleased, but had absolutely no guidance or suggestion to direct him. Behind one door was a hungry, man-eating tiger and behind the other a beautiful lady, dressed as a bride. If he opened the door which concealed the tiger he was at once devoured, and the operation of chance was judged to have proved him guilty; if he opened the door which concealed the lady, he was held to be proved innocent and was immediately married to her with great rejoicings. No previous ties were allowed to put a stop to this marriage. The disposition of the lady and of the tiger behind the two doors was subject to change on every occasion and was, of course, a profound secret. Now it happened that a young courtier of humble rank won the love of the king's daughter; and being detected by the king was imprisoned and brought to trial in the arena. The princess by means of gold and a woman's determination discovered behind which doors the lady and the tiger were to be placed. She went through a long and agonized conflict between horror at the thought of her lover's destruction by a ferocious tiger and jealousy at the idea of his possession by another, the fairest maid of honor of the court. At length her mind was made up. On the day of the trial she unobtrusively signalled to her lover, to open the right-

hand door. This he immediately did. The author does not undertake to say what
followed, but leaves the question to his readers: "Which came out of the opened
door,—the lady, or the tiger?" The force and succinctness of this story, the surprise
of the conclusion, and the piquancy of the concluding question (which has a parallel
in the *questions d'amour* of the mediæval courts of love) have made this tale justly
famous.

LADY ROSE'S DAUGHTER, by Mrs. Humphry Ward (1903). This is the story
of Julie le Breton, a brilliant and fascinating young woman who is introduced to the
reader as the companion and protégé of Lady Henry. The latter, an elderly and
infirm woman of domineering nature, who has been a social leader in her day, finds
her companion's tact and cleverness indispensable in the entertainment of the guests
who still flock to her house. Julie, whose antecedents are known to but few persons,
is really the daughter of Lady Rose Delaney, who left her uncongenial husband
and went away with an artist named Marriott Dalrymple. Julie was the child of this
union, which was never sanctioned by the marriage rite, and after the death of her
parents took the name of the governess in whose care she was left. Lady Rose was
the daughter of Lord Lackington, an habitué at Lady Henry's, who becomes very
fond of the charming Miss Le Breton; she finally makes known her identity to him
and he accepts her affectionately as his grand-daughter and provides for her at his
death. When upon his death-bed he exacts a promise from Julie to marry Jacob
Delafield, a nephew of Lady Henry's and the heir to a title and large estates. Delafield
has loved Julie for years but she has refused his offer of marriage and given her affection to Captain Warkworth, a handsome and selfish fellow, who is already engaged to
her cousin Aileen Moffatt. Julie does everything in her power to further Warkworth's
interests and through her influence with those in authority he is made a major.
He wins Julie's love under the guise of friendship and plays with her affection. When
the time comes for his return to the army, Julie feels she cannot give him up and
consents to meet him in France and stay with him till his departure. This plan
is frustrated by Delafield, who discovers her as she is alighting from the train at
Paris and telling her that her grandfather is dying escorts her back to his bedside.
Julie does not see Warkworth again and in time consents to marry Delafield, who in
spite of his knowledge of her previous experience remains true to her. Warkworth
dies of fever leaving his fiancée heartbroken and Julie crushed with grief. Her husband nobly comforts her and she begins to appreciate his sterling qualities. Delafield's cousin, the Earl of Chudleigh, dies leaving him his title and possessions and
Julie who has grown to love her husband is happy in the thought of the new life that
is opening for them.

LADY WINDERMERE'S FAN, by Oscar Wilde (1892). Lady Windermere quarrels
with her husband on the ground that he is paying undue attentions to another woman. The real fact is that this woman is her own mother whom she has not seen
since she was a child and whom she believes to have died long since. Lord Windermere has been trying to help her without revealing who she is. He invites her to his
house under an assumed name, whereupon Lady Windermere leaves him with the
intention of running away with a lover, Lord Darlington. She writes a letter to her
husband stating that she is leaving him, but her mother, Mrs. Erlynne finds it and
tears it up. She goes to Lord Darlington's room whither her daughter has gone and
persuades her to go back to her husband. She herself waits to meet Lord Darlington
and his friends including Lord Windermere, returning from their club. Lord Winder-

mere picks up his wife's fan on the floor and wrathfully asks how it comes to be in Lord Darlington's rooms. Mrs. Erlynne promptly says that she took his wife's fan in mistake and allows it to appear that she herself had come in secret to Lord Darlington's rooms. Lady Windermere is reconciled to her husband and Mrs. Erlynne marries Lord Augustus Lawton on condition that they live out of England. The play abounds in the wit which made Wilde the most brilliant talker of his time.

LALLA ROOKH, by Thomas Moore (1817) a series of Oriental tales in verse, enclosed in a prose framework. This latter relates the journey of Lalla Rookh, the beautiful daughter of the Emperor Aurengzebe, from Delhi to meet her betrothed, the young king of Bucharia, in the vale of Cashmere. On the way she and her train are entertained by four tales related by Feramorz, a beautiful young poet from Cashmere with whom she falls in love and who proves at the conclusion of the journey to be the king of Bucharia himself. A touch of humor is supplied by her chamberlain, Fadladeen, whose suspicion of the young poet's impression upon the princess finds voice in caustic criticisms of his verses, and who is astonished and discomfited by the discovery of the youth's identity. The first tale, which is in heroic couplets, treats of Mokanna, the 'Veiled Prophet of Khorassan,' a hideous impostor who by his magic arts gained control of that province, hiding his face from his devoted followers by a silver veil. To his haram he has enticed the beautiful Zelica a maiden of Bokhara, on the promise of admission to Paradise, where she hopes to be the bride of her lover, Azim, supposedly dead. Azim, however, returning from the wars in Greece, joins the veiled prophet. But when he finds his love, Zelica, wedded to Mokanna and cruelly treated, Azim deserts him and joins the invading army of the Caliph. The Veiled Prophet is defeated and kills himself by plunging into a vat of corrosive poison which consumes him. Zelica, who wishes only to die, puts on his veil, confronts the Caliph's army, and is slain by Azim, with whom she exchanges forgiveness in death. In the second story, 'Paradise and the Peri,' one of the airy spirits, offspring of the fallen angels, who live on perfume and perform beneficent tasks though excluded from Paradise, was promised admission by the angelic guardian of the portal if she could bring thither the gift most dear to Heaven. She brought first a drop of blood from a patriot dying to free India from a tyrant, then the last sigh of an Egyptian maiden, expiring of grief at the loss of her lover, whom she had nursed through the plague; and finally, from the valley of Balbec a tear of repentance dropped by an impious criminal as the result of a child's prayer. This penitent's tear, the gift most prized by Heaven, opens Paradise to the Peri. The metre of this second story is stanzaic, each stanza containing twelve octosyllabic lines, six rhyming in couplets, and the last four alternately. The third narrative, 'The Fire-Worshippers' deals with the Ghebers, or Persians of the old religion, who retained their ancient beliefs after the Mohammedans had conquered the country, keeping up a resistance in the mountainous districts. Hafed, their leader, falls in love with Hinda, daughter of Al Hassan, the Arabian emir who has come to root out these enemies of Islam. The young Gheber gains admission to her bower, incognito, and wins her love. Later she is captured by the Ghebers and learns that her beloved is their chieftain. In a sudden attack the Arabs defeat the Persians and Hafed immolates himself on a funeral pyre. Hinda who is being sent back to her father for safety's sake, leaps from a galley into the lake and is drowned. The metre of this and the succeeding tale is a varied one, like that of Scott's 'Lay of the Last Minstrel.' Fourth and last comes the story of the Sultana Nourmahal, the 'Light of the Haram' favorite wife of the Emperor Selim, son of the great Akbar. While they are celebrating the Feast of Roses in the

Vale of Cashmere she quarrels with her husband. In order to effect a reconciliation she persuades an enchantress, Namouna, to teach her a magic song. The singing of this by Nourmahal, masked, at the Emperor's banquet, wins back his love. The work is graceful in style, bright, sometimes luscious in coloring, occasionally over-sentimental and theatrical in incidents and dialogue, but unbroken in narrative interest. As an entertaining series of romantic tales it fully accomplishes its purpose, which can have been only to give pleasure.

LAMPLIGHTER, THE, by Maria Susanna Cummins, was the author's first book, and appeared in 1854, when she was twenty-seven. This simple home story secured an immediate popularity. The scene is laid in New York. Gerty, a forlorn and ignorant girl, spends her early years with Nan Grant, a coarse, brutal woman who abuses her. Her greatest pleasure is watching old Trueman Flint as he goes his rounds to light the city lamps. Trueman rescues the child, and although he is poor himself, adopts her. Under his loving care, and in association with his neighbors, — thrifty Mrs. Sullivan and her son Willie, a boy somewhat older than herself,— Gertrude grows into a happy and beautiful young girl, the great comfort of Uncle True. She is befriended by Emily Graham, a noble Christian character, the beautiful only daughter of a rich, indulgent father. Emily is blind as the result of a careless act of her young brother. Overcome by remorse, and embittered by his father's reproaches, this brother has disappeared, to Emily's great sorrow. Gerty is sent to school, where she is fitted to teach; but after Trueman's death she becomes a member of the Graham family. Willie Sullivan, the friend of her childhood, becomes a noble-minded and successful young man who falls in love with Gertrude. In Philip Amory, a high-minded man whom Emily and Gertrude meet while traveling, they discover the long-lost brother; and he proves in the end to be Gertrude's father, who for years has been vainly searching for her. The story is weak in plot and characterization; but the idyllic charm of its first hundred pages or so gave it for a few years a very extraordinary vogue. It is now little read.

LAND AND LABOR, 'Lessons from Belgium,' by Seebohm Rowntree (1910). "This book" (says its author) "is written in the hope of contributing to the solution of the problem of poverty in Britain by throwing some light on its relation to the system of land tenure." It records the results of four years' microscopic investigation (which could only have been undertaken by a very wealthy and disinterested man into all the main aspects of the social and economic life of Belgium. Part 1 is devoted to the history and constitution of the country, the history of land tenure, and the number of landowners in Belgium classified according to the size of their holdings. Three quarters of the landowners in Belgium had less than five acres each, 95% had less than 25 acres, and only 146 men more than 2500 acres each. Parts 2 and 3 deal with the industrial and agricultural conditions of Belgium, part 4 with the chief factors which account for its extraordinary productiveness before the war, whether in industry or agriculture and part 5 with the standard of life. No European country before the war was producing so much per capita either in industry or in agriculture. Detailed information is given as to methods of scientific farming, market gardening, afforestation, agricultural societies, and other activities. The means of transport in Belgium, whether by rail or water, were not only the cheapest but the most complete in the world, and had an extraordinary effect not only in industry and agriculture but upon the general life of Belgium. The volume as a whole is a model of disinterested, impartial, and thorough investigation.

LAND OF COCKAYNE, THE, by Matilde Serao (1891). A powerful study in fiction of the passion for gambling and the evil effect of the national lottery in Naples on all classes of society. The lottery is the joy and curse of the Marquis di Formosa as well as Gaetano, the glove-maker, Carmela, the factory girl and her insolent lover Raffaele. Cesare, the wealthy pastry maker, loses everything he has in the hope of getting money from the lottery for a new venture. The Marquis has ruined himself and is sacrificing his frail young daughter, the Lady Bianca, to his terrible passion. A medium whom he and his friends consult about winning numbers makes him believe that Bianca's innocence may call on the spirits to reveal lucky numbers, and the Marquis destroys her health and happiness trying to force the sensitive neurotic girl to see spirits for him. She loves Dr. Amanti, peasant born, but a great and wealthy physician, but her father, advised by the medium, forbids her to marry and she obeys. The idyllic love story of Bianca and Dr. Amanti has a tragic ending. Her father refuses her prayers to bring him to her until it is too late for him to save her life. All the characters lose money, honor, and self-respect through the curse of their obsession. The story is also a description of Naples, of its people and scenes at all times and seasons. The panorama of the procession of the festival of San Genaro is a vivid picture.

LAND OF COKAINE, THE. An old English poem, of a date previous to the end of the twelfth century, preserved, among other sources, in Hickes's 'Thesaurus' and the 'Early English Poems' of Furnivall. The name appears also in the French and German literatures, sometimes as 'Cocaigne,' again as 'Cokaygne.' In every instance it represents an earthly land of delight, a kind of Utopia. Dr. Murray thinks the name implies "fondling,"—a gibe of countryfolk at the luxurious Londoners.

The old English poem in question is a naïve description of the extremely unspiritual delights of a land on the borders of the earth, "beyond West Spain," where all the rivers run wine or oil, or at least milk, where the shingles of the houses are wheaten cakes, and the pinnacles "fat puddings," and where, — undoubted climax of felicity, — "water serveth to nothing but to siyt [boiling] and to washing."

In this fair land of Cokaine, where no one sleeps or works, and where men fly at will like the birds, stand a great abbey and cloisters both for nuns and monks. The ease and gayety of the religious vocation in this paradise of gray friars and white is depicted with the broad humor and exceeding frankness of our forefathers. It is a satire on the morals and pretensions of the ecclesiastical body; but, though the picture is painted in colors veiled by no reverence, they are mixed with little bitterness. The author laughs rather than sneers.

The French poem of the same name, 'Pays de Cocaigne,' differs from the English in that it lacks the whole satirical description of the cloisters.

LAND OF HEART'S DESIRE, THE, by W. B. Yeats (1894). A fairy play based on the legend that on May Eve the fairies may steal away a newly married bride if only she be tempted to give them, at their asking, fire and milk. Maurteen Bruin and Bridget his wife, Shawn, their son and his "newly-married bride, Maire," and the village priest, Father Hart, are sitting in the kitchen in the twilight. Old Bridget has been scolding her son's wife for reading a book about the fairies, instead of helping with the work. "A little queer old woman" knocks at the door begging "a porringer of milk," and the girl gives it to her in spite of Bridget's warning. Later she gives "a burning sod" to "a little old man" to light his pipe. To Bridget's reproaches she answers, in anger at her nagging tongue, that she calls on the fairies to take her from the dull house, where she is unhappy. They hear singing, and the father opens the door to a little child with red gold hair dressed in pale green. They play with her and pet her, thinking she is only a human child, and the priest takes down the crucifix from the wall because it frightens her. The child begins to dance and calls the young bride to ride upon the winds with her. The family, except Maire, gather around the priest in terror. Without the crucifix he is powerless. Shawn tries to keep his wife, reminding her of their love, and she turns to him, but the fairy child has lured her away. When the child leaves and Shawn crosses the primroses the child has strewn around the "newly-married wife," he clasps in his arms no more than "a drift of leaves, or bole of an ash-tree changed into her image."

LAND OF POCO TIEMPO, THE, by Charles F. Lummis (1893), is a delightful record of the author's travels in New Mexico; a land, as he describes it, of "sun, silence, and abode . . . the Great American Mystery — the National Rip Van Winkle." The different chapters treat of New-Mexican customs of the inhabitants, of the folk-songs, of the religious rites. Perhaps the most fascinating portion of the work is that devoted to the "cities that were forgotten"; those great stone ruins, rearing ghost-like from illimitable plains, with as little reason for being there as the Pyramids in the sands of the desert. The book is written in a pleasant conversational style, and with much picturesqueness of description.

LANDLORD AT LION'S HEAD, THE, by W. D. Howells (1897), is a subtle study of types of character essentially the product of present-day conditions of life in New England. It is a masterpiece in the sense of its having been written with the strong and sure hand of the finished artist. The author assumes complete responsibility for his work, and the reader is at ease. The story is concerned chiefly with the fortunes of the Durgin family, New England farm-people, who own little but a magnificent view of Lion's Head Mountain. By the chance visit of an artist, Westover, they are made to realize its mercantile value. Mrs. Durgin's ambitions, aroused by the success of her "hotel," are centred in her son, Jeff Durgin. The portrait of this country boy swaggering through Harvard, standing, but with a certain impudence, always on the edge of things, is drawn with wonderful clarity. Another admirable creation is Whitwell, a neighbor of the Durgins, a sort of rural philosopher, with a mind reaching helplessly out to the pseudo-occult, and to the banalities of planchette. His daughter Cynthia, the most hopeful figure in the book, is a sweet, strong mountain girl, "capable" in the full sense of the word. In strong contrast to her is the Boston society girl, Bessie Lynde, who flirts with Jeff for the sake of a new sensation. The scenes are laid partly in Boston, partly in the mountains. The vulgarity of certain aspects of both city and country life is mildly satirized. The novel is supremely American.

LANGUAGE AND THE STUDY OF LANGUAGE, by William Dwight Whitney (1867). This work attempts to answer the question, How did language originate? The growth of language is first considered, with the causes which affect the kind and the rate of linguistic change; then the separation of languages into dialects; then the group of dialects and the family of more distantly related languages which include English; then a review of the other great families; the relative value and authority of linguistic and of physical evidence of race, and the bearing of language on the ultimate question of the unity or variety of the human species: the whole closing with an inquiry into the origin of language, its relation to thought, and its value as an element in human progress. Professor Whitney's theory is that acts and qualities were the first things named, and that the roots of language — from which all words have sprung — were originally developed by man in striving to imitate natural sounds (the onomatopoetic theory) and to utter sounds expressive of excited feeling (the interjectional theory); *not* by means of an innate "creative faculty" for phonetically expressing his thoughts, which is Max Müller's view.

LAOKOON. Lessing's 'Laokoon,' written in 1766, marked an epoch in German art-criticism. It derives its title from the celebrated piece of sculpture by the Greek artists Polydor, Agesander, and Athenodor, which is taken as the starting-point for a discussion on the difference between poetry and the plastic arts. The group represents the well-known episode during the siege of Troy, when the Trojan priest, Laokoon, and his two sons, are devoured by snakes as a punishment for having advised against admitting the decoy horse of the Greeks into the town. In this group Laokoon apparently does not scream, but only sighs painfully. Virgil, who recounted the same episode in his Æneid, makes the priest cry out in his agony. Lessing asks why this divergence in treatment between the artist and poet? and answers — because they worked with different materials. The poet could present his hero as screaming, because the heroes of classical antiquity were not above such shows of human weakness. But the artist, in presenting human suffering, was limited by the laws of his art, the highest object of which is beauty; honco ho muot avoid all those extremes of passion, that, being in their nature transitory, mar the beauty of the features. He can reproduce only *one* moment, whereas the poet has the whole gamut of expression at command. This constitutes the radical difference between poetry and the plastic arts, related though they be in many ways. The plastic arts deal with *space*, and have for their proper objects bodies with their visible attributes; they may, however, suggest these bodies as being in action. Poetry deals with *time*, and has for its proper objects a succession of events or actions; at the same time it may suggest the description of bodies. Homer already knew this principle, for in describing the shield of Achilles he invites us to be present at its making. In like manner we know what Agamemnon wore by watching him dress. All descriptive poetry and allegorical painting is hereby ruled out of court. There is yet another difference. The plastic arts in their highest development treat only of beauty. Poetry, not being confined to the passing moment, has at its disposal the whole of nature. It treats not only of what is beautiful or agreeable, but also of what is ugly and terrible.

These principles, developed by Lessing in his small treatise, came like a revelation to the German mind. Goethe thus described the effect: "We heartily welcomed the light which that fine thinker brought down to us out of dark clouds. Illumined as by lightning we saw all the consequences of that glorious thought which made clear the difference between the plastic and the poetic arts. All the current criticism was thrown aside as a worn-out coat."

LA SALLE AND THE DISCOVERY OF THE GREAT WEST, see **FRANCE AND ENGLAND IN NORTH AMERICA.**

LAST ATHENIAN, THE ('Sidste Athenaren'), by Viktor Rydberg (1880), translated from the Swedish by W. W. Thomas in 1883. The scene of the novel is laid in Athens in the fourth century of our own era; and deals with the inner dissensions of the Christian church, the struggles and broils of the Homoiousians and Athanasians.

and the social and political conditions involved in or affected by these differences. The corruption of the upper classes, the lingering power of the old religion of Greece, the strange melée of old and new philosophies and erratic social codes, are presented by the introduction of many types and individuals. But a confusing multiplicity of interests and characters interferes with a clear view. The stage is too crowded. The parts of the plot are woven together about the love-story of Hermione, daughter of the philosopher Chrysanteus, and a young Athenian of the degenerate type, who from a promising youth passes into the idle and heartless dissipation of the typical Athenian aristocrat. Influenced by divided motives, he makes an attempt to regain his moral standing, and does regain Hermione's confidence; but on his wedding night, he is killed by the lover of a young Jewish girl whom he has betrayed and deserted. The famous historic figures of the epoch are all introduced into Rydberg's picture, — emperors and bishops, political schemers and professional beauties, soldiers and merchants, princes and beggars. Even St. Simeon Stylites on his pillar is painted in all his repulsive hideousness of saintly squalor. A pretty interlude to the development of the story is afforded by several charming interpretations of the old legend of Narcissus and the Echo.

LAST DAYS OF POMPEII, THE, by Edward Bulwer, Lord Lytton (1834). The characters and scenes of this story are in a great measure suggested by the peculiarities of the buildings which are still to be seen at Pompeii. The tale begins a few days before the destruction of Pompeii, and ends with that event. The simple story relates principally to two young people of Grecian origin, Glaucus and Ione, who are deeply attached to each other. The former is a handsome young Athenian, impetuous, high-minded, and brilliant, while Ione is a pure and lofty-minded woman. Arbaces, her guardian, the villain of the story, under a cloak of sanctity and religion, indulges in low and criminal designs. His character is strongly drawn; and his passion for Ione, and the struggle between him and Glaucus, form the chief part of the plot. Nydia, the blind girl, who pines in unrequited affection for Glaucus, and who saves the lives of the lovers at the time of the destruction of the city, by conducting them in safety to the sea, is a touching and beautiful conception. The book, full of learning and spirit, is not only a charming novel, but contains many minute and interesting descriptions of ancient customs; among which, those relating to the gladiatorial combat, the banquet, the bath, are most noteworthy.

LAST LETTERS FROM EGYPT, see **LETTERS FROM EGYPT,** by Lady Duff-Gordon.

LAST OF THE MOHICANS, THE, a novel of frontier life, one of the 'Leatherstocking Tales' by James Fenimore Cooper, published in 1826. During the siege of Fort William Henry on Lake George by the French and Iroquois under Montcalm (1757) two daughters of its commander, Colonel Munro, set out from the neighboring Fort Edward to join their father. They are accompanied by Major Duncan Heyward, and the singing master David Gamut, and guided by a renegade Huron, called by the French "Le Renard Subtil." The latter leads them astray with a view to betraying them into the hands of a wandering party of Iroquois. But his designs are foiled by the scout, Natty Bumppo (called "Hawkeye" in this story), and his comrades, the Mohican, Chingachgook, and his son, Uncas, who rescue the party from the scalping-knife and bring them safely to the fort. Soon afterwards Munro surrenders on honorable terms to Montcalm and is permitted to march out of the fort with arms and colors. The stragglers, however, are massacred by the Indian allies of the French, and in the confusion the two girls, Cora and Alice Munro, are again carried off by Le Renard Subtil. Munro and Heyward set out in search of them, aided by Hawkeye, Chingachgook, and Uncas. After a series of hair-breadth escapes and cunning ruses Alice is rescued but Cora is slain rather than become the wife of Le Renard Subtil and Uncas dies in avenging her. Lastly, Le Renard Subtil perishes by falling from a cliff.

LAVENGRO: 'The Scholar, Gipsy, Priest' (1851). **ROMANY RYE** (1857) (Sequel to Lavengro). By George Borrow. These books comprise a tale of loosely connected adventures introducing romantic, grotesque, and exciting episodes, and interwoven with reflections on the moral and religious condition of the world, with a large intermixture of mystic and philosophic lore. They suggest Le Sage's story; and like the 'Gil Blas,' the characters are drawn largely from Spanish sources. Gipsy life and legends form a kind of background to the writer's reflections on the men and morals of his time. The author, born in East Dereham, Norfolk, England, 1803, had been employed in 1840–50 as an agent of the British and Foreign Bible Society in distributing Bibles in the mountainous districts of Spain, and had met with hardships and rough usage which helped to embitter his feelings toward the Roman Catholic religion, at the same time that they afforded him glimpses of the simple life of the lower classes, and especially an acquaintance with the Gipsy tribe-life, which had a peculiar charm for him. "Lavengro" is depicted as a dreamy youth following the fortunes of his father, who is in military service. His visits are divided between the Gipsy camp, the "Romany chal," and the "parlor of the Anglo-German philosopher." The title "Romany Rye" (Gipsy Gentleman) is introduced in the verse of a song, "The Gipsy Gentleman," sung in Chapter liv. of 'Lavengro':—

> "Here the Gypsy gemman see,
> With his Kernan jib and his rome and dree;
> Rome and dree, rum and dry,
> Rally round the Romany Rye."

The song is sung by "Mr. Petulengro," the author's favorite Gipsy character. The hero's trials of mind and faith are depicted, when, at the age of nineteen, he is cast upon the world in London to make his living as a hack author. Meeting with success with one of his books, he leaves London to roam abroad, and becomes in turn tinker, gipsy, postilion, and hostler; but ever preserves the self-respect of the poor gentleman and the scholar in disguise. His object in writing is to show the goodness of God, and to reveal the plots of popery; he shows much contempt for the pope, whom he calls "Mumbo-Jumbo," and for all his ceremonies. He would encourage charity, free and genial manners, the exposure of the humbugs of "gentility," and the appreciation of genuine worth of character in whatever social station. The titles "Scholar, Gipsy, Priest," are not successive characters assumed by the author, but stand for these various types of humanity. A marked feature of these books is their use of elaborate fables for moral instruction. Such are those of the 'Rich Gentleman' and the 'Magic Touch,' the 'Old Applewoman,' and 'Peter William, the Missionary.'

LAWS OF ENGLAND, by Sir William Blackstone, see **COMMENTARIES ON THE.**

LAWS, THE (Leges), of Plato, translated by Benjamin Jowett. In the early years of life according to the doctrine contained in 'The Laws' education is wholly a discipline imparted by means of pleasure and pain. The discipline of pleasure is imposed chiefly by the practice of the song and dance. The forms of these should be fixed, for it would be political unwisdom to depend on the fickleness of the multitude. There should be choruses of boys and girls and grown-up persons, and all will be heard repeating the same strain that "virtue is happiness." The chorus of aged minstrels, who will sing the most beautiful and the most useful of songs will give the law to the rest.   Education is to begin at or rather before birth, to be continued for a time by mothers and nurses under state inspection and finally is to include music and gymnastics.   In the category of music Plato included reading, writing, playing on the lyre, arithmetic, and a knowledge of mathematics, enough to preserve the citizens in after-life from impiety, which to Plato meant either atheism or denial of Providence or grotesque and immoral superstitions.   Gymnastics, the primary aim of which was mental and not merely physical development, are to be practised in order that the pupil might acquire the due balance between mental and physical which would make him useful in war.

'The Laws' abounds in profound reflections which suggest principles that are only in the twentieth century beginning to be carried out by social and educational reformers.   "Cities will never cease from ill until they are better governed."   Education should begin with birth and even before it.   Wise policy must include a programme of sanitation.   These and other suggestive ideas make 'The Laws' even yet one of the stimulating treatises on education (circa 360–347 B.C.).

LAWS OF ECCLESIASTICAL POLITY, THE, by Richard Hooker (1593–97).   A learned and broadly rational treatise on the principles of church government, the special aim of which was to prove, against the Puritanism of the time, that religious doctrines and institutions do not find their sole sanction in Scripture, but may be planned and supported by the use of other sources of light and truth; and that in fact the Scriptures do not supply any definite form of church order, the laws of which are obligatory.   The course of church matters under Queen Elizabeth had so completely disregarded the views and demands of the Puritans as to give occasion for a work representing other and wider views; and Hooker's genius exactly fitted him to supply a philosophical and logical basis to the Elizabethan church system.   Of the eight books now found in the work, only four were published at first; then a fifth, longer by sixty pages than the whole of the first four, in 1597; and three after his death (November 2d, 1600), — the sixth and eighth in 1648, and the seventh in 1617. The admirable style of the work has given it a high place in English literature; while its breadth of view, wealth of thought, and abundant learning, have caused it to increase in favor with the advance of time.

LAY DOWN YOUR ARMS, see **GROUND ARMS.**

LAY SERMONS, ADDRESSES, AND REVIEWS, by Thomas Henry Huxley, a series of fifteen lectures and essays, written at various times between 1854 and 1870 and collected in the latter year.   Six of the individual essays or addresses are educational, pleading for the recognition of natural science as not only a utilitarian but also a liberal study.   Huxley had deep convictions on this subject, and strong opposition to overcome.   He writes, therefore, with great vigor and effectiveness, as also in the two articles defending Darwin's 'Origin of Species.'   Two of the lectures were delivered with the aim of popularizing scientific knowledge.   The address 'On the Physical Basis of Life' shows that every living creature is formed by different dispositions of one substance — protoplasm, and argues that this material substance is the source of all life; at the same time Huxley repudiates the charge of materialism on the ground that he makes no inquiry into the essential nature of protoplasm.

since that question is unanswerable. 'On a Piece of Chalk,' a lecture delivered to workingmen in Norwich, makes the chalk a text for a discourse on geology and the origin of species. The chalk, being composed of the shells of aquatic animals, naturally leads to these topics. An address on Descartes traces the influence of his philosophy through the two developments of idealism and scepticism, and a review of one of Huxley's hostile critics emphasizes the distinction between agnosticism and positivism. Finally, there are three presidential addresses, delivered before scientific societies, on evolution as applied to geology and to botany, and on spontaneous generation. The value and charm of these essays lie in their honesty, directness, simplicity, clearness, and incisive reasoning power.

LAZARILLO DE TORMES, formerly attributed to Diego Hurtado de Mendoza. This "picaresque" novel was first published in 1553, but was written when the author was a student at Salamanca (1520–23). Mendoza's authorship has been questioned, and it has been attributed to Juan de Ortega, and to certain bishops, who are said to have composed it on their way to the Council of Trent. Still, the probabilities are all in favor of Mendoza, and it is the work upon which his literary fame chiefly rests. The hero is a young rogue who begins his career as guide to a rascally blind beggar. The beggar ill-treats him, and he avenges himself cruelly but comically. He then passes into the service of a priest, a country squire, a "pardoner," a chaplain, and an alguazil. The author leaves him in the position of town-crier of Toledo. The story opened the way for the *novela picaresca*, i. e., the novel of thieves, to which we owe 'Guzman d'Alfarache' and 'Gil Blas'; and is one of the best of its kind. The author shows his originality by breaking away from the magicians, fairies, knights errant, and all the worn-out material of the Middle Ages, and borrowing his characters from the jovial elements to be found in the shady side of society. All his characters, as well as the hero, are vagabonds, beggars, thievish innkeepers, knavish lawyers, or monks who have become disreputable; and all throb with intense life in his brisk and highly colored narrative. Every episode in Lazarillo's checkered existence is a masterpiece of archness and good-humor. The work, which created an epoch in the history of Spanish prose, is, unfortunately, unfinished: the author, having apparently become a little ashamed of this offspring of his youth, refused to complete it. A second part was added by De Luna, a refugee at Paris, in the following century; but it is far from having the qualities of Mendoza's fragment.

LAZARRE, by Mary Hartwell Catherwood (1901). This romantic novel is founded upon the legend that at the time of the French Revolution, the Dauphin was spirited away to America by the court painter Bellenger. In the story the young Prince grows up among the Indians of the Northwest under the name of Eleazer Williams — softened by them to Lazarre. Having been reduced almost to imbecility by previous harsh treatment, the child at first believes himself to be the son of the Indian chief in whose care he has been placed. Under the healthful influence of the climate, he regains both mental and physical strength and, attracting the notice of the settlers, gains an education. While studying at the manor house, he falls in love with Eagle, Madame De Ferrier, who recognizes him as the Dauphin, seen by her years before in St. Bat's Church, London. When news is received from France of the death of Eagle's husband, Lazarre confesses his love and asks her hand in marriage. Though deeply attached to him, she tells him she cannot marry a King, and starts for France to reclaim her estates. He follows her to France and mingles in the brilliant court of Napoleon, making an unsuccessful plea for recognition to Louis XVIII. After various thrilling adventures he returns to his beloved wilderness in America, where, after years of waiting and searching, he finds Eagle for whom he renounces the crown, which is offered him by an envoy of the Bourbons, who turn to him as a last resource. The story is one of sustained interest and displays the author's knowledge of the wild country in the old time, as well as her fertile imagination. The character of the Prince is an interesting study and that of Eagle is drawn with remarkable charm and skill.

LEARNED LADIES ('Les Femmes Savantes'), a comedy by Jean Baptiste Poquelin, universally known as Molière, was first acted in 1672, when the author, although then in the last stages of consumption, played a leading part. One of the brilliant social satires, in which the great realist dared point out the faults and follies of contemporary society, it ridicules the pedantry and affectation of learning then fashionable among court ladies. Chrysale, an honest bourgeois, loving quiet and comfort, is kept in continual turmoil by his wife Philaminte — who affects a love of learning and refuses to keep even a kitchen maid who speaks incorrectly — and by her disciple, his foolish old sister Belise, who fancies every man she sees secretly in love with her. Chrysale and Philaminte have two daughters, — Armande, a pedant like her mother, who scorns marriage and rebuffs her lover Clitandre; and Henriette, honest and simple, who when Clitandre transfers his love to her, accepts it in spite of her sister's jealous sneers. Chrysale prefers Clitandre as son-in-law, but is too hen-pecked to resist his wife's will until spurred by the scorn of his brother Ariste. The plot is too complicated to be reproduced, and the strength of the play lies in its character-drawing. The wit with which Molière heaps scorn upon ill-founded pretension to learning, and his powerful exposition of vanity and self-love, have kept the play popular in France for over two hundred years.

LEATHERSTOCKING TALES, a series of five novels of frontier life by James Fenimore Cooper. The title is derived from one of the nicknames applied to the hero, Natty Bumppo, a brave pioneer and woodsman who appears in each of the stories. He is also called Hawkeye and Deerslayer. The novels were not written according to the chronological sequence of the hero's life. The earliest novel, 'The Pioneers'; or, 'The Sources of the Susquehanna' (1823) represents him as an old man, retreating across the Alleghanies before the advance of civilized settlement. In the next novel, 'The Last of the Mohicans, a Narrative of 1757' (published in 1826) he appears in the prime of life as a scout in the campaign of Fort William Henry. 'The Prairie' (1827), reverting to his old age, describes his further retirement to the western plains, and his death. Some years later Cooper returned to the subject and wrote two stories of Natty Bumppo's youth. In the first of these, 'The Pathfinder, or the Inland Sea' (1840) he appears as the lover of Mabel Dunham. The other, 'The Deerslayer, or the First War Path' (1841), though the latest of the novels, depicts incidents earlier than appear in any of the others. It describes Natty's first experience of Indian warfare. The order of publication and the fictitious chronology may best be indicated by the following table:

Order of Publication	Fictitious Chronology
'The Pioneers' (1823)	'The Deerslayer' ⎱ youth
'The Last of the Mohicans' (1826)	'The Pathfinder' ⎰
'The Prairie' (1827)	'The Last of the Mohicans' (prime of life)
'The Pathfinder' (1840)	'The Pioneers' ⎱ old age
'The Deerslayer' (1841)	'The Prairie' ⎰

The whole series forms an admirable picture of the period of settlement and Indian warfare and offers some excellent portrayals of character. For further details see under 'Deerslayer' and 'Last of the Mohicans.'

LEAVES OF GRASS, a collection of poems in free rhythms by Walt Whitman, first published in 1855, and re-issued with additional poems in 1856, in 1860, in 1866, in 1871, and in 1876. Whitman said that the purpose of the book was "to articulate and faithfully express in literary or poetic form, and uncompromisingly, my own physical, emotional, moral, intellectual, and æsthetic Personality, in the midst of, and tallying, the momentous spirit and facts of its immediate days, and of current America — and to exploit that Personality, identified with place and date, in a far more candid and comprehensive sense than in any hitherto poem or book." 'Leaves of Grass' is accordingly the frankest self-revelation, the fullest embodiment of American life, and the most original stylistic and metrical experiment of any poetical work ever published. Whitman portrays himself as a lover of life in all its forms, particularly of men and women, a wanderer of city streets, country roads, battlefields, and hospitals, eager to fraternize with people of every rank, and especially with the rough and poor. He is keenly sensitive to all the delights of life, physical, mental, and spiritual, and it is his cardinal doctrine that matter, mind, and spirit are equally noble; hence the extreme sensuousness of some of his poems never becomes sensuality but is a part of his faith in the goodness of life as a whole. But above all the joys of physical satisfaction, beautiful landscape, human comradeship, and spiritual contemplation, is the joy of self-consciousness, the feeling of his individual being. It is not conceit or exaggerated egotism but a delight in being alive, which turns impatiently from doctrines of asceticism and original sin to happy contemplation of self and the world. One of the longest poems of the collection is entitled 'Song of Myself,' and this title might have been given to the whole book. Again, Whitman is an American through and through, and his poems depict almost every conceivable type of American landscape, American social life, and American manhood and womanhood, as observed by a man who had mingled with it all in a human, democratic way. On the sea-beaches of Long Island, the crowded ferries and pavements of Manhattan, the farms and lumber-camps of the Alleghanies, the tents and battlefields of the Civil War, the plantations of the South, the prairies, the Rockies, the Pacific Coast, and hundreds of other typical American backgrounds he constantly portrays that sense of equality, comradeship, and confident hopefulness in pioneer enterprise which is the distinctive American characteristic. Most striking of all Whitman's peculiarities, however, is the freedom of his style and metre. Discarding all literary references and borrowings, all conventional and ornamental poetic diction, and all regular measures, he wrote in a style which, though fluent and exuberant in imagery, was clear and direct. His typical poetic form is a long rhapsody in lines of a length and metre varying with the emotional mood and of a rhythm exquisitely corresponding to it. The predominating line is very long, of six, seven, or eight stresses, and an indetermined number of unstressed syllables; such long lines are occasionally varied by the insertion of very short lines. Whitman's work is by no means to be called "prose poetry" for it has a very marked poetic though unstandardized rhythm; and, although the logical connection of his thought is not always fully expressed, each poem, and indeed the whole work, has an organic unity of idea and sentiment. Although the frankness of some of Whitman's verse injured his reputation among the more Puritanic of his fellow-countrymen, his powers were early recognized by men of letters, including Emerson. They were eagerly read in English and French intellectual circles and have been highly influential in the development of twentieth-century verse, English and American.

LECTURES ON ART, see **ART, LECTURES ON,** by H. A. Taine.

LECTURES ON HEAT, see **HEAT, LECTURES ON,** by John Tyndall.

LED HORSE CLAIM, THE, by Mary Hallock Foote. The scene of this charming romance is laid in a Western mining-town. On opposite sides of the Led Horse Gulch are the two rival mining-camps, the Shoshone and the Led Horse. Cecil Conrath, lately come to join her brother, superintendent of the Shoshone camp, while wandering alone one morning, finds herself, to her dismay, on Led Horse ground, and face to face with Hilgard, superintendent of the rival camp. He is a handsome and fascinating man, and the two young people rapidly fall in love with each other, though they meet but seldom, on account of the animosity existing between the two mines. From sounds that reach him through the rock, Hilgard discovers that Conrath has secretly pushed his workings beyond the boundary line, and that the ore of which the Shoshone bins are full is taken from the Led Horse claim. The case is put into the hands of lawyers; but before anything can be done, Conrath makes an attempt to jump the Led Horse mine. Hilgard has been warned; and with his subordinate, West, awaits the attacking party at the passage of the drift. Shots are exchanged, and Conrath is killed, whether by Hilgard or West is unknown. Though Hilgard has done but his duty in defending his claim, Cecil cannot marry the possible murderer of her brother. He returns to New York, where he would have died of typhoid fever, had not Cecil and her aunt opportunely appeared at the same hotel to nurse him back to life. In spite of the disapproval of her family, the lovers are finally married. This book was published in 1883, and was read with great interest, as being one of the first descriptions of mining life in the West, as it remains one of the best.

LEE, GENERAL ROBERT E., RECOLLECTIONS AND LETTERS OF, by his son, Captain Robert E. Lee, was published in 1904. It is a pleasant, intimate record of the great Confederate general from the point of view of his family. In an informal and conversational style the author gives his recollections of his father beginning with the earliest, and intersperses them with extracts from his letters and a running account of the various incidents of his career. The book thus conveys in its quiet way a very fair idea of what Lee accomplished and an admirable picture of his private life and character. This narrative confirms the general impression of his manliness, nobility, and simple dignity. Particularly interesting is the account of his work as president of Washington College in Virginia and its contribution to the reconstruction of the South.

LEIGHTON COURT, by Henry Kingsley (1866). This book is an interesting story of English social life at the time of the Indian mutiny. Robert, the younger brother of Sir Harry Poynitz, masquerading as a master-of-hounds under the name of Hammersley, is engaged by Sir Charles Seckerton to take care of his pack. He falls in love with Laura Seckerton, and at last tells her of his attachment, when she urges him to leave the country. The next morning Hammersley's horse is discovered drowned on the sea-shore, and his master is supposed to have shared the same fate. Laura, believing him dead, accepts the hand of Lord Hatterleigh. The plot now concerns itself with gambling debts, family quarrels, and intrigues social and financial, tale-bearings, challenges, and sudden deaths. It moves rapidly, however, to a proper ending. The author calls the story "a simple tale of country life." The character of Hatterleigh, with his sterling worth hidden under a rather dull and effeminate exterior, is very cleverly drawn, as is also Sir Henry Poynitz, with his life of apparent villainy and final justification.

LEILA, by Antonio Fogazzaro, see **THE PATRIOT.**

LEISURE CLASS, see **THEORY OF THE.**

LEO THE TENTH, THE LIFE AND PONTIFICATE OF, by William Roscoe. (2 vols., 1868). This work is a natural sequel to its author's 'Life of Lorenzo de' Medici,' which made his reputation. It was translated into French (1808), German (1818), and Italian (1816–17). Though the Italian version, Count Bossi's, was placed on the Index Expurgatorius, 2800 copies were sold in Italy. The work was severely criticized by the Edinburgh Review for an affectation of profundity of philosophy and sentiment, and for being prejudiced against Luther. On the whole, however, it is one of the best works on one of the most fascinating and instructive periods of human history, containing not merely the biography of Leo but to a large extent the history of his time; describing not only Cæsar Borgia and Machiavelli, but Wolscy, Bayard, and Maximilian. It was the first adequate biography of Leo X.; and its attempt to prove him widely influential in the promotion of literature and the restoration of the fine arts, as well as in the general improvement of the human intellect that took place in his time, is certainly successful.

LEON ROCH (La Familia de León Roch) by B. Pérez Galdós (1878). This novel is a painful study of the struggle which is to-day taking place between dogma and modern scientific thought. The field of battle is the family of Leon Roch, a young scientist, married to Maria, the daughter of the Marquis de Telleria. Leon thinks he will have no trouble in molding the young girl, but finds soon after marriage that she expects to convert him. When he laughingly asks her how, she tears a scientific book from his hand and destroys it. Knowing that his wife's confessor is responsible for her conduct, he offers to forsake his scientific studies if she will leave Madrid and confine her churchgoing to Sundays. She refuses; but when he insists on a separation, she consents. The visit of her brother Luis, a religious fanatic, prevents its accomplishment; and his death places an insuperable barrier between husband and wife.

From this event the story moves rapidly to a sad ending.

LETTERS CONCERNING THE ENGLISH NATION, by Arouet de Voltaire (1733). These letters were written by Voltaire while on a visit to London to his friend Thiriot. Though very simple in style and diction, they are graced by a certain charm and by delicate touches which are a constant delight.

They might be divided into four main sections. The Quakers, Presbyterians, Episcopalians, and Unitarians occupy the first seven letters, and are subjected to the witty but not biting remarks of the French critic. The second division discusses the government of England as a whole. The philosophy of Locke and the science of Sir Isaac Newton, with an interesting letter on Inoculation, including its history and uses, can be classed together in the third division. To all lovers of English literature, and especially of Shakespeare, the fourth division is of much interest. In his remarks on the English drama, Voltaire says of Shakespeare, "He was natural and sublime, but had not so much as a single spark of good taste."

In speaking of religion, Voltaire says: "Is it not whimsical enough that Luther, Calvin, and Zuinglius, all of 'em wretched authors, should have founded sects which are now spread over a great part of Europe, when Sir Isaac Newton, Dr. Clark, John Locke, and Mr. Le Clerc, the greatest philosophers as well as the ablest writers, should scarce have been able to raise a small handful of followers?"

LETTERS FROM A CHINESE OFFICIAL ('Being an Eastern View of Western Civilization') is a brief series of essays contrasting Chinese and Western life to the strong advantage of the former.   Originally published anonymously in England in 1902 and in America in 1903, they attracted wide attention by the pungency of their criticism, the boldness of their accusation of modern civilization, and the piquancy of their concealed authorship.   It was at first generally believed that they were actual products of a Chinese visitor; but it afterwards transpired that the author was Mr. G. Lowes Dickinson, a brilliant English essayist.   Writing with reference to the European reprisals against China after the Boxer uprising, the supposed mandarin sets forth an explanation of Chinese hostility to the Western peoples by pointing out the fundamental distinction between the two civilizations.   In China the typical community is agricultural, economically self-sufficient, and stable, governed by strong family obligations; in England, the prevailing type of society is urban, dependent on trade for the necessities of life, impelled primarily by individual self-interest and the love of gain.   The typical Chinese is industrious, contented, appreciative of beauty, able to enjoy life; the typical Westerner is restless, dissatisfied, striving for greater wealth, concerned with the means of life rather than its enjoyment.   The Chinese religion is a simple belief in human brotherhood and the dignity of labor and it is actually practised.   The Christian religion is a glorification of the spiritual at the expense of the physical, elevating human love and brotherhood but condemning all other worldly interests, all violence, aggressiveness, and selfishness.   But the Western nations though professing this creed, always evade it in practical life; as witness their treatment of the Chinese after the Boxer outbreak.   The Chinese government is decentralized but stable, resting on immemorial custom and family loyalty; Western government is highly developed but constantly changing, often with the overthrow of long-established institutions.   Chinese art and literary culture aim at the appreciation of beauty in the ordinary relations of life.   Western art is commonplace, choked by materialistic science and commercialism.   For all these reasons the Chinese prefer their own civilization; and it was their resentment at the attempt to force on them a culture inferior, as they believed, to their own which caused the Boxer uprising and its cruel suppression by the Western powers.   This little book is most effectively written and may be accepted as a faithful representation of the point of view which it pretends to give at first hand.

LETTERS FROM EGYPT, LAST, of Lady Duff-Gordon, to which are added 'Letters from the Cape.' (1875).   These letters, which cover the period from 1862 to 1869, are written in a free and familiar vein, at once engaging and frank.   The descriptions of travels, adventures encountered, people met, and sights seen, are written to give friends at home a gossipy account of all her movements, and with no view to publication.   But Lady Gordon, as Lucy Austin, had begun in early childhood to write fascinating letters, and these were too good to be withheld from the public.   They touch upon an endless variety of topics, with the readiness of a mind quick to observe, trained by happy experience, and always sympathetic with the best.

LETTERS OF F. M. DOSTOEVSKY (1915).   These seventy-seven selected letters cover forty years.   The first letter, written to his father when Dostoevsky was seventeen, is a pitiful appeal for money. The humiliating struggle with poverty continues all his life to be topic of his correspondence. When he leaves the army at twenty-three, he writes to his brother that he is in danger of imprisonment because he has not money to buy civilian clothes. The letters to his brother tell of his omnivorous reading of European literature. At twenty-four the publication of his first novel 'Poor Folk' brings him fame and, for a time, fortune. The four years' exile to Siberia follows this extravagant and unproductive period. He writes to his brother a vivid account of the journey of the political prisoners to Siberia, and the tragic suffering of his life in prison. At thirty-eight he was permitted to return to European Russia, but was obliged to leave finally to escape his creditors. For ten years he wanders, ill and unhappy, in Germany, France, Italy, and Switzerland, writing to make money to pay his debts so that he may return to Russia. Dostoevsky cannot work, cannot think, cannot truly live except on Russian soil and in Russian atmosphere. His passion for Russia makes him despise the culture of Germany and France. The letters show that his antipathy to Turgeneff was due to the latter's affectation of contempt for Russian ideals and achievement. Russia is always his inspiration. A month before his death, he writes, "I hold all evil to be founded upon disbelief," "and maintain that he who abjures nationalism abjures faith also." "The national consciousness of Russia," he says, "is based on Christianity." "The inmost essence and ultimate destiny of the Russian nation is to reveal to the world her own Russian Christ." The last ten years of his life he spent in Russia, recognized as a genius and enjoying great popularity.

LETTERS OF HORACE WALPOLE, fourth Earl of Orford (1798), are among the most brilliantly written correspondence of the eighteenth century; and new editions, with added pages, continued to appear down to 1847. Enjoying the income of three sinecures secured to him through his father, the thrifty Sir Robert, the elegant Horace dawdles through a charming society life, dilating, for the pleasure of the pretty women and fashionable men whom he chooses to favor with his observations, on the butterfly world of trifles and triflers in which he flutters his fragile wings. A fascinating chronicle of small-talk it is, which this busy idle gentleman has bequeathed to later generations. His own hobbies and fancies, as he indulges them in his Gothic villa at Strawberry Hill, he dwells upon with an indulgent smile at his own weakness; and he praises or condemns, with equal mind, the latest fashions of Miss Chudleigh's ball, the American war, or his own love of scenery. Witty, lively, thoroughly cheery, are his descriptions of his environment. "Fiddles sing all through them," says Thackeray; "wax-lights, fine dresses, fine jokes, fine plate, fine equipages, glitter and sparkle there: never was such a brilliant, jigging, smirking Vanity Fair as that through which he leads us." Perfectly heartless, quite superior to emotion, these gossipy pages of the "most whimsical of triflers and the wittiest of fops" have never failed to delight the literary public of succeeding generations, which enjoys seeing the eighteenth century reflected in the mirror of a life long enough to stretch from Congreve to Carlyle.

LETTERS OF MADAME DE SÉVIGNÉ, THE, first published about thirty years after her death at La Haye in 1676, compose the most famous correspondence of the seventeenth century. Contained in fourteen stout volumes, their copiousness alone implies an atmosphere of leisure. Most of the letters were written to her only daughter, after that young lady married and went to her husband's estates in southern France. Here are the lively records of her daily interests and occupations at the

Hôtel Carnavalet in Paris, at Livry, or at her country seat, 'Les Rochers,' in Brittany. She is now a financier, cramping her income to meet the reckless obligations of her son; now a fervent devotee, working altar-cloths with her own hands, and ardently in sympathy with the school of Port Royal and the Jansenists; now a noted beauty at court or a brilliant wit among the "precious ones" at the Hôtel de Rambouillet; at all times a fine lady, resourceful, gracious, captivating. Her affection for her daughter vents itself in a thousand reiterations of her desire to have her again at Paris; while passages of delightful gossip, always amusing, often pathetic, crowd the pages. Among her other correspondents, Madame de Sévigné reckoned the Duc de Roche-foucauld and the famous literary twins, Madame de La Fayette and Madame de Scudéry, all of them her intimate friends. Essentially intellectual, familiar with Quintilian, Tacitus, and St. Augustine, she greatly admired Corneille, while she merely tolerated Racine, whose pathos left her unmoved. Yet so vivid was her imagination that where she could not feel, she divined; and her literary judgments are thoroughly appreciative. This imaginative force in a naturally reserved temperament gives an extraordinary value to the pictures which she has drawn of the society of her time, admirably faithful to all its aspects and employments in the country, the domestic circle, at the play, at the court, in the undertaking of momentous social and political reforms. The literary charm and vivacity of the letters, where she lets the pen "gallop away with the bridle on its neck," make them classic in a literature rich in famous letters.

LETTERS OF OBSCURE MEN, see **EPISTOLÆ OBSCURORUM VIRORUM.**

LETTERS OF PLINY, a collection of ten books of letters by Pliny the Younger, published between 97 and 109 A. D. For a synopsis of their contents and a critical estimate see the LIBRARY under 'Pliny the Younger.'

LETTERS OF ROBERT BROWNING AND ELIZABETH BARRETT BROWNING, 1845-1846, THE, were published by Robert Barrett Browning, son of the two poets, in 1899. The two volumes comprise all the letters that passed between Browning and Miss Barrett from their first acquaintance to their marriage, September 12, 1846, and clandestine departure for Italy. Since they were never separated thereafter no other letters are in existence. The circumstances of the correspondence were unusual and romantic. Miss Barrett was an invalid, confined to the house and subject to the whims of a selfish and eccentric father. She was the best-known woman poet of her day, and much more famous than Browning, whose work was appreciated only by a few. Each was greatly impressed by the poetry of the other, and he fell in love with her before they met. After some months' correspondence they were brought together through the good offices of a common friend, and Browning was thereafter a weekly visitor. In the letters, which are almost daily through the eighteen months of their courtship, we read their discussions of one another's poetry, their expression of intimate friendship rapidly growing into love, their playful contention in unselfish devotion, their expression of all that love has effected in transforming and enriching their lives. As the correspondence continues we note the difficulty caused by the father's irrational opposition to the match, the daughter's final determination to act without his consent, the marriage concealed from him for a time, and the arrangement for Elizabeth Browning's departure with her husband for Italy—a step which in spite of her father's predictions of disaster proved the foundation of health and happiness, though it was never forgiven. At the time of publication some controversy arose as to the propriety of giving these letters to the world. It should be noted that Browning left them to his son to use as he saw fit, and that therefore he could not have objected to the idea of their publication. Moreover, although the reader sometimes has a feeling that he is an eavesdropper in a conversation sacred to two persons only, this feeling disappears in his enthusiasm at witnessing the idealizing power of love in its noblest form. To destroy the record of the love of two such highly-gifted natures, whose love was itself a poem, would have been a wrong to the world.

LETTERS OF THOMAS GRAY, THE, published after his death by his friend Mason in 1775, constitute not the least brilliant title of this author to the fame of a great letter-writer, in a century of letter-writers. The letters contain a series of minute sketches of the poet's life, and afford an insight into the endless choosing and refining of his supersensitive taste. His daily noting of the direction of the wind, his chronological lists, his confession that he would like to lie upon his back for hours and read new romances by Marivaux and Crébillon, his careful annotations in books, alternate with discussions of his own theory of verse and of poetical language, or criticisms on his friends. A certain playfulness, as distinct from humor on the one hand as from wit on the other, gives these epistles an air of careless ease and cheerfulness quite unique and individual. Writing to Walpole, a martyr to the gout, he says: "The pain in your feet *I* can bear." Concerning the contemporary French he says: "Their atheism is a little too much, too shocking to be rejoiced at. . . . They were bad enough when they believed everything." The pregnant *obiter dicta*, "Froissart is the Herodotus of a barbarous age," and "Jeremy Taylor is the Shakespeare of divines," are well-known illustrations of his keen critical perception. These letters have held their own, since they appeared, as models of epistolary style, easy, unaffected, and brilliant.

LETTERS TO AN UNKNOWN, by Prosper Mérimée, was published after his death, in 1873, under the editorship of Taine. The *Inconnue* was Mademoiselle Jenny Dacquin, the daughter of a notary of Boulogne, whose friendship with Mérimée extended over nearly forty years. For some time after the publication of the letters her identity remained a mystery to the public, as it had been to Mérimée during the first nine years of their correspondence.

The letters have a double value. They throw light upon two complex types of modern character. They record subjective impressions of contemporary persons and events — impressions all the more valuable because of the rare individuality that received them. They reveal a man whose intellect was not in league with his heart; who was as fearful of the trickery of the emotions as the English are of "scenes"; a man of the world who had a secret liking for other-worldliness; a cynic who made his cynicism a veil for tenderness.

The woman is a more elusive personality. She knew the power of mystery, of silence, of contradiction. She preferred to keep friendship by carelessness, than to lose it by intensity. The letters begin before 1842, and continue until Mérimée's death in 1870. They touch lightly and surely upon every event of importance in political, literary, and social circles. Many are written from Paris; many from Cannes; some from London; some from the Château de Fontainebleau. They mention everybody, everything, yet in a spirit of detachment, of indifference, sometimes of weariness and irony: — "Bulwer's novel 'What will He Do with It?' appears to me senile to the last degree; nevertheless it contains some pretty scenes, and has a very good moral. As to the hero and heroine, they transcend in silliness the limits of romance." "The latest, but a colossal bore, has been 'Tannhäuser.' . . . The fact is, it is prodigious. I am convinced that I could write something similar if inspired by the scampering of my cat over the piano keys. . . . Beneath Madame de Metternich's box it was said by the wits that the Austrians were taking their revenge for Solferino." These extracts fairly illustrate the keen observation and good sayings of the 'Letters.'

LETTERS TO DEAD AUTHORS, by Andrew Lang (1886), are little essays in criticism, addressed in a spirit of gentle humor to the "dear, dead women" and men of whom they treat. The ninth, to Master Isaak Walton, begins: "Father Isaak — When I would be quiet and go angling, it is my custom to carry in my wallet thy pretty book, 'The Compleat Angler.' Here, methinks, if I find not trout I shall find content." The letter to Theocritus is heavy with the scent of roses and dew-drenched violets. The author's pagan sympathies lead him to inquire — "In the House of Hades, Theocritus, doth there dwell aught that is fair? and can the low light on the fields of Asphodel make thee forget thy Sicily? Does the poet remember Nycheia with her April eyes?" To Thackeray he says: "And whenever you speak in earnest, how magical, how rare, how lonely in our literature is the beauty of your sentences!" And to Dumas: "Than yours there has been no greater nor more kindly and beneficent force in modern letters." Each letter gives the serene compliments of the author to the author on what was really best in his work. Each letter is gay and unassuming, but under the nonchalance is the fine essence of criticism. An odor as of delicate wine pervades the volume, the fragrance of an oblation to the great Dead, by a lover of their work.

LETTERS TO HIS SON, by Philip Dormer Stanhope, Earl of Chesterfield (1774). These letters were not written for publication, but were intended by Chesterfield to aid in training his son and forming his character; and were first given to the public after the Earl's death. They are characterized by a mixture of frivolity and seriousness, justness and lightness. Begun when the boy was but seven years old, the earlier ones are filled with rudimentary instruction regarding history, mythology, and the use of good language; later follows what has been called "a charming course of worldly education," in which mingle philosophical truths, political sophistries, petty details regarding wearing apparel, and so on. Almost every page contains some happy observation or clever precept worthy to be remembered. Chesterfield endeavors to unite in his son the best qualities of the French and English nations; and provides him with "a learned Englishman every morning, and a French teacher every afternoon, and above all, the help of the fashionable world and good society." In the letters the useful and the agreeable are evenly blended. "Do not tell all, but do not tell a lie. The greatest fools are the greatest liars. For my part, I judge of the truth of a man by the extent of his intellect." "Knowledge may give weight, but accomplishments only give lustre; and many more people see, than weigh." "Most arts require long study and application; but the most useful art of all, that of pleasing, requires only the desire." The letters show evidences of the lax morality of the times; but are remarkable for choice of imagery, taste, urbanity, and graceful irony.

LETTRES DE FEMMES, by Marcel Prévost (1892) was succeeded in 1894 by 'Nouvelles Lettres de Femmes' in 1894 and 'Dernières Lettres de Femmes' in 1897. The letters are supposed to be written by women to each other, the correspondent thinking no one but the recipient will see the letter. They are entertaining and gracefully written composed at mahogany desks in boudoirs, and are always intimate revelations of character and mood. The subject is invariably the writer's love affairs with husband, lover, or both. They are witty and ironic. The author has been heralded as the "master of feminism." They are written from the French standpoint of morals and taste.

LETTRES PERSANES, LES ('Persian Letters'), by Montesquieu, were at first published anonymously in 1721. The book is a piquant satire on French society during the eighteenth century, its manners, customs, oddities, and absurdities being exposed through the medium of a wandering Persian, who happens to find himself in Paris. Usbek writes to his friends in the East and in Venice. The exchange of letters with his correspondent in the latter city has for its object to contrast two centres of European life with each other and with Ispahan, the centre of social life in Persia. But Montesquieu is not only a keen and delicate observer of the fashionable world, — some of his dissections of the beaux and belles of his time remind one of Thackeray — but he touches with firmness, though with tact and discretion, on a crowd of questions which his age was already proposing for solution: the relations of populations to governments, laws, and religion; the economic constitution of commerce; the proportion between crimes and their punishment; the codification of all the laws of the various provinces of France; liberty, equality, and religious toleration. These questions were particularly menacing at the time the author wrote, and the skill with which he stated them through the mouths of his Persians had something to do with their ultimate settlement. The portraits of different types in the 'Lettres,' sketched with apparent carelessness, would not be out of place in the gallery of La Bruyère; they are less austere, but they reveal more force and boldness. The work is, unfortunately, disfigured by many scenes that are grossly immoral; and this fact had as much to do with its extraordinary success as its pictures of ideal social virtues. Its mysterious and incomplete descriptions of Oriental voluptuousness delighted the profligates of the Regency. To the *philosophes* and skeptics of the time, also, the 'Lettres' showed that Montesquieu was one of themselves; and they were happy to have an opportunity of laughing at the Christian religion, while pretending to laugh at the Mohammedan. Still, if the objectionable portions of the 'Lettres Persanes' were removed, there would yet remain enough matter to furnish a volume at least as wise as Bacon's Essays, and far more witty.

LEVIATHAN, or 'The Matter, Form, and Power of a Commonwealth, Ecclesiastical and Civil,' a political and sociological treatise by Thomas Hobbes, published in 1651. The book was written in defence of monarchy but its arguments were based not on divine right but on natural law. After a psychological analysis of man as an individual, in which all his powers and faculties are traced to natural sources, Hobbes asserts that the natural state of man in society would be one of war — "a war of every man against every man." To avoid this anarchy the individual must yield up his rights to one supreme individual or body, the 'Leviathan,' which should have supreme power to dispose the state as it sees fit; and this absolutism in the state must extend also to the church. This conclusion pleased neither the Puritans, who had overthrown King Charles, nor the Royalists, who believed that all rightful governments were divinely established. In deriving the power of a sovereign from an agreement made by the people Hobbes placed the ultimate power in their hands and thus prepared the way for the 'Social Contract' theory of the eighteenth century,

32

and for the French Revolution. The 'Leviathan' is noteworthy in an age of long periods and elaborate displays of erudition for the directness, concentration, and business-like plainness of its style. In the history of English thought it marks an important stage in the progress of naturalistic views.

LIARS, THE, a comedy by Henry Arthur Jones (1901). Young and pretty Lady Jessica resents the neglect of her husband, Gilbert Nepean, and indulges in a desperate flirtation with a distinguished diplomat, Edward Falkner, who adores her. She has met her lover at the "Star and Garter" but their little dinner is interrupted by the arrival of her brother-in-law, who threatens to tell her husband of her indiscretion. Lady Jessica and her sister and her cousin Dolly invent an elaborate maze of lies to save the situation. The husbands and men friends are dragged unwillingly into the conspiracy. All seems to go well until the lover arrives and tells the wrong lie, and then the truth "with a vengeance." Lady Jessica, irritated at her husband's attitude, is ready to elope with her hero, but yields to the persuasion of the wise family friend, Sir Christopher, who points out to her the social inconvenience of liaisons on this particular planet. She becomes reconciled to her thoroughly frightened husband, and the unhappy lover departs for the wilds of Africa.

LIBERTY, ON, by John Stuart Mill (1858). A small work on individual freedom under social and political law. It had been planned and written as a short essay in 1854, and during the next three years it was enlarged into a volume, as the joint work of the author and his wife; but according to Mr. Mill's protestation, more her book than his. His own description of it is, that it is a philosophic text-book of this twofold principle: — (1) The importance, to man and society, of the existence of a large variety in types of character, the many different kinds of persons actually found where human nature develops all its possibilities; and (2) the further importance of giving full freedom of opinion and of development to individuals of every class and type. Mr. Mill thought he saw the possibility of democracy becoming a system of suppression of freedom, compulsion upon individuals to act and to think all in one way; a tyranny in fact of the populace, not less degrading to human nature and damaging to human progress than any of which mankind has broken the yoke. A reply to Mill's views was made by Sir J. F. Stephen in his 'Liberty, Fraternity, and Equality' (1874). Stephen attempted to so re-analyze and re-state the democratic ideas as to show that Mill's fears were needless.

LIFE AND ADVENTURES OF GUZMAN D'ALFARACHE, see **GUZMAN D' ALFARACHE.**

LIFE AND ADVENTURES OF JACK OF THE MILL, see **JACK OF THE MILL.**

LIFE AND DEATH OF RICHARD YEA-AND-NAY, THE, by Maurice Hewlett (1900). A historical romance of the third Crusade. The story purports to be written by the Abbot Milo, confessor and friend of Richard Cœur de Lion called Richard Yea-and-Nay by Bertran de Born, the troubadour, because of the strange self-contradictions that mark this masterful ruler, "torn by two natures," "sport of two fates," "the loved and loathed," "king and a beggar," "god and man." Jehane Saint-Pol is the beautiful girl he loves and wrongs. He renounced her saying Nay to his heart, but stole her back from before the altar of her marriage with another saying Nay to his head. He crowned her Countess of Anjou, but repudiated the marriage when he becomes king, to make Berengère his queen in order to have her dowry to make his crusade to the Holy Land. He refused to be husband to the queen and was faithful to Jehane to the end. Jehane sacrifices all for the man she loves. She becomes a wife in the harem of the Old Man of Musse as the price of Richard's life. Richard dies in Jehane's arms, the romantic hero of chivalry. The pageant of this feudal age is reproduced in brilliant pictures.

LIFE OF JESUS, see JESUS.

LIFE OF THE BEE, THE ('La Vie des Abeilles'), a literary description of the social life of bees, by Maurice Maeterlinck, was published in 1901. An English translation by Alfred Sutro, to whom the work was dedicated, appeared in 1902. The author is familiar with all the scientific literature of bees and is himself an experienced apiculturist, but in this book he aims to present the facts not in the arid manner of the matter-of-fact scientist or writer of practical directions but with such literary charm as to bring out the romantic, poetic, and picturesque aspects of the subject and to show its appeal to the scientific and philosophic imagination. This end he accomplishes without any sacrifice of scientific truth and accuracy, all of his details being precise and proven fact being sharply distinguished from "pathetic fallacy." A meditative preface, 'At the Threshold of the Hive,' discusses the literature, general outlines, and philosophic bearings of the subject. 'The Swarm' traces the life of a hive from early spring to the establishment of a new colony. 'The Foundation of the City' describes the construction of the new home and the functions of the queen, workers, and drones. 'The Young Queens' pictures the rivalry between the queens, the elder of whom destroy the younger unless restrained by the workers in the interest of new colonies, and the process of parthenogenesis by which the queen lays eggs which develop only male bees or drones. In 'The Nuptial Flight' is described the remarkable union of one male bee and the queen. It can take place only at the summit of a lofty flight, where the queen is overtaken by the strongest male; it is immediately followed by the death of the male; and it suffices to fecundate the queen for life, enabling her to lay thousands of eggs which produce males, females, and workers. 'The Massacre of the Males' shows how the drones, useless encumbrances after the fertilization of the queen, are ruthlessly killed by the workers; and how the bees hibernate. The last chapter, 'The Progress of the Species,' is devoted to a demonstration of the thesis that bees have not a mere mechanical instinct but an active intelligence and are capable of material and social progress. The whole book is an admirable union of scientific accuracy and literary grace.

LIFE ON THE LAGOONS, by Horatio F. Brown (1890). Beginning where Nature began to hint at Venice, Mr. Brown describes the peculiar topography of the region: the deltaed rivers flowing into the broad lagoon; the Lidi, or sandy islands, that separate the lagoon from the Adriatic, and guard the city for seven miles inland, from attack by war-fleet or storm; and the Porti, or five channels that lead from the lagoon to the sea. When the reader knows the natural geography of Venice as if he had seen it, he may pass on and behold what man has done with the site, since the year 452, when the inhabitants of the near mainland, fleeing before Attila the Hun, the scourge of God, took refuge on the unattractive islands, amid six miles of shoals and mud-banks and intricate winding channels. The descendants of these fugitives were the earliest Venetians, a hardy, independent race of fishermen, frugal and hardworking, little dreaming that their children's children would be merchant princes, rulers of the commercial world, or that the queen city of the Middle Ages should rise from their mud-banks. Mr. Brown gives a concise sketch of the history of Venice, from its early beginnings to the end of the Republic in 1797, when Napoleon was making his new map of Europe. These preliminaries gone through (but not to the reader's relief, for they are very interesting), he is free to play in the Venice of to-day, to see all its wonderful sights, and read its wonderful past as this is written in the ancient buildings and long-descended customs. He may behold it all, from the palace of the Doges to the painted sails of the bragozzi. The fishing boats, the gondolas, the ferries, the churches, the fisheries, the floods, the islands across the lagoon, the pictures, the palaces, the processions and regattas, and saints' days, all have their chapters in "this spirited and happy book," as Stevenson called it. All the beauty and fascination of the city, which is like no other city in the world, have been imprisoned in its pages; and the fortunate reader, though he may never have set foot in a gondola, is privileged to know and love it all.

LIFE ON THE MISSISSIPPI, by Mark Twain (1883), is in part an autobiographic account of the author's early life, during which he learned and practiced a pilot's profession on the river, wholly unconscious of the literary channels in which his later course would be steered. It is prefaced by a graphic description of the mighty Mississippi, its history, its discovery by La Salle and others, and its continuous and wonderful change of bed, so that "nearly the whole one thousand three hundred miles which La Salle floated down in his canoes is good solid ground now." He relates his boyish ambition to be a steamboat-man, and how he attained it. His descriptions of his training and experiences before he became a full-fledged pilot are as characteristic and unique in handling as is the subject itself, which covers a long-vanished phase of Western life. The second half of the book recounts a trip made by the author through the scenes of his youth for the purposes of the work and the acquirement of literary materials: he enumerates the changes in men, manners, and places, which the intervening twenty years have brought about, and intersperses the whole with many lively digressions and stories, comments upon foreign tourists (Captain Hall, Mrs. Trollope, Captain Marryat, Dickens, and others); Southern vendettas; a thumbnail story, probably the nucleus of 'Pudd'nhead Wilson'; 'Murel's Gang'; the "fraudulent penitent"; and others. The book is especially valuable as the author's personal record of an epoch in the country's growth which has now passed into history.

LIGHT OF ASIA, THE, by Sir Edwin Arnold (1878). 'The Light of Asia' is a poetic exposition in eight books of the Hindoo theology. "It was," the author says, "inspired by an abiding desire to aid in the better mutual knowledge of East and West." Through the medium of a devout Buddhist, Arnold presents the life of the young Gautama, living in princely joy, shielded from every care and pain. He develops the wistfully dreamy character of the young prince into the loftiness of the noble, loving Buddha, who "cast away the world to save the world." The religious teaching is merely indicated, because of the limitations of the laws of poetry and the sacrifice of philosophical details to dramatic effect.

The Buddha of Arnold teaches that the way to attain Nirvana, the highest desire of every soul, is through four truths. The first truth is Sorrow: "Life which ye prize is long-drawn agony." The second truth is Sorrow's Cause: "Grief springs of desire." The third truth is Sorrow's Ceasing. The fourth truth is the way, by an eightfold path, "To peace and refuge"; to Nirvana, the reward of him who vanquishes the ten great sins. Nirvana, according to the poet, is not annihilation. It is the calm sinless state reached, by the suppression of all fond desires, through an existence continually renewed according to the law of Karma. The poem, which was published in 1878, is rich in sensuous Oriental pictures and imagery. It has been translated into many languages, both European and Asiatic; and has done much to create an interest in the religion of Buddha.

In 1890 appeared 'The Light of the World,' written, it was said, to silence the criticism that Buddha was Christ under another name, and to show the essential differences in the teachings of the two. The story follows the historical life of Jesus. It is divided into five sections, each of which sets forth a special aspect of the divine life. Despite its Oriental setting, the character of Christ remains simple and dignified. Like its predecessor, the book quickly became a popular favorite.

LIGHT THAT FAILED, THE, by Rudyard Kipling, appeared in 1890, and was his first novel. It is a story of the love of Dick Heldar, a young artist, for Maisie, a pretty, piquant, but shallow girl, brought up with him as an orphan. Dick goes to the Soudan during the Gordon relief expedition, does illustrations for the English papers, gains a true friend in Torpenhow, a war correspondent; and winning success, returns to London to enjoy it. But a sword-cut on his head, received in the East, gradually brings on blindness; and he tries heroically to finish his masterpiece, a figure of Melancholia, before the darkness shuts down, — the scene in which he thus works against the physical disability which means ruin, being very effective. When blindness comes, he is too proud to let Maisie know; but Torpenhow fetches her, and she shows the essential weakness of her nature by not standing by him when he is down in the world. Heart-broken, he returns to the British army in the East, and is killed as he sits on a camel fully exposed to the enemy's fire, as he desired to be. The sketch of the early friendship and love of Dick and Maisie, the vivid scenes in the Soudan, the bohemian studio life in London, and the pathetic incidents of Heldar's misfortune, are portrayed with swift movement, sympathetic insight, and dramatic force. The relation between Dick and Torpenhow runs through the tale like a golden strand. The dénouement here described is that of the first version, and preferred by Kipling; in another version Maisie remains true to Dick, and the novel ends happily.

THE LIGHTNING CONDUCTOR, by C. N. and A. M. Williamson (1903). This is a lively and entertaining description of a tour through France and Italy in a motor car. The story is told in a series of letters emanating from the pens of the principal characters, namely Miss Molly Randolph and the Honorable John Winston. The former, a pretty and attractive American girl with a rich father, who provides her with an unlimited letter of credit, is traveling in Europe with her aunt, Miss Kedison, as chaperon. While in England Molly is inspired with the idea of possessing a motor car in which to tour through France, and buys a second-hand machine of Mr. Cecil Landstown, who gives her to understand that it is in fine condition. Delighted with her bargain, Molly provides her aunt and herself with automobile outfits, engages a chauffeur and sets forth on her travels. Her satisfaction, however, is but short-lived as the machine proves to be an utter failure and accidents and catastrophes follow each other in rapid succession. The chauffeur proves incompetent and disagreeable and finally goes off to purchase a new crank for the machine with a five-hundred-franc note and never returns. At this point the Honorable John Winston, who is touring the same country in his new "Napier," is strongly attracted by the "beauty in distress," and wishing to keep near her, offers his services as chauffeur and is accepted. Under the name of Brown he proves a most valuable and efficient guide and is dubbed the "Lightning Conductor" by his vivacious mistress. A Frenchman named Talleyrand comes upon the scene and in order to get Molly to continue her journey in his automobile sets fire to her machine and destroys it. His deed is discovered, he is dismissed by Molly, and Brown substitutes his beloved "Napier" which he claims his late master, Mr. Winston, is desirous of renting. After a series of exciting and entertaining adventures the dénouement finally comes, Brown's real identity is revealed, and Molly forgives his deception and listens favorably to his declaration of love.

LIGHTS AND SHADOWS OF SCOTTISH LIFE, by "Christopher North" (Professor John Wilson, author of 'Noctes Ambrosianæ'). First published in 1822 in book form, and dedicated to Sir Walter Scott. The stories deal with the deepest and the simplest passions of the soul, — such themes as the love of man and maid, of brother and sister, of husband and wife; death, loyal-heartedness, and betrayal; of the Lily of Liddesdale (the shepherdess lassie), and how she overcame the temptation to be false to her manly farmer lover and marry a lord; of the reconciliation of two brothers over their father's grave; of the death in childbirth of a beautiful wife; of the reconcilement of a deserted betrothed girl to her lover by the girl's friend, who was herself on the morrow about to become his bride. The tales resemble a little Hawthorne's 'Twice-Told Tales,' but a good deal more the recent beautiful Scottish stories of the 'Bonnie Briar Bush' and 'Margaret Ogilvy' variety, though devoid of the Scotch dialect of these latter. Artless tales they are, full of tenderest emotion and pathos, dealing with lowly but honest family life. A little of the melodramatic order, with just a suspicion of a taste for scarlet and the luxury of tears (as in the story of Little Nell in Dickens), and written in a florid high-flown diction. Yet admirably wholesome reading, especially for young people, who have always passionately loved them and cried over them. They give also fine pictures of Scotch rural scenery, — mountain, heath, river, snow-storm, the deep-mossed cottage with its garden of tulips and roses, the lark overhead, and within, the little pale-faced dying daughter. Such a story as 'Moss-Side' gives as sweet and quiet a picture as Burns's 'Cotter's Saturday Night.'

LIN McLEAN, by Owen Wister (1897). This volume contains six sketches and a short poem; and in each of them the "charming cowboy," as the Vassar girls call him, is the central figure. The scene is laid in Wyoming "in the happy days when it was a Territory with a future, instead of a State with a past." Lin McLean is a brave boy and a manly man, who does right from inherent goodness, not because he is afraid of the law; and he is successful, whether he is trying to rope a steer or win a sweetheart. He has his troubles, too, but rises above them all, his imperturbable good-nature being a ready ally. The chapters are sketches, primarily, for those who are tired of the pavements and brick walls of cities; the air breathes of summer, and the little cabin on Box Elder is like the shadow of a great rock in a weary land. The most noteworthy of these sketches is 'A Journey in Search of Christmas'; others are: 'How Lin McLean Went East'; 'The Winning of the Biscuit-Shooter'; 'Lin McLean's Honeymoon'; 'Separ's Vigilante'; and 'Destiny at Drybone.'

LINCOLN, ABRAHAM, by Lord Charnwood (1916), published in the Makers of the Nineteenth Century Series. This "first considered attempt by an Englishman to give a picture of Lincoln" is the most successful interpretation of his character yet presented. Its originality lies in the perspective view probably impossible to an American writer. Lord Charnwood is an admirer of Lincoln, whom he ranks as one of the greatest men of our time, but he depicts with full candor the crudities and faults in his hero. He describes the frontier life of which he was a product, his originality of mind and persistent self-training, and the gradual development of a rare character, and its adaption to great events and demands, until his leadership is recognized by his country and he bears "on his shoulders such a weight of care and pain as few other men have borne." Writing for English readers, the author summarizes American history and conditions in order to give background to the biography. The second chapter traces the growth of the American nation through Colonial days, the Revolution, and the War of 1812, and discusses the Missouri Compromise, and leaders, parties, and tendencies in Lincoln's youth. He dwells at length upon the Lincoln and Douglas debates which brought Lincoln into prominence. A later chapter is devoted to Secession, and the case of the South against the Union. The last half of the book is the history of the Civil War. He discusses English opinion at the time of the war, regretting the "powerlessness to comprehend another country and a self-sufficiency in judging it" and explains that the case of the North was not apprehended. England was actuated by a "sincere belief that the cause of the North was hopeless and that intervention . . . might prove the course of honest friendship to all America." The British working people were persistently on the side of the North. Aside from the politicians for and against the war, Darwin and Tennyson are known to have taken the Northern cause to heart. Dickens, who hated slavery and "who in 'Martin Chuzzlewit' had appealed, however bitterly, to the higher national spirit which he thought latent in America, now, when that spirit had at last and indeed asserted itself, gave way in his letters to nothing but hatred of the whole country." Lincoln's claim to universal interest Lord Charnwood believes is that "he elected to fight the war not so much to preserve the United States government as because he believed that the preservation of that government was necessary to the triumph of democracy." His greatest deed "was the keeping of the North together in an enterprise so arduous, and an enterprise for objects so confusedly related as the Union and freedom." "He had been able to free the slaves, partly because he would not hasten to this object at the sacrifice of what he thought a larger purpose." He wrote before his presidency, "As I would not be a slave so I would not be a master. This expresses my idea of democracy." Full credit is given to Lincoln's administrative genius in his conduct of affairs, his recognition of public opinion, and the necessity of trusting subordinates, his neglect of the lesser for the greater, and his inflexibility on essentials. Lord Charnwood includes war. strategy as one of the subjects on which Lincoln exercised a masterly guidance. His picture of Lincoln is a convincing portrait of a forceful and charming personality, and a great statesman.

LINCOLN, ABRAHAM, A HISTORY, by John G. Nicolay and John Hay, was first published serially in the Century Magazine between 1886 and 1890 and then in a ten-volume edition, in which certain chapters on military and political events omitted from the magazine were printed in full. The work is profusely illustrated with portraits of Lincoln and of his contemporaries and with a few photographs of scenes and documents connected with his life. The authors were private secretaries to Lincoln, and were intimately associated with him from a time previous to his election to the presidency until his death. They knew his correspondence, were acquainted with his problems and anxieties, and had daily intercourse with his advisers both political and military. They also had charge of all of Lincoln's private papers after his death and conducted the widest researches into the diaries and records of the period. From all these materials they constructed not only the standard biography of Lincoln but a history of the Civil War. Although there is some natural exaggeration of the dominating influence of Lincoln and a tendency to find his judgment unerring in every instance and to exhibit his colleagues at a corresponding disadvantage, the work is based on honest convictions and gives a fair, reliable, and picturesque view of the great events of the period. It is a significant comment on Lincoln's personality that his two most intimate associates should have devoted so many years after his death to the erecting of such a monument to his memory.

LINCOLN, ABRAHAM, THE LIFE OF, by Ida M. Tarbell. (2 vols., 1900. New edition, 1917). The material for Miss Tarbell's biography was first published in a series of articles in McClure's Magazine in 1895 and 1896, the result of an attempt made by the publishers and the author to secure reminiscences of Lincoln from his surviving contemporaries. The value of the work is that it is to some extent based on independent research and new material. An appendix of 200 pages gives a miscellaneous collection of hitherto unpublished speeches, letters, and telegrams. It is a popular detailed biography presenting in an attractive series of pictures the leader who won the love of the people. The story of his early life and development is traced in more detail than in any other biography. Miss Tarbell corrects the commonly accepted story of the extreme poverty and unusual hardship of his boyhood as compared with average pioneer conditions. While Lincoln spoke of his life in Indiana as "pretty pinching times," his description of his youth was that of a happy joyous boyhood. The pioneer life was rude, but the pioneers were independent, self-reliant citizens enduring temporary hardship to accomplish their work of settling the new country. Documents are presented which show his mother to have been of good family and his father something more than a shiftless "poor white." Lincoln had few books of his own but they were the best, and he once told a friend that he "read through every book he had ever heard of in that country for a circuit of fifty miles." One of the books he read and studied when he was eighteen was the Indiana Statutes, which began with the Declaration of Independence, and the Constitution. Lincoln said later, "I never had a feeling politically that did not spring from the sentiments embodied in the Declaration of Independence." The author tries to do away with the legend of miraculous growth which has gathered about his remarkable career. To the later life of the President little that is new is added. Anecdotes of his relations with his associates, with the soldiers and office-seekers, present a clear picture of the real Lincoln. The illustrations include portraits of Lincoln at different ages. The new edition adds a new chapter and a twenty-page preface summing up recent publications on Lincoln and the effect of this new knowledge on our conception of Lincoln. She says: "He is to-day our national touchstone as well as the source to which liberal statesmen of all lands look for the most perfect understanding and expression of the spirit and aims of democracy."

LINCOLN, ABRAHAM; THE TRUE STORY OF A GREAT LIFE, by William Henry Herndon. (Second edition, 1892). This biography of the "foremost American" covers his life from birth to death, being extremely full with regard to his origin and early days. These first chapters contain many things that have been severely criticized as trivial, misleading, or false in effect if not in intention. Mr. Herndon was for twenty years President Lincoln's intimate personal friend as well as his law partner, and had perhaps a closer knowledge of his character and idiosyncrasies than any other man. Feeling, as he himself says, that "' God's naked truth ' can never injure the fame of Abraham Lincoln, " he told what he thought to be the truth unreservedly — even unsparingly. One of Thackeray's objects in writing 'The Virginians' was to draw George Washington as he really was, with the glamour of historic idealization stripped away. Criticism objected to Mr. Herndon's book that it would go nigh to prevent the process of idealization altogether as to Lincoln. Yet throughout its minute and often trifling details, as throughout its larger generalities and syntheses, it is evident that the biographer loved his hero, and meant to do him full justice; and that whatever shortcomings the history presents are due to the fact that the historian lacked the quality of imagination, without whose aid no object can be seen in its true proportions.

LINNET, by Grant Allen (1900). This is a romance of the Tyrol and its scenery and people are described in a manner both effective and pleasing. Two young English tourists come to a little mountain village where they find the Tyrolese in all their native simplicity; the young men, with the pride and aspirations of the hunter, who dance wildly and make love fiercely, and the maidens of easy virtue who tend their cows in the summer and serve a master in the village through the long winter. One of these is Linnet, the heroine, an innocent, modest girl among her bold associates, who possesses a marvelous voice. Both tourists are charmed with the lovely singer, but while one is selfish and conceited and pays her meaningless compliments, the other, who is quiet and undemonstrative, really wins her love. His friend, however, being more wise in worldly affairs than himself, persuades him of the folly of his course, and takes him away from the place. Linnet has other lovers, among whom is the taciturn inn-keeper, who is a musician and travels with minstrel troupes of his own training, and who means to marry her as a matter of business. He takes Linnet with him on his next tour and while she is rapidly becoming famous she again meets her "Englander" and the love which began in the Tyrolese mountain again assumes its sway. The love story is told with much charm and grace, and when the scene changes to London the contrast in character and national traits between that city and the land of the Tyrol is strikingly shown.

LION OF FLANDERS, THE, by Hendrik Conscience (1838). In this Flemish historical romance, among the best he has written, the author deals with one of the most glorious episodes in his country's history; the expulsion of the armies of Philip le Bel in the thirteenth century from Flemish soil by a rising of the common people. His hero is Robert de Bethune, the "Lion of Flanders"; whose father, Guy de Dampierre, had incurred the enmity of his French suzerain by siding with the English king. The story opens with a stirring picture of the turbulence and fury of the Flemings on learning of the approach of the French army. Conscience shows in this novel that he was a close student of Sir Walter Scott. He has a thorough knowledge of the manners as well as of the history of the period in which its scenes are laid, and he has been entirely successful in giving a faithful and lifelike conception of Flanders in the thirteenth century.

LITERARY AND SOCIAL ESSAYS, by George William Curtis. The nine essays which compose this volume were collected from several sources, and published in book form in 1895. Written with all the exquisite finish, the lucidity and grace which characterized every utterance of Mr. Curtis, these essays are like an introduction into the actual presence of the gifted men of our century in whose splendid circle the author was himself at home. Emerson, Hawthorne, and the placid pastoral Concord of their homes, are the subjects of the first three chapters and are treated with the fine power of apt distinction, with the richness of rhetoric and the play of delicate humor, which those who heard Mr. Curtis remember, and those who know him only in his published works must recognize. To lovers of Emerson and Hawthorne these chapters will long be a delight, written as they were while the companionship of which they spoke was still warm and fresh in the author's memory.

Equally interesting and valuable as contributions to the biography of American letters are the chapters on Oliver Wendell Holmes, Washington Irving, and Long-fellow. Perhaps no one has given us more intimately suggestive portrait-sketches of the personalities of these familiar authors than are given in these collected essays. Particularly interesting to American readers are the occasional reminiscences of personal participation in scenes, grave or humorous, where the actors were all makers of history for New England. The book contains Mr. Curtis's brilliant essay on the famous actress Rachel, which appeared in Putnam's Magazine, 1855; a delightful sketch of Thackeray in America, from the same source; and a hitherto unpublished essay on Sir Philip Sidney, which is instinct with the author's enthusiasm for all that is strong and pure and truly gentle.

LITERARY HISTORY OF THE AMERICAN REVOLUTION, THE. Vol. i., 1763–1776; Vol. ii., 1776–1783. By Moses Coit Tyler (1897). A work of great research and accurate learning, presenting the inner history of the Revolution period, 1763–1783, as set forth in the writings of the two parties in the controversy of the time. The Loyalists or Tories, as well as the Revolutionists, are heard; and all forms of the literature of the time have been made use of, the lighter as well as the more serious, poetry as well as prose, and in fact everything illustrative of the thoughts and feelings of the people during the twenty years' struggle for independence. The care and thoroughness with which neglected persons and forgotten facts have been brought into the picture make the work not only very rich in interest, but an authority not likely to be displaced by future research. A conspicuous feature of the work, on which the author lays great stress, and which is likely to give it increasing interest with the lapse of time, is the pains taken to show that the Revolution ought not to have created an almost hopeless feud between America and England, and that a correct understanding of its history is calculated to do away with this feud. The fascination of Mr. Tyler's history is greatly heightened by its spirit of charity and fairness, and by his suggestions looking to complete future reconciliation between America and England.

LITERARY LANDMARKS OF LONDON, by Laurence Hutton (1887). The author has not attempted to make of this either a text-book or biographical dictionary. It is a work which appeals to those "who love and are familiar with Pepys and Johnson and Thackeray, and who wish to follow them to their homes and haunts in the metropolis, — not to those who need to be told who they were and what they have done." The sketches are arranged in alphabetical order, beginning with Addison and ending with Young; and the rank of the poet or writer is not determined by amount of space. For instance, Wordsworth and Herrick have assigned to them but a few lines, for they were not poets of brick and mortar; while whole pages are given to half-forgotten authors of one immortal song, who spent all their days in London.

Full indices, local as well as personal, enable the reader to find what appeals to him most in whatever part of the town he may be. He can walk with Johnson and Boswell from the Club in Gerard Street, and call on the way on Dryden, Waller, Lamb, or Evelyn; stop for refreshments at "Will's" or "Tom's" with Steele, or, in the church of St. Paul, Covent Garden, pray for the repose of the souls of Butler, Wycherley, and "Peter Pindar" who sleep within its gates. London has no associations more interesting than those connected with its literary men, and nothing of moment connected with their careers in the city has been omitted. It is plainly evident that the author's chief aim has been completeness and exactness.

LITERARY LAPSES, by Stephen Leacock (1910). A collection of humorous sketches: 'Boarding-House Geometry,' the postulates and axioms of this story are reprinted in THE LIBRARY; 'How to Live to be 200,' 'How to Avoid Getting Married,' 'Men who have Shaved me,' 'Insurance up to Date,' 'Borrowing a Match,' etc. One of the most amusing is 'My Financial Career,' the experience of a shy young man who decides to deposit his fifty dollars a month salary in a bank. In 'Number Fifty-Six' a Chinese laundryman, a second Sherlock Holmes, deducts the character and history of a man from study of his weekly wash, a logical biography but unfortunately absurdly mistaken. 'A New Pathology' takes up the powerful reaction of clothes on the wearer, and the diagnosis and treatment of such common diseases as "Contractio Pantalunæ; or Shortening of the Legs of the Trousers," the painful malady of growing youth, and "Inflatio Genu; or, Bagging of the Knees of the Trousers," in which "the patient shows an aversion to the standing posture." The author's advice to those who fear germs and bacilli is: "If one flies into your room, strike at it with your hat or with a towel. Hit it as hard as you can between the neck and the thorax. It will soon get sick of that." "A, B, and C" are the heroes of the "short stories of adventures and industry with the end omitted" we meet as John, William, and Henry in early chapters of the arithmetic, and who conceal their identity as X, Y, and Z later in problems of algebra. These delightful absurdities are the 'Literary Lapses' of a professor of economics.

LITERARY MOVEMENT IN FRANCE DURING THE NINETEENTH CENTURY, by Georges Pellissier (1889. Authorized English version, by Anne Garrison Brinton, 1897). A work which Brunetière pronounced upon its appearance not less the picture than the history, and at the same time the philosophy, of contemporary French literature. It is without doubt the best history of French achievement in letters during the last hundred years. The list of authors, sixty in number, whose works are used as examples of the literary movement, begins with Rousseau and Diderot, and embraces all the names that are of greatest interest for their relation to developments subsequent to the Revolution. The chief conceptions which have held sway in France, creating schools of literature, are carefully studied; and the examples in writers of various types are pictured with felicitous insight. After the classic period had lasted from the middle of the sixteenth century nearly two hundred and fifty years, Rousseau and Diderot became the precursors of the nineteenth century, its initiators in fact. Then Madame de Staël and Châteaubriand preside at its opening. The founders of Romanticism, modern French literature begins with them. There still lingered a school of pseudo-classicists, and then Victor Hugo brings in the full power of Romanticism. There is a renovation of language and of versification, and a wide development of lyric poetry. The culmination of Romanticism is in the new drama, and again it renews history and criticism, and creates the novel. But half a century brought the decadence of Romanticism; and Realism, essentially prosaic, a fruit of the scientific spirit, succeeded. Its evolution, its effect on poetry and criticism, and its illustration in the novel and the theatre are carefully traced.

LITERATURE, by Hermann Grimm (1886), is a collection of scholarly essays, upon half a dozen of the great figures of literature. The book has a peculiar interest for Americans in its two essays on Emerson, whose genius Professor Grimm was the first German to recognize. Even to-day Emerson has not a large hearing in Germany, — his style is different and his ideas strange to the whole tone of German thought; and thirty-five years ago, when Professor Grimm had just discovered him, and went about sounding his praises and persuading his friends to read him, he (Grimm) was considered slightly mad. He persisted, however, in considering Emerson as the most individual thinker the world has seen since Shakespeare.

In two illuminative papers, the author undertakes to explain the most brilliant figure of eighteenth-century letters, Voltaire. In 'France and Voltaire,' he traces, from the time of Louis XIII., the governing ideas of French life, and their expression in the great writers, Corneille, Racine, Molière, and the rest, till Voltaire came to give voice to the new feelings that were surging up in the hearts of the subjects of Louis the well-beloved. In 'Frederick the Great and Voltaire,' he chronicles the stormy friendship of the erratic German genius for the erratic French one. 'Frederick the Great and Macaulay' treats of Macaulay's essay on that monarch, and incidentally Macaulay's theory of history. Other essays are on Albert Dürer, the great pioneer of modern artists; on Bettina von Arnim, the girl-friend of Goethe; on Dante; and on the brothers Grimm, father and uncle of Hermann Grimm, and known everywhere as the compilers of 'Grimm's Fairy Tales.'

LITERATURE OF THE SOUTH OF EUROPE, HISTORICAL VIEW OF THE, by Jean Charles Léonard Sismondi. L. L. de Loménie, in the 'Galerie des Contemporains Illustres,' calls Sismondi "the most eminent historian of the nineteenth century in everything relating to the science of facts"; and George Ticknor says his brilliant 'Literature of Southern Europe' will always be read for the beauty of its style and the richness and wisdom of its reflections. He was a man of enormous erudition (published sixty-nine volumes), and made truth his idol, he says. He lived eighteen months in England and five or six years in Italy, accompanying Madame de Staël on two Italian tours. His portrait shows a face strikingly like that of our Washington Irving. He was born in Geneva in 1773, and in 1811 gave there the lectures out of which the books we are considering grew. The lectures were published in four volumes (Paris), in 1813. The work is a little feeble in parts, but as a whole strikingly original. He begins with a full account of the Troubadour literature and of the Trouvères, with copious illustrative citations; and discusses with ample learning the work of Dante, Boccaccio, Tasso, Petrarch, and Alfieri. Then he gives rich tableaux of Spanish and Portuguese literature, — 'The Cid,' Cervantes, Camoens, and others. In his treatment of Spanish literature, he did not have access to all the original authors, but depended largely on his predecessor, Bouterwek. But Ticknor gives him very high praise for wide research and breadth of view.

LITTLE BAREFOOT ('Barfüssele'). From the German of Berthold Auerbach (1856). This Black Forest peasant story relates with rustic simplicity how two children, Amrie and her brother Danie, are left orphans with their home broken up; and how, not understanding what death means, they wander back night after night to the deserted woodcutter's hut where they lived with their parents, and lifting the latch, call again and again: "Father, Mother." They are separated, and brought up as parish orphans, Amrie living with brown Mariann, an old woman who is called a witch, but who is kind to her. The dreamy, imaginative child passes her lonely days on the common as goose-girl; and to save her earnings for her little brother Danie, goes without shoes, thus winning the name of "Little Barefoot." An old friend of her mother who has married the richest farmer in the adjoining district offers to adopt her; but on Amrie's refusing to forsake her brother, she hangs a garnet necklace round the child's neck, and tells her if she is ever in need of a friend to come to Farmer Landfried's wife. Amrie is promoted to be maid in the family of the rich peasant Rudel, whose daughter Rose treats her with scorn; but one day Rudel's young daughter-in-law takes pity on the pretty Barefoot, and dresses her with her own hands for a village wedding. Here Amrie dances with a stranger, a handsome youth, who has ridden to the Feast on a fine white horse, and who chooses no partner but her. She has one day of perfect happiness, and is still dreaming of her unknown partner when she sees him riding up to Farmer Rudel's door, having been sent by his parents, the wealthy Landfrieds, to seek a bride. They wish him to marry Rudel's Rose; but the youth, on beholding again his pretty partner, has eyes only for her, and finding that Rose treats her cruelly, he comes to the rescue and carries her off on his white horse. When they approach his father's farm to which he is expected to bring a less humble bride, John's heart fails him; but the brave "Little Barefoot" goes before him, charms his old father with her artless sweetness and tact, and showing his mother the necklace she once gave her, appeals to the kindness of her dead mother's friend. So the old people's hearts are melted, and they give her a grand wedding. Danie is made head dairyman on the great farm; and when Amrie's first child comes, she is christened Barbara, but is always called by her father "Little Barefoot."

LITTLE DORRIT, by Charles Dickens, was published 1856–57, when the author's popularity was at its height. The plot is a slight one on which to hang more than fifty characters. The author began with the intention of emphasizing the fact that individuals brought together by chance, if only for an instant, continue henceforth to influence and to act and react upon one another. But this original motive is soon altogether forgotten in the multiplication of characters and the relation of their fortunes. The central idea is to portray the experiences of the Dorrit family, immured for many years on account of debt in the old Marshalsea Prison, and then unexpectedly restored to wealth and freedom. Having been pitiable in poverty, they become arrogant and contemptible in affluence. Amy, "Little Dorrit," alone remains pure, lovable, and self-denying. In her, Dickens embodies the best human qualities in a most beautiful and persuasive form. She enlists the love of Arthur Clennam, who meantime has had his own trials. Returning from India, after long absence, he finds his mother a religious fanatic, domineered over by the hypocritical old Flintwinch, and both preyed upon by the Mephistophelian Blandois, perhaps the most dastardly villain in the whole Dickens gallery. The complications, however, end happily for Arthur and Amy. The main attack of the book is aimed against official "red tape" as exemplified in the Barnacle family and the "Circumlocution Office." It also shows up Merdle the swindling banker, "Bar," "Bishop," and other types of "Society." The Meagleses are "practical" people with soft hearts; their daughter is married to and bullied by Henry Gowan, whose mother is a genteel pauper at Hampton Court. Other characters are Pancks the collector, "puffing

like a steam-engine," his hypocritical employer Casby, the humble and worthy
Plornishes, the love-blighted and epitaphic young John Chivery, and the wonderful
Mr. F.'s aunt with her explosive utterances.

LITTLE FADETTE ('La Petite Fadette'), a novel by George Sand, appeared
in 1848.

It is one of George Sand's short studies of peasant life, considered by many critics
her finest work, in which she embodied loving reminiscences of her childish days in
the province of Berry.   It is a poetic idyl, recounted with a simple precision which
places the reader vividly in the midst of the homely incidents and daily interests of
country life.

To Père and Mère Barbeau, living thriftily upon their little farm, arrive twin
boys whom they name Landry and Sylvain.   As the boys grow up, they show an
excessive fondness for each other, which their father fears may cause them sorrow.
So he decides to separate them by placing one at service with his neighbor, Père
Cailland.   Landry, the sturdier and more independent, chooses the harder lot of
leaving home.   He adapts himself to the change and is happy; while Sylvain, idle,
and petted by his mother, suffers from the separation and is jealous of his brother's
new friends.   Later the two brothers both love the same woman, little Fadette.
The plot centers itself in the outcome of this situation.

LITTLE MINISTER, THE, by J. M. Barrie. (1891).   A love story, the scene
of which is laid in the little Scotch weaving village of Thrums at about the
middle of the last century.   Aside from its intrinsic interest, there is much skilful
portrayal of the complexities of Scotch character, and much sympathy with the
homely lives of the poverty-stricken weavers, whose narrow creed may make them
cruel, but never dishonorable.   The hero, Gavin Dishart, is a boy preacher of twenty-
one, small of stature but great in authority, and given to innocent frolic in exuberant
moments.   Grouped about him are his people, who watch him with lynx-eyed vigilance, ready to adore, criticize, and interfere; while an all-pervasive influence is the
mother love and worship of "soft-faced" Margaret Dishart.

Across the narrow path of the Little Minister, and straight into his orthodox
life, dances Babbie the Egyptian, in a wild gipsy frock, with red rowans in her hair.
Against the persuasiveness of her beautiful eyes and her madcap pranks, even three
scathing sermons against Woman, preached by Gavin in self-defense, are of no avail;
and the reader follows with absorbed interest his romantic meetings with the reprehensible Babbie, and the gossip of the scandalized community.   The rapid unfolding
of the story reveals Babbie's sorrowful and unselfish renunciation of Gavin, and her
identity as the promised bride of Lord Rintoul, who is many years her senior.   A false
report of Gavin's death brings the lovers together again on the eve of Babbie's marriage.   Fearing pursuit, she consents to a hasty gipsy marriage with Gavin in the
woods; and the climax is reached when a flash of lightning reveals the ceremony to
Lord Rintoul, two stern elders of the Kirk, and Rob Dow, who is seeking to save the
Little Minister from his wrathful people by killing the Egyptian.   In the flood that
follows, the chief actors in this dramatic scene are scattered; but Gavin and Babbie,
after many adventures, are reunited, a deed of heroism on the part of the Little
Minister having reinstated him in the love of his people.

The story is recounted by Dominie Ogilvy, who is at last revealed as the father of
Gavin.   It is lighted by touches of quaint humor that soften what might otherwise
seem stern and forbidding in the picture.   An instance in point is that of Tibbie

Craik, who would be "fine pleased" with any bride that the minister might choose, because she "had a magenta silk, and so was jealous of no one."

In 1897 the book was dramatized, with a violent wrenching of the plot to meet dramatic necessities.

LITTLE RED RIDING-HOOD, see FAIRY TALES.

LITTLE RIVERS, by Rev. Henry Van Dyke, D.D. (1895), breathes the very spirit of wholesome pleasure.   The book is called a record of profitable idleness, and describes the author's wanderings with rod and line, exploring the Adirondack woods, canoeing along the silver streams of Canada to the music of the old French ballads sung by the guides, tramping the heathery moors of historic Scotland, following the fir-covered banks of the Austrian Traun, and trying casts in the clear green lakes of the Tyrol.   Dr. Van Dyke has heard of people who, like Wordsworth, feel a passion for the sea or the mountains; but for his part he would choose a river.   Like David's hart he pants for the water-brooks, and asks for nothing better than a quiet stream with shady banks, where trout are not too coy.   He loves nature with the love of a poet and a close observer; the love of a man whose busy working-life is spent among bricks and mortar, but who has a country heart.   When he was a little boy, he slipped away without leave one day, with a heavy old borrowed rod, and spent a long delightful afternoon in landing three tiny trout.   Soon afterwards he was made happy by a rod of his own, and began to ply the streams with a zest that has never since failed. The good sport, the free, irresponsible, out-door life, and the beauty of wild nature are the subject-matter of the volume.   Bird songs and falling waters are the music, and happy summer sunshine lights its pages.   There is, says the author, very little useful information to be found here, and no criticism of the universe, but only a chronicle of plain pleasures, and friendly observation of men and things.

LITTLE SHEPHERD OF KINGDOM COME, THE, by John Fox, Jr. (1903). This is a story of Kentucky and the Civil War.   It opens in the mountain region, where Chadwick Buford, a small boy of unknown antecedents, finds himself suddenly homeless through the death of the kind mountaineer and his wife, with whom he has lived.   His only possession is a fine shepherd dog named Jack to whom he is devotedly attached, and with him for a companion he starts out in search of an abiding place. After much weary tramping he arrives at the settlement of Kingdom Come, where he is taken in and made welcome by a family named Turner.   "Chad," as he is called, makes himself useful in tending the sheep and Jack shows his wonderful ability in that line.

In the household is a pretty little girl named Melissa, an adopted waif, who forms a warm attachment for Chad.   He goes to school and becomes the protégé of the schoolmaster, Caleb Hazel, who appreciates his sterling qualities.   While on a logging trip with the Turners and Hazel, Chad becomes separated from them and is left behind in the city of Lexington.

He falls into the hands of Major Buford who becomes interested in his namesake and takes him to his home.

There Chad becomes acquainted with the Deans, the Major's neighbors, and finds in Margaret, the daughter of the house, the ideal of his life.   He soon finds out that his unknown pedigree causes him to be shunned by his companions, and, heartbroken, he steals away from the Major's house, and returns to the Mountains.

Later the supposed blot upon his birth is removed.   He is proved the Major's kinsman, and returns to college and occupies his rightful position. He becomes engaged to Margaret, but with the opening of the Civil War feels that his duty is towards the Union and enlists in that Army, thereby estranging himself from both Margaret and the Major. His career during the war is one of brave deeds and generous actions, and he risks his life to save that of his enemy, Daniel Dean. Melissa makes a hazardous trip at night to warn Chad that his life is in danger, and dies later as a result of her exposure on that occasion. When peace is finally declared, Chad returns home a Major, all is forgiven, and he and Margaret are re-united.

LITTLE WOMEN, by Louisa M. Alcott (1868–69). A story of the daily home life of four girls in a New England family of half a century ago. The March family is the author's own family, and the "little women" are herself and her sisters. In the first chapter Jo, the heroine, is fifteen, a lovable tomboy, with ambition to be a writer. The oldest sister, pretty Meg, is sixteen and aspiring to be a young lady. Beth is a shy timid little girl of thirteen, the saint of the family. Golden-haired Amy, the youngest, tells her sisters that her ambition is to be a great artist and to overcome her selfishness. Their mother is "a stout motherly lady," with a "can I help you" look about her, whom the girls know is the most splendid woman in the world. The girls go to parties, and jolly picnics, act out Pilgrim Progress to make their work more interesting, and take turns reading aloud to irascible old Aunt March. There are tragedies as when the proud Amy is obliged by the teacher at school to open her desk and throw two dozen delicious pickle limes out of the window and have her hands slapped with a ruler. See this sad chapter quoted in the LIBRARY. Jo writes wonderful melodramas in her den in the attic when genius burns, and the 'Witches' Curse' is acted by the sisters to an admiring audience of girl friends. Their best friend is Laurie, the boy who lives with his grandfather in the great house next door. Meg becomes engaged to Laurie's tutor and the first wedding in the family is a great event. It is a disappointment to girl readers that Jo will not marry Laurie. He decides to go to Europe to forget her, and says good-bye to them all racing down the stairs "as if for his life," turning back to ask once more "Oh Jo, can't you?" but she sends him away. Gentle Beth grows more frail and Jo loses her best loved sister. Aunt March prefers Amy's politeness to Jo's blunt manners and independent spirit and invites Amy to go to Europe. Jo struggles along with her stories and goes to New York to try her literary wings. She intends to be the old maid of the family, but instead falls in love with a middle-aged German professor, a striking contrast to the polished boyish Laurie. Laurie meets Amy in Italy and consoles himself with her. The charm and wholesomeness of the story made it a prime favorite with the last generation and it remains one of the best juvenile books ever written.

LIVES OF THE ENGLISH POETS, by Samuel Johnson. The first four volumes of this once very popular work were published in 1779, the last six in 1781. Macaulay pronounced them the best of Samuel Johnson's works. The style is largely free from the ponderous lumbering sentences of most of his other works, the narratives entertaining and instructive, and the criticisms often just, yet sometimes grossly prejudiced. The volumes were small in size, but Johnson had intended to make his sketches much smaller. They had been ordered by forty of the best booksellers in London to be used as prefaces for a uniform edition of the English poets. Johnson was peculiarly qualified for the work, deriving his material largely from personal recollections. The publishers, it is said, made $25,000 or $30,000, while the writer got only $2,000. The MS. of the work he gave to Boswell, who gives us certain variorum readings.

Johnson himself thought the life of Cowley, the best, and Macaulay agrees with him. The account of Pope he wrote *con amore* said that it would be a thousand years before another man appeared who had Pope's power of versification. In the sketch of Milton the old Tory spoke with scorn and indignation of that patriot poet's Roundhead politics, calling him "an acrimonious, surly Republican" and "brutally insolent," and poured contempt on his 'Lycidas.' Such things as this, with his injustice to Gray, called down on his head a storm of wrath from the Whigs; which, however, failed to ruffle in the least the composure of the erudite old behemoth. It is amazing to read the names of "*the* English poets" in this collection. Who now ever hears of Rochester, Roscommon, Pomfret, Dorset, Stepney, Philips, Walsh, Smith, King, Sprat, Halifax, Garth, Hughes, Sheffield, Blackmore, Fenton, Granville, Tickell, Hammond, Somerville, Broome, Mallet, Duke, Denham, Lyttleton?

LIVES OF THE HUNTED, by Ernest Seton-Thompson, was published in 1901, and has added a companion volume to his former successful book, 'Wild Animals I Have Known.' It is a collection of eight short stories and each one bears its underlying message of the kinship between man and animals, and shows that the enduring interests and passions, mother love, pride, and the desire of liberty, are shared alike by all living creatures. Five of the stories relate to the four-footed race and three to the birds, and they are all vital with interest and display the author's keen observation and his sympathetic knowledge of his subject. In the snowy ranges of the Northwest, we are shown Krag, the mighty Kootenay ram, delighting in his strength and beauty, who at last falls victim to man's desire for "trophies of the chase." In the guarded forests of the Yellowstone Park we see little "Johnny Bear" borne down in his struggles for existence, and Chink, the trembling little pup, who rises to the heights of dog-like fidelity and courage. In the sage-brush deserts of New Mexico, we follow the Kangaroo rat to the fairylike labyrinths of his underground kingdom, or view the experiences of Coyotito. Mother Teal, guarding her helpless brood against the perils of the world, Randy, the busy little cock-sparrow, and the chickadees of the North woods, are all pictured in a way that cannot fail to impress the reader. This book, like its predecessor, strikes a note that is clear and forcible as well as appealing, and will do more to change one's attitude towards the dumb animals than protective and preventive legislation could ever have accomplished.

LIVES OF THE PAINTERS, by Giorgio Vasari, more fully 'Lives of the most excellent painters, sculptors, and architects' was published in 1550, and in a revised and enlarged edition in 1568. This work is our chief source of information concerning the artists of the Italian Renaissance. Its author was himself an accomplished painter and architect, a sympathetic yet discriminating critic, and an excellent stylist. He had wide acquaintance among artists and wrote of them with delight, though somewhat too ready to accept unverified statements and to neglect accuracy of detail. Browning knew the 'Lives' well and drew from them the materials for his 'Fra Lippo Lippi' and 'Andrea del Sarto.'

LIZA-DVORYANSKOE GNYEZDO ('Nest of Nobles'), by Ivan Turgeneff (1858. English translation 1869). The story of this gloomy novel is not easily analyzed, but a bare statement of the plot would run thus: Maria Dmitrievna Kalitine, a rich widow living in a Russian provincial town, has a beautiful daughter Liza, who is deeply religious. Vladimir Nikolaevich Panshin, who pays court to her, is a young man with charming manners and an easy flow of egotistical talk. Presently appears

33

Fedor Ivanovich Lavretsky, a distant cousin of Maria Dmitrievna, who is known to live unhappily with his wife. Between his father, a despotic, narrow-minded egotist, and his aunt Glafira, a harsh, fierce old woman, Lavretsky's bringing-up has been a strange and solitary one; and at the age of twenty-three he naturally falls in love with the first pretty girl he sees, — Varvara Pavlovna Korobine, — whom he marries. As she detests Russia, they finally settle in Paris where he discovers her faithlessness and leaves her. Maria Dmitrievna receives him cordially, and he becomes a frequent visitor to the house. Little by little he and Liza fall in love; and upon the complications that thus arise, the interest of the story is founded. The difficult situations are skillfully managed, and the reader cannot resent the sadness of the tale as needless, because it results inevitably from the conditions. Like all Turgeneff's books, the chief interest of 'Liza' lies in its study of character.

LOG-BOOK OF A FISHERMAN AND ZOOLOGIST, by Frank Buckland (1875). The chapters of this book were originally published as articles in the periodical Land and Water. They all have some bearing on zoölogy; and possess such titles as 'Exhibitions Outside the Cattle Show,' 'King Charles the First's Parrot,' 'Foot of Napoleon's Charger,' 'Fish at Great Grimsby Docks,' 'Singing Mice,' 'Experience of a Whitstable Diver,' 'The Woodpecker and the Bittern,' 'Reminiscences of Natural History in Scotland,' 'My Monkeys,' etc. The book is agreeable light reading; always entertaining, and often instructive. In the chapter on 'Horseflesh Dinner at the Langham Hotel,' the author's opposition to hippophagy is recorded; while the chapter on 'Dinner of American Game at the Langham Hotel' is duly appreciative. The account of a fight between a scorpion and a mouse, in which the mouse comes off victorious, is very curious. The essayist is a firm believer in the value of observation. He thinks the education of the present day is too much restricted to book-learning, taking quite too much for granted the authority of whatever ideas and opinions obtain the authenticity of print. Adults, even more than the young he thinks, should be not only trained to observe and impress exact images of objects on the memory, but to use their fingers in analyzing and drawing, and above all, in dissecting beasts, birds, and fishes, so as to understand their wonderful structure and mechanism. Few naturalists have united exact knowledge and minute observation with so agreeable a faculty of description.

LOKIS, by Prosper Mérimée (1868), is one of the strongest and most skillfully constructed of his works. The motive is the almost universal belief that human beings may be transformed into animals. A German professor and minister, commissioned to make a new translation of the Scriptures into the Zhmud language, is invited by a Lithuanian nobleman (Count Szémioth) to reside at his castle and use his valuable library during his labors.

The Count's mother, on the day of her marriage, had been carried off by a bear, and when rescued, found to be hopelessly insane, even the birth of her son having failed to restore her reason.

The Professor finds the Count an agreeable companion, but observes in him certain strange and often alarming characteristics. The Count is in love with a beautiful, witty, but rather frivolous young girl, Miss Julia Ivinska, and the Professor goes with him several times to visit her at Doughielly. At last their engagement is announced, and the Professor is recalled to the castle to perform the marriage ceremony.

The next morning the bride is found dead, and the Count has disappeared.

The whole trend of the story, the incidents and conversations, often seemingly irrelevant, the hinted peculiarities of the Count, all serve to point, as it were inexorably, at the inevitable conclusion that the man has at last undergone the terrible transformation and become a bear, after killing and partially eating his helpless victim.

The perfect simplicity and naturalness of the language, the realism of its romance, the grace and wit of the dialogue, and the consistency of the characters, — particularly of the Professor, who narrates the story with the utmost plausibility, — give it the effect of history. While the supernatural is the most dramatic quality of the story, every incident in it might nevertheless be explained scientifically.

LOMBARD STREET, 'A Description of the Money Market,' by Walter Bagehot, is a lucid exposition of the English banking system published in 1873. The Bank of England, the Private Banks, the Joint Stock Banks and the bill-brokers are considered in turn, the main features of the whole system explained, and the problems arising from them discussed. "Two fundamental ideas run through the whole of Mr. Bagehot's book, of which the first is this: that it is wrong, unjust, and dangerous that the whole banking reserve of the kingdom should be kept in one bank, the Banking Department of the Bank of England. He points out in detail how all the country banks of Great Britain keep their cash resources in some one of the London banks, and how all of these London banks keep *their* cash resources with the Bank of England, so that the reserve of notes in this one institution constitutes the fund which must meet a sudden demand from all parts of the kingdom. . . . While admitting, however, the grave defects of the one reserve system as practised in England, Mr. Bagehot frankly states that it is useless to hope for or advocate any change. He treats the adoption of a many reserve system as wholly impracticable . . . confining himself to the consideration of what should be the proper management of the single reserve in the Bank of England." (Gamaiel Bradford in North American Review, vol. cxix, October, 1874). The second fundamental idea is that in a time of panic it is the true policy of a reserve-holding bank to be liberal in granting loans and discounts and not to be too rigid in scrutinizing security. Only thus can public confidence be maintained; otherwise the impression that money cannot be obtained will create a rush for money. The book is an admirable and rare example of business ability and experience united with literary skill, economic insight and the gift of clarity in exposition.

LONDON, by Sir Walter Besant (1892, New ed. 1894), is a comprehensive survey of the metropolis of the modern world from the Roman days to those of George the Second. The material is of course well worn, but the skill of the writer's method and the freshness of his interest make it seem new. He begins his tale with the occupation of the Romans, who appreciating the value of the river Thames, picked out a dry hillock in the great stretches of marsh along the stream, and founded the town of Augusta, — an isolated spot in the midst of fen and forest. After the Roman evacuation of Britain, no more is heard of Augusta; the town having been deserted or destroyed. It was a new settlement in the old spot that rose again to prosperity as Lud's Town. From the sixth century onward, the city, though ravaged by plagues, and more often by fires, always its bane, has grown steadily in population, wealth, and importance. Roman, Saxon, Danish, Norman, Plantagenet, and at last English, it has always been a city of churches and palaces. Its burghers have always been free men. owning no lord but the king; and its mayors have rivaled great nobles in power and splendor. Dick Whittington may not have made his fortune by selling a cat; but it is certain that when, as mayor of London, he entertained King Henry V., he burned £60,000 worth of royal bonds, as a little attention to royalty. The city's greatest mayor was Sir Thomas Gresham, who, in Elizabeth's Day, conceived the idea of transferring the center of the world's commerce from Antwerp to London, and to that end built the Royal Exchange. The record of each century is full of incident, story, and social changes. Mr. Besant is writing on a subject he loves, and spares no pains to lay before the reader a brilliant picture of the streets and buildings, businesses, customs, and amusements of the ever-flourishing, ever-changing city, now the great center of the financial, economical, and social world.

LONDON, see **LITERARY LANDMARKS OF,** by Laurence Hutton.

LONDON SOCIAL LIFE, see **IMPRESSIONS OF,** by E. S. Nadal.

LONELY WAY, THE ('Der einsame Weg') by Arthur Schnitzler (1904). The theme of the play is the inevitable emptiness and loneliness of lives devoted wholly to self-indulgence without regard to the welfare or suffering of others. In a succession of quiet conversations the characters reveal themselves and their relations to each other, which make the situation a tragedy. A young art student, Wegrath, takes his friend, Julian Fichtner, to visit his betrothed, Gabrielle. The fascinating Julian falls in love with her, and they plan to elope a week before the wedding. The night before they are to leave together, Julian decides that he wishes to be free from the ties and duties which marriage brings, and he deserts her. She marries Wegrath, who becomes a professor of art and president of the Academy. The oldest of her two children Felix, is Julian's son. The play opens just before Gabrielle's death when Philip is twenty-three. Julian has drifted about in pursuit of pleasure and has not fulfilled the great promise of his early years. His hope of solving the problem of the "lonely way" is to claim the love and companionship of his son Felix. Felix turns from him to the father he has always known and loved as his own. Von Sala, a middle-aged dramatic poet, who like Julian has lived for himself, disregarding human ties, points out to Julian that he had acquired no right of possession in Felix. He defines love as service. For those who will not serve, there lies ahead the "lonely way." The lonely are "their kind" who are free because they have never belonged to anyone but themselves. Johanna, the sister of Felix, loves Von Sala, and he commits suicide when he learns she has drowned herself for his sake. The characters of the two egoists, Julian and Von Sala, are brilliantly and consistently drawn.

LONG ROLL, THE, by Mary Johnston (1911). This is the first of two books dealing with the Civil War, and opens out before the secession has taken place. The scene is laid in Virginia and the opening chapters show how generally opposed the people are to war and how they hope for the preservation of the Union. When war is declared, however, all the loyal Virginians put their state first, and enter upon the great struggle. The book contains many stirring descriptions of battles and skirmishes and shows the sufferings of the soldiers and of those left behind. The family of General Warwick Cary figure prominently in the story and he and his son Edward are among the first to volunteer. There are three daughters the most beautiful of whom is Judith, whose romance is shadowed by the sadness of war. She has two suitors, Richard Cleave and Maury Stafford; the former is the chosen one, while the latter filled with jealous rage vows vengeance on his rival. Both men are officers in the Confederate army and during the conflict the moment comes when Stafford can gratify his evil desire. He is given a message by General Stonewall Jackson to convey to Colonel Cleave and he changes the order in such a manner that Cleave commits a great indiscretion which results in disaster to his troops. He is court-martialed, found guilty of disobedience to orders, and dismissed from the Army, a disgraced man. Though innocent of wrong-doing Cleave is unable to clear himself, as the man to whom Stafford gave the message to deliver verbally to him is dead. However, desirous of doing his duty against all odds Cleave changes his name and enlists as a gunner in the Artillery. Here he does notable service and is finally recognized by General Stonewall Jackson who has an explanation with him which clears up much that has been mysterious. The next day Jackson is shot in battle and subsequently dies, but before his death requests that Richard Cleave be given another trial. The story ends with the description of the funeral of Stonewall Jackson, the eccentric but beloved soldier, and the reader is convinced that Cleave's innocence will soon be acknowledged and that the faithful and devoted Judith who has been nursing the sick and wounded in the hospitals, will have her patience and loyalty rewarded.

LOOKING BACKWARD (1888), and **EQUALITY** (1897) by Edward Bellamy. Bellamy's nationalistic romance, or vagary, 'Looking Backward,' has had a sale of nearly 400,000 copies in ten years, and is still in demand. It recounts the strange experiences of Julian West, a wealthy young Bostonian, born in 1857, a favorite in the highest social circles, engaged to a beautiful and accomplished lady, Miss Edith Bartlett. West has an elegantly furnished subterranean apartment, where he is accustomed to retire for privacy and rest. In 1887 he is put into a hypnotic sleep.

In the year 2000, Dr. Leete, a retired physician, is conducting excavations in his garden, when West's chamber is disclosed. The doctor, assisted by his daughter Edith, discovers and resuscitates the young man, who finds himself in a regenerated world.

The changed appearance of the city, the absence of buying and selling, the system of credits, the method of exchanges between nations, the regulation of employment by means of guilds, all overwhelm him with surprise.

He notes no distinctions of rich and poor, no poverty, no want, no crime. All the people are mustered into an industrial army at the age of 21, and mustered out at 45.

The national system of dining-rooms, the condition of literary men, the abolition of middlemen, the saving of waste through misdirected energy, matters of religion, of love, of marriage, all open up lines of thought and of action new and strange to him; and falling in love with Edith, he finds he has fixed his affections upon the great-granddaughter of his old love, Edith Bartlett.

He falls asleep, and seems awake and finds himself back again in the old Boston with its monopolies and trusts and the frenzied folly of its competitive system, with its contrasts of living and its woe, with all its boundless squalor and wretchedness. He dines with his old companions, and endeavors to interest them in regenerating the world by well-planned coöperative schemes. They denounce him as a pestilent fellow and an anarchist, and he is driven out by them. He awakes from this troubled dream to find himself in harmony with the new conditions; and here 'Equality' takes up the story, and through the explanations of Dr. Leete and Edith, and through his own experiences, he learns how the crude ideals of the nineteenth century were realized in the year 2000.

The first step is substituting democracy for monarchy. To establish public schools is next, since public education is policy for the public welfare. It is further urged that each citizen be intrusted with a share of the public wealth, in the interests of good government. He will then no longer be a champion of a part against the rest, but will become a guardian of the whole.

Life is recognized as the basis of the right of property, since inequality of wealth destroys liberty — private capital being stolen from the public fund. Equality of the sexes is permitted in all occupations; even the costumes are similar, fashion having been dethroned.

The profit system is denounced as "economic suicide," because it nullifies the benefits of common interests, is hostile to commerce, and largely diminishes the value of inventions.

There is a common religion (based upon the doctrine of love); the old sects are abolished. "If we love one another, God dwelleth in us," is the keynote of the new dispensation.

There are no more wars; "Old Glory" now betokens that nowhere in the land it floats over is there found a human being oppressed or suffering any want that human aid can relieve.

Though written in form of a novel the author intended it "in all seriousness, as a forecast, in accordance with the principles of evolution, of the next stage in the industrial and social development of humanity," especially in the United States. He believes that the Golden Age lies before us and not behind us and is not far away. A number of clubs are devoted to achievement of the social and economic system advocated in this book.

LORD JIM, a romance by Joseph Conrad (1915). A promising young Englishman, son of a clergyman, becomes chief mate of the "Patua" before he has been tested by experience of the hardships of life at sea. He dreams of heroic deeds, but when the real crisis comes, panic seizes him, and he deserts the sinking ship with the other officers, leaving the eight hundred sleeping pilgrim passengers to their fate. The ship, by some miracle, keeps afloat, and is towed into Suez by a French man-of-war, and its officers are disgraced. The issue of Jim's honor is for him beyond the decision of any court of inquiry. Another chance must come to let him prove himself the hero of his romantic imagination. He tries to make a fresh start, but the wretched story follows him everywhere. Finally he accepts the position of trader in a remote Malay village, where as adviser, practically chief, he is loved, trusted, and admired by a savage tribe. By courage and self-sacrifice, he feels he has mastered his fate, and atoned for his moment of cowardice. Unfortunately his people endow him with supernatural power. He allows a band of pirates to go free after an attack on the village. They abuse his safe conduct, and kill the young son of Chief Dorian, his own closest friend. Instantly his prestige is gone. He is regarded as a devil who has brought about this dire misfortune. He refuses to fight for his life, leaves the girl he loves, and gives himself up to be shot by the aged Dorian. Descriptions of the calm moonlight night on the tropic sea in the "Patua" are quoted in the LIBRARY from the second and third chapters.

LORD ORMONT AND HIS AMINTA, by George Meredith (1894). In this novel the author deals with a weighty social question with a light and graceful touch.

Lord Ormont, a distinguished general, is the object of the hero-worship of two children: Aminta Farrell, called "Browny," and Matey Weyburn. When Aminta becomes a young lady, she marries Ormont, no longer a hero, but a mere civilian dismissed from his country's service, and soured by public neglect. To show the world how he despises its opinion, he refuses openly to acknowledge his marriage to

Aminta. She, of course, is the chief sufferer from this perversity of humor. Weyburn meantime becomes Lord Ormont's secretary, falls in love with his old playmate, and does not conceal his love. The ensuing scandal is less tragic than humorous. Matey and Browny betake themselves to the Continent; and, contrary to all precepts of conventional morality, "live happily ever afterwards." The novel is at once sprightly and judiciously sober. It is remarkable for one or two magnificent scenes, scarcely surpassed in the whole range of fiction. Nothing could be more beautiful and effective as a study of sky and sea, of light and air and out-door glory, than the scene where Aminta and Weyburn swim in the ocean together, creatures for the time being of nature, of love, and of joy.

LORNA DOONE: A Romance of Exmoor (1869), by R. D. Blackmore, is its author's best known work; and is remarkable for its exquisite reproduction of the style of the period it describes. "To a Devonshire man it is as good as clotted cream, almost," has been said of it; and it is Blackmore's special pride that as a native he has "satisfied natives with their home scenery, people, life, and language." But the popularity of the brilliant romance has not been local, and has been equally great on both sides of the Atlantic. Even without so swift a succession of exciting incident, the unhackneyed style, abounding in fresh simile, with its poetic appreciation of "the fairest county in England," combined with homely realism, would make it delightful reading. Much as Hardy acquaints us with Wessex, Blackmore impresses Exmoor upon us, with a comprehensive "Englishness" of setting and character. It is out-of-door England, with swift streams, treacherous bogs, dangerous cliffs, and free winds across the moors. The story is founded on legends concerning the robber Doones, a fierce band of aristocratic outlaws, who in revenge for wrongs done them by the government, lived by plundering the country-side. Regarding their neighbors as ignoble churls and their legitimate prey, they robbed and murdered them at will. John Ridd, when a lad of fourteen, falls into their valley by chance one day, and is saved from capture by Lorna Doone, the fairest, daintiest child he has ever seen. When he is twenty-one, and the tallest and stoutest youth on Exmoor, "great John Ridd" seeks Lorna again. He hates the Doones who killed his father, but he loves beautiful innocent Lorna; and becomes her protector against the fierce men among whom she lives. If slow to think, he is quick to act; if "plain and unlettered," he is brave and noble: and Lorna welcomes his placid strength. Scattered through the swift narration, certain scenes, such as Lorna's escape to the farm, a tussle with the Doones, the attempted murder in church, the final duel with Carver Doone, and others, stand out as great and glowing pictures.

LOST MANUSCRIPT, THE ('Die verlorene Handschrift') by Gustav Freytag (1865). The scene of this strong and delightful story is laid in Germany towards the middle of this century. A young but very learned philologist, Professor Felix Werner, goes with his friend Fritz Halm, also a learned man, in search of a lost manuscript of Tacitus, to the castle of Bielstein, near Rossau, where he supposed it to have been hidden by the monks in the sixteenth century. Though the quest is for the moment fruitless as regards the manuscript, the professor finds in Ilse, the beautiful fair-haired daughter of the proprietor of the castle, a high-minded and noble woman. He brings her home as his wife. Werner is professor at the university; and Ilse, though brought up among such different surroundings, adapts herself readily to her new life, and becomes very popular among her husband's colleagues and with the students. The reigning sovereign, hearing of Ilse's charms, invites the professor to pass, with his wife, some weeks at the palace; offering, as an inducement, all the aid in his power towards finding the missing manuscript. The invitation is accepted, and all at first goes well. Ilse is not long, however, in perceiving that while her husband is treated with marked distinction, she is shunned by the ladies of the court, the sovereign alone singling her out by his too marked attentions. Her position is equivocal. Werner, however, intent only upon his manuscript, is blind to the danger of his wife. During a temporary absence of her husband, Ilse, to save her honor, escapes to Bielstein. The professor, returning, misses his wife, and follows her in hot haste, and they are happily reunited. All hope of finding the manuscript proves vain, and the professor realizes with remorse that while pursuing this wild quest, he has risked losing what was dearest to him. The book is lightened by a humorous account of the hostility between two rival hat-makers: Herr Hummel, the professor's landlord, and Herr Halm, the father of Fritz Halm, who lives directly opposite. There is a subordinate love affair between Fritz Halm and Laura Hummel, the son and daughter of the rival houses, ending in marriage. The story, if not the most brilliant of Freytag's telling, is yet graphic and entertaining, and is a great favorite in Germany.

LOST SIR MASSINGBERD, by James Payn (1864). This novel, generally considered the best of this indefatigable novelist's stories, was one of the earliest. It is a modern tale of English country life, told with freedom, humor, and a certain good-natured cynicism. A bare synopsis, conveying no idea of the interest of the book, would run as follows: Sir Massingberd Heath neither feared God nor regarded man. His property was entailed, the next heir being his nephew Marmaduke, whom he tries to murder in order to sell the estates. Marmaduke is befriended by Harvey Gerald and his daughter Lucy, falls in love with Lucy, and finally marries her. Sir Massingberd in his youth secretly married a gipsy, whom he drove mad with his cruelty. She curses him: "May he perish, inch by inch, within reach of aid that shall not come." Sir Massingberd disappears, and all search for him in vain; many months later his bones are found in an old tree, known as the Wolsey Oak. It was supposed that he climbed the tree to look about for poachers, that the rotton wood gave way, and he slipped into the hollow trunk, whence he could not escape. Had he not closed up the public path which skirted the tree, his cries for help must have been heard. With his disappearance and death all goes well with the households on which the blight of his evil spirit had fallen, and the story ends happily.

LOTHAIR, by Benjamin Disraeli, Lord Beaconsfield (1870). The scene of this extravagant, but at the same time remarkable, story is laid chiefly in England about 1570, at the time when it was published.

The hero, Lothair, a young nobleman of wide estates and great wealth, is introduced a short time before the attainment of his majority. Brought up under the influence of his uncle, Lord Culloden, "a member of the Free Kirk," he has been surrounded by a Protestant atmosphere. When, in accordance with his father's will, he goes to Oxford to complete his education, his other guardian, Cardinal Grandison, determines to bring him into the Roman Church.

The story is a graphic description of the struggles of rival ecclesiastics, statesmen, and leaders of society to secure the adherence of the young nobleman.

On a visit to the ducal seat of Brentham, the home of Lothair's college friend Bertram, he falls in love with Bertram's sister, Lady Corisande, and asks for her hand, but is refused by her mother.

Lothair next comes under the influence of Lord and Lady St. Jerome, and Miss

Arundel. Charmed with the beauty and peace of their life, he is almost won over to the Romanist side. At the critical moment he meets Theodora, the wife of Colonel Campian, an American, "a gentleman, not a Yankee; a gentleman of the South, who has no property but land." Theodora is an Italian but not a Romanist, and the scale is turned toward the Protestant side. Colonel and Mrs. Campian are friends of Garibaldi; and through them Lothair is inspired to join the campaign of 1867 against the papal forces. He is severely wounded at Mentana, and is nursed back to health by Miss Arundel, who by degrees re-establishes her influence over him. Again he is saved by Theodora, who appears to him in a vision and reminds him of the promise given to her on her death-bed, that he will never join the church of Rome.

By a desperate effort, Lothair escapes the vigilance of his Romanist friends, and after travels in the East returns to London.

A second visit to Brentham renews his deep admiration for Lady Corisande, whose love he succeeds in winning.

The narrative of 'Lothair' never lags or lacks movement. The intervals between the adventures are filled with witty sketches of English society and portraits of English personalities. The character of Lord St. Aldegonde is perhaps the happiest of these. "When St. Aldegonde was serious, his influence over men was powerful." He held extreme opinions on political affairs. "He was opposed to all privilege and to all orders of men except dukes, who were a necessity. He was also strongly in favor of the equal division of all property except land. Liberty depended on land, and the greater the land-owners the greater the liberty of a country." "St. Aldegonde had married for love, but he was strongly in favor of woman's rights and their extremest consequences."

LOVE EPISODE, A, see ROUGON-MACQUART.

LOVE ME LITTLE, LOVE ME LONG (1857). In this story, Charles Reade turned away from his wonted exposition of social abuses to write a love story, pure and simple. It is a pleasant study of upper middle-class English life. Lucy Fountain, a young heiress, has two guardians, — her uncle Mr. Fountain, and Mr. Bazalgette, the husband of her mother's half-sister; and she divides the year between their two homes. She is pretty, charming, and useful; and both Uncle Fountain and Aunt Bazalgette want to establish her close at hand by choosing a husband for her. But Lucy is indifferent both to Mr. Hardy, the banker selected by her aunt, and Mr. Talboys, the man of ancient lineage who is favored by her uncle. She falls in love with David Dodd, a manly young sailor in the merchant service, who loves her, but who recognizes her social superiority, while he is forced to admit that his Lucy is freakish, — now kind, now cold. To escape importunity at home, she runs away and stays with her old nurse, where David discovers and wins her. They have a few blissful weeks together before David sails on the Rajah, of which through Lucy's influence he has been made captain. The story is simple, but full of homely incident, clever dialogue, shrewd character-drawing, and overflowing humor. With its sequel, 'Very Hard Cash,' it is considered among the best of Reade's novels. Lucy herself is the type of woman oftenest drawn by Reade, — pretty, emotional, noble at heart, but given to coquettish deceits and uncertain moods, until steadied by love.

LOVEL, THE WIDOWER, by W. M. Thackeray (1860). One of the great master's later books, written after his first visit to America, this simple story touches, perhaps, a narrower range of emotion than some of his more famous novels; but within its own limits, it shows the same power of characterization, the same insight into motive, the same intolerance of sham and pharisaism, the same tenderness towards the simple and the weak, that mark Thackeray's more elaborate work. Frederic Lovel has married Cecilia Baker, who dies eight years later, leaving two children, the little prig Cecilia and Popham. Their governess, Elizabeth Prior, wins the affection of the doctor, the butler, and the bachelor friend who visits Mr. Lovel and tells the story. Lady Baker's son Clarence, a drunken reprobate, reveals the fact that Miss Prior was once a ballet-dancer (forced to this toil in order to support her family). Lady Baker orders her out of the house; Lovell comes home in the midst of the uproar, and chivalrously offers her his heart and hand, which she accepts, and he ceases to be Lovel the Widower. Lady Baker, his tyrannical mother-in-law, has become immortal.

LOVE'S LABOUR'S LOST is one of Shakespeare's early dramatic productions, written about 1588 or '89, and has all the marks of immature style; yet its repartees and witticisms give it a sprightly cast, and its constant good-humor and good-nature make it readable. The plot, as far as is known, is Shakespeare's own. There is an air of unreality about it, as if all the characters had eaten of the insane root, or were at least light-headed with champagne. Incessant are their quick venues of wit, — "snip, snap, quick, and home." In a nutshell, the play is a satire of utopias, of all thwarting of natural instincts. Ferdinand, King of Navarre, and his three associate lords, Biron, Dumain, and Longaville, have taken oath to form themselves into a kind of monastic academy for study. They swear to fast, to eat but one meal a day, and for three years not to look on the face of woman; all of which "is flat treason against the kingly state of youth." But, alas! the King had forgotten that he was about to see the Princess of France and three of her ladies, come on a matter of State business. However, he will not admit them into his palace, but has pavilions pitched in the park. At the first glance all four men fall violently in love, each with one of the ladies, — the king with the princess, Biron with Rosaline, etc.: Cupid has thumped them all "with his bird-bolt under the left pap." They write sentimental verses, and while reading them aloud in the park, all find each other out, each assuming a stern severity with the perjured ones until he himself is detected. One of the humorous characters is Don Adriano de Armado, "who draweth out the thread of his verbosity finer than the staple of his argument." In him, and in the preposterous pedant Holofernes, and the curate Sir Nathaniel, the poet satirizes the euphuistic affectations of the time, — the taffeta phrases, three-piled hyperboles, and foreign language scraps, ever on the tongues of these fashionable dudes. The "pathetical nit," Moth, is Armado's page, a keen-witted rogueling. Dull is a constable of "twice-sodden simplicity," and Costard the witty clown. Rosaline is the Beatrice of the comedy, brilliant and caustic in her wit. Boyet is an old courtier who serves as a kind of usher or male lady's-maid to the princess and her retinue. The loves of the *noblesse* are parodied in those of Costard and of the country wench Jaquenetta. The gentlemen devise, to entertain the ladies, a Muscovite masque and a play by the clown and pedants. The ladies get wind of the masque, and, being masked themselves, guy the Muscovites who go off "all drybeaten with pure scoff"; Rosaline suggests that maybe they are sea-sick with coming from Muscovy. The burlesque play tallies that in 'Midsummer Night's Dream,' the great folk making satirical remarks on the clown's performances. Costard is cast for Pompey the Huge, and it transpires that the Don has no shirt on when he challenges Costard to a duel. While the fun is at its height comes word that sobers all: the princess's father is dead. As a test of their love the princess and Rosaline impose a year's severe penance on their lovers, and if their love proves true, promise to have them; and so do the other ladies promise to their wooers. Thus love's labor is, for the present, lost. The comedy ends with two fine lyrics, — the cuckoo song ('Spring'), and the 'Tu-whit, tu-whoo' song of the owl ('Winter').

LOVES OF THE TRIANGLES, THE, by George Canning. In 1797 George Canning then Under-Secretary of State for Foreign Affairs, planned in conjunction with George Ellis, John Hookham Frere, and others, the Anti-Jacobin, a political paper edited in the interests of the Tory party.

Satire and parody were the vehicles by which editors and contributors tried to effect their end; and among the various articles and poems, none were wittier than those written by Canning, then barely twenty-seven. One object of these contributions was to cast ridicule on the undue sentimentality of various literary men of the day, in their alleged false sympathy with the revolutionary spirit in France.

'The Loves of the Triangles' was presented as the work of a quasi-contributor, Mr. Higgins, who says that he is persuaded that there is no science, however abstruse, nay, no trade nor manufacture, which may not be taught by a didactic poem. . . . And though the more rigid and unbending stiffness of a mathematical subject does not admit of the same appeals to the warmer passions which naturally arise out of the sexual system of Linnæus, he hopes that his poem will ornament and enlighten the arid truths of Euclid and algebra, and will strew the Asses' Bridge with flowers.

This is of course a satire on the Botanic Garden of Dr. Darwin, to whom indeed the parody, 'The Loves of the Triangles,' is dedicated. Only about three hundred verses in rhymed iambics were published of this poem, forming one canto; yet argument, notes, as well as the body of the poem itself, are the perfection of parody, and in the midst of it all are several lines assailing Jacobins.

A portion of the invocation may serve as a specimen of the style: —

"But chief, thou nurse of the didactic Muse,
Divine Nonsensia, all thy sense infuse:
The charms of secants and of tangents tell,
How loves and graces in an angle dwell;
How slow progressive points protract the line,
As pendant spiders spin the filmy twine.
How lengthened lines, impetuous sweeping round,
Spread the wide plane and mark its circling bound;
How planes, their substance with their motion grown,
Form the huge cube, the cylinder, the cone."

LOVEY MARY, by Alice Hegan Rice (1903). This story continues the experience of "Mrs. Wiggs of the Cabbage Patch," and is written in the same entertaining vein. A new heroine, however, is introduced in the person of "Lovey Mary," who having begun life as a foundling, has spent her first fifteen years in a "Home." She has never known anything but rebuffs and cold treatment, and longs for affection and some of the good things of life. Her first real pleasure is derived from taking care of a child named Tommy, who is brought to the Home by his wayward mother Kate Rider, who has been a previous inmate. Lovey Mary, who has a deep aversion for Kate who has treated her unkindly in the past, is at first much opposed to the child who is put in her charge but soon overcomes this feeling and grows to love him passionately. After two years of devotion during which time Tommy has grown to return some of the affection which Lovey Mary lavishes upon him, she discovers that

Kate is planning to take her child and decides to prevent this calamity. Accordingly she slips away at early dawn with Tommy in her arms and at the end of a fruitless day finds herself at the "Cabbage Patch." Here she is met by the kind-hearted Mrs. Wiggs who immediately sets about making her comfortable. It is decided that she shall take up her location with Miss Hazy, a shiftless individual who is helped along in her struggles for existence by the inmates of the "Patch." Lovey Mary finds work in the factory and restores Miss Hazy's untidy abode to cleanly conditions. The matron of the Home discovers the whereabouts of her missing charge but instead of making the fact known decides to let Lovey Mary continue in the course she has chosen. However, Lovey Mary who has a well-developed conscience feels she is not really justified in keeping Tommy from his mother and finally decides to restore him; she goes to Kate who is sick in the hospital and after a reconciliation takes her home and nurses her till she dies. The reader takes leave of Lovey Mary and Tommy as they are starting off on a trip with their kind friends the Reddings, life having assumed a brighter aspect for the heroine than she had ever deemed possible.

LOYAL RONINS, THE, by Shunsui Tamenaga. This historical tale, translated from the Japanese by Edward Greey and Shinichiro Saito, was published in English in 1880. It relates to affairs that occurred in 1698. The book is profusely illustrated with characteristic Japanese pictures by Kei-Sai Yei-Sen of Yedo or Tokio. The graceful poetic style gives great charm to this naïve romance, the names of the characters are quaint even in translation, and the pictures of feudal Japan are vivid and fascinating. The Japanese atmosphere pervades the entire book. The main story is very simple, though there are numerous episodes touching or humorous. Lord Morningfield, Daimio of Ako, is condemned to commit hara-kiri (through the treachery and deceit of Sir Kira, master of ceremonies to the Shogun), and his property is confiscated. His widow, Lady Fair-Face, assumes the religious name of Pure-Gem and lives in retirement. Forty-seven of his retainers — now Ronins, or outlaws of the Samurai class — sign with their blood an agreement to avenge his death. Under the leadership of Sir Big-Rock, who divorces his wife and disowns his children, that they may not be punished for his deeds, the Ronins slay Sir Kira in his own house. After imposing ceremonies of respect at the tomb of their illustrious chief, the Ronins surrender themselves to the Council at Yedo. They are condemned to death and sentenced to commit hara-kiri. Forty-six forms clothed in pure white, headed by Sir Big-Rock, mount the hill of death, plunge into the dark river, and pass over to Paradise, where they are welcomed by the spirit of their beloved chief.

LUCK OF ROARING CAMP, THE, and other sketches, by Bret Harte (1870), have for their subjects strange incidents of life in the far West during the gold-fever of '49. The essential romance of that adventurous, lawless, womanless society is embodied in these tales. Representative members of it, gamblers "with the melancholy air and intellectual abstraction of a Hamlet"; all-around scamps with blond hair and Raphael faces; men with pasts buried in the oblivion east of the Mississippi; young men, battered men, decayed college graduates, and ex-convicts, are brought together in picturesque confusion, — their hot, fierce dramas being played against the loneliness of the Sierras, the aloofness of an unconquerable nature. 'The Luck of Roaring Camp' is perhaps the most beautiful of the sketches; 'The Outcasts of Poker Flat' is scarcely less pathetic. In 'Tennessee's Partner,' and in 'Miggles,' humor and pathos are mingled. The entire book is a wonderfully dramatic transcript of a phase of Western life forever passed away.

LYRICAL BALLADS, a collection of lyrical poems, mainly by William Wordsworth, but including 'The Ancient Mariner' and 'The Nightingale' by Samuel Taylor Coleridge, was first published in 1798. A second edition, with corrections and additions and a famous preface by Wordsworth, appeared in 1800. As originally planned the volume was to have been the joint production of Coleridge and Wordsworth, the former treating supernatural themes in such a manner as to create poetic belief, and the latter investing common incidents with an atmosphere of wonder and imagination. Wordsworth's superior industry and Coleridge's indolence brought it about that with the brilliant exception of 'The Ancient Mariner' the volume was confined to the second of these two objects. In his preface Wordsworth upholds his choice of ordinary events and humble life on the ground of the greater emotional sincerity and the more beautiful natural background afforded by them; and he defends the plainness and baldness of his style and metre on the ground that the language of poetry should closely approximate to the language of everyday life and that metre is not essential to poetry. (For Coleridge's criticism of these opinions, which are a natural reaction from the conventionality of eighteenth-century poetic diction, see the digest of his 'Biographia Literaria'.) Many of the 'Lyrical Ballads' like 'Anecdote for Fathers,' 'Simon Lee,' 'The Idiot Boy,' 'We are Seven,' and 'Lucy Gray' incurred ridicule through their simple ballad metre, the prosaic matter-of-factness of their expression, and the absence of externally striking incidents and climaxes; yet each of these poems, if sympathetically read, stirs the imagination and emotions of the reader and awakens him to the spiritual significance of the humblest and most commonplace events. More arresting but still simple in treatment are those rural tragedies 'Goody Blake,' 'The Thorn,' and 'Ruth.' The landscape beauty of the Lake District and the simple dignity of a humble life lived close to nature appears in 'The Old Cumberland Beggar' and in 'Michael,' both in blank verse. The poet's early love of his native dales, his moods of mystical insight, and his ties of kinship and affection are reflected in 'There was a Boy,' 'Nutting,' and 'Influence of Natural Objects' (all in blank verse, afterwards included in the 'Prelude'), 'Tintern Abbey' (a magnificent hymn to the immanent presence in nature), the address to his sister, Dorothy, in the same poem and in others, the Matthew poems dedicated to an old friend and the exquisite Lucy-poems, lamenting the loss of a real or ideal love, who had grown up under the influences of nature. Coleridge's 'Ancient Mariner,' by a marvelous *tour de force* creates and endows with reality a succession of fantastic adventures in the South Seas, involving a sailor who has incurred the enmity of the elemental spirits by killing an albatross. Spell-bound by the poet's consummate art we follow the mariner's punishment and purgation with a painful interest and a temporary conviction of reality; and are meanwhile delighted by a series of marvelous pictures, horrible and exquisite in turn. The 'Lyrical Ballads' began a new era in English poetry. They stirred contemporary writers to throw off the last restraints of conventional diction and to draw from the springs of sentiment, feeling, and imagination.

LYS ROUGE, LE, see **RED LILY.**

MACAULAY, LIFE AND LETTERS OF LORD, edited and arranged by his nephew, Sir George Otto Trevelyan (1876), is recognized as a biography of whose excellence English literature may boast. From the great historian's correspondence, private memoranda, and original drafts of his essays and speeches, and from the recollections of friends and relatives, the author has produced a model book. Macaulay's untiring patience of preparation, the tireless labor expended in collecting materials, his amazing assiduity in arranging them, his unequaled memory, and his broad popular sympathies, are sympathetically described, and reveal to us the most distinguished, progressive, industrious, able, versatile party leader of the first half of this century. The genuine honesty and worth of his character, and his brilliant scholarship, are as evident as his limitation in the fields of the highest imagination. Throughout the book Trevelyan suppresses himself conscientiously, with the result that this work ranks among the most faithful and absorbing biographies in English.

MACBETH, Shakespeare's great tragedy of ambition and retribution, was written about 1606. The prose story used was found in Holinshed's 'Chronicles.' The sombre passions of the soul are painted with a brush dipped in blood and darkness. In every scene there is the horror and redness of blood. The faces of the murdered King Duncan's guards are smeared with it, it stains the spectral robes of Banquo, flows from the wounds of the pretty children of Macduff, and will not off from the little hand of the sleep-walking Lady Macbeth. Banquo and Macbeth have just returned from a successful campaign in the north. On the road they meet three weird sisters, who predicted for Macbeth kingship, and for Banquo that his issue should be kings. 'Tis very late; the owl has shrieked good-night; only the lord and lady of the castle are awake. He, alone and waiting her signal, sees a vision of a phantasmal dagger in the air before him. He enters the chamber. "Hark! it was but the owl." — "Who's there? what ho!" — "I have done the deed: didst thou not hear a noise?" In the dead silence, as day dawns, comes now a loud knocking at the south entry, and the coarse grumbling of the half-awakened porter brings back the commonplace realities of the day. Macbeth is crowned at Scone. But his fears stick deep in Banquo, and at a state banquet one of his hired murderers whispers him that Banquo lies dead in a ditch outside. As he turns he sees the ghost of that noble-man in his seat. "Prithee, see there! behold! look!" — "Avaunt! and quit my sight! Thy bones are marrowless, thy blood is cold; thou hast no speculation in those eyes which thou dost glare with." — "Gentlemen, rise, his Highness is not well." Macbeth, deep in crime, has no resource but to go deeper yet and becomes a bloody tyrant; but ends his career at Dunsinane Castle, where the slain king's sons, Malcolm and Macduff, and ten thousand stout English soldiers meet their friends the Scottish patriot forces. The tyrant is fortified in the castle. The witches have told him he shall not perish till Birnam wood shall come to Dunsinane, and that no one of woman born shall have mortal power over him. But the enemy, as they approach, cut branches from Birnam wood "to shadow the number of their host." This strikes terror to Macbeth's heart; but relying on the other assurance of the witches, he rushes forth to battle. He meets the enraged Macduff, learns from him that he (Macduff) was ripped untimely from his mother's womb, and so is not strictly of woman born. With the energy of despair Macbeth attacks him, but is overcome and beheaded.

McFINGAL, by John Trumbull. The author of 'McFingal,' "the American epic," was a distinguished Connecticut jurist and writer. The poem aims to give in Hudi-brastic verse a general account of the Revolutionary War, and a humorous descrip-tion of the manners and customs of the time, satirizing the follies and extravagances of the author's own Whig party as well as those of the British and Loyalists. McFin-gal is a Scotchman who represents the Tories; Honorius being the representative and champion of the patriotic Whigs. McFingal is of course out-argued and defeated; and he suffers disgrace and ignominy to the extent of being hoisted to the top of a flag-pole, and afterwards treated to a coat of tar and feathers. The first canto was published in 1774, and the poem finally appeared complete in four cantos in 1782. The work is now unread and comparatively unknown, but its popularity at the time of its issue was very great; and more than thirty pirated editions in pamphlet and other forms were printed, which were circulated by "the newsmongers, hawkers, peddlers, and petty chapmen" of the day. It contains many couplets that were famous at the time, some of which are still quoted. The two that are perhaps the most famous, and which are often attributed to Samuel Butler, the author of 'Hudibras,' are —

> "No man e'er felt the halter draw
> With good opinion of the law."

and

> "But optics sharp it needs I ween,
> To see what is not to be seen."

'McFingal' was considered by many fully equal in wit and humor to its great prototype 'Hudibras'; and its subsequent decadence in popularity is thought not to be owing to any deficiency in these respects, but to a lack of picturesqueness in the story and of the elements of personal interest in its heroes.

MACHIAVELLI, LIFE AND TIMES OF NICCOLÒ, a biography by Pasquale Villari, published between 1877 and 1882, and in a complete English version by Linda Villari in 1898. In order to interpret and account for the doctrines of Machiavelli the author traces the history of his life in connection with the events of his time. The book is thus an extremely illuminating study of the Italian Renaissance as well as the fullest and best account of Machiavelli and his works. A general conspectus of the Italian states, and their literary and political condition at the close of the fifteenth century is followed by an account of the political career of Machiavelli, from his appointment as secretary to the Florentine Council of Ten in 1498 to his loss of office on the fall of the republic in 1512. A full history of his official activities is combined with an account of the political and military struggles of the period and of their effect upon Machiavelli's views. In particular he was impressed by the ruthless yet efficient policy of Cæsar Borgia in his conquest of Romagna, and took him as a model for his ideal 'prince. In the second book is described Machiavelli's literary career forced on him by his retirement from public life. 'The Prince,' 'The Discourses,' 'The Art of War' the comedies, and the 'Florentine Histories' are all analyzed and critically estimated. A concluding chapter sums up the chief events and the significance of Machiavelli. In Villari's opinion he was a great and original political thinker, who first frankly recognized the distinction between public and private morality and in a scientific and impersonal fashion (marred by too great moral insensibility) attempted to determine the principles of successful government. If he believed in doing unscrupulous acts for the sake of efficient government his aims were high and disinterested, embracing nothing less than the unity of Italy.

MADAME BOVARY, by Gustave Flaubert, appeared in 1856, when the author was thirty-five. It was his first novel, and is regarded as the book which founded the realistic school in modern French fiction, — the school of Zola and Maupassant. The novel is a powerful, unpleasant study of the steps by which a married woman descends to sin, bankruptcy, and suicide. It is fatalistic in its teaching, Flaubert's theory of life being that evil inheres in the constitution of things. Madame Bovary,

a doctor's wife, has been linked to him without really loving him; he is honest, uninteresting, and adores her. Reared in a convent, her romanticism leads her to
dream of a lover. She finds one, then another; spends money after the manner of a
light woman; and when she has involved her husband in financial ruin, kills herself
and leaves him to face a sea of troubles. The time is the first half of last century;
the action takes place in provincial French towns. The merit of the novel lies in its
truth in depicting the stages of this moral declension, the wonderful accuracy of
detail, the subtle analysis of the passionate human heart. Technically, in point of
style, it ranks with the few great productions of French fiction. It is sternly moral
in the sense that it shows with unflinching touch the logic of the inevitable misery
that follows the breaking of moral law.

MADAME CHRYSANTHÈME, by Pierre Loti (whose real name is Louis Marie
Julien Viaud), appeared in 1887, when he was thirty-seven. It is the seventh of the
novels in which Loti has tried to fix in words the color, atmosphere, and life of different countries. The scene of 'Madame Chrysanthème' is Japan, and the reader sees
and feels that strange land as Loti saw and felt it, — a little land of little people and
things; a land of prettiness and oddity rather than of beauty; where life is curiously
free from moral and intellectual complexities. Loti has but a single theme, the
isolated life of one man with one woman; but the charm of 'Madame Chrysanthème'
is not in its romance. The pretty olive-hued wife whom the sailor Loti upon his
arrival at Nagasaki engages at so much a month, conscientiously does her part. She
pays him all reverence, keeps the house gay with Japanese blossoms, plays her harp,
and is as Japanese a little oddity as he could find; but fails even to amuse him. She
is as empty of ideality as her name-flower is of fragrance, or as the little apartment
which he rents for her and for himself is of furniture. But the disillusion of Loti
himself, the mocking pessimism underlying his eager appreciation of the new sense-
impressions, and the exact touch and strong relief of his descriptions of exotic scenes,
exercise a curious magnetism.

MADEMOISELLE IXE, by Lanoe Falconer (1891). This short and vivid story gives
a graphic description of an episode in the life of a Russian Nihilist. Mademoiselle
Ixe, who is the principal figure in the tale, is first introduced as governess in an English family by the name of Merrington, where on account of her extreme reticence she
is regarded with some distrust. However, owing to her unquestionable ability, and
her satisfactory management of the children, she is retained in the household. She
wins the affection of Evelyn Merrington, the eldest daughter, a pretty and attractive
girl, who is just finishing her studies, and who has a devoted admirer in Parry Leth-
bridge, a young fellow of wealth, who is a constant visitor at the house. In the course
of time the Merringtons give a ball, and among the guests is a Russian count, who is
visiting in the neighborhood. Before the event Mademoiselle Ixe confides to Evelyn
that she has a message to deliver to the count, whom she has previously known. The
climax of the story is reached when the guests at the ball are startled by a pistol shot
and see the count stagger and fall, while Mademoiselle Ixe stands immovable with a
smoking pistol in her hand. She is immediately secured in her own chamber while
the police are sent for; but during this interval, Evelyn persuades her to escape, and
is assisted by Parry, who drives her in his dog-cart to the next town. Before her
departure Mademoiselle Ixe explains to Evelyn that it is for love of her country, and
from no personal motive, that she has tracked her victim to this place, and committed the desperate act. The count proves to be not seriously injured, and shortly

recovers, and Evelyn some three years later marries her devoted lover. Soon after her marriage she receives a pathetic letter from a Russian prison congratulating her on her well-deserved happiness and signed simply "X." The story is told in a very interesting vein, and has many interesting character-sketches and a decided touch of wit and humor running through the book.

MADONNA'S CHILD, by Alfred Austin. This romantic poem, which its author, later poet-laureate, calls the "firstborn of his serious Muse," was first published in 1872. The scene is laid at Spiaggiascura, on the Riviera; and Olympia, the heroine, "a daughter of the sunlight and the shrine," is sacristan of a little seaside chapel:

> "Sacred to prayer, but quite unknown to fame,
> Maria Stella Maris is its name. . . .
> Breaks not a morning but its snow-white altar
> With fragrant mountain flowers is newly dight;
> Comes not a noon but lowly murmured psalter
> Again is heard with unpretentious rite."

To this chapel comes a stranger, Godfrid, and surprises Olympia,

> "Atiptoe, straining at a snow-white thorn
> Whose bloom enticed but still escaped her hand."

He

> "deftly broke
> A loftier bow in lovelier bloom arrayed."

and gave it to her; and then accompanied her to the chapel, kneeling with her before the Madonna. Later, she finds to her horror that he is an unbeliever. To her supplications to —

> "Bend pride's stiff knee; no longer grace withstand,"

his answer is, "I cannot." With her he makes a pilgrimage to Milan. She leaves him with a priest who has been her adviser; but the old priest's efforts are in vain, and he tells her:

> "Through his parched bosom, prayer no longer flows.
> By Heaven may yet the miracle be wrought:
> But human ways are weak, and words are naught."

She decides that they must part, but he asks:

> "Is there no common Eden of the heart,
> Where each fond bosom is a welcome guest?
> No comprehensive Paradise to hold
> All loving souls in one celestial fold?"

She answers:

> "Leave me, nay, leave me ere it be too late:
> Better part here, than part at Heaven's gate."

MÆVIAD, THE, see **BAVIAD.**

MADRAS HOUSE, THE, by Granville Barker (1910). This play is a clever discussion of the woman problem, chiefly by a number of types of men, members of the firm of the Madras House, a great shop which caters to women. Act I. shows the

34

suburban home on Sunday where Mr. Huxtable, one of the owners, lives with six grown unmarried daughters. Society provides no real interests to take the place of husbands, children or work to mitigate the dullness of the lives of the Misses Huxtable. District nursing, foreign missions, and water-color sketching are not sufficiently engrossing. In Act II. we hear about a scandal in the store. Mr. Philip Madras, the young, progressive member of the firm, has to consider the slavery of the shop for the employees, and the difficulties in the way of a clerk who ventures to become an unmarried mother. Act III. is the business meeting to consider the proposition of an American millionaire to buy the store. The men discuss the position of women in modern life. Mr. Charles Madras, the head of the house, resenting the stimulating presence of women in politics, business, and art, has solved the problem for himself by retiring to a Mohammedan country where women are segregated. The models, parading before them in the new costumes, illustrate the sex appeal of dress. Act IV. introduces Jessica, the attractive modern woman, wife of Philip Madras. After the meeting at the store the young husband and wife talk together of the price to be paid for free womanhood, and the problem of making the world less of a "barnyard" in spirit.

MAGDA ('Die Heimat'), by Hermann Sudermann (1893). The high spirited Magda has been driven from home by the tyranny of her father, an ex-soldier, who rules his household with military despotism. She has sinned and suffered and worked, and at the opening of the play, returns to the home of her girlhood, after an absence of many years, a famous opera star. The pastor, Magda's rejected suitor, who still loves her, persuades her father to consent to receive her. She realizes that the free independent life of the artist has led her far beyond the petty bourgeois society and the commonplace family life, as well as the yoke of paternal authority. By mischance her father learns the secret of her past, and in a frenzy orders her to marry the father of her child, now a government councillor in the little town. The interview with her lover and her father is quoted in the LIBRARY. The former lover is willing enough to marry the rich woman and distinguished artist, and though she despises the man, Magda at first consents for love of her father and to give her son a name. When it transpires that the condition made is that she shall part from the child to avoid scandal, she spurns the marriage. The old soldier insists that the marriage shall take place to redeem the family honor. He threatens to take her life and his own if she persists in her refusal. In vain she tries to convince him that it is because she is now pure and true that she cannot act otherwise. As a last argument, she hints that she has had other lovers. As he is on the point of firing his pistol at her, he succumbs to apoplexy. Two types of conflict are presented, the struggle of the individual against the accepted rules of conduct, and the struggle between individual self-respect and the conventional ideal of absolute contrition and self-abasement for sins committed; but the success of the play depends upon its well-contrived situations and the opportunity it offers to a gifted actress.

MAGNALIA CHRISTI AMERICANA, by Cotton Mather. This 'Ecclesiastical History of New England, from 1620 to 1628,' treats more extensively of the early history of the country than its title seems to indicate, unless it is borne in mind that at this time the Church and State were so closely connected that the history of one must necessarily be that of the other. It was first published in London, in 1702, and is a standard work with American historians. It is divided into seven books: the first treating of the early discoveries of America and the voyage to New England;

the second is 'Lives of the Governors'; the third, 'Lives of many Reverend, Learned, and Holy Divines'; the fourth, 'Of Harvard University'; the fifth, 'The Faith and the Order in the Church of New England'; the sixth, 'Discoveries and Demonstrations of the Divine Providence in Remarkable Mercies and Judgments on Many Particular Persons'; the seventh, 'Disturbances Given to the Churches of New England.' In the sixth book, the author gives accounts of the wonders of the invisible world, of worthy people succored when in dire distress, of the sad ending of many wicked ones, and of the cases of witchcraft at Salem and other places. Of the last he says: "I will content myself with the transcribing of a most unexceptionable account thereof, written by Mr. John Hales."

The situation and character of the author afforded him the most favorable opportunities to secure the documents necessary for his undertaking, and the large portion of it devoted to biography gives the reader a very faithful view of the leading characters of the times.

MAHĀBHĀRATA OF KRISHNA-DWAIPAYANA VYASA, THE. This great Indian epic has been compared to a national bank of unlimited resources, upon which all the poets and dramatists of succeeding ages have freely drawn, so that scarcely a Sanskrit play or song lacks references to it. As the compilation of long series of poets, it contains not only the original story of the Kaurava-Pandava feud, but also a vast number of more or less relevant episodes: it is a storehouse of quaint and curious stories. It tells of the mental and moral philosophy of the ancient Rishis, their discoveries in science, their remarkable notions of astronomy, their computations of time, their laws for the conduct of life, private and public, their grasp of political truths worthy of Machiavelli. Stories and histories, poems and ballads, nursery tales and profound discourses on art, science, daily conduct, and religion, are all sung in sonorous verse. Written in the sacred language of India, it is the Bible of the Hindus, being held in such veneration that the reading of a single Parva or Book was thought sufficient to cleanse from sin. It has been translated into English prose by Kisari Mohan Ganguli, and published in fifteen octavo volumes. Sir Edwin Arnold has translated the last two of the eighteen parvas into blank verse; and in his preface he gives a succinct analysis of the epic which has been called "the Fifth Veda." To ordinary readers much of the figurative language of the 'Mahābhārata' seems grotesque, and the descriptions are often absurd; but no one can help being amazed at its enormous range of subjects, the beauty of many of the stories it enshrines, and the loftiness of the morality it inculcates. In grandeur it may well be compared to the awe-inspiring heights of the Himalayas.

MAID OF SKER, THE, by Richard D. Blackmore (1872), carries one through the last twenty years of the eighteenth century in England and Wales. "Fisherman Davy" Llewellyn, 'longshore sailor, and later, one of Lord Nelson's very bravest "own," — while fishing along the shores of Bristol Channel and Swansea Bay, finds in a drifting boat, which is carried by the seas into Pool Tavan, a wee two-year-old child asleep, — the Maid of Sker. "Born to grace," and very beautiful too, is this "waif of the sea," first known as "Bardie," then Andalusia; and last proved by the true Bampfylde peculiarity of thumbs, to be Bertha, the long-lost daughter of that aristocratic family. Brave Commander Rodney Bluett's proud relations do not therefore object to his marriage with the heroine. The old veteran's description of naval engagements, and his quaint views of "the quality" (the story is a first-person narrative throughout), makes it intensely dramatic. The death and disinterment of

"Black Evan's" five sons, smothered in a sand-storm; the villainy of giant Parson Chowne, and his savage death from hydrophobia; and the honest love of the narrator for Lady Isabel Carey, are prominent factors in the development of the plot. It is to the latter that old Davy, describing "the unpleasantness of hanging," remarks, "I had helped, myself, to run nine good men up at the yard-arm. And a fine thing for their souls, no doubt, to stop them from more mischief, and let them go up while the Lord might think that other men had injured them . . ." . . . In another place he is made to admit, "If my equal insults me, I knock him down; if my officer does it, I knock under . . ." These illustrations show something of the drollery of much of Blackmore's writing.

MAID'S TRAGEDY, THE, by Beaumont and Fletcher, was acted probably in 1610 and first printed in 1619. It is the most powerful drama of these authors. Evadne, a lady of the court of Rhodes, is the secret mistress of its king. To hide his guilt the monarch commands a young courtier, Amintor, to wed Evadne. Although Amintor is already plighted to another lady, Aspatia, whom he loves, he conceives it his duty to obey; moreover he is dazzled by Evadne's beauty. In the first act the wedding is being concluded by a masque, and amid many compliments the bride is escorted to the nuptial chamber. Bride and bridegroom are left alone; and then gradually, with a cold, contemptuous delight in the torture she is inflicting, Evadne reveals to Amintor that she is the king's mistress and that the marriage is to be a marriage in name only. Amintor submits to the principle of unswerving loyalty to the king; and in the morning they accept the railing congratulations of their friends as if they were an ordinary happy married couple. But Melantius, Evadne's brother, and Amintor's dearest friend, suspects from his bearing that something is wrong and gets the secret out of him. Being of a more resolute character he decides at once on vengeance. First he summons his relatives and friends for an attack on the king and makes arrangements to seize the fortifications. Then he goes to his sister, forces her to confess, and stirs her not only to repentance but to undertake in her own person to kill the king. After an affecting scene of contrition with her husband she goes off to perform this task. She dismisses the king's attendants, finds him sleeping, ties his arms to the bed, and then wakening him denounces his lust and cruelty before stabbing him to death. Meanwhile Melantius has seized the fort and holds it to obtain justification from the new king, Lysippus. At the same time Aspatia, eager for death, disguises herself as a youth and goes to Amintor, declaring herself a young brother of Aspatia who is seeking by single combat to avenge her wrongs. Forced at length to fight, Amintor mortally wounds her. At this moment Evadne enters, fresh from the king's murder, and begs Amintor to receive her as a wife. But he refuses, and Evadne kills herself. The dying Aspatia now reveals her identity and the two lovers are for a moment happily reconciled; but her death speedily follows and Amintor will not survive her. Melantius is prevented from following his example only by force and threatens to die of starvation.

Though over-sensational and lacking in consistency of characterization this play includes situations not only of tremendous theatrical effect but of real tragic pathos and horror.

MAIN CURRENTS IN NINETEENTH CENTURY LITERATURE, by Georg Brandes, a series of lectures originally given in Danish at the University of Copenhagen (published 1871–1890 under the title 'Hovedströmninger i det 19 de aarhundredes litteratur'; translated into German, 1894–1896 under the title 'Hauptström-

ungen der Literatur des neunzehnten Jahrhunderts'; and into English, 1901-1905).
The author's object was to trace the course of European thought in the first
half of the nineteenth century by describing the most important movements in
French, German, and English literature. In his view, these exhibit a reaction from
the revolutionary principles of the eighteenth century, followed by the gradual
emergence of the idea of progress in more vigorous form. Volume I., 'The Emigrant
Literature,' illustrates the first reactionary movement by essays on Chateaubriand,
Goethe's Werther, Senancour, and others. Volume II. is devoted to 'The Romantic
School in Germany' with its strong Catholic tendencies, its mysticism and mediæval-
ism. In Volume III., 'The Reaction in France,' the triumph of the Catholic Reaction
is illustrated by reference to Joseph de Maistre, Lamennais, Lamartine, and Victor
Hugo, when they supported the clerical party. Volume IV., 'Naturalism in England,'
shows how a naturalistic revolt against convention in literature led to a rebellion
against religious and political reaction, culminating in Byron, who gave the impetus to
a new progressive movement throughout Europe. Volume VI., 'The Romantic
School in France,' illustrates the effect of this movement in French Literature, from
the Revolution of 1830 to that of 1848, discussing such writers as Lamennais, Hugo,
and Lamartine in their later phases, Alfred de Musset, and George Sand. In Volume
VII., 'Young Germany,' a similar return to progressive ideas is traced in the works of
men like Heine, Börne, and Feuerbach, who prepared for the German uprising of
1848. Brandes is a critic of the school of Taine, and is fond of tracing the interrelations of literature, politics, philosophy, science, and religion. His style is made
eminently readable by his definiteness of opinion, forcefulness of statement, and
copiousness of citation and illustration.

MAINE WOODS, THE, by Henry D. Thoreau, was published in 1864. When the
first essay was written the author was forty-seven years old; but the whole book,
while filled with shrewd philosophic observations, has all the youthful enthusiasm
of a boy's first hunting expedition into the wilds of Maine. And it is this quality
that makes his experiences so charming alike to young and old. Lowell says, "among
the pistillate plants kindled to fruitage by Emersonian pollen, Thoreau is thus far
the most remarkable, and it is eminently fitting that his posthumous works should
be offered us by Emerson, for they are strawberries from his own garden. A singular
mixture indeed there is: Alpine some of them, with the flavor of rare mountain air;
others wood, tasting of sunny roadside banks or shy openings in the forest; and not a
few seedlings swollen hugely by culture, but lacking the fine natural aroma of the
more modest kinds. Strange books these are of his, and interesting in many ways,
instructive chiefly as showing how considerable a crop may be raised in a comparatively narrow close of mind." If the lovers of Thoreau count this judgment as less
than the truth, it nevertheless contains a truth. These sketches treat of expeditions
with the Indians among Maine rivers and hills, where unsophisticated nature delights
the botanist, zoölogist, and social philosopher. In the first essay are many shrewd
comments upon the pioneers as he sees them. "The deeper you penetrate into the
woods," he says, "the more intelligent, and in one sense the less countrified, do you
find the inhabitants; for always the pioneer has been a traveler and to some extent
a man of the world." . . . "There were the germs of one or two villages just
beginning to expand." . . . "The air was a sort of diet-drink!" . . . "the lakes,
a mirror broken into a thousand fragments and wildly scattered over the grass,
reflecting the full blaze of the sun." The book is full of strange doings of the
Indians who talk with the musquashes (muskrats) as with friends, of the varied

panorama of nature and the picturesque lives of the busy lumbermen and the hardy pioneers.

MAINTENON, MADAME DE, by J. Cotter Morison (1885), is a brief but capable effort to extricate the memory of the famous Frenchwoman from willful misrepresentation, either by her friends or by her enemies. This study is a strong and thoughtful presentment of her extraordinary career, beginning with poverty and humiliation; culminating as Queen of France, wife of Louis the Magnificent; and ending in dignified seclusion at the convent school of St. Cyr, which she herself had established for poor girls of noble birth. But it is not mere narration, for Madame de Maintenon's character is drawn with sympathy, and keen although not obtrusive psychological analysis. Through all her experiences, whether clad in sabots and guarding poultry for her unwilling guardian and aunt, Madame de Neuillant; or as wife of the crippled poet of burlesque, Paul Scarron; or in her subsequent glory, — she is a shrewd utilitarian, making the best of her present, and concerning herself little with the future. She successfully serves two masters, and by clever scheming and religious devotion lays up treasure both in this world and in the next. Her friends have declared her to be an angel of goodness; her enemies have accused her of great deceit and immorality. Both were wrong. She was not passionate enough to be wicked, and her head always governed her heart. "A wish to stand well with the world, and win its esteem, was her master passion"; and her other chief preoccupation was with spiritual affairs, which she treats "as a sort of prudent investment, — a preparation against a rainy day, which only the thoughtless could neglect." Her ruling characteristics were tact and good sense. They showed her how to make herself agreeable, and how to serve other people; and thus she gained the popularity she craved.

MAISON DE PENARVAN, LA, see **HOUSE OF PENARVAN.**

MAÎTRE DES FORGES, see **IRONMASTER.**

MAJESTY, by Louis Marie Anne Couperus (1894). This is one of the great works of modern Dutch fiction, said to be based on the life of the Tsar of Russia, Nicholas II. Othomar, Crown prince of Liparia, is the son of the Emperor Oscar and his wife Elizabeth. He is a delicate, nervous, morbid, over-conscientious boy, who loves his people, but dreads the responsibility one day to be his. Oscar, on the contrary, is confident that majesty is infallible; while Elizabeth lives in constant terror of an anarchist's bomb, not for herself, but for her husband and children. Othomar is led into a love affair by the Duchess of Yemena, a beautiful coquette, much older than himself. He falls ill, is sent away with his cousin Hermann, visits his grandfather (King of Denmark) Siegfried of Gothland, and is betrothed for state reasons to the Archduchess Valérie. He wishes to abdicate in favor of his younger brother, who however dies, and he is forced to take up his burden. Soon after his marriage, his father is assassinated and he is crowned. The story of his noble deeds (a romantic forecast) as Emperor is told in a second volume, called 'The Peace of the World.' Couperus was the leader of the Dutch "sensitivists" who revolutionized Dutch taste in the last twenty years of the nineteenth century. 'Majesty' may be regarded rather as a prose poem than as a novel.

MAKING OF A MARCHIONESS, THE, by Frances Hodgson Burnett (1901). The scene is laid in contemporary England, and the heroine is Emily Fox-Seton.

an amiable and unselfish young woman of good family who is obliged to support herself. She lives in inexpensive lodgings spending her slender earnings to the best advantage, and being possessed of a sunny and cheerful disposition, is contented with her lot. To her astonishment and delight she is invited by her patroness Lady Maria Bayne to make her a visit at Mallowe, her beautiful country seat. She is to be one of a large house party among whom is to be the Marquis of Walderness, who is considered the "catch" of the season. Emily finds an unselfish happiness in promoting the comfort and pleasure of Lady Maria's guests and is untiring in her efforts to add to their enjoyment. She keeps herself in the background never dreaming that she is herself an object of attention, but hoping with unselfish interest that the affections of the Marquis will be won by Lady Agatha Slade, a dainty and lovely girl, who is anxious to win a matrimonial prize. Nevertheless, the Marquis, who prefers beauty of character, to external charms, is impressed by Emily's noble qualities, and asks her to be his wife. The Marquis's proposal is such a complete surprise to Emily that at first she cannot believe her good fortune, but he soon convinces her that she is really the object of his choice and she accepts him with all the joy of a simple nature. Lady Maria greets this unexpected dénouement with remarkable composure and the story ends happily for all concerned.

MAKING OF AN AMERICAN, THE, an autobiography by Jacob A. Riis, was published in 1901, having previously appeared serially in the New York Outlook. In a delightful vein of conversational reminiscence the author describes his boyhood in the ancient Danish sea-port of Ribe, his attachment to the girl, Elizabeth, who was to be his wife, his varied experiences in America as factory-workman, ship-laborer, and canvasser, with seasons of unemployment and tramp life, and his entrance into journalism as reporter, editor of the Brooklyn News, and police editor for the Tribune. Meanwhile he had revisited Denmark and been happily married to the girl whom he had loved from boyhood. The latter half of the book describes his labors to improve the conditions of the New York slums, the success of his book 'How the Other Half Lives' in rousing the public to the horribly overcrowded and unsanitary condition of the tenements, and the destruction through his efforts of a squalid district called "Mulberry Bend," which was turned into a public playground. The account of the author's relations with Theodore Roosevelt, then Police Commissioner for New York, and a strong upholder of his efforts, is extremely interesting. A charming account of a visit to the old Danish home and of the happy domestic life of the family closes the narrative. There are many illustrations of Danish and American persons and places connected with the author, and the whole book has an intimate and homely personal touch.

MALADE IMAGINAIRE, LE, by Molière. This comedy is in three acts, and was first produced in Paris in 1673. It was the last work of the author; and in it, as Argan, he made his last appearance on the stage. Argan, who imagines himself ill, is completely under the dominion of Monsieur Purgon his physician. By his advice, he wishes to marry his daughter Angélique to Thomas Diafoirus, a young booby, just graduated as a doctor. Béline, his second wife, wishes him to oblige both of his daughters to become nuns, that she may inherit his property. Angélique is at first pleased, thinking that he wishes her to marry Cléante with whom she is in love. Argan insists upon the marriage with Thomas, whose studied oratorical speeches entirely captivate him.

Béralde, the brother of Argan, pleads for Cléante, and tries to convince his brother

of the charlatanism of his doctors and the selfish designs of his wife. Argan is deaf
to all reason; but to please his brother, asks the apothecary to defer the administering
of an injection. Purgon is indignant at this "crime of Lèse Faculté," and to Argan's
great despair, declines to treat him longer. Toinette, a servant-girl, disguised as a
traveling physician, examines into his case, and tells him the diagnosis of Purgon was
entirely erroneous. In her proper character she defends Béline, and to prove to
Béralde that his opinion of her is false, asks Argan to counterfeit death. He does so,
and learns the true character of his wife and Angélique's love for him.

He consents to her marriage with Cléante, with the proviso that he shall become a
physician. Béralde suggests that Argan himself become one, assuring him that with
the bonnet and gown come Latin and knowledge. He consents, and by a crowd of
carnival masqueraders is made a member of the Faculty. To the questions as to
what treatment is necessary in several cases, he replies: "Injection first, blood-letting
next, purge next." He takes the oaths to obey the laws of the Faculty, to be in all
cases of the ancient opinion, be it good or bad, and to use only the remedies prescribed by the Faculty, even though his patient should die of his illness. It was when
responding "Juro" (I swear), to one of these questions, that Molière was attacked by
a fit of coughing, causing the rupture of a blood-vessel, from the effects of which he
died a few hours later.

MALAY ARCHIPELAGO, THE, by Alfred Russel Wallace (1869), is divided into
five sections, each of which treats of a naturalist's travels and observations in one of
the groups of the Malay Archipelago. The sections are named: 'The Indo-Malay
Islands,' 'The Timor Group,' 'Celebes,' 'The Moluccan Group,' and 'The Papuan
Group.' The author traveled more than fourteen thousand miles within the Archipelago, making sixty or seventy separate journeys, and collecting over 125,000 specimens of natural history, covering about eight thousand species.

The records of these journeys, which are arranged with reference to material
collected, instead of to chronology, are delightful. Besides the valuable scientific
notes, there are most interesting accounts of the islanders and the dwellers on the
neighboring mainland, their manners and customs. The style is felicitous, making a
scientific treatise as fascinating to read as a story.

MALAYSIA AND THE PACIFIC ARCHIPELAGOES, see **AUSTRALASIA.**

MAN AND NATURE; or, PHYSICAL GEOGRAPHY AS MODIFIED BY HUMAN ACTION.
By George Perkins Marsh (1864). A work of great research and admirable exposition of interesting facts; showing how human action, such as the clearing away of
forests, the drainage of land, the creation of systems of irrigation, etc., very greatly
modifies the conditions belonging to the surface of the earth. Not only are the
matters treated of great practical importance, but the pictures of conditions and
changes in different lands, and over the many varieties of the earth's surface, are
very entertaining. The work became at once a standard with international recognition; a considerably enlarged Italian edition was issued at Florence in 1870; and a
second American edition, with further changes, appeared in 1874. In this final form
the title was altered to 'The Earth as Modified by Human Action.' The earlier
title was peculiarly appropriate; as it is not the earth only which the modifications
by the hand of man reach, but the course of nature, climate for example, in connection with the earth, or vegetation wholly created by human action. In every way the
book is a most suggestive one.

MAN AND SUPERMAN; a comedy and a philosophy, by Bernard Shaw (1903). Jack Tanner is Shaw's whimsical and paradoxical conception of the modern Don Juan, no longer the huntsman in the duel of sex but the helpless quarry. An attractive young English girl, Ann Whitefield, decides to marry Tanner. Her first step toward her "marked down victim" is to have him appointed her guardian by her father's will. Tanner objects violently to this responsibility, but predicts that Ann will do exactly as she likes, and she does like that "dear father's will" be carried out. He is panic-stricken when 'Enery, his chauffeur, opens his eyes to Ann's real intentions. Tanner considers his only hope of escape from marriage, the loss of his freedom, and individuality, is flight. He dashes off to Europe in his motor car, seeking a "Mohammedan country where men are protected from women." Ann, with a party of friends, pursues him in another car. The destined husband-to-be struggles in vain when Ann overtakes him in the mountains of Spain. He denounces her as a vampire, and declares he will not marry. Ann triumphs, because she is Everywoman, the Life Force incarnate, the instrument of Nature who brooks no defeat. The unwilling Tanner surrenders to the Life Force. The play gives the author opportunity for the expression of amusingly brilliant talk against existing social institutions. An interlude reprinted in part in the LIBRARY is Tanner's dream, in which he plays the part of Don Juan Tenorio, while the other characters appear in other rôles of the Don Juan legend.

MAN AND WOMAN, 'A Study of Human Secondary Sexual Characters,' by Havelock Ellis, was first published in 1894, in the 'Contemporary Science Series,' of which he is the editor. This impartial, detailed, and accurate comparison of the physical and mental qualities of the two sexes is of high value to all who are interested in the social and economic problems connected with the position of woman. After tracing the history of woman from savage days when she was a slave and a chattel, through mediæval times, when she was regarded as a necessary evil, down to the modern period of relative social equality the author proceeds to inquire what are the permanent distinctions between the sexes, confining himself to the secondary sexual characteristics (*i. e.* those not directly connected with sexual reproduction). Taking the child and the ape as standards of comparison he points out that women develop more rapidly than men but stop at an earlier stage, resembling that of the infant. This is no disparagement, however, as man's growth approximates him more closely to the ape. Though man is larger and stronger than woman, the formation of his skeleton is not markedly different from hers except in the case of the thigh-bone and, to some extent, of the pelvis. Man's brain is not relatively heavier than woman's. Contrary to the usual view woman's senses are less keen than man's, and women can endure a greater amount of pain. The popular mistake is due to the fact that sensibility is confused with affectability. Women perceive less quickly but react more strongly to perceptions and suggestions. Hence they are more emotional, more subject to hypnotism and nervous affections than men. As manual workers men surpass women in rapidity and perhaps in dexterity. Intellectually, women are more precocious and quicker than men, who are slower but more logical, and more capable of abstract thought. In business women are more docile and industrious than men. Woman's proverbial tendency to concealment and deception is, according to Mr. Ellis, a fact attributable to her restricted social position, to her comparative physical weakness, to her sense of modesty, and to the maternal instinct of protection. "The artistic impulse is vastly more spontaneous, more pronounced, and more widely spread among men than among women" although the latter excel in the less creative and more interpretative forms of art, as novel-writing and acting. Man, finally, is more variable than woman, producing more abnormalities, both geniuses and idiots; woman is more affectible than man, and hence more emotional and sensitive. "Woman is not undeveloped man, but diverse." Her different organization must be recognized as equally valuable with man's and equally entitled to development. The book is eminently fair and reasonable and free from arbitrary conclusions. Evidence is given in support of direct assertions, and where testimony is weak or conflicting that fact is noted.

MAN FROM GLENGARRY, THE, by Ralph Connor (1901). This is a tale of the life among the Canadian lumbermen, of their toil in the great forest and their work of floating the timber down the rivers. The book opens with a vivid description of a fight between "Murphy's gang" and that of Macdonald, at a tavern where the rival lumbermen are assembled. In this fight, "Black Hugh" Macdonald is fatally injured and one of the motives of the story is the subduing of his intense desire to be revenged upon his enemy Le Noir. His son Ranald Macdonald, "The Man from Glengarry," takes up the feud and the author depicts the mental conflict which he undergoes before he rises to the height of saving the life of his mortal foe. The character of Mrs. Murray, the wife of the Scotch Presbyterian minister, is interestingly presented in the description of her religious influence over Ranald Macdonald and the other rough lumbermen, "a hundred of whom are ready to die for her." The story traces the development of Ranald's character from his introduction as a lad of seventeen years, at the tavern brawl, through many thrilling adventures in the woods and on the river, up to the time that he becomes the educated and successful manager of the British American Coal and Lumber Company. The religious element in the book is a strong one and predominates over that of the love theme. Ranald's wild nature is strongly influenced by his love for the beautiful but ambitious Maimie St. Clair, whose life he saves, and who accepts his boyish devotion, but who later turns from him in order to make a brilliant match. Ranald in the end finds his true affinity in the loyal and sprightly Kate Raymond, Maimie St. Clair's intimate friend. The story has much force and graphic quality and the picture of the sturdy Glengarry men, led by the moral and physical giant Macdonald Bhain, is truthful and convincing, as are the descriptions of life in the backwoods and on the river.

MAN OF FEELING, A, by Henry Mackenzie. This short novel, published anonymously in 1771, is said to have created as much interest in England, when first published, as did 'La Nouvelle Héloïse' in France. It is remarkable for its perspicuity of style; though it shows the influence which Sterne exercised over the author Endeavoring to profit by the fact that the author was unknown, a clergyman of Bath, Mr. Eccles, claimed to be the author, presenting a manuscript with corrections, erasures, etc. Although the publisher then announced the name of the real author, on Eccles's tomb is inscribed: "Beneath this stone, the Man of Feeling lies." The story purports to be the remainder of a manuscript left after the curate had extracted several leaves at random for gun-wadding. Young Harley, who is in love with his neighbor's daughter, Miss Walton, sets out for London with the object of acquiring the lease of an adjoining property. His experiences on the trip make up several short stories. He is a great physiognomist, but is deceived by two plausible gamblers. He visits Bedlam Hospital; and the pitiable sights there seen are described. A very interesting chapter is that describing a dinner with a Misanthrope, in which the latter's complaints of his time seem to be the sempiternal ones of all nations. The story of his meeting with Miss Atkins, her rescue from a brothel and return to her father, is skillfully told. The cruelties of the press-gang, and of the treatment of East-Indian subjects, afford an opportunity for the "Man of Feeling" to condemn the East-Indian policy of the government. Upon his return, believing that Miss Walton is to marry another, he falls ill. She visits him; but her acknowledgment that she returns his affection does not come soon enough to save his life.

MAN OF THE HOUR, THE, by Octave Thanet (1905). This story deals with the labor problem and with socialistic efforts to solve it. The hero of the tale is John Ivan Winslow, the only son of a Russian mother and an American father. As a child he is sensitive and impressionable and imbibes the nihilistic views of his mother who is strongly in sympathy with her oppressed people. Before her marriage Mrs. Winslow had been the Princess Olga Galitsuin and had met her husband when he was on a business trip to Russia. Not till after their marriage did Mr. Winslow discover his wife's socialistic tendencies, and these in connection with her impracticability and foreign ways caused unhappiness between them which led finally to their separation. This was a great source of sorrow to Johnny-Ivan, as our hero was called, and the departure of his beautiful mother across the sea and her subsequent death almost broke his heart. Mr. Winslow had married a second wife, who was a noble woman, but John-Ivan had steeled his heart against her; after his father's death, which occurs after his leaving college, he is incensed at the division of the property. John-Ivan is left one hundred thousand dollars, while the rest of the large fortune goes to his stepmother, but this legacy is soon dissipated as he scatters it broadcast in his effort to aid suffering humanity. At the end of a year John-Ivan is penniless and seeks employment as a common workman in a factory. He sees life in all its phases, suffers many hardships, and meets with injuries and misfortunes. During this time his stepmother and his sweetheart, Peggy Rutherford, have been doing everything in their power to find him, but he has purposely hidden his identity. Peggy finally discovers his whereabouts and corresponds with him under the assumed name of Roger Mack, a boy he had once befriended. At length John-Ivan returns to his father's factory in order to assist in suppressing a labor uprising and is shot and seriously wounded. Upon his recovery his stepmother gives him a letter written by his father before his death, telling him that the legacy was given him as an experiment and the whole fortune is to be his eventually. By this time John-Ivan has realized the futility of his socialistic efforts and is ready to begin life anew with the faithful Peggy as his helpmate.

MAN ON THE BOX, THE, by Harold MacGrath (1904). Robert Warburton, the hero of this tale, handsome and fascinating, and of independent fortune, resigns his commission in the United States Army owing to a wound from an Indian bullet, which incapacitates him from service. He travels abroad, and one day in Paris is struck by the charm and beauty of an American girl whom he sees in a steamship office arranging for passage home, and he immediately books himself for the same steamer. He does not succeed in meeting the object of his admiration during the voyage as she and her father are very exclusive and avoid introductions. However, he learns that she is Miss Betty Annesley, an heiress, and her father, Colonel Annesley, recently retired from a responsible position in the War Department. Warburton goes to his brother's house in Washington and discovers that his sister Nancy is well acquainted with the Annesleys who are living in the same city. The evening of his arrival, in order to play a joke on his sister, he dresses in the clothes of the groom and plans to drive the family home from a reception. By mistake he gets the wrong carriage, drives the occupants at breakneck speed, and when terrified they call on him to stop, he jumps down and kisses the young lady who alights, who proves to be Miss Annesley. She has him arrested and he spends the night in jail, but the next morning she pays his fine and offers him a groom's position with her. He accepts and does the menial work that falls to his share, becoming meanwhile more and more deeply in love with her. Colonel Annesley has, by gaming, lost his daughter's fortune and to retrieve it has agreed to sell plans of his country's fortifications to a Russian, Count Karloff, who threatens to make the treachery known unless Betty agrees to marry him. At the critical moment Warburton interferes and saves the day. Betty, who has penetrated his disguise, owns up to her share of the deception and gives him her love for which he has not dared to hope.

MANDEVILLE, SIR JOHN, see **THE TRAVELS OF.**

MANNEQUIN D'OSIER, LE, see **L'HISTOIRE CONTEMPORAINE.**

MANON LESCAUT, by L'Abbé Prévost. This masterpiece was first published in Amsterdam in 1753, when its author was in exile. When but seventeen years old, the Chevalier Des Grieux, who is studying for holy orders, meets Manon Lescaut at an inn. She tells him she is being carried to a convent against her will. They elope; but Des Grieux's happiness is of short duration. A rich neighbor informs his parents of his whereabouts, and his father takes him home. Convinced of Manon's complicity in this, he resumes his studies. At the end of eighteen months, Manon, then sixteen years old, seeks him out, and they again elope.

When all their money is spent, he resorts to gambling, and she to the life of a courtesan. At this time, a wealthy prince offers to marry her; but pulling Des Grieux into the room, and giving the prince a mirror, she says: "This is the man I love. Look in the glass, and tell me if you think it likely that I shall give him up for you."

Soon after, they are both imprisoned. Des Grieux escapes, killing a man in so doing, and then assists Manon to escape. Dazzled by the offers of the son of her former lover, she leaves Des Grieux again. He finds his way to her, and is about to decamp with her and the riches which her last lover has showered upon her, when they are again arrested. By his father's influence he is released, but Manon is sent to America, and he goes with her on the same ship, which lands them in Louisiana. They are supposed by the Governor to be man and wife, and are treated as such. Des Grieux is about to marry Manon, and tells the Governor the truth of their relations; but Synnelet, the Governor's nephew, falls in love with Manon, and the Governor forbids the banns. Des Grieux and Synnelet fight, and the latter is wounded. The lovers try to make their way to the English settlements, but Manon dies, and Des Grieux buries her in the woods and lies down on her grave to die. He is found, accused of her murder, but acquitted and returns to France to find his father dead.

It is difficult to give any idea of the charm with which the author has enveloped these characters, and the censors of the book allege that in this very charm lies its insidiousness. It is a classic, and has served as model for many other books; some writers claiming that the authors of 'Paul and Virginia,' 'Atala,' and 'Carmen' have but clothed Des Grieux and Manon in other garments.

MANU, see **SACRED BOOKS OF THE EAST.**

MANUAL of Epictetus, see **MORALS.**

MANXMAN, THE, by Hall Caine, is a present-day romance, the scene of which is the Isle of Man. It was published in 1894; and was the most successful of the author's novels up to that time. Old Iron Christian, Deemster (or Judge) of the Isle, has two sons, Thomas and Peter. The elder, Thomas, marries below him and is disinherited. He dies, leaving a son, Philip, who is reared in the Deemster's house. The younger, Peter, has an illegitimate son, Peter Quilliam, who loves pretty Kate Cregeen, daughter of an innkeeper. The two lads grow up together as sworn friends. Peter and Kate are sweethearts, but her father objects to him because of his birth and poverty. Pete goes off to make his fortune, leaving Kate in Philip's charge. Philip, during his absence, wins her love and betrays her. Meanwhile tidings come of Pete's death. Philip cares for Kate, but feels that she is in the way of his ambition to become Deemster. He tells her that they must part; and on the return of Pete, who was falsely reported dead, she marries the latter out of pique, hoping until the last that Philip will interfere and marry her himself. She has a child by her husband, but is tortured by the thought that it may be Philip's. The shame of her loveless marriage nearly drives her crazy; and on Philip's return from abroad she runs away on the very day that he becomes Deemster, to live with him secretly, under an assumed name. The blow well-nigh crushes Pete when he returns to the empty house. He does not suspect that she has joined Philip; whom he tells that, solicitous for her health, he has sent her to England. To guard her good name he even receives mock letters from her, written by himself. Philip represents to Pete that she is dead. The husband never learns the truth, but leaves the island forever, placing the boy in Philip's keeping. Their guilty union so preys upon the conscience of both Philip and Kate, however, that the woman at last leaves him, and Philip offers what restitution he can. He makes a public declaration of his sin, resigns his high office, and takes in his own the hand of the woman he has loved and wronged, that they may begin life openly together. With this dramatic scene of the confession the story closes.

MARBLE FAUN, THE, by Nathaniel Hawthorne (1860). This is the last complete romance by the author, and was thought by him to be his best. It was composed carefully and maturely, Hawthorne not having published anything for seven years; and appeared simultaneously in Boston and London under different titles. The original name proposed was 'The Transformation of the Faun,' shortened by the English publisher into 'Transformation,' and changed in America by Hawthorne to 'The Marble Faun.' The scene is laid in Rome; the chief characters, four in number, are introduced together in the first chapter: Kenyon, an American sculptor; Hilda and Miriam, art students; and Count Donatello, an Italian friend. Hilda, blonde and gentle, with New England training and almost Puritanic feeling, is beloved by Kenyon. Miriam, dark and passionate, is admired by Donatello. An accidental resemblance of Donatello to the famous Faun of Praxiteles is used by the author to picture a corresponding human character, — beautiful, but heedless and morally unconscious, until brought into contact with sin and suffering. This "transformation" is occasioned by the persecution of Miriam by a mysterious person, accidentally encountered in the Catacombs, who thereafter attaches himself to her, haunts her, and dogs her footsteps. He finally intrudes himself upon her during a moonlight excursion to the Capitoline Hill; when Donatello, enraged beyond endurance and encouraged by a glance from Miriam, grasps him and flings him from the Tarpeian rock to his death. From that instant Miriam and Donatello become linked together by their guilty secret; and the happy, heedless, faunlike Donatello becomes the remorseful, conscience-stricken man. Hilda, meanwhile, is involved in the catastrophe. She has seen the deed committed, and is overwhelmed; she can neither keep nor betray her terrible secret, and breaking down under the weight of its oppression, the Puritan maiden seeks the bosom of the Roman Church and pours out her secret at the confessional. In the end Donatello gives himself up to justice, Hilda and Kenyon are married, and the unhappy Miriam disappears. The underlying interest of the book rests in the searching analysis of the effect of the murder upon the characters of those involved in the deed. Donatello is awakened from a blissfully immature unconsciousness of the world into a stern realization of crime, and its consequences, remorse and suffering; while Hilda is crushed with a sense of the wickedness which has been thrust upon her innocent vision. Incidentally the book is filled with the spirit of Rome and with Roman sights and impressions, which have made it the inseparable manual of every sojourner in the "Eternal City"; to each and all of whom is pointed out "Hilda's tower," where she kept the legendary lamp burning before the shrine, and fed the doves, until the day when another's crime drove her from her maiden refuge.

MARCELLA, by Mrs. Humphry Ward, is the writer's fourth novel, and was published in 1894, when she was forty-three years of age. It is the story of the life of the heroine from her girlhood, when she has vague dreams of social amelioration, is ignorant of facts and unjustly impatient with the existing order, especially with the upper classes. The story opens with scenes amidst the country gentry and their dependents. Marcella becomes engaged to Aldous Raeburn, the son of a nobleman, but breaks the engagement, partly through the influence of Wharton, a brilliant socialistic demagogue. She goes to the city, and by her intercourse with the poor, through her work as a trained nurse, she learns the difficulties in the way of enforced social reform, and gradually comes to a clearer appreciation of her early mistakes and the noble character of Aldous; with the result that she finally returns to him. The novel contains graphic sketches of the state of the lower classes in England, rural and urban, one of the dramatic incidents of the plot being the trial and execution of the poacher Hurd. The scenes in Parliament, too, where Wharton's knavery is exposed, are powerfully realistic and effective. Marcella evolves into a noble type of the higher womanhood, and the story is one of the strongest and most successful Mrs. Ward has written.

MARCO POLO, see **TRAVELS OF.**

MARGARET OGILVY, by Sir J. M. Barrie (1896). This is Barrie's loving tribute to the memory of his fond mother, who, according to an old Scotch custom, was called by her maiden name, Margaret Ogilvy. "God sent her into the world," he says, "to open the minds of all who looked to beautiful thoughts." Margaret was a great reader; she would read at odd moments, and complete, the 'Decline and Fall' in a single winter. It was her delight to learn scraps of Horace from her son, and then bring them into her conversation with "colleged men."

Barrie, after leaving the university, enters journalism, and his proud mother cherishes every scrap he has written. She laughs when she sees the title of 'An Auld Licht Community' in a London paper, and is eager to know if her son receives pay for such an article, being greatly amazed to learn that this is the best remunerated of all his writing. "It's dreary, weary, up-hill work, but I've wrastled through with tougher jobs in my time, and please God, I'll wrastle through with this one," said a devout lady to whom some one had presented one of Barrie's books. He feared that his mother wrestled with his writings in the same spirit.

Margaret was a great admirer of Carlyle, but her verdict of him was "I would rather have been his mother than his wife." She always spoke of "that Stevenson" with a sneer, but could not resist reading 'Treasure Island' and his other books. Barrie asks, "What is there about the man that so infatuates the public?" His mother's loyal reply is, "He takes no hold of me; I would hantle rather read your books." Margaret is greatly pleased and very proud to find herself so often depicted in her son's books. She affects not to recognize it, but would give herself away unconsciously. She says, chuckling, "He tries to keep me out, but he canna; it's more than he can do."

At the ripe age of seventy-five, Margaret Ogilvy peacefully passed away. Her last words were "God" and "love"; and her son adds, "I think God was smiling when he took her to him, as he had so often smiled at her during these seventy-six years."

MARIUS, THE EPICUREAN, a philosophical romance by Walter Pater, and his first important work, was published in 1885. The book has but a shadowy plot. It is, as the sub-title declares, a record of the hero's "sensations and ideas," a history of a spiritual journey. Marius is a young Roman noble, of the time of Marcus Aurelius. Like the philosophic emperor himself, he is the embodiment of the finer forces of his day; his temperament being at once a repository of the true Roman greatness of the past, and a prophecy of the Christian disposition of the New Rome. He seeks satisfaction for the needs of his soul in philosophy, the finer sort of epicureanism, that teaches him to enjoy what this world has to offer, but to enjoy with a certain aloofness of spirit, a kind of divine indifference. In his earliest manhood he goes to Rome, meets there the philosophic emperor, mingles in the highly colored life of the time, studies, observes, reflects. His closest friend is Cornelius of the imperial guard, a Christian who loves Marius as one in spirit a brother Christian. Through association with Cornelius, and by the law of his own character, Marius is drawn into sympathy with the new religion; yet, as becomes one who shares the indifference of the gods, he makes no open profession: but at a critical moment he lays down his life for his friend.

'Marius, the Epicurean,' is a remarkable story of spiritual development, as well as of the strange, luxurious, decaying Rome of the second century of the Christian era. Pater has drawn this panoramic background with the accuracy of the scholar and the sympathy of the artist. "The air of the work, the atmosphere through which we see the pictures pass and succeed each other, is chill and clear, like some silver dawn of summer breaking on secular olive-gardens, cold distant hills, and cities built of ancient marbles."

MARJORIE DAW, by Thomas Bailey Aldrich. The well-known story of Marjorie Daw is developed through the correspondence of two young men, named respectively John Flemming and Edward Delaney. The latter seeks to relieve the tedium of his friend's sick-room by a description of his neighbor, Marjorie Daw. He paints her charms in glowing colors, and enlarges upon her attractions, the wealth of her father, and the delightful colonial mansion in which she dwells. Flemming, who is com-

pletely fascinated with his friend's description, falls in love with the maiden, and
presses Delaney for more and more particulars, which he generously furnishes, until
he has convinced Flemming that Marjorie has been led to reciprocate his feelings.
The critical moment at last arrives when Flemming, having sufficiently recovered,
telegraphs that he intends to press his suit in person. His friend, now realizing how
serious the affair has become, endeavors frantically to prevent Flemming from carrying out his purpose; but finding his efforts unavailing, he departs hastily from town
leaving a note of explanation behind him. Flemming arrives, receives Delaney's
note, and encounters the surprise of his life. This short story was first published in
1873, and is a very characteristic piece of Aldrich's clever workmanship.

MARKETS OF PARIS, THE, see **ROUGON-MACQUART.**

MARRIAGE, THE HISTORY OF HUMAN, see **HUMAN,** etc.

MARRIAGE CUSTOMS IN MANY LANDS, by Rev. H. N. Hutchinson (1897).
A volume presenting for general readers a careful account of quaint and interesting
customs connected with betrothal and marriage among peoples and races in all parts
of the world, with a large number of carefully selected illustrations. The purpose of
the book is not to discuss the origin of the customs of various peoples, but to give a
picture of them, and thereby contribute a chapter to the story of the human race
as it is seen in all its varieties at the present time. A work adequately dealing with the
subject has become possible through the comprehensive character of the reports of
travel and observation which are now available, and Mr. Hutchinson has made
excellent use of these sources of information. A special value will attach to his work
from the fact that in many instances existing old customs have rapidly given way to
the spirit of modern change.

MARRIAGE OF FIGARO, THE, a comedy by Beaumarchais, written in 1776, first
acted in 1784, is a sequel to 'The Barber of Seville' (acted 1775). Figaro, confidential
servant of the Count of Almaviva, is engaged to Suzanne, waiting-gentlewoman to
the Countess. In promoting Figaro and paying Suzanne's dowry the Count intimates to her his wish to make her secretly his mistress, or as he puts it, to revive the
seignorial rights in the marriage of his vassals which he had renounced in marrying
the Countess. Suzanne reveals this proposal both to the Countess and to Figaro, who
plans an intrigue by which the Count, though duped in his pretensions to Suzanne,
may yet approve of her marriage. He proposes that Suzanne should give the Count
a rendezvous which should be kept by a young page, Cherubin, dressed in Suzanne's
clothes, and that the Count should then be surprised by his wife, Suzanne, and Figaro.
But while Cherubin is being dressed for the part by the Countess and Suzanne they
are surprised by the Count, who with some reason is jealous of Cherubin, an adolescent, in love with every woman he meets and worshipping the Countess, who in her
neglected condition has a sentimental tenderness for him. By Suzanne's cleverness he
manages to escape undetected, and the Countess now decides, without telling Figaro,
to keep the rendezvous herself. Meanwhile the Count, suspecting that Figaro and
Suzanne are plotting against him, resolves to prevent their marriage by favoring the
claims of Marceline, a lady no longer young, from whom Figaro has unfortunately
borrowed ten thousand francs on the promise of marrying her if he cannot pay.
Marceline now urges her suit, Figaro is unable to produce the money, and the Count
renders judgment that he must marry her at once; but from this fate Figaro is res-
sued by the opportune discovery that he is Marceline's son. Preparations for the

marriage of Figaro and Suzanne are now resumed; but the Countess resolves nevertheless to carry out the ruse already planned of meeting the Count in the guise of
Suzanne, hoping by this means to win back his love. Under her direction Suzanne
arranges a meeting with the Count in the garden during the wedding festivities.
Figaro, who is not in the secret but who accidentally learns of the assignation, believes Suzanne disloyal and goes to spy upon her. An entertaining series of meetings,
cross-purposes, and mistaken identities follows, in which the Countess, Suzanne,
Figaro, Cherubin, and other characters are concerned. In the end the Count and
Countess are reconciled and Figaro and Suzanne happily married. The interest of
this comedy is sustained throughout by the skilful conduct of a complicated intrigue,
the brilliance of the dialogue, the truth of the portraiture, and above all by Figaro's
denunciation of aristocratic pretensions which definitely foreshadows the Revolution.

MARRIAGE OF LOTI, THE ('Le Mariage de Loti'), by Louis Marie Julien Viaud
("Pierre Loti"), was first published in 1880 under the title 'Rarahu,' the name of its
heroine. While not one of Loti's strongest books, it shows his power of re-creating
the peculiar atmosphere of a remote island visited during his long connection with
the French navy. There is a curious mingling of fact and fiction, difficult to dis-
entangle, in this glowing study of Tahiti in the declining years of its Queen, Pomare
IV. A photograph of the South Sea maiden of fourteen, whose passion for Loti
neutralized his love for Princess Ariitea, and finally captured him, is still in existence;
and Rarahu's whole mournful history is traceable in the wistful features and flowing
hair. It is not so clear whether the large single blossom worn over one ear is the
hibiscus flower she had on when she first met the young officer, or the white gardenia
that became her favorite ornament. A victim of the extraordinary blending of primitive with conventional conditions that prevailed in the Society Islands in 1872, this
child of nature, strikingly beautiful, but still more remarkable for her poetic imagination and profound love for Loti, is placed for a while on a better social footing than
the usual so-called Tahitian marriage could give. Loti's sincere love for the half-
taught savage, able to read in her Polynesian Bible, and intelligent enough to be
saddened by the intellectual gulf between them, does not prevent him from laying
down laws for her conduct during his absence, without the slightest intention of
observing similar ones. If Loti is unconscious of the moral inconsistency, Rarahu is
not; and after his final departure she ceases — not indeed to pine for him, but to be
true to his memory and precepts. Ground between the upper and nether millstones
of desertion and temptation, she dies at eighteen of consumption, retaining only the
Queen's pity and the affection of her cat Turiri, — a good study of a cat by a true
philofelist, who has devoted a volume to his own cats. This Tahitian idyl is slight;
its charm lies in the delicate analysis of moods and emotions growing directly out of
island life and scenery. Its originality suffers somewhat in the reader's imagination,
after the classic 'Typee' of Herman Melville, whose voyage to the Marquesas was
made in the fifties; but its merits are its own.

MARRIAGE OF WILLIAM ASHE, THE, by Mrs. Humphry Ward (1905). This
is a story of English life, social and political. William Ashe, the hero of the tale, rich,
handsome, and well-born, heir to the title of Earl of Tranmore, and successful politician, makes a hasty marriage with Lady Kitty Bristol, the eighteen-year-old daughter of Madame d'Estrees (by her first husband, Lord Blackwater). Ashe first meets
Kitty at a reception given by her mother, who in spite of her questionable reputation
draws many influential men about her by her personal charm. Ashe proposes to

35

Kitty and is accepted, though she warns him that her hasty temper and uncontrollable nature may cause him to regret this step.   They are next seen three years later settled in a house in London where Kitty's love of excitement causes her to plunge madly into the social vortex.   Ashe proves a devoted and indulgent husband, allowing his wife every liberty which her unconventional nature demands.   They have one child, a partially crippled boy, who is a great disappointment to Kitty and whom she alternates in treating with affection and indifference.   Kitty's waywardness proves a serious drawback to her husband's promising political career; she alienates the friendship of Lord Parham, the prime minister upon whom Ashe's promotion depends, and enters into a violent flirtation with Geoffrey Cliffe, whose poetic and unprincipled nature has a strong fascination for her.   The death of her child, following a season of extreme gaiety, leaves Kitty a physical wreck; and Ashe takes her to Italy to try to win back her health.   Here she again meets Cliffe and eventually flees with him while her husband is in England endeavoring to suppress a scurrilous book which she has written.   The finale comes some two years later when Ashe and Kitty meet unexpectedly at a small inn in the Alps; the latter who has sustained many hardships is in a dying condition and passes away soothed and comforted by her husband's presence.

Mrs. Ward found suggestion for her fiction in historical persons.   Kitty is drawn from Lady Caroline Lamb, William Ashe from Lord Melbourne, and Cliffe from Lord Byron.

MARTHE, see **EN ROUTE.**

MARTIAN, THE, by George Du Maurier, his third and last novel, was published posthumously in 1897.   The hero is Barty Josselin, the story of whose life is told by his friend and companion, Robert Maurice.   The school life of the two lads in the "Institution F. Brossard," in Paris, is sketched in detail in Du Maurier's inimitable manner, the account being largely autobiographic.   Barty is from the start a handsome, high-spirited, mischievous, and gifted fellow, thoroughly practical, yet with traits that have in them a strange idealism.   After school, the boys return to England, and Barty goes into the army, but does not like it, and resigns.   Then his eyes give out; and he travels for a time, and consults various physicians, being helped finally by a celebrated German specialist, Dr. Hasenclover, who assures him that he will be blind in only one eye.   Before this, he has come to such melancholic discouragement that he intends suicide; being saved therefrom by discovering in a dream that he has a kind of guardian spirit, the Martian, a woman soul, who has undergone a series of incarnations, and is now an inhabitant of Mars.   She advises him about his eyes, and thereafter, for many years, she constantly communicates with him and helps him, using a kind of shorthand called *blaze*.   She inspires him to write wonderful books, whereby he becomes a famous author.   Against her advice, he obeys the dictates of his heart by marrying Leah Gibson, a noble Jewess, when the Martian would have had him choose Julia Royce, an English belle whom he meets in Germany. The marriage is so happy that the Martian acknowledges her mistake.   When Barty's daughter Martia is born, the Martian becomes incarnated in her form; and upon the young girl's death, the strange being from another world returns to Mars, whereupon Barty himself also passes away.   The charm of the story lies in the genial description of bohemian friendship and love, seen retrospectively in the half-light of illusion; and in the suggestive way in which the odd supernatural element is woven into the narrative

MARY BARTON, by Elizabeth Cleghorn Gaskell (1848), is a forcible tale of Manchester, at the time when the manufacturing districts suffered the terrible distress that reached its height in 1842. It deals with the saddest and most terrible side of factory life, and was one of the first English novels to attempt this subject.

John Barton, the father of Mary, is a weaver, an honest man, possessing more than the usual amount of intelligence of his class. When the story opens, he has plenty of work and high wages, which he spends to the last penny with no thought of the possible "rainy day." Suddenly his master fails, and he feels the effect of his improvidence. His wife and little son die from the want of ordinary necessaries, and Mary alone is left to him.

Mary's beauty has attracted the attention of young Mr. Carson, the son of a wealthy mill-owner. Meanwhile she is deeply loved by Jem Nilson, a man of her own class. In the distress of this time it is decided to send a petition to Parliament. John Barton is chosen one of the delegates to present it. The failure of the petition embitters him so that he becomes a Chartist. He further increases his morbid feelings by the use of opium to deaden the pangs of hunger. Young Mr. Carson has indulged in satires against the delegates, which unfortunately reach their ears and rouse their anger. They resolve on his assassination and determine the instrument by lot, which falls to John Barton. Suspicious circumstances lead to the apprehension of Jem Nilson. Mary suspects the truth, and determines to rescue her lover without exposing her father. At the trial Jem learns for the first time of Mary's love for him. John Barton disappears without rousing suspicion, and Jem is cleared through his ability to prove an alibi. The story ends with Barton's return to his home, and his death after a confession of his guilt. The chief interest of 'Mary Barton' lies in the touching simplicity of the descriptions of daily life among the artisan class. Their graphic power brings the reader into a vital sympathy with the life and scenes described. Some of the sad pictures of those toiling, suffering people are presented with intense pathos.

MASON-BEES, THE, a collection of essays on the chalicodomæ or mason-bees proper by Jean Henri Casimir Fabre, translated from the author's great work 'Souvenirs entomologiques' (1879–1905) by Alexander Teixeira de Mattos (1914). With another volume, 'Bramble-Bees and Others' (1915) by the same translator, this book constitutes a complete treatise on wild bees. The mason-bees were first observed by the author when he was teaching surveying to a class of boys on the open plains or "harmas" near Carpentras. Noticing that the boys would pause in their work to lick straws he discovered that they were eating honey from the clay nest of a large black bee. With these bees, the chalicodomæ, he performed a number of experiments, attempting to determine, by means of marking them with chalk, the limits and nature of their power to find their way to their hives. He found that a large percentage made their way back through any obstacles and in spite of being swung about in boxes and confused; but he could not explain their instinct of direction. Fabre is conservative as to the reasoning power of bees, as distinguished from instinct, and is extremely sceptical with regard to the Darwinian hypothesis of protective mimesis. The book consists largely of records of experiments, which must be carefully followed but well repay the effort by the fascinating pictures and truths which they reveal. Fabre's graphic style and absolute sincerity render his scientific observations more attractive than the picturesque fancies of humanizing naturalists. He unveils the romance and mystery of the actual insect world.

MASQUERADER, THE, by Katherine Cecil Thurston (1904). This is the story of two men of totally different characteristics and identical physical endowments, who bargain to exchange places. The exchange allows one the liberty to indulge his craving for opium, the other an opportunity to satisfy his ambition for statesmanship and a public career. John Chilcote, M.P., rich, aristocratic, and prominent in the social and political world, encounters by chance in a London fog his double, John Loder, poor, obscure, and without friends. The fragmentary conversation which takes place at their meeting reveals to Chilcote the other's ambition, and to Loder the secret of his companion's weakness for morphia. Then follow a series of exchanges. The likeness deceives every one, even Chilcote's lovely wife who has long shunned and despised her uncongenial mate but now sees an encouraging change of mood which indicates a struggle to regain lost ambition and interest. Loder throws himself heart and soul into the political world and rekindles the public faith in his double, as well as the faith of his wife who clings with more and more hopefulness to the bright image which is at intervals blurred by the return of Chilcote. The two men find it more and more difficult to return to their original spheres: Chilcote because of his craving for morphia; Loder because of his marvelous gift for oratory as well as his increasing love for Eve, his double's wife. The crisis comes after Loder has won fame by his brilliant Parliamentary speech and has called forth from the delighted wife a passionate response to his own love. Loder feels his position unbearable and determines to relinquish it for ever. Chilcote's excesses make his continuance of the deception necessary, however, and he determines to explain everything to Eve; she has meanwhile discovered his secret, but nevertheless begs him not to leave her. Loder convinces her that their duty lies in the way of renunciation and together they go in search of Chilcote. Upon reaching his lodging they find him dead. After the relaxing of the strain under which both have been laboring they hesitate as to their future decision. Loder suggests going away to win a new position for himself, but Eve points out to him that his duty lies in the direction of the discharge of those obligations and responsibilities which he has assumed so extensively and he acknowledges that he has now to consider the needs of his country which has honored him with its confidence, and of the woman who loves him.

MASTER, THE, by I. Zangwill (1895). This story is the biography of an artist; and in it the reader is led to an artist's London, and wanders through an artist's world. From early boyhood the ruling passion of Matthew Strang's life is a love of art and a desire to paint pictures. A poor boy, struggling against poverty and misfortune, he ever keeps this goal in view. Overwhelmed by want and suffering, he marries a young woman his intellectual inferior, but possessed of a small competency by which he is enabled to pursue his beloved vocation. He becomes a great artist; and the distance widens between him and his commonplace wife, who has no appreciation of his work or ideals. Matthew Strang is courted by distinguished people, and breathes an atmosphere that intensifies the contrast with his own home, which he rarely visits. He is thrown into the society of Eleanor Wyndwood, a beautiful and accomplished woman. She is his ideal, and he falls in love with her. He feels that inspired by her companionship he could achieve the highest success. Eleanor returns his love; and Strang is on the point of forgetting all but his passion for her, when he is suddenly awakened to the realization that his highest duty lies in the renunciation of his desires. He goes back to his nagging, prosaic wife, and irritating household, having bid farewell to his love and art. But the latter is not to be taken leave of; for, away from the whirl of society and in the solitude of his out-of-town studio, he toils to accomplish his best work. Here "the master" at last produces his greatest pictures; here he becomes not only master of his art, but "master of his own soul." Throughout the book the point of view is profoundly poetic, and the character of "the master" is developed with truly masterly skill: as are also the portraits of Billy, the artist's deformed brother; the sharp-tongued Rosina, his wife and his foster-sister, steadfast Ruth Hailey, whose gentle influence and self-effacing love are contrasted with the more selfish affection of the impressionable and impulsive Eleanor. The book is filled with clever epigrammatic phrases, and abounds in humor.

MASTER AND MAN, see **ROUGON-MACQUART.**

MASTER CHRISTIAN, THE, by Marie Corelli (1900). This book is an arraignment of the ecclesiastical system and of modern Christianity as typified partly by the Church of Rome and partly by the Church of England. The keynote is struck in the opening chapter, when the author describes the sensuous atmosphere of a great cathedral as the background for the ascetic figure of Cardinal Boupré, who typifies the simple-minded and saintly son of the church, and is contrasted with the Abbé Vergniaud and other ecclesiastics in the tale, who were both worldly and wicked. The book is for the most part a series of conversations carried on sometimes among the "servants of Christ," sometimes in fashionable society, while the motive running throughout all is the constant struggle of the spiritual against the material. The Cardinal has been present at a service in a Paris church during which the immoral Abbé is nearly murdered by his own natural son, and the Abbé's confession of his sin and acknowledgment of his child give great offense at Rome, whither the Cardinal is summoned. Here the principal characters of the story are assembled, among them Aubrey Leigh, an American actor and journalist, who is deeply pained by the pride and wickedness of the modern churches, and the Cardinal's beautiful niece Anglea, who has painted a wonderful picture which ultimately brings her under the ban of the church. A brief outline can give only a faint idea of the many subjects touched upon by Miss Corelli in this book; its six hundred pages contain her opinions on many of the topics of the day.

MASTER OF BALLANTRAE, THE, by Robert Louis Stevenson (1889), is a Scotch romance of the eighteenth century, beginning with the Stuart uprising of 1745. It is a sombre tragedy of the enmity of two brothers, of whom the elder, James Durrie the Master, takes the side of King Charlie; the younger, Henry, that of King George. Alison Graeme, a kinswoman with a fortune, is intended for the wife of the Master; but on his going to join the Stuart and being believed dead she is married to Henry, without loving him. The tale is narrated mostly by the steward of Ballantrae, John MacKellar, who is devoted to the house and to Henry Durrie, whose nobility, set beside the wickedness of his brother, he realizes to the full. After the marriage appears Chevalier Burke, a companion of the Master, to say that he is not dead; Burke narrates their wanderings, which include an episode on a pirate ship and adventures among Indians in the wilds of New York. MacKellar then takes up the tale, describing the persecutions suffered by Mr. Henry, whose brother first writes to demand a large sum of money; then returns, impoverished and disgraced, to his paternal home, where he foments trouble between Henry and his wife. Finally, goaded by the Master's insults, Henry fights a duel with him and leaves him for dead; but he is carried off to sea by smugglers and recovers, remaining away for some time, and traveling in India, as is communicated by Burke. Then the Master reappears with Secundra Dass, an East-Indian, whom he has made his creature; whereupon Henry and his wife and children betake themselves secretly to New York, where Mrs. Durrie owns an estate, leaving the Master at Ballantrae in the charge of MacKellar. James soon finds out his brother's whereabouts and pursues him, keeping to his tactics of persecution. Arrived there, he does all he can to harm Henry, who is installed in a position befitting his rank. False news from Scotland to the effect that the Master, though a rebel, is to have his title restored, which will cut off Henry's son from the succession, leads the younger brother to concoct a plan whereby James, who intends going to the northern wilderness to regain pirate treasure he has buried there, shall be led to his death. The Master for a time outwits the party of adventurers who attend him, with the purpose of first getting the treasure, then making away with their nominal leader. Finally, to escape them, he feigns death and is buried by Secundra Dass, who puts him in a state of suspended animation. When Henry and his party seek the grave, they find the Indian digging up the buried Master, who lives long enough to open his eyes, at which vital sign his brother falls dead. Thus the fraternal enemies lie at last in one grave in the western wilderness.

MASTERMAN READY; or, The Wreck of the Pacific, by Captain Marryat (1842). This book was written with a double motive: to amuse the author's children, and to correct various errors which he found in a work of a similar nature 'The Swiss Family Robinson.'

Mr. Seagrave and his family, returning to their Australian home after a visit to England, are shipwrecked on an uninhabited island with their black servant Juno, and Masterman Ready, an old sailor. As they see no signs of immediate relief, they build a house, and make themselves comfortable. They cultivate and explore the island, finding many animals of which they make use, and build a strong stockade around the house in order to be fortified in case of attack. It is not long before they are glad to avail themselves of its protection against a band of cannibals from a neighboring island. They beat off the savages again and again, but are kept in a close state of siege until their water gives out. Ready, attempting to procure some from an unprotected part of the inclosure, is severely wounded by a savage who has managed to steal upon him unawares. Another and more determined attack is made, which seems certain of success, when the booming of cannon is heard and round shot come plowing through the ranks of the terrified savages, who now think of nothing but safety. The shots come from a schooner commanded by Captain Osborn, the former master of the Pacific, who has come to rescue the Seagraves. Ready dies of his wounds and is buried on the island, and the survivors are carried in safety to Australia. The story is told in an interesting and entertaining manner, and is enlivened throughout by the many amusing experiences of Tommy Seagrave, the scapegrace of the family. The descriptions of the ingenious contrivances of the castaways are accurately given and form an interesting feature of the book.

MATHILDE, by Sophie Cottin, see her **ELIZABETH.**

MATING OF LYDIA, THE, by Mrs. Humphry Ward (1913). The scene of this story is laid in England, in the Lake country, and it deals largely with the affairs of a pretty and unworldly young artist named Lydia Penfold. She lives in a simple way with her widowed mother and her sister Susan, and ekes out the family income with her painting. By her charm and beauty Lydia wins the heart of Lord Tatham, a rich young land-owner who desires to marry her. Lydia, however, who is not dazzled by wealth or position, refuses his offer because she does not love him. She later becomes interested in a young barrister, named Claude Faversham, who is acting as private secretary for a rich and tyrannical old man named Edmund Melrose. Twenty years before, Melrose had brought to his Cumbrian estate an Italian wife, many years his junior, whom he had treated with harshness and cruelty. When no longer able to endure existence with him, Netta Melrose had taken her little daughter Felicia and fled with her to her own country. Since that time she had been forced to subsist on a pittance of eighty pounds a year which was all her millionaire husband would allow for the support of his wife and child. Melrose meanwhile, having a mania for collecting curios, had spent his money lavishly on his hobby. After having lived for years as a recluse, Melrose at last becomes interested in young Faversham, who having been thrust upon his hospitality by being brought to his house when seriously injured, finally becomes a necessity to him as a companion. Melrose makes Faversham manager of his estate, paying him a fabulous salary, and also makes him his heir on the condition he will not interfere with his own harsh measures to his tenants. Faversham, who is an honorable man and had hoped to better the terrible existing conditions, agrees to the management, feeling it will only be temporary as Melrose is aged and infirm. Lydia, however, is terribly disappointed in the man she had learned to love and refuses his offer of marriage. Melrose is secretly murdered by one of his ill-treated tenants and Faversham is accused of the crime. The real murderer confesses his guilt, Faversham is acquitted, and makes over all his inheritance to Melrose's wife and daughter who have reappeared upon the scene. Lydia then marries Faversham and Lord Tatham consoles himself with Felicia Melrose.

MATRIMONY, by W. E. Norris (1881). Mr. Norris's third novel is the story of the fortunes of a county family named Gervis, the scene being laid partly in Beachborough, an English county-town, and partly among an aristocratic half-bohemian set in Paris. Mr. Gervis, a brilliant diplomat, marries an Italian woman, by whom he has two children, Claud and Geneviève. His second wife is a Russian, Princess Omanoff, who has already been twice married, and has her own cynical views as to the blessings of matrimony. Mr. Gervis and the Princess maintain separate establishments, but are on friendly terms. When the story opens, Mr. Gervis, with his son Claud, after a long residence abroad, has just returned to England to take possession of a family estate, lately inherited. From this point the true story begins. Its complications arise from the love-affairs of Claud and his beautiful sister, from certain outlived episodes in the life of the Princess, and from the serious effects that spring from the frivolous cause of the Beachborough Club's reading-room gossip. Nothing is out of the common, yet the elements of disaster and of tragedy are seen to be potential in the every-day lives of the every-day characters. The book abounds in types of character done to the life. Even the callow club-house smokers have an individuality of their own; and French dandies, men of letters, gamblers, scoundrels, Russian adventurers, and backbiting ladies of quality, rowdies, and philosophic speculators on the cosmos in general, are each and all as real as the crowd in the street.

MAUREEN'S FAIRING, by Jane Barlow. This delightful collection of eight short stories, descriptive of Irish peasant life, first appeared in 1895, and its title is that of the first story. Maureen O'Dell is a blind girl with a brother Rody, who is not "too bad-manin' a poor lad whatever, but sorra the ha'porth of use. Moon-in' about the place from mornin' till night; but rael good he is to Maureen. He'd be hard set to make more of her if she could see from this to the land of Egypt and back again." It is his custom to sit with her and watch the wild rabbits coming out to play in the dusk, but he tells her they are fairies. On the night on which the story begins, he tells her they are holding "a cattle fair, no less, wid every manner of little baste a-dhrivin' out to it, only the quarest little bigness on them that ever you beheld. There's a drove of bullocks. The whole of them 'ud trot aisy on the palm of me hand. But what 'ud you suppose they've got be the way of cattle pens? The peelin's of the apple you had aitin' here last night." Rody's descriptions are interrupted by the arrival of Christy M'Kenna, who unwittingly destroys Maureen's belief in fairies and in Rody as well, by speaking of the rabbits. Grieved at his mistake, he tries to atone for it by describing his adventures at sea. Then he makes her a "fairing," or present, of a shell he had picked up on the beach at Jamaica, and promises to come the next day and show her others. A few weeks after, Mrs. O'Dell in telling of her good luck says: "Goodness help you lad, sez I, and what at all will you be doin' wid only a dark wife to keep house for you? And sez he to me, 'Bedad, ma'am, I'll tell you that aisy, if you'll tell me what I'm to do widout her; for me soul to the saints, if I know, be any manner of manes.' "

MAXIMINA, by Armando Palacio Valdés (1887). A vivid picture of modern Spain is shown in this interesting novel, the scene of which is laid chiefly in Madrid. Miguel de Rivera marries Maximina, a modest country girl. He brings her to Madrid and lives happily until he finds his fortune compromised. As editor of a Liberal newspaper, he signs notes to enable the paper to continue; with the promise of Mendoza, a politician and one of the backers, that they shall be taken up when due. When the Liberals come into power, the holder of the notes calls for payment. The responsible parties neglect to protect Miguel; and Mendoza suggests that he sign more notes to gain time, and be a candidate for Congress, so that by their united efforts they can force the minister to settle. Against his will he enters the contest, with a promise of government support; but is sacrificed for political reasons, and his entire fortune is swept away. A son is born to him at this time, and he finds himself without employment or funds. Maximina dies, and Miguel becomes secretary to Mendoza, who has become minister. The story of the unsuccessful attacks on Maximina by Don Alphonso, a fashionable roué, and his success with Miguel's sister, is interwoven with the main plot. The author introduces us to life behind the scenes at the newspaper office, and the halls of Congress, and shows the petty political intrigues of the rural districts of Spain, which are readily recognized for their fidelity by any one acquainted with the life depicted.

MAXIMS, or according to the original title 'Réflexions ou Sentences et Maximes Morales,' a collection of 504 brief observations by François, duc de la Rochefoucauld, published in 1665. They are the epigrammatically phrased experiences of a courtier and man of the world who has seen the weakness and selfishness of human nature. Their general character is indicated by the remark prefixed as a motto to the fourth edition: 'Our virtues are most commonly mere vices in disguise.' For a fuller characterization, see the LIBRARY, under 'La Rochefoucauld,' p. 12321.

MEASURE FOR MEASURE, written about 1604, is one of Shakespeare's later comedies, the outline of the plot taken from the Italian novelist Cinthio and from Whetstone's tragedy of 'Promos and Cassandra.' License has now for a long while in Vienna run by the hideous law, as mice by lions; and the sagacious but eccentric duke attempts to enforce it, especially against sins of lust. The scenes that follow are gloomy and painful, and search deep into the conscience; yet all ends happily after all. The motif is mercy; a meting unto others, measure for measure, as we would wish them to mete unto us. The duke feigns a desire to travel, and appoints as deputies Angelo and Escalus. They begin at once to deal with sexual immorality: Escalus none too severely with a loathsome set of disreputable folk; but Angelo most mercilessly with young Claudio, who, in order to secure dower for his betrothed, had put off legal avowal of their irregular relation until her condition had brought the truth to light. Angelo condemns Claudio to death. His sister Isabella, about to enter a nunnery of the votarists of Saint Clare, is induced to plead for his life. As pure as snow, yet, as her "cheek-roses" show, not cold-blooded, her beauty ensnares the outward-sainted deputy and "seemer," who proposes the release of her brother to her as the price of her chastity. Isabella has plenty of hot blood and moral indignation. She refuses with noble scorn; and when her brother begs his life at her hands, bids him die rather than see her dishonored. The duke, disguised as a friar, has overheard in the prison her splendid defense of virtue, and proposes a plan for saving her virtue and her brother's life too. It is this: There dwells alone, in a certain moated grange, forgotten and forlorn now these five years, Mariana, legally affianced to Lord Angelo, and who loves him still, although owing to the loss of her dowry he has cast her off. The friar-duke proposes that Isabella shall feign compliance, make an appointment, and then send Mariana in her place. Isabella agrees to risk her reputation, and the dejected grass-widow is easily won over to meet Angelo by night in his brick-walled garden, The base deputy, fearing Claudio's revenge if he frees him, breaks his promise and sends word to have him executed. The duke and the provost of the prison send Angelo the head of a prisoner (much like Claudio) who has died overnight; Isabella supposes her brother to be dead. The duke, entering the city gates in state, *in propria persona*, hears her petition for justice. Angelo confesses; and after (by the duke's order) marrying Marianna, is pardoned. Indeed, there is a general amnesty; and the duke takes to wife Isabella, who thus enters upon a wider sphere of usefulness than that of a cloister.

MECHANISM OF THE HEAVENS, THE ('Mécanique céleste'), by Pierre Simon Laplace. The first two volumes of this remarkable work were published in 1799, the third appeared in 1803, the fourth in 1805, and the fifth in 1825. The author has set forth in one homogeneous work the leading results which had been separately achieved by his predecessors, at the same time proving their harmony and interdependence. The entire work is divided into sixteen books, treating of: The General Laws of Equilibrium and Motion; The Law of Universal Gravity; The Form of the Heavenly Bodies; The Oscillation of the Sea, and of the Atmosphere; The Movement of the Heavenly Bodies on their Axes; The Theory of Planetary Movements; The Theory of the Moon; The Satellites of Jupiter, Saturn, and Uranus; Comets; The Form and Rotation of the Earth; Attraction and Repulsion of the Spheres; The Laws of Equilibrium and Movements of Fluids; The Oscillation of Fluids that cover the Planets; The Movement of Planets and Comets; and the Movement of Satellites. The work is very diffuse, and it is said that the author found himself at times obliged to devote an hour's labor to recovering the lost links in the chain of reasoning covered by the recurring formula, "It is easy to see." 'The Exposition of the System of the World,' by the same author, is a more popular dissertation on the same subject, disembarrassed of the analytical paraphernalia, of the greater work. It has been truly said that Laplace was not properly an astronomer, but rather belonged to that class of savants who, neglecting direct observation of phenomena, depend upon the observations of others, and discover by force of calculation and meditation those great laws of which the patient researches of observers have shown the elements, without suspecting the principle.

Translated by Mrs. Mary Somerville in England, and by Nathaniel Bowditch in America.

MEDEA, a tragedy by Euripides, acted 431 B.C. The play opens on the day when Jason, having put aside Medea, daughter of Œetes, King of Colchis, is to wed the daughter of Creon, King of Corinth. Medea, by her magic art had enabled Jason to win from her father the Golden Fleece, had joined him in his flight to Greece, had killed her brother, Absyrtus, who pursued them, had restored Jason to his kingdom of Iolcos by inducing the daughters of the usurper, Peleus, to murder their father, and had then accompanied Jason to Corinth, where she had borne him two children. Overcome with indignation at the faithlessness of her husband, she has now uttered threats against his proposed new bride. These have been reported to Creon, who at the beginning of the play punishes Medea by banishing her and her children. An introductory dialogue between Medea's nurse and the children's pedagogue puts these facts before the audience, and is followed by the entrance of the chorus of Corinthian ladies whose ode is frequently interrupted by the laments of Medea, hidden behind the scenes. There ensues a dialogue between Medea and Creon in which he agrees at her request to defer the exile for a day; a scene with Jason, who excuses his course on the ground of desire for royal authority to benefit his sons and Medea, attributes her exile to her own unrestrained tongue, and offers her money; a conversation with Ægeus, King of Athens, whom Medea induces to swear to give her an asylum; an explanation to the chorus of her plan of vengeance; and an episode with Jason in which she pretends to justify his conduct, urges him to plead with his new bride that the children may not be exiled, and sends her two sons to enforce this plea with a present of a crown and robes, both poisoned. The children soon announce the success of their mission. Medea bids them a tender farewell and sends them into the house, resolved to put them to death. A messenger now comes in reporting the death of the bride and also of Creon, through the poisoned ornaments. Medea now enters the house, whence are heard the death cries of her children as she murders them. Jason, coming in to rescue his children from the vengeance of the Corinthians, is horrified to learn that they have fallen by the hand of their own mother. He attempts to break into the palace; but Medea appears on the roof in a chariot drawn by dragons, and after bitterly denouncing her faithless husband departs for the asylum promised her in Athens. The chorus in this play is sympathetic with Medea, but shocked at her crime, which, however, it makes no movement to prevent. Like all the plays of Euripides, 'Medea' is full of rebellious questionings of the ways of God to Man. It excels in pathos and in psychological insight.

MEDECIN DE CAMPAGNE, LE, see **COUNTRY DOCTOR.**

MEDITATIONS OF MARCUS AURELIUS, a collection of ethical and philosophical reflections, written in Greek by the Roman Emperor, Marcus Aurelius (121–180 A.D.), at leisure moments during his campaigns against the tribes east of the Danube (c 170 A.D.). The book consists of detached paragraphs, some very short, others running to one or two hundred words in length, evidently set down at times of contemplation as a guidance to self-examination and an incentive to self-improvement. Marcus Aurelius is the most distinguished exponent of the Stoic philosophy. His book illustrates its practical working in a mind and character unusually pure, lofty, and humane and in a sphere of life offering the greatest opportunities for beneficent action. The leading ideas are that the universe is governed by Supreme Reason; that all things therefore are for the best; that we should not complain or be perturbed at suffering, or injuries which are not in our control, since these are evidently permitted by an all-wise Providence; that towards everything not in our power we should adopt an attitude of complete indifference; and that our one concern should be the attainment of virtue through the exercise of our free will. Virtue consists in the control of the lower appetites and passions, the maintenance of equanimity in all circumstances, however distressing, the performance of justice and charity to our fellowmen, and the reverencing of the Supreme Reason and its manifestations. The austerity of this creed is lightened up by the delicacy of the emperor's moral insight, his human sympathy, and the simple unassuming dignity of his character.

MEHALAH, by Sabine Baring-Gould, 1880, is a tale of the salt marshes on the east coast of Essex, England, a strange region, where even at the present day, when this story is dated, superstition is rife. Every character in the book is eccentric, the half-mad Mrs. De Witt with her soldier jacket and her odd oaths, Elijah Rebow, the fiery gipsy-beauty Mehalah, or Glory, as she is called. Mehalah loves George De Witt, but quarrels with him about Phœbe Musset. Elijah loves Mehalah, and vows to make her his wife. To do this, he robs her of her savings, burns the house over her head, and compels her to seek shelter under his roof with her sick mother. So, among this half-barbarous folk, go on the amenities of life; and the story grows more and more lawless to the end. It is a powerful study of primitive characters, never agreeable, but always absorbing. Its strength is in the skill with which the romancer environs his fierce human creatures with an equally untamable nature. "Wild, singular, and extraordinary as the conceptions and combinations of the author of 'Mehalah' are, they are almost, if not entirely, removed from the realm of imagination. It is on this fact that their value and their permanence as literature rest. They are bits of human history, studies of eccentric development, scenes from the comedy of unsophisticated life."

MELTING POT, THE, by Israel Zangwill (1910). The hero of this drama is a young Jewish musician, who has escaped to New York from the massacre of Kishenev and sees in America the great crucible, the melting pot, in which people of every race and creed are fused into one nation. He earns his living playing the violin in cheap music halls, and devotes all his spare time to the composition of a symphony 'America' which shall express his ardent patriotism. At the settlement he meets and loves Vera Revendal, also a Russian, but a Gentile and the daughter of a nobleman. She tries to interest Quincy Davenport, a spendthrift millionaire, in David's symphony, but David rejects this help and denounces him and his class as untrue to American ideals. His love for Vera causes his orthodox uncle to turn him out of his home. Davenport, who wants to divorce his wife and marry Vera, brings her father to America to prevent her marriage to a Jew. David recognizes in Baron Revendal the inhuman officer who directed the slaughter of his father, mother, and sister at Kishenev, and in a frenzy of remembrance renounces Vera. As his sym-phony is being played to the immigrants at the settlement on a Fourth of July, he realizes that he has been false to the ideals of his music; he returns to his concep-tion of the United States as the crucible that could melt all race differences and feuds, and the lovers are reunited.

MEMOIRS OF SHERLOCK HOLMES, see SHERLOCK HOLMES.

MEMORABILIA, THE. The 'Apomnemoneumata,' by Xenophon (c 434-c 355 B.C.), is generally known by its Latin title of 'The Memorabilia,'—an incorrect and somewhat misleading translation of the Greek word. This is the most important of the writings that the author has devoted to the memory of Socrates. Like Plato, he dwells principally on those doctrines of the master that harmonize with his own views. In the beginning, by way of preface, he replies to the positive accusations brought against the philosopher, Then he proceeds to develop his real purpose; which is to depict the true Socrates, not from the opinions of others, which are al-ways controvertible, but from his own words and actions, and in this way place under the eyes of the Athenians a correct likeness of the man they condemned because they did not know him. He next treats of the many examples of right living given by Socrates to his countrymen, and of the lesson of his life. After the lesson of his life comes the lesson of his discourses. This is embodied in a series of dialogues between Socrates and persons engaged in different occupations, upon the subjects which engrossed his whole attention: piety towards the gods, temper-ance, the duties incumbent on children with regard to parents, friendship, the po-litical virtues, the useful arts, and the science of dialectics. As it was Xenophon's object to create a feeling of love and veneration for his master among the Athenians, he touches chiefly on those points in the character of Socrates that he believed would conduce to this end. Thus he describes him as teaching that in matters of religion every one should follow the usages of his city. Socrates, he says, sacri-ficed openly and publicly; he not only consulted the oracles, but he strongly ad-vised his friends to consult them; he believed in divination, and paid close attention to the signs by which the divinity communicated with himself. More than half of the chapters in the third book are devoted to the conversation of Socrates with generals and hipparchs, and Xenophon attributes much of his own knowledge of military matters to his good fortune in having been acquainted with his master. The most beautiful dialogues, however, are those which deal with the feelings that ought to actuate the members of the same family,—the love of the mother for her child, and of brother for brother. The chapters which conclude the work are noted for deep feeling, tenderness, and elevation of thought.

MEN OF THE OLD STONE AGE: 'Their Environment, Life, and Art,' by Henry Fairfield Osborn (1915). The book is a history of the origin and develop-ment of man from the anthropoid apes to the Old Stone Age and the beginnings of the modern European races. The latest anthropological discoveries, includ-ing the various skeletons of primitive man found at Heidelberg and Neander-thal, and the later specimens of the more civilized Crô-magnon race, occurring in the valleys of Southern France and Northern Spain, are combined with the latest archæological and geological data relevant to the subject in a clear and orderly narrative of human development. The book is superbly illustrated with reconstruc-tions of early types of men and animals and reproductions of drawings of men, horses, fish, and other creatures, made on the walls of caverns in the regions mentioned by "upper palæolithic artists." These representations show considerable skill and appreciation of nature on the part of a race which existed at least 25,000 years ago. Abundant maps and diagrams accompany the text, which expounds the subject clearly, avoiding undue discussion of controverted points, and aiming at a straightforward presentation of admitted facts. As the writer lays no claim to authority as an anthropologist, and relies in part on the investigations of Cartilhac, Breuil, Obermaies, and others, the book is rather a compilation for the layman and a general conspectus for the scientist than a piece of original investigation; but it is an exceedingly valuable summary, skilfully arranged by an archæologist of distinction, of the latest conclusions as to the history of primitive mankind.

MENÆCHMI, a comedy by Plautus, the source of Shakespeare's 'Comedy of Errors.' A full summary of the Plautine comedy is given in the LIBRARY under 'Plautus,' pp. 11561–2. Shakespeare by representing the two servants as twin-brothers, doubles the fun and the entanglement. The play is an excellent example of classical comedy—its stock characters, its complicated intrigue, and its witty dialogue.

MERCHANT OF VENICE, THE, is a drama of Shakespeare's middle period (1597). The story of the bond and that of the caskets are both found in the old Gesta Romanorum, but the poet used especially Fiorentino's 'Il Pecorone' (Milan, 1558). An atmosphere of high breeding and noble manners enwraps this most popular of Shakespeare's plays. The merchant Antonio is the ideal friend, his magnificent generosity a foil against which Shylock's avarice glows with a more baleful lustre. Shylock has long hated him, both for personal insults and for lending money gratis. Now, some twenty and odd miles away, at Belmont, lives Portia, with her golden hair, and golden ducats; and Bassanio asks his friend Antonio for a loan, that he may go that way a-wooing. Antonio seeks the money of Shylock, who bethinks him now of a possible revenge. He offers three thousand ducats gratis for three months, if Antonio will seal to a merry bond pledging that if he shall fail his day of payment, the Jew may cut from his breast, nearest the heart, a pound of flesh. Antonio expects ships home a month before the day, and signs. While Shylock is feeding at the Christian's expense, Lorenzo runs away with sweet Jessica, his dark-eyed daughter, and sundry bags of ducats and jewels. Bassanio is off to Belmont. Portia is to be won by him who, out of three caskets,—of gold, silver, and lead, respectively,— shall choose that containing her portrait. Bassanio makes the right choice. But at once comes word that blanches his cheeks; all of Antonio's ships are reported lost at sea; his day of payment has passed, and Shylock clamors for his dreadful forfeit. Bassanio, and his follower, Gratiano, only tarry to be married, the one to Portia, and the other to her maid Nerissa; and then, with money furnished by Portia they speed away toward Venice. Portia follows disguised as a young doctor-at-law, and Nerissa as her clerk. Arrived in Venice, they are ushered into court, where Shylock, fell as a famished tiger, is snapping out fierce calls for justice and his pound of flesh, Antonio pale and hopeless, and Bassanio in vain offering him thrice the value of his bond. Portia, too, in vain pleads with him for mercy. Well, says Portia, the law must take its course. Then, "A Daniel come to judgment!" cries the Jew: "Come, prepare, prepare." Stop, says the young doctor, your bond gives you flesh, but no blood; if you shed one drop of blood you die, and your lands and goods are confiscate to the State. The Jew cringes, and offers to accept Bassanio's offer of thrice the value of the bond in cash; but learns that for plotting against the life of a citizen of Venice all his property is forfeited, half to Antonio and half to the State. As the play closes, the little band of friends are grouped on Portia's lawn in the moonlight, under the vast blue dome of stars. The poet, however, excites our pity for the baited Jew.

MÉRIMÉE, PROSPER, see LETTERS TO AN UNKNOWN.

MERRY WIVES OF WINDSOR, by Shakespeare (printed 1602), is a play written, according to tradition, at the request of Queen Elizabeth, who wanted to see Falstaff in love. With its air of village domesticity and out-o'-doorness is united the quintessential spirit of fun and waggery. Its gay humor never fails, and its readers alway wish it five times as long as it is. The figures on this rich old tapestry resolve themselves, on inspection, into groups. The jolly ranter and bottle-rinser, mine host of the Garter Inn, with Sir John Falstaff and his men, Bardolph, Nym, and Pistol; the merry wives, Mrs. Ford and Mrs. Page, and their families; then Shallow (the country justice), with his cousin of the "wee little face and little yellow beard" (Slender), and the latter's man Simple; further Dr. Caius, the French physician, who speaks broken English, as does Parson Hugh Evans, the Welshman; lastly Dame Quickly (the doctor's housekeeper), and Master Fenton, in love with sweet Anne Page. Shallow has a grievance against Sir John for killing his deer; and Slender has matter in his head against him, for Sir John broke it. But Falstaff and his men outface the two cheese-parings, and they forget their "pribbles and prabbles" in the parson's scheme of marrying Slender to Anne Page. But the irascible doctor has looked that way too, and sends a "challenge" to Evans. Mine host fools them both by sending each to a separate place for the duel. They make friends, and avenge themselves on the Boniface by getting his horses run off with. Falstaff sends identically worded love-letters to Mrs. Ford and Mrs. Page, hoping to replenish his purse from their husbands' gold. But Pistol and Nym, in revenge for dismissal, peach to said husbands. The jealous Ford visits Falstaff under the name of Brook, and offers him a bag of gold if he will seduce Mrs. Ford for him. Jack assures him that he has an appointment with her that very day. And so he has. But the two wives punish him badly, and he gets nothing from them but a cast out of a buck-basket into a dirty ditch, and a sound beating from Ford. The midnight scene in Windsor Park, where Falstaff, disguised as Herne the Hunter, with stag-horns on his head, is guyed by the wives and their husbands and pinched and burned by the fairies' tapers, is most amusing. During the fairies' song Fenton steals away Anne Page and marries her. The doctor, by previous arrangement, with mother Ford, leads away a fairy in green to a priest, only to discover that he has married a boy. And Slender barely escapes the same fate; for he leads off to Eton Church another "great lubberly boy," dressed in white as agreed with Mr. Page. Anne has given the slip to both father and mother, having promised her father to wear white for Slender and her mother to dress in green for the doctor.

METHODISM IN THE UNITED STATES, A HISTORY OF, by James M. Buckley (1897). A work of description and history, designed to present Methodism in comparison with other forms of American Protestant Christianity; to show its origins and follow its developments; to mark the modifications which it has undergone; and to note into what branches it has divided, through what conflicts it has passed, and what have been the controversies with which it has had to deal. Dr. Buckley is an accomplished journalist of his denomination, thoroughly familiar with the men and movements representing nineteenth-century Methodism, and not less with the history of other churches in America; and his story of the wide sweep and vast weight of the faith and fellowship running in the names of Wesley and of Methodism is as interesting as it is opportune.

METHODS OF SOCIAL REFORM, by William Stanley Jevons (1883). This volume appeared, with a preface by the author's wife, after his too early death in 1882, the papers composing it having already been published in the Contemporary Review. Professor Jevons takes the view that the possible methods of social reform are well-nigh infinite in number and diversity, becoming more numerous as society grows more complex, and that the recognized methods at any given time are to be used not disjunctively but collectively. In this volume, he considers Amusements, Public Libraries, Museums, "Cram" (in its university sense), Trades Societies, Industrial Partnerships, Married Women in Factories, Cruelty to Animals, Experimental Legislation, and the Drink Traffic, Systems of Conveyance of Documents, other than the Post-Office under government control, the Post-Office Telegraphs and their Financial Results, Postal Notes, Money Orders and Bank Checks, a State Parcel Post, the Railways and the State. His Inaugural Address before the Manchester Statistical Society, his opening address as president of Section C of the British Association, and a paper on the United Kingdom Alliance, economic science, and statistics, are also given. Libraries he regards as one of the best and quickest paying investments in which the public money can be used, attributing the recent advance in British library economics and extension largely to American example. The paper on "Cram" takes the view that while the method of university examinations is not perfect, it is the most effective known for enforcing severe and definite mental training, and of selecting for high position the successful competitors; while any system of preparation for the examinations that leads to success is a good system. He favors co-operation and profit-sharing, but opposes government ownership of the railways. In all his work, Professor Jevons has shown that his practical and exact mind is always informed by a spiritual and ethical influence that gives his conclusions a special weight on their moral side; and this work, written with great clearness and attractiveness, is no exception to the rule.

MICAH CLARKE, by A. Conan Doyle (1888), presents in the form of a novel a graphic and vivid picture of the political condition in England during the Western rebellion, when James, Duke of Monmouth, aspired to the throne, and when Englishmen were in arms against Englishmen. The story tells of the adventures of the young man whose name the book bears, of the many perils which he encountered on his journey from Havant to Taunton to join the standard of Monmouth, and of the valiant part he played in the final struggle, when the King's troops were victorious and hundreds of Protestants, who had escaped death on the field, were hanged for treason.

Through this melancholy but thrilling narrative runs a pretty vein of love-making. The gentle and innocent Puritan maid, Mistress Ruth Timewell, who had never heard of Cowley or Waller or Dryden, and who was accustomed to derive enjoyment from such books as the 'Alarm to the Unconverted,' 'Faithful Contendings,' or 'Bull's Spirit Cordial,' finds love more potent than theology, and prefers Reuben Lockarby, a tavern-keeper's son, to Master John Derrick, a man of her own faith.

But the climax of 'Micah Clarke' is reached in the description of the battle on the plain in the early morning, in which one learns what religion meant in England toward the close of the sixteenth century. Against the disciplined and well-equipped regiments of the King are opposed Monmouth's untrained and ragged forces—peasants, armed only with scythes, pikes, and clubs, but with the unfaltering courage of fanaticism in their hearts and with psalms on their lips.

'Micah Clarke' is a book for old and young; a book which instructs, while it quickens the imagination and stirs the blood.

MICHAEL AND HIS LOST ANGEL, by Henry Arthur Jones (1896). The play opens with a scene in which the Rev. Michael Faversham, an ascetic clergyman of the Church of England, who had taken vows of celibacy, insists that Rose Andrew, who had secretly given birth to an illegitimate child, and her father, who had been assisting her to deceive the public about this circumstance in her life, should confess their fault in public before his congregation. Michael's dearest aim at the moment is the restoration of the Minster, and he has just received a large anonymous contribution, which he suspects has come from Mrs. Lesden, a wealthy woman who has recently come to live in the district; and whom at first he dislikes on account of her apparent frivolity and insincerity. She persists in making excuses to see him and he gradually falls a prey to her fascinations and admits to her that he is enamored of her. In great mental agony he retires for meditation and prayer to St. Decuman's Island, an uninhabited island, where he had built a small cabin around the shrine of the saint. Mrs. Lesden had written to him that he is the only man living who can inspire her to attempt the life of a saint, but that the cost to him would be too great. He burns her letter and hopes that he has overcome the temptation, when a tap comes to the door and she appears. He persuades her to renounce their love, but finds that there is no means of return for her from the island that night. Afterwards Michael in the presence of Rose makes public renunciation of his fault in his own church. Going to Italy to spend his time in penance and retirement, he again meets Mrs. Lesden, wasted and dying, who has followed him and who dies in his arms.

MIDDLEMARCH, by George Eliot (1872). This, the last but one of George Eliot's novels, she is said to have regarded as her greatest work. The novel takes its name from a provincial town in or near which its leading characters live. The book is really made up to two stories, one centring around the Vincy family, and the other around Dorothea Brooke and her relatives. On account of this division of interest, the construction of the story has been severely criticized as clumsy and inartistic.

Dorothea Brooke, the most prominent figure on the very crowded canvas, is an orphan, who, with her sister Celia, lives with her uncle Mr. Brooke, a man of vacillating and uneven temperament. Dorothea's longing for a lofty mission leads her to marry an elderly and wealthy clergyman, Rev. Edward Casaubon, who has retired from the ministry to give his time to an important piece of literary work. Dorothea, though not yet twenty, hopes to be his amanuensis and helper; and is greatly grieved to find that her husband sets slight value on her services. In other ways she has been disillusioned before the death of Mr. Casaubon, a year and a half after their marriage. A rather insulting provision of his will directs that his widow shall lose her income if she marries Will Ladislaw, a young cousin of Mr. Casaubon's. Ladislaw is partly of Polish descent; and both his mother and his grandmother had been disinherited by their English relatives for marrying foreigners. Ladislaw owes his education to Mr. Casaubon; but not until after the death of the latter does the friendship between the younger man and Dorothea take the tinge of love.

Rosamond Vincy, who may be called a minor heroine, is the daughter of the mayor of Middlemarch. She is a beautiful girl, whose feeling that she is much more refined than her commonplace relatives, leads her to lofty matrimonial aspirations. She wins the love of Dr. Lydgate, who, though nephew to a baronet, has a hard struggle to establish himself as a Middlemarch physician, with Dr. Sprague and Dr. Minchin as rivals. Neither he nor his wife knows how to economize; and the latter, feeling her husband's poverty an insult to herself, is a hindrance to him in every way. The story of his efforts to maintain his family, and at the same time to be true to his ambition to add to the science of his profession, is a sad one. In the characters of Dorothea and Lydgate, George Eliot develops the main purpose of this novel, which is less distinctly ethical than some of the others. Her aim in 'Middlemarch' was to show how the thought and action of even very high-minded persons is apt to be modified and altered by their environment. Both Dorothea and Lydgate become entangled by their circumstances; though in his case the disaster is greater than in hers, and in each case it is a moral and not a social decline which is pointed out. Two secondary love stories in 'Middlemarch' are those of the witty Mary Garth and the spendthrift Fred Vincy, and of Celia Brooke, and Sir James Chettam. The chorus, which constantly reflects Middlemarch sentiment at every turn of affairs, is a large one, including Mrs. Fitchett, Mrs. Dill, Mrs. Waule, Mrs. Renfrew, Mrs. Plymdale, Mrs. Bulstrode, Mrs. Vincy; and among the men, Mr. Dollop, Mr. Dill, Mr. Brothrop Trumbull, Mr. Horrock, Mr. Wrech, Mr. Thesiger, and Mr. Standish.

More carefully drawn are the caustic Mrs. Cadwallader, the self-denying Mr. Farebrother, hypocritical Mr. Bulstrode, the miser Featherstone, and the honorable Caleb Garth and his self-reliant wife.

MIDSUMMER NIGHT'S DREAM, by Shakespeare, was written previous to 1598; the poet drawing for materials on Plutarch, Ovid, and Chaucer. The roguish sprite Puck, or Robin Goodfellow, is a sort of half-brother of Ariel, and obeys Oberon as Ariel obeys Prospero. The theme of this joyous comedy is love and marriage. Duke Theseus is about to wed the fair Hippolyta. Lysander is in love with Hermia, and so is Demetrius; though in the end, Demetrius, by the aid of Oberon, is led back to his first love Helena. The scene lies chiefly in the enchanted wood near the duke's palace in Athens. In this wood Lysander and Hermia, and Demetrius and Helena, wander all night and meet with strange adventures at the hands of Puck and the tiny fairies of Queen Titania's train. Like her namesake in 'All's Well,' Helena is here the wooer: "Apollo flies and Daphne leads the chase." Oberon pities her, and sprinkling the juice of the magic flower love-in-idleness in Demetrius's eyes, restores his love for her; but not before Puck, by a mistake in anointing the wrong man's eyes, has caused a train of woes and perplexities to attend the footsteps of the wandering lovers. Puck, for fun, claps an ass's head on to weaver Bottom's shoulders, who thereupon calls for oats and a bottle of hay. By the same flower juice, sprinkled in her eyes, Oberon leads Titania to dote on Bottom, whose hairy head she has garlanded with flowers, and stuck musk roses behind his ears. Everybody seems to dream: Titania, in her bower carpeted with violets and canopied with honeysuckle and sweet-briar, dreamed she was enamored of an ass, and Bottom dared not say aloud what he dreamed he was; while in the fresh morning the lovers felt the fumes of the sleepy enchantment still about them.

But we must introduce the immortal players of 'Pyramus and Thisbe.' Bottom is a first cousin of Dogberry, his drollery the richer for being partly self-conscious. With good strings to their beards and new ribbons for their pumps, he and his men meet at the palace, "on the duke's wedding-day at night." Snout presents Wall; in one hand he holds some lime, some plaster and a stone, and with the open fingers of the other makes a cranny through which the lovers whisper. A fellow with lantern and thorn-bush stands for Moon. The actors kindly and in detail explain to the audience what each one personates; and the lion bids them not to be afeard, for he is only Snug the joiner, who roars extempore. The master of the revels laughs at the delicious humor till the tears run down his cheeks (and you don't wonder), and the lords and ladies keep up the fun by a running fire of witticisms when they can keep their faces straight. Theseus is an idealized English gentleman, large-molded, gracious, and wise. His greatness is shown in his genuine kindness to the poor players in their attempt to please him.

MILL, JOHN STUART, AUTOBIOGRAPHY OF (1873). The reader who for the first time learns how John Stuart Mill was brought up by his father, James Mill, will perhaps wonder how the scholar ever survived so arduous a régime, so early imposed. Starting Greek at the age of three, he had read many works in that language before he began Latin in his eighth year. Numerous histories occupied a large part of the interval until his twelfth year, when he began logic, to which he added political economy a year later. Brought up by his father to think that nothing was known of the manner in which the world came into existence, he says of himself in this book that he had not thrown off religious belief, he had never had it, a circumstance which lends all the greater interest to views which he was elsewhere to express in 'The Utility of Religion and Theism.' He records the formation of the Utilitarian Society (whence the term Utilitarian passed into general use, though Mill had borrowed it from Galt's 'Annals of the Parish'), by himself and a group of other young men who took Utility as their standard in ethics and politics. Later he helped to found the Westminster Review as a Radical offset to the Edinburgh and Quarterly, then in the heyday of their power. At that time he and his fellow-workers based their political faith on representative government and complete freedom of discussion. His intercourse for twenty years with the lady who was afterwards, on the death of her first husband, to become his wife, was a source of profound intellectual stimulus to him and modified his views on religion, ethics, political economy and every subject which occupied his mind. It is interesting to note that the man who wrote a classic treatise 'On Liberty' could also epitomise in these words his own and his most intimate fellow-workers' views. "While we repudiated with the greatest energy that tyranny of society over the individual which most Socialistic systems are supposed to involve, we yet looked forward to a time when society will no longer be divided into the idle and the industrious; when the rule that they who do not work shall not eat, will be applied not to paupers only, but impartially to all; when the division of the produce of labour, instead of depending, as in so great a degree it now does, on the accident of birth, will be made by concert on an acknowledged principle of justice; and when it will no longer either be, or be thought to be, impossible for human beings to exert themselves strenuously in procuring benefits which are not to be exclusively their own, but to be shared with the society they belong to." The most poignant section of a pathetically interesting self-revelation is Mill's lament for the loss of his wife. "Her memory is to me a religion, and her approbation the standard by which, summing up as it does all worthiness, I endeavour to regulate my life."

MILL ON THE FLOSS, THE, by George Eliot (1860), one of the masterpieces of fiction, is like 'Middlemarch' a tragedy, though a tragedy destitute of the usual heroic setting and grandiloquent circumstances. The author found her tragic material in the commonplace lives of English working-people; and traced the workings of fate in the obscure development of a young girl, with passions no less strong than those of a woman in some ancient Greek tragedy, suffering in a magnificent environment, under the gaze of the world. Maggie Tulliver, the daughter of the Miller of Dorlcote Mill, is from childhood misunderstood and dominated by the coarse-grained well-meaning people about her. Her brother Tom, a hearty young animal, with selfish masculine instincts, accepts her devotion as he would that of a dog. He teases her because she is a girl. He hates her when she eludes him by going into her fairyland of imagination, whither he cannot follow her. She loves him devotedly; but to her love always brings suffering. She is ill regulated, and is therefore not a favorite with her aunts, Mrs. Glegg and Mrs. Pullet, who can see no trace of the respectable Dodson blood in her. Maggie's childhood is a series of conflicts with respectability. In her girlhood the passionate little heart is somewhat subdued to her surroundings. Family troubles are brewing. They culminate in the death of Mr. Tulliver, and in the sale of Dorlcote Mill. Maggie ceases to be a child, becomes a woman. The needs of her nature find satisfaction in the companionship of Philip Wakem, the crippled son of the lawyer who helped to ruin Mr. Tulliver. It is the old story of Verona, of the lovers whose families are at feud, translated into homely English life. Maggie must renounce Philip. Tom hates him and his race with all the strength of his hard-and-fast uncompromising nature. Maggie, starving for beauty, for the joy of love and life, seeks to satisfy her spiritual cravings in that classic of renunciation, the 'Imitation of Christ.' She feeds her rich nature with the thoughts of the dead. The next temptation in her way is Stephen Guest, betrothed to her cousin Lucy. Stephen represents to Maggie, although she does not know it, the æsthetic element that is lacking in her barren life. The two are thrown together. Their mutual passion masters them. Maggie almost consents to go away with Stephen, finds herself indeed on the journey; but at the last minute turns back, though she knows that she has endangered her good name. The worst interpretation is put upon her conduct. From that time on she faces the contumely of the little village community. Death, and death only, can reconcile her to the world and to Tom, who has stood as the embodiment of the world's harshest judgment. They are drowned in the great flood of the Floss: "Brother and sister had gone down together in an embrace never to be parted; living through again in one supreme moment the days when they had clasped their little hands in love and roamed the daisied fields together." The tragic atmosphere of the novel is relieved by passages of quaint, primitive humor, by marvelous descriptions of well-to-do rural types. The Dodson family is hardly surpassed in fiction.

MILLIONAIRE, THE, by Mikhail Artsybashev (1904). The three stories are painful Russian realism. The millionaire is the unhappy rich man, who cannot buy the love and friendship he longs to have. He suspects everyone who approaches him of a design to get money from him. His morbid obsession makes life a burden and he commits suicide by drowning. The story of 'Ivan Lande' is that of the man who tries to live on earth like Jesus. Ivan's first act is to try to give his inheritance of four thousand rubles to the starving families of the workmen who are out of employment, but he succeeds only in making his mother furious that the money which his father worked to save should go to a "pack of paupers." The church is against him because he disregards the letter for the sake of the spirit, and his refusal to fight the man who has struck him wins him only contempt. He dies miserably and alone. 'Nina,' called 'The Horror,' in Russian, is a story of criminal attack and murder of an innocent young girl. Because the murderers are a magistrate, a police commissioner, and a doctor, the Russian police shoot down the crowd who call for justice.

MILLIONAIRE BABY, THE, by Anna Katharine Green (1905). This is a detective story founded on the mysterious disappearance of Gwendolen Ocumpaugh, the only child of wealthy parents and heiress to a fortune which gives her the name of the "Millionaire Baby." She disappears from a bungalow on the family estate while in the charge of her nursery governess, Miss Graham. Mrs. Ocumpaugh is giving a large reception at the time the loss of Gwendolen is discovered and frenzied with grief she leads the search for the child. The river is dragged, at her suggestion, and one small shoe belonging to Gwendolen is found in the bushes and another in the river. However, Mr. Trevitt, the private detective, who is at work on the case, discovers that the two shoes are for the same foot and immediately scents a conspiracy and is convinced that the child has been abducted. In the next house to the Ocumpaughs lives an attractive widow, named Mrs. Carew, who on the day of the disappearance has been to the city and brought back with her an orphan nephew with whom she is to sail immediately for Europe. Mr. Trevitt explores the bungalow with Mrs. Carew as she will not permit him to go there without her, and he discovers a trap door under a rug which leads to a room underground and finds proof of Gwendolen's having been secreted there. He discovers a woman's footprints which he suspects are Mrs. Carew's but on interviewing Mrs. Ocumpaugh she breaks down and confesses that they are hers. She tells him that Gwendolen is not her own child but has been procured for her by a Dr. Pool who has aided her in deceiving her husband as to her real identity. Mr. Ocumpaugh being in Europe at the time of the abduction which was precipitated by the threats of Dr. Pool who would force her to give up the child, she had finally taken Mrs. Carew into her confidence and together they had planned for Gwendolen's disappearance. Mrs. Ocumpaugh herself hid her in the bungalow and later carried her to Mrs. Carew's where she was dressed as a boy, with her hair cut and darkened. The child Mrs. Carew had brought back from the city was surreptitiously carried away in a covered wagon and the servants were dismissed for the occasion.

Mrs. Ocumpaugh, who loves her husband devotedly, is almost crazed at the thought of his learning her duplicity, when Dr. Pool suddenly dies, and later developments show that Gwendolyn is Mrs. Carew's own child whom poverty has forced her to part with at her birth.

MILTON, JOHN, THE LIFE OF, 'Narrated in connection with the Political, Ecclesiastical, and Literary History of his Time' by David Masson (7 vols., 1858–94. Revised and enlarged edition of Vol. i., 1881). A thorough and minute 'Life of Milton,' with a new political, ecclesiastical, and literary history of Milton's whole time, 1608–74. The work embraces not only the history of England, but the connections of England with Scotland and Ireland, and with foreign countries, through the civil wars, the Commonwealth, the Protectorates of Oliver and Richard Cromwell, the period following of anarchy, and the first fourteen years of the Restoration. It claims to be, and unquestionably is, the faithful fulfillment of a large design to make a history of England's most interesting and most momentous period, from original and independent studies; not a mere setting for the biography of Milton, but a work of independent search and method from first to last, to which the inquirer can turn for accurate information in regard to any important fact of the entire Milton period.

The Pilgrim Fathers took refuge in Holland the very year of Milton's birth; the age was the age of Puritanism; Milton was the very genius of Puritanism, and largely too of broad Pilgrim character and mind; the Westminster Assembly, by which Scotch Calvinism was made dominant in England, was a notable fact, side by side with the Long Parliament from July 1st, 1643, to February 22d, 1649; Presbyterianism found advantage from this Assembly to plant its organization on English soil; the less vigorous and more truly English system of independency, conspicuously represented by the Pilgrims to New England, won a place in the history; and over all rose that Commonwealth, which runs in the name of Cromwell, and to the governing body of which—the great Council of State—Milton was secretary from March 15th, 1649, to December 26th, 1659. To all these large and significant matters Professor Masson addressed himself with masterly research; and in due connection brings upon the scene all the great figures of the time. He uses the utmost pains also to tell the story of Milton's powerful prose writings, his vigorous and independent thinking in those great works which are one of the richest mines of interest and inspiration in the whole of English literature. Not only has Professor Masson given everything knowable about Milton, but he has shown the truest appreciation of the mind and character of the great poet, and of the varied aspects of the great age in which he played so conspicuous a part.

MINISTER'S WOOING, THE, by Harriet Beecher Stowe. The scene of this interesting story is laid in New England, and deals with the habits and traditions of the past century. Mary Scudder, the only daughter of a widowed mother, has been reared in an atmosphere of religion and piety. Being of a naturally sensitive temperament, she lives up to their teachings with conscientious fervor. She is in love with her cousin, James Marvyn, but does not listen to his protestations, because he has no religious belief. He goes to sea, is shipwrecked, and supposed to be drowned; and Mary, in course of time feels it to be her duty and pleasure to become engaged to the venerable Dr. Hopkins, her pastor and spiritual adviser. The wedding-day is set, and only one week distant, when Mary receives a letter from James Marvyn, telling of his miraculous escape from death, his religious conviction, and change of heart, and his abiding love for her. He follows the letter in person, and presses his suit; but Mary, in spite of her inclinations, considers it her duty to abide by her promise to the Doctor. However, through the intervention of Miss Prissy Diamond, a delightful little dressmaker, who acquaints Dr. Hopkins with the facts of the case, this sacrifice is prevented. The good Doctor, at the cost of his own happiness, relinquishes Mary, and gives her to James. The central purpose in this story is to show the sternness and inflexibility of the New England conscience, which holds to the Calvinistic doctrines through all phases of life. The struggle that goes on in the heart of Mrs. Marvyn and of Mary, when James is supposed to be drowned unconverted, is a graphic delineation of the moral point of view at that time. All the characters in the book are well drawn and have striking individualities; Madame de Frontignac, Miss Prissy, and Candace, the colored servant, being especially worthy of note. The story was first published in serial form in the Atlantic Monthly in 1859.

MIRROR FOR MAGISTRATES, THE. This once popular work, the first part of which was published in 1555, and the last in 1620, was the result of the labors of at least sixteen persons, the youngest of whom was not born when the oldest died. It probably owed its inception to George Ferrers, who was Master of the King's Revels at the close of the reign of Henry the Eighth; and he associated with himself William Baldwin. Richard Niccols is responsible for the book in its final state; and in the interim, it was contributed to by Thomas Newton, John Higgins, Thomas Blennerhasset, Thomas Chaloner, Thomas Sackville, Master Cavyll, Thomas Phaer, John Skelton, John Dolman, Francis Segar, Francis Wingley, Thomas Churchyard, and Michael Drayton. It is a "true Chronicle Historie of the untimely falles of such unfortunate princes and men of note, as have happened since the first entrance of Brute into this Iland, until this our latter age." It was patterned after Lydgate's 'Fall of Princes,' a version of Boccaccio's poems on the calamities of illustrious men, which had been very popular in England. The stories are told in rhyme, each author taking upon himself the character of the "miserable person" represented, and speaking in the first person. The first one told by Ferrers is that of Robert Tresilian, Chief Justice of England, "and of other which suffered with him, therby to warne all of his autority and profession to take heede of wrong judgments, and misconstruing of laws, which rightfully brought them to a miserable ende." This book is of little value to-day except to collectors; but it was the intention of its authors to make of it a great national epic, the work of many hands.

MISER, THE, see **L'AVARE.**

MISÉRABLES, LES, by Victor Hugo, appeared April 3d, 1862. Before publication it was translated into nine languages; and its simultaneous appearance at Paris, London, Brussels, New York, Madrid, Berlin, Saint Petersburg, and Turin, was a literary event. It has since been translated into twelve other languages. Hugo's first novel, since his great mediæval romance 'Notre Dame de Paris,' published thirty-one years earlier, 'Les Misérables,' is a story of the nineteenth century. It gives a comprehensive view of Paris, and discloses the author's conception of the present time, and his suggestions for the future. Though a novel with a purpose, it is questionable whether the poet's feeling for the ideal and picturesque does not exceed the reformer's practical sense and science. 'Les Misérables' is often criticized for lack of unity and careless arrangement of its abundant matter; but its enormous knowledge of life and history, and its imaginative power, give it an irresistible fascination. The central figure of the five books which compose the story is Jean Valjean, a simple, hard-working peasant, who, stealing a loaf of bread for his sister's starving children, is arrested and condemned to the galleys for five years, a punishment lengthened to nineteen years by his attempts to escape. Cruelty and privation render him inert and brutish; and on his release the convict begs in vain, till the Bishop of D—— takes him in and gives him food and shelter. The aged Bishop is a saint, shaping his life in literal obedience to the divine commands; but in return for his kindness, Valjean steals his silver and escapes in the night. When the police bring the culprit back, the Bishop saves him by declaring that the silver had been a free gift to him. Touched to the heart, Valjean henceforth believes in goodness and makes it his law. His future life is a series of self-sacrifices, resulting in moral growth. He becomes in time a rich manufacturer, mayor of his town, and a noted philanthropist. Among other good deeds, he befriends Fantine, a grisette abandoned by her lover, and forced into a life of degradation to support her child. Fantine dies just as Valjean is arrested by Javert, an implacable detective who has recognized the ex-convict. Valjean temporarily evades him, but wherever he goes, Javert ferrets him out. Finally to save another man mistaken for him, Valjean surrenders himself and is returned to the galleys. He escapes, and rescues Fantine's child, little Cosette, from the cruel Thénardiers, sordid inn-keepers to whom her mother had intrusted her. She grows up a beautiful, loving girl, the solace of his life, and for her sake he accomplishes his supreme sacrifice. Marius, a worthy young man, falls in love with her. Valjean arranges the marriage, conceals her ignoble birth, and provides for her future. But Marius misjudges him, and believes him guilty of unworthy conduct; and for Cosette's sake, the old man leaves her. But he cannot live without her; and when Marius learns his mistake, discovers that he owes his life to Valjean, and hurries to him with Cosette, the patient hero is dying. In this complicated history, which involves many characters, chiefly types of the poor, the unfortunate, and the vicious of Paris, certain passages stand out with dramatic intensity; among them being the famous chapter of the battle of Waterloo; the description of the Paris sewers, through the intricacies of which Jean Valjean flees with wounded Marius; and of the defense of the barricade, where Gavroche, the best existing study of a Paris gamin, gathers bullets and sings defiantly as he meets death. The place of 'Les Misérables' is in the front rank of successful romantic fiction.

MISS BROWN, by Violet Paget ("Vernon Lee") (1884). The object of this satirical novel is to expose the falseness of the æsthetic ideal and its tendency to debase all who follow it; and it aroused the indignation of all the "æsthetes."

Miss Brown herself is a girl endowed with great beauty, who is discovered by Mr. Hamlin, an artist and poet of high reputation. At the time when he finds her, she is a nursemaid in the family of another artist in Italy, belonging to the same school. Mr. Hamlin determines to save her from the commonplace career before her. He therefore settles on her a fourth of his income, leaving her free to marry him or not after she has been educated. She goes to a school in Germany, where she receives instruction in the usual learning and accomplishments. Mr. Hamlin himself instructs her in his school of poetry, and writes to her long letters filled with his theories on art and life. Work as hard as she can, out of her love and gratitude for Mr. Hamlin, she cannot become the æsthete that he desires. After she discovers the true character of Hamlin, the thought of marrying him is revolting to her. She turns for interest to her cousin Robert, a radical, interested in the welfare of the lower classes. She now studies political economy with greater fervor than ever went to the art and poetry of Burne-Jones and Rossetti. She sees, with delight, Hamlin's growing attachment to another girl; but his failure to win her results in his utter debasement. Miss Brown then, in a spirit of self-sacrifice, claims Hamlin's promise to marry her, and allows him to think that she loves him. The character of Miss Brown, always a noble-minded and simple woman, is a strong and forcible creation, standing out vividly in the midst of her weak and emotion-loving companions.

MISS JULIA; 'A Naturalistic Tragedy,' by August Strindberg (1888). The romantic, headstrong daughter of a count, in the abandon of the Midsummer Eve festivities, flirts and dances with her father's gentlemanly valet, and gives herself to him when they have fled to his room to avoid being seen together in the kitchen. Jean, the valet, despises his neurotic young mistress for his easy conquest, and she hates herself and him. The excuse she offers for her rash conduct is false education and home training. Her mother, with ideas of woman's independence, has brought her up to learn everything that a boy is taught, in order to prove that a woman is as good as a man. Her father insisted on being master in his own house. His wife took her revenge by setting fire to the house and stable the day after the insurance expires, and contrived to have her husband borrow money from her lover to repair the damage. Julia learned from her mother suspicion and hatred of men, and from her father contempt for her own sex. She is the modern type of "man-hating, half-man, half-woman." She has just broken her engagement with a lover who refused to act her slave and jump over her whip like a dog. Jean is the type of self-made man, whose son may yet be a count as he boasts. He is the polished gentleman in imitation of his master. If he can shed the valet's livery and become a hotel keeper, he realizes that, in a different social environment, he could care for Julia, but in the count's house in the presence of the count's boots to be cleaned, he is the slavish servant, unable to surmount the social barrier to answer her appeal for a word of love. Julia must get the money to run away and start the hotel in Switzerland. She is unwilling to leave her pet bird behind, so the brutal Jean chops its head off before her eyes. As they are about to leave, the count returns and rings for his boots, and at the sound of the bell Jean is a menial again. He gives Julia a razor and, hypnotized by the suggestion, Julia goes out to end her life, since the aristocrat cannot live without honor.

MISS RAVENEL'S CONVERSION FROM SECESSION TO LOYALTY, by J. W. De Forest (1867). Dr. Ravenel, a Southern Secessionist, comes North at the beginning of the War, with his daughter Lillie; her Secessionism being more a result of local pride and social prejudice than of any deep-seated principle due to thought and experience. Her conversion is due, in part, to the influence of her lovers, John Carter and Edward Colburne, each in turn her husband,—the War making her a widow after a short period. With the inexperience of youth, carried away by the appearance rather than the reality of perfection, she makes a wrong choice in her life companion; but death steps in before her mistake is fully comprehended. The character of John Carter, who dies a Brigadier-General, is strongly drawn; his excesses of sensuality, his infidelities to his wife, his betrayal of the trust assigned him by his government for personal aggrandizement, all cloaked by the personal magnetism which blinds those near him, and makes him a popular commander and his death a national loss. In contrast to this is the equally strong picture of Edward Colburne, a dutiful son, a brave soldier, a faithful lover and friend; meeting his enemies in open warfare with the same courage that he displays on the less famous battle-ground of inner conflict, where he struggles against his disappointment in love, his loss of deserved promotion and distressing conditions after the war, lightened only by the tardy love of the woman to whom he has remained faithful. The love episodes are the least interesting of the narrative. There are graphic descriptions of battles, those of Fort Winthrop and Cane River being the most noteworthy; cynical annotations of the red-tapeism and blunders of the War Department; and humorous sketches of the social life in New Orleans during the Northern occupation, with race dashings of aristocracy, Creoles, invaders, and freed negroes, besides many amusing anecdotes and details of army life—all in De Forest's sharp black and white.

MISSISSIPPI, see LIFE ON THE.

MR. BRITLING SEES IT THROUGH, by H. G. Wells (1916). This novel is an account of the mind of England during the first two years of the war, in terms of the actual life of Mr. Britling and his pleasant family. Mr. Britling is a distinguished man of letters living at Matching's Easy, an English country place in Essex. He is a very real person, thinking and writing, entangled in his eighth love affair, absorbed in learning to drive a motor car, and devoted to his Sunday game of hockey. In a soliloquy he likens his mental processes to a "piece of orchestral music wherein the organ deplored the melancholy destinies of the race, while the piccolo lamented the secret trouble of Mrs. Harrowdean; the big drum thundered at the Irish politicians, and all the violins bewailed the intellectual laxity of the university system. Meanwhile the trumpets prophesied wars and disasters, the cymbals ever and again inserted a clashing jar about the fatal delay in the automobile insurance, while the triangle broke into a plangent solo on the topic of a certain rotten gate-post he always forgot in the daytime, and how in consequence the cows from the glebe farm got into the garden and ate Mrs. Britling's carnations." War comes with its shock, grief and disillusion. At first Mr. Britling conceives the idea that the war was brought about and carried on by a Prussian war party, then he speculates as to the end of the war and a Supreme Court of nations, and finally he begins to realize what the war is. The horror of war is brought home to him. His old Aunt Wilshire, staying at a small watering-place, is the victim of an air raid, blown to pieces by a Zeppelin bomb over her game of patience. His best loved son, Hugh, is killed in the trenches. In conclusion he writes and rewrites a letter to the parents of the lovable absurd German boy, who has been tutor in his family until called to the front to be shot in Russia; in this letter Mr. Britling comes to impersonal feeling beyond the borders of nationalism to find a meaning which will justify the sacrifice and a God who is not responsible for all the ills of humanity, of a God who is real and close.

MR. CREWE'S CAREER, by Winston Churchill (1908). Mr. Crewe's ardent and unsuccessful pursuit of political office is involved in a story of state politics controlled by a railroad. The real hero is Austen Vane, the only son of Judge Hilary Vane. The father, who is chief counsel for the railroad and boss of the political machine, is proud of the public service of the railroad and regards his own service as the part of high patriotism. The son stands unflinchingly for clean politics, and becomes the leader of the Opposition. He does justice to his father's personal integrity and point of view. He says to the New England farmers who appeal to him: "Conditions as they exist are the result of an evolution. The railroads, before they consolidated, found the political boss in power, and had to pay him for favors. . . . We mustn't blame the railroads too severely, when they grow strong enough, for substituting their own political army to avoid being blackmailed." Austen falls in love with Victoria, the charming daughter of the railroad president. Like her lover, she is forced to find her father's methods wrong in spite of her affection for him. The central incident is the campaign for governor. Mr. Crewe, the bachelor millionaire, thickly encased in the armor of self-conceit, pushes himself for the nomination, as a champion of the people against the railroad. Austen refuses to accept the nomination, out of respect for his father, and the railroad candidate wins an empty victory, since the handwriting on the wall is visible that the day of domination of the North Eastern railroads is past.

MR. DOOLEY, IN PEACE AND IN WAR, by F. P. Dunne (1898). This is a collection of papers containing the observations and reflections of Mr. Dooley, who is a character who will live for a long time in the memories of those who read his words of wisdom. Mr. Dooley is a Chicago Irishman past middle age, who lives in Archey Road, where he presides over a small saloon. Having left Ireland in his youth, he has witnessed, from his point of vantage, the events of the world's history, regarding which he has meditated deeply, and having done so is always ready to impart his impressions to his sympathetic friend and comrade, Mr. Hennessy, or to answer the searching questions of his neighbor, Mr. McKenna. Mr. Dooley has all of an Irishman's shrewdness, combativeness, independence, and appreciation of courage and loyalty, and his keen wit and picturesque phraseology make his reflections very entertaining reading. Mr. Dooley's national reputation was made at the time of the Spanish-American War, when his humorous comments with the underlying truth and common-sense which they contained were eagerly quoted over the whole country. Besides presenting his impressions of the war, Mr. Dooley deals with the various topics of the day, and draws amusing pictures of manifold celebrities from the "new woman" to the expert lawyer and modern child. His philosophy, full of wit and humor and yet often possessed of an undercurrent of pathos, covers a wide field, and in reading it one cannot fail to be impressed by its clear-sighted reasonableness and indomitable common-sense. The author of 'Mr. Dooley' has taken his rank among the noted humorists and has made a genuine contribution to permanent literature.

MR. ISAACS: 'a Tale of Modern India' (1882), Marion Crawford's first, and in some respects his greatest novel, is a study of the development of a man's higher nature through a woman. Mr. Isaacs, an exquisite instrument for another soul to play upon, is a high-bred Persian whose real name is Abdul-Hafiz-ben-Isâk. He is of a dreamy, spiritual nature, of a disposition lacking but one of the patents to nobility — reverence for women. As a professed Mussulman he is married to three wives, whom he regards with kindly contemptuous tolerance. The first person to suggest to him that women may have souls is Paul Griggs, the man who tells the story. He meets the beautiful Persian in Simla, India, becomes in a day his friend and confidant by virtue of some mysterious spiritual attraction. The lesson inculcated by Griggs is soon to be learned by Isaacs. He meets and loves a beautiful, noble Englishwoman, a Miss Westonhaugh. Each day draws him nearer to her; each day reveals to him the infinite as expressed in her fair soul. She returns the love of the mystical, beautiful Persian. The last test of the spirituality of his passion is her death. From her death-bed he goes forth with his face to the stars. "Think of me," he says, "not as mourning the departed day, but as watching longingly for the first faint dawn of the day eternal. Above all, think of me not as alone, but as wedded for all ages to her who has gone before me."

MR. MIDSHIPMAN EASY, by Captain James Marryat (1836), is one of the many rollicking tales by this author, who so well knows the ocean, and the seaports with their eccentric characters, and is only at home in dealing with low life and the lower middle-class. In this case we have the adventures of a spoiled lad Jack, the son of a so-called philosopher, who cruises about the world, falls in love, has misfortunes, and at last good luck and a happy life. The incidents themselves are nothing, but the book is entertaining for its "character" talk, and because the author has the gift of spinning a yarn.

MRS. CAUDLE'S CURTAIN LECTURES, by Douglas Jerrold, appeared first as a series of papers in Punch; and were published in book form in 1846. They gained at once an enormous popularity, being translated into nearly all European languages. The secret of this popularity is not difficult to discover. The book is a dramatic embodiment of a world-old matrimonial joke — the lay sermons delivered at night-time by a self-martyrized wife. Mrs. Caudle had little in this world to call her own but her husband's ears. They were her entire property. When Mrs. Caudle died, after thirty years of spouseship, the bereaved Job Caudle resolved every night to commit to paper one curtain lecture of his late wife. When he himself died, a small packet of papers was found, inscribed as follows:

"Curtain lectures delivered in the course of thirty years by Mrs. Margaret Caudle, and suffered by Job, her husband."

A single paragraph will suffice to show how Job suffered:

"Well, Mr. Caudle, I hope you're in a little better temper than you were this morning! There — you needn't begin to whistle. People don't come to bed to whistle. But it's like you. I can't speak that you don't try to insult me. Once I used to say you were the best creature living; now you get quite a fiend. *Do let you rest:* No, I won't let you rest. It's the only time I have to talk to you, and you *shall* hear me. I'm put upon all day long; it's very hard if I can't speak a word at night: besides, it isn't often I open my mouth, goodness knows!"

MRS. MARTIN'S MAN, by St. John Ervine (1915). Sixteen years before the story begins, James Martin deserted his wife, Martha, and his two children, and left for parts unknown. In time Mrs. Martin comes to regard herself as a widow. She buys a hardware shop, which prospers so exceedingly that when Martin comes home after a prolonged debauch of sixteen years, he finds his wife with a flourishing business and a much more comfortable home than he had ever made for her. He comes back filthy, ragged, and sodden. Mrs. Martin greets him without any display of emotion. She makes it plain to him that if he wants to bide in her house, he must stop drinking, keep himself clean, not swear before the children as he did before he went away, and save her the wages of a boy by doing small jobs in the shop. She gives him a little money to keep him from feeling wholly a pauper. Her drastic method is pretty nearly successful. James Martin becomes the devoted slave of his daughter Aggie, a pretty girl of seventeen, and rather than have her know his past, he keeps straight. Meanwhile Mrs. Martin has trouble with her sister, Esther. Before James went away, there had been a love affair between her and James. Discovery is what Esther fears most. She is thoroughly devoted to Jamesey, Mrs. Martin's son, and when Jamesey comes to know that his aunt Esther had been his father's "fancy woman," the boy becomes desperately ill. Finally Mrs. Martin brings him to see that he must forgive his aunt, unless he wants to kill her. Then as neither Esther nor Jamesey can remain at home with James Martin there, Mrs. Martin buys Esther a shop in Belfast, and arranges for Jamesey to lodge with his aunt back of the shop. All this done, Mrs. Martin settles down to life with James and Aggie. Though she has made life happier for four people, she has lost her own illusions. Her stoic philosophy is "things happen and they cannot be changed."

MRS. WIGGS OF THE CABBAGE PATCH, by Alice Caldwell Hegan (1901). This is the story of an optimistic woman who in spite of her many adversities is always able to look on the bright side of things. Mrs. Wiggs is a widow with a family of five children to support; her husband has died as the result of intemperance.

but instead of dwelling upon Mr. Wiggs's shortcomings, the widow always lays stress upon the "fine hand he wrote." The "Cabbage Patch" is not a real cabbage patch but a collection of remarkable cottages set down at random close to the railroad tracks. The scene of the story is laid in Kentucky and a true southern atmosphere pervades it. Mrs. Wiggs, whose originality displays itself in various ways, has chosen "geographical" names for her three daughters and they are called respectively "Asia," "Australia," and "Europena." Her oldest child is a boy named Jimmy who at the age of fifteen has worked so hard in his efforts to be a bread-winner for the family that he is completely worn out and dies soon after the story opens. His mother, whose courage has carried her through her other misfortunes is overwhelmed by this trouble but struggles bravely on. She is assisted at this sad time by Miss Lucy Olcott, a pretty and philanthropic young lady, who gets up a purse for the family and provides them also with food and clothing. She continues to be "their good angel" and in return they are instrumental in bringing about her reconciliation with her lover Robert Redding, as she and he meet accidentally in the Wiggs's cottage and settle a grievance which has parted them. The story is full of amusing incidents and Mrs. Wiggs's humorous and philosophical remarks are a great source of entertainment. Her cheerfulness under adversity, her unselfishness and sympathy for others in trouble, make her an example and an inspiration to all with whom she comes in contact. An especially amusing description is that of the "Annexation of Cuba," which tells how Mrs. Wiggs and her son Billy restore to life a half dead horse and after nursing him, make him a valued member of the family. The visit of Mrs. Wiggs and the children to the theatre through the kindness of "Mr. Bob," who provides them with tickets, is a great event in their lives and is set forth in a most entertaining manner.

MITHRIDATE, by Racine. This powerful and affecting tragedy was produced on the 13th of January, 1673, the day after the author's reception into the Academy. It seems to have been written in reply to those critics who asserted that the only character he was successful in painting was that of a woman. The scene is laid in Pontus, and the hero is the cruel and heroic king who was the irreconcilable enemy of Rome. Mithridates has disappeared, and is believed to be dead. His two sons, the treacherous Pharnaces and the chivalrous Xiphares, prepare to seize this crown and dispute the possession of his betrothed Monima. The old king returns, discovers by a stratagem that Xiphares has won the love of Monima, and swears to be avenged. Meanwhile he plans a formidable attack on Rome: he will ascend the Danube and burst upon the Romans from the north. Xiphares favors the project, but Pharnaces opposes it, and the soldiers refuse to follow their king. The Romans unite with the rebels; and in the battle that follows, Mithridates falls mortally wounded. Before dying, he joins the two lovers Xiphares and Monima. In his portraiture of Mithridates, Racine sometimes rises to the sublimity of Corneille. He has scarcely ever written anything grander than the speech in which the hero explains his policy to his two sons. The manner in which the complexity of Mithridates's character, his greatness and weakness, his heroism and duplicity, are laid bare, shows wonderful psychological delicacy and skill; and all this is finely contrasted with the simplicity and unity of the nature of Monima in its high moral beauty and unvarying dignity.

MOBY-DICK, by Herman Melville (1851), is the name by which a certain huge and particularly ferocious whale was known. This whale has been attacked many times, and has fought valiantly. Captain Ahab, of the whaler Pequod, has lost a leg in a conflict with this monster, and has vowed to kill him. The story tells how the captain kept his vow; and it serves not only for the relation of some exciting adventures in the pursuit of whales, but as a complete text-book of the whaling industry. Every species of whale is described, with its habits, temperament, and commercial value. Every item in the process of whale capture and preparation for the market is minutely described. Besides all this, the characters of the owners, officers and crew of the whaling ship are drawn with truth and vigor; and there is a good sketch of a New Bedford sailors' boarding-house.

The scene is laid first at New Bedford and Nantucket, and afterwards on those portions of the ocean frequented by whaling vessels, and the time is the year 1775. Probably no more thrilling description of a whale hunt has been written than that of the three days' conflict with Moby-Dick, with which the story closes, and in which the whale is killed, though not until he has demolished the boats and sunk the ship. 'Moby-Dick' is of increasing value in literature from the fact that it is a most comprehensive hand-book of the whaling industry at a time when individual courage and skill were prime factors, when the whale had to be approached in small boats to within almost touching distance, and before bomb-lances, steam, and other modern improvements had reduced whaling to the dead-level of a mere "business." It contains also the best rendering into words of the true seaman's feeling about the ocean as his home which has ever been written.

MODERN DEMOCRACY, PROBLEMS OF, by E. L. Godkin, see **PROBLEMS OF.**

MODERN INSTANCE, A, by William D. Howells (1881). The scene of the story is first laid in a country town in Maine, where Bartley Hubbard, a vain, selfish, unprincipled young man, is editing the local paper. He marries Marcia Gaylord, a handsome, passionate, inexperienced young country girl, and takes her to Boston, where he continues his journalistic career. As time goes on, the incompatibility of the young couple becomes manifest; Marcia's extreme jealousy, and Bartley's selfishness and dissipation, causing much unhappiness and contention. The climax is finally reached, when, after a passionate scene, Bartley leaves his wife and child, and is not heard from again for the space of two years. His next appearance is in an Indiana law-court, where he is endeavoring to procure a divorce from Marcia; but his attempt is frustrated through the intervention of her father, Judge Gaylord, who goes to the Western town and succeeds in obtaining a decree in his daughter's favor. At the end of the story Bartley is shot and killed in a Western brawl, and Marcia is left with her child, dragging out her existence in her native town. Ben Halleck, who is in love with Marcia, figures prominently throughout the book, and the reader is left with the impression that their marriage eventually takes place. If the novel can hardly be called agreeable, it proves Mr. Howells has penetrated very deeply into certain unattractive but characteristic phases of contemporary American life; and the story is told with brilliancy and vigor.

MODERN PAINTERS. The first volume of 'Modern Painters' appeared in 1843, when Ruskin was but twenty-four years old. In this book the young author challenged the verdict of his age and placed himself in direct antagonism to its standards of taste, and estimates of truth, by refuting the adverse criticism of Turner, which was then rife. At first this defiant note excited merely wonder and curiosity, but it was soon found that this new authority in the field of art was able successfully to champion the cause that he had undertaken, and on the appearance of his second volume of 'Modern Painters,' Ruskin's position as prose writer and art critic was assured and the throne of Turner was secure.

The five volumes of 'Modern Painters' cost their author over twenty years of labor, during which time Ruskin's ideas changed considerably, which fact must account for some seeming contradictions in the various volumes, — contradictions which bespoke the broadening and maturing of the writer's point of view.

The principal argument and illustration of 'Modern Painters' is hinged upon *nature-truth* and its appearance in the paintings of Turner, although the work was also an inquiry into the object and means of landscape painting and the spirit which should govern its production. The author discourses upon the appearance of nature, and enters exhaustively into the discussion of what is true in art as revealed by nature. In this eloquent setting forth of what he believed to be the truth, Ruskin has produced his most forceful work, and one which sparkles with brilliant prose passages and offers keen observations upon nature and art. It has been said that there are many who never saw the beauty of cloud form, or knew the majesty of the hills, or felt the sweetness of the meadows until taught by Ruskin in 'Modern Painters.'

With the completion of 'Modern Painters,' Ruskin ended the cycle of work by which he is popularly known as a writer upon art; in his later works art was sometimes his text, but rarely his theme.

MODERN RÉGIME, THE, by H. A. Taine (1891). This is the third and concluding part of Taine's 'Origins of Contemporary France,' of which his 'Ancient Régime' and 'French Revolution' were the first and second. While based on the fullest and minutest research, and giving a striking picture of the new régime following the Revolution, it is less impartial than the previous parts of the work. The indictment of Napoleon is as bitter as the picture of his almost superhuman power is brilliant; and whatever the Revolution produced is referred to mingled crime and madness. Taken together, the three works show Taine at his best of originality, boldness, and power as a writer.

MODESTE MIGNON, by Honoré de Balzac (1846). The heroine of this romance, Modeste Mignon, lives in a small city in northwestern France. She has the religious faith of a child, while her mind is exceptionally well informed in many ways. The machinery of the story is slight. The young girl, daring in her simplicity, writes to a famous author to thank him for his books. A friend of that author, charmed by the freshness of the letter, replies; and a pretty love story is the result. Many characters appear, and there are fresh and dewy pictures of rural France. The great whirlpool of Paris does indeed devour its allotted victims; but the atmosphere of the book, as a whole, is tranquil, and its influence not uncheerful.

MOLIÈRE, HIS LIFE AND HIS WORKS, 'a Critical Biography,' by Brander Matthews (1910). The author's aim is to give a plain statement of the dramatist's life, free from the distortions of unproved slander; to exhibit his gradual development in dramatic power and to estimate his achievement; and finally to explain his relation to his times. By rejecting the scandals in regard to Molière's marriage, he renders Molière a more respectable, though less interesting figure. His criticism of the dramatist's failings is incisive, but his general valuation of the plays is extremely high. Molière he regards as the best representative of the French mind, the greatest figure in French literature, the founder of modern high comedy, and the rival of Shakespeare. As a background to Molière's life and work the author has drawn an interesting picture of the age of Louis XIV., keeping it in due subordination and relation to the central theme. The book is not only a valuable source of information to those unable to consult the French authorities, but an aid to all serious students of Molière.

MOLINOS THE QUIETIST, by John Bigelow (1882), is a little volume, narrating in the tone appropriate to the subject the eventless history of Michel de Molinos, a priest of Spanish descent, who was the originator of one of the most formidable schisms that ever rent the Latin Church. 'Il Guida Spirituale,' the book containing the obnoxious doctrine of quietism, appeared at Rome in Italian in 1675; and in six years went through twenty editions in different languages, an English translation appearing in 1699. The main points of the doctrine are thus described: The human soul is the temple and abode of God; we ought therefore to keep it unspoiled by worldliness and sin. The true end of life is the attainment of perfection, in reaching which two stages exist, meditation and contemplation. In the first, reason is the faculty employed; in the second, reason no longer acts, the soul merely contemplates the truth in silence and repose, passively receives the celestial light, desiring nothing, not even its own salvation, fearing nothing, not even hell, and indifferent to the sacraments and all practices of external devotion, having transcended the sphere of their efficacy. Sixty-eight of the propositions in this work were condemned as heretical at Rome in 1687; and its author was imprisoned for life, dying in confinement in 1697.

MONASTERIES OF THE LEVANT, by Robert Curzon, see **VISITS TO THE.**

MONDAY-CHATS, see **CAUSERIES DU LUNDI.**

MONEY, see **ROUGON-MACQUART.**

MONK, THE, by Matthew Gregory Lewis, was published in 1795, when the author was twenty years old. The book is one of the "dime novels" of English literature; a fantastic medley of ghosts, gore, villains, cheap mysteries, and all the stage machinery of flagrant melodrama. Like Mrs. Radcliffe's novels, it belongs to the class of the pseudoterrific. At the time of its publication, however, its exaggerations were not so apparent. Horace Walpole's 'Castle of Otranto' and Mrs. Radcliffe's 'Mysteries of Udolpho' had popularized the mock-heroic. The air was full of horrors. 'The Monk' seemed to contemporary readers one of the great books of the day. That it was not without merit was proved by the verdict of no less an authority than Sir Walter Scott, who styled it "no ordinary exertion of genius." So great was its fame, that the author to the day of his death was called "Monk" Lewis. The hero, Ambrosio, is the abbot of the Capuchins at Madrid, surnamed "The Man of Holiness." His pride of righteousness opens him at length to spiritual disaster. An infernal spirit assuming the shape of a woman tempts him, and he falls. One sin succeeds another until he is utterly ruined. Upon the fabric of the monk's progression in evil the author builds wild incidents of every degree of horror.

MONNA VANNA, by Maurice Maeterlinck (1902). At the end of the fifteenth century, when the play opens, Pisa is besieged by the Florentine armies led by

Prinzivalle, a hired mercenary. Guido, the governor, has sent his aged father to the enemy's camp to ask the terms of capitulation. Marco, the father, returns with the message that Prinzivalle, already betrayed by the Florentines, is in turn, ready to betray his masters, and to send ammunition, wagons of provisions, and herds of cattle to the starving Pisans on one condition. The condition is that the beautiful Monna Vanna, wife of the governor, shall come for one night to his tent, alone, clad only in her mantle. Monna Vanna, to save the doomed city, accepts the condition, in spite of her husband's prohibition of the sacrifice. Prinzivalle, unknown to Monna Vanna, had known and loved her years before, and when she comes to his tent, he reveals himself to her and proves the nobility of his love by his respect for her. Their conversation is interrupted by the news of the arrival of the Florentines who will proclaim Prinzivalle a traitor. She urges him to return with her and take refuge in Pisa. Within the rejoicing city — now furnished by Prinzivalle with arms and provisions — her father and husband receive them. Guido repulses her and refuses to believe that she is not dishonored. He insists that she has lured Prinzivalle to Pisa to revenge herself upon him. Recognizing the lack of faith in her husband and the perfect trust of her lover, she tells the lie her husband wishes to believe to save Prinzivalle from death. As Prinzivalle is led away to the dungeon of which Vanna alone shall hold the key for her revenge, we know that she loves the greater man and will free him and escape from her husband to share his exile. The conventional honor of the husband, his false pride and selfishness are contrasted with Monna Vanna's heroism in giving herself for her country and her truth in protecting even by untruth the man whose surety she has made herself.

MONSIEUR BEAUCAIRE, by Booth Tarkington (1900). In this sparkling and graceful story the author presents a supposed episode in the life of Louis Philippe de Valois, cousin of Louis XV. of France, who is masquerading as Monsieur Beaucaire. This accomplished prince, bent upon adventure and desirous of having perfect freedom in the choice of a bride, goes to England in the suite of the Marquis de Mirepoix disguised as a barber. Arrived at Bath he assumes the rôle of gamester and, while amusing himself, falls in love with the beautiful Lady Mary Carlisle. The Duke of Winterset, who is paying his addresses to this lady, is trapped by Beaucaire while cheating at cards, and fearful of exposure consents to introduce the supposed barber as his friend, the Duke de Chateaurien, at Lady Malbourne's ball, where he charms all by his grace and elegance, and is favored by a rose from Lady Mary. His social success is assured from that time and his suit for the hand of the fair Mary prospers until he is suddenly set upon by the jealous Duke of Winterset and his confederates. Brutally attacked by them in the presence of his lady love, who has but just assented to his proposal, Beaucaire is accused of being a low-born lackey. After displaying his skilled swordsmanship against overwhelming odds, he is borne off by his servants wounded and too faint to justify himself in the eyes of Lady Mary, who now turns coldly from him. The climax of the tale is reached one week later in the Assembly Room, where a brilliant throng gathers to greet the ambassador of Louis XV. and other French nobles. Here, Beaucaire, hailed as the Duke of Orleans by his respectful countrymen, confronts those who have scorned and derided him and tells his story in the presence of the humiliated beauty and the disgraced Duke of Winterset. Then, after announcing his intention of wedding his sweet cousin in France, whose devotion he has previously failed to appreciate, Beaucaire takes leave of the chagrined Lady Mary, who regrets her lamentable mistake.

MONSIEUR BERGERET À PARIS, see **L'HISTOIRE CONTEMPORAINE.**

MONTCALM AND WOLFE, see **FRANCE AND ENGLAND IN NORTH AMERICA.**

MONUMENTS OF NINEVEH, see **NINEVEH AND ITS REMAINS.**

MONTCALM, LE MARQUIS DE, a biography by Thomas Chapais (1911). The author admits in the preface that the subject has been often treated before, particularly by Francis Parkman and the Abbé Casgrain. But he believes that his access to fresh historical evidence justifies him in an attempt at reinterpreting the achievements and personality of the great French chieftain. The result of an unprejudiced study of the documents has been, he maintains, to rank Montcalm even higher than previous historians have placed him and in particular to prove him superior to the Governor-General, Vaudreuil. After a chapter on Montcalm's earlier career and another on the relations between England and France from 1748 to 1756, the book is devoted to Montcalm's exploits as commander of the French army in Canada from the outbreak of the Seven Years' War to his defeat and death at Quebec in 1759. The various battles are carefully discussed and graphically portrayed; the greatness of Montcalm's achievement is fittingly praised; and his noble and courageous acceptance of defeat receives its due tribute. The book reflects the French-Canadian reverence for the memory of Montcalm whom the writer characterizes as "un honnête homme, un chrétien sincère, et un grand Français." There is also generous appreciation of the bravery and chivalry of Wolfe.

MOON HOAX, THE, by Richard Adams Locke (1859). This pretends to announce the discovery of a vast human population in the moon. Its contents appeared originally in 1835, in the New York Sun, under the title, ' Great Astronomical Discoveries lately made by Sir John Herschel,' increasing the circulation of that paper, it was said, fivefold. The skit was soon afterward published in pamphlet form, the edition of 60,000 being sold in less than a month. This account pretended to be taken from the supplement to the Edinburgh Journal of Science, and was most circumstantial and exact. The discovery was asserted to have been made at the Cape of Good Hope, by means of a new and vastly improved telescope invented by the younger Herschel. The article described beaches of gleaming sand; lunar forests; fields covered with vivid rose-poppies; basaltic columns like those of Staffa; rocks of green marble; obelisks of wine-colored amethyst; herds of miniature bisons, with a curious fold or hairy veil across the forehead to shield the eyes from the intolerable glare of light; troops of unicorns, beautiful and graceful as the antelope; and groups of some amphibious creatures, spherical in form, which rolled with great velocity across the sands. Moreover, the telescope discloses the biped beaver, which constructs huts like the human savage, and makes use of fire; a semi-human creature with wings; and a race about four feet high, and very unpleasant in appearance, which certainly has the gift of speech. After observations which fill many pages, the account goes on to explain that an unfortunate fire has destroyed the telescope, and that the expedition could not make the discoveries certainly at that time imminent. The sensation produced by this nonsense was widespread and profound. The press took sides for and against its authenticity, and for some time a large public credited the statements made. Of course the absurdity of the tale soon revealed itself, and then the whole matter became known as the "Moon Hoax." But the whole invention was set forth with the most admirable air of conviction, and the book takes its place among the best of Munchausenish tales.

MOONSTONE, THE, by Wilkie Collins (1868), is one of the best examples of the author's general purpose to mystify the reader. At the storming of Seringapatam, a holy city of India, by the British in 1799, a certain John Herncastle possessed himself, by the massacre of its keepers, of a large and peculiar diamond known as the moonstone. With his dying breath, one of the Brahmins cursed the Englishman, declaring that the diamond would bring disaster and misfortune to its unlawful possessors. The story treats of the mysterious disappearance of the stone, bequeathed by Herncastle to his niece, Miss Verinder, and of the tragedy that ensued before the guilty persons could be with certainty apprehended. The closing lines of the story find the moonstone once again in India, fixed as formerly in the forehead of an idol.

MORAL TALES, by Miss Edgeworth (1801), have been translated into many languages, and have retained their popularity in England and abroad. As the title denotes, these stories have a didactic purpose, and although intended to amuse young people, would insinuate a sugar-coated moral. The character-drawing is capable and shrewd; and the fluent, animated style makes them easy reading. The seven stories comprising the volume have a sensible, matter-of-fact, thoroughly eighteenth-century quality. Miss Edgeworth inculcates nobility, generosity, and sincerity; but above everything else, she inculcates good sense. It is not enough for young Forester to be brave and talented. He is held up to ridicule for his uncouth ways and disdain of conventions, until he learns the wisdom of conforming to social usage. Evelina is a feminine Forester, and learns the same lesson. Tact is a favorite virtue with Miss Edgeworth. It is by carefully consulting the individual tastes of her pupils that "The Good French Governess" reforms Mrs. Harcourt's family. Tact is the secret of the "Good Aunt's" success in her educational experiment. Miss Edgeworth teaches boys and girls to despise self-indulgence and uncontrolled emotion; and to mistrust appearances. Her model hero is young Mr. Mounteagle, the matrimonial prize in 'Mademoiselle Panache,' who, momentarily attracted by the beauty of Lady Augusta, has the sense to perceive her inferiority to the sensible, domestic, and amiable Helen Temple.

MORALS, THE, OF EPICTETUS (c. A. D. 60), consisting of his 'Manual' and 'Discourses,' are the sole writings preserved to our age, through the assiduity of his pupil Arrian. Published in the early second century, they afford our only record of the doctrines of the greatest of the Stoics. The 'Manual,' still a favorite with all thoughtful readers, is a guide to right living. Its tone is that of a half-sad serenity that would satisfy the needs of the soul with right living in this world, since we can have no certain knowledge of the truth of any other. "Is there anything you highly value or tenderly love? estimate at the same time its true nature. Is it some possession? remember that it may be destroyed. Is it wife or child? remember that they may die." "We do not choose out our own parts in life, and have nothing to do with those parts; our simple duty is to play them well." The 'Discourses,' also, display a simple, direct eloquence; but they introduce frequent anecdotes to enliven an appeal or illustrate a principle. Both disclose the Phrygian freedman, as a singularly noble soul, unaffected, pure, self-centred, supremely gentle, and winning.

MORALS OF LUCIUS ANNÆUS SENECA, THE (Philosophica c. 4 B.C.–65 A.D.). is the general title given to twelve essays on ethical subjects attributed to the great Roman Stoic. They are the most interesting and valuable of his numerous works. Representing the thought of his whole life, the most famous are the essays on 'Consolation,' addressed to his mother, when he was in exile at Corsica; on 'Providence,' "a golden book," as it is called by Lipsius, the German critic; and on 'The Happy Life.' The Stoic doctrines of calmness, forbearance, and strict virtue and justice, receive here their loftiest statement. The popularity of these 'Morals' with both pagan and Christian readers led to their preservation in almost a perfect condition. To the student of Christianity in its relations with paganism, no other classic writer yields in interest to this "divine pagan," as Lactantius, the early church father and poet, calls him. The most striking parallels to the formularies of the Christian writers, notably St. Paul, are to be found in his later works, especially those on 'The Happy Life' and on 'The Conferring of Benefits.'

MORE, SIR THOMAS, see **HOUSEHOLD OF.**

MORGESONS, THE, Elizabeth Barstow Stoddard's first novel (1862). The plot is concerned with the fortunes of the Morgeson family, long resident in a seacoast town in New England. Two members of it, Cassandra, by whom the story is told, and her sister Veronica, are girls of strange, unconventional nature, wholly undisciplined, who live out their restless lives against the background of a narrow New England household, composed of a gentle, fading mother, a father wholly absorbed in business and affairs, and a dominant female servant, Temperance. When Cassandra returns home from boarding-school, she finds Veronica grown into a pale, reticent girl, with unearthly little ways. Veronica's own love-story begins when she meets Ben Somers, a friend of her sister. Both girls are born to tragedy, through their passionate, irreconcilable temperament; and the story follows their lives with a strange, detached impartiality, which holds the interest of the reader more closely than any visible advocacy of the cause of either heroine could do. 'The Morgesons' is rich in delineation of unusual aspects of character, in a grim New England humor, in those pictures of the sea that are never absent from Mrs. Stoddard's novels. Suffusing the book is a bleak atmosphere of what might be called passionate mentality, bracing, but calling for a sober power of resistance in the reader.

MORMON, THE BOOK OF, Translated by Joseph Smith, Jr. Division into chapters and verses, with references, by Orson Pratt, Sr. Salt Lake City Edition of 1888: copyright by Joseph F. Smith, 1879.

The title-page bears also a particular statement of the character and origin of the 'Book,' a part of which runs as follows:

"An account written by the hand of Mormon, upon plates taken from the Plates of Nephi. Wherefore it is an abridgment of the record of the people of Nephi, and also of the Lamanites; written to the Lamanites who are a remnant of the house of Israel; and also to Jew and Gentile: written by way of commandment, and also by the spirit of prophecy and of revelation. . . .

"An abridgment taken from the Book of Esther also; which is a record of the people of Jared: who were scattered at the time the Lord confounded the language of the people when they were building a tower to get to heaven; which is to show . . . that JESUS is the CHRIST, the ETERNAL GOD, manifesting himself unto all nations."

The scheme of the book is that of the visions and dreams and prophesyings of Lehi, who dwelt at Jerusalem all the days of the reign of Zedekiah; and of the life and doings of Nephi, son of Lehi; and of the preaching of Jacob, a brother of Nephi; and of the events under Mosiah, king over the Nephites, and in whose days Alma founded their church; and of an account by Alma's son Alma, of a period of rule by judges; and of a record by Helaman, grandson of the last Alma, and by his sons, of wars and prophecies and changes down to the coming of Christ; and of a book by a son of Helaman, Nephi, covering the life of Jesus; and of still another book of Nephi, continuing the story after Christ for about three hundred years; and finally of a book by Mormon himself, giving, at the end of a thousand years from Lehi under Zedekiah, the final story of the Nephi records and traditions. These successive books fill 570 of the 632 pages of the Book, and tell a story of events from 597 B.C. to the days of Mormon, about 350–400 A.D. The work concludes with a book of ancient history by Moroni, son of Mormon, and finally with a book of last words by the same Moroni. In the scheme thus outlined, use is made of some of Isaiah's prophecies, freely quoted, and of a good deal of the life of Jesus in the Gospels, with changes freely made. Two formal attestations are given, in one of which three persons testify that they had seen metal plates containing the originals of the entire work, and knew them to have been translated by the gift and power of God (out of "the reformed Egyptian"); and in the second of which eight persons bear witness that they had "seen and hefted" the plates, "and know of a surety that the said Smith has got the plates of which we have spoken." A characteristic word of the spiritual higher teaching of the book, on its final page, reads as follows: "Come unto Christ and be perfected in him, and deny yourselves of all ungodliness, and love God with all your might, mind, and strength." Certain features of the system later developed are unknown to the Book.

MOROCCO, ITS PEOPLE AND PLACE, by Edmondo de Amicis (1875), a book of travel and description. As a member of the Italian ambassador's suite, the author enjoyed unusual facilities for observing the manners and customs of Morocco, while he received constant courtesies at the hands of the natives. Many unfamiliar phases of life and character are treated; the countryside, as well as all the large centres of population, receiving attention. The narrative is full of incident and worldly philosophy; and without pretending to be formally historic, vividly portrays the religious life and racial problems of this Moorish land.

MORTAL ANTIPATHY, A, the third and last of Oliver Wendel Holmes's novels, was published in 1885, when he was in his seventy-sixth year. Like the two preceding works of fiction (to which it is inferior), it is concerned with a curious problem of a psychological nature. Maurice Kirkwood, a young man of good family, suffers from a singular malady, brought on by a fall when a child. When very small, he was dropped from the arms of a girl cousin. Ever after that, the presence of a beautiful woman caused him to faint away. A love story is interwoven with the story of his cure.

MORTE D'ARTHUR, a prose compendium of the Arthurian romances, made by Sir Thomas Malory, knight, who completed it in 1470, the year before his death.

It was published by Caxton in 1485. The prose romance of Merlin by Robert de Baron, the English metrical romances 'La Morte Arthure,' and 'Le Morte Arthur,' the French romances of Lancelot and Tristan formed the basis of the work. Starting from the obscure figure of a British chieftain, a *dux belloum*, against the Saxons, King Arthur had developed into a world-monarch, the centre of an intricate cycle of stories. To the marvelous tales of his birth, marriage, Round Table, conquests, and death, had been added the loves and adventures of his knights, Gawain, Lancelot, Tristan; and the mystical Christian legend of the Holy Grail; and all these stories had been told again and again in many languages and in ever-varying forms. From this confused exuberance of material, Malory, by selection and alteration, produced in reasonable compass a unified and fairly complete version of the whole cycle. The convenience of this version and its transparent, picturesque, and expressive style have made it popular ever since, and it has been the source of practically all subsequent literary redactions of the Arthurian legend. The general scope of the narrative may be indicated under the following heads: 1. THE BIRTH AND EARLY EXPLOITS OF ARTHUR. The magician Merlin plays an important part in this division of the story. It is Merlin who makes possible the clandestine union between King Uther Pendragon and Igrayne, Duchess of Cornwall, of whom Arthur is born. Merlin too provides for the boy's education and through his arrangements Arthur afterward becomes king. Through Merlin he obtains the sword Excalibur from the Lady of the Lake. Merlin is his constant mentor, and the chief prop of his throne. Arthur's marriage to Guinevere, daughter of King Leodegran, and his various struggles with discontented subjects, invading kings, giants, and the Roman Emperor Lucius, who sends to Britain to demand tribute, make up the principal exploits of this period. 2. THE PASSION OF LANCELOT AND GUINEVERE. Lancelot du Lake occupies in Malory and in the later French romances the position of leading knight at Arthur's court, earlier held by Arthur's nephew Gawain. In Malory, Gawain is represented as cruel, fickle, and a light-of-love — traits which Tennyson has retained. Lancelot, on the other hand, is "the gentlest knight that ever ate in hall among ladies, the sternest to his mortal foe that ever put spear in rest." Yet he continues for years, without Arthur's knowledge, an intrigue with Guinevere. This is finally revealed to the king by the traitor Mordred. Lancelot escapes, afterwards rescues Guinevere from execution by burning, and retires with her to his castle of Joyous Gard; but at the order of the Pope he yields Guinevere to Arthur. After the death of the king, both Lancelot and Guinevere take monastic vows and retire from the world. 3. THE PASSION OF TRISTRAM AND ISOULDE. This famous love story is less brilliantly told by Malory than by the Norman Thomas or the German Gottfried, its interest being subordinated to that of Lancelot and Guinevere. Tristram of Lyonesse by a combat with Sir Morôlt of Ireland, frees his uncle, King Mark of Cornwall, from paying tribute to the Irish king. Wounded by his opponent's poisoned spear, he goes to Ireland, where he is healed by Isoulde, daughter of the Irish king. Afterwards he goes to woo her for his uncle, King Mark; but as he is conducting her to Cornwall, they drink a potion, which makes them lovers till death. Their clandestine meetings after her marriage to Mark are at length discovered. Tristram is exiled to Brittany, where he marries the king's daughter, Isoulde of the White Hands. But the tragic ending of the story is not given by Malory, who, though he conducts Tristram through many other adventures, does not mention his death. 4. THE QUEST OF THE HOLY GRAIL. Arthur's knights set out to find the Holy Grail, the cup in which the Lord's Supper was instituted, and which had been brought to England by Joseph of Arimathæa. The quest is achieved by Sir Galahad, the maiden knight, a son of Sir Lancelot. Accompanied by Sir Perceval and Sir Bors he crosses the sea to the holy city of Sarras, where, after receiving the Sacrament from the Grail, he dies and the Grail is caught away to Heaven. 5. THE PASSING OF ARTHUR. When Arthur is making war upon Lancelot, his natural son, Mordred, made regent in his absence, raises a rebellion in the hope of seizing the crown. After a bloody battle, Mordred mortally wounds Arthur and is himself slain by him. Arthur then departs in a barge to the Valley of Avilion to be healed of his wound. Malory's narrative is characterized by a love of chivalric and aristocratic ideals, and an English preoccupation with questions of morality.

MOSSES FROM AN OLD MANSE is the title of Nathaniel Hawthorne's second collection of tales and sketches (1854). The Old Manse, Hawthorne's Concord home, is described in the opening chapter of the book. The remaining contents include many of Hawthorne's most famous short sketches, such as 'The Birth-Mark,' 'Roger Malvin's Burial,' and 'The Artist of the Beautiful.' These stories bear witness to his love of the mysterious and the unusual; and their action passes in a world of unreality, which the genius of the author makes more visible than the world of sense.

MOTHER, by Kathleen Norris (1911). This is the story of the Paget family, who live in a small town called Weston, a few hours out of New York. Mrs. Paget, the central figure of the story and from whom the book derives its title, is a woman of great character, devoted to her family and untiring in her services to them. Her husband and her seven children are her world, and with very limited resources she makes for them a cheerful and happy home. Margaret, the eldest daughter, is possessed of great beauty and charm but is forced to teach school to eke out the family income. She chafes under the drudgery of her daily life and is longing for a change of environment when the opportunity suddenly comes to her. Mrs. Carr-Boldt, a rich society woman of New York, is passing through Weston in her motor-car when one of the school children suddenly dashes in front if it and is run over. Excitement prevails until Margaret appears upon the scene and displaying much presence of mind, disperses the crowd and quiets the child who is but slightly injured. Mrs. Carr-Boldt is immediately attracted by her beauty and capability and before leaving the town asks her to become her private secretary. Margaret goes to New York and lives with her benefactress in her luxurious home, the magnificence of which is in great contrast to the simple one she has left behind. She goes abroad with Mrs. Carr-Boldt and while there meets Dr. John Tenison, a young American professor, rich, handsome, and talented. He and Margaret are mutually attracted to each other but are obliged to part hastily and do not meet again till they do so in Margaret's own home to which she has returned for a short visit. She fears the impression he will get from seeing the shabby and meager appointments of her home and of being in the confusing atmosphere of a large family, but on the contrary he is struck with the wonderful qualities of her mother. He proposes to Margaret and before leaving tells her that having seen her mother he now realizes where she has derived the traits which have won his love. Margaret, who has always loved her mother devotedly, now realizes how much happier she is in her life of loving service than is Mrs. Carr-Boldt with all her riches.

MOTHER, by Maxim Gorky (1906). An intimate picture of the lives and world of a group of socialists in Russia, who face danger and death for the sake of their ideal, the liberation of the working people from "the narrow dark cage" of ignorance and oppression. Until the death of her brutal husband, the mother lives in fear, "in anxious expectation of blows." She is described as a dazed cowed creature, beaten into a dumb acceptance of her lot. Her son Pavel begins to drink like his father and the other factory workers, but by some hidden way the "forbidden" socialist books get to him, and change his life. When he tells his mother his purpose to "study and then teach others," to help his fellow-workers to understand why life is so hard for them and to fight with them against its injustice, she is at first terrified for his safety. Gradually her mind stirs in response to his, and she grows in courage and understanding. Her son is sent to prison for leading a First of May parade, and she goes on with his work, distributing the forbidden literature in the factory. She becomes the heart of the group of which he is the intellect. There are arrests, escapes, speeches, encounters with spies, and finally the Mother, who is watched as a suspicious character, is arrested with the papers she is carrying. A gendarme beats her and chokes her to death as she tries to say a last word for the Cause. The son is sentenced to exile in Siberia.

MOTHER GOOSE'S MELODIES. Few books in the English language have had so wide-spread a circulation as the collection of nursery rhymes known as 'Mother Goose's Melodies.' Indeed the child whose earliest remembrance does not embrace pictures of 'Little Boy Blue,' 'The House that Jack Built,' 'Who Killed Cock Robin,' 'Baa, Baa, Black Sheep,' and 'Patty Cake, Patty Cake, Baker's Man,' has sustained a loss of no small magnitude. In 1860 a story was started to the effect that "Mother Goose" was a Boston woman; and she was identified as Elizabeth Goose, widow of Isaac Vergoose, or Goose, and mother-in-law of Thomas Fleet, a well-known Boston printer, said to have issued a collection of the 'Melodies' in 1719. There is an entire lack of evidence, however, to support this assumption; although Boston has a true claim upon the fame of "Mother Goose," because two Boston publishers issued the book in 1824. But it is now conceded that "Mother Goose" belongs to French folklore and not to English tradition; and some writers even connect her with Queen Goosefoot, said to be the mother of Charlemagne. Charles Perrault, born in Paris in 1628, was the first person to collect, reduce to writing, and publish the 'Contes de ma Mère l'Oye,' or 'Tales of Mother Goose'; and there is no reason to think that "Mother Goose" was a term ever used in English literature until it was translated from the French equivalent, "Mère l'Oye." It is probable that her fame first reached England in 1729, when 'Mother Goose's Fairy Tales' were translated by Robert Samber. The original 'Mother Goose's Melodies' was not issued until 1760, when it was brought out by John Newbery of London. While "Mother Goose" herself is of French origin, many of the 'Melodies' are purely of English extraction, some of them dating back to Shakespeare's time and earlier.

Famous writers of fiction "may flourish and may fade," great poets pass into distant perspective; but until time has ceased to be, it is certain that 'Mother Goose' will reign in the hearts and murmur in the ears, of each succeeding generation.

MOTHS, by Louise De la Ramée ("Ouida") (1880). This novel depicts the corruption (springing from idleness and luxury) of modern European society, especially of the women of rank, who are compared to moths "fretting a garment." The first chapter presents such a woman, Lady Dolly, a fashionable butterfly with an ignoble nature. Her daughter by a first marriage, Vera, joins her at Trouville. The girl has been brought up by a worthy English duchess, who has instilled into her mind the noblest traditions of aristocracy, and has developed a character unworldly, high-spirited, and idealistic. The plot turns on her tragic conflict with a false and base social order. Like Ouida's other novels of high life, it unites realism with romance, or with a kind of sumptuous exaggeration of the qualities and attributes of aristocracy, which, to the average reader, is full of fascination.

MOUNTAINEERING IN THE SIERRA NEVADA, by Clarence King (1872). Mr. King is so well known a scientist that the government very properly long ago annexed his services. It is therefore to be taken for granted that the geology and geography of this volume are above suspicion. But what delights the unlearned reader is not its scientific accuracy, but its nice observation, its vivid power of description, its unfailing humor, its beautiful literary art. The official mountaineer in pursuit of his duty ascends Mount Shasta and Mount Tyndall, Mount Whitney and the peaks of the Yosemite, and gathers all the data for which a distant administration is pining. But on his own account, and to the unspeakable satisfaction of his audience, he "interviews" the Pike County immigrant, the Digger, the man from Nowhere, and the Californian; and the reader is privileged to "assist" with unspeakable satisfaction on all these social occasions, and to sigh that there are not more. A joy forever is that painter of the Sierras whom the geologist encountered, painting on a large canvas, who accosted him with "Dern'd if you ain't just naturally ketched me at it! Git off and set down. You ain't goin' for no doctor, I know"; and who confesses that his aim is to be "the Pacific Slope Bonheur." His criticisms on his fellow artists are more incisive than Taine's. "Old Eastman Johnson's barns and everlasting girl with the ears of corn ain't life, it ain't got the real git-up." Bierstadt's mountains would "blow over in one of our fall winds. He hasn't got what old Ruskin calls for." The concluding chapter is given to California as furnishing a study of character. Forced to admit the conditions on which she has been condemned as vulgar and brutal, he yet perceives that *being* is far less significant than *becoming*, and that her future is to be not less magnificent than her hopes.

MOUNTAINS OF CALIFORNIA, THE, by John Muir, a work describing the geology, the flora, and the fauna of the California mountains, was published in 1894, and in an enlarged edition in 1911. In the opening chapter the topography of the state and the relation of its two mountain systems, the Sierra Nevada and the Coast Range, are graphically set forth, and a broad picture of these two parallel ranges and the intervening Central Valley is indelibly impressed on the reader's mind. At the same time a number of skilfully chosen details add such life and color as to inspire a longing to see the reality. Then follow a chapter on the Glaciers, illustrated by records of personal explorations; chapters on the Snow, on the High Sierra, on the Passes, on the Glacier Lakes, and on the Glacier Mountains. All are the work of a geologist, who not only knows the mountains scientifically, but loves them and can describe them poetically. A long chapter on the Forests gives individual attention to the various types of trees, giant and otherwise. The chapters on the Douglas Squirrel, the Water Ouzel, which swims under water, the Wild Sheep, which jump down precipices one hundred and fifty feet high and escape unhurt, and on the Bee Pastures, or meadows full of marvelous wild flowers, show the keenest appreciation for animal and plant life as well as for scenery. "The River Flood" exhibits the Californian mountains in their wilder moods. The book is the work of an enthusiastic nature-lover, but without rhapsodizing or sentimentality, and checked by sober scientific observation. As a word-painter and as a revealer of the rich treasures of beauty in the wonderful mountain-world of California, he merits the highest praise.

MOURNING BRIDE, THE, by William Congreve. This, the only serious play written by Congreve, was produced in 1697, and was most successful. Lugubrious is a cheerful term by which to characterize it. Almeria, the daughter of Manuel, King of Granada, while in captivity marries Alphonso, the son of Anselmo, King of Valencia. In a battle with Manuel, Anselmo is captured, Alphonso drowned, and Almeria returned to her father. He insists upon her marriage with Garcia, the son of Gonzalez, his favorite. Manuel captures Zara, an African princess, and with her two Moors, Osmyn and Heli. Almeria finds that Osmyn is Alphonso; and Zara, overhearing them, is led by her jealousy to induce the King to allow her mutes to strangle him, and to give orders that none but her mutes shall have access to him. Gonzalez, to secure a mute's dress, kills one, and finds on him a letter from Zara to Alphonso, telling him she has repented and will help him to escape. Manuel orders Alphonso to be executed at once; and to prove Zara's treachery, places himself in chains in Alphonso's place to await her coming. Gonzalez, to make sure of Alphonso's death, steals down and kills him. Meeting Garcia, he learns that Alphonso has escaped, and that he has killed the King instead of Alphonso. The King's head is cut off and hid, so that his death may not be known. Zara, thinking that it is the body of Alphonso, poisons herself; and Alphonso, storming the palace, reaches Almeria in time to prevent her from taking the remainder of the poison. Two quotations from this play have become almost household words: the first, "Music hath charms to soothe a savage breast"; and the second, "Heaven has no rage like love to hatred turned; nor hell a fury, like a woman scorned."

MUCH ADO ABOUT NOTHING, by Shakespeare, was first published in 1600. The mere skeleton of the serious portions of the drama he took from Bandello, through Belleforest's translation; the comic scenes are all his own. In the portrayal of Beatrice, Benedick, and Dogberry, he lavishes all his skill. The constable Dogberry is hit off to the life, with his irresistibly funny malapropisms. He is a lovable old heart-of-gold, who is always taking off his hat to himself and his office, and absurdly pardons every crime except the calling of himself an ass. The scene is laid in Messina. Benedick is just home from the wars. He and Beatrice have had some sparring matches before, and thick and fast now fly the tart and merry witticisms between them, — she "the sauciest, most piquant madcap girl that Shakespeare ever drew," yet genuinely sympathetic; he a genial wit who tempts fate by his oaths that he will never marry. From the wars comes too, Claudio, brave, but a light-weight fop, selfish, and touchy about his honor. He loves Hero, daughter of Leonato. Beatrice is the latter's niece, and in his house and orchard the action mostly takes place. The gentlemen lay a merry plot to ensnare Beatrice and Benedick. The latter is reading in the orchard, and overhears their talk about the violent love of Beatrice for him, and how (Hero has said) she would rather die than confess it. The bait is eagerly swallowed. Next Beatrice, hearing that Hero and Ursula are talking about her in the garden, runs, stooping like a lapwing, and hides her in the honeysuckle arbor. With a strange fire in her ears she overhears how desperately in love with her is Benedick. The bird is limed; she swears to herself to requite his devotion. Hero's wedding-day is fixed: Claudio is the lucky man. But the villain Don John concocts a plot which has most painful results — for twenty-four hours at least. He takes Claudio and his friend Don Pedro to the orchard, and shows them, as it seemed, Hero bidding John's follower Borachio a thousand good-nights: it is really her maid Margaret in her garments. Claudio in a rage allows her to go to church, but before the altar scornfully rejects her. Her father is in despair, Beatrice nobly indignant and incredulous. Hero swoons, and the officiating friar advises the giving out that she is dead from the shock. Claudio believes it, and hangs verses on her tomb. Meantime Dogberry's famous night-watch have overheard Borachio confess the villainous practice of John and himself. Then Hero's joyful friends plan a little surprise for Claudio. Leonato makes him promise, in reparation, to marry a cousin of Hero's, who turns out to be Hero herself come to life. A double wedding follows, for Benedick willingly suffers himself to be chaffed for eating his words and becoming "the married man." Yet both he and Beatrice vow they take each other only out of pity.

MUNCHAUSEN, BARON, see **TRAVELS AND ADVENTURES OF.**

MURRAY, JOHN, MEMOIR AND CORRESPONDENCE OF. With an Account of the Origin and Progress of the House, 1768–1843. By Samuel Smiles. (2 vols., 1891). The history of as great a publisher as literature has ever known, and a most notable example of devotion to the production of books of character and value, irrespective of mere mercenary considerations. The foundation of the great London house of Murray was laid in 1768, by a John Murray, who retired from service as a lieutenant of marines, and bought out a bookselling business at No. 32 Fleet Street. The second and the great Murray was a boy of fifteen at his father's death in 1793, but two years later he began his publishing career, at first with his father's shop man as a partner; but "a drone of a partner" was not to his mind, and from March 23d, 1803, he was alone. His first attempt to deal with an author gave the keynote to a career of unexampled distinction, when he wrote: "I am honestly ambitious that my first appearance should at once stamp my character and respectability; . . . and 'I am not covetous of gold.'" The tradition thus started, of weighing the character of a work and the credit of publishing it, and letting the chance of making money by the publication pass as of secondary importance, was for forty years the glory of the name of Murray. "The business of a publishing bookseller," he said, "is not in his shop, or even in his connections, but in his brains." A man of fine taste and broad culture, possessing moreover innate generosity and magnanimity, his dealings with authors were frequently munificent; and in notable instances he counted the honor before the profit. He started the Quarterly Review, in February, 1899, as a Tory organ, and carried it at a loss for two or three years. Nothing characterized him more than his steady confidence in the success of the best literature; and in proportion as a publication was of high character, he was determined and lavish in pushing it to success. Nor was he for this any the less a consummate man of business, achieving extraordinary success as a merchant prince at the head of the London book trade. To a large extent he depended on his own judgment in accepting books for publication. His most famous engagements were with Scott, Southey, Byron, Moore, Lockhart, and the Disraelis. To the younger Disraeli, then only twenty, he owed the one wholly damaging venture of his career, — an attempt in daily journalism which ignominiously failed at the end of six months, with a loss to Murray of £26,000.

MUSIC AND MUSICIANS, DICTIONARY OF, by Sir George Grove. (5 vols. 1904–10), edited by J. A. Fuller Maitland. Sir George Grove's Dictionary, the first instalment of which appeared in 1878, was intended as much for the general reader as the trained musician, and indeed to a great extent owed its success to this very fact. The new edition, edited by Mr. Fuller Maitland, has endeavored to adhere to the same principle, as far as the limits of space have allowed. The monumental articles on Beethoven, Mendelssohn and Schubert of the original edition, which are Sir George Grove's chief contributions to musical literature, are retained, with only such additions and corrections as met with the writer's own wishes. In its revised form the work, not only explains the meaning of musical terms, but of words, like acoustics, for example, which have come into use in the more penetrating and scientific study of music. It now includes not only modern and mediæval, but ancient music. In a work of such scope, limits of space have made it impossible to include the name of every musician who might be held to deserve mention. Whether executants or composers, only those have been admitted who have attained to real eminence, and whose reputation extends beyond the country of their birth or adoption. In the case of all composers of real importance, their works have been catalogued systematically under their opus-numbers, if such exist, and so much criticism, even of living people, has been admitted into the text as will explain the general characteristics of the musicians under discussion. It is sufficient to add that the widest and most impartial catholicity has been shown in the choice of contributors and that the work is now everywhere recognized as a classic.

MUSIC, THE HISTORY OF, by W. S. Pratt (1907). This work, as the author explains in the preface is rather a book of reference for students than a critical survey of a few salient aspects of the subject, or a specialist's report of original research. The leading tendencies or movements of musical advance are thrown into relief, reference being made to particular styles and composers as illustrations. The need of such a study arises from the fact that amid the general progress of historical investigation the history of music has been almost neglected, partly because of the lack until recently of adequate text-books and partly because of the insufficient recognition of the fine arts as essential parts of anything that deserves the name of culture. This neglect is all the more remarkable because however far back investigation into the history of even the most primitive races has gone, there appears to have existed "the spontaneous use by all races of song, dance, and instrument as a means of expression, amusement, and even discipline." The division of subject is into primitive or savage music, Greek and Roman; mediæval, including the rise of Christian music and covering the period to the fifteenth century; the Venetian and Roman Schools and the Church and secular music of the sixteenth century: the early musical drama and the rise of dramatic music in the seventeenth century; the early Italian opera of the eighteenth century, which was also to produce the masterpieces of Haydn, Gluck, and Mozart; the early and middle nineteenth century with the names of Beethoven, Schumann, Mendelssohn, Wagner: the later nineteenth century of which perhaps the most conspicuous figure was Richard Strauss. The work is not a history of instruments, but it contains 110 illustrations of selected specimens from the Metropolitan Museum in New York and the University of Michigan at Ann Arbor. These are of the most varied interest and value and range from the stone flute of Alaska, the Hindu sarangi, the ancient Irish harp, to the elaborate sarussophones of the present day.

MUSIC, THE OXFORD HISTORY OF, see **OXFORD.**

MUTABLE MANY, THE, by Robert Barr (1896). This is one of the many accounts of the struggle between labor and capital. The scene is London, at the present day. The men in Monkton and Hope's factory strike. Sartwell, their manager, refuses to compromise with them, but discusses the situation with Marsten, one of their number, who clings to his own order, at the same time that he avows his love for Sartwell's daughter Edna. Sartwell forbids him to speak to her. The strike is crushed, Marsten is dismissed, and becomes secretary to the Labor Union. He sees Edna several times, she becomes interested in him, and her father sends her away to school. Marsten visits her in the guise of a gardener, offers her his love, and is refused. Barney Hope, son of her father's employer, a dilettante artist of lavishly generous impulses, also offers 'himself to her and is refused. Later, he founds a new school of art, becomes famous, and marries Lady Mary Fanshawe. Marsten brings about another strike, which is on the eve of success, and Sartwell is about to resign his post. Edna, seeing her father's despair, visits Marsten at the Union and proposes to marry him if he will end the strike and allow her father to triumph. He declines to sell his honor even at such a price. The members of the Union, seeing her, accuse Marsten of treachery, depose him from office, and so maltreat him that he is taken to the hospital. His successor in office is no match for Sartwell, who wins the day. Edna goes to Marsten, and owns at last that she loves him.

MUTINEERS OF THE BOUNTY, THE, by Lady Belcher (1870). This latest published account of a long unsolved ocean mystery and of a unique settlement on a South Sea island, written in the prosaic style of an official document, amply substantiates the old adage, "Truth is stranger than fiction." The most vivid imagination would fail to conceive the plot of a tale more varied and more exciting in its details.

In 1789 H. M. S. Bounty, Lieutenant Bligh commanding, while sailing in the South Seas was captured by mutineers, and the commander with eighteen of the crew were set adrift in the cutter. The ship sailed to Tahiti. There dissensions arose among the mutineers. Half of them, accompanied by a score of native men and women, sailed away, and all trace of them was lost for many years.

Lieutenant Bligh reached England, returned to Tahiti, captured the mutineers who were on that island, and after many disasters and shipwreck conveyed them to England. A sensational trial ensued. Two of the mutineers were pardoned. The others suffered the extreme penalty of the law. Then a reaction in public sentiment set in, and it was generally conceded, even in official circles, that the insolent and overbearing conduct of the commander warranted the course of the mutineers.

Some twenty years later, a British vessel happened accidentally to stop at Pitcairn's Island. The officers were amazed to meet young men who spoke excellent English, and to find a prosperous and happy Christian community, largely descendants of the mutineers.

They learned that the Bounty sailed directly from Tahiti to Pitcairn's Island, where the mutineers made a settlement. Four years later, on account of a quarrel over a woman, the natives murdered all but four of them. Then two of them contracted such beastly habits of intoxication that one died in delirium tremens and the other was put to death as a measure of public safety.

One of the survivors, John Adams, remembering his early Christian training, established the principles of the Christian religion so firmly in this peculiar community that the almost unknown island in the South Seas became a conspicuous example of an earthly paradise.

This community, maintaining its essential characteristics, still occupies Pitcairn and Norfolk Islands. Its members carry on a constant correspondence with relatives and friends in England. Many photographs of the islanders, reproduced in this book, represent a people prepossessing in appearance and apparently comfortable and prosperous.

MY ARCTIC JOURNAL, by Josephine Diebitsch-Peary. In 'My Arctic Journal,' Mrs. Peary describes her experiences as a member of an exploring expedition sent out by the Philadelphia Academy of Natural Sciences. Besides her husband (the commander), Lieutenant Robert E. Peary, U. S. N., there were five other men in the party. These were Dr. F. A. Cook, Messrs. Langdon Gibson, Eivind Astrup, John T. Verhoef, and Michael Matthew Henson, Mr. Peary's colored attendant. The steam whaler Kite, in which they sailed, left New York June 6th, 1891, and returning, reached Philadelphia September 24th, 1892.

In her journal, which covers the whole of this period, Mrs. Peary not only records the ordinary events of each day, but gives many valuable accounts of the scenery of Greenland and of the habit of the Eskimos whom they met. She gathered eiderdown; shot wild ducks; cooked the meals for the party; cut out new garments, and showed the native women how to sew them; took care of her husband's broken leg, and nursed others when ill; and patiently bore whatever discomfort came to her. The expedition accomplished several of the objects which it had in view, — proving, for example, that Greenland is an island, discovering the ice-free land masses to the north of Greenland, and delineating the northward extension of the great Greenland ice-cape. After twelve months on the shores of McCormick Bay, the party set out on the return in company with the relief expedition led by Professor Heilprin, in good health and spirits. Mrs. Peary was as cheerful as the others, and the one cloud on the homeward journey was the mysterious disappearance of Verhoef.

Mrs. Peary's 'Journal' is written in pleasant style, and in two ways has a definite value. First, it shows that the terrors of an Arctic winter, even in the neighborhood of latitude 78°, have been greatly magnified; and second, it adds much important information to our stock of ethnological knowledge.

To her published journal Mrs. Peary has added a chapter giving her impressions of Greenland when she revisited it in the summer of 1893.

MY CHILDHOOD, by Maxim Gorky (1915). This autobiography begins with the boy's first memories, his father's death and the birth of a brother, and ends with his seventeenth year. He defends the unflinching realism of his story, saying, "I am writing not about myself but about that narrow, stifling environment of unpleasant impressions in which lived — aye, and to this day lives — the average Russian of this class." He asks himself near the end of the book whether it is worth while to describe "these oppressive horrors of our wild Russian life" and answers in the affirmative, because "the Russian is still so healthy and young in heart that he can and does rise above them." He writes impersonally about his own life as a spectator of the "cruelty of the drab existence of an unwelcome relation" in his grandfather's house at Nijni Novgorod. His grandfather, tugging barges along the Volga, has come to own barges in his old age, and is in fairly comfortable circumstances, but his miserly character and tyranny make his entire household wretched. The child, Alexei, learns pity for all suffering from the floggings he receives from this inhuman grandfather. His two uncles are cruel and wicked, keeping the household in continual brawl with their violent quarrels. He hears how they had tried to kill his father one time by pushing him into a hole in the ice, and stamping on his fingers when he attempted to save himself. He watches his grandfather beat his grandmother. The boy tries to stab his stepfather when that unpleasant youth kicks his mother. The only attractive character is his gentle old grandmother. He says "her disinterested love for all creation enriched me and built up the strength needful for a hard life." Her memory was stored with rhymed folk-tales and fairy tales, which she would recite to the boy. Deeply religious, her prayers were a poetic adoration of beautiful phrases and metaphors to which he loved to listen. She saw angels, and at times, when she was drunk, most entertaining fiends. His mother stays away from the intolerable home, and Alexei gradually comes to understand her passionate erring nature. One of the houses they live in is packed full of lodgers, and has a tavern on the ground floor. Alexei watches the drunken men "crawling out of the taven and staggering up the road, shouting and tumbling about." Another home is next a slaughter yard with its noise of bellowing cattle, and the smell of blood so strong it seemed to Alexei that it "hovered in the air in the shape of a transparent purple net." When he is not in school he earns money by collecting bones, rags, paper, and nails in the street. After his mother's funeral, his grandfather says to him, "Now, Lexei — you must not hang around my neck. There is no room for you here. You will have to go out into the world." So Alexei went out into the world. A year after 'My Childhood' Gorky published IN THE WORLD (1917) which continues the experiences of his early life up to his fifteenth year, and is a series of pictures of the every day life of Russian working people, artisans, small shopkeepers, sailors, and soldiers. He is first doorboy in a shoe shop, then drudge in the house of a draughts-man where he expected to be taught a trade, but instead was employed as a scullery boy by the quarrelling women. He ran away and became a dishwasher on a Volga steamer. His experience is always coarse and brutal, but he is saved from it by his own "fastidious dislike," by the teaching of his old grandmother, and above all by his escape into the world of books. Books were literally the boy's salvation from the senseless cruelty and viciousness of the life about him, which he recognized as the result of dreariness, boredom and ignorance. A cook on the Volga steamer lent him books, Balzac, Scott, and Turgenieff. From that time he begs, buys, and borrows all the books he can get hold of, and thinks of the "great world," of "foreign countries where people lived in a different manner." He says, "Writers of other countries depicted life as cleaner, more attractive, less burdensome than that life which seethed sluggishly and monotonously around me. This thought calmed my disturbed spirit and aroused visions of the possibility of a different life for me." "The more I read, the harder it was for me to go on living the empty, unnecessary life that most people live." He works in an icon-maker's shop. Again and again he returns to his old grandmother "more consciously charmed by her personality" but realizing as he grows older "that that beautiful soul, blinded by fanciful tales, was not capable of seeing, could not understand a revelation of the bitter reality of life," and cannot help him in his restlessness and perplexity. At last he thinks, "I must do something for myself, or I shall be ruined." The narrative closes as he goes to Kazan in the secret hope of finding some means of studying at the academy.

MY NOVEL; or, VARIETIES IN ENGLISH LIFE, by Sir Edward Bulwer-Lytton (1853). This novel presents an intimate and faithful picture of the English life of Bulwer's day. The scenes are laid partly in the village of Hazeldean, where a number of the characters are first introduced, and partly in London. Among the types of English-men and foreigners presented are Squire Hazeldean; Parson Dale, a simple Church of England clergyman; Audley Egerton, a politician of fame; Baron Levy, a money-lender; Harley, Lord L'Estrange, who is perhaps the hero of the book; Leonard Fairfield, a poet; and Dr. Riccabocca, a political exile, who is really an Italian Duke,

As a picture of English life in the first half of the century, 'My Novel' is remarkable for its realism. It is perhaps the strongest of Bulwer's novels in its breadth of view, and in its delineation of many varieties of character.

MY OFFICIAL WIFE, by Colonel Richard Henry Savage (1891). This clever skit is permeated by a Russian atmosphere, in which visions of the secret police, the Nihilists, and social life in St. Petersburg, are blended like the vague fancies of a troubled dream.

Colonel Arthur Lenox, with passports made out for himself and wife, meets at the Russian frontier a strikingly beautiful woman whom he is induced to pass over the border as his own wife, who has remained in Paris.

At St. Petersburg, Hélène, the "official wife," receives mail addressed to Mrs. Lenox, shares the Colonel's apartments, and is introduced everywhere as his wife. But he has learned that she is a prominent and dangerous Nihilist, and is in daily fear of discovery and punishment.

Lenox frustrates her design to assassinate the Emperor; after which Hélène escapes by the aid of a Russian officer whom she has beguiled. Meantime the real wife has come on from Paris, and endless complications with the police ensue. The Colonel secures his wife's release by threatening the chief of police that otherwise he will inform the Tsar of the inefficiency of the police department, in not unearthing the scheme for his assassination.

MY SCHOOLS AND SCHOOLMASTERS, by Hugh Miller (1854), is one of the most delightful of autobiographies as far as it goes. (It stops with Miller's assumption of the editorship of the Edinburgh Witness in 1840 — after which he was teacher rather than pupil.) The author desired it to be regarded as "a sort of educational treatise, thrown into the narrative form, and addressed more especially to workingmen"; but men and women of all classes find it good reading. For seventeen years covered by this volume, he worked at the trade of stone-mason, — though he had been carefully educated by his two uncles, and possessed an extensive knowledge of English language, history, and literature, — spending his spare time in geological research and in reading. His remarkable powers of observation he must have developed early: he speaks of remembering in later life things that only a sharp eye would have noted, as far back as the end of his third year. Having disposed of his parents' biography in the first chapter, the work narrates his earliest recollections of his own life, his school days, his youthful adventures, the awakening of his taste by one of his uncles for the study of nature, his first attempts at authorship, visits to the Highlands, choice of a trade, moving to Edinburgh, religious views, illness, receiving an accountantship in a branch bank at Cromarty, marriage, the death of his infant daughter, etc. It abounds in stories, interesting experiences, keen observation of natural objects, and anecdotes of prominent men, — all in an admirable style.

MY STUDIO NEIGHBORS, a volume of sketches, by William Hamilton Gibson. Illustrated by the author (1898). The titles of these sketches are: 'A Familiar Guest,' 'The Cuckoos and the Outwitted Cow-bird,' 'Door-Step Neighbors,' 'A Queer Little Family on the Bittersweet,' 'The Welcomes of the Flowers,' 'A Honey-Dew Picnic,' 'A Few Native Orchids and their Insect Sponsors,' 'The Milkweed.' Nobody since Thoreau has brought a more exact and clear observation to the study of familiar animal and plant life than the author of these sketches, and even Thoreau did not always see objects with the revealing eye of the artist. Mr. Gibson has the "sharp eye" and "fine ear" of the prince in the fairy tale; and his word pictures are as vivid as the beautiful work of his pencil. To read him is to meet the creatures he describes, on terms of friendship.

MY STUDY WINDOWS, by James Russell Lowell (1874) contains a series of biographical, critical, and poetical essays, in whose kaleidoscopic variety of theme continual brilliancy illuminates an almost perfect symmetry of literary form. The charming initial essay, 'My Garden Acquaintance,' treats of the familiar visits of the birds at Elmwood. This is followed by a similar essay entitled 'A Good Word for Winter.' 'On a Certain Condescension in Foreigners' is the third; and a review of the 'Life of Josiah Quincy' follows. Then come critical essays upon the lives and works of Carlyle, Abraham Lincoln, James Gates Percival, Thoreau, Swinburne, Chaucer, Emerson, Pope, and the early English authors, or rather upon some of their critics and editors. Characterizations like these abound: 'I have sometimes wondered that the peep-shows, which Nature provides in such endless variety for her children, and to which we are admitted on the one condition of having eyes, should be so generally neglected." "He (Winter) is a better poet than Autumn when he has a mind; but like a truly great one, as he is, he brings you down to your bare manhood, and bids you understand him out of that, with no adventitious helps of association, or he will none of you." "All the batteries of noise are spiked!" "The earth is clothed with innocence as with a garment; every wound of the landscape is healed. . . . What was unsightly before has been covered gently with a soft splendor; as if, Cowley would have said, Nature had cleverly let fall her handkerchief to hide it." The essay upon Chaucer was always a favorite with that admirable critic, Prof. F. J. Child; and to him Lowell dedicated the volume.

MYCENÆAN AGE, THE, 'a Study of the Monuments and Culture of Pre-Homeric Greece,' by Dr. Chrestos Tsountas and J. Irving Manatt. With an introduction by Dr. Dörpfeld. (1897. 7th edition, 1899). A most valuable summary of the discoveries of twenty years, from Schliemann's first great "find" at Mycenæ to 1896. Dr. Tsountas was commissioned in 1886, by the Greek government, to continue Schliemann's work; and after seven years of explorations, he brought out a volume on 'Mycenæ and the Mycenæan Civilization,' in which he undertook a systematic handling of the whole subject of prehistoric Greek culture in the light of the monuments. This was written in Greek and published at Athens. Dr. Manatt, of the Greek chair at Brown University, undertook, on his return from a four-years' residence in Greece, to prepare an English version of Tsountas's work; but later, in view of three years' rapid progress of explorations, and with the aid of new materials furnished by Tsountas, he made a largely new work, bringing the Mycenæan story up to date. This story is "a great chapter of veritable history newly added to the record of the Greek race." It "covers the period approximately from the sixteenth to the twelfth century B.C." It had been taken for granted that the time of Homer represented the earliest known stage of Greek civilization, the childhood of the race. But Homer lived in Ionia of Asia Minor, as late at least as the ninth century B. C.; and the new discoveries show the Mycenæan civilization widely spread in Attica and central Greece, and Crete even, seven hundred years before Homer. Of the life and culture of this pre-Homeric Greece, the story told by Drs. Tsountas and Manatt gives a full, exact, and richly illustrated view.

MYSTERIES OF UDOLPHO, THE, by Mrs. Anne Radcliffe (1795). Like the famous 'Castle of Otranto' of Horace Walpole, this story belongs to the school of limelight fiction. Udolpho is a mediæval castle in the Apennines, where, during the seventeenth century, all sorts of dark dealings with the powers of evil are supposed to be carried on. The love-lorn lady who is more or less the victim of these supernatural interferences is an English girl, Emily St. Aubyn, and her noble and courageous lover, who finally lays the spell, is the Chevalier Velancourt. The plot, such as it is, is quite indescribable; and the interest of the book lies in the horrors which accumulate on horror's head. Modern taste finds the romance almost unreadable, yet Sheridan and Fox praised it highly; the grave critic and poet-laureate Warton sat up all night to read it; and Walter Scott thought that, even setting aside its breathless interest as a story, "its magnificence of landscape, and dignity of conception of character, secure it the palm"; while the author of 'The Pursuits of Literature,' a distinguished scholar, who knew more of Italian letters than any other man in England, discourses on "the mighty magician of 'The Mysteries of Udolpho,' bred and nourished by the Florentine Muses in their sacred solitary caverns, amid the paler shrines of Gothic supersitition and in all the dreariness of enchantment: a poetess whom Ariosto would with rapture have acknowledged."

NABOB, THE, by Alphonse Daudet (1877). This romance is one of the most highly finished of the author's works. Jansoulet, the Nabob, has emigrated to Tunis with but half a louis in his pocket. He returns with much more than twenty-five millions; and becomes at once the prey of a horde of penniless adventurers, whose greed even his extravagant generosity cannot satisfy. His dining-room in the Place Vendôme is the rendezvous of projectors and schemers from every part of the world, and resembles the Tower of Babel. Dr. Jenkins, the inventor of an infallible pill, persuades him to endow his famous Asile de Bethléem, hinting to him that the Cross of the Legion of Honor will reward his benevolence; but it is the doctor, and not the poor Nabob, who is decorated. Montpavon, an old beau, saves a bank, in which he is a partner, from insolvency with the money of the multi-millionaire; the journalist Moessard receives a liberal donation for a eulogistic newspaper article: in short, Jansoulet becomes the easy dupe of all who approach him. 'The Nabob' is a romance of manners and observation; and it blends successfully many of the qualities of both the naturalist and the romantic schools. It exhibits a singular faculty for seizing on the picturesque side of things, and a wonderful gift of expression. Although several models among the French commercial classes must have sat for Jansoulet, most of the other characters are prominent figures in Parisian life, very thinly veiled.

NANA, see **ROUGON-MACQUART.**

NAPOLEON I., THE LIFE OF, 'Including new material from the British Official Records,' by J. Holland Rose, was published in 1902. This is one of the first English books in which Napoleon is treated with due appreciation and at the same time judicially. Napoleon's military genius and his great achievements as a statesman receive adequate recognition though without hero-worship. A study of the documents in the British War, Admiralty and Foreign Offices has enabled the author to contribute materially to our knowledge of Napoleon's policy and of British diplomacy. In particular he reveals the complicity of the British government in a plot against Napoleon's life in 1803–1804. The work is a singularly well-proportioned presentation of the essential facts of Napoleon's career, embodying and clearly expressing the results of many minute and particular investigations. The military campaigns are clearly set forth, the political events skilfully untangled, and the signi-

594
THE READER'S DIGEST OF BOOKS

ficance of Napoleon's character and career keenly estimated. The author has achieved historical impartiality in a field particularly difficult for an Englishman, even a century after Napoleon's defeat.

NAPOLEON BONAPARTE, THE LIFE OF, by William Milligan Sloane, professor of history in the University of Columbia, appeared serially in the Century Magazine in 1894–96, and in four volumes in 1897. While the author began his task with the consciousness that "Napoleon's career was a historic force, and not a meteoric flash in the darkness of revolution," he has not attempted to enter into the labyrinth of a general history of the times, except as a necessary background for his portraiture. He carries the reader in narrative over the now well-trodden path from Corsica to St. Helena, with a scholar's precision as well as a lively interest, and in a way to dissolve the illusions and establish the facts of the Napoleonic period. In accomplishing this purpose, Professor Sloane has had the great advantage of adding to his abilities as a historian the invaluable factor of an impartial mind. He has drawn the most prominent figure of the French revolutionary times with an American perspective, entirely free from the prejudices and passions that still survive in Europe. The most original portion of this monumental work is the study of Napoleon in his Corsican home, and the demonstration that the man was already prefigured in the unruly boy. This careful study of the youth of this military genius does more to illuminate his subsequent career than any other investigation that has been made. The boy was literally the father of the man. The author gives a striking summary of his character as he was at the age of twenty-three: "Finally there was a citizen of the world, a man without a country: his birthright was gone, for Corsica repelled him; France he hated, for she had never adopted him. He was almost without a profession, for he had neglected that of a soldier, and had failed both as an author and as a politician. He was apparently, too, without a single guiding principle; the world had been a harsh stepmother, at whose knee he had neither learned the truth nor experienced kindness. He appears consistent in nothing but in making the best of events as they occurred. . . . He was quite as unscrupulous as those about him, but he was far greater than they in perspicacity, adroitness, adaptability, and persistence."

NAPOLEON BONAPARTE, MEMOIRS OF, by Louis Antoine Fauvelet de Bourrienne. (1829–31; New York, 4 vols., 1889). An exceptionally entertaining narrative of the career of Napoleon, from his boyhood and school days in Corsica to his final overthrow in 1815; the work of a schoolfellow of the young Bonaparte, who became in April, 1797, the intimate companion and private secretary of the then successful general in Italy, and continued in this close and confidential position until October, 1802, but then suffered dismissal under circumstances of a bitterly alienating character, and finally wrote this history of his old friend under the pressure of very mixed motives, — pride in accurate knowledge of many things in the earlier story, and in his early companionship with Napoleon; desire, perhaps, to come much nearer to true history than the two extremes of unqualified admiration and excessive detestation had yet done; and no small measure of rankling bitterness towards the old comrade who never relented from that dismissal with discredit in 1802, nor ever again permitted a recurrence of personal intercourse.

Metternich said at the time of their publication that Bourrienne's 'Memoirs,' though not brilliant, were both interesting and amusing, and were the only authentic memoirs which had yet appeared. Lucien Bonaparte pronounced them good enough as the story of the young officer of artillery, the great general, and the First Consul, but not as good for the career of the emperor. The extreme Bonapartists attacked the work as a product of malignity and mendacity, and a suspicion in this direction naturally clings to it. But whether Bourrienne did or did not inject convenient and consoling lies into the story of his long-time friend and comrade, whose final greatness he was excluded from all share in, and whether he did or did not himself execute the 'Memoirs' from abundance of genuine materials, the book given to the world in his name made a great sensation, and counts, both with readers and with scholars, as a notable source of Napoleon interest and information. "Venal, light-headed, and often untruthful," as Professor Sloane pronounces him, Bourrienne nevertheless remains one of the persons, and the earliest in time, who was in the closest intimacy with Napoleon; and his history might have given us even less of truth if he had kept his place to the end.

NARRATIVE AND CRITICAL HISTORY OF AMERICA, THE, edited by Justin Winsor. This history was prepared upon a co-operative plan (which the editor had previously adopted for his 'Memorial History of Boston'), of dividing historical work into topical sections, and assigning these divisions to different writers, each eminent in his own department, all of whom worked synchronously, thus bringing the whole work to rapid and accurate completion. Each chapter has two parts: first a Historical Narrative which groups the salient points of the story, and embodies the result of the latest researches; second, a Critical Essay by the editor, which, with the appended notes on specific points, is a new procedure in historical methods. In these critical essays are set forth the original sources of the preceding narrative, — manuscripts, monuments, archæological remains, — with full accounts of their various histories and locations; the lives of those who have made use of them; the writers who are authorities upon the several subjects; societies interested in them; and critical statements of existing knowledge and the conditions bearing upon future study. The work is chiefly designed for, and chiefly useful to, writers rather than readers of history: to each of the former it may save months or perhaps years of search for materials, and the constant duplication of such researches already made. It is in fact a co-operative bureau of first-hand sources. It begins with the earliest facts known about the whole continent and its aboriginal inhabitants, including a discussion of the pre-Columbian voyages; describes the different discoveries and settlements by European nations, — Spanish, English, French, and Dutch; and the rise and history of the United States, down to the close of the Mexican war and the end of the year 1850. For the rest of the continent the history is continued down to about 1867. The authors engaged in this work are distinguished each in his own field of study, and much valuable material of an archæological and genealogical character was furnished to them by the leading learned and historical societies. In bibliography there is, along with other important matter, a careful collation of the famous "Jesuit Relations"; and in cartography — a subject of which Mr. Winsor had long made a special study — the work is noticeably strong. The publication extended over the years 1884–89.

NASKS, see SACRED BOOKS OF THE EAST.

NATHAN BURKE, by Mary S. Watts (1910). The nominal autobiography of Nathan Burke, "hero of Chapultepec" in the Mexican war, written for his grand-children, is the life of an American youth in Ohio in the forties. Nat, with his only property, his father's old musket, walks fifteen miles from the backwoods to begin his career as chore-boy for Mr. Ducey, in Columbus, the capital city. He is promoted to clerk in the grocery store, studies law evenings, and is admitted to the bar. He volunteers for service in the Mexican war, distinguishes himself, and returns to marry Francie, the niece of his first employer, and become a prominent citizen. It is an old-fashioned leisurely tale of a bygone day, presenting a great variety of interesting characters, the homespun Lincoln-like hero, Mrs. Ducey, the transplanted southerner, who treats her self-respecting "help" like slaves, and is blindly devoted to her vicious son, George, who deserts the army and owes his good-for-nothing life to Nathan's intercession, old George March, Mrs. Ducey's uncle and rough cross-grained bene-factor, and Nance, the beautiful backwoods girl who is forced into the streets because Mrs. Ducey cannot recognize truth and loyalty outside her own class.

NATHAN THE WISE, by Gotthold Ephraim Lessing. In this book we see embodied Lessing's ideal of the theatre as the pulpit of humanity. The theme is the search for truth under all creeds, the protest of natural kinship against the artificial distinctions and divisions of mankind on religious grounds, and the elevation of neighborly love to the highest place in the Divine favor. The play is called 'A Dramatic Poem in Five Acts.' The scene is in Jerusalem. The plot turns upon the fortunes of a certain Christian knight in wooing for his bride Recha, the supposed child of the Jew Nathan. He had saved her life in a conflagration, and the Jew in gratitude assents to the knight's suit; knowing, as the knight does not know, that his ward is a bap-tized Christian child. The Patriarch, learning of the Jew's concealment of Recha's Christian origin, and of her attachment to Nathan and his faith, is ready to have the Jew committed to the flames for this crime against religion. The matter is brought before the Sultan Saladin for adjustment; and the moral of the drama is focused in the beautiful story related by the Jew to Saladin, of 'The Father and his Ring.' A father had a certain very precious ring, which on dying he bequeathed to his favorite son, with the instruction that he should do likewise, — that so the ring should be owned in each generation by the most beloved son. At length the ring comes into the possession of a father who has three equally beloved sons, and he knows not to which to leave it. Calling a jeweler, he has two other rings made in such exact imita-tion of the original one that no one could tell the difference, and at his death these three rings are owned by the three brothers. But a dispute very soon arises, leading to the bitterest hostilities between the brothers, over the question which of the rings is the first and genuine one; and a wise judge is called in to settle the controversy. Seeing that the rings only breed hatred instead of love, he suggests that the father may have destroyed the true one and given them all only imitations; but if this be not so, let each one of the brothers vindicate the father's honor by showing that the ring he owns has truly the power of attracting not the hatred but the love of others. The magnanimity and justice of the Sultan suggest that he is the judge prefigured in the legend; but the moral of the play points to the one Divine Arbiter, who alone can read the motives and know the true deserts of men and declare who is the possessor of the father's ring.

The play was performed in Berlin two years after the author's death, and was coolly received; but it was brought out with success by Goethe and Schiller in Wei-mar in 1801, and has long since taken its place among the classics of German literature.

NATURAL HISTORY, by Georges Louis le Clerc de Buffon. The Jardin des Plantes in Paris will ever be associated with the name of Count Buffon. In what was then called the King's Garden, the greatest naturalist of the eighteenth century, as superintendent under appointment by Louis XV., accomplished the two colossal undertakings of his life, — the re-creation of the garden itself, and the production of 'L' Histoire Naturelle.' The latter work, published between 1749 and 1804, in forty-four volumes, ranges over the entire field of natural history, from minerals to man. Although borrowing largely from the studies of Aristotle, Descartes, Leibnitz, and others, Buffon introduced an entirely new conception in the treatment of his subject. He cast aside the conjecture and mysticism that had been so long a barrier in the path of pure science, and resorted to observation, reason, and experiment. To him belongs the honor of being the first to treat nature historically, to make a critical study of each separate object, and to classify these objects into species. But at this point Buffon's researches came to a stop. He was too much of an analyst and not enough of a philosopher to catch the grander idea of later scientists, — the relation of species to each other and the unity of all nature. Some of the best results of his work are contained in the enumeration of quadruped animals known in his time, and the classification of quadrupeds, birds, fishes, insects, plants, of the American continent, all unknown in the Old World. One of his most valuable contributions to science is his history of man as a species. Man had been studied as an individual, but to Buffon belongs the credit of having discovered the unity of mankind. The author of this great collection of data, which served as a foundation for the comparative sciences of the nineteenth century, has been called "the painter of nature," because of the magnificence of his style, a style so attractive as to set the fashion in his day for the love of nature, and to inspire all classes with a passion for natural history.

NATURAL HISTORY AND ANTIQUITIES OF SELBORNE, THE, by Gilbert White, was published in 1789. It is a leisurely account, by an old-fashioned naturalist, of the general topography, physiography, meteorology, fauna, and flora of a single parish, Selborne, which "lies in the extreme eastern corner of the county of Hampshire, bordering on the county of Sussex, and not far from the county of Surrey; is about fifty miles southwest of London, in latitude 51, and near midway between the towns of Alton and Petersfield." White was an Oxford fellow and an ordained clergyman, who after some years of residence in college and clerical work, removed to Selborne, his native place, in 1755, inherited the family property there in 1763, and remained in the village the rest of his life, without any regular ecclesiastical duties and devoting his time to reading, writing, and scientific observation. His love of birds, of plants, and of the sights and sounds of field and wood suggested to his mind the writing of a history of the locality which should deal, not with its annals or antiquities but with its natural features. In an age when the chief interest of the country gentleman was in his dogs and gun and of the scholar in his books this was an innovation. White kept a careful record of the weather, the first appearance of various species of birds, the behavior of different animals, and many other details of interest to the lover of nature. These notes he arranged in a series of discursive letters, addressed to his friends, Thomas Pennant, and the Honorable Daines Barrington. The letters were completed in 1787 and published two years later as 'The Natural History of Selborne.' They are brief, entertaining, and written in an easy graphic style which breathes the quiet refinement of an eighteenth-century scholar and gentleman who can quote Virgil or Milton to illustrate his statements. Though the method is conversational and desultory, the different letters have each a unity of topic and the careful records of birds and animals, some now extinct in England, are of scientific worth even to-day. The book is also valuable as a stimulus to nature-study as a means of cultivation and enjoyment.

NATURAL HISTORY OF PLINY, an encyclopædia of mathematical, geographical, anthropological, zoölogical, botanical, and mineralogical knowledge, with concluding sections on sculpture, painting, and other fine arts. It was completed and dedicated to Titus, heir of Vespasian, in 77 A.D. There is a quaint English translation by Philemon Holland, published in 1601. For bibliography of later translations and for a synopsis of the contents of the book, see the LIBRARY under 'Pliny the Elder.'

NATURAL SELECTION, CONTRIBUTIONS TO THE THEORY OF, by Alfred Russel Wallace (1870). A volume of essays, ten in number, which were first published in 1855, 1858, 1864, 1867, 1868, and 1869. The first and second of these, 'On the Law which has Regulated the Introduction of New Species,' and 'On the Tendency of Varieties to Depart Indefinitely from the Original Type,' give an outline theory of the origin of species as conceived by Wallace before he had any notion whatever of the scope and nature of Darwin's labors. One or two other persons had propounded, as Darwin admits, the principle of natural selection, but had failed to see its wide and immensely important applications. Wallace's essays show that he had not only noted the principle, but had fully grasped its importance. To some extent Wallace's essays, published before Darwin's work on 'The Descent of Man,' showed a marked divergence from Darwinian views. In a later reprint, 1891, of his 'Contributions,' Wallace made alterations and considerable additions. In his 'Darwinism,' 1889, Wallace gave an admirably clear and effective exposition of Darwin's views, with much confirmation from his own researches.

NATURE AND ELEMENTS OF POETRY, THE, by Edmund Clarence Stedman. The lectures contained in this volume, published in 1892, were delivered by the author during the previous year at Johns Hopkins University, inaugurating the annual lectureship founded by Mrs. Turnbull of Baltimore. Mr. Stedman treats "of the quality and attributes of poetry itself, of its source and efficacy, and of the enduring laws to which its true examples ever are conformed." Chapter i. treats of theories of poetry from Aristotle to the present day; Chapter ii. seeks to determine what poetry is; and Chapters iii. and iv. discuss, respectively, creation and self-expression under the title of 'Melancholia.' These two chapters together "afford all the scope permitted in this scheme for a swift glance at the world's masterpieces." Having effected a synthetic relation between the subjective and the objective in poetry, the way becomes clear for an examination of the pure attributes of this art, which form the themes of the next four chapters. Mr. Stedman avoids much discussion of schools and fashions. "There have been schools in all ages and centres," he says, "but these figure most laboriously at intervals when the creative faculty seems inactive." This book constitutes a fitting complement to Mr. Stedman's two masterly criticisms on the 'Victorian Poets' and the 'Poets of America.'

NEIGHBOR JACKWOOD, by J. T. Trowbridge, an anti-slavery novel, was published in 1856, when its author had been turned into an "anti-slavery fanatic," as he called himself, through seeing the fugitive slave Anthony Burns marched from the Boston court-house to a revenue cutter in waiting for him by the President's orders at Long Wharf, and thus returned by the Commonwealth of Massachusetts to his Virginia bondage. "The story finished, I had," says Mr. Trowbridge, "great trouble in naming it. I suppose a score of titles were considered, only to be rejected. At last I settled down upon 'Jackwood,' but felt the need of joining to that name some characteristic phrase or epithet. Thus I was led to think of this Scriptural motto for the title-page: "A certain woman went down from Jerusalem to Jericho, and fell among thieves"; which suggested the question, "Who was *neighbor* unto this woman? and the answer, 'Neighbor Jackwood.' And I had my title." Like his juvenile stories, this novel for grown folks is crowded with incident and dialogue, — homely and true to life in part, and in part melodramatic. The heroine, Camille, — a fugitive "white" slave under the alias "Charlotte Woods," — is sheltered by the Jackwoods in their Green Mountain farmhouse, and meets thereabouts the hero, Hector Dunbury. Their mutual love, darkened by the dangers and distresses which multiply about the path of the fugitive, and almost thwarted by a passionate and unscrupulous rival for the girl's hand, who knows her secret, is happily crowned at last by marriage, though the husband has to purchase his wife from her Southern master. The story was dramatized and played in Northern theatres with some success; sympathy for the maiden overcoming the prejudice against its abolitionist bearing, and the mésalliance of Hector and Camille.

NEIGHBORS, THE, by Fredrika Bremer (1837). The scene of this every-day romance is laid in Sweden, and the descriptions give a delightful glimpse into the domestic life of that country. Franziska Werner tells the story by a series of letters to a distant friend. She has lately married "Bear," a country doctor; and the first letters describe her impressions of her new home, her neighbors, and her stepmother-in-law. "Ma chère mère," as she is called, is an eccentric woman possessed of great ability and an iron will. Years before she and her own son Bruno had quarreled, his fiery temper had clashed with hers, and he ran from home with his mother's curse ringing in his ears. After fifteen years of dissipation, he returns under an assumed name and settles at Ramm, as a new neighbor, hoping to win his mother's forgiveness. He is discovered by Franziska and her husband; and at their house he renews his love for Serena, his childhood's friend. She is pure and good, and his passionate, stormy nature is quieted by the strength and beauty of her spiritual one. She loves him, but feels that her duty lies with her aged grandparents; and despite his violent love-making, remains firm in refusing him. At the risk of his life, Bruno saves his mother by stopping her runaway horses, and a reconciliation is brought about at last. Bruno next saves Serena's life, and they become engaged. Hagar, a Hebrew woman, who loves Bruno and has followed him to Ramm, is jealous of Serena and attempts to kill her. Failing in this she tries to take her own life, and dies confessing her sin and clearing Bruno's character. Serena and Bruno marry, and the letters again continue in a pleasant domestic vein. There are many interesting situations in the book, much poetry of thought and feeling, besides an atmosphere of country life that is most refreshing. Miss Bremer has been called the Jane Austen of Sweden.

NELSON, THE LIFE OF, by Captain A. T. Mahan. This monumental biography is a sort of supplement to the author's 'Influence of Sea-Power.' He considers Lord Nelson as "the one man who in himself summed up and embodied the greatness of the possibilities which Sea Power comprehends, — the man for whom genius and opportunity worked together, to make the personification of the navy of Great Britain the dominant factor in the periods hitherto treated." Earl Nelson arose, and in him "all the promises of the past found their finished realization, their perfect fulfillment." Making use of the materials of the many who have written biographies of this fascinating personality, and even richer materials that came into his possession, it was Captain Mahan's object "to disengage the figure of the hero from the glory that cloaks it." His method is to make Nelson "describe himself, tell the story of his own inner life as well as of his external actions." He therefore extracts from the voluminous correspondence extant passages that enable him "to detect the leading features of temperament, traits of thought and motives of action, and thence to conceive within himself, by gradual familiarity even more than by formal effort, the character therein revealed." In the same way as he thus reproduces his individuality, so he treats of his military actions; showing not merely what he did, but also the principles that dominated him throughout his life. The author's logical faculty stood him in good stead in thus concentrating documentary evidence to bear on mooted points, and he most skillfully unravels tangled threads. At the same time his vivid and richly embroidered style, combined with just the right degree of dignity, makes his presentation of mingled biography and history as interesting as a romance and as satisfying as history. The two stately volumes are adorned with numerous portraits and engravings, and with maps and plans explanatory of the battles and engagements described.

NELSON, THE LIFE OF, by Robert Southey (1813). The life of Nelson, written to provide young seamen with a clear concise account of the exploits of England's greatest hero, is a model among short biographies, and a classic in English literature. It is considered the author's masterpiece. "The best eulogy of Nelson" Southey writes, "is the faithful history of his actions; the best history that which shall relate them most perspicuously." A special edition was published by the American government and a copy issued to every seaman and every officer in the American navy. Nelson's splendid career is the very stuff of biography. The story begins with anecdotes of his boyhood which give proof of his courage and indomitable will. He was twelve years old when he first went to sea with his uncle Captain Suckling. His life was an uninterrupted effort to be the best man at his work, and his promotion was rapid. He was a captain when he was twenty-one, and an admiral before he was thirty. Nelson never had good health and on a voyage to India he was so affected by the climate that he was obliged to return home. On this return voyage one day after a long and gloomy reverie, he experienced a sudden glow of patriotism and exclaimed, "I will be a hero! and confiding in Providence brave every danger." The incidents of his life reveal his fascinating personality, his devotion to his country and to his men, and his heroism and leadership in battle. The three greatest naval successes, the battle of the Nile, the victory of Copenhagen, and of Trafalgar, when Nelson received his death wound, are fully and interestingly described. Napoleon had transported the best French army to Egypt for Eastern conquest, depending on his fleet for his means of communication. Nelson destroyed thirteen out of the seventeen French ships, rendering the army in Egypt useless. The victory of Copenhagen shattered the Northern coalition and freed England from pressing danger. The incident of Nelson clapping his telescope to his blind eye in order not to see the signal to cease firing is a story of the Copenhagen attack. Trafalgar was the battle which rendered an invasion of England by Napoleon impossible and made England mistress of the seas. It was at Trafalgar that he made his famous signal before going into action, "England expects that every man will do his duty," the signal which Southey says so truly "will be remembered as long as the language, or even the memory of England shall endure." The story of his personal life is his marriage and his romantic attachment to the beautiful Lady Hamilton for whose sake he separated from his wife. Nelson died in the hour of victory. With characteristic self-forgetfulness, he insisted that the surgeon should leave him and attend to those to whom he might be useful, for he said, "you can do nothing for me." His

last words were, "Thank God, I have done my duty." "So perfectly, indeed, had
he performed his part, that the maritime war, after the battle of Trafalgar, 'the most
signal victory that ever was achieved upon the seas,' was considered at an end: the
fleets of the enemy were not merely defeated, but destroyed," and by the destruction
of this mighty fleet, "all the maritime schemes of France were totally frustrated."
It is a clear and charmingly written narrative, perhaps never surpassed for the
perfection of its prose style.

NEMESIS OF FAITH, THE, by James Anthony Froude.   A small book published
in 1849, but purporting to review the experience at Oxford in 1843 of a student of
that time, in whose mind doubts arose which led him to give up the ministry of
religion in the Church of England.   It in fact reflects Mr. Froude's own experience,
so far as relates to the departure of the hero of the story from orthodoxy of belief, and
his relinquishment of the clerical profession.   The thread of story in the book is only
just enough to enable Mr. Froude to make an imaginary character speak for him,
first in a series of letters, and then in an essay entitled 'Confessions of a Sceptic.'
The free-thinking is that of a mind wishful to live by the ideal truths of the Bible
and the spirit of Christ; but unable to believe the book any more divine than Plato
or the Koran, or Christ any other than a human teacher and example.   Both Romanist and English Church teachings are keenly criticized, with special reference to John
Henry Newman, who was at first a singularly eloquent preacher in the university
pulpit, and later a convert to Romanism.   "That voice so keen, so preternaturally
sweet, whose every whisper used to thrill through crowded churches, when every
breath was held to hear; that calm, gray eye; those features, so stern and yet so
gentle," — these words picture Newman as he preached at St. Mary's, the principal
university pulpit.

NERO, by Ernst Eckstein (1888).   Translated by Clara Bell and Mary J. Safford.
This historical romance calls up the Rome of ancient days, when the imperial city
was at its greatest in power, magnificence, and brutality.   The principal characters
in the story are the well-known Emperor; his wife Octavia, the chaste and beautiful;
the gentle, infatuated Acte; the base and scheming Agrippina, mother of Nero;
Poppæa, the shameless, cruel, intriguing mistress; Nicodemus, the fanatic; and the
grasping pagan, Tigellinus.
   These characters are woven into a complicated but fascinating plot, in which vice
and virtue, honor and crime, Christianity and heathenism, are in perpetual conflict.
   The author, while allowing himself the usual license of the novelist for scope and
imagination, is generally faithful to the history of the period.   And while he has
drawn many graphic pictures descriptive of that terrible age, — such as the popularly conceived brutal character of the Emperor, the burning of Rome, and the
illumination by human torches of Nero's gardens, — his real purpose has been more
to indicate the stages that lead up to these fatal tragedies, than to portray the
tragedies themselves.

NET, THE, by Rex Beach (1912).   This story opens in Sicily where a young American
named Norvin Blake had gone to attend the wedding of his friend Martel Savigno.
The two men had met in Paris and had become such warm friends that Blake had
taken this long journey in order to be Martel's best man.   Upon meeting his friend's
fiancée, Countess Margherita Ginini, Blake is impressed by her great beauty and
charm, and a feeling is aroused within him which no other woman had ever evoked.
As the days go by he finds himself deeply in love with his friend's fiancée, but en-

deavors to smother his traitorous feelings. On the eve of the wedding while Blake, Martel, and his steward are returning home, they are attacked in a lonely place by members of the Mafia Society, whom Martel has offended, and he and his steward are killed. Blake escapes, but blames himself for cowardice in not having been able to help his friend. The Countess Margherita is heart-broken at the loss of her lover and declares that she will find the murderers and avenge Martel's death. Blake is recalled to America by the illness and death of his mother and when he returns to Sicily eight months later, finds Margherita gone, having left no clue to her whereabouts. Blake starts an unsuccessful search, but finding she has sailed for America he returns to his own country. After four years of unavailing search Blake is found living in New Orleans, rich and much sought after socially. He becomes interested in a young and fascinating girl named Myra Bell Warren and enters into a semi-serious engagement pact with her. Meantime he is engaged in the hunt for Martel's murderers and discovers that they are in New Orleans carrying on their deadly work. He receives anonymous letters which put him on track of the villains and finally they are hunted down and lynched by the angered populace. Blake discovers Margherita disguised as a nurse and under an assumed name living in New Orleans. He learns that she has written the anonymous letters warning him of danger and he declares his love for her. On account of Myra Bell, Margherita refuses Blake's advances but when the former elopes with another man, she surrenders, and acknowledges her love for him.

NEW ENGLAND, A COMPENDIOUS HISTORY OF, by the Rev. John Gorham Palfrey, D.D. This history is the chief and monumental work of its author, a distinguished scholar and divine. It embraces the time from the first discovery of New England by Europeans down to the first general Congress of the Anglo-American colonies in 1765. But a supplementary chapter has been added, giving a summary of the events of the last ten years of colonial dependence down to the battles of Lexington and Bunker Hill. The four volumes were originally issued at intervals from 1865 to 1873. A revised and final edition was issued in 1883, after the author's death. Dr. Palfrey divides New England history into three cycles of eighty-six years each. The first, dating from the Stuart accession to the throne of England in the spring of 1603, ends on April 19th, 1689 when the colonists, betrayed by Joseph Dudley, imprisoned the royal governor Andros, thus marking the First Revolution. The Second Revolution was inaugurated April 19th, 1775, when, betrayed by Governor Hutchinson, the people rose and fought the battle of Lexington and Concord. The Third began on April 19th, 1861, when the first blood in the revolution against the domination of the slave power was shed in the streets of Baltimore. Palfrey's history embraces the first two of these periods, and covers the physical, social, and political conditions which have determined the growth and progress of the New England people. The author has treated this subject with wider scope and greater detail than any other writer. He has handled it with a force and vivacity of style, and with a careful minuteness of investigation combined with a discriminating spirit of inquiry, which have elicited the admiration of every scholar who has entered the same field. Some of Dr. Palfrey's judgments have been disputed, but his great work as a whole remains unchallenged as a valuable contribution to American history.

NEW ENGLAND PRIMER, THE. This famous work, the earliest edition of which known to exist was published in Boston in 1727, has passed through various changes of form and text.

An eighteenth-century edition contains the alphabet and syllabarium, followed by several columns of simple words. Next appears

"THE DUTIFUL CHILD'S PROMISE.

I will fear God, honor the King,
I will honor my Father and Mother,
I will obey my superiors."

The alphabet rhymes, illustrated by crude wood-cuts, follow. Among the most atrocious of these is the picture of the man of patience, spotted with sores, accompanied by this rhyme:—

"Job feels the rod,
Yet blesses God."

There is said to have been a picture of the Crucifixion in an earlier edition, with appropriate rhyme; which our rigid Puritan ancestors discarded in favor of Job, claiming that it smacked of papacy.

Among other curious rhymes may be quoted:—

"Proud Korah's troop
Was swallowed up."

"Peter denies
His Lord, and cries."

"Whales in the sea
God's voice obey."

"Time cuts down all,
Both great and small."

The last rhyme is illustrated by a picture of the Grim Destroyer mowing a broad swath with an old-fashioned scythe.

After the Lord's Prayer and the creed is an illustration of John Rogers surrounded by blazing fagots, guarded by the sheriff, with his wife and "nine small children and one at the breast" gazing upon his martyrdom. There is an account of John Rogers, and a copy of his rhymed address to his children.

An Alphabet of Lessons next appears, beginning with

"A wise son maketh a glad father, but a foolish son is the heaviness of his mother";

and closing with

"Zeal hath consumed me because my enemies have forgotten the word of God."

The Shorter Catechism (Westminster), with a few hymns, occupies the remaining half of this little book of 64 pages, having only 3½ by 2¼ inches of printed matter on each page.

In 1897 Mr. Paul Leicester Ford prepared a complete history of the New England Primer, fully presenting the subject historically and bibliographically in an illustrated duodecimo volume of 354 pages.

NEW ESSAYS: OBSERVATIONS, DIVINE AND MORAL, collected out of the Holy Scriptures, Ancient and Modern Writers, both Divine and Human; as also out of the Great Volume of Men's Manners; tending to the furtherance of Knowledge and Virtue. By John Robinson (1624). A volume of sixty-two essays, on the plan of Bacon's, but at greater length, and in ethical, religious, and human interest more like Emerson's 'Essays' in our own time: the work of an English clergyman and scholar, in exile at Leyden in Holland, under whose ministry and through whose counsel the Pilgrim Fathers developed religious liberalism and executed the earliest planting of New England.   He was the Joshua of the religious exodus from England.

Montaigne's use of the word had suggested to Bacon the use of the term "essays" to designate "certain brief notes, set down rather significantly than curiously."   The earliest 'Bacon's Essays,' published in 1597, was a little book of ten short essays, in barely twelve pages (of a recent standard edition).   The second enlarged edition, in 1612, was only thirty-eight essays in sixty-four pages.   The final edition, 1625, had fifty-two essays in two hundred pages.   As pastor Robinson died in March, 1624, he cannot have seen any but the second edition.   To note his relation to Bacon's work he called his book 'New Essays.'   He doubtless thereby indicated also his consciousness that his views were of new departure.   He was in fact an initiator of new liberty and liberality in religion, new breadth and charity and freedom in church matters, and new democracy in political and social order, on grounds of reason and humanity.

In the preface to his 'New Essays,' pastor Robinson says that he has had first and most regard to the Holy Scriptures; next, to the memorable sayings of wise and learned men; and lastly, "to the great Volume of Men's Manners which I have diligently observed, and from them gathered no small part thereof."   He adds that "this kind of meditation and study hath been unto me full sweet and delightful, and that wherein I have often refreshed my soul and spirit amidst many sad and sorrowful thoughts unto which God hath called me."   The study of human nature, the sweetness of spirit, and the scholarly eye to the world's best literature, mark a rare mind, a prophet of culture in church and commonwealth.

NEW FREEDOM, THE, 'A Call for the Emancipation of the Generous Energies of a People,' is a collection of political essays put together by William Bayard Hale from speeches delivered by Woodrow Wilson during his campaign for the Presidency in 1912 and shortly after his election.   In a clear, direct style with homely and concrete illustrations they present certain principles of democratic government as evolved by the author during his experience with trusts and professional politicians when governor of New Jersey.   These principles he applies to the issues of the 1912 campaign, representing the Republicans and the Progressives as supporters of monopoly, special privilege, and government by trusteeship and the Democrats as the defenders of individual opportunity, fair competition, and direct popular government.   The trust, the tariff, and the political boss are the three institutions which are subjected in this volume to a trenchant and vigorous attack.   While praising the legitimate co-ordination of business enterprises in the interests of economy and efficiency Mr. Wilson denounces those combinations which aim simply at the increase of private gain through the suppression of competition and actually weaken efficiency by refusing to adopt new inventions lest they involve the alteration of existing machinery. He maintains that such trusts must be made impossible by public investigation and control.   As to the protective tariff, he denounces not its principle but its abuse for the benefit of trust and monopoly.   Tariff taxes enable manufacturers to escape foreign competition; as a result they are unchecked in the formation of illegal combinations and are enabled to raise the prices to the consumer and to reduce wages to the laborer.   All tariff schedules should be revised with a view to withdrawing protection from such industries but not to destroying the principle of protection itself. Finally the bosses and the political machines which they have created so operate as to take the control of affairs away from the parties and from the people, and to lodge it with a small group of corrupt interests.   For this abuse Mr. Wilson's remedies are the initiative, the referendum, and the recall. These enable the people on the petition of a reasonable number to intervene when legislatures and officials have become tools of the bosses, to introduce or to veto legislation, and to remove persons who have been unfaithful to their trust. These rights, however, he thinks need not be often invoked, and need not extend to the judiciary. In attacking these abuses just outlined the author is especially aiming at the tendency of all business and all politics to fall under the control of a small group of wealthy men, who have constituted themselves trustees for the people and desire to organize and direct their economic, social, and legislative activities. Against this tendency Mr. Wilson sets the old American principle of freedom and individual opportunity, showing, however, that in this new age new conditions of business have arisen which make necessary a revision of the laws and legislation by which freedom and opportunity are secured. "The new freedom" is to be won by "taking common counsel," *i. e.*, by open democratic discussion, by the revival of a sturdy spirit of independence and self-reliance, and by adequate policing and publicity on the part of the government against those who would bring the American people under their tutelage.

NEW GRUB STREET, a novel by George Gissing (1891). The author paints on a broad and diversified canvas the struggle for existence in the English literary world of his day. The general conception is that in the modern Grub Street success is assured only by adopting the most frankly utilitarian and mercenary ideals. The author must write what the public wants and is willing to pay for, without consulting his artistic conscience; and he must employ every art of self-advertisement and of acquiring influential friends in order to gain that apparent prosperity which alone can win him a fair hearing. The encumbrance of marriage to a woman of no fortune is not to be thought of. Poverty, in fact, is regarded in this book as an unmitigated evil, a hindrance to physical cleanliness and health, domestic happiness, personal amenity, and the development of a fine character and creative artistic work. The *dramatis personæ* include representatives of various types who labor under the dome of the British Museum, in cheerless garrets and narrow middle-class, lodgings, — novelists, reviewers, literary hacks, writers of books about books, literary advisers unable to write successfully themselves—all with the self-conscious introspection common to literary men and many with their bitter enmities. The two most prominent characters are Jasper Milvain, a clever reviewer and essayist, who frankly accepts the materialistic standards of the New Grub Street and wins social and literary success; and Edwin Reardon, a highly "temperamental" and conscientious novelist, who refuses to sacrifice his artistic ideals to the popular taste, writes two fine but unappreciated books, and then through financial worry and his wife's lack of sympathy with his resolute stand against cheapening his art, falls into a condition of nervous depression which not only makes work impossible but leads to the separation of husband and wife and his death from privation and despair. A legacy which comes to his wife and an ensuing reconciliation with her come too late to restore him to health. Jasper is an admirer of Mrs. Reardon's cousin, Marian Yule, daughter of Alfred Yule, a literary editor and reviewer of the old stamp, immensely learned and industrious but pedantic and without brilliancy, and embittered by his lack of recognition, which is due in part to his having married beneath him. Marian has been brought up to assist her father and spends her time working in the British Museum. She loves Jasper, and a sum of £5000 to which she falls heir makes it seem possible to him to propose to her without injury to his literary career. The legacy, however, proves to have been in large part exhausted by bad investments; and her father, becoming blind, needs to be assisted with what remains. Jasper, therefore, having first unsuccessfully made advances to an heiress without the knowledge of his fiancée, withdraws from the engagement and at length marries Amy Reardon, widow of his friend the unsuccessful novelist. From the same source as Marian she has inherited £10,000 which remain intact, and the couple enter on a social career which bids fair to end in high literary distinction. Interesting minor characters are Milvain's two sisters, Maud and Dora, who come to London to support themselves by writing children's books. They make marriages, the first to a man of some wealth and the second to Whelpdale, a literary adventurer whose experiences as a writer for American newspapers are borrowed from those of Gissing himself. Another character, Harold Biffen, a penniless scholar, lives in destitution and supports himself by tutoring poor clerks for civil-service examinations. He is a man of fine, generous temperament, keen literary sensibilities, and excellent classical scholarship, and he loves life in all its manifestations. He is at work on a novel entitled 'Mr. Bailey, Grocer,' which is without plot or embellishment, but sets forth "absolute realism in the sphere of the ignobly decent." The formula might well stand for much that is characteristic of Gissing's own work. After long months of hunger and privation the book is finished, rescued by Biffen from a fire, and submitted to the publishers, one of whom pays a small sum for it. With the public it is a failure. Biffen is a faithful companion of Reardon in his miseries and is present at his death, which occurs at Brighton just after the reconciliation with his wife. Later, Biffen, overcome by the beauty of Amy Reardon and her sympathy for him, falls hopelessly in love with her, and feeling himself alone in the world and without object in life, takes poison and dies on Putney Heath. The book is somewhat ill-constructed as regards temporal sequence and the shifting of point of view from one group of characters to another. Nor will it appeal to those who enjoy a cheerful atmosphere and a happy ending. But it is a powerful picture of a phase of life, which it treats with sober and convincing realism; and it contains some exceedingly human personages, a number of absorbing events, and many thorough analyses of character and temperament.

NEW MACHIAVELLI, THE, by H. G. Wells (1910). This is the autobiography of a man named Richard Remington, who at the age of forty-three reviews his past experiences in a most detailed manner. Born in Kent, England, the son of an unconventional father, and a narrow and strait-laced mother, the boy grows up amid conflicting influences an introspective and studiously inclined youth. Orphaned at the age of sixteen, he works out his later career with little interference from outside sources; he goes to college, and develops a taste for writing, and early becomes a successful author. He marries a rich and attractive girl named Margaret Seddon, who is deeply in love with him, and who willingly overlooks his past affairs with women which he confesses when he proposes to her. Margaret is a sweet and high-minded woman with ambition to aid her husband in his career. Assisted by her money and influence, Remington secures a seat in Parliament as a Liberal. Margaret is deeply interested in this party and is greatly disappointed when later her husband swings over to the Conservative side. This causes a widening of the breach which has been growing up between them, as Remington's love for his wife has been gradually lessening in spite of her devotion to him. A new interest has come into his life through his friendship with Isabel Rivers, a brilliant and independent girl, whom he had known in her school-girl days and had seen blossom into womanhood. Isabel's advanced thought and strong and impulsive nature appeal strongly to Remington, who soon finds himself passionately in love with her, and she reciprocates his feelings.

They succeed in keeping their secret for some time, but finally it becomes a public scandal and they realize that their relations must cease if Remington is to continue his public career. They decide not to meet again, and Isabel is on the point of marrying another man, when their infatuation reasserts itself and they are unable to resist it. They elope, and fly to a foreign land, and by so doing, Remington sacrifices his political career which had promised to bring him honor and glory, and while he can but look back with regret to the busy world that he has relinquished he contents himself with his overmastering passion for Isabel.

NEW REPUBLIC, THE, by William H. Mallock. This satirical work (published in England in 1876) attracted much attention for a time. Its sub-title, 'Culture, Faith, and Philosophy in a Country House,' gives an idea of its scope. The author, a nephew of the historian Froude, introduced to his readers the principal literary characters of the day under very transparent masks. The scene is laid in an English villa; and the chapters are made up of conversations between the guests, who are spending a quiet Sunday with their host, Mr. Laurence. While arranging the menu cards, it occurs to him to lay out a series of topics to be discussed at his table; for, said he, "It seems absurd to me to be so careful about what we put into our mouths, and to leave to chance to arrange what comes out of them." More things in heaven and earth than are usually discussed at such times are thus brought forward by the author, whose skill in parody is manifest. It was soon an open secret that "Luke" was Matthew Arnold; "Rose," Walter Pater; "Lord Allen," Lord Rosebery; "Herbert," Ruskin; "Storks," Huxley; "Stockton," Tyndall; "Jenkinson," Professor Jowett; "Saunders," Professor Clifford; "Mrs. Sinclair," Mrs. Singleton ("Violet Fane," to whom the book is inscribed); "Lady Grace," Mrs. Mark Pattison; and "Miss Merton," Miss Froude. The personal flavor of Mr. Mallock's satire caused the book to leap into instant popularity. The foibles and hobbies of his models were cleverly set off; and though the fun was sometimes bitter, it was rarely ill-natured. The central figure of the group was Mr. Herbert, in whose poetical imagery the great word-painter was not unfairly represented. Matthew Arnold was ridiculed unsparingly. One sentence, descriptive of Laurence has been widely quoted: "He was in many ways a remarkable man, but unhappily one of those who are remarkable because they do not become famous — not because they do."

NEW WAY TO PAY OLD DEBTS, A, by Philip Massinger (1625). Massinger's style, in the opinion of Charles Lamb, "was the purest and most free from violent metaphors and harsh constructions of any of the dramatists who were his contemporaries." As to sustained excellence and general competence, Professor Saintsbury declares that "unless we are to count by mere flashes, he must rank after Shakspere, Fletcher and Jonson among his fellows. The present play, his masterpiece, which was probably first produced in 1625, was revived by Garrick in 1748 and long kept its place on the English stage. The chief character, Sir Giles Overreach, Massinger's best creation, is an unscrupulous, relentless usurer who compasses his own nephew's ruin by encouraging his spendthrift habits and then screwing bonds and mortgages out of him. He tries to lure his neighbours into law that he may ruin them and get possession of their lands. He employs someone to tempt his nephew whom he has ruined to commit the gravest crimes. The goal of all his ambition, he says is

> "to have my daughter
> Right honourable; and it is a powerful charm
> Makes me insensible of remorse, or pity,
> Or the least sting of conscience."

The nephew invents "a new way to pay old debts" by inducing Lady Allworth, a wealthy widow, to ask him to dinner and pay attentions to him in the presence of Marrall, a tool of the usurer's. Marrall then tells Overreach that she is about to marry his nephew. Tom Allworth, son of the widow, and page to Lord Lovell, is in love with Overreach's daughter Margaret, whom her father desires to marry Lord Lovell. The latter pretends to make love to her in order that Tom Allworth, as his page, may gain admission to Margaret. Marrall tricks his master out of his bond, Lord Lovell and Lady Allworth marry each other, Margaret is united to her lover, and Overreach goes mad when he finds his deep laid schemes are overthrown.

NEW WORLDS FOR OLD, by H. G. Wells (1908), is a popular exposition of socialism for the general reader. The author is a moderate socialist, believing in the gradual introduction of socialism though government control of industry not with Marx in an immediate economic revolution. He advocates the taking over by the government of all public utilities, the heavy taxation of large fortunes, the establishment of a minimum wage, and the assumption by the state of full responsibility for the care of children, including education, and vocational training, for the support of expectant mothers, and aged persons, for attendance upon the sick. Yet he would not do away with the family or with private property, and he believes that the advantages of both these institutions would be much more widely and equally distributed under the system that he proposes than at present, when such a large proportion of families live in filth, penury, and demoralizing conditions and when the majority of people are constantly haunted by the fear of poverty. The various stock objections to socialism, as for example its opposition to the biological law of the survival of the fittest and to the acquisitive instincts of human nature, are effectively answered; and an excellent case is made out for the progressive administrative socialism in which the author firmly believes. The positions taken are supported by many interesting citations from sociological investigations among the poor and other data of a statistic kind. The fluent, informal, conversational style and the ready illustration of principles by instances and topics of homely, every-day occurrence make the book eminently readable. It is inspired by a real enthusiasm and by faith in the power of science to solve sociological problems, and it gives a very good idea of the essence of socialism.

NEWCOMES, THE, by W. M. Thackeray (1854), one of the few immortal novels, has many claims to greatness. It not only presents a most lifelike and convincing picture of English society in the first half of the century, but it excels in the drawing of individual types. Colonel Newcome, perhaps the most perfect type of a gentleman to be found in the whole range of fiction, sheds undying lustre upon the novel. Ethel Newcome is one of the rare women of fiction who really live as much in the reader's consciousness as in the conception of the author. Clive Newcome is also possessed of abundant life. His strong and faulty humanity is the proof of his genuineness.

All the world knows his story, beginning with the bravery of boyhood just released from the dim cloisters of Grey Friars. His father, Colonel Newcome, has come from India to rejoice in him as in a precious possession, and to renew his old associations in London for the sake of his son. Clive's career, on which so many hopes are built, is marred with failures. He loves his cousin Ethel Newcome, but she is hedged from him by the ambitions of her family. He himself makes a wretched marriage. His dreams of success as an artist fade away. The Colonel loses his fortune, and in his old age becomes a pensioner of Grey Friars. The quiet pathos of his death-bed scene is unique, even in Thackeray. With the word "Adsum" upon his lips, the word with which he used to answer the roll-call as a boy at school, he passes into peace. Clive and Ethel, each free to begin the world again, meet at his death-bed. The novel closes upon their chastened happiness. No words of praise or criticism, no detailed description, can convey the sense of the light and sweetness of 'The Newcomes.' As a novel of English upper and middle class life, it remains without a rival.

NEWPORT, by George Parsons Lathrop (1884). 'Newport' is a story of society,— the intrigues, adventures, and superficialities of one summer affording the author opportunity for many epigrammatic remarks, vivid descriptions of the principal places of local interest, and photographs of men and women of the leisure class. The love affair of a charming widow, Mrs. Gifford, and a widower, Eugene Oliphant, incidently engages the reader's attention; a love affair which, after a slight estrangement and separation, is ended by a sudden and incredible catastrophe, an unexpected finale strangely out of harmony with the preface of elopements, Casino dances, polo games, flirtations of titled heiress-hunters, and other trivialities of social existence. The characters are well chosen and very well managed, the individual being never sacrificed to the type, though the reader is made to feel that the figures are really typical. In no other piece of fiction has the flamboyant and aggressive life of Newport — that life wherein amusement is a business, and frivolity an occupation — been more vividly painted.

NIBELUNGENLIED, THE, an epic poem in Middle High German, composed by an unknown poet at the end of the twelfth or the beginning of the thirteenth century. Earlier ballads or lays furnished the basis of the story, which is now regarded, however, as the unified production of a single author not a conglomeration of individual poems. The theme, which originated in the primitive folk-lore of the Teutonic peoples and the internecine warfare of the Period of the Migrations, was known by all the Germanic nations, and received literary treatment in the Scandinavian eddas and sagas as well as in the Nibelungenlied. Siegfried, a warrior endowed with surpassing bravery and magic powers is treacherously slain by Hagen at the instigation of Brunhild in vengeance for the deception by which Siegfried had obtained her as wife for King Gunther of Burgundy. Siegfried's widow, Kriemhild, sister of Gunther and Hagen, marries Etel (Attila), King of the Huns, invites her brothers and their train to the court of Attila, and there has them massacred, falling herself in the mêlée. The poem consists of nearly 2400 four-line strophes, the first line rhyming with the second and the third with the fourth. The lines are divided by a caesura into two halves, each half containing three accented syllables, with the exception of the last half of the fourth line, which contains four accented syllables. The language of the Nibelungenlied differs from Modern High German about as that of Chaucer does from Modern English. The best translations into Modern High German are those by Simrock and Bartsch. Some English versions are W. N. Lettsom's (1850, new ed., 1903), Foster-Barham's (1887), Alice Horton's (1888), Birch's (1895), G. H. Needler's (1905 — reproducing exactly the original metre), D. B. Shumway's (1909 — in archaic prose), and A. S. Way's (1911 — in Morris's long couplets without strophes).

NICK OF THE WOODS; or, THE JIBBENAINOSAY, by Robert Montgomery Bird. M.D. (1837). This is a tale of Kentucky during the "dark and bloody" days.

and was especially popular about the middle of the nineteenth century. A play, founded upon this narrative, was received with boundless applause, held the stage (a certain grade of stage) for many years, and was a forerunner of the dime novel in stimulating an unhealthy desire among boys to run away from home and go West to kill Indians.

From that fateful day in his boyhood, when he saw his home destroyed and his relatives and friends brutally butchered by red fiends, Nick devotes his life to revenge. Eventually he kills every member of the band of Indians that desolated his home, while hundreds of other savages also fall by his hand. He marks each victim by a rude cross cut upon the breast. The red men look upon him as the Jibbenainosay, an Indian devil; believing that such wholesale slaughter, by an unseen and undetected foe, must be the work of supernatural powers.

The author has been taken to task by critics who complain that he pictures the red man upon a plane far below that of the noble savage described by Cooper and others. Bird replies that he describes the cruel, treacherous, and vindictive Indian as he exists, and not the ideal creation of a novelist. Experienced frontiersmen, with practical unanimity, indorse the estimate of Indian character presented in this book; but it must be said that neither portrait of the North-American Indian does him justice. Perhaps some educated Red Man will one day draw the picture of the "frontiersman."

NINETEENTH CENTURY IN ENGLAND, by John Ashton, see **DAWN OF THE.**

NINETEENTH CENTURY LITERATURE, by Georg Brandes, see **MAIN CURRENTS IN.**

NINETY-THREE ('Quatre-vingt-Treize'), by Victor Hugo, bears the sub-title: 'Premier Recit. La Guerre Civile,' and was intended to form the first part of a trilogy. It was published in 1874. The edition of 1882 contains several remarkable designs signed by the author. The story deals with an episode of the Vendean and Breton insurrection; the scene opening in a wood in Bretagne where a woman, driven distracted by the war raging around herself and her three children, encounters a body of republican soldiers. During this time, a band of émigrés are preparing to land under the command of a Breton nobleman, the Marquis de Lantenac. The English government, though it has furnished them with a ship, informs the French authorities of their design, and a flotilla bars their passage. The émigrés, after securing the escape of Lantenac, who is commissioned to raise Bretagne, blow up the vessel. After landing he learns that a price is set on his head. A number of men come towards him and he believes he is lost, but bravely tells his name. They are Bretons, and recognize him as their leader. Then ensues a conflict in which the marquis is victorious, and in which no quarter is given except to the three children, whom the Bretons carry to La Tourgue as hostages. La Tourgue is besieged by the republican troops under Gauvain, the marquis's nephew, assisted by the ex-priest Cimourdain, a rigid and inflexible republican who has trained Gauvain in his own opinions. The besieged are determined to blow up the tower and all it contains, if they are conquered. When their case is desperate and the tower is already on fire, an underground passage is discovered, and they can escape. Lantenac is in safety, but he hears the agonizing shrieks of the mother, who sees her three children in the midst of the flames. Moved with pity, he returns, saves them, and becomes a prisoner. When he is about to be executed, Gauvain covers him with his own cloak, tells him to depart, and remains in his place.

A council of war condemns Gauvain; and at the moment he mounts the scaffold, Cimourdain, who was one of his judges, kills himself. Hugo incarnates in his three principal characters the three ages of human society. Lantenac the monarchic chief personifies the past; Cimourdain, the citizen priest, the present; and Gauvain, the ideal of mercy, the future. Although the descriptions and disquisitions are sometimes wordy and tedious and there are many improbabilities in the romance, the picture of the three little children tossed about in the revolutionary hurricane will always be considered one of the loftiest achievements of Hugo's genius. The account of the convention of 1793, and the conversations of Marat, Danton, and Robespierre, also show the hand of a master.

NINEVEH AND ITS REMAINS (1849). **MONUMENTS OF NINEVEH** (1853). By Austen Henry Layard. A highly interesting narrative of the earliest of the discoveries which had laid open to historical knowledge the civilization, empire, and culture of Babylonia (and Assyria), back to about 4000 B. C., and which already promise to make known history beginning as early as 7000 B. C. Layard, in traveling overland from London to Ceylon, passed ruins on the banks of the Tigris which tradition pointed out as marking the site of Nineveh; and the desire which he then felt to make explorations led him to return to the region. He made some secret diggings in 1845, and in 1846 and 1847 pushed his excavations to the first great success, that of the discovery of the ruins of four distinct palaces, one of which, supposed to have been built by Sardanapalus, yielded the remarkable monuments which are still a chief attraction of the British Museum. Beside the bas-reliefs and inscriptions which had covered the walls of a palace, there were the gigantic winged human-headed bulls and lions, and eagle-headed deities, which are among the objects of Assyrian religious art. As an opening of a story of discovery hardly surpassed in the annals of modern research, the work reported in Layard's books is of the greatest interest.

NIPPUR; or, EXPLORATIONS AND ADVENTURES ON THE EUPHRATES. 'The Narrative of the University of Pennsylvania Expedition to Babylonia, in the Years 1888-90.' By John Punnett Peters. Vol. i.: First Campaign. Vol. ii.: Second Campaign (1897). The latest and most remarkable story of Babylonian exploration and discovery, carrying back to a most unexpectedly early date the distinct records of human history and of developed culture. In the lower valley of the rivers Tigris and Euphrates, both civilization and religion, literature and science, had four conspicuous seats in cities which flourished not less than eight thousand years ago. They were Eridu, the most southerly and westerly, the seat of the worship of Ea, a god of Beneficence, and of Merodach his son, especially known as a god of Mercy; Ur, the seat of the worship of the moon-god, Sin, one of whose seats was Sinai, and especially a god of goodness, the moon-deity being regarded as the Father-God, to whom the sun is a son and the evening star a daughter; Erech, farther north, the seat of the worship of Ishtar, the evening and the morning star, conceived as the equal of her brother, the sun, and the magnificent ideal of female character at the highest level of divinity; and Nippur, the most northerly and easterly, and the seat of the worship of Bel, or the sun, — conceived, not as son to the moon-god, but as a supreme god, represented by the setting sun, and most especially revealed in the flaming redness of his setting in times of excessive heat and drought; the Angry En-Lil, or "Lord of the Storm," who caused all the weather troubles of mankind, — desolating winds, violent storms, floods, drought, and all injuries. It was by him that the Deluge was brought, and for it the good Ea, and kindly Sin, and Merodach the

Merciful, charged him with cruel injustice; and the Babylonian Noah, making a
sacrifice after the flood, invited all the gods except En-Lil. As god of the red sunset
the nether-world was his, ruled by a son who was of like cruel temper with his father.

Nippur is thus the original seat of the conception of a god of anger and a religion
of fear. It was a great and flourishing city as long before Abraham as Abraham is
before our day. Its temple, commonly known as the House of En-Lil, Dr. Peter
says (just as the temple at Jerusalem was called the House of Yahweh) had stood
about five thousand years, when it fell into ruins about or before 150 B. C. Dr.
Peters speaks of "the close connection existing between Babylonian and Hebrew
civilization, legends, myths, and religion." He states also that "the new vistas of
ancient history opened by the work recently done in Babylonia have shown us men in
a high state of civilization, building cities, conducting conquest, and trafficking with
remote lands, two thousand years before the period assigned by Archbishop Ussher's
chronology for the creation of the world." The culture was Babylonian, and Nippur
was its darkest development.

NOÉMI, by S. Baring-Gould (1895), is a tale of Aquitaine, during the English occupation, in the early fifteenth century. The country was in a state of civil war; and free
companies, nominally fighting for French or English, but in reality for their own
pockets, mere plunderers and bandits, flourished mightily. The most dreaded freebooter in the valley of the Dordogne was Le Gros Guillem, who from his stronghold
at Domme sweeps down upon the farms and hamlets below; till at length the timid
peasants, finding a leader in Ogier del' Peyra, a petty sieur of the neighborhood, rise
up against their scourge, destroy his rocky fastness, and put his men to death or flight.
Guillem's daughter, Noémi, a madcap beauty, joins her father's band of ruffians; but
soon sickens of their deeds, and risks her life to save Ogier from the oubliette, because
she loves his son. The book is filled with thrilling and bloody incident, culminating
in the storming of L'Eglise Guillem, as the freebooter's den is ironically called, and
the strange death of the robber chieftain. The descriptions of the wild valley of the
Dordogne, and the life of the outlaws, are striking; and the pretty love story, set
against this background, very attractive. As a picture of a fierce and horrible
period, it is hardly less vivid than the 'White Company' of Conan Doyle.

NORTH AMERICAN ARCHÆOLOGY, INTRODUCTION TO THE STUDY OF,
by Cyrus Thomas (1898). This résumé of the progress made to the date of publication in the investigation of North American archæology is an introduction to the
study of the people and monuments of the prehistoric period. The writer does not
believe that the existence of glacial or palæolithic man has been scientifically established for North America. Moreover, the difference between the monumental remains of the Old World and the New, in his opinion, demands a different method of
study and a different classification of periods. For the purposes of his volume he
divides the North Atlantic Continent into three sections, the Arctic, the Atlantic, and
the Pacific divisions, and discusses the implements, ornaments, dwellings (caves,
cliffs, huts, or houses), and the mounds of each. He is of opinion, largely from the
evidence of burial and other mounds, that there is nothing to support the view that
any race other than the Indians ever occupied the North American continent until its
discovery by Europeans.

NORTH POLE, THE, a narrative of adventure and discovery by Robert E. Peary,
published in 1910, with a laudatory introduction by Theodore Roosevelt, and a
Foreword, briefly tracing the history of arctic explorations in search of the North Pole,

by Gilbert H. Grosvernor, of the National Geographical Society. The volume is splendidly illustrated by photographs made during the expedition, many of them at the Pole, and by an excellent map, clearly indicating the route followed and its relation to those of other explorers. The author describes in a full and interesting manner his final and successful expedition to the North Pole, beginning with his departure from New York on July 8th, 1908, narrating his arrival via Sydney, and Etah, at Cape Sheridan on September 5th, his setting out by sledge from Cape Columbia, March 1st, 1909, to cross the Polar Ocean for the Pole, his arrival at the Pole on April 6th, and his return to Cape Columbia on April 23d. The elaborate preparations, perfected through the experience of previous voyages, the curious customs of the Esquimaux, whose co-operation made success possible, the excitement of musk-ox and walrus-hunting, the occupations of the long arctic night, the difficulties and perils of dog-sledging across the rough and broken ice of the arctic sea, the tension of the last stages, and the exultation at the discovery of the Pole are all graphically portrayed. A tragic incident is the death of Professor Ross G. Marvin, the meteorologist and tidal observer of the expedition, who was drowned by breaking through young ice which had formed over "lead" or stretch of open water, on April 10th, 1909. The statements of the route followed and of the goal attained are validated by facsimiles of the original records made during the sledge journey to the Pole, by Peary, Marvin, and Captain Bartlett, commander of Peary's steamer, the "Roosevelt."

NORTH-WEST PASSAGE, THE, "Being the record of a voyage of exploration of the ship Gjöa, 1903–1907, by Roald Amundsen" was published in 1908. In two handsome volumes replete with maps and illustrations the explorer narrates his journey in a 47-ton yacht, the Gjöa, with the double purpose of locating the North Magnetic Pole and of accomplishing the North-West Passage. He left Christiania on June 16th, 1903, established headquarters on the south-east coast of King William Land, September 12th, and spent nearly two years there, making many excursions and observations. He was able to locate the Magnetic Pole, but proved that it has no constant position, meanwhile. One of his lieutenants, Hansen, charted the east coast of Victoria Land. On August 13th, 1905, Amundsen set sail in the Gjöa to make the North-West Passage, which he accomplished by traversing Simpson Strait and the channel under various names which divides Victoria Land from the mainland. He reached King Point at the mouth of the Mackenzie River early in September, and here he wintered, making a trip inland to the Yukon. Next summer on July 23d the Gjöa again set sail and reached Nome, Alaska, on August 30th, 1906, completing the North-West Passage. The book gives a most entertaining account of the incidents of the voyage and land expeditions. There are many interesting illustrations and anecdotes of the Esquimaux, and the writer's sense of humor enlivens the narrative. THE SOUTH POLE (1913) records Amundsen's success only a short time before the ill-fated Scott expedition reached the same goal. Having projected another northern enterprise and failed to obtain sufficient funds he nevertheless sailed from Norway in Nansen's ship, the Fram, August 9th, 1910, and announced to his party his resolution to attempt the South Pole. They landed at the Bay of Whales on the Antarctic Continent on January 14th, 1911, established a camp for the antarctic winter on the great ice barrier, and then traversed the plateau of the continent, discovering many mountain ranges as high as 16,000 feet. On December 16th, 1911, he and four comrades attained the South Pole. The volumes are profusely illustrated and there is a long appendix of scientific records and observations.

NOSTROMO; A TALE OF THE SEABOARD, by Joseph Conrad. The scene of this tale of silver mine, buried treasure, and revolutions is a South American republic. The silver mine was a government concession forced upon an English family living in Costaguana. Charles Gould, the last of the family, brings foreign capital, builds a railroad, takes the state politicians on his unofficial pay-roll, and makes the family white elephant a valuable property. The political party out of power dislike the reign of law and order, which follows, and start a revolution in a desperate attempt to gain possession of the mine, now the "treasure house of the world." Silver enough to buy a kingdom is waiting shipment at the wharf, and to prevent it becoming spoils to the invader, Charles Gould decides to hide the ingots on one of the islands at the entrance of the harbor. The man chosen for this enterprise is Nostromo, an Italian sailor, foreman of the wharf. Nostromo has come to Costaguana to make his fortune, and thus far his fortune is his good reputation. His pride and joy is to be "well spoken of." He is the hero of the populace of Italians and natives and has the confidence and esteem of the English and Spanish residents and officials. To his romantic imagination this will be the most famous and desperate affair of his life, which will be talked about "from one end of America to the other." His boat is nearly run down in the night by the steamer bringing the attacking soldiers, but he succeeds in getting to the island and burying the treasure. When he returns the rebels are in possession and he finds himself a political fugitive and penniless. It is assumed by the Goulds that the silver has been lost at sea, and Nostromo realizes that the buried treasure is his secret. Charles Gould saves the Gould concession, the development of which has become the ruling passion of his life, by presenting the winning argument of tons of dynamite ready to blow up the silver mountain in case of attack. Nostromo is entrusted with the dangerous mission of getting help from the government troops. He makes a spectacular dash from the town on an engine up the mountain, over the mountains on horseback to the capital, and returns with the soldiers by sea in time to save the day. Nostromo visits his treasure island at night, and carries away the silver ingots, which he disposes of in distant ports. A lighthouse is built on the island, but Nostromo arranges that his old friend, Viola, shall be the keeper. Nostromo loves Giselle, Viola's younger daughter, but is betrothed to the older daughter, Linda. As soon as he has removed a fortune from the buried treasure, he expects to run away with Giselle. He cannot resist coming to the lighthouse at night to see his sweetheart, and is shot by Viola who mistakes him for a night prowler. The once "incorruptible" Nostromo dies a thief, and the inevitable curse of buried treasure is thus fulfilled.

Such in brief is the main plot of the novel, but it is not merely the story of Nostromo and his life but it rather includes the stories of all concerned with the silver mine, Conrad's power of realizing the intricacies and entanglements of both character and incident is nowhere better displayed than here in this amazing creation of a South American State.

NOTRE-DAME OF PARIS, by Victor Hugo (1830), relates a romance growing up in and around the cathedral of that name. More than this, the mighty building, dating back at least to the eleventh century, and enriched with thirteenth-century glass, seems to fill the author's vision and dominate his mind from beginning to end; just as it dominates, from its immemorial island, the overflowing city for which he wrote. Among his different conceptions of Notre-Dame—folding over and fitting into each other—he brings out most clearly of all the truth that the cathedral of the Middle Ages was the book of the people: and that since the dawn of printing, books have taken the place of those marvelously involved and inexhaustible carvings, where the smoldering passions of the multitude, their humor and irreligion as well as their religion and poetic emotion, found continual expression. Even necromancy and astrology wreathed themselves in fantastic figures around the great doorway of Notre-Dame.

To the reader who loses himself in the atmosphere thus created, the world is France, France is Paris, Paris is the cathedral. He is taken through the aisles and galleries, out on the roof, up in the towers, and into every nook and corner of the church; then lovingly, faithfully, scrupulously through the squares or cross-roads of the old city, along crooked streets that have vanished, and thoroughfares still existing, like Rue Saint-Jacques or Rue Saint-Denis, which it calls the arteries of Paris. Thus it may be taken as a fifteenth-century guide-book of the town, answering all the purposes of a Baedeker; not only giving the general topography but touching on nearly every structure then standing, from the Bastile to the gibbet of Montfaucon.

To Quasimodo, the deaf and deformed bell-ringer of the cathedral, "stunted, limping, blind in one eye," the great church is an object of extravagant devotion and superstitious awe. Its arch-deacon alone had pity on him when he lay, a miserable foundling, at its door; it is all the home he has ever known, and he leads a strange existence among the statues and gargoyles within and without. Sometimes, when he is skulking among them, the great interior seems alive and trembling, like some huge animal—an elephant, perhaps, but not an unfriendly one. In such passages the poet romancer gives his wild fancy full rein.

No less than 'Faust,' the story is a phantasmagoria, in which a learned goat has a rôle of importance, everywhere accompanying the heroine, Esmeralda, a beautiful, innocent, and incorruptible singer and dancer of sixteen summers.

This many-sided book may also be regarded as an eloquent condemnation of capital punishment; of all forms of capital punishment, perhaps, or the writer would hardly say in 1831 that the vast resources of the chamber of torture have been reduced in his day to a sneaking guillotine that only shows its head at intervals. Or, quite as fairly, the book may be regarded as a sermon against celibacy, since it never loses sight of the effect of monastic vows on the ardent though ascetic archdeacon of the cathedral, Claude Frollo. The avowed motive of the story is the workings of fate, in whose toils nearly all the chief characters are inextricably caught. The keynote is given in the word *anágke*, the Greek equivalent of *kismet* or *fate*, which the author—if his introduction is to be taken seriously—found rudely scrawled on the wall of a cell in one of the cathedral towers. Like Walter Scott's 'Quentin Durward,' and Théodore de Banville's exquisite play of 'Gringoire,' 'Notre-Dame' contains a searching study of the treacherous but able monarch, Louis XI., and his barber Olivier-le-Daim.

NOUVEAUX LUNDIS, a continuation of the 'Causeries de Lundi' by Sainte-Beuve. These were literary reviews of moderate compass (usually between six and eight thousand words) appearing every Monday (with some interruptions) between 1849 and 1857 in a Parisian newspaper ('Le Constitutionnel' up to 1852, then 'Le Moniteur'). The second series, entitled 'Nouveaux Lundis,' was published regularly in 'Le Constitutionnel' from 1861 until Sainte-Beuve's death in 1869. The former series was collected in fifteen and the latter in thirteen volumes. A man of voluminous reading, receptive disposition, delicate insight, and personal experience in creative work, Sainte-Beuve was admirably prepared to interpret literature.

He does not, like the critics of the classical period, bring all works to the test of some previously arranged standard and condemn them if they depart from it. Instead he attempts to determine what the author intended to do when he composed the work and whether he succeeded in his aim. This method necessitates an impartial study of the author and everything that influenced him; the result is that Sainte-Beuve's 'Causeries' present us with a series of vivid and truthful portraits of great writers and an explanation of their work as determined by their personality and environment. Mingled with the biography, gossip, and analysis with which the essays are necessarily filled there flash out here and there many discriminating judgments, all the truer because they are founded on the sympathetic and minute portrayal of the author. The subjects of the 'Lundis' not only range over French literature, classic and contemporary, but include many figures from England, Germany, Italy, and the ancient classics.

NOVUM ORGANUM, THE, by Francis Bacon. The 'Novum Organum,' or 'New Method,' forms the second part of Lord Bacon's great philosophical work entitled 'Instauratio Magna,' 'The Great Restoration' of Science. The first part, entitled 'De Augmentis Scientiarum,' is an extension of the previous work on the Advancement of Learning. The third part is the 'Historia Naturalis.' The 'Novum Organum' contains the outlines of the scientific and inductive method; viz., that of proceeding from facts to general laws, instead of inferring facts from assumed general principles which have never been proved. This latter, the philosophical and metaphysical method, was repudiated by Bacon, and together with the "superstitions" of theology, was declared to have no place in the new learning. The 'New Method,' therefore, is an attempt at an interpretation of nature from direct observation. "Nature," says Bacon, "we behold by a direct ray; God by a refracted ray; man by a reflected ray." At the beginning of the 'Novum Organum' we read this first of the series of 180 Aphorisms of which its two books consist: "Man, the minister and interpreter of Nature, can do and understand only so much as he has observed in her: more he can neither know nor do." As obstacles to correct observation and inference from nature, he mentions the four kinds of "Idola," or preconceptions which prejudice the mind at the outset and which must, therefore, be removed: the Idola Tribus, or the misconceptions growing out of our nature as man; the Idola Specus, those growing out of our individual or peculiar nature or surroundings; the Idola Fori, misconceptions imbibed through common speech and opinions leading to much idle controversy; and finally the Idola Theatri, or fables and fictions of tradition that continue to be sources of error. He refers contemptuously to the Greek Sophists, and quotes the prophecy of the Egyptian priest concerning the Greeks: "They are always boys: they have neither the age of science nor the science of age."

The second part begins with the Aphorism, "It is the work and intention of human power to generate and superinduce a new nature or new natures upon a body already given: but of a nature already given to discover a form or a true difference, or a nature originating another nature (naturam naturantem) or a source of emanation, this is the work and intention of human learning." The study of forms is therefore the object of the new method; and the remainder of the work is devoted to illustrating, particularly by observations of the action of heat, the true mode of making and comparing observations of natural occurrences. In conclusion the author refers to man's fall from a primitive state of innocence and his loss of his dominion over nature. This is however capable of restoration first by religion and faith and then by the arts and sciences. For labor is not always to be a curse, but man shall "eat his bread in the sweat of his brow," not indeed in vain disputations and idle ceremonies of magic, but in subduing nature to the uses of human life.

NUMA ROUMESTAN, by Alphonse Daudet (1880). The author at first intended to call his romance 'North and South'; a title indicative of his true purpose, which is to contrast these two sections of France, not at all to the advantage of the one in which he was born. Numa Roumestan is a genuine Provençal; a braggart, a politician, a great man, and a good fellow to boot. He appears in the opening pages at a festival at Apt, where he is the choice of his adoring fellow-countrymen for deputy. Congratulations, embraces, hand-shaking, and requests for offices, are the order of the day. He promises everything to every one,—crosses, tobacco, monopolies, whatever any one asks,—and if Valmajour, the tambourine player, come to Paris, he will make his fortune. A friend remonstrates with him. "Bah!" he answers, "they are of the South, like myself: they know these promises are of no consequence; talking about them will amuse them." But some persons take him at his word. The story is intensely amusing, and there is not a chapter which does not contain some laughable incident. The mixture of irony and sensibility which pervades it is Daudet's distinguishing characteristic, and reminds the reader of Heine. There are some scenes of real pathos, such as the death of little Hortense. Daudet describes the early career of Gambetta in the chief character. Gambetta was his friend, but Daudet never shrank from turning his friends into "copy."

OBADIAH OLDBUCK, ADVENTURES OF MR., by Rodolphe Töpffer. This series of 184 comic drawings, illustrating the wonderful exploits of Obadiah Oldbuck in search of a sweetheart, with text explaining each sketch, first appeared in French in 1839, under the title of 'M. Vieuxbois,' and is the first of a series of like sketches illustrating other stories. The work won for its author high praise, and was originally drawn for the amusement of his young pupils. Obadiah, in despair at not having received an answer from his sweetheart, determines on suicide; but the sword luckily passes under his arm. For forty-eight hours he believes himself dead, but returns to life exhausted by hunger. He tries to hang himself, but the rope is too long. He fights with a rival, and after vanquishing him is accepted by his sweetheart. He is arrested for hilarity, and the match is off. He drinks hemlock, but is restored to life. He becomes a monk, but escapes; and finding a favorable letter from his sweetheart, elopes with her. He is recaptured by the monks, and throws himself from a window; but his life is saved by the index of a sun-dial. He escapes, and is to be married, but is late and finds neither parents nor bride; throws himself into a canal, but is fished out for his wedding clothes. He is buried, and dug up by birds of prey, and frightens his heirs, who have him arrested, and he is sentenced to a year's imprisonment. He escapes, and, finding himself on a roof, lets his dog down a chimney to sound it. The dog lands in the fireplace of his sweetheart's house, and she embraces the dog. Obadiah pulls and hauls up his sweetheart and her father and mother. Just as they reach the top of the chimney, the rope breaks and Obadiah falls, but is saved by falling into a street lamp. After many other ludicrous adventures he is married to his lady-love.

OBLÓMOF, by Ivan Goncharóf (1857). A study of a curious state of inertia, difficult for the western mind to understand, but recognized and given a name in

Russia. Oblómof, the hero, is intellectual, and has a generous heart, but is incapable of decision or action. He dreams away his life, in spite of the efforts of his friends to rouse him. Olga, the girl he loves and who loves him, almost succeeds in awakening him, but he sinks back to apathy and his dressing-gown and slippers. One of his day dreams is the vivid remembrance of his happy childhood in the country, a picture of the idle life on a large Russian country estate. His energetic friend Schtoltz who marries Olga, manages his affairs, and tries to induce him to live in his manor in the country, but Oblómof is unable to change his passive life. His landlady marries him and takes care of him until his prolonged inertia, the sluggish gliding from day to day, ends quietly in death. The portrait of a failure, the story however leaves a sense of the essential worth of human nature. The Oblómof family are comic but lovable in spite of their bovine content and stupidity. See the LIBRARY.

OBSERVATIONS ON POPULAR ANTIQUITIES. By John Brand. An entirely new and revised edition, with the additions of Sir Henry Ellis (1887). A work devoted to popular explanation of the customs, ceremonies, superstitions, etc., of the common people. It is at once instructive and very entertaining.

OCEANA; or, ENGLAND AND HER COLONIES, by James Anthony Froude (1886). This is the record of a journey made by the author via Cape Town to Australia and New Zealand, and home by way of Samoa, the Sandwich Islands, San Francisco, Salt Lake, Chicago, and New York in 1884–85. Of the places visited he gives historical sketches, his own observations, personal experiences, and speculations as to the future, describes the sights, etc.; all his records being interesting, and most of them valuable. He makes his visit to Cape Town the occasion of a résumé of not only its history and condition, but of his own connection with South-African affairs in 1874. In Australia he is struck by the general imitation of England, and asks, "What is the meaning of uniting the colonies more closely to ourselves? They *are* closely united: they are ourselves; and can separate only in the sense that parents and children separate, or brothers and sisters." Here too he sees that the fact that he can take a ticket through to London across the American continent, to proceed direct or to stop *en route* at will, means an astonishing concordance and reciprocity between nations. In the Sandwich Islands he finds "a varnish of Yankee civilization which has destroyed the natural vitality without as yet producing anything better or as good." He pronounces the Northern men of the United States equal in manhood to any on earth; has no expectation of Canadian annexation; thinks the Brooklyn Bridge more wonderful than Niagara, New York almost as genial as San Francisco, and New York society equal to that of Australia, though both lack the aristocratic element of the English. In conclusion he states his feeling that as it was Parliament that lost England the United States, if her present colonies sever the connection, it will be through the same agency; but that, so long as the mother country is true to herself, her colonies will be true to her. Mr. Froude, as is well known, is no believer in the permanence of a democracy, and on several occasions in this work expresses his opinion of its provisional character as a form of political life.

OCTOPUS, THE, 'a Story of California,' by Frank Norris (1901). This book has for its central motive Wheat, the great source of American power and prosperity, and also the literal staff of life. The volume deals with the production of wheat and pictures a corner in California, the San Joaquin valley, where a handful of ranchmen are engaged in irrigating and ploughing, planting and reaping and harvesting. While performing all the slow arduous toil of cultivation they are at the same time carrying on a continuous warfare against the persistent encroachment of the railroad, whose steel arms are reaching out, octopus-like to grasp, encroach upon, and crush one after another all those who venture to oppose it. The novel typifies on a small scale the struggle going on between capital and labor, the growth of centralized power, and the aggression of the corporation and the trust. But back of the individual and back of the corporation is the spirit of the nation, typified in the wheat, indomitable, rising, spreading, gathering force and carrying with it health and sustenance to other nations. Throughout the book the two underlying thoughts are kept before the reader,—that of the railroad, insistent and aggressive, and that of the wheat, powerful and life-giving. The most dramatic scene in the book is that in which S. Behrmann is struck down at the very summit of his ambition, caught in a trap by his own wheat and pictured miserably writhing and choking to death in the dark hold of the ship, while the pitiless hail of grain pours down upon him from the iron chute.

ODD NUMBER, THE, an English translation by Jonathan Sturgis, of thirteen stories by Guy de Maupassant, appeared in 1889. Each tale is an admirable example of the literary art which made Maupassant the acknowledged master of the short story. All show an acute realization of the irony of life, and are written in a pessimistic strain. The unerring choice of words, the exquisite precision of the descriptive touches, carry home the sensation which Maupassant wished to convey. Many kinds of life are revealed.

In 'The Piece of String,' we have the petty shrewdness, thrift, and obstinacy of the Norman peasant. Maître Hauchecorne, on his way to the market-place, is seen to pick up something from the ground and thrust it into his pocket. Thereupon he is accused of stealing a missing purse. His find was only a bit of string; but neither his guilt nor innocence can be proved, and he rests under the imputation all his days. In time he himself is almost persuaded of his guilt.

'La Mère Sauvage' is a study of the primitive passions of an old peasant woman, who, learning that her son has been killed by the Prussians in battle, avenges him by burning to death the four kindly young Prussians who have been quartered upon her.

'The Necklace' is a picture of bourgeois life. Monsieur Loisel, a petty official, and his pretty young wife, are honored with an invitation to an official reception. On their return, Madame Loisel loses the diamond necklace which she has borrowed from her rich friend, Madame Forestier. Without mentioning the loss, they make it good, thus incurring a debt which burdens the rest of their lives. It takes ten years to pay it; and they become inured to work and poverty, and prematurely old. Meeting Madame Forestier one day, Madame Loisel tells her the whole story. "My poor Mathilde!" says her friend, "My necklace was paste, worth at most five hundred francs." There is something poignant about the continual revelation of needless pain in these tales; but their brilliancy, their vividness, their admirable art, and unerring sense of "values," will long compel a hearing for them.

ODYSSEY, THE, an epic poem in Greek hexameters, once attributed unquestioningly to Homer, the reputed author of the 'Iliad' (*q. v.*), but now thought by many to be a somewhat later work than the 'Iliad' and by a different hand or hands; for the theory that the 'Iliad' is a combination of various individual lays has also been applied to the 'Odyssey.' The 'Odyssey' is a sequel to the 'Iliad' and narrates the ten years' adventures of Ulysses during his return journey from Troy to his own kingdom, the island of Ithaca. Not only a brave warrior but the most prudent and crafty of the Greek chieftains, he is conducted through a series of adventures that test all his courage and skill. Many of these are akin to the marvels of later European fairy-tales. Ulysses and his men visit the Lotos-eaters, who feed on a plant which makes them forget their homes; they are imprisoned by a one-eyed giant, who devours some of them and whom they at last blind and outwit; many are transformed to beasts by a potion offered by Circe, an enchantress; they are rescued from her by a talisman revealed to Ulysses by a god; their leader visits the underworld and speaks with the shade of Achilles; they are lured by the sirens, who correspond to the Teutonic mermaids; in passing through a narrow strait they barely avoid two monsters, Scylla and Charybdis; the men all perish at sea through an offence to the sun deity; and Ulysses, having been cast ashore and detained for a long time by the nymph Calypso, at length gets away through the intervention of Athene, but is again shipwrecked by the enmity of Poseidon and drifts to the land of the Phæacians. The king's daughter, Nausicaa, takes pity on him and escorts him to the palace of her father, Alcinous, who feasts Ulysses, hears his story, and sends him home to Ithaca. Here he finds his palace beset by the petty chieftains of the island, who, supposing him dead, are wooing his wife, Penelope, and, while she defers making the choice in the hope of her husband's return, are living in the palace and wasting his substance. His son, Telemachus, having vainly tried to stir the people against these chieftains, has gone under the conduct of Athene, who assumes the guise of an old chieftain, Mentor, to look for his father; and after visiting the courts of Nestor and Menelaus has learned through a soothsayer of the place of Ulysses's confinement and of his speedy return. Ulysses, advised by Athene, disguises himself as a beggar, gets admission to his own palace without detection, except by one or two of the servants, conspires with them and with his son who has returned; and getting possession of a mighty bow slays all the suitors and disloyal servants, reveals himself to his wife, and aged father, and receives the submission of the people. Unlike the 'Iliad,' which is martial and impassioned, the 'Odyssey' contains comparatively little fighting and no pitched battles. It deals with the marvelous, the romantic, the pathetic, and the domestic; for this reason it has a somewhat more modern tone and appeal. The best English translations are Chapman's (1614–1615) in heroic couplets, Pope, Broome, and Fenton's (1725–26) in heroic couplets, Cowper's (1791), in blank verse, William Morris's (1887), in a long ballad measure, William Cullen Bryant's (1871), in blank verse, Butcher and Lang's prose version (1879), and Samuel Butler's prose version (1900).

ŒDIPUS AT COLONUS, by Sophocles. This was the author's last tragedy, and was not presented until some years after his death. It has very little action, but nowhere has Sophocles risen to higher poetic grandeur. His drama is a magnificent hymn in honor of Athens and of his birthplace Colonus, in which the purest moral ideals are expressed in the sublimest language. The poet depicts the glorious end of Œdipus, who finds an asylum on Attic soil, and vanishes mysteriously in the sacred grove of the Eumenides, to become henceforth the protecting hero of the land. The incidents are made up of the violence of Creon, the abduction of the daughters of Œdipus, their touching deliverance, the imprecations of the old man against his unfilial son Polynices, and his sublime dramatic apotheosis. But the beauty of the tragedy consists especially in the ideal representation of the noblest sentiments: the majesty of the aged hero, now reduced to beg for bread; the gentle piety of Antigone; the artlessness of the rustic chorus, at first appalled by the mere name of the stranger, but soon, at the request of Theseus, to give him a most gracious and hospitable reception; finally, the luminous background where Athens appears to the patriotic eyes of her poet in all her dazzling splendor. Œdipus, the victim of his sons' ingratitude, has sometimes been compared to Shakespeare's King Lear. But while the two characters are almost equal in tragic grandeur, there is always a reserve, a self-restraint, in the stormiest scenes of the Greek dramatist which is absent from the English play.

ŒDIPUS THE KING, by Sophocles. Aristotle, whose rules for the conduct of the tragic poem are mainly based on the 'Œdipus,' regarded it as the masterpiece of the Greek theatre. It is certainly, if not the finest, the most dramatic of the author's works. The opening scene has an imposing grandeur. The Theban people are prostrate before their altars, calling on their gods and on their king to save them from the terrible plague that is desolating their city. Creon returns from Delphi with the answer of the oracle: — The plague will continue its ravages as long as the murderer of Laius, their former ruler, remains unpunished. Œdipus utters the most terrible imprecations against the assassin, declaring he will not rest until he has penetrated the darkness that enshrouds the crime. He thus becomes the unconscious instrument of his own destruction; for he himself is the involuntary slayer of his own father, the unwitting husband of his own mother. The spectator is hurried on from incident to incident, from situation to situation, until at last the sombre mystery through which the hapless king has been blindly groping is lit up by one revealing flash, and Œdipus rushes into the palace, exclaiming, "O light of day, I behold thee for the last time!" There is no character in ancient tragedy that excites so much human interest as Œdipus,—an interest made up of anguish and compassion; for unlike the heroes of Æschylus, he is neither Titanic nor gigantic. He is an ideal man, but not so ideal as to be entirely exempt from weakness and error; and when he suffers, he gives vent to his agony in very human cries and tears. The other persons in the drama—the skeptical and thoughtless Iocasta; the choleric soothsayer Tiresias; Creon, who appears to more advantage here than in the 'Antigone' and 'Œdipus at Colonus'; even the slave of Laius—are all portrayed with the most consummate art and distinction of style. The choral hymns and dialogues have an ineffable tenderness and sublimity. The 'Œdipus' has been imitated by Seneca in Latin, Dryden and Lee in English, Nicolini in Italian, Corneille, Voltaire, and several others in French; but none of these imitations has even a faint reflection of the genius of the original.

ŒUVRE, L', see ROUGON-MACQUART.

OFF THE SKELLIGS, by Jean Ingelow. This story was published in 1872, and has been much praised, though its rambling and disconnected style makes it very different from the intense and analytic novel of to-day.   There are bright dialogues and good descriptions, the scenes at sea and in Chartres Cathedral being especially well done.

Dorothea Graham loses her mother in early childhood, and comes into the care of an eccentric old uncle, who keeps her in school for nine years, and then takes her on board the yacht that is his home. While cruising off the Skelligs, they rescue a raft-load of perishing people who have escaped from a burning vessel. Dorothea nurses one man whom she considers a sailor, but who proves to be Mr. Giles Brandon. On his recovery he invites Dorothea and her brother to his home, where she meets Valentine, Mr. Brandon's volatile young stepbrother. He is very friendly to Dorothea, and makes love to her in jest, which finally becomes earnest, though he makes no pretense at passion. As his health is delicate, he is going to settle in New Zealand, and begs Dorothea to marry him and accompany him. Being abandoned by her uncle and brother, and having no friends, the girl consents, but on the wedding day Valentine does not appear. He has fallen in love with another girl, and wishes to break the engagement with Dorothea, who is naturally shocked, though fortunately her heart is not deeply involved. Mr. Brandon shows her all sympathy, and soon explains that he has loved her from the beginning, but has supposed that she cared for Valentine. She can hardly accept him at once when she has just been ready to marry another, but as her feelings subside she grows really to care for him, and they are married in the end.

OGIER THE DANE. This story of the paladin of Charlemagne has appeared in many different forms; but the earliest manuscript is a *chanson de geste*, or epic poem, written by Raimbert de Paris in the twelfth century. The subject is still older, and Raimbert is thought to have collected songs which had been sung in battle years before. The first part is entitled 'The Anger of Ogier,' and is descriptive of the feudal life of the barons of Charlemagne. In a quarrel over a game of chess, Charlot, the son of Charlemagne, kills Beaudoin, the son of Ogier. Ogier demands the death of Charlot, but is exiled by Charlemagne, whom Ogier would have killed but for the protection afforded by the barons. Ogier flies to Italy, and Charlemagne declares war against his harborer. Ogier shuts himself up in Castelfort, and withstands a siege of seven years; at the end of which time, all his followers having died, he makes his way to the camp of Charlemagne and enters the tent of Charlot. Throwing his spear at the bed where he supposes Charlot to be asleep, he escapes into the darkness, crying defiance to Charlemagne. Afterwards he is captured while sleeping, but by the entreaties of Charlot the sentence of death is changed to that of imprisonment. The country is invaded by Brahier, a Saracen giant, seventeen feet tall and of great strength. Ogier is the only man fit to cope with him, and he refuses to leave his prison unless Charlot is delivered up to his vengeance. Charlemagne accedes, but Charlot's life is saved by the miraculous interposition of Saint Michael. The poem ends with Ogier's combat with the giant, who is conquered and put to death. Among the tales in which Ogier figures there is a romance called 'Roger le Danois,' the 'Orlando Furioso' of Ariosto, and the 'Earthly Paradise' of William Morris.

OLD GREEK EDUCATION, by J. P. Mahaffy (1881), considers a subject which is not often presented systematically. The author traces the development of Greek youth from the cradle to the university; thus leaving off where most writers on Greek life and customs begin. In this obscure field, his scholarship presents much that is unfamiliar to the general reader. The successive chapters treat of the infancy and earlier childhood of Grecian boys, of their school-days, of the subjects and methods of education, of military training, of the higher education, of theories of education, and of university life. These subjects are considered in a familiar, popular manner, designed to bring the reader closer to the ancient civilization, to enable him to appreciate it upon its every-day side. The work is valuable as a preparation for a wider study of Greek customs, manners, and institutions. It is written with a nimble pen, and its entertainingness is not eclipsed even by its scholarship.

OLD HOUSE, THE, by Feodor Sologub (1915). The story of "The Old House" tells about a young student, Boris, led into revolutionary activities by a spy, betrayed and hanged. His grandmother, mother, and sister left alone in the "Old House" refuse to believe that he is dead, and keep up a pretense of awaiting his return, refusing to remember his tragic fate. All the other stories are uncanny and mysterious, either about the supernatural, or obsessions which lead to happiness in madness. In one story a ragged old man watches a little boy playing with a hoop. He finds the hoop of an old barrel and takes it to the woods, where unseen he imitates the boy, and plays at being a child again, "small, beloved, and happy." The story of 'Lights and Shadows' tells of an imaginative child who plays at making shadows on the wall with his fingers until he loses interest in everything else. His mother plays with the shadows with him in the evenings to induce him to study his lessons later, and she also becomes the prey of the "persistent, importunate shadows." 'The White Mother' in the story with this title is the dead sweetheart of a bachelor, to whom she appears in dreams. He adopts a little boy who resembles her and finds happiness again.

OLD RÉGIME IN CANADA, THE, see **FRANCE AND ENGLAND IN NORTH AMERICA.**

OLD ST. PAUL'S, by William Harrison Ainsworth. This historical story, dealing with the horrors of the plague which depopulated London in 1665, was published in 1841. The old cathedral of St. Paul's is made the scene of various adventures. The plot recounts the many attempts of the profligate Earl of Rochester to obtain possession of Amabel Bloundel, the beautiful daughter of a London grocer. The hero is Leonard Holt, an apprentice of the grocer, who is in love with Amabel but is rejected. The Earl is finally successful and carries off Amabel, to whom he is married. She, like many of the other characters, dies of the plague.

Leonard Holt frustrates the Earl's attempts until he is himself stricken with the plague; but he recovers from it and lives to save the life of King Charles during the great fire of London, of which historical event a graphic description closes the story. Leonard, in return for his services to the King, is created Baron Argentine; and marries a lady of title, who at the opening of the story is supposed to be the daughter of a blind piper, and has loved him patiently all through the six volumes.

OLD SIR DOUGLAS, by the Hon. Mrs. Norton (1871). The thread of plot which this story follows is this: By the death of his father, a Scotch gentleman, Douglas Ross comes into possession of a large estate; and by the death of his only brother immediately afterwards, is made the guardian of a nephew, Kenneth, legitimatized on that brother's death-bed. The boy inherits his father's profligate tendencies, and as he grows to manhood becomes a daily anxiety to his uncle. It is in Italy, where he has been called by Kenneth's bad conduct, that Sir Douglas meets and marries Gertrude Skifton, who has already refused Kenneth, and is made most unhappy by his unkindness. The scene changes to Glenrossie, the Scottish home where the conditions are not improved, but made harder by the presence of a malignant stepsister. Good deeds, however, bear fruit as surely as evil ones. From this point the complications multiply, and many calamities threaten; but the blameless lives of Sir Douglas and his gentle wife do not close in darkness. The story is one of the battle of life waged in an obscure corner of the world: interesting because it is typical; realistic almost to the point of offense, were it not that its realism is not willful but subserves an end.

OLD STONE AGE, THE, by H. F. Osborne, see **MEN OF THE.**

OLD STORY OF MY FARMING DAYS ('Ut Mine Stromtid'), by Fritz Reutei, appeared in Olle Kamellen (1860–64). The 'Stromtid' — the best known novel of the noted Platt-Deutsch humorist — is considered by competent critics to equal the best productions of our great English humorists, Sterne and Dickens, and is thoroughly fresh, sound, and hearty in tone. Its characters are masterpieces of delineation, and have become familiar to readers of many tongues. The delicious creation of the inspector emeritus, Uncle Zacharias Bräsig, is one of the triumph? of modern humor; and it is not only in the Low German speech that quotations are made from "de lütte Mann mit den rötlich Gesicht und de staatsche rode näs" (the little man with the reddish face and the stately red nose). One of the best portions of the book is his speech before the Rahnstadt Reform Club, on the subject, "Whence arises the great poverty in our city?"

Almost equally popular characters are Hawermann, "un sin lutt Dirning" (his little maid), and Triddelfitz. The quaint oddity of the Platt-Deutsch lends itself peculiarly well to the quality of Reuter's humor, and the material of his story shows by its vivid reality that it was drawn from the personal experience and observation of the author. The 'Stromtid' was the last and best of Reuter's novels founded on life in the Low German countries.

OLD TOWN FOLKS, by Harriet Beecher Stowe. This work was published in 1869. The scene is Old Town; the time, a period just succeeding the Revolution. A description of Natick, the old Indian Mission town, and its famous Parson Lothrop,—whose stately bearing, whose sermons in Addisonian English, and whose scholarly temperament, marked him as a social and intellectual leader,—introduces the story.

"Lady" Lothrop, the parson's wife, at the time of her marriage stipulated that she should be permitted to attend Episcopal services on Christmas, Easter, and other great days of the church. Horace Holyoke, nominally author of the book, is left an orphan when a mere boy. He tells how the views of Calvinists and Arminians, and great questions of freedom and slavery, were freely discussed at the village gatherings.

Henry and Tina Percival, English orphans, were consigned respectively to old Crab Smith and to Miss Asphyxia Smith, illustrations of the malign influence of a misplaced adherence to the old theology. The children are ill-treated and run away, taking refuge in the deserted Dench house (the estate of Sir Charles Henry Frankland), where they are found and returned to the village by Horace's uncle and Sam Lawson, the village do-nothing, a quaint character whose droll actions and sayings enliven the whole book.

Tina is then adopted by Miss Mehitable Rossiter, daughter of the former clergyman of the parish, while Harry is under the patronage of Lady Lothrop.

On Easter Sunday, the children, with Horace, are taken in her great coach, by Lady Lothrop, to Boston, where they attend service at King's Chapel, and meet prominent people in the city. They make the acquaintance of Ellery Davenport, a former officer in the Continental army whose characteristics closely resemble those of Aaron Burr. He recognizes the Percivals as belonging to an excellent family, and finally secures a valuable English inheritance for the children. Henry, after leaving college, returns to England to manage his estate, and finally takes orders in the Church of England. Tina is married to Ellery Davenport; but immediately after the ceremony Emily Rossiter, whose mysterious disappearance some years before was a cause of intense grief to her family, returns from Europe, confronts Ellery, and tells how he allured her from home to live with him out of wedlock. Tina adopts Emily's daughter, and goes abroad with her husband. After their return to America, Ellery devotes himself to public affairs, and is eventually killed in a political duel. Two years later, Horace Holyoke, is united to his first love, Tina. The story chiefly lives in the character of Sam Lawson.

OLD WIVES' TALE, THE (1908), established Arnold Bennett's reputation as a novelist; in solidity of construction and carefulness of detail it surpasses anything he has done since. Its heroines, the sisters Constance and Sophia, are typical of the English lower middle class about the middle of the last century; their home is at Bursley, one of the "Five Towns" Mr. Bennett has made famous. When the girls leave school it is their mother's wish that they should both go into the shop which supports the family. Constance agrees placidly, but Sophia rebels and trains for teaching. By accident she meets Gerald Scales, a flashy young commercial traveler, who makes love to her. One afternoon when Sophia is chatting with Gerald, her paralytic father, by whose bed she had been enjoined to sit, slips from his pillow to the floor and dies instantly. Sophia feels herself responsible for his death, and suffers keenly from remorse. Eventually, however, she elopes with Gerald and severs all connection with her family. As soon as Gerald's supply of money begins to fail, he deserts her in Paris. When she recovers from the dangerous fever brought on by the shock, she finds herself in the house of Madame Foucault, an irresponsible demi-mondaine. Out of gratitude to Madame, who has nursed her back to health, Sophia buys the Foucault furniture when it is attached for debt and when Madame runs off with a lover, Sophia takes over the house. Through Chirac, a journalist friend, she secures a houseful of eminently respectable gentleman lodgers who pay well for comfortable and efficient housekeeping. Sophia buys so shrewdly before the Siege of Paris and makes so much money that after the Commune she is able to buy the Pension Frensham, a well-established house for English tourists. Here she grows into middle age and prospers by her solid business ability, highly respected by all who have to do with her. Meanwhile Constance has been leading a quiet and uneventful life in Bursley. Her mother and aunts have died and she has been married and widowed. Her eighteen-year-old son has gone up to London to study art, and with the departure of the boy Constance is left without companionship and without interest in life; even the shop has passed from her control. After twenty odd years, news of Sophia comes to Five Towns through a Bursley man newly returned from Paris. Constance writes to her sister and urges her to come to Bursley for a visit. Sophia makes the journey all in a flutter and the two lonely sisters set up house together in the district in which they spent their childhood. Before they have settled down comfortably to everyday life, news comes from Manchester of the illness of Sophia's long lost husband. She hastens to his bedside only to find him already dead. Soon after her return to Bursley she succumbs to the shock and a cold brought on by the long automobile drive home. Her death leaves Constance quite alone, for her son Cyril is studying abroad and before he returns her death follows, so that the only real mourner at the funeral is her old poodle, Fossette.

OLIPHANT, LIFE OF LAURENCE, AND OF ALICE OLIPHANT, HIS WIFE, THE, by Margaret O. W. Oliphant (1891), one of the most fascinating and satisfactory biographies in the English language, has made luminous and intelligible a character that might be readily misunderstood or misinterpreted. Laurence Oliphant, a thorough product of his century, combined its most diverse forces: its scientific spirit and its mysticism, its brilliant and thoughtful worldliness, and its passionate idealism. In him the mystical at last predominated, and wrapped him as in a cloud from the comprehension of his fellows. His biographer has traced this spiritual development side by side with the events of his outward life,—a life of unusual picturesqueness and depth of color. His travels in Russia, in America and Canada, in China, in the Crimea, and in the Holy Land, form a striking background to that other journey towards "lands very far off," from which he never rested. His spiritual pilgrimage and its unearthly goal gave reason and coherence to his life. Many of his letters are collected in this biography, throwing additional light upon a nature made for the intimacies of affection, for the revelations of friendship.

OLIVA, PALMERIN DE, see **PALMERIN.**

OLIVER TWIST, by Charles Dickens (1838). This story shows in vivid colors the miseries of the pauper's home where the inmates are robbed and starved, while the dead are hurried into unhonored graves; the haunts of villains and thieves where the wretched poor are purposely made criminals by those who have sinned past hope; and one wrong-doing is used to force the victim deeper in vice. With such lives are interwoven those of a better sort, showing how men and women in all grades have power on others for good or ill.

Oliver Twist — so called because the workhouse master had just then reached the letter "T" in naming the waifs — was born in the poorhouse, where his mother's wanderings ceased forever. When the hungry lad asked for more of the too thin gruel he was whipped. Bound out to work, he runs away from this slavery and goes to London. The Artful Dodger takes the starving lad to the den of Fagin the Jew, the pickpocket's school. But he will not steal. He finds a home. He is kidnapped and forced to be again with the bad ones, and to act as helper to Sykes the robber in house-breaking. Nancy's womanly heart, bad though her life may be, works to set him free. Once more good people shelter him, rescuing him without assistance of the Bow Street officers, who make brave talk. The kind old scholar, Mr. Brownlow, is the good genius who opens before him a way to liberty and a life suited to his nature. The excitable country doctor deceives the police, and saves Oliver for an honest career. The eccentric Mr. Grimwig should not be overlooked. The mystery of his mother's fate is solved, and he finds a sister. Although the innocent and less guilty suffer, the conscious wrongdoers are, after much scheming and actual sin, made to give back the stolen, repair — if such can be — the evil done, and pay the penalty of transgression. They bring ruin on their own heads. There are about twenty prominent characters, each the type of its kind, in this life-drama; separate scenes of which we may, as it were, read in our daily papers, so real are they. The author says that as romance had made vice to shine with pleasures, so his purpose was to show crime in its repulsive truth.

ON HEROES, see **HEROES AND HERO WORSHIP.**

ON LIBERTY, by J. S. Mill, see **LIBERTY.**

ON THE EVE, by Ivan Turgeneff (1589). In this tale which is devoid of plot, but full of Turgeneff's charm of style and delicate character-drawing, he seeks to show the contrast between the dilettante trifling or learned pedantry of young Russia, and the intense vitality of conviction in the youth of other nations. He first introduces two young Russians, André Bersieneff, a doctor of philosophy from the Moscow University, and Paul Schubin, a gay and pleasure-loving artist, who has been modeling the bust of a beautiful girl, Elena Strashof, whose charms he dwells upon. She is the daughter of a dissipated noble; and her mother, a faded society belle, has left her to the care of a sentimental governess. The ardent girl, filled with high aspirations, rebels at the prosaic routine of her life, and longs for intercourse with nobler natures. Both the young men are in love with her, but she despises Shubin as a trifler; and just as she is beginning to be interested in the young philosopher Bersieneff, the real hero appears on the scene. This is Dmetri Insarof, a young Bulgarian patriot, whose life is devoted to freeing his country from the yoke of Turkey. His mother has fallen a victim to the brutality of a Turkish aga, while his father was shot in trying to avenge her; and he is now looked upon by his compatriots as their destined leader in the approaching revolt. His tragic story and his high aims appeal to Elena's idealism; but Insarof, finding that "on the eve" of the great conflict, he is distracted from his mission by love for Elena, has resolved to leave her forever without a farewell. She, however, seeks him out, and avows her devotion to him, and her willingness to abandon home and country for his sake. In his struggle between his passion for her and his dread of involving her in perils and hardships, he falls dangerously ill. His comrade and former rival Bersieneff nurses him with disinterested friendship until he is partially restored to health, when he and Elena are married secretly, owing to the opposition of her family to the foreign adventurer. They start together for Bulgaria to take part in the struggle for his fatherland, but have only reached Venice when Insarof dies in his young wife's arms. Elena, in a heart-broken letter, bids her parents a last farewell before joining the Sisters of Mercy in the Bulgarian army, as she has now no country but his. Thus ends the life story of the noblest and most ideal pair of lovers the great Russian novelist has ever drawn.

ON THE FREEDOM OF THE WILL, by Jonathan Edwards, see **FREEDOM.**

ON THE HEIGHTS ('Auf der Höhe'), by Berthold Auerbach (1865), is considered the author's finest work. The charm of the story is not conveyed in a synopsis of the plot. Countess Irma von Wildenort has been placed by her father, Count Eberhard, a recluse, at a German court. Her beauty and intellectual vivacity attract the King, somewhat wearied by his Queen's lofty and pious sentiments and her distaste for court festivities. Early in the story the Queen gives birth to the Crown Prince, for whom a wet-nurse is found in the person of Walpurga, an upright, shrewd peasant woman, who, for the sake of her child's future benefit, reluctantly accepts the position. She is full of quaint sayings, and her pious nature finds favor with the Queen. Her naïve descriptions of court life are very entertaining. From the same mountain district as Irma, Walpurga acquires some influence with her, and she quickly detects the unspoken love of the King for her; but Irma disregards

her friendly warnings. The Queen is apparently unaware of their increasing infatuation. Irma, becoming restless and unsettled, visits her father, who solemnly
warns her against the temptations of court life. She is drawn back irresistibly to
court, and the King reveals his passion for her by kissing the statue of which she is
the model. Irma, in a sort of ecstasy, submits for a moment to his caresses.
For a time she lives as though in the clouds. The Queen's friendship for her increases,
and her Majesty resolutely banishes her occasional suspicions of evil.

Walpurga returns home laden with gifts and money, and she and her husband,
Hansei, buy a farm on the mountain. Irma's father meanwhile receives anonymous
letters, wrongfully representing her as the King's mistress. The shock of the accusation mortally prostrates him, and Irma is summoned in haste to his death-bed.
Unable to speak, he traces one word on her forehead and expires. She falls unconscious. Letters of condolence arrive from their Majesties; the King's inclosure one
of passionate longing; the Queen's so full of affection and confidence that remorse
seizes Irma. She writes her guilt to the Queen, and resolves to drown herself. In
her wanderings she comes unexpectedly on Walpurga and her family, on the way
to take possession of their new home. She implores protection from herself; and
in the care of Walpurga and the grandmother, she lives for a year "on the heights,"
writing a journal of philosophical and religious rhapsody.

Tormented by remorse, she grows weaker in body, while her soul becomes purified of its earthly passion. Gunther, her father's friend, absolves her from his curse;
and, her spirit freed, she passes away in the presence of the King and Queen, now
happily reconciled.

ON THE REPLY OF THE HARUSPICES, by Cicero, see **HARUSPICES.**

ONE OF CLEOPATRA'S NIGHTS ('Une Nuit de Cléopâtre'), by Théophile Gautier.
In this charming short story, published in 1867, in a collection of 'Nouvelles,' the
author shows the exhaustive study which he had made of Egypt and its ancient
customs. He introduces Cleopatra to his readers as she is being rowed down the
Nile to her summer palace. In describing the cause of her ennui to Charmian,
Cleopatra graphically pictured the belittling, crushing effect of the gigantic monuments of her country. She bewails the fate of a Queen who can never know if she
is loved for herself alone, and longs for some strange adventure. She has been followed down the Nile by Meïamoun, a young man who is violently infatuated with
the Queen, but whom she has never noticed. That night she is startled by an arrow
which enters her window bearing a roll of papyrus on which is written, "I love you."
She looks from the window and sees a man swimming across the Nile, but her servants are unable to find him. Soon after, Meïamoun dives down into the subterranean passage which conducts the waters of the Nile to Cleopatra's bath; and the
next morning, as she is enjoying her bath, she finds him gazing at her. She condemns him to death, and then pardons him. He begs for death, and she yields,
but tells him he shall first find his most extravagant dream realized: he shall be
the lover of Cleopatra. "I take thee from nothingness; I make thee the equal of a
god, and I replunge thee into nothingness." "It was necessary to make of the life
of Meïamoun a powerful elixir which he could drain from a single cup." Then
follows the description of the feast. After a night of magnificent splendor, a cup of
poison is handed to him. Touched by his beauty and bravery, Cleopatra is about
to order him not to drink, when the heralds announce the arrival of Mark Antony.
He asks: "What means this corpse upon the floor?" "Oh! nothing," she answers;

— "a poison I was trying, in order to use it should Augustus make me prisoner. Will it please you, my dear, to sit by me and watch the dancers?"

ONE SUMMER, by Blanche Willis Howard (1875). This light but refreshingly humorous little romance opens with the quasi-pathetic picture of Miss Laura Leigh Doane, a city girl, imprisoned by the rain in a New England farm-house, and suffering from loneliness and ennui. "I would like to be a man," she cries, "just long enough to run down to Pratt's for that book; but no longer, oh no, not a moment longer!" Unable to bear the dullness, she finally ventures alone on this errand; and in the dark, while charging against the wind around a corner, runs into Philip Ogden, and thrusts the ferule of her umbrella stick into his eye. She leads him home; and he (assuming that she is a girl of humble station) hands her two dollars. Chagrined, she demurely takes this punishment, having learned that he is an old chum of her brother's, also spending his vacation here — but she resolves never to forgive him. Many scenes of pleasant comedy ensue, both before and after the arrival of her brother Tom, with his wife and the baby; the romantic Bessie, at what she regards as critical moments, tragically warns her droll but marplot husband against spoiling it all. A charming description of a yachting trip to Mt. Desert is introduced; the "log" of which is said to have been furnished by another hand. The finale is in exact accordance with poetic justice: Miss Laura and Philip become engaged. The story, after a time, attained wide popularity in consequence of its breezy situations, sparkling conversations, and bright descriptions, and has been republished with illustrations.

ONE WOMAN'S LIFE, by Robert Herrick (1913). The heroine of this story is a selfish woman who accomplishes her own ends regardless of the consequences to her friends. Milly Ridge is but a girl of sixteen when the story opens in Chicago, where, with her father and grandmother, she is about to move into a new home. The family have come from another western city, and Milly, who has social ambitions, is much disappointed to find that her father has chosen an unattractive house in an unfashionable quarter. Mr. Ridge is a man without culture or polish, who has never been successful financially, and is dominated by his pretty and self-willed daughter; the latter, overcoming her disappointment as best she can, sets about gaining an entrance into society, and through connecting herself with a certain church, makes influential friends, who aid her social career. She becomes engaged to a rich man, for whom she does not care, but throws him over, and later marries Jack Bragdon, a poor young artist, for love. This marriage is regarded as most quixotic by her friends, who know her extravagant tastes and love of society. A legacy of $3,000 left by her grandmother, coming shortly after her marriage, enables Milly and her artist husband to go to Paris, where the latter desires to study. Here, a daughter is born to them, and although Milly had not cared to have a child, she becomes a devoted mother. Bragdon, whose affection for Milly had been absolute up to this time, becomes entangled with a Russian baroness, whose portrait he is painting; and from this time Milly's faith and love are shattered. They return to New York, where Milly plunges into society and incurs expenses far beyond their means. Bragdon works hard to keep the "pot boiling," and then dies leaving his wife nothing but debts. With the help of friends Milly keeps along for a while and then becomes housekeeper and companion for a business woman, named Ernestine Geyer, who is charmed by her winning personality. Miss Geyer makes a good living out of running a laundry and has laid up $10,000, which, later, Milly persuades her to invest in starting a cake-shop with herself. This proves a financial failure, and at this crisis Milly marries an old-time admirer, a rich ranchman, and leaves without a scruple the friend who has lavished both money and affection upon her.

ONESIMUS: MEMOIRS OF A DISCIPLE OF ST. PAUL, by the author of 'Philochristus: Memoirs of a Disciple of the Lord,' appeared in America in 1882. The story is told in the language used in the English version of the Acts of the Apostles and is placed in the first century of the Christian era.

Onesimus, who himself tells the story in the first person, is one of the twin sons of a noble Greek. Stolen from his parents in childhood, he is sold as a slave, and becomes one of the household of Philemon, who is represented as a wealthy citizen of Colossæ. Falsely accused of theft, Onesimus runs away. It is then that he meets "Paulus" (the Apostle St. Paul), and becoming a convert to the Christian faith, is sent back to Philemon, his master, with the letter which figures in the New Testament as 'The Epistle to Philemon.' Onesimus becomes a minister, at length, and suffers martyrdom for his faith.

A prominent character in the narrative is St. Paul, into some passages of whose life the author enters with picturesque minuteness, dwelling upon his final ministry and martyrdom at Rome. Thus is attempted a faithful and realistic view of the early Christian faith and apostolic times, introducing Nero and several other historical characters. The entire narrative is founded upon statements of the Scripture records, but some liberties are taken as to both characters and scenes. However, the author has gathered much of his material from such sources as are generally recognized as authentic, even embodying the substance of passages from these "authorities" in the descriptions and conversations. The whole difficult subject is handled in a striking manner; the tone is reverent; and the treatment is eminently artistic, and quite winning in its simple, dignified beauty.

ONLY A GIRL, by Wilhelmine von Hillern (1865). This book is the romance of a soul; the agonies, the sickness unto death, and the recovery, of a noble mind. Ernestine von Hartwich, embittered by the fact that she is "only a girl," a shortcoming which has caused her father's hate and mother's death, determines to equal a man in achievement, — in scientific attainments and in mental usefulness, — that her sex shall no longer be made to her a reproach and even a crime. This desire is taken advantage of by an unscrupulous uncle who will profit by her death. Secluding her from the world, he attempts to undermine her health by feeding her feverish ambitions. Her mind is developed at the expense of very human feeling, every womanly instinct, and every religious emotion. She is shunned by women, envied and humiliated by men, regarded by her servants and the neighboring peasantry as a witch. It is through the door of love, opened for her by Johannes Mollner, that she finally leaves the wilderness of false aims, unnatural ambitions, and unsatisfactory results, to enjoy for the first time the charm of womanhood, human companionship, and belief in God. The story is overloaded with didacticism; its logic fails, inasmuch as the poor girl is an involuntary martyr; and its exaggeration and sentimentality do not appeal to the English reader. But the book was a great favorite in Germany, where it has been considered a powerful argument against what is called the higher education of women.

OPUS MAJUS, of Roger Bacon (A.D. 1267). Newly edited and published, with introduction and full English analysis of the Latin text, by J. H. Bridges. (2 vols.

:897). An adequate publication, after 630 years, of one of the most remarkable productions of the human mind.

The work is an exhortation addressed to Pope Clement, urging him to initiate a reform of Christian education, in order to establish the ascendency of the Catholic Church over all nations and religions of the world. Its author wished to see recognition of "all the sciences," since all are parts of one and the same complete wisdom. He first gave experiment the distinct and supreme place which was later revived by Descartes, and carried out in modern science. He formed a clear conception of chemistry, in his day not yet separated from alchemy; and of a science of living things, as resulting with chemistry from physics. "The generation of men, and of brutes, and of plants," he said, "is from elemental and liquid substances, and is of like manner with the generation of inanimate things."

The central theme of his work was the consolidation of the Catholic faith as the supreme agency for the civilization and ennoblement of mankind. For this end a complete renovation and reorganization of man's intellectual forces was needed. The four principal impediments to wisdom were authority, habit, prejudice, and false conceit of knowledge. The last of these, ignorance under the cloak of wisdom, was pronounced the worst and most fatal. A striking feature of this scheme of instruction was its estimate of Greek culture as providentially ordained not less than Hebrew, and to be studied the same as Hebrew. In view of the corruption of his own times, Roger Bacon said: "The ancient philosophers have spoken so wonderfully on virtue and vice, that a Christian man may well be astounded at those who were unbelievers thus attaining the summits of morality. On the Christian virtues of faith, hope, and charity, we can speak things of which they knew nothing. But in the virtues needed for integrity of life, and for human fellowship, we are not their equals either in word or deed." A section of his moral philosophy Roger Bacon devotes to the first attempt ever made at the comparative study of the religions of the world.

His protests against the intellectual prejudices of the time, his forecasts of an age of industry and invention, the prominence given to experiment, alike as the test of received opinion and the guide to new fields of discovery, render comparison with Francis Bacon unavoidable. In wealth of words, in brilliancy of imagination, Francis Bacon was immeasurably his superior. But Roger Bacon had the sounder estimate and the firmer grasp of that combination of deductive with inductive method which marks the scientific discoverer.

The competent editor, whose judgments we give, has furnished analyses of Bacon's Latin text which enable the English reader to gather easily his leading ideas.

OREGON TRAIL, THE, 'Sketches of the Prairie and Rocky-Mountain Life,' by Francis Parkman, was first published in 1847, in the Knickerbocker Magazine, then in book form in 1849 under the title 'The California and Oregon Trail'; in later editions the book reverted to its old title. It is a graphic and highly entertaining account of a journey undertaken by Parkman and his friend Quincy Adams Shaw, both fresh from college, in the summer of 1846. Already dedicated to the task of writing the history of England and France in the New World, Parkman wanted experience at first hand of the unsettled wilderness and its aboriginal inhabitants. The friends decided to journey from the Missouri to the foot-hills of the Rockies, following the settlers' route to Oregon, which then included the whole territory west of the Rockies from Mexico to the fiftieth parallel. Leaving St. Louis on April 28th they proceeded by steamer to a point near Kansas City. From here they set out with a guide, a muleteer, five horses, and three mules. Traveling with a party of Englishmen for company and for part of the way with a small troop of emigrants, they traversed what is now the state of Kansas and then followed the valley of the Platte. The way was enlivened by heavy windstorms, by the appearance of Indians, and by an exciting buffalo hunt. Leaving their companions at the forks of the Platte they followed the North Fork, entered what is now the state of Wyoming, and reached Fort Laramie, then a trading-post. Here they remained for several days, fraternizing with a village of Sioux Indians encamped near-by. Though weakened by serious illness, Parkman determined to join one of the bands of Sioux who were planning to take the war-path against the Snake Indians. By a series of misunderstandings, they missed the party which they were seeking, but Parkman would not agree to turn back, and taking another guide pushed on alone in pursuit, promising to meet Shaw and the rest of the party at Fort Laramie on the first of August. A ride through a wild and mountainous part of Wyoming, infested by hostile Indians, brought Parkman to the band of Sioux, whom he was seeking. They were none too trustworthy, and it is probable that only an iron resolution and the suppression of all signs of weakness due to a severe illness, preserved Parkman from a treacherous assault. He feasted the Indians, was feasted by them in return, smoked the peace-pipe with them, made them a set speech, and gave them presents. Though he did not see any battles he took part in several buffalo hunts, witnessed a serious quarrel which almost came to bloodshed, collected some Indian folk-lore, and of course lived intimately with the tribe, sharing their lodges and buffalo robes, and getting a valuable insight into their character. He rejoined his party at Fort Laramie shortly after August 1st, and the return journey was made without incident. Although this journey played its part in undermining his health, it was of inestimable value to Parkman as an historian, and was the occasion for one of the most delightful books of travel in the language. The picture of the American prairies in the old savage days before the advent of the railroad and the barbed-wire fence, is historically priceless; and the author's adventurous enthusiasm and indomitable resolution give the autobiography intense interest.

ORIENTAL RELIGIONS: INDIA, CHINA, PERSIA, by Samuel Johnson. Mr. Johnson's labors in producing this trilogy extended over many years. The first volume, India, appeared in 1872, the second, China, in 1877; and the last, Persia, in 1885, after the author's death. The volumes, although separate, really constitute one work, the underlying idea of which is that there is a Universal Religion, "a religion behind all religions"; that not Buddhism, not Brahminism, not Mahometanism, nor even Christianity, is the true religion; but that these are only phases of the one great religion that is back of them all and expresses itself, or various phases of itself, through them all. And he maintains that the "Universal Religion" is revealed and illustrated in the Oriental religions. This thesis pervades the whole work and is present in every chapter. It presides over the search for facts and the selection and combination of facts, and is defended with skill and enthusiasm. The work is therefore not really a history, or a compendium of Oriental philosophy, but the exposition of this theory to which the author had devoted the study of a lifetime. Mr. Johnson was a sound scholar, a deep thinker, a patient investigator, and an earnest and eloquent writer. It is not necessary to accept his estimate of the relative values of Christianity and the religions of ancient life in Asia; but this whole work taken together, certainly forms a valuable contribution to the elucidation of the thought expressed by Chevalier Bunsen in the title to one of his works, 'God in History.'

ORIGIN AND ORGANIZATION OF THE INQUISITION, see **INQUISITION OF THE MIDDLE AGES.**

ORIGIN OF CIVILIZATION AND PRIMITIVE CONDITION OF MAN, ON THE, by Baron Avebury (John Lubbock) (1870). The aim of this volume is to provide a description based on the evidence of a large variety of travelers and observers, of the social and mental conditions of undeveloped races, their religions, arts, and laws; their ideas of morals, and their systems of marriage and relationship. The careful study of these aspects of primitive life will eventually help to solve many complex problems of ethnology, but the difficulty of obtaining reliable evidence is uery great, owing to the unwillingness or incapacity of primitive peoples to make themselves understood by travelers or missionaries, and the absence in their languages of words to express abstract ideas or large numbers. Primitive religion is an affair of this world, and not of another and higher existence; it has little or no connection with morality; its deities are mortal, a part not the author of nature, and can be forced into compliance with the will of man. Nevertheless the scientist can trace in the various forms of primitive religious belief a gradual rise from lower to higher conceptions of God, man, and the world. The earliest traces of art as yet discovered belong to the Stone Age, and sometimes take the form of sculpture and sometimes of drawings or etchings made on bone or horn with the point of a flint. The strongest proof, however, that the race has evolved from lower to higher types is the history of the ideas of marriage, at first a purely physical and temporary relation, devoid of any notion of morality, affection, or companionship. Lord Avebury is of opinion that the varied evidence which he has brought together in his book strongly supports the doctrine of development. He therefore concludes that existing primitive peoples are not, as used sometimes to be asserted, the descendants of civilized ancestors; that the primitive condition of man was one of utter barbarism, and that from this condition various races have independently raised themselves.

ORIGIN OF SPECIES BY MEANS OF NATURAL SELECTION, ON THE, or 'The Preservation of Favored Races in the Struggle for Life,' by Charles Darwin, was published in 1859. Though without exception the most influential book of the nineteenth century it is indebted to Lamarck and Lyall for the conception of the evolution of species, and its special hypotheses of natural selection and survival of the fittest were formulated simultaneously by Alfred Russell Wallace. But the patience and thoroughness with which they were worked out by Darwin, the mass and skilful arrangement of his evidence, the clearness and persuasiveness of his argument, and the quiet beauty and power of his style gave the theory general currency and made the book a classic. The fundamental position of the book is that the various species of organic beings are the result not of special creation, but of a gradual process of evolution, one species insensibly developing from another. This process he describes as a result of *natural selection*, which includes the infinite *variation* of the individuals of a species, the *struggle for existence* — that is, the competition between these individuals for the limited opportunity of survival, the *survival of the fittest*, that is of those best adapted to their environment, and the *transmission* of their distinctive qualities to their descendants. In this way new species gradually arise out of the old. Or, as Darwin puts it in his concluding paragraph, all the elaborately constructed organic forms that we see about us have been produced by laws. "These laws, taken in the largest sense, being Growth with Reproduction; Inheritance, which is almost implied by Reproduction; Variability, from the indirect and direct action of the conditions of life, and from use and disuse; a Ratio of Increase so high as to lead to a Struggle for Life, and as a consequence to Natural Selection, entailing Divergence of Character and the Extinction of less-improved forms. Thus from the war of nature, from famine and death, the most exalted object which we are capable of conceiving, namely, the production of the higher animals, directly follows." The facts and experiments upon which this theory is based, are recorded in the main body of the book. They include his observations, made during a tour of the world as naturalist on H. M. S. Beagle and a series of investigations into the breeding of domestic animals made at his home in Kent. Further evidence was adduced in later works, and the implications of the doctrine as applied to the origin of man were stated in 'The Descent of Man and Selection in Relation to Sex' (1871). Although the book was bitterly attacked by the supporters of traditional theology and by those who feared it would promote materialism, and although recent scientists have questioned the details of its hypothesis, particularly as regards the survival of the fittest and the transmission of acquired characteristics, yet its main position has won practically universal acceptance, and has influenced every field of thought, including religion, sociology, philosophy, history, and literary criticism.

ORIGINS OF CONTEMPORARY FRANCE, see **ANCIENT RÉGIME: MODERN RÉGIME: FRENCH REVOLUTION.**

ORISSA, see **ANNALS OF RURAL BENGAL.**

ORLANDO FURIOSO, by Ludovico Ariosto, a romantic epic of Charlemagne and his peers, published in forty cantos in 1512, revised and enlarged to forty-six cantos in 1532. The poem is a continuation of the 'Orlando Innamorato' of Matteo Maria Boiardo (1434–1494), a great feudal noble of the court of Ferrara, where the French romances of chivalry were as much in fashion as the newer classical studies. His epic, left unfinished in 1494, published in 1506, recounts the wars of Charlemagne and the Saracens with emphasis, not on the religious and heroic motives of the early French epic, but on the love-affairs of the warriors, who have become as polished and as susceptible as the knights in the Arthurian romances. Ariosto carries on the story with greater finish and maturity but less spontaneity. The background of his narrative is the driving out of France of the army of Saracens, which at the beginning is besieging Paris under Agramante, King of Africa, aided by Marsilio, King of Spain, and two formidable champions, Rodomonte and Manricardo. But the ambuscades, stratagems, single combats, and pitched battles, necessary to drive them out, are less emphasized than the love of warriors on each side for ladies on the other. The central theme is the love of Ruggiero, a youth of Christian descent, brought up among the Saracens, and one of their champions, for a maiden warrior, Bradamante, sister of Rinaldo, one of the Paladins of Charlemagne. As a compliment to his patrons, Ariosto represents this hero and heroine as ancestors of the House of Este, the ducal family of Ferrara. The numerous vicissitudes of this love-story are due to the opposing nationality of the lovers and to the schemes of a magician, Atlante, who wishes to remove his pupil, Ruggiero, from the dangers of war. At the opening of the story, for instance, Ruggiero is released by Bradamante from a tower in which Atlante has confined him; but immediately afterwards he has the imprudence to mount his tutor's hippogriff, and is carried by this creature to the island of the sorceress, Alcina. Fascinated by her beauty and enchantments, he remains here as her paramour until released by the seer, Melissa, who annuls Alcina's spells and exposes her in her true ugliness. After a visit to the abode of Logistilla, or wisdom, Ruggiero departs on his hippogriff, intending to return to Bradamante. But in passing a small island, he sees a beautiful woman, exposed to a sea-monster and rescues her, by means of the dazzling rays of a magic shield. The woman is the beautiful Angelica, beloved of Orlando, and almost all the Paladins and their opponents but obdurate to all. Even Ruggiero forgets his plighted troth and begin to make love to her. But by means of an enchanted ring she becomes invisible and escapes him. After other obstacles have been placed in his way by Atlante, Ruggiero again meets Bradamante, who forgives his infidelities but insists on his baptism before she will accept him. Ruggiero gives his promise, but is delayed in its execution by the feeling that he should not desert Agramante, his leader, while the war is going badly for him. Further complication is introduced by Marfisa, a female warrior on the Moorish side, who becomes attached to Ruggiero and is an active rival of Bradamante, until it is discovered that Ruggiero and Marfisa are brother and sister. Again Ruggiero is required to meet Rinaldo, brother to Bradamante, in single combat; but the outcome is a close friendship. Finally the objections of the lady's father are met by the chivalrous withdrawal of the Emperor Leo, his choice for his daughter's hand; and Ruggiero's slaying of Rodomonte, who rebukes him for his apostasy, is followed by the marriage of the lovers.

Though the madness of Orlando gives the poem its name, this is in reality a brilliant episode. Orlando and Rinaldo have been prominent among numerous rivals for the hand of Angelica, daughter of Galafron, King of Cathay, have followed her to her own country and return to France just when Paris is besieged. Through the operation of two magic springs in the forest of Arden, Angelica now hates Rinaldo, and he passionately loves her, though previously, and by operation of the same springs Rinaldo hated her and she loved him. Orlando (the Roland of the French epic) has loved her from the first, unrequited. In the first cantos of Ariosto, Angelica is successively pursued by various suitors and at length carried off by sailors to be exposed, as already explained, to a sea-monster. Rescued from this fate by Ruggiero and from Ruggiero by her magic ring she returns to Paris, where, among the Saracen wounded, she finds a beautiful youth, Medoro, whom she nurses back to health in a herdsman's cottage. She has fallen in love with him, and on his recovery they are married. After a month of idyllic happiness they set out for the coast of Spain to embark for Cathay. Meanwhile Orlando in his search for Angelica comes to the grove where Angelica and Medoro used to meet and notices their names carved on the trees and stones. The cottager confirms his worst fears. He rushes again into the woods where long brooding gives way to violent madness. He tears up the trees, breaks the rocks with his sword, chokes the stream, and having thus devastated the whole scene, tears off his clothes and lives a wild man, feeding on roots and raw flesh and offering violence to all who approach him. A dramatic incident is his meeting with Angelica and Medoro on the coast of Spain, as they are about to sail for Cathay. He does not recognize Angelica, but he pursues her and is foiled only by her swiftness. She and Medoro thus escape and sail for her kingdom, while Orlando crosses into Africa. Here he later meets and attacks some of the Paladins, one of whom, Astolfo, has a cure for his malady. Having got possession of Ruggiero's hippogriff, Astolfo, among other strange adventures, has soared to a mountain-top which proved to be the Earthy Paradise and there met the Evangelist Saint John, by whose aid he ascended in Elijah's fiery chariot, to the moon. Here in a valley containing everything lost on earth, he found the wits of Orlando enclosed in a great jar. This jar he now has in this tent and a direct application of it to Orlando's nostrils restores the madman to his senses. His love is forgotten, and in a great final combat he does Charlemagne a great service, by slaying Agramante, the African king. Rinaldo too is cured of his infatuation for Angelica by a second drink of the spring which causes hatred.

Infinite variety of incident, unwearied zest for life, rich sensuous color, as in the canvases of Rubens and Veronese, ease and copiousness of diction, are the leading qualities of 'Orlando Furioso.' More worldly and satirical than Spenser, Ariosto lacks his spirituality and seriousness and is much less allegorical; but the general effect of the two poems is not unlike.

ORLOFF AND HIS WIFE; tales of the Barefoot Brigade, by Maxim Gorky (1901). Realistic sketches of the under-world of Russia, of tramps and outcasts, the degraded, hopeless, and vicious. Orloff, the cobbler, loves his wife, but beats her in sheer boredom from the dull life of continual tedious work in their cellar. When she reproaches him, he blames fate and his character. "What can you say to a man if life has made a devil of him?" or, "Am I to blame if I have that sort of character?" Orloff and his wife become acquainted with a medical student inspector and are hired to help fight the cholera epidemic in the hospital. Orloff is happy at first in the new environment. He wonders why so much trouble and expense is permitted for men who are to die. "Couldn't that same money be used for improving life?" he asks. Praise of his industry transforms him. He longs to be a hero, to attract attention to himself by brave and generous deeds. A quarrel with his wife starts him on a drunken spree and he returns to his old ways of life, but she escapes and is helped by her friends in the hospital to teach her cobbler's trade in a trade school. The wretched daily and nightly toil in a bakery is the scene of 'Konováloff.' Konováloff is the only character in the book who does not throw the responsibility of his bad luck on Fate or other people. In arguments with his fellow workman he persists in his own guilt toward himself and life. "Every man is the master of himself" and "none is to blame if I am a scoundrel," he says. These self-questionings of Gorky's characters and their curiosity about the meaning of life never leads to regeneration, but serve as excuses for vice. "Men with Pasts" are outcasts who live at the night lodging house. Their hatred of life is born of failure. What power they have is always evil, working toward their own undoing. Those men, who through idleness or cowardice, have fallen from a higher class, are more debased than nature's true vagabonds, whose instinct for liberty makes them the outcasts from society. The novel, 'Varenka Olessova,' which concludes the book, recounts the interminable conversations of a conceited pedant, with Varenka, a fresh, natural young girl, while he is making a visit in the country. He is attracted by her, but cannot make up his mind whether he is in love with her or not, and the end of the story leaves him still in a state of indecision.

ORME DU MAIL, L', see **L'HISTOIRE CONTEMPORAINE.**

ORPHEUS C. KERR PAPERS, THE, by Robert Henry Newell (1862–68). The 'Letters' composing this book appeared originally in the daily press during the Civil War. Narrating the history of a fictitious and comic "Mackerel Brigade" [Mackerel = "Little Mac," McClellan's well-known popular nickname], they purported to be written from the scene of action; were devoted to the humors of the conflict; and were widely read at the time throughout the North. In a sense they are historic. Their gibes and bitterly humorous shafts were directed chiefly against the dishonest element of society that the upheaval of the war had brought to the surface, the cheating contractors, the makers of shoddy clothing, imperfect arms, scant-weight ammunition, and bad supplies for the army in the field, as well as towards the selfish and incompetent general officers and office-seekers. Much of the fun of the letters is to-day unintelligible, some of the satire seems coarse; but there is no doubt that the author did immense service in creating a better sentiment as to the offenses that he scored, and to open the way, among other benefits, for the improvement which was to be known as "civil-service reform."

ORTHODOXY, a series of essays by Gilbert K. Chesterton (1908). The book presents the positive side of the thought, advanced in 'Heretics,' namely that definite convictions and a serious theory of the universe are an essential to sane and happy life. In 'Orthodoxy' Chesterton, in response to a challenge, states his own philosophy, showing the stages by which he has been led to an acceptance of orthodox Christianity. After brilliantly ridiculing the determinists, the sceptics, the pragmatists, the worshippers of will, the Tolstoyans, and other modern thinkers because they deprive life of a solid, intelligible purpose and sacrifice wholesome sanity to logic, Chesterton outlines the development of his own belief. In 'The Ethics of Elfland,' he derives from the fairy-tales learned in childhood the conviction, first, that scientific laws do not establish inevitable connection between phenomena and that miracles are conceivable; and, secondly, that incomprehensible happiness might depend on an incomprehensible condition, e. g., some apparently irrational taboo or formula; in other words, that there is in the universe a personal will in distinction to an impersonal law. In 'The Flag of the World' the contradictory tendencies of optimism and pessimism are shown to be reconciled by Christianity, which, while affirming the existence of God and the wickedness of suicide, also affirms the separation of the world from God and the glory of martyrdom. The author's desire to love the world without trusting it was met by the Christian doctrine of the Fall; and this once grasped every other detail seemed to fall into place. 'The Paradoxes of Christianity' adduces other examples of conflicting tendencies allowed a certain amount of free play by Christianity; for example losing one's life and saving it, dignity and humility, mercy and anger, valor and non-resistance, asceticism and marriage; and in this skillful combination the author finds a proof of its truth. In 'The Eternal Revolution' Chesterton points out how the desire for progress towards a fixed ideal is met by the doctrine of the Fall of Man and the scheme of salvation. 'The Romance of Orthodoxy' is an attack on the modernist doctrines of the impossibility of miracles (which is a denial of God's freedom), the divine immanence (which practically means pantheism), unitarianism (which means an Oriental and tyrannical idea of God), universalism (which makes moral effort less urgent and the struggle of life less critical), the regarding of sin as disease (which destroys free-will), and the denial of the divinity of Christ (which derogates from the dignity of suffering). In 'Authority and the Adventurer' Chesterton meets the objection that the moral effects of Christian belief do not prove its objective truth by a brief confutation of modern sceptical views and a statement of the arguments for the positive truth of Christianity. The negative arguments are that men are a superior variety of beasts, that religion arose from fear, and that it promotes gloom; that Christianity inculcates weakness, is a product of the dark ages, and promotes suspicion and unprogressiveness. After vigorously confuting these arguments, Chesterton gives as the positive arguments which appeal to him that by reliable human testimony miracles do happen, that Christian dogma satisfies the instincts of our nature, and that however dissatisfied we may be with the imperfections of life, Christianity teaches us to enjoy life as a whole. The book irritates many readers by its constant striving after paradox and epigram, but its defense of orthodoxy and conservatism is a strong and apparently a sincere one.

OTHELLO, THE MOOR OF VENICE (written about 1604), ranks with 'Hamlet,' 'Lear,' and 'Macbeth,' as one of Shakespeare's four great masterpieces of tragedy. The bare outline of the story came to him from Cinthio's 'Il Moro di Venezia.' It is the story of "one who loved not wisely, but too well; of one not easily jealous, but being wrought, perplexed in the extreme." Othello has a rich exotic nature, a heroic tenderness, quick sense of honor, child-like trust, yet fiercest passion when wronged in his soul. In Iago we have a villain to whom goodness is sheer silliness and cruel craft a fine prudence. The Moor has wedded Desdemona, and from Venice sailed to Cyprus, followed by Roderigo, who is in love with her and is a tool of Iago. Iago hates Othello for appointing Cassio his lieutenant, leaving him to be his humble standard-bearer. He also suspects him of having cuckolded him, and for mere suspicion in that kind will diet his revenge by trying to pay him off wife for wife, or failing that, to poison his happiness forever by jealousy. And he wants Cassio's place. He persuades Roderigo that Cassio and Desdemona are in love, and that if he is to prosper, Cassio must be degraded from office or killed. The loyal Cassio has a poor brain for drink, Iago gets him tipsy and involved in a fray, and then has the garrison alarmed by the bell. Othello dismisses Cassio from office. The poor man, smitten with deep shame and despair, is advised by "honest" Iago to seek the mediation of the divine Desdemona, and out of this he will work his ruin; for he craftily instills into the mind of Othello that his wife intercedes for Cassio as for a paramour, and brings him where he sees Cassio making his suit to her, but retiring when he perceives Othello in the distance. "Ha! I like not that," says Iago. And then, forced to disclose his thought, he reminds the Moor that Desdemona deceived her father by her secret marriage, and may deceive him; also tells a diabolically false tale of his sleeping with Cassio, and how he talked in his sleep about his amour with Desdemona. Othello had given his wife a talismanic embroidered handkerchief, sewed by a sibyl in her prophetic fury. Iago had often urged his wife Emilia to steal this "napkin," and when he gets it he drops it in Cassio's chamber. The Moor sees it in his lieutenant's hands, and further sees him laughing and gesturing about Bianca, a common strumpet, and is told by Iago that Desdemona and his adventures with her were Cassio's theme. When, finally, the "honest," "trusty" Iago tells him that Cassio had confessed all to him, the tortured man throws his last doubt to the winds, and resolves on the death of Cassio and Desdemona both. Cassio is only wounded; but the gentle Desdemona, who, all heartbroken, and foreboding, has retired, is awaked by Othello's last kisses (for his love is not wholly quenched), and after a terrible talk, is smothered by him where she lies, — reviving for a moment, after the entrance of Emilia, to assert that Othello is innocent and that she killed herself. The Moor avows the deed, however, both to Emilia and to two Venetian officials, who have just arrived on State business. In the conversation Iago's villainy comes to light through Emilia's telling the truth about the handkerchief; she is stabbed to death by Iago, while Othello in bitter remorse stabs himself, and as he dies imprints a convulsive kiss on the cold lips of Desdemona. Iago is led away to torture and death.

OUR DAILY BREAD (Das tägliche Brod), by Clara Viebig-Cohn (1900). A realistic picture of lower class life in Berlin in the experiences of a servant-girl, whose life is one long struggle against poverty and circumstance. Her sturdy character saves her from tragedy and the story from unrelieved gloom. Mina comes from the country to her uncle in Berlin with great expectations that her relatives will help her to get a good situation. Her uncle keeps a small green-grocer's shop, and her aunt a registry office in which the servant girls of the neighborhood gather in their free time to gossip and to flirt with Arthur, the son. Her aunt makes her do the rough work of the house while she waits for a situation, and charges her board and lodging fee. She gets a situation and toils from morning until night, overworked, underpaid, and underfed. In her loneliness she turns to Arthur who is glad to go to the park with her on Sundays as she has her wages to spend for his entertainment. She soon expects to be the mother of his child. Arthur is weak but not vicious, and so incapable that he is always out of work. Mina first tries to board her baby, and finally goes home to her parents for help, but is turned away in disgrace. She tries to abandon the little girl in the public park, but her courage fails and she goes back to her. Resolved that the only course for her is to make Arthur acknowledge the child and marry her she goes to him and insists on her rights, in the face of his mother's abuse. She is no longer an inexperienced girl to be frightened and driven away. She is a mother, with legal redress, fighting for her child. After their marriage the struggle with poverty goes on, as Arthur cannot keep at work. She lives under the shop in the cellar with his family, and her work by the day is the sole support of six people. Through the kindness of her old employers a post as porter is found for Arthur, their daily bread seems assured, and the book ends with a more hopeful outlook.

OUR MUTUAL FRIEND, by Charles Dickens. "In these times of ours," are the opening words of this book, which was published in England in 1864-65. The scene is laid in London and its immediate neighborhood. All the elaborate machinery dear to Dickens's heart is here introduced. There is the central story of Our Mutual Friend, himself the young heir to the vast Harmon estate, who buries his identity and assumes the name of John Rokesmith, that he may form his own judgment of the young woman whom he must marry in order to claim his fortune; there is the other story of the poor bargeman's daughter, and her love for reckless Eugene Wrayburn, the idol of society; and uniting these two threads is the history of Mr. and Mrs. Boffin, the ignorant, kind-hearted couple, whose innocent ambitions, and benevolent use of the money intrusted to their care, afford the author opportunity for the humor and pathos of which he was a master.

Among the characters which this story has made famous are Miss Jenny Wren, the doll's dressmaker, a little, crippled creature whose love for Lizzie Hexam transforms her miserable life; Bradley Headstone, the schoolmaster, suffering torments because of his jealousy of Eugene Wrayburn, and helpless under the careless contempt of that trained adversary—dying at last in an agony of defeat at his failure to kill Eugene; and the triumph of Lizzie's love over the social difference between her and her lover; Bella Wilfer, "the boofer lady," cured of her longing for riches and made John Harmon's happy wife by the plots and plans of the Golden Dustman, Mr. Boffin; and Silas Wegg, an impudent scoundrel employed by Mr. Boffin, who is, at first, delighted with the services of "a literary man with a wooden leg," but who gradually recognizes the cheat and impostor, and unmasks him in dramatic fashion.

As usual, Dickens finds occasion to incite his readers to practical benevolence. In this book he has a protest against the poor-laws in the person of old Betty Higden, whose dread of the almshouse haunts her dying hours. By many, this volume, published among his later works, is counted as among the most important.

OUR NEW ALASKA; or, THE SEWARD PURCHASE VINDICATED, by Charles Hallock (1886). In the preface, the author explains that the special object of the book is "to point out the visible resources of that far-off territory, and to assist their laggard development; to indicate to those insufficiently informed the economic value of important industries hitherto almost neglected, which are at once available for immediate profit." In thus considering the industrial and commercial aspects of Alaska, the author does not neglect its natural beauties, nor the peculiarities of the inhabitants and their customs. Because of the variety of his observation, the work is never lacking in interest, and the reader is made to share the pleasure of the traveler in his voyage of discovery.

OUR OLD HOME, a series of English sketches by Nathaniel Hawthorne. This volume of charming sketches was published in 1863, and (in the words of the author) presents "a few of the external aspects of English scenery and life, especially those that are touched with the antique charm to which our countrymen are more susceptible than are the people among whom it is of native growth." The opening sketch on 'Consular Experiences' gives interesting glimpses of Hawthorne's own life as consul at Liverpool; and among other entertaining chapters are those designated 'About Warwick,' 'Pilgrimage to Old Boston,' 'Some of the Haunts of Burns,' 'Up the Thames,' and 'Outside Glimpses of English Poverty.' In that entitled 'Recollections of a Gifted Woman,' he recounts his acquaintance with Miss Delia Bacon, who was then deep in her 'Philosophy of the Plays of Shakespeare'; an absurd book, for which Hawthorne wrote a humorous preface. These, and other English sketches included in Hawthorne's note-books, were at first intended by him to be used as a background for a work of fiction which he had partially planned; but what he calls "the Present, the Immediate, the Actual," proved too potent for him, and the project was given up and only the sketches were published. This volume holds its popularity not simply because of the incomparable charm of the manner in which it is written, but because of its faithful delineation of nature, life, and manners in England. There are clues to English character to be gathered from 'Our Old Home,' which could not otherwise be obtained save by protracted association with the English people at home.

OUR VILLAGE, by Mary Russell Mitford, was one of the first books written which show the poetry of every-day life in the country; and Miss Mitford may fairly be called the founder of the school of village literature. There is no connected story, but the book contains a series of charming sketches of country scenes and country people. The chronicler wanders through the lanes and meadows with her white greyhound Mayflower, gossips about the trees, the flowers, and the sunsets, and describes the beauty of English scenery. The chapters on The First Primrose, Violeting, The Copse, The Wood, The Dell, and The Cowslip Ball, seem to breathe the very atmosphere of spring; while others tell interesting stories about the people and village life. In her walks, the saunterer is accompanied by Lizzy, the carpenter's daughter, a fascinating baby of three, who trudges by her side, and is a very entertaining companion. Descriptions of the country are dwelt on more frequently than descriptions of the people, but there is a capital sketch of Hannah Bint, — who showed great judgment in setting up as a dairy-woman when only twelve years old, — besides various short discourses on schoolboys, farmers, and the trades-people of the town. The scenes are laid in "shady yet sunny Berkshire, where the scenery, without rising into grandeur or breaking into wildness, is so peaceful, so cheerful, so varied, and so thoroughly English." The first series of sketches in 'Our Village' appeared in 1824.

OXFORD HISTORY OF MUSIC, THE, edited by W. H. Hadow (6 vols., 1901–05). The *motif* of the above volumes and the justification of their existence are well explained in the editor's preface. "The history of an art," he says, "like the history of a nation, is something more than a record of personal prowess and renown. The great artist has commonly inherited a wealth of past tradition and effort which it is at once his glory and his privilege to administer." Moreover of all the arts music has exhibited the most continuous evolution. Therefore there is every justification for a treatise, which deals with the art rather than the artist, which shall follow its progress through the interchanges of success and failure, of aspiration and attainment, which shall endeavor to illustrate from its peculiar conditions the truth of Emerson's profound saying, "that the greatest genius is the most indebted man." Of the six volumes the first two deal with the music of the Mediæval Church, from the rise of discant or measured music to the work of Palæstrina (d. 1594), the composer to the Papal Choir at Rome, and his successors. The third traces the evolution of music in the seventeenth century from Josquin and Arcadelt to Purcell; the fourth devotes special treatment to the works of Bach and Handel and the harmonic counterpoint characteristic of their time; the fifth has as its theme the rise and progress of the Viennese School, and the development of the great instrumental forms from Haydn to Schubert; the sixth and last discusses the formative influences which inspired Weber in the theatre, Schumann and Chopin in the concert room. To a later generation is left the task of assigning their due places in the history of music to Brahms and Wagner, Tschaikovsky and Dvořák and Richard Strauss and the still more difficult task of explaining and appraising the tendencies which supply the sole key to the interpretation of these composers. This work admittedly belongs to the same category as Grove's Dictionary, and like it should find a place in every well-chosen library.

OXFORD REFORMERS OF 1498, THE: JOHN COLET, ERASMUS, AND THOMAS MORE: A history of their Fellow-Work, by Frederic Seebohm (1867, 1887). A work not designed to offer biographies of the persons named, but to study carefully their joint work at Oxford. John Colet, a son of Sir Henry Colet, a wealthy merchant who had been more than once Lord Mayor of London, and was in favor at the court of Henry VII., had come home from study in Italy to Oxford in 1496; and, although he was not a Doctor, nor even a deacon preparing for full clerical dignity, he startled the conservatism of the church and the university by announcing a course of public free lectures on the epistles of Paul. It was a strikingly new departure, not only in the boldness of a layman giving lectures on religion, but in new views to be brought out. What was called the New Learning, starting from study of Greek, or the world's best literature, was taking root at Oxford. Two men of note, Grocyn and Linacre, who had learned Greek, were working hard to awaken at Oxford interest in the study of Greek. And among the young students Colet found one, not yet of age, who showed the finest type of English genius. He was called "Young Master More."

The fine quality of his intelligence was even surpassed by the sweetness of his spirit and the charm of his character. He was destined to be known as Sir Thomas More, one of the great historic examples of what Swift, and after him Matthew Arnold, called "sweetness and light." Colet was thirteen years older than More, but the two held close converse in matters of learning and humanity. They were Humanists, as the men of interest in all things human were called. Colet and More had been together at Oxford a year when a third Humanist appeared upon the scene in 1497, the year in which John Cabot discovered North America. This was Erasmus, who was already a scholar, after the manner of the time, in Latin. He came to Oxford to become a scholar in Greek. He was scarcely turned thirty, — just Colet's age, — and had not yet begun to make a great name. The story of the three men runs on to 1519, into the early dawn of the Lutheran Reformation. Colet becomes a Doctor and the Dean of St. Paul's Cathedral in London (1499), and on his father's death (1510), uses his inherited fortune to found St. Paul's School, in which 153 boys of any nation or country should be instructed in the world's best literature, Greek as well as Latin; and not monkish church Latin, but ancient classical Latin. Colet declared that the "corrupt Latin which the later blind world brought in, and which may be called Blotterature rather than Literature," should be "utterly banished and excluded." Erasmus wrote a work 'On the Liberal Education of Boys.' It was in line with the new learning, that Erasmus edited, and secured the printing of, the New Testament in Greek, hoping it would lead, as it later did, to an English version. He said of "the sacred Scriptures: I wish these were translated into all languages, so that they might be read and understood. I long that the husbandman should sing portions of them to himself as he follows the plow, that the weaver should hum them to the tune of his shuttle, that the traveler should beguile with their stories the tedium of his journey." It was in the same humanist spirit that More wrote his 'Utopia,' published in 1516, and embodying the visions of hope and progress floating before the eyes of the three "Oxford Reformers." More was about entering into the service of Henry VIII.; and he wrote the introduction or prefatory book of the 'Utopia,' for the express purpose of speaking out boldly on the social condition of the country and on the policy of the King.

PAGAN AND CHRISTIAN ROME, by Rudolfo Lanciani (1893). A most richly illustrated account of the changes at Rome, by which it was gradually transformed from a pagan to a Christian city. Discoveries recently made show that Christian teaching reached the higher classes at a very early date, and even penetrated to the palace of the Cæsars. Long before the time at which Rome is supposed to have favored Christianity, there had been built churches side by side with the temples of the old faith. Tombs also bear the same testimony to gains made by Christianity in important quarters. Great names in the annals of the empire are found to be those of members of the Christian body. The change in fact which was brought to maturity under Constantine was not a sudden and unexpected event. It was not a revolution. It had been a foregone conclusion for several generations, the natural result of progress during nearly three centuries. It had come to be understood before the official recognition of it by Constantine. A great deal that was a continuance of things pagan in appearance had in fact received Christian recognition and been turned to Christian use. Institutions and customs which still exist originated under the old faith, and were brought into the service of the new. Far more than has been supposed, the change was due to tolerance between pagans and Christians. By comparing pagan shrines and temples with Christian churches, imperial tombs with papal tombs, and pagan cemeteries with Christian, Lanciani at once discloses the wealth of art created in Rome, and proves that pagan and Christian were allied in its creation.

PAGE D'AMOUR, UNE, see **ROUGON-MACQUART.**

PAHLAVI TEXTS, see **SACRED BOOKS OF THE EAST.**

PAINTERS, see **LIVES OF THE PAINTERS,** by John Ruskin.

PAINTING, by Leonardo da Vinci, see **TREATISE ON.**

PAINTING, HISTORY OF, by Dr. Alfred Woltmann and Dr. Karl Woermann (English translation, with preface by Sidney Colvin. 2 vols., 1880). This monumental work of two great German savants is a fine example of German Gründlichkeit. The first volume, the work of Dr. Woltmann, deals exhaustively with the history of ancient, early Christian, and mediæval painting. The earliest works of known date in ancient Egypt; the tile-paintings of Assyria and Babylon; the vase-paintings, mosaics, miniatures, mural paintings, of ancient Greece and Rome; the beginnings of Christian art in the catacombs; the illuminated manuscripts of early mediæval Ireland; the miniatures, panel paintings and paintings on glass of the central mediæval period (950–1250); the transformation in the thirteenth century from Romanesque to Gothic influences; the predominance of Italy in the fourteenth century — all these are treated with fullness of detail, clarity, and an abundance of apt illustrations from originals. The second volume, by Dr. Woermann, is devoted to the Renascence, not in the sense merely of a Revival of Antiquity, but in the deeper signification of "a new birth of Nature; a resuscitation and restoration of Nature to the human soul," by which Nature was no longer regarded as sinful and reprobate, and Art gained the power of seeing things as they are. The glory of Flemish painting in the fifteenth century and of the Flemish and Dutch schools of the early sixteenth; Dürer, Cranach, and Holbein in the sixteenth century in Germany; the flowering of Italian art in the Renascence period and the exuberance of its golden age, the days of Leonardo, Michael Angelo, and Raphael, — such are the themes of the second volume, which is even more richly illustrated than the first.

PALACE OF PLEASURE, THE, by William Painter. This famous collection of tales was first published in 1566; and its great popularity is proved by the fact that six editions were issued within twenty years after its first appearance. 'The Palace of Pleasure' was the first English story-book that had for its object purely the amusement of readers, and it aroused to life imaginations which had been starved on theological discussions. The stories are translated, some from Livy's Latin or Plutarch's Greek, others from French translations of the original tongues; still others from the Italian collections of Boccaccio, Bandello, and Marguerite of Valois. They are admirably selected to represent the higher class of stories current at the time of the Italian Renaissance. They are simply told, without much of the morbidness of the Italian originals, and with all their beauty. There is no attempt at the conciseness which is now considered essential in a short story, but rather a tendency to dwell on details, — to make the sweetness long drawn out. The style has a delicate prettiness which does not take away from it sincerity and clearness.

Despite the great charm of the tales in themselves, the chief interest in them lies in the fact that the collection was used as a storehouse of plots by the Elizabethan dramatists. Shakespeare took from it the stories of 'Timon of Athens,' 'Romeo and Juliet,' 'The Rape of Lucrece,' and 'Giletta of Narbonne' (from which he gained the main plot of 'All's Well That Ends Well'). Webster found here the plot of 'The Duchess of Malfi'; and Marston, Shirley, and Peele, all took plots from these tales. Painter is responsible for many of the Italian scenes and names that fill the early plays, and for many of the fantastic situations. For these two reasons, then, Painter's book is interesting: for itself, as the first English story-book, and for its influence on others, as the source of many plots.

PALACE OF THE KING, IN THE, by F. Marion Crawford (1900). This story opens in the old Moorish palace to which King Philip the Second had brought his court when he finally made Madrid his capital. Don John of Austria (Philip's half-brother), who has just returned from the conquest of Granada, is deeply in love with the beautiful Maria Dolores de Mendoza. She has been forbidden by both her father and the king to marry him for reasons of state, but is determined to do so, and in this is abetted by her blind sister. After a struggle to overcome her father's opposition, Dolores is ordered to retire to a convent where she is to be imprisoned until after Don John shall have made another marriage. Dolores is locked into her chamber, from which she escapes disguised as her blind sister and seeks Don John in his apartment in the palace, in order to throw herself upon his protection. Thither come her father and the king, and high words ensue between the monarch and his half-brother. Philip in sudden anger draws his sword and seems to thrust Don John through the heart, and is then overcome by the realization of the consequences which such a deed must necessarily bring upon him. Old Mendoza, aware of the terrible position of the king, offers himself as a sacrifice, and before the courtiers assembled in the ball-room announces himself as the slayer of Don John. Mendoza is at once condemned to death, but Dolores who has been a concealed witness of the deed rushes to the king and succeeds in obtaining her father's release. Returning to the body of her lover she finds that he is still alive, his wound proving but a slight one. Then follows the marriage of the devoted lovers.

PALMERIN DE OLIVA is a romance of chivalry, a feeble imitation of 'Amadis of Gaul,' which was first published in Salamanca in 1511. It has generally been considered to be of Portuguese origin; but Ticknor, in his 'History of Spanish Literature,' asserts that the author of it was a carpenter's daughter in Burgos. This is one of the books against which Cervantes inveighs as responsible for the mental condition of Don Quixote; and in the famous scene of the burning of the books of chivalry, he says: "This Oliva, let it be hewn in pieces and burnt, and let not the very ashes be left." The hero was the grandson of a Greek emperor in Constantinople; but on account of his illegitimacy, was deserted by his mother and left on a mountain, where he was found in an osier cradle, among the olive and palm trees. He was named Palmerin de Oliva, from the place where he was found. He soon gives tokens of his high birth, and makes himself famous by his prowess against the heathen, enchanters, etc., in Germany, England, and the East. He at last reaches Constantinople, where he is recognized by his mother, and marries the daughter of the Emperor of Germany, who is the heroine of the story. A continuation by the same author called 'The Second Book of Palmerin,' which treats of the adventures of his sons, Primaleon and Polendos, appeared later.

PALMERIN OF ENGLAND ('Palmerin de Inglaterra'). This is a romance of chivalry, after the style of 'Amadis of Gaul,' and in this class of literature regarded as second only to it in point of merit. This is the book, which, with 'Amadis,' Cervantes saves from the holocaust in Don Quixote, as he says, "for two reasons: first, because it is a right good book in itself; and the other, because the report is that a wise King of Portugal composed it. All the adventures of the castle of Miraguarda are excellent, and managed with great skill; the discourses are clear, observing with much propriety the judgment and decorum of the speaker." It was long supposed to be the work of Francisco Moraes, a Portuguese, who published it in 1567 as a translation from the French. In 1807 Southey published an English translation, attributing the original to Moraes, and credited him with modesty in not claiming the authorship. It has since been found to have been the work of Leon Hurtado, and to have been published originally in Spanish, in Toledo, in 1547. In it are recounted the exploits of the son of Don Duarde, or Edward, King of England, and Flerida, a daughter of Palmerin de Oliva; consisting of jousts in tournaments, battles with giants and Saracens, and adventures in the Castle of Miraguarda. This story is in some respects a continuation of Palmerin de Oliva.

PAMELA, or, VIRTUE REWARDED, by Samuel Richardson, is the first work of fiction by an author who began what is called the modern analytic novel. It was published in 1740, and won instant applause and a wide circle of readers in all classes of society, women especially following with bated breath the shifting fortunes of Pamela Andrews. She is a serving-maid whom the son and heir of the family dishonorably pursues. She indignantly repels his advances and leaves the house, only to be followed by her tormentor. Finally, being truly in love with her, Mr. B—— decides to overlook their difference of station and marry her. The second part of the novel, which appeared the following year and narrates Pamela's life after this union, is less interesting. The story is told in the form of letters — a form used in all Richardson's fiction. The moral standard — which is that of English society in all the first half of the eighteenth century — seems to the modern reader disgraceful. Mr. B—— acts toward Pamela as only a profligate and rascal would to a girl of his own station; yet Pamela, in the true spirit of caste distinction, extols him, when he at last condescends to wed her, as not only the greatest but the best of men. There is much human nature, however, in the book; and the interest is strong and well maintained. Richardson did a new thing in novel-writing when he chose a girl of the humble class for heroine, and made use of every-day contemporaneous persons and scenes for the purposes of fiction. Thus the story of incident and the analysis of character came into English fiction; and thus the Modern Novel traces its development from Richardson.

PAN MICHAEL, see WITH FIRE AND SWORD.

PANAMA ('The Canal, The Country, The People'), by Arthur Bullard appeared first as successive articles in various magazines and was published in book form in 1911. In entertaining journalistic fashion the reader is conducted by steamer to Colon, with brief pauses at several of the West India Islands and picturesque descriptions of the scenes and incidents of the journey. The canal zone and its inhabitants are then depicted after which follows an entertainingly written account of the early history of the country from the days of Spanish discovery and colonization. The attempts of the French to build a canal and the revolution which established the Republic of Panama and gave the United States possession of the canal zone are next narrated; and the book closes with an account of the building and completion of the canal, a tribute to the Chief Engineer, Colonel, now General Goethals, and an interesting explanation of the extermination of yellow fever by the Chief Sanitary Officer, Colonel Gorgas. Relief and outline maps of the canal and the isthmus and photographs of men and places add to the value of the book.

PANDECTS, THE, of Justinian. This digest was an attempt to form a complete system of law from the commentaries of the great jurists on the Roman law. The work was done by a committee of seventeen famous lawyers; it was begun in 530 A. D. and completed in 533. The magnitude of the task becomes apparent when we hear that there are 9,123 extracts in the Pandects (the word " Pandects" is from the Greek Pandecton, which means all-receiving). The extracts were made from 2,000 treatises; one-third of them come from Ulpian, one-sixth from Paulus, and the rest from thirty-six other writers.

The Pandects, with the Codex Justinianus, became the law for the Roman Empire. When the Lombards invaded Italy in 568, they overturned almost all the few remaining Roman institutions, the law-courts among them. In Ravenna, however, the Roman law was still taught; and the Lombards allowed their Roman subjects to be judged according to the Roman law. The Codex, which begins with an invocation to the Trinity, and contains a great deal of legislation on ecclesiastical matters, was always held in esteem by the clergy; but the Pandects were ignored, as being the work of pagan jurists.

In the last part of the eleventh century there was a great revival of the study of Roman law. There has always been a tradition that this revival was caused by the discovery at Amalfi of a copy of the Pandects; but the Pandects had never been really forgotten. The revival of the Roman law was a kind of advance guard of the Renaissance movement. Irnerius of Bologna, the greatest teacher of his time, revived the study of the Pandects, which, together with the Codex, became the basis of all mediæval legislation.

In the Eastern, or Byzantine, Empire, the Pandects, under the name Basilica, were statute authority even down to 1453, when Constantinople was captured by the Turks.

In practice, however, it was superseded in the tenth century by Ezabiblos, which was to a slight degree an epitome of the Basilica. The Ezabiblos survived even the invasion of the Turks in some parts of the Empire, and was adopted as the statute law of the kingdom of Greece in 1835.

PAOLA AND FRANCESCA, by Stephen Phillips (1897). The play opens with the arrival of Francesca, "dreaming from her convent," escorted from Ravenna by the fair young Paolo to be the bride of the Lord of Rimini, the stern, serious Giovanni, in the "gray of life." It is the story of Dante retold, except that the author introduces an embittered widowed cousin, Lucrezia, who warns Giovanni that "Youth goes toward youth," and later conspires to betray Paolo and Francesca. The aged nurse sees in second sight the woe that Destiny is bringing. "Unwillingly he comes a wooing: she unwillingly is wooed: yet shall they woo. His kiss was on her lips ere she was born." Paolo struggles loyally against his growing fatal passion for Francesca. He implores his brother to allow him to leave Rimini to join his troops starting at daybreak for war, but Giovanni commands him to be present at the marriage feast, and Francesca innocently entreats Paolo not to leave her alone among strangers. They meet and love, and Giovanni is told of their meetings by the watchful Lucrezia. His heart is torn between the remembrance of his affection for his younger brother and his jealous hatred for his betrayer. Paolo resolves to put an end to his life with poison but to look once more on Francesca. Francesca turns to Lucrezia and in a touching scene asks her to be a mother to her; and the childless Lucrezia at last loves her, and tries to save her, but it is too late. Paolo finds Francesca alone in spite of Lucrezia's precautions, and in an ecstasy of love they defy fate. Giovanni returns and kills them locked in each other's arms.

PARADISE LOST, an epic poem by John Milton, published in 1667, is in style the loftiest and in subject the most sublime of all epics since Homer and Virgil. It preserves for modern readers the stately dignity of classical verse and the Puritan view of the relations between God and Man. It abounds in the most powerful delineations of character, the most exquisite imagery, and the most delicate and varied metrical effects and verbal felicities. Every line reflects the personality of a poet somewhat hard and austere but inspiring in his devotion to purity and duty. That the poem is now seldom read as a whole is due to the fact that its theology does not satisfy our age, that when Satan is withdrawn from the scene our interest flags, and that long paraphrases of Scripture make the closing books tedious.

The subject of 'Paradise Lost' is the Fall of Man, its causes and consequences. This is a theme which not only embraces the entire history of the world but extends from a period before the world's creation until after its dissolution. Yet in treating this vast subject Milton has reduced every part to due proportions and has related it clearly to the central action; and in accordance with the practice of the classical epic poets he has obtained variety by departing from temporal sequence and by delegating part of the story to characters in the poem instead of narrating it in his own person. Thus he opens not with the rebellion of Satan, which imitates the whole action, but with the moment of his recovery after his defeat and fall from Heaven to Hell. From this point the story is conducted in unbroken sequence through the first four books. Satan and the other fallen angels rise from the burning lake and assemble in a powerful army. After addressing his troops in a spirit of resolute defiance against God he summons their leaders (afterwards the gods of the heathen) to a council in the newly-erected palace of Pandemonium (Book I). Their deliberations as to further war result in Satan's undertaking to discover the newly-created world and to seduce its inhabitants to rebellion. At the gates of Hell, Satan is checked by two horrible guardians, Sin and Death, his own unnatural progeny; but he placates them with the promise of abundant prey in the event of success in his mission; and after a perilous journey through chaos he arrives on the opaque outer surface of the mundane universe (Book II; for the cosmographic scheme, see the LIBRARY, under 'Milton'). Observing this flight, God the Father informs the Son and the good angels of the coming success of Satan's enterprise and of the necessity of a redeemer for Man. This office is freely accepted by God the Son. Meanwhile Satan, disguised as an angel of light, enters the universe, wings his way to the Sun, inquires of the archangel Uriel, its guardian, the way to the Earth, and flying thither alights on Mount Niphates (Book III). Here in soliloquy he finally renounces good for evil and then entering Paradise observes in various disguises the happiness of Adam and Eve and makes an attempt to corrupt the latter by means of a dream, but is foiled by a band of guardian angels under the archangel Gabriel (Book IV).

This is the finest part of the poem, the most striking and original in its incidents, the richest in simile, metaphor, and allusion and the most delightful in word-pictures.

In the next four books Milton takes advantage of the pause just reached to turn back, explain the causes of Satan's fall from Heaven, and describe the creation of the world. This information he does not impart in his own person but puts it into the mouth of the archangel Raphael, who has been sent by God to warn Adam and Eve against disobedience, and to answer their inquiries. He tells of the original revolt of Satan and his followers against God's conferring of supreme authority upon the Son, and of the bravery of Abdiel in reproving his rebellious fellows (Book V); of their three days' battle with Michael and the good angels, ended by the intervention of the Son of God, who drove the rebels over the battlements of Heaven and pursued them with thunder to the place of punishment provided for them (Book VI); of the creation of the world by the decree of the Father and by the operation of the Son in order that its inhabitants might ultimately attain Heaven in the place of the fallen angels (Book VII). In the eighth book, to give further variety to the method of narration, the creation of Eve and the injunction against eating of the tree of the knowledge of good and evil are recounted to the archangel, by Adam himself; and by warning Adam against inordinate desire for knowledge, and inordinate affection for Eve, Raphael foreshadows the coming catastrophe and puts him on his guard against it.

In these four books the interest of the poem somewhat falls off, owing partly to the materialistic character of the war in Heaven, partly to the fact that Book VII follows the narrative of Genesis too closely, and partly to the absence of Satan from this and the following book.

The last four books relate the catastrophe and its consequences. In Book IX Eve, who has a touch of wilfulness, resolves, against the advice of Adam, to work in the garden by herself. Satan, taking the form of a serpent, tells her that he, the serpent, has obtained the power of speech by eating of the tree of knowledge of good and evil, and assures Eve that by following his example she will attain a similar increase of power and enlightenment. Convinced by his specious arguments that disobedience will be no sin in this case, she eats the fruit, and in the ensuing false sense of exaltation urges Adam to eat also. Though he realizes her delusion Adam complies out of love for her, choosing to disobey God and perish with her; but after eating he shares in her intoxication and approves of her crime, thus making it his own. Book X relates the condemnation of the guilty pair by the Son of God, and the arrival in the Universe of Sin and Death, who have followed in Satan's wake, building a causeway from Hell to the World, and who proceed to destroy much of the fertility and beauty of creation. Satan, whose future punishment has been foretold by God the Son, receives earnest of it, when at the moment of his announcement of victory to his followers in Hell, he and they are temporarily transformed to serpents. In Books XI and XII, on the occasion of expelling Adam and Eve from Paradise, God sends the Archangel Michael to inform them that their punishment will finally be removed by the sacrifice of the Son of God. Michael then reveals to Adam, first by a series of visions, and then by narration, the effect of his sin upon the course of history from the murder of Abel to the Second Advent. Comforted by the assurance of ultimate restoration Adam and Eve are expelled from Paradise.

This final section of the poem often attains the epic grandeur of the first books. The narrative of the Fall is marked by the re-appearance of extended similes. The arrival of Sin and Death and the transformation of Satan are finely conceived. The prophetic outline of the world's history is prosaic; but the account of Adam's and Eve's expulsion from Paradise by the flaming sword is one of the greatest artistic triumphs in literature.

PARADISE REGAINED, an epic in four books, published in 1671, is not a sequel of Paradise Lost,' which includes in its scope the recovery of Paradise, but the development into brief epic form of an episode which Milton considers essential to that recovery. This event is not the passion of Christ, nor his resurrection, but his temptation. This made clear the Saviour's perfect obedience to God, which not only counterbalanced Adam's disobedience but also showed that Christ was ready for the sacrifice necessary to atone for Adam's sin. Milton adheres to the main outline of St. Luke's account of the temptation, using less ornate and figurative language than in 'Paradise Lost,' but adding long descriptions and much detail foreign to the simple Biblical narrative. Satan's appearance as an old pilgrim in the desert is dramatically set forth; the temptation to turn stones into bread is supplemented by the laying out of a sumptuous banquet fit for a Roman epicure; and the view from the mountain is made the occasion of a fine description of the Roman Empire in Christ's day. Milton's Arianism appears in the words of God the Father with reference to the Saviour: "This perfect man *by merit called my son*." The poet's hardness and austerity are reflected in the somewhat cold and unsympathetic personality of Christ as presented by him. Though absolutely characteristic of its author the poem, on account of its severity and restraint, has never been as popular as 'Paradise Lost.'

PARADYSE OF DAYNTY DEVISES, THE. This quaint old book is set forth as "conteyning sundry pithy preceptes, learned counsels, and excellent inventions, right pleasant and profitable for all estates." It is a collection of sixteenth century poetry, by M. Edwardes, W. Hunnis, the Earl of Oxford, R. Hill, Saint Barnarde, Lord Vaux, Jasper Haywood, D. Sand, F. Kindlemarsh, M. Yloop, Thomas Churchyard, and various anonymous writers. There were editions published in 1576, '77, '78, '80, '85, '96, 1600, and 1606. A reprint was made in 1810, by Sir Egerton Brydges, and again in 1865, by J. P. Collier. The last was made from Heber's unique copy of the 1578 edition. This collection is especially interesting, because it contains poems not in any other impression. A poem headed 'No Pleasure Without Some Payn' is assigned to Sir Walter Raleigh, and one by George Whetston occurs in this volume which is nowhere else to be found. It was very popular, and the name has been used for similar but less valuable miscellanies.

PARIS IN AMERICA ('Paris en Amerique'), by Édouard René Lefebvre Laboulaye. This satirical romance was first published in 1863. Through the wonderful adventures of a Parisian doctor of the conventional type, who with his whole family is spirited away to America by a sorcerer, Laboulaye sets forth an amusing contrast between many customs and institutions of the New World and those of his own "belle France." The whimsical conceit of this old Frenchman suddenly become in appearance and environment an American, while retaining his memory and his hereditary prejudices and opinions, serves Laboulaye as a means of expressing himself pungently on many points wherein his own country might well learn of a younger nation.

The first bewildering change which greets the metamorphosed physician is the exceeding comfort of his household arrangements, with the unfamiliar baths and heating apparatus; the next is the affectionate and unrestrained attitude of his wife and children. A thunderbolt falls upon him when he finds his daughter engaged to a man who has not previously asked his consent, and who makes absolutely no inquiries about a dot. An equal surprise is the career of his son, who at sixteen chooses a business, finds an opening, and departs, like a man for the Indies.

Then in a succession of humorously interesting chapters the author takes his hero through the civil world of America as it was in the sixties; he makes him a volunteer fireman, shows him the inner workings of the free American Press, initiates him into the bitter knowledge of what it is to be a candidate for office. And the whole is told with the would-be grumbling tone of an old fellow who wants to believe in the superiority of his adored country in every particular over this "land of savages."

But alas when the sorcery is undone, and the Parisian reawakes in fair Paris, with an unmistakable French family about him, he would fain have remained under the enchantment. His son is no longer self-reliant; his daughter blushes and is shocked to tears at his suggestion that she shall marry the man of her heart; and his wife is indignant that he should suppose his daughter so ill-bred as to have a choice. There is a keen reproach for France in the mockery of the finale, which pictures the doctor in an asylum, where in the estimation of his countrymen, his strange ideas fit him to be an inmate.

PARLIAMENTARY NOVELS, by Anthony Trollope. These are: 'Phineas Finn,' 'Phineas Redux,' 'The Prime Minister,' and 'The Duke's Children.' Trollope tells us in his autobiography that in 'Phineas Finn' he began a series of semi-political tales, because, being debarred from expressing his opinions in the House of Commons, he could thus declare his convictions. He says: "I was conscious that I could not make a tale pleasing chiefly by politics. If I wrote politics for my own sake, I must put in love, sport, and intrigue, for the benefit of my readers. In writing 'Phineas Finn' I had constantly before me the need of progression in character, — of marking the changes naturally produced by the lapse of years. I got around me a circle of persons as to whom I knew not only their present characters, but how they would be affected by time and circumstance." 'Phineas Finn' was completed in May, 1867, and its sequel, 'Phineas Redux,' not until 1873. The former traces the career of an Irishman, young and attractive, who goes to London to enter Parliament, leaving behind his boyish sweetheart, Mary Flood-Jones. He is admired by many, especially by Lady Laura Standish, who is succeeded by another love, Violet Effingham, and she by a charming widow, Marie Max-Goesler. In time he gives up politics, goes home, and becomes Inspector of Poor-Houses in County Cork. Trollope says: "I was wrong to marry him to a girl who could only be an incumbrance on his return to the world, and I had no alternative but to kill her." Phineas Redux goes back to Parliament, has more sentimental experiences, and makes a still higher reputation. A political enemy of Phineas is murdered, and he is accused of the crime, but is acquitted, largely through the efforts of Marie Max-Goesler. 'The Prime Minister' is chiefly devoted to the unhappy marriage of Emily Wharton and Ferdinand Lopez, a Portuguese adventurer, and to the affairs of the prime minister and his wife. The latter couple are known to readers of Trollope's earlier novels as Planty Paul and Lady Glencora, now Duke and Duchess of Omnium. The duke is sensitive, proud, and shy, and feels the burden of his responsibility, while his wife is forever working for his advancement. He goes gladly out of office at last. We hear little of Phineas Finn, save that his second marriage is happy, and that he is made Secretary for Ireland and then Lord of the Admiralty. Trollope tells us that the personages of these books are more or less portraits, not of living men, but of living political characters. 'The Prime Minister' is his ideal statesman. He says: "If my name be still known in the next century, my success will probably rest on the characters of Plantagenet Palliser and Lady Glencora." This volume was published in 1876, and the series was finished in 1880 with 'The Duke's Children.' This opens with the death of the duchess, and relates the further history of her children. The duke's sons and daughter are a deep disappointment to him. His heir, Lord Silverbridge, is dismissed from college, and enters Parliament as a Conservative, whereas the family has always been Liberal. His daughter insists upon marrying a poor commoner, and his heir upon marrying an American girl, while his younger son is idle and extravagant. In the end, however, he accepts the choice of his children, and the book closes with his return to politics. Phineas Finn and his wife reappear in these pages, he still devoted to politics, and she the faithful friend of the duke and his daughter.

PARLIAMENTARY REFORM, a volume of essays, by Walter Bagehot, appeared in 1884. Its most striking and valuable feature as permanent literature is the historical review of the function of "rotten boroughs," from the accession of the Hanoverian dynasty to their abolition by the Reform Bill of 1832. He does not share the popular disgust for them, though he admits that by 1832 they had survived their usefulness. He shows that the system amounted simply to giving the great Whig families a preponderating power in Parliament, which for many years was the chief bulwark against a restoration of the Stuarts, the small squires and the Church being so uneasy at casting off the old house that there was always danger of their taking it back. See also 'English Constitution,' by Walter Bagehot.

PAST AND PRESENT, by Thomas Carlyle. This treatise was published in England in April, 1843; in May it was published in America, prefaced by an appealing notice to publishers, written by Ralph Waldo Emerson, to the effect that the book was printed from a manuscript copy sent by the author to his friends, and was published for the benefit of the author. Mr. Emerson somewhat optimistically hoped that this fact would "incline publishers to respect Mr. Carlyle's property in his own book."

'Past and Present' was written in seven weeks, as a respite from the harassing labor of writing 'Cromwell.' In 1842, the Camden Society had published the 'Chronicles of the Abbey of St. Edmund's Bury,' written by Joceline de Brakelonde, at the close of the twelfth century. This account of a mediæval monastery had taken Carlyle's fancy; and in 'Past and Present' he contrasted the England of his own day with the England of Joceline de Brakelonde. Englishmen of his own day he divided into three classes: the laborers, the devotees of Mammon, and the disciples of dilettanteism. Between these three classes, he said, there was no tie of human brotherhood. In the old days the noble was the man who fought for the safety of society. For the dilettantes and the Mammonites he preached the "Gospel of Work." For the uplifting of the class of laborers, for the strengthening of the tie of human brotherhood, he proposed what seemed chimerical schemes in 1843; but before his death some of his schemes had been realized. He attacked the "laissez faire" principle most fiercely; he advocated legislative interference in labor, sanitary and educational legislation, an organized emigration service, some system of profit-sharing, and the organization of labor.

In 1843, 'Past and Present' was regarded as forceful, rousing, but not practical. It had, however, a great effect on the young and enthusiastic; and is now looked on as one of the best of Carlyle's books, and as the expression of a political philosophy which, however violently expressed, was at bottom sensible and practical.

PASTON LETTERS. This is a most interesting and valuable collection of letters, written in the reigns of Henry VI., Edward IV., Richard III., and Henry VII. They were handed down in the Paston family, till the male line became extinct in 1732, and eventually came into the hands of Sir John Ferris, who first published them.

He brought out two quarto volumes in 1787, two in 1789, and left material for a fifth, which appeared in 1823. He gave the letters in two forms, one an exact copy, retaining the old and variable spelling, the other with the spelling modernized, and obsolete or obscure words explained. He also prefixed to the separate letters valuable historical notices, and subjoined facsimiles of the seals and signatures. These quartos were, however, very expensive; so in 1840, Ramsay brought out a popular edition with some corrections and condensations: more recently other editions have appeared.

The letters themselves present very clearly the manner of life and thought of the middle classes during the Wars of the Roses. They incidentally throw light on historical personages and events; but their chief concern is with the everyday affairs of the Paston family of Norfolk. They show how exclusively the wars involved the nobility and their retainers, and how the commoners carried on their affairs undisturbed by bloody battles and subsequent beheadings. We learn from the letters of the dress, food, and social customs of the day, and some things appear strange to us, — as the great formality of address, and the humble deference shown to parents by their children and to husbands by their wives; but we are chiefly impressed by the fundamental fact that human nature was then very much what it is now.

PASTOR FIDO, IL, by Giovanni Battista Guarini. This pastoral drama, which was first produced in 1585, is the masterpiece of the author, and its influence can be seen in all subsequent literature of this class. It is a most highly finished work, after the style of Tasso's 'Aminta,' but lacks its simplicity and charm. It ran through forty editions during the author's life, and was translated into almost all modern languages. The scene is laid in Arcadia, where a young maiden is sacrificed annually to the goddess Diana. The people can be freed from this tribute only when two mortals, descendants of the gods, are united by love, and the great virtue of a faithful shepherd shall atone for the sins of an unfaithful woman. To fulfill this condition, Amarilli, who is descended from the god Pan, is betrothed to Silvio, the son of Montano, the priest of Diana, and a descendant of Hercules. Silvio's only passion is for hunting; and he flees from Amarilli, who is beloved by Mirtillo, the supposed son of Carino, who for a long time has lived away from Arcadia. Amarilli reciprocates the love of Mirtillo, but fears to acknowledge it, as falseness to her vow to Silvio would entail death. Corisca, also in love with Mirtillo, learns of it, and by a trick brings them together and denounces them. Amarilli is condemned to death; and Mirtillo, availing himself of a custom allowed, is to be sacrificed in her place, when Carino arrives, and Mirtillo is found to be the son of Montano. In his infancy he was carried away in his cradle by a flood, and had been adopted by Carino. As his name is also Silvio, it is decided that Amarilli in marrying him will not break the vow which she had made to Silvio, and by this marriage the decree of the oracle will be fulfilled.

PATHFINDER, THE, see **LEATHERSTOCKING TALES.**

PATIENCE, see **PEARL.**

PATRINS, by Louise Imogen Guiney (1897), is a collection of twenty short essays on things of the day, with one disquisition on King Charles II. The little papers are called 'Patrins,' from the Romany word signifying the handfuls of scattered leaves by which the gipsies mark the way they have passed; Miss Guiney's road through the thought-country being marked by these printed leaves. The essays are distinctly literary in form and feeling; the style is grace itself; the matter airy yet subtle, whimsical and quite out of the common. 'On the Delights of an Incognito,' 'On Dying as a Dramatic Situation,' 'An Open Letter to the Moon,' 'A Bitter Complaint of an Ungentle Reader,' are some of the fantastic and alluring titles. 'An Inquirendo into the Wit and Other Good Parts of his Late Majesty King Charles the Second' attempts for the Merry Monarch what Froude attempted for Henry VIII. The piece is in the form of a dialogue between a holder of the generally accepted view of the Second Charles's character, and a devoted admirer of that sovereign, who wears a sprig of green in his hat on the anniversary of the Restoration, and feeds the swans in St. James's Park, because his Majesty once loved to do so. This apologist considers Charles II. as the last sovereign with a mind; and for that merit, he can find it in his heart to forgive much to that cynical and humorous gentleman.

PATRIOT, THE ('Piccolo mondo antico') by Antonio Fogazzaro (1896) is the first of a trilogy introducing the Maironi family, Franco and Luisa, the father and mother of Piero Maironi, who is the "Sinner" in 'Piccolo mondo moderno,' and becomes the "Saint" in 'Il Santo.' The scene of 'The Patriot' is Valsolda on the beautiful Lake Lugano, during the years of Austrian oppression preceding United Italy. The story is the conflict between the religious nature of Franco and the scepticism of his wife, Luisa, which later accounts for the warring elements in the temperament of their son. Franco is cast out by his wicked old grandmother, the Marchesa Maironi, because he will marry the lovely Luisa, who, as the daughter of a teacher, is not his equal in rank or fortune. His strength is blind faith in the religion and practice of the Catholic Church. On the eve of his departure to Piedmont to join the patriots, Luisa confesses to him her rationalist beliefs. Their devoted love for each other does not fail but they are separated in spirit by their different views of life. They have one child, Maria, whom they adore. The child is drowned, and Luisa's grief almost destroys her reason. Franco returns too late to see his child, and is nearly captured by Austrian spies. As the war for freedom begins, Luisa is persuaded to leave the grave of her child to say goodbye to her husband. The vision of war and death to come brings her to herself, and the child is conceived who is to fight the battle of the modern world.

THE SINNER ('Piccolo mondo moderno') (1901) begins when this child, Piero, is a man. He is bound to an insane wife, but loves a beautiful married woman, Jeanne Dessalle, who is separated from her vicious husband. His conscience forbids this intrigue while his reason claims his right to happiness. In Piero, the profound faith of his father strives against the intellectual unbelief of his mother. Even while he resolves to "travel the path of an apostate in the cause of social justice," he has mystic premonitions of some high spiritual destiny. He considers giving up the world for the ascetic life, but has chosen Jeanne instead when he is summoned from her to his wife's death-bed. Elisa, his young wife, recovers her reason in this last hour, and he is overwhelmed with love and conviction of sin. In a night vigil in the chapel, adjoining the asylum, he has a prophetic vision of his future life as a servant of God. He gives away his property and disappears from the world and Jeanne. The nobility of the provincial town with their shabby liveries and petty household economies, the smart set who attend the reception at the Villa Dessalle and the household dependents are interesting types of modern Italian society.

THE SAINT ('Il Santo') (1901). After three years, Jeanne's husband is dead, and she searches for her lost lover. She finds him as Benedetto, a humble lay brother at a Benedictine monastery. He has served his apprenticeship of penance and fasting, and spends nights on the mountain in prayer, already the "Saint" who is to reform the Catholic church. His unorthodox views drive him from the monastery to the hills of Jenne, where he becomes known as the "Saint of Jenne" for his good deeds and holy life. The superstitious peasants hail him as a miracle worker; pilgrimages are made to his hermitage; and his notoriety rouses the jealousy of the priests who drive him forth again. In Rome he finds disciples and friends among the liberal Christian democrats. Of this group, Don Clemente, his beloved confessor of the monastery is a leading spirit, and Selva, a writer on Catholic theology the leading intellect. He preaches mediæval faith with the accepted truths of science, and emphasis on the essential and eternal in religion, right living as more important even than right belief, or practice of devotion. He has a dramatic interview with the Pope, in which he denounces the four spirits of evil in the church, the spirits of falsehood, of clericalism, of avarice, and of immobility, and tries to persuade the Pope to leave the Vatican. The Pope is sympathetic and friendly, but points out that he has few saints in his church but many Scribes and Pharisees to reckon with, and is powerless to help him. The clericals of the Vatican are disturbed, and make terms with the government in the matter of an episcopal nomination, on condition the government will get the troublesome Maironi out of Rome. Pressure is brought to bear on those who give him shelter. Jeanne, sternly forbidden his presence, protects him through her friends. Broken in health by the severity of his mortifications of the flesh, he escapes persecution only in death, at the house of a friend, Professor Mayda, an agnostic. On his death-bed he sends for Jeanne and holds out to her his crucifix, which she accepts as a sign of her adoption of his faith. The novel attracted great attention as a conscientious and devoted endeavor to present in fiction the attempt to reconcile Roman Catholicism with modern science and to reform the Church.

LEILA (1910). Leila, a high-spirited girl, is the adopted daughter and heiress of Signor Marcello, to whose son she had been betrothed. He had wished to have her constantly with him in memory of his dead son, and had bought her from her sordid disreputable father. Leila was glad to escape from the home of her father, ruled over by a vulgar housekeeper, though it was a severe trial to her pride to enter her new home "as a thing bought and paid for." As the story opens Signor Marcello is expecting a guest, Massimo Alberti, a young Milanese doctor, his son's intimate friend. After he sees the young man he forms the opinion that Massimo would be a desirable and suitable husband for Leila, whom he dreads to leave to the mercies of her parents in the event of his own death, which he believes to be close at hand. Massimo falls in love with Leila, but is scorned by her as a fortune hunter brought by Signor Marcello to woo the heiress. She considers herself the victim of a plot and will have none of him, refusing to own to herself that she loves him. Signor Marcello dies suddenly and as Leila is a minor her obnoxious father arrives to take possession. The priests scheme to induce Leila to retire to a convent and thus divert her money to the Church. Donna Fedele, the friend of the family, and of Massimo, succeeds in convincing the proud wayward Leila of her mistaken judgment of Massimo. Overcome with remorse for her treatment of her lover, Leila runs away to join him at Valsolda, and offers herself to him. Donna Fedele gives up the surgical operation which would prolong her life to follow her and chaperone her protégés until the marriage can take place. As in other works by this author, there is a vivid religious background, in which the doubts and beliefs of each character are set forth. Massimo was a favorite disciple of Benedetto, "the Saint," but like Leila nearly loses his faith in the Church because of the unworthiness of some of its members. The last chapter

is the burial of Benedetto beside his parents at Valsolda. Jeanne Desalle attends the
funeral service.

PATRONAGE, by Maria Edgeworth (1814). This novel was written for a purpose;
and the moral is apparent throughout, and amply illustrated in almost every character in the book.

Mr. Percy, a sensible English gentleman of the present time, brings up his sons
and daughters to depend upon themselves for success in life, and not upon the
patronage of influential persons. The result is most gratifying: the sons all succeed
in their different professions by their own efforts, and the daughters marry well
through no efforts of their own, but according to their merits. Mr. Falconer, Mr.
Percy's ambitious cousin, also has a large family; but he seeks the patronage of Lord
Oldborough to further the advancement of his sons, and uses various diplomatic
means to establish his daughters well in the social world. In spite of the unceasing
efforts of Mr. Falconer, and the decidedly questionable proceedings of his wife, none
of their children do them credit; and patronage without earnestness of purpose and
high ideals proves a failure.

PATTY, by Katherine S. Macquoid (1871), is a story of English middle-class contemporary life. Patty Westropp, the pretty and ambitious daughter of a gardener
inherits a fortune, changes her name, attends a fashionable French school, and presently emerges from her chrysalis state a fine lady. Her beauty and her money
enable her to marry an English gentleman of good family; and the chief interest of
the story lies in the complications which spring from the contact of a nature ruled by
crass selfishness and vulgar ambition, with nobler and more sensitive spirits. The
character study is always good, and the novel entertaining.

PAUL AND VIRGINIA, a novel by Bernardin de Saint-Pierre, was published in 1788.
The scene is Port Saint Louis in Isle de France, now Mauritius, and the story is
narrated to a visitor by one of the colonists, a friend of the persons concerned. In a
beautiful wooded valley lived two women, each with her child and servant, and each
in her own cottage, but cultivating the land jointly and living on terms of the closest
intimacy. One of these women was Madame de la Tour, a widow disowned by her
noble family in France for marrying beneath her. She had a daughter, Virginia, born
after the death of her husband, and a negro slave-woman, Marie, married to the
negro, Domingo, the farm laborer of the two properties and the slave of Marguerite,
the owner of the other cottage. Marguerite is a Breton peasant girl betrayed by her
lover, and has sought refuge from slander in this distant colony. Her child, Paul,
completes this little circle, which lives in idyllic peace and content. Strongly influenced by Rousseau's 'Émile,' the author paints an existence of ideal simplicity,
in which the elders support themselves by wholesome labor and the children grow up
in innocent, healthy activity, ignorant of books, but skilled in useful arts, in knowledge
of the external world, in admiration for the gorgeous scenery of the island, and in an
atmosphere of natural piety and affection. The domestic scenes, and the episode
of the children's wandering through the forest on a humanitarian errand and losing
their way, are prettily narrated. Rousseau's 'Nouvelle Héloïse' furnishes the suggestion for the scenes of passion and renunciation which follow and for the emotional
and pictorial descriptions of nature with which they are surrounded. As the children
grow up they begin to feel an affection for one another different from the brotherly
and sisterly feeling of their earlier years. The mothers notice this and discuss their

marriage, which Madame de la Tour would defer until the children are older. Word now comes from France that Madame de la Tour's aunt, to whom she had formerly applied in vain for assistance, is willing to forgive her and to make Virginia her heir. At the urgent advice of the governor of the island M. de la Bourdonnais and of her confessor Mme. de la Tour accepts the offer, and after declaring her love for Paul and promising to be his wife, Virginia sails for France. In a year and a half she writes that her aunt has sent her to a convent to be educated and keeps her under severe restrictions. More than two years later a French ship is sighted and a message comes in the pilot's boat from Virginia that she has been disinherited by her aunt for refusing a marriage arranged for her and is now on board the ship and immediately to return to her mother and Paul. But a hurricane wrecks the ship before it can land, and Virginia, refusing to remove her clothes or accept the aid of a naked sailor who offers to take her to shore, is washed overboard and drowned. In attempting to swim out to her, Paul is hurled back upon the beach, wounded and senseless. He recovers, but all efforts to comfort him are vain; and two months after the death of Virginia he himself dies of grief, soon followed by his mother, and by Virginia's. The death of the old negro couple leaves only the aged settler, who tells the story and who was the intimate friend of both families, to keep alive their memory. For the modern reader the book is spoiled by a tendency to sentimentality, an absence of realism, a reliance on theatrical effects, an excessive penchant for moralizing, and the prudery of the motive responsible for Virginia's death. There is nevertheless a simple attractiveness about the youthful figures, set off by the romantic beauty of the tropical scenery and the passionate intensity of their love.

PAUL CLIFFORD, by Bulwer-Lytton (1830). Lord Lytton's object in 'Paul Clifford' was to appeal for an amelioration of the British penal legislation, by illustrating to what criminal extremes the ungraded severity of the laws was driving men who by nature were upright and honest. To quote from Clifford's well-known defense when before the judges: "Your laws are of but two classes: the one makes criminals, the other punishes them. I have suffered by the one — I am about to perish by the other. . . . Your legislation made me what I am! and it now destroys me, as it has destroyed thousands, for being what it made me." The scene of the story is laid in London and the adjoining country, at a period shortly preceding the French Revolution. Paul, a child of unknown parentage, is brought up by an old innkeeper among companions of very doubtful character. Arrested for a theft of which he is innocent, he is sentenced to confinement among all sorts of hardened criminals. He escapes, and quickly becomes the chief of a band of highwaymen. In the midst of a career of lawlessness, he takes residence at Bath under the name of Captain Clifford and falls desperately in love with a young heiress, Lucy Brandon, who returns his affection; but realizing the gulf which lies between them, he resolutely takes leave of her after confessing vaguely who and what he is. Shortly after this he robs, partly through revenge, Lord Mauleverer, a suitor for the hand of Lucy, and intimate friend of her uncle and guardian, Sir William Brandon, a lawyer of great note, recently elevated to the peerage and soon to be preferred to the ministry. Brandon has had, by a wife now long since lost and dead, a child which was stolen from him in its infancy. His secret lifework has been to find and rehabilitate that child, and so preserve the family name of Brandon. As a result of the robbery, two of Paul's associates are captured. He succeeds in liberating them by means of a daring attack, but is himself wounded and taken prisoner. Judge Brandon presides at the trial. At the moment when he is to pronounce the death sentence, a scrap of paper is passed him revealing the fact that the condemned is his own son. Appalled at the disgrace which will tarnish his brilliant reputation, he pronounces the death sentence, but a few minutes afterward is found dead in his carriage. The paper on his person reveals the story, and Clifford is transported for life. He effects his escape, however, and together with Lucy, flees to America, where his latter days are passed in probity and unceasing philanthropic labors.

PEARL, a poem of the fourteenth century, a link between the 'Canterbury Tales' and the work of the early Saxon poets, Cædmon and Cynewulf, was written by a contemporary of Chaucer, whose name is unknown. Hidden from the world of letters for many centuries, this jewel of old-English verse appeared in modern setting in 1891. The edition is the work of Israel Gollancz of Christ's College, Cambridge. Prefixed to it is the following quatrain by Tennyson: —

> "We lost you — for how long a time —
> True pearl of our poetic prime!
> We found you, and you gleam reset
> In Britain's lyric coronet."

A manuscript of the Cottonian collection at Oxford contains 'Pearl,' with three other poems, — 'Gawain,' 'Cleanness,' and 'Patience,' — each a gateway into the visionary or romantic world of the fourteenth century. In the opinion of the editor, all four poems are by the same unknown author, and antedate Chaucer's work. The intervening centuries have swept away every evidence of this author's name and place; but his works reflect a vivid personality, making himself seen even through the abstractions of mediæval allegory. The editor endeavors to trace the outlines of this personality, guided, as he says, by "mere conjecture and inference." There is no decisive evidence whether 'Gawain' or 'Pearl' was the first written of the four poems; the editor believes, however, that 'Gawain' was first. Its date is approximately determined by the connection the editor traces between the Gawain romances, so popular in the fourteenth century, and the origin of the Order of the Garter. In the poem 'Gawain,' a fair young knight of Arthur's Round Table is protected in a combat with the Green Knight by a mystic girdle, the gift of his hostess, the wife of the Green Knight. In the three days preceding the combat, she had tempted him three times, and three times he had resisted the temptation. To reward him for his chastity, the Green Knight permits him to keep the mystic circlet, and to wear it as an honorable badge, as well as a protection from injury. In the editor's opinion, these incidents of the poem refer directly to the adventure of King Edward III. with the Countess of Salisbury, and to the subsequent founding of the Order of the Garter. The contemporary poets thus sought to honor the King by comparing him with Gawain, the very flower of courtesy and purity; the conception of Gawain as a false knight "light in life" belonging to a later day.

To pass from 'Gawain' to 'Pearl' is to pass from earthly to heavenly romance. 'Gawain' reflects the gay chivalry of the fourteenth century, 'Pearl' its disposition to see visions and to dream dreams. Before Chaucer, the Muse of English verse had closed eyelids. A brilliant example of the mediæval dream-poem is found in 'Pearl.' It is an ancient 'In Memoriam,' a lyric of grief for the poet's dead child Margaret; and it finds its truest counterpart in the "delicate miniatures of mediæval missals, steeped in richest colors and bright with gold." The poem consists partly of a Lament over the loss of a gem too fair to be hidden in earth, and partly of a Vision of the child's bliss with God. Throughout, the symbol of the Pearl is used the type of Margaret, the type also of perfect holiness. The 'Vision' is rich in gorgeous imagery, as if the poet had drawn his inspiration from the Apocalypse. He is carried in spirit to a land of unearthly beauty, where he beholds his daughter clothed in shining garments sown with pearls. She tells him of her happiness, reveals to him the heavenly Jerusalem, and so comforts him that he becomes resigned to his loss. Recent critics have raised the question whether the poem treats of a real child or is entirely allegorical.

The poems 'Cleanness' and 'Patience' are, in the opinion of the editor, pendants to 'Pearl.' 'Cleanness' relates in epic style the Scriptural stories of the Marriage Feast, the Fall of the Angels from Heaven, the Flood, the Visit of the Angels to Abraham, Belshazzar's Feast, and Nebuchadnezzar's Fall. The poem 'Patience' relates episodes in the life of Jonah. A vivid, childlike description is given of Jonah's entrance into the whale's belly and his abode there. The artistic form of these poems represents a compromise between two schools: the East Midland school which produced Chaucer and looked to French literature for inspiration, and the Saxon school of the West-Midland poets, "whose literary ancestors were Cædmon and Cynewulf." It would seem "that there arose a third class of poets during this period of formation, whose avowed endeavor was to harmonize these diverse elements of Old and New, to blend the archaic alliterative rhythm with the measures of Romance song. 'Pearl' is a singularly successful instance of the reconciliation of these two widely diverse forms of poetry.

PEARL OF ORR'S ISLAND, THE, by Harriet Beecher Stowe. This story gives a truthful and interesting picture of the people in a Maine fishing hamlet. Mara Lincoln, the "Pearl," a beautiful girl, has been brought up by her grandparents, Captain and Mrs. Pennel; her father having been drowned and her mother having died at her birth. Moses, the hero of the book, shipwrecked and washed ashore upon the island when very young, is brought up and cared for by the Pennels; and bears their name. The result of this is the mutual attachment of the young people, which is at first more strongly felt by Mara. Moses accepts Mara's devotion as a matter of course, and does not awaken to the fact that he is in love with her until piqued by the attentions bestowed upon her by Mr. Adams of Boston. Then, prompted by jealousy, he pays marked attention to Sally Kittridge, a bright and attractive girl, Mara's dearest friend; but Sally, always loyal to Mara, makes Moses realize the true state of his feelings. .

The descriptions of the picturesque scenery of the island are graphic and accurate; and the Pennel house, now known as the "Pearl house," and the "grotto," where Moses and Sally are shut in by the tide, are objects of interest to visitors. The spicy sea-yarns of Captain Kittridge, and the quaint sayings of Miss Roxy and Miss Ruey Toothacre are entertaining features of the book. 'The Pearl of Orr's Island' was not published until 1862, although it was begun ten years before that time.

PEAU DE CHAGRIN, LA ('The Wild Ass's Skin'), by Honoré de Balzac (1831). This forms one of the 'Philosophic Studies' of the great Frenchman. In 1829 a young man, in despair because of failure to succeed in his chosen career, tries the gaming table. He meets an old man, who revives his interest in life by showing him a piece of skin, bearing in Arabic an inscription promising to the owner the gratification of every wish. But with each request granted the skin becomes smaller. The life of the possessor is lessened as the enchanted skin diminishes. The unknown young man seizes the skin, crying "A short life but a merry one!" Scenes in Paris

ass before us, taken from lives of artists, journalists, politicians. We meet again
Canalis, a chief character in 'Modest Mignon.' One chapter is entitled 'The Heart-
ess Woman.' Raphael by virtue of the talismanic skin becomes rich. Pauline loves
im. Life smiles on them. Yet the fatal skin is brought to his eyes, casting a gloom
ver everything — scientific work, salons of painting and sculpture, the theatre —
mbittering all. He brings the skin to Lavrille, a savant, for examination. "It is
he skin of an ass," is the decision. Raphael was looking for some means to stretch
he skin, and thus prolong his life. He tries mechanical force, chemistry; but the
kin becomes less and still less — till he dies. Through all we feel the author's tone of
ony toward the weakness and sins of society. Some twenty principal personages are
itroduced.

PEDAGOGICS OF THE KINDERGARTEN ('Die Pädagogik des Kindergartens'),
collection of essays on the education of young children, written by Friedrich Froebel,
ollected and published in 1861. Proceeding from a sympathetic consideration of
he child's physical and mental impulses Froebel shows how its play may be so
irected from the earliest stages onward as to develop harmoniously the various
onceptions, and reasoning processes incident to education. For instance, the ball
atisfies the child's desire to grasp at things and by playing with it he gets the con-
eption of unity, while the cube with its various faces and corners teaches him the
onception of variety in unity. Touching these things suggests to him that they are
ot himself and thus inculcates the distinction between subject and object. When the
ube is cut up into eight small cubes he learns the difference between the part and
he whole, outer and inner. Arithmetical processes are also suggested by putting
ogether these small cubes. Various games with the ball attached to a string teach
he ideas of movement, space, and time. Then the imagination is stimulated by
naking believe that the ball and cube are living things. Thus the child's mental
owers are naturally unfolded in accordance with his normal instincts; and education
ecomes a co-operation with nature. The book ends with a concrete illustration —
he teaching of a little girl to read and write by the observing of the sounds and the
imultaneous forming of the symbol. The universality of the kindergarten at the
present day is the best comment on the influence of this book.

PEER GYNT, by Henrik Ibsen (1867). Peer Gynt is the victim of an overmastering
magination. He brags of wonderful deeds true only in his childish dreams. At a
wedding he steals the bride to prove himself a daredevil to the guests who ridicule
his lying tales. His ideal of himself as self-sufficient is only self-indulgence and self-
eeking. After a series of adventures in the mountains, a meeting with "The Boyg"
he spirit of compromise, for whom he turns aside, typical of the obstacles he goes
round and never surmounts, and an amour with the foul daughter of the troll-
king, typical of his sensuality, he leaves Solveig, the young girl who has followed him
to the mountain and goes to seek his fortune in America. Trade in slaves, idols,
Bibles, and rum makes him wealthy. Some companions maroon him on a desert
shore in Africa. He finds the Sultan's white horse and robes, and is acclaimed a
prophet by the Arabs, until he loses all through infatuation for a dancing girl. His
answer to the riddle of the sphinx is his solution of life, egotism. He is crowned
emperor of himself by the inmates of a madhouse. Returning to Norway, he is
shipwrecked but escapes death by pushing another man from the boat. However,
Death is waiting for him at the cross roads in the guise of the Button Molder who
will melt him back to nothing. Hell will not receive him since "it needs strength and

earnestness to sin." Solveig has waited for him all the years. In her memory he ha lived in faith and hope and love, "as in God's thought." The lesson is as in Bran self-realization through self-surrender.

PEG WOFFINGTON, Charles Reade's first novel, was published in 1852, when h was thirty-eight. This charming story of eighteenth-century manners has bee dramatized under the title 'Masks and Faces.' It opens in the green-room of Cover Garden, where the Irish actress, Margaret Woffington, in the hey-day of her fam and beauty, tricks the entire dramatic company, including Colley Cibber the famou playwright and comedian, by personating the great tragic actress Mrs. Bracegirdl At the same time she achieves the conquest of a wealthy and accomplished Shropshir gentleman, Ernest Vane, who is presented to her by a London fop, Sir Charle Pomander. Vane besieges her with flowers and verses until he arouses the jealous of Sir Charles, who is also her admirer. In the midst of a banquet which Mr. Van is giving in honor of the actress, his lovely country bride appears unexpectedly upo the scene. Peg Woffington, who had believed Vane to be a single man and her loya suitor, hides her grief and resentment under a guise of mockery; but the innocent youn wife faints away on finding out how she has been betrayed. Peg Woffington nex appears in the garret of a poor scrub author and scene-painter, James Triplet, whom she has befriended by sitting to him for her portrait. Here, after fooling a party c her theatrical comrades and would-be art critics, who have come to abuse the pictur by the ingenious device of cutting out the painted face and inserting her own in th aperture, she practices the same trick upon Mabel Vane, Ernest's wife, who has sough refuge with Triplet from the persecutions of Sir Charles Pomander. Mabel, seein the image of her rival, pours forth to it a pathetic appeal that Peg will not rob he of her only treasure, her husband's heart; when to her dismay, she perceives a tea upon the portrait's face, which reveals the *real* woman: and a touching intervie follows, in which the courted actress begs the simple young wife to be her friend Then comes on the scene Sir Charles Pomander, in amorous pursuit of Mabel; closel followed by her husband, whom Triplet has summoned to the rescue. A reconcilia tion between the married pair results, and Sir Charles retires discomfited. Woffingto takes an affectionate leave of the Vanes, who soon return to their Shropshire hom and domestic bliss; while the noble-hearted Peg, after a few years more of stag triumphs, retires before her bloom has faded, to a life in the country, and there end her days, "the Bible in her hand, the Cross in her heart; quiet; amidst grass an flowers, and charitable deeds."

PELHAM, by E. Bulwer-Lytton (1828), appeared anonymously; and it had reache its second edition in 1829. It belongs to the writer's initiatory period, being the firs novel that gave promise of his ability.

Henry Pelham, having taken his university degrees and enjoyed a run to Paris returns to his native England, and takes an active part in the political events of hi time. In accordance with the sub-title of the book, 'The Adventures of a Gentle man,' the hero endeavors to realize Etherege's ideal of "a complete gentleman; who according to Sir Fopling, ought to dress well, dance well, fence well, have a genius fo love letters, and an agreeable voice for a chamber."

Pelham becomes especially useful to his party; but on account of jealousies and intrigues his merits are not properly acknowledged.

Meantime he has yielded to the charms of the wealthy and accomplished siste of his old schoolmate and life-long friend, Sir Reginald Glanville. Glanville is sus-

ected of the murder of Sir John Tirrell, whom he had threatened because the latter
ad been guilty of atrocious conduct toward a lady who was under Glanville's protec-
ion. A terrible network of circumstantial evidence causes Pelham to feel certain of
is friend's guilt. Glanville tells the whole story to Pelham, and protests his inno-
ence. By the aid of Job Johnson, a London flash man whom Pelham recognizes as a
ool fitted to accomplish the results he desires, a boozing ken of the most desperate
uffians in the city is visited; and Dawson, the confederate of Tom Thornton who
ad committed the murder, is released. Dawson's testimony convicts the real
murderer, and of course exonerates Glanville.

Political honors are now thrust upon Pelham, who disdains them; while his happy
marriage with the lovely Ellen Glanville is the natural sequence to the tale.

ELLE THE CONQUEROR, by Martin Andersen Nexø (1913–16).   The life story of
elle challenges comparison with Jean Christophe. Pelle represents the will-to-
ower in the labor movement. He is a peasant boy on a bleak Danish island, work-
ng his way by helping his delightful old father the cow-herd, Lasse. He escapes the
qualor of the farm life to become apprentice to a shoemaker in the provincial town.
Ie discovers that he cannot make his way by energy and good will because labor is
xploited. With high-hearted youth he seeks his fortune in the capital. His history
s that of the labor party, first the sweat shop, then the labor union. He finally
ecomes the leader of the shoemakers. He dreams of federation of all trades, and
ads a strike of all the workers to victory. The "Great Struggle" has been long
nd his wife, Ellen, his children and his old father have been sacrificed to the Cause.
t the moment of his triumph he discovers that Ellen has sold herself to buy bread
or her children. As leader of the Union he is a marked man and on a plausible
riminal charge is sent to prison for a term of years. When he is free again the age of
machinery has come with its changes. There are new leaders and new ideas. Ellen
s unchanged and in mutual forgiveness they are happily reunited. He has gained
roader vision and works out a plan of co-operative organization of industry in new
ervice to his fellows. His final program is a co-operative workmen's village.

ENDENNIS, by W. M. Thackeray (1850), is more simple in plot and construction
han his other novels. It is a masterly study of the character and development of one
rthur Pendennis, a hero lifelike and convincing because of his very unheroic quali-
ies and faulty human nature. He begins his career as a spoiled, somewhat brilliant
oy, adored by a foolish mother, and waited upon by his adopted sister Laura. From
his atmosphere of adulation and solicitude, Pendennis goes to the university; but
ot before he has fallen in love with an actress ten years older than himself. He owes
is escape from his toils to the intervention of a worldly-minded uncle, Major Pen-
ennis, a capitally drawn type of the old man-about-town. At the university he
lossoms into a young gentleman of fashion, with the humiliating result of being
plucked" in his degree examination, and having his debts paid off by Laura. His
manliness reawakens, and he goes back to have it out with the university, returning
his time a victor. Then follows a London career as a writer and man of the world.
The boy just misses being the man by a certain childish love of the pomp and show
f life. Yet he is never dishonorable, only weak. The test of his honor is his conduct
owards Fanny Bolton a pretty girl of the lower class, who loves him innocently and
whole-heartedly. Pen loves her and leaves her as innocent as he found her, but un-
appy. His punishment comes in the shape of Blanche Amory, a flirt with a fortune.
The double bait proves too much for the boy's vanity. Only after she has jilted him are

his eyes opened to the true value of the gauds he is staking so much upon. The whole
some lesson being learned, he marries Laura and enters upon a life of new manliness.

His character throughout is drawn with admirable consistency. He is perhaps the
most commonplace, and the most thoroughly human, of Thackeray's men.

PENGUIN ISLAND ('Île des Pengouins'), by Anatole France (1909). This ironical
satire is an allegorical history of France. A zealous Christian missionary, St. Mael
mistakes an island of Penguins for primitive heathen people, and as the birds listen
attentively to his preaching, he baptizes them all in three days and three nights.
An assembly of learned doctors in heaven consider the consequences of this unfortunate error of age and blindness, and it is decided that the untoward baptism is
valid, and the only thing to do is to give the Penguins human souls. St. Mael tows
the island to the coast of Europe and the Penguins begin their human history. Along
with souls they acquire clothes, with the lamentable consciousness of feminine charm
and masculine license (see chapter quoted in LIBRARY) and all the drawbacks of
civilization one after another. They create law by biting and cudgelling one another.
They lay the foundations of property by appropriating the earth with violence, the
strong trampling upon the weak, and the strongest Penguin of them all founding a
noble house. Taxation follows its historical course, the burden falling on the poor,
the rich and noble declare themselves exempt. The chapter on the Middle Ages and
the Renaissance satirizes superstition in religion, the religious wars and massacres.
The art critics who laud primitive painting to the skies receive attention. Modern
times relate the glories of Trinco (Napoleon) who conquers half the world, annexes it
and loses it, the Pyrot (Dreyfus) affair, under the title "The eighty thousand bales of
hay" and the industrial wars in distant parts of the planet, cotton, coal, and iron
wars, in which thousands are killed to secure orders for umbrellas and rubbers. The
Penguins have trusts, and sky-scrapers, and perfect the manufacture of explosives
so that finally a small revolutionary minority is able to destroy wealth by blowing
up the world, and grass grows again on the site of Paris. In the last chapter the
author prophesies history without end for the Penguins, a succession of cycles of
civilization, war, and destruction.

PENROD, by Booth Tarkington (1914). The chapters are a series of adventures
and misadventures which occur in the life of Penrod, aged twelve. No one really
understands Penrod except perhaps his great aunt Sarah, who asked him to return
to his father the sling shot she had taken from that dignified gentleman thirty-five
years before. Penrod's father accepted the gift thoughtfully and for once Penrod
escaped deserved punishment. Certainly the author and manager of 'The Children's
Pageant of the Table Round' did not know the real Penrod when she selected him
to appear as the "Child Sir Lancelot," in the pageant to recite lines unworthy of
man's dignity. Penrod is the author of a blood-curdling work of fiction entitled
'Harold Ramorez, the Road Agent; or, Wild Life among the Rocky Mountains.'
His riotous imagination is always getting him into mischief. He is always found out
and invited to the woodshed by an irate father. It is not safe to call him "little
gentleman" while there is a cauldron of tar in the neighborhood. The chapter ". A
Boy and his Dog" is quoted in the LIBRARY.

'PENROD AND SAM' (1916) continues the story of Penrod's adventurous career,
opening with his experiences as a militarist, and closing with a children's party. He
is ably assisted in his exploits by his friend Sam Williams, and by the faithful Herman
and Verman.

NSÉES PHILOSOPHIQUES ('Philosophical Thoughts'), by Denis Diderot 46), which are said to have been put on paper in the space of three days, and at bidding of one of the philosopher's feminine friends, have been compared with scal's 'Thoughts' in point of force and eloquence. But though the comparison y be made of the manner, it does not hold of the matter; for Diderot expended this ammunition of wit and intellect in demolishing the foundations of all religious ch, and the monuments built to it in the shape of sacred books. His statements made with such entire confidence, that it is easy to believe the work to have im-ssed its readers with faith in the infallibility of its author. It was very widely d and exceedingly popular among the fashionable world at the time of its pearance.

NSÉES SUR LA RELIGION et Quelques. 'Thoughts on Religion and on Certain er subjects by M. Pascal; being writings found among his papers after his death,' a collection of meditations, the preliminary stages of an 'Apology for the Christian eligion,' which Pascal did not live to complete. On his death in 1662 they came o the hands of his colleagues, the Jansenists of the Abbey of Port Royal, who blished them in 1670 with some alterations. The exact text was not printed until e nineteenth century. As left by Pascal the manuscript consisted of disconnected editations, some of them only half-completed, others much corrected, interspersed th notes of the general plan of the work. Most of the editors have grouped the rious thoughts into a logical sequence in accordance with this plan. Pascal's m was to establish the truth of Christianity in face of the scepticism and religious difference which were the fruits of the Renaissance. He begins by emphasizing an's restlessness without God, his constant search for new pleasures, new sensa-ons, new occupations, without attaining peace. Man wishes for diversion in order avoid thinking about himself, because when he looks within he finds a want which thing earthly can satisfy. Man is a chaos, an enigma, a being placed midway etween the infinitely great and the infinitely little, and unable to understand either, ith a reason which raises him above the inanimate universe around him but which nnot explain its inner meaning, with aspirations for good and for truth which he nnot realize. So far Pascal agrees with the sceptical analysis of Montaigne; but here the latter tolerantly accepts these conditions, Pascal seeks relief from them a force beyond nature. In Christianity he finds a revelation which accounts for an's discontent by the doctrine of the Fall and brings happiness through the sub-ission of the will and conscience to God as revealed in Christ. That this religion contrary to reason is an argument in favour of its truth since it claims supernatural rigin and might therefore be expected to clash with the natural and normal view. hristianity, it is true, as Pascal conceived it, demanded the absolute submission to od of man's will of his independent judgment, and his love of worldly pleasure. But he believed that the absolute expediency of such a course could be mathematically emonstrated. In accepting Christianity we sacrifice a finite good on the chance of aining infinite happiness. Should Christianity be true our gain is infinite; should it e untrue our loss is nothing; for finite goods give only a fleeting pleasure. This is Pascal's celebrated "wager," which he enforces by urging the power of habit to econcile us to the sacrifice. Finally he considers the evidence of Christianity from he fulfilment of prophecy, the records of Christ's life, the remarkable spread of he Church, and the beauty of the Christian type of character.

The work abounds in penetrating and incisive observations on man as an in-dividual and in society (for example, the reduction of all wars to the quarreling of two children for a "place in the sun"). Its combination of mathematical precision, philosophic grasp, epigrammatic skill, and the deepest religious insight and feeling is unique. Pascal's clear, idiomatic, nervous style with its absolute command of close reasoning, irony, sarcasm, apt illustration, and telling simplicity absolutely set the standard for the French prose of the great writers of the later Seventeenth Century and has never become obsolete.

PENSÉES SUR L'INTERPRÉTATION DE LA NATURE ('Thoughts Concerning the Interpretation of Nature'), by Denis Diderot, afterward printed under the title 'Étrenne aux Esprits forts,' was written in 1754, and forms a prelude to Diderot' 'Système de la Nature.' It is a rather fantastic attempt to "interpret" nature, and contains a mingling of profound and shallow observations, the whole rendered obscure by a mass of verbiage. As one critic says: "The reader must be patient who wins an occasional glimpse of illumining beauty or interest. To very few would the work prove a real interpretation of nature."

PEOPLE OF THE UNITED STATES, A HISTORY OF THE, by John Bach McMaster. An important work in eight volumes (1883–1913). It is, as the title declares, a history of the people. It describes the dress, amusements, customs, and literary canons, of every period of United States history, from the close of the Revolution to the Civil War. Politics and institutions are considered only as they affected the daily life of the people. The great developments in industrial affairs, the change in manners and morals, the rise and progress of mechanical inventions, the gradual growth of a more humane spirit, especially in the treatment of criminals and of the insane, are all treated at length. It is a social history: it aims to give a picture of the life of the American people as it would seem to an intelligent traveler at the time, and to trace the growth of the influences which built up out of the narrow fringe of coast settlements the great nation of the Civil War.

The book is always entertaining, and is a perfect mine of interesting facts collected in no other history; but the author shows too much love of antithesis, and no doubt will reconsider some of his conclusions.

PEPACTON, by John Burroughs. This book was published in 1881, and is one of the most pleasing of the many delightful collections of papers on outdoor subjects that Mr. Burroughs has given us. It takes its title from the Indian name of one of the branches of the Delaware; and the first paper gives an account of a holiday trip down this stream in a boat of the writer's own manufacture. In the next he tells us many interesting facts about springs, and their significance in the development of civilization. Indeed, in all the papers he shows himself not only the close scientific observer, but the poet who sees the hidden meanings of things. Perhaps he is most interesting when he combines literature with nature, as in the essay on 'Birds and the Poets,' in which he shows that most of the American poets have been inaccurate in their descriptions of nature. As he says, the poet deals chiefly with generalities, but when he descends to the particular he should be accurate. Longfellow has erred most in this respect, while Bryant, Emerson, and above all Whitman, have been more careful. The rhyme for "woodpecker" seems to trouble the poets; as Mr. Burroughs puts it:

> "Emerson rhymes it with bear,
> Lowell rhymes it with hear;
> One makes it woodpeckair,
> The other woodpeckear."

In another paper he demonstrates Shakespeare's surprisingly accurate knowledge
nd use of natural facts, and that the close observer and analyst of the human heart
ad an equally keen sense for the doings of birds and flowers. There is also an
ttractive study of our fragrant flowers, and of the origin and propensities of weeds.
The Idyl of the Honey-Bee' almost sends one to the woods bee-hunting, in general
he writer's enthusiasm for outdoor things is contagious. For this reason the essays
re more than a charmingly written record of the author's own observations, —
hey are an inspiration to search out the secrets of nature at first hand.

PEPITA JIMENEZ, by Juan Valera (1874). The scene of this vivid story is in
Andalusia. Pepita Jimenez, when sixteen years old, is married to her rich uncle,
Don Gumersindo, then eighty years old. At the end of three years, she finds herself
widow, with many suitors for her hand, among them, Don Pedro de Vargas. At this
ime his son Luis comes to pay him a visit before taking his last vows as a priest.
Having lived always with his uncle, he is learned in theology and casuistry, but little
ersed in worldly affairs. The acquaintance with Pepita arouses sentiments which
e had never known; and he soon recognizes that he loves her, and that she returns
is affection. Horrified at his position, both in regard to his profession and to his
ather, he resolves never to see Pepita. Visiting the club, he meets Count de Genaza-
ar, a rejected suitor of Pepita, who speaks slightingly of her. He expostulates with
im on the sin of slander, but is only derided. The expected departure of Luis has
o affected Pepita that she is ill; and her nurse, Antonona, goes to Luis and obliges
im to come to bid farewell to her mistress. He goes at ten o'clock at night, and is
eft alone with Pepita. She tries to convince him that he is ill adapted for a priest.
f he has allowed himself to be charmed by a plain country girl, how much more are to
e feared the beautiful, accomplished women he will meet in future life. Her self-
ondemnation causes him to praise her; and when he leaves her, at two o'clock in the
norning, he is obliged to confess his own unworthiness. He learns that Genazahar
wes Pepita a large sum of money; and goes to the club, where he finds him gambling.
He enters the game and finds a chance to insult him. In a duel they are both wounded,
he Count, dangerously. When Luis recovers he marries Pepita.
The novel is regarded in Spain as a modern classic.

PEPYS'S DIARY, a private journal in short-hand kept from January 1st, 1660, to
May 31st, 1669, by Samuel Pepys, clerk of the Navy Board. The manuscript was
eft with the rest of his library to Magdalene College, Cambridge, where it was
eciphered by the Reverend John Smith between 1819 and 1822. The first edition,
dited by Lord Braybrooke, appeared in 1825; fuller editions were published in 1828,
848–1849, 1854, and 1875–9; the standard edition by H. B. Wheatley in 1893–1899.
Pepys was the son of a London tailor, and a student of St. Paul's School and Magda-
ene College, Cambridge. He was married early to the daughter of a Huguenot
efugee. Through his cousin, Edward Montagu, afterwards Earl of Sandwich, he
vas a passenger on the ship that brought Charles II. home from exile, obtained his
lerkship in the Navy Office and gained access to the Restoration court. During
he nine years in which he kept his diary he was a busy and valued public servant
teadily increasing in wealth and prosperity. His diary is an intimate record of his
aily business, recreations, personal likes and dislikes, and domestic affairs. Its
ccounts of the various political and social changes of the Restoration, of the intrigues
nd corruption of the English Navy in the days of the Dutch war, of the great plague
nd fire of London, and of the social habits and customs of the people, especially

the middle and upper classes are of the highest value to historians.   Pepys was one o
those sociable people who are never weary of attending functions of all kinds, an
whose zest for life renders nothing human uninteresting to them. Thus the mer
record of a family dinner party, a visit to a country village, or a walk on London bridg
is full of a gusto which makes the language forceful and the details interesting
Again, he was writing for no eye but his own and consequently set down with absolut
frankness instances of his own foolishness, selfishness, cruelty, and sensuality, whic
most men would carefully conceal even from themselves. Pepys was, however, n
villain.   He was a respectable London householder, an able official, respected by h
colleagues, a lover of music and an antiquarian, a collector of old ballads; but ther
was a streak of coarseness in him, though no more than we should expect in a
"homme moyen sensuel" of the Restoration period. He took bribes, ate and dran
too much, admired the dissolute ladies at the court, flirted with pretty girls, was cru
to his servants, and jealous of his wife, though unfaithful to her, and did not observ
consistency between his religious moods and his practice.   The frankness, naïvet
and unconscious humour with which he sets down these sins and peccadilloes ha
a strange fascination for the reader. Of course part of the piquancy of the boo
comes from the fact that the reader is overhearing something which the writer neve
intended him to know.   The diary was kept up for nine years, when the weakness o
Pepys's eyes forced him to relinquish it.   Had it never been discovered he would sti
have been remembered as an antiquarian and historian of the Navy, but one of th
most interesting and spontaneous revelations of a personality in all literature woul
have been lost.

PÈRE GORIOT, by Honoré de Balzac (1834).   This story is one of the most painf
that the master of French fiction ever forced upon a fascinated but reluctant reade
It is the history of a modern Lear.   Père Goriot, a retired manufacturer of vermicell
having married his daughters, Anastasie to the Count de Restaud, and Delphine t
the Baron de Nucingen, is abandoned by them after he has settled on them his who
fortune.   Even to see them he is reduced to the extremity of watching on the street t
get a glimpse of their beloved faces as they drive by.   In the wretched pension whe
he lives he meets Eugène de Rastinac, whose distant relationship to the Viscountes
de Beauséant enables him to frequent the select society of the Faubourg Sain
Germain.   He there makes the acquaintance of Père Goriot's daughters, and becom
the cavalier of Delphine.   The daughters, mere devotees of fashion, treat the po
old man with increasing barbarity, until, knowing that he is on his death-bed, the
both attend a ball, though he beseeches them to come to him.   He is buried b
charitable acquaintances; and as the body is brought from the church, the empt
coaches of the daughters fall in behind and follow it to the grave.   Crowded wit
incidents, and made profoundly interesting by its merciless fidelity of characteriza
tion 'Père Goriot' compels attention; while in style it is one of the most brilliant
Balzac's long succession of novels.

PERICLES, PRINCE OF TYRE, a play published in 1608, written in part by Shake
peare.   His part in it begins with the magnificent storm scene in Act iii., — "Tho
god of this great vast, rebuke these surges," — "The seaman's whistle is as a whisp
in the ears of death, unheard," etc.   The play was very popular with the mass
for a hundred years.   Indeed the romantic plot is enough to make it perenniall
interesting and pathetic; the deepest springs of emotion and of tears are touched b
the scenes in which Pericles recovers his lost wife and his daughter. — After certai

strange adventures Pericles, Prince of Tyre, arrives with ships loaded with grain at Tarsus, and feeds the starving subjects of King Cleon and Queen Dionyza. Afterwards shipwrecked by Pentapolis, he recovers from the waves his suit of armor, and buying a horse with a jewel, goes to King Simonides's court and jousts for his daughter Thaïsa's love. He marries her, and in returning to Tyre his wife gives birth, in the midst of a terrible storm, to a daughter whom he names Marina. The mother, supposed dead, is laid by Pericles in a water-tight bitumened chest, with jewels and spices, etc., and is thrown overboard by the sailors, but cast ashore at Ephesus and restored to life by the wise and good physician Cerimon. Pericles lands with his infant daughter at Tarsus, where he leaves her with his old friends Cleon and Dionyza. The pretty Marina grows up, and so excites the hatred of the queen by outshining her own daughter, that she tries to kill her; but the girl is rescued by pirates, who carry her to Mitylene, where she is bought by the owner of a disreputable house, but escapes to take service as a kind of companion in an honest family. The fame of her beauty and accomplishments spreads through the city. One festal day comes Pericles, sad and ill, in his ship to Mitylene, and meeting with Marina, learns from her her story. His joy is so great that he fears death. By Diana's command, revealed to him in a vision, he goes to Ephesus to confess before the people and before her priestess the story of his life. The officiating priestess turns out to be his wife Thaïsa, who went from the physician's house to become a ministrant in the temple of the goddess of chastity.

PERKIN WARBECK, by John Ford (1634). "In the whole of our dramatic literature," says Prof. A. W. Ward, "no plays except Marlowe's 'Edward II.,' the anonymous 'Edward III.,' and this isolated effort by Ford, can prefer any claim to notice by the side of Shakespere's national historic dramas." 'Perkin Warbeck' is the most perfect in form of Ford's plays, well conceived and written on a high level of literary skill. It describes how James IV. of Scotland, having taken sides with Perkin Warbeck, who claimed to be Richard, Duke of York, the second son of Edward IV., marries Warbeck to his kinswoman, Lady Katharine Gordon, against the wishes of her father, the Earl of Huntley, who wished her to marry Earl Dalyell, though formerly for ambitious reasons he had frowned upon the latter's addresses. Ford is careful not to present the King in an unfavorable light, and even the impostor Warbeck is never allowed to betray himself. Huntley and Dalyell are simple, sincere, and convincing characters.

PERSONAL RECOLLECTIONS OF JOAN OF ARC, see **JOAN OF ARC,** by Mark Twain.

PERU, see **CENTRAL AMERICA, NOTES ON.**

PERU, CONQUEST OF, see **CONQUEST OF.**

PETER IBBETSON, by George Du Maurier. In 'Peter Ibbetson' romance and realism are so skillfully blended that one accepts the fairy-tale element almost unquestioningly. The book is a prose poem, and carries its reader into a new world of dreams and ideal beauty.

The first chapters tell the hero's life as a child in the country near Paris, where he lives happily with his parents and his delicate little friend Mimsey Seraskier, until his father and mother die, and he is taken away by his uncle. The next years are spent at school in England; then Peter quarrels with his bad, ill-bred uncle, and becomes a lonely, hard-working architect. He falls in love at first sight with Mary, the Duchess of Towers: "It was the quick, sharp, cruel blow, the *coup de poignard*, that beauty of the most obvious, yet subtle, consummate, and highly organized order, can deal to a thoroughly prepared victim." Afterwards he has a strange, sweet dream of his boyhood, where Mary is the only living reality; and she tells him how to "dream true," and thus live over again his happy life as a child in France. Finally Peter meets Mary face to face; they discover, he that she is Mimsey Seraskier, and both that they have dreamed the same dream together. After this interview they part forever. Peter hears that his uncle has told infamous lies about his mother, and in justified rage kills him, more by accident than design. On the night that he is sentenced to be hanged, Mary comes into his dream again and tells him that the sentence will be commuted, and that after she is separated from her wretched husband she will make his life happy. Then comes an ideal dream-life of twenty-five years, that must be read to be understood and appreciated, during which Mary's outward life is spent in philanthropy and Peter's is spent in jail. When she dies, and their mutual dream-life ends, Peter becomes wildly insane. She visits him once after her death, and gives him strength to recover and write this singular autobiography. He dies in a criminal lunatic asylum, we are told, and whether he was mad, or the story is true, is left to the imagination.

'Peter Ibbetson' was published in 1891, and was the first novel of the famous English artist.

PETER PAN, by Sir J. M. Barrie (1904). This is a children's play. Peter Pan overheard his parents discussing what they would make of him when he became a man, and was so alarmed at the prospect that then and there he determined never to grow up, but to run away to the fairies in the Never-Never-Never land. He likes to listen outside of the nursery window when Mrs. Darling is telling stories to her children, and one day when Nana, the dog who acts as nurse to the children, shuts the window suddenly he loses his shadow. Peter comes back the next night to look for his lost shadow, which Mrs. Darling has laid away in a drawer. The Darling children, Wendy, Michael, and John, asleep in the nursery, wake up and see Peter. He tells them about his home with the lost children in the trunks of trees, and asks Wendy to come and be a mother to them. He teaches the children how to fly and they sail away together. Then begins the finest kind of adventure with Indians, and with Pirates led by the bloodthirsty Captain Hook, who has a fearful iron hook in place of a hand. A crocodile has eaten the hand and so enjoyed the taste, that he follows Captain Hook always, hoping to finish his meal, but the hungry crocodile never succeeds in his pursuit, because unfortunately he had once swallowed an eight-day clock which ticks loudly and warns Captain Hook of his approach. The children are guarded from the pirates by Tiger Lily, the Indian princess, and her braves. Peter has a fairy companion, Tinker Bell, seen only as a flickering light, who saves his life by drinking the poison Captain Hook has prepared for him, and is herself saved only by Peter's appeal to the audience to believe in fairies. Once the children, except Peter, are captured by the pirates, but the wily Peter provides himself with a clock and frightens Captain Hook into hiding from his enemy, the crocodile, while he arms the boys, and the children takes possession of the pirate ship, and make the pirates walk the plank. Wendy has to return home, but it is arranged that she shall visit Peter every spring to attend to the housekeeping in his little home in the tree top with the fairies.

PETER SCHLEMIHL, by Adelbert von Chamisso.   This tale, written in 1814, has attained world-wide fame.   The theme is the old popular superstition that the Devil can take a man's shadow without being able to control the man himself.   The setting, however, is modern, and the extravagant plot is developed with straight-forward simplicity.   Peter Schlemihl, being in reduced circumstances, encounters a mysterious gray man, to whom he surrenders his shadow in return for Fortunatus's purse.   His boundless wealth, however, brings him little satisfaction, as people regard his shadowless estate with aversion and horror.   He is constrained to shun even the moonlight, and passes most of his time in forced seclusion.   Finally his unpopularity drives him from the town, and he takes up his residence in a remote spot.   Here, by means of the greatest caution, his secret remains for a time unguessed; and on account of his wealth and liberality he is regarded as a nobleman.   He finds his greatest satisfaction in the society of the innocent and affectionate Mina, a forester's daughter; and is about to marry her when his misfortune is betrayed by a faithless servant, and Mina's father bids him begone.   The gray man then reappears, and offers to restore the shadow at the price of Peter's soul.   The broken-hearted man has the strength of will to refuse, and relinquishes all hopes of earthly happiness rather than endanger his eternal welfare.   He throws the purse into a fathomless cavern, and wanders about in poverty till by chance he gains possession of the Seven-League Boots.   He is thus enabled to travel over all the surface of the earth, except, for some mysterious reason, Australia and the neighboring islands.   He makes his headquarters at ancient Thebes, and enters upon the career of a scientific explorer, taking refuge in the world of nature, since the world of men is forever closed to him.

PETITE FADETTE, LA, see **LITTLE FADETTE.**

PHALARIS, DISSERTATION ON THE EPISTLES OF, by Richard Bentley (1699). 'The Letters of Phalaris' was a Greek work purporting to be real correspondence of a ferocious Dorian tyrant of Sicily in the sixth century before Christ.   The educated world of Swift's time accepted them as genuine; and Sir William Temple, in a pamphlet assuming the literal truth of many of the wildest legends and myths of antiquity, and setting the ancients in general above the moderns in a series of comparisons curiously naïve for an educated man, had extravagantly lauded them.   This led a young Oxford man, Charles Boyle, to edit the 'Letters' for English readers of Greek; and in doing this he used an insulting expression with regard to a fancied wrong done him by Bentley, who had just then (1694) become librarian to the King.   Bentley had promised a friend who wished to take the other side in the discussion with Temple, an essay on the Phalaris letters; and in this he showed clearly that they were a clumsy forgery by a Greek rhetorician of about the time of Christ.   Boyle took offense in connection with the appearance of Bentley's essay, and with the help of several Oxford wits brought out a sharp reply, January, 1698.   It was to dispose of this that Bentley, fourteen months later, March, 1699, published his 'Dissertation'; not merely a crushing reply to Boyle, but in matter and style, on lines which were then new, a masterpiece of literature.   It was a brilliant piece of criticism, based on accurate historical research; it presented on several points, which are still of interest, stores of learning rarely ever equaled; and it abundantly testified Bentley's genius as a controversialist.   As a scholar, a learned critic, and a university educator, Bentley stands not only at the highest level, but at the head of the stream which has come down to our time.   There began with him a broad and thorough scholarship in Greek and

Latin literature, which before him was only beginning to get under way. He is thus to scholars one of the great names of learning and of letters.

PHASES OF THOUGHT AND CRITICISM, by Brother Azarias, of the Brothers of the Christian Schools (Patrick Francis Mullany), 1892. A book of search for the ideal in thought, with special reference to the cultivation of religious sentiment on the basis of the Catholic faith. The writer states the principles for which he contends, and what may be called the logic of spiritual discernment, and then makes an application of them in very carefully executed studies of the 'Imitation' of À Kempis, 'The Divina Commedia' of Dante, and the 'In Memoriam' of Tennyson. These three studies show the author at his best, as an ardent traveler on "the road that leads to the Life and the Light." The last of the three is the most elaborate; and in it the zealous expounder of spiritual method "watches a great modern poet wrestling with the problem of bridging the chasm which yawns between agnosticism and Christianity."

PHEIDIAS, ESSAYS ON THE ART OF, by Charles Waldstein (1885). A volume of great importance, consisting of nine essays, of which the first and second are introductory; one on the province, aim, and methods of the study of classical archæology and the other on the spirit of the art of Pheidias, in its relation to his age, life, and character. These two essays aim to bring into view the nature and causes of Greek genius for art, and the character of the art of the greatest of Greek sculptors, who ranks in the art of Greece as Æschylus does in its drama. The five essays which follow deal with the sculptures of the Parthenon in the order of time of their production, and of the growth of the artist's own development. Of the two remaining essays, the first deals with the gold and ivory statues; the Athene of the Parthenon, over forty feet in height, and the incarnation in ivory and gold of overpowering majesty and spiritual beauty; and the Zeus at Olympia, a seated or throned figure, forty-two feet in height, a marvel of construction and decoration, and beyond all comparison impressive, to give the idea of the King of the gods.

The last essay considers the influence of the work of Pheidias upon the Attic sculpture of the period immediately succeeding the age of Pericles. The sculpture of Pheidias was that of idealism, divine and religious sculpture, serving to portray forms worthy of indwelling divinity. Dr. Waldstein's discussion not only brings out the fact that Pheidias was the greatest creator of ideals or creative thinker of the Greek race, — the Greek Shakespeare, one might say, — but it touches as well upon Greek art generally; and with a view to his wider study some important papers are added in an appendix.

PHILASTER, or, Love Lies a Bleeding, a romantic drama by Beaumont and Fletcher, first published in 1620 but acted not later than 1610. The King of Calabria offers the hand of his daughter, Arethusa, and the succession to the kingdoms of Calabria and Sicily, to Pharamond, Prince of Spain. The princess, however, loves Philaster, the rightful heir to Sicily, whose popularity will not permit the king to exclude him from his court. They plight their troth, and Philaster gives Arethusa a page named Bellario, as a messenger and reminder of their love. Pharamond, meanwhile, assured of her hand but annoyed by her coldness and by the time that must elapse before his marriage, seeks comfort in a liaison with Megra, a frivolous court lady. Detected in this intrigue, Megra spitefully accuses the princess of a similar offence with the page. The nobleman, Dion, and others friendly to Philaster. thinking his alliance with Arethusa undesirable, not only accept this story but inform Philaster that they can witness to its truth. That prince credits the accusation, questions and dismisses Bellario, and violently rebukes Arethusa. During a hunting party, the princess, not caring where she goes, loses her way, faints, and is comforted by Bellario, who has been wandering about the forest. Philaster, coming upon them, thinks his accusations confirmed. Driving off the page he offers the princess his sword with the request to kill him and on her refusal wounds her. But a peasant, seeing a man with his sword drawn upon a woman, intervenes. He wounds Philaster, who runs off, pursued by the king and courtiers. Coming again upon Bellario asleep by a spring he wounds him also, in order to defleet the pursuit upon him, and then hides under a bush. But when he hears the page take the wounding of Arethusa upon himself, Philaster, now convinced of the boy's loyalty, crawls from his hiding-place, and proclaims his own guilt. Both are arrested; but Arethusa begs the custody of them and promptly marries Philaster. Condemned to death by the irate king she and Philaster are saved by an uprising of the people, who love the prince. The king, now repentant, accepts Philaster as his son-in-law and dismisses Pharamond with Megra. The latter, however, renews her accusation against Bellario and Arethusa. To get at the truth the king orders the page to be tortured, and it now transpires that this page is the lady Euphrasia, daughter of Dion, who had conceived a deep passion for Philaster, and out of pure devotion to him had entered his service disguised as a boy, letting her father suppose that she was on pilgrimage. She is urged to accept from the king a husband and dowry, but declares that she has vowed never to marry but to serve the princess. The drama ends with the departure of Pharamond and Megra and the blessing of Philaster and Arethusa as heirs of Sicily and Calabria. There is affiliation between this play and the later romances of Shakespeare, and the character of the woman-page, Bellario, has a grace, a pathos, and a poetic charm of expression which rivals Shakespeare's Viola and Imogen.

PHILIP AND HIS WIFE, by Margaret Deland (1895). This book might well be called a study in selfishness, although its emphasis seems to bear upon marriage and the marriage laws; concerning which the author propounds certain theories and problems, without offering any direct solution. Philip Shore, an unsuccessful artist, marries Cecilia Drayton, rich, beautiful, and accomplished, but soulless, and finds himself face to face with the question: "Is not marriage without love as spiritually illegal as love without marriage is civilly illegal? And if it is, what is your duty?" The story of 'Philip and his Wife' is painful and almost tragic, but it is set against a background of charming variety and richness of color. The plot is simple. Philip and Cecil come to open dispute regarding the bringing-up of their only daughter, Molly. They can agree to separate, but neither will divorce the other. Who shall have the care of Molly? In the end Cecil surrenders the child to Philip, who goes his way, while his wife departs on hers. Each has failed in a different way; he because of his lonely spiritual selfishness, she because of her light-minded, superficial, and perilous frivolity. The subsidiary characters are drawn with great skill and charm. Roger Carey, crude and uncompromising, is engaged to the dainty Alicia, Cecil's younger sister. The engagement is broken because of her devotion to her invalid mother, the querulous Mrs. Drayton, whose selfishness is all-devouring, while she prays devoutly and quotes Scripture without ceasing. Carey falls under the influence of Cecil Shore's beauty, which for a time captivates him, despite his recognition of her true character. His manliness asserts itself at last, and Roger returns to Alicia, in whom he finds his ideal helpmeet. Dr. Lavendar, the honest, blundering old rector, and his amiable brother, are cleverly depicted; as are also Susan Carr, in her goodness of heart and soundness of sense; Mrs. Pendleton, with her "literary" affectations; and Molly in her weird precocity. All these, down to the drunken brute Todd and his tearful Eliza, are portrayed with exquisite comprehension and unfailing felicity of humor. There are some scenes of great dramatic power, and the background of village life in southern Pennsylvania is pictured with much charm.

PHILIP VAN ARTEVELDE, a tragedy, by Sir Henry Taylor (1834). One of the best English tragedies since Shakespeare, by an author distinguished for his protest, in the spirit of Wordsworth, against the extreme sentimentalism of Byron. His 'Isaac Comnenus' (1827) — a drama picturing the scene at Constantinople when the hero was Roman (Byzantine) emperor there (1057–59, A.D.) — was mainly a preliminary study for his masterpiece, the 'Van Artevelde'; in which, with noble thought and admirable power, he brings back the stress and storm of fourteenth-century life. The father of Philip, the great Jacob van Artevelde, an immensely rich brewer, eloquent and energetic, had played a great part as popular leader at Ghent, 1335–45; and it fell to his son to figure similarly in 1381, but to be slain in a great defeat of the forces of Ghent the next year. Taylor's tragedy recalls the events of these two years. Two songs—

"Quoth tongue of neither maid nor wife—"

and

"If I had the wings of a dove—"

have been pronounced worthy of Shakespeare, although his lyrical efforts generally were laboriously artificial. He had very little eye to the stage, — was in fact more a poet than a dramatist, and a poet of thought especially, — but he used great care in his studies of character.

PHILISTINES, THE, by Arlo Bates (1889), a story of fashionable Boston society, takes its title from Matthew Arnold's name for the rich and self-satisfied classes of the community, to whom money, and the good of life expressible in money, are all. Arthur Fenton, a painter of great promise, gives up original work to paint the portraits of rich men, and marries the niece of Boston's greatest art patron, a high-minded but somewhat narrow girl, with whom he is totally out of sympathy. The story traces his gradual deterioration; and his outlook on life becomes more and more worldly. In short, the motive of the book is the illustration of that dry-rot of character which is certain to seize on its victim when wealth, or ease, or any external good, is made the end of existence. It shows the remorselessness of nature in insisting on her penalties when her laws of development are disregarded. Yet the story never degenerates into an argument, nor is it loaded with a moral. Several of the personages have epigrammatic tendencies, which make their society entertaining. "People who mean well are always worse than those who don't mean anything." "He was one of those men who have the power of making their disapproval felt, from the simple fact that they feel it so strongly themselves." "Modern business is simply the art of transposing one's debts." "A broad man is one who can appreciate his own wife." "A woman may believe that she herself has accomplished the impossible, but she knows no one of her sisters has." "Conventionality is the consensus of the taste of mankind." "The object of life is to endure life, as the object of time is to kill time." Society matrons, maids, and men, are delineated with the sure touch of one who knows them; and receptions, Browning Clubs, art committees, business schemes, and politics, form a lively background for the story.

PHILOBIBLON. An enthusiastic Latin eulogy of books and learning by Richard Aungerville, — called Richard de Bury from his birthplace (1287): St. Edmund's Bury, *i. e.*, Burg, England. He was a true thirteenth-century brother of Magliabecchi, Dibdin, or D'Israeli the elder. He was Bishop of Durham and Lord High Chancellor and Treasurer under Edward III. In one of his chapters he tells how, his hobby for books becoming known, rare books flowed to him from every side: he was always purchasing and always on the search at home and abroad. In Chapter xix. he tells of the loan library, or book hall, he endowed at Oxford, with five salaried scholars in charge. No book was loaned except upon security, and when a duplicate copy was owned. The chapter on the cleanly handling of books is rigorous and amusing: he hates the dirty cleric who will eat fruit and cheese over a book; in winter allow ichor from his nose to drop upon it; twist it, wrench it, put in straws for marks, press flowers in it, and leave it open to collect dust. Bonaventure's cardinal's hat came to him when he was washing dishes; but look out that the scullion monk washes his hands before reading a book. Weak men are writing books, but the choicest trappings are thrown away upon lazy asses. Let the wisdom of great books breathe from us like perfume from the breath of the panther. No man can serve both books and mammon.

PHILOSOPHY OF THE INDUCTIVE SCIENCES, see **INDUCTIVE SCIENCES.**

PHINEAS FINN, see **PARLIAMENTARY NOVELS,** by Anthony Trollope.

PHINEAS REDUX, see **PARLIAMENTARY NOVELS,** by Anthony Trollope.

PHRA THE PHŒNICIAN, THE STRANGE ADVENTURES OF, by Edwin Lester Arnold (1890), is a fantastic story that recounts the adventures of Phra through recurring existences extending from the earliest Phœnician period to the times of Queen Elizabeth. Through all these lives Phra retains his individuality, though adapted to varying times and places. The story opens with an expedition of Phra as a Phœnician merchant to the "ten islands," or "Cassiterides." He reappears in the early British days, the slave consort of his Druid wife, and changes into a centurion in the house of a noble Roman lady. At his next appearance Phra is again a Briton, and serves under King Harold at Hastings; he is successively a Saxon thane, and an English knight under King Edward III., before his final incarnation during the reign of Queen Elizabeth, when he writes of his various adventures. From act to act of his existence Phra is followed by Crecy, a damsel who renews her life as he does and constantly seeks his love. She dies to save one of his numerous lives on a French battle-field where Phra is serving under Edward III.

PHROSO, by Anthony Hope (Hawkins) (1897), is the story of one Lord Charles Wheatley — told by himself — and his experiences in taking possession of the small Greek island, Neopalia, which he has purchased from Lord Stefanopoulos. Denny Swinton, his cousin, Hogoardt, a factotum, and Watkins, his servant, accompany him. The natives, under Constantine, Lord Stefanopoulos's nephew, violently oppose them and threaten their lives. They all escape from the island by a secret passage to the sea, except Wheatley, who is imprisoned. He is about to be stricken to death before the populace, when Phroso, the "Lady of the Island," leaps to his aid, declaring that she loves him better than life. Wheatley shows the people that Constantine has lately assassinated his uncle and is now plotting the murder of his own (secret) wife, Francesca, that he may be free to marry Phroso, heiress to the island

Constantine becomes the prisoner and Wheatley the Neopalians' favorite, since Phroso, their dear lady, loves him. His joy, however, is not unmixed, — he is betrothed to Beatrice Hipgrave in England. Nowraki, a Turkish Pasha, arrives and woos Phroso, greatly complicating matters and nearly demolishing Wheatley's plans. After many exciting exigencies, the brave Wheatley weds the lovely Phroso; but not till Constantine, Mouraki, and Francesca are slain, and Miss Hipgrave is found to be already consoled. Plot is rapidly succeeded by counterplot throughout the story, which is written in the characteristic romantic style of the author.

PHYSIOGNOMY: FRAGMENTARY STUDIES (1775–78), by Johann Caspar Lavater. The author, who was preacher, scholar, philanthropist, and philosopher, called his work 'Physiognomical Fragments for the Promotion of a Knowledge of Man and of Love of Man.' There are four duodecimo volumes, making in all a little more than a thousand pages. The numerous and varied illustrations cover, in addition, about one hundred pages, besides those occurring in the text. The subject is treated profoundly and widely — including studies of the bony basis of form, in lower animals and man. Thence we rise to classes of humanity, with portraits of eminent characters from all epochs of historic time. Reproductions of famous paintings are given to make clearer the features upon which are printed, by nature's unerring finger, the language Lavater would have us all to read. Thus could we learn to know congenial spirits at a glance; see honest minds indicated in form, feature, and gesture; and be enabled to "sense" where Satan leads, ere our lives be marked forever by the contact of evil. Physiognomy, in such relation, is meant to include all means by which the mind of man reveals itself to his fellows: face, body, hands, all, from the hairs of the head to the soles of the feet, show expression in motion, standing, speaking, writing; examples of each being given in this monumental work. The fourth volume contains the author's portrait and biography.

PHYSIOLOGUS ('The Naturalist'). A very remarkable book of animal allegories, some fifty or sixty in number, produced originally in Greek at Alexandria, as early probably as the final completion of the New Testament, or before 200 A.D., and in circulation for many centuries, in many languages, as a kind of natural Bible of the common people; more universally known, and more popularly regarded, than the Bible even, because so familiar in the memories of the masses and not dependent upon written copies.

So entirely was it a book of tales and traditions of the uneducated mass, more often told to hearers than copied out and read, that any one who made a written copy varied the text at will, enlarging or abridging, and inserting new ideas or Scripture quotations at pleasure. It was in this respect a reflection of the literary method of the Græco-Hebrew writers of the time of Christ and the Greek Christians of the New Testament age, 50–150 A.D. It was the lesson only of the story, not its exact text, which was regarded; facts were of less account than the truth meant to be conveyed. Some of the animals of the stories were imaginary; and with animals were included the diamond, the magnet, the fire-flint, the carbuncle, the Indian stone, and such trees as the sycamore and one called peridexion. The facts in each story were not those of science, given by Aristotle or any other authority; but those of folk-lore, of popular tradition and fable, and of frequent touches of the imagination. It mattered little as to the facts, if they were of startling interest: the important thing was the spiritual lesson. Thus the one horn of the unicorn signifies that Christ is one with the Father; the wonderfully sweet odor of the panther's breath, attracting all other animals except the serpent, signifies Christ drawing all unto him except the Devil. The riot of legend and fable, which ran under "Physiologus says," took the popular fancy in proportion as it was wild; and credulity thus stimulated was the strongest belief. The ideas thus taught passed into all the literatures of Europe, and found incessant expression in art, and in emblems carved upon churches and even upon furniture.

The Greek text of 'Physiologus,' and versions in great variety, have been printed; and in the 'Geschichte des Physiologus,' by F. Lauchert, 1889, a full account of the origin, character, and diffusion of the work is given, with the Greek original and a German translation. See also 'Animal Symbolism.'

PICKWICK PAPERS, THE, by Charles Dickens. 'Posthumous Papers of the Pickwick Club' is the one novel of Dickens that abounds neither in pathetic, grewsome, nor dramatic passages. It is pure fun from beginning to end, with a laugh on every page. It was published in 1836, and aided by the clever illustrations of Hablot Brown, or "Phiz," it attained immediate success and laid the foundations of Dickens's fame. The types illustrated are caricatures, but nevertheless they are types: Mr. Pickwick, the genial, unsophisticated founder of the club; and that masterly array of ludicrous individuals drawn from all classes high and low.

Although the whole book is exaggerated comedy, there is no other that has furnished more characters universally known, or given to common English speech more current phrases. Many sayings and events are still in the "Pickwickian sense"; Sam Weller and his admirable father are still quoted; Mrs. Leo Hunter is still a feature in social life; Bardell trials occur occasionally; and there are many clubs as wise as Pickwick's.

PICCOLO MONDO ANTICO; PICCOLO MONDO MODERNO, see **THE PATRIOT.**

PICTURES OF TRAVEL ('Reisebilder'), by Heinrich Heine (1826). The appearance of the first book of these sketches of travel marked an epoch in the development of German literature. It was read with avidity by the public, and so strong was its influence that it gave the first serious check to a prevailing tendency in the world of letters, — the romantic tendency. The power of the Romantic School was broken by the vivid realism of Heine's 'Hartz-Journey.' The keen observation of the great lyrist and satirist, his brilliant searching criticisms of men and institutions, his stinging sarcasms poured out on existing conditions, were entirely opposed to the spirit of Romanticism; and the work marked if it did not initiate the reaction from that school.

Its author attained at once, upon its appearance, to almost as wide-spread a recognition as he was ever to reach among his countrymen. And indeed these prose pictures from the Hartz region are peculiarly illustrative of the many-sided nature and genius of Heine, who was at once a master of polemic prose and a lyrist of unsurpassed melody, a robust humorist, and a merciless satirist. The brilliancy and the bitterness, the sweetness and the mockery, of his strange nature, are all brought into play in this, his first prose work of significance.

Descriptions of nature, vivid pictures of the social and political aspects of the country, bitter polemics against certain of the Romanticists, especially Platen, sudden flashes of a wit always keen but not always delicate, are woven together in a style unfailingly brilliant. Interspersed with the prose are a few fugitive lyrics; among them some of the most exquisite of the songs of Heine.

PIERS PLOWMAN, see **VISION OF.**

PILGRIMAGE OF ANACHARSIS THE YOUNGER, THE ('Voyage du Jeune Anacharsis'), by the Abbé Barthélemy. The hero of the story is a descendant and namesake of the Thracian king who arrived in Athens 600 B. C. and became the friend and adviser of Solon. Anacharsis is supposed to have traveled through Greece and to have finally settled in Athens some years before the death of Alexander the Great. From Athens he makes several journeys to neighboring countries, observing everywhere the usages and manners of the natives, taking part in their festivals, and studying the nature of their governments. At other times he devotes his leisure to philosophical investigations, or converses with the great men who then flourished at Athens: Phocion, Xenophon, Plato, Demosthenes, etc. The work is preceded by an introduction, in which allowance being made for the progress of the historical and archæological sciences during the present century, the reader will find an exhaustive account of the arts, manners, literature, government, and general history of Greece, from the earliest times until its subjection by Philip of Macedon. The author also enters fully into the civil, literary, and philosophical history of all the other enlightened nations of antiquity. The work is a masterpiece of style as well as of erudition; and the numerous abridgments of the 'Anacharsis' that have appeared at various times have been failures, because they lack the charm of the author's style. The Abbé Barthélemy spent thirty years in composing his romance, which appeared in 1779.

PILGRIM'S PROGRESS, THE, an allegory by John Bunyan (1678). Under the similitude of a pilgrimage the story describes the Christian life. The hero, Christian, carrying a burden of sins and terrified by the Biblical announcement of judgment to come, leaves the City of Destruction to find Zion the City of God. Directed by Evangelist to the Wicket-Gate of conversion, he is involved in the Slough of Despond and led astray by Mr. Worldly-Wiseman to seek salvation in the village of Morality. Terrified by thunders from the neighboring Mount Sinai (*i. e.* the Law), he is rescued by Evangelist, enters the gate, and begins his journey. At the Interpreter's house he is instructed by pictures, and other graphic means, in the central doctrines of Christianity, particularly that of justification of faith. Coming then to a cross he is released from his burden; clothed in fresh garments, sealed on the forehead, and given a roll of instructions and advice. Encountering various pilgrims who represent different varieties of error in the Christian life he continues his journey, climbs the Hill Difficulty, sleeps in an arbor and loses his roll, recovers it, faces the lions, is entertained in the House Beautiful, fights Apollyon in the Valley of Humiliation, traverses the Valley of the Shadow of Death, is joined by Faithful, is imprisoned with him by the people of Vanity Fair, escapes after the martyrdom of Faithful, gets another companion, Hopeful, turns into Bypath Meadow, is imprisoned by Giant Despair, escapes from his Doubting Castle by the key of Promise, views the Celestial City from the Delectable Mountains, crosses the Enchanted Ground, enters the Country of Beulah, crosses the River of Death, and is received into the Holy City. As a concrete embodiment of the essentials of universal Christianity the book is treasured by Christians of every shade of opinion and dogmatic affiliation, all over the world. Its homely, direct style, and arresting incidents added to its graphic presentation of spiritual truths make it, outside of the Bible, perhaps the most absorbing of all narratives.

In the Second Part, published in 1684, we read the adventures of Christian's wife,

Christiana, her four sons, Matthew, Samuel, Joseph, and James, and her friend, Mercy, who are all travelling to the Celestial City, following the example of Christian. Like most sequels this story is not equal to the first part, but it contains some striking and entertaining figures and episodes—Mr. Greatheart, the conductor of the party, a valiant fighter, Mercy's suitor, Mr. Brisk, the eldest boy, Matthew, who is made ill by eating fruit from Beelzebub's orchard, and other bits of genuine character-portrayal.

PILOT, THE, by James Fenimore Cooper, written in 1823, was a pioneer in genuine sea stories. Walter Scott's 'Pirate' had just been published, and was discussed at a New York dinner-table where Cooper was present. The guests generally expressed the opinion that it could not have been written by Scott, who was suspected to be the author of Waverley, because Scott never had been at sea. Cooper said that for that very reason he thought Scott wrote it, and added that he would undertake to write a real sea story. 'The Pilot' was the result.

Paul Jones's adventures suggested the plot; which is, in brief, an attempt during the Revolutionary War to abduct some prominent Englishmen for exchange against American prisoners. An American frigate, purposely unnamed, with the schooner Ariel, appears off Northumberland and takes on board a mysterious Pilot, who is intended to represent Paul Jones. A heavy gale arises; the frigate is saved only by the Pilot's skill and knowledge. Near by, at the "Abbey," lives Colonel Howard, a self-expatriated American loyalist, with his nieces, Cecilia Howard and Katherine Plowden; also a relative, Christopher Dillon, a suitor of Cecilia's and the villain of the story. The girls' favored lovers are Griffith, first officer of the frigate, and Barnstaple, commander of the Ariel. The girls discover, and Dillon suspects, the proximity of their lovers. Griffith, disguised and with a small support, reconnoitres the "Abbey," and is overpowered by troops obtained by Dillon; but he is rescued by reinforcements brought by the Pilot, whose own mission has failed. Colonel Howard and family are taken aboard the frigate. Meanwhile Barnstaple has fought and captured the British cutter Alacrity. Finding Dillon aboard of her, he sends him on shore, under parole, together with the coxswain, "Long Tom" Coffin. "Long Tom," with his inseparable harpoon, is Leatherstocking in sea-togs. Dillon betrays his trust, and orders a neighboring battery to fire on the Ariel. Tom, informed and aided by Katherine, drags Dillon back to the Ariel, but too late to save her. Crippled by the battery, she is wrecked; Tom refuses to leave her, Dillon is left aboard to punish his treachery; — both are drowned. The frigate takes off the survivors, gallantly runs the gauntlet of an English fleet, and lands the Pilot in Holland, his mission ended though not accomplished. After the war the four lovers are happily united.

PILOT AND HIS WIFE, THE, by Jonas Lie (1874). This story is of Norwegian simplicity. The scene is laid partly in Norway, partly in South America where the hero goes on his voyages. Salve Kristiansen loves Elizabeth Raklev, whom he has known from her childhood, which was spent in a lighthouse on a lonely island, with her grandfather. Salve is a sailor, later on a pilot. He hears that Elizabeth is engaged to a naval officer named Beck, and in a rage goes on a long voyage. Later he finds the report false; she confesses her love for him, and they are married. He is of a jealous, suspicious nature, and fierce in temper. She is often unhappy, but at last she sees that it is useless to submit passively; that there can be no happiness without mutual trust: so she reclaims and shows him the letter in which she refused to marry Beck "because my heart is another's." Convinced at last of her loyalty, Kristiansen after a struggle conquers his jealousy, and life is happy at last.

PIONEERS, THE, see **LEATHERSTOCKING TALES.**

PIONEERS OF FRANCE IN THE NEW WORLD, by Francis Parkman, a history of colonizing enterprises in North America in the sixteenth and early seventeenth centuries, was first published in 1865 and in revised form in 1885. The work is divided into two parts, the first of which narrates the unsuccessful attempts of the Huguenots to found a Protestant colony in Florida. After recounting the failures of Villegagnon in 1558 and Ribaut in 1563, Parkman tells the tragic story of Laudonnière's settlement at the mouth of the St. John's River, the massacre of its garrison by the Spaniards under Menendez de Avilés (1565), and the vengeance taken by the French privateer, Dominique de Gourges (1568). The second part, after an opening chapter on the explorations of Verrazzaro and Cartier, is almost entirely devoted to the colonizing efforts of Samuel de Champlain, the Father of New France. First we hear of his experiences with de Monts, at the ill-fated colony of St. Croix in Acadia (1604–1605), and with Lescarbot and Poutrincourt at Port Royal during the happy winter of 1606–1607. Then follow the wranglings that ensued between adventurers and Jesuits, the destruction of the colony by the unauthorized intervention of the governor of Virginia in 1613; Champlain's new colony at Quebec in 1608, his expedition to the lake that bears his name in 1609, and his journeys up the Ottawa, through Lake Nipissing to Lake Huron, and thence by the Severn and Trent rivers and a chain of lakes to Lake Ontario in 1615; his campaign against the Iroquois in this and the following year; his gradual development of a permanent colony at Quebec, 1616–1627; the capture of Quebec by Kirke in 1629, its restoration to France and Champlain's death as governor of the colony in 1635. This work, the initial volume in Parkman's monumental narrative on the struggle of England and France for North America, has all of Parkman's brilliance and vigour of narrative, his careful reliance upon original sources of information, and his illuminating indication of the effect of old-world movements and tendencies — such for example as the Reformation and the Counter-Reformation — upon the colonists and natives of the new world.

PIPING HOT, see **ROUGON-MACQUART.**

PIT, THE, by Frank Norris (1903). This book, which was published after the death of the author, was the second of the trilogy entitled 'The Epic of the Wheat,' which he was intending to complete. It deals mainly with the wheat markets and speculative greed of Chicago and describes in a forcible manner the mighty whirlpool, the Pit. The central figure in the story is Curtis Jadwin, a typical Chicago wheat trader, whose masterful nature makes him a leader among men. He is daring and lucky and possesses a clear, far-seeing brain and unlimited confidence in his own judgment and good fortune. In the beginning of the story he is one of three suitors for the hand of Laura Dearborn, a beautiful girl, who has recently moved to Chicago from her home in the east. The other two, Sheldon Corthell, a rich young artist, and Landry Court, a clever young trader, woo her unsuccessfully and Jadwin carries off the prize. Laura, who is at first somewhat unresponsive to the strong affection which Jadwin lavishes upon her, gradually awakens to an appreciation of his character and learns to love him deeply. Her husband's success in business is regarded by her as a misfortune as it takes so much of his time and thought that she is forced to spend many lonely hours. Although provided with every luxury that money can supply she allows herself to become very unhappy because she cannot command her husband's entire attention. Upon the return of Corthell, after an absence of several years in Europe, she finds in his homage and admiration a solace for her loneliness and drifts into an "affair" with her old-time admirer. Jadwin's business at this time has reached a crisis as he has been speculating extensively and losing heavily. He makes one grand final effort to carry the market and regain his fortune and face the "ravening wolves" alone, but meets his Waterloo and is a ruined man. His defeat causes a physical breakdown and he returns to his home a shattered wreck. Laura, who is on the verge of going away with Corthell, is aroused from her folly by her husband's condition and from that moment has no thought except for him. She nurses him through a long illness and the story closes with their departure for a new country, to begin a new life.

PLAIN DEALER, THE, by William Wycherley (1674). "The author of 'The Plain Dealer," said Dryden, "has obliged all honest and virtuous men by one of the most bold, most general, and most useful satires which has ever been presented on the English theatre." The theme, however, and the manner in which it is treated confine this comedy to the category of plays which are to be read and not acted. Manly, "of an honest, surly, nice Humour" is a ship's captain who chose a sea-life to avoid the world. He is beloved by Fidelia, who for his sake gives up a large fortune and follows him to sea in male attire. Together they plot against Olivia, who had been Manly's mistress. The litigious widow Blackacre and her son Squire Jerry are the forerunners of Goldsmith's better known characters Mrs. Hardcastle and Tony Lumpkin. The idea of a line in the prologue, "and with faint praises one another damn," is more commonly remembered in Pope's unconscious reproduction "Damn with faint praise." The sentiment in Manly's mind when he said "I weigh the man, not his title; 'tis not the king's stamp can make the metal better or heavier" was later to find immortal expression in Burns:

"The rank is but the guinea stamp,
The man's the gowd for a' that."

PLASHER'S MEAD, by Compton Mackenzie (1915). Guy Hazelwood, an Oxford friend of Michael Fane's (see 'Sinister Street'), decides to retire from the world to make poetry his career. He rents a quaint old house in the country, called "Plasher's Mead," which he and Michael have discovered together on a vacation ramble. The first evening of his seclusion he meets in the moonlit meadow his neighbors, the three lovely daughters of the rector, Monica, Margaret, and Pauline. He falls in love with Pauline, a gay young girl whom Michael Fane describes as a faery child. The unworldly rector takes his mind off his garden bulbs to help publish the poems which are to be a great success, and make the happy marriage possible. Love's young dream is a prolonged engagement of two years of constant companionship, of nursery teas, birthday parties, music at the rectory, and walks about a romantic countryside. The perfect months in twenty-four chapters end in a parting, as there seems no prospect of living on poetry. Guy would postpone the delightful dream of marriage indefinitely, but Pauline, come to womanhood, is unhappy with the strain of hope deferred; she takes on herself the responsibility of the decision that she is not essential to Guy's happiness and gives him his freedom. He goes to Italy and meets Michael Fane about to enter a brotherhood in Rome.

PLAYBOY OF THE WESTERN WORLD, THE, by J. M. Synge (1907). The hero of this drama is Christie Mahon, the timid son of a small farmer, who is a bully and a tyrant. The lad's life is intolerable, and when he is bidden to marry an elderly widow he rebels.   In the quarrel he hits his father on the head with a spade ana thinking he has killed the old man, runs away across the country to a distant village. Here he tells his tale of persecution and parricide, and finds himself suddenly converted into a hero.   He enlarges on the original story each time he tells it.   Pegeen, the romantic daughter of the keeper of the public house, falls in love with him and dismisses her accepted suitor, the cowardly Shawn Keogh.   The Widow Quinn, a modern Irish Wife of Bath, tries to win him from Pegeen.   The girls from the neighborhood bring him presents.   In the height of his glory his father appears in the flesh in search of his son, none the worse for the wound in his head which had felled him and proceeds to beat Christie with his stick.   Immediately all his admirers, Pegeen included, turn upon him as a wretched impostor.   He tries to live up to his former reputation by a real attempt to slay his father and is surprised and disillusioned to find that the villagers have turned from admiration to horror and are ready to hand him over to the police.   His father appears again to defend him and they go away together; but Christie has found himself and is master now.   The hero worship has made another man of him.   During his short stay he has won all the prizes at the local games and though he has told Pegeen a string of lies, he has talked poetry and love so irrisistibly that she laments at the end of the play that she has lost the only Playboy of the Western World.   It is a delightful comedy in exquisite poetic diction. There is no reason for regarding this satire as directed against the Irish nation, although at its first performance in Dublin and its subsequent reproduction in New York and Philadelphia, it was the occasion for popular demonstrations of disapproval.   Scenes from the play are reproduced in the LIBRARY.

PLUTARCH'S LIVES, a series of forty-six biographies of famous Greeks and Romans, arranged in pairs.   Sir Thomas North's translation (1579) is in vigorous Tudor English and is interesting as the source of Shakespeare's Roman plays.   Modern translations are afforded by the Bohn Library and the Loeb Classical Library. For a synopsis and criticism see the LIBRARY under 'Plutarch.'

POE, EDGAR ALLAN, by George E. Woodberry (1897).   In preparing this biography of Poe, the author carefully reviewed all previous biographies and essays bearing upon his subject, rejecting all statements not fully authenticated.   He also had recourse to recently furnished documents from the U. S. War Department, and also to personal letters from friends and relatives of Poe.

Woodberry dwells upon Poe's brilliancy, originality, and ability as a critic as well as an author.   He admits Poe's inexcusable habit of passing off his own old productions as new articles, often with little or no revision, but defends him against the charge of plagiarism.   In fact, he notes that Poe's lack of continuous application and absolute want of mental and moral balance alone prevent him from being the peer of the ablest authors of his time.   It is the best life of Poe extant and may be considered final.

POET AT THE BREAKFAST TABLE, THE, by Oliver Wendell Holmes.   'The Poet,' like its predecessors, 'The Autocrat' and 'The Professor,' was first printed as a series of papers in the Atlantic Monthly, making its appearance in 1872.   In merit it is somewhat superior to 'The Professor,' but hardly equal to 'The Autocrat'; and though containing the familiar 'Aunt Tabitha,' and 'Homesick in Heaven,' has nothing to be compared with 'The Chambered Nautilus' or 'The One-Hoss Shay.'

Like the earlier volumes, it consists of rambling, discursive talks on many subjects.

— religion, science, literature, — with a frequent excursion into the realm of philosophy. The local flavor is very strong, as usual with Holmes; and probably the papers will always have a greater attraction for New-Englanders than for those to whom the local allusions are pointless, and the setting alien. Nevertheless, the author's sympathies are as wide as humanity itself; and he gives many a hard hit at prejudice and intolerance. Moreover he says repeatedly that his chief object in writing is to meet some need of his fellow-creatures, to strike some chord that shall wake a responsive note in some kindred soul. Certainly this wide-reaching human kindliness is not the least charm of this delightful book.

The principal persons at the table are the Poet; the Old Master, a scholarly philosopher; the Scarabee, a withered entomologist; the poetic young astronomer; Scheherazade, a young girl who writes stories; and the Lady. All of these occasionally take part in the conversation, but frequently the writer in his own person addresses the reader directly. In whatever guise he appears, however, we cannot help recognizing the genial personality of Holmes himself. As he says in the verses subjoined as epilogue to the series:—

"A Boswell, writing out himself!
For though he changes dress and name,
The man beneath is still the same,
Laughing or sad, by fits and starts,
One actor in a dozen parts,
And whatsoe'er the mask may be,
The voice assures us, This is he."

POETRY, NATURE AND ELEMENTS OF, by E. C. Stedman, see **NATURE,** etc.

POETS, see **LIVES OF THE ENGLISH POETS,** by Samuel Johnson.

POETS OF AMERICA, THE, by Edmund Clarence Stedman (1885), a work of the same general scope and design as the 'Victorian Poets,' and a kind of sequel to it, is written in the belief that "the literature — even the poetic literature — of no country during the last half-century is of greater interest to the philosophical student, with respect to its bearing on the future, than that of the United States. American poetry, more than that of England during the period considered, has idealized, often inspired, the national sentiment, — the historic movements of the land whose writers have composed it." After introductory chapters on 'Early and Recent Conditions,' and on the 'Growth of the American School,' the author considers critically the work of Bryant, Whittier, Emerson, Longfellow, Poe, Holmes, Lowell, Whitman, and Taylor, — concluding with a chapter on the poetical outlook. These essays are sympathetic and scholarly, showing fine insight not only into the nature and character of American verse, but into the environment also of which it was a product.

POLITICAL ECONOMY, PRINCIPLES OF, by J. S. Mill (1848). This book was written with the idea of giving to the world a work similar in object and conception to Adam Smith's 'Wealth of Nations' which Mill believed to be "in many parts obsolete, and in all imperfect." It was Mill's desire to present purely economic phenomena in their relation to the most advanced political ideas of his own. The book is a kind of fusion of the economics of Ricardo in which he had been brought up and the ideas which had come to him as a result of his intense desire to ameliorate the condition of the masses. He accepts the older theory of rent and profits, the doctrine of the wages fund, which few would now maintain, and, with many exceptions, the principle of laissez faire.   In his later years he recognized that much of his economic teaching was inconsistent.   The great merit, however, of the work, which made an immense impression on his own time, and held a most important place in the world of economic thought, was its conspicuous candor, its uprightness of purpose, and its inflexible determination to stimulate sincere thinking.   The great protest of the book is against the notion that "wealth consisted solely of money; or of the precious metals, which, when not already in the state of money, are capable of being directly converted into it."   To a present-day reader, perhaps the most valuable chapter is that entitled "On the probable futurity of the laboring classes," in which Mill maintains that the theory of dependence and protection is no longer applicable in modern society and that the social independence of woman would raise the general intelligence of society.

POLITICIAN, THE ('Daniele Cortis'), by Antonio Fogazzaro (1885).   Daniele is a statesman with ideals in advance of his time for the social regeneration of Italy. When he says that "the progress of modern society demands the assistance of religion and liberty," the report is spread abroad that he is a clerical.   When he suggests that the clergy should return to "poverty and evangelical humility" and be forced "to study and to lead blameless lives," the priests of his own parish denounce him as anti-Catholic and forbid the people to vote for him.   He proposes to establish a new party to be represented by a progressive journal.   The love story is his devotion to his cousin the Baroness Elena, who has made a disastrous marriage.   Di Santa Giula, the senator, her husband, involved in dishonorable debt, is on the verge of criminal prosecution.   Elena's uncle, the head of the family, will provide the money to save her husband's honor and liberty on condition that he emigrates to America.   Elena, unknown to her uncle, promises to accompany him, thus giving up her family and the man she loves, to be faithful to her ideal of her marriage vows.   At the last, the sacrifice seems too hard to bear, but Daniele's uncompromising ideal of duty for himself and for her holds her to her decision to go with her husband.   As in other novels by this author the hero draws the heroine from religious doubt to his own faith.   At the tragic parting, of intense suffering to both, he assures her: "They are wedded not with flesh but with heart.   Thus also are wedded the stars and planets, not with their body, but with their light; thus also the palm-trees, not with their roots, but with their summits."   He returns to Rome to the battlefield of politics, and she, leaving a letter of farewell for her uncle and her frivolous vulgar-hearted mother, joins her husband at the port of Venice.

POLYOLBION, by Michael Drayton.   The 'Polyolbion' appeared first in 1613, early in the reign of James I.   It is a poetical gazetteer of England apparently based on Camden's 'Britannia.'   It contains about 100,000 verses, divided into thirty books of uneven lengths.   Its enormous length has always kept it from popularity, even among the readers of the seventeenth century, who had time and willingness to read long books.   The account is based on a journey of the Muse, which takes her up and down the various rivers of England; and throughout, all the countries, mountains, rivers, cities, towns, and fields are described in full, as well as the birds and beasts that inhabit them.   At appropriate points, such as battle-fields, landing-places of great men, homes of poets, and graves of heroes, the Muse pauses long enough to give the reader a full account of the event or the man for which the place is memorable.

    The verse consists of monotonous Alexandrine couplets, seldom relieved by any striking passages. Drayton obviously takes great enjoyment in full-sounding names of places and people, and in references to classic authors.   There is, however, no inspiration in the work. Even the patriotic admiration for England, characteristic of the time, does not amount to a passion with him. Still, the whole poem is a patriotic attempt to glorify England in every aspect.

POPULAR ANTIQUITIES, by John Brand, see **OBSERVATIONS ON.**

POPULAR TALES FROM THE NORSE, by Peter Christian Asbjørnsen (1858). This is a collection of Norse folk-tales, translated by George Webbe Dasent. The stories in this compilation are the Norse versions of the stories which have been floating all over Europe for so many ages. There is nothing in these tales of the heroic doings of Odin and Thor, of Volsungs and Vikings, that we associate with Norse stories. The only supernatural beings are the Trolls, a dark, ugly race, ill-disposed to mankind. The favorite story seems to be the adventures of some poor youth, who starts out to seek his fortune, and meets with many strange happenings, but usually ends by winning a princess and half a kingdom. There are many old friends under different names: 'Cinderella,' 'The Sleeping Beauty,' 'Tom Thumb'; and one story, 'East o' the Sun and West o' the Moon,' is a combination of the old tale of 'Cupid and Psyche' and 'Beauty and the Beast.' The old pagan customs and legends show through the veneer of Christianity, as in 'The Master-Smith,' where the blacksmith, who has angered the Devil, goes to make his peace with Satan after he has lost his chance of heaven, because he does not want to be houseless after death: he would prefer to go to heaven; but as he cannot, he would prefer hell to a homeless fate.
The stories are prefaced by an essay written by Mr. Dasent, in which he traces many of them from their Sanskrit originals through Greek to German mythology.

PORTION OF LABOR, A, by Mary E. Wilkins (1901). The scene of this story is laid in an industrial centre of New England and all the characters depicted are more or less closely connected with a great shoe factory. Andrew Brewster, the heroine's father, is a patient, gentle New Englander, dignified in the presence of adversity, yet keenly sensitive withal, while his wife, who is of coarser fibre and somewhat vulgar, is redeemed by her fierce pride in her beautiful daughter. Ellen Brewster stands out a delicate flower, from the coarser growth around her, and the author traces her development into womanhood, while her aspirations and creeds as a young girl are resolved into a spiritual force, which sends her into the factory with uplifted head and exalted soul and makes her the backbone of her father, and the stern judge of her homely lover. The author draws in Ellen, a creature of grace, daintiness, and refinement, who is gifted with spiritual and intellectual strength and who assumes the rôle of an industrial Joan of Arc, playing an important part in initiating a strike and later in advocating its termination. She rejects her gentle but commonplace lover and in the end contracts a love-match with a rich and eligible man. The keynote of the story seems to be that of the ideal womanhood finding its highest development and recompense in fulfilling with dignity and devotion a commonplace and unlovely destiny. And the author aims to bring the reader to a realization of the thought that to be a part of labor is greater than to be the highest product of labor.

PORTRAIT OF A LADY, THE, a novel by Henry James (1882). The heroine, whose portrait is drawn with remarkable elaboration and finish, is an American girl, Isabel Archer, beautiful, intellectual, of a clear-cut character, and her own mistress. The elements in her nature that make her a lady are emphasized by her experiences with men. When the story opens she is a guest in the home of an aunt, Mrs. Touchett, whose husband, an American banker, has been settled for many years in England. They have one son, Ralph, a semi-invalid.

A neighbor, Lord Warburton, wishes to marry her, but she refuses him because she does not love him, and because she wishes to have more experience of the world as a single woman. In the same fortnight she rejects another suitor, Caspar Goodwood, an young earnest New Englander, who has followed her to England. She misses in him the romantic element, and will not accept his virtues in exchange. By the death of her uncle she finds herself a great heiress; half of Ralph's patrimony being willed, at his own request, to her. In the weeks of her uncle's illness, she forms a friendship with Madam Merle, a guest of Mrs. Touchett's, a thorough woman of the world, who finds that she has uses of her own for Isabel. A far different friend is a country-woman, Henrietta Stackpole, a correspondent for a home paper. She is sincere, democratic, loyal to her national traditions and desirous that Isabel should be so. She wishes therefore to bring about a marriage between Goodwood and Isabel. After her uncle's death, Isabel goes to Italy. There, through the offices of Madam Merle, she meets Gilbert Osmond, a man without rank or fortune, but of unerring tastes, and of an exquisite manner of life. His possessions are limited to a few faultless works of art and a little daughter, Pansy, just out of a convent. The lady in Isabel is attracted by Osmond's detailed perfections. Against the wishes of her friends she marries him. With marriage comes disillusionment. Isabel finds that she is smothered in the airless life of barren dilettantism; she finds that her gentlemanly husband is soulless and venomous. He wishes to force his daughter, Pansy, into a loveless marriage, and sends her to a convent until she shall show worldly wisdom through mere pressure of ennui. During her exile Isabel discovers that Pansy is not the child of Osmond's first wife, but of Madame Merle, his former mistress. Being summoned at this time to England, to the death-bed of Ralph Touchett, she regards her departure from her husband's house as final. The book closes with the intimation that she will take Pansy under her protection, and will not marry Caspar Goodwood.

POT-BOUILLE, see **ROUGON-MACQUART**.

POTIPHAR PAPERS, by George William Curtis. This brilliant satire on New York society was published in 1856, and is still read, though it has partly lost its point owing to changed conditions. The papers are something in the manner of Addison's satires on the pretensions and insincerities of society; but at times the bitterness becomes more scathing, and reminds one of Thackeray in its merciless analysis of folly and ignorance. The writer divides the society of which he speaks into three classes: the newly rich, who have acquired wealth but not culture; the descendants of the old families, who make the glory of their ancestors serve instead of any manliness or worth of their own; and the dancing youths into whose antecedents or characters nobody inquires, so long as they enliven the ball-rooms, and constitute eligible partners for the young ladies. A description is given of Mrs. Potiphar's ball, where dresses are ruined by careless waiters, and drunken young fellows destroy valuable property, and hosts and guests are thoroughly miserable while pretending to enjoy the occasion. In the account of the Potiphars in Paris we see how wealthy Americans, when lacking innate breeding and refinement, make themselves ridiculous in the eyes of foreigners. The gilded youth of the day, as well as the shallow and flippant women, are held up to derision, while our sympathies are aroused by the poor, toiling, unaspiring fathers, who are not strong enough to make a stand for their rights. In reading these papers we can only be glad that the persons described by the author are no longer typical of American society. One of the enduring characters is the Rev. Cream Cheese, who sympathetically advises with Mrs. Potiphar as to the color of the cover of her prayer-book.

POVERTY, A STUDY IN TOWN LIFE, by Seebohm Rowntree (1901). The author of this work, a manufacturer of the city of York, England, here records the results of an exhaustive inquiry into the social and economic condition of the wage-earning class in York. The standard of life as regards food and housing, the proportion of the population below "the poverty line," the immediate causes of poverty, and the relation of poverty to the standard of health are treated in detail. Poverty is defined as the condition of those "whose total earnings (including those of grown-up children living at home) are insufficient to obtain the minimum necessaries for the maintenance of merely physical efficiency." After arriving at a scientific estimate of the minimum required for that purpose even if the poor could obtain their food at contract prices, and were fed no better than the inmates of public institutions (e. g. prisons and workhouses), Mr. Rowntree shows that nearly thirty per cent. of the total population of the city were living in poverty, the most potent cause of this depressed economic condition being lowness of wages or other causes over which the individual worker has little or no control. The main conclusions of this book have not been shaken. It carries a little further the methods adopted by Charles Booth in 'Life and Labour of the People in London,' and by independent investigation arrives at almost exactly similar results. These two books may be said to have revolutionized the whole method of approach to the study of the problem of poverty, and later investigations for other cities in England and in the United States have merely served to confirm the correctness of their conclusions.

PRAGMATISM, 'a new name for some old ways of thinking,' by William James, is a series of eight lectures delivered in Boston in 1906 and published in 1907. James begins by distinguishing two types of philosophical thinkers, the rationalists and the empiricists, the "tender-minded" believers in an ideal unity beneath shifting phenomena, and the "tough-minded" deniers of any reality except that of individual things and of any predetermined harmony in the universe. As a method of settling the dispute James offers *pragmatism* or the method of testing the truth of philosophic theories by their *practical* action, by the way in which they *work*. (From the Greek πράγμα, action, from which our words "practice" and "practical" are derived.) The word was introduced into philosophy by Charles Pierce in 1878 but was unnoticed until 1898, when James's use of it in a philosophical address gave it currency. The intellectualist view is that ideas are true according as they agree with the absolute and eternal realities; the pragmatist on the other hand believes that the ideas are true according to their effect upon our other ideas and upon our conduct. "True ideas are those that we can assimilate, validate, corroborate, and verify. False ideas are those that we can not." "Truth *happens* to an idea. It *becomes* true, is *made* true by events. Its verity *is* in fact an event, a process: the process namely of its verifying itself, its veri-*fication*. Its validity is the process of valid-*ation*." "The true is only the expedient in the way of our thinking, just as 'the right' is only the expedient in the way of our behaving." Pragmatists, in denying the existence of abstract truth, resemble the mediæval nominalists, who refused to admit the reality of general conceptions except as inherent in particular facts.

The two first lectures state the alternative of rationalism and empiricism and offer pragmatism as the solution.   In the third, the problems of substance and accident, of matter and spirit, of materialism and spiritualism, of design and unconscious evolution, of free-will and determinism are all weighed by the pragmatic method, by inquiring what practical effect these beliefs have on men's moral and mental attitude. The fourth chapter discusses the question of monism and pluralism, of "the one and the many."   The powerful appeal of the theory that the universe is absolutely *one* is illustrated by quotation from a modern Vedantist philosopher; but by the pragmatic method it is shown that neither absolute monism nor absolute pluralism is in agreement with the facts of experience.   In 'Pragmatism and Common Sense' our commoner ideas are explained as a number of successful hypotheses which have worked well, as adaptations to reality not revelations of some mystic world-truth.   In 'Pragmatism's Conception of Truth' the method is further elaborated and is defended against the intellectualist position that truth is not made but absolutely obtains. 'Pragmatism and Humanism,' with reference to the teachings of F. C. S. Schiller, shows how pragmatism leads to the position that truth is largely a human product, since our sensations and judgments enter so profoundly into its determination.   In 'Pragmatism and Religion' James reminds us that pragmatism is a method not a philosophy, and that it excludes neither the rational nor the empirical thinkers, neither the "tender-minded" nor the "tough-minded" but only strives to determine what views man can best live by.   It does not shut its eyes to disagreeable evidence, nor on the other hand does it exclude theism, meliorism, and a belief in moral freedom and effort.

The practical appeal of James's theory and the lucidity, concreteness, and literary grace with which he sets it forth have won it many adherents, have made "pragmatism" a household word, and have done much to popularize the study of philosophy. James's influence on and affiliations with the modern French thinkers like Bergson and Boutroux and the philosophic innovators in other modern countries, is deep and wide.   Pragmatism has also stirred up vehement opposition among the rationalists. Whatever the merits of the contending parties there can be no question of the value and fruitfulness of James's ideas.

PRAIRIE, THE, see LEATHERSTOCKING TALES.

PRÉCIEUSES RIDICULES, LES, by Molière.   No one of Molière's comedies is better known than this famous satire on the 'Précieuses,' which was produced for the first time in 1659.   It can almost be entitled a farce, being an exaggeration of an exaggeration.   It is in one act, and is a satire on a style of speech, and an affected taste in art and literature, prevalent among a certain class at that time.   It is said that when writing it, Molière had in mind the literary lights who assembled at the Hôtel de Rambouillet.   The story is of two country ladies, Madelon and Cathos, just arrived in Paris, who reject two suitors proposing marriage, unless they first serve a long apprenticeship of courtship and gallantry as do the heroes in 'Artemène' and 'Clélie,' two novels by Mademoiselle Scudéry, much in vogue at that time. In revenge, the rejected suitors clothe their valets, Mascarille and Jodelet, in rich dress, and send them to masquerade as the Marquis de Mascarille and Vicomte de Jodelet.   They are warmly welcomed by the ladies, who are charmed with Mascarille's expressed intention of writing the history of Rome in the form of madrigals.   Mascarille composes a ridiculous impromptu of four lines, which he dissects word by word, calling attention to the many esoteric beauties, invisible except to the veritable

"Précieux." The deception is kept up until their masters come and despoil them of their rich clothes, leaving them in their servant's dress. Molière, in his preface, says the piece was printed against his better judgment, as much of the success which it attained depended upon the action and tone of voice. The justice of this remark is appreciated if one has seen its performance at the Comédie Française, where tradition has preserved intact all the original "business" of the piece.

It was a great success; and as his attacks on quackery had made possible a reform in medicine, so this comedy rendered ridiculous the name "Précieux," which had before been considered a distinction.

PREHISTORIC EUROPE, by James Geikie (1880). "Prehistoric" in this volume is used to mean the whole period disclosed to us by means of archæological evidence, as distinguished from what is known through written records, and the purpose of the book is to present in outline what appear to have been the most considerable physical changes experienced in the European continent since the beginning of the Pleistocene period. In the latter category Dr. Geikie includes the Preglacial, Glacial, and Interglacial deposits. Under "Postglacial" he classifies the accumulations which are of later date than the last great extension of glacier ice in Europe. He accepts the current division of prehistoric time into three periods, — the Stone Age, when weapons, implements, and ornaments were made exclusively of stone, wood, horn, or bone; the Age of Bronze, when cutting instruments began to be made of copper or bronze; and the Age of Iron, when bronze gave place to iron. The Stone Age, with which geologists chiefly have to do, is usually, after Lord Avebury, divided into the Palæolithic and Neolithic periods. During the Palæolithic Age, the beginning of which, according to Dr. Geikie, must go back at least 200,000 years, the lion, the hippopotamus, the rhinoceros, the mammoth were contemporaneous with man in Europe, and lived together under a climate which for one period was extremely equable and genial. At a later stage in this period Pleistocene Europe suffered extreme conditions. Arctic animals lived in what is now the South of France, and the mammoth ranged in Spain and Italy. During this period, when the climate of Europe underwent violent changes, the alluvial and cave deposits were formed and the flora and fauna were compelled to migrate over vast distances. During the last glacial epoch of the Pleistocene period, Britain and the southern portion of the Scandinavian peninsula, which had been depressed, were gradually re-elevated. Spitsbergen, Greenland, Iceland, and the Faroe Islands, which at this period formed a portion of the mainland, were eventually isolated, but before the North Sea was formed Neolithic man had entered Europe and crossed into Britain. Less clement conditions succeeded the genial climate, and a still later change during the Age of Bronze brought about a condition of humidity. In the Age of Iron this humidity disappeared and the sea retreated to its present level.

PRELUDE, THE, or, GROWTH OF A POET'S MIND; an Autobiographical Poem, by William Wordsworth, was begun in 1799, completed in 1805, but not published until 1850. It was intended as preliminary to a great philosophical poem enunciating Wordsworth's views of man, of nature, and of society, to be composed in three parts under the general title of 'The Recluse.' Of this projected poem only the second part, called 'The Excursion' was completed (see the digest of 'The Excursion'). The first book of the first part was posthumously published in 1888 under the title of 'The Recluse.' In 'The Prelude' which, Wordsworth said, stood to the greater poem in the relation of an ante-chapel to a cathedral, the poet gives an account of the development of his own mind and heart under the influences of education, nature, and society, with the aim of proving to himself and others his fitness for the work he is undertaking. Though numbering fourteen solid books partly on abstract topics in sober blank verse the poem has intense interest, not only on account of its beautiful descriptive passages, but from its masterly analysis of the poetic gifts and the influences which foster them. In the two first books, 'School-Time,' Wordsworth vividly sets forth the unthinking physical joys of his youthful out-door sports and his moments of calm intuition of a spiritual presence in nature; 'Residence at Cambridge' describes the idleness and aimlessness of the poet's first college days roused only by the memory of great Cambridge men like Newton. The book entitled 'Summer Vacation' records the renewed spell exercised on the poet by his native landscape on his first return to it and his first semi-deliberate self-consecration to the task of poetry. In Book V. he begins to be influenced by Shakespeare, Milton, and other great poets, and in the sixth walks with a friend across the Alps and is impressed by nature on a grander scale than in the English Lake region. In the eighth book, on the occasion of his return to London, he shows how his love of nature had fostered his love of man by investing man with a dignity drawn from the noble landscapes against which the poet had first noted him; and how this dignity, first recognized in the shepherds of the Lake District clung to Wordsworth's conception of man even when he saw his petty and ugly side in the London crowds. In Books IX. and X. Wordsworth describes his visit to France between November, 1791, and December, 1792, recounting how his zeal and enthusiasm for the Revolution were stimulated by his friendship for Captain Michel Beaupuys, an enlightened patriot whose acquaintance he made at Blois early in 1792. He then describes the excitement of his sojourn in Paris in the days that followed the September massacres, and his narrow escape from involvement in the fate of the Girondins, through the necessity of his leaving France at the close of the year. Book XI. recounts the moral crisis through which Wordsworth passed on his return, a republican, from a country which was abandoning her republican ideals, to his own country which was attacking them by warring against the Revolution. From despair he is redeemed by the counsel and influence of his sister, Dorothy, and by his love for nature. His renewed confidence and joy in poetic production are analyzed in the next two books: 'Imagination and Taste, how Impaired and Restored,' and in the 'Conclusion' we have a general analysis of the poet's ripened powers and a picture of his settlement at Alfoxden in company with his sister Dorothy and in the neighborhood of Coleridge, ready to begin his poetic production.

PRIDE AND PREJUDICE, by Jane Austen. The story of 'Pride and Prejudice' is extremely simple: it is a history of the gradual union of two people, one held back by unconquerable pride and the other blinded by prejudice; but in spite of little plot, the interest is sustained through the book. The characters are drawn with humor, delicacy, and the intimate knowledge of men and women that Miss Austen always shows. Mr. Bennet, amiable and peace-loving, leaves to Mrs. Bennet, his querulous, ambitious, and narrow-minded wife, the difficult task of marrying off his five daughters. Her daughter Elizabeth, though not so beautiful as Jane, is the brightest and most attractive member of the family. She has a lively disposition, frank, pleasing manners, and a warm heart; and though bitterly prejudiced against Mr. Darcy, the wealthy, dignified hero, his excellent qualities and faithful devotion win her at last, and she forgives the pride from which he stooped to conquer her. Among the minor characters are George Wickham, fascinating and unprincipled, who elopes with Lydia Bennet; Mr. Bingley, Darcy's handsome friend, who marries Jane Bennet: and Mr.

Collins, a small-souled, strait-laced clergyman. The scene is laid in England in the country; and the characters are the ladies and gentlemen Miss Austen describes so well in her novels. 'Pride and Prejudice' was published in 1813. It was Miss Austen's first novel, and was written when she was twenty-one years old, in 1796.

PRIME MINISTER, THE, see **PARLIAMENTARY NOVELS,** by Anthony Trollope.

PRIMITIVE MAN, by Louis Figuier. Revised Translation with Thirty Scenes of Primitive Life and 233 Figures of Objects belonging to Prehistoric Ages (1870). A clear popular manual of the facts and arguments going to show the very great antiquity of man. It presents the evidence of actual relics of prehistoric life, with special attention to those found in France. At the time of its publication English readers were familiar with the views advocated by Lyell and Lubbock, and knew less of the results of French research, on which prehistoric archæology very largely rests. In the scheme of this startlingly interesting science the history of primitive mankind is divided into two great periods or ages: (1) The Stone Age, divided into three epochs; and (2) The Age of Metals, divided into two epochs. The story of these ages is the story of primitive man. Man first appeared in the epoch of those gigantic animals which became extinct long ages ago, the mammoth and the great cave-bear. He could dwell only in caves and hollows of the earth; and his clothing was made from the skins of beasts, or was of skins not made at all. The few simple tools or weapons which he contrived showed one chief material, except wood for handles, and that was stone. Horn and bone came into use for some minor implements, but stone was the material mainly employed for tools and weapons. Manufactures consisted chiefly in making sharp flakes of stone, some with edges for knives or hatchets, and others with points for a thrusting tool or weapon. If fire was known, and the potter's art also of molding moist clay into shapes and baking them to hardness, this added not only to the comfort but to the implements of primitive man; and shells perforated and strung made jewelry. If there was any money it was shell money. Bone and horn served to make implements such as arrow-heads, and bodkins, man's earliest needles. If a use like that of paper was known, a flat bone, like a shoulder-blade, served. The first art was with a bodkin, scratching on the flat of a bone the outline of the head of a favorite horse, or of a reindeer captured for a feast. Burial customs arose, and funeral feasts; and there seem to be indications of belief that the dead were not so dead but that they would need food and tools and other means of life.

The name given to this earliest Stone Age epoch is that of the Mammoth and Cave-Bear, the conspicuous representatives of the gigantic animals of that time. It was a time of fearful cold, in one of the ages of ice which played so large a part in the early history of the globe.

The second of the Stone Age epochs is called that of the reindeer, because this animal existed in great numbers, and with it the horse, various great cattle, elk, deer, etc., in place of the mammoth, cave-bear, cave-hyena, cave-lion, etc. The intense glacial cold of the first epoch was gone. Forests instead of ice clothed the earth. But these earlier Stone Age epochs are a dark dismal night hard to penetrate. A third Stone Age epoch followed, called the Polished Stone epoch, because of the great improvement effected in implements by polishing or smoothing the stone parts. Other advances were made in every department of early rude life. It was the age of many tamed animals.

The Stone Age was succeeded by the Age of Metals, in which there first came the Bronze epoch; and after it the Iron epoch, each being marked by knowledge of the use of the metals named.   The details, and the exact facts as to the type of man in each of the earliest epochs, can be made out but imperfectly; and since Figuier wrote, not a little has been added to our knowledge; yet the story as far as given is of extreme interest.

PRINCE, THE ('Il Principe'), a political treatise by Niccolò Machiavelli, written in 1513 but not printed until 1532.   The author, whom the restoration of the Medici in 1512 had deprived of his office of secretary to the council of the Florentine Republic, devoted his enforced leisure to the writing of a treatise on the ideal prince.   This he dedicated to one of the Medici, Lorenzo son of Piero, nephew of 'Il Magnifico,' and afterwards Duke of Urbino (1492–1519), partly in the hope of employment with the new government but mainly because he sincerely believed that a prince of the Medici might if wisely counseled bring unity to an Italy parcelled into small states and humiliated by foreign conquests.   Beginning with an enumeration of the different types of princes he distinguishes hereditary principalities, partly hereditary principalities (*i. e.*, including inherited and conquered territories), newly acquired principalities, some won by personal valor like that of Francesco Sforza, some acquired by fortune and by the arms of others, like that of Cæsar Borgia, some obtained by crime, and some by the favor of one's fellow citizens; and finally, the Papacy.   Incidental to this list are many illustrations, both from Machiavelli's classical reading and from his diplomatic experience, teaching by example the wise and the inefficient methods of princely rule.   Machiavelli then denounces the system of hiring mercenary soldiers to defend the state, maintaining that they are unreliable, a danger to the prince, a damper on the warlike spirit of the people, and a needless expense; and he strongly advocates national armies.   Then follows the main part of the book, namely a series of rules and principles to guide the prince's conduct.   These are introduced by the remark that since so many of the prince's subjects are evil he must learn to use evil as well as good in order to maintain a strong government.   It is better for a prince to be reputed miserly than to waste the resources of the principality; but a man may be lavish in order to secure power, especially if he can be generous at the expense of other people.   Clemency is better than cruelty, but cruelty is sometimes necessary; and if a prince cannot be both feared and loved, it is better for him to be feared. Fidelity to promises is good; but owing to the unruly nature of a prince's subjects it is sometimes impossible.   A wise prince should not keep his faith to his own disadvantage and when his reasons for pledging it are no longer existent.   But he should hide this infidelity by means of simulation and dissimulation, putting on a mask of piety, humanity, and above all of religion.   To deprive his subjects of their goods or of their wives is bad policy; a contented people and vigorous repressive measures against rebels secure a prince against uprisings.   The remaining chapters deal with the use of fortresses, the way to avoid flatterers, the proper use of counsellors and secretaries; and the book ends with an impassioned plea for the unification of Italy. This was indeed Machiavelli's one aim; and his one dominating principle of government is that the end justifies the means.   Italy could not be unified without a strong government; this could at that period be set up only by an autocrat; he could not maintain himself without sometimes disregarding moral principles.   Such was Machiavelli's position.   He has the merit of stating openly and fearlessly what every prince was practicing or endeavoring to practice; and his principles have a remarkable affinity with a view of the state widely current to-day.   In relentlessly applying scientific principles to public policy he is a true representative of the modern world then just born.

PRINCE AND THE PAUPER, THE, by Mark Twain (1881). The plot of this interesting story hinges on the remarkable resemblance of a poor street boy to the young English prince afterward Edward VI. Tom Canty, the pauper, looking through the iron gates of the royal court-yard, is ordered away by the guard. The young prince, overhearing the command, invites him in; and for amusement, changes clothes with him. While dressed in rags he sees on Tom's hand a bruise inflicted by the guard, and burning with indignation, he rushes alone from the palace to chastise the man: he is mistaken for Tom and driven away. He falls in with Tom's family, and is so badly treated that he runs away with Sir Miles Hendon, a disinherited knight, who takes pity on him, thinking his frequent assertions of royal birth a sign of madness. They wander about the country, having one adventure after another, and finally return to London just before Tom Canty's coronation.

Meanwhile Tom, in his changed condition, also undergoes many trials on account of his uncouthness of manner and ignorance of court etiquette; which, added to his apparent forgetfulness of the whereabouts of the "Great Seal," convince those around him that he has become demented. Gradually he grows accustomed to his position, and acquires sufficient knowledge of polite behavior to reassure the nobles regarding his mental balance; while he becomes less and less anxious about the disappearance of the real prince, which at first caused him much regret.

On the morning of the coronation Edward eludes his protector, and hastening to Westminster Abbey, forbids the ceremony. The hiding-place of the "Great Seal" is made the final test of his claims; and, assisted by Tom Canty's timely suggestions, he reveals it. He is then crowned in spite of his rags, and soon after rewards Tom Canty for his loyalty, and Sir Miles Hendon for his faithful services. All his short reign is tempered with the mercy and pity which in his misfortunes he so often desired and so seldom received.

PRINCE OF INDIA, THE, by Lew Wallace (1893). Both the title of this book, and the locality chosen by its author as a background for the story, awaken the interest of the reader. 'The Prince of India' is no scion of those ancient families that held sway over the country of Golconda, but is a Jewish shoemaker condemned by our Lord to wander over the earth until his second coming. This "Wandering Jew" is first introduced at the hidden sarcophagus of Hiram, King of Tyre, which he has not visited for one thousand years. Ten centuries before, he had found this mine of priceless jewels, and had concealed the spot for future exploration. He pays a short visit to Byzantium, where he possesses another treasure vault, and then departs for China for a fifty-years' stay. It is after the expiration of this period that he assumes the title of "Prince of India." He is filled now with the purpose of teaching men that God is Lord under whatever form worshiped, and that all men should be united by the bond of brotherly love. The Mohammedans do not accept his teaching, and he next goes to Constantinople to reveal it to the Greek Church, though he is at this time in league with the heir-apparent of the Turkish empire. The thread of romance here appears in the love of the young Turk for the Princess Irene, a relative of Constantine, Emperor of Byzantium, and also in the fondness of the "Prince of India" for a little Jewess named Lael, whom he adopts. The "Prince" is unsuccessful in his mission at Constantinople; and in rage and disappointment at the treatment he receives, he sets fire to his possessions and flees to the side of Mohammed, the heir of the Turkish empire. Then follows the capture of Constantinople, which is graphically set forth by the author. The fiery Mohammed weds the beautiful Irene, who tempers the victor's enthusiasm by her spirit of Christianity. "The Prince of India," borne down on the battle-field and supposed to be dead, rises with renewed youth to wander forth again, an outcast and stranger to his generation. In many ways this book resembles 'Ben-Hur': it covers a period of many years, and its plot is built by putting together historical and geographical facts, and weaving in a thread of romance. The "boat-race" introduced in this story suggests the famous "chariot-race" in 'Ben-Hur.' The book has a value in awakening an interest in a fascinating period of history, and in fixing in the reader's mind many historic events and customs, while its treatment of the religious questions involved is broad and comprehensive.

PRINCESS, THE; A MEDLEY, a romantic narrative poem in blank verse with intervening lyrics, written by Alfred Tennyson and published in 1847. The story is set in an attractive framework. Seven college friends are visiting one of their number at the estate of his father, Sir Walter Vivian, who happens to be entertaining his tenants with a garden party. During the afternoon a group of privileged guests, ladies from neighboring estates, and the collegians, assemble on the greensward in the court of a ruined abbey adorned by a broken statue of an ancestor of the family, Sir Ralph. After some bantering talk between young Walter Vivian and his sister Lilla regarding woman's social position, it is suggested that the company should be entertained by a story told in seven parts by each one of the men in succession. The ladies are to fill the pauses of the narrative by singing ballads. Taking his suggestion from a remark of Lilla's that if she were a great princess she would found a college for women, the first narrator (who has been describing the occasion in the first person) begins a tale which is a fantastic medley of classical, mediæval, and modern elements. A prince of a northern kingdom is betrothed as a child to Ida, a princess of the neighboring realm to the south (the locality and the period are left vague). When the time comes for the fulfilment of the marriage the princess, influenced by two advisers, Lady Psyche and Lady Blanche, forswears the company of men and establishes a great university for women, excluding all men on pain of death. Her father, King Gama, refuses to compel her to fulfil her contract; and the prince, anticipating his father's intention of declaring war, makes his way with two companions, Cyril and Florian, to the southern kingdom, where they gain access to the new University in the disguise of women. Here they are soon detected by the tutors, Lady Psyche, a charming widow with an infant daughter, Aglaia, and Lady Blanche, an older woman with a beautiful daughter, Melissa. But these, for their own reasons, keep silence, Psyche because she is Florian's sister, Blanche because she hopes to profit by her knowledge, and Melissa because she sympathizes with the young men. After a day of attendance at lectures and inspection of the wonderful gardens and buildings, the three supposed maidens accompany the princess on a geological excursion in the neighboring hills. On the way, the prince, in the character of a maid of honor from the northern court, pleads his own cause with the princess, but in vain; she is devoted to the cause of woman's emancipation, and will not think of marriage. At supper that evening, in a tent beside a waterfall, the visitors are requested to sing. The prince's falsetto and a ribald song by Cyril, who is reckless and flushed with wine, betray the sex of the visitors. The princess and her train at once take horse. In her haste and anger she falls from the bridge and is rescued by the resolute action of the prince, who plunges into the swift current and draws her out. Lady Psyche and Cyril escape, Lady Blanche and Melissa are dismissed, and the prince and Florian are ridiculed and thrust out by the angry princess, who retains Lady Psyche's child. But in the meantime the northern king has invaded the realm, captured Gama, and invested the university lands. The three companions and Lady Psyche find refuge in his camp. King Gama's three sons now coming up with a large army, it is arranged that the question of the princess's contract be decided by a tournament, fifty champions to fight on each side. The champions of the princess are headed by her brother, Arac, a jovial and gigantic warrior who strikes down the prince but spares his life. Her side being victorious, the princess is now freed from her obligation. But in gratitude for his rescue she offers the use of her university buildings to nurse him and the other wounded men back to health. The university becomes a hospital. With the days of convalescence many of the wounded men become enamoured of the maidens who are caring for them. Among others, Florian wins Melissa; Cyril, who had persuaded the princess to return Psyche's child, is accepted by Psyche as her husband; and finally the Princess Ida yields to the prince's suit.

The poem is rich with color and melody, the imagery being almost luscious in its beauty and the verse in its smoothness. The interspersed lyrics are not only suited to their context but are among the most passionate and spontaneous that Tennyson ever wrote. To the present age the theme absolutely lacks the daring novelty that it presented to Tennyson's readers in 1847, but the character of Princess Ida is of permanent interest and appeal.

PRINCESS ALINE, THE, a novelette by Richard Harding Davis, was published in 1895. The hero, Morton Carlton, is a young artist with an international reputation, wealth, and high social position; altogether, a most fortunate young gentleman. At the time the story opens he takes passage for Europe, because he has fallen in love with the Princess Aline of Hohenwald, or rather with a picture of her; and is determined to meet her, and by the help of the gods to woo her.

On the steamer New York, going over, are a Miss Morris and her aunt. Carlton finds them very pleasant people, desirable to know; he confides the object of his trip to the younger lady. She is at once in sympathy with the romantic, impossible project. The three float around Europe in the wake of the Princess. The book is written in a clever, crisp style, and shows much worldly knowledge.

PRINCESS CASAMASSIMA, THE, by Henry James, a novel of modern life, and a study in fiction of socialistic questions, was published in 1886. A motley collection of persons are brought together in it, united by their common interest in socialism. The scenes are laid for the most part in the east side of London. The majority of the characters are of the working-classes. Two, the Princess Casamassima and Lady Aurora, are women of rank and wealth. Both classes are represented in the hero, Hyacinth Robinson, the child of a certain immoral Lord Frederick, and his mistress, an ignorant Frenchwoman. Hyacinth, in whom the aristocratic nature predominates, is reared by a poor dressmaker, among forlorn east-side people. His sympathy for their condition makes him an easy prey of certain workingmen with strong socialistic tendencies. In a moment of blind enthusiasm he gives his word that he will perform, when called upon, an act which may cost him his life. About this time he meets the beautiful Princess Casamassima, separated from her husband, living in London that she may study the lower classes.

The novel has a rambling and diversified plot, concerned with other people besides the Princess and Hyacinth, clearly defined and cleverly drawn characters. A certain satirical element in the treatment of the theme imparts an atmosphere of comedy to the book, despite its tragic ending.

PRINCIPIA, NEWTON'S, more fully 'Philosophiæ Naturalis Principia Mathematica' ('The Mathematical Principles of Natural Philosophy'), by Sir Isaac Newton, was first published in 1687. In this famous treatise Newton's law of gravitation was set forth and mathematically demonstrated. The work consists of a series of definitions, laws, corollaries, rules, and propositions supported by diagrams, mathematical proof, and in the last book, records of observation. The first book is concerned with the motion of particles or bodies in free space and in it Newton formulates the law of gravitation — that every particle of matter in the universe attracts every other particle with a force which varies directly as the product of their masses and inversely as the square of the distance between them. The second book considers motion in a resisting medium and the laws of hydrostatics and hydrodynamics with reference to waves, tides, and acoustics. In the third book Newton applies the laws just demonstrated to the explanation of the solar system, showing that all the motions of the planets and their satellites are accounted for by the law of gravitation.

PRINCIPLES OF MORALS AND LEGISLATION, AN INTRODUCTION TO THE, by Jeremy Bentham (1780). This, Bentham's greatest work to which he had devoted the labor of many years, is the most concise statement of the principles by which his name is best known. Though originally written with the limited design of serving as an introduction to a penal code, it took on a much wider scope and serves as the clearest explanation of the author's principle of utility. "Nature," he says "has placed mankind under the governance of two sovereign masters, pain and pleasure. . . . On the one hand the standard of right and wrong, on the other the chain of causes and effects are fastened to their throne." Utility he defines as follows: "that property in any object, whereby it tends to produce benefit, advantage, pleasure, good, or happiness (all this in the present case comes to the same thing) or (what comes again to the same thing) to prevent the happening of mischief, pain, evil, or unhappiness to the party whose interest is considered: if that party be the community in general, then the happiness of the community: if a particular individual, then the happiness of that individual. Bentham attacks the principles of asceticism (approving of actions in so far as they diminish happiness), sympathy, and antipathy, principles opposed to that of utility. Utility is the sole standard by which the moralist must shape his rules and the legislator his laws. "The general object which all laws have, or ought to have in common, is to augment the total happiness of the community: and therefore, in the first place, to exclude, as far as may be, everything that tends to subtract from that happiness: in other words, to exclude mischief. But all punishment is mischief: all punishment in itself is evil. Upon the principle of utility, if it ought at all to be admitted, it ought only to be admitted in as far as it promises to exclude some greater evil." The author's aim is to apply this principle to legislation, to distinguish "cases unmeet for punishment," to establish some sort of proportion between the punishment and the crime, to determine the classes of crimes, and to delimit the respective spheres of ethics and jurisprudence. Never before had English institutions been subjected to so rigorous, comprehensive, and impartial an analysis, and no other work perhaps has been so prolific in suggestion to legislators or has had such an influence in the clarification and development of British legislation.

PRISONER, THE, a novel, by Alice Brown (1916), opens with the home-coming of its hero, and its theme is his spiritual development in the course of his readjustment to everyday living. Jeffrey Blake, known as Jeff, has been serving a term for the misappropriation of funds, and returns to his native town to find his old father awaiting him. The elder man has for years been faithfully guarded by the two pretty daughters of his second wife now dead, whom he married late in life; the two girls, Anne and Lydia, are united with the father in their desire to make Jeff's reëntry into life a triumph over the past tragedy; their first impression that he must succeed in making money gives way to their recognition of his higher needs. Jeff's wife, Esther, a heartless beauty, who lives nearby, has fascinated two of the eligible townsmen, Alston Choate, a lawyer, and Reardon, a rich clubman, who in years past had been Jeff's friend and an instrument in his financial downfall. Jeff's first hope of a reconciliation with his wife is swept away by her repudiation of him, and in a revulsion of feeling he reacts to his devoted step-sister Lydia, who though in love with him, determines to remain only his guardian angel; Jeff is equally firm in his desire not to spoil her future. Esther's eccentric aunt, Mme. Beattie, returns from Europe and reveals to Lydia the story of her diamond necklace, in years past stolen by Esther and presumedly lost. In order to shield his wife and pay for the gems Jeff had plunged into the speculation which had ruined him. Mme. Beattie, who has returned to extort more money, threatens to publish the story of Esther's theft in the local paper. The necklace, which has not been lost, is found by Lydia in Esther's hand-bag, and she rushes back to Jeff with it; he returns it to Mme. Beattie in the presence of his wife and Choate, thus humiliating Esther in the eyes of this admirer. Esther turns to Reardon for consolation, and plans an elopement with him after having tried in vain to effect a reconciliation with Jeff, who, hearing of her plan, stops her flight at the station and takes her home with him. After listening to the friendly protestations of the family she retires to her room for the night, but later slips from the house and catches the midnight train to join Reardon. The book closes with the suggestion that when a legal separation has been accomplished Jeff and Lydia will be united, as Anne and Alston Choate are to be.

PRISONER OF ZENDA, THE, the best known of Anthony Hope's romances (1894), relates the picturesque adventures of Rudolf Rassendyll, an English gentleman, during a three months' sojourn in the Kingdom of Ruritania.

He arrives upon the eve of the coronation of King Rudolf, whom he meets at Zenda Castle. In a drinking bout the king is drugged, and cannot be aroused to reach the capital Strelsau in time for the coronation. This treachery is the work of the king's brother, Duke Michael, who wishes to usurp the kingdom. To foil his designs, Colonel Sapt and Fritz von Tarlenhem successfully assist Rassendyll to personate the king. He is crowned, plays his part without serious blunders, and then sets about accomplishing the king's release, — a task rendered dangerous and difficult by the cunning and prowess of Michael and his followers. Rassendyll loves and is loved by the Princess Flavia. She is also beloved by the king and his brother. Only the release of the monarch — accomplished in a series of dashing dramatic episodes — prevents Rassendyll from wedding Flavia. The story is told with wonderful vim and spirit, and with a freshness and healthfulness of feeling remarkable in an era of morbid fiction. The novel has been dramatized in a successful play of the same name.

PRIVATE GASPARD, a Soldier of France, by René Benjamin (1916). The Prix Goncourt has been awarded to this war novel, which records the everyday experience of a civilian soldier. Gaspard, the snail seller from Paris, is mobilized with his regiment of peasants, mechanics, and tradesmen, shoulder to shoulder with journalists and savants. He is the traditional Frenchman, the Gallic cock of legend, the incarnation of esprit. In the picturesque argot of Paris, he scoffs at the enemy, cheers the men with his irrepressible gayety, and tries out the joke of the end of the war before it has begun. His pals are blown to pieces beside him, and he himself is wounded. In the hospital, as in the freight cars with the troops, or on the march, his cheerfulness makes him the life of the place. A dying companion believes he will live if he can only hold out until morning. During the night he asks every few minutes if it is not yet four o'clock, and refuses to be deceived because he cannot hear the cocks crowing. Gaspard slips out of the ward and immediately afterward a cock crows lustily, and the poor fellow recovers his confidence and dies with a smile on his face. Gaspard's wound opens as a result of his exertion, and he has to remain in the hospital many weeks longer. His winter campaign lasts just twenty-two hours, fighting with an unseen enemy, and he is back in the hospital again with only one leg. We leave him hobbling up the Avenue Alexandre III. with undaunted spirit, a small Gaspard skipping at his side.

PROBLEMATIC CHARACTERS ('Problematische Naturen'), a romance by Friedrich Spielhagen (3 vols., 1860). For this, his first important production, Spielhagen chose as motto a quotation from Goethe, in which is to be found the underlying thought of the romance: "There are problematical natures which are not equal to the conditions among which they are placed, and whom no conditions satisfy. Thence arises the monstrous conflict which consumes life without enjoyment." In the narrative, the strongest illustration of this class of persons is the character of Oswald Stein, the hero. He is introduced as private tutor in a noble family; as a man of good, honorable, and kindly intentions, and of much personal charm. But the development of the story shows him to lack one essential trait, in the absence of which his courage and his warmth prove insufficient to the demands of duty; he is inconstant. The three volumes lead him from one experiment in the realm of sentiment to another, — his most striking experience involving Melitta, a beautiful and warm-hearted lady of rank in the neighborhood. Oswald proves himself incapable of a real fidelity and lasting affection towards any of the fair beings who lavish their hearts upon him. One of them says of him that he is fickle simply because he forever pursues an unattainable ideal, and is forever disappointed! This aspiring and sympathetic soul arouses sympathy, however, only in his character of faithful and brotherly friend to his charge, Bruno. Bruno himself is another problematic character, but he is not called upon to set his fitful temper and stormy heart against the hard necessities of life: he dies while still a loving, heroic, moody boy, little understood, and loved by few. At his death, Oswald departs for fresh scenes; and the conclusion of the romance is not at all a conclusion of the action, which is reached in a later novel.

PROBLEMS OF MODERN DEMOCRACY, by Edwin Lawrence Godkin (1896). This collection of eleven political and economic essays, on subjects connected with the evolution of the republic, belongs among the most thoughtful and most interesting books of its class — with Lecky's, Pearson's, Stephen's, Fiske's, and Lowell's. From the first one, 'Aristocratic Opinions of Democracy,' published during the last year of the Civil War, to the last, 'The Expenditure of Rich Men,' thirty-one years elapse; yet the comment of time simply emphasizes the rightness of Mr. Godkin's thinking. He states the aristocratic objections to democracy with absolute fairness, concedes the weight of many of them, is even ready to admit that to some degree democracy in America is still on trial. But he maintains that the right-hand fallings-off and left-hand defections with which its opponents tax our political theories, are really due to quite other causes, — causes inseparable from the conditions of our existence.

Thus thoughtfully he considers ethics, manners, literature, art, and philosophy, public spirit and private virtue; and his conclusion is that the world's best saints of the last hundred years have come out of the Nazareth of democracy, — issuing from the middle and lower classes in Europe, from the "plain people" in America. 'Popular Government' is a review and refutation of much of the doctrine of Sir Henry Maine, in his volume on that subject. 'Some Political and Social Aspects of the Tariff' deals with the subject in its industrial and ethical applications, and concludes that the "independence of foreigners" which a high tariff is supposed to secure, must be the result simply and solely of native superiority, either in energy, or industry, or inventiveness, or in natural advantages. The papers on 'Criminal Politics,' 'Idleness and Immorality,' 'The Duty of Educated Men in a Democracy,' 'Who Will Pay the Bills of Socialism?' and 'The Real Problem of Democracy,' are lay sermons of so vigorous an application that the most easy-going political sinner who reads them will not be able to escape the pangs of conscience. The final paper on 'The Expenditure of Rich Men' is a disquisition on the difficulty of real sumptuosity in America.

PRODIGAL SON, THE, by Hall Caine (1904). The scene of this story is laid in Iceland, a part of the world not often chosen by the novelist. It deals mainly with the lives of two brothers, Magnus and Oscar Stephenson, the sons of the Governor-General. Magnus, the elder, is engaged to be married to Thora Neilson, the daughter of Factor Neilson, the leading merchant of the place and his father's lifelong friend. The match is most satisfactory to both families and all goes well until the return of Oscar from college after an absence of six years in England. He has there acquired a manner and air which combined with his handsome face and figure make him seem irresistible to the simple home people. His career at Oxford has been a failure owing to the weakness of his character but his shortcomings are overlooked in the light of his buoyant spirits and genial ways. He soon wins away Thora's affection and marries her, leaving the faithful Magnus heart-broken. Before the marriage Oscar's fickle heart had been drawn to Thora's younger sister, Helga, whose unprincipled nature had led her to use all her fascinations to win away her sister's lover. She continues in this course, and their mutual love of music, which brings them together, causes Oscar to fall completely under her sway. Thora is crushed with grief and Magnus who is maddened by the turn of affairs tries in vain to keep his brother true to his wife. A daughter is born to Thora and she is filled with joy, but Helga convinces Oscar that the babe is not safe with Thora and gets him to put her in her charge. Thora crazed with grief steals from her sick-bed, gets the child and brings it home, then dies as the result of her exposure. Oscar, overwhelmed with sorrow and remorse, buries in his wife's grave his musical compositions which he feels have taken the time and thought which should have been given her and swears he will never write another note. The day following the funeral Oscar is found guilty of forging his father's name for a large sum of money, and to save the family from disgrace the Governor mortgages everything that he possesses. Oscar goes abroad at once promising his father he will never see Helga again, but the promise is broken and he and she unite again on their musical careers.

Oscar has his manuscripts exhumed from his wife's grave and making a big success with his music becomes a rich man. After years he returns to his home under an assumed name, pays off the mortgage, which is about to be foreclosed, and leaves a fortune for his daughter Elin, now grown. He slips away unrecognized, but after having gone a short distance, is overtaken by an avalanche on the mountain, and his eventful career is ended.

PROFANE STATE, THE, see **HOLY STATE,** by Thomas Fuller.

PROFESSOR BERNHARDI, a comedy by Arthur Schnitzler (adaptation in English by Mrs. Emil Pohli, 1913).   Professor Bernhardi, a Jewish physican of distinction, is the director of a large charity hospital, the "Elizabethinum." A patient, a young girl, is dying with septicæmia as a result of malpractice. She does not realize her condition, believing herself perfectly well, and is happy in the delusion that her lover is coming to take her away with him. A Catholic nurse, Sister Ludmilla, the only woman who appears in the play, advised by an officious medical student, sends for a priest. Dr. Bernhardi forbids him to see the patient and make her last hour of life unhappy. The priest insists that it is his duty to bring the unrepentant girl to conviction of sin and save her immortal soul. Sister Ludmilla tells the dying girl the priest has come, and she dies at once from the shock. The enemies of Dr. Bernhardi magnify his refusal of the last consolations of religion to a dying patient. At a stormy board meeting, Dr. Bernhardi is forced to resign his position as head of the hospital. The clerical party take up the affair, and Dr. Bernhardi is indicted and sentenced to a term in prison. The Jewish counsel for the defense is so afraid of appearing biased in favor of his own race that he loses the case. The twelve doctors of the hospital staff, Jews and Gentiles, impartially and humorously presented represent different types of character and prejudice. Prince Constantin is ill, and has need of the services of the great physician, Dr. Bernhardi. He is released from prison and escorted home in triumph by the enthusiastic medical students. The priest stated at the trial that he did not believe Dr. Bernhardi had intended to insult religion, but was following the dictates of his professional conscience. For this piece of honest testimony he is removed from his parish by his superiors and sent to a remote Polish town. He calls on Dr. Bernhardi to say that he thinks the doctor was in the right in this special case, but that he could not acknowledge this publicly in court, because the admission might be misunderstood and misconstrued by enemies of the Church. The nurse, Sister Ludmilla, confesses that she gave false testimony at the trial, and Dr. Bernhardi's friends urge him to demand a revision. He refuses to consider taking any revenge. One of his colleagues says of him, "You begin to understand — to pardon everything, — and then where is the charm of life, if you cannot love or hate any more?" A sincere individualist, Dr. Bernhardi claims only that he did what he considered right in a special case. There is nothing in the play which would cause offence to either race or religion.

PROFESSOR'S LOVE STORY, THE, by Sir J. M. Barrie (1894).   Professor Goodwillie, in the absence of his watchful sister, employs a charming young lady as private secretary, and falls in love with her without knowing it. He believes he is suffering from some fatal brain malady because he is so absent-minded and unable to concentrate on the scientific book he is writing. The physician is baffled by his old friend's condition, and irritated by the amusement of the young lady, Lucy White, at his efforts to understand the case; but the truth dawns on him and he tells the professor he must have fallen in love. The professor is alarmed and decides to run away from London to escape the unknown woman and join his sister in the country, and of course takes his secretary along with him. Lucy White really loves the man she has bewitched, and resents his sister's treatment of her as a designing adventuress. Lady Gilding, a dowager, who is a "marrying woman," determines to entrap the professor and ignoring the possibility of the secretary as a rival, confides her plans to the "simple, little Lucy thing." Lucy acts out the Dowager's plan herself, pretending to faint in the professor's arms. Having awakened him to realization of his love for her, she is ashamed of her duplicity and refuses to marry him. An old love letter found in the mailbox restores Miss Goodwillie's faith in her dead lover and changes her attitude toward the lovers. She brings Lucy and her brother together again.

PROGRESS AND POVERTY, by Henry George. Single taxers hold this, the chief work of the author, to be the Bible of the new cult. It was written in the years 1877–79, and the MS. was hawked about the country and refused by all publishers till the author, a practical printer, had the plates made, doing a large part of the composition himself. It was then brought out by Appletons in 1879. He seeks, in the work, to solve a problem and prescribe a remedy. The problem is: "Why, in the midst of a marvelous progress, is grinding poverty on the increase?" In the solution he begins with the beginning of political economy, takes issue with accepted authority, and claims that the basis law is not the selfishness of mankind, but that "man seeks to gratify his desires with the least exertion." Using this law as physicists do the law of gravitation, he proceeds to define anew, capital, rent, interest, wealth, labor, and land. All that is not labor, or the result of labor, is land. Wealth is the product of labor applied to land. Interest is that part of the result of labor which is paid to capital for its use for a time; capital is the fruit of labor, not its employer; rent is the tax taken by the landholder from labor and capital, which must be paid before capital and labor can divide. The problem is solved, he declares, when it is found that the constantly increasing rent serves so to restrict the rewards of capital and labor that wage, the laborer's share of the joint product, becomes the least sum upon which he can subsist and propagate. The laborer would refuse such a wage; but as it is the best he can do, he must accept. Were the land public property he could refuse, and transfer his labor to open land and produce for himself. As he cannot do this, he must compete with thousands as badly off as is he, hence poverty, crime, unrest, and all social and moral evils.

The remedy is to nationalize the land, — make it public property; leaving that already in use in the possession of those holding it, but confiscating the rent and abolishing all other forms of taxation. He declares taxation upon anything but land to be a penalty upon production; so he would tax that which cannot be produced or increased or diminished, — i. e., land. This, he claims, would abolish all speculation in land, would throw it open to whomever would use it. Labor, having an opportunity to employ itself, would do so, or to a large enough extent to increase production; and as man is a never-satisfied animal, increased production would bring increased exchange; hence prosperity, health, wealth, and happiness.

PROMETHEUS BOUND, a drama by Æschylus (B. C. 525–456), the most sublime of Greek tragedians, presents the contest between Zeus and the Titan, Prometheus, whose counsels had set Zeus upon his throne, but who had incurred that deity's displeasure through giving the use of fire to man. At the beginning of the play he is nailed to a mountain-peak by Hephæstus at the order of Zeus as a punishment for his presumption. Here he is visited by the daughters of Oceanus, who sympathize with him, and by their father, who counsels submission to Zeus but in vain. Another victim of Zeus now enters in the person of Io, who has been transformed by the god into the form of a heifer and is being driven from land to land by the jealousy of Hera, and the persecutions of Argus, who is tormenting her in the shape of a gad-fly. Prometheus tells her that she shall be restored to her own shape and bear a son, the father of a royal race, one of whom, Hercules, shall free the Titan from his bonds.

Moreover he prophesies that Zeus shall make a marriage, the son of which shall dispossess his father. Zeus now sends Hermes to demand particulars of this coming danger. Prometheus defiantly refuses to reveal what he knows; and in punishment Zeus cleaves the rocks with his thunderbolts and sinks his enemy beneath the earth.

In the lost 'Prometheus Unbound,' which was perhaps the third member of a trilogy, it is conjectured that a reconciliation was brought about by the intervention of Hercules. Prometheus was released and revealed his secret that Zeus must refrain from marriage with Thetis. Thus the theme of the entire work was not rebellion, but justification of the ways of God to man.

The grandeur of the scenario and the superhuman magnitude of the characters — all of whom but Io are deities — illustrate the Titanic quality of this dramatist's imagination.

PROMETHEUS UNBOUND, a lyrical drama by Shelley, written at Rome in 1819, is an independent treatment of the theme of Æschylus (see the synopsis of his 'Prometheus Bound') by a revolutionary poet who could not accept the possibility of a reconciliation between the rebel, Prometheus, and his tormenter, Zeus. The scenario, however, and the conception of the defiance of Prometheus, owe much to the Greek play. When Shelley's drama opens Prometheus has been for ages chained to the rock, attended and comforted by the Oceanids, Panthea and Ione. With the passing years his hostility to Zeus has become less bitter though still determined, and he cannot recollect the curse which he pronounced upon the tyrant until it is repeated to him by a phantasm of Zeus himself, raised by Earth, the mother of Prometheus, at his earnest request. Prometheus says he would gladly recall this curse but he knows nevertheless that Zeus must fall. In a last effort to learn the secret Zeus sends down Hermes and the Furies, threatening the Titan with further tortures if he will not tell what he knows. On his refusal the Furies subject Prometheus to the moral torture of hearing the woes that man has suffered and then leave him. After comforting Prometheus Panthea and Ione depart to reassure their sister, Asia, Prometheus's love, in her retreat in the Indian Caucasus. Meanwhile the day of Prometheus's deliverance has arrived, and voices summon Asia down to the abode of Demogorgon, a personification of that ultimate Power which the Greeks thought of as behind and above the gods, and which typifies for Shelley the all-pervading soul of all things. She there learns of the resistless force of this Power and of the imminent freedom of Prometheus and then ascends in one of the chariots of the Hours to witness his deliverance. Zeus has just wedded Thetis, Demogorgon ascends to Olympus, becomes incarnate in the child that is born, and casts Zeus from the battlements of Heaven. Prometheus is freed from the rock by Hercules, is reunited to Asia, and retires with her to a grotto, which they make their home. Earth, Heaven, Air, and all the powers of the universe break out into pæans of joy and praise to salute the new reign of peace and fraternity, and in this burst of lyric rejoicing the poem closes. The 'Prometheus' is imbued with Shelley's pantheistic and anarchistic views, his belief in the essential goodness of human nature, his hatred of dogmas and tyrannous government, and his noble humanitarian enthusiasm. Perhaps none of his poems so well illustrate his exquisite and melodious lyric gifts, his marvelous power of painting mountain scenery and atmospheric effects, and his lack of appreciation of ordinary earthly scenes and human characters.

PROMISE OF AMERICAN LIFE, THE, 'a treatise on social and political science' by Herbert Croly (1909). He begins by analyzing the conception of America as the land of promise and distinguishing between the uncritical anticipation of continued prosperity and the responsible effort to ensure the fulfilment of this hope by the attempt to realize an ideal. Many Americans do not make this distinction; and those who make it do not all recognize that a change of conditions has made necessary a revision of the American ideal. The original ideal was one of political and economic freedom and independence, finding expression in universal competition; and its effects were good since it was a stimulus to activity and exploitation of the sources of wealth; but with the increase of population and the seizure of natural resources into a few hands has come a "morally and unsociably undesirable distribution of wealth." This must be regulated by the state, if the "promise of American life" is to remain valid for the masses; and thus the old untrammeled individual freedom must give way to social control. These opinions are enforced by a review of American political and economic history, outlining the struggles of Federalists and Republicans, Whigs and Democrats, Slavery men and Abolitionists, and after 1870, the growth of specialized scientific political, commercial, and business interests, which destroyed the homogeneity of American life and brought about the need of a renewed solidarity. Four typical reformers, Bryan, Jerome, Hearst, and Roosevelt, are then subjected to analysis and criticism. The author now gives his own proposals for reform. Democracy must be interpreted not merely as the securing of equal rights for all but as the insuring of well-being and social improvement to the various types of individuals who constitute the state. The capitalists and the masses must be so regulated as to insure the economic and social improvement of all, without doing violence to the principle of private property or of nationality. Particular problems of international policy and administrative and industrial reform are then considered, and the book closes with a discussion of what the individual can do to insure the success of the public measures proposed. The book is a carefully reasoned presentation of the altered political and social theories made necessary by the advent of a new era in the history of America.

PROMISED LAND, THE, by Mary Antin (1912). This is an autobiographical study of the immigrant, of what he brings to America, and what he finds here, and in it the author presents the case of the Russian Jew's American citizenship in a new and vivid light. The book opens with the child's early life in Polotzk, where the Jews are enduring many persecutions and where they are forced to live within the "Pale" set apart for them. Thus shut out from the national existence they had retained many quaint and mediæval customs and curious religious ceremonies described by the little Jewish girl, who at an early age began to pen this story of her life. When the writer was but ten years old her father emigrated to America, later sending for his family to join him in the new world. The writer gives a touching description of the uncomfortable exodus from the old world and their adventures on the way to their new home in the north end of Boston. Here the advantages of the "Promised Land" awaken wonder and delight and the child begins at once to profit by the free education which may be enjoyed by all. Her story contains many pictures of the problems and perplexities faced by this Jewish family in their endeavors to assimilate themselves with the life of their adopted country. While seeing life from the slums of the city the writer sets forth her gradual advance towards taking possession of all the heritage offered in this new land. Passing with honors through the public-schools, aided by sympathetic teachers, and by the clubs and settlement-homes open to her, the young girl develops into the thoughtful and cultured woman, who shows in this story of her own development the possibilities open to all the aliens who come with the earnest intention of profiting by the advantages which all may share alike in this land of the free. Having traced the story of the child through her school-days and watched her gradually expand under the influence of teachers, friends, free libraries and lecture halls the reader takes leave of her as she is about to enter the college gates which have just opened to admit this pilgrim who has learned to grasp all the best treasures offered in the "Promised Land."

PROOF OF THE PUDDING, THE; a novel, by Meredith Nicholson (1916), is a study of the development of the character of Nan Farley, and the scene is laid in a town in Indiana. An orphaned child of humble lineage, Nan at an early age is adopted by Timothy Farley and his wife who lavish upon her wealth and affection. Being selfish and pleasure-loving, Nan, upon reaching young ladyhood falls in with a fast set, and against her father's wishes joins in their frivolities. She accepts the attentions of Billy Copeland, who has divorced his wife, Fanny, a charming and capable woman, in order to gain Nan's affections, but Nan's father, who is in failing health, tells her he will disinherit her if she marries him. Nan has a warm friend and admirer in Jerry Amidon, a clever young business man, straightforward and honest, who knew her before her adoption. Copeland's passionate wooing strongly influences Nan, and though she does not really love him she is on the point of eloping with him when his appearance in an intoxicated condition saves her from this folly. Mr. Farley dies suddenly, and after the funeral Copeland urges Nan to destroy her father's will, in which case she will be sole heir to his property, as Mrs. Farley has died previously. Nan has a night of temptation, but finally her better self triumphs, and she realizes her past short-comings and decides in future to lead a better and more unselfish life. The next day she confides her experience to Cecil Eaton, a family friend and adviser, and tells him she has decided not to accept a cent of the Farley money as she feels she is unworthy of it. Wishing to be self-supporting, she joins Fanny Copeland, who bears no ill-will against her, in the management of her dairy farm. Copeland meanwhile has been indulging in dissipation and become financially embarrassed, but is extricated from the latter position by the united efforts of Eaton and Fanny, who still loves him. Nan marries Jerry Amidon, and the Copelands become reunited, after Billy's reformation, which is brought about by Eaton, who has always unselfishly loved Fanny. Mr. Farley's will is proved invalid, and the bulk of the property goes to Nan, who expresses the desire to use it wholly for charitable purposes.

PROVERBIAL PHILOSOPHY, by Martin Farquhar Tupper. Tupper's 'Proverbial Philosophy' is a book of essays, or poems in blank verse, dealing with almost every emotion and condition of life. The author begins thus: "Few and precious are the words which the lips of wisdom utter"; and he proceeds to compile a work filling 415 pages.

The poems or meditations were published between 1838 and 1867; and are in two series, dealing with over sixty subjects. The book contains many wise sayings, but it is mostly padded commonplace. For many years it was in great demand, but lately it has been subjected to ridicule.

PRUE AND I, by George William Curtis. These charming papers were published in 1856; and have been popular ever since, as the subject is of perennial interest, while the treatment is in the author's happiest vein. They are a series of sketches or meditations showing the enjoyment to be derived from even the most commonplace existence. The spires and pinnacles of the sunset sky belong to every man; and in the fair realm of Fantasie all may wander at will. The papers are supposed to be written by an old bookkeeper, who strolls down the street at dinner-time, and without envy watches the diners-out. His fancy enables him to dine without embarrassment at the most select tables, and to enjoy the charming conversation of the beautiful Aurelia. He owns many castles in Spain, where he can summon a goodly company, Jephthah's daughter and the Chevalier Bayard, fair Rosamond and Dean Swift, — the whole train of dear and familiar spirits. He goes for a voyage on the Flying Dutchman, and finds on board all who have spent their lives on useless quests, — Ponce de Leon, and the old Alchemist. He gives us the pleasant dreams and memories roused by the sea in those who love it, and tells the simple, pathetic history of 'Our Cousin the Curate.' He also lets his deputy bookkeeper Titbottom tell the story of the strange spectacles, which show a man as he is in his nature, — a wisp of straw, a dollar bill, a calm lake. Once the owner was in love, and, looking through his spectacles at the girl he adored, he beheld — himself. But whatever the suggestive and genial old bookkeeper is thinking or relating, his heart is full of his Prue; from beginning to end it is always "Prue and I."

PSYCHOLOGY, THE PRINCIPLES OF, a scientific treatise by William James, was published in its complete form ('Advanced Course') in 1890 and in an abridged form ('Briefer Course') in 1892. The work is introduced by a chapter entitled 'The Scope of Psychology' followed by two chapters on the structure and functions of the brain. Then follows a series of somewhat loosely connected chapters (some of them originally published in learned reviews) dealing with the methods of psychological investigation, rival theories of the mind, and such indispensable topics as habit, the stream of consciousness, attention, association, memory, imagination, the perception of space and time, instinct, the emotions, and the will. James employs both introspection and experiment as instruments of psychological research. He refuses to trench on the province of metaphysics by discussing anything but thoughts, feelings, volitions, and their relation to the brain, yet he is no materialist. His clearness of statement and picturesqueness of illustration make this the most attractive of psychological text-books.

PSYCHOPATHOLOGY OF EVERYDAY LIFE ('Psychopathologie des Alltagslebens') a psychological treatise by Sigmund Freud, published in 1904 and in an English translation by A. A. Brill in 1914. The general thesis is that the pschopathologic effects which appear in neurotic conditions may also be observed, though in a lesser degree, in normal persons. For example, the common occurrence of forgetting a well-known name with or without substituting some other for it is due to its direct or indirect suggestion of some idea which is disturbing to the mind and which is being unconsciously repressed. The connection may be discovered by analyzing the ideas passing through the subject's mind, some of which by their associations will probably point to the name required. A similar explanation is offered for our apparently unmotivated slips of the tongue or pen, absentminded actions and omissions to act, misplacing or loss of objects, abstracted or mechanical movements, and errors or blunders. All are accounted for by some unconscious but strong impulse to avoid something disagreeable or to indulge some hidden desire — an impulse which in our conscious life is forgotten or repressed. There is no room for chance in these apparently trivial actions; all are determined by our psychic life and may yield the richest information to the psycho-analyst. On the other hand the coincidences of foreboding and disaster, of omen and fulfilment are not, on present evidence, to be attributed to supernatural origin but to some unrecognized association of ideas. The book is an exceedingly stimulating and helpful analysis of a widespread group of phenomena of high interest, and its conclusions are based on strong evidence. One feels however, that some of the associations are forced, and that there is too great readiness to find evidence of the "sexual complex."

PUBLIC FINANCE, by C. F. Bastable (1892). Every governing body or "State" requires for the due discharge of its functions repeated supplies of commodities and personal services, which it has to apply to the accomplishment of whatever ends it may regard as desirable. For all States, whether rude or highly developed, some provisions of the kind are necessary, and therefore the supply and application of State resources constitute the subject-matter of a study which is best entitled in English, 'Public Finance.' The author discusses the general features of State economy, the cost of defense, the expenditure involved in the maintenance of justice and security, the relations of the State to religion, education, industry, commerce. The second part is devoted to public revenues, their forms and classification, whether agricultural, industrial, or capitalist; the third and fourth to the principles of taxation, and the different kinds of taxes; the fifth to the relation between expenditure and receipts; the sixth to the preparation, collection, control, and audit of the budget. "Prudent expenditure," says Professor Bastable in conclusion, "productive and equitable taxation, and due equilibrium between income and outlay will only be found where responsibility is enforced by the public opinion of an active and enlightened community."

PUCK OF POOK'S HILL, by Rudyard Kipling (1906). This volume comprises a set of fantastic tales, juvenile in character. Two children Dan and Una amuse themselves by enacting portions of 'A Midsummer Night's Dream' which they do on Midsummer Eve, in the middle of a Fairy Ring, on Pook's Hill in old England. Suddenly Puck appears beside them and after instructing them in fairy lore joins them in a series of adventures. In the successive chapters which are pervaded by historic personages as well by the influences of the fairies and People of the Hills, the reader is introduced to the most important epochs in the development of England's history; the children are instructed by Puck regarding the heroes of Asgard and various other traditional happenings and in their sylvan exploits in his company they constantly encounter the famous personages under discussion. They learn of the adventures of King Philip's fleet as they tramp through the pastures through which the great guns were once carried to the sea-coast. As they fish in the brook, they are instructed regarding the "Domesday Book" and the ownership of the land where they rest under the trees. The woods speak to them of the doings of the Saxons and with nimble Puck at their side they follow the footsteps of those early warriors; they note where the Northmen fled, and where Alfred's ships came by. King John and his Magna Charta is introduced to them and Roman Legions appear before them, under the guidance of Cæsar. King Arthur and his Knights of the Round Table flit before their curious gaze and when in the final chapter Una and Dan take leave of Puck, they have learned from their fantastic guide the substance of all the vital events which have played the principal part in their country's development and have been impressed with the spirit of true patriotism. Each chapter is prefaced by a song, lyric, or ballad, in keeping with the character of the text which is to follow, as for example 'The Runes on Weland's Sword,' 'A British-Roman Song,' 'A Pict Song,' 'A Smuggler's Song,' and others of varying theme.

PURCHAS HIS PILGRIMES. This remarkable and rare book was published in 1619. It is a compilation by Samuel Purchas, a London divine, of the letters and histories of travel of more than thirteen hundred travelers. It consists of a description of travel in Europe, Asia, Africa, and America; and the later editions of 1625 and 1626 contain maps, which are more diverting than instructive. In this work the author allows the travelers to speak for themselves; but in 'Purchas his Pilgrimage,' published in 1613, he himself gives the "Relation of the World and the Religions observed in all ages and places discovered, from the Creation unto this Present."

More accurate and extensive knowledge has to-day supplanted these books, and they are rarely consulted except by those curious to know the ideas in regard to the rest of the world, which then obtained in England. The world, however, is the authors debtor for his four-years' labors; and it is sad to think that the publication of these books was the cause of his death, if not in a debtor's prison, at least in want.

PURITAN IN HOLLAND, ENGLAND, AND AMERICA, THE, by Douglas Campbell (1892). This historical survey of Puritanism in its ethical, social, and political aspects is strikingly original, since it seeks to demonstrate, with much strength and clearness, that the debt of the American nation for its most radical customs and institutions is not to the English at all, but to the Dutch. It endeavors to prove that the very essence of Puritanism came originally from Holland, leavened the English nation, and through the English nation, the embryonic American nation. Some of the most common of American institutions, — "common lands and common schools, the written ballot, municipalities, religious tolerance, a federal union of States, the play of national and local government, the supremacy of the judiciary," — all these came directly from Holland.

Mr. Campbell's work is most valuable as an introduction to the study of American history, or in itself considered as a scholarly though not always impartial monograph.

PURPLE ISLAND, THE (called also the Isle of Man), by Phineas Fletcher. This poem, in twelve cantos, published in 1633, describes the human body as an island. The bones are the foundation; the veins and arteries, rivers; the heart, liver, stomach, etc., goodly cities; the mouth, a cave; the teeth are "twice sixteen porters, receivers of the customary rent"; the tongue, "a groom who delivers all unto neare officers." The liver is the arch-city, where two purple streams (two great rivers of blood) "raise their boil-heads." The eyes are watch-towers; the sight, the warder. Taste and the tongue are man and wife. The island's prince is the intellect; the five senses are his counselors. Disease and vice are his mortal foes, with whom he wages war. The virtues are his allies. All is described in the minutest detail, with a rare knowledge of anatomy, and there is a profusion of literary and classical allusion.

PUSS IN BOOTS, see **FAIRY TALES.**

PUT YOURSELF IN HIS PLACE, by Charles Reade (1870) is a dramatic novel with a purpose. The scene is laid in Hillsborough, an English manufacturing city; and the story relates the struggles of Henry Little, workman and inventor, against the jealousy and prejudice of the trades-unions. Because he is a Londoner, because he is better trained and consequently better paid than the Hillsborough men, because he invents quicker processes and labor-saving devices, he is subjected to a series of persecutions worthy of the Dark Ages, and is ground between the two millstones of Capital and Labor; — for if the workmen are ferocious and relentless, they have

45

learned their villainy from the masters and bettered the instruction. This stern study of social problems, however, is nowhere a tract, but always the story of Henry Little, who is as devoted a lover as he is honest a workman, as thorough a social reformer as a clear, practical thinker, and the hero of as bitter a fight against prejudice, worldly ambition, and unscrupulous rivalry outside the mills, as that which he wages against "The Trades." Among the notable figures in the book are Squire Raby, Henry's uncle, a gentleman of the old school; Jael Dence, the country girl, simple, honest, and strong; Grotait, the gentlemanly president of the Saw-Grinders' Union, with his suave manners and his nickname of "Old Smitem"; and Dr. Amboyne philanthropist and peacemaker, who maintains that to get on with anybody you must understand him, and when you understand him you will get on with him. His favorite motto is the title of the book. Like all of Charles Reade's stories, 'Put Yourself in His Place' has a wealth of dramatic incident, and moves with dash and vigor.

QUABBIN: 'The Story of a Small Town, — with Outlooks upon Puritan Life,' by Francis H. Underwood (1893). It is the biography of a New England town, and is dedicated "to those, wherever they are, who have inherited the blood and shared the progress of the descendants of Pilgrims and Puritans." No detail of village and farm life has been left out as too homely; and familiar scenes, outdoors and in, are described in 'Quabbin' with that care which writers often reserve for the novel aspects of some foreign land. This quality lends the book its interest. The social characteristics of a New England town are graphically noted; the minister's revered chief place; "general-training day"; the temperance movement, started at a time when drunkenness from the rum served at ministerial "installations" was not infrequent, and ending in the total-abstinence societies, and in rigid no-license laws for the town. With the railroad came "improvements," including comforts that were unknown luxuries before; and to-day, "with morning newspapers, the telegraph, and three daily mails, Quabbin belongs to the great world."

QUEECHY, by "Elizabeth Wetherell" (Susan Warner). 'Queechy' was written in 1852, and sold by the thousand in both England and America; being translated into German, French, and Swedish. Mrs. Browning admired it, and wrote of it to a friend: "I think it very clever and characteristic. Mrs. Beecher Stowe scarcely exceeds it, after all her trumpets." The story takes place chiefly in Queechy, Vermont. Fleda Ringgan, an orphan, on the death of her grandfather, goes to her aunt Mrs. Rossiter, in Paris, under the care of Mrs. Carleton and her son, rich English people. Every man who sees Fleda, from the time she is eleven, falls in love with her; but she loves only Carleton, whom she converts to Christianity. The Rossiters lose their money, and return to Queechy, where Fleda farms, cooks and makes maple-sugar, to support her family. Carleton revisits America, and is always at hand to aid Fleda in every emergency; although he never speaks of love until they are snowed up on a railway journey. He saves her from the persecutions of Thorn, a rival lover. His mother takes her to England. They are married, and do good for many years.

QUEED, by Henry Sydnor Harrison (1911). This is the story of the evolution of Mr. Queed from a dried up and eccentric little person, who is all intellect, to a normal human being, who developes his muscles and falls in love with a charming girl named Sharlee Wayland. At the opening of the story Mr. Queed has a humiliating encounter with Miss Wayland's big dog who knocks him down on a crowded thoroughfare and kindles his indignation. Later he encounters Miss Wayland at her aunt's boarding-house where he is living and toiling day and night over a monumental work on Sociology. Miss Wayland becomes gradually interested in Mr. Queed as an intellectual curiosity, who is sadly in need of humanizing influences as well as remunerative labor; she secures him a position on a daily paper where he exercises his intellectual powers effectively but where he discovers that he is physically a weakling, when he is attacked by an irate proof-reader. From this time Mr. Queed sets out to develop his muscles and consorts with a pugilistic friend named Klinker, who introduces him to athletic circles. By degrees the life around him begins more and more to reach him, first at one point and then at another, until in the course of time he develops a normal and rounded manhood. The mystery which has surrounded his birth is in the end cleared up, and he discovers that he is the son and heir of Henry G. Surface, whom he had known under the name of Professor Niclovius. The chance discovery of a letter bearing the name of Surface reveals the Professor's identity, and the young man confronts him with the fact and he confesses that he is the hated and despised being who has won a dishonorable notoriety in years past, and who has betrayed the friendship of Miss Wayland's father and looted her own fortune so that she is forced to earn her living. Not until after the death of the supposed Professor does Queed learn that he is in reality Henry G. Surface, Jr. This discovery causes him to at once set about righting the wrong done by his father. He turns over his estate to Miss Wayland who promptly refuses it, though she shows her partiality for its owner. In the end a compromise is arranged and she accepts the money with the understanding that she shall use it to endow a Reformatory which she calls the Henry G. Surface, Junior Home. The young people are united and Mr. Queed becomes editor-in-chief of an important paper.

QUENTIN DURWARD, by Sir Walter Scott (1823). The scene of this exciting story is France during the reign of Louis XI., and its main outline is this: Quentin Durward, a brave young Scot, having a relative in the Scottish Guards of the French king, comes to France to seek his fortune. The crafty and superstitious Louis is pleased with the youth, and sends him on a strange errand. Under the royal protection are two vassals of the Duke of Burgundy, the lovely Isabelle of Croye and her scheming aunt. Charles of Burgundy is too formidable an enemy, and Louis decides to make Isabelle the wife of William de la Marck, a notorious brigand, who is quite able to defend his bride. The unsuspecting Quentin is sent to conduct the ladies to the Bishop of Liège, the plan being that William shall attack the party and carry off his prize. Quentin, discovering the king's treachery, succeeds in delivering his charge to the bishop; but even here she is not safe. William attacks the castle of Liège and murders the bishop, while Quentin and Isabelle escape. She returns to Burgundy, preferring her old persecutor to the perfidious king. But that wily monarch has already joined forces with the bold duke, to avenge the bishop's death and to besiege De la Marck. Charles offers the hand of Isabelle as a prize to the conqueror of William, and Quentin bears off in triumph a not unwilling bride.

Among the chief characters introduced are the Burgundian herald, the Count of Crèvecœur, and Le Balafré of the Scottish Guard, Quentin's uncle. The figure of Louis is well drawn in his superstitions, his idolatry of the leaden images that garnished his hat-band, in his political intriguing, and in his faithlessness and lack of honor. The book made a sensation in France, and its first success was on foreign shores. It was written at the flood-tide of Scott's popularity at home; the ebb began with 'St. Ronan's Well,' published six months later. The principal anachronisms are noted in the later editions.

QUICK OR THE DEAD?, THE, a novelette by Amélie Rives, was first published in 1883 in Lippincott's Magazine. It attained at once great notoriety in this country and in England, because of the peculiar treatment of the subject, the strangeness of its style, and the flashiness of the title, which has become one of the best known in fiction. Its hysteria, its abundant and bizarre use of adjectives, and its innocent treatment of passion, betrayed the youth and inexperience of the author; yet it is not without traces of genius. The heroine, Barbara Pomfret, is a young widow, whose husband, Valentine, has been dead two years when the story opens. In the first chapter she is returning to the old Virginia homestead, where she has passed the few months of an absolutely happy married life. There everything reminds her of her lost love, awakening the pain that she had sought to lull to sleep. She has not been long among the familiar scenes, when Valentine's cousin, John Dering, who has come to the neighborhood, calls to see her. His remarkable resemblance to Barbara's dead husband, in appearance and speech and manner, is at first a source of suffering to her. After a time, however, this resemblance becomes a consolation. Yet she rebels against her new feeling as disloyal to Valentine. She struggles to keep the identity of the two men distinct. She hates herself because she cares for her cousin. Yet her love for him grows stronger, as his passion for her becomes more imperious. She strives to resist it, to be true to the dead. Finally she gives herself up to her love for the living, but her abandonment to her overmastering passion is of short duration. She believes that she is more bound to the dead than to the living, and sends John away at the last, that she may be faithful to her first love. 'The Quick or the Dead?' is morbid and immature to a high degree; yet as a psychological study of a sensitive woman's conflicting emotions it is not without interest and significance. The style is impressionistic. "In the glimpsing lightning she saw scurrying trees against the suave autumn sky, like etchings on bluish paper." "A rich purple-blue dusk had sunk down over the land, and the gleam of the frozen ice-pond in the far field shone desolately forth from tangled patches of orange-colored wild grass." "She threw herself into a drift of crimson pillows . . . brooding upon the broken fire, whose lilac flames palpitated over a bed of gold-veined coals."

QUINCY ADAMS SAWYER, by Charles Felton Pidgin (1900). This novel recounts the experiences of Quincy Adams Sawyer of Boston, the son of a millionaire and a graduate of Harvard College, who spends two years in the country town known as Mason's Corner, where he finds many quaint country personages. Sawyer, while recuperating his health, enters into the life of the place and attends the singing-school, husking-bees, and surprise-parties with various village belles, finally falling in love with Miss Alice Pettengill, who develops into a talented poet and author. The book breathes the atmosphere of familiar country scenes and quaint characters, among whom may be mentioned Obadiah Strout, the singing-master of the town, who has composed a new national air which he prophesies will be sung when the 'Star-Spangled Banner' and 'Hail Columbia' "are laid upon the shelf and all covered with dust." Hiram Maxwell, another original character, blessed with a great appetite, remarks, "I've got only one way of tellin' when I've got enough, — I allus eats till it hurts me, then I stop while the pain lasts."

Sawyer marries Miss Alice Pettengill, who for a time becomes blind, but whose sight is in the end restored. The object of Mr. Pidgin in the production of this story is twofold — to give a realistic picture of New England life of twenty-five years ago and at the same time to paint the portrait of a true American gentleman.

QUINTUS CLAUDIUS, by Ernst Eckstein. (Translated from the German by Clara Bell.) This story, which appeared originally in 1881, is 'A Romance of Imperial Rome' during the first century. The work was first suggested to the author's mind as he stood amid the shadows of the Colosseum and the earlier scenes are largely laid in the palaces and temples that lie in ruins near by this spot. The central motive of the book is the gradual conversion to Christianity of Quintus Claudius, son of Titus Claudius, priest of Jupiter Capitolinus; his avowal of the same, and the consequences that flow from it to himself, his family, and his promised wife, Cornelia. The time of the story is 95 A. D. at the close of the gloomy reign of Domitian; and the book ends with that Emperor's assassination and the installation of Nerva and Trajan. The story enjoyed a wide popularity in its day.

QUO VADIS (1895) perhaps the most popular novel of the Polish master in fiction, Henryk Sienkiewicz, is, like the "trilogy," historical; it deals, however, not with the history of Poland, but with that of Rome in the time of Nero. The magnificent spectacular environment of the decaying Roman empire, the dramatic qualities of the Christian religion, then assuming a world-wide significance, offer rich material for the genius of Sienkiewicz. He presents the background of his narrative with marvelous vividness. Against it he draws great figures: Petronius, the lordly Roman noble the very flower of paganism; Eunice and Lygia, diverse products of the same opulent world; Nero, the beast-emperor; the Christians seeking an unseen kingdom in a city overwhelmed by the symbols of earthly imperialism; and many others typical of dying Rome, or of that new Rome to be established on the ruined throne of the Cæsars. The novel as a whole is intensely dramatic, sometimes melodramatic. Its curious title has reference to an ancient legend, which relates that St. Peter, fleeing from Rome and from crucifixion, meets his Lord Christ on the Appian Way. "Lord, whither goest thou?" (Domine, quo vadis?) cries Peter. "To Rome, to be crucified again," is the reply. The apostle thereupon turns back to his martyrdom. While 'Quo Vadis' cannot rank with the "trilogy," it is in many respects a remarkable novel.

QUR'ÂN, see **SACRED BOOKS OF THE EAST.**

RAB AND HIS FRIENDS, by Dr. John Brown (1855), a short story by a well-beloved Edinburgh physician, is in its way a classic. Rab is a sturdy mastiff — "old, gray, brindled, as big as a little Highland bull" — with "Shakespearean dewlaps shaking as he goes." His friends are his master and mistress, James Noble, the Howgate carrier, "a keen, thin, impatient, black-a-vised little man"; and the exquisite old Scotchman, his wife Ailie, with her "unforgettable face, pale, serious, lonely, delicate, sweet," with dark gray eyes "full of suffering, full also of the overcoming of it." Ailie is enduring a terrible malady; and her husband wraps her carefully in his plaid and brings her in his cart to the hospital, where her dignified patient lovableness through a dangerous operation moves even the thoughtless medical students to tears. She is nursed by her husband. "Handy, and clever, and swift, and patient as any woman, was that horny-handed, snell, peremptory little man"; while Rab, quiet and obedient, but saddened and disquieted by the uncomprehended trouble, jealously guards the two. Perhaps no truer, more convincing dog character exists in literature than that of ugly faithful Rab.

RAIDERS, THE, by Samuel R. Crockett (1894), the best story by this author, is an old-time romance, dealing with the struggles with the outlaws and smugglers in Galloway early in the eighteenth century. It is a thrilling tale of border warfare and wild gipsy life, and it embodies many old traditions of that time and place. The hero, Patrick Heron, is laird of the Isle of Rathan, — "an auld name, though noo-a-days wi' but little to the tail o't." He is in love with May Maxwell, called May Mischief — is a sister of the Maxwells of Craigdarrock, who are by far the strongest of all the smuggling families.

Hector Faa, the chief of the Raiders, sees May Mischief, and he too loves her in his wild way. The Raiders are, for the most part, the remnants of broken clans, who have been outlawed even from the border countries, and are made up of tribes of Marshalls, Macatericks, Millers, and Faas. Most conspicuous among them are the last-named, calling themselves, "Lords and Earls of Little Egypt." By reason of his position and power, Hector Faa dares to send word to the Maxwells that their sister must be his bride.

"The curse that Richard Maxwell sent back is remembered yet in the Hill Country, and his descendants mention it with a kind of pride. It was considered as fine a thing as the old man ever did since he dropped profane swearing and took to anathemas from the psalms, — which did just as well."

The outlaws then proceed to attack the Maxwells and carry off May Mischief. Patrick Heron joins the Maxwells in the long search for their sister. After many bloody battles and hair-breadth escapes, he is finally successful in rescuing her from the Murder Hole. This he accomplishes by the aid of Silver Sand, the Still Hunter, a mysterious person who "has the freedom of the hill fastness of the gipsies." He has proved himself the faithful friend of Patrick Heron. He turns out to be John Faa, King of the Gipsies.

RALPH ROISTER DOISTER, by Nicholas Udall, was the first English comedy, although not printed until 1556, and probably written about 1541. At this time Nicholas Udall, its author, was headmaster of Eton school; and the comedy was written for the schoolboys, whose custom it was to act a Latin play at the Christmas season. An English play was an innovation, but 'Ralph Roister Doister' was very successful; and though Nicholas Udall rose in the Church, reaching the dignity of canon of Windsor, he is chiefly remembered as the author of this comedy.

Roisterer is an old word for swaggerer or boaster; and the hero of this little five-act comedy is a good-natured fellow, fond of boasting of his achievements, especially what he has accomplished or might accomplish in love. The play concerns itself with his rather impertinent suit to Dame Christian Custance, "a widow with a thousand pound," who is already the betrothed of Gavin Goodluck. But as Gavin, a thrifty merchant, is away at sea, Ralph Roister Doister sees no reason why he should not try his luck. His confidant is Matthew Merrygreek, a needy humorist, who undertakes to be a go-between and gain the widow's good-will for Ralph. He tries to get some influence over the servants of Custance; and there is a witty scene with the three maids, — Madge Mumblecrust, Tibet Talkapace, and Annot Allface. The servants of Ralph — Harpax and Dobinet Doughty — have a considerable part in the play, and the latter complains rather bitterly that he has to run about so much in the interest of his master's flirtations.

Dame Custance, though surprised at the presumption of Ralph and his friend, at length consents to read a letter which he has sent her, or rather to have it read to her by Matthew Merrygreek. The latter, by mischievously altering the punctuation, makes the letter seem the reverse of what had been intended. Ralph is ready to kill the scrivener who had indited the letter for him, until the poor man, by reading it aloud himself, proves his integrity. While Dame Custance has no intention of accepting Ralph, his suit makes trouble between her and Gavin Goodluck, whose friend, Sim Suresby, reports that the widow is listening to other suitors. There is much amusing repartee, several funny scenes, and all ends well.

RAMBLES AND STUDIES IN GREECE, by J. P. Mahaffy (1876, 7th ed., 1913). A record of what was seen, felt, and thought in two journeys to Greece, by a man trained in classic knowledge and feeling. By many critics it has been preferred to the author's 'Social Life in Greece.' The titles of some of the chapters, 'First Impressions of the Coast,' 'Athens and Attica,' 'Excursions in Attica,' 'From Athens to Thebes,' 'Chæronea,' 'Delphi,' 'Olympia and its Games,' 'Arcadia,' 'Corinth,' 'Mycenæ,' 'Greek Music and Painting,' etc., show something of the scope of the volume. From his study of the ancient Greek literature, Professor Mahaffy had reached the conclusion that it greatly idealized the old Greeks. In his 'Social Life in Greece,' 1874, he described them as he thought they actually were; and this description very nearly agrees, he says, with what he found in modern Greece. He judges that the modern Greeks — like the ancients as he sees them — are not a passionate race, and have great reasonableness, needing but the opportunity to outstrip many of their contemporaries in politics and science. The volume reveals the acute observer whose reasoning is based on special knowledge.

RAMONA, by Helen Jackson (1885). This story is a picturesque, sympathetic, and faithful picture of Spanish and Indian life in California. The scene opens upon an old Mexican estate in Southern California, where the Señora Moreno lives, with her son Felipe, and her adopted daughter Ramona, a beautiful half-breed, Scotch and Indian. Ramona betroths herself to Alessandro, a young Indian of noble character. Señora Moreno forbidding the marriage, they elope, to face a series of cruel misfortunes. The Indians of Alessandro's village are deprived of their land by the greed of the American settlers; and wherever they settle, the covetousness of the superior race drives them, sooner or later, to remoter shelters. The proud and passionate Alessandro is driven mad by his wrongs, and his story ends in tragedy, though a sunset light of peace falls at last on Ramona. So rich is the story in local color, — the frolic and toil of the sheep-shearing, the calm opulence of the sun-steeped vineyards, the busy ranch, the Indian villages; so strong is it in character, — the bigoted just châtelaine, the tender Ramona, the good old priest, — that its effect of reality is unescapable; and Californians still point out with pleased pride the low-spreading hacienda where Ramona lived, the old chapel where she worshipped, the stream where she saw her lovely face reflected, though none of these existed save in the imagination of the author.

RAVENSHOE, by Henry Kingsley (1862). The "House of Ravenshoe" in Stonington, Ireland, is the scene of this novel; and the principal actors are the members of the noble family of Ravenshoe. The plot, remarkable for its complexity, has three stages. Denzel Ravenshoe, a Catholic, marries a Protestant wife. They have two sons, Cuthbert and Charles. Cuthbert is brought up as a Catholic and Charles as a Protestant. This is the cause of enmity on the part of Father Mackworth, a dark, sullen man, the priest of the family, who has friendly relations with Cuthbert alone. James Norton, Denzel's groom, is on intimate terms with his master. He marries Norah, the maid of Lady Ravenshoe. Charles becomes a sunny, lovable man, Cuthbert a reticent bookworm. They have for playmates William and Ellen, the children of Norah. Two women play an important part in the life of the hero, Charles, — Adelaide, very beautiful in form and figure, with little depth, and lovely Mary Corby, who, cast up by shipwreck, is adopted by Norah. Charles becomes engaged to Adelaide. The plot deepens. Father Mackworth proves that Charles is the true son of Norah and James Norton, the illegitimate brother of Denzel; and William, the groom foster-brother, is real heir of Ravenshoe. To add to the grief of Charles, Adelaide elopes with his cousin Lord Welter. Charles flees to London, tries grooming, and then joins the Hussars. Finally he is found in London by a college friend, Marston, with a raving fever upon him. After recovery, Charles returns to Ravenshoe. Father Mackworth again produces evidence that not James Norton, but Denzel is the illegitimate son, and Charles, after all, is true heir to Ravenshoe. The union of Charles and Mary then takes place.

REAL FOLKS, by Mrs. A. D. T. Whitney (1871). Mrs. Whitney explains the real folks she means in the saying of one of her characters: "Real folks, the true livers, the genuine *neahburs* — nighdwellers; they who abide alongside in spirit." It is a domestic story dealing with two generations. The sisters Frank and Laura Old-ways, left orphans, are adopted into different households: Laura, into that of her wealthy aunt, where she is surrounded by the enervating influences of wealth and social ambitions; Frank, into a simply country home, where her lovable character develops in its proper environment. They marry, become mothers, and reaching middle age come, at the wish of their rich bachelor uncle Titus Oldways, to live near him in Boston. The episodes in the two households, the Ripwinkleys and Ledwiths, so widely divergent in character, complete the story; which, while never rising above the ordinary and familiar, yet, like the pictures of the old Dutch interiors, charms with its atmosphere of repose. It is a work for mothers and daughters alike. It exhibits the worth of the domestic virtues and the vanity of all worldly things; but it never becomes preachy. Its New England atmosphere is genuine, and the sayings of the characters are often racy of the soil; while the author's sense of humor carries her safely over some obstacles of emotion which might easily become sentimentality.

REAL WORLD, THE, by Robert Herrick (1901). In this story, the author presents an interesting study of American social conditions, as viewed through the eyes of his hero, Jack Pemberton, three phases of whose life are depicted, "childhood," "youth," and "manhood." Pemberton's early days are darkened by poverty and family dissensions and, amid discordant surroundings, he begins to realize that most individuals create for themselves an unreal environment in which they live, mistaking their own shadowy creations for reality; he determines to find for himself the "real world," and the author traces his gradual awakening to ambition for success in the social and material universe, and his final recognition that the "reality" he seeks must be upon a higher plane. While acting as clerk at a summer hotel, Pemberton makes the acquaintance of Elsie Mason, a brilliant, impulsive, and ambitious girl who becomes his youthful idol and who shares with him her worldly wisdom. She fires him with aspirations for the world she seeks to conquer, and his love for her forms the ruling motive of his early career. She continues to influence him strongly, even after her mercenary marriage with a rich man, until he awakens to a realization of the utter frivolity of her character and discovers that she, too, is a phantom. In the end he wins the love of the sweet and conservative Isabelle Mather, who has passed through an unfortunate engagement with Elsie Mason's dissipated brother, and who helps him to attain his "real world." The author follows Pemberton's career as a poor boy, a hotel clerk, a student at Harvard College, and takes leave of him as a successful lawyer, who has passed through many trials and struggles which have developed in him a strong, upright character.

REBECCA OF SUNNYBROOK FARM, by Kate Douglas Wiggin (1903). This is the story of a quaint and original little girl, whose trite sayings are a constant source of amusement to the reader. Rebecca Randall is one of seven children and their mother being a widow with nothing but a mortgaged farm for their support, they have known little besides work and privation. Nevertheless, Rebecca, blest with an optimistic spirit, sees the silver lining in the clouds and makes the best of her surroundings. At the age of ten she leaves home to go to live with her mother's two unmarried sisters, Miranda and Jane, who are to take charge of her and send her to school. Rebecca makes the journey to Riverboro' alone by stage and in so doing wins the heart of the stage-driver, Mr. Cobb, who becomes her staunch friend. Her life in her new home is full of trials as her aunt Miranda is severe and unreasonable, but Rebecca by her winning ways practically softens her hard nature. At school Rebecca finds a friend and congenial spirit in Emma Jane Perkins and their intimacy continues throughout the story. Rebecca's aptness at her lessons and her originality of thought and expression arouse the interest of her teacher who does all she can to aid her progress. In Mr. Adam Ladd, a kind and generous young man, Rebecca finds the prince of her fairy tales and she calls him "Mr. Aladdin," after that hero of romance. Mr. Ladd does much to add to Rebecca's happiness and his interest in her becomes so deep that at the close of the story it is plainly seen that his feelings have turned to something more serious. The reader takes leave of Rebecca after her graduation from the seminary, on which occasion she is class poet and carries off many honors. Aunt Miranda, after a long and tedious illness, dies, leaving her house and land to Rebecca, who is made happy by the thought that it is in her power to bring comfort and happiness to her mother and brothers and sisters.

RECENT RESEARCH IN BIBLE LANDS, by H. V. Hilprecht, see **BIBLE LANDS,** etc.

RECHERCHE DE L'ABSOLU, see **ALKAHEST.**

RECORDS OF A GIRLHOOD, by Frances Anne Kemble (1879). This work gives the history of the life of a great actress, member of a family of genius, from her birth up to the time of her marriage (1809–34). Her incorrigible childhood, her school-days in France, her first visit to the theatre, her early efforts at authorship, her distaste for the stage, her first appearance on it, her successes there, the books she has been reading, her first visit to America, her comments on American life, which, to her, is so primitive as to seem barbarous, — all this is duly set forth. Among those of whom she relates memorable recollections or anecdotes are Lord Melbourne, Rossini, Weber, Fanny Elssler, Sir Walter Scott, Talma, Miss Mitford, Theodore Hook, Arthur Hallam, John Sterling, Malibran, Queen Victoria, George Stephenson, Lord John Russell, Edmund Kean, Chancellor Kent, Edward Everett, Charles Sumner, and a hundred other personages of equal fame. She knew everybody who was worth knowing, was petted and spoiled by the highest society, and reigned as an uncrowned queen in whatever circle she delighted by her presence. She declares it to be her belief that her natural vocation was for opera-dancing; and says that she ought to have been handsome, and would have been so, had she not been disfigured by an attack of small-pox at the age of sixteen, whose effects never wholly disappeared.

The book is brightly written, is full of well-bred gossip, and always entertaining.

RECORDS OF LATER LIFE, by Frances Anne Kemble (1882). This volume resumes its author's history at the point where 'Records of a Girlhood' leaves it — namely, at her marriage with Mr. Pierce Butler in 1834; and ends with her return to America in 1848, and her success in earning by public readings a home at Lenox, Massachusetts. With the exception of two visits to Europe, the first two-thirds of the book are given to her life in America; the last third, to her stay in Europe (1845–48). The record begins by describing some of the points at which her English ideas disagree with American ones. It is full of amusing comments on our life, — its crudeness, unhealthiness, lack of leisure, and extravagance, and the discomforts of travel. She speaks with evident pleasure of her American friends, sets down many observations and plans for the abolition of slavery, as she studies it on her husband's plantation in Georgia, and makes, in short, a vivid picture of American social life in the first half of the century. She gives specific studies of Philadelphia, Niagara Falls, Rockaway Beach, Newport, Boston, Lenox, Baltimore, and Charleston. Though she has faith in American institutions, she is not without intelligent misgivings: "The predominance of spirit over matter indicates itself strikingly across the Atlantic, where, in the lowest strata of society, the native American rowdy, with a face as pure in outline as an ancient Greek coin, and hands and feet as fine as those of a Norman noble, strikes one dumb with the aspect of a countenance whose vile, ignoble hardness can triumph over such refinement of line and delicacy of proportion. A human soul has a wonderful supremacy over the matter which it informs. The American is a whole nation, with well-made, regular noses; from which circumstance (and a few others), I believe in their future superiority over all other nations. But the lowness their faces are capable of 'flogs Europe.'" Her strictures on the English aristocracy, and middle and lower classes, are equally severe. In the last third of the book are described her return to the stage and her appearance as a public reader in England, in 1847. In 1841 she was on the Continent, and in 1846 in Italy. Most of this history is told in the form of letters written at the time, wherein her literary opinions and speculations on life and philosophy are freely expressed. Her anecdotes of Dr. Channing, Grisi, Lord and Lady Landsdowne, Sydney Smith, Lady Holland, Rogers, Wordsworth, Mrs. Somerville, Follen, Taglioni, Liszt, Mendelssohn, Fanny Elssler, Mrs. Grote, Jenny Lind, Moore, Macaulay, Dickens, Dr. Arnold, Bunsen, Thackeray, etc., are always entertaining and often most illuminating.

RED AS A ROSE IS SHE, by Rhoda Broughton (1870). This commonplace love-story is very simply told. The scene is laid in Wales. The heroine, Esther Craven, promises to marry Robert Brandon, "to keep him quiet," though caring much less for him than for her only brother. But on a visit she meets the heaven-appointed lover, and notwithstanding her engagement the two at once fall in love. Interested friends, who do not approve of the affair, plot and bear false witness to break it off. Esther confesses to Brandon her change of feeling, and he is man enough to release her. Then ensues a period of loneliness, misunderstanding, and hardship for the heroine, whose character is ripened by adversity. When happiness once more stands waiting for her, she has learned how to use its gifts. The story moves quickly, and is entertaining.

RED BADGE OF COURAGE, THE, by Stephen Crane, was published in 1895. It attracted a great deal of attention both in England and America, by reason of the nature of the subject, and of the author's extreme youth. It is a study of a man's feeling in battle, written by one who was never in a battle, but who seeks to give color to his story by lurid language. Henry Fleming, an unsophisticated country boy, enthusiastic to serve his country, enlists at the beginning of the Civil War. Young, raw, intense, he longs to show his patriotism, to prove himself a hero. When the book opens he is fretting for an opportunity, his regiment apparently being nowhere near a scene of action. His mental states are described as he waits and chafes; the calculations as to what it would all be like when it did come, the swagger to keep up the spirits, the resentments of the possible superiority of his companions, the hot frenzy to be in the thick of it with the intolerable delays over, and sore doubts of courage. Suddenly, pell-mell, the boy is thrown into battle, gets frightened to death in the thick of it, and runs; after the fun is over, crawls back to his regiment fairly vicious with unbearable shame. The heroic visions fade; but the boy makes one step towards manhood through his wholesome lesson. In his next battle courage links itself to him like a brother-in-arms. He tests and is tested, goes into the thick of the fight like a howling demon, goes indeed to hell, and comes back again, steadied and quiet. The book closes on his new and manly serenity.

"He had rid himself of the red sickness of battle. The sultry nightmare was in the past. He had been an animal, blistered and sweating in the heat and pain of war. He now turned with a lover's thirst to images of tranquil skies."

RED COCKADE, THE, by Stanley J. Weyman (1896). This is a romance filled with exciting incidents of the stormy times of the French Revolution. The hero, the Vicomte de Saux, is one of the French nobility. His sympathy with the troubles of the French peasants leads him to adopt the Red Cockade, notwithstanding his ties of blood and his engagement to marry a young woman of a prominent Royalist family. He is constantly torn between loyalty to his convictions and to the woman that he loves, and is often placed in situations where he is obliged to save Mademoiselle de St. Alais from the rage of the mob.

As the Vicomte de Saux refuses to join the Aristocrats, the mother and one brother of Mademoiselle de St. Alais denounce him utterly. But Dénise herself, after having been saved by him from her burning château, loves him intensely and is true to him, though her relatives have betrothed her to the leader of the Royalists. The other brother Louis, from his old friendship for the Vicomte, upholds his sister. The book closes with a scene in the room where Madame de St. Alais lies dying from wounds received at the hands of the mob. Her elder son has been killed by the revolutionists. With the mother are Dénise and Louis, and also the Vicomte de Saux. In her last moments she gives Dénise to her lover. After their marriage the Vicomte and his bride retire to their country place at Saux. The man to whom Dénise was betrothed out of vengeance to her lover, disappears after the overthrow of his party.

RED LAUGH, THE, fragments of a discovered manuscript, by Leonidas Andreief (1904). A soldier's diary during a disastrous campaign in Manchuria at the time of the Russo-Japanese war. It is an indictment of war, and a study in morbid psychology. "Horror and madness," the two opening words of the book express the theme. The "red laugh" is the symbol which to him expresses the wounded, torn, mutilated bodies. "It was in the sky, it was in the sun, and soon it was going to overspread the whole earth — that red laugh." The common soldiers go mad from the horror of the battlefield, and the terrible fatigue of incessant marching. The doctors go mad at sight of suffering they are unable to relieve. Students detailed to help bring in the wounded lose their reason and commit suicide. At home a mother receives letters from her son for a month after the telegram has announced his death, and when the letters stop coming she goes mad. The dead write to the dead. In the confusion two regiments mistake each other for the enemy, and the writer of the diary loses both legs. He goes back to his family glad to be alive but looks sadly at his bicycle. A journalist, he tries to write the story of the war, and becomes insane over it. His brother tries to complete the narrative from the notes, and he also sees the "red laugh," "something enormous red and bloody" "laughing a toothless laugh." The physical horror becomes mental to him also, and ends in the inevitable madness.

RED LILY, THE ('Le Lys rouge'), by Anatole France (1894). The story of an emotional Frenchwoman's liaisons with two men. Madame Therese Martin-Bellème was married by her father to an elderly count, a government minister. After two years of this marriage of convenience she and her husband are strangers in the same house. The beautiful young countess is loved devotedly by Robert Le Menil, and she accepts his love, the first she has known, not because she loves him, but because she is carried away by his love for her. Three years later, she leaves the lover she likes for a lover she loves, Dechartre, a sculptor. She tells him truly that she has never loved another. Le Menil refuses to accept his dismissal by letter and comes to Florence where she is visiting. Dechartre hears of his presence and suspects their former intimacy, but she denies all. Later, in Paris, he hears her name coupled with that of Le Menil, and is tortured with jealousy. She is possessed by the one idea that she must not lose him, the man she loves with all her heart, and tells him again that he is her one lover. Le Menil had gone away to forget her in vain. He returns and follows her to the theatre with reproaches and entreaties which Dechartre overhears. She is obliged to tell her lover the truth. Dechartre refuses to understand that she is not a light woman, or believe her avowals that she has loved him alone, and in a pathetic last interview she realizes that her happiness is at an end. The pictures of Florence and Paris add charm and the minor characters are of interest as personal sketches of the author himself and his contemporaries. Choulette, the anarchist and mystic, an old vagabond full of delightful enthusiasms, is probably a portrait of Verlaine. Miss Bell, the English poetess, has been identified with Miss Mary Robinson (now Madame Duclaux); De Chartre is supposed to represent the passionate side of Anatole France's nature, Paul Vence, the artistic and intellectual side; Schmoll is the Jewish scholar, Oppert.

RED ROBE, THE ('La Robe rouge') by Eugene Brieux (1900). This is a scathing satire on the law and lawyers, the clumsy and inefficient machinery of justice, especially the French judiciary which makes advancement depend upon success in winning convictions. In the hope of winning the red robe of a judge, the "juge d'instruction," Mouzon, and the prosecuting attorney, Vagret, both try to convict a man of murder, whose guilt is extremely doubtful. Lesser men who have influential friends and relatives have been promoted over Vagret and this notorious case is his great chance to distinguish himself. In time to save the accused peasant, Etchepars, he realizes that his desire to win has been stronger than his zeal for truth and sacrifices his chance of advancement. Promotion comes to the unscrupulous Mouzon, who has bent all his energies to weaving a net of circumstantial evidence around Etchepars, regardless of truth. In order to discredit Yanetta, the wife of the accused, as a witness, he ferrets out a scandal of her girlhood in Paris, which is unknown to her husband. In the trial, her character as an honest woman is taken from her; her husband repudiates her and takes away her children. In revenge she stabs and kills Mouzon, the lawyer who has brought about her misery. This last dramatic scene is quoted in the LIBRARY.

RED ROCK, by Thomas Nelson Page, was published in 1899. It is entitled 'A Chronicle of the Reconstruction,' and is a faithful portrayal of the political and social conditions which existed during that era. The scene is laid "partly in one of the old Southern States and partly in the land of memory" and opens just before the war. Red Rock is the name of a plantation which has been owned and occupied by the Gray family for many generations, and which takes its name from a rock with a huge red stain upon it, which was believed to be the blood of the Indian chief who had slain the wife of the first Jacquelin Gray. The present Jacquelin, the central figure of the story, is a young lad at the time of the breaking out of the war, and, after the death of his father in battle, he enlists, at the age of fifteen, to fight for the South. After many trying experiences, in which he shows great nobleness and courage, he returns home at the close of the war seriously wounded. He finds desolation and ruin all about him and is forced to witness his mother's death and her burial in alien soil, as their home and patrimony have been wrested from them by dishonest means. Jacquelin has always loved Blair Cary, the companion of his childhood days, but he holds aloof from her, thinking that she is in love with his dashing cousin, Steve Allen, and his suit does not prosper. After many thrilling episodes with "Carpet-baggers," Ku Klux raids, and law-suits, Jacquelin at last comes into his own, winning back the estate of his father and the hand of the girl he loves. Steve Allen, the hero of many exciting adventurers, marries Ruth Welch, a charming Northern girl who has come to make her home in the South. Dr. Cary, who figures prominently in the story, is a noble character and spends his last strength in visiting the bedside of his enemy Leech, the villainous overseer, who has everywhere worked havoc and desolation.

RED ROVER, THE, by James Fenimore Cooper (1827). This story relates to the days before the Revolutionary War; and is one of Cooper's most exciting sea tales. Henry Ark, a lieutenant on his Majesty's ship Dart, is desirous of distinguishing himself by aiding in the capture of the notorious pirate, the Red Rover. With this in view he goes to Newport, disguised as a common sailor under the name of Wilder, and joins the Rover's ship, the Dolphin, which is anchored there awaiting the de-departure of a merchantman, the Caroline. The Captain of the Caroline meets with an accident and Wilder is sent by the Rover to take his place; shortly after he puts to sea followed by the Dolphin. A storm arises, and the Caroline is lost; the only survivors being Wilder, Miss Gertrude Grayson, a passenger, and Mrs. Wyllys, her governess, who are rescued by the Dolphin. Not long after, a royal cruiser is sighted. This proves to be the Dart; and the Rover, going on board of her in the guise of an officer in the royal navy, learns by accident of Wilder's duplicity. He returns to the Dolphin, and summoning his first mate accuses him of treachery; Wilder confesses the truth of the charge, and the Rover, in a moment of generosity, sends him back to his ship unharmed, together with the two ladies, without whom Wilder refuses to stir. The Rover then attacks the Dart, and takes it after a hard fight. He is about to have Wilder hanged, when it appears that he is a son of Mrs. Wyllys whom she has supposed drowned in infancy; and the Rover, unable to separate the new-found son from his mother, sets them all off in a pinnace, in which they reach shore safely. After the close of the Revolutionary War a man is brought to the old inn at Newport in a dying condition: he proves to be the Red Rover, who, having reformed, has served through the war with credit and distinction.

The book holds the interest of the reader throughout; and the descriptions of the storm and battle are very vivid.

REDGAUNTLET, by Sir Walter Scott. Sir Alberick Redgauntlet, ardently espousing the cause of the Young Pretender in 1745, pays for his enthusiasm with his life. The guardianship of his infant son and daughter is left to his brother, outlawed for violent adherence to the House of Stuart; but the widow, ascribing her bereavement to the politics of the Redgauntlets, desires to rear her children in allegiance to the reigning dynasty. The little girl having been kidnapped by her guardian, the mother flees with her boy; who, ignorant of his lineage, is brought up in obscurity under the name of Darsie Latimer. Warned by his mother's agents to shun England, the young man ventures for sport into the forbidden territory, and is seized by Redgauntlet. Detained as a prisoner, Darsie at length learns his true name and rank, and meets his sister, now grown up to charming womanhood. Redgauntlet, a desperate partisan, endeavors by persuasion and threats to involve his nephew in a new plot to enthrone the Chevalier, and conveys the youth by force to the rendezvous of the conspirators. Meanwhile, Darsie's disappearance has alarmed his devoted friend, Alan Fairford, a young Scotch solicitor; who, in spite of great danger, traces him to the gathering-place of the conspiring Jacobites. The plot, predestined to failure through Charles Edward's obstinate rejection of conditions, is betrayed by Redgauntlet's servant, and the conspirators quickly dispersed, their position rendered absurd by the good-natured clemency of George III. Redgauntlet, chagrined at the fiasco, accompanies the Chevalier to France, and ends his adventurous career in a monastery. Darsie, now Sir Arthur Redgauntlet, remains loyal to the House of Hanover, and bestows his sister's hand upon Alan Fairford (in whom, according to Lockhart, Scott drew his own portrait).

Sixteenth in the Waverley series, 'Redgauntlet' was issued in 1824, two years before the crash that left Scott penniless. Though showing haste, the tale does not flag in interest, and even the minor characters — notably Peter Peebles the crazy litigant, Wandering Willie the vagabond fiddler, and Nanty Ewart, the smuggler — are living and individual.

REDS OF THE MIDI, THE ('Les Rouges du Midi'), by Félix Gras, translated into English by Mrs. Thomas A. Janvier, is a strong story of the French Revolution, published in 1896. One Pascal La Patine, in his old age, night after night, in the shoemakers shop, tells the story of his youth. His father was killed by the gamekeeper of the Marquis; he himself was forced to fly for his life. Longing to be revenged upon the aristocrats, he joins the "Reds of the Midi" (the insurgents of Southern France), goes to Paris, sees all the horrors of the Revolution, rescues the daughter of the Marquis from the guillotine, loves her in silence, enlists in Napoleon's army, and after fighting in Spain, Egypt, and Russia, returns to his native village of Malemort to end his days, firm in the faith that Napoleon has never died. It was in Malemort that Gras was born: the Prologue is pure autobiography, and many of the characters are drawn from life. There is a vivid picture of the famous Marseilles Battalion, "who knew how to die," and a passing glimpse of Napoleon.

REEF, THE, a novel by Edith Wharton (1912). An American diplomat in London, George Darrow, meets his first love, Anna Leath, who had married abroad, and is recently a widow. Darrow is on his way to her in France, when he receives a telegram asking him to postpone his visit. Chilled and disappointed, and uncertain how to spend his holiday, he chances to meet Sophie Viner, a young American acquaintance, companion to a Mrs. Murrett in London, who has turned her adrift almost penniless. She is on her way to friends in Paris, and her courage and gay youth appeal to him. When they discover her friends have left Paris, he follows his impulse to give her a little of the pleasure she has missed, and they drift into a temporary and irregular connection. This episode becomes the "reef," which wrecks their later lives. Darrow visits France as Anna's fiancé, several months later, and finds Sophie Viner installed in the household as governess to Anna's daughter, and engaged to be married to Owen, her stepson. The secret of their former acquaintance is discovered. Sophie loyally throws up her prospects and goes back to the service of Mrs. Murrett, to keep the memory of Darrow, whom she loves. Anna comes to understand and forgive Sophie and Darrow, but jealousy of their past intimacy makes it impossible for her to marry him. The author's well-known powers of psychological analysis have full scope in the distinction of the characters and the delicate situations which result.

REFLECTIONS OF A MARRIED MAN, by Robert Grant. These entertaining "reflections" chronicle in a humorous manner the various experiences, perplexities, and amusing episodes, which occur in the daily life of a married couple at the present day. The husband reflects that at the age of thirty-five, being happily married, his entire point of view has changed since the days of his bachelorhood. Instead of speculating on the soulful subjects which agitated his mental faculties at that time, he finds himself hopelessly entangled with the butcher, the baker, the candlestick-maker, the school-teacher, and the clergyman, and is particularly interested in the size of his quarterly bill for boots and shoes. The experiences of the couple when they are first married and go to housekeeping are described in an amusing way, and the trials caused by Mary Ann and the cook are most realistic. A clever point in the story is where a second wedding journey is undertaken, but under decidedly different conditions, as there are now four vigorous children to be left behind. The husband and wife anticipate the freedom from care which their outing will afford them; but while deriving enjoyment from the trip, they both acknowledge that they are counting the days until their return home. The reflections close with the hope expressed by the head of the family that the children may be as happy as he and his wife Josephine have been, despite the fact that their careers have been so much more commonplace and prosaic than they had anticipated in their youthful days. The 'Reflections' were published in 1892, and followed by 'The Recollections of a Philosopher,' which continue the family chronicles.

REFLECTIONS ON THE REVOLUTION IN FRANCE, a political essay in epistolary form, originally intended simply as a private letter to a young friend in France but expanded during composition into a treatise and published in 1790. Although an ardent champion of liberty in the cases of America, Ireland, and India, Burke was vehemently opposed to the Revolutionists in France. He had always advocated a "manly, moral, regulated liberty"; they favored the wholesale abolition of old institutions. The English Revolution of 1688 involved no break with the past but was rather a return to the sound constitutional principles of an earlier time, the interdependence of king, lords, and commons in one nicely-poised scheme. The

French Revolution of 1789 was based on the right of the people to cut loose from all established institutions and to introduce an entirely new philosophy and method of government. The result was a loosening of the bonds that make society possible — of chivalry, of loyalty, of decency, of self-restraint, of subordination, of reverence, of discipline. This Burke illustrates by reference to the abolition of the nobility, the confiscation of the Church, the disorganization of the army, and, in a passage famous for its eloquence, by a description of the insults heaped upon the King and Queen when they were brought forcibly from Versailles to Paris. He also makes the remarkable prophecy that the revolution will end in a military dictatorship. The depth and power of Burke's ideas on political philosophy and his ability to apply them to a great contemporary crisis and to comprehend its underlying tendencies are superbly illustrated in this profoundly thoughtful and passionately eloquent polemic.

REFORMATION OF THE CHURCH OF ENGLAND, History of the, by Bishop Burnet (3 vols., 1679, 1681, 1714); and 'History of his Own Time' (2 vols., 1723, 1734), are English standard books of high character and value. The second of these works is of great intrinsic worth, because without it our knowledge of the times would be exceedingly imperfect. For the first the author was voted the thanks of both houses of Parliament. Burnet was bishop of Salisbury, 1689-1715; and in 1699 he brought out an 'Exposition of the Thirty-nine Articles' which became a church classic in spite of high-church objection to his broad and liberal views. He was from early life a consistent representative of broad-church principles, both in politics and divinity. His tastes were more secular than scholastic. Of bishops he alone in that age left a record of able and conscientious administration, and of lasting work of great importance. Although bitterly attacked from more than one quarter on account of the 'History of His Own Time,' the best judgment to-day upon this work is that nothing could be more admirable than his general candor, his accuracy as to facts, the fullness of his information, and the justice of his judgments both of those whom he vehemently opposed and of those whom he greatly admired. The value of the work, says a recent authority, "as a candid narrative and an invaluable work of reference, has continually risen as investigations into original materials have proceeded." The best edition of both the Histories is that of the Clarendon Press (1823-33; 1865).

REIGN OF FERDINAND AND ISABELLA, History of the, by William Hickling Prescott (1837). This is the earliest of the books of Prescott. Circumstances had enabled the author to command materials far beyond those of any previous writer, and he had fine talents for the task. The main story told by him was preceded by a view of the Castilian monarchy before A. D. 1400, and of the constitution of Aragon to about A. D. 1450. The work then proceeded through twenty chapters, to near the middle of the second volume, with 'The Age of Domestic Development, 1406-92,' and on to the end of the third volume, twenty-six chapters, with 'The Age of Discovery and Conquest, 1493-1517.' To near the middle of the third volume, "a principal object" of the history had been "the illustration of the personal character and public administration" of Isabella, whom Mr. Prescott pronounced "certainly one of the most interesting personages in history"; and into the second half of the work came the story of Columbus. No writer of judicious history has left Columbus on a more lofty pinnacle of moral greatness, as well as fame, or more carefully held a screen of admiration, and almost of awe, before actions and aspects of character which were of the age and of Spain and not of the ideals of man at his best. The Portuguese pursuit of discovery for a hundred years from 1418, which reached out a thousand miles into the Atlantic and carried the Lisbon ships round the south point of Africa to the real India and which in 1502 made an independent discovery of the south continent, Mr. Prescott took hardly any note of. But within the limits of his picture he wrought most admirably, to interest, to instruct, and to leave in literature a monument of the Catholic Queen and of Columbus.

REJECTED ADDRESSES, by James Smith and Horace Smith. This volume of poetical parodies was issued anonymously in 1812, and met with great success, both the critics and the public being delighted with the clever imitations; though, strange to say, the authors had much difficulty in finding a publisher for the book. The 'Rejected Addresses' were the joint work of the brothers James and Horace Smith, who wrote them as a burlesque upon the many prominent and unsuccessful competitors for the reward offered by the management of the Drury Lane for an address to be delivered at the opening of the new theatre. The 'Rejected Addresses' were begun at this time, and were completed in a few weeks. Among the imitations set forth in the volume, the following are the work of James Smith: 'The Baby's Début' (Wordsworth), 'The Hampshire Farmer's Address' (Cobbett), 'The Rebuilding' (Southey), 'Play-House Musings' (Coleridge), 'The Theatre' (Crabbe), the first stanza of 'Cui Bono' (Lord Byron); the song entitled 'Drury Lane Hustings'; and 'The Theatrical Alarm-Bell,' an imitation of the Morning Post; also travesties on 'Macbeth,' 'George Barnwell,' and 'The Stranger.' The rest of the imitations are by Horace Smith. The 'Rejected Addresses' were widely commended in their day, and still hold a high place among the best imitations ever made. Their extent and variety exhibited the versatility of the authors. Although James wrote the greater number of successful imitations, the one by Horace, of Scott, is perhaps the best of the parodies; and its amusing picture of the burning of Drury Lane Theatre is an absurd imitation of the battle in 'Marmion': —

> "The firemen terrified are slow
> To bid the pumping torrent flow,
> For fear the roof would fall.
> Back, Robins, back; Crump stand aloof!
> Whitford, keep near the walls!
> Huggins, regard your own behoof,
> For, lo! the blazing rocking roof
> Down, down in thunder falls!"

RELIGION, ANALOGY OF, by Joseph Butler, see **ANALOGY**.

RELIGION OF THE ANCIENT EGYPTIANS, by Alfred Wiedemann (1897). A work designed to set before the reader the principal deities, myths, religious ideas and doctrines, as they are found in Egyptian writings, and with special reference to such facts as have important bearings on the history of religion. It is based throughout on original texts, of which the most significant parts are given in a rendering as literal as possible, in order that the reader may judge for himself of their meaning. Dr. Wiedemann expresses the opinion that the essays of Maspero, in his 'Études de Mythologie et de Religion' (Paris, 1893), are far weightier for knowledge of the subject than any previous writings devoted to it. Maspero especially condemns the point of view of Brugsch, who attempts to prove that Egyptian religion was a coherent system of belief, corresponding somewhat to that imagined by Plutarch in his interesting work on Isis and Osiris.

We may speak of the religious ideas of the Egyptians, he says, but not of an Egyptian religion: there never came into existence any consistent system.   Of various religious ideas, found more or less clearly represented, it cannot be proved historically which are the earlier and which are the later.   They are all extant side by side in the oldest of the longer religious texts which have come down to us, — the Pyamid inscriptions of the Fifth and Sixth dynasties.   Research has determined nothing indisputable as to the origins of the national religion of the Egyptians, their form of government, their writing, or their racial descent.   The more thoroughly the accessible material, constantly increasing in amount, is studied, the more obscure do the questions of origin become.

Ancient Egypt was formed by the union of small States, or districts, which the Greeks called Nomes: twenty-two in Upper Egypt, and twenty in Lower Egypt. Each nome consisted of (1) The capital with its ruler and its god; (2) the regularly tilled arable land; (3) the marshes, mostly used as pasture, and for the cultivation of water plants; and (4) the canals with their special officials.   Not only did each nome have its god and its own religion regardless of neighboring faiths, but the god of a nome was within it held to be Ruler of the gods, Creator of the world, Giver of all good things, irrespective of the fact that adjacent nomes similarly made each its own god the One and Only Supreme.

There were thus many varieties and endless rivalries and conflicts of faiths, and even distinct characters attached to the same name; as Horus at Edfu, a keen-sighted god of the bright sun, and Horus at Letopolis, a blind god of the sun in eclipse.   If a ruler rose to royal supremacy, he carried up the worship of his god.   From the Hyksos period of about six hundred years, the origin of all forms of religion was sought in sun worship.   Dr. Wiedemann devotes chapters to 'Sun Worship,' 'Solar Myths,' and 'The Passage of the Sun through the Underworld,' tracing the general development of sun worship and the hope of immortality connected with it.   Then he sketches 'The Chief Deities'; 'The Foreign Deities'; and 'The Worship of Animals,' which was due to the thoroughly Egyptian idea of an animal incarnation of deity.   He then reviews the story of 'Osiris and his Cycle,' and the development of 'The Osirian Doctrine of Immortality,' — "a doctrine of immortality which in precision and extent surpasses almost any other that has been devised."   This doctrine, Dr. Wiedemann says, is of scientific importance first from its extreme antiquity, and also from its many points of affinity to Jewish and Christian dogma.   The whole cult or worship of Osiris, of Isis, and of Horus, with some other related names, forms a study of great interest.   Dr. Wiedemann concludes his work with chapters on 'Magic and Sorcery,' and 'Amulets,' features in all ancient religion of the practical faith of the masses.

REMARKABLE PROVIDENCES, by Increase Mather.   In 1681, when the agitation in the Massachusetts Bay Colony over the questions respecting the imperiled colonial charter was rapidly approaching a climax, and the public mind was already feverishly excited, the ministers sent out a paper of proposals for collecting facts concerning witchcraft.   This resulted three years later (1684) in the production of a work by President Increase Mather of Harvard College, which was originally entitled 'An Essay for the Recording of Illustrious Providences.'   Into this book President Mather had gathered up all that was known or could be collected concerning the performances of persons supposed to be leagued with the Devil.   It is rather remarkable to learn from this work that modern spiritualistic performances — rappings, tippings, trances, second sight, and the like — were well known to the grave fathers of New England, although they unfortunately looked upon them as far more serious matters than do their descendants to-day.   The book also contains a remarkable collection of wonderful sea-deliverances, accidents, apparitions, and unaccountable phenomena in general; in addition to the things more strictly pertaining to witchcraft. Palfrey the historian believes that this book had an unfortunate effect upon the mind and imagination of President Mather's son, the Reverend Cotton Mather; and that it led him into investigations and publications supposed to have had an important effect in producing the disastrous delusion which followed three years later, in which Cotton Mather was so lamentably conspicuous.

RENAISSANCE IN ITALY, THE (1875–86), the most comprehensive work of John Addington Symonds, was published in five volumes, each dealing with a different phase of the great era of New Life in Italy. Vol. i., 'The Age of the Despots,' presents the social conditions of the time, especially as they were embodied and expressed in the cultured despots of the free cities. In Vol. ii., 'The Revival of Learning,' the brilliant mundane scholarship of the era is exhaustively considered. Vols iii. and iv. are devoted to Literature and the Fine Arts as reflecting the spirit of the times. Vol. v. treats of the Catholic reaction, the revulsion of feeling, the reversal of judgment, which followed when the magnificent materialism of the Renaissance overdid itself. The work as a whole is a wonderfully sympathetic and scholarly record of one of the most fascinating periods of Italian development. It is adapted at once to the uses of the scholar and to the general reader.

RENÉ, by François Auguste Châteaubriand, published separately in 1807. 'René' and 'Atala' are the fruits of Châteaubriand's American travels, and they abound in the exquisite description of natural scenery for which he is noted.

'René,' an episode of the prose epic 'Les Natchez,' is in effect a monologue of the young European of that name, who has fled to the New World and its solitudes; and who relates to his adopted father Chactas, and the French missionary Father Souël, his previous life and the causes of his self-exile. Seated under a great tree in the haunts of the Natchez Indians, of whose tribe Chactas is a chief, the young man tells his listeners the story of his boyhood, and his restless wanderings from land to land in search of mental peace. He has passed through ancient countries and modern, has studied humanity in its earliest monuments and in the life of his own day, and finding no satisfaction in any phase of life, has remained long in forest solitudes, — only to meet there thoughts of death.

He tells further how he was rescued from this temptation by the love of his sister Amélie, who came to him and led his mind back to life, then disappeared from his sight forever in the living death of a convent, where she hid a heart oppressed by a feeling for René too strong for her peace. The tragedy of his sister's confession has driven René to these wildernesses.

The episodes of René and Atala are beautiful in melody and description, but inevitably unreal in their suggestions of Indian life and character.

REPRESENTATIVE GOVERNMENT, Considerations on, by J. S. Mill (1860). This work, though written in 1860, is still the best statement in English of the case for representative government. The author, being of opinion at the time the book was composed that both Conservatives and Liberals had lost confidence in the creeds which they nominally professed without having made any progress towards providing themselves with a better, attempts to state a doctrine which is "not a mere compromise, by splitting the difference between the two, but something wider than either, which in virtue of its superior comprehensiveness, might be adopted by either Liberal or Conservative without renouncing anything which he really feels to be valuable in his own creed." The keynote of the book is that political institutions are the work of men and owe their origin and their whole existence to human will. Similarly as they were first made by men, so they have to be worked by men and even by ordinary men. It is plain, therefore, that they can be altered or removed by human will, but whatever alteration or change is made must be of such a character as to suit existing conditions. "The most important point of excellence," he says, "which any form of government can possess is to promote the virtue and intelligence of the people themselves. The first question in respect to any political institution is, how far they tend to foster in the members of the community the various desirable qualities, moral or intellectual." The ideally best form of government, whereby Mill means the one which is practical and eligible under the circumstances, is the representative because "the rights and interests of every and any person are only secure from being disregarded, when the person interested is himself able, and habitually disposed to stand up for them" and because "the general prosperity attains a greater height, and is more widely diffused, in proportion to the amount and variety of the personal energies enlisted in promoting it."

REPUBLIC, THE, of Plato (c. 398–360 B. C.), translated by Benjamin Jowett (1891–92). The 'Republic' of Plato is the first and perhaps the greatest treatise on education. He is the first writer who has a distinct grasp of the thought that education should comprehend the whole of life and be preparatory to another in which education is to begin again. True knowledge is not something which is to be imposed from without but elicited from within, and education will implant a principle of intelligence which is better than ten thousand eyes. The Platonic conception of education is not as it were to fill an empty vessel, but to turn the eye of the soul towards the light. The child is first to be taught the simple religious truths, which are only two in number, that God is true and that he is good. It follows, therefore, that children should not be taught the old mythology, which largely consists of descriptions of the treacherous and scandalous conduct of the gods. After these religious truths come moral truths and unconsciously the child will learn what are the most important things next to religion, good manners, and good taste. The work of education is to be carried on not only in an atmosphere of desire for truth, but of repose. Children, therefore, should not be taken to dramatic entertainments, which are exciting for young people. Education should be a harmonious growth, in which are learnt the lessons of temperance and endurance, and the body and mind develop simultaneously in equal proportions. The great principle to be recognized in all art and nature, and the principle which must dominate education also, is simplicity.

The next stage of education is gymnastic, which, however, is not primarily a training of the body, but of the mind. Its aim should be to discipline the passionate element in human nature, as the purpose of music, which should follow gymnastic, is to restrain the acquisitive and draw out the rational within us. After music and gymnastic, which should make the training of the mind their chief aim, education should begin again from a new point of view. "True knowledge" (says Jowett) "according to Plato is of abstractions, and has to do, not with particulars or individuals, but with universals only; not with the beauties of poetry, but with the ideas of philosophy, and the great aim of education is the cultivation of the habit of abstraction. This is to be acquired through the study of the mathematical sciences. They alone are capable of giving ideas of relation, and of arousing the dormant energies of thought." See also 'Dialogues' of Plato.

RESEARCH MAGNIFICENT, THE, by H. G. Wells (1915). William Benham at an early age realizes that there are certain bounds to the attainment of what he calls "aristocratic living " The First of these is Fear. It comes to him when as a little boy he is shut in a field with an angry bull; and when he is "dared" to deny God in a thunderstorm. As he grows older, Benham takes heroic methods to overcome fear, both physical and mental. Knowledge of the Second Limit, Indulgence, comes to him as a grown man. He realizes it indirectly through his friend Prothero's struggles against temptations and through a knowledge of his mother's past. The experience comes to him directly through his entanglement with a fascinating widow, Mrs. Skelmersdale. Weary of her blandishments, he goes on a walking tour. In a particularly lovely part of England, he meets, wooes, and marries Amanda Morris. With her he continues his search for the best in life. Amanda is occasionally bored. It is evident that she would have preferred a rational honeymoon to dangerous jaunts in Arabia and Asia Minor, probing into the hearts of men. Before long she inveigles her husband back to London and tries to break him into fashionable life. Benham refuses to quit his research and goes abroad again, this time with his friend, Billy Prothero. While the young men are studying Russia in revolution, word comes to Benham that his wife has been untrue to him. A hasty trip to England confirms the rumor. It is at this juncture in his career that Benham discovers the Third Barrier—Jealousy. After a hard fight he conquers his mad rage, settles a comfortable sum on Amanda, offers her a divorce, and leaves England, this time for good. In the course of his wanderings over the globe, Benham formulates a Fourth Limit to the "aristocracy" he wants to achieve—Prejudice: prejudice against a man because he is of a different color, or of a different degree of intelligence. He dies in Johannesburg in an attempt to obliterate this barrier: seeing a troop of English soldiers firing on insurgent natives, he puts himself in the way and dies in the arms of his friend, White, to whom he entrusts the formulating of the ideal for which he was striven.

RESEARCHES INTO THE EARLY HISTORY OF MANKIND, by E. B. Tylor, see **EARLY HISTORY, ETC.**

RESURRECTION, by Count Lyov N. Tolstoy, published in 1900, presents in the author's usual powerful vein the absorbing theme of the development of a great character, besides offering a picture of Russian society, from the wealthy office-holding circle, to the peasants and common soldiers, jailers, and criminal classes. Nekhludoff, a well-to-do Russian noble, who enjoys his money and his superficial society existence and takes his views of life without questioning, from the atmosphere around him is one day called on for jury duty. One of the cases he has to try is that of a woman who is accused of poisoning a merchant for his money. Nekhludoff, to his horror, recognizes in the prisoner a girl from his aunt's estate with whom he had fallen in love as a young man and seduced. He is overcome by the realization of his personal responsibility for the crime in question, a responsibility which he is conscious of holding first towards the girl and second towards the community at large. Through the technical ignorance of the jury Katusha is condemned to penal servitude in Siberia, and Nekhludoff makes up his mind to follow her, win her back to a true life, and marry her. The story is a study of his gradual winning of a higher life for himself by coming in contact with the peasants and exiles with whom he must needs associate in his endeavor to do right by Katusha. Thus in his effort to right the wrong he has done to another, he unconsciously rights the wrong done in himself by the false social outlook and inadequate education which had made him what he was.

and he constructs for himself a new and broadly human creed of living.   In this story
Tolstoy reveals his wonderful power of handling innumerable details and of presenting a supremely realistic picture of Russian life.

RETURN OF SHERLOCK HOLMES, see **SHERLOCK HOLMES.**

RETURN OF THE NATIVE, THE, by Thomas Hardy, was published in 1878, being
his sixth novel.   The scene is laid in Southern England, in the author's "Wessex
country," the district of which he has made an ideal map for the latest edition of
his works.   The hero of the book, the "native," is Clym Yeobright, formerly a
jeweler in Paris, but now returned to the village of his birth, on Egdon Heath.   The
giving up of his trade is due to his desire to lead a broader, more unselfish life.   He
plans to open a school in the village, and to educate and uplift the rustics about him.
His Quixotic schemes of helpfulness are upset, however, by his falling in love with
Eustacia Vye, a beautiful, passionate, discontented woman, "the raw material of a
divinity."   His marriage with her is the beginning of a troubled life, severed far
enough from his ideals.   Her self-sought death by drowning leaves him free to begin
again his cherished career of usefulness.   As an open-air preacher he seeks an outlet
for his philanthropic spirit.   The story of Yeobright and Eustacia is not the exclusive
interest of the book.   Many rustic characters, drawn as only Hardy can draw them,
lend to it a delightful rural flavor which relieves the gloom of its tragic incidents.

RÊVE, LE, see **ROUGON-MACQUART.**

REVENGE OF JOSEPH NOIREL, THE ('La Revanche de Joseph Noirel'), by Victor
Cherbuliez (1870).   A lively and skillful character sketch by this master of literary
portraiture; who here, as in 'Jean Teterol's Idea,' takes for his theme the moral
unrest caused by social class distinctions, but carries the development of his theme to
a tragic extreme.   The scene is laid at Mon Plaisir, near Geneva, the villa-home of
the well-to-do bourgeois manufacturer, M. Merion, whose wife has social ambitions
of which the daughter Mademoiselle Marguerite is made the innocent victim.
Given in a *mariage de convenance* to M. le Conte d'Orins, she finds the unhappiness of a union without love intensified into horror and dread by the suspicion
that her husband has been guilty of a hidden crime.   Meanwhile the hero of the
story, Joseph Noirel, is the trusted overseer in the works of M. Merion; having
been gradually promoted to this position of responsibility and esteem from that of
the starving child of disgraced parents, whom the village crier had rescued and introduced as an apprentice in the factory.   On Mademoiselle Marguerite's returning
from her years of training in the convent for the aristocratic life to which her
mother had destined her, Joseph is captivated by her beauty; and after being thrown
together by the accident of a storm, he becomes the hopeless victim of a devouring but
unrequited love for her.   The marriage with the count having taken place, Joseph
becomes aware of the crime of which the husband is guilty, and informs Marguerite,
who flees for refuge to Mon Plaisir.   The count meanwhile creates the suspicion
that it is a guilty attachment on the part of Marguerite for Joseph which has brought
her there, and her parents indignantly reject her plea for their protection.   A word
from her would reveal her husband's crime and would cost his life.   Meanwhile
Joseph has already resolved to end his hopeless misery by taking his own life.   Marguerite maintains her silence, obeys her husband, and leaves her father's house.   She
asks Joseph to become the instrument of her death before taking his own life, and

under circumstances that would imply guilt, while yet she remains innocent, and the savior of her husband's life and honor. The narration of this climax of the story's action is in the highest plane of dramatic writing, and is a remarkable exhibition of the author's power of reserve, and of his ability to suggest the hidden reality beneath expressed unreality.

REVERIES OF A BACHELOR: OR, A BOOK OF THE HEART, by "Ik Marvel," pseudonym of Donald Grant Mitchell. The Bachelor's first Reverie was published in the Southern Literary Messenger in 1849, and was reprinted the following year in Harper's New Monthly Magazine. It represents the sentimental Bachelor before a fire of oak and hickory in a country farmhouse. He broods through an evening of "sober and thoughtful quietude." His thoughts are of matrimony, suggested by the smoke — signifying doubt; blaze — signifying cheer; ashes — signifying desolation. Why should he let himself love, with the chance of losing? The second Reverie is by a city grate, where the tossing sea-coal flame is like a flirt, — "so lively yet uncertain, so bright yet flickering," — and its corruscations like the leapings of his own youthful heart; and just here the maid comes in and throws upon the fire a pan of anthracite, and its character soon changes to a pleasant glow, the similitude of a true woman's love, which the Bachelor enlarges much upon in his dream-thoughts. The third Reverie is over his cigar, as lighted by a coal, a wisp of paper, or a match, — each bearing its suggestion of some heart-experience. The fourth is divided into three parts, also: morning, which is the past, — a dreaming retrospect of younger days; noon, which is the Bachelor's unsatisfied present; evening, which is the future, with its vision of Caroline, the road of love which runs not smooth at first, and then their marriage, foreign travel, full of warm and lively European scenes, and the return home with an ideal family conclusion. These papers, full of sentiment, enjoyed a wide popularity.

REVOLUTION IN FRANCE, by Edmund Burke, see **REFLECTIONS ON THE.**

REYNARD THE FOX. This is one of the cycle of animal-legends which are generally supposed by scholars to be of Oriental origin, and which have been adopted into most of the Germanic languages. The group of stories clustering about the fox as hero, and illustrating his superiority over his fellows, as cunning is superior to strength, first appeared in Germany as Latin productions of the monks in cloisters along the banks of the Mosel and Maas. This was as early as the tenth century, and France knew them by the end of the twelfth under the name of 'Le Roman du Renard.'

In 1170 the material took definite shape among the secular poems of Germany in the hands of Heinrich der Glichesâre, who composed an epic of twelve "adventures" in Middle High German, on the theme. In all the old versions there is a tendency toward satirical allusions to the ecclesiastical body, and toward pointing a moral for society through the mouths or the behavior of the animals. After traveling into the Flemish tongue, the adventures of the fox came back into German speech; this time to appear in Low German as the famous 'Reinke de Vos,' printed in Lübeck in 1498.

Nearly three hundred years later, 1793, Goethe turned his attention to the long-popular subject, and gave the animal epic its most perfect form in his 'Reinecke Fuchs.' In the twelve cantos of the 'Reinecke Fuchs,' which is written in hexameters, Goethe gives an amusing allegory of human life and passions, telling the story of the fox and his tricks in a more refined tone than his early predecessors, but losing something of their charm of naïve simplicity.

The drawings of the noted German artist, Wilhelm Kaulbach, which illustrated an edition de luxe of recent years, have renewed the interest of the reading public in Goethe's poem. Perhaps the most familiar trick of Reynard is the story of how he induced the bear to put his head in the crotch of a tree in search of honey, and then removed the wedge which held the crotch open, leaving the bear a prisoner, caught by the neck.

RICHARD II., by Shakespeare (printed 1597). This drama (based on Holinshed's 'Chronicle') tells the story of the supplanting, on the throne of England, of the handsome and sweet-natured, but weak-willed Richard II., by the politic Bolingbroke (Henry IV.). The land is impoverished by Richard's extravagances. He is surrounded by flatterers and boon companions (Bushy, Bagot, and Green), and has lost the good-will of his people. The central idea of 'Richard II.' is that the kingly office cannot be maintained without strength of brain and hand. Old John of Gaunt (or Ghent) is loyal to Richard; but on his death-bed sermons him severely, and dying, prophesies of England, — "this seat of Mars,"

> "This fortress built by Nature for herself
> Against infection and the hand of war,
> This happy breed of men, this little world."

Richard lets him talk; but no sooner is the breath out of his body than he seizes all his movable or personal wealth and that of his banished son Bolingbroke, to get money for his Irish wars. This step costs Richard his throne. While absent in Ireland, Bolingbroke lands with a French force, to regain his property and legal rights as a nobleman and open the purple testament of bleeding war. The country rises to welcome him. Even a force in Wales, tired of waiting for Richard, who was detained by contrary winds, disperses just a day before he landed. Entirely destitute of troops, he humbly submits, and in London a little later gives up his crown to Henry IV. Richard is imprisoned at Pomfret Castle. Here, one day, he is visited by a man who was formerly a poor groom of his stable, and who tells him how it irked him to see his roan Barbary with Bolingbroke on his back on coronation day, stepping along as if proud of his new master. Just then one Exton appears, in obedience to a hint from Henry IV., with men armed to kill. Richard at last (but too late) shows a manly spirit; and snatching a weapon from one of the assassins, kills him and then another, but is at once struck dead by Exton. Henry IV. lamented this bloody deed to the day of his death, and it cost him dear in the censures of his people.

RICHARD III., by Shakespeare (printed 1597), the last of a closely linked group of historical tragedies. (See 'Henry VI.') Still a popular play on the boards; Edwin Booth as Richard will long be remembered. As the drama opens, Clarence the brother of Richard (or Gloster as he is called) is being led away to the Tower, where, through Gloster's intrigues, he is soon murdered on a royal warrant. The dream of Clarence is a famous passage, — how he thought Richard drowned him at sea; and in hell the shade of Prince Edward, whom he himself had helped to assassinate at Tewkesbury, wandered by, its bright hair dabbled in blood, and crying: —

> "Clarence is come; false, fleeting, perjured Clarence."

Gloster also imprisons the son of Clarence, and meanly matches Clarence's daughter. The Prince Edward mentioned was son of the gentle Henry VI., whom Richard stabbed in the Tower. This hunch-backed devil next had the effrontery to woo to wife Anne, widow of the Edward he had slain. She had not a moment's happiness with him, and deserved none. He soon killed her, and announced his intention of seeking the hand of Elizabeth, his niece, after having hired one Tyrrel to murder her brothers, the tender young princes, sons of Edward IV., in the Tower. Tyrrel employed two hardened villains to smother these pretty boys; and even the murderers wept as they told how they lay asleep, "girdling one another within their innocent alabaster arms," a prayer book on their pillow, and their red lips almost touching. The savage boar also stained himself with the blood of Lord Hastings, of the brother and son of Edward IV.'s widow, and of Buckingham, who, almost as remorseless as himself, had helped him to the crown, but fell from him when he asked him to murder the young princes. At length at Bosworth Field the monster met his match in the person of Richmond, afterward Henry VII. On the night before the battle, the poet represents each leader as visited by dreams, — Richmond seeing pass before him the ghosts of all whom Richard has murdered, who encourage him and bid him be conqueror on the morrow; and Richard seeing the same ghosts pass menacingly by him, bidding him despair and promising to sit heavy on his soul on the day of battle. He awakes, cold drops of sweat standing on his brow; the lights burn blue in his tent: "Is there a murderer here? No. Yes, I am: then fly. What, from myself?" Day breaks; the battle is joined; Richard fights with fury, and his horse is killed under him: "A horse! a horse! my kingdom for a horse!" But soon brave Richmond has him down, crying, "The day is ours: the bloody dog is dead."

RICHARD CABLE, by S. Baring-Gould (1888). Richard Cable is the keeper of a light-ship on the coast of Essex, England. He is a widower, and father of a family of seven children, all girls. During a storm Josephine Cornellis, a young lady of the neighborhood, whose home is not particularly happy, is blown out to the light-ship in a small boat, and rescued by Cable.

Richard, being a moralist, gives advice to Josephine, who loses her heart to him. Events so shape themselves that she places herself under his guidance, and the two are married; but almost immediately Richard finds himself in a false position owing to the fact that he is not accustomed to the usages of society, and Josephine too feels mortified by her husband's mistakes. A separation takes place, Richard sailing round the coast to Cornwall, and taking his mother, the children, and all his belongings. Josephine repents; and as she cannot raise him to her sphere, decides to adapt herself to his. She goes into service as a lady's-maid. More complications ensue, and Richard, who has become a prosperous cattle-dealer, appears opportunely and takes her away from her situation. While he still hates her, he desires to provide for her. This she will not allow; but is anxious to regain his love, and continues to earn her living and endeavor to retrieve her great mistake. Eventually, at his own request, they are re-married.

There are several other interesting characters necessary to the working out of a plot somewhat complicated in minor details, but the burden of the story is concerning ill-assorted marriages and ensuing complications, —hardness of heart, pride, malice, and all uncharitableness.

RICHARD CARVEL, by Winston Churchill (1900). The characterization of this hero of the Revolutionary period is undoubtedly one of the best of its type in recent fiction. Richard Carvel spends his early life in Maryland, where he is brought up by his grandfather, an ardent supporter of King George. Here begins his varied and romantic career, as does his devotion for the lovely Dorothy Manners, who is shortly

removed to London, where it is hoped she will contract a brilliant marriage.   Through
the instrumentality of a rascally uncle, Carvel is kidnapped by pirates and is later
captured by Paul Jones, with whom he casts in his fortunes; they become fast friends
and together experience many vicissitudes.   In London, the hero undergoes trials and
privations and suffers the humiliation of being detained in the debtor's prison, from
which he is rescued by Dorothy Manners.   His subsequent career in London is
distinguished by steadily increasing success and he enjoys the friendship of Horace
Walpole, George Fox, and other prominent men.   Carvel frustrates the plan of Mr.
Manners to make a match between his daughter and the miserable Duke of Charter-
sea, and soon after learning of the death of his grandfather and of the fact that he has
been defrauded of his rightful inheritance, returns to America.   Here he finds an
occupation in taking charge of the lands of a worthy lawyer and patriot, until the
breaking out of the Revolution, when he enlists and serves with Paul Jones.   The
great climax of the story is reached in the brilliant description of the victory of the
Bon Homme Richard over the Serapis, in which battle Carvel is severely wounded;
he is taken to England where he is nursed by Dorothy, who at last consents to become
his wife, and returns with him to America, where his heritage is finally restored to
him.

RICHARD YEA AND NAY, see LIFE AND DEATH OF.

RIDDLE OF THE UNIVERSE, THE ('Die Welträsel'), a metaphysical and scientific
treatise by Ernst Haeckel, was published in German in 1899 and in an English translation by Joseph McCabe in 1901.   An eminent and prolific scientific investigator,
a passionate admirer of Darwin, and uniting power of minute research with bold
metaphysical speculation, Haeckel put forth this book at the close of a long career of
biological discovery, in defense of the extremest form of materialistic monism.   From
the chemical law of the indestructibility of matter and the physical law of the conservation of energy he formulates the law of substance or "law of the persistence
of matter and force"; and he strives to prove that this law is sufficient in itself to
account for all known phenomena, material, mental, and spiritual.   He holds with
Spinoza that matter and energy "are but two inseparable attributes of the one
underlying substance."   The dualistic idea of a personal God above or outside of
Nature, of an immortal soul distinct from the body, and of the freedom of the will
undetermined by causality, he regards as delusions, due to a false conception of the
central importance of man in the cosmos.   An eternal process of evolution and
devolution is constantly producing and then destroying the various planetary systems;
on one of these planets, the earth, and possibly on all the others, life has arisen and
developed, the lower species gradually evolving into higher—all under the impulse of
purely mechanical and material forces.   Consciousness is a vital property of every
living organism and is a purely natural phenomenon.   Man's body and soul have
arisen by a process of natural evolution from the lowest forms of existence.   Ethical
principles have evolved from the social necessities of man in association with his
fellow men.   Dogmatic religion is a hindrance to man's progress, a cause of unhappiness and misery, and above all a delusion.   There can be no compromise between
Christianity and modern science; the former is based on a mistaken dualistic view of
the universe and is essentially hostile to worldly learning, happiness, and progress.
Idealistic philosophy and all dualistic systems are equally untenable.

Haeckel is the ablest defender of the materialistic attitude since Darwin, Huxley,
and Tyndall, and goes beyond them in the sweeping and positive nature of his opinions.

He has a patience of investigation and a wealth of detailed information equal to that of Darwin and a greater metaphysical tendency than his English masters. His great defect is a dogmatism and intolerance quite as marked as that which he attacks. His book has too much the air of having completely solved the whole riddle of the universe. One cannot fail to be impressed, however, with his statement of what materialistic science has accomplished and with the range and grasp of thought with which he marshals it all into a philosophic system. As a writer of polemic he is quite the equal of Huxley and has widely and profoundly influenced German thought.

RIDERS TO THE SEA, by J. M. Synge (1904). In a cabin in an island off the west of Ireland, Cathleen, a girl of about twenty, finishes kneading cake and sits down to the spinning wheel. Nora, a young sister, puts her head in at the door, and takes from under her shawl a bundle given her by the young priest. In it are a shirt and stocking "got off a drowned man in Donegal." The priest has given them to her to find out if they belong to her brother Michael, who has been missing. Her father and four other brothers have all been drowned fishing. Maurya, the mother, tries to dissuade her last surviving son, Bartley, from putting to sea when a storm is threatening. "It's hard set we'll be surely the day you're drowned with the rest. What way will I live and the girls with me, and I an old woman looking for the grave?" Bartley insists on going and when he is gone, Maurya, who had gone down to the well tells her daughters that she had seen Bartley riding past, followed by his brother Michael. The girls tell her that Michael's body has been found in "the Far North" and while they are keening for him, through the open door voices are heard. "They're carrying a thing among them and there's water dripping out of it and leaving a track by the big stones," says Nora. It is the body of Bartley, whom his gray pony has knocked into the sea. "They're all gone now, and there isn't anything more the sea can do to me. . . . They're all together this time, and the end is come. . . . No man at all can be living forever, and we must be satisfied," are Maurya's concluding words.

RIENZI, THE LAST OF THE ROMAN TRIBUNES, by Sir Edward Bulwer-Lytton (1848), is one of the author's most famous historical romances. It is founded on the career of Cola di Rienzi, who, in the fourteenth century, inspired by visions of restoring the ancient greatness of Rome, made himself for seven months master of that imperial city, and after nearly seven years of exile and excommunication, during part of which he was a prisoner, repeated the triumph, finally dying at the people's hands in 1354. Bulwer was so impressed with the heroism and force of character of his hero, that at first he meditated writing his biography, instead of a romance founded on his life. The story adheres very closely to the historical facts. To secure accuracy and vividness of setting, the novelist went to Rome to live while writing it. Rienzi's contradictory character, and above all, his consummate ability, and the ambitious and unprincipled yet heroic nature of his rival, Walter de Montreal, are skillfully drawn. Among the lesser personages, Irene, Rienzi's gentle sister, and Nina, his regal wife, with her love of the poetry of wealth and power; Irene's lover, Adrian di Castello, the enlightened noble; Cecco del Vecchio, the sturdy smith; and the ill-fated Angelo Villani, are prominent. Many of the situations and scenes are very strong. The treatment is epic rather than dramatic; and the splendid yet comfortless civilization of the Middle Ages, so picturesque and so squalid, so ecstatic and so base. is vividly delineated.

RIGHT OF WAY, THE, by Sir Gilbert Parker (1901). In this powerful story the author has set forth with a master's touch the study of a man's soul. "Beauty Steele," the brilliant barrister, who is thought to have been wiped out of existence in a drunken brawl, awakens in absolutely new surroundings and as Charles Mallard begins a new life, which, though unhampered by previous ties and associations, is ever menaced by old tendencies to vice. The metamorphose from the drunken fop to the well-loved tailor is attained through a sequence of natural events, none of them beyond the pale of possibility, and the working out of the story to its unexpected conclusion is natural, just what might have happened under the same circumstances in real life. The atmosphere of a quaint little Canadian village, with its simple folk and simple ways, is a pleasing background for the story of this man's duplex life, filled as it is with its tragic problems of love and sorrow. The character of Rosalie Evanturel, the lovely daughter of the village postmaster, is delightfully fresh and original. In her, Charles Mallard finds his real affinity, and his love for her becomes the ruling motive in his second existence. The story, while psychological, is full of dramatic interest and yet carries to the end a perfect sense of proportion and a wonderful resemblance to nature. Mr. Parker handles his problem of presenting this double existence with the greatest skill, and, with a true artistic touch, does not, even at the end, lift the curtain which separates the new life from the old. Kathleen, once the wife of "Beauty Steele," whose arrival on the scene gives her an opportunity to enter the chamber of death and recognize the erstwhile brilliant barrister, goes away unenlightened as to his prolonged existence, leaving Rosalie Evanturel kneeling by his bier.

RIGHT STUFF, THE, by Ian Hay (1910). The scene of this story is laid in Great Britain and shifts from Scotland to England. The hero of the tale is a young Scotsman named Robert Fordyce, familiarly called Robin. When first introduced to the reader he is on his way to Edinburgh to try for a scholarship which will enable him to attend the University. Born and bred on a farm and reared by sober and God-fearing parents, Robin has the big physique and honest nature which usually results from such environment. Successful in his efforts he passes his examinations and wins the highest honors, goes through the University and prepares to study for the ministry, when his brother's failing health causes him to abandon his career in order to help support the family. He takes up journalism and labors at it faithfully for three years but relinquishes it gladly to become private secretary to Adrian Inglethwaite, M. P. While occupying this position Robin lives in his employer's family and is thrown in daily contact with Mrs. Inglethwaite's pretty twin sisters named respectively Dolly and Dilly. These two fascinating damsels are so exactly alike that they puzzle even their own family and they amuse themselves by mixing up their various admirers. To their great surprise Robin discovers a slight difference in them upon their first meeting and never thereafter mistakes one for the other. Dilly marries Richard Lever and on the night of her wedding Robin tells Dolly of his love for her but says he shall not propose to her until he has become worthy of her. This original method of love-making is new to Dolly and at first she does not know just how to take it. Time goes on, however, and just as a critical election is in progress the Inglethwaite's little girl Phyllis is taken seriously ill. This crisis brings the love affair to a climax and though the election is lost, Phyllis recovers, and Dolly acknowledges her love for Robin before he has reached the point of claiming her. The reader takes leave of them fifteen years later when Robin has become the Right Honorable Sir Robert Fordyce, Privy Councillor and Secretary of State.

RIGHTS OF WAR AND PEACE, by Grotius, 'De Jure Belli ac Pacis.' With Translation and Notes, by Dr. William Whewell. (3 vols., 1853. Translation alone, 1 vol.)   One of the most interesting, most significant, and most permanently important of books.   Its importance, to the present day as in the past, is that of the earliest and greatest work designed to apply the principles of humanity, not only to the conduct of war but to the whole conduct of nations, on the plan of finding these principles in human nature and human social action.   The works of Albericus Gentilis (1588), and Ayala (1597), had already dealt with the laws of war.   To Grotius belongs the honor of founder of the law of nature and of nations.   The significance of the original work, published at Frankfort in 1625, when the Thirty Years' War was making a carnival of blood and terror in Europe, is the application of Christian humanity to the conduct of war, and to the intercourse of nations, which Grotius proposed.   The work is one of immense learning, in Roman law especially; and although executed in one year, with his brother's aid in the large number of quotations, it in fact represented the studies of twenty years, and filled out an outline first written in 1604.   The whole history of the author is of exceptional interest.   A most versatile scholar at an early age, a translator of Greek poetry into Latin verse of high poetic quality, a Dutch historian in a Latin style worthy of Tacitus, and a Christian commentator and apologist of broadly humanist enlightenment, superior even to Erasmus, he was also one of the most attractive characters of his time.

RIGHTS OF WOMEN, by Mary Wollstonecraft, see **VINDICATION OF THE RIGHTS OF.**

RIIS, JACOB A., see **MAKING OF AN AMERICAN.**

RIME OF THE ANCIENT MARINER, THE, by Samuel Taylor Coleridge, first appeared in 'Lyrical Ballads' (1798).   It is one of the most fantastic and original poems in the English language.   An attempt at analysis is difficult; for, as has been happily said: "The very music of its words is like the melancholy, mysterious breath of something sung to the sleeping ear; its images have the beauty, the grandeur, the incoherence, of some mighty vision. The loveliness and the terror glide before us in turns, with, at one moment, the awful shadowy dimness, at another the yet more awful distinctness, of a majestic dream."   A wedding guest is on his way to the bridal festivities.   He hears the merry minstrelsy, and sees the lights in the distance. An old gray-bearped man — the Ancient Mariner — stops him to tell him a story, and although the wedding guest refuses to listen, he is held by the fixed glance of the mysterious stranger.   The Ancient Mariner describes his voyage, how his ship was locked in the ice, and how he shot with his crossbow the tame Albatross, the bird of good omen which perched upon the vessel.   The entire universe seemed stunned by this wanton act of cruelty: the sea and sky sicken, the sun becomes withered and bloody, no winds move the ship, "idle as a painted ship upon a painted ocean"; slimy things creep upon the slimy sea, death-fires dance about the vessel; and the Albatross hangs around the neck of the Ancient Mariner.   A spectre ship appears, and the crew die, leaving the graybeard alone.   After a time he is moved to prayer, whereupon the evil spell is removed.   The Albatross sinks into the sea, and the Mariner's heart is once again a part of the universal spirit of love.   After hearing this story, the wedding guest "turns from the bridegroom's door." and

"A sadder and a wiser man
He rose the morrow morn."

The weird ballad is capable of many interpretations; for the Ancient Mariner is nameless, there is no name for the ship, and her destination is vague. In its small compass it contains a tragedy of remorse, and of redemption through repentance. The imagery is wonderful, and the poem is pervaded by a noble mystery. Words-worth, Coleridge affirms, wrote the last two lines of the first stanza of Part iv.

RING AND THE BOOK, THE, by Robert Browning. This dramatic monologue, the longest and best sustained of Browning's poems, was published in four volumes in 1868–69, and is his greatest constructive achievement. This poem of twenty-one thousand lines contains ten versions of the same occurrence, besides the poet's prelude. It presents from these diverse points of view the history of a tragedy which took place in Rome one hundred and seventy years before. Browning, one day in Florence, bought for eightpence an old book which contained the records of a murder that of the olden time in Rome, with the pleadings and counter-pleadings, and the state-ments of the defendants and the witnesses; this Browning used as the raw material for 'The Ring and the Book,' which appeared four years later. The story follows the fate of the unfortunate heroine, Pompilia, who has been sold by her supposed mother to the elderly Count Guido, whose cruelty and violence cause her eventually to fly from him. This she does under the protection of a young priest named Giuseppe Caponsacchi, whom she prevails upon to convey her safely to her old home. She is pursued by the Count, who overtakes her and procures the arrest of the two fugi-tives, accusing her and Caponsacchi of having eloped. They are tried; and the court banishes Caponsacchi for three years, while Pompilia is relegated to a convent. Having at a later period been removed from there to her former home, she is sud-denly attacked by the Count and several hired assassins, who brutally murder her and her two parents; then follows the Count's trial and condemnation for the murders, and (even in Italy) his final execution. The events of the tragedy are enumerated by the Count, Pompilia, Caponsacchi, the Pope, and others, each from his or her peculiar point of view; and two opposing aspects of the case as seen from outside are offered by "Half Rome" and "The Other Half." Browning in conclusion touches upon the intended lesson, and explains why he has chosen to present it in this artistic form. The lesson has been already learned from the Pope's sad thought: —

> " — Our human speech is naught,
> Our testimony human false, our fame
> And human estimation words and wind."

The Pope's soliloquy is a remarkable piece of work, and the chapters which contain the statements of Pompilia and Caponsacchi are filled with tragic beauty and emotion. The thought, the imagery, and the wisdom embodied in this story, make it a triumph of poetic and philosophic creation.

RISE OF ROSCOE PAINE, THE, by Joseph C. Lincoln (1912). This is the story of a young man named Roscoe Paine who on account of his invalid mother is spending years of enforced idleness in a little town on Cape Cod. Six years pre-viously Mrs. Paine had been stricken with a severe illness which had made her helpless, and dependent upon the companionship of her only son, who had given up a position in the banking-house in the city, which he had held since leaving college, and had settled down in the town of Denboro, to lead the life of a recluse and an idler. The son of an embezzler who had ruined his family, and deserted them, and committed suicide when exposure threatened, Roscoe felt that his father's disgrace had cast a blot upon his life which could never be erased. Accordingly he and his mother had hidden themselves from the world and under an assumed name were trying to live down their affliction. The arrival in Denboro of a rich New York financier named Colton, who builds himself a palatial residence causes a stir in local circles. Mr. Colton has an only daughter named Mabel who is a most attractive girl. She has an accidental meeting with Roscoe whom she takes for a "native" and treats as such. Later on, Roscoe several times comes to her rescue and saves her from disasters of various kinds, and she begins to appreciate his strength and character. Mr. Colton desires to buy a strip of land belonging to Roscoe and offers a fabulous sum for it, but he refuses to sell, wishing to retain the land as a convenient thoroughfare for his neighbors. Finally, however, he is obliged to relinquish it in order to procure money to save a friend from disgrace. Mr. Colton is taken suddenly ill and while unconscious a crisis arises in his affairs which is successfully met by Roscoe. Before his illness Mr. Colton had offered Roscoe a position in his business but the latter had declined not wishing to reveal his identity. Mr. Colton becomes convalescent and renews his offer so urgently that Roscoe decides to tell him everything. When Mr. Colton learns that he is the son of Carleton Bennet whom he had known before his downfall, he becomes even more interested in Roscoe and gives his daughter to him in marriage though the latter had felt that in his position he had no right to aspire to her hand.

RISE OF THE DUTCH REPUBLIC, THE: 'A History,' by John Lothrop Motley. First printed in 1856, at the author's expense, — because the great publishers, Mr. Murray included, would not risk such an enterprise for the unknown historian, — it proved an immediate popular success; and was followed by a French translation (supervised with an introduction by Guizot) in 1859, and soon after by Dutch, German, and Russian translations. James Anthony Froude, in the Westminster Review, characterized the new work as "a history as complete as industry and genius can make it . . . of the first twenty years of the Revolt of the United Provinces; of the period in which those provinces finally conquered their independence and established the Republic of Holland." Of the ten years' preparation, half were spent by the author with his family abroad, studying in the libraries and State archives of Europe. Writing from Brussels to Oliver Wendell Holmes, he says: "I haunt this place because it is my scene, — my theatre . . . for representing scenes which have long since vanished, and which no more enter the minds of the men and women who are actually moving across its pavement than if they had occurred in the moon. . . . I am at home in any cemetery. With the fellows of the sixteenth century I am on the most familiar terms. . . . I go, day after day, to the archives here (as I went all summer at The Hague) studying the old letters and documents. . . . It is, however, not without its amusement, in a moldy sort of way, this reading of dead letters. It is something to read the real, bona-fide signs-manual of such fellows as William of Orange, Count Egmont, Alexander Farnese, Philip II., Cardinal Granvelle, and the rest of them. It gives a 'realizing sense,' as the Americans have it." This "realizing sense" is what Motley put into his published record of the struggles of the Protestant "beggars of Holland" with the grandees of Spain, throwing off the yoke of their bigoted ruler, Philip, in spite of the utmost cruelties of mediæval warfare and the Church's Inquisition practiced by Philip's favorite general, the notorious Duke of Alva.

RISING OF THE MOON, THE, by Lady Gregory (1907). A one-act comedy dealing with the relations existing between the peasants and the police at the time of the Fenian period in Irish history. There are four characters, a police sergeant, two policemen, and a political prisoner who has broken gaol. At the opening of the play, the sergeant and his two assistants are pasting up placards describing the fugitive, offering a reward of one hundred pounds for his capture. The sergeant decides to watch the quay himself, in case the escaped prisoner should come there to meet a boat. As he walks in the moonlight meditating on the "spending" there must be in a hundred pounds, the prisoner comes along in the guise of a ballad singer. At first he is an object of suspicion, but he ingratiates himself with the sergeant by telling him he knows the man he is looking for, would recognize him a mile off. He offers to share the watch, and asks nothing of the reward, for a poor man like him "going on the roads and singing in fairs" could not afford "to have the name on him, that he took a reward." He dilates on the ferocity of the missing man until the sergeant is glad of his company, and they sit back to back on a barrel, on which one of the notices is pasted, the better to watch in two directions. The supposed ballad singer sings some of the old songs awakening tender memories of the sergeant's unofficial youth. They become involved in speculation as to the accidents of life that make the sergeant a constable instead of a Fenian patriot. A boat approaches and the signal, verses of the rebel song "The Rising of the Moon," is answered by the rowers, and the sergeant recognizes he has been duped. The prisoner appeals to the sergeant not to betray him, and hides as the policemen return. The sergeant resists the temptation of the reward and lets him escape. Left alone he thinks of the one hundred pounds and wonders if he is as great a fool as he thinks he is.

RIVALS, THE, by R. B. Sheridan (1775). 'The Rivals' Sheridan's first dramatic effort which met with instant success and has remained a favorite on the stage ever since, was written when he was but twenty-four. It contains a whole gallery of characters which have become household words. Sir Anthony Absolute is a variant of the hackneyed character, the angry father. Sir Lucius O'Trigger hits off the dueling habits of his fellow-countrymen of that time. Bob Acres is perhaps the best known blockhead on the comic stage. Mrs. Malaprop's "derangement of epithets" is a never-failing source of amusement. Lydia Languish, that extraordinary compound of extravagance and simplicity, who wanted a husband but thought it would be tame to have one without an elopement is the most attractive of maidens. Faulkland is the personification of perversity, who always has a grievance and never loses an opportunity of making himself and other people miserable. The interest in the plot of the play never flags, and the wit and brilliance of the dialogue are sustained throughout. The characters bear strong resemblances to figures in plays by earlier authors, but to use the words of Hazlitt it "appears to have been the peculiar forte and the great praise of our author's genius, that he could imitate with the spirit of an inventor."

ROBBER COUNT, THE ('Der Raubgraf'), by Julius Wolff (1890). The scene of this romantic German story, which has enjoyed immense success, is laid in the Hartz Mountains, in the fourteenth century. From the heights of his mountain stronghold, Count Albrecht of Regenstein, the robber count, overlooks the whole surrounding country, including the castle of the bishop of Halberstadt, his sworn enemy, and the town and convent of Quedlinburg, of which he is champion and protector. The abbess of this convent, which shelters only the daughters of royal and noble houses, and is subject to no rules of any order, is the beautiful and brilliant Jutta von Kranichfeld. This woman loves Count Albrecht with all the force of her imperious nature, and he returns the passion in a lesser degree, until the unfortunate capture by his men of Oda, countess of Falkenstein. Oda is already loved by the count's younger brother, Siegfried; and Albrecht detains her in the castle with a view to furthering his brother's wooing, and also to wrest from his enemy, the bishop, her confiscated domains of Falkenstein. This capture is disastrous to all. Oda and the count fall in love with each other. Siegfried finds this out, and purposely gets killed in a fray. Albrecht, overcome by the strength of his enemies, is captured, and tried in the market-place of Quedlinburg. His life is saved by Jutta's intervention with the Emperor; but when in spite of this service he marries Oda, the wild jealousy of the rejected princess knows no bounds. At her instigation, the count is set upon and killed by the bishop's men. She then takes the veil for life.

ROBBERY UNDER ARMS, by "Rolf Boldrewood" (1888). This story of life and adventure in the bush and in the gold-fields of Australia gives a most vivid picture of bush life; and purports to be the history of the Marston family of reprobates, told in a straightforward, unaffected style by Dick Marston while he is awaiting execution in jail at Sydney. It shows how the boys, led on by their father, became first cattle robbers, then bank robbers, and regular bush-whackers. There are encounters of travelers with the police, holding up of stage-coaches, storming of houses. and many other thrilling adventures. The reader is given an excellent picture of the gold diggings and every feature of colonial bush life and scenery.

There is no regular plot. Most of the robber gang are killed in one way or another; but the book ends happily, for the hero is reprieved, and marries the girl who has been true to him in spite of all his misdeeds, and who has continually urged him to lead a better life. The adventures of the Marston family under the leadership of Captain Starlight rival those of Jack Sheppard or Dick Turpin, with the advantage to the reader that they bring on the scene a new country, with a new people, new conditions of life, and new customs.

ROBERT ELSMERE, by Mrs. Humphry Ward (1888), is a successful example of the embodiment in a work of fiction of intellectual problems of contemporary interest. It recounts the struggles of a young clergyman who cannot accept all the miracles and dogmas of Christianity, yet is in deep sympathy with its spirit. The scene is laid partly in a country village in Surrey, partly in London. The chief character is Robert Elsmere, a young, sensitive clergyman, fresh from the Old-World environment of Oxford. He marries Catherine Leyburn, a woman of mediæval faith, who loves him intensely, but is incapable of sympathizing with him in the struggle through which he is to pass. Robert, in his country rectory, begins a mental journey, the goal of which he dares not face. He realizes after a time that he can no longer accept the conventional conception of Christianity, and must, therefore, leave the church, to preach what seems to him a more liberal gospel, better fitted to the needs of the century. His wife is heart-broken by his apostasy; but she accompanies him when he goes to London to work among the poor of the East side, and to found a new brotherhood of Christians.

Other persons and scenes relieve the tension of the plot: Rose, Catherine's beautiful, willful sister; Langham, the withered Oxford don, cursed with indifference and paralysis of the emotional nature; Newcombe the wan, worn High-Church priest; the cynical Squire Wendover; the gay society folk of London, — these all playing their several parts in the drama make up a well-rounded whole. 'Robert Elsmere' had a phenomenal success, partly owing to the nature of its subject, and partly to its genuine literary merit. Aside from its intrinsic value, the sensation it produced entitles it to rank as one of the most remarkable books of its generation.

ROBERT FALCONER, a story, by George Macdonald (1875). Robert Falconer is brought up by his grandmother in a little Scotch town. His mother had died when he was too young to remember her. His father was worthless and dissipated, and had left home when Robert was a mere child. The most vivid impression of Robert's youth, an impression that colored the whole course of his life, is his grandmother's anguish over her son; whose soul, according to her rigid Scotch theology, is lost forever. Robert grows up with the settled purpose of finding and reclaiming his father. His youth is outwardly uneventful, but he early revolts against the theology of his grandmother, and his doubts of the existence of God cause him great mental struggles. His neighbor, Mary St. John, a calm, high-souled woman, exerts a great refining influence over him. He develops a talent for music, and learns secretly to play on his grandfather's violin; but Mrs. Falconer, his grandmother, finding the violin in Robert's possession, burns it as an instrument of the Devil. When Robert goes to Aberdeen to college, his protégé, a poor boy nicknamed Shargar, follows him, and the two live together with the rigid economy so frequent among Scotch students. In Aberdeen, Robert meets the man who has the deepest influence over him, Eric Ericson, and his father's friend Dr. Anderson. Eric is troubled by the same doubts as Robert; and being of a more sensitive, fiery nature, is even more distressed thereby. Eric wins the heart of Mary St. John, who has always been Robert's divinity; but he dies before they can be married. Robert travels, and studies medicine for five years. Dr. Anderson, at his death, has left Robert his property; and the latter returns to Scotland, and then goes to London. There he spends his time and money helping the poor, and soon has a company of earnest men and women to help him, with Mary St. John at their head. After waiting so many years, he at last finds his father, sunk to the lowest depth of poverty and degradation. He gradually wins his affection, and restores him to health. They start for India together; but the ship is lost, and they are never heard from again.

This is not at all a story of action, nor is it told with great skill: it is mainly an account of the growth of Robert's soul. His strong good-sense, courage, and helpfulness, are shown. The story has the decided metaphysical character of all Macdonald's stories.

ROBINSON CRUSOE, by Daniel Defoe (1719). This world-famous tale of adventure is supposed to have been suggested by the real experience of Alexander Selkirk, who was shipwrecked and lived for years on a desert island. Robinson Crusoe, a young Englishman, goes to sea in his youth, is captured by the corsairs, is shipwrecked and washed ashore on an uninhabited island, recently satisfactorily identified with Juan Fernández Island in the Pacific Ocean off the coast of Chile, South America. The narrative consists of a careful description of his adventures and experiences during the twenty-eight years of his exile. It tells of his ingenious contrivances for his comfort, how he builds him a habitation, procures food to sustain life, and makes a raft by which means he gets to the shipwrecked vessel, and succeeds in getting many articles that are of use to him. An exciting incident in the story is when, after eighteen years of solitude, he comes across the imprint of a human foot in the sand, and in consequence of this discovery is thrown into a state of terror and consternation. He lives for a long time in great suspense, as he finds evidence that the island is visited by cannibals; but it is not until six years later that he encounters them. On this occasion one of their victims escapes, and Crusoe saves his life and keeps him for a servant and companion. He names him Friday, and teaches him civilized ways. He proves honest, devoted, and reliable, and shares Crusoe's life and duties until, a few years later, they are rescued and taken from the island on an English ship. Crusoe eventually returns to England, where he marries and settles down to enjoy the wealth that he has accumulated during his strange adventures. The first volume ended at this point, and met with such remarkable success that the author, four months later, brought out a second volume entitled, 'The Farther Adventures of Robinson Crusoe'; and this in turn was followed, one year later, by a third relating his 'Serious Reflections' during his wanderings. The simplicity of style, and the realistic atmosphere which pervades the narrative, have caused the popularity of this book to remain unimpaired.

RODERICK RANDOM, a picaresque novel by Tobias George Smollett, was published in 1748. The hero, whose experiences are founded on those of Smollett himself, is the son of a Scottish gentleman, who has incurred the displeasure of his father by marrying Charlotte Bowling, a poor relation and dependent of the family. After giving birth to Roderick Random she dies, and her husband, disinherited by his father, leaves England. Roderick is brought up at his grandfather's, where he is contemptuously treated by his relatives, endures much cruelty from the schoolmaster, and is finally left without a shilling at the squire's death. But his uncle, Lieutenant Tom Bowling of the navy, enables him to pursue his education for three years, until, having killed his captain in a duel, Bowling is forced to escape to the French West Indies. Roderick now apprentices himself to an apothecary. Then, accompanied by an old schoolfellow, Hugh Strap, he undergoes various adventures with highwaymen, sharpers, and practical jokers, both on the road and in London. He qualifies as a surgeon's mate for the navy, but fails to get an appointment, and becomes a journeyman apothecary. He is pressed as a common sailor, and shipped on his uncle's old vessel, H. M. S. Thunder, where he makes a good friend in the sailor, Jack Ratlin, and the surgeon's mate, Thomson, who procures for Roderick a similar appointment. He goes through a campaign against the Spaniards in American waters, including the siege of Cartagena (1741), experiences much squalor, disease, and suffering, returns to England in another vessel, and is shipwrecked on the coast of Sussex. Robbed of his money, he is relieved by a kindly old lady, who procures him a post as footman to an eccentric, blue-stocking, maiden lady of the neighborhood. Random, who conceals his identity to avoid pursuit by one of the naval officers who has an enmity against him, falls in love with Narcissa, the niece of his employer, and on rescuing her from the embraces of a brutal suitor, Sir Timothy Thicket, informs her of his love and of his gentle birth. Encouraged by the lady but forced to escape from the vengeance of his rival, he is carried by smugglers to France, meets and relieves his uncle, Tom Bowling, who has made his way there and is living in destitution, and being robbed by a rascally friar, enlists in the French army, and fights at the Battle of Dettingen. Returned to France he meets at Rheims his old friend Strap, who has inherited some money from his late master, a French nobleman, and is able to procure Roderick's discharge and to fit him out as a fine gentleman in order that he may make a wealthy marriage in England. Thither he goes accompanied by Strap, who puts his money and services at his friend's disposal. Roderick pays his addresses to a Miss Melinda Goosetrap, who, however refers him to her mother whom he cannot deceive into thinking him a man of property. Other attempts are equally unfortunate and he is at length reduced to gambling in order to retrieve his fortunes.   Through a friend he is introduced to a wealthy and witty but deformed lady, Miss Snapper, whom with her mother he escorts to Bath in the hope of making a marriage with her.   But at Bath he encounters Narcissa whom he again wooes and who vows constancy.   Her brother the squire, however, wishes her to marry Lord Quiverwit, and Melinda who is at Bath, circulates reports as to Roderick's character. He defeats the nobleman in a duel, but Narcissa is carried off by her brother and Roderick in despair, loses his money at play, becomes surgeon to the vessel now commanded by Tom Bowling, and makes a voyage to the Guinea coast and to Buenos Ayres, where he meets a wealthy English trader called Don Roderigo.   This man proves to be Roderick's father, who by a series of vicissitudes had made his way to that country in the train of a Spanish grandee and had grown rich through his favor.   They return to England where Roderick is happily married to Narcissa, and Strap to her attendant, Miss Williams.   Roderick's father purchases his paternal estate from the heir, who is encumbered with debt, and the family settle themselves there.   Though there is much coarseness and brutality in Smollett's work and his hero, like others of the *picaro* class is a libertine and not scrupulous about paying cheats in their own coin, there is a wholesome cheerfulness about him and a vigorous realism in the whole story.

ROLAND, see **CHANSON DE ROLAND.**

ROLAND, MADAME, is a biographical study by Ida M. Tarbell (1869).   Having had access to much theretofore unpublished material, the author has presented the characters of M. and Madame Roland, Buzot, Louis XVI., and others, in strong new light.   There is everywhere evidence of the most painstaking research, and broad knowledge of the genius and characters of the Revolution; while many passages exhibit a fine appreciation of the remarkable subject of the study, which is wholly admirable.   The presentation of the material regarding Mademoiselle Phlipon's relations with M. Roland, and their subsequent marriage, and the story of her efforts at title-hunting, are particularly new.   The pictures throughout are vigorous and fascinating, and the work is by many regarded as the most satisfying presentation of the subject which has yet appeared.

ROMAN AFFAIRS ('Les Affaires de Rome'), by Félicité Robert de Lamennais (2 vols., 1836), was written after the rupture of the author with the Papacy.   It contains an account of his journey to Rome, with Montalembert and Lacordaire, and their efforts to obtain a decision on the orthodoxy of the doctrines inculcated by their journal L'Avenir (The Future), which held that the Church should put herself at the head of the democratic movement.   The book contains also, under the caption Des Maux de l'Église et de la Société, what the author considered a faithful picture of the Catholic Church throughout the world, as well as of the state of society.   He indicates remedies to cure the evils of both, while affirming that there is a complete antagonism between the Church and the people in every country, an antagonism growing ever more acute.   The Church of the future will not be, he maintains, that of Rome whose day is past, nor will it be that of Protestantism — an illegitimate, illogical system that, under the deceptive appearance of liberty, has introduced the brutal despotism of force into the State and is the source of egotism in the individual. What the future Church is to be, however, Lamennais does not make clear.

ROMAN DE BRUT, see **BRUT, ETC.**

ROMAN EMPIRE, DECLINE AND FALL, see DECLINE, ETC.

ROMAN LITERATURE, A HISTORY OF, by A. C. T. Cruttwell (1878). This study of classic literature is founded on the monumental work of Teuffel; and in its smaller space, treats its subject with equal accuracy and discrimination, and with more charm. Its abstracts are more interesting, and its characterizations are often done not only with exactness, but with a picturesque touch that gives the subject a contemporary interest, and makes Horace or Virgil or Cicero a personal acquaintance. The literary criticism is excellent of its kind, and the book is as valuable a companion to the reader for pleasure, as to the student with a purpose.

ROMAN POETS, THE, by W. Y. Sellar. Vol. i., The Poets of the Republic; Vol. ii., Virgil; Vol. iii., Horace and the Elegiac Poets (1863–97). The entire work forms one of the most scholarly, complete, and interesting contributions to the history of literature ever written. The author is not only a classical critic of the first order, of ripe scholarship and fine literary taste, but his appreciation of Roman culture, profound and exact, and his exceptional power of lucid exposition, have enabled him to give Roman intellectual culture of the finer sort its due, in comparison with Greek, to an extent not elsewhere done. Largely as Roman genius in Latin literature was fed from Greek sources, it was yet more original and independent than has been commonly supposed. The whole level of Latin culture is at once lifted and illuminated in Dr. Sellar's wonderfully rich and glowing pages. The volume devoted to Virgil is unsurpassed in any language as a masterpiece of interpretation and of delightful critical praise. The writer's outlook is not that of a Latin chair alone: it is that of humanity and of universal culture; that of Greek and English and European history; to bring Roman mind into comparison with all the great types of mind in all lands and of all ages. To know what the deeper spiritual developments of the Roman world were when Christ came, what were the rays of light and the clouds of darkness at the dawn of the new faith, readers can hardly find a better guide than this study of the Roman poets.

ROMAN SCENES OF THE TIME OF AUGUSTUS, see GALLUS; OR, ROMAN SCENES.

ROMAN SINGER, A, by Francis Marion Crawford (1884). Nino Cardegna, the Roman singer, is the adopted son of Cornelio Grandi, who tells the story. Cornelio is the last of the Conti Grandi, and has been forced to sell his estate at Serveti and pursue a professor's life at Rome. Nino has the audacity to fall in love at first sight with Hedwig, daughter of Count von Lira. Won by the beautiful tenor voice, Hedwig fully returns his love. They arouse the suspicions of the father, a "cold, hard, narrow man," who secretly carries his daughter to an obscure castle in the Abruzzi.

Nino searches Paris and London in vain for a trace of Hedwig. Meanwhile his father gets a hint of the probable whereabouts of the Liras, and immediately starts on a search for them. Careful inquiries extract the desired information. He takes up his abode near the castle, and at last, by enormous bribes to a servant, secures an interview with Hedwig. From her he learns of her great unhappiness; of her father's purpose to keep her a prisoner until she consents to marry Benoni, a rich Jew; and of her own determination never to yield.

When Nino arrives he seeks the count, and asks for his daughter's hand. He is refused, and thereupon determines to take her away without her father's consent, if it is her own wish. Hedwig succeeds in escaping to Nino by an unused stair and door. On mules that are in readiness they climb the Abruzzi to points that horses cannot reach. After being married at a little village in the mountains, they return to Rome, where there are interesting scenes with the old count, who refuses to be reconciled, and with Benoni, who turns out to be insane.

The story ends with the prospective return of Grandi to his old estate at Serveti. The charm of this book is in its good, healthy romance, its honest, straightforward love-making without mawkish sentimentalism. With its strong Italian atmosphere, and its ingenious situations following one another in quick succession, it carries us quite out of ourselves. The characters are strongly and consistently drawn.

ROMANCE OF A MUMMY, THE, by Théophile Gautier. In this remarkable novel, first published in 1856, is contained almost all then known of the life and customs of the ancient Egyptians. It will probably never be popular with the general reader, because of its too local color; and few can appreciate the amount of study necessary to write such a book. There is an exuberance of minute details about the architecture and inside decorations and furnishings of the palaces, founded on accurate studies. The author has chosen for the date of his story the time when, according to the Bible, Moses led the Israelites out of bondage; and from the same source and without any help from Egyptian records, he gives an account of the events that lead to the drowning of the host of Pharaoh in the Red Sea. The story treats of the love of Tahoser, daughter of the Theban High Priest, for Poëri, a young Jew who is steward of Pharaoh. He is in love with Ra'hel, and escapes across the Nile every night to meet his beloved, who lives in one of the mud huts where the Jews, reduced to slavery, are baking bricks in the sun for the building of the Great Pyramids. Tahoser disguises herself as a servant, and enters the service of Poëri. She swims the Nile one night, following him, and finds him with Ra'hel. Falling ill with a fever, she is cared for by Ra'hel, and upon her recovery is to be married to Poëri; but Pharaoh learns of her hiding-place and takes her to his palace. After his death she reigns, and is buried in his tomb. The papyrus, which the novelist says was found with her body, discloses the story of her life.

ROMANCE OF A POOR YOUNG MAN, THE, by Octave Feuillet. This very popular novel, which first appeared in 1857, is one on which the attacks of the followers of the school of "naturalism" have most heavily fallen. They claim that the plot is exceedingly improbable and melodramatic. Maxime Odiot, Marquis de Champcey, by the rash speculation of his father, is left without fortune. Through the intercession of his old notary, he becomes steward of the Château des Laroque. His intelligence wins the esteem of all; but leaving all in ignorance of his noble birth, he confines his intimacy to an old lady, Mademoiselle Porhoël Goël, an octogenarian. Marguerite, the daughter of Laroque, treats him with the greatest consideration; but he professes the greatest indifference for her. Finally, through the machinations of Madame Aubry and Mademoiselle Hélonin, suspicions are raised as to the loyalty of Maxime's intentions. Marguerite is made to believe that Maxime seeks to make himself the heir of Mademoiselle Porhoël Goël, and is warned that he may so compromise her as to oblige her to marry him. Entering the tower of an old ruin one evening, she there finds Maxime. After conversing with him, she seeks to go, and finds the door locked. She believes that Maxime hopes to compromise her by obliging her to remain with him all night in the tower, and accuses him of treachery. He acknowledges his love for her; but to save her honor, leaps from the tower, in spite of her attempts to detain him. It is found that Marguerite's grandfather had formerly been the steward of Maxime's family, and had enriched himself from the estate during the Revolutionary period. Madame Laroque restores the fortune to Maxime, and he marries Marguerite.

ROMANCE OF DOLLARD, THE, by Mary Hartwell Catherwood, appeared in 1888. It is a romance of New France in 1660, and breaks new historic ground for romantic treatment. Louis XIV. of France has sent out a shipload of stolid peasant girls, as wives for the settlers in New France. In the same ship goes Mademoiselle Claire de Laval-Montmorency, young and very beautiful. When she reaches Quebec, she is unable to explain her purpose in coming out to that wild new country quite to the satisfaction of her uncle, the Bishop of New France. Pending further examination by the bishop, she goes to the marriage market, where the shipload of girls is to be disposed of, to see the strange sight, and to encourage her own maid, who is to choose a husband. There she finds the Sieur des Ormeaux, Adam Dollard, — the commandant of Montreal. Dollard has loved her in old France; and, at this unexpected meeting, pursues his wooing to such good advantage that they are married at once, before news of the strange proceeding can reach the ears of the stern bishop. Accompanied by Claire's maid, Louise, and Dollard's servant, Jacques, who had chosen each other in the marriage market, Claire and Dollard go by canoe to Montreal.

The Iroquois, the dreaded Six Nations, are moving on the settlements: there are two bands of them; and if these can be prevented from joining forces, New France may still be saved. Adam Dollard, with sixteen others, has sworn to go out and check them, giving and taking no quarter. Dollard, heartbroken at the pain he must cause Claire, and filled with remorse at having so selfishly married her and marred her peace when he knew the fate in store for him, starts off without telling her. Then, ashamed of this cowardice, he returns. She bears the news bravely, as becomes a daughter of the house of Montmorency, and begs to go with him. He cannot grant her prayer; and leaves her with the nuns of the Hôtel-Dieu in Montreal. Claire steals out from the convent in the night, with Massawippa, an Indian girl, whose father, a Huron, had joined Dollard's expedition. With wonderful courage, they fight their way through the wilderness to the little fort which Dollard is defending. Dollard and his men hold the fort eight days against the horde of the Iroquois; then the fort is taken, and all perish. This is a story of heroism, simply told; the truth of the main incidents is vouched for in a preface by no less a historian than Francis Parkman.

ROMANCE OF THE ROSE, THE ('Roman de la Rose'). This allegorical poem is one of the earliest works in the French language. It is in two parts: the first, consisting of four thousand verses, was written some time during the thirteenth century, by Guillaume de Lorris; while the second, containing about nineteen thousand verses, was written by Jean de Meun, who lived somewhere about 1320. The introductory lines of the first part tell us that in this 'Romance' is inclosed all the art of love. L'Amant dreams that he finds an immense garden, surrounded by a wall, on which are painted pictures of Hate, Felony, Covetousness, Avarice, etc. Inside, he finds Cupid, Beauty, Riches, Courtesy, and other graces. He chooses an opening rosebud, but finds it surrounded by a thick hedge of thorns. "Kind Welcome" allows him to kiss the rose, but "Evil Mouth" gossips so much about it that Jealousy confines the Rose in a tower, guarded by Danger, Fear, and Shame. L'Amant, separated from his

Rose, abandons himself to despair. At this point the romance of Lorris ends. By the aid of Cupid, Venus, Nature, and her confessor Genius, the tower of Jealousy is forced to capitulate, and L'Amant is at last permitted to gather the Rose. The first part is a eulogy of women and chivalrous love, while the second seems to be almost a satire on the first; for Meun reduces love to the pleasure of the senses, and respects nothing that the Middle Ages were accustomed to venerate. Meun is less of a poet than Lorris, but the former is the more erudite, and the second part is encyclopædic in its references, ranging from Latin quotations to the Philosopher's Stone, and the complaints of the lower classes. This work has excited almost as much adverse criticism as praise, the priests at one time thinking there was something in the allegory derogatory to dogma. It enjoyed great popularity when allegory was esteemed, and had considerable influence upon the work of Chaucer, who translated part of it.

ROMANCES OF THE EAST ('Nouvelles Asiatiques'), by Count Joseph Arthur de Gobineau (1876). In both style and matter, these stories are among the gems of the world's literature: their penetrating insight, their creative portrayal of character, their calm irony, their exquisite grace and charm of expression, set them quite apart. The author was a man at once of affairs, of the world, and of letters, an acute thinker and close observer, who applied a literary gift of the first order to wide experience and digested speculation. In these 'Nouvelles' he had a theory to uphold, — that of the essential diversity of human nature, in opposition to that of its essential unity, — but it does not obtrude itself. He was for several years French minister at the court of the Shah of Persia; and instead of embodying his views of Oriental character in the form of essays, he conceives a set of characters displaying their racial traits in action. The first of the stories is 'The Dancing Girl of Shamakha'; a study in the racial traits of the Lesghians of the Caucasus, with side-lights on Russian frontier life, the slave-trade, and other things. Next follows 'The History of Gambèr-Aly,' illustrating the unstable, volatile, fanciful Persian character, at the mercy of every passing gust of emotion and wholly given over to it while it lasts. Third and grimmest of all is 'The War against the Turkomans'; the same theme continued, but with special reference to the utter corruption of the governmental fabric, based wholly on personal influence, with neither public spirit nor even ordinary forecasting commonsense. Both these shed a flood of light on Persian social life; a significant feature, as also in the next, is the supreme power of the women in it, exercised with as little conscience as the men exercise their public functions — naturally. The impression left would be most depressing and rather cynical, were it not that in the last two he gives with fairness another and nobler side of the Oriental nature. 'The Illustrious Magician' shows the passionate longing of the Eastern mind for the ultimate truths of the universe and of God, its belief that the crucifixion of sense and steady contemplation by the soul can attain to those primal secrets, and its willingness to pay that price for knowledge. The final story, of great tragic force but sweet and uplifting, is of Afghan life, — 'The Lovers of Kandahar.'

ROMANS, CONSIDERATIONS ON THE GREATNESS AND DECAY OF THE, see **GREATNESS, ETC.**

ROMANY RYE, see **LAVENGRO.**

ROME, A GENERAL HISTORY OF, from the foundation of the city to the fall of Augustus, 753 B. C.–476 A. D., by Charles Merivale (1875). A work specially designed for the general reader seeking to be informed of the most noted incidents, the most remarkable characters, and the main course of events, together with their causes and consequences. The three principal stages separately noted are that of the antiquities; that of the marvelously rich "dramatic" period, crowded with the great figures of the best age of Rome; and that of the dissolution of ancient society and the changes wrought by the influence of Christianity. It is this third stage which Dr. Merivale considers of most vital interest, and his treatment of which gives to his work an exceptional value.

In his earlier and larger work, 'A History of the Romans under the Empire' (8 vols., 1865), Dr. Merivale exactly filled, with a work of the highest authority and value, the gap between Mommsen and Gibbon, 60 B. C.–180 A. D.

ROME, GREATNESS AND DECLINE OF, by Guglielmo Ferrero, see **GREATNESS,** etc.

ROME, HISTORY OF, by Victor Duruy. This 'History des Romains,' first published in 1879 in Paris, is the most elaborate and complete of the works of Victor Duruy. It is the result very largely of original research. The edition of Mahaffy, published in 1883, has no superior, and perhaps no equal, as a popular history of Rome. The modern edition, as published in 1894, is very attractive; having over three thousand well-selected engravings, one hundred maps and plans, besides numerous other chromo-lithographs.

This work covers the whole subject of Roman history, and is the best work of reference; having, unlike the works of Merivale and Gibbon, a general index, which enables the ordinary reader to find any fact required. Unlike Mommsen, Duruy sifts tradition and tries to infer from it the real value of Roman history. In regard to the illustrations, Duruy's book stands alone; giving the reader all kinds of illustration and local color, so as to let him read the history of Rome with all the lights which archæological research can afford.

Beginning with a speculative description of the geographical, political, and religious conditions of Italy before the establishment of Roman power, the history of Rome is traced in eight volumes, each of which has two sections, from its founding, 753 B. C., to its division and fall in 359 A. D. The history has fourteen main periods; the first being 'Rome under the Kings,' 753–510 B. C., and the 'Formation of the Roman People'; and the last, 'The Christian Empire from Constantine to Theodosius' (306–395 A. D.).

ROME, PAGAN AND CHRISTIAN, by Rodolfo Lanciani, see **PAGAN,** etc.

ROMEO AND JULIET, by Shakespeare, was first published in 1597. The plot was taken from a poem by Arthur Brooke, and from the prose story in Paynter's 'Palace of Pleasure.' The comical underplot of the servants of Capulet *vs.* those of Montagu; the fatal duels, the deaths of Mercutio and Tybalt; the ball where Romeo, a Montagu, falls in love with Juliet; the impassioned love-scenes in the orchard, the encounter of the Nurse and Peter with the mocking gallants; the meetings at Friar Laurence's cell, and the marriage of Juliet there; Romeo's banishment; the attempt to force Juliet to marry the County Paris; the Friar's device of the sleeping-potion; the night scene at the tomb, Romeo first unwillingly killing Paris and then taking poison; the waking of Juliet, who stabs herself by her husband's body; the reconciliation of the rival families, — such are the incidents in this old Italian story, which has touched the hearts of men now for six hundred years. It is the drama of youth, "the first bewildered stammering interview of the heart," with the delicious passion, pure as dew, of first love, but love thwarted by fate and death. Sampson bites his thumb at a Montagu; Tybalt and Mercutio fall. Friar John is delayed; Romeo and Juliet die. Such is the irony of destiny. The mediæval manners at once fierce and polished, — Benvenuto limns them. We are in the warm south: the dense gray dew on leaf and grass at morn, the cicada's song, the nightingale, the half-closed flower-cups, the drifting perfume of the orange blossom, stars burning dilated in the blue vault. Then the deep melancholy of the story. And yet there is a kind of triumph in the death of the lovers: for in four or five days they had lived an eternity; death made them immortal. On fire, both, with impatience, in vain the Friar warns them that violent delights have violent ends. Blinded by love, they only half note the prescience of their own souls. 'Twas written in the stars that Romeo was to be unlucky: at the supper he makes a mortal enemy; his interference in a duel gets Mercutio killed; his overhaste to poison himself leads on to Juliet's death. As for the garrulous old Nurse, foul-mouthed and tantalizing, she is too close to nature not to be a portrait from life; her advice to "marry Paris" reveals the full depth of her banality. Old Capulet is an Italian Squire Western, a chough of lands and houses, who treats this exquisite daughter just as the Squire treats Sophia. Mercutio is everybody's favorite: the gallant loyal gentleman, of infinite teeming fancy, in all his raillery not an unkind word, brave as a lion, tender-hearted as a girl, his quips and sparkles of wit ceasing not even when his eyes are glazing in death.

ROMOLA, by George Eliot (1864). The scene of this one historic romance of the author is laid in Florence at the end of the fifteenth century, and its great historic figure is Savonarola. The civic struggle between the Medici and the French domination, the religious struggle between the dying paganism and the New Christianity, crowd its pages with action. The story proper follows the fortunes of Tito Melema, — a Greek, charming, brilliant, false, — his fascination of Romola, his marriage, his moral degradation and death. The incidents are many, the local color is rich, but the emphasis of the book is laid on the character of Tito.

The working out of this is a subtle showing of the truth, that the depression of the moral tone by long indulgence in selfish sin is certain to culminate in some overshadowing act of baseness. "Tito was experiencing that inexorable law of human souls, that we prepare ourselves for sudden deeds by the reiterated choice of good or evil that gradually determines character." This is the key to the book, which is strongly ethical; but which is not the less profoundly interesting as a story. In Florence as in Loamshire, the lower classes are to the novelist unceasingly picturesque; and the talk of the crowd, in the squares and streets, full of humor and reality. In 'Romola' appears her one attempt (in the case of Savonarola) to show a conscience taking upon itself great and novel responsibilities. Always studies of conscience, her other books depict only its pangs under the sting of the memory of slighted familiar obligations. Her own saying that "our deeds determine us as much as we determine our deeds," is the moral lesson of Romola.

RORY O'MORE, by Samuel Lover (1836). In 1797, De Lacy, an officer of the French army, volunteered in the interest of universal liberty to investigate the prevalence of revolutionary tendencies in England and Ireland. Falling sick in the house of a well-to-do Irish peasant, Rory O'More, he found his host the soul of wit, honor, and hospitality. Rory, undertaking the delicate mission of forwarding De

Lacy's dispatches, fell in with a band of insurgents, who, though calling themselves United Irishmen, desired the reign of license rather than the freedom of Ireland. One of their number, Shan Regan, was Rory's sworn enemy, having been rejected by his sister, and through this feud the hero met with unpleasant adventures, in which his quickness of resource served him well. At last, however, chivalrously defending an unpopular collector from Shan's ruffians, Rory was secretly shipped to France with the man whom he had befriended. Rumor spread that he had killed the collector, and absconded; and on his return a year later, Rory was confronted with the charge of murder. The opportune reappearance of his supposed victim on the very day of O'More's trial alone saved him from the halter. Meanwhile, a rebellion in Ireland had been crushed; and the unhappy people, disappointed in expected aid from France, lost hope of independence. Rory with his impoverished household, and the disheartened enthusiast De Lacy, hopefully turned their faces towards America. In spite of its stilted style and improbable incidents, this story is valuable in its delineation of Irish character, and in its picture of the Irish uprisings at the close of the eighteenth century.

ROSARY, THE, by Florence L. Barclay (1910). The scene of this story is laid in England and opens during the progress of a house-party at the beautiful estate of the Duchess of Meldrum. Among the guests are her niece Jane Champion and Garth Dalmain, the latter a talented young artist, rich, handsome, and well-born. Jane is a woman of thirty, of large physique and with very plain features of which she is painfully aware. She has a fine nature and is generally popular, being considered in the light of a good comrade by most of her men friends. Having an independent fortune she has not lacked matrimonial opportunities but has never been really loved. Jane has a great musical ability and a wonderful voice which owing to her modesty has not been heard by her friends. The Duchess who knows of her niece's talent asks her to fill the place of a prima-donna who was to have sung "The Rosary" at a large musical she has planned for her guests. Jane sings the song, and not only electrifies her audience but wins the heart of Garth Dalmain, who realizes she is the one woman in the world for him. He proposes to Jane who reciprocates his love, but feeling sure that his artistic taste will tire of her plain looks, she refuses him on the score of his youth, as he is three years her junior. Garth is heartbroken but devotes himself to his art, and although greatly sought after, remains true to Jane, who spends three years in travel and philanthropic work. At the end of this time, while sojourning in Egypt, she hears that Garth has been accidentally shot and has become blind. She hastens to him at once and nurses him back to health pretending that she is a stranger to him. He is struck by the similarity of his nurse's voice to Jane's, but she keeps up the illusion explaining that this fact had been frequently noted by others. After some weeks, when Jane feels convinced that his love for her is unshaken she again sings "The Rosary" and he at once recognizes her and realizes that his faithful nurse and his beloved Jane are one and the same. They are immediately married and enter into their happiness which had been achieved through so much suffering.

ROSE AND THE RING, THE, by W. M. Thackeray (1854). In the prelude to 'The Rose and the Ring' the author, "M. A. Titmarsh," welcomes young and old to what he calls a "Fireside Pantomime." The story grew out of a set of Twelfth Night pictures that the author was requested to make for the amusement of some young English people in a "foreign city," supposed to be Rome.

The story is a delightful fairy-tale, with a very quiet satire. It is essentially a "funny book," not a philosophy in humorous guise.

The Rose is a magic rose belonging to Prince Bulbo, of Crim Tartary, and makes its possessor appear always lovable. The Ring is a fairy ring given to Prince Giglio of Paflagonia by his mama. It also has the property of making the wearer seem beautiful to all and beloved by all.

Prince Giglio and the Princess Rosalba, of Crim Tartary, are deprived of their rightful thrones by their guardian uncles, who wish to place in power their own children, Angelica and Bulbo. Rosalba is an outcast from her own kingdom, and reaches the capital of Paflagonia, where she becomes maid to the lazy Angelica, cousin of Giglio.

Giglio and Rosalba are the favorites of the Fairy Black Stick; although at their christenings she has given to each, as her best gift, a little misfortune. This fairy is all-powerful, as is shown by the terrible fate of old Gruff-a-Nuff, who, when he refused to admit the fairy to Angelica's christening, was turned into a brass knocker on the hall door. She never forgets Giglio and Rosalba, nor deserts them in their troubles; but finally brings a happy issue out of their misfortunes. This most delightful of books of its kind was illustrated by the author's own drawings, which interpret the story and are an essential part of it.

ROSE GARDEN, see GULISTAN.

ROSE OF THE WORLD, THE, by Agnes and Egerton Castle (1904). The first scene of this story is laid in India where Lady Rosamond Gerardine is living in splendor with her second husband Sir Arthur Gerardine, who is Lieutenant-Governor. She receives a visit from Major Raymond Bethune, comrade of her former husband, Harry English, who tells her that he wishes to write a biography of his dead friend and asks her to allow him to look over his papers. She peremptorily refuses and Bethune, who does not know what to make of her behavior, appeals to her niece Aspasia and to Sir Arthur, to aid him in getting her to alter her decision. The latter accedes to Bethune's desire and tells his wife he wishes her to assist him in his work. Lady Rosamond becomes much overwrought and so ill that her husband sends her back to England in the company of her niece and Bethune. She goes to the home of her dead husband and there opens the box of letters which she has never touched until now. She had avoided reading these letters to save herself the pain which they might cause her, but now upon perusing them a deeper love for English is awakened than she had ever felt for him in his lifetime. This feeling becomes so intense that she takes an utter dislike to Sir Arthur and everything connected with him; she dresses herself in weeds, mourns unceasingly, and calls herself Harry English's widow. Sir Arthur returns from India and thinking his wife is becoming insane is on the point of consulting a brain specialist when his Hindoo secretary throws off his disguise and proclaims himself the man so long mourned as dead. After having been severely wounded in battle he had been held a prisoner for five years and upon finally making his escape had returned to find his wife married to another man. He had entered their household in disguise in order to find out whether or not she was happy in her present condition. Rosamond is so completely overcome by the shock of English's return that a long and alarming illness ensues during which her hair turns snow white. She eventually recovers and English is rewarded by her love after his long period of waiting. Bethune marries Aspasia and Sir Arthur withdraws from the field.

ROSMERSHOLM, by Henrik Ibsen (1886). Beata, the sickly, commonplace wife of the master of Rosmer, has committed suicide by drowning herself in the mill stream. Since her death, Rebecca West, a clever, interesting young woman, has been mistress of the manor and friend and companion of Rosmer, the husband. Rosmer is a conservative aristocrat, a retired clergyman, but inspired by Rebecca's ideas, he has become a freethinker in religion and radical in politics. As soon as he announces his change of views, he is attacked by his former friends, not by a challenge of his beliefs, but by scandalous insinuations in regard to the position of Rebecca in his household. His eyes are opened to his love for Rebecca and he asks her to marry him, though he now is overwhelmed by the suspicion that his unhappy wife had seen his interest in Rebecca, and he is thus responsible for her death. To "give back his innocence," Rebecca confesses her guilt. She had known that Beata stood in the way of his intellectual freedom and her own ambition to make him a man of action and leader of men. She had influenced Beata to dwell on her childlessness. Finally, the hint that Rebecca is Rosmer's mistress drives the deluded woman to believe it her duty to remove herself to save the ancient family name from disgrace. Rosmer's faith in himself and his borrowed ideals is destroyed with his discovery of Rebecca as a designing adventuress. Rebecca has been ennobled by her association with Rosmer, and on the eve of her departure she reveals to him her unselfish devoted love, changed from the sensual passion which had not stopped at crime. With the lust for expiation and sacrifice of his former priestly ideals, he asks her to prove her love and restore his faith in her by doing what his wife did for him. Although resenting the superstition that claims him and kills the possibility of happiness, she consents, and together they leap into the mill-stream.

ROUGES DU MIDI, see **REDS OF THE MIDI.**

ROUGHING IT, by Samuel L. Clemens (1872). Mark Twain's droll humor is constantly flashing out as he describes a long and eventful journey from St. Louis across the plains, in the early "sixties," to visit the mining camps of Nevada. He notes the incident of a barkeeper who was shot by an enemy, adding, "And the next moment he was one of the deadest men that ever lived." Interesting incidents of Mormon life and customs are given. Brigham Young's sage advice to an Eastern visitor was: "Don't incumber yourself with a large family; . . . take my word, friend, ten or eleven wives are all you need — never go over it." Mark Twain failed to meet the Indian as "viewed through the mellow moonshine of romance. . . . It was curious to see how quickly the paint and tinsel fell away from him and left him treacherous, filthy, and repulsive." Describing an absurd adventure that happened to his party, the author says: "We actually went into camp in a snow-drift in a desert, at midnight, in a storm, forlorn and helpless, within fifteen yards of a comfortable inn."

He tells interesting stories of life in the mining camps, of the frenzied excitement, of great fortunes made and lost, of dire poverty, and of reckless extravagance; instancing a case when he refused to cross the street to receive a present of a block of stock, fearing he would be late to dinner. And that stock rose in value from a nominal sum to $70 per share within a week.

Going to San Francisco, the author witnesses the great earthquake, of which he relates amusing incidents. He then goes as a reporter to the Sandwich Islands, the land of cannibals, missionaries, and ship captains. He does not enjoy the native food, poi, which too frequently used is said to produce acrid humors; "a fact," says

Twain, "that accounts for the humorous character of the Kanakas." Obtaining a large stock of rich material for stories, the author returns to San Francisco, and acquires notoriety and wealth in the lecture field. "Thus," said he, "after eleven years of vicissitudes, ended a pleasure trip to the silver mines of Nevada, which I had originally intended to occupy only three months. However, I usually miss my calculations further than that." The volume is a mine of the frontier slang, such as the author utilizes in 'Buck Fanshawe's Funeral.'

ROUGON-MACQUART, LES, by Émile Zola. There is perhaps no literary work of the last part of the century that has caused so much comment as this series of twenty novels, relating the natural and social history of a family under the Second Empire. It is a phenomenon that cannot be ignored in a history of literature, not only because of the variety of subjects treated, but from the fact that the author, being the acknowledged head of the so-called school of naturalism, has carried his theories farther than any of his disciples. In 1869 he began his task, — a study in hereditary influence, with a complete genealogical tree, and a plan for twenty novels, — from which very little variation is seen when the series is completed twenty-two years after. Beginning with the Coup d'État in 1852, he ends his series with the downfall of Napoleon III., adding 'Doctor Pascal,' which is a résumé of the series. With the ancestors whom the author chooses for his characters we should perhaps expect that animal passion would be the motive of most of these novels; but one must charge M. Zola with poor judgment or a departure from the scientific spirit, when he places a character, which by his own deductions seems to show no trace of the family "lesion," in 'La Terre,' the coarsest one of the series — for Macquart is the most decent of the entire community. Whatever may have been the author's intention, the general public does not read his books as a study in heredity. Each one is complete in itself; and while in 1896 the first novel of the series had reached a sale of only 31,000 copies, there had been sold 113,000 copies of 'La Terre,' 176,000 of 'Nana,' and 187,000 of 'La Débâcle.' The first to appear was 'La Fortune des Rougons' (The Rougon Family: 1871). Adelaide Fouqué, whose father was insane, was married in 1786 to Rougon, a dull, easy-going gardener. After her husband's death she had two illegitimate children, Antoine and Ursule, by Macquart, a drunkard and a smuggler. The offspring of the marriage was Pierre Rougon. By chicanery, Rougon obtains possession of the property, sells it, and through marriage with a daughter of a merchant, enters into an old business firm. Ursule is married to an honest workman named Mouret; and Antoine, who inherits his father's appetite for drink, marries a market-woman, also intemperate.

'La Curée' (Rush for the Spoil: 1872) is a study of the financial world of Paris at the time Haussmann laid out the boulevards. Aristide, son of Pierre, who has changed his name to Saccard, becomes immensely wealthy by political intrigue, — acting as straw-man for the government in the purchase of the property needed to lay out the new boulevards. He is helped by his elder brother Eugène, who has entered political life.

'La Conquête de Plassans' (The Conquest of Plassans: 1874). The struggle for the control of a village in which the Abbé Faujas obtains complete ascendency over Marthe Rougon, who is married to François Mouret. The latter, accused of insanity, is placed in an asylum, and finally becomes insane. Escaping, he sets fire to his house, destroying himself and the abbé therein.

'Le Ventre de Paris' (The Markets of Paris; or, Fat and Thin: 1875). Lisa Macquart is the member of the family who, as a market-woman, furnishes opportunity for a detailed study of the markets. Zola looks upon this work as a sort of modern Iliad, the song of the eternal battle between the lean of this world and the fat. Of this book a prominent critic said that he had been able to read it only by holding his nose.

'La Faute de l'Abbé Mouret' (The Abbé Mouret's Trangression: 1875). A study of the clergy, religious life, and mysticism, in which Serge Mouret is the leading character. It is almost needless to say that the abbé does not resist temptation; but by repentance he is able later to perform, with little perturbation, the burial service over the woman he had loved.

'Son Excellence Eugène Rougon' (His Excellency Eugène Rougon: 1876). A story of political life, in which are realistic descriptions of the Imperial Court, of the functions of Prime Minister (Rougon) and his cabinet, and a careful pen picture of Napoleon III., his manners and customs.

'L'Assommoir' (The Dram Shop: 1877). A story of life among the workmen of Paris, and of the killing effect which the cheap drinking-shop has on them. Gervaise the daughter of Antoine, is the character around whom the scenes revolve. It was this work which brought Zola his reputation and fortune. The chief figure, Gervaise, a daughter of this family driven from home when fourteen, and already a mother, goes with her lover to Paris. There he deserts her and her two children. She afterwards marries a tinsmith, Coupeau. The beginning of their wedded life is prosperous; but as the years go on, vice and poverty disintegrate what might have been a family into mere units of misery, wretchedness, and corruption. Zola traces their downfall in the pitiless and intimate fashion characteristic of him, and not difficult with characters created to be analyzed. The book is a series of repulsive pictures unrelieved by one gleam of a nobler humanity, but only "realistic" as scraps: the life as a possible whole is as purely imaginative as if it were lovely instead of loathsome.

'Une Page d'Amour' (A Love Episode: 1878). A physical and psychological study of the various phases of a woman's passion. The struggle is between her love for her child and her passion for a doctor who has saved the child's life. The night on which she cedes herself to the doctor, the child, looking from an open window for her return, contracts a sickness from which it dies. Hélène, the daughter of Ursule, is the family representative. There are fine descriptions of Paris seen from a height, varying with the spiritual phases of the characters.

'Nana' (1880). A study of the life of a courtesan and actress. Nana is the daughter of Gervaise and the drunkard Coupeau. She grows up in the streets and disreputable haunts until she comes under the notice of a theatre manager. Her great physical beauty attracts men of all classes, and none resist her. The grandest names are soiled; and those who do not leave with her their fortunes, leave their honor or their life. The greatest fortunes are dissipated by her, and yet at her door is heard the continual ring of the creditor. She contracts the black smallpox, and dies deserted and wretched. The description of her appearance after death is a shocking contrast to the pictures of voluptuousness in the other scenes.

'Pot-Bouille' (Piping Hot: 1882). A study of the life of the bourgeoisie. Octave, the son of François Mouret, comes to Paris determined to make his fortune through women's love for him. A study of life in the tenement flats, where the skeletons of the different family closets are made to dance for our amusement, to the music of the servants' quarrels ascending from the kitchens.

'Au Bonheur des Dames' (The Ladies' Paradise: 1883). A study of the mammoth department stores. Octave, by his marriage with the widow Hedouin, and her subsequent death, becomes proprietor of the shop. A description is given of the growth of the business, of the struggle for existence by the smaller stores and of their being swallowed up by the giant, and of the entire routine of a great store.

'La Joie de Vivre' (How Jolly Life Is: 1884). Pauline Quenu, the daughter of Lisa, is a foil to the character of Nana: a woman of well-balanced mind, giving up her lover to her friend, and upon their separation, taking their child and becoming its true mother. Always triumphant and smiling, she is ever sacrificing herself to the selfish whining egoism of those who surround her.

'Germinal' (Master and Man: 1885). A study of life in the mines. The illegitimate son of Gervaise, Étienne Lanier, a socialist, is forced to work in the mines. Low wages and fines cause a strike, of which Lanier is one of the leaders. He counsels moderation; but hunger drives the miners to desperation, and force is met by force. Several are killed, Lanier is deported, and the miners fall back into their old slavery. This work is generally considered to be the author's best.

'L' Œuvre' (Work: 1886). A study of artist life. Claude Lanier, illegitimate son of Gervaise, a painter with a vivid power of conception, lacking the power of execution; and, in despair of attaining his ideal, hangs himself before an unfinished picture.

'La Terre' (The Soil: 1888). A study of peasant life and the greed for land; a greed which causes hatred between sisters, neglect of parents, and ends in the murder of Jean Macquart's wife by her sister. This story abounds in vulgarity, and the brutish instincts of the peasants make them lower than the beasts that surround them. It has aroused more opposition than any other of his works.

'Le Rêve' (The Dream: 1888). This has been likened to a fairy story; and it is said Zola wrote it in deference to the sentiment against his admission to the Academy, to show that his strength did not wholly lie in "realism." Angelique, the illegitimate daughter of Sidonie Rougon, is placed in a foundling asylum, and adopted by a family whose occupation is the making of church vestments. She dreams of her prince, who soon presents himself in the person of a painter of church windows, who is really the son of a bishop who took orders after his wife's death. He opposes his son's marriage to a woman of the lower classes; but consents when called to administer the last sacrament to Angelique, and she dies in her husband's arms.

'La Bête Humaine' (Human Brutes: 1890). A study of railway life, in which Jacques Lanier, a locomotive engineer, inherits the family "lesion" in the form of a maniacal desire to murder women. There is a stirring description of a struggle on a moving locomotive between Lanier and his drunken fireman, in which both are precipitated under the wheels and the express train is left to drive along without check.

'L'Argent' (Money: 1891). A study of stock speculation and "wild-cat" companies. Aristide Saccard, having lost his wealth, starts the "Banque Universelle" for the exploitation of different schemes in the Orient. A description is given of the unscrupulous methods employed to float great schemes. Saccard's bank becomes the leading institution of the stock exchange. Subscriptions pour in by the million, — widows, orphans, and millionaires fighting to get the shares; and Saccard is the financial ruler, rolling in wealth and luxury. Then comes the struggle with the "bears" the final defeat, and the ruin of the investors.

'La Débâcle' (The Downfall: 1892). A powerful novel of the Franco-Prussian war, and the siege of Paris. It portrays with strength and boldness, on a remarkable breadth of canvas, the incidents of that great campaign. Intermingled with the passions of war are the passions of love; the whole forms a pageant rarely surpassed in fiction. The principal characters are Jean Macquart, a corporal in the French army, who had fought at Solferino; Maurice Levasseur, a young lawyer enlisted as a private in Macquart's command; Delaherche, chief cloth manufacturer of Sedan; Henriette Weiss, sister of Maurice, and wife of an accountant; Honoré Fouchard, quartermaster-sergeant; and Silvine, Honoré's betrothed, who has been betrayed by one Goliah, on whom she later takes terrible vengeance. The story is concerned chiefly with the friendship of Macquart and Levasseur, and the love of Macquart and Henriette, who is left a widow during the siege of Sedan. This terrible siege forms the dramatic centre of the story. The book ends tragically with the death of Maurice Levasseur by the hand of Macquart, who had bayoneted him not knowing that it was his friend. With this shadow between them, Jean and Henriette feel that they must part. "Jean, bearing his heavy burden of affliction with humble resignation, went his way, his face set resolutely toward the future, toward the glorious and arduous task that lay before him and his countrymen, — to create a new France."

'Le Docteur Pascal' (1892). Pascal Rougon, son of Pierre, has collected all the data relating to his family, and sums up their history. Adelaide Fouqué is insane; Eugène, a deputy to Congress; Seccard, an editor; Octave, a successful merchant; Jean Macquart, married again and father of a healthy family. Doctor Pascal diagnoses his own mortal disease, hour by hour; and as he feels the last moment approaching, jumps from his bed, adds the date and cause of his death to the genealogical tree, as well as the birth of his illegitimate child by his niece, in the words, "Unknown child to be born in 1894. What will it be?"

ROUNDABOUT PAPERS, THE, by William Makepeace Thackeray. Thackeray undertook the editorship of the Cornhill Magazine; in the year 1859. 'The Roundabout Papers' were sketches for the magazine, coming out simultaneously, between 1859 and 1863, with 'Lovel the Widower' and 'The Adventures of Philip.' They represent Thackeray's best qualities as an essayist, and cover a wide range of subjects. Some of the titles are: 'On Two Children in Black,' 'On Screens in Dining-Rooms,' 'On Some Late Great Victories,' 'On a Hundred Years Hence,' and 'A Mississippi Bubble.' One of the papers, 'The Notch on the Axe,' displays the author's peculiar genius for burlesque story-telling. It is a dream of the guillotine, occasioned by his grandmother's snuff-box and a sensational novel. The essay 'On a Joke I Once Heard from the Late Thomas Hood' is a cordial tribute to that poet's memory, and in it the joke is not repeated. One of the most noteworthy of the papers is called 'On Thorns in the Cushion.' The task of editing a magazine was irksome to Thackeray's kindly and sensitive nature. "What, then," he writes, "is the main grief you spoke of as annoying you, — the toothache in the Lord Mayor's jaw, the thorn in the cushion of the editorial chair? It is there. Ah! it stings me now as I write. It comes with almost every morning's post. . . . They don't sting quite so sharply as they did, but a skin is a skin, and they bite, after all, most wickedly. . . . Ah me! we wound where we never intended to strike; we create anger where we never meant harm, and these thoughts are the thorns in our cushion." Thackeray, in fact, resigned the position of editor in 1862, though he continued to write for the magazine as long as he lived.

RUBÁIYÁT OF OMAR KHAYYÁM, THE, a sequence of quatrains, rhyming *aaba,* selected and freely translated by Edward Fitzgerald from the 'Rubái'yát' or detached quatrains of the Persian scholar and poet, Omar Khayyám, who was born at Nasháipúr in Khorassán, became astronomer-royal to the Sultan at Merv, and died at Nasháipúr, probably in 1123 A. D. He was a distinguished astronomer and mathematician, an enemy of bigotry and fanaticism, a free-thinker in matters of religion, and, it is said, a lover of pleasure.   Some think that his praises of love and the wine-cup have a religio-symbolical meaning as in the writings of the Súfis and in the orthodox interpretation of the Song of Solomon; but the weight of opinion inclines to the theory that he really sought in these delights to forget the injustices and per-plexities of existence.   His Rubái'y, or quatrains, of which over 1000 are extant, are separate poems each of a single stanza and deal with various topics.   In making them known to the Western world Fitzgerald selected or adapted seventy-five of these stanzas on related themes and wove them into a single connected poem, preserving the metre, the thought, and the atmosphere of the original.   This translation was published in 1859, a second edition, enlarged to one hundred and ten stanzas, appear-ing in 1868.   The evanescence of beauty and worldly glory, the impotence of learn-ing to solve the mystery of life, the domination of man's will by forces outside of himself, the injustice of the doctrine of eternal punishment, and the wisdom of a sceptical attitude towards the unseen and an epicurean acceptance of the joys of love and wine are the principal thoughts of the poem.   Their affinity with the pessimism, agnosticism, religious revolt, and indifferentism of the latter half of the nineteenth century, combined with the exquisite oriental imagery of the poem, its felicitous metre and diction, and its arresting phraseology, have given the Rubáiyát an extraordinary vogue.   Few poems in English literature are more widely quoted and parried or have entered so deeply into the public consciousness.

RUDDER GRANGE, a humorous story by Frank R. Stockton, appeared serially in 1879.   It was the first of the author's books to establish for him a wide reputation. A slight thread of story suffices to connect a series of humorous episodes which result from the efforts of a young couple — Euphemia, and her husband who tells the story in the first person — to establish themselves in a summer home at once desirable and inexpensive.   They hit upon the plan of securing an old canal-boat, which they fit up and name Rudder Grange.   The droll sayings and original doings of Pomona, the servant; the courting of Jonas, her lover; the unique experiences of the boarder; the distresses of Euphemia and her husband, are told in a manner which is irresistibly funny.   The same characters reappear in several of Mr. Stockton's later stories, the longest of which is 'Pomona's Travels.'

RUINS, by Constantin François Volney.   These meditations upon the revolutions of empires were published in Paris in 1791, and have for their theme the thought that all the ills of man are traceable to his abandonment of Natural Religion.   The author, who was an extensive traveler, represents himself as sitting on the ruins of Palmyra, dreaming of the past, and wondering why the curse of God rests on this land.   He hears a voice (the Genius of the Tombs), complaining of the injustice of men, in attributing to God's vengeance that which is due to their own folly.   Love of self, desire of well-being, and aversion to pain, are the primordial laws of nature.   By these laws men were driven to associate.   Ignorance and cupidity raised the strong against the weak.   The feeble joined forces, obliging the strong to do likewise.   To prevent strife, equitable laws were passed.   Paternal despotism was the foundation of that of the State.   Tiring of the abuses of many petty rulers, the nation gave itself one head.   Cupidity engendered tyranny, and all the revenues of the nation were used for the private expenses of the monarch.   Under pretext of religion, millions of men were employed in useless works. Luxury became a source of corruption. Excessive taxation obliged the small landholder to abandon his field, and the riches and lands were concentrated in few hands. The ignorant and poor attributed their calamities to some superior power, while the priests attributed them to wicked gods. To appease them, man sacrificed his pleasures. Mistaking his pleasures for crimes, and suffering for expiation, he abjured love of self and detested life; but as nature has endowed the heart of man with hope, he formed, in his imagination, another country. For chimerical hopes he neglected the reality. Life was but a fatiguing voyage, a painful dream, the body a prison. Then a sacred laziness established itself in the world. The fields were deserted, empires depopulated, monuments neglected; and ignorance, superstition, and fanaticism, joining their forces, multiplied the devastation and ruins. The Genius shows him a revolution, where Liberty, Justice, and Equality are recognized as the foundation of society. Before accepting a religion, all are invited to present their claims for recognition. The result is not only dissensions among the different religions, but between the different branches of the same religion, each one claiming that his is the only revealed religion and that all the others are impositions.

RUINS AND EXCAVATIONS OF ANCIENT ROME, see **ANCIENT ROME.**

RURAL RIDES, by William Cobbett (1830). 'Rural Rides' consists of the accounts of a series of political tours on horseback which Cobbett took through many English counties for some years before 1830. His impressions were published regularly in his paper the "Political Register," which enjoyed a huge circulation and exercised immense influence. Published in collected form under the present title, they form an extraordinarily vivid picture of the social and domestic life in the agricultural England of Cobbett's day. The modern student is not so much concerned with the fact that Cobbett was the foremost journalist in the struggle for parliamentary reform, as with his shrewdness, his homely eloquence, his independence of thought, with which was combined a perfectly sincere interest in the welfare of the poor, especially of the agricultural laborer, whose condition at that time and indeed for generations afterwards was a scandal to England. The book is not only remarkable as a vivid picture of the life of certain strata of society at a particular epoch, but from the literary point of view, its descriptions of rural scenery are in many ways unsurpassed, and it is one of the best examples of the use of terse, vigorous, direct, and unadorned Anglo-Saxon which the language has to show. In this case the style is, indeed, the man, fearless, pugnacious, homely, in every line breathing the love of his fellow-men and a consuming hatred of oppression.

RUSH FOR THE SPOIL, see **ROUGON-MACQUART.**

RUSSIA, see **UNDERGROUND RUSSIA,** by Stepniak.

SACRED AND LEGENDARY ART, by Mrs. Jameson (1848). This, perhaps the best-known and most valuable of Mrs. Jameson's numerous volumes is not only a mine of interesting and often out-of-the-way information brought together by accurate research, but it is also marked by a genuine feeling of artistic sympathy with the subject. The authoress modestly says in the preface that the book "has been written for those who are, like myself, unlearned." Nevertheless its width and sureness of reading is as remarkable as the skill and gracefulness of the arrangement. The legends of the angelic hierarchies, cherubim, seraphim, and choirs; of angels, whether as ministers of wrath or of grace; of the archangels, seven or four or three, are here recalled, in so far as they have been represented in art. The four evangelists, the twelve apostles, the doctors of the Church, the patron saints of Christendom, the martyrs whether of Greece and Rome, or of Lombardy, Spain, and France; the early bishops, and the saints whether hermits or warriors, who have inspired the great masters of art, all have their appropriate place in a unique catalogue.

SACRED BOOKS OF THE EAST, THE. Translation by Various Oriental Scholars, and Edited by Max Müller. (First Series, 24 vols., 1879–85. Second Series, 25 vols., 1886–95.)

An attempt to provide, by means of a library of selected works, a complete, trustworthy, and readable English translation of the principal Sacred Books of the Eastern Religions, — the two religions of India, Brahmanism and Buddhism; the religion of Persia, the Parsee or Zoroastrianism; the two religions of China, Confucianism and Taoism; and the religion of Arabia, Mohammedanism. Of these six Oriental book-religions, Brahmanism was started by Brahman or priestly use of a body of Sanskrit poetry. The other five started from the work of personal founders: Buddha, Zoroaster, Confucius, Lao-tze, and Mohammed. In Buddha's case, the book of his religion came from his disciples. Zoroaster produced a small part only of the Parsee books. Confucius produced the sacred books of his religion; but mainly by compiling, to get the best of the existing literature. Lao-tze produced one very small book. The Koran or Qur'an was wholly *spoken* by Mohammed, not written, — in the manner of trance-speaking; and preserved as his disciples either remembered his words, or wrote them down.

The oldest writings brought into use as scriptures of religion were the Babylonian, dating from about 4000 B. C. The Egyptians also had sacred writings, such as the 'Book of the Dead,' which may have had nearly as early an origin. India comes next to Egypt and Babylonia in the antiquity (perhaps 2000–1500 B. C.) of the poems or hymns made into sacred books and called the Veda. Persia follows in order of time, perhaps 1400 B. C. To the Greeks, from about 900 B. C., the Homeric poems were sacred scriptures for many centuries, very much as in India Sanskrit poems became sacred. The Chinese scriptures date not far from 600 B. C., and the Buddhist about a hundred years later. The Hebrews first got the idea at the last end of their history, when in exile in Babylon; and they not only borrowed the idea, but borrowed stories and beliefs and religious feelings. Under the direction of Ezra, a governor sent from Babylon, they publicly recognized writings got together by the priestly scribes as their sacred scriptures. The exact date was 444 B. C. The idea of scriptures of religion is a universal ancient idea, similar to the idea of literature in modern times. It in some cases grew very largely out of belief that the trance inspiration, which was very common, was of divine origin. The Koran, or Qur'an, which came very late, 622 A. D., was wholly the product of the trance experiences of Mohammed; and as such it was thought to be direct from God. The trances in which Mohammed spoke its chapters were believed to be miraculous. He did not know how to write; and while he made no other divine claim, he pointed to the trance-uttered suras or chapters of the Koran as manifestly miraculous.

The sacred books of the East do not come to us full of pure religion, sound morality, and wise feeling. They rather show the dawn of the religious consciousness of man, rays of light and clouds of darkness, a strange confusion of sublime truth with senseless untruth. Their highest points seem to rise nearer to heaven than anything we can read elsewhere, but their lowest are dark abysses of superstition. What may seem, however, on first reading, fantastic phraseology, may prove upon sufficient study a symbol of deep truth. But it is chiefly as materials of history, records of the mind of man in many lands and distant ages, and illustrations of the forms taken by human search for good, aspiration for truth, and hope of eternal life that all the many books of old religions and strange faiths are full of interest to-day.

In the list of separate works which follows, the books of the different religions are brought together. The figures in Roman are the numbers under which the volumes have been published. The Oxford University Press is about to bring out a greatly cheapened popular edition of the entire double series.

BRAHMANICAL

'Vedic Hymns.' Part i.: Hymns to the Maruts, Rudra, Vâyu, and Vâta. Translated by F. Max Müller. Part ii.: Hymns to Agni. Translated by Hermann Oldenberg. (2 vols. xxxii., xlvi.)

The hymns of Rig-Veda are something over a thousand in number, divided into ten Mandalas, or books. Rig-Veda means Praise-Veda. The other three Vedas, placed side by side with the Rig-Veda, on the top shelf of Veda Literature, are the Sama-Veda, the Yajur-Veda, and the Atharva Veda. But they are not collections of hymns. The Sama-Veda is a liturgy, to be used in connection with a kind of sacrament, in which a liquor prepared from the Soma plant and used in aid of inspiration was employed. It was made up mostly by quotations from the Rig-Veda. The Yajur-Veda was another liturgy, to be used in connection with sacrifices and made up partly by quotations from the Rig-Veda, and partly by prose directions (yajus) for the sacrifices. There was thus a first Veda of the poets, and a second and third of the priests. To some extent at least the poets had been priests also, in the simple days before the age of priests or Brahmans. The fourth Veda was like the first in being a literary collection, but hardly at all another book of hymns. It had some poetry, but more prose, and was more a book of thoughts than of song. But it made the fourth of the original Vedas. Its hymns are given in Vol. xlii., 'Hymns of the Atharva-Veda.' The reader will easily see that these Atharva-Veda hymns represent a different and much later stage of culture from that seen in the Rig-Veda.

The word Veda means knowledge; and it was carried on to cover several stages of development or successive classes of productions, such as the Brahmanas, the Upanishads, the Sutras, the Laws, and many more. Not only the four Vedas, but the Brahmanas and the Upanishads, are included under Sruti, — something heard, absolutely divine; while later productions are classed as Smriti, something handed down, tradition of human origin.

The Maruts were the Storm-gods, the wild forces of nature, and to these the first volume is almost wholly devoted. To give, however, at the opening, an example of the very best, Max Müller places at the head of his collection a hymn containing the most sublime conception of a supreme Deity. The second volume contains the greater part of the Agni hymns of the Rig-Veda. The two volumes make a very valuable study in translation of selected parts of the earliest, most original, and most difficult of Vedic books, the Rig-Veda.

The volume of hymns from the Atharva-Veda, translated by Maurice Bloomfield, includes very extended extracts from the Ritual books and the Commentaries; making, with the translator's notes and an elaborate introduction, a complete apparatus of explanations. Most of the hymns are for magical use, — charms, imprecations, etc., with a few theosophic and cosmogonic hymns of exceptional interest.

'The Satapatha-Brahmana,' according to the Text of the Mâdhyana School. Translated by Julius Eggeling. (5 vols. xii., xxvi., xli., xliii., xliv.)

An example of the ancient theological writings appended to the original four Vedas by the Brahmans, or priests, for the purpose of very greatly magnifying their own office as a caste intrusted with the conduct of sacrifices of every kind. There are some thirteen of them, with attachments to different parts of the original four Vedas. The title given above is that of the most important and valuable. It is called Satapatha, or "of the hundred paths," because it consists of one hundred lectures. It has a very minute and full account of sacrificial ceremonies in Vedic times, and many legends and historical allusions. Nothing could be more wearisome reading; yet the information which can be gleaned in regard to sacrifices, the priestly caste, and many features of the social and mental development of India, is very valuable. A devout belief in the efficacy of invocation and sacrifice appears in the Vedic hymns. This was taken advantage of by the Brahmans to arrange a regular use of these hymns in the two liturgical Vedas, and to establish a proper offering of sacrifices conducted by themselves. The Brahmanas are their endlessly repeated explanations and dictions about sacrifice and prayer.

The third, fourth, and fifth books of the great work presented in these five volumes deal very particularly with the Soma-sacrifice, the most sacred of all the Vedic sacrificial rites. It concerns the nature and use of "a spirituous liquor extracted from a certain plant, described as growing on the mountains." "The potent juice of the Soma plant, which endowed the feeble mortal with godlike powers and for a time freed him from earthly cares and troubles, seemed a veritable God, — bestower of health, long life, and even immortality." The Moon was regarded as the celestial Soma, and source of the virtue of the plant.

Another branch of the story of sacrifices relates to the worship of Agni, the Fire. It fills five out of fourteen books, and the ideas reflected in it are very important for knowledge of Brahman theosophy and cosmogony. The ritual of the Fire-altar was brought into close connection with that of the Soma "fiery" liquor.

'The Upanishads.' Translated by F. Max Müller. (2 vols. i., xv.)

Philosophical treatises of the third stage of the Veda literature, designed to teach the spiritual elements, the deepest thoughts, and the purest wisdom of Vedic religion. The first stage was the Veda, or the four Vedas, in the limited sense. The second was the Brahmanas or priestly commentaries on the four Vedas. The third stage was the Upanishads looking in a very different direction from that of the priests and the pious offerers of sacrifice; works for thinkers. They were produced, to the number of 150 to 200, in the long course of time; but of the most ancient, older probably than 600 B. C., the list is short. They mostly grew up in close connection with Brahmanas, in a sort of appendix to them called the Aranyakas (forest-books).

In Max Müller's two volumes, twelve representative ones are given. As early as the reign of Akbar at Delhi in India (1556-86), translations of fifty Upanishads were made; and in 1657 Dârâ Shukoh, a grandson of Akbar, and Shâh Jehân's eldest son, brought out a translation into Persian, a language then universally read in the East, and known also to many European scholars. This act of religious liberalism, like that of the great Akbar, was made a pretext in 1659, by Aurangzib, the son of Shâh Jehân, who had succeeded to the empire, for putting to death the scholar brother who wished to bring Mohammedans and Hindus into one broad faith. In 1775 one of the manuscript copies of this Persian translation came into the hands of Anquetil Duperron, a French scholar famous also for his discovery of the Zend-Avesta, or Zoroastrian scriptures of ancient Persia; and he brought out a translation into

Latin, one volume in 1801 and a second in 1802. Although the Latin was very hard to understand, and this was a specimen of the utterly unknown Sanskrit literature, done first into Persian in 1657, Schopenhauer, since known as one of the most eminent of German philosophers, said: "I anticipate that the influence of Sanskrit literature will not be less profound than the revival of Greek in the fourteenth century." He also said of the Upanishads as he read them: "From every sentence, deep, original, and sublime thoughts arise, and the whole is pervaded by a high and holy and earnest spirit. And how thoroughly is the mind here washed clean of all early engrafted Jewish superstitions, and of all philosophy that cringes before those superstitions. In the whole world there is no study so beneficial and so elevating. It has been the solace of my life, and will be the solace of my death."

The two volumes here given contain eleven of the Upanishads, which Max Müller calls "the classical or fundamental Upanishads of the Vedânta philosophy," and which the foremost native authorities have recognized as the old and genuine works of this class.

'The Vedânta-Sûtras,' with the Commentary by Sairkarâkârya. Translated by G. Thibaut. (2 vols. xxxiv., xxxviii.) Sutras are short aphorisms, a collection of which contains a complete body of teaching. One class of sutras contains concise explanations of sacrificial matters, designed to give in brief what the Brahmanas give at interminable length. Another class are designed to give in the same way concise, clear explanations of the philosophy taught in the Upanishads. They deal with such topics as the nature of Brahman or the Divine, the relation to it of the human soul, the origin of the physical universe, and the like. Sutra writings form the fourth stage of Veda.

'The Grihya-Sûtras,' Rules of Vedic Domestic Ceremonies. Translated by Hermann Oldenberg. (2 vols. xxix., xxx.) These treatises giving rules of domestic ceremonies reflect in a very interesting way the home life of the ancient Aryas. In completeness and accuracy, nothing like the picture which they give can be found in any other literature. They are a secondary class of Sûtras; based, in the case of those here given, on the Rig-Veda, and on one of the Brahmanas. They presuppose the existence of "Srauta-sûtras," dealing with such more important matters as the great sacrifices. Their object was to deal with the small sacrifices of domestic life.

'The Sacred Laws of the Aryas,' as taught in the schools of Apastamba, Gautama, Vâsishtha, and Baudhâyana. Translated by Georg Bühler. (2 vols. ii.: xiv.) The original treatises showing the earliest Aryan laws on which the great code of Manu, and other great codes of law by other lawgivers, were founded. As a revelation of the origins of law and usage in the early Aryan times, these treatises are of great interest. They overthrow the Brahmanical legend of the ancient origin of caste, and carry sacred law in India back to its source in the teaching of the schools of Vedic study; proving that the great law codes which came later, and claimed to be revealed, were a literary working-over of older works which made no claim to be revelation. The laws that are brought to view are of the nature of Sûtra teaching in regard to the sacrifices and the duties of the twice-born.

'The Insut11tes of Vishnu.' Translated by Julius Jolly. (vii.) A collection of legal aphorisms, closely connected with one of the oldest Vedic schools, the Kathas, but considerably added to in later time. The great work of Manu is an improved metrical version of a similar work, the law-book of the Manavas. Both the Manavas and the Ka*th*as were early schools studying the Yajur-Veda in what was known as its Black form; Black meaning the more ancient and obscure; and White, the corrected and clear. The 'Institutes,' in one hundred chapters, were put under the name of Vishnu by a comparatively late editor.

'Manu.' Translated, with extracts from seven Commentaries, by Georg Bühler. The celebrated code of Manu, the greatest of the great lawgivers of India. The translation is founded on that of Sir William Jones, carefully revised and corrected with the help of seven native commentaries. The quotations from Manu, which are found in the law-books now in use in India, in the government law courts, are all given in an appendix; and also many synopses of parallel passages found in other branches of the immense literature of India. Manu is the Moses of India. His laws begin with relating how creation took place; and chapters i.–vii. have a religious, ceremonial, and moral bearing. The next two chapters deal with civil and criminal law. Then three chapters relate again to matters chiefly moral, religious, or ceremonial.

'The Minor Law-Books.' Part i. Nârada: Br*i*haspati. Translated by Julius Jolly. (xxxiii.) A volume of law-books of India which come after Manu. The first is an independent and specially valuable exposition of the whole system of civil and criminal law, as taught in the law-schools of the period; and it is the only work, completely preserved in manuscript, which deals with law only, without any reference to ceremonial and religious matters. The date of Manu being supposed to be somewhere in the period 200 B. C. to A. D., Nârada is supposed to have compiled his work in the fourth or fifth centuries A. D. The second part of the volume contains the Fragments of Br*i*haspati. They are of great intrinsic value and interest, as containing a very full exposition of the whole range of the law of India; and they are also important for their close connection with the code of Manu.

ZOROASTRIAN

'The Zend-Avesta.' Part i.: The Vendidad. Part ii.: The Sîrôzahs, Yasts, and Nyâyis. Translated by James Darmesteter. Part iii.: The Yasna, Visparad, Âfrînagân, Gâhs, and Miscellaneous Fragments. Translated by L. H. Mills. (iv., xxiii., xxxi.) The Parsee or Zoroastrian scriptures. The three volumes contain all that is left of Zoroaster's religion, the religion of Persia under Cyrus, Darius, and Xerxes; which might have become, if the Greeks had not defeated the Persian army at Marathon, the religion of all Europe. The Mohammedans almost blotted it out in Persia when the second successor of Mohammed overthrew the Sassanian dynasty, 642 A. D. To-day the chief body of Parsees (about 150,000 in number) are at Bombay in India, where their ancestors found refuge. Though so few in number, they have wealth and culture along with their very peculiar customs and ideas. Only a portion of their sacred writings is now extant, and but a small part of this represents the actual teaching of Zoroaster. The Parsees are the ruins of a people, and their sacred books are the ruins of a religion; but they are of great interest as the reflex of ideas which, during the five centuries before and the seven centuries after Christ, greatly influenced Judaism, Christianity, and Mohammedanism.

'Pahlavi Texts.' Translated by E. W. West. (3 vols., v., xviii., xxiv., xxxvii.) A reproduction of works, nine in number, constituting the theological literature of a revival of Zoroaster's religion, beginning with the Sassanian dynasty. Their chief interest is that of a comparison of ideas found in them with ideas adopted by Gnostics in connection with Christianity. They form the second stage of the literature of

Zoroastrianism. The date of origin of the Sassanian dynasty, under which the Pahlavi texts were produced, is 226 A. D. The fall of the dynasty came in 636-651 A. D.

'The Contents of the Nasks,' as stated in the 8th and 9th books of the Dinkard. Translated by E. W. West. (2 vols. xxxvii., xlvii.) The Nasks were treatises, twenty-one in number, containing the entire Zoroastrian literature of the Sassanian period. The object of the present work is to give all that is known regarding the contents of these Nasks, and thus complete the earlier story of the Zoroastrian religion.

'The Bhagavadgîtâ, with the Sanatsugâtîya, and the Anugîtâ.' Translated by Kâshinâth Trimbak Telang. (viii.) The earliest philosophical and religious poem of India. It is paraphrased in Arnold's 'Song Celestial.' Its name means the Divine Lay or the Song sung by the Deity. The work represents an activity of thought departing from Brahmanism, and tending to emancipation from the Veda, not unlike that represented in Buddha and his career.

BUDDHIST

'Buddhist Suttas.' Translated from Pâli by T. W. Rhys-Davids. (xi.) A collection of the most important religious, moral, and philosophical discourses taken from the sacred canon of the Buddhists. It gives the most essential, most original, and most attractive part of the teaching of Buddha, the Sutta of the Foundation of the Kingdom of Righteousness, and six others of no less historical value, treating of other sides of the Buddhist story and system. The translator gives as the dates of Buddha's life of eighty years about 500-420 B. C.

'Vinaya Texts.' Translated from the Pâli by T. W. Rhys-Davids and Hermann Oldenberg. (3 vols., xiii., xvii., xx.) A translation of three Buddhist works which represent the moral teaching of Buddhism as it was definitively settled in the third century B. C. They belong to that part of the sacred literature of the Buddhists which contains the regulations for the manner of life of the members of the Buddhist Fraternity of monks, nearly the oldest and probably the most influential that ever existed.

'The Dhammapada.' A collection of verses; being one of the canonical books of the Buddhists. Translated from Pâli by F. Max Müller. And 'The Sutta-Nipata.' Translated from Pâli by V. Fausböll. (x.) Two canonical books of Buddhism. The first contains the essential moral teaching of Buddhism, and the second an authentic account of the teaching of Buddha himself, on some of the fundamental principles of religion.

'The Saddharma-pundarîka; or, The Lotus of the True Law.' Translated by H. Kern. (xxi.) A canonical book of the Northern Buddhists, translated from the Sanskrit. There is a Chinese version of this book which was made as early as the year 286 A. D. It represents Buddha himself making a series of speeches to set forth his all-surpassing wisdom. It is one of the standard works of the Mahâyâna system. Its teaching amounts to this, that every one should try to become a Buddha. Higher than piety and higher than knowledge is devoting oneself to the spiritual weal of others.

'Gaina-Sutras.' Translated from Prâkrit by Hermann Jacobi. (2 vols. xxii., xlv.) The religion represented by these books was founded by a contemporary of Buddha; and although in India proper no Buddhists are now found, there are a good many Gainas, or Jains, holding a faith somewhat like the original Buddhist departure from Brahmanism. The work here translated is their bible.

'The Questions of King Milinda.' Translated from the Pâli by T. W. Rhys Davids. (2 vols. xxxv., xxxvi.) A work written in northern India, but entirely lost in its original form. It was translated into Pâli for the Buddhists of Ceylon, and is held in great esteem by them. It is of such a literary character as to be pronounced the only prose work composed in ancient India which would be considered, from the modern point of view, a successful work of art. It consists of discussions on points of doctrine between King Milinda and an Elder. There is a carefully constructed story into which the dialogues are set.

'Buddhist Mahâyâna Texts.' Translated by E. B. Cowell, F. Max Müller, and J. Takakusu. (xlix.) Several works of importance for the history of Buddhism. The first is a poem on the legendary history of Buddha. The second is a group of Japanese Buddhist works, such as 'The Diamond Cutter,' one of their most famous Mahâyâna treatises; 'The Land of Bliss,' which more than ten million Buddhists — one of the largest Buddhist sects — use as their sacred book; and 'The Ancient Palm Leaves,' containing fac-similes of the oldest Sanskrit manuscripts at present known. The third is another Japanese work, in the form of a 'Meditation' by Buddha himself. Japan received Buddhism from China by way of Corea in 552 A. D. The present volume gives all the sacred books in use by the Japanese Buddhists.

'The Fo-sho-hing-tsan-king: A Life of Buddha,' by Asvaghosha Bodhisattva, translated from Sanskrit into Chinese by Dharmaraksha, 420 A. D., and from Chinese into English by Samuel Beal. (xix.) A Life of Buddha rendered into Chinese for Buddhists in China. It contains many mere legends, similar to those which appeared in apocryphal accounts of the life of Jesus.

CHINESE

'The Sacred Books of China. The Texts of Confucianism.' Part i. The Shû King, the Religious Portions of the Shih King, and the Hsiâo King. Part ii.: The Yî King. Parts iii. and iv.: The Lî Kî, or Collection of Treatises on the Rules of Propriety, or Ceremonial Usages. Translated by James Legge. (4 vols. iii., xvi., xxvii., xxviii.) The productions of Confucius; not original compositions, but a variety of compilations, designed to present the best practical wisdom as of authority, because it was old as well as because it was good. Not only was Confucius not the founder of a new religion, but his aim was to make a system of good conduct and proper manners which would leave out the low religion of spiritism and magic and priestcraft, as the mass of the Chinese knew it, and in fact still know it. The volumes named above are a complete library of the teaching of Confucius.

'The Shuh' is a book of historical documents covering the period from the reign of Yao in the twenty-fourth century B. C., to that of King Hsiang, 651–619 B. C. As early as in the twenty-second century B. C., the narratives given by Confucius were contemporaneous with the events described.

'The Shih' is a Book of Poetry, containing 305 pieces, five of which belong to the period 1766–1123 B. C. The others belong to the period 1123–586. The greater number describe manners, customs, and events, but the last of the Four Parts is called 'Odes of the Temple and the Altar'; and many other pieces have something of a religious character. The Hsiao is a work on Filial Piety, and one of great interest.

'The Yî,' called the Book of Changes, was originally a work connected with the practice of divination. It is obscure and enigmatical, yet contains many fragmentary physical, metaphysical, moral, and religious utterances very suggestive of thought, and in that way peculiarly fascinating. It was highly prized by Confucius as fitted to correct and perfect the character of the reader. The Sung dynasty, beginning 960 A. D., based on it what has been called their "Atheo-political" system. An outline of this is given in an appendix to the translation of the Yî.

'The Lî Kî' is the Record of Rights, in 46 books, filling two large volumes in translation. They belong to the period of the Kau dynasty, about 1275 to 586 B. C.; and so far as they reflect the mind of Confucius, it is at second-hand through the scholars, who gathered them up centuries after his death, in the time of the Han dynasty.

'The Sacred Books of China. The Texts of Tâoism.' Translated by James Legge. (2 vols., xxxix., xl.) The scriptures of the second of the two practical philosophic religions which originated in China about the same time, that of Confucius and that of Lao-tze. The latter philosopher was the more transcendental of the two, and in its pure form his teaching was a system of lofty thought. But Tâoism long since underwent extreme corruption into a very low system of spiritism and sorcery. What the real thoughts of the great master were, these volumes show. They first give the only work by the master himself, the Tâo Teh King, by Lâo-tze. Next follow the writings of Kwang-tze, of the second half of the fourth century B. C. There is given also a treatise on 'Actions and their Retributions,' dating from the eleventh century of our era, about which time the system changed from a philosophy to a religion. Other writings are added in elucidation of the Taoist system, and its degradation to a very low type of superstition.

MOHAMMEDAN

'The Qur'ân.' Translated by E. H. Palmer. (2 vols. vi., ix.) A translation of the utterances of Mohammed, which were brought together into a volume after his death, and thereby made the sacred book of Mohammedanism. There is no formal and consistent code either of morals, laws, or ceremonies. Given, as it was, a fragment at a time, and often in view of some particular matter, there is no large unity either of subject or treatment. The one powerful conception everywhere present is that of God, his unity, his sovereignty, his terrible might, and yet his compassion. There is also an impressive unity of style, a style of free and forcible eloquence, which no other Arabic writer has ever equalled. The earlier utterances especially, made at Mecca, are in matter and spirit the mighty words of a most earnest prophet, whose one and steady purpose was to so proclaim God as to reach and sway the hearts of his hearers. In his later Medinah period, the prophet had his peculiar gift more under control. He would calmly dictate more extended utterances, to be written down by his hearers. At his death no collection of the scattered utterances of the master had been made. Zaid, who had been his amanuensis, was employed to collect and arrange the whole. This he did, from "palm-leaves, skins, blade-bones, and the hearts of man." Some twenty years later the Caliph Othman had an authorized version made, and all other copies destroyed. This was 660 A. D., about 50 years after the first attack of convulsive ecstasy came upon Mohammed.

SADDHARMA-PUNDARÎKA, see **SACRED BOOKS OF THE EAST.**

SAINT, THE, by Antonio Fogazzaro, see **THE PATRIOT**

SAINT-SIMON, MEMOIRS OF THE DUKE OF, a voluminous autobiographic history of the reign of Louis XIV. from 1691 to his death in 1715, and of the Regency to 1723. The author, Louis de Rouvroy, Vidame de Chartres and, after 1693, Duke of Saint-Simon, a noble of ancient family and high rank, was in constant attendance at Versailles from 1702 to 1721, during which time his powers of observation procured him an intimate acquaintance with the ceremonies and intrigues of the court and the character of its frequenters.   Retiring in 1723 on the death of the Regent, he resided on his country estates and completed his memoirs.   On his death in 1755 the manuscripts were seized by his creditors.   In 1760, through the intercession of his family, they were confiscated by the government to save them from dispersion; but permission to examine them was sparingly granted.   An incomplete edition was published in 1789; but the entire work was not released for publication until 1829, when it appeared in forty volumes.   The definitive text was published from 1856 to 1858. A noble of the old régime intensely occupied with questions of privilege and precedence and with a keen eye for the outer and inner traits of men and women, Saint-Simon left the world a priceless record of the most brilliant and powerful court of Europe. It is true that his personal experience of that court did not include its most glorious days but covered only the period when it was overshadowed by a reactionary religious policy and by the steadily diminishing prestige of French arms during the war with William III. and the ensuing war of the Spanish Succession.   Nevertheless Saint-Simon's daily association with the nobles, gentlemen, great ecclesiastics, and brilliant men of letters who thronged the palace yields a series of historical portraits, groups, and scenes of the most representative character.   The portraits of the king, of Madame de Maintenon, of the princes and princesses of the royal family, of the nobles and attendants, of the typical activities of the court, and of the characters and events which influenced the development of public policy are of the highest value to the historian, to the writer of historical fiction, and to the lover of entertaining gossip about old-world society.   The unsparing revelations of the seamy side of life in the days of the *Grand Monarque*, the photographic realism of the portraiture, and the revelation of the author's aristocratic prejudices, cool assurance, and piercing insight are particularly admired.   The style has not the classic finish of the great prose masters of the age but belongs to an earlier, less disciplined period.   It can be forceful but is often loose in construction.   The memoirs are tedious in certain passages, and these are omitted in the convenient English translation by Francis Arkwright (1915).

SALAMMBÔ, by Gustave Flaubert (1864).   This historical romance was the fruit of Flaubert's visit to the ruins of old Carthage, and is a kind of revivification of the ancient capital and its people.   The scenes testify to the great erudition of the author, but critics complain that the picture has too little perspective.   All is painted with equal brilliance — matter essential and unessential.

The sacred garment of Tanit is made the object around which the action revolves; and the fate of Carthage is bound up in the preservation of this vestment within her walls.   The central point of the story is the boundless passion of Matho, a common soldier among the mercenaries, for Salammbô, the beautiful daughter of the great Hamilcar; and the fate of the vestment of Tanit continually overshadows the fate of his love.   By a mad act of daring, he gets possession of the carefully guarded treasure, and through its influence on the popular mind, heads a rising of the troops, who proceed against Carthage.   Urged on by the High Priest, Salammbô is persuaded that it is her sacred duty to recover the stolen vestment, and so bring back the protection of the goddess to the arms of Carthage.   Under his instruction, she is led secretly by night to the tent of Matho to obtain the vestment.   Obedient to the pontiff, she endures the soldier's wild transports of joy, and succeeds in carrying away the vestment, which in his self-forgetting adoration he has wrapped about her

Fortune returns to the Carthaginians, the rebellious leader is taken, and Salammbô's wedding to the man of her father's choice is made the scene of Matho's martyrdom. Looking down at the torn and dying man, whose eyes alone retain the semblance of humanity, Salammbô suddenly recalls the tender babble of those agonized lips, the adoration of those eyes on that night in his tent. She realizes what this man has suffered for love of her, and her heart breaks. In the act of drinking the wine her bridegroom offers, she sinks back dead. And thus the two beings whose touch has profaned the garment of Tanit pass from the earth. The most brilliant of romances dealing with the classic world, this story holds its place through all variations of popular taste, among the masterpieces of fiction.

SALVATION NELL, by Edward Sheldon (1908). The scene of this realistic play of the slums is the Cherry Hill district on the upper West Side of New York City. Act I. takes place in a bar-room where Nell Sanders, the heroine, is a scrubwoman. She is Jim Platt's "girl" whom he has lately neglected, beyond pocketing her earnings, for some woman in a house across the street, which is presently raided. Another loafer tries to embrace Nell, and Jim nearly kills him in a fight, and is sent to prison for a term of eight years as a result. The showily dressed Myrtle Odell, who has escaped arrest in the raid, urges Nell to follow in her footsteps. She describes graphically the life in the sweat shop from which she has escaped, the endless sewing on of buttons and the hundreds of pairs of pants to be stitched, "those eternal pants." Nell hesitates, but rejects the affluence of vice to follow "Hallelujah" Lieutenant Maggie O'Sullivan of the Salvation Army. In the second act, eight years later, Nell has risen to be a captain in the Salvation Army. The brutal Jim gets out of prison, and after a long search finds her living alone with her child in the tenement. He is ready to resume their old relations, but Nell, though she discovers that she still loves him, has changed. He wants her to go West with him after he has made a successful theft of diamonds. She warns him that she will inform the police about the diamond robbery. She tries to save him from a criminal life and apparently fails. The last act shows a street scene in Cherry Hill. Jim hangs around on the outskirts to hear Nell make a Salvation Army speech, and is converted by her eloquence. He begs her to help him see things as she does. There is a large cast of well-known types, the saloonkeeper, policeman, delicatessen dealers, hokey-pokey men with their wares, street Arabs, gangs of "bad men," loafers, and the Salvation Army girls, reproducing faithfully the environment of squalor, vice, and crime.

SAMUEL BROHL AND COMPANY, a novel, by Victor Cherbuliez (1879). One of the most entertaining productions of a writer who excels in delicate comedy, and has given readers an agreeable change from the typical "French novel"; though it has little substance or thought. The action occurs during the year 1875, in Switzerland and France. Samuel Brohl, a youth of lowest origin, is bought by Princess Gulof, who educates him, and then makes him nominally her secretary. He tires of her jealous tyranny and runs away, assuming the name and history of Count Larinski. Antoinette Moriaz, an heiress of romantic notions, who undervalues the love of honest Camille Langis because "there is no mystery about him," supposing Samuel to be the Polish hero he impersonates, thinks she has found the man she wants at last. Madame de Lorcy, her godmother and Camille's aunt, suspects "Count Larinski" of being an adventurer; and is finally helped to prove it by the Princess, Samuel's former mistress, who recounts to Antoinette how she bought him of his father for a bracelet, which bracelet Samuel has given the girl as a betrothal gift. Disillusioned, she breaks with Samuel, saying pathetically, "The man I loved was he whose history you related to me" (i. e., Count Larinski). Camille visits Samuel to get back Antoinette's letters and gifts, contemptuously refuses a challenge, and buys the keepsakes for 25,000 francs. The bargain concluded, Samuel theatrically thrusts the bank-notes into a candle flame, and repeats his challenge. In the resulting duel, Camille is left for dead by Samuel, that picturesque scamp fleeing to America. Camille recovers, and eventually his devotion to Antoinette meets its due reward.

SAND, GEORGE, L'HISTOIRE DE MA VIE. This work was begun in 1847, and completed in 1855. It was published in Paris at the latter date, and republished, essentially unchanged, in 1876.

The four volumes of autobiography, comprising over 1800 pages, deal with the first forty years of the author's life, and close twenty-one years before her death. The first and second may be styled the introduction to the story; being devoted mainly to the antecedents of the writer, her lineage, her father's letters, and to a running commentary on the times. The autobiography proper begins in the third volume. Here the extremely sensitive nature, and vivid, often wild, imagination of a girl, may be seen unfolding itself in continuous romance, sufficient in quantity and quality to foreshadow, if not to reveal, one of the most prolific novelists in French literature.

In these pages, the writer portrays a genius in embryo fretting over its ideals, — in the passion for study and observation; in the convent experience of transition from realism to mysticism; in domestic hopes and their rapid disillusioning. In the last volume appear the beginnings of the George Sand of our literature, — the mystic transforming into the humanitarian and the reformer; the dreamer subdued by many sorrows; the new novelist happy or defiant amidst her friends and foes.

As a work of art and as an autobiography, 'L'Histoire de Ma Vie' is defective in the lack of proportion involved by overcrowding the story at the beginning with extraneous matter and childhood experiences, to the exclusion of important episodes of maturer years, and the abrupt ending of the narrative where the author has just entered upon her literary career.

But taken as a whole, the autobiography is an invaluable contribution to the French literature of the first half of the nineteenth century. Outside of contemporary interests, we have, with a few reservations, the frank, vivid portraiture of a child both of kings and toilers; a woman of the convent and of bohemia; a genius in literature striving for the welfare of her kind.

SANDFORD AND MERTON, by Thomas Day. The history of Sandford and Merton has afforded entertainment and instruction to many generations of boys since its first publication about 1780. Portraying the social ideas of the English of more than a hundred years ago, it can hardly be regarded, in the present day, as exerting a wholesome influence, — in fact, it is chiefly remarkable for its tone of unutterable priggishness.

Master Tommy Merton in this story is the son (aged six) of a wealthy gentleman who dwells chiefly in the island of Jamaica. Tommy's short life has been spent in luxury, with the result that he has become an unmitigated nuisance. Harry Sandford, on the contrary, though the son of a poor farmer, was even at an early age replete with every virtue; and when the two boys are placed under the instruction of a Mr. Barlow, an exceptionally wise and good clergyman, he is continually used as an example to the reprehensible Tommy. Morals are tediously drawn from every incident of their daily lives, and from the stories which they read in their lesson books. 'The Gentleman and the Basket-Maker'; 'Androcles and the Lion'; 'History of a Surprising Cure of the Gout,' and other stories of a like nature, form the food on which these young intellects are nourished.

Not the least remarkable feature of the book is the polished language used by these children of six years of age; and this juvenile can now only be regarded as an excellent example of the literature with which our grandfathers and great-grandfathers were regaled in their youth.

SANDRA BELLONI, by George Meredith. This novel was first published in 1864, under the name of 'Emilia in England.' The Greek Pericles, ever in search of hidden musical genius, finds it in the voice of Emilia Sandra Belloni, while visiting Mr. Pole. Pole has squandered the money held in trust for Mrs. Chump, a vulgar but kindhearted widow, and is therefore forced, with his children, to submit to her attentions. Wilfred Pole, his son, loves Emilia, but means to marry Lady Charlotte. Discovering this, Emilia wanders away, loses her voice, and is rescued from starvation by Merthyr Powys, who has long loved her. He goes to fight for Italy. The Poles are brought to the verge of ruin by Pericles. Emilia's voice returns. Pericles saves the Poles, on her signing an agreement to study in Italy for three years and sing in public. Wilfred hears her sing, casts off Lady Charlotte who favors the Austrians, and throws himself at Emilia's feet. She now realizes his inconstancy and Merthyr's nobility, writes to the latter that she loves him, and will be his wife at the end of the three years for which she is pledged. The story contains all of Meredith's marked mannerisms; but also flashes with wit, and is full of life and vivacity.

SANDY, by Alice Hegan Rice (1905). This is the story of a young Irish boy named Sandy Kilday, who at the age of sixteen, being without home or relatives, decides to try his luck in the new country across the sea. Accordingly he slips aboard one of the big ocean liners as a stowaway, but is discovered before the voyage is half over and in spite of his entreaties is told he must be returned by the next steamer. Sandy, however, who has a winning way and sunny smile, arouses the interest of the ship's doctor, who pays his passage and gives him some money with which to start his new life. On the voyage Sandy has made friends with a lad in the steerage named Ricks Wilson, who earns his living by peddling, and he decides to join him in this career. Sandy has also been deeply impressed by the face of a lovely young girl who is one of the cabin passengers and when he discovers that she is Miss Ruth Nelson of Kentucky he decides to make that state his destination. He and Ricks remain companions for sometime although Sandy's strong sense of honor causes disagreements as to the methods of their dealings. Sandy finally becomes disgusted with this life and after catching a glimpse of Ruth at a circus, where he is dispensing his wares in a humorous manner, he decides to abandon it altogether.

He parts from Ricks and falling ill by the roadside is picked up by a colored woman called Aunt Melvy, who is in the employ of Judge Hollis. The latter takes Sandy to his home and his wife nurses him through a long fever and then, as they are childless, they adopt him into their household. The Judge gives Sandy a good education, sends him to college, and he becomes a successful lawyer. All this time his love for Ruth has been unswerving though she has not responded to his advances. Judge Hollis is shot by an unknown assassin and Sandy, who discovers the assailant to be Ruth's dissipated brother Carter, refuses to give evidence against him. Sandy is kept in jail until freed by Ruth's intervention, Carter having confessed his crime to his sister before his death. The Judge recovers from his wound and Sandy and Ruth are happily married to the satisfaction of all concerned.

SANTO, IL, see THE PATRIOT.

SARAGOSSA, by Benito Perez Galdós (1879).   This novel gives a dramatic picture of the valor of the Spaniards defending their national existence against Napoleon's generals.   The brave citizen, Don José de Montorio, gives his services, his wealth, and his sons to his country.   Candiola, the miser, rouses Don José's anger by his refusal to give his stores of flour to maintain the army.   The wretched Candiola has a beautiful daughter, Mariquilla, who loves Augustine de Montorio, not knowing he is the son of the man who has denounced her father.   A Spanish Juliet, she brings food to her Romeo and binds his wounds.   Another brave woman, Manuela, the "Maid of Saragossa," encourages the men with brave words and herself fires a cannon all day in the trenches until she falls wounded.   It is discovered that Candiola has revealed to the enemy a secret passage into the city, and he is condemned to be shot. Augustine is the gaoler of his sweetheart's father.   Mariquilla, beside herself with grief and terror, implores him to let her father escape.   Augustine cannot make her understand that she is asking the impossible.   Finally the city, a mere heap of dust and ashes and dead, agrees to an honorable capitulation.   Augustine finds Mariquilla dead, and goes from her grave to a monastery.

SARTOR RESARTUS, by Thomas Carlyle, first appeared in Fraser's Magazine, in 1833–34, and later in book form.   It is divided into three parts, — introductory, biographical, and philosophical.   The first part describes an imaginary book on 'Clothes: Their Origin and Influence' by Diogenes Teufelsdröckh, Professor of Things in General at Weissnichtwo in Germany.   The book, the editor complains, is uneven in style and matter, and extraordinarily difficult to comprehend, but of such vigor in places that he is impelled to translate parts of it.   The book begins with a history of clothes: they are co-existent with civilization, and are the source of all social and political distinction.   Aprons, for example, are of all sorts, from the smith's iron sheet to the bishop's useless drapery.   The future church is shown in the paper aprons of the Paris cooks; future historians will talk, not of church, but of journalism, and of editors instead of statesmen.   Man is apt to forget that he is not a mere clothed animal, — that to the eye of pure reason he is a soul.   Still Teufelsdröckh does not counsel a return to the natural state, for he recognizes the utility of clothes as the foundation of society.   Wonder, at himself or at nature, every man must feel in order to worship.   Everything material is but an emblem of something spiritual; clothes are such emblems, and are thus worthy of examination.

The autobiographic details sent to the editor which fill Book ii. came to him on loose scraps of paper in sealed paper bags, with no attempt at arrangement anywhere. A mysterious stranger left Teufelsdröckh, when he was a helpless infant, at the house of Andreas Futteral, a veteran and farmer.   Andreas and his wife Gretchen brought the boy up honestly and carefully.   As a child he roamed out-doors, listened to the talk of old men, and watched the sunset light play over the valley.   At school he learned little, and at the gymnasiums less.   At the university he received no instruction, but happened to prefer reading to rioting, and so gained a great deal of information.   Then he was thrust into the world to find out what his capability was by himself.   He withdrew from the law, in which he had begun, and tried to start out for himself.   The woman whom he loved married another, and he was plunged into the depths of despair. Doubt, which he had felt in the university, became unbelief in God and even the Devil, — in everything but duty, could he have known what duty was. He was a victim to a curious fear, until one day his whole spirit rose, and uttering the protest of the "everlasting yea," asserted its own freedom. Life came to mean freedom to him; he felt impelled to "look through the shows of things to the things themselves," — to find the Ideal in the midst of the Actual.

The third book, which deals with the philosophy itself, is much less continuous and clear. In the first chapter, he praises George Fox's suit of leather as the most remarkable suit of its century, since it was a symbol of the equality of man and of the freedom of thought. Religion is the basis of society: every society may be described as a church which is audibly preaching or prophesying, or which is not yet articulate, or which is dumb with old age. Religion has entirely abandoned the clothes provided for her by modern society, and sits apart making herself new ones. All symbols are valuable as keeping something silent, and, at the same time, as revealing something of the Infinite. Society now has no proper symbols, owing to over-utilitarianism and over-independence. Still a new society is forming itself to rise, Phœnix-like, from the ashes of the old. Mankind, like nature, is one, not an aggregate of units. The future church for the worship of these mysteries will be literature, as already suggested by the prophet Goethe. Custom makes nature, time, and space, which are really miracles, seem natural, but we must feel wonder and reverence at them. Our life is through mystery to mystery, from God to God. The chief points, in concluding, to be remembered are: All life is based on wonder; all clothes, or symbols, are forms or manifestations of the spiritual or infinite; cant and hypocrisy everywhere should be replaced by clear truth.

The book is written in Carlyle's most characteristic style and contains remarkable passages of romantic autobiography.

SATAPATHA-BRAHMANA, THE, see **SACRED BOOKS OF THE EAST.**

SATIROMASTIX, by Thomas Dekker (1602). As late as 1599 Dekker and Ben Jonson had collaborated in two plays, but they quarrelled before Jonson (in 1600) had brought out 'Everyman out of his Humor' and 'Cynthia's Revels' both of which contain satirical allusions to Dekker. In 1601 Jonson made a merciless onslaught on Dekker and Marston in the 'Poetaster,' to which Dekker made a vigorous, but good-humored reply in 'Satiromastix,' or the Untrussing of the Humorous Poet.' Horace (Ben Jonson) is commissioned to write a nuptial song in honor of the marriage of Sir Walter Terill and Caelestine. Horace first appears "sitting in a study behind a curtain, a candle by him burning, books lying confusedly: thereafter follows a labored address to himself by Horace, which is meant to suggest that Jonson's style is slow and heavy in workmanship. Not only Jonson's vanity, irritability, spleen, and perversity are ridiculed, but also his old clothes and other personal peculiarities. The names Horace, Crispinus (Marston), and Demetrius Fannius (Dekker) are borrowed from Jonson's 'Poetaster.' The best character in 'Poetaster' is a certain Captain Tucca, and critics are divided as to the success of Dekker's artifice in borrowing Tucca and employing him in his own play to pour out brutal and foul-mouthed epithets upon the head of Horace.

SCARLET LETTER, THE, the novel which established Nathaniel Hawthorne's fame, and which he wrote in the ancient environment of Salem, was published in 1850, when he was forty-six years old. Its simple plot of Puritan times in New

4C

England is surrounded with an air of mystery and of weird imaginings. The scene is in Boston, two hundred years ago: the chief characters are Hester Prynne; her lover, Arthur Dimmesdale, the young but revered minister of the town; their child, Pearl; and her husband Roger Chillingworth, an aged scholar, a former resident of Amsterdam, who, resolving to remove to the New World, had, two years previously, sent his young wife Hester on before him. When the book opens, he arrives in Boston, to find her upon the pillory, her babe in her arms; upon her breast the Scarlet Letter ' A " ("Adulteress"), which she has been condemned to wear for life. She refuses to reveal the name of her partner in guilt, and takes up her lonely abode on the edge of the wilderness. Here Pearl grows up a wild elf-like child; here Hester makes atonement by devoting her life to deeds of mercy. Her husband, whose identity she has sworn to conceal, remains in the town, and in the guise of a physician, pries into and tortures the minister's remorse-haunted soul. Hester, knowing this, forgetting aught but love, proposes flight with him. He wills to remain, to reveal his guilt publicly. Confessing all, after a sermon of great power, he dies in Hester's arms, upon the platform where she once stood condemned. A wonderful atmosphere of the Puritan society bathes this book, its moral intensity, its sensitiveness to the unseen powers; while forever pressing in upon the seething little community is the mystery of the new-world wilderness, the counterpart of the spiritual wilderness in which Hester and Arthur wander. This great creation is one of the few "classics" that the nineteenth century has added to literature.

SCHILLER, FRIEDRICH, LIFE AND WORKS OF, by Calvin Thomas (1901). The aim of this, one of the latest and ablest of Schiller biographies is to interpret the works of the poet "as the expression of an interesting individuality and an interesting epoch," to see the man as he was and to understand the national temperament to which he endeared himself. At Ludwigsburg in Würtemberg Schiller "got his first childish impressions of the great world: of sovereignty exercised that a few might strut in gay plumage while the many toiled to keep them in funds; of state policies determined by wretched court intrigues; of natural rights trampled upon at the caprice of a prince or a prince's favorite." Partly educated at the Karlschule at Ludwigsburg, — an institution founded to gratify a fad of Duke Karl, and intended to serve as a training-ground for future servants of the state — for at least part of his time at school he got the reputation of a dullard. But his poetic powers were ripening, and first took shape in an important work in 'The Robbers' (1780) which was read secretly to a knot of admiring school-mates. The success of this play, one of the most significant of the eighteenth century, led Schiller on to other and still more successful efforts in drama—'Fiesco' and 'Cabal and Love.' The most prolific period of his literary life was the time of his close association with Goethe at Weimar from 1794 until Schiller's death in 1805. The verdict of this biographer is that while Schiller lacked the supreme qualities of a great world-poet, he was great as a man, and his life of passionate striving for the ideal is a splendid model for all intellectual work.

SCHOLAR AND THE STATE, THE, and other Orations and Addresses; by Henry Codman Potter (1897). A volume of thoughtful papers, of which the first, giving the volume its title, was delivered as the Phi Beta Kappa Oration at Harvard in 1890, and the second, on 'Character in Statesmanship,' was the address of April 30th, 1889, at St. Paul's Church in New York, which carried off the chief honor of the celebration of the one hundredth anniversary of the first inauguration of Washington as President of the United States. There are seventeen papers altogether, and they constitute a conspicuous illustration of the best type of churchman: a bishop of New York, who was in every secular respect an eminent citizen, and an author of wise counsel in matters of political and social interest.

SCHÖNBERG-COTTA FAMILY, see CHRONICLES OF THE.

SCHOOL FOR SCANDAL, THE, by R. B. Sheridan (1777). Sheridan's dramatic masterpiece 'The School for Scandal' narrowly escaped suppression as a license to perform it was refused, and it was only through the author's personal influence with the Lord Chamberlain, Lord Hertford, that the license was granted on the very day fixed for its performance. "It is," says Hazlitt, "if not the most original, perhaps the most finished and faultless comedy which we have." It is also the wittiest and most deadly attack that has ever been made in English on the organized hypocrisy of society. Joseph and Charles Surface present the contrast between shameless hypocrisy and reckless good-nature. Sir Peter Teazle, the most miserable dog ever since six months previously Lady Teazle made him the happiest of men, and his perpetual squabbles with his young wife: the scandal scene in which Sir Benjamin Backbite, Lady Sneerwell, and Mrs. Candour strike "a character dead at every word"; the scene in which Charles sells all the family pictures but those of his uncle who is the purchaser in disguise; and the discovery that it is Lady Teazle and not a little French milliner who is behind the screen are so familiar as to have become household words; and the play is as popular on the stage as ever. It is said that 'The Rivals' was prepared in great haste in response to stimulus from the company who were to play it, and that when it was completed the author wrote on the last page: "Finished at last, Thank God! R. B. Sheridan." To which one anxious official added: "Amen! W. Hopkins the Prompter!"

SCHOOL FOR WIVES, see L'ECOLE DES FEMMES.

SCIENCE OF ENGLISH VERSE, THE, see ENGLISH NOVEL, by Sidney Lanier.

SCIENCE OF THOUGHT, THE, by F. Max Müller (1887). This is a work which may be read as the intellectual or philosophical autobiography of the great scholar, wise thinker, and delightful writer, whose name it bears. The author says that he has written it for himself and a few near friends; that some of the views which he presents date from the days when he heard lectures at Leipzig and Berlin, and discussed Veda and Vedanta with Schopenhauer, and Eckhart and Tauler with Bunsen; and that he has worked up the accumulated materials of more than thirty years. The views put forth, he says, are the result of a long life devoted to solitary reflection and to the study of the foremost thinkers of all nations. They consist in theories formed by the combined sciences of language and thought; or, he says, in the one theory that reason, intellect, understanding, mind, are only different aspects of language. The book sets forth the lessons of a science of thought founded upon the science of language. It deals with thought as only one of the three sides of human nature, the other two being the ethical and the æsthetical.

SCOTT, SIR WALTER, LIFE OF, by J. G. Lockhart (1838). Lockhart's 'Life of Sir Walter Scott' is by many placed second, as Boswell's 'Johnson' first, in the list of great biographies. His intimate relation to Sir Walter, his sympathy with the subject, his extensive acquaintance with the persons and events associated with Sir Walter's name, lastly, his own literary bent combined to make Lockhart an ideal biographer. Scott's activities as advocate, clerk of session, and sheriff; his success as the author of the 'Lay of the Last Minstrel' and 'Marmion'; his work as reviewer and editor; the instantaneous popularity of 'Waverley' and a long and rapid succession of novels; best of all his extraordinary charm as host and conversationalist, are described by the most faithful, sympathetic, and discerning of chroniclers. It must have been most difficult to deal justly with Scott's unfortunate business connections with the publishing firm of Ballantyne, which left him liable for a debt of £130,000. Scott's noble refusal to take advantage of the bankruptcy laws and to accept the many offers of private assistance which he received,—this, with his gallant attempt, which finally broke even his vigorous constitution, to clear off the mountain of debt that had been accumulated through no fault of his, makes the story of his life both heroic and pathetic. Lockhart's intense devotion to Scott has led him into no blind idolatry, and it is now commonly agreed that in these pages he has done substantial justice not only to the poet and novelist, but to the Ballantynes.

SCOTTISH CHIEFS, THE, by Jane Porter. This spirited historical romance was first published in 1809, and has enjoyed unceasing popularity. It gives many pictures of the true knightly chivalry dear to boyish hearts, and is historically correct in all important points. The narrative opens in 1296 with the murder of Wallace's wife by the English soldiery, and shows how, fired by this outrage, he tried to rouse his country against the tyrant Edward. He gathers about him commons and nobles, and gains especial favor with venerable Lord Mar. Lady Mar is impressed by his beauty; and when he scorns her dishonorable passion, she proves his worst enemy, and incites the nobles to treason. He also wins the heart of the lovely Helen Mar, who respects his devotion to his dead wife, and does not aspire to be more than his sister. Wallace effects the capture of the castles of Dumbarton, Berwick, and Stirling, and fights the bloody battles of Stanmore and Falkirk. But as soon as he becomes prominent, petty jealousies spring up among the nobles; and when in spite of his inferior birth he is appointed regent, their rage knows no bounds. He has continually to guard against treachery within as well as foes without, but his intrepid spirit never fails. He goes in the disguise of a harper to the court of Edward, and rouses young Bruce to escape and embrace his country's cause. Bruce and Wallace go to France to rescue the abducted Helen Mar, and while there meet Baliol, whom Edward had once adjudged king of Scotland. On returning to his own country Wallace finds the English in possession of much of the territory he had wrested from them, and by a series of vigorous movements regains the mastery. But internal feuds and jealousies are too strong for him, and on Edward's second invasion Wallace is abandoned by his supporters. He flees and long eludes his pursuers, but is finally betrayed, taken to London, and brutally hanged and quartered. But the fire that he had kindled did not altogether die out, and Edward was obliged to treat Scotland with respect even after he had murdered her hero.

SCOTT'S LAST EXPEDITION, an account of the attainment of the South Pole by Robert Falcon Scott and of his death from cold and starvation, with a record of the scientific achievements of the enterprise, edited by Leonard Huxley and published in 1910. The first volume includes the journals of Captain Scott and the second the scientific records by Dr. E. A. Wilson and other members of the expedition. There are fine portraits, reproductions in color from Dr. Wilson's drawings, and many photographs and maps, and the chronology is carefully indicated. Scott's expedition established a base at McMurdoo Sound on the Antarctic Continent, from which various important voyages of discovery were undertaken, and much valuable material obtained. The journey for the South Pole was begun in 1911 and the goal was reached on January 18th, 1912. Amundsen had been there five weeks before, and had left a flag, a tent, and other objects. Thus although Scott did not win the race his journey was valuable as a corroboration of Amundsen's discovery. On the return journey, severe weather, an insufficient supply of food, and an accident to Lieutenant Evans greatly delayed the party. Evans finally died, another member, Oates, weakened by exposure wandered off into the snow and perished rather than be a hindrance to his comrades, and the remaining members of the party, Scott, Wilson, and Bowers, were caught by a blizzard on March 21st, only eleven miles from the next supply-depot, and being insufficiently provided with food and fuel, were frozen to death, March 29th, 1912. The journal, recovered when the bodies were found eight months later, is the record of a courageous English gentleman who from the first faced the prospect of death and who from his entries in this journal seems to have felt it closing in upon him, but who to the last retains his quiet self-control and unswerving devotion to duty. His last written words were a tribute to his comrades and a plea for adequate provision by the nation for their families and his own.

SCOURING OF THE WHITE HORSE, THE, by Thomas Hughes (1859). The colossal image of a white horse, hewn upon the chalk cliff of a Berkshire hill, is a lasting monument of the battle of Ashdown. It was constructed in the year 871, by King Alfred the Great, marking the site of the turning-point of the battle, and is the pride of the county.

The "pastime" of the scouring of the white horse was inaugurated in 1736, and has been held at intervals of from ten to twenty years ever since. The whole countryside makes of it the grand holiday of Berkshire. The farmers for miles around, with pick and shovel, remove the accumulations of soil from the image, so that it stands out in bold relief, clear and distinct as when first completed.

After this is accomplished, the two succeeding days are devoted to athletic sports, — horse and foot races, climbing the greased pole, wrestling matches, and backsword play. The hill is covered with booths of showmen and publicans, and rich and poor alike join in the festivities of the occasion.

The particular "pastime" recounted in this book occurred in 1857; and the experiences of a prosperous Berkshire farmer and his guest, a former schoolmate, lend a personal flavor and interest to the story.

The book is made for boys, and no writer excels Hughes in the vivid description of manly sports: like his exciting accounts of the cricket match and the boat-race in his famous 'Tom Brown' stories, and 'The Scouring of the White Horse.'

SEA POWER, THE INFLUENCE OF, UPON HISTORY, by A. T. Mahan, see **INFLUENCE etc.**

SEA POWER, THE INTEREST OF AMERICA IN, by A. T. Mahan, see **INTEREST etc.**

SEA WOLF, THE, by Jack London (1904). This is a sea-story and depicts life under most brutal and revolting conditions. The hero and narrator of this tale is Humphrey Van Weyden, a literary critic and a man of leisure, who is wrecked in a fog while crossing San Francisco Bay in a ferry boat. He is carried out to sea and is picked up by a sealing-schooner named the "Ghost," which is outward bound. The captain, "Wolf Larsen," so called on account of his fiendish cruelty and furious outbursts of temper, refuses to put Humphrey ashore and forces upon him the duties of cabin-boy. Van Weyden is robbed and abused by Mugridge, the cook, but obtains no satisfaction from the captain, who is a curious mixture of brutality and self-culture, and amuses himself by discussing life and literature with Humphrey when he is not tormenting him physically. On various occasions the crew, driven to desperation by the brutal treatment they have received from the Sea-Wolf, endeavor to take his life, but each time are foiled by his indomitable strength with dire results to the leading conspirators. A beautiful girl named Maude Brewster who has been wrecked at sea is rescued by the "Ghost" and both Humphrey and the Sea-Wolf are captivated by her. This is a dangerous complication, and leads to many trying situations in which Humphrey finds himself in danger of the Sea-Wolf's vengeance. Finally the "Ghost" is wrecked and Humphrey and Maud get away in a small boat and reach a desert island where they manage to exist for some time. The hulk of the ship is washed ashore, its only occupant being the Sea-Wolf, who has become blind and helpless and has been deserted by all his men. Humphrey and Maud endeavor to make repairs on the damaged vessel in the hopes of thereby getting away from the island, but Larsen whose ugly nature is unchanged tries in every way to frustrate their efforts. He tries to kill Humphrey but does not succeed and soon becomes paralyzed as well as blind. His companions tend him until the hour of his death, which finds him unsoftened. The lovers who have endured such terrible hardships are finally rescued by a revenue cutter and their sufferings are over.

SEABOARD SLAVE STATES, A JOURNEY IN THE, by F. L. Olmsted, see **JOURNEY** etc.

SEATS OF THE MIGHTY, THE, by Gilbert Parker (1896), is a historical romance, of which the scene is laid in Quebec at the critical period of the war between the French and English. It is a rapid succession of exciting adventures wherein figures prominent in history play their part with the creations of the author.

Captain Robert Moray, of Lord Amherst's regiment, is a hostage on parole in Quebec. On a false charge of being a spy he is imprisoned. His death, however, is prevented by Doltaire, an instrument of La Pompadour, who has brought Moray into these straits for purposes of his own: by keeping him alive, that is, Doltaire hopes to obtain papers in Moray's possession that are of great importance to La Pompadour. Moreover, he suspects Moray of affection for Alixe Duvarney, whom he himself loves, and would torture his rival with the knowledge of his own success.

The monotony of the imprisonment is varied by interviews with Gabord the jailer, "who never exceeds his orders in harshness"; and by occasional visits from the brilliant Doltaire, or from Vauban the barber, who is the connecting link with Alixe and her world.

Of two attempts to escape, the first is frustrated by Doltaire; the second, a year later, meets with better success. Gabord has been induced to bring Alixe to her lover, and a marriage ceremony is performed by an English clergyman who has been smuggled into the quarters. That night Moray and five other prisoners make their escape, and in a few days succeed in reaching the English lines.

Moray's information as to the condition of the city, and the pass by which the Heights of Abraham may be reached, is invaluable.

After the battle and the capture of the city, Moray begins the search for Alixe.

Accidentally he learns of the death of Doltaire. He finds Alixe at last in the mountains above the city, where she had taken refuge from the persecutions of Doltaire, Here she tends her wounded father, and has for her companion Mathilde, the poor, demented sweetheart of Vauban. The characters are well drawn.

SECOND BLOOMING, THE, by W. L. George (1914). The theme might be "No, people are not happy ever after" or, the futility of the lives of leisure-class women without responsibility of children or household cares. Three married sisters take different paths to solve the unrest of their thirties. Grace is the wife of a facetious barrister, who still calls her "Gracie-Bracie" and "girlie" after years of married life. Her two children do not need her since they are cared for by efficient servants. Art and isms do not fill her life; interest in dress is an absorbing phase of her development, and a very amusing clever bit of psychology on the part of the author. She finds her great adventure in the passion and danger of a secret love affair. Clara, the elder, who is married to a Tory baronet, blooms again in a feverish activity in politics and philanthropy. Mary, the youngest, begs the question, by having an unfashionably large family, which leaves her no surplus energy to expend outside her home. In the last chapter the sisters compare notes on their views of life. Clara, recovering from a nervous breakdown, enjoys the memory of her past triumphs. Grace, beautiful and unrepentant, clings to the store of memories of her lover, and asserts that "to want things, to have them, and to pay for them is to become bigger and finer." Mary, the model mother of eight, thinks "all you can do in life is to suffer what you've got to and to enjoy what you can" and that "there's hope for everybody, even for wives."

SECOND MRS. TANQUERAY, THE, by Sir A. W. Pinero (1893). Pinero and Wilde were the earliest of the later nineteenth-century dramatists who attempted to do for England what Ibsen had done. Boldness in treating actual problems of every-day life went with an equally bold use of modern stagecraft. Aubrey Tanqueray, a well preserved and handsome widower of forty-two informs his old friends Misquith and Jayne, both men of the world and older than himself, that he is about to marry again, but refrains from telling them the lady's name. Paula (the second Mrs. Tanqueray), a beautiful, fresh, innocent-looking young woman of twenty-seven (who nevertheless has had a past), is cold-shouldered by some of Aubrey's former society lady friends. He married her in the honest belief that if he were kind to her (as her former male acquaintances had not been) she would be a reclaimed woman. She speedily finds her position unbearable, because she is ignored by local society, and also because she is unable to win the affection or confidence of Ellean, a young girl of nineteen, a daughter of Aubrey's by his first marriage. He himself is unwilling that the second Mrs. Tanqueray should be the mentor of his daughter, and gives his consent to Ellean's going to Paris with Mrs. Cortelyou. In Paris Ellean meets and becomes engaged to Captain Ardale, who had formerly been intimate with Paula. Paula feels it to be her duty to inform Aubrey of their relationship. He forbids Ellean to see Captain Ardale again. Ellean now admits that from the first meeting she had guessed what sort of woman Paula was. Paula in wild despair, though Aubrey offered to go away and start a new life with her elsewhere, killed herself. "Killed herself? Yes. Yes. So everybody will say. But I know — I helped to kill her. If I'd only been merciful!" says Ellean in the concluding words of the play.

SECRET WOMAN, THE, by Eden Philpotts (1905). A tragedy of Dartmoor country folk with the background of the landscape of the moor in wonderful contrasts of season. Handsome, affectionate Anthony Redvers turns from his stern cold wife, Ann, the mother of his two grown sons, in passionate desire to Salome Westaway, a young girl with whom his elder son, Jesse, is innocently in love. Ann discovers her husband's intrigue with an unknown woman. In a passion of anger and jealousy she strikes him, pushing him into the well to his death. Jesse urges her to confess her guilt, as she longs to do to expiate her sin, but Michael, the younger son, who worships his mother and condemns his father, threatens to take his own life unless she keeps the secret that Anthony's death was not an accident. Salome, heartbroken at the loss of Anthony, cares nothing for Jesse, but becomes engaged to him in order to have his help for her father, whose easy-going ways have mortgaged the farm. The cheerful Mr. Westaway, with his love-your-neighbors-as-yourself philosophy, and Nat Tapps's hell-fire religion, relieve the gloom of the story. Jesse tells Salome of his mother's deed, and she at once reveals herself to the widow to denounce her cruelty. Salome's passion gives way before Ann's remorse, and forgiveness is mutual. Jesse throws himself over the quarry when he learns that Salome was his father's "secret woman." Ann gives herself up to justice, and Michael, with beautiful devotion, waits for his mother to serve her prison term.

SELBORNE, see **NATURAL HISTORY AND ANTIQUITIES OF.**

SELF-HELP, by Samuel Smiles. This book, first published in 1859, has held its popularity down to the present. It was the second of a series of similar works.

'Self-Help' is a stimulating book for young people, written in an interesting manner; and while full of religious feeling, is free from cant. The tenor of the work may be judged by a quotation from the opening chapter: "The spirit of self-help is the root of all genuine growth in the individual; and, exhibited in the lives of many, it constitutes the true source of national vigor and strength. Help from without is often enfeebling in its effects, but help from within invariably invigorates." The book abounds in anecdotes of celebrated men, — inventors, scientists, artists, soldiers, clergymen, and statesmen: Minton and Wedgewood the potters; Arkwright Watts, and Peel; Davy, Faraday, Herschel, and many others, among scientists; Reynolds, Michael Angelo, Haydn, Bach, Beethoven, and others in the arts; Napoleon, Wellington, Napier, Livingstone, as examples of energy and courage. The various chapters dwell upon National and Individual Self-Help; Application and Perseverance; Helps and Opportunities; Industry, Energy, and Courage; Business Qualities; Money, its Use and Abuse; Self-Culture; and Character.

SERAPH, by Count Leopold Sacher-Masoch. This delightful story by the great German novelist, who has been called the Galician Turgeneff, was translated into English in 1893. As a frame for a charming tale, the author gives a vivid description of Hungarian life and customs. We are introduced to Seraph Temkin, as he is about to shoot at a card held in his mother's hand. She tells him she has educated him with one object in view, the revenge of a wrong done her by a man whose name she now gives — Emilian Theodorowitsch. Seraph journeys to the Castle Honoriec, and gives his name and his mother's to Emilian. To his surprise, Emilian says he has never heard of Madame Temkin, but insists on Seraph accepting his hospitality. He remains, and learns from everybody of the tenderness, generosity, and nobility of his host. Emilian tells Seraph the story of his life. He had married a woman accustomed to command and be obeyed. An estrangement sprang up between them, and when a son was born, a handsome nurse came into the house. His wife became jealous but persisted in keeping the nurse. One night the nurse began to coquet with Emilian. He upbraided her, whereupon she fell at his feet and began to weep. He raised her up, and his wife, entering, found the nurse in his arms. Taking the child, she escaped, and he had never been able to find a trace of her. Another charm of the castle for Seraph is Magdalina, Emilian's adopted daughter, with whom Seraph is in love. Running after her one day, she flees into the chapel. He finds her hiding in the confessional, and kneeling down at the wicket, he tells her of his love. He is interrupted by his mother in disguise, who upbraids him for his delay; and when he asks her what relationship existed between her and Emilian, she answers "none," and escapes. Magdalina tells him this woman reminds her of a portrait in an abandoned part of the castle. She leads him there, and he is struck with the familiarity of the scenes. He rushes to a clock, pulls a string, and hears an old familiar tune; and in the next room finds his mother's portrait. He thinks of but one way in which his mother could have been wronged, in spite of Emilian's very suggestive story; and going down stairs he insults Emilian and challenges him to a duel, in which Seraph is shot. When he recovers from his swoon, he finds himself again at the castle with Magdalina watching over him. He sends for Emilian, and tells him of the portrait; and the father clasps his long-lost son in his arms. The reconciliation of the husband and wife ends the story.

SERPENT SYMBOLS, ooo CENTRAL AMERICA, NOTES ON, by E. G. Squier.

SERVANT IN THE HOUSE, THE, by Charles Kennedy (1907). The theme of this symbolic drama is the brotherhood of man. The vicar has appealed for funds to rebuild his crumbling church. His brother, the Bishop of Benares, whom he has not seen for many years, has promised to help him. His wife has succeeded in interesting her worldly brother the Bishop of London in the plan, because he believes that the name of the Bishop of Benares, who is famous for his piety and good works, will bring in millions, which the ambitious prelate wishes to divert to his chief interest in life, the Society for the Promotion and Preservation of Emoluments for the Higher Clergy. Both bishops are expected on the same morning. The vicar has another brother, Robert, who is a drunkard, disowned by the family. The childless vicar and his wife have adopted Robert's daughter Mary, who has never known her father. The vicar's conscience tells him that he is a hypocrite to preach the spirit of brotherhood in his pulpit and refuse to help his own disreputable brother, who has become a scavenger. His worldly wife feels that Robert has only his deserts and opposes her husband's wish to gain peace of mind by receiving Robert at the vicarage. Into this troubled household comes the Bishop of Benares, disguised as Manson, the new butler. When Robert, rough, uncouth, cursing at the injustice of the world, comes to claim his daughter, Manson quiets him, so that he hides his identity from Mary to save her dream of a father, brave and beautiful and good. The Bishop of London arrives, and with physical and spiritual blindness and deafness combined, mistakes Robert for the vicar, and reveals his own hypocrisy to Manson. Through Manson's influence, Mary is led to think about her father and ask the vicar about him, and in spite of his wife he tells her the truth. Robert, whose business is drains, has gone under the foundations of the church to find the source of corruption, a vault under the very pulpit, symbolizing the dead body of tradition and convention which poisons those who would worship God in spirit and in truth. He sets about the work of cleaning it out in such brave spirit that his daughter recognizes him as her dream came true, and his brother throws off his clerical coat to work with him. Manson orders the pompous

Bishop of London, the servant of Mammon, out of the house, and reveals himself to his brothers. The character of Manson is a replica of Jesus Christ. It is suggested that he may be the Messiah. His presence brings truth and harmony into the tangled lives of the vicar's household.

SEVEN CHAMPIONS OF CHRISTENDOM, THE, by Richard Johnson. This is a romance of chivalry, which was one of the best known and most popular books of its time. The oldest known edition is dated 1597. In it are recounted the exploits of St. George of England, St. Denis of France, St. James of Spain, St. Anthony of Italy, St. Andrew of Scotland, St. Patrick of Ireland, and St. David of Wales. St. George kills the dragon, and after seven years' imprisonment escapes, marries Sabra, and takes her to England. He draws the sword of the necromancer Ormandine from the enchanted rock, rescues David, who had been unable to draw the sword and kills Ormandine. St. Denis, after an enchantment of seven years in the shape of a hart, rescues Eglantine from the trunk of the mulberry-tree. St. James, by knightly prowess, wins the love of Celestine. St. Anthony kills the giant Blanderon and rescues Rosalinde; but her six sisters remain enchanted, in the forms of swans. St. Andrew forces the father of Rosalinde to become a Christian; and God, in recompense, restores the daughters to their former shapes. St. Patrick rescues the six sisters from the hands of satyrs. The Seven Champions collect immense armies from their native countries to attack the Saracens; but St. George is called to England to defend Sabra, who has killed the Earl of Coventry in defense of her honor. He defeats the champion of Coventry and returns to Egypt with Sabra, where she is crowned queen. Going to Persia, he finds the other champions under the spell of the necromancer Osmond, devoting themselves to the love of evil spirits, who are in the form of beautiful women. He breaks the spell, and the armies of the champions defeat those of the Saracens. The second part relates the achievements of St. George's three sons, and the rest of the noble adventures of the Seven Champions; also the manner and place of their honorable deaths, and how they came to be called the Seven Saints of Christendom.

SEVEN LAMPS OF ARCHITECTURE. The 'Seven Lamps of Architecture' by John Ruskin appeared in 1847. In this book architecture is regarded as the revealing medium, or lamp, through which flame a people's passions, and which embodies their life, history, and religious faith, in temple, palace, and home.

The first Lamp is "Sacrifice," or the offering of precious things because they are precious, rather than because they are useful or necessary. Such a spirit picks out the most costly marble or the most elaborate ornamentation simply because it is most costly or most elaborate, and is directly opposed to the prevalent feeling of modern times which desires to produce the largest result at the least cost.

Next comes the "Lamp of Truth," or the spirit of reality and sincerity characteristic of all noble schools of architecture. Ruskin here condemns all falsity of assertion in architectual construction, in material, in quantity of labor, and in the substitution of effect for veracity, and traces the downfall of art in Europe to the substitution of *line* for *mass*, and of mere expression in place of the general principles of truth.

The third and fourth Lamps are those of "Power" and "Beauty," or the expression in architecture of the sublime and the delightful; the sublime, indicating man's power to *govern;* the delightful, man's power to *gather.* The former ability shows itself in form, situation, and line, and the latter in ornamentation.

Then follows the "Lamp of Life," which is the spirit of originality that seizes upon substances, alike in use and outward form, and endows them with its own energy, passion, and nobility, until rough stones come to life. This spirit of Life is distinguished from the spirit of death by its power to animate. The spirit of death may act and imitate, but it is powerless to inspire.

The last two Lamps are those of "Memory" and "Obedience"; the one ever burning brightly and steadily among those peoples who reverence the past, and flaming forth in buildings erected to commemorate national achievements; while the other, the "Lamp of Obedience," reveals strict conformity in architecture to its laws, which should be no more disregarded than the laws which govern religion, politics, or social relations.

Ruskin affirms that "the architecture of a nation is great only when it is as universal and established as its language, and when provincial differences in style are nothing more than so many dialects."

SEVEN WHO WERE HANGED, THE, by Leonid Andreyev (1908). The fear of death, the horror and iniquity of capital punishment, is the theme of this powerful study of the character, thoughts, and feelings of men and women condemned to die. Five of the prisoners are revolutionists who have attempted to assassinate a high official in Russia, two are common peasant murderers. They wait in solitary confinement for seventeen days after the judgment, and are finally summoned to ride in the dark to midnight execution. The young soldier, Sergey, fights successfully the fear of death that takes possession of his sound strong body, but he is tortured with dread of the farewell visit from his stricken father and mother. The strong characters, Werner, the leader of the terrorists, and the young girl, Musya, are able to bear the thought of inevitable death, he with enlightened mind, and she by her innocent purity and conception of immortal life. Musya goes to the scaffold supporting the ignorant terrified murderer with her beautiful courage and humanity. The author aims through his art to destroy the "barriers which separate one soul from another," and helps us to realize sympathetically the humanity of even the lowest criminal.

SEVENTEEN, by Booth Tarkington (1916), is a humorous and entertaining description of a boy of seventeen named William Sylvanus Baxter. Called "Willie" by his family and "Silly Bill" by his schoolmates, he appears before the reader in the various moods and situations to which a youth of that age is heir. Though pretending to be indifferent to feminine charms he falls an easy victim to the fascinations of Miss Lola Pratt, a pretty, insipid young girl who is visiting her friend May Parcher. Lola has for a constant companion a little lap-dog named Flopit to which pet she talks an endearing species of baby-talk; she uses the same style of language when conversing with her friends, a method which proves very fascinating to the callow youths by whom she is surrounded. Willie, who endeavors to appear at his best before his charmer, borrows his father's dress suit, and all goes well until the fact is discovered by his mother, who is aided in her efforts by Willie's sister Jane. The latter, a sagacious and knowing child of ten, is a constant thorn in the flesh to her brother, as she finds out all his secrets, and through her intervention most of his plans are frustrated. Many incidents are amusingly described which are of serious moment to the hero of the tale. The disappearance and enlargement of his father's dress-suit which causes the cessation of his evening visits to Miss Pratt; his non-appearance at a tea given by his mother for the charming Lola, and his inability to get a dance with her at the last party of the season, prove most entertaining reading. The misery of Mr. Parcher whose roof is sheltering the lovely visitor, and who has neither peace nor happiness in his own home owing to the continual presence of the youths who swarm about Miss Pratt until the "wee sma' hours," is most graphically described, and when her departure finally takes place, his happiness is complete. William, on the contrary, witnesses her going with the deepest sorrow and regret, and expresses his sentiments in a poem which he encloses with his picture in a box of candy as a parting token of his affection.

SEVIGNE, MADAME DE, see **LETTERS OF.**

SEWALL, SAMUEL, AND THE WORLD HE LIVED IN, by N. H. Chamberlain (1897), is an account of one of the most notable of the early Puritan worthies, who was graduated from Harvard College in 1671, only fifty-one years after the landing of the Pilgrims at Plymouth. Sewall came of a good family of English nonconformists, who came to this country when he was a boy of nine. He grew up to be a councilor and judge, highly esteemed among his contemporaries; but his fame to-day rests not on his achievements in his profession, but on the remarkable diary which he kept for fifty-six years, chronicling minutely the events of his daily life. He saw all there was to be seen in public and social life. As a man of position, connected with the government, he made many journeys, not only about the colony but over seas to court. As a judge, he knew all the legal proceedings of the country, being concerned, for example, in the Salem witchcraft trials. No man of the time was better furnished with material to keep a diary, and his was well done. Its pages afford many a vivid picture of the early colonial personages, — their dress and their dinners, their funerals and weddings, their town meetings, their piety, their quarrels, and the innumerable trifles which together make up life. Mr. Chamberlain finds this diary a match for Evelyn's and Pepys's, and unique as far as America is concerned. He has drawn most of the material for his book from the three huge volumes of the journal, following the career of the diarist from his first arrival in the colony to his death in 1729. The pages are studded with quotations delightfully quaint and characteristic; and the passages of original narrative nowhere obscure these invaluable "documents."

SHADOW OF DANTE, A, by M. F. Rossetti, see **DANTE.**

SHAKESPEARE, WILLIAM, A LIFE OF, by Sidney Lee (1898). The motto of this book would appear to be that which was said (by one of them) to have animated the contributors to the English Dictionary of National Biography: "no flowers, by request." The purpose of the writer has been to provide a book which "shall supply within a brief compass an exhaustive and well-arranged statement of the facts of Shakespeare's career, achievement, and reputation, that shall reduce conjecture to the smallest dimensions consistent with coherence, and shall give verifiable references to all the original sources of information." By common consent he has abundantly succeeded in this aim. He traces the parentage, childhood and education of the poet; his early days at Stratford and first appearances as an actor on the London stage; the first dramatic efforts which, notwithstanding the poet's unique originality and fertility of invention, took the form of adapting familiar Ovidian fables for English readers; his amazing fluency of composition, which made Ben Jonson say of him that "whatsoever he penned he never blotted out a line." The whole of Shakespeare's dramatic work was probably begun and ended between his twenty-seventh and forty-seventh year. The student of human nature will also notice that his noblest literary efforts during the latter portion of these years coincide with certain shrewd business transactions which re-established him as a man of property in his native Stratford, where he spent his concluding days. An extraordinary variety of information is conveyed not only in the chapters which deal with Shakespeare's life and works, but in the sections which deal with autographs, portraits and memorials, bibliography, and the poet's posthumous reputation. As a perfect example of the terse, restrained, and judicial criticism of the true scholar, students should note the chapter (only two pages in length) in which Sir Sidney Lee attempts a general estimate of the poet, and which thus begins and ends. "In knowledge of human character, in wealth of humour, in depth of passion, in fertility of fancy, and in soundness of judgment, he has no rival. . . . To Shakespeare the intellect of the world, speaking in divers accents, applies with one accord his own words: 'How noble in reason! how infinite in faculty! in apprehension how like a god!'" The new edition of 1911 contains a great deal of additional matter, based largely on recent researches into the history of the theatre and theatrical companies of Shakespeare's time.

SHALLOW SOIL, by Knut Hamsun (1893). A satirical picture of a group of mediocre young writers and artists, whose pretensions are taken seriously by an admiring community. Contrasted with them are two sterling young merchants, Henriksen and Tidemand, who are despised by the clique as "peddlers," and "hucksters," and tolerated for the sake of the money, wine, and suppers they are willing to provide for impecunious artists. Tidemand's wife, Hanka, has an intrigue with Irgens, the shallow, selfish poet, who takes her money and devotion until he tires of her. The two friends, Tidemand and Henriksen, talk over their affairs in the office at the back of Henriksen's great warehouse, in the fragrant atmosphere of spices, coffee, and wines. Tidemand has a pathetic faith that sooner or later he and his wife will be happy together again. Henriksen confides to Tideman his love for his betrothed, Aagot, a beautiful young girl from the country. The unsophisticated Aagot is Irgens's next victim. He gradually wins her from her fiancée and under his corrupting influence she loses her innocence and purity. An interesting character is Coldevin, Aagot's tutor, who worships her and tries to show her the sham of the worthless poet and his circle. Hanka's eyes are opened to her husband's noble character; convinced of her love, he forgives her, and takes her back. Henriksen commits suicide, unable to endure Aagot's downfall.

SHE, by Sir Rider Haggard (1887). This is a stirring and exciting tale. Mr. Haggard has pictured his hero as going to Africa to avenge the death of an Egyptian ancestor, whose strange history has been handed down to him in an old manuscript which he discovers. His ancestor, a priest of Isis, had been slain by an immortal white sorceress, somewhere in Africa; and in the ancient record his descendants are exhorted to revenge his death. The sorceress, no other than "She," is discovered in a remarkable country peopled by marvelous beings, who, as true servants of the sorceress, present an exaggerated picture of the barbaric rites and cruelties of Africa. To this strange land comes the handsome and passionate Englishman, with two companions who share his many thrilling experiences. A mysterious bond exists between the young Englishman and the sorceress: the memory of the ancient crime and the expectation of its atonement. The climax of the story is reached when the travelers and the sorceress together visit the place where the mysterious fire burns which gives thousands of years of life, loveliness, strength, and wisdom, or else swift death. "She" for the second time dares to pass into the awful flame, and so meet her doom, being instantly consumed.   The weird tale does not lack a fitting background for its scenes of adventure, the author choosing an extinct volcano for the scene of the tragedy; so vast is its crater that it contains a great city, while its walls are full of caves containing the marvelously preserved dead of a prehistoric people.   Haggard's practical knowledge and experience of savage life and wild lands, his sense of the charm of ruined civilization, his appreciation of sport, and his faculty of imparting an aspect of truth to impossible adventures, find ample expression in this entertaining and wholly impossible tale.

SHE STOOPS TO CONQUER, by Oliver Goldsmith (1773).   Sheridan and Goldsmith were the only dramatists of their century whose plays are acted to-day. 'She Stoops to Conquer,' though the manager had to be won over to make the attempt to produce it, was a huge success on the first night.   It attained, to use the words of Dr. Johnson, "the great end of comedy, making an audience merry," and it has been making audiences merry ever since.   Hardcastle who loves "everything that's old: old friends, old times, old manners, old books, old wine" (but whose wife objects to being put in the category of old things which her husband loves); Mrs. Hardcastle, who spoils their son, Tony, a constant frequenter of "The Three Jolly Pigeons"; and Miss Hardcastle, whom her father wishes to marry to young Marlow, "one of the most bashful and reserved young fellows in all the world," have all taken their places among the best beloved characters on the comic stage.   The idle yet mischievous, cunning yet stupid Tony Lumpkin, with his associates at "The Three Pigeons" one of whom is a showman who declares that his bear dances to none but the genteelest of tunes, is another unforgettable character.   One of the most ably-conceived figures in the book is young Marlow, whose bashfulness in the presence of Miss Hardcastle and freedom when in the company of the supposed maid-servant who was really Miss Hardcastle in disguise, combine to make up a remarkable piece of character-drawing.

SHELBURNE ESSAYS, by Paul Elmer More, a collection of literary essays in seven volumes, the first series published in 1904, the second and third in 1905, the fourth in 1906, the fifth in 1908, the sixth in 1909, and the seventh in 1910.   Most of them had previously appeared in briefer form in the New York Evening Post and other journals and periodicals.   The title, as the first essay explains, is derived from the village of Shelburne in the valley of the Androscoggin in Maine, where the author spent two years of retirement and became convinced of his vocation as a critic.   The essays cover a wide range of literature from the Bhagavad Gîtâ to Tolstoy.   The greater number, however, are concerned with the writers of the nineteenth century, and a goodly proportion deal with the great writers of America.   One volume, the sixth, is devoted to great religious thinkers—among them—Saint Augustine, Pascal, Bunyan, and Plato — who are grouped under the sub-title, 'Studies of Religious Dualism.'   The author is a stimulating and suggestive critic, who emphasizes particularly the necessity of a revival of classicism in an age of romantic disintegration.

SHENANDOAH, by Bronson Howard (1888).   A military drama of the Civil War. The first scene is a Southern home in Charleston in the early morning hours after a ball.   Lieutenant Kerchival West, a Northern officer, is making a declaration of love to Gertrude Ellingham, a Southern girl.   As he awaits her answer the first shot is fired by the Confederates upon Fort Sumter in Charleston harbor, beginning the war which makes the North and South enemies, and he accepts his dismissal. The second and third acts take place at the Ellingham homestead in the Shenandoah valley. Gertrude Ellingham is captured and brought a prisoner before Lieutenant West just after she has succeeded in carrying dispatches to Thornton in the Confederate lines. Thornton, the villain of the piece, is also captured later. Lieutenant West had fought a duel with him for insulting his colonel's wife, Mrs. Haverhill, with his attentions. Thornton springs at Lieutenant West, wounding him seriously. He accuses the unconscious man to Colonel Haverhill of being Mrs. Haverhill's lover. Gertrude, forgetting her devotion to the South, kneels beside West, confessing her love. Colonel Haverhill's son, Frank, has led a wild life, and has been disowned by his father. He joins the army under an assumed name, and accepts from his father, as commander, the dangerous mission of going through the enemy's lines to get the signal code of the Confederates. He captures the code, but is mortally wounded. His father attends the funeral, doing honor to his bravery, not knowing the young officer was his own son. There is a thrilling scene when the Union army is in retreat, and General Sheridan rides to the rescue turning the retreat to victory. The last act is in Washington after Lee's surrender. A long delayed letter written by his dead son explains to Colonel Haverhill how the miniature of his wife had come into Lieutenant West's possession. All the various lovers are reunited.

SHERLOCK HOLMES, ADVENTURES OF, by Sir A. Conan Doyle (1892), consists of twelve sketches, purporting to have been recorded by Dr. Watson, a friend and coadjutor of Sherlock Holmes. In each narrative Holmes figures as a scientific amateur detective of remarkable skill, unraveling the most intricate criminal snarls. Enslaved to cocaine, eccentric, brusque, he nevertheless is a patient and untiring student, having developed his penetrative faculties to an amazing degree. His forte is *a posteriori* reasoning, which enables him so to group apparently unimportant effects as to uncover the most remote and disconnected causes. As an analytical chemist he classifies many varieties of cigar ashes, mud, dust, and the like; collates endless data, and constructs chains of evidence with a swift accuracy which results in the apprehension and conviction of criminals only less gifted than himself. The sketches are: 'A Study in Scarlet'; 'A Scandal in Bohemia'; 'The Red-Headed League' (given in this LIBRARY); 'A Case of Identity'; 'The Boscome Valley Mystery'; 'The Five Orange Pips'; 'The Man with the Twisted Lip'; 'The Blue Carbuncle'; 'The Speckled Band'; 'The Engineer's Thumb'; 'The Noble Bachelor'; 'The Beryl Coronet'; and 'The Copper Beeches.' All are full of bizarre and often of grewsome details, and all are unrivaled as specimens of constructive reasoning applied to every-day life. Sir Conan Doyle was still writing the adventures of Sherlock Holmes in 1917. Later books are 'Memoirs of Sherlock Holmes' (1893) and 'Return of Sherlock Holmes' (1905), 'His Last Bow' (1917).

SHERMAN MEMOIRS OF GENERAL W. T., written by himself (4th ed., 1891). In this autobiography General Sherman tells the story of his life up to the time of his being placed on the retired list in 1884; a final chapter by another hand completes the story, and describes his last illness, death, and funeral. Beginning with a genealogical account of his family, the work describes his boyhood, his appointment to and course at West Point, his assignment to a second lieutenancy in the Third Artillery, stationed in Florida, his experiences in California in 1846–50, his marriage in Washington to a daughter of Secretary of the Interior Ewing, in 1850, his resignation from the army in 1853, and engaging in business, law, and teaching; then comes the account in his own words of the part he played in the Civil War, which all the world knows. The tour in Europe and the East is dismissed in three short paragraphs. The whole is told simply, frankly, and in a matter-of-fact way, in English that is plain, direct, and forcible, if not always elegant. The famous "march to the sea" he describes in a businesslike style, that, when supported by accomplished facts, is beyond eloquence. Sherman himself regarded it as of much less importance than the march from Savannah northward. The chapter on "Military Lessons of the War" is interesting, especially to military men. Some of his conclusions in it are that volunteer officers should be appointed directly or indirectly by the President (subject to confirmation by the Senate), and not elected by the soldiers, since "an army is not a popular organization, but an instrument in the hands of the Executive for enforcing the law"; that the country can, in case of war in the future, rely to supplement the regular army officers on the great number of its young men of education and force of character. At the close of our Civil War, some of our best corps and division generals, as well as staff-officers, were from civil life, though "I cannot recall any of the most successful who did not express a regret that he had not received in early life instruction in the elementary principles of the art of war"; that the volunteers were better than the conscripts, and far better than the bought substitutes; that the greatest mistake of the War was the mode of recruitment and promotion; that a commander can command properly only at the front, where it is absolutely necessary for him to be seen, and for his influence to be felt; that the presence of newspaper correspondents with armies is mischievous. He closes his book in the justified assurance that he "can travel this broad country of ours, and be each night a welcome guest in palace or cabin."

SHERWOOD, MRS. MARY ELIZABETH WILSON, see **EPISTLE TO POSTERITY.**

SHIPS THAT PASS IN THE NIGHT, by Beatrice Harraden. This sad little story achieved notoriety when it was published in 1894, largely on account of its taking title. The scene is laid in a Swiss winter-resort for consumptives. Bernardine, a pathetic worn-out school-teacher, of the new-woman type, who has had hitherto little human interest, finds herself one of the 250 guests of the crowded Kurhaus at Petershof. Her neighbor at table is Robert Allitsen, a man whom long illness and pain have rendered so brusque and selfish, that he goes by the name of the "Disagreeable Man." He declares that he has no further duties towards mankind, having made the one great sacrifice, which is the prolonging, for his mother's sake, of a wearisome and hopeless existence. These two people strike up a close comradeship, and Bernardine discovers unsuspected depths of kindness and tenderness under the gruff exterior of the Disagreeable Man. Her own nature is insensibly softened and enriched by the sight of the suffering around her. At the end of the winter Bernardine's health is re-established, and she returns to the old second-hand book-shop where she lives with her uncle. Robert Allitsen parts from her with scarcely a word; but when she has gone, he pours out in a beautiful letter all the love he feels for her, and has fought so hard against. The letter is never sent. Bernardine confides to her old uncle her love for this man. In the meantime Mrs. Allitsen, his mother, has died; and shortly after, Robert Allitsen appears in the old book-shop. Bernardine requires him to continue the sacrifice now for her sake. That same day she is killed by an omnibus: and the "Disagreeable Man" goes back to Petershof to live out his lonely life. A sad picture is given of the thoughtlessness of the caretakers who accompany the invalids.

SHIRLEY, Charlotte Brontë's third novel, was published in 1849. The scene is laid in the Yorkshire country with which she had been acquainted from childhood. The heroine, Shirley, was drawn from her own sister Emily. The other characters include three raw curates, — Mr. Malone, Mr. Sweeting, and Mr. Donne, through whom Charlotte Brontë probably satirized the curates of her own acquaintance; Robert Moore, a mill-owner; his distant cousin, Caroline Helstone, whom he eventually marries; his brother, Louis Moore, who marries Shirley Keeldar, the heroine, and a number of others, including workingmen and the neighboring gentry. The story, while concerned mainly with no one character, follows, to some extent, the fortunes of Robert Moore, who, in his effort to introduce new machinery into his cloth mill, has to encounter much opposition from his employés. In her childhood while at school at Roe Head, Charlotte Brontë had heard much of the Luddite Riots which were taking place in the neighborhood, and which furnished her later for the descriptions of the riots in Shirley.

The book faithfully reproduces the lives of country gentlefolk, and is richer in portrayal of character than in striking incident. Wholesome and genial in tone, it remains one of Charlotte Brontë's most attractive novels.

SHOEMAKER'S HOLIDAY, THE, or, The Gentle Craft, by Thomas Dekker (1600). This, the most frolicsome picture of life in London in the time of Elizabeth, is from the pen of a playwright who was born in the metropolis of unknown parentage, who was frequently in prison for debt, and whose very varied and vigorous literary activity seems rarely to have supplied him with the means of a decent living. Notwithstanding his struggle with fortune, he was, at his best, on a level with the best that the Elizabethan drama has to show. One of his earliest, and, perhaps his best play, is the present comedy, which depicts the manners and customs of "the gentle craft" of shoemaking. The prologue of this "merrie conceited Comedie" informs us that "nothing is purposed but mirth," and the argument is thus stated by Dekker himself. "Sir Hugh Lacy, Earl of Lincoln, had a young gentleman of his own name, his near kinsman, that loved the Lord Mayor's daughter of London; to prevent and cross which love, the Earl caused his kinsman to be sent Colonel of a company into France; who resigned his place to another gentleman his friend, and came disguised like a Dutch shoemaker to the house of Simon Eyre in Tower St. who served the Mayor and his household with shoes. The merriments that passed in Eyre's house, his coming to be Mayor of London, Lacy's getting his love, and other accidents." Simon Eyre with the unceasing flow of staccato phrases which he pours out upon all and sundry from the King to his wife Margery, the "wench with the mealy mouth that will never tire" is Dekker's best creation and one of the most irresistibly comic characters in English literature. Acted in 1599 as 'The Gentle Craft,' published in 1600 under this title.

SHORT HISTORY OF FRENCH LITERATURE, A, by George Saintsbury, see FRENCH, ETC.

SHORT HISTORY OF THE ENGLISH PEOPLE, A, by John Richard Green (1874), is perhaps the most popular history of England ever written. The author had consulted a vast number of sources, and collected his material at first hand. The process of fusing it into a highly vitalized continuous narrative he performed with wonderful skill, sympathy, and acumen. The period covered in the first edition is from the earliest times to the ministry of Disraeli in 1874. The distinction of this great work is that it is really a history of a people, and of their evolution into a nation. It is not primarily a record of wars and of the intrigues of courts, but of the development of the important middle class, the rank and file of the nation. The 'History of the English People,' in four volumes (1877–80), is an amplification of the earlier work, and both have undergone revisions and additions.

SHORT STUDIES IN LITERATURE, see **ESSAYS OF HAMILTON WRIGHT MABIE.**

SHORT STUDIES ON GREAT SUBJECTS, by James Anthony Froude (2 vols., 1877–82). The peculiar charm of Froude as an essayist and historian lies in his picturesque and almost romantic manner, making past events and persons live once more and move across his pages. The graphic scenes in these 'Short Studies' are highly effective, though preserving no logical sequence or relation to one another. The first volume begins with a treatise on 'The Science of History'; and the fourth ends with the social allegory called 'On a Siding at a Railway Station,' where the luggage of a heterogeneous group of passengers is supposed to be examined, and to contain not clothing and gewgaws, but specimens of the life-work of each passenger or possibly nothing at all, — by which he then is judged. The very discursiveness of these studies enables one to find here something for various moods, — whether classic, moral, or æsthetic; whether the thought of war be uppermost in the reader's mind, or of travel, or science, or some special phase of the conduct of life.

SHUTTLE, THE, by Frances Hodgson Burnett (1907). This is the story of an American girl who sells herself for a title and finds her experience dearly bought. Rosalie Vanderpool, a pretty butterfly, indulged from infancy by her wealthy parents and surrounded by every luxury that money can provide, marries Sir Nigel Anstruthers, a dissipated, degenerate Englishman, who visits New York for the purpose of securing an heiress to restore his shattered fortunes. Before the waning of the honeymoon Rosalie has discovered her terrible mistake and when her husband takes her home to his dilapidated estates and she is confronted by his mother, who equals him in coarseness and brutality, she realizes the horror of her position. Sir Nigel refuses to allow his wife any communication with her family and they, thinking she has lost her affection for them, consider her as lost to them. Twelve years elapse, and then Rosalie's younger sister Betty, who has reached the age of twenty years, and is a beautiful girl of great force of character, decides to visit her sister and find out what has caused the separation. She arrives unexpectedly at Stornham Court and is confronted by a haggard and shabby woman and a hunch-backed boy, who prove to be Rosalie and her eleven year-old-son, Ughtred. Betty learns with horror of her sister's terrible experiences, and hears of the brutal blow which caused her child's deformity and also of the making over of her money to her husband who has used it all for his own purposes. Sir Nigel being absent for a stay of several months Betty at once sets to work to improve matters. She repairs the house and grounds, buys new clothes for her sister and restores to her as much as possible her lost youth and happiness. Betty becomes deeply interested in Lord Mount Dunstan, a neighbor, who is living on his impoverished ancestral estates. Dunstan is a man of strong character and loves Betty but will not declare himself while he is poor and she is rich.

Sir Nigel returns from his holiday and fixes his degenerate eye on his attractive sister-in-law, who, when in a most critical position, is rescued from his clutches by Mount Dunstan. The latter horsewhips the brutal coward, as he deserves, and tells Betty of his love, to her great happiness. Sir Nigel dies of a paralytic shock and Mr. and Mrs. Vanderpool at last visit the home of their long-lost daughter.

SIBERIA, see TENT LIFE IN, by George Kennan.

SICILIAN VESPERS, THE, by Cassimir Delavigne. This tragedy in five acts, first performed in Paris in 1819, is only memorable from its subject, the "Sicilian Vespers," that being the name given to the massacre of the French in Sicily, in 1282, the signal for which was to be the first stroke of the vesper-bell. John of Procida returns from a visit to secure the aid of Pedro of Aragon in liberating Sicily from the French. His son Loredan has become the fast friend of Montfort, the representative of Charles of Anjou. Montfort asks Loredan to intercede for him with Princess Amelia, heir to the throne of Sicily, unaware that she is his betrothed. Procida orders his son to slay his friend, who is also his country's foe. Amelia warns Montfort, whom she loves despite her betrothal. Montfort, learning Loredan's claims upon her, upbraids him and banishes him; but his nobler impulses triumph, and he pardons him. Night falls; the massacre breaks out. Under cover of darkness, Loredan stabs his friend, who forgives him with his last breath. Loredan cries, "Thou shalt be avenged," and kills himself. His father exclaims, "O my country, I have restored thy honor, but have lost my son. Forgive these tears." Then, turning to his fellow-conspirators, "Be ready to fight at dawn of day." And so the play ends.

SIERRA NEVADA, MOUNTAINEERING IN THE, see MOUNTAINEERING, ETC.

SIGNOR IO, IL, by Salvatore Farina (1880). This story of the egoism of Marco Antonio Abaté, professor of philosophy in Milan, is charmingly told. In the first three chapters, the Professor, in the most naïve manner, tells of his detestation of egoism, and how he has sacrificed himself by allowing his dead wife, and living daughter Serafina, to make themselves happy by waiting on him. Iginio Curti, an opera singer, is the wolf who breaks up his happy home by marrying Serafina. Many letters from his daughter he returns unopened to Curti. Tiring of his solitary life, he advertises for a wife. In one of the answers, signed Marina, the writer says she is a young widow. He recognizes the handwriting of his daughter and writes for her to come home. She does so; and he finds Curti has told her nothing about the return of the letters, but has given her many presents, which, he said, came from her father, in place of letters.

Thinking Serafina ill, her father obliges her to go to bed; and he goes to bring the granddaughter, whom Serafina had left at home. His surprise is great when he finds Curti alive and healthy, and that Marina is an opera singer for whom Serafina had written the letter. When he discovers that Curti not only deceived his daughter as to her father's selfishness, but that his little granddaughter believes him to have sent her many presents, he says that hereafter he will teach his pupils that above all the treatises on philosophy, there is one that must be studied early and to the last day of our lives, self — Il Signor Io.

SIGNS AND SEASONS, by John Burroughs. This pleasing book of nature-studies was first published in 1886, and consists of thirteen essays. The first, entitled 'A Sharp Lookout,' treats of the signs of the weather and many other curious discoveries which the keen observations of the author have brought to light. He says: "One must always cross-question Nature if he would get at the truth, and he will not get at it then unless he questions with skill. Most persons are unreliable observers because they put only leading questions, or vague questions. . . . Nature will not be cornered, yet she does many things in a corner and surreptitiously. She is all things to all men; she has whole truths, half truths, and quarter truths, if not still smaller fractions. One secret of success in observing Nature is capacity to take a hint. It is not so much what we see as what the thing seen suggests. We all see about the same: to one it means much, to another little." The author is not one of those who preaches what he does not practice, and he gives the reader the result of his studies: the signs of the weather, the shape and position of plants and flowers, the habits of animals, birds, and bees, with apt quotations from other authors showing their opinions on the same subjects. One cannot read this book without wondering how he could possibly have passed so many things without noticing them; and the next walk in the woods will be taken with greater pleasure, because of the curiosity awakened by the author's observations. The other essays are entitled: 'A Spray of Pine,' 'Hard Fare,' 'The Tragedies of the Nests,' 'A Taste of Maine Birch,' 'Winter Neighbors,' 'A Salt Breeze,' 'A Spring Relish,' 'A River View,' 'Bird Enemies,' 'Phases of Farm Life,' and 'Roof-Tree.'

SILAS MARNER, by George Eliot (1861). This story of a poor, dull-witted Methodist cloth-weaver is ranked by many critics as the best of its author's books. The plot is simple and the field of the action narrow, the strength of the book lying in its delineations of character among the common people; for George Eliot has been truly called as much the "faultless painter" of bourgeois manners as Thackeray of drawing-room society. Silas Marner is a handloom weaver, a good man, whose life has been wrecked by a false accusation of theft, which cannot be disproved. For years he lives a lonely life, with the sole companionship of his loom; and he is saved from his own despair by the chance finding of a little child. On this baby girl he lavishes the whole passion of his thwarted nature, and her filial affection makes him a kindly man again. After sixteen years the real thief is discovered, and Silas's good name is restored. On this slight framework are hung the richest pictures of middle and low class life that George Eliot has painted. The foolish, garrulous rustics who meet regularly at the Rainbow Inn to guzzle beer and gossip are as much alive as Shakespeare's clowns; from the red-faced village farrier to little Mr. Macey, the tailor and parish-clerk, who feels himself a Socrates for wisdom. But perhaps the best character in the book is Dolly Winthrop, the wheelwright's wife, who looks in every day to comfort Silas, — a mild soul "whose nature it was to seek out all the sadder and more serious elements of life and pasture her mind on them"; and who utters a very widely accepted notion of religion when she says, after recommending Silas to go frequently to church, as she herself does, "When a bit o' trouble comes, I feel as I can put up wi' it, for I've looked for help i' the right quarter, and give myself up to Them as we must all give ourselves up to at the last; and if we've done our part, it isn't to be believed as Them as are above us 'ud be worse nor we are, and come short o' Theirn." "The plural pronoun," adds the author, "was no heresy of Dolly's but only her way of avoiding a presumptuous familiarity."

SILENCE OF DEAN MAITLAND, THE, by "Maxwell Grey" (Miss Mary G. Tuttiett) (1886). Cyril Maitland, a young clergyman of the Church of England, accidentally kills the father of a village girl whom he has led astray. The man's body is found, and circumstantial evidence points to Henry Everard, Cyril's lifelong friend and the lover of his twin sister. Cyril is silent; allows his friend to be sentenced to penal labor for twenty years. His sensitive soul suffers torture, but he cannot bear to lose the approval of man, which is very life to him. His little sister gives unconsciously the keynote of his character: "I think, papa, that Cyril is not so devoted to loving as to being loved."

Endowed with a magnetic personality that fascinates all, with a rare voice, and with wonderful eloquence, Cyril Maitland who becomes almost an ascetic in his penances and self-torture, gains great honor in the church, becomes dean, and is about to be appointed bishop. Life has proved hard to him. His wife and all his children, save one daughter and a blind son, have died, and the thought of his hidden sin has never left him.

On the day before that in which he is to preach the sermon that will put him in possession of the highest place in the church, he receives a letter from Everard who is out of prison after eighteen years of suffering, telling Cyril that he knows all, but forgives freely. This breaks the dean's heart. The next day he rises before the great audience of the cathedral and confesses all, — lays his secret soul bare before them. In the awful pause that follows the benediction, they approach Cyril, who has fallen into a chair, and find him dead.

The book falls just short of being great; it reminds one of 'The Scarlet Letter,' though it lacks the touch of the master hand.

SILENT WOMAN, THE, see EPICENE.

SIMPLE LIFE, THE, by Charles Wagner (1902). This book was translated from the French by Mary Louise Hendee, and opens with an introduction and biographical sketch of the author by Grace King. The title, 'The Simple Life,' gives at once the keynote to the contents of the volume. The author, who is deeply impressed with the increasing complexity of living, and the shams and worldliness of the present day, sets forth in a forcible manner the advantages to be derived from plain living and high thinking. He dwells upon the useless expenditure of time, strength, and money, upon those unnecessary things which instead of adding to one's happiness, increase one's cares and responsibilities. In describing the Complex life, which most people are striving to attain, Mr. Wagner shows how much valuable energy is wasted on the unimportant details of daily living, and how much better and happier people would be if they would only content themselves with simpler methods. After considering simplicity in a general way the author shows how it may be applied to "thought," "speech," "needs," and "pleasures." The mercenary spirit of the day and its attendant evils, pride and the love of notoriety, are dwelt upon and strongly denounced by the apostle of simple living. He recommends doing away with all that is artificial, and quenching the desire for wealth and power. He dwells upon the importance of the life in the home, and shows how necessary it is that the right thought and influence should prevail there. The home life, Mr. Wagner claims, is the germ of the whole social organism, and if the atmosphere can be kept free from worldliness the result will be felt in all social institutions. With regard to describing simplicity in any worthy manner the author declares his inability to do so, for he claims that all the strength, beauty, and joy of life come from that source.

SIMPLE STORY, A, by Mrs. Inchbald. 'A Simple Story' was written, as the preface to the first edition tells us, under the impulse of necessity in 1791. It is divided into two parts, and relates the love affairs of a mother and her daughter. In the first part, Miss Milner is left by her father under the guardianship of Mr. Dorriforth, a Catholic priest. To his displeasure, she leads a life of great gayety, surrounded by numerous suitors, among whom is prominent one Sir Frederick Lawnley. At the instigation of another priest, Sandford, who is irritated by Miss Milner's lack of stable virtue, Dorriforth removes with his ward to the country. There he urges her to declare her true feelings toward Lawnley. In the presence of Sandford she denies all interest in the young man; but the next day, on hearing that Dorriforth had, in a moment of anger, struck Lawnley for presuming to pursue her, and had thus exposed himself to the necessity of a duel, she decides that her profession of indifference was false. Still she refuses absolutely to continue her acquaintance with Lawnley. To Miss Woodley, her friend, she furnishes a key to her contradictions by declaring that she really loves Dorriforth. Miss Woodley, shocked at such a passion for a priest, insists on her departure to visit some friends. During this visit, Dorriforth becomes Lord Elmwood, and obtains dispensation from his priestly vows. On hearing, through Miss Woodley, of the true state of his ward's feelings, he declares himself her lover; but her frivolity and disregard of his wishes make him break the engagement. Her sorrow at his departure for Italy, however, is so great that Sandford, convinced of their mutual love, marries them, and dismisses the carriage which was to take him away.

During the interval between the first and second parts of the story, Lady Elmwood, led astray by Sir Frederick, has been banished with her daughter from her husband's presence, and his nephew Rushbrook is adopted as his heir. At the death of his wife, Elmwood consents that his daughter Matilda and the faithful Woodley may live in his country house, provided that he never see his daughter or hear her name. Rushbrook falls in love with Matilda, and almost incurs his uncle's extreme displeasure by his hesitation to confess the object of his love. At last Matilda meets her father quite by accident on the stairs, and is banished to a farm near by. Here she is consoled by frequent visits from Sandford, who intercedes with her father for her as far as he dares. At length Lord Margrave, a neighboring peer, attracted by her beauty, carries her to his house by force. News is brought to Lord Elmwood, who pursues, rescues, and restores his daughter to her rightful position. Out of gratitude for his compassion when she was unfortunate, she accepts Rushbrook's love with the happiest results.

The characters are often inconsistent; they are cruel or kind, they weep, faint, curse, without any apparent motive. At the end, the author declares that the object of the tale is to show the value of "a proper education."

SIN OF JOOST AVELINGH, THE, by "Maarten Maartens" (1890). This writer's real name is J. M. W. Van der Poorten Schwartz. Although he is a Dutchman, his stories are all written in English, and afterwards translated into Dutch for home use. The scene of this is Holland. Joost is an orphan, shy, morbid, and misunderstood. His uncle, with whom he lives, forces him to study medicine, which he hates, and forbids him to marry Agatha van Hessel. As Joost is driving him to the notary to change his will, he dies of apoplexy. Joost inherits his money and marries Agatha. Ten years later, Arthur van Aeveld, the next heir, meets the servant who sat behind the carriage on the night of the Baron's death, and persuades him to swear that Joost murdered his uncle. At the last moment, he confesses his perjury. Joost is acquitted, and made a member of the States General. He declares that though not actually a murderer, he is guilty, in that he hated his uncle, did nothing to help him in his extremity, and drove straight on in spite of the old man's appeal to him to stop. With his wife's concurrence, he gives up his money and political position, becomes clerk to a notary, and is happy on a small salary.

SINGULAR LIFE, A, by Elizabeth Stuart Phelps (1896). This is the story of Emanuel Bayard, a young man of noble character, and deeply religious nature, who having been brought up among luxurious surroundings, chooses to give up all for the cause of Christ. Being an orphan, he has lived from childhood with his rich uncle, Mr. Hermon Worcester, who intends to make him his heir. Bayard goes to the Theological Seminary at Cesarea where he cannot sincerely subscribe to some of the doctrines and is accordingly judged "unsound," and thereby wins the disapproval of the faculty and also of his uncle, who is one of the trustees of the seminary. He accepts a call to a small parish in Windover, a seaport town, where he ministers with great patience and self-sacrifice to a congregation made up from the roughest and lowest elements of society. While in Cesarea, Bayard had gained the friendship of Helen Carruth, the daughter of the professor of Theology, a handsome and brilliant girl, whom later he passionately loves; he undergoes many struggles before he can convince himself that it is right for him to marry, or to ask Helen to share his poverty, but finally his great love, which she reciprocates, conquers all obstacles. Bayard's uncle dies and leaves him a small legacy, which is however sufficient to make him independent, and he and Helen are married. They return from their wedding trip for the dedication of Bayard's new chapel for which he has labored untiringly and which is called the Church of "Christlove." As they are leaving the chapel after the service, Bayard is struck by a missile from the hands of a miserable wretch named Ben Trawl. The blow proves fatal and after a week of suffering, borne with fortitude and courage and tended by his heartbroken wife, Bayard dies, leaving behind him the legacy of an unselfish and noble life.

SINISTER STREET, by Compton Mackenzie (2 vols., 1913-1914). The first volume was published in the United States under the title 'Youth's Encounter,' and is the story of a boy's encounter with life from his childhood to his eighteenth year. The sympathetic analysis of his thoughts and feelings and the detailed account of the most trivial incidents of his days give this study of the mind of childhood and youth reality and absorbing interest. From his own childish point of view, and with immature defective reasoning about his surroundings, he tells how his adored mother is almost always abroad, and he and his baby sister, Stella, are left to the indifferent care of a succession of incompetent and drunken servants. His lonely dreary childhood ends with the arrival of a governess, who is hereafter always a friend and protecting influence in his life. The chief incidents of the development of Michael's adolescence are his interest in religion and his amorous adventures. The mystery of his mother's long absences from home is now explained. Lord Saxby is killed in the South African war and Mrs. Fane tells Michael and Stella that he was their father. His wife had refused to give him a divorce, so that he can only leave his fortune to Michael, who is illegitimate, and cannot inherit the title.

In the second volume Michael begins life all over again in the undergraduate world of Oxford. The first part of this volume, 'Dreaming Spires,' the minutely detailed picture of these Oxford years is a complete novel in itself. The second part, 'Romantic Education,' is Michael's experiences in "Sinister Street," the underworld of London, in quixotic search of his boyhood sweetheart. Lily, whom he undertakes to rescue and redeem. He learns the underworld very thoroughly before he finds Lily, and gains knowledge of many types of women, the lodging-house keeper, the lodger in the basement den, Miss Poppy Grace, who is insulted because he offers her a present of money but declines the favors she is willing to give in exchange, and Daisy Smith, with whom he succeeds in establishing friendly relations. The beautiful, languid Lily at last reappears, but slips back to her old ways before he can marry her. Michael takes his broken heart to Rome, and there is a hint that he may find a purpose in life in the Catholic church. The author says, "My intention was not to write a life, but the prologue of a life. The theme of 'Sinister Street' is the youth of a man who presumably will be a priest."

SINNER, THE, by Antonio Fogazzaro, see **THE PATRIOT.**

SIR CHARLES DANVERS, see **THE DANVERS JEWELS.**

SIR CHARLES GRANDISON, Samuel Richardson's third and last novel, was published in 1754, when the author was sixty-five years of age. In it he essayed to draw the portrait of what he conceived to be an ideal gentleman of the period, — the eighteenth century. The result was that he presented the world, not at all with the admirable figure he had intended, but with an insufferable prig surrounded by a bevy of worshiping ladies. The novel, both in character-drawing and story-interest, is much below his earlier work. 'Sir Charles Grandison' shows his genius in its decline, after the brilliant earlier successes. The plot is neither intricate nor interesting. It centres in the very proper wooing of Harriet Byron by the hero; who wins her, as the reader has no doubt he will, and who in the course of his wooing exhibits towards her and her sex an unexampled chivalry which strikes one as unnatural. Grandison has everything in his favor, — money, birth, good looks, high principle, and universal success; and one cannot help wishing this impossible paragon to come down off his high horse, and be natural, even at the expense of being naughty. The novelist overreached himself in this fiction, which added nothing to the fame of the creator of 'Pamela' and 'Clarissa.' Richardson had sympathy for and insight into the heart feminine, but for the most part failed egregiously with men, — though Lovelace in 'Clarissa Harlowe' is an exception. Like all his novels, 'Sir Charles Grandison' is written in epistolary form.

SIR GEORGE TRESSADY, by Mrs. Humphry Ward, is in some sense a sequel to 'Marcella,' since that heroine's life after marriage is traced in it, and she is the central character of the story. It was published in 1896, two years after the earlier book. Its hero, however, is Tressady, a young baronet and owner of an iron mine. He becomes engaged to a pretty, light chit of a girl, and marries her, without any deep feeling of love or serious consideration of the bond. He then falls under the influence of Marcella, now Lady Raeburn, who likes him and hopes to win his political support for her husband, Aldous Raeburn, a prominent statesman. The feeling deepens to love on Tressady's side; but he is saved from himself by the nobility of Marcella, who gently rebukes her lover and is steadily loyal to Aldous. Through her mediation a better relation is established between Tressady and his wife, who is soon to become a mother. But Tressady's career is brought to an untimely and tragic close. During the labor troubles in his mines, he descends a shaft and is killed in an explosion. Burning questions of politics and political economy are ably handled in the story. which also, as a chief motive, deals with woman's relation to

politics and public place.   On the whole, it is of a more sombre cast than 'Marcella';
but it is interesting, for its presentation of modern problems.

SIR NIGEL, by A. Conan Doyle (1906).   This is a historical romance and tale of
adventure, the scene of which is laid in England in the fourteenth century.   In
prefacing the story, the author asserts that he has taken great pains to make the local
coloring correct and has studied many authorities in order to make the book an
authentic historic reproduction.   The hero of the tale is Nigel Loring, the descendant
of a noble family and the last of his race.   In the opening chapters he is living alone
with his aged grandmother, Lady Ermyntrude Loring, upon a small remnant of their
great estate which has been devastated by pestilence and wrested from them by law.
Even this small holding is in danger of passing out of their hands, as for years a feud
has existed between the monks of Waverley and the house of Loring, and the former
are endeavoring to make the impoverishment of the Lorings complete.   King Edward
and his suite pay a visit to Tilford Manor House, the Loring home, and in order to
provide for his entertainment Lady Ermyntrude sells a jewelled goblet, a bracelet,
and a golden salver that are her choicest possessions.   The King is pleased with
young Nigel, and when the latter sues to be taken into his service, he makes him
squire to Sir John Chandos, one of his principal knights.   The financial embarrassment of the Lorings is relieved by the King and he settles the difficulties that over
shadow their estate.   Nigel fits himself with armor and goes to join the King after
having taken leave of his sweetheart Mary Buttesthorn, daughter of Sir John Buttesthorn, a neighbor and friend.   Nigel's military experiences are both varied and
eventful.   He is involved in adventures of all kinds but his courage and intrepidity
bring him safely through his many perils.   The climax of Nigel's military career is
reached when he is fighting against the French under the Black Prince with his
beloved master Chandos and plays a prominent part at the time of the surrender of
King John.   For his valor on this occasion he is knighted by the Black Prince and
returns home as Sir Nigel Loring to wed his faithful lady-love.   The experiences
recounted in this volume are prior to those related in 'The White Company,' a
previous publication.

SIR RICHARD CALMADY, THE HISTORY OF, by Lucas Malet (1901).   This
powerful story opens with a picture of the ancestral home of the Calmadys, in which
the hero's father seems destined to enjoy, with his young wife, complete and lasting
happiness.   Then follows an accident in the hunting field and Sir Richard is brought
home mangled; he dies despite the efforts of the surgeons to save him by amputating
his injured legs.   A few months later the hero of the book is born, a beautiful healthy
child in all respects save one — the lower part of each leg is missing, the feet being
attached at the point where the knees should be.   As child and young man, Sir
Richard Calmady behaves in the most exemplary manner, despite his misfortune
and the constant reminders of it, from which his wealth and position cannot shield
him.   Lady Calmady's life is devoted to her son, and some of the scenes between the
two are the best in the book.   The young man wishing to marry, selects a sweet but
stupid little scion of the nobility, who at the eleventh hour begs to be released in order
to marry another.   Sir Richard now undergoes a moral revolution and gives himself
up to dissipation.   He succumbs to the wiles of a fair and wayward cousin, only to
be afterward insulted and maltreated at the hands of one of her cast-off lovers.
Nursed back from the resulting fever by his neglected mother, who hastens to his bedside in Naples, he at last returns home, a confirmed misanthrope and misogynist

Becoming convinced, however, of the wrongfulness of this attitude of mind, he turns his attention to charity and founds a home for cripples, and as a reward wins the heart and hand of a handsome and admirable woman, with whom his acquaintance has hitherto been a superficial one. The book abounds in epigram, allusion, and vivid character-painting, but its unshrinking realism is sometimes repellent.

SLEEPING BEAUTY, see **FAIRY TALES.**

SMOKE BELLEW, by Jack London (1912). This is a tale of wild adventures in the Klondike, in which Christopher Bellew, nicknamed "Smoke" proves himself the hero of countless marvelous exploits. Bellew, who has drifted into journalism in San Francisco, is invited by his uncle to take a short trip to the gold-region, the elder man deploring the "softness" of his dilettante nephew, who seems to have degenerated from the hardihood and physical prowess of his race. At the first taste of the wild life, however, the young man's inheritance asserts itself and he decides to remain in the Klondike instead of returning with his uncle. He immediately plunges into the strenuous activities of the North and in a short space of time trains himself to battle successfully with the elements and to endure the terrible hardships of the country. At the outset he is spurred on by an encounter with a spirited girl named Joy Gastell, whose father is an "Old-timer" and who from childhood has been accustomed to cast her lot in with the hardy explorers. From time to time Bellew encounters this daring beauty, who aids him at several critical junctures and to whom he is able to render important services in return. In company with his special chum "Shorty," Bellew works his way up to Dawson and subsists for some time by hunting and trading in moose-meat. The friends join an exciting stampede to Squaw Creek to take out claims, but are outwitted by Joy Gastell, who, in the interest of her father leads them on to a wrong trail. Later she makes amends for this trick by offering Bellew a chance to secure another claim to acquire which he has a neck-and-neck race with a formidable rival "Big Olaf"; the result is a tie which causes the two to divide the claim. Bellew has a thrilling escape from death on a glacier where in order to save his companion he cuts loose from the rope which is attached to the other; he outwits a coterie of gamblers at Dawson and thereby amasses a large sum of money and after many experiences he is captured by a tribe of Indians and forced to remain in their isolated settlement. He finally makes his escape in company with the daughter of the chief, who is a white man; the girl has fallen in love with him, and heroically aids him in his return to freedom, herself perishing from starvation just as the goal is reached; here Bellew once more meets the faithful "Shorty" with whom he hastens back to join Joy Gastell whom he has long loved and who is impatiently awaiting his return.

SNOW-BOUND, 'a Winter Idyll,' by John Greenleaf Whittier, was published in 1866. It is described by him as "a picture of an old-fashioned farmer's fireside in winter." The metre resembles that of Scott's 'Lay of the Last Minstrel'; iambic tetrameter couplets predominate, but occasionally, alternating or interlacing rhymes are introduced to vary the movement. In depicting a New-England family gathering on a snowy winter evening Whittier is describing his own home circle as it was in his boyhood at East Haverhill, Massachusetts. After an account of the farm-house shut off from the world by a roaring blizzard — an account made particularly vivid by a wealth of homely and expressive detail — Whittier shows the group about the blazing oak fire. The father tells of his wanderings in Canadian forests and lumber camps and his labors on the marshes and fishing-grounds of the New England coast. The mother describes Indian raids and massacres during the French wars in New Hampshire or reads from old Quaker books of martyrology and religious experience. The uncle delights the children with his rich lore of hunting and fishing, and the aunt describes the huskings and apple-bees of her girlhood. The village schoolmaster speaks of "classic Dartmouth's college halls," plays the fiddle, and tells of his experiences at parties in country settlements. There is present a guest, Harriet Livermore, a religious enthusiast, a traveler, and a woman of the world. Her complex and unstable temperament and her charm of personality are brilliantly portrayed by the poet. Fraternal tributes are also paid to Whittier's brother and two sisters. The storm keeps the party snow-bound for a week, during which the various occupations and amusements of the farm are described with the poet's usual fidelity. 'Snowbound' is a characteristic product of rural New England — its scenery, types of character, mode of life, and ideals are thoroughly representative of the soil. The absolute truth and sincerity of the poem, its pictorial power, and its family loyalty and affection are its outstanding merits.

SOCIAL CONTRACT, THE ('Contrat social'); or, PRINCIPLES OF POLITICAL RIGHT, by Jean Jacques Rousseau. In French this is a masterpiece of style. The principle that "Will, not force, is the basis of the State" has never been more effectively proclaimed. 'The Social Contract' was published in 1762, and was regarded as the catechism of the French Revolution. Its influence on European life and thought was enormous. Rousseau's aim was to guarantee individual rights and social liberty by transforming existent States; and in explaining this he dwelt upon the rightful authority of the general will. 'The Social Contract' has little or no claim to originality, but the borrowed doctrines are strikingly presented. The work is divided into four books, treating respectively of — (1) The origin of civil society in a contract; (2) the theory of sovereignty and the general will; (3) the constitution of a government; and (4) civil religion. It overthrows the old conception that property and birth should alone give a title to political power, and upholds the claim of the toilers to share in the government of the State which they sustain by their productive labor.

SOCIAL EQUALITY: 'A Short Study in a Missing Science,' by William Hurrell Mallock (1882). This original and acute work asserts the need of a new science, applicable to that field after considering which modern democracy declares social equality to be the only hope of mankind. This science is the "science of human character"; and Mr. Mallock aims to point out its limits, and the order of facts of which it will take cognizance, reviewing the most important of these and stating the chief general conclusion that will result from them. His main points are as follows: That human character naturally desires, as soon as seen, inequality in external circumstances, or social inequality (a condition which not only produces this desire, but in turn is produced by it). All labor is caused by motive, lacking which man is not a laboring animal; and motive is the resultant of character and external circumstances, i. e., of a desire for social inequality, and of a social inequality answering the desire, — respectively the subjective and the objective side of the same thing. Inequality supplies the motive, not indeed of all human activity, but of all productive labor, except the lowest. Social inequality, then, Mallock asserts, has been, is, and so far as we have any opportunity of knowing, ever will be, the divinely appointed means of human progress — whether impersonal as expressed in enterprises, discoveries. and inventions, or personal as expressed in the social conditions under which the enterprises, discoveries, and inventions have been made and utilized. Social equality he regards as a hindrance to progress, and a cause of retrogression. He thus joins issue squarely with the socialists, strives to confute them even out of their own mouths, and asserts that facts, reason, and science, lie not with them but with the present order of society. The book is written with great clearness and directness, and an abundance of illustrative instances. It is the work of a scholar, and of a keen and vigorous thinker; and is an admirable text-book for conservatives.

SOCIAL LIFE IN GREECE FROM HOMER TO MENANDER, by John Pentland Mahaffy (1874. 3d ed., 1877), is a delightful and instructive book which aims at presenting to us not so much petty details as the large and enduring features of the life of the Greeks, — enough, certainly, about their food, their dress, and their houses, but especially "how they reasoned, and felt, and loved; why they laughed and why they wept; how they taught and what they learned." The picture, of course, is mostly Athenian, since only Athenian colors exist for the painting. The result is not only of literary and antiquarian, but also of practical value, as showing how high a civilization was attained by a people that had to contend with a worthless theology, with slavery, and with ignorance of the art of printing. Professor Mahaffy writes in no mere archæological spirit, but with his eye always on the present and the future, — as where he refers to the present French republic, the theory of "might being right," and the cause of the Irish. The topics treated are: 'The Greeks of the Homeric Age'; 'The Greeks of the Lyric Age'; 'The Greeks of the Attic Age'; 'Attic Culture'; 'Trades and Professions'; 'Entertainments and Conversation'; 'The Social Position of Boys in Attic Life'; 'Religious Feeling'; and 'Business Habits.'

SOCIAL LIFE IN OLD VIRGINIA BEFORE THE WAR, by Thomas Nelson Page (1896). This little volume, which in a way recalls Washington Irving's 'Sketch Book,' is a sympathetic sketch of Southern ante-bellum plantation life, portraying a state of society incredible to those who had no experience of it, and probably to-day all but incredible to those who once knew it best. Beginning with the "great house," its grounds, gardens, and outbuildings, the personality and life of the mistress, of the master, and of their daughters and sons, first pass before us. Then come portraits of those august functionaries: the "carriage driver," the butler, and "mammy" the nurse; even the gardeners, the "boys about the house," the young ladies' "own maids," and the very furniture, are not forgotten. The description embraces both great house and cabins. The mysteries of "spending a month or two," of "spending the day" (i.e., dining), and of Sunday hospitalities, are dissolved; the varying seasons, the fox hunt, Christmas festivities, the ladies' "patterns" and the gentlemen's politics, — all sides of that complex existence appear. And the conclusion of the whole matter is, that while the social life of the Old South had its faults, "its graces were never equaled."

SOCIAL LIFE OF THE CHINESE, 'With Some Account of their Religions, Governmental, Educational, and Business Customs and Opinions,' by Justus Doolittle (2 vols., illustrated. 1865). The author of this valuable work was for fourteen years a member of the Foochow mission of the American Board, during which time he had abundant opportunity of studying the Chinese. The work is somewhat loosely written, most of it being in the form in which it was originally published as a series of letters in the China Mail of Hong Kong; but it is one of the best of the few authorities on "the inner life of the most ancient and populous, but least understood and appreciated, of nations." Though it has special reference to Foochow and it: vicinity, the description of many of the social and superstitious customs is applicable to other parts of the empire, though sometimes customs vary greatly in the different Chinese provinces. It treats of agriculture and domestic matters, betrothal and marriage, married life and children, treatment of disease, death, mourning and burial, ancestral tablets and ancestral halls, priests, popular gods and goddesses, mandarins and their subordinates, competitive literary examinations, established annual customs and festivals, superstitions, charitable practices, social customs, charms and omens, fortune-telling, opium-smoking, etc. Altogether it is a treasury of information about Chinese life, and may be considered trustworthy in its statements.

SOCIAL PROBLEM, THE; 'a Constructive Analysis,' by C. A. Ellwood (1915). A rapid change of opinion has taken place during the last generation in the way of approach to social problems. Dr. Ellwood's volume, which is chosen because it is a fair sample out of a large number dominated by the same social philosophy, is dedicated "to the far-thinking men and women of the twentieth century, who must solve the social problem." Its aim is to present not only a brief analysis of the many-headed social problem as we see it in Western States, but an outline sketch of a social philosophy which shall serve as a basis for well-ordered progress. The social problem is considered in its historic, physical, biological, economic, and spiritual aspects, for it contains factors which belong to each of the categories mentioned, and no analysis which fails to take account not only of each of them, but of their relation to one another can be considered adequate. "The solution of the social problem," says Dr. Ellwood, "requires neither superhuman intelligence nor superhuman character." Nor will it come about by concentration on mere externals, or mere machinery, nor yet by sudden catastrophic change, or methods of violence. Social evils will gradually disappear before better education, better environment, and the development of a well-balanced program of social progress. This well-balanced program will be based upon certain broad principles, which are more and more coming to be accepted, as for example, "Business is for social service, and not for private profit." The policy of industrial insurance and legislative protection must be developed and extended. Dr. Ellwood, moreover, strongly maintains that "scientific reform of taxation is probably the most important administrative method by which the injustices and inequalities of our present economic system can be overcome."

SOCIAL SILHOUETTES, by Edgar Fawcett (1885), is a series of gracefully ironic sketches upon New York society. Mr. Mark Manhattan, born among the elect, related to most of the Knickerbocker families, and blessed with an adequate income, amuses his leisure by a study of social types. He introduces us to the charmed circle of Rivingtons, Riversides, Croton-Nyacks, Schenectadys, and others, all opulent, all sublimely sure of their own superiority to the rest of humanity. With a serene pity born of intimate knowledge of society's prizes, he watches the rich parvenu, Mrs. Ridgeway Bridgeway, push her way to recognition. There is the young lady who fails because her evident anxiety to please repels with a sense of strain all who approach her. There is the young man who succeeds because he makes no effort, and although able to express "nothing except manner and pronunciation," has name and dollars. Mr. Bradford Putnam is another type, an egotistic nonentity without a thought in his mind or a generous sentiment in his heart, who arrogantly enjoys what the gods have provided. Mr. Mark Manhattan does not think that "the brave little Mayflower steered its pale, half-starved inmates through bleak storm of angry seas to help them found an ancestry for such idle dalliers." He is a kindly cynic with sympathy for those who suffer in intricate social meshes, and with contempt for all false standards and hypocrisy. He is not a reformer, but an indolent spectator with a sense of humor, who, after all, enjoys the society which he wittily berates.

SOCIALISM, 'a Critical Analysis,' by O. D. Skelton (1911). This analysis of Socialism is distinguished by wide knowledge of the multifarious literature of the subject, by thorough grasp of political science in general, and by a willingness to see what is good in Socialists and Socialist programs. This can be said of few books written by way of examination of the proposals of the Socialists who have usually, during the last generation, had by far the best of the argument. Professor Skelton's work is one of the ablest works on the anti-Socialist side which have appeared in English. He states and criticizes the Socialist indictment of society, and subjects to a patient and thorough analysis the theory of Karl Marx that the economic factor in history has been the most important, that a class struggle between capitalist and proletarian has arisen out of economic conditions, and that capitalist development, based on the exploitation of surplus value, leads inevitably to the breakdown of capitalism and the establishment of socialism. The last two chapters discuss the modern socialist ideal and the modern socialist movement, as exemplified in Germany, France, the United Kingdom, and the United States. There is a valuable bibliography of books and current periodical literature.

SOCIALISM, FABIAN SOCIETY ESSAYS IN (1889). The Fabian Society is an organization of intellectual Socialists, having their headquarters in London with affiliated but independent branches in other parts of Great Britain and Ireland. It includes a large number of extremely thoughtful, well-informed, and energetic members, whose influence on the thought and life of the country has been out of all proportion to their numbers. The present volume consists of eight essays. Sidney Webb discusses the historic, William Clarke the industrial, Sydney Olivier, the moral, and G. B. Shaw, the economic basis of socialism. Graham Wallas has a paper on property, and Mrs. Annie Besant one on industry under socialism, while G. B. Shaw outlines the "Transition to Social Democracy" and Hubert Bland estimates the outlook for Socialism. Each of the seven writers here mentioned, though little known at the time of the publication of these essays, has since made a mark either in the field of sociology, political science, administration, or journalism, and the essays, of which scores of thousands of copies have been sold, have had an extraordinary influence in the shaping of political thought and development during the last generation.

SŒURS VATARD, LES, see **EN ROUTE.**

SOHRAB AND RUSTUM, a narrative poem by Matthew Arnold, first appeared in a volume of his poems published in 1853. In the sub-title he calls it 'An Episode,' evidently intending it as an imagined extract from a long epic poem in the Homeric manner. Its rapidity, simplicity, vividness, and nobility are all in accordance with his views of Homer's style, and the epic similes, proper names, and descriptive details are so selected as to suggest by their local color the Asiatic background. The story — that of a combat between a father and a son who do not know one another — is a well-known theme of heroic poetry, occurring in the Old High German 'Hildebrandslied' and in the Persian poet Firdausi's epic, 'Shah Namah,' the ultimate source of Arnold's poem. Rustum, the mightiest chieftain of the Persians, in the course of his wanderings, marries the daughter of the king of Ader-baijan, but leaves her in order to continue his military exploits. She bears him a son named Sohrab, but fearing that the father will take him away to be a warrior sends Rustum word that the child is a girl. Sohrab, grown to young manhood and longing to find his father, takes service with the Tartar king, Afrasiab, hoping to draw the attention of Rustum by his feats of arms. As a means of quicker fame he takes occasion of an impending battle between the Tartars and the Persians to challenge the bravest Persian champion to single fight. Rustum, who is with the Persian army, though retired like Achilles on account of the Persian king's neglect, yields to the entreaties of his fellow-chieftains and accepts the challenge, but in plain armor and without announcing his name. When Sohrab first sees his antagonist he has an intuition that it is Rustum and eagerly inquires if this is not so. But Rustum, ignorant of his motive and suspecting him of seeking some pretext not to fight, refuses to reveal his identity and dares Sohrab to come on. In their first encounter, after an exchange of spears, Sohrab cleverly evades his opponent's club, by the weight of which Rustum loses his balance and falls; but Sohrab courteously refrains from this advantage and offers truce. Rustum, however, is enraged at his downfall and renews the struggle with fury. The fight is long and close and made more dreadful by a sand-storm which envelops the combatants. At length Rustum, hard-pressed, shouts his own name with the effect that Sohrab, in bewilderment, ceases to fight and is pierced by his father's spear. Dying on the sand he declares that Rustum, his father, will avenge his death; and in the affecting scene which follows, the truth at last comes out by means of a seal pricked on Sohrab's arm by his mother. At the close of the poem the father is left mourning over his son by the banks of the Oxus; and the poet's description of the river's northward course under the stars and moonlight to the Aral Sea affords a welcome relief from the emotional tension of the story.

SOIL, THE, see **ROUGON-MACQUART.**

SOLDIERS OF FORTUNE, by Richard Harding Davis (1897), is a spirited novel of adventure. The scene is laid in Olancho, the capital of a little seething South-American republic, on the eve of one of its innumerable revolutions. The hero is Robert Clay, a self-made man, an engineer, general manager, and resident director of the Valencia Mining Company in Olancho. Although the novel is full of adventure, it is primarily a study of two types of women, two sisters, the daughters of Mr. Langham, president of the company. The elder is a New York society girl of a most finished type, — self-possessed, calmly critical, with emotions well in check, noble, but not noble to the point of bad form. Her sister Hope, not yet out, is enthusiastic, generous, sweet. Robert Clay meets the elder, Alice Langham, at a dinner just before he sails for South America. He has long known of her through portraits in the society newspapers. He has an ideal of her as a woman unspoiled by wealth and position. He half confides to her his admiration of her. Later when he learns that she and her sister, with their father, are coming to Olancho to visit their brother and to see the mines, he is wild with delight. But he is doomed to disappointment in the character of Alice. Appreciative and sensitive as she seems, she has herself too well under control, is always afraid of going too far, is never quite sure of Robert Clay's desirability as a husband. Her coldness chills and alienates Clay. Hope, on the other hand, gives expression to her genuine enthusiasm. She is delighted with the strangeness of the life, is as interested in the mines as if she herself were a director. In the dangers and excitements of the revolution, which breaks out during her visit, she displays courage, nerve, and womanliness. The nobility in Clay's nature draws her to him. He loves her and claims her for his wife. Alice is left to marry a conventional society man of her own type. 'Soldiers of Fortune' is well written and readable. Full of excitement as it is, the dramatic incidents in it are yet subordinated to the delineation of character.

SOLL UND HABEN, see **DEBIT AND CREDIT.**

SOMERVILLE, MARY, PERSONAL RECOLLECTIONS OF, 'With Selections from her Correspondence,' by her daughter, Martha Somerville (1874).

Never has the simplicity of true greatness been more clearly shown than in the life of Mary Somerville, the life of a woman entirely devoted to family duties and scientific pursuits; whose energy and perseverance overcame almost insuperable obstacles at a time when women were excluded from the higher branches of education by prejudice and tradition; whose bravery led her to enter upon unknown paths, and to make known to others what she acquired by so courageous an undertaking. After a slight introduction concerning her family and birth, which took place December 26th, 1780, the 'Recollections' begin in early childhood and continue to the day of her death. She lived to the ripe old age of ninety-two, preserving her clearness of intellect to the end; holding fast her faith in God, which no censure of bigot, smile of skeptic, or theory of science could shake; adding to the world's store of knowledge to her final day, — her last work being the revision and completion of a treatise on the 'Theory of Differences'; and leaving behind for the benefit of the new generation annals of a life so wonderful in its completed work, so harmonious in its domestic relations, so unassuming in its acceptance of worldly distinctions, that the mere reading of it elevates and strengthens.

There are charming descriptions of childhood days in the Scottish home of Burntisland; days of youth when she arose after attending a ball to study at five in the morning; a delicate reticence concerning the first short-lived marriage with her cousin Craig, succeeded by the truer union with another cousin, the "Somerville" of whom she speaks with much tenderness; domestic gains and losses, births and deaths; the beginnings, maturings, and successes of her work; trips to London and the Continent; visits to and from the great; the idyllic life in Italy, where she died and is buried: loving records of home work and home pleasures; sorrows bravely met and joys glorified, — all told with the unaffectedness which was the keynote to her amiable character. Little information is given of the immense labor which preceded her famous works. The woman who, as Laplace said, was the only woman who could understand his work, who was honored by nearly every scientific society in the world, whose mind was akin to every famous mind of the age, so withdraws her individuality to give place to others, that the reader is often inclined to forget that the modest writer has other claims to notice than her intimate acquaintance with the great. And as in many social gatherings she was overlooked from her modesty of demeanor; so in these 'Recollections,' pages of eulogy are devoted to the achievements of those whose intellect was to hers as "moonlight is to sunlight," while her own successes are ignored, except in the inserted letters of those who awarded her her due meed of praise, and in the frequent notes of her faithful compiler.

SON EXCELLENCE EUGÈNE ROUGON, see **ROUGON-MACQUART.**

SONG OF SONGS, THE ('Das Hohe Lied'), by Hermann-Sudermann (1908). This detailed life story of the downfall of a weak and unfortunate woman is a merciless analysis, step by step, of gradual degeneration of character and degradation. Lily Czepanek, left without protectors, is foredoomed to shipwreck by her romantic, impulsive disposition. Her father, a musician and composer, deserts his family when she is fourteen, and two years later her mother is placed in an insane asylum. Lily has to give up school and go to work in a circulating library. Her teacher, to whom she is devoted, warns her to be on her guard against qualities which may be her undoing. He tells her she has "three kinds of love: love of the heart, love of the senses, and love springing from pity." He says, "Two are dangerous. All three lead to ruin." She longs always to be a rescuing angel to the people around her. In the circulating library her beauty brings her to the notice of the officers of the regiment in the town. The Colonel, an aristocratic libertine, marries her. A young officer, member of the household, whom she tries to reform, seduces her, and she is divorced by her husband. She tries to earn her living by painting china, encouraged by a man who finally allows her to discover that he is her only buyer. She becomes his mistress. When she is twenty-five she meets a young man whom she loves and who loves her and wants to marry her. She tries to write him a letter giving a true account of her life. The letter makes her appear a low-lived adventuress. She tears it up and writes another in which she seems a noble woman deceived. She realizes that neither is the truth. Her associations have so degraded her that though her lover is willing to condone the past, this last chance of regeneration proves impossible. She tries to commit suicide, but has not the courage, and returns to her former lover, who marries her to keep her. Her self-analysis in dialogue with her conscience, her fits of repentance, and struggles to escape from her weakness, and her final self-recognition and submission to circumstance make an interesting though repellent psychological study.

SONG OF THE LARK, THE, by Willa Sibert Cather (1915), is the story of a poor young girl who becomes an opera star. Thea Kronborg is the daughter of a Swedish minister in Moonstone, Arizona, who has a large family and small means. At an early age Thea shows a talent for music and her mother contrives that it shall be cultivated. When she is sixteen she receives a legacy of six hundred dollars and with this money she goes to Chicago to continue her study of the piano. Here she is advised to take up voice-culture, and this she does with the result that she develops a phenomenal voice. She meets a wealthy young brewer named Fred Ottenburg, who becomes much interested in her and furthers her career by assisting her socially and financially. Ottenburg has been unhappily married, and is separated, but not divorced, from his wife. Thea, who is ignorant of his past, becomes deeply attached to him and accepts his invitation to a ranch in the Arizona mountains owned by his father. She joins him there, and he later persuades her to journey with him to New Mexico, after which he tells her that he is not free to marry her, much as he desires to do so. Thea refuses to accept any more aid from him, and as soon as she reaches New York sends for an old friend, Dr. Archie, who advances her the funds necessary to enable her to study in Germany. There she spends ten years perfecting her art, at the end of which time she returns to New York a successful prima donna, and sings the leading rôles in Wagnerian opera. Eventually Thea marries Ottenburg, who is at last free. The story presents a vivid picture of American life and is a searching study of the career and temperament of the professional musician.

51

SONIA, by Henri Gréville (1878). This is a powerful and impressive, and at the same time charming and refined, story of Russian life. Sonia is a poor little slave girl, who is knocked about and abused by the brutal aristocrats, bearing the name of Goréline, whom she serves. The cruel treatment continues until a young tutor, named Boris Grébof, comes to the château to give lessons to Eugène and Lydie, the son and daughter of the household. He pities Sonia and is kind to her; and she in return feels for him the deepest affection. Boris falls in love with Lydie, who is a very pretty girl, and wins from her a promise of marriage; but as soon as Madame Goréline discovers the attachment, she is filled with rage and at once dismisses the tutor. He takes Sonia, who has also been driven from the house, to his home, where she remains in the employ of his kindly aged mother for several years. Boris continues to cherish his affection for Lydie all this time, and she allows him to consider himself engaged to her; although she, being weak and fickle, is constantly on the lookout for a chance to make a more brilliant match. Eventually she casts Boris off; and he, discovering the falseness of her nature, is consoled, and in course of time marries his faithful serving-maid, Sonia, who has become a handsome and capable girl, and has acquired under his tuition considerable education. This story gives a distinct picture of home life in Russia, where Madame Gréville resided for many years, and where she was enabled to master all phases of Russian character.

There is much in the book that is bright and noteworthy, and the character of Sonia is developed with much delicacy and originality.

SOUL OF THE FAR EAST, THE, by Percival Lowell (1886). The Far East whose Soul is the subject-matter of this sympathetic study is principally Japan, but China and Korea are considered also. Among the traits of character and the peculiarities of usages distinguishing all Far Eastern peoples, the author classes the far less pronounced individualism of those races, as compared with Westerns: Peoples, he says, grow steadily more individual as we go westward. In the Far East the social unit is not the individual but the family: among the Easterns a normally constituted son knows not what it is to possess a spontaneity of his own. A Chinese son cannot properly be said to own anything. This state of things is curiously reflected in the language of Japan, which has no personal pronouns: one cannot say in Japanese, I, Thou, He. The Japanese are born artists: to call a Japanese cook an artist is to state a simple fact, for Japanese food is beautiful, though it may not be agreeable to the taste. Half of the teachings of the Buddhist religion are inculcations of charity or fellow-feeling: not only is man enjoined to show kindliness to fellowmen, but to all animals as well. The people practice what their Scriptures teach; and the effect indirectly on the condition of the brutes is almost as marked as its more direct effect on the character of mankind.

SPANISH CONQUEST IN AMERICA, THE, by Sir Arthur Helps, was published in four volumes, in England, from 1855 to 1861. Its sub-title, 'Its Relation to the History of Slavery and the Government of Colonies,' conveys a more adequate idea of the theme.

While Sir Arthur was laboring upon his compendious work, 'Conquerors of the New World' (1848–52), his interest in Spanish-American slavery so increased that he visited Spain, and examined in Madrid such MSS. as pertained to the subject. As a result the present work appeared. The author had spared no pains to render his work absolutely trustworthy, eschewing the picturesque method wherein he might have excelled, in order to attain to absolute accuracy, — a rare virtue in historians. The result was that the work, written with an obtrusive moral purpose, and devoid of literary brilliancy, was not a success. Frequently the author suspends the onward movement of the narrative while he pauses to analyze motive and investigate character. Seeing that his elaborate work lacked popularity, Sir Arthur broke up much of the biographical substance into 'Lives,' which appeared later: 'Las Casas, the Apostle of the Indians' (1868); 'Columbus' (1869); 'Pizarro' (1869); and 'Hernando Cortes' (1871). All these became justly popular; and while the parent work is valuable chiefly to students of the period, its progeny still delight the general reader.

SPANISH LITERATURE, THE HISTORY OF, by George Ticknor (1849). This work was the fruit of twenty years of study and labor. It is divided into three parts: Part i., beginning with 'The Cid' and the chronicles, and ending with the death of Charles V.; Part ii., treating of the golden age of the drama, the lyric, and the novel; and Part iii., making a study of the conditions of the literary decadence. The translations used were original; and the book remains an authority and a classic. Hallam declared that "It supersedes all others, and will never be superseded." Translated into many tongues, its profound learning, its modesty, and its forcible style, make it as agreeable as it is valuable.

SPANISH VISTAS, by George Parsons Lathrop (1883) "Unless he be extraordinarily shrewd," says the author, "a foreigner can hardly help arriving in Spain on some kind of a feast-day." Perhaps it is that all days in that land of romance seem like red-letter days to one who has come from the workaday world and the unshaded vistas of reality. Spain, to the general observer, is a field scarcely more known than Italy was a few decades ago; but each year the interesting peculiarities of the people are becoming modified, at length to entirely disappear; so the chapters which preserve the actual appearance of the Spain of to-day have the additional value of a probable future reference. There is no attempt to review political events in the work, only to present a striking and faithful photograph of the essential characteristics of the country, and catalogue particular and local features. If one were forced to select among a number of delightful pictures, perhaps the chapter on 'Andalusia and the Alhambra' would be chosen; but to that on 'The Lost City' the eye turns again and again with ever renewed interest. The last pages are devoted to 'Hints to Travelers,' and are useful in supplying certain information not to be found in the usual guide-book, and condensing this in a very convenient form.

SPEECH ON CONCILIATION WITH THE COLONIES, see **CONCILIATION** etc.

SPEED THE PLOUGH, by Thomas Morton. To this comedy, first produced in 1796, we owe one of our best-known characters, — the redoubtable Mrs. Grundy. Here as elsewhere she is invisible; and it is what she may say, not what she does say, that Dame Ashfield fears. Farmer Ashfield has brought up from infancy a young man named Henry, whose parentage is unknown. Sir Philip Blandford, Ashfield's landlord, is about to return after many years' absence, to marry his daughter Emma to Bob Handy, who "can do everything but earn his bread." Sir Abel, Bob's father, is to pay all Blandford's debt. In a plowing-match, Henry wins the prize, and Emma bestows the medal. It is a case of love at first sight. Sir Philip hates Henry, and orders Ashfield to turn him from his doors, but he refuses. Sir Philip is about to force Ashfield to discharge a debt, when a man named Morrington gives Henry the note of Sir Philip for more than the amount.   Henry destroys it, when Sir Philip declares that Morrington, whom he has never seen, has by encouraging Sir Philip's vices when young, possessed himself of enough notes to more than exhaust Sir Philip's fortune.   Sir Philip confides his secret to Bob.   He was to marry a young girl, when he found her about to elope with his brother Charles.   He killed Charles, and hid the knife and a bloody cloth in a part of the castle which he has never visited since.   Sir Abel, in experimenting with a substitute for gunpowder, sets the castle on fire. Henry saves Emma from the flames; and breaking into the secret room, brings forth the knife and cloth.   Morrington appears, and proves to be Sir Philip's brother and Henry's father.   To atone for the wrong done his brother, he had gathered all the notes which his brother had given to usurers, and now gives them to him.   Bob marries Susan, Ashfield's daughter, whom he was about to desert for Emma; and the latter is married to Henry.

SPIRIT OF LAWS, THE ('Esprit des Lois'), by Montesquieu (1748).   The work of a French baron, born just 100 years before the French Revolution of 1789, has the double interest of a singularly impressive manifestation of mind and character in the author, and a very able study of the conditions, political and social, in France, which were destined to bring the overthrow of the old order.   In 1728, after an election to the Academy, Montesquieu had entered upon prolonged European travel, to gratify his strong interest in the manners, customs, religion, and government to be seen in different lands.   Meeting with Lord Chesterfield, he went with him to England, and spent nearly two years amid experiences which made him an ardent admirer of the British Constitution, a monarchy without despotism.   Returning thence to his native La Brède, near Bordeaux, he gave the next twenty years to study, the chief fruit of which was to be the 'Esprit des Lois.'   As early as 1734 he gave some indication of what he had in view by his 'Considerations' upon Roman greatness and Roman decline.   The 'Esprit des Lois' appeared in 1748, to become in critical estimation the most important literary production of the eighteenth century, before the 'Encyclopédie.'   Its purpose was research of the origin of laws, the principles on which laws rest, and how they grow out of these principles.   It was designed to awaken desire for freedom, condemnation of despotism, and hope of political progress; and this effect it had, modifying the thought of the century very materially, and raising up a school of statesmen and political economists at once intelligent and upright in the interest of the governed.

SPLENDID SPUR, THE, by Sir A. T. Quiller-Couch (1890).   The scene of these thrilling adventures is England, in the days of King Charles.   Jack Marvel overhears Tingcomb, Sir Deakin Killigrew's steward, plotting with the villainous Settle to destroy his master's son, Anthony, and seize the estate.   He warns him, but too late; sees him die, receives from him the King's letter to General Hopton, is himself pursued, escapes, rescues Sir Deakin and his daughter Delia.   Sir Deakin dies from exposure, and Delia sets out with Marvel to deliver the King's letter.   Adventures follow thick and fast: they are captured, and escape again and again, finally reaching Cornwall, Delia's home.   She falls into Settle's clutches; and Marvel is wounded and nursed by Joan, a wild Cornish girl, who conveys the King's letter to Hopton.   Marvel recovers Delia; they are hard pressed by the foe, but Joan, in Marvel's clothes, leads them astray, receives a fatal wound, and dies for Marvel's sake.   Tingcomb, the wicked steward, falls headlong from a precipice, the stolen property is regained, and Delia decides to seek a safer shelter in France. Marvel remains to fight for King Charles. Delia, seeing that he loves her not less, but honor more, exclaims, "Thou hast found it, sweetheart, thou hast found the Splendid Spur."

SPOILERS, THE, by Rex Beach (1905). The scene of this story is laid in the Klondike while the gold fever is at its height. The central figure in the narrative is Roy Glenister, a man of powerful nature, whose theory of life is that force can accomplish anything. He and his partner Bill Dextry are returning to Klondike after an enforced absence and as their ship is about to sail their attention is drawn to a beautiful young girl who is endeavoring to evade the quarantine officers and board their steamer. Glenister exerts himself in her behalf and succeeds in rescuing her from her pursuers. Her name is Helen Chester and her rescuer falls in love with her on the voyage and endeavors to force her to reciprocate his affection. Instead, however, he wins her scorn by kissing her against her will and she vows she will never forgive him. Upon reaching Klondike Glenister finds that there is litigation over his claim, which contains a valuable gold mine, and he must fight to keep it in his possession. His principal enemy is a political boss named McNamera who does everything in his power to ruin him. Glenister's love for Helen proves a deep influence in his life and softens and refines his nature, though she remains obdurate to his suit. McNamera, who is also a rival in love, succeeds in getting Helen to look favorably upon his proposal. Helen has brought with her to Klondike papers, the contents of which she is ignorant of, but which prove to be the instrument by which Glenister's claim is to be proved invalid. They are held by an unscrupulous lawyer who bargains to reveal the contents to Helen in return for her love. She accedes to his proposition but is rescued from his clutches by a notorious gambler called Brancho Kid, who proves to be her wayward brother whom she has not seen for years. Glenister conquers McNamera in a fierce weaponless duel and the latter is proved to be a scoundrel. Helen gives Glenister the papers but he refuses to make use of them as by so doing he would ruin her uncle Judge Stillman, who is criminally involved with McNamera. This generous action which culminates a series of sacrifices made by Glenister for Helen causes her to appreciate his true character and she confesses her love to him.

STANDARD OIL COMPANY, THE HISTORY OF THE, by Ida M. Tarbell, was published in 1904, having previously appeared serially in McClure's Magazine. The author had made a thorough study of all documents connected with the subject, including testimony before legislative and judicial investigating bodies, newspapers, pamphlets, periodicals, and private correspondence; and she had conversed with many persons involved in the struggles evoked by the company, including many of their own officials. Her book is thus founded on a critical examination of a great mass of contemporary evidence. After a brief introductory chapter on the early days of the oil industry in Pennsylvania from the digging of the first oil-well in 1859 to the rise of a great industrial community, Miss Tarbell narrates the first business experiences of John D. Rockefeller, his entry into the oil business in 1862, and his founding of the Standard Oil Company in 1870, its defeat of competitors by means of obtaining rebates from the railroads, the overcoming of legislative and popular opposition, the gradual absorption of rival organizations, and the development of an organization controlling the entire oil industry of the country. "To-day, as at the start, the purpose of the Standard Oil Company is . . . the regulation of the price of crude and refined oil by the control of the output; and the chief means for sustaining this purpose is still that of the original scheme — a control of oil transportation giving special privileges in rates." Though remorselessly exposing its evils, Miss Tarbell is not without admiration for this great organization. "If it has played its great game with contemptuous indifference to fair play, and to nice legal points of view, it has played it with consummate ability, daring, and address. The silent, patient, all-seeing man who has led it in its transportation raids has led it no less successfully in what may be called its legitimate work. Nobody has appreciated more fully than he those qualities which alone make for permanent stability and growth in commercial ventures." Miss Tarbell's work is eminently readable and is a valuable contemporary historical authority on the most striking example of the most important industrial and financial movement of the nineteenth century.

STANDISH OF STANDISH, by Jane G. Austin (1890). This is called "a story of the Pilgrims"; and with this charming and authentic narrative the author begins her series of tales relating to the Plymouth Colony. The book is full of romantic and dramatic episodes, all of which are founded on fact, and are therefore doubly interesting. In the opening chapters the Pilgrims are first pictured on board the Mayflower, lying at anchor, where they are passing the dreary weeks until the pioneers of the colony can decide on a suitable place for a settlement. At last the location is chosen; and the few log cabins which serve as abiding places for the Pilgrims prove foundation stones for the flourishing town of Plymouth. Throughout the story Miles Standish, who can rightfully be called the hero of this tale figures prominently. His manliness and courage in overcoming obstacles and adversity, his tenderness and kindness to the sick and suffering, and his deep love and devotion for sweet Rose Standish, form a striking picture. Her death, which occurs soon after their landing, causes him the deepest sorrow, but he eventually feels it his duty to marry again; and John Alden's interview with Priscilla Molines in his behalf is picturesquely described. His subsequent marriage to his cousin Barbara Standish, which occurs after a stormy courtship, ends this interesting narrative. Throughout the story the privations and sufferings of the Pilgrims, which they bear with such courage and fortitude, are pictured in the most graphic manner. Governor Carver and his gentle and delicate wife; John Harland, their faithful friend and helper; and Mary Chilton, who has historic interest as being the first woman to step on shore, are also charmingly portrayed.

STEIN, LIFE AND TIMES OF: or, GERMANY AND PRUSSIA IN THE NAPOLEONIC AGE, by J. R. Seeley, regius professor of modern history in the University of Cambridge (3 vols., octavo, 1878). Professor Seeley's object in writing this valuable if rather lengthy biography was primarily, as he states in his preface, to describe and explain the extraordinary transition period of Germany and Prussia, which occupied the age of Napoleon (1806–22), — and which has usually been regarded as dependent upon the development of the Napoleonic policy, — and to give it its true place in German history. Looking for some one person who might be regarded as the central figure around whom the ideas of the age concentrated themselves, he settled on Stein. Biographies of other prominent persons — as Hardenberg, Scharnhorst, etc. — are interwoven with that of Stein. The work is divided into nine parts: (1) Before the Catastrophe (*i.e.*, the Prussian subjugation by Napoleon); (2) The Catastrophe; (3) Ministry of Stein, First Period; (4) Ministry of Stein, Transition; (5) Ministry of Stein, Conclusion; (6) Stein in Exile; (7) Return from Exile; (8) At the Congress; (9) Old Age. It is clearly and picturesquely written, and springs from a statesmanlike and philosophical grasp of its material. Stein's great services to Prussia, and indeed to the world (the emancipating edict of 1807, his influence in Russia, at the Congress of Vienna, 1814, etc.), have never elsewhere been so convincingly stated. The author indeed confesses, that while at starting he had no true conception of the greatness of the man, Stein's importance grew on him, and he ended by considering the part which the chancellor played an indispensable one in the development of modern Germany. Many extracts are given from Stein's letters and official documents, which make his personality distinct and impressive. The politics and social conditions of Russia, Austria, and France, and the effect which these produced in Germany, are made both clear and interesting. A multitude of anecdotes and personal reminiscences adds the element of entertainment which so serious a biography demands. But its great merit is that nowhere else exists a more judicial and philosophic estimate of Napoleon's character and policy than in the chapters devoted to his meteoric career.

STEVEN LAWRENCE, YEOMAN, by Mrs. Annie Edwards (1867). Katharine Fane, rich, beautiful, good, engaged to Lord Petres; and Dora Fane, poor, frivolous, and heartless, — are cousins. Dora sends Katharine's picture to Steven Lawrence, in Mexico, as her own He falls in love with it, returns to England, discovers his mistake, but is beguiled by Dora into marrying her. They are not happy. Dora persuades him to take her to Paris, where she leads a life of frivolity. Katharine, who loves Steven, though she will not admit it, is his friend, now as ever. She goes to his aid, and fancying him a prey to evil companions, sends him to England. He returns unexpectedly, finds his wife at a ball in a costume he had forbidden her wearing, and casts her off; she elopes, Katharine follows and brings her back. Steven declines to receive her; Katharine takes her to London, where she dies, frivolous to the last. A few days before the time set for her marriage to Lord Petres, Katharine hears that Steven has been thrown from his horse and is dying. She hastens to his bedside, breaks her engagement — and he recovers. He prepares to sell out and go back to Mexico; but Katharine stoops to conquer, begs him not to leave her, and wins the happiness of her life. It is an entertaining story, of the common modern English type.

STICKIT MINISTER, THE, by S. R. Crockett (1893). The short stories, by S. R. Crockett, contained in the collection called 'The Stickit Minister, and Some Common Men,' were first printed in a newspaper.

These stories of "that gray Galloway Land," as the author calls it, are told in a very simple, pathetic way. The "stickit minister" is a young divinity student, who learns that he must die in a few years from consumption. He and his younger brother have inherited but a small property; so, in order that his brother may study to become a doctor, he leaves college and goes home to cultivate the farm. It is generally supposed that he has failed to pass his examination, whence the name "stickit stuck fast minister"; and even his brother treats him with coldness and ingratitude.

The second story, 'Accepted of the Beasts,' tells of a pure-hearted, noble young clergyman, who is turned out of his church because of certain unfounded accusations brought against him by the machination of an evil-minded woman. Next morning a farmer discovers him singing "He was despised and rejected of men" to a herd of cattle, which press about him to listen. A few hours later he is found lying dead.

'A Heathen Lintie' is the story of a middle-aged Scotch woman, who has secretly written and has had published a volume of poems. She watches anxiously for the paper which is to contain a review of them. At last it comes; but she dies before she is

808 THE READER'S DIGEST OF BOOKS

able to read enough of it to discover that what she believes is praise is in reality cruel, scathing criticism.

Some of the stories — as 'A Midsummer Idyl,' 'Three Bridegrooms and One Bride,' and 'A Knight-Errant of the Streets' — are less pathetic and more humorous.

STONE AGE, THE, see **MEN OF THE OLD STONE AGE,** by H. F. Osborn.

STONES OF VENICE, by John Ruskin, in three volumes, appeared in the years 1851 and 1853. This work treats of the archæology and history of Venice, and unfolds the causes of her strength and glory, her downfall and decay. The author aims to show that the Gothic architecture of Venice was the expression of a state of national virtue and pure domestic faith, while its Renaissance architecture had arisen from a condition of concealed national infidelity and domestic corruption.

The first volume, entitled 'The Foundations,' presents the principles of all noble building and describes the virtues of architecture as threefold: first, the end should be accomplished in the best way; second, it should say that which it was intended to say, in the best words; and third, it should always give pleasure by its presence. Ruskin next considers his subject in its two great divisions of Strength and Beauty, or as constructive and ornamental architecture. The volume is prefaced with an outline of the history of the city and her Doges, and concludes with a brilliant description of the drive from the gates of Padua to Mestra, and thence by gondola along the dark waters to Venice.

The second volume, entitled 'Sea Stories,' is devoted to a study of the buildings marking the Byzantine and Gothic periods; the one characteristic of the earlier, the other of the crowning era of Venetian life.

The third volume, entitled 'The Fall,' offers an analysis of Renaissance architecture, or that of Venetian decline. This era is divided into three periods, distinguished as the Early, the Roman, and the Grotesque, each marking a distinct phase of degeneracy in Venetian life. In the last two volumes of this work Ruskin shows how Venetian architecture was ever subject to the temper of the State, rising and receding with the growth of the moral or the immoral dispositions of the people. The last period of decline, styled by Ruskin "Grotesque Renaissance," was the outcome of an unscrupulous love of pleasure, and its features were the worst and basest of all preceding styles; with it closed the career of the architecture of Europe. In the 'Stones of Venice,' its author demonstrates the truth that a nation's history, though unwritten by any historian's pen, is yet inscribed distinctly and lastingly on the blocks of stone that tell of her home life, her manufactures, and her religion.

STORY OF A BAD BOY, THE, by Thomas Bailey Aldrich (1870), is a fresh, humorous story, that has long been popular with children of all ages. Its opening sentences tend to explain the dubious title: "This is the story of a bad boy. Well, not such a very bad, but a pretty bad boy; and I ought to know, for I am, or was, that boy myself. . . . I call my story the story of a bad boy, partly to distinguish myself from those faultless young gentlemen who generally figure in narratives of this kind, and partly because I was not a cherub. . . . In short, I was a real human boy, such as you may meet anywhere in New England; and no more like the impossible boy in a story-book than a sound orange is like one that has been sucked dry." The story is autobiographical in so far as suited the author's purpose. Rivermouth, where the so-called bad boy of the story was born and brought up, after spending a few of his earliest years in New Orleans, stands for Portsmouth, New Hampshire; just as his name, Tom Bailey, stands as a part, not even disguised, of the author's own. Tom Bailey's temperament and appetites were wholesome; his boyish pranks were never vicious or mean, though he frankly "didn't want to be an angel," and didn't think the missionary tracts presented to him by the Rev. Wibird Hawkins were half so nice as Robinson Crusoe, and didn't send his "little pocket-money to the natives of the Feejee Islands, but spent it royally in peppermint drops and taffy-candy." The author, disgusted with the goody-goody little hypocrite of an earlier moral tale, created this boy of flesh and blood, to displace the moribund hero of "Sandford and Merton"; though, as Mr. Aldrich has since remarked, "the title may have frightened off a few careful friends who would have found nothing serious to condemn in the book itself." The story has been translated into French, German, Spanish, Danish, Swedish, and Dutch.

STORY OF A COUNTRY TOWN, THE, by E. W. Howe (1883), is a tale of the monotonous unlovely life of a small, hard-working, unimaginative Western village. The story is told in the first person by a boy who has never known any other life, and whose farthest goal of experience is the neighboring town. It is a masterpiece of modern "realism," the life and events of the place being described with a marvelous fidelity. Yet the test of veracity fails in the unrelieved gloom of the story, which is bereft of all sunshine and joyousness, and even of all sense of relation to happier things. The town of Twin Mounds seems as isolated and strange as if it were in another world. Even nature is utterly cheerless and human life apparently without hope. The narrative itself is loose and rambling, centering about the domestic troubles of Joe Erring and his wife, and culminating in dreary tragedy. The book has a grim fascination; and at least one extraordinary character, Lyth Biggs, whose cynical philosophizing leaves the reader fairly benumbed by the chill of its candor.

STORY OF AN AFRICAN FARM, THE, a novel published in 1883 under the pseudonym of "Ralph Iron," really by Olive Schreiner. On a realistic background of South African landscape and farm-life the author depicts the aspirations and disillusionments of youth in an age of disintegrating faith and ideals. Waldo and Lyndall, the central personages of the story, are brought up on a Boer farm, in Cape Colony, Waldo being the son of the German overseer and Lyndall, an orphan girl, cousin of Em, who is stepdaughter to Tant' Sannie the Boer mistress of the farm. The two girls were left in the guardianship of Tant' Sannie at the death of Em's father, an Englishman, the Boer woman's second husband. Although Tant' Sannie is ignorant and selfish the children lead a life of happy companionship at the cabin of the overseer, a kindly, simple-hearted South German of a childlike trust and piety. On this idyllic scene arrives a clever scoundrel named Bonaparte Blenkins who by the grossest flattery gets the confidence of Tant' Sannie, induces her to turn away the German who had befriended him, and on his death, subjects the boy Waldo to the most malignant persecution and finally to a cruel beating. Shortly afterwards, through indiscreetly making love to another Boer woman, Tant' Sannie's niece, Blenkins is driven from the farm. The sufferings that Waldo has endured and the revelation of evil which the experience has brought have utterly destroyed his former childlike faith in God. Contact with modern thought in the books that he procures deepens his confusion. His life becomes an aspiration for a knowledge of truth which experience will not give him. This aspiration becomes defined by an allegorical tale related to him by a stranger, a man of the world, who happens to be resting at the farm and is interested by the boy's face and words. Waldo determines to seek work in the cities, to read, and to see life. While he seeks knowledge, Lyndall yearns for power. Possessed of unusual beauty and charm and great force of personality she succeeds in making her guardian send her to school at Cape Town. Disregarding the conventional studies there, she reads and thinks as she pleases, and in four years becomes an accomplished woman, the writer of a number of successful novels and plays, and an ardent upholder of woman's independence. Being extremely beautiful and attractive, she has many admirers. With one of these she forms a connection which she will not permit to be made permanent by marriage, because she feels that the man's love is one merely of possession and that he appeals only to half of her nature. Returning home she finds Tant' Sannie about to be married again, thus leaving the farm to Em, who has just become engaged to a girlish young Englishman, Gregory Rose, lessee of half the farm. Lyndall and Waldo in several long colloquies exchange experiences in a mood of absolute comradeship, not as woman and man but as spirit and spirit. He then departs for the cities on his search for a knowledge of life. Meanwhile, though Lyndall scorns Gregory's femininity, he has become fascinated by her; and when released by Em, who sees how matters stand, declares his love. Lyndall, who expects soon to become a mother, scornfully tells him he may give her his name; but her lover having followed her to the farm and again offered marriage, she clandestinely departs under his protection, though still refusing any legal tie. They go to the Transvaal, where they soon quarrel and separate. Lyndall gives birth to a child, which dies a few hours afterwards. She is cared for until her death, which soon follows, by her rejected suitor, Gregory, who has traced her to the inn at which she is staying, and who attends her with devotion and tenderness, in the disguise of a nurse. Meanwhile, Waldo, after months of wandering, varied employments, reading, and meditation, returns to the farm, hoping to hear something of Lyndall. The news of her death deprives him of any further instinct for existence. He dies peacefully, sitting in the sun on a lovely summer afternoon. The marriage of Gregory and Em closes the story.

STORY OF BESSIE COSTRELL, THE, by Mrs. Humphry Ward (1895). In this story Mrs. Ward has depicted life among the working classes under most painful and trying conditions. Bessie Costrell is the niece of John Bolderfield, an old man who, by dint of scrimping and saving for many years, has accumulated by hard labor enough money to support himself for the remainder of his life. This wealth, the acquirement of which has been the one ambition of his life, has been kept hoarded in an old trunk; and this he confides to the care of his niece, before leaving his native town for a period of some months. Bessie is much delighted to be given charge of the money, and at first only regards it with honest feelings of pride; but eventually the temptation becomes too strong for her, and her natural extravagance asserting itself, she opens the chest and spends part of the money in a reckless way, drinking and treating her friends. At length her free use of money begins to arouse suspicion; and she takes alarm and goes to the chest to count the balance, when she is caught in the act by her husband's profligate son, who assaults her and robs her of the remainder. Matters have reached this crisis when John returns home and, to his horror and consternation, finds his money gone. He is at first prostrated by the terrible discovery; but on recovering consciousness, he accuses Bessie of the theft, which she strenuously denies. John then sends for the constable, who succeeds in proving her guilt. Bessie's husband, Isaac Costrell, a stern, hard man, who is a leader in the church, is overcome with horror on learning of his wife's dishonesty, agrees that she will have to go to prison, and tells her that he will have nothing more to do with her.

The wretched woman, overwhelmed with terror and grief, drowns herself in a well, and the narrative ends leaving the husband filled with remorse, and John brokenhearted and penniless. The story is told in a realistic manner; and although many of the situations arc unpleasant, it bears the mark of a master hand.

STORY OF GÖSTA BERLING, THE, by Selma Lagerlöf (1894). Translated in 1898, by Pauline Bancroft Flach. This work, which won for its author the Nobel Prize in 1909, depicts life in the province of Värmland, in Southern Sweden, at the beginning of the last century. Miss Lagerlöf, who has grown up in the midst of the wild legends of her country, embodies them in her story, which abounds with incidents which have actually occurred among these primitive and superstitious folk. Gösta Berling is a handsome and dashing youth, who begins his life as a preacher among the rude mining folk; he is endowed with a magnetism and eloquence which carry all before them, but at the opening of the story he has fallen from grace and is to be dismissed from his parish for drunkenness. By an inspired burst of eloquence he forces his flock to reverse their verdict, and the Bishop, who has come to unfrock him, departs with words of approbation. His moment of exaltation is swiftly followed by one of despair and self-accusation, and feeling convinced that he will be implicated in a wild prank played upon the Bishop by a dissolute companion, he rushes away to resume his dissipated career. Having reached the lowest depths of degradation he crawls into a snow-drift to end his life, when he is forcibly rescued by the Major's wife of Ekeby, a power in the land and a mine-owner. She awakens in him his lost sense of honor, and he goes with her to Ekeby to become one of the many pensioners upon her bounty. Gösta Berling's passionate and impulsive nature leads him into one love affair after another; all women adore him, and he seems to bring misfortune to all with whom he comes in contact. He wins the affection of the lovely young countess Ebba Dohna, who dies from the shock of learning his past history. He elopes from a ball with the beautiful Anna Stjärnhok, but they are pursued by wolves, and being convinced that the powers of evil are following them he drives her to the family of her betrothed whom she was about to forsake. The capricious Marianne Sinclair next stirs his heart, and having brought down her father's wrath by making love to her at a ball he finds her shut out of her own home on a winter's night. He rescues her and carries her to Ekeby, where she is betrothed to him, but on her returning to her father's house without leaving him a message Gösta Berling repudiates her and declares his love dead. He is befriended by the young countess Elizabeth; wife of the stupid Henrik Dohna, and becomes her abject slave, but does not presume to lift his eyes to her whom he regards as an angelic being; he is unjustly accused of making love to her, and she is finally driven from her home by her jealous mother-in-law and enraged husband. After much suffering she and Gösta Berling are at last united, the countess having previously been cast off by her husband and her marriage with him annulled. Having left behind them the hollow joys of wealth and luxury the couple begin a new life dedicated to the welfare of their fellow beings. The book contains many vivid character studies and powerful descriptions of the mingling of the elements with the passions of men.

STORY OF MARGARET KENT, THE, by Ellen Olney Kirk. This book was published in 1886, under the signature of Henry Hayes. The scene of the story is laid in New York, where Margaret Kent, an able and fascinating woman, is supporting herself and her little daughter by means of her pen. At a very early age she has married a man who has proved to be weak and a spendthrift; and who, after dissipating both their fortunes, had left her, six years before the story opens, to go to South America. From the time when Margaret establishes herself in the city, the story concerns itself with the suitors who suppose her to be a widow, and with the sudden complications introduced into her life by a rumor that she is playing a false part and is not free.

The story is well told, and full of grace and color. The character of Margaret is distinctly portrayed; while the dry speeches of Miss Longstaff, the quaintness of little Gladys, and the kindness of Mr. Bell, Margaret's elderly admirer, afford interesting passages.

STORY OF THE C. W. S., THE, by Percy Redfern (1913). This jubilee history of the Co-operative Wholesale Society (1863–1913) is a fully documented record of an organization which has grown from the humblest beginnings till it has become a huge trading concern with an annual turn-over (in 1912) of more than 750 million dollars. The aim of the English co-operative pioneers was to establish a system of mutual shop-keeping by which the customers estimate their own demand, provide their own store from which to supply it, and retain for themselves what otherwise would be "profit," but is in this case a saving upon a domestic business conducted within the consumers' own circle or club. In addition the Pioneers hoped that eventually the control of industry would pass into the hands of the working class. The student of political development in democratic countries cannot afford to neglect the growth of working-class organizations like the British co-operative societies, which besides their economic effects upon the life of the nation, have been a training in affairs and in citizenship for large numbers of the population. Moreover, the example of the British co-operative societies, like the wholesale, which now engage not only in many forms of production but in banking and insurance, is being copied by other countries. The book is clearly and candidly written and abounds in photographic illustrations of the prominent activities or personalities of the society.

STORY OF THE HEAVENS, THE (1894), by Sir Robert S. Ball, professor of astronomy in the English University of Cambridge.

This large work, revised to represent recent progress, brings within a single volume all the principal facts of the magnificent story of the sun and moon, the solar system, the laws which rule it, the planets of our system, their satellites, the minor planets, comets, and shooting stars; and the vast depths of the universe filled with suns which we see as stars. The special questions of the star-land known by the telescope and the spectroscope are all carefully treated. Ball wrote many other works on astronomy and was the acknowledged authority of his time.

STOWE, HARRIET BEECHER, LIFE AND LETTERS OF, by Annie Fields, appeared in 1897. It is the best life of the author. Written in a most entertaining style, with just enough of personal reminiscence and anecdote to quicken interest, it is a discreet and satisfying biography. The reader comes into closer acquaintance with Mrs. Stowe in the perusal of her letters, of which Mrs. Fields has made wise and varied selection. Living through, and herself so potential a factor in, the days of the anti-slavery movement, Mrs. Stowe naturally was in more or less intimate correspondence with the reformers, agitators, statesmen, clergymen, and littérateurs of her own stormy era. The selections made from this correspondence form most interesting reading, and add greatly to the value of the biography.

STRANGE STORY, A, a novel by Bulwer-Lytton (1862), deals with that order of occult phenomena which includes mesmerism, hypnotism, clairvoyance, and ghost-seeing. The story is told by one Dr. Fenwick. His professional rival in the town in which he settles is a Dr. Lloyd. He comes into direct opposition to him when the latter becomes a disciple of Mesmer, and seeks to heal the sick by mesmeric influence. Fenwick directs a vigorous pamphlet against Lloyd's pretensions, treating the whole matter as child's-play, beneath the notice of science. On his death-bed Lloyd sends for Fenwick, accuses him of having ruined him by his attacks, and intimates that he will be forced to acknowledge the existence of supernatural forces. The narrative that follows relates the fulfillment of Lloyd's dying threat. Curious occurrences force Fenwick into the consideration of occult phenomena. He becomes at last a believer in the existence and power of unseen forces. 'A Strange Story' combines romance with science, scholarship with mysticism. It is one of the most fascinating embodiments in fiction of the occult philosophy.

STRENUOUS LIFE, THE, by Theodore Roosevelt (1900). This is a collection of thirteen essays and addresses on various subjects. The book takes its title from the first of the series, which is an exposition of that ideal of character and that theory of life of which Mr. Roosevelt himself is such a conspicuous example. Two of the papers are admiring biographical studies of Grant and Dewey and the others are along ethical, political, and civic lines. One essay on 'The American Boy' contains much in the way of valuable suggestions and advice. The author tells the youth that if he would turn out a good American, he must not be a coward or a bully, a shirk or a prig. He must work hard and play hard, be clean-minded and clean-lived, and able to hold his own under all circumstances. The following quotation perhaps gives the key to the sentiment which runs through the book: "I wish," says the author, "to preach that highest form of success which comes, not to the man who desires mere easy peace, but to the man who does not shrink from danger, from hard-ship, or from bitter toil, and who, out of these, wins the splendid ultimate triumph." Among the subjects ably treated are "Expansion and Peace," "Civic Helpfulness," "Character and Success" and "Military Preparedness and Unpreparedness."

STRIFE, by John Galsworthy (1909). The conflict in this drama is between capital and labor. A strike has been in progress at the Trengartha Tin Plate Works for months, until the men and their wives and children are starving, and the corporation is on the verge of bankruptcy. Both sides are disheartened, and ready for compromise, but the strike is prolonged by fanatical leaders who represent the extreme types of capital and labor. David Roberts, leader of the strikers, has a grievance against the company because it has underpaid him for a valuable invention, but he is fighting not for himself, or even for the other strikers, but for the future against the master, Capital, beating the life out of Labor. His demands are excessive, and he has therefore lost the support of the trade union, which represents the spirit of compromise. The directors are led by John Anthony, the founder of the company, and for thirty-two years its president. He is determined to fight and win, as he has so often fought and always won. To the remonstrances of his son and daughter, who sympathize with the men, and to the timid expostulations of the directors who, like the strikers, are fighting only for the welfare of themselves and their families, he replies in terms of the future. Capital and Labor are at war, and the defeat of Capital means mob government. Every concession will be but the prelude to more extravagant demands. The second act reveals in one scene the sufferings of the women and in another scene

the turbulent disaffection of the men.   Roberts, in a fiery speech, has won the strikers
over to the side of strife, when news is brought to him that his wife has died of her
enforced privations.   The meeting, bereft of his presence at the crucial moment, votes
for conciliation.   The last act shows John Anthony voted down by his directors and
forced to resign the presidency of the company.   The secretary of the corporation
and the union leader discover that the terms of settlement are identical with the ones
offered at the beginning of the fight so that nothing has been gained by either side,
through all the months of strife and misery and economic waste, except that the best
man of each side has been broken irretrievably.   The author conceives the leader of
capital in as generous a spirit, and in as true a light as the leader of labor, great figures,
worthy of each other's steel, akin to each other, towering head and shoulders above
the men who desert and betray them.

STRINGTOWN ON THE PIKE, by John Uri Lloyd (1909).   In this story the author
describes the inhabitants of the rolling land which lies between the Ohio and Kentucky
rivers.   The Stringtown people are a rugged, narrow folk, suspicious in their intercourse with strangers, yet at heart loyal and sturdy.   The story opens with a curious
maze of negro-lore, and Cupe, an old darky living with his wife in a cabin on the outskirts of Stringtown, foretells in a mysterious way the events which are to follow.
Cupe's master, the Corn Bug, a social pariah, ignorant and steeped in debauchery,
comes into possession of certain papers, which establish his claim to all the region
about Stringtown.   The papers are submitted to Judge Elford, who officially expresses the opinion that the claim if pressed would be almost certain of success, and
that the land would revert to the drunkard.   It is then that the Corn Bug, rising to a
fine height, burns the papers and goes back to his life of privation and hardship.
The romance of the tale centres about Susie Manley and her lover Samuel Drew, who,
after an absence of some years, returns to be professor of chemistry in the University
on the Hill.   The character of the Red Head Boy is drawn in direct contrast to that
of his rival and foe, Drew.   He is a combination of generosity and maliciousness and
forms the dominating influence in the story.   Mr. Nordman, the uncle of Red Head,
has died under suspicious circumstances, and his nephew is charged with the murder.
Drew accepts the invitation to testify as a chemical expert in the case, and on his
evidence, which is based upon an error, the prisoner is sentenced to death upon the
gallows.   He is not however allowed to be unjustly executed.

STUDENT'S HISTORY OF THE ENGLISH PARLIAMENT, see **ENGLISH
CONSTITUTION,** by Walter Bagehot.

STUDIES NEW AND OLD IN ETHICAL AND SOCIAL SUBJECTS, by F. P.
Cobbe, see **ETHICAL etc.**

STUDIES OF THE GREEK POETS, by J. A. Symonds, see **GREEK etc.**

STUDIES ON HOMER AND THE HOMERIC AGE, by W. E. Gladstone, see
HOMER.

SUBJECTION OF WOMEN, THE, by John Stuart Mill (1869).   An able essay
designed to explain the grounds of the early and strong twofold conviction: (1), that
the principle of woman's legal subordination to man is wrong in itself, and is now one
of the chief hindrances to human improvement; and (2) that it ought to be replaced

by a principle of perfect equality, placing no disability upon woman, and giving no exclusive power or privilege to man. After reviewing the conditions which the laws of all countries annex to the marriage contract, Mill carefully discusses the right of woman to be equal with man in the family, and her further right to equal admission with him to all the functions and occupations hitherto reserved to men. He concludes with a strong chapter on the justice, mercy, and general beneficence, of a social order from which the slavery of woman shall have entirely disappeared.

SUNKEN BELL, THE, by Gerhart Hauptmann (1896). A romantic fairy drama staged in the German forest. Heinrich, the artist, has cast a wonderful bell. The mischievous wood spirits loosen a spoke of the wheel in the wagon carrying the bell to the church, and the bell crashes down the mountain side into the lake. The master bell-founder pursues his bell, and Rautendelein, the nymph, finds him lying half-dead in the woods. He is carried home in delirium by the villagers. Rautendelein has fallen in love with him and for her sake he leaves his wife and children to follow her up the mountain. With her help and the dwarfs he sets to work making a new and more wonderful bell. The pastor climbs the mountain to rebuke Heinrich and persuade him to return to his home. Heinrich answers him with his vision of the perfect bell, not designed for a church but all humanity, and his worship of the Sun as the symbol of Nature. The artist reaches his ideal on the height, but his humanity forces him to descend to the plain. His forsaken wife, Magda, throws herself into the lake, and he hears the bell at the bottom of the lake rung by her dead hand. His children appear to him carrying an urn filled with their mother's tears. He curses the lovely Rautendelein and goes back to the world of men. He finds no peace, and returns to the mountain, but Rautendelein in her despair has parted with her humanity and become the sad bride of the frog king. She rises out of the well to bring her lost lover the goblet of death, which Heinrich demands.

SUPERSTITION AND FORCE, by H. C. Lea (1866). A volume of learned and interesting essays on certain subjects of special importance in the history of the Middle Ages. They are: 'The Wager of Battle,' 'The Wager of Law,' 'The Ordeal,' and 'Torture.' The writer treats of them as 'Methods of Administering Injustice.'

SURGEON'S STORIES, THE, by Zakarias Topelius (1872–74). Topelius was a Finn; and his wonderful series of historical tales, although written originally in Swedish, exploit the fortunes of a Finnish family for six generations, from 1631 to the latter part of the last century. The stories are ostensibly related by Andreas Back, a quack doctor, whose career is humorously set forth in the introduction, and whose characteristics are portrayed in the prelude to each cycle of tales. He was born on the same day as Napoleon. According to his own account he had saved the Swedish fleet, and the lives of Gustavus III. and Arnfelt (or he would have done so had they listened to him); he had been granted an audience with Bonaparte, and had pulled a tooth for Suvorof; and he liked to relate his experiences with just a tinge of boastfulness, but when he was once started on his narrations he quite forgot himself, and was carried away by the exciting events of the past. It was his pleasure to gather around him in his dusty attic a little bank of listeners; — we see them all, the postmaster and the old grandmother and the schoolmaster and the rest. "His memory," says his chronicler, "was inexhaustible; and as the old proverb says that even the wild stream does not let its waves flow by all at once, so had the surgeon also a continually new stock of stories, partly from his own time, and still more from periods that had long since passed. He had not a wide historical knowledge; his tales were desultory character-sketches rather than coherent description: . . . what he had was fidelity, warm feeling, and above all, a power of vivid delineation." The connection between the fifteen stories that make up the six volumes is maintained by a copper ring with runic inscriptions, which is first seen on the finger of Gustavus Adolphus, and is popularly supposed to protect him so long as he wears it, from iron and lead, fire and water. This ring he had received from a Finnish maiden; and it is his son by this Finnish maiden who founds the family of Bertelskjöld, in whose possession the amulet descends with many adventures through generation after generation. The titles of the six cycles hint at the chronological development: Times of Gustavus Adolphus; Times of Battle and Rest (1656–97); Times of Charles XII.; Times of Frederick I.; Times of Linnæus; Times of Alchemy. These stories, with their vivid descriptions, their wonderful pictures of battle and intrigue, their rose-colored touches of romance, take rank among the ablest works of historical fiction.

SWISS FAMILY ROBINSON, THE, or Adventures in a Desert Island, by J. R. Wyss (1813). This book was originally written in German, was translated into French, and afterwards into English. It is an entertaining tale written for young people, after the style of 'Robinson Crusoe,' from which the author is supposed to have derived many of his ideas. It deals with the experiences of a shipwrecked family, a Swiss clergyman, his wife and four sons, who, deserted by the captain and the crew of the vessel on which they are passengers, finally reach land in safety. They exhibit wonderful ingenuity in the use they make of everything which comes to hand, and manage to subsist on what articles of food they find on the island, combined with the edibles which they are able to rescue from the ship. They have various experiences with wild beasts and reptiles, but emerge from all encounters in safety. They build a very remarkable habitation in a large tree, which is reached by means of a hidden staircase in the trunk; and in this retreat they are secure from the attacks of ferocious animals. They continue to thrive and prosper for several years, until finally a ship touches at the island, and they are once again enabled to communicate with the mainland. By this time, however, they are so well pleased with their primitive life that they refuse to leave the island home. The story was left in an unfinished condition by the author, but several sequels to it have been written, all of which vary in their accounts of the doings of this interesting family. The book has long enjoyed a well-deserved popularity, and in spite of various anachronisms is enjoyable and entertaining reading.

SYMBOLIST MOVEMENT IN LITERATURE, THE, a volume of critical essays by Arthur Symons, published in 1899. In the introduction, symbolism is defined as "a form of expression, at the best but approximate, essentially but arbitrary, until it has obtained the force of a convention, for an unseen reality apprehended by the consciousness"; or in the words of another writer, "A symbol might be defined as a representation which does not aim at being a reproduction." The author then goes on to explain the rise of the conscious symbolist movement at the close of the nineteenth century as a reaction from the realistic school — Flaubert, the Goncourts, Zola, Leconte de Lisle, de Hérédia — who aimed at the exact representation of the visible world in impeccable style. Putting aside this love of pictorial description, this rhetorical finish, this materialistic point of view, the symbolists strive by means of suggestion, and association to convey a sense of that spiritual presence which they apprehend as underlying all appearances. The first thorough symbolist, though ante. rior to the rise of the school, was Gérard de Nerval (1808-1854). An erratic and bohemian genius, he suffered from attacks of madness, the abnormal mental associations of which suggested to him new and startling combinations of ideas and quickened his power of using words to evoke feelings and sentiments impossible to communicate directly. His sonnets are the first examples of symbolism. Count Villers de l'Isle Adam (1838-1889), noted for his pride of race, his Catholicism, his admiration of the Middle Ages, and his hostility to modern science, was an early symbolist, whose brilliant dramas, novels, and satires gathered about him a group of admiring younger men. Arthur Rimbauld (1854-1891), vagabond, adventurer, successful Eastern trader and explorer, was a poet at seventeen. His poems are few but startling, full of the wildest combinations of imagery and the most unexpected identifications of incongruous ideas. A curious sonnet in which he assigns a color-value and a set of associations to each of the vowels illustrates that blending of different sensations and ideas which is characteristic of the symbolists and often seems akin to madness. There is a fine essay on Paul Verlaine, skilfully interpreting his moral instability, sensitiveness to beauty, physical and spiritual, alternation between sensuality and religious sentiment, mystical insight, and preference of the suggestive to the rhetorical. Jules Laforgue (1860-1887) is the satirist of the group, writing with a half-sad, half-amused irony in a precise yet colloquial style. Stephane Mallarmé, whom Symons knew intimately, left an interesting account of his poetic procedure. Having in mind a certain effect of mystery, for example the silence of the forest, he would concentrate on this effect until words spontaneously presented themselves, which he would afterwards revise, so that the colors and the notes suggested would be absolutely in harmony with the impression to be produced; but logical consistency and coherence were neglected. The pictorial symbolism of Huysmans, a master of gothic word-painting, and the mystical symbolism of Maeterlinck are then illustrated. In the 'Conclusion' the author contends that mysticism, the faith of the symbolist, is the surest remedy for the despair which comes with a sense of life's transiency. No better interpreter of the symbolists could be found than Arthur Symons, who had personal friendship with many of them, enthusiastic appreciation of their work, admirable critical discrimination, and an eminently readable style.

SYNNÖVE SOLBAKKEN, by Björnstjerne Björnson. This story, which was the first to reveal to the world at large the genius of the author, was brought out in 1857, in a Norwegian newspaper, and was not translated into English until 1870, although it had previously appeared in French, German, Spanish, and Russian. The scene of the narrative is laid among the Norwegian hills, which are minutely and picturesquely described. Synnöve, the daughter of a well-to-do farmer, is a pretty and charming girl, idolized by her parents and beloved by all who know her. She loves her early friend and schoolmate Thorbjörn Granliden, who is generally considered a rough and vindictive fellow. He is the son of worthy parents, but his father, by over-severity towards him in his childhood, has inculcated in him the very traits he has endeavored to overcome, and Thorbjörn grows up aggressive and reticent. He is deeply in love with Synnöve, but does not dare to confess his feelings to her family; nor does she allow him to visit her, on account of the reputation in which he is held. He finally promises her he will mend his ways and become more respected, when he unintentionally becomes entangled in a brawl, and is stabbed and seriously wounded. This catastrophe causes a change in him for the better; and by the time of his recovery he is much softened and improved. His father at the time of his son's illness realizes

52

how deep his affection is for him, and a reconciliation takes place between them which is the beginning of their final understanding of each other. After his return to health, his father goes with him to Solbakken and asks for the hand of Synnöve in marriage, which is granted by her parents. The story has been called one of Björnson's masterpieces; and shows his fine perception of human nature, and his skill in revealing the traits and characteristics of the peasantry of his native country. The development of the savage beauty of Thörbjorn's character, and the strong scene at the church door, where he becomes reconciled to his former enemy, show the marvelous power of the author.

TABLE TALK, or, ORIGINAL ESSAYS, by William Hazlitt, was originally published in two volumes, the first in 1821 and the second in 1822. Among its thirty-three essays may be mentioned 'On the Pleasures of Painting,' which sets forth with the author's usual romantic gusto the delights of the artist both in observation and in creation; Hazlitt's personal interest in art also appears in the essays on Sir Joshua Reynolds's 'Discourses on Painting' and on a landscape by Nicholas Poussin. In 'The Indian Jugglers' he contrasts the marvelous perfection attained by these entertainers, by rope-dancers, and by professional sportsmen like Cavanagh, a fives-player of his acquaintance, with the relative inadequacy of the work of painters, essayists, and poets; yet he concludes that the latter, having set themselves the harder task, are worthy of greater honor. 'On Going a Journey' reveals Hazlitt's fondness for solitary walking and for the comforts of good food and a snug inn. It records the luxurious sentiment with which he recalled the surroundings and details of some roadside meal with a favorite book in his youthful days. A number of the essays are on the usual general topics, e. g., 'On Genius and Common Sense,' 'On Vulgarity and Affectation.' These are treated in Hazlitt's characteristic sinewy style, with an abundance of apt quotations, particularly from Shakespeare, Spenser, and the early dramatists, and not infrequently a line from Wordsworth or Coleridge. Dramatic criticism is represented in 'Whether Actors Ought to Sit in the Boxes' (at intervals during the performance) — a question answered in the negative because the practice destroys illusion; and literary criticism appears in the essays on 'Familiar Style' and 'Milton's Sonnets.' On the whole, this volume is pretty broadly representative of Hazlitt's personality and genius.

TALE OF A TUB, A, a prose satire by Jonathan Swift, written about 1696 and published in 1704. A fifth edition with the author's apology and with notes appeared in 1710. Though the chief topics for ridicule are the bigotry of warring religious sects and the pedantry of dishonest critics the satire is broader in its scope and extends to the whole of human life. The book was issued anonymously and is provided with an elaborate machinery of apology, dedications, preface, introduction, digressions, and conclusion. The apology, prefixed to the fifth edition, explains the circumstances of composition and defends the author from the charge of irreverence. The dedication to Lord Somers and the epistle dedicatory to His Royal Highness, Prince Posterity, are extremely brilliant satires on the love of fame. In the preface the treatise is represented as an empty tub thrown to the Leviathan of skepticism to toss and play with until a scheme might be devised to check its dangerous activities. (The title also means "a cock and bull story.") This preface also ridicules the professed modesty of authors. The main purpose of the introduction is to satirize oratory under the three heads of the pulpit, the ladder, and the theatre. The first digression contrasts the true critic, who detects faults and the false critic who points out his own excellences. In the second, Swift attacks Bentley and Wotton the opponents of his patron, Sir William Temple, in the controversy as to the relative merits of ancient and modern writers. Brilliant pieces of satiric writing are the 'Digression in Praise of Digressions,' the 'Digression concerning Madness in a Commonwealth'; and in the conclusion Swift shows his literary virtuosity by writing upon nothing, "when the subject is utterly exhausted to let the pen still move on." In the main body of the book, which these chapters enclose and set off, the corruptions of the ancient church and the fanaticism of the Puritans are graphically represented by the story of three brothers, who inherit from their father three suits of clothes and a will which gives directions for the care of them. The clothes represent the Christian faith and the will the Scriptures. After seven years have passed (representing the first seven Christian centuries), the brothers desire to adorn their suits in the latest fashion; and in spite of the prohibitions of their father's will they contrive to torture it into a justification of disobedience. Peter, the eldest brother, who takes the lead in this equivocation, stands for the Church of Rome, which justifies the use of images and ceremonies on the ground of expediency and tradition. Later he makes himself heir of a wealthy man (the donation of Constantine), insists on homage from his brothers (papal supremacy), and develops other tyrannical practices which in a manner more vigorous than reverent typify the doctrine of Purgatory, auricular confession, the sale of indulgences, the use of holy-water, the issuing of papal bulls, the celibacy of the clergy, and the doctrine of transubstantiation. At length the two younger brothers rebel against Peter, get copies of their father's will (translation of the Scriptures), and resolve to reform their procedure (the Reformation). One of them, Martin (the Lutheran and Anglican churches), removes some of the ornaments from his clothes, but will not tear them all off lest he destroy the clothes too. The other, Jack (the Calvinists and kindred Protestant sects), passionately rips off every decoration (iconoclasm), tears and spoils his clothes, and makes his father's will a fetich, refusing to use an expression which does not occur in it or to do anything which it does not sanction (bibliolatry). He founds the sect of the Æolists, or believers in mystic inspiration, Swift's account of whom is a savage and coarse attack upon the enthusiasts of the extremer Puritan bodies. An appendix entitled 'The History of Martin' traces the history of the Church of England from the reign of Henry VIII. to that of Queen Anne under the continued employment of the characters of Peter, Martin, and Jack. In pungency of style and exuberant satiric power the book is unsurpassed.

TALE OF TWO CITIES, A, by Charles Dickens (1859), differs essentially from all his other novels in style and manner of treatment. Forster, in his 'Life of Dickens,' writes that "there is no instance, in his novels excepting this, of a deliberate and planned departure from the method of treatment which had been pre-eminently the source of his popularity as a novelist." To rely less upon character than upon incident, and to resolve that his actors should be expressed by the story more than they should express themselves by dialogue, was for him a hazardous, and can hardly be called an entirely successful, experiment. With singular dramatic vivacity, much constructive art, and with descriptive passages of a high order everywhere, there was probably never a book by a great humorist, and an artist so prolific in conception, with so little humor and so few remarkable figures. Its merit lies elsewhere. The two cities are London and Paris. The time is just before and during the French Revolution. A peculiar chain of events knits and interweaves the lives of a "few simple, private people" with the outbreak of a terrible public event. Dr.

Manette has been a prisoner in the Bastille for eighteen years, languishing there, as did so many others, on some vague unfounded charge.   His release when the story opens, his restoration to his daughter Lucie, the trial and acquittal of one Charles Darnay, nephew of a French marquis, on a charge of treason, the marriage of Lucie Manette to Darnay, — these incidents form the introduction to the drama of blood which is to follow.   Two friends of the Manette family complete the circle of important characters: Mr. Lorry, a solicitor of a very ancient London firm, and Sydney Carton, the most complete gentleman to be found in Dickens.   Carton has wasted his talents, leading a wild, bohemian existence in London.   The one garden spot in his life is his love for Lucie Manette.   To this love he clings as a drowning man to a spar.   For this love he lays down his life.   At the breaking out of the French Revolution, Darnay hastens to Paris to aid an old family servant who is in danger of losing his life.   His wife and his father-in-law follow him.   Gradually the entire circle of friends, including Mr. Lorry and Sidney Carton, find themselves in the horrible environment of the Paris of the Terror.   Darnay himself is imprisoned and condemned to death, by the agency of a wine-seller, Defarge, and his wife, a female impersonation of blood and war.   To save the husband of the woman he loves, Carton by strategy takes his place in prison.   The novel closes with the magnificent scene where Carton goes to his death on the scaffold, redeeming a worthless life by one supreme act of devotion.   Only the little sewing-girl in the death-cart with him knows his secret.   As he mounts the guillotine there rises before him the vision of a redeemed and renewed Paris, of a great and glorious nation.   There rise before him many memories and many dead hopes of his own past life, but in his heart there is the serenity of triumph: "It is a far, far better thing that I do than I have ever done; it is a far, far better rest that I go to than I have ever known."

TALES FROM SHAKESPEARE, by Charles and Mary Lamb (1807).   This modest volume, which was to prove Charles Lamb's first literary success, was written at the desire of William Godwin, as one of a series of children's books published by him. It consists of the plays of Shakespeare transposed into narrative form — the comedies by Mary Lamb, and the tragedies by Charles, and preserving as far as possible the original language of the poet's blank verse.   Prepared for children, its entire simplicity proved an added charm for readers, young and old.   The scholarship and literary taste of its authors, meanwhile, could but produce not a mere prose version of the plays for juvenile amusement, but a critical introduction to the study of Shakespeare, in the finest sense.

TALES OF A TRAVELLER, by Washington Irving (1824), is a delightful medley of humorous and tragic elements.   The genial humorist himself declares them to be "moral tales," with the moral "disguised as much as possible by sweets and spices." Sometimes sportive, abounding in mockery which although keen is never bitter, they are again weirdly grotesque or horrible, like the work of Poe or Hoffmann. Always they have the individual flavor and easy grace characteristic of Irving. The volume is divided into four parts.

In the first, a nervous gentleman and his friends, guests of a jovial fox-hunting baronet in his "ancient rook-haunted mansion," become reminiscent of family ghost-stories and vie with each other in wild romances, the actors in which cannot rest, but frighten would-be sleepers from their former haunts.

In Part ii., Buckthorne, ex-poor-devil author and actor, become a comfortable country squire, narrates the ups and downs of his varied career.

Part iii. is a succession of adventures with Italian banditti, recounted by a group of travelers gathered in an inn at Tarracina. Among them is a pretty Venetian bride who shudders to hear of the wild horde infesting the Apennines, always ready to attack and rob defenseless parties, and carry them off in the hope of extorting ransom. Another and more incredulous listener is a young Englishman, whom the bride dislikes for his insensibility. The next day he is taught a practical lesson in the existence of brigands; and by rescuing the fair Venetian from their hands, reverses her opinion of him.

In Part iv., Irving collects the romantic legends concerning Captain Kidd and his fellow buccaneers, and the treasure they are supposed to have secreted in the neighborhood of Hellgate. There are other legends too, involving the compact with the Devil, which tradition has made an inevitable condition of the securing of illegal gains. All these varied scenes of England, Italy, and America, Irving presents in happy incidental touches which never clog the action with description, yet leave a vivid picture with the reader.

TALKS TO TEACHERS ON PSYCHOLOGY, by William James (1899). The aim of these addresses is to make teachers conceive, and, if possible, reproduce sympathetically in their imagination, the mental life of their pupil as the sort of active unity which he himself feels it to be. "Psychology," says James, "is a science, and teaching is an art, and sciences never generate arts directly out of themselves. An intermediary inventive mind must make the application, by using its originality. To advance to that result, we must have an additional endowment altogether, a happy tact and ingenuity to tell us what definite things to say and do when the pupil is before us." The professional task of the teacher consists mainly in "training the pupil to behaviour," in the sense of the widest possible fit reaction to the circumstances into which the vicissitudes of life may lead him. Education is "the organization of acquired habits of conduct and tendencies to behaviour." There is no reception in the mind of the child without reaction, and no impression without a corresponding expression. There is only one way of insuring a pupil's interest and that is that the teacher before beginning to talk should make sure that the scholar has something in his mind to attend with. Once started, the subject must be made to suggest new aspects of itself and to prompt new questions. "I cannot but think," the author says in conclusion, "that to apperceive your pupil as a little sensitive, impulsive, associative, and reactive organism, partly fated and partly free, will lead to a better intelligence of all his ways. Understand him, then, as such a subtle little piece of machinery, and if, in addition, you can also see him *sub specie boni*, and love him as well, you will be in the best possible position for becoming perfect teachers."

TALMUD, BABYLONIAN, New Edition of the. English Translation; Original Text Edited, Formulaetd, and Punctuated: by Michael L. Rodkinson. Revised and Corrected by the Rev. Dr. Isaac M. Wise, President Hebrew Union College, Cincinnati, Ohio. 20 vols. in 10 (1896–1903). An edition in English translation of the whole Talmud thoroughly cleared of confusion and corruption, and brought into a readable and intelligible form, in which it can be understood in its vast range of interest, and judged upon its real merits as the great Jewish encyclopædia of religion, ethics, education, law, history, geography, medicine, mathematics, and in fact knowledge and opinion on every branch of thought and action. Dr. Wise speaks of the work as "Rodkinson's reconstruction of the original text of the Talmud"; which is confessed to have been in a very bad state, from irrelevant matter thrust in by later hands and even by hostile hands, and from corruptions such as works existing for ages in manuscript, and successively copied by scribes sometimes careless of accuracy and often free with changes or additions, are liable to. Dr. Rodkinson's perfect mastery of the Hebrew, and his comprehensive knowledge of the true Talmudical facts, with his admirable grasp of high ideals, and confidence that they are the ideals of his race and of the Talmud, have enabled him to reconstruct the original text and to give a clear and readable rendering of it in English, by which for the first time the Talmud is made as accessible to Anglo-Saxon readers as the books of the Old Testament. In his representation, "the Talmud is not a commentary on the Bible." It is not a body of dogma to be enforced, but of opinions to be considered; "not the decisions, but the debates, of the leaders of the people"; "not a compilation of fixed regulations," but a book of "liberty, both mental and religious," knowing "no authority but conscience and reason." The extreme freedom of suggestion and statement used by those who speak in it, the special reasons for many of its laws, such as the desire to break from the neck of the people the yoke of the priests, and the vein of humor running through much that seems most objectionable, are insisted on by Dr. Rodkinson as showing that "nothing could be more unfair, nothing more unfortunate, than to adopt the prevailing false notions about this ancient encyclopædia."

Dr. Rodkinson's work is thus not only a definitive English-Hebrew Talmud, for popular reading as well as for study of Jewish lore of every kind, but it is an interpretation to the modern mind of a vast monument of Hebrew life and thought, the value of which cannot be exaggerated. Vols. i. and ii. give 'Tract Sabbath,' in 390 pages. Vol. iii. gives 'Tract Erubin,' of 250 pages, in which are embodied the famous Rabbinical devices for getting round the prohibitions of 'Tract Sabbath.' Vol. iv. has 'Tract Shekalim,' which is all about a sacred half-shekel tax, paid by every Israelite at twenty years of age; and 'Tract Rosh Hashana' (or New Year), 232 pages. There are twelve of these 'Tracts,' forming the first section of the entire work, called 'Moed' (Festivals). The whole of Dr. Rodkinson's colossal task includes a new Hebrew text; some parts of which, to fill gaps in the commentary sections, he has himself composed from materials given in the Palestinian Talmud or in Maimonides. The entire work is sufficiently advanced to make its early completion secure. The reader of Dr. Rodkinson's own writings easily recognizes in his mastery of English style, and his high mental and ethical qualifications, ample assurance of his ability to make his Reconstructed Talmud an adequate text-book of the learning and the liberal spirit of modern Reformed Judaism. To Christian scholars, teachers, and students of liberal spirit, his work must be most welcome.

It may be briefly added here that there are two forms of the Talmud; namely, the Babylonian and the Palestinian. There first grew up a body of explanations and supplementary ordinances called Mishna, or teaching, designed to mark the application of Mosaic law or to supplement it. The impulse to this Mishnic development began in Babylon, during the exile there; it dominated the return to Jerusalem under Ezra; and it was brought to a final result by Rabbi Jehudah Hannasi, about 160 A. D. After the conclusion of the Mishna, there grew up two bodies of further explanation, called Gemara, one at Babylon and the other in Palestine. The Mishna thus came to exist in three greatly differing forms: Mishna by itself, and Mishna as embodied with Gemara in the Talmud of Babylon or that of Palestine. Dr. Rodkinson deals with the Babylonian form of Mishna and Gemara.

TAMING OF THE SHREW, THE (first printed in 1623), partly by Shakespeare and partly by an unknown hand, is a witty comedy of intrigue, founded on an old play about "the taming of the shrew" and on Ariosto's 'I Suppositi'; and is preceded by another briefer bit of dramatic fun (the "induction") on a different topic, — *i. e.*, how a drunken tinker, picked up on a heath before an alehouse by a lord and his huntsmen, is carried unconscious to the castle, and put to bed, and waited on by obsequious servants, treated to sumptuous fare, and music, and perfumes, and told that for many years he has been out of his head, and imagining that he was a poor tinker. "What! am I not Christopher Sly, old Sly's son of Burton Heath? . . . ask Marian Hacket, the fat ale-wife of Wincot, if she know me not." At length this Sancho Panza, who still retains his fondness for small ale, sits down to see the laughter-moving comedy 'The Taming of the Shrew,' enacted for his sole benefit by some strolling players. The brainless sot found its delicious humor dull; not so the public. Baptista, a rich old gentleman of Padua, has two daughters. The fair Katharina has a bit of a devil in her, is curst with a shrewish temper; but this is partly due to envy of the good fortune of the mincing artificial beauty, Bianca, her sister, whose demure, gentle ways make the men mad over her. Yet Kate, when "tamed," proves after all to be the best wife. The other gallants will none of her; but the whimsical Petruchio of Verona has come "to wive it wealthily in Padua," and nothing daunted, wooes and wives the young shrew in astonishing fashion. The law of the time made the wife the chattel of her husband, otherwise even Petruchio might have failed. His method was to conquer her will "to kill her in her own humor." He comes very late to the wedding, clothed like a scarecrow, an old rusty sword by his side, and riding a sunken-backed spavined horse with rotten saddle and bridle. His waggish man Grumio is similarly accoutred. At the altar he gives the priest a terrible box on the ear, refuses to stay to the wedding dinner, and on the way to his country-house acts like a madman. Arrived home, he storms at and beats the servants, allows Kate not a morsel of food for two days, preaches continence to her, throws the pillows around the chamber, and raises Cain a-nights generally so that she can get no sleep, denies her the bonnet and dress the tailor has brought, and so manages things as to seem to do all out of love to her and regard for her health, and without once losing his good-humor. In short he subdues her, breaks her will, and makes his supreme; so that at the end she makes a speech to the other wives about the duty of obedience, that would make the "new woman" of our time smile in scorn. Of Bianca's three suitors the youngest, Lucentio, gets the prize by a series of smart tricks. Disguised as a tutor of languages he gets her love as they study, while his rivals, "like a gemini of baboons," blow their nails out in the cold and whistle. Lucentio at the very start gets his servant Tranio to personate himself, and an old pedant is hired to stand for his father; and while Baptista, the father of Bianca, is gone to arrange for the dower with this precious pair of humbugs, Lucentio and his sweetheart run off to church and get married. The arrival of the real father of Lucentio makes the plot crackle with life and sensation.

TANTE, by Anne Douglas Sedgwick (1911). This is the story of the part played by Madame Okraska, a great pianist and musical genius, in the life of her ward Karen Woodruff and the latter's husband Gregory Jardine, a well-to-do barrister. While for the first time listening to the celebrated pianist, Jardine's interest is awakened in a charming young girl who follows every movement of the musician with absorbed attention, and who proves to be Madame Okraska's ward. He subsequently meets her at the home of a mutual friend, where Madame Okraska (called by her ward "Tante") is receiving a throng of devotees, and where Jardine awakens the antipathy of the elder woman by his failure to accord her the admiration she exacts from all. Tante goes on a tour to America leaving her ward to vegetate in the country with Mrs. Talcott, an elderly retainer. Here, Jardine wooes and wins the unusual girl who has been brought up in an unconventional world wholly apart from his own social standards. Although loving and docile, Karen is obdurate at any suggestion that is not in harmony with her guardian's ideas, and withholds her promise of marriage until Tante has cabled her consent. The marriage takes place and the young pair enjoy wedded bliss until the return of Tante to the field. Her jealous nature resents Karen's devotion to another, and Jardine's antipathy to her, which he tries to conceal, evokes her bitter hatred. She does everything in her power to build up a barrier between husband and wife and finally succeeds in working sufficiently upon Karen's overwrought sympathies to cause her to desert Jardine and fly back to her adored guardian. Her flight is ill-timed, as she arrives at a moment to interrupt an affair which Tante is carrying on with a young poet, named Drew. Drew, who is wearying of the elder woman, begins to pay attention to Karen and is discovered by Tante when protesting his passion for her ward. In a burst of anger, which for the first time reveals her true character to the deluded Karen, she orders the girl from the premises after overwhelming her with abuse. Karen wanders away, and is picked up ill and half-crazed by an old admirer, whose protection is misunderstood by the deserted husband. Through the good offices of Mrs. Talcott the misunderstanding is finally explained, and Karen, her eyes opened to the perfidy of her once adored Tante, is restored to her long-suffering husband.

TARAS BULBA, by Nikolai F. Gogol (1839). This is a gruesome story of Cossack life in the fifteenth century. Ostap and Andrii, the sons of Taras Bulba, a Cossack leader return from school; and he takes them at once to the Setch (a large Cossack village) to present them to his brothers in arms. There they drink, carouse, and quarrel, until a new ataman is elected and an expedition is sent against Kief. Andrii is taken into the city by the maid of the Voivoid's beautiful daughter, his sweetheart in student days. The city is given over to famine; he feeds his love, and for the sake of her beauty turns traitor and joins her party. The Voivod goes out to attack the Cossacks; and Taras Bulba, in his righteous wrath, slays his son. His other son Ostap, is captured, and he himself is wounded. On recovering, he bribes a Jew to take him in disguise to Warsaw, where he sees Ostap tortured to death. He raises an army, fights, and spares none, shouting as he burns and slays, "This is a mass for the soul of Ostap." Finally he is captured, however, thirty men falling upon him at once. He is bound to a tree; fagots are placed at the foot of it and preparations are made to roast him. He sees that his Cossacks are lured into a trap, and shouts a warning; they fly over the precipice on their horses, and plunge into the river, across which they swim and escape. Taras perishes, but his Cossacks live — to talk of their lost leader.

TARTARIN OF TARASCON, by Alphonse Daudet (1872). Daudet's exquisite portrayal of mock adventures of the boastful Tartarin is a delightfully entertaining specimen of the finest quality of French humorous writing. Tartarin of Tarascon, to whom the adulation of his fellow-townsmen is as necessary as the breath of life, is animated by the spirit of a big-game hunter and a love of adventure. On Sundays, accompanied by his fellow-sportsmen of Tarascon, he goes just outside the town, and in lieu of other game, long since fled, tosses his cap into the air and riddles it with shot. At this noble pastime Tartarin is without a peer. His study walls are thickly hung with such trophies of his skill. He has long been the absolute king of Tarascon sportsmen. To assure this position among his townsmen, who are beginning to doubt his prowess, he starts for Algiers on a real lion hunt.

With innumerable trunks filled with arms, ammunition, medicine, and condensed aliments, arrayed in the historic garb of a Turk, Tartarin arrives at Algiers. An object of much curiosity and speculation, he at once sets out for lions, but returns daily, disheartened by his fruitless quest. He is himself bagged by a pretty woman, Baya, in Moorish dress. One day he meets Barbasson, a native of Tarascon, captain of the Zouave, plying from Marseilles to Algiers. Barbasson tells him of the anxiety and eagerness for news of him at Tarascon.

At this, Tartarin deserts Baya, and starts south for lions. After many adventures in the desert, he finally kills the only lion he has seen, — a poor, blind, tame old lion, for which he has to settle to the amount of all his paraphernalia and money. The lion's skin is forwarded to Tarascon, and Tartarin tramps to Algiers, accepts passage from Barbasson, and at last reaches home, where he is greeted with frenzied applause. His position has been made secure by the arrival of the lion's skin, and he again assumes his place in Tarascon. Evenings, at his club, amid a breathless throng, Tartarin begins: "Once upon an evening, you are to imagine that, out in the depths of the Sahara — ."

TARTUFFE, by Molière (Jean Baptiste Poquelin). This most famous comedy, once performed under the title 'The Impostor,' was published complete in 1669. The principal characters are: Madame Pernelle; Orgon, her son; his wife Elmire, his son and daughter; and a friend, Tartuffe, who stands forth as a type of the religious hypocrite. The old lady is very devout, but uses plain words when scolding the grandchildren. Orgon, the husband, on coming home hears that his wife is ill; but immediately inquires about Tartuffe, seeming to think of no else. This honey-lipped egoist is chosen by the father as the proper person to whom he should marry his daughter.

But she thinks not so. Those who are forced to marry against their will do not make virtuous wives. The modesty of Tartuffe is easily shocked; yet he would examine closely the material of the dress of Elmire, to whom he pays court, telling her that to sin in secret is not to sin at all. Elmire risks her reputation a little to unmask the vile deceiver in the eyes of her husband. Through fear of hell, Tartuffe yet rules the husband, gets his property by scheming, and has him arrested as a traitor. At last the king acts; and Tartuffe is led off to prison. This is a striking presentation of the manners and morals of the people and times.

TASK, THE, a descriptive and reflective poem by William Cowper, published in 1785. It was begun at the instance of the poet's friend, Lady Austen, who playfully asked him to write a poem in blank-verse about a sofa. Accepting the challenge Cowper traces in about one hundred Miltonic lines the evolution of the sofa from the stool. He then proceeds discursively to enlarge on the pleasures of country walks, the delights of gardening, and the coziness of the winter fireside, mingling these descriptive passages with autobiographic records of religious experience, satirical attacks on the luxury of cities, the corruption of politicians and the worldliness of the clergy, pietistic denunciations of deism, skepticism, and natural science, and outbursts of humanitarian sympathy for slaves, dumb animals, and all who are oppressed. These and other topics occupy six books entitled respectively: 'The Sofa,' 'The Time-Piece' (i.e., the omens of future judgment), 'The Garden,' 'The Winter Evening,' 'The Winter Morning Walk,' 'The Winter Walk at Noon.' 'The Task' reflects the enthusiasm for natural scenery, the impulse to self-revelation, and the eagerness to relieve suffering, of the later eighteenth century. The author is a refined, sensitive Christian gentleman with a gift of easy, graceful expression, and a nature of fine sensibility and quiet humor. The morbid strain which so sadly affected his peace and happiness left no trace on this poem.

TATLER, THE, a collection of periodical essays, 271 in number, which originally appeared in the form of a penny journal, issued three times a week, from April 12th, 1709, to January 2d, 1711, and were reprinted in four volumes, 1710–1711. Richard Steele was the originator of the publication and the writer of at least 188 of the papers; Joseph Addison was the author of 42, and collaborated with Steele in 36; Swift had part in about a dozen numbers, and there were a few minor contributors. The venture was originally intended as a magazine of general news. Each number consisted at first of several sections. Accounts of gallantry, pleasure, and entertainment were dated from White's Chocolate House; discussions of poetry, from Will's Coffee House, of learning, from the Grecian, of miscellaneous topics from the editor's apartment; and of foreign and domestic news, from St. James's Coffee House. The latter item consisted mainly of dispatches and comments concerning the War of the Spanish Succession, then raging, and was a result of Steele's official position of Gazetteer, which gave him access to recent information. After the eightieth number, however, these news-items seldom appear. With the ninetieth, instead of containing three or four brief essays, each number includes one substantial article, on the model afterwards continued by the same writers in 'The Spectator.' Like those of the latter periodical, the articles are concerned exclusively with the criticism of manners and the promotion of culture and morality. Discussions of public behavior, of costume, of sports and entertainments, of vices and frivolities, of duties and obligations, of drama, poetry, and the standard of taste, make up the bulk of the contents. Gaming and duelling are denounced, chivalry upheld, and womanly modesty and seriousness urged. As in 'The Spectator,' a number of fictitious personages add life and interest to the essays and give opportunity for interesting character-sketches. The writer of the papers is supposed to be Isaac Bickerstaff, an old philosopher and astrologer of sixty-four. He is borrowed from the pamphlets in which Swift writing under this pseudonym denounced and hoaxed the impostor, Partridge (1708–1709). Other personages are Bickerstaff's familiar servant, Pacolet, his half-sister, Jenny Distaff, her husband, Tanquillus, and their three boys. The members of his club, the Trumpet, in Fetter Lane, forestall the better known Spectator's Club. They are Sir Geoffrey Notch, a decayed gentleman, Major Matchlock, a veteran of the Civil War, Dick Reptile and his nephew, and a Bencher of one of the Inns of Court. Among Addison's contributions to the portrait-gallery of 'The Tatler' are Ned Softly, the poetaster, and Tom Folio, the pedant. As the Spectator is usually credited to the genius of Addison so the Tatler may be regarded as chiefly the product of Steele. The two differ as exquisite polish and logical completeness differ from careless spontaneity and incidental meditation.

TECHNIQUE OF THE DRAMA, an analysis of dramatic principles by Gustav Freytag, published in 1863, translated by Elias J. MacEwan in 1895. The author, himself a successful dramatist, seeks to determine the laws according to which great plays are composed, supplementing the rules of Aristole's ' Poetics ' by reference to the works of Shakespeare, Lessing, Goethe, and Schiller. In the first section of the book, ' Dramatic Action,' Freytag shows how the central idea of a play is selected and developed from the raw material of experience or reading, defines the dramatic as emotion leading to action, or action producing emotion, explains dramatic unity as the result of the adequate motivation of every action, emphasizes the need of probability, magnitude, and progressive interest in the actions chosen, and discusses the nature of the "katharsis" or emotional renewal effected by tragedy. The second part 'The Construction of the Drama' represents every tragedy as made up of a rising and a falling movement, distinguishing the exposition, the initial impulse, the ascending action, the climax, the entrance of a tragic force, the descending action, the final reaction or possibility of a happy outcome, and the catastrophe. This helpful formula is then applied to the Greek and the Teutonic drama and is shown to be the basis of the division of plays into five acts. Effectiveness in the structure of scenes whether including few persons or large masses is then happily illustrated from Shakespeare (Section IV). In the fourth section, 'The Characters,' Freytag emphasizes the need of unity, consistency, proper relation to the action, and consonance with the age in which the personages are supposed to live. Questions of versification and of method in composition occupy the short fifth and sixth sections. The book has had wide currency and considerable influence. Its scheme of dramatic structure is certainly valuable to the student of the classic plays, ancient and modern.

TELEMACHUS ('TÉLÉMAQUE'), ADVENTURES OF, by Fénelon, is a French prose epic in twenty-four books, which appeared in 1699. Having been shipwrecked upon the island of the goddess Calypso, Telemachus relates to her his varied and stirring adventures while seeking his father Ulysses, who, going to the Trojan war, has been absent from home for twenty years. In his search the youth has been guarded and guided by the goddess Minerva, disguised as the sage Mentor. This recital occupies the first six books, the remaining eighteen containing the hero's further remarkable experiences, until at last he returns to Ithaca, where he finds Ulysses already arrived. On the way thither occur his escape from the island of Calypso, whose love for Telemachus prompts her to detain him on her fair domain, and his visit to the infernal regions, in search of his father, whom he believes to be dead. This romance of education, "designed at once to charm the imagination and to inculcate truths of morals, politics, and religion," has always been regarded as a French classic. It is still much used in English-speaking schools, as a model of French composition. The author has borrowed from, and imitated, the Greek and Latin heroics with undisguised freedom, and has succeeded in imparting to his work their antique air and flavor.

TEMPEST, THE, one of Shakespeare's very latest plays (1611), written in the mellow maturity of his genius, is probably based on a lost Italian *novella* or play, though certain incidents are borrowed from three pamphlets on the Bermudas and Virginia and from Florio's Montaigne. The scene is said to be laid in the haunted island of Lampedusa in the Mediterranean. In the opening lines we see a ship laboring in heavy seas near the shore of an island, whose sole inhabitants, besides the spirits of earth and air typified in the dainty yet powerful sprite Ariel, are Prospero and his lovely daughter Miranda, and their slave, the deformed boor Caliban, an aborigine of the island. The grave and good Prospero is a luckier castaway than Robinson Crusoe, in that his old friend Gonzalo put into the boat with him not only his infant daughter, but clothes, and some books of magic, by the aid of which both men and spirits, and the very elements, are subject to the beck of his wand. He was the rightful Duke of Milan, but was supplanted by his brother Antonio, who with his confederate, the king of Naples, and the latter's son Ferdinand and others, is cast ashore on the island. The shipwreck occurs full in the sight of the weeping Miranda; but all hands are saved, and the ship too. The humorous characters are the butler Stephano, and the court jester Trinculo, both semi-drunk, their speech and songs caught from the sailors, and savoring of salt and tar. Throughout the play the three groups of personages, — the royal retinue with the irrepressible and malapropos old Gonzalo, the drunken fellows and Caliban, and Prospero with his daughter and Ferdinand, — move leisurely to and fro, the whole action taking up only three hours. The three boors, fuddled with their fine liquor and bearing the bark bottle, rove about the enchanted island, fall into the filthy-mantled pool, and are stoutly pinched by Prospero's goblins for theft. The murderous plot of Antonio and the courtier Sebastian is exposed at the phantom banquet of the harpies. Spellbound in the linden grove, all the guilty parties come forward into a charmed circle and take a lecture from Prospero. General reconciliation. Then finally, Miranda and Ferdinand are discovered playing chess before Prospero's cell, and learn that to-morrow they set sail for Naples to be married.

TEMPLE HOUSE, the third and last novel of Elizabeth Barstow Stoddard, was published in 1867. The scene is laid in a forgotten, decaying seaport town of New England. The plot follows the fortunes of one family, the inmates of Temple House — a homestead of dignity in the prosperous days of the town, but now tarnished and forlorn. It shelters Argus Gates, a retired sea-captain, a lover of solitude; his sister-in-law Roxalana, an ineffective, dreamy, silence-loving soul; and her child, Tempe, an elf of a girl who marries John Drake, a neighbor, almost before she is out of short dresses. He dies soon after, the young widow going back to Temple House. By a shipwreck another unusual character, Sebastian Ford, is added to the Temple House circle. The Spanish blood in his veins tinges his least act with romance. He proves his devotion to his rescuer, Argus Gates, by defending the honor of the woman he loves, Virginia Brande, the daughter of a wealthy neighbor. The book closes upon the happiness of Virginia and Argus, a kind of subdued happiness in accordance with the autumnal atmosphere of the story. The slumberous haze lifts only to reveal two or three spirited scenes connected with Virginia's love-story.

TEN THOUSAND A YEAR, by Samuel C. Warren (1841). This story, though regarded by critics as "ridiculously exaggerated and liable to the suspicion of being a satire on the middle classes," has held a certain place in fiction for more than half a century. Tittlebat Titmouse, its hero, is a vulgar and conceited young clerk in the London shop of Dowlas, Tagrag, Bobbin & Co. Through the machinations of Messrs. Quirk, Gammon, and Snap, Solicitors, who have discovered a flaw in the title of an old and rich family, he finds himself put in possession of an estate yielding £10,000 a year. Hitherto abused and bullied by everybody, he is now flattered and invited by his former master, Tagrag, by Quirk of the great law firm, and by the Earl of Dredlington, each anxious to secure him as a son-in-law. Titmouse marries Lady Cecilia, and takes his seat in Parliament in place of Charles Aubrey, dispossessed of the estate, his election being secured by scandalous corruption and a reckless expenditure of money. The Earl of Dredlington, finding a deed by which his son-in-law settles £2,000 a year on Gammon, learns that it is hush-money; and that Titmouse, proving to be an illegitimate child of the great house, has no right to the estate he enjoys. In consequence the attorney-general fixes a charge of conspiracy upon Quirk, Gammon, and Snap. Quirk and Snap are imprisoned, while Gammon escapes only by suicide. The Aubreys' rights are restored. The wretched Titmouse goes through insolvency; and his mind having become unbalanced by his overthrow, he passes the remainder of his miserable life in a lunatic asylum. The story has no literary standing, and is verbose and overloaded with irrelevant matter. But the plot is ingenious, the legal complications are managed in a way that won the admiration of accomplished lawyers, and the story with all its faults contrived to arouse and maintain the reader's interest.

TEN YEARS' DIGGING IN EGYPT, 1881–1891, by W. M. Flinders Petrie, published in 1892, is an informal, non-technical account of the labors of this great Egyptologist, illustrated by numerous wood-cuts from sketches of his own. He begins by telling of his season at the pyramids, 1881–1882, which he carefully measured, making many discoveries as to their departure from exact symmetry and as to the tools and methods of their construction. In the next expedition, that of 1884, he unearthed at Tanis an interesting portrait-statuette and a collection of papyri with a key to the hieroglyphics. In 1885 he discovered some Greek inscriptions, coins, and vases in the Greek colony of Naukratis. Several months of 1886 were devoted to the twin Greek colony of Daphnæ, the Biblical Tahpanhes, where both Egyptian and Greek relics were found; near by was a place called Tell Nebesheh, where the explorer unearthed a statue of Rameses II. and a temple. In 1887 Petrie made a voyage up the Nile to Thebes, Assuan, and Esneh, where he copied many hieroglyphic inscriptions and made ethnographic studies of the faces on the monuments. In the following year he was at work on the pyramid at Hawara, and remained in that district for three years, making examinations of many pyramids and discovering many domestic implements and other relics. To these records of exploration Petrie adds some interesting chapters on general topics. In Chapter XI. he traces the history of art and civilization in Egypt from the earliest times. In Chapter XII. he explains how excavations are made, showing the need of imagination in choosing a site, of following a general plan, of training workmen to be careful of their finds and to report on where they found them, of rejecting useless objects, and of safely packing the objects discovered. The last two chapters describe respectively the character of the Egyptian fellah, and the necessities of the traveler who would live cheaply in Egypt. The book is entertainingly written, reflecting the enthusiasm of the scholar and the practical knowledge of the experienced traveler and man of the world.

TENNYSON, ALFRED, LORD, A MEMOIR, by his son Hallam Tennyson (1897). This great biography is exceedingly full and circumstantial, progressing from year to year of Tennyson's life, letting it tell itself for the most part through letters. A great number of these were given to the world for the first time, together with many poems not before printed. Appended to the second volume are a number of personal recollections of the poet, by men distinguished as statesmen and men of letters.

TENT LIFE IN SIBERIA, by George Kennan (1870). The author of this book of exploration and adventure was employed, in 1865–67, by the Western Union Telegraph Company, in its audacious scheme of building an overland line to Europe by way of Alaska, Bering's Strait, and Siberia, — a futile project, soon forgotten in the success of the Atlantic Cable. He tells the story of the undertaking from the side of the employees, — a story known to few even of the original projectors. It is a record of obstacles well-nigh insuperable met and overcome with astonishing patience and courage; of nearly six thousand miles of unbroken wilderness explored in two years, from Vancouver's Island to Bering's Straits, and from Bering's Straits to the Chinese frontier; of camping in the wildest mountain fastnesses of Kamtchatka, in the gloomy forests of Alaska and British Columbia, and on the desolate plains of Northeastern Siberia; of the rugged mountain passes of Northern Asia traversed by hardy men mounted on reindeer; of the great rivers of the North navigated in skin canoes; of tents pitched on northern plains in temperatures of 50 and 60 degrees below zero.

Though the enterprise failed in its special aim, it succeeded in contributing to our knowledge of a hitherto untraveled and unknown region. Its surveys and explorations are invaluable. The life and customs of the natives are minutely described; while the traveler's sense of the vastness, the desolation, and the appalling emptiness of this northern world of snow and ice conveys a chill almost of death to the sympathetic reader. The book is written in the simple, business-like style that, when used by men of action to tell what they have done, adds a great charm of reality to the tale.

TERRE, LA, see **ROUGON-MACQUART.**

TESS OF THE D'URBERVILLES, a remarkable novel by Thomas Hardy (1891), is an embodiment in fiction of the Tragedy of the Woman, — the world-old story of her fall, and of her battle with man to recover her virginity of soul. Tess, a beautiful village girl, is a lineal descendant of the ancient D'Urberville family. Her far-off gentle blood shows itself in her passionate sensitive nature. By a mere accident she becomes the prey of a young man of gross instincts, returning to her home soiled and dismayed. Her child is born and dies. "Her physical blight becomes her mental harvest"; she is lifted above the groping mental state of the people about her. This etherealization has fatal results. As she was once the victim of man's vices, she is destined to become the victim of his conventional virtues. At a farm far removed from the scene of her sufferings, she meets Angel Clare, a gentleman's son. Their mutual love ends in marriage. On their wedding-day Tess tells Clare of her past. From that hour she ceases to be for him "enskied and sainted," becoming a mere soiled thing which had drifted in its perilous beauty across his path. He leaves her; and her struggle with her anguish of spirit, with her poverty, and her despair, has a fearful ending: "The President of the Immortals" had finished his sport with her. 'Tess' is well-nigh primeval in its treatment. A novel created apparently by inexorable forces of nature, it is joined by its strength and pitilessness to the blind powers of the world. Yet it is not without sunny spaces, revelations of warm nooks of earth hidden from the blasts of the tempest.

THADDEUS OF WARSAW, by Jane Porter (1803), is an "old-time" romance. Thaddeus, a young Polish nobleman, — last in the line from John Sobieski, the famous king of Poland and conqueror of the Turks,—leaves home with his grandfather, count palatine, to serve under King Stanislaus in repelling an invasion by Russia and her allies. Defeated after gallant fighting, the old count is slain, and Thaddeus flies to the defense of his mother in their castle. She expires in his arms; Thaddeus is driven forth, and sees Warsaw and the Sobieski castle burned. The renowned General Kosciuszko, the king's nephew Prince Poniatowski, and other historic characters, figure prominently in the tale. After the partition of Poland the exiled Thaddeus reaches England, where a cloud on his birth is lifted, showing him a scion of the Somerset family; his marriage with a high-born English girl makes a happy ending. This was the earliest of Miss Porter's historical novels, and it appeared some years before Scott's 'Waverley.' Having seen and talked with many poor and proud, but noble, Polish refugees in London, Miss Porter wrote with a pen "dipped in their tears," representing a pure and generous ideal, — the nobles as mostly noble, and the serfs like Arcadian shepherds.

THAIS, by Anatole France (1890). Thais was a famous courtesan in Alexandria about the fourth century. Paphnutius, a holy man, who had retired to the desert to live the monastic life, has a vision of the beautiful actress and is inspired to convert her and save her from sin. He returns to Alexandria, the scene of his profane youth, borrows a rich embroidered garment from his former school friend, Nicias, and presents himself at the house of Thais. The fear of death and age had lately oppressed Thais, and she listens to his talk of eternal life and of spiritual love, which appealed to her all the more, because as a child she had been baptized by a Christian slave. Paphnutius persuades Thais to renounce her profession, to make a bonfire of all her riches, costly cups, priceless statues, jewels and furniture and carpets, and to follow him to a nunnery in the desert. He leaves her in the care of the abbess, and returns to his cell and his disciples, but he is unable day or night to banish from his mind the lovely image of Thais. He goes forth again and becomes a stylite, living on the top of a pillar, to separate himself from the world. Finally he hears that Thais, the penitent and saint, is dying. He regrets that even at the price of damnation he has not possessed one moment of her love. He hastens to Thais, whom he finds at the point of death, and in a frenzy tries to win her from the vision of the life eternal. She pays no attention to his pleadings and to his earthly passion, and dies in sanctity. The face of Paphnutius is so disfigured by his sensual desire that the nuns shrink from him as from a vampire. "He had become so hideous that as he passed his hand over his face he felt its brutality."

THEOLOGICAL AND LITERARY ESSAYS, by Richard Holt Hutton (1875). The two volumes of this work contain nine theological and nine literary papers. Among the first are 'The Moral Significance of Atheism,' 'The Atheistic Explanation of Religion,' 'Science and Theism,' 'What is Revelation?' 'M. Renan's Christ,' etc., etc. Mr. Hutton is a theist, owing his belief in theism to his study of the religious philosophy of F. D. Maurice. After he has spoken of skepticism and dogmatism as but different forms of the attempt to accommodate infinite living claims upon us to our human weakness, he says: "It seems to me that it has been the one purpose of all the divine revelation or education of which we have any record, to waken us up out of this perpetually recurring tendency to fall back into ourselves," — i. e., to self-forgetfulness, and self-surrender to a Higher than ourselves. Among the names and subjects considered in the literary essays are Wordsworth, Shelley, Browning, the poetry of the Old Testament, Clough, Arnold, Tennyson, and Hawthorne. As a whole these are marked by depth of insight, breadth of view, and nicety of judgment. They show high scholarship, and an innate gift for criticism highly trained; and they are very interesting reading.

THEORY OF THE LEISURE CLASS, THE, 'An Economic Study of Institutions' by Thorstein Veblen (1899). It is a merciless analysis, from the strictly economic point of view, of the claims of the leisure class to be a valuable factor in modern life. He finds that this class originated in the stages of savagery, when the men of the tribe devoted themselves to predatory acquisition, leaving the productive work to women and slaves. In the barbaric stage, which followed, the control of wealth and freedom from labor marked the nobility and work was regarded as a badge of social inferiority. This feeling continued when the growth of industrial activity led to the modern struggle for wealth; and the ruling classes who emerged from this struggle were characterized by two distinctive features: "conspicuous leisure and conspicuous consumption." By the first term the author means the tendency of the upper classes to avoid menial labor and associations, to cultivate manners and modes of speech which suggest a life of elegant refinement, and to indulge in such activities as government, war, sports, and devout observances but not in productive labor; by "conspicuous consumption" he means the desire to avoid the appearance of poverty and to convey an impression of pecuniary strength by spending money in extravagant and wasteful ways. The author's interpretation of the term "waste" is a narrowly economic one, anything which contributes merely to subjective satisfaction and not to definite physical needs being regarded as wasteful; and he carries his theory too far in attributing practically every non-utilitarian desire of the leisure class to the impulse to show one's financial superiority. But he is a keen observer, with an incisive, critical mind, who sees through many insincerities and veiled predatory instincts, and few of the leisure classes can read the book without feeling uncomfortable. This discomfort is not lessened by his occasional rather elaborate protests that of course he is speaking purely in the economic sense and that no doubt these activities may have a high cultural value, but that he is concerned with very practical realities. Defenders of the classics are particularly irritated by his treatment of this subject as a mere conventional badge of the leisure classes without any practical use and hence an admirable example of "conspicuous waste." Religion, the law, business, and sports, fare no better. But he has done the leisure classes an admirable service in allowing them to see themselves as the industrial classes probably view them. The style is unadorned, unemotional, detached, and coolly remorseless.

THEOLOGICAL AND LITERARY ESSAYS, by Richard Holt Hutton (1875).

THESE LYNNEKERS, a novel, by J. D. Beresford (1916). The seven Lynnekers are the rector, his ineffectual wife, and their five children. Strictly speaking, the story is concerned with Richard, really the cleverest of the sons. When Dick fails in the classics at the Oakstone School, the Rector feels justified in putting him into the Medboro' Bank, instead of sending him to Oxford. He is totally unaware that Dickie is a mathematical genius. Dickie's job means something like a hundred and fifty pounds in the exchequer. On the strength of the saving, everybody spends more money, particularly Mrs. Lynneker. Meanwhile Dickie is bound to the bank for five years. But by studying evenings he works out an education for himself; he reads mathematics, history, economics, literature, and theology, and his great desire is "to get at the bottom of things." Meanwhile Mrs. Lynneker draws on the funds of the Coal Club for family expenses. To hide her defections, she borrows thirty pounds from the Medboro' Loan Company. When the company fleeces her, rather than go to her husband, she tells Dickie, who succeeds in driving the Loan Company out of town. At the end of five years, Dickie has made himself so indispensable that he is offered the position of bank-manager. But he prefers "to get into the game" in a large city. Just at this juncture, Martyn Lynneker, a distant cousin, comes down to see the family. He is so impressed by Dickie's power of thinking for himself that he offers him a legal education and a possible seat in Parliament. After some thought, Dickie refuses the offer because he sees in it a barrier to his own political independence. Instead he goes into the business office of a financier.

The family, which has been much disappointed in Dickie's treatment of Martyn, is delighted with his engagement to Sybil Groome, the bishop's niece. But even in the flush of his first love, Dickie has to yield to the demands of his family, and when the rector is stricken with paralysis, Dickie sacrifices everything to be with him. In his last days, the rector realizes for the first time that Dickie is the tower of strength of his family. The others all fail to the end to appreciate the solidity of his character and what he has done for them.

THOUGHTS, see **PENSÉES,** by Denis Diderot.

THOUGHTS CONCERNING EDUCATION, SOME, by John Locke (1693). Locke's work, which has its place among the classics of education, originally consisted of letters addressed to his friend Edward Clark about the care of his son. It is not, and does not profess to be, a treatise on education in general, but only the advice of one friend to another about the individual education of a gentleman's son. At school and university he had strongly disapproved of the educational methods in vogue in his time. In this work he propounded views which are even yet the aspiration rather than the achievement of educational reformers. He taught that a sound basis for education should be laid by training the child in healthful habits of eating, sleep, cleanliness, and exercise. Children should be hardened by exercise in the open air, and by robust treatment instead of being enervated by luxuries and delicacies. On the other hand they should not be harshly used and beating should be reserved only for obstinacy and untruthfulness. Upon the foundation of bodily health should be built up a training in character and intelligence,—"virtue, wisdom, breeding, and learning." The teacher must have wisdom rather than mere learning. "The great business of all" (for both teacher and pupil) "is virtue and wisdom. Teach him to get a mastery over his inclinations, and submit his appetite to reason. This being obtained, and by constant practice settled into habit, the hardest part of the task is over." He strongly recommends that the young gentleman "should *learn a trade, a manual trade;* nay two or three, but one more particularly," that in after life he may have the means of useful diversion in leisure hours. Education should be a natural enjoyment, not an unwelcome task, and should fit the pupil for a life of moral usefulness.

THREE DAUGHTERS OF M. DUPONT, THE ('Les Trois Filles de M. Dupont') by Eugène Brieux (1897). A social drama dealing with the theme of the French marriage of convenience, arranged by the parents. The play opens as Julie, the youngest daughter of M. and Mme. Dupont, is about to be betrothed to Antonin Mairaut. The discussion of the proposal of marriage is given in the LIBRARY. Julie's father allows her fifteen minutes to make up her mind about her future husband, and reminds her of her older sister Caroline's unhappy life in the household as an old maid. The parents on either side deceive each other about the dowry and settlement, and the marriage is arranged. Julie finds her husband a selfish tyrant who is determined to make her the slave of his pleasure. Antonin, for reasons of expense, refuses to allow her the motherhood she had looked forward to for her happiness in the marriage. They quarrel violently, and she makes up her mind to leave him. The oldest sister, Angèle, the victim of seduction in her youth, is a demi-mondaine in Paris. An aunt leaves a legacy to Caroline and Angèle, and Angèle comes home after eighteen years' absence for the legal formalities. Caroline longs to be married and turns over a part of her inheritance to her father's clerk to win him for a husband, not knowing he is already bound to another woman. The two older sisters advise Julie from their bitter experience not to divorce her husband, but to live on with him, for of the opportunities open to the average girl in provincial French society, as illustrated in the lives of the three sisters, the loveless marriage is the least intolerable. Julie returns to her husband, resigned to the inevitable, saying, "I had romantic ideas, I saw marriage as it is not. Now I understand it. In life it is necessary to make concessions." She determines to console herself with a lover like the rest. The play is a plea for a marriage of love, reiterated by the dramatist, in another play 'La Française.'

THREE ENGLISH STATESMEN, by Goldwin Smith (1867), is a course of lectures delivered during his professorship of history at Oxford University, on Pym, Cromwell, and Pitt. The clear and brilliant style of the book, vigorous and simple, at once enchains the attention and wins from the reader an absorbed interest in the author's theories of politics and politicians. He has the rare faculty of condensing whole chapters of history into a few words, and of presenting in one vivid picture the complicated state of nations. In his essay on Pym, he is able in a few pages to detail the problems and grievances that had beset the English people, and indeed the Continental nations, ever since the first outbreaks against the absolute power of the Church. He recognizes that the Reformation in England was by no means accomplished when Henry VIII. chose for his own ends to defy the pope; that this upheaval was precisely the old struggle of the people against tyranny whether of the Church or State. When, after eleven years of royal government without a Parliament, Charles I. was forced to call one, Pym became its leader. It was he who brought to book the great Duke of Buckingham, he who dared to impeach Strafford and Laud. The lampooners spoke a true word in jest when they called him "King Pym." Pym died early in the great fight; and the soldier, Cromwell, came to the front as the leader of republican England. Mr. Smith admires Cromwell as a genius and a high-minded man; yet he deprecates Carlyle's essay upon him as crass, undiscriminating worship. The soberer writer sees Cromwell's faults and deplores them. He does not excuse the execution of the King, or the massacres in Ireland; but he holds that Cromwell, to maintain his control over the thousands of reckless fanatics who had made him their leader, was forced to deeds of iron. As Protector, he was one of the strongest and wisest rulers England ever had. The last and longest paper is that on Pitt, the great statesman of the eighteenth century, who was prime minister at twenty-four, and the champion of free trade, a reformed currency, religious toleration, colonial emancipation, abolition of the slave-trade and of slavery. Pitt's espousal of the cause of the colonies in Parliament especially commends this study of him to American readers.

THREE MUSKETEERS, THE ('Les Trois Mousquetaires'), by Alexandre Dumas (1844). 'The Three Musketeers' is the first novel of Dumas's famous trilogy, of which the others are 'Twenty Years After' and 'The Vicomte de Bragelonne.' The three stories together cover a space of time from 1625 to 1665, and deal with the life of a Gascon adventurer named D'Artagnan, from his arrival in Paris on a rawboned yellow pony with three crowns in his pocket, to his death as Comte D'Artagnan, Commander of the Musketeers and Marshal of France.

On his first day in Paris, the young D'Artagnan, who desires to enter the famous corps of Louis XIII.'s Musketeers, contrives to entangle himself in three duels, with three of the most dreaded members of that body, who are known by the pseudonyms of Athos, Porthos, and Aramis. By his pluck and spirit, he wins all three for friends; and the four of them from that time share their fortunes, good and bad, and become the heroes of many stirring events. The novel throughout is highly dramatic and of absorbing interest.

THREE YEARS OF ARCTIC SERVICE, 'An Account of the Lady Franklin Bay Expedition of 1881–84, and the attainment of the Farthest North,' by Adolphus W. Greely (1886). A popular account, drawn from personal diaries and official reports, of one of the most remarkable of the Arctic expeditions, and one with scarcely a parallel in the terrible sufferings through many months from which the party were at last rescued. The primary object of the expedition was a scientific one; and the utmost care was given to physical observations, from July 1st, 1881, at St. John, Newfoundland, to June 21st, 1884, forty hours before the rescue of the survivors. The wealth of interest thus created, with that of the remarkable experiences of the party, and the range of travel achieved, make the work one of unique and lasting value.

THROUGH NIGHT TO LIGHT ('Durch Nacht zum Licht'), by Friedrich Spielhagen (3 vols., 1861), a conclusion of the romance 'Problematische Naturen' (Problematic Characters).

The promise of the title is not fulfilled by the course of this story or its conclusion. Oswald Stein, the hero of the preceding narrative, is to be brought "through night to light" in this work, but he does not accomplish this transition. The same inconstancy, the same facile impressibility, and the same transitoriness of impression, are brought out by similar sentimental experiences to those narrated in 'Problematic Characters.' Indeed, the hero is even less admirable than in his hot youth, since his experiments are no longer entirely innocent. The solution offered to the puzzle of his life is Oswald's heroic death on the barricades of Paris; but this suggestion of "light" is inadequate in view of the darkness of the preceding "night."

The story is usually regarded as an attempt to effect a compromise between the realistic tendencies of the late nineteenth century, and the idealism of an earlier school. It is rich in single episodes of interest or beauty; and its various heroines, Melitta, Hélène, Cécile, are well drawn. As a whole, however, and looked at from the point of view of its purpose, 'Through Night to Light' is not a powerful or convincing statement of the problem which the novelist has propounded.

THROUGH THE DARK CONTINENT, by Henry Morton Stanley, appeared in 1878. It is a graphic narrative of his dangers and remarkable experiences in traversing the African continent, from the eastern shore to the Atlantic Ocean. Already distinguished as an African explorer, he had told the story of his earlier trips in 'How I Found Livingstone'; and the latter's death in 1874 made him anxious to continue his unfinished work. The London Daily Telegraph and the New York Herald combined to organize an expedition of which he was appointed chief. Its objects were to solve the remaining problems of Central African geography, and to investigate the haunts of slave-traders.

Before beginning his own narrative, Stanley sums up all that was previously known about the Nile and great central lakes; and the achievements of his predecessors, Speke, Burton, and Livingstone; and shows that the western half of the continent was still practically a blank.

He reached Zanzibar Island in September, 1874, where he engaged Arab and Wangwana porters, and brought supplies of cloth, beads, and provisions. Upon November 12th, he embarked with three young English assistants and a company of 224 men for the mainland in six Arab dhows. From that day until his triumphal return to Zanzibar in a British steamer, over three year later, with the survivors of his company, he describes a long contention with famine, disease, insubordination in camps, war with hostile natives, and other dangers. After pushing inland, he turned northward to Lake Victoria, which he circumnavigated in the Lady Alice, a barge constructed so as to be portable in sections. Upon this trip he met Tsesa, the then king of Uganda, whom he says he converted to Christianity, and in whose domains he was royally entertained. The party then proceeded to Ujiji, on Lake Tanganyika, at which point Stanley again embarked with a picked crew, and sailed around the lake. In his subsequent march across country, he heard rumors of Dwarfland, which he afterwards visited, and had dangerous skirmishes with cannibals. He reached the Luama River, and followed it 220 miles until it united with the Lualaba, to form a broad gray river which he knew as the Livingstone, or Congo. Along its many windings, sometimes delayed by almost impassable rapids, through the haunts of zebra and buffalo, and of friendly and hostile natives, he persuaded his weary men, until they reached cultivated fields again, and a party of white men from Bornu came to greet him. Even then his troubles were not over, for the sudden relaxation from hardships caused illness among his men, from which several died.

According to his promise, he took his company all the way back to their homes in Zanzibar; and saw their happy meeting with the friends who welcomed them as heroes.

The Anglo-American Expedition had succeeded, and after its work the map of Africa was far less of a blank.

THROUGH THE LOOKING-GLASS, see **ALICE'S ADVENTURES IN WONDERLAND.**

THUS SPAKE ZARATHUSTRA, 'A Book for All and None' ('Also Sprach Zarathustra'), is a philosophic treatise by Friedrich Nietzsche, published in 1884. An English translation appeared in 1911. It consists of a series of rhapsodic discourses in impassioned and poetic prose, supposed to be addressed by a Persian sage, Zarathustra, to his disciples and to the people. The discourses, which are divided into four books, are provided with striking and romantic titles of a mystical suggestiveness, e. g., 'The Three Metamorphoses,' 'The Flies in the Market-Place,' 'The Thousand and One Goals,' etc. The general position of the book is that good and evil are purely relative and that there is one morality for the strong, vigorous, efficient man, and another for the weak, average, subordinate man. The first or "master-morality" is governed by the "will to power" and justifies the strong man in dominating over his inferiors and giving free scope to the development of his personality. The second, or "slave-morality" produces pity, submission, humility — all instincts which appeal to the weak and sickly who need protection. This latter passive and degenerate morality is the basis of Christianity. Thus must give way before a revival of the Pagan code, which is active, creative, and which leads to the evolution of a higher order of being, the Super-man. A natural corollary of this belief is a hatred of democracy and a passionate advocacy of aristocracy. For a full exposition and estimate of Nietzschism see the introductory essay and the selections from Nietzsche in the LIBRARY.

TICKNOR, GEORGE, LIFE, LETTERS, AND JOURNALS OF (2 vols., 1876). The story of the life of a private gentleman is here delightfully told through his journals and letters to and from friends; his daughter, with excellent taste, having joined the history which these documents reveal, by the slightest thread of narrative. The birth of George Ticknor in Boston in 1791, his education in private school and college, his deliberate choice of the life of a man of letters as his vocation, his four years of study and travel abroad, from the age of twenty-three to that of twenty-seven, his work at Harvard as professor of French and Spanish, his labor upon his 'History of Spanish Literature,' his delightful home life, a second journey in Europe in his ripe middle age and still a third, full of profit and delight, when he was sixty-five, his profound interest in the war for the maintenance of the Union, and finally the peaceful closing of his days at the age of seventy-nine, — these are the material of the book. But the reader sees picture after picture of a delightful existence, and is brought into intimate relations with the most cultivated and agreeable people of the century. George Ticknor had the happiness to be well born; that is, his father and mother were well educated, full of ideas and aspirations, and so easy in circumstances that the best advantages awaited the boy. With his inheritance of charming manners, a bright intelligence, a kind heart, and leisure for study, he was certain to establish friendships among the best. The simple, delightful society of the Boston of 18,000 inhabitants, where his boyhood was passed; the not less agreeable but more sophisticated Boston of 40,000 citizens that he found on his return from Europe, a traveled gentleman; and the Boston of three times as large a population, where still his own house afforded the most delightful hospitality and social life, among many famous for good talk and good manners, — this old town is made to seem worthy of its son. The papers recording Mr. Ticknor's visits abroad are crowded with the names of men and women whom the world honors, and who were delighted to know the agreeable American: Byron, Rogers, Wordsworth, Hunt, Lady Holland, Lady Ashburnham, Lord Landsdowne, Macaulay, Sydney Smith, Jeffrey, Lockhart, Châteaubriand, Talleyrand, Madame de Staël, Goethe, Herder, Thorwaldsen, Manzoni, Sismondi, and in later years, every man of note in Europe. Of all of these, most interesting friendly glimpses are given in letters and journals. Mr. Ticknor's characterizations of these persons are admirable, always judicious and faithful, and often humorous. With his strong liking for foreign men and things, he was one of the best Americans, seeing the faults of his country, but loving her in spite of them. Happily he lived to see a reunited Union, and to cherish the loftiest hopes for its future. The young American who looks for fine standards of intellectual, moral, and social achievements will find his account in a study of the life of this modest, accomplished, genial, hard-working, distinguished private gentleman.

TIDES OF BARNEGAT, THE, by F. Hopkinson Smith (1906). The scene of this story is laid in a sea-faring town called Barnegat, where Jane Cobden and her sister Lucy have been born and bred. They are the last of their race and are looked upon as the aristocrats of the village. Jane is a beautiful and unselfish character and idolizes her sister who is many years her junior. Lucy, who is of a very different nature, is vain, selfish, and unprincipled and when just blossoming into womanhood allows herself to be led astray by Barton Holt, the son of Captain Holt, a life-long friend of the family. The secret is known only to the Captain and Jane, and he, horrified at the discovery, turns his son out of his house and disowns him, while Jane grief stricken, hastens with Lucy to Paris, where they are lost to the sight of their friends for several years. At the end of that time Jane returns to her home accompanied by a small boy by the name of Archie, whom she has adopted. The child is something of a mystery to Jane's friends and neighbors but she does not satisfy their curiosity in any way. Before the trouble Jane had become engaged to the village doctor, a fine man loved and esteemed by all and affectionately designated as "Dr. John." He is anxious to marry Jane but in order to keep her secret she refuses to comply with his desire. Lucy marries a Frenchman and after years returns home a widow with one daughter. She is as frivolous as ever, caring only for admiration and show, and contemplates a second marriage with a man from whom she is most desirous of hiding her past. Archie grows to be a fine and muscular young man and joins the life-saving staff under the direction of Captain Holt. Barton Holt, who had been considered dead for years, writes his father he is alive and coming back to visit him. The ship on which he is a passenger is wrecked by a frightful storm when they are in sight of land. Archie risks his life with others of the life-saving crew and is drowned in the act of rescuing the father who is unknown to him. Barton also perishes, and over his dead body, his father to the horror of Lucy makes public the story. Jane is at last free to marry "Dr. John" and learns he has all the time been aware of the truth.

TILL EULENSPIEGEL. The origin of this book of the adventures of Till Eulenspiegel is doubtful. It is supposed that these stories were collected and first published in Low Dutch, in the year 1483. The hero of them, whose first name was Till or Thyl, was a traveling buffoon, who, besides presenting farces and the like, was a practical joker. The name of Eulenspiegel probably comes from a picture or coat of arms which he left after perpetrating a joke, which consisted of an owl (Eule) and a mirror (Spiegel), and which is to-day shown, on what is said to be his gravestone, in Lüneburg.

The motive of many of the jokes is the literal interpretation by Till of what he is told to do; something after the style of Handy Andy, except that Till's misinterpretations are not the result of simplicity. Many of them are very filthy, while others would to-day be considered crimes and not jokes. It is difficult to understand how this book could have had a popularity which has caused it to be translated into many languages. It is to-day only appreciated as a curious picture of the taste and customs of its time. It differs from like books of southern Europe in that none of the stories are founded on amorous intrigues.

TIMBUCTOO THE MYSTERIOUS, by Felix Dubois. Translated from the French by Diana White (1896). The story of a long journey inland in French Africa: from Dakar, the port of Senegal, by rail above 170 miles to St. Louis, the capital of Senegal; thence by river steamer on the Senegal eight days to Kayes, the capital of French Sudan; then by rail part of the way, and by caravan the remainder, to the Niger at Bammaku; and, last of all, on the vast sea-like breadth of the Niger to Timbuctoo. The story of French occupation; of improvements recently made; of the great river and the country through which it flows; and of the remarkable city once a great seat of Mussulman culture, and in French hands not unlikely to become a centre of European civilization and science in the heart of Africa, — is one to reward the reader, and one also to form a valuable chapter in the history of European conversion of the Dark Continent into a land of light and of progress. A special interest in the book is the discovery in Jenne and Timbuctoo of ancient Egyptian architecture, leading to the belief that the ancient empire of Sangird was founded by emigrants from the Nile.

TIMON OF ATHENS (first printed in 1623) is by Shakespeare, either in whole or in part. It is a bitter satire on friendship and society, written in the stern sarcastic vein of Juvenal. The sources of the plot seem to have been Paynter's 'Palace of Pleasure,' Plutarch's 'Life of Antony,' and Lucian's 'Dialogue on Timon.' Shakespeare's "Timon" is unique both in his ostentations and indiscriminate prodigality and in the bitterness of his misanthropy after his wealth was gone. Yet he was of the noblest heart. His sublime faith that his friends were as generous as he, and that they were all brothers, commanding one another's fortunes, was a practical error, that was all. Men were selfish wolves; he thought them angels. His bounty was measureless: if a friend praised a horse 'twas his; if one wanted a little loan of £5,000 or so, 'twas a trifle; he portioned his servants and paid his friends' debts; his vaults wept with drunken spilth of wine, and every room blazed with lights and brayed with minstrelsy; at parting each guest received some jewel as a keepsake. When all was gone, full of cheerful faith he sent out to his friends to borrow, and they all with one accord began to make excuse. Not a penny could he get. Feast won, fast lost. The smiling, smooth, detested parasites left him to his clamorous creditors and to ruin. The crushing blow to his ideals maddened him; his blood turned to gall and vinegar. Yet he determined on one last banquet. The surprised sycophants thought he was on his feet again, and with profuse apologies assembled at his house. The covered dishes are brought in. "Uncover dogs, and lap!" cries the enraged Timon. The dishes are found to be full of warm water, which he throws in their faces, then pelts them with stones and drives them forth with execrations, and rushes away to the woods to henceforth live in a cave and subsist on roots and berries and curse mankind. In digging he finds gold. His old acquaintances visit him in turn, —Alcibiades, the cynical dog Apemantus, his faithful steward Flavius, a poet, a painter, senators of Athens. He curses them all, flings gold at them, telling them he gives it that they may use it for the bale of man, pronounces his weeping steward the only honest man in the world, builds "his everlasting mansion on the beached verge of the salt flood," where "vast Neptune may weep for aye on his low grave, on faults forgiven," writes his epitaph, and lies down in the tomb and dies.

TITUS ANDRONICUS (1593) —A repulsive drama of bloodshed and unnatural crimes, now believed to have been written by Shakespeare, since it often is included in the original Folio Edition of 1623. No one who has once supped on its horrors will care to read it. Here is a specimen of them: Titus Andronicus, a Roman noble, in revenge for the ravishing of his daughter Lavinia and the cutting off of her hands and tongue, cuts the throats of the two ravishers, while his daughter holds between the stumps of her arms a basin to catch the blood. The father then makes a paste of the ground bones and blood of the slain men, and in that paste bakes their two heads, and serving them up at a feast, causes their mother to eat of the dish. Iago seems a gentleman beside the hellish Moor, Aaron, of this blood-soaked tragedy.

TO HAVE AND TO HOLD, by Mary Johnston (1900), was one of the most popular books of the year. It is a historical romance and deals with life in the Virginia colonies in the early part of the 17th century. Ralph Percy, the hero of the tale, an Englishman of birth and breeding, is leading a life of adventure in Virginia, when a cast of the dice decides him to choose a wife from among the shipload of maids who have just arrived from England. He hastily marries a proud and lovely maid who proves to be none other than Jocelyn Leigh, the King's ward, who had fled the country disguised as a serving-maid, in order to escape marriage with Lord Carnal, the King's favorite, whom she despised. Carnal traces her and follows her to Virginia, where he does everything in his power to get possession of her, and uses every foul means possible to rid himself of her husband. Percy and Lord Carnal, who are bitter enemies, have various encounters, in all of which the former succeeds in getting the best of his rival. News comes from England that Jocelyn and her husband are to be brought back there, by order of the King and the latter imprisoned, while the former is forced to comply with his Majesty's wishes. Jocelyn and Percy flee in the night, pursued by Lord Carnal, and set sail in a small boat accompanied by Jeremy Sparrow, the minister who married them and who has been their staunch friend, Diccon, a servant, and Carnal, who by this means is kept in their power. They are wrecked and cast upon a desert island, where Percy encounters a band of pirates who have come ashore to bury their Captain. He conquers them, assumes the character of Kirby, a famous pirate, and becomes their commander. Percy and his companions remain upon the pirate ship until his orders against attacking an English merchantman cause rebellion, and during the fracas Sparrow seizes the wheel and runs the ship upon the rocks. After their rescue Percy is sentenced to be hung as a pirate, when Jocelyn's pleading for his life saves him and reveals how much she has grown to love the man whom she married so hastily. The ship returns to Virginia where, after long separation and many thrilling experinces, Percy and Jocelyn are at length re-united and Carnal, a physical wreck, takes poison and thereby ends a life of baseness and disappointed hopes.

TOADS AND DIAMONDS, see FAIRY TALES.

TOGETHER, by Robert Herrick (1908). The theme of this picture of American life is mismated marriage. The brilliant wedding of Isabelle Price and John Lane begins a frank intimate study of their married life and that of their friends. Isabelle and her husband drift apart as he becomes absorbed in business, and she cultivates false ideals of social self-realization and freedom. A minor character, Dr. Renault, states the cult of the ego of the American woman. He tells Isabelle that women of her class pride themselves on their culture, individuality, cleverness, development, leading their own lives, but, call it what they will, it is the same, "the inturning of the spirit to cherish self." Woman, the spender, "sees in marriage the fulfilment of her heart's desire — to be queen, to rule and not work." "So long as she may but please this lord of hers, so long as she may hold him by her mind or her body, she will be queen. She has found something softer than labor with her hands, easier than the pains of childbirth." Only one of the couples, Alice and Steve Johnson are truly mated. Their wholesome comradeship, many children and commonplace poverty make them heroic and happy, but not interesting or successful. Robert Falkner, married to the frivolous Bessie, loves sensitive high-souled Margaret Pole, who yields to one idyllic week-end with him but refuses to marry him. Margaret's marriage with the weak Larry, is "one of the millions of mistakes women make out of the girlish guess," mistakes growing out of "blind ignorance of self and life." The ambitious Conny Woodward sacrifices her husband to her will for power. The story is also an indictment of modern business. Isabelle's husband is the scapegoat in the courts for the illegal methods of the railroad of which he is vice-president. There is a happy ending with Isabelle and her husband beginning a new partnership, living together in mutual confidence and affection, but the picture of American life and womanhood presented is far from flattering.

TOILERS OF THE SEA ('Les Travailleurs de la Mer') (1866). A novel by Victor Hugo, which possesses double interest: first, in the story; secondly, in its bold descriptions of the colossal and secret powers of the elements. In time it followed after the still more famous 'Les Misérables.' The scene is laid in Germany; and the book is dedicated to the "Isle of Guernsey, severe yet gentle, my present asylum, my probable tomb." The heroine, Deruchette, is the niece of Lethierry, who has invented a steamboat, La Durande, which plies between Guernsey and St. Malo, and which is the wonder of the Channel Islands. His partner, Rantaine, disappears with a large sum of money, and is succeeded as captain of La Durande by Clubin. The latter has friends among the smugglers, and with their assistance finds Rantaine, who has escaped in the guise of a Quaker. Clubin obtains this booty and determines to keep it. He plans to wreck La Durande on the rocks known as "Les Hanois," and then to swim ashore and escape. From this point, the story is full of the excitement and terror of the life of the sailor. The descriptions of the sea, the wind, and the mysteries of the ocean-bed, are wonderful. Among the most striking scenes is the encounter of Gilliatt, the real hero of the book, with an octopus which lurks in a rocky cavern beneath the sea. Penetrating into the shadows of this submarine crypt, whose arches are covered with seaweed and trailing moss, Gilliatt soon finds himself in the embrace of the gigantic and slimy monster, whose gleaming eyes are fixed upon him. Of this story George Henry Lowes said that it had "a certain daring inflation about it which cannot be met elsewhere; and if the splendor is barbaric it is undeniably splendid. Page after page and chapter after chapter may be mere fireworks which blaze and pass away; but as fireworks, the prodigality is amazing." He also says that the author has given "a poetical vision of the sea, which is more like an apocalypse than the vision of a healthy mind."

TOM BROWN'S SCHOOL DAYS, the finest and most famous example of stories depicting English public-school life, was written by Thomas Hughes, and published in 1857, when the author was a young barrister of three-and-thirty. It leaped at once into a deserved popularity it has never lost. Tom is a typical middle-class lad with the distinctive British virtues of pluck, honesty, and the love of fair play. The story portrays his life from the moment he enters the lowest form of the great school, a homesick, timid lad, who has to fag for the older boys and has his full share of the rough treatment which obtained in the Rugby of his day, to the time when he has developed into a big, brawny fellow, the head of the school, a football hero, and ready to pass on to Oxford, — another story being devoted to his experiences there. A faithful, lifelike, and most entertaining picture of the Rugby of Dr. Arnold is given; its social habits, methods of teaching, its sports, beliefs, and ideals. The wide influence of that great man is sketched with hearty appreciation; and in another figure — that of the gentle, high-charactered lad Arthur — one may recognize Dean Stanley in his student days. Individual scenes, like the bullying of Tom when he is green in the school, the football match, and the boat race, will always cling in memory for their graphic lines and fullness of life. An honester, manlier story was never written, for the author had been through it all, — the novel is "by an old boy," the title-page declares; moreover, it teaches, by the contagion of example, those sterling virile virtues which have made the English one of the great dominant races of civilization. To read 'Tom Brown' is to have an exhilarating sense of the vigorous young manhood of that nation, its joy in fruitful activity.

TOM BURKE OF " OURS," by Charles Lever (1844). This is one of Lever's characteristic stories of an exiled Irish patriot, who wins glory and preferment under the banners of France. Tom Burke, the son of an Irish gentleman, being orphaned runs away from home to escape the persecutions of his father's attorney. He falls in with Darby the "Blast," a shrewd, odd character, who is prominent among the United Irishmen. They reach Dublin, where Tom meets Charles de Meudon, a young French officer, who gives him a letter to the Chef of the Polytechnique at Paris, where he is to become *un élève*. On graduating from the military academy, Tom becomes an officer in the Eighth Hussars; but from an accidental acquaintance with the Marquis de Beauvis, a Bourbonist, he unconsciously becomes involved in a political intrigue, and his actions are closely watched by the police. In aiding De Beauvis to escape, Tom is himself arrested and imprisoned for treason. Through the intervention of General D'Auvergne and Mademoiselle Marie de Meudon, the sister of Charles, with whom he has fallen in love, Burke is set free. Troops are ordered to the front, and Napoleon invades Germany and Austria. After meritorious service at Austerlitz, Tom Burke, whom General D'Auvergne has made aid-de-camp, is promoted to a captaincy and takes part in the battle of Jena. But, disgusted at having constant watch over his actions, he throws up his commission and quits the service. On reaching Dublin Tom is arrested on old scores; but is acquitted through the testimony of Darby, and comes into his inheritance, an estate of four thousand pounds a year. For several years Burke leads a lonely life: but finally returns to France and again enlists, also aiding the Napoleonic cause with money. On the field of Montmirail, Burke is reported to the Emperor, and for an attack on the Austrian rear-guard at Melun he is made colonel. After his gallant conduct at the Bridge of Montereau, where he leads the assault, Burke is given the Emperor's own cross of the Legion. Napoleon's doom is sealed, and he is exiled. Tom, refusing to serve under the Bourbons, though offered the grade of general, throws aside all thought of military ambition, marries Marie de Meudon, and retires to private life.

TOM CRINGLE'S LOG, by Michael Scott. This work was originally published as a series of papers in Blackwood's Magazine, the first of them appearing in 1829. They were afterwards published (in 1834) in two volumes; and have enjoyed a wide and well-sustained popularity, not only among English speaking people but on the continent of Europe also. During the publication of these papers Mr. Scott preserved his incognito even towards his publisher. The author spent some sixteen years of his life (1806 to 1822) in the West Indies, in connection with a mercantile house in Kingston, Jamaica. The travels among the neighboring islands and to the Spanish Main, gave him not only great familiarity with the social life of the West Indies, but also a knowledge of the wild and adventurous nautical life of the times, and of the scenes and aspects of a tropical climate which he has so faithfully and vividly portrayed. There is no plot; but the book contains a series of adventures with pirates, mutineers, privateersmen, and men-of-war, storms, wrecks, and waterspouts, interspersed with descriptions of shore life and customs. The time chosen is one full of historical interest; for the book opens with an adventure in the Baltic in which the reader is brought into contact with Napoleon's army, and later on there are adventures with American men-of-war and privateersmen, during the War of 1812, — the celebrated frigate Hornet playing a small part.

Few, if any, sea writers have exhibited such a remarkable power of description; and the book will stand for many years as one of the most accurate pictures of West Indian life, both afloat and on shore, during the early part of the nineteenth century.

The publication of 'Tom Cringle's Log' was followed in 1836 by 'The Cruise of the Midge'; and these two were the only books written by Michael Scott, who died in 1835, before the publication of the latter work.

TOM GROGAN, by F. Hopkinson Smith (1895), is a spirited and most entertaining and ingenious study of laboring life in Staten Island, New York.

Tom Grogan was a stevedore, who died from the effects of an injury. With a family to support, his widow conceals the fact of her husband's death, saying that he is sick in a hospital, that she may assume both his name and business.

She is thenceforth known to every one as 'Tom Grogan.' A sturdy, cheery, capable Irishwoman, she carries on the business with an increasing success, which arouses the jealous opposition of some rival stevedores and walking delegates of the labor union she has refused to join.

The story tells how, with marvelous pluck, Tom meets all the contemptible means which her enemies employ in order to down her, they resorting even to the law, blackmail, arson, and attempted murder. In all her mannish employments her mother-heart beats warm and true; and her little crippled Patsy, a companion to Dickens's Tiny Tim, and Jenny the daughter with her own tender love affair, are the objects of Tom's constant solicitude.

The author has given a refreshing view of a soul of heroic mold beneath an uncouth exterior, and a pure life where men are wont to expect degradation.

TOM JONES, by Henry Fielding, conceded to be that writer's masterpiece, and deemed by some critics the greatest English novel, was published in 1749, when the author was forty-two. He had, however, been long at work upon it. The story is Fielding's third piece of fiction, and represents the zenith of his literary power; 'Amelia,' which followed two years later and was his last novel, having less exuberance and happy invention. 'The History of Tom Jones, a Foundling,' is the full title of the book; Tom is the foundling, left on the doorstep of a charitable gentleman, Mr. Allworthy, who gives him a home and rears him with care, but, grieved by his wild conduct as a young man, repudiates him for a time. Tom is a high-spirited, handsome fellow, generous and honest, but perpetually in hot water because of his liking for adventure and his gallantry towards women. He loves Sophia Western, whose father, Squire Western, an irascible, bluff, three-bottle, hunting English country magnate, is one of the best and best-known pieces of character-drawing in the whole range of English fiction. The match is opposed strenuously by the squire; and Tom sets out on his travels under a cloud, hoping to win his girl in spite of all. He is accompanied by his tutor, the schoolmaster Partridge, a simple-minded, learned man, very lovable, a capitally drawn and amusing figure. Another character sympathetically sketched is that of Blifil, the contemptible hypocrite who seeks Sophia's hand and tries to further his cause by lying about Jones. Tom has many escapades, especially of the amatory sort; and his experiences are narrated with great liveliness, reality, and unction, the reader being carried along irresistibly by the author's high good spirits. No other eighteenth-century story gives such truthful, varied, and animated scenes of contemporaneous life in country and town. Jones finally triumphs over his enemies, is reconciled with his guardian, the blot on his birth is removed, and he wins his Sophia. He is throughout a likable fellow, though his ethics are not always agreeable to modern taste or conscience.

TOMMY AND GRIZEL, by Sir James M. Barrie (1900). This is a clever and baffling character-study of Thomas Sandys (whom the author first introduced to the public under the guise of "Sentimental Tommy"), and of Grizel, who adores him and studies his every act and motive. Tommy is a unique and original creation possessed of a genius which unfits him for practical life. He is a creature of ever-varying moods who may be loved but never understood and still less approved of. Grizel, who is a paragon, is destined to have her career blighted by her love for this erratic genius, with his gift at writing and his fatal gift of making-believe. She realizes that Tommy does not love her, and yet she loves and honors him for his effort to make her think he does. To Tommy "all the world's a stage" and he is cast for leading lover. He knows by instinct how to make direct appeal to every woman's heart and he cannot resist the constantly recurring temptation to exercise his power. The reader follows his brief career with scorn and sympathy, as he writes matchless love scenes and then endeavors to materialize them by flirting with the London ladies, as he struggles to return Grizel's ideal love in kind, and having primed himself with high resolves, immediately makes love to shameless Lady Pippinworth, almost breaking poor Grizel's heart. The author paints his abject misery at the realization of the harm his selfishness has wrought, his hasty marriage with the distraught Grizel, and his devoted nursing of her back to health and happiness, and finally his weak indulgence of his former passion for the tantalizing demon embodied in Lady Pippinworth, who lures him to follow her into the garden and is the cause of his being impaled upon the picket fence, where he meets his tragic end.

TONO-BUNGAY, a novel, by H. G. Wells (1908). This romance of modern advertising follows the fortunes of George Ponderevo, and his uncle, Edward Ponderevo, a chemist, inventor of a quack patent medicine "Tono-Bungay," which brings him a colossal fortune. George begins his autobiography with reminiscences of the "Great House," where his mother was housekeeper. He is banished in disgrace for thrashing a young nobleman, and goes to live in the neighboring town with his uncle, the chemist. The money that his mother left in trust for his education is lost in the bankruptcy which follows his uncle's foolish speculation, but George wins a scholarship in the University of London. Edward Ponderevo, now a druggist's clerk, launches his patent medicine and asks his nephew to join him to "make Tono-Bungay hum." George knows that the concoction is a swindle, but he wants money to get married and accepts the offer. Their success is due to his business ability as well as his uncle's genius for advertising Tono-Bungay, which its creator comes to believe in by the mere reiteration of his own brilliant assertions; he builds a great "property out of human hope and a credit for bottles and rent and printing." George's marriage is a failure, and after divorce from Marion, his insipid wife, he gives his time and interest to inventing airships, neglecting to keep the business humming. There are digressions and monologues on all subjects bearing on George's intellectual and spiritual development. He meets and loves his old playmate of the "Great House," Lady Beatrice, too late to win her from a clandestine relation with another man. A mysterious trip to Africa in search of a radio-active substance fails to save Tono-Bungay from bankruptcy. George rescues his dying uncle from the criminal consequences of his imagination by flying across the channel with him in his airship. As in other books by Mr. Wells, the story is the framework for the author's views of the springs of conduct and belief.

TORY LOVER, THE, by Sarah Orne Jewett (1901). The scene of the story is laid in Berwick, Maine, on the Piscataqua River, and deals with the period of the Revolution. Roger Wallingford, the hero of the tale, is a fine fellow of Tory ancestry, who, through his love for Mary Hamilton, a beautiful girl, joins the cause of the Patriots. Mary, whose brother Colonel John Hamilton warmly espouses this cause, is herself fired with enthusiasm and patriotic fervor, and urges her childhood's friend to identify himself with those seeking independence. Through her influence over Captain Paul Jones, who is her brother's guest, and who is enthralled by her beauty, a commission is obtained for Wallingford and he ships on the Ranger. This course, Mary hopes, will insure the safety of Roger's mother, Madam Wallingford, whose loyalty to the King places her in a perilous position. Such a step, however, fails to satisfy the people and Madam Wallingford is forced to leave the country. At this time bad news concerning Roger has been received and he has been accused of treachery and desertion and no trace of him can be found. Mary, who is confident of Roger's integrity, accompanies his mother to England, determined to do everything in her power to find him and clear his name. After many disheartening disappointments, Mary's efforts are at last crowned with success and, through the assistance of Paul Jones, Roger is found at a country inn, where he, as an escaped prisoner of war, has taken refuge disguised in the costume of a drover. It is proved that Roger has been the victim of a conspiracy and the mystery is cleared up by the confession of the villain who has caused it and who meets with well-deserved punishment. The lovers are happily united.

TOTTEL'S MISCELLANY, a collection of lyric poems published by Richard Tottel in 1557 under the title 'Songs and Sonnets, written by the right honourable Lord Henry Howard, late Earl of Surrey, and others.' The volume preserves the best work of the court poets of the early English Renaissance including Sir Thomas Wyatt (1503–1542), Henry Howard, Earl of Surrey (1516–1547), Nicholas Grimald (1519–1562), and Thomas, Lord Vaux (1510–1556). Wyatt, the pioneer of the new poetry, is represented by about thirty sonnets and a number of graceful and charming lyrics. Like his master, Petrarch, he sings almost entirely of the beauty and cruelty of his mistress and of the joys and pains of love; and beneath the ingenious and varied metaphors of the Petrarchian self-analysis runs a strain of genuine feeling. Particularly original are the lines in which he describes his lady's former kindness, and makes a vigorous renunciation of further slavery. In the sonnet, which Wyatt introduced into English poetry, he adopted the Petrarchian form with modifications, changing the sextette into a quatrain followed by a couplet. Owing to the alterations in English accentuation and inflection since Chaucer's time he had difficulty in achieving metrical smoothness; and some of his lines will not scan properly; but with practice he attained true rhythm and thus initiated the reform of English versification from the chaos of a century. His lyrics, like 'Awake, my lute' and 'And wilt thou leave me thus?' positively sing themselves; and in his epistle to Poins, containing the fable of 'The Town Mouse and the Country Mouse' he shows power as a humorist, a narrator, and a satirist. Surrey, the disciple of Wyatt, but placed first in the collection because of his rank, is represented by sonnets and songs of love, with a few epigrams, an elegy on Wyatt, and some descriptive and dramatic pieces. Though less original than Wyatt he is more smooth and finished, and, owing to the romance attaching to his love for the fair Geraldine and to his tragic death, is a more appealing personality. His sonnets and lyrics are of the same general character as those of Wyatt, and he is an equally close follower of Petrarch's lyrical method. His sonnets, however, depart from the Petrarchian arrangement of octave and sextette, and consist of three quatrains, each with its own alternate rhymes, and a concluding couplet. This form of the sonnet was adopted by Shakespeare. Surrey's elegy on

Wyatt, his epigram on the Happy Life, and his dramatic complaint of a lady whose husband is at sea, illustrate other sides of his genius. An extensive contributor to the Miscellany is Nicholas Grimald. His poems, and those of the anonymous lyrists who make up the volume, include love-songs, moral reflections, pastorals, complaints, and elegies. They prove the existence at the court of Henry VIII. and his successors of a considerable number of practised writers, who had mastered a number of lyric forms. Of these one of the most typical, now archaic, is the so-called "poulter's measure," an alternation of hexameter and heptameter lines often with a hobbling movement very tedious to the modern reader. One of the minor contributors, Lord Vaux, is remembered for his poem 'The Aged Lover Renounceth Love,' fragments from which are sung by the Grave-Digger in Shakespeare's 'Hamlet.' The popularity of 'Tottel's Miscellany' is proved by the numerous editions through which it ran (1559, 1565, 1567, 1574, 1585, 1587), by contemporary reference, and by the appearance of other miscellanies of similar title and content: 'The Paradise of Dainty Devices' (1578); 'The Gorgeous Gallery of Gallant Inventions' (1578), 'A Handful of Pleasant Delights' (1584); 'The Phœnix Nest' (1593); 'England's Helicon' (1600); 'England's Parnassus' (1600); and 'Davison's Poetical Rhapsody' (1602).

TRACTATE ON EDUCATION, by John Milton (1644). Milton's famous letter on Education was addressed to Samuel Hartlib, a Pole by birth, who settled in England and devoted himself to philanthropic schemes for the benefit of his adopted country. It is a protest on behalf of the youth of his time against "the asinine feast of sow-thistles and brambles which is commonly set before them as all the food and entertainment of their tenderest and most docile age." His definition of "a complete and generous education" is "that which fits a man to perform justly, skillfully, and magnanimously all the offices, both private and public, of peace and war." A knowledge of things was to be substituted for the mere knowledge of words. The Greek, Latin (and even Hebrew, Syriac, and Chaldee) authors prescribed were chosen not for their form but for their subject matter. The pupil was to acquire (for practical and utilitarian purposes) a comprehensive acquaintance with the science of his time — "geography, trigonometry, fortification, engineering, navigation." Later would come comedies and tragedies, Greek, Latin, and Italian, and the study of law-givers from Moses, Lycurgus, and Justinian to the common or statute law of England. In their hours of exercise the youth were to learn, also with the utilitarian aim in view, fencing, wrestling, music, riding, sailing. Fortunately Milton had sufficient sense of humor to see that all this prodigious curriculum "is not a bow for every man to shoot in that counts himself a teacher, but will require sinews almost equal to which Homer gave Ulysses." Nevertheless though as an ideal for everyday use the precepts of the book are impractical of accomplishment, it is still full of valuable suggestion.

TRACTS FOR THE TIMES. These papers, published at Oxford between 1833 and 1841, have become part of English history; for it meant much to the English people, who held that their liberties were concerned with the limitation or extension of ecclesiastical power. The Church, in its reaction against Romanism, became, in many instances, negligent in ritual and meaningless in decoration. There were no pictures of saints, but memorial busts of sinners; no figures of martyrs, but lions and unicorns fighting for the crown; and Tract 9, on 'Shortening the Service,' says "the Reformation left us a daily service, we have now a weekly service; and they are in a fair way to become monthly." The impetus to the Tractarian movement was given partly by the changes contemplated in the Irish episcopate. The British Parliament, which was all-sufficient to pass the Act of Uniformity in 1662, was, in the minds of the Tractarians, incompetent to modify that act in 1832. The so-called Tracts varied from brief sketches, dialogues, etc., to voluminous treatises like those on Baptism and (No. 89) "On the Mysticism Attributed to the Early Fathers," which make about a volume each. The fight for the standard occurred around Dr. J. H. Newman's famous No. 90, "On the Thirty-nine Articles of the English Church," which aroused the English public. It states that "The English Church leaves marriage to the judgment of the clergy, but the Church has the right to order them not to marry." The strong point with the Tractarians was that the Prayer Book was not a Protestant book, but was framed to include Catholics; and the leaders determined to push this point. Newman, in No. 90, says, with pitiless logic and clear statement, that "The Protestant confessions were drawn up to include Catholics, and Catholics will not be excluded. What was economy with the first Reformers is a protection to us. What would have been perplexing to us then is perplexing to them now. We could not find fault with their words then; they cannot now repudiate their meaning." As an example of skill in dialectics, these Tracts are worth studying. They were the utterances of master-minds dead in earnest. The leaders were such men as Keble, author of the 'Christian Year'; Dr. Pusey, Regius Professor of Hebrew; Dr. J. H. Newman, R. H. Froude, Rev. Isaac Williams; and Rev. Hugh Rose, of Cambridge.

The Tracts have done much to restore artistic symbolism as well as earnestness to the Church; on the other hand they have alienated the bulk of Protestant Dis-senters, who are willing to admit the claims of the Tractarians to rule the Church of England, but not to rule them. Fellowship with the pope was earnestly deprecated by the Tractarians, who have done good work in the Anglican Church since; but Newman and some others found their way to the Roman communion, and gave some color to Punch's Puseyite hymn: —

> "And nightly pitch my moving tent
> A day's march nearer Rome."

TRADES UNIONISM, HISTORY OF, by Sidney and Beatrice Webb (1894). This model example of meticulous investigation in a field almost unexplored until its publication is the result of seven years' unremitting labor among original records, fugitive pamphlet literature, the archives of trades unions, illumined by intimate acquaintance with the actual working of existing trade unions. "In spite of all the pleas of modern historians for less history of the actions of governments, and more descriptions of the manners and customs of the governed, it remains true that history, however it may relieve and enliven itself with descriptions of the manners and morals of the people, must, if it is to be history at all, follow the course of continuous or-ganizations. The history of a perfectly democratic State would be at once the history of a government and of a people. The history of trade unionism is the history of a State within our State, and one so jealously democratic that to know it well is to know the English working man as no reader of middle-class histories can know him." The origins of trade unionism and the struggle for existence during the first quarter of the nineteenth century, the revolutionary period of the next score years, the gradual change from the old unionism to the new, which might be assigned to the years between 1875 and 1889, are traced with amazing skill. This work is not only the classic history of British trade unionism, but it is a model to all social investigators, combining the most conscientious and painstaking capacity for the discovery of facts with superb skill in co-ordination and explanation.

TRAFALGAR, a tale, by Benito Perez Galdós (1879). The first of a series of historical novels dealing with the Spanish War of Independence. Gabriel, the youth who tells the story, is with his master on the largest man-of-war of the Spanish fleet, a witness to the battle. The vessel surrenders to the English after a desperate fight. English and Spanish take to the boats to escape from the sinking ship. Gabriel notes the humanity of the English and asks himself, "Why are there wars? Why cannot these men be friends under all circumstances of life as they are in danger? Is not such a scene as this enough to prove that all men are brothers?" They reach another captured Spanish man-of-war, also "in desperate situation, floating at the mercy of the wind and waves and unable to make any course." They find on board, Don Rafael Malespina, the lover of Gabriel's young mistress, Rosita. The idea of being taken into Gibraltar as prisoners was intolerable to the Spaniards. They outnumber the English, and by a sudden rush disarm their conquerors and take command of the ship. They suffer shipwreck in a tempest which forbids help from shore but are rescued by another vessel. Don Rafael recovers from his wound and marries Rosita, and Gabriel, who worships her from afar, runs away to further adventures.

TRAGIC IDYLL, A ('Une Idylle Tragique'), by Paul Bourget (1896). M. Bourget declares that in life there are two types of beings corresponding to tragedy and comedy, to one of which great departments each belongs, generally with no mixture. "For one, the most romantic episodes end as in a vaudeville. For the other the simplest adventures end in drama; devoted to poignant emotions, cruel complications, all their idylls are tragic idylls." With this idea in mind the author pictures the young Provençal Vicomte de Carancez, a true D'Artagnan, *un gourmand de toutes les gourmandises,* who has run through his inheritance of 600,000 francs; and contrasts him with his friend Pierre Hautefeuille, a genuine, sweet-tempered, chivalrous, and chaste (at least, comparatively chaste) provincial gentleman. The light, fickle, astute, and clever adventurer, whose very title is in question in searching for means to recoup his fortunes deliberately falls in love with a rich widow, the Venetian Marchioness Andriana Bonaccorsi; and successfully carries his romantic plan into execution, cleverly parrying all the attempts of her Anglomaniac brother to get rid of him by sixteenth-century methods of poison and assassination. Pierre on the other hand falls under the seduction of the beautiful and passionate morganatic wife of an Austrian archduke; and though their liaison reaches the last development, its guilty fruit is utter wretchedness for both, — not, as an Anglo-Saxon moralist would have pictured it, from the breaking of any moral law, but because a former lover of the Baroness Ely de Sallach-Carlsberg is Pierre's most intimate friend; their passions cross each other and clash, and ultimately lead to the death of Olivier du Prat, who in a moment of exaltation and moral despair sacrifices himself to save his friend, though he knows that this friend is playing him false and breaking a solemn oath. This dead friend becomes the living remorse that prevents the two passionate lovers from ever again meeting.

The story opens at Monte Carlo, the heated unwholesome life of which is set forth in the most brilliant colors. It is like a historical painting, so many portraits are introduced. The description of the sea trip to Genoa, whither the beautiful yacht of the American millionaire carries most of the personages of the story, is also most vividly told, and the episode of the secret marriage is like a canto of a poem. Surely no ceremony in Genoa had ever been more remarkable: "This great Venetian lady had come from Cannes on an American's yacht to marry a ruined gentleman of dubious title from Barbentane, assisted by a young American girl and an Austrian lady, a morganatic archduchess, who in her turn is accompanied by a Frenchman of the simplest, the most provincial French tradition."

The poetry of the idyll is not to be gainsaid, or its fascinating interest, or its dramatic power. Its tenuous moral is thoroughly French, but is based on this epigrammatic exclamation: —

"Ah! demain! ce dangereux et mysterieux demain, l'inevitable expiation de tous nos coupables aujourd'huis. (Ah to-morrow, that dangerous and mysterious to-morrow, the inevitable punisher of all our guilty to-days!)"

To an American reader an element of comedy is introduced in the author's amusing portrayal of Marsh the American railway magnate. More realistic is his account of the half-mad scientific Archduke, who hated his wife and yet was jealous of her.

TRAVELS AND ADVENTURES OF BARON MÜNCHHAUSEN, THE, by R. E. Raspe, published in England (1785), was founded upon the outrageous stories of a real man, one Baron Karl Friedrich Hieronymus von Münchhausen, born at Boden-werder, Hanover, Germany, 1720; died there, 1797. He had served in the Russian army against the Turks. Later his sole occupation seemed to be the relation of his extraordinary adventures to his circle of friends. Raspe purported to have preserved these tales, as they came hot from the lips of the inimitable Baron. They are monuments to the art of lying as an entertainment. On one occasion, the hero, being out of ammunition, loaded his gun with cherry-stones. With these he shot at a deer. Coming across the same deer some time afterwards, he sees a cherry-tree growing out of his head. The Baron's other adventures are on a par with this; and his name has become a synonym for magnificent, bland extravagance of statement.

TRAVELS IN FRANCE, by Arthur Young, is more fully entitled 'Travels during the years 1787, 1788, 1789, and 1790, undertaken more particularly with a view of ascertaining the Cultivation, Wealth, Resources, and National Prosperity of the Kingdom of France.' Young was an English country gentleman who had had considerable experience in agriculture and had written books which were looked upon as authoritative on the agrarian resources of England, Wales, and Ireland. With a view to furnishing similar information concerning France he made a three years' tour of that country, visiting the most remote districts and making the most minute inquiries into the agricultural resources and organization of each locality. His experiences and conclusions are recorded in the 'Travels' in the form of a journal. Not only does he describe the nature of the soil and the crops, but the pay of the laborers, the relations of landlord and tenant, and the social customs and mental attitude of the people, and he enlivens his pages with the incidents, amusing, curious, and exciting which befell him on the road. A foreigner traversing France in the revolutionary period on a novel mission was naturally looked upon suspiciously; but he bravely faced the dangers and came through them without mishap. His book is of high value for the historian, as a record of the economic and social conditions which led to the French Revolution and of the sentiments of the French people at the time.

TRAVELS OF MARCO POLO. The record of the adventures of the Venetian merchant Marco Polo, as dictated by him to a fellow-prisoner in Genoa, is one of the most remarkable books of travel ever written. Marco Polo was born at Venice about 1254. His father, a man of noble rank, in 1275 had taken young Marco with him on a trading expedition to China and the East. The youth of twenty entered the service of the Emperor of China, and traveled extensively through the neighboring regions. Returning later to Venice, he was captured in the struggle between that city and Genoa. It was in the year 1298 that Rusticiano or Rustichello of Pisa wrote for him the history of his wanderings.

The "young bachelor's" experience made an interesting book. "Ye shall find therein" (says the prologue) "all kinds of wonderful things. . . . Some things there be indeed therein which he beheld not; but these he heard from men of credit and veracity."

It is said that a French version of the book was made under his direction. Though his narrative made a great sensation, it was for many years regarded as a mass of fabrications and exaggerations. It had an undoubted effect, however, upon exploration; and later researches have confirmed the truth of many of the author's descriptions. This may be taken as a sample of its style: —

"Book iii., Chap. ii. DESCRIPTION OF THE ISLAND OF CHIPANGU.

"Chipangu is an Island toward the east in the high seas, 1500 miles distant from the continent; and a very great Island it is.

"The people are white, civilized, and well-favored. They are idolaters and are dependent on nobody. And I can tell you the quantity of gold they have is endless. . . .

"I will tell you a wonderful thing about the Palace of the Lord of that Island. You must know that he hath a great palace which is entirely roofed with gold. . . . Moreover, all the pavement of the palace, and the floors of its chambers, are entirely of gold, in plates like slabs of stone, a good two fingers thick, . . . so that the richness of this palace is past all bounds and all belief."

The work was published in English in 1818. The most valuable edition to the student is that of Colonel Henry Yule, in two volumes, London, 1875.

TRAVELS OF SIR JOHN MANDEVILLE, THE, a prose narrative of eastern travel written in French about 1357 and afterwards translated into Latin, into English, and into other modern vernaculars including Italian, Spanish, German, Dutch, and Danish. The earliest manuscript of the French version is dated 1371. There were five independent Latin versions, only one of which, extant in fifteenth-century MSS., has been printed. Of the three English versions, all in fifteenth-century manuscripts, one made from a defective French MS. was printed in 1499 by Wynkyn de Worde and frequently thereafter; the versions represented by the Cotton MS. (printed by Halliwell, 1839, and modernized by A. W. Pollard, 1900) and by the Egerton MS. published by the Roxburghe Club in 1889, are fuller and more accurate. That the French and not the Latin or the English is the original version is clearly proved by internal evidence as well as the plain statement of the French version which one English version (the Cotton) mistranslates and distorts so as to state that the Latin is the original. In the opening chapter the author asserts that his name is Jehan de Mandeville, that he was born and brought up in England, that he left that country at Michaelmas, 1322, that he made extensive journeys, traversing Turkey, Armenia, Tartary, Persia, Syria, Arabia, Egypt, Lybia, Ethiopia, Chaldea, Amazonia, and India; and that he gave up travel owing to the gout and wrote this account of his adventures in 1356 or 1357. None of these statements can be accepted. The travels have been proved to be derived from various earlier books of travel. The first part, which describes the Holy Land, is based on the narrative of a German knight, William of Boldensele, whose book was written in 1336. This information is supplemented by many details from earlier writers on the Crusades and on the Saracens. The description of Asia, which occupies the second part of the book, is taken from the narrative of Friar Odoric of Pordenone, who visited India, China, and Tibet about 1316–1318. This is filled in with alleged facts from mediæval encyclopædias, with details from a history of the Mongols, and with extracts from the spurious Epistle of Alexander to Aristotle and the Epistle of Prester John. The whole book is a mass of hearsay, fable, and prodigy, drawn from every literary source available and very cleverly woven into an apparently personal narrative. The author's name is equally suspicious. There is no evidence in the book, except his own assertion that he was an Englishman. There is no record of a Sir John Mandeville. It is true that a chronicler resident in Liège, Jean d'Outremeuse (1338–1399) asserts in his 'Myrur des Histors' that the author of the 'Travels' had lived at Liège from 1343 to 1372 as a philosopher and physician under the name of "Jean de Bourgogne dit à la Barbe" and that on his death-bed in the latter year he revealed himself to his friend, Jean d'Outremeuse, as "Jean de Mandeville, chevalier, comte de Montfort en Angleterre et seigneur de l'isle de Campedi et du Château Perouse." But this title does not sound convincing. Some think that Jean d'Outremeuse invented this character and compiled the travels himself. Others believe that he did know a Jean de Bourgogne, the writer of the travels, and identified him with a certain follower of Baron Mowbray in the reign of Edward II. All that we can be sure about is that the 'Travels' are a clever, literary compilation by a man who was probably not an Englishman, not named Mandeville, and not a traveler.

The book itself is one of the most entertaining of all mediæval prose works. Its easy, simple style and the naïveté with which it recounts the marvels of the court of Prester John and of the Cham of Tartary, of the earthly paradise and the hills of gold guarded by ants, its vegetable lambs and generating diamonds are balanced by a certain artful moderation by which the author pretends to withhold greater marvels lest he be called a liar, and occasionally states that he did not see this particular prodigy but had heard of it from someone who had been there and had narrated all the details — which are then given in full. The book was valued in its day as a treasury of information on eastern travel, and is now esteemed as a storehouse of interesting mediæval lore.

TRAVELS WITH A DONKEY IN THE CEVENNES, by Robert Louis Stevenson, is one of the author's earliest works, published in 1879 when he was under thirty. It is an account of his journeyings, for health's sake, in the mountains of southern France with a diminutive donkey, Modestine by name. It is full of charming descriptions of the native population and of nature, and has lively fancy, frequent touches of poetry and sparkling humor, making it one of the most enjoyable of Stevenson's autobiographic writings. The sketch of the seemingly meek but really stubborn and aggravating donkey, whom he becomes fond of in spite of himself, is delicious.

The itinerary is described under the headings: 'Velay,' 'Upper Gévaudan,' 'Our Lady of the Snow,' and 'The Country of the Camisard.' Quotable passages abound: — "Night is a dead monotonous period under a roof, but in the open world it passes lightly, with its skies and dews and perfumes, and the hours are marked by changes in the face of nature. What seems a kind of temporal death to people choked between walls and curtains, is only light and living slumber to the man who sleeps afield."

After camping out in a pine wood over night: "I hastened to prepare my pack and tackle the steep ascent before me, but I had something on my mind. It was only a fancy; yet a fancy will sometimes be importunate. I had been most hospitably received and punctually served in my green caravanserai. The room was airy, the water excellent, and the dawn had called me to a moment. I say nothing of the tapestries or the inimitable ceiling, nor yet of the view which I commanded from the windows; but I felt I was in some one's debt for all this liberal entertainment. And so it pleased me, in a half-laughing way, to leave pieces of money on the turf as I went along, until I had left enough for my night's lodging."

At the end of his trip he sold Modestine: "It was not until I was fairly seated by the driver . . . that I became aware of my bereavement. I had lost Modestine. Up to that moment I had thought I hated her, but now she was gone. . . . For twelve days we had been fast companions; we had traveled upwards of 120 miles, crossed several respectable ridges, and jogged along with our six legs by many a rocky and many a boggy by-road. After the first day, although sometimes I was hurt and distant in manner, I still kept my patience; and as for her, poor soul! she had come to regard me as a god. She loved to eat out of my hand. She was patient, elegant in form, the color of an ideal mouse, and inimitably small. Her faults were those of her race and sex; her virtues were her own. Farewell, and if forever —."

TREASURE OF THE HUMBLE, THE ('Le Trésor des Humbles'), a series of essays by Maurice Maeterlinck (1896), makes its appeal to the God which is in man. The writer of soul-dramas here presents his mystical, twentieth-century philosophy in concrete form. This mysticism seems the direct fruit of modern science, which has so completely disproved the existence of the soul that a new immortality is henceforth insured to it. But the converts of the end of the century, among whom Maeterlinck may be numbered, find that they must establish the claims of the spirit on no superficial or acknowledged grounds. "We do not judge our fellows by their acts — nay, not even by their most secret thoughts; for these are not always undiscernible and we go far beyond the undiscernible. A man shall have committed crimes reputed to be the vilest of all, and yet it may be that even the blackest of these shall not have tarnished for one single moment the breath of fragrance and ethereal purity that surrounds his presence; while at the approach of a philosopher or a martyr, our soul may be steeped in unendurable gloom." These essays go, indeed, far beyond the undiscernible; whether the author write of 'Mystic Morality,' of 'Women,' of 'The Tragical in Daily Life,' of 'The Invisible Goodness,' or of 'The Inner Beauty.' Some spiritual experience is needed to comprehend; otherwise they will seem but words full of sound and fury, signifying nothing. They are not addressed to the intellect primarily, but to the universal soul of man. "It is only by the communications we have with the infinite that we are to be distinguished from each other." "To love one's neighbor in the immovable depths means to love in others that which is eternal; for one's neighbor in the truest sense of the term is that which approaches nearest to God." "Nothing can separate two souls which for an instant have been good together." "I know not whether I would dare to love the man who had made no one weep."

TREATISE ON PAINTING ('Trattato della Pittura'), by Leonardo Da Vinci. This famous treatise was probably written before the year 1498. It has survived in two editions, of which the first is in an abridged form, and contains only three hundred and sixty-five chapters; while the other is a detailed one, and is comprised in nine hundred and twelve chapters. The early and abridged edition was issued in France in 1651, about one hundred and thirty years after Leonardo's death, and an English edition appeared the same year; since when, it has been published in most of the languages of Europe. Knowledge of the more exhaustive version of the treatise is owing to Manzi's discovery in 1817 of a transcript of the original in the Vatican library. According to this manuscript, the 'Trattato della Pittura' is divided into eight books, which are designated: —

1. The Nature of Painting, Poetry, Music, and Sculpture.
2. Precepts for a Painter.
3. Of Positions and Movements of the Human Frame.
4. Of Drapery.
5. Light and Shade and Perspective.
6. Of Trees and Foliage.
7. Of Clouds.
8. Of the Horizon.

This 'Treatise' may be termed an encyclopædia of art: it is clear and concise, and is to this day of great value to those studying art, although there is a lack of coherence between its sections. Rubens wrote a commentary on this 'Treatise'; Annibale Caracci used to say that if during his youth he had read the golden book of Leonardo's precepts, he would have been spared twenty years of useless labor; while Algarotti declared that he should not desire any better elementary work on the art of painting. Among the subjects treated in the abridged edition of the 'Treatise' are: 'What the young student in painting ought in the first place to learn'; 'How to discern a young man's disposition for painting'; 'That a painter should take pleasure in the opinions of everybody'; 'The brilliancy of the landscape'; 'Painters are not to imitate one another.' There are many pungent epigrams and clever philosophical sayings scattered throughout the 'Treatise,' which are frequently quoted. No other old master left behind so many valuable manuscripts as did Leonardo; but owing to the difficulty of deciphering his handwriting, very little is yet known of many of the most important ones.

TRENCK, BARON, LIFE OF (1787), is the autobiography of Baron Friedrich von Trenck, whose life was a succession of adventures scarcely less marvelous than the romantic and highly colored account he gives of them. He entered the Prussian service while still a mere boy, and stood high in Frederick the Great's favor, until, through his love affair with the King's sister, he incurred the royal displeasure, which caused his first imprisonment, the beginning of no end of misfortunes: loss of property, numerous imprisonments and attempts at escape, dangerous wounds, and perils of all kinds. These are all most graphically described in a manner that reminds one of Münchhausen's marvelous tales. The anecdotes interspersed give, whether true or false, a vivid picture of the turbulent condition of court life at the time of Frederick the Great and Maria Theresa, under whom Baron Trenck later served. His restless adventurous temperament led him to Paris, when the Revolution was in full swing; he was there accused of being a secret emissary of foreign powers, and was beheaded by Robespierre's order in July, 1794.

His cousin, Baron Franz von Trenck, an equal hero and swashbuckler, has also written an autobiography, which however has not attained the celebrity of Baron Friedrich's wonderful mixture of fact and imagination.

TRICK TO CATCH THE OLD ONE, A, by Thomas Middleton (1608). Professor C. H. Herford describes this sprightly play as "the strongest of Middleton's comedies of intrigue." Witgood, a spendthrift and profligate, is ruined by his uncle, a usurer named Lucre. Indeed he maintains that it is "a principle in usury" for a man's "nearest kin" to fleece him in preference to a stranger. Witgood is driven to live upon his wits — "Are there not a million of men in the world that only sojourn upon their brain, and make their wits their mercers," he asks himself. He pretends that he has won the affections of a rich widow, whom he induces a courtesan of his acquaintance to personate. Lucre, hoping that the supposed widow as well as his nephew, will fall into his net, immediately makes a show of kindness to them. Then another usurer, Hoard, who had an old grudge against Lucre, makes up his mind to have revenge of his old enemy by seizing this new prize. Witgood connives at this new manœuvre with the result that in the end he is freed from his financial obligations to his uncle and Hoard takes the pretended widow off his hands. "Here for ever," says Witgood, "I disclaim the cause of youth's undoing. . . . Lend me each honest hand, for here I rise a reclaim'd man, loathing the general vice."

TRILBY, by George Du Maurier (1895), is a story of English and Continental art life and literary life of a generation ago, narrated by one who participated in the scenes and recalls them in memory. The action is chiefly in Paris. Trilby is a handsome girl whose father was a bohemian Irish gentleman and her mother a Scotch barmaid. Trilby is laundress and artist's model in the Latin Quarter. She is great friends with three artists who are chums: Taffy, a big Yorkshire Englishman; the Laird, a Scotchman; and Little Billee, an English fellow who has genius as a painter, and whose drawing of Trilby's beautiful foot is a *chef d'œuvre*. He loves her, and she returns the feeling, but Little Billee's very respectable family oppose the match, and Trilby, after saying yes, decides it to be her duty to refuse, which drives her lover into a brain fever. Amongst the bohemians who frequent the studio is Svengali, an Austrian Jew, who is of repulsive character but a gifted musician. He is attracted by Trilby, and discovers that she has the making of a splendid singer. He half repels, half fascinates her; and by the use of hypnotic power forces her to go away with him. She wins fame as a concert artist, always singing in a sort of hypnotic trance under his influence. The three artists, visiting Paris after a five years' absence, attend one of these performances, and are astounded to recognize Trilby. Svengali, now rich and prosperous, dies suddenly at a concert while Trilby is singing; and she, missing his hypnotic influence, loses her power to sing, goes into a decline, and dies surrounded by her old friends. Little Billee, heart-broken, also dies, though not before he has won reputation as an artist. The final pages form a sort of postscript twenty years after, telling of the fate of the subsidiary characters. The main interest is over with Trilby's death.

TRISTRAM SHANDY, by Laurence Sterne. The Life and Opinions of Tristram Shandy, Gent., is "a heterogeneous sort of whimsical humorous memoirs." The first volume appeared January 1st, 1760, when Sterne was forty-six. Up to this time he had lived the life of an easy-going fox-hunting churchman, utterly obscure; but this, his first effort, so amused the public, that he was persuaded to compose further in the same strain; and he published in all nine volumes, the last in January, 1767. The work is full of domestic comedy, "characters of nature," "the creations of a fine fancy working in an ideal element, and not mere copies or caricatures of individualities actually observed," like those of Dickens. Here live old Uncle Toby, Corporal Trim, Dr. Slop, and the Widow Wadman; and who does not enjoy their garrulous gossip, and that of Sterne himself in his frequent whimsical digressions, so full of keen observation and gentle ridicule? Sterne had evidently studied the humorists well: 'Tristram Shandy' reminds us, now of Cervantes, now of Rabelais, now of Swift; but it is *sui generis* nevertheless. Coleridge praised especially Sterne's power of giving significance to "the most evanescent minutiæ in thought, feeling, look, and gesture." The work has always been popular, perhaps never more so than to-day, when the development of realism in English fiction is receiving so much attention.

TRIUMPHANT DEMOCRACY, by Andrew Carnegie (1886). This book is an "attempt to give Americans a better idea of the great work their country has done and is still doing in the world." Mr. Carnegie says that "in population, in wealth, in annual savings, and in public credit, in freedom from debt, in agriculture, and in manufactures, America already leads the world"; and this statement he proceeds to prove by an overwhelming array of statistics. The book is a glorification of democracy; and admitting frankly the many evils and corruptions in America, asserts that in no country is the common man so free, so able to make his way. The growth of the West and its enormous food-producing capacity are treated at length. Manufactures, mining, agriculture, pauperism, and crime, railways and waterways, are all considered in detail, with a wealth of statistics to support every statement. There is a tendency to make the American eagle scream a little louder than is usual nowadays; but on the whole, most Americans would agree heartily with Mr. Carnegie's pride in American institutions. Mr. Carnegie is so optimistic that he will not admit that even the horde of immigrants pouring in on us from Europe is anything but an unmixed blessing. Two chapters are devoted to literature and art, but it is evident that the material prosperity of the country is the main idea of the book.

TROILUS AND CRISEYDE, by Geoffrey Chaucer (1380). This narrative poem is partly translated and partly adapted from the 'Filostrato' of Boccaccio. 'Il Filostrato' numbers 5700 lines, 'Troilus and Criseyde,' 8240. It is the first great love poem in the English language. Troilus, a prince of the royal house of Troy, scoffs at love and lovers until one day he sees the beautiful Criseyde, a young widow, at the Temple of the Palladium, and falls madly in love with her. Pandarus, her uncle, and Troilus's friend, coaxes his secret from the timid youth and promises to help him with his niece. Pandarus finds Criseyde sitting with her women "with-inne a paved parlor" poring over tales of chivalry. He represents Troilus as dying of love for her. After he leaves, a ballad sung by Antigone sets her dreaming of love. At this moment of destiny, Troilus, the brave young warrior, rides by her window, returning from battle with the Greeks, amid the shouts and praises of the people. On the next day Pandarus returns with a letter which Criseyde at first refuses to receive but at last consents to answer. Pandarus persuades his niece to go to the palace on a plausible pretext, and contrives to have the lovers meet. He next invites Criseyde to supper at his house, telling her that Troilus is away, and cannot be there. A thunderstorm aids his plans. Criseyde is induced to spend the night at her uncle's house. Pandarus comes to her room with the news of Troilus's unexpected arrival, and she consents to see him and yields to his love. Criseyde's father is a traitor in the Greek camp. He sends for his daughter on an exchange of prisoners. The lovers are heartbroken at the parting, but Criseyde with vows that "shake the throned gods" swears to return in ten days. She soon discovers that no pretext for return will avail, because her father, the priest, has foreknowledge that the city is destined to destruction. Diomede, a young Greek, pays court to her and wins her, though she

grieves for Troilus, the truest lover woman ever had, and laments her own inconstancy. Since it is no use for her to repent, she will make amends by being true to
her new lover. When Troilus can no longer continue to believe Criseyde faithful, he
seeks death in battle and is slain by Achilles. The name, Criseyde, has become a by-
word for faithlessness in love, as Troilus stands for all time for the faithful lover.
Chaucer's Criseyde is a masterpiece of sympathetic portrayal, full of charm in spite
of her fickleness, in marked contrast to the wanton Cressida of Shakespeare. Ten
Brink says of her, "The English Criseyde is more innocent, less experienced, less
sensual, more modest than her Italian prototype." He speaks of the trickery and
intrigue which was necessary to bring her at last to Troilus. Pandarus is a genial,
humorous character, a masterpiece of comic art, a clever manager of men, where
Boccaccio's Pandaro is an unprincipled young gallant and go-between for the lovers,
and Shakespeare's Pandarus is senile and repulsive.

TROILUS AND CRESSIDA (1609) is one of the later products of Shakespeare's
pen. Whether he got his facts from Chaucer, or from mediæval tales about Troy, is
uncertain. The drama is his wisest play, and yet the least pleasing as a whole,
owing to the free talk of the detestable Pandarus and the licentiousness of the false
Cressida. Some have thought the piece to be an ironical and satirical burlesque of
Homer. There is very little plot. The young Trojan, Troilus, in love with Cressida,
is brave as a lion in battle and green as a goose in knowledge of women. (But "to
be wise and love exceeds man's might.") His amour, furthered by Cressida's uncle,
Pandarus, is scarcely begun when Cressida is exchanged for a Trojan prisoner and
led off by Diomed to the Greek camp. On arriving, she allows herself to be kissed
by the Greek generals, whom she sees for the first time; as Ulysses says, "There's language in her eye, her cheek, her lip." She has just vowed eternal loyalty to Troilus
too. But she is anybody's Cressida; and with anguish unspeakable, Troilus later
overhears her making an appointment with Diomed, and sees her give him his own
remembrance pledge. By gross flattery of the beef-witted Ajax, the wily Greek
leaders get him to fight Hector. But Hector and he are related by blood, and after
some sparring and hewing they shake hands. Hector is then feasted in the Grecian
tents. The big conceited bully Achilles, "having his ear full of his airy fame," has
grown "dainty of his worth"; and finding his reputation "shrewdly gored" by his
long inactivity, and by the praise Ajax is getting, and especially spurred on by the
death of Patroclus, at length comes into the field, but plays the contemptible coward's
part by surprising Hector with his armor off and having his Myrmidons butcher him.
Thersites is a scurvy, foul-mouthed fellow, who does nothing but rail, exhausting the
language of vile epithets, and hitting off very shrewdly the weak points of his betters,
who give him frequent fist-beatings for his pains. The great speeches of Ulysses,
Agamemnon, and Nestor all breathe the selfsame tone of profound sagacity and
insight into human nature. They have the mint-stamp of but one soul, and that
Shakespeare's. Homer's sketches of the Greek leaders are the merest Flaxman
outlines; but Shakespeare throws the Röntgen rays of his powerful analysis quite
through their souls, endowing them with the subtlest thoughts, and through their
masks utters such sentences as these:—

> "The ample proposition that hope makes
> In all designs begun on earth below,
> Fails in the promised largeness."

> "*One* touch of nature makes the whole world kin,—
> That all with one consent praise new-born gauds."

"Keep then the path;
For emulation hath a thousand sons
That one by one pursue: If you give way,
Or hedge aside from the direct forthright,
Like to an entered tide they all rush by
And leave you hindmost."

There are no other scenes in Shakespeare so packed with sound and seasoned wisdom as the third of Act i. and the third of Act iii. in 'Troilus and Cressida.'

TROIS FILLES DE M. DUPONT, LES, see **THREE DAUGHTERS OF M. DUPONT.**

TROPICAL AFRICA, by Henry Drummond, was published shortly after the author's return from his African explorations in 1886; several of the chapters having appeared as magazine articles before their publication in book form. There is considerable breadth of subject-matter; but the man of science, pervaded by a robust, religious spirit, speaks in every chapter.

From the geographer's view-point, the volume possesses greatest value as outlining the water-route to the heart of Africa, by way of the rivers Zambezi and Shire, and as describing some of the great inland lakes. The "geological sketch" and the "meteorological note" are admirable in their way, and the observations upon the white ant, and the mimicry of African insects, evince the gifts of the painstaking and ingenious observer. But the author speaks his most earnest word when he treats the "Heart-Disease of Africa [the slave trade], and its Pathology and Cure." Professor Drummond severely arraigns the "Powers" for tolerating the inhuman enormities of this hideous traffic. The language of the volume throughout is vivid though simple; and the quaint humor, now and again appearing, adds zest and flavor to the interesting narrative.

TROUBADOURS AND TROUVÈRES, by Harriet Waters Preston (1876), is an account of the poetry of Provence, old and new. The earlier essays describe the work of the two best-known of the "Félibres," as the school of modern poets of the South of France is called: men who write in the old "langue d'oc," or Provençal dialect, in opposition to the "langue d'oïl," or French tongue, which they do not acknowledge as their language. Miss Preston makes many translations of their verse, which give a vivid presentment of the fire and color and naïve simplicity of the originals. Another poet of the South of France, neither Provençal nor French, was Jacques Jasmin, who wrote in the peculiar Gascon dialect, with all the wit and gayety of his race. The forerunners of all these men were the old troubadours, who flourished from the driving out of the Saracens to the end of the crusades, during the "age of chivalry," and who spent their lives making love songs for the ladies of their preference. Their chansons, or songs, so simple and so perfect, were invariably on the one theme of love; occasionally they wrote longer pieces, called "sirventes," which were narrative or satiric. Many charming translations illustrate their manner. The book closes with a chapter on the Arthurian legends, showing what these owe to Geoffrey of Monmouth, to unknown French romances, to Sir Thomas Malory, and finally to Tennyson. Miss Preston's excellent scholarship and rare literary gift combine to make a most entertaining book.

TROY AND ITS REMAINS, by Dr. Heinrich Schliemann (1875). A work offered to the reader as 'A Narrative of Researches and Discoveries made on the Site of

Ilium and in the Trojan Plain.' It is a graphic story of most remarkable discoveries on the spot which tradition, from the earliest historic age of Greece, has marked as the site of Homer's Ilium. Through ruins piled to the height of fifty feet Schliemann dug down to the fire-scattered relics of Troy, and brought to light thousands of objects illustrating the race, language, and religion of her inhabitants, their wealth and civilization, their instruments and appliances for peaceful life and for war. The discoveries at the same time throw a new light upon the origins of the famous Greeks of history, and open somewhat the not before known history of the primitive Greeks of Asia. The wealth of detail in the narrative, with the map, plans, views, and illustrative cuts, representing 500 objects discovered on the site, give the work an extraordinarily readable character.

TRUE RELATION, THE, by Captain John Smith. This famous work was published in London, in 1608. The full title is, 'A True Relation of such occurrences and accidents of noate as has hapned in Virginia since the first planting of that Collony, which is now resident in the South part thereof, till the last returne from thence. Written by Captain Smith, Coronell of the said Collony, to a worshipfull friend of his in England.' The account was also called 'Newes from Virginia.' It relates the founding of Jamestown, from January 1st, 1607, when three ships sailed from England for Virginia, to May 20th, 1608. Dealings with the Indians, especially with "the great emperour Powhatan," occupy the greater part of the pamphlet. The style is straightforward, and the whole tone exceedingly naïve. Captain John Smith has always been one of the few picturesque figures in early colonial history, and the writers of school histories have always made the most of him; his veracity was unquestioned, until Mr. Charles Deane, in the preface to an edition of 'The True Relation,' published in 1880, pointed out that the story of the rescue of Captain Smith by Pocahontas makes its first appearance in Smith's 'General Historie,' published in 1624, and no such romantic incident is hinted at in 'The True Relation.' Mr. Deane charges Captain Smith with having magnified his own share in the doings of the colony; and it cannot be denied that all through 'The True Relation,' Captain John Smith is the central figure. But making all reasonable allowances for self-conceit and self-glorification, there is no doubt that the settlers would have starved the first winter, if John Smith had not had his own energy and all they lacked into the bargain.

TRUTH, THE, by Clyde Fitch (1906). The scene opens at the house of Mrs. Warder. a young married woman, who is given to systematic lying, and who has been carrying on with Fred Lindon a flirtation which she wishes people to believe is merely harmless and amusing.

Mrs. Lindon, a handsome, but nervous and overstrung woman, informs Warder that his wife meets her husband every day. Warder questions his wife, who involves herself in such a maze of lies that his worst suspicions are justified, and he declares that he will live with her no longer, though now, in penitence and sincerity she protests her love for him. She goes to stay with her father Roland, an impecunious and shifty person, who is constantly in debt to his landlady, and who has frequently wheedled money out of her husband through her. She upbraids her father for allowing her to grow up in the habit of telling lies, and is trying to break off the habit when he concocts a telegram to her husband asking him to come at once to her, as she is dying. Roland tries to make the parlor look like a sick-room, but the landlady tells Warder when he comes that his wife has not been ill at all. Mrs. Warder protests to her husband that now, even if she tells lies, she has learned to loathe them and be afraid of them. "We don't love people, because they are perfect, we love them because they are themselves," he says, as he is reconciled to her.

TRUTH AND POETRY FROM MY OWN LIFE, see GOETHE'S AUTO-BIOGRAPHY.

TURKISH SPY, THE ('L'Espion Turc'). 'Letters Written by one Mahmut, who lived Five-and-Forty Years undiscovered at Paris. Giving an Impartial Account to the Divan at Constantinople of the most Remarkable Transactions of Europe, and covering several Intrigues and Secrets of the Christian Courts (especially that of France) from the year 1637 to the year 1683. Written originally in Arabic. Translated in Italian and from thence into English, by John Paul Marana. In 8 vols. London: 1801.'

The contents of this remarkable work are quite fully described by the above lengthy inscription on the title-page. A romance, really written by Giovanni Paolo Marana, but pretending to be the confidential communications of a refugee Turk, to his friends, — this performance is an ingenious and witty comment on the political and social conduct of Christian Europe during the seventeenth century, as viewed by a pretended outsider. The writer himself inclines to the philosophy of Descartes; he is not given to credulity, but in no case yields up his loyalty to the faith of Islam. He keeps himself in hiding from the detectives of Cardinal Richelieu in Paris from 1641 to 1682; and employs his time in writing lengthy epistles to the Sultan, to friends in Vienna, to Mahomet, a eunuch exiled in Egypt, and others. Among the personages and topics commented on are Charles II. of England, Philip II. of Spain, the Religious War in Germany, "Gustavus, King of Swedeland," and in France the course of affairs during the reign of the house of the Medici. His resources in classical lore are extensive. Alexander the Great comes under his review with sovereigns of later times. To his friend the eunuch in Egypt he writes in friendly confidence; towards the close of the long record admitting that he has loved a woman for thirty years, only at last to be deceived in her and to learn the folly of earthly love. "Let us therefore," he counsels his friend, "reserve our love for the daughters of Paradise!"

TURMOIL, a novel by Booth Tarkington (1915). The scene of this novel is a smoky industrial city of the Middle West whose God is Big Business, and old Sheridan of the Sheridan Trust Company, the biggest of its kind, is the city incarnate. He had come from the country crossroads to the pleasant little town and done more than one man's share to make it big and smoky. He loved the smoke, calling it prosperity. His two older sons, Jim and Roscoe, are young business men after his own heart. The youngest son, Bibbs, who hopes to be a poet, is a disappointment. His father's efforts to have him learn the business from the ground up results in prolonged nervous prostration. Later he finds out that it is possible to feed zinc to a chopping machine crashing sixty-eight times a minute quite happily if one has a friend like Mary Vertrees to think about. Jim is killed by the collapse of a building of his own faulty construction. Roscoe's wife's unworthiness leads him to weakness and failure. Sheridan's daughter runs away with a fortune hunter. It is to the despised Bibbs that the father has to turn, and Bibbs responds honorably, proving himself the best of the family. Mary Vertrees had believed it her duty to marry Jim for the sake of her family. She learns to love Bibbs in failure and success, and together they will reduce even Big Business to the level of common humanity.

TURN OF THE SCREW, THE, by Henry James (1898).   A terrifying ghost story about two children, haunted by the evil spirits of a man and a woman, former servants, who are determined to gain possession of the souls of the little boy and girl.   Their young governess encounters the spectres, and gradually discovers the mysterious power which they exert over the children, who try to conceal their intercourse with their sinister companions.   The efforts of the loyal governess to protect her charges, the supreme struggle between the living woman, and the spectre villains is a thrilling drama, which ends in victory for the governess, though Miles, the boy, dies in her arms in the act of turning from the evil.   Flora, the beautiful little girl, is still obsessed by the influence of the dead Miss Jessel, even after her removal from the haunted house.   The mystery, the face at the window, the vision seen across the lake, the meeting face to face on the stairs with the dreadful spectre of Peter Quint, conveys an eerie atmosphere which constitutes the power of the book.

TURNSTILE, THE, by A. E. W. Mason (1912).   This is a story of English political and social life the opening chapters of which are laid in South America.   It is here that Cynthia Daventry, the heroine of the story, is first introduced to the reader.   She is the adopted daughter of a rich and childless couple who had left their native home, England, in their early married life to build up their fortunes in a new country.   This they succeeded in doing, and upon reaching middle life adopted from a foundling asylum, a lovely little girl of three years, who had been put there by her father, James Challoner.   He was the profligate son of an old English family, whose wife had been killed by an earthquake.   Until Cynthia's seventeenth birthday she is ignorant of her parentage and then her bad and dissolute father appears on the scene and claims her.   The only alternative for the Daventrys, who love Cynthia as their own, is to flee with her, and the next day they sail with her for England.   Here they settle in Warwickshire, Daventry's old home, and after three years the elderly couple die, leaving Cynthia heiress to a large fortune.   She is beautiful and has many suitors but none touch her heart.   She becomes interested in Captain Harry Rames, an Arctic explorer, who has given up the Navy and gone into politics.   He is clever and ambitious and realizes he must marry money to further his career.   He is attracted to Cynthia and proposes to her though he does not feel a deep love for her.   Cynthia realizes this but decides to marry him as she thinks the furthering of his political career will be an interesting experience for her.   Their married life goes on for some time in a commonplace fashion and then Cynthia realizes that she is in love with her husband; at the same time she feels there is some shadow between them and fears she has a rival.   This however proves to be the call of the sea, and exploration, which has re-asserted itself in Rames, and which he is trying to hide from her.   When the secret is out, the husband and wife understand each other at last and acknowledge their mutual love, and Cynthia consents to Rames's conducting an expedition which will take him from her for three years, though the parting causes her deep sorrow.

TWELFTH NIGHT, or, What You Will, by Shakespeare, is a delightfully humorous comedy.   An item in the manuscript diary of John Manningham shows that it was played February 2d, 1601, in the fine old hall of the Middle Temple, London, — a hall still in existence.   The twelfth night after Christmas was anciently given up to sport and games; hence the name.   The fresh, gay feeling of a whistling plowboy in June was the mood of the writer of 'Twelfth Night.'   Tipsy Sir Toby's humor is catching; his brain is like a bottle of champagne; his heels are as light as his head, and one feels he could cut a pigeon-wing with capering Sir Andrew "to make all split," or sing a song "to make the welkin dance." The scene is a seaport city of Illyria, where a sentimental young duke is fallen into a love-melancholy over the pitiless lady Olivia. Now the fair Viola and her brother Sebastian, — strikingly alike in feature,—unknown to each other reach the same city, Sebastian in company with his friend Captain Antonio. Viola enters the service of the duke as a page, in garments such as her brother wore. With the rich Olivia dwell her Puritanical steward Malvolio, her kinsman Sir Toby Belch, and her maid Maria, and other servants. Olivia has a suitor, and Sir Toby an echo, in the lean-witted Sir Andrew Aguecheek. Malvolio is unpopular: he thinks because he is virtuous there shall be no more cakes and ale; but Maria lays a trap for his vanity, which is fathoms deep. She drops a mysterious letter in Malvolio's path, penned in Olivia's hand ("her very C's, her U's, and her T's"). The letter begins with "M O A I doth sway my life," bids him be opposite with a kinsman and surly with servants, recall who commended his yellow stockings and wished to see him cross-gartered, and remember that some have greatness thrust upon them. He swallows the bait, and makes himself such a ridiculous ass that Olivia thinks him out of his wits, and Sir Toby has him bound and put into a dark room. Malvolio has called the clown "a barren rascal," and this keen-witted lovable fellow now has a delicious bit of retaliation. Assuming the voice of the curate Sir Topas, he assures him that until he can hold the opinion of Pythagoras that the soul of his grandam might haply inhabit a bird, he shall not advise his release. Then resuming his own voice he indulges in more excellent fooling. When last seen Malvolio is free, and bolting out of the room swears he will be "revenged on the whole pack" of them. To return: Viola (as "Cesario") becomes the duke's messenger to woo Olivia by proxy. Olivia falls desperately in love with the messenger; and when Aguecheek spies her showing him favors, he is egged on by roguish Sir Toby to write him a challenge. But Cesario is afraid of the very sight of naked steel, and Sir Andrew is an arrant coward. Sir Toby, after frightening each nearly out of his wits with stories of the other's ferocity, at length gets them for form's sake to draw their swords; when in comes Captain Antonio, and mistaking Cesario for Sebastian, takes his part. In the meantime, Olivia has married Sebastian by mistake for Cesario, and the two knights both get their heads broken through a similar misunderstanding; for however it may be with Cesario, Sebastian is "a very devil incardinate" with his sword. Presently Sebastian and Cesario meet, and the mystery is solved: Viola avows her sex, and marries the duke, whom she ardently loves.

TWENTY YEARS AFTER ('Vingt Ans Après') by Alexandre Dumas (1845) is a story of the "Fronde," — the uprising of the people of Paris against Cardinal Mazarin, prime minister of France and reputed husband of Anne of Austria, the regent, mother of the boy king Louis XIV. D'Artagnan, who has never left the Guards, and Porthos, who has returned to that company with the hope of being made a baron, find themselves pitted against Athos and Aramis, who have emerged, one from his country-seat, the other from his convent, to take a hand in the Fronde. After much skirmishing, which gives us a brilliant account of the warfare of the Fronde, Athos and Aramis go to England on a commission from Henrietta Maria, exiled in France, to her husband Charles I.; and presently Porthos and D'Artagnan are sent by Mazarin with dispatches to Cromwell, in company with a young Englishman named Mordaunt, who is the son of an infamous beauty of the Court. Athos and Aramis are captured by the Parliamentary army. This is but the beginning of a long series of dramatic adventures. The exciting story draws to a close with the ending of the Fronde.

TWENTY YEARS AT HULL-HOUSE, by Jane Addams, an autobiographical account of her career as a social reformer, was published in 1912. The early chapters relate her bringing up at Cedarville, Illinois, her education at Rockford, Illinois, where she obtained the degree of B.A. in 1881, her illness followed by two European journeys in which she became awake to the miserable lot of the poor, and her decision in 1888 to take up settlement work, for which she made preparation by a visit to Toynbee Hall in London. Then follows an account of the establishment of the Hull House Settlement in 1889. The building, an old family mansion, in the centre of Chicago, was at first sublet from the tenants, and afterwards presented to the settlement by the owner. The present thirteen buildings represent the increase of the work since that time. Miss Addams's associates, the diversified array of settlement visitors, and the varied social and educational activities of the organization, are described in the ensuing chapters. Her active interest in strikes, labor legislation, and problems of immigration is the subject of the three absorbing chapters which follow. A visit to Tolstoy and a criticism, sympathetic yet discriminating, of his thorough-going solution of the labor problem occupies another chapter. Miss Addams's contributions to civic betterment as an inspector of garbage-removal, and a member of the Board of Education are also recorded; and the book closes with a general exposition of the educational value of a settlement in the socialization of democracy. Informal and anecdotal in method the book sets forth entertainingly and in a concrete way a great and fruitful social ideal and describes a life of beneficent effort for the cause of mankind.

TWENTY YEARS OF CONGRESS: FROM LINCOLN TO GARFIELD, with a Review of the Events which Led to the Political Revolution of 1860 by James G. Blaine, with portraits. (2 vols. 1884–86). Mr. Blaine's unrivaled opportunity of knowing the period treated of in this work makes it an important contribution to history. It is clear, interesting, and brilliantly written. A large part of the first volume is devoted to a review of the events which led up to the Civil War. Beginning with the original compromises between the North and the South embodied in the Constitution, it proceeds with the Missouri Compromises of 1820 and 1821, the origin and development of the Abolition party, the character of the Southern leaders, the Mexican War, origin and growth of the Republican party, the Dred Scott decision, the debate between Douglas and Lincoln, the John Brown raid, and Lincoln's election. Then follow two chapters on Congress in the winter of 1860–61; after which the course of affairs during the War and down to the inauguration of President Johnson occupies the rest of the volume. Mr. Blaine shows himself to be a warm admirer of Henry Clay, contrasting him very favorably with Webster, and saying of him: "In the rare combination of qualities which constitute at once the matchless leader of party and the statesman of consummate ability and inexhaustible resource, he has never been surpassed by any man speaking the English tongue." Of General Grant he speaks in the most appreciative terms. The picture of Lincoln's character is strongly drawn and glowing. Volume ii. covers the period from the beginning of Johnson's administration to the year 1881. The disbandment of the army, reconstruction, the three amendments to the Constitution, the government's financial legislation, Johnson's impeachment, General Grant's two terms, the Geneva award, Hayes's administration, the fisheries question, and Garfield's election, are among the topics treated. In conclusion, the author alludes to the unprecedented difficulty of the legislative problems during the War, and briefly notes the course of Congress in grappling with them, reviews the progress of the people during the twenty years, claiming credit for Congress for the result, and asserts that "No government of modern times has encountered the dangers that beset the United States, or achieved the triumphs wherewith the nation is crowned."

TWICE-TOLD TALES, by Nathaniel Hawthorne. (First series, 1837; second series, 1847). The 'Twice-Told Tales' took their title from the fact of their previous publication in various annuals and magazines. The book was favorably noticed, although the quality of the author's genius was not then widely appreciated. The tales are national in character, and the themes are chosen from among the many quaint and interesting traditions of New England. Told with a felicity and repose of manner that has not been surpassed in our literature, they reveal a power of imagination, a knowledge of the obscurer motives of human nature, and a spiritual insight, which marked a distinct epoch in American literature. The second series of 'Twice-Told Tales' begins with the four 'Legends of the Province House,' — tales which, especially characteristic of the author's genius, at once added to the romantic glamour which surrounds the Boston of Revolutionary days. Throughout, the 'Tales' are characterized by Hawthorne's beauty of style, — smooth, musical, poetical. He looks upon all things with the spirit of love and with lively sympathies; for to him external form is but the representation of internal being, all things having life, an end, an aim. The sketch entitled 'A Rill from the Town Pump' is perhaps the most famous in the collection, which contains here and there themes and suggestions that Hawthorne later elaborated in his longer stories; notably the picture of a beautiful woman wearing an embroidered "A" upon her breast, who afterwards reappears in 'The Scarlet Letter.' 'The Great Carbuncle' was especially admired by Longfellow, who commends its poetic beauty. The 'Tales' have often a sombre tone, a fateful sense of gloom, weird and sometimes almost uncanny; but they possess an irresistible fascination. Among those best known are 'The Gray Champion,' 'The Gentle Boy,' and the 'Wedding Knell.'

TWO CHIEFS OF DUNBOY, THE, by James Anthony Froude (1889). This is the only novel written by Froude, whose book on 'The English in Ireland in the Eighteenth Century' had already established him as an authority on Irish matters.

The scene of the story opens on the banks of the Loire, near Nantes, France; where one Blake, a ship-owner and Irish exile, fits out a vessel as a pirate to prey upon British shipping, and persuades Morty Sullivan, one of the chiefs of Dunboy and an Irish exile, to take the command. The chief action of the plot takes place at or near the village of Castleton in Bantry Bay, Ireland: where Colonel Goring, the other chief of Dunboy, an Englishman, has established a Protestant settlement for the purpose of working the copper mines, establishing a fishery, and protecting the coast from smugglers. The time is the middle of the eighteenth century. Goring is a magistrate, and is feared and hated by the Irish peasantry. He is fearless in the discharge of what he believes to be his duty, in which he receives but slight support from the government. He is eventually killed treacherously by Morty Sullivan and some accomplices. Sullivan, who has visited Ireland for the purpose of estimating the chances of success in case the French should land troops, is killed in an attempt to escape from the government forces. The story gives opportunity for the relation of many thrilling adventures, such as the chase of the privateer by a British frigate, the drilling of Irish rebels by moonlight, and the prevention by the coast-guard of the landing of ammunition. The questions of the relation of landlord and tenant, of church, education, industries, and government, are discussed with great lucidity, and the national characteristics of the Irish are shown: their love of that which has existed for centuries, their opposition to improvements, and their instability and lack of cohesion. That incomprehensible machine, the government, is shown in a part of the story of which Dublin is the scene; and there is a description of a riot which is suppressed by the dragoons.

The book carries that interest which is always felt in a well-told historical story, and the descriptions of Irish scenery are vivid.

TWO GENTLEMEN OF VERONA (first printed 1623), one of Shakespeare's earliest and least attractive comedies, for the plot of which he was slightly indebted to Bandello, to Sidney's 'Arcadia,' and to Montemayor's 'Diana Enamorada.' The scene is laid alternately in Verona and in Milan. The noble Valentine of Verona remarks to his friend Proteus that "home-keeping youths have ever homely wits"; hence he will travel to Milan, with his servant Speed. Proteus, a mean-souled, treacherous, fickle young sprig, is in love with Julia, or thinks he is. His servant's name is Launce, a droll fellow who is as rich in humor as Launcelot Gobbo of the 'Merchant of Venice.' Julia is the heroine of the piece; a pretty, faithful girl. Proteus soon posts after Valentine to Milan, and at once forgets Julia and falls "over boots in love" with Silvia. Julia also goes to Milan, disguised as a boy, and takes service with Proteus. The latter treacherously betrayed Valentine's plan of elopement with Silvia to the duke her father, who met Valentine, pulled the rope ladder from under his cloak, and then banished him. As in the play of 'As You Like It,' all the parties finally meet in the forest where Valentine has been chosen leader by a band of respectable outlaws. Julia confesses her identity; Valentine, with a maudlin milk-sop charity, not only forgives Proteus (whom he has just overheard avowing to Silvia that he will outrage her if he cannot get her love), but, on Proteus repenting, actually offers to give up Silvia to him. But Julia swoons, and Proteus's love for her returns. A double marriage ends this huddled-up finale. Launce affines with Touchstone, Grumio, Autolycus, and the Dromios. He is irresistibly funny in the enumeration of his milkmaid's "points," and in the scenes with his dog Crab. This cruel-hearted cur, when all at home were weeping over Launce's departure, and the very cat was wringing her hands, shed not a tear; and when, in Madam Silvia's dining-room, he stole a chicken-leg from the trencher and misbehaved in an unmentionable manner, Launce manfully took a whipping for him. Nay, he stood on the pillory for geese Crab had killed, and stood in the stocks for puddings Crab had stolen. Crab enjoys the honor of being the only dog that sat to Shakespeare for his portrait, although others are mentioned in his works.

TWO MEN, Elizabeth Stoddard's second novel, was published in 1865. As in her two other stories, the scene is laid in a New England seaport town; the characters being the members of one family, all of them of strongly marked individuality. The head of the house is Sarah Auster, whose husband Jason, once a ship-carpenter, is overshadowed by her aggressive nature, and by the great wealth which is hers from her grandfather, and which she hopes will descend undivided to her son Parke, — a beautiful, sweet-natured boy, untainted by his mother's strange perverse disposition. There is another heir, however, — her cousin Osmond Luce, a seaman. After a long absence he suddenly appears with his little daughter Philippa. He resigns his rights in his child's favor, and goes to sea again. Sarah takes unwilling charge of Philippa, who grows into a strange, silent girl. She loves her cousin Parke with a grave, intense love, but he knows nothing of it. He is attracted only by brilliant colors of character, or by beauty of form. He entertains a wayward love for a beautiful girl, Charlotte Lang, in whose veins is negro blood. The shadow of their relation crosses at last the threshold of Parke's home. His mother dies of her grief. Charlotte dies at the birth of her child. Then Parke sails away from the scene of his tragedy, leaving Philippa and Jason alone in the old homestead. In time they love and are married. 'Two Men' is written in the clear, remote style of Mrs. Stoddard, its stern realism being relieved by passages of quaint humor.

TWO NOBLE KINSMEN. A most noble and pathetic drama, founded on Chaucer's 'Knighte's Tale,' and first printed in 1634, with the names of Shakespeare and Fletcher on the title-page as authors. The grand passages suggest the style of 'Coriolanus' and of 'The Tempest,' and seem beyond Fletcher's powers: e. g., the magnificent description of Arcite's horse, worthy of the Panathenaic frieze; the Meissonier portraits of the champion Knights' assistants, — the stern, brown-faced prince with long, black, shining hair and lion mien, the massive-thewed blond, and the rest, the portrait of Arcite himself, his eye "like a sharp weapon on a soft sheath," "of most fiery sparkle and soft sweetness"; or of Palamon's brown manly face and thought-lined brow. And how Shakespearean that phrase applied to old men nearing death, — "the gray approachers"! And who but Shakespeare would have written the lines (so admired by Tennyson) on Mars, —

> "Who dost pluck
> With hand omnipotent from forth blue clouds
> The mason'd turrets"?

The under-plot about the jailer's daughter, who goes mad for Palamon's love, is a weak and repulsive imitation of the Ophelia scenes in 'Hamlet.' The play is about the tribulations of two noble youths who both love the same sweet girl, "fresher than the May," — Emilia, sister of Hippolyta, wife of Theseus. Their love separates them; they were a miracle of friendship, they become bitterest foes. By Theseus's command they select each three friends, and in a trial by combat of the eight champions, Arcite wins Emilia, but is at once killed by his horse falling on him, and Palamon secures the prize after all.

TWO YEARS BEFORE THE MAST, by Richard Henry Dana. This personal narrative of a sailor's life is probably the most truthful and accurate work of its character ever written. Although originally published in 1840, the production of a youth just out of college, it still holds its charm and its popularity in the face of all rivals and successors. The author, upon graduating from Harvard College in the year 1837, at the age of twenty-two, was forced to suspend his studies on account of an affection of his eyes. Having a strong passion for the sea, he shipped "before the mast" upon the brig Pilgrim for a voyage around Cape Horn on a trading trip for hides to California. After rounding the Horn the Pilgrim touched at Juan Fernandez; the next land sighted being California, then inhabited only by Indians and a few Spaniards. She visited Monterey, Santa Barbara, San Pedro, and finally San Diego, the depot of the business. Here Dana remained several months ashore, handling and curing hides. He did not return home in the Pilgrim, but upon the arrival of the ship Alert, consigned by the same owners, he procured an exchange to her. The voyage home in this vessel is graphically described. While aboard of her Dana touched at San Francisco, where, except the Presidio, there then existed one wooden shanty only. This was afterwards rebuilt as a one-story adobe house; and long remained as the oldest building in the now great city.

The book contains a straightforward and manly account of the life of a fore-mast hand at that date; and it gives in detail the adventures, hardships, and too often brutalities, which accompany a seaman's life. Mr. Dana sets forth from his own personal experience the thoughts, feelings, enjoyments, and sufferings, as well as the real life and character, of the common seaman. In reading it one finds more than the ordinary record of a sea voyage; for there runs through the simple and lucid narrative an element of beauty and power which gives it the charm of romance. The book was immediately successful, passed through many editions, was adopted by the British Board of Admiralty for distribution to the navy, and was translated into many Continental languages. In 1869 the author added a supplementary chapter giving an account of a second visit to California, and the subsequent history of many of the persons and vessels mentioned in the original work. William Cullen Bryant, who procured the first publication of the book, recommended it to the publishers as "equal to Robinson Crusoe"; and the event has justified his forecast, with the additional merit that the story is absolutely real and truthful.

TYPEE and **OMOO**, by Herman Melville (1846, 1847). The first-named work, 'Typee,' a famous book, the forerunner of all South-Sea romances, the most charming of all, and the source of many new words in our vocabulary, like *taboo*, is a narrative of the author's enforced sojourn, in the summer of 1842, among the cannibal Typees on one of the Marquesas Islands. It appeared simultaneously in New York and London, and won everywhere the highest praise. With Toby, another young sailor, Melville deserted from the steamship Dolly, in Nukaheva Bay, intending to seek asylum with the friendly Happars; but they missed their way and arrived in Typee Valley. They were well received there, however, were given abundant food (eaten under some apprehensions that they were being *fattened*), and except that their attempts to depart were frowned on, they had no cause to complain. After about a month Toby became separated from his comrade, and was taken off the island in a passing ship. For four months Melville lived an indolent, luxurious life in a sort of terrestrial paradise, with nothing to do, plenty to eat, waited on by a body servant Kory-Kory, petted by a score of beauteous dusky damsels, and especially adored by the incomparable Fayaway. But discontent lurked in his bosom; and at length, to the sorrow and even against the will of his hosts, — poor Fayaway was quite inconsolable, — he contrived to make his escape on a Sydney whaler which was short of men.

'Omoo' (The Rover) continues our author's adventures, changing the scene to Tahiti, whither the steamer Julia proceeded. While in Papeetee harbor Melville and a new friend, Dr. "Long Ghost," joined some malcontents among the crew, who had a grievance against the captain, and were put ashore. Wilson, the high-handed English consul, ordered them into the "calaboza," where, with not too much to eat they stayed several weeks under the benevolent custody of Captain Bob, an old native. They were finally helped away to Imeeo, a neighboring island, by two planters who wished to engage them as farm hands. Digging in the ground with primitive hoes proved not to their tastes, however; and they soon departed for Taloo, where they were hospitably treated by "Deacon" Jeremiah Po-Po, a native convert. They attended church, participated in a feast, visited a royal palace under care of a pretty little maid of honor, caught a glimpse of Queen Pomaree, and otherwise enjoyed themselves, until, a Vineyard whaler appearing, Melville bade farewell to Dr. "Long Ghosts" and sailed away. In these two books the author has succeeded in his stated purpose of conveying some idea of novel scenes that frequently occur among whaling crews in the South Pacific, and in giving a familiar account of the condition of the converted Polynesians.

UARDA, by Georg Moritz Ebers (1876). This is a study of ancient Egyptian civilization in the city of Thebes, in the fourteenth century before Christ, under Rameses II. A narrative of Herodotus, combined with the Epos of Pentaur, forms the foundation of the story. We have a minute description of the dress, the food, the religious customs and wars of the ancient Egyptians. There are three separate love stories: that of Bent-Anat, daughter of Rameses, who loves Pentaur, the poet-priest; that of Nefert, wife of Mena, the king's charioteer; and that of Uarda herself, who has many adorers, for only one of whom she cares, — Rameri, the king's son. Pentaur is sent into exile, rescued by Uarda, following in Bent-Anat's train. He saves the king in battle, and is rewarded with the princess's hand. Nefert is pursued by Paaker, but is true to her husband. Paaker plots to betray Rameses, and perishes in his own trap. It then becomes known that he is the son of a gardener, and Pentaur the true son of the noble, they having been exchanged at birth. Uarda (The Rose) proves to be grandchild to the king of the Danaids, her mother having been taken captive many years before. She marries Rameri; and after her grandfather's death, they rule over many islands of the Mediterranean and found a famous race.

UNCLASSED, THE, by George Gissing (1896), is a study of the lower London life, written with moderation and sincere sympathy with the sinful and the poor. There is no shirking of unpleasant details, but the author does not throw any glamour over the lowest life of the streets. It is rather a study of conditions than of character, although the personages of the story are distinctly drawn. In the dénouement it appears that the "unfortunates" may climb back to a decent life if social conditions favor.

UNCLE REMUS, 'His Songs and His Sayings.' By Joel Chandler Harris (1880). These quaint and humorous folk-lore fables "are told night after night to a little boy by an old negro who has nothing but pleasant memories of the discipline of slavery, and who has all the prejudices of caste and pride of family that were the natural results of the system." The animals talk and show their native cunning,—Brer Rabbit, Brer Fox, Brer 'Possum, and the rest. These characters, as delineated by Mr. Harris, have won world-wide fame, and are familiar in all literature and conversation. Their adventures seem directly drawn from the darkey's vivid and droll imagination; though in the preface Mr. Page gives data received from ethnologists, which seem to prove the existence of like stories—some of them identical—among Indian tribes in both North and South America, and the inhabitants of India, Siam, and Upper Egypt. But in his preface to a later collection of 'Uncle Remus Stories' Mr. Harris lightly scoffs at such learned dissertations; and suggests one's pure enjoyment, like his own, of the stories for themselves.

UNCLE TOM'S CABIN, by Harriet Beecher Stowe. This world-famous story was written in 1851, and appeared originally, from week to week as written, in the National Era, an abolition paper published at Washington. Brought out in book form when completed as a serial, its popularity was immediate and immense. Its influence during the last decade of slavery was great, and its part in the creation of anti-slavery sentiment incalculable.

It opens in Kentucky, and closes in Canada. The chapters between are chiefly located in Ohio, in New Orleans, beside Lake Pontchartrain, and down upon the Red

River.   Their chief purpose is to depict slavery, and the effects of it, by portraying the experiences of Uncle Tom, and of those with whom he was more or less connected, through the space of some five years.   Their chief personages, rather in the order of interest than of introduction, are Uncle Tom, the pious and faithful slave, and little Eva, to whom he is devoted; Augustine St. Clare, father of Eva, and his complaining wife; Mr. and Mrs. Shelby, from whose "old Kentucky home" Uncle Tom is sold South; George Shelby, their son, who finally seeks him for repurchase, and finds him dying of brutality on that remote Red River plantation; Simon Legree, who bought Tom after St. Clare's death (which followed not long after that of Eva), who owns him when he dies, and who represents the brutal slaveholder as St. Claire represents the easy and good-humored one; Cassy, once Legree's favorite, now a half-crazed wreck of beauty; Emeline, bought to succeed her, but who escapes with Cassy at last; Eliza, who proves to be Cassy's daughter, and to whom she is finally reunited; George Harris, Eliza's husband, who follows her along the "Underground Railway" in Ohio, after her wonderful escape across the Ohio River on the ice, carrying her boy Harry; Tom Loker, Haley, and Marks, the slave-catchers, who hunt these runaways and are overmatched; Simon Halliday and Phineas Fletcher, the Quakers, with their families; and Senator and Mrs. Bird, and John Van Trompe, all of whom assist the fugitives; Miss Ophelia, the precise New England spinster cousin in St. Clare's home; Topsy, the ebony "limb of mischief," who never was born but just "growed"; and Aunt Chloe, Uncle Tom's wife back there in "old Kentuck," whose earnings were to assist in his return to her, but to whom he never returns.   Other but incidental characters, field and household servants, swell the number to fifty-five.

In a 'Key to Uncle Tom's Cabin,' its author gave matter to sustain both the severe and the mild pictures of slavery which her story had drawn.

UNDER THE TREES AND ELSEWHERE, see **ESSAYS OF HAMILTON WRIGHT MABIE.**

UNDER THE TRICOLOUR ('Barnavaux et Quelques Femmes') by Pierre Mille (1915).   Tales of military life in the African possessions of France, told by a French Mulvaney, named Barnavaux, a soldier in a regiment of territorial infantry.   Most of the episodes are slight, but with humor and pathos vividly reproduce the life of the French soldier on foreign service, and his relations to the natives.   Barnavaux has a dominant pride in the white race, loyalty to his corps, courage, simplicity of heart, and all the vices of a strong man. He reflects on European law as dealing with native customs, and raises interesting questions of justice and commonsense in startling anecdotes from his experience.   "Marie-Faite-en-Fer," the heroine of the first story is the mistress of a French garrison.   She survives the climate, nurses the soldiers through an epidemic, and is tender mother of the regiment, possessing all the virtues, save one.   'The Dead Ship' is a remarkable description of the horrors of the deep sea, the brief resurrection during a storm of an old slave ship, with its chained oarsmen.   'The Leper's Island,' called "Felicite" on the maps, is a tale of horror, of the cold vengeance of a proud native girl on a too bold white man.   'The Man Who Saw the Sirens,' has an amazing love affair with a mermaid.   The joyous humor of 'Barnavaux Victorious' describes an encounter of wits between a zealous policeman, and the tipsy marines whom he endeavors to entangle in the meshes of civil law and order.

UNDER THE YOKE ('Pod Igoto'), by Ivan Vazoff (1893), is the best-known piece of literature Bulgaria has produced.   It was written during the author's unmerited exile in Russia; and the sensation it created brought about his recall to Bulgaria. As a record of one of the series of revolutions that completed the nation's release, in 1878, from the Turkish yoke, it will always be dear to his countrymen. As a tale of love and war in equal parts, embroidered upon the sombre background of the central Balkan, it passes the limits of local interest, appealing to all lovers of liberty. Humorous passages and delicate touches abound. Vazoff is not only a natural story-teller, but a poet of a high order. Like Chaucer and Ronsard, he found his native tongue in a state of transition and fermentation, that, on the whole, rendered the opportunities greater than the drawbacks. He was first in a rich field; and in this novel the embarrassment of material is evident from the beginning. In an early chapter the celebration of a domestic event has brought together the descendants and connections of the conservative, morose, and unpopular Diamandieff. He has an irrepressible married daughter, whose sallies keep her husband in subjection and her guests in fits of laughter. Then there is Diamancho Grigoroff, the story-teller, with his look of intense cunning, whose rambling narratives and flagrant exaggerations command the utmost attention. Monastic restrictions are more honored in the breach than in the observance, for nuns of the Greek Church are not wanting to the feast. There are young men dressed in the fashions of Paris and belonging to the *jeunesse dorée* of Bulgaria. Lalka, the host's pretty daughter, pale with grief at the arrest of a young physician of revolutionary tendencies, and Rada, a beautiful orphan in black, to whom no one pays the slightest attention as she moves about with the after-dinner coffee, but who is the heroine of the story, complete the charm of a scene in which the characters are pointed out somewhat after the orderly methods of the prologue. Taciturnity is not a national trait, and the characters have plenty to say, but say it with more or less reserve according to their proclivities; one or two of them, ripe for a revolt against Turkish authority, hardly daring to commit themselves. The outrages attributed to the Turks, although grewsome reading, furnish a perfect parallel to those still inflicted upon Armenians. The book would therefore be useful to a student of the Armenian question.

UNDERGROUND RUSSIA, by Stepniak. The former editor of Zemlia i Volia (Land and Liberty), who for many years hid his identity under the pseudonym of "Stepniak" (freely translated "Son of the Steppe"), wrote in Italian a series of sketches of the revolutionary and Nihilistic movement in which he had taken such an important part. The introduction gives a succinct history of the individualistic propaganda which resulted in Russia in a certain measure of freedom for women, and which, at the expense of much suffering and many young lives sacrificed, spread a leaven of liberalism through the vast empire of the Tsars. Stepniak traces the successive changes that have taken place in the attack on Autocracy before and since 1871. He defends even the Terrorism that leveled its weapons against the lives of the highest in power. He who had himself been delegated to "remove" certain of the enemies of liberty, could not help arguing in favor of assassination as a political resource. Under the sub-title of 'Revolutionary Profiles,' he draws pen-portraits of some of his acquaintances among the Nihilists. Stepanovich, Dmitri Clemens, Valerian Ossinsky, Prince Kropotkin, Dmitri Lisogub, Jessy Helfman, Viera Sassulitch, and Sophia Perovskaya. The last half of the volume describes various attempts at assassination, and of escape from prisons or Siberia. As a description of the propaganda and methods of the revolutionists in attempting to free their country from governmental tyranny, and as a statement of their aims and purpose, this little work, of one of their number, desultory and inartistic as it is, will be invaluable to the future historian. It will at least show the desperate earnestness and self-sacrificing spirit of some of Russia's noblest sons and daughters. For English readers, the work has the disadvantage of spelling Russian names in an unfamiliar (that is, in the Italian) manner. It was written in 1881; and the year after was published in England, with a preface by Pavel Lavrof.

UNDINE, by De La Motte Fouque (1814). This is a fanciful German tale, well known for its beauty of conception and expression. Sir Huldbrand of Ringstetten is obliged to explore an enchanted forest to win fair Bertalda's glove. At the end of a day full of mysterious adventures in the forest, he rides out upon a lovely promontory of land, where an old fisherman and his wife give him shelter. Years before they had lost their own child by the lake, and afterwards a beautiful little girl had come to them: it was the water-spirit Undine. She is now eighteen years old; and when she sees the handsome knight she falls in love with him, and causes the elements to detain him days at their cottage. The storms send a priest to land, and he marries Undine and Sir Huldbrand. Undine had been a lovely but irresponsible creature to the day of her wedding, but after her marriage she becomes possessed of a soul through their mutual love. The waters having subsided, Sir Huldbrand carries his bride back to the city, where Bertalda and Undine become warm friends. The water-spirit Kühleborn warns Undine against Bertalda; but when it is discovered that Bertalda is the fisherman's daughter, Undine pities her, and takes her home to the castle at Ringstetten. There Bertalda wins Huldbrand's heart from Undine, and she is very unhappy. Undine tries to save her husband and Bertalda, but the water-spirits become enraged against him; and when they are all in a boat sailing to Vienna, Undine vanishes under the water. On the night that Huldbrand marries Bertalda, Undine arises from the fountain in the court, sweeps into his room, and fulfills the laws of her destiny by a fond embrace that takes his life; and he dies in her arms. A little spring ripples beside the grave of the knight; and in the village the people believe it is poor Undine, who loved too faithfully and suffered so much. 'Undine' is considered the author's masterpiece.

UNDISCOVERED COUNTRY, THE, by W. D. Howells (1880), is a favorite with many of the author's lovers. The central figure, Dr. Boynton, an enthusiastic spiritualist, is an admirable study of a self-deceiver, an honest charlatan. He is a country doctor, who has become a monomaniac on the subject of spiritualistic manifestations, and has brought up his daughter, a delicate, high-strung, nervous girl, as a medium. His attempts to take Boston by storm end in disaster. He is branded as a cheat, his daughter is believed to be his confederate, and he and Egeria seek refuge in a community of Shakers, whose quaint and kindly ways are portrayed with a loving pen. The peaceful monotony of the daily life, its plain plenty, its orderliness, its thrift, is constant and unoppressive industry, the moral uprightness of the broad-brimmed and straight-skirted community, the strangeness of the spiritual culture which forbids the sowing of any seeds of sentiment, the excellence of character which is so perversely one-sided and ineffective—all these conditions and effects are so vividly reported that the reader seems to behold with his bodily eyes the long barns bursting with harvests, the bare clean rooms of the houses, and the homely pleasantness of every-day activity. In this islanded tranquillity Egeria blossoms into beautiful womanhood, and her supernatural powers vanish forever. A happy life opens before her; but the eyes of the poor visionary, her father, cannot turn away from the Undiscovered Country. Unbalanced trickster that he is, little Dr. Boynton is yet a lovable and pathetic figure, honestly a martyr to his cause. The story is told with an unfailing humor and sympathy, which make the Shaker settlement seem almost a place of pilgrimage.

UNITED NETHERLANDS, HISTORY OF THE, by John Lothrop Motley. This work was published in four volumes in London in 1860, in New York in 1868. It covers the period from the death of William the Silent to the year 1609; and like 'The Rise of the Dutch Republic,' to which it is immediately sequent, it has become one of the classics of English historical narrative. There are later works on the same epoch that have changed received opinion on some minor points of character and event, but Motley, in his volumes of Dutch history, has no rival in his power of reviving the age and its heroes for the reader, in his scholarly analysis of remote causes and in his clear and convincing style.

UNITED STATES, HISTORY OF THE, FROM THE COMPROMISE OF 1850, by James Ford Rhodes, an account of the period between the Missouri Compromise of 1850 and the inauguration of Rutherford B. Hayes to the Presidency in 1877. At the beginning of the first volume (1893) the historian announced his intention of covering a period of thirty-five years, extending to the election of Grover Cleveland in 1885 but the seventh and last volume (1906) ends with the return of the Democrats not to national power but to control of the Southern states. The author's own summary of the period is as convenient as any that could be made: 'the compromise on slavery devised by great statesmen, its upsetting by an ambitious Northern senator, the formation of the Republican party; the agitation of slavery; Southern arrogance and aggression; the election of Lincoln; the refusal of the South to abide by the decision of the ballot-box, the Civil War; the great work of Lincoln, the abolition of slavery; the defeat of the South; Reconstruction based upon universal negro suffrage; the oppression of the South by the North; the final triumph of Southern intelligence and character over the ignorance and corruption that so long had thriven under Northern misconceptions.' This is the most authoritative history of the period with which it deals and is characterized by fairness, accuracy, thoroughness, and narrative interest. Its treatment of the politics of the Reconstruction period is unequalled by any other history.

UNITED STATES, A HISTORY OF THE PEOPLE OF THE, by J. B. McMaster, see **PEOPLE, ETC.**

UNLEAVENED BREAD, by Robert Grant (1900). In this clever story, the author paints with consummate skill the portrait of one special type of American woman. Selma White, bred in a small country village where there are no class distinctions, gradually develops the most intense social ambition for the gratification of which she is ready to sacrifice everything, even her husband's honor. Selma is endowed with beauty, an active brain, and a pleasing conviction of her own superiority to nearly everyone with whom she comes in contact, yet she is very crude and excessively ignorant. Her first realization of social distinction comes after her marriage with a "hustling" varnish manufacturer with whom she makes her home in the small western city of Benham. Here as Mrs. Lewis J. Babcock she discovers that there are persons who affect a social superiority over her. While professing to denounce such a thing upon impersonal and democratic grounds, it in reality becomes her special grievance. Having been divorced from her husband, she marries a professional man of a very different type, a man who thinks that she is the woman to share his ideals, but wh-awakens to disappointment, which is shared by his wife who finds that in New York she is unable to gratify her social ambition. At this point Mr. Grant introduces Flossy Williams and her husband, two social climbers, whose characters are delightfully drawn. Selma, in her endeavors to carry out her social schemes, hounds her husband unceasingly; he later dies an overwrought and worn-out man. Selma then marries a lawyer and rising politician, and begins again to climb the social ladder; she sets her heart upon becoming the wife of a senator and determines to leave no stone unturned towards compassing this end. Her husband is finally elected Governor, as the result of a private transaction with a representative of a great corporation, and when one of the state senators dies the way is opened for him to become senator. He has given his promise to sign a certain bill in order to secure his governorship and he now realizes that his chances for the senatorship hang upon his failure to keep his promise. His wife comes forward and convinces him that he is under no obligation to keep his word and that in the interest of American ideals he must forget his obligations and secure the senatorship. Together they play the hypocrite and the bill is vetoed and the coveted senatorship won. In his creation of this persistent, unscrupulous social climber, Dr. Grant scored a notable success.

UP FROM SLAVERY, by Booker T. Washington (1901). This is one of the most remarkable autobiographies ever written and reads like a romance. Its author was born at Hale's Ford, Virginia, "about" 1858, was a slave until freed by the Emancipation Proclamation, and never knew who was his father. As a child he was buffeted about, enduring poverty and privations, his life of drudgery in the "nigger quarters" of the Malden family, whose property he was, being a trifle more comfortable than his existence in the poorhouse to which his mother took him in West Virginia. As a child he worked in the salt furnaces and then in the mines, during which time he had a chance to get a few months' schooling every year. Later he secured employment with a New England woman, and was enabled to attend night school, and then at odd times he worked and studied, until in 1871 he started for the Hampton school of which he had heard so much. He became the star pupil of the place and was graduated with honors, although he was obliged to work his way through. After spending some time at Hampton as a teacher, he founded the now famous institution at Tuskegee, Alabama, which must always be a notable monument to his energy and enthusiasm for the work of uplifting his race. The college was started in 1881 in a shanty, under the most inauspicious circumstances and at a time when the idea of a higher school for the "blacks" was treated with derision. The story of Booker Washington's career is told with much grace and simplicity as well as extreme modesty. It would be difficult to parallel this instance of a man born a slave and beginning his life in the most miserable and desolate surroundings, who became within forty years one of the world's effective workers, commanding the attention of pulpit and press, welcomed in the homes of greatness and having won for himself universal respect.

UPANISHADS, THE, see **SACRED BOOKS OF THE EAST.**

UTOPIA, by Sir Thomas More. This book, which was written in Latin in 1615, is the source from which have been taken many of the socialistic ideas which are to-day interesting modern thinkers. At the time it was written, the author, fearing to acknowledge these ideas as his own, attributed them to a mythical person, Raphael Hythloday, lately returned from America, whither he had gone with Amerigo Vespucci.

In describing a country which he had visited, called Utopia (meaning in Greek "no place"), he calls attention to abuses then prevalent in England; among them the punishment of death for theft, high rent of land, the number of idle retainers, the decay of husbandry, the costliness of the necessities of life, and the licentiousness and greed of the rich, who, by monopolies, control the markets.

In 'Utopia' the government is representative. The life is communism. No man is allowed to be idle; but labor is abridged, and the hours of toil are as brief as is consistent with the general welfare. All are well educated, and take interest in the study of good literature. Such a lessening of labor is gained by a community of all things that none are in need, and there is no desire to amass more than each man can use. Gold and silver are only used for vessels of baser use, and for the fetters of bondmen. Happiness is regarded as the highest good; but that of the body politic is above that of the individual. Law-breakers are made bondmen.

There are few laws; for it is not just that men should be bound by laws more numerous than can be read, or more complex than may be readily understood. War is abhorred; it being most just when employed to take vacant land from people who keep others from possession of it. There are many religions but no images. They thank God for all their blessings, and especially for placing them in that state and religion which seemeth best; but they pray, if there be any better state or religion, God will reveal it unto them.

Many reforms which More suggested are no longer considered Utopian; among them, entire freedom in matters of religion, in support of which he lost his life.

VALENTINE VOX, THE VENTRILOQUIST, by Henry Cockton (1840). This novel has enjoyed popularity since the time of its publication. Its hero, Valentine Vox, a young English gentleman living at home with his mother, a rich widow, is struck with admiration of the ventriloquism of an itinerant juggler and magician who visits his native place. To his delight, he finds that he himself possesses the ventriloquial power; and by a diligent course of training he perfects himself in it. On a trip to London Valentine visits the House of Commons, the opera, Gravesend, the British Museum, Guildhall, a masquerade at Vauxhall, the "Zoo," the Ascot races, etc.; and wherever he goes he indulges his propensity for practical joking to the fullest extent. One adventure follows another with breathless rapidity. With the whole is inwoven a love story, not of a very profound nature. There is no plot; and the incidents are a harum-scarum collection of disjointed happenings, while the book has little literary merit. But the roistering and uproarious fun that fills the thick volume make it a welcome companion to most young people "from sixteen to sixty."

VALLEY OF DECISION, THE, by Edith Wharton (1902). A summing up of the Italy of the latter half of the eighteenth century. The hero, Odo, Duke of Pianura, represents the mind of his time, inheriting the conservative tradition of the past, and awakening to the modern spirit of scientific inquiry and political free thinking. The heroine, Fulvia Vivaldi, stands for the new order of ideas. Her father, a professor of philosophy, is exiled for his views. Odo rescues Fulvia from imprisonment in a convent and is escaping with her to Switzerland, when he learns that his cousin's death has made him Duke of Pianura. His duty is to return and devote his life to giving liberty to his people. Soon after his accession he marries the duchess, his cousin's widow. Fulvia returns to encourage his plan to give the people the liberal constitution for which unfortunately they are not yet ready. In the riots which follow she is killed by the shot intended for Duke Odo, her lover. After her death he withdraws the constitution and accepts defeat. When the ideas they had striven for are at last triumphant he has returned to the beliefs and tradition of his caste, and is driven into exile. The historical background is a panorama of the petty principalities, court intrigue, the misery of the peasants, the strolling players, the Jesuits, Illuminati, and the learned literati working in secret for progress.

VAN BIBBER AND OTHERS, by Richard Harding Davis (1890) is a collection of short stories that appeared originally in the magazines. The central figure in the majority of them is Van Bibber, a young New Yorker of the mythical "Four Hundred," a charming fellow, combining the exquisiteness of the aristocrat with the sterling virtues of the great American people. His tact is consummate, his ideals of good form unimpeachable, his snobbery entirely well-bred. Having plenty of money, and nothing to do but to be "about town," he is in the way of adventures. Some of these are funny; one or two are pathetic. They all serve to throw high light upon Van Bibber in his character of a swell. The stories are well written, and show the author's equal acquaintance with Fifth Avenue and with the East Side.

VANITY FAIR, by W. M. Thackeray (1847-48) is one of the few great novels of the world, and perhaps the only novel of society that ranks as a classic, as a perfect and complete embodiment of those peculiar forces and conditions embraced in the term "fashionable." As the sub-title states, it is "without a hero"; but not, however, without a heroine. The central figure of the book is that chef-d'œuvre, the immortal, inimitable, magnificent Becky Sharp, the transcendent type of social strugglers, the cleverest, most unmoral woman in the whole range of fiction. From the hour when she tosses Johnson's Dictionary, the last gift of her teacher, out of the window of the Sedley coach, to her final appearance on the stage of the novel, she never falters in the bluff game she is playing with society. Her victims are numerous, her success, with slight exceptions, is unimpeachable. In constant contrast to her is pretty, pink-and-white, amiable Amelia, all love and trust, Becky's school intimate and first protector. On Amelia and Amelia's family, Becky first climbs towards the dizzy heights of an assured social position. Rawdon Crawley is her final prey, the successful victim of her matrimonial ventures. Having secured him, she is more at liberty to be herself, to cease the strain of concealing her real nature, in her home at least. To the world she is still an actress, and the world does not find her out until it has suffered by her.

The environment in which she is placed—fashionable England of the beginning of the century—offered a great field for the genius of Thackeray. He portrayed it with marvelous, sustained skill through the long, leisurely, many-chaptered novel. Not a foible of fashionable life escaped him; not one weakness of human nature, not one fallacy of the gay world. His satire plays like searching light upon the canvas. His humanity does not miss the pathos sometimes lurking under the hard, bright surface of events. He does not forget that some women are tender, that some men are brave. Neither does he pass eternal judgment upon his characters. In his dealings with these frequenters of 'Vanity Fair,' there is something of the indifference of the gods, something, too, of their chivalry.

VATHEK, THE HISTORY OF THE CALIPH, by William Beckford (1786). This imaginative and gorgeous story first appeared in French. "Vathek bears such marks of originality," says Lord Byron, "that those who have visited the East will have some difficulty in believing it to be more than a translation." Vathek, ninth Caliph of the race of the Abassides, is the son of Motassem, and the grandson of Haroun al Raschid. Though a Prince Charming, he is yet a capricious ruler, indulging his desires in the most extravagant manner and falling into illness when his will is crossed. His troubles begin when he meets a Giaour, who obtains a strange influence over him; and after leading him into shocking enormities, induces him to abjure Mohammedanism and call upon the Prince of the powers of the air. In this course Vathek is encouraged by the queen-mother, Carathis, whose incantations produce the most appalling results. He sets out to meet the Giaour, to obtain from him the treasures of the pre-Adamite Sultans, with other much-desired gifts. But on his way he meets and falls in love with the beautiful young Nouronihar, and spends many days in wooing her. At last, with the maiden, he proceeds upon the journey, and enters the awful Hall of Eblis, filled with ineffable glories. Here he receives indeed all that is promised him, but deprived of any wish to possess it or capacity to enjoy it; and learns that his self-seeking and heartless service of his own appetites has drawn upon him the punishment of eternal torment and remorse; a doom which includes the loss of "the most precious of the gifts of heaven,—Hope."

VEDÂNTA-SÛTRAS, THE, see **SACRED BOOKS OF THE EAST.**

VEDIC HYMNS, see **SACRED BOOKS OF THE EAST.**

VENTRE DE PARIS, LE, see **ROUGON-MACQUART.**

VERA VORONTSOFF, by Sonya Kovalevsky (1896). Sonya Kovalevsky, whose father was a general at the head of the Russian artillery, adopted the Nihilistic procedure of making a fictitious marriage, for the purpose of securing her intellectual freedom. She became one of the most famous mathematicians of Europe, won the Bordin prize, and was for ten years professor of mathematics in Stockholm University. Her marvelous achievements in science did not prevent her from suffering on the womanly side of her complex nature. Undoubtedly something of her own life history is to be read between the lines of her novel, 'Vera Vorontsoff,' which she is said to have written in Swedish. It relates simply but effectively the story of the youngest daughter of a Russian count, ruined partly by his own extravagances and partly by the emancipation of the serfs. The girl grows up with little training until Stepan Mikhailovich Vasiltsef, a professor from the Polytechnic Institute of Petersburg, removed from his position on account of seditious utterances, comes to reside on his little neighboring estate and teaches her. They end by falling in love; but Vasiltsef, who inclines to take the side of the peasants in their differences with their former masters, is "interned" at Viatka, and dies there of consumption. Vera sacrifices herself by marrying a poor Jewish conspirator, condemned to twenty years' imprisonment, and thereby commuting his punishment to exile to Siberia, where she joins him. The character of Vera is carefully drawn in the genuine Russian method; she is the type of the self-sacrificing maiden of gentle birth, of which the annals of Nihilism are full. There are a few pretty descriptions, as for instance, that of the approach of the spring on the steppes; but the force of the story lies in its pictures of life at the time of the liberation of the serfs. It has been twice translated into English.

VERDANT GREEN, MR., AN OXFORD FRESHMAN, THE ADVENTURES OF, by "Cuthbert Bede" (Rev. Edward Bradley). Since its publication in 1853-

57, this story has taken a certain place as an English humorous classic, comparable in some sort to Kortum's famous 'Jobsiad' in German (though one is in prose, the other in doggerel verse), but on the whole *sui generis*. It narrates the university adventures of an innocent and simple young Englishman of family and position, brought up in the bosom of an adoring family; the pranks his fellow undergraduates play on him; the rather severe "course of training" they put him through, in order to remove his "home-feathers," and the result finally achieved. Humor and fun abound in it; and though much of the fun is mere horse-play, and much of the humor of a kind which a later literary taste finds happily out of fashion, the book still gives pleasure to the whole English undergraduate world, and to a smaller American contingent.

VIA CRUCIS, a romance of the Second Crusade, by F. Marion Crawford (1900). The story is placed in the twelfth century and deals with the doings of the Crusaders, a particularly effective subject for a romance. The scene is first laid in England, then shifts to the French Court, and from thence to Rome, then back again to France and from there to the arid sands of Syria. The hero, Gilbert Ward, is a brave English knight, half monk and half barbarian. His father is treacherously killed by Sir Arnold de Curboil, who marries his victim's wife within a month after her husband's death. Gilbert, foully wounded by Sir Arnold and cheated of his heritage, is forced out into the world as an adventurer. Arriving at the French Court, his great torso and gentle manner win him the love of the beautiful Queen Eleanor, who is the central figure of the story. Her passion for the English knight is so strong that with her bold and masterful nature, she almost causes him to falter in his loyalty to Beatrix de Curboil, his step-sister, whom he really loves. However, the efforts of the amorous queen finally prove fruitless in winning him from his allegiance to his early love, and he remains steadfast against temptation. Gilbert leaves the Court and wends his way to Rome, where in the struggle for possession of the Holy Sepulchre he gains distinction and renown. The disinherited Norman boy, the savior of the army and the hero of the day, becomes the Guide of Aquitaine and marries the faithful Beatrix. Freed from the spell which the Queen had in the past woven around him, Gilbert at last kneels calmly at her feet uttering the words, "I cannot love you, but in so far as I may be faithful to another I give you my whole life." This romance, which belongs essentially to the life of the old world, is well constructed and well told, and the Queen's generous renunciation of her love for Gilbert renders her figure in the story a dramatic one.

VICAR OF WAKEFIELD, THE, Oliver Goldsmith's famous story, was published in 1766. Washington Irving said of it: "The irresistible charm this novel possesses, evinces how much may be done without the aid of extravagant incident to excite the imagination and interest the feelings. Few productions of the kind afford greater amusement in the perusal, and still fewer inculcate more impressive lessons of morality." The character of the Vicar, Dr. Primrose, gives the chief interest to the tale. His weaknesses and literary vanity are attractive; and he rises to heights almost sublime when misfortune overtakes his family. The other actors in the simple drama are Mrs. Primrose, with her boasted domestic qualities and her anxiety to appear genteel; the two daughters, Olivia and Sophia; and the two sons, George, bred at Oxford, and Moses, who "received a sort of miscellaneous education at home" —all of whom the Vicar says were "equally generous, credulous, simple, and inoffensive." Squire Thornhill resides near the family, and elopes with Olivia, to the great distress of the Vicar. He suspects Mr. Burchell, who turns out to be Sir William Thornhill, the uncle of the young Squire. Sir William asks for Sophia's hand, and sets right the family misfortunes. Numerous pathetic and humorous incidents arise out of the story. Among the latter is that of the family picture, which, when finished, was too large for the house. Mrs. Primrose was painted as Venus, the Vicar in bands and gown, presenting to her his books on the Whistonian controversy; Olivia was an "Amazon sitting upon a bank of flowers, dressed in a green joseph richly laced with gold, and a whip in her hand; Sophia a shepherdess; Moses, dressed out with a hat and white feather"; while the Squire "insisted on being put in as one of the family in the character of Alexander the Great, at Olivia's feet.' Austin Dobson says that the 'Vicar of Wakefield' "remains and will continue to be one of the first of our English classics."

VICOMTE DE BRAGELONNE, THE; or, TEN YEARS AFTER (1848–50). This, the last novel of Dumas' 'Three Musketeers' series, is the longest and in many ways the most powerful of the three. Some parts of it have been published as separate novels. Those chapters devoted to the king's love for Mademoiselle de la Vallière have been issued under the title of 'Louise de la Vallière'; while the ones dealing with the substitution of Louis XIV.'s twin brother for himself have appeared as 'The Man in the Iron Mask.' The romance in full presents a marvelously vivid picture of the court of Louis XIV., from a time shortly before his marriage to Maria Theresa to the downfall of Fouquet. The Vicomte de Bragelonne is the son of the famous Athos, of the 'Three Musketeers'; the best type of young nobleman, high-minded, loyal, and steadfast, who cherishes from his boyhood an unwavering love for Mademoiselle de la Vallière, which ends only in his death on a foreign battlefield after she deserts him for the king. The four old comrades, Athos, Porthos, Aramis, and D'Artagnan, all reappear: Athos the perfect gentleman, big Porthos, so simple and kind-hearted, Aramis a bishop and schemer, and D'Artagnan a soldier still, quick-tempered and outspoken as ever, but withal so full of loyalty and kindliness that his very enemies love him. The chief plot of the book relates the struggle of Colbert to supplant Fouquet as Superintendent of Finances; and the struggle of Aramis, who has become General of the Jesuits, to keep Fouquet in power.

Aramis discovers the existence in the Bastille of the twin brother of Louis XIV., exactly like him in person, who has been concealed from his birth for reasons of State. Aramis conceives the glorious idea of carrying off Louis XIV., and setting up a king who will owe his throne to him, and in return make him cardinal, prime minister, and master, as Richelieu had been. This plot he and Porthos (who does not understand the true situation in the least) carry out with the utmost success, deceiving even the king's own mother; but the affair is frustrated by the fidelity of Fouquet, who, on learning the substitution, rushes to free the real king. Aramis and Porthos fly across France to Belle-Isle in Brittany, where they are besieged by the king's ships, and Porthos meets a tragic death. Aramis escapes to Spain, and, being too powerful a Jesuit to be touched, lives to an honored old age. Louis XIV. meantime imprisons his brother in the famous iron mask; and arrests Fouquet, who had been a bad minister, but at the same time such a gentleman that D'Artagnan says to him: "Ah, Monsieur, it is you who should be king of France." Athos dies heartbroken, after learning of the death of his son; and last of all, D'Artagnan falls in the thick of battle in the musketeer's uniform he had worn for forty years. Even those who have least sentiment over the personages of fiction can hardly part with these familiar and charming old friends without a pang.

VICTORIAN POETS, THE, by Edmund Clarence Stedman (1876). A book of literary and biographical criticism, and, at the same time, a historical survey of the course of British poetry for forty years (1835-75), showing the authors and works best worth attention, and the development through them of the principles and various ideals of poetic art as now understood and followed. It forms a guide-book to 150 authors, their lives, their productions, their ideas and sympathies, and their poetic methods. The author had contemplated a survey of American poetry, with a critical consideration of its problems, difficulties, failures, and successes; and to prepare himself for this, and make sure to himself correct ideas of the aim and province of the art of poetry, that he might more certainly use wisdom and justice in studying the American field, he undertook first the thorough critical examination of the English field, of which the present volume was the result. The book, therefore, may be viewed as the earlier half of a large work, of which 'The Poets of America,' published in 1885, is the later half; and this conception by Mr. Stedman of the unity in historical development of English and American culture attests, as the entire execution of his task everywhere does, the clearness and breadth of his insight, and the value of his guidance to the student of poetry. The distinction, in fact, of Mr. Stedman, shown in all his work, and marking a stage in the larger progress of American culture, is his rank as a scholar and thinker in literature, broadly conscious of all high ideals, and thereby superior to the provincial narrowness of uninstructed Americanism. He thus has no theory of poetry, no school, to uphold; but favors a generous eclecticism or universalism in art, and extends sympathetic appreciation to whatever is excellent of its kind.

VICTORY, by Joseph Conrad (1915). Axel Heyst is committed to a profound mistrust of life by his father, an expatriate Swedish nobleman and pessimistic philosopher. He deliberately chooses to escape life by drifting through the world as an onlooker. The islands of the South Pacific, he finds ideal for the scene of his wanderings. His unfailing courtesy, however, betrays him into casual acts of kindness, and the consequences of action seem always to be more action. He befriends an English trading captain, and to escape his gratitude becomes manager of a bogus coal company which fails and leaves him stranded on an island more disgusted with the world of action than ever. Unconsciously he has incurred the dislike of a ruffianly German hotel-keeper, named Schomberg. This dislike is fanned into hatred when in a moment of compassion he carries off a forlorn English girl, member of a traveling orchestra, to his island hermitage to save her from the odious advances of Schomberg. In spite of this decisive act he remains the son of the father who warned that "he who forms a tie is lost" and "of the stratagems of life the most cruel is the consolation of love," and cannot believe in his happiness with Lena. Schomberg, cheated of his prey, finds instruments of revenge in two most dreadful villains, the truly gentlemanly Mr. Jones, and his follower Ricardo. He wishes to rid his hotel of these gamblers, and stuffs them with lying tales of hidden ill-gotten treasure hoarded by Heyst on his solitary island. This piratical adventure appeals to plain Mr. Jones, "the insolent spectre on leave from Hades." Heyst and Lena are trapped and the tale ends in a welter of tragedy, but not before Lena has met the ordeal, bested the feral Ricardo, and justified love and life to Heyst.

VIE DE JESUS, LA, by Ernest Renan, see **JESUS.**

VILLAGE COMMUNITIES, see **ANCIENT LAW,** by H. S. Maine.

VILLAGE COMMUNITY, THE ENGLISH, by F. Seebohm, see **ENGLISH,** etc.

VILLAGE LABOURER, THE, by J. L. and Barbara Hammond. "Many histories," say Mr. and Mrs. Hammond, "have been written of the governing class that ruled England with such absolute power during the last century of the old régime. . . . One history has only been sketched in outline; it is the history of the way in which this class governed England. The writers of this book have here attempted to describe the life of the poor during this period. It is their object to show what was in fact happening to the working classes under a government in which they had no share." Besides supplying the best picture which recent times have produced of the life of the poor in England at this epoch, this volume discusses fully for the first time the actual method and procedure of the Parliamentary Enclosure of common fields, and the laborers' rising of 1830. This rising, like most others, was due, as is here proved, to the existence of intolerable grievances, which have sown the seeds of problems unsettled even in the first two decades of the twentieth century. The burden of its message appears in these concluding words: "Amid the great distress that followed Waterloo and peace, it was a commonplace of statesmen like Castlereagh and Canning that England was the only happy country in the world, and that so long as the monopoly of their little class was left untouched, her happiness would survive. That class has left bright and ample records of its life in literature, in art, in political traditions, in the display of great orations and debates, in memories of brilliant conversation and sparkling wit; it has left dim and meager records of the disinherited peasants that are the shadow of its wealth, of the exiled labourers that are the shadow of its pleasures, of the villages sinking in poverty and crime and shame that are the shadow of its power and its pride."

VINAYA TEXTS, see **SACRED BOOKS OF THE EAST.**

VINGT ANS APRÈS, see **TWENTY YEARS AFTER.**

VIRGIN SOIL, by Ivan Turgeneff (1876). Turgeneff gives in 'Virgin Soil' a graphic picture of the various moral and social influences at work in the modern Nihilistic movement in Russia. The motive of the story is deep and subtle, and is developed with masterly skill and refinement. The hero Neshdanoff, a young university student of noble but illegitimate descent and in poor worldly circumstances, has his sympathies roused for the depressed peasantry of Russia, and with romantic ardor enters into the secret conspiracy for their relief. In the house of a government official where he is engaged as tutor, he meets Marianne, a relation of the family, who is also secretly an enthusiast in the Nihilistic cause, and, irresistibly drawn to her, he elopes with her, and seeks employment with a machinist and manufacturer, Solomine. The effort to descend to the level of the peasants, to enter into their life, and to rouse them to a united movement for liberty, is met with a stolid apathy and lack of intelligence on their part, that dampens his ardor and makes his effort seem to him like the merest sentimentalism, that can never yield any real result. This loss of faith in himself and in his own sincerity impels him to break his promise of marriage with Marianne, and, commending her to marry Solomine, the machinist and manufacturer, to take his own life in despair of finding a sphere in the world for his genius,—a mixture of inherited aristocracy and purely romantic democracy. In Solomine is depicted the real reformer, the man without "ideals" and elegant phrases, who, in his honest dealings with those under him and his recognition of the true dignity of labor and of neighborly service, is exerting the redeeming force that can gradually introduce a new manhood into the laboring classes, and so enable them to appreciate and aspire to the practical and the heroic elements of a true freedom.   In the marriage of Solomine and Marianne is seen the union of reform, as distinguished from the ineffectual idealism of an aristocracy that lacks the practical knowledge and the social deviation of a middle class.

VIRGINIA, by Ellen Glasgow (1913).   Virginia is the perfect flower of the tradition of womanhood of an earlier generation in the South.   The first book of the novel is the idyllic picture of her girlhood, of first love and romantic courtship.   Her education is "founded on the simple theory that the less a girl knew about life, the better prepared she would be to contend with it."   She feels ardently but does not think or read.   Reading is a luxury for the idle.   She is trained to ideals of gentleness and self-sacrifice as the crowning virtues for woman.   The standards her mother passes on to Virginia on her wedding day are that her husband's will must now be hers and that whenever their ideas conflict, it is the woman's duty to give up.   Oliver, her husband, an ambitious young playwright, is not at first successful, and her intellectual limitations prevent her from understanding his life-work.   At forty, he is a young man with a future, while she has flung her youth and beauty into past service of wifehood and motherhood.   Her daughters are self-sufficient in an age of self-assertive feminism.   Her husband leaves her for the actress who shares his success.   She finds herself a failure in the changed habitat of the modern world with demands on women beyond self-forgetfulness and gentleness.   Her one consolation is the devoted affection of her brilliant young son.

VIRGINIAN, THE, by Owen Wister (1904).   This is a story of the West and tells of ranch life and cowboy doings.   The hero of the tale "the Virginian," by which title alone he is known to the reader, has left his native state at an early age to try his fortunes in the western country.   After roughing it in various places, he is finally established on Judge Henry's cattle ranch in Montana, where the owner regards him as his right-hand man.   He is twenty-seven years of age and strikingly handsome, and though unversed in the ways of the world and ignorant as to book learning, he has a character and personality which inspire respect from all who know him.   His high sense of honor, his dauntless courage, and his sympathy for the weak, are constantly shown in the various episodes which occur throughout the story.   In Miss Molly Wood, a Vermont girl, who tries school-teaching in the West in order to get a change of environment, he sees his ideal, and from the moment of his first meeting with her, makes up his mind to win her for his wife.   He wooes her faithfully for three years, during which time she gives him books to read and helps him to become better acquainted with the world in which she lives.   The difference in their positions and education seems an unsurmountable barrier to Molly and she is on the point of returning to Vermont, when she discovers her lover in the woods wounded and unconscious, with no succor at hand.   She manages to revive him somewhat, gets him on his horse, and supports him while she leads the animal a distance of five miles to her home.   The wound proves to be a serious one, but the Virginian is brought through by Molly's devoted care and nursing and when he is convalescing he is made happy by her confession that at last love has conquered.   They are married and after a blissful honeymoon spent camping in the hills, Molly takes her cowboy to visit her relatives, an ordeal through which he passes most creditably.

VIRGINIANS, THE, by William Makepeace Thackeray (1859) is a sequel to 'Henry Esmond,' and revives a past society with the same brilliant skill. The chivalric Colonel Esmond, dear to readers of the earlier novel, goes to Virginia after his marriage with Lady Castlewood, and there builds a country-seat, which he names Castlewood in remembrance of his family's ancestral home in England. In the American Castlewood his twin grandsons are reared by their widowed mother, Madame Rachel Warrington, that sharp-tongued colonial dame so kind and generous to her favorites, so bitter and unjust to all who oppose her. She is a loving but tyrannical mother; and, after the Colonel's death, exercises autocratic rule over the Castlewood domain. Among her frequent visitors is young Colonel Washington, a brave, attractive figure, with fame yet to win.

Virginian life in pre-Revolutionary days is made very real to the reader; and is clearly distinguished from the English life upon which young Harry Warrington enters after his brother's supposed death in a disastrous campaign of the French and Indian War, upon which he has accompanied Colonel Washington. The lavish and generous young Virginian is at first repelled by the cold courtesy and selfish thrift of his Old World cousins. But his fortune soon wins him favor; and, too simple to detect mercenary motives, he plunges into social dissipation under the direction of Baroness Bernstein, an antiquated egotist, whom his grandfather had loved as the beautiful and coquettish Beatrix Esmond. He is deep in debt, and has promised to marry an elderly cousin, when he is rescued from his folly by the arrival of his shrewd and generous brother George. George resumes his heirship, and Harry is no longer a prey for cupidity. In the story of their subsequent adventures, the exposition of social baseness and hypocrisy would be gruesome if it were not for the kindly humor which mollifies the satire.

VISHNU, INSTITUTES OF, see **SACRED BOOKS OF THE EAST.**

VISION OF PIERS PLOWMAN, THE, an English poem of the fourteenth century, is ascribed, chiefly on the ground of internal evidence, to William Langland, or Longland, a monk of Malvern, in spirit a Thomas Carlyle of the Middle Ages, crying out against abuses, insisting upon sincerity as the first of virtues.

This poem belongs to the class of the dream-poem, a characteristic product of his century. Dante had seen all heaven and hell in vision. Gower and the author of 'Pearl' had dreamed dreams. 'The Vision of Piers Plowman' is a curious amalgamation of fantastic allegory and clear-cut fact, of nebulous dreams and vivid pictures of the England of the day. The author is at once as realistic as Chaucer and as mystical as Guillaume de Lorris, the observant man of the world and the brooding anchorite; his poem reflects both the England of the fourteenth century and the visionary, child-like mediæval mind.

Internal evidence fixes its date about 1362. Forty manuscript copies of it, belonging for the most part to the latter end of the fourteenth century, attest its popularity. Three distinct versions are extant, known as Texts A, B, and C. The probable date of Text A is 1362–63; of Text B, 1376–77; of Text C, 1398–99. The variations in these texts are considerable. An imitation of the poem called 'Piers Plowman's Crede' appeared about 1393. The author of 'Piers Plowman' represents himself as falling asleep on Malvern Hills, on a beautiful May morning. In his dreams he beholds a vast plain "a feir feld ful of folk," representing indeed the whole of humanity: knights, monks, parsons, workmen singing French songs, cooks crying hot pies! "Hote pyes, hote!" pardoners, pilgrims, preachers, beggars, jongleurs, who will not work, japers, and "mynstralles" that sell "glee." They are, or nearly so, the same beings Chaucer assembled at the "Tabard" inn, on the eve of his pilgrimage to Canterbury. This crowd has likewise a pilgrimage to make. . . . "They journey through abstract countries, they follow mystic roads . . . in search of Truth and of Supreme Good."

This search is the subject of an elaborate allegory, in the course of which the current abuses in Church and State are vigorously attacked. The poet inveighs especially against the greed and insincerity of his age, personifying these qualities in Lady Meed, who leads men astray, and tricks them into sin. The poem throws much light upon social and religious institutions of the day. These revelations must, however, be sought for among the strange mist-shapes of allegory.

The poet's vocabulary is similar to that of Chaucer. Several dialects are combined in it, the Midland dialect dominating. The metre is alliterative, long lines, divided into half-lines by a pause. Each line contains strong, or accented, syllables in fixed number, and weak or unaccented syllables in varying number.

About 'Piers Plowman' there had grown up a considerable body of editorial commentary and of learned discussion in which Professor Manly's theory of divided authorship holds the leading place.

VISITS TO THE MONASTERIES OF THE LEVANT, by Hon. Robert Curzon, (1851). Beginning in 1833, the author's travels covered a period of four years, in which time he visited many curious old monasteries, and secured a number of rare and valuable manuscripts. He gives his impressions of the countries through which he wandered, and devotes some space to the manners and customs of the people in each, brightening his narrative by occasional anecdotes and noteworthy facts gleaned by the way.

The volume is divided into four parts. Part i. deals with Egypt, where Mr. Curzon visited the famous Coptic monasteries near the Natron Lakes. These, he tells us, were founded by St. Macarius of Alexandria, one of the earliest of Christian ascetics. The members of the Coptic orders still dwell in the old houses, situated amid fertile gardens on the crowns of almost inaccessible precipices. The ruined monastery of Thebes, the White Monastery, and the Island of Philæ, the burial-place of Osiris, were also visited.

Part ii. describes the visit to Jerusalem and the Monastery of St. Saba. This house was named for the founder of the "Laura," the monastic rule which Charles Kingsley uses to such excellent effect in the opening chapters of 'Hypatia.' The "Laura" still exists where the rocky clefts and desert wastes of Asia and Africa offer suitable retreats for the ascetic monks.

Mr. Curzon devotes some time to the Jews of Jerusalem—enough to show their prevailing characteristics and he also notes the interesting fact of his rediscovery of the "Apple of Sodom," long supposed to be a creation of fictitious character. It is, he says, a juicy-looking plum-like fruit, which proves to be a gall-nut filled with dry, choking dust.

Part iii. opens with the writer's impressions of Corfu and his visit to Albania, whence he leaves for Meteora, a grassy plain surrounded by tall peaks of rock, where, in apertures like pigeon-holes, the monks have had their dwellings. On top of the rocks are left some of the buildings of St. Barlaam. To reach them the traveler was forced to climb some rickety ladders over a tremendously steep declivity, because he disliked the other mode of reaching the top—being drawn up 230 feet in a net attached to a mended, weather-worn rope. Subsequently, he visited Hagios Stephanos, Agio Triada, Hagia Roserea, and finally the great monastery of Meteora.

Part IV. gives the trip from Constantinople to Mt. Athos; up the Sea of Marmora, through the Archipelago to Lemnos; thence to Mt. Athos and the monastery of St. Laura, full of rare old paintings. The other monastic houses of the neighborhood, from Vatopede to Caracalla, were also visited; and Mr. Curzon returned to Constantinople, having purchased a number of valuable manuscripts, including an Evangelistarium in gold letters, on *white* vellum, of which sort there is but one other known to exist.

VOLPONE; or, THE FOX, by Ben Jonson (1605). Volpone which had been acted at the Globe Theatre in 1605 or 1606 and repeated at both Oxford and Cambridge was printed in 1607 with a dedication "To the most Noble and most Equal Sisters, the Two Famous Universities." The dedication denounces the license of protesters and sets up in contrast the ideal for the true poet. "If men will impartially, and not asquint, look toward the offices and function of a poet, they will easily conclude to themselves the impossibility of any man's being the good poet, without first being a good man." The true poet is "able to inform young men to all good disciplines, inflame grown men to all great virtues, keep old men in their best and supreme state, or, as they decline to childhood, recover them to their first strength"; he "comes forth the interpreter and arbiter of nature, a teacher of things divine no less than human, a master in manners." The comedy, the scene of which is laid in Venice, is a picture of depravities common in all countries at that age, and a vigorous satire upon these vices. The story is of a scoundrel magnifico of Venice, who in order to attract gifts from friends and followers feigned deadly sickness. He and his parasite (Moscha or fly) persuade each of these friends Voltore (vulture) Corbuccio (crow), and Corvino (raven), that he is to be the heir of Volpone. All grovel and fawn upon him but all are in turn deceived. In the end the parasite rounds upon his master, and justice is meted out to all the party. The play long kept its place upon the stage, but the depravity of the life depicted makes it unpalatable to modern readers. Coleridge, while acknowledging its "fertility and vigor of invention, character, language, and sentiment" declares it impossible "to keep up any pleasurable interest in a tale, in which there is no goodness of heart in any of the prominent characters."

VOYAGE AROUND MY CHAMBER, by Comte Xavier de Maistre (1874). A charming group of miniature essays, polished like the gems of a necklace, the titles of which were suggested by the familiar objects of the author's room. It was written during his confinement for forty-two days under arrest in Turin, while holding the position of an officer in the Russian army. He treats his surroundings as composing a large allegory, in which he reads the whole range of human life. He depicts with delight the advantages of this kind of "fireside travel," in its freedom from labor, worry, and expense; and then he shows under the vast significance of such objects as the Bed, the Bookcase, the father's Bust, the Traveling-Coat, and the instruments of Painting and Music, the wide range of reflection and delight into which the soul is thus led. The bed is the beginning and the end of earthly life; the library is the panorama of the world's greatest ideals; and here he reflects on the grandeur and attractiveness of Lucifer as depicted by Milton. The traveling-coat suggests the influence of costume on character, which is illustrated by the effect of an added bar or star of an officer's coat on the wearer's state of mind. 'The Animal' is the heading of the chapter defining the body as the servant of the soul, a mistress who sometimes cruelly goes away and neglects it, as when, while the mind is absorbed in some entrancing thought, the hand catches up heedlessly the hot poker. The most subtle of these interpretations is that of the portrait of a fair lady whose eyes follow the gazer; but foolish is the lover who thinks them bent on him alone, for every other finds them gazing equally at him even at the same moment.

VOYAGES OF CAPTAIN COOK AROUND THE WORLD, THE THREE FAMOUS.

The accounts of Captain Cook's three voyages were written by as many hands: the first by Dr. Hawkesworth (1773); the second by Cook himself (1773); while Lieutenant King prepared the third from Cook's notes, and completed the narrative (1784).

The first voyage was undertaken in 1768, to observe the transit of Venus. Having made successful observations at Otaheite in the Society Islands, Cook explored the South Sea, and determined the insularity of New Zealand, which had been considered part of a great Antarctic continent. He discovered the straits named after him, and amid great dangers explored the eastern coast of Australia, hitherto unknown. In 1772 he started on a second voyage, to explore the hypothetical Antarctic continent. He investigated the specified latitudes, and sailed farther south than any previous navigator. Having satisfied himself that no such continent existed, he turned eastward and discovered New Caledonia, Georgia, and other islands. On his return he received many honors, and was elected to the Royal Society. His third voyage was in search of the Northwest Passage. Sailing about in the Pacific, he discovered the Sandwich or Hawaiian Islands; and then, having explored the unknown coast of North America, he passed through Bering's Strait, and surveyed the coast on both sides. Baffled in his attempt to reach the Atlantic, he returned to winter near Honolulu in the Sandwich Islands, where he was treacherously murdered by the natives in 1779.

The narrative is especially important because Cook was animated by the scientific spirit, and made valuable observations in many departments of science. Throughout the book appear the resources and courage of the man, and his humane discretion in dealing both with his sailors and with the savages; while its publication gave a new impetus to discovery and exploration.

VINDICATION OF THE RIGHTS OF WOMEN, by Mary Wollstonecraft (1792).

The object of the book was to overthrow the current opinions that women were created simply for the enjoyment of men, that a woman's supreme object in life should be to get a husband, and that in order to attain this end she should affect an indifference to it while secretly pursuing it. The author attacks the idea that girls should avoid the appearance of physical robustness, liveliness, and independence and should affect delicacy and weakness. Out-of-door exercise and a wholesome honesty of deportment are advocated instead. A woman's rights involve duties, to herself first of all, then to her husband, to her children, and to the state. These duties cannot be fulfilled without the development of the mind and character, which contemporary ideals hindered. Instead of being confined to one career, namely marriage, woman should be admitted to such others as she is fitted for. She would thus be a better wife, a better mother, and a better citizen. For the avoidance of the social evil the author urges the application of one standard of sexual morality to men and women, the education of girls and boys in the same schools, and the determination to regard woman as the comrade and not the plaything of man. The book is a strong and vigorous plea for a cause then in its infancy. It anticipated many of the arguments and appeals of later reformers and in its ardent revolutionary zeal exercised considerable influence in favor of woman's rights. The author showed her independence in the fact that though a disciple of Rousseau she mercilessly criticized his principles and practice in regard to woman's privileges.

WAGES OF SIN, THE, by "Lucas Malet" (1890), is a study of character rather than a novel of incident. The leading personages stand in high relief against a background of commonplace English prosperity. Mary Crookenden, the heroine, is a charming English girl; beautiful, spirited, and an heiress. Her cousin, Lance Crookenden, who is a few years older, has loved her from childhood; but she accepts his devotion as an agreeable matter-of-course, and in spite of his wealth and good looks, regards him with a tinge of affectionate contempt. Mary has many suitors; among them a young clergyman, Cyprian Oldham, and an artist, James Colthurst. She engages herself to Oldham, but finds him too conventional to be sympathetic; and becomes fascinated by Colthurst, the most gifted and most earnest man she knows, who loves her passionately. But a sin of Colthurst's youth lays a heavy hand upon him, pushing away his love, interdicting his happiness, and laying a curse upon those who are dearest to him. The innocent suffer for the guilty, and the wages of sin is death.

WALDEN, an autobiographic narrative by Henry D. Thoreau (1854). A sturdy individualist, and lover of nature Thoreau retired from the world to live a hermit-like existence on the shores of Walden Pond, near Concord, Massachusetts. For two years, from 1845 to 1847, he lived in a cottage built by himself at a cost of $28.12½. He subsisted on the plainest food, mostly corn meal, rice, potatoes, and molasses, tilled his own soil, and spent his leisure hours in botanizing, observing animal life, enjoying the scenery, reading, and meditation. The book is a discursive record of his experiences, under such headings as 'Economy,' 'Where I Lived and What I Lived For,' 'Sounds,' 'Solitude,' 'The Bean-Field,' 'The Ponds,' 'Winter Animals,' 'Spring.' Thoreau was a keen observer of birds, fish, animals, and flowers, and has described them with truth and attractiveness. He loved to support himself by hardy out-door toil in a country civilized enough to be cleared for cultivation; he did not enjoy the wilderness, but preferred the proximity of man. His philosophy is a combination of stoicism and asceticism, with an epicurean fondness for the beautiful in natural scenery and a Yankee shrewdness, practicality, and humor. His style has the purity and simplicity of Emerson's without its abruptness.

WALLENSTEIN, an historical drama by Friedrich Schiller, first acted in 1799 and published in 1800. There are three divisions: 'Wallenstein's Camp' (a brief prologue in one scene); 'The Piccolomini' (in five acts); and 'Wallenstein's Death' (in five acts). The first of these is written in irregular rhyming verse and the others in iambic pentameter. The play is based on Schiller's own 'History of the Thirty Years' War' (1791–1793) and on further investigations. The events, apart from certain alterations for dramatic effect, are essentially historical. The theme is the fall and death in 1634 of Count Albrecht Wenzel Eusebius von Wallenstein, Duke of Friedland, and commander of the military forces of the German emperor, Ferdinand II. Desirous of strengthening the empire by centralizing its power he had with the emperor's consent raised a great army, crushed the Protestant states, and repelled the invasion of the Swedes under Gustavus Adolphus. In order to strengthen himself against intrigues of jealous enemies at the emperor's court he now opened negotiations.

with the Swedes; and when the emperor discovered them he deprived Wallenstein of his command, undermined his authority over his army, and procured his assassination at Eger in Bohemia, February 25, 1634. 'Wallenstein's Camp' introduces us to the army of the Duke of Friedland encamped at Pilsen in Bohemia on the 22d of February, 1634. Various types of soldiers — cuirassiers, jägers (or mounted riflemen), dragoons, sharpshooters, uhlans, arquebusiers, artillerymen — from all parts of the empire and from beyond it — Croatia, Tyrol, Lombardy, the Netherlands, Scotland, Ireland — are mingled with camp hangers-on — a sutler-woman, a preaching friar, a peasant with loaded dice. The variegated movement and color of the scene suggests the size of the army and the field from which it has been drawn and for which it is fighting. The general's growing estrangement from the court is reflected in the talk of the soldiers. Wallenstein has been requested to furnish an escort for the new Spanish regent of the Netherlands on his way from Italy to his new government. The army feel that the execution of this order would weaken them and that their best interest lies in remaining with Wallenstein, upon whose power depends their hope of pay and plunder. They resolve to petition him through one of their generals, the younger Piccolomini, not to send any of them to the Netherlands. The scene ends with a spirited soldier's chorus praising the military life as the only free and noble one.

At the beginning of 'The Piccolomini' Wallenstein's fortunes are approaching a crisis. Count Questenberg has come from the emperor with a commission deposing Wallenstein from his command and appointing his Lieutenant-General, Octavio Piccolomini, in his stead. This commission he makes known to Piccolomini, who, however, conceals it until Wallenstein's opposition to the emperor shall grow more pronounced so that his officers may be induced to abandon him. On the same day Colonel Max Piccolomini arrives in camp, escorting Wallenstein's duchess and their daughter, Thekla. The duchess's sister, Countess Tertzky, has arranged this step, hoping that Max will fall in love with Thekla and thus become bound to the fortunes of Wallenstein. Her schemes are to a certain point successful. Max and Thekla become plighted lovers; but deeply as Max honors and reverences her father he is loyal to the emperor and has as yet no thought that Wallenstein entertains any treasonable intentions. These he first begins to suspect at a banquet held that evening by Count Tertzky, when the officers are induced by Wallenstein's confidant, Illo, to sign a pledge of devotion to their general from which a proviso safeguarding their loyalty to the emperor has been clandestinely removed. The rest, flushed with wine and stirred by Wallenstein's defiance of the emperor's orders earlier in the day, willingly sign. Max, who has just come from his interview with Thekla, and is therefore *distrait*, postpones signing until a remark of Illo's, under the influence of wine, shows him that a deception is being practiced. This gives Octavio Piccolomini, his father, who has himself signed for form's sake, a chance to reveal to Max what he knows of Wallenstein's negotiations with the Saxons and Swedes and of the emperor's intention to depose him. Max indignantly refuses to believe in Wallenstein's treason unless it is confirmed by his own lips. Meanwhile news comes to Wallenstein that the man who carried his dispatches to the Swedes and Saxons has fallen into the emperor's hands. At the urgent insistence of Tertzky and Illo and against his inclinations — he determines on a definite act of rebellion. He arranges with Wrangel, the Swedish envoy, to yield certain territory to the Swedes in return for their support. To this final step he is at length brought by the impassioned eloquence of Countess Tertzky, who sees in submission to the emperor the Duke's speedy ruin. Max, on the other hand, does all he can to make Wallenstein retract. Yet he hesitates to abandon him though Octavio Piccolomini and all the officers who signed the declaration of loyalty plan to do so. With the parting of father and son this division of the play closes.

In the opening act of 'Wallenstein's Death' the Duke of Friedland receives the news of the defection of the greater part of his army. Colonel Butler remains but he, as we have learned in a previous scene of 'The Piccolomini,' has been led by Octavio to believe that Wallenstein hindered his promotion and insulted him. He therefore stays in order to gain revenge. In the second act he manages to precipitate Wallenstein's fall by announcing to a deputation of a regiment which has not yet seceded and which the Duke is attempting by exhortation to keep faithful that Tertzky's troops have torn down the imperial ensign. The soldiers leave at once. Max now comes in to bid farewell to Thekla before leading off his regiment to join the imperial troops. Wallenstein at first attempts to detain him by force and then by persuasion. Max is tempted to go over to his side; but he appeals to Thekla whether he could retain her love and prove false to his inner conviction of duty to the emperor; and she says that he could not. They bid each other farewell and Max is carried off by his regiment, which has in fact invaded the castle in search of him.

The Duke gives orders that his remaining troops should retire to Eger. Here they learn that the Swedes have defeated the imperial forces and will effect a junction with Wallenstein on the morrow. Butler determines to lose no time; and in spite of the protests of Colonel Gordon, the commander of the citadel, he resolves to kill Tertzky, Illo, and Wallenstein that very night, and suborns a number of officers and soldiers for that purpose. Meanwhile news has come of the death of Max Piccolomini in a fierce battle between his regiment and the Swedes, at Neustadt. Thekla, who faints at the first shock, bears the news heroically, and learns from the Swedish messenger the full story of her lover's brave death. Then she hastens to die at his tomb. The same evening Tertzky and Illo are murdered at a banquet. Wallenstein, ignorant of their fate and of his daughter's, has a final interview with Countess Tertzky and Gordon, who vainly tries to induce him to return to his allegiance. He retires to his room, and is there murdered by Devereux and Macdonald, Butler's subordinates. Countess Tertzky, refusing to survive the downfall of her family, takes poison; and Octavio Piccolomini comes in at the close to regret his rival's death and to accept the fruits of it.

The dramatic skill with which Schiller has moulded an unwieldy mass of historical data into a unified structure with constantly heightening interest; his insight into the spirit of the times and into the leading characters of the period; his ability to embody his philosophical ideas as to freedom and necessity, the real and the ideal, in concrete and living personages; and the eloquent and melodious poetic diction in which his thoughts are clothed — these are some of the elements of greatness in Schiller's 'Wallenstein.'

WALKS IN ROME, by A. J. C. Hare, see **DAYS NEAR ROME.**

WALPOLE, HORACE, see **LETTERS OF.**

WANDA, a romantic novel by "Ouida" (1883). It has a picturesque and extravagant plot and setting. Wanda, the heroine, a beautiful woman of high rank and wealth, is the possessor of a magnificent ancestral castle in the mountains of Austria. There the nineteenth century meets the Middle Ages. Wanda is herself steeped in old-world traditions of honor and chivalry. She will not marry until she loves and she does not love readily. One stormy night a stranger is rescued from drowning in the lake beside the castle. He calls himself René, Marquis de Sabran-Romaris, but he is really the natural son of a great Russian noble by a peasant girl. Yet he is the son of the father rather than of his mother; he has lived so long in the atmosphere of aristocracy that he almost believes in himself. The ancient family from which he stole his title is extinct. The world accepts him as its last representative. By temperament and training he is in every way a man suited to Wanda von Szalras. She loves him in spite of herself. He on his part loves her honestly for herself alone; loves her so much that he cannot tell her the true story of his birth, and that he was once Vassia Kazán, a serf. Only one person lives who remembers Vassia Kazán. This is Egon Vàsàrhely, Wanda's cousin, who cherishes for her a hopeless love. As a boy guest in the house of Prince Zabaroff, Vassia's father, he had quarreled with Vassia, and had wounded him with a knife.

The Marquis of Sabran marries Wanda; children are born to them; their married life is wholly happy. After several years, Egon is prevailed upon to visit them. The beautiful features of Wanda's husband awaken strange memories of a boyish quarrel. By a long chain of circumstances, Sabran is at last forced to tell Wanda of his deception. She sends him from her, and for three years lives in solitude and bitterness. She forgives him only when he saves the life of their eldest son. But he has given his own life to do this, living only eleven days after the rescue of the child. "In the heart of his wife he lives forever, and with him lives a sleepless and eternal remorse."

WANDERING JEW, THE, by Moncure D. Conway (1881), traces through all its forms and changes, to its sources as far as can be perceived, the marvelous legend which won such general belief during the Middle Ages. The first appearance of the story written out as narrative occurs in the works of Matthew Paris, published 1259, wherein is described the visit to England, thirty years before, of an Armenian bishop. The prelate was asked whether he knew aught of the Wandering Jew. He replied that he had had him to dinner in Armenia shortly before; that he was a Roman, named Cartaphilus, door-keeper for Pilate. This ruffianly bigot struck Jesus as he came from the hall of judgment, saying, "Go on faster; why dost thou linger?"

Jesus answered: "I will go; but thou shalt remain waiting till I come."

Therefore Cartaphilus has lived on ever since; never smiling, but often weeping and longing for death, which will not come. In the sixteenth century there are accounts of the appearance of the Wandering Jew in German towns. His name is now Ahasuerus; his original occupation that of a shoemaker. In the seventeenth century he is heard of again and again, — in France, Spain, the Low Countries, Italy, and Germany. Many solemn and learned treatises were written in Latin on the subject of this man and his miraculous punishment. The various stories of him quoted are so graphically related that it is a surprise to follow Mr. Conway into his next chapter, in which he sets down the myth of the Wandering Jew with that of King Arthur, who sleeps at Avalon, and Barbarossa of Germany, who slumbers under the Raven's Hill, both ready to awake at the appointed hour. Every country has myths of sleepers or of wanderers who never grow old. The Jews had more than one: Cain, who was a fugitive and a vagabond on earth, with a mark fixed on him that none might slay him; Esau, whose death is unchronicled; Elias and Enoch who never died, in the ordinary way. Barbarossa, Arthur, Merlin, Siegfried, Tannhäuser, Lohengrin, — the Seven Sleepers, the Flying Dutchman, — all these are variants of one theme. Judas has had the same fate in legend. So has Pilate; so has Malchus, the servant of Caiaphas. Mr. Conway presents the theory that all these tales have their root in the primitive myths of savage peoples, perhaps in sun-myths; but he does not pursue this rather futile speculation, devoting himself rather to the story in its special form of the Wandering Jew, and tracing its development, and its expression in folk-lore, poetry, and fiction. The book is a fascinating study of the curious and unusual, scholarly in substance but popular in treatment.

WANDERING JEW, THE ('Le Juif Errant'), by Eugene Sue (1845). This curious rambling episodic romance is written from an extreme Protestant point of view, and introduces the character of Ahasuerus, who, according to legend, was a shoemaker in Jerusalem. The Saviour, bearing his cross past the house of the artisan, asks to be allowed to rest an instant on the stone bench at his door. "Go on!" replies Ahasuerus. "*Thou* shalt go on till the end of time," answers the Saviour — and so the Wandering Jew may never find home, or rest, or even pause. The scene of this romance is laid chiefly in Paris, in 1832. One hundred and fifty years prior to this date, Count Rennepont, a descendant of the sister of the Wandering Jew, who is also condemned to wander, professed conversion to the Catholic faith in order to save his property from confiscation. His ruse was discovered, however, and the whole estate given to the Jesuits. But Rennepont succeeded in secreting 150,000 francs, which he caused to be invested, principal and interest to be divided among such of his heirs as should present themselves at a certain rendezvous in Paris, after the lapse of a century and a half. Then comes an intensely dramatic description of the espionage to which the heirs have been subjected, and the successful machinations of the Jesuits in order to obtain this money. While they succeed by the most reckless acts of persecution and violence in preventing six of the seven heirs from presenting themselves to claim the vastly increased inheritance, they produce the seventh heir, Gabriel Rennepont — a virtuous young Jesuit priest, who has already made over his worldly goods to his Order — to claim the inheritance. A codicil to the will, found in a mysterious manner, postpones the day for delivering over the funds, and temporarily defeats these designs. But now, by adopting utterly conscienceless means, the heads of the Society of Jesus lead on the six heirs to their deaths before the arrival of the day which has been finally set for the partition of the millions. In the end, however, by an unforeseen catastrophe, the purposes of the Order are foiled. Rodin, a remarkable character, a little, cadaverous priest of marvelous energy and shrewdness, engineers the cause of the Jesuits; and by his diplomacy not alone lures the heirs to their ruin, but himself reaches the coveted post of General of the Order, though judgment finally overtakes him also. The story is very diffuse, and the episodes have only the slightest relation to each other. It is melodramatic in the extreme, and the style is often bombastic, while the personages have little resemblance to human beings in human conditions. But when all abatement is made, 'The Wandering Jew' remains one of the famous books of the world, for its vigor, its illusion, its endless interest of plot and counterplot, and its atmosphere of romance.

WAR AND PEACE, by Count Lyof Tolstoy (1864–69), perhaps the greatest of his novels, deals with the stirring conflict between Napoleon and France, and Koutouzoff and Russia, beginning some years before Austerlitz. As might be expected of one of the most mystical of modern writers, war is treated not alone as a dramatic spectacle, but as a symbol of great social forces striving for expression. The novel is a combination of mysticism and realism. Tolstoy has portrayed the terror of battle, the emotions of armies in conflict, with surpassing skill and power. The book as a whole leaves an indelible but confused impression upon the mind of the reader, as if he had himself passed through the din and smoke of a battle, of which he retains great dim memories. But above all is the impression of fatality, and the part that accident plays in all campaigns.

WARFARE OF SCIENCE WITH THEOLOGY IN CHRISTENDOM, A HISTORY OF THE, by Andrew Dickson White (1896. New ed., 1913). The work grew out of a lecture on 'The Battlefields of Science,' delivered by the author in reply to clerical and orthodox strictures upon the non-sectarian principles of Cornell University, of which he was president. Coming to believe that interference with science in the interests of dogmatic theology had always proved harmful not only to science but also to religion, and that all free scientific investigation had ultimately benefited religion, he proceeded to illustrate this conviction by a book entitled 'The Warfare of Science' (1876), a series of magazine articles, 'New Chapters in the Warfare of Science,' and at length by the present work. The plan of the book is to take up in succession various scientific theories and to trace their progress against vehement theological opposition to the time of their general acceptance. Among these theories are, the evolution of all species, including man, from lower forms; the sphericity of the earth; the heliocentric theory of the universe; the antiquity of the earth and man as demonstrated by fossils, weapons, implements, and skeletons, and other geological and anthropological discoveries; the gradual moral evolution of man, the attribution of witchcraft and insanity to psychic abnormality instead of diabolic influence; the bacterial origin of disease; and the human authorship of the Scriptures. In each case the dogmatic view is clearly stated, the growing opposition to it accurately traced, the effect of the struggle estimated, and the triumph of the scientific view recorded. Full references are given in support of all statements and there is an excellent index, but the book is so written as to appeal to the general reader as well as the scholar. It is an impressive piece of writing, unified by a great conception.

WAVERLEY, by Sir Walter Scott, the first of the world-famous series of romances to which it gives the title, was published in 1814. The author withheld his name at first, from doubt as to the success of the venture. The continuance of the concealment with subsequent issues followed perhaps naturally; Scott himself could give no better reason afterwards than that "such was his humor." Although the authorship of the series was generally credited to him, it was never formally acknowledged until the avowal was extorted by his business complications in 1826. 'Waverley' is a tale of the rebellion of the Chevalier Prince Charles Edward, in Scotland in 1745. Edward Waverley, an English captain of dragoons, obtains a leave of absence from his regiment for the purposes of rest and travel. His uncle, Sir Everard, whose heir he is, gives him letters to a Scotch friend, Baron Bradwardine of Tully-Veolan, Perthshire, who is a quaint mixture of scholar and soldier, and a strong Jacobite. He has a beautiful and blooming daughter Rose. During Waverley's visit, a party of Highlanders drive off the Baron's cattle; and Waverley offers to assist in their redemption from Fergus Mac Ivor, "Vich Ian Vohr," the chief of the clan. Waverley accompanies Fergus's messenger first to the island cave of Donald Bean Lean, the actual robber, and thence to Fergus's home, where he meets the chief himself and his brilliant and accomplished sister Flora. Waverley falls in love and offers himself to Flora, who discourages his addresses. Joining a hunting party, he is wounded by a stag and detained beyond his intended time. Meanwhile the rising of the Chevalier takes place; and Donald Bean, assuming Waverley to be a sympathizer and desiring to precipitate his action, intercepts Waverley's letters from home and uses his seal (stolen from him at the cave) to foment a mutiny in Waverley's troop. This and his unfortunate delay have the double effect of causing Waverley to be dishonorably discharged from his regiment for desertion and treason, and of inducing him in return to join the rebellion in his indignation at this unjust treatment. He first, however, attempts to return home to justify himself; but is arrested for treason, and rescued by the Highlanders when on his way to the dungeons of Stirling Castle. He serves at Preston Pans, where he saves and captures Colonel Talbot, who proves to be a family friend who had come north to help him. He procures Colonel Talbot's release and sends him home; after which events march rapidly. The Chevalier is defeated at Clifton, and Fergus is captured. Waverley escapes, conceals himself for a while, and later makes his way to London; where Colonel Talbot shelters him, clears his name from the false charges, and obtains his pardon, and that of Baron Bradwardine who had also joined the rebellion. Fergus is executed, and Flora retires to the Benedictine convent at Paris. Waverley wooes and marries Rose Bradwardine, and rebuilds Tully-Veolan, which had been destroyed in the campaign.

WAY OF ALL FLESH, THE, by Samuel Butler (1903). A brilliant satirical novel written in the eighties, attacking the institution of the family, especially the relations between parents and children, and the religion of the Scribes and Pharisees in the Anglican church and its clergy. The life history of the hero, Ernest Pontifex, begins with his great grandfather, the carpenter. This attractive old man and Ernest's Aunt Althea are his only agreeable relatives. His father, Theobald, has not one redeeming feature. He enters the church without vocation because of family pressure, He marries without love, and has children whom he dislikes, but he is so self-deceived that he regards himself as a model husband and father. Christina, Ernest's mother, believes Theobald everything he claims to be. Her satisfaction in herself and Theobald, and the dreams of greatness she indulges in for such deserving people, make her the most entertaining character in this amazingly entertaining book. Ernest is in complete subjection to his parents, but his instinctive knowledge and hatred of his father is the saving grace which keeps him from becoming a like prig and hypocrite, and makes Theobald see him as an ungrateful child who does not love his father as he ought. Butler attributes the unhappy relations which exist between parents and children in part to the Church Catechism "written too exclusively from the parental point of view" and quite evidently not the work of one who likes children. Ernest escapes from family prayers and Sundays and beatings to school, where he is treated with stupidity and brutality by teachers who like teaching because it is tyranny made easy. He goes to Cambridge and takes deacon's orders. Ernest's career in the Church is cut short by six months in jail for making improper advances to a respectable young lady. It is a profitable time of reflection and mental growth. He casts off Theobald and Christina for a fresh start in life, and marries Ellen who had been his mother's maid. They set up a second-hand clothing shop which prospers until Ellen goes back to drinking. He rejoices to find himself a bachelor again when he learns that she has another husband. The fortune his Aunt Althea left him, to be made known to him when he is twenty-eight, gives him financial independence, and he comes through his varied experiences a happy and dignified human being.

WAY OF THE WORLD, THE, by William Congreve (1700). Congreve, said Voltaire, "raised the glory of comedy to a greater height than any English writer before or since," and Swinburne called 'The Way of the World' "the unequalled and unapproached masterpiece of English comedy." The play was coolly received on its

first production, and Congreve told the audience bluntly that they could save themselves the trouble of disapproving, as he did not mean to write any more. The chief
character in the play is Millamant an accomplished elegant lady, who hopes and
fears nothing and whose law of life is her own caprice. Her conquests have ceased
to surprise or interest her. "What is it that a lover can give?" she asks, "Why one
makes lovers as fast as one pleases, and they live as long as one pleases, and they die
as soon as one pleases; and then if one pleases, one makes more." One of Congreve's
best known lyrics is Millamant's song:

> "Love's but the frailty of the mind
>   When 'tis not with ambition join'd.
>
> If there's delight in love 'tis when I see
>   That heart, which others bleed for, bleed for me."

WEALTH AGAINST COMMONWEALTH, by Henry D. Lloyd (1894). This
treatise begins with an epigram and ends with a promise. "Nature," says Mr.
Lloyd, "is rich; but everywhere man, the heir of Nature, is poor." Why is this so?
Because the people who are all the time helping Nature to produce wealth are the
blind agents of a few enlightened but selfish schemers. The great natural monopolies
which ought to be the property of a nation, are allowed to be controlled by private
individuals. Coal and oil, lumber and iron, and hundreds of indispensable commodities, are produced by "trusts"; and the result is that the few are constantly growing
richer and the many are finding the battle of life an ever-increasing defeat. Mr.
Lloyd shows with unsparing detail and with unimpeachable accuracy the working
of the various "trusts," and the tyranny which they stand for in a so-called land of
liberty. He believes that the people, who after all are the fountain-head of power,
have the right to regulate all these immense questions. "Infinite," he says, "is the
fountain of our rights. We can have all the rights we will create. All the rights we
will give we can have. The American people will save the liberties they have inherited by winning new ones to bequeath. With this will come fruits of a new faculty
almost beyond calculation. A new liberty will put an end to pauperism and million-
airism, and the crimes and death-rate born of both wretchednesses, just as the liberty
of politics and religion put an end to martyrs and tyrants." With a view of educating
the people to a knowledge of their rights, Mr. Lloyd marshals his appalling array of
facts, and points out a way for improvement in an unparalleled condition of things.
The book is marked by the serenity of optimism; for the author sees that the methods
employed by "trusts" in production work for greater economy and for greater
advantage in production: but he believes that those who create wealth should share
in the wealth; and that the so-called "fortunate few," who possess without having
helped to create, should realize their selfishness and become henceforth the servants
of those whom now they make serve. Mr. Lloyd's indictment of our modern civilization is said to have had a great influence on the altruistic thought of the day.

WEALTH OF NATIONS, An Enquiry into the Nature and Causes of the,
by Adam Smith (1776). A treatise of economic research, of great breadth; but
specially designed to show the wisdom and justice of free trade among nations. In
the very wide range of subjects dealt with are found social history, the politics of
commerce, rules of taxation, and educational theories now generally accepted; but
the chief burden of the book is freedom of trade among all nations. Its note is international, never considering how one nation may promote its own wealth at the
expense of other nations. The work is full of facts, shows wealth of varied reading,

and remarkable sagacity in the use of very imperfect data. The style of the work is diffuse, and the arrangement of materials irregular and loose; more in the manner of a great study than of a perfectly finished work. To a very large extent it drew from the work already done in France by the economists of the "Encyclopédie" school; first among whom stood Turgot, whose 'Sur la Formation et la Distribution des Richesses' supplied Smith with passages of his first book very closely following the divisions and arguments of Turgot. Smith had visited France at the close of the Seven Years' War, had spent a year in Paris, and had seen much of the economists there. He had returned home in October, 1766, and settled in retirement at Kirkcaldy, where he gave ten years to the production of his book. Five English editions of the work appeared during its author's life, and it was translated into many modern languages. It is at once a great English classic and a landmark in economical science. The earlier life of the author had been that of a professor at the University of Glasgow, where he was given the chair of logic in 1751, and that of moral philosophy the next year. In 1759 he published 'A Theory of the Moral Sentiments,' of which there were six editions during his life. It was his custom to give some attention to political economy in his Glasgow lectures; and he then drew those inferences on behalf of freedom of trade which he afterwards expanded into his 'Wealth of Nations.' In 1763 Smith resigned his chair to take charge of the education of the son of the Duke of Buccleugh; and it was on a pension of £300 a year, given him by the duke, that he retired to Kirkcaldy. It is said that Pitt thought well of Smith's free-trade views, and might in happier times have adopted a free-trade policy; but it was reserved for the school of Cobden to induce England to act on them.

WEAVERS, THE ('Die Weber') by Gerhart Hauptmann (1893). The starving weavers, cheated and underpaid, are shown receiving their wages from a bullying cowardly manager. He calls in his vulgar, rich, capitalist master who makes a speech to them showing how much they are to be envied and himself pitied, since he has all the anxiety to bear and all the capital to provide. A young soldier returning from the army, indignant at the misery he sees, stirs the weavers to revolt. A bright lively scene in the cheerful public house is interrupted by the noise of the crowd outside. The mob of strikers go to the house of the capitalist to find that he and his family have been warned and made their escape. They break the furniture and destroy the pictures. The last scene begins with family prayers in an old weaver's home. As there is no food, they begin the day's work fasting. News is brought that the house of the capitalist has been torn down, and the soldiers called to stop the uprising. A stray shot comes through the window and kills the old weaver at his loom, the only man who has kept out of the strife. It is a gruesome picture of terrible conditions, one of the first modern plays that deals with the life of the proletariat.

WEBSTER, DANIEL, by Henry Cabot Lodge (1883). This forms Vol. viii. of the 'American Statesmen' series. Mr. Lodge disclaims all credit for original research among MS. records in preparing this life of Webster; and is content to follow in the footsteps of George Ticknor Curtis, to whose "elaborate, careful, and scholarly biography" of the great statesman he frankly acknowledges his indebtedness for all the material facts of Webster's life and labors. But on these facts he has exercised an independent judgment; and this biographical material he has worked over in his own way, producing an essentially original study of the life of Webster. In considering the crises of Webster's life as lawyer, orator, senator, statesman, he in a few brief chapters brings the man before us with striking vividness. To portray Webster as a lawyer, his part in the Dartmouth College Case is recounted; for there his legal talents are seen at their best. The chapter on this case is a model of clear and concise statement. Webster as an orator is the subject of another chapter, dealing with his speeches in the Massachusetts Convention of 1820, and his Plymouth oration, and their effects upon the auditors. His part in the tariff debates of 1828 in Congress, his reply to Hayne, and his struggle with Jackson, occupy two chapters, in which Webster's extraordinary powers of reasoning and of oratory are analyzed. Mr. Lodge seems to judge without partisanship Webster's Seventh of March speech, and the dissensions between him and his party. He recognizes in Webster, above all, "the pre-eminent champion and exponent of nationality."

WEIR OF HERMISTON, an unfinished romance by Robert Louis Stevenson, the last novel he wrote, was published in 1896. A fragment, it gave promise of being his best work. An appended editorial note by Sidney Colvin tells how the plot was to be carried out. Nine chapters only had been written, the last on the very day of Stevenson's death. The whole action passes in Edinburgh and the lowlands of Scotland; the time is the early nineteenth century. Weir is a Lord Justice Clerk, a stern, silent, masterful man, noteworthy for his implacable dealings with criminals; his wife is a soft, timid, pious creature, whose death is told in the first chapter. Their son Archie is of a bookish turn, high-spirited, sensitive, idealistic, growing up with little attention from his father. But gradually Weir comes to care for his son, who is so revolted by the father's relish of his function in hanging a malefactor, that he cries out against the execution while it is taking place. This incenses the judge, who sends him to his moorland country estate of Hermiston to learn to be a laird. There he falls in with Kirstie Elliot and wins her love, and is tended by her aunt Kirstie, a dependent of the Hermiston house, who cares for Archie (as she did for his mother) with almost maternal affection. A visit from Frank Innes — an Edinburgh schoolmate of Archie's, and a shallow, vain, but handsome fellow — makes trouble; for he maligns Archie to the country folk, and seeks to win the younger Kirstie away from him. Kirstie the elder has an interview with Archie, in which she brings him to a sense of his wrong in making love to a girl out of his station, and he has a stormy meeting with his sweetheart — at which point the novel breaks off, all the elements for a tragedy having been introduced. The plot as planned by Stevenson involved the betrayal of the young Kirstie by Innes, although she is faithful in heart to Archie, who kills his rival and is condemned to death by his own father, the judge. Kirstie's brothers, known as the "Four Black Brothers," seek to take vengeance on Archie as the betrayer of their sister; but on learning the true state of the case, they rescue him from prison, and the lovers flee together to America. Here was splendid material for dramatic handling, and Stevenson would have made the most of it. The novel is written in the finest vein of romance; and the drawing of such characters as the judge — whose historic prototype is Lord Braxfield — and Kirstie the elder, is unsurpassed in his fiction. The Scotch coloring is perfect.

WESLEY'S JOURNAL, 'An Extract of the Reverend Mr. John Wesley's Journal' was published at intervals by Wesley from 1738 to 1791, as a kind of 'Apologia' of his life and doctrine. He explains in the preface that about fifteen years before he began to keep a daily record of his conduct for the purposes of religious self-examination; and that on leaving on his mission to Georgia in 1735 he had broadened its scope to include the description of interesting events in his experience, persons whom he had met, and meditations on various topics of general appeal. After an introductory letter written in his Oxford days and descriptive of the religious austerities and philan-thropics which won for his circle the name of Methodists he proceeds with the Journal, the first book of which describes his voyage to Savannah, his labors among the Indians his interest in the doctrines of the Moravians, and his bickerings with the colonists. In the second book he records his conversion from reliance on the diligent perfor-mance of religious labor and self-denial to a conviction of his personal salvation and justification through faith alone; and he shows the influence of his Moravian friends in bringing him into this frame of mind. He also describes the founding of the first Methodist society in Fetter Lane for the exchange of counsel and advice in spiritual experience. The remaining books are a record of Wesley's marvelous activity, his daily preaching and journeying, his overcoming of fashionable prejudice and brutal violence, his establishment and pastoral care of a multitude of societies, and, at last his founding of a new church. The entries present an attractive picture of Wesley's character and personality. They reveal a man of cultivation, literary taste, human sympathy, and catholicity, yet with a supreme all-pervading missionary purpose, a deep conviction, and a clear and powerful method of setting it forth. Though the religious aim predominates, the book contains many observations of a secular charac-ter on men and literature, and is a valuable historical commentary on the eighteenth century.

WHAT SOCIAL CLASSES OWE TO EACH OTHER, by William Graham Sumner. This work, published in 1883, was written by the professor of political economy in Yale University, and was intended to explode the fallacy of regarding the State as something more than the people of which it is composed. Every attempt to make the State cure a social ill, Mr. Sumner says, is an attempt to make some people take care of others. It is not at all the function of the State to make men happy; to say that those who by their own labor and industry have acquired or augmented a fortune shall support the shiftless and negligent, is to strike at the liberty of the industrious. Evils due to the folly and wickedness of mankind bear their own bitter fruit; State interference in such cases means simply making the sober, industrious, and prudent pay the penalty which should be borne by the offender. The type and formula of most philanthropic schemes is this: A and B put their heads together to decide what C shall do for D. Poor C, the "forgotten man," has to pay for the scheme, without having any voice in the matter. "Class distinctions simply result from the different degrees of success with which men have availed themselves of the chances which were presented to them. In the prosecution of these chances, we all owe to each other good-will, mutual respect, and mutual guarantees of liberty and security. Beyond this nothing can be affirmed as a duty of one group to another in a free State."

Professor Sumner's book is a useful antidote to many of the futile and dreamy socialistic schemes now afloat. A process warranted to regenerate the world in a day always has its attractions. Professor Sumner, however, is a more thorough-going supporter of the "laissez-faire" doctrine than most economists of the present day. Besides, he disregards the very dishonest means by which wealth is often attained. His defense of the capitalist class is not quite reasonable: not all capitalists, we know, are the despicable villains described by the extreme socialists; but neither could all of them be regarded as men who have simply made legitimate use of "the chances presented to them." However, Professor Sumner's protest against the insidious attacks on the liberty of the majority, under the specious guise of legislative aid for the weak, is straightforward and convincing.

WHEEL OF LIFE, THE, by Ellen Glasgow (1906). The scene of this story is laid in New York and it deals with the marital difficulties of the men and women who people its pages. The principal characters are Roger Adams, a man of sterling qualities, who is married to a shallow and frivolous wife; Gerty Bridewell, whose rich husband causes her much unhappiness on account of his fondness for other women; Arnold Kemper, a man of the world who is divorced from his wife, and Laura Wilde who is attractive, intellectual and unmarried. Laura, who lives in an old-fashioned house in Gramercy Park with her aged uncle and aunt, is a warm friend of Gerty whom she has known since her school-days. The two women are a great contrast to each other, as Laura is of a thoughtful nature, with high ideals which find their vent in poetry, while Gerty, who is a great beauty, is frivolous and worldly. Laura has had many suitors but her heart has remained untouched until her meeting with Arnold Kemper. She becomes engaged to him, but breaks off the match on the eve of her marriage, owing to an affair of Kemper's with an opera singer which causes Laura's disillusionment. After breaking her engagement Laura rushes away from the house in an agony of grief, and hides herself from her friends among strangers in an outlying suburb. In her trouble she turns to Roger Adams who has been her warm friend for years and asks him to come to her. Roger, in the meantime has buried his wife, Connie, whose life of frivolity had led her finally to drugs and disgrace. Roger had cared for her tenderly throughout her downward career but in spite of his efforts was unable to save her from ruining her life. Connie, after having left her husband and living a life of shame, finally returns to him in a dying condition and passes away in a hospital shielded and ministered to by Roger until the last. Laura gradually awakens to the fact that her feeling for Kemper was but a dream and finds in Roger the ideal she had sought.

WHEN KNIGHTHOOD WAS IN FLOWER, by Edwin Caskoden (1898). This is a historical romance of England in the sixteenth century, which describes the courtship and marriage of Mary Tudor, sister of Henry VIII., and Charles Brandon who is far below her in the social scale. In this romantic love-story the reader is introduced into the intrigues and follies of the court and is shown how a willful princess obtains her own way. Brandon's strength, comeliness, and courage win him favor in the eyes of the King and the love of Mary Tudor, for whom he cherishes a seemingly hopeless passion which almost works his ruin. King Henry determined to use his sister for purposes of political advancement, arranges a marriage for her with the old French king, promising that after his death she shall marry whom she likes. To this promise she later holds him when she confesses her marriage to Brandon. Besides King Henry, there are various historic personages introduced, among them Cardinal Wolsey, the Duke of Buckingham, and Jane Bolingbroke, who with her dove-like gentleness is a contrast to the brilliant, flashing, ever-changing Mary Tudor, whose picture is a clever piece of character drawing. The scene in which she coaxes the King to bestow the title of Duke of Suffolk upon her lover is one of the most effective. The quality of the book is dramatic, and the court and its doings are described in the language of to-day, except for occasional extracts from an old family chronicle of the narrator. The story carries the reader forward rapidly and his interest in the fortunes of the beautiful heroine and her trio of friends continues without a break until the happy conclusion, when the Princess attains her heart's desire.

WHEN VALMOND CAME TO PONTIAC, a novel by Gilbert Parker (1895), has for its motive the Napoleonic glamour which still enchants simple folk on the outlying borders of the French nation. Into the little French-Canadian village of Pontiac comes Valmond, a mysterious stranger, bearing about him the atmosphere of a great, dead world. In form and manner he recalls Napoleon. Though but a youth of some twenty summers, he seems the heir of magnificent memories. Little by little he steals into the hearts of the simple villagers. Little by little he wins them to the belief that he is the son of Napoleon. Even Sergeant Lagroin, a veteran of the Old Guard, coming to challenge his pretensions, is won to him by his manner of authority, and his utterance of watchwords thought to be buried forever within the dead lips of the great General. The Sergeant's complete surrender to this strange young Napoleon establishes his claim with the village-folk. Valmond has dreams of reconquering France. He forms his adherents into a little army. The movement attracting the attention of the government, soldiers are sent to demand the surrender of Valmond and Lagroin. The latter dies under the fire of their rifles, refusing to the last to wake from his beautiful dream.

"Valmond stood over his body, and drew a pistol.

"'Surrender, Monsieur!' said the officer, 'or we fire!'

"'Never! A Napoleon knows how to die!' came the ringing reply, and he raised his pistol at the officer.

"'Fire!' came the sharp command.

"'Vivé Napoléon!' cried the doomed man, and fell, mortally wounded."

Valmond also, refusing to surrender, is shot. Dying, he confesses that he was the child of Italian peasants, reared as a page in the house of Prince Lucien Bonaparte. After his death, however, it is discovered that he was really what he made pretense of being, the son of Napoleon, born at St. Helena.

WHIP AND SPUR, by George E. Waring, Jr. This series of interesting personal experiences of the War of the Rebellion was first published in the Atlantic Monthly. It was reprinted in book form in 1875. Colonel Waring was attached to the 4th Missouri Cavalry, and the scene of his service was chiefly in Missouri, Arkansas, Mississippi, and Tennessee. While there is very little fighting recorded, other no less interesting features of the War are related without any attempt at dramatic effect. He tells the stories and paints the characters of various horses that he owned, Vix, Ruby, Wellstein, and Max. The two last chapters give a vivid picture of fox-hunting in England. The volume shows that Colonel Waring is as clever in handling the pen as in managing the great problem of cleaning the streets of a great city.

WHIRLIGIGS, by "O. Henry" (1910) are incidents in the merry-go-round of life, presenting the dramatic surprise of the unexpected in men and affairs. A man and woman, outcasts in South America, believing themselves murderers, are betrothed, and count the world well lost if they are together. The man he had struck down in a quarrel arrives on the boat which brings the woman the news that her husband is alive, and without farewells they start for home. In another story the youngest cub-reporter deciphers a cable dispatch smuggled past the censor from the war front in Japan, which has baffled the entire editorial staff, and gives his paper the biggest "beat" of the war. In a third a trader on a trip across the mountains rescues an opera singer who has been kidnapped by the Indians. In the environment of the snow-capped Andes, the woman is a goddess singing te deums and misereres. As they descend to the tablelands his divinity becomes more an earth woman. At the sea level she sits on the table singing coon songs, and the mystery of romance takes flight. In still another story two would-be kidnappers capture a "Tartar" in an active, imaginative small boy, whom they are glad to return to his parents with a bonus of two hundred and fifty dollars. These little ironies of life are told with humor and pathos in O. Henry's picturesque American slang.

WHITE APRONS, a romance of Bacon's Rebellion, by Mrs. Maud Wilder Goodwin (1896) is a story of the struggle in Virginia between popular rights and aristocratic privilege a hundred years before the Revolution. The hero, Bryan Fairfax, is sent by Bacon to bring to his camp several ladies, adherents of his opponent, Governor Berkeley. Among them is Penelope Payne, with whom the young soldier speedily falls in love. Bacon sends Penelope to Jamestown to inform Berkeley that if he attacks before noon, the women will be placed in front of Bacon's uncompleted works. Penelope taunts Bacon with cowardice, and tells him that he and his followers shall be known as White Aprons. The tide of war turns, Bacon dies, and Fairfax is taken prisoner by Berkeley, who becomes an unbearable tyrant. When Fairfax is put on trial for his life, Penelope, to the surprise of all, comes forward to testify in his favor, and openly confesses her love for him. Berkeley in a frenzy of rage condemns Fairfax to death, but consents to his reprieve for three months. Penelope straightway sets out for England to seek a pardon from the King. She goes to the house of her uncle, the historic Samuel Pepys, and there she meets Dryden, Buckingham, and various other wits and beaux. The beauty of her portrait, painted by Kneller, obtains her an audience with the King; who, after a trial of her constancy, grants her the pardon, with which she makes all speed home, arriving at the critical moment when Fairfax is on the scaffold. The story ends as it begins, with the burden of an old song: "Love will find out the way." Though slight in texture, the work is very daintily executed, and the spirit of colonial Virginia is well suggested.

WHITE COMPANY, THE, a romantic tale of the fourteenth century, by A. Conan Doyle (1891). Alleyne Edricson, a gentle, noble-spirited youth, who has been sheltered and educated among a company of white-robed Cistercians in England, leaves the abbey to make his way in the world. Together with two sinewy and gallant comrades, Hordie John and Samkin Aylward, he attaches himself to the person and fortunes of Sir Nigel Loring, a doughty knight, the mirror of chivalry, ever in quest of a passage-at-arms for the honor of his lady and his own advancement in chivalry.

In vigorous phrase and never-flagging interest, the tale rehearses how that Sir Nigel heads the "White Company," a band of sturdy Saxon bowmen, free companions, and leads them through many knightly encounters in the train of the Black Prince, in France and Spain. The story rings with the clash of arms in tourney lists, during wayside encounters and on the battle-field, and reflects the rude but chivalric spirit of the century.

Many characters known to history are set in lifelike surroundings. The movement is rapid, stirring episodes follow each other rapidly and withal there is presented a careful picture of the tumultuous times in which the varied scenes are laid.

It is in Spain that Sir Nigel's young squire, Alleyne, wins his spurs by gallant conduct, thrillingly told in a passage which will rank with the author's ablest efforts. Alleyne lives to return, with a few comrades of the decimated White Company, and claims the hand of Lady Maude, Sir Nigel's daughter, who has long loved the young squire, and gladly weds him as a knight.

WHITE DEVIL, THE; or, VITTORIA COROMBONA by John Webster (1612). "By Shakespeare alone among English poets," says Swinburne speaking of this play

THE READER'S DIGEST OF BOOKS 899

"have the finest scenes and passages of this tragedy been ever surpassed or equalled in the crowning qualities of tragic or dramatic poetry — in pathos and passion, in subtlety and strength, in harmonious variety of art and infallible fidelity to nature." The heroine of the play, Vittoria Corombona, wife of Camillo, has an intrigue with Duke Brachiano and in the first scene in which she appears she tells the Duke of a dream which is to incite him to murder her husband and his own duchess. Camilio is murdered and his body so laid as to conceal the crime. The Duchess is slain by poison, the portrait of her husband, which she used to kiss, having been infected by Doctor Julio with poisoned oil. Vittoria at her trial for the murder of her first husband confronts her judges and accusers with cold and unmoved scorn. Flamneo, brother of Vittoria, and secretary to Brachiano, murders his brother Marcello, attendant on Francisco de Medicis, Duke of Florence. Over his bier Cornelia, mother of Vittoria, speaks the exquisitely beautiful dirge, than which there is nothing finer outside Shakespeare:

> "Call for the robin-redbreast and the wren
> Since over shady groves they hover.
> And with leaves and flowers do cover
> The friendless bodies of unburied men."

Brachiano is assassinated at the instigation of Francisco. Vittoria bravely fronts the murderer's knife, yet utters the hopeless cry,

> "My soul, like to a ship in a black storm
> Is driven, I know not whither."

WHITE ROCKS, THE ('Les Roches blanches') by Édouard Rod (1895). In the Bois-Joli belonging to the Swiss commune of Bielle are two great rocks, called Les Rochers Blancs, about which twines a romantic legend. A noble lord who had loved a woman kept from him by some unknown barrier had entered a Trappist monastery; the woman at the same time became a nun. But they met every night in the pine-trees of the Bois-Joli. They were faithful and loyal, and kept their vows; and just as they had bidden each other an eternal farewell, they were stiffened into stone side by side. History repeats itself in the life of the peasant pastor of Bielle, M. Trembloz. Among his parishioners is an aristocratic family, consisting of M. Massod de Bussens and his wife: "Madame de Bussens was not precisely beautiful, but she had a wealth of thick silky hair, which set off a forehead of exceeding purity; large sky-blue eyes, from which flashed at moments a repressed inward light; a charming mouth formed for smiling, but rarely seen to smile"; young in appearance, and slender as a girl. Her husband is a sanctimonious tyrant who has crushed out whatever love she may once have felt for him. M. Trembloz is simple-hearted, but gifted with marvelous eloquence; he sees that she suffers; he understands her, and it is only a question of a few meetings when they find themselves deeply in love. But like the mythical lovers of the White Rocks, they resolve to meet no more. Unfortunately, their secret is discovered and reported to M. de Bussens, who charges her with unfaithfulness. She confesses that she loves the pastor. Her husband is implacable, and sends her away, depriving her of their charming son Maurice, who loves her and is desperately afraid of his father.

M. Rod raises the eternal question of what shall be done with incompatible marriage, but makes no attempt to cut the Gordian knot. The petty society of a Swiss provincial town is graphically depicted; but perhaps the cleverest portrait in the book is the keen, ambitious Madame Trembloz, the mother of the pastor, who in her way is as much of a tyrant as is M. de Bussens in his. The episode of the young gi-

Rose Charmot, who is brought before the directors of the Orphan Asylum and charged with having gone astray, brings to light all the narrowness of the self-righteous and Pharisaical spirit rampant in such a provincial town, and forms a background for the nobleness of the pastor and Madame de Bussens, who alone take the girl's part. The story is written in a fascinating style.

WICKER-WORK WOMAN, THE, see **L'HISTOIRE CONTEMPORAINE.**

WIDE, WIDE WORLD, THE, by "Elizabeth Wetherell" (Susan Warner: 1851). It is a study of girl life, which reached a sale of over 300,000 copies. The life of the heroine, Ellen Montgomery, is followed from early childhood to her marriage, with a fullness of particulars which leaves nothing to the reader's imagination. Her parents going to Europe, she is placed in the care of Miss Fortune Emerson, a sharp-tempered relative of her father's. Amid the sordid surroundings of her new home, her childish nature would have been entirely dwarfed and blighted had it not been for the good offices of Alice Humphreys, a sweet and lovable girl, who with wise and tender patience develops the germs of Ellen's really excellent character.

At length both Mrs. Montgomery and Alice Humphreys die; and after some years, Ellen comes to take up a daughter's duties in the home of her kind friend. The scenes and episodes are those of a homely every-day existence, which is described with a close fidelity to detail. Ellen's spiritual life is minutely unfolded, and the book was long regarded as one of those which are "good for the young." The criticism of a later generation, however, pronounces it mawkish in sentiment and unreal in conduct. It stands among the fading fancies of an earlier and less exacting literary taste.

WIFE OF SIR ISAAC HARMAN, THE, a novel by H. G. Wells (1914) is the history of the development of a woman's individuality. Beautiful and still very much of a child in spite of her twenty-four years, Lady Harman finds herself the mother of four children with whose bringing up she is not permitted to interfere, and the mistress of an uncomfortably ornate mansion which she is not allowed to manage. Her husband, the fabulously rich Sir Isaac Harman, owner of the International Bread and Cake Stores, controls her as absolutely as he does his other possessions. Through her seamstress, Lady Harman hears that her husband's Stores have sent smaller dealers into bankruptcy; she also learns that his waitresses get too little to permit them to live decently. On a house-hunting expedition, she meets an entirely different sort of man, Mr. Brumley, the owner of Black Strand, a pretty country place; he is a man of letters and a bit of a sentimentalist, and on business connected with the sale of the house to Sir Isaac, he calls on Lady Harman. Through him she meets a number of pleasant women, but Sir Isaac disapproves of her new friends and orders her not to receive or visit them. For the first time in her life, Lady Harman is defiant; she steals out of the house to keep a dinner appointment with Lady Beach-Mandarin. Maddened by her disobedience, Sir Isaac whisks his household from Putney to Black Strand, shuts his wife up, and gives it out that she is ill. Goaded past endurance Lady Harman runs away. She falls in with a band of militant suffragettes, and breaks a window in the Jago Street Postoffice. After Sir Isaac's tyranny she finds prison a relief. When she leaves the Holloway Gaol, she finds Sir Isaac very ill and penitent. He bestows on her four great hostels in which the waitresses from the Stores are to be housed at a moderate rate. But as time goes on, he manages to circumvent Lady Harman's desire to make the hostels real homes, by turning them into institutions with unfriendly matrons, stiff rules and fines for misdemeanors. As his illness grows, he becomes more disagreeable and suspicious and has Lady Harman and the innocent Mr. Brumely followed by a detective. Finally Lady Harman is advised to take her husband to Santa Margherita. While they are there Sir Isaac opens a letter from Mr. Brumley to his wife. From that letter he learns of the admiration and affection Mr. Brumley has for her and he berates Lady Harman in hideous terms, threatening to disinherit her. He works himself into such a frenzy that he suffers a stroke and dies. According to the terms of an old will, Lady Harman is to have the Hostels, as long as she remains unmarried. Returning to England, she finds Mr. Brumley most desirous of wedding her, but she refuses. The story ends, however, leaving the reader with the conviction that Lady Harman will lose the Hostels after all.

WILD ASS'S SKIN, THE, see **PEAU DE CHAGRIN.**

WILD DUCK, THE, by Henrik Ibsen (1884). The characters in this drama are the Ekdal family and their connections. Many years before the play opens the father was ruined by Werle, his wealthy partner, who reaped the profits of a fraudulent business contract for which Ekdal was sent to prison for a term of years. Werle provided the money to furnish a photographer's shop for Hjalmar, Ekdal's son, and encouraged him to marry Gina, a servant who had been Werle's mistress. Hjalmar is a lazy poseur. He pretends he is working on an invention which will restore the family name and honor, and leaves all the work of the photograph shop to his amiable devoted wife, and the gentle loving child, Hedwig, whom he believes to be his own daughter. The father, the disgraced old man, with some discarded Christmas trees has made an imitation forest out of the attic, where he plays at hunting a few rabbits and pigeons. Hedwig has a lame wild duck which is the pride of the preserve. They are a happy family circle in spite of their misfortunes, until Gregers, the son of Werle, with a bigoted zeal for truth, decides it his duty to thrust the unpleasant facts of Gina's past upon his former friend, Hjalmar, and thus, as he thinks, lay the foundation of a true marriage. The worthless Hjalmar declaims in theatrical fashion about his shattered honor, though he is presently willing to accept a money allowance for his father and Hedwig from the elder Werle. Gregers talks to the sensitive, wounded Hedwig of the nobility of sacrifice, and suggests that she give up her most cherished possession, the wild duck, to prove her love for Hjalmar. She goes to the attic, but instead of killing the bird shoots herself. Contrasted with Gregers is the family friend, Dr. Relling, who wishes to make the world happy by fostering illusions, and who tries to prevent the tragedy. The lame wild duck with its clipped wings may represent any or all of the Ekdal family, except Gina, whose practical common sense is contrasted with the frothy idealism of the rest of the household, and of Gregers Werle.

WILD IRISH GIRL, THE, by Lady Morgan (1801). Sydney Owenson, afterwards Lady Morgan, was born at Dublin in 1783. She was still a young woman when she had earned her rank as the first patriotic Irish romancer of modern times. She was "quoted with respect by Byron." 'The Wild Irish Girl,' one of her earliest tales, instantly became a favorite. In England it went through seven editions in less than two years, and in 1807 it had reached its fourth American edition.

The story recounts the adventures of the son of an English nobleman, banished for a season to his father's estate in Ireland, in order that he may give up his frivolous dissipations and begin a more studious life. Here he meets the Prince of Inismore, one of the old Irish nobility, and his daughter Lady Glorvina, the wild Irish girl. Her wildness seems mild to the reader of to-day. She was clad "in a robe of vestal white enfolded beneath the bosom with a jeweled girdle. From the shoulder fell a mantle of scarlet silk, while the fine-turned head was enveloped in a veil of point lace." The Englishman has a fall, and spends some days of convalescence as the Prince's guest, concealing his identity and the fact that he is the "hereditary object of hereditary detestation." Glorvina, who plays delightfully upon the harp, exerts an irresistible fascination. He has nearly declared himself her lover when he learns that he has a rival in a mysterious stranger. Events prove that the stranger is none other than the hero's father, to whom Glorvina feels herself bound in gratitude if not in love. The magnanimous parent, however, gives up his claim in favor of his repentant and grateful son.

The story is in the form of letters, and suffers from the consequent limitation; but the sketches of Irish life are curious and picturesque.

WILHELM MEISTER'S APPRENTICESHIP. The first part of 'Wilhelm Meister' was finished in 1796, after having occupied Goethe's attention for twenty years. The central idea of this great novel is the development of the individual by means of the most varied experiences of life. There is no plot proper, but in a series of brilliant episodes the different stages of the hero's spiritual growth are brought before the reader. Wilhelm Meister is a young man with many admirable qualities of character, but passionate and emotional, somewhat unstable, lacking reflection and proper knowledge of the world. The son of a well-to-do business man in a small German town is traveling for his father's house when he falls in with a troupe of strolling comedians. From earliest boyhood he has been devoted to the theatre, a passion which has been nourished by puppet-plays and much reading of dramatic literature and romances. Disgusted with the routine of business, and eager for new experiences, he joins the players, determined to become an actor himself. His apprenticeship to life falls into two periods. The first comprises the lessons he learned while among the players. Brought up in comfort in a respectable, somewhat philistine household, he enjoys at first the free and easy life of his new companions, though as a class they had at that period hardly any standing in society. He becomes passionately attached to Marianne, a charming young actress, who returns his love, but whom he leaves after a while, because of ungrounded jealousy. For a time he thinks he has found his true vocation in the pursuit of the actor's art. But ill-success on the stage, and closer acquaintance with this bohemian life of shams and gilded misery, disillusions him, and reveals the insubstantiality of his youthful ambitions. Leaving the actors, he becomes acquainted with some landed proprietors belonging to the lesser nobility of the country. And here the second period of his apprenticeship begins. Meeting people of culture and position in society, he comes into closer touch with real life, and is initiated into the ways of the world. His development is further hastened by finding his son Felix, whom he has never acknowledged. What women and society are still unable to teach him, he now learns from his own child. The awakening sense of his parental responsibilities is the final touchstone of his fully developed manhood. Having thus completed his apprenticeship to life in a series of bitter experiences, he now marries a lady of rank, and turns landed proprietor. The scheme of the novel gave Goethe opportunity to bring in the most varied phases of society, especially the nobility of his time, and the actors. He also discusses different æsthetic principles, especially the laws of dramatic art as exemplified in 'Hamlet.' He also touches on questions of education and religious controversy, and satirizes somewhat the secret societies, just then beginning to spring up in Germany. 'Wilhelm Meister,' in short, gives a richly colored picture of the life of Goethe's time.

WILHELM TELL, a historical drama by Friedrich Schiller, first acted in 1804. The theme is the struggle of the three so-called forest-cantons (Waldstätte) of Switzerland — Uri, Schwyz, and Unterwalden — to win complete autonomy under the German emperor. Their confederacy for this purpose in 1291 was the nucleus of the modern Swiss republic; and their independence was assured by their victory at Morgarten over the Duke of Austria who had invaded their country in 1315. About these events a series of legends gradually accumulated which were first recorded in the fifteenth century and were incorporated into sober history by the sixteenth-century Swiss chronicler, Ægidius Tschudi, in his 'Chronicon Helveticum,' and by the eighteenth-century Swiss historian, Johannes von Muller (1752–1807). These two authorities were the main sources of Schiller's play. According to them the Habsburg Emperor, Albrecht, placed cruel governors over the forest cantons with the aim of reducing them to absolute subjection. These governors inflicted various cruelties upon the people, as a result of which they rose in rebellion, drove out the governors, and destroyed their castles, in the year 1308. The assassination of the Emperor, in the same year, freed the Swiss from the danger of reprisal. A leading figure in the uprising was William Tell, a hunter living at Altdorf in the canton of Uri. Forced by Gessler, the cruelest of the governors, to shoot an apple from his son's head and afterwards imprisoned for admitting his intention to shoot Gessler in case of failure, he escaped, shot the governor from an ambush, and thus gave the signal for general revolt. The absence of any contemporary reference to the cruelties of the governors, and the occurrence of the apple-shooting episode in ballads and folk-tales all over the world, throw discredit upon the historicity of these events; but from the sixteenth century onwards they were firmly believed in by the Swiss people. Accepting these data as true for purposes of poetic creation, Schiller built up a great drama on the broad, free lines of a Shakespearian chronicle-history, unified by the conception of the bravery and solidarity of the whole community. In this picture of a whole society striving towards one aim, no touch of individual or class characterization and no local color is forgotten. We are shown the governors, brutal and ruthless; the native nobility, inclining towards the Emperor, but won at last to full co-operation with the people, the burghers, conscious of their unbroken past of freedom under the empire and determined to maintain their privileges; the humbler peasants, hunters, herdsmen, and fishermen, bound by the same sacred ties; and lastly the sturdy, resolute Tell, embodiment of the individual frankness, integrity, and efficiency without which the coalition would fall to pieces. The action is loosely knit, a series of scenes rather than a tissue of closely related events.

WINDOW IN THRUMS, A, by Sir James M. Barrie (1889), is a continuation of the 'Auld Licht' series. Its scenes are confined mainly to the interior of the little Scotch cot in "Thrums" where lived Hendry and Jess McQumpha, and their daughter Leeby. In Mr. Barrie's later work, 'Margaret Ogilvy,' an affectionate and artistic picture of his mother, we discern that in Jess and Leeby his mother and sister sat for the portraits. Jess is a quaint figure. A chronic invalid, yet throbbing with interest in everybody and everything, she sits at the window of her cottage, and keeps up with Leeby a running fire of terse and often cutting comment upon village happenings, and thus holds herself in touch with the life and gossip which she knows only through the window. Barrie's sympathetic ability to see how inseparable are humor and pathos makes his characters living and human. Tammas Haggart, the humorist, at much pains to understand and dispense the philosophy of his own humor; the little christening robe which does the honors for the whole village, and which is so tenderly revered by Jess because it was made for her own babe, "twenty years dead," but still living for her; the family pride in Jamie, the son who has gone to London, in whom we may see "Gavin Ogilvy" (Barrie's own pseudonym); and finally, Jamie's homecoming to find Hendry, Jess, and Leeby gone to the long home, are absolutely real. And if the reader laughs at the whimsicalities of the village folk, it is because he loves them.

WINGS OF A DOVE, THE, by Henry James (1902). The heroine of this novel, Kate Croy, has before her, as object lesson, an impossible father and a complaining widowed sister who warn her from their experience that poverty is the worst possible evil. Her wealthy aunt, Mrs. Lowder, has taken up her handsome niece with the understanding that Kate shall reward her by making a marriage worthy of her aunt's social ambition for her. The man selected is Lord Mark. Kate is secretly engaged to an impecunious young journalist, Merton Densher, and she hopes time will, in some way, make it possible for her to marry the man she loves. An American heiress, Milly Theale, comes to London with a chaperon who is an old school friend of Mrs. Lowder's, and the two girls become friends. Milly has met Densher in New York and fallen in love with him. As Milly is found to be stricken with a mysterious mortal malady, Kate conceives the plan that Densher shall make Milly happy by his attentions for the short period of life left to her, even to the point of marrying her, in order to inherit her wealth for himself and Kate. Densher has left their affairs to Kate, recognizing her "talent for life," and he is thus committed to the part of init-mate devoted friend to Milly before he fully realizes Kate's plan. The great London doctor recognizes that Densher is the man to make Milly happy and prolong her life, and the deception seems to become the path of kindness and duty. Densher follows her to Venice and with growing distaste plays his rôle. The fact of Kate and Densher's engagement is maliciously betrayed to Milly by Lord Mark, who discovers their relations, and she pathetically gives up her struggle for life. She dies and leaves her millions to Densher. He asks Kate to choose between the money which he will turn over to her, or marriage with him without the money, which he refuses to accept. She demands from him an assurance that he is not in love with Milly's memory, and he declines to give it, offering again to marry her at once. "As we were?" asks Kate. "As we were," he reiterates. "But she turned to the door, and her headshake was now the end. We shall never be again as we were!"

WINNING OF BARBARA WORTH, THE, by Harold Bell Wright (1911). The scene of this story is laid in Rubio City, a town of comparatively recent birth, on the banks of the Colorado River. The opening chapters describe the perilous journey across the desert of a party of travelers who encounter a terrible sand-storm and narrowly escape death. The principal member of the party is Jefferson Worth, bank president and leading citizen of Rubio City, and he is accompanied by a clever young engineer called the "Seer," who figures quite prominently throughout the story. After the furious sand-storm has abated, traces are seen of lost travelers and soon the dead body of a woman is discovered and nearby is found a lovely little girl of less than four years. No clues to the child's identity are to be found and she is cared for by the rescuing party and is later adopted by Worth who has no children of his own.   Barbara Worth becomes a beautiful and accomplished woman with a strong and generous nature and is beloved by rich and poor alike. Her influence over her stern and cold father, who idolizes her, is most remarkable and at her bidding he becomes considerate and kind.   The arrival upon the scene of Willard Holmes, a young engineer from New York, produces a distinct impression upon Barbara, who up to this time had been fancy free.   Holmes is college bred, of good lineage and character.   He has come to Rubio City to represent a New York company's interest in the irrigation of a part of the desert called "King's Basin," which is the very place where Barbara was found and in which she feels a vital interest.   In course of time Holmes and Barbara fall in love with each other, but the match is strongly opposed by the former's guardian, James Greenfield, a rich and aristocratic bachelor, who loves Willard as his own son and objects to his marriage with a girl of unknown origin. However, during the work upon "King's Basin," a casket is found containing the proofs of Barbara's identity and she is found to be the child of Greenfield's own brother, who was lost on the desert many years before while traveling with his young wife and child.   Before these proofs are found, however, Holmes has declared himself true to Barbara though his marriage to her means the loss of his inheritance.

WINNING OF THE WEST, THE, by Theodore Roosevelt (1889-96).   Four volumes each complete in itself, and together constituting a study of early American develop ments; to be placed by the side of Parkman's 'France and England in North America.' It treats what may be called the sequel to the Revolution; a period of American ad- vance, the interest and significance of which are very little understood.   Washington himself prophesied, and almost planned, the future of the great region beyond the Ohio.   When, at the close of the war, there was no money to pay the army on its disbandment, he advised his soldiers to have an eye to the lands beyond the Ohio, which would belong not to any one State but to the Union; and to look to grants of land for their pay.   Out of this came the New England scheme for settlement on the other side of the Ohio.   The promoters of this scheme secured the passage of the Ordinance of 1787, which made the Ohio the dividing line between lands in which slaves might be held to labor, and those in which there should be no slavery, and which broadly planned for the education of all children on a basis of equality and free schools.   To an extent without parallel these actions of a moment fixed future destiny.   How the course of events from 1769 brought about those actions, and the progress forward for twenty years from that moment, is the subject of Mr. Roosevelt's carefully planned and admirably executed volumes.   The mass of original material to which Mr. Roosevelt has had access, casts a flood of new light upon the field over which he has gone, with the result that much of the early history has had to be entirely rewritten.   It is in many ways a fascinating narrative, and in every way a most instructive history.

WINTER'S TALE, A (printed in 1623), one of the last dramatic pieces from Shake- speare's pen, has the serene and cheerful wisdom of 'Cymbeline' and 'The Tempest.' It is based on Greene's 'Pandosto' (1588).   In this story, as in Shakespeare, Bohemia is made a maritime country and Delphos an island.   The name 'Winter's Tale' derives partly from the fact that the play opens in winter, and partly from the resemblance of the story to a marvelous tale told by a winter's fire.   Like 'Othello,' it depicts the tragic results of jealousy,—in this case long years of suffering for both husband and wife, and the purification of the soul of the former through remorse, and his final reconciliation with his wronged queen.   Leontes, king of Sicily, unlike

Othello, has a natural bent toward jealousy; he suspects without good cause, and is grossly tyrannical in his persecutions of the innocent. Hermione, in her sweet patience and sorrow, is the most divinely compassionate matron Shakespeare has delineated. Polixenes, king of Bohemia, has been nine months a guest of his boyhood's friend Leontes, and is warmly urged by both king and queen to stay longer. Hermione's warm hospitality and her lingering hand pressures are construed by the king as proof of criminality: he sees himself laughed at for a cuckold; a deep fire of rage burns in his heart; he wants Camillo to poison Polixenes; but this good man flies with him to Bohemia. Leontes puts his wife in prison, where she is delivered of a daughter. He compels Antigonus to swear to expose it in a desert place, and then proceeds with the formal trial of his wife. His messengers to Delphi report her guiltless. She swoons away, and Paulina gives out that she is dead. But she is secretly conveyed away, after the funeral, and revived. Her little son dies from grief. Sixteen years now elapse, and we are across seas in Bohemia, near the palace of Polixenes and near where Hermione's infant daughter was exposed, but rescued (with a bundle containing rich bearing cloth, gold, jewels, etc.) by an old shepherd. Antigonus and his ship's crew were all lost, so no trace of the infant could be found. But here she is, the sweetest girl in Bohemia and named Perdita ("the lost one"). A sheep-shearing feast at the old shepherd's cottage is in progress. His son has gone for sugar and spices and rice, and had his pocket picked by that rogue of rogues, that snapper-up of unconsidered trifles, Autolycus. The dainty Perdita moves about under the green trees as the hostess of the occasion, giving to each guest a bunch of sweet flowers and a welcome. Polixenes and Camillo are here in disguise, to look after Polixenes's son Florizel. After dancing, and some songs from peddler Autolycus, Florizel and Perdita are about to be betrothed when Polixenes discovers himself and threatens direst punishment to the rustics. The lovers fly to Sicily, with a feigned story for the ear of Leontes; and the old shepherd and his son get aboard Florizel's ship to show the bundle and "fairy gold" found with Perdita, expecting thus to save their lives by proving that they are not responsible for her doings. Polixenes and Camillo follow the fugitives, and at Leontes's court is great rejoicing at the discovery of the king's daughter; which joy is increased tenfold by Paulina, who restores Hermione to her repentant husband's arms. Her device for gradually and gently possessing him of the idea of Hermione's being alive, is curious and shrewd. She gives out that she has in her gallery a marvelous statue of Hermione by Julio Romano, so recently finished that the red paint on the lips is yet wet. When the curtain is drawn by Paulina, husband and daughter gaze greedily on the statue, and to their amazement it is made to step down from its pedestal and speak. They perceive it to be warm with life, and to be indeed Hermione herself, — let us hope, to have less strain on her charity thereafter.

WITCHING HOUR, THE, by Augustus M. Thomas (1907). Jack Brookfield, a professional gambler, in whose rooms the play opens, is believed by his friends to be possessed of an extraordinary personal magnetism. It is said that this gift is shared by his sister, Mrs. Campbell and her daughter Viola. The interior decorations of Brookfield's magnificent house have been planned by Clay Whipple, who is in love with Viola. On seeing that a rival of his is talking earnestly to her at the opera, he proposes to her and is accepted. He kills a man accidentally at the house of Jack Brookfield, and is charged with murder by Frank Hardmuth, the assistant District Attorney, who had been talking to Viola at the opera, and who now asks Jack Brookfield for support in his love suit. Brookfield declines to attempt to influence his niece. In a first trial Clay is convicted, but he is able to secure a second. While the jury are deliberating, Brookfield attempts to concentrate the psychic force of the community upon them with the object of securing an acquittal. Before the trial, which resulted in an acquittal, had come to an end, Brookfield had caused to be published a charge against Hardmuth of having planned and procured the assassination of the governor of Kentucky, whose place he is now anxious to secure. Hardmuth rushes to meet Brookfield and points a Derringer at him but by hypnotic influence is forced to drop it. In the end Brookfield, as he feels that he himself has often been acting against the law, and that his success at cards has been merely due to his hypnotic powers, decides to help Hardmuth, of whom the police are in search, across the line.

WITH FIRE AND SWORD (1890), **THE DELUGE** (1891), **AND PAN MICHAEL** (1893), a trilogy of magnificent historical novels, by Henryk Sienkiewicz, treats of that period of Polish history which extends from 1648 to the election of Sobieski to the throne of Poland as Yan III. It thus embraces the most stirring and picturesque era of the national life. The first of the trilogy deals with the deadly conflict between the two Slav States, Russia and Poland. It is an epic of war, of battle, murder, and sudden death, of tyranny and patriotism, of glory and shame. In 'The Deluge,' two great events of Polish history form the dramatic groundwork of the novel: these are the settlement of the Teutonic Knights in Prussia, and the union of Poland with Lithuania and Russia through the marriage of the Polish Princess Yadviga with Yagyello, Grand Prince of Lithuania. The war between Poland and Sweden in 1665, brought on by the action of the Teutonic Knights, is described in this novel. Like its predecessor, it treats of battles, of sieges, of warriors, of the suffering and glory of war. A knowledge of Polish history is almost essential to the understanding of its intricate and long-drawn-out plot. In Pan Michael the story of Poland's struggle is continued and ended, its general lines being the same as those of the first two novels.

In the historical fiction of this century nothing approaches the trilogy of Sienkiewicz for magnificent breadth of canvas, for Titanic action, for an epical quality well-nigh Homeric. The author's characters are men of blood and iron, heroes of a great dead age, warriors that might have risen from huge stone tombs in old cathedrals to greet the sun again with eagle eyes. These novels as history can be best appreciated by Sienkiewicz's own countrymen, since they appeal to glorious memories, since they treat of the ancestors of the men to whom they are primarily addressed.

But the novels belong to the world; they are pre-eminent in the creation of characters, of humorous fighters, of women to be loved like the heroines of Shakespeare, and of such men as Zagloba, a creation to rank with Falstaff.

WITH THE PROCESSION, by Henry B. Fuller (1895), is a story of modern Chicago life, conceived in a gayer spirit than the author's painful study of 'The Cliff-Dwellers.' This tale occupies itself with the social rather than the business side of society, and takes upon itself the function of the old French comedy, — to criticise laughingly men and morals. The Marshalls belong to a family as old, for Chicago, as the Knickerbockers for New York or the Howards for England. They have had money for thirty years, and can count themselves as belonging to the *ancien noblesse* of the city, the race whose founders can remember the early settlers. But the father and mother have not taken advantage of their opportunities. They are old-fashioned people, who despise modern society because they do not understand it, and who keep on living in the primitive ways of forty years ago. The eldest son goes into business; the eldest daughter marries. on the social level of green rep furniture and Brussels carpets of floral design. The second daughter, Jane, full of energy, and ambition, wreaks herself on charities or clubs. But the younger son, Truesdell, is educated abroad; and the youngest daughter, Rosy, goes to school in New York. Truesdell returns home in a few years an alien; with a dilettante knowledge of music, art, and literature, and a set of ideas and ideals wholly Continental, and wholly foreign to anything his family has ever heard of. At the same time, Miss Rosamund Marshall emerges from school, a willful, shrewd, self-sufficient beauty, who is irrevocably determined to win a proud position in Chicago's best society. A new day dawns for the Marshall family: they can rusticate no longer amid the city's clangor; they must take their place "with the procession." Mrs. Granger Bates, the envied society leader, becomes their pilot, and they are fairly launched on the great social sea. The author's irony is pervasive but never bitter, though sometimes it gives us a sharp surprise. There is so much of tragedy as inheres in the deliberate choice of low aims and material successes over noble efforts and ends. Rosy makes the match she hopes for, sacrificing her family to it. Poor Mr. Marshall, who cannot keep up with the pace of the crowd, falls under their heedless and merciless feet. The character-drawing is admirable: Mrs. Granger Bates, the multi-millionaire who lives in a palace, keeps up all her accomplishments, and neither forgets nor conceals the happy days of her youth when she washed "Granger's" shirts and cooked his frugal dinners; Jane Marshall, the embodied common-sense and good feeling of feminine America; the pushing little widow, her aunt, determined to obtain social recognition; the cad, Truesdell; the pathetic, ineffectual "Pa"; the glaringly vulgar Mrs. Belden, — all these and a dozen more are as typical and indisputable as they are national, and impossible in any other land. The story is extremely entertaining, and carries conviction as an authentic picture of a certain phase of our chaotic life.

WITHOUT DOGMA, a novel of modern Polish high life, by Henryk Sienkiewicz (1891), was published in an English translation in 1893. Unlike his historical novels, this book has few characters. It is the history of a spiritual struggle, of "the battle of a man for his own soul." Leon Ploskowski, the hero, young, wealthy, and well-born, is of so overwrought a temperament that he is depressed by the very act of living: "Here is a nature so sensitive that it photographs every impression, an artistic temperament, a highly endowed organism; yet it produces nothing. The secret of this unproductiveness lies perhaps in a certain tendency to philosophize away every strong emotion that should lead to action." Leon tells his story himself, in the form of a journal. His relatives wish him to marry a beautiful young cousin, Aniela, who loves him with a whole-souled affection. Being sure of her love, he is disposed to delay his marriage, that he may have time to analyze his emotions in regard to her. While absent in Rome, he drifts into an unworthy passion for a married woman, a Mrs. Davis; yet, so peculiar is his temperament, the thought of Aniela is rarely absent from him. In the sultry air of passion, he longs for the freshness and fragrance of her purity. But even the knowledge that she is soon to be out of his reach does not steady his nobler purposes. The fortunes of her family being now at a low ebb, Aniela is forced into marriage with a rich Austrian, Kromitzki, a commonplace man incapable of appreciating her fine nature. So soon as she is thus out of reach, Leon, whose moral nature goes by contraries, becomes passionately in love with her, and tries with subtle art to make her untrue to her husband; but dear as Leon is to her, Aniela remains faithful to her marriage vows. Unlike Leon, she is not "without dogma." She clings to her simple belief in what is right throughout the long struggle. Her delicate organism cannot stand the strain of her spiritual sufferings. The death of her husband is soon followed by her own death.   In her last hours she tells Leon, as a little child might tell him, that she loves him "very, very much."   The last entry in his journal implies that he will follow her, that they may be one in oblivion, or in another life to come.   The journal of Leon Ploskowski reveals the wonderful insight of Sienkiewicz into a certain type of modern character.   The psychological value of the book is pre-eminent, presenting as it does a personality essentially the product of nineteenth-century conditions, — a personality upon which hyper-cultivation has acted as a subtle poison.

WIVES AND DAUGHTERS, by Mrs. Gaskell (1865).   This is a delightful story of country life in England.   It follows Molly Gibson through all the various experiences of her girlhood, beginning with her life as a child alone with her father, the doctor, in the village; describing her visits and friendships in the neighborhood, and finally after her father has married again, her new life with the second Mrs. Gibson and her daughter Cynthia.   The characters are unusually interesting and well drawn, with humor and sympathetic understanding.   There is the old Squire of the town, with his two sons: Osborne, the pride of his heart, who has married secretly beneath his social standing in life; and Roger, a fine, sturdy fellow, who bears the burdens of the family, and upon whom every one relies.   There is the great family at the Towers, the members of which patronize the villagers, and furnish them with food for speculation and gossip; and then, besides the doctor and his family, there is Miss Browning, Miss Phœbe, and the other funny old ladies of the town.   Mrs. Gibson's character is wonderfully depicted.   She is one of those delicate, yielding women, with an iron will carefully concealed; and she is diplomatic enough to feign a sweetness of disposition she does not possess.   She has little heart or sense of duty; and her child Cynthia, though fascinating and brilliant, is the sort of girl one would expect from careless bringing up and continued neglect.   Molly's untiring patience towards Mrs. Gibson, and her generous devotion to Cynthia, even at the expense of her own happiness, endear her to every one; and though Mrs. Gaskell died before the completion of the story, we are told that she intended Roger to marry Molly.   As Molly has long loved him, we may suppose that her troubles at length end happily.

WOMAN IN THE NINETEENTH CENTURY, by Margaret Fuller Ossoli (1844). A book of special interest from the remarkable character and intellectual ability of its author, and from the representative position which it holds as an early prophecy of the now broadly developed recognition of women as aspirants for culture, and as applicants equally with men for positions and privileges in the various fields of human activity.   After actively participating in the celebrated Brook Farm experiment of idealist socialism, where she thoroughly wrought out for herself new-departure convictions in religion, and having served a literary apprenticeship of note as a translator from the German, and as editor for two years of The Dial, a quarterly organ of New England Transcendentalism, she brought out in 1844 her 'Summer on the Lakes,' and the next year the 'Woman in the Nineteenth Century,' — a considerably enlarged reproduction of an essay by her in The Dial of October, 1843, where she had used the title, 'The Great Lawsuit; or, Man as Men, Woman as Women.' By adding a good deal to the article during a seven weeks' stay at Fishkill on the Hudson (to November 17, 1844), she made what was in effect a large pamphlet rather than a book adequately dealing with her subject, or at all representing her remarkable powers as they were shown in her 'Papers on Literature and Art.'   To do her justice, the book, which was her prophecy of a movement which the century is fulfilling, should be taken as a text, and her later thoughts brought together under it, to have as nearly as possible a full indication of what, under more favorable circumstances, her genius would have given to the world.

WOMAN IN WHITE, THE, an early and notable novel by Wilkie Collins, was published in 1873. Like his other works of fiction, it is remarkable for the admirable manner in which its intricate plot is worked out. The narrative is told by the different characters of the story in succession. The first narrator is Walter Hartright, a drawing-master, who has been employed by Mr. Frederick Fairlie of Limmeridge House, in Cumberland, England, to teach drawing to his niece, Laura Fairlie and her half-sister Marian Halcombe. Laura bears a strange resemblance to a woman who had accosted him on a lonely road near London, — a woman clothed entirely in white; who, he afterwards discovers, is an Anne Catherick, supposed to be half-witted, and, when he met her, just escaped from an asylum. In her childhood Anne had been befriended by Laura's mother, Mrs. Fairlie, because of her resemblance to Laura, and by her had been dressed in white, which Anne had worn ever since in memory of her benefactress. Hartright discovers also that there is some mystery in the girl's having been placed in an asylum by her own mother, without sufficient justification of the act.

Walter Hartright falls in love with Laura Fairlie; but she is betrothed to Sir Percival Glyde of Blackwater Park, Hampshire. Sir Percival has a close friend, Count Fosco, whose wife, a relative of Laura's, will receive ten thousand pounds on her death. The marriage settlements are drawn up so that Sir Percival himself, in the same event, will receive the whole of Laura's fortune. Laura had pledged her dead father to marry Sir Percival, but she has no love for him. Marian Halcombe goes with her to Blackwater Park. There, in the form of a diary, she carries on the narrrative where Walter Hartright discontinued it. A plot is hatched by Count Fosco, who is a strong villain, and by Sir Percival, who is a weak one, to get Laura out of the way and obtain her money, by taking advantage of the resemblance between her and Anne Catherick, who at the time is very ill. By a series of devices Laura is brought to London, and put into an asylum as Anne Catherick; while the dying Anne Catherick is called Lady Glyde, and after her death buried as Lady Glyde. These events are told by the various actors in the drama. By the efforts of Marian, who does not believe that her sister is dead, she is rescued from the asylum. Walter Hartright, seeking to expose Sir Percival's villainy, discovers that he is sharing a secret with Anne Catherick's mother; that Anne knew the secret, and had therefore been confined in an asylum by the pair: the secret being that Sir Percival had no right to his title, having been born out of wedlock. Before Hartright can expose this fraud, Sir Percival himself is burned to death, while tampering with the register of the church for his own interest. In the general clearing-up of affairs, it becomes known that the Woman in White was the half-sister of Laura, being the natural child of her father Philip Fairlie.

The story ends with the happy marriage of Laura to Hartright, and with the restoration of her property.

WOMAN KILLED WITH KINDNESS, A, by Thomas Heywood (1603). Of this writer Lamb speaks as "a sort of prose Shakespeare: his scenes are to the full as natural and affecting. But we miss the Poet, that which in Shakespeare always appears out and above the surface of the nature." Though later critics than Lamb are less enthusiastic in their praise, all accord to Heywood the merit of naturalness and pathos. 'A Woman killed with Kindness' has been called by Symonds "the finest bourgeois tragedy of our Elizabethan literature." Heywood discusses the problem of the unfaithful wife in a way very unusual in Elizabethan drama, and arrives at a solution not out of accord with modern ethics and sentiment. Master Frankford, an English gentleman, wealthy, cultured and well connected has married the sister of Sir Francis Acton, who as he supposes is "a fair, a chaste, and loving wife; perfection all, all truth, all ornament." Wendell, well-born but unfortunate and poor, is generously treated by Sir Francis, and basely requites his patron's confidence by debauching his wife, who gave way rather from weakness than sinfulness. Instead of taking her life, Frankford resolves to "kill her even with kindness," and sends her loaded with every provision for her needs to a lonely manor-house, but forbids her to look on him or on her children again. Solitude and remorse break her heart, but, as she lies on her deathbed, the husband whom she had sent for to ask his forgiveness gives her his blessing.

WOMAN MOVEMENT, THE, by Ellen Key, was published in Swedish in 1909, and in an English translation by Mamah Bonton Borthwick in 1912. After tracing the gradual emancipation of woman from the extension of her civil rights, through her admission to equal educational advantages and to most vocations open to men, to her approaching achievement of the right to vote, the author goes on to point out the need of further liberation of a spiritual kind, her idea being that woman should have the right to the free development of her nature without conformation to masculine standards. For this consummation certain socialistic alterations in the organization of society would be necessary, giving woman, if she desires it, a right to motherhood and adequate opportunity to rear her children. Some interesting observations as to the effect of the emancipation of woman upon the comradeship of young people, upon the relations of man and wife, and upon those of mother and daughter, conclude a stimulating and timely study.

WOMAN OF NO IMPORTANCE, A, by Oscar Wilde (1893). This successful drama is more remarkable for the brilliance of its dialogue than for the coherence and credibility of its plot. Twenty years before the play begins, Lord Illingworth, then George Harford, betrayed an innocent girl, whom he had promised to marry. The girl, to him, was "a woman of no importance." Her son, Gerald Arbuthnot, an underpaid bank clerk in a provincial town, meets Lord Illingworth, who takes a fancy to him, and offers to make him his secretary. Mrs. Arbuthnot recognizes the man who as George Harford ruined her life, and refuses her consent to her son's appointment. Gerald cannot understand her change of mind, and is unwilling to give up this promising opportunity. Lord Illingworth tells her that he considers Gerald's future more important than her past, and dares her to tell her son the truth. She tells Gerald her own story as that of another woman, but his answer is to condemn the woman. "No really nice girl," he says, "would go away from home with a man to whom she was not married." Gerald argues that he will be in a position to ask Hester, the American girl he loves, to marry him. Mrs. Arbuthnot withdraws objection rather than give her real reason. One of the guests at this week end house party has dared Lord Illingworth to kiss the puritanical Hester. Hester rushes in from the terrace crying out to Gerald that Lord Illingworth has insulted her. Gerald, beside himself with anger, springs at Lord Illingworth. "Don't hold me mother," he cries. "I'll kill him." His mother stops him with the confession that Lord Illing-

worth is his father. Gerald's first idea is that Lord Illingworth must make reparation by marrying his mother. She refuses to consider the hideous mockery of such a
marriage. While Hester and Gerald are in the garden, Lord Illingworth comes to
Mrs. Arbuthnot to try to make arrangements to keep his son. He offers to marry
her, but she tells him he has come too late. When the lovers return Gerald asks his
mother if she has had a visitor. She replies, "No one in particular, A man of no
importance."

WOMAN THOU GAVEST ME, THE, by Hall Caine (1913). The father of Mary
O'Neill, bitterly disappointed that she is not a son to inherit the title and property
of Lord Raa of Castle Raa, wholly neglects her. Her mother is an invalid and the
child is unkindly treated by her Aunt Bridget who has charge of the household. When
she is seven years old she is sent to a convent in Rome, and remains there until she is
eighteen, only once being allowed to visit her island home. It is her mother's dying
wish that she should become a nun, but her father suddenly takes her away and
proposes to marry her, against her wishes, to the distant cousin who has become
Lord Raa. Before she leaves Rome she meets her childhood friend, Martin Conrad,
who is about to sail on an expedition to the Antartic. He tries to prevent the marriage, but in vain. Lord Raa and his bride start on their honeymoon in a raging storm
which is symbolical of their married life. Mary refuses to allow her husband to
come near her. Lord Raa despatches a messenger to her father, who sends her Aunt
Bridget and the priest, Father Dan, to reason with her. It is finally arranged that
Lord Raa shall not force her to obey him until she comes to love him. On the steamer
going to Marseilles they meet Alma Lier, an American girl, who had been at the
convent with Mary and is now a handsome, fashionably attired woman, the divorced
wife of a bogus Russian count. Alma plans Mary's ruin. After endless mortifying
experiences in various cities, Mary and her husband return home to Castle Raa, where
Lord Raa plans to have a house-party and Alma is invited. While in London Mary
tries to see if she can secure a divorce from Lord Raa, but neither Church nor State
will countenance it. She meets Martin again, and Lord Raa invites him to visit
them. Alma plans that while the rest of the party are away on a yachting cruise,
Mary and Martin shall be left together. Martin begs Mary to flee with him, and
defy the law. She refuses and he leaves her to go on his expedition to the South
Pole.

Some weeks later while Lord Raa is in London Alma discovers Mary's delicate
condition and announces it to Lord Raa and Mary's father. The father is delighted
and plans a great celebration. Lord Raa is furious, charges Mary with being unfaithful to him and strikes her. Mary decides to flee the castle and with the help of
her maid leaves that very night and goes to London with very little money. She keeps
in hiding, but hears the report that Martin's ship has been lost. No maternity
hospital in London will take her without knowing the name of the prospective child's
father, so she has to remain in cheap lodgings with insufficient food and care. After
the birth of the baby girl she boards her with a poor woman and works day and night
sewing for a greedy Jew. When the Jew discovers that she has a baby he discharges
her. The baby sickens from lack of care and from soothing-syrups and Mary is in
despair. Half-crazed she dresses up in her one fine gown still remaining and goes out
on the street. As she wanders about she falls into the arms of Martin, who has returned and had been searching all London for her. Mary is unconscious for two days.
By means of a letter found in her pocket the baby is recovered, is taken to a good
home in the country, and is restored to health. Mary is taken back to her island

home, to Martin's father, who is a doctor. Lord Raa obtains a divorce from her and marries Alma. Martin is knighted by the king and plans to marry Mary and take her to the Antarctic with him, but the exposure and deprivations she has undergone prove too much for her, and she dies before the time for him to leave.

WOMEN, see **SUBJECTION OF WOMEN,** by J. S. Mill.

WOMEN, VINDICATION OF THE RIGHTS OF, by Mary Wollstonecraft, see **VINDICATION, ETC.**

WONDERFUL ADVENTURES OF NILS, THE, by Selma Lagerlöf (1906). A cruel selfish boy is changed into an elf as punishment for a mischievous trick. He travels on the back of a goose with the wild ducks all over Norway, learning kindness and helpfulness in fellowship with the birds and animals, his friends. This fairy tale is the result of years of study of animal and bird life by the author to make an interesting nature book for the public schools. She has woven legend and folktales into the story of little Nils' journey, which has become a children's classic. As "Thumtietot" the elf, he sees farms, manors, castles, cities, logging camps, and mines, and has thrilling adventures with bears and eagles and reindeer. At the end of the sequel 'Further Adventures of Nils' (1907) he returns home and finds himself a human boy again when he knocks at the cottage door.

WONDERFUL MAGICIAN, THE, 'El Magico Prodigioso,' a drama by Pedro Calderón de la Barca, first published in 1637. The theme is the martyrdom of Saint Cyprian and Saint Justina in Antioch, 290 A.D. Cyprian, a noted scholar of Antioch, is visited by a demon, in human guise who attempts to entangle him by a discussion of the nature of God. Finding this vain he determines to attain the ruin of Cyprian by inspiring him with love for Justina, a poor Christian girl already the subject of Satanic temptations. An occasion is presented when Lelius, son of the governor, and Florus enter and proceed to fight a duel for her hand. Cyprian intervenes in the dispute and proposes to go to the lady as intermediary. On his arrival at the house of her foster-father, Lysander, he promptly falls in love with her himself and is as promptly rejected, the lady having fixed her affections only on Heaven. The demon now causes trouble by appearing in the form of a man descending from her window in the sight of Lelius and Florus, who have come up from different directions to watch her house, and each of whom takes the intruder for the other. Encouraged by their withdrawal from the suit of one whom they now believe wanton, Cyprian, in handsome clothes, again wooes Justina and is again rejected. In desperation he declares that he would willingly sell his soul to possess Justina, and is at once confronted by the demon in the form of a magician, who makes a formal contract with him, sealed in blood, to give him Justina in exchange for his soul. To compass his desires a year of instruction in a subterranean cavern is necessary; and at the end of that time Cyprian prepares his spells to draw Justina to his embraces. The demon by a chorus of spirits and by violence attempts to bring her in person. She appears touched at first but her virtue and Christian principles come to her aid and she not only rejects his advances but successfully resists his attempts to carry her off. The demon then has recourse to illusion, creating a phantom figure of Justina which responds to Cyprian's invocations. But by divine grace it turns to a skeleton just as he is about to embrace it. Cyprian is profoundly stirred and repentant, as he realizes that it is the Christian God who has saved Justina and who may yet save him. Meanwhile the Christians are arrested while at worship, Justina among the rest; and the governor who fears her influence over his son, condemns her to death. Cyprian appears at her side, relates his commerce with the demon and his salvation from his compact, avows himself a Christian, and goes forth to martyrdom with Justina.

An incongruous comic interlude is furnished by the rivalry of Cyprian's two servants for the hand of Justina's maid and the bargain by which each is to have her on alternate days.

In its piety, exaltation of personal honour, and fine lyrical passages the play is characteristic of Calderón.

WONDERFUL YEAR, THE, by W. J. Locke (1915). The wonderful year is the year before the war. Martin Overshaw, the hero, is an impecunious young English schoolmaster. In Paris for the first time for a holiday, he meets the equally impecunious Corinna. As they sit at dinner in a little restaurant in the Latin quarter, Corinna confesses that though she has studied art for three years she "cannot paint worth a cent," that she has spent all her money, and has to go home to England. Corinna calls to the table a newcomer, Mr. Daniel Fortinbras, whom she introduces to Martin as a "Marchand de Bonheur," a dealer in happiness at five francs a consultation. They ask his advice as "candidates for happiness." He sends them off on a bicycle trip together to his brother-in-law, Bigourdin the innkeeper at Brantôme. This unconventional prescription does not cause the hero and heroine to fall in love as they should. Corinna returns to England to become a failure as a professional suffragette, since her enthusiasm is not sufficient for imprisonment and hunger strikes. Martin remains at the inn as waiter and friend of Bigourdin and his lovely niece, Félise, rather than return to the drudgery of teaching the "drybones of examination French." He is led away from the inn by the lure of an American guest, Lucilla Merriton, and on the last of his savings becomes a fashionable tourist in Egypt. Failing to win Lucilla, he starts back by steerage via Hongkong and India and arrives in France just as war is declared. He finds he has really left his heart at the inn with Félise and at the end of the wonderful year, he enlists with Bigourdin to fight for France. The last chapter of the story takes him back to Félise, a hero with an empty sleeve. Corinna receives a love letter from Bigourdin wounded at the front, discovers her heart, and goes to him and then to Brantôme to await his homecoming. The "Marchand de Bonheur" gives his blessing to the happy couples.

WOODSTOCK, by Sir Walter Scott (1826). 'Woodstock' is an English historical novel of the time of Cromwell; the events occurring in the year 1652, immediately after the battle of Worcester. The scene is laid chiefly in the Royal Park and Manor of Woodstock, — "Fair Rosamond's bower." In addition to King Charles II., disguised as Louis Kerneguy, a Scotch page, the leading personages are Sir Henry Lee, the royal ranger of the Park; his son Albert, a royalist colonel; his daughter Alice; and Colonel Markham Everard, who is high in favor with Cromwell. The Lees and Everards have been intimate friends before the war separated them politically; and Markham and Alice are lovers. Other principal actors are Roger Wildrake, a dissipated but brave and loyal Cavalier; Joceline Joliffe the underkeeper, and his pretty sweetheart Phœbe Mayflower; and Joseph (miscalled "Trusty") Tomkins, a Cromwellite soldier and spy. The story opens with service of a warrant by Tomkins upon Sir Henry Lee, ordering him to surrender the Park Lodge to a Parliamentary Commission, charged with sequestrating the property. Colonel Everard sends Wildrake to Cromwell, and procures the revocation of the order. Dr. Rochecliffe, a scheming royalist, is in hiding in the secret passages with which the Lodge is honey-combed, and terrifies the commissioners with nocturnal noises and other annoyances, which they believe to be the work of the Devil; and they gladly withdraw. Colonel Albert Lee arrives with Charles disguised as his page; and Alice's loyal devotion to the King, coupled with the gift of a ring from him, arouses Everard's jealousy. He challenges his Majesty; the duel is prevented by Alice, but in such a manner as further to inflame Everard and confirm his suspicions. To save Alice's honor and happiness, the King avows his identity, throwing himself upon the honor of Everard, who accepts the trust. Tomkins is soon after killed by Joliffe for undue familiarity with Phœbe; but has already made reports which bring Cromwell to the spot with a detachment of soldiers. The King and Albert exchange clothes, and the former escapes, leaving Albert to simulate him. Cromwell besieges and storms the Lodge and captures Albert, but the delay has saved King Charles. Cromwell is furious at the successful deception, but finally relents, and releases Albert, who goes abroad, where he subsequently dies in battle. Everard and Alice are married. The book ends with a sort of epilogue, in which Sir Henry, old in years and honors, presents himself at the triumphal progress of Charles at the Restoration, eight years later; he is recognized and affectionately greeted by the King, and passes away in the shock of his loyal joy, murmuring *Nunc dimittis.*

WOOLMAN, JOHN, 'A Journal of the Life, Gospel, Labours, and Christian Experiences of John Woolman' was published in 1774. Woolman was born in Northampton, New Jersey, in 1720. Becoming an earnest member of the Society of Friends in 1721 he devoted his life to religious exhortation, travelling from one settlement to another and supporting himself by work as a tailor or a merchant's clerk. He married in 1749 and until 1756 kept a store at Northampton, though his principal concern was for his missionary journeys. Having won considerable influence in the Society he undertook in 1772 a voyage to England, where he visited various Quaker meetings. He died of small-pox in the city of York, October 7, 1772. Woolman's journal is characterized by absolute simplicity and sincerity. The language is plain and unadorned and there is an utter absence of pose, of garrulousness, and of striving for picturesqueness of effect. Quiet humility, delicate consideration for others, and unaffected sense of the divine presence breathe through every line of the book. Another characteristic is a sensitiveness though not a morbidity of conscience and a quiet moral resoluteness in following its dictates. Woolman disapproved of slavery as an institution, did all that he could to discourage it among the Quakers, and refused to countenance it in any way, direct or indirect. He had a similar feeling towards the exploitation of the poor and the use of luxuries and scrupulously avoided any action which might in any way be interpreted as encouraging such wrong-doing. For instance, he refused to sell merchandise of a frivolous or unnecessary kind, and he shipped to England in the steerage because the cabin accommodations seemed to him needlessly luxurious. His piety is without fanaticism or hypocrisy and the record of it is one of the most attractive of Christian biographies.

WORK, see **ROUGON-MACQUART.**

WORKERS, THE, by Walter A. Wyckoff (1897-99). These remarkable personal reminiscences describe the experiences of a young college graduate who in order to solve for himself some of the social problems of the day, goes out into the world in the guise of a day laborer. He starts from Philadelphia without money in his pocket and only the clothes upon his back, and prepares to work his way across the country in the rôle he has assumed. 'The Workers' is in two volumes and in the first entitled 'The East,' we are told of the difficulties attending the adjustment of the writer to his new conditions, and are given a detailed account of his experiences as a day laborer, a hotel porter, a hired man, and a farm hand. The first volume closes with a description of his life in a logging camp, and in this first part of his work he has dealt entirely with rural conditions; he has been a laborer in an un-crowded market and has been in close contact with poverty, but not despair. In his second volume, however, entitled 'The West,' he gives a graphic picture of the misery and suffering of the vast army of the unemployed in the crowded labor mar-ket of Chicago, and his own experiences are most thrilling. As a factory hand he has a chance to study organized labor in a big factory, he analyzes the social dis-content of the anarchists, and works as a road builder on the grounds of the World's Fair. He works his way to California through the great wheat farms, toils in the mines, and drives a burro across the desolate plains. After a year and a half spent amongst these conditions, the author reaches his destination, the Pacific coast; his experiment is at an end and one of the most striking narratives ever written by a scholar comes to a close.

WORLD AS WILL AND IDEA, THE, a philosophical treatise by Arthur Schopen-hauer, first published in four books in 1819, and enlarged in the editions of 1844 and 1859 by chapters supplementary to each of these books. Beginning with Kant's theory of the purely subjective character of our acquaintance with the world he proceeds to inquire whether it is not possible to determine the nature of reality. And he answers that the fundamental fact in the universe is *will*. This will is a blind, unconscious tendency to live and propagate itself, inherent in everything, animate and inanimate, in nature, in the mineral, vegetable, and animal kingdoms, and in all the physical processes of man's body, and arises to consciousness only in his deliberate acts. But, inasmuch as all life is full of rapine, cruelty, and suffering, and of desires the satisfaction of which brings nothing but new desires, disillusion, or *ennui*, this instinctive will to live is an evil. It may be overcome in two ways: by means of the enjoyment of art which is the representation and contemplation of the idea of the beautiful which the world is trying to express, and which lifts man into a serene passionless atmosphere; or by the denial of the struggle for existence, the renunciation of all desires, and the attainment of a state of peaceful resignation akin to the Buddhist *Nirvana*. A fuller statement of Schopenhauer's philosophy is given in the introduction to the extracts in the LIBRARY and in the extracts them-selves. Kant, Plato, and the Hindu religious writings are named by the philosopher as the three chief influences which helped to fashion his thought. His brilliant originality, unusual range of information and culture, and exceptional literary gifts make him one of the most widely-read of philosophers. His pessimism reflected certain prevalent tendencies of nineteenth-century thought but had had less influ-ence on philosophic development than his doctrine that everything is reducible to a manifestation of will. This latter doctrine is developed by Hartmann, Nietzsche, and the Pragmatists.

WRECK OF THE GROSVENOR, THE, by W. Clark Russell (1874). This story of the British merchant marine is notable amongst sea novels for its fidelity to the life, some phases of which it vividly portrays; and is the best by this author. The story is told by the second mate of the ship Grosvenor; and it relates the causes of dissatisfaction amongst the crew, and the harsh treatment of the men by a brutal and inhuman captain and chief mate. The troubles reach their climax in a mutiny, in which the captain and mate are killed by the crew. The mutineers finally desert the ship near the coast of America, and are lost in a gale. The ship also goes to the bottom; but the second mate and the few who were faithful to him are rescued when almost at the last gasp, by a passing steamer.

The gallant rescue from a sinking vessel in mid-ocean, of a beautiful and wealthy young lady with her father, brings into the story the necessary element of romance, and provides the second mate with a satisfactory partner for life.

The chief value of the book lies in the fact that it deals in a plain, straightforward manner, and without exaggeration, with some of the most glaring evils of the mercantile marine. Events like those recorded are familiar to every man who sailed the seas during the middle and even the latter part of this century, and they show to what an extent the power given by the law may be abused when placed in the hands of ignorant and brutal officers.

'The Wreck of the Grosvenor' is said to have been a powerful factor in reforming the laws relating to the merchant seamen in Great Britain. Apart from its humanitarian motives, it is interesting for the excellent descriptions with which the sailor has to deal.

WRECKER, THE, by Robert Louis Stevenson, was written in collaboration with his stepson, Lloyd Osborne, when the author was a little over forty, and published in 1891–92. It is one of the best of Stevenson's adventure stories, and full of exciting incident, quick action, and vivid characterization. The scene is modern, and shifts from land to sea. Preliminary chapters depict student life in Paris; but the main story begins in San Francisco, with the purchase of the wrecked ship Flying Scud by Loudon Dodd and Jim Pinkerton, and with their voyage in quest of its supposed treasure. No treasure, but a ghastly tragedy, is revealed as the tale goes on. The Flying Scud has been sunk and her name changed, in order to hide a wholesale murder, while her crew have assumed the names of the doomed men for the same reason. The unraveling of the dark mystery is most ingeniously conducted, and the sea life and the pirate spirit are indicated with gusto and vigor. So cunningly is the plot constructed that not until the very end is the key furnished. The characters of several of the seamy mariners, and especially that of Pinkerton, a typical western American with no end of energy and brass, are capitally drawn.

WUTHERING HEIGHTS, the one novel written by Emily Brontë and the work which exhibited the remarkable quality of her genius was published in December, 1847, only a year before her death, when she was twenty-eight years old. The scene of the tale is laid in the rugged moorland country in the north of England, with which she was familiar from childhood; the persons are drawn from types only to be found perhaps in that country,—outlandish characters in whom gentility and savagery are united. The hero of 'Wuthering Heights' is Heathcliff, a man of stormy, untrained nature, brought as a child to Wuthering Heights, the home of the Earnshaw family, by Mr. Earnshaw, who had picked him up as a stray in the streets of Liverpool. He is reared with Earnshaw's two children, Hindley and Catherine; for the latter he conceives an intense affection, the one gleam of light in his dark nature. Catherine returns his love; but Hindley hates him. Hindley is sent away to college, but returns on his father's death, bringing with him a wife, who afterwards dies at the birth of a son, Hareton. Catherine meanwhile has made the acquaintance of Edgar and Isabel Linton, gentleman's children, living at Thrushcross Grange, not far from Wuthering Heights. In course of time Catherine marries Edgar, though she loves Heathcliff. Isabel falls in love with Heathcliff, who marries her in the hope of revenging himself thereby on the Linton family. His cruel treatment drives her from him. She gives birth to a son, Linton; Catherine to a daughter, Catherine. The elder Catherine's death is precipitated by Heathcliff's stormy avowal of his continuing passion for her. Long after her death he plans to marry his son Linton to Catherine's daughter, because he hates them both, children as they are of marriages that should never have been. In this he is successful; but Linton dies, leaving Catherine a very young widow in the house of her dreadful father-in-law. Hareton Earnshaw, Hindley's son, and another object of Heathcliff's hate, is also one of the household. With the death of Heathcliff, and the union of Hareton and Catherine, the story ends. Heathcliff is buried by the side of his beloved Catherine. The greater part of the narrative is related by Nellie, the housekeeper at Thrushcross Grange, the old nurse in the Earnshaw family. Among the minor characters is Joseph, a servant in the same family, whose eccentric character is drawn with marvelous skill. The entire book remains a monument of unmodified power,—of strength without sweetness. Only at the close of the book, the tempest ceases, revealing for a moment the quiet spaces of the evening sky. The one to whom the strange troubled story had been related, seeks the graves of Heathcliff and Catherine:

"I lingered round them under a benign sky; watched the moths fluttering among the heath and harebells; listened to the soft wind breathing through the grass; and wondered how any one could ever imagine unquiet slumbers for the sleepers in that quiet earth."

YEMASSEE, THE: 'a Romance of Carolina,' by William Gilmore Sims (1835). This is an American romance, the leading events of which are strictly true. The Yemassee are a powerful and gallant race of Indians, dwelling, with their tributary tribes, at the time of the action, in South Carolina. Their hunting grounds are gradually encroached upon by the English colonists, who, by purchases, seizures, and intrigues, finally change the feeling of friendship with which their advent was greeted, into fear, and finally into savage revolt. It is during this period of war-fare (the early part of the eighteenth century) that the scene of the romance is laid. Mingled with the description of the life of the primitive red man is a stirring account of the struggles of the early colonists. The romance culminates in a realistic account of the attack by the Yemassee, in conjunction with neighboring tribes and Spanish allies, upon a small band of colonists, who, after a fierce conflict, finally defeat them. Interwoven with the scenes of savage cruelty, Spanish intrigue, and colonial hardship, is the love story of pretty Bess Matthews, daughter of the pastor, and Gabriel Harrison, the savior of the little band; who later, as Charles Craven, Governor and Lord Palatine of Carolina, claims her hand. If the narrative seems often extravagant in its multiplicity of adventures, hair-breadth escapes, thrilling climaxes, and re-current dangers, it is to be remembered that it depicts a time when adventure was the rule, and routine the exception; when death lurked at every threshold, and life was but a daily exemplification of the "survival of the fittest."

Some of the principal characters are Sanutee, chief of the Yemassee; Matiwan, his wife; Occonestoga, his son, slain for betrayal of his tribe; Richard Chorley, the buccaneer; and the trader Granger, and his wife,—the latter a type of the woman, brave in spirit and keen of wit, whom the early colonies developed.

YESTERDAY, TO-DAY, AND FOREVER, 'a poem in twelve books,' by Edward Henry Bickersteth (1866). A work in blank verse, 10,750 lines in length, devoted to imaginative journeyings after death in Hades, Paradise, and Hell, with a review of creation, the Fall, the empire of darkness, redemption, the war against Satan, the victory over Satan, the millennial Sabbath, the Last Judgment, and heaven's many mansions. The author, who was made bishop of Exeter in 1885, has been in his generation, as his father was in the previous generation, a chief representative in the Church of England of profoundly Evangelical, anti-Romanist, and anti-liberal, pietism and teaching,—a very emotional and earnest pietism and intensely orthodox Low Church teaching. The 'Christian Psalmody,' compiled by the father in 1832, which went through 59 editions in seven years, was the most popular hymn-book of the Evangelical school in the Church. The 'Hymnal Companion,' prepared by the son (final revised and enlarged edition, 1876), is in use in thousands of churches in England and the colonies. It was to impressively invoke divine and eternal auspices for the doctrines and pietism of the Evangelical party, and to feed Evangelical faith and enthusiasm, that the younger Bickersteth, with Dante and Milton in view, essayed his ambitious task, and executed it with very fair success, at least as to teaching and emotion.

YESTERDAYS WITH AUTHORS, by James T. Fields. With the exception of Miss Mitford's letters and some paragraphs of other matters, the contents of this book first appeared in the Atlantic Monthly, during the year 1871, in a series of papers called 'Our Whispering Gallery.' The 'Yesterdays' are spent with Pope, Thackeray, Hawthorne, Dickens, Wordsworth, and Miss Mitford. With all but the first of these Fields had a personal acquaintance; with Hawthorne, Thackeray, and Dickens, a warm friendship which lasted until their deaths. The relation between publisher and author is of a delicate nature, having in it elements of mutual interest and enforced intimacy; when to this is added the tie of kindred mind and personal predilection, the record of it is noteworthy. The title is particularly applicable to the subject-matter. The remembrance of the day before is so potent in the present; yesterday and to-day are so allied in sentiment, that in reading these charming recollections, conversations, letters, anecdotes of work and play, one feels that the veil has been withdrawn, and those to whom we owe so much entertainment and instruction are still with us, not merely portraits in a picture gallery revivified by the touch of the artist. The author's recollections of Dickens are exceptionally interesting. To him is accorded a major portion of the book, as in life was accorded a greater share of time and affection.

YONE SANTO, 'a Child of Japan,' by Edward H. House (1888). This pathetic little story of life in Tokio appeared first in the Atlantic Monthly, and met with much favor. Its author was an American journalist and critic long resident in Japan. Yone Santo is a lovely Japanese girl, with a thirst for knowledge, and a genius for self-sacrifice rare in any country. The victim of cruel tyranny in her own home she wins the compassionate interest of Dr. Charwell, who helps her to get an education, and tries to shield her from the misdirected zeal of certain women missionaries. Brought up to accept without question the authority of her older relatives, the gentle Yone had been married to a coarse, ignorant old boat-builder; and afterwards she meets the handsome young Bostonian, Arthur Milton, who wins her love for his own careless pleasure. Her childlike confidence in the good doctor saves her from trusting herself to Milton's treacherous schemes, and she lives out her short though **not**

unhappy life under the protection of her Western friends. Her lover, penitent and remorseful, returns to receive her dying blessing; and at last this long-suffering white-souled little pagan saint found rest.

The story excited resentment for its bitter arraignment of missionaries.

YOUTH'S ENCOUNTER, see **SINISTER STREET.**

YUCATAN, TRAVELS IN, see **CENTRAL AMERICA, INCIDENTS OF TRAVEL IN,** by J. L. Stephens.

ZARATHUSTRA, see **THUS SPAKE ZARATHUSTRA.**

ZEND-AVESTA, THE, see **SACRED BOOKS OF THE EAST.**

ZINCALI, THE, by George Borrow. This account of the gipsies of Spain appeared in England in 1842, and quickly ran through three editions. Borrow evinced in early life a roving disposition and linguistic ability. In 1835, at the age of thirty-two, he undertook to act as the agent of the British and Foreign Bible Society in Spain, and accomplished his perilous mission with the devotion of an apostle and the audacity of a stage brigand. He was all things to all men, especially to gipsies; and in 'The Bible in Spain,' his first book, he relates his amusing and interesting adventures. 'The Zincali' grew out of this journey, and deals with the gipsies alone. The charm of the book, which is full of anecdote, lies in its graphic fidelity. The Spanish gipsy, as described by Mr. Borrow, differs in many respects from the gipsy of romance. His hardihood and wretched mode of life; his virtues, his faults; his devotion to family and kindred; and his inveterate dishonesty, are faithfully portrayed. The very same gipsy woman, who, being waylaid and robbed, is heroic and unconquerable, in defense of her own virtue, and, stripped of her property, makes her weary journey 200 miles on foot with her poor children, is absolutely vile in leading others into infamy to recoup her finances. A chapter on gipsies in various lands depicts the universal gipsy, the product of the mysterious East. Mr. Borrow gives many illustrations of his popularity with the gipsies; one at Novgorod, where one sentence spoken by him in Romany brings out a joyful colony of gipsies in song and loving greeting. His love of adventure, of unconventional human life, and of philology, went hand in hand and reinforced each other.

ZURY; THE MEANEST MAN IN SPRING COUNTY, a Novel of Western Life, by Joseph Kirkland (1887). 'Zury' is a tale of the life and society, of the struggles, reverses, and disappointments, of those who, at the period immediately preceding our Civil War, journeyed in prairie schooners to the settlement of the great West.

The story is almost entirely in the form of dialogue—the peculiar patois of the backwoods—and of such a construction that it must be followed word for word for the successful unraveling of the plot. There are no tiresome descriptions, and but little narrative, where one so usually finds a résumé of what has passed and a brief prospectus of what he may expect; so that the careless reader, who glances at the beginning, takes a peep or two at the middle, and then carefully studies the last two chapters, will certainly find himself quite nonplussed.

Zury (an abbreviation for Usury) Prowder arrives, while still a child, in the wild forests of Illinois, there to grow up with the country. One by one his little sister

his father, and mother give up and die; but still the boy continues to live on, and in
the end carves riches out of poverty.   To do this he has suffered extreme privations,
and reduced the science of economy to such a degree that he has earned the distinction of being the meanest man in the county.   At the juncture when Zury owns
half the town, and holds mortgages on the other half; when he is the whole municipal government and most of the board of public education, a young woman from
Boston, Miss Ann Sparrow, appears upon the scene to take charge of the "deestrict"
school.   Henceforth the interest in the two is paramount, and through the now
humorous, now pathetic struggles of the girl, at first for recognition, then for success,
we see of what delightfully superficial nature Zury's meanness was after all; and
once more find an illustration of the wonders that a little of the sweetness and light
which accompany education may accomplish, even in the wilderness.

SUPPLEMENT

SUPPLEMENT

THE READER'S DIGEST OF BOOKS

ABLE McLAUGHLINS, THE, by Margaret Wilson (1923). The McLaughlin clan live in the Iowa prairie. Wully McLaughlin was a member of a Union regiment in the Civil War. Half of the regiment had been made prisoners and on the march toward a train, Wully is left lying helpless by the roadside, a guard over him, waiting for the wagon to pick them up. He makes his escape and reaches his home. Five families of Covenanting Scotch in the neighborhood were deserting the principles of their forefathers and taking out naturalization papers, hoping to "vote for Lincoln." Wully begins to help in the fall ploughing. He meets Chirstie, a girl he had known, and tells her that she is his "lassie." He receives a notice asking the scattered men of his regiment and paroled soldiers to report at headquarters. After three months in the hospitals, he is discharged and returns home. "Five years ago, he had gone away a strong, high-spirited lad, and now he dragged himself brokenly around the dooryard, the wreck of a man." Peter Keith is a cousin of Chirstie's and also of Wully's — "the smallest adult of Wully's seventy-one cousins . . . and by far the most worthless of them." While Wully was in the hospital, Peter has betrayed Chirstie. Wully suspicions it and Peter admits it. Wully's first impulse is to kill him, but he decides that this would only make Chirstie notorious. "The way he saw was better than that." Peter had always been talking about running away to the West. "A situation hideous forced upon them, a thing which had to be faced out, like the war, from which there was no escape but victory. If he got rid of Peter, why should he not have her [Chirstie]?" He manages to see Peter. "He spoke to his cousin only a few sentences. . . . Then he turned, and rode swiftly away." He came to Chirstie's. "I know the whole thing!" he whispered. "I've got it all settled. . . . It's all right. He'll never frighten you again. You can't get away. I've come for you!" At their marriage, Chirstie falters in her responses and faints at the end of the ceremony. After her marriage, she dreads the time when the truth about herself will be known, but she and Wully go to live with his family — his mother and father and "the hilarious young McLaughlins." "Her life expanded in all directions to make room for the three great loves that came to her — the first and greatest, her redeeming husband, the second, her little son, and the third, her mother-in-law, who overcame her by the most insidious kindness, by such a simplicity that the charitableness of her deeds became apparent only upon later reflection." But Chirstie, the more that her appreciation for her mother-in-law deepened, the more intolerable did the deception become, and she begs Wully to tell the truth. He is impatient with her — insists that they leave things as they are. The secret must be kept even from his mother. The only thing that could make him hate Chirstie would be for her to betray him, now after it was all over. A few days before her confinement, Peter's mother, who is Chirstie's "Aunt Libby," returns from Chicago, where she had gone, hoping to find tidings of Peter who had never communicated with any of his family.

Libby's husband had been told by a stranger that he had seen Peter in a livery stable in Chicago. Failing to find Peter, Libby comes home again, pouring out her restlessness to Isobel McLaughlin, Wully's mother, and to Chirstie. After she goes, Chirstie gives way to tears and tells her mother-in-law that her baby is not Wully's. She begs her not to let Wully know that she has told the truth at last. Isobel decides that Peter is the father of the child and tells her husband. Both of them accept the situation with thanks to God that it was not Wully that had done "so ill a thing." They think that it was a grand thing for him to have married Chirstie — "She's a good girl — we'll have to just bide our time. But I'm glad I've no son like that lad Peter!" Chirstie's baby is born, and while the infamy of her condition has become known, it had scarcely been less interesting than "the scandal of Isobel McLaughlin's attitude towards it." Wully and Chirstie and their "bonny wee Johnnie" move into their new house. "The baby had just naturally become Wully's child." Then Peter returns and goes to see Chirstie. Her husband is in the fields, and she runs screaming to him. She tells him that Peter came to the door and laid hands on her. She shows him her torn sleeve. "Rage came over him like a fever mounting." He could not believe that Peter had so underestimated him as to return. He had been a fool to let him go unpunished. But all he needed was one more chance at him. "He lusted for his gun." He returns with Chirstie to the house, but they find no trace of Peter. But John, Wully's younger brother, has seen Peter — "drinking away as usual at O'Brien's"— and had brought him as far home as the McTaggerts' corner. Wully is determined to have it out with Peter and goes over to the Keith's. But Libby, his mother, has not seen him. Nobody has seen anything of him. As the news spreads that he has been in the neighborhood and disappeared the men start a hunt for him. Wully is forced to join them. The whole neighborhood gathered at the alarm. By noon Wully's father and mother were at the Keith's, and the heads of families for miles around. Up and down the road the boys and younger men were halloing and beating about, and in the kitchen the wise old heads were holding a consultation. They organize the search. As the days pass, and the excitement dies out, the members of the clan return to their neglected fields. Peter's mother loses her mind, but Squire McLaughlin "vowed he would never stop hunting." Wully's belief grew constantly stronger that Peter had simply gone back to wherever he had come from. To Peter's distracted mother, he affirmed that Peter was alive; and to his dreading wife he proclaimed that certainly he was dead. But the whole desire of his life was to know which statement was true. Then one day Wully and Chirstie go to Chicago and Chirstie buys a new cloak. They have a great lark. They are preparing to return home, when a strange man accosts Wully, and Chirstie sees him and Wully turn and walk down the street. When Wully returns, Chirstie knows by his face that he has seen Peter. But they start home. Wully tells her that Peter is dying in a livery stable. "They were looking for some one to take him home." They had asked Wully to bring him out and he had refused. Chirstie told Wully that they ought to go back and get Peter — "If he's dying, Wully. And Auntie waiting there for him." Wully says he will not go back, and Chirstie tells him that if he won't, she will. "He made me do evil once. You made me do evil once. But nobody can make me do it again!" She had jumped out of the wagon by this time and down the road she ran. "I'm going back to him!" she cried. And Wully told her to go on, "if she liked him so well." Wully drives on, the baby on his lap. "He was glad to think of Peter Keith dying there, lonely, shrunken, filthy." To escape meeting some one on the road, he turns back and drives in the direction that Chirstie has gone. She suddenly turns back and climbs into the wagon.

"You know I don't want to go back to him! . . . If you want to know how much I hate him, I'll tell you. It was me that shot him that time. It wasn't his foot I was aiming at, either." But they go back and bring Peter home. And at the terrible sight of Peter's face, Wully pities his enemy. "When he saw that face — it was the last thing in the world that he intended doing — but someway, in spite of himself, he achieved generosity. . . ."

ABRAHAM LINCOLN, an American chronicle play in six episodes, by John Drinkwater (1919). Written by an Englishman who expressly disclaims any attempt to achieve a "local color" of which he has no experience, or an "idiom" to which he has not been "bred." The author follows Lord Charnwood's biography of Lincoln for the essential facts of his life. The first episode is the notification to Lincoln of his nomination for president of the United States. On an evening in the spring of 1861 some of the neighbors have called at his home in Springfield, Illinois, to be the first to congratulate him. He tells them that he will accept the high office, because of an "inner conviction" of destiny. He makes clear to the delegation who come to offer him the nomination that if the South should claim the right to secede he will fight for the Union, and that he is against slavery. The second episode takes place ten months later in Washington. A commission representing the Confederate States of the South are having an interview with Mr. Seward, Secretary of State, to urge compromise, and to propose that the forces at Fort Sumter be withdrawn. Lincoln comes in and to their proposals he answers that if the South remains loyal to the Union it can fight for slavery by all constitutional means, and avoid civil war. Summoning a Cabinet meeting to discuss the relief of Fort Sumter he overrides the vote of the majority, and orders immediate relief of the fort. The third episode takes place in a reception room in the White House nearly two years later. The wife of a war profiteer, Mrs. Goliath Blow, has called to tell the President that she and Goliath believe "those Southern brutes must be taught a lesson." Mrs. Otherly, a widow whose son has been killed at the front, asks the President if the war must go on. "Isn't there some way of stopping it?" He answers her that he has put the question daily to himself, but though war is an evil thing the cause of the Union is just. He refuses his hand to Mrs. Blow when she leaves, telling her that he is ashamed of her and her kind who dishonor the cause for which the North is fighting, preaching hatred, destruction, and revenge. The people of the South are mistaken, but are honest in their belief in their cause. The President sends for an aged negro preacher, William Custis, to whom he tells his intention of emancipating the slaves. In the fourth episode a Cabinet meeting shows Lincoln, cheered with good news of victories in the field that will probably end the war, in jocose mood not appreciated by his critical associates. At the close of the meeting Lincoln reads them his Emancipation Proclamation. There are protests, and counsel for delay, but Lincoln is firm. Hook tenders his resignation in anger, begging to be excused from the formality of shaking hands. The fifth episode is the surrender of General Lee to General Grant. Lincoln comes on an unexpected visit to General Grant in his headquarters in a farmhouse near Appomattox. The Confederate Army is practically surrounded, and word comes that Lee has asked for an armistice. In the early morning the orderly finds Lincoln asleep stretched out on two chairs. General Meade comes to confirm the report of the surrender. Lincoln and Grant know that the moment they have hoped for during four long years has come at last. The President leaves with a last word of caution against reprisals and orders to be "merciful." General Lee arrives and agrees to the "magnanimous" terms upon which surrender will be accepted. When he offers his sword to General Grant, the conqueror bids him return it to its "rightful place" in its scabbard. They shake hands and gravely salute each other as the curtain falls. The sixth episode is at Ford's Theater just outside the President's box on the evening of April 14, 1865. The crowd in the darkened theatre, seen through the door of the box demands a speech from the President. The author has grouped in this speech some of the most characteristic of Lincoln's spoken words. The play is resumed after the cheering dies away. Suddenly John Wilkes Booth appears making his way to the door of the box. He opens the door, fires a revolver and rushes away with an officer in close pursuit. Through the open door Mrs. Lincoln is to be seen kneeling beside the President. Secretary Stanton steps from the box and raises his hand for silence. "Now he belongs to the ages," he says.

ACROSS ARCTIC AMERICA: NARRATIVE OF THE FIFTH THULE EXPEDITION, by Knud Rasmussen (1927). The book is the story of a 20,000 miles' journey starting from Greenland and covering a large part of Arctic America. The official name of the expedition was: "The Fifth Thule Expedition, — Danish Ethnographical Expedition to Arctic North America, 1921–24." The author, whose father was a missionary among the Eskimos, and whose mother was part Eskimo, spoke the Eskimo language as his native tongue, and so was particularly fitted for the expedition. His childhood playmates were Eskimos and in his earliest days he "played and worked with the hunters, so that even the hardships of the most strenuous sledge-trips became pleasant." When he was eight years old he drove his own team of dogs and at ten had a rifle of his own. As he grew older and learned of the interest which the history of the Eskimo held for science, he spent eighteen years in Greenland, studying the culture and history of one tribe of Eskimos. Thus he laid the foundation for a comprehensive study of all the tribes. In 1910 he established in collaboration with M. Ib Nyeboe a station in North Greenland for trading and study and to this was given the name of "Thule." This station became the base for his subsequent expeditions. By 1920 the program in Greenland was completed, and in the summer of 1921 began the expedition which went from Greenland to the Pacific Ocean. At first they worked from a base on Danish Island, west of Baffinland, excavating the ruins of a former Eskimo civilization and studying the primitive Eskimo of the so-called Barren Grounds. Later with two Eskimos as companions he travelled by dog sledge across the continent to the Behring Sea. On the way they visited the various tribes, lived on the land, shared the life of the people, and inquired into their culture and history. Because of his knowledge of the language and the people he was always a welcome guest, joining in the hunts like a member of whatever tribe he happened to be visiting at the time. His observations on this trip constitute the book. The other members of the expedition, among them some Danish scientists of note, "did notable work in mapping territory known before only in a vague way." Accounts of their work are excluded from this book because full reports of their work have been issued elsewhere. He makes the Eskimo himself the hero of this book. "His history, his present culture, his daily hardships, and his spiritual life constitute the theme and the narrative. Only in form of telling, and as a means of binding together the various incidents is it even a record of my long trip by dog sledge." The Eskimos are widely scattered from Greenland to Siberia along the Arctic circle. There are about 33,000 in all. Evidence points to the fact that "at least 1500 years have elapsed since the various tribes broke off from one original stock," and yet Rasmussen found that his Greenland dialect served to gain him an entrance and understanding in all these scattered tribes. "The most primitive Eskimos, a nomadic tribe who lived in the interior and hunted caribou, had almost no knowledge of the sea, and their customs and tabus were limited accordingly. Nothing in their traditions or implements indicated that they had ever been acquainted with marine pursuits. But the folklore of the sea-people, in addition to being unique in its references to ocean life, was in many other respects identical with that of tribes that had never been down to sea. The conclusion was inevitable that originally all the Eskimos were land hunters, and that a portion of them later turned to hunting sea-mammals. The latter people retained all their old vocabulary and myths, and added thereto a nomenclature and a folklore growing out of their experience on the water."

ADAM AND EVE, by John Erskine (1927). This is a modernized version of the Biblical account of Adam and Eve in the Garden, and also takes into account the legend of Lilith —"the creature" whom Adam saw on the fourth day after his creation — the "beginning of his maturity." The story begins with Adam's "social life" before he met Lilith. Summed up in broad outlines, he admired the landscape, observed certain animals switching away at flies — "he suspected cows" — and more fields, more maples, and one apple orchard. In the course of his observations, he discovers a horse and a dog and a "fuzzy elastic something which moved by humping itself up and then stretching again." His impressions of the things that he comes upon, as he stops for berries along the road, feels the first drop of rain, or sees the sunlight on the orchard, and his reactions to flowers or food, to water leaping up in a spring, fill up his days and nights until Lilith crosses his path, and then "he made the effort of his life to be on his guard." He tells her that the animals were there when he arrived — animals first — then man. "And then woman," said Lilith. She made him irritable and sarcastic. "Obviously the woman had a bad effect." She was no proper companion. He would stay away. He gathered berries and ate them, all by himself. Having met Lilith, he had acquired a dead past. Lilith follows up the acquaintance. She built an addition to her house and Adam moves into it. "How wise she was! But perhaps he would never feel at home with her kind of wisdom — as he never would feel at ease with nature, if what she said of nature was true." Eve appears just when Adam and Lilith are having a colloquy over a dead cow. She accuses them of neglect — the cow should have been put in a barn. Adam takes her home — she lives in the orchard. Lilith takes the calf. Adam tells Lilith that he will be "back in ten minutes." He had not intended to stay, yet he had not entirely intended to go. "This woman made a new kind of appeal. Perhaps it was the emphasis she put on manners. What she said about eating was much to the point. Of course one didn't go to dinner in order to eat — not unless one was an animal. The object was to talk, in between eating." "If any one had told him yesterday that in the next twenty-four hours he would wait on a strange female as though he were her servant, build a house for her, get her meals, sleep outside the door to assure the tranquillity of her mind — he would have jeered at the prophet." Now — "just how had he got into this fix? And what sort of creature was this? . . . Lilith had come first — and she was perfection . . . In certain regards Eve did indicate advance. She was inclined towards spiritual things, and away from nature," but "there were two dark consequences of her superiority. She wasn't entirely pleasant to get on with. She had expressed satisfaction in very little he had done for her, in very little life had brought her." "Don't be too difficult, Eve." But they decide to make a garden — together. "Not in front of the house where it would spoil the view, but off to the left." "That suits me," said Adam. Lilith comes to see them and Adam goes home with her. The author calls this part of the story, "The Fall of Man." Adam begins to worry about Eve and returns. Eve was sitting on the ground, feeding a small fire with sticks. "Would you mind standing on the other side? You're blocking the breeze," was her greeting. "Yes, she was his wife," he mused. "It was the sort of truth Lilith used to refer to, the kind you can't put into words, but which you experience. Each moment he spent with Eve he became more her husband. He hadn't planned it, but perhaps it was one of those relations you are born to. Eve didn't seem to be getting any happiness out of it, either." Eve warns Adam against Lilith, and when the three have an encounter she expresses her views on life, food, clothes and the like — and the home. "If men live your way, there can never be a settled home, nor sound society nor —" Lilith walked back, and raised her hand to interrupt. "I needn't remind you, Eve, of the possibilities in your settled society. You will be Lilith to some other man. They looked at each other, for once in complete understanding." "I don't see that, Lilith," said Adam. "I happen to be the only man." Both women laughed. "Goodby," said Eve. "Come on, Adam." Adam sees Lilith once more. She was sitting in front of her door, elbows on knees, and chin in hand, gazing off into the landscape. As Adam drew nearer, he felt rather self-conscious. "What's the news?" asked Lilith. "It's come. I'm a father." "All this fuss, Adam, over just another man? Didn't you say once this silly repetition would make life endlessly monotonous?" "That facetious remark," observes the author, "was the final error." "To ask a new father whether his progeny was making life monotonous proved how far out of touch she was with the higher concerns of the soul." Adam returns to Eve. "Eve, I hope you don't mind my saying it so often, but I'm glad it wasn't a girl. After all, this is a man's world."

ADVENTURES IN ARABIA, by W. B. Seabrook (1927), is not only an account of vivid, colorful adventures in a strange land, but it is filled with mature, understanding comment on the character and customs of the tribes who live in Arabia. Through a friendship with Daoud Izzedin, a Druse studying in this country and his father, the author met Amir Amin Arslan, a city Arab powerful among the desert tribes. So he sent Seabrook as a guest protected by the sanctuary laws into the black tents of one of the chief tribes of desert Bedouins, the Beni Sakhr, whose sheik, Mitkhal Pasha became his friend. He was entertained in the spacious and luxurious tent of the sheik upon roast mutton served whole surrounded by rice and gravy on a huge platter from which all the guests dipped in turn. He rode with Mitkhal Pasha, on swift white horses, and on the white racing camels which are the pride of their owners. Dirt of a healthy sort was everywhere, most of their ablutions were a kind of dry cleaning done with sand, but no filth or vermin were to be seen. The sheik's wives lived on the other side of the curtained tent in the harem. These he made no attempt to meet although it would have been quite possible. Bedouin women in the desert go about freely unveiled. One day his friend gave judgment to a young sheik and his wife who came complaining because her husband would not take another wife; the burden of being a sheik's only wife was too great and beside she was lonely for another woman of her own kind. On another occasion he was taken to visit a beautiful Bedouin girl of high birth who regaled them with stories while she made the best of the opportunity to torment a lover who waited upon her. Mansour, the gorgeous black slave who always attended Mitkhal Pasha, was himself the possessor of much land and cattle, the gift of his master when the slave had saved his life. Such as Mansour never cared to take the freedom that could easily be theirs by riding to any British post and claiming it. Later Seabrook was allowed to ride in ghrazzu with the Beni Sakhr. Mitkhal's flock of white camels had been reported insufficiently guarded and these had aroused the greed of the Sirdieh. A camel rider brought in the news of the proposed raid and the next morning the warriors lay in ambush when the flock went as usual to graze. This rough ghrazzu is really a game, not war in which, although lives may be spent, slaughter is not the object but stealing camels and other herds, the prize. Definite rules are honorably observed and captives are treated as guests. But the author not accustomed to the hardships of the long days in saddle found it almost too much for his endurance. Nor were the Arabs without their tale of a beautiful woman, Gutne, who caused as much despair and bloodshed between tribes as ever Helen of Troy. But Seabrook visited other tribes. Daoud takes him to the castle of Sultan Pasha Atrash. The story of the Sultan Pasha's attack on a French tank during the war is told. With a learned man among the Druses he discusses their religion and the significance in relation to it of the golden calf, which missionaries allege they worship. Furthermore he learned something of the tests that a candidate must pass before he can be admitted as an akil or elder. Finally Daoud takes him to see his cousin, the famous "Veiled Lady of Mukhtara," the most powerful woman among the Druses to-day. In the palace of the Melewi he is lavishly entertained and later learns something of the mysteries of their religion, how through rhythm they come first to the state of simple bliss, then to power and finally to a state of positive unity in which the soul creates conscious visions of beauty and glory, and he watches the whirling dervishes in their sacred dance. Finally he visits the Rufai or howling dervishes, a sect very different from the whirling Melewi. Several of these dervishes were in the mystic state. That night, stepping back a thousand years apparently, in the Rufai Hall of Torture he saw the dancing, howling dervishes slash and burn themselves in their religious frenzy. Afterward he ascertained that, while the wounds and burns were actual, they had not been deep and the subject made a normal recovery. His last trip was to the mountain of the Yezidees, a mysterious sect who were reported to be worshippers of Satan. He explores their sacred temple on Mount Lalesh and he is even permitted to see something of those caverns beneath the temple where ancient altars of sacrifice were said to be, but he found no evidence of these. Further up the mountain he entered the gleaming white tower where Yezidee fakirs came to make magic. This was his final visit before departing from a land where the people so hospitably shared with him the intimacies of their life and religion.

AGE OF INNOCENCE, THE, by Edith Wharton (1920). A picture of the artificial, conventional society of the New York of the eighteen-seventies. Ellen Olenska, born in the inner exclusive circle which rules Fifth Avenue, had lived abroad and married a Polish count. She has been obliged to leave her dissipated husband, and has returned to the protection of her relatives in New York. At the time Ellen appears in the family opera box the engagement of her cousin, May Welland, is about to be announced to Newland Archer, a young lawyer. He and his mother are able to arrange that their relatives, the van der Luydens, socially supreme in New York, shall entertain the Countess at a dinner party they are giving for a visiting Duke, and thus prevent lesser social arbiters from ostracizing her, because of certain stories of her flight with her husband's secretary. The Duke knew Ellen in Europe, and accustomed to the free European intercourse with writers, painters, musicians and diplomats, they scandalize their hosts by attending a Bohemian Sunday evening party, given by the new rich Mrs. Struthers. Ellen's family dread the publicity of the divorce court and ask Archer to persuade her to stop proceedings, and she sadly consents. In friendship with Ellen, Archer is happy in a world of ideas and opinions at variance with the dull narrow circle of which his beautiful fiancé is the perfect flower, but he discovers his love for Ellen too late to withdraw decently from marriage with May. Ellen has moved to Washington before May and Newland Archer return from their continental tour. She is presently in disgrace with the family because she refuses to listen to overtures from her husband. Her grandmother, Mrs. Manson Mingott, the head of the clan, is talked into cutting down her allowance, but after a stroke sends for her favorite to come and live with her, and it is Archer who meets Ellen at the station. Ellen decides that the situation is impossible and that she will live in Paris, and May gives her a farewell dinner. Archer, surrounded by the family, realizes "that to all of them he and Madame Olenska were lovers. . . . He guessed himself to have been for months the centre of countless silently observing eyes and patiently listening ears . . . and that now the whole tribe had rallied about his wife on the tacit assumption that nobody knew anything, or had ever imagined anything, and that the occasion of the entertainment was simply May Archer's natural desire to take an affectionate leave of her friend and cousin . . . the way of people who dreaded scandal more than disease, who placed decency above courage, and who considered that nothing was more ill-bred than 'scenes'." He makes the best of his married life, and never sees Ellen again, though many years later he goes to Europe with his son and gets as far as her door, but decides not to give up his youthful memory of her for the reality.

ALICE ADAMS, by Booth Tarkington (1921), is the revealing story of a small town girl. Her father, Virgil Adams, is recovering from a serious illness when the story opens. The business of convalescing is difficult, at best; but when complicated with the reiterations of the nurse, her face mismodelled by sleep, who persists in assuring him that he has had a wonderful night's rest, not to mention the sprightly prophecies of his wife, that he will soon be able to look for more remunerative work, Virgil finds the road to complete recovery singularly beset. Alice, the adored daughter, attempts to soothe Virgil with bright chatter and caresses. She also urges her mother to show more tactful consideration of her father, but the day for a perfect understanding between her parents is past. Mrs. Adams allows no chance to escape in which to prod Virgil into resigning from the "old hole," as she characterizes his position with the Lamb Company, where he has been for so many years. She has no sympathy for the tender glamour which he throws about his work, but urges him to set about the making of quantities of money to which, in some mysterious way, she feels that they are entitled. When Alice is in her own room, she spends much time in posturing before her mirror, trying out the effect of sauciness, smiling weariness or scornful toleration. She saw herself constantly as in a picture and rehearsed gestures of greeting. In her made-over organdie, Alice goes with her brother Walter to Mildred Palmer's dance, where she discovers that hers is the only organdie frock, amid clouds of chiffons and taffetas. Walter dances the first dance dutifully with his sister, only to desert her afterwards with the injunction that she "flag" one of the "long-tailed birds" to take her on for the next dance. Alice, whose only other partner is Frank Dowling, who has pantingly escorted her through one dance, sits alone, constrained to keep up the merry fiction of waiting momentarily while her partner is absent. Finally, in desperation, she resorts to sitting with one of the chaperones, who in time turns a conspicuously deaf ear to Alice's prattle. When Arthur Russell, Mildred's reputed fiancé, is brought up for introduction to Alice, she dances with him, although fearing that he has been asked to give a wall-flower a good time. At the close of their dance, she suggests that he find Walter for her. He does so, only to discover him casting dice with the colored men around the place. Alice attempts to throw over this incident the bright cloud of fiction that Walter chooses to consort with odd characters owing to his literary aspirations. When Alice reaches home, after assuring her mother that she has had a splendid time, she bursts into tears. As events gather for a catastrophe, Mrs. Adams continues her efforts to push Virgil into starting a glue business, the recipe for the glue having been confided to him years before by Mr. Lamb. Virgil, from uttering dismal wails of "Oh, my, my," finally entertains the thought and writes a letter to Mr. Lamb, severing his connection with the firm. Anxiously he awaits the reaction of his chief, but for some time nothing happens. In the meantime, Alice receives the attentions of Arthur Russell. Unconsciously she builds her little fiction of herself as the pampered daughter of an indulgent father. She begs Arthur to listen to no word spoken of her by any of the townspeople. Jokingly, he promises, but it is impossible to avoid the Palmers who inadvertently drop the news that Virgil Adams has done a dishonest thing. He has started a glue factory with a stolen process involved. They speak slightingly of Alice as a girl who pushes herself and does not last. Arthur, red and miserable, keeps silent. That night he is invited to dinner at the Adams' house, but although extra help has been hired and flowers are bought to grace the occasion, the dinner is a failure. Arthur does not seem to see Alice, nor does he taste the food which Mrs. Adams has so painstakingly prepared. Alice, with some queer clairvoyance, knows that this is their last five minutes together, for he will never come again. The straggling little flowers die upon the hot white cloth, as romance dies out of the life of Alice. They are interrupted by the arrival of a friend, who announces to Virgil that his son Walter is short in his accounts at the Lamb Company. Heart-brokenly Virgil declares that we "don't know enough to live until it is time to die." The father goes to his glue factory, to ascertain how much he can borrow on it to save his son's honor, only to find that opposite his piece of ground stands the completed factory of J. Lamb, who will rival him in the manufacturing of glue. It is only after Virgil suffers another stroke that friendly relations are resumed by the two older men and Lamb offers to buy out Virgil's factory and refrain from prosecuting the son. Virgil says, "You think you're going to be pushed right up against the wall; you can't see any way out, or any hope at all; you think you're gone — and then something you never counted on turns up; and while maybe you never do get back to where you used to be, yet somehow you kind of squirm out of being right *spang* against the wall. You keep on going — maybe you can't go much, but you do go a little. See what I mean?" And Alice takes the step that all along she knew she would be doing. With her mother's acceptance of boarders in the home, Alice turns to the stairway that leads to Frincke's Business College — the "very doorway she had always looked upon as the end of youth and the end of hope . . . where pretty girls turned into old maids of a dozen different types, but all looking a little like herself." "Well, here she was at last! She looked up and down the street quickly and then with a little heave of the shoulders she went bravely in, under the sign and began to climb the wooden steps. Half-way up the shadows were heaviest, but after that the place began to seem brighter. There was an open window overhead somewhere, she found, and the steps at the top were gay with sunshine."

ALICE SIT-BY-THE-FIRE, by Sir J. M. Barrie (1905). The author describes this comedy as "a page from a daughter's diary." The children of an Anglo-Indian colonel and his wife are awaiting the return from India of the parents who are almost unknown to them. Cosmo, thirteen, a naval cadet, is afraid that his father will kiss him, and rehearses greetings intended to ward off this disgrace to his manly feelings. Amy, his sister, is seventeen, and has just put up her hair. She wonders whether father and mother will talk like the characters in plays from which she has derived her knowledge of "Life." With her dearest friend, Ginevra, she has seen five "serious" plays in the last week, "always about a lady and two men," in the situation called "the odd, odd triangle." When the parents arrive everything seems to go wrong. The nurse, who has had the baby for seventeen months, is fearful that she will be displaced by what she calls a black "yah-yah," regards the mother as her natural enemy, and warns her that the baby does not like "to be touched by strangers." Sure enough the baby cries and will have nothing to do with Alice. Cosmo has the "happy notion" of interposing the tea-tray between himself and his father's greeting. His mother, who is almost hysterical with excitement, embraces Cosmo, and he likes it, but his conversation discourages her to the point of tears. The Colonel warns her not to be too demonstrative with Amy, so she is reserved with her daughter, who is chilled and bewildered. A young bachelor friend, Steve Rollo, who has known Mrs. Grey, as "the belle of the Punjaub" comes in to see his friends. Alice is thankful to have someone in the house who is glad to see her. Steve kisses her cheek and finds it wet. He is amazed to hear that the children do not adore her on sight, as everyone always has. The Greys promise to come around to his rooms after dinner. As he is leaving Amy in the hall hears him say to Alice as he kisses her good-by, "And you'll come to me after dinner to-night, Alice?" The stage-struck Amy recognizes at once that this is an "assignation," and that her mother is an "erring wife." "She knows that under such circumstances she must play the part of the devoted friend who 'saves' the heroine compromised by being discovered in the bachelor's rooms." She puts on her best party frock and proceeds to do her duty. Steve is completely mystified by her melodramatic talk and her demand for "the letters." When Colonel Grey is announced, Amy hides in a cupboard. Alice arrives later in a state of gloom. She tells them that Cosmo had been sulky at dinner, and Amy said she had a headache, and went to bed. By chance Alice discovers Amy in the cupboard, and tries to get her husband away in order to conceal their daughter's indiscretion. All her efforts are in vain as Amy comes out and declares that Steve is her "affianced husband." The Colonel is not deceived by any of the explanations, and Steve is convinced that Alice must "love him not wisely but too well." Alice insists on being left alone with her daughter, and is able to piece together the absurd misconceptions in Amy's mind. She decides to play the part and allow the silly Amy to think she has saved her mother. Steve is allowed to come to say good-by to Alice in Amy's presence, and he fatuously tells Mrs. Grey, as her chaperone prefers to have him call her, that he had not realized before to-day what her feelings for him were. Colonel Grey sends Amy to bed, and to the bewilderment of Steve, the father and mother rock with laughter. Steve comes down to earth again, and to understanding of the fool he has made of himself. Alice has won her children, but she promises her husband that Amy shall hear the whole true story before she sleeps. She herself has learned that she is now the mother of a grown daughter, and says farewell to the "Alice that was." It is to be "Alice Sit-by-the-fire henceforth."

ALL GOD'S CHILLUN GOT WINGS, by Eugene O'Neill (1923). This drama of the marriage of a white woman and a negro is a tragic and beautiful love story which ends in frustration and madness. In the opening scene Ella and Jim are children playing together on the street in a mixed neighborhood in New York. The awkward, ambitious colored boy sees all beauty and perfection in the undeserving Ella, who, as she grows older, develops prejudice of race and scorns his mute adoration. She takes up with Micky, the ward bully, and it is when he discards her and her illegitimate child dies, that she accepts Jim's protection as her only refuge. The slow-witted Jim has graduated from high school, and aspires to be a lawyer. They are married and go to Europe where they are happy for a time. Ella loves Jim for his goodness, but unconsciously she recoils from contact with blacks, and on their return she gradually loses her reason. His kind mother and educated sister see that she has no sympathy with his studies to pass the bar examination. Ella tries to kill her husband; though she fails in her attempt she is able to prevent him from sleeping and reading his law books, so that he fails to pass the examination, in her mad desire to "look down on him." She returns to the stored-up memories of childhood, and wants Jim to play with her again, and loyal Jim accepts the kind of love she has to give him, and asks God to let his suffering purify him of selfishness, and make him worthy "of the child you send me for the woman you take away."

AMERICA COMES OF AGE, by André Siegfried (1927) describes the American people, perplexed with domestic problems of no mean importance, being suddenly thrust into maturity through the industrial development in this country that came of the Great War. Mass production in industry is introducing a new civilization with a higher standard of living than any hithertofore known. "American industry," says the author, "is evolving a school of thought which will throw light on the fundamental conditions of its existence, on the methods that have been worked out by experience, and on the moral factors which will determine its place and its mission in the community. It is an important moment in the development of the nation, for it signifies that it has now reached maturity." The character of the American people has been visibly altered in the nineteenth century by the changing tides of immigration. So great is this change that the question arises whether America will remain Protestant and Anglo-Saxon. The Protestants of Nordic origin who have come to these shores have been readily assimilated. Individuality due either to racial or religious traits that remain distinct after several generations prevent the Latins, the French, the Finns, the Mexicans, the Irish Catholics and the Jews from complete assimilation. The moral and political ideas, the religious, intellectual and artistic traditions of these imperfectly Americanized peoples are either passively opposed or actively in conflict with those of the old native stock. The feeling of social obligation is typically Anglo-Saxon, while that of Latin democracies is individualistic and negative. The heart of the American religious problem, however, is in the conflict between the Modernists, whose chief characteristics are moral sincerity and this traditional Anglo-Saxon concern for the social welfare, and the Fundamentalists, who are the spiritual descendants of Cromwell, hostile to the broader conceptions of social welfare and hypnotized by the literal preservation of dogma. "The mysticism of success is perhaps their genuine religion, and with it is combined a certain guileless optimism, as well as the utilitarian outlook of Bentham." The Catholic Church is a thing apart in the heart of the American body politic. Neither the Protestant nor the Catholic Church is so much threatened by aggressive disbelief as by the prevalent, everyday materialism, the obsession for tangible and

material accomplishments which dominates American life in every field. Both
the recent agitation over the teaching of evolution in the schools and the legislation against liquor are characteristic of these Anglo-Saxon Americans who think of
themselves as the moral élite, justified in imposing their customs on the rest of the
country. The stimulating climate of America, in contrast with the oppressive
atmosphere of the British Isles which necessitates some outside stimulant for the
people to keep them up to a normal level of vitality works in favor of the prohibi-
tionist's program. The American has no need for such a stimulant. Beside this
the sentiment of the Protestants for moral uplift, expressed through numerous reform
organizations and the attitude of the important employers of labor, knowing the
disastrous consequences of heavy drinking in industry, favor prohibition. The problem of the colored race in America is peculiarly difficult of solution. The South
takes a paternalistic attitude toward them, but refuses, for the most part, to give
them either equal justice in the courts, or political and economic equality of opportunity. In 1917 a large northward movement of the discontented negroes was
started. The more primitive of these went toward the manufacturing cities of the
Middle West, the more educated negroes to the large cities of the Atlantic sea-board.
Although the Northern attitude is traditionally more liberal, social separation of the
negro is as real as in the South. The best type of intellectual negroes to-day are
working for their racial rights as men but do not favor assimilation. In tune with
the dominant American sense of racial superiority is the favor with which the eugenic
movement has been received here. The effect of such a movement, if once generally
accepted, would be to create a new eugenic conscience and code of morals. The
European immigrants in the country being individualists resent such interference
with their intimate relations, as they have the prohibition movement. The present
restrictive immigration laws limiting the supply of unskilled labor will force the
country further along the road of standardization of industry making for more
specialized mass production. But this is conducive to the maintenance of a high
standard of living. The Ku Klux Klan movement is the resort of certain of the
middle class native born Americans to protect themselves against the threats inherent in these problems that have been discussed, by using illegal direct action.
Its danger is that, however high its idealism, it is unjust to certain elements in the
country, dangerous because it is certain to attract to itself violent and lawless elements, and weak because it has proven incapable of carrying out constructive work.
American trade is still largely interested in the home market which is able to absorb
most of her products and she has almost every natural resource she requires. As
long as this remains true her policy will remain protectionist in regard to foreign
trade. In finance, however, since the War, her interests have become international.
She has a monopoly of the gold supply of the world. The sovereign independence of
Europeans is threatened by a new and subtle imperialism, unlike anything we have
known before, depending on how America decides this problem of international responsibility. The effects of this large gold supply was in part counteracted by the
expansion of national production, and any further disastrous effects due to its presence in this country as well as the necessary deflation following the War were well
taken care of by the policy of the Federal Reserve Banks which preserved the stability
of the business world. Conflict in American political life more often concerns itself
with sectional issues, or propagandist causes within the parties than with a conflict
of opposing political principles between the parties. The final chapters discuss
America's relations with Great Britain, France, the Orient and a concluding contrast between American and European civilization. In America France is either

enthusiastically loved or severely judged. The relationship is essentially a sentimental one. The English and Americans may often act as enemies but they are always brotherly enemies. "France can arouse great enthusiasm at times in the United States, England never; but the English position is much stronger . . . it is based on the solid foundation of family relationship." Between the United States and Canada the relationship is more intimate. The same civilization, the same language, the same customs and standard of living are riveted together through sharing the same menace on their Pacific Coast. For the peril from the peaceful invasion of economic and social life by the Chinese and Japanese concerns both equally. The Pacific Coast is a world frontier between the white and yellow races, and in view of this the English and Americans of the Far West truly feel an international solidarity. The old European civilization, says Siegfried, did not really cross the Atlantic. The American civilization is marked by the creation of new conceptions. The luxury and wealth of America, which is the result of high-speed mass production do not compensate in the eyes of this trained observer from France for the sacrifice of one aspect of civilization, originality and individual development in art, science and literature.

AMERICAN ADVENTURE, THE, by David Saville Muzzey (2 vols., 1927) covers the period from its earliest launching on these shores to the present administration of Calvin Coolidge. The urge of adventure, commercial rivalry, economic pressure and the Stuart trend toward absolutism both political and religious were the stimulants which resulted in permanently transplanting English institutions to the new world. The distance of the colonists from England, their habit of independence and local self-government inherited from seventeenth century England all intensified in the colonists those traits of courage, endurance, self-reliance, equality of opportunity, and jealousy of privilege conspicuous in the earliest settlers. The conflicting authorities of Crown and Parliament made England in the seventeenth century weak in her colonial policy, nor was she ready to extend to the colonists the principles and privileges of the Revolution of 1689. England persisted in viewing the colonies primarily as economic assets and in following up this mercantile policy the alienation between England and the American colonies originated. After the rejection of the Declaration of Rights and Grievances the Continental Congress which met the following spring still delayed the Declaration of Independence. Apathy and disunion indeed persisted long after independence was declared and made Washington's task of raising and sustaining troops fit for service an almost impossibly difficult one until the Battle of Trenton, a critical action of the War which encouraged the forlorn Revolutionary army with hopes of ultimate victory. The English Whigs, in opposition to the king, sympathized with the colonists to a degree. Whether Howe, who was a Whig, was acting under the influence of English politics in failing to press Washington too closely after the Battle of Long Island and in refusing to join the army of the Tory Burgoyne as planned, is not known. The French Alliance and further successes of the Continental army aroused England to a more active prosecution of the War. But for diplomatic successes scored by Benjamin Franklin and others on the continent and a change back to a Whig ministry in England, Cornwallis' capitulation at Yorktown need not have been irretrievable, the final act of the Revolution.

The struggle which had torn England since the days of Queen Elizabeth was, at bottom, a conflict of Prerogative against Democracy. This same struggle was carried over into subsequent American history. Owing to the magnitude of the subject only the three major paths of this American Adventure which Dr. Muzzey has cleared, together with such minor movements as are the outcome of them, will be traced here. These were: the struggle of Democracy against Prerogative; the constant westward pressure of the frontier; and the development of the Monroe Doctrine from its originally simple statement of a passive attitude through increasingly complex situations to a definitely aggressive policy.

The marvellous mineral and agricultural resources of the West became the basis of prosperity after the Civil War. Transcontinental railroads linked Atlantic and Pacific and the electric cable joined the Old World and the New. Only the South, kept prostrate by the vengeful spirit that possessed Congress, could not recover. This spirit in Congress gave support to the pernicious activities of carpet baggers from the North who exploited the South through the negro vote. Under Grant a more liberal Republican policy was adopted, favoring home rule for the South. With the close of the Reconstruction period coinciding with the close of Grant's administration, the Democrats for the first time since the War gained control in Congress. Third parties appeared to voice the revolt of the Farmers, Laborers, Prohibitionists, Greenbackers and others. The contested election of Hayes, says the author, showed a nation so firmly rooted in Democracy and orderly self-government that such a crisis could be carried off without conflict. The first successful attempt of the government to control economic interests was the Cullem Act of 1887 for the regulation of Interstate Commerce. Prerogative was now being attacked under the form of monopoly. The Sherman Anti-Trust law of 1890 was the next step. The triumph of Cleveland's second term was the recognition by Great Britain of the Cleveland-Olney extension of the Monroe principle as applied in the Venezuela boundary dispute. Cleveland admitted that "It established the Monroe Doctrine on lasting foundations before the eyes of the world." The election of 1896 "was the most important in our history since the Civil War." It marked the end of organized politics' effort of the past twenty years toward currency inflation and paternalistic legislation. It again emphasized the firmness of the Union, for Bryan in his wildest flights never considered the possibility of leading a secession; and it ushered in the triumph of big business under Hanna's skilful leadership. The outcome of the Spanish War resulted in a curious combination of two major trends of our history, the habit of expansion and the development of the Monroe Doctrine. The political protectorate of Cuba led to other responsibilities and established our supremacy in the Caribbean. A violent conflict of opinion between our historic instinct for expansion and a newly awakened fear of imperialism followed our acquisition of the Philippines. The reëlection of McKinley in 1900 became a referendum in which the people pronounced for expansion. Porto Rico came willingly under the protection of the United States and soon evidenced that social and economic progress already seen in the Philippines. Roosevelt's policy in the Caribbean grew increasingly aggressive until, under the flimsiest of pretexes he cut the Gordian knot at Panama by seizure of the Isthmus at that point where the canal was to be dug. In the early years of Roosevelt's first administration, Venezuela again figured in an incident that enhanced the prestige of the Monroe Doctrine. The fight of Democracy against Prerogative again came to the fore in Roosevelt's administration. Industrial democracy was the keynote of the period after the Civil War. But a new popular movement was now under way. The boss-ridden convention gave way in many states to the direct primaries. The initiative and referendum, the recall, city managers, and commission form of government were tried first in Wisconsin, Oregon, North Dakota and other western states. Taft succeeded only in keeping pace with this movement for direct government. Although, in some cases he actually accomplished more in the prosecution of the laws against monopoly than Roosevelt, he was too deliberative and legalistic to lead the movement. So the new Progressive Movement, pledged to the control of the trusts, labor legislation, tariff revision, graduated income tax, conservation, direct primaries and the recall naturally turned to Roosevelt as its leader. Wilson's principles were progressive but he stressed the emancipation of the people rather than their protection. He criticized Roosevelt and Taft as ready to act for the people but not through them. His attack on privilege was initiated with the Underwood-Simmons bill drastically revising the tariff downward and compensating for the loss of revenue by a graduated income tax. His second attack on privilege was through the Federal Reserve Act. The Sherman Anti-Trust Act had been found inadequate for the curbing of the trusts so the Federal Trade Commission Act was designed to establish more equitable relations with business through the courts. This was not like the Sherman Act a penal statute, but the Clayton Act, which supplemented existing laws against unlawful restraints and monopolies was penal in nature. In his Mexican policy, Wilson used the Monroe Doctrine to protect them against internal disturbance when he refused to recognize a government not regularly elected by the people. Our neutrality in the Great War was first that of indifference to the political and military aspects of the struggle, then, insistence on the full preservation of our rights and privileges, followed by emphasis on preservation of American property and lives, changing into a period of preparation if necessity should force us to take up arms and ending with the Sussex ultimatum. After the War entrance to the League became the issue of the next campaign; Harding, the anti-League Republican, was elected. The outstanding event of his term, before his sudden passing left Calvin Coolidge at the head of the government, was the Washington Conference on the Limitation of Armament. Coolidge's economical administration in the interests of good business assured his popular reëlection. From the crime wave, the disregard of the law even among the better classes due to divided opinion on the Prohibition Amendment, the unequal distribution of wealth, the private exploitation of natural resources, the continuing antagonism between capital and labor, Dr. Muzzey concludes that our real need and hope lie in the education of public opinion in the appreciation of our common responsibility for the success of democratic government. He quotes in conclusion from the President's last message that our duty now is to give stability to the world and for that we need idealism.

AMERICAN CIVILIZATION, THE RISE OF, by Charles A. and Mary R. Beard, see **RISE OF.**

AMERICAN DRAMA, A HISTORY OF THE, FROM THE BEGINNING TO THE CIVIL WAR, by Arthur Hobson Quinn (1923). Bibliography — pp. 395–416. A List of American Plays — pp. 419–462. Index — pp. 465–486. Guided by a study of unpublished manuscripts relating to the early American theatre, the desire of the writer of this history is to present a helpful survey rather than worship of mere uniformity. "Certain of the playwrights have their special significance, but as the subject develops, the type of play becomes usually of more importance than the individual playwright. . . . The drama has been considered throughout as a living thing. No attempt has been made to treat the unacted drama except incidentally, and except for the Revolutionary satires, attention has been concentrated upon the plays which actually reached the stage." Under this category the plays of writers born abroad but identified with the American stage are included. Among the topics and writers surveyed are: the drama and the theatre in the colonies; the drama and the Revolution; the coming of comedy; English models; William Dunlap, playwright and producer; first native negro character; James Nelson Barker (1805–1825); John Howard Payne and the foreign plays; Robert Montgomery Bird and the rise of the romantic play (1825–1850); Indian plays; Abolition plays; American comedy types (1825–1860); George Henry Baker and the later romantic tragedy; the influence of Dion Boucicault's introduction of the travelling company with one play. Though the writer of the history believes that the roots of the modern American drama lie deep in the early days, he attributes to Boucicault's invention the gradual decline of the stock repertoire company and the simultaneous rise of the latter day dramatist.

AMERICAN DRAMA, A HISTORY OF THE, FROM THE CIVIL WAR TO THE PRESENT DAY, by Arthur Hobson Quinn (2 vols., 1927). Bibliography, Including a List of American Plays — pp. 255–335. Index — pp. 339–359 (Vol. 2). These two volumes continue Arthur Hobson Quinn's history of the American drama written for the professional theatre. The preface to the first volume specifies three objects: "The first has been to paint a picture of the drama, not only in its loftiest moments, but also in those no less significant stretches of achievements in which it has been one of the most potent forces in our social history. The second has been to point out among the playwrights of the period the prevailing types and tendencies so that some coherent progress might be apparent. The third has been to indicate the relative merits of the dramatists, not only from my (the author's) point of view but also from that of the effect of their plays upon the discriminating criticism of their time." From Augustin Daly to Clyde Fitch (Volume 1) the dramatists are treated historically, as well as critically, and a complete record of their achievement is attempted. From the death of Moody to the present day (Volume 2) the playwrights are treated more selectively in separate chapters, or "grouped according to the kind of play for which they have been distinguished." Though the plays surveyed are set against the background of the American theatre, and though dramatic conditions are explained in terms of the local theatre, no detailed discussion of Little Theatres or Community Theatres is undertaken. The book is thus primarily a history of the American drama, and not of the American theatre. The table of contents lists chapters on: Augustin Daly; Bronson Howard; William Dean Howells and the approach to realism; Edward Harrigan, Charles Hoyt and the comedy of types; the drama of the Frontier; James A. Herne and the realism of character; David Belasco and his associates; William Gillette and the realism of action; Augustus Thomas and the picture of American life; Clyde Fitch and the development of social comedy; William Vaughn Moody and the drama of revolt; Percy Mackaye and the drama of spectacle; Rachel Crothers and the feminine criticism of life; Langdon Mitchell, Jesse Lynch Williams, and the later social comedy, including A. E. Thomas, Thompson Buchanan, Philip Barry; Edward Sheldon; the height of melodrama; George Ade, George Cohan, Winchell Smith, Frank Craven, Anne Nichols; Tarkington, "The Yellow Jacket," Philip Moeller, Edna Millay, Charles Rann Kennedy and other Romance playwrights of the Twentieth Century; the rivalry of the motion picture, the decline of the travelling company and the rise of the independent theatre; Eugene O'Neill, poet and mystic; the new realism of character as exemplified in the plays of Owen Davis, George Kelly, Sidney Howard and Maxwell Anderson; the drama of the provinces, Paul Green, L. Vollmer and Hatcher Hughes.

AMERICAN FRONTIER, HISTORY OF THE, by Frederic L. Paxon (1924). This author reviews the period from 1763 to 1893 and shows the proportions of the whole story. The American frontier took shape in the final years of the century of colonial wars, and upon the return of peace started upon the conquest of the continent. "Its British origins survive to mould its life, but its destiny and its spirit have become American." He sees as the result of the European settlement in 1763 the greatest military effort that Britain ever made in America, but he notes also that the peoples of the British colonies who were ceasing to be British, were assuming the new aspect of American. He discusses here the racial strains, in proportion to population — the Germans, the Scotch-Irish, the Irish, with the subsequent change and spread of population. At this period the Appalachian valleys felt the touch of Americanization, and the writer considers that these valleys stayed the course of westward advance. Colonial tendencies are shown to have merged into a common nationality, and in the proclamation of George III., dated October 7, 1763, which added to the original list of colonies, which now stretched between the new dominions of Quebec and Florida, the colonists found not only the beginnings of an ordered policy but a starting point for the winning of the West. From this point, events are reviewed dealing with the great Indian barricade, the Indian frontier line, land disputes, the formation of land companies, the adjustment of the Pennsylvania boundary-line, the French and Indian Wars, and the effect of Braddock's defeat in 1755. The extension of settlements into the Shenandoah country and the Tennessee valleys,— that period when the "speculators were thinking in terms of huge provincial grants and the frontier farmers continued steadily at their task of clearing lands —" the factions in North Carolina politics which produced the insurrection, with its culminating conflict in 1771, the Transylvania speculation, connected with the movement of new colonies, the negotiations of Daniel Boone and James Robertson which marked the road from the settlements into the Kentucky Valley and the Blue Grass Region — are treated in detail, and the author sees at this stage a new sort of imperial expansion in these varied movements. Frontier influences after the Revolution are discussed. "The strongest of the slender bonds that held the States together until common interest grew sufficiently close to dominate the local, are to be found in the opportunities created and the duties entailed by the huge areas of open land, extending along the rear of every State, and filling the unoccupied expanse between the ill-fated Proclamation Line and the Mississippi River. Easy access to the land was indispensable to frontier communities, and common interest here engendered common purpose." The author adds that the frontier as a *region* was that area of the United States in which the frontier process was going on at any moment. He also observes that the American frontiersman had to erect, in the course of a lifetime, all the institutions of private or public life that he desired. The aspects of the national land system reveal the Ordinance of 1787 as a great constructive measure. Its policy was to be carried out by Washington, who, at the end of his administration, secured possession of the whole American territory — "the new government was a going institution." The formation of the new States and the political theories of the frontier are discussed, with the conclusion drawn from the result of constitution making in the United States, that it "affords a measure of popular ideas of government such as no other community possesses." The period of Jefferson Democracy is here reviewed, the social, religious and political aspects, with certain changes observable in American relationships. The clash of principles in Ohio, the Louisiana Purchase, and the problems of the Southwest border are also reviewed, and the author here turns to the significant events which were to affect the future of the West. After following the progress on the border, the Indian problem claims attention. It is not, however, until after the victory of 1812, that the frontier becomes more stabilized; and the subsequent period of the great migration, with the forces which produced it, brings forward all the factors of progress which with the growth of population, and the admission of new states, constitute some of the features and phases of the vast development. The slavery question is here reviewed. Frontier finance is discussed, and outstanding changes, such as the American system, the anti-tariff land controversy of the Jacksonian period, Federal improvements, canal engineerings, land booms, the status of Indian policy, frontier activities, the settlement of Oregon, the war with Mexico, the conquest of California, the railroad age, land grants and western roads; mining development, overland routes, the theory of land grants and the demand for more liberal land policies; the effect of the Civil War on the United States, with the complete survey of every phase of the frontier, are treated as a continuous influence. The disappearance of the frontier was marked by "the transmutation into agrarian influence, and the struggle was henceforth to be less a contest between the older sections and the young, and more a struggle of the agricultural element of society against the industrial." The author says that the first century of American independence was dominated by the influence of the frontier; "its second seems likely to be shaped by industry and the pressure of the outside world."

AMERICAN IN THE MAKING, AN, THE LIFE STORY OF AN IMMIGRANT, by M. E. Ravage (1917). Born in Vaslui, Rumania, of Jewish parents, the author knew very little of America until the return of a distant relative from that more distant land. Couza arrived in a burst of glory, bringing presents for all the family: a safety razor, a fountain pen, a music box! His stories of the new land and his own importance were marvellous and were received with openmouthed wonder. In the minds of his family and friends he was elevated to great positions; he did not deny that he might be an American Ambassador. Shortly after Couza's return to America there began an exodus from Vaslui to America and among them went the young Ravage. Arrived in America almost penniless he went to visit his gorgeous relative, foreman of a factory, and was not made very welcome, but in the house of a cousin he found sanctuary. It was in 1900 that Mr. Ravage came to America as a lad of sixteen and settled among his own country people in the Rumanian section of New York City. His first attempt to make a living was as a pedler of candies; his second was in an East Side barroom as tap-boy. In the saloon the boy got his first conception of opportunity; he learned much and not all of it was bad. His next place was in a sweatshop and here began his real intellectual start. There were intelligent young immigrants in the shop who attended lectures; read at every spare moment; argued and talked and settled the affairs of the universe to suit their own tastes almost daily. They showed him the way to the public library, the intellectual theatres and educational clubs. "Nothing in the way of thought-interest was too big or too heavy for this intelligentzia of the slums." He went to evening school; prepared for college; took his examination for a scholarship at Cornell and failed. All this time he was living as an immigrant among immigrants; his Americanization had not yet begun. After his failure to enter Cornell young Ravage decided to enter the University of Missouri and gallantly set forth. It was a far cry from the Ghetto to the comparative conventionalism of the West and the boy had a hard time at first. For one thing his finances were extremely low and he was compelled to live with a roommate. But he never succeeded in keeping a roommate long. It became almost a game with him to see how long it would be ere his current roommate would look the other way when they met. The arguments were so different from the East Side; these people were too polite to say what they really thought, and yet they whistled indoors; they were very elaborate in their introductions, too, but they threw biscuits at one another at table! In every way young Ravage tried to get in touch with these strange contradictory young people. He read Mark Twain aloud to get the sound of the vernacular; he even joined the cadet corps and attended chapel regularly although it bored him. Then he made one college friend and some of the loneliness abated. Summer came and he joyously set out for New York to revisit his family. But he found that he had outgrown them; the very things he had longed for in his lonely college days now seemed trite to him. He went to a lecture with a girl friend and did not enjoy it as of yore. When the summer ended he returned gladly to Missouri. His friend met him at the station; men spoke to him on the campus, some even thumped him on the back. His heart was glad; at last his dream was realized. He was an American.

AMERICAN ORCHESTRA AND THEODORE THOMAS, THE, by Charles Edward Russell (1927). The career of Theodore Thomas and the results of his efforts to mould musical taste in this country are reviewed by this author who sees a stupendous work in the forty-three years of ceaseless and often desperate struggle which passed between the time when the orchestral leader first raised his baton over a concert orchestra and the time when he laid it down forever, and notes, as the result, that music became a pervasive influence in thousands of American homes. Thomas came to this country in 1845. His birthplace was Esens, the capital of the great marshy East Friesland province of Northwest Germany. He had already become a musician of ability and some renown. "He was mad for music and indifferent to everything else, including the school to which he was early sent in the old red brick building back of the Lutheran church." He reached New York at a period when brass bands were in demand — an age of political military parading. The Philharmonic Society, "destined to play so noble a part in the development of metropolitan culture," had been launched three years before the arrival of the Thomas family, but orchestral music left New York cold indeed. The theatres had their orchestra for overtures and incidental accompaniment, and the biographer says that "the first really coercive incident in the career of Theodore Thomas was when he secured a place in one of these theatre orchestras." Thomas's father later enlisted in the United States Navy as a musician, becoming the first horn blower in the Navy band at Portsmouth, Virginia, and he obtained in the brass choir a place for his son who at that time was about fifteen years old. From that experience the real struggles of Theodore Thomas began, and the author pictures him going forth as a violin virtuoso, without accompanist, backer or guide, travelling from town to town, giving public performances for what money he could take in at the door of a hotel dining room or public hall. "He was his own manager, ticket collector and press agent. Often he travelled on horseback from town to town — preferably at night and alone!" In 1850, he returned to New York to find the musical situation much changed, but he never had a thought at that time, says his biographer, of another metier than that of violinist and composer. Fate hurled him into something wholly different. He was unexpectedly called upon to conduct the opera, "The Jewess," at the old Academy of Music, and achieved such success that he was made permanent conductor. "Instead of one instrument on which to express his ideas, he had forty or fifty." He renounced his cherished plans of a virtuoso's career, and resolved to make the cultivation of musical taste in America his life work. His biographer considers that this was the infantile stage of musical development, not alone in New York but in other cities, but says that Thomas had a basic belief in music as an ethical force. "To his mind the beauty of music and the beauty of conduct were akin; ethics and æsthetics were inseparable." He is quoted as saying, "What our overworked business and professional men most need in America is an elevating mental recreation that is not an amusement." He felt that what was required was something that would appeal to and arouse the spiritual nature, and for that purpose was nothing in the world comparable to music. Not music that consisted of a mere concourse of agreeable noises, but music that had spiritual significance and message. "The summit of such music," says the biographer, "was to be found in the symphony, which Thomas deemed the highest achievement of the human mind and the greatest expression of the aspiration of the human soul, so that when a symphony had been heard with understanding and knowledge it conferred upon the hearers a wealth of the purest emotions, cleansing and uplifting." The prejudice that he met only emphasized the hardness of his task, for against the mere name of a symphony existed a prejudice that amounted to a phobia. "Symphony"— that meant something technical, remote, darkling, abstruse, and beyond the comprehension of any except long-haired experts, music cranks, of whom the perfectly sane might well beware. "It was upon this field that Theodore Thomas, aged twenty-seven ventured that May night at the old Irving Hall, Fifteenth Street and Irving Place, with an orchestra of about forty men, made up chiefly from the opera where he had been conducting, and a program of his own peculiar constructing. The artistic results, if not the money receipts, encouraged Thomas in the belief that he had chosen the right way. In taking upon himself the responsibilities of the Theodore Thomas Orchestra, he assumed that the rich men of America would do for the American public what the governments of Europe did for the European public. His work at this time is likened to the siege of a fortress. "No matter how many times Thomas might have conducted a Beethoven symphony, whenever it recurred upon one of his programs he gave to it as much intensive study and thought as if he had not before seen it." He was reputed, recalls the biographer, "to be the coolest and most self-possessed conductor that ever raised a baton." The outstanding appointments which came to him afford many pages of comment, as do his work at the American Centennial in 1876; his summer night concerts at Central Park Garden, in New York; his concerts under the auspices of the Cincinnati Festival Committee and others. A tempting offer came to him when he was asked to become head director of a great national school of music, to be established in Cincinnati, and he now felt that he had before him the work he had always wished most to do. The biographer reviews the contentions which resulted in Thomas's severing his connection with the school and his subsequent return to New York, where he accepted the conductorship of the Philharmonic. There now followed "fruitage of his sowing." The Boston Symphony Orchestra was formed, "the spacious result of the demand he had fostered and the public taste he had led." Chicago wanted him back for more summer concerts; and throughout the memorable year he was preparing for another service to the musical cause. Of this part of his work, the biographer says: "He had long known as other musicians had known, that the concert pitch of all the orchestras in America, his own, no less, was too high. It was a thing that no one was to blame for, a universal condition that in his judgment deprived the orchestra of some of its rightful accuracy, power, and effect. He made up his mind when, for the second time, he took the direction of the Philharmonic, that so far as that organization was concerned he would, within the next two years, bring its pitch to accuracy. Therefore, he gave all his players notice that at the end of that time the pitch of the orchestra would be lowered nine sixteenths of a tone, and all were instructed to prepare for the change, securing new instruments if necessary, or altering the old. When the time came the revolution went into effect without a hitch." He virtually effected the same change in every musical instrument in America. The new pitch was scientifically correct. The full tide of Thomas's success is considered to have been in the years when he had the New York Philharmonic, the Brooklyn Philharmonic, his own orchestra, the New York and Brooklyn choral societies, his regular orchestral seasons in New York and Brooklyn, a series of popular concerts at Steinway Hall and a special series in New York with Raphael Josephy as soloist. He also embarked on a musical enterprise of such purpose and dimensions as to take him on a transcontinental tour which involved fourteen thousand miles of travel, and he undertook to extend his musical ministry by giving a series of concerts for young people and for workingmen. "And then from this pleasing summit and goodly prospect, he was cast of a sudden into the depths of defeat and disaster." This part of his career brings his biographer to the organization of the American Opera Company, which Thomas directed, and which at the end of its season, was so much in debt that its incorporators and backers refused to meet the obligations or to contribute any farther to its existence. But the "Waterloo" of Thomas's career is described in the experiences related by the biographer in the chapter entitled "Waterloo at the World's Fair." He recalls that Thomas took the directorship of music at the Chicago Fair against his judgment, and he considers that the controversy there which created such a storm all over the country and lessened his prestige for the time, was so serious in its effect as to make him a changed man. "Strange are the ways of the fate that hounded him." Chicago has erected upon its beautiful lake front a monument to his memory. The biographer sees as a result of Thomas's career tangible and permanent movements that may be translated into practical statistics: "On May 13, 1862, there was in the United States, besides the band before him, one orchestra entitled to be called of the due symphonic quality, and that feeble and dubious, with five concerts a year. When he left New York for Chicago, 1891, there were in addition to his own, three others of assured and definite basis and one that led a fitful existence. Twenty-one years after his death, I count in the United States fifty-one grand orchestras giving regular and competent seasons and hundreds of excellent smaller bands in the picture houses and hotels playing a grade of music that but for his sowing and the produce thereof would have been impossible. When he began, a knowledge of the joy of great music was the possession of a cultural sect so small as to seem now a thing for ridicule. Twenty-one years after his death a perception of such joys was becoming a national possession. When he began, a single movement of but one symphony was a sign for revolt to the handful of persons that had been tricked into hearing it. In December, 1926, by means of the joining of a grand orchestra and the radio, an audience estimated at two millions heard the whole of Beethoven's Fifth." The book is the story of the American orchestra since about 1846 as well as the record of the successes and failures of Theodore Thomas.

AMERICAN PAINTING, THE HISTORY OF, by Samuel Isham. New Edition, with Five Supplementary Chapters by Royal Cortissoz (1927). In this book, Samuel Isham, Associate of the National Academy of Design, Member of the Society of American Artists, traces the history of painting through three periods: The Colonial, The Provincial, and The Cosmopolitan. The supplementary chapters, by Royal Cortissoz, Member of the American Academy of Arts and Letters, brings the survey down to date. Isham discusses the development of the art through the comparatively short course of its growth in America. At first such art as the struggling colonies possessed came from visiting English craftsmen, usually of the most unskilful type. Soon, however, talent developed among the native born, of whom some of the most promising and enterprising went to England to perfect themselves. Two or three of these men were of quite exceptional ability, for example Copley, Stuart and West. Intellectual dependence on the mother country naturally lasted long after the political ties were broken, but finally separation, the social changes resulting from the change of government and the ruder, more isolated life incident to the development of the country, weakened the influence of English art. In its place came all manner of strivings of native talent to satisfy the æsthetic cravings of native taste, crude at first, but gradually improving under the influence of Düsseldorf, Rome, and later of Paris. One interesting result of this movement, which Mr. Isham points out, was the development of a native landscape school. With the conclusion of the Civil War came another change. Under the author's guidance we watch and see the reasons for the departure for Europe almost in a body of the succeeding generation of artists. They studied in the best *ateliers* of the Old World, side by side with the men who were the leaders of European art; they accepted European standards of workmanship and also to a great extent, European tastes and interests. Even after their return, when they had begun half unconsciously to reflect native ideas in their work, they still tested it by comparison with what was being done elsewhere. The old period of isolation was past. Mr. Isham emphasizes the fact that it is along these latter lines that our painting is developing, adapting itself to native needs and to a new-found native taste with a rapidity that precludes any adequate record. The author believes that a history of American painting should have its importance not through its descriptions of isolated men or their works, but as a record of the growth of the country in intelligence and culture — in other words, a sort of History of Taste. The lives of the early painters have consequently been given in some detail so that it might be seen not only what manner of men they were, but also how they were formed by their surroundings and the sort of public to which they catered. For the same reason, an attempt has been made to note the rise and growth of the different art organizations and their social and intellectual character, and also to give some record of the foreign influences that have been brought to bear upon them. As the author himself says: "It is this development of painting and of the appreciation of painting which it has been the aim of this book to trace, and mention of the lives and works of individual painters has been made as they seemed to illustrate such development. The ungrateful and impossible task of recording the names and works of every meritorious painter has not been attempted." In the five supplementary chapters Mr. Cortissoz discusses the various influences that have, during the past twenty-five years, developed the public taste; the revival of experimentation and individualism in art; the persistence of the decorative motive and the work of Charles W. Hawthorne and others; the realistic movement, with Luks, Bellows, John Sloan, and others; recent developments in mural painting; the landscape painters, the portrait painters, impressionism, and modernism. There are thirty-two chapters in all, bearing chapter headings such as the following: The Primitives; Copley and His Work; Career of Benjamin West, Decline of English Influence; New York Becomes the Art Center; Culmination of Early Landscape School; Increase of French Influence; LaFarge and Whistler; Recent Landscape Painting in America; The Modern Portrait Painters and Recent Mural Decorations. The book contains one hundred and forty-one illustrations in the text, and twelve photogravures.

AMERICAN PORTRAITS, 1875–1900, by Gamaliel Bradford (1920). This is the first of a series of interpretative portraits in which the author expects to cover American history. He is "concerned with their souls . . . with their work only as their souls are illustrated in it." The men he chooses for this period are Mark Twain, Henry Adams, Sidney Lanier, James McNeill Whistler, James Gillespie Blaine, Grover Cleveland, Henry James, and Joseph Jefferson. He begins, "When I was a boy of fourteen, Mark Twain took hold of me as no other book had then and few have since. . . . The criticism of life, strong and personal, if crude, the frank, vivid comments on men and things, set me thinking as I had never thought, and for several years colored my maturing reflection. . . . " In this later judgment he places Mark Twain with the satirists, Molière, Ben Jonson, and Swift rather than with the great comic writers of the world. "His thought was bitter because it was shallow," and "his theoretical conclusions were Nihilistic," a "dogmatic religion of negation." He made men laugh, and "used his terrible weapon of satire to demolish meanness, greed, pettiness, dishonesty," but the final impression is "desolating." When he "had fairly got through with the shams, the trouble was that there was nothing left." His irreverence stripped all the illusions from life. The great charm of his personality made his influence overwhelming. "When he clasps your hand and lays his arm over your shoulder, and whispers that life is a wretched, pitiable thing, and effort useless, and hope worthless, how are you to resist him?"

Mr. Bradford finds in Henry Adams a "lack of seriousness" that he considers the clue to his "whole colossal search for education," and the failure of "the universe, after the most humiliating efforts" to educate him. "He approaches the profoundest questions of life and death in an attitude of amused curiosity." "Smothered with education" he came "to despise it altogether." "He spent his life tramping the world for education; but what he really needed was to be de-educated. . . . He needed not to think, but to live. . . . It was easier to sit back and proclaim life unworthy of Henry Adams than it was to lean forward with the whole soul in a passionate, if inadequate, effort to make Henry Adams worthy of life."

"To Mark Twain thought was an amusing diversion, to Henry Adams it was a splendid stimulant of curiosity, to Lanier it was a despotic master. . . . He believed that the secrets of God could be wrestled for, that every good thing was an object of combat and conquest. . . . He thought with passion . . . fiercely determined to get rid of the rags and shroudings of tradition and convention and thrust way down to the solid structure of naked verity." "His thinking life was one long effort to solve problems, to break through difficulties instead of dodging them, to reach the last analysis of his own soul and the souls of others." Mr. Bradford considers that it is his poems not his prose writings that give him a permanent place in American literature. "But to one who comes to the poems fresh from the close study of Lanier's inner life," they are disappointing. "Why could he not put his soul into them?" He attributes this failure to Lanier's "instinctive reserve."

His "glorious spirit, ever toiling, ever hoping, giving up all material success for the long pursuit of an ideal, was the very stimulus that the young men of the South needed above all others."

In dealing with Whistler, his problem is "to reconcile a great artist with a little man; or, if not a little man, an eccentric man" . . . to whom laughter and fighting were diversions, and drawing and painting his serious business. "No matter how much Whistler may have attitudinized in life, in art he was sincere and genuine." "In short, those who judge him by his quarrels and his bickerings and his flippancy and his odd clothes get no idea of the deep, conscientious earnestness of the artist."

For the study of Blaine he has Mrs. Blaine's delightful letters which reflect the whole course of her husband's career . . . and no picture of him would be complete which did not show his affection for his family and theirs for him. "He was born to mix with men, to please them, and to succeed with them. . . . He could sway great masses of men by his personality. . . . Even his enemies felt it difficult to resist his charm." His mastery of words played a large part in his life, and Mr. Bradford believes he was the victim of "the fatal, delusive power of words," when he defended his business morality, and dubious speculation. "Unquestionably he even excused to himself the complicated course of shuffling and concealment by which he endeavored to hide all his proceedings . . . his own private concerns . . . long past and buried. . . . " "With pretty much all the virtues, all the graces, all the gifts of genius, he will be remembered in his country's annals as the man who lost the presidency because he was suspected of financial dishonor."

Grover Cleveland succeeded by great industry and tireless work with very little talk. The author pictures him as a great moral force expressing himself chiefly in a will to veto.

James, he represents, as "a man whose whole life was in art," and "life was chiefly interesting, not in itself, but as matter for art." "His real humanity, his essential, vivid, passionate existence, was in his art." One of his characters says, "What's art but an intense life — if it be real?"

He shows Jefferson rich in human traits, and that his cheerfulness and optimism were "not a matter of temperament, but a matter of will." Jefferson "loved to sum up his own and all life in a phrase of Seneca: 'Life is like a play upon the stage; it signifies not how long it lasts, but how well it is acted.' "

AMERICAN REVOLUTION, THE, by Charles Howard McIlwain (1923). The aim of this author is to give a constitutional interpretation of the issues involved in the American Revolution. He traces what he considers the whole train of continuous constitutional development which led directly to the struggle. This train of events, he holds, had a definite and discoverable beginning, and once begun, it led straight to revolution. "Revolution occurred in 1776, but the direct and continuous causes of it definitely began neither later nor earlier than May 19, 1649. On that day the Parliament passed the act establishing the Commonwealth." The claims made, — a right to bind the colonies in "all cases whatsoever," — formally asserted for the first time, marked the beginning, from this author's viewpoint, of the constitutional issue that led directly to the Revolution. To show its important bearing upon the subsequent action on the part of the colonies, the author discusses, in the following arrangement, the antecedents of this act, the earliest resistance to its central principle, the historical and constitutional justification of this principle, and of the objections made to it, and, lastly, the historical connection of this important act with the later part of the constitutional struggle in the colonies. The conclusions assume that the American opposition lost its "constitutional character in 1776, and became a subject no longer susceptible of constitutional treatment." In making clear what the constitutional position was prior to the Revolution, the author enumerates an infringement of the colonial charters, a violation of the law of nature and a breach of the constitution of the British Empire, and it is this last count which he considers the most far-reaching, and which "offers a complete justification of the whole of the American demands." In the views of the author, upon this pivotal question, he admits his divergence of opinion from other historians, whose viewpoints stress the nationalistic characteristics of the colonies as making independence "inevitable." He, therefore, divorces from his own treatment what he calls the "network of causes, economic, social, or political," and considers them at the background rather than in the foreground, where he puts the constitutional phase of the struggle.

AMERICAN SCULPTURE, THE HISTORY OF, by Lorado Taft. (New Edition, 1924.) I. The Beginnings of American Sculpture, 1750–1850; II. Middle Period, 1850–1876; III. Contemporary Sculpture, 1876–1923. The author makes quite clear the drawback to American sculpture of working in a country without tradition, but he recognizes that the third, or contemporary period, has brought a new revelation of the beautiful in nature, and is showing to the people of this country the possibilities of sculpture. In this period it has reached for the first time national expression — something neither Anglo-Saxon, nor Italian nor French, but a fusing of all these elements into an art which is vital and significant, the true product of the country and the age which has given it birth. Portions of Mr. Taft's introduction will serve best as a means of summarizing the content of this book: British sculpture scarcely existed at the time when the American colonies were in process of making. Thus it came about that our ancestors here in America were without sculptural tradition. Moreover, in large measure they were of a humble class — working people unacquainted with the arts. It is not surprising, then, that stock of this character, transplanted to an unsettled and inhospitable shore, should have been practically immune from artistic inspirations, and that two whole centuries were to elapse before sculpture should make a shy appearance. Until the third decade of the nineteenth century there was no real native sculpture. Our first professional sculptor was born in 1805. It is difficult to realize that our actual achievement from the very kindergarten stage of an unknown art to the proud position held by American sculpture in the Paris Exposition of 1900 was the work of threescore years and ten. As beginners seldom attempt groups, but work timidly on single figures, so the beginnings of American sculpture are discovered in isolated workers appearing here and there in the most unexpected localities: Rush in Philadelphia; Augur in New Haven; Frazee in New Jersey. Then with the opening years of the last century, came the first Americans destined to make sculpture a profession: Greenough in Boston, Crawford in New York, Powers in Cincinnati. To-day our sculptors thrive in groups; the isolated practitioners of the art are few. Almost without exception these sculptors of the first half of the century were animated by a single desire — to get to Italy as soon as possible. The reasons for this are not far to seek. Their own country afforded neither sculptural instruction nor examples. Those who went abroad remained there; hence no returning current of helpful knowledge and counsel came to aid those left behind. Another sufficient reason for the unanimous hegira of this time lay in the dearth of good materials in this country. It must be acknowledged that up to the time of the Centennial but little significance had crept into American sculpture. It was impersonal — expressing in no way the spirit of the people. The lyric strain was almost unknown; our sculptors were executants, not composers. With the Centennial Exposition of 1876 came an artistic quickening such as this country had never known before. It began with the recognition of our own shortcomings as compared with other lands. France in particular made a strong appeal to our newly awakened tastes, and the work of one or two Americans who had studied in Paris had great influence. The demand for a better and more forceful art was not long to remain unanswered. With the advent of Saint Gaudens there came a notable change in the spirit of American sculpture. Though we owe this change largely to Paris, the result has not been French sculpture. Paris has vitalized the dormant tastes and energies of America — that is all. A pronounced and helpful feature of the new order is the fact that as a rule the Parisian-trained sculptors do not remain abroad, they return to America, and, like their French masters, they delight in teaching. The influence of such a man as Saint Gaudens becomes incalculable when multiplied through the pupils whom he had brought up to share his triumphs. Thus the art schools of America are at the present time in a flourishing condition, and the opportunity for study from nature is so abundant in all our large cities that it is no longer necessary for a student of sculpture to go abroad excepting for travel and observation. Hands have grown skilful and eyes discerning here in America, while not a few of our sculptors have learned the art of thinking and expressing themselves in truly sculptural terms, — something which is quite different from realistic imitation. The author, a leading member of the Sculpture Society, who is also an instructor in the Art Institute of Chicago, traces this history of development in twenty-eight chapters, the headings of some of which are: Early Efforts in Sculpture; Greenough and His Times; Crawford and Sculpture at the Capitol; Early Women Sculptors, Augustus Saint Gaudens, Daniel C. French, Frederick MacMonnies, The Younger Generation in New York. The book contains 128 plates and illustrations.

AMERICAN TRAGEDY, AN, by Theodore Dreiser (2 vols., 1925) reveals the pitiful life of a boy of the lower middle classes, Clyde Griffiths, born of a father mentally weak and a strong though untrained mother, both of that peculiarly narrow religious zealotry manifest in itinerant street preachers. The boy early rebelled against his abnormal life, seeking first in miscellaneous jobs, then as an assistant at a soda fountain and finally in the unexpected splendor of the Hotel Green-Davidson as a bell-boy work that would bring him some of the comfort and fun that other boys have, as well as relief from family life. The other bell-boys soon initiated Clyde, who had a winning personality, into their escapades outside of hours — dinners in which the habits of these men of the world they had seen pass through the Green-Davidson doors as to wine, women and song were faithfully copied. Joy rides too, when one of their friends could borrow from his father's wealthy employer his best car and take them and their girl friends out. But on one such ride, in speeding back lest they be late in going on duty, they ran over and killed a little girl. Seeking to escape the police the car was wildly smashed into some obstacle and all not too wounded, escaped. After some hardships, Clyde made his way to Chicago where, after various experiences he again met one of the other bell-boys and so found a place at the Union League Club. There he met his uncle, Samuel Griffiths, a very successful collar manufacturer from Lycurgus, New York, in the city on business. After a talk that interested his uncle in him — the families had not been in touch for years — he received word to come on to his uncle's home town if he cared to work into some position in his factory. This was just what Clyde had been longing for. He was too ambitious to pass his life as a bell-boy. But on his arrival it appeared that his uncle's family did not care to encourage his ambitions, particularly in a social way, for they represented the exclusive upper social life in Lycurgus. Clyde did, however, meet that fascinating and modern young woman, Sondra Finchley, in their home. Later, to spite his cousin Gilbert, whom Clyde closely resembled, Sondra took Clyde up and introduced him to all their mutual friends. Previous to this belated social acceptance Clyde had spent much time in loneliness which had been somewhat eased of late since a new, and lovely little country girl, Roberta Alden, had come into the stamping department of the factory where he was now foreman. They had in fact become lovers although it was strictly against the rules of the factory for any of the foremen to have anything to do with the girls who worked under them outside of hours. As Clyde's intimacy with Sondra progresses more rapidly than his happiest dreams, his need and desire for Roberta grow less. Then she tells him that he must help her find a way to prevent their child from being born. For a time the tension increases. Clyde wavers distracted between Roberta's claims and Sondra's more openly expressed favor. The newspaper account of a boating accident in another state leads to dark thoughts in the young man's harassed mind. How simple things would be if Roberta should drown on some such excursion and he escape to happiness with Sondra! At intervals diabolic voices seem to whisper the details of the murder into his shrinking ears. Roberta becomes importunate in her anguish. He takes her on an excursion to Grass Lake and Big Bittern in the Adirondacks. In the solitude of the south shore of that lonely lake his fiendish plans materialize. Then, when the moment arrives he shrinks from it and hates the girl the more because he knows himself too weak to find his freedom this way. A discussion arises and she creeps toward him in the boat, which tips dangerously. With his camera in hand he instinctively strikes to ward her off and she falls back. His sudden movement to save her throws them both into the water as he had previously planned. Although he is a good swimmer and she is not twenty feet away and unable to swim, his former resolution revives and he swims for the shore leaving her to drown. There he picks up the suit case he has hidden, changes into a dry suit, and makes his escape to Sondra and their friends who are soon off on a gay camping tour of Bear Lake. Not long after he is traced through letters found in Roberta's suit case, left at Big Bittern, in spite of the various aliases which he had used, and arrested. The dramatic and romantic interest of this case arouses widespread interest. Samuel Griffiths, more for the sake of his own good name than out of regard to Clyde, furnishes him with excellent counsel but to no purpose. The pathetic letters which Roberta had been writing him contrasted with the carefree nature of Sondra's letters. The evidence of the affair being planned in advance, outweigh the claim of the defence that Roberta's death was due to an accident. Clyde's own mind continues to be confused as to the preponderance of guilt in his motives. His mother comes on and endeavors, by addressing public meetings in her son's behalf to raise the money for an appeal of the case, for Samuel Griffiths and his family have withdrawn their interest and moved away from Lycurgus to escape the notoriety. That fails as well as an appeal to the new Governor made by Mrs. Griffiths and the Rev. McMillan, a minister with the spirituality of the old saints, who had interested himself through the mother's appeal in Clyde's case. When all hope is gone this man becomes the source and means of a growing spirituality and strength of character in this boy now for the first time fitted to live rightly but forced instead, to pay the last penalty to the State for a crime committed out of weakness and undisciplined greed for happiness, one of the many derelict through inadequate character training and the lack of the normal joys of youth.   The social apathy and irony of life are seen in the final scene laid in a western city at night wherein the opening is repeated.   Another young lad, this one Clyde's nephew, forms a part of an identical street mission under the leadership of the aged grandfather and grandmother, another American tragedy in the making.

AMERICANIZATION OF EDWARD BOK, THE, the autobiography of a Dutch boy fifty years after (1920).   Edward Bok came from Holland with his parents in 1870 when he was six years old.   He and his brother went to the public school in Brooklyn without knowing a word of the English language.   The fortunes of the transplanted family did not flourish, and Edward looked for some work outside school hours to add to the family income.   One afternoon a baker noticed the hungry boy looking in his window at the buns.   "Look pretty good, don't they?" he asked.   "They would if your windows were clean," the Dutch boy answered, and got his first job washing windows for fifty cents a week.   Later he helped as clerk in the bakery afternoons, delivered newspapers Saturday mornings, and peddled ice-water and lemonade to the thirsty passengers on the trolley cars to Coney Island in the afternoons.   He also reported the children's parties he attended to a Brooklyn newspaper.   Poverty forced him to leave school when he was thirteen and become an office-boy with the Western Union Telegraph Company.   With his schooldays ended the question of self-education became an absorbing question to him.   He decided to read about the lives of successful men who had not had the advantages of a college education, and saved his luncheon money and carfare until he was able to buy a set of Appleton's Encyclopedia.   After he read the articles he wrote to some of his heroes for further information as to certain points, with the result that he made an interesting and valuable collection of autograph letters, and gained the friendship of President Garfield, General and Mrs. Grant, Jefferson Davis, President and Mrs. Hayes, and on a trip to New England following his correspondence met Oliver Wendell Holmes, Louisa Alcott, Phillips Brooks, Wendell Phillips, and others, talked with the failing Emerson, and went to the theatre with Longfellow.   His first editorial venture was in his twenty-first year when he started the "Brooklyn Magazine" with a distinguished list of contributors through his acquaintance with so many celebrities.   Two years later he sold out and founded one of the first newspaper syndicates.   In 1882 he obtained a position as stenographer with the Henry Holt Company, and in 1884 with the Scribner firm, and was later placed in charge of the advertising department.   In 1889 he became editor of the "Ladies Home Journal" and the rest of the story is the development of this magazine. Through his editorial position he was able to accomplish a great many reforms: cleaning up of cities, abolition of the public drinking cup and a crusade against patent medicines.   He describes the inauguration of the various departments of his magazine such as, Side Talks with Girls, The King's Daughters, and Questions and Answers for Young Mothers, the foundation of free scholarships in colleges, his cooperation with prominent architects to publish a series of plans for houses which could be built at a moderate price, and his similar work for gardening and interior decoration.   The last chapter on Where America Fell Short with Me contains some interesting suggestions for the treatment of the foreign-born.

ANNA CHRISTIE, by Eugene O'Neill (1920). Originally titled Chris Christopherson, it is as much the drama of the old sailor, Chris, as of Anna, his daughter. Chris has two passions, hatred of the sea, whose service he cannot escape, and love for his daughter, whom he has sent to inland relatives in order that she may escape the sea's curse. When the play opens Anna has just arrived at the quayside saloon where Chris spends his time when he is not aboard the coal barge which he captains. After years of separation the daughter is still to the father an innocent young girl representing all the perfection his sailor's life has never known. In reality she has been soiled and shamed by her farmer cousins, and has been living in a "house." She lives happily on the barge with her father, and the clean peace of the wide sky and water, which Chris knows is only the deceptive calm of "de old Davil" sea, works her regeneration. A boat from the open sea filled with wrecked sailors comes out of the mysterious fog, and brings the Irish stoker. Mat Burke, to fall in love with Anna. He defies her father to keep him from marrying her. Anna, inately honest, stops their fight to decide her future with the story of her life. Burke and Chris each go his own way to forget their misery in drink, and unknown to the other the two sign up for a voyage on the same ship. Burke rebelled against marrying a woman with such a past, but his love for Anna brings him back to her.

ANNETTE AND SYLVIE, see **THE SOUL ENCHANTED,** by Romain Rolland.

ARCHITECTURE IN AMERICA, STORY OF, THE, by Thomas E. Tallmadge (1927). A popular survey of the art in which American supremacy is recognized at the present time. An introductory chapter traces architecture from its beginnings down to its appearance in Colonial America. Beginning with the Colonial period (1630–1800) the author reviews in turn the overlapping post-Colonial or Transitional period (1790–1820), the Greek revival (1820–1860), the Parvenu period (1860–1880) after the Civil War, the Romanesque revival (1876–1893), the period of Richardson, World's Fair of 1893, the turning point in our architectural story, and the modern period since that time marked by Eclecticism, or the art or philosophy of selecting from every school, the free borrowing from many sources. The homes of the colonists copied the houses of the same period in England. Mr. Tallmadge divides this period into the Early American, 1630 to 1700, and the Georgian, 1700 to 1800. The carpenter-architects, like Samuel McIntire of Salem, depended on well-known architectural handbooks, and memory. The early part of the Georgian period was dominated by Sir Christopher Wren, and the latter by the designs of Inigo Jones and Robert and James Adam. Of churches the author describes the Virginia type, the New England meeting-house, and the "full-blown Georgian church" of which Christ Church, Philadelphia, is the best example. The post-Colonial he declares was the "personal property of Thomas Jefferson" in the plans he sent from Paris for the Capitol of Virginia at Richmond, and in the buildings of the University of Virginia. Differing from other authorities who would make Jefferson the sponsor of the Greek revival that followed, he describes the buildings that Jefferson inspired as a French version of the Roman. Benjamin H. Latrobe was the architect who brought the Greek revival from England to America. A chapter on Spanish and Creole architecture gives credit to the important influence of the missions of California and Louisiana on our architectural history. The influences of the Parvenu period were the Victorian Gothic and the French style of the Third Empire, and the insignia of the mansions of the wealthy were mansard roof, cupola and porches, oriels, bays, port-cochères, policed by the cast iron dog with his companion the deer in the days of Elsie Dinsmore and Uncle George and his nephew, Rollo. A mélange of the Gothic and that of Charles L. Eastlake's designs became known as the "Queen Anne" style. Richard M. Hunt was a distinguished architect though he lived in this dark period. The Romanesque Revival was the first important movement that was original to America, and its architect was Henry Hobson Richardson, and Trinity Church, Boston, is his greatest work. The Classic style was adopted for the buildings of the exposition of 1893, and the spectacle was so beautiful that layman and professional alike were convinced of the superiority of the art of Greece and Rome. The Transportation Building designed by Louis Sullivan and admired by European visitors expressed his rationalist idea that the form should express the function. His disciples challenged the Beaux Arts, the great architectural school in Paris, with their originality. Since 1893 important schools of architecture have been founded in universities. Charles Follem McKim was the leader of the college bred and technically trained and equipped architects of the period following the World's Fair. The firm of McKim, Mead and White designed the Boston Public Library, the buildings of Columbia University, and the J. Pierpont Morgan Library, New York, and the Pennsylvania Terminal Station in New York City. Next to McKim in the æsthetics of Eclectic architecture Mr. Tallmadge ranks Ralph Adams Cram and Bertram Grosvenor Goodhue who followed the Mediævalists as McKim the Classicists. Of the development of American types, Mr. Tallmadge takes up the different styles under the headings, houses, churches, schoolhouses, universities, apartments and hotels, railway stations, banks, clubs, stores, theatres, factories, and the influence of city planning. The last chapter "Today and Tomorrow" is devoted to the praises of the skyscraping office-buildings of which the Woolworth Tower is supreme, and the influence of the designs of Eliel Saarinen. The author is himself a practicing architect.

ARCTURUS ADVENTURE, THE, by William Beebe (1926). "An account of the New York Zoological Society's First Oceanographic Expedition." The avowed objects of the Expedition were the investigation of the Sargasso Sea — that floating continent of seaweed, and the study of the Humboldt Current. But "owing to continual storms the former was in such a disintegrated condition that I (Dr. Beebe) soon decided to postpone detailed study until a more favorable time. In the Pacific, to our surprise, we found there was no trace of the Humboldt Current about the Galápagos. The inexplicable absence of this great, cold, Antarctic current was more than made up for by the presence of equally unexpected natural conditions." The "unexpected natural conditions" referred to were rare and unusual forms of marine life, some of which had never before been recorded, so that the expedition combined exploration with scientific research. The "Arcturus" was a well equipped floating laboratory, carrying a complete staff of research scientists and artists, and it boasted some features which no other ship ever before claimed. One of these was the "pulpit," a cage of three-man capacity, which when lowered over the bow of the ship afforded the occupants excellent opportunity for observation of marine life ahead of the ship. Amusing contretemps are recorded by Dr. Beebe, resulting from the "pulpit" before the novelty wore off. He states that "it was some time before the crew learned to distinguish between cries for appreciation and yells for help." Another extraordinary feature of the "Arcturus" was the Fourth Dimension — so-called — a contrivance consisting of a combination of rigging and boardwalk which, extending from the side of the ship out over calm water, permitted eager scientists to note piscatorial activities beyond the region disturbed by the engines. In addition to these oddities the "Arcturus" carried trawls, nets and dredges suspended to various depths, as well as adequate diving apparatus. In his account of the Expedition, Dr. Beebe takes his tone from the title he gave the book: the "scientific" is never allowed to outweigh the "adventure," so that the result is a nice blending of erudition and irony. Varying the routine of classification, analysis and in some cases christening of specimens secured, all of which are duly set down, with care towards the minimizing of technicalities, so as not to confuse the layman, the members of the "Arcturus" expedition had the almost unparalleled experience of beholding the birth of a volcano, the actual eruption of a volcanic island from the surrounding sea. The book is profusely illustrated, with color-plates, photographs and black-and-white drawings. Shrimps and squids and flying-fish, sharks and albatrosses and many more make vivid the pages, maintaining a constant variety of interest.

ARIEL, THE LIFE OF SHELLEY, by André Maurois, translated by Ellen D'Arcy. (1924.) An introduction addressed to the "benevolent" reader explains that the author has cast his biography in novel form and yet has not permitted himself to ascribe to Shelley a line or an opinion not authenticated by his letters, those of his friends, or his published poems. The story is of Shelley, the rebel against conventional society, his friends and his loves, the perplexities and tragedies that beset him, how he lived not how he wrote. At home and at school "the smallest threat of authority threw him into a passion of resistance." Shelley was "sent down" from Oxford for expressing his views in a pamphlet on atheism, and with him his friend, Hogg, for trying to defend him. Alone in London, without friends, at war with his father, Percy's young sisters kept him from starvation by sending him pocket-money by their pretty schoolmate, Harriet Westbrook. Harriet's older sister, Eliza, and her father, the retired publican, saw the advantages of an alliance with the handsome young heir to a fortune and a title, and encouraged their intimacy. Harriet was unhappy in school and in love with Percy, while he felt the responsibility for the mind he believed he had formed, and it ended in the trip to Scotland to be married, a mad freak of mistaken chivalry. They were not happy together for long. Eliza fostered Harriet's discontent that she was not received by the Shelley family, and had not the luxury and position of the wife of a future baronet. Harriet grew cold to Shelley, and he came to believe that she was unfaithful to him. A constant visitor at the Godwin home Shelley fell in love with Mary Godwin, lovely in mind as in person. Then follows the elopement of Shelley and Mary to the continent accompanied by her sister, Jane Clairmont, afterwards called Claire. Godwin refused to have anything to do with them on their return. Nevertheless when Shelley came into his inheritance on his grandfather's death, the mean, rapacious Godwin persisted in borrowing money of him. After Harriet's suicide enabled Percy to marry Mary, Godwin's smug satisfaction that his daughter would one day be Lady Shelley "inspired his ex-disciple with further contempt for his character." The passionate and predatory Claire, realizing the impossibility of taking Shelley from her sister, decided to expend her unemployed affections on Byron, and in the face of repeated rebuffs succeeded in becoming his mistress. Byron first appears on the scene at Geneva where Shelley, Mary and Claire were spending a few weeks. He is shown in his relations with the Shelleys and as the profligate, and the vain play-actor, in contrast to the mystical, sincere, high-minded Shelley. Byron's conception of life pained Shelley, the moralist, while his brilliant paradoxical defence of his point of view delighted Shelley, the artist, and the two men were excellent company for each other. Claire's love affair did not prosper. Byron did not feel "in any way bound to this young woman who had thrust herself upon him with such pertinacity." He consented to provide for their child, Allegra, after she was a year old, but refused to ever see Claire again. The Shelleys bought a house in England, but later decided to go to Italy to live. "The ties of family, of friendship, of business, had raised round him intangible walls behind which he was stifling." His generosity to the Godwin family continued, and Claire and Allegra were dependent upon him. His new friend, Leigh Hunt, with a wife and five children, needed help. "Life had brought him so much suffering, his good intentions had been repaid by such evil results . . . the regeneration of the real world now appeared to him so unrealizable that he . . . . sought satisfaction . . . in the more docile and malleable world of the imagination." He felt "that in a new country his life would be like a sheet of white paper on which he could compose a new existence in the same way that he could compose a poem." They finally settled in Pisa, and found themselves the center of a gay and pleasant circle of friends. Here Shelley had his Platonic love affair with the beautiful Emilia Vivani. Mary consoled herself with the thought that he was addressing his impassioned verses to "the divine essence of Emilia . . . and not to a very pretty girl with black eyes" and also that the poet was "so engrossed in the ardor of composition that he had no time to go and see the poem's heroine." Emilia disillusioned him herself by making a worldly marriage. Their two children died, and a son, Percy Florence, was born. In spite of Claire's entreaties Byron had placed Allegra in an Italian convent where she caught a fever and died. The book ends with the sudden tempest and Shelley's funeral pyre on the beach.

ARROW OF GOLD, THE, by Joseph Conrad (1919). This novel revolves around "Ulysses," a young adventurer and sympathizer with the Carlist movement in Spain, and a beautiful and fascinating woman, Dona Rita, who, after years of companionship with a man of great wealth, Henry Allègre, finds herself at his death, again in Paris, where she has taken up her residence among the treasurers of art in that "Pavillion which became well known to the élite of the artistic, scientific, and political world." She was in a fair way to become a celebrity, but something checked it — some sort of gossip. It becomes known to some of the Royalists that the "heiress of Mr. Allègre is contemplating a secret journey." Among the Royalists is a Madame Blunt, an aristocratic old lady who takes advantage of this opportunity to send a message to her son, John Blunt, a Captain of Cavalry in the Army of Legitimists. There were no regular postal communications with France, but Dona Rita was able to get anything that she liked. "She could get a whole army over the frontier if she liked. She could get herself admitted into the Foreign Office at one o'clock in the morning if it so pleased her. . . . Doors fly open before the heiress of Mr. Allègre." But despite her success, she suffered from a strange sense of unreality. The only feeling that she was positive of was — fear. Dona Rita acts as the intermediary in a number of affairs. "Every bald head in the Republican Government got pink at the tope whenever her dress rustled outside the door." They bow with immense deference when the door opens but the bow conceals a smirk because of those "Venetian days." Her movements were commented on in exclusive drawing-rooms and also in other places where the gossip took on another tone. They said that she had a "coup de cœur" for some one. Blunt falls in love with her. On a carnival night, in company with his friend, Monsieur Mills, he arranges for a meeting. Ulysses has seen Mills in one of the Legitimist drawing-rooms. They now arrange to meet at Dona Rita's villa. She casts an enchantment over Ulysses, who is now merging into the idea of the Legitimist Principle, although he considers his act an independent assertion. Among Dona Rita's acquaintances was an international politician and financier named Azzolati. He has promised to do anything in the world for her provided that he would never find her door shut against him as long as he lived. She had commanded him to "take himself off instantly." Dona Rita now decides to adopt the name of "Madame de Lastaola." She considers that she has been precipitated into the crowd of mankind, with an enormous fortune flung brutally at her head, but she has not forgotten her younger days when she tended the goats, and one of the neighbor's sons — a distant cousin — had pursued her into a hole and sat outside with stones in his determination to win her promise to be his wife. Her house in Marseilles is now being used by Carlist officers on leave or on a mission, and she has put her sister, Therese, in charge. Dona Rita calls "Ulysses" Monsieur George, and he is told that she is "both flesh and shadow." "She is for no man. She would be vanishing out of their hands like water that cannot be held," Madame Leonore warns him whenever he goes to her café. Monsieur George's services to the Carlist movement are immensely appreciated. Madame Blunt, who has lived through the Commune, hears of him, and when she crosses the frontier to see her son wants Monsieur George presented to her — she had an insatiable curiosity for anything that was rare. "Are you complex, with unexpected resistances and difficulties in your être intime — your inner self? I wonder now . . . " she said to him. "Madame, I have never tried to find out what sort of being I am." His intercourse with Dona Rita has now become very close and confidential and Madame Blunt who knows of it, tells him that she has been preoccupied a long time with Dona Rita. "It arose from a picture, from two pictures and also from a phrase pronounced by a man, who in the science of life and in the perception of æsthetic truth had no equal in the world of culture. He had said that there was something in her of the women of all time. . . . Such women are not born often. They never develop. They end obscurely. Here and there one survives to make her mark — even in history. And even that is not a very enviable fate. They are at another pole from the so-called dangerous women who are merely coquettes. A coquette has got to work for her successes. The others have nothing to do but exist." Dona Rita's great fortune protected her in a certain measure. Madame Blunt tells Monsieur George what she knows of "Madame de Lastaola's" history. After the death of Henry Allègre, she made "one mistake." When she discovered it, she sent away the man in love with her directly she had found out that his love was not worth having; that she had told him to go and look for his crown; and after dismissing him, she had remained generously faithful to his cause, in her person and fortune. This cause if successful would put Don Carlos de Bourbon on the throne of Spain, and the plan which the Legitimist sympathizers have very much at heart, is to organize a supply by sea of arms and ammunition to the Carlist detachments in the South. And in the person of the eccentric youngster, "Monsieur George," both Monsieur Mills and Captain Blunt believe they have found the very man to put it through. They rely upon Dona Rita to persuade him, and after meeting her, he plunges into the long adventure. It was an ugly and desperate enterprise. Just before he leaves on one of his expeditions, Dona Rita's maid tells him that there is a man who is everlastingly trying to see "Madame" alone — that "Madame" must have given him a hold on her in some way. So far, the maid has managed to keep him off. "Monsieur George" believes that the man is mixed up in the Carlist intrigue. The unlawful trade which "Monsieur George" now enters upon becomes more dangerous and he scents treachery. When his craft is fired upon, he escapes, and at the moment of danger finds that his mind had been fixed on the memory of an arrow of gold, feathered with brilliants and with ruby gleams all along its shaft, a jeweled ornament which Dona Rita wears. Often he had dreamed of it — that Dona Rita herself had raised a perfect round arm to take an arrow of gold out of her hair to throw it at him by hand, like a dart. He always woke up before it struck. Everything slips now out of his grasp — the vessel has to be destroyed and he is thrown on shore after the shipwreck. He returns to Marseilles and notifies the Carlist agent of the sudden ending of his smuggling activities. The man asks him to meet an agent, José Ortega, who is arriving that morning, and tell him the news of the disaster. Ortega will take it to headquarters at Tolosa. "Madame de Lastaola" will also be at Tolosa. "Monsieur George" discovers that Ortega is the man of whom Dona Rita is afraid. Ortega discloses that he knows all about her — they are distant cousins. "Monsieur George" decides from Ortega's actions that he is half-mad, but he takes him to the Consul's house and puts him up for the night. Therese, who makes his bed, recognizes him. Two hours earlier, Dona Rita had arrived from Paris — she decided not to go to Tolosa. "Monsieur George" tells Therese that he will not sleep in the house that night — he does not know that Dona Rita is there. But before he leaves, he hears her voice and enters her room. He tells her that Ortega is under the same roof. Through Therese, Ortega learns of the presence of Dona Rita. He is fully crazed by this time, but tries to reach her room. "Monsieur George" and Dona Rita hear a noise. Ortega calls to her and shakes the door handle. He bangs on the door and raves. Dona Rita and "Monsieur George" take refuge in the darkness and silence. Ortega continues to make an uproar. When he finds that he cannot break down the door, he rushes off to kill Therese, and falls headlong in the hall, where "Monsieur George" finds him, and sends for the doctor. Rita disappears. Years afterward, her lover fights a duel with Captain Blunt who has openly said that "Madame de Lastaola" had become the prey of a young adventurer who had exploited her shamefully. She had sent the arrow of gold to "Monsieur George" as a keepsake, and to prevent him from dreaming of her. Then, years later, he is deprived even of the arrow. It was lost to him in a stormy catastrophe, "but it had not been a thing that one could leave behind one for strange hands"— like the old King Thule with the gold goblet of his mistress, he would have had to cast it into the sea before he died.

ARROWSMITH, by Sinclair Lewis (1925). A satire on the medical profession, and the kind of science that aims for quick material results, commercial gain and publicity. Martin Arrowsmith is a young medical student at a Middle-West State University with a passion for pure science, in contrast to his classmates who "argue about whether they can make more money in a big city or a town, and is it better for a young doc to play the good-fellow and lodge game, or join the church and look earnest . . . get an office on a northeast corner, near a trolley car junction." Martin confides to the admiring "co-ed," Madeline Fox, that he thinks he will be a ship's doctor because at least he would not have to spend his time "trying to drag patients away from some rival doc that has an office on another deck." His friend, Angus Duer, already sees himself as "a brilliant young surgeon," and does not hesitate to say that he is out to make money. Fortunately for Martin there is one old German professor of bacteriology, Max Gottlieb, dedicated to patient, accurate, scientific investigation, who becomes his friend and scientific conscience. At the Zenith Hospital a chance encounter introduces him to Leora, and he deserts the cultured

Madeline for this gay comrade who ruffles his dignity, but is never "improving" or demanding. When she goes home to North Dakota he follows her and they are married, and to support a wife, the disciple of Gottlieb has to give up dreams of working in a laboratory "for the thrill of uncharted discoveries." After his interneship at the Zenith Hospital, he becomes a general practitioner in Wheatsylvania, a small North Dakota town, where ignorance and hypocrisy make life unbearable. Leora's child is stillborn, and they learn that she can never have another. Martin gets the opportunity to take a position as public health officer in Nautilus, where equal disillusionment awaits him. His superior, Dr. Pickerbaugh, is a pompous booster, and organizer, holding strongly to the belief "that a rapid and noisy moving from place to place is the means (and possibly the end) of Progress." Leora tells him that she sees that he is to work twenty-eight hours a day, and then if there is any time left he can work in his laboratory. "You belong in a laboratory," she said, "finding out things, not advertising them." Dr. Pickerbaugh is elected to Congress, and Martin has a chance to make some experiments and write a paper that gains the attention of Max Gottlieb, now with the McQuirk Institute in New York. The invitation to join Gottlieb comes to Martin in Chicago, where he has a routine position as pathologist with Angus Duer in the Rouncefield Clinic, after being accused of "radical" sympathies, and forced out of the office at Nautilus. Eventually Martin makes a great discovery in bacteriology, but is anticipated by a member of the Pasteur Institute, and incurs the disfavour of his director, who would have had him publish his notes six months earlier before they were complete and substantiated. He devotes himself to the study of the effect of "phags" on germs, and goes out to the West Indian Island of St. Hubert, to test his "phags" on the victims of an epidemic of plague which has broken out there. His plan is to give his treatment to selected cases only, verifying by comparison with uninoculated patients the value of his serum. Leora insists on going with him, and through the carelessness of a servant dusting, picks up a cigarette soaked with plague germs, and Martin finds her dead. This breaks his morale, and he gives the serum to everyone, and thus betrays his scientific ideals, and perhaps humanity, to save life. When the plague ceases it now is not possible to tell whether the "phage" had checked it or it had run its course. After a time Martin marries the wealthy widow, Joyce Lanyon, whom he had met at St. Hubert. She becomes the mother of the son that the lovely, generous Leora could not give him, but she has no interest in his work, and is angry when he misses a dinner engagement to stay at the laboratory. The baby, Martin feels, will grow up to be an aristocrat like his mother, and one day condescend to him. Being the husband of a rich wife makes his work impossible, and he breaks away to join his friend, Terry Wickett, who is doing independent research in a place of his own in the woods in Vermont. Martin is happy to carry on experiment for the sake only of the ultimate truth. He says to Terry, "We'll plug along on it (the new quinine stuff) for two or three years, and maybe we'll get something permanent — and probably we'll fail."

ART, A HISTORY OF, by Joseph Pijoan (3 vols., 1927) is a survey of the whole art history of mankind from the Neolithic Age to the present with many illustrations. It covers not only the accepted masterpieces of painting, architecture and sculpture, but also weaves into the story, the development of the minor arts such as pottery, clothing, jewellery, ceramics and embroidery. The author has drawn upon the new knowledge available in the general field of history through recent excavations. Thus through the exercise of the historic sense the chief art production of each period is given its proper perspective and place. Such chapters as those on modern painting and architectural form are interesting as art criticism. Volume one covers primitive art, and that of Egypt, Babylonia, the Mediterranean Colonies and the Far East. Both children and savages reproduce an object not as it is but according to their picture of it. The art of the aborigines is better than that of children because they add observations of nature to their repertory of mental images. The first step is usually ornamentation of the body, then sculpture of varying kinds including masks for dancing, then painting. Architecture among the aborigines is rudimentary, for the tomb was the only monumental building of predynastic art. The structural technique of Egyptian temples is poor. Persian art showed itself eclectic, but assimilated what it took. Their isolation from the Græco-Roman world preserved the Oriental character of their art which was handed down in Arabian culture. Alexander's invasion of India left a Græco-Buddhist art that was a conglomeration of forms. The Chinese surpassed in painting. Ægean art emphasized the palace whereas in classical Greece the temple was more important. Circular structure at Epidaurus characterized the fourth century B.C. but after the death of Alexander Ionian tastes predominated in architecture. The Augustan period at Rome marked the triumph of Hellenistic art. The period of the Roman supremacy was characterized by bridges and aqueducts. The art most peculiar to the Romans was, perhaps, that of the legionaries which was modified by the different provinces in which it appeared. In the aboriginal civilizations of America there was a noticeable cultural unity. The temples and palaces were the most striking forms in the Maya cities. Their ceramic art was also important. The second volume opens with a study of early Christian art. Enamels and other rich decorations characterized the art of Byzantium. Its earlier patterns were Persian and Coptic but later Byzantine art developed a style of its own. The Germanic tribes showed a love of the goldsmith's art. Of Merovingian monuments little remains but two illuminated manuscripts which date from the Visigothic occupation. Except for ivory carvings no sculptures of the Carolingian period have come down to us. The Arabs had no art traditions before the time of Mahomet. Moslem countries are most famous for their industrial art. The Romanesque applies to the art derived from the Latin which arose subsequent to the Carolingian period. Out of the Romanesque grew the Gothic style which was chiefly famous for the beauty of its cathedrals, the most important of which were built in the thirteenth century. With the end of the thirteenth century a school of painting developed at Sienna in complete independence of Florence which was then preëminent in all art matters. Tuscan sculpture originated at Pisa and developed a local character in Florence during the fifteenth century. About the middle of the fifteenth century in Florence a liberal tendency was manifest in a desire for novelty both artistic and literary. Botticelli is representative. The third volume begins with the sixteenth century. Florence took second place, for this was the golden age of the Roman Renaissance, under Julius II, and Leo X. The church of Saint Peter was the great work of this period. It was planned but not finished by Bramante. Michelangelo gave the cupola its definite form. Now painting centred in Rome drawing artists like Leonardo from their native provinces. During the first half of this century the work of Michelangelo overshadowed the entire field of art. Venetian painting began about the end of the fifteenth century with Gentile and Bellini. Titian also was of this period. In the reign of Ferdinand and Isabella, German and Burgundian artists imported a flamboyant Gothic style into Spain. The Burgundian sculptors of this reign executed marvels. The Reformation gave no great impulse to art, although two painters, Dürer and Hans Holbein were outstanding figures. Little is known of the Baroque style, which consists in the employment of unsuitable or extravagant forms, from the time of Michelangelo until the middle of the eighteenth century. In painting the Bolognese school sought eclectic perfection. Versailles is typical of French architecture under the Bourbons which tended toward the Baroque. Velasquez and also Murillo were trained in the school of Seville. The great Renaissance architects of England were Inigo Jones and Sir Christopher Wren. The Baroque period was the golden age of Flemish and Dutch painting; Rembrandt was the master of the Dutch; Van Dyck and Reubens of the Flemish school. Then a reaction against the Baroque set in. Napoleon encouraged classical forms. An interesting feature of the nineteenth century romantic architecture is the rehabilitation of the Gothic as natural and adapted to the requirements of modern times. Rodin and Meunier were the great masters of sculpture after the romantic period. At the end of the nineteenth century, fatigue with realistic art is represented by the work of the impressionists. The objective of the new movements, seems to be pure, abstract form. The Russian ballet as painting in movement, with literature and music assisting, points toward the future of modern art.

AT MRS. BEAM'S, a comedy, by C. K. Munro (1921). At Mrs. Beam's boarding house in London are gathered a group typical of the "permanent" inmates of such establishments. There is the inquisitive and garrulous spinster, Miss Shoe, old Miss Cheezle interested in nothing but her game of Patience, the Irish widow, Mrs. Bebb, a bridge expert, her boorish young son, James, always at the graphophone, two giggling young women, Mrs. Stone and her friend, Miss Newman, and the middle-aged, unsuccessful Mr. Durrows, appealed to by all the ladies as a masculine authority on every topic of conversation. Miss Shoe makes up her mind that two new arrivals from Paris are the "French Bluebeard," who has been featured in the newspapers recently, and his next victim, doomed to disappear in the large trunk they have brought with them. Mr. Dermot and the fascinating Laura, are wanted by the police of three countries, and are temporary boarders on their way to South America. Laura tells Miss Shoe that she is the daughter of Viscount Bix. In their room the next morning Mr. Dermot provokes a quarrel with Laura, who throws things at him and overturns the furniture, so that the noise brings Miss Shoe to the door, ostensibly to borrow some coals, but really to satisfy her insatiable curiosity. Later Laura overhears Dermot trying to induce Mrs. Stone to become his secretary, and becomes furiously jealous. She makes up to a Mr. Langford, and answers Miss Shoe's guarded criticism of her behaviour as not quite "nice" with the information that her husband is on intimate terms with many other women, thus confirming Miss Shoe's worst suspicions of him. Miss Shoe's detective work brings out the fact that they are not married, and that Laura is terrified of Dermot sometimes. This is all a preconcerted plan to provide for their ejection from the respectable boarding house. The landlady asks them to leave the next day. Dermot gets permission to say a few words to the boarders in farewell after dinner, and keeps them engaged while Laura goes through their rooms for money and jewellery to put in the trunk. He thanks Miss Shoe particularly for her kindness to the "innocent" Laura, all the while emphasizing his remarks by brandishing a large scimitar at the terrified woman, encouraging her in the Bluebeard fiction to the last. With a flourish he gives her the knife as a farewell present "out of that famous trunk," telling her that though it is not itself a "dead female," he has been assured that it has been the means of making some. Mr. Durrows arrives, very drunk, wearing Miss Shoe's chain, which

Dermot had given him at the bar, and claims the scimitar as his own. Follows the announcement by Mrs. Beam that the police have just rung up to say that Dermot and his friend are international thieves, and the discovery that they have taken everything in the house of any value.

AXE, THE, by Sigrid Undset (1928).   This book is the first volume of " The Master of Hestviken," the setting, Norway of the lawless thirteenth century.   The first chapters are the story of Steinfinn, one of the body-guard of the young King Magnus, who fell in love with Ingebjörg, betrothed by her father to Mattias Haraldsson. Steinfinn rode away with her one day after the manner of young Lochinvar, after her father had refused his consent to their marriage.   Seven years later Mattias came to their house with an armed band, and took his vengeance by shaming them with taunts that he allowed them to remain man and wife henceforth "by his favor."   In revenge for this humiliation Steinfinn with his kinsmen and servants made a raid on Mattias when he returned to the country, and fought him to the death.   Steinfinn came home to die of his wounds.   Olav, the foster-son of Steinfinn, had been betrothed to Ingunn, his oldest daughter, when the two were children. After the fight with Mattias Olav tried to get Steinfinn's consent to their immediate marriage.   The greedy half-brothers of Steinfinn became the guardian of his children at his death, and had other plans for Ingunn.   Olav took her for his wife and appealed to the Bishop to defend their rights.   Provoked into a fight with a cousin of Ingunn's, Olav killed his tormentor, and escaped to his mother's kin in Denmark. Ingunn remains at the home of Arnvid, Olav's friend, until her relatives insist that she come to her grandmother's home.   Olav and Ingunn are married in the sight of the powerful mediæval Church, yet without the sanction of the Church, or the consent of Ingunn's guardians.   The delicate, nervous girl is unhappy in the group of her prosperous, unsympathetic relatives.   She has to defend herself against the suitors favoured by the family, who are hostile to Olav.   Olav is in the service of the Bishop, now in exile, until his death, and then becomes the vassal of a powerful Earl, able to promise to obtain for him a bought peace, so at last he comes to Ingunn's uncle to negotiate his atonement, and sees Ingunn but without claiming her for his wife.   All too soon he has to leave her to brooding and lonely dreaming.   It is fifteen frustrated unhappy years that they are separated before Olav is able to recover his inheritance and become Master of Hestviken.   A young travelling clerk, Teit, has made friends with Ingunn, and seduced her one night, so that when Olav comes to take her home she is with child.   He is beside himself with grief and anger at her confession, and rides away again.   Her aunt finds a foster-mother for the child when it is born, and Arnvid comes from Olav to tell her that he will return to fulfil the marriage, and is able to prevent Ingunn from suicide.   Olav meets the clerk, Teit, who wants to marry Ingunn, and kills him in a duel with axes in a lonely mountain hut.   The book takes its title from the axe, named Kin-fetch, which Olav had inherited from his father, a weapon that had been in the family more than one hundred years.   Olav believed that its match was scarce to be found in Norway. Ingunn and Olav first recognized their love for each other on a day's journey through woods and streams to take the axe to a smith.   The resentment that Olav feels toward Ingunn is less than the protective love and tenderness he has had for her since she was a child, and though the chastened woman, in her disgrace and remorse would have him leave her, they are bound together by the past, and are not divided by their sorrow and misfortune.   Vivid idyllic and realistic description of Norwegian life and character.

THE READER'S DIGEST OF BOOKS

BABBITT, by Sinclair Lewis (1922). A satire of the American business man, the
story of how the Booster's Club, the Athletic Club, and the Good Citizens' League,
of the commercial city of Zenith, combine with the real estate business to standardize
George F. Babbitt by offering the rewards of good fellowship and popularity.
George is forty-six years old, married, has three children, and lives in a standardized
house in the best residence section, Floral Heights.   In the language of the author
he is a booster, a joiner, a hustler, full of push, punch, and pep.   At home with his
family, at the club luncheons, in his office, we hear George expounding the gospel
of business and expressing his second hand opinions gleaned from newspaper edi-
torials, his suspicion of anything "high-brow," all a composite of slangy trivial
commonplaceness, though pitifully human.   He praises the laws against fast driving
even if he never obeys them, believes in prohibition but does not practise it, resolves
to give up smoking, and does everything except stop smoking.   The dinner-party
for the McKelveys is a masterpiece of description of a social failure.   Later at a
hotel in Chicago, George meets the English guest of the McKelveys, Sir Gerald
Doak, and after various suggestions for the evening which he thinks suitable for the
entertainment of the aristocracy, he discovers that Sir Gerald is a congenial spirit,
an English "Babbitt" with a new title bought by business success in Nottingham,
and they spend the evening at the movies with real talk afterward about business,
most enjoyable to the English visitor after weeks of hostesses who like Lucile Mc-
Kelvey had asked his opinion about polo and picture galleries in Italy.   In spite
of his jovial bluster George is discontented, a rebel at heart.   A girl had wept on
his shoulder because she had not been invited to a party, and the decent, soft-hearted
George found himself engaged and presently married and obliged to give up his
cherished plan to study law to support a family by "selling houses for more than
people could afford to pay."   He longs for romance and idealism and secretly rebels
against the crooked business methods and political deals of his father-in-law and
partner, Henry Thompson, and makes feeble, futile struggles to revolt, only to
succumb in the end.   His sensitive friend, George Riesling, is destroyed in the
conflict, shoots his nagging wife, Zilla, and goes to prison.   Zilla refuses to get a
pardon for him, because she wants to make an example of him.   Deprived of this
friendship, "passing the love of women," George tries to find the "fairy girl" of his
dreams in the flesh.   He makes tentative advances to his stenographer, and learns
from a manicurist that he is not "gay and valliant" but the old bore who is to be
endured as the price of a large dinner.   Mrs. Tanis Judique asks him to find a flat
for her and then to come and see her in it, and in later hints to his wife about his
relations with Tanis and "the Bunch" this dull affair led her to believe that "a
Wicked Woman had captivated her poor George."   George's attempts to be independent and liberal ended in complete surrender to the Good Citizens' League,
"trapped into the very net from which he had with fury escaped and, supremest
jest of all, been made to rejoice in the trapping" under the strain of ostracism by
his kind.   Ted Babbitt, motor-mad, elopes with lovely Eunice Littlefield, movie-
mad, on a total capital of six dollars of which the preacher took five to tie the knot.
His father rejoices that his son knew what he wanted to do and did it, and says
pathetically: "I've never done a single thing I've wanted to in my whole life. . . .
Don't be scared of the family.   No, nor all of Zenith.   Nor of yourself, the way
I've been."

BACK TO METHUSELAH, a metabiological pentateuch, by Bernard Shaw (1921).
In a succession of scenes and a preface of a hundred pages, Mr. Shaw writes a drama

of creative evolution. His thesis is that death comes to man just as he reaches maturity and wisdom, and that unless man can train his will to enable him to extend his span of life to at least 300 years, the force back of evolution which proceeds by trial and error will discard the human race along with other experiments like the mastodon and the megatherium in favor of a more competent and ingenious species. The first of the five plays under the title begins in the Garden of Eden, and introduces Adam and Eve and the Serpent. Adam is profoundly disturbed to see a fawn fall and break its neck, and is led thus to think about death and eternity. The Serpent tells the curious Eve about Lilith, alone in the Garden until she conquered death by achieving birth and produced Adam and Eve. First in creation comes imagination; "you imagine what you desire; you will what you imagine; and at last you create what you will." Death does not matter if birth brings other Adams and Eves. The Serpent tells Eve how it gathered a part of life in its body, and shut it into a tiny white case made of what it had eaten, and instructs her in the mysteries of procreation. Adam chooses to live a thousand years. In the second act a few centuries later, Eve is spinning and Adam is tilling the soil of an oasis in Mesopotamia. The first murderer, Cain, comes to see his parents. He has become a warrior since he killed Abel, and scorns the simple pastoral life of Adam and Eve. Eve reproaches her son for his laziness, selfishness, fighting, and boasting. In self-defence he asks them who invented death for man. They confess that they could not face the prospect of living forever. Cain's excuse then is that he acts only as the minister of death. Eve rejoices that some of her children are dreamers and thinkers. The second play is called "The Gospel of the Brothers Barnabas." The two prime ministers, Lubin and Burge, caricatures of Asquith and Lloyd George, make a political call on Mr. Barnabas, which occasion gives the author an opportunity to satirize the politics of the present day. Conrad Barnabas, a professor of biology, tells them about his new book dealing with longevity. He says that the political and social problems of modern civilization cannot "be solved by mere human mushrooms who decay and die when they are just beginning to have a glimmer of the wisdom and knowledge needed for their own government." Each of the prime ministers, at this point, states why he thinks the other is not capable of governing England. Burge and Lubin think that the scientist has a new patent medicine in mind, and are ready to draft a bill to restrict its use to the best people, but lose interest when they find he is talking about a biological thesis, though Burge thinks he can use the idea as an election slogan. The third play is "The Thing Happens." The scene is the official parlor of the President of the British Isles in the year 2170. The government is administered by efficient Chinese and Negro ministers and secretaries, with a mere figurehead for president, a descendant of both Burge and Lubin. The Barnabas of the day is the accountant general, the greatest living authority on the duration of human life. A book by an American describes an invention of breathing under water which if put into effect will upset his estimates and his pension system, since it is pointed out that an extraordinary number of prominent persons have died by drowning in the last two centuries. The cinema pictures of these persons displayed for the entertainment of the visiting American prove beyond a doubt that the archbishop is the same man who has been two previous archbishops, a president and a general. The archbishop, the young minister who had married the niece of the first Conrad Barnabas, has succeeded in living nearly three hundred years. To avoid embarrassing questions about his age he has staged his death by drowning, to begin another career. The Domestic Minister, Mrs. Lutestring, joins the group, and reveals herself to the archbishop as the parlor maid at the house of Conrad Barnabas, two centuries before. The fourth play is the "Tragedy of an Elderly Gentleman." It is the year 3000. The capital of the British Empire is now Bagdad, and the British Isles has been abandoned to the long-livers. The elderly gentleman has accompanied his son-in-law, the prime minister, Mr. Badger Bluebin, his daughter and granddaughter on a pilgrimage to Ireland, as Bluebin wishes to consult the oracle maintained by the long-livers. The strain of talking with a man and a girl of the long-livers drives the elderly gentleman almost to madness, and the girl long-liver to join the Island political party which stands for extermination of the short-livers. With the party is Cain Adamson Charles Napoleon, Emperor of Turania, the leading general of the time, the man of destiny. His philosophy of war is the logical extension of the ideas of his first ancestor, and it becomes necessary to isolate him by wireless to keep him quiet. The oracle is conducted with the mummery appropriate to the immature short-livers. The British envoy's question as to the "destiny of English civilization" resolves itself into an inquiry as to which party will win at the next election, and elicits from the oracle the reply, "Go home, poor fool," which it appears was the same answer given to another politician, an illustrious predecessor, who also consulted the shrine. The politician therefore can go back to his constituents with this assurance. The elderly gentleman is so influenced by the proposed misrepresentation, and the atmosphere of truth on the Island that he asks to remain there, and is killed by a compassionate glance from the oracle. The last play is "As Far As Thought Can Reach." In the year 31,920 men and women are born from eggs at the age of seventeen, spend four years of youth in dancing, and singing, and mating, and then become Ancients who spend adult centuries in contemplation of reality, and in the study of abstruse mathematical problems. They have conquered the need to eat or sleep, and their great ambition is to dispense with bodies altogether, to become a vortex of pure intelligence. A newly born girl springs from the egg. Other youths near their fourth year leave their friends to join the Ancients. A youthful Pygmalion moulds two statues of human beings, a man and a woman, and a young chemist gives them life. Their reactions of cruelty, and stupidity, and jealousy are intended as contrast to the long-livers. In the epilogue the ghosts of Adam, Eve, Cain, the Serpent and Lilith appear to express their judgment of life. Eve thinks all is well since her clever ones have inherited the earth. Cain sees that there is no place in the universe for him and his "splendid game." Adam is stupid as ever and can make nothing of it. Lilith waits with patience for the time to come when they will have "disentangled their life from the matter that has always mocked it."

BARE SOULS, by Gamaliel Bradford (1924). A succession of spiritual portraits of men of letters who were also notable letter writers, and therefore afford, the author says, "the most satisfactory clues for the naturalist of souls." All but Fitzgerald remained unmarried, and he was a benedict for only a short time. He takes up their habits of work, their attitude toward money and fame, their relations in love, politics, and friendship. The clue to Voltaire he finds in the intense and enormous vitality of spirit of the man, his zest for life, wide range of interests, deep-seated sympathy for humanity and zeal to improve the lot of mankind. Mr. Bradford considers him "the greatest spiritual influence of the mid-eighteenth century." The conservatives of his time condemned him as a destroyer, and his admirers stress the continual warfare of his ironic mockery of "the rotten social world" into which he was born. Gray was a shy, semi-recluse, spending his days reading and thinking, impressed with the "terrible insignificance of great peoples and great doings" in the mood of his Elegy. He was rarely ill but never quite well "probably because of the constant use of his brain and very moderate use of his muscles . . . with the mental depression naturally consequent." He delighted in Italian art, Gothic architecture, gardens, the changes of the seasons, the coming of the birds, and was never quite in touch with "the wild outdoors," though the Alps and the Scottish Highlands gave him "a delicious shudder." When he refused the laureateship he declared that he had "no relish for any other fame than what is conferred by the few real judges that are so thinly scattered over the face of the earth." Horace Walpole, an intermediary between the world of letters and the world of affairs, "held a mirror to the faults and follies and fascinations of the great world. He devoted his time mainly to keeping the mirror bright, polished, and gleaming. . . ." The son of a famous prime minister he lived in the atmosphere of kings and courts, took life with nonchalance and ease, and "made his letters next to Voltaire's, the most remarkable epitome of a historical epoch that has ever come down to us." He took a theatrical delight "in the vast disordered show to which he had such intimate access," and portrays the actors and scenes in picturesque anecdote. All his life he was a dilettante, "that is, a person who somehow takes great matters by their petty aspects because he is incapable of taking them in any other way. . . ." At twenty-four he admits that he is not interested in love, and his friendship with Madame du Deffand came when he was fifty and she was seventy, and devoted to him with the ardor of a girl of sixteen. The mild and domestic Cowper was convinced that he had committed the unpardonable sin, and was inescapably damned. The torment of his melancholy was likely to become actual derangement under any unusual strain. He "dodged hell in every sort of a mild and sinless diversion," and speaks of "dancing all night and shooting half the day." "Walking was at all times his resource and joy." Like Gray he was fond of gardens and the pleasant prospects of a landscape, but "a wild outlook oppressed him." Lamb, "a creature of whim and frolic fancy" Mr. Bradford believes comes near to embodying the exquisite court fool or clown of Shakespeare, all merriment and mockery, yet all tenderness and love and wisdom. Drink was his natural enemy and dearest foe, because "his light, fine, unstable, fantastic brain was too easily overset." There was his "untiring devotion to the few whom he loved." Thackeray called him "Saint Charles," and "to those who feel that the insoluble mystery of the universe is in no way better solved than by the two delicately related keys of love and laughter," he may well be so considered. Keats, he portrays as "a sane, sound, normal human being," not a visionary, or "crack-brained dreamer," while he had the health to enjoy his life. He had unique imaginative faculty, and the madness of genius. Keats said of himself, "I carry all matters to an extreme; so that when I have any little vexation, it grows in five minutes into a theme for Sophocles." His love for Fanny Brawne, prevented from fulfillment by his illness, tortured his last hours, and Mr. Bradford believes that love and glory killed him, that if he could have lived "a fat easy Philistine life . . . tuberculosis might well enough have let him alone." Flaubert's high ideals kept him searching for the right word. "A sentence sometimes cost him hours, even days of toil." His art was his life, and "Madame Bovary" is the triumph of his art, and his letters are the triumph of the artist. Edward Fitzgerald was the connoisseur, and made little use of his great talents because he was the pattern of an idler. "For all this idle ease," he writes, "I think I must be damned." Bradford reviews the careers he might have chosen. Instead he "walked a little, thought a little, scribbled a little, as he would have said of himself, smoked a great deal, and died."

BARNUM, by M. R. Werner (1923). The material in the several editions of the autobiography of P. T. Barnum has been coördinated in this volume which interprets the story and character of the man whom the author considers one of the most typical Americans and whose influence and position in American life were important. It is as the Connecticut Yankee that Barnum is introduced in these pages. He worked on his father's farm, had some schooling, was a Universalist, and found ways for making money during his boyhood. He was early attracted to the possibilities of the lottery business. "Lotteries at this time were permitted by the state and often indulged in by churches and educational institutions." He was also employed in his father's country store, and, as the author unfolds the story of those activities, Barnum's abilities and the power to attract by the "unusual" were early manifested in an age and in an environment which produced him. "In his mind," says the author, "was the fixed idea that if he could get something to exhibit to the New York amusement-loving public, he would succeed." The first adventures of Barnum in New York began with his American Museum, on Broadway and Ann Street, where his gradual acquisitions included stuffed animals, a tame alligator, a live anaconda, and freaks, together with a free exhibition of pictures, — a collection which attracted a public which would now patronize the Zoological Gardens and the American Museum of Natural History. "It was Barnum's aim to make the Museum the talk of New York, and he used every available means of advertising, creating means when they were not available." The list of notorious curiosities and the character of the programs are recalled against that decade of New York life when visitors to the city went to Barnum's museum before breakfast, and when Tony Pastor and E. H. Southern were receiving their early dramatic training under the Barnum patronage. Barnum's connection with a group of famous midgets, and his travels with General Tom Thumb, when he was received at Buckingham Palace, are recalled in detail, as throwing light upon the methods of advertising and the amazing abilities of Barnum to capitalize every exploitation, no less than his keen understanding of what the public would want. In 1846 Barnum, who had selected Bridgeport for his home, duplicated the Brighton Pavillion, "the gorgeous memorial to his extravagance built by Queen Victoria's uncle, George IV.," and "Iranistan," built at Bridgeport, appealed, as the author points out, "to his spectacular imagination." The walls in Barnum's private study were brocaded with orange satin, and adjoining the study was a bathroom, with a shower of hot and cold water. "An enthusiastic New York visitor to "Iranistan" said that inside it was as 'elegant as a steamboat.'" Barnum is shown to be something of a dictator of public amusements. In what was called his Moral Lecture Room, he enacted melodrama, dealing with the evils of drink, and gained world-wide publicity for his advocacy of temperance. The master stroke of Barnum, as shown in this study, was the importing of Jenny Lind, —"the greatest musical wonder of the world." He turned impresario, and the tickets to the first concert at Castle Garden were auctioned. "Credit must be given to Barnum for the impetus to musical enterprise in the United States, even though his intentions were not purely educational or philanthropic." The author adds that it would be a mistake to say that music in America depended for its success on Barnum, "but it was his ability as a publicity entrepreneur that caused thousands to realize for the first time what pleasure they had been missing in their ignorance of music." He created a large scale demand, the satisfaction of which was carried out by men of superior musical judgment, "but music in the United States was advanced many years in its progress by Barnum's daring importation and unique exploitation of Jenny Lind." Barnum's next venture was the organization of the "Great Asiatic

Caravan, Museum, and Menagerie"—the forerunner of his exploits in the three-ring circus. The final chapters in the life of this "Prince of Humbugs," as Barnum called himself, when he himself was humbugged and bankrupt, bring in his association with celebrities who had admired him in the days of his reputation; and the author recalls the negotiations by which Barnum reopened old enterprises, from which he derived profit, and entered upon new schemes for exhibiting sensations. What is called the Barnum revival shows that above the art of money-getting that character-ized Barnum's success was a marvellous energy which, as this volume stresses, was unassuaged by travel and entertainment, and insisted upon a wider outlet. In the immense traveling show, combining all the elements of the museum, menageries, and variety performance, "the greatest show on earth," Barnum's genius for astute show-manship found its final expression,—the ultimate outcome of the group of ideas which the author holds has interested the world in Barnum.

BARREN GROUND, by Ellen Glasgow (1925). The Virginia countryside is the background of this epic novel in which the heroine, Dorinda Oakley, the daughter of an ineffectual "poor white" farmer, rescues the barren acres of her father's farm from the invading broomsedge, and becomes a rich, successful woman. At twenty Dorinda went to help Nathan Pedlar at the village store during the illness of Rose, his pretty consumptive wife. The romantic Dorinda fell in love with Jason Grey-lock, the son of the doctor, back from New York to help his dissolute old father in his practice. The savings she had gathered to buy a cow for her parents go for a blue dress instead, which her lover said would match her eyes. She is betrayed and jilted on the eve of her wedding since Jason is forced to marry another girl, Glauce, by outraged brothers at the point of a gun. Dorinda goes to New York to hide her shame, and a street accident there prevents her motherhood, and brings her a friend, the surgeon in attendance, who gives her a home and work for two years. A summons to the death-bed of her father brings Dorinda home again. Her dis-illusion has brought her to believe "that as long as she could rule her own mind she was not afraid of the forces without." With money borrowed from her northern friends, hard labor in the fields, courage, and iron determination, she makes the un-profitable farm into rich pasturage, and thirty years later her scientific dairy has brought her wealth. She renounced love with her youthful disaster, and "put her heart into the land" with the self-surrender that marked her brief romance. Her mother, Eudora Oakley, a religious fanatic, spends herself in a frenzied activity of futile work, and becomes an invalid. Rufus Oakley, her brother, spoiled and self-indulgent, kills a man and escapes a prison sentence by his pious mother's falsehood. After the death of her half-demented mother Dorinda marries Nathan Pedlar, the homely, honest, loyal friend of her girlhood, to make a home for his children. He is killed in a railroad wreck in heroic rescue work. The heavily mortgaged farm of her former lover comes into her possession, and she takes Jason now destitute and sodden with drink, from the poorhouse, and allows him to remain under her roof in peace and decency until his death. There are interesting minor characters, the scandal-loving old Mother Fairlamb, reminiscent of Thomas Hardy's rustic char-acters, and the sensible and competent negro, Fluvanna. The humor of the colored folk of the old and new types lightens the sombre narrative.

BATOUALA, by René Maran (1922). This book by a French West Indian negro gives a picture of life in a native village in the Congo, their customs, habits, ways of thought and superstitions. Batouala, the chief, renowned in the village for his vigor and prowess in running, wrestling, and throwing the javelin, wakes in his hut to the monotonous jungle day. He reflects on the inferior white man who is afraid of scorpions and the heat of the sun, and must get natives to do heavy work for him, to tire oneself with work, squandering health in the pursuit of intangible, imaginary ends for the acquisition of stupid money. "To do nothing was simply to profit by everything that surrounds us," differing from laziness. The booming of the tom-tom drums calls the people to the ceremony of the feast of the circumcision. The naked youths and maidens come dancing to the knives of the older men and women. Anyone who shows pain is unworthy of life and may be struck down. All is a preparation for the dance of love, when all are permitted to indulge in debauchery. Suddenly in the midst of the frenzy Batouala sees the young, handsome Bissibingui going off with his favorite wife, Yassiguindjia, whom he had bought "with seven waist-cloths, a box of salt, three copper collars, a bitch, four pots, six hens, twenty she-goats, forty big baskets of millet, and a girl slave." His revenge is prevented by the news that the white men are returning, and in the general stampede only one man is left behind, the father of Batouala, who "had crossed the black brush for the faraway village whence no one has ever returned." Bissibingui and Batouala sit together apparently reconciled at the funeral, but each knew the other was plotting his death. The sorcerer declares that it is Yassiguindjia's fault that Batouala's father died, that she had sent him an evil spirit, and she asks Bissibingui to save her from being put to the tests and the torture. In the meantime the hunt is in progress. The brush is fired, the animals are driven out to fall before the javelins of the hunters. Bissibingui takes the precaution to refuse the food and drink Batouala offers him and while they wait for the game listens to the stories the chief tells of the tribal legends of the discovery of fire, and the enmity of the sun and moon, and is saved for the moment by the presence of witnesses. Batouala's javelin thrown at Bissibingui misses him as he throws himself on the ground to escape the attack of a panther, and Batouala receives a mortal blow from the beast. Carried back to the hut he lingers through the ceremonies of the sorcerers trying to drive away the evil spirits, and dies overcome by a last effort to separate Bissibingui and Yassiguindjia.

BEASTS, MEN AND GODS, by Ferdinand Ossendowski (1922). The author, a distinguished Polish scientist, was living in the Siberian town of Krasnoyarsk on the shores of the Yenisei River in the beginning of the year 1920. One afternoon while he was at the house of a friend he learned that the Red soldiers had surrounded his own house. He knew that his arrest by the Bolshevik Government would be followed directly by his execution as a counter-revolutionist, and that he must flee for his life. A peasant on the road drove him twenty miles from the town to a forest, and he started on the long adventurous journey through Mongolia and Tibet to get to China and India where he would be safe and could communicate with his friends. During most of the winter Dr. Ossendowski lived in a mud hut built around the roots of a fallen cedar tree, hunting to provide himself with food and furs for warmth. Bands of the Red soldiers were searching the forest for fugitives and constant watchfulness was necessary to escape them. In the spring when the ice broke on the Yenisei River he saw hundreds of mutilated bodies of officers and soldiers of the Kolchak army borne along with the current. Another fugitive, a Russian agricultural expert joined him, and later they had the company of a number of "White" officers who were also trying to escape from the Bolsheviki. They travelled on foot, on horseback, by boats, and on camels as opportunity offered and always in imminent danger of capture and death. On the border of Tibet they had a fight with bandits in which six of the men were killed, and they were forced to turn back over the difficult and dangerous trail to find another route to the Pacific through Manchuria. They crossed mountains and deserts hiding from people, making short stops in the most desolate places, and fed for weeks on raw, frozen meat because they were afraid to attract attention by the smoke of fires. They met friends and foes among the peasants and wandering tribes. He reports the conditions in Mongolia in this eventful time. In the course of the journey he met the Russian Kalmuck, Tushegoun Lama, the leader of many tribes, and the fanatical Baron Ungern, a convert to Buddhism and eager for the liberation of Mongolia, fighting for the Allies. He helped him to get to Urga, to escape assassination by Sepailoff, and to reach a station on the Chinese Eastern Railway from whence Dr. Ossendowski was able to get to Pekin in May, 1921. At Urga he had several interviews with the Living Buddha, and the last section of the book describes the city of the Lamas, and their rites, and hypnotic powers. Throughout the book is continuous description of the country and birds and beasts.

BEECHER, HENRY WARD, an American portrait, by Paxton Hibben (1927). This biography is an interpretation of the facts of Beecher's life in the light of the new biography, and is also a vivid picture of the social and political background of the mid-nineteenth century. His father, the Rev. Lyman Beecher, was a stern type of Calvinist, and his household agonized and wept over the salvation of their souls. "God was indeed an infinite detective watching children from above." By the time Henry was eight he knew more about "decrees, foreordination, election, reprobation, and the excellent prospects of an unsaved child than most theological students even of that day." This son, regarded by his father as his most unpromising child, grew up to discard the religion of Hell and make a great success as a preacher of a God who loved sinners. The shy, awkward young preacher in Indiana discovered that people responded more quickly to emotional appeal than to the metaphysics of his father. His power as an orator grew until he could sway thousands by his spoken words, and personal magnetism. Henry C. Bowen and David Hale wanted to make Plymouth Church a business success, and they found in Beecher the popular preacher who made their investment pay, and gave the church the publicity it needed, for in those days "church-going was the only amusement permitted the godly, and divine services received the attention from the press later accorded theatres and social activities." Beecher's name was an asset to "The Independent," and "The Christian Union," the religious journals of the day. He preferred the good, but his ruling passion for success, his sentimentality and lack of definite convictions made him continually palter with evil. In Indiana he tried to avoid expressing himself on the subject of slavery as he had no sympathy with the Abolitionists, and his appeal for funds to buy the freedom of two mulatto girls, the Edmonson sisters, was he explained "an act of Christian philanthropy divorced from the general question of slavery." However as the agitation against slavery grew strong in the North he became a late convert, declared the system of slavery accursed by God and man, and now shares the fame of William Lloyd Garrison. Whenever an idea or a movement became popular Beecher became its spokesman, even though he had previously been in the ranks of the opposition. He had been hostile to Lincoln, but received the credit of swaying British sentiment in his favor in his speeches in Liverpool and Manchester, when in fact the sympathy of these cities for Lincoln made them give Beecher a cold reception in view of his well-known opposition to Lincoln, and his attitude after the Trent affair. He wrote to Theodore Tilton of his

English experience as the triumph he wanted to believe it, and Theodore spread the news in his journal and in the newspapers. Before Beecher's return the country was ringing with the account of his taming of the British. When Lincoln acknowledged one of Beecher's many letters with a courteous note, Beecher spoke in Plymouth Church of "the last letter I received from him," as part of an intimate and confidential relationship. He was in Washington just at the right moment to appear with Lincoln at a window of the White House, and shared the cheers of the crowd who probably considered him responsible for the President's policies. He was widely known as a supporter of President Johnson, but when the leaders of Plymouth Church repudiated their pastor's stand he made public statement that he was not a "Johnson man in any received meaning of the term," and retained his popularity. Beecher was so connected with the vested interests that he could not be allowed to be disgraced by the scandal of his relations with Mrs. Tilton. "The truth must not come out — think of the influence on society, said the Hon. Benjamin F. Tracy." The jury disagreed, and Beecher was given an ovation by the crowded and enthusiastic Plymouth congregation. Mr. Hibben shows Beecher in the character of Synge's Playboy. In an appendix are notes for each chapter giving documents to prove his statements.

BEGGAR ON HORSEBACK, a fantastic comedy, by George S. Kaufman, and Marc Connelly (1924). An impecunious young composer, Neil McRae, is on the verge of a nervous collapse from overwork and trying to earn enough money to keep soul and body together. Gladys Cady, the "flapper" who wants to marry him, is bringing her vulgar rich parents and her brother, Homer, to tea in the afternoon. After the Cadys, who are from Neil's home town, come and go, all talking at once, all the time, Neil's friend, Dr. Albert Rice, prescribes rest for Neil, and advises him to be practical and marry the willing Gladys for the sake of his music. Neil scorns the suggestion until Cynthia Mason, the girl he loves, who lives across the hall and is as poor as himself, comes in for her tea things, and agrees with Albert that Neil had better marry Gladys. Believing that Cynthia does not care for him he becomes engaged to Gladys when she telephones to him a few minutes later. As the jazz orchestra across the square plays a version of Lohengrin's wedding march Neil falls asleep, and most of the play is a dream in which his future as the husband of Gladys Cady is caricatured in a series of fantastic episodes. A double procession advances down the two aisles of a theatre, the one headed by Mr. Cady in golf knickers carrying a tall silk hat, with Gladys on his arm in the costume of a bride carrying a bouquet made entirely of banknotes, and the other led by Mrs. Cady and Homer. The ushers wear wedding veils over their otherwise impeccable garments. Neil, still in his bathrobe, is reminded by Albert, the minister, that this is his wedding day. The couple proceed to the living room of their new home, filled with marble columns and voluminous crimson curtains, with innumerable butlers, who announce hosts of guests for tea who are totally invisible to the bewildered Neil. He tries to play for them and all his music turns to jazz. Neil's father-in-law takes him to his "widget" factory to learn the business. Neil starts his business career by trying to get a pencil with the assistance of two stenographers, Miss Hey, and Miss You, filling out a requisition form which asks his age and sex, etc., and what he did with his last pencil. He delivers a pompously inane but much applauded speech in a "business conference," and is handed checks for a million dollars. Gladys takes him to a restaurant where she dances off with the head waiter, strangely like Dr. Albert Rice, leaving Neil to dream of love in a cottage with Cynthia. Albert advises him to murder all of his new family-in-law. One after the other the Cadys fall before Neil's paper cutter grown to the dimensions of a scimitar. The reporters come to him for the story and he invites them to attend his trial. Newsboys appear with the latest illustrated news about the murder. The second act is the trial. Judge Cady enters to the tune of the soldier's chorus from "Faust" wearing a red robe over his golf costume. Homer reads the charge. Neil wants to prove that he has a right to kill anyone who interferes with his music. He calls Cynthia to help him, and she suggests that he play the pantomime they are working on together, "A Kiss in Xanadu." It tells the tale of a prince and a princess who each search for romance on a moonlight night. Disguised they meet on a bench where they kiss and exchange flowers for tokens, and then steal back to their canopied, curtained beds. The next morning the princess looks sadly at her rose, and does not let the prince glimpse it. He hides his token from her. They never know that to each of them the other was the romantic lover of the hour in the moonlit garden. The verdict of the jury sentences Neil to work in the Cady Consolidated Art Factory, where novelists, artists, poets, and now a musician turn out their products to order from behind the bars. Neil prefers to die, and calls Cynthia to help him prepare for his execution. Just then he wakes up, and Cynthia comes in to tell him that she will marry him, and that she knows that there are things that would be worse than poverty for his art. Gladys decides that she and Neil are not really suited to each other, and she has just met one of her oldest boy friends who is waiting for her downstairs.

BEHAVIOURISM, by John B. Watson (1924). The behaviourists define their mission as an observation and control of human behaviour. It is a reaction against introspective psychology depending on the field of consciousness as subject matter, and the use of such vague terms as "the mind," "the will," "perception," "image," "sensation," which the behaviourist does not include in his scientific vocabulary. The new psychology is a purely objective, experimental branch of natural science, and the behaviourist "wants to control man's reactions as physical scientists want to control and manipulate other natural phenomena." The control is to be exercised through "conditioned responses." For example, if a child is feeling of a piece of fur and a loud sound is made which frightens him, he will become afraid of the fur which he associates with the sound. By artificially forming new associations the child can be "re-conditioned" so that fur might be associated with something pleasant like a stick of candy. Lecture 2 gives methods and examples of stimulus and response in test cases with individuals and dogs, and discusses such social experiments as prohibition and the destruction of the monarchy in Russia. Lectures 3 and 4 describe the human body, the mechanism through which control is to be exercised. Lecture 4 is on the rôle the glands play in everyday behaviour. Lectures 5 and 6 dismiss the whole concept of instinct as academic and meaningless. He asks the question, "is the unlearned birth equipment of man . . . the same wherever he is found, be it in Africa or in Boston . . . in the year six million B.C. or in 1925 A.D.? Has he the same unlearned equipment, whether born in the cotton fields of the South, in the Mayflower or beneath the silken purple quilts of European royalty?" Lecture 6 is on what the study of the human young has to teach, including a summary of unlearned equipment. Lectures 7 and 8 take up the emotions, rage, love, fear, etc., contending that "man's emotional life is built up bit by bit by the wear and tear of environment upon him." Mr. Watson suggests that the methods of the behaviourist will "enable us to substitute natural science in our treatment of the emotionally sick in place of the . . . method now known as psycho-analysis." Lecture 9 discusses our manual habits, the human being's enormous capacity for forming finger, hand, arm, leg and trunk habits, habit growth and formation in infants, animals, and adults, as in the learning curves in typewriting and telegraphy, and the tendency to "stop improving at the lowest economic level that enables an individual to get along in his group." Lectures 10 and 11 on talking and thinking present the thesis that our whole body is implicated in our thinking. Thinking is talking to ourselves, and for the most part to be identified with verbal organization, but sometimes also with manual and visceral organization, hence the formula of the conditioned reflex can be applied to thinking habits also. "Language . . . gives us a manipulable replica of the world we live in." Lecture 12 on personality, "the outgrowth of the habits we form," presents "man as an assembled organic machine ready to run," in spite of "our constant strife to become kings and queens," our "infant carry-overs," and other ills. The author bases his case on experiments conducted under his own supervision, and used in this book in a wealth of illustration.

BETROTHAL, THE, a fairy play, by Maurice Maeterlinck (1918). A sequel to "The Bluebird." Tyltyl is now seventeen. In his morning dreams the fairy Bérylune comes to help him choose "the great and only love" of his life. At her bidding six village girls with whom he has exchanged glances or greetings come to the woodcutter's cottage, and as the fairy has lent him the green hat with the jewel its magic divests them of false modesty and jealousy, and they woo him with the frankness of dream maidens. Tyltyl is greatly disturbed to choose only one. The fairy tells him that the choice must be made not by him, but by his ancestors and his posterity. A miser is converted to generosity by the sapphire, to provide the gold for the journey to discover the rightful bride. Guided by Light, and also Destiny, a colossal figure who shrinks to the size of an ordinary man at the sight of Light, they proceed to the Abode of the Ancestors. Here Tyltyl is greeted by his grandparents and then by a motley crew of his forbears, including rich men, poor men, beggars, and thieves, a murderer, a drunkard. His grandmother explains that for several generations the family were beggars, father and son succeeding one another in the same church and in the same doorway, which brought to their posterity "patience, resignation, endurance, temperance and the habit of never catching cold." The Great Ancestor, and spokesman for the rest is a cave man. The girls pass in review before them and none of them gain recognition as the bride to be. The ancestors are interested in a white veiled figure accompanying the group, who pleads mutely with extended hands, but Tyltyl cannot remember, so she remains like an unfinished statue. The last resource is the children to be born who may know their mother. It is a long climb up the Milky Way to the Hall of the Unborn children, "near to the stars and yet within yourself," Light tells Tyltyl. Some children greet Tyltyl as grandpapa, but it is his own six children who must make the decision. The girls pet the children and Tyltyl thinks they must be hard to please to reject all of his lovely friends. The littlest one of all picks out the white veiled figure and brings her to life with his caresses, and even then Tyltyl cannot remember her. Destiny has now shrunk to a babe in arms that the girls take turns carrying, "a dear, sweet, obedient little thing," they call him. Wakened by his mother Tyltyl helps to tidy up the cottage for expected visitors, old neighbors. When they come in Tyltyl recognizes the beautiful unknown girl of his dream, who is Joy, the child to whom he had given his bird long ago. The mothers and fathers find them kissing each other when they open the door.

BEYOND THE HORIZON, by Eugene O'Neill (1918). Of two brothers on the Mayo farm Andrew is a son of the soil like his father, and Robert is delicate and of the intellectual type. On the eve of his departure for a sea voyage with an uncle, Robert Mayo suddenly decides that he loves Ruth, the daughter of a neighbor, and that he will remain on the New England farm. Andrew had hoped to marry Ruth, and in spite of his father's anger sails with the uncle. Three years bring Robert only disillusion, and failure on the farm he hates. His child is his only comfort. Ruth has soon discovered that the marriage was a mistake, and thinks that she is in love with Andrew. When Andrew returns for a brief visit he completes the disillusion of his brother and the woman he had once loved. Robert hoped his brother would bring some romance from his adventurous seafaring, but finds him only dull and commonplace, untouched by his experiences. Ruth, who had believed that Andrew still loved her, learns that she has been easily forgotten. Every character in the play, but most poignantly Robert, is obsessed with desire for what lies "beyond the horizon." Andrew leaves his mother, now a widow, to make his "pile" in the Argentine. After five years he comes home again. The child is dead, Robert is ill with tuberculosis, while the farm has gone from bad to worse. Andrew has made a fortune in grain, speculated, and lost most of it. Robert tells him, "I'm a failure, and Ruth's another . . . but you're the deepest-dyed failure of the three, Andy . . . gambling with the thing you used to love to create. . . ." He dies telling them that he is happy at last, freed from the farm, that he has won his trip"— the right of release — beyond the horizon."

BIRTH, by Zona Gale (1918) is a novel whose power and poignancy grow from the accumulation of innumerable small details. Little Pitt, the fruit and pickle salesman, is a most unpromising hero. Through compassion he drifts into marriage with Barbara Ellsworth, the pretty and insipid village belle of Burage. On account of her father's long illness, he had died leaving their tiny home and paper-hanging business covered with mortgages. Barbara appreciates having a husband to shoulder these burdens, even so maladroit a little man as Marshall Pitt but not the social humiliation attendant on being married to one whom her village chums all looked upon as a regular stick. Miss Arrowsmith, the fine lady of the town and the kindly neighbor at whose home the young couple had been married, tried to help Barbara stand by her husband. For Pitt's native goodness was so evident that the girl did try, until a handsome young bandmaster, Max Bayard, beguiled her when the tent show came to town during one of Pitt's absences in Chicago working for Strain. Then she left him, taking her six months' old baby with her to Chicago, to meet her lover. Nonplussed and with his better nature touched, Bayard tells the young mother to go back to her husband. Barbara does return and leaves the baby with Miss Arrowsmith but feels too shamed to remain, so she disappears. Pitt leaves Burage too, convinced by his neighbors that he is not competent to bring up his child, first to try in the city, and later in the gold fields of Alaska to earn a living for little Jeffery. Miss Arrowsmith did not have the strength of will to carry out her wish to adopt Jeffery, against her invalid mother's objections. So it is to Mis' Hellie Copper that Pitt sends his regular pittance for his son's upbringing. She becomes a widow; and when nothing is heard of Pitt for a long time, the young lad goes to work for Beck, an unscrupulous individual who soon wheedles the widow into investing some of her insurance money in his business. He fails and young Pitt and Mis' Hellie argue that a bill owing to Beck which comes into Jeffery's hands after Beck had fled and left his affairs in the hands of a receiver, belongs of right to them as reimbursement for their losses through him. Soon after, Pitt reappears and he and Jeffery settle down to a life which is happiness to the father since his loneliness and hardships in Alaska, but which means irritating disappointment to the son who had dreamed of a far more heroic appearing father during the long years of separation. Miss Arrowsmith has returned from abroad to find the sensitive and promising little boy she had left grown into a young man without confidence in himself or moral convictions due to the inadequate training he had received during his impressionable years. She joins Marshall Pitt in urging Jeffery to develop his natural gift for drawing. But the boy refuses both the financial help which she offers him and the sum obtained years ago from the sale of Barbara's little house which Pitt had saved against her return. Mournfully Pitt tells Miss Arrowsmith that he has failed with Jeffery as he did with Barbara, "he acts kind of the way Barbara used to. Not cross — patient on purpose! That's a terrible thing. . . ." And later, urging the boy, with wistful yearning that his son may have an easier and happier life than his own, "I've never known how to do anything right, seems though. Ain't they something could tell a person how, if they could get ahold of it?" Finally death comes to him as he rushes into a burning building to save a little dog who had shown devotion to him in his lonely craving for understanding. It was after he was gone that Jeffery for the first time felt the quality of his father's courageous struggle, and follows his father's wish that he make reparation to Beck. About the unraveling of Pitt's sorry existence, its casual blundering achievements, its inevitable fiasco Zona Gale has suggested an eternal viewpoint. She has torn aside the ludicrous mask of personality that was Marshall Pitt and revealed the spiritual hero in the little man.

BIRTH AND GROWTH OF RELIGION, THE, by George Foot Moore (1924). "The universality of religion within the range of our knowledge," observes the author, "warrants the inference that it has its origin in a common motive, and the identity of the elementary notions that everywhere go with it implies that they are man's natural response to his environment and experience." The origin of religion, he holds, being inaccessible to historical investigation, is to be approached by a psychological inquiry. In discussing the antecedents and rudiments of religion, he surveys the phenomena of religions that he considers accessible to observation and gives his findings: man believes that there are powers, however conceived, upon whose behavior toward him his well-being is in manifold ways dependent; he believes that these powers are actuated by motives like his own, and therefore comprehensible; he believes that it is possible for men, in some way or other, to work upon the powers so as to keep them from doing harm or make them serve him; and, finally, he acts on this belief. The author proceeds then to the task of showing what men first imagined the powers to be like, and what they did in consequence of these notions. Under the subject — souls and spirits — and the emergence of gods, the various factors which have contributed to worship and myth, — rituals, invocations, offerings, sacrifices, and other things of a sacramental character, are reviewed. "The constant elements in the *cultus* of the gods are offering and prayer." Discussing morals and religion, the author says, "Religion was not made ethical, but morality religious, and religion thus often interposed a formidable obstacle to moral progress. This is peculiarly the case where the law is fixed in sacred scriptures containing a closed canon of revelation, which admits no addition or subtraction, no change, and thus gives the stamp of finality to the institutions, laws, and moral standards of a past which religion is thus forbidden to outgrow." The religions of a higher civilization provide the author with instances which, he considers, illustrate in different ways the reciprocal relations between religion and culture, and which show how knowledge and thought may outrun religion, which then, as by an instinct of self-preservation, becomes a retarding or even a reactionary force. The philosophers, Plato and Aristotle, he points out, on the one hand, and the Stoics on the other, endeavored to make religion rational and ethics scientific. The author considers in this study the first religions which he says may be called natural religions, in the sense that what men seek in them are natural goods, the good things of this life; and in the closing chapters he turns his attention to what he terms the supernatural religions, inasmuch as they answer man's desire for the good things of another life, "goods beyond the nature we know." They have been called "redemptive religions," but the author holds that in the meaning naturally put on the word "redemptive" Christianity is the only one of them properly so called. In the concluding chapter on salvation, religion and philosophy, he says that philosophy began in India as well as in Greece, with the problems of the physical universe — cosmological problems to which theology had led the way. Following its course, he finds that "historical Christianity is, therefore, a cord of three strands, Jewish ethical monotheism; Hellenistic soteriology, profoundly modified by the Jewish element; and Greek philosophy, which not only constituted the formal principle of Christian theology but made large contributions to the material element." He concludes that the intellectual victory of Christianity over all the rival salvations of the time was due to the fact that it alone offered not merely a way of salvation but a philosophy of salvation.

BISMARCK, THE STORY OF A FIGHTER, by Emil Ludwig (1927). Bismarck is depicted as "a character filled with pride, courage, and hatred — the basic elements from which his actions resulted." The author believes that "by the beginning of the thirties Bismarck's inner development was practically finished. . . . All that followed, throughout his career, was no more than a deepening of the elementary lines already traced," and therefore he deals at considerable length with his rebellious youth, resentful of all control, undisciplined at home and at school and college, and too proud to accept the initial drudgery of a career. Bismarck says of himself that he was born to give, not to obey, orders, and unable to endure a superior he could not keep any of the positions obtained for him through the influence of his family. "The Mad Junker" experienced conversion through the influence of Marie von Blanckenburg, and his pious fiancé, Johanna von Puttkamer. The year of his betrothal, 1847, he began his political career as deputy in the United Landtag. As statesman and ambassador his ambition was to consolidate the German States into a great Empire governed by Prussia, and to establish the Hohenzollern dynasty in its divine appointment. With infinite patience and skill Bismarck led William to take the measures he considered necessary for the welfare of the country. Neither of the two men, whose characters were so utterly different, could get on without the other, and it is difficult to say which of them had the harder task. Ludwig asks, "Was it harder for an elderly gentleman of moderate gifts though of royal blood to put up with a comparatively young man as minister, a man who was only a Junker, but happened to be a genius; or, for a bold statesman to put up with a perpetually hesitating king?" All great decisions had to be suggested by Bismarck to William by slow degrees and subsequently wrested from him. "Bismarck came to regard the king as his liege lord and as a sort of father," which enabled his pride to endure the position he was placed in. His fearlessness made him disregard "the threats of the Chambers, the king's mistrust, the queen's influence working against him, the malice of the courts, the intrigues of the envoys, the death sentences passed on him by foreign revolutionists, and, ere long, the revolvers of fanatical idealists." He had to fight for his great aims against lack of comprehension, pettiness, anti quated ideas, and class prejudice of men and parties. Bismarck says, "Foreign affairs are, for me, an end in themselves, more important than anything else in the world." The fundamental idea of his policy as chancellor, the author states, was to make his own nation great and to prevent anti-German coalitions. "He never made wars for the sake of conquests." "In old age," Bismarck "often asked himself whether the unification of Germany might not have been effected without the three wars. . . ." After the proclamation of the United German Empire William I refused to shake hands with Bismarck, publicly slighting the "man whose creative mind" had made him emperor, because he was not eager to accept the dignity, and because he preferred the title "Emperor of Germany" instead of "German Emperor." Scarcely one of Bismarck's friends and associates did not sooner or later incur his hatred. He never tolerated the slightest rebellion against his own imperious will, and "heaped persecution upon all of another way of thinking than himself." He could recognize only two reasons why anyone should differ from him in opinion: malice or place-hunting. The fight against the bourgeoisie brought Bismarck into association with Lassalle, like Bismarck animated with pride, courage, and hatred, and "less inspired by sympathy with the fourth estate than by dislike of the third," and Bismarck became the first State socialist in Prussia. Bismarck believed that force was the sole method of ruling a great people. In 1862 the Prussian Parliament which he hated refused to vote the funds necessary for the reorganization of the army. It was then that Bismarck made the speech declaring that the great questions of the day could not be settled by rhetoric and decrees but by "blood and iron," the phrase which outraged his friends and foes alike. He failed to appreciate the growing power of democracy until too late, but it was the German people who were to save his work from destruction. For fifty-eight years his power was almost absolute until disagreement with William II, who rebelled against his tutelage and forced his retirement.

BLACK APRIL, by Julia Peterkin (1927). A story of negro life on an isolated South Carolina plantation visited by its owners only during the shooting season. There is not a single white character in the book. April, the foreman, rules his people like a tribal chief. "Li'l Breeze" one of April's illegitimate children is born on Sandy Island. Granny puts the plough and the axe under his mother's bed to cut the "birthing pains." "The buckra (quality white folks) leave their children money; the black folk leave their children signs" the lore of unnumbered beliefs in the potency of charms. When Breeze was twelve his mother, deserted by the husband she had married after her disgrace was forgotten, gave him to Cousin Big Sue, the cook at the "big house." From this point the story is told through the impressions his new life made on the sensitive child. The powerful April takes an interest in the boy. Big Sue does not lick him when April is there. Leah, April's wife, crazed by jealousy of her handsome and popular husband, quarrels continually with the other women, particularly Big Sue and Zeda. Sherry, the son of April and Zeda, grows up to rival and quarrel with his father until there is not room for both of them on the plantation, and April orders Sherry off the place. Big Sue's daughter, Joy, has been away four years studying to get a "depluma." She returns and is unhappy to hear that Sherry is gone, and frightened at April's bold admiration. Big Sue and Leah fight each other, and Leah receives her death blow before they can be pulled apart. There is no letter from Sherry and after a time Joy elopes with April. Instead of meeting the news with an outburst of grief Big Sue is delighted that her daughter has caught the finest man on the plantation. Three months after the marriage Joy gives birth to Sherry's son. April falls ill and by the time they take him to the hospital gangrene has made it necessary to amputate his legs. No charm can help him. The cotton crop is threatened by the boll-weevil, and they send for Sherry to be foreman, and every man, woman and child works in the fields to help him. Sherry is kind to the broken April, but he becomes Joy's lover again, and April loses courage under his misfortunes, and dies asking them to bury him in a "man-size-box" as if he were still "six feet-fo."

BLACK OXEN, by Gertrude Atherton (1923). The title of this book is taken from a quotation from W. B. Yeats, about "the years" which "like great Black Oxen tread the world." Lee Clavering is the most quoted, omniscient young columnist in New York, and his friends of the brilliant group of artists and intellectuals whom he has nicknamed the Sophisticates expect him to write a great play some day. One evening at the opening night of an indifferent play he is aroused from boredom by his interest in a beautiful young woman who rises and faces the house, surveying it leisurely through her opera glasses after the custom of Europe. Wandering up the aisle he meets his elderly relative, Charles Dinwiddie, who tells him that he has seen a ghost. The unknown woman is the image of his old sweetheart, Mary Ogden, who married Count Otto Zattiany and went to Hungary to live thirty years ago. He can only conjecture that she must be Mary's "left-handed" daughter. The resourceful Clavering manages to meet her, and she tells him that she is the Countess Josef Zattiany, and a cousin of Mary Ogden, and that she is obliged to spend some time in New York on business, and has reasons for remaining obscure. Her beauty, her strange resemblance to Mary Ogden, whose house on Murray Hill she is living in, and the fact that she has presented no letters of introduction to any of Mary Ogden's friends, make her the most discussed woman in town. Mrs. Oglethorpe, leader of New York society, and one of Mary Ogden's most intimate friends, calls and is not received. Lee falls in love with her and she with him, and she promises to tell him the truth about herself. First she sends for Mrs. Oglethorpe to make her apologies. She gives up her masquerade as the Countess Josef Zattiany, as she is really Mary Ogden, rejuvenated by the treatment of her glands at a famous sanitarium, and now physically no older than the twenty-eight that she looks. It is a shock to Lee that she is old enough to be his mother, but he adores her and wants to marry her. Her life as a great lady in the diplomatic world in Europe had ended with the War and war work in the hospitals. Among her lovers had been a Prince Hohenhauer whom Mary had not named, but Lee recognizes from her description when the newspaper headlines announce his arrival in New York. He knows that all her interest is in her relief fund and the world of Europe, that when they are married she will not be happy in New York, and that they will have to divide their time between his world and hers. He does not want Mary to meet the Prince who would remind her of the past, and probably claim her interest in some important mission which had doubtless brought him to Washington. Quickly he makes plans for a house party in the Adirondack camp of his cousin, Mr. Dinwiddie, and rushes Mary off the next morning. They announce their engagement, and he gets her consent to marry him in two weeks. She becomes completely Mary Ogden, instead of the Countess Zattiany, and they spend happy days together banishing the sense of coming disaster that had depressed them both. A telegram comes to Mary from Prince Hohenhauer that he must see her, and she decides to drive to the railway town to meet him to prevent him from coming to the camp. One of the most important men in Europe, with limited time at his disposal, would not take the trip without reason, and though she hates to deceive Lee she does not want him to accompany her and tells him that she is going to sign some business papers. She does not return. The Prince convinces her that she is needed in Austria, and for that reason, not because of their long past love, he asks her to marry him. As the wife of an American, Mrs. Lee Clavering, she would have no position or influence to play the part in Austria that could be hers with her beauty, her gifts, her political experience. He appeals to her as the European she is, and to her love of power against the dream of young love, that to her old mind now seems trivial and insignificant in comparison. Lee realizes her boundless ambition and her devotion to Austria, and follows her to New York, and as he fears finds not Mary Ogden but the Countess Zattiany. She loves Lee but will not marry him, and dismisses her probable marriage to the Prince as so purely incidental that it is not worth talking about. Lee, bitter and stricken, bids her a formal good-by.

BLISS, and other stories, by Katherine Mansfield (1920). These short stories without plot are pictures which reveal the characters in moments of emotion, love, happiness, hatred or sorrow. In the title story, "Bliss," a young couple are having some friends in to dinner. The pear tree in the garden "in fullest richest bloom" seems in its perfection symbolic of the wife's happiness. She suddenly falls passionately in love with her husband, only to discover as the guests are leaving and she sees them together in the hall that her new and adored friend is her husband's mistress. Disillusioned she ran over to the long windows. "'Oh, what is going to happen now?' she cried. But the pear tree was as lovely as ever and as full of flower and as still." A tree is used again to represent a state of mind in "The Escape," in which a husband is able to attain mental escape from the nagging of his neurotic, selfish wife. "The Little Governess" is travelling on the Continent for the first time to get to a new position at Munich. A benevolent old gentleman, her travelling companion, offers to show her the city. He suddenly becomes a beast, and the pretty English girl runs away from him back to her hotel, too late for her appointment, and is left stranded in Munich. All this happens because of the ill-will of the porter, who placed the man in her carriage marked "Ladies Only" because she had not given him a large enough tip. "Je Ne Parle Français" is the story of how an Englishman ran off to Paris with a girl, and then leaves her there alone as soon as they arrive at the hotel on account of his greater love for his mother, told in the chatter of the Frenchman who meets them at the station, in his revery long after as he sits in a café. "Psychology" is afternoon tea, a man and woman talking beside the fire trying to keep their frank, intellectual friendship from becoming something more, avoiding the silences which threaten them with emotional complications. "Pictures" shows Miss Ada Moss, a middle-aged, second-rate singer, at the moment when she is at the end of her resources with only a shilling and thrippence in her vanity bag, after having vainly climbed the stairs of theatrical agents in search of work. She sits down in the park to read the form handed her in the film office, "Can you aviate — high dive — drive a car — buck-jump — shoot?" and has a "good cry." Her landlady has given her until eight that night to pay the rent of her room. She imagines herself in the Café de Madrid. "They have concerts there in the evenings. . . . Why don't they begin? The contralto has not arrived . . . 'Excuse me, I happen to be a contralto; I have sung that music many times.'" The respectable

Miss Moss walked into the café, and she had hardly sat down when a stout gentleman took the chair opposite. Five minutes later she follows him out of the café. "Prelude" is the doings of a quite ordinary family to whom nothing important happens, but the unimportant things vividly present the characters of Linda Burnell, Stanley, her husband, her sister Beryl, the ideal Grandmother, and the children, Kezia, Lottie, and Isabel, first leaving the old home, a picture of a house stripped and desolate seen through the eyes of a child, and then beginning life in the new house. The delicate Linda thinks of her mixed feelings for her husband, her love and admiration and respect and hate. He is full of energy and plans and devotion to Linda. Beryl admires herself in the looking-glass and watches herself playing the part of the lovely young girl, and gives orders to Alice, the servant, in a special voice.

BONDS OF INTEREST, THE (Los intereses creados). A comedy in a prologue and three acts by Jacinto Benevente was translated from the original Spanish by John Garrett Underhill (1917). It is one of the great Spanish dramatist's best known plays. The comedy is a satire on the duality of human nature. The prologue is spoken by Crispin who tells that it is a play of puppets, impossible in theme, without any reality at all. In the first act, Leander and Crispin arrive penniless at an inn in a strange city. Handsome young Leander is weary, and Crispin, a wily, self-appointed rogue of a servant, assures him that by taking advantage of their talents and effrontery all will be well. He gives bold advice and proceeds to call the innkeeper berating him for keeping them waiting. He persuades him that Leander is a great notable traveling incognito, and demands the best service. Harlequin and The Captain, two other vagabonds, appear, one boasting of his poems and the other of his sword. The innkeeper seeks to drive them away but Crispin commands that they be served and that money be advanced to them from Leander's account, thus winning them to Leander who has assumed the air of a grandee. Act two opens in the garden of the impoverished Dona Sirena. She and Columbine, her servant, enter. The mistress is in a fury because the tradesmen are refusing to serve without payment and she is having a great fête that evening. Columbine suggests that her friend Harlequin, the poet, can provide entertainment. When she leaves the garden, Crispin appears and informs Columbine that a great gentleman has arrived in town and is sending a marvelous entertainment for the fête. Music is heard in the distance and Dona Sirena comes to inquire about it. Crispin explains and hands her a paper from his master. She reads that if through her help Leander wins the daughter of Polichinelle, he will pay her one hundred thousand crowns. Crispin has discovered that others seek her influence and has far outbidden them. Leander enters and Dona Sirena is much impressed. Guests begin to arrive, all talking of the mysterious personage who has come to town. When the wealthy Polichinelle enters with his wife and daughter Silvia, Sirena leads the girl off to dance with Leander. When her father will follow them Crispin detains him. He reveals that he knows of Polichinelle's criminal past and then warns him against Leander. Polichinelle rushes out to get Silvia. Leander enters, deep in despair. He has fallen truly in love and regrets the deception. Crispin tells him that he has put the father against him knowing it would make Silvia love him madly and win the mother as an ally. Silvia enters and the act ends with the lovers in embrace. The third act takes place in Leander's house which has been obtained on credit. Crispin is vividly describing to Harlequin and the Captain an attack on Leander by ruffians hired by Polichinelle. Columbine comes with the message that Silvia has fled to Dona Sirena's home and vows she will marry Leander. When they leave, Leander accuses Crispin of hiring the assassins. Crispin assures him that love requires deceit and tells him their creditors are about to come down upon them. Doña Sirena enters and warns them that their subterfuges are known but she is still willing to help them and has brought Silvia. When she enters and finds Leander unwounded he tells her of the deception. While they talk Crispin announces that Polichinelle and others are coming. The lovers disappear and Crispin faces the irate father and band of angry creditors. After much clever discussion he convinces the creditors that Leander's marriage to Silvia is the only solution, whereupon they all turn against Polichinelle. Leander returns with Silvia, and her mother and the lovers announce that they scorn Polichinelle's money and will live in poverty. But they are persuaded otherwise. Crispin tells Leander he is leaving him but that he should remember that "the ties of love are as nothing to the bonds of interest."

BRED IN THE BONE, AND OTHER STORIES, by Elsie Singmaster (1925). Ten sketches of a Pennsylvania Dutch community of Mennonites, Dunkers, and other narrow religious sects. Five of the stories are about two old maids, the Shindledecker sisters, stout, practical Betsey, and thin "crowd shy" Tilly. Their peaceful home is invaded by two men canvassing for votes for a new constable who promises to clear a gang of bootleggers out of the neighborhood. Through a crack of the door Betsey says that they are plain people and will have nothing to do with such worldliness. In the night Betsey hears a noise in their woods and goes out followed by her sister to tell the bootleggers that they must keep off the property. They find a large truck of cases of liquor stuck at the edge of the "sink hole" of quicksand. Resolutely they push the truck into the quicksand, and calmly return home, and the next day forget all about it in the daily round of kitchen tasks and quilting. A strange dog whines and scratches at the door of the comfortable old house. At about the same time they receive unwelcome visits from an antique collector, Cora, who manages to get inside the house, and tries to make friends in order to persuade them to part with their priceless old furniture. The sisters, who distrust all strangers, are warned by the neighbors of Cora's intentions, and determine that she shall not enter the house again. When Cora and her friends arrive with a great van in hopes of booty, the dog comes to Betsey's side and frightens them away, and thus wins his position of a "man in the house." Eleazer Herr, also a member of the Mennonite meeting house, comes to tell the sisters that the end of the world is coming on Wednesday night at midnight. Betsey devoutly prepares her ascension robes, but Tilly is sceptical. While Betsey is clearing a path in the snow to get to the hill, Tilly visits the kitchen of the thin, ascetic Eleazer, and before he returns from work she has prepared for him a rich indigestible dinner, such a meal as he had never had before in his whole life. Late that night they call for him to accompany them to the top of the hill and cannot rouse him from deep slumber to further consideration of the day of wrath that is on hand. Several years later tragedy enters the life of the sisters when Tilly finds that she is no longer able to sew fine, neat stitches on quilts. The doctor tells her that she is threatened with blindness and must wear a black bandage for several months. There follow difficult useless days for Tilly and nerve-racking days for patient Betsey. Finally Tilly confesses that she wants Betsey to read to her — not from the Bible nor the Hymn Book nor the Martyr Book — but from a "world's book" forgotten by the doctor on one of his visits. Betsey yields to her; but overwhelmed by conscience she rises in open meeting to confess her sin. All understand, of course, that the sin is for Tilly's sake and are unconsciously fascinated by Betsey's naïve narrative of the novel as far as she has read. One by one the members of the Mennonite meeting arrive at the Shindledecker house Sunday afternoon to hear the end of the story of the "Courier of the Czar." In the last account of the Shindle-deckers, old age is making them wonder what is to become of the little house, the cat and the dog, and all the furniture and beautiful quilts, the labor of their own hands and of generations before them. Their problem is solved by a strange legacy of a little baby girl, left to Betsey by a poor young woman to whom she had been kind one market day on the street car. This child they will love and care for and educate in modest useful Mennonite ways to be like the embroidered motto in the kitchen: "Little and unknown, loved by God alone." Another modest Mennonite is William Hershey. Threatened with dire poverty, and the foreclosure of the mortgage on his farm, he goes one evening to his creditor, Calvin Weikert, to beg him to be lenient, and receives a harsh refusal. The following day William hears that Calvin has been accused with strong circumstantial evidence of the murder of Job Sharretts, whose land Weikert had long coveted, on Wednesday evening between seven and seven-thirty. William remembers that this was the evening and the time when he had seen and talked to Calvin. He dreams of nothing but telling the truth. His evidence is unquestionable and Weikert is dismissed. William's mortgage is torn up, but William never knows that Calvin actually was guilty. William had mistaken the day. Isidore Bornot, of French origin, has nothing but his blacksmith shop and his dreams. He is so given to day-dreaming, that his dream-life, in which he is always a hero, means more to him than reality. One of his favorite dreams is of saving the lives of many thousands of people in a church about to collapse. On Memorial Day Isidore walks to town to the celebration, dreaming as he walks. He stands outside by the new monument outside the crowded church. He gazes so intently at the spire that actually it does seem to sway. Believing that he is predestined to this moment, Isidore enters the church and informs the congregation that the spire is about to crash. In the rush to safety several are killed, hundreds wounded. Isidore escapes to the woods. His dream world struggles with reality and finally he resigns from reality by plunging into a dark pool. Among the other simple Quaker-like sects in the community are the Dunkers and the Amish. Thomas Bashore is a Dunker, whose splendid simple nature is bitterly hurt and whose life is almost ruined by the selfishness of his young wife, of "the world's people," who flouts him, insults him and wounds him, finally deserting him to return to movies and automobiles and gaiety. Martin Ebersole, the Amishman, is spared such a miserable marriage with an admired yellow-haired "unbeliever." He returns to marry the sweet blue-eyed Sallie Funk of his own sect, and to follow the peaceful ways of his fathers and neighbors. In the story "Bred in the Bone," Lydia Reinecker finally pays for her superstition with the life of her husband. In her girlhood Lydia drives four miles in the night to bring the powwow doctor to say incantations over her sick mother. Her mother recovers and she believes that it is due to the charms not the doctor's care. After Lydia is married to Alfred Frantz, a successful lawyer, she takes her baby suffering from underweight to the powwow doctor and the child seems to improve. The children of Lydia and Alfred grow up and marry, and the time has come when Alfred means to take life more easily. They have the companionship of their early married life. Then Alfred is ill, and though the doctor assures Lydia that he is getting better, she does not believe it. In desperation Lydia calls in the powwow doctor while the nurse is out of the house and her husband is sleeping. When the nurse returns she finds everything quiet but Alfred has had some kind of a shock and has died of heart-failure.

BRIDAL WREATH, see **KRISTIN LAVRANSDATTER,** by Sigrid Unset.

BRIDGE OF SAN LUIS REY, THE, by Thornton Wilder (1927). "On Friday noon, July the twentieth, 1714, the finest bridge in all Peru broke and precipitated five travellers into the gulf below. . . . It had been woven of osier by the Incas more than a century before . . . a mere ladder of thin slats swung out over the gorge, with hand rails of dried vine . . . St. Louis of France himself protected it . . . it was unthinkable that it should break." It happened that Brother Juniper, a Franciscan monk, in Peru to convert the Indians, was a witness of this accident. The thought came to him: "Why did this happen to those five? . . . Either we live by accident and die by accident, or we live by plan and die by plan." He resolved to place theology among the exact sciences by using this Act of God as the perfect laboratory afforded to justify the way of God to man. His laborious investigation into the lives of these five people, to prove that in each case death at that moment was best, published in an enormous book, was pronounced impious by some judges and ordered to be burned with its author in the public square, so "leaning upon a flame" Brother Juniper smiled and died. The stories of the five, and of the great actress La Périchole are as follows: Dona Maria, marquesa de Montemayor, was cursed with an ugliness and awkwardness that antagonized every one, even her exquisite daughter, Clara, upon whom her mother fastened an idolatrous love. The mother could not "prevent herself from persecuting Dona Clara with nervous attention and a fatiguing love." "From the offers of marriage that fell to her Dona Clara deliberately chose one that required her removal to Spain." For the Marquesa "letter writing had to take the place of all the affection that could not be lived." She forced herself to go into society, taught her eye to observe, and read the masterpieces of her language that she might write entertaining letters to her daughter. Pepita, a little girl from the Convent, came to be her companion. The child had been selected by the Abbess to carry on her own work, a burden beyond her years. On a pilgrimage to a shrine with the Marquesa who wished to offer prayers for the health of her daughter about to give birth to a child, Pepita wrote a letter to the Abbess telling of her difficult life with the Marquesa and her longing to see the Abbess. The Marquesa read the letter which Pepita refused to send because it was not brave enough. The old lady reflected that she herself "had never brought courage to either life or love," and resolved to learn "to permit both her daughter and her gods to govern their own affairs." Two days later they started back to Lima and crossed the bridge at the time of the accident. Manuel and Esteban are twin brothers, foundlings, brought up in the Convent by the Abbess. The word "love is inadequate to describe the tacit almost ashamed oneness of the brothers." A shadow across this unity was Manuel's infatuation for the actress, Camilla Périchole, who employed him to write letters for her. When he saw that it disturbed his brother, "in one unhesitating stroke of the will" he removed the disturbing woman from his heart. Manuel dies, and Esteban is alone. The Abbess arranges with Captain Alvarado that Esteban shall go on a voyage in his ship, and at the last the Captain prevents him from hanging himself in his despair. He asks the Captain to take the wages due to him to buy a present for the Abbess, because she has suffered in the loss of Pepita. As they start on the journey Esteban crosses the river by the bridge, and is one of the five to die. Camilla Périchole is the greatest actress in the Spanish world, and the delightful adventurer Uncle Pio is her trainer, her singing master, her reader, her maid, her errand boy, and her banker. He discovered the child singing in the cafés. and with his selfless passion for beautiful women, and his love for Spanish literature, he created the artiste. The Viceroy made her his mistress, and she had three children. After the theatre the Viceroy invited the exiles from Spain, Captain Alvaro, Uncle Pio, and the Archbishop, who had read all the literature of antiquity and forgotten it, except "a general aroma of charm and disillusion," to midnight suppers, where Camilla was the queen of the feast. Uncle Pio had taught her how great ladies carry themselves on great occasions; the Viceroy taught her how they relax, and her art gained new finish from the association. Camilla became ambitious to achieve social position and respectability, and left the theatre. An epidemic of smallpox destroyed her beauty, and she lived thereafter brooding in seclusion, refusing to see even Uncle Pio. He gained an interview with her by artifice, and persuaded her to let him have her beautiful and delicate son, Jaime, for a year, and as they cross the bridge the accident happened.

BRIMMING CUP, THE, by Dorothy Canfield (1919). The fortunes of Neale Crittenden and Marise Allen are glimpsed again in the prelude of this book at that moment of union where the story of "Rough Hewn" closes on the Roman Campagna. This story opens over a decade later when Marise Crittenden, lonely now that her youngest boy has passed out of her constant care with the beginning of school years, receives a call from her new neighbor, Mr. Welles, who has recently retired from business, and his guest, Vincent Marsh, son of his former employer. Marsh, a prosperous and cultivated man of the world, at once recognizes an unusual personality in Marise. The succeeding chapters are rich in flavor of Vermont country life, such as the neighborhood gatherings to dance the old square dances, or to view the opening of the night blooming cereus. Against the background of these scenes Vincent Marsh proceeds with his usual headlong directness to win Marise from husband and children for himself. The children, sturdy and alluring little individuals, he looks upon as tiresome little leeches taking their gifted mother's best time and strength. Marise and Vincent find themselves deeply congenial in their love of music and before long they are caught in the swirl of an adult passion whose power and danger they fully recognize. Insidiously the duel between the two progresses and along with it, its humbler and more simply tragic counterpart is enacted in the lives of beautiful Nellie Powers, her husband Gene, and Frank Warner, the lover. Neale, although preoccupied with his business affairs, is aware of how matters stand between Marise and Vincent and one morning in the wakeful hours before dawn he fights his own battle for the woman who sleeps by his side. The issue of that battle is his decision that he must remain loyal to their old compact on the Roman Campagna and to his own ideals. He will make no move to hold his wife; she knows what he means in her life, and must remain free to make her own choice. Coercion would be fatal to the spirit of their love. Marise's old school friend of French and Roman days, Eugenia Mills, returns for a visit and throws her influence with Vincent in arousing Marise to resent the drudgery of her days. Actually, by misrepresenting to Marise some of Neale's business dealings, she hopes to lessen the husband's influence and through Marise's defection, gain Neale's attention for herself. Vincent presses Marise for a return of his passion, confident of his success. Just at this time, Marise's old aunt Hetty, who has been a second mother to her, dies. From her temporary doubt of her husband Marise realizes how much more important to her is his integrity than the love of the other man. Sorrow, too, helps dissipate the fog of infatuation, and Marise wins her way to true maturity through facing the warring elements in her nature. She sees that, just as, having had real children she could never go back to playing with dolls, so having grown into the richly varied interests of adult life she could not return to the period of all absorbing singleness of passion. The true mate for her maturity she finds not in the man who would selfishly absorb her in his passion even though he understands so perfectly her love of music and can, besides, give her the delights of the great world; but rather in the man who looks upon her as his equal in strength though he perceives her finer quality, and whose pride will make no claims on her except those she allows voluntarily. The author has analyzed and portrayed the maturity of a subtle woman's passion with the same power she has shown in the stark, primitive story of the Powers family which is complementary to it. Such is her range that she delights with the perfect understanding of the simplicities of children at the same time that she interprets the storms of maturity successfully.

BRITISH HISTORY IN THE NINETEENTH CENTURY, by George Macaulay Trevelyan (1922). This author aims "to give the sense of continuous growth, to show how economic led to social, and social to political change, how the political events reacted on the economic and social, and how new thoughts and new ideals accompanied or directed the whole complicated process." He begins with the year 1782 when England was on the eve of the industrial revolution, but first draws the picture of the village and agricultural communities of the England of the early years of George III. He notes economic and social changes perceptible between 1750 and 1770, with the unchallenged position of the upper classes — a position of social and political supremacy which has "never been seen in any other age or land." The historian's comment is that no aristocracy has ever better fulfilled the functions for the performance of which aristocracy specially exists — the intelligent patronage of art, philosophy and literature, and the living of a many-sided and truly civilized life by means of wealth and leisure well applied. The influence and social status of the clergy, who were more identified with the squirearchy than ever before, the reaction of the new fact — Methodism — on the gentry, the decay of Oxford and Cambridge, the criminal laws, prisons, the opening of British Colonies to Scottish trade, the turnpike movements in both countries, are discussed with other striking characteristics of the age. The course of events brings the historian to his appreciation of Edmund Burke and Charles Fox, Shelburne and Pitt, with surveys of India, the slave trade, Wilberforce and the Evangelicals, Australia and Canada. The reactions on England of economic changes and of the French Revolution, the anti-Jacobins and Democrats — the movement to introduce democracy following upon the publication of Paine's "Rights of Man," — made for the new proletariat as well as the new middle classes which the Industrial Revolution was creating. The historian reveals the mood of the nation — the main stream of English opinion and that of the French people which culminated in the catastrophe — the "metaphysical war" between the ideas of Rousseau and the ideas of Burke, and which drew Great Britain into the field of war. The historian follows the course of the war — its four periods — which ended with the collapse of the Second Coalition, with Napoleon nominally First Consul, and Britain standing alone once more. The war with Napoleon, the final settlement of Europe, with its merits and defects, are treated in their relation to British security, which the author considers was England's for a hundred years of progress in liberty and high civilization — the merits of the great settlement associated with the names of Wellington and Castlereagh. Politics and economics, material and moral influences on the new society, popular education, coal-mining, the coaching days, the prize-ring, the infancy of athletics, supply the historian with abundant material during the years immediately preceding the outbreak of war between Great Britain and the United States. The causes of war are discussed, with phases of action, the aspects of the Treaty of Ghent and Castlereagh's American policy. The historian follows the history of Great Britain through the period dominated by such figures as Brougham, Bentham, Owen, and Cobbett, and discusses the radical movement and the second repression. In 1820 the famous Cato Street conspiracy — "as bloody in its intention as the Gunpowder Plot"— was submerged somewhat by the trial of Queen Caroline, which sank deep into men's hearts and prepared the way for change. The period of liberal Toryism; Canning, Peel, Huskisson, Francis Place, and the Combination Acts; Canning's foreign policy; Spain, America, Greece, the Holy Alliance; religious equality, and Catholic emancipation are treated as separate developments, and problems of the newer age, with the middle classes moving rapidly toward Parliamentary Reform, and which afford the historian an opportunity for reviewing the difference of opinion as to economic cure for the distress of the time. "The basis was laid of the Whig-Liberal party that dominated the next generation, the Government was beaten in the Commons on the Civil List; Wellington resigned, and the King sent for Lord Grey." The Grey ministry, the Belgian crisis, the main provisos of the English, Scottish and Irish Reform Acts, and other movements, including trade unions and socialism, the abolition of slavery, the great Trek to the Colonies and the tide of emigration to the United States, are but a few phases of the time which the author discusses. The historian comes in 1837 to the reign of Queen Victoria, "which associated itself in the public mind with a new set of ideas." Peel's budget; Disraeli's imperialism; the expansion of trade and enterprise; and the outstanding features of Victorian prosperity, with the later evolution in the Church; Gladstone's ministries; Mill, Darwin, and the new era; Chamberlain and Churchill; the Salisbury ministries; Parnell, Cecil Rhodes, and the Robert's campaign, are a large part of this scholarly unfoldment of English conditions in the nineteenth century, which the historian considers closed with the death of Queen Victoria.

BROADWAY, a comedy by Philip Dunning and George Abbott (1926). The scene of this play written in the racy dialogue of a group of cabaret performers and their friends, the bootleggers, takes place in the private back room of the Paradise Night Club in New York City. The one thing that matters to Roy, the chorus man, besides getting on in his "art," is Billie, his chosen partner. The middle-aged Greek proprietor, Nick, is angry because she is late, but he calms down when she comes in with his patron, Steve Crandall, the bootleg king. Roy asks Steve to "lay off" Billie. Steve would resent his interference in his affairs if he did not consider the dancer beneath his notice. With Roy "pacing" them, the chorus girls prance out of the room to the stage in the cabaret. As soon as they are alone Steve and Nick discuss the business affairs of "the second biggest industry in the U.S.A." Steve makes Nick, who is a regular customer, buy a truck load of liquor "highjacked" from the "Scar" Edwards' gang the night before, though Nick protests that he does not want to become involved in the war between the rival bootleggers. "Scar" comes in looking for Steve to protest his encroachment on the territory above 125th Street. In the quarrel that follows Steve shoots "Scar" in the back. As Roy and Billie come down from their dressing rooms they see Steve and his henchman, Dolph, going out the door with an apparently drunken man between them. Roy calls, "Who's the drunk?" Steve answers, "Just one of the boys we're helping home," and "the death march continues." Steve later takes the precaution of warning Billie not to say anything about what she had seen, as his drunken friend was a big politician, and it might make trouble. He gives her a diamond bracelet which she does not think she ought to accept, but her act is on and she has to go before she can return it. Roy begs her to give it back to Crandall. He loves her and wants her to marry him, and accuses her of being a "gold digger" and preferring to marry a "rich guy." Billie decides to stay after the show to Steve's party just to prove to Roy that he cannot tell her what to do and what not to do. Dolph is worried to see Dan McCorn of the homicide squad outside in the cabaret. Presently Dan comes into the back room and jokes with Steve and the others. Casually he lets them know that the body of "Scar" Edwards has been found. Dan interrupts Pearl trying to telephone, and she confides to him that she is "Scar's" girl, at the Paradise to watch his interests. They are going to be married as soon as he gets his divorce. "Scar" had told her that he was coming around to have a "show-down" with Steve, to-night, but she has not seen him. Dan does not tell her of the murder, but later she hears Steve say that "a local nuisance named 'Scar' got bumped off to-night." She almost faints but pretends it is nothing, and goes on with the others for the "pirate dance." Steve's party is a rough one, and Billie comes to Steve for protection from some of his Chicago friends. Roy has had a fake telegram sent to Billie saying her mother is ill, but his ruse is found out, and Billie is indignant at his attempt to get her to go home. Dan walks in again just as Steve and Roy are fighting, and Roy has managed to get Steve's gun away from him. The policeman arrests Roy ostensibly for breaking the law by carrying a weapon, but really because he wants to examine Steve's gun and thinks Roy will be safer in jail at the moment. Roy thinks Steve has "framed" him, and in revenge tells Dan about the "drunk" with the scar on his face. Billie, called as a witness, at a look from Steve denies that she saw anything. Roy is led away in a frenzy of grief that he cannot protect Billie from Crandall. "She's only a kid. She don't know what she's up against." The next night Roy and Billie practise the steps of their new act, and come to a better understanding. Dan McCorn warns Nick that he is waiting for Steve. In the office Steve confesses to Nick his need to get out of the country. He asks Nick to borrow a car for him since his own is too well known, so he can take Billie and some of the girls for a joy ride after the show. He can get rid of the girls he does not want later outside the city. The instant Nick goes out Pearl, who has been listening behind the door, appears with a pistol in her hand. She tells Steve, "the last thing you see before you go straight to hell is Jim Edwards' woman. . . ." With the silencer the shot makes no noise, and Pearl hides the weapon in her hand-bag and runs upstairs as Nick falls out of sight through the office door. Dan McCorn advises Nick to tell him where Steve is if he knows or worse things will happen to him, and they find him dead. Nick accuses Roy, but Dan who guesses that justice has been done says he shall report it to the office as a suicide. As he goes out the door he mutters under his breath to Pearl, "Pull yourself together, kid." Roy and Billie get an offer from a vaudeville manager to put on their act in "Chambersburgh and Pottsville," and announce joyfully that they are "going on the matrimonial circuit" also. Nick sends them all off to the cabaret, and crossing himself leans half fainting against the locked door of the office waiting for the return of Dan with the coroner.

BUDDENBROOKS, translated from the German of Thomas Mann, by H. T. Lowe-Porter. (2 vols. 1924.) This chronicle of four generations of the Buddenbrook family begins in the year 1825 with a house-warming party given by old Johann and his wife to celebrate their removal to the large house in Meng Street, with offices on the ground floor for their prosperous grain business. The second generation is represented in Johann, junior, the Consul. The author describes the company of grandchildren, poor relations, dependents, friends, their clothes, the furniture, the courses of the dinner, and the conversation which goes back to memories of Napoleon, with the same detail. It is a picture of German social life of the period reflected in the fortunes of the family. Gotthold, the oldest son who has married against his father's wishes, writes protesting that he is practically disinherited. The decline of the family and the business begins with the Consul, who is arrogant, self-satisfied, and pious, without the initiative, daring, and vision of his father. His children are Thomas, who follows his father as head of the business, the indolent, irresponsible Christian, who fails repeatedly in business ventures, and Antoinette, impulsive, and frivolous, destined for disaster. The unattractive, elderly Herr Grünlich wins her father's consent to his suit, but not hers. Sent away to the shore to recover her health and spirits and come to a proper view of her duty to the family, Tony falls in love with a young medical student, and promises to wait for him. The great black book of the family genealogy impresses her childish mind and increases her sense of importance, and with her own hand she adds her betrothal to Herr Grünlich. The husband turns out to be a bankrupt who had plotted to bolster up his fortunes by the alliance with the Buddenbrooks, and the Consul brings Tony and her daughter back home again. Christian goes to London to a business firm, friends of the family, and Thomas to Amsterdam, where he marries Gerda, a wealthy heiress. On a visit to Munich, Tony meets Herr Permaneder, and makes a second marriage, which is also a failure, and she comes back to her family. She decides to get a husband for her daughter, and is even less fortunate than in her own case. Erica's husband is jailed for fraud. Thomas alone upholds the honor of the family. He is made consul and elected senator. His mansion in Fisher Street surpasses the Meng Street house. But Thomas 'tells his sister, Tony, that he knows from life and from history that "often the outward and visible material signs and symbols of happiness and success only show themselves when the process of decline has already set in," and so it is. There are business failures which make it necessary to economize at home. Gerda, his wife, becomes too much interested in Herr Lieutenant von Throta, who shares her interest in music. Johann, his son, the last of the family, is a delicate, dreamy, sensitive child, with a gift for music. Thomas dies, and then Johann, of typhoid fever in his young manhood.

CAPONSACCHI, by Arthur Goodrich and Rose A. Palmer (1926). This play, in three acts, prologue and epilogue, is based on Robert Browning's poem, "The Ring and the Book." The scene of the prologue is a Court of Justice in the Vatican, 1698. The "soldier-saint," Canon Caponsacchi, had been accused of seducing Pompilia, the lovely young wife of Count Guido Franceschini. Guido, in the rôle of outraged husband, has slain Pompilia and her father and mother. His defense to the Judges is calumny of Caponsacchi and Pompilia. Caponsacchi's defense forms the play. The Pope, the final arbiter, seeks "the truth that lies in the hearts of men," and to that end secretes himself in an anteroom where he can hear the proceedings of the trial. Act One takes place at Arezzo eleven months earlier at the time of the Carnival. From the comments of the crowd one learns that the wicked Count Guido has married the seventeen-year-old Pompilia for her wealth, is treating her shamefully, and is seeking to rob her parents of their entire fortune. There is talk of the popular Canon Caponsacchi, and rumor that he and his companion Conti, a Falstaffian monk who provides the comic relief in this tragedy, are coming to the Carnival in disguise. Garbed as fortune-tellers the two clerics make merry, and moved by the distress of Pompilia's father and mother, take up a collection to help them get to Rome to escape Guido's persecution. The Archbishop brings news of Caponsacchi's preferment and that he is to go to Rome, and Caponsacchi and Conti go to their cells to remove their motley garments. Pompilia appeals to the Archbishop for protection in vain, and falls into the clutches of the Governor, a corrupt official in league with Guido, who pretends to advise her and tricks her into meeting her husband. Caponsacchi returns and Pompilia looks in his eyes and derives comfort from his answering looks even while Count Guido is dragging her away. All of Caponsacchi's chivalrous pity is roused by her sad plight. The first scene of the second act is Caponsacchi's cell. Guido plots to compromise his wife and Caponsacchi, and sends him passionate letters imploring his assistance, and writes her letters purporting to be from Caponsacchi. Neither Pompilia nor Caponsacchi are deceived. He learns that Pompilia can neither read nor write. Gerhardi, a friend of Caponsacchi, brings a true message from Pompilia that she is in great distress, and Caponsacchi determines to take her to Rome with him to her parents, even though by so doing he wrecks his career. In the second scene Pompilia from her balcony tells him that she had not cared what happened to her and would have welcomed death, but that she knows that she is to have a child now, and would save its life and her own. Guido overtakes them at a wayside inn only one short stage from Rome. He bribes the landlord to place incriminating letters in the bedroom where they will be found. When they arrive, Caponsacchi carries the exhausted Pompilia upstairs for a rest while the horses are changed, discovers Guido when he comes to urge the grooms to haste, and is prevented from giving him his just punishments by the guards. Moved by Caponsacchi's stand upon his right as a priest to be tried in the Vatican, the crowd forces Guido to carry his case to Rome. The Judges at the Vatican find Caponsacchi's story "hard to believe, but possible," but they dare not acquit him outright lest they be charged with winking at scandal in the Church, so he is banished for eight months. Pompilia is sent to her parents. Eight months later on Christmas Eve Conti comes to say that Caponsacchi is free and will come to pay his respects to Pompilia that evening. Pompilia's child is two weeks old, and has been sent to the nuns for safety. After Conti leaves to get Caponsacchi, Guido and three hired assassins break into the house. He has heard of the birth of the child, and comes to claim his son as the heir to the gold he still covets. In order to make Pompilia confess, Guido slays first her mother and then her father, and stabs Pompilia. Caponsacchi knocks and Guido's henchmen take to their heels, leaving Guido to reckon with Caponsacchi, while Conti goes for the guards. Pompilia revives for a moment to tell Caponsacchi of her love and faith in God's help. The epilogue is the same scene as the prologue in the Court. Caponsacchi has just finished speaking. The Judges are influenced by the shouts of Guido's followers without, and Caponsacchi's tale is unsubstantiated, as Conti has been poisoned, and his friend, Gerhardi, is mysteriously missing. It seems that the Count will win the case. Then the Pope draws the curtains and orders Guido to be executed for his crime with his accomplices, and to Caponsacchi he gives his blessing with the words, "Well done."

CAPTAIN'S DOLL, THE, by D. H. Lawrence (1923). These three novelettes deal with conflict in love in subtle ways which a summary can reproduce only partially in outline of external happenings. In the title story the English Captain Hepburn on duty in a foreign city is infatuated with an Austrian refugee, Countess Johanna von Rassentlow (Hannele). She is supporting herself designing dolls, which have become quite famous, and has made one, a life-like portrait of the Captain. His wife, who has not seen him for more than a year, hears rumors of his love-affair, appears unexpectedly, comes to the studio as a casual customer, and wants to buy the doll. Later she meets Hannele and suggests that she is able to use her influence with the British commander to deport women who may be dangerous to the soldiers. Then an accident occurs, Mrs. Hepburn falls out the window at the hotel and is killed. Captain Hepburn goes back to England to attend to his affairs and place his children in school. After several months of silence he writes Hannele, but receives no answer. In Munich he hears that she is in the Tyrol, and of her engagement to an elderly Austrian, the Herr Regierungsrat Trepte. The Herr Regierungsrat is a "real old Roman of the Empire," "with the witty volubility of the more versatile Austrian." "No one had ever quite kissed her hand as he kissed it." He made her feel like a queen in exile. Captain Hepburn invites her to go on an excursion to the glacier. On the long walk up the beautiful mountain they recognize the power each has over the other in "a sort of silent hostility." In the past his wife, he tells her, had made a doll of him in her mind, as Hannele had in a portrait. He believes that is what a woman does with love, and he will have none of it again. He will be honoured and obeyed or nothing, and love and cherish a wife as such in the sense of the words of the marriage service. She finally consents to be his wife on his terms. "The Fox" is the story of two girls, Miss Banford and Miss March, and their chicken farm, and their enemy the fox. The fox is symbolic as is the doll in the earlier story. One night, a young man, Henry Grenfel, a returned soldier, whose grandfather had owned the farm, knocks at the door. It is too late for him to get to the village, and they invite him to spend the night. He stays on, and falls in love with March, who identifies him in a way with the fox. Banford becomes furiously jealous, and tries to persuade March not to marry him, and to his despair almost succeeds. Henry kills the fox. After Henry has gone back to camp March writes him that she cannot leave her friend. At the farm he finds them trying to fell a tree. He offers to finish it, and half accidently and half on purpose kills Miss Banford with the falling tree, and there is no obstacle to their marriage. "The Ladybird" is the title used for the English edition of this book. Lady Beveridge has lost her sons and her brother in the War. In the hospital where the enemy prisoners are interned she finds Count Johann Dionys Psanek, whom she had known as a boy, and who had visited her with his wife in the spring of 1914. Her daughter Lady Daphne, a society beauty, accompanies her mother to the hospital, and goes again because the Count awakens a part of her nature which her husband's devotion has never touched. The ladybird is his crest. Her husband's adoration idealizes her, and is tiring to her. The Count goes away never to return, but the bond between them is so strong that they are not separated in spirit.

CAPTIVE, THE, by Edouard Bourdet, translated from the French by Arthur Hornblower, Jr. (1926). A play dealing with the theme of sex inversion. Irene de Montcel, a beautiful, cultured young woman, refuses to leave Paris, when her father, a member of the Foreign Office, is ordered to Rome for the winter. He insists that she shall accompany him, and tells her that he will never see her again or allow her to see her young sister, Giselede, unless she can give some explanation of her strange conduct. She then tells him that she is on the point of becoming engaged to the young lawyer, Jacques Virieu, and asks Jacques, who loves her and wants to marry her, to pretend to be her fiancé. Jacques finds out that she is spending all her time with some new friends, a Monsieur and Madame d'Aiguines. Unable to gain Irene's confidence he sends for Monsieur d'Aiguines, whom he believes to be her lover, and discovers that he is a friend of his school-days. Monsieur d'Aiguines reveals that it is his wife whose dangerous charm holds Irene in bondage and urges him to give up Irene and cure himself of loving her. His own life has been ruined because his wife cares only for other women. After this interview Irene comes to him as a "petitioner for mercy and pity rather than respect," and asks him to marry her to protect her. They are married and travel for a year. On their return to Paris Irene tells Jacques that the sinister Madame d'Aiguines is trying to see her again. She meets her by accident and comes home completely dominated by her warped infatuation, but suggests that they go away for a time. Jacques tells her that he recognizes that she has made every effort to make their marriage a success without love. The encounter with Madame d'Aiguines has changed her from a statue into a glowing, living woman. He will make no effort to hold her. She leaves him, and presently a servant announces that Madame has gone out. He goes also, to Françoise Mcillant, who loves him, and had been his mistress.

CAPTIVES, THE, by Hugh Walpole (1920). The heroine, Maggie Cardinal, has lived for nineteen years in a remote country village, neglected by her miserly, dirty father, the vicar. At his death she goes to London to make her home with her aunts, members of a fanatical religious sect awaiting the second coming of Christ. The head of the Kingscote Brethren is Mr. Warlock, and Martin, his son, is the other captive. Martin's father and Maggie's Aunt Anne are determined to offer these two to God when he descends as they believe he may do at any moment in his chariot of fire. To the young people their elders stand for a mysterious force against which they revolt, but they feel it is always lying in wait for them and will one day claim them. Thurston, half-charlatan, half-fanatic, says to Martin, "You are a religious man really — can't escape your destiny, you know. . . . It's like 'aving a 'are lip — you'll be bothered with it all your life." Martin has returned home from years of wandering in Spain and France and South America to the religious atmosphere of his childhood because of his love for his father. Maggie and Martin fall in love almost at first sight. They meet every day to walk and talk together until they are seen by some of the Brethren, and Maggie is kept a prisoner by her aunts. He has told Maggie the secret that he is married to a Frenchwoman who has left him. The saintly Mr. Warlock bids the congregation prepare for New Year's Eve at midnight as the time of God's coming, and the little group of disappointed women and broken men who have "passed the adventurous period of life and passed it without adventure" gather under the hissing gas jets in the ugly chapel eager "for some revelation that was to answer all questions and satisfy all expectations." God does come but in the guise of the Angel of Death to take the minister, and leave the flock without a shepherd. Martin comes to say good-by to Maggie, and she is prevented by Aunt Anne from following him. After she recovers from brain fever she plans to get away from the unnatural household and try to earn her living. A friend, Mrs. Marks (Katherine Trenchard of "The Green Mirror"), invites her to visit her. Here she meets the Rev. Paul Trenchard and his sister Grace staying with their relatives. Paul is attracted to Maggie, and she consents to marry him. They live at Skeaton, a horrible seaside place full of gossip in winter and sand trippers in summer. Grace, a detestable person who is jealous of Paul's increasing love for his wife, makes her marriage more difficult and her life in the community a failure. They both had thought of Maggie as a child they would mould and guide, and her independence in thought and action is a surprise. Called to London to see her Aunt Anne before her death she hears from Amy Warlock that her brother had written a number of letters to Maggie which she had destroyed. Later she learns that Martin is ill in London, and leaves her husband to take care of him. "There were many difficulties ahead for her. She had still to deal with Paul: Martin was not a perfect character, nor would he suddenly become one. Above all that strange sense of being a captive in a world that did not understand her, some one curious and odd and alien — that would not desert her."

CARAVAN, by John Galsworthy (1925) is sent out by its author, "bearing merchandise of sorts . . . through the desert of indifference toward the oasis of public favor." It is a complete collection to the date of publication in which an early tale is paired with a later one having some likeness or contrast of theme or mood. "A Stoic" better known from its stage rendering, "Old English," portrays the crucial moment in the life of old Heythrope. Financially he has reached the limits of his creditors' patience and is threatened with bankruptcy and the loss of his various directorships which now are his sole source of income. He sees himself relegated to the keeping of his coldly self-righteous daughter who will effectively restrain him from any liberty of enjoyment, even the satisfaction of his appetite for good food which remains to him after all the others are gone. He determines to spite her and the doctor and enjoy one epicurean meal though it be his last. So he goes to his last sleep, a man who has never been afraid to enjoy all life's frills and flavor to his very last moment. In contrast to this, "Salvation of a Forsyte" is the story of Swithin Forsyte, who on his death bed realizes that he has never tasted life to the full, for he looks back on his one near romance when, as a young man traveling on the Continent he fell in love with a charming little Polish patriot and very nearly committed himself to an affair, but just in time the prudence of his family blood restrained him. In "Quality" an old bootmaker who cared more for his craftsmanship than success or life itself reveals the same sterling trait of character in a tradesman that appears in a man of good family in the tale, "The Man Who Kept His Form." All through school, and later in his struggle for success on a fruit farm in Australia, through the loss of his wife, and the hardships of the War and his subsequent poverty, he keeps his form, never fails to exact of himself, as he does of others a measuring up against the highest standards, the only endurable ones to his mind, without whimpering. "A Man of Devon" and "The Apple Tree," among the longest of these stories, sound a purely lyrical note. Zachary Pearse, the man of Devon, whose piratical ancestors went out with Drake, conceives a modern gun-running, buccaneering scheme to be pulled off on the coast of Morocco. He means to take with him on this adventure as his bride, Pasiance Voisey, granddaughter of John Ford, a sternly puritanical man of the neighborhood. So closely is the girl subjected to the old man's will that, for freedom's sake, she secretly marries Pearse. Then, when it seems necessary to leave her behind she wanders about the cliffs disconsolate until she falls and dies after a few days' suffering. The soft Devonshire setting is as lyrical in mood as the spring idyll in "The Apple Tree" of Frank Ashurt's first love for lovely Megan David, a Celtic girl he found in a farm house where he was resting during a walking trip with a college chum. Many years afterward, coming back with a wife of his own class he dreams of that early love, "the apple tree, the singing and the gold" and the temptation to illicit love he had so valiantly overcome, only to find Megan's grave at the cross-roads where only suicides are buried. "The Pack" and "The Dog It Was That Died" illustrate the power of mob psychology. The first is among college students against one of their number who will not conform; the other of a man who in spirit is a throw-back to the old

Ironsides of Cromwell's time. His true nature appears for the first time during the War when he becomes the fanatical spy hunting leader of all those who persecute and intern the Germans living in England. In "A Miller of Dee" a man who is the outcast of a small town, where he lives as a ferryman, because he suspects every one of unfriendliness, keeps his young wife from all neighborly contacts as well. Then his petty suspicions centre on the young woman. He becomes convinced that she means to be unfaithful to him and kills her. "Late –299," in contrast, is the story of a man also ostracized, but in his case because his every attitude and motive are nobler than the world, or even his family can credit. Only the blind old barber, whittling his figures of the Christ, to whom he goes to read after his release from prison sympathizes with his sufferings and touching his face that he may the more easily model the face of the Christ, understands that here is one who has shown a martyr's pride and endurance of sorrow.

CATHEDRAL, THE, by Hugh Walpole (1922). The cathedral "so beautiful, so lovely . . . so haughty, so jealous . . . become a god demanding its own rites and worshippers." The domination of the cathedral is expressed in the words of the half-mad painter Davray, "This place can bide its time. Just when you think you're master it turns and stamps you out." Archdeacon Brandon is often called the "King of Polchester," such is his position in the town and in the affairs of the chapter. A new canon, Ronder, a round, obese, purring gentleman, with a passion for intrigue, finds in Polchester a situation exactly suited to his powers. His opinion of the handsome archdeacon is that he is after all "a stupid, autocratic, retrogressive, goodnatured child," and he decides that he shall no longer have everything his own way. While stressing his admiration of Brandon's fine character, the clever Ronder begins to stir up opposition in the chapter. The conservative archdeacon represents the old ideas, clings to old forms and rituals. A living in the town of Pybus St. Anthony falling vacant gives Ronder the opportunity to contest the archdeacon's choice for the appointment. An ordinary, well-connected, safe young man, Rex Forsyth is the candidate. Ronder favors the brilliant, and revolutionary Wistons, to the simple-minded archdeacon almost an atheist. In the meantime things are not going well in the archdeacon's family. His son, Falk, is sent down from Oxford, arriving on the same train that brings Canon Ronder. Mrs. Brandon has hated her husband for years because he has not satisfied her demands for attention and love. This silent lonely woman is passionately attached to one of the local clergy, Mr. Morris, and hesitates to go away with him only on account of her love for her son. Falk, occupied with his infatuation for Annie Hogg, the daughter of the local publican, has no time to think about his mother. The town gossips are whispering about their meetings but the family know nothing until Falk, in spite of his love for his father, and the knowledge of the blow it will be to him, takes the "reserved, proud, honest Annie" to London to be married. An inefficient librarian dismissed because of the archdeacon's complaints intercepts a letter of Mrs. Brandon's to Mr. Morris and brings it first to Canon Ronder, and then to Archdeacon Brandon. Mrs. Brandon confesses her infidelity to her husband, accuses him of pride and conceit, and reproaches him that he has never thought of her except as a piece of furniture in his house. She goes away with Mr. Morris leaving a cruel note, hoping that he will realize that loneliness is worse than any other hell, "the kind she has suffered for twenty years." Only his daughter Joan is left to him. The family have never paid any attention to her, but she is lovely and dependable, and postpones her engagement to Johnny, Lord St. Leath, to give all her thought to

her father.   Brandon and Ronder meet at lunch with the bishop, and come to open
violent quarrel on the drive home about the Pybus St. Anthony living.   The archdeacon even insists on getting out of the wagonette and walking home rather than
ride with his enemy.   Ronder is driven to remorseless implacable anger, and Brandon's hatred of Ronder becomes an obsession that brings him to the verge of insanity.
At the meeting of the chapter the archdeacon makes his plea for Forsyth.   He
begs them to think only of the good of the cathedral not of their personal feeling
about himself, but he fails, and dies of his defeat, protesting like Job that he has
served his God.   The injury to Canon Ronder who has used Wistans as a weapon
to crush the man who held the power he wanted is more insidious but hardly less
fatal.   There is a hint that Wistans will eventually be the means of Ronder's downfall.

CATHERINE THE GREAT, by Katherine Anthony (1925), is the biography, written
in the psychoanalytic tradition, of the German Lutheran princess who became
the Empress of the vast Russian empire.   Born in 1729 in the garrison town of
Stettin where her father, Prince Christian August of Zerbst-Dornburg, was commander of a regiment, the future empress was christened Sophie Auguste Friedrike.
The little girl was called Fike.   Her mother, the enterprising Princess Johanna
Elizabeth of Holstein-Gottrop, despising the life in the poverty-stricken household,
made as many visits as possible each year to her more well-to-do relatives and always
took Fike with her.   Fike's governess was a Frenchwoman, Babet Cardel, of enlightened views and to her teachings can be traced, Miss Anthony thinks, much of
the realism which later astonished the world in the Empress of Russia.   "The
princes of Anhalt-Zerbst were a pious line," so Fike received instruction in religion
also from Pastor Wagner, whom Fike refused to swallow whole.   So Babet had to
make peace continually between the clever young princess and her religious adviser.
Fike was a plain girl but she knew that eventually a marriage must be made, so
she was not surprised when she was fourteen to learn that she had been invited
with her mother to make a visit to the Russian court.   The Empress Elizabeth's
invitation was a command to the ambitious mother and overcoming all difficulties
the visit was made.   Shortly Sophie of Zerbst was betrothed to the Grand Duke
Peter, heir to the Russian throne; she gave up her Lutheran religion to become a
member of the Greek church; and had her name changed to Catherine.   Nine years
of unhappy married life with the half-witted Grand Duke followed and the Empress
Elizabeth clamored in vain for an heir to the throne until one of the court ladies
advised Catherine that by transgressing her marriage vows a son might be born.
Catherine's first lover was Sergei Saltikov, a young chamberlain of the Grand
Duke.   In 1754 Catherine bore a son, whom the Empress Elizabeth had christened
Paul and immediately took him in charge taking all care of him.   Catherine was
not even to care for her own son.   In 1761 the Empress Elizabeth died and was
succeeded upon the throne of Russia by her weak and more than half mad nephew,
who ruled as Peter III.   During the six months of his reign Catherine lived in strict
retirement, while the emperor was growing more and more unrestrained.   In June,
1762, Catherine as Colonel of the Guard, riding a white horse and wearing oak leaves
in her hair, leading her loyal troops, became Catherine II and the ex-emperor was
imprisoned.   Shortly afterwards the news was given out that Peter had died of a
hemorrhoidal attack.   From then on until her death Catherine II, who had come to
Russia as a poor little princess without even a bridal chest of linen, ruled supreme
in Russia.   She put through the partition of Poland, made a fixed code out of the

tumbled mass of Russian laws, gained the Crimea and Georgia for Russia, and by acclaim of her subjects became Catherine the Great. Miss Anthony explodes the theory or myth of the three hundred lovers of Catherine, and numbers them as twelve, excluding the Grand Duke, her husband. One lover always succeeded another, some lasting many years. Potiomkin, who held the chief place in her affections for fifteen years and shared her dreams of driving the Turk from Europe, was an old friend who had helped her seize the throne. With the death of Potiomkin the Empress seemed to fail. Her lovers grew younger and younger until it began to be said that she would end in the arms of a boy. Catherine the Great had three great fears: she feared venereal disease, smallpox, and ignorance. She was an intelligent ruler in a court of nobles almost as ignorant as her peasants; while she herself was a friend and correspondent of such men as Grimm and Voltaire. She had three thirsts: to enlighten her people, to liberate her own mind through science and literature, and to extend the boundaries of Russia. She was the leader in the partition of Poland and upon the throne of Poland she placed one of her former lovers. "Because she had come without sheets to Russia," says Miss Anthony, "she was obliged to put through the partition of Poland." Catherine was a prodigious writer. She left a library of her own writings, many of which were not printed in Russia until just before the Great War. Manifestos, ukases, political pamphlets, and her correspondence with Grimm and Voltaire took up a large part of her time, but she also wrote tales for her grandchildren, two volumes of a history of Russia, and two sets of her own memoirs. The first set she wrote in her youth; but the other was written many years later and the two do not always agree.

CAT'S CRADLE, by Maurice Baring (1926). The story begins in Rome. Blanche, the only child of an Englishman, Henry Clifford, the younger son of a peer, and the last of an old Whig family, is sent to Rome to recover from an attachment to a penniless subaltern by her selfish father who is ambitious to have her make a marriage in keeping with her great beauty and position. Persuaded by her father, Blanche breaks off her engagement to Sydney Hope, and marries Prince Guido Roccapalumba, a wealthy nobleman. Guido's mother, the Princess Julia, rules the household. He is afraid of her and Blanche soon realizes that she herself cannot persist in any line of conduct that is not approved by her mother-in-law. Blanche becomes a Catholic, and her religion is a solace to her. She discovers that her husband is narrow, meticulous, tortuous, self-centred — insanely jealous, and intensely secretive. As time passes, her life grows more and more difficult. Guido has infatuations which torment her; and the admiration which she arouses everywhere results in scenes with Guido. Blanche's father believes that one of her "affairs" has become too serious; her mother-in-law has sown the seed of this idea. At a great ball in Rome, Blanche promises this new lover, Alfredo Chiaromonte, that she will leave her husband. She hears that Guido has been taken ill, that he has left the ball suddenly. This illness turns out to be a "seizure," and Blanche gives up Alfredo. Fourteen years pass. Guido's illness has remained a mystery. The doctors can do nothing, and conclude that his malady is all imagination and nerves. Guido receives his friends, converses himself, but no one is permitted to speak to him. If they do, he feels the effect afterward. Blanche has devoted her life to him. Guido lies on a sofa — for months he does not even move. Blanche meets Bernard Lacy, an officer in the Cold Stream Guards. He has just recovered from a love affair with an actress — he had refused to go anywhere, the only person in whose society he seemed to find any pleasure was Walter Troumestre. Bernard first saw Blanche in Paris. Meeting her again in Rome, he is interested in her peculiar situation, and the mystery of Guido's invalidism. He hears of an incident which makes him believe that Guido is shamming. A portrait of Blanche, painted by a French artist, arrives. Guido has had a bad day and refuses to look at it. The picture was put in the *salotte* next to his room. The next morning it was not in the same place. The servants had not removed it; no one had been in the room, but somebody had looked at the picture, had lifted it to look at it, and had not put it back exactly in the same place. A member of Guido's household was convinced that Guido, out of curiosity, had risen from his bed to look at Blanche's portrait. The theory of his illness is that on discovering that Blanche did not love him — never, never could love him — he could not forgive her for marrying him, or rather for not loving him, and was determined she should never love any one else. "A man like Guido, from revenge or jealousy, would be capable of doing anything." Bernard now becomes a frequent visitor at the Palazzo Fabrini, during the hours when Blanche receives for the entertainment of her husband. Their intimacy, progresses, and, during a confession of their love, Guido surprises them, and has Blanche put out of the house. Bernard returned to London; Blanche moved into a small apartment. Half of Rome blamed her — Guido's friends and relatives; the other half did not blame her at all. "What sort of marriage was it to be tied to a man who spent his life on a sofa in a semi-darkened room?" Blanche later goes to London and keeps house for her uncle and his young daughter, Rose Marie, who becomes something of a ward to Blanche. Bernard meets her in London. Guido is dead, and Blanche and Bernard see each other frequently. Bernard and Rose Marie meet frequently, too, in Blanche's house. Blanche discovers that Bernard and her ward are falling in love with each other. Blanche is fifteen years older than Bernard, and although he is aware of it, she still has a fascination for him. But it is Rose Marie that he loves. When he tries to tell Blanche that he wants to marry her ward, she subtly leads him into a confession and a proposal to herself. They are married and settle down in London. Rose Marie knows that Blanche is an incurable flirt, a coquette, who "couldn't help enslaving every man she came across." Walter proposes to Rose Marie, and she accepts. After the marriage, they go to Constantinople, where Walter collects material for a book. When they return to England, Bernard invites them to live at Dower House. For the first time since their marriage, Blanche, Bernard, Rose Marie and Walter meet. Rose Marie hates Blanche.   "She hated Blanche not as Iseult of Brittany, Iseult, the lily-handed, had hated Iseult of Cornwall; but she hated Blanche, as Iseult of Cornwall hated Iseult of Brittany. She felt certain that her right was the greater, not because she loved Bernard more, but because she knew that Bernard loved her and did not love Blanche, and had never really loved Blanche. It had been for him a passing fancy, a *coup de tête;* he had given in to her love — the love of an older woman at the height of her dazzling beauty for a young man." Bernard is now obsessed with Rose Marie; Blanche makes a close friend of Walter. Rose Marie broods over the situation. "Blanche was behaving abominably — inexcusably; Blanche was false to the core; she professed virtue and did worse than practice vice; she did not even practice vice; if she did, she would have been a better woman; as it was, she led people on and left them high and dry." But the result of this brooding was that Rose Marie, instead of keeping in the background, "advanced into the glare of the footlights." Blanche now feels that she is reaping the reward of everything that she has done and through a spiritual crisis, in which she admits her mistakes, and from an act of inner self-sacrifice, finds peace. After her death, Bernard appears wretched. Walter goes to the front when the war between Bulgaria and

Turkey and Serbia breaks out, and never returns. In the end Bernard marries Rose Marie.

CERTAIN RICH MAN, A, by William Allen White (1909) is a story of the forty years following the Civil War and the changes they wrought in a little frontier town of Kansas. Sycamore Ridge, the town, really stands as a microcosm of the whole country and one sees in its long struggle up out of the mire and muck of war the true background of the early twentieth century America. The story opens in 1857 when John Barclay was a boy of seven years. Four years before his father had been killed for preaching an abolition sermon, and his widowed mother, a splendid type of pioneer woman, bravely facing the future had become a washerwoman to support herself and her son. But the culture of her former life was not forgotten and John was raised in accordance with the traditions of New England. The Civil War began when he was eleven years old and when the local company marched away to join the army, John Barclay and his playmate, Bob Hendricks, went too, hidden under a load of saddles. When discovered they became great favorites with the soldiers and before arrangements could be made to send them back, the boys witnessed the horrors of battle. John's foot was wounded and throughout his life he limped. When he was sent home he found that his mother was to be the teacher of the local school. After the war was over the Sycamore Ridge heroes returned to become the respected citizens of the fast-growing town. John was now sixteen. Under his mother's guidance he had read widely and had developed a passion for music. Bob Hendricks and he continued to be inseparable friends and Ellen Culpepper, his playmate for years, was now his sweetheart. Before he and Bob went to the State University he confessed his love to Ellen who promised to wait for him. Her sister, Molly, became engaged to Bob. The boys left with the good wishes of all their fellow townsmen. John worked his way through the University and a sharp trait of getting more than his bargain began to show in his dealings. It worried Bob but John scoffed. He seemed hard except in his devotion to Ellen and for her his soul yearned. One day a letter announced her death and the best in John seemed to pass with her. In 1872 he returned to Sycamore Ridge, a full-fledged young man. He became the law partner of his old friend, General Ward, and their offices were over the bank which Bob's father directed and where Bob, too, was now installed. John's sharp methods worried his partner, who was a true idealist, but the young man had started on a course from which he would not turn. Continually he thought out schemes for making money, and ever to his advantage. In 1873 he married Jane Mason, a charming girl from a neighboring town. The panic of that same year closed the Hendricks bank temporarily so Bob and Molly delayed their wedding. Then John sent Bob east to manage the sale of stock in a big wheat land scheme. It was hard for the lovers to part, for Molly loved Bob with a passion as deep as his own. John's operations became more and more extensive and he was growing richer and richer. But this prosperity did not extend to his friends. One by one he sacrificed them. To protect his interests he kept Bob in New York several years and in the interim under the pretext of saving Bob and his father and her own father, beloved Colonel Culpepper, from ruin he persuaded Molly Culpepper that she should marry Adrian Brownell, a new editor of the local paper to whom they owed money. It was John's overdrafts that had brought the danger about. General Hendricks' bank was left but a husk and when John forced the old man to a forgery on his books, it killed him. After Bob's return home he soon discovered the truth and his soul burned with rage. He refused to join in any of John's schemes and entered into the struggle for good government and clean politics while John carried his operations to the great cities of the East. Year by year his wealth increased. He built a magnificent home in Sycamore Ridge for his mother, wife and daughter, who preferred the little town and their old friends to all the advantages of wealth. John Barclay's daughter, Jeannette, fell in love with Neal Ward, son of old General Ward, so her father took the young man as his secretary, while Jeannette and her mother were sent abroad. His power was extending and he was known as one of the wealthiest men in the country. But the corrupt methods of its attainment could not ever remain hidden and in 1903 John Barclay was indicted by the United States government. Neal Ward was required to give damaging testimony, so this ended his engagement to Jeannette. John escaped prison through legal trickery. He retained his wealth but a realization of his moral failure was beginning to dawn upon him. His old friend Bob Hendricks, who had bravely fought for the interests of the people and who had remained true to Molly through all the years, was murdered by her husband as a result of political intrigue, instigated through information supplied by John. Shortly after the death of his boyhood friend, John Barclay's wife died. All this and his daughter's unhappiness weighed heavily upon him. Finally a new faith was awakened in him and he disposed of his great wealth to the joy of his aged mother, Jeannette, and his old friends in the town. Jeannette's marriage to Neal followed and happiness reigned. Several years later John Barclay died in an attempt to rescue a poor woman from drowning. Throughout the book, the author's portrayal of the local characters who form the background of the story is particularly excellent.

CHAINS, by Theodore Dreiser (1927) is a collection of lesser novels and stories varying in mood between the realistically normal and the abnormal, sometimes the supernormal. "Chains," the title story of the collection, is one of the longer stories of an elderly man of wealth and station, Garrison, who, as he was nearing fifty was attracted to a beautiful young woman, a stranger to him who was injured in a street accident. The story is told in an unusual form which is also employed in another story of this collection, "Fulfillment." The action develops as Garrison meditates on the past and the character of this lovely woman, Idelle, whom he has rescued and married. But at intervals the reverie is broken into by a sentence or paragraph descriptive of the journey from a business engagement in a distant city back to his wife. His infatuation for her is detailed along with the unworthy incidents and lovers which she has told him were in her past. The recurring refrain of what he is noting with his eyes but oblivious to in his mind is first poetic in mood, growing more concrete as he nears his home. Finding that again, as he had feared, she is not awaiting him he is first angry and defiant, then submissive as he jumps in his car again to go and find her for he knows he cannot do without her youth and beauty in his home, no matter what the price. "Fulfillment" is the record of a beautiful and successful woman's reflections as the refrain of action marks her departure from a beautiful home, her impatience over her wealth, the announcement of the return of her old husband whose business trip is ended and bringing him back to her earlier than she had hoped, while she directs the chauffeur to drive her down into the East Side where she lived when married to a poor artist, the man she had really loved until his early death. During the ride other reminiscences of early lovers and her struggle for success also flit across her mind. In "Sanctuary" a young girl of the streets is shown in the hopeless struggle for love and romance. Her sordid home life and the weary burden of a mother half-drunk all the time. the loss of one job after another,

her betrayal by a handsome young groceryman, her detention for a time in the house of the Sisterhood of the Good Shepherd, her marriage, after she is out again, to a worthless wastrel who forces her to go on the streets again but whom she loves in spite of all until he puts her out on the street, and finally her return to the good sisters while still but a young woman utterly tired of life and glad to find refuge in this sanctuary is a pitiful story. "The Hand" is one of the most impressive of these tales. It is the story of the horror that follows and finally gets the better of Davidson. In his mining days Davidson had needed to be rid of his partner Mersereau and he had "fixed" him. Only he could never forget the gruesome big, rough, bony right hand of this man as it had reached out toward him while he had glared at him with glazing eyes. Under dates of a few months apart Davidson notes the successive reappearance of that awful hand, sometimes it appeared on the ceiling of his bedroom, formed by the rain dripping down, sometimes after Pringle has been telling him of the evil spirits who follow drunkards and degenerates, he hears knocking and the voice of his old mining mate saying he will never leave him. He develops the obsession that his food is being poisoned by these evil ones and particularly the ghost of Mersereau who he believes is trying to choke him to death. Ultimately he does die suffocated, not knowing that it is his own hand has done the choking. For he was a victim of tuberculosis of the throat, which was so painful at times that it led to his constant desire to clutch at his throat. His dislike of food the doctor explains as another symptom of his disease; what the doctor found it impossible to explain was Davidson's delusion that he was persecuted by an evil spirit. Other stories illustrating the inevitabilities of our fate, "Love and hope, fear and death, interwoven with our tasks, inhibitions, jealousies and greeds," as he mentions them in his foreword, are "Typhoon," "Khat," "The Shadow," "Phantom Gold," "The Mercy of God," "Convention," and others.

CHANGING WINDS, by St. John G. Ervine (1917). This story begins in Ulster, on a small estate in County Antrim, where the owner, an Irish gentleman by the name of Quinn, passes his days in agricultural pursuits. He has a very strong feeling for Ireland and Irish ways, is a Unionist, a Protestant, hates the English accent, all of which decided him to have his son, Henry, educated in Ireland. "Anyway," he said to the lad, "you'll have an Irish tongue, whatever else you have!" Henry is nervous and self-conscious — is lacking in courage, and his sudden accessions of fright puzzle his father. At school, he has three close friends, Gilbert Farlow, Ninian Graham and Roger Carey. During an Easter vacation, Ninian takes Henry to Devonshire, to the Graham estate, where Henry first meets Mary, Ninian's sister. The boys plan out their lives. They want to go to Cambridge, and when they come down from Cambridge, the proposal is that they all live together in London, take a house and get some girl to look after them. Gilbert did the planning, and he and Ninian and Roger went to Cambridge, but Henry did not go with them. "It was Mr. Quinn who upset the plan." He makes up his mind that Henry is to spend several months at home, under the tutelage of John Marsh, and then proceed to Trinity College, Dublin. Henry acquiesced in his father's wishes — reluctantly. He and Marsh work together, making "Irishry," as Marsh called it, and through Marsh's influence a Gaelic revival is started — Gaelic games, songs, dances and literature. Henry meets Sheila Morgan, a village girl, who came into the schoolroom one night "out of a drift of rain." Her effect upon him puts all thought of Mary out of his head. They have a love affair, but Sheila knows that Henry is above her station in life and refuses to marry him. After his graduation from

Trinity, Henry settles down in London with his former schoolmates. Gilbert is a dramatic critic, and playwright, Ninian is with a firm of engineers in London, Roger goes off every day to his chambers in the Temple, — "four bright lads simply bursting with brains," — Gilbert said of them, for Henry takes up writing seriously and is at work on a novel. When they are not talking of themselves, they talk of England and public affairs, trade unions, Ireland and Home Rule, sex, the origin of the Fabian Society, social reforms and improved Toryism, but their days are spent in work, and their recreation takes the form of visits from Chesterton and Wells and other celebrities. They gather about them a group of friends, each of whom has distinguished himself in some fashion at his college. Gilbert meets the sister of one of them, Lady Cecily Jayne, a beauty in English society, whose husband permits other men to make love to her. Gilbert is one of her victims. So is Henry. But Gilbert makes up his mind to save his friend from the greedy Cecily and carries Henry bodily off to Ireland. "We can become something better than one of Cecily's lovers, can't we?" is the way he looks at it. The World War now draws the four friends from their daily absorptions into its wave of patriotism. Three of them go into it blithely — but with Henry the old fears and precautions hang over him. Besides, he has another novel coming out . . . and he thinks it utterly absurd that Gilbert should become a soldier, that "his sensitive mind should be diverted from its proper functions to the bloody business of war." To which Gilbert replies: "Fightin's such a filthy job that it ought to be shared by everybody that can take a hand in it at all. It does not seem right somehow to do your fighting by proxy." Gilbert enlists. Henry stays in Ireland — completing his sixth novel. At Christmas, his father dies, and he is left alone to manage the place. Then in the midst of his perplexities and feelings about the War, the Irish rebellion breaks out, leaving him stunned. But when it collapses, Henry's way is clear. He must go to the front. Gilbert, and Ninian, and Roger have given up their lives. "They had not sought to escape from destiny or to elude death." And John Marsh had been killed in the rebellion. "It was foreordained that old men would make wars and that young men would pay the price of them . . . and it is of no use to try to save oneself." There was still time for him to live on the level of his friends. He would marry Mary and then he would take her to his home, and when he had given his house to her, he would enlist as a soldier. He obtains a permit to go to England. Beyond England he knew lay France and Flanders. The story ends with his departure.

CHILDREN AND FOOLS, by Thomas Mann (1928) is an offering of nine significant stories covering a wide range both in mood and technique and representing his artistic growth, or at least mutations, over almost the entire period of his literary career. It is interesting therefore to consider them in their historical sequence. The most recent story, "Disorder and Early Sorrow," does not set forth the delicate nuances of emotion any more exquisitely than those early ones, "Tobias Mindernickel," "Little Louise" and, best of all, "Little Herr Friedmann," which is the title story of an earlier collection. These stories are all of types which are aberrations from the normal. The first three mentioned are studies in the refinements of cruelty. "Tobias Mindernickel," a grotesque old man, the butt of the children in the shabby neighborhood where he lives, is mentally malformed. He cannot look at man or even inanimate life with a level eye. His complete lack of personal assurance cripples him mentally. Only when he is ministering to the suffering does he discover the normal dignity and self-possession of a human being. He acquires a playful little dog which he is happy with when it is injured and he can nurse it. So one day when it is frisking about, fully recovered, he intentionally wounds it that he may enjoy again that pleasure of superiority he finds in alleviating pain but he goes too far in this and the little dog dies. "Little Louise" is another tragedy of personality, the story of a man grotesque in his fat and fatuous devotion to a beautiful wife. She arranges with her lover an entertainment in which the husband, as the climax of the evening, appears as a little girl dancer in a red silk dress. As the dance progresses he grows increasingly conscious from the tension of the on-lookers of the true state of affairs and finally succumbs to a stroke of apoplexy before the merrymakers. In "Little Herr Friedmann" a boy grows up hunch-back through the carelessness of a nurse in his babyhood. But he develops a beautiful and sane spirit, learning with epicurean taste to enjoy the delights of literature, music and the drama, making a success of his life in spite of his heavy handicap, because he wisely realizes his physical limitations — knows that love is not for him. Then at thirty all his careful defences against fate are wrecked by his love for a woman whose elementally passionate nature lets no man alone, even so pitifully brave a man as little Herr Friedmann. Compared with these subtle and sincerely poignant but ruthless studies, the stories of his middle period are of less value. "The Path To The Cemetery" and "The Infant Prodigy" are rather fantastical sketches, and the abnormal qualities are of a more superficial type. "How Jap Fought Do Escobar" written in 1911 and "Disorder and Early Sorrow" written in 1926 apply the same searching sensitiveness exhibited in the early group to studies of precociously developed children. The little boy who watches Jap fight with Do Escobar is presented as precociously English in his appreciation of virility and sport, while himself but a delicate child. In "Disorder and Early Sorrow" a lovely little girl, Lorie, while yet but a child, feels the first touch of passion when one of the young men attending her elder sister's party shows her attention. The tumult of passion and despair which shakes her infantile heart falls from her in the peaceful winged sleep of childhood, from which she awakens with all feeling obliterated ready to again play the fascinating game of five gentlemen with her father and little brothers. It reveals a mood of childhood with fastidious precision that does not overstep the boundaries of careful psychology.

CHORUS GIRL, THE, by Anton Chekhov (1927). The author includes in this volume a group of short stories of which "The Chorus Girl" is the first. Pasha, with her adorer, Nickolay Petrovitch Kolpakov, is surprised by a visit from Nickolay's wife. Nickolay disappears inside, and Pasha denies that he is there. His wife demands the return of the presents which her husband has made Pasha. He has taken money which did not belong to him to buy these gifts. If the money can be raised, he will avoid arrest. Pasha says that she has never given her anything. When his wife insists that she knows better and begs her to save Nickolay by giving up the presents, Pasha gives her the trinkets which Nickolay has given her and other articles which her admirers have bestowed upon her. The wife departs, after breaking into sobs. "If you like it I will go down on my knees! If you wish it!" she had cried. Pasha feels that the lady is trying to humiliate her by exalting herself. After the lady goes, Nickolay comes out and moans that his wife has humiliated herself to Pasha. "Get away from me . . . you low creature!" he cried with repulsion. "Verotchka" — the second story, is the name of Ognev's daughter — Ognev Kuznetsov — at whose house Ivan Alexeyitch Ognev lives for several months during which time he is busy preparing a statistical report. Ivan finishes his work and prepares to return to his home in Petersburg. He bids Ognev good-by, and leaves "his respects" to Vera, the daughter. On his way to the station he encounters her, and she confesses her love for him.   He feels for her an inward revulsion.   In declaring her love for him, she had cast off the aloofness which so adds to a woman's charms, and she seemed to him plainer and more ordinary.   The story deals with his reactions to the situation.   He frankly tells her that he has no love for her — only respect. But he rages inwardly at his coldness and stupidity with women.   Vera leaves him and returns to her home alone.   Tormented by his conscience, Ivan feels that he has lost something very precious, something very near and dear which he could never find again.   Before he journeys on to the town, he returns to Vera's house and stands under her window.   After he reaches the town, he sat in his room and gazed a long time at the light.   "Then he tossed his head and began packing."   The third story, entitled "My Life" represents a clash between a father and son — the Poloznevs — the elder Poloznev is a successful architect, and considers that his son is a burden upon him, because he has no regular position in society; the younger Poloznev believes that what his father calls a position in society is the privilege of capital and education. "Those who have neither wealth nor education earn their daily bread by manual labour, and I see no grounds for my being an exception."   The father argues with irritation that his son has the "divine spirit, a spark of the holy fire, which distinguishes him in the most striking way from the ass or the reptile, and brings him nearer to the Deity."   This fire is the fruit of the efforts of the best of mankind during thousands of years.   If his son persists in doing manual labor it will mean that he is putting out the sacred fire which the Poloznevs have guarded.   But the son — Misail — becomes a workman, and renounces his inheritance.   He no longer lives in Great Dvoryansky Street, but in a suburb.   His sister begs him to reform his ways.   Misail's ideas are that everyone should engage in manual labor, so that the strong should not enslave the weak, the minority should not be a parasite on the majority, nor a vampire forever sucking its vital sap; that is, all without exception, strong and weak, rich and poor, should take part equally in the struggle for existence, each on his own account, and that there was no better means for equalizing things in that way than manual labor, in the form of universal service, compulsory for all.   Blagovo, who is in love with Misail's sister, argued warmly with him, and his family beg him to alter his line of conduct and return to duties in keeping with his rank.   Mariya Viktorovna and Misail have ideas in common, and after their marriage, live on an estate where they continue to work out their ideas of self-improvement.   In the end they find that their own successes have not had any perceptible influence on the life around them.   Misail's wife leaves him, becomes a singer and goes to America. His sister decides that she must also lead an independent life, but, deserted by her lover, falls ill.   Blagovo becomes absorbed in his profession.   And Misail finally returns to his old home for a talk with his father, who blames him for everything. Misail turns on him: "How is it that in not one of these houses you have been building for the last thirty years there has been anyone from whom I might have learnt how to live, so as not to be to blame?"   The next story — "At a Country House" — concerns itself with the effect of a conversation between Pavel Ilyitch Rashevitch, the owner of the house, and his guest, Meier, the deputy examining magistrate, in which Pavel has been incautious and tactless enough to raise the subject of "blue blood," without finding out beforehand what his visitor's position was.   Pavel's two daughters overheard the conversation.   They know that their "egoist-father" finds pleasure in chattering and displaying his intelligence — that this is more precious to him than his daughters' happiness.   Meier has said that his father was in the artisan class and that he was proud of it.   Whereupon, he had left abruptly.   In the district Pavel is called the "toad."   After Meier leaves, Pavel feels a remorse.   Somehow or other, by some fatality, it always happened that he began mildly, amicably, with good intentions, but without being himself aware of it, gradually passed into abuse and slander. He asks himself the question if he "could be possessed by some devil which hated and slandered in him, apart from his own will?" The next morning he wrote a letter to his daughters, in which he begged them to forget him, and to bury him in a plain coffin or send his body to the dissecting theatre. But he feels that what he has written reeks of malice and affectation. He hears from the next room the word, "The toad!" "A Father," one of the stories in this collection, recounts the tragedy of a drunken father, who lives apart from his children, in a disreputable locality. He intrudes himself on one of his sons, in the latter's summer villa, and borrows money from him to pay for his lodgings. The son supplies him with a ten-rouble note and takes him back to his lodgings, but the father stops on the way to buy drink at the various taverns. The story is of the conversation between the two. The father asks his son to be allowed to see Sonya, the daughter. He plans out how it can be done — he will keep away from spirits for three days, then his son can lend him a suit — then he will come to his son's flat and he can bring Sonya there. The son promises him that he will let him see her. "On the Road" is a story of travellers meeting in the "travellers' room" at the tavern, kept by the Cossack, Semyon Tchistopluy. Mademoiselle Ilovaisky is one of the travellers; another is Grigory Petrovitch Liharev, — the third, Sacha, Petrovitch's little daughter. Petrovitch tells his story to Mademoiselle Ilovaisky. He has endured privation, prison. He had plunged into Nihilism — was a fervent devotee of Russian life. "I have been a misfortune to all who have ever loved me." He finally tells her that he is on his way to the coal mines — he has a position as superintendent. She knows the mines — they are owned by her uncle — and he is a maniac, a despot, a bankrupt. She tells Petrovitch that he must not go — it is worse than exile. Having suffered enough, he is thankful for "coal mines." She leaves the tavern, but in the look that he sees in her eyes — "if his finely intuitive soul were really able to read that look, it suddenly began to seem to him that with another touch or two that girl would have forgiven him his failures, his age, his desolate position, and would have followed him without questioning or reasonings." There are four other stories in the collection: "Rothschild's Fiddle," "Ivan Matveyitch," "Zinotchka," "Bad Weather," and "A Trivial Incident," written in lighter vein.

CHRIST, LIFE OF, by Giovanni Papini (1923). Freely translated from the Italian by Dorothy Canfield Fisher. The narrative begins with a description of the stable where Jesus was born — a real stable, not the bright, airy portico which Christian painters have created. And the author says that it was not by chance that Christ was born in a stable. "What is the world but an immense stable where men produce filth and wallow in it? Do they not daily change the most beautiful, the purest, the most divine things into excrements?" After the birth of Jesus — "born of a stainless Virgin, armed only with innocence" — the animals were the first to worship him, and after the animals came those who care for animals — the shepherds. As they were watching their flocks in the long winter night, they were shaken by the light and by the words of the Angel. "Fear not, for behold I bring you good tidings of great joy. . . . Glory to God in the highest and on earth peace to men and good will." The author follows their steps into the dim light of the stable, tells of their gifts — "that little which is so great when offered with love." In their steps, too, he brings the wise men from Chaldea, as they knelt before the Child. "Mounted on their camels with their fullstuffed saddle bags, they had forded the Tigris and the Euphrates, crossed the great desert of the Nomad tribes, followed along the Dead Sea. They were guided to Judea by a new star, they had come to adore a King. When the wise men left Christ, persecutions began — the persecutions by those who were to hate Him to the day of His death. When Christ appeared upon the earth, criminals ruled the world unopposed. He was born subject to two sovereigns, the stronger far away at Rome, the weaker and more wicked close at hand in Judea. In vain Virgil, the loving pious Virgil, had foretold a new order and a new race, a kingdom of heaven less spiritual, less brilliant than that which Jesus was to announce. Augustus Caesar saw in these words only a pastoral fancy. In Herod the Great, this author sees a monster — "one of the most perfidious monsters of the many which have sprung from the burning deserts of the East." "He was not a Jew, nor a Greek, nor a Roman." To quote the description: "He was an Idumean, a barbarian who prostrated himself before Rome, and aped the Greeks the better to secure his dominion over the Jews." Superstitious like all Orientals, credulous of presages and soothsayers, he readily believed the three wise men when they said that, led by a star, they had come from the interior of Chaldea toward the country which he had fraudulently stolen. The massacre of the Innocents was the last act of Herod. The author sees a tremendous mystery in this blood-offering of the pure, in the death of so many of Christ's contemporaries. They belonged to the generation which was to betray and crucify Him. There follows the story of the flight into Egypt — Mary going to the west, crossing the old land of Canaan and coming by easy stages to the Nile, to that country of Mizraim which had cost so many tears to her ancestors fourteen centuries before. The parallel is drawn of Jesus carrying on the work of Moses and at the same time demolishing the work of Moses, going back over the route taken by the first redeemer. Moses led the Jews from Egypt toward Canaan. Now the greatest of liberators in danger of his life went back to the banks of that river where the first Saviour had been saved from the water and had saved his brothers. The short exile in Egypt, the return to Nazareth, the celebration of the Passover at Jerusalem, where Mary searched for the Child and found Him the centre of the circle in the Temple, are described, the author turning next to the period of Christ's life when as a man he worked with material things. "Three teachers He had: work, nature and the Book." His trade is one of the four oldest and most sacred of men's occupations and it taught Him, this author says, "that to live means to transform dead and useless things into living and useful things; that the meanest material fashioned and shaped can become precious, friendly, useful to men; that the only way to bring salvation is to transform." The early influences are discussed; and Jesus is pictured in the house at Nazareth as meditating on the Commandments of the Law; in the fiery laments of the Prophets He recognizes His destiny. At the beginning of His thirtieth year, when He presented Himself to men as the Son of Man, He knew what awaited Him, even to the last; His life to come is already set down day by day in pages written before His earthly birth. While Jesus, in the poor little work-shop at Nazareth was handling the axe and the square, a voice was raised in the desert toward Jordan and the Dead Sea. Last of the Prophets, John the Baptist called the Jews to repent. In that dark age of the Herods, old Judea profaned by the Idumean usurpers, contaminated by Greek infiltration, scorned by Roman soldiery, obstinately hoped for a great vengeance, and it willingly lent an ear to the voice of the desert. John the Baptist saw in the Messiah soon to appear a "master of flame." — "The new King will be a fierce husbandman. Every tree which bringeth not forth good fruit is hewn down and cast into the fire. He will thoroughly purge His floor and gather His wheat into the garner, but he will burn up the chaff with unquenchable fire. He will be a baptizer who will baptize with fire —" The author quotes explicit texts as Jesus presents Himself to be baptized of John. He says that there was not even an appearance of a conversion in Christ's life. "He begins with frank absolute certainty, with the recognizable authority of purity." "The three remaining years of His life, after His baptism, are the most brightly lighted by the words of the four Gospels," but in the story of Jesus no sign of a different way of life before conversion ever shows itself in any allusion or in any implicit meaning, is not recognizable in the smallest of His acts, in the most obscure of His words. After the baptism, the author considers that Jesus begins a new epoch in His life. Christ now goes into the desert — puts the desert between Himself and humanity. The picture of Him alone in the desert is contrasted with His life in the fields of Galilee and in the green meadows along the Jordan; and the forty days of solitude are recalled as the last of His preparation. The temptation is told of, the two challenges which He refused. The tempter asked for material bread and a material miracle of Him and promised material power. Jesus did not take up the challenge and refused what was offered. His return among men is here described. At Jerusalem lived the powerful of the world, the Romans, masters of the world and of Judea, with their soldiers in arms. Jerusalem was ruled by the representatives of the Caesars; of Tiberius, the drunken assassin, the perfidious heir of Augustus. At Jerusalem lived the High Priests, the old custodians of the Temple, the Pharisees, the Sadducees, Scribes, the Levites and their guards, the descendants of those who pursued and killed the prophets, the petrifiers of the Law, the bigots of the letter, the haughty depositories of arid fanaticism. At Jerusalem are the treasures of God, the treasures of Caesar, the guardians of the treasure, the lovers of wealth; the Publicans with their excise men and parasites, the rich with their servants and their concubines, the merchants with their crowded shops; money bags clinking with shekels in the warmth of the bosom above the heart. "Jesus comes to combat all these." The author follows His steps from Jerusalem to Galilee where, entering into the Synagogue, Christ begins to teach. His message now is that "The Kingdom of God is at hand; repent and believe the Gospel." The author finds Him often at Capernaum — situated on the caravan route which from Damascus crosses Iturea and goes toward the sea. It was a commercial centre of some importance. Artisans, bargainers, brokers, and shopkeepers had come there to stay; men of finance — publicans, excise men and other fiscal tools. The little settlement, half-rustic, half a fishing village, has become a mixed and composite city, where the society of the times — even soldiers and prostitutes — was fully represented. There, in the Synagogue, Jesus is described as reading from one of the scrolls of the Scriptures. Nobody in Capernaum could remember having heard such a Rabbi. The fisherman came to hear him; the peasants of the neighboring countrysides; the gentry; the poor. And when He came out from the Synagogue all those stood waiting in the streets to see Him again. The author recalls that it was among the fishermen of Capernaum that Christ found his first disciples. One morning two boats came back toward Capernaum while Jesus standing by the lake was talking to the people who had gathered around Him. He entered into one of the boats and asked the fishermen to put it out a little from the land so that He might not be pressed upon by the crowd. "Up right near the rudder He taught those who had remained on the land, and when He had left speaking He said to Simon, 'Launch out into the deep, and let down your nets for a draught.' And Simon answered, 'Master, we have toiled all the night and have taken nothing, nevertheless at thy word, I will let down the net.' " The author tells of the miracle; and quotes Christ's words: "Follow me, and I will make you fishers of men."

Again Jesus is pictured as he sat on a little hill in the midst of the first apostles, surrounded by hundred of eyes. From the Mount, you could see only the plain, calm under the loving sunset light; on one side the silver-green oval of the lake, and on the other the long crest of Carmel. The nine Beatitudes which Christ delivered here are given and discussed and the author says that from that point, when Jesus spoke on the Mount, a new phase of the human education began. "He understood that the old law was doomed, drowned in the stagnant swamps of formalism; the endless work of the education of the human race was to begin over again, the ashes must be brushed away, the flame of original enthusiasm must be blown into it, it must be carried through to its original destination which is always metanoia, the changing of the soul." The author holds that the most stupefying of Jesus's most revolutionary teaching was his definite repudiation of the old law of retaliation. Christ's answer, when questioned about prayer, is also given in the light of contrast to the "tiresome blandishments" of Oriental prayers. The Lord's Prayer — the Pater Noster — taught by Jesus on the Mount, is "a prayer neither literary nor theological — neither bold nor servile. It is one of the simplest prayers in the world — the most beautiful of all prayers." The miracles are recalled; and the parables by which he taught. "Jesus never wrote — once only he wrote on the sand, and the wind destroyed it." At the beginning of His work, He had explained how the soul must be transformed to found the Kingdom; and as He approaches His death, He taught what the punishments of the stubborn would be and in what manner He would come again. This discourse on the "Last Things," the author considers a second Sermon on the Mount. Christ's prophecies are shown to have been fulfilled years after his death. The narrative passes now to the preparations for His condemnation. "To have an idea of the hatred which the upper classes of Jerusalem felt toward Jesus, priestly hatred, scholastic hatred and commercial hatred, we must remember that the Holy City apparently lived by faith, but in reality on the Faithful. The priestly caste got their living from the tithes in kind, from the taxes of the Temple from the payments for the first-born. . . . A net-work of self-interest thus bound to the Herodian edifice all the inhabitants of Jerusalem, down to the vendors at fairs and the sandal-makers." Jesus with his Gospel threatened directly the position and fees of these classes. For some time His life had not been safe. "If we are to believe John, the order was given to certain guards to capture Him." Time pressed; Jerusalem was full of foreigners and many were listening to Him. The author follows step by step the entire narrative of the last days. The Sanhedrin, the supreme council of the aristocracy which ruled the capital; the betrayal on the part of one of the "Twelve"; the Last Supper with those who had been sharing His life; the Passion in the Garden of Gethsemane; the disappearance of the disciples; the "infamous procession"; with Jesus face to face for the first time with the religious head of his people — the High Priest, a Sadducee, head of one of the most aggressive and wealthy families of the ecclesiastical patriarchate; the four authorities who questioned Him in the space of a few hours; two rulers from the Temple; Annas and Caiaphas; and two temporal rulers, Antipas and Pilate. The trial, the degradation and the final condemnation to death as a "blasphemer and false prophet"; the "comedy of legal pretense played to an end," the ratification from the Procurator, the swiftness with which the death sentence was executed are all told; together with the account of Christ's reappearance to the women in the garden and to his disciples and His Transfiguration. And the Transfiguration forecasts the Ascension. The author believes the "solution of the evil of the world is the transformation of human souls" by religion, and the perfect religion taught by Christ.

CHRISTIANITY, PAST AND PRESENT, by Charles Guignebert (1927). An analysis of the origin and development of the Christian religion by the Professor of the History of Christianity at the Sorbonne. The author takes for his point of departure the idea that "not only in its dogmas, but also throughout the ramifications of its whole organism, a religion undergoes the process of evolution." And so Christianity grew by successive adaptations to environment. The twenty-four chapters are grouped under three main divisions: Part I, Christianity in Classical Times: The Creed and the Church; Part II, The Middle Ages: Theology and the Papacy; Part III, Modern Times: Politics and Roman Catholicism. An analysis of each chapter, following its heading in the contents, is of value in giving an idea of the variety and scope of the subjects treated. The outline of Chapter I, Jesus' Initiative, will suggest the thoroughness with which the book has been prepared: I. The Jewish origin of Christianity. Jesus the Nazarene; paucity of our information respecting him. How and why his history soon gives place to legend. Tradition and the sources of our Gospels. How these Gospels were composed. The gaps in the narrative filled in by faith. How the problem of Jesus' rise presents itself. II. The sphere from which Jesus issued. The country of the Jews and its surroundings; the vast amount of religious material at the disposal of a fresh syncretism. Jesus' training entirely Jewish. The Palestinian world in the time of Herod the Great. The priestly hierarchy and worship; the scribes and legalism; the people and the religion in force. The expectation of the Messiah. Characteristic features of Galilean Judaism. III. The theory which accounts for Jesus' rise. The Messianic hope. Jesus in relation to the Baptist. The themes on which he preached: the coming of the Kingdom and repentance. Did he believe himself the Messiah? The bearing of the Gospel designations Son of God, Son of David, Son of Man. Various difficulties and probabilities. Jesus a Jewish prophet. After Jesus' apparent failure to fulfil his mission, followed by his ignominious death, "what could possibly remain of him except some moral maxims, valuable certainly, but less original than they are ordinarily said to be, and the touching recollection of his virtues and personal charm? Logic answers: Nothing. Nevertheless, the history of events seems to prove logic wrong." Dr. Guignebert traces the rise of Gentile Christianity, the work of Paul, the triumph of Christianity in its keen competition with rivals from which it made large appropriations of doctrine and ritual, the origin of the Papacy, the development of scholasticism, the emergence of humanism, the Protestant Reformation, and the conflict with science. This history of development is recorded and commented on under chapter headings such as the following: The Work of the Apostles; The Foundation and Organization of the Church; The Conflict with the State and with Society; The Origin of Papacy; Scholasticism; The Opposition to the Church in the Middle Ages; The Catholic Reform; the Jesuits and the Council of Trent; The Age of Enlightenment; Liberalism, Criticism and Science versus Theology. Following Spengler, Professor Guignebert considers that religions like civilizations pass through a cycle of evolution and devolution — birth, growth, decay and death. He closes his history with the pessimistic prophecy that "all religions end, religions which, like living organisms, are born of a need, nourished upon death, die day by day of life, and finally lapse into the eternal crucible."

CIRCLE, THE, by W. Somerset Maugham (1922). The play begins thirty years after Lady Kitty has deserted her husband and five-year-old son, Arnold, to run away with Lord Porteous, a distinguished politician, thereby ruining his career. Arnold has been married three years to Elizabeth, who is now in love with Teddie

Luton, about to return to his plantation in the Malay States, and determined to take Elizabeth back with him. Elizabeth has invited Lady Kitty and Lord Porteous to spend the week-end with them, in spite of Arnold's misgivings. The situation becomes more complicated by the unexpected arrival of Arnold's father, Clive Champion-Cheney. He has grown philosophical with the years, however, and is more tolerant toward his erring wife than is his son, and less perturbed at the prospect of meeting her again. He warns Elizabeth that her romantic idealization of Kitty and Porteous as the great lovers who sacrificed the world for each other is as exaggerated as Arnold's self-righteous disapproval. Teddie is urging his suit with Elizabeth, telling her of the hardships of colonial life, when Kitty and Porteous arrive. Elizabeth is shocked by the affected, silly, painted Kitty, behaving as if she were twenty-five, and the frankly grumpy old age of Porteous. Clive Champion-Cheney tells the disillusioned Elizabeth that Lady Kitty's "soul is as thickly rouged as her face." Her false position in the social world, her lack of opportunity to lead a normal life have ruined her. Teddie assures Elizabeth that he would love her just as much if she were old and ugly, and also that he likes her tremendously. She decides that nothing else in the world matters, and they plan to go away together in spite of the disastrous experience of their elders. Instead of leaving a note on the pincushion as did Lady Kitty, Elizabeth tells Arnold that their marriage is not a success and she wants her liberty. When she makes him realize that she is in earnest and will leave him, he asks her if she wants to be a pitiful wreck like Lady Kitty, and declares that he will never consent to a divorce. In the drawing-room that evening the elder Champion-Cheney shows Elizabeth an album in which she finds a picture of Lady Kitty, so young and lovely that she does not recognize her, and Lady Kitty is affected to tears at this reminder of her lost youth. Porteous comforts his wife with real affection and she regains her spirits. She tries to dissuade Elizabeth with her own story. "The first two years were wonderful. People cut me, you know, but I didn't mind. I thought love was everything. . . . One sacrifices one's life for love and then one finds that love doesn't last. The tragedy of love isn't death or separation. One gets over these. The tragedy of love is indifference." Coached by his father, Arnold changes his tactics and weakens Elizabeth's resolution by overwhelming her with generosity. He will let her divorce him and not stand in her way if she must go. Since Luton is a poor man, he will give her a generous allowance, as his love cannot allow her to want for anything. She wavers and asks Teddie how she can desert Arnold when he is so decent. She could not forgive herself if she profited by his generosity. Porteous and Kitty want to save these two young things, but in the end they offer them not common sense, but their motor car. Porteous moralizes, "If we made rather a hash of things perhaps it was because we were rather trivial people. You can do anything in this world if you're prepared to take the consequences, and consequences depend on character." As the lovers run away through the garden Clive Champion-Cheney comes in, and holds forth to his former wife and her husband anent his knowledge of women's psychology. His advice to Arnold has prevented the elopement. He has kept Elizabeth by offering her freedom. He begins to laugh and the others join in laughter at his complacency and ignorance of the fact accomplished, and the curtain descends on this amusing situation.

CIRCUS PARADE, by Jim Tully (1927). The author writes these stories of circus life from the basis of his own experiences as a hobo travelling with a third-rate circus of ten cars in the Southern states. The series of incidents and character portraits of the performers, hangers-on, trailers, pickpockets, and gamblers, are a sordid, brutal picture from behind the scenes. He joins "Cameron's World's Greatest Combined Shows" as assistant to the lion tamer, who is killed by the brown bear one day when he slipped and fell in the cage. Old Cameron, the owner, dreamed always of a larger show, and cheated the public and his helpers to hoard the money for his circus. By keeping back the first month's pay out of kindness, he explained, in order to be sure that no one who worked for him would finish the season "broke" he was able to cheat them out of the money by forcing them to desert by bad treatment or by "red-lighting" them. "Red-lighting" was an ancient and dishonorable circus custom which consisted in opening the side door of a moving car near the red lights of a rail-road yard, and kicking the undesired traveller out. The high class gamblers, known as the "Bob Cameron men," were the ticket sellers who made short change, and the loaded dice experts. They received no salary and gave ten per cent of their earnings to Cameron. One night the oil workers who had been short-changed charged the tent and fought in a bloody riot until the circus hands won by turning the elephants on the crowd. The strong woman, Lila, weighed four hundred pounds, and spent her money on the fluffiest of dresses and beribboned hats to make herself as dainty as other smaller women. Incurably romantic from reading paper-backed novels, she was an easy prey for Anton of the human pyramid, who made love to her and dis-appeared with the earnings she entrusted to him to buy a farm for their home. After he left her they found her dead in her crumpled finery with a little blue bottle clenched in her right hand. Goosey, the elephant trainer, had been round the world seven times, always in charge of elephants, and once spent a year in Africa with a hunter and watched the herds he loved by the hour. He had many stories to tell about his charges. There was much argument as to whether the lion or the tiger would win in a fight, and one night a deserting trainer opened the cage door to find out. In the end Cameron and his dishonest associates are "red-lighted" and robbed by men whom he had previously served the same way. The big tent is burned and the gilded circus wagons go into winter quarters black from heat and smoke.

CLAIRE AMBLER, by Booth Tarkington (1928). Claire Ambler was a flirt. She combined instinctively, in her own proper person, all the sophistication of Cleopatra, and all the innocence of Juliet — and she was beautiful. Until she was eighteen she did not have a thought in her head; instead "she had feelings that she believed to be thoughts; she had likes and dislikes that she believed to be thoughts; she had impulses that she believed to be thoughts; her mind was full of shifting and flying images that she believed to be thoughts; it was also full of echoes of what she had heard and read, and these she usually believed to be thoughts original to her." That was Claire at eighteen. The book is divided into three parts, each treating of a climactic episode in her life. Part I, "The Birth of Thought," relates how Claire, going out with one swain in his canoe, allows herself to be transferred to another swain's more reliable motor-boat. Swain the first shortly upsets, and is obliged to swim for shore only a short and nervous distance ahead of three hungry sharks. Claire's sole reaction is to wonder what folks would have said about her if he had drowned. Whereupon the disgusted youth hurls the most opprobious epithet in his vocabulary: "Prom-trotter!" And, "Oh, my goodness!" she whispered. "He was right!" Claire had had a thought. The scene of Part II is a resort on the Italian Riviera, three years later. An Italian prince is dangling after Claire, so she perversely seeks to attract a veteran-invalid of the War. Playing with fire once too often, Claire gets herself badly scorched: she falls in love with Charles Orbison, who is slowly and courageously dying. Then, to save him what pain she can, Claire rises to one of the most gallant acts of her life: she leaves Raona without letting him know she cares. It is in this section of the book that the princeling, Arturo, sums up bitterly Claire's salient characteristic: "You like men to be in love with you, but not to trouble you by telling you." Part III is laid in New York, a few weeks before Claire's twenty-fifth birthday. Twenty-five looms ahead of her as the first milestone of spinsterhood. Already all of her contemporaries are married — many of them to her own rejected suitors. She is panic-stricken, but refuses to surrender to mob-instinct. Resolutely she gives Walter Rackbridge, the most persistent of her remaining suitors, her decisive "No." He has announced that this time he will take her answer seriously. He pays attention to a younger girl, and Claire, with the clear-sightedness she has acquired through her love for Orbison, realizes what Rackbridge means to her, and hastily reclaims him. As she goes up the aisle to him, her indomitable two-mindedness overtakes her — a trait which lets her see herself as others see her; a sort of stage-manager to all she does. This self-consciousness wonders whether she really loves Walter or is marrying him to save her own face. With a thrill she acknowledges to herself that at last she cares more for someone than for herself — the egoist in her is finally submerged. *Omnia vincit amor.*

CLARENCE, an American comedy, by Booth Tarkington (1919). The hero, Clarence, a young entomologist, just demobilized from the American army after the War, is trying to get a civilian position. The opening of the play finds him waiting in the outer office of a financial magnate, Mr. Wheeler. The millionaire's efficient secretary regards him as most unpromising, and is trying to get rid of him, but at the same time she wants to be kind to a soldier. As a soldier, Clarence has had no opportunity to be a hero. He spent his year of service in a Texas training camp driving a mule, and the only wound he received was at target practice. It happens that the Wheeler family is in the throes of domestic difficulties, and Mrs. Wheeler, the two children, and the governess choose this day to come to see Mr. Wheeler at the office. Cora and Bobby are at the boarding school age, and both are suffering from puppy-love. Cora imagines herself in love with a middle-aged grass widower, Herbert Stem, who is paying attention to her in order to spend as much time as possible in the society of her charming governess, Miss Violet Pinney. Bobby has been expelled from three exclusive preparatory schools in the East, and considers he is entangled in an "affair" after he has forcibly kissed Della, the housemaid. While Miss Pinney is in the office talking with Mr. Wheeler about Cora, the children confide in Clarence. Cora assures the secretary that she would be glad to let Clarence have an interview with her father in her stead. When Bobby is left alone with Clarence he tells him that Miss Pinney, whom he has known four days, is the great passion of his life. Mrs. Wheeler, the young second wife, who thinks Violet Pinney much too attractive to be a governess, arrives, and does not notice Clarence so that he is forced to hear her troubles. Mr. Wheeler and Miss Pinney come out of the office with the weeping Cora, and by the time the family have been sent home, the distracted Mr. Wheeler decides to employ Clarence at his house, since he has learned so much about the family, and he considers that his experience in driving mules may be helpful. In the Wheeler home Clarence takes dictation from Mr. Wheeler, tunes the piano, mends the hot-water pipes, and is comforter and friend to all the family. His appearance in new civilian clothes drives all remembrance of Mr. Stem out of the romantic Cora's heart. He has a benign influence on Mrs. Wheeler, rousing Mr. Wheeler to jealousy. Even the servants become the slaves of Clarence. Mr. Wheeler reflects that he engaged Clarence without knowing anything about him, and is not sure of his last name. Violet is as certain that it is "Moon" as he is that it is "Smun," and as Mr. Wheeler is not accustomed to contradiction, he thinks her an obstinate young woman. Mr. Stem comes in to ask if Clarence is not the Charles Short advertised in the newspaper as a deserter from the army. It turns out that his name is Clarence Smith, and that he is an entomologist, a Ph.D., and an authority on coleoptera mentioned in "Who's Who," that he had told Della he worked in a laboratory, not a lavatory. The mail brings him his reappointment to his old position, and he prepares to leave the now united and peaceful Wheeler family, taking Violet with him. Cora and Bobby are left disconsolate at this ending of romance for them, and the prospect of school the next week.

CLEVELAND, GROVER, THE MAN AND THE STATESMAN, by Robert McNutt McElroy (1923), is an authorized biography of Grover Cleveland by a professor of history at Princeton University. The biography is also a political history of the United States during the years while Cleveland was serving as Mayor of Buffalo, Governor of New York, and President of the United States. The book has an introduction by Elihu Root. Genealogical studies were a matter of indifference to Grover Cleveland; he showed a total lack of interest even in his own ancestors, but others more interested have discovered that the first Cleveland in America was Moses Cleveland, an indentured apprentice, who landed in Massachusetts in 1635. Grover Cleveland's father, Richard Falley Cleveland, was a minister whose first pastorate was at Windham, Connecticut. His mother, Ann Neal, was of Irish and French descent. She was born in Baltimore in 1806 and in 1829 married Richard Cleveland. In 1837, while his father was pastor at Caldwell, New Jersey, Stephen Grover Cleveland was born. In 1841 the Reverend Richard Cleveland accepted a call to the church in Fayetteville, New York. The family went thither on a slow Erie canal boat. In this quiet village Cleveland spent the early years of his boyhood and received his first schooling. In 1851 the family moved to Clinton where the educational advantages were greater, but Cleveland in his heart turned to the simpler life in the little village. Years afterward when he was President he visited Fayetteville and made a speech in which he said in part: "If some of the old householders were here I could tell them who it was that used to take off their front gates. I mention this because I have been accused of so many worse crimes since I have been in Washington that I consider taking off gates something of a virtue." The dream of his life as a boy was to go to Hamilton College, but his dream was never realized. The family was too hard pressed for money, so Cleveland went back to Fayetteville to work in a store for fifty dollars a year, with board and room. He arose at five in summer and five-thirty in winter, went out to the pump each morning to wash, then returned to the store to "open up, sweep out, build the fire, dust up, lay out the goods." When he was sixteen his father died and Grover found a position in the New York Institute for the Blind, where he remained for one year. From there he went to Buffalo, where he secured a clerkship in a law firm and in 1863 came his first public office: Assistant District Attorney of Erie County. He won the confidence of all with whom he came in contact. In 1869 he became a member of the firm of Lanning, Cleveland, and Folsom. In 1870 he was elected Sheriff of Erie County, where his reputation for honesty grew even greater. In 1881 he was elected Mayor of Buffalo, where he was called the "veto mayor" from his habit of putting his veto on anything he considered dishonest or not above-board. As Mayor of Buffalo he first saw the executive office, when with others he went to see Governor Cornell to ask that the death sentence of one Flanagan be commuted, because the sentence instead of being for murder in the first degree should have been for manslaughter. The case did not impress the Governor, but Cleveland sprang to his feet saying: "We came to you as to a King, pleading for mercy. It is your duty to hear us to the end." The sentence was commuted. Later the Governor spoke of him as "a remarkable man in Buffalo." Before his term as Mayor was finished the "veto mayor" was elected Governor of New York. Very shortly the new governor was anathema to the spoilsmen. He refused to appoint men to office on any other grounds than fitness for the place. When it became his duty to veto the Five Cent Fare bill he was sure that he had made himself the most unpopular man in New York, but he had not, although the audience in an Albany theatre rose and hissed him a few days later. He had done the right thing and a brave one and public opinion veered to his side. Before he had finished his term as Governor he was nominated for the presidency, much against the wishes of Tammany Hall. The convention hall resounded to General Bragg's tribute, "We love him for the enemies he has made." Cleveland was the first Democratic president since the Civil War. The Bible upon which he took the oath of office was given him by his mother. He always kept it by him; during the years of his presidency the Bible lay in an upper drawer of his desk. Cleveland despised filling offices and did not hesitate to say that "reward for partisan activities is one mode of misappropriation of public funds." This, of course, was a weird idea to the party leaders, and the appointments he did make were often displeasing to them and to others. He made mistakes, and began anew, but altogether he struck a high average of excellence in his appointments. In 1886 he married Frances Folsom, the daughter of his old law partner. This union proved so happy, despite predictions to the contrary, that Chauncey Depew wrote: "My only regret about it is that it will be so much harder for us to win against both Mr. and Mrs. Cleveland." But Mrs. Cleveland's charm did not serve to keep her husband in the White House when he dared to urge tariff reform and so he lost the next election. He went to New York City and took up again the practice of law. He remained here for the next few years. In 1892 he was again elected to the presidency. The Free Silver question with Bryan as its apostle and the Democratic party hard in tow arose early in this term. Cleveland was always against it and his firm stand and his strengthening of the gold standard stood the country in good stead during the financial crisis of 1893 and saved it from ruin. As president, Cleveland's veto power was still in strong evidence and in all he struck down one hundred and eight pension bills. His foreign policy was analogous. He blocked "manifest destiny in Hawaii" and kept Germany out of Samoa. But when England questioned the Venezuela boundary he dropped the veto and seized the Monroe Doctrine. Near the end of his second term a treaty was made. Europe was startled to learn that the United States was a factor to be reckoned with in world politics. In 1897, at the end of his second term as President, Cleveland retired to his home in Princeton and watched the political game from the sidelines. On June 24, 1908, he died at his home as he had so often wished, with his wife near him. His last words might be called the key to his whole life: "I have tried so hard to do the right."

COLD HARBOUR, by Francis Brett Young (1925). The Cold Harbour district was a strip of sloping country between the main road that runs from the Severn to North Bromwich and the edge of the Black Country. From the South it is isolated by hills along the base of which straggles a remnant of Mercian forest, now a preserve for pheasants. No road enters it from that side but the half-hearted cart-track. . . . On the North it is bounded not by the black country — but by a zone that was black a hundred years ago, riddled with colliery workings, scattered pit-mounds, utterly useless for farming or afforestation; abandoned; dead. An ancient house at Cold Harbour is occupied by a queer couple — the Furnivals. The story tells of the experiences of the Furnivals and of the visitors to the house, and of the apparitions which have caused the place to be considered "haunted." These apparitions are associated with scenes of blood, violence and horror and the influences which are apparently evident are definitely and actively evil. Ronald Wake, a physician, interested in psychical research, makes a study of the apparitions — an investigation. He offers to find some explanation, but Furnival himself objects to any investigation. Mrs. Furnival is an invalid. Furnival tries to leave the impression upon Wake that his wife is insane. Wake believes that the spirit of the righteous who have found rest in God are never concerned in these manifestations, are never "earth-bound." When cases of the Cold Harbour type have been investigated, to the extent of arriving at an explanation, he has been convinced that the spirits concerned in them are those of men and women who have died violent deaths, with some weight of sin or anxiety on their mind that has been sufficient to exclude them from the peace of Heaven. He is of the opinion that an active spirit opposed to the light of Christianity, a hostile and jealous spirit, has been allowed to exercise its power. He works out his theories upon the established fact that Cold Harbour has had an unsavory history for centuries and that this accounts for the ghostly phenomena. His explanation is that the ether is supposed to be capable of receiving and retaining impressions of light and sound at certain times when the event from which these impressions arise are intensified by some extremity of emotion in a human soul. "It's only in such emotional extremity as is reached at the moment of death that the soul is able to implant these impressions on that everlasting and unchanging medium." But the power of hypnotism finally supersedes the other theories in the mind of Wake, who concludes that Furnival discovered his "unique power," and then went from strength to strength, from audacity to audacity, until he knows that the minds of sixty per cent of the people who enter the door of Cold Harbour are potentially in his power. "He grafted phantoms on their brain." Cold Harbour is destroyed by fire — burnt and guttered, with the Furnivals in it. But through Mrs. Wake's clairvoyant brain the end of the story — the night of the fire — is told. Furnival is murdered by his wife, and Mrs. Wake, over whose mind the horror holds sway, describes the events in detail.

COLONIAL MIND, THE, by Vernon Louis Parrington (1927). This volume carries the account of the development of America from early beginnings in Puritan New England to the triumph of Jefferson and back-country agrarianism. The author explains that such a study necessarily deals much with intellectual backgrounds, and "especially with those diverse systems of European thought that from generation to generation have domesticated themselves in America, and through cross-fertilization with native aspirations and indigenous growths, have resulted in a body of ideals that we reckon definitely American." He designates as "Carolinian liberalism" the thought which gave a special cast to the New England mind, for in its deeper purpose Puritanism became a frank challenge of the traditional social solidarity of English institutional life. He discusses this thought as a Puritan heritage against English backgrounds. He presents John Cotton as the most authoritative representative of the ideal of priestly stewardship in New England; John Winthrop, as magistrate, is considered to have represented the ideal and polity of the theocratic magistracy. Other ideas are discussed other than those of Winthrop and Cotton, — ideas which the reviewer considers fruitful or feculent, but which came out of England in the teeming days of the Puritan revolution to "agitate the little settlements." The influence of

Thomas Hooker and Roger Williams — with their contributions of independency — is recalled, with the conclusion that "England gave her best when she sent us Roger Williams" — the repository of the generous liberalisms of a vigorous age. "Other dreamers in Israel" are recalled, with the later terror of witchcraft, when superstition and bigotry succeeded the period of creative vigor of the ministry. The author gives much study to the Mather "dynasty." Of the early and middle eighteenth century, he says "a new psychology was created, which spread among a vigorous people — a psychology of democratic individualism," and from this determining influence he holds that the creative outlines of our history took shape. He sees that immigration in the eighteenth century was almost wholly economic in motive, and of the different racial strains that mingled their blood with the earlier English — Irish, Huguenot-French, German, Scotch-Irish — the last, he says, was by far the most important. He writes also of the frontier, which exercised so creative an influence in shaping American character and institutions. The career of Jonathan Edwards is reviewed — "the reactionary Calvinist and philosophical recluse — who became the intellectual leader of the revolutionaries." In the career of Benjamin Franklin, the author sees a singularly dramatic fitness. The American Revolution, after a hundred and fifty years, he still finds somewhat a puzzle, although he accepts John Adams' thesis that the "revolution was in the minds and hearts of the people." The argument, the propaganda and the final social consequences are discussed, as are the American Tory and the American Whig, and the anti-Federalism of Samuel Adams. There is a chapter on "Literary Echoes," of the Revolutionary upheaval. Reviewing the period which the close of the War brought, with its emphasis upon the form and control of the new political state to be erected, the author finds that American political thought followed an independent path, and in spite of its English origin came to conclusions that differentiated it broadly from the old-world theory. In this connection he analyzes the character of the leading political thinkers — first the English group — Hamilton, Jefferson, and others; and then the French group represented by Thomas Paine. The impact of the French Revolution is also discussed in relation to its effect upon the political democracy which was getting under way. But he sees with the triumph of Jefferson in the great struggle of 1800 the winning of the first democratic battle, although he admits even then the forces which were at work preparing a different pattern of life for America unlike that of the simple agrarianism with its domestic economy, which Jefferson represented.

COMEDIANS, THE, a story of ancient Rome, by Louis Couperus (1926). The tale of a band of actors who come to Rome to perform for the feast of the Megalesia in the reign of the mad emperor, Domitian, in the first century. The actors are "despised 'histriones,' without any right of citizenship, the scorned entertainers of the crowd . . . jeered at in the street and the forum . . . but within, most of them felt a mysterious pride at being artists, exponents of the age-old comedies of Plautus and Terence." Lavinius Gabinus is the master of twenty-six perfectly trained slaves, of whom the most engaging are the youthful twins, Cecilius and Cecilianus, who play the women's parts. They are the children of a lady of the court, Crispina, whose brother, Crispinus, is high in favor with the emperor. She had given the boys to Lavinius when they were three years old, and dependent on the whims of Domitian as she is, she may not recognize them now, as to do so would be to make known her liaison with her former lover, Manlius. The company of actors arrive at the low tavern of Nilus, the Egyptian, in the Suburra, already crowded with a motley company of sailors, thieves, murderers, Christians, and the dirty, beggar-priests of

Galli, with the image of their goddess Rhea Cybele, whose feast is about to be celebrated. Two patrician women in disguise, "sensation-seekers," enter the tavern,
Nigrina, of a famous Roman family herself, and the wife of a senator, she has entered
the arena as a gladiator, and Fabulla, the young niece of the empress. Fabulla sits
on the knee of the gladiator, Colosseros, and forgets "her everlasting fear of being
seized by Domitian's executioners . . . for no reason . . . because she had laughed
or not laughed." The happy-go-lucky twins make friends with her and everyone
else. They dance at a feast at which the urbane Pliny entertains Juvenal, Tacitus,
and Suetonius, among other friends, at his magnificent villa, and ride back to Rome
in the litter with Martial, summoned to the emperor, and composing "impromptu"
epigrams on the way. Crispina hires them from Lavinius at great cost to have them
with her in her home, where they are bored and long for the freedom of their Bohemian life. The emperor has seen them play in the "Bacchides" and Crispinus,
to entertain his master, takes Cecilius to the palace. The twins are separated for the
first time in their lives, and Cecilianus becomes ill with grief, and Cecilius dances in
the hall of mica until he faints from fatigue. Martial moves Cecilianus to his villa
and sends for the gladiator, Carpoforus, "with the eyes of a gentle beast," to cheer
him. The two friends meet a band of Christians led by Saint John, who stops to
speak words of comfort to the boy. Fabulla has joined the Christians after her
friend, Nigrina, has been murdered, and she now tells Cecilianus that she has seen his
brother at the palace and that he still lives. Carpoforus, who is the emperor's favorite
gladiator, gains an audience with him, and is granted the favor he asks: freedom for
Cecilius. Pliny hires them from Lavinius to keep them at his villa. The house
where the troupe is housed tumbles down and most of the band are killed. Lavinius
succeeds in buying and hiring a few comedians, and after a farewell feast at Nilus's
tavern, they start out in a travelling cart to play at Naples, and Syracuse and Carthage, just as the murder of Domitian is announced, and their friends, the gladiators,
rush to the palace to avenge his death. It is a frank picture of Roman manners, and
of the dissolute, persecution-mad Domitian and his time.

COMMAND, by William McFee (1922). An adventure story of the sea, of conspiracy, shipwreck, and romance in the Near Eastern seas. During the War Reginald
Spokesby, second officer of the "S. S. Tanganyika" in the British merchant service, on
leave in England, becomes engaged to Ada Rivers, "a fine girl," "a bargain" for
him her fiancé admits. Mr. Spokesby tries to make himself worthy of her by a
course of lessons with the London School of Mnemonics, "endorsed by kings, and
emperors, merchant princes and famous mezzo-sopranos." "By means of this
system, learned in twelve lessons, you trebled your intellectual power," and "quad-
rupled your earning power." His friend, Archie Bates, the chief steward, making
money by smuggling hashish, introduces Spokesby to Mr. Dainopoulos, a Greek,
one-time waiter in New York, now winning the War for himself in many devious
ways in Saloniki. Spokesby meets his English wife and her friend, Evanthia Solaris,
a young and beautiful Balkan adventuress, who makes him forget the adoring Ada.
Evanthia is in despair because with the departure of the enemy consuls she has lost
her lover, the German vice-consul, Fridthof Lietherthal. She cannot read or write,
but she speaks six languages, and her mental processes would have evoked the admiration of the London School of Mnemonics. Both Mr. Dainopoulos and Evanthia
decide to use Spokesby for their own purposes. Mr. Dainopoulos needed a skilled
navigator to insure the safe conduct of a steamer into an enemy port, and Evanthia
wished to follow her lover to Smyrna. The "Tanganyika" is torpedoed, and Mr.

Dainopoulos offers the unsuspecting Spokesby a post on his boat, the "Kalkis." Evanthia makes Spokesby believe that she will marry him if he will take her with him. "She was aware that this man come up out of the sea like some fabled monster of old to do her bidding, was the victim of her extraordinary personality, yet she never forgot that his admiration, his love, his devotion, his skill, his endurance were no more than her rightful claim. Incomparably equipped for a war with fate, she regarded men always as the legionaries of her enemy." Her war cry was, "Je deteste les hommes." The "Kalkis" is rammed and Spokesby, transformed by the sea, responsibility, and love, shows himself efficient, and masterful. They arrive safely at Smyrna and Spokesby discovers that he has been "running a cargo" for the enemy. The ruthless Evanthia, true only to herself, finds her German lover, and Spokesby goes off alone in the night to save his boat. He never attains the supreme command to which he aspired. Returning to England he finds that Ada has married a wealthy manufacturer of munitions. After the War he takes a harbor-mastership in the West Indies. He regrets nothing and feels that "He could go forward now into the future, armed with knowledge and the austere prudence that is the heritage of an emotional defeat." Lieutenant Lietherthal is a most interesting character with his wit and philosophic nihilism. "A nation of mongrels who think of nothing but thoroughbred horses and dogs" is the description of the English this former Rhodes scholar gives to Evanthia. He looks forward to the end of European civilization, "a vast cesspool of republicans engaged in mutual extermination" when the yellow man from Asia and the blacks from Africa will overrun Europe. Deserted by her lover, Evanthia, with a refugee ticket pinned to her blouse, returns to her friend, Madame Dainopoulos, now living in the costly Villa Dainopoulos at San Stefano. She never told her adventures, but as she "lay in a silken hammock in the great houseboat by the breakwater" or wandered through the orange groves, she murmured, "Je deteste les hommes."

COMSTOCK, ANTHONY, ROUNDSMAN OF THE LORD, by Heywood Broun and Margaret Leech (1927). The modernist authors of this biography portray Comstock as a fanatic, and an ignorant zealot, but though they have no sympathy with his point of view, they confess to an admiration for the courage and sincerity of the man. He was a crusader against vice, and in spite of his reputation, did very little damage to sincere art and literature. He lived and died a poor man uncorrupted by bribes which would have made him rich as in the case of the Louisiana Lottery cited. His death at seventy-one was the result of "over-doing in a purity convention." The diary kept when he was in the army shows him to have been more interested in getting up prayer meetings and church services than in the struggle between the North and the South. He writes, February 28, 1864, "Would gladly go without eating Sundays if we might have a 'Chaplin' and Sunday worship." He also speaks of his own sinfulness in speaking harshly to the cook. "Should have kept nearer Jesus." He was not popular with the soldiers who twitted him with being a Christian, and working too hard. Frequently he speaks of being severely tempted by Satan, but is reticent as to the nature of the temptations, to which he does not "yield," "by God's grace," though he sometimes admits failure. The illiterate farmer boy came to New York after the Civil War to make his fortune selling drygoods. He is shocked at the drinking, gambling, and general loose living of the clerks of his acquaintance, and the display of pornographic literature on the newsstands. This book is a social history of the time, and it is shown that there was a wave of reform and that behind Anthony was a solid army of Puritans who supported his later work, of whom many were reluctant to have their names connected with the fight against obscenity but were with him in spirit. He had married a quiet, self-effacing woman ten years older than himself, Margaret Hamilton, "Maggie," and is very happy in his home life. The violation of the Sunday closing law by the saloons in his neighborhood gives him a chance to fight the demon rum. He is able to secure a conviction and push the case through apathetic court proceedings in which the case is continually adjourned. There were laws on the statute books against the traffic in indecent books and pictures, and the interest of the Y. M. C. A., roused by Comstock's revelations, sent Messrs. Whitehead and Brainerd to Albany to secure the passage of a saloon bill, and a bill on the suppression of obscene literature, which passed in 1868, and enabled the obscure young salesman, Anthony Comstock, to use his superfluous energy to hunt the publishers and the book-dealers who sold erotic literature, and drive them out of business. The Y. M. C. A. appointed a Committee for the Suppression of Vice, and secured Anthony's services "to engage in a still-hunt against the business." These Christian laymen had reckoned without their lieutenant, whose zeal made his efforts a matter of public notoriety and ridicule. The name of Anthony Comstock became a synonym for prudery, Puritanism and officious meddling, especially after the publicity of his controversy with the "lady brokers," Woodhull and Claflin, and George Francis Train. His greatest triumph was the passage of his anti-obscenity bill by Congress. At midnight on a Saturday the bill had not yet been passed. He argued with his conscience the expediency of staying to watch the bill, and did break the Sabbath by remaining for half an hour before he went to his room to pray for the bill. He received a commission as Special Agent from the Postmaster-General, and returned home to his wife in triumph, in the early morning of his twenty-ninth birthday. His work against fraudulent advertising and the quackery of patent medicine was a great achievement. In an interview two years before his death he boasted that he had caused the conviction of enough persons to fill a passenger train of sixty-one coaches, and destroyed one hundred and sixty tons of obscene literature. However, he never knew the difference between postcard-mongers and sociologists, did not grow wise with experience, and was probably more intolerant in the end than when he began his work. His assaults on the liberal-minded brought him deserved unpopularity, and it was true that he was too ignorant to discriminate between a frankly pornographic book and a medical publication of an educational character. He failed to recognize that freedom of thought and speech was a part of the tradition of America guaranteed by the Constitution. His methods of getting evidence by writing to his destined victims under an assumed name, and masquerading as a free-lover and labor reformer, in the case against Ezra Heywood for example, were much criticized. He thought that the pictures exhibited in the Paris Salon were hung in a saloon. His raid of the Art Students' League because they published a pamphlet containing reproductions of sketches made by the students in the life classes almost cost him his government position. In his last days one of his admirers said that he was like an old prophet, an angry prophet still making threats, and referring in his reports to Sodom. "Imagine the worst" is a favorite phrase. He believed in himself and the holy cause to the end. The last chapter by Mr. Broun is an essay on censorship.

CONQUEST OF CIVILIZATION, THE, by James Henry Breasted (1926). The author aims to present a connected story of the development of civilization from its beginnings in the rude implements of the Stone Age to the period of the supremacy of Rome. "The Ordeal of Civilization," by J. H. Robinson, follows this book with the history of the civilization of Western Europe, continuing the story to modern times.

"In dealing with each civilization," Dr. Breasted includes "a sufficient framework of political organization and of historical events . . . but the bulk of the space has been devoted to the life of man in all its manifestations — society, industry, commerce, religion, art, literature — ." in order to show how one age has grown out of its predecessor, and each civilization has profited by that which came before. Part I gives a short sketch of man's prehistoric progress as it went on for probably several hundred thousand years after he began making stone tools and weapons. In the Orient men slowly built up a high civilization (4000 to 3000 B.C.), while the men of the Late Stone Age in Europe lived without metals or writing. As they gradually acquired these things civilized leadership shifted slowly from the Orient to Europe. Part II begins with the historic epoch of the earliest civilization in Egypt, its decline and fall, the civilization of Babylonia which followed a few centuries later, the rise of the Sumerians and their struggle with the Semites, which ended with the disappearance of the Sumerians. There follows the story of the early Assyrians and their rivals, and the rise of the Assyrian and Chaldean Empires. Part III opens with the Indo-Europeans, who were to a large extent the ancestors of the present peoples of Europe, in their original home on the grassy steppes of the region east and northeast of the Caspian Sea. About 2000 B.C. some of the Aryan tribes of this group wandered eastward to India, and others keeping the name "Aryan" or "Iran" pushed west and southwest to establish eventually the powerful empires of the Medes and Persians. Persia was the last of the great Oriental powers, and as it declined after 4000 B. C. its civilization gave way before the Greeks, another Indo-European people. There is a chapter on the Hebrew Kingdoms, their destruction by Assyria and Chaldea, the "Exile," and their deliverance and restoration to Palestine by the Persians. The ancient Oriental civilizations "gave the world the first highly developed practical arts, including metal work, weaving, glass-making, paper-making. . . . To distribute the products of these industries among other peoples and carry on commerce, it built the earliest seagoing ships and it made the first roads and bridges. . . . The Orient also gave us the earliest architecture in stone masonry, the colonnade, the arch, and the tower or spire. It produced the earliest refined sculpture, from the wonderful portrait figures and colossal statues of Egypt to the exquisite seals of early Babylonia. It gave us writing and the earliest alphabet. In literature it brought forth the earliest known tales in narrative prose, poems, historical works, social discussions, and even a drama. It gave us the calendar . . . made a beginning in mathematics, astronomy, medicine . . . produced governments on a large scale . . . [and] finally, in religion, the East developed the earliest belief in a sole God. . . ." The dawn of European civilization is the rise of an "Ægean World" in the islands of the eastern Mediterranean which in time extended to the mainland. The civilization of the "Grand Age" of Crete was overthrown and destroyed by the Greek barbarians. Then follows the rise of the Greek civilization to the high level of the city-states, which surpassed all the cultures which had preceded it in the period which followed Pericles in Athens. This civilization was preserved by the Roman conquerors when it otherwise would not have survived the descent of more Indo-European barbarian tribes from the North. Alexander the Great by his conquests gained the leadership of the Greek world for Macedonia. The civilization of the western Mediterranean is the story of Rome and the development of the Christian Church. Rome fell before the German barbarians, but Mediterranean civilization spread northward to transform the life of the conquerors. "Thus enough of the civilization which the Orient and the Greeks had built up was preserved so that after long delay it rose again in Europe to become what we find it to-day."

CONRAD, JOSEPH, LIFE AND LETTERS, by G. Jean-Aubry (1927). The Polish years of Conrad begin at the time when hope began to rise again in those who, "for three generations had not ceased to dream of regaining national independence." The policy of Count Alexandre Wielopolski had just succeeded in obtaining mitigation of Russian tyranny in Poland, and Conrad's parents, upon the solicitation of friends in both political groups, went to Warsaw, where, in the "white and scarlet salon," little Conrad saw people with grave faces enter and disappear. These were the first meetings of the National Committee which led to the exile of the family to Vologda, where, bereft of his mother, Conrad spent his early childhood. In those tragic surroundings, the biographer sees an unconscious training in a secret and inflexible fidelity to ideals disassociated from hope. "There was only one door open to him leading from the world in which he lived, one escape for his lively imagination — reading." He lived in close companionship with a father to whom death was a familiar thought, and for whom life had no longer any attraction, and the child was driven to live in a world created by his own imagination. The book that directed his imagination toward the sea, according to this biography, was Victor Hugo's "Travailleurs de la Mer." After his father's death, Conrad was placed "en pension" with M. Georgeon at Cracow, where he attended classes, and where his "strange, new project of being a sailor" was most surprising to his family, whose traditions were exclusively military or literary and those of an inland race. His first glimpse of the sea was from the Lido, and his determination to go to sea, which sprang from an impulse deep within him, remained unshaken. The French days of Conrad now begin, and his biographer turns to his life at Marseilles, where Fate played into the hands of the Polish boy, both in the companions he knew and the adventures upon which he embarked — adventures "whose dangers and indeed because of them, had left a sense of exaltation which remained for him the most glorious moment of his youth." The Singapore and Borneo voyages, where Conrad came across men from whom he created some of his heroes, are recalled as affording him an opportunity to obtain all the information he could about the people in this corner of the world, "where the clash of two races and many religions, the passions, follies, principles, and failures of men wove those intricate plots of which he was to become the astonishing dramatist." His biographer considers this part of Conrad's life to have been richer in literary fruit than even the second half of 1887, with the possible exception of the second half of 1890, which he passed in the Congo, although the former believes that the journey to the Congo, even with its unfortunate consequences in its effect upon Conrad's health for the rest of his life, "gave us the great writer." "It may be said that Africa killed Conrad the sailor and strengthened Conrad the novelist." After Conrad ceased to make any effort to return to his first vocation and confined himself entirely to his literary work, his labors are considered to have been particularly fruitful. Stressing the difficulties of that time, among them illness and money troubles, the biographer gives surprising proof of Conrad's energies in the production of novels and short stories, and in the collection of intimate letters which these volumes contain.

CONRAD IN QUEST OF HIS YOUTH, by Leonard Merrick (1919). When Conrad was thirty-seven his Aunt Tryphena died, and left him everything. Liberated by "everything," he starts on a sentimental journey to recapture the past. In his old haunts in the Latin Quarter in Paris "the ardor of the students left him chilly," and he felt a hundred years old at the close of his stay there. The idea comes to him to revisit Sweetbay by the sea, where he had spent a happy summer of childhood with three cousins, and had his first sweetheart, Mary Page. He takes a house there and invites his cousins to join him, but the whole adventure is a dismal failure, and Mary Page has moved away. The quest of Mary Page brings him to Redhill and the wrong family of Pages. The old vicar puts him right and he writes to Mary, now Mrs. Barchester-Bailey, and receives a formal note from her in which she addresses him as "Dear Sir." His call on her destroys the memory of this romance, and he escapes the boredom of her conversation about how she "has woke up Tooting" with her "Thursdays" with the consolation only that "she thought he admired her very much." At the theatre the scent of a woman's handkerchief recalls his adoration of a young married woman, Mrs. Adaile, when he was seventeen in Rouen. After weeks of search he finds her at a hotel in Ostend, to find her altered from the girl of twenty years ago, still attractive, but rather stout. Nevertheless, he makes love to her, and persuades her to come to his room to kiss him good-by, but alas for romance, she finds him asleep, and pins a message on the curtain, "Dreamer. Goodbye. There is no way back to Rouen." However, "for an instant the spirit of youth flashed so close that he nearly captured it." The last adventure is at a small provincial town where he plays the part of "angel" to a company of actors who have been cheated and left stranded by a rascally manager. The Countess of Darlington, once the popular Miss Rosalind Heath of the stage, chose this particular time to look up her old chum, Tattie Lascelles, and revisit the light-hearted world of the "profession" she had forsaken. Society, she says to Tattie, is dull for her as she never rehearsed for it and is not easy in the part of high-class comedy. Conrad meets her as "Miss Daintree" and, by the time the manager has bolted, he also is almost a member of the company. In order to avoid Conrad's generosity, Rosalind has to confess that she is not on the stage now and is a married woman, but he has a kiss to remember her by. She gives him Tattie's address in London as the girls are staying there together as long as Rosalind's husband is away and her holiday lasts. His note inviting her to lunch goes astray and he suffers hope, suspense, and desperation, until he hears from her, and as her cab comes around the corner at last he realizes that "he has made his great discovery — that a man is young as often as he falls in love."

CONSTANT NYMPH, THE, by Margaret Kennedy (1924). The story begins in the châlet in the Austrian Tyrol where Albert Sanger, an eccentric musical genius, lives with the seven noisy, brilliant children of his two wives and his mistress. The wild brood of children were known as the "Sanger Circus" from their wandering life over Europe with their father. The few months that Sanger spent at home he invited all the world to visit him, ignoring his poverty, and lack of accommodation. Odd strangers of all classes and nationalities, whose very names Sanger had forgotten, would turn up unexpectedly. Lewis Dodd, a disciple of Sanger, on his way to the châlet, found himself in the company of a Jewish manager who had arranged a ballet for an opera of Sanger's, and received his invitation on the strength of it. The two older children, Kate and Caryl, were fortunately practical and domestic. The next four, Antonia, Teresa, Paulina, and Sebastian, were the children of Evelyn Churchhill, of good English family, who had fallen in love with her music teacher, and made the mesalliance which brought her poverty and hardship until she died when she was thirty. After her death Sanger had taken up with blonde, common Linda, who had one vulgar child, Susan. In that house music was the one sacred thing. The children were careless of obedience, self-command, manners, but took their music seriously. Even Susan had a little of the Sanger talent, and with her facility, self-confidence and showiness, she had a certain cheap effect, which her disgusted father realized might eclipse the industrious talent of Caryl and Kate, and the fine brilliance of Evelyn's children. Lewis Dodd had written a one act opera for the family to perform for Sanger's birthday, and they rehearsed and concocted words for the libretto. At supper Sanger made his appearance, and his friends saw with shocked surprise that he was very ill. The meal was a gloomy one with Linda quarrelling about Antonia who had run away for a week and had been staying with Jacob Birnbaum, a rich young Jew, whose interest in music brought him into the Sanger household. Sanger guessed that Birnbaum had seduced his daughter and that Trigorin would presently succumb to Linda's languishing glances, but he could not rouse himself to express his resentment. After supper for an hour he was his old brilliant self, and the visitors felt "that they were assisting at something epic and earning a sort of immortality simply by listening to Sanger and laughing with him." The child-woman Teresa, only fourteen, loved the selfish, moody artist, Lewis. He really had both heart and imagination, but spent his life running away from them and had cultivated a kind of cruel arrogance to defend his sensitiveness against the world. He is sorry about Antonia, caught by life, and unhappy, and comforted Teresa, sad for her sister, until she danced along the path of the mountain beside him with all her usual lightheartedness. Teresa had come upon Lewis in a distraught frenzy of creation, and knew what ailed him, since she lived in a family of artists, and "rated the writing of music as an atrocious and painful disease." As for Teresa, innocence was the only name that Dodd could find for the wild, imaginative solitude of her spirit, which the impudence of her manners could not hide. He wished he could safeguard her youth, and wondered if he could persuade Sanger to put the girls in a convent school. That night Sanger died, and the news of the calamity reached the two distinguished scholars, who were Evelyn Churchill's brothers, in England. A week later they received letters from Caryl, from Jacob Birnbaum, and Lewis Dodd asking what to do with the penniless children. Robert Churchill and his niece, Florence, started for Switzerland to take charge of their young relatives. Into the casual Sanger family comes the pink and white, well-bred, conventional Florence, like a visitant from another world, like nothing the children had ever seen. Florence knows about Dodd's symphonies, and finds out that the father of this rough genius is a member of Parliament, Sir Felix Dodd. She marries this black sheep of the family, and they all go to London, except Antonia, who marries Jacob Birnbaum. Back in her own environment in England it seemed to Lewis that Florence had changed oddly. She is so assured and domineering. The undisciplined Sanger children run away from the school which promises to "turn out a splendid type," and find Lewis alone, as Florence is spending a week-end with her father. They bring back to Lewis a vivid realization of the life he has left behind, and recollection of the genius to which he may be untrue in the stuffy life of Strand-on-the-Green. The schools refuse to receive the children back again, and Florence has to keep these aliens in her house. The fondness of Lewis for Teresa brings out everything mean in Florence's nature, and her persecution of the fifteen year old child thoroughly antagonizes Lewis. Florence is angry that she cannot understand her husband whom she wants to lionize, while these preposterous Sanger children are one with him. Jacob Birnbaum and Antonia come to London, and Jacob arranges for a concert for Lewis. Florence's father discovers her jealousy of Teresa, and her dislike of Teresa's popularity with Dodd's musical friends, and decides to take Teresa to live with him. Florence's unkindness to Teresa makes Lewis aware of his own feelings for Teresa, and he asks her to run away with him after the concert, but she refuses out of loyalty to

Florence. Lewis tells Teresa that he intends to leave on the boat for Brussels after the concert and urges her to join him. He begs Florence to be kind to Teresa after he has gone. This drives Florence to such insult to Teresa that the girl decides there is nothing left for her to do but go away with Lewis. The trip across the channel makes Teresa ill, and almost as soon as they arrive at the boarding-house in Brussels the effort of trying to open a window brings on a heart attack, and she dies.

CONSTANT WIFE, THE, by W. Somerset Maugham (1926). The theme of this comedy is the single moral standard. The charming Constance has been married fifteen years to John Middleton, an eminent London surgeon. She knows that he is having an affair with her best friend, Marie Louise, and is determined that her family and friends shall not tell her the gossip about it. Mother, sister, and business woman friend all fail to break through her clever inability to listen. The business woman, Barbara, suggests that if Constance ever wishes to be financially independent she would welcome her as a partner in her interior decoration shop, and Constance is flattered but not interested. There enters Marie Louise, who admits that she has been lunching with a beau, and presently John comes in. It is perfectly obvious that they have not only lunched together but are planning to dine together as well. When the rest go, Constance's mother lingers, hoping to give aid and council, but the only confidence she can elicit is that Constance expects a caller, Bernard Kersal. Her mother must remember him; Constance probably would have married him if he had not so openly adored her. Now he is returning after fifteen years in Japan, and Constance is a little flurried. Her mother must stay until he arrives. If he is impossible they will talk about the weather until he leaves. If he is nice Constance will place a handkerchief on the piano to signal for her mother's departure. Bernard is clearly the kind of man with whom Constance would enjoy a tête-à-tête, and it takes three successive handkerchiefs on the piano to effect the elder lady's departure. Bernard assures Constance that he is as much in love with her as he ever was, but promises not to talk about it again. If Constance will give him her friendship and let him see as much as possible of her during the year he is in England he will not presume on it or make a nuisance of himself. The act ends with the introduction of the virtuous lover to the philandering husband. A fortnight later Bernard has called to take Constance to a polo game. Marie Louise stops in to tell John that she is worried about her husband's strange behavior, and believes he suspects something, but John laughs her fears away. John complains that he has lost his gold cigarette case. At this moment Mortimer Durham, Marie Louise's husband, is announced. He says to Constance, "I thought you might like to know that your husband is my wife's lover." He produces the gold cigarette case with John's initials which he had found under his wife's pillow as proof. The imperturbable Constance saves the situation by explaining in elaborate detail how it happened that she herself had left the cigarette case in Marie Louise's room. She convinces Mortimer that he has made a mistake and extracts apologies from him for herself and Marie Louise. She finally sends him off to buy a pearl necklace to appease the wounded feelings of his unjustly suspected wife. After the departure of the humiliated Mortimer, Constance has finally to confess that only by the greatest effort has she kept her friends and relatives from telling her what she herself had observed for the last six months. Bernard takes the crestfallen Marie Louise to her car. John is more worried and upset by his wife's calmness than if she had reproached him and made the conventional scene. Her mother and sister are also mystified at her attitude. She tells John that theirs has been a perfect marriage because they had five years of exquisite happiness, and then ceased to love at the same moment, and thus escaped the recriminations and quarrels of a one-sided passion. Bernard returns with renewed protestations of devotion and offers of marriage, and to him she expounds further her philosophy of marriage. She thinks that the modern wife in her class is a parasite. "Her house is managed by servants, nurses look after her children . . . and as soon as they are old enough she packs them off to school." She will not be less than the conventional wife as long as John provides her with all the necessities of existence. Left alone at last, she telephones Barbara that she will accept her business offer. After a successful year in business, Constance is planning a six weeks' holiday in Italy, and tells John that she is going with Bernard. She has paid into John's account at the bank a thousand pounds for her board and lodging for the year. At the end of six weeks of romance Bernard will sail for Japan and she will return to her home and husband. She may be unfaithful, but she is the "constant wife." She knows that her husband will not divorce her for doing no more than he did himself. John breaks a large vase to relieve his outraged feelings but asks her to come back.

COUNTERFEITERS, THE (Les faux-monnayeurs), translated from the French of André Gide, by Dorothy Bussy (1925). A novel of the development of a group of young fellows through their experience with and influence upon one another, and each in contact with someone older. The chief character, Edouard, may be taken as a prototype of the author, though Gide speaks through other characters as well. Edouard is writing a novel to be called "The Counterfeiters," which, he says, will tell "everything I see, everything I know, everything that other people's lives and my own teach me." Edouard has come to Paris in answer to a letter from Laura asking his help, as she is about to become the mother of a child not her husband's, and her lover has deserted her. Her betrayer is Edouard's nephew, Vincent, whose weak nature makes him the victim of the brilliant, shallow pervert, Count Robert de Passavant, and his mistress, Lillian, Lady Griffiths. He gambles and loses the money he had promised to Laura, and wins it back too late to help her. With Lillian he sails for Africa, finally murders her, and goes insane. Shyness and misunderstanding keep Edouard and his young nephew, Olivier, from declaration of their mutual love. Bernard picks up Edouard's suitcase check, and in it finds his Diary and Laura's letter. He gets in touch with Edouard and Laura, and travels to Switzerland with them. The sensitive Olivier feels himself supplanted in Bernard's affection, and in Edouard's. Jealousy drives him to the companionship of Count Robert seeking his friendship through Vincent, who well knew the character of the man to whom he introduced his young brother. Bernard gains stability and self-understanding from his experiences and his adoration of Laura, and returns to his home and his school. Laura is still unhappy because of her unrequited love for Edouard, but goes back to her husband. Olivier leaves the Count and is happy with Edouard. His friend Armand Vedel takes Olivier's place as secretary to Count Robert and his magazine. There are sketches of many minor characters, Sarah Vedel, who revolts against the moral code of her family, has an affair with Bernard, and runs away to England, slowly mastered by her selfishness, the old master, La Perouse and his lovely grandson, Boris, and Olivier's younger brother, George. George falls into the bad company of Ghéridanisol, a bully in the school, and engaged at the instigation of his villainous uncle, Strouvilhou, in the circulation of counterfeit coins. This course in unwholesome worldliness ends with the episode of the shocking death of little Boris in a cruel game planned by Ghéridanisol, who was responsible for the crime, which turned George from admiration to horror of his leadership.

CRADLE SONG, THE (Canción de cuna), by Gregotio and Maria Martinez Sierra. Produced in Madrid in 1911, in New York, 1921 and 1926. The action of the play takes place in a Convent of Enclosed Dominican Nuns in Spain. The nuns and novices have gathered for a simple celebration of the birthday of their beloved prioress. Sister Joanna of the Cross has written some verses to commemorate the day. As a special dispensation the novices are allowed to talk together. Sister Joanna of the Cross tells the others of her love for her baby brother, and how he cried when she left home to come to the Convent. They ask Sister Marcella, who is the latest from the world outside, and so young she cannot seem to cure herself of liking to climb trees, to tell them a story, but she refuses as she is afraid one of them might tell the Mother Mistress on her, as has happened before. In the midst of their chatter the bell of the Convent door rings. Sister Marcella sees through the wicket that no one is there, but there is a basket on the revolving "wheel" which she turns inward, and in the basket is a baby girl, with a letter to the Reverend Mother, asking that this child of an erring woman may be brought up in the Convent as God's child. The prioress is inclined to accept the baby as a gift of God. The Vicaress thinks it will lead to "dissipation and more dissipation," that the Scriptures says God is a jealous God, and they have renounced all worldly attachments. The little novices are all excitement and eager to keep the baby. Their friend, the kind doctor, who is a bachelor, offers to adopt the child to comply with the legal formalities, and entrust her to their care. They decide she can live with the gardener's wife until she is old enough to decide whether or not she will adopt the cloistered life. The curtain falls with Sister Joanna of the Cross kneeling alone beside the basket, while the other nuns go to prayers inside the cloister, crooning tenderly to the child instead of remembering to join in the responses. Eighteen years have passed when the second act begins, and the child, Teresa, has grown to girlhood, and is going to be married, and go to America to live. She is pretty and gay and the joy of her adopted mothers, who are now making her an exquisite trousseau. The Vicaress does not approve that the pretty clothes are in the latest fashion according to the patterns, as she is sure "there are fashions in hell." Antonio is coming for her, and Teresa asks that the Prioress will allow him to see and thank the nuns who have done so much for her and whom she loves so fondly. In the last moments before Antonio arrives Teresa and Sister Joanna of the Cross are alone together, and speak for the first time of the bond of motherhood which has been between them from the beginning. Now Antonio is seen outside the grill. He stands in the sunlight and cannot see them in the darkness. Teresa calls to him, and he thanks Sister Joanna for her care of his bride. The Prioress and the other nuns come in, and the young man greets them with reverence and charming shyness. He promises to take good care of their child in the great new world of America, where he has an assured position as an architect. Growing bolder, he asks the favor that they will allow him to see them face to face, and the Prioress graciously permits Teresa to draw the curtains. He will send them a radio from the ship. This sounds to the sisters like the works of the devil. Sister Inez has the happy thought that they can sprinkle any telegram that comes with holy water. The nuns sadly embrace the weeping Teresa in farewell. The doctor, now an old man, comes to take his adopted daughter from the home of her happy girlhood, and promises Teresa that he will always care for the nuns. The chapel bell rings calling the nuns to service.

CRAIG'S WIFE, a drama, by George Kelly (1925). The scene is the living room in the home of Walter Craig. Mrs. Craig cares more for her immaculate, beautiful house than she does for the happiness of anyone in it. She is so particular that a succession of servants refuse to stay with her. There are no roses in the garden because the petals would clutter up the lawn and the floors. Mrs. Craig has just returned from a visit to her sister in Albany, who is seriously ill, bringing her niece, Ethel Landreth, with her, as she thinks the sick woman will be better alone, though Ethel is worried, and feels she ought to have stayed with her mother. It is on Ethel's mind that she has not told her mother that she is practically engaged to marry Professor Fredericks at her school, as she knows it will please her. Her aunt advises her not to marry a professor who has his way to make, and tells her that what a woman should seek from marriage is independence and security rather than romantic love. Mr. Craig wanted a wife and a home; and he has them. Her guarantee of the permanence of the home for herself is "the control of the man upon which they are founded." While Ethel is resting in her room there is a long distance call on the telephone from Mr. Fredericks, which Mrs. Craig answers, informing him that her niece is lying down and cannot be disturbed. Mrs. Craig is annoyed to hear that Mrs. Frazier, a neighbor, is upstairs visiting with Miss Austen, her husband's aunt, who lives with them. Walter Craig comes home and is pleased to see his wife and that Mrs. Frazier is calling on his aunt. His wife makes disagreeable insinuations about the kindly, harmless Mrs. Frazier's "highly premeditated" campaign to force her way into the house to satisfy her prying curiosity. After Mrs. Frazier's departure she scolds Miss Austen for encouraging Mrs. Frazier to come into the house while she was away. Miss Austen answers that she knows that Mrs. Craig does not want anybody in her house, and that she is leaving herself. She explains to her nephew the reasons why she must go, that the house is Harriet Craig's, and that her husband is a "regrettable necessity" tolerated only for its upkeep. She has discouraged the visits of his friends, and as they now reckon without him in their social life, presently they will reckon without him in business life. Craig cannot believe that his wife is as selfish as she is pictured, but he admits that he would not have gone to Fergus Passmore's house to play cards the night before if Harriet had been home. An accident happens that shows Harriet to her husband in her true colors. Birkmire, another friend, comes in great excitement to tell Craig that Fergus Passmore and his wife have been found dead in their library, and, according to the papers, the police are looking for a man who left the house shortly after midnight. The man is of course Craig. He goes off with Birkmire to find out what has happened and to tell what he knows at Police Headquarters. Mrs. Craig has just read of the tragedy in the papers when detectives arrive to trace an inquiry that was made from the house about the Passmore telephone number. She had asked information regarding the number to check up on Walter's movements while she was away, and now lies about it, partly to avoid any connection with the Passmore case, and partly to hide from Walter that she has been spying on him. For the same reasons she refuses to let Craig telephone to the police when he arrives. Is her name to be mixed up with a scandal like this? If she had not been away he would not have been out with his friends again and she admits that she has been able to get rid of visitors. Did he think she wanted her house turned into a tavern? The housekeeper reveals that it was Mrs. Craig who had asked for the Passmore number. The next morning Mrs. Craig comes down to find that Walter has spent the night in the living room smoking and scattering cigarette ashes and stubs over her rugs, and she thinks he is crazy when he shows her that he has smashed the ornament on the mantlepiece. He tells his wife that the police have found a note in which Passmore, who was known to be insanely jealous, confesses to murder and suicide. Miss Austen goes to the hotel, and the housekeeper, who is leaving, goes with her. The cook has left, and Harriet has discharged the housemaid, Mazie, the night before. Professor Fredericks, not able to get in touch with Ethel on the telephone, comes to see her, and goes with her to her home. Craig proves to his wife that he is not the "romantic fool" she has thought him by telling her what he now sees their marriage has been. He will join his aunt at the hotel, and leave her the house she married him for. If the affair at Passmore's had not revealed her, something else would, so his going may as well be now as later. A telegram comes that her sister is dead. Mrs. Frazier comes in to bring some roses for Miss Austen, and Mrs. Craig tells her she will give them to her, keeping up appearances to the last. As the curtain falls she is left alone in the house for which she has sacrificed so much.

CRANE, STEPHEN, a Study in American Letters, by Thomas Beer, with an introduction by Joseph Conrad (1923). A sympathetic portrait of Crane written like a realistic novel against the background of the America of the eighties and nineties. He was born in Newark, New Jersey, the son of a Methodist minister. The boy must have heard much talk of the Civil War from the soldiers. It is told that he was spanked for playing at burying and digging up a little friend in the sand at Asbury Park, who was supposed to be a soldier whose comrade remembered that he had had a flask of whiskey on his person before he was buried. Another story of the boy was that he fought and lost a tooth at school to back up his assertion that Tennyson was "swill." He went to college at Syracuse, New York, and had a position as Syracuse correspondent of the "New York Tribune" which impressed his classmates. The author says that he always wrote too well to be a good newspaper man. "His visual sense was unique in American writing," Mr. Beer says, "and his mind by some inner process had stripped itself of all respect for those prevalent theories which have cursed the national fiction." Richard Watson Gilder was shocked at his ironic novel, "Maggie," that Crane wrote about the Bowery he knew so well, and when Gilder was asked in 1904 why Morrison's "Child of the Jajo" did not offend his taste, he answered: "But Mr. Morrison's an Englishman." Crane was in advance of his generation, and consequently an outlaw. Hamlin Garland appreciated the genius of the shabby boy, and sent a copy of "Maggie" to Howells, advised him about literary markets, and fed him beefsteak. Howells, the first critic in the land at the time, was delighted with Crane's book, and tried to help him sell it. When he was twenty-five the "Red Badge of Courage" made him famous. With his success began the stories of his drinking and taking drugs, and general immorality, which Mr. Conrad and Mr. Beer deny as having no foundation in fact. Richard Harding Davis publicly thrashed a man about town for repeating these slanders in his presence. He was also falsely accused of borrowing from French and Russian literature. Hearst sent him to report the Græco-Turkish War, and he stopped in London, where he met and made friends with Harold Frederic. He married an American woman, older than himself, who had followed him to Greece, and they set up housekeeping in England. The Spanish-American War broke out, and Crane went home to offer his services, and went to Cuba as correspondent for "The World" when the naval recruiting bureau would not accept him after a physical examination. He writes that the whistling of the American soldiers in Cuba was "a jumble of Chinese lanterns in a fog." Fever wrecked Crane's health, and he died a year later in England. There are a number of minor portraits of the people whom Crane liked and disliked, and stories of his experiences in New York and London. He disliked Stevenson, Mrs. Humphry Ward, Lillian Russell, and Frances Willard. He did not dislike Henry

James because he was so kind. Conrad says of him that his greatest extravagance was hospitality, and there was much company always in the English home.

CREAM OF THE JEST, THE, a comedy of evasions, by James Branch Cabell (1917). The story begins with a bit of "dream-stuff" out of Felix Kennaston's romance of the world's youth in the country of Storisende when, in the character of Horvendile, the clerk, he has rescued his heroine, the lovely La Beale Ettarre, by slaying the brigand who would prevent her from marrying Sir Guion. He tries to tell his characters that they are puppets of his fashioning in a world he has created. It is not possible for them to believe him, and he says, "It may be that I, too, am only a figment of some greater dream. . . . It may be the very cream of the jest that my country is no more real than Storisende. . . ." In his twentieth century existence which has grown tedious and humdrum to him he has achieved fame as a novelist, a fortune, and a wife, Kathleen, he is fond of. By gazing at half of a broken disc covered with strange hieroglyphics which he picks up in his garden, "the sigil of Scoteia" Ettarre had given him in the story, he is able to escape into adventure with her in a dream world in which he is both spectator and actor of many parts. "The Wardens of Earth unbar strange windows" to him. He found himself often in Paris and Constantinople, Alexandria, Rome and London in different epochs. Thus, he was in Jerusalem on the day of the Crucifixion, in London in 1649, in Troy when Priam was a lad playing marbles, with Napoleon on the evening of his coronation, talked with Shakespeare, and Oliver Cromwell, and rode with Ettarre to the guillotine of the French Revolution. The dream ends if and when he touches the inaccessible Ettarre. Kennaston's love affairs in the flesh with a number of lovely women had brought him only disappointment and vexation and regret. Ettarre embodied all he was "ever able to conceive of beauty and fearlessness and strange purity, all perfections . . . for which he must always hunger in vain." She is "that ageless lovable and loving woman of whom all poets had been granted fitful broken glimpses. . . ." The talisman turns out to be the fragment of the decorated cover of a cold cream jar, the other half of which he finds on his wife's dressing table. "Many thousand husbands may find at will among their wives' possessions just such a talisman. . . ." On the occasion of this discovery he thought he caught a glimpse of the ageless woman in Kathleen's eyes imprisoned in the flesh as Horvendile; the ideal lover was one with the solid, respectable citizen who was Kennaston.

CREATION BY EVOLUTION. Edited by Frances Mason (1928). "A Consensus of Present-Day Knowledge as set forth by Leading Authorities in Non-Technical Language that All may Understand." The twenty-four eminent scientists of Great Britain and America whose articles form the content of this book all agree as to the definition of evolution. To them all it means the universal fact of change. Each scientist discusses this phenomenon as it appears in his particular field, and the result is a piling up of conclusive evidence as to the truth of the belief that creation is a gradual process of transformation, or evolution, according to natural laws. As Frances Mason, the editor, says in her foreword: "The book does not attempt to explain the origin of life, or to determine the causes that lie behind the changes in living things from age to age. It attempts to show that there are changes and to describe how they come about."

A sentence or two summarizing each article will perhaps be the best method of summarizing the book:

EVOLUTION — ITS MEANING, by David Starr Jordan. — By evolution is meant the universal process of orderly change — change which is never the result of accident or caprice. Creation by evolution reveals a "godhead infinitely worthy of obedience and adoration."

WHY WE MUST BE EVOLUTIONISTS, by J. Arthur Thomson. — Though we must admit uncertainty as to the *causes* of evolution, we cannot hesitate in regard to the *fact* of evolution which is proved to us by the record of the rocks, by geographical evidence, by anatomical evidence, and by embryological facts. The argument for evolution is cumulative. "All the lines of facts meet in the same conclusion — the present is the child of the past."

CAN WE SEE EVOLUTION OCCURRING? by Herbert Spencer Jennings. — "Geological time is enormously long and evolution is prodigiously slow." However, it is possible to see, in the amoeba, for example, that from a single race there are produced many hereditarily diverse races, differing slightly. This same fact of change has been observed, though with great difficulty, in higher organisms.

VESTIGIAL ORGANS, by George Howard Parker. — "Vestigial organs are those that are quite useless." They have been observed in snakes, in birds, in mammals and in man, both in his embryonic and his adult state. No advocate of the theory of special creation can explain their existence. On the other hand, from an evolutionist's standpoint they are seen to be organs in process of disappearance. They are signs of the past and "they afford us as indisputable proof of the correctness of the evolutionary view as can be reasonably expected."

EVOLUTION AS SHOWN BY THE DEVELOPMENT OF THE INDIVIDUAL ORGANISM, by Ernest William MacBride. — "The embryological argument for evolution rests on the hypothesis that every animal, in its growth from the egg to maturity, recapitulates the history of the race." In other words, "every animal begins its development in the egg, which is a single cell comparable in structure to the lowest forms of life known to us, and as it grows to the adult form, it sketches in broad outlines the whole story of its evolution."

EMBRYOLOGY AND EVOLUTION, by Edwin Grant Conklin. — "Individual development everywhere consists of progress from a relatively simple to a relatively complex form. Development is not the unfolding of an infolded organism; it is the formation of new structures and functions by combinations and transformations of the relatively simple structures and functions of the germ cells."

THE GEOGRAPHICAL DISTRIBUTION OF ANIMALS, by William Berryman Scott. — "The arrangement of living things on the surface of the earth is the necessary outcome of the whole vast series of changes — geographical, climatic and biological, through which the earth has passed during unimaginably long periods of geological time." Each individual species does not represent a separate act of creation, but is the result of evolution — a new form rising by modification of older ones.

THE RECORD OF THE ROCKS, by Francis Arthur Bather. — The record of the rocks shows a "gradual change from the oldest to the newest forms, and at no point is it possible to say that there was an entirely new creation. . . . For these reasons palaeontologists are bound in honesty to accept evolution" though they do not yet profess to know all its laws and causes.

THE NATURE OF SPECIES, by John Walter Gregory. — The use of the word "species" implies the idea of fixity. "The circulus provides a nomenclature which is consistent with the view that evolution results from changes affecting the mass of individuals belonging to a group."

THE PROGRESSION OF LIFE ON EARTH, by Sir Arthur Smith Woodward. — "If we compare the various groups of animals of the present day, we shall find that they can be arranged in a series that gradually leads from the simplest to the most complicated — from the lowest to the highest   No conflicting evidence to this slow and regular advance of the world of life has thus far been discovered."

THE EVOLUTION OF PLANTS, by C. Stuart Gager. — "The plants of one geological period have been derived from those of a preceding period by a process of descent with gradual modification.   This is what is meant by organic evolution.

THE STORY TOLD BY FOSSIL PLANTS, by Edward Wilber Berry. — Fossil plants illustrate the fact that "plants underwent a gradual transformation from simplicity to complexity and were differentiated in both structure and habit in successively higher groups, thus exemplifying the universal principle of evolution.

BUTTERFLIES AND MOTHS AS EVIDENCE OF EVOLUTION, by Edward Bagnall Poulton. — Change of color, mimicry and rudimentary wings in butterflies and moths serve to illustrate the truth of the evolutionary principle.

THE EVOLUTION OF THE BEE AND THE BEEHIVE, by Sir Arthur Everett Shipley. — How has the wonderful socialistic life of the honey-bee come about?   If we trace the social bees and wasps back to solitary bees and wasps, we can see a steady growth of complexity which is another illustration of the evolutionary principle.

THE EVOLUTION OF ANTS, by William Morton Wheeler. — The study of the anatomy of ants, of their distribution, of their modifications, and their habits has convinced all competent biologists in the reality of the evolutionary process as illustrated by them.

THE EVOLUTION OF THE HORSE AND THE ELEPHANT, by Frederic Brewster Loomis. — The most notable changes of an evolutionary nature in the horse consist of an increase in size, changes in the size and structure of the teeth, and most conspicuous of all, changes in the form of the foot.   Likewise, "the story of the elephant is sufficient in itself to prove the evolution of that particular order of mammals and a similar story could be told of other orders of that class, and of many other groups, both high and low."

THE EVOLUTION OF THE BIRD, by David Meredith Seares Watson. — "Comparative anatomy, embryology and palaeontology agree in testifying that the bird is a highly specialized descendant of some reptilian ancestor."

CONNECTING AND MISSING LINKS IN THE ASCENT TO MAN, by Richard Swann Lull. — "That the evidence for organic continuity seems meagre is due in part to our lack of perspective, in part to our prepossession with false conceptions or pseudo-conceptions, and in part to our proneness to magnify imperfections that merely mar but do not destroy a most magnificent, clearly unified, and deeply impressive moving spectacle of creation, which at length makes Man the heir of all the ages."

THE LINEAGE OF MAN, by William King Gregory. — In this article Dr. Gregory discusses the origin of the vertebrates; the earliest chordates; early evolution of the fishes; origin of the amphibia; origin of the reptiles; the mammal-like reptiles; origin of the egg-laying mammals; origin of the placental mammals; and the origin and evolution of the primates, including man.

THE HUMAN SIDE OF APES, by Samuel Jackson Holmes. — "In man and animals love and antipathy, courage and cowardice, self-sacrifice and selfishness, loyalty and deception, play much the same part in determining behavior.   We play the game of life less simply and crudely than the animals, but our fundamental interests in life are much the same."   A clearer appreciation of this general fact is gained by a careful study of our next of kin in the animal world — the ape.

THE EVOLUTION OF THE BRAIN, by G. Elliott Smith. — "The only reasonable and satisfying explanation of such close resemblances, both in structure and in function.

of the brain of some creatures, like the chimpanzee and gorilla, to the brain of man is the inference that (a) these other creatures have the undeveloped germs of a mind similar in kind to man's (one, however, that has definitely lost the power of significant development or further progress of the kind distinctive of man's immediate ancestors), and (b) that both the brain and the mind of man are the results of a long process of development from ancestors common to those of other living creatures having brains of the same essential type.

PROGRESS SHOWN IN EVOLUTION, by Julian Sorrell Huxley. — "The forces which we can actually detect operating in the evolution of plants and lower animals are automatic and non-conscious; whereas those operating on the human level, as we can again obviously verify for ourselves, are in part conscious and include ideals of truth, beauty and morality. We may even say that the forces of evolution conspire to act as 'a power, not ourselves, which make for righteousness.'"

MIND IN EVOLUTION, by C. Lloyd Morgan. — The concept of evolution means upward and progressive advance through many grades reaching its culmination in the highly developed mind.

CUMULATIVE EVIDENCE FOR EVOLUTION, by Horatio Hackett Newman. — All evolution is in the end one vast universal coördinated process.

The book is amply illustrated and at the end of each article is to be found a bibliography of books and articles on that particular phase of the subject.

CREATIVE CHEMISTRY, by Edwin E. Slosson (1919). In these fourteen chapters, which, as he says, originated "in a series of articles prepared for 'The Independent' in 1917–18 for the purpose of interesting the general reader in the achievements of industrial chemistry," Dr. Slosson has given a group of concise, lucid expositions of various chemical phenomena continually recurring in everyday life, which the layman is inclined to take for granted. The Introduction by Professor Stieglitz defines chemistry as "the fundamental science of the transformation of matter." Professor Slosson calls "creative" chemistry those achievements in chemical research which result in something absolutely new and unprecedented in nature. There are, he says, two chief divisions of chemistry: analytic (taking apart) and synthetic (putting together again), and as Virgil saw so long ago, the former is infinitely easier than the latter: "Facilis descensus Averno." The achievements Dr. Slosson lists range from synthetic flavors to the products of rubber; from coal-tar colors (aniline dyes) to high explosives. He analyzes the necessity for feeding the soil, and explains where, how, and how much it is needed. He paints a picture of the waste formerly and extravagantly thrown away in the destructive distillation of coal and then goes on to explain some of the manifold uses to which that waste has been and can be put. No longer is it necessary to ransack the far corners of the earth for colors naturally produced: the chemist from his laboratory can give you an aniline dye of any color or combination of colors in the rainbow. Another use to which the once despised coal-tar is put is the manufacture of synthetic scents. Whereas formerly one of the rarest of perfumes was derived obscurely from the civet-cat, a source of which as Dr. Slosson says, "The least said the better," through the manipulations of the chemist that identical scent can now be derived as a by-product of coal. The next subject to occupy Professor Slosson's attention is cellulose, or paper. He makes an imposing list of the objects that can be successfully made from paper, and more broadly from fibrous material, wood and cotton, one of which is synthetic silk, and he proves that it is chemically possible to make a nourishing food from sawdust, though, as he says, "You probably would not like it." He then turns to the synthetic plastics, the most common of which is celluloid. Others becoming popular because of their superior hardness and non-inflammability are bakelite (named from Dr. Baekeland, the Belgian chemist who discovered it) and galalith, a French compound which is nothing but casein hardened by formaldehyde. Discussing rubber, Dr. Slosson admits regretfully that there has been discovered so far no satisfactory synthetic substitute for the original, and urges greater cultivation of rubber plantations, as well as the retention by the Powers (including the United States) of control over those tropical countries yielding rubber. Three chapters on alimentary subjects deal respectively with "The Rival Sugars," beet and cane; "What Comes From Corn," which, as a diagram shows, is everything from corn syrup to corn starch, from oil to laundry starch; and "Solidified Sunshine," which is oil: cottonseed, linseed, peanut and cocoanut, and the various margarins. The chapter on "Fighting With Fumes" deals with the attainments of the chemists in making gas for the gas attacks of the war. The next to the last chapter, "Products of the Electric Furnace" is, as Dr. Slosson admits, somewhat outside the realm of chemistry proper, but then, if it had not been for furnaces capable of achieving temperatures up to 14,000 degrees F., the chemist would not rejoice as he does in fireproof test-tubes, and few of the other steps in his progress would have been made. The last chapter, "Metals, Old and New," concerns primarily iron — the most vitally important of all — and the products to be derived from it; also the rarer metals: tungsten, manganese, platinum, radium, and others. The book is illustrated with photographs and diagrams, and at the end is appended a brief bibliography, arranged by chapters, for those who wish to pursue the subject further.

CREWE TRAIN, by Rose Macaulay (1926). The heroine, Denham Dobie, a girl of nineteen, has lived alone with her father in the comparative savagery of the Republic of Andorra. After his death she is transplanted to London to the sophisticated society of her mother's relatives, the Greshams. She is unsocial, "a savage captured by life trying to grasp its principles," with endless question of the meaningless intricacy of the conventional life that is forced upon her. Peter Gresham, her uncle, his wife, Aunt Evelyn, her cousins Audrey, Catharine, Noel, Guy, and Humphrey all seem strange, attractive creatures with their continuous talk about books, and plays, and pictures, and people, talk for the sake of talk. Denham liked to eat and drink and play like a boy of twelve and lie down to rest when she was tired, and, above all, not to be called on to express opinions about anything. Life she discovers is largely one boring occupation after another. She cannot understand the "curious desire" which people who had plenty to eat at home and servants to do the work had to eat meals in houses other than their own. It was a part of the "mysterious secret that other people had . . . obviously part of the good life . . . that she, too, must learn to desire." Arnold Chapel, the junior partner of the Gresham publishing house, is attracted by her unlikeness to "the jolly, knowledgeable, companionable girls who made his world," falls in love with her dark beauty, and they are married. Living up to Arnold is even more difficult for Denham than living up to the Greshams. Arnold loves society as much as she loves solitude. Aunt Evelyn has told her that if she goes out to dinner she must talk, that it is not fair to the hostess or the men next her if she does not. "If you can't talk, you mustn't go out. Women who can't or won't speak when they're out are a public nuisance." Denham had read a book on the diseases of dogs, and at dinner when her neighbor said to her, "Did you see the Guitrys last week?" she answers "in the manner of Ollendorf," "No, but the hair of my dog is coming out," and after exhausting this topic the conversation languished.

"The affirmative which was, for others, the beginning of a flow of comment and exchange of ideas was to her merely a bald affirmation of a fact, the shutting, not the opening of a door." "What's your favorite pudding?" Denham asked her right-hand neighbor, and they really conversed, since he "did not make his answers closed doors . . . and being what is called a highbrow, he liked to talk about puddings, films and music-halls. On puddings the high and the low of brow can meet." Aunt Evelyn had told her that one could go away after dinner at half past ten, so she insisted on leaving. "To Arnold the question had always been how late after dinner one could stay." When they gave dinners themselves Denham asked Arnold why they could not save time, trouble, and service by putting all the food on the table at once and using only one plate. Arnold publishes a novel, and has to turn to Audrey, who also works in the publishing office, for sympathy about his first review, as Denham "couldn't see that it mattered what other people wrote, said, or thought about one's books, or about anything else." Denham had a respite from the "Polite Life" on a holiday in Cornwall, especially after she discovered a secret passage from a cave by the sea up to the cellar of a cottage which Arnold rented for her. Here she could be as untidy as she liked, and if visitors approached she could retreat to her cave. Unfortunately, Arnold tells the secret to the garrulous, gossiping Aunt Evelyn, and a newspaper article attracts curious sightseers. Denham goes riding alone around the countryside on her motorcycle to the scandal of her conventional relations. In the end Arnold compromises by getting a house outside the London Denham detests, but within reach of it. Denham "settles down" to be a proper wife and mother. She is subjugated by the bond of love. "What was the good of revolt? Life was too strong; it forced one. . . . One was trapped by love. . . . If you had never loved, you could be happy, loafing idle and alone, exploring new places, sufficient to yourself. . . . Love was the great taming emotion. . . . It defeated all other desires in the end. . . . Life itself was the trap, and love the piece of toasted cheese that baited it, and, the bait once taken, there was no escape." Even when the bait has lost some of its savor, it has done its work; "these two were safe and snug in the trap, and had no more need of toasted cheese."

CROME YELLOW, by Aldous Huxley (1922). Crome is the name of the country house of Henry and Priscilla Wimbush, where Denis, a self-conscious young poet, is a guest at a house-party. There is almost no action, only a great deal of the most modern kind of talk. The story begins with the arrival by train of Denis, is concerned with his timid, hopeless love for Anne, the delightful niece of the host, and ends with his departure, sadder and wiser, a victim of jealousy. The middle-aged Mrs. Wimbush, with a coiffure "of a curiously improbable shade of orange," gambles on the races and football with the aid of the stars. She spends her time casting the horoscopes of the players on both sides. "A match between the Spurs and the Villa entailed a conflict in the heavens so vast and so complicated that it was not to be wondered at if she sometimes made a mistake about the outcome." Her husband has a passion for Italian primitive art, and is engaged in writing a history of his ancestors. He reads two episodes from his manuscript to the guests, romantic tales written in the manner of the eighteenth century. Another member of the household is Jenny Mullion, a spinster of thirty, who retires into her "ivory tower" of deafness, and makes caricatures of the others in her private notebook. Mr. Scogan, a contemporary and schoolfellow of Henry Wimbush, who looks "like one of those extinct bird-lizards of the Tertiary," is a rationalist who discourses to Denis on the theoretical State, when he would rather be wooing Anne. Anne has an ironic turn of mind with her doll-like beauty. She thinks Denis too absurdly young to be considered as a lover, and is interested in the artist, Gombauld, who is painting her portrait. Denis talks to her about the futility of life, in contrast to the world of ideas where everything is clear. Her philosophy is that "one enjoys the pleasant things, avoids the nasty ones." Mary, a serious innocent of twenty-three, with her short hair "hung in a bell of elastic gold about her cheeks," discusses Malthus, modern divorce, psycho-analysis, cubism, and is worried about her repressions. She and the engaging youth, Ivan, sleep on opposite towers on the warm summer nights, and with him Mary abolishes her repressions, but "far from bringing the expected peace of mind," she has nothing "but disquiet, a new and hitherto unexperienced misery" when Ivan departs to another house-party. There is a village dance and Henry Wimpole, "the gentle aristocrat with the face like a grey bowler" and his interest in the past, remarks that "if all these people were dead this festivity would be extremely agreeable," for then one could read about them, and almost persuades us that the proper study of mankind is books. Denis sees Anne and the Byronic Gombauld embracing in the garden after the dance, and climbs the tower intent on suicide, but finds Mary there, and they confide their sorrows to each other. She advises him to go away, and he sends himself a telegram cancelling his stay. Anne, now wearying of Gombauld, expresses disappointment at his departure, and he bitterly regrets having taken this step, and reluctantly says good by.

CROSS, THE, see **KRISTIN LAVRANSDATTER**, by Sigrid Unset.

DAEDALUS, OR, SCIENCE AND THE FUTURE, by J. B. S. Haldane (1924). The author states his opinion that the centre of scientific interest in the past has been in physics and chemistry, but that biological discoveries will dominate the future. Of important biological inventions he enumerates only six of importance of which four are older than history. In the field of physics he speculates on the practical consequences of Einstein's discovery, and prophecies that the present age of materialism will be replaced by Kantian idealism first as a basal working hypothesis for the physicist and then for all educated men. Another "safe prophecy" is that "in 50 years light will cost about a fiftieth of its present price. . . ." A lamp as a source of light he considers as wasteful of energy as to burn down one's house to roast pork. He expects that we shall derive mechanical power from the wind and sunlight, and thus perhaps shift the centre of industrial gravity to well-watered mountainous tracts in India, British Columbia or Armenia. Foodstuffs we shall build up from such sources as coal and atmospheric nitrogen, and do away with agriculture. Mr. Haldane reproduces some extracts from the essay of an undergraduate at Cambridge University in his first term about one hundred and fifty years from the present time. In 1940 a purple alga has been invented which so increased the production of wheat that the agricultural states were ruined by the fall in food prices. A strain escaping into the sea increased the fish population so that England was rendered self-supporting in respect of food. The color of the sea changed from blue to purple. In 1951 the first ectogenetic child was produced. France was the first country to adopt ectogenesis, and by 1968 was producing sixty thousand children annually by this method. As a result of selective breeding he foresees election placards such as, "Vote for Smith and more musicians," "Vote for O'Leary and more girls," or "Vote for Macpherson and a prehensile tail for your great-grandchildren." These examples of a biologist's imagination will show why Mr. Haldane regards the biologist "as the most romantic figure on earth at the present day." Science is "the free activity of man's divine faculties of reason and imagination," the "answer of the few to the demands of the many for wealth, comfort and victory," and "finally, it is man's gradual conquest. first of space and time, then of matter as such, then of his own body, and those of other living beings, and finally the subjugation of the dark and evil elements in his own soul."

DAMAGED SOULS, by Gamaliel Bradford (1922). Psychological portraits of men prominent in American public life, "a group of somewhat discredited figures." Mr. Bradford qualifies his use of the word "damaged" in a prefatory article. The seven selected are Benedict Arnold, Thomas Paine, Aaron Burr, John Randolph of Roanoke, John Brown, Phineas Taylor Barnum, and Benjamin Franklin Butler. Mr. Bradford does not intend "in any way to rehabilitate or whitewash, but to bring out their real humanity and show that, after all, they have something of the same strength and weakness as all of us." A common characteristic of the varied group he believes to be lack of analysis of their own motives and natures coupled with limitless discussion and explanation of their conduct. All have a facility, if not felicity, with words, except Arnold and Brown, who were above everything men of action. They were busy, practical men, to whom words were tools, no more, but very ready, handy, terrible tools, with which they obtained results. The essays give the reader an insight into the thoughts, motives, moral qualities, and purposes which guided the lives of each one. Arnold fought bravely for his country at Saratoga and Lake Champlain, though Congress slighted him in promotions, "to the surprise and disgust of Washington, who repeatedly recommended him." As military governor of Philadelphia he was in the midst of an old aristocratic society, became intimate with loyalists, and it was probably his "love of display and the desire to assert his great position," which led him into extravagance and debt. He was not strong enough to endure lack of appreciation and injustice, or to withstand money and position offered him by the British. The great contribution Tom Paine made to the cause of American freedom is stressed. The pamphlet "Common Sense" ranks with the Declaration of Independence as an inspiration to his fellow citizens, and sold by the hundred thousand. His later political writings and especially his attacks on religion discredited the one-time popular idol. The rebels of yesterday are the conservatives of to-day. "In the light of the changes that have taken place since his time, it is difficult to find anything in his general principles that accounts" for the "storm of obloquy" that came upon him. His "dangerous, treacherous pen" slipped too easily into violence and abuse. The bitterest enemies could establish nothing against his character except that he sometimes drank and that he was not clean. Roosevelt called him a "filthy little atheist." However unpractical and misdirected some of his efforts, "through discomfort, through penury, through obloquy, he toiled for an ideal. . . . And Paine's work was inspired by the love of humanity." "Such a life has a far nobler strain in it than the self-seeking and self-indulgent career of a man like Aaron Burr." Burr "came into the world to amuse himself, and he early conceived that the richest sources of masculine amusement are the love of women and the domination of men." Mr. Bradford admits that Burr "had murdered his rival, conspired against his country, deserted his followers, robbed his friends, made a plaything of female virtue . . . yet he had done it all in the most amiable spirit." His daughter believed him superior to all other men. John Randolph, he characterizes as "a furious negative," always denouncing something or somebody, but a true patriot, who had lost faith in his world, and his fellow men. The condition of his nerves, and his depression, drove him to resort to drink and in later years to morphine. A man who "was a slave-holder and a lover of liberty . . . an aristocrat and a lover of democracy" must be pitied for the conflicts within himself which he could never reconcile. John Brown was a fanatic, who identified his own will with the will of God, but his sincerity and singleness of purpose are unquestionable. His enemies grew to respect him, and his spirit of sacrifice. The exuberant showman, Barnum, thought that "mankind liked to be humbugged and always would be, that some humbug was legitimate and delightful, and that precisely such was his." In actual business transactions his honesty seems beyond dispute. He loved notoriety and was a great pioneer advertiser. Of the vainglorious politician, Butler, he says he was an efficient and successful organizer in politics, and war, and his wife loved him.

DANCE OF LIFE, THE, by Havelock Ellis (1923). Essays on the art of dancing, of thinking, of writing, of religion, of morals. The author's thesis is that life as a whole, not isolated parts of it, should be regarded as an art. "Religion or the desire for the salvation of our souls, art or the desire for beautification, science or the search for the reasons of things — these conations of the mind, which are really three aspects of the same profound impulse, have been allowed to furrow each its own narrow separate channel, in alienation from the others. . . ." He regards the civilization of to day as "a classic mathematical Renaissance," and the dance its symbol. "The dance is the rule of number and of rhythm and of order, of the controlling influence of form, of the subordination of the parts to the whole." The movements of the waves on the shore, the combination of the elements into compounds, the motions of the stars, the feet of children at play all conform to the laws of rhythm. He claims that dancing springs from the most fundamental impulse of being, namely, the impulse for expression. Hence, dancing is not primitive but fundamental. "The art of dancing, moreover, is intimately entwined with all human tradition of war, of labour, of pleasure, of education, while some of the wisest philosophers and the most ancient civilisations have regarded the dance as the pattern in accordance with which the moral life of men must be woven. To realize, therefore, what dancing means for mankind . . . we must survey the whole sweep of human life. . . ." He draws on a wealth of erudition to illustrate his points. In "The art of thinking" he points out that the distinction between science and art is modern, that the sciences are to-day as in the Middle Ages "the arts of the mind," "that the true man of science is an artist," as Sir William Osler has said, "the student is 'of imagination all compact.' " "Matter is a fiction, just as the fundamental ideas with which the sciences generally operate are mostly fictions, and the scientific materialization of the world has proved a necessary and useful fiction. . . ." (Vaihinger). "Thinking in its lower grades is comparable to paper money, and in its higher forms it is a kind of poetry." Ellis stresses imagination, a "faculty" much undervalued. "Action is the last end of thinking, which reversed is to say that thought is action — rhythmic, harmonious action." For the art of writing "the law of the logic of thought" is more important than the "conventions and decorums of style," and the writer must be prepared to cast aside "all conventions of a past age that were once beautiful because alive, and now false because dead," but "there is a decorum and orderliness without which all written speech must be ineffective and obscure." In the hands of great writers "such observance was not a servile and rigid adherence to external rules, but a beautiful convention, an instinctive fine breeding. . . ." He believes the core of religion to be "the art of finding our emotional relationship to the world conceived as a whole," and "best termed mysticism, the relationship of the Self to the Not-Self." . . . The opposition between science and religion he considers the result of "dead tradition" and "dead metaphysics" on both sides. The art of religion is a way of life. The great artist in religion is the mystic, the great artist in morals is the stoic, like Marcus Aurelius. The practice of morals lies in strenuous action; the "collective community, at any time and place in its moral aspect . . . an army on the march along a road of life more or less encompassed by danger." "What we call morals is simply blind obedience to words of command — whether or not issued by leaders the army believes it has itself chosen —. . . and beyond this the duty of keeping in step with the others, or of trying to keep in step, or of pretending to do so." The two roads which man may travel are the road of tradition, of the many, and the road of reason, sought out by the few. "Morality is the necessary restraint on the necessary biological instinct of possession," which in its exaggeration leads to the development of civilization. The possessive instinct when pushed too far becomes the cause of the ruin of that civilization. The achievement of a stable and abiding form of civilization depends on preservation of the creative as against the possessive instinct, a society of quality instead of quantity.

DARK LAUGHTER, by Sherwood Anderson (1925). A "flighty," irresponsible Chicago reporter, John Stockton, leaves his wife, Bernice, who has become a successful writer of cheap short stories, changes his name to Bruce Dudley, and starts off down the Illinois River in a boat. He imagines himself saying to his friend: "Do you know, I've a notion to leave my wife. Well, you see, she's more interested in other things than being a woman. . . . I'm setting out on a little voyage of discovery. I've a notion that Myself is a land few men know about. I thought I'd take a little trip into Myself, look around a little there." When his money gives out he takes a job painting wheels in a factory in the town of Old Harbor, where he once lived with his father and mother. He is fortunate to have a place in the shop next to Sponge Martin, a delightful old craftsman, who had been an independent carriage painter in the days before factories and automobiles. Several times a year he and his companionable old wife go on a fishing trip, make a bonfire and have a picnic, with a bottle of corn whiskey to make them feel like kids again. The heroine is Aline, the wife of their employer, Fred Grey. Her story is told in retrospect in the few minutes she sits in the car waiting for her husband to come out of his office. Aline's father is rich enough to pay $5,000 apiece for the family portraits. He allowed his daughter to go to Paris with the artist and his wife to attend art classes. "Fred had been a young American in an Eastern college, an only son of a rich father, then a soldier in France." In the Bohemian crowd in Paris he recognized Aline as a "nice girl," the sort he would marry at home. After the "Quat'z Arts Ball" they spend one night of courtship riding around Paris, while Fred pours out to Aline his experience in the trenches, and they are married the next day. Aline longs for the perfect lover and a child, and Fred wants the affection and comfort of a mother in his home as he forges ahead in his business. He cannot accept Venus but wants the Virgin. As Bruce with Sponge Martin passes Aline their eyes meet and both recognize mutual attraction. He answers her advertisement for a gardener, and on Armistice Day while Fred is on parade they become lovers. She tells Fred that she expects to have a child. Bruce had gone away, but returns and Aline tells Fred that they are going away together. The action is slight. The author is interested in depicting what his characters feel and think, their reaction to each other and to their surroundings. The "dark laughter" is "that of the singing, chuckling, care-free sub-chorus of negroes," just outside the scene of action. "When a negro woman wants to go live

with another man, she does. Negro men and women 'takes up' with each other."
"In the road before the house one of the negro women now laughed. . . . . 'I knowed
it, I knowed it, all the time I knowed it,' she cried, and the high shrill laughter ran
through the garden and into the room where Fred sat upright and rigid in bed." He
is left alone to face his loss and the disgrace that the wife of a Grey of Old Harbor
should run away with a common laborer.

DAUGHTER OF THE MIDDLE BORDER, A, by Hamlin Garland (1921). A
sequel to the author's "Son of the Middle Border." These autobiographical reminiscences continue the story of the Garland family after their return from North
Dakota to the "final Garland homestead" in West Salem, Wisconsin. The author
makes his home in Chicago in order to be near his mother, the "Daughter" of the
title. His circle of friends in the Chicago of 1893 include Eugene Field, Lorado Taft,
George Ade, John T. McCutcheon, Henry B. Fuller, Opie Read, and others of an
interesting group. His work takes him to New York and Washington, and to England for a visit to meet the English friends, Henry James, Barrie, Shaw, Zangwill,
and Doyle, won for him by his book "Rose of Dutcher's Coolly." He visits the Indian
reservations in the West to get material for a new book. Another trip is with his
childhood friend, Burton Babcock, grown to a grizzled mountaineer, into the wilderness of British Columbia and Alaska. He marries Zulime Taft, the sister of his
friend Lorado Taft, a Kansas girl who has just returned from four years' art study
in Paris. Their honeymoon takes them to the Indian country, and after a visit to
the homestead, to the East for a few months to see publishers and old friends. A
legacy from Aunt Susan Garland enables his father to give up his farm in North
Dakota. He says, "It released him from the tyranny of the skies. All his life he
had been menaced by the 'weather.' Clouds, snows, winds, had been his unrelenting
antagonists. Hardly an hour of his past had been free from a fear of disaster. The
glare of the sun, the direction of the wind, the assembling of clouds at sunset — all
the minute signs of change, of storm, of destruction had been his incessant minute
study. For over fifty years he had been enslaved to the seasons. . . . He agonized
no more about the fall of frost, the slash of hail, the threat of tempest. . . ." The
earlier story tells of Garland's life as a son of a pioneer. This book deals with his
later years as husband and father and with his literary work, and the literary circle
of his friends, and of the West of the Indian frontier. After his mother's death he
and his wife and their two daughters, spend half their winters in the East, where they
have pleasant relations with St. Gaudens, Theodore Roosevelt, the Setons, the Gilders,
William Dean Howells, Edward McDowell, the Pages, Frank Norris, and others.
After his father's death the family give up the homestead, which the son had provided
for the declining years of his parents among their old friends and kinsfolk, and
Hamlin Garland and his wife and children move to New York.

DAUGHTER OF THE SAMURAI, A, by Etsu Inagaki Sugomoto (1925). Autobiography of a Japanese woman of the ancient feudal order of the Samurai. She
was born in the cold northern province of Echigo, "considered by the Government
only a frozen outpost suitable as a place of exile" for political offenders. Her father
held the office of daimio, and had fought to uphold the Shogun power. Only an
eleventh hour pardon had saved him from execution. Her mother burned their
castle to save it from falling into the hands of their enemies, and disguised, hid her
son in a temple, and her daughters in poor farmhouses. The background of her
story is the thoughts and customs of a Samurai household. The old grandmother

sealed the Buddhist family shrine with "the pure paper of protection" when the "strength-giving foreign food," meat, was cooked in the house for the first time. She told the children, "I would rather not grow as strong as a Westerner — nor as clever. It is more becoming for me to follow the path of our ancestors." Their neighbor, Mr. Toda, trying to become progressive with the times, ventured into the business world as dairyman and butcher. The disgrace to the family name was so keen to his grandmother that she made the sacrifice of death in protest. Etsu's brother was disowned by his parents for refusing to marry the bride of their choice. After years in America he returned to be the head of the family at his father's death. A marriage for Etsu is arranged with his friend in America, Matsuo, and the two families celebrate the betrothal ceremonies. The grandmother tells her, "where you live is a small matter. The life of a Samurai, man or woman, is just the same: loyalty to the overlord; bravery in defense of his honour. . . ." Then Etsu is sent to Tokyo to the mission school for an English education, and becomes a Christian. She goes to America to meet her unknown husband, and they find a happy home with some American friends. The delicate and significant anecdotes of Japanese life give place to her impressions of American life and its contrast to her home. Two daughters are born, and she takes them back to Japan on her husband's death. Her own position is very humble in the family, for a son's widow is an unimportant person in Japan. She is granted the unheard-of request to the family council to be allowed the privilege of guiding their studies, as Matsuo had expressed in his will a desire that, since he had no son, his daughters should receive the liberal education that had been planned for them in America. When her oldest daughter, Hanano, is fifteen, and the dreaded question of her marriage comes up, she gains the consent of the family to take the children back to America for a few more years of study. The story ends on the eve of their departure, and with the saying of her grandmother, "Little Grand-daughter, unless the red barbarians and the children of the gods learn each other's hearts, the ships may sail and sail, but the two lands will never be nearer." This book is a contribution to this better understanding.

DAVID, a play, by D. H. Lawrence (1926). The drama, written in all the varieties of Biblical, strongly cadenced prose, interspersed with simple rhymes indicative of celebration and primitive exuberance in the group scenes, closely follows the several Bible episodes. Saul, in Gilgal, is rejected by the prophet Samuel from the kingship of Israel, because he has not followed the Lord's command as to the complete destruction of the Amalekites (Scene 1). Samuel, never again to see his king, retires to Ramah to mourn him and to await God's word (Scene 2). In Bethlehem, at the house of Jesse, the youngest son, David, is anointed future leader of his people by Samuel (Scenes 3 to 4). With Saul, in Gilgal, the boy-harper soothes the God-rejected king and becomes friend of Jonathan, the king's son (Scenes 5 to 6). The Israelites are now at war with the Philistines. The giant Goliath has defied Israel and gone unchallenged, but David, armed with faith and subtlety, slays him (Scene 7). Jonathan and David now swear covenant. Saul, brooding and afraid of David's triumph, attempts his life. The king fails. When his madness leaves him he promises David his daughter Merab, but finally marries him to the younger Michal (Scenes 8 to 12). Their love only makes Saul the more afraid. He again attempts David's life. David leaves the court and seeks Michal. Jonathan ordered to pursue refuses, and with Michal speeds David's escape to Samuel in Ramah, where the prophet gives him his blessing. Saul follows only to miss David, and now in Ramah, on the prophet's hill, madness leaves him, and he strips naked to the peace of God's glory (Scenes 13 to 15). Peace between the father and son-in-law is not to be, however. Once again Jonathan warns David of Saul's anger, and the friends renew their covenant and part (Scene 16). This Bible narrative serves Lawrence in his exegesis, essentially the probing of two mysteries: love, and the nature of the great Lord of life. Love is evil unless it is of the unseen Almighty that keeps pure. Three lines of the Bible text are thoroughly interpreted: "But the spirit of the Lord departed from Saul, and an evil spirit from the Lord troubled him. . . . And David behaved himself wisely in all his ways; and the Lord was with him. Wherefore when Saul saw that he behaved himself very wisely, he was afraid of him." It is the prudent recognition of the Almighty in people as in things which leads David to them triumphant. It is the sick heart's attention to the heart's desires of the limited ego which the Almighty rules but as madness that destroys the house of Saul. The king, jealous of the praise of his people and the affection of his people for David, thus loses the magnanimity proper to the Lord's anointed. Again Michal and Jonathan are happy in their affection for David only in the absoluteness of their mutual consent to protect each other as the Lord willed it, and not in their love become merely a matter of personal possession. Yet in David's very prudence, and in the ease with which he retains his triumphs and his loves, is his weakness. Innocent, David remains to the end a grown youngster. There is no struggle in his love, no consequent need for sufferance. The conflict to realize the Lord's flame and the failure to do so, integrally in the blood and spirit of Saul's household, is a foreign conflict to David. Never touching it, he never approaches in comprehension of the nature of the universe which is of oblivion, before the Beginning, before men's and David's concept of God. Youthful bargainer with his Lord for to-morrow's glory, David will never know the faceless flame of his strength, the passion of Saul, and of Saul stripping naked on the prophet's hill in Ramah. Putting the Lord inside a house, the temple of Judah to come, and singing to Him his clean psalms full of worldly wisdom, David must always partake of the commonplace, or at best of the successful poet. And the commonplace is its own destroyer, as Jonathan makes clear in the closing speech of the play: "I would not see thy new Day, David. For thy wisdom is the wisdom of the subtle and behind thy passion lies prudence. And naked thou wilt not go into the fire. Yes, go thou forth, and let me die. For thy virtue is in thy wit, and thy shrewdness. But in Saul have I known the magnanimity of a man. Yes, thou art a smiter down of giants, with a smart stone. Great men and magnanimous, men of the faceless flame, shall fall from Strength, fall before thee, thou David, shrewd whelp of the lion of Judah. Yet my heart yearns hot over thee, as over a tender, quick child. And the heart of my father yearns, even amid its dark wrath. But thou goest forth, and knowest no depth of yearning, thou son of Jesse. Yet go. For my twilight is more to me than thy day, and my death is dearer to me than thy life. Take it. Take thou the kingdom, and the days to come. In the flames of death where Strength is, I will wait and watch till the day of David at least shall be finished, and wisdom no more be fox-faced, and the blood gets back its flame. Yea, the flame dies not, though the sun's red dies. . . ."

DAWN, A LOST ROMANCE OF THE TIME OF CHRIST, by Irving Bacheller (1927). This story is presented as having been discovered when some ancient sheets of vellum were treated with acid. They revealed a contemporary record, written by Doris of Colossae, which covers events from the sixteenth year of Tiberius to the period of Domitian and gives a vivid portrayal of early days of Christianity. A frightful desert storm left Doris, a beautiful young girl, the only survivor of a band of Greeks. Rescued by roving Ishmaelites, she later escaped with another captive, the young Jew, Apollos, who is a follower of Jesus. They grow to love one another, but he remains true to his wife. After many hazardous adventures they reach Jerusalem, where he leaves her with his old aunt and goes on to his home. Doris attends the secret meetings of the Christians, and one night they are attacked, many being killed. She escapes and finds refuge with Nicodemus. Being a foreigner, she is required to report to the Roman officials, and Vespasian, the handsome young centurion, whom she and Apollos encountered on their journey, wishes to marry her. She refuses, but later is forced into a union with him and bears him a son. Tiring of her, he agrees to let her take her child and go in search of Apollos, whose wife has died. Many vicissitudes befall her and for a time she is the concubine of a Roman general. She escapes and in the course of her wandering, comes upon a vast crowd on a hillside. Then she beholds Christ, witnesses a miracle and all her paganism is swept away. She is befriended by some kindly country folk until gossip, started by a wealthy Pharisee whom she had scorned, forces her away. She is captured and led to the Temple, cast before Jesus and accused of adultery. Then he uttered the famous words, "He that is without sin among you, let him cast a stone at her." From that time on she becomes one of the bravest spreaders of Christ's gospel. On her journeys she meets many of the personages mentioned in the Bible. Saul of Tarsus is deeply in love with her, but harshly persecutes her until he is converted. Several times she faces martyrdom but never falters in her faith. Vespasian, who has become commander of the legions, saves her on one occasion and takes their son to Rome with him. He also promises to obtain pardon for Apollos who is in prison for preaching Christ's doctrines. Many months elapse before the lovers are finally reunited. After their marriage they continue to spread the Gospel in spite of persecution. When Paul is imprisoned in Rome, Apollos leaves Doris to go and testify for him, and never returns. She witnesses the destruction of Jerusalem and then goes to Colossae, where she continues to win converts to Christ. Her record closes with the coming of the imperial soldiers to arrest her and lead her to her martyrdom. Mr. Bacheller has skilfully woven innumerable historic events into this moving love story in which he revivifies the time of Christ with rare fidelity.

DAYBREAK (Spiel im Morgengrauen), by Arthur Schnitzler (1927). His orderly wakes Lieutenant Willi Kasda Sunday morning to receive a call from his former friend and fellow officer, Otto von Bogner, who had been obliged to leave the army because of debts. In his civilian position as cashier of an electrical company von Bogner has borrowed nine hundred and sixty gulden from funds of the firm and must replace it before the expected visit of the auditor. He entreats Willi to lend him the money. Willi explains that he has only one hundred gulden, and that his Uncle Robert Wilram has discontinued his allowance and for some unknown reason refuses to see him. However, he tells his friend that he plays cards on Sunday afternoons with some friends in Baden, and will risk the money he has to try to win the necessary amount. Willi has lunch with some friends, the Kessners, having a flirtation with both mother and daughter, Emily, until it is time to meet his friends at the café. They play baccarat, and Willi is lucky enough to win several hundred gulden more than the sum he had undertaken to win. Returning to the Kessners he finds they have all gone out to supper. He goes back to the café and joins the game again, and wins two thousand gulden. They have supper, and then as Willi leaves to take the train back to his barracks he sees the Kessner family at another table, stops to speak to them, and so misses his train by half a minute. Again he goes to the café and this time possessed by a feverish desire to play on, wins and loses, and wins, and though his friends beg him to stop, the old man, Consul Schnabel, his opponent, urges him on. At the end of the game he is in debt to the amount of eleven thousand gulden to the Consul, and obliged to pay it by noon on Tuesday. Consul Schnabel tells him that he is leaving the country Tuesday evening, and unless the money is forthcoming he will report him to the commander of his regiment, which means disgrace and loss of his commission. Willi is forced to apply to his uncle, who explains that he has married Leopoldine Lebus, a prostitute, whom he sees only at stated intervals, that she has control over his money. He receives an allowance from her. Willi remembers Leopoldine as a flower girl he has had an affair with himself, and without telling his uncle his intentions, resolves to ask her for the money. She receives him kindly, and promises to send her answer by a responsible person. That evening she comes herself, accepts his invitation to dinner, and spends the night. In the early morning she leaves him, laying a single bill for one thousand gulden on the table as "payment for the entertainment," as he had paid her for entertainment long ago when she loved him and he had left her and forgotten her. Angered and mortified he yet sees the "hidden, inescapable justice" which has ensnared him, "not only in this sorry adventure but in the very essence of his life." Folding the bill in an envelope, he addresses it, and sends it by his orderly to Otto von Bogner. The army doctor who had been one of the group at the café calls to see Willi at the same time that the grateful von Bogner arrives. There is no answer to their knock. They force the lock and find Willi dead with his pistol in his hand. His uncle arrives too late with the money which Leopoldine has sent to save him.

DEAR BRUTUS, by Sir J. M. Barrie (1922). This comedy is inspired by the lines of Shakespeare, "The fault, dear Brutus, is not in our stars, but in ourselves, that we are underlings." As one of the characters, Mr. Purdie, says, "It's not Fate. Fate is something outside us. What really plays the dickens with us is something in ourselves. Something that makes us go on doing the same sort of fool things, however many chances we get." Puck from "Midsummer Night's Dream" is disguised as an eccentric old bachelor, Mr. Lob, who admits that he is all that is left of Merry England. He has invited a week-end party of guests to his country house for Midsummer Eve, and has chosen a group of people who have one thing in common, the desire for a second chance. There is the philanderer, Mr. Purdie, whose wife, Mabel, catches him kissing his affinity, Joanna Trout, in the garden, the comfortable, contented Mr. and Mrs. Coade, the aristocratic and snobbish Lady Caroline Laney, and an unsuccessful artist, Mr. Dearth, with his handsome, discontented wife, the model he had married. Mr. Dearth has been driven to drink by the disdain of Alice, Mrs. Dearth. She regrets that she did not marry the Honourable Freddy Finch-Fallowe, whose present attentions her husband warns her are dishonorable. There is talk about a mysterious wood which the villagers believe springs up on Midsummer Eve which Lob wants them to find. Dearth draws aside the window curtains, and they see that the garden has vanished, and in its place is an endless wood of great trees, and one by one the guests go out to discover What Might Have Been. The second act in the magic wood finds Purdie married to Joanna, and making love to Mabel, his former wife, while the disconsolate Joanna follows them to overhear their exchange of endearments. Matey, the thieving butler, has become a dishonest captain of finance, and the money-hunting beauty, Lady Caroline, who had tried her best to send him to jail in the first act, is now his admiring wife. Mr. Dearth, has found his inspiration and incentive to paint in the companionship of Margaret, his daughter-that-might-have-been. "She has as many freckles as there are stars in heaven. She is as lovely as you think she is, and she is aged the moment when you like your daughter best. To this ideally happy pair comes a vagrant, starving woman, to whom they give some money. She tells them that she is the wife of the Honourable Freddy Finch-Fallowe, and curses his name. The sight of the forlorn woman upsets Dearth, and he leaves his beloved child for a moment, in spite of her frightened protests, to go to a house to get food for the beggar woman. The forest fades into black nothingness and with it disappears the little daughter that never was. Purdie and Mabel, still under the spell of the wood, are the first to return to the house, where they find Lob asleep in his chair. When Joanna arrives he is still offering Mabel, "the dog-like devotion of a life-time," but breaks off as he comes back to his real self to ask, "Which of you was I saying that to?" The conceited Purdie is dismayed to realize that he is not the fine fellow he had thought himself. The trio anticipate some amusement in seeing the return of the others. Matey is the next one, "the James Matey," he informs them, "a name not, perhaps, unknown in the world of finance." Lady Caroline's "Jim" encounters the tray containing coffee cups, somehow feels at home with it in his hands, and presently retires to the pantry. Coade, who had always thought he "could do things" if he had a second chance, has been dancing through the wood whistling a tune, and now proposes to his own wife. The Honourable Mrs. Finch-Fallowe appears with a story about giving her sandwiches to a poor girl and her father whom she met in the wood, and without waiting for consent seizes the cake on the tray. Then Dearth comes in to tell these strangers that he and his daughter had just met in the wood a poor woman famishing for want of food, and asks for something for her. Memory comes back to them, too. Dearth does not join in the anger of the others at Lob. Rather he thanks him for that happy hour. As they sit down to breakfast the Dearths go out together on a painting expedition. Two of Lob's guests have responded to the magic of his spell.

DEAR OLD TEMPLETON, by Alice Brown (1927). John Templeton, at forty was a fairly successful author, but his success has been due more to his personality than to his stories. He was born with a "vulnerable face." Editors were pained when they put him off with rejection slips. "Unless you were too obtuse to human values ever to feel those things, you knew he could be hurt tremendously. Something childlike in him, something doglike and dumb, you didn't know." That was what made his worried editor hate to refuse his stories and caused more men than one to fall into the habit of "Dear Old Templeton." But it is Templeton himself who decides that his best work lies behind him, that, in fact, he has "written out," and on the afternoon that he arrives at this conclusion he impetuously proposes to his editor a return of a story which has already been accepted and a speedy parting. What he wants now is to "live" — something he has really never done. He has a sharp conviction that he might, "even against reason," live now. Mrs. Templeton had nothing in common with her husband. She possessed the "farsight that takes only the international into account and fails to salute the duster under her nose." In consequence, "Red House," where the Templetons live, in a village near New York City, was unkempt. Templeton attended to the housekeeping. At the moment that he is awakening to the need of escaping and exploring a new universe in solitude, Sally Templeton, the only child of the Templetons, a charming girl, arrives from Europe, after tramping around with a schoolgirl chum. Templeton's brother, Pat, who is also a writer, comes home with her. Mrs. Templeton takes Sally off to lectures and clubs and the house is not "licked into shape," as Templeton hoped it would be with Sally's return. But it is Mrs. Templeton who suggests that her husband employ the Hilliards, Eunice and Elizabeth, mother and daughter, who live in the neighborhood, to help in the emergency. Elizabeth is a schoolteacher, removed by "unscalable barriers from the class of 'help,'" but as she had gone through hardships to get herself educated she accepts Templeton's offer. Under her management, the domestic skies in the Templeton household clear miraculously. "Old Stephen Calvert" and his son, Champney, are neighbors. Champney fought in the War, and returned sobered by his experiences. He spends his time in his workshop, working out his plan to rebuild London. When he and Sally meet, he is being pursued by a girl who is not welcomed at the fine old house of the Calverts, but Champney finds himself drifting into a bond which he has half accepted as inevitable. Elizabeth enters whole-heartedly into her work at the Templetons, whom she looks upon as "intellectuals," but she is being slowly crushed under a suspicion which has been aroused by the relations of her mother with Jim Blaisdell, a married man. She spies upon their movements and after she knows that the two are meeting secretly, openly accuses her mother. Eunice retaliates by accusing Elizabeth of loving Templeton. Elizabeth is angered for herself, and for Templeton. The distrust between the two women widens. Templeton, to his amazement, finds that his books are selling, his royalties mounting higher and higher, and that for some unaccountable reason he is becoming a literary celebrity. In his work, he had aimed at being a realist, but he is now being discussed as a great American satirist. But he considers it a calamity to be hailed as a prodigy. Pat and Mrs. Templeton have been managing his affairs for him. Pat informs him that he has been telling the public about him — he has lectured and talked before Mrs. Templeton's clubs, on Templeton and his satires; the public needed to be told. Templeton is aghast, but as the wave of popularity continues to rise, as the result of Pat's publicity, he decides that after all, Pat, instead of being the unpractical Bohemian he had always considered him, was the best of business men. As a further example of Pat's ideas of modern professional ethics, he deliberately makes a modernized version of one of Templeton's "plays" and sells it. When Templeton learns of it his reaction is the same, "only his starved heart seem to be crying within him." To Sally he says, "It's nothing, dear, nothing. It's of no consequence. That's what we're taught to say, aren't we, when somebody trips us up? 'Never mind! It's of no consequence.'" Templeton awakens finally to the situation between Sally and Champney. Champney breaks with Irene, who attempts to kill herself by a plunge of her car over an embankment. Her courage fails her and in averting a tragedy for herself her car knocks down a woman walking above the embankment. Irene learns from Champney that she has maimed Mrs. Templeton for life. But Champney is now free to tell Sally of his love. The story ends with their complete understanding, and with Templeton, "book in hand," reading to the helpless Mrs. Templeton. "There's no place on earth that I want to be except right here. . . . Make a tryst with me somewhere, sometime, when we're young again, and we'll get a job of reporting and go from star to star." Sally has given her verdict of Elizabeth to Templeton. "Send her off, if you can manage it." And Elizabeth had gone, taking her dream with her — back to her teaching. And Eunice had broken off her relations with Blaisdell. Templeton settles down to his calm, detached philosophy of life. Nothing will surprise him now. "Old Stephen Calvert" out of his "lonely magnificence" comes over to "Red House." "Templeton," he announces, "I want to come and live with you." "Now Templeton was indeed surprised — almost knocked off the base of his composure." "But now he saw too plainly how contrary the winds are in mortal affairs, and how they shift,

with no warning, and blow all sorts of cluttering débris over the castles of the credulous mind, until the doors are sealed up by rubbish and the windows darkened against
even the sunrise of a dream."

DEATH COMES FOR THE ARCHBISHOP, by Willa Cather (1927). Fiction,
which is in essence part of the history of America. The story of two missionary priests
who carry the Cross "into territories yet unknown and unnamed" in New Mexico
and Colorado. Jean, Father Latour, successively bishop, and archbishop of Santa
Fé for thirty-eight years, is a French aristocrat and scholar. His Indian guides love
him for his good manners, for his unostentatious courage, and for the respect with
which he listens to their tales of the old religion. On his first journey across the
desert the young bishop blots out the pain of his own fiery thirst in meditation on
the passion of Jesus. His companion, Father Vaillant, is a simple, peasant type,
with practical faith in God, who gave him feather beds and an ox cart for his mission
to Colorado, and whose zeal for saving souls gives him no rest. The two devoted
friends make long, arduous journeys over their territory of romantic scene and legend.
Once in a blizzard the Indian guide takes Father Latour into an ancient cave of fear
and superstition swearing him to secrecy. There is no plot, only the life histories of
Father Latour and his intrepid vicar, Father Vaillant, character sketches of the
people with whom they come in contact, the Mexicans, the Indian chief and his son,
who become the friends of Father Latour, the Indian guides, the Spanish gentleman,
and his wife who would decline a fortune because it involved admitting that her age
was over fifty, "Kit" Carson, the American guide and agent, and the recital of
miracles and of saints' legends. There is the story of the priest who made a beautiful
rock garden, invited his friends to feast on his fresh vegetables, and paid for his
gluttony with his life, because he struck and accidentally killed his serving boy for a
mishap, and was tossed over the cliff by the Indians. At his death, mourned by all
his people, "the old archbishop lay before the high altar in the church he had built."

DEATH IN VENICE, translated from the German of Thomas Mann, by Kenneth
Burke (1925). Three long short stories of the artistic temperament. The title
story is of the last days of Gustav von Aschenbach, a distinguished novelist, spending
his holiday in Venice. In the lounge of the hotel on the Lido he notices a group of
Polish children with a governess, three nun-like girls, and a handsome boy of about
fourteen. Aschenbach is "astonished, terrified even, by the really godlike beauty
of this human child." Unobserved, he watches the boy at the hotel, on the sands, in
the streets, and on the boats, "continually rediscovering with new pleasure all this
familiar beauty, and his astonishment at its delicate appeal to his senses was unend-
ing." The cholera appears in Venice, and the elderly novelist, knowing the danger,
deliberately refrains from warning the Polish family, and remains himself for the
sake of his obsession. He does not feel well, and dies suddenly on the day that the
Polish family are leaving. The action of the second story, "Tristan," takes place in
a sanitarium for consumptives. Herr Klöterjahn, a German merchant, brings his
beautiful young wife, Gabriele, who has not been strong since the birth of her son, to
the cure. Herr Spinell, a young writer, spends much time talking with her. The
doctor has forbidden her to play the piano, but he induces her to play Tristan and
Isolde to him, and after that day she is not so well, and soon her husband and the
bouncing, exuberant child are sent for, and she dies. Tonio Kröger of the last story
resembles his dark, emotional Italian mother, rather than his father, the Consul.
He writes verses, which seem illicit and improper to his schoolmates and teachers.

His best friend is Hans Hansen, his exact opposite, a fine scholar and a good fellow besides, popular with everyone. At sixteen he is in love with blonde Ingeborg Holm. Long years after he has a reputation as a writer, he takes a journey to Denmark and stops on the way at his native town and visits his old home, which is now converted into a public library. Concealed on the piazza of a hotel at a Danish resort, he watches his childhood friends, Hans and Ingeborg, dancing in the ballroom, but does not make himself known to them. He takes stock of himself and calls his life a failure, because his preoccupation with art has made their simple joys impossible to him, and "excited by this festival in which he had taken no part, he was tired out with envy." He realizes that he has given up the possibility of life and love in order to understand them more completely.

DEBONAIR, by G. B. Stern (1928). Subtitled "The Story of Persephone," this novel is a modern version of the capture of Demeter's daughter by Pluto, who, moved by a mother's pleadings, permits Persephone's return to earth for half the year. In this case, Persephone is Loveday Trevelyan, Demeter is her widowed mother, and Pluto is represented in general by all the forces that seek inevitably to draw Loveday away, and in particular by Charles Elvaston, whom she loves. According to Mrs. Trevelyan's fond impression for the last year Loveday, alone in London, has been studying art under quite respectable auspices and severe chaperoning. Actually, she has been doing nothing of the sort: that is, for the last ten months of the year. Tiring of her art and her impeccable auspices, Loveday had struck out for herself, taking up dancing as a profession and dropping it, living as a gold-digger (much on the lines of Lorelei Lee and her friend Dorothy), precariously, but protected by her own fastidious distaste for being "mauled," finally meeting Charles Elvaston and his mother, whom he idolizes, but with whom Loveday feels stifled. All this is told in retrospect after Loveday has joined her mother at an unfashionable resort on the Italian Riviera. After a brief stay, Loveday and her mother get on each other's nerves, and Loveday runs away to visit her friend, Judith Maitland, a much older woman, but more sympathetic with Loveday than Mrs. Trevelyan. While at the "House of the Seven" Loveday hears that Charles's mother "Petal" has married again, so Charles is free. She makes an abortive attempt to go back to England, then returns to her mother. Eventually she and Charles meet and are reconciled — presumably they are — to "live happily ever after," keeping Mrs. Trevelyan with them part of the time. The book is written in a super-subjective, psychoanalytical vein that gives the effect of unreality. One feels as though moving in a dream — recognizing that it is a dream, yet powerless to break the transparent shell of illusion, or knowing that even if one did break it another would replace it, and the mad fantasy continue dreamlike.

DECLARATION OF INDEPENDENCE, THE, by Carl Becker (1922). An exhaustive interpretation of this historic document is made from several viewpoints which take into consideration the various forms by which the framers presented their case. "Having formulated a philosophy of government which made revolution right under certain conditions, they endeavored to show that these conditions prevailed in the colonies, not on account of anything which the people of the colonies had done, or had left undone, but solely on account of the deliberate and malevolent purpose of their king to establish over them an 'absolute tyranny.' The people of the colonies must, accordingly (such is the implication), either throw off the yoke or submit to be slaves. As between these alternatives, there could be but one choice for men accustomed to freedom." In its first part, the author holds that the Declaration formulates, in general terms, a democratic political philosophy; and in the second, enumerates the specific grievances against the King of Great Britain, which, ostensibly, are presented as the historical causes of the Revolution. From this point, the author holds that, superficially, the Declaration seems chiefly concerned with the causes of the Revolution, with the specific grievances; but in reality, it is chiefly, one might say solely, concerned with a theory of government — with a theory of government in general, and a theory of the British empire in particular. Seeing in what he calls "eighteenth-century thinking" the common understanding of a natural order of things, the author mentions the group of writers of that time whose books may have influenced Thomas Jefferson, notably Locke's second treatise on government, which the Declaration, in its form, in its phraseology, is claimed in this volume to follow closely. The channels through which the philosophy of Nature and Natural Law made its way in the colonies in the eighteenth century are noted, with special acknowledgment to English literature, steeped in this philosophy, and the author concludes that the "Americans did not borrow it." "They inherited it." The author traces the first tentative steps to find a theory that would meet the emergency — the new emergency that faced the colonists. From 1764 to 1776, the colonists are shown, step by step, to have modified their theories to suit their needs until they finally shaped what was the thought of the age — the idea of natural law and natural rights. The various drafts of the Declaration are given, with the list of signatures. The literary qualities of the document are discussed, what is called "Jeffersonian felicities" — phrases which bear the stamp of Jefferson's mind and temperament. In his concluding chapter, the author treats of the philosophy of the Declaration which may still be seen, he observes, in the state constitutions, perfunctorily safeguarding the liberties of mankind.

DECLINE OF THE WEST, THE (Untergang des Abendlandes), by Oswald Spengler. Authorized translation by Charles Francis Atkinson (1926). The German work comprises two volumes, of which only the first, subtitled "Form and Actuality," is covered by this translation. The work was conceived as early as 1912, according to the author, but was not finished until 1917. Published in 1918, certainly some of its popularity in Germany is due to the fact that the German defeat by the Allies may be considered as only a part of the predestined fall of Western civilization. "In this book" says Spengler, "is attempted for the first time the venture of predetermining history, of following the still untravelled stages in the destiny of a Culture, and specifically of the only Culture of our time and on our planet which is actually in the phase of fulfilment — the West-European-American." Historians of civilization in the past, he says, have made history a process of evolution of "ancient-mediæval-modern history." He asserts that there is no "civilization" though there have been a number of equally important "civilizations," each an organism born to flourish in a spring and summer and decay in an autumn and winter of old age. He regards his system as the "Copernican discovery in the historical sphere, in that it admits no sort of privileged position to the Classical or the Western Culture as against the cultures of India, Babylon, China, Egypt, the Arabs, Mexico — separate worlds of dynamic being which in point of mass count for just as much in the general picture as the Classical, while frequently surpassing it in point of spiritual greatness and soaring power." What have been called historic causes are really aspects, features or symbols, and historians have recorded "things become" rather than "things becoming." "There is not one sculpture, one painting, one mathematics, one physics, but many.

. . . ." "Present-day historians think they are doing a work of supererogation in bringing in religious and social, or still more art-history details to 'illustrate' the political sense of an epoch." They forget the "soul" of which visible history is the expression, sign and embodiment. "A Culture is born in the moment when a great soul awakens out of the proto-spirituality (dem urseelenhaften Zustande) of ever-childish humanity. . . . It blooms on the soil of an exactly-definable landscape, to which plantwise it remains bound. It dies when this soul has actualized the full sum of its possibilities in the shape of peoples, languages, dogmas, arts, states, sciences, and reverts to the proto-soul." In this process the living Culture hardens into a static Civilization. A Civilization is an organic structure and is subject to laws of birth, growth, and death, inherent laws which cannot be altered. To support his thesis, he compares classical and modern civilization with a detailed examination of different periods from the point of view of mathematics or concepts of time and space, the arts, architecture, sculpture, painting, music, drama, ethics, and natural science. Each Culture begins with an intuitive, religious Spring, and grows toward a Winter of liberalism and rationalism and city-mindedness. Thus our Western Culture, which came into existence about 900 A. D., is not on the threshold of continuous progress, but began to decline at the end of the eighteenth century. The present imperial system will be destroyed by wars of annihilation, and will be succeeded by a period of "Caesarism" about the year 2000. (See charts at end of volume.) We must face the fact that we are as near the end of an era as the Romans were in the days of Augustus. The course of history is predetermined by Destiny. "Cultures are organisms, and world history is their collective biography." He applies his "morphological" canons to the great Cultures, the Apollonian (Classical), Magian (Arabian), and the Faustian (our own), of which Goethe's "Faust" is, in his opinion, the most perfect symbol.

DEIRDRE, by James Stephens (1923). In this novel James Stephens writes of his native Ireland, not in sly humor, as in his "Crock of Gold," but in romantic saga. Conachúr, after being deserted by his queen, Maeve, whom he had married against her will after she had struck and killed his wife, Clothru, her sister, decides to remarry. His love fixes on the beautiful Deirdre. All of her sixteen years the charge of the aged Lavarcham, the king's "conversation woman," the maid has been reared supposedly hidden from the eyes of men. Secretly, however, she has been outside the women's chambers, and has consorted with the young hero, Naoise, the king's nephew, who was wont to spend the nights in the adjacent woods, around the campfire with his brothers, Ainnle and Ardan, all sons of Uisneac. With Naoise and his brothers, Deirdre escapes to Scotland, a week before the celebration which would proclaim her marriage to the king. This event marks the earliest fulfilment of the magician Cathfa's prophecy that Deirdre, the Troubler, as her name signified, would bring civil strife to Ulster. For seven years the three boys and the girl run wild in the woods, hunt, and fight the Scots for their lives. At the end of this time, Conachúr, who still loves and broods bitterly on his disappointment, plots vengeance, and under the pretence of a pardon successfully induces the lovers to return to Ireland. As protector of the unsuspecting lovers, Conachúr sends Fergus mac Roy, his stepfather, whom the queen, Nessa, had married on the condition that he would yield the throne to her son, Conachúr, for the first year of their marriage. In the time that followed, however, the people grew used to Conachúr, and would not have Fergus for king. Conachúr had always wished to do away with Fergus, though his stepfather had accepted a subordinate rôle and had remained loyal. The story tells further of

Fergus's dilemma on his way to Ireland with Deirdre and the sons of Uisneac; how he was detained by Borach in his island kingdom to feast for one week on sharks, in spite of the fact that his promise to Conachúr compelled immediate return, and thus obliged to turn over his charges to his sons, Buinne and Iollan, for the journey. The king has contrived that Fergus shall unwittingly betray them, and Deirdre has misgivings in spite of his assurances that his sons represent him. Deirdre and the young men arrive safely at Conachúr's palace. They are not received by the king, but are sent to the fort of the Red Branch for hospitality. In the night, driven by his consuming hunger for Deirdre, Conachúr surrounded his nephews in the fort with his soldiers. They withstood his battalions in single combat; one son of Fergus, Iollan, fought with them, while Buinne fought against them. Following a progression of battles, the impending defeat of Conachúr turns to victory when he sets fire to the Red Branch, and with the aid of the magician, Cathfa, causes the waters of the sea to rise around the sons of Uisneac. Forced to swim, they forsake their arms, are caught by Conachúr's men, and are slain by Mainè Rough-Hand by the king's command, though he had promised Cathfa to spare his grandsons, the sons of Uisneac. "Deirdre knelt by the bodies, and she sang their keen, beginning: 'I send a blessing eastward to Scotland.' When she had finished the poem she bowed over her husband's body; she sipped of his blood, and she died there upon his body." The last line of the novel reads: "So Far, the Fate of the Sons of Uisneac, and the Opening of the Great Tain."

DELECTABLE MOUNTAINS, THE, by Struthers Burt (1927). Stephen Londreth belongs to an aristocratic, old Philadelphia family against whose traditions he is a rebel. After he graduated from college he bought a ranch in Wyoming and made his home there, and a success of cattle-raising. His sister Molly, however, is the black sheep of the family whose name is never mentioned. She had married a blackguard, and then disgraced her family by divorcing him. From the Riviera she writes to Stephen to ask him to help her to get the money from her father for the necessary "dot" to marry a Frenchman with whom she is in love. She receives an annual sum from her father, and wants to have the capital that would represent her allowance for fifteen years. Stephen goes home to urge Molly's claim to happiness, and finds his father and mother unsympathetic, and has a quarrel with his father. The next day he leaves for New York to visit his friend, Vizatelly, who had been his English instructor at college, and is now doing musical criticism for a newspaper, and occasional brilliant essays. At Vizatelly's studio he meets Mercedes Garcia (née Wiggins), a dancer in a Broadway theatre. They meet again later in the evening at a Greenwich Village ball, and Stephen falls in love and proposes to her. When he comes back from Panama in three months they are married. He takes her first to Philadelphia to see his family for a day and then to the lovely western country. They are both deeply in love, and are happy for a time, but each expects too much of the other. Stephen corrects his wife's use of slang, and she resents his superiority, and she has not enough to do. The servants attend to the housekeeping. A friend of his sister Joan's, Mary Ward, a cold-hearted, sophisticated flirt, comes to visit them at the ranch, and tries to add Stephen to her collection of lovers. Mercedes had never before met a girl of Stephen's class, and learns a great deal. She tells Stephen that she wants to return to New York and the stage for a time. He goes home to Philadelphia into the family business, and writes her that he will come to New York to see her. Mercedes cannot get back her dancing position, and has to live in a cheap boarding house, as she has refused to let Stephen give her money.

An artist, Charles Hastings, gets her a chance to work in the movies, and she is able to carry on. The kind and clever Mr. Vizatelly seeks out Mercedes and lectures her, and is troubled about his two friends, and also at the attention that Hastings is paying to Mercedes. When Stephen comes at the New Year, Mercedes takes a suite in a hotel in order to make him think that she is successful and prosperous. They both long for explanations and understanding, but each is too proud to take the first step toward a reconciliation. Stephen returns to Philadelphia and does not come to see Mercedes again. She happens to be out for dinner and the theatre the night that Stephen is in New York on his way to Europe after his father's death. Stephen makes it possible for Molly to marry her lover, de Sauvigny, by making over half of his large inheritance to her. Mercedes is about to take Hastings as a lover because he loves her so much, and she is grateful for his kindness to her. Vizatelly appeals to Hastings not to accept her sacrifice because she loves her husband, and will never marry him, and they will all be unhappy. However, other factors were to decide what would happen to Mercedes. She finds that she is going to bear Stephen a child, and, homesick for the protection of the encircling mountains and solitude of her western home, she goes to the ranch. Against her express orders, Jean, in charge of the ranch, writes Stephen the letter that brings him back. He tells Stephen that Mrs. Londreth is a very proud lady, but that he is sure that she wants her husband. Two men on horseback are seen coming in the distant valley, and soon Stephen and Mercedes are together again. There is the background of the Wyoming country and ranch life, the world of the theatre, and Bohemian New York, and the society of the Londreth family in Philadelphia.

DESIRE UNDER THE ELMS, by Eugene O'Neill (1924). Passing over the scenes which show Ephraim Cabot's two older sons leaving for California (it is 1850) and those which are designed to elucidate the character of Ephraim, the drama is wholly centred upon Abbie, Ephraim's third wife. Ephraim is the kind of New England farmer who bases his life on a belief in a hard and cruel religion. He brings to his upland farm Abbie Putnam, thirty-five and half his age. The only son remaining at home is Eben, thirty-two, who believes that the farm belongs to him. Fearing to lose it to the woman, he greets Abbie with a hate which is worthy of his father. But Abbie is equally greedy and more clever. She tells the aged Ephraim that she believes it is possible for them to have a child and in his delight he promises, if so blessed, to make over his property to the new heir. Abbie then cold-bloodedly proceeds to seduce Eben, who has never known kindness or affection, and falls easy prey. When Abbie's son is born, Ephraim exults and Eben, tortured in the grip of an impossible situation, tells him the truth. But meantime Abbie, with all her cleverness, has reckoned without her own passions. She finds herself blindly in love with Eben and, in order to prove to him that she loves him more than the farm for which they have fought, she strangles their child. The play ends with Abbie and Eben led off to jail, happy and exultant in their complete acceptance of and absorption in one another. They have passed through and beyond sin and tragedy and found light beyond the evils of cruelty and repression. Whether one disagrees with the philosophy of the play, whether, even, one finds distasteful, as many have, the brutal frankness of many of the lines, no one can deny the clarity, the strength, and the strange, almost unearthly beauty which O'Neill has brought to pass on such barren ground.

DEVELOPMENT OF THE UNITED STATES, by Max Farrand (1918). This interpretation reaching from 1607 to 1917 emphasizes national character and eco-

nomic development rather than political events.   The expansion of the few thousand
colonists, scattered along the Atlantic coast in the early seventeenth century, into a
population of over one hundred millions, occupying the whole central portion of the
North American continent, and holding outlying possessions, forms the early theme
of these studies; while from early colonization, with its expansion and contacts, to the
period of independence, which definitely revealed the important difference between
American and British institutions — making a condition, rather than a cause, the
reason for the inevitable struggle — to the steps taken when the problems of making a
government work confronted the American people, these studies discuss the various
factors and influences which were responsible for putting the government on a more
stable basis.   "The Constitution was floated on a wave of commercial prosperity."
In certain phases of development, the author sees the results of expansion.   "The
acquisition of Louisiana, like the Declaration of Independence, and the Ordinance of
1787, and the Federal Constitution, was an epoch-making event in American history.
In the first place, it doubled the area of the United States, thereby increasing enormously the natural resources of the country."   The author reviews the period of liberal
government, which preceded the War of 1812, the significance of the Treaty of Ghent,
and the stimulating forces which made for the new America.   From that "nervous,
hurried energy of the American people," which the author considers is ascribable to
the period after that war, the study goes beyond that democratic era into the Jacksonian epoch, and the subsequent movements which were forerunners of an intellectual awakening, as well as philanthropic and humanitarian — a national spirit appeared immediately after the War of 1812.   Slavery and the Civil War are reviewed,
and the reconstruction and adjustment period receive discussion.   The growth of the
West, events which made for industrial history, the labor question, immigration,
business and politics, the adoption of the Australian ballot, are interpreted from the
author's viewpoint of their respective significance; while of the new order it is emphasized that the essence of American idealism, as seen through the entire progress of
the United States, is service to mankind.   America as a world power, with a united
people putting forth the "ultimate and unknown strength of the whole United
States," is discussed in the final summary.

DICKINSON, EMILY, LIFE AND LETTERS OF, by her niece, Martha Dickinson
Bianchi (1924).   The biographical sketch, an outline of less than one hundred pages,
precedes the letters, some of which are published for the first time.   Emily Dickinson's father was a prominent lawyer in Amherst, and the treasurer of Amherst College.   Her mother, Emily Norcross, of another old New England family, sent her
bridal silver and mahogany to her new home in an ox-cart, as there was no railroad
to Amherst.   Emily had one sister, Lavinia, the Vinnie of the letters, and a brother,
Austin, who married her dearest friend and confidante, Susan Gilbert.   She was
educated at Miss Lyon's Female Seminary at South Hadley, which announced as
one of its leading aims, the training of "mates for the missionaries sent out to the
foreign field."   It was here that Emily protested against keeping Christmas as a day
of fasting and mortification, and was sent home for a time in consequence.   Letters
written from school reveal her high spirits and gay humor.   Later at the Amherst
Academy she was the wit of the school.   Though this gifted girl was devoted to her
family, she was an alien spirit in the God-fearing household, as she was also in the
bleak Puritanical society of her time.   "The church dominated all life, social and
public," and Emily's unconventional religion, her intimate feeling for a loving God,
and refusal to consider "herself as hateful in his sight," led her to flout the gloomy

religious atmosphere and doctrines. She wrote to a friend of family worship, "They are religious except me, and address an eclipse every morning whom they call their 'Father.' " When her father was elected to Congress he took his family with him to Washington for the winter. On a visit from there to Philadelphia she met and fell in love with a man, already married, and at once hastened home, followed by her lover, who begged her to run away with him. She refused to take her own happiness if by so doing she wrecked another's life. From this time she lived the life of a nun secluded in her home and garden. Shyness and sensitiveness made her become more a recluse in the years following. More and more she communicated with her friends and even with her beloved sister-in-law, Sue, by little notes and poems. Of her friends she says, "I never sowed a seed in childhood — unless it was perennial — that is why my garden lasts." These friends included Helen Hunt Jackson, J. G. Holland, Judge Otis P. Lord, the Bowles family of Springfield. The family discovered only by accident that Emily was writing poetry. She would allow nothing she wrote to be published, and left directions that her poems should be destroyed with her letters at her death. To Thomas Wentworth Higginson she did send some poems for criticism, and, though it is not apparent that she adopted any of his suggestions, they became warm friends, and a number of the letters are to him. She writes, "You ask of my companions. Hills, sir, and the sundown. . . ." Her poetry expresses her ecstasy in living, in the joy of sunsets, the hemlocks in snow, the murmur of bees, her flowers. There are references to her unhappy love affair, and the later poems deal with the problems of death and immortality. Many of the letters are notes of condolence on some bereavement. Someone said of her, "Physically timid at the least approach to a crisis in the day's event, her mind dared heaven and earth." The letters close with the note to the Norcross cousins the day before her death, "Little Cousins — Called back." The collection of letters is incomplete, because she had exacted the promise from her most intimate friends to destroy her letters.

DISENCHANTMENT, by C. E. Montague (1922). The British writer and soldier has set forth in this book some of his experiences, and those of his companions, together with his impressions of, and reactions from, the World War. "Now that most of our men in the prime of life have been in the army we seem to be in for a goodly literature of disappointment," he says in his opening paragraph of his chapter, "The Vision." "All the ungifted young people came back from the War to tell us that they were 'fed up.' That was their ailment, in outline. The gifted ones are now coming down to detail. They say that a web has been woven over the sky, or that something has made a goblin of the sun — about as full details of a pain as you can fairly expect a gifted person to give, although he really may feel it." He adds that no doubt disenchantment has flourished before and that the young melancholiasts are only less good at their craft. From the viewpoint of the young recruit — the volunteer, he sees as the result of his first early experience in army discipline, a peace that comes only to a man who suddenly finds all his maturity's burdens to have dropped from him by some magical change, in the new order of things in which all was fixed from above, down to the time of his going to bed and the way he must lace up his boots. His vow of willing self-enslavement has immersed him in the Dantean repose of obedience, and he saw that everything that God had made was very good. "That was the vision." This mental peace, the physical joy, the divinely simplified sense of having one clear aim, the remoteness of the rest of the world, all favored a tropical growth of illusion. "Here were hundreds of thousands of quite commonplace persons rendered, by comradeship in an enthusiasm, self-denying, cheerful, unexacting, sanely exalted, substantially good. To get the more quickly 'fit to be used, men would give up even the little darling vices which are nearest to many simple hearts. . . . Where, then, did the first shiver of disillusion begin?" he asks. "Perhaps with some trivial incident." But he makes it clear that no matter what may have "changed the first lyric-hearted enthusiasm," one thing that held fast was the men's will to win. There are chapters devoted to the talk in the trenches, to Agincourt and Ypres, and to that long tedium when "time and place came when the spirit, although unbroken, went numb: the dull mind came to feel as if its business with ardor and choric spheres and quests of Holy Grails, and everything but the rest, had been done quite a long while ago." And this of the influence of religion: "if any official religion could ever refine the gold out of all that rich alluvial drift of 'obstinate questionings of sense and outward things,' now was its time." Nobody used it: the tide in the affairs of churches flowed its best, but no church came to take it. But the brigade chaplains came, and under their influence, "the shy and uncouth muse of our savage theology unfolded her wings and flew away." There follows some description of warfare — the Flanders battle of July 31, 1917, and the reaction upon the physical senses of modern fighting, as the author feels it. "As you gaze from the top of a tree or a tower behind your own front, in a modern war, all the landscape beyond it looks as if man had perished from the earth, leaving his works behind him. It all looks strangely vacant and dead, the roofs of farms and the spires of churches serving only to deepen your sense of this blank deletion of man, as the Roman arches enhance the vacuous stillness of the Campagna." And finally — the last thrill of the War — the first stroke of eleven o'clock, on the morning of Armistice Day, on the town clock of Mons, only captured that morning. And this, at the end: "for the moment, no doubt, war has gone out of fashion; it pines in the shade, like the old horsehair covers, or antimacassars of lace. . . . But may it not come into fashion again? Do not all the great fashions move in cycles, like stars?"

DISRAELI, A PICTURE OF THE VICTORIAN AGE, by André Maurois, translated by Hamish Miles (1928). The author begins with Disraeli's Jewish forbears, and then shows Benjamin in his home, the oldest son of a disciple of Voltaire, and the author of "Curiosities of Literature," and in "the turmoil of the little schoolboy world" where he makes himself leader of a "modernist" group, and is expelled for organizing a dramatic club. The "impertinent young man," devoured with ambition, makes friends with Lockhart and Sir Walter Scott through John Murray, his father's publisher, in plans for a newspaper, which end in fiasco. After two years of travel in Europe he returns to startle London with his gay waistcoats, his jewellery, and his epigrams, and to put his adventures and dreams into novels, while he tries to get into the political world through the world of fashion. The indiscreet adventurer gradually learns wisdom and responsibility, gains his seat in Parliament, and the respect of a hostile majority, and the confidence and affection of Victoria, who had earlier despised and distrusted him. He stands at last preëminent among the statesmen of Europe, the one man Bismarck acknowledged his equal. In Maurois's account he is always the play-actor to whom an audience is indispensable. Sarah, his sister, is the first of many women to whom he pours out his confidences and the devotion of his affectionate heart, Mary Anne, his wife, Mrs. Wyndham Lewis, the Sheridan sisters, Lady Blessington, Lady Dorothy Nevill, Mrs. Brydges Williams, and the Queen, to all of whom he writes hundreds of letters in ardent, florid, Oriental phrases. Gladstone is his foil in this biography. "To Disraeli, Gladstone was a man of assumed piety, who cloaked his skill in manœuvres with feigned scruples. To Gladstone, Disraeli was a man without religion and without political faith." Disraeli is reported to have said of Gladstone: "My only difficulty with him is that I have never been able to understand him." The well-known stories, the long duel with Peel, the struggle with Gladstone, the Suez Canal coup, management of the affair with Russia, the triumph of the Congress of Berlin, are effectively retold. The romance of the rise of this Jewish soldier of fortune to be the grand vizier of the greatest sovereign in the world is best expressed in his own conception of the most desirable life: "a continued grand procession from manhood to the tomb."

DR. ADRIAAN, by Louis Couperus, translated by Alexander Teizeira de Mattos (1918). The fourth and last volume of the "Book of Small Souls," the chronicle of a neurotic, inbred, Dutch family, the Van Lowes. Adriaan, the son of Constance and Henri Van der Welcke, is the big soul that appears at last among so many small ones, devoted to petty self-interest and grievances. From childhood he has been the comfort and companion of his half-estranged father and mother. When he is sixteen they move to the gloomy old house of his father's family at Dreibergen. At once he proposes that they shall provide a home for his widowed Aunt Adeline, and her nine children, Guy, Gerdy, Alex, Jan, Constance and the rest. He is like a brother to his heedless, childlike father. Adriaan breaks away from family traditions and refuses to enter the diplomatic service because he prefers to study medicine and serve all humanity. However well he knows what is best for others in body and soul, he is not a good judge of what is best for his own private interests. He marries too coldly a handsome girl of the bourgeoisie, Mathilde, attracted to her because she is healthy and normal in contrast to the morbid strain of his mother's family, and will have healthy children. He can give her only half of himself, and she comes to realize it, and resent his devotion to his large adopted family, who understand him better than she does and share his feelings. Mathilde is fond of Adriaan, and she had liked the idea of writing Baroness Van der Welcke on her calling cards, and escaping from the genteel poverty of her home. She wants her husband to give up his large, unremunerative practice at Dreibergen and become a fashionable physician at The Hague. The family dislike her as an alien in their midst. At a ball she meets Johan Erzeele, a friend of her girlhood with whom Gerdy is now in love, and encourages his attentions. Adriaan makes the sacrifice of giving up his own life to please her and they go to The Hague to live. Mathilde had been a superficial, rather vain young woman, with a few vulgar aspirations. Now that she has the life she had wanted she is not happy, for though she had not appealed to Adriaan's family or they to her, her environment has changed her, and she has grown more like the people and things that surrounded her. She now suffers from a refinement of soul, senses and nerves through a perception that Adriaan had thought she would never have. She no longer puts the question to Adriaan whether he really loves her, but asks herself if she loves him, and also if she loves Johan. She tells Constance that she was too different from them all at Dreibergen to be at home, and that Adriaan is too far above her, that he oppresses her with his lofty ideals of self-sacrifice and doing good. Adriaan sees her with Johan and senses the situation between them. He decides to return to Dreibergen and leave her and his children at The Hague until she has time to decide whether or not she loves Johan and wants a divorce. The book closes with the death of the old grandmother, Constance's mother, the last of the older generation; characteristic of the author there is no conclusion only as in life an ending which is perhaps a beginning.

DRUMS, by James Boyd (1925). A novel of character in the historic setting of the American Revolution. Johnny Fraser is the son of a Scotchman who had been out at Culloden, and a daughter of the old English plantation aristocracy. At the opening of the story they send their son from the pioneer country home to the town of Edenton to receive the education of a gentleman with the scholarly old rector, Dr. Clapton. Here he meets the colonial gentleman, the sterling though slow-witted Sir Nat, interested in his horses and racing, Wylie Jones, the clever, courtly young friend of his mother's, concerned with politics, and the British Captain Tennant and his charming London bred daughter Eve, with her fine manners, who almost wins his heart away from the sturdy Sally Merrille, the rustic beauty at home. Johnny is a fine young gentleman after three years when the war between England and the Colonies breaks out. His father sends for him to come home to avoid the troubles of the times, and he says good-by to Eve on her way to safety with friends in New York, and indignantly watches roughs stone the old captain, her father, as he leaves the town on order of Mr. Teague Battle representing the Continental Congress, who restrains Johnny for his own safety from going to his friend's assistance. At home Sally is taken up with the soldiers going off to war and cool to Johnny, especially after her brother, Job, joins the army. His father, mindful of Culloden, and representing the opinions of many Colonials, says to Johnny ready to join the Provincials, "There's no glory to war except i' the silly dreams of children or the false memories of old men. It's bloody, and no good comes of it. And as for rebellion, if rebels against Great Britain could ever succeed, we should have . . . (at Culloden). What chance then have these provinces wi' a dozen different nationalities within their borders, wi' thousands honestly loyal tae King George and tens of thousands indifferent? . . . And if against all reason it should succeed, what have ye got? . . . Ye've merely traded a government of tinsel fops for a government of fustian demagogues." His father had lost his home and all he had through rebelling against British rule once, and he persuades his son to go to England to work in the exporting house of friends until the war is over. Young Johnny meets Eve in London and the fashionable circle of her friends. It is necessary for her to make a brilliant marriage before the Tennant funds are exhausted, but she is kind to young Johnny as long as is possible. On an errand to Scotland for his friend, Wylie Jones, to take money to Mrs. Jeannie Paul, the mother of Paul Jones, regarded by the British as a pirate and fugitive from justice, the sound of North Carolina voices in a coast raid to burn British ships gets Johnny out of bed in the night and off to Captain Jones's ship with his compatriots. He waits in Paris for Jones to get a ship, has a visit with his old friend, Sir Nat, until that simple, lovable man is provoked into a quarrel about America and killed in a tavern riot. In the fight between the "Bonhomme Richard" and the "Serapis" Johnny serves in the fighting foretop, is wounded and invalided home. As soon as he is well again he joins the ragged, starving army of Commander Daniel Morgan to fight Tarleton's dragoons, is again wounded, and goes home. The book closes with the passing of the Continental army on their way to the final victory, which, of course, the watching, crippled Johnny can not foresee. A call from Mrs. Merrille reassures him about Sally's feelings toward him, and all his troubles are ended.

DUSTY ANSWER, by Rosamund Lehmann (1927). A quotation from Meredith,

"Ah, what a dusty answer gets the soul,
When hot for certainties in this our life!"

states the theme of "Dusty Answer," a novel by Rosamund Lehmann. Judith Earle was hot for certainties, the certainties that mean so much to youth, delight in all active life, and desire for affection and love. The thought of the children who lived next door with whom she played in childhood, pale Mariella, and her four boy cousins, Charles and Julian, Roddy and Martin, became the glowing memory of her lonely girlhood. After they returned to London, Judith had only one glimpse of them, when they came down for a skating party during a winter of their late 'teens. This brief return served but to brighten the aura of dreams with which the imaginative girl had surrounded them since their departure. Of them all, Charles, with his angelic, girlish beauty, had held first place in her shy thoughts. Then the report came of his marriage to Mariella just before he left for the front. He never came back, but one summer after the war Mariella, the girl widow, came back with little Peter, Charles's baby son, and opened the old place to receive the others, since the grandmother was gone. As the summer passes, Judith overcomes her first shyness to enjoy an intellectual companionship with Julian, who has returned from the War strange and stern, seeming to care only for his brother Charles's little son. She plays with Martin, who has become a splendid athlete. His devotion to her is no less than in the days when he used to send her smudgy scrawls in school. Again she wins Roddy's lazy regard. His personality it was which had always held the most mystery for her from the earliest days. In the dark mazes of his nature she found something akin to her own. The close of this summer of reunion with her old playmates finds her starting her life at Cambridge bereft of the gentle protection and guidance into college ways which she had expected from her father. Then, one of those engrossing friendships that sometimes develop between two girls brought her intimacy with Jennifer, whose bright vivacity was the antithesis of her own dusky introspective ways. This girl-love continued serene for a time and running parallel to it was her growing love for Roddy, whom she saw only at intervals. Roddy is a well-drawn type of the man whose charm piques and lures his friends to extravagant lengths of devotion, although he neither seeks it nor claims the qualities adequate to satisfy such emotions. The attraction and jealousy felt by the two girls for each other, or by Tony, a young poet devoted to Roddy, for Judith, whom he looks upon as a rival for his friend's affections marks well the delicate parallelisms and distinctions in such youthful affairs. Although Roddy has as fine a gift for drawing as Charles or Julian for music, his really important gift is for expressing personality. In her naïve, straightforward way Judith responds to this appeal. She is proud of a love which, when Roddy comprehends its true nature, annoys and antagonizes him. About the same time Jennifer mysteriously disappears with another girl. When Judith discovers that Roddy holds their mutual passion so lightly, and is disappointed in her friendship with Jennifer as well, she turns in a revulsion of feeling to Martin, and accepts his love and his sincere if unalluring offer of marriage, only to find that she cannot carry her promise through to fulfilment. Judith leaves with her mother for a trip on the continent. Julian joins them abroad and, but for Martin's sudden death by drowning, would have persuaded Judith in her search for some meaning, some certainty in life, to try unconventional love with him. On this note the book closes as Judith, recalled by faithful Martin's death, turns back, ever seeking, but with only a dusty answer. The acclaim with which this first novel by an unknown author has been received is due not so much to the depth or power of the characters drawn as to the quality of personality in its more elusive tones that is revealed. More than all Rosamund Lehmann has succeeded in evoking the atmosphere of youth in its idealism, its ardent seeking for meaning in life, its cynical recoil from reality and its entirely youthful note of finality in having achieved all experience before the journey is well begun.

DYBBUK, THE, a play, by S. Ansky. Translated from the original Yiddish by Henry G. Alsberg and Winifred Katzin (1926). Founded on an old superstition that when a young person dies before his time, his soul returns to earth to complete its span, and may enter the body of a living person in the form of a Dybbuk. It becomes necessary to exorcise the invading spirit, and this is done in a ceremony conducted by the rabbi and assistant judges. The people in this story belong to the intensely religious Chassidistic sect among the Russian Jews. The scene of the first act is "a wooden synagogue of venerable age," in the town of Brainitz. Three batlonim, or professional prayermen, and six or seven students are chanting the Talmud. Channon, a devout student, stands absorbed in meditation. There is also present a mysterious stranger known only as the Messenger. The prayermen are hungry and hope that the wealthy merchant, Sender, will succeed in getting a bridegroom to suit him for his pretty daughter, Leah, for then there will be feasting and cheer. Chennoch tries to induce his fellow student, Channon, to give up his meddling with the mystic rites of the Kabala to the neglect of his Talmudic studies. Presently Leah with her nurse, Frade, and her companion, Gittel, enter the synagogue. Channon gazes raptly at her, and is so agitated that he can hardly reply when she greets him. The news comes that Sender has failed again, the fourth time, to bring home a bridegroom for Leah, because the bridegroom's father refuses to board the couple for ten years. Sender himself arrives with the glad news that the match has been arranged, and the feast is to be prepared. Let everyone make merry. Channon cries out in despair that all his fasts and ablutions and spells and symbols have been in vain, and falls dead before the altar. The second act takes place in the courtyard of Sender's house on the day of the wedding. According to custom, all the poor people of the village have been summoned to the wedding feast lest they cast an evil spell. The beggars claim their right to dance with the bride. Leah goes to the graveyard to ask her mother's spirit to come to her wedding, and she also asks Channon. Menashe, the bridegroom, arrives before Leah returns. Though he is the son of a wealthy farmer, the conspicuous duties of bridegroom fill him with terror, and he is stupid and clownish, a sorry contrast to the brilliant student, Channon. Leah is seated in the bridal chair, but instead of accepting the timid Menashe, she rises and cries out in a strange voice, "No. You are not my bridegroom." As the curtain falls the Messenger says, "Into the bride has entered a Dybbuk." The third and fourth acts take place in the house of the Rabbi Azrael. Sender has brought Leah to the holy man to drive out the Dybbuk, whom they know by his voice is the student, Channon. The city rabbi, whose permission is required for the exorcism, relates that the dead father of Channon has visited him in dreams asking that he summon Sender before the court for trial for mortal injury done another. The exorcism is postponed until after the trial to be held between the living and the dead. A messenger is sent to the graveyard to summon Channon's father, and after a time it is apparent that the dead man is in the court behind the sheet, and within the holy circle drawn by Azrael's staff. The proceedings reveal the fact that Channon and Leah had been promised to one another at birth. Sender had grown rich and had wanted a bridegroom of high estate and great possessions for his daughter, and had broken his pact. Sender is responsible for the death of Channon, and "of his son's sons to the end of all generations." The Court decides that Sender is guilty and he is ordered to give half his possessions to the poor, and to light the memorial candle for Channon and his father each year for the remainder of his life, as though they were his kindred and to pray for their souls. The exorcism of the rabbi forces the Dybbuk to depart from Leah, and the coming of the bridegroom is announced. In the moment that Leah is alone the soul of Channon calls to her and she is united to her predestined bridegroom in death.

EARLY AUTUMN, a story of a lady, by Louis Bromfield (1926). The third story in a study of periods of American life. This is a picture of decadent New England. The theme is the same as in the earlier novels, "The Green Bay Tree," and "Possession," the effort of the individual to escape from the domination of the family and tradition, and live freely. The Pentland family have been resident at Pentlands for some three hundred years. The heroine, Olivia, is an outsider of Scotch-Irish extraction, married to Anson Pentland, and daughter-in-law of John Pentland, "the last of the Puritans," of a family whose "prestige had once been of national proportions." Anson is a bloodless weakling occupied in writing a genealogy. Jack, their young son, is an invalid. Sybil, the daughter, is a charming girl of eighteen. When the story opens Olivia, nearing her fortieth birthday, is in love for the first time in her life with a self-made Irish politician, Michael O'Hara, who has come to live in the neighborhood. The romantic Irishman worships the great lady that the lovely Olivia is in very truth. He rides with Sybil in the early mornings and induces Olivia to join them. The others of the family are Mrs. John Pentland, hidden away in the north wing with a trained nurse, since she has been insane most of her married life, meddlesome, hypochondriac Aunt Cassie, Mrs. Struthers, swathed in crêpe, living a vicarious existence spying on Olivia and gossiping about Sybil, and Sabine Callendar, a divorced cousin, who has brought her young daughter, Thérèse, from Paris to visit her old home. The family have not a drop of the Pentland blood in their veins as Olivia discovers from reading some correspondence between Sabina Pentland, the beauty of the family portraits, and her cousin Toby Cane, but they do not know of the ancient bar sinister, and are true to what they believe themselves to be. Sabina hates all the family except Olivia and her children, and with the passion for vicarious experience which she shares with Aunt Cassie determines to be the *deus ex machina* to help Olivia and Sybil to freedom and happiness, and bring the little world of Pentlands down about the heads of the others. She encourages O'Hara, and invites Jean de Cyon, Lily Shane's son, from Paris to visit her. The death of Jack draws old John Pentland and Olivia, always sympathetic, even closer together. He has loved Mrs. Soames, now the aged remains of the beauty she once was, and tells Olivia that he has never been unfaithful to his wife, in spite of the gossip about their relations. Gradually John Pentland shifts to the dependable Olivia the duty and burden of the charge of the family, making her the unwilling victim of a tradition not her own. Before he rides to his death on the back of his wild red mare he has made Olivia the real Pentland of his own ideal, convinced that, as he says, "There are things which people like us can't do." Persuaded to give up her chance of happiness with O'Hara, she connives at the elopement Sybil and Jean plan with the aid of Sabina, and like the rest of the Pentlands lives vicariously in their escape. She is left to the daily, tiresome visits of Aunt Cassie, and the society of the dreary Anson, her weak and shifting ally, imprisoned in their code of the past. The story is told from the point of view of Olivia, and is a record of mental reflections and mental attitudes.

EARLY CIVILIZATION, by Alexander A. Goldenweiser (1922). Man's unity is the first principle established by the author in his examination of early civilizations. Man is one, and civilizations are many; both are affected by local conditions of life. Civilization, it is further established, is a social heritage of ideas and institutions, due to individual minds and perpetuated by society. With reference to the evolutionary theory, the author points out that modern archæology and anthropology have upset the conclusions of Spencerian evolutionists: evolution in early civilizations seems to be neither uniform, nor gradual, nor progressive. The author then proceeds to illustrate early civilization by an historical survey of representative examples. He selects the Tlingit, Haida, Eskimo, Baganda, and Arunta as illustrating three American tribes, one African, and one Australian. He exposes in great detail the case of environmental adjustment presented by the Eskimo; the hunting-and-fishing civilization of the Northwest Tlingit and Haida, with a digression on the Iroquois matriarchate showing a typical form of social organization; next, the well-rounded civilization of the Baganda inhabitants of Uganda, with their large-scale cattle-breeding, agriculture and manufacture; finally, the magic-ridden community of the central Australian Arunta, devoid of agriculture, manufacture and domestication. In his conclusions the author points out that, viewed historically, his five examples have illustrated the fundamental aspects of all civilization: religion, art, social and political organization, economic pursuits and ideas. His studies also lead him to conclude that diffusion is as great among primitive tribes as among ourselves. But he notes the lack of disinterested science and of individual freedom. Every local civilization, he concludes further, is in some respects like all civilization, in others like all primitive civilizations, still in others like the civilization of a certain geographic area, in some like that of a smaller area, and finally it is like itself in some specific aspects. This generalization Mr. Goldenweiser explains by two principles: (1) the origination of peculiar cultural features by individuals in a tribe; and (2) their spread through contact, historically, with other tribes. Having studied primitive civilizations historically, the author now approaches the same facts in their functional aspects. Economic conditions and industry are everywhere the result of solving the problem of life by the invention of weapons and tools. Invention, however, though common to all tribes, is not professional or exclusive. It is at best the reproduction of an accidental discovery. Illustrations are furnished by Kwakiutl woodwork, Hopi pigments, and Tewa ethnobotany. Art appears wherever industry is developed. Objects in themselves offer opportunity, and primitive art is expressive rather than exclusively imitative. Symbolism is widespread and has a religio-mythological value. In North America, religion and magic centre most often about the idea of the Guardian Spirit, not necessarily personal, who represents the inclusive supernatural power. Ritual concerns itself with adolescent initiation, through solitary communion. Melanesian Mana and fetich worship substitute a wholly impersonal power for animism, while anthropomorphism and the All-Father belief include universal personification. Chuckee supernaturalism and Bella Coola cosmology furnish examples. Society as an aspect of primitive civilization is rooted in the fact that man is localized and that life in groups involves problems to be regulated by law or custom. Group subdivision is almost everywhere the case, starting with the family, based on blood-relationship, and extending to the clan (or gens), the class, and the moiety. Within the functions of these groups is that of regulating intermarriage. In social organization, age is of great importance. Precedence is given to the old men (sometimes women) of the tribe, in many matters of social significance. Some tribes exhibit social disabilities of women, mainly political. The author concludes from his facts that racial factors are not correlative with civilizational characteristics, and that environmental factors are not all-explanatory. Historico-geographical diffusion must be invoked to supply the deficiency. Environment gives the material and not the form of civilization. The formative factors are: (1) individual creativeness; (2) social and psychological inertia; (3) historical interrelations of groups. There follows a criticism of Graebner and Rivers' thoroughgoing diffusionism. Finally, the author closes with a comparative estimate of the theories held concerning Early Man. He reviews the contributions of Spencer, Frazer, Durkheim, Wundt, Lévy-Bruhl, and Freud, agreeing rather with the latter three in ascribing to the pragmatic attitude of early man his lack of rational thought, his limited technical achievements, and his failure to create a cosmos ruled by other forces than magic.

ECONOMIC CONSEQUENCES OF THE PEACE, THE, by J. M. Keynes (1920). Mr. Keynes was the official representative of the British Treasury at the Paris Peace Conference and sat as deputy for the Chancellor of the Exchequer on the Supreme Economic Council until his resignation of these positions on June 7, 1919, because he disapproved of the terms of the Treaty with Germany. In this book he states the grounds of his objections to the decisions of the Conference in regard to the economic problems of Europe. Chapter 2 is an analysis of the economic interdependence of the States of Europe before the War. Chapter 3 on the Conference is a brilliant and humorous characterization of Clemenceau, Lloyd George and Wilson, and describes the procedure by which the President, without a definite and detailed program and by reason of his temperament, was, in Mr. Keynes's opinion, manoeuvred by his more adroit associates into the acceptance of a Treaty which was a violation of the Armistice based upon the Fourteen Points. Chapter 4 on the Treaty begins with an account of the preliminary negotiations between the Allied and Associated Powers and Germany, and then discusses the chief economic provisions of the Treaty. Chapter 5 discusses Reparation under four headings, (1) Undertakings given prior to the Peace Negotiations, (2) The Conference and the terms of the Treaty, (3) Germany's capacity to pay, and (4) The Reparation Commission. Chapter 6, Europe after the Treaty, is a pessimistic prophecy of the disintegration of Europe. Chapter 7, Remedies, is Mr. Keynes's program, which includes revision of the Treaty of Versailles, the cancellation of inter-Ally indebtedness, an international loan and the reform of the currency. In this chapter he discusses the relations of Central Europe to Russia. He believes that the economic clauses of the Treaty cannot be enforced, that the claims against Germany are exaggerated, that the inclusion of pensions and allowances in the claims was a breach of faith, and that the legitimate claim against Germany was within her capacity to pay.

EDUCATION OF HENRY ADAMS, THE, by Henry Adams (1918). This autobiography, written in the third person, is the author says "the story of an education," and the persons who figure in it "are supposed to have value only as educators or educated." By education he means Henry Adams's adjustment to the world, and the one thing he asks of education is that it shall be adequate preparation for life. From time to time he speaks of his experiences as an education that did not educate, and of himself as a failure from the point of view of his own high standards. The grandson of one president and the great-grandson of another, he was born in 1838, and the first chapters are a picture of the New England environment of his boyhood, his home in Boston, his grandfather's home in Quincy, where the family spent the summers, and a study of New England character and temperament. The influences on the mind of the boy were political and literary, and the ideas, those of the eight, eenth century, no real guidance for the future. Then come four years at Harvard College, which he considers time wasted for his purpose. He regrets that he had no instruction in the modern languages, and in mathematics, that would have been invaluable to him in later life. To his own surprise he was chosen class orator. The class saw him as most representative of themselves, and he saw them, his judges, as so many mirrors of himself and his shortcomings. He remembers that one of his illustrious uncles remarked that the oration was singularly lacking in enthusiasm, and that another commented on his perfect self-possession. The next winter he enrolled at the University of Berlin to study civil law, and criticizes the German lecture system as the method of the thirteenth century in its deadliest form. He attended an elementary high school to learn the German language. Mediæval Rome he finds fascinating, but not the place to teach nineteenth century youth what to do in a twentieth century world. At Naples he heard that Garibaldi and his Thousand were about to attack Palermo, and managed to get sent to the seat of war with despatches. He came home in the midst of the presidential campaign of 1859, and voted for Lincoln and started to read law the same day. His father was elected to Congress, and Henry Adams went to Washington with him to act as his secretary. President Lincoln appointed Charles Francis Adams his minister to England in 1861, and Henry Adams, as secretary, analyzes that critical period of negotiations over the Trent Affair, the sailing of Confederate privateers, and the prevention of the recognition of the Confederate States by the British Government, hostile to Lincoln and Seward, and in the face of Gladstone's public announcement that Jefferson Davis and the southern leaders had made a nation, "one of the most perfect educational courses in politics and diplomacy that a young man ever had a chance to pursue. The most costly tutors in the world were provided for him at public expense — Lord Palmerston, Lord Russell, Lord Westbury, Lord Selborne, Mr. Gladstone, Lord Granville, and their associates, paid by the British Government; William H. Seward, Charles Francis Adams, William Maxwell Evarts, Thurlow Weed . . . employed by the American Government. . . ." The book gives brilliant characterizations of the men Henry Adams was associated with at home and abroad. He meets Swinburne at a house-party, and listens astonished far into the night to his original, wildly eccentric, gifted talk. The Adams family returned to America after seven years' absence, and Henry Adams went to Washington to await the announcement of Grant's Cabinet, which put an end to his hopes of a political appointment. The simplicity of Grant fretted and irritated Adams. He had met one other man of the same type, Garibaldi, also an enigma to him, in whom likewise intellect counted for nothing, only energy. The two articles on British finance and banking which he had expected would lead to a post in the Treasury Department, had been sent from London to the "North American Review." He became a member of the staff of this magazine, and spent the years 1869–1870 in Washington writing and watching the chaos of politics. The next summer he went to England, and was in Paris at the outbreak of the war with Germany. In 1871 he accepted an assistant-professorship at Harvard to teach mediæval history, and "of all his many educations, Adams thought that of school-teacher the thinnest." A year or two as editor of the "North American Review" satiated his desire for education in that profession. He had no time to write, and ironically measures the success of an editor by the number of advertising pages he can secure. The story then continues in a chapter called "Twenty Years After" (1892). As soon as Grant's administration ended in 1877 he had returned to Washington, to follow "the current of his time" as he had determined when, a young man in England, he had become a Darwinian for fun whether it was true or not, and settled on writing as a career. He held no public office, but followed with sympathetic interest the world diplomacy of his friend, John Hay, and the politics of other friends, Senator Cameron, Cabot Lodge, and Theodore Roosevelt, while he wrote his histories.

The last chapters expound his dynamic theory of history, and the development of a law of acceleration, mathematical and relative, the movement from unity to multiplicity. Progress is the development and economy of forces. He uses as a formula the coal output of the world, which doubled every ten years between 1840 and 1900, in the form of utilized power, and might be measured in terms of twenty-five and fifty year periods back to 1400, and in longer periods before 1400 until the movement became infinitely slight. At the rate of progress since 1800 he prophesies that the man of the year 2000 would know how to control unlimited power, and think in complexities unimaginable to an earlier mind. This book is a sequel to the author's "Mont-Saint-Michel and Chartres," which he calls "a Study of Thirteenth-Century Unity," as he calls this autobiography, "a Study of Twentieth-Century Multiplicity." It was privately printed in 1906 to the number of one hundred copies, and sent to persons interested for correction and suggestions. The author considered it incomplete and unfinished, and would not consent to its publication during his lifetime.

EDWARD VII, KING, a biography by Sir Sidney Lee (2 vols., 1927). It was at the request of King George V that Sir Sidney Lee undertook the writing of this life of Edward VII, and a great deal of important unpublished material was placed at the author's disposal. The book is based on documents in the royal archives at Windsor and at Marlborough House, and on numerous collections of letters addressed by the late King to personal friends and to men of prominence in official life. Sir Sidney Lee is solely responsible for the plan and execution of the biography. The first volume, "From Birth to Accession," covers the period from November 9, 1841, to January 22, 1901; the second volume, "The Reign," the nine years to May 6, 1910. The background is the history of England and Europe. The Prince Consort was responsible for the stifling system of education to which the Prince of Wales was subjected. Baron Stockmar, his trusted mentor, called the attention of Queen Victoria and Prince Albert to the disreputable career of King George IV as a horrible example of defective education and the "moral ruin overtaking royal heirs who were left in youth at the mercy of flatterers seeking favour by pandering to vice and self-indulgence," with the result that the Prince was not allowed to have the companionship of boys of his own age except on rare occasions in the presence of his father, and a succession of "tutors" and "governors" crammed the unhappy youth with information, and enforced the rigorous code of disciplinary rules drawn up by Prince Albert. At Oxford and Cambridge his father demanded that he should live "in an entirely separate establishment" under the strict supervision of his governor instead of in a college, so that he was not able to have the ordinary experiences of an undergraduate. Fortunately, Prince Albert believed in the educational value of travel, and the Prince toured England and the Continent, and visited Canada and the United States in his eighteenth year. His governor, Colonel Bruce, complained that his charge had no respect for learning, and "tended to exaggerate the importance of dress and etiquette," but speaks of his charm of manner. A cousin of Queen Victoria, Prince von Hohenlohe, says of the boy that he gave "an impression of good breeding," and deplores his "nervous awe of his father." After his father's death, Victoria's loyalty to the memory of her husband led her to continue his methods of repression and systematic scheme of education. She admitted that the Prince ought to become more acquainted with affairs, but treated him as incapable of responsibility and confidence, and denied her heir any share in her constitutional duties. Out of a list of eligible brides prepared by his Uncle Leopold, King of the Belgians, the Prince chose the Princess Alexandra, daughter of Prince Christian, afterward King Christian IX of

Denmark. Victoria's retirement from society made it inevitable that the Queen's Court should be largely replaced by that of the Prince and Princess of Wales. She also allowed her son to take a leading part in the reception of foreign sovereigns and diplomats who visited England. Foreign affairs became his great interest, and though the Queen refused him access to the official papers which were distributed to the Cabinet officers, ministers of state on their own responsibility gave him information in spite of her efforts to keep him a cipher in political affairs, and foreign diplomats credited him with influence that he did not have and talked with him freely. It was not until his personal friend, Lord Rosebery, became Foreign Secretary in 1886, when the Prince was in his forty-fifth year, that the foreign despatches were forwarded to him, and he was over fifty before the Queen's reluctant permission allowed him to read the reports of cabinet meetings. Though he was not an intellectual man, he had a retentive memory, and acquired a knowledge of men and affairs which made him a great influence in his time. Denied a military career by his mother, he had hoped for a government position. The proposal by ministers that the office of Lord Lieutenant of Ireland should be conferred on the Prince was vetoed by the Queen. This book reveals his important work in philanthropy, and his continued interest and activity in politics in spite of Victoria's prohibitions. He turned to society for recreation, and is best known before his accession to the throne as the leader in society and sport. From boyhood he had shown social gifts, and his friends ranged from the proletariat to royalty. Disraeli once spoke of him as "one who has seen everything and knows everybody." Queen Victoria looked with misgiving on his departure from the social exclusiveness of her husband's era. He loved good company, and was devoted and loyal to his friends. Friends introduced him into racing circles, and he ultimately had a large stable at Sandringham, and was twice the winner of the Derby. He was devoted to the theatre and a lover of good music. In his early years he formed a close intimacy with the great financiers of the Rothschild family. He ruffled the susceptibilities of the Austrian Court by his visit to that country to enjoy the hospitality of his Jewish friend, Baron Hirsch. There were few clubs in London of which he was not a member or a guest. He continued to enjoy foreign travel, and spent much time in France. In the War of 1870 the Queen was pro-German, and the sympathies of the Prince were with the French. His chivalrous offer of a home to the fugitive Empress was rated by the Queen as a piece of "presumptuous indiscretion." After his accession to the throne he was able to turn English policy from an Anglo-German entente, and achieve the Anglo-French entente. Much space is given to an unflattering picture of his nephew, William II of Germany, and the antagonism between the two men. The Kaiser was jealous of his uncle's influence and popularity, and they were continually in conflict. The resumé of the times takes up in detail the Samoan and Moroccan affairs, the efforts of William to provoke distrust between England and Russia, and his unfriendly conduct during the Boer War. In Edward's skilful handling of European international relations he rendered the greatest service to his country, though it is evident he was never his "own foreign minister," and acted within the limits of the constitution. The chapter on "The King and the Constitution" is an essay on the royal prerogative in English history. In spite of his popularity with his subjects, he found himself out of sympathy with many of the democratic tendencies that asserted themselves in the latter part of his brief reign. The character study of the King shows him to have been an honest, courageous, and kind English gentleman, and a hard worker. It is a laudatory biography, but the author does not disguise his subject's limitations, his preoccupation with matters of ceremony and dress, and his indifference to books and learning. This book denies that Edward had any intention of isolating and encircling Germany, as his German critics claimed, and insists that Edward ever worked for the peace of Europe, though Sir Sidney tells of his disapproval of the proposed Hague Conference, and notes his disgust with Campbell-Bannerman's article in "The Nation" in which he urges that Great Britain should propose an "arrest of armaments" at the Conference.

ELDER SISTER, THE, by Frank Swinnerton (1925), is a novel involving the customary triangle with some ramifications. Vera and Anne Treacher were sisters, both pretty typists with large firms in the West End of London, both in love with Mortimer, a handsome clerk of a suburban bank, both loved by men in the firms where they worked, to whom they were indifferent. Anne, the elder sister, although possessed of good brains and an admirable will power, a naturally friendly girl, was of a placid, unimaginative, almost stolid temperament. In contrast, Vera was serious, often moody, sometimes vivacious and always impulsive in her reactions toward life. Mortimer was weak but good natured, with little control over his inward life and impulses. Secret currents pulsed between the three friends, but each understood little of the baffling mystery that was in the hearts of the others. Vera's main preoccupation during business hours in Blankenburg's Universal Stores was in scorning the inane and plain typists who worked in the room with her and in evading the attentions of Mr. Harrow, a lanky and unprepossessing individual, whose admiration of her knew no discouragement. Mr. Sims, the active and determined new managing partner in Kilburn's publishing house, for all his air of a man about town, developed no less an appreciation of the elder sister's pleasant presence in his office. Then, restless, morose young Mortimer, vaguely jealous of Mr. Sims, and feeling the need of Anne's strength and repose of character, asked her to marry him. To Vera this meant the end of all her dreams of love. But the honeymoon was hardly over before Mortimer realized his mistake. Anne's equable love was no longer enough. He wanted the stimulation of Vera's passionate resistance and submission, the sense of being able to dominate and mould her life. Anne's strength antagonized him. Weakly he succumbed to the fire and challenge of Vera's personality. Shrewd and sympathetic little Mum suspects the tragic struggle of her daughters, but finds no way to avert the impending catastrophe. The characters of the three, no longer friends, are revealed with a fine precision; a wealth of delicate and subtle nuances differentiate them. Impetuously and uncontrollably Mortimer turns from the friendly love of his bride to the passionate prospects that Vera's presence inspires. That which quiet, wise little Mum fears comes to pass on a night when Mortimer and Vera treacherously meet. The ensuing disaster shows each in their true color. Mortimer and Vera run away selfishly certain of their right to happiness and the suffering, unselfish elder sister is left to recover from the shock to her love and faith. But she finds reassurance in the resources of her own character and the possibilities of a happier future under the management of Mr. Sims appear a not improbable dénouement.

EMERGENCE OF MODERN AMERICA, THE, by Allan Nevins (1927). The dozen years of reorganization and readjustment which followed the Civil War are here reviewed as marking the emergence of the new and modern Republic which, with one great era in American life at an end, struggled through a period of bewildering chaos, each section of the country making its own contribution to the national culture, to economic growth, intellectual life and social idealism. From 1865 to

1878 this narrative draws the picture of the changing conditions. The author finds the South, from Virginia to Texas, "dotted with towns which had been partly or completely ruined; business sections laid waste by fire; cities plundered; a chaos of crumbling walls; rotting wharves; smouldering wastes; transportation broken down; destitution; and with the new condition of freed negroes, a social revolution "the most sweeping and sudden that has ever affected a large part of the American population and an almost unique event in history." He follows the rapidly changing conditions of land tenure and labor, the struggle of the white ruling class to preserve its control, and sees in the late sixties, which he considers the "darkest days in the South," a social readjustment that was surer and more continuous than the political readjustment, with traces of the conflict, little by little, being erased. Simultaneously, the industrial boom in the North "pressed forward with a speed which seemed to leave all old landmarks behind and which year after year wrought new social changes." The development of the Pennsylvania oil fields, the manufacture of ready-made clothing, the enlarged output of cotton mills and of iron furnaces; the expansion of financial institutions; the stream of European immigration; the building of railways; the establishment of long-distance trunk lines, and the inexorable conquest of "lake and canal business" are all a phase of this period of thriving industry and post-War prosperity. As a result of this expansion, the author sees the rise of the American city to a new importance in American life. Urban modes and manners are discussed, "more and more the texture of American civilization was becoming urban in character." The author also turns his attention to the taming of the West, where, after the building of the transcontinental railway, and with the Indians pushed aside and pacified, cities sprang up as if by magic on the central plains. "Everywhere was heard the strident voice of the boaster." Stock breeding and agriculture are shown as the chief concern of the settlers in the region between the Mississippi and the Rockies, in the period under review, and the picturesque and hardy type of manhood in the cowboy made for a powerful influence upon the national character — a service which the range performed for American life. The author considers that the Far West gave national life a sense of spaciousness and adventure that it would otherwise have lacked. Stagecoach and immigrant train, mining rush and cattle round-up, Mexican mission and salmon fishery, Chinatown and Indian agency, made up a varicolored panorama that added breadth and brightness to the American scene. The revolt of the farmer forms a phase of this narrative which deals with the economic evils of various sections — a revolt which helped to create a class consciousness. But from the confusion and unsettlement, and a hurried, aggressive growth, the historian finds the birth of an alarming public and private corruption, which brought about "a moral collapse in government and business." The manners and morals of the times are discussed, and a review is made of the influences which made for the broadening and deepening of American culture, together with the tendencies which remoulded American life.

EMIGRANTS, THE, by Johan Bojer, translated from the Norwegian by A. G. Payne (1925), tells the story of the Norwegian pioneer settlers in America. The book opens in Norway with the roofing of a new house for farm hands at Dyrendal. Following a Norwegian building custom, a celebration is held. Miss Else, daughter of the Colonel of Dyrendal, spends much time with Ola Vatne, who is employed by her father. He is a young man of questionable reputation, so that night the Colonel dismisses Ola without an explanation. A few hours later a fire breaks out in the new building and destroys it. The farm foreman visits Ola Vatne at his home, asks him to put his hand on the Bible and swear he is innocent. He cannot, so the next day the sheriff drives out with handcuffs to arrest him but finds Ola gone. After a few nights the sheriff's place is set on fire. There is a rumor that Ola had said he would have every farm in the parish in ashes. The people are alarmed and keep the farms so well guarded after dark that it is dangerous for any outsider to go near them. The search for Ola continues for days. Finally two wood-cutters find him lying on the ground almost unrecognizable. He goes with them and is turned over to the sheriff. The Colonel is a witness during the trial and recommends mercy for Ola, saying the whole affair is a boyish prank. Partly due to this intercession, Ola gets only one year of imprisonment. Weeks later the Colonel learns from his daughter that she is determined to marry Ola when he comes out of prison. The return of Erik Foss from America, after seven years' absence, arouses much enthusiasm in the community. His marvellous tales of land to be had for nothing and easy to cultivate inspire the farmers. He offers to assist any who care to return with him and many respond. A varied group set out with him for America, among them Ola Vatne just out of prison. Unknown to her family, Else too accompanies the emigrants, as she and Ola have planned to be married by the captain of the ship when at sea. Their first year is spent in Wisconsin, where the men work in a sawmill and the women do the washing, cooking, and other household labors. But they are eager for their own land and soon go on to Northville, Dakota, which is still a territory, where Erik Foss has taken a claim on a quarter section, one hundred and sixty acres, for each of them. After securing their outfits, they start on their long ride over the prairie with ox teams to the land that now is theirs. The bare, bleak prairie so vastly different from their native country disheartens the pioneers, but soon the rich soil stimulates them to long hours of ploughing and they bravely face the struggle with the long, cold winters, the drought, the prairie fires, the locusts and the loneliness. But it is not of these hardships that they write to their friends in Norway. To them they tell of the wonderful possibilities in the new land, of the absence of class distinction, and their enthusiasm soon brings more emigrants to America. Erik Foss died during the first winter after the group had settled in Dakota and the leadership fell on Morten Kvidal. His love for his homeland still dominates his life and he longs to return to Norway and repurchase his father's home. Finally he goes, but soon realizes that his interest in the little settlement where he is recognized as leader is greater than his home ties, so after a time he returns. He finds Nidaros, which is the name the emigrants gave to their settlement, growing rapidly. The railway is soon to reach there. A bank and a hospital are planned. With the help of his wife, Else, Ola Vatne overcomes his weakness for liquor, and makes his farm one of the finest in the district. He becomes an ardent advocate of prohibition and makes speeches in favor of it, but dies before it is adopted by the state. Else has proved an admirable pioneer and is foremost in promoting the interests of the settlement. The emigrants feel a righteous pride in the great farms they won from the barren prairies. They appreciate the privilege of voting and becoming a part of the development of America, knowing that every opportunity lies open to their children.

EMINENT VICTORIANS, by Lytton Strachey (1918). Clear-cut, witty, unsentimental portraits of Cardinal Manning, Florence Nightingale, Dr. Arnold, and General Gordon, in which the interest is divided between the form and the subject. Includes sketches of many of their contemporaries, Newman, Gladstone, Clough, Sidney Herbert, Lord Panmure, and Lord Cromer. The author gives an outline of the events of the lives, the positions they filled, and through the intimate revelation of letters and diaries, discovers the forces and impulses that made them what they were. Manning at nine years old "devoured the Apocalypse," and never through his life forgot "the lake that burneth with fire and brimstone." The bankruptcy of his father prevented him from realizing his ambition for a political career. His father wished him to take orders, "but the thought disgusted him. The church was suggested to him as a field of work," but "it was only when the offer of a Merton Fellowship seemed to depend upon his taking orders that his heavenly ambitions began to assume a definite shape." He became a great politician and statesman, first in the Anglican and then the Catholic Church. "I am conscious of a desire," he wrote in his diary after he had become a Catholic, "to be in such a position (1) as I had in times past, (2) as my present circumstances imply, (3) as my friends think me fit for, (4) as I feel my own faculties tend to." Over and over again he vows to Heaven that he will seek nothing, "But, if something came to him — ? . . . he had not vowed not to take. Might it not be his plain duty to take? Might it not be the will of God?" Cardinal Newman is his foil in this study. He is able to prevent papal recognition of the one figure which "seemed to challenge the supremacy of his own." "The nature of Newman's influence was impossible for him to understand, but he saw that it existed . . . that singular, that alien, that rival renown" that "must be silenced at all cost." The popular conception of Florence Nightingale, the "saintly, self-sacrificing woman, the delicate maiden of high degree who threw aside the pleasures of a life of ease to succour the afflicted" is replaced by a more interesting figure than the legendary one, though one that is less agreeable. A nurse in her time meant a disreputable Mrs. Gamp, unable to carry out the simplest medical duties, and the change in this state of things was due to Miss Nightingale. Her opportunity came with the Crimean War and the complete breakdown of the medical service at the seat of War, through incompetent officials, lack of supplies at the hospitals, and incredible absence of cleanliness. "It was not by gentle sweetness and womanly self-abnegation that she . . . brought order out of chaos . . . and spread her dominion over the serried and reluctant powers of the official world; it was by strict method, by stern discipline, by rigid attention to detail, by ceaseless labour, by the fixed determination of an indomitable will." Her demoniac activity drove Sidney Herbert to his death, and the benevolence and public spirit and service of her long life were only equalled by her ruthlessness and acerbity. The headmaster of Rugby, whose character is chiefly known from the testimony of his remarkable influence on a great many distinguished men, to which Strachey also bears witness, gains nothing in reputation from this essay. The public schools of his day are described as "a spectacle of disorder and brutality," and "the very seats and nurseries of vice." Public opinion demanded a more liberal curriculum and a higher moral tone. In his plan for reform, Dr. Arnold decided "to treat the boys at Rugby as Jehovah had treated the Chosen People; he would found a theocracy." The elder boys deputed to keep order in the class-rooms were his "Judges of Israel." The curriculum continued to be essentially the teaching of Latin and Greek. His ideal was to make his students Christian gentlemen, and he was the founder of the worship of athletics, and "good form." "Chinese Gordon" was the hero of the hour, but for his distinguished services in China the English authorities rewarded him with an obscure post at Gravesend, supervisor of the erection of a system of forts. Later as governor-general of the Sudan he spent six years in "extraordinary, desperate, unceasing, and ungrateful labour." His last great adventure was occasioned by the revolt of the Mahdi. . The enthusiast, fighter, and bold adventurer was sent on a mission to conduct an inglorious retreat from the

Sudan, a policy which Gordon believed could not be justified. He remained in Khartoum until he forced the English Government, in spite of Gladstone's opposition, to send a force for his relief which could crush the Mahdi and retain the Sudan, but, due to political delay, the relief expedition did not arrive in time to save him. Gordon, like Manning, Miss Nightingale, and Dr. Arnold, identified his own indomitable will with the will of God.

EMPEROR JONES, THE, a play, by Eugene O'Neill (1921). An ex-porter on an American railroad, Brutus Jones, negro, escaped from prison, has made himself ruler of a tribe of blacks on an island in the West Indies, "from stowaway to Emperor in two years," he boasts. He tells his subjects that he bears a charmed life; only a silver bullet can kill him. In the first scene in the palace Henry Smithers, a mean cockney white trader finds out that while their emperor is asleep, his subjects have gone up to the hills to prepare for revolt. He convinces Jones that his Emperor days are over, and while they are talking the sound of the tom-tom starts in the distance. Jones has worked his subjects hard to put money in foreign banks for his return to civilization. His philosophy of life, learned from listening to "white quality talk" on the Pullman cars, he tells Smithers is "For de little stealin' dey gits you in jail soon or late. For de big stealin' dey makes you Emperor and puts you in de Hall of Fame when you croaks." He has to cross the forest to reach the refuge of a French gunboat. The next scenes are in the forest, where he loses his way and becomes hungry and afraid. He discards his fine uniform and the polished shoes which hinder his progress. The ghost of Jeff, Pullman porter, throwing dice in the game in which he had slashed him with a razor appears, and he fires at him, and for answer the beat of the tom-tom becomes more rapid. He tells himself that he is a member of the Baptist church and that it was hunger that made him imagine he saw the ghost. Then he has a vision of the convict gang and guard working on the road, relives the scene, and, having no shovel to fell the guard this time, fires another bullet. In terrified obsession he sees himself on an auction block of pre-war times with a group of southern planters bidding for him. "I shows you I'se a free nigger, damn yo' souls," he shouts, shooting at the auctioneer. In the next scene he is a galley slave rowing in a boat with other slaves. At five in the morning Jones is seen kneeling before an altar howling for mercy to a Congo witch-doctor, who in pantomine shows that the forces of evil demand sacrifice, pointing to a huge crocodile which appears in the river. Jones fires his last bullet at the crocodile. In the final scene the bad white, Smithers, taunts the blacks with their failure to pursue Jones, "wastin' the 'ole bloomin' night beatin' yer bloody drum and castin' yer silly spells." Shots are heard in the forest, and presently the soldiers come in with Jones's body riddled with silver bullets.

ENCHANTED APRIL, THE, by Countess Von Arnim, later Countess Russell (1922). An advertisement in the "Times" describing a small mediæval Italian Castle to be let furnished for the month of April captures the imagination of Mrs. Wilkins and Mrs. Arbuthnot, dutiful wives who need a vacation from homes and husbands. After a rainy day of shopping in London they find the picture of "Wistaria and Sunshine" too alluring to be resisted. To lighten the expense of the trip they in turn advertise for two other ladies to join them, and secure the company of Lady Caroline Dester, a young society beauty surfeited with the attentions of family and suitors, and an elderly widow, Mrs. Fisher, whose sole interest in life is celebrated Victorians she had known "when she was little." Mrs. Wilkins tells her husband that she has an invitation to visit a friend, and when he disbelieves her statement she is able to convince him by producing the Madonna-like Mrs. Arbuthnot. Rose Arbuthnot is the victim of a supersensitive conscience. Frederick, her husband, under the pseudonym of Ferdinand Arundel, writes popular memoirs of the mistresses of kings, and his wife has to live on the proceeds of the abandoned behavior of the ladies Du Barry, Montespan, and Pompadour. The fact that she and Frederick "draw their sustenance from guilt, however much purged by the passage of centuries, was one of the secret reasons of her sadness," and had estranged her from her husband. He lived in rooms in London, often not coming home to Hampstead for weeks at a time. She gave the money to the poor of the parish whose boots were therefore "stout with sins." The beauty of San Salvatore has an almost instant effect. Lotty Wilkins is so filled with love and unselfishness that she wants to share her happiness with the husband she had run away from, and writes to him to come to the Castle. Mr. Wilkins recognizes Lotty's new friend Lady Caroline as of the old and wealthy Droitwiches family, most desirable acquaintance and possible business connection for an ambitious lawyer, and arrives directly. He is on his best behavior even to his wife, the friend of Lady Caroline, and makes a conquest of the self-centred Mrs. Fisher, with his attentions and interest in her anecdotes of Carlyle, Tennyson, and the other great ones, as she also is a woman of wealth and might sometime need assistance in her affairs. The spell of the place and Lotty's joy makes Rose believe that San Salvatore might affect Frederick, and they might come to a better understanding, and she writes to him. Possibly her obstinate strait-lacedness about his books and absorption in good works has been a mistake. He comes to call on Lady Caroline, who knows him well as Mr. Arundel. Rose takes him to her heart as the answer to her letter, and Lady Caroline does not make any complications when she meets him at dinner as Mr. Arbuthnot by mentioning that they had ever met before. Love seemed to bring happiness to everyone but herself, thought Lady Caroline. She is kind to Mr. Briggs, the owner of the castle, when he comes to call on them, and falls instantly in love with her, as it is a pity anything so young and boyish should not be happy, and the buoyant Lotty sees the end from the beginnings of that affair, though Mellersh, her husband, is shocked that she should believe a Dester should so condescend.

EPISODES BEFORE THIRTY, by Algernon Blackwood (1924). An autobiography of vivid adventure and almost melodramatic incident. As the son of the widowed Duchess of Manchester and Sir Arthur Blackwood, once known in fashionable circles as "Beauty Blackwood," the knowledge of the world of the class in which he belonged was attributed to the boy of twenty sent to Canada to make his fortune. However, it happened that his parents had renounced the world to become leaders in a narrow evangelical sect, and their children were "cut off from the amenities of the social life" to which they were born in a home where a guest might be invited to lead in prayer or was liable at any moment to be asked if he "had given his soul to Jesus." He missed a position on the Canadian Pacific Railroad because at the first ball he had ever attended he "had not the slightest idea that the correct and polite thing to do was to ask each young lady for the pleasure of a dance," and thus offended a high official of the road who considered he had snubbed his sister. With his "unique ignorance of life" he became easy prey to a swindler who induced him to invest in a dairy business. When this failed he went into partnership with his friend, John Kay, in the purchase of a small tavern in Toronto, which went bankrupt in six months. His father, a temperance reformer, hearing of this latest venture, told his brother with tears in his eyes that Algie had gone to hell, his soul was lost. The two friends took a delightful holiday of several months in the primeval woods of a Canadian island lake before they started for New York to find work. New York is the scene of the greater part of the narrative. Three Englishmen, all over six feet in height, lived and starved in a small hall-bedroom in a cheap boarding house in East 19th Street. Blackwood secured a position as a reporter on the "New York Sun" at $15 a week, the only certain source of income for them all. They learned to cook porridge over the gas jet, and discovered that to eat strips of dried apple followed by a drink of hot water was most economical food, as the false repletion lasted longer. Blackwood became ill from undernourishment. All this time a sense of pride prevented him from letting his family know how his affairs stood, and his belief in Karma (he had become a Buddhist at seventeen) led him to accept his painful experiences as his due with a kind of indifferent resignation. Kay had left with a theatrical touring company. Blackwood was alone, dependent on his other friend, Arthur Boyde, and the kind German doctor, Otto Huebner, victim of the drug habit, his only comfort the reading of his copy of the Bhagavad-Gita. A young English actor whom he had met but once pawned his overcoat to buy food for Blackwood. Through him he learned what he had begun to suspect that his companion Boyde was a criminal who had "spotted" Kay and Blackwood from the start as inexperienced and generous, and good for a free lodging. They forced him to a confession and gave him another chance, which he used to borrow money for himself in Blackwood's name, pretending that he was paying the expenses of his illness. He stole some money given to Blackwood and left him alone and helpless in bed for four days without food while the funds lasted. Boyde finally left in the night with every possible pawnable article including Blackwood's clothes. Blackwood determined to put Boyde where he could no longer harm himself and others, and swore out a warrant for his arrest on a charge of forgery and theft, and after a long chase he ran him down in a saloon and had him convicted. He and Kay escaped from the city on a wild-goose chase for gold into Ontario, a glorious interlude to the nature loving Blackwood. After two and a half years reporting on the "New York Times," Blackwood's first good fortune came with the position of secretary to James Speyer, pleasant work, a good salary, and a friendly employer. The story ends just before his thirtieth birthday with his return to England.

ESCAPE, an episodic play, by John Galsworthy (1926). A war hero, Captain Matt Denant, sitting on a bench in Hyde Park, London, in the evening, drifts into casual conversation with a young woman of the streets. As Denant strolls away, a detective who has been watching them, arrests the girl. Denant comes to her defense to protest that she had neither "accosted" nor "molested" him, gets into an argument with the officer who threatens to arrest him also, and knocks him down. The man strikes his head against an iron rail as he falls and they find he is dead. Denant is sentenced to prison for five years for manslaughter. The nine succeeding episodes of the play are the story of his attempt to escape from prison as he had done from a German prison camp. In the first episode he is picking potatoes on the prison farm at Dartmoor, and takes advantage of the fog to jump over the wall. Two wardens almost catch him on the road that night in the darkness, but find they are struggling with each other, and that he has slipped away. The next night he manages to get into the Inn and conceal himself under a bed, intending to be off again by daybreak, but he oversleeps and apologizes for his presence to the young married woman whose room it is when she sees him behind the door. She has heard of the famous case, and knows that he is not an ordinary criminal. The situation appeals to her sporting instincts and she helps him to escape in her husband's fishing clothes, giving him chocolate, a flask, and some money. Fishing on the bank of a stream, he meets a retired judge who recognizes him, discusses the case, and admitting that the detective was doing his duty, still questions the danger of giving the police discretion on morals, considering that most human beings have no discretion and the rest lack morals. The kindly old gentleman calls him by name as he says good-by, and wishes him a pleasant journey. His next encounter is with a group of lower middle-class picnickers, whose reaction to the news that there is an escaped convict abroad is that of human bloodhounds. With their Ford car Denant would have a chance to get away if there were not constables stationed on the road ahead. A couple he asks for directions have different points of view. The pompous husband wants to hand him over to the police and the wife would like to drive him past the constables to safety. The exhausted fugitive takes refuge in a gravel pit on the edge of the moor, where he is found by two laborers and a farmer. He manages to give them the slip, and the little girl with the farmer, attracted by his pleasant manner, gives the constable a misleading direction to prevent his capture. Two maiden ladies are having tea as Denant jumps in their window and with a gesture of appeal hides from his pursuers behind their window curtain. Miss Dora gives him a cup of tea and both the sisters lie to save him, the one gladly and the other reluctantly. He leaves the safety of their cottage as they quarrel about giving him shelter, and reaches the vestry of the village church just before evening service. The parson tells him he cannot give him the sanctuary he claims, but he can rest in the church. Denant does not make the problem any easier by asking what Christ would have done in this situation. It is his own peace of mind and his influence in the parish that troubles the parson, he confesses. There is a loud knocking on the locked door, and the parson hides Denant in a closet behind the surplices and cassocks. His rough parishioner, the farmer Browning, asks the parson whether on his honor as a Christian gentleman he has or has not seen the escaped convict, and after a moment of silence Denant comes out and gives himself up to avoid incriminating the parson. He says to him, "It's one's decent self one can't escape." The parson agrees and convicts himself as a coward.

ETERNAL HUSBAND, THE, by Fyodor Dostoevsky (1917), is a story whose tragedy is subtly concealed under the surface flow of events. Velchaninov, a man of the world grown a little weary as he nears his fortieth year, is dawdling through the summer in St. Petersburg held there by a lawsuit upon the settlement of which his future fortune depends. His restless, depressed mood worries him until he traces it to the effect on him of a man with crêpe on his hat who has dogged his steps for some days. One night this man reveals his identity. He is Pavel Pavlovitch Trusotsky, husband of that Natalya Vassilyevna whom Velchaninov had loved in the provincial town of T—— some ten years before. Velchaninov remembered the woman as hardly beautiful except when she became animated. She was very thin, not very well educated, though a woman of intelligence, determination and considerable artistic taste. Velchaninov had passed a very happy year there, continuing on friendly terms with the husband, who remained unaware that he had become the wife's lover. And then she abruptly dismissed him. Later Velchaninov discovers that Pavel Pavlovitch has a little girl, Liza, with him in St. Petersburg. From something that Trusotsky lets fall he believes Liza really to be his own daughter, born some months after his departure. He becomes intensely interested in her. Suspecting the man of a malicious feeling toward the girl, Velchaninov prevails on him to allow her to go to his old friend, Klavdia Petrovna, to be cared for with her own family in their summer villa until Trusotsky finishes his business in St. Petersburg. Liza mourns so for the man she looks upon as her father that, when he does not come to see her, she falls ill of a fever and dies. It is with the greatest difficulty that Velchaninov finds Trusotsky among the low companions to whom he has in his morbid mood resorted, in time to procure the proper legal forms for the child's burial. Velchaninov had dreamed that through loving and caring for Liza he might retrieve an idle and dissipated life and is stunned by her loss. Some time afterward Trusotsky reappears prosperous and well-clothed and announces that he has been accepted by the parents of a young girl of good family as her betrothed. Her childlike innocence is her chief attraction for him. The girl refuses to have anything to do with him and shows marked preference for Velchaninov at a party to which Trusotsky dragged him. That night Trusotsky stays with Velchaninov and devotes himself to the relief of the man he calls his friend when he has a severe attack of illness, until Velchaninov is eased into slumber, when he attempts to stab him. Velchaninov wakes in time to struggle for his life. Later as Trusotsky is leaving for his province, he sends Velchaninov an old yellowed letter found after his wife's death which reveals the fact that he has known Liza was not his but Velchaninov's child since that time. Pavel Pavlovitch Trusotsky appears to Velchaninov as the type of the eternal husband, a man whose real qualities can only appear in their normal balance in his character when he has a wife whose innocence he can protect and care for. Without a wife he is lost, has no object in life. But his boundless devotion is such that he is always doomed to be betrayed. When Velchaninov last meets him he is at a provincial railway station travelling with a fussy woman, whom he introduces as his wife, and a younger man. The triangle, Velchaninov notes, is again complete.

EXPRESSING WILLIE, by Rachel Crothers (1924). Willie Smith, a newly rich young man from the Middle West, has built an Italian palace on Long Island, which is so palatial that his mother does not find it homelike. She sees that Willie is falling into the clutches of a group of parasites and cheating, self-expressionists, and is likely to marry Frances Sylvester, a fascinating divorcée, who has serious designs on the fortune that Willie has made in toothpaste. Determined to rescue her son, she invites Minnie Whitcomb, the home-town music teacher, who had been Willie's sweetheart in the old days in Tuckerville, to come and stay with them. Minnie arrives on the eve of a week-end party, happy that Willie, whom she adores, has thought of her again. Willie hears about Minnie's visit for the first time from his mother while Minnie is in her room changing for dinner. He rises to the situation, and introduces her to Taliaferro, the noted painter, the first of the guests to arrive. The timid, shrinking girl listens to the glib talk about the necessity of expressing one's self, and is greatly impressed. She has been awkward and measured her length on the polished floor when she tried to play for them, and is at first mortified and unhappy. An instant convert to self-expression, she rallies after dinner, and plays as one inspired, astounding the others with her genius. She now wants to help Willie to express himself, and goes to his room at a late hour to talk with him. There is a knock at the door and Willie hides her in a closet, and locks the door. Frances Sylvester comes to borrow one of Willie's "delicious cigarettes," and then settles down to enjoy it. She is most seductive in her negligée, but Willie is in an agony of embarrassment at Minnie's presence in the closet. When she can stand it no longer, Minnie pounds to be let out. Frances implies the worst about Minnie, and declares that she will leave in the morning rather than stay in the house with her. Minnie says that she will tell everything to the other guests, Taliaferro, Mr. and Mrs. Cadwallader, and Willie's mother. Dolly Cadwallader has known Frances long and well, and senses that there is something wrong since Frances is so anxious to prevent Minnie from telling the story. Mrs. Smith calls Minnie "a little fool." The Cadwalladers offer Willie their congratulations on his engagement to Frances. Taliaferro's praises of Minnie, who he thinks may become a great musician, shows Willie his own feeling for Minnie, and rouses him to a realization of her genuine honesty and worth. He proposes to her, kisses her, and when she protests that he must marry Frances and continue to express himself, he answers: "I'm expressing myself all right — and I'm going to keep right on." This nice, commonplace young man, who had been uncertain, as Mrs. Smith said, "whether he's God — or a tadpole" had found himself.

FABULOUS FORTIES, THE, 1840-1850, a presentation of private life, by Meade Minnigerode (1924). This decade in America, the author says, "was a brilliant three ring circus, filled with marvellous side shows and prodigious natural curiosities, glittering with mirrors and chandeliers, thunderous with brass bands and fireworks, choked with the dust of glorious caravans." From contemporary newspapers and books he reconstructs this "awkward age" of New York manners, what people wore, what they ate, the books they read, what they saw at the theatres, and the social events of the day. In 1842 the stores advertised "Muslin for Ascension Robes" for the Millerites preparing for the Day of Judgment. On Broadway, the "most fashionable of all American streets," expensively dressed women in furs, and satins, with ostrich feathers in their pink and blue rohan bonnets were "escorted by beaux in Byron collars and richly tasseled cloaks, with whiskers under their chins — stepping over the pigs." There was no finer hotel in the country than the Astor House, and the Hoboken House at "beautiful, rosy Hoboken" was a favorite summer resort. The election of 1840 was won for "Tippecanoe and Tyler too" by General Harrison, on the slogan of the log cabin without any party platform, against Martin Van Buren, described in the press as "a monarchist in principle, a tyrant and a despot in practice." Parades in every city had canoes and log cabins on wheels as the chief feature of the candidacy of the plain man against "the Wall Street cliques." Woman's sphere was the home, and the perfect lady was "equally capable of entertaining in the parlor and managing in the kitchen." Social functions were rated successful on the basis of the amount of money expended and represented. The social news reports, "Probably at no recent soirée have so many fine fortunes and pretty women been present. At a fair valuation about $4,500,000 of property in stocks and real estate at present prices were represented by the fair ones present." Ferdinand, Prince de Joinville, third son of Louis Philippe, came to America, and was entertained with balls and banquets. Fanny Essler, the dancer, made a triumphal tour of the country. Another visitor, Mr. Charles Dickens, was "the literary guest of the nation," and subsequently wrote his "American Notes" which roused a tempest of resentment. The polka was introduced to fashionable society by Mr. Korponay, a retired officer in the Hungarian army, became the rage all over the country, and was rated as an indecent "introduction of foreign licentiousness and corrupt manners." Mr. Barnum began his career with a museum, in which he exhibited his freaks. The most popular entertainments of the Forties were negro minstrels and lurid melodrama at the theatre. There was a great civic celebration of the completion of the Croton Aqueduct, "the proudest day for the city that its inhabitants had ever seen since the discovery of this part of the world by Hendrick Hudson, and perhaps since the fast anchored isle of Manhattan emerged from the general deluge." The festivities began with the firing of cannon at dawn, and ended with a magnificent parade. The last chapter, "Ho for California," describes the settlement of California, and the discovery of gold there. Extracts from the letters of a pioneer give details of the risks of the journey and the rough life of the Forty-niners' San Francisco.

FAINT PERFUME, by Zona Gale (1923). Leda Perrin, a young writer sentenced to a year of rest because of neuritis in her arm, returns from New York to her father in the country rectory at Prospect. He has invested in a copper mine in Montana, talks of a trip to Sicily on the fortune that he is going to make, and then dies after a fortnight's illness, never knowing that he has left his daughter penniless. She is obliged to make her home with her uncongenial cousins, the Crumbs. There is Orrin, the travelling salesman, hail-fellow-well-met, exuding *epprit*, with his continual advice to his women-folk to stop their jangling, and his commonplace wife, Tweet, whose solicitude for others is a sort of meddlesome envy. Tweet longs to adopt a six-year old girl with curls, because she would like to make her pretty dimity dresses, but has no interest in her own nephew of that age. Mrs. Crumb, the mother, Pearl, her daughter, of an "over-ripe sweetness," and the pathetic Grandfather Crumb, lonely in the noisy, vulgar circle, make up the family. The sensitive Leda has nothing in common with them, and refuses to quarrel or answer back, so that they dislike her superiority. She is glad to hear that the beauty of the family, Richmiel, is coming home for a visit, with her husband, Barnaby, a writer, though she cannot picture Barnaby, whose distinction she remembers though she had seen him only once at the wedding nine years before, in the stifling atmosphere of the Crumb household. Her expectation is disappointed as Richmiel, and her son, Oliver, arrive alone. Barnaby and Richmiel have arranged a divorce in Paris, but Richmiel says that Prospect folk can be told that Barnaby was not able to get away. A telegram comes from Barnaby that he is coming to Prospect. He misses Oliver, who adores his father, and is able to persuade Richmiel to let him have the child part of the year, as she cares only for herself, and had intended to leave Oliver with her family while she spent the winter in California. Barnaby recognizes Leda's fine quality, and there arises between them love which is peace, harmony and completion. She goes to Chicago to the studio of a friend, and Barnaby comes to see her to ask her to marry him. The telephone rings announcing the arrival of Orrin and Tweet in search of Pearl, who has run away with the postman. Richmiel is with them, and asks why Barnaby is there. She refuses to allow Barnaby to have Oliver if he marries Leda. They are obliged to renounce their happiness to her selfishness for the sake of the child, who cannot bear the separation from his father. The deceived Pearl comes to Leda, who manages to shake her complacent composure and take her back to Prospect, where she tells the family she has been in Chicago for a day's shopping. Poor old Grandfather Crumb, who alone had made the house bearable to Leda, finds out that he is going blind, and drowns himself rather than be dependent. Barnaby follows Leda to Prospect and they part again secure in their love and understanding. He thinks it may not be for long, as Richmiel will probably marry, and be glad to be finally rid of the boy, but Leda's greater courage faces the truth that there is little chance of escape for her, and that she will have only the "faint perfume" of romance instead of the fruition of love.

FAR AWAY AND LONG AGO, A HISTORY OF MY EARLY LIFE, by W. H. Hudson (1918). The naturalist's childhood and youth were spent on the pampas of

South America, and he describes the great grassy plains dotted with small islands of trees. The house where he was born was called "The Twenty-five Ombú Trees," named for the surrounding gigantic indigenous trees, the branches of which made a playhouse for the children as well as a nesting place for the birds. "My feathered friends," he says, "were so much to me that I am constantly tempted to make this sketch of my first years a book about birds and little else." He says that he himself was "just a little wild animal running about on its hind legs amazingly interested in the world in which it found itself." A great adventure was his first sight of flamingos, and when he was older the hunting of wild ducks, and golden plover. Every aspect of the plains is described, the changes of the seasons, "the water-like mirage" of the rainy season, the giant thistles, great pampero storms of hail, and fierce winds, and fires in the grass. The writer describes the plantation life, the herds of cattle and wild horses, and the cruel sports of the gauchos who herded the cows, with character sketches of typical heroes such as Barboza, the great fighter, and singer of ballads of his own composition. The observant little boy tells about the adventurers of this remote region who came to his father's hospitable home, the blind beggar on horseback who levied tribute for his support, the insane hermit doing penance for some crime, the succession of tutors for the children, Mr. Trigg, the actor, a tyrant in the schoolroom, but the delightful comrade and entertainer of the family until his weakness for drink put an end to his stay, the unholy priest, the English and Spanish neighbors, Mr. Royd, and Don Gregorio, with his passion for piebald horses, Don Anastacio, devoted to pigs, Don Evaristo Peñalva, the grand old man of the plains, the husband of six wives. He recalls his first visit to the city of Buenos Ayres, one of his earliest memories. The fall of the tyrant, Rosas, led to troublous times for the country. The death of an old dog friend gives him his first thoughts of death and immortality, and a later illness, which did not prove fatal as the doctors prophesied, turned his mind to religion and the working out of a philosophy of life.

FATA MORGANA (Mirage), a comedy, by Ernest Vajda (1925). Fata Morgana is the Italian name of the fairy, Morgan le Fay, step-sister of King Arthur and pupil of Merlin, and her name is used to designate the mirage which she is supposed to create. The author of this play calls his heroine, Mrs. Fay. She comes to spend the night in the country with some relations of her husband in order to attend the Anna Ball, a village celebration and all-night dance. The Budapest coquette arrives on the same train that the family take to go on to Gabroc for the ball, and she finds only George, the eighteen year old student left at home for punishment. The telegram announcing her visit has not been sent from the local post office, there are no more trains that night, and no carriage for her to take as even the servants have gone to the Anna Ball. George falls in love at sight with his beautiful cousin, Mathilde, as she asks him to call her. She is pleased with her conquest of the charming boy, so different from her admirers at Budapest. George is enchanted not to be treated like a child. Mathilde leads him on to make love to her and gayly promises to divorce her husband and marry him. She sends him to bed and then opens the door and goes to him. The next morning the family return, and bring Gabriel, Mathilde's husband, who had been in Gabroc on business. He has a surprise for his wife, the gift of the fee from his client, which means to her the coveted trip to Ostend at the height of the season, and the latest things in clothes to wear. Sparkling with joy she changes her mind about staying in the country and plans to return home that day with Gabriel. George, still under the spell of the night before, almost ruins everything for her, by declaring to Gabriel that Mathilde is his fiancée, and that she is going to get a divorce and marry him. To save herself Mathilde says that George is mad and lying about her. This ending to his romance is George's first bitter lesson of disillusion. Mathilde tells George that she must have "the city, clothes, and jewellery, books and the theatre, conversation," and appeals to the chivalry of the proud, sensitive boy not to make her pay for one evening with her entire life. For her sake he tells Gabriel that nothing he said was anything but his own imagination, and thus sacrifices to Mathilde his pride and sense of honor. The jealous Gabriel is appeased, and reconciled to his wife, and they take the train for Budapest. George's father understands the tragedy that has happened to George and realizes that he is no longer a child. As the play ends George thanks his father for permission to take a trip if he likes, and begins to study the lesson Mathilde had interrupted two nights before.

FATHERS OF THE REVOLUTION, by Philip Guedalla (1924), presents, in the new psychological manner of interpretation, sketches of a few scenes in the lives of twelve men each connected in some way with the American Revolution. "H. M. King George III" pictures the king as a mild, domestic, inquisitive person, brought up by a careful mother. He attended to his kingly duties punctiliously and went the even tenor of his way, in war or peace, until he died at seventy, insane and muttering gently. "H. M. King Louis XVI" he says was "a little dull." Stupidly he went about his duties and his pleasures, always responding a little vaguely to the promptings of his ministers and attendants. "The Right Hon. Lord North, K. G.," who looked so much like King George III, whose friend he was until the end of his life, was Prime Minister of England before and during a part of the Revolution. He was an accomplished and agreeable man, with an unprepossessing countenance and was "(with his sovereign and General Washington) the official architect of the Republic." "The Right Hon. Earl of Chatham" believed "that the Parliament has a right to bind, to restrain America," and that "we may bind their trade, confine their manufactures." But he insisted "that this Kingdom has no right to lay a tax upon the colonies." As a result that man of illnesses and oddities and strangely unlogical sayings was very popular in America. "The Right Hon. Edmund Burke," who supported the colonies in the days of the Revolution "became more American than the English and far more English than the Americans." He lived to see all his predictions about America come true. "Lieutenant-General John Burgoyne" had much experience of war both in theory and practice. He had a marvellous theory about coming down from Canada with his forces and uniting with General Howe's forces at Albany, and with their combined soldiery he intended to cut the colonies into two factions. His orders were signed and he departed on his errand, but unfortunately Howe's orders never reached him. So Burgoyne met his defeat and laid one more paving stone in the path to American independence. "Lieutenant-General Earl Cornwallis," pompous and suave, lost at the siege of Yorktown and laid the final stone in the path to American success. In after years he was active in many of Britain's foreign affairs and forgot the fall of Yorktown. But all his other deeds are forgotten and the failure at Yorktown is still remembered by the world. "General Washington" is pictured as a gentleman of the true English tradition; stately, a little stiff, fond of fox hunting and even conducting battles in the traditional fashion. He lived in that grave tradition of good manners; and "in it, with an unwavering finger on his pulse, he gravely died." "Dr. Franklin" in contrast to Washington was the first American. Simple, witty, unpretentious, he nevertheless had great influence in the foreign affairs of his country both before and after the Revolution. Though he never expected to stand before kings he actually stood before five before his work was finished; and as Washington was the father of his country Franklin was the "father of American humour." "Mr. Samuel Adams" had a "harsh and sometimes halting voice" and yet it was "the first voice of the Revolution." As early as 1769 he was urging revolt and freedom from the mother country. He was always talking and talking in his peculiar voice and the burden of his talk was always the same. "If the Revolution dawned in Boston, Mr. Adams was its morning-star." "Mr. Alexander Hamilton," the little lion from the West Indies, had so often wished there was a war. He finally had his wish and fought in the Revolution and when "his elders had drummed out the king Hamilton played in the new Republic." And he played his part well in the Treasury of the new country; he founded a bank, consolidated debts and encouraged commerce as an item in the national accounts. "One can almost say that the United States were a product of his bookkeeping." "M. de La Fayette" was looking for adventure, and romance was dead in France. So he embarked for the country across the *triste plaine* of the North Atlantic for here was a country which had declared its independence. He knew little about it except that there was a war. Valiantly this boy of nineteen served the country without pay through some years of the war, winning respect and honor from the colonists. Always in his after-life he viewed all wars as like the Revolution in America and went his high-minded way to fight them.

FIRST AMERICANS, THE, by Thomas Jefferson Wertenbaker (1927). That period of history from 1607 to 1690 supplies the material for this era of American development in which the author traces the historical sequences of the thirteen English colonies, when the English people "first planted themselves in the New World" and thus became our "First Americans," and on through the seventeenth century, — in the interval, the "tender plant of European civilization taking firm root." The author treats of the causes which led to the American Revolution and holds that the separateness of Britain and her colonies was based upon distance, upon soil, climate and geography, all of which shaped the destiny, in his opinion, of the colonies. The story of English expansion, the economic phases of the great undertaking of the London Company, are treated as an interesting experiment in the history of colonization, and as a background for the economic and social structures of the colonies. The tobacco colonies are shown to have introduced a system of immigration which became the foundation of economic life for almost a century. The establishment of the Puritan settlements in Massachusetts and the economic and social fabric of New England, together with the beginnings of its industrial system and other distinctive features of life, are contrasted with the community organization of the South. The "old school churchmen" and the part they played in civil government gave way to the ideas which the author discusses under liberalism and the widening of human sympathies which marked, in his opinion, the fall of the New England theocracy. Of the transplanted Anglican Church to Virginia, the author discovers profound changes which were wrought in this institution. Of witchcraft, he discusses the New England excesses, which finally led to the reaction which he calls the growth of rationalism which was destined eventually to sweep the civilized world. The author also deals with the dangers to which the colonists were subjected through ignorance of hygiene, and the contagious diseases which surrounded them, together with the lack of competent medical assistance; "colonial medicine was less efficient in 1690 than in 1640, for the physicians of the second generation had a more imperfect training than those who migrated from England." He holds that the advance in medicine in Europe found no reflection in America.

Special chapters are concerned with the rigid code of personal conduct and the crude ideas concerning crime and its punishment which the colonists held, with the conclusion that, measured by contemporaneous European standards, the "settlers were notably humane." The beginnings of an intellectual life and the establishment of schools, from the author's viewpoint, were of slow growth by reason of the large degree of isolation and the fact that no leisure class existed in what was still British America. The colonists, both in Virginia and New England, "were still in the stage of accumulation." In the judgment of the author, neither books nor schools shaped the education of the Virginian or Marylander as much as life upon the plantation. Of the planter and Puritan, and the differences in the motives of their emigration, it is shown that their tastes and deportment were very similar. But the two sections developed on different lines. The social instincts and the various forms of recreation of the Southern colonists are contrasted with the more circumscribed pleasures of the New Englander. The homes of seventeenth-century Americans are shown to have been simple but not crude, the mode of transportation to have been largely by boat. In all the colonies the ordinary or tavern was a centre of life, but the history of architecture and travel during the seventeenth century illustrates, in the words of the author, the play of forces in the transit of civilization from the Old World to the New. The colonists are shown to have clung to the practices of the mother country, but the forces which were operating to change them from Englishmen to Americans are summed up in the outstanding accomplishments which the author lists in his final observations of the progress of the century.

FISHMONGER'S FIDDLE, by A. E. Coppard (1925) is a collection of seventeen simple tales most of which deal with homely events in the lives of English country folk. The characterizations are excellent and the situations whether comic or tragic are described with rare skill. "Old Martin" the first tale, tells of a retired old sea captain pursued by a belief in a superstition that the last person to be buried in a graveyard must slave for the other lost souls. After the death of his niece he finds no rest until another death occurs in the village. In "The Little Mistress" the charming wife of a busy doctor loses interest in her lover because her stupid servant-maid secretly reads and revels in the love letters he sends her. "Willia Waugh" is a short character sketch of a stubborn man refusing to do a favor for a neighbor and later forcing it on him. "The Higgler" tells of a simple young dealer in poultry and eggs who marries a poor girl although he has been asked by a rich farmer woman to marry her daughter. He admires the daughter greatly but feels that since she is so above him there must be some insidious reason for the unusual proposal. Later the mother dies and he learns that she had made the request only because her daughter loved him and wanted to marry him. "The Jewel of Jeopardy" is a tragic tale of a "calamitous girl." From her birth calamity followed in her wake, bringing death or misfortune to anyone with whom she was associated. Her only love affair ended in tragedy and later she became blind and was still pursued by her Nemesis. In "The Watercress Girl" Mary MacDowall, a country maid, betrayed by a young villager, threw acid on the girl he later planned to marry and disfigured her for life. Mary is imprisoned for months and when released, her former lover seeks her and plans to disfigure her. But seeing her in all her beauty and learning that she had borne him a child which had died, he is again attracted to her. "A Wildgoose Chase" tells of Martin Beamish, who, at thirty-five, desires freedom and suggests to his wife that they separate for a while. She demurs but finally agrees and goes to Italy. Soon he tires of his freedom and wishing her back, follows her to Italy. But she has found happiness and refuses to return with him. "Dumbledon Donkey" describes the amusing capture and later the burial of an old donkey by some rustics. In "A Three Handed Reel" the wife of a soldier involves him in a murder while attempting to shield him from arrest for desertion. "The Snare" relates the advice given by an innkeeper to a traveller that all women are snares. "Fishmonger's Fiddle," the title story, tells of Maxie Morrisgarde, who, deserted by her husband, found refuge with a very strait-laced aunt and uncle. When a young fiddler falls in love with her, she longs to go with him but cannot face divorce nor the disapproval of her relatives, so solemnly promises never to see him again. In "A Little Boy Lost" the parents of a timid child try in every way to interest him in games or toys but he remains apathetic. He grows up listless and useless and ends as a helpless invalid. "A Diversion with Thomas" tells how a holiday journey to an historical old town is utterly ruined by a band of schoolboys. "Mr. Lightfoot in the Green Isle" describes intimate encounters during a visit to Ireland.

FOREVER FREE, a novel of Abraham Lincoln, by Honoré Willsie Morrow (1927). This historical novel, carefully documented, deals with the plots, counterplots and undercurrents of hostility and treachery that surrounded Lincoln from the moment of his taking office in March, 1861, until the issuing of the final Emancipation Proclamation, New Year's Day, 1863. The author introduces a beautiful Southern spy, Miss Annabel Ford, into the Lincoln household as Mary Lincoln's social secretary, to guide her skilfully among the rocks and reefs of supercilious Washington society. Miss Ford is a passionate Confederate, devoted to the maintenance of the institution of slavery, and perfectly frank about expressing her sentiments. Her outspoken partisanship amuses Lincoln. For a while she gulls completely, not only the Lincolns, but John Hay and George Nicolay, the Executive Secretaries. Little Willie Lincoln dies in her arms. Mary Lincoln depends on her in all things. Miss Ford falls in love with Lincoln, and becomes his bitter enemy when he does not respond to her advances. So successfully does she insinuate herself into the good graces of the White House family and staff that it is a long time before they can believe that she is guilty of treachery. Disguised as a colored waiter she gets back to the White House to try to assassinate Lincoln before he signs the Emancipation Proclamation, and is killed in a fracas with a servant before the detectives discover her identity. Lincoln orders a coffin and decent funeral at his expense for his "evil genius." The historical characters in the book are Horace Greeley, General McClellan, William Russell, General Fremont, Stanton and many others.

FORSYTE SAGA, THE, by John Galsworthy (1906–1920). Includes three books, 'The Man of Property," "In Chancery," and "To Let," with two new "interludes" linking them together, "The Indian Summer of a Forsyte," and "Awakening," making the history of a typical upper middle-class family of the Victorian era and the first twenty years of this century. According to the family tree appended, the founder of the family was a certain Jolyon Forsyte, farmer, born in 1741. His grandchildren are the old people of the present generation, Jolyon, James, Swithin, Roger, Nicholas, Timothy, and four sisters, "Aunt Juley," "Aunt Hester," "Aunt Susan," "Aunt Ann." The clan have gathered at tea at the house of "Old Jolyon" in June 1886 to celebrate the engagement of his granddaughter, June Forsyte, to a young architect, Philip Bosinney. June's father, young Jolyon, had left his wife, now dead, to run away with a foreign governess, and they had been married now for six years and had two children. Soames Forsyte, son of James, is "the man of property," the most progressive of the family, which young Jolyon, not true to type, describes "as the pillars of society, the cornerstones of convention. . . . They possess . . . the power of never being able to give yourself up to anything soul and body, and the sense of property." The story develops the struggle between the ideas symbolized by Soames and those symbolized by Irene, his wife, and young Jolyon, rebels against ownership. Irene, the author says, is "a concretion of disturbing Beauty impinging on a possessive world." She had been unhappy with a stepmother, and yielded to Soames' persistent courtship, and has tried for three years to make the best of her mistake. She wants the personal freedom that Soames had promised her but refuses to give. The architect, Bosinney, is building a house for Soames in the country. He and Irene fall in love and June's engagement is broken. Soames forcibly asserts his rights of possession in Irene, and brings suit against Bosinney for money expended beyond contract for the house to ruin him, and the young man in distraction of mind is either a suicide or killed by accident crossing the street. Irene leaves Soames and supports herself by giving music lessons. In "The Indian Summer," old Jolyon is reconciled to his son and happy with his grandchildren. June and young Jolyon are away, and the lonely old man is happy to meet Irene on the grounds of the house he has bought from Soames, where she had come for memory's sake. The last weeks of his life are filled with joy and peace by her companionship and charm. "In Chancery," twelve years later, Soames is troubled by the realization that he has no son to inherit his property. He goes to see Irene and tells her that she is still his wife and tries to induce her to return to him. She turns to Jolyon, who looks after the income his father left her, for protection, and advice. Soames has her shadowed, follows her to Paris, and practically forces her into the relation of corespondent with Jolyon, in order to get a divorce. At the last he comes to Jolyon's house where Irene is staying and threatens to bring them to court with every circumstance of disgrace unless they will swear not to see each other again. Of the younger generation, Val, the son of Soames' sister Winifred, meets Holly and Jolly, Jolyon's children, and makes love to Holly and fights with Jolly. The two boys join the Yeomanry and are off to South Africa to fight the Boers. Val is wounded, and Jolyon does not forbid Holly to go out to marry him, though he tells her that he does not like that branch of the family. Jolyon's son dies of the fever. Soames marries Annette, a French girl, as soon as he gets his divorce, and is bitterly disappointed that their child is a girl, but the sight of the baby, whom they call Fleur, gives him a triumphant sense of possession. A son is born to Irene and Jolyon the same year. In "To Let," the two young people, Fleur and Jon, ignorant of their parent's past, meet and fall in love. They keep their Romeo and Juliet idyl secret because Fleur senses that there is opposition, and gets the truth about the family feud. She is a Forsyte, and though exquisite and charming, is her father's daughter, determined to have what she wants at any cost to others. Jon is old fashioned, sensitive, and loyal, and will not marry her as she urges without telling his mother, whom he adores. Holly warns Jon, "You are a giver, she is a taker." Jolyon writes Jon a letter to put before him the barrier the past has made between him and Fleur. Irene tells Jon not to think of her, that she will always love him, and he will lose nothing. Fleur sends Soames to plead for her, and it is seeing his mother in Soames' presence as she refuses to take his hand that makes him definitely decide to give up Fleur. Jolyon goes to British Columbia where his widowed mother joins him, and Fleur marries Michael Mont, the son of a baronet. After the wedding Soames reflected on the changes that had come with the years. "To Let" — the Forsyte age and way of life, when a man owned his soul, his investments, and his woman, without check or question. And now the State had, or would have, his investments, his woman had herself, and God knew who had his soul." The new kind of individualism asserted the worth not of what you have but what you are.

FOUNDING OF NEW ENGLAND, THE, by James Truslow Adams (1921). For a background, typically American, this volume, as an approach to the colonization period of the New England group, deals first with the classification of the Indian tribes at the time of the first settlements. The aborigines of that section are described as possessing a high degree of unity when the original settlers came to New England, and the status of the tribes controlled what the author calls their "foreign policy" which, with their "whole complex of cultivation" was of profound importance to those early voyagers, an account of whose seafaring to the New World is given, and treated as "business ventures of groups of individuals or joint stock companies . . . episodes in the expansion of English commerce." The author does not consider that there was any break at the beginnings of American history, but holds that the English colonies were by-products of British commercial activity, and that English "colonial policy" was but a mere phase of her commercial policy. From that point of view he estimates the development of events with which the book deals. Three factors are stressed in the history of New England colonization — geographical environment, the Puritan movement in England, and the Mercantile Theory. From the geographical side, the struggle against environment is shown, — its effect upon the colonists; and in the aspects of Puritanism which the author discusses, this movement is revealed as a movement of protest, and largely negative. In following its various phases, "religious, patriotic, or worldly," the author concludes that Puritanism became the "reasoned expression of the middle-class state of mind." An account of the first permanent settlements, the entire Pilgrim movement to America, including the famous Mayflower Compact, the hardships of life at Plymouth, are considered in detail and in relation to the later development, which by 1622 meant other beginnings along the coast and the great migration into Massachusetts Bay in 1630. The author observes that the more important elements in that larger migration, — "the bringing of families to form permanent homes, the peculiar form of church government, the individual ownership of freely acquired land, and the severing of business and legal relations with any company in England" followed the ways laid out by the simple founders of Plymouth. The trying period of the colonists during their religious differences with England, the influence of Roger Williams and Ann Hutchinson, with the establishment of what the author calls "A New England Oligarchy," are treated at length in the citation of events dealing with the struggle between religious freedom and intolerance and the suppression of free speech. The author sees in the struggle for civil freedom, which continued, the "sole contribution of the colony to human progress." He follows the course of this progress along the frontier, in the colonies of Rhode Island and Connecticut, with the whole westward movement of New England and its additional new communities and influences, together with the inevitable contest between the settlers and the Indians as the American frontier advanced, with the resultant attempts to unify New England — her scattered settlements which made up a continuous line of English colonies. The cross-currents in the Confederacy are revealed in their effect upon the political and intellectual life of America; while the defeat of the theocracy, the history of which is recalled in many contemporary evidences of the persecution of ministers and magistrates, is given as a concrete instance in the dramatic period under discussion of the great forces which ultimately made for intellectual freedom in America. "The contest was fought out on religious lines, because it was an age of religious interests." The author takes also the entire colonial organization into account, and in his appraisals of England and her colonies discusses the essential features of the Mercantile Theory, as applied to economic doctrine and state policies, showing it to be, in his opinion, a process of state-making and national-economy-making which he considers gives it a heightened meaning. But the theory of empire, the entire imperial scheme over which the later clash came, constituted the real problem, however, which the author considers was most disturbing to the colonists who had to bring local institutions into working relations with the sovereign power which, after the Restoration, reasserted its imperial control. The removal of the Indian menace from the borders, after a furious struggle and inevitable conflict, is shown to have been a permanent gain to the colonists. Their later dissensions and the rise of opposing groups among themselves made for the distinctions which, so the author says, had a marked effect on colonial life. The early educational system of Massachusetts is reviewed, with its immediate historical bearings. In the extension of the influence of the colonists, this review sees, as a particularly New England effort, the church, the common-school, and the town-meeting, and in this impulse, liberalized as it was destined to be, the colonists moved on to the development of their liberties when the work of the founders was over.

FOUR HORSEMEN OF THE APOCALYPSE, THE ("Los cuatro jinetes del Apocalipsis"), from the Spanish of Vicente Blasco Ibañez (1918). A novel of the Great War culminating in the Battle of the Marne. At the outbreak of war one of the characters says, "God is asleep, forgetting the world . . . while he sleeps the four feudal horsemen of the Beast will course through the land as its lords." The story of the Desnoyers family begins in the Argentine whither the Frenchman, Marcelo Desnoyers, a young man, had emigrated in 1870 to escape the war with Prussia. He became overseer of the vast lands of the millionaire ranchman, Julio Madariaga, the tireless "centaur," a good-natured, eccentric tyrant, ruling his hundreds of men by the capricious system of a blow followed by a gift. In time Desnoyers married his employer's eldest daughter. The younger daughter married a German employee, Karl Hartrott. After the death of the cowboy father-in-law, in the saddle on his horse as he had lived, the Hartrott family left the Argentine to live in Germany. Their letter about gay social life in Berlin stirred Madame Desnoyers and her son Julio, and daughter Chichi, to envy, and Desnoyers allowed himself to be persuaded to return to Paris. The old man rented an ostentatious house and bought the historic castle of Villeblanche-sur-Marne, which he filled with antiques. The acquisition of the castle led to friendship with his neighbor, Senator Lacour, whose son, René, later became Chichi's fiancé. Julio is a disappointment to his father. He gives up the study of engineering to set up a studio to paint, but distinguishes himself in nothing but dancing the tango. Through the Lacours Julio meets a young married woman, Marguerite Laurier, becomes her lover; and she takes the first steps toward a divorce in order to marry him. Then the War puts an end to the life of light pleasures. Marguerite's husband is one of the first to go to the front, is wounded and blinded, and the frivolous girl, who really loves Julio, goes to Lourdes to nurse her husband and they are reunited. Desnoyers is ashamed that his son does not enlist. He goes to his castle at Villeblanche, is forced to entertain the Germans who are advancing toward Paris, witnesses the execution of the mayor and the curé, and sees the scientific spoliation of the village and the castle. They use huge trucks to carry away all his furniture which they do not destroy. His nephew, Otto von Hartrott, rescues him from the cottage of the keeper where he has taken refuge and is thankful to get a few crusts of bread, and brings him to lunch with the German officers, a stranger at his own table. Under the protection of the Red Cross flag flying over the castle the Germans make an artillery attack on the French. After the retreat of the German troops and the arrival of the French he is able to return to Paris. Left stranded by Marguerite's desertion Julio forgets that he is a citizen of the Argentine, and comes to say good-by to his proud father wearing the uniform of France. Senator Lacour is able to arrange a trip to the front to see René and Julio. Desnoyers finds Julio "a man at last . . . tasting the delights of knowing that he was a useful being, that he was good for something, that his passing through the world would not be fruitless." When Julio is invalided home for a fortnight his father has the joy of walking the streets of Paris with a hero, and then Julio returns to the trenches and is killed. Julio did not reveal that in the fortunes of war he had killed one of his cousins. The psychology of the French and the Germans is contrasted on the ranch in the Argentine, in visits of the relatives in Berlin and in Paris, and during the War.

FRÄULEIN ELSE, a novel, by Arthur Schnitzler, translated from the German by Robert A. Simon(1925). The young girl, guest of her rich aunt at an Alpine resort, receives a telegram from her mother advising her of an important special delivery letter to follow. Her father, a clever lawyer, is always in difficulties because of his passion for gambling. This time he has embezzled a large sum of money, and asks Else to try to borrow it from an elderly sensualist, Herr von Dorsay, mentioned in her letters as staying in the same hotel, to save her father from prison. She dislikes the man and dreads the ordeal of making the request. He has helped her father once before as he points out to Else. The price he asks for his assistance now is that she shall come to his room at midnight to gratify his desire to look at her beauty. The entire action is the record of the thoughts in the mind of this sensitive girl, made ill by shame, her feelings of impotence and despair visualizing the scene with Dorsay, her memories in these last hours of her life before she takes veronal. When other characters speak to her italics mark their words in the midst of her own secret revery.

FRANCE, ANATOLE, HIMSELF, a Boswellian record by his secretary, J. J. Brousson (1925). The author came from a provincial university to help Anatole France with his "Joan of Arc." For eight years he kept records of the daily conversations and anecdotes which make up this book. His aim was to show "the Master" on his "intimate side without the trappings that almost all men put on for the public." He reveals that the illustrious author had two kinds of conversation, one sort for the public and another in private soliloquy. At Madame's receptions he regaled his admirers with selected anecdotes which had been carefully rehearsed beforehand. In his private conversation he is "laborious, uneasy, grating, breathless, full of contradictions," the exact opposite of the "official fireworks," but though the beginning may be heavy and awkward gradually his intellectual confidences become a stream of brilliant reminiscences, quotations, epigrams, and analogies often lasting several hours. M. France tells the new secretary that the references for his book must be put in order "to shut the mouths of those who maintain that he is only a novelist." Josephine, the servant, drags in a huge quantity of manuscript pinned tightly into a sheet with safety-pins, and presently the carpet is covered with note-books, scraps of notes and bills on which are scrawled hasty references, newspaper cuttings, and letters. "Aren't they talking of canonizing the holy girl?" says M. France. "We must be ahead of them, and race them to the church door." The point with him is to finish his book, a "liberal and republican monument" before the priests make a saint of her. Josephine and "Madame," his Egeria, tyrannize over him. Madame kept him working at his books. She would ask him at lunch how many pages he had written that day, and call him a lazy school-boy when he insisted on a holiday. On his way to a luncheon party with "Ma-dame" Josephine runs after him, and drags him back into the house by his coat-tails to change his shirt, and put on his morning coat, calling the idlers at the gate to witness how he had tried to slip away to meet ministers, and countesses, and actresses in his nightshirt. At the last Josephine is obliged to pass "the cere-monial article, all starched and stiff, over the nocturnal garment." His method of work was to write on odds and ends of paper, and send the scraps and scrawls to the printer without any correction. With the proofs in hand he would cut out each sentence even extract single words with a pair of archaic scissors. Thirty times he would rebuild a paragraph, taking each sentence, one by one, to recom-bine the whole, as if he were playing a game of Patience. The sixth proof he called "almond icing," otherwise, "the factitious, the adventitious." He now adds no more to the manuscript, but "throws cargo overboard." He scolds the secretary when he cannot find a lost reference, and when the passage at last is found he embraces him, and presents him with the wing of a Spanish altar-screen of gilt wood, and statuettes of Tanagras. "The Master" haunts the curio and print shops to add antiques to his collections. His comments on women are incessant with the frank-ness and sensuality of his "Red Lily." If he could preserve only one book it would be a fashion magazine. "Their ribbons and bibbons," he says, "would tell me more about future humanity than all the philosophers, novelists, preachers, and men of science." There are some autobiographical fragments about his father, the pompous Legitimist bookseller; and his witty, sceptical mother, who loved flowers, and prided herself on her perfect cooking. His mind plays on every topic and whether he is discussing love or Napoleon his remarks are equally heterodox from the conventional and Puritanical standpoint. References to death depressed the old Pagan. One day he astonished his secretary by raising his hat with osten-tation as a funeral passed by. He said, "It is my own destiny that I have saluted. . . . Let us live in peace that we may die in peace. The difficulty is not to die, but to live. Let me have no tedious priest at my death-bed, but a pretty woman, and may the hands be fair that close my eyes for the great sleep."

FRANKLIN, BENJAMIN, by William Cabell Bruce (1917). In this voluminous study the life of Benjamin Franklin stands out upon a European as well as an Amer-ican background. "In America," observes the author in his introduction, "he was such a thorough American in every respect that Carlyle is said to have termed him on one occasion, 'The Father of all the Yankees.' In England he was English enough to feel the full glow of her greatness and to see her true interests far more clearly than she saw them herself. He had too many Anglo-Saxon traits to become wholly a Frenchman when he lived in France, but he became French enough to truly love France and her people and to be truly loved by them. In the opinion of Sainte-Beuve he is the most French of all Americans." Franklin's moral standing and system are studied and analyzed from his autobiography, as expounding his doctrine in regard to the virtues which were classified under thirteen heads which the author discusses in his opening chapter, — Franklin's moral practices improving, he concludes, largely as the result of age and wisdom. Closely akin to Franklin's system of morals were his views about religion, and numerous extracts, selected from his writings, are given to indicate his belief in the hand of Providence, while the author holds that other expressions furnish a "religious or quasi-religious setting to Franklin's thoughts upon his own dissolution." Franklin as a philanthropist and citizen is shown to have made a religion of his zeal to promote the welfare of his fellow-creatures, and his various projects of a public nature, among which the Philadelphia City Library was the first, are recalled, and reveal, with the expanding horizon which the author says came to Franklin in 1757, his activities when he was drawn off into the world-currents of his time. "He was both by nature and training at once a philosopher and a philanthropist." The author next turns from Franklin's philanthropic zeal and public spirit to his happy and more intimate personal and social traits. His rare qualities for making enduring friendships is also revealed, in chapters which the author devotes to Franklin's American friends, to his British friends, and to his French friends. "Wherever he happened to be," observes the writer, "he was too exempt from local bias, thought thoughts, cherished feelings and spoke a language too universal not to make a strong appeal to good will and friendship." The explanation of the "great concourse of friends that Franklin drew about him," was found, this volume points out, in his robust, honorable character and mental gifts. The various business enterprises which engaged Franklin's attention, the opening of printing offices in different colonies, and the history of his partnerships which enabled him to branch out still more, together with the political consequence of such moves that led to his appointment of Postmaster at Philadelphia, are discussed in the light of his personal exertions which enabled him at an early age to obtain the leisure for the rest of his life which he so much desired for philosophical studies and amusements. Entering next upon the career of Franklin as a statesman, the author recalls the conspicuous part the eminent American played when the opportunity presented itself in the "stirring transactions which ushered in the American Revolution." While he had no hand in the preparation of the Declaration of Independence, the author points out the active part taken by Franklin in the adoption of the Articles of Confederation. In tracing the events in historical sequence which were to culminate in Franklin's memorable third visit to France and his success at the Court of that country, the author sums up the outstanding triumphs which came to the illustrious ambassador through the great institution of learning which honored him with academic degrees, both in this country and abroad. These events in his life were of no slight importance, as viewed by the author of this biography, who sees the era one which readily regarded a man like Franklin as a true citizen of the world. The closing chapters deal with Franklin as a man of science and as a writer. In the former rôle, the author's conclusions are that "the scientific conjectures of Franklin may not always have been sound, but they are invariably so readable that we experience no difficulty in understanding why the Abbé Raynal should have preferred his fictions to other men's truths. Of Franklin as a writer, the author agrees with Hume that Franklin "was the first great man of letters for whom Great Britain was beholden to America."

FRANKLIN, BENJAMIN, the First Civilized American, by Philips Russell (1927). In this biography the author does much to correct the ignorance in regard to the life of Benjamin Franklin deplored by Rupert Hughes in his recent life of Washington. Hughes comments on the failure of the American people to revere Franklin "as one of the major gods of America," although the French put him among the four or five greatest men of all time. From a study of fresh documents in London and Paris and the State department in this country, Russell makes clear how deep his roots went into the intellectual life of the eighteenth century. He believes that Franklin's much reading of "The Spectator" in his youth, shaped his character after the sturdy, independent, kindly figure of Sir Roger de Coverley. Differences between the young Benjamin and his elder brother, James, to whom he was early apprenticed as a printer, caused him to take a hasty leave of home and Boston, but not before he had acquired experience as a printer and editor of his brother's paper, "The Courant." He comes to New York smuggled aboard ship by a friend and thence afoot he makes his historic entry into Philadelphia, eating a bun before the eyes of pretty Deborah Read, his future wife, as he passes her door. Through friends made in New York he obtains work with a printer. Later Governor Keith of Pennsylvania takes an interest in him and sends him to England to choose the printing outfit with which the Governor has promised to set him up in business, for Philadelphia lacks an able printer. The trip proves of great value to him although he learns how little confidence is put in Governor Keith's promises by those who know him. Working for large English printing firms, Franklin perfects his trade, sees something of the world and forms contacts with friends which prove of lifelong value. On his return he launches the Junto Club whose purpose is "to seek truth, promote good fellowship and realize the benefits of occasional wine and song." This becomes the parent of many like organizations, the first civilizing influence started by Franklin for his fellow men. During this period he draws up his simple and unorthodox creed and personal liturgy. His autobiography lists thirteen personal virtues he hoped to acquire and his struggles over them. At twenty-four, says Russell, he becomes head of his own printing business without having lived up to any of the maxims for which he became renowned. After long waiting on the lady's part, he marries Deborah Read and settles down. Under his management the books owned by the Junto Club become the nucleus of the first subscription library later to become the Philadelphia Library. That same year, 1732, Washington was born. He publishes his first number of "Poor Richard's Almanac" the broad plebeian humor, pithy and thrifty sayings of which strike a popular note. At about the same time he becomes owner of the first Pennsylvania newspaper started a few months earlier by a competitor, "The Pennsylvania Gazette." These publishing ventures and other wise investments give him a comfortable income. Philips Russell accuses the "Almanac" of being the foundation of the great American philosophy of Get-On. "It established a rock of philosophic materialism. . . . It well nigh drove out from the spirit of the American people all tendency to a love for leisure and a cultivation of the graceful arts, made its literature didactic and its art timid." But later on he says that, "It is greatly to Franklin's credit that he nowhere claims that his prosperity was due exclusively to his own efforts." As Russell fills in the picture of Franklin's life, he appears a curious combination of a great man. With the gusto and versatility of the Renaissance, he devotes his gifts to practical ends that are characteristically American. His superiority of mind lay not in its originality but in the quality of keeping his eyes open and of putting two and two together. He did not discover electricity but showed more clearly than others that lightning was a manifestation of it. "He could not only do things but get publicity for them." Thinking to retire from business with a comfortable fortune at forty, he planned to give his time to his scientific experiments. But he is now drafted into the pub-

lic service. Responsibility and reverence attended Franklin from his first civic
efforts in Philadelphia. Not only did he establish the first subscription library in
the city, he organized the first fire company, founded an academy which later grew
into the University of Pennsylvania, started a newspaper and magazine, raised
the funds for the first hospital, induced the city to clean and light its streets, invented
the Franklin stove, made numberless experiments in soil cultivation and manures.
"For my own part when I am employed in serving others, I do not look upon myself
as conferring favors, but as paying debts," he wrote to Whitefield. After service
as Postmaster-General during which time he introduces postal reforms and starts
the first penny post, and after other years in the Assembly, he enters upon his long
period of foreign service. He represents first the Pennsylvania Assembly and later
the interests of the colonies at the English court before the Revolution and then
rounds out a full life with his invaluable services as Commissioner at the French
Court during the Revolution and after. Whether we consider him as printer or
publicist, humor enters into his solution of the problems life sets him. Sometimes it was broad as in his earlier contributions to Boston and Philadelphia
papers and in certain of his letters; sometimes it served a serious purpose as in
his newspaper hoaxes in London when, in the famous "Edict of the King of
Prussia" he endeavored by mirthful means to help England see herself as the
Colonies saw her; at other times he was witty as in his letters to Madame Brillon
or those gay and graceful bagatelles that so delighted his French friends. Both
his humor and his suave gallantry to lovely ladies were more in tune with the
times as they were lived abroad then in the colonies. John Adams and his wife
Abigail and others prone to Puritanism were outraged by those very qualities which
endeared him to his cosmopolitan friends. They did not see that the sincerity
and sweetness of these qualities rooted his great nature deep in common humanity
and so made him strong and serene under the stress of his heavy labor for his country
during his years abroad. Philips Russell does not minimize the quality of this
service. From his middle forties on he speaks of this great early American as a
genuinely civilized human being.

FREE THOUGHT IN THE SOCIAL SCIENCES, by J. A. Hobson (1926). Before applying his critical rule to current theories of economics, politics, and ethics,
the author describes what he considers the art of free thought, that is to say the
discovery and rigorous elimination of bias and ulterior motives from scientific
thinking. He uses the terminology of modern psychology to distinguish between
the interested and disinterested pursuit of knowledge, to caution us against the bias
of metaphor to which we are subjected by the use of language, and to shake off some
of the taboos which have grown up in the social sciences to the detriment of further
progress. Finally, he shows by common sense how personal and economic biasses
will affect, consciously or unconsciously, the investigations and the theorizing of the
best equipped and most sincere observers. In the second part of the book, Mr.
Hobson reviews the rise of political economy as a science, and shows how from the
start it was oriented to secure the acceptance and, later, the maintenance of an economic order benefiting a certain group of persons, namely, the mercantile and industrial class. Although Adam Smith's survey of the economic order was comprehensive
and very possibly not intended as a tract for the furtherance of specific economic
interests, it was the source-book of the major classical economists, who were plainly
endeavoring to justify the laissez-faire system, as most profitable to their interests.
In neo-classical economics, — represented by the Cambridge school with its

doctrine of marginalism, — the same analysis may be made, and the interests of a capitalist class fearful of an alteration of the status quo may be plainly discerned. This analysis Mr. Hobson makes, showing the contradiction and inapplicability of the marginal theory which presupposes infinitesimal quantities of both economic wants and goods as the translation of qualitative preferences, which are in fact unconsciously arrived at without any mathematical evaluation of desirability. This exposure of neo-classical economics is followed by a similar treatment of proletarian economics which demonstrates that corresponding biasses, instincts, and wilful blindness operate to distort to the same degree the proletarian view of the economic world. In an economics of human welfare, the author concludes, no illusion should be entertained that exact quantitative measurements may be obtained. The problem of determining the utility to the consumer and the disutility to the producer, — which is the crucial problem in any economic melioration, — must always involve some psychological factors not amenable to measurement. But social standards need not for that reason be discarded, and if used with a consciousness of their approximativeness, they may serve as leads and direction-posts to a rational and non-partisan meliorism. In the third part of "Free Thought in the Social Sciences" the author deals with politics and ethics, showing that the art of politics has always been directed to the securing and maintenance of power by some group or combination of groups, and that theories have been simply rationalizations of that accomplishment. This leads him to a consideration of the theory of nationalism and patriotism which is at the basis of the modern national state, with its characteristic doctrines of sovereignty and self-preservation. These doctrines in turn involve a treatment of race-eugenics as a method of political and national safeguard, since both within the nation and in the society of nations, group leadership seems to have shifted its centre of gravity, by reason of the so-called race-suicide among the Nordics, as well as by the heavy toll which the last war took from that group. Mr. Hobson shows that on this ground race-eugenics is essentially harmful since it furnishes no disinterested standard of human fitness; and since it appears to place a premium on qualities of adventuresomeness and restlessness which may not necessarily be the most useful or valuable. Moreover, the complete lack of control of environmental factors under modern conditions invalidates all such tests and all such hypotheses. In ethics, it is shown that both the capitalist and proletarian groups use the system of conduct most pleasing to their prejudices and passions, regardless of inconsistencies with any other doctrines they may happen to hold in respect of economics or politics. And at the root of all proposed changes may be found some new set of biasses and interests. Though Mr. Hobson does not expect that the acquisitive impulses of nations and individuals will abate, he believes that human nature is not on that account "immutable and intractable." What it needs is a greater realization of its own biasses and a keener appreciation of the art of free-thinking. Free-thought, he maintains, has a survival power superior to all conceivable perversions of the sciences to "interested" purposes and "ulterior" motives.

FRÉMONT, by Allan Nevins (2 vols., 1928), is an attempt, says the author "at an honest and impartial biography of a man who has been the subject of excessive laudation and excessive detraction." John Charles Frémont was born out of wedlock to a mother, Anne Whiting Pryor, who belonged to one of the best families of Tidewater Virginia. She had fled from her elderly husband to Charles Frémont, a dashing but impecunious emigré from the French Revolution, who appeared in

Richmond about 1810. After a few years of wandering the father died leaving three children, and the mother moved to Charleston. John Mitchell, a lawyer, fancied bringing him up to the law and with that in view sent him to an excellent Scotch preparatory school. In a year·he was ready to enter the Junior class of Charleston College. At this time his salient traits, ardor, imagination, ambition, quickness, endurance and reckless impetuosity were well established. Joel Poinsett, an ardent Democrat and Unionist, became his next benefactor. Through him Frémont received an appointment as teacher of mathematics aboard the sloop "Natchez" when it left Charleston harbor after the Nullification troubles had been adjusted, on a cruise to South America. But the opportunity to help survey the route of a projected railway between Charleston and Cincinnati led him to refuse a permanent appointment for teaching mathematics in the Navy. Captain Williams, under whom this work had been done, was ordered to make a military reconnaissance of the mountainous country of the Cherokees in Georgia by President Jackson with a view to transferring these tribes beyond the Mississippi, and he asked Frémont to assist him. Secretary Poinsett understood the young man's tastes and had him commissioned a second lieutenant in the Topographical Corps and ordered to Washington. Thereupon his kind guardian further arranged to have him included in a much larger expedition under the distinguished foreigner, Jean Nicholas Nicollet, which was to survey the country between the upper Mississippi and Missouri rivers. Senator Benton was opposed to Frémont's marriage to his daughter, Jessie, on account of their youth and the poverty that would be theirs, but when separation proved of no avail and their runaway marriage was announced, he received them into his home. At twenty-nine the government sent Frémont out at the head of his own first expedition. This lasted three and a half months and accomplished all the objects of the government, exploring the Kansas River Valley, then over to the Platte, reaching their main objective, the South Pass of the Rockies on August 8th, 1842. The most spectacular feat of this trip was the ascent of that peak of the Central Rockies now known as Frémont's Peak. On this trip he first met and engaged Kit Carson, with whom he was to be frequently associated later. Jessie's literary skill in writing up this expedition combined with the adventurous and scientific appeal of the report and its practical value to the stream of westward roving pioneers made it widely read. He set out on his second expedition in 1843 with thirty-nine men, well armed. They went up the Kansas River to the head of the Arkansas. At Great Salt Lake many new and valuable scientific observations were made. Then they visited Dr. Whitman's mission in Oregon and started to cross the Sierras in winter. As the men came out on one of the wintry peaks they found themselves looking down on the glowing spring in the valley of Lake Klamath. In characteristically headlong fashion, Frémont took his men across the Sierras into California where they were hospitably entertained and allowed to reëquip at Sutter's Fort. In June 1844 they reached Pueblo, having returned by the Wasatch Mountains and over the Continental Divide. The Third Expedition in the midsummer of 1845 was arranged, says Frémont, with regard to the possibilities of war with Mexico. There were sixty well armed men suitable to any emergency. The first objective was that section of the Central Rockies in which the Arkansas, Rio Grande and Colorado all find their sources, then to further examine Great Salt Lake and survey the vast chains of mountains west of the Rockies, the Sierras, and the Cascade Range, and to discover passages through them to the Pacific. In December, 1845, he again reached Sutter's Fort in northern California. No proper scientific report, beyond the maps, was ever made of this third expedition so crowded was it by major political events soon to follow. Here he found the stage all set for his dramatic foray which was to end in his espousing the cause of the militant American settlers of California, clashing with Castro, and, after the arrival of Lieutenant Gillespie of the Marine Corps with secret, partly verbal instructions, taking an active part in the coming revolution. For a time he played a waiting part against the desire of the Americans who were anxious for a stable government. But he saw the need of forestalling England and being the first to get a foothold in California. And the government despatches which were directed to the Consul, Larkin, while emphasizing this fear of English aggression, urged a policy of friendly concession toward the Californians but no suggestions warranting the use of armed force. These verbal instructions, as reported by Frémont later, warned him that Polk desired that he "should not let the English get possession of California, but should use any means in his power, or any occasion that offered, to prevent such a thing." It was not long before a pretext occurred which justified Frémont in his own eyes in assuming a leading rôle in events about to be enacted. His hardy force became the nucleus for the California Battalion in that uprising against the Mexican government known as the Bear Flag War. Commodore Stockton left in command of the American ships on the Pacific Coast by Commodore Sloat was seen in friendly coöperation with Frémont, whose battalion was taken into the naval service. Before Sloat's departure news had arrived of the outbreak of hostilities between the United States and Mexico so that the Bear Flag War was now over, further hostilities being merely an extension of the general conflict with Mexico in California. Acting with Commodore Stockton, a force of three hundred and sixty men took Los Angeles, and California was declared a possession of the United States under martial law. While Frémont went north to the Sacramento Valley to recruit his forces, Gillespie, left in charge in southern California lost Los Angeles to the aroused Californians. Before Frémont with unusual caution had assembled a suitably equipped army to come to the relief of Gillespie, General Kearny had set out from Santa Fé under government orders to conquer California. Meeting Kit Carson with despatches, he forced him to turn back with him. In a skirmish after reaching California, Kearny was worsted. Then, meeting with Stockton at San Diego, the two subdued the insurrection, leaving Frémont, who arrived from the north soon after the reoccupation of Los Angeles, to cope with the sporadic fighting by the Californians. At first Kearny generously waived Stockton's offer of the supreme command but later assumed it. Stockton had already promised Frémont the governorship of California and this Frémont accepted choosing to obey the orders of his old friend when the question arose whose authority was paramount. For a time both General Kearny and Frémont were acknowledged as governor in different parts of California. Not long after this dispute arose Kearny received orders from Washington which he concealed from Frémont, upholding his authority. Frémont was finally brought East by Kearny as a virtual prisoner under charges of mutiny and insubordination. No sooner were the principals to this quarrel both in Washington than the irate Senator Benton insisted on a court-martial to clear his son-in-law. This famous case aroused intense public interest for a time, public sympathy being generally on the side of the young explorer. When the verdict was given against him there was a general feeling that he ought to have been cleared but for the usual jealousy of West Pointers against an outsider. President Polk did modify the verdict by pronouncing him not guilty of mutiny and allowing him to remain in the army, but this Frémont refused to do. The early fall of 1848 found the Frémonts en route to California to make a new start in that promising land. He hoped to push west from the headquarters of the Rio Grande along the thirty-seventh parallel looking for a pass over the Sierras that could be used as a practicable, direct railroad route to the coast. The bitter midwinter weather made it, in his estimation, all the better test. So fierce were the storms as they approached the Great Divide that most of their provisions were lost and the men were so nearly starved that they were forced to turn back, but too late to prevent a disastrous toll of lives and terrible suffering to the survivors. On his last trip to California, Frémont had left $3000 with the American consul to purchase a small ranch. Instead he had bought Mariposa, a wild tract of land in the Sierra foothills. The Frémonts reached California just as the famous gold rush of '49 was starting, in which, for a time, they found themselves engulfed. Gold was found on Mariposa and Frémont immediately became a man of large affairs. Soon he was sent East again as Senator from the new state on a free soil platform. He sat in Congress only three weeks as this was a short session and did not return for he was defeated by the pro-slavery forces. The Mariposa estate now dominated his life for a time. Mariposa business as well as search for health and rest after the ordeal of the two fires of 1851 in San Francisco which had affected Jessie's health, sent them to Europe, where they enjoyed many delightful experiences, being received everywhere. Frémont returned to head his fifth and last expedition to find a route for a Pacific railway at his own expense. The matter was being considered by the government and Jefferson Davis, a West Pointer and Secretary of War, had passed over Frémont's qualifications and appointed other men to head the several government parties sent out on the same quest. The route surveyed for a railroad was never used. Certain leaders believed that Frémont should head an alliance between the Native American party and the Democrats as their presidential candidate for 1856. This he refused to do but his sentiments and personality were such that he was named as the popular choice of the new Republican party. Frémont always believed that if a running mate had been chosen more acceptable to the Pennsylvania voters he might have won the election. After long litigation, Frémont's title to the Mariposas was now confirmed and he pushed rapidly the physical development of the estate. Just after Lincoln's election, Frémont stopped in New York, on his way to Europe, and enjoyed a brief and cordial interview with the president elect. On the outbreak of war he offered his services and was called home to become one of the ranking Union generals, the Commander of the Department of the West. He arrived in Missouri at a critical time when the state was torn between Unionist and Secession sentiment. He was much criticized later on for the extreme and expensive measures he took in fortifying St. Louis and in intimidating the rebels, which measures proved, however, immediately salutary. Affairs were in great confusion. It was the eve of the dramatic "hundred days in Missouri." General Prentiss was in a desperate situation at Cairo, a key position on the Ohio and Mississippi. So Frémont came to his relief with thirty-eight hundred men, ordering Lyon, who was also menaced by a large Confederate army, to fall back on his base at Rolla. Instead Lyon fought and lost in a disastrous engagement at Wilson's Creek. Frémont's failure to support him swelled the bitter criticism, although it was later proved that he had not had a large enough force to meet both situations and the Government demands for troops in addition. Frank Blair, who had headed the Unionists in their first resistance to Secession, was a member of a family, politically powerful throughout the State and very friendly with Lincoln. Frémont refused to show this family undue preferment and the conflict between them grew rapidly. Throughout the Blair circle, reports were circulated accusing Frémont of extravagance in administration and an exclusiveness that made approach to him very difficult. There were many armed rebels within the State, and because of these Frémont issued a military proclamation freeing all slaves who were the property of armed rebels without consulting the administration at Washington. Frémont's arduous efforts at organization of the department were just beginning to bear fruit. He was pursuing Price's fleeing army, hoping by a successful engagement to turn against the Confederates on the Mississippi and so right himself with Lincoln and his critics, but he was weakened by the insubordination of his generals, Pope and Hunter, and the malicious exaggeration of his defects due at least in part to hasty organization of affairs which were in a chaotic state on his taking up the command and which had to be carried through in the presence of an active enemy. Frémont's army was encamped just beyond Springfield, in good field condition and and with the spirit of the troops high believing a battle imminent, when Lincoln's patience wore out and Frémont lost his command. So strong was public sentiment in his behalf that Lincoln gave him another chance, the command of the newly created Mountain Department in western Virginia. Here he failed to reinstate himself in Lincoln's eyes and finally resigned, although many facts are brought to show that the action expected of him in that campaign was not possible of accomplishment under the conditions he faced. As Lincoln came up for reëlection, a strong party of radicals gathered about Frémont. But in the end he abdicated in Lincoln's favor, not, as he frankly stated, because he favored the policies of the administration but because the other candidate, McClellan, if elected, would bring back slavery. The Blairs had by this time lost public favor and were out of public life. The years until his death in 1890 showed the usual fluctuation of his fortunes. He lost his holdings in the Mariposa estate. With what little money remained from this he went into railroad developments in the Southwest, which ended so disastrously that he and Jessie were plunged into poverty. Then his loyal and talented wife who had, for so many years lived the life of a *grande dame*, showed her quality and for a time supported them by her magazine writings. He was at length reinstated, through the influence of friends, as a major general on the retired list. With life again promising comfort for both in old age this gallant and gifted Pathfinder of the West died suddenly of peritonitis. His best epitaph is that written by his wife, "from the ashes of his campfires have sprung cities."

FRIENDLY ARCTIC, THE, by Vilhjalmur Stefansson (1921). The opening chapters are concerned with the fundamental aspects of Polar exploration and of the Polar regions. The author describes in detail the experiences of the explorers in the grip of the ice, in their ship, the "Karluk," wedging its way among cakes and floes, and the final tragedy of being held in fetters of ice. "Drifting in the pack is a tense game. In the beginning you have a certain amount of discretion in choosing your berth. After that it is luck upon which the life of your ship depends. And luck may change at any time. A day or two after we were beset it began to freeze. In four or five days young ice had formed in every little open space where irregular floes did not fit exactly against each other. . . . By this time I had made up my mind that the "Karluk" was not to move under her own power again and that we were in for a voyage such as that of the "Jeanette" or the "Fram," drifting for years, if we had the luck to remain unbroken, eventually coming out somewhere towards the Atlantic, either we or our wreckage." The explorers left their ship and camped on the ice, and the "Karluk" disappeared. The account of the dangers of travelling by land under the guidance of the Eskimos, describes the dangers attending the explorers, who found the first human habitation among the Colville River people. The customs, beliefs and modes of thought of the Eskimos are explained in the light of their effect upon the task of the explorers. Section by section of the Arctic regions is described and the problems of the North, as fought and overcome — "cold and hunger, wet and starvation" and all that goes with them in those forbidding regions, together with the ills of the body, which the explorers endured, typhoid, pneumonia and pleurisy — are discussed in these pages which record new experiences in those great northern territories which the author holds should have the effect of changing many preconceived ideas. The Arctic Circle is shown to be a landscape not different in appearance, except for the absence of trees, from prairie or meadow. This account shows that animal life is abundant on many portions of the land and nearly everywhere in the ocean. Birds and insects are in evidence. The season for travel in the Arctic regions is in mid-autumn and the end of early spring — the gay social season among the Eskimos is in the winter months. The author proves that in the farthest Arctic the sea supplies food even more abundantly than the land. The unknown regions which he explored, by which thousands of square miles were added to Canada, and which the explorer considers have given "a few more spots of color to our maps and forms," are told of in his first impressions of the land — its vegetable and animal life. The equipment — the sledge pulled by dogs, the skis, the rotting of the dog harness, the thaws, which converted most of the ice into what was known as "needle ice," are incidental features of the account, but the author repeats again and again that hardships are not necessarily involved in the work of the Arctic explorer. The outstanding discoveries which form the conspicuous features of the narrative are described at length, with surveys of the coast; Arctic housebuilding is told of, and Arctic phenomena; while ethnological information gained from the Eskimos, the physical characteristics of the natives, Eskimo tales, and the succession of adventures which led the travellers into the footsteps of earlier explorers, geological knowledge and information of the natural history, together with the experiments in hydrographic work, in surveys, and in magnetic declinations, the numerous soundings, which outline the "continental shelf from Alaska to Prince Patrick Island and disclose the submarine mountains and valleys of the bed of Beaufort Sea," are all part of this Arctic record. And by a new departure in Polar exploration, the return after the fifth winter in the Arctic is recalled vividly as one of the most interesting and important that the expedition undertook.

FROM IMMIGRANT TO INVENTOR, by Michael Pupin (1922) is the autobiography of a Serbian peasant boy who rose from poverty to a high position, as inventor and college professor, known and honored internationally. Born in the tiny village of Idvor in Banat, of old Serbian stock, the boy was brought up in the traditions of his race. His father, a sturdy peasant, was several times knez (chief) of the village; his mother could neither read nor write but she was a remarkably intelligent woman and probably to her the author owes his investigative turn of mind. He early outgrew the village school at Idvor and was sent to a higher school some miles away where he first saw a simple electric apparatus and heard the story of Franklin and the kite. His father scoffed at the idea of the kite which drew lightning from the sky, but his mother believed and urged him to learn more. During the summer months the boy returned to his native village and with other boys was set to guard the cattle at night. In order to learn of the approach of Roumanian cattle thieves the boys thrust their knives into the hard ground and used them as listening posts. Thus early in life the future inventor learned the principle of some of his inventions. It was in these days, too, that the question of light began to intrigue him. "What is light?" he asked. Nobody knew. In 1874, after a year's schooling in Prague, during which time his father died, the young Michael came to America and landed at Castle Garden with no other possessions than the suit he wore and five cents. His first job was driving mules on a Delaware farm. The daughter of the house became interested in him and taught him his first English and pronounced him "smart." Leaving this farm to find a higher and better place he wandered about a bit and finally came to New York. Here he had various odd jobs until he arrived at a cracker factory where he stayed some time and learned much. The fireman at the factory gave him many hints of practical philosophy, and his friend Bilharz, a young Continental intellectual, taught him Greek and Latin. Working by day and studying by night at Cooper Union, Pupin prepared himself to enter Columbia University, which at that time was located at 50th Street. Besides the Columbia faculty his greatest teacher was Henry Ward Beecher, then pastor of the Plymouth Church in Brooklyn, whom the boy heard as often as possible. He had long been an admirer of Beecher's sister, Harriet Beecher Stowe, and had read "Uncle Tom's Cabin" in translation before coming to America. Any relative of hers was sure to be worth hearing in the boy's estimation. When he had been a time at Columbia Pupin began to coach the backward sons of New York's aristocracy and his money worries grew less. After a brilliant graduation he went to Cambridge and Berlin to study under eminent scientists the subject "What is light?" During these years he made a return visit to his native land where he revived the beautiful memories of his boyhood years and saw again his wonderful mother, grown older but keen as ever that her son should learn to understand the world she admired but did not know. In 1901 Pupin returned to Columbia as professor of electro-mechanics. In the early years there he had his troubles with the heresy hunters. The two methods of electrical power distribution, the direct and alternating current, were being discussed. The young professor eulogized the latter system and offended some of the "big" men of the electrical industries, who hinted that he had better resign. But the Columbia authorities were not perturbed and so he stayed. Pupin is an idealist in science and the main object of his narrative was "to describe the rise of idealism in American science, and particularly in physical sciences and the related industries." A proof of his idealism is in his gift to the United States government of the use of his invention eliminating static interference with wireless transmission.

GALAHAD, Enough of his Life to Explain his Reputation (1926). The story begins four years after Arthur's marriage to Guinevere. Arthur and Lancelot had cleared the country of dragons, and ogres, and caitiff knights before Guinevere came to the court, and Arthur, content to rest on his laurels, is busy with the affairs of the kingdom. Guinevere is the old-fashioned woman who wants to inspire men to great deeds, and she therefore turned to Lancelot to fulfil her dreams and ambitions. She tells Lancelot that she "could love only one kind of man — the kind that makes a difference in the world, who builds something, who always goes on." Lancelot like Arthur is the simple loyal soldier type admirable as long as there is plenty of fighting to be done. He is bewildered by the exacting Guinevere's demands. It is after one of her numerous quarrels with him that he goes on an errand for Arthur to King Pelles and meets his daughter Elaine. King Pelles is a model of propriety, but Elaine is a reckless young thing with no inhibitions, and advanced views about self-expression and living a full life. She is the woman Lancelot ought to have loved and married. He is of course devoted to Guinevere and refuses to have anything to do with Elaine when she falls in love with him and declares her passion.

Through the jealousy of Elaine's rejected suitor, Sir Bromel, a garbled story of the affair gets to the court. The kindly Arthur thinks the match would be a good one for Lancelot, and sends him on another errand to King Pelles to aid his wooing. Lancelot goes reluctantly because of Arthur's command, the more so because Guinevere does not wish him to visit Elaine again. He is relieved to find that King Pelles has sent his wilful daughter away to visit relatives. By a trick Elaine gets Lancelot to come to her at night, and tempts him to stay with her. She thinks that she can win him if she bears him a child. Arthur invites Elaine to court after Galahad is born, but Lancelot, true to his love for Guinevere, will have nothing to do with her. Guinevere drives Lancelot to madness with her reproaches, and he wanders about the country, and finally is cared for by Elaine and comes to himself again. Summoned by Guinevere to combat with a false knight who has accused her, he returns to the court and happiness with the beautiful queen. When Galahad is seventeen Elaine sends him to his father at the court. The handsome, brave youth is a godsend to Guinevere who determines to form his character to carry out her ideals. After his first successful tournament she upsets his belief that in trial by combat the innocent man can win against the one who is in the wrong by pointing out that victory comes to the strongest arm, skill and experience, and the freshest horse, and fires him with ideas of right and wrong. She succeeds in making Galahad the perfect prig. When he finds out that his father and mother are not married as he had supposed, he judges them unworthy of his society, and the fact that his queen and pattern of virtue has been unfaithful gives him no choice but to repudiate them all or be false to his ideals. He leaves to search for the Holy Grail. Once again Lancelot is the victim of his own charm with another Elaine, the lovely young daughter of Sir Bernard of Astolat. On the way to join Arthur at a tournament Lancelot is their guest for the night, and like the first Elaine this girl offered herself to him, heart and body, and when he refuses she dies of love. The jealous Guinevere hears the story and will not believe that there are two Elaines and that Lancelot is faithful until she sees the young girl dead in the chapel, and then it is too late as she has sent Lancelot away. Before Lancelot went to the abbey to enter the religious life, he confessed to Arthur, that he had loved his wife too well, and heard from his friend that he had known about it for a long time. Soon after their wedding Arthur had discovered that Guinevere married him to reform him, and was relieved when she gave it up and turned her attention to Lancelot, and condoned the affair because he understood Guinevere so well. Arthur had never cared for the theory that women should be an inspiration to men, and thinks they had much better confine themselves to inspiring each other.

GALLIONS REACH, by H. M. Tomlinson (1927). James Colet, "Jimmy," a city clerk in London, after twenty years in the great shipping firm of Perriam Limited, was goaded by insult to strike his chief, who fell over dead from heart failure. Jimmy went out into the night, and walked as far as Gallions Reach, the Thames waterfront in the Limehouse district. He intended to go to the office in the morning and give himself up to the police, but chance led him into the company of Captain Hale and to his ship, the "Altair," sailing for Far Eastern ports, and he decided to stay on board. The freighter is wrecked by a storm in the wild Indian seas, and after heroic days in the life-boats, the survivors are picked up by an ocean liner. The hero of this adventure story is a passive dreamer whose response to extraordinary experience and peril on sea and land shows his own fine spirit. The rescue takes him to Rangoon, and from there into the jungle with Norrie, a geologist and prospector. They meet Mr. Parsell, a distinguished ethnologist, so obviously in need of a keeper to get him safely back to civilization, that Colet goes on with him instead of returning with Norrie. They also meet wild elephants and prowling tigers, and tropical storms. In search of a tribe of original men, "almost virgin documents . . . not obscured by the palimpsest of many civilizations," Mr. Parsell eludes their watchful care and disappears in the night, so Colet and the Malay guides break camp and find their way to the sea again. At the hotel he meets his friend Sinclair, officer of the "Altair" and sails with him back to Gallions Reach to lay the ghost of old Perriam.

GARDEN PARTY, THE, and other stories, by Katherine Mansfield (1922). "At the Bay" is a day at the shore with the Burnell family of "The Prelude," and lovely pictures of the sea. Stanley, the man of action, prides himself on being first in the water. He rushes off to the city, and the family settle down to quiet and peace. Linda, his wife, dreaming in the hammock, thinks of her love for Stanley in "breathing spaces of calm," but most of the time "it was like living in a house that couldn't be cured of the habit of catching on fire, on a ship that got wrecked every day. And it was always Stanley who was in the thick of the danger. Her whole time was spent in rescuing him, and restoring him, and calming him down, and listening to his story. And what was left of her time was spent in the dread of having children." This is "her real grudge against life." Her new baby lying in the grass smiles at her and she is forced to recognize that she does love her children. The women and children go in bathing. Beryl, longing for a lover, goes out in the moonlight, and meets wicked handsome Harry Kember, but she is strong and wrenches herself free from his embrace, and it does not seem to matter afterward as the sea murmurs in the stillness. "The Garden Party" given on a perfect day is a most successful affair, but in the midst of the preparations Laura hears that a man has been killed near by, and her pleasure is spoiled. She wants her mother to stop the party and the band playing. Afterward in her picture hat and shining dress she goes to the cottage with a basket of sandwiches and cakes. The dead man sleeps peacefully, remote from garden parties and baskets and lace frocks. "Isn't life . . . " she sobs to her brother, "but what life was she couldn't explain." "The Daughters of the Late Colonel" want the funeral to be "a good one that will last," as if they were buying a nightgown. After his tyrannical rule is over the two elderly spinsters are still obsessed by his presence "in the top drawer with his handkerchiefs and neckties, or in the next with his shirts and pyjamas, or in the lowest of all with his suits. He was watching there, hidden away — just behind the door-handle — ready to spring." They worry about the nurse staying another week with her laugh "like a spoon tinkling against a medicine-glass" and "simply fearful about butter," whether to give the porter his top-hat, and whether Cyril, his grandson, ought to have the Colonel's watch. They think over their drab lives wondering if everything might have been different, and each tries to say something frightfully important to the other about the future, but neither can capture the wandering thought. The "Life of Ma Parker," brave old charwoman, kitchen-maid at sixteen, married to a baker, seven of her thirteen buried, "if it wasn't the 'ospital it was the infirmary you might say," and of the other six, "emigrimation" for the boys, and "going wrong" for the girls, in spite of their mother's struggles. Ethel, the youngest, married a good-for-nothing waiter who died the year Lennie, her grandson, was born. Lennie was gran's boy from the first, but "taking him to the cemetery, even, never gave him a colour; a nice shake-up in the bus never improved his appetite."

When Lennie dies she feels that the time has come when she must have a "proper cry," "but where?", "There was nowhere." "She couldn't go home. . . . It would frighten Ethel . . . she couldn't sit on a bench anywhere; people would come arsking her questions. She couldn't possibly go back to the gentleman's flat; she had no right to cry in strangers' houses. If she sat on some steps a policeman would speak to her." "Marriage à la Mode" tells the story of William, the loving, fine-natured husband of the silly, shallow Isabel, who has turned from him to a group of sham poets and painters. He goes home for the week-end and never sees her alone. He remembers the holidays they used to have with the children when Isabel had been the miracle of loveliness and kindness William thought her. He writes to her: "My darling, precious Isabel . . . " a despairing love letter, and she reads it aloud to her horrid, jeering friends on the lawn. For a moment, alone in her room, she knew herself for what she is, "vile, odious, abominable, vulgar," but also "shallow, tinkling, vain," and when they call to her to go in bathing with them, she goes, "laughing in the new way." "Miss Brill," the English governess, spends her Sunday afternoons listening to the band concert at the Jardins Publiques. She is wearing her cherished fur neckpiece with its dim eyes and battered nose for the first time in the season. A young girl gayly tells her companion, "It's her fu-fur which is so funny. It's exactly like a fried whiting," and Miss Brill goes home to cry, forgetting even to buy her Sunday treat, a slice of honey-cake at the baker's. In "The Stranger," Mr. Hammond meets his wife who has been in Europe for ten months on a visit to their eldest girl. She tells him of the stranger, the young man, who had died "of heart" in her arms the night before. For his jealous, loving nature it is unendurable. Janey says, "It hasn't made you sad? It hasn't spoilt our evening — our being alone together?" "Spoilt their evening. Spoilt their being alone together," he thinks: "They would never be alone together again."

GIANTS IN THE EARTH, a saga of the prairie, by O. E. Rolvaag (1927). Five families of Norwegian pioneers cross the plains in their wagons in 1873 to settle on the bank of a stream in Dakota Territory, far from neighbors, and timber. The resourceful, energetic Per Hansa has only thirty dollars, hardly any tools, and only porridge for food for his family. They build sod huts, and raise crops to barter for supplies. Per builds the largest hut, and goes on the long trip to Sioux Falls with his ox-team to get willow poles to thatch his roof. He ploughs the first crooked furrow in the new land, and sows the first wheat in the spring. It is a dramatic adventure story with few actual happenings. Indians pass near the little settlement, and Per makes friends with them by caring for the wounded hand of one of them. The great events are the journeys to the village of a dozen shanties and two stores when supplies are needed, the bartering of potatoes, the snaring of ducks for winter food, and the catch of fish in the net Per made, and the great winds and blizzards of the winter. Per and the two boys are happy in the new home. Beret, his wife, hates the hard life, and fear of the immense open spaces and the solitude drives her into a kind of madness. She believes her third son, Peder Victorius, who has not been properly christened, is a lost soul. A minister comes to visit them, and after a time Beret is better. Religion becomes her comfort and grows to be an obsession. Their friend, Hans Olsa, on his death bed because of exposure in a blizzard trying to shelter his cattle, longs to see the minister. Beret insists that Per shall go to the distant settlement for the minister, and against his own better judgment he starts off on skiis, and never returns. It is a story of endless toil, of hardship, of famine, and plague of locusts, and of dauntless courage and the early rites of civilization.

GOLDEN DAY, THE, a Study in American Experience and Culture, by Lewis Mumford (1926). According to this arraignment of industrial civilization America has deserted culture for the idea of progress, and makes an end in itself of instrumentalism. The pioneer unconsciously followed Rousseau "back to nature," but bartered his heritage for gaslight and paved streets and ultimately skyscrapers. "We are living on fragments of the old cultures, or on abortions of the new, because the energies that should have gone into the imaginative life are balked by the persuasive instrumentalism of the environment." The "Golden Day" is the period of the ascendency of New England, 1830 to 1860, which ended with the Civil War. The Puritan seaboard communities were "outposts of Europe: they carried their own moral and intellectual climate with them"; there was no native literature, only a Jonathan Edwards, a Benjamin Franklin, and a Thomas Paine. In the pioneering period America ceased to be an outpost of Europe. "The movement into backwoods America turned the European into a barbarian." Emerson was the leader in the first indigenous American literature. For him matter and spirit were not in conflict; he achieved the synthesis of physical and spiritual. His worthy followers were Thoreau and Whitman. Hawthorne represents "the twilight of Puritanism as a spiritual force," still concerned with "sin, death, eternity." Herman Melville continues the tradition in "Moby Dick." The Civil War "was a struggle between two forms of servitude, the slave and the machine. The machine won, and the human spirit was almost as much paralyzed by the victory as it would have been by the defeat." The period of Elizabethan daring on the sea, well-balanced adjustment of farm and factory, the lecture-lyceum, were replaced by the exploitation of oil, gas, coal, and industrialism that created the unscrupulous profiteer. Culture could not flourish in this "Gilded Age." Henry James fled to Europe. William James stayed at home, and evolved a philosophy of compromise and acquiescence which he called pragmatism. Mr. Mumford quotes Mark Twain's letter to Walt Whitman on his seventieth birthday in praise of industrialism. Mark Twain accepted his environment, and viewed man as "an automaton, a mere creature of the forces that worked upon him," and partly hid his despair by his humor. John Dewey developed the ideas of pragmatism, or "instrumentalism" as he prefers to call it, and for him, like the pioneer, happiness means a preparation for something else. Happiness "is found only in success; but success means succeeding, getting forward, moving in advance." The deficiencies of Mr. Dewey's philosophy, Mr. Mumford considers, are the deficiencies of the American scene. "A Goodyear and a Morse seem to him as high in the scale of human development as a Whitman and a Tolstoi. . . ." Mr. Dewey's justification of art is that it is in his own words "peculiarly instrumental in quality. . . . The creators of such works are entitled, when successful, to the gratitude that we give to inventors of microscopes and microphones; in the end they open new objects to be observed and enjoyed." A detailed criticism of instrumental philosophy ends with a quotation from Emerson: "Things are in the saddle and ride mankind." Mr. Mumford thinks that we must overthrow the rider, and recover the horse, "for otherwise, horse and rider may drive to the devil."

GOOD WOMAN, A, by Louis Bromfield (1927). The fourth of a series of novels beginning with "The Green Bay Tree," which the author says may be considered as a single novel with the title "Escape." In this story Philip struggles to escape from the domination of his mother, Emma Downes, the good woman. Her easygoing, drinking husband, Jason Downes, had deserted her when Philip was two years old, leaving a note, "explaining that it was impossible for any man to continue living with so much virtue." Emma told the world that Mr. Downes had gone to China on business, and after "a year had passed, during which she constantly spoke of his letters and doings in China," she gave out that she had not heard from Jason for so long that she feared something had happened to him, and invoked the Government to investigate his disappearance. "In due time Mrs. Downes put on mourning and the derelict husband became enveloped in the haze of romance which surrounds one who apparently has met his death among the bandits of the Manchurian mountains. . . . She had always been rather vague about geography, and from time to time distributed his remains over half of Asia." She started a bakery and later a lunch-room which was a great success. Her greatest success is her son Philip, whom she moulds to her own perfect satisfaction. At one time he had expressed a "foolish" desire to be an artist, but she had persuaded him to be a minister instead, married him to Naomi Potts, "known throughout the churchgoing world as 'the youngest missionary of God,'" and given him to the work of the Lord in blackest Africa. There was no bond between Philip and Naomi save their work. Emma had explained to Philip that they could not live together as man and wife as long as their minds and bodies were devoted to their work. The beauty of the tropical jungle after a time dims the image of the mother who has "done everything" for him, and Philip begins to think for himself. Emma, returning from reading "one of my son's interesting letters" at the meeting of the Woman's Christian Temperance Union, receives word that Philip and Naomi are on their way home, and are not going back. Philip writes that he has made a mistake in his calling. After his return Philip goes to work in the mills with "the Hunkies and Dagoes," and Emma and Naomi fight his rebellion which they keep a secret as long as they can, finally telling the church people that his health will not allow his return. Naomi is happy only in the life she knows in the missionary field, and is thwarted in her domestic surroundings. Bovine Aunt Maybelle tells her that she must have a child to win Philip's love, and even Emma now urges the use of this weapon. When her twins are born they do give her a claim on Philip. Just as Emma is about to marry a Congressman, Moses Slade, her graceless husband returns. Gradually the mother he has respected and admired disintegrates as Philip sees the real Emma reveal herself, hard, vain, self-righteous, ready to sacrifice everything and everybody to appearances, to her position in the community. Religion in her hands became "a political business-like instrument of success." Mary Conyngham, his real mate, the childhood friend his mother had separated him from, arranges with her friend, Irene Shane, to have Philip use the stable at Shane Castle for a studio. Naomi finds him there drawing the mysterious, beautiful Lily Shane, and sees herself suddenly as "dowdy, and ridiculous," "a pale, thin, freckled woman, with sandy hair, dressed in funny clothes." She tells the tale of her misery to the tired, middle-aged preacher, the Reverend Castor, wretchedly unhappy with a nagging, invalid wife, and they run away together to try to find the happiness life has denied them. In a few days they are found dead in a rented room where they turned on the gas. Philip is free to marry Mary, and haunted by the memory of the weird procession of black virgins celebrating the adoration of the god of fertility, he returns to Africa to paint, and dies of the fever, before he can accomplish his destiny. Emma allowed people to think that he had gone back to his old work, and so to certain death and martyrdom, and recaptured the glory of having given a son to foreign missions. Emma received the news of Jason's death from his Australian wife who enclosed a photograph of herself and Jason with their five children. It was a little more than a year later that Moses Slade and Emma Downes were married in Washington. Emma blossomed out into "a national figure, concerned always with moralities and reforms," and as "chairman," or member of a dozen committees and movements against whisky and cigarettes, and for Sunday closing." During the War she wore herself out making the speech that began on a quavering note: "I had a son of my own once, but he gave his life as a martyr in Africa. . . ." At her funeral service the minister said, "She was a good woman."

GRANDMOTHERS, THE: A FAMILY PORTRAIT, by Glenway Wescott (1927), a novel. This novel subtitled a family portrait begins with the pioneer days of the family in Wisconsin and parallels, in part, the author's adolescence. The first chapter deals with Alwyn Tower as a small boy, the house in Hope's Corner, his grandmother Tower's keepsakes. The second chapter generalizes on Alwyn's knowledge of America — in retrospect, while in Europe. "Alwyn daydreaming in Austria, a little self-consciously a poet. . . . And for a moment the well-bred voices, the philosophies, the orchestras were swept away. For a moment all Europe seemed less significant than the vicissitudes of pioneers, men who were anonymous unless they were somebody's relatives. He did not quite like their suffering, their illiterate mysticism, their air of failure; but he understood them, or fancied that he did. It did not matter whether he liked them or not — he was their son. . . . Among them of their marriages and love affairs there had also been born a composite character, the soul of a race that was not actually a race; something so vague that one recognized it only as an atmosphere, a special brightness, or a peculiar quality of the temperaments and customs and fortunes of Americans." Alwyn Tower saw these pioneers "disillusioned but imaginative, going through the motions of hope. Pretenders to royal blood, the site of whose kingdom has long been forgotten. . . . And as he thought of their lives, he was surprised by regret (their regret) which weakened and then strengthened his will: regret that the time for laughter and ease, even for him seemed never to come, while work never came to an end." The chapters following are about these ancestors as Alwyn remembers them through stories, through boyhood acquaintance or from daguerreotypes. This is a chapter on his grandfather, Henry Tower, a fragment of his autobiography on his early pioneer experience; and the rest of his story, service in the Civil War, the death of his first wife, Serena Cannon, and their only son Oliver; the story of his second marriage to Rose Hamilton, his brother Leander's former sweetheart; of his lifelong disappointment in his work, in his children, and in his aspirations. There is a chapter on his wife, her early rejection by Leander, her later compromise with what her days brought her, and the stories which she told Alwyn. There is a chapter on Alwyn's Great Aunt Mary Harris, who later married Henry's brother Harrison — her previous marriage to Dr. Brandom, his death in Missouri during the border raids, her marriage to Cleaver, their separation as a result of his trouble with the Unionists, her world-wide travels after her widowhood. There is a chapter on Alwyn's great-Aunt Nancy Tower's unhappiness at being married to Jessie Davis, a farm-hand and insensitive, and their son Timothy whom she managed to educate in the refinement of her own way. After her death, her son Timothy was adopted by Alwyn's great uncle Leander, a bachelor, who had rejected love (to Rose Hamilton) and was later to be rejected when Timothy departed his own way to California. All his life Leander bears, in addition, the sorrow of his brother Hilary's disappearance in the Civil War — his brother of sixteen who would rather have suffered death than a life of separation from Leander by Leander's engagement to Rose Hamilton. The story of the older generation is completed with a chapter on Alwyn's maternal grandparents — Ira and Ursula Duff — their unhappy marriage, and Ursula's madness in the end, her words to Alwyn: "you are my sweetheart, you know." Several people, anonymous, or almost so, are remembered in a chapter on the dead: a beautiful boy whose name had been forgotten, as well as the hired man who ate skunk. The story of Alwyn's parents' generation portrays the story of his father, his mother, his uncles James and Evan and his aunt Flora. His mother's girlhood includes the story of her rejection of Paul Fairchild, her illness, her happy marriage to Ralph Tower, Alwyn's father, who continued to work the soil with his father, Henry. Alwyn's Uncle Jim becomes a minister and marries the wealthy Caroline Fielding. His life is not disappointing, but it might have been different had his father allowed the son's marriage to the musical Irene Geiger. Alwyn's Aunt Flora dies at the age of twenty-nine, after her refusal of the love tendered her by Richard Wallace and Herbert Ruhl. Alwyn's Uncle Evan, who goes under the name of John Craig, lives a prosperous rancher in New Mexico with his wife Susanne Orfeo, a woman of French and Italian parentage, and their son Leander Orfeo — years after Evan's desertion in the Spanish-American War and his stay in London where he met Susanne in her father's gem shop. The final chapter of this saga of a family tells of his parents' removal to Brighton, of his grandmother Tower's death, and of Alwyn's understanding of her life's meaning for his own life, scarcely begun, which would repeat the life of those who had gone before him, all the surprises to come being merely the result of earlier combinations. The grandmothers thus remain a symbol of a "continual bridge from the past, across a sort of abyss in the dark, to the future, a certain knowledge of at least one side of the abyss (the side from which Alwyn came) and a certain knowledge of other bridges."

GREAT AMERICAN BAND WAGON, THE, by Charles Merz (1925). Modern American customs, enthusiasms, idiosyncrasies and foibles are portrayed in a humorous, penetrating, kindly critical manner in seventeen chapters, each concerned with some salient feature of Young America's manner of living. "The Once Open Road" describes the restlessness of John Smith, Jr., who drove off from the old home in Connecticut back in 1791, in a wagon loaded to the breaking point with a "wife, two barrels of flour, a Bible, three muskets, a Governor Winthrop desk, six volumes of Jonathan Edwards, and a cask of rum" into the far-away State of New York, and carries the story down to John Smith, 5th, who lived in Iowa in this century. This latest descendant of the Smith family had none of the desks or clocks or casks of rum of his ancestor, but "he had a block of stock, a six cylinder coupé and a barrel of phonograph records for his daughters." The constant urge to go pioneering is an American urge. The chapter, "Sweet Land of Secrecy," is devoted to secret societies. Mr. Merz says, "We join everything"; how we join, and what illustrious and resounding titles we apply to our otherwise plain business man selves. Radio is the subject of a chapter. "This is our counterpart of the drum the black man beats when the night is dark and the jungle lonely. Tom-tom." Who has not listened to a radio far into the night? Who has not tuned in (and out) of a hash of political speeches, soprano solos, jazz bands, bedtime stories, sermons and what not, without thinking some of the same things that Mr. Merz has written down here? "Thirsty? Try Our Cherry Split." This and various other signs greet the patron of "The New American Bar" — which is just the author's name for our modern soda fountain. One never realized what an artist a soda clerk is until reading how he pumps the chocolate, spurts the syrup on to the side of the glass — not the bottom — and thrusts the concoction under the electric mixer to complete the process of serving an ice-cold drink. And so on through "Bigger and Better Murders," the great American game of golf, education on a large scale, or, "Roll Your Own Diploma," through present day styles in homes, business men's interest in bathing beauties, American tourists "doing" Europe, the movies — down to public opinion, "Head-line Heroes" and "The Attack on New York." His observations on the "New America" are thought provoking. Is this what we really are? Throughout his book he characterizes us as "a restless people, with a great store of curiosity and an immense reserve of energy, a heritage of youth and a tremendous will to go somewhere."

GREAT GATSBY, THE, by F. Scott Fitzgerald (1925). Jay Gatsby is a mysterious young man who emerges from nowhere and buys a great estate at West Egg, Long Island, and entertains there on a lavish scale. The guests at his parties are often unknown to their host. They drink his champagne, walk and dance on his velvet lawns, and discuss the wild rumors about Mr. Gatsby.. Is he a bootlegger, a German spy, a cousin of the ex-Kaiser? The story is told by Nick Carroway, a man in whose tolerance all sorts and conditions of men confide. He happens to take a cottage on the edge of Gatsby's grounds, and gets to know and like him. Gatsby has invented a character for himself out of the romantic material of cheap fiction, and is faithful in playing the part of this Platonic conception. His real name is James Gatz, and his family are shiftless farmers in a small town in Minnesota. The boy, making his living digging clams, rows out to Dan Cody's yacht, is taken aboard, and becomes secretary and companion to the millionaire for five years until his death. At the beginning of the War Gatsby was stationed at Camp Taylor, near Louisville. Daisy, Nick's cousin, the prettiest and most popular girl in town, and the first "nice girl" Gatsby had ever met, is a revelation to him. They become secretly engaged, but before Gatsby can get back from France after the Armistice, Daisy has grown tired waiting, and marries a wealthy man of her own world, a "great, big, hulking specimen," football player at Yale. Gatsby returns penniless, determined to make a fortune, and win Daisy again. When the story opens Gatsby has made his money in shady, unscrupulous business and has bought the show-place at West Egg because Daisy and Tom live at East Egg. He entertains for all the world in the hope that Daisy will appear some evening among the guests. Nick invites Daisy to tea to meet Gatsby, and he tries to recapture his lost romance. He wants Daisy to leave Tom, and go back to Louisville to be married to him, just as they had planned five years before. Daisy is bored and neglected by Tom, who has a mistress in town, Myrtle Wilson, who lives with her simple, unsuspecting husband over his garage on the road to New York. Just at this time when Tom sees that Daisy is infatuated with Jay Gatsby, Mr. Wilson finds out that his wife is having an affair with some man, and tells Tom of his decision to move back to the West. Tom has insisted on driving to New York in Gatsby's yellow car with Jordan Baker, Daisy's friend and bridesmaid. On the return trip Gatsby has his own car, and Daisy is driving. Mrs. Wilson rushes out to intercept Tom, and is run over and killed. Mr. Wilson starts out to find the man who drove the yellow car, gets Gatsby's name from Tom, and shoots Gatsby and then himself. Gatsby is the victim of chivalry, and pays for his dream, not for his sins. He has no friends, only business associates, and of the crowds who enjoyed his hospitality, only one man joins Nick and Gatsby's father at the funeral. Tom and Daisy have gone away, leaving no address. The book is a fantastic satire, a detective story ending in melodrama.

GREAT GOD BROWN, THE, by Eugene O'Neill (1925). The drama is based on the idea that everyone has a multiple personality and that we all wear masks, when self-revelation is too painful to ourselves or others. The chief characters have each his or her mask to represent the face turned to the world, and "to dramatise changes and conflicts of character." In soliloquy or when talking with someone who understands and values the true self the mask can be removed. The two friends, Dion Anthony and Billy Brown, both love the same girl, Margaret. She marries the artistic, poetic Dion, whose mask of Pan she loves, though she does not know the real man underneath. Dion tries to show her his real self, but has to give it up. His inner nature is thus thwarted in self-expression, and his outward self becomes transformed from laughing Pan to mocking Mephistopheles. In spite of his gifts Dion is unsuccessful, and at Margaret's intercession, Brown offers him the position of architect in his firm. A letter to the papers by the author confesses "the mystical pattern which manifests itself as an overtone . . . dimly behind and beyond the words and actions of the characters." Dion Anthony is Dionysus and St. Anthony, a representative "of the eternal war between the creative pagan acceptance of life and the self-denying spirit of Christianity." Margaret is "the direct descendant of the Marguerite of 'Faust,' the eternal girl-woman." Brown represents "the visionless demigod of our new materialistic myth, success, building his life of exterior things, inwardly empty and resourceless." Cybel, the prostitute, to whom Dion can reveal his real self, and who gives him the understanding his wife's devotion has not had, is "the incarnation of Cybele, the earth mother." Brown still loves Margaret and in order to keep Dion faithful to her, he takes over Cybel, providing for her munificently. At Cybel's house Dion and Brown meet. Dion falls at Brown's feet and dies. As Mephistopheles he condemns "Brown to destruction by willing him his mask, but this mask falling off . . . it is the Saint who kisses Brown's feet in abject contrition and pleads as a little boy to a big brother to tell him a prayer. Brown has always envied the creative life force in Dion — what he himself lacks. When he steals Dion's mask of Mephistopheles he thinks he is gaining the power to live creatively, while in reality he is only stealing that creative power made self-destructive by complete frustration. The devil of mocking doubt makes short work of him." He can no longer be himself to anyone in this Jekyll and Hyde existence. Margaret accepts and loves him as Dion, and to the world he is "forced to wear a mask of his Success, William A. Brown . . . and in the end out of his anguish his soul is born." He becomes Dion and is accused of murdering Brown, whose mask is found dead. In a sense he has killed Brown, and so it is nothing which is shot by the police in Cybel's house. In the epilogue Margaret, an old woman, masked to her three sons, speaks to them of their father.

GREAT HUNGER, THE, by Johan Bojer, translated from the Norwegian by W. J. Alexander Worster and C. Archer (1919). Peer Holm, the illegitimate child of a Norwegian officer, is brought up in the family of a fisherman. The story begins with the adventure of fishing with the big deep-sea lines which the boys were forbidden to touch when the men of the village were away, because what may not a deep-sea line raise to the surface, and this time it brought a Greenland shark, the fiercest monster of the northern seas, into the boat, and a fight for life to Peer, and Peter, and Klaus, the doctor's son. Though Peer knows he is "a sinner now, and a wild young scamp," he dreams of becoming a priest, and sometimes a bishop who will "lift up his finger," and all the stars will break into song. This career is closed to him by poverty. He goes to the city to work his way through the technical school. Grief at his sister's death makes him turn from a pitiless God who seemed to protect and care only for those "who have parents and home and brothers and sisters and worldly goods. . . . But here's a boy alone in the world, struggling and fighting his way on as best he can — from him I will take the only thing he has. . . ." His faith in science is now everything to him, and he resolves to "be one of the sons of Prometheus, that head the revolt against the tyranny of Heaven." Ferdinand Holm, his friend, tells him that the modern technician is a priest, a descendant of Prometheus, and that every victory which the spirit of man wins over nature wrenches something of their omnipotence from the hands of the gods. He joins Ferdinand and Klaus in Egypt, builds the Nile barrage and railroads in Abyssinia, and returns to his native land wealthy and famous. In conversation with a friend who hails him as a missionary of culture he speaks his disillusion: "I believe that fire and steel will soon brutalize men. Machines kill more and more of that which we call the godlike in us." Then he marries a lovely wife, Merle, has three children, and thinks he has found happiness in the joy of living in his great house with his family. On another dam he does brilliant work, but an unexpected vein of water appears in the tunnel, his engineers make costly mistakes, and he loses his fortune and ruins his father-in-law, who had gone bond with him. His invention, a mowing machine, is complete except for one detail, but he has worked too hard and his health breaks, and a competitor steals his idea. The engineer of the Nile barrage is reduced to living in a peasant's hut, earning his living as a blacksmith when he is able to work. Two of his children have to be sent to relatives of his wife, and the third is bitten to death by a churlish neighbor's dog. Struck down by misfortune Peer finds his spiritual hunger satisfied by the discovery of the divinity of man. He writes to his friend Klaus: "I sat alone on the promontory of existence, with the sun and the stars gone out, and ice-cold emptiness above me, about me, and in me, on every side . . . by degrees it dawned on me that there was still something left. There was one little indomitable spark in me, that began to glow all by itself — it was as if I were lifted back to the first day of existence, and an eternal will rose up in me. and said: Let there be light . . . and more and more it came home to me that it is man himself that must create the divine in heaven and on earth — that that is his triumph over the dead omnipotence of the universe." Man can be greater than his fate.

GREEN BAY TREE, THE, a novel, by Louis Bromfield (1924). The story begins in a Middle Western town which has changed from a frontier settlement to an industrial city within the lifetime of the heroine, Lily Shane. Her father, John Shane, a worldly adventurer, came from Europe just before the Civil War, built a bizarre Gothic-Georgian house, "Cypress Hill," called by the town, "Shane's Castle," married Julia Barr, a farmer's daughter, and sent her to Paris to school for two years to train her to be mistress of this home. Before his death, the mills and the slums where the millworkers lived had reached the gates of the estate. "Shane's Castle" was no longer an island surrounded by marshes but by great furnaces, steel sheds and a glistening maze of railway tracks." Lily, a beautiful girl in her early twenties, loved by the governor of the state, refuses to marry him even though she expects to be the mother of his child, because she distrusts her own passion for him, though she cannot tell why she is sure she would not be a good wife. It is arranged that Lily shall go to Paris to Madame Gigon, retired teacher of the school both Lily and her mother had attended at St. Cloud. Madame Gigon's father had been ruined by the collapse of the Second Empire, and she is highly respected "in the circles which moved about the aging figure of the Prince Bonaparte." Here Lily passes for a widow and her son Jean is born. Her younger sister, Irene, made hysterical by the discovery of Lily's unconventional morals, wants to become a nun, but her mother wins her promise not to leave her during her lifetime, and shrewdly arouses her interest in the families of the millworkers and the Welcome House Settlement. After four years Lily returns to visit her mother, and "Cypress Hill" is gay again with a dinner party and a ball. Willie Harrison, the young mill owner, representative of the industrial aristocracy, courts Lily, and takes the sisters over the mill where Lily sees Stepan Krylenko, the young Ukrainian labor leader whom Irene has taught to speak English. Lily returns to Paris to her son and to her lover, Cesaire, the baron, cousin to Madame Gigon. She makes it possible for her young relative, Ellen Tolliver, to come to Paris to study to become a great pianist. Lily goes home once more when her mother is dying and arrives in the midst of the steel strike. After the funeral, alone in the house at night, Lily watches the strikers hold a meeting. There is a fight with the police and later Krylenko escapes to the house. She hides him and cares for his wounds, talks with him, and is stirred to infatuation for the young blond giant, grown to be a man of power and ideals under Irene's tutelage. Irene finds them together, senses the situation and the sisters are forever estranged. Lily goes to her comfortable, luxurious life in Paris and Irene to the convent. Her lover, Cesaire, is killed in the War and her son maimed. After the War she marries M. de Cyon, an old friend, a cabinet minister. Watching the parade of the soldiers among a group of Americans she encounters the governor, now a senator, to whom the years seem to have brought nothing of wisdom, of humor, or gentleness, "only a certain vulgar shrewdness." She realizes "for the first time, what in the unwitting cruelty of her youth she had never known . . . that he had really suffered." Lily, with her courageous flair for life continues to flourish like a green bay tree, though as she tells the governor, she no longer thinks that it is possible to live by one's self alone — without touching the lives of others. The abnormal, repressed Irene dies in a French convent. Stepan Krylenko, deported to Russia, dies of typhus in Moscow.

GREEN HAT, THE, by Michael Arlen (1924). A boy and girl love between Iris March and Napier Harpenden is thwarted by his overbearing father, Sir Maurice, who wants his son to marry a rich girl, and considers Iris and her twin brother, Gerald, the last of an old family, as bad stock. Iris, starved for love, marries Boy Fenwick, madly in love with her. The handsome Boy Fenwick just down from Oxford appears to "have been the most beloved of the beloved young men" of his time. On the "dawn of his wedding night" he is found lying dead below the window of his room in the courtyard of the hotel at Deauville. "Mrs. Boy Fenwick had seemed to feel most deeply her responsibility to Boy's memory and to his friend's love for him." She says that it was her fault, that he had died "for purity," without any further explanation, letting it be believed that he had committed suicide "in the despair of the disenchantment of an ideal." Her brother who has worshipped Boy Fenwick is lost without his hero, and completely estranged from his sister. He lives a solitary life and takes to drink like his father, who died of it. The writer of the story sees Iris for the first time when she comes to see her brother, who lives in the same house. She is wearing a green hat, hence the title. Two older men, Guy and Hilary, friends of the March family, tell him her tragic story. Four years after Fenwick's death she married Captain Storm, who was killed by Sinn Feiners in Ireland. Iris is beautiful, courageous, a loyal friend, but she is what they call "déclassée." She comes to see Gerald another time and the writer discovers that Gerald has committed suicide and sends her away without telling her. Guy goes to see her the next day to break the news to her. Three days before Napier marries Venice Pollen he meets Iris for the first time since Fenwick's death, and makes her tell him the truth about Fenwick's unworthiness and the remorse which caused him to end his life, but it is too near the wedding day for Napier to break with Venice. On Napier's honeymoon the writer takes him to see Iris, who is near death in a nursing home in Paris. After a time the lovers meet again and decide with Venice's knowledge and sympathy to go away together. Sir Maurice sends for Iris to come to see him, determined to make one last effort to interfere, and she asks the writer to accompany her. Guy and Hilary are there and presently Napier and Venice arrive, and there are mutual recriminations, explanations, and Sir Maurice apologizes to Iris for accusing her of being the cause of Fenwick's death. She jumps into her car, sends Napier back, and drives violently into a tree, making the last sacrifice, and choosing the way to make her death seem an accident. Napier goes to India, and Venice awaits his return. The interest is not in the story so much as in the manner of the telling of it, and the dialogue.

GREEN MIRROR, THE, by Hugh Walpole (1917). The Trenchards are an upper middle-class family of the early part of the century, self-sufficient, and completely indifferent to the rest of the world. Into this complacent circle, interrupting the celebration of Grandfather Trenchard's birthday, a more important event than Christmas, comes an outsider, Philip Mark, who proceeds to fall in love with Katherine, the eldest and favorite daughter. Philip "isn't quite an Englishman, you know. Been abroad so long." No Trenchard ought to marry a man who thinks of Russia as a fine country. Mr. Trenchard accepts him on what is virtually a year's probation. Millie, the younger daughter, just back from school in Paris, stirred by a world outside the family, is the only one of them to welcome Philip and consider Katherine's happiness. Mrs. Trenchard determines that Katherine shall never leave her, that she will either get rid of Philip or that he shall be absorbed into the family. They all secretly dislike and distrust him, but the conflict is with Mrs. Trenchard, whose inflexible, unconquerable hatred and opposition to Philip is difficult to realize because of her silent inertia. All the Trenchards are devoid of imagination, and Katherine, devoted to her family, is slow to understand that she must choose between Philip and her mother. Philip is amiable and susceptible to the domination of stronger wills. In Russia he had a mistress, Anna, a ghost of the past almost symbolic of Philip's life outside the Trenchard circle, ready to reclaim him. His last hope is that Mrs. Trenchard will find out about this affair and cast him out, and he knows that in this event Katherine would go with him. Henry, the young blundering brother, hears about Anna, tells Aunt Aggie, the malicious old maid, and she springs it on the family at Sunday night supper. It turns out that Mrs. Trenchard has known all along, and Philip's last defense breaks down. Rather than lose Katherine he will give up his own life and become a Trenchard. Katherine had thought she loved Philip for his strength, but discovers that she loves him for his weakness. She proves herself to be more of a woman than a Trenchard, and plans escape for them both by the evening train to London. Her mother never forgives her, and refuses to have any relations with them afterward. The green mirror which hangs in the drawing-room of the London house has reflected generations of the family. It "gave to the view that it embraced some comfortable touch so that everything within was soft and still and at rest." Henry, symbolic of the younger generation, throws a book at Philip, the invader, and instead of hitting Philip breaks the mirror, and "instantly the whole room seemed to tumble into pieces . . . and with the room, the house . . . and Trenchard traditions. . . ."

GROWTH OF THE SOIL, THE (Markens Grede), by Knut Hamsun (1920). An epic of the peasant pioneer who goes into the wilderness, clears the land for his farm, makes a sod hut for shelter, then a house of logs, establishes a family, and becomes prosperous by his efforts. Isak's only companions during the first winter are his three goats. In the spring, Inger, a girl who has no suitors because of her harelip, comes to help him. They work hard and are happy together. She goes to visit her home and brings back her cow, which is a great and wonderful event. When their first child is a year and a half old they make the trip to the village to have him baptized and to be married. An elderly widow, relative of Inger, comes to see them and envies their happiness. She sends a Lapp with a hare in his bag which he manages that Inger carrying her third child shall see, and true to the superstition as to prenatal impressions the baby is born with a harelip. Inger has always contrived to be alone at the critical time fearing that her children may inherit her deformity. She makes way with the infant to save it from the suffering she has endured herself. The malicious Oline comes to see them, ferrets out the secret and tells the story. Isak pities Inger and does not reproach her. She is sentenced to eight years in prison, but the intercession of their friend, Geissler, the former sheriff, brings about her release, and she comes back with the little girl born in the prison. An operation had left only a tiny scar to mark her harelip. She has learned dress-making, become citified, and finds her home lonely. For a time she is unfaithful to Isak with a workman in the neighborhood. Eleseus, the oldest boy, attracts the attention of an engineer, who takes him to the city to work in his office. He is not successful and is spoiled for the farm. "So Eleseus departs for America. He never comes back." Copper on the land makes Isak more prosperous. Other settlers come. Axel Strom hires Barbro, the pretty daughter of Brede, to help him. They live as husband and wife, and Axel is pleased that Barbro is to have a child which will hold her to him. She has lived in the city as a servant and does not want to have any ties so drowns the child, claiming that it is an accident. A champion of woman's rights, Mrs. Heyerdahl, pleads her case with the court and she goes free. Mrs. Heyerdahl takes her into her household, but Barbro cannot go straight, and goes back to Axel because she is again to have a child. His only concern is that she will be no help to him at harvest time.

GUARDSMAN, THE, a comedy by Franz Molnar (1924). A popular Viennese actor has been married for six months to his beautiful actress wife. Noticing that she seems abstracted and spends much time playing the melancholy and romantic music of Chopin, he fears that she is tired of him and would welcome a lover. He devises a ruse to test her love for him by playing the part of an admirer. Dressed as a Russian guardsman he walks in front of her window, and sends her flowers, which she tells her husband are from a silly girl. Next he writes asking permission to call, while her husband is fulfilling an engagement in another city. The actor leaves to get his train and then returns in the disguise of the guardsman, and declares his passion for the actress. She invites him to join her in her box at the opera that evening, and he leaves tormented as a husband by the success of his courtship, yet pleased with the triumph of his art as an actor. At the opera he gets from her the admission that while she loves her husband she is not in love with him. Still prais-

THE READER'S DIGEST OF BOOKS

ing her husband's intelligence she leads on the supposed Russian Prince to renewed protestations of love. They are joined by their mutual friend, the critic, Dr. Bernhard, to whom the husband has confided his plan to test his wife's fidelity. In an aside the actor tells him that he is convinced that all is well, since as he says, "a woman who can be true to her husband when I am the lover will be true always." His self congratulations come too soon however. She responds to his ardent suit and they kiss in the anteroom and make an appointment to meet the next day. He returns home unexpectedly as his wife is expecting the visit from the guardsman, dresses behind the screen, and confronts her with his masquerade. She gayly announces that she has seen through his disguise from the first, and was merely playing the part he expected of her, to tease him. At the end the husband and the reader are both in some doubt as to the truth of her story.

HAIRY APE, THE, by Eugene O'Neill (1921). The play opens in the stokehole of a transatlantic liner, where Yank, by his tremendous strength and his good-natured bullying reigns supreme. He is completely satisfied with the narrow little world of coal and steel in which he "belongs," and does not envy the passengers on the promenade deck, who to him are mere baggage. The fabulously rich and beautiful Mildred Douglas pays a slumming visit to the depths of the ship, and shrinks fainting from the sight of the grimy, half-naked Yank with horror and contempt. The action of the drama now takes place in the consciousness of Yank, who is roused to a vague discomfort and curiosity as he senses that there is a world in which he does not "belong." In successive scenes aboard the ship and in port in New York Yank attempts to win recognition as a human being. The final blow falls when he wanders on Fifth Avenue during the Easter Parade, and all the gay self-satisfied throng turn toward him blank, unseeing, inhuman masks. He jostles and pushes them, creates a disturbance, and gets himself beaten and carried off by the police. The prisoners to whom he tells his wrongs advise him to join the I. W. W., but no talk about class consciousness and orderly revolution can help him. His tragedy reaches its fulfillment at the monkey house in the Zoo, where in the darkness Yank meets his death in the embrace of that other and stronger Hairy Ape whom he had been said to resemble, and whom he had been curious therefore to see. Then again he "at last belongs . . . perhaps."

HAPPY MOUNTAIN, by Maristan Chapman (1928), is a novel about the hill-folk of the Tennessee Mountains. The story centres about Wait-still-on-the-Lord Lowe, or Waits Lowe as he was commonly called. Waits was a mountain boy who longed to see the rim of the world; to see of what cities were made and to get books into his hands, with their multitude of words which were of curious fascination to him. In the springtime, when the hills were dusky purple and the tickling in his heels became unbearable, Waits bade good-by to Dena, the girl who loved him, and slipped at daybreak from the home of his father and mother to start afoot over the edge of the mountain. Romance danced ahead of Waits, as it led him through fields and towns and fertile valleys, where he is stunned by the lack of manners of the low-people who, when asked for food, hand him scraps of "leftments," wrapped in newspaper and bid him be gone. Words swirled through Waits' brain, "a power o' words, hard words made outen iron 'n' brass; an' soft words, like corn-silk, an' proud sharp words, like frost on a sapling branch, an' pretty, kind words, like blue flowers comin' out o' the black swamp dirt." While in the "outlands," picking up odd jobs of work, in order that he may buy his food and not be dependent, Waits purchases a fiddle, which he calls Venger, with which he attempts to learn self-expression. After weeks of wandering, blown along like an irresponsible leaf before the wind of his imagination, Waits meets with a conductor of a train which has stopped at his home town daily for years, and is amazed to learn that the train had another terminus as well as Glen Hazard and that he is only a day's journey away, whereas it has taken him weeks of foot-travel to reach this place. The conductor tells Waits some home gossip and something of Dena, who has looked, so it was rumored, with favor upon the fiery-headed stranger with silky-soft eyes and hands like the claws of a son of Satan. Without more ado, after asking the fare to Glen Hazard, Waits makes ready to go home, where he must win Dena all over again. In his own words, he feels for her "as the dew for the grass and the blue wood-smoke for the still air at night-time." A prayer of Waits', of singular beauty, is "God — here's my torn-up-ness lying spread out before you — do you aim to take 'n' mend it?" Dena finally accepts Waits, after some difficult days, saying as she hands the fiddle back to him, "Take him an' let him talk, efn he's so minded. I guess the three of us'll get along." Waits took his homeward way, letting Venger have his head. "And the hills heard and the mountains knew and were filled with the sound of gladness."

HARMER JOHN, by Hugh Walpole (1926). Subtitled "An Unworldly Story," this novel is one of the 'Polchester' tales and a companion-piece of "The Cathedral." It is in miniature a retelling of the coming of a Christ: a rephrasing of the age-old fable of Socrates, of Jesus, of any and every great reformer who by being in advance of his time and his environment incurs first the admiration and then the hate of the people: since it is human nature to fear and hence hate that which we do not understand. "Harmer John's" real name was Hjalmar Johanson. His father was Swedish, his mother a native of Polchester, and the son comes to the Cathedral Town to set up as a gymnastic instructor. He preaches the gospel of the healthy mind in the healthy body, and the eternal beauty and glory of God manifested in physical perfection. He is simple as a child, strong as an elephant, and utterly naïve. He falls in love with Maude Penethen, the daughter of his landlady, pretty as a doll, and as shallow. He makes friends with the Reverend Tom Longstaffe, whose daughter Mary is about to come home with her illegitimate child. He sets up in business and for a while he prospers greatly: due partly to personal magnetism, partly to the influence of various prominent Canons of the Cathedral, and partly to the novelty and freshness of his views and methods. Then his spontaneous and instinctive championship of the under dog leads him to denounce the hideous slums of Seatown. His outspoken frankness makes enemies for him. Maude, fickle little weathercock, jilts him. "From him that hath not is taken away" until he is stripped bare. Still he struggles to bring light to those who are wilfully blind. Alone he advocates the destruction and reconstruction of Seatown. Finally in a riot down there he is killed by the very folk he sought most earnestly to benefit. A bitterly sardonic note is struck in the concluding chapter, laid several years later, wherein Gabrielle Midgeley, a little dried up spinster, through whose eyes most of the story is told, comes back to Polchester on the anniversary of Harmer John's death. His cherished reforms are now an accomplished fact, and the pious folk of Polchester have erected a tablet to his memory. He is fast becoming a legend. Thus it is with the giants of the earth. We like to admire them, but we find them inconvenient until safely and innocuously dead. Whether the cult they sponsor be wisdom as with Socrates, or valor as with Jeanne d'Arc, or beauty as with Harmer John, it is all one. Folk prefer to pluck the beams from their own eyes, and resent officious suggestions.

HE WHO GETS SLAPPED, a tragi-comedy, by Leonid Andreyev (1922). In the greenroom of a provincial circus the dissipated Count Mancini, the alleged father of the lovely bare-back rider, Consuelo, is trying to borrow a few francs from "Papa" Briquet, the proprietor of the circus. He threatens to take Consuelo, their star, away, and Briquet and his wife, Zinida, the lion-tamer, are sufficiently impressed with his talk to give him twenty francs. Into this tawdry little world so sufficient unto itself comes a stranger from "out there." He is expensively dressed and obviously a gentleman, and yet he asks to be taken on as a clown. He proposes that they shall call him "He Who Gets Slapped," and the amusement of the company suggests that it is a good idea worth trying out. Briquet insists on knowing his real name on account of the police before he will agree to engage him. "He" gives him a card which he says is "just a check for an old hat." The real identity of "He" as they call him is never revealed, but it is evident that he is a well-known if not distinguished person. His wife and his best friend have been false to him, and the friend in addition to stealing his wife has appropriated his ideas which he has published in a popularized vulgar form. Disguised in the ridiculous garb of a clown "He" tells the crowd his wise and beautiful thoughts and gets himself laughed at and slapped jesting at their expense. Everyone in the circus loves the dainty child, Consuelo, and the stranger also falls in love with her. The Count confides to him that he intends to sell her to the highest bidder to repair his fortunes, and that he is certain that he will be able to get Baron Regnard to marry her. Consuelo and her partner, Bazano, are unconsciously in love with each other. "He" appeals to Bazano to rescue her from the dissolute baron with his "convex spider-like eyes," but Bazano is too proud to acknowledge his love. Zinida is in love with Bazano, who will have nothing to do with her. She becomes possessed with the idea of making her lions love her, and holds the audience spellbound with her daring. The innocent Consuelo asks "He" what this "love" is that everyone talks about, that this fat baron offers her, whose "honest, faithful wife" she will be, though of course she does not love him. "He" tries to answer her query by telling her fortune in the lines of her hand. She cannot understand his warnings. He declares his own love for her, but she will not listen, and in quick temper slaps him soundly. He pretends that he was only playing his part of clown to her queen. The friend who has robbed "He" of everything sees him at a performance and comes behind the scenes to talk to him. "He" is believed to be dead, and the traitor asks if he will ever come back, confessing that he is unhappy and unable to enjoy the fruits of his treachery. "He" dismisses him with the answer that he will never return to the world. At Consuelo's last performance before her marriage to the Baron the ring where she rides is carpeted with the roses he brings to her; the audience cheer but there are no laughs for the clowns; everyone is too sad to say good-by to Consuelo. In the greenroom the circus folk drink her health with the Baron's champagne. The performers go back to the ring, and Consuelo tells "He" she is frightened. "He" offers to take her away but she says "it is too late." She asks him not to talk to her but to drink to her happiness. "He" gives her a glass in which he has put poison, and says, "Drink to your happiness, to your freedom," and asks her to save half its contents for him. The Count chides her for keeping the Baron waiting. She says she is tired, and everyone gathers around her in sympathy. "The clowns play a little tune on their pipes to cheer her." Consuelo becomes silent and quiet, and they realize that something serious is happening. "He" tells them it is death. To Consuelo, who is frightened, he says, "Don't you feel that you are in the foam, white sea-foam, and you are flying to the sun?" She answers, "I am flying. I am the sea-foam and this is the sun," and dies in his arms thinking it all a joke. "He" turns away to "struggle lonesomely with the torpidity of coming death." The Count is hysterical, and the Baron rushes out for the police. A shot is heard from outside the door. The Baron has committed suicide. "He" struggles to his feet, and speaks "strongly and indignantly": "You loved her so much, Baron? And you want to be ahead of me even there? No! I am coming! We shall prove then whose she is to be — forever ——"

HELL BENT FER HEAVEN, a play, by Hatcher Hughes (1923). The scene is the interior of a cabin in the Blue Ridge Mountains. Old David Hunt and Meg, his daughter-in-law, are waiting for Matt and Sid to return. Sid has come back from overseas with the A. E. F., and Matt has driven to the railroad station to meet his son. The central character is the young Rufe Pryor, a religious fanatic, "hell bent fer heaven," who justifies his selfish and malignant doings by representing them as the will of God whose divine instrument he is. He has been helping Matt in the store while Sid was away. Meg feels sorry for him because the men are always "a-pickin' on 'im," and tries to take his part. Matt says he is not worth his salt, and he is tired of his "bellyachin'." Sid, a handsome boy, excited to get home again, begins to talk war with his grandpap, who "fit" with Stonewall Jackson and Robert E. Lee. He and Meg persuade Matt not to send Rufe off for another month. The pious Rufe warns Matt that he may bully him about the things of this world, but he cannot keep him from loving Matt's immortal soul. Just as Sid is asking about his sweetheart, Jude Lowry, her brother, Andy, the mail-carrier comes in, and the friends greet each other warmly. There had been a feud between the Hunts and the Lowries, but the two families have been at peace for half a century, and the marriage of Sid and Jude will further strengthen the bond of friendship between them. Rufe, who is in love with Jude, plans to stir up the old feud to get rid of his rival. After getting Andy drunk he cunningly rouses him to ugly feelings against Sid, by making him think that Sid has been boasting that there were three more Lowries than Hunts killed in the blood feud. He advises Andy to pocket his pride however and live at peace with Sid if he can, as the Hunts are dangerous folk. He insinuates that Andy is afraid of Sid, with the result that Andy forces Sid to dance at the point of his pistol, until Jude comes in and interferes between them. David is convinced that Rufe is to blame for what has happened. Sid interrupts Rufe declaring his love for Jude, and tells him to get it straight that he is going to marry Jude, and alone with Sid, Jude agrees that she will be his wife. She brings Andy in to apologize, and Sid starts off to ride a part of the way home with Andy, while Jude remains at the cabin because a storm is threatening. A shot is heard, and Sid's horse comes back without his rider. The Hunts and Jude go out to look for Sid's body. Sid escaped the shot, and comes in on Rufe left alone, and by his questions gets him confused, and finds out most of the truth in spite of Rufe's lies. Rufe tries to prevent Sid from going to the dam to telephone to head off his father and grandfather on their way to the Lowries. In the midst of a prayer of advice to God how to treat Sid, Rufe bethinks him that he can get some dynamite from the store and blow up the dam. He tells God that while Sid is under the dam telephoning "the waters o' your wrath'll sweep over him like they did over Pharaoh an' his hosts in olden times." Rufe returns to find grandpap guarding Andy, and presently Jude and Meg are back from their search, sick with grief and anxiety. At Rufe's suggestion they put Andy in the cellar, where he tries to bargain with him not to tell his part in the affair. The flood waters recede so that Rufe cannot hope that Andy will drown in the cellar. Just as Rufe has decided that the Almighty intends to use him as an instrument of vengeance to kill Andy, Sid comes up behind him. Impersonating his own ghost he manages to worm a complete confession from Rufe. With everything explained the only thing that worries the Hunts and the Lowries is what to do with Rufe. The women cannot believe such a good Christian can be guilty of such dastardly deeds, though Rufe assures them that God moves in a mysterious way. Rufe dashes for the cellar to get away from Andy, and David facilitates his escape. They are well rid of Rufe, and Grandpap David has "saved a lot of folks from a run-in with the sheriff."

HER SON'S WIFE, by Dorothy Canfield Fisher (1926). Mary Bascomb is a middle-aged gentlewoman, a widow, who supports herself and her only child, Ralph, by teaching school. She idolizes her son, a grown man now, but since she still thinks of him unconsciously as a little boy, it is a tremendous shock to her when he wires that he has married his landlady's daughter, adding, "Lottie isn't your kind, Mother, but she's all right." Ralph and his wife come home, and Lottie in Mrs. Bascomb's eyes is impossible — pretty in a way, but loud, slangy, vain, without a thought in her head. Ralph is too weak to control her, and is jealous of her flirtations. On Mrs. Bascomb devolves the augmented care of the household, and, in great measure, of the baby that soon comes. Realizing reluctantly that Ralph will never amount to anything very much, Mrs. Bascomb vows passionately that the baby shall not be ruined through Lottie's influence the way Ralph has been. It is Lottie's inordinate vanity that gives Mrs. Bascomb her great idea. Lottie grows stout, and as she insists on wearing shoes that are too small for her, she has a "perfectly terrible" time with her feet. Playing on her self-pity, Mrs. Bascomb persuades her that she is really much worse than is the case, and gradually Lottie begins to keep to her room. She loves to be fussed over, and Mrs. Bascomb is only too willing to fuss over her if by so doing she can rescue "Dids" (christened Gladys, a name Mrs. Bascomb loathes). Dids grows up to healthy-minded, healthy-bodied girlhood, her inheritance from her grandmother predominating, so that when she leaves for college, one of the many questions in the air is "Where did you put that volume of Masefield?" After she has gone the house is curiously empty, and with a pang Mrs. Bascomb turns to Lottie, who is "all she has left now." She had thought that Dids' departure for college would be the end. But "this was not the end, at all. It was only at last, the beginning." And it was strange that "utter humility and remorse could have so sweet a savor. . . . Was it because they were now perfumed with pity and love?" The book raises an interesting ethical question: had Mrs. Bascomb the right, in order to save her granddaughter, to curtail her daughter-in-law's life within the confines of a neurotic invalid's room, even though that room were made as pretty and comfortable and attractive as was humanly possible? Does the end justify the means? The book does not answer this question definitely, but it does undoubtedly give one "furiously to think."

HIGH PLACE, THE, A Comedy of Disenchantment, by James Branch Cabell (1923). Florian, the ten year old son of the third Duke of Puysange in the land of Poictesme in early eighteenth century France, has two dreams. In the first he meets the Princess Mélusine in the forest, and goes with her to the "high place" under the spell of her enchantment, and sees her sister, Melior, the sleeping beauty. In the second dream he is the reigning duke, and is riding toward Storisende to marry his fifth wife, Mademoiselle Louise de Nérac, having disposed in Bluebeard fashion of her predecessors. He first offers a prayer at the church of his patron saint, the Holy Hoprig, for the success of his new venture in matrimony. Janicot, the Prince of the World, "adversary of all the gods of men" turns him from his journey with the promise that he will give him Melior, his ideal of beauty, instead, if he will deliver their first child to Janicot. It is also agreed that Melior must then vanish, and the life of "the greatest man living in France" is to be a Christmas present to Janicot from Florian. Florian kills the monsters which guard the palace, and asks for the hand of the princess. In the company of King Helmas, her father, he finds Hoprig who has been canonized by the Christian Church by mistake, and all the while that Florian had been under the impression that the saint had been looking out for his interests in heaven, he had been snoring in an enchanted sleep. After marriage Florian discovers that though of incomparable beauty his wife is stupid and garrulous, and in intelligence seems to him to "rank somewhere between a magpie and a turnip." He is insufferably bored with her, and only too eager to get rid of her by carrying out his diabolical bargain with Janicot. By an unexpected turn of affairs the greatest man of France at the Christmas season is his friend, the Duke of Orléans, and he goes to Paris reluctantly to poison him and to get a pardon for killing his brother, Raoul, in a duel. The scorned fiancée, Mlle. de Nérac, having no male relatives, had to be avenged by his loved brother, Raoul, the husband of her sister. When Melior's child is born he learns that he is not after all the father. Hoprig had made use of his sainthood to extract from the recording angel a copy of Florian's bargain with Janicot, and prevented him from giving the Devil his due by becoming the father of Melior's child himself. His boyish ideals of beauty and holiness have connived to trick and disillusion him. Melior declines to vanish since she is now a Christian. Florian challenges Hoprig to combat to avenge his wounded honor, and the saint promptly summons St. Michael to aid him. Michael arrives very indignant that a prince of heaven should be invoked to settle private quarrels. Janicot joins them, and Florian begs for a compact to be rid of Melior on any terms. Hoprig and Melior return to the "high place" and the "old time" on "the last cloud going west." The romantic Florian tells his father how in his dream there seemed to be no logic or reasonableness anywhere, and that "the people that wanted things did not want them any longer once they had got them. They seemed rather to dislike them." His father counsels him, "To submit is the great lesson. I too was once a dreamer: and in dreams there are lessons. But to submit, without dreaming any more, is the great lesson; to submit, without either understanding or repining, and without shirking the fact that this universe is under no least bond ever to grant us, upon either side of the grave, our desires . . . to do that is wisdom." To the boy this seems "stupid and unaspiring advice," but he agrees that in practice the one rule to follow is: "Thou shalt not offend against the notions of thy neighbor." Janicot talking with Michael, "furnishes a key to Poictesme: it is a country in which men, fettered as they may be by space and time, by good and evil, dream triumphantly beyond them."

HILL COUNTRY, by Ramsay Benson (1928), is the winner of the Stokes-Forum prize for the best biographical novel of 1928. The story is unique of its kind in that James J. Hill, whose personality dominates the story, never appears on the scene in person; nor is any one man hero. First one, then another is in the limelight, perhaps young Sven Opsahl most of all; but each and all feel the influence of that unseen power which is Hill in accord with his purposes. The story opens when Pick Overturf chooses the site for a homestead which in time develops into the town of Gumbo on the Minnesota prairies. The main branch of the railroad that James J. Hill is building up the Red River Valley toward the North comes through Gumbo. Hill's influence is first seen when clever little Weese Overturf writes for, and receives from Hill, a contribution of a hundred dollars for the school library. Hill writes her that if she will read as many books as a hundred dollars will buy she will have the foundation of a liberal education. He suggests further that her townspeople be hospitable to the Swedes, who are settling among them in great number — a suggestion that is disregarded for some years during which political and other feuds are waged before Yankee and Swede settlers learn to live in harmony, pitting common interests as farmers against the world, and finally in the Farmers' Alliance, against J. J. Hill. Andy Maguffin, a Yankee with the bark on, in other words, the town's bad man, furnishes considerable interest in his courtship of the Widow Larkin when he isn't baiting the Swedes. When Eric Odquist becomes his rival, matters develop to an exciting and surprising climax in which the widow is left to live happily ever after — with the right man. Sven Opsahl, an orphan, works for Clewel, editor of the "Voice," a man of little principle, but brilliant promises. By the time his promises have completely collapsed and the paper is put up at public auction, the boy is able to purchase it and soon makes a local success of it, particularly when he espouses the side of the Alliance against J. J. Hill, whose gift of blooded stock to the farmers to encourage stock raising does not convince Sven of his good intentions. For Clewel had taught young Sven how to marshal statistics proving that Hill was robbing the farmers through extortionate freight rates. On the basis of certain facts sent him anonymously, which Sven attributes to Weese, he learns that Hill is endeavoring to gain the control of another railroad through a certain bill that is to come up in the next Legislature. He wins the contest for a seat in the Legislature against Pick Overturf, Hill's man. Overturf fails to get money from Hill to tide over the affairs of the bank whose funds have been lost through an investment that had Hill's backing. Life in St. Paul convinces Sven that few of the men who seem to oppose Hill are sincere. He suspects even the best of them has his price when Hill cares to pay it. His own convictions in regard to the bill he has opposed are confused and rendered dubious by a clever lawyer in the Hill interests. Then Hill comes to the rescue of the Gumbo bank, thus saving the honor of Overturf, whose daughter, Weese, Sven marries. The book is exceedingly well written. It is a real life seen in perspective and on many sides, through the eyes of various people, and as impossible of set classification as is ever the case with life. The pioneer setting is done in a compact, comprehensive and workmanlike manner that alone would give it high place among novels of this genre.

HIND LET LOOSE, A, by C. E. Montague (1924). The author sets the mood for his story by calling it an "Immorality." "Nearly all my people are no better than they should be; they 'lie and cog, and flout, deprave, and slander, and yet no one is properly whipped at the cart's tail in the end.'" And he adds that no excuse occurs to him, except that life is so. The setting is in England, in Halland, which, like some others, is the second city in the Empire, and the story revolves around a brilliant young Irish journalist and his relations with two rival editors of the two daily papers, published in Halland, and whose animosities made Halland's world go round. Brumby is editor of the "Warder," Conservative, and Pinn is the ruling power of the "Stalwart," Liberal. Fay is secretly in the employ of both editors and writes the leaders for the two papers. To Pinn, he is known under the name of Maloney. Fay worked on the theory that most leaders were made for all times and all themes and the use of any party to any of earth's quarrels. Concert notices and art criticisms were treated the same way. He kept an assortment of them. When Brumby asked for a "lead" on Lord Albry's speech, Fay supplied it without even the necessity of reading the speech, and when he hears that the office of the "Stalwart" has been destroyed by fire and that the editor must have a leader on the Albry's speech at once, as the paper had to be "got out" that night, he meets the emergency by getting back his leader for the "Warder" before it has been set up and saves the day for the "Stalwart." He "riggs out" something else for Brumby. In the meantime, Pinn comes to the office of the "Warder" to ask Brumby to print the "Stalwart." "The plant's a scrap-heap, — red-hot." Brumby condescends to help out in the mechanical difficulties, but learns that the leaders on the "Stalwart" are written by a journalist — Maloney, and not by Pinn himself. The climax comes while Pinn is arranging for his staff to bring over the "rescued copy" to the office of the "Warder," and Fay appears. "There are things not to be put on the stage." "So be it unsaid here how it looked, how it sounded, when Pinn and Brumby found tongue and took turns to give Fay gigantic pieces of their mind." Two weeks later they each hire him again in the same capacity and Fay gives in. Neither Pinn nor Brumby know what the other has done. Albry is speaking again and Fay's leaders are needed. But he is also waiting to see a third editor — Roads, who has just launched a penny paper, and wants Fay to write the leads. He tells Fay confidentially that both Pinn and Brumby have informed him that they had "sacked" him, and had warned him of his tricks. Fay acquiesces in the plan — he will write the leaders provided that he can do so in his own time. The story ends with his secret connections with all three papers — the "Warder" and the "Stalwart" fighting each other, and the "Eye-Opener" fighting them both. It is Mrs. Fay alone who fears for the outcome. She voices her apprehension: "Colum, you have a great turn for the writing. Don't use it to do wrong." "Is it" — comprehension dawned — "harm Ireland?" And when she tells him that he might some time or other be seeing the thing would be good for England to do for herself and not for Ireland, and "saying it, perhaps, before he knew." his answer is: "Ah, then, I'm not that bad."

HISTORY, OUTLINE OF, THE, by H. G. Wells (1920). This far-ranging work places in their proper relationship the gradual changes which all manifestations of life on this universe have undergone. It treats of the ages and nations and races and, in the words of the author, traces a steady growth of the social and political units which men have combined. "In this 'Outline' we have sought to show two great systems of development interacting in the story of human society. We have seen, growing out of that later neolithic culture, the heliolithic culture, and arising out of this in the warmer alluvial parts of the world, the great primordial civilizations, fecund systems of subjugation and obedience, vast multiplications of industrious and subservient men. We have shown the necessary relationship of those early civilizations to the early temples and to king-gods and god-kings. At the same time we have traced the development from a simpler neolithic level of the wanderer peoples, who became the nomadic peoples, in those great groups the Aryans and the

Hun-Mongol peoples of the northwest and the northeast and (from a heliolithic phase) the Semites of the Arabian deserts. Our history has told of a repeated overrunning and refreshment of the originally brunet civilizations by those hardier, bolder, free-spirited peoples of the steppes and desert. We have pointed out how these constantly recurring injections have steadily altered the primordial civilizations both in blood and in spirit; and how the world religions of to-day, and what we now call democracy, the boldness of modern scientific inquiry and a universal restlessness, are due to this 'nomadization' of civilization." According to the "Outline," the origin of man is still very obscure, but what the author calls this new thing "life" crept, he says, in the shallow waters and intertidal muds of the early Palæozoic period and, he suggests, was perhaps confined to our planet alone in all the immensity of space, although he further points out that because of modification and differentiation of species being extremely rapid, life had already developed a great variety of widely contrasted forms before it began to leave traces on the rocks. The author does not consider those periods, the Azoic or Archæozoic age (primordial life), or the Proterozoic age of animalculæ, or the early Proterozoic period, before the appearance of any vertebrate animals, or subsequent ages as "a mere swift prelude of preparation," but prefers for them to loom large in perspective. His general statement concerning all geological records is that it is a story of widening range. "Classes, genera and species of animals appear and disappear, but the range widens. It widens always." The "Outline" says with equal certainty that there is no break, no further sweeping away of one kind of man and replacement by another kind "between the appearance of the Neolithic way of living and our own time. There are invasions, conquests, extensive emigrations and intermixtures, but the races as a whole carry on and continue to adapt themselves to the areas into which they began to settle in the opening of the Neolithic Age," — the Neolithic phase of human affairs which had its beginning in Europe ten or twelve thousand years ago. The author observes that there is no real break in culture from their time onward until we reach the age of coal, steam, and power-driven machinery that began in the eighteenth century. "But up to a few hundred years ago mankind has on the whole been differentiating." The "Outline" holds that the species has differentiated into a very great number of varieties, many of which have reblended with others, which have spread and undergone further differentiation or become extinct. The "Outline's" approach to the language of mankind "rings the changes upon a number of common roots," and as the author points out, with the discovery of language, a new source of knowledge was added to the dug-up remains and vestiges upon which we have had to rely in answering the questions regarding the prehistoric Aryans, "those Nordic Aryans who were the chief ancestors of most Europeans and most white Americans and European colonists of to-day, as well as of the Armenians, Persians, and high-caste Hindus." "Step by step man made his way from barbarism to civilization at Old-World centres," observes the author. "Chinese civilization came into history 2000 years B.C., the result of a long process of conflicts, minglings and interchanges between a southern and a northern culture." In the thousands of years, what was happening to the rest of the world? "From the Rhine to the Pacific, the Nordic and Mongolian peoples were learning the use of metals; to the south of the civilized zone, the negro was making a slow progress under the stimulation of invasion of whiter tribes from the Mediterranean regions. In North America a group of Mongoloid tribes were spreading southward; in South America, two civilizations were to be builded, Mexico and Peru. The early American civilization is considered as a separate development. Of Greek civilization that grew up in South Italy and Greece and Asia Minor, the "Outline" has this to say: It was not their own; they wrecked one and put another in its place. The intellectual outbreak in Athens was not a general movement. It was a movement of a small group of people. From the mental and moral activities of Athens and Alexandria, the author turns to the growth of human ideas in the Mediterranean world and to what he calls the "almost separate intellectual life of India, and the rise and spread of Buddhism. He then takes up the history of the two Republics, Rome and Carthage, the political structure of the Roman Empire, and recognizes a parallel in many respects of a modern flavor, as events lead to his comparison of the subsequent Roman Republic with a modern state. His observations cover the entire period of Roman history, from the fifth century B.C. to the end of the republic. Then follows a "catalogue" of the emperors, with Roman civilization at its zenith, the stir of what the "Outline" groups as the "great plains," the crumbling of the Roman empire with a review of the revived Hellenic Empire. This brings the author to the Christian Era. After establishing its definite entry "upon the stage of human affairs," the "Outline" tells also of the rise of Islam in the world and completes a survey of Asia in the dawn of the seventh century. It then turns again from what the author calls "the intellectual renascence on the cradle of the ancient civilizations" to the affairs of the Western world; the Feudal system, the Frankish Kingdom of the Merovingians; Charlemagne, the Normans, the Saracens, the Hungarians, and the Seljuk Turks; the story of the Crusades, and gives a list of leading Popes. The dawn of Communism, the reawakening of science, exploration and mercantile development, according to the "Outline," absorbed the intellectual energies of Western Europeans, in the fading of mediæval ideas. "There came now an interregnum, as it were, in the consolidation of human affairs, a phase of the type the Chinese annalists would call an 'Age of Confusion.'" The author considers the age of the great powers — princes, parliaments, and powers — of the seventeenth and eighteenth centuries — the story of Britain and the Netherlands, the rise of Prussia as a great power, and France's "Grand Monarchy." "Phantoms, these powers which rule our minds and lives to-day, they are things only of the last few centuries, a mere hour, an incidental phase in the vast deliberate history of our kind," comments the author, as he turns to the discovery of the continent of America, which, according to the chronological arrangement of the "Outline" now becomes a part of the phase of expansion to become, in the language of the "Outline" a western European civilization that had broken free from the last traces of Empire. America, before and after the revolt, and the French Revolution, are taken full account of, together with the effect upon the world's history of the subsequent Napoleonic period. A general review of the Nineteenth Century brings the author to discuss the "most salient turning-points that finally led the toboggan of human affairs into its present swift ice-run of progress." The mechanical age, beginning with the discovery of the use of steam, is held by the "Outline" to constitute a fresh phase of history. Modern invention, in the space of a century, made a stride in the material conditions of life vaster than anything that was accomplished during the whole long interval between the Palæolithic stage and the age of cultivation, or between the days of Pepi in Egypt and those of George III. The "Outline" takes up "the broad features of the project which is called Socialism." It concerns itself with the political changes and conflicts and new alliances in both Europe and America, and the author says: "Interest in this game of European diplomacy shifted to Germany"; and of the discord in interests between the northern and southern states of the American union, "the economic differences based on slavery had at last led to open war";

and of the British Empire, "it was and is a quite unique political combination." And of the strong "flowing tide of imperialism" which the author considers characterized the Germany in the post-war days, Germany's influence upon the public mind is given in this outline, the author finding interesting contrasts in the operation of the forces which throughout the centuries produced "the expansive imperialism of Europe." The "Outline" takes into consideration the fundamentally different institutions and traditions which explain the attitudes of the various governments, and, in the final chapters, examines the state of mind of Europe and America in regard to "international relation in the years that led up to the catastrophe of 1914." The author reviews the main phases of the world struggle, bringing, in his concluding chapter, the "Outline of History" up to our own times, and also setting forth what he believes will be the broad fundamentals of the coming world state.

HOME TO HARLEM, by Claude McKay (1928). A story of the night-life of Harlem's negro population by a negro writer. The time is just after the War in the last days before Prohibition. Jake found that his day dreams of going over the top were to end in toting lumber in Brest, so he took a chance to go to London and found plenty of work there as a docker. At last he is homesick for the brown boys and girls in Harlem, and stokes his way back. In a cabaret he dances with Felice, and loves her, and loses her the next day, and finds her again after a time. Zeddy, his buddy, warns him that he must look out as the Government is looking for deserters. He works longshore until he finds out that there is a strike and he is scabbing. Then he is third cook on a dining-car on the Pennsylvania railroad, and makes a new friend, Ray, whom the other men call "the professor" because he is an educated Haytian. He tells Jake the story of Hayti and of Toussaint, called L'Ouverture. They bunk together in the filthy quarters assigned to the railroad crew in Pittsburgh. There is the tale of the long war between the chef and the pantryman on the car. Jake finds favor in the eyes of women and could be a "sweetman" kept by the earnings of women, and live a lazy comfortable life if he liked. For a while he lives with Rose, who sings and dances at the Congo cabaret, but he never took money from her. Zeddy lives with "Gin-head Susy," a New York cook, who has a little apartment in Brooklyn, where she gives parties for her friends to play cards, and drink, and dance to the "Tickling Blues" on the phonograph. She belonged to the ancient aristocracy of black cooks, and her art is cream tomato soup, ragout of chicken giblets, Southern fried chicken, candied sweet potatoes, and rum-flavored fruit salad waiting in the ice-box. There is much dancing, singing, fighting, drinking, and loving in these pages. Jake "had always managed to delight in love and yet steer clear of the hate and violence that govern it in his world." Zeddy quarrels with him about Felice and he just escapes a fight, and Zeddy accuses him of gunning at him but running away from the Germans for all the dance hall to hear. They make it up, but Jake thinks it will be better for him and Felice to leave Harlem and not take any chances after what Zeddy has said about him. They leave for Chicago, which Jake has heard is "a marvelous place foh niggers."

HOTEL, THE, by Elizabeth Bowen (1928). A psychological novel of undercurrents, ripples below the surface in the lives of a group of English people wintering in a hotel on the Italian Riviera. The characters are varied types but they have in common a consuming interest in each other's affairs. Their thoughts, emotions, and reactions are treated as of the paramount importance they are to themselves.

A moody, difficult young girl, Sydney Warren, on the verge of a nervous breakdown as a result of her university examinations, is the guest of her cousin, Mrs. Bellamy, an amiable chronic invalid. Sydney's infatuation for a middle-aged widow, Mrs. Kerr, becomes the subject of comment at the hotel. We first see Sydney unable to play her usual brilliant game of tennis because Mrs. Kerr is among the spectators. Mrs. Kerr's effortless charm makes the young girl her slave, running her errands and jealous of her thoughts of others, her son Ronald and various friends Mrs. Kerr mentions vaguely as charming or attractive. Mrs. Kerr is not described except in her effect on Sydney and Ronald who unexpectedly comes to visit his mother. Mrs. Kerr deserts Sydney after her son arrives, and leaves her bitter and resentful of this treatment, and the outspoken sympathy of the other hotel guests. James Milton, an Anglican clergyman some years older than Sydney, falls in love with her, and asks her to marry him. She refuses at first, and then suddenly accepts him as an escape in her disillusion. He realizes that Mrs. Kerr is his rival, especially when Mrs. Kerr, feeling secure in her domination of her adolescent son, again takes up Sydney. For a time Sydney and James are happy, and the hotel guests are happy watching them. On a drive with Mrs. Kerr and Ronald they are in danger for a moment on a curve on the mountain, and Sydney's vivid realization of possible death makes her understand how slight is her feeling for her fiancé, and she breaks the engagement. She breaks away from Mrs. Kerr also, however, and they all leave the hotel. Mr. Milton and Ronald are the first to go in enforced companionship on the same train to Italy. Mrs. Kerr is expecting to join another young girl, Margot Emmery, in Paris. The other guests include a pensioned Anglo-Indian, Colonel Duperrier, married to a neurotic and complaining wife, jealous of the innocent pleasure her husband takes in the society of the young girls; Mr. Lee-Mittison, always botanizing and arranging picnics, and his devoted wife urging him to tell his best stories. The younger generation besides Sydney, audacious, naïve, and sophisticated, are the three Lawrence girls, and Veronica is a typical "flapper." She becomes engaged to the only young man, an ex-soldier, Victor Ammering, unable to get work now that he must adjust himself to civil life. Eileen Lawrence is also in love with Victor. Their father proposes to remove his family from the hotel and Victor's society. There are a pair of spinster friends, Miss Pym and Miss Fitzgerald, who quarrel and are reconciled again to roam the hills and paint bad pictures of the scenery, and gossip about their fellow-guests. The Honorable Mrs. and Miss Pinkerton spend their time in complaining to the management of the public use of a bathroom across the hall allotted to them. These chance and transient relationships are amusing, and the novel is social comedy in spite of the main theme of inversion which runs through the book.

HOUSE MADE WITH HANDS, THE (1927) is an early novel, hitherto unpublished in America, by the anonymous author of "Miss Tiverton Goes Out" and "This Day's Madness." The book is said to be largely autobiographical. It is the story of the life of an intensely sensitive English girl from her babyhood until early middle age. The youngest of four children, Babette or Barbara, who was the only child born in the "house made with hands," came to love it with an all-absorbing love. To her the house and the members of her own family were all that mattered. Every separation from the house or its inmates was torture to her. Sent to a boarding school in the neighborhood she was so miserable that she arose from a sick bed to fly for protection to her home. The family, loving and cherishing Barbara, built up around her a sanctuary from which she never afterward seemed able to escape.

But it was the house which brought to her the strongest feeling of protection; away from it she was not happy. When love came to her in the person of a quiet, devoted bachelor, known by the nickname Julius Caesar, Barbara refused his devotion to remain in the only environment she had ever loved. Gradually her loved ones departed from the house; her father and mother died, her sister married, one brother was killed in the War, but Barbara stayed on, investing the house itself with the feeling of safety which her family had woven around her. Even the World War and air raids in the immediate vicinity could not shake her faith. When all London was terrified, Barbara was sure. There came a night when the raid was very close at hand and at last a feeling of awe came over Barbara. She had just received a letter from Julius Caesar and her thoughts played with the possibility of a new home with him. The raiders came nearer. In terror at last Barbara fled from room to room, arousing old memories, trying to find safety and protection when at last none was to be found. In desperation she ran out into the garden and "Something black moved across the moon in the direction of "The Chestnuts." She watched it in a profound detachment — that fussy, destructive, yet futile atom. And the house before her tottered, the earth slid from under her, the skies fell." But not before there had come to Barbara an understanding of that other house of which her loved ones had vainly tried to teach her "the house not made with hands."

HOW MUSIC GREW, (from prehistoric times to the present day), by Marion Bauer and Ethel Peyser (1926). Beginning with the earliest times, over one hundred thousand years ago, the origin of music is described in the prayers and dances which our distant ancestors made to their gods when they wanted rain or food, or in celebrating festive occasions. The American Indian's music is given interesting treatment, with both an account of the songs and the instruments the Indians used. The Egyptians, Syrian and Hebrew nations, with their peculiar scales; the Greeks and Romans with their advancing musical forms and Pythagoras's theory of tone relationship; the Orientals with eighty-four scales on down to Troubadours and Minnesingers, folk music and, finally, our modern music, this book describes without too much detail yet without omitting any important points the development of the musical art through the various peoples of the world. For a history of Church music, begin with the chapter on "What Church Music Imported from Greece" and follow on through succeeding chapters at various points. One may gain an understanding of the words "Madrigal" and "Motet." One may come to appreciate the great church organs of our time through knowing of their development from small, inefficient and difficult instruments to the modern electrical console and organ of stupendous proportions with ease of manipulation and perfect control. The first attempts to combine music and drama — i.e., early ballets and plays called pastorales — beginning in Italy in the second half of the sixteenth century led to the beginnings of opera. This book tells of the development of the opera in the various European countries. When "music comes of age" and "dance tunes grow up" into suites and violin makers produce that superb instrument, the Cremona, then we begin to come down to the place where we ourselves have played the music the authors tell about. The introduction to Haydn and Mozart, Beethoven and Wagner makes these musical figures stand out clearly in their relationship to the whole field of music. The aim of the book is to give an appreciation of our modern music, and a more definite idea of what modern music really is. The last pages are devoted to America's entrance into the field and "Twentieth Century Music." Such terms as "plyform music," "Multi-rhythms" are here briefly explained.

HOWE, JULIA WARD, by Laura E. Richards and Maud Howe Elliott (2 vols., 1915). The life and times of Julia Ward Howe, who wrote the "Battle Hymn of the Republic," are set forth in these volumes. The childhood of this noted woman was passed in New York, the city of her birth, in a home erected by her father, a leading banker, and described as a "large house on the Bowling Green, a region of high fashion in those days." After the death of her mother, who was Julia Rush Cutler, the family removed to Bond Street, then at the upper end of New York City. "Julia and her sisters sometimes went for a drive in pleasant weather, dressed in blue pelisses and yellow satin bonnets to match the chariot; they rarely went out on foot; when they did, it was in cambric dresses and kid slippers; the result was apt to be a cold or sore throat, proving conclusively to the minds of their elders how much better off they were within doors." Her first lessons were from governesses and masters and she was placed at the age of nine in a private school. She could speak French fluently, was reading "Pilgrim's Progress," and counted it, later in life, as one of the books which had most influenced her. At seventeen, she was reading Gibbon's "Decline and Fall of the Roman Empire." She began at an early age to write verse. Her biographers allude frequently to her love of music, which became one of the passions of her life. Her habits of study are shown to have been of the most methodical character. She mastered four languages, and it was mathematics only for which she had no gift. Her first literary venture was a translation of Lamartine's "Jocelyne." Julia's marriage to Samuel Gridley Howe in 1843 transferred the scenes of her life from New York to Boston, where Dr. Howe was Director of the Perkins Institution for the Blind, and was known, as the biographers point out, throughout the civilized world as the man who had first taught language to a blind deaf mute (Laura Bridgman). The Howes travelled extensively abroad and on their return to America took up their residence at the Perkins Institute. Numerous letters, which this biography contains, fill in the picture of a time which in her later years Mrs. Howe looked back upon as one of the happiest of her life. These letters refer to her meetings with Emerson, the Russell Lowells, the Whittiers, the Hawthornes, Charles Sumner, Oliver Wendell Holmes, Longfellow and other literary men and women of the time. The Howes later removed into their own home, "Green Peace," and letters to her sisters give glimpses of Mrs. Howe's life during the years of 1845 to 1850. Her literary output during this period included verse and plays. Her biographers give the stirring account of the episodes which inspired the writing of the "Battle Hymn of the Republic," which was "sung, chanted, recited, and used in exhortation and prayer on the eve of battle." It was printed in newspapers, in army hymn-books, on broadsides; "it was the word of the hour, and the Union armies marched to its swing." The later phases of her development as a literary figure are considered by her biographers as broadening her outlook through personal contact with her audiences, which she now reached in intimate gatherings in her home on the occasions of which she read aloud her philosophical essays. "That same winter saw the birth of another institution which was to be of lifelong interest to her, the New England Woman's Club." The Club movement was to be henceforth one of her widest interests. This biography gives also the story of Mrs. Howe's leadership in the Peace Crusade of 1870, her activities in the pioneer society for the Advancement of Women, and her "call to preach." In the continued story of Mrs. Howe's life are found the interesting and varied experiences encountered when she revisited Europe, her later work in connection with the New Orleans Exposition, and the events of her last years. She received the degree of Doctor of Laws from Smith College just before her death in her ninety-first year.

HUMANIZING OF KNOWLEDGE, THE, by James Harvey Robinson (1924, 2d revised and enlarged Edition, 1926). The author shows that one of the great problems of education is to make the results of scientific research available to the average man. In this age of specialization it is essential that the prejudice against the popularizer shall be overcome, and that knowledge be rehumanized. Heretofore the ideal of the scientific student has been to dehumanize investigation in order to escape from the mediæval tendency to consider natural phenomena in terms of human interest. Laborious observations have accumulated a mass of new knowledge of which the majority of mankind remains ignorant or regards with indifference and even hostility, except in those cases where the inventor or engineer has worked with the business man to apply knowledge to industry and intercommunication, and thus make research benefit our daily life and environment. Dr. Robinson suggests that in anthropology, history, philosophy, psychology, and economics much that has passed for truth will in the light of new scientific knowledge be discovered to be as obsolete as the scholastic philosophy which was supplanted by experimental science. He urges reconsideration of old beliefs and traditions in the scientific mood of "wonder, curiosity, and inquiry. . . . The scientific mood is but another name for intelligence." The great bulk of scientific knowledge is hidden in scholarly monographs and the transactions and proceedings of learned societies, written in technical language that is unintelligible to the general reader. As an example of the difficulties which beset the seeker after knowledge he quotes from an article in the "Encyclopædia Britannica" on the polarization of light: "A stream of light coming directly from a natural source has no relation to space except that concerned in its direction of propagation, round which its properties are alike on all sides." His comment is that "like the lovers in Dante's "Commedia," the simple inquirer is likely to read no farther that day." Science as set off against traditional belief and lore of various kinds "should include all the careful and critical knowledge we have about everything of which we can come to know something." The author gives the striking illustration of the conscious and unconscious confusion of mind and misunderstanding of even intelligent laymen on the subject of Darwinism and evolution as an example of the ineffectiveness of present methods of popularizing scientific discoveries. So-called controversial matters are carefully excluded from the curriculum of schools and colleges. How are young people to be placed in a position to form an intelligent opinion if they are trained "in an utterly unscientific confidence in ancient lore regarding, let us say, religion, race, business, heredity, and sex?" Dr. Robinson recommends that one should choose for instruction "some phase of human interest rather than some field of scientific investigation, select the book that treats it best, and then bring to bear all the available knowledge by way of criticism or elaboration that may be found. . . ." "Minds of the requisite temper, training and literary tact must be hunted out, encouraged, and brought together in an effective, if informal, conspiracy to promote the diffusion of the best knowledge we have of man and his world."

ICEBOUND, a drama, by Owen Davis (1921). A New England story of a prodigal son. The Jordan family have lived on the same farm in Veazie, Maine, for over one hundred years. They are hard as the rocky soil they have tilled. The only pleasant person in the family connection is young Jane Crosby, a poor relative, who has lived in the family since she was fourteen. The family sit stiffly in the parlor of the old homestead while Mrs. Jordan, their mother and grandmother, lies dying upstairs. There are Henry, the oldest son, a tight-lipped man of fifty,

Emma, his spiteful wife, and her pretty, vain daughter by her first husband, Nettie, Sadie, a widowed daughter, and her son Orin, and Ella, the sour-faced spinster daughter. The selfish, exacting old mother has been alienated from children as selfish and narrow as herself, but has cherished a secret tenderness for her youngest son, Ben, an ex-soldier, the black sheep of the family. Ben is under indictment for setting a neighbor's barn on fire in a spirit of revenge. The family are united only in their contempt for the absent Ben, and their dislike for Jane, whose company Mrs. Jordan has preferred to that of themselves. Their chief interest is their prospective shares in the estate. The first thing they will do after the funeral is to send Jane away. To their surprise, Ben walks in the door, reckless and at odds with all as ever. He has risked arrest to come home to see his mother. It seems that Jane has sent him some money of her own to pay for his railroad ticket from Bangor, because she knew his mother would die happier if she saw him. He is too late, as the word comes that Mrs. Jordan is dead. Henry, at the bidding of the women, tells Jane that she need not expect to stay at the farm after the funeral. She answers that she is glad to go, that she hates them all and longs to get away from them. Judge Bradford, the family lawyer, then announces that Mrs. Jordan has left all her property to Jane, except a hundred dollars to each of her children. The family threaten to go to law, but the Judge assures them that he is a good enough lawyer to prevent them from breaking the will. When the sheriff comes for Ben, Jane offers to put up his bail, as Henry has refused, if he will do as she says until his trial is called in the spring. She needs his help on the farm. Though Ben is more like his mother than the other Jordans, he is sufficiently "icebound" to distrust her kind action. Some months later the family are again gathered in the sitting-room of the old home. Each one has some favor to ask of Jane. Ella wants funds to buy a partnership in a dressmaking business. Sadie has to have some money to pay her rent. Nettie can not go to a party without a new dress. Jane has helped them all so many times already that she will not listen. Ben is inclined to take her part until they tell him that she has made him the laughing-stock of the town. They call him "Jane Crosby's white slave." When he hears Jane is calling him, he refuses to go, and says she can send for the sheriff. She comes in then to tell him that one of the horses is sick, and he forgets his resentment and hurries out to the barn. The Jordans, Ben tells Jane, are "half-froze" before they are born, mean and hard so that they can live the mean hard life they have to live on a farm that is frozen half the year. "Icebound, that's what we are — all of us — inside and out." Judge Bradford comes in to see Jane and she gets him to promise that he will try to save Ben from prison. She gives him the letter Mrs. Jordan had left to Jane with the will, asking her to try to reform and marry Ben, whom they both love. Nettie puts on the blue dress Jane had bought for herself to wear on her birthday, and gets the notice and interest from Ben that Jane had hoped to win. Jane calls the family together once more to turn the Jordan estate over to Ben, and tell them that she is going away. Ben has learned to work and will keep on working the farm. He is not to go to prison, because the indictment is to be dismissed. Nettie who had given up going with Ben because she just couldn't bear the thought of the way people would laugh at her after he went to jail, turns toward him now, as do all the rest. Henry reminds him that they are brothers, and Ben agrees to endorse his note, but as the head of the family he warns them that he intends to be a real Jordan. The Judge refuses to accept Ben's thanks for his kindness, and tells him all is due to Jane. Ben tries to find out from Jane why she has done so much for him and now leaves him when he most needs her. He had never cared for Nettie. That sort of thing is not his idea of love. At last she shows him the letter from his mother, and Ben breaks through the ice of the Jordan reserve to tell Jane his love for his mother, and for her, and Jane is ready to take her chance of happiness with him, and stay.

IF WINTER COMES, by A. S. M. Hutchinson (1921). Mark Sabre, lovable, sensitive, unconventional, has the capacity for seeing the other person's point of view clearly and even sympathetically, which enables him to understand Nona, the girl he loves when she marries the brilliant, handsome Lord Tybar, as graceless as he is fascinating, and to make excuses for Mabel, the woman he marries, a model housewife, but convention-ridden, mean, without humor, and a snob. She grows to hate Mark because she cannot follow his mind, his humor seeming to her sarcasm. She objects to his whimsical nicknames for the servants, the tall Rebecca Jinks and the short Sarah, as High Jinks and Low Jinks. Mark, with his temperament, should have derived amusement from detached contemplation of life, instead of allowing his kind heart to involve him in the muddled affairs of others. He goes to the War and returns with his health broken, and a shattered leg, and is badly treated by his business firm. He befriends Effie, with her war baby, which gives Mabel the opportunity to blacken his character and sue for divorce. The young girl he takes into his home at the cost of ostracism, kills herself and the baby, and his former partner, Twyning, whose son is really the father of the child, manages to get Mark accused of murder. Mark, acquitted by the court with censure for his conduct, has a hemorrhage of the brain. His real mate, Nona, now a widow, comes to take care of him, and the tardy spring is not far behind at the end of the story, though he has destroyed Effie's letter which would have publicly cleared his good name, out of sympathy for the bereaved father when Harold Twyning is killed in France.

IMMORTAL MARRIAGE, THE, by Gertrude Atherton (1927) is a re-creation of the historic love story of the Athenian leader, Pericles and Aspasia of Ionia. When Axiochus, father of Aspasia, died he left her under the guardianship of Hippodamus, an architect of high repute. Being young, beautiful, and intellectual, Aspasia determines to live in Athens where she can come in contact with the great minds of the day. She overcomes all of her guardian's objections and leaves with him and his family for Athens. As they enter the city they see great numbers of men listening to Pericles, who is telling of the wonders of Athens. Aspasia immediately becomes interested in the leader, but when she learns from an aunt of the law passed by him, that all children not born of two Athenian parents are cast out of the tribe and placed on a lower social scale, she refuses to meet him. She considers the law unjust as she sees the unhappiness it has caused in her aunt's home. Distinguished men of the period become regular callers at the home of Hippodamus and Aspasia holds daily counsel with such personages as Sophocles, Pausanias, Socrates and Phidias. They were fascinated by her beauty and intellect. Pericles, hearing of her charms, wishes to meet her, but she refuses until Anaxoras, who has taught both her and Pericles, arranges a meeting and she welcomes him to her circle. Olympias, the wife of Pericles, by whom he had two sons, had recently divorced him and left his house. At this time he was called to the north to subdue an uprising and was away for several months. Upon his return he again sought Aspasia with whom he was now deeply in love. Although they realize that a marriage between them will not be recognized as legal because Aspasia is not an Athenian, they decide to marry and soon Aspasia is established in the home of Pericles. The Oligarchs, jealous of Pericles' success, attempt to drive him out, accusing him of wasting public money and denouncing his democratic form of government. But Pericles is again elected to lead and Athens prospers. The great men of the day now hold daily discourse with Pericles and Aspasia. However by the great numbers of Athenian citizens she is considered a hetæra — a courtesan, and is liable to attack in public. In spite of Pericles' fears she attends the theatre to hear Sophocles' "Antigone" but is unmolested. She bears a son to Pericles and they now feel the effect of the law to keep Athenian blood pure. A revolt in Samos calls Pericles to war for several months. Aspasia has opened classes for the women of Athens, and is teaching them to read and write. However the Oligarchs, powerful socially, no longer call at Pericles' house and refuse to permit their wives to attend the classes. When Pericles returns victorious Athens is grateful but the resentment against Aspasia continues. The Comic Poets ridicule both in their plays, accusing Aspasia of seeking revenge and claim that if Athens is plunged into war it will be her fault. Samos again revolts and Pericles leads the troops to victory. He excludes the Megarians from trading in Athens, and they, seeking revenge, bring about a war with Sparta. The dreaded plague becomes prevalent and many die, among them one of Pericles' legal sons. Pericles is blamed for the war and plague and is not reëlected. Within a short time Athens regrets the loss of his leadership and asks for his reëlection, but he refuses to accept office. Finally he agrees to reënter public life if his son by Aspasia be declared legitimate. They comply with this request and Pericles is elected. But that night he is stricken with a wasting disease and dies within a short time, acclaimed by Athens as greater than any of his ancestors. Mrs. Atherton gives the reader a vivid realization of life in the brilliant age of Pericles.

IMPERIALISM AND WORLD POLITICS, by Parker Thomas Moon (1926). The fact that "more than half of the world's land surface, and more than a billion human beings, are included in the colonies and 'backward countries' dominated by a few imperialist nations" in Western Europe and North America, makes imperialism "the most impressive achievement and the most momentous world-problem of our age." Professor Moon begins with a description of mercantilism, an earlier form of imperialism, the creed of princes in the sixteenth and seventeenth centuries and of merchant princes in the eighteenth century and its decline. The discovery and prompt exploitation of "darkest Africa," the new economic situation toward the close of the nineteenth century, the competition for markets and raw materials, and improved communications bring about a revival of interest in colonies and national-empire. He assigns the determinant rôle in empire-building to the interested national and international groups of exporters, importers, bankers, and shippers helped by the explorers and missionaries, and military and naval advocates of imperialism for strategic defense, and enumerates the motives of altruism, economic nationalism, national honor, surplus population, etc., which are rallied to their support. The regions in Africa, Asia, the Near East, the Far East, the islands in the Pacific, and in Latin America, which have been the scene of imperial conquest and development are taken up in turn, both from the standpoint of the imperialist country and the subject peoples. The closing chapters are "nationalism versus imperialism in Europe," "the League and its mandates," and "conclusions," an analysis and summary of the various aspects and problems of imperialism, the good and the evil, the conflicting interests and ideals, and the possible development in the future. The author believes the solution of the problem will come through the creation of more effective forms of international coöperation, and the development of an "international mind."

IN ABRAHAM'S BOSOM, the biography of a negro in seven scenes, by Paul Green (1926). A drama of the struggles and defeat of a negro who tries against heavy odds to rise above his condition as a laborer in the turpentine woods of North Carolina, the time being about forty years ago. Abraham McCranie dreams of arousing his own people to a sense of racial dignity, and to this end he tries to educate himself in his free moments in order to teach in a colored school. The white people are against a school, and the negroes do not want it. His fellow laborer says, "Give a nigger a book and des'well shoot him. All de white folks tell you that." Colonel McCranie, the kindly owner of the plantation, promises to help him realize his ambition, but Abe, angry at postponement, argues with the Colonel and strikes Mr. Lonnie, the Colonel's son, who warns him not to answer back and to keep his place, and is lashed with the whip for lifting his hand against a white man. He marries Goldie and becomes ugly and sullen with disappointment and bad luck with his crops, and the loss of two babies. The Colonel, who it is known is Abe's father, comes to tell him that he has made arrangements for the school, and gives him a deed to the house and land. After the Colonel's death Mr. Lonnie does not support him. Abe antagonizes his neighbors by whipping an unruly student, and the school is closed. Abe goes to the city to work, and spends fifteen years making speeches to further his ideas, driven from one place to another as his wild talk angers his employers. He tells his people that "men is men," "color hadn't ought to count," and in his vision of the future sees even a college for negroes. His son, Douglas, whom he had dedicated to the service of his people, grows up worthless and stupid. At last Abe decides to go back to his old home to live. Douglas, released from prison, comes back just as he is going to hold a meeting of the negroes to try to start another school, and with his careless talk betrays his father's plan to the white men. Before Abe gets to the meeting-place, the negroes have been driven away by a mob of masked white men. On the way home, beaten, his clothes torn, he meets Mr. Lonnie, who scolds him and tells him he is going to take his crop away, and Abe, enraged beyond endurance, kills him. His last words when the mob come to his cabin to shoot him as he stands in the doorway are parts of his speech, "We got to be free, freedom of the soul and of the mind. Ignorance means sin and sin means destruction. Freedom. Freedom. . . ."

INDIAN JOURNEY, by Waldemar Bonsels (1928), is no surface search for the merely picturesque. Nor is he concerned with making an objective study of social or economic conditions in this ancient land. It is rather, in subjective, and deeply acceptive mood that he ponders the meaning of life in jungle and society and appraises its natural beauty in sensitive and poetic terms. After a long stay in Cannamore, in the province of Malabar, he journeys across the Valarpattanam lagoon by boat, thence into the hills, and so by boat again down the Netraviti to the ancient seaport of Mangolore. During the course of this journey through little known parts of India he observes the dread doom of the cobra's bite; he wins the confidenec of an old monkey in the hills; shoots a panther prowling about their camp and admires the beauty of the great cat stretched on the ground — "the thorny, bluish-green leaves of the aloes contrasted with the yellow tint of the panther's fur." As he descends from the hills he sees a tiger in the open on a rocky upland. Then

Panya, his servant, points out the distant blazing of the steppes afire. Twice
Panya saves his life when he falls ill of jungle fever. Then, while negotiating with a
native kinglet of the Shamadjii, he discovers one of the ruler's wives imprisoned in
a vile hut, tormented by ants, and procures her release, only to find that she has little
use for unaccustomed liberty and is glad to return to her despotic lord. During
a prolonged stay through the rainy season in Mangolore he is introduced by the
English Collector to a radical Brahmin, Mangeshe Rao, and through intimacy with
him becomes somewhat involved in his unhappy fate. This is the culmination, not
only of his actual journey, but of that spiritual adventure which is the more significant part of the book. Schiller's words, "What we have felt as beauty will some day
confront us as truth" became Waldemar Bonsel's guiding motto. So, in the spirit of
surrender that he finds in all things Indian, he absorbs from Huc, his tame monkey,
and old Gong, a wild monkey of the hills, from dawdling and dreaming along the sea-
shore and in converse with the natives, a sweet and sensuous joy in nature, a serene
love of existence that fills his being and causes him to discard the western ideal of salvation through struggle. When, during his journey along the lagoons, fever dreams
come, he believes himself dead and surrenders to the throbbing, thrilling beat of earth
until he sinks into a deep and blissful oblivion. In the ancient city of Bijapur,
whose inhabitants have all died of the plague he comes to see death as a duty just
as much as life, realizing that those who have understood life will understand death
likewise. The tiger on his rocky pedestal reminds him of the sphinx and those
composite statues of Egypt whose bodies are partly human, partly bestial. Such
statues, placed among their deities, showed that the Egyptians recognized in such
forms their own dual nature. So he comes to understand better this worship of the
beast mentioned by St. John in the Book of Revelation which has so pervaded the religions of antiquity. The highest form of this Oriental abdication of the self he finds in
the mystic valor and devotion of Mangeshe Rao, the Brahmin who adds western learning to the culture of his caste that he may be the better fitted to lead his people toward a united India, only to be betrayed by suspicious members of his own caste.
His Indian travels teach him that, "you will be disappointed wherever you go, if you
think you can experience something genuine unless you, yourself are genuine. The
mystical is not the dark or the obscure; it is not the fantastic portent of incomprehensible or mysterious processes. The mystical, in its profoundest sense, involves
rather a certitude of eternal truths operating beyond our ken." So through the
beauty of India he comes to a better understanding of its truth.

INTRODUCTION TO SALLY, by "Elizabeth" (1926). Sally Pinner, christened
Salvatia as a compromise for Salvation, by her God-fearing parents, became "Sally"
despite their struggles to prevent it; they thought "Sally" common. The child
grew so amazingly pretty that the Pinners' pride in her became anxiety and their
chief concern how best to keep her hidden from the world. Mr. Pinner, the grocer,
knew about the world from the "movies" and the Sunday newspapers — beauty's
lure, and the woman pays. Even the clergy, it was evident, came to the shop not
to buy currants but to look at Sally. Other grocers accused him of using his daughter as a decoy for trade. After her mother's death Mr. Pinner felt the responsibility
of the protection of his innocent daughter so strongly that he decided to move from
London to the quiet country village of Woodles, lived in as he discovered practically
exclusively by ladies. The first weeks the village had been quiet as he could have
wished, but toward the end of January there was hardly an afternoon that young
men did not appear hurrying through Woodles on bicycles, horses, and in cars, and

he became aware of Cambridge, ten miles away, a place "where toffs were taught."
Then one afternoon in March Jocelyn Luke came into the shop to ask for petrol.
Mr. Pinner answered, "No, sir," as quickly as possible, hoping that the young man
would go away without seeing Sally, standing on some steps rummaging aloft among
the tins. As for Jocelyn, he wished to use his brains in the pursuit of scientific
truth, and had been proof against every distraction from his purpose until he saw
Sally. Mr. Pinner need not have been worried and angry, because if he had only
known it he was looking at his future son-in-law, who would solve his problem and
leave him to the peaceful life he coveted by taking over the responsibility of Sally.
As soon as young Luke mentioned marriage Mr. Pinner stopped sending Sally out
of the shop when he came and nearly fell on his neck. "If your intentions is honorable" — said Mr. Pinner, and then invited him into the back room, which Sally
lit up like a lamp with the beauty which left Jocelyn dumb and gaping. Jocelyn
asked Sally to marry him and the obedient girl having been told by her father that
Heaven had sent Mr. Luke for that purpose, replied amiably that she didn't mind
if she did. She had always done as she was told, and liked the looks of the young
gentleman who so unexpectedly was to become her husband. Jocelyn had lived
with his mother, a widow, whose single pride and joy was her son. The letter from
Jocelyn telling her that he has given up his career and is going to earn his living in
London to support a wife comes as a dreadful shock. Her neighbor, Mr. Thorpe,
has made up his mind that she is just the woman to sit at the head of his table when
he has friends to dinner. He advises her that what's been done can't be undone,
and proposes to console her for the loss of her son, and in her disappointment she
decides to accept him. Jocelyn has begun to take Sally in hand. He started by
attacking her h's, whose absence had early become acutely distressing to him.
Every day he devoted an hour the first thing after breakfast to them. But he had
found her most obtuse. And when he finally takes Sally to visit his mother, both
of them begin to deal with the situation. Jocelyn's mother is somewhat restored
by the shock of Sally's loveliness. It is finally arranged that Jocelyn is to go off
to Cambridge, find a suitable little house for them all, but his mother privately is
bent on staying where she is and of keeping Sally with her. When Sally is told
that her husband is going away — finds that he has really gone, she has puzzled
thoughts. She had understood from her study of the Bible that husbands should
cleave to their wives. Till death, the Bible said. Nobody had died. It wasn't
cleaving to go away to Cambridge and leave her high and dry with a lady. Sally
decided to run away from her mother-in-law. Mr. Thorpe lends her his car and she
surprises her father with a call. But Mr. Pinner's notions will not permit him to
harbor any runaway wives and he insists upon her returning to Almond Tree Cottage. On the train Sally meets the Lady Laura Moulsford and tells her her story.
The Lady Laura, bored with her charities and clubs and authors and artists, is
delighted over what she calls her "find" in the person of such a beauty as Sally.
She takes her to her London house, and to the theatre, and Sally makes a sensation. "Indeed, the way Sally was disturbing everybody was most unfortunate."
All Laura's brothers fall in love with her, and when Charles takes her down to the
ancestral place, his father, the old Duke, who is ninety-four, falls in love, and wants
to make a legal arrangement which will permit Sally to live under his roof while
her husband is at Cambridge. Laura decides that Sally and Jocelyn must be reunited, and takes Sally to Cambridge, where Sally gets things done her way. And
Jocelyn discovers in all the arrangements for Sally's happiness, including the fact
that they are to be permanent guests of a duke, and that Sally is expecting a baby,

that after all instead of his moulding Sally, she was moulding him without any intention or desire of her own.   All that had happened to him in the brief weeks since he had added Sally to his life was that she was moulding him into a cat's paw. And Sally refused to live in the Duke's castle — refused to live anywhere except in the four-roomed cottage in the corner of the garden.   On this one point she was like a rock; a polite rock.   She had been brought up to believe only in "elbow-grease"; and refused to use any modern labor-saving devices; and the Duke, much concerned at first, settled down to this determination of Sally's, explaining it to himself by remembering Marie Antoinette.   She had her Trianon.   He was sure that some day Sally would grow up and then she would find Versailles ready for her.

ISRAFEL, THE LIFE AND TIMES OF EDGAR ALLAN POE, by Hervey Allen (2 vols., 1926).   A detailed factual biography of the objective events of Poe's life, without literary criticism and almost without character analysis.   The method of the author "has been to disregard, for the most part, the findings of all other biographers who have worked in the field, and to depend totally upon source material drawn from contemporary documents, letters, and the evidence given by those who saw, talked with, and, to some extent, knew the man."   Former biographers, because of the inaccessibility of material which has recently become available, have had to struggle with contradictions and concealments, so that this is the first biography to tell the complete story of the man.   At the death of his actress mother, the child, Edgar Poe, was taken into the Allan household at the insistence of Mrs. Allan with the reluctant consent of the hard-headed Scotch merchant, John Allan.   The author notes the indulgence of Mrs. Allan as compared with the severity of her husband to the boy, though Mr. Allan evidently had some fondness for Edgar while he was still a child.   His boyhood up to the age of fifteen years was perfectly normal; and if he had been legally adopted by his foster parents his feeling of inferiority against which he built up a morbid pride would not have existed, and he would not have invented some of the adventures that made such difficulties for his biographers. As it was, Mr. Allan "never allowed him to lose sight of his dependence on his charity."   After Edgar's return from school in England he is pictured as a clever, attractive boy, popular in the best society of Richmond.   At the University of Virginia Poe was not provided with sufficient funds for his necessary expenses by his guardian, now one of the richest men in Virginia.   Poe resorted to gambling to try to get money to pay his debts.   The author says of the stories of his drinking at this time that it "was not habitual but rare," and was noted for its unusual effect rather than for its frequency.   Later in his despondency he resorted to alcohol and drugs, but at first it was not excessive drinking, but the disastrous effect of a casual glass on his sensitive nervous system.   The record of his scholarship was good.   It was the harshness and niggardliness of Mr. Allan which ended his college life and led him to run away from home.   He enlisted in the army under an assumed name. This "enlistment is significant of the fact that he already found himself unable to cope with the world in civilian life.   His tender rearing, his education, his desire for leisure and solitude, and, above all, his nervous, impulsive and erratic characteristics . . . now began to be tremendous handicaps" in the "Middle American" period, which despised a dreamer, and put "a premium on physical endurance and insensibility."   Mrs. Allan's "frantic requests" to see her foster-son before her death were granted too late for him to get to Richmond, but Mr. Allan's promise not to abandon Poe resulted in efforts to get him into West Point as a final solution of his ward's future.   While waiting for his appointment, Poe lived with his poverty-stricken relatives in Baltimore, his aunt, Mrs. Maria Clemm, her daughter, Virginia, and his brother, Henry Poe. At this time he was without proper clothing and almost starved as repeated appeals to Mr. Allan brought only meagre and delayed assistance. "From the West Point period, the beginning of Poe's physical troubles definitely dates." The "long continued regimen of drill and exercise must have left him morose and unstrung." The time and privacy necessary for writing was lacking. John Allan's second marriage and the birth of legitimate heirs destroyed Poe's hopes of further assistance from him, and he left the Academy procuring his discharge by a studied neglect of duties since Mr. Allan would not give his permission to have him withdraw from the course. Ill and starving in New York he again wrote desperate letters to Mr. Allan to which he received no answer. He went to Baltimore to Mrs. Clemm, and for the rest of his life he depended on that devoted woman for sympathy and the comfort of a home. Poe married his cousin, Virginia, "the prototype of his heroines." At this time he earned a precarious living for all of them by work for various magazines, and the publication of his poems and stories which brought him fame but very little money. "Other writers of the age avoided poverty by various expedients: Longfellow was a professor, Emerson was a minister, Holmes was a doctor, Hawthorne found refuge in a minor government employ. . . . Poe alone of his generation, unable to long cope with the world in any practical way" was dependent on his pen. The author proves that Poe worked desperately hard at his profession by citing the mere bulk of his published work. Mrs. Clemm sometimes kept a boarding-house, and while they lived in Philadelphia both Mrs. Clemm and Virginia took in sewing, and Mrs. Clemm always borrowed and begged for the family. Poe arrived in New York in April 1844 with only $4.50 in his pockets. The great ambition of his life was to be the owner of a literary journal, but this opportunity was frustrated for lack of $140. In Virginia's last illness Poe began his friendship with Mrs. Frances Sargent Osgood, which the author says was the first of a "series of hectic, platonic friendships that succeeded and overlapped each other." After his wife's death he was devoted to the kind nurse, Mrs. Shew, and became conditionally engaged to Mrs. Helen Whitman. He returned to Richmond and was about to be married to Mrs. Elmira Shelton, his early love, at the time of his death. Even on the eve of marriage to another woman he felt that he must live near Mrs. Annie Richmond. "All the realities of life lay, for Poe, in the realm of the imagination. . . . Love, like everything else, could be perfect for him only imaginatively. . . . Every woman whom he loved was exalted into the dream angel whom he could worship imaginatively, rather than physically enjoy," and during the "celestial episode" with the "angel in paradise" of the moment, there would be "a great deal of mundane talk," which "involved him in ludicrous and petty squabbles and predicaments." On the journey from Richmond to Philadelphia where he was going to do some editorial work on a book he stopped at Baltimore. There was an election in progress, and it is believed that Poe was a victim of one of the lawless political gangs of the day, and was kept by them "docile with drugs and whiskey," and "voted" repeatedly at the polls. He was found delirious in a tavern, and died after a few days' illness in the hospital in Baltimore, where his friends took him.

JACOB'S ROOM, by Virginia Woolf (1923). This novel is the first written in Miss Virginia Woolf's later "stream of consciousness" manner exemplified by "Mrs. Dalloway" and "To the Lighthouse." The departure from the more formal narrative design of the author's earlier "Night and Day" results in a development of narrative reminiscent of Sterne's meandering through memory in "Tristram Shandy." Characteristic, also, is the writer's aim toward a lyrical fictional form approximating for twentieth century English literature the inclusiveness of the emotional and poetic values of Elizabethan drama for its time. Jacob's room is, therefore, a novel with transitions of story omitted. Only the high lights of Jacob's life are presented, and their changes made without warning. In contrast, episodes which have no relation to Jacob's immediate fate are included, such as the reveries of the poor, who, though they do not enter Jacob's middle class society, are yet properly a part of the novelist's poetic rendering of Jacob's complete existence. The story is of Jacob's room, in which he was brought up with his brothers Archer and John, which was filled with the memories of their mother when they had grown up and left it, and which, in the end, contained almost nothing but Jacob's letters "strewn about for anyone to read." For Jacob had fought for his country in the War, and had died. Jacob's mother was Betty Flanders. Her husband, Seabrook, was dead, and her brother, Morty, lost — perhaps in Australia. So she sometimes spent her vacations on the seacoast of Cornwall, but most of her days in Scarborough, which overlooked the circle of the old Roman camp. With Rebecca, the maid, Betty "plotted the eternal conspiracy of hush and clean bottles" — that is, milk bottles for the children. Betty, then "half-way between forty and fifty," never remarried, though Captain Barfoot, who was older and whose name described his lame leg "called every Wednesday, as regular as clockwork," and was admirable. The Rev. Andrew Floyd, who was going to teach the boys Latin, proposed to her, but "how could she think of marriage!" Instead, he was made Principal of Mansfield House and married to Miss Wimbush of Andover, but before he left Scarborough he let Archer have the paper knife, Jacob, the works of Byron in one volume, and John, the kitten. In October, 1906, Jacob Flanders, aged nineteen, went up to Cambridge. Cricket and the days of a boy after butterflies were over. Followed Sunday luncheon with the don, Mr. Plumer, whose wife believed in Shaw and Wells, and, in contrast, friendship with that holiday companion, Timmy Durrant, and with Richard Bonamy, another contrast, who had the Wellington nose and maybe "wanted to write poetry, too, and to love — oh, the brutes! It's damnably difficult." And "Bonamy knew practically everything — not more about English literature than Jacob — but he had read all those Frenchmen." Round the Scilly Isles with Timmy Durrant on his yacht, and Jacob then met Timothy's sister, Clara. Maybe she loved him, but did not have the courage — certainly did not have the courage — to ask him. Timothy's mother thought Jacob awkward but distinguished looking. Of all women, Jacob, in his mind, honored Clara most. After that a little of everything happened, but the substance of Jacob's thought might have been Mrs. Plumer's: "What was at the top of the ladder? A sense that all the rungs were beneath one apparently." So Jacob lived in London, spent hours on the text of Marlowe in the British Museum and cared very little for the agnostic and the feminist studying beside him, and loved the not too faithful Florinda, and then Laurette, and wrote home more casually. Fanny Elmer loved Jacob to desperation, but Jacob had grown to be a man. He would forget her — going to Paris on his way to Greece with a book in his pocket. And he did, and met Sandra Wentworth Williams, who looked in the mirror and thought — "I am very beautiful." In Jacob, however, were "the seeds of extreme disillusionment which would come to him from women in middle life." So he left her to her husband, — Sandra with Jacob's copy of Donne. In England, again, the glory of the Acropolis, and one evening there with Sandra remained in Jacob's mind a glow to be repeated. He was in love. Bonamy knew as much, for Jacob did not seem over glad to see him.   This was perhaps as it should be.   For what did even Bonamy matter as against love, and as against sudden battle which was to consume even Greece, even Sandra.   "Such confusion everywhere," exclaimed Betty Flanders.   "What am I to do with these, Mr. Bonamy?" She held out a pair of Jacob's old shoes.   1914, and English youth, such as Jacob, had died in the War fighting its own disillusion.

JALNA, by Mazo De La Roche (1927).   The family home of the Whiteoaks in Canada is named "Jalna," in memory of the Indian station where Philip and Adeline Whiteoaks met and married.   Adeline has survived her husband, and is determined to celebrate her hundredth birthday.   Her two sons, Ernest and Nicholas, old men themselves, are children in the eyes of the despotic old matriarch.   Nicholas has his dog and his piano and memories of a gay past in London, and Ernest is making notes for a critical work on Shakespeare which will never be finished.   Of the next generation, the red-headed, dominant Renny is head of the house, and his sister, Meg, is the housekeeper.   There are four younger half-brothers.   Eden, the eldest of these, is twenty-three, Piers, Renny's right-hand man on the farm, twenty, Finch, a shy, awkward youth of sixteen, and Wakefield, a precocious child of nine. Piers defies the family by eloping with Pheasant, the illegitimate daughter of a neighbor, Maurice Vaughan, whose engagement to Meg had been broken off twenty years before by his affair with the village girl, Pheasant's mother.   The masterful Renny settles the noisy, violent quarrel that ensues when Piers brings home his unwelcome bride.   "He had said that Piers was not to be cast out from the tribe, and the tribe had listened and accepted his words as wisdom. . . . They depended on him, from savage old Gran down to delicate little Wake," able always to wheedle his stern brother with his facile tears.   "He had only to shut his eyes tightly a moment and repeat to himself, 'Oh, how terrible.   How terrible,' and in a moment the tears would come."   Now Piers smiled at Pheasant, who was from henceforth one of them.   Eden incurs the family disapproval by writing poetry instead of taking an interest in raising apples and horses.   At his publisher's in New York he meets the cultured, intellectual Alayne Archer, an admirer of his poetry, and in two weeks they are engaged.   He brings this daughter of a college professor home with him, wondering what she will think of his amazing family and the graceless old tyrant, Gran.   She does find Gran almost unendurable at first, but comes to share the family pride in the spoiled old lady.   Piers is unfriendly, jealous for Pheasant of her reception by the others, and considers Eden a good-for-nothing loafer.   Alayne is puzzled by these new connections who are everything that is different from her home circle.   "Even while their conduct placed her past life on a plane of dignity and reticence, their warmth and vigor made that life seem tame and colorless." Eden is not diligent in trying to find a position, and Alayne has a vision of him as he would be as an old man staying on at Jalna, content without hope or ambition like his uncles.   He resents her bothering him about work like the petulant child that he is, and turns to Pheasant for entertainment.   Alayne and Eden both find out that it was his poetry that she loved, not himself.   Renny and Alayne fight against a devastating attraction for each other, and avoid being together.   Finch comes on Eden and Pheasant in the woods and tells Piers who goes in search of them.   Eden runs away, and Alayne plans to return to New York.   Meg refuses to live in the house with Pheasant, and sulks in a hut on the place until Maurice Vaughan solves the problem of her stubbornness by proposing to her again.   The last chapter is the birthday party for Gran, which her sons and grandson spared no pains to make memorable, with music and bonfires in the evening. Pheasant is happy again, glad that she is at home with Piers, not off with Eden as he had urged. "Eden was not among them, but the vision of his fair face, with its smiling lips, mocked each in turn." To Renny it said: "I have shown you a girl at last whom you can continue to love without possessing, who will haunt you all your days." To Alayne: "I have made you experience in a few months love, passion, despair, shame, enough for a lifetime. . . ." To Piers: "You sneered at me for a poet. Do you acknowledge that I am a better lover than you?" . . .

JANE CLEGG, a domestic drama, by St. John Ervine (1913, 1920). In a comfortable but undistinguished living room typical of the lower middle class, Jane and her mother-in-law are waiting for Henry Clegg, who is late coming home from work. Jane and Henry have been married twelve years, and have three children. Jane has no illusions about Henry, who is an "absolute rotter," a liar, stupid, and unfaithful. The two women discuss his shortcomings. His doting mother is sentimental and querulous. She has never been able to say no to her son, but cannot understand what she calls Jane's lack of firmness with him. The least Jane should have done the time he went after that other woman was to "'ave tore 'er 'air off." Jane explains that she would have left Henry then except for the simple fact that she could not, with the children so small and no money of her own. Now that her Uncle Tom has left her some money it is very different. The old lady thinks it "unnatural" that Jane should talk calmly about leaving her husband when the Bible says, "Till death do you part." The delayed Henry arrives full of excuses for being late, and changes the subject by repeating his demand for a loan of Jane's money, which he tells her he could have doubled three times over for her. She wisely refuses to let him have a penny of the money she intends to save for her children's education. Henry really wants the money to pay a "bookie" who is dunning him, and to give to his "fancy woman," Kitty, who is going to have a child. Mr. Munce, the "bookie," calls to ask Clegg to pay him, and will not believe that Henry cannot get hold of his wife's money. Henry tells him his troubles, and that he wants to get away to Canada with Kitty. Munce threatens to tell Clegg's wife and his employer what he knows unless he gets his money. Chance puts a check due the firm for which Henry travels into his hands, and he becomes more deeply involved. The cashier at Henry Clegg's place of employment comes to wait at the house for Henry, who has not been in that day, to ask an explanation about the check which he has not turned in. Henry returns and is obliged to confess that he has cashed the check. The two women entreat Mr. Morrison, the cashier, not to tell his employer, and Jane offers to pay the money back to save her children's father from prison. Mrs. Clegg tells Jane it is the hand of Providence that she is able to use her Uncle Tom's money to save her husband's good name instead of hoarding it up. Henry has a plausible tale of getting behind in his expenses on the road and his employer's meanness in making his travellers bear the bad debts of their customers. It has been agreed that the Cleggs are to go to Canada. When Mr. Morrison calls for the money Mrs. Clegg's defence of her son reveals the lies he has told the two women, and the cashier makes it clear that there is some other explanation of his debts. Henry confesses that he has lost the money gambling. No sooner has Morrison left than Munce comes in. Jane refuses to pay his twenty-five pounds, because Henry had told her he stole the money from his employer to pay Munce. Munce sees that his one chance to get his money is to tell Jane what he knows about Clegg, and the truth comes out at last. Henry admits that he has spent the money for tickets to Canada, and that he and Kitty are leaving in the morning, and is surprised that Jane takes the news so calmly. He knows he is weak and mean, but it has been too hard on a chap to live with a woman who is his superior. Jane is a finer woman, but Kitty is more comfortable. Jane sends her undesirable husband off to his "fancy woman." "It wouldn't be decent . . . it would be like committing a sin" to let him stay the night with her. She is left saddled with Henry's nagging old mother, who spoiled him, and is now doing her best to ruin his children.

JAVA HEAD, by Joseph Hergesheimer (1918). A story of old Salem in the days when the town was noted for its trade with China and the East Indies, and the newfangled clipper ships were supplanting the old bowed sailing vessels. Jerry Ammidon, the head of a family of merchants and merchant-captains, had named his house "Java Head," after the high black rock of the Sunda Strait, the "symbol of the safe and happy end of an arduous voyage." He lived now in his rich memories of the sea, in following the voyages of his son, Gerrit, on the map, and had a secret contempt for his land-loving son, William, the shrewd business man, but also good husband and father to his four daughters. The family are anxious about Gerrit, whose ship is long overdue from China. He returns, bringing a high-born Chinese wife, whom he has married under strange circumstances to save her from death. The gracious Rhoda, William's wife, welcomes her for the family as the men are stricken dumb with surprise. Taou Yuen is a miracle of Oriental charm and elegance, and impassive dignity, but the situation is difficult. As Rhoda says of her, "She is very gorgeous and placid, superior on the surface; but the heart — that isn't made of jade and ivory and silk." With her simplicity of spirit and the few simple ideals of conduct which generations of ancestors have bred in her blood as well as her mind, Taou Yuen gives an impression of living with fundamentals and essentials, in the midst of a society preoccupied with trivial externals. Gerrit has been in love with Nettie Vollar, an outcast in Salem circles, because she was born out of wedlock. Her uncle, Edward Dunsack, an unsuccessful trader, demoralized by smoking opium in China, sees in Taou Yuen the princess of his opium dreams. He hopes to use Nettie's love for Gerrit as a lever to estrange Gerrit from the Chinese wife he covets for himself. Through Edward Taou Yuen learns about Nettie, and goes to see her. While she is calling on Nettie, who is ill, Edward comes into the room, and locks the door. To escape the pollution of his touch, Taou Yuen chooses death by swallowing opium pills. Old Jerry finds out that without his knowledge two of the company's vessels are engaged in the opium trade, and dies of the shock. Gerrit marries Nettie and sails away on his ship, "The Nautilus." Sisdal, Rhoda's lovely young daughter, is sent to Lausanne to school, away from her romance with Roger Brevard.

JEFFERSON, by Albert Jay Nock (1926). This is an intimate study of the life of Thomas Jefferson. It reviews the period of his youth, when he was a student at the College of William and Mary, in Williamsburg, and the beginnings of his life at Monticello, where, after his marriage, he set up housekeeping. His personal tastes as reflected in the furnishings and the architecture of his home are told of, together with his habits and interests in his farm, his family and his books. His service in the Virginia Assembly and certain of his bills, which the author considers marked a great advance, are a part of this early record, with brief allusion to the work of Jefferson in the Continental Congress, and the Declaration of Independence.

The items of his work on the Virginia statutes are discussed in relation to the spirit of the country at that time, — "they had to run the gauntlet of a small and compact opposition, in which a number of motives had place, and as many prejudices, social, economic and religious." Great emphasis is put on Jefferson's attitude toward farming — his paramount interest, which the author says governed his estimate of politics, of trade and commerce, of banking and manufacturing. "The greatest service which can be rendered to any country is to add a useful plant to its culture, especially a bread grain; next in value to bread is oil." This dry but fundamental truth, to quote the author, seems to have never been far out of Jefferson's mind. Numerous instances and examples of Jefferson's inclinations and practical ideas are given to show that while his devices and efforts "netted him nothing, they were of great benefit to the nation at large." The author tells of the failures of Jefferson which he attributes to the uncommon difficulties attending the practice of farming, but gives credit to his management, to his treatment of slaves, and to his special "technique" which represented his ideas "that the human being is not for all purposes a machine." Jefferson's inventions are mentioned; among them the leather-top buggy and the swivel-chair. The period of his ambassadorship, his later work in the Cabinet of President Washington, his legislative differences with Alexander Hamilton on the latter's fiscal system, which placed him before the country as a doctrinaire advocate of State rights and of strict Constitutional construction, "whereas he was really neither," to the return of Jefferson to Monticello, form many pages of this study; Jefferson's position on the issues of the times being clearly stated with those of his contemporaries. His career as vice-president under Adams, and the two Jefferson administrations, characterized as eight years of "splendid misery," are told of in relation to the processes of political development which the author points out was not distinguished by Mr. Jefferson, even though it went on before his eyes. "He had a fanciful theory of his own concerning the natural division of parties." Jefferson is shown to have lacked the perception to see an economic interest in the factional divisions among Republicans and in their tendency to amalgamate with the Federalists. "The opinions of men are as various as their faces, and they will always find some rallying principle or point at which those nearest to it will unite, reducing themselves to two stations with a common name for each." "And yet," adds the biographer, "curiously no man ever drew a clearer picture of economic motive in party affiliation than Mr. Jefferson." The financial embarrassments of Jefferson after leaving the Presidency are recalled in the final chapter, which tells of his death at Monticello.

JEFFERSON AND HAMILTON, by Claude G. Bowers (1925), is the story of the struggle that developed the principles of the Democratic party as opposed to the aristocratic or Federalist party. John Fiske's statement that, "All American history has since run along the lines marked out by the antagonism of Jefferson and Hamilton," and his insistence on the picturesqueness of the spectacle that these two giant antagonists presented, state the author's theme. Pronounced statements of any kind are always carefully documented by references to sources. Hamilton and Jefferson were not only antagonists but antitheses in many things beside their political creeds; first in their birth and early training. Hamilton, a poor boy whose parentage is uncertain, born in a little isle of the West Indies, first came to America through funds raised by friends who admired his precocious description of a hurricane which swept his native isle. By this means he was educated at King's College, now Columbia, where his brilliance and personal charm early won him friends among those of high birth and powerful position. He never exerted himself to charm those of any other rank in life. Jefferson, through the Randolphs, his mother's family, was descended from gentlemen of title who traced their pedigree far back in England and Scotland. But this fact did not seem to greatly impress this illustrious descendant. Brought up on his father's thousand acres at Shadwell, he received from that democratic pioneer and farmer, the training of the wilderness. Thrown into the aristocratic society of college at Williamsburg he found himself, "at heart a western man with Eastern polish." Jefferson understood the spirit of the American Experiment. Hamilton, because of his arrogant attitude toward the common people, failed in understanding. Early and late in his career he complained, "that this American World was not made for me." It is a curious paradox that most of the leaders of Federalism — Hamilton, Fisher Ames, and even Adams — were men of modest birth, who yearned to introduce the pomp and circumstance of the Old World into our early institutions: while the leaders of Democracy, Jefferson, Edward Livingston, Albert Gallatin, were men of gentle birth who had broken away from old traditions. Full justice is done Hamilton as a young man. Bowers finds him at his best as a journalist. "One of the fathers of the American editorial. His perspicacity, penetration, powers of condensation and clarity of expression were those of a premier editorial writer." Nor is the "Force, clearness . . . 'logic on fire'" of his eloquence ignored. Hamilton is given his full due for the part he played in making the constitutional convention possible, but Bowers disclaims some of the Hamiltonian myths. He played no active part in the Convention itself, and the records are indisputable that the Constitution as adopted was in direct contradiction to Hamilton's plans. He had hoped for a president elected for life, senators for life, too, if possible, and electors with a property qualification. When he saw it was a choice of accepting the Constitution or facing anarchy, he subordinated his personal preference and supported it with all the strength of his brilliant intellect. Eventually his perception of the need of a vigorous central government fortified the Federal power sufficiently so that it safely weathered the diplomatic and civil storms of those early years. Bowers acknowledges the great benefit to the newly formed nation of the financial stability which Hamilton secured. He believes, however, that, "having been unable to introduce a class influence into the Constitution, by limiting the suffrage . . . with a property qualification, he hoped through his financial system to accomplish his purpose in another way." While Bowers is scrupulous to do justice to the brilliant genius of Hamilton, his natural sympathies make him the better interpreter of Jefferson. He is presented not only as the far-sighted statesman, the resourceful politician, the amateur of art and science, the accomplished scholar and writer, but more than this, the philosopher who almost alone made his way through the hysteria and turbulent partisanship of the period without losing his serenity and poise. Even in those last trying days when he, as vice-president, presided over the Senate and announced the electoral votes between himself and Burr to be a tie, he did it with his usual unruffled composure. While Hamilton and Jefferson do occupy the foreground, this is more than a dual biography. There is no impressionistic slurring of backgrounds, whether human or social, but a clean-cut delineation. The picture of New York streets after dark in the days of the first Congress is one instance, and that of Philadelphia in the heyday of its power as the nation's capital is equally vivacious and picturesque. It is a book with as intricate an unravelling of plot as appears in any novel. In a period when the tension between the parties favoring England or France was tightening, it was said of Adams that he alone was neither pro-English nor pro-French but aggressively American. By successive stages the struggle approached a climax. First the efforts of the Federalists for funding and assumption of the state debts; then the Alien and Sedition Acts; Hamilton's war complex and Adam's unexpected assertion of his will in sending a minister to Paris after the furor occasioned by the X. Y. Z. papers; the disruption of the Federalist party and the plots within plots resulting in the final dénouement when Hamilton threw his influence against Burr and for his long time antagonist Jefferson; here is dramatic conflict vividly rendered. Hamilton's reason in so doing throws a last kindly light on a career approaching its close: "If there is a man in the world I ought to hate, it is Jefferson. With Burr I have always been personally well. But the public good must be paramount to every private consideration." If Jefferson is primarily a humanitarian ahead of his time, Hamilton, too, "thought in terms of world politics," while their fellow-country-men remained provincial in their thinking. One understood the viewpoint of the farmer and the pioneer who formed the body of the Democratic party, the other the viewpoint of the mercantile and leisured classes.

JEFFERSON, THOMAS, LIFE AND LETTERS OF, by Francis W. Hirst (1926). Colonial Virginia in the middle of the eighteenth century, "The Old Dominion" as it was called, with its tidewater country and its "Piedmont" country, supplies the historic atmosphere for the beginnings of this biography, which takes into account the boyhood of Jefferson and his earliest environment. His tastes and interests as a boy, his hobbies and scientific pursuits, his unusual talents and exceptional industry are considered by this author to have been no less astonishing than the variety of his aptitudes; a gift for languages, a gift for mathematics and mechanics, a profound interest in law and customs, a passion for music and architecture are qualities which are cited as proof of Jefferson's versatility. Proof, too, the biographer gives of Jefferson's habits and methods at William and Mary College. "For," he writes, "we shall never understand Jefferson if we leave out his inexhaustible appetite for knowledge; nor appreciate his consistency and idealism, if we forget that he was well versed in Sidney and Locke before he plunged into politics." Jefferson's rise as a barrister, his marriage, and early life at Monticello are briefly sketched as a rare combination of circumstances. "Everything now seemed to promise prosperity and happiness." The rights and wrongs of America are next considered by the author, who reviews the grievances supplied by George III and his ministers. "During 1773, when fresh commotions arose in New England, Jefferson had stepped forth as one of the originators of the Committees of Correspondence." Jefferson's first pamphlets are given, containing the development of his historical theory on which the Continental Congress should base its claims in negotiating with Britain. The biographer adds that thus did Thomas Jefferson "lay the axe of political freedom at the root of arbitrary power and imperial domination." With the outbreak of the War in 1775, Jefferson headed the poll when Albemarle County elected its Committee of Safety. The biographer says also that Jefferson's account books show his work in organizing a supply of powder for the militiamen of Virginia and collecting money for the Bostonians. On May 7, he left Monticello for Philadelphia. "Within a few days of his arrival Congress committed to him the glorious task with which his name and fame will forever be linked." This biographer quotes from the authentic account of Jefferson of the proceedings in Congress and Congressional Committee from June 7, when the delegates from Virginia moved the Resolution, to July 4, when the Declaration of Independence as amended was reported, ratified, and signed. Jefferson's career after the momentous occasion at Philadelphia is next considered. He returned from Congress and took his seat in the House of Representatives at Williamsburg. "To democratise, liberalise, and humanise the laws and their administration was the task of a reformer whose ideals were equality of political rights and equality of economic opportunity. To this task Jefferson brought a marvelous consortium of talents and qualifications." His various reform bills are cited, notably the Magna Charta of religious liberty, entitled a "Bill for Establishing Religious Freedom." Jefferson, as governor of Virginia, is again revealed as the super-man, confronting desperate difficulties, with Virginia at the mercy of British raids. Extensive notes on the Virginia of this period reveal Jefferson, in the years following his governorship, as an author, at work upon his first and last book, described as being animated by the politics of the day and abounding in characteristic judgments vigorously expressed not merely on Virginia questions but on all things human and divine which came into his mind as he wrote. His biographer discusses at length the work of Jefferson and the main features of his scheme on which the American monetary system was founded by his scientific genius. In 1784, Jefferson was appointed a Minister Plenipotentiary to France, to assist Benjamin Franklin and John Adams in negotiating Treaties of Commerce with foreign nations. The biographer now writes of Jefferson in the rôle of diplomat and traveller, and of his part in the early scenes of the French Revolution. On his return to America, Jefferson was made Secretary of State in Washington's Cabinet. His political duel with Alexander Hamilton is shown to have helped to create two opposing systems and parties. Jefferson's foreign policies, his four years as Vice-President of the United States, and the years which intervened before he became President, together with his first and second administrations, his views on the acquisition of the Louisiana territory, form the main material from which the biographer draws at this period for his life of the "Sage of Monticello," of whom he writes, in the concluding chapter, "Of all the monuments left by Jefferson none is so truly characteristic as the University of Virginia. Until you have seen it and Monticello you have not known Jefferson."

JEREMY, by Hugh Walpole (1919). The story begins on Jeremy Cole's eighth birthday, and continues the tale of the adventures of his eighth year. He is a sturdy, self-willed, imaginative boy, living in the cathedral town of Polchester with his father, the narrow-minded, unimaginative minister, his placid mother, and his two sisters, Helen, with whom he makes terms, and Mary, whose adoration makes her his willing slave. Helen is pretty and intelligent, charming to strangers, and the queer curates who come to the house. Mary is the ugly duckling, plain, sensitive, and jealous, especially of Jeremy. There is also a silly old maid, Aunt Amy, with whom Jeremy is constantly at war, and an understanding Uncle Samuel, an artist, who lives on the bounty of his rather stupid sister and brother-in-law, though he despises them. The most important member of the family to Jeremy is his mongrel dog, named Hamlet by Uncle Samuel. "The Jampot," the children's cross nurse, gives her ultimatum that either the dog goes or she gives notice, and won't take it back even if they ask her on their bended knees, and they don't, so she departs weeping to give way to Miss Jones, the governess. The children drive Miss Jones almost to distraction with persecution that is a game to them until she appeals to Jeremy's kind heart, and flatters him by talking to him as if he were a grown person, and then all goes well. The family go to a farm near the seashore for the vacation. Mary shuts Hamlet in a barn on a walk hoping to lose him. She is jealous because Jeremy prefers the company of the dog to her own society.

Jeremy gets lost in the wood at night going to find him, and sleeps under a tree until he is found. The Coles return to Polchester, and Jeremy runs away to the Fair, and rides on the merry-go-round. The story ends as the family say good-by to Jeremy going away to school.

JEREMY AND HAMLET, by Hugh Walpole (1925), continues the account of the joys and sorrows of Jeremy at school and at home. On his return in the vacation he finds that his dog, Hamlet, pampered by the cook, has degenerated into a lazy kitchen dog. He wins him back to become a real boy's dog again, the boon companion of his master's wanderings, and later the victor in a fight with the canine bully of the town. Christmas is spoiled for Jeremy by his father, who is unjust because he has forgotten that he himself ever was a child. After a week of disgrace and unhappiness, Uncle Samuel comes home to straighten things out with his understanding sympathy. There is a party, and Jeremy dances with a lovely young lady, who asks him about his football, and makes him think seriously about matrimony for the first time. Uncle Percy, his father's brother from New Zealand, comes to make a visit, and Jeremy hears his Olympian father laughed at and contradicted when he speaks with his usual voice of authority, and suddenly feels a great dislike for his uncle and loyalty to his father. On one vacation he makes the discovery that his tiresome sister, Mary, might be a real companion. At school Jeremy befriends a snivelling, sneaking new boy who dogs his footsteps until his protégé shows a positive genius for cricket, and then snubs his champion. Jeremy makes good at football and the story ends at Magg's after the game when everyone is spending his Saturday pocket-money for doughnuts, and the boys call "Three cheers for Stocky, the football hero," and Jeremy's leg stops hurting with the pleasure of it all.

JEREMY AT CRALE, by Hugh Walpole (1927). Jeremy Cole is now past fifteen, and has arrived at the dignity of sharing a study with two other upper-class boys, Marlowe and Gauntlet. Marlowe, a quiet studious boy, nicknamed "The Sheep," took no interest in games. Jeremy's greatest ambition was to make the first football team. Gauntlet, born for intrigue, becomes the friend of Staire, whom Jeremy cannot "stick." Staire's father is a baronet, a retired diplomat, and Jeremy resented his "attitude of Grand Seigneur to his rightful peasantry." Jeremy was democratic, from laziness and easy good-humor. In the school it was the "swell" thing to be a follower of Staire and "the rebellious and defiant thing to believe in Stocky Cole." Before the third day of the new term the two rivals had had a rough and tumble row because Staire made fun of Uncle Samuel's painting that Jeremy had brought back with him to Crale. All the younger boys took sides, and one new boy, Charles Morgan, was so bullied by Baldock and Crumb, the friends of Staire, for his allegiance to Jeremy, that he ran away from school. The master blames Jeremy for doing nothing to stop a small, new boy from being tormented, and Jeremy feels that he has been a coward in his efforts to keep out of a fight in order to keep his place safe for football. The Morgan boy was found and brought back, and became a popular hero because he did not tell on his tormentors. Meanwhile as bullying was out of favor, Crumb and Baldock blackened Jeremy's character. Parlow, one of the masters, who had always been Jeremy's friend, called him a bullier of small boys, and the injustice of it all made Jeremy very unhappy. Uncle Samuel came to Crale for an afternoon, and Jeremy talks out his troubles to him, and feels better. He tells Gauntlet boldly that he knows the lies that are being made up about him and the Morgan boy, and passes the old traditional word, "Behind Runners," to Staire to challenge him to fight. Staire is the better fighter but Jeremy wins by pluck and rage, and recovers all his former prestige and popularity. In the great game between Crale and Callendar Jeremy plays on the First Fifteen, and helps to beat the rival school.

JEST, THE (La cena delle beffe), a tragi-comedy, by Sem Benelli (1919). The scene is laid in Florence in the days of Lorenzo the Magnificent; the theme is revenge. Giannetto, the gifted young painter of madonnas, sensitive, and frail, with all the graces except courage, has been tormented since childhood by Neri, a captain of the mercenaries, and his brother, Gabriello, both brutal bullies. On the night before the play opens they had traced grotesque designs on his back with a dagger, and then thrown him into the river. After this dreadful experience Giannetto determines to gain the revenge he cannot get by physical strength with his superior wit. He invites the brothers to a banquet given in his honor by his friend, Tornaquinci. As the play opens he is telling his host the story of his persecution and the "jest" he plans to trap his enemies. His gayety is a mask, he tells his friend, which hides the dull ferocity of his consuming hate. Have they not heaped cruelties and indignities upon him past endurance? Did they not rob him of his chosen bride, Ginevra, the night before the bans were published? "They paid her father fifty ducats and carried her away." She is a toy, a slave, in Neri's great rich house. The doors are opened to admit Neri, Gabriello, and between them, Ginevra, all "smiling and very splendid." At dinner after much drinking, Giannetto leads the talk to a challenge of Neri's boasted courage. He wagers twenty ducats that Neri dare not go to a certain wine shop and insult the innkeeper. Sending Ginevra home with scant courtesy, Neri dons borrowed armor, and strides off in a drunken rage. In Neri's doublet, left behind, Giannetto finds the key to Ginevra's house, "the key to Paradise." He sends his dwarf to spread the news that Neri has suddenly gone mad, and asks Tornaquinci to tell the Magnificent that his vengeance has begun. The second act takes place in Ginevra's house the next day. Cintia, Ginevra's' maid, rouses Ginevra to report that Neri is mad, and has been locked up by Lorenzo's guards. Ginevra replies that it is Cintia who is mad, that she has just left Neri sleeping. When the sleeper appears at the door it is Giannetto. As he is wooing Ginevra they are warned of Neri's escape from his captors, and the noise of his furious approach sends Giannetto into hiding behind a secret door, and Ginevra to crouch behind the bolted door of her bedroom. Neri has almost battered the door down before the soldiers of the Medici swarm into the room and bind him again. Giannetto calls Ginevra to look at her fallen lover, and goads Neri to fury, telling him that he will cheer and comfort his mistress. The third act is in the dungeon where Neri is imprisoned. Giannetto comes with the doctor to bait his victim. For the ordeal of confrontation Giannetto has brought three women whom Neri had ruined and discarded, "three mildewed rags that once were clean as snow," to stir up the devil in him that the doctor may drive it forth. Lisabetta contrives to be alone with Neri, and advises him to feign madness, so that she may help him to escape. The ruse is successful, and the guards are convinced that Neri is witless and harmless. Giannetto knows he is shamming, but is willing to cry quits. He humbles himself before Neri to ask for reconciliation and peace between them, but Neri will only babble meaningless nonsense in reply. Giannetto orders the guards to free Neri, warning him that when he is free he will walk again into the web and be destroyed. He whispers to him that they will meet that night at Ginevra's house.

In the fourth act Neri has pulled himself up to Ginevra's window, and made the terrified girl agree to his plan to murder Giannetto. He forces her to prepare to receive her lover, and hides behind the curtain. Giannetto sends Gabriello, who also loves Ginevra, to her bedroom, wearing Giannetto's white mantle. It is Neri's own loved brother that is his victim. When Neri comes from the bedroom laughing savagely with the bloody dagger in his hand he sees Giannetto smiling at him, learns the truth, and becomes forever a madman. Giannetto kneels at the shrine of the Virgin to pray for them both.

JOAN AND PETER, by H. G. Wells (1918), is a novel that makes education a concrete motive through the lives of two young people, Peter and Joan. Master Peter Stubland, for whom the sunshine was made as Dolly, his whimsical young mother, admitted to her cousin, Oswald Sydenham, was born in the early years of the twentieth century. Oswald thought of Peter's father as a blonde young man with a tenor voice, who punched copper. Thus did jealousy affect a young man who at twenty-one had won the V.C. and adjusted his life to carry on courageously in spite of a scar that obliterated half of his formerly handsome young face. On Oswald's next return from Uganda, where the interests of the Empire were keeping him so active that he was beginning to forget his mutilation, he found Peter had a new playmate, little Joan, the illegitimate baby daughter of Dolly's brother who had died. When Dolly and her husband were drowned off Capri, the guardianship of the children according to the father's will was left to four people, Arthur's two sisters, Phyllis and Phoebe, who were in the van of the Pre-Raphaelite movement, Oswald, and his aunt, Lady Charlotte, an emphatic Victorian lady of the old school. For a time the children went to a school selected by their aunts, where all the educational fads of the day flourished. Then Lady Charlotte took them away from their flighty aunts to sound public schools of the regular sort. Peter's vigorous, unfettered mind was soon in conflict with the foggy pretence at learning and the deadening discipline and routine of High Cross School. He ran away, and fortunately for him Oswald Sydenham was invalided home from Africa because of recurrent bouts with fever and now took over the children's education, for it had been discovered that Dolly had survived her husband from the report of witnesses so that her will, making Oswald the sole guardian, held good. Oswald himself had specialized in biology in school and after a disheartening looking about, he found schools for the two where their intelligence was respected and trained according to the latest scientific theories of the day. Both finished at Cambridge. The frank, gay, irresponsible years of adolescence were passing. Peter was engrossed in an intrigue with a light girl which was slackening his moral fibre and hurting the brilliant record he was making at Cambridge. Joan was moody, engrossed in a dark quarrel with her beloved "Petah," growing reckless as she watched Peter. Oswald found himself pondering "the generations running to waste like rapids." The trouble he found with these modern youngsters was that they were well educated physically and mentally but "it had left their wills as spontaneous, indefinite and unsocial as the will of a criminal." Not their ideas but their wills were confused, their impulses not focussed. Shortly after their trip to Russia, during which Oswald observed and compared Peter with the young people about them, he led a German of Peter's age to speak of the ambitious destiny of his nation. He realized that this boy had his definite place in an imperial dream, that he was indeed but a German version of himself in youth believing in an imperialism for his nation that would bring order and civilization to the world; in this case it was German Kultur und Ordnung.

Then the War was upon them. At first Peter and his friends could not believe that such dwarfish and comic characters as politicians and kings could launch disaster on a whole world. Peter went to the front as an aviator, Joan became a member of the motor corps at home. It was a common occurrence now to hear that this friend and the other had "gone West," in soldier parlance. Peter was badly wounded in an air fight and after his recovery could only serve in a balloon as an aerial intelligence to the forces below. During his convalescence at home Joan determined to make him realize that, although she was a foster sister, her feelings toward him were not at all sisterly. This extremely modern awakening to love ended in a wartime marriage before his return to the front. After he was brought down by a German, with his leg shattered and so no longer fit for active service, he returned to England and Joan, ready at last to start a new home with her. With what they had of training from schools and experience they were building a new life together in which Peter would do research while Joan was going into business to build better homes for the common people. So Oswald found his task at last accomplished. He realized that he had been learning all the time as he helped these children grow. He had learned, as he had stripped off more of the external and superficial from his life, that there were always deeper reserves and no limit to that which the human spirit is able to endure.

JOAN OF ARC, by Albert Bigelow Paine (2 vols., 1925). This life of the Maid of France embraces the entire record. Beginning in Domremy, the story threads its way from a tiny stream, "which holds a place to-day, in human memory and grave debate, because it flowed by the birthplace of a little girl who only a few years later would change the destinies of France," over hills, through tangled forests, and a land laid waste by war, to the coronation of a king, ever following the armored figure, "riding by command of celestial Voices," through imprisonment, torture, and the trial, the stake. The story ends at last in Rouen when Joan had been dead a hundred years. Every known utterance of Joan herself is preserved in this biography, which also contains her letters, the testimony of witnesses on oath, the questionings of the doctors, priests and judges who tried her, and the story of the Rehabilitation. "Of Joan's infancy there is not even a tradition," says this biographer, "but of no other childhood of five hundred years ago is the record so faithfully preserved. At her trial Joan herself furnished some of the details, and at the Process of Revision, or Rehabilitation, twenty-five years later, her playmates and neighbors completed the simple story. It was given under oath, and the clerks carefully set it down. "There are some confusions of memory, but the picture is fresh and clear. Nothing else in history compares with it." Joan's peasant home is shown to have been in no way different or superior from those of the neighbors. If Joan's parents, Jacques d'Arc and Isabelle Romée, brought any fortune to Domremy, the biographer found no mention of it. Joan's mother, in her sad later years, pleading for a revision of the verdict at Rouen, said: "Joan of Arc was my daughter; I raised her in the fear of God and in the traditions of the Church, according to her age, and according to the circumstances, which required her to be of the meadow, and of the field." The biographer dwells on this matter, as he explains, to help a little to keep the record straight. Here he introduces the testimony of Hauviette and Mengette, two of Joan's childhood companions, who at the Revision, told of her industrious habits. "Jeanette spun, did the housework, harvested, and, in all the seasons when it was her turn, sometimes guarded the flocks, her distaff in her hand." Upon the Tree — the notable landmark in the village, associated with romance and possible enchantments, the biographer also dwells "not only because of its importance in Joan's childhood, but in the days ahead." Before her judges, Joan spoke of it as the "Ladies" or "Fairy Tree." She had gone there, according to her testimony, and had twined the wreaths for the picture of the Virgin at Domremy. "Certainly the children loved the Tree and it could be seen from many directions, and whatever the parents might think of fairies, the children had no doubts on the subject." The little dreamer and mystic had none. But she had grown up, as the biographer points out, knowing that not far away, beyond the hills, France was torn by fierce struggles; that bloodshed and famine were everywhere; that their hereditary King was not really a king, never having been crowned, but was next to being a fugitive, secluded in some still unconquered corner of his kingdom, below the river Loire. Domremy is pictured as having plenty of news of these things. Dwellers in that quiet land along the Meuse knew that the world was stricken; they prepared for the worst. Even the children were familiar with the politics of their country. "They knew the unworthy queen-mother, Isabeau of Bavaria, had disowned her son, sold his birthright in a treaty with England, thus plunging France into still deeper ignominy. Almost to a child they were in sympathy with the fugitive King. Philip, Duke of Burgundy, had allied himself with England; Maxey, the village across the river, was Burgundian. The boys of Domremy would occasionally invade Maxey, and Joan saw them 'return much bruised and wounded.' She was thus, in a way, already part of the struggle for the Dauphin, as Charles VII was then known to her." Joan told her judges that she had had a great and warm zeal that the King should recover his kingdom. When she was well into her thirteenth year, she received her first intimation of the work she was to do. This was the year following the battle of Verneuil which had brought overwhelming defeat to the French forces. The biographer gives this picture: "On a summer day, at the hour of noon, in her father's garden, as she later testified, she saw toward the church a great light, and heard a Voice. At that hour she would hardly be spinning or sewing. It would be when dinner had been prepared and she was waiting a little in the shade for her father and brothers to come to the fields. The Voice came from the direction of the light, 'a worthy voice, full of dignity.'" Always she held resolutely to the statement, "that after hearing it three times she recognized the Voice to be that of an Angel, which eventually she knew to be Saint Michael, though at first she had great doubts." The light and the Voice came often, "she was told to be a good child and that God would help her, and that she would go to the rescue of the King." "The Voice also told her that Saint Catharine and Saint Margaret would come to her, to comfort and counsel her in what she had to do." "To her saints Joan pledged her maidenhood 'for so long as it pleased God'; that is, until her mission should be ended." The visions and the Voices continued to come during four years or more before Joan was ready for the work assigned her. She was brought face to face with this work when the news of the siege of Orleans reached Domremy. Orleans was the key to the country below the Loire. If the English captured it, France would be no longer France, but a province of England and the King would end his days in exile. The biographer again quotes from Joan's testimony before her judges: "Two or three times a week this Voice exhorted me to go to France. . . . The Voice kept urging me; I could no longer endure it. It told me that I would raise the siege of Orleans." The biographer believes that she departed near the end of December, 1428, within a week of her seventeenth birthday. Joan's interview with Sire de Baudricourt at the palace in Vaucouleurs, as given at the Revision, mentions only one important detail, but

Durand Laxart, her uncle, who gave it, recorded Joan's words: "I have come to you on the part of my Lord, in order that you may send word to the Dauphin, to hold fast, and not to cease war against his enemies." The Dauphin would be made King and "it is I who will conduct him to the coronation." It is shown that de Baudricourt gave her a sword and his blessing. Into the winter mist and gloaming, the biographer gives that next glimpse of Joan and her little army riding through the *porte de France* — remaining now almost intact, "its arched gateway as perfect as that great moment when they set their faces toward Chinon, where, in as hollow a court as France has ever seen, a disowned and discouraged king dallied among empty-hearted triflers, little dreaming that a peasant girl was on her way to bring him a crown." The story of Charles and his court is reviewed, with the Valois dynasty standing against the intermittent warfare which England had maintained with France for nearly a hundred years to support "a shadowy claim on the throne." Joan, and apparently her Voices, knew nothing of electorates or the will of the people. "The 'gentile Dauphine,' as she called the King, duly crowned and consecrated, would at once become the symbol of a peaceful and united France." The biographer recalls that Joan, in her audience with the King at Chinon, pledged him to rule righteously, and that she insisted before all upon his coronation. The siege of Orleans must be raised, the way made safe to Rheims. These things at least must be done in the brief time allotted her. The evidence is that she was held at Chinon and at Poitiers for examination. After the findings are considered by the King, Joan was accepted legitimately — the permission given for her to conduct a troop of soldiers to Orleans, for "nothing had been found in her that was not of the Catholic faith and very reasonable." The biographer draws a picture of the "busy and happy days of preparation at Tours." He quotes from Joan's testimony at Rouen the description of her banner, sown with lilies, of her pennant, on which was pictured the Annunciation, with an angel holding a lily. It is from Father Pasquerel, Joan's chaplain, that the brief details of the departure are known: "The day we quitted Blois to go to Orleans, Joan had all the priests assembled. The banner at their head, they opened the march. The soldiers followed. The cortège left the city by the side of the Solonge (the country to the south of the Loire) chanting, 'Veni Creator Spiritus' and several other anthems." The biographer sees in that picture a likeness to the Crusades as a military spectacle. For the full details of Joan and her army marching on Orleans, the "Journal of the Siege" is relied upon — and this also supplies the story of the vigorous warfare when Joan, in white armor and carrying her banner, led her army safely past the forts where were Talbot and the English, and of the "great day which closed with the ringing of bells and rejoicing in the streets of Orleans, sounds that fell ominously on English ears. "Joan of Arc, a peasant girl of seventeen, had been in battle and given her soldiers victory." The Voices had revealed a casualty to Joan — a wound in her shoulder. It was cured in a fortnight, she told her judges, adding that in the meantime she "had not ceased to ride." Swept now by the flame of Joan's faith, the hazardous journey to Rheims is taken, with Joan side by side with her King, setting out to complete her mission. The Coronation on July 17, 1429, is described, with a review of events which led to Joan's final determination to see Paris at closer range that she might restore to the King all his kingdom. Charles's stand is here discussed, as revealing to Joan for the first time that she no longer had even the King's good will in her enterprise. In the attempt to describe the attack on Paris, this biographer considers it best merely to reconcile the varying accounts of those actually present, holding that their testimony, with Joan's few answers before her judges, constitute all the evidence worth while.   Joan told her judges that she did not assault Paris by command of her Voices, but by request of the nobles, who wished to engage in a skirmish or demonstration of arms.   The result of that assault, the manner in which Joan received her wound, and the failure of the Maid to reach Paris, together with the unforgettable scene when she "laid her armour complete before the image of Our Lady and the relics of the abbey at St. Denis," are described in the final chapters of Volume I.   The second volume considers the last campaigns of Joan, her captivity, the trial at Rouen, the last scenes at the stake, when the executioner abated the flames to let the people see that she was dead.   "That which had been Joan of Arc, she who in silver armour had conquered at Orleans and led the King to Rheims, had become no more than a heap of charred cinders, which the executioner carried to the Seine, in order that no relic of her might be preserved."   This second volume also contains the "supplementary report, remorse and rumours of marvels," and an account of the Rehabilitation.

JOANNA GODDEN by Sheila Kaye-Smith (1921) is the study of a woman, whose character has so much of sturdy simplicity, sincerity and sweetness that she becomes typical of the farmers of the Three Marshes of Sussex without losing those qualities that link her to womanhood the world over.   At her father's death, Joanna Godden took over the management of his farm, "Little Ansdore" and the keeping of her younger sister, Ellen, regardless of the consternation and critical amusement that this occasioned on the Marsh.   Public opinion held that Joanna's proper course was marriage with the devoted Arthur Alce.   But she had other plans, some of which failed.   Among these was her choice of a looker for her sheep.   Dick Socknersh was a fine figure of a man.   He had beside a certain tenderness with the lambs, and an instinctive subservience to her will that Joanna found gratifying after the insubordination of her other men-servants.   She realized, after a disastrous attempt at crossbreeding Spanish sheep with the Marsh variety, that he would have been a better shepherd if he had opposed her ignorant enthusiasm in this matter.   When her own instinct told her that popular gossip was right in declaring that it was Dick Socknersh's merits as a man and not as a looker that kept him there, hurt pride in herself led her to dismiss him savagely.   Although Joanna knew she was not herself acceptable to higher social circles, such as Dungemarsh Court, she resolved to educate Ellen as a lady.   Then handsome young Martin Trevor came to live with his father, Sir Harry Trevor, at North Farthing.   Her forthright admiration challenged his interest and finally won his passionate love.   She had always been considered a fine woman with her ruddy coloring and richly moulded figure.   During this lyric interval when her love for Martin blossomed, she lost her intense ambition to be a successful farmer.   Contact with a finer personality softened her.   When Martin, who had come down to the country to live because of poor health, took a severe cold and died suddenly, she plunged into work for "Little Ansdore" and Ellen to keep from despair.   Her experiments in raising wheat on the Marsh were successful.   In the years that followed she added "Great Ansdore" to her other holding and was now known all over the Marsh as the successful if eccentric mistress of the Manor of Ansdore.   She wore her prosperity in a manner as flamboyant as before Martin's death but always with a secret loneliness at her heart.   Nor was Ellen's affection any alleviation.   For her education only dissatisfied her with life at Ansdore despite its newly acquired splendor.   Martin's father, a gentleman who refused to grow old emotionally, roused Ellen from a stodgy marriage with Arthur Alce, Joanna's discarded lover.   Although

Joanna was outright in condemning the wanderer, she received her again in her home in her usual warm-hearted fashion. Then, just as Ellen, through her graceful passivity was about to marry into the smaller gentry, Joanna herself went beyond the conventions with a man who recalled Martin dimly in certain superficial traits only, but soon proved himself of far different quality. With all the impetuous honesty of her nature, Joanna discarded this caddish lover when she most needed his protection and Ellen, herself reëstablished, withdrew in disdain from her sister. So Joanna bravely sold her beloved Ansdore and retired to the home of a maid, who had worked for her and whom she had befriended in similar predicament, there to await the coming of her child.

JUDGE, THE, by Rebecca West (1922). The story begins in Edinburgh where Richard Yaverland, home from years in South America and Spain, meets and falls in love with Ellen Melville, the seventeen-year-old stenographer at his lawyer's office. To Ellen, longing for adventure, the name of Andalusia sounds like Treasure Island. She listens entranced to the tale of his adventures which he spins out for her benefit. This shy Scotch girl, who lights up the dull office with her beauty and her gay spirit, is an ardent suffragist. Richard sees her standing on the corner selling papers for the Cause on Saturday afternoon, and buys a ticket for a suffrage lecture in order to see her again. He has had many affairs with women, but finds himself humble before Ellen's innocence and purity. Their engagement is almost coincident with her mother's death. He sends Ellen to his mother in Sussex until he can finish his business and come there himself to marry her. The second half of the book is dominated by Richard's mother, Marion, and the love of Richard for Ellen is overshadowed by his far deeper devotion to his mother. Marion would like to be tender and loving to Ellen, and she admits to herself "that while she desired to hurt the woman whom he (Richard) had loved, she would gladly have murdered the woman who had refused to love him." She suffers from insomnia, and in the reveries of her sleepless nights the story of her life is told, and her unwillingness to give up Richard to Ellen. Richard is the son of the young squire, Sir Harry, who betrayed her passionate love. She broods over the disgrace and the cruel treatment she had received from the villagers when she brought Richard into the world while Sir Harry was away on a trip and did not hasten his return to come to her in her great need of him. The boys had stoned her in the streets. Sir Harry's butler, Peacey, offered to go through the form of marriage with her to protect the terrified girl, and then after Richard was born and she was too weak to withstand him had forced the consummation of the marriage. She bore a second son, Roger, whom she tried to love but could only pity and loathe, and finally send away from her to his father. Now from time to time the worthless Roger comes to her for money to get him out of some scrape, and she bears with him patiently. Sir Harry settled a large sum of money on her and Richard before his death. The author makes her text: "Every mother is a judge who sentences the children for the sins of the father." Richard returns and Ellen loses her vivacity, and is bewildered and miserable in the face of his absorption in his mother, and jealousy of the memory of his father. Marion desires Richard's happiness but he is to her both lover and son and she cannot control her jealousy of Ellen. Roger appears with his fiancée, Poppy, a woman of the streets and member of the Salvation Army band that Roger has joined. He adores Marion though for years he has realized her aversion for him. Marion walks off the pier into the river one night, leaving a note scribbled on the blotter: "This is the end. Death. . . . Give him to Ellen. I must die."

As Richard reads it, his half-brother makes an insulting remark about Richard and Ellen, and Richard stabs him to death with the bread knife from the table. He sighs with relief, saying, "Well, it's all cleared up now. It is as if she had never seen Peacey. . . ." Richard takes Ellen to an island hut to hide, and before he is taken by the police she is calmly wondering whether her child will be a son or a daughter.

JUNGLE DAYS, by William Beebe (1923) is the colorful record of observations made by the author in British Guiana. His work table, upon which much of life's tragedies is noted, is of mahogany because in the jungle that is the cheapest material in the form of boards, with a crab-wood top whose first ruddy-brown cells were fashioned from the water and earth and sun at least a century and a half ago. Mr. Beebe notes that the magic of his table is always apparent in one way or another. The thoughts which it generates and the happenings on its surface are vivid and memorable. "It is an event to hurry out to in the early morning, it is a regret to leave for jungle tramps and for meals, it is only exhaustion which excuses its midnight abandonment." The first magic which it made was to prove to be alive. The legs had been made from freshly cut saplings, and were set in cans of water to discourage ants. Mr. Beebe, in putting his hand down one day, discovered a soft tissue, something like moth's wings or a tangle of cobwebs. To his surprise, upon investigation, he found that the table was sprouting leaves. Picturesquely, Mr. Beebe imagines his table as growing higher and higher upon its living legs, until he would be forced to mount with the table. The author imagines us all as links in a tremendous chain, from the first smallest nucleus, to the editor who publishes his book and the reader who purchases the same. One day, Mr. Beebe wished to study the head of a yellow vulture which he had just shot. Upon investigation he finds it covering with its wide sweep of wings, the huddled forms of a spectacled owl and an anaconda, wrapped in a death grip. The anaconda, in crushing the life from its victim had unwittingly pressed deeper into its own body the beak of the owl which had stabbed the snake, so that death for both resulted. Mr. Beebe dissects the body of the snake and finds the silvery form of a fish, the basha, which the snake has swallowed. Upon further exploration he finds within the body of the basha the comparatively huge form of a frog. Hopeful to the last, with scalpel and scissors he penetrates to the intestines of the frog where upon some mucous scraped from the food canal and placed in a drop of water under a microscope, Mr. Beebe finds Opalina, the last — or first — link in the endless chain. Opalina is a tiny oval being, covered with a fur of flagella with which it whips itself through the water. It is able to elongate itself, until like a broken hour-glass it subdivides and becomes two new entities, which in their turn will subdivide until the last two-hundredth part of a nucleus is ejected from the body of the frog. This infinitesimal being, in all likelihood, will be swallowed by an inch-long tadpole. Opalina will start life anew in a tiny tube, in the body of the tadpole. It will live upon minute particles and fragments of black leaf mold and mud, which come down the spiral stairway or tube. Mr. Beebe pictures the life of Opalina as similar to that of the prisoner in one of Poe's tales, in which he finds the confining walls growing hourly closer and closer. As the tube shortens it contracts and straightens out, while the supply of rations is cut off. "A dark curtain of pigment is drawn across the epidermal periscope and as books of dire adventure say, the 'horror of darkness is added to the terrible mental uncertainty.'" When the tadpole becomes a frog, Opalina may then feast upon bits of half-digested ants, beetles, thousand-

THE READER'S DIGEST OF BOOKS

legs and worms rolled along in the dense gastric stream. "A strange choice of home for one of our fellow living beings." The book graphically describes the tiny shock administered to the author by the electric eel, which draws into the waters the lightning to be redistributed at his fishy will. It relates the strategy of the giant wood roach, brown and gray with marbled wings which had flown through the rain in at the window. The roach was in dire extremity, being in the grasp of a two-inch ctenid spider. Slipping a deep glass dish over the conflict, Mr. Beebe left them for a space of fifteen minutes. Upon returning, he found that the roach had accomplished her revenge. "Barely alive and still in the grasp of the spider, she had changed from a strong virile creature to an empty husk, dry and hollow, while over her and the spider, over glass and table-top scurried fifty active roachlets. They had burst from their mother fully equipped and ready for life, leaving her but a vacant, gaping shell; a maternal shell, the ghost of a roach. The spider grasped in vain at the diminutive forms, as tiny, transparent, fleet they raced back and forth over him, as he grasped the dying, flavorless shred of the mother; holding fast as though he hoped that this unnatural miracle might reverse itself at any moment and his victim again become fat and toothsome." There is the description of the cuddlesome baby sloths, hanging upside down to the fur of their mothers, or to the branch of a tree; there is detail of mangrove jungles, of thrips and of the life of apes. There is also the story of a mother wasp which deposits her eggs within the pearly egg of a scarlet and black butterfly. In a few days the eggs become tiny mummies, leaning in a heap in the centre of the egg, with the exception of one which is isolated from the rest and leans toward the wall of the cage. Shortly after this, Mr. Beebe observed that the mummy cases were discarded in the centre of the shell and the tiny wasps were milling about, trying to find an exit. One, which he calls the Gnawer, stronger than the others makes every effort to break through, but having no leverage he fails until two or three of the others coming close behind him, he presses against their faces and bodies with his hind legs and finally succeeds in breaking the tough wall. He emerges and runs away to a near-by leaf; then, to Mr. Beebe's astonishment, he returns to the hole, wipes it carefully around the edges and waits. His sisters emerge, one at a time, with whom he mates quickly, when they fly away to the farther side of the deep dish where they have been under observation. The book, with its thrilling life studies, is as absorbing as a novel. You marvel at the gallant fight of the white mole cricket, who loses a leg but hops cheerfully away to dig himself into the sands before the incoming rush of tide. You wonder at the adaptability of the jungle creatures, who, with the color and markings of the vegetation to shield them from enemies, live quietly their loves and hates and fulfil their destinies.

JURGEN, a Comedy of Justice, by James Branch Cabell (1921). This epic of eroticism is classic in form, romantic in style, and wittily satirical in diction. Cabell has invented his own mythology, while borrowing freely from legend and literature, so that along with his own creatures we encounter such familiar figures as Guinevere and Helen of Troy, Satan and the "God of Jurgen's Grandmother" who is a peer of Anatole France's God in "Penguin Island." The story goes that Jurgen, a prosaic pawnbroker of fifty, comes upon a monk who has stubbed his toe on a stone and is cursing the Devil who put it there. Jurgen remonstrates with him, perversely praising the Devil. Whereupon his Satanic Majesty manifests himself and thanks Jurgen — and rewards him by removing his wife, Dame Lisa, "a high-spirited woman, with no especial gift for silence," no one knows whither. For a time Jurgen is whole-heartedly glad to be rid of her, since as with all good things it was possible to get too much of Dame Lisa. But conscience, speaking as ever through the opinions of his neighbors, instructs Jurgen that it is his duty to go and look for her. He sets out, meets the Centaur Nessus, who gives him a bright shirt, his lost youth and — a shadow which writes down in a notebook everything he does and says. Finding himself once more twenty-one, of personable appearance and inquiring disposition, Jurgen proceeds to act just as one would expect — though, like his shadow, one cannot be too sure of all his doings "since in the dark no one can see what happens." Enough that it is Jurgen's avowed intention "to deal justly by everyone" — particularly pretty women. In this he is joyously unmoral, not, as the Censors have claimed, immoral — a distinction of value to be remembered. So he meets his old sweetheart — and sees through her. He rescues Guinevere from her Sleeping Beauty enchantment, in the traditional way — and subsequently grows sufficiently tired of her to regard her bridal procession to King Arthur with equanimity, not to say relief. He encounters Anaïtis, who bears a suspicious resemblance to Queen Morgan le Fay, and whose exclusive preoccupation with priapean indulgences at first interests him, then bores him. (The moral here is obvious: no man wants permanently a life of perpetual, unmitigated license.) He meets and marries a hamadryad, who is properly jealous when he acknowledges himself attracted by Helen of Troy. He goes to Hell and marries a vampire. He goes to Heaven and holds metaphysical converse with the God of his Grandmother. Finally he seeks out Koshchei (a superhuman, not to say diabolic gentleman who defies analysis, being strictly *sui generis*) and announces that he has had enough: he would just as soon be Jurgen the pawnbroker, aged fifty, henpecked husband of Dame Lisa, if you please. The transformation is duly effected and Jurgen goes home — presumably to live happily ever after. Through the book there runs the theme of Jurgen's scepticism, which he is willing to express on any and every occasion: "Of course you may be right; and certainly I would not go so far as to say you are wrong, but still at the same time——!" It is this scepticism, with its basis of sardonic wit, that saves the book from being outrageous, and justifies the saying of Hugh Walpole in his introduction that "for those who have the key to Jurgen's world here is a world indeed!"

KEATS, JOHN, by Amy Lowell (2 vols., 1925). Miss Lowell has written this biography to place in "a chronological pattern" new material relating to Keats from the collections in American libraries, including her own, the Morgan Library, and others noted in the preface. Another reason for writing this book is her opinion that the authors of previous books on Keats belong to the nineteenth century, in attitude if not in fact, and that she can write from the point of view of the twentieth century. Her thesis is that Keats was the forerunner of modern, contemporary poetry, a man whose "life was one long struggle to outdistance his mental environment." "I do not mean," she says, "that he wrote as the modern poets do, but he thought as they do, and as his contemporaries most emphatically did not." This modernity she finds especially in his letters as compared with the stilted correspondence of his age. Her "endeavour has been to show him as a particular poet, hindered and assisted by his temperamental bias as a man, writing in a certain *milieu*." She considers "no detail which could add vividness to the picture is unimportant, nothing which could clarify his psychological processes too slight to be mentioned," and follows his short life with the minute detail of a daily record as far as is possible, supplemented by conjecture based on her sources of his life and the time. The biography begins with the marriage of Thomas Keats and Frances Jennings, the poet's father and mother. From an unpublished memoir compiled by Keats's publisher, Taylor, after a conversation with Richard Abbey, the dull, unsympathetic guardian of the Keats children in later years, she quotes a pleasant picture of their grandmother, Mrs. Jennings, a malicious one of Mr. Jennings, and of Thomas Keats, and a scandalous description of the poet's mother, whom Abbey evidently cordially detested. "Abbey distorts facts with a diabolical cleverness," she proves in her defence of Keats's parents from other contemporary testimony. For Keats's schooldays Miss Lowell follows the account by Cowden Clarke, and the letters of his brother, George Keats, with more detail than the Colvin biography. She reproduces in imagination the family conclave on what career John should follow, and gives a description of the position of surgeon's apprentice in those days. With Keats's exceptional mind and capacity he became a good doctor, and in the case of his own fatal illness later his diagnosis was right and those of his attending physicians wrong. The medical record of his illness shows that he was the victim of the medical science of his day, which hurried the naturally strong young man to his grave by every device of mistaken practice. The tuberculosis which caused his death was a sufficient explanation of the psychoses which made his mental and emotional attitude to Fanny Brawne so extreme and abnormal. The poet at twenty studying medicine in London was "a conundrum to fellow-students, a perturbing pleasure to Mathew, a petted protégé to Cowden Clarke, a flame-winged phœnix to his brothers, and a jolly good fellow to the rest of his small circle." Severn speaks of the "eagle" appearance of Keats, and the "wine-like lustre" of his eyes. Bailey says that "the form of his head was like that of a fine Greek statue." Miss Lowell's avowed purpose is to fill out and complete the picture of Keats and the group of his friends given in other books. Woodhouse she considers to have been "the most worthy and disinterested of all Shelley's friends." Bailey was too much the "pedant and prig." Though she gives Severn credit for his devotion to Keats in his last illness in Rome, she denies that he was an intimate of the poet before this time, and accuses him of making capital of this companionship in his own interest in after years. She quotes Charles Lamb, Hazlitt, Crabb Robinson, and Haydon to attest the charm of Hunt whom she believes to have been a constructive critic to Keats. Haydon overestimated himself as a painter but he was an extraordinary man. Keats did not like "poor, iconoclastic, circumstance-baffled Shelley," as Miss Lowell calls him. She approves Max Beerbohm's estimate that, apart from his poetry, Shelley was "a plain, unadulterated crank." She does not think that Brown "entirely justified Keats's love for him." Mr. Abbey had the opinion that a man who could fling away a profession to become a poet was almost an abandoned character, and therefore did his best to keep him away from his young sister, Fanny, whom Keats dearly loved. Miss Lowell has taken pains to defend the character of the maligned Fanny Brawne, unjustly accused of frivolity, disloyalty, and lack of intelligence. The evidence seems conclusive that Fanny endured patiently the unreasonable jealousy of Keats, and was considerate of a lover, ill and despondent. "She was well educated for a girl of her class and period," a voluminous reader, was interested in politics, and in later life, she wrote for "Blackwoods." The story of Keats's life is accompanied by a critical commentary of his poetry. In Keats's own words, it was "the principle of beauty" that he loved. Miss Lowell, herself an imagist poet, dwells on his appreciation of form and color. She denies that his poems have any symbolism or allegory or mysticism. Her analysis of "Endymion" occupies about one hundred and fifty pages, including a study of its sources, of which she considers Drayton's "Endymion and Phoebe" the most important. The book is a storehouse of information about Keats. The Appendix contains (A) Chronological List of Keats's Poems, compiled according to later information, (B) the "Gripus Fragment," of a play which may or may not be by Keats, (C) Annotations and underscored passages in books owned or borrowed by Keats, (D) a Fragment of the Journal-Letter to George and Georgiana Keats.

KEATS, JOHN, HIS LIFE AND POETRY, HIS FRIENDS, CRITICS AND AFTER-FAME, by Sir Sidney Colvin (1917). This study of the poet's life "crowded with imaginative and emotional experience" is based on materials available in 1917. The author quotes from poems and letters of Keats in order that some of the story may be told in his own words, and traces the sources of his inspiration in literature, art, and nature, "of ancient Greece, of mediæval romance, and of the English woods and fields." His mother's father, John Jennings, owned a livery stable, carrying on a large business in London and the suburbs, the management of which he left to his son-in-law, Keats's father. After the death of his grandfather and of both his parents Keats's grandmother made Richard Abbey, a tea merchant, trustee of the estate and guardian of the children, John, George, Tom, and Fanny. The boys were sent to Clarke's school at Enfield, and his friend, Cowden Clarke, the son of the head-master, is the source of information for this time of Keats's life. He shows him to have had an intense affection for his mother and brothers, to have been a favorite at the school, to have had a fiery temper, with a "terrier courage," which made him a great fighter. It was Cowden Clarke who first introduced him to the works of Spenser which had so great an influence on his genius. He also brought him to see his friend, Leigh Hunt, who became Keats's friend, and printed a sonnet of Keats in his paper, the first appearance of the poet in print, "and a decisive circumstance in his life." After Keats left school he was apprenticed to a surgeon, Thomas Hammond, and later was a pupil at Guy's Hospital, and obtained a license from the Court of Apothecaries to practise. Colvin quotes accounts of Keats at this time, written by fellow medical students. He gave up his medical course because he decided to dedicate his life to poetry. He said to Cowden Clarke of his unfitness for the profession, "The other day during the lecture, there came a sunbeam into the room, and with it a whole troop of creatures floating in the ray; and I was off with them to Oberon and fairy-land." The story of his life is his relations with his friends, the Hunts, Charles Brown with whom he lived after his brother Tom's death, and the companion of the walking tour in Scotland and Ireland, Charles Wentworth Dilke, their friend and neighbor, Benjamin Haydon, the sound critic but mediocre artist, John Hamilton Reynolds and his sisters, Charles Lamb, who recognized his genius, and Wordsworth, whom Keats admired though he was chilled by his egotism, "vanity and bigotry." Keats "did not take to Shelley as kindly as Shelley did to him," says Hunt. Colvin writes that "Keats, with the rich elements of earthly clay in his composition, his lively vein of every-day common-sense and humour, his keen, tolerant delight and interest in the aspects and activities of nature and human nature as he found them, may well have been as much repelled as attracted by Shelley. . . ." The first volume of Keats's verse was published in 1817, and was launched, to quote the words of Cowden Clarke, "amid the cheers and fond anticipations of all his circle," but, he continues, "the book might have emerged in Timbuctoo with far stronger chances of fame and appreciation. The whole community as if by compact, seemed determined to know nothing about it." The notices in the reviews were not such as to help a new writer to fame or his book to sale. Keats found other publishers for his next work, and made new friendships with the publisher, John Taylor, and Richard Woodhouse, a young solicitor, literary adviser to the firm. Colvin summarizes the history of English poetry in his study of Keats's poetry. There are two chapters on the story of "Endymion," its sources, plan, and symbolism, its technical and poetical qualities and its relation to the works of certain other poets and poems of Keats's time. He retells the facts about the attacks on Hunt and Keats by "Blackwood's (Edinburgh) Magazine," and the "Quarterly Review," and contradicts the views of Keats's friends that it was the cruelty of these criticisms that killed him. His sudden fall from robustness and high spirits at this time was due to the beginning of tuberculosis. Keats wrote Woodhouse, "the attempt to crush me in the 'Quarterly' has only brought me more into notice. . . . I think I shall be among the English poets after my death. . . ." However in spite of the "flint and iron" of his disposition, Keats had always to fight fits of depression and self-torment, and a year or two later when he realized the harm these reviews had done to his material prospects, these consequences did prey on his mind, and "conspired with the forces of disease and passion to his undoing." It was after his brother Tom's death and George's emigration to America that Keats met and fell in love with Fanny Brawne. His friends regarded the attachment as a misfortune to him. Colvin pays tribute to her kindness, and constancy in essentials to her lover, and her patience with his "wild outbursts of jealousy and suspicion," but does not think she was capable of appreciation of the "manner of man he was." The "tortured, terrifying vehemence" of Keats's passion for her was a love that though requited could have no fruition, because of his poverty and fatal illness. After Keats became too ill to be left alone he accepted the invitation of the Hunts to live with them, and then stayed with the Brawnes the last weeks before he went to Italy, the verdict of the doctors being that a winter in the South was his only chance of health. The artist, Joseph Severn, accompanied him, the first impulse of devotion to his friend strengthened, on reflection, by the plan to work in Rome for the travelling studentship of the Royal Academy. On the voyage to Italy Keats wrote to Mrs. Brawne, "I dare not fix my mind upon Fanny. I have not dared to think of her." He writes to Brown of Fanny, "To receive a letter from her — to see her handwriting would break my heart . . . to see her name written, would be more than I can bear." Severn's care of Keats is written in his letters to the friends in England who hoped for his recovery, though Severn and Keats both knew there was no hope. The last chapter is an epilogue which traces the slow growth of Keats's fame after his death.

KING'S HENCHMEN, THE, by Edna St. Vincent Millay (1927) is a lyric drama of three acts, the first from the pen of this well-known poet. In the first act Eadgar, King of England, is discovered seated in his hall at Winchester surrounded by his loyal henchmen. The ladies of the court are seated in the background. All are listening to the tale Maccus, the harper, is singing, their favorite saga of the glory and death of Cynewulf, King of Wessex. It is five o'clock in the morning and all are awaiting the coming of Aethelwold, who is about to set out on a mission for the king. Meantime the ladies' gossip reveals the situation at court. Eadgar, the king, is weary of his widowed lot. He has heard much of the beauty of Aelfrida, daughter of the Thane of Devon. So he has decided to send Aethelwold, his foster brother and trustiest henchman, to see the maid and if she be as beautiful as it is rumored, he is to woo her for the king and bring her back with him. The act closes with Aethelwold's departure accompanied by Maccus, and all the court with Eadgar at their head, bidding him farewell. Act two opens in a forest in Devon, a month later, on the evening of All Hallow Mass. Aethelwold and Maccus are lost in the wood which is filled with mist. They chaff each other on the errand which has brought them there, for Aethelwold has but little liking for women of any sort and the dubious nature of the road induces the question whether, if he follow it, he will not find it leads to Hell and he be obliged to woo a daughter of the Fiend. So with light hearts they part. Presently Aelfrida enters with Ase, her servant. Instructed by the maid, Aelfrida seeks in the woods on All Hallow's Eve to discover by spell and rune her lover that is to be. Ase departs and the girl chants the rune of "Whitethorn and blackthorn," while she goes forward holding the torch behind her. So she comes upon Aethelwold asleep in the wood. Under the glamor of the moon on this mysterious night they hail one another as lovers destined for one another. As Aelfrida departs Aethelwold learns her name and station, for she is that maid he must woo for his king. In despair he sends Maccus back to the king with the message that the beauty of the Thane of Devon's daughter is nothing much for a king, but that he, being poor, will stay there and wed the girl since her father is rich in lands and kine. In the third act Aelfrida and Aethelwold are found in the house of Ordgar the Thane of Devonshire, where they have remained since their marriage, for Aelfrida still keeps her father's house. It is the following spring and Aelfrida is full of discontent for she cannot understand why her husband, who is such a favorite of the king, will not take her to his court at Winchester. Then Maccus comes with word that the king, when riding into Wales, has come by the shore out of love and desire to see Aethelwold. That wretched man seeks to save his life and love, although his honor is gone, by having his beautiful wife disguise herself as a loathsome hag, and remain in her bower whither he will lead the king for a secret visit. As they approach, the door opens and Aelfrida steps forth regal in her loveliest robes. When she had learned from her husband the king's early intentions toward her, wounded ambition and self-love prove stronger than her love for Aethelwold. Seeing her thus faithless, and himself bitterly shamed for his faithless treatment of his king, Aethelwold stabs himself. Sternly Eadgar refuses to interfere until the tragedy is consummated. Then he rebukes the perfidious Aelfrida, "Thou hast not tears enow in thy narrow heart to weep him worthily. Wherefore have done." While loyal Maccus waves her back from her slain lord with bitter scorn, "I would not have thee foul this blood." The lyric mood is held throughout the entire play. The lament for the Untimely Dead at the end with its refrain, "And thou liest here," in its mood is reminiscent of such early English poems as "Deor's lament." A moving and beautiful work!

KISS FOR CINDERELLA, A, by Sir J. M. Barrie (1916). This modern Cinderella is a little London slavey, Jane, sometimes called "Miss Thing," who spends her days cleaning in a studio building for one pound and seven shillings a week. A policeman comes to Mr. Bodie to warn him that he is showing too much light, as it is the period of the War and German airplanes are abroad. He hears Cinderella tell Mr. Bodie that she has a great wish to go to a ball, and to see Buckingham Palace, and does not comprehend the romantic notions that make her want to dodge the police guardians of the king's home. He trails Cinderella home, and finds that at night she is the proprietress of a penny emporium named "Celeste et Cie." after a shiny Bond Street window front. She sells shaves for a penny, does odd jobs of tailoring, and for her share of war work maintains a little group of war orphans, one English, one French, one Belgian, and the fourth, Gretchen, "who is not Swiss." All the potatoes go to the little waifs so that she goes hungry herself. Miss Thing tells her babies the story of Cinderella, and plays makebelieve with them until she really almost believes that she is Cinderella. It is to amuse the children that she goes out to sit on the steps of her shanty, half pretending and half expecting the visit of the fairy godmother and the invitation to the ball. The kindly policeman wraps his muffler around the little drudge, and she falls asleep to dream that she is Cinderella at the ball. The king and queen like the pictures on her dingy pack of cards hold a gorgeous court. They sit on gold rocking-chair thrones, and personally dispense ice cream in golden cones from a golden push cart. The king's speech is a page out of a city official's pompous address at a charity festival. There follows a contest for the hand and heart of the prince, none other than the friendly police-man. One by one the famous beauties from the studio walls pass before the prince in the hope of rousing his languid interest, the smiling Mona Lisa, the dashing Gainsborough lady, the flashing Carmencita, and the Girl with the muff, but in vain. Fair they may be, but have they perfect feet? And what are "uppers" without the feet? Cinderella of course meets the test. The Prince and Cinderella are married, and they are all dancing to the music of the hurdy-gurdy when the stroke of midnight makes an end to the revels, and Miss Thing wakes up in the hospital. "An angel" is standing by her bed with a boiled egg on a tray. At first she thinks it is the egg you always get with your tea in the workhouse the day before you die. In this convalescent home by the sea Miss Thing recovers from undernourishment and exposure to await the coming of her policeman. He has written her a letter in which he tells her that he prefers her company to that of thirty-four policewomen. At her request he proposes a second time, and thus gives her the chance to accept in the grand phrases she has been "keeping handy" just in case. As Miss Thing knew all along in her valiant heart every story about Cinderella must have a happy ending.

KRAKATIT, by Karel Capek (1925). Engineer Prokop completes the invention of a new explosive which he calls Krakatit. He has evolved it out of his obsession that all matter is highly explosive and only held together until some disturbing ele-ment releases its energy in an explosion. A small quantity of his Krakatit explodes, apparently of itself, on Tuesday night, and with his already mutilated chemist's hand again wounded, his brain inflamed from exhaustion and the exaltation of a successful inventor, mixed with horror at the realization of the destructive possi-bilities of his explosive, Prokop rushes to Prague. There, George Thomas, an old Polytechnic classmate, finds him wandering, weak and feverish, in the streets and takes him home to his apartment smelling of cigarettes and women. Thomas extracts the formula for Krakatit from his unconscious guest and leaves him saying that he is going to his father in Tynice to borrow money. The next morning a beautiful young girl, heavily veiled, comes to the apartment with a package for Thomas. She fears that he has gone to commit suicide and Pro-kop, overcome by her beauty, promises to deliver the package. He manages to reach Tynice in his delirious state and collapses at the house of Dr. Thomas, George's father. In the peaceful country life of the doctor's home Prokop's health and weakened memory are slowly restored. His inventor's enthusiasm reawakes, but alternates with his growing attraction toward young Annie, the doctor's daughter. On suddenly reading the following advertisement in the newspaper: "Krakatit! Will Eng. P. send his address? Carson, Poste Restante." his passion for science takes precedence of his love affair, clears his memory and starts him off after Thomas, whom he now realizes has possession of the Krakatit formula and he believes that this Carson must be in touch with him. Involved in these thoughts is the desire to find the beautiful veiled girl to return the package to her and save her from Thomas. In Prague there is no trace of Thomas, but Prokop learns, through reading his mail in his luxurious apartment, that Thomas is engaged in every dishonest scheme imaginable and in many love affairs, but that the veiled unknown is only the sister of one of the infatuated women. On going to his own hut workshop the engineer finds it cleaned out, but Carson turns up quite at home there. He informs Prokop that he has all his possessions in safety and will restore them and give him a large sum of money in return for the process of making Krakatit. It comes out that Thomas is working for Carson, so far unsuccessfully, in the Balttin factory, on the formula, but that anarchists are in possession of the small quantity of Krakatit which Prokop had left in his workshop. Carson has discovered that the anarchists have a secret wireless station through which, on Tuesday and Friday evenings, they disturb the electromagnetic climate, produced by wireless stations, which holds Krakatit together, and it then disintegrates, causing frightful explosions. He appeals to Prokop to help against this anarchist power, but Prokop's one idea is that Krakatit must no longer exist in order to save humanity. Unable to find the veiled girl, Prokop follows Carson to Balttin to find Thomas and learn the girl's address. He is imprisoned immediately on his arrival in the castle of Balttin until he shall make Krakatit for them. He works, in the perfect laboratory provided for him, on other inventions, lives in the castle and becomes involved in a passionate love affair with the young Princess, his hostess. He makes mad efforts to escape, but ends by offering to give up humanity to destruction through Krakatit if he may marry the Princess. She will not accept the sacrifice and forces him to escape with her help. Then he falls into the hands of the anarchists, who have his snuffbox of Krakatit and wish more. At an anarchist meeting they start fighting for the explosive powder and the old man, the anarchist leader, and a beautiful girl help Prokop escape. The old man takes him to the anarchist wireless station, that in some mysterious way is also Prokop's old workshop. By manipulating the electricity the old man causes the explosion of the Krakatit at the anarchist meeting and then tells Prokop that all the power is now in his hands. This drives Prokop once more to search for Thomas to stop him from making Krakatit, which will only be exploded through the anarchists' machine. Intermingled with his wish to save mankind is still the desire to find the veiled girl. He fails to reach Thomas and thousands are killed in the explosion which follows immediately on Thomas's successfully completed manufacture of Krakatit. Fleeing once more from an explosion, Prokop finds refuge with a curious old man, who wanders about the countryside with his old horse and wagon and a little lighted peep-show of pictures of the world. He also reads the stars and tells fortunes. The old man tells Prokop: ". . . You will not achieve the highest and you will not release everything. . . . You wanted to do great things, and you will instead do small ones. . . . He whose thoughts are full of the highest turns his eyes away from the people. Instead you will serve them." Now Prokop understands that it is God the Father speaking.

KRISTIN LAVRANSDATTER, a trilogy translated from the Norwegian of Sigrid Unset, by C. Archer and J. S. Scott (1923–1927), under titles, Volume 1, The Bridal Wreath; Volume 2, The Mistress of Husaby; Volume 3, The Cross. A domestic and psychological novel of the first half of the fourteenth century, with Kristin, the heroine, as daughter, wife and mother. Her father, Lavrans Bjorgulfson, has followed knightly pursuits in his youth, but has now settled on his manor, the leader in his part of the country of the landed aristocracy, a kind of peasant nobility peculiar to Norway. The story begins when Kristin is seven years old, and the landmarks in her life are the journeys out of her home valley with her father, on horseback up to their mountain saeter, and to his distant southern manor, and to Oslo, where she hears mass in the cathedral. The year that Kristin is fifteen, her father agrees that she shall marry Simon, son of a neighbor, but the betrothal feast is postponed pending the settlement of the lands. Her childhood foster-brother, Arne, who loves her, is killed in a quarrel with a fellow who had given Kristin an ugly fright, and because of this unhappy experience, Lavrans and Simon take her to Oslo to the Convent to school for a year. In Oslo she meets Erlend Nikulausson of Husaby, kinsman to the King and his mother. They fall in love, and for his sake Kristin is "led into sinful revolt against all of whom God had set over her," even though she knows the fascinating and impulsive Erlend has had a disgraceful entanglement with another woman, by whom he has had two children. She becomes his mistress and finally his wife, after a long struggle by passive resistance with her beloved father. At the wedding she wears the golden wreath, token of maidenhood, though she is soon to become a mother, an affront to her family and all her kinsmen, and even to the hereditary servants and vassals, all of whom are dishonored by Kristin's lapse. Kristin had persuaded Simon to break the tryst between them, and before her father had given his consent to her marriage with Erlend, Simon had married a widow, older than himself. In "The Mistress of Husaby," Kristin undertakes to set her husband's manor in order, her own house and thirty farms, since the easygoing Erlend has had no care for his estate. She lives an intense secret life of shame, and fear and doubt until her first child is born, and then makes a pilgrimage to do penance for her sin, twenty miles barefoot, in shirt of sackcloth, carrying her child. Seven sons are born to Kristin and Erlend in quick succession. Erlend becomes a captain and a warden and is often away on his ship. Seeing a long-desired chance to serve Norway, he conspires against his sovereign, King of Sweden, who held Norway in fief, is thrown into prison and is on trial for his life. Simon become a widower, married Ramborg, Kristin's young sister, though he continues to love Kristin. It is Simon, who for Kristin's sake, saves Erlend by persuading the intercession of powerful kinsfolk. This treachery cost Erlend his estates, and in Volume 3, "The Cross," the family live in Jorundgaard, Kristin's childhood home, which had become hers after the death of her father. Both Kristin and Erlend are unwelcome to the householders and neighbors because of their past misdeeds. Never a farmer, Erlend spends his time hunting, and leaves the burden of the management of the estate, the only heritage for their seven sons, to Kristin. Overwrought with responsibility Kristin reproaches Erlend in words he cannot forgive, and in the night he rides away to his own mountain farm, Haugen, where he lived alone regardless of appearances. Ulf, Erlend's rough, faithful kinsman, the first to support her at Husaby, is her steward at Jorundgaard. Once Kristin went to Erlend to entreat him to return, and to carry a death-bed message from Simon, who had been estranged from Erlend, and from that meeting another son is born. Erlend leaves her to bear alone the scandal that comes when the child is born in his absence. When the child dies and Kristin is openly accused of adultery with Ulf and of causing the death of the child, he rides down from the mountain to defend her honor and receive his death wound. The love story of Kristin and Erlend, and the conflict of her ambition, and steadfast, unbending integrity against his wilful recklessness is a dramatic story. Too late Erlend sees life as he has made it, and says "God help me. I have been an unwise man," and Kristin realizes how the strife of their parents has affected the lives of her sons. Two older sons become monks, and Gaute, now head of the house, brings home a fair bride "taken from her father by the strong hand," and there is another gathering of the kinsmen to set this right. The story ends with the advent of the terrible Black Death, which finds Kristin in the Convent to which she has retired. Ulf walks with her on her errand to bring a poor woman who has died of the plague to the town for Christian burial, and carries her back to the Convent mortally stricken herself.

LABRADOR DOCTOR, A, by Wilfred Thomason Grenfell (1919). The autobiography of Dr. Grenfell leads from the heather-clad hills of Heswall and the Sands of Dee, "every inch dear to me," through London, and to his North Sea work, "thirty-two years spent in work for deep-sea fishermen," and through holiday time in Asia Minor, to close range of the World War, and back again to the far-away section of the world which gives the title to his book. Of his birthplace, Parkgate, near Chester, England, he recalls the early days and impressions, his parents, brothers, and home life, the humble neighbors who lived by the seafaring genius "which we ourselves loved so much," the great salt-water marshes which seemed so endless to "our tiny selves," the fascination of the Sands, greatly enhanced by the numerous birds in search of the abundant food which lay buried along the edges of the muddy gutters. At the age of fourteen Grenfell entered Marlborough School in Wiltshire, where his own bent was not of the things of the land . . . "boats were the things which appealed to me most." Of his school life, one of the impressions recorded is that "form" is a part of the life of all English schools, and "the boys think much more of it than sin." He began here to collect and study natural objects . . . "stealing into the great forest, my butterfly net under my coat, to try and add a new specimen to my hoard." At college he found his real interest when he was shown a "pickled human brain." He had never thought of a man's body as a machine. The idea attracted him as did the "gramophone, the camera, the automobile." The opportunity came at this time for him to go to London with his father and take up work in the London Hospital and University, preparatory to studying medicine. Of his impressions of the methods of teaching, he says, "there was practically no histology taught, and little or no pathology;" *materia medica* was almost identical and "while we had better fortune with physiology, no experience and no apparatus for verifying its teachings were ever shown us." They attended the dispensary. "Personally, I went once, fooled around making an eggnog, and arranged with a considerate druggist to do the rest that was necessary." He adds that he satisfied the examiners at the College of Physicians and Surgeons, and those of the London University at the examinations for Bachelor of Medicine. He speaks here of hearing D. L. Moody, the evangelist. "His practicality interested me, and I stayed the service out. When eventually I left, it was with a determination either to make religion a real effort to do as I thought Christ would do in my place as a doctor, or frankly abandon it. That could only have one issue while I still lived with a mother like mine." Dr. Grenfell recalls his experiences at the London Hospital, where there were now and again fishermen from the large fishing fleets of the North Sea, and he applied to go out. "There was never any question as to the real object of the Mission to Deep-Sea Fishermen. The words, 'Heal the sick,' carved in large letters, adorned the starboard bow. 'Preach the Word' was on the port, and around the brass rim of the wheel ran the legend, 'Jesus said, Follow me and I will make you fishers of men.'" He says, "these 'leep-sea fisheries were a revelation to me. . . . It was amazing to find over twenty thousand men and boys afloat — the merriest, cheerfulest lot which I had ever met. . . . Clothing, food, customs, were all subordinated to utility." Dr. Grenfell says that they embodied all the traits of character that make men love to read of the stories of the buccaneers and other seamen of the sixteenth-century period. He considered that the field of work offered him aroused his ambitions sufficiently to make him believe that his special capacities and training could be used to make new men as well as new bodies. The North Sea work grew apace. Vessel after vessel was added to the fleet. Her Majesty, Queen Victoria, became interested. An Institute at Yarmouth for fishermen ashore and a dispensary vessel to be sent out each spring among the thousands of Scotch, Manx, Irish, and French fishermen who carried on the herring and mackerel fishery off the south and west coast of Ireland, were new ventures; a dispensary and social centre at Crookhaven, just inside the Fastnet Lighthouse, and another in Tralee on the Kerry coast, north of Cape Clear, were established. "Gatherings for worship and singing were also held on Sundays on the boats, for on that day neither Scotch, Manx, nor English went fishing. The men loved the music, the singing of hymns, and the conversational addresses." "The opportunities for both holding simple religious services and rendering medical help from our dispensary were numerous . . ." He tells of establishing a small mission room in the harbor. "Twenty years have passed away," he writes of the "Lure of Labrador," and the first day that he saw the island, — "but still its events stand out clear and sharp." Dr. Grenfell reviews the conditions at that time, the more striking features of native life — the undrained and dirty huts. Two islands were chosen for cottage hospitals, and the experiment was repeated on a larger scale on his return in the spring. Among the Eskimos he found a great deal of tuberculosis and much eye trouble. The average life was short and infant mortality high. He describes life in the White Bay — the desolation of Labrador in those years. His work lay almost entirely among the white population of the Labrador and North New England coasts, but he came in contact with the native races and rendered them such service, medical or otherwise, as lay within his power. The Eskimos suffered one year "heavily from an epidemic of influenza." "Like all primitive people they had no immunity to the disease." "It was a pathetic sight as the lighter received its load of rude coffins from the wharf, with all the kindly little people gathered to tow them to their last resting-place in the shallow sand at the end of the inlet." Lecturing and cruising, Dr. Grenfell learned to know the Labrador people and to love them. "I have sailed the seas in ocean greyhounds and in floating palaces and in steam yachts, but better than any other I love to dwell on the memories of that summer, cruising the Labrador in a twenty-footer." The dangers of the seal fishery are discussed; the later work which was opened in Iceland, the story of the first winter at St. Anthony, the hardships of winter travelling on this coast, and the final establishment of the hospital. The coöperative movement — the organizing of stores which afforded a solution of some of the problems — is reviewed with the progress of the work and the writer holds that the industrial mission, the educational mission, and the orphanage work at least rank with and should go hand in hand with hospitals in any true interpretation of a gospel of love. He pays tribute to his coworkers, to their vision, ability and devotion. The problems of education as observed in Newfoundland and Labrador are discussed; the awakening of interest in Labrador conditions, the "reindeer experiment" by which it was proved "that the deer can live, thrive, and multiply on the otherwise perfectly valueless areas of this North country, and furnish a rapidly increasing domesticated 'raw material' for food and clothing supply to its people." The "ice-pan adventure," and other important and significant movements are told of in detail. In 1915, Dr. Grenfell joined the Harvard Surgical Unit for a proposed term of service at a base hospital in France. In the concluding chapters of his biography, he writes of the future of the Labrador mission to which he believes that the "Strathcona" — the hospital ship — is the keystone. Of himself he says, "I do not feel that it mattered much whether I chose medicine for an occupation, or law, or education, or commerce, or any other way to justify my existence by working for a living as every honest man should. But if there is one thing about which I never have any question, it is that the decision and endeavor to follow the Christ does for men what nothing else on earth can."

LADY INTO FOX, by David Garnett (1925). England in the nineteenth century is the scene of this strange event described in circumstantial detail. A country gentleman, Mr. Tebrick, was walking with his young wife, Sylvia, to see the hunt, and suddenly, "where his wife had been a moment before was a small fox." Her husband's love was equal to the demands put upon him by this amazingly difficult situation. He shot his two dogs, dismissed the servants, and they settle down to the life of a correct English country household as well as they are able. In the beginning little but the lady's body seemed changed, and he believed they could be happy enough if they could live secluded from the world. Sylvia wore a dressing gown for the sake of modesty and walked self-consciously on her hind legs, but in spite of his efforts she gradually lost interest in books and music and playing cards with him. She lapsed in attention to the story of Clarissa Harlowe, which her husband was reading aloud to her, and fixed her gaze with a strange intentness on the bird in its cage. After the terrible moment when he left her alone a moment with a rabbit and a bunch of snow drops and came back to find her devouring the rabbit she repented, and "motioned to the portable stereoscope, and . . . they spent the rest of the afternoon together very happily looking through the collection of views which he had purchased of Italy, Spain, and Scotland." However with each lapse she grew wilder and more impatient of her husband's control until she finally escaped to the woods. Sylvia's unfortunate husband found solace in playing with the litter of cubs, whose paternity was to him a source of only momentary if acute jealousy. The hounds tear her from his arms at last.

LAST OF MRS. CHEYNEY, THE, a comedy, by Frederick Lonsdale (1925). Mrs. Cheyney, "a wealthy widow from Australia," is giving a charity concert in the garden of her home at Goring, England. In the drawing-room, George, the cockney page, tells Charles, the butler, that the garden is full of "swells." He has called everybody "my lord," and has not been contradicted once. Charles reveals that "the old party they call Maria," is Lady Frinton, who met his mistress at Cannes, and then introduced her to her set of friends. "The old one with the painted face and the pearls" is Mrs. Ebley, once a beauty with many lovers. "She kept her pearls, but became respectable," and to-day her house is the most exclusive of all English homes. The presence of Lord Elton, "a rich eligible bachelor, an intimate friend of royalty," is a triumph for the attractive hostess, as he seldom goes anywhere. Lord Arthur Dilling is young, rich, clever, cynical, and also a bachelor. The guests enter the room and put an end to the conversation of the servants. The talk is about the success of the party. the infatuation of the gay Lord Dilling and the pompous Lord Elton for Mrs. Cheyney. The perfect manners of Charles are the subject of comment. Lord Dilling asks him if he has not met him somewhere before, and if he was ever at Oxford, but the incomparable Charles has no such recollection, and answers that he came from an employment agency in London. With the departure of the guests the servants join Mrs. Cheyney and appear to be thoroughly at home. Their chief topic of conversation is Mrs. Ebley's pearls, and it becomes apparent that the group have designs on the necklace. Mrs. Cheyney tells them that she has received an invitation to stay with Mrs. Ebley for the week end. She admits that she is thinking of refusing the invitation. "The idea of persuading perfectly charming people into inviting you to their house for the purpose of robbing them," she says, is rather distasteful to her. The suave Charles is able to overcome her scruples. The next acts take place at Mrs. Ebley's house party. The charming Mrs. Cheyney is in the garden with Lord Elton, and Lady Joan believes he has proposed. Lord Dilling confesses that he is in love with Mrs. Cheyney, and that she will not have anything to do with him. Later in the evening Mrs. Cheyney refuses Lord Dilling's offer of marriage to his surprise and dissatisfaction. Mrs. Cheyney pleads a headache and goes to her room after Mrs. Ebley has told her if she wants aspirin to come to her for it. Charles arrives with a cablegram enclosed in a parcel for Mrs. Cheyney, and Lord Dilling, who has his suspicions about the perfect butler, opens the parcel and reads the message before it is delivered. He arranges with Mrs. Ebley to change bedrooms for the night as he has not been sleeping well, and hers is quieter. As he expects Mrs. Cheyney comes in to get the pearls, and finds Lord Dilling waiting for her. She pretends at first that she has come for the aspirin, but gives up the pretence. If she agrees to stay with him, Lord Dilling will say nothing about the affair, but she convinces him that she is not the kind of woman he thinks she is by choosing rather to ring the bell and arouses the house. He tries to protect her by saying that he tricked her into coming to the room, but Mrs. Cheyney tells the truth. They all agree to wait until morning to decide what to do about it. In the morning they discuss sending Mrs. Cheyney, and her accomplice, Charles, to jail, but dread the resulting scandal. Lord Elton had proposed to her in a letter, in which he had expressed freely his private opinion of his hostess and her friends. Dilling has told him that "if it were his letter and he were her, he wouldn't sell it for twenty-five thousand pounds." A copy of the letter makes Lord Elton most unpopular with his fellow guests, and convinces them of the awkward position they are in. They must buy the letter back to save their reputations. Mrs. Cheyney and Charles seem quite determined to go to jail unless Lord Elton will pay ten thousand pounds for the letter, which Mrs. Cheyney will regard not as blackmail but as evidence of breach of promise. Lord Elton protests but writes the check which Mrs. Cheyney tears to bits, as she hands him an envelope containing the letter also in small pieces. Charles is reduced almost to tears at the sight. They ask her why she tore it up, and she gives the credit to her sense of decency, which is stronger than her dishonest inclinations. She is not a widow, and not from Australia, just a London shopgirl, wanting beauty and attractive things, and the easiest way to get them seemed to be to become a pupil of Charles. Lord Elton offers to set her up in a shop of her own, and they all promise to be her customers. They are curious about Charles, who did spend three years at Oxford, and offers now to return the watch he took from Lord Dilling five years before, but Lord Dilling asks him to do him the favor of keeping it. Charles is now going to parts unknown and says goodby. Now Lord Dilling tells Mrs. Cheyney that he has told his father, the bishop, all about her, and this understanding parent is waiting to give them his blessing. This is "the last of Mrs. Cheyney," and "the beginning of Lady Dilling."

LAST POST, THE, by Ford Madox Ford (1928). Mark Tietjens was a member of an ancient family who owned an immense estate, "Groby," somewhere in the North. He had worked with the Transport Department in the War Office of England, had built it up from the day of his entrance, thirty years ago, to the day of his resolution never more to speak word nor stir a finger. The last word he had ever spoken had been on the day that one of his colleagues at the Ministry had telephoned him the terms of the Armistice. Marie Leonie, who had lived with him for twenty years, had received the message that the Allies did not intend to pursue the Germans into their own country. Mark's exact remark — in English — she could not remember definitely — he had been recovering from double pneumonia at the time — but in effect, of this she was certain, he would never speak again. "For the betrayal of France by her Allies at the supreme moment of triumph had been a crime news of which might well cause the end of the world to seem desirable." When this story opens Mark lies in bed, staring at the withy binders of his thatch shelter, a hut that has no sides; only his eyes moved with unusual vivacity, all the life of the man being concentrated in them and their lids. The doctor has given orders that Mark must never be left alone. In his opinion, if the man ever moved — physically — there was danger that the lesions, if there were any in his brain, might then be restarted with fatal effects. They never let him out of their sight. Mark's brother, Christopher, will inherit "Groby." His marriage to Sylvia has proved unhappy. To prevent trouble in the future over the estate Mark makes legal provision for Marie Leonie. As Madame Tietjens, Marie is better prepared to face her legitimate sister-in-law. Sylvia had an intimacy with Mrs. Millicent de Bray Pape, an American, whose husband had olive-tree plantations in the United States, and who claimed a spiritual affinity with Madame de Maintenon. Mrs. Pape wanted to hire "Groby" furnished, and with Sylvia's illegitimate son by a Field Marshal, whom Christopher has accepted as his own, and who is known as "Mark Tietjens," goes to see Mark to make the arrangements. They do not know of his determination never to speak. Sylvia had circulated the report that Mark's physical condition was due to the sins of his youth, and Mrs. Pape accepts it. All that she wants from the "libertine" is his permission for her to live in semi-regal state at "Groby," and to explain about the "great Groby tree" — the symbol of the Tietjens — which Sylvia had wanted to cut down because the old house was unlettable, darkened as it was by the funeral plumes, and to spite Christopher. Between the two brothers there was an old score to be settled. Mark had accused Christopher of living on the immoral earnings of Sylvia, and Christopher had from that time on refused to accept a penny from the Groby estate, and was making his living from selling antiques. He had a broker in America. Mark had proposed the annulment of Christopher's marriage. With Sylvia out of the way, Christopher could legitimize his relations with Valentine Wannop, with whom he had lived for years. Valentine, on the night before the Armistice, had gone through some terrible experience with Sylvia. That was the night when the band had played the "Last Post" for the Dead, and Christopher had stopped the bugle because its sound was intolerable to Mark. Sylvia had been informed that Christopher and Valentine were in communication. Valentine had come to Mark for protection — the day that the news of the Armistice came, which finished Mark with the Ministry, with the Government, with the nation, with the world. Sylvia returns to her affair with the Field Marshal, and proposes marriage to him as the father of her son "Mark Tietjens." — Christopher can be divorced; he has settled down into a tranquil devotion to his brother, and Valentine has supplanted her. But her case in court turned out a fiasco. At "Groby," Mrs. Pape has had the great tree cut down, and a part of the old house fell with it. She faces a damage suit, although Mark does not interfere. Christopher's mind is weakened, as he peddles his antiques about the country, and Valentine is awaiting a child. Sylvia tells Valentine that it was she who had the Groby Tree cut down as a revenge on the Tietjens, but that now she is "leaving her husband to her." And Mark gets her message — she is going to divorce Christopher and dissolve her marriage with the sanction of Rome, because of Mark's unforgettable services to the country. Mark has had a fear that Valentine was Christopher's half-sister. This weight is finally lifted, and with the great Groby Tree down the curse was perhaps off the family. As death approaches, Mark breaks his long silence by whispering into Valentine's ear the words of an old song. . . . "Never let thy bairnie weep for thy sharp tongue to thy goodman."

LAZARUS LAUGHED, by Eugene O'Neill (1927). The play begins just after the miracle of the resurrection of Lazarus from the dead by Jesus, after Jesus has gone away. The message Lazarus brings from beyond the grave is that "there is no death." With "God's eternal laughter" on his lips he asks the people to laugh with him that death is dead. He says: "There is Eternal Life in No, and there is the same Eternal Life in Yes. Death is the fear between. . . ." The neighbors remember that Lazarus used to be pale even when he worked in the fields, and now he is brown and young. The followers of Lazarus dance and sing while they are ploughing the earth and tending the flocks. His house in Bethany comes to be called the House of Laughter. At the news of the crucifixion of Jesus, the Nazarenes and the Orthodox battle with each other, and the father and mother of Lazarus and his two sisters, Mary and Martha, are trampled and killed. He says: "Sometimes it is hard to laugh — even at men." A centurion comes to bring Lazarus to Rome. Tiberius Caesar has heard of him, and hopes that the Jew has some secret or nostrum to restore his youth. At Athens they tell of Lazarus that to look in his eyes is to forget sorrow. "It is as if a heavy weight you had been carrying all your life without knowing it suddenly were lifted. . . ." Caligula meets Lazarus, and against his will, is affected by his strange power. He plots to have the crowd of the followers of Lazarus killed by the Roman legions when they reach Rome to see if Lazarus will betray grief, and they die laughing, and Lazarus laughs with them. At his audience with Tiberius, Pompeia gives poison to Miriam, his wife, to see if Lazarus can save her from death. Because he cannot learn the secret of youth from Lazarus, Tiberius has him burned in the amphitheatre. He asks Lazarus for assurance of hope for himself, Tiberius Caesar. Lazarus answers: "What is — you? But there is hope for Man. Love is Man's hope — love for his life on earth, a noble love above suspicion and distrust. . . ." Pompeia throws herself into the flames to laugh and die with Lazarus. Caligula comes rushing to save Lazarus, and slays Tiberius. He then stabs Lazarus, calling out: "I have killed God. I am Death. Death is Caesar." The fear by which a people is governed is thus restored by Caesar. Caligula sinks to his knees and asks Lazarus to forgive him and save him from fear and death, and the last words of Lazarus come with a faint dying note of laughter: "Fear not, Caligula. There is no death." Caligula tries to hold the remembrance but forgets. As Lazarus has said: "It is too soon."

Men still need their swords to slash at ghosts in the dark. . . ." There is a continual chorus, after the manner of Greek tragedy, first of the Old Men in the house of Lazarus, and then of his followers, and the Greek and Roman crowds.

LEE, A DRAMATIC POEM, by E. L. Masters (1926). The characters are General Lee, Mrs. Lee, General Longstreet, General Pickett, soldiers, a mountaineer, Ormund and Arimanius, who take the place of a Greek chorus, the South, Virginia, and the Republic. The leader of the Confederacy is taken as a symbol of the free soul battling vainly to retain conditions of freedom. The Civil War becomes an issue between the old way of life as against the new slavery of industrialism. In the prologue, the time is April 17, 1861. Ormund and Arimanius, eternal types, walk at the foot of the uncompleted Washington Monument in Washington, continuing a discussion of plans being made in heaven for war on earth. Arimanius complains that always the friends of Liberty "partake of crime" and God accepts the burnt offering of Abel, the commercial North, rather than the fruit and flowers of Cain, the farming South. He foresees a race which now follows John Brown's soul, living in the future to enslave another brown race. Ormund reminds him of the prophecy that John Brown's soul shall hunt the soul of Lee. Arimanius argues that the Union is a lesser thing than the growth of Liberty. Ormund foretells Lincoln's lofty place in the future untouched by slander and to Arimanius' question: "And what for Lee?" prophesies "dark despair" and "Fates that ruin and renew him." The two then draw near to Arlington across the river to counsel Lee, who has passed the night in prayer.

*   *   *   *   *   *   *   *   *

Lee in his chamber still strives to learn the will of God, to know if Duty be only to fulfil higher laws which do not seem to serve an earthly purpose. Mrs. Lee comes after a sleepless night to counsel peace. He sees the South as seceding for civil liberty, not for slavery. Mrs. Lee asks "How will it stand in history?" Lee answers: "God is a God of truth." Mrs. Lee reminds him of happiness and honor, but he has decided with the clearing light of dawn to stand by Virginia, as Washington stood by his country, at the risk of "fortune, fame and traitor's fate."

*   *   *   *   *   *   *   *   *

Ormund and Arimanius have listened pityingly to Lee's struggle and see the future suffering on the battlefields. Then they cross the river to the Washington Monument again to listen to the Republic's wrath. The Republic relates how "Destiny, named also God," breathed upon the waters and deeps of life and stirred men with visions that they might discover and conquer America for her. She condemns the South as living in a dead past, sheltered by the hardworking North and says the disobedient shall be broken. She calls the roll of states to learn where they stand and coming to Virginia appeals to Lee as her "soldier son." Lee replies that he cannot turn against his state and kin and the blood of his sire "whose sword for Revolution was unsheathed." The soul of Washington is his guide against the growth of Tyranny for an issue not "Slavery but Gold." The Republic asks him if he will misguide flaming youth into catastrophe and Lee says that the stock bred of eagles are spirits needing no leading to enroll in the cause of Liberty. Then the Republic invokes Jehovah, the Lord of Hosts, to lay waste the South and its people and cities, and calls on the sea and rivers and the mountains to overthrow the South. Arimanius and Ormund turn away, the former condemning Jehovah's Book and curses invoked by the North. Ormund reminds him that the South will also invoke them. At night, Ormund and Arimanius, on an eminence above the battlefield of Gettysburg, review the past victories of tho South and foresee future defeat, while the soldiers sing "Stonewall Jackson is sleeping in the cold, cold ground." Later in the night Ormund and Arimanius, near Round Top, speak of the accident caused by need of shoes which has made Gettysburg the battleground in spite of Lee. They go to Lee's tent. Longstreet and an officer are discussing Lee's unusual rest-lessness. Lee tells General Longstreet that he is resolved to make a grand assault on the Ridge at dawn. Longstreet protests, but will obey. Arimanius and Ormund ascend an eminence to watch Lee limp into Grant's trap. Arimanius describes the taking of the Ridge by Pickett and its loss. That night Ormund and Arimanius hear voices singing, "John Brown's soul has conquered Capt. Lee."

A deserting Confederate seeks refuge with a Union-sympathising mountaineer. The soldier is overcome with grief that he has deserted Lee, but he was driven almost mad by the letters of suffering from his family and the loss of the Ridge. He tells of all the young Southern gentlemen, fresh from college, inspired to fight for Liberty by Greek ideals and the Bible. The mountaineer points out that the South has been conquered by soft living while the North succeeds because it has gained strength in conquering the mountains and the West. A Horseman appears announcing that the War is over, and Lee surrendered at Appomattox. Ormund and Arimanius speak of the North inflamed at Lincoln's assassination and blaming Lee, when both "but did the work before them." Then they go to give courage to Lee. While Lee sleeps in a farmhouse a soldier and the farmer talk of the tragedy of Lee's surrender and of his refusal to go to Oxford, taking upon himself instead the hardship of the headship of the small University at Lexington, in order to build up again the young lives he led to ruin. Lee comes out and mounts his horse, Trav-eler, bids the soldier go home and "forget the hatred of the War" to build a new America, which he says "is my work and yours." Lee meditates aloud to Traveler as he approaches Lexington and the Blue Ridge Mountains. He thinks of the terri-ble beauty of battle left behind and the dull life of service and duty before. He rides into the welcoming city and Arimanius says that he is entering a trap which will suffocate and immolate him now that the "imperial bigotry of old John Brown, miscalled the Union," has defeated the South. Ormund replies that it is not a trap, but that losing life for duty "Lee shall find life." Arimanius says he sees the Repub-lic "angry and majestic" approaching Lexington.

The Republic comes from her "obedient domain," which has forgotten the words, "Let us have Peace," and subjects the conquered South to ignominy. The South protests that she should be treated according to the "laws of War in honor," but the Republic still insists that it was "vile conspiracy" and "foul rebellion." They argue about secession, and Virginia defends Lee . She says that the Republic's head "must yet be bowed to honor Lee," and that in Time a Nation may go but "the gift of Truth, or Duty, Courage, Sacrifice, or Thought shall last." A Messenger brings word that Lee has died whispering, "Strike the tent!" The last scene is the dirge of the students who carry Lee to his grave.

LETTERS OF GERTRUDE BELL, selected and edited by Lady Bell (2 vols., 1927). "Scholar, poet, historian, archæologist, art critic, mountaineer, explorer, gardener, naturalist, distinguished servant of the State," and "recognized by experts as an expert in them all." Thus Lady Bell writes of the extraordinary career of her dis-tinguished step-daughter. The letters, which begin in 1874, when Gertrude Bell was six years old and end in 1026, just before her death in Bagdad, are almost all written to her father and his wife. In the first chapter one of her college friends writes of the gayety and untiring energy with which Gertrude threw herself into every activity of college life, tennis, hockey, dancing, dramatics, at the same time that she put in seven hours a day of hard study that won for her a brilliant First Class in the School of Modern History. She went to parties in London and hunted in the country. In 1892 Lady Bell's brother-in-law, Sir Frank Lascelles, was appointed minister to Persia, and Gertrude made her first journey to the East to visit the Lascelles at Teheran, and wrote home of the wonder of the desert and the gardens and the bazaars like the Arabian Nights. Twice she made the trip around the world. In 1897 she is staying at the Embassy in Berlin, is presented at Court, attends two Court balls, and was at tea with the Emperor and Empress when the Emperor received a sheaf of telegrams announcing the mobilization of Bulgaria and Servia. Her first desert journeys were made from Jerusalem. She is learning Arabic and is interested in the inscriptions. She writes vivid, entertaining descriptions of the country, and her camping experiences, and the wild-looking Dervishes she has made friends with in Jerusalem. The letters of 1901 and 1902 describe amazing feats of mountain climbing in the Alps. In 1905 and 1907 she is travelling in Asia Minor copying inscriptions, and impressed with the Roman roads she sees telling the story of former domination. She writes her father of copying a queer inscription, all curious rabbit-headed things and winged sorts of crosses and arms and circles which Sir William Ramsay identifies as Hittite, the very thing he had most hoped to find in this unknown country. They arrive at a village and ask for inscriptions, and are told by the villagers that there are none, and then after much argument someone admits that that there is a written stone in his house, and then everyone has a written stone somewhere, and all must be looked at though ninety-nine per cent are worthless. In the fierce Druze country she heard one evening the letting off of guns which is the call to arms, and was allowed to ride up the mountain to the bonfire, where the men and boys stood in a circle to sing their war song, and dance the sword dance, before the two thousand horsemen rode out in the morning to kill and die. Of her journey to Hayil in Arabia, just before the War, Sir David Hogarth writes that it was a pioneer venture which put a line of wells before unknown on the map, and that she accumulated information about the tribes which T. E. Lawrence made signal use of in the Arab campaigns of 1917 and 1918. The first year of the War she worked in England and France. In November, 1916, she was sent to Cairo, and eventually to Bagdad, to put her intimate knowledge and understanding of the Arabs at the service of the British Intelligence Office, trying to unite the tribes to fight on the side of the Allies against the Turk. She helps to make Feisal king, and writes home that she will never engage in creating kings again; it is too great a strain. She describes the vivid picture of the enthronement ceremony, and all Iraq, from North to South, gathered together for the first time in history. She chronicles the making of history on one page of her letter and gives thanks on the next for a blue dress and cloak sent from home. Of King Feisal she says he knows that one or two of us would go to the stake for him, and tells of many talks together, and of their complete sympathy. The old sheiks came in from the desert to ask her counsel. She writes her father that she is happy in feeling that she has the love and confidence of the whole nation, and that she is sure that no Bagdad citizen cares half as much as she does for the beauty of the river and the palm gardens. In the official notice of her death the High Commissioner says of her work in the East: "She had for the last ten years of her life consecrated all the indomitable fervour of her spirit and all the astounding gifts of her mind to the service of the

Arab cause, and especially to Iraq." Two historical summaries written by Sir Percy Cox and Sir Henry Dobbs of her work with them are interpolated in the second volume of letters.

LETTERS OF HENRY JAMES, THE, selected and edited by Percy Lubbock (2 vols., 1920). The letters begin in 1869 when James was twenty-five years old, and take up the story of his life at the point to which he brought it in his reminiscences "Notes of a Son and Brother." They are arranged in groups chronologically, and each group is prefaced with a biographical sketch by the editor. In an introduction the editor says that to those who did not know Henry James the letters will give an impression of his talk. In a letter to Miss Grace Norton, James himself says, "what are letters but talk . . ." and, "It is indeed, I think, of the very essence of a good letter to be shown — it is wasted if it is kept for one." The letters are to his family, to whom he was devoted, and his many intimate friends, impressions of the social scene of which he was an interested spectator, and talk about books. Some of his correspondents are W. D. Howells, Edmund Gosse, Robert Louis Stevenson, Charles Eliot Norton, Mrs. Humphry Ward, H. G. Wells, Mrs. Edith Wharton, T. S. Perry, Hugh Walpole, Compton Mackenzie, and Edward Marsh. It was in 1875 that he came to Europe with the intention of settling in Paris. At this time he wrote "Parisian Letters" for the "New York Tribune." Ivan Turgenev introduced him to Gustave Flaubert, Edmond de Goncourt, Alphonse Daudet, Guy de Maupassant and others. However, he found the circle of literature closed to any foreigner. He writes to W. D. Howells, "I don't like their wares, and they don't like any others." To his brother, William, he expresses his desire to go to London, and early in 1877 he is in England. Before he had been a year in London he writes to Miss Norton, "I feel now more at home in London than anywhere else in the world," and to C. E. Norton, "I am attached to London in spite of the long list of reasons why I should not be; I think it on the whole the best point of view in the world." The young author went everywhere and met everybody. The letters tell of his country house visits, and dinners, one hundred and seven in one season. A letter to William James in 1877 speaks of "seeing a bit of Huxley" at his house Sunday evenings, and dining with Lord Houghton — with Gladstone, Tennyson, Dr. Schliemann (the excavator of old Mycenae, etc.) and half a dozen other men of "high culture"; sitting next to Tennyson who talked with a "strange rustic accent" about port and tobacco. The winter of 1881 to 1882 James spent in Boston, New York and Washington. His mother, to whom he was deeply attached, died in February, 1882. He returned in December, arriving too late to see his father before he died. This was his last visit to America for more than twenty years. Alice James, his sister, and an invalid, came to London to live near her brother from the fall of 1884 until her death in 1892. Her companionship was a great pleasure to him. When she was at Bournemouth in 1885 he spent several weeks with her and made an intimate friend of another invalid imprisoned there, R. L. Stevenson. James called himself a "cosmopolitanized American." He spent part of every year in France and Italy, and found a delightful old eighteenth-century house at Rye, where he could retire from London for quiet and freedom of interruption in his work. From 1889 to 1894 James tried to become a playwright, and gives as his reasons that he wanted to make a kind of financial success that his novels did not achieve. The failure of the plays he writes of in detail to his brother, William, the "abominable quarter of an hour during which all the forces of civilization in the house waged a battle" of applause against the jeers of the gallery. Answering a letter from Howells he says that he feels that he has "fallen upon evil days — every sign or symbol of one's being in the least wanted, anywhere or by anyone, having so utterly failed. A new generation, that I know not, and mainly prize not, has taken universal possession." However, he had the greatest confidence in his art, and in the manner of writing more than the matter. He writes Wells: "It is art that makes life, makes interest, makes importance, for our consideration and application of these things, and I know of no substitute whatever for the force and beauty of its process." Literary style is so much to him that he scores "Tess of the d'Urbervilles" to Stevenson as "vile," and speaks of the "abomination of the language." Ibsen, he considers "ugly, common, hard, prosaic, bottomlessly bourgeois." He urges Walpole never to believe that "Form is [not] substance to that degree that there is absolutely no substance without it. . . ." and deplores the "lack of composition" in the novels of Tolstoi and Dostoievsky. In 1904 James visited the United States again and travelled west to California for the first time. In 1910 he had an illness partly physical and partly nervous that made it impossible for him to work. William James and his wife came to stay with him and help his recovery by their beloved presence. When they returned to America he could not bear to be separated from them and sailed with them. William, the dearest friend of his life, died soon after they arrived. On his seventieth birthday, April 15, 1913, two hundred and seventy of his friends paid him honor in a letter and the present of a golden bowl, an exact reproduction of a piece of old Charles II plate, and asked that he permit Sargent to paint his portrait. The last letters cover the period of the first years of the War, which stirred James to passionate loyalty to England. On July 26, 1915, he became naturalized as a British subject. Among the "honours of the New Year" there was announced the award to him of the Order of Merit, and the insignia was brought to him in his last illness by Lord Bryce, his friend of many years. He died within two months of his seventy-third birthday on February 28, 1916.

LETTERS OF WILLIAM JAMES, THE, edited by his son, Henry James (2 vols., 1920). The letters to family and friends are divided into chronological groups with explanatory biographical comment by the editor connecting the groups. Technical and polemical letters have been omitted. An introductory chapter gives a sketch of his ancestry, a portrait of his philosopher father to whom William owed much, his gentle mother, and a brief character study of James and an account of the years before the first letter written in 1861 when he was a student of chemistry and comparative anatomy in the Lawrence Scientific School at Harvard University. "Ardently adventurous and humane" is the phrase which the son uses to describe his father's vivid personality. The family lived in London, Paris, Boulogne-sur-Mer, and Geneva for differing periods while the children were growing up, and William at nineteen was a wide reader in three languages. Their father, says E. L. Godkin, was a "formidable master of English style." He loved to stir up discussion and the family meal was like a debating society, "the business of outdoing the head of the family in the matter of language" being a joyous exercise to the children. William James tested several fields before he found himself as writer and professor of philosophy. In his teens he studied art for a year in the studio of William Hunt, with John La Farge as stimulating fellow-pupil. The following year, 1861, he turned to science, and Charles W. Eliot, then in charge of the chemical laboratory, speaks of his unusual mental powers, remarkable spirituality, and great personal charm. In 1863 he writes to his mother that he feels that it is important that he should make a final choice of a profession. He cites the advantages of medicine, but wonders about the prospects of a naturalist. Later he interrupted his medical studies to join the expedition which Agassiz was taking to the Amazon River. At the end of nine months he had decided that the excursion had been a mistake. He writes to his father that he is convinced that he is "cut out for a speculative rather than an active life." William's delicate health did not allow him to take part in the Civil War. After Lincoln's death he writes from Brazil to his parents: "Poor old Abe. What is it that moves you so about his simple, unprejudiced, unpretending, honest career? . . . albeit unused to the melting mood, I can hardly ever think of Abraham Lincoln without feeling on the point of blubbering. Is it that he seems the representative of pure simple human nature against all conventional additions?" . . . In the spring of 1867 James interrupted his medical course again to go to Germany for eighteen months, partly on account of his health, and partly because of a desire to learn German and to study physiology in the German laboratories. In spite of his illness and depression the letters home are full of wit and cheer, and those to his little sister, Alice, are delightful nonsense. He thanks her for her letter, and says that if at the time he received it she felt herself "strongly hugged by some invisible spiritual agency, you may now know that it was me." The letters to his friends, O. W. Holmes, Jr., and to Thomas W. Ward and Henry P. Bowditch, describe his doings, the people he meets, and his views of life. In November, 1868, he returned home to Cambridge, where the family now lived, and took his medical degree in June, 1869. The chapter of the next four years is entitled "Invalidism in Cambridge." In spite of the fact that he could use his eyes only a short time every day he did a great deal of reading of German literature and philosophy. James was appointed instructor in anatomy and physiology at Harvard in 1872. He passed thence to psychology and then to philosophy, and was a professor at Harvard for thirty-five years. Early in 1876 he met Miss Alice H. Gibbens, and the next day he wrote his brother Wilky that he had met "the future Mrs. W. J." They were married in 1878 after a short engagement, and the marriage was an unusually happy one. One month before his marriage he contracted to write a book on psychology for the "American Science Series." He spent twelve years of critical study and original research in its preparation, and this monumental work established his reputation in Europe and America. Still handicapped by ill health he spent much time in Europe with his family to relieve the strain of his teaching. Lectures helped to eke out his salary and give him leisure to write and think. After a week at Chautauqua he writes to his wife that he will be glad to "get into something less blameless but more admirationworthy. The flash of a pistol, a dagger, or a devilish eye, anything to break the unlovely level of 10,000 good people — a crime, murder, rape, elopement, anything would do." Lectures at San Francisco were ended by the earthquake. The Gifford Lectures given in Edinburgh were published as "The Varieties of Religious Experience." The "Talks to Teachers" and other works by James were the result of lectures. The cottage in the Adirondacks was always a refuge when "his sleep went to pieces." Mrs. James managed to keep him from giving himself too generously to his students and many friends. The intimate letters to Josiah Royce, Henry L. Higginson, E. L. Godkin, Miss Frances R. Morse and many others reveal his genius for friendship. A last letter to his father pays tribute to the debt he owed him and speaks his affection. The letter to Mr. Godkin about the review of his father's book ought to be read by all reviewers of books. He was quick to appreciate and praise the works of contemporary literature and philosophy, Howells, Richard Jeffries, Santayana, H. G. Wells, Hugo Münsterberg, Dickinson S. Miller, Kipling. There are letters to Theodore Flournoy, F. C. S. Schiller, Henri Bergson, and to Henry Adams. James went to Europe in 1910 to consult a Paris specialist about his heart and take a course of baths at Nauheim. Too much "sitting up and talking" with friends in

Paris tired him, and the baths proved debilitating. He reached home in August, 1910, and died at Chocorua, New Hampshire, his summer home, on the 26th.

LETTERS TO HIS CHILDREN, THEODORE ROOSEVELT'S, edited by Joseph Bucklin Bishop (1919). Letters to and about his five younger children, dating from the Spanish-American War in 1898 when Roosevelt was in service in Cuba to his African hunting trip in 1909 to 1910. Before the youngest were able to read he sent them so-called "picture letters." He addresses each one of the children from five-year-old Quentin to Ted, freshman at Harvard, as his equals. To Ted he writes of football and his standing in his studies, and sympathizes with the annoyances of the publicity incident to being the son of the President. When he finds it necessary to advise or criticize he does so directly and affectionately, usually with an apology for his "preaching." He writes to Kermit: "I would rather have a boy of mine stand high in his studies than high in athletics, but I could a great deal rather have him show true manliness of character than show either intellectual or physical prowess. . . ." There is much about the children's pets, guinea pigs, dogs, kittens, rabbits, the pig, named Maude, at the ranch, a cougar and lynx hunt in Colorado, description of Thanksgiving and Christmas celebrations at the White House, pillow-fights, the President's visit of inspection of the Panama Canal. He writes Archie about Quentin bursting into the room to show him three snakes Mr. Schidt of the animal store had lent him to play with, interrupting an interview with the Attorney-General. The President sent him into the next room where four Congressmen were waiting until Mr. Roosevelt should be at leisure to see them, which considerably enlivened these gentlemen when they discovered the snakes were alive. Roosevelt was always the playmate and boon companion of his children. "Describing a romp in the old barn at Sagamore Hill in the summer of 1903, he said in one of his letters that under the insistence of the children he had joined in it because: 'I had not the heart to refuse, but really it seems, to put it mildly, rather odd for a stout, elderly President to be bouncing over hayricks in a wild effort to get to goal before an active midget of a competitor, aged nine years. However, it was really great fun.' " He was the keenly interested companion in the reading of books, and the discussion of politics and public affairs as the children grew older.

LIFE, by Johan Bojer (1920), is a Norwegian romance. A company of young men and girls are on their way to spend Easter at the home of General Bang in the mountains. Paul Tangen, the artist, coaxed Jorgen Holth to drop his teaching and other duties and come with them. The General's eldest son, Reidar, was to go with them, and his daughter, Inga, with her friend, Astrid Riis, a girl with golden hair and a pretty figure, who had been a pupil of Holth's. As a further inducement to get him to leave his studies he was told that Astrid admired him. Holth was older than the other men, disappointed in his career because he had had to give up other gifts to teach, for he had a family and was poor. The jolly Easter party in the fresh mountain air did him good and he was particularly happy when he thought of the good times he had had with Astrid. But Astrid was unhappily in love with Reidar Bang. This she knew could never come to happy conclusion because her father, a retired captain, fancied he had suffered great wrongs from General Bang; was certain that it was the General's influence which had kept him from promotion. Since his retire-ment he had been at work on a plan for the reorganization of the army which he felt certain would right him in the eyes of all. Later in the summer the young people were playing on the tennis courts and occasionally Astrid was able to slip away, after her work was done and her father cared for, to have a little fun with the others. On one occasion, Reidar helped her on with her tennis shoes and lost his heart when he noticed a little hole in the heel of her stocking. But she let the elderly teacher, Holth, take her home rather than the young man whose love she feared. Holth now began to make opportunities to go to walk with her; even tried to fancy he was making love to her when caressing his tired wife. He was hungry for youth now that he had almost lost it. Astrid's brother had been driven away from home by his father's harshness and was living a wild life. From all this sordidness and gloom Astrid was glad to get away. When she was with Holth she dreamed it was handsome Reidar Bang instead, whom she always thought of as she had seen him at Easter leaping into the air on skis. Out boating one night, she allows herself to be hypnotized with thoughts of love so that Holth grows over bold in his love making and returns to his home intoxicated with his supposed conquest. But now Astrid realizes that it was no dream of love but of horror for her. She forbids Holth to ever see her again. Reidar dreams that the girl he is falling in love with is in some danger and one day he seeks her out to help her. She meets him but after they have clung together she pushes him away telling him it is too late. In terror of her father she forces him to leave. Her brother, about to leave for America where he is hoping to make a fresh start, stops in to say good-by and she tells him of her love for Reidar and how she fears her father. The young man faces the father and accuses him of all the trouble and gloom he has brought upon them and tells him of his sister's engagement. Astrid is put out of doors by the irate old captain so she goes to her lover. Her brother had just told her of their mother's love of sunshine in the open and how she escaped the gloom her husband cast on their home life by an unhappy love affair which had a tragic end. Astrid feels that her fate is to be the same as her mother's but first she will marry Reidar and for a little while have the happiness of being with him. Her father, finding his plans for the reorganization of the army refused, sits alone, after she has left and thinks over his life. He decides that perhaps he has thought too much of himself and makes up his mind to go to the grand wedding which General Bang is preparing for Reidar and Astrid and to forgive the General. The young couple live happy for a time in their mutual love, despite Astrid's strange sadness which puzzles her husband. Then comes a message to Reidar at his office from their home saying that Astrid had taken a boat out on the bay one gusty autumn day and has not returned. She had lived out her mother's fate to its sad climax.

LIFE AND DEATH OF HARRIET FREAN, by May Sinclair (1922), is a poignant psychological portrait of a woman's life from childhood to death. An only child, Harriet Frean was worshipped by her parents and she idolized them. She loved to be good, for being good was being beautiful like Mamma. Once she disobeyed and the unhappiness it gave Papa and Mamma made her resolve to always behave beautifully. At school her particular friend was Priscilla, a thin, shabby, high-strung girl from another city, who adored Harriet. Priscilla vowed eternal devotion and promised never to marry. Years passed and Harriet grew up. She loved the evenings at home with her parents, the trips to London to hear lectures or concerts. She went to some of her friends' parties but nothing ever happened. Priscilla wrote of her engagement. Her fiancé was working in London and came to see Harriet. They fell deeply in love with each other and Robin begged Harriet to marry him. But she refused. She said it would hurt Priscilla. Papa and Mamma said she had done the right thing, but for weeks she cried herself to sleep. Then they took her to Italy and gradually she recovered. Her father published a book and contributed to "The Spectator". Each year they went abroad and always they read together, the best books. Harriet felt quite superior to her friends. When she thought of Robin she felt a thrill of pleasure at her sacrifice. Five years after his marriage he wrote that Priscilla was paralyzed. Harriet visited them but was glad to leave in a few days. She could see Prissie was jealous. When Harriet was thirty-five her father lost all his money and died shortly afterward. Her mother had a small income so they moved to a cottage at Hampstead — each trying to please the other. Life went on as usual until Mamma became very sick and died. For a while Harriet secluded herself. Then the emptiness appalled her. She called on her friends. For the first time in her life she did things on her own initiative. She gardened. She read novels. Robin wrote of his wife's death and again of his marriage to the nurse who had attended Priscilla. It had been her dying wish. Harriet knew it was jealousy. She was now forty-five and growing gray. She visited the seaside and saw Robin and his wife. He was a querulous, complaining invalid but his wife was devoted to him. Harriet felt sorry for her. She could not go on loving Robin so; it hurt her self esteem. His wife told Harriet that Priscilla had not been paralyzed but had developed her illness to keep a hold on Robin and that he had used up all his moral capital in living with her. She returned to her cottage and life went on. A niece of Robin's called frequently and one day announced her engagement to a man who had been engaged to her dearest friend. Harriet deplored Mona's defence of her act and told her what another girl had done in a similar case. Then the girl bluntly told Harriet that she had been responsible for all the illness and unhappiness. She could no longer think of her act as beautiful and uplifting. The years passed. One by one her idols crashed. When she was sixty-eight she became ill. She had "what Mamma had" and died after an operation calling for her mother.

LILIOM, a legend in seven acts and a prologue, by Franz Molnar (1908, 1921). Liliom, whose name may be translated in Viennese idiom as "tough," is the braggart barker at a cheap amusement park frequented by the servant class. On the merry-go-round he flirts with Julie and her friend, Marie, until Mrs. Muskat, the proprietress, is aroused to order the girls to leave. In the quarrel Liliom takes Julie's part and asserts his own independence of the jealous Mrs. Muskat, who discharges him. Marie goes home, but Julie waits for Liliom to get his things, and they sit down together on a park bench. Julie has stayed out so late by this time that she knows she has lost her situation. Her admiration and innocence somehow attract the child-like Liliom, and though she does not say she loves him she cannot leave him. In the next act they are living together in the "dilapitated hovel" of Julie's aunt, Mrs. Hollunder, who with her son has a photographer's "studio" on the edge of the park. They are as inarticulate as ever, ashamed of the love they cannot express or understand. Though Mrs. Muskat begs Liliom to come back to his old job, which has been his pride and his "art," he will not give up Julie. Never having learned a trade, he is idle and angry with himself and the patient, submissive Julie. She understands that he beats her because he is unhappy not to be at work, as she tells Marie. Mother Hollunder wants Julie to marry a carpenter, a widower with two children, able to support her, and urges her to leave the good-for-nothing Liliom. Mrs. Muskat comes again for Liliom, and he listens to her until Julie insists she must tell him something. When he learns that he is to be a father, he is thrilled at the prospect, and sends Mrs. Muskat away. His friend, "the Sparrow," will help him to get the money he needs for the baby, and they will go to America, where he thinks vaguely he can make good. The plan is that they shall waylay a cashier of a certain factory carrying the payroll when he gets to a lonely place on the railroad embankment. Liliom is to accost him to ask what time it is, and Sparrow will knock him on the head from behind. Julie is suspicious of "the Sparrow" and tries to keep Liliom at home. Marie and her husband are coming to have their pictures taken. At the embankment they play cards as they wait. Liliom is so nervous that he does not realize that "the Sparrow" is cheating him. Soon he has lost all the money he has, and the prospective gains from the robbery they have not yet committed. The hold-up is a failure as the cashier is armed and too quick for them. "The Sparrow" wrenches himself free before the police get there, and Liliom stabs himself to escape capture. The police ambulance brings him back to the studio to die. Julie understands all that he tries to say to justify himself to her, that he was not "mad" when he struck her, only he had to because she cried, and he could not bear it, and that he could not be a caretaker, though she can answer only "yes." He tells her he is not afraid of the "police up there." Alone with her dead she is able for the first time to speak her love. The carpenter comes to offer sympathy and marriage, but she refuses. Presently two policemen from "up there" appear to take Liliom to give an account of himself at the court of heaven. The defiant Liliom will not express regret for any part of his life on earth. The celestial magistrate sentences him to sixteen years in the crimson fire to burn out his pride and stubbornness. Then he will be allowed to return to earth for one day to expiate his sin of striking his wife by doing something good for his daughter. In the final scene sixteen years later the two "heavenly policemen" bring Liliom as far as the hedge outside "the tumble-down house" where Julie and her daughter Louise are living. The woman and the girl are sitting at a table in the garden having their midday meal. They give the supposed beggar a plate of soup. In answer to his questions Louise tells him that her father died in America long ago, and that he was handsome and good. The stranger says he knew Liliom and that he was something of a bully, and had beaten her mother. Julie denies this and orders him to go away, and not to slander their dead. He calls to Louise and tries to give her a present, a star he has stolen from the heavens for her. Louise points to the gate, and in his despair and frustrated love, he strikes her hand. The policemen shake their heads deploringly and follow Liliom as he walks forlornly away. Louise asks her mother, "Is it possible for someone to hit you — hard . . . and not hurt you at all?" Julie answers, "It is possible, dear — that someone may beat you, and beat you, and beat you — and not hurt you at all."

LILLECRONA'S HOME, by Selma Lagerlöf (1926), like the "Saga of Gösta Berling," depends for its mood of rich folk beauty on the wild, native legends of Värmland. Against this background is set a peasant romance told with the simplicity of "little maid's" devotion to Mamselle Maia Lisa, her mistress. Being third in line of the beautiful pastor's daughters who are successively the heiresses of the rich peasant holding of Lövdala, when her father marries again, Mamselle Maia Lisa becomes a Swedish Snow White. In spite of the intimacy that father and daughter had enjoyed, it takes little time for the woman who has insinuated herself into the father's good graces to wreck all this happiness. Not content with misrepresenting his daughter's intentions to the father, she succeeds in estranging the girl from the man she loves, Lillecrona, a handsome young pastor of another province. There is a tradition that, when the waters of Black Lake receded, three things remained, the cold breeze that always blew through the fertile valley, the cold fog that came in the autumn, and a cruel water-sprite who tried from time to time to find a home in the hearts of men. As the stepmother's treachery closes about

Maia Lisa, the author charms us into believing, along with the childlike peasants, that the cold stepmother can be no other than the cruel water-sprite. Humorous episodes abound that relieve this mood of gloom. One, in true folk vein, is the adventure of "Big Billy," the pet goat when he laps up the dregs of the brandy left outside the brew house to cool and sets the household in an uproar with his antics. Another, showing that there is humor as well as honor among thieves, relates the story of Vetter, a light-fingered neighbor who spent much of his time in prison because he could never, for long, resist practicing his profession. "He was as proud of his clever thefts as the pastor's wife was of her fine cooking." The next morning after she had put a stout new lock on the larder, she found its entire removable contents arranged neatly on the larder steps. Vetter sent her his respects and said she must know that he never stole from his neighbors but she need not think any of her locks were good enough to keep him from getting anything he wanted. The stepmother's meddling results in Lillecrona's making a sad mistake, plunges the once blithe Maia Lisa into a melancholy decline, and so bewilders and betrays the gentle old pastor that he dies of grief. But at length the stepmother's malign influence is revealed as that of the wicked water-sprite, and Maia Lisa, through the help of "little maid," saves her lover from desperate remorse to the true home for which his spirit longs, her love and the melodies which he again calls from his violin. Thus, as in so many of Selma Lagerlöf's delicate fantasies, pure romance is thrown like a rainbow bridge from the storms of life to its deeper reality.

LINCOLN, ABRAHAM, THE PRAIRIE YEARS, by Carl Sandburg (1926), is a poet's prose portrait of our great Civil War President, differing little in its effect from Edwin Markham's poem, "Lincoln, The Man of the People." Not the reiteration of well-known facts, but a sympathetic placing of the man in his years of growth on his native prairies among the plain people who knew him as a friend and whose garnered anecdotes testify to his human worth, is what makes this book valuable. In a cabin on Nolin's Creek in Hardin County, Kentucky, he was born of Tom Lincoln and Nancy Hanks. His mother died when only thirty-six years old, "a pioneer sacrifice," and he grew up in their new Indiana home, mothered by Sarah Bush Johnston, his father's second wife. All his life Abraham Lincoln was good to this woman, who said of their relationship, "His mind and mine, what little I had, seemed to run together." Jesse Fell of Pennsylvania first suggested to Lincoln his eligibility for the nomination by the new Republican Party as president and asked for a sketch of his early life and schooling. Lincoln's summing up of those early years is modest, "There is not much of it for the reason I suppose, that there is not much of me." Of his schooling he comments, "Of course when I came of age I did not know much. Still, somehow, I could read and write and cipher to the rule of three, but that was all. I have not been to school since. The little advance I now have upon this store of education, I have picked up from time to time under the pressure of necessity." That necessity is an excellent as well as an exacting school teacher is seen in the years so modestly alluded to by Lincoln. He learned geography at first hand, studied men and manners and made note of his first impressions of slavery when he took a flat boat down the Mississippi to New Orleans at the age of nineteen. The ventures as storekeeper and postmaster at New Salem which resulted from this service with Daniel Offut, disastrous as they were financially, brought him in contact with Mentor Graham, the schoolmaster, and others who appreciated his possibilities and helped him on in his career, and gave him the opportunity for much reading. Appointed deputy surveyor of Sangamon County, under Mentor Graham's guidance in six weeks he went so far beyond his modest ciphering to the rule of three, as to make himself sufficiently familiar with the higher mathematics involved in surveying. Later in life, the logical method of deduction learned from these studies he applied to his study of political problems. Herndon, his law partner, often found him vexatiously sceptical, never satisfied with anything unless it could be demonstrated. In the same way he mastered grammar. Years later, when a successful lawyer, he advised a young man desiring to study law in his office, that the shortest and most satisfactory way of becoming a lawyer was to read the necessary books and pass the law examinations, as he had done, by himself. Early he learned to organize his mind and life and was known by his intimates as a learner all his life. For Herndon the phenomenon of Lincoln's constant growth was close to a miracle. Lincoln himself speaks of his mind as like steel, very hard to make any impression on but once a thing was impressed on it, never lost. He learned slowly. The Judds of Chicago in an evening's conversation with Lincoln after he had become well known sectionally, expressed their surprise over his scholarly cultivation. Life even more than necessity was his teacher. After the wider, more stimulating contacts gained during his term as Congressman at Washington, the breadth and certainty with which he handled a subject was noticeably augmented. Although Lincoln's personal sincerity and honesty forced him to take a position in regard to the Mexican War that lost him his constituency, the glow of this same quality of sincerity grew steadily throughout the debates with Douglas, in marked contrast with the dubious standards of his opponent. The country at large, following these debates with Douglas, who was already a national figure, became thus familiar with Lincoln's name and possibilities. The picture of this period, when he ran for United States Senator against Douglas, and made his celebrated house divided against itself speech that did so much to put him to the forefront of his party, does justice to his aspect as a practical politician, for Sandburg makes clear that, "Outside of the right and wrong of any issues of justice and humanity in politics, Lincoln enjoyed it as a game." Although this fondness for politics took much time from his law practice, his increased reputation made him the responsible and sought-after lawyer for more important cases when his attention was again focussed on his private affairs, in spite of his notorious lack of money sense where his private interest was concerned. Full recognition by thoughtful men of his claims to the presidential nomination followed soon after his Cooper Union speech. The radical utterances of Seward and Channing, hitherto better known, in regard to slavery formed an unfavorable contrast in the minds of the country at large to Lincoln's more moderate attitude full of patient understanding of the situation in the South as well as in the North. For Lincoln, through friendships in the South, and through closer knowledge of economic conditions there, believed that, if Northern capital was as tied up in slaves and was as dependent on slavery for development of its resources as was the case in the South, the Northern attitude toward it would be no different from the Southern. Yet the suffering and injustice to the black man always saddened him and he expressed himself as satisfied that he had contributed somewhat to the betterment of the world if, through his opposition to Douglas, he had done something to stay the further growth of slavery in new territories. The range of emotions from tragic to comic that animated the mobile contour of his face captivated those who knew him, particularly women. According to Herndon, melancholy dripped from him in his darker moods. Sandburg does not exaggerate sentimentally the effects of his early loss of his sweetheart, Ann Rutledge, in his life, but he allows the inference that this early grief forced open channels that made his personality sensitive and tender and through which penetrated the injustice, suffering and despair of slavery. Gradually from these accumulated memory sketches of friends expressed through the poetic mood of the author the humanity of Lincoln emerges. — first the gawky length of him, the rugged weather-beaten mask of him, the sincere and indomitable mind of him, until all these are merged in "the illuminated, mysterious, personality," the prophet and spokesman of a time whose objectives were still shrouded in mystery.

LINDA CONDON, by Joseph Hergesheimer (1919). Until Linda is fourteen she spends her life with her gay, pretty mother in hotels, Florida in winter, Lake George in summer, in a setting of plush chairs, palms, and white marble columns. The other women disapprove of Mrs. Condon; and Linda understood that it was because they are jealous that men like her mother and pay her so much attention. Linda is dark, with agate blue eyes, and a strange, ill man, unlike the usual hotel guests, once called her Bellina, and told her something like a fairy tale about the worship of beauty in the Middle Ages, quoting the line, "La figlia della sua mente, l'amorosa idea." She is a grave, aloof child, and older than her years. Her mother instructs her that she must never marry a poor man, and that love and marriage are two different things, and Linda never doubts her mother's correctness and wisdom. A permanent wave ruins Mrs. Condon's beautiful golden hair, and she decides to accept middle age and marry a rich and persistent suitor, Moses Feldt. The stepfather is kind, and Linda likes him, but does not care for his daughters, Judith and Pansy. With Judith at a studio party, she meets the sculptor, Dodge Pleydon, who leaves the Russian singer he has brought with him to look long at Linda. He takes her home and kisses her good-by. She promises to send him word if she changes her address while he is away in South America. After a concert a woman asks her name, and tells her that she is her father's sister, Amelia Lowrie. An invitation comes to her to visit her aunts in Philadelphia, and, in spite of her mother's anger, Linda insists on going to stay with them, and is at ease and happy in the social world of her father. The house is as different as possible from the elaborate hotels and gigantic apartments, the "tropical interiors" of her New York life. Dodge Pleydon comes to see her, and is accepted by the Lowries when they learn that his mother was a Dodge. He asks Linda to marry him, but the violence of his love frightens her. She is disappointed in herself that she is so cold and unresponsive. Her mother has come to dislike Linda, so superior, like her father, Bartram Lowrie, and with the youth and beauty the older woman envies. Arnaud Hallet, the distant cousin she had met in Philadelphia, twice her age, adores her, and she finally turns to his affection and kindness to escape from her mother's aversion and Dodge's passion. Marriage and her two children do not change Linda, and she condemns herself as an unsatisfactory wife and an unnatural mother, though she tries desperately to be more than a spectator of life. Her beauty has inspired Pleydon to become a great sculptor. When his masterpiece is destroyed by a drunken mob she is shaken to the depths of her being for the first time in her life. Knowing that Pleydon has expressed his vision of her in the statue, she feels as if she, too, had been dragged from a pedestal and shared its fate. Linda determines to leave Arnaud and go to Pleydon and give him the remainder of her life. He has lived so long with the vision of her that it is more to him than the reality, and she realizes that she can bring him nothing more than he already has. She quietly returns home to her husband, who never knows that she had intended to leave him. The children grow up and marry, and Linda's beauty fades. After Pleydon's death she goes to the Massachusetts town to see the replica of the statue, and understands at last what Pleydon had vainly tried to explain to her of her part in his success, which until now she had felt had belonged exclusively to him. She sees that he has preserved her spirit, her secret self, from destruction by death and time and is comforted.

LITERATURE, THE OUTLINE OF, edited by John Drinkwater (3 vols., 1923). The purpose of this history is given in the Editor's Introduction: "The present outline has two functions. First, it is to give the reader something like a representative summary of the work itself that has been accomplished by the great creative minds of the world in letters. But, also, it aims at placing that work in historical perspective, showing that from the beginning until now, from the nameless poets of the earliest scriptures down to Robert Browning, the spirit of man when most profoundly moved to creative utterance in literature has been and is, through countless manifestation, one and abiding. It aims not only at suggesting to the reader the particular quality of Homer and Shakespeare and Goethe and Thomas Hardy, but also at showing how these men and their peers, for all their new splendours of voice and gesture, are still the inheritors of an unbroken succession. . . . The comparison of one age's literature with that of another in point of merit is as little profitable as the comparison of one individual writer with another. The fine attitude towards art, as toward anything else, is to be grateful always for the good and beautiful thing when it comes, without grudging and without doctrinaire complaint that it is not something else. It does not help anybody to say that eighteenth century English poetry is inferior to that of seventeenth century, or that Fielding was a better novelist than Meredith. All these things alike are the great glories of a race, the one as honourably to be kept in memory as another." The first volume is a popular study of world literature from the beginnings to the time of the Renaissance. The remaining two volumes form primarily an outline history of English literature. The scope of the work is indicated in the table of contents.

Volume 1, Chapter I — The First Books in the World (a brief note on the early art of writing, and the communal beginnings of literature); II — Homer; III — The Story of the Bible (by E. W. Barnes); IV — The English Bible as Literature; V — The Sacred Books of the East; VI — Greek Myths and the Poets; VII — Greece and Rome; VIII — The Middle Ages; IX — The Renaissance. Volume 2, X — William Shakespeare, by Harley Granville-Barker; XI — Shakespeare to Milton; XII — John Milton, by John Drinkwater; XIII — Marvel and Walton; XIV — John Bunyan; XV — Pepys, Dryden, and the Restoration Drama lists; XVI — French Literature of the Age of Louis XIV; XVII — Pope, Addison, Steele, Swift; XVIII — The Rise of the Novel (in England); XIX — The Eighteenth Century Poets (English); XX — Dr. Johnson and His Circle; XXI — Edward Gibbon and Other Eighteenth Century Prose-Writers (English); XXII — Robert Burns; XXIII — The Literature that made the Revolution (Voltaire, Diderot, Beaumarchais, Rousseau); XXIV — Goethe, Schiller and Lessing; XXV — Wordsworth, Coleridge, Southey and Blake; XXVI — Byron, Shelley, Keats. Volume 3 — XXVII — Scott, Dumas and Hugo; XXVIII — Early Nineteenth Century Essayists (English); XXIX — Victorian Poets; XXX — Dickens and Thackeray, by G. K. Chesterton; XXXI — The Victorian Novelists; XXXII — The New England Writers (including Poe, Whitman, Mark Twain and Joel Chandler Harris); XXXIII — The Nineteenth Century French Writers; XXXIV — The Great Victorians; XXXV — Modern Writers, American and European (American Writers by Henry James Forman); XXXVI — Some Later Victorians; XXXVII — Dramatic Literature (Sheridan, Ibsen, Strindberg, Pinero,

Jones, Shaw, Barrie); XXXVIII — English Poetry Since Swinburne, by Gilbert Thomas; XXXIX — Later Day Writers (English).

Each chapter is supplemented with a general bibliography, and appended to the entire work is an index of nineteen pages.

LITTLE FRENCH GIRL, THE, by Anne Douglas Sedgwick (1924). The story of Alix de Mouveray and her mother, the beautiful and charming Madame Vervier, whose mode of life is a succession of lovers. Alix is sent to the English home of one of the lovers, Captain Owen Bradley, killed in the War, because her mother hopes to arrange for her in England the suitable marriage which she herself has made impossible for Alix in France, and at the same time to free "Maman" from her daughter's innocent and embarrassing presence. The background of the story is the contrast between the English and French social character and standards and in particular their different attitude toward love and marriage. Giles, an Oxford student, has guessed the relation between Madame Vervier and his brother, and does not want his mother or his brother's fiancée, Toppie, whose real name is Enid Westmacott, to learn the truth. The friendship of Toppie and Alix is the beginning of a series of complications that makes them both understand the situation. The exquisite Alix never fails in loyalty to her mother, and makes her brave adjustment, with the help of Giles, who has grown broad-minded and understanding from his association with Alix and the group around Madame Vervier, which includes a distinguished archæologist and an actress. The aged Monsieur de Maubert discusses with Giles the difference between love and affection and the position of Madame Vervier and the future of Alix, and they agree to differ, each sorry for the other. Lady Mary Hamble comes to call on Mrs. Bradley to explain to her why her son Jerry must not marry Alix. Jerry is faithful, and Giles goes to France to plead his cause with Alix, with full knowledge that what Toppie and Jerry have both said to him is true, that he loves Alix himself. Madame Vervier tells Giles that Jerry is the man that will give Alix security, position and wealth, that she is bewildered at the English ideas her child has adopted that she should refuse to accept her mother's decision in the matter of her marriage. André, her mother's lover, urges his suit for Alix to Giles. Instead of the marriage of convenience Alix chooses the marriage of love with Giles, who had not believed he had a chance with her, the man who understands all about her life and will make her happy.

LOLLY WILLOWES, by Sylvia Townsend Warner (1926), is a delicate fantastical tale which might be called the Odyssey of an old maid. Even to-day, while the species is by no means extinct in rural regions, it already has a quaintness of flavor as of a bygone time. Lolly Willowes came of an old English family of long established customs. Her father had moved the family seat to Ladysmith, where his brewery was established. There she grew up with a feeling for the land and for nature very different in quality from that of Joanna Godden; for the pagan love of natural life was not so much in her blood as in her spirit. After the death of her father and mother, she passively allowed her brother James who lived in London to take charge of her life. There the serene routine of the days drifted smoothly along disturbed only in the autumn of the year by an inexplicable restlessness that returned to her with every season. One day, lured to a small green-grocer's shop where were displayed all manner of country goodies and flowers, she carried home all the heavy headed chrysanthemums on sale and with them a spray of beech leaves the owner of the shop had thrust into her arms with the flowers. They were grown in the Chilterns.

he said. Studying a map of the region, a wild out-of-the-way country village, Great Mop took her fancy. Long years enough she had given over her own tastes and helped rear her brother's family. Now they were grown and she meant to live the life she pleased. Life in Great Mop was so natural and happy she could listen with disdain that was almost patience to the remonstrances of her family. An inexplicable quality in the place with its ancient beech woods, charmed her. The inhabitants, too, on closer acquaintance proved to be of different nature from most villagers. Long cross country walks and the reading of some curious old books revealed more clearly, not only the nature of the charm that this region held for her but more about that strange restlessness which had troubled her for so long. She discovered that, like her neighbors, she was in sympathy with nature, not only in its open, natural manifestations, but in those curious occult aspects that connoted witchcraft. Then, Mrs. Leak, her landlady, took her to a witches' sabbath. It turned out as disappointing as other social affairs she had been forced to attend in the past, that is, until she met a gentlemanly chap whom she knew at once must be Satan himself. As she talked with Satan she realized that, at last the strange restlessness was gone. She understood why so many women have been witches, women who had lived drab lives settling down into dust covered age, "to show our scorn of pretending life's a safe business, to satisfy our passion for adventure. . . . One doesn't become a witch to run around being harmful, or to run around being helpful either, a district visitor on a broomstick. It's to escape all that — to have a life of one's own, not an existence doled out to you by others, charitable refuse of their thoughts, so many ounces of stale bread of life." She acquired a "familiar" in the shape of a kitten called Vinegar, and went peacefully and contentedly about the life she had chosen.

LONG JOURNEY, THE (Fire and Ice), by Johannes V. Jensen (1923). This chronicle records the long journey travelled by mankind from primitive times to modern civilization. Parts One and Two are entitled "Fire and Ice." In the age of fire, and in Norna Gest as a figure, the Northern spirit yearns beyond the North. Norna Gest outlives his generation and seeks it in the Land of the Dead. North and South, which since the Lost Country have been sundered worlds, come together again. Weaving his plot through the ages, the author pictures the Cimbrians and Teutons moving southward in Norna Gest's footsteps and the first clash taking place between Northern "barbarians" and ancient civilization. He shows that later, when Christianity began to penetrate the North, it met the people streaming southward; "the Christian belief in immortality directly revives the memory of the Lost Country; from this union of South and North springs the most beautiful myth of the Middle Ages — the Virgin Mary, Goddess of Spring, the soul of Northerner and the art of the Ancients in one, blossoming into its highest consummation at the Renaissance." Continuing the plot, the ring is completed — an imaginary ring, but it is within this circle that the author wishes "The Long Journey" read. Fyr, the Prometheus of the Forest Folk, and the Danish word for fire, is interpreted as a fiery, impetuous figure. Carl's story reveals him as "the one-eyed All-father of Northern mythology, whose chariot, the Carl's wain, is conspicuous in the sky." "Mam," the Danish for Moa, was named by her children with the first syllable they could utter; "Vaar" (Spring) is shown to be the original name of May. Of Fyr, the author says that the Forest Folk thought that he was the sun; "dazzling and generous he moved each day upon the heavens, sowing his light over the world." The moon was his mother Woe; "she goes after him and follows all his doings with pallid face; now whole, now half, she gives away pieces of her heart for him." This chronicle also records the coming of ice upon the world. "One morning down in the valleys the hunters and the hunted see a white hood, with a strange, hard gleam, like a lifeless eye, lying upon the head of Gunung Api; the first forerunner of the Ice Sheet." The general theme is that Man had his origin in the great northern forest before the Ice Age, that he came out of the primeval together with the beasts, shared their life and became transformed with them. In a forest in transformation, with herbs on the way to become trees, one species growing beyond itself and into another, the beasts found sustenance and changed after their manner, one leaving another and on the way to become a third; as the foremost creature among the beasts, though by no means the strongest, but the richest in possibilities, Man arose.

LONG JOURNEY, THE (The Cimbrians), by Johannes V. Jensen (1923). This chronicle forms the third and fourth parts of the historical cycle. Book I records the birth of Norna Gest in Sealand and follows his wanderings from the settlement which the men of the Stone Age had created, and his development as he matures into taking part in men's life. Through the symbolical figures of Norna Gest and Dart and Skur, man moves on. Either in a craft of his own making, or roving on the road like sibyls, a traveller with no hearth of his own, Norna Gest is revealed as coming and going as inconstantly but as surely as the seasons. Thousands of years pass, and he comes again into his native valley and finds the clans different, with no living memory of the clans from which they descended, and "yet they were the same people"; the big red fishers of the Stone Age as well as the sturdy husbandmen of the Bronze Age lived again in them, but their tradition did not even go back as far as the Bronze Age; they were now living in the Iron Age and had no conception of men ever having lived another sort of life. Norna Gest now becomes the wandering scald, with a harp of his own making. "Beloved and almost feared was Norna Gest's harp." His songs treated of the Volsungs, "the wild obscure lays of the Migrations." The author tells of the Migrations and Norna Gest's part in them; of Sweden and of the Island of the Dead, the shores of the Mediterranean, the coasts of the sun; Norway — where Norna Gest spends the last years of his life — living in his memories which belonged to the morning of his life when he and his companion, Dart, "the first human couple," had shared a tree with the squirrel. These memories were blended in his mind with the myths of other races, races which had wandered as far from their early home as he, and preserved an early memory as clouded as his, the "myth of Ygdrasil, the great world-tree, the origin of all life." In Book II the author takes up the story of the Cimbrians, and again the figure of Gest is seen wandering among the fjords of Jutland, on his way to visit the Cimbrians up in the out-of-the-way tracts on the Limfjord. The heart of the Cimbrians' land was a highland. "At a distance the first impression of life was the graves of the ancients." But if the heights and horizons were given over to departed generations, the living dwelt down in the valleys, in hereditary homesteads lying far apart. The Cimbrians were great cattle breeders; for half the year they moved about with their herds, and in winter they stayed at home on their farms, where they carried on agriculture. Book III treats of "The Raid." The Cimbrians had left their country, through great disasters, threatening all with destruction and drowning. Vedis and Glum, Ingvar, Boierik and Tole are among the symbolical figures. The Cimbrians finally enter the country between the Danube and the Eastern Alps, and Norna Gest follows them as far as their first collision with the Romans. "The external destiny of the Cimbrians, when from an obscure past they entered the light of annals, is a theme which extends from that time to all times, the ghost-world of history; henceforth it is this we follow in following them."

The advance-guard of the Cimbrians, according to this chronicle, ate the bread of captivity and punishment until they died under the far-famed Southern sky. The small second generation propagated a smaller third; the remainder were lost among the heterogeneous bastards of the Roman people. "The first unhappy generation of captives wore their chains smooth in the slaves' quarters of many a Roman establishment, till age, affliction and harsh treatment put an end to their sufferings. . . . Of the youngest brood, and perhaps of some descendants of their elders, we hear something later when the slaves' revolt broke out in Italy, under its leader Spartacus. . . . The Romans submitted his dead body to torture. . . . On the highway between Rome and Capua a horseman might enjoy riding along on an avenue of six thousand crucified slaves. Among them some of the last of the Cimbrians expired, nailed up in the blazing sun."

LONG JOURNEY, THE (Christopher Columbus), by Johannes V. Jensen (1924). This is the fifth and concluding part of Jensen's historical cycle. "The great Migrations had brought their ancestors from forgotten shores by the Baltic, straight through the countries of the Old World and all the turbulent centuries of the Middle Ages, as far as the Mediterranean — now Columbus was to carry the migration farther. The history of the Longobards then is the history of Columbus's past; in his blood, though the origin is forgotten, he inherits profound and powerful promptings from wandering forefathers." Columbus is shown to have completed the Northern migration, and he is treated as a symbol of the restless skipper-soul who is condemned to sail the seas until the Day of Judgment, and the Santa Maria is the phantom ship in which he sets sail. He centred his religion upon a beautiful ancient devotion to Woman, and in her honor his imagination refashioned his Forest and his Ship into a Cathedral. "Columbus was a child of the Gothic; we must seek its genesis if we would know how his nature came about; we must go backward in the youth of the race to the prototype of the myth of God's Mother, the heart of the Gothic. Columbus inherited it in the form of universal longing: the eternal feminine; the Holy Virgin was the woman in his life. Santa Maria was the name of his ship." The author follows the adventures of Columbus to his discovery of the new continent and takes up again the connection between the forest man and the man of the Ice Age, that part of mankind which had remained in the North and had changed instead of leaving: the descendants of Carl. Centuries before, relates the chronicle, there had been a man on these shores who had left deep traces in the life of the inhabitants, and had bequeathed to them an obscure but powerful memory, the legend of the "White God." This is the figure of Norna Gest over which ages had passed; he had become a myth. The tradition lived that the "White God" would return. Columbus found this situation when he opened up the way from Europe to the new countries in the West. This chronicle also touches upon the epoch of Cortez and the conquest of Mexico; Cortez's advance on the plateau, the conspiracy of Cholula, Malina's service and the massacre, the entrance into Mexico and Montezuma's captivity in his own city, his death and the disastrous retreat from Mexico, the famine among the natives, and their surrender. Of the New World, the author says that after the discoverers and adventurers came the settlers. He views this movement as the great book of the Emigrants. "The emigration was divided into main streams: one from Southern Europe which was to settle Latin America, Norman at the top, the Migrations filter through the South, and Romance at the bottom; but the other later stream came from the North of Europe, the very source of the Migrations, and from it have come the United States." Book III treats of the "Phantom Ship."

"But the Santa Maria continued her ghostly voyage south of Cape Horn, round the Cape of Good Hope, across the oceans, round the world, into every remote channel, past every island, as she must so long as the yearning lasts which once fitted her out to sail for the Lost Country. . . . And there they are, all the yearners and discoverers who craved to see the earth, the great names — nothing but vocal sounds, like an organ pealing in the soul, but true music — Columbus, Vasco de Gama, Bartolomeu Diaz, Cabral, Balboa, Cabot, Magellan, Frobisher, Hudson, Cook!" But all the voyages of discovery, which were the work of many, the author of this chronicle holds are inevitably connected with Columbus as their central figure.

LOST LADY, A, by Willa Sibert Cather (1923). A novel of the Middle West in the last days of the pioneer railroad builders, "great-hearted adventurers who were unpractical to the point of magnificence." The home of the Forresters was known from Omaha to Denver for its hospitality "even after the retirement of Captain Forrester and the sacrifice of his wealth to depositors of a certain bank in Denver who trusted in his name." His young wife, Marion, of surpassing charm, courage and gayety, represented a refinement of civilization which save in her had not yet reached the town. Neil Herbert, an admiring boy, tells the story, and it is for him that she is "lost" when he discovers that his ideal of perfection is as frail in morals as she is fair. Her bluff old husband appreciates her affection and devoted care, and understands her love of beauty and pleasure. Even while he lives she has a lover in one of his friends, a hero of many ambiguous stories, the "prince of good fellows" type of bachelor. A boy searching for rabbits sees their sleigh in the woods when they run away from the house-party, but keeps the secret. "Mrs. Forrester had never been too haughty to smile at him when he came to the back door with his fish. She never haggled about the price. She treated him like a human being. His little chats with her, her nod and smile when she passed him on the street were among the pleasantest things he had to remember." After her husband's death and her lover's marriage, Ivy Peters, rude town boy grown to be an unprincipled lawyer who takes advantage of everyone's necessity, becomes tenant of her fields, business adviser, and so intimate that Neil is disillusioned. This common fellow finally marries and buys the Forrester place, giving Mrs. Forrester the means to go West to her girlhood home. Many years later Neil heard once more of his long lost lady, who had become to him a "bright, impersonal memory," that she died the cherished wife of a wealthy Englishman in South America. Neil had seen the end of an era, the sunset of the pioneers. What he could not forgive Mrs. Forrester was "that she was not willing to immolate herself, like the widows of all these great men, and die with the pioneer period to which she belonged: that she preferred life on any terms," when "only the stage-hands were left to listen to her. All those who had shared in fine undertakings and bright occasions were gone."

LOYALTIES, by John Galsworthy (1922). The play opens at the country house of Charles and Lady Adela Winsor who are entertaining guests during the races. A rich young Jew, Ferdinand De Levis, finds that £1,000 has disappeared from under his pillow late at night. He had received this money from the sale of a horse, "Rosemary," which another of the guests, Ronald Dancy, a retired army captain and D.S.O., had given him earlier in the year, as "a dud," in order to save its keep. Dancy is not well off, and naturally resents this transaction, as De Levis is wealthy and has won two races that day. De Levis believes that Dancy, who had won a bet from him earlier in the evening by doing a high jump, had leaped from one balcony to another to enter his window, since the door was locked. He informs Winsor of the theft, and insists that the servants shall be cross-questioned, and the police called in to investigate. Later when De Levis names Dancy to Winsor and General Canynge they are indignant that an officer, a gentleman, a member of their set should be accused by this outsider who is received only because of his money. General Canynge, the soul of honor, discovers by chance that Dancy's sleeve is wet, as if he had been out in the rain, and keeps quiet about this damaging fact. He is able to prevent De Levis from making the charge public at the time. Three weeks later De Levis, blackballed for the Jockey Club, blames Dancy's friends, and insists that the affair shall be brought before the law courts. Dancy has called him a "damned Jew," and he has called Dancy a thief. Dancy is not enthusiastic about pressing the charge for defamation of character. He suggests to his bride, Mabel, that they get out of the country and forget it, but she insists on seeing it through. While the case is being tried the missing banknotes are traced by their numbers to an Italian wine merchant, Ricardos, who confides to Dancy's lawyer that he received the money from Dancy in part payment of a debt of honor in which his daughter is concerned. All the characters are loyal to the best traditions of their class. Winsor is true to his ideal of hospitality; Canynge to the esprit de corps of a British army officer; Mabel to her wifely loyalty to her husband; Dancy to his own daring and reckless bravado. De Levis has his racial pride. He says, "My lace was old when you were all savages." He wants his name cleared and nothing more. That a warrant is issued is not his doing. He does not want to send Dancy to jail, and refuses to take the money. Twisden, Dancy's lawyer, drops the case because of loyalty to his profession. He advises Dancy to leave the country, and his devoted wife forgives him and tries to help him to escape to Morocco. She keeps the police inspector back until a shot is heard from the adjoining bedroom. Dancy takes his own life as the only means of escape from disgrace. The play ends with the words of the society girl, Margaret Orme, "Keep faith. We've all done that. It's not enough." Loyalty has not proved itself a sufficient guide for the complex affairs of life.

LUMMOX, by Fannie Hurst (1925). The Scandinavian servant, Bertha, called by every one "the lummox" because she is big and clumsy, is shown in a series of the "situations" which make up her hard life. She works for sixteen hours a day in the homes of the rich in New York City with devotion and self-sacrifice, exploited by both her employers and her fellow-servants. In each place Bertha helps someone in a crisis of life. When the book opens she is a young girl at the home of the Farleys, the willing slave of their selfish poet son, Rollo. He is her lover for one night, and the emotional experience stimulates him to write one remarkable poem that brings him fame. Crouched behind the door, Bertha hears him read it to the girl he is going to marry. Bertha goes to the rough sailor's lodging-house, which is the only refuge she knows when she is out of work, and toils in offices as a charwoman until Rollo's son is born. For the child's sake she gives it to a wealthy couple, Mr. and Mrs. Bixby, for adoption. Later the Bixbys move to New York and Bertha lives with Willy, their man-servant, provides a home and comfort for him in order that she may hear about her boy. The concertina she sends to the child by Willy is his favorite plaything. He develops a talent for music, and is taken to Europe to study by his adopted parents. Years afterward chance brings Bertha outside the hall where her son is to play, and she is present at the triumph of his debut. In service with the Musliners, the neurotic bride is brought into right relations with her husband by Bertha's kind mothering. Her only reward is dismissal with a month's wages, because Mrs. Musliner is embarrassed to have been so intimate with a servant. She befriends Helga, the pretty young girl who had worked with her at the Farleys, taking her from a "house" to a place with her in the household of the despotic Mrs. Oessetrich. The daughters, ruled, crushed, and thwarted by their mother, find the quiet Bertha a refuge and help, until she is discharged for theft by Mrs. Oessetrich because of the things Helga had hidden in their room before she died of pneumonia in the hospital. In the next few years she is the comforter of the old Jewish mother-in-law in the incessant conflict with her son's Christian wife in the Wallenstein household. Bertha refrains from giving the old woman her heart medicine so that she may never know that her adored son is going to send her away to an institution to please his wife. Again at the lodging-house she takes care of Chita, the little "slavey" with her body covered with bruises where her drunken parents have beaten her. To protect the girl from the drunken sailors, Bertha brings the "Society" to rescue the unwilling child. Coincidence brings Bertha scrubbing floors at a settlement to see her receive a certificate to teach in kindergarten, when the little waif has become transformed into a neat, pretty young girl. It is hard for the middle-aged Bertha to find a place, and she has to work by the day when she can get the chance. At last in a bakery she is hired by the proprietor, Meyerbogen, a good-hearted widower, to clean his house, and finds home and employment caring for his five children, who adore her.

MAGIC MOUNTAIN, THE (Der Zauberberg), by Thomas Mann (1927). The scene is the Alpine Valley of Davos, and the "magic mountain" is the symbol for an international sanitarium for tubercular patients who come as a precaution for a month and linger within the magic circle losing all count of time. It is a detailed study under the microscope of the routine of life and the treatment in a typical institution. Hans Castorp, a young engineer from Hamburg, ready to take his first position with a firm of ship-builders, comes to spend his vacation with his cousin, Joachim, a patient at the institution. In the rarefied atmosphere Hans feels fatigued, develops a slight cold, takes the examination included in the rates, and convinces himself he needs the cure. He stays seven years instead of the three weeks' visit he had planned, losing all contact with the outside world, leaving at last only when the "thunder clap" of the War breaks the magic spell. Joachim breaks away at the end of a year after a stormy interview with the director, only to return to die after a few months. The story is the mental and spiritual development of the youthful Hans as he is absorbed into his surroundings, and takes stock of himself, his position in the world and the meaning of the world to him. He falls in love with a beautiful Russian, Madame Chuchat, and finds courage to declare his passion on the night of a carnival ball before her departure from the sanitarium the following day. There are long discussions with the other patients on every conceivable subject, including history, philosophy, religion, love, death, alchemy, masonry, and politics, the modern equivalent of a Platonic dialogue. Hans becomes reflective and learns to express himself in argument with his older friend, the Italian, Herr Settembrini, a liberal democrat who stands for reason and enlightenment, and the latter's adversary, the subtle Jesuit, Herr Naphta, urging faith and submission. Madame Chuchat comes back as she had promised her lover, but accompanied by the aged Herr Peeperkorn, whose commanding personality makes him the ruling spirit in the group. Hans with his craving for personal experience becomes friends with her protector in spite of his love for the woman. After the death of Herr Peeperkorn Madame Chuchat goes away again. Herr Naphta shoots himself in a duel with Herr Settembrini, who, true to his convictions, refuses to fire at his opponent. The "seven-sleeper" Hans, roused, goes off to the soldier's camp. He had come to the sanitarium a raw, ignorant, inexperienced youth, and he leaves with a trained mind and a full experience.

MAIN CURRENTS IN AMERICAN THOUGHT, by Vernon Parrington, see **COLONIAL MIND; ROMANTIC REVOLUTION.**

MAIN STREET, the story of Carol Kennicott, by Sinclair Lewis (1920). The small town of Gopher Prairie is typical of "ten thousand towns from Albany to San Diego," and Main Street of the story is the "continuation of Main Street everywhere." In every town we may find the same "Farmer's National Bank," the same type of "Howland and Gould's Grocery," the same "Axel Egg's General Store," and the prototype of the Widow Bogart, piously moralizing and spreading scandal, with her son, Cy, the town's bad boy, Dave Dyer, the druggist, repeating the same joke day after day and year after year, and Ezra Stowaway, the banker, foreclosing mortgages in order to inculcate respect for the law. The names of the characters vary in the different towns, but the characters themselves are the same. We see Gopher Prairie through the eyes of Carol, the city girl who is the bride of Dr. Will Kennicott, as she rebels against the drab monotony and pettiness of her environment and makes futile efforts to change things. Her kind, wholesome husband is proud of her and does his best to make her happy, but resents her attitude of superiority to his friends and his town. Miss Vida Sherwin, the high school teacher, whom the doctor describes as "a regular wonder — reads Latin like I do English," says to Carol of Gopher Prairie, "They don't think it's ugly. And how can you prove it? — matter of taste." Carol gives a party, providing other entertainment than the well-worn stunts, and other refreshment than angel cake, which is a daring innovation. She tries to get public interest to build a new city hall to replace the "bleakly inconspicuous," "liver-colored frame coop" which serves the purpose, a new schoolhouse, a Little Theatre. She pleads with the dreary company of the Thanatopsis Club for scientific help for the poor. Her young friend, Fern Mullins, the teacher, loses her position, and is hounded out of town by Mrs. Bogart, as a scapegoat for her son, Cy, who gets hold of liquor at a party and tells his mother that Fern dared him to take a drink. Taking an interest in her husband's practice adds to her appreciation of Will. Her baby, Hugh, made her a part of the town for a year or two, as with "nine-tenths of her emotion concentrated on him" she had no time to criticize the shops, and the streets, and the people she knew. Bea, her Swedish servant, seems most like the girls Carol had known at college, and Carol creates a servant problem by paying too high wages, and by treating her like a companion. Miles Bjornstam, the anarchist, marries Bea, and for the sake of his wife and baby, Olaf modifies his wild talk. The town society is slow to accept an ex-hired girl married to an "irreligious socialist." Just as Miles decides to begin life over again in another place, Bea and the baby die of typhoid. Another friend is Guy Pollock, the lawyer, stranded in Gopher Prairie, longing "to go back to an age of tranquility and charming manners." Carol meets another alien, Eric Valborg, apprentice to the tailor and suspected by the town of being a poet, and falls in love with him. She finally gives up the struggle, and goes to Washington to a position in a government office. The thing she gained in the two years of work was renewed courage, and that "amiable contempt called poise," which enabled her to return to Gopher Prairie with a fairer attitude toward the town as a toiling new settlement. In the book the author is the champion of his heroine against the commonplace town. The play, adapted from the book, ridicules Carol's idealism expressing itself in a desire to read Dunsany and Maeterlinck to Gopher Prairie's struggling citizens.

MAN COULD STAND UP, A, by Ford Madox Ford (1926). The author's reaction to war is summarized in his introductory letter to Gerald Duckworth, Esq.: "This is what the late war was like: this is how modern fighting of the organized, scientific type affects the mind. If, for reason or gain or, as is still more likely, out of dislike for collective types other than your own, you choose to permit your rulers to embark on another war, this — or something very accentuated along similar lines — is what you will have to put up with!" On the day of the Armistice, when the story opens, Valentine Wannop, a physical instructress at an English public school, who imagined her life had been nun-like and restrained, decides that now she can "let out the good little Cockney yelps that were her birthright." "As she might have expected she got it in the neck immediately afterward — for over cockiness." Through Lady Macmaster she hears of the return of Captain Christopher Tietjens from the front, and that he is half mad and destitute at the Lincoln Inn. Lady Macmaster, "in remembrance of old times wants to be the means of bringing the two together again." Christopher has a wife and child. Two years before he went to the front he had met Valentine. Mrs. Tietjens has affairs with other men. Once Christopher's General had been quartered at "Groby," the Tietjens' estate. Whether his wife had become the General's mistress or not, Tietjens did not know, but he did know that the General had sent another lover of Mrs. Tietjens' to the front to get him killed, and that he had sent him, too, to get killed, that he had withheld from him his decorations, and had unjustly dismissed him, simply because he had wanted Sylvia Tietjens. Valentine goes to the Inn and finds Tietjens a victim of shellshock. All that he wants is to take Valentine away. He can not divorce his wife — she's the mother of his child. He can not live with her, and he can not divorce her. And he has lost all chance of distinction, command, pay, cheerfulness, even equanimity, all because of his General. Lady Macmaster circulates the report that Tietjens and Valentine have had a liaison lasting for years. Valentine's mother attempts to interfere. She is a novelist. "Novelists live on gossip." Tietjens and Valentine prepare to celebrate Armistice Day together. They are joined by some of Tietjens' comrades. "But I'm not mad. I'm not destitute." He had run out to get money to celebrate with her. He had meant to go and fetch her, to celebrate that day together. "In one heart-beat a piece . . . they had been made certain that their union had already lasted many years." The War had made a man of him. "It had coarsened him and hardened him. There was no other way to look at it. What he had been before, God alone knew. . . . But to-day the world changed. Feudalism was finished; its last vestiges were gone. It held no place for him. He was going . . . to make a place in it for. . . . A man could now stand up on a hill, so he and she could surely get into some hole together!"

MAN WHO CONQUERED DEATH, by Franz Werfel (1927). The story of Herr Fiala, who in former days stood as gate-keeper to the National Treasury Office in Vienna clad in a sumptuous uniform trimmed with fur, wearing a three-cornered hat bright with silver lace and carrying a long black staff topped with a silver ball but who was now, in his old age after the War, glad to serve as part time watchman in a warehouse. He lived in a small, drab flat in the Josefstädterstrasse. Every dark room of it must do full time service for, while he and his good wife Marie occupy the bedroom, Klara, her sister, sleeps on a mattress in the kitchen, and their epileptic son Franzl must use the sofa in the dim dining-room. Klara is a disappointed and vixenish old maid. It was, therefore, a comfort when the old couple were able to celebrate his name day with a rare little feast of coffee and cakes before her return.

Frau Fiala brought out the best red linen tablecloth and fine china saved from more prosperous days. The picture of Herr Fiala, standing in uniformed dignity between the two councillors who had graciously consented to pose with him, dominates the room, and represents the high-water mark of their lives, something to be remembered and lived up to. Every evening on his return from duty at the warehouse Herr Fiala would go and stand before it and think of the past. It was, perhaps, the sight of it that prompted his wife's lavish celebration in his honor. Herr Fiala had always provided for his family, nor was he without thought for their future. He shared with Herr Schlesinger, the insurance agent, a secret whereby his good wife, Marie, would be made comfortable, their pitiful son Franzl would be saved from the asylum, even the cantankerous Klara need not want when he no longer watched over their welfare. A goodly sum would be theirs if he survived his sixty-fifth birthday. The sharing of this secret with Marie crowned their celebration of his sixty-fourth year. The sordid life of the flat went on. Hopeless Franzl continued his daily, fruitless search for work. Klara continued to hoard worthless scraps purloined from the houses where she worked and to vent her rage and malice on any who disturbed her. The old man kept steadfastly to his duty as watchman in all kinds of weather. Then one day, when Marie and Klara had foregathered with old cronies at the cemetery, whither they had gone to celebrate All Souls' Day, Herr Fiala sent Franzl, who had watched his father for some time with anxiety, to go and find him a bed at the hospital. This was in the November before his sixty-fifth birthday, which came early in January. Thereupon began the old man's desperate struggle with disease. He amazed the doctors and nurses by his pertinacious grip on life when fatally stricken. It was necessary to keep guard yet some weeks if their future was to be assured. His face became a mask of death. In the dying man's last dream the gruesome fight lost its seeming horror, for he believed himself back in his old gorgeous habiliments, standing under orders, a glorious feeling after being in the kitchen with the women these past years. With all the loyalty and fortitude of his early military training and of his great days as gate-keeper, he closes with death in a final fight of intolerable anguish. Out of the squalor of these pitiful lives rises the spirit of the old watchman significant of indomitable humanity with one shout voicing his victory over death, thus summing up the motives of pride and fortitude that recur with rhythmical precision throughout the story. Werfel has written in a mood of pity that understands and so is without condescension.

MÅRBACKA, by Selma Lagerlöf, translated from the Swedish by V. S. Howard (1924). Autobiographical reminiscences of the author's childhood at Mårbacka, the novelist's family home since the days of her great-great-grandfather, Pastor Morell. In each generation something was added to Mårbacka. Pastor Lyselius built the stable for ten horses and a cow-house for thirty cows, and the granaries, storehouses, and sheds needed. Pastor Wennervik built a new house, and laid out gardens, and the pretty white fences and gates that made the peasant farm into a beautiful home. He had been a tutor in his youth and had fallen in love with the rich, high-born young lady, the sister of his pupil. They exchanged vows in the bowers of the manor park, but one day their trysting place was discovered, and the tutor was dismissed. In his last days he married the cross old housekeeper who was a cruel stepmother to his lovely daughter, Lisa Maja, especially after her father's death. Lisa Maja refused to marry the clergymen selected for her, and broke the family tradition by her marriage to the paymaster of the regiment, Daniel Lagerlöf. The peasants at first did not like him because he had upset the old order and married the parson's daughter, but his forbears had all been clergymen, and though he had not inherited the gift of speechmaking he knew how to rule the community well and wisely. The romance of his courtship and married life is one of the stories the children hear the housekeeper tell, and they are delighted to listen, and have the grandfather who had been to them no more than a wooden image come to life. The stories of the household are divided into five groups. The first group tells of the illness like infantile paralysis which came to Selma when she was three years old. The children's nurse, a peasant girl, Back-Kaisa, had been faithful and was to be depended on, but had shown no affection for the children, never played with them, and knew no sagas and songs. When she washed them the soap always got into their eyes, and she combed their hair with hard pulls. Selma's helplessness brought out her tenderness and changed her from the cross nurse into the devoted friend. The family spent a summer at the shore for the benefit of Selma's health. Lieutenant Lagerlöf, her father, made friends with everyone in the place, the fishermen, retired sea captains, and all the people, high and low, succumbed to the charm of his breezy personality. The second and third groups of stories are the tales of the family and the past told by the old housekeeper, and of the neighbors, Colour Sergeant Karl von Wachenfeldt, once the handsomest man in Värmland, and the idol of the ladies, who had married the sister of Lieutenant Lagerlöf, and now in his lonely old age is still received kindly at Mårbacka, and of the blighted romance of Aunt Lovisa. "The New Mårbacka" tells of the changes that Lieutenant Lagerlöf made in the gardens, and the new barn he built that only lacked a steeple to look like a church, and his plan for a second story for the house, the dream that never materialized. The last group, "Workdays and Fête Days," is the picture of the happy life of the novelist's childhood, the games with her brothers and sisters and cousins, the joy and work when the fisherman brought the first fish in the "slom" season, until they grew so plentiful that the housemaids had to leave off spinning and weaving to help in the kitchen, and the little girls came from the schoolroom to help the grown-ups. On the Lieutenant's birthday the family kept open house, and all the neighborhood talent came to make music and improvise plays for the celebration, and dance in the garden lighted with paper lanterns.

MARCHING ON, by James Boyd (1927), is a story that conveys the reality of the Civil War with the same sensitive fidelity that characterized the picture of the Revolution in "Drums." James Fraser, son of a poor white farmer of North Carolina, falls in love with Stewart Prevost, the daughter of a wealthy planter living at Beaumont, a nearby estate, while he is hauling rails ordered by the Colonel from his father's farm. Stewart is friendly to his timid advances but her father repulses the young man. Pride in his descent from an earlier Fraser, a hero of the Revolution, strengthens his resentment at the Colonel's affront and drives him to leave his father's home and find his future in railroading. The early railroading and industrial conditions of the South before the War are vividly set forth. Then comes the Civil War and James enlists in young Charles Prevost's company, the Cape Fear Rifles. Their regiment is in only one brief action before winter sets in and they build their huts in sight of the Blue Ridge where the Yankees linger. During that winter's encampment Captain Prevost takes him along on many of his foraging trips for the troops. On one of these, skirmishers from the Union lines shoot Stewart's gallant and popular brother. In their last meeting before the company left home Stewart had begged James Fraser to guard her brother. Though without blame in the matter of her brother's death, it is not until he receives her letter that the sense of responsibility for her brother's untimely end leaves him. There is so much marching that James Fraser figures that the history of the time was written by and on his feet. They are in great battles, but the War as a whole is viewed as those of a latter day look upon it, as a drab and gruesome affair, an endless marching on of troops so weary that they often sleep as they march. The events are seen and felt through a film of fatigue. In a later battle many of his friends are killed and James is taken a prisoner to a Yankee camp. The horrors of the next two years have almost unsettled his mind when Stewart prevails on her father to arrange his exchange and he turns his weak and stumbling feet toward home. There, before he has fairly recovered his strength, the Yankees take Fort Fisher. Stewart flees with him as her acknowledged lover to his parent's humble farm. True to the tradition of his class, Colonel Prevost remains to arrange for the safety of those dependent on him and meets his death at the hands of Northern desperadoes, in the attempt to rescue his wife's picture from their desecrating hands. Sincerity and simplicity give power to this panoramic portrayal of the Civil War.

MARIA CHAPDELAINE, a tale of the Lake St. John country, by Louis Hemon (1921). The simple story of simple pioneering folks. The passion of Samuel Chapdelaine's life was to "make land" — to force a comfortable farm from unbroken forests. But he could not stay and enjoy the comforts after they were accomplished. Always he must move on farther north to the wide stretches of forest and again conquer. With his wife and six children he is wresting a home in the parish of Peribonka, miles from the little village in which the story opens. Maria Chapdelaine had been on a visit to some relatives and her father has come to the village to meet her. It is Sunday and after mass as they leave the little wooden church they exchange greetings with the few of the parishioners they know. The young men gaze favorably upon Maria and lament that she lives so far from the village. A handsome young trapper, François Paradis, halts her and her father and is recognized as a former neighbor. His admiration for Maria is evident and he promises to call within a few weeks. Maria treasures the promise. They bid adieu to their simple-hearted friends and start on their long drive over ice and snow to their home. Maria was eagerly welcomed by her mother, her younger brothers, and little sister. Every little item of her visit must be told. So seldom did their lives touch the outer world that her journey to a neighboring parish seemed a wondrous event. After dinner their only neighbor, Eutrope Gagnon, called. All knew that it was Maria he came to see, but his remarks were directed to her father. The coming of spring which meant a vigorous period of work was the main topic of conversation that evening. As the days passed they watched for the various signs that tell of the end of their long winter. And Maria watched for François. Late one night he appeared and Madame Chapdelaine and the children hailed him with joy — a visitor is such a rare occurrence. He tells them his many experiences and tries to win a glance from Maria, but she keeps her eyes modestly lowered. Even when he left she feared it would be bold to look into his eyes and felt ashamed at the beating of her heart. In June the two eldest boys returned home from the shanties where they had worked all winter and soon with their father and younger brother were hard at work "making land." Day after day they felled trees and unearthed stumps, while Maria and her mother prepared hot meals for them and praised them for their labor. On the feast of Saint Anne they planned a holiday to go picking blueberries. The night before was a memorable one, an evening of company such as they never had before. Eutrope Gagnon came; then later, an old friend and his nephew, Lorenzo Suprenant from the United States. When the happy welcome to these was finished, who appeared but François Paradis — and Maria was overjoyed. Lorenzo sought to interest her in his stories of the great cities but her thoughts were all for François. The others left but he stayed overnight and the next day picked berries with Maria. He told her of his love and promised to return the next spring, so their vows were plighted. Through the busy summer she thought ever of him. September brought frosts and soon winter set in. So severe was it that the Chapdelaines had to forego the great event of the year, the midnight mass on Christmas eve, so dear to the French-Canadian. Maria's regret was deep as she had planned to offer so many prayers before the altar. The family made merry Christmas Day but she, in order to win divine favor, spent the day reciting a thousand Aves. New Year's Day was celebrated by making candy. No visitors came until Eutrope Gagnon appeared in the evening. He bore sad news. He told that François Paradis in an attempt to reach there to spend Christmas had been lost in the snow. Maria was sore stricken. Her parents sensing her sorrow promised to have masses read for his soul, but for weeks she was sad and dejected. In February her father drove her to the church and after mass they visited the Curé to whom all his flock brought their troubles. He talked to Maria and bade her not to grieve so deeply and to fulfil her duties. March brought Lorenzo Suprenant again to their home and this time he asked Maria to marry him, to leave the dreary forests for the comforts of the United States. But as she could not decide he promised to return again for his answer. When Eutrope Gagnon heard of his visit, he came quickly to offer himself to Maria. Marriage with him meant the hard life of the forest which she had always known. However, she would be near her people. But she could not promise, for her heart still longed for François. Then came tragedy to the Chapdelaines, for their mother became ill and, although the doctor was brought from miles away — she died after much suffering. Eutrope helped much during this time and the household burdens fell upon Maria. As she sat by her mother's dead body she realized what a splendid sacrifice her mother's life had been — passing all her days in lonely places, spending all her strength in a thousand heavy tasks. And the recompense? Maria asked herself why she should stay and give up the delights of the city which Lorenzo offered her. But as she pondered, the joys of life in the open, of nature's unfolding each spring, of the intimacies of home, of the ties of race, welled within her and she knew that she would stay. So she gave her promise to Eutrope Gagnon to marry him as soon as her younger sister could take care of the household duties.

MARTHA AND MARY, by Johannes Anker-Larsen, translated from the Danish by Arthur G. Chater (1926). The motherless little daughters of Nils Anderson are devoted to each other, and together bear courageously the coming of a stepmother with her own five children, who starves Martha and Mary of food, and their father of affection. Nils tries to escape his misfortunes in drink, and finally hangs himself in the barn. His brother Johann comes to the funeral, and takes Mary home with him, as she is less useful on the farm than the practical Martha. Martha is to be sent for later if his wife approves, and if it is too hard for her at home. He never sends, and kind neighbors find a friendly home for her. Later Martha's foster-mother dies, and her foster-father starts for America, but dies on the way before they have left Denmark. Martha gets work on a farm. Her employer's son, Frederick, loves her, and it is hard for Martha that he is too much under his mother's thumb to keep his promise to her. There are plenty of places open to the capable Martha, and she gives notice, saying, "Where I myself am not good enough, my work's not good enough either." At her next place, a coöperative dairy, she meets Knud Lindberg, and after Frederick's marriage to the girl of his mother's choice, she marries him. After her confirmation Mary becomes maid and foster-daughter to Pastor Nyeland and his wife. In the meantime she has heard that her sister has gone to America. Mary lives in the dream world of her childhood, seeing the marvels of the cosmos in a piece of clover or a pebble or broken twig, and the sun, "a gold plate on the blue cloth of the sky." Then one day Karl Hjellesmark, friend from her old home, and now a student, comes riding to the parsonage on the first bicycle seen in the neighborhood, and she sees the sunlight of her dreams in his eyes. Their love is so assured that they leave it unspoken when he returns to Copenhagen for his studies, promising to come back next summer. Annette Preisler, studying to be an actress, makes him forget Mary. A fellow-student, Visby, wins Annette for his mistress, when her actor-lover leaves her, and Karl turns to politics and marries the daughter of a manufacturer. The pastor has always loved Mary, and when his wife dies and there is gossip about Mary staying on at the parsonage he asks her to marry him. She thinks of him as a kind, elderly friend, while for him it is a time of awakening of youth and passion, and the marriage is not a happy one. They have one lovely daughter, Inger, who learns to know her mother's friends, the flowers, and grows up to be her companion. When Inger is eighteen, she goes for a visit, and is found drowned after a social gathering where her innocence is betrayed by a young lieutenant. The theme in the stories of the two sisters is the quest of a personal religion, a faith sublime enough to satisfy the highest form of spiritual aspiration and simple enough to afford a rule of conduct in the workaday world. Mary reassures her husband, troubled by his study of the higher criticism of the Bible. She says, "Why fear the progress of science as a hindrance to faith. Can science ever discover any truth that is not God's truth?" Mary and Martha represent two different angles of approach to religious truth. Martha one day defined her philosophy of life: "If anybody set out to be just simply good, they'd have a hard time of it. But somebody must. I will." The background of the story shows the development and progress of social life in Denmark from the stage of tallow dips in the charming picture of the little sisters on the farm to coöperative dairies and electricity and post-War profiteering. Martha's husband becomes a rich squire, and in her new automobile she starts out to search for her sister Mary. Martha's daughter, Lisa, is worthy of her; the sons are "wasters." When Lindberg loses his money, the sons take positions as chauffeurs, and Martha and her husband become caretakers to a delightful old aristocrat Mr. Bay, whose son later marries Lisa, who works in his office. Some of the money is saved, and Martha, now a widow, is well off, but continues to work in Mr. Bay's garden. She tells him of her one wish to see her sister Mary again, and with the help of a directory and a telephone he is able to find Mary living in Copenhagen since the pastor's death, and the sisters are reunited.

MARY ROSE, by Sir J. M. Barrie (1920). The play contains a fairy tale and a ghost story set in the ordinary lives of everyday people and everyday life. Mr. and Mrs. Morland are devoted to their only daughter, Mary Rose. She is nineteen and has just fallen in love with the young midshipman, Simon Blake, her playmate, who has grown up and asked her to marry him. When he asks her parents' consent they tell him of a strange thing which had happened to Mary Rose seven years before when the family were spending a holiday in the outer Hebrides. While her father was fishing he was accustomed to leave Mary Rose on a tiny treeless island

called by a name which meant "The Island that Likes to Be Visited." One day
she waved to him as usual from the island, but by the time he had reached the island
in the boat she had mysteriously vanished. They learned that the natives had a
superstitious dread of the island. On the thirtieth day after her disappearance the
Morlands on the mainland saw her again on the island just where they had left her.
She was completely unconscious of the interval of time that had passed, and they
never told her. Four years later Simon and Mary Rose with their baby, Harry,
go to the same place for a vacation, and picnic on the little island. As Simon's
back is turned stamping out their fire she hears "the call of the island" again, and
is gone. Simon tries to laugh off his terror, but he knows the truth, that he will not
find her. After twenty-five years have passed the Morlands sadly admit that they
have almost forgotten Mary Rose. Simon is now a successful, middle-aged captain.
Harry has grown up and run away to sea years before. A telegram comes from Cameron, the student who had rowed Simon and Mary Rose to the island and is now the
minister in his native place, that Mary Rose has come back, and that he is bringing
her home. When she arrives she is still the girl of twenty-three in all her bloom and
beauty. She does not understand the change the years have made in the others. She
asks, "Where is my baby?" She runs to the room that had been hers and then his,
and we gather that the shock of the discovery of the truth causes her death. Many
years later Harry, the son, now a rough Australian soldier, back in London after the
Great War, comes to the deserted old home haunted by the ghost of Mary Rose still
seeking her child. The terrified old caretaker unwillingly shows him through the
rooms. While she is getting him a cup of tea he sees the scenes of the happy and
troubled past enacted. He takes a candle and goes into the little room and finds
Mary Rose. She asks him confidentially, "Would you mind telling me why everyone is so old?" Harry tries to comfort her, and succeeds in breaking the spell that
binds her to the past, by unknowingly fulfilling her wish of long ago, that her baby
might one day be big enough to take her on his knee as she had held him on hers.
She hears the "call" of the island once again, and gladly responds, this time never to
return.

MATRIARCH, THE, a chronicle, by G. B. Stern (1925). A history of the Rakonitz
family of international Jews from the year of Austerlitz to the present. Simon,
whose father had obtained for his people the right to use a surname, and who himself
won for the Ghetto folk the privilege of the vote in Pressburg, married blue-eyed
Babette Weinburg, the schoolgirl, who was the only person in town able to interpret
between Napoleon and his polyglot Hapsburg subjects. They became the ancestors
of a large family with blue eyes, straight, delicate noses, with the lightness and brightness of their native Vienna in their blood, and noted for its masterful womenkind.
Anastasia, the oldest daughter of their oldest son, insisted on marrying her cousin,
Paul, and became the first matriarch, deciding thereafter where and with whom the
"enormous amounts of aunts and cousins and great uncles and so forth" were to live
and to marry. For example, Susie Lake, the English girl who married Bertrand,
her son, and became the mother of Toni, one day to succeed her grandmother as
matriarch, longed above all things to have her own home, and instead she found
herself living with Anastasia, completely dominated by her mother-in-law. The
family had moved to London at the time of the French Revolution, Anastasia's
unmarried brothers, Albrecht, Maximilian, and Louis were making fortunes for the
family in rubies and sapphires. The hospitable Anastasia entertained for all of them,
and her house was headquarters for the others of the family who lived in Paris or

Vienna, or Constantinople. Danny Maitland came to live in the house when his mother, Sophie, died, and he and Toni grew up together in love and conflict. To Danny, "the matriarch was someone who interfered and gave orders, and exulted in power like some wicked old Roman emperor." Just when he was happy at his jolly, ordinary boy's preparatory school in London, she arranged for him to go to Vienna to the Rakonitz relations to go to school with foreign boys, and three years later when he had learned to adore Vienna he was summoned back to school in England. Toni, with her own tireless spirit and zest for pleasure, admired her gay, warm-hearted grandmother, and knew all the family traditions by heart. The end of the family prosperity came when the brilliant Uncle Maximilian staked their all in a gamble on a sapphire mine in Siam, which proved to be a swindle. Uncle Maximilian, who might have made another fortune, died of heart failure. Bertrand, Toni's father, who in all his easy-going, selfish existence had cared deeply only for one person, Maximilian, threw himself under a train, and Albrecht died that night of a stroke. Only Uncle Louis was left to bear the burden. This disaster left Anastasia with only a small inheritance left by her husband, more eccentric and extravagant than ever, and as always the prey of every plausible claimant for charity. Susie Lake escaped from the matriarch's tyranny at last, but only to extreme poverty with her own mother. The delicate Toni secured a post with an expensive modiste in Bond Street, graduated into the wholesale costume trade, and made a success of it. Danny, back from the War, wants to marry Toni, who will not have him because they are cousins, and it is because Anastasia married her cousin that the family and especially Toni herself are not strong. He unexpectedly meets his artist father who had deserted his mother, and finds out that he was not Sophie's child, is not a Rakonitz and therefore free to marry Toni. Then suddenly he realizes that he must give up Toni or continue to be enslaved to the family. She has made her cousin, Derek, give up his own plans for happiness to pay a family debt with all the ruthlessness of the matriarch. He tells her that she will be the bully of the family like her grandmother, and in spite of her protests, he kisses her and goes away. Val and the other women of Toni's generation are also successful in business. The family tree in 1925 shows that Toni has married a Maurice Goddard, and is the mother of three children.

MAUVE DECADE, THE, by Thomas Beer (1926). "American life at the end of the nineteenth century," the decade of the World's Fair in Chicago in 1893 ending with the Dewey Parade with Theodore Roosevelt riding at the head of the New York State Militia in 1899. The book opens with Emerson's funeral in 1882 as noted in Miss Louisa Alcott's diary, with a picture of Bronson Alcott, the last of the Transcendentalists, standing beside the grave, his employment gone now that he can no longer have a new phrase of Emerson to reflect "in the shallow pool of his intelligence." The author states: "All that had been finely stalwart in the Bostonian age had vanished, the reckless courage and self-willed individualism of Emerson, Thoreau, and Channing, the deliberate cultivation of research into the motives, not the manners of human action. The confusion of morals with manners . . . had helped . . . to destroy what was honorable in the Bostonian tradition, and from the remains of that tradition welled a perfume of decay, cants, and meaningless phrases: 'the nobility of democracy,' 'social purity,' and the like." For a motto he quotes Mr. Whistler's phrase, "Mauve is just pink trying to be purple . . ." and illustrates his points with humorous anecdote and cynical comment of the bad taste and foibles of the period. The first chapter, "The Titaness," is an arraignment of American women, their attitude of moral superiority and efforts to dominate literature, art, and the stage in the interests of the purity of the home. Louisa Alcott escaped from the drudgery of the household of her idle old father by writing "moral pap for the young" to use her own words. The servant question begins to make life in the city more attractive than the country, though Frances Willard, that guardian of public morals, deprecates the frivolities of the cities. "The Hon. George Hoar begged the men to let female superiority purify politics by voting." It was the time of the Trilby craze. Then the American Girl was invented, the Gibson Girl, the Christy Girl, and others, though Grant Allen referred coldly to "American girls indulged by 'poppa' and spoiled beyond endurance by 'mamma.' . . ." "Wasted Land" is a sketch of the great Pullman strike and the panic of 1893 to 1894, and Coxey's Army in Washington. This chapter includes a description of the last raid of the Dalton gang. Mark Hanna made a president. In the chapter, "Depravity," Anthony Comstock and Miss Frances Willard are introduced, and Oscar Wilde is the villain of the piece. A young Mr. Armstrong, studying in Paris, wrote home that he had met Oscar Wilde, and was ordered home by cable within five minutes of the arrival of his letter. There was an idea that the city was wicked and the country pure and unsullied. In the play, "Fashion," it is a noble farmer who saves the depraved people of the city. The civilization that Frances Willard foresaw was "a sterile meadow, dangerless, sprinkled with folk wearing white ribbons." "Dear Harp" is a discussion of the position of the Irish Americans, their political supremacy and their social inferiority, and the Protestant prejudice against Catholics. "The Unholy Ghost" sums up the authors and literature of the period. Professor Harry Thurston Peck wrote about the size of sleeves, and every other thing in the "Bookman" with a lightness of manner that distinguished the magazine from the pretentious heaviness of earlier literary magazines. The editors refused one of his articles praising Nietzsche, saying, "We are the last people on earth to condemn Mr. Peck for his interest in European literature." A woman writer says of Mr. Peck, "He takes so much unnecessary trouble in dragging out the foreign writers." Other writers discussed are Kipling, Stevenson, Barrie, Bangs, Henry Adams, and Stephen Crane. The last chapters are "The American Magazines," and "Figures of Earth."

MEANWHILE, by H. G. Wells (1927). In young Philip Rylands' beautiful Italian villa is gathered a week-end party. Lord and Lady Tamar, fresh from their work at Geneva, are the internationally minded young people who would bring salvation to the world by legislation. Colonel Bullace and his wife are traditionally minded Tories, "full of ready-made opinions." Geoffrey Rylands, Puppy Clarges, Mr. Haulbowline and the Mathisons are different names and shapes for "Stupids"; people whose only idea is to waste time effectively or picturesquely in tennis, dancing and bridge. There is Mr. Plantagenet-Buchan, an American Petronius and natural epicurean; Lady Catherine, a dusky beauty whose time is the present, a present made more radiant for conquest by the background of a dimly suggested past. She is a woman of passionate intuitions rather than intelligence. Cynthia Rylands, wife of Philip, is intelligence alert, waiting for leadership. She had grown up with the idea that there is "something eminently desirable that you got from the literature of the world, that was conveyed insidiously by great music and by all cared-for and venerated lovely things . . . an inward and spiritual grace " that made life worth while. Philip Rylands on the other hand is intelligence dormant, one whose magnificent vitality and luxurious life have formed a splendid cocoon around his intellectual and spiritual life. Into this week-end party, Philip's restless curiosity drags Mr. Sempack, a social philosopher, and to a certain extent, incarnation of Wells. He is described as a large dispersed individual with ungainly limbs, looking like a dissenting minister painted by Augustus John; sometimes known as a Utopographer. Mr. Sempack is reported to be a brilliant conversationalist as well as a profound writer. Mrs. Rylands loves good talk and conspires with Lady Catherine, who is developing a prospective interest in Mr. Sempack, and Mr. Plantagenet-Buchan, to draw him out at dinner that night. So Mr. Sempack becomes the amiable despot of the dinner table and the result is an evening of Great Talk. This talk, of a kind familiar to readers of Wells's other books, dwells much on the present social status of the world, a world in which we live provisionally: a world we blunder through by instinct, where work is necessary but happiness must be taken for the wild flower it is. The best most of us can do in this sort of world is to compromise. Meanwhile, Mr. Sempack's talk intensified in Mrs. Rylands the feeling that "they were living without quality." The Bullaces and Mathisons, needless to say, do not allow Mr. Sempack's large assumptions to go unchallenged. It has been said that nothing is more dangerous than ideas. Out of the ideas launched at this dinner table various consequences flow. Philip Rylands is a man of exuberant vitality which must find some outlet. In the life of the rich, normal outlets fail and he finds himself, to his own distgust and to his beautiful young wife's disillusionment, involved in an intrigue with another member of the house-party, Puppy Clarges, "a girl who denies all the accessories of sex and is sex unadulterated." Mrs. Rylands secludes herself and begs of Mr. Sempack, whose philosophical calm is much disturbed just then by Lady Catherine's reaction to his ideas — and person, for advice in this crisis of her life. Mr. Sempack helps Mrs. Rylands to understand that her husband has not been unfaithful in mind or spirit, but that he needs understanding love and direction not condemnation or even forgiveness from a superior moral altitude. During the dinner from which Mrs. Rylands pleads for excuse the delicate condition of health, as a reason for absence from her duties as hostess, the conversation turns to religion. Of this Mr. Sempack says, "By no means to be despised. . . . But in the cold, clear light of our increasing knowledge today, these consolations fade. . . . We cannot keep them if we would. We strain to believe and we cannot do it. We are left terribly to the human affections in all their incompleteness — and behind them what remains for us? Endurance. The strength of our own souls." But while Mr. Sempack's stoicism recognizes the increasing loneliness of those who give up craving for individual recognition, he finds compensations in vigorous literary and scientific work, in building the way for a better life here on this planet by taking on the real job at hand, that of reconstructing people's ideas. Meanwhile, Mrs. Rylands decides that her husband's place is in London, where the great strike is on and where he must find his place and part to play in affairs, since he is one of the great coal owners. There Philip goes and endeavors to apply reason and Mr. Sempack's principles to the chaos of the great strike. So much space is given to this strike because it is a concrete instance of the wasteful Old World order. As Mrs. Rylands awaits in the beautiful villa the coming of her child, a new sense of God comes to her. "He had dawned upon her, not as a dawn of light, for she knew no more than she had ever known, but as a dawn of courage. She perceived she could as soon have called him 'Courage' as called him 'God.'" Thus the relation of husband and wife is tested and a better focus of their mutual love and of their purpose in life is gained.

MEMORIES OF TRAVEL, by James Bryce (1923), is the record of journeys through Iceland, Poland, the Alps, the Southern Pacific Isles, the Altai Mountains and North America. These travels covered a period of some sixty years between

1872 and 1921, comprising an extraordinary variety of climate, scenery, vegetation and customs, with ample proof of the author's exceptional powers of observation. It was Lord Bryce's expressed desire to share some of these experiences with those who had not had a like privilege, so that the book is invested with a sincerity and informality of choice of material. His impressions of Iceland are told, to some extent, in terms of the negative, its absence of trees, of crops, of habitation — as we know the word — and of color. He dwells upon the grandeur of the vast stillnesses and of Iceland's frozen desert wastes. There are, besides the white of the snow mountains, two colors and no more; intense volcanic black, changing in some atmospheres to richest purple or violet and the pale yellowish-green of the marshy plains. There are no reds, either of earth or rocks or heather bloom; no blue-gray of limestone; no dark blue of slate; or young green of fir or beach or hazel copse. The shadows of cloud sweeping over the broad expanse of plains and the stern black crags jutting into the sky are described with great beauty. In Iceland Lord Bryce found entertainment in the commodious wooden house of his host, whose nearest neighbor was fifteen miles distant. In this home were daughters with ability to play several different musical instruments and to speak and sing in at least four languages. Simple hospitality, with the desire to give of their best without stint, was evident. The peasant's house is customarily built of sod, with a few blocks of basalt supporting the upper walls. From a distance it resembles a little hillock, so that one is in some danger of riding over it and finding the horse's foot half-way down the chimney. Inside the cottage is a labyrinth of low, dark passages, with tiny chambers which are seldom, if ever, cleaned, so that there is an overpowering reek of dried fish and other unpleasant odors. One understands why the first thing to be done upon entering is to light a pipe and smoke furiously until the room is in a cloud. The furniture and internal appurtenances are scant, but there are always three things no Icelandic farm lacks — books, a coffee-pot and a portrait of Jon Sigurdsson, the illustrious leader of the patriotic party. The Icelandic farmer has little ready money, but he is a person of substance and is the owner of horses, sheep, oxen and probably broad lands, which his family have held for centuries, with a pedigree often going back further than that of all but three families in England.

* * * * * * * *

The mountains of Poland, with their grandeur, their rugged crests stabbing the sky like giant teeth, their valleys with small, sparkling lakes afford a striking contrast to Iceland's desolate wastes. The houses are mostly of unhewn logs, the interstices stuffed with moss or mud and standing not in regular lanes but at all angles. Each dwelling has its hay-house, its cow-house and sometimes a tiny garden of two or three yards "wattled" in with a rowan bush, a tansy and a poppy growing inside.

* * * * * * * *

The third subdivision of the book is the description of the county of the Zipps, the peasants in their gayly striped costumes, their activities and for background the most charming scenery within the compass of the Hungarian Mountains. The Tatra Mountains, part of the Carpathian Range, which is not continuous as the geographers would lead us to believe, is a ridge of granite six thousand feet in height upon which are set like turrets of a city wall a row of sharp and savage peaks, the highest of which reaches eighty-seven hundred feet. Lord Bryce describes the climbing of mountains, the guide who danced airily over the rocky face of the cliffs where there was apparently nothing but the friction of the body to keep one from hurtling off into space, steep snow-slopes with their "grace of contour, a furry tenderness of surface, a pearly play of light and color where the sun strikes its crystals, its blue and violet shadows."

*   *   *   *   *   *   *   *

While describing North America, the author, to use that famous phrase of Alexander Hamilton, "tries to think continentally." He reviews the rivers, lakes and mountains of the country, stressing the mountains as of most scenic value since any body of water depends to great extent upon the character of their banks, whether these be low and monotonous or bold and varied. He makes comment on the beauty of Indian summer in Eastern America, a season scarcely known in Europe excepting in Italy and Greece, with its superb crimsons and scarlets of maples, the many-tinted yellows of beech and birch and the deep tender green of the white pines. In richness of colors, whether we think of the autumn woods of Maine or the rocks of the Western Canyons, America stands preëminent.

SUVAROFF'S ALPINE CAMPAIGN

In this account Lord Bryce gives us an entirely new picture of the short campaign of the Russian Suvaroff in the heart of Switzerland in September and October, 1799. Very little has heretofore been written regarding this short though remarkable campaign involving a march from Airolo, at the south foot of the St. Gotthard to Ilanz in the valley of the Vorder Rhein. Suvaroff, so Bryce points out, was the only really great commander Russia has produced and was the equal of many European generals, excepting of course Napoleon and Wellington. By the example of his boundless courage, his passionate patriotism and a readiness to share all their hardships, he won the universal admiration of his troops who responded to his every appeal. He was thus able to accomplish results in spite of hardships which were seemingly beyond human endurance. By traversing the entire region himself and describing the difficulties encountered in passing from mountain peaks to valleys, avoiding deep precipices, cliffs and cataracts which were difficult of accomplishment by his party in August properly equipped as they were with food, boots and alpenstocks and the assistance of a guide, he shows by contrast how heartbreaking was the task of the Russian soldiers who were half-starved and carrying muskets, ammunition and knapsacks and hampered by the necessity of moving artillery and cavalry through the snow, being hard pressed by the French on all sides. We are lost in wonder and admiration for this great general carrying out the plans of the general staff, which possibly a more skilful tactician would have refused to undertake and who by sheer force of character and influence over his troops, rescued an army from such perils.

MEN WITHOUT WOMEN, by Ernest Hemingway (1927). Short stories of striking variety in most of which as the publisher states "the softening feminine influence is absent — either through training, discipline, death or situation." They are told in compact dialogue. "The Undefeated" is the sordid and heroic story of Manuel Garcia, a bull-fighter past his prime, just out of the hospital and trying to get an engagement. The manager offers him a substitute position, and he is obliged to take it for very little money. In the café he asks his friend, Zurito, the picador, to pic for him. Zurito has retired from the ring himself, and tries to dissuade Manuel from fighting. There is a vivid description of the bull-fight. The bull gores and tosses Manuel, and the crowd is unfriendly, but Manuel kills his bull in the end, and then goes to the hospital again. "The Killers" are two gunmen who come into a small restaurant where they expect a man, Ole, will have his dinner. They talk aimlessly with the proprietor and then line him up with the waiters whose hands they tie as one of the gunmen takes them to the kitchen. George, the proprietor, asks what it is all about. They say they are going to kill Ole just to oblige a friend. They have never seen him or he them, and he is only going to see them this once. Ole, the Swede, does not come this particular night, and the two go away. A boy from the restaurant warns Ole lying on his bed at the rooming-house. Ole says nothing and makes no move to escape. He knows they will get him sooner or later. "Fifty Grand" is a boxing story. Jack is training at a health farm for a fight with Walcott. He is not in good form and has no heart in the fight, is troubled with insomnia and worries about his wife. Jerry, the trainer, and Danny Hogan, proprietor of the farm, discuss his chances. After a secret conference with his managers Jack tells them that he is betting on Walcott "fifty grand," that he has to take a beating, and is going to make money enough to retire on his last fight. Both the fighters are betting against themselves. In the ring Walcott hits below the belt, but Jack, though cruelly hurt, calls to the crowd that it was an accident, as he does not want to stop the fight and lose his money. He then fouls Walcott so badly that though he does not want to give up he is obliged to do so. "A Canary for One" is a conversation on a train. An American woman is taking a canary in a cage to her daughter in Italy. She tells her fellow travellers that American men make the best husbands. Her daughter fell in love with a Swiss in Vevey, but her mother would not allow them to marry. They talk of shops, and hotels and clothes and the train arrives in Paris. The American husband and wife to whom she has been talking are returning to Paris to set up separate residences. "A Simple Inquiry" is the question of a major to a soldier about his love affairs in which the soldier either does not understand or purposely misunderstands the suggestion that is left unsaid. "Ten Indians" tells the disillusion of an adolescent boy with the Indian girl he is in love with. "Now I Lay Me" is the reverie about his boyhood fishing and other episodes of a soldier suffering from insomnia.

MERTON OF THE MOVIES, a comedy, by George Kaufman and Marc Connelly, based on the novel of the same name by Harry Leon Wilson (1922). Merton Gill, is a fifteen-dollar-a-week clerk in the general store in Simsbury, Illinois, is ambitious to be a movie actor. He has consecrated himself to the uplift of the movies. His one sympathetic friend in the village is Tessie Kearns, the milliner and would-be scenario writer. Together they look at the photographs which Merton has had taken in every kind of outfit from cowboy to polo player. Tessie particularly admires the "still" of Merton in a dress suit in which Merton looks so much like the famous screen star, Harold Parmelee. Merton confides to Tessie that he has two hundred and seventy dollars saved and as soon as he gets three hundred he is going to start for Hollywood. Later when the store is closed, Merton practises with the "support" of the lady-dummy in the checked gingham dress labelled "Our Latest for Milady only $6.98," and the gentleman-dummy in the raincoat. Acting as the hero, Merton is about to throw the villain in the raincoat over the cliff when Amos Gashwiler, his employer, comes in to put a stop to the "riotin." Merton will have to give up the movies or leave Mr. Gashwiler's emporium. Merton decides to "follow his star," though Mr. Gashwiler thinks it is not likely that "a boy from Simsbury" can ever be a successful actor. Merton gives the finishing touch to his imaginary triumph in an interview, which he concludes with the familiar words of the screen magazine, "Perhaps I owe most, however, to . . . my wife. She is more than a wife. She is my best pal, and, I may say, my severest critic." He pulls his cot out from under the counter, and kneels down in the moonlight. "Oh God," he prays, "make me a good movie actor. Make me one of the best. For Jesus' sake, Amen." Three weeks later Merton is listening to the conversation of his fellow applicants in the waiting room of the Holden lot in Hollywood. He is annoyed to hear a girl of the soubrette type talking flippantly about Beulah Baxter, to Merton "the wonder woman of the screen." She speaks of starring with Beulah, and Merton is sure she was joking, because his "wonder woman" had said in an interview that if she ever used a "double" she would feel "that she was not keeping faith with her public." The Montague girl is interested in the "nice kid" who is so "awful green," and his pathetic illusions. She introduces him to Jeff Baird, the slapstick comedy king, but Merton does not appreciate the honor; he prefers "something of a finer nature." A moment later his chance comes to be an extra with the great Parmelee in the filming of Robinson Crusoe. A society scene is to be interjected into Crusoe's adventures. The scene develops with skilful satire directed against movie "bunk." Merton is the first to volunteer to pick up the book from the centre table, and is so awkward and scared that the director shouts at him: "It's a book. Not a rattlesnake. . . . Didn't you ever see a book before?" Merton is paid off, and remains alone on the lot, because he is afraid that if he leaves he can never get in again. He brushes away a tear and plays the book scene over again as the curtain falls. At the end of another week a very seedy, hungry Merton is still on the lot. The admirer of Beulah Baxter hears his "wonder woman" quarreling with the director, Mr. Rosenblatt, her fourth husband since she started counting. As he watches a new "Hazard of Hortense" in the making, Hortense, pursued by the villain, leaps from the ship into the sea, and the Montague girl "doubling" for Beulah comes dripping out of the water at his feet. She sends for sandwiches and coffee and after the fourth sandwich Merton gives up his dignified aloofness, and tells her all about the correspondence course he has taken with the moving picture acting school in Stebbinsville, Kansas, and the photograph that so markedly resembles Harold Parmelee. The Montague girl persuades Jeff Baird to give Merton a chance to burlesque the actor he most admires in a leading rôle in what Merton believes is a serious picture. Out of Merton's deadly earnestness they make a hilarious comedy, and he does not know until the film is completed that he is a great success in the "low comedy" which he abhors. Other directors come to him with flattery and offers of large salaries. Mr. Gashwiler, who is in California on a trip, hails him as a great man, and tells him he is going to have a brass plate put up in his store in Simsbury, "Here worked Merton Gill." Merton turns for comfort and understanding to the Montague girl , though he first tries to pretend he knew all along what they were doing, but his play-acting breaks down, and he hides his face in her lap. Called to the telephone to give an interview to a screen magazine, he says, "What? No, I'm not yet, but I'm going to be. Miss Montague. . . . More like a pal. And I might also add, she's my severest critic." Merton of the Movies had "arrived."

MESSER MARCO POLO, by Donn Byrne (1921), recounts the love story of Marco Polo and the daughter of Kubla Khan. Malachi Campbell, a grand old Ulster Scot who had fought in wars the world over and was wiser than the scholars, at ninety years of age, proud and undaunted, arrives in New York and calls on a clansman who as a boy had listened to his stories in the glens of Antrim. That evening to a group of friends he tells the "real story of Marco Polo" and brings back the glorious past with all the magic of his Irish imagination: it is nearing night on the first day of spring and soft breezes float over Venice. Young Marco Polo threw down his quill in the counting house where he was learning his trade. He felt a stirring within him that called for neither the grand lady to whom he wrote verses nor the little gown-maker whose affection was lavished upon him. He left his desk and strolled through the city. Everywhere were fine shadows and the splashing of oars. A great admiral's galley was ready to put to sea, a merchantman from Africa. Along the canals "all the people in the world, you'd think." A Frenchman with silks, a Spaniard with his long, lean sword, a Greek courtesan enthroned in her gondola, a Muscovite, Moorish captains, Crusaders, Scots and Irish mercenaries. This was Venice — the Pride of the West, the Jewel of the East. Marco Polo wandered on to a wine shop where gathered the foreign people and entered. Men from all parts of the world were there. A Hindoo performed magic. An Irish chieftain stabbed an insulting German trooper. A great commotion ensued, but Marco Polo noticed a strange sea-captain sit bland and unmoved and knew him to be a Chinaman. Marco talked to him and asked if he had ever seen his father and uncle who had travelled to China several years before and learns that they are on their way home. The glories of China are described to the youth, but he scoffs at the idea that any place could hold more beauty and treasure than Venice. Then the sea-captain told him of Golden Bells, the lovely little princess, daughter of Kubla Khan. Time went on but Marco could not forget. Ever a bell was ringing in his heart and he knew he must go to China. When his father and uncle return he plans to go with them on their next expedition. Now it was the time when the Christian people felt that they must spread the truth which only they knew. No one but Christians could be saved and the light must be spread. Kings were becoming saints, and saints, kings. Kubla Khan in far China had heard of the religion and had charged the Polos to have the Pope send some theologians to explain it and its wonders. Now Marco Polo had the faith of the young and to think that lovely little Golden Bells would be damned if the true religion was not brought to her was beyond endurance. So gladly he accepted the mission to spread the truth in China and with the blessing of the Pope he set forth with his father and uncle. With their caravan of camels and donkeys they passed through many strange countries. Eastward ever eastward and then the terrors of the desert. The demons and war-locks tormented them. Nearly all the servants deserted and finally buffeted by a stinging sand storm Marco Polo lay down to die, calling for little Golden Bells. Now Malachi tells of Golden Bells in her Chinese garden. There she was, slim little princess, with Li Po, the great poet, who instructed her, and a magician, the Sanang, who was to amuse her. Sanang called her to watch the rare sport in the crystal globe. There they see the warlocks of the desert tormenting Marco Polo who lies dying. She cries and demands to have him saved. So all the Sanang's magic is put to use and Marco Polo is saved. Soon he arrives at the great palace of Kubla Khan. There on the throne beside the great ruler is little Golden Bells and both are smiling. So then Marco Polo remembers his mission and he tells them of the Lord Jesus. Golden Bells wept to hear of the crucifixion and when he told of the Resurrection then Kubla Khan gave a great shout and hoped that Christ then showed them His power. But learning the facts the great Khan and the assembly became quiet and polite and Marco Polo's heart fell. All were dismissed and Kubla Khan talked with Marco telling him that all the teachings of Christ were in their books and that their thinkers and magicians could work greater wonders, so for him not to try and convert the country but to stay and be his guest. Little Golden Bells comforted him and assured him she was a convert and so he stayed to instruct her. Day after day they sat in the garden and she learned of Christ and all the saints, and then Marco said he must go. But there was no going from Golden Bells, so Li

Po wrote a marrying song and Marco Polo stayed. Now you must see him seventeen years later and fourteen years after his wife, Little Golden Bells, had died. A tall, lean figure, hair streaked with gray, a hard, lean face and savage eyes — the great Khan's bravest warrior who administered justice to everyone. But never did he mention Golden Bells. Now Kubla Khan was very old and Li Po, the poet, was gray and frail, and one day they came to Marco and told him he had best go back to Venice. The great ruler feared that after his death, rivals would treat Marco Polo unkindly. But he refused to leave the garden and his memories of Golden Bells. "I've forgotten Venice. I've even forgotten my God for her," he said. Then the old Sanang works magic and Li Po sings a song and little Golden Bells appears in the garden and tells him to go. And so he went.

MICROBE HUNTERS, by Paul de Kruif (1926). A popular and dramatic account of the discoveries and investigations of celebrated bacteriologists. The story begins with Leeuwenhoek, the Dutch dry-goods merchant, and janitor of the City Hall in Delft, who had a passion for grinding lenses, and accumulated microscopes to satisfy his insatiable curiosity about the "sub-visible" world of bacteria. He found in a drop of rain water what he described as "little animals, a thousand times smaller than any creatures which we can see with our eyes alone," that "tumbled about and sidewise, this way and that." When Leeuwenhoek was born in 1632 there were no microscopes, "only crude hand-lenses that would hardly make a ten-cent piece look as large as a quarter." The cheese mite was believed to be "the smallest creature God had created." He found these "little animals" in the secretions of his mouth, and as years went on he discovered them in the intestines of frogs and horses. In the tail of a little fish he was the first man to see the circulation of the blood in the capillary blood vessels. The next of the microbe hunters was the Italian Spallanzani, born in 1729, who proved by his experiments, in opposition to the popular theories of his time, that microbes must have parents, that life can only come from life. He was the first to segregate a single microbe and watch it divide into two. Louis Pasteur began his scientific work as a chemist, but was diverted to bacteriology to study yeast and ferments to help the wine distillers of France. These experiments led to the method now called "Pasteurization," killing germs by heating almost to the boiling point. When he met the Emperor Napoleon III he told him that his greatest ambition was to find the microbes that were the cause of disease. His contemporary, Robert Koch, discovered and isolated the bacilli of tuberculosis and cholera, and proved that microbes are our most deadly enemies. Pasteur discovered and perfected a vaccine against anthrax, and then, haunted by his childhood memory of the death in his village of the victims of a mad wolf, turned his attention to the study of rabies. Experiments with dogs enabled him to achieve the vaccine that prevented hydrophobia. Roux and Behring discovered the antitoxin for diphtheria. There is a chapter about that strange genius, Metchnikoff, and his work with phagocytes and theory of immunity, and his invention of the famous calomel ointment to cure syphilis. The next chapters are given to the scientists who studied the diseases carried by insects. Theobald Smith hatched ticks in an incubator and after years of laborious experiment in the field and in his laboratory answered all the questions about Texas or Southern cattle fever. David Bruce, in Africa, proved that the tsetse fly carried the sleeping sickness. Ronald Ross in India and Battista Grassi in Italy, working independently, yet aiding each other, located the mosquito as the criminal messenger of malaria. Finally, "that there is now scarcely enough of the poison of yellow fever to put on the points of six pins" we owe to the tireless research and heroism of Walter Reed, Jesse Lazear, James Carroll and certain enlisted men of the United States Army, who in their self-sacrificing zeal "in the interest of science, and for humanity" determined definitely that it was a mosquito that carried yellow fever. To their efforts is owed the fact that Havana to-day is as it is, instead of the pest-hole it was in 1900. The last of the microbe hunters discussed by Dr. de Kruif is Paul Ehrlich, who opened up a new era in microbe hunting by his chemical research to discover a compound capable of curing syphilis. Dr. de Kruif calls the compound of Dr. Ehrlich (which went by the name of 606, the number of experiments it took to find it) a "magic bullet." Thanks to Ehrlich's efforts, Dr. de Kruif is able to conjecture hopefully of an age when bacteriology and chemistry will work hand in hand.

MIND IN THE MAKING, THE, by James Harvey Robinson (1921, Revised Edition, 1923). In a preface H. G. Wells says of this book that it takes much that was "latent and crude" in his mind and gives it "texture and form and confidence." The author states that "if some magical transformation could be produced in men's way of looking at themselves and their fellows, no inconsiderable part of the evils which now afflict society would vanish away or remedy themselves automatically." He would "raise men's thinking onto a plain" which would "enable them to fend off or reduce some of the dangers which lurk on every hand." In order to forward this change of mind Dr. Robinson has brought together the facts now accepted among the scientifically minded which cast light on the "nature of mind" and its past doings. The title of his book is a statement of his conviction that those processes of thought which we call mind have been developing during hundreds of thousands of years, at first very slowly, recently with surprising rapidity. The making of the mind consists in the accumulation of knowledge and its applications and can therefore go on indefinitely in the future as it has progressed in the past. The second chapter is "On Various Kinds of Thinking." First is "the reverie," that stream of spontaneous thought "far too intimate, personal, ignoble, or trivial to permit us to reveal more than a small part of it . . . in many cases an omnipotent rival to every other kind of thinking." Its chief preoccupations are "self-magnification and self-justification." Then there is the thinking which takes the form of everyday planning. The third kind of thinking comes when anyone questions our beliefs and opinions. We hastily fabricate a defence of our convictions, many of which were acquired in childhood and have not since been revised. This is called "rationalizing" by modern psychologists. It "is the self-exculpation which occurs when we feel ourselves, or our group, accused of misapprehension or error." ". . . Most of our so-called reasoning consists in finding arguments for going on believing as we already do." Opinions which are "the result of experience or honest reasoning do not have this quality of 'primary certitude.'" But sometimes, the author says, "under Providence, the lowly impulse of resentment leads to great achievements. Milton wrote his treatise on divorce as a result of his troubles with his seventeen-year-old wife, and when he was accused of being the leading spirit of a new sect, the Divorcers, he wrote his noble "Areopagitica" to prove his right to say what he thought fit, and incidentally to establish the advantage of a free Press in the promotion of Truth." It is possible that future generations may brush aside "almost all that had passed for social science, political economy, politics, and ethics . . . as mainly rationalizing." Lastly is "creative thought" which "transforms the world." This represents a rare type of curiosity and wide range questioning characteristic of the ancient prophets and the scientific minded of to-day. "For this kind of meditation begets knowledge, and knowledge is really creative inasmuch as it makes things look different from what they seemed before and may indeed work for their reconstruction." Creative ideas have to be "worked up" and then "put over" to "become a part of man's social heritage." Dr. Robinson gives as an example of this kind of curiosity and creative intelligence Galileo's observation of the swinging of the lamps hanging by long chains in the cathedral and his subsequent invention of the pendulum clock, and the productive reveries of poets and dramatists and novelists. The chapters following give the historical and psychological backgrounds which have gone into the making of the twentieth century mind. The "four historical layers underneath the minds of civilized men" are "the animal mind, the child mind, the savage mind, and the traditional civilized mind." Like animals we learned by "trial and error" or "fumbling and success" as Dr. Robinson prefers to call it since it is "the success that establishes the association." Differing from animals man is "co-operative and cumulative" and the experience of one man could profit another. Personification "one of the most virulent enemies of clear thinking" we share with our savage ancestors when our newspapers state that "Berlin says" or "America so decides." Modern "principle" is "too often only a new form of the ancient taboo, rather than an enlightened rule of conduct." After reviewing early "types of mind" the writer discusses the beginnings of critical thinking among the Greeks, their achievement limited because "Greek civilization was founded on slavery and a fixed condition of the industrial arts." Experiment leading to increased knowledge was associated with the servant or slave and held in contempt. The Greeks had sought salvation through intelligence and knowledge. The world of the Middle Ages was dominated by religious and mystical thought, an uncritical faith and reliance on authority. The author points out that the Middle Ages being much nearer to us in time have still an influence on human thought and morals far greater than the ideas of the Greeks. An account of the scientific revolution follows beginning with Francis Bacon. This has brought about such changes in our environment that "since the Middle Ages, and especially in the past hundred years science has so hastened the process of change that it becomes increasingly difficult for man's common run of thinking to keep pace with the radical alterations in his actual practices and conditions of living." "We might think in terms of molecules and atoms, but we rarely do." There follows some account of "our present plight in the light of history," and the fact that modern inventions brought about such an overwhelming importance to "business for business' sake" that it has become a sort of new religion, and those that impugn it are subject to suspicion. The writer closes with a reference to a passage in Goethe's "Faust" where he likens History to the Book with Seven Seals described in Revelation. He suggests that the seals were "seven great ignorances." "No one knew much (1) of man's physical nature, or (2) the workings of his thoughts and desires, or (3) of the world in which he lives, or (4) of how he has come about as a race, or (5) of how he develops as an individual from a tiny egg, or (6) how deeply and permanently he is affected by the often forgotten impressions of infancy and childhood, or (7) how his ancestors lived for hundreds of thousands of years in the dark ignorance of savagery. The seals are all off now. The book at last lies open before those who are capable of reading it. . . ." In an early chapter on "Methods of Reform" Dr. Robinson recommends the "liberation of Intelligence" as yet "an untested hope in its application to the regulation of human relations. . . . It has not been tried on any large scale outside the realm of natural science. There, everyone will confess, it has produced marvellous results . . . it has completely revolutionized men's notions of the world in which they live, and of its inhabitants, *with the notable exception of man himself.*"

MIRROR FOR WITCHES, A, by Esther Forbes, a novel (1928). Reminiscent of Cotton Mather's "Wonders of the Invisible World," the fiction in this book has its setting in a world of understanding of Manichean distinctions, and of a Puritan God who logically implies his opposite the Devil. To render the contemporary scene, Salem during the witchcraft days of the seventeenth century, the style assumes appropriate archaisms of narrative, and reproduces the court trial of a witch in a long conversational passage between Magistrate and Examinate. A child is picked up by the English skipper, Jared Bilby, in Brittany at Mont Hoël, just after her parents have been burned as witches. He adopts her and takes her with him, first to England, and then to Salem in the New World. Doll, as she is called, grows to womanhood haunted by the memory of her parents' tragedy, and the harrowing belief, which her Puritan surroundings do not attempt to mitigate, that her soul has been signed away to the Devil. Jared Bilby loves his charge, but his wife Hannah mistreats her continually. As a way out, Bilby proposes her marriage to Titus Thumb, son of the Deacon. The young man, indeed, looks upon Doll with favor, but his better nature is under the influence of the town rumors that Doll is an imp and a witch. His suspicions are further increased when she succeeds in rescuing his father's runaway bull, riding him, so he thinks, in the transformed presence of an Indian who is mortally wounded by his bullet and at once transformed again into Doll unharmed. Yet, though Titus suspects that the bull is Doll's "Familiar," the ban announcing the marriage is proclaimed. Doll, however, protests in church against the union with Titus, her behavior causing mortal illness to her foster-father. Before his death, nevertheless, he swears to her spiritual innocence and exonerates her from the charge of witchcraft. Doll is fated not to escape. In her isolation she plays with the Thumb children, Sorrow and Labour. They eat the dolls of corn husks and pumpkin seeds which she has given them to play with, and in their consequent illness they accuse Doll of having bewitched them. Brought up for trial in Salem, Doll innocently lured by the hope of pardon, proclaims her virtue in the case of the Thumb children but confesses to her love for a Demon; the latter is really no other than the pirate Shadrach Greene, who has turned the girl's imagination with the mysteries of Hell and the Devil before being publicly executed. Though the mother of the pirate, Goody Greene, is witness to the fact of her son's seduction of Doll, her testimony is rejected by the court. Doll is imprisoned pending the confirmation of her death sentence. Half crazed she is consoled by the preacher Zacharias Zelley, an Oxford graduate with rationalistic leanings, who has himself been heavily burdened by the injustice of her persecutors. At the advent of the pirate-Demon's child, Doll dies, her mind still captivated by the hallucinations of a Hell where she will meet her love and exist happy in a state unshadowed by the terrors of righteous malice.

MISS LULU BETT, by Zona Gale (1920), is the poignant story of six months of a woman's life. The woman is Lulu Bett, who, with her mother, lives in the home of her sister's husband, Herbert Deacon. Herbert was a widower with one daughter, Diana, when he married Ina Bett and now there is a second daughter, Monana, a spoiled darling who frequently refuses the family bill of fare, preferring that Lulu should arise from the table and prepare a special dish of milk toast for her. Herbert Deacon rules his little household of women with a firm hand, permitting no extravagant gestures, either with money or emotions. At the beginning of the story, Lulu is taken to task for having purchased a flowering plant when, if Herbert is not mistaken, she has given them the impression that she is wholly without means. Lulu, with unwonted spirit, throws the offending plant upon the wood-pile in the shed

Later, she rescues the one blossom, pinning it upon her dress, which further affronts Herbert. Herbert is afflicted with a large facetiousness, which he en.ploys to his own delight and to the terror of his women-folk. His one tenderness is the love which he bears for the woman who reared him, whom he calls Ma. He also indulges Mother Bett when she retires during one of her "tantrims," which are a periodic affair when she refuses to eat or converse with the family. Lulu is the inevitable maid-of-all-work in the house; cooking the meals, serving the table, attending to the whims of the child Monana and becoming the butt of most of Mr. Deacon's pointed and cruel gibes. Apparently, it has never occurred to Lulu that she might fill any other niche in life than that of fifth wheel in Ina's family, with only the individuality of an automaton. There comes a letter announcing the approaching visit of Herbert's brother Ninian, whom Lulu has never met, although she has studied his photograph at odd moments on the parlor shelf. Now it is no longer merely a photograph, but a new personality which will come into the house, so that she sees it in a different relation to herself. When Ninian arrives unannounced at the back door, he finds Lulu baking pies. She has no time to surround herself with her customary timid reserves, as Ninian proceeds at once to become acquainted, throwing the spell of his warm masculinity about Lulu, who has known no men excepting Herbert. Lulu responds with unexpected sallies of wit which delight Ninian and astonish Lulu herself. Dazzled with her own ability, Lulu unfolds during Ninian's visit, so that she is quite mistress of herself and the occasion when Ninian invites Lulu, Ina and Herbert to go on a two hours' ride to the city for a theatre party, which exceeds even Lulu's wildest ideas of adventure. After the play while they are having a gay little supper, Herbert brightly suggests that someone dance upon the table, or otherwise amuse them, else the other diners would begin to read a funeral service over them. Ninian, not to be outdone, inquires why not a wedding service? Upon being questioned, Lulu painfully admits that she is not familiar with the service, so could not repeat the lines. Ninian elucidates by declaiming, "I, Ninian, take thee, Lulu, to be my wedded wife." They dare Lulu to say it. So that other Lulu, who has come so strangely to the surface since Ninian's arrival and who sometimes fought the battles of plain Lulu, says, "I, Lulu, take thee, Ninian, to be my wedded husband." Suddenly Herbert Deacon, who is the village justice of the peace as well as dentist, shows a shocked face to the others. They have undoubtedly undergone a civil wedding service, by the law of the state, which he says must immediately be annulled. Lulu, dumfounded, looks at Ninian, who non-chalantly accepts the situation, admitting that he hopes it is legal and binding, if Lulu does not mind. To everyone's amazement, Lulu realizes that she does not mind, so the two go off on their wedding journey, while Ina is left to break the news to Mrs. Bett and to prepare to take care of her own home. After an interval of perhaps two weeks, Lulu returns alone to the Deacon home, in a pitiful array of new clothes. Ninian, after they have reached Savannah has told Lulu that he has been married before and that although he hopes his wife has passed on to her reward, yet he has no definite proof that he is free to marry. Caring for Lulu and regretting the necessity of telling her, Ninian still prefers to be straightforward about it. Lulu accepts the story and returns home, but Herbert insists that the townspeople shall never know the truth. Far better that they believe that Ninian tired of Lulu than that the crime of bigamy should be connected with the family name. Lulu protests her faith in Ninian, which is finally justified by Herbert's receiving a letter from Ninian enclosing proofs of his early marriage, with the additional information that his first wife is still living. Consequently he must remain away from Lulu. For Lulu home conditions have become well-nigh intolerable, and she decides to find employment

THE READER'S DIGEST OF BOOKS

elsewhere. On her way to the bakery where she intends to work, she talks with Cornish, the town's small music dealer, who longs to practise law. His sympathies have been aroused by Lulu's struggle for independence and he has learned to care for her in his gentle, middle-aged fashion. Therefore, as counter-inducement to the job in the bakery, he asks Lulu to marry him. Lulu, who has not really loved Ninian, but had been carried away by the delight of being cherished, accept's his offer of himself, his little business and his large sympathy and understanding.

MISTRESS OF HUSABY, see **KRISTIN LAVRANSDATTER,** by Sigrid Unset.

MR. FORTUNE'S MAGGOT, by Sylvia Townsend Warner (1927). For many years Mr. Fortune had been a bank clerk, and few people would have suspected that he concealed beneath a prosaic exterior the "maggot," which the author defines on the title-page as "a nonsensical or perverse fancy." When his godmother died and left him one hundred pounds he left England to be a missionary at St. Fabien, a port on an island in the Pacific. The archdeacon discovered that Mr. Fortune was the best man to keep the accounts, and carry the subscription list to the English visitors, which was not what he had come to the East for. After ten years he felt a call to carry the Gospel to the small and remote island of Fauna, and though the archdeacon disapproved, a call is a call, and not to be disregarded. With the remains of his legacy he outfitted himself with tinned meats, tea, soap, a gentleman's housewife, a second-hand harmonium, a lamp, and rolls of white cotton and a sewing machine to make clothes for the natives. On Sunday in Fauna as he knelt before an improvised altar his first convert joined him, Lueli, a handsome, slim brown boy. Lueli remained his only convert. The natives liked Mr. Fortune, and listened politely to his exhortations, but slipped away at the first opportunity. He lived happily with Lueli, his "man Friday," who though so recently a heathen displayed all the Christian virtues, and he came more and more under the spell of the island, with its care-free, childlike inhabitants. Urged on by the archdeacon, he made Lueli a pair of trousers, but his effort was a failure. One day Mr. Fortune discovered Lueli's idol decked with fresh flowers hidden in an arbor. He brought it back to the hut and sternly ordered the unwilling Lueli to destroy it. That night an earthquake rocked the island. Lueli dragged Mr. Fortune to safety, but the idol was burned with the hut. Without a god Lueli knew that he must die, and no efforts of Mr. Fortune could dispel his melancholy. He tried teaching him higher mathematics, which had been a delight of his own youth, and drove Lueli to attempt suicide. It was during this lesson that he mentioned an umbrella, and in answer to Lueli's question described it as "the shell that would be formed by rotating an arc of curve about its axis of symmetry, attached to a cylinder of small radius whose axis is the same as the axis of symmetry of the generating curve of the shell. When it is not in use it is properly an elongated cone, but it is more usually helicoidal in form." Mr. Fortune knew that his mission had not been a success and he had come to believe that the natives were better off without conversion, and the organized ritual of the church. Before he left the island he wanted to make a new idol for his friend Lueli. The disillusioned missionary carved a god in imitation of the others he had seen, placed wreaths of flowers around its neck, and sent Lueli out to it. When he heard the boy talking with soft, happy voice to his idol the new completely heathenized Mr. Fortune knew that his part in Fauna was done. He could not trust himself to stay without trying to alter these unspoiled children of the woods and waters. He tells Lueli that he also lost his God the night of the earthquake, and that when he himself goes away his God will remain on the island where he lost him, and with him a part of Timothy Fortune will remain also, so that he will not leave his friend utterly.

MR. PIM PASSES BY, a comedy, by A. A. Milne (1919).   A charming widow, Olivia Telworthy, has been married for five years to George Marden, of Marden House, Buckinghamshire.   Her first husband had been a rascally promoter from whom she had been separated for years before his death in Australia was announced in the newspapers.   The other member of the family is George's niece, Dinah, about to be engaged to a young artist, Brian Strange.   Brian has gone out to the farm with George in order to ask his consent to the marriage.   Dinah, waiting for them to return, receives a caller, an old gentleman, Mr. Pim, who has come with a letter to her uncle from a mutual friend, to ask for an introduction to a man in London.   The young girl introduces herself to the kindly, gentle Mr. Pim, and explains that George is her uncle, not her father, and then how glad she was to have him marry such a lovely person as Olivia Telworthy.   Mr. Pim is from Australia he tells her, which is where the unpleasant Telworthy drank himself to death after serving a prison sentence, and they comment on the unusual name, "Telworthy."   As Mr. Marden does not return, Mr. Pim decides to go to the village and send a telegram, and come back again.   In the meantime Dinah and Brian tell the sympathetic Olivia of their engagement.   George is opposed to the marriage.   They are too young, he does not like Brian's futuristic painting, and does not believe that he could support a wife, and will not take Olivia's suggestion that he give Dinah an allowance until she comes of age.   They are in the midst of this family disagreement when Mr. Pim returns. In the course of conversation with George and Olivia, the garrulous stranger tells them of the odd coincidence of his encounter on the boat from Australia with a drinking ne'er-do-well once in his employ who had been in prison for some kind of fraudulent company-promoting, named Jacob Telworthy.   The conventional George is horrified to think that, as he puts it, their union has been unhallowed by the Church and the Law.   What seems wrong to Olivia is that she lived five years with a bad man she did not love, not that she has lived five years with a good man she does love.   If she belongs to anyone but herself it is certainly not to Jacob Telworthy but to George.   As George becomes more miserable and involved in consideration of the situation, Olivia becomes more mischievous.   She urges him to ask his Aunt Julia what the County will think about it, and asks if she shall still call her Aunt. He sends to the Trevors where Mr. Pim is lunching, and asks that gentleman to come and give further details.   Aunt Julia is amazed to find out that Olivia is a bigamist. Olivia waits for George to get round to saying that he loves her and shall keep her with him in spite of all the Telworthys in the world.   Mr. Pim adds to his story that the Telworthy he had met died in Marseilles.   George is now happy and thankful, and asks Olivia to go up to London and be married at a registry office.   She has other ideas, however, and George has to propose to her again, and before she will accept him, he finds himself committed to give his blessing to Dinah and Brian, to agree to the purchase of new curtains and carpet and a honeymoon in Paris.   Mr. Pim returns to tell Mrs. Marden how it happened that he had been impressed by the name of Telworthy by his chat with Dinah, when all the time he knew the man's name was Henry Polwittle, and that he had never known anyone named Telworthy.   Mrs. Marden does not tell her husband of this later call from Mr. Pim, and prepares to go on to London to be married as planned.   Mr. Pim appears at the window once more to whisper to Olivia that he has remembered that it was Ernest Polwittle — not Henry, and goes happily away at last with an easy conscience.

MR. WADDINGTON OF WYCK, by May Sinclair (1921). A study of an ego with all Malvolio's pompous conceit and belief in his all-conquering eye. Horatio Bysshe Waddington is able to keep the illusion of his noble character and mental and spiritual superiority through the pity and kindness of his charming wife, Fanny, because she thinks it is partly her fault, that he might have been different if she had ever really loved him. We see him chiefly through the eyes of Barbara, his young secretary, and Ralph Bevan, Fanny's cousin, his former secretary, with whom Barbara checks up her impressions. To all of them as to the reader the sight of his solemn satisfaction with himself is a continuously entertaining spectacle. He starts a branch of the National League of Liberty at Wyck in order to unite England against Bolshevism that she may continue to be a free country, and manœuvres to have himself elected president, to the delight of Sir John Corbett, who sees through his pretence of indifference. At the first meeting he makes a speech which is a masterpiece of patriotic bunk. His young son, Horry, who has his mother's sense of humor, comes home from school on purpose not to miss seeing the pater "going it." Ralph had been discharged for trying to write Horatio's book, "Ramblings Through the Cotswolds," for him. In this "projection of his ego" instead of rambling around the country Mr. Waddington is really rambling round and round himself, and the narrative is a jungle of darkness and confusion due to his treatment of the map of Gloucestershire entirely with reference to Wyck-on-the-Hill to which naturally all roads lead. Barbara is more tactful than Ralph, and learns to write with a "Waddington twist" so that Mr. Waddington's chief contribution to the book comes to be photographs of the author, on the Tudor porch, in his library, on his horse, in fishing costume, etc. As he loses youth he clutches at romance and is the easy prey of a dubious war widow, Mrs. Levitt, for whose sake he turns an old servant out of his home that she may occupy it rent free. Barbara, acting as secretary, cleverly saves him from blackmail after he has made himself ridiculous in a declaration of love. Unfortunately, his fatuity mistakes Barbara's kindness for love for himself. He dons a canary yellow waistcoat, and proposes to take her to Italy or the Riviera until he can get a divorce. Even after she tells him of her engagement to Ralph, he thinks he has driven her to take this step, because of jealousy of Mrs. Levitt, and loyalty to Fanny. "It was Barbara's virtue, not Barbara, that had repulsed him. This was the only credible explanation of her behaviour, the only one he could bear to live with." Fanny confesses to Barbara that she had known all the time that he was "head over ears in love," and was glad in the hope that "he could have one real feeling . . . care for something or somebody that wasn't himself." She had thought it would cure him of trying to be young. Horatio goes to stay with his mother "to be made young again." To her he never was a day older than twenty-five.

MRS. DALLOWAY, by Virginia Woolf (1925). The story deals with the events of a single day in the life of Clarissa Dalloway, but the present is revealed and enhanced by the past in a record of the thoughts and memories passing through her mind. The other characters shown in their relation to her are her amiable, commonplace husband, Richard, a member of Parliament, who has missed being a cabinet minister, Peter Walsh, her lover of thirty years ago, just returned from India, her daughter, Elizabeth, her daughter's embittered friend and tutor, awkward, unattractive Miss Kilman, making her last tense effort to snatch Clarissa's lovely daughter for herself from her worldly mother's influence, Sally, Lady Rosseter, the intimate friend of her girlhood and Peter's friend and confidant of that long past time when Clarissa had chosen the successful Richard instead of the lovable Peter, Lady Bruton, who cannot write a letter to the "Times," with whom Richard and the priggish Hugh have lunch. The day the author has chosen, Clarissa, "the perfect hostess," is giving to preparations for a party in the evening. She goes out to buy some flowers. Peter comes to call on her in the morning, and attends her party in the evening, and in the interval we have an analysis of his recollections and feelings, and his love for Clarissa. The tragic story of the shell-shocked soldier, Septimus Warren Smith, and his young Italian wife, Lucrezia, is interpolated. Peter sees the couple sitting in the Park and thinks they are having a lover's quarrel. Sir William Bradshaw, the distinguished specialist, is late for Clarissa's party, because of the suicide of Septimus. Clarissa reflects on the tragedy of this life thrown away and talked about at her party as somehow "her disaster — her disgrace." "She had schemed; she had pilfered. She was never wholly admirable. She had wanted success . . . and once she had walked on the terrace at Bourton" with Peter. The party is a success because of the attendance of a prime minister, and the day comes to an end as the guests depart and Peter waits for a last word with Clarissa. "'What is this terror? what is this ecstasy' he thought to himself. 'What is it that fills me with extraordinary excitement? It is Clarissa,' he said. For there she was."

MODERN DEMOCRACIES, by James Bryce (2 vols., 1921). In these surveys of the countries which Lord Bryce considers in his analysis of Democracies, the reader is taken on a voyage of discovery among the materials most easily available; and the aim of the book, as set forth by the author, "is to present a general view of the phenomena hitherto observed in governments of a popular type, showing what are the principal forms that type has taken, the tendencies each form has developed, the progress achieved in creating institutional machinery, and, above all — for this is the ultimate test of excellence — what democracy has accomplished or failed to accomplish, as compared with other kinds of government, for the well-being of each people." Six countries, where democracy exists, are selected for treatment: two old European States, France and Switzerland; two newer States in the Western hemisphere, the American Union and Canada; and two in the Southern hemisphere, Australia and New Zealand. Descriptions of these modern democratic governments are given, the author dwelling upon those features which he considers illustrate their democratic character. Other chapters classify and compare the "phenomena which the examination of these governments reveals and set forth the main conclusions to which they point." In the author's review of certain factors which he says are generally operative, are to be found the influence of education, of religion, of the newspaper press, of tradition, of party spirit and party organization, and of public opinion as a ruling force. Lord Bryce discusses the diverse experiments among peoples of various types and under various physical and mental conditions and holds that new ideas inspire new political aspirations and find their expression in politics. The author also holds that of all modern countries the United States supplies the most abundant data for the study of popular government. Canada, whose economic and social conditions resemble those of the United States, but whose political institutions are different, presents, from Lord Bryce's viewpoint, better than perhaps any other country, the working of the English system, which can be judged in its application to the facts of a new and swiftly growing country, thoroughly democratic in its ideas and institutions. In Switzerland, the fusing power of free institutions is noted and the author observes that "diverse as are the human beings in other respects, they have been, for the purpose of politics, melted together in one crucible and run into one mould." Discussing what democracy has done for France, Lord Bryce holds that no modern country has done more, if indeed as much, to originate and develop philosophic thinking on politics, but adds that "the greater part of these stores of knowledge and wisdom are not used in political life." In recalling the situation in France of a few years ago, when foreign observers thought that the flame of national life flickered low, he cites the effect of the War which suddenly brought the French people to confront the national peril and "showed that the old spirit of France had lost nothing of its fervour." In the newest of all the democracies — Australia — the author finds the best example of the "unlimited rule of the multitude." He takes into consideration her economic influences and conditions, the executive and the civil service, local government, commonwealth parties, labor organizations, industrial disputes, and the characteristics of Australian democracy, together with its formative influences. New Zealand's steps toward democracy and its political awakening form the subject of a large part of these studies which analyze the results of its democratic government. From the light of the facts described in the survey of six democratic governments the author concludes with observations on what he calls certain "phenomena" which bear on the working of democracy everywhere, together with general reflections on the present and future of democratic government. "Democracy has become, all over Europe and to some extent even in North America, also, desired merely as a Means, not as an End, precious in itself because it was the embodiment of Liberty."

MONT-SAINT-MICHEL AND CHARTRES, by Henry Adams (1905). Originally printed for limited circulation under the title of "Travels France." "The Education of Henry Adams" (1906, 1918), which followed the "Mont-Saint-Michel and Chartres" in expository sequence, defined history as the historian's interest in "the law of reaction between force and force — between mind and nature." Adams attempted the early volume to show that the mind's reaction to force in the eleventh, twelfth, and thirteenth centuries was coherent and uniform, in the later volume, that the growth of mechanical force over a period of seven hundred years since the Middle Ages compelled a philosophy of multiplicity and a science of insoluble abstractions and theory. The unity of spiritual instinct which, to Adams, informed the various spheres of mediæval activity is analyzed in the sixteen chapters of the "Mont-Saint-Michel and Chartres" with reference to the several phases of church architecture, literature, history, and philosophy. The exposition is accomplished in order of time, so that the first chapter begins with the Norman art of the eleventh century — specifically with "Saint Michiel de la Mer Del Peril." To Adams, the archangel who loved heights stands for the church and state militant, the spirit of the Norman Conquest and the first Crusade. "Here we do not feel the Trinity at all; the Virgin but little; Christ hardly more; we feel only the archangel and the Unity of God. We have little logic here, and simple faith but we have energy." The architecture is thus a static reproduction of the general life of the eleventh century, and the "Chanson de Roland," discussed in the second chapter, a manifestation of the same life in poetry, in fact of the qualities and intensities brought forth in the architecture. The transition from the Norman style to the Gothic and the meaning of this transition is presented in the third and fourth chapters on "The Merveille of the Mount" and the cathedrals of Coutances, Bayeux, Caen, and Rouen. "What the Roman could not express flowered into the Gothic; what the masculine mind could not idealize in the warrior, it idealized in the woman; no architecture that ever grew on earth, except the Gothic, gave this effect of flinging its passion against the sky." "The difference of sex is not imaginary." "In 1058, when the triumphal columns (of Mont-Saint-

Michel) were building, and Taillefer sang to William the Bastard and Harold the Saxon, Roland still prayed his 'mea culpa' to God the Father and gave not a thought to Alda, his betrothed. In the twelfth century Saint Bernard recited 'Ave Stella Mario' in an ecstasy of miracle before the image of the Virgin, and the armies of France in battle cried 'Notre-Dame — Saint-Denis — Montjoie.'" The next five chapters (V to X) are on the Chartres cathedral — its towers and portals, roses and apses, twelfth-century glass, legendary windows and "Court of the Queen of Heaven" — and show the significance of this idealization of the feminine in relation to the Church and the full dedication of the cathedral to the Virgin. "Wherever we find her (the Virgin) at Chartres and of whatever period she is always Queen. Her expression and attitude are always calm and commanding. She never calls for sympathy by hysterical appeals to our feelings; she does not even altogether command, but rather accepts the voluntary, unquestioning, unhesitating, instinctive faith, love, and devotion of mankind." This twofold manifestation of unifying force, the superiority of the feminine in the central rôle of the Church (including the State) is further enlarged on in the remaining six chapters of the volume; in the chapter on the "Three Queens," which shows the importance of medieval woman in the State; in the chapter "Nicolette and Marion," which gives the history of the school of "courteous love"; in the chapter, "Les Miracles de Notre Dame," which tells of the complete redeeming power of the Virgin; in the chapter, "Abelard," treating the problem of unity and how it could produce diversity as expressed in the Trinity; in the chapter, "The Mystics" (Adam de Saint-Victor, and Saint Francis) and their implicit faith; and, finally, in the chapter on Saint Thomas Aquinas in which the Church is explained in terms of theology. The author concludes. "The theology turns always into art at the last and ends in aspiration. The spire justifies the church." "The architects of the twelfth and thirteenth centuries took the Church and the universe for truths, and tried to express them in a structure which should be final. Knowing by an enormous experience precisely where the strains were to come, they enlarged the scale to the utmost point of material endurance, . . . the result was an art marked by singular unity, which endured and served its purpose until man changed his attitude toward the universe. The trouble was not in the art nor in the method of the structure, but in the universe itself which presented different aspects as man moved. Granted a church, Saint Thomas's Church was the most expressive that man has made and the great Gothic cathedral its most complete expression. . . . The delight of its aspiration is flung up at the sky. The pathos of its self-distrust and anguish of doubt is buried in the earth as its last secret."

MOODY, D. L., A WORKER IN SOULS, by Gamaliel Bradford (1927). Dwight Lyman Moody was an unlettered man, who was convinced that his most important mission in life was to save souls from hell by the method of conversion. The author says that a generation ago he was "an immense, magnificent agency for bringing men to God." Henry Drummond is quoted as declaring that Moody was "the greatest man this century had produced." The chronology of his life in brief outline is that he was born in Northfield, Massachusetts, in 1837, started selling shoes in Boston in 1854, sold shoes in Chicago for a few years, and then gave up a business in which he was a success after a severe struggle with himself to devote all his time to religious work. In the church which he joined on going to Chicago he was rejected as a Sunday-school teacher. In those days he could not read the Bible without stumbling over the hard words. He discovered his gift of speaking at a Sunday-school convention. The other speakers had not appeared, and he was called on, and after that all he needed was opportunity and practice. He later snowed great talent for executive management. For training for his work he read the Bible, and said frankly that he read no book unless it would help him to understand "the Book." The author has read Moody's writings, and what others have written about him in order to discover and interpret his purpose, his methods, and his personal character. The sincerity of the man, his tremendous energy, simplicity, and determination have manifestly appealed to Mr. Bradford. His preaching was restrained, and conversational in tone, though his spirit was intense, and like Phillips Brooks he used an astonishing rapidity of utterance. In the chapter on Moody the preacher, Mr. Bradford considers his use of words, and the effect he had on audiences, and their effect on him. His great success as a speaker did not affect Mr. Moody's modesty, humility, and self-effacement. "Heaven and Hell" is a discussion of his theology, and of revival meetings in general, Mr. Moody's methods, and his belief in prayer. The supreme question with him was: "Are you a Christian?" His was a personal religion in which creeds were secondary, and though a Protestant he refused to be labelled by a sect, and even subscribed to the building of a Roman Catholic Church. In his home he was sunny and sweet, and his family adored him. The house was usually full of guests, and there are many anecdotes of his wit and kindness. He disapproved of the theatre, dancing, cards, all sports that encroached on the Lord's Day, and condemned the Sunday newspaper. There is a chapter on his association with Mr. Sankey, one on the man of business, which shows his mighty and magnificent power of making men do his bidding, which leads Mr. Bradford to speculate what he might have done in the field of politics or business with his insight into character and power of organization. "Great men bowed down to him, learned men deferred to him, rich men opened their purses freely." He was a man's man, and unlike so many leaders he would not put up with "a train of adoring women." From the time that he gave up the shoe business in Chicago he depended on voluntary contributions of his friends for money to live, and while enormous sums of money passed through his hands for his work he left no estate when he died.

Mr. Bradford makes an interesting comparison of the intellectual equipment of Moody and Lincoln, since both these men began at the bottom of the ladder, and made their way up by sheer personal power without formal education. To the Bible Lincoln added Shakespeare, and Shakespeare, says Mr. Bradford, "sums up all that was outside of Moody's world." The author also adds some autobiographical passages which state some of his own conceptions of religion and the universe.

MOON AND SIXPENCE, THE, by W. Somerset Maugham (1919). A seemingly commonplace stockbroker, Charles Strickland, suddenly deserts his wife and children, leaving them unprovided for, and goes to Paris to study art. The friend who tells the story, finds him living in poverty in an attic, brutally indifferent to news of his family, happily striving to paint the inexpressible. Of his wife, he writes, "God damn my wife. She is an excellent woman. I wish she was in hell." She would have taken him back if he had run away with another woman, but is insulted that he has left her merely because of a passion for art, and hopes that he will rot with some loathsome disease, and eventually he does. A Dutch painter, Stroeuve, recognizes his genius, and saves his life by nursing him through an illness in his own studio, against the wishes of his wife who hates and fears him. When he recovers he seduces Madame Stroeuve, now passionately in love with him, and then leaves her to poison herself when he is tired of her. He says, "Blanche Stroeuve didn't commit suicide because I left her, but because she was a foolish and unbalanced woman. . . . She was an entirely unimportant person." He drifts to Marseilles, goes as a stoker on a boat to Tahiti, and lives there in a bungalow in the woods with a native girl until he dies of leprosy. The French doctor found the walls of his room "from floor to ceiling covered with strange and elaborate compositions . . . primeval and terrible . . . beautiful and obscene." His black wife tells the doctor that he had ordered her to burn the house when he died. "He had made a world and saw that it was good. Then, in pride and contempt, he destroyed it." He never tried to sell his paintings. After his death his pictures were bought by collectors and museums at fabulous prices. It is the biography of a genius, sacrificing everything and everybody to artistic creation, preferring to seek the moon instead of the proverbial sixpence.

MOON CALF, by Floyd Dell (1920). "Felix's world was a world of dreams." The youngest child of poor parents in a small town in southern Illinois, he moons and blunders along in the hostile workaday world, living his real life "in the day-dreams which books unfolded for him," and some way learning to think, and talk and write, and escape the life of a factory worker. Rose, the imaginative daughter of an actress, is a congenial playmate for a time. The story of his adolescence and youth is the record of his enthusiasms and love affairs. He works in a candy factory in the school vacations, plays at atheism and socialism, and finds happiness writing poetry, "the solace of magic words." The teacher, who admires his poetry, introduces him, to a group of mediocre, middle-class people. He outgrows her, and the dallying lady of thirty-five with a rondeau for his villanelle, and even tires of his own indifferent verse. At the end of the book he has advanced from feeding the press machine to reporting for the newspaper, and meets Joyce, a girl who can be kissed on a roller-coaster, and yet share with him the pleasure of a Shaw play. Their trysting place is an island cabin, where they play at housekeeping, and yield to the "Life Force." He loses his job, and goes to the country home of his friend Tom to write a novel. Joyce misunderstands, and he is too self-absorbed to notice the danger signals in her letters, so loses her to a young man in her own Philistine world, whom she decides not to burden with the tale of her pre-marital intimacies. This affair sends Felix to Chicago. "The Briary Bush," a sequel, takes up his adventures there as reporter and dramatic critic, and marriage to Rose Ann. The young hero sets out to be a realist and face the hard facts of life, and instead of the difficulties he anticipates, at every turn, success, friends and opportunities crowd upon him.

MOTHER, THE, by Grazia Deledda, translated from the Italian, by Mary G. Steegmann (1923). The scene of this psychological story is a remote Sardinian hill village, and the entire action takes place within two days. The mother, Maria Maddalena, a humble servant, has made every sacrifice that her son might achieve the peasant's ambition to become a priest. She has the happiness of returning with him to their own village, "grown wild and uncivilized, without faith" for lack of a priest. The former priest had practised sorcery in his old age, and his parishioners believed he was protected by the devil in person. For ten years no priest was willing to live there because his spirit returned to haunt the presbytery. For a time all goes well, until Paul falls in love with Agnes, the lonely lady of the manor. He had "made his vows whilst still too young to understand all that he was professing and renouncing. . . . Taught that divine love was all-sufficing . . . when human love overtook him he was too inexperienced and too weak to have any chance in the struggle for victory — and he desperately trusted to the hazard of events to save him when his own self-deception and cowardice had failed — when confronted with the greater strength and moral

honesty of the woman." His mother follows him when he goes out at night and discovers the romance. The story is told chiefly in her emotional reactions on the situation. Her simple mind is filled with terror lest Paul shall break the laws of the Church,
and her heart yearns over the unhappiness of her son. In a dream the old priest
comes to see her, and tells her that she had better have brought up her son to follow
his father's trade, that her ambition to come back as mistress where she has lived
as servant has brought trouble upon Paul. He threatens to drive both of them out
of the parish, and advises her to let Paul follow his destiny in the world God created
with all its beauty and gave to man for his pleasure. Urged by his mother to renounce Agnes and save both their souls, Paul gives up the plan of going away with
Agnes, and writes her a note breaking off their relations. He goes up the mountain
to administer the last rites to the old hunter who has turned solitary through dread
of men, accompanied by the delightful boy sacristan, Antiochus, and the domineering
keeper with his dog. Antiochus insists on dedicating his life to the Church just at
this moment when Father Paul is most bitterly regretting his own immature vows.
The night comes and Paul goes to a last interview with Agnes who reproaches him,
and tells him that she will come to Mass the next morning and denounce him publicly.
Paul warns his mother of what Agnes plans to do, and they go to the service. Agnes
listens to the singing of the women and the old men, her own people, who look up to
her as their mistress, and cannot denounce herself with the man whom she wishes to
punish. Paul sees her advance to the altar steps and thinks the moment he has
dreaded has come, but Agnes crosses herself and turns toward the door. The congregation smiled at her and blessed her with their eyes as a "symbol of beauty and of
faith, so far removed from them and yet in the midst of them and all their misery,
like a wild rose amongst the brambles." Her gaze fell on his mother whose will
pitted against her own has won the battle for the Church she mystically seems to
represent. They discover that she is dead, and Paul knows instantly that the "shock
of that same grief, that same terror which he had been enabled to overcome" has
killed her.

MOTHER AND SON, see **THE SOUL ENCHANTED,** by Romain Rolland.

MOTHER'S RECOMPENSE, THE, by Edith Wharton (1925). Kate Clephane
had revolted against the stifling oppression of her married life, and run away with
Hylton Davies, to her, less a lover than the "agent of her release." She had not
realized that her husband would not allow her to see her baby daughter, Anne,
again until she had made many vain attempts. After two years she had left Davies,
and lived the life of the expatriates in Europe, wandering from one dingy hotel to
another. When she was thirty-nine she had met Chris Fenno, an artist ten years her
junior, and in her love for him "her real self had been born." When the book opens
Kate is forty-five, still charming, and hoping that Chris, whom she has not seen for
several years, will come back to her. There is an ironic picture of the society of the
French Riviera where the exiles have partially rehabilitated themselves by their
war work, and fill their days with engagements to kill time. Two cablegrams come
to Kate, one announcing the death of her mother-in-law, and the other from Anne
asking her to come home. Anne and her guardian, Fred Landers, an old friend of
Kate's, meet her at the pier in New York, and take her to the remembered Fifth
Avenue home. Her daughter is lovely and devoted, and Kate is happy in her affection. A more tolerant New York society accepts her as a woman who has once
"stooped to folly," but has wiped out the indiscretion by years of rectitude. Her

affair with Chris had been on the eve of the Great War, and had never been known. She now meets Chris again as the friend of her daughter, and presently Anne tells her that they are engaged to be married. He later tells Kate that he had not known that she had a daughter. She makes him promise to give up Anne and go away. Anne thinks that it is her money that has made him give her up, but finds out that her mother had been to see him, and makes her confess that she has tried to prevent the marriage. Anne's love and uncommon strength of will bring him back to her, and Kate cannot bring herself to tell her that he has been her lover. Anne must have her happiness at any cost. She tells Anne that she has decided to accept Fred Landers after the wedding, but she cannot go through with it, and the last chapter finds her back on the Riviera in a better hotel planning to fill the empty hours so that there shall be no time for introspection and remembrance.

MY ANTONIA, by Willa S. Cather (1918). This story of pioneer life in Nebraska purports to be the memories of a successful lawyer, Jim of the book, about his boyhood friend, the Bohemian immigrant girl, Antonia. Her father, a musician and a dreamer, has brought his family to America at the insistence of her vulgar, ambitious mother. Unequal to the struggle against homesickness and want he commits suicide. Antonia has her father's sensitive fineness, but also strength of body and gay, courageous spirit to carry her through hardship and cruel circumstance. The first years of her girlhood she works as a farmhand exploited by her brother. Then the American friends arrange that she shall work as hired girl in the Harling family in the town. The dances are the undoing of Antonia. The kind Harlings want her to stay at home in the evenings and she leaves their protection. She escapes the schemes of her next employer for her ruin with Jim's help. Larry Donovan, passenger conductor, "a kind of professional ladies' man," deceives her with a promise of marriage, and when she joins him in another city fools and betrays her. As soon as her money is gone he deserts her, and she returns to hard labor on the farm and the disgrace of a fatherless child. After twenty years the writer visits Antonia, "battered but not diminished," married to a commonplace farmer of her own race, and mother of a large family of healthy, happy children. There are also the stories of the other immigrant girls, Antonia's friends, Lina Lingard, who becomes a fashionable dressmaker, and Tiny Soderball, the successful business woman.

MY GARDEN OF MEMORY, an autobiography, by Kate Douglas Wiggin (1923). The author tells not the story of her life but stories about her life. It begins with "when I was a little girl" which is "a chronicle of a child's life in a Maine village more than fifty years ago." For Kate and her sister Nora there were simple household tasks and simple pleasures, and the joys of books. On a railway train Kate makes the acquaintance of Charles Dickens on a lecture tour of the United States. She explains to him that her mother and cousin had gone to his reading the night before but that she could not go as three from the same family would have been too expensive. The great author is amazed that such a child should have read all his books and her favorite and his, "David Copperfield," six times. "Of course," Kate conscientiously explained, "I do skip some of the very dull parts once in a while. . . ." The little girl felt that she had never known anyone so well and intimately and so easy to talk to. The family move to California for the benefit of her stepfather's health. Life in Santa Barbara is gay with dancing and horseback riding for the girls, and Kate's charm of personality and genius for friendship bring her happy times. The singer, Annie Louise Cary, invites her to visit her in San Francisco, and gives

her a view of the world behind the footlights that is the beginning of an interest in
amateur theatricals.   Hard times followed the death of her stepfather, due to unfortunate land speculations.   While they "were eating up the horses and carriages
and harnesses" Kate sent her first story to the "St. Nicholas Magazine" in New York
and was amazed to receive a check of one hundred and fifty dollars for the manuscript.   The eldest of the family, she feels that she must find some way to earn a living.   A friend, Mrs. Caroline Severance, invites Kate to spend a year with her in
Los Angeles to take the kindergarten course with Miss Marwedel, and the family
manage to raise the money for her tuition.   Felix Adler forms a Free Kindergarten
Association in San Francisco and Kate is called to organize its first school in the slums
in Silver Street.   She tells the story of this successful undertaking and the three
years of "happy, useful, hopeful days" until her marriage with Samuel Bradley
Wiggin, a childhood friend, interrupts her work, though after her marriage she continues to lecture in the Training School.   Her first books, "The Birds' Christmas
Carol" and "The Story of Patsy," were written to get funds for the benefit of the
Silver Street Free Kindergartens.   The books, she says, brought her friends in many
places.   She is cordially received in England, where she lectures and gives readings.
Her husband died in 1889 in New York.   On the voyage to England in the summer of
1894 she meets George C. Riggs and they are married the next spring.   A chapter on
the wedding journey tells of coöperative housekeeping on an island near Venice
with Mr. and Mrs. Laurence Hutton, Mr. and Mrs. Charles Dudley Warner, and
Mrs. Clement Waters.   They rent a house near Washington Square, in New York,
and give their first dinner for Sir Henry Irving and Ellen Terry, the other guests
including Mark Twain, Clyde Fitch, Mr. W. D. Howells, Mrs. Craigie (John Oliver
Hobbes).   Her husband's business interest in Great Britain took them abroad for a
few months every year, and England seemed a second home.   In 1900 she was the
guest of Alexandra College, Dublin, during Queen Victoria's visit.   In 1906 she
spent a week at the Vice-Regal Lodge, the guest of the Lord Lieutenant of Ireland
and his wife, the Earl and Countess of Aberdeen.   She is presented at Holyrood
Palace and in the haste of departure forgets to exchange her comfortable black
"reform model" bedroom slippers in which she had been practicing her curtsy for
her white satin shoes, and has to give her entire attention to concealing her feet.
The list of her friends is a catalogue of the most gifted and interesting men and women
of her time.   Mrs. Riggs writes of her books and their backgrounds, of translations
and collaborations, and her writing habits.   The rest of the story is her life in Maine
at her house "Quillcote" in her childhood home with her neighbors to whom she is
less the author than the daughter, sister, and wife, and active member of the Dorcas
Society.   A chapter on "The Barn That Came to Life" as a sort of "Hall of Happy
Hours" at Quillcote for the village, opened with a neighborhood dance at which
three ladies between seventy and eighty joined in the old-fashioned reels and polkas.
The dramatization of "Rebecca of Sunnybrook Farm" takes Mrs. Riggs to New York
and London and many friends help to celebrate her triumph as a playwright.   She
expresses her conviction that the reason autobiographies are written and this one
came to be is that "the song is never ended."

MY HEART AND MY FLESH, by Elizabeth M. Roberts (1927).   Theodosia Bell
was the granddaughter of Anthony Bell, who came of a proud old Kentucky family
and was himself a gallant figure.   Theodosia's girlhood was passed happily under
his care after the death of her mother.   She shared his ambition for her success as a
violinist.   Although two of her lovers attracted her, she cared more for her music.

Then suddenly her girlhood came to an end with old Anthony's last illness. Searching one day among his papers she discovered what her father had been and the secret sorrow of her mother's life. When she spoke of this to the old man, he only rebuked her angrily, "Enough virtue in a Bell, in a Montford, to carry along a little excess weight." But the excess weight that this knowledge brought was not so easily carried by a young girl. Both lovers, to whose claims her awakening maturity was beginning to respond, were lost; one through death, the other through the aggressive tactics of another girl. Then came disillusion in regard to her possibilities as a musician. She had the temperament, but not the hand of a great violinist, said her teacher. Losing wealth and established position she searches life consumed with a desire to understand these mulatto half-sisters and brother whom her father's incontinence had caused to touch her own life. With the fascinated repugnance of the girl, the reader is dragged through the lower depths of Kentucky small town life. A long illness separates her from the lurid torture of these experiences, only to bring her to livid anguish of another sort. Worn thin by illness, she goes to an old aunt for recovery. The old woman, who has forgotten all but the motions of life, lives in the country surrounded by her old hounds. Here the girl hears voices, almost loses her reason and all desire for life, until the desperate tie is broken and she finds herself free of her nightmare existence. In the Spring River Valley community she finds work, a renewal of life and the coming of satisfying love. Perhaps the greatest single episode in the book is that of Theodosia's last visit to the cabin of Americy and Lethe, her half-sisters. In these mulatto scenes Miss Roberts rivals Sherwood Anderson in "Dark Laughter," particularly in the loathsome power of that last scene when Theodosia, her early disappointments in love aggravated by morbid mood, foregoes her aversion and joins Lethe in a threnody of hate. Theodosia finds her fulfilment after experience has developed her perception of fundamental values, and her knowledge of her own limitations. She turns to the new life as school teacher in the quiet fertile farming section of Spring River Valley, with health and sanity regained. She learns from Caleb Burns, master of beautiful blooded stock, how simple and serene and natural love may be.

MY LIFE AS AN EXPLORER, by Sven Hedin. Translated by Alfrild Huebsch (1925). The first part of his book shows him a boy of fifteen standing on the quay at Stockholm watching Nordenskjöld's ship the "Vega" steam into the harbor after his hazardous completion of the Northeast passage. The shouts of the multitude assembled to greet the Arctic explorer roused in him a keen desire "to return home that way." A journey to Baku on the Caspian Sea in his twentieth year to tutor the son of a Swedish engineer turned his interest to Asia. When his work was finished he spent the money he had earned on a journey through Persia and Mesopotamia to Bagdad and thence "through the desert, through unsafe Kurdistan and western Persia to Teheran." A few years later he was sent to Persia by the King of Sweden to act as interpreter for a special mission to the Shah. At twenty he had learned the Tatar and the Persian languages, and later he lectured and wrote in German, English and Russian. Again after his work was done he went on an adventurous trip through Caucasia, Mesopotamia, Persia, Russian Turkestan and Bokhara, into Chinese Turkestan. After two years' study of Asiatic geography he set out again on a journey that lasted three and a half years and covered "a distance greater than from pole to pole." Robbers set upon him. Sand-storms threatened to wipe out the caravans with which he travelled. He found himself penniless in strange lands. But always good fortune attended him; and he was a resourceful man of great

physical endurance.   On the desert all of his camels and half of his men died of thirst
as they used up their supply of water, and he and two others were saved by mere
chance.   One night he found a small pool of water in the bed of a dried up stream
just in time to save his life.   With recovered strength he went back for the other men.
His fourth journey into the heart of Asia was in 1899 with the backing of King Oscar
and material help from the Czar of Russia.   Disguised as a pilgrim he attempted to
reach the holy city of Lhasa.   Though he succeeded in traversing parts of Tibet
never before reached by a white man he was prevented from getting to the forbidden
city.   His final Asiatic expedition took him again to unexplored Tibet over the mountains from India.   His trail was often a "death-strewn retreat" through the high
passes.   Animals and men succumbed to the unaccustomed altitude, the battle with
the blizzards, and the bitter cold.   The food supply gave out.   The explorer pressed
on against every obstacle pitting his perseverance and strength against imminent
death.   Political opposition from England, China, and Russia hindered his progress.
He discovered the source of the Indus, and explored "inaccessible" regions disguised
as a shepherd until he was taken captive by the Tibetans.   Hedin finally made his
way out through India.   He and his men crossed the boundary from Tibet to India
on a cable stretched over a deep gorge.   Men, horses, dogs, boxes were all pulled
over on a wooden yoke fitted over the cable.   From Simla Hedin went to Japan
where began the series of "splendid receptions by Academies, Geographical Societies,
Kings and Emperors" that had been the dream of his boyhood.   He describes
pomps and customs of a vanished past such as the court ceremonies of the Shah's
palace.

MY MOTHER AND I, by E. G. Stern, with a foreword by President Roosevelt
(1917).   E. G. Stern begins by telling how a visit from her mother opened the door
of the past and led her to write this book.   She begins with a description of the
"kitchen" in their Ghetto home in a sorry district in a middlewest town.   When
the author was two years old she came with her mother and baby sistsr, Fanny,
from their Russian Polish cottage to join her young rabbi father.   The "kitchen"
was a basement room, and their only one, leading up to an alley and then up into a
courtyard, where all the neighbors' children played until tired, scolding mothers,
who thought playing a sin, drove them out.   Her mother only pretended to scold,
to the horror of the other mothers.   In this "kitchen" was a gas stove, a table, a
huge bookcase, holding the rabbi's many Hebrew books, two chairs, a trunk covered
with steerage labels, a cot, a box, a big kitchen clock with the Statue of Liberty
painted on it and her father's stovepipe hat, used to hold the onions.   She remembers
her father best with his haggard, bearded face bent over a book and his bearded
friends coming to talk with him and to listen reverently to his reading of the Talmud.
Her mother is pictured in her memory as small and plump and redcheeked, always
bent either over the stove or rocking the cradle with the baby of the year, who always
died, and sewing and sewing aprons to be sold.   She told the children stories of the
woods and fields of her old home and never let them see her grief.   She shared their
scanty food with others who needed it and taught her children never to repeat what
went on in their home.   When E. G. Stern was old enough she helped her mother
sew, rocked the babies and played games with the boys on the street.   Besides this
she loved to write Yiddish letters for the illiterate neighbor women, and even the
men, to their European relatives and in this way she learned much of their lives.
At home she was brought up in the Hebrew traditions and at school found much to
contradict them, even her arithmetic problems, which, like all her lessons she shared

with her mother, had no relation to their Ghetto life. She went also to a Hebrew school. At grammar school the national holidays were celebrated without conveying anything to the little immigrant. Her first comprehension of America and patriotism came from the son of her Hebrew teacher who gave her a little metal American flag when he enlisted in the army? When the family moved to a new home of three rooms the child received her first knowledge of the fact that all the world of America was not a dirty Ghetto. An old lady living across the way in a nice, little house told how the streets now so dingy had once been lined with trees. At this time she found "Little Women" in the garret of an old ragshop and from this made her first picture of an American home and the life of its children. Later her teacher gave her library books and she soon lived in a world far from the noisy, dirty Ghetto. Her mother helped her to buy more books and listened eagerly as her daughter translated them for her into Yiddish. Her mother also managed to pay for piano lessons for her. Her father had had to take to manual labor, though he was delicate, in order to support his family and they now bought a house and rented one floor. They even had a bathtub to which all the neighbors came with their soap and towels on Fridays and often were given half the Sabbath chicken and stuffed fish. At school she was continually learning new ways and her mother would try anything she asked if it did not "irritate father." But while her mother's uncomprehending sympathy followed her daughter, the father's did not, and only the mother's intervention permitted E. G. Stern to go to High School. There she made American friends and became accustomed to the life of American homes. While her sixteen-year-old neighbors were marrying and settling to hard lives she won a scholarship and was allowed to go to college. She worked her way through and the life was a revelation and joy to her. Only at night, when she returned to town, did she think of the Ghetto. Her mother now had a negro woman to help her and the mother and daughter saw little of each other and were fast growing apart. At last she loathed her home and its surroundings and with her small savings went to New York. There she studied and worked and lived in an American home. But her money gave out and she wrote to her mother for help. She says that she will never forget the answer and her mother's joy at being close to her daughter again through helping her. Later she went home to receive her American lover in her old surroundings. Then she and her mother drew closer again as she was shown the lace and linens which the mother had spent years in preparing for her daughter's trousseau. After this she married and went away. Until the Stern's son was born she was out of touch with her mother. But the thought of the first grandchild brought her mother to visit. The sight of the small boy in his white nursery, fed and handled only at regular intervals, so unlike the Ghetto babies, made clear the unbridgeable distance between their lives. She had helped to make her daughter an American, but she could not understand the new standards which separated them.

MYSTERIOUS STRANGER, THE, by Mark Twain (1916). This posthumous work presents an aspect of Mark Twain's nature which in life he rarely revealed — his pessimism, more explicitly, his resignation to the absurdities of the human race and the illogicality of the universe. With this resignation goes laughter, not the usual "sense of humor" before stupid incongruity which deceived humanity deploys as its virtue, but laughter which destroys injustice. In one instance, the story tells of the dog forgiving the man who had wronged him, so that God would maybe accept the man's absolution. The story is told by Theodore Fischer of the mediæval village of Eseldorf, Austria. To Theodore and to his friends, Nikolaus and Seppi, appears the mysterious stranger, the angel Satan, dream of their imaginative excitement. He stays with them, and each time that he alters the fated course of a human life the mystery of the universe is revealed. At first he merely complies with the wish of the three boys and fills their pockets with sweets. Then he makes birds out of clay and sets them free, so that they fly away singing; and, afterward, he creates a miniature castle with hundreds of wee folk whom he destroys almost as soon as he creates. The parable implicit in his deeds becomes clear only when he pursues the range of his activities among the villagers. Father Peter has been accused of stealing by the Astrologer and Father Adolf. To save the innocent, Satan confounds the false accusers and sets the innocent crazy, since earthly happiness seems possible to him only when accompanied by insanity. The angel does further good: Nikolau's first act on earth so determined the chain of all his other acts that he was destined to live a long life as an invalid; the angel drowns him, as an act of kindness. "He had such strange notions of kindness," complains Theodore. Yet Satan explained to him that Nikolaus had a billion possible careers and that none of them was worth living. The mysterious stranger liked Theodore and his friends, but then he could also destroy them without compassion. For "he always spoke of men in the same old indifferent way. He didn't mean to hurt us, you could see that; just as we don't mean to insult a brick when we disparage it; a brick's emotions are nothing to us; it never occurs to us to think whether it has any or not." For to Satan it was evident that man had the Moral Sense but that God and his angels were indifferent. Satan knew no space, nor time, nor good nor evil — all human distinctions and human vanities. With these distinctions men invented wars, and destroyed each other; burned innocent people at the stake and invented hell; raised a few over many and kept these many in chains. Such was the history of human progress, of a race afraid and led by usurping minorities. After many months Satan came less frequently, and finally appeared to make his farewell. For by this time Theodore was beginning to guess what the angel was to verify. Satan would dissolve into the nothing out of which Theodore had made him. For nothing existed save empty space, and Theodore or merely the thought of Theodore. All the illogicalities of existence, a god who tortured yet commanded worship, an angel who was kind yet helped people only by killing them or turning them insane, bore the stamp of a dream which had no future life or heaven — "The silly creation of an imagination that is not conscious of its freaks."

NAPOLEON, by Emil Ludwig (1926). A study of the character and genius of Napoleon by a German writer, which, however, leaves out no incident of importance, though the biographer considers the course of battles and the contemporary position of European states irrelevant, and relegates dates to a prefatory outline. In his analysis Herr Ludwig takes in turn the three forces which he believes drove Napoleon forward — self-confidence, energy and imagination — and illustrates his points with hundreds of examples. He considers his dominant trait to be inordinate egotism. Madame de Staël says of Napoleon that he was unique; he neither hated nor loved. "For him no one exists but himself," she said. At school in France he was a devoted Corsican and hated his adopted country. Later self-interest turned him against Corsica and his father's old friend, the patriotic Paoli. After a year in the Paris Cadet's School he is a sublieutenant, and his examiners say of him that he is "extremely egotistical," has "much self-love, and overweening ambition." The author recalls that one of the believers in the young man's star called him "a mathematician or a visionary." His "constant deliberation builds up something within him which he names 'the spirit of things' . . . the thinking in numbers, to which he ascribes part of his success and for which he has to thank his mathematical training. There is nothing too small for this brain; for the sum total of millions of details is a plan whose scope is world embracing." From boyhood "his self-esteem is nourished on historical parallels." He compares himself to Caesar and Charlemagne. It was the Revolution and its doctrine of equality that gave him his opportunity to rise to a leading position. The biography tells of his marriage with Josephine and the triumphant campaign in Italy which made him the idol of Paris, the Egyptian expedition, and his struggle for supremacy with the directors and the coup d'état of the Eighteenth Brumaire. Napoleon had himself elected First Consul in 1799, his term of office extended for life in 1802, and took the Roman imperial title of emperor that his dictatorial nature craved in 1804. For ten years to come he showers honors, wealth, crowns and territories on his brothers and sisters, who repay him with ingratitude, quarrelling about titles and precedences. Instead of allowing the Pope to crown him Napoleon placed the golden circlet of laurel leaves on his own head, thus reducing to a mockery the legitimate formalities of coronation that he seemed to copy. But the crown inoculates him with the virus of divine right and legitimacy in course of time, and he divorces Josephine to marry Marie Louise in order to have an heir. On the field of battle the disastrous Russian campaign is followed by Dresden, his last great victory, and Leipzig, his first great defeat, and in a few weeks Napoleon is beaten by the Allies, exiled to Elba, and deserted by Marie Louise. His self-esteem made it impossible for him to see his defeat except as a decree of fate, the working of destiny. The dream of peace in Europe led Napoleon to incessant warfare, exhaustion and downfall. While he would have been glad enough to lay down the sword in victory he could not drop it in defeat. The author discovers in Napoleon a pan-Europa pioneer, quoting him as saying that "Europe would soon have become one nation, and anyone who travelled in it would always have been in a common fatherland. . . . Sooner or later, this union will be brought about by the forces of events . . . after the fall and disappearance of my system it seems to me that the only way in which an equilibrium can be achieved in Europe is through a league of nations." Napoleon was a foreigner always and therefore never a nationalist. The Bourbons were unpopular and Napoleon returned to France for the Hundred Days which were the happiest of his life. The author draws a harrowing picture of the exile at Saint Helena, the bickerings of his companions in exile, and the harshness of the governor. In the epilogue Herr Ludwig points out that Napoleon's renown will rest on his administrative acts when interest in his battles has faded. There are interesting accounts of his meetings with Goethe and Müller. Talleyrand is portrayed as a self-seeking monster ever betraying his chief.

NATIONALISM, ESSAYS ON, by Carlton J. H. Hayes (1926). Professor Hayes makes a distinction between nationalism, the historic development of the modern national state, and nationalism as a belief, an "emotional fusion and exaggeration . . . of nationality and patriotism" which has become a religious worship of the state, "a reaction against historic Christianity," and a return to an earlier idea of a tribal god and a chosen people. He reviews recent world history to trace the growth of national consciousness in Europe in the "literary, political, economic, and religious differentiations in the sixteenth and seventeenth centuries," and its transformation "into nationalism at the close of the eighteenth and opening of the nineteenth century by the French Revolution, the Industrial Revolution, and the vogue of romanticism." The book deals chiefly with the evil aspects of nationalism masquerading as patriotism and fostering intolerance, militarism, and war, which, unless abated or modified, bids fair ultimately to destroy all civilization.   This new religion of the *patrie* has its ritual of the flag instead of the cross, which is the object of ceremonies devised for "saluting" the flag, for "dipping" the flag, for "lowering" and for "hoisting" the flag.   "Men bare their heads when the flag passes by," and children in the schools pledge allegiance.   It imperils freedom of thought by employing the educational machinery to inculcate "a spirit of exclusiveness and narrowness which thrives on, and in turn nurses, a smugness that is laughable, an ignorance that is dangerous, and an uncritical pride that can be reduced, if at all, only by a beating."   "My country, right or wrong, my country" declaims the faithful nationalist. . . . ." Contemporary nationalism "places a premium on uniformity," and represses criticism.   "Individual differences, class differences, religious differences, are alike deemed unfortunate; and the individual of genius is suspect, especially if his genius displays itself in criticism of national uniformity."   Masquerading as irredentism it has struggled to enlarge the area of national country by enforcing obsolete historic claims or aspirations, regardless of the wishes or interests of the population.   The remedy the author believes is to be found in a combination of nationalism with internationalism.   The Industrial Revolution, recognized as an important factor in the development of nationalism, has been laying the foundations of world citizenship. "Under existing economic conditions, no nationality can be entirely self-sufficing, no national state can be really sovereign and independent of the rest of the world." "In this industrial age it is impossible . . . to restrict either experimental science or applied science to any particular nationality."   "The first successful steamboat was invented by an American of Irish stock, the first telephone by an American of Scottish stock, and the first successful airplane by Americans of English stock, but airplanes, telephones, and steamboats are now operated in all civilised countries."   For our knowledge of germs we are indebted to a French scientist, and for our enjoyment of the radio we are under obligations to an Italian.   The author concludes with the statement that "nationalism when it becomes synonymous with the purest patriotism, will prove a unique blessing to humanity and the world."

NED MᶜCOBB'S DAUGHTER, a comedy, by Sidney Howard (1926)   The first act takes place in a restaurant which is a cheaply constructed additional room to an old Maine farmhouse.   Carrie, Captain Ned McCobb's daughter, is expecting her father and her husband, George Callahan, to come off the ferry for dinner.   Two neighbors, prohibition agents, are eating at a table.   Carrie is bargaining with the carpenter about the building of a kitchen for her "spa."   While Carrie is in the house with her two children, sick with the measles, a young man, who is evidently from East Side New York, comes in asking for George Callahan.   The Federal agents think that he must be the man they are looking for, and leave to arrange to have someone come to town to identify him.   When Carrie returns, the stranger introduces himself as George's brother, Babe.   She tells him that George is working on the ferry with her father, and that she has never told the Captain that George had been in prison for a year for driving the taxi in a hold-up.   While the family are at dinner Carrie sees her brother Ben, the Federal agent, and Lawyer Grove coming into the yard, and it is noticeable that George looks sick at the news.   They have come with a warrant of arrest for George who has been holding back fares on the ferry.   The Company will not prosecute if George can pay back the sum of two thousand dollars by noon the next day.   Alone with the family, George angers the Captain by telling him that the honest McCobbs will have to go with him as accessories if he goes to jail, because they have had the use of the expensive car he bought with the money. Carrie blames herself for concealing George's bad record and lack of character from her father. Just as Captain McCobb is telling Carrie that he had never told her that he had given George a thousand dollars to get him out of a scrape, the old man has a stroke resulting in his death? In the next act Jenny, the young mill girl who helps Carrie in the restaurant, is sitting in the parlor as far from the coffin as possible, while Carrie is doing some work outside. George is asking her to run away with him, and threatens to tell Carrie of their relations in the past if she refuses. Lawyer Grove calls to see Carrie, and she asks him to give her more time to get the money, as she will have to mortgage the farm. She had intended to get the money for her new kitchen with a mortgage, but will have to give up that plan now, especially as Nat Glidden, the carpenter, cannot begin the work without money. The lawyer tells her what her father was beginning to say when he died, that the house is mortgaged already. She asks George what he did with the thousand, and he swears on the Bible that it was for doctor's bills for his mother's last illness. Babe finds out privately from George that he had used the money to send Jenny to a doctor in Boston when she was going to have a child. He calls Carrie and tells them both that he is in the bootlegging business, and will give Carrie the two thousand if he can use the farm for his operations. She is obliged to consent as there is no other way to save George from prison. The Federal agents appear in the yard, and George is ready to betray his brother now that they have the two thousand, but Carrie will not let him do such a mean trick, and sends them off. The third act opens the next morning early. George pries open the drawer of the desk and would have escaped with the two thousand if Jenny had not called Carrie to prevent the theft. Babe tells Carrie what he knows about George and Jenny, which is the last straw for Carrie. She tells them both to get out of the house. She then learns that she is practically going to run a bootlegger's boarding house, that Babe will leave his pal, Eustace, and his girl, on the farm while he is in the East, and there will be seventy men running the trucks for her to take care of. She speaks of the necessity of sending her children away, and he brutally insists that he will not allow it, as they will be good "blinds" riding the hay wagons on top of the liquor. The threat to misuse her children rouses this shrewd Yankee woman to use her wits to free herself and them. She gets the money for her kitchen extension from him, and gives him a note for the sum at six per cent, and then tells him to get out, that the Federal agents are in the restaurant within call, and Babe confesses that he is beaten, and hurries out the front door. The Federal agents come in at her summons, and turn out to be only Nat Glidden and her brother, Ben, playing the part, and Carrie and her children are saved.

NEW DECALOGUE OF SCIENCE, THE, by Albert Edward Wiggam (1922). This author holds that Science has supplied man with a true technique of righteousness, and that the time has arrived for a "new Decalogue, a new Sermon on the Mount, a new Golden Rule." These new codes of conduct, as he unfolds them, have none of the absolutism of the old, yet they are filled with warnings of wrath, both present and to come, for the biologically ungodly, as well as with alluring promises for them who do His scientific will. The first warning which biology gives is that the advanced races of mankind are going backward; that the civilized races of the world are, biologically, plunging downward. The argument deals with the great physiological diseases of man's body, which are on the increase, and the functional neuroses, the diseases that affect man's mind and behavior, which are probably all increasing. The findings of various organizations of research, and the opinions of leaders in this field, are cited in the examples given of deficiency, where intelligence and physique are rated. Heredity and not environment is emphasized as the chief maker of men, and the social and political import of this reasoning is that nearly all the happiness and nearly all the misery of the world are due, not to environment, but to heredity; "that the differences among men are, in the main, due to the differences in the germ cells from which they are born; that social classes, therefore, which you seek to abolish by law, are ordained by nature; that is, in the large statistical run of things, not the slums which make slum people, but slum people who make the slums." The author considers that the warning of biology proves that charity and philanthropy have failed to improve the human breed unless they have at the same time improved the quality of life. Medicine, hygiene and sanitation have weakened the human race unless they have upbuilt by selection the health, energy and sanity that are already present in the stream of human protoplasm. Morals, education, art and religion are not directly improving the inborn capacities. In trying to settle what the author calls the vast moral dilemmas of a new world, incomplete or else discredited methods of the old have been used. Three great phases or ideas have run through all history — the idea of one God; the extension of this unified conception of God. From these conceptions developed a great code of morals. Of the modern period of life, it is held that the human mind has gone through vast developments, as the result of the revelation of natural law. One of these consequences is classified as a new scripture — the Decalogue of Industry. The author holds that when completed it will give us an industrial order made for men, instead of using men to promote an industrial order, and that it will transform industry from a mere scheme of production into a scheme of life. Science must usher in a new ethics, a new way in which human beings will regard one another and their duties toward one another, a new sense of what God and life and birth and death really mean, to every man, woman and child. "For if science combined with that spirit of Christ which does run through all religions and all spiritual aspiration cannot save the world nothing else can." Under the control of such agencies as the author views from their positive side, eugenics is discussed as the first commandment of science. "It is not a mere program, — it is a change in the perspective of civilization, character and life. It is a new kind of humanism." From the author's viewpoint, it is simply conscious, intelligent organic evolution, which furnishes the final program for the completed Christianization of mankind. The duty of scientific research — not to become rich, but to become righteous — is shown in its effect upon the universe, as setting evolution going forward again. From the program outlined, the author believes that the psychologists and biologists can contribute and out of this *entente cordiale* between theory and practice, between experiment and management there will emerge a new and sound philosophy, not doctrinaire but dynamic, not about hypothetical men, but actual man. The duty of preferential reproduction of the human herd is measured in the light of science and statistics; slow race-improvement through the lowly-born and the increase of the well-born. Continuing his comments upon life and the state, the author reasons that if our social orders are to endure, the ethics of the microscope and the chemist's tube, the religion of the mathematician's honesty and rigidity of logical process; the philosophy of intelligently thought-out possibilities of this existent world may be used as "methods for making over and improving it."

NEW VIEWPOINTS IN AMERICAN HISTORY, by Arthur Meier Schlesinger (1922). This volume discusses in its opening chapters the profound influence which immigration has exerted on the development of American institutions, political ideals, and industrial life, and the deep impression made by various racial strains upon the early history of the country. The author holds that immigration entered a new phase in the years following the Civil War, as prior to that time the immigrants had been of racial strains very closely related to the original settlers who were responsible for the Revolution. He places the responsibility for the accelerated growth of political and industrial radicalism upon the immigrants, and traces the beginnings of organizations and parties formed by various groups. Discussing the heterogeneous ingredients of the "American," he says, "that American manners and culture owe much to this admixture there can be little doubt though such influences are pervasive and intangible and their value not easy to assess. Of the older racial strains, the irrepressible good humor and executive qualities of the Irish, the solidity and thoroughness of the Germans, the tenacity and highmindedness of the Scotch-Irish, the law-abiding qualities of the English, and the sobriety and industry of the Scandinavian have undoubtedly made important contribution to our national character." The geographic factors are also considered in the light of crumbling barriers of distance, which have brought about new conditions in the former isolated position of the United States, with the result that America, in the opinion of the author, faces new international duties and responsibilities. The economic influences, "arising from the possession of property, or from the desire for such possession, or from the use of such property as a lever of political or social power," are treated with a view of showing transition and change through successive periods. The author considers that the story of the struggle of the aristocracy against democracy is a complex one, which touched the life of the past generations; the decline of aristocracy in America is shown and the moral drawn from the democratic ideal in regard to its steady advance over all forms and traditions of aristocracy. The rôle played by women in American history is consistently treated and their status, politically and economically, are given tribute in strengthening the author's claim that whatever affects the position of women in America will affect the entire people of which they are so intimately a part. The American Revolution and the economic aspects of the movement for the Constitution, the significance of Jacksonian Democracy, and the Doctrine of States' Rights are studied in relation to "time and circumstance." The author maintains that the history of the white man in America, painted upon a smaller canvas than that of European history, which "reaches back into the dim mists of antiquity," makes the total period of time embraced comparatively short; therefore, in his approach to the modern era he views it independently of the corresponding period in Europe in his examination of what he considers were the foundations of modern America — beginning with the revolution in transportation and agricultural systems, and on through the transformation of the industrial system. America's foreign relations and certain aspects, classed as material and political development, the strides made by science and other interpretations of what the author calls the "Modern scene" are treated of as new impulses and in the general summary of research. The rival political parties are also considered with studies of their leading representatives and declarations of party belief.

NEW WORLD, THE, problems in political geography, by Isaiah Bowman (1921, Revised edition, 1926). The author is Director of the American Geographical Society of New York, and was chief territorial expert of the American Commission to Negotiate Peace at the Paris Peace Conference in 1919. This book, with two hundred and thirty-eight maps, and sixty-five photographs, is discussion and statement of the changes made by the World War in boundaries, spheres of influence, mandates, protectorates, and colonial possessions. Several of the maps have been engraved several times to show different decisions of the Conference and Treaties. There are descriptions of individual countries and peoples, their problems, resources, commerce, shipping, history, with summaries of various treaties which have determined their boundaries in the past. The importance of oil and coal is discussed with illustrative maps. The chapter on the "African Colonies and the European Powers" takes up the problems of race and religion, the penetration of Africa by the white races, colonial rivalry, international agreements respecting liquor traffic, slave trade, and protection of wild animals, as well as a detailed statement on each country. Latin America is included, with a statement as to the various boundary disputes. This edition contains a supplement of seventy-five pages on the United States including sections on foreign relations, American interests in the Philippines, the Washington Conference of 1921–1922, Inter-Allied indebtedness and reparations, the merchant marine, and frontiers. There is an additional chapter of notes which add information to the edition of 1921. A bibliography for each chapter gives a valuable selected list of references. An appendix gives an outline of treaties and resolutions adopted by the Conference on the Limitation of Armament, and the Tacna-Arica Protocol. The index is detailed and adequate.

NEXT AGE OF MAN, THE, by Albert Edward Wiggam (1927), is a discussion, in a non-technical way of some of the simpler aspects of eugenics. The author has touched purposely upon a number of the social forces at work in national life in order to show that they all bear very directly upon the biological constitution of the race. He first questions whether that degree of civilization which has appeared from time to time in the history of the world has been retained as a permanent improvement in man's natural traits and capacity. He sees civilization itself as a gigantic and never ending tinkering with the human germ plasm upon which evolution depends. Two of the greatest problems of our time, prohibition and tuberculosis, he discusses as concrete illustrations of how important it is to apply science to our social undertakings. Alcohol, he believes, is a curse that need be prohibited to only a small percentage of the human race, who are psychopathic whether they drink or not. The study of the inner life problems of the heavy drinker by an expert in clinical psychology would do more to solve this problem than prohibition. Three world possibilities lie just ahead for civilized men. The first that men will mutually destroy each other on the battlefield, the second that men will go through a long period of social, economic, and political muddling without any clear idea of what they want or where they are going, and the third world possibility is that men may begin to apply human intelligence to human affairs. He believes the highest education of the best people is the only way to breed better people and in this way to make a permanently better world. Four men he finds impossible for this work, the professional economic and political optimist, the pessimist, who also seeks relief from the dilemmas of life by an extreme defence mechanism, in his case by saying there is no solution, the conservative who believes that nothing should ever be done for the first time, and the radical who believes that nothing should ever be done except for the first time. The new liberal is the man best fitted to solve this problem. The old liberal under Rousseau freed men's minds from many errors and gave them free education and suffrage even though most of their ideas are not accepted by the scientifically trained liberal of to-day. So he formulates the question of the modern world. "Will science enable men to build a civilization which, by its social customs, its educational meth-

ods, its religious and ethical idealism and taboos, its economic adjustments and its
political procedures — its essential structure, its inherent drive and dynamics —
. . . will force the human race biologically upward; or will science be only a new and
more terrible instrument . . . by which they will be forced biologically downward?"
Eugenics, he contends, is simply the new social, educational, religious, industrial and
political statesmanship. Its problem is to correlate social evolution with biological
evolution. Two objectives are before eugenists, to preserve the race from deterioration in the midst of a stimulating, happy environment and then to improve them.
Four cornerstones or principles prevail in eugenics; the first that the mental, temperamental, and spiritual traits of man are inherited by the same mechanism and in
the same degree as his physical traits; as man rises in the scale there is an increased
ability to control his environment but his environment does not always bring out all
the traits which are latent in his nature through heredity; the second "the non-
inheritance in any large, wholesale way of what is commonly called 'acquired' characters," which prevents the germinal stream from being burdened with the passing
fads and follies of man; the third that "good qualities tend to be associated with one
another in the natural make-up of men and women," which leads him to believe that
intelligent people are more moral, live longer, are more healthful and beautiful; the
fourth the tendency of like to marry like or assortive mating. He finds progress is not
a product of the masses, but the creation of a few unusual individuals who have very
little relationship biologically to the rest of the population. Then he examines how
the general population grows and spreads over the planet and how many people there
are likely to be on the planet. As wealth grows and new interests develop so that
people are lifted above the brute struggle for existence, the birth rate which has been
rising begins automatically to decline until the population becomes stationary. The
type of education offered women by the colleges attracts a class of whom at least half
are not a marrying type. Longevity he classes as a purely inherited trait and the
longer potential life a woman has, the greater will be the number of children she pro
duces. In the past those leaders who largely determine a civilisation have come
largely through the chance mating of excellent strains so that a combination of qualities results which appears in a leader of genius. Out of the tendency of like to mate
with like and to produce children of like qualities develops a social conification in
which they tend to pyramid their biological as well as their social gains. Yet in so
far as democracy works successfully it defeats its own end biologically for as leaders
from the laboring class rise they marry into the upper classes and thereby intensify
the talents which enabled them to rise. "So wealthy families today, are building up
financial genius, just as in past ages military genius has been built up, by intermarriage and conification." Four new goals of education which will help better the
race he announces, first the measurement of the mind, next the measurement of educational progress, third the adjustment of men and women in industry, and in
economic and political life and last the measurement and education of moral character.
Not only the kind of education man gets but his environment, the character of his
leadership, the kind of government he has, the way he makes his living and the economic conditions that surround him, it is these which improve him biologically or
deteriorate him. The author believes that there is a rising tide of biologic capacity
and quotes Dr. Raymond Pearl on "The Differential Fertility of the American People"
to show that the future American people are going to come mainly from the farmers,
factory workers and miners who show the greatest fertility relative to the total population. It is right then that every effort should be made to improve the general capacity of these groups. But it is from these cones of leadership thrown up within the

mass of the population that the largest single factor will come in creating a naturally civilized world. Various rude methods of birth control have been practised in the past, but these have more often than not operated to reduce the fertility of the upper classes, and the lowest classes, being ignorant and careless of these methods, have threatened to swamp those better elements from whom leaders most often come. One of the most hopeful factors for the future is the research now being conducted by biochemists which will lead to such simple and safe methods of birth control that soon such knowledge may be within the reach of all grades of society. .So he foresees a peaceful and benign natural selection which will arise to replace the old bloody natural selection of the jungle in which the relatively superior elements of the population whose power of parental instinct is strongest will be the most fertile because they will best appreciate the privilege of parenthood. These will usher in that great race which under these conditions we may expect in the next age of man.

NIGGER HEAVEN, by Carl Van Vechten (1926). This novel of negro life has its setting in the Harlem of to-day. Mary Love and Olive Hamilton occupied an apartment together. Neither of the girls earned very much money, they mingled with, but did not entertain, the richer social set that lived in the splendid row of houses Stanford White had designed on One Hundred and Thirty-Ninth Street, or in other pleasant localities. They took in most of the good plays and musical shows, revues and song recitals, usually sitting in the balcony to save expense, although "Olive was light enough and Mary's features were sufficiently Latin so that they were not rudely received when they asked at the box office for places in the orchestra." But there had been embarrassing situations. Howard Allison, a negro whose father had been a slave, has just begun the practice of his profession, law. He is a friend of the two girls and interested in the perplexing phases of the Negro problem. Richard Fort Sill, who was so "white that below the line he was never taken for a Negro," is another friend. Howard resents the invasion of the white people who come up to the Harlem cabarets. "Why, in one or two places they've actually tried to do a little jim crowing!" He looked upon it as a bore, "to have them all over our places while we are excluded from their theatres and restaurants merely on account of our color, theatres and restaurants which admit Chinese and Hindus — if I wore a turban or a burnous I could go anywhere — and prostitutes of any nationality. Why, a white prostitute can go places where a colored preacher would be refused admittance." Mary expresses the opinion that the best of the colored race object to intermingling — to mixed marriages. Harlem, to her, was a sort of Mecca, where it was an advantage to be colored. Howard believes that the solution is economic, that when the negroes, in the mass, become rich enough, they will become powerful. Randolph Pettijohn, a negro in the Harlem set, loves Mary, but when he asks her to marry him, she refuses. She tells one of her friends, Adora, that she does not love Randolph. "Rannie didn't care whether you loved him or not," Adora told her. "He wanted a respectable woman for a wife, somebody to give him a decent show-window, so he could go about a little more with the swells. He's dead cut up about it." "I'm sorry," Mary responded. "I can't help it. I just couldn't do it." Mary "cherished an almost fanatic faith in her race, a love for her people in themselves, and a fervent belief in their possibilities." She felt at times that they were all savages and recalled what she had been told — and her reason informed her that it was probably the truth — "the Negroes never premeditate murder; their murders are committed under the reign of passion. If one made a temporary escape from a man bent on killing, it was likely to prove a permanent escape. The next morning, in another mood, probably he would have forgotten his purpose. There had never been, her information assured her, a Negro poisoner. Negroes use the instruments that deal death swiftly: knives, razors, revolvers." Howard and Olive marry; and Mary meets Byron Kasson, a writer. The story revolves around their relations. They are both in love with each other, and both feel the social humiliations which they encounter in New York. Mary wonders why they are subjected to insults. Byron tells her of his experiences in trying to get work. "I answered advertisements for clerks, for secretaries. I'm insulted by office-boys, even, by our own people; porters, elevator boys." "Nigger Heaven," he moaned. "That's what Harlem is. We sit in our places in the gallery of this New York theatre and watch the white world sitting down below in the good seats of the orchestra. Occasionally they turn their faces up towards us, their hard, cruel faces, to laugh or sneer, but they never beckon. It never seems to occur to them that Nigger Heaven is crowded, that there isn't another seat, that something has to be done. It doesn't seem to occur to them either," he went on fiercely, "that we sit above them, that we can drop down things on them and crush them, that we can swoop down from this Nigger Heaven and take their seats. No, they have no fear of that! Harlem! The Mecca of the New Negro!" Lasca Sartoris is an exotic figure, who flits from Paris to Harlem. Byron comes under her influence and leaves Mary. Lasca tires of him and deserts him for Randolph Pettijohn. Mary, who still loves Byron, tries to console him, but his pride created a new belligerency and he sends her away. After she has gone, he makes a swift decision. He knows that he loves Mary, but he resolves "that he can't go back to her until he has proved how much he hates Lasca" . . . his hand crept slowly toward the object concealed beneath the pillow. At one of the Harlem resorts he sees Lasca and Randolph. He reaches for his pistol, but before he attempts to shoot, another shot is heard and Randolph is killed. Another negro, Anatole Longfellow, whom Lasca had cast aside, kills him, and makes his escape. Byron sees Randolph "in a pool of blood under the amber moon." Fascinated, he crept slowly towards it. Suddenly, he stamped on the face with the heel of his boot, and drew his revolver and shot once, twice into the ugly black mass. Immediately his anger left him. "Mary," he cried aloud, "I didn't do it! I didn't do it!" He was curiously conscious that a white hand was reaching for the gun. He looked up to face a coat of blue buttoned with brass.

NO MORE PARADES, by Ford Madox Ford (1925). "In this novel the events," says the author, "such as it treats of, are vouched for by myself. There was in France, at the time covered by this novel, an immense base camp, unbelievably crowded with men whom we were engaged in getting up the line, working sometimes day and night in the effort. That immense army was also extremely depressed by the idea that those who controlled it overseas would — I will not use the word betray, since that implies volition — but 'let us down.' We were oppressed, ordered, counter-ordered, commanded, countermanded, harassed, strafed, denounced — and, above all, dreadfully worried. The never-ending sense of worry, in fact, far surpassed any of the 'exigencies of troops actually in contact with enemy forces,' and that applied not merely to the bases, but to the whole field of military operations. Unceasing worry! We took it out in what may or may not have been unjust suspicions of the all-powerful ones who had our lives in their hands — and seemed indifferent enough to the fact. So this novel recounts what those opinions were: it does not profess to dictate whether those opinions were or were not justified." Christopher Tietjens, of Groby, an English officer, and a godson of General Campion, is at a base, packed with men "tighter than sardines." Sylvia Tietjens, his wife, "had been excruciatingly unfaithful. He could not be certain that the child he adored was his own." Three months before the story opens, they had parted — or he thought they had parted. She could not, thank God, get into France — to that place. Yet she could make scandals in the papers that every Tommie read. There was no game of which she was not capable. He had had a very painful morning with her three months ago — the pain coming from a suddenly growing conviction that his wife was forcing herself into an attitude of caring for him. She was perfectly capable of forcing herself to take that attitude if she thought that it would enormously inconvenience himself. Tietjens has long known Valentine Wannop, the daughter of his father's oldest friend, who was also an old friend of General Campion. He forms a violent attachment for her, and, although they had exchanged no confidences, he is sure that his feelings are returned. When he goes out to France for the second time, he invites Miss Wannop "to become his mistress." Sylvia has threatened to ruin him in the Army, and writes to General Campion that her ducal second-cousin, the "lugubrious Rugeley," highly disapproved of Tietjens' being in France at all. A later despatch from Havre informs the General that Sylvia will arrive on the noon train. Campion despatches a furious note to Tietjens, who has also been told that Sylvia has reached the base, although he does not know what his wife's errand in France is. He gets marching orders — he is to be sent up the line. He swears that he will not go at the bidding of "a hog like Beichan," whose real name was Stavropolides, formerly Nathan, and complains that the Army is reeling at the base because of the continual interferences of civilians, and that it was absolutely impossible to get through his programs of parades because of the perpetual extra drills that were forced on them at the bidding of civilians. Tietjens calls on Sylvia at her hotel, but she sends him word that she is "engaged." With her at the time is Major Wilfrid Perowne, "whose affair with her might have been something to boast about, had he been boastful." Sylvia tells Perowne that she has come to France to be reconciled with her husband. Tietjens and Sylvia meet at a tea at Lady Sachse's. "It almost broke Sylvia's heart to see how exactly Christopher did the right thing." In order to take him down a peg or two in General Campion's estimation, she tells the General that her husband is a Socialist. The General says that he is going to have Tietjens drummed out of the service. She has already told him that Tietjens has seduced Valentine Wannop. She explains that her husband is heir to one of the biggest fortunes in England, for a commoner, but refuses to touch a penny. "He desires to model himself upon our Lord," and the General says that he always knew that Tietjens had a screw loose. Sylvia permits Perowne to come to her room at her hotel, and she expects Tietjens also. General O'Hara also comes. Tietjens shuts the door on Perowne and orders a subaltern to take General O'Hara away — O'Hara is drunk. After settling certain details with Sylvia, Tietjens goes up to his camp and sees the draft off. Tietjens' troubles shake up General Campion, but Tietjens tells him that Sylvia is to have "Groby" and that he can use it as his headquarters. The General is at a loss where to send Tietjens. The latter has lung trouble and cannot go up the line. He wants to be put in command of divisional transport for two reasons — one that that employment would put Valentine Wannop's mind at rest. Tietjens will not use the money that was left him because of the way it was left. His father had committed suicide because he believed things said of Tietjens by a stranger. The General discusses all of these things with him. He tells Tietjens that when a man finds his wife unfaithful to him he should "divorce the harlot or live with her." Tietjens' answer is: "Still, sir . . . there are . . . there used to be . . . in families of . . . position . . . a certain . . ." He stopped. The General said: "Well . . ." Tietjens said: "On the part of the man . . . a certain . . . call it . . . parade!" The General said: "Then there had better be no more parades. . . ."

NOCTURNE, by Frank Swinnerton (1917). The two girls, Jenny and Emmy, live with their half-paralyzed father in the poorer district in London. Jenny works in a millinery shop. The older Emmy, who stays at home to do the routine of drudgery of the house and take care of Pa, envies the greater freedom of her sister. She sees the years slipping by without bringing her the husband and children she would be content to work for. The romantic Jenny rebels against the drabness of life. She is dreaming about Keith Redington, a sailor that she has met, but is glad to go to the movies with the commonplace Alf for lack of anything better to do. In their sphere politeness is ranked as an affectation so there is nothing to prevent the sisters, with their clashing temperaments, from continual quarrelling. Emmy reproaches Jenny for her scorn of Alf, whom Emmy herself adores. When Alf comes with tickets for the movies Jenny generously manoeuvres to make the reluctant swain take Emmy instead of herself, to his discomfiture and Emmy's delight. After Pa is put to bed Jenny sits discontentedly trimming her hat, thinking "What a life." She considers Emmy's jealousy of her and Alf, and her own feeling that love is giving not getting, and has nothing to do with envy or hating people or being jealous. In answer to her wish that something new and exciting would happen there is a knock at the door. Keith has sent a motor car with a letter asking her to come to supper with him on the yacht of which he is captain, as he is not free to come to her. Conscience stricken she realizes that it is a breach of duty to leave Pa, but she cannot miss this chance for happiness. Pa promises to be a good boy, and she goes to her lover. She has her hour of the luxury she craves. She and Keith quarrel and make up again, and he assures the doubting girl of his good faith, and asks her to marry him when he returns in three months. She yields herself completely to his love. At the theatre and on the walk home afterward Emmy and Alf discover that they are admirably suited to each other. Alf comes in "for a bite of supper" and they find Pa lying unconscious on the kitchen floor, where he had fallen and cut his head trying to reach to the top of the cupboard to get his beer. Just at this moment Jenny comes in, and they do not guess that she has been out of the house. After Pa is back in bed and Alf leaves, Jenny confesses that she has been with Keith. Emmy does not believe that Keith will marry Jenny, but her own love affair is too new to allow her to be unkind or even to think much about her sister. Alone in her room with the self-reproach that she had deserted Pa and the knowledge that she has irretrievably consigned her future happiness and freedom to Keith, all Jenny's doubts of Keith return. She struggles for composure and to get back to her old gay way of looking at everything. In a forlorn, quivering voice she ventured: "What a life. Golly, what a life," and buried her face in the pillow.

NOVEMBER NIGHT, by the anonymous author of "The House Made with Hands" (1928). A psychological novel about Denise, the supersensitive, self-centred wife of Horace, the rather prosaic business man she has married for his money. She seems to resent her husband's very existence, and spends her time brooding over the memory of Roland, her lover, who was killed in the War. In an illness before her marriage she lost her voice, which put an end to a promising musical career. "The

book is really the defence of Denise in all the wrong things she does to her relations
and her husband: things that she does by the light of her uncompromisingly truthful,
wholly unmoral nature." She despises her well-meaning mother, Mrs. Vynor, and
her sister, Pansy, but is fond of her clever brother, Martin, who is charming and weak.
He leaves his wife, Amy, and four children, pretends that he is in Canada on business,
while he really is in London with another woman. He speculates with his mother's
small fortune, and Amy's inheritance from her father, so that they are left penniless.
Horace gives tens of thousands of pounds to save the family from the disgrace of
Martin's speculations, and makes the condition that he shall leave the country.
He makes great sacrifices in his business to do this, because he loves his beautiful
wife deeply, though he understands her attitude toward him, and for the sake of the
child that Denise is expecting. Denise eagerly awaits the child that she can love and
give everything that was her lover and her art. She hates to share the child with
Horace, and considers the affectionate interest of her mother and sister an intrusion.
At a Watch-Night service she attends on New Year's Eve to escape from Horace and
her mother-in-law, she is attracted by the exaltation of motherhood in the Catholic
Church, and determines to become a Catholic in order to possess her child more
completely. At this time she goes away from home to a friend's cottage to be by herself for long periods, because Horace has asked her mother to stay with them since Mrs.
Vynor now has not money enough to keep up her home. She postpones going to see
Horace's mother, who is ill and has asked to see her, until it is too late, and does not
even go to the funeral. When she tells Horace that she is going to join the Catholic
Church he definitely refuses to allow her to bring up his child in an alien faith. He
says: "I thank God there's going to be something in my life, now my mother's gone,
that won't be insulted by me — loving it." Kind and forbearing as he is, he refuses
to be done out of just the one thing that his marriage has brought him, the child he
longs for. The story ends with the birth and death of the baby, while Denise is
delirious, and it is doubtful whether she will die or live to be a better wife to Horace
whom she has at the last come to appreciate. In the first chapter, Charles, Martin's
little son, gives Denise a cocoon on her birthday, which becomes to her a kind of
mascot, and is a symbol of her selfishness. She tends it carefully until the first time
she goes away from Horace when her neglect causes the death of the moth. For a
moment before her delirium she sees that she has treated everyone to whom she
owed affection and sympathy, and especially Horace, with the same neglect that had
killed the moth.

O GENTEEL LADY, by Esther Forbes (1926). A young lady of the eighteen-fifties,
Miss Lanice Bardeen, in crinoline, seed pearl brooch, and costly mink pelisse, boards
the train to Boston, to run away from her home, and her fiancé in Amherst and launch
herself on a career. Her lovely, heedless Mamma has disgraced the family by
running away first to Italy with one of her husband's students, Roger Cuncliffe, and
thus made Amherst an impossible place for her daughter to live. As for Mr. Augustus
Trainer, it was one thing to be angry at one's Mamma but quite another for Augustus
to sneer. Lanice telegraphed Cousin Pauline Poggy that she was coming, and her
cousin met her at the station with the family barouche to drive to the Poggy home on
Beacon Street. Pauline is a young lady of lofty principles devoted to many causes,
but particularly the rights of women. It was decided that Lanice should study art,
and in her spare hours act as amanuensis to her uncle, the old, retired merchant, who
for years had been writing an historical study of Salem witchcraft. Augustus followed Lanice to Boston to renew his suit, but she begs him to believe that she can

never be more than a sister to him. Her uncle's publisher offers Lanice work on his magazine, "Hearth and Home," and though her plain cousin suggests that the brown merino dress is more suitable to wear, and looks much more like cultured Boston, Lanice prefers to go to the editorial office in green trimmed with fur, looking her charming self. She meets Mr. Whittier, and Mr. Emerson, Dr. Holmes, and Professor Longfellow at the publisher's, and one day Lanice had her wish to meet "strangers coming from far lands and fine adventure." Professor Sears Ripley presents to her a wild young Englishman, Anthony Jones, whose book on his travels in Arabia was to be brought out by the firm. He sees in Lanice the likeness to a type of Persian princess, and he does not tell her "how his restless eyes had roved over the earth looking for this evasive beauty in the flesh." Sears Ripley also appreciated Lanice's haunting beauty, and regrets that he has introduced these two friends. Captain Anthony asks to have Lanice's services as secretary and makes love to her that is very different from the little furtive advances of Augustus's courtship. Now he could tell her of the "undeviating devotion he had always borne for the Persian princesses of the Mughal Court, dead for centuries." There was a piquancy to him "in never knowing whether you held in your arms an editoress or the reincarnation of a Persian princess." When the book was completed the fascinating Mr. Jones kissed Lanice good-by and went back to England. The "Hearth and Home" stories seemed tame and artificial to Lanice now, and she can scarcely bear to go on with her work. A cable announces the death of her mother in Italy, and she decides that she must go over and bring her back home. Her father gives her an introduction to Roger Cuncliffe and to the American consul, and Mr. Fox gives her letters to Mr. and Mrs. Browning, and Mr. Tennyson, Mr. Dickens, Mr. Thackeray and other celebrities, and offers to pay part of her expenses if she will write about them for his magazine. Mr. Cuncliffe sent his servant to Marseilles to meet her. She finds it impossible to harden her heart against the charm and courtesy of Roger, soon to die of tuberculosis, and she grows fond of this girl who had come into the midst of his affairs and asked him an answer to all the riddles of life. In England Professor Ripley takes her to see George Eliot and goes with her to Cornwall. She hears that Anthony Jones is in England and is staying at the God-Begot House in Winchester, and thinks that she must go there and say to him, "Anthony, I've come thousands of miles just to say good-by." It is after her visit to the Tennysons at the Isle of Wight, and she tries to compose her mind to write about the "black and tousled and rough" laureate "brooding over his clay pipe," but at the last minute her pride weakens and she goes to Winchester. The maids at the hotel forget to call her in time and she misses Anthony, and felt she had always known that she would never see him again. The comprehending Professor Ripley comes to find and console her, and rejoices that she was too late. After she gets back she tells Pauline how Anthony had seemed to pull down her "whole house of life," and the wise and understanding Roger had someway built it up again, and that now she thinks she could marry someone whom she cared about who understood her, but would not carry her off her feet. That afternoon Sears Ripley proposes and is accepted. They spend their honeymoon on Cape Cod where Ripley's eccentric friend, Thoreau, finds a paradise for them. In the last chapter the contented Mrs. Ripley sits holding her child in her arms and thinks of the girl she had been once.

OF HUMAN BONDAGE, by W. Somerset Maugham (1915). A realistic presentation of the mental and spiritual development of the hero, Philip Carey, from childhood to about thirty years of age, and of the various forces and circumstances which make him.   Left an orphan, the child Philip goes to live with his selfish, hypocritical uncle, the Reverend William Carey, and his old-maidish wife, Aunt Louisa.   Philip is handicapped by a club-foot, which makes him painfully sensitive and self-conscious. At school he becomes more shy and solitary, mocked by unfeeling playmates because of his deformity.   One master calls him a club-footed blockhead.   All through his life when anyone wishes to be unkind it is by reference to his foot.   He drifts through unhappy years, a disappointment to himself and others.   His uncle had expected him to enter the University and to be a clergyman.   Instead he loses his faith in religion and goes to Heidelberg for a year of study.   When he comes home, an elderly governess, Miss Wilkinson, visiting his uncle and aunt, falls in love with him, and he gets the experience he craves of women in a liaison with her.   He goes to London to an office to learn to be an accountant, but is a failure, and decides to study art in Paris.   The group of art students discuss their work, and their mistresses.   Cronshaw, an older man, a poet, lives in squalor with a slatternly woman who deceives him, and spends his evenings in brilliant talk at the café.   Philip hears the creed of the artist: "An artist would let his mother go to the workhouse, let his wife and children starve, sacrifice everything for the sake of getting on to canvas with paint the emotion which the world gave him."   At the art school he meets the unattractive Fanny Price, with a false faith in her own genius, starving in order to go on painting, who hangs herself when she comes to the end of her resources.   After two gay years he returns to the rectory, a failure as an artist, but with an enhanced sense of beauty, and a deeper philosophy of life.   Again he starts for London, this time to study medicine like his father.   His loneliness leads him into an enslaving infatuation for Mildred, a common, vulgar waitress in a tea-shop.   He wants to marry her, but she prefers Emil, a married man, and goes away with him.   Nora Nesbit, making a precarious living writing penny novelettes loves Philip, and becomes his companion and mistress, until Mildred, deserted by Emil, comes back.   Philip loves her as much as ever and provides a home for her until her baby is born, when she rewards his devotion by running away with his friend and fellow-student Griffiths, who also deserts her.   She becomes a prostitute, and Philip again gives her a home, though he no longer loves her.   She resents his indifference, though she has never cared for him, wrecks his furniture, and leaves him.   He takes in Cronshaw, the poet, dying and penniless.   His depleted inheritance is wiped out by an unlucky venture on the Stock Exchange, and he has to give up his medical studies, and find work.   Thorpe Athelney, his kind journalist friend, rescues him from starvation and sleeping on park benches, takes him into his family, and finds a position for him in the shop where he himself is press agent.   Philip spends two terrible years as shopwalker and window designer at six shillings a week, "and found."   Then his uncle dies and leaves him enough money to finish his medical course.   In the vacation he takes a post as substitute assistant to a country physician in Dorsetshire, and is offered a partnership, which he refuses, because he wants to travel.   On a holiday hop picking with the Athelney family he seduces the oldest daughter, the amiable, buxom Sally.   He does not love her, but is fond of her, and decides to marry her and take the country practice.   He concludes "that the simplest pattern, that in which a man was born, worked, married, had children and died, was likewise the most perfect" life.

OLD COUNTESS, THE, by Anne Douglas Sedgwick (1926).   The wicked, pathetic, painted old woman who gives the story its title is a faded beauty of the Second Empire.   English visitors to the Dordogne Valley, an artist, Dick Graham, and his wife,

Jill, meet this strange old woman, Madame de Lamouderie. The Countess comes upon Dick as he sits painting the menacing, precipitous cliffs, and the torrent of the river, and invites him and Jill to tea at the musty old manor house above the village of Buissac. She is extravagantly glad to see these young people from a world from which she has long been an exile, and is infatuated with the handsome, mocking Dick. He promises to do her portrait when they return in the spring. Jill is a dependable, outdoor girl, who has left her country life and following the hounds for love of her husband. The temperamental Dick finds rest and refuge in his tranquil wife, whom he loves devotedly. When they return to Buissac they find with the Countess, the young mistress of the manor, the tragic, saint-like Marthe Lédurac, whom the jealous Madame de Lamouderie disparages to the Grahams, hoping to discourage them from friendship with her. Jill is greatly attracted by Marthe, and, though at first the timid, repressed French girl avoids her, she at last accepts Jill's friendship, and tells her the sad story of her life. Her mother had killed her father in love with another woman, and, as there were extenuating circumstances, she had been allowed to go free after the trial, half mad with grief and remorse, and dependent on the constant companionship of her daughter until her death a few years before. Marthe had then given the destitute Madame de Lamouderie a home just as she lavished love and care on all the stray suffering animals in the neighborhood. The winters Marthe spends in the city playing the harp and teaching music. From the first Dick and Marthe feel a powerful attraction for each other, which they both strive to conquer. The vain old Countess wants Dick's attentions, and tries to keep him for herself by lies about Marthe, misrepresenting her kindness to a poor soldier during the War to make Dick believe her the mistress of many lovers. The comprehending love of Jill makes her realize that Marthe and Dick are destined lovers, and she goes on loving them both, and makes up her mind to give Dick his freedom. A great storm floods the river and the country, and the Countess hoping in her jealous fury to get rid of Marthe carries a little kid to the island, soon to be inundated, ties it there, and counts on Marthe's devotion to her pet to send her to its rescue and her death. Dick doubts the confused statements of the old woman about Marthe and goes to the island to find her. On the roof of the cabin with the waters rising and death imminent Marthe speaks her love for Dick. Jill comes in a boat to get them, and Dick is saved, insensible, but Marthe slips or falls into the water and is lost. In an epilogue two years later Jill comes back to Buissac to dedicate a memorial fountain to Marthe. Dick is recovering from the long illness that followed the tragedy, and has begun to paint again. Jill and Dick are together as Marthe had intended they should be. The old Countess had died calling on Marthe, her benefactress, for intercession with "le bon Dieu."

OLD ENGLISH, by John Galsworthy (1924). The dominant character in this play, Sylvanus Heythorp, chairman of The Island Navigation Company, an unscrupulous egotist, is nicknamed "Old English" by his associates, who admire the pluck which enables him, now that he is over eighty and not able to get up from a chair without help, to make his creditors and the stockholders of the company do his bidding. The fees he receives from directorships, conferred upon him because of his recognized business ability and supposed probity, enable him to pay an annual interest to his creditors and fend off bankruptcy. He advises them not to press for payment of the principal, and thus kill the goose that lays the golden eggs, as even the house he lives in is the property of his daughter. In order to provide for Phyllis and Jock, the children of his illegitimate son, he urges the Company to buy four ships from his friend, Joseph Pillin, for sixty thousand pounds, and blackmails his friend into giving him a commission of ten per cent, arranging safely within the law to have the money settled by Pillin on Rosamund Larne, the children's mother, until they are of age. Mrs. Larne writs stories for the newspapers to supplement the money Mr. Heythorp is able to give her, but is always in difficulty with tradesmen, and though she has promised not to say a word about the matter, she now calls up her lawyer to see if she can borrow some money on her expectations. The lawyer, Charles Ventnor, one of Mr. Heythorp's creditors, is able to get enough information from the foolish Mrs. Larne to guess what has taken place, and then prove his suspicions to be true. He has already tried to induce Mr. Heythorp to pay him privately behind the backs of the other creditors to prevent him from making trouble for him. With the information he now has he goes to Mr. Heythorp to threaten him with exposure unless he gets his money. Mr. Heythorp defies him to do his worst, and has the servant put him out of the house. Then on the last day before he is disgraced and dependent on the daughter he despises, Miss Adela, given to piety and good works, he orders a good dinner, and induces the servants who adore him to give him the champagne, and port, and brandy, which the doctor has forbidden, to drown care, and so dies of apoplexy. The charming Phyllis comes in after the theatre with young Bob Pillin to show "Guardy" the new dress she has bought with the money he gave her, and her lover takes her away before she can discover that "Old English" is not merely asleep in his chair.

OLD LADIES, THE, by Hugh Walpole (1924). At the top of a creaky, rickety old lodging-house in the cathedral town of Polchester three old ladies lived in genteel poverty. Mrs. Amorest had railway stocks that did not pay dividends, though she saw that the trains always seemed to be full whenever she went near a railway station. Her husband had been a well-known poet. Her son, Brand, from whom she had had no word for years, is in America trying to make a fortune. The author sees that Mrs. Amorest has "eyes bright as the sea with sun on it and a smile both radiant and confiding," but Archdeacon Brandon says of her, "Who was that shabby little woman?" A wealthy cousin already on his death-bed promises to provide for her in his will, and on the strength of these expectations the gay, courageous old lady recklessly buys a little Christmas tree to entertain her two acquaintances. Miss May Beringer, stupid and timid, lives in the past, consoled by her little dog and a beautiful ornament of amber given to her years before by a woman friend whose affection is her most precious memory. The other old lady, Agatha Payne, greedy and self-centred, tells fortunes on her cards all day long and broods over the possessions of her two acquaintances which she covets for herself. She considers herself defrauded when Mrs. Amorest's hope of a legacy from her cousin is disappointed. Then her roving fancy becomes set on Miss Beringer's piece of amber, "dragging her out of her lethargy and idleness, possessing all that was left of her imagination and lustful desires." She perceives that the other woman is afraid of her, and as the mouse is to the cat, so was timidity to Agatha Payne. She felt she must see the amber often every day, and that she could frighten May into changing her mind about parting with it. She begins a systematic persecution of her victim. Miss Beringer becomes ill and begs her to leave her alone. She tries to leave the town but misses the train. The dreadful Agatha finally literally frightens her to death. Mrs. Amorest's son arrives rich and full of remorse for his lack of consideration and takes his mother away from the cheerless house. It is a sympathetic picture of the pathos of deserted old age.

OLD NEW YORK, by Edith Wharton (1924). Four historical novelettes dealing respectively with the "forties," the "fifties," the "sixties," and the "seventies." In the first, "False Dawn," young Lewis Raycie leaves his father's country house on the Sound, "a convenient driving distance from his town house on Canal Street," to complete his education by making the "grand tour" of Europe. Lewis gets up before daybreak to say good-by to his sweetheart, Beatrice Kent, "Treshy," a poor relation and ward of a distant cousin, and therefore not the bride his pompous, domineering father would choose for him. He meets his sister stealing out of the house with a basket of provisions for that poor young Mrs. Edgar Allan Poe, dying in poverty in a cottage near their mansion. Mr. Raycie gave his son a princely allowance for travelling expenses, and commissions him to buy a collection of "recognized" Old Masters for a "Raycie Gallery," for which he allows five thousand dollars. In Switzerland Lewis met a pleasant young Englishman, John Ruskin, and with this kind friend to guide his choice his eyes were opened to a new world of art. Instead of the Guido Renis and Carlo Dolces his father expected, he brought home a collection of Italian primitives, "with not a full-bodied female among 'em." The picture of the princess looked to Mr. Raycie like a portrait of plain Treshy Kent. A year later Mr. Raycie died and all New York agreed that it was the disappointment about the pictures that had killed him. He disinherited his son, but bequeathed the pictures to him. With money from his mother, Lewis was able to marry Treshy, and open the Raycie Gallery to public exhibition for the New York of the day to laugh at. Years afterward this collection which had brought its collector only pain and humiliation was found in an attic, sold at auction for five million dollars, and provided pearls and Rolls-Royces for a descendant of the family.

The second, "The Old Maid," is the tragedy of an unmarried mother in the repressed fifties. Delia Lovell had stifled a romantic preference for her cousin, Clem Spender, the impecunious artist, and married James Ralston of the rich, conservative Ralston family of New York, and at twenty-five is the mother of two children, and one of the handsomest and most popular "young matrons" of her day. Her cousin, Charlotte Lovell, is about to marry Joe Ralston, a cousin of James. The Ralston family want Charlotte to give up a day nursery for poor children, which she has kept up ever since her return from the South, where she spent a year in the care of an old family governess recovering from a threatened attack of consumption. Delia agrees with the Ralstons that Charlotte should not run the risk of infection for her children-to-be, and Charlotte confesses that one of the little girls is her own child, and that its father is Clem Spender. He had loved Delia, but after her wedding had turned for a time to Charlotte who loved him. Delia takes control of the situation, and tells Joe that he can not marry Charlotte because she has had a recurrence of her former illness. She installs Charlotte in a farmhouse up the river, and arranges that she shall have the little foundling girl with her. After six years when James dies the generous Delia invites Charlotte and the little girl, Tina, to come and live with her. Tina grows up a charming young girl, and loves Delia, whom she calls mamma, more than her Aunt Chatty. The maternal passion of Charlotte makes the situation unendurable to her, and all Delia's kindness turns to venom in her soul. In order to make Tina eligible to marry Lanning Halsey, the man she loves, Delia formally adopts Tina, and Charlotte is grateful, though at first she is almost ready to sacrifice her child's happiness to her own pride before she can give her consent. The night before Tina's wedding Charlotte accuses Delia of leaving nothing undone to divide her from her daughter, and of doing everything for them both for the sake of Clement Spender. Delia is filled with compassion for Charlotte, and only hopes that she will not trouble the happy Tina with her jealousy. Poor Charlotte sees that Delia has become Tina's real mother and that she herself is the old maid that her child thinks her, and allows Delia to go to Tina waiting for her good night.

"The Spark," the third of the series, has for the leading character, Hayley Delane, a simple, chivalrous, elderly gentleman belonging to the sixties rather than to the polo-playing, racing, dancing, card-playing, sporting set of the nineties. He is married to a selfish, philandering wife, Leila. The younger friend telling the story rejoices when Delane thrashes a man guilty of ill-treating a pony at the polo game, though, as the man is his wife's admirer, Delane is obliged to apologize in order not to have his action misunderstood and provoke scandal. Delane had been in the Civil War and had apparently "stopped living," or rather growing mentally, at nineteen. Wounded and in the hospital in Washington, he had come in contact with a man, "a spark," whose influence remained with him always, and who became to Delane a kind of advisory conscience in moments of crisis. He insists on bringing his wife's disreputable old father home to spend his last years, though Leila is against it, because he thinks his friend of the hospital visits would think it right. One day a picture in a book reveals that the friend was Walt Whitman.

"New Year's Day" is a New Year's Day of the seventies. Lizzie Hazeldean had once been Lizzie Winter, the daughter of a discredited minister, a penniless girl of uncommon charm, rescued from humiliating dependence on a capricious older relative by marriage to the promising young lawyer, Charles Hazeldean. They had six years of perfect happiness and success. Then Charles became an invalid with an obscure disease of the heart. Lizzie had all the "helpless incapacity" of her time and her class, and knew no way to get money for the heavy expenses of nurses and specialists except by her graces, so she gave the husband she adored a last year of life of ease of mind by carrying on an affair with a lover, Henry Prest, to get the money she needed. On New Year's Day a fire in the Fifth Avenue Hotel drove her and Mr. Prest out the front door of the hotel in the sight of people who knew them. Charles Hazeldean died the next week, and Lizzie went abroad for six months. When she returned she rejected the proposal of marriage of Henry Prest, and explained the motive for her acceptance of his love in the past. After her one great courageous action she lives an outcast in the rigid and self-sufficient society of New York of her day and generation.

ON THE TRAIL OF ANCIENT MAN, by Roy Chapman Andrews (1922). This preliminary narrative of the field work of the Central Asiatic Expeditions of 1922 "makes no attempt to give the full scientific significance of our discoveries," says the author, who early gives the reader intimate glimpses of the vast preparations for his scientific program and the ground plan upon which the Expedition was organized. He then outlines some of the objectives of the Expedition, notably that of obtaining the rare and typical large mammals of Asia for exhibition in the new Hall of Asiatic Life of the American Museum of Natural History, which was his particular work as a zoölogist. The Expedition, which finally got under way at Peking, "made a very imposing spectacle with seven cars. . . . Above us loomed a rampart of basalt cliffs crowned with the Great Wall of China which stretched its serpentine length along the broken rim of the plateau. Roaring like the prehistoric monsters, the bones of which we had come to seek, our cars gained the top of the last steep slope and passed through the narrow gateway of the wall. Before us lay Mongolia, a land of painted deserts dancing in mirage. . . ." It is through numerous and similar descriptive bits that the author prepares the reader for the great moments of discovery when he gives in detail the finding, for example, of the reptilian bone, the dinosaur, which he considers added an entirely new geological period to the knowledge of the continental structure of Central Asia and opened up a palæontological vista dazzling in its brilliance. This, with the other previous findings, indicated to the scientist that the theory upon which the expedition was organized might be true; that "Asia is the mother of the life of Europe and America." The most important find, from the scientist's viewpoint, was the skeleton of a Baluchitherium, the discovery of which the author considers has a very important bearing on the general theory of evolution and is favorable to the supposition that the "ancestors of man may also be found in this same country." The scientist describes his personal experiences and reactions, together with those of his companions, through the long months of discovery, when new specimens were being constantly added to his collections— skulls, skeletons, and the "first dinosaur eggs ever seen by human eyes." His conclusions, however, accord to the discovery of archaic mammals the greater scientific importance, as the author holds that probably after the dinosaur eggs have been forgotten these little skulls will be remembered by scientists "as the crowning single discovery of research in Asia." The scientist, in his search for ancestral stock, and the place of its development, believes that it is only by finding skeletons or skulls that he can definitely correlate Asiatic primitive men with those of Europe, and he sees in their "culture," the types of implements which they made, and the methods of shaping the stone tools a relationship which strengthens his contention that there was a common origin for the European and Asiatic cultures. In addition to the scientific discoveries of the Expedition, the information gained of the flora of the country, the members of the party spending many days in botanizing, shows it to be much like that of American lakes. This, with the findings of the geologists, as well as the contributions of the palæontologists, and the studies of animal life in the desert, supply the material in this volume of illuminating clues for the archæologist.

ONE MAN'S LIFE, by Herbert Quick (1925). An autobiography which had reached the author's twenty-eighth year when his death at sixty-three left it unfinished. His father and mother, of Dutch extraction, were early pioneers to the Middle West from New York State. He tells as if it were part of his own experience of the train of three ox teams that reached Dubuque, Iowa, in the rainy season of 1857. The fowls were in crates tied to the back of the wagon. Their one cow his father had named Shakespeare. At district school later Herbert was puzzled to find pages of blank verse apparently "written by our old cow — or, anyhow, with her name signed to them," in his Fifth Reader. His father and mother were married in "mid-voyage" of the prairie schooners. The rains had made the Iowa River impossible to cross, and so the family settled in a log house at Steamboat Rock. They lived that bitterly cold winter on the deer that were trapped by the deep snow. Herbert Quick's father was an excellent sawyer, and there was a great demand for men of his ability. From this log house the family moved to a farm on the prairie, where Herbert was born in 1861. He had infantile paralysis when he was two years old, and, though he recovered his general health, it was a trial for him to wear shoes and his share of the farm work was physical torture to the "pale, awkward, clumsy boy." He always had a slight lameness, and the world of the intellect became of necessity the only realm in which he had any chance to succeed. At school he was recognized as a tow-head prodigy. He pays tribute to the virtues of the McGuffey readers which gave his young mind the experience of real literature. From the First and Second Readers he learned to know Mary's Lamb by heart, and that George

Washington could not tell a lie about the cherry tree. The Third Reader included beautiful selections from the Bible, and introduced him to such writers as Croly, Irving, Scott and others. The Fifth Reader contained selections from Shakespeare, Byron, Milton, Johnson, Bryant, and Addison. The small boy found a tune for Browning's "How They Brought the Good News from Ghent to Aix," so that he could sing it at the top of his voice as he followed the cows or the plough or the harrow. The story of his childhood runs parallel with the description of the prairie, the changes of the seasons, the grass high enough to hide a tall man walking through in the swales, hunting for the eggs of the prairie chickens after a fire had bared the ground, fishing in the many little brooks with a hook made from the ribs of a discarded parasol. The birds and animals and flowers of the Iowa prairies were a joy to the imaginative boy. He watched the sand-hill cranes dance with odd mingling of awkwardness and grace, and hunted for wild geese. The western meadow lark he believes to be an eastern bird "which migrated to the prairies and learned in the great open spaces to give forth a broader and fuller message than that which it brought from the forests." The people who migrated he judged went through the same sort of change. The house he lived in was of thin, unpainted basswood, and with no coal, and only the wood hauled from the timber, the winters were a test of endurance. During the cold waves and blizzards many people froze to death in their beds, and he remembers hearing his father tell of the freezing of live stock. The family moved farther west to Colfax Township. The chapter on the "Chronicle of Wheat" tells of raising wheat before and after machinery was invented to help the farmer, and the "Tragedy of Wheat," the appearance of rust and blight which forced a change of crops. The corn and hogs came to pay as little as had wheat after a time. The summer before Herbert's fifteenth birthday the Grange movement turned to politics and anti-monopoly to the wrath of Governor Clarkson. A six weeks' course at a teacher's institute gained the youth of sixteen a certificate to teach school. He hoped to earn money to go to college, but the money was always needed at home, and he had to give up that dream. At one time he applied for admission to West Point to get an education, and was debarred because of the traces of his infantile paralysis which would have made long hours on his feet, marching, impossible. At Mason City, Iowa, he taught school and studied law at the same time. A girl from Syracuse, Ella Corey, came to visit, and two years later when he had been admitted to the bar, he made his first visit East to see her again, and brought her back with him. The book contains portraits of pioneer characters as well as the pioneer life, old "Doc Wright," who worsted a grizzly bear in a hand-to-hand fight, the Rainsbarger gang of terrorists who appear in his novel "The Hawkeye" as the Bushyagers, and Klinefelter, the friend of the author's early days as a schoolteacher, his father who never read a book after he became a pioneer, the Van Sweringens, and others. The last chapter tells of his introduction to the theories of Henry George.

ORDEAL OF CIVILIZATION, THE, by James Harvey Robinson (1926). The author, a leader of the new and humanistic school of historians, begins this history of Europe and its civilization with an introduction on history as "something far more vital than the record of bygone events and the description of extinct institutions." Those events and situations which promise to forward the understanding of how the ideas, institutions, and ideals that make our Western Civilization have come about rather than what were those of our predecessors have been selected from the record of the past. The book is more than a sketch of the history of Europe since during the past two or three centuries the civilization of Western Europe has spread itself over the world "as no other civilization in the history of mankind has done," because modern science and invention have developed unprecedented methods of intercommunication and transportation.   Therefore the history of Western Europe is "the background of contemporaneous ways of doing and thinking" in North and South America, Australasia, and latterly of India, Japan, Western Asia and Africa. The story begins with the decline and break-up of the Roman Empire.   Dr. Robinson stresses the importance of the fact that we do not inherit our civilization directly from the Roman Empire, because the intervening Middle Ages "emphasized habits of thought and institutions . . . which form in a peculiar sense the background of our prevailing civilization."   The review of events continues with the Germanic invasions and succeeding age of turmoil, the subsequent rise of towns, the spread of trade, the rôle of the Church, the revival of higher education, the substitution of the kingly state for the feudal baronies, the Renaissance, the Protestant Reformation, the French Revolution, the development of the modern states, the Industrial Revolution, Great Britain and her Empire, the expansion of European influence in the nineteenth century through international trade and competition and imperialism, the partition of Africa, European interference in China and Japan, rivalry of Japan and Russia, Russia and the Near Eastern question.   The last chapters are the World War, and Europe since the World War, including the settlement of the Treaty of Versailles, changes in the map of Europe, the League of Nations, and plans to abolish war.   The author then returns to the subject of his introduction in a chapter dealing with "the present trend of human affairs" and "the importance of being historically minded."   He points out that it was "the students of nature rather than historians who first appreciated the tremendous advantage of finding out how things had come about in order to comprehend the more fully how they are," and thus furnished a new setting and a new starting point for human history.   Civilization may be "measured by the degree in which it transcends the possibilities of our animal progenitors and all our animal relatives."   The discoveries of behaviorist psychology in experiments with babies and children contribute to an understanding of the life of adults.   A survey of the knowledge of the world and its inhabitants, that is now available, leads the writer to reflect that we continue to think of new things in the old ways and are really far more old-fashioned than we realize, that while Knowledge increases at a rapid pace Wisdom tarries far behind.   The answer to many of our present problems could be found in the understanding of the past in which they had their beginnings.   Man is too apt to accept without question the habits and beliefs of the group in which he happens to be reared.   Advance in intelligence depends upon ability to question and reconsider what we have taken for granted.   We should summon prejudices and carelessly formed convictions to the bar of judgment and trace their history and analyze their hold upon us.   "Precedent, however venerable, must be reinspected before it is accepted."   History might become "the sovereign solvent of prejudice and the necessary preliminary to readjustments and reforms" in the field of politics, economics, education, and our social relations.   Dr. Robinson suggests that it might have a chastening effect on "an ardent Marxian socialist to realize that Marx's theories were a mid-Victorian product, the counterpart of the classical, Manchester school of defenders of things as they were."   He would have every school child read the Madison Papers and "realize the groping, the compromises, the British and French influences" that went into the making of our Federal Constitution.   The growth of "historical-mindedness" will "enable future writers to give history far more importance than hitherto in the useful enlargement of our memories by showing not so much how things were as how they came about.   The author gives many illustrations of the value of this emphasis on the interpretation of what is now known of the past. He considers the "appreciation of the current discoveries in regard to man's nature contributed by biologists and psychologists and reënforced by anthropologists" a sign of progress.

ORIGIN AND EVOLUTION OF LIFE, THE, by Henry Fairfield Osborn (1917). The author is president of the American Museum of Natural History and research professor of zoölogy at Columbia University. The theory here presented is that of "action, reaction and interaction of energy." The first half of the volume is "devoted to what we know of the capture, storage, release, and reproduction of energy in its simplest and most elementary living phases; the second half is devoted to the evolution of matter and form in plants and animals, also interpreted largely in terms of energy and mechanics." "The demonstration of evolution as a universal law of living nature" is accepted as "the great intellectual achievement of the nineteenth century," but the writer stresses the wide diversity of opinion on the *causes* of evolution. He believes that although "we know to some extent *how* plants and animals and man evolve; we do not know *why* they evolve," and that naturalists have failed "to make progress in the search for causes . . . because they have attempted to reason backward from highly complex plant and animal forms to causes . . . thinking from matter backward into energy rather than from energy forward into matter and form." He would "reverse our thought in the search for *causes* and take steps toward an energy conception of the origin of life and an energy conception of the nature of heredity." Starting from Newton's three laws of motion, Dr. Osborn develops the idea that in addition to the physico-chemical laws of action and reaction between organisms and their environment there are also laws of interaction between the parts of the organism. "In each organism the phenomena of life represent the action, reaction, and interaction of four complexes of physico-chemical energy, namely, those of (1) the Inorganic Environment, (2) the developing Organism (protoplasm and body-chromatin), (3) the germ of Heredity-chromatin, (4) the Life Environment. Upon the resultant actions, reactions, and interactions of potential and kinetic energy in each organism Selection is constantly operating wherever there is competition with the corresponding actions, reactions, and interactions of other organisms." Thus every living plant and animal is plastically moulded by four sets of energies. The following chapters consider in order, "first the evolution of the inorganic environment necessary to life; second, theories of the origin of life in regard to the time when it occurred and the accumulation of various kinds of energy through which it probably originated; and, third, the orderly development of the differentiation and adaptation of the most primitive forms." There follows a survey of the development of life-forms from the bacteria to the highest mammals, covering a period of "perhaps a hundred million years." In his introduction he quotes Aristotle as essentially right when he said that "Nature produces those things which, being continually moved by a certain principle contained in themselves, arrive at a certain end." The writer aims to discover what this internal moving principle may be.

ORPHAN ANGEL, THE, by Elinor Wylie (1926). For purposes of fiction the author assumes that Shelley was not drowned, but instead was rescued by a Yankee brig just off Leghorn Harbour, and carried to America, not unwillingly, as he suspected that Mary no longer cared for him. There is no answer to the letter he sends her from Boston, and he does not know that the ship was lost on the return voyage, and Mary never received any word from him. His rescuer, David Butternut, had killed one of the crew, Jasper Cross, in self-defence. The conscience-stricken David believes Shiloh (the Scriptural name he mistakes for Shelley), who resembles Jasper, to be sent by God to take Jasper's place and save him from being a murderer, and the captain rejoices that he can satisfy the authorities of the port of Boston that he has brought home the same number of crew that shipped on sailing. David confides to Shiloh that he feels that he must go to Kentucky in search of the unknown sister of Jasper, Silver Cross, to make atonement. The quest of an injured woman, beautiful, alone, and perhaps in peril, appeals to Shiloh's poetic fancy. They start the long journey on foot from Boston through the forests and pioneer settlements of the romantic, free America of Shelley's dreams. The charm of Shiloh's serious grandiloquent manner and conversation and his physical beauty win friends all along the way, and the common sense of the rough, kindly David saves the pilgrimage from coming to an untimely end. In Louisville they find out that Silver had moved years before to St. Louis, and as there is no letter from Mary, Shiloh goes on with David, happy in the fiery joy of being free. Shiloh saves the lovely child, Melissa, from drowning herself to get away from her drunken father, though as she says, "I reckon you can't fix a man's hog-meat and mush for seven years without getting mighty attached to him, spite of being hanged about a bit when the corn liquor's entry powerful in his sperrit." It is arranged that Judge Poindexter shall take the granddaughter of his old friend to live in his home, and the champions of the distressed damsel are able to start on their way again. Shiloh's zeal to help women in trouble is equalled only by his greater zeal to leave them when they inevitably fall in love with him. At the Ohio River they join Captain Appleby and Professor Lackland going to the Professor's wedding on a flat boat, and the time passes pleasantly as Shiloh and the Professor discuss philosophy and David plays checkers with the Captain. The bride, Miss Rosalie Lillie, weeps for love of Shiloh as she prepares for the wedding festivities. Silver, a poor little Cinderella, has left St. Louis to go live with her rich, arrogant, Spanish relatives in California. Her kind old godfather, Monsieur Saint Ange, has received a legacy since her departure and proposes that Shiloh and David shall bring her back to him or at least see how it fares with her, and for Silver's sake, the proud Shiloh permits him to loan them money to provide the equipment of pack mules and saddle horses for the long dangerous trail across the plain, and over the Rocky Mountains. They are captured by Indians, but Anne, a white girl, adopted daughter of the chief, saves them just as the fire is kindled at the foot of the stake to which Shiloh is bound, and brings him to banquet with her father, a noble brave, who talks like Horace Walpole. He says, "It will give me great pleasure to make you known to certain of our more distinguished chiefs to-night; you must be sick of the society of women and social inferiors." Shiloh thanks him, but protests, "I cannot agree to your strictures upon the opposite sex, and I have never agreed to any theory whereby society is arbitrarily divided by certain rules inadmissible to an enlightened mind." Anne, in anger that Shiloh's couch is covered with furs other than sable and beaver, declares that she will strip the skin off her body and stretch it for the comfort of this man she loves with the "ultimate fervor of her soul," and her father says, "Gently, gently, my dear little girl; it is quite unnecessary to become so emphatic about a mere matter of bedding." He sends her to her room for punishment of her "egregious folly." David thinks it might pass the time "to go to their party," and "to see all them solemn old mummies setting round in their Sunday shawls, and then handing a long painted pipe about in the silliest way I ever see in all my born days." The way across the desert is beset by many strange adventures, but at last Shiloh, in the costume of a Spanish gentleman, calls on Don Narciso de Coronel, and finds Silver, Silvie la Croix, lovely as her miniature, sitting under a rose tree in the garden.

ORPHAN ISLAND, by Rose Macaulay (1924). In the year 1855 a company of orphans gathered from East London and, bound for an asylum in San Francisco, together with a governess, Miss Charlotte Smith, a dour Scottish nurse, Jean, and the ship's doctor, O'Malley, an Irishman, are shipwrecked, and cast away on an uninhabited, tropical island in the Pacific. The treacherous ship's mate, Thinkwell, who left the party to their fate, prospered in Australia. He left a written confession of his misdeed and a chart, showing the location of the island, which many years later came into the hands of his grandson, a Cambridge don, who decides to set out with his sons, Charles and William, and his daughter, Rosamond, on a rescue expedition in 1922. They land on the Island and find Miss Smith, aged ninety-eight, reigning over a population of over a thousand souls. Miss Smith had reconstructed on her coral reef the social order of Victorian England. She had married the bibulous, satirical O'Malley, after the Scottish rite, and had ten children, remaining in ignorance of the fact that he has a wife in Ireland until just before a hungry shark put an end to him and his stream of Latin quotations. The Smiths, her offspring, are the landed gentry, the aristocracy of Smith Island, and the orphans and their progeny furnish the working class, the hewers of wood and drawers of water. The daughter of an evangelical clergyman, Miss Smith established the Church of England, with Sunday services and Sabbath prohibitions. Education is based on what she herself had learned and taught in former days. Conduct is modelled on the precepts of Miss Smith, and a book of etiquette saved from the ship. There is a daily "press" written on the sands of the beach, and read sociably by the assembled community. Miss Smith calls her eldest son, Albert Edward, and her dwelling "Balmoral," and uses the royal "we" when conversing with her subjects. There is a rebel group in one corner of the Island which provides its Irish problem. The Thinkwells have an audience with Miss Smith, who warns them not to put notions in the heads of the orphans about leaving the island. However, a number of the orphans want to be rescued, and see the world, and Miss Smith plots to prevent this emigration. During the festivities of the "Royal Birthday" the convicts, acting on secret instructions from their "sovereign," seize the ship and sail away, and the Thinkwells and the captain are marooned with the rest. Old Jean is cruelly disappointed to lose the chance which she has cherished for so many years of returning to Scotland, and for revenge on Miss Smith tells the Islanders that Miss Smith was "ne'er the honest wife of the doctor." Miss Smith has a stroke and dies from rage and excitement. The orphans rebel and throw off the "Smith yoke," declare a republic, change the name of the Island to Orphan Island, and ask Mr. Thinkwell to head the government. He faced the task of bringing the Island from the stage of knowledge of the Victorian era of 1855 up to the Neo-Georgian period of 1923, and found it more interesting than his work in Cambridge. For Rosamond it was a dream come true to live on the lovely Island. The scientific William "had occasional desires to increase his stock of knowledge at European sources," but "these are counterbalanced by the greater freedom and peace of his present life." Charles, in love with Flora Smith, is unhappy when she marries Peter Connoly, her island lover, but he is made a professor of literature, and finds "as much pleasure in writing for this island public as for his public (nearly as small and much less appreciative) in England." The story is an entertaining satire on the Victorians, the moderns, and the whole human race.

OSLER, THE LIFE OF SIR WILLIAM, by Harvey Cushing (2 vols., 1925). Here is a record of the significant achievements in Canadian, American and British medical history from 1870 to 1920 — a record animated by Osler's personality and testifying fully concerning the important part he played in medicine during this half century. The author, himself a distinguished surgeon and neurologist, explains in a foreword that "because of Osler's interest in the history of his profession the effort has been made — to bring him into proper alignment with that most remarkable period in the annals of medicine through which he lived and of which he was part. The reader of the biography is further told that "here are merely the outlines of the final portrait, to be painted out when the colours, lights and shadows come in time to be added. . . ." The biographer, as far as possible, lets Osler tell his own story by means of extracts from his writings and addresses and through a recital of the manifold activities which crowded his life. The first volume, which treats of Osler's early life and of his work in Canada and the United States, covers the most active years of his professional career. The son of an Episcopal clergyman from Cornwall, the youngest of nine children, born in the wilderness of Upper Canada in 1849, came to medicine through his interest in natural history and science. When Osler wrote his text-book, "The Principles and Practice of Medicine," in 1891, he dedicated the volume to three men: William Arthur Johnson, James Bovell, and Robert Palmer Howard. Johnson was Warden of the preparatory school attended by young William Osler and was an ardent student of natural history; Bovell was Dean and Professor of the Institutes of Medicine at Trinity College, Toronto; Howard was Dean of the Medical Faculty at McGill University. They were apparently the three who did most to shape the scientific and professional ideals of William Osler. In his early twenties, while acting as clerk in the Montreal General Hospital, Osler read and made part of his working creed the sentence from Carlyle: "Our main business is not to see what lies dimly at a distance, but to do what lies clearly at hand." Putting this precept into vigorous practice, he devoted the next ten years to study, both at home and abroad; to lecturing on physiology at McGill; to a more intense and intelligent application of the microscope to the problems of disease than it had hitherto been put on this side of the Atlantic; to the production of innumerable and well-written articles on various phases of medical research; and to practical work in the wards and the post-mortem room, whereby "he laid the foundation of his subsequent brilliant career as a clinician." Perhaps Osler's most far-reaching influence upon American medicine, following his acceptance of a post as Professor of Clinical Medicine at the University of Pennsylvania, lay in his frank criticism of the lax standards existing in most of the medical schools of the United States during the eighties. His power as a teacher and inspiring director of medical research was already being widely felt, and his boyish gaiety and capacity for friendship were making him as well liked in Philadelphia as he had been in Toronto and Montreal. As Physician-in-Chief to the Johns Hopkins Hospital in Baltimore Osler continued his contributions to medical teaching and research in the United States. During the next fifteen years, or up to the time he was called to Oxford in 1905, he did a number of notable things. He wrote his text-book of medicine; he instituted the method of bedside teaching in the wards for the benefit of medical students; he made important studies of typhoid fever and tuberculosis; he gained increasing prestige as a teacher, lecturer, and writer; and at the end of this strenuous period, spurred on by his wife, Grace Revere Gross, descendant of Paul Revere, he decided that the call to Oxford as Regius Professor of Medicine was an opportunity he could not let pass. In the second volume Osler is taken through his quieter, English period — a period in which he devoted himself more and more to books and reading, although taking an active part in Oxford teaching and English medical work. All sorts of honors came to him in these later years. He was painted by Sargent as a member of that notable group which includes three other renowned physicians, Welch, Halstead, and Kelly. He was made a delegate of the University Press and became one of the Curators of the Bodleian Library. The Athenaeum Club conferred membership upon him, likewise the Bibliographical Society. He delivered numerous lectures at famous institutions and became Sir William in 1911, when the new King George made him a baronet. As for his work, he was active in bringing about the success of the Oxford Fund campaign and in working for broadening reforms in the University curriculum. He continued his fight against tuberculosis, allied himself energetically with public health propaganda in England, and was of great service to medical education in the kingdom. He was a champion of preliminary science courses "properly given" in the public schools, even though such work might endanger the ancient prestige of classical studies. The last five years of Osler's life were shadowed but ennobled by sacrifices to war. While he was performing professional service of great importance to the English army, as an active Colonel in the Medical Corps and as a research worker, both Lady Osler and he were living in constant apprehension that their son and only child, Revere Osler, lieutenant of artillery, would not survive the constant fighting in which his battery was engaged. He was killed by shell-fire in August, 1917, back of Ypres. During the next two years Osler devoted himself chiefly to writing. He died of pneumonia December 29th, 1919.

OUR SOCIAL HERITAGE, by Graham Wallas (1921). Our social heritage consists of that portion of acquired characteristics derived from teaching and learning. It is the distinguishing feature of man as a civilization-building animal, and man has in a sense become dependent upon his social heritage to the extent that, deprived of it, he would either perish, or vegetate for thousands of years in semi-animal barbarity. The fact that our social heritage is constantly increasing necessitates its continuous criticism and improvement. We acquire, as individuals, a part of our social heritage from the power, inculcated in childhood, of making sustained muscular and mental efforts. Will and impulse are differentiated and controlled, resulting in the ability to use for a long period of time processes which are naturally intermittent, like working and thinking. We manufacture motives and drives that impel us in these activities by suppressing inattention, fatigue, and the desire for variety. These artificial intellectual and muscular methods have had the most successful results in the physical sciences, but now the effort seems to be directed to the moral sciences, with possible consequences to educational technique. Our social heritage involves group action, or rather, group coöperation, which is based, like individual work, on a combination of biologically inherited instincts and socially acquired habits. Language is an integral part of group coöperation and our impulses in a group involve the intermittent desire to lead and to follow. Using language as a means of controlling and expressing these impulses we derive social discipline, discussion, and dissent, although at times of emotional stress, social expedients are likely to be replaced by reversion to primitive instinct. The unit of social coöperation in modern times is the nation. But the nation is an artificial grouping more dependent on social heritage than ordinary group coöperation. The nation is an abstract intellectual entity, and one the formation of which has been left to chance or to untrustworthy professional moulders of opinion. But we should try to form a rational idea of the nation and make this formation a conscious process. Without this conscious process we are not likely to realize that permanent unity within a modern industrialized nation must be based on contentment. Contentment, in turn, depends on the highest possible social equality, on an understanding of economic facts, and on the greatest possible adaptation of each individual to his work. This adaptability and consequent liking will result rather from educating to realize differences among human beings than from inculcating identity. The coöperative activities of nations during the nineteenth century proceeded haphazard by means of two instruments: the territorial state and capitalism, both of which are now under the fire of both criticism and unreasoned opposition. Progressive opinion now favors vocationalism. Considered critically, vocationalism must, to justify itself, offer a sufficiently varied life, refrain from strengthening professional conservatism, permit the integration of labor, and be compatible with the accumulation of capital for future work. Experience on all these points tends to show that the modern democratic state takes the more socially desirable, and modern vocational organization the less socially desirable side. An examination of the Trades Unions, which are the most highly organized vocational organizations of to-day, supports this view. From a psychological point of view, the obstruction of human impulses depends for its results rather on the nature of the obstructing cause than on the nature of the obstruction. Hence the principle of liberty must be based on psychological insight. The author finds that the acumen of Pericles on this point was far greater than that of Mill and the Liberal Party in the nineteenth century, and that the future of Liberalism depends on its ability to modify for modern use the viewpoint of Pericles. As psychological entities of the same power are natural rights, honor, and independence, and a practical examination of their value will lead to discrimination in their use as records parliamentary government, the press, in fact, all the agencies of modern government. No abstract consideration will avail. From national coöperation to world coöperation is not a mere extension. It involves a change in the process of coöperation, since socially desirable national habits, say of defence, may interfere in the wider sphere of international coöperation. But world coöperation is essential to the survival of the species, since wars are becoming more and more destructive and comprehensive in their scope. Only a strict historical and scientific attitude toward the concepts of nationality, equality, liberty, etc., will pave the way to international coöperation. Intellectually, science and the scientific attitude have involved us personally in the dilemma of free-will and determinism. However we seek to escape it, it reacts unfortunately upon our conduct. Simpler motives seem more "scientific" than less simple motives. Likewise, the materialistic interpretation of history has been since 1848 a revolutionary economic force, at the same time that Darwinian determinism has offered an apparent explanation of wars, making them more likely. Individually, determinism lessens initiative and responsibility. Loose thinking on scientific versus non-scientific motives should therefore be carefully controlled. In this problem what part has the Church, a socially inherited factor of great importance, been able to play? In wars, its effect has been absolutely nil. In the English Church the failure is ascribed to defects in metaphysical and psychological insight. Everywhere the substitution of ritual for ethics seems to be the rule. Clerical professionalism and vivifying intellectual activity are incompatible, and the latter will not necessarily follow from the former as a result of the disestablishment of the Anglican Church. Organized emotion, in an intellectual rebirth, will probably take a radically different form from that we have associated with the Church.

OUR TIMES, by Mark Sullivan (2 vols., 1926–1927). The first volume, "The Turn of the Century," is the history of the first twenty-five years of the twentieth century after the manner of McMasters, whose lead he follows, since his main concern is with the occupations, the amusements, the literary canons of the times, the changes of manners and morals whereby he traces the growth of the human spirit. No longer is the main emphasis on the wars that have occurred, nor the leaders that have arisen from time to time. With his long experience as a newspaper man, Mark Sullivan brings a new point of view to the appraisal of history. The newspaper virtues of conciseness, accuracy, and sense of dramatic display are here, but back of these qualities stand more substantial ones, an equally modern conception of the forces below the surface. The forces of unrest, and sympathy with the under dog prevalent before 1900, that brought about the fall of the great trusts and the period of muck-raking which contributed to the rise of Roosevelt; these are enunciated clearly as the mood of the people at the dawn of the new century. A first glance at this book with its curious juxtaposition of bright and dark patches makes it appear a veritable crazy quilt of history, its facts flung on paper with the seeming irrelevance of any masterpiece of cubist art. The manners and customs and the clothes that accompanied them are reproduced with careful fidelity. The old files of "The Ladies Home Journal" and "Butterick" are drawn upon to illustrate these and incidentally the fact brought out that a long step toward the emancipation of women was achieved when they were freed from the weight and waste of clothes that swept the ground. No less clearly the gradual freeing of thought from the fetters of nineteenth century provincialism is traced not only in more liberal customs and manners but in the art and literature of the period. The quality of the best sellers in fiction, the folk humor, the popular music of 1900 is contrasted with that of 1925. Out of the mood and manners of 1900 have grown the principles and practice of 1925. While the people, their temper and their tastes, is his theme, out of the people have come three leaders who have moulded the people to their will, Bryan, Roosevelt, and Wilson. Mr. Sullivan speaks of these men as a contemporary who has watched them in the making. His anecdotes of them will be a source for future historians. Particularly characteristic of the person and the period is the story of Roosevelt's rise to power by means of, and finally over the heads of, the bosses, Platt and Hanna. Other backgrounds he gives us, those of the great inventions of this quarter of a century which have so markedly changed life for the man in the streets. The use of typewriters was more than trebled. In 1925 the use of the telephone was fifteen times what it was in 1900. The radio was unknown in 1900, did not come into general use until 1920 and then there were only five thousand sets used by the technically expert. By 1924 there were about two million five hundred thousand receiving sets in use. The perfecting of the vacuum cleaner and the electric iron, thinks the author, may have meant as much to the average woman as the bringing of the suffrage. The story of the automobile is told in full together with those inventions which preceded it that are used in its construction. "The automobile was no more than a coördination and adaptation of old ideas and inventions, some of which, like the wheel, mingled their origins with the mists of antiquity." This book is based, not only on a new attitude toward history, the emphasis on the people and their progress; there is also a new attitude toward the importance of wars. "The losses occasioned by the War were far outbalanced by the salvaging of life effected by new discoveries in medical science and the application of new principles in sanitation." There is besides a new emphasis on what makes life richer for the average man. His material enrichment and comfort he gives in detail, but Mark Sullivan questions, "whether he was spiritually enriched also; what use man made of his increased years upon the earth, his increased leisure. . . . Of this it is not possible to speak so confidently. . . . He got more goods, more things, but also he became more enmeshed in the anxieties of a complex and hurried way of life. He missed the chance of making a possible more satisfying use of the release from physical labor that electricity brought." Then there is a new attitude toward heroism. When he discusses the achievements of scientists, particularly of those martyr doctors, Lazear, Carroll, Finlay and Reed, who succeeded in stamping out yellow fever in Cuba, of Colonel Goethals and Gorgas in Panama he finds the true heroes of the modern spirit.

The second volume, "America Finding Herself," although it does not have the attraction of novelty in historical writing as the first volume had, holds the interest as well and is as full of characteristic detail as the first. The American mind is revealed through the forces that formed it. Since the average American active during the first twenty-five years of the twentieth century acquired his stock of ideas, his cultural background before 1900, the principal source of that culture was the country school. The readers, particularly McGuffey's, were the main textbooks in use, and these formed the literary taste of the pupils, as they gave them some familiarity with the English classics. The history taught was mainly American. Historical perspective and balancing of values were sacrificed to an aggressive national complacency. The geographies were behind the time and no less liable than the histories to teach the inferiority of other races and countries. Singing geography was a quaint custom of this period. Education started as a religious conception and was predominant in the schools. Its influence continued for a long time to be felt in secular studies. Arithmetic, spelling and fine Spencerian handwriting held an important place in the curriculum of every school, as well as elocution and public speaking usually of a flamboyant type. The economic aspects of the first five years of the century show a change from one-man business enterprises to large corporations and the growth of these into trusts. Dodd was the man who took the word trust in its biblical meaning and perverted it to its modern connotation. The oil trust and the steel trust, so different in their methods of operation, and the men who made them what they were, Rockefeller and Carnegie, are carefully analyzed. The picture drawn is careful to overlook no details however incriminating, yet is full of those extenuations of these men and their work due to the trend of the times in which they lived. Then Roosevelt is pictured going into action. The surprise of the conservative rich men, among whom he belonged by birth, when his policy of fair play for all who are Americans without fear or favor to any, is put into practice, is vividly brought out. The complexities of the labor situation and of the anthracite coal strike whose settlement so increased Roosevelt's prestige, are explained. How Roosevelt freed himself from political vassalage to Mark Hanna brings out the character of two men born to rule according to their different standards in a manner that does justice to both. Since, however, the purpose of the author in this history is to tell the story of the average man in America, neither the complete story of the trusts is told nor a detailed picture of Roosevelt's career given. There follows a chapter on the pure food agitation, its inception in the furor that followed the publication of Upton Sinclair's novel "The Jungle," its development by such experts as Dr. Wiley, and Miss Alice Lakey, and its successful conclusion after seventeen years' delay by lobbyists and politicians. No less dramatic than the story of Roosevelt in the political arena and Wiley on the pure food crusade is that narrating the patient struggle of the Wrights and their predecessor, Langley, for mastery of the air. An exceptionally acute analysis of the result gained by the perfect coördination of their mental qualities working together, helps to make their success more easily understood. The final chapters deal with such minor but important matters to the average man as the changing fashions in clothes, the popular literature and the drama of the period.

OUTWARD BOUND, a drama, by Sutton Vane (1924).   For the thread of the story the author uses the myth of Charon's ferry on the river Styx.   The ferry boat is changed to a modern ocean liner, and the action takes place in the lounge room. Five of the seven passengers do not realize the momentous change which has overtaken them, though they are vaguely puzzled that they cannot remember just how they came on board, or what port they are bound for.   Ann and Henry, a pair of young lovers who have become passengers by their own act, know how and why they are there, and now fear nothing but separation.   The other passengers are a snobbish, middle-aged woman, Mrs. Cliveden-Banks, who is taking the trip to join her husband, Tom Prior, a young wastrel, who all his life has "started to face facts by getting drunk," William Duke, "a sincere, earnest, young clergyman," Mr. Lingley, a pompous, self-made millionaire and member of Parliament, and Mrs. Midget, a worn, gentle little charwoman who had once had a lodging house of her own.   It is Prior who first discovers that there seem to be no officers or crew aboard except the elderly steward, Scrubby, and that there are no port or starboard lights on the boat.   He overhears Ann and Henry talking about turning on the gas, and he remembers that the husband Mrs. Cliveden-Banks expects to meet died a month ago.   The steward answers his question, "Yes sir, we are all dead.   Quite dead. They don't find out so soon as you have as a rule."   Scrubby tells him they are sailing for heaven and hell too.   "It's the same place, you see."   With difficulty Tom convinces the other passengers of the truth.   He is panic-stricken as he thinks of his wasted life.   His mother had made every sacrifice to educate him at Oxford and to make a "gentleman" of him, and he has come to nothing.   Mr. Duke, released from the prohibitions and inhibitions of his church, becomes innocently frolicsome, recalling limericks he has overheard his choir boys reciting, and addressing Mrs. Cliveden-Banks as "Banky."   She is certain that nothing unpleasant can happen to one of her important social standing.   Mrs. Midget is concerned only for her unacknowledged son, Prior.   Scrubby tells them that when they reach the harbor an examiner will come on board.   Mr. Lingley, the promoter, calls a meeting to draw up an address, but his usual go-getter methods receive no support.   Duke tells him that he is trying to impress the examiner with his business importance and his "supposed interest in his fellow creatures" to save his own skin.   The examiner turns out to be the genial clergyman, Rev. Frank Thompson, who greets the surprised Duke as an old friend, and wants to hear all the news about their mutual friends.   There is a parish waiting for Duke, and he can begin his work right away by assisting in the examination of his fellow passengers.   The selfless Mrs. Midget passes immediately to her reward.   She is allowed to give up the little cottage with a garden by the sea that is waiting for her to act as housekeeper for her erring son, Prior, who must live and work in the slums.   "Oh sirs, ain't it wonderful?" she says.   "He doesn't know me, and I've got him to look after at last — without any fear of me disgracing him.   It's 'Eaven. . . ."   The foundations of Lingley, Limited, resting on the plans of a turbine engine stolen from the inventor who died in poverty, are well known to the examiner.   Mrs. Cliveden-Banks is condemned to live with her high-souled husband and be a wife to him until she learns to be a good wife.   Her punishment will be to "stand the look in his eyes" which she never was able to meet.   The examiner takes no notice of Ann and Henry who are not on the passenger list.   They are "half-ways" like Scrubby, condemned to remain on the ship until their time comes.   They tell Scrubby that they are unmarried lovers, that they had been brave, but the malicious gossip of their friends had gradually beaten them down. They had turned on the gas to end it all. Henry is worried about their dog, and longs to go back to life — just for a little while. He goes up on deck alone, and disappears. Scrubby thinks that probably the dog outside broke the window, and Henry lives again. Ann calls and Henry comes back to fetch her home. "We've such a lot to do, my love," he says, "and such a little time to do it in. Quick. Quick."

PAGE, THE LIFE AND LETTERS OF WALTER H., by Burton J. Hendrick (2 vols., 1924). The story begins when Page was a ten-year-old Southern boy at the end of the Civil War, but all but one hundred and thirty pages of the two volumes are devoted to his life as ambassador to Great Britain from 1913 to 1918, and especially to the period of the War. He was the youngest of a group of twenty students chosen to inaugurate the new Johns Hopkins University for graduate study. From 1878 to 1913 Page was engaged in newspaper work in various parts of the United States, and as editor successively of the "Forum," the "Atlantic Monthly" and the "World's Work." A Democrat, and life long friend and admirer of Woodrow Wilson, he worked for his election to the presidency. It was Page who introduced Col. House to Mr. Wilson. One day the telephone rang and Col. House's voice came over the wire, "Good morning, Your Excellency." He had been authorized to offer Page the post of ambassador to Great Britain. Then begin the letters about his life and work in England, with the sketch of the diplomatic and political conditions under which the letters were written by Mr. Hendrick. There is hardly anything else to compare with these brilliant, illuminating comments on public men and policies except the letters of the Adams family written at several different periods in our diplomatic history. Theodore Roosevelt wrote to Page in 1918 expressing his belief that Page had represented America during those trying years "as no other ambassador in London has ever represented us, with the exception of Charles Francis Adams during the Civil War." His theory of the office as a "kind of listening post on the front of diplomacy" impelled him to write the President regularly with "a frankness which Mr. Wilson's friends regarded as almost ruthless." A much larger number of letters are addressed to Col. House, many to his family, and some to friends. Wilson said of the letters, "They are the best letters I have ever read." They furnish a life-like portrait of a cultured gentleman of intellectual power and the capacity and genius of a statesman in frank intimate letters touched with a delightful sense of humor. Social functions were a part of his work and he regales the President with descriptions of them at great length, as for example the state dinner to the King of Denmark. The letters about the affair of the British recognition of Huerta as president of Mexico, and the correspondence which led to the repeal of the tolls act in re the Panama Canal are of great historical interest. In the first years of the War he performed exacting duties on behalf of the Central Powers with conscientious fidelity and observed scrupulous public neutrality. "Neutrality," he once exclaimed, "there is nothing in the world as neutral as this embassy. Neutrality takes up all our time." Col. House had been in Europe in 1914 on a secret peace mission to Germany, France, and England, and it was his revelations of failure of negotiations in Germany which convinced Page that Germany was the aggressor in the War. He believed that British-American friendship and coöperation were of the greatest importance to mankind, and differed sharply with Mr. Wilson's policy of neutrality. The letters tell of his difficulties with Mr. Bryan and Mr. Lansing in the State Department, which left his letters unacknowledged and unanswered. He had a great admiration for Sir Edward Grey whom he compares to Lincoln. His arduous duties to which he gave himself without stint made him a victim of the War just as surely as was any man who died in the trenches.

PARTY, AND OTHER STORIES, THE, by Anton Chekhov (1917).

THE PARTY. — Olga Mihalovna, expecting a baby in two months, entertains the guests gathered to celebrate her husband's "name-day" and hopes that they will leave before midnight. All her thoughts and emotions, especially about her husband, Pyotr, are accentuated by her discomfort. Her misery and temporary dislike of her guests grow all through the afternoon's picnic tea, music and supper. That night, after much pain, the baby is born dead and too late her husband regrets that they had not given up everything to take care of the baby.

TERROR. — The writer tells of Dmitri Petrovitch Silin, whom he likes and whose philosophy he enjoys, but whose protestations of friendship embarrass him. He visits him often on his farm and is much attracted by the beauty of Silin's wife, but is not in love with her. One evening Dmitri Petrovitch pours out to him all his inner terror and incomprehension of life. His supposed friend listens only to the fact that Silin's wife does not love her husband. That night he makes advances to the wife, who spends the night with him. In the morning he goes away forever, asking himself: "Why have I done this?"

A WOMAN'S KINGDOM. — Inheritor of a big estate and a factory, Anna Akimova wakes on Christmas Day full of undefined anticipation. She is always uneasy in her conscience about her suffering dependents, but does nothing. All day she receives guests and gives out gifts of money. She is handsome and respected by her large household and by her dependents, but unmarried and dissatisfied. She remembers her early life of poverty and regrets the lost freedom, thinks longingly of marrying anyone, even a peasant. She ends the day in weeping with her maid, who is disappointed in love.

A PROBLEM. — Outside the study door sits Sasha Uskov while inside his three uncles discuss endlessly his crime of cashing a false promissory note and what must be done to save the family honor. His maternal uncle, kind Ivan Markovitch, prevails on the other two to give him another chance and joyfully leads his nephew away, only to have him demand the loan of a hundred-rouble note under threat of repeating his former crime. The nephew returns to his dissipations.

A KISS. — During the War an Artillery Brigade is quartered in a village and a resident general dutifully invites the officers to tea. Among them is a little man, Ryabovitch, with spectacles and red lynx-like whiskers, who is too shy to take part in the conversation. He loses his way in the big house and in a dark room a woman kisses him by mistake. On this kiss he builds up in his imagination a whole love affair and lives happily in it until the Brigade returns later to the little village and nothing really happens. His imaginary romance ends with the feeling that "the whole of life . . . is an aimless jest. . . ."

ANNA ON THE NECK. — As eighteen-year-old Anna goes off on her wedding day with her fifty-two-year-old husband he tells her the story of a man who received the order of Saint Anna of the second grade. It seems that this man had a quarrelsome and frivolous wife so that when His Excellency presented the order he said: "So now you have three Annas: one in your buttonhole and two on your neck." The bridegroom tells his young bride that he hopes His Excellency will never have occasion to say the same to him. At first the young bride is timid and afraid to ask for money for herself and her lovable drunkard father, but, after a success at a dance, followed by the devotion of a number of men, she feels her power and lives a life of continual pleasure, sending her bills to her husband. When the husband comes to receive the order of Saint Anna His Excellency repeats the remark about the three Annas.

THE TEACHER OF LITERATURE. — The teacher, Nikitin, is happily in love and leaves his bachelor quarters with the geography teacher, Ippolit Ippolititich, who always talks of what everybody already knows, to be happily married. His wife, Masha, is young and everything that she does pleases him, but the dogs and cats, which are part of her dowry, annoy him. One night, as he plays cards with some friends, one of them speaks of his having "pots of money," referring to his wife's money. He is stirred by this to complete discontent with his lot and thinks he will take a holiday and go to his old lodgings in Moscow.

NOT WANTED. — Zaikin, coming out to his summer villa, exhausted and hungry, meets a stranger in ginger-colored trousers and they exchange views on the expense of summer homes and say that "Summer holidays are the invention of the devil and of woman." He finds no one but his little boy in the villa, dinner unprepared, and his wife and daughters out rehearsing for a play. His wife returns with noisy guests, who stay so late that they have to spend the night, and Zaikin finds himself giving up his bed. He wanders out for air and meets his acquaintance, Ginger Trousers, also turned out because of guests.

TYPHUS. — Lieutenant Klimov, travelling from Petersburg to Moscow, feels a growing hatred for a Finn travelling companion. It comes from a developing illness, which becomes worse and worse. He can only lie on his seat and suffer, thinking of the comfort of being at home in his own bed and cared for. At home he recovers from typhus and wakes filled with a sensation of infinite happiness and joy which does not at first let him realize the sad news of his sister's death from the contagion.

A MISFORTUNE. — The lawyer, Ilyin, is spending the summer in the neighborhood, tormented by his love for Madame Lubyantsev. She tells him that she loves and respects her husband and she feels most self-righteous, though the lawyer tells her that she is insincere. He makes love to her and she discovers that she is really a low creature and ends by going to him.

A TRIFLE FROM LIFE. — Nikolay Ilyitch Belyaev goes to see his mistress and finds only her young son at home. He amuses himself talking to the child, and after promising on his honor not to tell anyone, receives the information that the child visits his deserted father. As soon as Belyaev's mistress returns, he betrays the child's trust in a selfish rage, though the boy, horrified and unbelieving, tries to stop him.

PASSAGE TO INDIA, by E. M. Forster (1924). The story opens with an argument in the casual conversation of a group of educated Indians as to whether or not it is possible to be friends with an Englishman, and it is the misapprehension on both sides that makes the situation that is the theme of the book. Dr. Aziz, a young Indian surgeon and poet, meets Mrs. Moore in a mosque. He is delighted with her because she has taken the trouble to remove her shoes, and because she talks to him as to an equal without race consciousness. She is charmed with the volatile, exuberant youth. Mrs. Moore is the mother of Ronny Heaslop, the young city magistrate at the small city of Chandrapore, and she has come out to visit him bringing with her, Adela Quested, the girl whom Ronny hopes to marry. Adela wants to see India and Ronny at his post before she decides to marry him and spend her life in India. Both the women are eager to know the real India beyond the Anglo-Indian colony, the Burtons, the Lesleys, and the Callendars, who shun social intercourse with the natives. The collector, Mr. Turton, offers to give a "bridge-party" for them, "not the game, but a party to bridge the gulf between East and West," he explains. The party is not a success as the hostess makes no effort to entertain her Indian guests, and Mrs. Moore and Adela are shocked to see that the natives are not treated with common politeness. Ronny, who is a Babbitt-like type of official copying his superiors in the traditional attitude, tells his mother that he is "not a missionary or a Labour Member or a vague, sentimental literary man . . . just a servant of the Government." He does not intend to be pleasant in India. He has something more important to do. Fielding, the schoolmaster, makes friends with Dr. Aziz, and invites him to tea to meet Mrs. Moore and Miss Quested. They arrange to go on a picnic together to the mysterious Marabar caves in the hills, "a group of fists and fingers thrust up through the soil" above "the sun-baked, flat expanse about Chandrapore." Dr. Aziz takes charge of the expedition, and spares no pains and expense to make it a success. It turns out disastrously. The first cave gives Mrs. Moore an indescribable feeling of fright and depression. Miss Quested goes into one of the caves alone and comes out with the hallucination that Aziz has followed and insulted her. This incident and the subsequent arrest of the sensitive Dr. Aziz arouse conflicting storms of racial passion. Mr. Fielding keeps his head and his belief in Aziz' innocence. "He had not gone mad at the phrase 'an English girl fresh from England,' he had not rallied to the banner of race. He was still after facts, though the herd had decided on emotion." The Europeans put aside their normal personalities and sunk themselves in their community. They ostracize Mr. Fielding for taking the part of the Indian. Mrs. Moore also believes Aziz innocent, and leaves India in the hot season before it is wise to travel to avoid the trial. The Indians consider the false accusation as a pretext for new humiliations and exactions. There is hysterical talk at the Anglo-Indian club, and bazaar talk, told in detail with humor and insight; legends multiply and there is even a small riot. At the trial under cross examination Miss Quested admits that she has made a mistake, that Aziz did not follow her into the cave, and withdraws the charge. The Anglo-Indians continue to believe that Aziz is guilty, and will have nothing more to do with Adela, who has let them down. The kindly Mr. Fielding allows her to remain at the school until her return to England. Mrs. Moore died on her way home, and "a legend sprang up that an Englishman had killed his mother for trying to save an Indian's life — and there was just enough truth in this to cause annoyance to the authorities." Ronny is transferred to another province, and Fielding given a position that takes him out of the district. Aziz had been annoyed that Fielding should give protection to Miss Quested, and persuade him to give up a counter-suit, and their friendship comes to an end in spite of Fielding's efforts at the time, and later when they meet again outside British India in the native state where Aziz makes a new home, they both want to be friends but the time is not yet ripe. Every influence in the land seems to say, "Not yet."

PASSION FLOWER, THE ("La malquerida"), translated from the Spanish of Jacinto Benavente (1913, English translation, 1926). A drama of peasant life in a Spanish village. Acacia, the beautiful daughter of Raimunda, has celebrated her betrothal to Faustino. She had discarded a former lover, her cousin Norbert, because of a rumor of his attentions to another girl. The step-father, Esteban, Raimunda's second husband, offers to accompany Faustino and his father, Tio Eusebio, part of the way as they return to their village. Presently he returns in great agitation with the news that Faustino has been killed by a shot from ambush and the murderer has escaped. Suspicion falls on Norbert, but he is able to establish his innocence to the satisfaction of the Court with proof that he was in another place at the time of the murder. Tio Eusebio and his other sons are convinced that Norbert hired an assassin to do the deed, and swear vengeance. Fleeing from them Norbert comes to his aunt, Raimunda, for protection. He tells her that Rubio, the servant of Esteban, has been showing rolls of bills and drinking in the tavern, and that he has boasted that he is the real master of the house. In the village they are singing a song about Acacia, calling her the "passion flower," because of the evil love her step-father bears her, which had made Esteban frighten Norbert away from her, and pay Rubio to kill Faustino. Acacia has never disguised her aversion for Esteban. Raimunda is passionately in love with her second husband, and accuses Acacia of being the cause of this dreadful situation because she had never treated Esteban like a father. The sons of Tio Eusebio shoot and wound Norbert, and the men of the village stop their work to talk about the affair. Esteban, driven from home by Raimunda's reproaches, had spent the night in the hills among the goat-herds in a hut with Rubio. Now he returns and begs his wife to pity him. He has struggled against his passion for Acacia who has always hated him. Her hate has become a part of his life that he could not bear to live without. The infatuated Raimunda forgives him, and plans to send Acacia away to the convent or to an aunt to make a good marriage. They will forget what has happened. She insists that Acacia shall call Esteban father and embrace him. Forced into his arms Acacia discovers that the great passion that had appeared to her to be hate is love. They cling together as Acacia tells him that he is the man she loves. Raimunda denounces Esteban, calling everyone to come and take the murderer, and disowns her daughter. Acacia urges Esteban to escape, but he refuses to go without her, and shoots Raimunda, who blocks their way. Acacia turns from Esteban to her dying mother, and Raimunda is satisfied.

PEACE CONFERENCE, A HISTORY OF THE, published under the auspices of the Institute of International Affairs, edited by H. W. V. Temperley. (6 vols., 1920–1924.) The first five volumes were planned by George Louis Beer and Lord Eustace Percy, the chapters being allotted to various experts under the general editorship of Mr. Temperley. The first volume is preliminary to the work of the Conference, dealing with the military defeat of Germany, the German Revolution, the Armistice negotiations with texts, the War aims of the belligerents, and of labor, the material effect of the War upon neutrals and belligerents, the organization of the Conference, the Council of Ten, of Four, or Five, the work of the Armistice Commission at Spa, the Supreme Economic Council, dealing with problems of food and relief, and the maintenance of the authority of the Conference in Germany, Poland, and Hungary. A chapter on the legal basis in treaties, conventions, and pre-Armistice agreements of international relations prior to the reëstablishment of peace by the peace treaties is concluded in the second volume. The second and third volumes are devoted to analysis and comment on the German Treaty, which is printed in full with the official index in the third volume. The military occupation of Germany is taken up in connection with the military clauses, and Chapter 7 describes the new Germany since 1918. A chronological summary of the years 1914–1918, and of the Peace Conference, 1919–1920, precedes the documents in the third volume, which include the new German constitution and the Treaties of Bucharest and Brest-Litovsk. The fourth volume tells of the military defeat of Bulgaria, the military and political collapse of Austria-Hungary, the Armistice, and the subsequent problems of the new states. Chapter 5 takes up the Treaty of London and the obligations it imposed on the Allies.

Chapter 6 the plebiscites held in connection with the peace treaties. The fifth volume discusses the reparation and financial clauses in the Austrian, Hungarian, and Bulgarian Treaties, and the economic clauses, including enemy property, debts and contracts in all the treaties, economic reconstruction in Europe, and the problem of racial and religious minorities, with text of minorities treaties, and peace treaties. An additional sixth volume deals with various aspects of the treaties in Northern and Eastern Europe, including Poland, the Baltic settlement and Russia, and outside Europe, the Turkish Empire, and Turkish Treaty, the development of nations and nationalities within the British Empire, Egypt, Iraq and Mosul, Palestine and Zionism, and Persia, Shantung, the United States Senate and the German Treaty, the establishment of the League of Nations, the mandate system with texts of typical mandates, and the Permanent Court. International labor at the Peace Conference is taken up in connection with the labor clauses in the second volume. The sixth volume deals with the International Labour Office, and the labor conferences in Washington, 1919, Genoa, 1920, and Geneva, 1921 and 1922. The documents include the Treaty of Peace between the United States and Germany, drafts and revised Covenant of the League, and the twenty-one demands of Japan, 1915. This work is continued by "The World After the Peace Conference," and the "Survey of International Affairs" for 1920–1923, and 1924.

PEASANTS, THE, A TALE OF OUR OWN TIMES, in 4 volumes: Autumn; Winter; Spring; Summer; translated from the Polish of Ladislas Reymont by Michael H. Dziewicki (1924–1925). The chief peasant of the village of Lipka, Matthias Bornya, a widower, sixty years old, plans to marry Yagna, the prettiest girl in the village, partly to cheer his declining years, and also to spite his married children who are eager to divide his beloved land among themselves. His daughter, Yuzka, is too young to manage his household, and Hanka, Antek's wife, cares only for her husband's interests. In the ceremony of the proposal, Yagna accepts Bornya by drinking the vodka brought by his friends in a truly Shakespearean scene. The wily blacksmith, Michael, husband of Magda, incites Antek to protest because six acres of the farm are given to Yagna as marriage settlement, and after a furious quarrel, in which Antek, who is Yagna's secret lover, names her wanton, Bornya turns his son and his family out of the home. Roch, the beggar apostle, friend of the peasants, with some of the neighbors, tries in vain to reconcile father and son. The wedding festivities of dancing, games and feasting described in detail last several days. Yagna refuses to have her hair cut, thus turning a symbol of submission into the symbol of her own inner freedom. The Christmas ceremonies at the church bring Antek and Yagna together again, and Hanka learns from a spiteful neighbor the explanation of Antek's moods of apathy and violence, and of his fight about Yagna with Matthew, another of her lovers, at the saw mill where he works. Bornya makes common cause with the half-starved Hanka against the lawless lovers. He comes near to murdering his son and his young wife by setting fire to the hay stack where they meet secretly. Antek rebuked by the priest before the congregation becomes a sullen outlaw in the community. In Bornya's house, Yagna, no longer petted and spoiled, works as a servant when she is brought back from her mother's cabin. The winter ends with a battle between the peasants of Lipka and some peasants who have been sent by the squire to cut down the forest in which the villagers have communal rights. Antek rushes to aid his father struck down by the forester, and in the moment they are reconciled, and return to simple relation of father and child. Agata, the old crone who begs alms over the countryside in the winter, returning in the spring that she may die like a good wife on her own feather bed among her relatives, finds the women doing the field work while the men are in prison waiting trial for the affair of the forest. Bornya lies in bed dying, while Hanka, back again in the home, runs the farm competently, guarding Antek's heritage, taking directions from him in the important matter of killing the pig. Yagna, loathing her husband and careless of her honor, drinks at the tavern with the Voyt, the headman of the peasants, now her lover. All the men return home except Antek, held for the death of the forester. The government forces a school on the reluctant people. A company of Germans come to buy the squire's land, are warned, persecuted, and finally driven out by the peasants who want the land themselves. Bornya dies just before Antek comes home on bail. The old man walked out to his fields in the night "like a spirit blessing every clod of earth, every ear of corn," "sowing empty-handed as though he were now sowing his very being in those fields of his fathers — all the days he had lived, all that life he had received, and was now giving back (a sacred harvest) to the Everlasting Lord." He sees the Heavens open and God "seated on a throne of wheat-sheaves" stretches out his hands to him. Antek returns determined to take his father's place on the farm and in the community. Yagna, now in love with Yanek, the organist's son who is studying to be a priest, will have nothing to do with him. The Voyt is in disfavor with the peasants for his mismanagement of their affairs, and the deficit in their funds which they claim he has spent on Yagna. Yanek's mother and the Voyt's wife accuse Yagna, stirring up the peasants to beat her and drive her out of the village. Her brother Simon, married against his mother's unkind will and driven from home, provides a refuge for her and his mother who comes to her, in his hut built far out on the new land. In each volume the season and the country described with lyric beauty serves as relief to the poverty-stricken struggle of the characters who are the slaves of their land. The book is a complete panorama of the life of a Polish peasant in description of the community, of customs and observances, and of the Catholic Church in its personal relation to the people at weddings, funerals, christenings and saints' days.

PERENNIAL BACHELOR, THE, by Anne Parrish (1925). The story of the decadence of an American family, the Campions, and an ironic picture of an age in America, its manners, clothes, games, food, and songs. It begins just before the Civil War when the family are well-to-do and living in their fine house, The Maples, somewhere in Delaware, and ends in the present when the hero is an old beau, laughed at by the modern, emancipated, sophisticated younger generation. The dashing, masterful Victor Campion married his wife, Margaret, because she was so sweet, and pure, and timid, and not "strong-minded." There are three children, Maggie, ten, May, six, and Lily, two, and they hope that the baby that is expected will be the longed-for son and heir. Mr. Campion is thrown from his horse and killed, and the child, named Victor, is born that night. Some of Mr. Campion's investments have been ill-advised, and the rest of the property is mismanaged by his widow, who continues to live in the way in which she has always been accustomed. The life of the family revolves around Victor, pampered and spoiled. The soldiers of the Civil War march past The Maples, but they are not as important as Victor's teething. The little girls play croquet in hoopskirts and pantalettes. In the seventies Victor wears jackets with braid looped all around the edges, "as if someone had been practising writing letter l's," and the girls go to picnics in "blue flannel boating costumes," and laugh immoderately at "the word spoon, the sight of a spoon." Mrs. Campion is an attractive woman, and is courted by a neighbor. She tells the worshipped

Victor that he is going to have a new father, and the boy shouts, "No, No," until she consents to send her suitor away. Maggie is the real "man" of the family, with her father's brains, and she also sacrifices her life to Victor. Her lover, Edward, wants her to marry him and go to South America. She gives him up, as she feels responsible for Victor after her mother's death. To pay for Victor's education the girls have no lessons except with their mother, and wear turned dresses. Victor goes to Harvard and is expelled. He falls in love with a heartless flirt, Lucy Hawthorne, who corresponds with him while she is on the Grand Tour, and then writes him that she is to marry a French count. He "accepts a position" with a real estate firm, and Maggie takes boarders to support the family. May, the beauty, does not marry, and her thwarted desires lead to delusions, and queerness, and finally suicide when some one sends her a cruel, old-maid valentine. Victor had made fun of the last man who had paid her attention, and spoiled that belated romance. They sell The Maples, and move into a small house. Maggie discovers that she has a cancer, and dies with the patient heroism that has marked her life. The amiable, selfish Victor never knows that he has ruined the lives of the women of the family. In the last chapter Victor goes to call at The Maples, and the young people who are dancing stop the music as they see him coming, and keep quiet while the butler says "not at home." Lily, standing at the window waiting for him to return home, runs to the door to let him in. She says: "Oh, Victor, you did look so nice coming along the road. I always think there's no one in the world looks as nice in a silk hat as you do."

PHILOSOPHER'S STONE, THE, by Johannes Anker-Larsen, translated from the Danish by Arthur G. Chester (1926). The search of man for God is the theme of this story of the development of two young men of different temperament from childhood to maturity. It begins with a picture of a dozen Danish children in the schoolyard, and proceeds to show what in the course of years life makes of them all. The "professor," a man who has gathered wisdom from much wandering about the world, is the mouthpiece of the author. The imaginative child, Jens Dahl, has the vision of heaven on earth of Wordsworth's famous ode. He sees heaven and hell reflected in the sexton's pipe-lid, and the elderberry tree speaks to him and his baby brother in the language of heaven. The "professor" only among the grown-up people understands his "gift," as does his friend, Christian Barnes, the pastor's son. The most important of the large group of minor characters is Holger, a great hulking boy, gentle and kind except when aroused to terrible wrath by cruelty or wrong. When the miller's man seduces his lovely schoolmate, Hansine, he is thrown into such a mental tumult that he ravishes and kills her, and then tries to hang himself. Jens, grown to be a dissipated student, tries to recapture consciously the mystical world of his dreamy childhood. He discards the established creeds, tries theosophy and occultism, experiments described in detail of emotional extravagance, and hallucination, which finally drives him to suicide. His first love, Tine, marries Peter, and is happy with him and her children, helped over a difficult time in their lives after she sees Jens again, by the "professor." Katharina, who believes that "if one is in this world one ought to be here," courts the metaphysical Jens in vain. He and Mai Skaarup fall in love at first sight, but their idyll ends with her death. Early in Christian's childhood, hidden in a barn, he had seen a housemaid in the act of being tumbled by a farmer. This experience he tells Jens has affected his character. Miss Dale, an American mystic, trains him to normal manhood in her school for mental hygiene in Los Angeles. For part of his development she turns him over to a cowboy to be punched into shape on a ranch. He returns to Denmark to take his university degree, and marry Helen, his schoolgirl sweetheart, now separated from her dissipated husband. The "professor" helps Holger, released from prison, to make a place for himself in the community and to accept God's way with him.

PHILOSOPHY, THE STORY OF, by Will Durant (1926). This representative selection of lives and opinions of great philosophers does not attempt to furnish a complete history of philosophy, but to give a fairly continuous account of certain lines of thought pursued by speculative thinkers from Plato to William James and John Dewey. Plato receives first attention not only as an individual thinker, but as a representative of, and the culminating point in, Greek thought. The problems of ethics, politics, and psychology which were of interest to the Greeks that preceded and were contemporaneous with him are treated in the light of their cumulative solutions expressed by him. In fact Socrates is as much the subject of this introductory chapter as Plato. With the death of the former, an era in idealistic and non-pragmatic thinking is held to be closed. His antithesis and pupil, Aristotle, is then considered as the founder of logic, the organizer of science, and the first encyclopædic mind, interested as much in knowledge gathered from observation and classification as in speculation and deduction. His ideas are presented in the light of his personal and political background, and some idea of his importance in later mediæval thought is given. The treatment of that relation of Plato and Aristotle to scholasticism is very brief, however, and the next figure dealt with is Francis Bacon. After the customary resumé of his life, his works are discussed one by one and the significance of each in relation to the method of induction in philosophic thinking, and of experimentation in scientific work, is pointed out. Next, the unrelated and out-of-the-stream philosophy of Spinoza is expounded in terms of his Jewish ancestry and education, and estimated in the light of its effects on later thinkers. In this connection, especially, the influence of his pantheism on such poets as Goethe, Coleridge, and Wordsworth, and such thinkers as Lessing, Herder, Schleiermacher, is shown to have been of great and generally underestimated importance. From Spinoza the story carries us to Voltaire as the archetype of the rationalistic *philosophe* of the French enlightenment. Voltaire's hectic career, his multifarious productions, his ubiquitous curiosity, are shown to be characteristic. In opposition to the supremacy of reason and common sense, resulting in the vindication of natural law and the dogma of science, Rousseau is discussed as the exponent of a reaction based on sentiment and a feeling for Nature substituted to an intellectual perception thereof. The path from Rousseau to Kant is then traced, with due regard to the influence of Voltaire on Kant's method, and of Locke on his ultimate data. The character of Kant himself and an estimate of his scientific training as reflected in his works supplement an analysis of the two "Critiques" as the foundations of German idealism, by which English and French thought were in their turn affected through Hegel, Carlyle, Wallace, Schopenhauer, Bergson, and others. Stemming from Kant, the voluntarism of Schopenhauer is shown to be directly related to the events of his time, the desolation following the Napoleonic Wars and the system of political reaction in Europe. Combating a purely economic determinism and emphasizing the need for appreciation of art and encouragement of genius, he advocated at the same time a restrained and controlled existence which allows circumstance no hold to affect the will and happiness of the individual. Herbert Spencer next passes in review as the major philosophic exponent of his time, the gatherer of threads spun out by individual thinkers, the synthetizer of positivism, evolutionism, and liberalism. His quick eclipse by the return-tide of English Hegelianism and the growing forces of paternalism and Marxism are demonstrated to have overemphasized his inaccuracies to the detriment of his genuine contributions in the field both of erudition and of speculation. Friedrich Nietzsche closes the list of individual philosophers treated in the entirety of their contribution. His unsystematic criticism of institutions, opinions concerning art, especially Greek and Romantic art, his extension of evolutionary philosophy to include the purpose of man surpassing himself in progressing, are described as having cleared and freshened the philosophic atmosphere. "The Story of Philosophy" closes with two chapters, one on living European philosophers, including Henri Bergson and the revolt against materialism; Croce and the philosophy of the spirit as self-expression; Bertrand Russell as the logician and scientist turning his mental activity to practical reform; and a second, on contemporary American philosophers, from William James with the theory of Pragmatism and Pluralism in a materialistic universe, to George Santayana with his modernized naturalism and rationality, concluding finally with John Dewey's instrumental application of James's pragmatism to the problems of economics, democracy, and education.

PINCKNEY'S TREATY: A STUDY OF AMERICAN ADVANTAGES FROM EUROPE'S DISTRESS, 1783-1800, by Samuel Flagg Bemis, belongs to the series of Albert Shaw Lectures on Diplomatic History and was awarded the Pulitzer prize for 1926. This book, together with the author's "Jay's Treaty," presents a review of the beginnings of the foreign policy of the United States. The treaty, signed at San Lorenzo on October 27, 1795, by Thomas Pinckney, on behalf of the United States, and by Manuel de Godoy, called Prince of the Peace, on behalf of Spain, does not deserve, strictly speaking, the author points out, to be called Pinckney's Treaty. The credit belongs rather to William Short, the predecessor of Pinckney at Madrid, who after years of patient diplomacy was removed from office, due to a whim of Godoy's, just as the treaty was about to be negotiated. By the Treaty of 1763, at the close of the Seven Years' War, Great Britain received Florida and all of Louisiana to the east of the Mississippi except the marshy lands south of Iberville and the island of New Orleans. These exceptions left both banks of the Mississippi for about two hundred miles in French hands; but a separate article provided for free navigation to the French and English. In 1762 Louis XV of France gave Louisiana to his cousin of Spain and the privilege with it, but the Spaniards refused to allow the British ships to moor along their shores. Finally the Treaty was cancelled on the outbreak of war between England and Spain in 1779. The Mississippi problem was made more complicated by the indefinite boundaries between the British and Spanish possessions east of the river. These problems Great Britain handed over to the United States in 1783. The peace settlement of 1783 "closed without Spanish recognition of the United States, without a settlement of the Mississippi question, and without an agreement on the Spanish American boundary in the southwest." The purpose of this book is to trace the history of these issues between Spain and the United States and other problems hinging on them. The Mississippi River was the only outlet for the products of the American settlements in the West and its closure would be fatal to expansion. The Spaniards with this in view sought to detach Kentucky from the eastern states. The people of Kentucky at one time seriously thought of setting up a separate state, and there was a plot on foot to place this state under the sovereignty of Spain. The chief conspirator was Brigadier-General James Wilkinson, Washington's second in command, whose secret correspondence with Spain has recently been unearthed. This is dealt with at some length by Mr. Bemis. The movement only came to an end when the politicians in the East recognized the importance of the Mississippi question to the United States as a whole and set out to secure a settlement. The main points in the Treaty were the guaranteeing to the United States the freedom of navigation and commerce along the Mississippi, the settling of the boundaries between the United States and the Spanish colonies, and the settling of the boundaries of West Florida. The author's method of organization is, substantially, to show how the question of the boundary and the navigation of the Mississippi arose; he traces the early negotiations, bringing out the characteristics of the chief actors on both sides, especially the Indians and Wilkinson; he portrays the effect of Jay's Treaty, the work of Short at Madrid, and the crowning achievement of Pinckney and the signing of the Treaty.

The appendix contains the text of the Treaty in both Spanish and English. The book was written largely from sources, much of it from the Spanish archives at Madrid. There are five excellent maps.

PITIFUL WIFE, THE, by Storm Jameson (1924). Trudesthorp, the great Manor House built by Sir Nicholas Trude in 1820, stood in the midst of the Yorkshire Moors. From him it had descended to his grandson, John Trude, a reckless, cruel, young giant, who deserted the place for years and returned when near his fiftieth year a hardened, dissipated man. Attracted to a beautiful young girl, he married her, although she cared nothing for him. Their first child was Jael, a shy, sensitive little girl, who worshipped her mother. Jael was eight years old when her brother was born, and on this occasion John Trude began a lusty drunken brawl which caused his wife to seek release from him in death. The boy was named Judas. Their father procured a woman to take charge of the children and then proceeded to ignore their existence. They occupied the left wing of the house and seldom came in contact with their father, who lived in drunken debauchery. Deserted by all his servants except one old witch of a woman, he let his estate go to ruin. Theodocia Trewin, the nurse, loved the children and cared for them tenderly. They grew up, always together, wandering over the moors, recklessly riding their pony, or absorbed in mediæval romance which Jael read avidly. She was about fourteen when one day she encountered young Richmond Drew in the woods. He was the grandson of the artist who had done the magnificent carvings in Trudesthorp, and he, too, was learning to be a sculptor. The two were strangely attracted to one another, but the boy soon left to live in Switzerland. He was nineteen when he returned and he and Jael fell ecstatically in love. Within a few months they were married and lived in exultant happiness. They stayed on at Trudesthorp as Jael could not bear to leave little Jude, who had been crippled in one leg when fleeing from his drunken father. Richmond turned one of the old Trudesthorp barns into a fine atelier and worked seriously at his sculpture, creating some excellent work. Jael posed for him and helped all she could. A son was born to them, and when David was two years old Richmond went off to serve in the War. For five years, except for two short visits, he was away. Toward the end of the War he was stationed near London and Jael went to him, but David became sick and she had to return home. When the War was over and Richmond returned, Jael sensed a difference in him. He was often moody and morose and Jael suffered keenly. There were quarrels and then tempestuous love scenes. They could not overcome their deep attraction for one another. There was no demand for sculpture now, so finally Richmond decided to reclaim the vast fields of Trudesthorp that were but tangled waste. Through a ruse he got drunken John Trude to sign the land over to him. This angered Jael, who felt he had cheated

Jude of his birthright, but Jude, the embittered youth, felt no anger and agreed to help in any way he could to restore the property. Richmond decided to go to a splendid farm in Kent and learn farming. He and Jael parted in a quarrel. When he arrived at the farm Buddy Marsh, the daughter of the owner, was there to greet him. She had been his mistress during the War, and was still deeply in love with him. At first he resisted her appeals, but eventually he succumbed although in his heart he dreaded being unfaithful to Jael. He had planned to stay five months but returned unexpectedly at the end of two, much to Jael's joy. He then set to work on the land and soon many improvements were made. One day a letter came to him from Buddy saying she was in the village nearby and wanted to see him. He went and met her and together they strolled through the very places so beloved by Jael. Richmond was fond of the girl who loved him so but feared that Jael would discover their relations. He promised to see her in London soon and returned to Jael. She was happy in having Richmond seemingly so content at Trudesthorp and they loved each other passionately, although she felt that there was some insurmountable barrier between them. During one of his visits to London she accidentally came across a letter from Buddy to Richmond. She did not read it but felt it was a clue to her unhappiness. Upon his return his joy at being with Jael quite overcame her fears. Then soon came a letter from Buddy and she recognized the writing. That night she could no longer restrain herself, so she slipped into his room while he slept and took the letter to her room and read it. Pain and desolation almost overcame her. The night was one of terror and misery and the next day Richmond found her hurt beyond belief. Nothing he could say could lessen her agony. Her whole life had been built on her dream of him and now this was shattered. He tried to make her understand that the affair was over and had meant little to him. He abased himself, suffering torment and gradually alleviated her sorrow. That night David was taken very ill and in saving him, Richmond and Jael again found each other.

PLAY'S THE THING, THE, by Franz Molnar (1920). Adapted from the Hungarian by P. G. Wodehouse (1926). This play within a play opens in a castle on the Italian Riviera. Albert Adam, the young composer, and his two sponsors, the collaborating playwrights, Turai and Mansky, have just arrived at the castle several days before their visit is expected as a happy surprise for the actress, Ilona Szabo, to whom Adam is betrothed. They are disappointed to find that the beautiful Ilona, with the other guests, is away on a picnic. The three artists spend the time talking "shop" while they wait for the party to return. The two older men are displeased to hear that Almady, an elderly actor, who had given Ilona her start and to whom she had been in the past indiscreetly grateful, is one of the guests. Adam knows nothing of the affair which his friends had thought all over and done with long ago. Ilona's apartment is next to theirs, and with the thin walls and the excellent carrying quality of professionally trained voices, they presently realize that she has returned but not alone. They overhear a passionate and compromising dialogue between Ilona and Almady, her former lover. Almady describes himself as a "squeezed lemon" which she wants to throw away, and Ilona assures him of her love, and evidently yields to his entreaties to remember the past. Her fiancé is heartbroken at this proof of her perfidy. Almady says, "that perfect shape, the rose flush of that skin . . . how round it is, how smooth, how velvety, how fragrant." To which Ilona's voice replies, "Don't bite." Adam permits Mansky to lead him off to bed, feeling that not only his love, but his career, life itself is over. Turai has an inspiration born of his desire to put together the shattered pieces of the lost romance. He plans to make Adam believe that the love passages to which he had listened are part not of life but a play. At the early hour of six next morning Turai is dressed and having his breakfast. He summons the sleepy Ilona and then the histrionic Almady to a conference, and has no difficulty in convincing them both that they are ruined without his help. Ilona's lover and Almady's wife and four children are more important in the sober light of day than what Ilona describes as her "sentimentalism." She thinks she might as well kill herself, and Almady says that he would like to die with her. She prefers to die alone, however. Turai presents the manuscript of the play which he has written during the night. They two are to act in it at the concert that evening. It is, he informs them, the one act play which they were rehearsing after their return from the picnic last night. They will recognize the lines. To their chagrin, they do. He sends them off to learn their parts, remarking to Ilona that he doubts if any play were ever written from more altruistic motives. Turai then persuades the miserable Adam to behave as if nothing had happened to avoid an open scandal during their visit. He calls Ilona on the telephone to announce their arrival, and she joins them, assuming surprise, and joy, and excitement. The third act is the rehearsal of the "play from the French." Turai has kindly consented to give Ilona and Almady the benefit of his professional advice, and to act as manager. Adam is induced to act as prompter. The play is the farcical tale of the insane jealousy of an old nobleman, played by Almady, for his beautiful and virtuous young wife, played by Ilona. He accuses her of infidelity, and the proof is a peach, the first to ripen that year in France, which she has sent to his hated rival, whom he knows now is her lover. He has intercepted her maid on the road carrying the peach, which he now produces. The husband is satisfied that he is mistaken by an excessively simple explanation. His wife agrees to forgive him, but as a punishment for his unjust suspicions, she forbids him to eat the peach. Up to this point Adam and Mansky have been bored and half-hearted listeners, their thoughts on the tragedy in real life in which they are all actors. Now they exchange glances. The lines sound familiar. The words which had sounded so shocking and revealing describe the "round, smooth, rose-skinned, fragrant peach," which Almady "must not bite," and the "play's the thing." Adam and Mansky go into fits of relieved laughter. Turai has an opportunity to tell the grateful Ilona that it was hard to find an object which had all those qualities, and was still respectable. Adam and Ilona embrace as they leave for dinner.

PLUTOCRAT, THE, by Booth Tarkington (1927). Earl Tinker, the plutocrat, is an American millionaire from the Middle West on a Mediterranean tour with his wife and daughter, Olivia. Olivia is being taken to Europe to cure her of an unfortunate infatuation. Mr. Tinker is blatant, and jovial, and dominates the transatlantic liner as he does his home city. The story is told from the standpoint of Laurence Ogle, a young playwright whose "Pastoral Scene" has just appeared on Broadway, and who now sees his vacation and first trip to Europe spoiled by enforced association with the obnoxious Mr. Tinker. Mr. Macklyn, poet for the few, and Mr. Jones, painter for the few, share his dislike for "just such fellows as that who make cultivated foreigners think what they do think of Americans." The cultivated foreigner they have in mind, and for whose benefit they are posing in the smoking-room, is a beautiful French woman, Madame Momoro, described by the poet as "carved out of an Hellenic stillness." Laurence Ogle feels that the success of his whole adventure to foreign lands depends upon meeting this lady. She is kind to him, but to his chagrin obviously prefers the society and conversation of Mr. Tinker.

When they reach Africa Ogle continually runs into Mr. Tinker, riding in barbaric splendor at the head of a caravan, surrounded by bowing hotel managers, distributing largesse to the populace, the companion of titled Europeans, always the centre of the scene.   Madame Momoro with her son, Hyacinthe, consents to be Ogle's guest on a motor trip over the mountains to Tunis.   Later he realizes that she has used him to follow Mr. Tinker to ask him for money to help her son in a business enterprise, and free them from the household of Mademoiselle Daurel, whose tyranny they had endured in Algiers in the hope of Hyacinthe's adoption and prospective inheritance. Ogle reproaches Madame Momoro, and she tells him some truths about himself as compared with the amiable and forceful Mr. Tinker before she leaves him.   There is a scene with Mrs. Tinker after she discovers that her husband has gone out to dinner with Madame Momoro, and Ogle tries to help Olivia save her father from her mother's anger at his innocent flirtation.   A letter from his New York manager informs Ogle that his play has been withdrawn after the second week, and he finds himself with only a few dollars left and no assets, and no alternative but to appeal to Mr. Tinker for money for his passage back to America.   Madame Momoro had told him that Africa changed people strangely, and he felt that his self-esteem had vanished in proportion as the figure of Mr. Tinker had become colossal.   An archæologist at the ruined Roman city of Timgad pointed out to him that Mr. Tinker was a new Roman. The Greeks and the civilized Orientals had laughed at the old Romans as the cultured Europeans now laughed at Mr. Tinker, but they respected their force and ability. At the hotel in Tunis he sees the Tinker family in the dining room, and "with no other help visible in heaven or earth, he definitely abandoned that appeal to Mr. Tinker which was the purpose of his journey," because he knew he had fallen in love .with Olivia.   At this critical moment when all seemed lost a letter arrives containing a check for the moving-picture rights of his play, and he stops tearing his hair to brush it and go down to dance with Olivia.   Mr. Tinker is not overjoyed to receive Ogle as a son-in-law, but has attributed his coldness to timidity and modesty, and accepts his daughter's choice, and Laurence accepts the archæologist's estimate of his prospective father-in-law.

POE, EDGAR ALLAN, LIFE AND TIMES, see ISRAFEL

POLITICAL AND SOCIAL HISTORY OF THE UNITED STATES, THE, by
Arthur M. Schlesinger (1925).   The birth and growth of Jacksonian democracy — a period of unrest and revolt — "the passion for democracy and the longing for nationality" — form the influences from which the author discusses the rise of the common man and the opening of a new era in America.   Jackson's fight for nationality, the differences between the Democrats and the Whigs, the upheaval in the realm of politics, which the author views as one phase of the demand of the common people for larger rights and opportunities; the struggle for free public schools; the beginnings of woman's suffrage; social reform, the flowering of American literature, the various movements of the era just prior to the discussion of the slavery issue, are treated as important phases of development.   The slavery controversy and sectionalism, the drift toward disunion, the movement for Southern independence, and the war of "American Nationality," the wartime problems of the North and the South, and the post-war South, are reviewed.   The derangement of Southern economic life, with its subsequent industrial reorganization, are shown to have been a phase of the great economic revolution that affected the entire country.   Upon the heels of the new era of growth, the author follows the agricultural revolution and the vanishing frontier, the opening of the West, and the outstanding achievements in transporta-

tion, mining and communication. The political trend from 1872 to 1885, with the scandals of the Grant administration, the "greenback question," the platform of the two parties, are recalled; as well as the moral agitation and humanitarian endeavor of that period, which the author alludes to as the "renascence of the woman's-rights' movement." The organization of the Red Cross, the intellectual revival in educational opportunities, the rise of organized recreations and sports, notably baseball, are discussed in their relation to national development. The growth of railway consolidation, the evolution of "big business," and the movement for concentration in manufacturing, industrial combinations, the Standard Oil Company's policies, are reviewed. "The trend toward consolidation in transportation and manufacturing was symptomatic of a similar irresistible movement in almost every sphere of commercial activity." The growth of labor solidarity, with the chief industrial conflicts, the political aspects of the labor movement, is discussed, together with the legislative changes in manufacturing states. Other social forces are reviewed in those periods of the country's progress when certain issues occupied the centre of the stage, notably the "Silver Crusade"; and the author considers these movements to have sprung from economic difficulties, a product of a complication of causes. The enormous material development of the country is shown in its effect upon the world's markets, for, although the aggressive policy of overseas expansion "ran counter to the temper of the American people, it gained momentum from its own success." The author sees the United States as a world power before the close of the McKinley administration, with "insular possessions in two hemispheres and a potential voice in the affairs of Asia, Africa and Europe." America's policy toward Latin America, the Cuban problem, the Spanish-American War, the annexation of the Philippines, the American program in China, the Panama "outbreak," and the building of the Canal, form the material which the author draws upon for his account; and as he approaches what he considers the dawn of a new epoch in America certain social and economic legislation which were the beginnings of the progressive or "Rooseveltian" movement are described. The author reviews the Wilson administration, and the concluding chapters are devoted to a study of the development of a colonial empire which resulted in completing the forty-eight states; to America and the World War, the problems of peace, and the administration of Coolidge.

POLYGLOTS, THE, a novel by William Gerhardi (1925). The time is immediately after the Armistice of 1918. "The world had got unhinged and was whirling round in a pool of madness, and those few lunatics were whirling independently within ours: wheels within wheels! So sensible and nice and relevant they were in their own little world of delusion that we, big lunatics, who were engaged in making war and revolution, allowed the little lunatics to roam in peace at large: out of a latent instinct of proportion that it would have been absurd to lock them up in the face of what was being done by admittedly sane people in our midst. Asylums and prisons were open: indeed, not in Russia alone. To give Europe her due "retail murderers had been invited to vacate their prison cells to participate in the wholesale murder going on galore upon the battlefields." Yet for the most part gaiety runs a fast race. For the scene is international, and the narrator-hero, "sleek black hair and all that sort of thing," travels, first on a liner, then on a transport, from the European front to Japan, thence past Vladivostok to Harbin, a Russian concession on the Chinese Eastern Railway, south to Shanghai, Hongkong, Singapore, Ceylon, Perim, Heliopolis, on to Gibraltar, and, finally to England. In English uniform is Captain George Hamlet Alexander Diabologh, and with him travel the polyglots, members of his

THE READER'S DIGEST OF BOOKS

family, like himself, speaking several languages, unlike himself, alien to their native English, married to aliens impoverished in the after-War confusion. "In the World War, the Russian Revolution, things had taken place, strange shiftings of families and populations, of which little has been heard as yet but the effect of which will tell one day." George himself is English out of profoundest desire to be identified as one thing or another. He writes of himself, "If you had been born in Japan and brought up in Russia and called Diabologh into the bargain you would want to be English." But he is also a Diabologh, and not for nothing. His uncle Lucy married three times, and could not count his children on the fingers of both hands. His father, Aunt Teresa told him, had had innumerable love-affairs. Twenty-three, he loves Sylvia Ninon Thérèse Anasthatia Vanderflint, who out of the kindness of her heart gives herself to him on the first night of her marriage to the inconsequential Gustave Bollanger. The latter stays behind in Harbin while his wife and her mother Teresa set sail for England, to escape the ghost of Uncle Lucy who hung himself in his sister's apparel after the bankruptcy of his Russian business during the Revolution. Death travels with the polyglots on a number of occasions. Aunt Teresa loses her son, Anatole, and her brother, Lucy. The Negodyaevs, friends of the Vanderflints, lose their little daughter, Natàsha. But the desire of the polyglots remains the desire of Sylvia: "Jesus!" she purls, "how I want to go on living forever!" So the selfish, hypochondriac aunt goes on living, and so her husband, Emmanuel, of whom George says: "I may be a cynic; but he is worse: he does not know he is a cynic. His daughter! His daughter! But the daughter wanted me to love her, and her father meantime loved other men's daughters. So why does he squeak and squeal, this censor of films? But what do you want, as Uncle Emmanuel might say, it's life." And since George is a novelist as well as a captain, he writes of them all at great length — "a novel is not the same as a short story." Here are Major Beastly, "What I always say is: one man's as good as another and a damned sight better"; Captain Negodyaev, suffering from persecution mania, having his family dress for flight from the Bolsheviks and then saying, "All Clear," and repeating again and again, "I have two daughters, Màsha and Natàsha, Màsha is married and lives with her husband Ippolit Sergèiecl Blagovèschenski, and this is Natàsha"; and the Russian generals of innumerous oppositions, among whom is one overbearing name, General Pshemovich-Pshevìtski; and the children, hosts of them, Uncle Lucy's, with clear brows, one with forget-me-not eyes. The premature death of Natàsha and her burial at sea cast a profound shadow over George's final pages of narrative. "She had seen Princess Mary's photograph in the 'Graphic' and had fallen in love with her. Now she found the page. 'Look! Oh, how beauty!' she said. 'Oh, what a lovely — Princess Mary!' . . . And again: 'Oh, you are my uncle. Oh, stop with me. Uncle Georgie I love you, I love you, Uncle Georgie, Uncle Georgie: I love you, stop with me.'" And then, according to Berthe, who nursed all the polyglots, the little one was very bad. George, whom Russia had bitten much too deeply, "who was also called Hamlet, and who was an intellectual" though he often fell asleep meditating the philosophic difference between the "subjective" and the "objective," reflected, brooding on her, "a little Russian girl in the deep vastness of the Indian Ocean. . . . A crowd of bewildered spirits caught upon a planet. We merely brush against each other's surfaces, and something deep down, unexplored, is ignored or dismissed." Previously he had reflected on love: "And what does love reveal? That concavities are concave, and convexities convex. Son of man! Is that all there is for you? Will it ever be so? There is little to choose between hunger and satiety." And later on humor: "Humour is when I laugh at you and laugh at myself in the doing (for laughing at you), and laugh at myself for laughing at myself, and thus to the tenth degree."

POOR WHITE, a novel, by Sherwood Anderson (1920). A story of the evolution of the hero from the decadent, poor white group, and the beginnings of modern industrialism in the transition of an agricultural community into a manufacturing centre. Hugh McVey and his shiftless, drunken father sweep saloons and clean out-houses in the little Missouri River town when hunger compels them to work instead of sit in the sun and do nothing. The wife of the station agent, an energetic New England woman, Sarah Shepard, interests herself in the boy, who comes to work for her husband. She scolds him and teaches him "to keep his naturally indolent body moving and his cloudy, sleepy mind fixed on definite things." When the Shepards leave the town he is able to take the place of telegrapher and station agent. The ambition to amount to something, which Sarah Shepard has aroused, leads him to work his way eastward as far as the town of Bidwell, Ohio. He invents a cabbage planting machine which, though it is not successful and has to be scrapped eventually, is the first industrial enterprise in Bidwell, and his later invention of a corn-cutting machine brings wealth to him and the town. Success does not change the dreamy, tongue-tied, lonely Hugh. Clara Butterworth, daughter of the richest man in town, who has made his money out of Hugh's invention, decides it is time for her to marry, and takes him for her husband. Pages are devoted to the story of Clara's development, first a hoydenish girl on the farm, then a dissatisfied student at the coeducational college with her masculine friend, Kate, and her awakening to ideas of sex. Hugh has always been attracted to women, but is afraid of them, and, seized with panic, runs away on his wedding night. His father-in-law brings him back the next day to the wife he had proposed to on an impulse of courage, and whom he has scarcely spoken with before. The story of the old harness maker, Joe Wainsworth, and his revolt against the machine, and the account of the first strike are interesting chapters.

PORGY, by Du Bose Heyward (1925). This story of negro life has its southern setting in the Charleston of to-day, in a century-old section, once frequented by governors, who had come and gone, and where "ambassadors of kings had schemed and danced." "Now before the gaping entrance lay only a narrow, cobbled street, and beyond, a tumbled wharf used by negro fisherman." Catfish Row, where Porgy lived, was a great brick structure that lifted its three stories about the three sides of a court. He was a cripple and earned his livelihood by begging. He could be seen any morning against the wall of the old apothecary shop that stands at the corner of King Charles Street and The Meeting House Road, "as consistent in the practice of his profession as any of the business and professional men who were his valued customers." Porgy's one vice was gambling, and his luck at throwing the dice caused the negroes with whom he played to believe that he "witched dem." A negro stevedore, Crown, Robbins, another companion, and Porgy play nightly under the beetling walls of the tenement. Crown and Robbins have a fight and Crown kills him. Before the police arrive, Crown makes his escape and hides in a palmetto thicket. Porgy, when questioned, denies any knowledge of the crime, and the police are satisfied. But they terrify old Peter, who lives in the tenement, and he tells them that he saw Crown kill Robbins. Porgy has been dependent upon Peter to help him out on the street, and realizes his helplessness when Peter is taken to jail as a witness. He invests some of his hard-earned money in a goat wagon, an inverted packing case, with lopsided wheels, improvised shafts and a patriarchal goat, which "tugged with the dogged persistence of age." In this "chariot," Porgy continued to beg. Bess, known as "Crown's Bess," comes to Catfish Row, looking for Crown. Finding Porgy prosperous from his gambling, she accepts him for a lover. Both of them undergo a subtle change. The dwellers in the tenement admit that Bess makes him a good mate. Another negro, Sportin' Life, taunts Bess with her old life and love of "dope," and she yields to the temptation when he offers to supply her with dope and pays him with Porgy's earnings. Then she finds Crown in the thicket and gives herself to him. Porgy questions her, and she tells him the truth. When the cotton comes in, she and Crown are going away together. "Ef dey warn't no Crown?" Porgy whispered. "Ef dey wuz only jes' de baby an' Porgy, wut den?" Bess tells him that away from Crown's influence, she could be good and happy. She pleads with Porgy to keep Crown away from her. And Porgy reassures her: "Yuh ain't needs tuh be 'fraid. Ain't yuh gots Porgy?" Their life goes on happily in Catfish Row, but when the cotton comes in, Crown ventures out of the palmetto swamp and goes to get Bess. Porgy hears him in the court and stabs him. The body is found across the street. Porgy is wanted at the inquest — to identify the murdered man. He has not the courage to look upon Crown and disappears in his goat-wagon. The police overtake him and he is sent to jail for contempt of court. When he is released and comes home to Catfish Row he learns that Bess, despondent and uncertain of his return, had taken liquor from the river gang and been carried away by them to the Southern cotton plantations.

PORTRAIT OF THE ARTIST AS A YOUNG MAN, A, by James Joyce (1916), a novel. "Once upon a time and a very good time it was there was a moocow coming down along the road and this moocow that was down along the road met a nicens little boy named baby tuckoo. . . ." This story told by Simon Dedalus, ex-medical student, oarsman, tenor, amateur actor, shouting politician, small landlord, small investor, bankrupt good fellow and praiser of his own past, to his son Stephen as an infant, portends in its essential language the future Stephen, artist as a young man. After infancy there is no escape but through passion and bitterness, through growing isolation in which even love is a bad dream. So one durance leads to another, the class of elements in Clongowes Wood College and Stephen's persecution by his school companions and the prefect, Father Dolan, to the tense atmosphere of an Irish family at strife over Parnell and the Church; his life at Blackrock to school again at Belvedere. Early love for Emma, and the obstructions of youth. — A degrading visit to Cork with his father — "The memory of his childhood suddenly grew dim; he tried to call forth some of its vivid moments but could not. He recalled only names — Dante (Miss Riordan) Parnell, Clane, Clongowes. . . . He had not died but he had faded out like a film in the sun. He had been lost or had wandered out of existence for he no longer existed. . . . Nothing stirred within his soul but a cold and loveless lust." He gave himself to it after wandering into a maze of narrow and dirty Dublin streets. The struggle of Catholic conscience brings grace for a while to Stephen, even obedience and contrition, and the possibility of joining the Jesuit order in which he has been raised. But when the moment for supreme obedience comes he turns aside, "his soul risen from the grave of his boyhood, spurning his gravecloths." The rest is but cleaving from the past, the birth of song in him for his earliest love of childhood, the purification in his mind of Emma's innocence which for over ten years he had sullied. The university, too, with its captious argumentative students is something to forget. He will not serve what he no longer believes in: home, mother, fatherland or church. He is not afraid to be alone or to be spurned for another or to leave whatever he has to leave, whether it is his friend Cranly or his mother praying for his return to faith. Away from home, he goes to find the loveliness which has not yet come into the world, to recreate life out of life.

POSSESSION, by Louis Bromfield (1925). Ellen Tolliver, poor relation of Lily Shane of the author's earlier novel, "The Green Bay Tree," dreams of escape from the ugly Middle West mill town and her mother's possessive love to become a great musician. As her pioneer forefathers restless and eager for conquest came to the West, her ambition reaches out to the East and Europe. To get to New York to study, she elopes with Clarence Murdoch, a travelling salesman, bent on escape from her friend, May Seton, whose father, the corset-manufacturer, has asked him his intentions. The ruthless Ellen regards Clarence "as a nice, kind, good man whom one tolerated," the first stepping-stone in her career. His clinging, humble adoration, and valiant struggle to be worthy of her, to make her care for him is a new domination, "the terrible power which the weak have over the strong." Through her music teacher Ellen has the opportunity to play at an evening reception given by Mrs. Callendar, and thereafter on many evenings as artist to entertain, and later as guest at dinner as well as performer. The handsome young millionaire, Richard Callendar, is passionately attracted to her and she to him. His wise old mother of Greek and Levantine extraction wishes him to marry the wealthy, ultra-sophisticated Sabine Cane, and sends for Ellen to talk over the situation. Thus Richard learns of the existence of Clarence, and urges Ellen to get a divorce and marry him. Clarence hears from his jealous friend, Mr. Wyck, of Ellen's meetings with Richard, and sees that she is unhappy. The day of Richard's marriage to Sabine, Clarence shoots himself, leaving a pitiful note of apology to Ellen, revealing this knowledge, and the fact that they have lived beyond his income and he has misappropriated some money. Ellen has just enough money left to get to Paris to her cousin, Lily Shane, who recognizes her gift and wants to help her. On the boat she meets Rebecca Schönberg, a Jewess, who later becomes invaluable as her manager. The luxury of Lily's household does not possess Ellen, who works without ceasing for her début in London. The War prevents her from continuing her triumphal progress to Vienna and Berlin, and she comes to America instead. Sabine, unloved and unhappy, is urged to a divorce by her mother-in-law, disappointed that the heir of the vast Callendar fortune is a girl. Ellen goes back to France and marries Richard. Her two brothers are killed in the War, her father is dead, so Ellen sends for her mother to come to Paris. When her son is born she turns him over to his grandmother and goes back to the waiting Rebecca and the concert stage. Her second marriage lasted only six months, since she finds Richard possessive and unfaithful, and in the conflict between love and her career, the career wins. She is "freed at last of all those old bonds, possessed now only by the beauty of the sounds she made."

POWER (Jud Süss), by Lion Feuchtwanger, translated by Willa and Edwin Muir (1925). The central scene of this historical novel of the middle of the eighteenth century is the Duchy of Württemberg, but the vast canvas covers the whole of Germany, the politics of the German States, and of the Empire, and the Papacy, the Courts and the life of the common people, including the Jews, during the period of Karl Alexander's rule in Swabia. The story begins with the incident of the trip of Duke Eberhard Ludwig to break with his mistress, the Countess, on the occasion of reunion with his wife. The great figure of the Jew, Süss, who dominates the book, is a young man, who has attached himself to Karl Alexander, an obscure princeling,

while Eberhard Ludwig is still Duke. A sudden whim of destiny removes the immediate heirs, and Karl Alexander succeeds to the ducal throne, and Süss becomes
the real ruler of the Duchy. His one objective is power, and he allows nothing to
stand in the way. At a time when his race is persecuted and isolated in ghettos,
the brilliant, courtly young Jew by his genius for government and finance makes his
name synonymous with power. He is always servile to his master because it is to
his own advantage. Karl Alexander embarks on a career of debauchery, and Süss
procures money and mistresses for him. Now and again the Jew goes to the little
white house in the forest, where his lovely and innocent daughter, Naemi, lives with
his Cabbalist uncle, Rabbi Gabriel. Prelate Weissensee, whose daughter, Magdelin
Sibylle, had been betrayed to Karl Alexander by Süss when her piety changed to
passion for the Jew, seeks his revenge by leading the Duke to pursue Naemi, who
falls to her death escaping from him. Süss has paid the supreme price for power.
He lives now only for vengeance. First a party to the Catholic plot against Swabia,
he then betrays the plot, and Karl Alexander, and delivers himself into the hands of
his enemies. They hang him on the public gallows after a long imprisonment. His
body is rescued by his fellow Jews and hidden in a place of safety. There are plots
and counter plots, and innumerable portraits, as of Isaac Landauer, the clever Jewish
financier, and the Duchess Marie Augusta, with her indolent contempt for mankind
and love of political intrigue, interfering in everything "with blind and amiable
industry."

PRECIOUS BANE, by Mary Webb (1926), is a strange, sombre novel of Shropshire
country folk. The story is told in the Shropshire dialect by Prue Sarn, and many
fascinating old customs are described. The Sarn's home stood near the mere, a
desolate lake shunned by the country folk after dark. Old Sarn, father of Gideon
and Prue, was strict and severe with his children, and their mother, a fearsome little
woman, stood in awe of him. One night, enraged at Gideon, he was about to punish
him, when the boy bumped into him and the father fell and died. Gideon, who at
seventeen was already showing signs of greed for money, had refused his mother's
plea — for a Sin-eater to take their father's sins upon him as was the custom. During
the funeral he offered to be the Sin-eater if she would give him the farm, to which she
gladly assented. So he ate the bread and took over his father's sins. That night
he told his young sister, Prue, of his plans for their future, to work with utmost
might and make a great fortune from their place so they could eventually move into
the town and have a grand house and servants. He had her pledge herself on the
Bible to serve and slave for him until this was accomplished. So she could keep his
accounts she was to learn reading and writing from the Wizard Beguildy, which
delighted her, as she longed for this knowledge. None of the farmers knew how to
read or write. She had to pay for her lessons by working in the field but this she
did not mind. Wizard Beguildy worked cures and charms for the countryside but
was otherwise avoided, as a wicked man, as were his wife and beautiful daughter,
Jancis. But Prue was fond of them and enjoyed going to her lessons. Gideon
worked furiously and kept Prue and his mother both slaving for him, and at the end
of four years the farm had greatly increased in value; but this only stirred him to
greater effort. About this time he began to call on Jancis, who was deeply in love
with him, and soon they were "promised," but old Beguildy hated Gideon and vowed
he would not permit the marriage. He planned to sell Jancis to some wealthy young
man. She and her mother connived to have him called to town and her "love-
spinning" ensued, to which came all the farmer women of the district. Prue was

happy over the engagement, but mourned that she could never know such joy, for she had a hare-lip, which was looked upon as a great affliction by the people and some called her a witch. To the "love-spinning" came the Weaver, Kester Woodseave, who was to weave the bridal linen, and when Prue saw him she fell deeply in love but kept herself hidden from him. Ever thereafter she thought of him during all the work at which Gideon kept her mercilessly. His ambition never faltered and he held her to her vow. Their poor mother grew worn and pitiful, but he kept her tending the pigs. To further his ends he refused to marry Jancis as yet, and did not oppose her father's hiring her as a dairy maid to a distant farmer. She pleaded against this but to no avail. All the countryside attended the hiring fair and plans were made for a bull baiting. The men had fierce dogs ready to attack a small bull when young Weaver Woodseave interfered. He persuaded the bull's owner to take it away and then offered to chain the dogs one by one. Prue, who was watching, sensed the danger, ran for the doctor and returned in time to save the Weaver from being torn to pieces. Later when he came to their house she kept out of sight until he was gone. Jancis had been away for nearly two years, when one night, just before Christmas, she appeared, wretched and worn, having run away from the farm. Prue comforted her and persuaded Gideon to treat her kindly, though he was angry to think she had lost all right to the wages she had earned. They were happy together and Prue got a farmer not so distant to hire Jancis for six months. Then she and Gideon were to be married. The next summer Prue was in the woods near the lake when suddenly Kester Woodseave appeared. This time he did not let her run away and talked with her, making her happier than she ever had been. When the harvest came, Gideon's fields gave a wealth of corn. All the neighbors came to help and to celebrate the "love-carriage," for Gideon and Jancis were soon to wed. The Weaver came, too, and Prue was happy. He told her he was off to London to learn a new weaving but would return to her. The day ended merrily for all. Only old Beguildy was missing. He still opposed the marriage and cursed Gideon. His wife made desperate plans to get him out of the way until it was over and persuaded a relative in the city to send for him. He was to be gone for a week, then the wedding would be over. Gideon, eager to have Jancis, persuaded her and her mother to let him come and take his bride before the wedding. Beguildy heard of this and returned, surprising them all. His anger was great and he vowed revenge. The next night he set fire to Gideon's stacks of grain and all was lost. Gideon's rage was boundless. He refused to see Jancis again and became hardened and cruel. Prue pleaded, but in vain, and she was forced to work harder than ever. Their mother became ill and Tivvy, a young woman, came to take care of her. Gideon resented the money spent on his mother. One day he had Tivvy give her foxglove tea and soon she died. Prue knew nothing of all this and mourned for her mother. Tivvy was in love with Gideon and planned to marry him through her hold on him. One night Jancis came stumbling into the house, carrying a baby, and sank at Gideon's feet. He refused to speak to her and left the house. Prue persuaded her to rest, but Tivvy tried to interfere. She blurted out the truth about poisoning the mother and Prue was aghast. Then she drove her out of the house and, leaving Jancis and the baby to rest, went out to seek Gideon. She accused him of his mother's death and said she would no longer stay with him. She returned to the house and found Jancis and the baby missing. Terrified, she sought them everywhere and finally found them drowned in the mere. After this a change came over Gideon and he began to see the ghost of Jancis everywhere — until one night he drowned himself in the mere. Prue disposed of the household things and the stock, and was about to leave when some cruel farmers accused her of being a witch and causing all the misery. She was saved by the Weaver, who appeared just in time and took her off with him to live happily ever after.

PREFACE TO A LIFE, by Zona Gale (1926). A novel of frustration. Bernard Mead has had a position in Chicago for six months and wants to make his own way and escape the .family lumber business that his father is determined shall keep him in the small Wisconsin town. On a three days' visit home he becomes engaged to Laura Hawes, his old sweetheart returned from school in Switzerland, and promises his father on his death bed that he will carry on the business. Laura's mother is ill, and she cannot leave the town. After he has proposed to Laura he meets Alla Locksley whom he instantly recognizes as the woman he loves. She tries to save him from the network of circumstance that has enmeshed him, but he has not the courage to break away from what is expected of him by his family and the town. He marries Laura and settles down to humdrum small-town life, and makes a success of the lumber business. After eleven years he has a visit from his college friend, Belnap, now an artist. Belnap reveals that he had married Alla knowing that she loved Bernard, and that they had separated, as the marriage had not been a success. He has come to see the man who had Alla's love, and had not loved her in return. Bernard explains that he had loved Alla, but that love was not everything, and that he had to consider obligation and responsibility. This visit of his friend rouses Bernard from placid contentment to reflect on what life had brought him. He writes to Alla and she arranges a visit to his aunts, her old friends, and in the few days that she is in his home, he realizes that his world is empty without her. The days of routine and repetition prey on his mind. For four months he was away from home in France during the War. At Alla's Paris address he learned that she was in India. After twenty-five years he takes stock of life again. His children, Helen, Bernard, and Hazel, are a disappointment. The boy, who at ten had been all eagerness to be in business with his father, had proved himself incapable in the office at twenty, and at twenty-four has no initiative or purpose, and is living at the club "playing a bit" before settling down, as he says. Bernard feels that life is tasteless, and that he is someway drying up and dying without finding out what it is all about. Suddenly one evening while a Mr. Barling is singing to Laura the music seems to make the lines and surfaces of the room move and change, and he attains to a kind of cosmic consciousness, which he can only explain to himself as "microscopes in my eyes, and in my ears." A minuteness of perception enables him to visualize the harmony of the infinitesimal threads that make up a coat, the perfection of color and form that compose a flower. His efforts to explain the flux and flow of the life that he sees about him frighten his family, who think him insane, and send for an alienist. The physician diagnoses his condition as repressed imagination and too close attention to business. Alla had always known him better than he knew himself, and he goes to her for understanding. She welcomes him as her lost lover, but he is not interested in love. Can't men and women do anything but love and beget, he asks. "Why don't they start to build?" He tries to tell her that everything in the world is moving, and shining, and building except people, who move but do not "build anything inside." A look of fear comes into her eyes, and she leaves him as he talks of his experience. The six women of his family welcome him home, and he braces himself to the isolation of his secret life. "After all he was only fifty-two, there would be eight years before he was sixty, and there would be time . . . time enough to find out everything." All that had gone before was merely a preface to a life.

PRESIDENT IS BORN, A, by Fannie Hurst (1928). At Thanksgiving dinner the Schuyler family, wives, husbands and children, twenty-two strong, come from as far as St. Louis and Springfield to the home where six of the children and several of the grandchildren were born. Henry and Matilda had come from Europe to Centralia, Illinois, when they were first married. Henry is now called the Old Gentleman, as there is his son, Henry, widely known in the State, who has twice been asked to run on a Republican ticket, once for Congress, and once for District Attorney, but has preferred to remain a country lawyer. Rebekka is the best man of the family with her pioneer passion for the land, and her model farm. Into this clan David, the late child of Henry and Matilda, is born, destined to be a great President of the United States. He spends a happy, normal childhood with sisters and brothers old enough to be his uncles and aunts. They are devoted to their small, sturdy brother, and see no signs of his future career, though Henry says of him once, "The kid's got the trick-combination of leadership, imagination tempered by a level head and a level heart. Man-of-the-people stuff." The scene is laid in two periods, the actual time of the story in the early years of the twentieth century, and fifty years later when David is President, set forth in footnotes supposedly from the diary of his sister, Rebekka. David has the experience of life on a farm, and after his father is financially ruined by signing a note for a friend, knows poverty in a small town. He owes much to his philosophical brother, Henry, who guides his reading and thinking, and his practical sister, Rebekka, disappointed in her own children, and happy to mother her brother, David. The child is self-reliant and has intellectual curiosity. He learns compromise and conciliation from the quarrels of the large family, and the arguments between his reactionary father and his progressive brother, Henry, and has the honesty of the Old Gentleman and the patient unselfishness of his peasant mother. The story ends when David is eighteen and leaves home to work in a wholesale grocery firm and go to evening law school. He has won his childhood sweetheart, Dora, and stops dreaming like the passive Henry to make money and position to get married. The footnotes refer to his achievements, his protective laws for the benefit of the negroes, Indians, and yellow races, his solution of the prohibition question, his Super-state policy, and the saving of the nation from "the allied international peace fiasco at Moscow."

PRIMITIVE RELIGION, by Robert H. Lowie (1924). The author states explicitly in his introduction that "this work does not purport to be a handbook of either the theories broached on the subject of primitive religion or of the ethnographic data described in hundreds of accessible monographs. . . . My purpose is to provide an introduction to further study in which other than the traditional topics shall assume a place of honor." Pursuant of this intention Professor Lowie declares his treatise to be "dedicated to the discussion of those cultural phenomena of the simpler societies which center about or are somehow connected with the sense of mystery or weirdness." The book is divided into three parts.

Part I consists of four "Synthetic Sketches" wherein by selecting and describing four striking instances of four types of primitive religions, Professor Lowie enables the reader to become conversant with the salient characteristics of a broad and fertile subject. Of the instances he chooses the first is that of the Crow Indians of eastern Montana, "because this tribe exemplifies one particular conception of the Extraordinary, a conception, moreover, typical of many other North American aborigines." The second is that of the Ekoi, horticultural natives of Southern Nigeria, "because these West Africans represent a wholly different attitude toward the Supernatural and neatly set off some of the features which distinguish Old World from New World belief and ritual." The third is that of the Bakaua and their neighbors the Jabim and Tami "about the shores of Huon Gulf, New Guinea" who "while showing some of the Africans' notions exhibit and stress still other methods of reaction toward the Extraordinary and exhibit one form of widespread ceremonial with great clarity." The last is "finally, the Polynesians" who "display an incomparable elaboration of what exists in germ not only among the Bakaua, but in a wider sense, in the primitive world at large."

Part II is a Critique of Theories. In three brief and lucid essays, Professor Lowie discusses successively Animism, Magic and Collectivism.

Part III treats of Historical and Psychological aspects. Some of the chapter headings are "Historical Schemes and Regional Characterization"; "Woman and Religion"; "Individual Variability"; and "Religion and Art."

The book is extensively and carefully annotated, and the competent bibliography at the end is a mine of material for anyone who cares to delve deeper into the subject. As it stands, "Primitive Religion" is a concise and readable summary for the layman.

PRIVATE LIFE OF HELEN OF TROY, THE, by John Erskine (1925). After the fall of Troy Menelaus brought Helen, "unrepentant, too beautiful to kill," back home to Sparta, according to this author. Helen has intelligence and imagination as well as beauty, and is able to twist her outraged husband around her little finger, but she is not so successful with her serious-minded and scandalized daughter, Hermione, grown to a young lady, and in love with her cousin, Orestes. Hermione had tried to protect her mother's reputation by spreading the story that Paris carried Helen off by force and that she did not go to Troy with him, but remained in Egypt until Menelaus came for her. The frank Helen hears this story from Charitas, her girlhood friend, and at once denies it. She does not consider that she was to blame for falling in love with Paris. It was fate, and she could not do otherwise than follow him. She thinks it was pride and lack of imagination that made Menelaus bring on a great war, destroy a city, and take hundreds to their death just because his wife ran away. The greater part of the story is told in conversations between Helen, Menelaus, Hermione, and Eteoneus, the old gate-keeper, about their theories of life, love, marriage, and human motives and impulses. Helen induces Menelaus to invite Pyrrhus, Achilles' son, to visit them in order that Hermione may see some other man before she definitely decides to marry Orestes. While the family are quarrelling over a husband for Hermione, the entire cycle of the Æschylean trilogy is enacted — the murders of Agamemnon, Ægisthus, Clytemnestra — announced to their relatives from time to time by messages brought in by the gate-keeper. Agamemnon had sacrificed his daughter, Iphigeneia, to get a favorable wind from the gods for the fleet to sail to Troy. Clytemnestra felt that she was justified in leaving Agamemnon, and bound to avenge her daughter's death. She lived openly with her lover, Ægisthus, introducing him to everyone as her "true husband" in the eyes of the gods. Menelaus had been favorable to Orestes, but thinks nothing can be decided until Agamemnon returns to put his house in order. Helen says of Orestes that he is incurably serious, with absolutely no sense of humor, will do his duty at any cost to others, and insist on carrying out what he thinks is the will of heaven even if he has to kill somebody. Agamemnon comes home to his wife, who greets him cordially, and then kills him as soon as he has removed his armor. The shocking news is brought that Orestes has avenged his father by killing his mother and her lover. Menelaus forbids Hermione to see Orestes again. Hermione replies that her father may be adventurous in battle, and her mother adventurous in love, but she will be adventurous in duty to Orestes. Hermione elopes with Orestes, but returns to tell her parents that before they were married they met Pyrrhus on the road, that the two men fought, and Orestes killed Pyrrhus. Helen points out to her husband that this man who has violated the laws of hospitality in such a terrible way is still his daughter's husband, and at last persuades him to be reconciled to them. Orestes comes under Helen's sway so noticeably that the cautious Hermione, on her father's advice, avoids a second meeting before they start on their pilgrimage to the oracle at Delphi In the last chapter Telemachus comes to the house to ask for tidings of his father, Ulysses, and at the sight of Helen the young man forgot his father, and his mother, and the suitors, as he gazed at her beauty.

PROFESSOR'S HOUSE, THE, by Willa Cather (1925). At the time the story opens the two great experiences of Professor St. Peter's life are in the past. His history, "The Spanish Adventurers," has made his reputation and given him financial independence. Tom Outland, his dearest friend and the only first-rate mind that ever came into his classes, has been killed in the War. His wife, Lillian, younger and gayer with prosperity, is more interested in the admiration of her two devoted sons-in-law than in her husband. The family in different ways are preoccupied with the material things that to him mean so little. The patent of Tom Outland's invention willed to Rosamond, his fiancé, the professor's oldest daughter, and commercialized by Louis, the clever, florid Jew, she married, has made them rich and envied. Kathleen, his younger daughter, is the wife of Scott McGregor, a journalist, wasting his talent on the successful "good cheer" articles he loathes to write, but which have enabled him to marry. The story is the inner rebellion of St. Peter, who has not "learned to live without delight," against the changes wealth has brought, the worldliness of his wife, the antagonism between his daughters, Rosamond's hardness and meanness, Kathleen's pettiness, and the vulgarization of Tom Outland's memory by Louis. When the family move into the new house the professor refuses to give up his inconvenient room under the eaves of the dismantled old house, which he has used as a study, and shared with Augusta, the German seamstress, and her "ladies," an armless torso covered with black cotton, and "a full length female figure in a smart wire skirt in a trim metal waistline . . . its bosom resembling a strong wire bird cage." Augusta, not a reader of Anatole France, considers these "unsuitable companions for one engaged in scholarly pursuits," and is bewildered when he keeps them, and makes her buy new ones for the new house. Except for Augusta's interference he would have let the old gas stove in his study blown out by the wind, blow him out, too, rather than take up his life again with his wife returning from a trip to Europe with Rosamond and Louis. The interpolated story of Tom Outland is his discovery with his pal, Roddy Blake, of an ancient Indian cliff city, and their year on the solitary blue mesa exploring the remains of a past civilization.

PROMETHEUS; OR, BIOLOGY AND THE ADVANCEMENT OF MAN, by H. S. Jennings (1925). In this exposition of the relations of heredity and environment the author protests against the assumption of eugenists and others anxious to better the human stock that there is a sharp distinction between heredity and environment. As he shows in the chapters on the biological background, "organisms are like other objects . . . what they do or become depends both on what they are made of and on the conditions surrounding them. The dependence on what they are originally made of we call heredity. But no single thing that the organism does depends alone on

heredity or alone on environment: always both have to be taken into account."
Heredity is not an "entity, a force, something that itself does things." The cell
from the very beginning is affected by its environment, which means only that the
cell will adapt itself to the environment in which it finds itself. As the human being
develops what was true at first is true all through life. He gives many illustrations
of the extreme complexity of the human egg. Many necessary factors enter into the
situation which produces so simple a feature as a red eye instead of a white one, and
if any one of them is absent the red color of the eye is not produced. "Not only
what the cell within the body shall become, but what the organism as a whole shall
become, is determined not alone by the hereditary materials it contains, but also by
the conditions under which those materials operate; or by other materials that may be
added later. Under diverse conditions the same set of genes will produce very diverse
results. It is not true that a given set of genes must produce just one set of characters
and no other. . . . It is not true that what an organism shall become is determined,
foreordained, when he gets his supply of chemicals or genes in the germ cells, as popular writers on eugenics would have us believe." "Every creature has many inheritances; which one shall be realized depending on the conditions under which it
develops; but man is the creature that has the greatest number of possible heritages."
It is ignorance of biology that leads to the exclusion of certain types of immigrants
under the impression that heredity is all powerful. In Part 3, "The Advancement
of Man," he denies that man is degenerating as is claimed by some writers because
people who had not survived in more strenuous life are being preserved by modern
scientific knowledge. There is no reason to suppose that biologically man may not
develop better under more favorable than less favorable circumstances. Historically,
the process of giving weaker members of the group a chance began with the discovery
of fire and the invention of clothing, and social organization, which did more to keep
the weak members of the race alive than any discoveries since made in saving tuberculosis patients or fending off typhoid or yellow fever. After discussing some of the
many problems of the eugenist, he concludes that "so long as biparental inheritance
is kept up, the variety . . . among the fruits of the human vine will continue.
Capitalists will continue to produce artists, poets, socialists and labourers; labouring
men will give birth to capitalists, to philosophers, to men of science; fools will produce
wise men and wise men will produce fools. . . ."

PROMISED LAND, THE, by Ladislas Reymont (1927), continues the prose epic
of the husbandmen for which "The Peasants" received the Nobel prize. This is
the story, for the most part the tragedy, of the peasants transplanted to a great manufacturing centre, Lodz, the promised land where, freed from the bondage of the soil,
they are hoping to make their fortunes. The life of Lodz is presented here in its
every aspect through those individual lives of which it is constituted. Here are
humble tragedies of unbearable poignancy, little ones dying from the diseases of the
slums, workmen mangled and thrown aside while their families are left to starve.
Here are grasping millionaires become expert in timing their fraudulent bankruptcies
and incendiary fires. Fortunes are made from the exploitation of workmen and the
production of shoddy goods that bring heavier profits than the proceeds of honest
work. Lodz is in microcosm typical of the ruthless competition of commercial life
going on all over the world. But a balance between the sordid and the spiritual, true
as in life, is maintained in the realism of this book. Beside the shady Shaya Mendel-
sohn, the orthodox Jewish manufacturer at the top, and Vilchek, son of a poor peasant
whose rascally operations raise him to affluence; beside Grosglik, the banker-extor-

tioner, and Kessler, the satyr mill-owner, are told the stories of lovely Mela Grun-span's sacrifice for her lover, the idealistic young doctor, Vysocki, and the noble love of Count Travinski for his fastidiously beautiful wife Nina. There is the father of Max Baum who fails in his one man struggle to adhere to his old craftsman's ideal of honest handweaving; and old Mr. Adam the upright and humorous old father of Charles Boroviecki, who becomes another victim to industrialism, nor must Anne, cousin and fiancé of Charles, be forgotten. She loses her place in Charles' life because she is the embodiment of that simplicity and dignity of life on the soil as a country land-owner, which he has given up. Out of this thronging drama of people gracious or greedy according to their natures, emerges the dominating personality of Charles Boroviecki, an expert in chemical dyes and printing, who has become manager of the greatest factory in Lodz. At first he appears one of those charming gentlemen, blessed at birth by all the fairies save only the malicious thirteenth, a man who coolly accepts as his right the love and good fortune that have always been his. Most of the women of Lodz are in love with him either actually or potentially. An amusing instance of this appears when Lucy Zucker, wife of a wealthy Jewish manufacturer, wins his devotion for a time. Basing her appeal to him on opulent, Oriental charms, chemically pure of gray matter, she lacks the wit to realize that a man of Charles's nature, engrossed in an ambition to establish his own factory and win success thereby, soon tires when asked to play the youthful fool. In his struggle for success, through racial antagonisms, treachery of friends and passionate dalliance, Charles finds himself so surrounded by enemies that he must forfeit the queen if he would not be completely check-mated. So he passes by his old sweetheart, Anne, to marry the millions coming to Mada Muller, the daughter of a wealthy but ignorant German factory owner. In the end Charles finds futility and ennui the price he must pay for his devotion to a too material success. Aside from the wealth of characters each completely individualized in this industrial epic, Reymont displays distinguished ability in depicting widely varied scenes. With equal ease he portrays the lyrical beauty on the old estate at Kurov, Boroviecki's wild rush by special train through the snow storm, "the Corybantic minstrelsy of the fire" which burned down his factory, or the terror and power of the death struggle between Kessler and the father of Sophy Malinovski whom he wronged.

PROPOSED ROADS TO FREEDOM, by Bertrand Russell (1919), is divided into two parts, the first an exposition of the historical phases of socialism, anarchism, and syndicalism, the second into a study of the problems of the future that have to do with work and pay, government and law, international law, science and art under socialism, and closes with a view of the world as it could be made, based on the principles of guild socialism with a strong anarchistic trend. All these movements form a democratic attempt at abolishing every kind of privilege and artificial inequality as understood by the present capitalistic system. Socialism advocates the communal ownership of land and capital but it formed no stable political party until the time of Marx. Marx collaborated with Engels in formulating the socialistic doctrine, first, in his Communistic Manifesto of 1848, then in his great book, "Capital," and finally in his later years through the formation of the International Working Men's Association. His philosophy is derived from Hegel. As the French Revolution marked the rise of the bourgeoisie against feudalism, so he believes the wage-earners or proletariat will rise against the bourgeoisie to establish the socialistic commonwealth. Anarchists are opposed to every kind of forcible government for they fear that when the state becomes all powerful it will inherit the tyrannical propensity of private capital. So, Bakunin, the founder of anarchism, in his best known work, "God and the State," represents belief in these as the greatest obstacles to human liberty. Kropotkin produced a more finished body of doctrine than Bakunin in his work, "Fields, Factories and Workshops," and "The Conquest of Bread," in which he devotes much time to technical questions of production. His main idea is that work should be made pleasant. Socialism became strong in Germany, while in England an attenuated form of it arose, which threw overboard the social revolution, the Marxian doctrine of value and the class war, only retaining a state socialism to be attained through "permeation" of civil servants. The Labor Party was formed in England in 1900 out of the trades unionists and the political socialists. In France socialism was affected by the social and political situation so that it took the form of syndicalism which upholds the viewpoint of the producer as opposed to the consumer. It aims at the organization of men not by party, but by occupation. The class war and direct action by means of the strike, boycott, the label and sabotage are its essential doctrines. The solidarity of all workers in a locality and of all workers in a trade are combined under a Confédération Générale du Travail. In this way industry is made self-governing. They would destroy the state and substitute ownership by organized labor. Anarchism is sympathetic to syndicalism except that the goal of the syndicalists, the general strike, is not accepted as a substitute for the violent revolution that the anarchists desire. Syndicalism stands for industrial unionism which is also accepted by the I. W. W.s of America, who practise a policy of militant action. The skilled native American workingman, representing the aristocracy of labor arrayed against the unskilled immigrants, stand for craft unionism. The Guild Socialists of England aim at autonomy in industry with curtailment but not abolition of the power of the state. They would reconcile the attitude of state socialism which thinks of men only as consumers with that of the syndicalists which considers them only as producers. In part two, various principles above expounded are examined for their practicability and the author evolves his own compromise system. He finds the anarchist plan of the free sharing of the elementary necessities of life has the possibilities of success but he does not think it so probable that it would be wise to try it. He believes with the anarchists that, if the greed and wastefulness of capitalism were done away with, it would be possible to supply the elementary necessities of life to all, but he doubts whether they are right in thinking no obligation to work should be imposed on any one. The fact that most people would prefer to work in moderation seems to be true since it so often happens that the man with a small income from investments which barely suffice for his most elementary needs usually prefers to work to supplement this with the means for some luxuries, yet he admits that the anarchist attitude would weaken the motives for work and might induce idleness. All above absolute necessities he thinks should be worked for. Work that is more skilled and more socially useful compensates the worker since it is more interesting and more respected and does not necessarily need the recognition of higher wages. The anarchist view that society can dispense with central authority he does not find reasonable, because theft (induced by envy of the luxuries of others, if not forced by starvation), crime, and the creation of organizations that might arise to subvert the anarchist régime by force must be regulated by a government backed by force. Guild Socialists have developed the syndicalist idea of making industries self-governing units so far as internal affairs are concerned into that of the Guild Congress with chosen representatives from these units to represent producers which would be an adequate check on the old Parliament elected on a territorial basis that represents consumers. The desire of finance to find new fields for investment, the power of the press used to influence public opinion as capitalists desire, and the pugnacity inherent in the uncontrolled habit of command among capitalists, all these are factors producing war, though capital alone is not responsible for war. The instinct of race hostility must be overcome, armaments reduced and international good will be born, if the League of Nations is to be effective. Competition, love of power and envy must be removed by more education and a better political and economic system. He considers education should be compulsory for every child up to sixteen years, and available for all who wish for it up to twenty-one years. Advanced technical training and scholarly advantages more than these, as well as the opportunity to devote their lives to work not productive of immediate values, such as scientific research, and the pursuit of the arts and literature later in life, would be injured by such patronage in a socialistic state as necessitated the standardizing of creative effort. A vagabond wage, covering the barest necessities of life might be made available to all who cared for such a life with the option of spending part or all of their time in some necessary work for any who wanted more than this; for if art and science are to flourish in a state, training, freedom and appreciation by the understanding should be guaranteed. With the removal of the fear of destitution, work would be freed of hateful drudgery, the expense of children would devolve on the state and women in the home, as well as those otherwise employed and men receive recognition for their work. This reorganization of society aided by science and education would bring about a world in which the creative, constructive spirit would be alive, affection would have free play and love be purged of its selfish instinct for domination. Life would become, in that possible world, an adventure full of joy and hope.

PROVINCIAL SOCIETY, by James Truslow Adams (1927). American social life from 1690 to 1763 is depicted in this volume. At the opening of the period the author deals with a widely scattered and mainly agricultural population and emphasizes the solidarity of family life, due to the parochial existence in solitary farms and hamlets. There was no fully differentiated American life, according to the author's observations, no American people. Social as well as political life was centred in England. But it is shown that from the very beginning of the settlements there had been marked social distinctions between the colonists. The advantages of the men of wealth in the colonies were becoming more fixed and definite, although the author considers the democratic and levelling tendencies of the frontier. The houses and way of living reflected, to a large extent, according to his conclusions, the influence of the various nationalities of the builders and bespoke in many instances excellent craftsmanship, if a lack of sanitary arrangements. "Tubs were unknown in America for a century and a half after our period." Contrasts are given between the attire of the moneyed class and the poor. The food and beverages of the period and the primitive methods of preparing them, and the general surroundings of the home life and its routine are later shown in the light of what the author says was a break with established customs and hereditary duties, although in many points the ways of life in the old country were reproduced. The aristocrats composed the small group which exerted great influence, but this study deals also with the larger class made up of small merchants, pioneers, fishermen, free day laborers, indented servants and slaves, who, like the farmers and tradesmen, "insisted just as rigidly upon distinctions among themselves." Snobbishness, says this author, has never been more rampant anywhere in America than it was in the small Puritan villages of New England. The main groups of colonial society are viewed and, as the century advanced, the author discovers a sharp alignment between all classes and sections. The intellectual outlook from 1690 to 1713 is shown to possess new movement and the author considers it as the beginning of a distinctly colonial culture. The art impulse of the period, revealed in painting, carved utensils, and in the minor arts, such as decorative weaving, needlework, and iron work, showed an individuality which the author considers lent a charm wholly submerged in the stock manufactured article of to-day. Silversmithing also made an advance. Music and the theatre were negligible. The sectarian aspects of religion, in the period under review, reveal two conflicting tendencies at work, one "toward a greater toleration and the other toward the setting up of established churches and even toward persecution." The new social structure which is portrayed drew heavily upon Europe for sustenance, but, the author finds, was American in origin. The infusion of new blood, the gradual spread of settlement, as the long line of pioneers plunged into the wilderness beyond, are treated as a growing complexity of colonial life, and the restless intercolonial movements of the times are compared with the development of the frontier region which, with its Scotch and German settlements, began an American life "divorced from the Old World." From 1713 to 1745, the author reviews life in the changing South, its economic condition under the system of land grants and the absence of an adequate labor supply. Of the factors which created a new social structure, the author sees the greatest impetus as the result of the later illimitable labor supply produced by the development of the slave trade. This leads him to a discussion of the great cleavage between the bond and the free, which he claims tended fundamentally to obliterate the lesser one of differing wealth and social position among the free whites. It created, in his opinion, a gulf between the white who owned even one or two slaves to toil for him, and the farmer or mechanic who labored for himself. "Aside from its effect upon the blacks, it was probably this influence upon the whites which was one of the most evil effects of the 'peculiar institution.'" Two contrasted types of culture are revealed to have existed in all the colonies. In the period reviewed which saw the development of commerce, piracy, privateering and smuggling are shown as factors that were not only highly speculative but highly adventurous, but fundamental causes are also shown which later concentrated commerce at larger centres. All of the social and commercial movements are reviewed in the final examination on the author's part of the forces which he says developed from the rise of an indigenous colonial culture and which tended to "unite the various colonists by a common intellectual outlook." From this development, a "native-born culture" comes into its own in the provincial society of the several colonies.

PUBLIC MIND, THE, by Norman Angell (1927). An analysis of the factors which constitute public opinion, enable it to be controlled and regulated in times of war or political contests, and an estimate of the results to government and society arising from its malleability. The thesis of the volume is that Society having become more complex and more vulnerable, owing to the spread of democratic government, the evils attendant upon the control of the public mind by demagogy, yellow journalism, and propaganda of all sorts are the most serious in our economic and political system. In the first part of the book, the author sketches a picture of the Public Mind as revealed (1) in an election, showing how catchphrases and coarse sarcasm are more likely to capture popular fancy than serious discussion of issues, (2) as it was revealed during the War, in the form of ready credibility given to atrocity stories, to anti-German and anti-Allies propaganda, on both sides of the conflict, with a resultant intolerance and ferocity that was only augmented by the utterances of the press, pulpit, and political platform, (3) as it revealed itself at the Peace, when war hatred turned to revenge, and absurd demands of reparations and retaliation against Germany were made on the governments of all nations, — twenty-four thousand million sterling and hanging the Kaiser, — at the same time as the contradictory demand of keeping Germany down economically was advocated with equal fervor, by the same uninformed Public Mind. Analyzing this Public Mind, it is found that Education and Religion, so far from alleviating the evils of its blindness by disseminating information and tempering the passions, only increases the violence of prejudices by inculcating ready-made notions of patriotism, nationalism, loyalty, antagonism, and vindictiveness, in the face of facts and the laws of evidence. The problem of public opinion is therefore a vicious circle: it cannot become more enlightened until it is better informed and cooler in viewing facts, and yet it will not even look at the facts, when they are available, from sheer passion and prejudice.

The second part of the volume shows that, in the final analysis, all governments being dependent upon the consent of a large group, be it a democracy or a dictatorship, the movements and beliefs of the public mind *do* matter in the final decisions and actions of national groups. And what is more, the ruling classes, sharing themselves the prejudices and blindness of the mob, are no more capable of securing wealth and peace and prosperity in the face of facts than the public itself. This was shown in the economic and social disaster of the last war. The argument, therefore, that it matters little what the people think, since the rulers control policies anyway, is utter nonsense. There must be, however, some solution to this situation. The author attempts to point the way to it in the third part of his work. Dictatorship, he says definitely, is not the solution, since no dictator can exist without the support of a large body of the population, or at least cannot exist against the will of that body. Only one possibility lies open. It must be squarely admitted that the voice of the people is not the voice of God, but usually the voice of Satan. Democracy is defended, then, not on the principle that popular judgment is right, but that in the long run it will dictate, even to dictators. It must therefore be taken into consideration and its defects remedied by consciously corrective methods. Of these there are three. The existing political instrument of democracy must be adapted to changed conditions of modern life, and the notion of the expert, or the group of experts, substituted for the notion of the elected representative unqualified to deal with one-tenth of the problems of government. Election, therefore, is to apply to a group of men, preferably small, who then choose suitable specialists to carry on the functions of government, — the commission or city-manager plan of government. Over a period of years, the public is able to judge whether the management has been capable and satisfactory. But it is totally unfit to judge on the basis of stump-speeches, which of two individuals is fitter to be city engineer or public health commissioner. Education is the second means of arriving at a more conscious habit of Social Judgment, based on the art of thinking about common facts correctly. For in the majority of cases it is not about abstruse or technical matters that the public goes wrong, but about very simple questions of fact: *this* being given, can *that* situation, in the name of common sense, be so? It is not ignorance of facts, but ignoring facts which is the habit to be destroyed. Finally, developing a moral sense of obligation to be intelligent, to rise above "instinct, temper, passion" is the third and most difficult, painful procedure to which we must subject ourselves if we are to avoid the costly mistakes that have characterized the activities of the Public Mind in the past.

PUBLIC OPINION, by Walter Lippmann (1922). In introducing his subject, the author posits the principle that for all of us there exists an objective world which we see, however, only in terms of the pictures we have formed of it. These do not necessarily correspond with the facts, the pictures in other heads, or the general opinion. All problems of public opinion, then, are involved in approaching the world outside. These approaches to the world outside are, in the modern world, affected by numerous and powerful factors. There is, in time of national danger, and even in peace, organized censorship of certain kinds of news. The author illustrates this point plentifully with war communiques and propaganda. Then there is the principle of privacy, which operates to cut off sources of news concerning private persons and public officials. All that happens is not for publication, and publication, as of "diplomatic illnesses," is not necessarily a guarantee of truth. Approaches to facts are guarded also by the factors of contact and opportunity. Everyone is not in the official family of a public personage, in a social set where the affairs of the world are common property, or in journalistic circles where news is available before modified publication. Lastly, time and attention also regulate our knowledge of what is going on. Some of us read carefully and at length a number of newspapers and periodicals. Others uncritically absorb the headlines of tabloids. Concerning the world outside, in any case, we think largely in terms of stereotypes. Stereotypes are central images formed on any given topic, and around which cluster any number of true or false associations. Now it is notorious that, except for observant minds and trained senses, the world of facts is most unreliably depicted in people's heads. Court testimony supports this generalization. It is impossible therefore that every individual should have a clear and organized picture of what is going on around him. At best, he will have points of cognition amid a sea of confusion. Stereotypes, as such, save time, serve as a means of defence against the new and bothersome, and permit straightforward action where more thorough investigation would paralyze effort. But in addition to permitting action, stereotypes and groups of stereotypes affect the direction of action. When gathered in what we term moral codes, stereotypes determine our responses to new situations, our attitude toward ideas, men, and things. Most often we share these codes with others, members of our family, profession, economic and social class. The codes, in turn, do not comprise *the* facts, but merely a *set* of facts; and since everyone assumes that *his* code embraces all the facts, we have in the resultant divergences the contradictions of public opinion. This is the theory suggested by Mr. Lippmann. On the basis of its analysis, the problem of public opinion is to detect stereotypes, by comparison, investigation, and introspection. There is, in the first place, the detection of language symbols and visual stereotypes; then, there is the discovery of vested interest and the investigation of the causes of different "self-interests" which are based, not so much on differences of actual as of imagined or ideal interest. In forming a common will, therefore, all these factors are not only at work, but consciously used by the so-called leaders of opinion, ranging from international statesmen to ward politicians. Wherever a common will has to be crystallized for making a decision, says the author, there is some conscious agent making use of the levers of common opinion. Democracy being based on the assumption of an active public opinion, Mr. Lippmann studies the origins of that assumption and analyzes its actual operation, comparing the nature of individual opinion with the ideal of a completely informed and thoroughly rational expert on matters governmental. The influence of leaders, of force, patronage, and privilege, is reviewed and forms a critical estimate of our present form of government, with its coerciveness, inefficiency, and aggressive spirit, internal and external. With this he compares the Guild Socialism of G. D. H. Cole, pointing out that there is no difference between the two, save in details of organization. From the comparison the author deduces the democratic fallacy to have been preoccupation with the source of government rather than its processes. The assumption that everyone is capable of self-government or is primarily interested in obtaining it, he says, is contrary to experience; but with its acceptance comes the inevitable control of the instruments of government by a self-centred few. "Public Opinion" closes with a common sense analysis of newspapers as an agency for the control of public opinion, including selection, distortion, and suppression of news, appeal to emotions and prejudices, devices to arouse and keep public interest, and final correlation of news with truth. Pointing the way to organizing intelligence, Mr. Lippmann advocates expert, scientific dissemination of information, appealing to the public, not by burdening it with specialized information but, on the contrary, by relieving it, and shifting the burden to the proper administrator. The network of intelligence bureaus necessary for canalizing this information would, if properly manned and organized, connect academic social scientists with governmental functions, and produce something like a reasonable opinion-forming agency.

RAIN, a drama, by John Colton and Clemence Randolph (1922). Founded on the story, "Miss Thompson," by W. S. Maugham. The scene is an island in the South Pacific where a party of travellers are marooned by quarantine measures for two weeks during the rainy season at Joe Horn's general store and hotel. Joe is an amiable hedonist who has retired from his native Kansas to this "last remaining bit of earthly paradise" to read Samuel Johnson in a comfortable wicker chair waited on by his native wife. The travellers are Dr. McPhail and his wife, two missionaries, the Reverend and Mrs. Davidson, and one second class passenger, the gay, slangy Sadie Thompson, whose free and easy manners scandalize the missionaries. Mr. Davidson is perverted by his own repressions into a continuous warfare on the sins of others. He proudly tells Dr. McPhail how he has had to teach the ignorant natives what sin is by fining those who did not wear trousers or a mother hubbard. Anyone who did not come regularly to church might be expelled from membership and thus from any share in the general catch of fish, so that they had to make the choice between religion and starvation. He used his power as missionary to "break" any trader who dared oppose him. He decides that Sadie must be a prostitute from Honolulu and therefore a brand to be plucked from the burning. His first step is to coerce the governor, by threat of the political influence of the missionary societies with Washington, into ordering Miss Thompson to be deported to San Francisco on the next boat. Her new friend, O'Hara of the Marines, has suggested that she go to Australia, instead of to the position promised her in Apia, to his friends, Biff and his wife, Maggie, until he can get out there. O'Hara asks the doctor to intercede with the missionary in Sadie's behalf. His intercession only rouses Davidson's suspicions as to why the girl does not want to go to San Francisco. The bewildered victim of his persecution herself appeals to Mr. Davidson, and he finds out that she had run away from the penitentiary, where she had been sent by the "frame-up" of a politician, not because she had done anything wrong. Sadie breaks down, and calls Davidson a "miserable witch burner." The persistent rain and the continuous prayers of the missionary at last bring the unhappy Sadie to a hysterical conviction of sin. O'Hara, confined in the barracks for four days by Davidson's report that he had seen him drinking, comes too late to her rescue. Joe tells him that "there hasn't been such a casting out of devils since the first chapter of Exodus." The marines are ready to put her aboard the boat for Sydney that night, but she refuses to leave. Mr. Davidson has told her that she must go back to the States to "accept an unjust punishment by man as a sacrifice to God." Davidson feels that he now has proof that Sadie is saved. His exalted state turns to a struggle between Davidson, the man, and Davidson, the missionary, and finally he deliberately opens Sadie's door and goes in. In the morning they find Davidson has committed suicide on the beach. The raucous sound of Sadie's phonograph is heard in her room, and presently she comes out dressed in her gaudy, cheap finery, bold and defiant and expressing her cynical opinion of men. She is not going to San Francisco but to Sydney if the offer still holds. She forgives Davidson when she hears what has happened. As Mrs. Davidson goes up the stairs Sadie says, "I guess I'm sorry for everybody in the world. . . ."

RAINBOW, THE, by D. H. Lawrence, a novel (1915). "And the rainbow stood on the earth. She knew that the sordid people who crept hard-scaled and separate on the face of the world's corruption were living still, that the rainbow was arched in their blood and would quiver to life in their spirit, that they would cast off their horny covering of disintegration, that new, clean, naked bodies would issue to a new germination, to a new growth, rising to the light and the wind and the clean rain of heaven. She saw in the rainbow the earth's new architecture, the old, brittle corruption of houses and factories swept away, the world built up in a living fabric of Truth, fitting to the over-arching heaven." This is the vision of Ursula Brangwen after her love for Anton Skrebensky has failed; explicitly, after his abject failure to satisfy her. Another of the many products of empire, he can only command as part of a political machine, not meet love in its desire for fulfillment. "As she grew better Ursula sat to watch a new creation. . . . There would be no child: she was glad. If there had been a child, it would have made little difference, however. She would have kept the child and herself, she would not have gone to Skrebensky. Anton belonged to the past. There came the telegram from Skrebensky: 'I am married.' An old pain and anger and contempt stirred in her. Did he belong so utterly to the cast-off past? She repudiated him. He was as he was. It was good that he was as he was. Who was she to have a man according to her desire? It was not for her to create, but to recognize a man created by God. The man should come from the Infinite and she should hail him. She was glad she could not create her man. She was glad she had nothing to do with his creation. She was glad that this lay within the scope of that vaster power in which she rested at last. The man would come out of Eternity to which she herself belonged." This is Ursula after her escape from everyday edification, — her love, her own contests with teaching school, misleading friendship and home. But her struggle to stay free in her intensity, simultaneously a struggle to approach others' intensity, and her expectation that others shall meet her and yet remain free in their turn is only the struggle of her ancestors. The legend of free presence seeking presence and the tragedy of submission and withering go back to her people and to their life on the Marsh Farm in the shadow of the church tower at Ilkeston in the 1840's. It is the story of how Tom Brangwen married the Polish lady, Lydia Lensky, how he compelled his stepchild, Anna, to love him as a father, how Anna in her turn grew up and married Will Brangwen, the son of Tom's brother Fred, how Anna and Will in love often indistinct from hate begot Ursula and her sisters and brothers. The sensations of these people are in the blood and their blood pulses with the rhythm of the earth-sphere. Secret forces draw them to earth and the same earth bound through the infinite buoys them toward heaven. "Yet she broke away, and turned to the moon, which laid bare her bosom, so she felt as if her bosom were heaving and panting with moonlight. And he had to put up her two sheaves which had fallen down. He worked in silence. The rhythm of the work carried him away again, as she was coming near." In this constant "intimacy of embrace and utter foreignness of contact" among the lovers of successive generations of Brangwens each previous generation, whether it is Tom Brangwen drowned in the flood, or his son, Tom, burying his strange passions in stranger hegira, is forgotten, while the rainbow reveals again the "strength and patient effort of the new germination."

RECOLLECTIONS, by John, Viscount Morley (2 vols., 1917). This book gives Morley's life as a student, a man of letters, and a statesman, and is not a personal biography. In the introduction he says, "A personal story is soon told. . . . It has been my fortune to write some pages that found and affected their share of readers; to know and work on close terms with many men wonderfully well worth knowing; to hold responsible offices in the State; to say things in popular assemblages that made a difference. . . ." He writes of men and events interesting from the point of view of literature and politics. Book I, "The Republic of Letters," gives brief facts about his early life, his choice of journalism as a career after he graduated from Oxford, his connection with the publishing house of Macmillan, and early friends and teachers. When he came to London at twenty-five George Meredith, ten years his senior, gave animating counsel to the "junior in whose future usefulness he had faith." Morley speaks of Meredith's rare moral and intellectual force, buoyant energy, sincerity of vision, spaciousness of mind and outlook, and faith in the good. Another early friend was John Stuart Mill, and the portrait of this leader ends with notes of a day in the country with Mill, a walk and talk about Goethe. Of foreign admirations, Morley writes of Victor Hugo, Mazzini, and George Sand. A chapter on leading contemporaries and their contribution to the thought of his generation describes Herbert Spencer, Leslie Stephen, Henry Sidgwick, and Matthew Arnold, a good talker, "the most pleasing and sociable of companions." Book II, "Public Life," records his entry into Parliament, and a political career, and tells of his new friend, Joseph Chamberlain, his character and characteristics. Later political differences never interfered with their friendship. Gladstone appointed Morley Secretary of State for Ireland in 1886. Huxley said: "Ah, he is sending you, my dear friend, to Ireland, as he sent Gordon to Khartoum." The Belfast riots were his first experience of Ireland. His position in Ireland brought him in intimate contact with Lord Acton, and Morley gives testimony of the value he set on "intercourse with this observant, powerful, reflective, marvellously full mind." A chapter on Parnell gives an account of his relations with the revolutionary leader. Book III, "Three Years in Ireland," deals with the period, 1892 to 1895. Morley was Secretary a second time. The "Recollections" continue the story of the Home Rule controversies. In 1894 when Gladstone's reign came to an end, Morley, invited to dinner with the Gladstones, was embarrassed to find that Mr. Gladstone had arranged to have him break the news to Mrs. Gladstone. Rosebery, the new premier, insisted that Morley should keep his post as Irish Secretary. A chapter on "Visits in Ireland" describe conditions in that country. Book IV, "Policies and Persons," covers the period 1895 to 1905. Morley opposed the Boer War in speeches and articles. At the end of 1904 Morley accompanied his friends, the Carnegies, to America, walked through the streets of Washington with Walt Whitman, and confessed himself most impressed with President Roosevelt and Niagara Falls. "An Easter Digression" is a ten-page study of Lucretius. Book V, "A Short Page in Imperial History," covers the years 1905 to 1910 when Morley was head of the India Office. His weekly letters to Lord Minto, the Viceroy, follow the course of events in India and relevant discussions in Parliament. Book VI, "A Critical Landmark," discusses the admission of Irishmen to electoral power in the House of Commons on the same terms as the other nationalities of the United Kingdom, and the measure which limited the veto of the Lords. Morley resigned his post at the India Office in 1910, but remained in the Cabinet as Lord President of the Council. This book ends with the events of the year 1911, and an epilogue reflecting on life, and death, and history. In the Introduction Lord Morley begins by saying: "The War and our action in it led to my retirement from public office." There are apt quotations at the head of each chapter selected from the author's wide reading. In the book proper he comments on the work of other authors in more detail than on his own writings.

RECONSTRUCTION IN PHILOSOPHY, by John Dewey (1920). In these lectures delivered at the Imperial University of Japan in 1919, Professor Dewey seeks not so much to express his own point of view on modern problems of philosophy as to present a general picture of the modes of thought and changed attitudes characteristic of present-day philosophy. He begins by showing the changed attitude to philosophy itself, explaining its origin in imagination and memory, which differentiate man from the lower animals, and the concomitant growth of matter-of-fact knowledge which conflicts with the former basis of speculation. From these two sources, all subsequent philosophies have derived. Classical philosophy stems from the first, and is dialectically formal, concerning itself with superior, or ideal Reality. Contemporary thinking accepts as evidence the data of matter-of-fact knowledge and dedicates philosophy to social functions rather than to the discovery of absolute Truth. Historically considered, the new philosophy begins with Francis Bacon, who was one of the first to conceive of knowledge as power, as the result of coöperation in research, and as testable by social progress. In the reconstruction of philosophy, therefore, scientific factors have played an important part, since science is the extension and verification of matter-of-fact knowledge. In the fulfilment of these functions, Science has changed our idea of the order of Nature. It is no longer finite and fixed, neither as to the cosmos nor as to the species which inhabit it. Change and motion are the guiding principles of the new order, and these, when controlled by man, open the door to progress. Nature as a concept having been revolutionized, experience and Reason, deriving from it, have likewise become new and different concepts. The latter have been made possible by two factors, connected with the scientific movement, the first an actual change in the data of experience resulting from the activities of science itself; the second, the development of an experimental psychology rooted in biology, which has swept away all rationalistic notions of how we think and how we acquire knowledge. With these new instruments or concepts it is not strange that notions of the Ideal and the Real should change. Previously, the Ideal had been based on escape from the disagreeable, true reality being ideal, changeless, and perfect. But with the notion of progress, mobility, incompleteness are the very factors which permit of melioration, and the ideal becomes simply the goal toward which conscious human effort is directed to make of the present data, or Real, the next Reality. In the process of accomplishment it is the Ideal. The problem of methods brings up questions of logic, a field which we would naturally expect to have been affected by new notions of philosophy. The purposes of science requiring constant comparison of theories with facts, the origin of thinking in conflicts is found in experimentation. Observation, exact and impartial, is necessary, but facts must be correlated. Hypotheses must therefore be formulated which fit them and are consistent with other hypotheses elsewhere devised to cover other groups of facts. Truth, in consequence, is no longer an abstract entity or thing, but the relation between definitions, or hypotheses, and facts. The true is the verified and workable. Such a notion of truth naturally implies a changed conception of ethics and morals. Since every moral situation requires forethought and choice before action, the question is whether the decision will be made on *a priori* principles of the good, or on specific observation, analysis, and prevision of consequences. Actions are always specific, and hence the new philosophy demands that judgments on moral questions be specific. Hence the old distinction between intrinsic and instrumental ends is swept away, and both social and individual purposes are regarded as equally intrinsic, and not as ends to be achieved and indulged in forever after, but as processes, activities, or directions. Growth is the only "end." And conscious growth implies meliorism. The volume closes with an examination of social and political institutions of the present in terms of the new philosophic concepts of truth, ideality, and growth.

RED SKY AT MORNING, by Margaret Kennedy (1927), like her first success, "A Constant Nymph," is a novel depicting the isolation surrounding the children of a genius. The Crowne twins, Emily and William, had beauty and wealth and the promise of gifts that might equal those of that ill-fated poet, their father. Although the celebrated trial of Norman Crowne for murder ended in an acquittal, the world did not, for a long time, cease to savor the scandal which wrecked his life. Together the twins combined to show a courageous front to the world to conceal their great sensitiveness so that no one guessed how vulnerable they were. While still innocent infants in the home of their aunt, Catherine Frobisher, who brought them up along with her own children, Charlotte and Trevor, they felt their separateness. In pathetic little ways they sought to establish their sense of family solidarity against a suspiciously sympathetic world. When they were very little they would crook their fingers together; later, when Trevor taunted them with their father's case, William ferociously attacked the older boy, abetted by Emily. When the War was over, they went to London to live together as they had always planned and became a brilliant focus of social success. Then a Polish-French adventuress, Tillie Van Tuyl, found William's wealth and naïve sympathy more indispensable than the intrigue she would have enjoyed better with Trevor. Her marriage to William was made more easy of accomplishment since the entente between brother and sister was broken by Emily's defection. For motives of self interest, Tillie had connived with Baxter, a popular producer, to take William's play, "The Seven Dawns," a closet drama, and give her a prominent part in it. On the first night, Emily attended with Philip Luttrel, the rector of her aunt's parish, a man much older than herself who had loved her happily and without desire of possession, since her childhood. Behind them in the darkness Emily hears not only adverse criticism of her brother's play, but the open statement that the speaker was one of those who had been present at her father's trial and never meant to miss a Crowne show. "Emily's radiance was a torch, deliberately brandished, not so much in defiance of external dangers as against some half-realized, inward doubt." Her long, desperate defiance of prejudiced public opinion crumbles at this and she seeks to lose her identity by becoming the wife of her elderly lover, to his private consternation. Monk's Hall, Mrs. Frobisher's old home, now occupied, despite scandalized whispers by her brother Bobby, a retired Indian military man and his mistress, Lise, becomes the scene of Part II. William has bought the old place on a generous impulse to save the old home to the family and to establish there a community of indigent artists collected by Trevor, who has himself been debarred from his mother's home because he will not devote himself to some regular profession. William soon discovers how hopeless his own marriage is and, like his father, finds release from unpleasant reality by living in a world of his own from which he only emerges in a rage when recalled by some more than usually irritating actuality.   Tillie and Trevor, meanwhile, renew their intrigue to the scandal of the community.   The dénouément shows William following relent-lessly the path his father had taken before him.   While the tragedy lacks power of portrayal, the high level of the earlier success is maintained by the brilliant epigram-matic characterization.   Catherine Frobisher's character is summed up in the opening paragraph, "she was one of those women who are more conspicuously successful as widows than as wives."   If the twins themselves seem too much creatures of air and fire rather than of solid earth to enlist sympathy for their fate, the human qualities of plain Charlotte, who accepts her lot in life with cheerful philosophy, and of Trevor, whose life is one long rebellion, early expressed against too much ancestor worship in his mother's attitude toward their father, and the matter-of-fact romance of Bobby and Lise, all these are made understandable and arouse interest through the author's delicate and meticulous artistry.

RELIGION, THE BIRTH AND GROWTH OF, by G. F. Moore, see **BIRTH.**

RELIGION IN THE MAKING, by A. N. Whitehead (1926).   Religion, on its doc-trinal side, according to Whitehead, can be defined as a "system of general truths which have the effect of transforming character when they are sincerely held and vividly apprehended."   Hence his starting-point in "Religion in the Making" is a study of religion in history.   He finds the source of religion in solitariness.   Religion is what the individual does in isolation.   As it finds expression in human history, however, religion exhibits four factors, or aspects, of itself.   These factors are ritual, emotion, belief, rationalization.   Ritual is the tendency of living organisms to repeat their own actions.   It is exhibited even by animals and the term as such may be applied to other than religious performances.   The use of ritual, however, evokes emotion, by its pragmatic success or for its own sake.   Play and religion therefore have the same origin.   But ritual and emotion cannot long continue without intel-lectuality.   Myths then both explain ritual and satisfy emotion.   All three inter-acting, increasing in number and complexity, lead to organization and rationaliza-tion.   The attempt here is to make a coherent order of life.   Religion, — and this is one of the central doctrines of the book, — stands between abstract metaphysics and the special principles regulating certain experiences of life.   Based on intuition and rationalization, the last stage of religion tends toward individualism at the same time as toward world-consciousness.   Social consciousness is displaced and principles are then judged no longer by pragmatic right, or use, but universal right, or truth.   Of the religions of the world the two great catholic examples are Chris-tianity and Buddhism.   In the endeavor to reach general principles, rationalized religion comes in contact with the problem of evil.   And it is in dealing with this problem that Buddhism and Christianity fundamentally differ.   Buddhism advo-cates escape from evil through release from the individual personality which experi-ences it.   But this release is not to be had through mere physical death, which fact discloses the metaphysical assumption of Buddhism.   Christianity follows the opposite principle: it is rooted in the experience of great lives, and has no definite metaphysic.   Thus it retains a wide scope of development, though it has always sought metaphysical backing.   To describe great moments of religious experience as precise truths is to formulate dogmas.   These are necessary as a basis of appeal for common agreement.   Though in the last analysis all religious experience is admittedly of intuitive and personal nature, the distinction is made that the intuitions emerge under special circumstances, but once formulated help us all to apprehend the nature of the truth thus revealed. To-day, according to the author, the one religious dogma in debate is the meaning of "God." He distinguishes three concepts: the Eastern Asiatic concept of an impersonal order to which the world conforms, which implies complete immanence; the Semitic concept of a personal individual entity, which implies complete transcendence; the Pantheistic concept in which the world is a phase of the ultimate individual entity, and which implies extreme monism. Christianity has not adopted any one of these concepts, keeping metaphysics subordinate to religious facts. But to find God, which the author believes is the problem of the modern world, some notion of the metaphysical implications of the three possible concepts must be had. In point of tone-feeling, he believes that the modern world will find God through love, and not fear. He continues with a description of the metaphysical backing possible for modern religion. Considering the universe as 1, the actual world, in time; and 2, the elements which go to its formation, analysis reveals those formative elements to be, 1, the creativity whereby the actual world has its character of temporal passage; 2, the realm of ideal forms exemplified in everything that is actual; and 3, the actual but non-temporal entity by which creative indetermination is made determinate, that is to say, God. God, therefore, enters into every occasion made actual and determinate; and here the metaphysical analysis might stop were it not for the fact that it leaves evil unaccounted for. At the present stage of analysis, evil in the world would be in conformity with the nature of God. Now evil is described as an unstable destructive agency, which promotes its own elimination either by destruction or by elevation. But God being actual, and being also the measure of esthetic consistency in the world, if we trace evil to the determinism derived from God, the inconsistency in the world is derived from the consistency of God. The world therefore exhibits two sides of which one, evil and incomplete, is to be construed in terms of additional formative elements not definable in terms applicable to God. Seeing the universe as an esthetic order, of which the moral order is only a phase, then, establishes the metaphysical assumption that the universe exhibits an infinite freedom of creativity and a realm of form with infinite possibilities, both being dependent for achievement in reality on the "completed ideal harmony, which is God."

REMEMBRANCE OF THINGS PAST (A La Recherche du Temps Perdu), by Marcel Proust (8 vols., 1918–1927). The book is written in the form of an imaginary autobiography, and is described by the translator as "a continuous novel." The narrator says, "When a man is asleep, he has in a circle round him the chain of the hours, the sequence of the years. . . ." Time and space are equally annihilated in the mind that recalls past experience with present associations, which is the method of this author. The first part, "Swann's Way," begins when the hero is a small boy spending the summer with his father and mother and aunts at his grandfather's house in the town of Combray in Normandy. The child cannot bear to go to sleep without his mother's good-night kiss. One night when M. Swann has come to dinner and he is therefore sent early to bed, his misery is so great that he determines to sit up until his parents come upstairs, though he is in an agony of fear that he will be punished. His father realizes that the child is exceptionally sensitive, and does not scold him, but advises his mother to comfort him and spend the night in his room. There follows a description of the household and a number of the people of the provincial town, in addition to the picture of Swann as seen through the eyes of the boy.

An unhappy old music teacher and composer, M. Vinteuil, avoids everyone he knows and spends his days in the cemetery at his wife's grave until he dies of a broken heart because his cherished daughter has a disgraceful friendship with another woman. The two walks that the boy takes with the family at Combray are "Swann's Way," past the estate of their friend, and the "Guermantes way" along the river toward Guermantes itself, the residence of the Duc and Duchess de Guermantes. The "ways" come to symbolize the different social groups of the Guermantes, who stand for the old order of the aristocracy founded on tradition, and Swann, the brilliant man of the world, a rich and cultivated Jew, member of exclusive clubs, and friend of the Comte de Paris and the Prince of Wales. The family do not walk in M. Swann's park any more because he has made a mesalliance with a beautiful and wanton cocotte, Odette, whom they cannot recognize. One day the boy sees Madame Swann and her daughter, Gilberte, through the hedge, and he meets the girl again in Paris in the Champs Élysée in the winter, and becomes her adoring playmate. The reminiscences of the boy now gives place to the story of Swann's amour of thirty years before with Odette. Swann sees her resemblance to the women of Botticelli, and identifies his passion for her with his artistic, esthetic tastes. She brings Swann to dinner with her friends, the Verdurins. They are vulgar bourgeoisie who pretend to despise the society to which they have not the entrée. That evening he hears the andante movement of Vinteuil's sonata, music which is to become famous. He meets the tiresome, punning Dr. Cottard, who becomes a celebrated surgeon, and Elstir, later a painter of genius, and whom the hero meets at Balbec. Odette soon tires of Swann, and he is tormented by jealousy of her relations with other men. At an evening party given by a Mme. de Sainte-Euverte, he hears the Vinteuil sonata played again, and recalls sadly the time when Odette had been kind and loving, and had not deceived him. He is glad of the wealth that enables him to keep her dependent on him in some measure. The story of the love affair of this sensitive man for the stupid, uncomprehending Odette is an epic of jealousy paralleled by the love of the young hero for Albertine, described in later volumes. Swann's friend, the Princess des Launes, meets him at Mme. Sainte-Euverte's reception at which she had condescended to appear, and is distressed that he looks so unhappy. She thinks that it is absurd that a man of his intelligence should let himself suffer at the hands of such a woman. The author says she feels "that a clever man ought to be unhappy only about such persons as are worth his while; which is rather like being astonished that anyone should condescend to die of cholera at the bidding of so insignificant a creature as the common bacillus."

The second part, "Within a Budding Grove" (A l'Ombre des Jeunes Filles en Fleur) returns to the reverie of the hero. Odette is now Mme. Swann, and the story begins to tell of her gradual social progress. Her husband continues to see his old friends of the Faubourg Saint-Germain, but cultivates the society of officials and politicians who will receive Odette. The boy admires Odette and loves Gilberte, and is a visitor at their house in Paris. His eagerness to be with her is so excessive that Gilberte becomes indifferent to him, and in his wounded pride he refuses to see her again, though they exchange letters. Two years afterward he has forgotten her, when he goes with his adored grandmother to Balbec, and admires a group of young girls on the beach, especially their leader, Albertine, whom he sees first as a profile outlined against the sea. Through the painter, Elstir, he meets her and her friends. A school friend of his grandmother's, Mme. de Villeparisis, of the Guermantes family, takes them to drive around the country. Her young relative, Robert Saint-Loup, comes to visit her, and the two young men become intimate friends. Sometime later, the hero, called by name, Marcel, first in the next part of the book, visits Saint-Loup at the town where his regiment is quartered, and meets Rachel, the young Jewish actress, who is his friend's mistress. She despises her lover as a mere man of the world, as she cannot appreciate the simplicity and breeding, and good taste, that places him above the circle of esthetic charlatans she considers his superiors. He suffers from jealousy even as Swann and Marcel in their love affairs. Baron de Challus, nephew of Mme. de Villeparisis, the sinister figure, who dominates the later volumes, "Cities of the Plain," joins his aunt, Mme. de Villeparisis, at Balbec. Marcel is puzzled by his strange, contradictory personality.

The third part, "The Guermantes Way," (Le Côté de Guermantes) is devoted to the experiences of the hero in the fashionable world of the Guermantes family, the illness and death of his delightful and unselfish grandmother, and his liaison with Albertine. The snobbishness and essential vulgarity of the Faubourg Saint-Germain are satirized as in the salon of Mme. Verdurin the affectations and shams of artistic pretensions were exposed. At the Champs Élysées Marcel and his grandmother hear the woman who tends the toilet say to the keeper of the grounds: "I choose my clients. I don't receive everybody in what I call my salons." The grandmother remarks: "It sounded exactly like the Guermantes and the Verdurins." She keeps her face turned from her grandson to try to keep him from seeing that she has had a paralytic stroke. Marcel admires the Duchesse de Guermantes, and courts her notice, and asks his friend, Saint-Loup, to speak well of him to his aunt. In this story of about 800 pages, 133 are given to description of an afternoon tea with Mme. de Villeparisis, and 184 pages to a dinner-party with the Duchesse de Guermantes. At Balbec he had thought Mme. de Villeparisis the "great lady" with her anecdotes of distinguished people who came to her father's house. Now he learns that she had married beneath her, and is almost déclassée in her own social world, though the Guermantes relatives continue to visit her. Another glimpse of Mme. de Villeparisis is through the eyes of a neighbor from Combray, who asks to have pointed out to her the "most beautiful woman of her time" for whom her father had ruined himself, and is shocked to see "a dreadful blowsy little hunched-up old woman." On another occasion he overhears a casual conversation between Mme. de Villeparisis and his father's friend, the ambassador M. de Norpois, which reveals to him that the old diplomat has been her lover for many years. This method of building up the personality of his characters by a series of impressions of the same person at different times is characteristic of the author. The last episode of this story is that Swann tells his friends, the Duc and the Duchesse de Guermantes, just as they are starting for a dinner, that he will not be able to take a trip to Italy with them as planned, because the doctor has warned him that he has only a few months to live. They are so preoccupied as ever with their social relations that they pretend that they think he is joking in order to avoid talking about his illness and making themselves late to dinner.

The fourth part, "Cities of the Plain" (Sodome et Gomorrhe), is a study of sexual inversion, and begins with the meeting of M. de Charlus and the tailor, Jupien, as seen by Marcel. There is an evening reception given by the Prince and Princess de Guermantes. Swann is not well received by the other guests because he is a Dreyfusard. The Prince discusses the case with him and asks his opinion, as he also believes Dreyfus innocent. Marcel sees Albertine in Paris, and at Balbec where he goes again for his health. Mme. Verdurin has inherited wealth, and entertains M. de Charlus at her Wednesdays, and Morel, nephew of the valet of Marcel's uncle, who has supplanted Jupien in the Baron's erotic affections. Marcel tires of

Albertine and is about to break off his relations with her, but in jealous suspicion of her preference for the society of other women after he discovers she has been the friend of Mlle. Vinteuil, he decides that he cannot live without her.

The last volumes soon to be translated are "Le Prisonnière," "Albertine Disparue," and "Le Temps Retrouvé." While his mother is at Combray Marcel brings Albertine to live with him in the family apartment in Paris, where he is alone with the old family servant, Françoise. His jealousy and suspicion of her Lesbian tendencies keep her practically a prisoner, and she finally runs away to her aunt at Balbec. When she had been with him he had doubted his love for her, but now he is miserable without her and questions her reasons for leaving him. Suddenly he hears that she has been killed by a fall from her horse. After her death he receives her letter promising to return to him. His analysis of his feelings toward her continues, as if she was innocent he had wronged her, and if she was guilty of perversion, he blames himself that she returned to a life she dreaded. He forgets her in the distractions of the social world that he reënters. M. de Charlus has a party given at the Verdurin's house at which the unpublished quartet of Vinteuil is played for the first time, and members of the illustrious Guermantes family are present. This happens as the author points out, because of the relationship of Charlus and Morel, the musician, whom he adores. The narrator retires to a sanitarium, but returns to Paris after the War. The salon of Mme. Swann has become one of the most elegant in Paris, and the Duchesse de Guermantes who had once in years past left the drawing-room of Mme. de Villeparisis in order to avoid meeting the wife of her friend, Swann, is now one of her guests. Robert Saint-Loup, the heir of the Guermantes family, has married Gilberte, who repudiated her fine old father in the hope of furthering her social ambitions. Saint-Loup is killed in the War. The Prince de Guermantes, ruined by the War, marries the wealthy Mme. Verdurin. Marcel recollects his childhood and youth, and the sight of Gilberte's daughter makes him realize that he himself is old, a hypochondriac like his Aunt Léonie described in the first chapters about the family life at Combray.

RESCUE, THE, by Joseph Conrad (1920), concerns the adventures of Captain Tom Lingard of the brig "Lightning" on that coast of an island in the Malay Archipelago known to adventurers of the eastern seas as "The Shore of Refuge." Rajah Hassim, nephew of one of the greatest chiefs of Wajo, and Tom Lingard had become friends after Hassim had saved Lingard from a treacherous stab in the back when they had met as seaman-traders in New Guinea. Later King Tom, as he was known on those seas, saved the young rajah and his sister, Immada, when he found them in a desperate situation. After his uncle's death an usurper had become chief and driven Hassim and his sister out. Feeling responsibility for the lives he had rescued, King Tom devoted his time and all his resources to the restoration of the exiled prince and princess to their kingdom. All his plans were matured. Men, arms and ammunition had been gathered in sufficient amounts to insure success, and Lingard was hastening to the agreed spot on the shore of refuge to take charge of the revolt when a yacht was discovered aground in the vicinity. It was owned by Mr. Travers, a rich Englishman, who, with his wife and a Spanish guest, d'Alcacer, was aboard. Travers will not credit Lingard with disinterested intentions when he warns him of the danger the yacht's company run on such a coast. Then Travers and d'Alcacer, out for a stroll on the beach, are taken captive by Daman's forces, natives whom Lingard had engaged along with other forces under Belarab for the coming revolution. The two white men are released on Lingard's pledged word and the whole party reassemble on board the

"Emma." The "Emma" had been towed up a creek and run aground on the shore of a lagoon opposite Belarab's settlement in the forest, under guard of Jörgenson, himself a derelict of the East, to be used as an arsenal and storehouse of supplies for the coming revolution. Young Carter has been left in charge of the brig and the yacht while this has been going on. Youthfully anxious to acquit himself well he fires on the natives in their war canoes about the shore and thus, unaware of the white men's whereabouts and of the circumstances of Lingard's pledge, breaks the truce. Lingard accompanies Travers and d'Alcacer back to Belarab's stockade where, according to agreement, they must be returned. Meanwhile Rajah Hassim and Immada are taken by Daman, who is jealous of Belarab's influence with Lingard. Jaffir, a native runner, brings the Rajah's ring to Jörgenson. Only Lingard would understand that the sending of the ring is a final call for assistance when Hassim is in desperate straits. Jörgenson decides that Mrs. Travers stands the best chance of taking the ring to Lingard without molestation. But she is distrustful of Jörgenson and does not deliver the ring, although she is glad of the opportunity of joining Lingard. For between herself and King Tom, the romantic adventurer, is a passionate attachment, which is avowed when she joins him within the stockade. Jörgenson and Hassim and Immada, threatened by Daman's men, await Lingard's help. When it seems that he has failed them, the gallant old adventurer throws his lighted cigar into the powder magazine rather than allow all the ammunition stored in the "Emma" to fall into the hands of Daman's crowd. With Hassim and Immada's death the reason for King Tom's whole enterprise fails and Belarab sends the white men back to their ships, glad to be rid of them for he desires nothing but peace for his people. On the sandbar at dawn Captain Tom Lingard and Edith Travers bid each other farewell. The brig "Lightning" takes its way due north as the yacht sets a southern course.

REVISION OF THE TREATY, A, by J. M. Keynes (1922). A sequel to the author's "Economic Consequences of the Peace." Mr. Keynes believes that the disaster prophesied in his earlier book has not come to pass because no serious attempt has been made to enforce the economic clauses of the Treaty of Versailles. He gives a summary of relevant events of the two previous years to December, 1921, and reviews the inter-Allied conferences of 1920 and 1921. There is a section on coal which corrects and amplifies some of the statements in his first book, and a section on the legality of the occupation of Germany east of the Rhine, and of the claim for pensions. In the discussion of the reparation bill he uses French official statistics to show that the French claims drawn up by interested creditors were based on an over-valuation. The Belgian claims he finds exaggerated, and the British estimate in respect of shipping losses very high. The claim for pensions and allowances is "nearly double that for devastation." He considers the cancellation of the Reparation and inter-Allied debts essential. In his proposed revision of the Treaty he would reduce the assessment from one hundred and thirty-eight milliard gold marks to thirty-six milliard gold marks, which he estimates as within Germany's capacity to pay, and explains his plan for the payment and division of this sum. The Appendix gives the documents embodying the agreements reached at the various conferences, the German Counter-Proposals of 1921, and tables of inter-governmental indebtedness.

REVOLT IN THE DESERT, by T. E. Lawrence (1926). The book is the history of the revolt of the Arabs against Turkish rule organized and inspired by Lawrence "through two years of bitter and weird adventure," from October 1916 to September

1918. The first book of 400,000 words was written, lost, rewritten again from memory, and published in a limited edition under the title "Seven Pillars of Wisdom." This is an abridgment. In an introduction the publishers tell how "in 1914, T. E. Lawrence was serving as a more or less unnoticed assistant in the British Museum's excavation of Carchemish on the Euphrates. . . . He knew the Near East intimately. His first direct knowledge of the complicated peoples of Arabia had been gained while he was still an undergraduate at Oxford, when he is said to have undertaken, alone and in native dress, a two-year expedition among the tribes behind Syria in order to gather material for his thesis on the military history of the Crusades." In its present form the book opens with his arrival at Jeddah on a "joy ride" in quest of a leader to carry the Arab revolt beyond Hejaz. At the end of a long camel ride he comes to Feisal, son of Hussein of Mecca, and writes, "I felt at first glance that this was the man I had come to Arabia to seek. . . ." A later picture of Feisal reads "he was a man of moods, flickering between glory and despair, and just now dead-tired. He looked years older than thirty-one; and his dark, appealing eyes, set a little sloping in his face, were bloodshot, and his hollow cheeks deeply lined and puckered with reflection. His nature grudged thinking, for it crippled his speed in action: the labour of it shrivelled his features into swift lines of pain. In appearance he was tall, graceful, and vigorous, with the most beautiful gait and a royal dignity of head and shoulders. . . ." Lawrence adopted the native dress in place of his uniform of the British Intelligence Office at Feisal's suggestion, since the Arabs associated khaki with the hated Turks. He passed into the Arab world, imitated their ways of thinking and acting, and made their cause his in order to make them identify his cause with theirs. The account of his adventures reads like an extract from the "Arabian Nights." The narrative is almost in the form of a diary, recounting the daily movements, the character of the innumerable miles of country crossed by camel and car over the burning desert in summer, and sharp, broken ice in winter, with the ordeal of hunger and thirst. His achievements made him a legendary figure, his title among the Arabs being "Wrecker of Engines," and he does mention toward the end of the book that "this bridge (was) my seventy-ninth." As the Turks set a price on his head he gathered about him a bodyguard of picked daredevils who were proud to be in his service, and "made boast throughout the army of their pains and gains." He won the confidence of the British Staff in the Near East, and the coöperation of General Allenby as well as the Arab Sheiks, Auda abu Tayi, Nuri Pasha Said, Nuri Shaalan, Talal el Hareidhin. Feisal was the prophet of the movement, laboring at his politics, "putting together and arranging in their natural order the innumerable tiny pieces which made up Arabian society, and combining them into his one design of war against the Turks. There was no blood feud left active in any of the districts through which he had passed, and he was the Court of Appeal, ultimate and unchallenged, for western Arabia. . . . No Arab ever impugned his judgments, or questioned his wisdom and competence in tribal business. By patiently sifting out right and wrong, by his tact, his wonderful memory, he gained authority over the nomads from Medina to Damascus and beyond. He was recognized as a force transcending tribe, superseding blood-chiefs, greater than jealousies. The Arab movement became in the best sense national. . . ." Auda was the greatest fighting man in northern Arabia. "He saw life as a saga. All the events in it were significant: all personages in contact with him heroic. His mind was stored with poems of old raids and epic tales of fights, and he overflowed with them on the nearest listener. If he lacked listeners he would very likely sing them to himself in his tremendous voice. . . . He spoke of himself in the third

person, and was so sure of his fame that he loved to shout out stories against himself
. . . yet . . . he was modest, as simple as a child, direct, honest, kind-hearted. . ."
The story ends with the triumphant entrance into Damascus. The author is alone
in his room, "working and thinking out as firm a way as the turbulent memories of
the day allowed, when the Muedhdhins began to sound their last call of prayer
through the moist night over the illuminations of the feasting city. One, with a
ringing voice of special sweetness, cried into my room from a near mosque. . . .
'God alone is great: I testify there are no gods, but God: and Mahommed is his
Prophet. Come to prayer: come to security. God alone is great: there is no god —
but God.' His voice dropped two tones, almost to speaking level, and he added
softly: 'And He is very good to us this day, O people of Damascus.' The clamour
hushed, as every one seemed to obey the call to prayer on this, their first night of
perfect freedom." The book is illustrated with prints of original drawings by various
English artists of prominent people in the story, and is furnished with a map of some
of Lawrence's journeys, and an index.

REVOLUTIONARY NEW ENGLAND, 1691–1776, by James Truslow Adams, is a
continuation of the author's "The Founding of New England" (1923). The first book
was concerned chiefly with the origins of colonial life. The present volume carries
the story from 1691 "the approximate date of the close of the narrative in the preceding to the Declaration of Independence and the ending of the colonial status of
the New England settlements." Mr. Adams styles this whole period revolutionary
and goes back to the early decades to find the origin of the grievances of the colonies,
the slow growth of revolutionary tendencies, and the rise of a radical party. In ,
an introductory chapter the author sketches the character of the eighteenth century, the rise of classes, the political effects of the Revolution of 1688, the effects
of frontier life on the colonists and the difficulties of the imperial problem. He then
traces the beginnings of the differences in questions of political philosophy of the
colonies and the mother country; the movement toward revolution, regarding the
whole not in the sense of a quarrel between two countries, but as a phase of the world's
advance during these years. Under the heading of the machinery of Empire, Mr.
Adams outlines the organization of England's colonial administration in America
and the causes of inefficiency, and shows the effect of the system and especially the
influence of the military operations on the colonists. With the dawn of the century
he takes up the state of culture in the colonies, the religious attitude, morals, laws of
the day and discusses the West Indian trade. Realizing the inability of the colonies
to ward off their enemies when fighting as separate units, an attempt at unified control
was made and the witty Irish Earl of Bellomont was sent as Governor General to try
his hand. His efforts were valiant but unavailing since he attempted to control
privateering, which last had been a legitimate business since the Peace of Ryswick.
His successor was Joseph Dudley, during whose governorship there was renewed war
with the French, and several unsuccessful attempts at coöperation between the
colonies and the imperial government. Early in the eighteenth century there came
a time of land speculation in the old colonies with a resulting expansion of the frontier.
The introduction of paper money without sufficient metal to back it plus the rising
cost of living were results. There were three main spheres of diverging interest between the Englishmen of old England and New England: the "divergence between
the newly developing sections and classes in New England itself, and the conflict of
material interest between those colonies and the Sugar Islands . . . and the beginning of marked class conflict in the mother country herself." With the expansion

in land holdings and the rise of capitalism there came a growing tendency toward secularism in contrast to the earlier strict puritanism. The New England of 1750 was still loyal to England, but it was no longer the New England of 1740. The capture of the fortress of Louisbourg and its subsequent return to France had taught the colonists that in the matter of promised financial aid for the carrying on of wars England was not a very strong reed on which to lean. "In the closing three years of the [Seven Years'] war, from the capture of Montreal in 1760, to the peace of Paris in 1763, the colonials, to a great extent, lost interest in its operations, the theatre of which, so far as America was concerned, was shifted from the continent to the West Indies." The colonists were interested in making money and resented England's attempts to take away any part of it with taxes. There was a large and lucrative trade between New England and the West Indies. Molasses imported from the West Indies was made into rum which became the currency of the day. The Molasses Act took large tolls of the profits of this trade and was one of the direct causes of the Revolution. Every attempt by England to tax the colonies met with disaster. Next came the question of quartering royal troops in Boston. The local authorities could not maintain order; the Crown tried it and the Boston Massacre resulted. There followed the battles of Lexington and Concord. The colonies were determined now on freedom from all overlordship on the part of England. Civil war had come.

REYNARD THE FOX, by John Masefield (1919). A narrative poem in two parts, written in octosyllabic couplets with line variants of seven to eleven syllables. In the manner of the Prologue to Chaucer's "Canterbury Tales" the first part of the narrative is a progressive description of about forty characters assembled for the fox-hunt at the Cock and Pye, a three-hundred-year old inn of the English countryside. The second part is devoted entirely to the story of the chase from the point of view of the pursued fox. Together both parts of the poem make a composite picture of one of England's oldest sports, neither a defence nor an attack of the fox-hunt. A number of the characters are reminiscent of types found in Chaucer, Fielding and other earlier English writers, the traditional jolly parson, and his sporting wife, the squire, small in brain, great in courage. "Two things he failed to understand, the foreigner and what was new." Masefield is abreast of his time in his description of the modern girls who sing ragtime, and win at tennis "the silver-cigarette-case-prize." Major Howe's mustache is clipped "tooth-brush-wise." Tommy Crowmarsh rides with the sonnets of Heredia on his lips. The names are interesting in themselves: John Restrop, John Pym, John Hankerton, Joan Urch, Charles Copse, Sir Button Budd, Robert Thrupp, Bill Ridden, Tom See, Bill Ripple, Sir Peter Bynd. The interest in character and name is not merely limited to what meets the eye. Masefield's descriptions are accompanied by an intent to get at English character and mind, especially at:

> "Great kindness, delicate sweet feeling
> Most shy, most clever in concealing
> Its depth for beauty of all sorts;
> Great manliness, a love of sports,
> A grave wise thoughtfulness and truth,
> A merry fun, outlasting youth,
> A courage terrible to see
> And mercy for his evening."

The animals are pictured as faithfully as the assembled hunters, the horses, eating, whinnying and ramping to see other horses in the adjacent stalls, of mounts, Stormalong, by Tempest out of Love-Me-Long, the hounds, Arrogant, Daffodil,

Queen, keen on the scent, the terriers fighting. The hunt is visualized: riding, working, talking, the kissing glasses clinking, the thought, "Life loves to change," over the face of them.

In Part Two the fox is hunted in broad autumn daylight through domestic garden patches, over English hill, heath, and into the woods of Mourne End. The verses follow the fox in his sleep, his day-dreams hearing the life of the woodland, seeking food and mate, in his scent, which is part of his sight and sound, in his going up-wind, escaping his pursuers, in his disappointed, winded attempts to find rabbit furrows to hide in. In the end, the fox escapes by a hairbreadth. A fox-terrier interfering on the hounds changes the scent, and another fox is slain in his stead. The fox lies still at nightfall, while the hounds return homeward, "all rank from a fox they'd eaten." The first whip, Tom Dansey, and Robin Dawe, the master of the hunt, deceived as to the real identity of the hound's prey, drink the triumph of the run. The hounds and mounts are cared for. Not many hours later the church bells recalling England chime midnight in the moonlight in which hunters and hunted sleep.

RHAPSODY, by Arthur Schnitzler, 1927, a dream novel, along Freudian lines, relates the experiences of a husband and wife. They had attended a masquerade ball the preceding evening and were relating their adventures when the talk drifts to those hidden wishes from the mysterious regions of which they are hardly conscious. They tell each other of an experience each had the preceding summer at a Danish watering place, when the spirit of adventure and freedom that for the moment possessed them, united though they were in thought and feeling, revealed something of those hidden currents of their being. Their confidences are interrupted at this point when the doctor is called to attend a dying patient, so he bids his wife good-night. While he is keeping the dead man's daughter, Fräulein Marrianne, company until the arrival of her fiancé, she tells him that she dreads leaving town after her approaching marriage because it is a comfort to her to be near the doctor whom she loves. On the arrival of the fiancé the doctor escapes. He is unwilling to return home immediately for the experience he has just been through and the mild spring night has made him restless. A woman of the street accosts him and coaxes him to her home but the image of his wife forces him to leave her in pity. He turns next, into a night restaurant, where he meets Nachtigall, an unfortunate musician whom he had known in his student days when they were both studying medicine. Through him he gains access to a Vienna night club of high society forbidden under mysterious penalties to all but the initiated. On the way there he surmises an adventure lurking in the shop where he procures his costume. After a hectic though seductive glimpse of debauchery practised as a fine art, he finds himself forcibly expelled. When he returns home and awakens his wife, she tells him of a strange dream she has had during his absence, the details of which he believes reveal a nature so faithless and cruel that his own experiences of the night pale to insignificance. That day, feeling absolved of all fealty to his wife, he determines to retrace his steps of the preceding night and see each of his abortive adventures through to the end. He first tries to find the unknown lady whose good will had saved him the night before. He reads of the suicide of a woman of high rank in the papers and investigation convinces him that the lady is his unknown benefactress who has thus been forced by her friends to pay the ultimate penalty for her defection from their club. Nor do any of his other adventures come to a satisfactory conclusion. That night on his return he finds the mask he wore at the strange club, lying on his pillow. He breaks down and tells his wife all of his experiences hoping that, remembering her own dream, she will forgive him. She, smiling, tells him that they ought to be grateful to have come unharmed out of all their adventures, whether real or only a dream, for surely not the reality of one night or even of a whole lifetime is the whole truth. And no dream, he answers, is ever entirely a dream.

RICEYMAN STEPS, by Arnold Bennett (1923). In this character novel the author develops the theme of miserliness, and a picture of the relations of husband and wife and servant, with humor and pathos. A middle-aged London bookseller, Henry Earlforward, in whom avarice has become a passion and a fine art, marries an almost equally penurious widow, Violet Arb. Mr. Earlforward buys the wedding ring from the proceeds of the sale of his bride's first one, as of course she could not use two, and gives her the change remaining from this transaction, for though he is a miser he is not a thief. Their honeymoon is a visit to Mme. Tussaud's Waxworks, where Henry's pleasure is spoiled by the discovery that some of the exhibits require an extra fee. Elsie, their young charwoman, becomes general servant in the living quarters over the dusty bookshop. For Elsie "kindness had a quality which justified it for its own sake whatever the consequences of it might be." She is unselfishly devoted to her employers and to her shell-shocked lover. The couple sacrifice their comfort to economy in fires and food, and the half-starved Elsie is driven to stealing from the larder at night. Preoccupied with their efforts to add to their hoard of money, nothing is too small to be taken into account, manœuvres to save gas, and minutiæ of daily tragedies and comedies about food, with the result that they both die within the year as a result of undernourishment. Mr. Earlforward disregards the doctor's warnings as an attempt to extract money for attendance. Mrs. Earlforward has not the strength to recover from an operation. Joe, who has disappeared after one of his spells, returns to Elsie, and she cares for him and Mr. Earlforward until the latter's death. In a collection of short stories, "Elsie and the Child," the first, the title story, is an epilogue, in which Elsie and Joe are married and in the service of Joe's former employer, the doctor. The child is the twelve-year-old Eva Raast, so devoted to Elsie that she at first refuses to go away from home to school, and thus throws the household into confusion. Elsie's management of the difficult Joe and the differences between life upstairs and below stairs make the story.

RIGHT OFF THE MAP, a novel, by C. E. Montague (1927). A satire on war in the story of two imaginary modern states, Ria and Porto, which divide between them the territory of a tropical island. The boundaries are a chain of mountains and a desert, and the cause of war is the ill-defined desert frontier where gold has been discovered. A dishonest business man, Mr. Bute, who remains off-stage, desires the war, and buys the press of both countries to support it. The editor of the "Voice," the only independent paper in Ria, is Cyril Burnage, an orator with "plush brains" and no convictions, the slave of public opinion. He is opposed to war, and holds out against it until he hears that Mr. Bute has obtained a controlling interest in his paper, and then tricked into making a speech by his beautiful, neurotic wife, Rose, who wants excitement, he responds to the sentiment of the crowd for war, and sends his friend, Willan, the hero of this story, and thousands of other men to be killed and wounded as a result of his golden words spoken to win the capricious approval of the wife he adores. Willan is a soldier of fortune who enjoys war as the best sport there is, and goes rejoicing with a clear conscience into this one, because, not able to distinguish between sincerity and bunk, he is inspired by Cyril. The army is not prepared for war, and the Colonel has had no experience in command. There was nothing furtive about the approach to the unseen enemy. The Colonel pointed with pride to a young officer standing on a high rock "like Michael Angelo's David," and even as Willan, the graduate of Sandhurst and veteran of the World War, looked the figure was suddenly brushed from the top of the stone like a golf ball swept off a tee by an invisible driver, and the war began. Other uplifted figures of Rian were swept from their pedestals, and there followed a desolating spectacle of heroism as officers rushed into the open leading little bodies of troops into the range of the guns. "That damned gallantry again," Willan groaned to himself. Line after line of Rian troops went down, and not an enemy head bobbed up. The rest learned to be soldiers, and by night, Willan, the highest officer left, commanded the remnants of the army, and led them into retreat high over a goat path into the mountains and down again into a secluded valley to rest and recuperate while they wait for new boots to be made to replace the bad ones sold to the army by its evil genius, Butc. Merrick, also a World War veteran, undertakes the great risk of getting through the enemy lines to let the besieged Rians know that the army is coming to the rescue. In the meantime the rout of the Rians is kept out of the papers which print false reports of victory as long as it is possible to make the people believe them. The Bishop, who had been glad to share the applause with Burnage in the balcony the day of his moving speech, and had blessed the departing troops, now tells Burnage that the country must "insist on a stern reckoning with all who have exposed it to so appalling a danger as insufficient preparation renders a war." Rose is delighted at the idea of a siege "as long as we go down with spirit." Her ardor is dampened by short rations, and the irregularity of the milkman, and her zest for nursing is spoiled by hearing herself so continually referred to as "a ministering angel." She is relieved from this rôle shortly for leaving her ward alone and causing the death of a soldier by her negligence. Her adoring husband thinks the strain of the siege is too hard on her, that she is looking pale and under-nourished, and decides to vote for capitulation to the Portans. Merrick gets through with his message to Burnage too late, but does not know it as he dies in the hospital. The expected attack by Willan and his men is repulsed, and Willan is tried by court-martial as a traitor, and hung. Burnage casts the vote against his friend, and thereby prevents the more realistic Portan on the Tribunal who believes Willan a good man from saving him. Willan is nursed by the girl he loves, Clare, also a realist, and has his last hour of happiness with her. At dawn Clare was only the chief mourner in a mourning city for somehow the truth of Willan's story became known.

RIGHT YOU ARE (IF YOU THINK SO), (Cosiè, se vi pare), a parable, by Luigi Pirandello, (1922). In this drama the people in a small Italian town become so curious about the relations of a certain Signor Ponza with his wife and his mother-in-law, Signora Frola, that finally the prefect is asked to find out the truth. Signor Ponza has been appointed to a government clerkship in the office of Commendatore Agazzi. He takes an apartment for himself and his wife on the top floor of a cheap tenement on the outskirts of the city, but settles his mother-in-law in the expensive apartment house where the Agazzi family live. His wife never leaves her home and sees no one but her husband. She appears on an iron balcony to talk with her mother in the courtyard below, and lets down a basket in which they exchange daily letters. The wife and daughter of Commendatore Agazzi call on Signor Frola, and are not received. Signora Frola comes to make an apology for her discourtesy to Signor Agazzi. In answer to their insistent questions she assures them that no girl ever had a more affectionate husband than her daughter, and that her son-in-law is most kind and solicitous for her own comfort, that the three of them are in perfect agreement, and she and her daughter refrain from visiting each other of their own accord, though it is no slight sacrifice. Signor Ponza calls to say that he cannot consent to have his mother-in-law pay or receive visits. With great reluctance he explains that Signora Frola has been insane since the death of her daughter, his first wife, four years before. His second wife, Julia, pretends that she is Lena, to humor the old lady who has the delusion that she is her daughter. His wife, however, cannot accept the caresses intended for another woman, a dead woman. He has been obliged to make this public explanation and have Signora Frola call, because of Commendatore Agazzi's complaint of impolite treatment of his wife and daughter, and because he cannot have them suppose that as Signora Frola gives out he is keeping a mother from seeing her own daughter out of jealousy. As it is he has to maintain two houses on his small salary. Signora Frola returns to convince the Agazzis that she is not a lunatic as she knows her beloved son-in-law believes. Her explanation is that Signora Frola, her daughter, fell ill of a contagious disease and had to be taken from home to the hospital. Signor Ponza became so over-wrought at this enforced separation, that he broke down nervously and had to be put under restraint. He became obsessed with the idea that his wife had died in the hospital, and when she recovered he could not recognize her again. To have him accept her they were obliged to pretend, with the collusion of the doctors, to have a second wedding. She thinks that he does not now believe that her daughter is his second wife, but seems to feel a need of maintaining the pretence. Signora Frola resents the curiosity that has forced these revelations, and threatened to destroy the structure of unreality which they have so painstakingly constructed. The village where Signor Ponza and his family lived has been destroyed by an earthquake, so there are no records to prove which story is true, to decide whether it is Signor Ponza or Signora Frola, that is suffering from a delusion. They try the strategem of bringing the two together, but in the presence of Signor Ponza, Signora Frola agrees with everything he says, that her daughter's name was Lena, and that his present wife's name is Julia, and they are no nearer the truth than before. It is suggested that the prefect in his official capacity shall summon Signor Ponza's wife to tell the true story, since the others are either unwilling or incapable of doing so. Signor Ponza is so indignant at this further intrusion into his private affairs that he offers to resign his position. Signora Frola comes to tell them that she will be obliged to leave the town and never see her daughter again even at a distance unless people will let her son-in-law alone. Signora Ponza herself comes in, a black-robed, veiled figure of mystery. To the impertinent strangers who question her, she answers that she is the daughter of Signora Frola, and the second wife of Signora Ponza, and for herself, she is nobody, or "whoever you choose to have me." She withdraws. Nothing is explained. The implication is that truth is relative, and the test to each man is "right you are if you think you are."

RISE OF AMERICAN CIVILIZATION, THE, by Charles A. and Mary R. Beard (2 vols. 1927). This survey of American history differs from most textbooks and treatises on the same subject in that it places equal stress on political, economic, social and cultural factors. The necessity in which the authors are placed of analyzing these four elements for every period does not mar, however, the continuity of the narrative. The latter begins a little in advance of the usual account, with a consideration of " England's Colonial Secret " in terms of mercantile imperialism, lateness of participation in colonial rivalry, naval strength, and able financing of civilian settlement overseas. The forms that the English establishments in the New World took are next discussed as revelatory of the structural bases of the republic-to-be. The fact that women joined the men in colonization, that something like a sufficient labor supply, including negro slaves, was secured, and that each section found some staple product on which to build its economic prosperity, immediately differentiated the American colonies from the Spanish and the French. Within the colonies themselves, the authors study differences between North and South, finding their origins in economic, religious, geographic and ethnic causes. But there was intercolonial migration, and soon, purely English immigration gave way to an influx of inter-European colonists, both factors helping to break down local differences, and leading to the assumption of power and commonalty which resulted in the American Revolution. This power, of course, was based on economic strength and aspirations to its expansion. Agriculture, shipping, and manufacture kept growing apace, hampered by restrictions from the Mother Country, yet were serious enough to threaten her monopoly and thus justify those restrictions. With this expanding power came a subtle change in the intellectual life of the colonies. Hitherto led by theologians of English formation, thought now fell into secular hands, and lawyers and publicists replaced the New England divine. The sources of inspiration, too, were different,— Voltaire, Diderot, d'Alembert, Montesquieu. Political and social thinking, immediate human welfare, superseded interest in religious thinking and the preoccupation in future salvation. Dealing next with the American Revolution, the authors brush aside the older theories of an indignant uprising of outraged virtue against oppression and of a successful insurrection of smugglers led by unemployed pettifoggers. It is mainly in mercantile and industrial rivalry that the causes of the separation are to be found. England found it necessary to protect her merchants and manufacturers at home by restrictive laws. These were difficult of enforcement; and all attempts to tighten the control only increased the natural friction arising from competition. Add to this, the unfortunate manner in which the ministers of George III went about clamping down colonial commerce, and the conflict becomes wholly explicable. The War was not conducted with the unity of purpose and loyalty to its cause which are generally assumed. Unsurmountable obstacles of intersectional jealousy, fear of military power, and personal rivalries interfered at almost every step. It is surprising indeed that a unified command and a successful campaign were at last achieved. But immediately after the stress of war and circumstance, the old jealousies reappeared and the semi-anarchical chaos of the Articles of Confederation followed the success of independence. Localism was the distinguished feature of the period. Fear of centralization, of dictatorship by any legislative or judicial body, and of any individual who might occupy the executive prerogatives that had belonged to the Crown, was embodied in the Articles. The classes most harassed by this ineffectual system of government by supplication were the financial, commercial, speculating interests of the country; and it was they who led the movement toward re-centralization. Concomitantly there was a populist movement, led by Daniel Shays, seeking to better the economic condition of the debtor agrarian class by paper money, scaling down the state debt, and abolishing property privileges embodied in the Articles. The repression of this movement in its culmination as Shays' Rebellion did not solve the situation, and the Congress being powerless to remedy it internally or to establish national sovereignty in foreign relations, the natural outcome was an extra-legal attempt to revise drastically the Articles of Confederation. The resulting Constitution was not so much a revision as an entirely new plan of government with the leading interests of the country compromising and sharing benefits among themselves in proportion to their influential strength. Already in these compromises are seen the germs of the conflict between the manufacturing and industrial North, in need of protection and mercantilist favors, and the free-trade, slave-labor South. The document as we know it to-day was finally drafted and proposed to the electorate, which divided, as was to be expected, along economic lines. But the opposition of the small farmers, laborers, and the debtor class generally, was unavailing against wealth, industrial and commercial. It was natural that after its adoption, the Constitution should be put into practice by its most ardent promulgators, and party division arose, as contemplated in " The Federalist," once more on the basis of economic interests. The Hamiltonian financial and commercial measures especially aroused opposition, in which was mixed a good deal of the theoretical and dialectic fervor of disciples of the French political *philosophes*. The debate was soon embittered by the French Revolution itself and the insecure position in which it placed the United States, torn between loyalty to a former ally and self-interest, the former dictated by the growing mass of Jeffersonian Republicans, the latter by the exigencies of governing a by no means unified country. The problems of the fledgling republic were not settled nor its unrest forever appeased by Jefferson's eventual victory. Foreign diplomacy was as dangerous and western agitation as clamorous under the Republicans as they had been under the Federalists, and concessions contradicting theories had to be made by Jefferson in both fields of government. First, he bought almost against his will the immense territory of Louisiana, and second, he passed the semi-pacific measure called the Embargo Act to attempt to bring France and England to terms in respect to American commerce. Pursuing this policy much longer was impossible, and under Jefferson's successor, Madison, the United States waged her first war, against the nation that had been her enemy before nationhood. Ineffectual as the war was, it served internally to intensify the differences between the commercial and agricultural interests. The Federalists, and the North generally, were against the war and saw in it nothing more than the self-interest of the southern and western states. Unable to recapture power, however, the Federalists continued as critics of an Administration which was being forced by events to adopt federal measures, culminating in the happy formulation of the Monroe Doctrine as an instrument of "sweeping nationalism." In the meanwhile, agricultural interests were augmenting in power, and a huge domain, favored by fertility and made profitable by migratory labor, arose in the West, that was to upset the original balance of power in the name of Jacksonian Democracy. The well-known effects of that triumphant farmer-labor party on the machinery of government are described by the authors, with an account of the actual events that featured Jackson's administrations. Then follows a flash-back to the cultural and intellectual elements involved in the fact of launching a new republic. With the establishment of the frontier at the Middle-West, it was natural that the next step should be to push onward to the Pacific. The story of Texas, California, New Mexico and Oregon is recounted in detail, with especial attention to the economic and political motives that prompted the parties opposed on the issue of annexation. The sweep of economic forces that were constantly changing under the impact of changing territorial extent, changing modes of locomotion, and changing governmental and political institutions, impelled the nation to the catastrophe of the Civil War which has been termed the "irrepressible conflict." The authors review the politics of the pre-War period, showing the futility of the compromises effected. Before going on to a consideration of the conflict itself, there is a chapter concluding this first volume on the Agricultural Era, that discusses the contrasting spectacles of Democracy: Romantic and Realistic. The part assigned to each, its manifestations in thought and literature, the creation of a distinctive culture, are the questions raised and discussed.

The second volume, treating of the Industrial Era, opens with an approach to the irrepressible conflict in terms of its proximate causes and manifestations, centring about slavery. The war itself, the authors term the Second American Revolution, and they deal with it in terms of its social, economic, and foreign implications rather than of its military history. The subsequent rounding out of the continent at the hands of the victorious farmers and capitalists occupies the next chapter, with an account of railroad development, re-alignment of economic forces and political parties, that prepares the picture of continental United States as we know it to-day. The civilization of the period exemplifies in every respect the triumph of business enterprise. It is the period of large-scale financing, oil prospecting, railroad scandals, and panics. Beneath this structure of wealth and success, however, the authors discern the rise of a national labor movement, parallel with, and unable to combat, business enterprise. It was only by indirect seepage that socialistic ideas spread, and at the point of necessity that social legislation favorable to labor found its way in the statute books. Since the Civil War, another factor had been at work changing the economic status of the country. This was the revolution in agriculture. Agriculture was becoming scientific, capitalistic, and productive of a surplus for export. Cotton was being overshadowed by grain, and the political oracles were now being inspired by the great Middle West for their legislative programs. Still the two-party system persisted, and the machinery of government adapted itself to rapidly changing conditions with the least amount of danger or disturbance. With the renewal of the Hamiltonian system of capitalist protection internally, conditions were suitable for a renewal of vigorous foreign policy destined to encourage commerce. One by one, Samoa, the Philippines, Hawaii, the Caribbean Islands, fell under the sweep of Manifest Destiny, until to-day the United States stands revealed as an imperialist power of the first rank. At the same time, the rapidly accumulating prosperity of the industrial and commercial classes was creating a new aristocracy of wealth which gave the tone to the entire "Gilded Age." Nouveaux-richism was rampant, exhibited itself in the most tasteless manner, and sought to acquire culture overnight by drawing a check. Between this class and the toiling masses residing in squalor and poverty, stretched the numerous professional and mercantile classes in whom Puritan sobriety survived to the greatest extent. Genuine culture progressed, though it did not keep pace with the extraordinary development of pure and applied science that was increasing secularization at the expense of religion. With the present century, the problems of imperialism come to the fore. The campaign of 1900 was waged on the principle of straightforward pacification and protection by war. Won by McKinley, the principle vindicated was pursued by Roosevelt, supported by the Supreme Court in the Insular Cases, and by Congress in Porto Rico and the Philippines. Hay and the Open Door declaration furnished the beginning of a Chinese policy adequate for the needs of our increasing trade there, a policy which was continued up to the Wilson administration. In the Caribbean, especially in connection with the Panama Canal, American interests were not more backward; and, again, until the Wilson régime, Mexico was kept under strict surveillance. Under the system of acquisition and enjoyment itself, however, unforeseen forces were beginning to brew that were to challenge the existing order. These are embraced under the chapter heading of "Towards Social Democracy," which includes the organization of industrial workers, woman suffrage, the civil service reform movement, the direct primary agitation, popular election of Senators, and government control of railroads and industries. The volume concludes with an account of the United States in the War and in the peace, as holder of the balance of power, and as the foremost exemplification of the machine age in all its aspects of mass production, speed, undigested comfort, irrational and amorphous mass opinion, plutocratic prosperity, and declining religious sentiment. The effect of the system on philosophy and the social sciences is briefly discussed, and the work closes on a note of optimistic contingency, based on the material possibilities the age and its system offer.

RISE OF THE COMMON MAN, THE, by Carl Russell Fish (1927). This volume treats historically of that period in American life which was dominated by a new generation which came into power in 1830 and which the author considers stamped the period with an outstanding Americanism. "As our story begins," he says, after an allusion to the decorum of colonial life which still remained on the surface, "the economic control by this aristocracy was limited, and affected life only at certain points. Of the natural resources of the land, in so far as they were used at the time, they controlled very little; they were distinctly an aristocracy by prestige based on the service of their fathers or themselves. In the years following, however, they became to some extent amalgamated with a rising moneyed class." The new impulses of the period are described and contrasts shown between the New England countryside and that of the Berkshires, or of the Dutch in the Valley of the Hudson and the Quakers in that of the Delaware or of the Germans in those of the Susquehanna and the Mohawk. The civilization of the middle region and the sweeping tide which "transported whole plantations from Virginia toward the South" are treated of from the viewpoint of social inheritance and, in the movements which he discusses, the author finds social orders "more purely American than anything which had previously existed." Industry, invention and trade completed the revolution in living which the author also holds this generation began in America. The manners and morals of the time, the diversions and preoccupations and the leading religious movements; the progress of education, art, science and literature, — the outstanding developments of the age, — composes the material which the author enlarges upon and maintains was distinctively American. Transportation and shipping, the labor movement of the period, agriculture and the public lands, immigration in the thirties and forties, and humanitarian reform, are also considered in this history of an era which the author holds ended its cycle in 1850. His conclusion is that "the generation of the thirties and forties did not evaluate, it destroyed taste; it produced, and let time value its products. It saw the acme of a particular development of individualism which had for some time been gaining ground and from which there was to be a rapid change to a more rigid system of community control. It presents one of the outstanding instances in history of the working of individuals trammelled by a minimum of law and convention. Its accomplishments were almost unprecedentedly the work of individuals, for leaders had little to enforce their leadership; they were the result of the independent work of more individuals than had ever before been free to work by and for themselves, at what they chose, and how they pleased."

ROAD TO ROME, THE, a comedy, by Robert Emmet Sherwood (1927). The historical incident upon which this play is based is the story that Hannibal, after having marched his army of Carthaginians three thousand miles and conquered the Alps in order to destroy Rome, turned back from the gates of the beleaguered city without the victory that was in his grasp. The first act takes place in the courtyard of the villa of Fabius Maximus on the day that he has been appointed dictator. Amytis, his beautiful young wife, is late for dinner because she has been dickering with a travelling merchant from Antioch for a green robe and an embroidered Phœnician nightgown. Her husband and his mother, Fabia, think she is not properly impressed with the dignity of being the wife of the first citizen of Rome. Fabia suggests that after all she is only a Greek like her mother, and does not understand the honor that has come to her husband. "Fabius is a typical senator — pompous, unctuous, consciously important and one hundred per cent Roman. His most casual utterance is delivered, as it were, from the eminence of the rostrum." He is shocked to find that Amytis knows nothing about Hannibal, but she reminds him that he had confessed he had never heard of Aristotle. His wife's lightness and gaiety and intelligence seem to him merely frivolity and flippancy. Hearing of the exploits of Hannibal she concedes that he must be a clever man though he has not contributed anything to the arts and sciences. Her husband tells her that she must set the example of "respectability, modesty, economy, duty, reverence, chastity," to the Roman matrons, and Amytis adds, "and mediocrity." At this moment Scipio, a Roman officer, comes to report to Fabius that Hannibal has defeated the Roman army, and is now encamped at the gates. The Romans are ready to meet their fate bravely. Amytis thinks she loves her life even if it is boring, and decides to go to her mother at Ostia on the sea coast. They notice as she leaves that she is wearing her new green dress, which is a strange costume for travelling. The scene of the second and third acts is the temple where Hannibal has his headquarters, now decorated with rich oriental hangings. The rough, humorous talk of the soldiers of the guard of two thousand years ago seems very like that of the soldiers of to-day. Hannibal enters, and it is clear that the soldiers respect and admire their quiet, dignified general, and that his word is law. Hannibal's young brother, Mago, remains with him to talk about a letter from their mother at home. Mago is alone when the soldiers bring in Amytis and her two devoted slaves. She says they are refugees from Rome who have lost their way. Mago commands that the three prisoners shall be executed as spies. He is in charge of the elephants and thinks it would be nice to show them to the charming Amytis. Hannibal enters while they are having a friendly conversation together. She tells Hannibal who she is and charms Hannibal into treating her as his guest for supper, and postponing her execution. What she really wants to know is his motive for fighting wars and winning battles. He admits that he has often asked himself the same question. That from childhood he had been consecrated by his father to the task of the destruction of Rome she considers is an excuse not a reason. To her war is futile and irrational. She asks him to be for once victor over his own victory. He grants her request that she may not die until morning, and they spend the night together. In the morning Hannibal offers Amytis her freedom to either return to her husband or to remain with him. He is still determined to attack Rome, but finally offers to give up Rome if she will go away with him. She will have him conquer himself, not for her sake, but for his own. "I want you to believe that every sacrifice made in the name of war is waste. When you believe that, you'll be a great man." Her husband and Scipio and Drusus come as a delegation from Rome to parley with Hannibal. Hannibal places Amytis under guard and tells Fabius that his soldiers have taken her prisoner, that she came to the camp concerned for her husband's safety. Fabius is delighted with this display of affection and courage in Amytis, whom he had deemed lacking in Roman qualities. Hannibal informs them that he has decided not to attack the city. He tells his soldiers that he has had instructions from the gods to proceed to Capua instead. It is, the author has said, his gesture of understanding of the force of the argument Amytis has presented. As the Carthaginians march away, Amytis waves Hannibal a silent farewell.

ROMANTIC COMEDIANS, THE, by Ellen Glasgow (1926). Judge Gamalial Bland Honeywell, twelve months after the death of his wife, "finds himself searching in vain for a living image of his Cordelia," and reflecting what Spring can do to one even at sixty-five —"a young sixty-five." He had married when he was a young man and, "Though he had lived all his life in Queensborough, where society had never outgrown an early stage of arrested development, his reputation as a lawyer had extended beyond his native Virginia, and many well-spent summers abroad had cultivated in him what he was fond of calling 'an international mind.'" His twin sister, Mrs. Edmonia Bredalbane, after one early scandal, "had indulged herself through life in that branch of conduct which was familiar to ancient moralists as nature in man and depravity in woman." Before his marriage, thirty-seven years ago, Judge Honeywell had been engaged to Amanda Lightfoot. After a lover's quarrel, she had broken the engagement, and he had walked into Cordelia's waiting arms. Amanda —"fifty-eight if a day, but marvellously preserved"— is supposed to have stayed single on account of this early affair. Now that the Judge is free, Queensborough society feels that after thirty-seven years' of waiting — during which period Amanda has shown the strain — the old love affair will materialize; and in the twelve months of his bereavement, Judge Honeywell has perceived that public opinion has been firmly but delicately pushing him and Amanda together, and makes up his mind that he will refuse to be pushed. Bella Upchurch and her young daughter, Anabel, are cousins of the Judge's late wife. Anabel has had an affair with Angus Blount, who left her, and went to Paris. Anabel is the type who, instead of "keeping her suffering to herself, worked it off by telling everybody." Judge Honeywell listened to her in distress and felt such a heavy sense of responsibility that he began to wonder what he could do "to mend the poor child's broken faith." He decides that he could make her happier than a younger man could ever have done and proposes. Anabel is positive that she can never be happy again and — decides to be "comfortable." "It's this horrible poverty that I can't bear. It's bad enough to be poor when you're happy, but to be poor when you're unhappy is too much to endure." Before she tells Judge Honeywell that she will marry him, she has a talk with Amanda about the old romance; and in one of her "dangerous impulses," she begs Amanda to "marry him now." Amanda laughs at the idea, and Anabel realizes that she will never know whether Amanda is sincere or not, for the "virtue of perfect behavior lies, not in its rightness, but in its impenetrability." She concludes that Amanda was only being noble in thought and attitude on a hard Victorian sofa. Anabel and the Judge are married and go abroad on the honeymoon. The rest of the story is concerned with Anabel's behavior after her marriage and with the Judge's conclusions that his marriage was a mistake. Anabel falls in love with Dabney Birdsong and is discovered in his arms by her husband, who rushes off, in despair, to his mother-in-law. Mrs. Upchurch wonders why it was that Anabel, with all the wealth she could desire and an adoring husband, who lived but to gratify her whims, should have scarcely recovered from one painful affair before she was plunging with unslacked ardor into another. "None of this would have happened if he had married me," thought Mrs. Upchurch. Anabel and Dabney run off to New York together. The Judge pursues them and tells Anabel that if she will return home he will agree to any conditions. "But you can't," she told him, "there aren't any conditions." "Of course, I shall give you your freedom," he said. She smiled triumphantly. "I am free." The Judge returns to his home and has a desperate illness. Mrs. Upchurch consoles him, and tells him that he is too fine a man to have his future ruined by any woman. There ought to be years of happiness ahead of him yet. "After all he is in the prime of life." She feels that possibly Amanda's long-awaited hour is dawning at last. But Judge Honeywell says that his life is over, that he has one foot in the grave already. After she goes, the young nurse — whom Dr. Buchanan had sent to him — suddenly engages his thoughts. "Swifter than light, swifter than inspiration, while he followed her with his eyes, the thought darted into his mind: "There is the woman I ought to have married!" . . . "Spring is here, he thought dreamily, and I am feeling almost as young as I felt last year."

ROMANTIC REVOLUTION IN AMERICA, THE, by Vernon Louis Parrington (1927). "This volume," says the author, "is the second in a proposed study of the main tendencies of American thought as expressed in our literature." He treats of the period which he holds hastened the development of nineteenth-century ideals by reason of the disturbing influences of the War of 1812 and later, the period which witnessed the uprooting of certain of the crasser growths by the Civil War of those vigorous years. He begins with the Virginia Renaissance — that last half of the eighteenth century which he considers marked the transition from middle-class to plantation ideals — and he holds that this transition was given intellectual stimulus "by the libertarian natural-rights philosophy that in England and France was undermining the old order." In its social and political philosophy, Virginia became increasingly libertarian, and the author quotes Alexander H. Stephens: "No people ever lived more devoted to the principles of liberty, secured by free democratic institutions, than the people of the South." In 1800 Jeffersonianism seemed to be a "comprehensive social philosophy peculiarly adapted to their needs." Discussing the "heritage" of Jeffersonianism as an expression of native conditions, interpreted, in terms of Physiocratic agrarianism, the author approaches the battle of ideas which followed the conflict of interests. In the struggle between the capitalistic and agrarian economics, Virginia is shown to have been the leader in the latter movement. The career and influence of John Taylor, "whose theories were founded in Physiocratic doctrine," the principles of John Adams and Alexander Hamilton, and the strategic position of John Marshall, are reviewed, as the author approaches the literary renaissance in the late twenties, which he says was an English romantic movement which reached the quiet plantations in Virginia. Book I of this study confines itself to "The Mind of the South," drawing as a background the "older plantation mind" which accepted the materials at hand, and "transmuted the easygoing plantation life into enduring romance." The author says that the work was begun by Kennedy in his idyllic "Swallow Barn." Caruthers applied stronger colors; John Esten Cooke, completer form; while Thomas Nelson Page refashioned the materials to suit the taste of a later day. But at a time when the romantics were beginning their work of constructing the plantation tradition the intellectual renaissance of Virginia was passing, and with the fading of the French influence, according to the opinion of this author, came increasing isolation and a conscious sectionalism. "If Virginia escaped the curse of industrialism it lacked the intellectual stimulus that came to New England with the rise of the textile mills." From what is described as "this slovenly background of aristocratic Virginia, with its liberalisms and conservatisms running at cross purposes" the enigmatical figure of Edgar Allan Poe emerged to "vex the northern critics." Of Poe, the author says: In the midst of gross and tawdry romanticisms he refused to be swallowed up, but went his own way, a rebel in the cause of beauty, discovering in consequence a finer romanticism than was before known in America. Coming now to southern imperialism, the author sees as early as 1824 a change that was to affect profoundly the course of southern thought in regard to her peculiar institution — the renaissance of slavery. He sees an abandonment of the Jeffersonian equalitarianism that had been deeply rooted in the southern mind from Kentucky to Georgia, and the casting aside of the agrarianism of John Taylor and the older Virginians; and the setting up in place of these congenial conceptions the alien ideal of a Greek democracy. Charleston, he says, was the intellectual capital of southern imperialism, but its numerical strength lay in the Black Belt, a compact territory, the heart of which was Georgia, Alabama, Mississippi and Louisiana. From this environment arises the vigorous new group which, he holds, largely created the new southern psychology — Bob Toombs, Alexander H. Stephens, L. Q. C. Lamar and Jefferson Davis. The author considers that the greatest figure in that long controversy was John C. Calhoun, who, with his dream of a Greek democracy, "steered his beloved South upon the rocks." Treating the various political doctrines of that time in relation to the influence of their leading exponents, the author approaches the drift of southern thought in the years immediately preceding the Civil War. He holds that the inadequacy of southern thought was identical with that of northern; blinded by sectional economic interests, they saw only half the truth. "Adventures in Belles Lettres" afford a picture of old Charleston, with its distinguished society, — "the capital of the planters, aristocratic, Puritan, Victorian, and old-fashioned culture, and the traditional home of Federalism." William Crafts — a southern Robert Treat Paine — is described as seeking to domesticate Boston culture in Charleston; the career of Hugh Swinton Legaré — the intellectual — a southern Puritan, is recalled, as well as the virile figure of William Gilmore Simms. The southern frontier in letters, the author says, established the tradition of frontier humor that flowered at last in Mark Twain. Book II of this study treats of "The Mind of the Middle East." "The literature of the Middle East during the years of the romantic revolution, unlike contemporary letters North and South, revealed no coalescing unity of spirit and purpose; it was rather the casual and somewhat fortuitous expression of two cities, both of which were divided by language and custom into fairly equal groups, and neither of which developed a homogeneous native culture." He says there were no intellectual hinterlands to Philadelphia and New York, as there were to Boston, and Charleston, and Richmond. He finds in Irving and Paulding and Cooper and Melville and Whitman a lack of strong community taste and purpose that marked the Concord group, or the Boston-Cambridge group, or even the Charleston group. "They expressed no common culture. . . . They stand on their own feet, and to understand them requires no critical examination of a complex cultural background." He finds that despite the extraordinary upheaval in economics and politics that New York unfortunately underwent no corresponding intellectual revolution. The ground was unprepared for the new philosophies. Of the two Knickerbocker "romantics," Washington Irving and James Kirke Paulding are treated in separate reviews; the detachment of Irving; Paulding's distrust of the middle class and his defence of America against the English critics. The work of James Fenimore Cooper, "a barometer of his generation," is reviewed, with his later political philosophy and his growing realism. The author considers that the literature of New York was heavily indebted to New England. William Cullen Bryant, Halleck, Willis, Greeley, Beecher, Curtis, Tuckerman, Park Benjamin, Stedman and Stoddard were "products of that more serious-minded world that was to create transcendentalism and issue in strange projects of social reform." Book III continues the studies in relation to "The Mind of New England." "The New England renaissance was tardy in appearing and of brief duration, yet in the few years of its extraordinary vigor it imparted a stimulus in American life that its historians have not greatly exaggerated." "Old Boston" is shown in its reaction from the revolutionary enthusiasm of '76. The movement of liberalism in New England was more pronounced because long restrained, and was ethical rather than economic. Liberalism and Calvinism; liberalism and the social conscience; Brook Farm — an attempt at an economic solution of social maladjustments; the awakening of the New England conscience to the evil of slavery; the character of certain militants — William Lloyd Garrison, Whittier, and Harriet Beecher Stowe, form the subject of many pages in this illuminating study, which later brings the author to his presentation of the transcendental mind, with the theories of Emerson, of Thoreau, of Theodore Parker and Margaret Fuller Ossoli. Other aspects of the New England mind culminate in the outstanding group to which Nathaniel Hawthorne, Oliver Wendell Holmes and James Russell Lowell belong.

ROOSEVELT, THEODORE, AND HIS TIME, Shown in His Own Letters (1920). Joseph Bucklin Bishop, who edited the letters, and wrote the connecting sections, was intimately associated with Roosevelt throughout his life, and was selected by him to write this history of his public service. All his personal and official correspondence together with other material was turned over to Mr. Bishop. After his graduation at Harvard in 1880, Roosevelt began to study law in New York and joined the Republican Club of his district. In January, 1882, at the age of twenty-two he entered the New York legislature as a member of the Lower House. From the first he took a commanding position among his associates. His first speech attacking a "deal" between the machine Republican members and a group of Tammany members created a sensation and throughout the term his courageous stand on important measures won praise from the press and the general recognition of both parties that here was a man of power. He was reëlected to a second term by an increased majority and his speech supporting Governor Grover Cleveland's veto of a bill to reduce the elevated railway fare was one of the most characteristic utterances of his career. Veteran politicians considered it and other of his acts "suicidal" to his political career. However, in spite of some opposition in his own party, he was elected to a third term. During this session he was the leader in putting through a number of important reform bills. By the end of this term his fame extended over the country. He was appointed delegate to the Republican National Convention in 1884, and here made a speech which won great applause. During his first term in the Legislature, Roosevelt published in May, 1882, "The Naval War of 1812." At the close of the campaign in 1884 he returned to his ranch in Dakota and varied his duties as ranchman with hunting trips and writing magazine articles and books. In 1889, President Harrison appointed Roosevelt a member of the United States Civil Service Commission and he immediately began a fight for reforms that brought a storm of wrath from his own party as well as from the Democrats. In spite of their opposition he accomplished much before he resigned in 1895, to accept the position of Police Commissioner of

New York City. Because of corrupt practices in the Police Department he faced a heavy task. But it was a fight to his liking and he immediately began reforms, the first closing saloons on Sunday, which brought the liquor interests to use all their forces against him. In 1897 he was appointed by President McKinley to the post of Assistant Secretary of the Navy. With his usual thoroughness he instituted changes in the Navy and within a short time the wisdom of these were shown by our victories in the war with Spain. In a letter written at this period of his career he states, "Germany is the power with whom I look forward to serious difficulty," and in another that Russia "will some time experience a red terror which will make the French Revolution pale." He pleaded for a larger Navy and when the "Maine" was sunk was eager for war to be declared. Desiring to enter active service he accepted an appointment as Lieutenant Colonel, and thus became the leader of the famous Rough Riders. Upon his return from Cuba, he was at once nominated for Governor of New York, won the election and was inaugurated in 1898. His struggles with Senator Platt continued throughout his term but he never compromised in any of the battles. The Franchise Tax was one of his important triumphs. In spite of his strenuous objection, he was nominated for Vice-President through opponents in his own party who were against his reforms. "If I have been put on a shelf, my enemies will find that I can make it a cheerful place of abode," he wrote at the time of his election. The tragic news of President McKinley's death came to him when he was tramping in the Adirondack Mountains. He went at once to Buffalo where he took the oath of office. In reply to a statement that he could be certain of the office for seven years he said, "I'd rather be full President for three years than half a President for seven years." Everyone was certain that a new epoch of our national history was opening. Favor seekers soon found that merit was the only standard Roosevelt would recognize in making appointments. Powerful financial interests sought to modify his views in regard to trusts and kindred matters. But early in 1902 he began the famous suit against the Northern Securities Company. News of it came as a bomb to Wall Street. After many legal battles the Supreme Court gave a decision against trusts. Writing to a friend, Roosevelt said, "It is above all to the interests of the men of great wealth that the people at large should understand that they also have to obey the law." The settlement of the coal strike of 1902 was another victory as was the affair with Kaiser Wilhelm over Venezuela. During these years he was making speeches throughout the country and carrying on correspondence with noted personages — Secretary Hay, Nicholas Murray Butler, Owen Wister, Elihu Root, Lord Morley, Rudyard Kipling. The year 1903 marks what Roosevelt considered the most notable and widely beneficent of his Presidential career, the possession of the Isthmus of Panama and the consequent construction of the canal across it. He easily won the nomination in 1904, and was elected by a great majority. "I am stunned by the overwhelming victory" he wrote to his son Kermit, who was in school at Groton. The year 1905 was most eventful for him. He arranged the Portsmouth Peace Conference which put an end to the war between Japan and Russia, and the Algeciras Convention which prevented war between France and Germany over possessions in Morocco. He took charge of affairs in Santo Domingo. He personally directed the preparations for building the Panama Canal. Many other lesser affairs were successfully carried out. His letters reflect his abnormal energy, mental and physical, and his broad insight into world affairs. There are letters to and from King Edward, Kaiser Wilhelm, Czar Nicholas, and noted diplomats of the period. Nineteen hundred and six saw him plunged in home affairs. Among other measures, the Railway Rate Bill and the Pure Food and Drug Act were put through. In 1907 came a panic, but in spite of severe criticism from friends and foes alike, Roosevelt refused to drop the suits against the Standard Oil Company and the Harriman lines which were then in progress. This same year he sent the battle fleet on a world tour for which he was again criticized but which proved a triumph when the ships returned in 1909. His letters through these years continue to exhibit his wide range of interest, encouraging authors, commenting on books, personages and events of all ages; describing birds, designing coins, his versatility was amazing. His letters to Sir George Trevelyan, the English historian, are of special interest. In 1908 he persistently refused to consider a third term and began to plan his African trip for which he departed in March, 1909. Before returning to America, in 1910, he visited the important cities of Europe, where he received the attentions of royalty. His famous letter "From Khartoum to London" is quoted in full and describes his triumphal European tours. A tremendous welcome was given him upon his return. Disappointed with President Taft's policies he finally consented to be a candidate in 1912. Through the famous "Steam Roller" method Taft won the party nomination, which resulted in the Third Party movement with Roosevelt as candidate. He made a vigorous campaign. In Milwaukee he was shot by a half-crazed fanatic but insisted on making his speech before going to the hospital. This ended his campaign but he won a large majority of the Republican votes in the election which made Woodrow Wilson president. The next few years he devoted to writing and hunting but at all times kept up his interest in affairs of State. From the outset of the War in 1914, his letters indicated his ardent desire that the United States should join the Allies. He wrote continuously and made speeches to further our entry and harshly condemned President Wilson's course. He advocated military training camps and with General Wood sponsored several of them. He refused to be a candidate in 1916 and strongly supported Hughes. When President Wilson declared war he immediately offered to raise a division and was bitterly disappointed when he was refused, for thousands of men planned to join him. He continued to speak and write in favor of a vigorous prosecution of the War. The death of his son Quentin saddened him but did not lessen his efforts. In November, 1918, he became ill and on January 5, 1919, he died at his home at Oyster Bay.

ROUGH HEWN, by Dorothy Canfield (1922), is the story of the romance between Marise Allen, an American girl brought up in France, and Neal Crittenden, whose parents are among the pioneer suburbanites of New Jersey. It precedes in time the story of "The Brimming Cup," which was published first. In the opening chapters the author presents the important events of a small boy's life sympathetically and consistently from that young person's own viewpoint. There is the shiny new hockey stick and the efficient use he makes of it in a gang battle between the Union Hill élite and the Hoboken Micks from the Jersey flats. His parents, immersed in their own adult interests do not see below the smiling small boy exterior to the gory satisfaction with which he examines the new stick in hopes he may find there a drop of blood as evidence of the recent battle. Later Neal's delight in reading is aroused and his interest swings between that and the out-of-door delights of bicycling and tennis. He learns the principles of real sport in playing tennis, but first meets disillusion when his chum shows himself a bad loser. His university life at Columbia is evidence of Mrs. Canfield's intimate and humorous understanding of the limitations and the zest that a course in the humanities may hold for a husky young man who majors in football. Interpolated, and contrasted with these early chapters revealing the life of a happy, average middle-class American boy run those chapters dealing with Marise Allen's French-trained girlhood. Business, and the craving for culture, which his wife Flora felt in the air of France, brought Horace Allen and his wife and child to Bayonne. The vivid pictures of life among the small town French bourgeoisie as well as the pictures of tourist life in Rome, later in the book testify to the author's careful observation during the years she herself lived in France and Italy. In Marise's early education is balanced her gain in concentrated application and mastery of detail as it is taught in the French schools against the loss due to a too early sophistication that infects her intimacy with Jeanne, the devoted Basque cook and nurse of her childhood. Flora Allen, her mother, is a latter day rendering of David Copperfield's Dora, a child who, in her desire for the thrill she has never felt in companionship with her husband, becomes involved in a tragic affair with Jean-Pierre Garnier, a young Frenchman but recently returned to his native town from America. Marise gets her first impression of this tragedy from the nurse Jeanne, although her good music teacher, Mademoiselle Hasparren and her father think they have saved her the shock of the scandal which the old nurse's ill-timed devotion has started. The effects of this early emotional shock on a high-strung and naturally pure girl are traced with discriminating care as revealed in Marise's later attitude toward men and life. The ensuing distrust of life would have resulted in complete cynicism if it had not been for the curative effects of music to which she devotes years of study. Then Neal and Marise, whose destinies nearly crossed when Neal spent some time learning the lumber business in the Vermont home of his great uncle at Ashley while Marise was visiting her aunt in the same town, meet in a Roman tourist pension. To their awakened love, Neal, handicapped only by excessive shyness and the traditional reticence of the Crittendens, brings the faith of a child whose parents have lived in happy union to heal and win back to a faith in love the girl whose knowledge of it in her parents' lives has brought such disillusion. Neal has revolted from too early success seeking for something more to life than the New York business game, which he had mastered early and easily, because of his intensive football training. Among the Roman ruins and on the romantic Italian compagna the two seekers find in each other the completion each needs and turn back to a happy new life in Ashley.

"ROVER, THE" (1923), is the last complete novel written by Joseph Conrad. It is a land, rather than a sea, story of old citizen Peyrol, formerly a master gunner of a vessel of uncertain reputation, which brought in a prize from the eastern seas in the period just after the French revolution. Old Peyrol finds his way to a safe harbor in the farmhouse on Escampobar Peninsula, the attic room of which looked out like a lighthouse over Hyères Road and on to the distant Mediterranean. It was apparent that some mystery attached to citizen Scevola, an ex-sansculotte and the ostensible owner of the farm and husband of the elusive young girl, Arlette. After a time a young officer of the French navy, Lieutenant Réal, also became a lodger. Then one day Peyrol discovered an English corvette in the roadstead where no English vessels had been seen since Toulon was evacuated by them some years before. Réal recognizes Peyrol as an old sea bandit and the very man to do a difficult and dangerous deed ordered by Napoleon through the admiralty. A small vessel carrying dispatches purporting to show that the French fleet assembled in Toulon harbor is destined for Egyptian waters, must be captured so that the English will carry this false information to Nelson. Meanwhile matters have changed within the farmhouse since Peyrol made it his home. Arlette, whose parents were killed during the reign of terror, had been rescued by Scevola. But the horror of the terrible experience that the young girl had been through had left her in a dazed, apathetic condition mentally, which could not be alleviated by the tender care given her by her old aunt Catherine. Peyrol's presence had been the first to rouse her, then her growing love for Lieutenant Réal completed her cure. Peyrol, through latent jealousy, and Catherine oppose her love for Réal, who himself hesitates, thinking her mind still clouded. So great is his wretchedness on this account, for he realizes that he returns her love, that he decides to himself do the deed ordered by the admiralty. At the final moment Arlette interferes and while Réal carries her back to Catherine, old Peyrol, realizing that his day is over, slips away with his faithful follower, Michel, carrying Scevola captive in the tartane bound on their dangerous enterprise. By simulating suspicious actions the tartane engages the attention of the British sloop, Amelia, before noticed in the roadstead, and chase is given. As the sun goes down the sloop fires on the tartane to prevent her probable escape under cover of dark, and all three men aboard her are killed. But the ruse has been successful, the false dispatches reach Nelson while a brave and free old spirit finds an appropriate end.

ROYAL ROAD TO ROMANCE, THE, by Richard Halliburton (1925). The author, the son of a rich American, refused the offer of his family of a *de luxe* trip around the world as a present when he graduated from Princeton, and with a college roommate shipped as seaman on a freighter, going to Hamburg in quest of romance and adventure, planning to pay his way by magazine and newspaper articles describing his adventures. Arrived in port they buy second-hand bicycles, choose their destination by the chance of placing a blind finger on the map of Europe, and start for Rotterdam on the road to romance. Though neither of the youthful adventurers have ever done any mountain climbing they persuade the Swiss guides to make the ascent of the Matterhorn late in the season by tales of their prowess on the Palisades in New York, and his first article is the description of this thrilling climb. After a gay time in Paris, Irvine leaves Richard to go to Italy, and Richard gives dancing lessons to get funds for a bicycle trip through the chateau country in France, to Carcassone. November finds him crossing the Pyrenees to reach the quaint little republic of Andorra. The president of the republic invites him to warm his toes at the fireplace in the kitchen of the executive mansion, and dresses in his Sunday best to have his picture taken. In Spain he finds another companion, Paul, studying architecture, who travels with him for a time. Part of the romance of adventure is to either travel on the railroad without tickets or at least to travel first class on a third class ticket by outwitting the guards. Always he has a schoolboy delight in doing the forbidden thing. At Gibraltar he finds himself in jail for taking pictures of the fortress for illustrations for his story, but his new friend, Paul, comes to his rescue, and a British officer lends him the money to pay his fine. He loses money at the gaming tables in Monte Carlo, swims the Nile, climbs the great pyramid, Cheops, at midnight, sails in a "butterfly" boat from Luxor to Edfu with an Arab boatman friend, and at Cairo earns some money by acting as guide for two American men who wanted to be "protected from mosques, and bazaars, and cemeteries." At Port Said he signs on the American oil tanker "Gold Shell" bound for Calcutta, and in need of a seaman. He hunts tigers and panthers, spent a day and a moonlight night in the garden of the Taj Mahal, visits the Vale of Kashmir with another friend of the road, David, and the "topsy-turvy, half-lost plateau of Ladakh far up in the heart of the Himalayas." They had the good fortune to be in Leh at the time of the inauguration of the child "Skushok," the living incarnation of the highest lama of the district, and Richard gives the baby god his supper of barley porridge and rocks him to sleep after the ceremony. He has a narrow escape from death from a cobra in the jungle, tramps over mountains, makes one long train trip in the cab of an engineer when he is put off the train by irate guards when he has no money to pay his fare, visits Rangoon, Bangkok, the temple of Angkor in the fabulous ruined city of the ancient Khymers, and spends an idyllic week in Bali, an island of the Dutch East Indies as yet unspoiled by civilization. With the family of a native salt-collector he sees the fantastic ceremony of the funeral and cremation of a native ruler. His boat to Macao is held up by Chinese pirates, a "jolly adventure." He arrives at Pekin in time for the wedding of the boy emperor. The last great adventure is the ascent of Fujiyama in mid-winter alone, as it had never been done before, and the guides refused to go with him. He manages to get a photograph of the snow-capped crater to prove that he has succeeded in this mad exploit. Then he ships to Seattle as one of the crew of the "President Madison," and home to Tennessee, finding editors in Portland, Denver and Kansas City to buy his Fujiyama story and thus pay his way home on an extra-fare train.

"R.U.R.," a fantastic melodrama, by Karl Capek, (1922). "Rossum's Universal Robots" is the name of the company, known as "R.U.R.", which manufactures artificial men and women, soulless machines, with no will of their own, no sense of joy or sorrow, or right or wrong, perfectly adapted to do the mechanical work of the world. The factory is located on a distant island where the original Rossum, a young scientist, retired in the year 1920, to make experiments. A bitter materialist, he "wanted to become a sort of scientific substitute for God." His son, an engineer, joined him, and with his father's formula, created the creatures he named "Robots," with all the best features and none of the disadvantages of human workers. At the opening of the play, Helena Glory, the attractive daughter of the president of the company, has come from Europe on a visit of investigation. She comes as a member of the Humanity League, organized to free the Robots from slavery, and give them the benefits of civilization. Harry Domin, the manager, tells her the story of the invention, and convinces her that Robots are not human beings. Domin's ideal for which he works is "to turn the whole of mankind into an aristocracy" freed from poverty by the work of the Robots. He introduces the other directors who are delighted to meet a beautiful woman. While they are alone for a few minutes, Domin asks Helena to marry him. The second act takes place ten years later, in 1943. The sympathetic Helena has persuaded Dr. Gall, the chemist, experimenting with the formula, to endow the Robots with intelligence and capacity for enjoyment, and these more nearly human Robots lead their kind in revolt against man. The Governments of Europe have bought millions of Robots for their armies and taught them the use of fire arms. One of the directors of the Frankenstein factory remarks that they have made a mistake to manufacture Universal Robots, that National Robots who would hate each other would have been better. There are so many Robots that man has become superfluous, almost extinct. Nana, Helena's old nurse, reads an item in the newspaper stating that "during the past week there again has not been a single birth recorded." Helena senses disaster, though they conceal the state of things in Europe from her, and go on with preparations for the celebration of the anniversary of her coming to the island. Her present from her husband is the new boat she sees riding at anchor, which looks like a gunboat. Domin confesses that there has been no news from the outside world for a week. The builder, Alquist, is more communicative, and admits that he thinks the destruction of mankind is at hand. Radius, a super Robot, says to Helena, "You are not as strong as the Robots."

You are not as skilful as the Robots. The Robots can do everything. You only give orders. You do nothing but talk." Helena begs Domin to leave the island and close the factory. Convinced that the manufacture of Robots must come to an end, she gets the papers containing the secret formulas from the safe and burns them in her grate. The directors see the mail boat coming in, and think the danger is over. They tell Helena that in case the rebellion had spread to the island they had planned to escape on the new boat, and that they could dictate their own terms to the Robots, because they have the Rossum manuscript. When the Robots understand that unless they have possession of the formula they cannot manufacture Robots, and that in twenty years the present lot will be worn out, and "there will not be one living specimen of a Robot that you could exhibit in a menagerie," they will be glad to compromise. The mail boat brings only more Robots distributing leaflets ordering Robots throughout the world to unite and kill all mankind. The house is surrounded, and Helena begs their forgiveness for the destruction of the priceless formula. From the drawing room window they see solid, motionless, silent masses of Robots, and the new boat is in their possession, with its guns trained on the house. Everyone is killed except Alquist, whom they spare because he is a workman like themselves. In the epilogue a year later the Robots entreat Alquist, the one man left on earth, to try to rediscover the formula, but he cannot help them. They propose that he dissect some of them to try to find out how they are made. Two young Robots, the last made by Dr. Gall, Helena and Primus, enter the laboratory, and Alquist is startled to hear the sound of human laughter. He questions them and puts their dawning feeling for each other to the test, and as they embrace, he hails them as a new Adam and Eve.

SAILOR, THE, by J. C. Snaith (1916). The story of a genius, who wins through bitter and degrading circumstance and environment to literary success in London. We first see Henry Harper, a puny newsboy, crouched in terror against a wall in a blind alley, with "Auntie" standing over him, whip in hand, taunting the child before she strikes him. Somehow Henry manages to dodge away and over the wall. He tries to die on a railroad track, but the train goes by on a switch. He climbs aboard a freight car, and gets away to six years of hardship and cruelty at sea on an old sailing vessel, the "Margaret Carey." His nickname of "the sailor" has been given him in irony, as he has no love for the sea though its beauty gives him ecstatic moments, and he never becomes a first-rate seaman. He lacks initiative to leave the ship he hates but is forced into another environment when the "Margaret Carey" is declared unseaworthy. Befriended by "Ginger" Jukes he becomes a professional football player, and is a great success until the day of the defeat of the Blackhampton Rovers by Duckingfield Britannia, when "Sailor" "sold the match." His interest had been diverted to a new world opened to him by laborious days of learning to read and write and spell. He drifts to London and Bowdon House, "sixpence a night, nightgowns a penny" and meets there Mr. Esme Horrobin, formerly fellow and tutor of Gamaliel College, Oxford. This strange bed fellow takes an interest in Henry, and sends him to Mr. Rudge, bookseller on Charing Cross Road. For forty-two years Mr. Rudge has been taking notes for his "History of the World" and he takes Henry as assistant in order to devote more time to this work. Inspired by a story of the sea he discovers in the bookshop, Henry writes one himself, and sends it to Edward Ambrose, the kind editor who eventually pays three hundred pounds for the serial rights of this masterpiece for his magazine. A child in the ways of the world Henry, through a desire to behave correctly, is fooled into marriage with vulgar Cora Dobbs, who turns out to be a prostitute.

Edward Ambrose introduces the genius to Mary Pridmore, a beautiful girl of good family, whose sailor brother, "Klondyke," had been a friend to Henry on the "Margaret Carey." Henry goes on a sea voyage to escape from Cora and his love for Mary. Cora drinks herself to death, and Mary marries him in time to save him from literally dying of love for her.

SAINT JOAN, a chronicle play, by Bernard Shaw (1924). The play opens at the castle of Vaucouleurs in the year 1429. Joan has come from Domremy to ask the captain in command, Robert de Baudricourt, to give her armor, a horse, and some soldiers, and send her to the Dauphin. The captain has refused to be bothered with her, and ordered that she be sent home to her father. His steward tells Robert that the hens will not lay because the maid has been kept waiting at his door for a week. In the meantime Joan has been winning the soldiers to belief in her mission to raise the siege of Orleans and drive the English out of France. When Robert sends for her she meets his bullying with frank good nature and insists that "voices" from God bid her crown the Dauphin in Reims Cathedral. The fact that his two companions-at-arms, Bertrand de Poulengey, and John of Metz, have enough confidence in her to be willing to accompany her to the Dauphin has more weight with him than her assertions that St. Catherine and St. Margaret talk with her every day. Bertrand considers that nothing but a miracle can rescue Orleans, and is in favor of giving Joan the chance to see Charles. The French soldiers are beaten, Joan says, because they are fighting only to save their skins, and that is easier done by running away, and the knights only for pay, and she must teach them to fight that "the will of God may be done in France," and God's French king may rule. However when the steward brings the news that the hens have returned to their duty, Robert thinks perhaps there is something to her claims. In the second act at Chinon Joan has her audience with the weak-minded, insignificant Dauphin. They arrange a test by seating Gilles de Rais on the throne to receive her, while Charles hides behind the courtiers. She detects the imposture, and searches out Charles. Her simplicity and faith as she kneels before the Archbishop gain the support of that sceptical prelate, which someone whispers is her first miracle. He tells her that she is in love with religion. At her request the silly and insolent courtiers are dismissed, and she pleads with the spiritless and protesting Charles until he makes her commander-in-chief of the army. The French army under Dunois is encamped on the bank of the Loire waiting for the wind to change so that he can ship his soldiers across the river and upstream to attack the English in the rear. The impatient Joan would storm the bridge at once, but Dunois welcomes her as a saint rather than a soldier, and entreats her prayers for a west wind. As they start for the church the wind changes, Dunois gives Joan his allegiance, and they rush to the attack. In a tent in the English camp Richard de Beauchamp, Earl of Warwick and the chaplain, John de Stogumber hold a conference with Cauchon, the bishop of Beauvais. The maid has led the soldiers to victory and Charles is to be crowned in Reims Cathedral. The fanatical chaplain is sure that Joan is a sorceress, else how could she have beaten an English army, and taken the great Sir John Talbot prisoner. Cauchon declares that the devil is using Joan to set the country above the Church, and she must be dealt with as a heretic. He will try to save her soul if it lies in his power to do so. The Church has had to stand aside while this presumptuous woman brings messages from God to Charles, usurping the power of the Pope himself. Warwick represents the secular power of the feudal aristocracy which Joan's direct dealing with the king has likewise disregarded. The churchman and the nobleman give up their differences as to whom God gives the power to rule in the face of this common enemy, the "Protestant" and the "Nationalist." Cauchon says, that to Joan, "the French-speaking people are what the Holy Scriptures describe as a nation." These subtleties bewilder Joan. "'England for the English,' goes without saying: it is the simple law of nature." This woman would deny England her legitimate conquests, and her "peculiar fitness to rule over less civilized races for their own good." After the coronation Joan is praying in the cathedral. The ungrateful Charles accuses Joan of self-conceit for the reason that she wants to continue fighting to take Paris. Even the faithful Dunois is of the opinion that God is on the side of the big battalions. The English have offered a large sum for her capture, and the day that Joan is dragged off her horse by a Burgundian and the man is not instantly punished by God, the soldiers will lose their faith in her. Her little hour of miracles is over. The Archbishop rebukes her for pride and disobedience, and says that her "voices" are the echo of her own wilfulness. The fourth act is the trial at Rouen. The Burgundians have sold Joan to the English. The Inquisitor commands that all minor charges such as praying at haunted wells and dancing around fairy trees shall be dropped for the one serious charge of heresy. Heresy almost always begins as in this case with vain and ignorant persons who set up their own judgment against the Church and take upon themselves the interpretation of God's will, believing honestly that their diabolical inspiration is divine. In terror of burning at the stake since if the charges were not true God would not allow the funeral pile in the market place, Joan recants, but tears up the paper she has signed when she finds that she is sentenced to life imprisonment. She is then formally condemned and led away to the executioner. John de Stogumber returns from the auto-da-fé overcome with remorse, calling himself a Judas. In an epilogue twenty-five years later, the King, now Charles the Seventh of France, receives the news that Joan's sentence has been reversed, and rejoices that people can no longer say that he was crowned by a witch and a heretic. The ghosts of Joan, Warwick, Dunois, Cauchon, and the others, visit Charles in his dreams. A cleric of the year 1920 joins them to announce her canonization, and they all kneel before Joan, who is the same downright, merry young girl they all knew.

SANDOVAL: A ROMANCE OF BAD MANNERS, by Thomas Beer (1924). Several years before the opening of this story, when New Orleans, a "mad and sulking city," was in possession of the Union Army, under General Butler, a group of Secessionists, believing that Louis Bonaparte, then on the throne of France, was favorable to their cause, attempted to send a bribe to one of Bonaparte's favorites, — "a lady in Paris." The plan is conceived at the house of Pierre Coty, a member of an old French family, and the uncle of Christian Coty de Sandoval, an officer in the Confederate Army. Coty and his friends stuff a huge bronze statue, a Hercules, with money and gold, wrapped in wax and cotton, and ship it to St. Louis where an English shipping agent, an Edward Ross, employed by Almy and Company, a New York banking firm, signed a receipt for it and took it on another boat. This "gift to a lady in Paris" was not looked at on the transport boat. "Soldiers scratched the matches of their pipes on its legs." Ross wrote to Coty that the statue had sailed from New York. But beyond this assurance, the Confederates heard nothing further — not a word from "the lady in Paris." The very nature of the transaction enjoined them to secrecy. Either Ross or somebody for whom he had acted had Coty and his friends in their power. Just before the statue had left New Orleans, Coty had befriended a youthful Federalist in the person of Christian Gaar, who had made himself a hero at sixteen by pushing a raft of burning cotton away from the sides of the "Oneida" in the New

Orleans harbor. Afterward, on a tour of the city, he had been set upon by drunken ruffians, from whom he had been rescued by Sandoval, who took him to his uncle's house. Christian awakened in a luxurious bed-chamber that opened into a garden where candles burned in silver holders on a marble console and a blue statue of the Virgin could be seen between frail trees. Indignant voices reached him from the garden. "This ought to wake Bonaparte up!" "An army had seized the city of these people and they grieved." But when the men strolled in from the garden to look at him, the elder Coty ordered a mulatto to serve coffee before taking him back to his anxious officers. Sandoval took him in the family carriage to the levee and turned him over to a guard. But the name — Christian Gaar — struck in Sandoval's memory. Christian had imparted the information to Sandoval's family that his father, Charles Gaar, was secretary to Mr. Robert Almy, the banker of New York. Apparently, this information carried no weight at the time. The Gaars were then living at Number 5 Bank Street, so Christian had informed the aristocratic Cotys, and Mr. Almy was one of the richest men in New York or the world. Years afterward, when the story opens, the announcement of Christian Gaar's engagement to May Almy, daughter of the late Robert Almy, supplies a long-awaited clue to the Sandoval family. Sandoval's memory was good. Gaar was a queer name and there could be but one Christian Gaar, the boy whose life he had saved and whose father was secretary to Robert Almy and whose man, Ross, had come to New Orleans only a few weeks after Christian had been in the house of Sandoval's old uncle. Sandoval had searched Paris for the missing Hercules, only to be laughed at, but, his memory now fully awakened by the announcement in the society journals, he leaves his unhappy and ruined family to find the proofs of the embezzlement on the part of Almy and Charles Gaar of the gold which Ross knew, he was now convinced, was secreted in the empty bronze statue. In 1864, Almy had made Gaar a partner, and the Gaars had built a showy house at Dobbs Ferry. Christian Gaar divided his time between the "palace" at Dobbs Ferry and his rooms in Grand Street, New York City, and candidly preferred the life of rich idleness in town. His younger brother, Thorold, shares the same view of the absurd ostentatiousness of the Gaars' way of living. The two brothers have a mutual distrust of their father. The newly-acquired wealth was attributed to the ability of the elder Gaar to secure raw cotton for Liverpool clients during the Civil War. Sandoval intrudes himself on the Gaar family. From Christian himself, he could learn nothing, but he makes him his confidant. From the police he finds that Ross is dead, but that counts for nothing, as Ross acted for another. He would have liked to have found Ross and taken him to this great thief's family and said: "Here! This is the witness of all!" A superb sweep of his hand told Christian just how he would have done it. Sure of his prey, Sandoval delights in keeping Christian in suspense. Never once does he mention the name of his father, until at the last, when he faces Christian with the precise details of the crime. The elder Gaar, he tells Christian, can make the arrangements he desires and without embarrassment to the "relatives." He has promised his family in New Orleans that he will recover some of the money. There is no need of hurry. Christian's father can examine the books of the bank and will be able to tell Miss Almy that at such and such a date of 1864 her father entered sums. Christian's engagement to Miss Almy has been broken — Mrs. Almy had a dislike of Christian's father. After all, he had once been only a clerk in her husband's bank. Sandoval knows how matters stand. "A cheque and all will be over, without words." Or a list of the gentlemen to whom her father owed the money could be sent to Miss Almy. "Better let Mr. Gaar handle this for you, Sandoval," said Christian. "I suppose you'll be at the hotel after dinner?" And he added, "I see now why you came to me in this muss — I wondered." "I'll have to talk to Father," Christian told Thorold. "Sandoval's so crazy he might go and see May." Thorold still saw pictures of a tramping statue, a black Hercules, stalking into the cellar of Almy and Company and finally up to the gymnasium in Fourteenth Street, conducted by his mother's twin brother. He had seen it, and it was hollow. "Uncle Pat's got a hollow statue — a Hercules — up at his place and Father gave it to him!" Christian was a white statue between the curtains of his bedroom. After his talk with his father, who "did not get mad," Christian goes to see the Hercules in his uncle's gymnasium. Then he and Thorold go to see Sandoval. Thorold remains downstairs with the crowd. It was Thorold who saw Sandoval's dead body beside a chair beneath the balustrade over which it had fallen. He supposes that Christian has killed him — flung him over the balustrade. When the police question him, he tells them that he saw Sandoval when he fell. The verdict is "suicide" and the affair is hushed up. Christian escapes to his rooms in Grand Street and Thorold goes to him. "Listen, Thor, and see what you think I'd better do." Sandoval had been gracious. He would wait Mr. Gaar's leisure. He wanted to see what the attitude of the Almys would be, and he had sent a letter by messenger to Miss Almy. "A pale streak went past Christian's eyes." He had turned upon Sandoval and accused him of a loss of honor. Sandoval had struck him across the mouth. Christian, "done with him now," had returned the blow. Sandoval, shaking with rage and with a gesture of outraged vanity, had retreated through the door and onto the balcony. Christian saw him as he fell over the balustrade. Thorold exclaims, "Then he killed himself, Christy!" "Trailing silver passed in my head with a tone of music and the sense of some lost fight in a nightmare. We had been beaten in a battle of shadows, honorably."

SARD HARKER, by John Masefield (1924). Chisholm Harker, nicknamed Sard for sardonic, is chief officer, of Captain Cary's ship, "The Pathfinder," now off the Central American State of Santa Barbara. He has had a dream that at a house, named Los Xicales, on the coast, he will meet again a girl he had known and loved in England ten years ago. He goes to the house which is closed, and the negro caretaker knows of no one of the name of Juanita de la Torre. At a boxing match he overhears two roughs talking about a plot to kidnap an English girl, Miss Kingsborough, for a Mr. Sagrado B. Though the ship is sailing that night he gets permission from Captain Cary to try to warn Miss Kingsborough. An employée at the club tells him that Hilary and Margarita Kingsborough have rented Los Xicales, and lends him a bicycle to ride out to see them. Mr. Kingsborough listens to his story of threatened danger and does not take it seriously. After Sard has gone he tells his sister, and she remembers that Sagrado means holy, and that a man named Hirsch, who practised infamous magic rites, had tried to make love to her once in Paris, and thinks it would be well to take Mr. Harker's advice and return to the hotel in the town. Before they can leave the house a gang of ruffians seize Margarita and knock Hilary senseless. In the meantime Sard Harker discovers that his bicycle has been stolen from where he left it at the gate, and starts to walk to get to his ship, which is the beginning of an epic journey through swamp, over mountains, across a desert, at incredible hazard of life, and hardship. He wins through by the heroism of a "simple mind, a strong body, and a strong will." Going through the woods toward the coast he flounders in a swamp and nearly loses his life in a quicksand, then injures his foot by treading on a sting-ray, and crawls along the beach until he is captured by rum runners. He escapes with his life through the intervention of one of the men, and is put on a silver train going inland to the mines. When the train arrives at the mining town he is thrown into prison as a thief. He manages to escape and starts to climb the snow-capped mountains to walk the hundred miles to the sea over a trail deemed impassable. Nature and man do their utmost to destroy him, but he gets safely to the town, and finds out that his ship has been wrecked, and Captain Cary is dead. He meets Hilary Kingsborough searching for his sister, and they hear her cry for help as they are talking together outside a house. She is chained to a pillar in the house guarded by Indians and in the power of the villainous Hirsch. Of course Margarita is Juanita, who has taken the name of her step-father, Hardy Kingsborough, and uses her own second name, Margarita, because it is easier for the English to pronounce. Hirsch has Sard Harker chained to another pillar, and taunts them with their fate. Hilary has managed to break a window in the struggle, and calls for help, which brings Don Manuel, the Dictator, and his guard to the rescue in time to save them from sacrifice to the Prince of Darkness. Hirsch is an ancient enemy of Don Manuel, had killed his betrothed, Carlotta, and it was in the ensuing revolution that the young sailor, Sard Harker, had helped Don Manuel to escape. Sard's dream of his lost sweetheart has come true. The Dictator offers him work, and all is well with him at last.

SASHKA JIGOULEFF, by Leonid Andreyev, 1925. is the story of Sashka Pogodin, son of a Russian general who changed his name to Sashka Jigouleff when he turned dreaming revolutionary and bandit, and is based on the life of a seminarian of that name active during the stormy years 1905–1907. Sashka, and his merry and versatile little sister, Lina, were brought to a provincial town to live after the father's death as Elena Petrovna hoped thus to keep her son safer from harm and longer for her own consolation by removing him from the dangers of Saint Petersburg. The children had a wholesome, and passively happy childhood. Although their temperaments were in such vivid contrast, the brother and sister were wrapped up in each other. His mother felt that Sashka's quiet manner and lack of talent placed him at a disadvantage before outsiders until he opened his mysterious deep eyes, so full of weariness and sorrow even when he smiled, that she feared he would not live long. The beauty of their home and of the life she made for them there attracted their school friends and made it a popular resort until the revolutionary spirit seized the group. Russia was going through troublous times. Beside oppression and tyranny everywhere, there was the war with Japan. Then Kolesnikoff, a man many years older, of peasant origin obtained an influence over Sashka. He was an honest man but easily carried away as a lawyer friend warned the boy. About this time Elena Petrovna confessed to her son her true relations with his father; how she had loved him and suffered from the general's abuse when he was drunk; how they had separated and then become reunited when he had overcome his drunkenness just before his son was born, but he had always resented her insistence on his reform so that, when he died they parted as enemies. Sashka felt that it was an intuition of his father's character which had been the cause of his sorrowful mood in childhood. Resentment toward his father personally, and the dominant military class he represented combined with a romantic devotion for his suffering country, made it easy for Kolesnikoff to draw the boy into his visionary plan for revolution. The man knew his own revolutionary ardor and intelligence was not enough to fit him to be the leader since he was at heart a peasant, and, when away from cities was liable to share the brutal nature of a beast. He must have someone who was young, pure and devoted, able to command and one whose sacrifice would be considered as a propitiatory offering for the sins of his fathers.   Such a one was Sashka Pogodin.   Together they rallied to their cause a group of peasants who called themselves brothers of the wood and the pale-faced, mystic-eyed youth who now called himself Sashka Jigouleff became their leader.   Although but a slight organization was attempted, the aristocratic aloofness and a certain sense of authority that settled on the maturing form of the young leader kept him in complete control of the rough rabble.   Success was with them for some months.   Unflinching sternness alone kept his followers from degenerating into bandits rapacious for personal gain and full of lust.   Few understood or approved the sacrificial fervor of the young commander.   Pretenders sprang up who permitted these excesses, and his own following dropped away.   After Kolesnikoff's death he went about in a stupor until he awoke to realize that he had sacrificed personal happiness in his mother's beautiful home and the love of charming young Jenny Egmont, for a dream that the people were too bestial and sordid to help him bring to pass.   At last, knowing he had not much more time to live he went back for a last look at his home only to find his dear ones gone.   His mother had been warned that her son would be taken if she allowed him to find her in the old home and so she had moved away.   So Sashka Jigouleff returned to die a terrible and solitary death with murderers whose fate he had chosen to share.   This penetrating yet poetic study of a sensitive boy, whose purest instincts, so characteristic of the heroic and romantic mood of youth, are his undoing is the only novel written by this artist of Russian letters.

SATURDAY'S CHILDREN, a comedy, by Maxwell Anderson (1927).   In the dining room of a typical city apartment, Mrs. Halevy and her married daughter, Florrie, discuss the fact that Bobby, the younger daughter, is still unmarried at twenty-three.   The nice O'Neill boy in Bobby's office must be made to propose and prevented from going off to South America.   The calculating Florrie answers the telephone when Rims O'Neill calls up Bobby, and makes up a tale about another suitor, Fred, with whom Bobby is going to a dance that evening, but perhaps if he would come around she would have time to see him.   Bobby comes in from dinner with Mr. Mengle, her employer.   She scorns Florrie's plans, but Florrie persists in advising her how to bring Rims to a proposal, and writes out in shorthand just what Bobby should say to Rims.   As soon as Rims arrives Florrie gets the rest of the family to go to a band concert, so that the lovers may be alone.   Bobby succumbs to the temptation to use her sister's notes when she finds that this boy she loves so much is actually going away, and tricks Rims into a proposal.   South America, he concludes, can go to the devil.   Five months later Rims and Bobby are living in a tiny flat in the Bronx trying to make his salary of $40 a week cover their budget, and romance seems to have flown out the window.   Everything is fuel to the flame of their quarrels, the rent, cigarettes, Bobby's relatives, Rims' card playing.   In a moment of mutual contrition they agree, "nobody ever loved anybody the way I love you."   Rims says, "I think about you all day long.   And then I come home at night . . . and we get into some goddam mess. . . . "   Bobby's scheming sister advises Bobby to get the upper hand over Rims by having a baby; it has worked with her Willie.   Father Halevy, who comes in later, is not sure that this is a good idea.   "The ribald advice and evil councilling" which she gets from her radical father when she insists on pinning him down is only a regret that a girl must marry in order to have an affair, and lose the romance and acquire the grocery bills.   Bobby finds an I.O.U. which Rims has dropped.   He comes back from his card game to get it, and accuses her of deliberately going through his pockets to discover it.   She is dismayed to learn that Rims owes more than the amount due from the I.O.U. he has won. With angry but mutual consent they agree to part. Rims dashes out the back door, and Bobby goes out the front. A moment later the back door slams; Rims is back calling penitently to Bobby, but there is no answer, and he leaves dejectedly. Bobby comes back calling softly to Rims, but Rims has gone and she too leaves the flat. In the third act, three weeks later, Bobby is working for Mr. Mengle again, and living in a respectable but dingy boarding house. Her father and Rims come to see how she is getting along. Rims has trailed her home one night. He is furious because she has been going out with her old employer, and has even had him calling at the house. Her father waits to ask her to come home again, which she is not willing to do. Rims returns to beg her to come back to him. Mr. Mengle's chauffeur arrives with what looks like a box of flowers. Bobby laughingly explains to Rims that it is not flowers but a bolt for the door to prevent the woman that keeps the boarding house, who thinks that young ladies who have callers should leave their doors open, from walking in. Rims puts the worst possible interpretation on the fact that Bobby has allowed Mr. Mengle to send her the bolt. Bobby, realizing how much Rims means to her, is patient with him and finally convinces him that she is able to take care of herself, and also that she loves him. She will not go back to the flat. She wants her love affair again. "Hurried kisses, clandestine meetings, a secret lover." Rims is obliged to leave her at the sound of the ten o'clock bell which means "callers out." Bobby starts listlessly to get ready for bed, and lies sobbing miserably. There is a noise at the window, and Rims climbs in from the fire escape, and begins busily to fit the bolt on the door. The curtain falls as Bobby's wish for romance is fulfilled.

SCHOOLMASTER OF THE GREAT CITY, A, by Angelo Patri (1917). Angelo Patri came to this country as an immigrant, bringing with him memories of the hero tales of Italy and stories of the Crusades, told by his father as he and his family and neighbors gathered round their fireplace. In New York the Patri family became a part of the tenement house life and Angelo went to school. He was not accustomed to sitting still and the restraint and routine often made him ill. His memory of his school years is of sitting still, repeating words, and then, as a reward, obtaining one minute of freedom to leave the room. By sitting still and learning words he went through school and to college. When Patri's father fell from a ladder the son went to work teaching. Remembering his own experience he was determined to discipline as he had been disciplined. In this he was so successful that the principal appointed him to an unruly class of fifty children. Here discipline did not work. In his desperation he recalled the tales which his father had told him and he told his pupils of his own childhood in Italy and also the hero stories. The children listened breathlessly. Next he bargained with them, exchanging stories for good work, until at last discipline was restored. Now he had time to be troubled by the rigid routine laid down for teachers and pupils by the principals. Each lesson was laid out for them, just so much work in just so many minutes. He soon learned ways of accomplishing the required results with a minimum of effort, but ended by doubting the value of this kind of learning for the children. After two years he returned to college to learn what education really is. There he discovered that "conduct, not ability to recite lessons, was the real test of learning and the sign of culture." He also learned that discipline is not passive obedience, but something active on the part of the child. From now on, though discouraged by principals, Patri tried to put life and action into teaching and learning. His motto became "I serve children." At last he was made a principal and proudly spoke of "My school." But almost at once he found that the teachers and children feared him and could not work with him, so it was not really his school yet. In time he led the teachers to understand what he was working for, but it was not yet his school for now he found that the parents were not with him. By having entertainments and meetings he worked to bring them in touch with the school. At last they came to see their children perform. Soon there were regular parents' meetings, conducted by parents, proud to be able to coöperate with the school in helping the children to better playgrounds, medical care and better moral training. They worked with the school to win what was needed from the city politicians. Patri had now brought the community into the school, but found that it must be held back from going out again through overorganization. He felt that now "My school" had become "Our school." Inside the school the form of teaching began to have more life. Individual types of children, mentally and physically handicapped, were given individual care, clubs were formed for all the children under the direction of teachers who particularly loved music, art, and nature. In the morning assemblies love of literature was fostered through study and recitation of special authors. But even with all this Patri found that only the individual handicapped children were learning by personal experience. "Our school" was "still in the grip of tradition, rules, records, and endless routine." "My school" was still a dream school though he had succeeded in humanizing it through socializing it. Angelo Patri closes his book looking forward to his school as an ideal attainable in the future. In it the elementary classes are to come into their own with the finest teachers and equipment, the three R's will accord with social needs and be dynamic, the teacher will experiment boldly, remembering that he is "a greater artist than he who paints a picture" or carves a statue or writes a book because he is the creator of human conduct! He ends by saying: "I feel that the attitude toward the school and the child is the ultimate attitude by which America is to be judged. Indeed the distinctive contribution America is to make to the world's progress is not political, economical, religious, but educational, the child our national strength, the school as the medium through which the adult is to be remade. What an ideal for the American people!"

SCIENCE, THE OUTLINE OF, edited by J. Arthur Thomson (4 vols., 1922). The author of this introduction to the whole field of science is regius professor of natural history at the University of Aberdeen. His aim is to present the modern knowledge of science in untechnical language for the information of the general reader, to do for science what Wells, J. H. Robinson, and Van Loon have done for history. The thirty-eight chapters illustrated profusely with half-tone and color plates are essays usually complete in themselves. Volume 1 begins with astronomy, the beginnings of life on earth, the story of evolution, and tells of the struggle for existence, the anatomical, physiological, and embryological proofs of man's relation to a simian stock, of the emergence of primitive types of man, with pictures and descriptions of the fossil remains known as the Pithecanthropus erectus, the Homo heidelbergensis, the Homo neanderthalensis, and other later stone-age ancestors. The section on "Evolution Going On" gives representative examples of the changes in animal and plant life with such illustrative pictures as "the Australian frilled lizard which is at present trying to become a biped." A chapter on the emergence of mind treats of experiments with animals and birds, and points out that man's advance in intelligence and from intelligence to reason is closely connected with his power of speech. The last chapter on "The Foundations of the Universe" includes sections on the discovery of X-rays and radium, of electrons, and the electron theory. Volume 2, Chapter 1 tells of the discovery of the invisible world by the invention of the microscope. Chapter 2 describes the human body as the perfect machine, and names the discovery of the ductless glands 'devoted to the manufacture of hormones' as one of the most remarkable discoveries of recent years. A chapter on Darwinism concludes that "if Darwinism means the general idea of evolution or transformism — that higher forms are descended from lower — that it stands to-day more firmly than ever." But if it is taken to mean "the particular statement of the factors in evolution which is expounded in 'The Origin of Species,' 'The Descent of Man,' and 'The Variation of Animals and Plants under Domestication,' then it must be said that while the main ideas remain valid there has been development all along the line. . . ." This volume contains chapters on the natural history of birds, mammals, and insects, and closes with a chapter on the new psychology, psychoanalysis, and the theories of Professor Freud. In Volume 3 Sir Oliver Lodge contributes a chapter on the progress of physical research; Julian S. Huxley is the author of the chapter on biology. There are chapters on botany, meteorology, and chemistry. The reader is referred to Dr. Edwin Slosson's "Creative Chemistry" for the story of the chemist's achievements "as a creator," the making of wealth out of what was formerly waste material, the invention of coal-tar colors, etc. Applied science tells the marvels of the electrical age, what electricity is, how it is generated and transmitted, and describes great electrical feats, the electrification of railroads over the Rocky Mountains and the Alps, and the utilization of the water power of Niagara Falls; the progress in the wireless telegraph and telephone; the trans-Atlantic flights. Volume 4 has a chapter on bacteria by Sir E. Ray Lankester, one on "What Science Means to Man," by Sir Oliver Lodge, and a last chapter by the Editor on "Science and Modern Thought." "The Making of the Earth and the Structure of the Rocks" discusses mountains, earthquakes and volcanoes. "The Science of the Sea" answers the question why the sea is salt, discusses its depth and temperature, pressure, the floor of the sea and other matters of oceanography, and marine life. Other chapters are "Ethnology," "Domesticated Animals," "The Biology of the Seasons," and "The Science of Health." Bibliographies at the ends of the chapters indicate "first books" to read on the subjects, and appended to the last volume is a "Classified Bibliography."

SCIENCE AND THE MODERN WORLD, by A. N. Whitehead (1927). Starting with the origins of modern science in the sixteenth century in western Europe, the author traces the relation which philosophy has had to the discoveries of modern science which we have come to adopt as dogma and faith. He prefaces his analysis with a definition of the function which philosophy has in respect to science, namely the coördination of its factual and hypothetical concepts to conform with our non-detailed inspection of things in general, intuitively perceived. That is to say the assumptions which the science of any era is forced to make to carry on its investigations should be mutually consistent and systematic in the formation of a system of nature as we perceive it directly through our senses. After a resumé of the importance of mathematics in the history of thought, as a means of exact and yet non-specific generalization, Professor Whitehead goes on to discuss what he calls the "Century of Genius," — the seventeenth, — which produced such men as Bacon, Harvey, Kepler, Galileo, Descartes, Pascal, Huygens, Boyle, Newton, Locke, Spinoza, and Leibnitz. The epoch thus signalized opened with a revolt against the "rationalism" of the mediæval thinkers, and the vindication of induction as the intellectual methodology of modern science, that is to say, the inference from characteristics of the immediate occasion of similar characteristics in future occasions. That century also set the tone of quantitativeness to science, a tone which it has not lost to this day. Instead of describing the quality or assigning the place of the object, it and its relations to other objects were measured. From these principles and the fact of their success in the hands of such investigators as Newton, the present basis of science was confirmed as that of a mechanistic materialism. There followed, according to Whitehead, a reaction in the Nineteenth Century, not in the field of science, but in that of philosophy and poetry. Already Hume in the middle Eighteenth had pointed out the shortcomings of a mechanistic materialism, and Kant pursued his line of reasoning. But especially in such poets as Wordsworth and Shelley, we find an expression of the sense of Nature intuitively perceived which runs counter to the thoroughgoing acceptance of a purely mechanistic universe. That the Eighteenth Century did not perceive the contradiction is due to the fact of its confident and superficial rationalistic activity, working upon the data of the preceding century and continuing its work of classification, measurement, and analysis with little regard to the philosophical bases and assumptions that these activities implied. As the Nineteenth Century progressed, however, the interest in science, shifting from the purely physical sciences to the biological, developed the theory of evolution to account for phenomena not amenable to exact measurement, or repetition over short periods of time in the laboratory. The theory, however, like previous scientific *convenances*, took no account of the coeval philosophic background of "materialism" with which, Professor Whitehead points out, it is wholly incompatible. For, it is clear that in a mechanistic universe, changes that occur must be purposeless and unprogressive, and evolution then becomes merely the name for a set of relations that have already been described in other connections. But Evolution appears to be more, namely a progressive and purposeful changing of complex organisms into higher, more complex organisms. Therefore, says the author, it "cries aloud for a conception of organism as fundamental for nature." This concept of organism, or better organization, the author goes on to discuss in relation to the modern theory of relativity, with which it fits in, though the latter is not essential to its acceptance. Organism supposes "events" grasping into unity a pattern of aspects, in which time and space are necessarily coördinated, though differentiated by the fact that the pattern endures and exhibits itself through any part of its total life-history. But the space-time system is unique to each event, and we must distinguish when we deal with any system or any event their relations to other systems, other events, and to the event itself at different stages of its life-history. This multiple space-time system, however, implies that time is atomic in its succession, since temporalization being part of the event, or realisation, the event requires duration exhibited as a whole. Time, therefore, is the succession of elements divisible in themselves, though the event temporalized is itself divisible. Professor Whitehead next relates this theory of time-space to the Quantum theory, which is of such importance in modern science in dealing with electrons and protons, that is to say the ultimate constituents of matter. For dealing with them, some theory of discontinuous existence is necessary to fit recorded observations, and this space-time concept, in which organisms correspond to the primary electron or proton, coincides with the theory developed, — the Quantum theory. The author concludes with an examination of the relation of science and his theory to the field of metaphysics, God, and Religion, with a final summary of the requisites for social progress in terms of intellectual activity and æsthetic awareness.

SECOND EMPIRE, THE, Bonapartism — The Prince — The President — The Emperor, by Philip Guedalla (1922). The first chapters are a prologue tracing the growth of the Napoleonic legend out of the propaganda manufactured by the first Napoleon at St. Helena, after the sword had failed him, to provide a happy ending for the drama left unfinished at Waterloo by making a path to the throne for a younger Bonaparte. The author denies that Napoleon I had any interest in the liberal ideas of the French Revolution except the doctrine of equality. "One could not manoeuvre a troop of horse in which each rank enjoyed a peculiar privilege, and the nation which made equal units of its citizens would march more promptly to its master's orders than any Old-World welter of castes and classes. To that extent and for reasons comprehensible to any drill sergeant Napoleon was an egalitarian." Napoleon III, in exile and imprisonment for many years, was a student, and cherished modern ideas of nationality, self-determination, and believed in the method of international conference. For example in the affair of Schleswig-Holstein "he had a vague notion that the population of the Duchies was predominantly German; if that were so, intervention on the Danish side would be a sin against the doctrine of nationality." At Chiselhurst in 1872 he talked about abolishing war, and had ideas about "a Council in regular session to settle the world's affairs, and an Assembly of the nations meeting to legislate in terms of international law." Mr. Guedalla suggests that the chief tragedy for Napoleon III was to succeed in his purpose, "which was to establish the Empire; that purpose once achieved, he no longer knew what he had to do." He believed in predestination, and became an opportunist without a policy. "He had followed a star; and a King, a Republic, and seven millions of men had gone down before the inevitable event," and he drifted along trusting to his star to light the way. This story of Napoleon III is a combination of history and biography, beginning with the childhood of the son of Hortense Beauharnais and Louis Bonaparte, his adventures with his brother and the Carbonari in Italy. The death of his brother made him the Pretender to the throne of France, in succession to the Duc de Reichstadt, and the journey from Italy to Paris taught him that the memory of the Empire was not dead, and made him a Bonapartist. The sufferings and horror of the wars were forgotten, and the splendor of the Empire was remembered as time passed. "France under Louis Philippe was haunted by the little figure of the Emperor; one could catch on every wind the echoes of old names, and men turned to the crude memories of the Empire for an escape into romance." The old King was himself forced to become a Bonapartist, to dedicate the Arc de Triomphe, and send to St. Helena for the bones of Napoleon to carry out his wish to be buried in France. The first attempt of Prince Louis to capture the French throne caused his exile to New York, the second from England to Boulogne landed him in the French fortress of Ham for six years. He escaped in disguise to England, and lived for two years as "a man of fashion" in London, until the Revolution of 1848 made his return to France possible. M. Louis Bonaparte became a candidate for the Presidency and was elected by a large majority, and Victoria wrote to her Uncle Leopold, "it will, however, perhaps be more difficult to get rid of him again than one may at first imagine," and so it proved. France's part in the Italian war for liberation is an important chapter, and was the prelude to the Second Empire. "On December 20, 1851, the French electorate affirmed by plebiscite the conversion of the Second Republic into the Second Consulate. . . . The Senate petitioned for the Empire. . ." and on November 21, 1852, another plebiscite approved the change. Napoleon III married the beautiful Eugenie, and took her to England on a royal visit. Victoria was fascinated with Napoleon III, a monarch who was also a gentleman, considering her "acquaintance with countless half-educated, clanking, military persons from the Courts of Europe," but amid the ecstasies of her diary she writes, "How far he is actuated by a strong moral sense of right and wrong is difficult to say." Napoleon III reigned eighteen years, and the personalities of the time crowd the pages of this book, a complete picture of the Empire. The elements which caused the overthrow are analyzed, the paradox of the Emperor's system that "preached liberty to foreign countries and maintained reaction in his own," the emergence of Prussia like a "bad fairy," the hostility of the younger generation and Paris to the Empire, the defeat of the French Army in 1870, the surrender of the stricken Emperor, and the end at Chiselhurst. The story ends with the death of the son of Napoleon III and Eugenie, the last Napoleon, in the service of England in South Africa in war against the Zulus. "Only the Empress lived on." Mr. Guedalla's style is the vivid narrative of a witness of the events.

SECRETS OF POLAR TRAVEL, THE, by Rear Admiral Robert E. Peary (1917). The discoverer of the North Pole, who for twenty-three years studied the problem of Arctic exploration from every angle and finally reached his goal, has written an account of his equipment. "The Roosevelt," the ship in which the successful trip to the Pole was made, was a specially stout ship planned by Peary and built to his specific orders. Two of the main requirements of a polar ice-fighter are, according to Peary, a rounded model which will rise steadily when squeezed in the ice, and there must be no projection of keel or other part to hold the ship from rising or give the ice an opportunity to get a grip. Also the ship must be most heavily braced and trussed to enable it to withstand the pressure of the ice floes. "For ramming she must have a sharply raking stern, which will rise on the ice at each blow." Profiting by all the mistakes of his predecessors and using all his ingenuity Peary made a ship which not only withstood the terrific use and misuse of the polar trip, but has been sold and resold and used in many lines of work since. In the matter of personnel Peary suggests small numbers and men of small, wiry build. On all his polar trips he made as great use as possible of the Eskimos. They with their knowledge of the north and its conditions have proved invaluable. Supplies, naturally, must be carefully figured out, both as to quantity and weight and containers. Square tins and boxes are the best, round tins take up too much room, especially on sledge trips. Placing the boxes of provisions on board ship was worked out "almost as carefully as would be the builders' plans of the blocks in a granite building." Furthermore the most crucial provisions are so placed that a ton or so could be thrown out on the ice in case of accident to the ship. There must be a variety of provision in order to keep up both interest and vigor. "Pemmican is the only food for dogs on a polar sledge journey." Winter quarters for an Arctic expedition were made according to the Eskimo plans. The houses were built of different materials: stone, wood, ice and snow, with the supplies used as part of the walls when possible. Stoves and lamps for warmth and light and bunks built in true Eskimo fashion, with a few books usually completed the houses. They were built, as a rule, for the winter season, in case at any time fire or ice might ruin the ship and the supplies. Clothing is an item of the greatest importance and many different kinds have been tried by the various explorers and discarded. Bearskin for the outer garment, with woolen undergarments and deerskin mittens, have been found good by several explorers. Peary advises this outfit. Peary's belief in the Eskimo as guide and helper on Arctic trips is implicit. "In powers of endurance, in ingenuity and intelligence in adapting themselves to their surroundings and in using to advantage every one of the all too few possibilities of their land, they are, in my opinion, unequalled by any other aboriginal race. With their wonderful knowledge of ice technic and their ability to handle sledges and dogs, the Eskimos were really more necessary as members of individual parties than the white men; for although they were not qualified to lead, they could follow another's lead and drive dogs much better than any white man." The resources of the country can be used largely in the matter of fresh meat. Fish, flesh and fowl in considerable variety abound in many localities. Musk-ox, reindeer and polar bear are all edible; walrus, whales, and seals are used. The Eskimo comes in for a large share of the taking of these on account of their superior knowledge. The matter of sledge equipment is of the utmost importance and on account of his careful planning and execution of every detail probably Peary owes his successful dash to the Pole.

SHACKLETON, THE LIFE OF SIR ERNEST, by Hugh Robert Mill (1923), is divided into three sections. Book One, called "Equipment" describes Shackleton's childhood, education, and early days at sea. Book Two, "Achievement" covers the years 1906 to 1910, the "Nimrod" voyage, his year in the Farthest South and the expedition to the Pole which just failed of success. Book Three, "Bafflement," portrays him in the days of unrest on shore and his last voyage. Descended from an old Yorkshire family settled in Ireland, Sir Ernest Shackleton was born in Kilkee, Ireland, in 1874. He was never a brilliant scholar, but he had a fine imagination and while still at school became obsessed with a desire to go to sea. At the age of sixteen his life on the sea began when he went as ship's boy on an old sailing vessel. Rough times were his lot here, both from the sea and from his companions, but he determined to carry on and rise in his chosen profession. He served his apprenticeship, secured certificates as mate and master, and passed from sailing vessel to steam vessel, and from a tramp ship to a mail boat. During the South African War he was third officer on a troop ship and in collaboration with Dr. McLean, the ship's surgeon, wrote an account of the voyage. It was in 1900 that Shackleton first had the idea of Polar exploration. At this time the news came that Borchgrevink, the Norwegian explorer, had reached the Great Ice Barrier and had found that its position was thirty miles south of that recorded by Ross fifty-eight years before. Shackleton knowing that a national Antarctic expedition was being planned, began to inquire about a possible post. In 1901 he obtained his wish and was appointed junior officer of the "Discovery," the ship in which Captain Scott was to make his first voyage to the South. With Scott and Dr. Wilson, the scientist, Shackleton was one of the three who on November 2, 1902, left the "Discovery" on the dash to the South Pole. Owing to terrible privations the attempt was abandoned 463 miles from the goal and Shackleton's health was so impaired that he was invalided home. Being the first to return from the expedition Shackleton was made much of and received a great ovation. There was a young lady who for several years had been the inspiration of Shackleton's career and, in order to make marriage possible, he took up journalism and for a time was on the staff of Sir Arthur Pearson's "Royal Magazine." Next he became secretary of the Royal Scottish Geographical Society. For a time, too, politics called him. When he was selected as Conservative candidate for Dundee in 1906 he conducted a breezy campaign but did not secure enough votes. Throughout all this time the idea kept recurring that his road to success ran via the South Pole. In 1909 he found a man who was willing to furnish financial backing for a new Polar expedition under the leadership of Shackleton. It was on this trip that he accomplished his great feat of reaching a point 96 geographical miles from the South Pole. This expedition had many important results for science: the discovery of the Beardmore Glacier, the ascent of Mt. Erebus over 13,000 feet high, and the determination of the south magnetic pole. But the chief thrill of the expedition came from the gallant attempt of Shackleton and three of his companions who so nearly reached their goal and then had to turn back because of lack of food. The next expedition which Shackleton led was in 1914 to 1916. He set out in the ship "Endurance" to cross the Antarctic, but the ship was caught in the ice and sank. There followed a period of horror when the leader faced hunger, disease, madness, and sudden death, but through it all he went with a spirit of marvellous fortitude and saved the lives of all of his men. Despite the loss of the ship this expedition was important scientifically, although it was not appreciated at the time because of the interest in the World War. During the rest of the War Shackleton was in South America sent by the British government for purposes of propaganda. There he received a commission as major in the British army. On January 4th, 1922, his ship, the "Quest," lay in the harbor of Grytviken, South Georgia, at the beginning of the last great cruise of his life. The last entry in his diary ended: "In the darkening twilight I saw a lone star hover gem-like above the bay." Then he lay down to sleep and never arose. He died of an attack of angina pectoris worn out with his struggles against the ice floes of the Antarctic and his struggles to raise money to lead more expeditions thither. He is buried under a great cairn at Grytviken.

SHADOW LINE, THE, by Joseph Conrad (1917), is subtitled "A Confession," so it may be inferred that this record of an experience that changed one young man from boyhood to adult, however it may have varied in outward detail, really portrayed some inner experience of Conrad's own life. The intimacy of tone in the text more than the subtitle or the fact that the first person is used in narrating the story bears out this theory. The restless discontent of youth leads the writer to give up suddenly a good berth on an eastern trader. While lounging in the Officers' Home ashore, through the friendly officiousness of Captain Giles, semi-retired authority on eastern navigation, an insignificant plot on the part of the club steward is discovered. For purposes of his own he had intended to withhold from the young man a message from the Harbour Office, asking him to take command of a ship whose captain had died at sea. The young man's elation over thus fortuitously receiving his first command is somewhat tempered when he boards the ship and learns from Mr. Burns, the first mate, the mysteriously vicious nature of the captain whose successor he was, and the unhealthy condition of the crew. Although the steward was put ashore with symptoms of cholera, and the humane doctor of the port advised against going to sea with an ailing crew, the impatience of the young commander over delay and his hope that the open sea would restore the crew to health decided him. For days they lay becalmed within sight of land, or were tossed in a circle by contrary winds. Nor were the crew free of the tropical fever. The chief mate, whose piteous plea had induced the captain to bring him along, grew steadily better although wasted by sickness and still under the obsession that the former captain was exerting an evil influence on the ship, but the men became worse although their gallant attempts to do their regular work filled the young captain with remorse. For they were without quinine, so essential to men in their condition, due to the fraudulent action of the former captain. The young captain blamed himself for not having personally verified the completeness of the medical supplies. With the help of Ransome, who had joined as a cook because of his bad heart, the two struggled for seventeen days with their inadequate though heroic crew, and adverse sailing conditions. Finally the mate gathered strength to come on deck and defy the malign influence with a burst of maniacal laughter. A favoring wind finally enabled the worn young commander to return to the port from which he had departed with such high hopes with his sickly crew. Captain Giles conceded his approval of one who had learned what so few youngsters understand, that a man must not be faint-hearted, but "stand up to his bad luck, to his mistakes, to his conscience and all that sort of thing."

SHELLEY, ARIEL, THE LIFE OF, by André Maurois, see **ARIEL.**

SHELLEY, HIS LIFE AND WORK, by Walter Edwin Peck (2 vol. 1927.) An exhaustive biography of the poet by a recognized Shelley scholar who has had access to the Shelley manuscripts in collections in England and the United States. Appendices covering one hundred and fifty pages include among hitherto unpublished material letters of Elizabeth Hitchener and William Godwin. The author's attitude to Shelley is sympathetic but dispassionate, notably in the discussion of his relations with his first wife, Harriet Westbrook. Shelley's rebellion against authority is shown successively at home, at Eton, and at Oxford. The early and continued influence of the philosophy of William Godwin is stressed. Shelley wrote to Godwin when he was leaving England that he respected him as the philosopher who first awakened and still regulated his understanding, though he deplores "the part of his character which is least excellent," referring to his unforgiving treatment of Mary and Percy who had carried out his principles in practice. Godwin's injured feelings as a father did not prevent his continual application to the Shelleys for money to pay his debts. Of love, Shelley writes to Peacock, "I think one is always in love with something or other; the error, and I confess it is not easy for spirits cased in flesh and blood to avoid it, consists in seeking in a mortal image the likeness of what is perhaps eternal." "Deep-rooted and enduring was the love" of the poet for his cousin, Harriet Grove, which Professor Peck considers "one of the most powerful forces in his life." The next Harriet threw herself on his protection against the persecution of her father, and threatened suicide. The secret of Shelley's attraction to her remains to the author an unanswered question, but she was a disciple, and he believed he had converted her to "infidelity," and therefore made the society of her former friends uncongenial. Of Shelley's abandonment of his wife, Professor Peck writes that it "had been sudden, deliberate, selfish," and that Shelley was responsible "for the state of the spirit" which drove her to her death. He finds Shelley's reactions to this tragedy expressed in the poems rather than in the letters to Mary. Mary belonged to Shelley's world, and he tells Peacock, "Everyone who knows me must know that the partner of my life should be one who can feel poetry and understand philosophy." She was persecuted by her stepmother, and in her turn threatened to die, according to Harriet's story, and by Shelley's own description we get a picture of an ardent sympathetic, yet thoughtless youth, finding a new plea for knight errantry. . . ." Harriet would not listen to his proposals for a "combined household to embrace his wife and the sister-of-his-soul," and his love for Mary triumphed. For the story of the elopement Professor Peck used three sources not hitherto employed in lives of Shelley. Claire, "silly, impulsive, wilful, and sentimental to a degree" accompanied the Shelleys on their travels and though Shelley was warmly attached to her she was "the bane" of Mary's existence. The "Epipsychidion" was written to Emilia Viviani, whom he idealized until she disillusioned him by her loveless marriage with the man of her father's choice. To Jane Williams he addressed more lyrics than to any other woman, and Professor Peck believes her to have been of great importance in "the history of Shelley's love-life, and the development of his lyric genius."

THE READER'S DIGEST OF BOOKS 1329

Shelley's political and social theories and his passion for reform are discussed in the analyses of his prose and poetry. Composing "Prometheus Unbound" Shelley could say, "I consider poetry very subordinate to moral and political science, and if I were well, certainly I would aspire to the latter; for I can conceive a great work, embodying the discoveries of all ages, and harmonizing the contending creeds by which mankind have been ruled." Parallels in the appendices show Shelley's indebtedness to earlier romances and contemporaries. The book begins with Hogg's memories of Shelley's early life and closes with Trelawney's description of his meeting with "the mild-looking, beardless boy," reading Plato, Sophocles, or Spinoza, and the account of the last year of his life reading and writing in the solitude of the woods, his selflessness, his devotion to his friends, his indifference to the prospect of death, and the last voyage and burial.

SHOW BOAT, THE, by Edna Ferber (1926). A popular feature of Mississippi River life in the eighteen-seventies was the floating theatre, presenting such old favorites as "East Lynne," and "Tempest and Sunshine" in one night stands. River travel had fallen off with the coming of the railroads, so Captain Andy Hawks, river pilot, decided to buy a show boat, "The Cotton Blossom," as "to leave the river — to engage, perforce, in some landlubberly pursuit — was to him unthinkable." The actors lived on board under the rule of gay, whimsical Captain Andy and his wife, the shrewish uncompromising Parthenia. Magnolia, her father's daughter in her love for the pageant of the river and the stage, grows up to be leading lady of the troupe in spite of her mother's opposition. Gaylord Ravenal, a debonair gambler out of luck, comes aboard to act for love of her. "No oriental princess was ever more heavily chaperoned than was Magnolia," but they managed to outwit Parthenia and get married. Kim, their daughter, is born in an hour of storm and flood on the river. Another stormy night Captain Andy danced over the side of the boat in sheer excitement as he had often done before and been fished out, but this time in the fog the Mississippi had her way with him. The stern Parthenia ran the boat like a female seminary after her husband's death. Gaylord brought Magnolia and Kim to Chicago where they settled down to the life of a professional gambler and his family, feast or famine, one day rooms at the Palmer House, the next in cheap lodgings. Magnolia's letters to her mother, especially in lean times, were triumphs of lying pride. "Sentimental Tommy's mother, writing boastfully home about her black silks and her gold chain, was never more stiff-necked than she." Gaylord loved his wife but the reform administration in Chicago and the prospect of a visit from Parthenia were too much for him, and he went away "for a few weeks" and she never saw him again. Magnolia placed Kim in a convent school and went on the stage where her rare smile and interpretation of negro spirituals win her a place among the great artistes. Later Kim is also a successful artist in New York, in the new manner, trained in a dramatic school. The word of Parthenia's death takes Magnolia back to the river and the "Cotton Blossom," and she stays there. The background of "Gambler's Alley" in earlier Chicago is a picture like the panorama of the gay, careless, Bohemian days on the show-boat, and the river towns.

SHOW-OFF, THE, a transcript of life, by George Kelly (1923). The Fisher family are united in lack of appreciation of Amy Fisher's suitor, Aubrey Piper, "the boy from West Philly" as he calls himself. He is a clerk at a salary of $32.50 a week in the freight offices of the Pennsylvania Railroad, but tries to give the impression that he is head of the department and a man of large affairs to anyone who can endure to listen to his continuous conversation about himself. When he calls, Mr. Fisher goes out to avoid being slapped on the back, Joe retires to the cellar to work on his invention, and Aubrey talks on, laughing boisterously at his own jokes as all his audience except Amy, who thinks he is wonderful, leave the room. After Aubrey takes his "reluctant leave" at midnight in high and noisy spirits, Amy's mother warns her that if she marries him she need not come crying around to her father to support her. The curtain goes down on Amy alone gazing raptly at the reflection of the light of the lamp on the diamond in her engagement ring. In the next act Amy and Aubrey have been married five months. Aubrey comes in hoping to find Amy with her mother. He has borrowed a friend's car, and wants to take his wife to the Automobile Show. He leaves and Amy appears tired out from looking for a house, and complaining of the high rents. Her mother asks her how they can consider increasing their expenses when they are not able to make ends meet without borrowing from her with only the rent of two rooms to pay for. Clara, her married sister, tells Amy that Aubrey has been borrowing money from her husband, Frank Hyland, and that she intends to put a stop to it. Amy refuses to believe it, but is afraid that it is true. Joe brings the bad news that Mr. Fisher has had a stroke at the factory where he works, and has been taken to the hospital. Just as they are leaving the house to go to the hospital, Aubrey walks in with a bandaged head. It seems that he came to grief in his borrowed car, ran into a trolley car and broke the arm of the traffic policeman. Frank Hyland has had to put up bail of one thousand dollars for him at the police station. According to Aubrey everyone else was in the wrong, and he was all right, and had a few things to say about the condition of traffic in the city. A workman from the factory stops at the house to bring home some of Mr. Fisher's things. Aubrey regrets that his car is laid up so that he cannot run him home, and talks grandly about the house of his father-in-law, in which he hopes to be given shelter in his poverty and irresponsibility, as if it were his own, that he had generously invited his wife's father and mother to share with them when he married Amy. A telephone message brings word that Mr. Fisher is dead, and Aubrey drops his showing-off to comfort Amy sincerely. In the third act Mrs. Fisher has received one thousand dollars from the insurance agent with which she presently pays Aubrey's fine for "recklessness, disregard of traffic signals, and operating an automobile without a license." Clara, whose husband does not love her, feels that the fact that Aubrey adores Amy makes up for some of his many deficiencies. Mrs. Fisher had declared that she would never have Aubrey in the house, but agrees to let them come home to live since Amy is going to have a baby. In a serious talk with Aubrey, Clara asks him to stop telling lies and showing-off, and tells him that his stay in the house will be dependent on his behaviour, as her father has left Clara the house so that she may protect her mother. She adds, "The very first time I hear that you've told anybody that this is your house — I'll see to it that you get a house that will be your own." Joe, whom Aubrey has called the "radio kid" and the "boy inventor," perfects an invention that makes his fortune. The company he works for signs a contract for a hundred thousand dollars for the rights. It seems that Aubrey had heard the talk about it, and representing himself as an official of the Pennsylvania Railroad and the head of the family since Joe's father's death, insisted that he would not permit "his ward" to deal with them unless they made the contract one hundred thousand instead of the fifty thousand they had offered Joe at his first interview with them, and for once his bluff had worked. Amy, her pride justified, tells Aubrey how wonderful he is.

SILENT STORMS, by Ernest Poole (1927). The story of the international marriage of a conservative American financier, Barry McClurg, forty-nine years old, and Madeleine de Granier, a brilliant young French girl, intensely interested in the French Fascist movement. There are two problems which they have to meet: the conflict of different civilizations as represented in entirely different backgrounds and ideas, and the disparity in their ages. Barry had married the young daughter of Charlotte Wheelright, a friend of his own age, who herself would have made him an excellent wife. His wife died soon after their marriage and he was left with his club and his friendship for his mother-in-law as his two chief interests outside the absorbing world of Wall Street, which is to him almost a religion. And then everything changes for him. Bob, his nephew, whom he has educated and sent abroad to prepare him for a place in Wall Street, returns and comes to live with him. He brings with him youthful enthusiasm, and a passion for "L'Europe nouvelle." It is Bob who introduces him to Countess Marie Madeleine de Granier, lecturing in America upon conditions in Europe and the need for American help. She is fascinated by his quiet power and wealth, which she desires to help her country and its youth. Barry's attitude toward post-war Europe has always been rather grim. He distrusts it, and does not understand it, but he falls in love with its eager young champion. Finally in spite of all reasons to the contrary, Barry and Madeleine are married. The difference in their ages turns out to be a problem of much less import than the differences in their cultural background and their outlook. Naturally the young wife, with her multi-racial ancestry, French, Italian, and Russian, finds America somewhat crass in spite of its charm. She is in her way exactly as insular as her husband. Finally they go to France to visit her Catholic family. The chateau is saturated with the rich oldness of life. Barry is not at home in it, or with her aristocratic parents or her uncle, the cardinal, and when a cablegram urges his immediate return to Wall Street, he goes, feeling that he could never give in to his wife's demand that he should live at least a part of each year in France, and perhaps even establish a great Paris office for his firm. His plans are more simple. He is content to continue adding to his fortune and to build, in time, a house in town and one on Long Island where his beautiful young wife would bear him children — real American children, with money behind them, and the bluest blood of Europe in their veins, — but not too visible. After their return to America a child is born — and dies, and the French girl, in her homesickness, grows farther and farther away from her husband, with intermissions of repentence when she seems to love him as much as ever. Barry sees a separation as the only solution of her unhappiness, and he urges his nephew, Bob, wholly suited to her in age and interests, to again become a frequent guest at their apartment. That the marriage should have failed is inevitable. Neither Barry nor Madeleine can be blamed. The novel ends with Madeleine sailing for Paris. "I shall never come back," she tells Barry when she leaves. He returns to his office to indorse a foreign loan which he has formerly rejected.

SILVER CORD, THE, a comedy in three acts, by Sidney Howard (1926). A study of possessive mother love. Mrs. Phelps, a wealthy widow, turns to her sons, David and Robert, for compensation, after her brief unhappy married life. With an unusual capacity for self-idealization, and self-pity, she creates a legend for her boys of maternal sacrifice and unselfishness, and talks of her weak heart regardless of the doctor's opinion that there is nothing the matter with it. David, the oldest son, returns home after two years of study abroad, with a wife, Christina. Robert, who has been in love several times and involved in a scandal which cost his mother twelve thousand dollars, is engaged to a charming young girl, Hester, now on a visit to her prospective mother-in-law. In her maternal obsession Mrs. Phelps determines to separate these young couples so that she can keep her sons for herself. Her greetings to her new daughter-in-law are belated and insincere. Christina is a biologist and has a position waiting for her at the Rockefeller Institute in New York. Mrs. Phelps is furious to learn from Christina that David is expecting to go into an architect's office in New York instead of remaining at home to build houses on the estate as she had planned, and accuses her of sacrificing her husband to her own scientific career. When Christina and David tell the family they are going to have a child, Hester is the only one to express congratulations. Alone with Robert, his mother persuades him that he is not in love with Hester or she with him, and gets him to promise to break the engagement. After dinner she makes the opportunity for him to jilt Hester, who is heartbroken and grows hysterical as she understands that his mother has come between them. Mrs. Phelps at first denies it, and then admits that she has advised Rob to break with her, and says that Robert told her that Hester had misconstrued his friendship and that he had never wanted to marry her. Hester does not believe this lie. She tries to call a taxi to leave the house, and is prevented by Mrs. Phelps who breaks the telephone cord, because for the sake of "appearances" she prefers to have Hester remain until morning. Christina now fully realizes the enmity and hypocrisy of her husband's mother, and her selfish domination of David. She has the key to the queer, arid places in his relation to her and to his work, a sort of "No-Man's Land" that she knows now is his mother's influence. Mrs. Phelps had placed David and his wife in separate rooms, and she now comes to his bedside for one of her old-time talks, in which she works on his feelings with the pride, affection, weak heart, and sacrifice themes until Christina comes in and she grudgingly leaves them alone, though in the next room she can hear every word they say as Christina suspects. Christina talks to David about the cruel treatment Hester has received, about their own love and relations as husband and wife, and her discovery of his mother's hold on him. David thinks it is all morbid rot, and believes that he can still "do what's right" for both his mother and his wife. His mother comes in again and gets the last word and her son's assurance that he will build her houses in Phelps Manor. Christina returns to call the men to prevent Hester, beside herself with grief, from drowning herself in the pond. Mrs. Phelps shouts out of the window to her boys to come back for their coats; they will get pneumonia. In the morning Mrs. Phelps defends herself to Robert against "the unreasonable attitude" Hester has taken toward her. She will tell everyone that Hester is insane. She plans to take Robert to Europe to avoid the talk about the affair. Now she asks David to help her with Robert, to leave Christina long enough to take them to Europe. David is anxious "to do the right thing," and says he will talk to Christina about it. Christina enters the room dressed for travelling and asks him to decide whether he will leave with her as a husband or remain with his mother as a son, since his mother will not allow any division of his affections. With ruthless candor and the frankness of the biologist she explains why Mrs. Phelps is not fit to be any one's mother. The "professional mother," as Christina calls her, defends her point of view. David is distracted by the conflict between the old ties and the new, but in spite of his mother's appeal he runs after Christina and Hester and joins them at the car. Mrs. Phelps is left with the weak Robert kneeling at her feet completely engulfed while she repeats to him that "mother love suffereth long and is kind; envieth not, is not puffed up. . . ."

SILVER SPOON, THE, by John Galsworthy (1925). This book continues "The Forsyte Saga," following "The White Monkey." The symbol of the disillusioned monkey representing the later Forsytes and the younger generation after the War is replaced by the silver spoon. The beautiful, spoiled Fleur was born with one in her mouth. Her doting father, Soames Forsyte, had put it there. Michael Mont, her husband, has left the publishing house and is a member of Parliament. He is seriously interested in promoting social reform, in helping the unemployed, and in an imperial policy of emigration named Foggartism after its author, old Sir James Foggart, who has written a book on "The Parlous State of England." The thesis is that England can no longer support herself and must depend on the Dominions to make the demand equal the goods she can supply. He advocates the emigration of children of from fourteen to sixteen years in large numbers. The hostility of the people in the Dominions toward the British immigrant due to their distrust of the usefulness and adaptability of adult immigrants would vanish if they had malleable youth to deal with. Fleur is absorbed in building up a salon to aid her husband in his career and satisfy her own social ambitions. The plot of the story grows out of a trumpery quarrel between Fleur and Marjorie Ferrar. Soames overhears Marjorie call Fleur a snob and lion-hunter, charges her publicly with slandering her hostess and asks her to leave the house. Fleur writes letters to several women calling Marjorie "a snake in the grass," and adds that "she hasn't a moral about her." Marjorie's father, Lord Charles Ferrar, like his daughter always in debt, advises her to bring an action for slander and get a settlement out of court with heavy damages. In a moment of discouragement Marjorie had become privately engaged to Sir Alexander MacGown, Member for a Scottish borough, and he takes up the quarrel, insulting Michael in the House. Soames, retired from business life without enough to occupy his mind, worries about the affair which his action has precipitated unaware that in Society everyone is slandered daily without hard feeling. Marjorie is one of the most talked-of young women in the fast set in London. Her creed is, "Not to let a friend down; not to give a man away; not to funk; to do things differently from other people; to be always on the go; not to be 'stuffy'; not to be dull." Her motto is, "Live dangerously." She is half in love with the young American, Jon's brother-in-law, Francis Wilmot, and encourages his devotion in spite of Sir Alexander's protests. Francis tries in vain to make peace between his two friends. Soames sees the lawyer about a settlement, but they will not accept the money without the apology which Fleur will not make. As Marjorie tells her grandfather, the marquess, "She won't, unless I do, and I won't unless she does." Marjorie begins to resent the way the case which she had initiated takes charge of her, and deprives her of initiative. Once the machinery of the quarrel is put in motion nothing can stop its revolutions. When the case comes to trial the defence is a clever arraignment of the modern view of morals in terms of personal antagonism. Marjorie is practically forced to admit that she has had a liaison, and her lawyers ask for a settlement on the basis of costs. Fleur has won the case in court, but Society resented moral superiority and sympathized with the victim; so Marjorie wins the battle though her engagement is broken. Fleur's heart had been in her collection of celebrities and her powers as hostess, and her social defeat makes her morbidly sensitive. She asks Michael to give up politics, the career that has his interest but to her is just a stunt, and take her for a trip around the world. She will not wait until the long vacation when he would be free to go, and he decides that he can not leave while Parliament is in session. It is decided that Soames shall take Fleur, and Michael shall join them later. There is another woman, Nora Curfew, who is unselfish and of superior character in contrast to the shallow, vain Fleur. Fleur resents Michael's admiration for her. The book ends with the departure of Fleur and Soames, and Michael returning to the empty house.

SIX CHARACTERS IN SEARCH OF AN AUTHOR, (Sei personaggi in cerca d'autore), a comedy in the making, by Luigi Pirandello (1922). A company of actors are rehearsing a play on the bare stage of a theatre when the play opens. They are interrupted by the entrance of six characters, a father, mother, son, stepdaughter, and two younger children, a boy and a girl. The father acts as spokesman and tells the manager that the author who created them either no longer desires to put them in a drama, or is unable to do so, and they wish to enact the tragedy which exists only in them. The characters contradict each other as they try to outline the plot of the play they ask the company to perform. Each character has a different conception of the way things happened, the truth from his point of view. The father and stepdaughter were evidently more nearly completed than the others in the author's mind, and dominate the scene. Before their play begins the mother had fallen in love with her husband's secretary, and her husband sent her away to live with him, rather than have her moping at home. She left her baby son with his father, and the secretary was the father of the three younger children. The son was educated away from home and has grown up almost a stranger to his father. The father had been interested in the other family, and had tried to get acquainted with the stepdaughter, so they had moved away to another city to hide from him. Recently the secretary had died leaving his family in poverty, and they had returned to their old home. The mother did sewing for a fashionable dressmaker, Madame Pace, who gave her the work in order to get in touch with the eighteen-year-old stepdaughter, who acts as intermediary between them. The play the family group represents begins with the scene in Madame Pace's establishment with the Madame's introduction of the father to the stepdaughter. The mother arrives in time to prevent her husband from making illicit love to her daughter. The father brings the mother and her children home to live with him. The father complains to the manager of the injustice that fixes him in a situation when he is discovered in a place where he should not have been in a moment which should have remained hidden. The manager decides to rehearse their play with his company, using the six characters as the manuscript of the uncompleted book, which the prompter shall take down in shorthand as the scenes are acted. The arrangement of the stage to look like Madame Pace's shop brings her to join the group, and she begins her preliminary conversation with the stepdaughter. The mother, overcome with indignation, and sorrow as she watches them, protests against re-living the torture of the spectacle. The actors then take their places to re-enact the scene, but this is not satisfactory to the characters, who feel that their reality is misrepresented. It is finally arranged that the characters shall go through the parts, and the company shall make their own artistic representation of the play afterward. The manager has to tell the father and stepdaughter that on the stage each character can not tell all his troubles to the audience in a monologue like an hour's lecture. The stepdaughter accuses the father of wanting to get his "noble remorses" and "moral torments" all acted. She continually questions his interpretation of his motives, and insults the son, who tries to separate himself from the family whom he regards with disdain and contempt. The son says that he stands for the will of the author, who decided not to put the characters on the stage and show everyone their shame. The father drives the manager distracted with discussion of the difference between illusion and reality.

He contends that the reality of the characters is immutable, forever attached to this scene the author had in his mind, while that of the manager and company is "a mere transitory and fleeting illusion, taking this form to-day and that to-morrow," according to changing conditions and circumstances. In spite of the continuous conversation between the characters and the manager the play goes on. The little girl is drowned in the fountain, and the little boy shoots himself. The intruding characters carry the boy off the stage, and the mystified and enraged manager curses them and the day he has lost over their play. The author discusses the problems of dramatic art and its representation in the theatre as well as the antithesis between life and art in the satiric dialogue of this play.

SKIN GAME, THE, a tragi-comedy, by John Galsworthy (1920). The theme is the class spirit, illustrated in the contest between an aristocratic English county family, the Hillcrists, and the pushing manufacturer, Hornblower. Hillcrist, hard pressed for money, had sold a piece of land to the newcomers. His wife refused to call on them, and the people that count follow her example. Hornblower decides to drive the Hillcrists out by extending his potteries to within three hundred yards of their house, with the purchase of a neighboring estate. If the Hillcrists will agree to treat his family as social equals he will reconsider putting chimneys on the Centry estate. War is thus declared; as Mr. Hornblower has broken his word about evicting the tenants on the property he already owns, Mr. Hillcrist would not trust him to keep his word. The two youngest members of the respective families, Jill Hillcrist and Rolf Hornblower, are friendly and regret the "war." Miss Mullins, who owns the Centry, decides that she can get a high price for the coveted property by selling at auction, and letting the Hornblowers and Hillcrists bid against each other. The estate is run up to three times what it is worth, and sold to Mr. Hornblower, who gets a stranger in the rear of the room to make the last bid for him, and the Hillcrists believe that the Duke has bought the place until Hornblower undeceives them. In the meantime Mrs. Hillcrist has sent Dawker, their lawyer, to London, to look up some damaging facts about Chloe, the Hornblower daughter-in-law. She notices at the auction that Chloe is visibly affected at the sight of Dawker talking with a strange man. She warns Mr. Hornblower that as he fights foul, so must they. Mrs. Hillcrist explains to her husband the weapon she proposes to use against the Hornblower family, and at first he refuses to use a piece of knowledge about the character of a woman, but finally agrees to allow Mrs. Hillcrist to tell Mr. Hornblower, but the information is to go no further. Mrs. Hillcrist writes a note asking Mr. Hornblower to call at eleven, and arranges with Dawker to be present with his London agents, and the proof of Chloe's guilt. Chloe suspects what is happening and sends for Dawker, and tries to bribe him to silence. She adores Charlie, her husband, and begs him not to spoil her life, but he tells her she is only a pawn in the game. In the morning Hornblower hears from Mrs. Hillcrist that Chloe had been employed in divorce cases as a professional corespondent. He does not believe it and brings Chloe to deny it, but when the proofs are laid before her she breaks down. Her own thought is that Charlie must not know, that she is faithful to him, and she asks Hornblower to keep the secret for the sake of the grandchild soon to be born. He calls Mrs. Hillcrist back and asks her terms. She demands that he sell them the Centry at the original low price, and when the deed is signed she and Dawker both swear that they will not tell what they know. The victory brings little joy to Jill and her father. Jill declares her intention of going to call on Chloe to show that she is friendly, though her father and mother try to dissuade her. She reports that

Chloe looks like a lost soul. Chloe herself comes in the French window to ask them to make up some story to tell Charlie, who suspects there is something, and has threatened to come to the Hillcrists for an explanation. Charlie Hornblower is announced, and Chloe stands outside the window. They try telling him that his wife had been accused of taking money as a clerk. He tells them he has just heard the truth from Dawker. As Charles leaves, Hillcrist and Jill go out to find Chloe. Mr. Hornblower arrives to demand the deed which he tells Mrs. Hillcrist and Dawker was won from him by "false pretenses and treachery," since even his own servants know about it. He makes a grab for the deed in the lawyer's pocket, and the two men are struggling together, when Hillcrist and Charlie Hornblower come in bringing Chloe from "the gravelpit" — just breathing. Hornblower refuses their aid, telling his sons to take her to the car. The Hornblowers are beaten and driven out, but at the cost of violating every principle of consideration and decency. Mr. Hillcrist says, "When we began this fight we had clean hands — are they clean now? What's gentility worth if it can't stand fire?"

SKYWARD, by Richard Evelyn Byrd (1928). The author's public reputation is due largely to his two spectacular flights to the North Pole and across the Atlantic Ocean. This book tells the story of the years of preparation that brought him to success and testifies that exploring the air and experiments by scientifically-trained men has made commercial flying safe. Many fatal accidents in the past were due to pioneering work, flights made for the promotion of aviation, part of the progress of any form of science. For ten years prior to his trans-Atlantic flight he had studied weather conditions over the North Atlantic, and on this trip he learned that his information was still defective. Aviation's greatest enemy "fog" is being conquered by science. The increase of landing fields throughout the country is a great factor of safety. His first experience in flying was at the naval flying station at Pensacola during the World War. He tells of the thrill of his first flight, and then of his first flight alone. In August, 1918, he was sent to Nova Scotia as commander of the United States Naval Air Station at Halifax. This was a disappointment as he had made application to fly one of the NC flying-boats across the Atlantic. After the War when the flight was undertaken men who had had foreign duty were not permitted to be members of the expedition. Byrd was one of the eight men formed into the "Trans-Atlantic Flight Section of the Bureau of Aeronautics," and helped plan for this first crossing, and through the efforts of Commander Towers was permitted to go with him in the NC-3 to assist in navigation "in the first two legs of the flight," as far as Newfoundland. He requested permission of the Navy Department to fly alone across the Atlantic but was dissuaded by the acting Secretary, Theodore Roosevelt, from making the attempt, in view of the fact that the airplane engine of that time was still unreliable in long flights. In 1921 he was detailed to join the ZR-2 (or R-38, as the English called her), the great dirigible which exploded over the Humber River on a trial flight. By missing the train he arrived too late to get a place on the ship and thus his life was saved. With the MacMillan expedition to Greenland in the summer of 1925 he did his first exploring in the Arctic Regions, and met Floyd Bennett, who became his friend and later his pilot, when he organized his own expedition to the Pole. The story of this thrilling adventure is told in detail from the financing of the expedition to the "non-stop flight around the world" made in the few minutes in which the "Josephine Ford" circled the Pole. The book quotes President Coolidge's speech at the presentation of the medals to Byrd and Bennett in which he calls attention to the progress of science since Peary's expedition in 1910. "Then Peary's trip to the Pole on dog sleds took about two-thirds of a year. He reached his goal on April 6. It was September 6 before news of the achievement reached the outside world. The naval officer of 1926, using an American invention, the airplane, winged his way from his base, at King's Bay, Spitzbergen, and back again in less than two-thirds of a day; and a few hours later the radio had announced the triumph to the four quarters of the earth. . . . " The chapter, "This Hero Business," describes his reception in New York and Washington after this spectacular success. The trans-Atlantic flight in 1928, was undertaken in the interests of science, not in competition with the planes in the race to be the first to reach Paris. Byrd used a three-engined plane and carried a crew of three men, Acosta, Balchen, and Noville, and about eight hundred pounds of scientific equipment. They arrived over Paris in a dense fog which prevented them from making a landing, and were forced to come down on the sea near a lighthouse on the French coast. The extra men to make observations and prove that passengers could be carried and the weight of the equipment made it impossible that fuel enough could be carried to keep the plane in the air over France until morning made a safe landing possible. Byrd sets forth his plans for the Antarctic expedition on which he plans to embark in September, 1928. In the preface, Admiral Moffett gives Byrd credit for a large part in the achievement of a Bureau of Aeronautics for the Navy. The chapter, "Political Interlude," is Byrd's description of the fight between the conservatives and General Mitchell, the radical, who wanted the separate air service, which Byrd believed that aviation was not sufficiently advanced to justify.

SO BIG, by Edna Ferber (1924). Selina's father, a professional gambler, gave his daughter her philosophy of life. He said to her, "I want you to realize that this whole thing is just a grand adventure. . . . The trick is to play in it and look at it at the same time. . . . The more kinds of people you see, and the more things you do, and the more things that happen to you, the richer you are. Even if they're not pleasant things. . . . " At his death she left Miss Fister's school in Chicago, and started to earn her living teaching a country school in a Dutch farming settlement on the outskirts of the city. Her gay spirit saw beauty in the fields of red and green cabbages like burgundy and jade, and gradually she grew into sympathy with her environment and abandoned all her girlhood dreams to marry Pervus De Jong, an illiterate truck farmer to whom cabbages were cabbages and nothing more. Her life became the monotonous routine of cooking, cleaning, mending, scrubbing and even work in the fields. When her husband died she drove her wagon of produce to the market in Chicago with no protection but her little son Dirk. The buyers refused to purchase of a woman, so she tried the round of private houses, until a policeman stopped her for peddling without a license. Her school friend, Julie Hempel, now Mrs. Arnold, rescues her, and August Hempel, once the butcher but now a great packer, provides the financial backing that enables Selina to make her farm a success. Her toil sends Dirk, nicknamed "So Big" from his baby measurement, to college, and makes an architect of him. Paula, Julie's daughter, loves Dirk though she prefers to marry a millionaire. Her influence leads him to give up architecture to get rich quick selling bonds. Roelf Pool, Selina's young boy friend of her first year in High Prairie, who shared her love for beauty, comes back from Paris a great sculptor. When Dallas O'Mara, the artist Dirk wants to marry, prefers Roelf, he sees his own failures, and through their eyes the success his mother has made out of the everyday business of living. He says at the end, "You're nothing but a rubber stamp, Dirk De Jong."

SON OF MAN, THE, by Emil Ludwig (1928).　The times are out of joint.　Jew hates Gentile: Roman conqueror, Greek merchant, Samaritan countryman.　The priestly Jewish overlords have conformed only in letter to the will of their victors.　At least, so with the Sadducees.　The lower house of the Sanhedrin is not so easily quelled or converted.　Conservatism pitched against Radicalism, yet even their radicalism tempered by the fanatical, self-righteous airs of "those set apart" or the "pure."　From their ranks only one "pure in heart" has stepped forth: Hillel, greatest of the Pharisees.　Of late Philo, the Greek-Jew, has elaborated Hillel's teachings and attained some popularity.　Still the promise of a redeeming Messiah appeals most to the Chosen Children of Israel, and they dream nightly of His coming deliverance.

A stripling moons and dreams about the hillside near his home town of Nazareth.　He is later to dwell again on this same hillside in reminiscence, as any normal being takes pleasure in recalling memories of early environment.　A few years and a peculiar unrest seizes the lad of nineteen, an unquiet sense of responsibility that dares him to impart his conclusions about politics, and man's worldly estate as well as his conduct in life, to more than the select few intimates in whom he has hitherto confided.　He hears of John the Baptist, the man who deigns to live with and benefit his fellowmen (so different from the Essenes of the selfish hermitage).　Jesus goes on pilgrimage to Jordan and is baptized in its waters.　Here first, in conjunction with an act of John, he takes his departure from the easy life of a self-sufficient carpenter.　Instead of returning in caravan to Nazareth, Jesus secludes himself in the fastnesses of the desert, there to commune with himself and that inner voice of promise.　Some times another prompting, equally enticing at first, begs him to forego such sacrifice in service to his fellowmen; eggs him on to individual worldly success.　Even in later days as prophet this harassing devil tempts him to tread circumvently, that he may avoid the scourge of the priests.　This theme of recurrent temptation — Ludwig makes plain the choice of two courses open to Jesus as to every other great leader — portrays him far more humanly than other biographers have dared to, while subtracting nothing from him as the Superman.　The evolution of Jesus into Christ is dwelt upon.　Each crucial point in that development is attributed to John's influence over him — he would seem peculiarly dependent on signs as the Baptist occasions them: John's capture opening the field to him; John's death necessitating an avowal of his rôle of Messiah.　Jesus is a changed man in temperament.　No longer the gentle expositor, he becomes proud enough, for all his humility, to outface his mother and disown her; to confound his simple followers with his words and then belabor them for their imperfect comprehension.　But there are recompenses in the metamorphosis.　He so far forgets the commandments bred into him, a true Jew, as to finally bring his healing mission to heathen, too.　He is transformed into a man for many races.

SON OF THE MIDDLE BORDER, A, by Hamlin Garland (1914).　An autobiography which is the story of two pioneer families, the Garlands and the McClintocks, in the Middle West of the years following the Civil War, a picture of a heroic period of frontier life in the annals of American history.　The author's father, Richard Garland, New England born, returned from the War eager for new lands and distant horizons.　The family migrate from Wisconsin to Iowa, to Minnesota, and finally South Dakota, the home-loving wife and sons sharing the wanderings of the pioneer father though not his enthusiasm. Richard Garland's father and mother came west by way of the Erie Canal, and it was Hugh McClintock, the father of Richard's future wife, who cared for the new arrivals in a lonely cabin at the edge of the Wisconsin village when it was discovered that their twelve-year-old daughter, Susan, was ill with small-pox. The large McClintock family were "sons of the border bent to the work of breaking sod and building fence quite in the spirit of sportsmen . . . reaping was a game, husking corn a test of endurance and skill, threshing a 'bee'," with barn-raisings, harvestings, and rail-splittings, and music and singing and dancing to cheer the evenings. The Garland family and David McClintock together leave this pleasant community life to take up farms on the distant prairie. Hamlin at ten years of age does a man's work on the new farm, driving the plough and breaking the soil for ten hours a day through the months of October and November. In the winter he goes to the country school, and has for seat-mate, Burton Babcock, who becomes his chum and life-long friend. The Garland boys, Hamlin and Frank, rose at 5 A.M. before daylight to milk the cows and curry the horses before breakfast. The author describes the beauties of the prairie in the different seasons, the wheat field, "the corn-field, dark-green and sweetly cool," the charm of the great open spaces, and the birds and wild life, but emphasizes the ceaseless round of unremitting toil. With good crops the farmers bought more land and more farm machinery, doubling the labors of planting and harvesting, and the drudgery of the housewife's dishwashing, cooking, sewing and churning did not lessen. There were neighborhood gatherings for singing, and the social life of the Grange. At the end of Hamlin's schooldays he and his brother Frank make a pilgrimage eastward to see Boston, New York, and Washington, working on farms as they tramped through the country to help pay the way. The family moved to new land in Dakota, and the horrors of the winter in a pine shanty on the plains decide Hamlin to break away from the farm and go to Boston to some way prepare himself to be a teacher. Then follows his struggle to establish himself in Boston first as a teacher, and then as a writer. The days of the first winter he spends reading in the Public Library, his only exercise an occasional slow walk, since he could not afford to waste his scanty food in physical effort, and he was too thinly clad to go out except when the sun shone. He attended free lectures at the Young Men's Union, and regardless of his poverty paid thirty-five cents for standing place to see Edwin Booth in Shakespeare's plays. Just as his money gives out and he is going to look for carpenter work to earn some more comes his opportunity to teach. He sends for his brother to join him, and Frank works as an accountant, and later goes on the stage in James Herne's company. One more summer he works on the Dakota farm, and sees Nature as beautiful as ever, but "all the gilding of farm life melted away" to the friends of his youth as well as to himself. Mr. Howells encourages him to use his city-trained pen to depict the sordid monotony of farm life and the enforced slavery of the pioneer. The book closes when the author is thirty-three with the return of his broken though undaunted parents to the home village in Wisconsin from which their pioneering twenty-five years before had begun, to a home their son has provided for their old age. A sequel to this book is "A Daughter of the Middle Border."

SONS AND LOVERS, by D. H. Lawrence (1913). A story of the relations of a mother and a son, and a picture of the life of a coal-miner's family. Mrs. Morel is a woman of superior breeding married to a drinking, brutal miner. She lives in her children, and they idolize her. After the death of her oldest son, William, she sets her affections on Paul, her second son, whose life, mental, spiritual, and physical, is minutely described. Arthur and Annie are the two younger children. There is an interesting description of Lily Western, "Gyp," the shallow girl to whom William was engaged. Paul has the artistic temperament and a talent for drawing. As soon as he is old enough he becomes a junior clerk in a factory, and studies art in his free time. Part 2 of the book deals with his love affairs with Miriam and Clara. They fail to satisfy him as his mother absorbs everything in him except his passions. Miriam is a shy, beautiful girl, who idealizes him, and is interested in his art work. She battles valiantly for him against his mother, and in spite of her nun-like purity gives herself to his desire, but can not hold him even by this sacrifice. He drifts into a passionate friendship with Clara Dawes, separated from her husband, and working in the factory with him. The puritanical Mrs. Morel condones this affair with a married woman, because it will not take her son away from her. Mrs. Morel dies after a long painful illness, and Paul is left alone in a derelict state. Miriam had not the courage to "take him and relieve him of the responsibility of himself," though she would sacrifice herself for him, and that he did not want.

SORRELL AND SON, by Warwick Deeping (1926). A story of the perfect comradeship between a father and son. The War has ruined the business in which Captain Stephen Sorrell, M.C., had a clerical post; his wife has deserted him. When the story opens Sorrell is leaving sordid Lavendar Street in London to go to the cathedral town of Staunton, where he has been promised employment in an antique shop. His one ambition is to give his schoolboy son, Christopher, a better preparation for the battle of life than he has had himself. Arrived in Staunton with only a few shillings left he finds that Mr. Verity, the antique dealer, has died suddenly. Without means to return to London he resolves to take any work that offers to support the boy, and becomes porter in a third-rate hotel conducted by handsome, vulgar, sensual Florence Palfrey, who delights in humiliating him because he is a gentleman. He bears her insults with dignity and performs the menial tasks assigned to him with stoical resignation. Another ex-officer, Tom Rolland, arrives at the Inn, makes friends with Sorrell, and meets Christopher. Rolland, musician and dilettante, is about to open a hotel at Winstonbury, and he asks Sorrell to be a second porter at the Pelican. Life at the Pelican is pleasant until the arrival of Buck, the head-porter, an ex-service man who had saved Rolland's life. After a few months Rolland discovers the kind of mean bully Buck is and discharges him. Sorrell is now head-porter and able to save more money for Christopher's education. Christopher leaves the town school and the genial, unconventional curate, Robert Porteous, takes him as a pupil. The fortune of the Pelican is made by the arrival of a honeymoon couple, the famous screen stars, Ethel Frobisher and Duncan Scott. Rolland respects their desire to avoid publicity. However, as they are leaving the hotel their car has a collision with a motor lorry and Ethel is injured and brought back. Her life is saved by a great surgeon and fourteen-year-old Kit decides he will study medicine. The Pelican becomes well-known and popular over night. Kit wins his scholarship at Cambridge and Sorrell is made manager of the Pelican and co-director of Rolland's other hotels. Dora, Kit's mother, now the widow of two wealthy husbands, seeking a new interest, makes advances to her young son, but fails to turn him from his devotion to his father and his work. He is successful in his medical studies in London, and popular with his fellow-students. A love affair with Mary Jewett, who sells programs in the theatre where one of Rolland's musical comedies is a success, puts an end to his restlessness of sex. She dies in his arms in the hospital!

after a street accident. Christopher receives a hospital appointment, performs his first major operation in the crowded amphitheatre, and goes on to success. Sorrell has plenty of money to provide for his son and has insisted that he need not be self-supporting until he has finished his studies. Mrs. Rolland presents Christopher to Molly Pentreath, the sister of his college friend, and he finds the tomboy of thirteen has become a most attractive young woman and a successful novelist. He can not understand her modern ideas of independence but loves her and fights her determination not to marry and to consider sex a mere incident. Sorrell understands her keenness for her work and insistence upon individual freedom. Kit admits to his father that he is jealous of her career but he contends that she should not bargain and hang back. If she would trust him she would find him a comrade not "a little petty domestic bore." Molly's surrender comes when Kit cuts his left hand through the rubber glove when he is operating and gets septic poisoning. She gives him the will to live that makes him fight for his life and win. Sorrell, selfless as always, lets them go away for a honeymoon without spoiling their happiness by letting Christopher know that he is ill. When Kit returns it is too late to operate for cancer. The young people reproach themselves for their blindness, but Sorrell is cheerful and indomitable in suffering. A new humility softens Molly's modernity; a new understanding enters Kit's seriousness. They have the courage and wisdom to put an end to the pain for Sorrell.

SOUL ENCHANTED, THE, by Romain Rolland (Vol. I. Annette and Sylvie, 1925; Vol. II. Summer, 1925; Vol. III. Mother and Son, 1927), is the life record of Annette Rivière. Not as a thesis nor a theory does the author claim attention for this story, rather, "Behold in this work merely the inner history of a life that is sincere, fertile in joys and sorrows, not exempt from contradictions, abounding in errors, yet always struggling to attain, in default of inaccessible Truth, that harmony of spirit which is our supreme truth." This struggle of a woman to realize her own soul possibilities opens in her father's home in Paris, six months after his sudden passing. Raoul Rivière, a well known architect and man of the world, is comfortably off. In these last two years of the illness which was to be his last, he had demanded a large share of his motherless daughter's attention. He was used to being the centre of attention with women, and now that there were no others he exacted from that blooming sprig of womanhood in her early twenties, a devotion she was only too happy to give him. Looking over his papers after death as she needs must, being sole heiress to his estate, she discovered, among other letters from light loves, a series extending over a long period of years, part of which were from one who signed herself Delphine and the remainder from a young girl, Sylvie, who called him father. Shaken thus rudely out of her sorrow and jealous that another had shared with her that place in her father's heart which she had believed hers alone, Annette seeks Sylvie, and after a few jealous manœuvres, the two half-sisters become close friends. Although certain characteristics of the father in each proclaim their common parentage, the girls are very dissimilar. Sylvie is lithe, graceful, sometimes a sleeping cat, sometimes watchful, malicious, a biting cat. She was a girl with all the gamin impudence and charm of the Parisian lower classes. Annette in contrast was big of bone and body, fresh of skin and naïve of heart, a sheltered girl of the upper bourgeoisie. Sylvie was self-contained, gave a due proportion of herself to her work, her lovers, her sister, but greater-hearted Annette could do nothing by halves, must give herself wholly to those she loved. So the younger girl soon enjoyed the ascendency in their relationship. Nor would she consent to let Annette share her home and fortune with her in any degree until she became ill and then, in convalescence, she did come to live with her sister for a time. During a trip to the mountains the two sisters almost become enemies, for both attract a handsome young Italian, Tullio, staying at the same hotel. Sylvie's gayety and daring prove more successful with the young man than Annette's proud dignity despite the advantage she possessed as a good sportswoman. Just in time to save their friendship the sisters depart but not before the incident has aroused Annette's sleeping passion. She goes into society again and is courted by two young men, Marcel Franck and Roger Brissot. Annette's preference for the latter is skilfully turned into an engagement by his mother almost before the girl realizes. For a time she believes herself contented with this handsome young man, obviously already on the road to political success. Her estate is contiguous with that of his family. In every way they seem fitting mates. Then, on a visit to his people Annette realizes that her personal life will be completely swallowed up in his; his clients and career, his party and its dogmas, his family and its traditions, his world. She, who had her own life, her own world, must give it all up. They go for a walk and she tells him her decision to part. He is so disconsolate that the girl's pity and then her passion for him is aroused, for she had cared for him that way. Even when in their youthful anguish this breaks all bounds, she will not consent to marry him. She returns to her home on the Quai de Boulogne there to await the coming of her child. Sylvie, who has enjoyed her lovers as she has her life from day to day, is astounded at Annette's lack of discretion, and urges her to leave the city for the next few months. So in the neighborhood of the Savoyard lakes she passes the winter until her child is born. Even before she lost her fortune through trusting too entirely to the good faith of M. Grenu, her attorney, she found she was unable to cope with the hostility of outraged bourgeoise respectability nor did she like better the assumption of freedom with which her former admirer, Marcel Franck, treated her. She now made her home with Sylvie, spending her days giving lessons to private pupils. Into this dreary routine, came a former schoolmate, a studious man who loved her and would have married her. But, though she suspected that he did not wish to hear the whole truth about her past, nothing but a complete revelation would satisfy her honest nature and this was more than his strictly Catholic conscience could condone. Marcel Franck now came back into her life after some years of separation. In his maturity she found him a mellow, genial comrade as they worked together over a catalogue of a collection of art of which he had charge. But Franck respected nothing in life. "Annette could more easily endure not being respected than losing respect — her own — for life." They parted. Marc, Annette's little son, had been much in the charge of his aunt Sylvie as he was growing up. Then Sylvie's little girl, Odette, was born. The child showed a great fondness for her aunt Annette. One day, left in the other room alone she fell from the window and was killed. Sylvie lived in stony despair until she found relief, first through séances in which she believed she again conversed with her little girl and later through a superficial cynicism and enhanced frivolity. Through friends Annette now met a doctor, Philippe Villard, and his wife, a woman who affected a doll-like lack of intelligence. Philippe, who had known a hard struggle before success was reached respected Annette's integrity of purpose, her courage and her matured loveliness. It was not long before the two became lovers. Annette felt that this Indian summer passion was hers, that Philippe was the man to whom she might fully surrender. Then his wife, knowing that she would never receive her rights through appealing to her husband, shrewdly threw herself on Annette's magnanimity and succeeded in winning her pledge that she would give up

Philippe. Marc, while knowing nothing of this, with adolescent sensitiveness perceived that there was mystery and tragedy in his mother's life. Annette now turned hungrily to the young boy for love. He had never made his mother as much his confidant as his aunt who better understood his temperament. The wealth of his mother's love threw him back on himself, made him all the more reticent. For a time after the War broke out, Annette, overcome with the morbid miasma that had spread all through the house where they lived, and wishing to take her boy from the city streets at such a time, sought a teaching post in a college in central France. Marc preferred to be shut up in a boys' school rather than go with her. When the boy escapes surveillance and runs wild in the city night, his aunt finds him and takes charge of him. Meanwhile Annette has become the friend of Germain, a wounded young officer of a noble family in the district where she teaches. In the name of their friendship and because he can not live long he begs her to be the intermediary between himself and a former German friend, Franz, now in a detention camp. The two young men loved each other as Damon and Pythias. As death approached, Germain goes to the mountains of Switzerland and there, with the help of Pitan, a socialist workman who lives in her house, at considerable risk to both, Annette succeeds in bringing Franz. Germain dies happy at seeing his friend and filled with love for the noble woman who has done so much for him. As Annette consoles Franz she loses her detached affection. She returns to Paris where Sylvie and Marc have become very anxious about her. Pitan had taught young Marc something of his gentle socialism and even better than that had awakened the boy's pride in the strange and courageous woman who is his mother. For so many years he had shut her out of his love and confidence and now it seemed to the lonely boy she had filled her life with the interests of others. He feared he had lost her forever. On her first return from Switzerland he is hurt by her withdrawal. Then she leaves him again for Franz. But Franz has recovered from his grief with the help of the two ladies of a near-by chalet, with the younger of whom he appears to be in love. Although Annette reëstablishes her power over him, she decides that she will give up this young man whom she has grown to love. Her return to Marc brings her the reward of years of struggle. The barriers of diffidence and reserve between mother and son are broken down. He asks about his father and when she tells him, seeks out Roger Brissot whose success as a socialist politician and speaker attracts the boy. But he never tries to know him further after listening to that polished demagogue addressing an audience. He calls his mother both father and mother. She has the happiness of knowing that he has become a man of sincerity and a courage which she doubts not will surpass her own in time of trial.

SOUL OF AN IMMIGRANT, THE, by Constantine M. Panunzio (1921). In his foreword Constantine Panunzio explains that he is writing the story of his experiences as an immigrant to suggest "what helps or hinders the many in or from becoming useful American citizens." Panunzio spent his early boyhood in his birthplace, Molfetta, a town in ancient Apulia. His grandmother decided to bring him up to follow in his patriot grandfather's footsteps, to become "First a priest, than a teacher, and at last a patriotic statesman." Though happy in the Italian life, celebrating the many feast days in a large circle of relatives, the strict upbringing imposed upon him, by both grandmother and father, together with an increasing love for ships and the sea, finally led him at thirteen to enrol as a sailor boy on a coasting schooner. When Panunzio was eighteen he took ship for America, which he imagined a vast beautiful country, "covered with forests, leisurely-winding rivers and great stretches of farm lands," with perhaps a few cities. He found it a place where foreigners were not made welcome and his only wish was to make enough money for his return passage. An American "padrone" hired him and his French sailor friend, Louis, to work with "peek and shuvle," which was the only work available for Italians, they were told. Soon they realized that all their money went to the "padrone" and the company store, so they found new work in a factory full of Russians. The Russians called them "dagoes" and forced them out. Next they fell into the clutches of the peonage system in a Maine lumber camp. Here the southern Italian suffered terribly from privation and cold until he and Louis escaped and separated. Very lonely without his only friend in a strange land, Panunzio found work in a Maine village of the type which led him to wonder why people speak of cities as being the centres of vice. Here he learned bad English, bad manners and in his innocence became involved in bootlegging. He was not able to collect his pay and in trying to reach an Italian lawyer was arrested for stealing a ride on a train. He supposed the policeman who arrested him was going to help him, but he was locked in a cell without explanation and spent a night of misery and homesickness. The kind judge somewhat restored his faith in mankind, but he was sent back to his former place. Through a kind old woman he at last escaped and went to a fine type of Yankee home. Inspired by one of the daughters, a school teacher, he decided to go to school. After a number of difficulties he was kindly welcomed into the Maine Wesleyan Seminary. During three years he worked his way through the four-year course and lived down the prejudice against a "dago" in order to take part in the school activities. He succeeded in this so well that he was elected to represent the school at the State University interscholastic oratorical contest, which he won. He went through Wesleyan University in Connecticut and entered Boston University School of Theology. He speaks with warm enthusiasm of his teachers as types of American gentlemen. During his school and college years he learned to appreciate American fair play. He feels great admiration for American life and institutions, but sums up what he has lost in this country as follows: loss of trustful simplicity, manners and respect for law, health, from overwork, and loss of thoroughness and exactness in work because of "the rush" of American life. In the spring of 1914, Panunzio became a naturalized American citizen after struggling through "the barbed wire entanglement" of requirements and delays, which seems to him almost insurmountable for an average immigrant. He found the treatment by officials most discourteous, but was impressed by the dignity of the judge when it came to the final oath. Panunzio's first experience in the work to which he later devoted himself occurred in his preparatory school days when he took a summer position in an Italian mission. In college he did more work on these lines and conducted an Americanization class in a factory town. His endeavor to expound the principles of democracy received little attention because the Italian factory hands had no interest in "talk" while the boss in the factory kicked them and called them "dagoes." For four years he served as pastor in American churches, but failed to obtain the pastorate of an old Boston church because of his race. Then he became the head of a Protestant Mission in the heart of the Italian tenement house district in North Boston. Here he received support and comfort from a man whom he calls his American "Big Brother." He learned the inner difficulties of the life of these segregated colonies and worked particularly with children. He comes to the conclusion that the problem of helping these people to become Americanized is an extremely difficult one and still to be solved. When the Great War came, Panunzio, unable to get into the army, went across with the Y. M. C. A. and gave many talks about America's coming into the, war to encourage the Italian soldiers at the front. It was while he was in Italy that he learned once and for all that America was home to him.

SOUTH, THE STORY OF SHACKLETON'S LAST EXPEDITION, 1914–1917, by Sir Ernest Shackleton (1926). In his preface Sir Ernest Shackleton explains that this Expedition was planned on a scale never before attempted in a Polar Expedition and was to be carried out under the British flag. The intention was to cross the Antarctic continent for the first time, a distance of some 1800 miles, the first half over unknown ground, from the Weddell Sea to the Pole. Every step of the trip would be to advance geographical science. Two sledging parties were to operate from the Weddell Sea base, studying fauna, meteorological conditions, making observations and collecting geological specimens. From the opposite side of the Pole another party was to start from the Ross Sea Base and push south to await the Transcontinental party on the top of the Beardmore Glacier. The former party was to start from Buenos Ayres, the latter from Tasmania. Money for the Expedition came from many sources in England, such as the Government, private individuals and schools. Just as they were prepared to start, the World War broke out and the Expedition offered its services to the Government but were told to go ahead as no one expected the War to last. Shackleton and his party on the "Endurance" left South Georgia on December 5, 1914, headed for the Weddell Sea. They travelled slowly southwest through new and old ice packs, seeing many sea birds, blue whales and seals. Often they had to change their course to avoid freezing in the floes in the unseasonably cold Antarctic summer. Some days they passed as many as five hundred icebergs, the highest about one hundred and fifty feet. When they stuck for a time in the ice the men played football and exercised the dogs brought for the sledges. The scientists studied such specimens as they could find. In January they sighted the land discovered by Dr. Bruce, but could not escape the icedrift. They struggled on with coal supply falling low and the dogs ailing until February when hope of reaching land before winter was given up and they built igloos and "dogloos" on the floe or took shelter in the ship's cabins. Now they began to drift northwest. All efforts to get in touch with wireless stations were unsuccessful. The men and dogs exercised and kept up their courage though the sun set for the winter on May first; it appeared in a mirage later. The moon circled in the sky for a while, giving a little light and the Aurora Borealis and mirages played on the horizon. The "Endurance" drifted, wedged in the pack, until September when the melting ice began to pile up and threaten to crush the ship. In October leakage, caused by pressure, became so dangerous that they abandoned the vessel and camped a mile and a half away, taking three small boats, four sledges and all supplies possible with them. In December Shackleton had to make the decision to march westward over the floe in the hope of reaching some island. After advancing seven miles in seven days they gave up the attempt and settled down with rapidly diminishing food. By now blubber had become acceptable nourishment. The men complained very little. After being carried out of reach of the desired land, in April, they decided to take to their boats to avoid being carried into the open Atlantic and out of reach of help. Continually soaked through, half starved and frozen, with lips cracked with thirst, they managed to reach the uninhabited Elephant Island in their little boats. There the men nearly went crazy with joy at being on solid earth again. With winter coming on once more and no hope of anyone looking for them on this island, Shackleton determined to go for help. He started with five men on the eight-hundred-mile trip to South Georgia in a twenty-foot boat. For fourteen days they constantly faced death from violent seas, exposure and cold.   But finally landed in King Haakon Bay on the west coast of South Georgia.   Then Shackleton and two men crossed glaciers and mountains and startled the whalers on the east coast by appearing in their long beards and filthy clothes.   They were made welcome with food and baths and learned that the War, which they had imagined over, was still raging and that the Ross Sea party was marooned.   Help was at once sent to the other three men on the island and then Shackleton went to attempt the rescue of the twenty-two men left on Elephant Island.   In his fourth attempt the ice opened just long enough for them to get through and rescue the survivors on the verge of starvation.   After the South American welcomes were over Shackleton hurried to New Zealand to help the Ross Sea party.   The Ross Sea party in the "Aurora," under Capt. Aeneas Mackintosh, sailed from Tasmania, December 24, 1914, to the Ross Sea.   All the ground, over which they were to lay out stations for Shackleton's party, had already been traversed.   They started from the ship in McMurdo Sound and the Great Ice Barrier, where stores and equipment were landed.   The ship went along the coast and started three sledging parties, which began erecting and stocking rock cairns to guide the Shackleton party.   They found signs of the Scott Expedition at different points. They suffered many discomforts as the dogs were not well trained, and also died, and food ran short.   Though the "Aurora" was fastened by hawsers and anchors, she broke loose and disappeared, leaving ten men and only a few supplies ashore.   In spite of insufficient clothing and food, scurvy, snow blindness and shortage of dogs they accomplished their allotted task and carried the dépots to Beardmore Glacier and left all in readiness for Shackleton.   One man died of illness and Mackintosh and another were lost on thin ice, when attempting to cross alone.   In the meantime the "Aurora" drifted from May to the following April, helpless in the ice and in constant danger, until they were towed into New Zealand.   In December Shackleton arrived in New Zealand in time to join the rescue party that brought back the seven survivors of the Ross Party.   Though the Expedition failed, owing to overwhelming natural obstacles, a large amount of important scientific work was carried out.   The members of the Expedition went into the World War on their return.   The Appendices contain an outline of the scientific work.

SOUTH WIND, by Norman Douglas, a novel (1917).   The vine, the sirocco and good conversation compose a hegemony in the island of Nepenthe.   Villainy, too, is frequently in ascendance, and not a very pretty thing, but to the cultured inhabitants filled with "a clear-cut all-convincing sense of the screamingly funny insignificance of everything" what is villainy?   Often, charm and power, as the visiting Bishop, Mr. Heard of Bampopo, learns during his stay of a fortnight.   Consequently everything of importance equivalent to nothing of importance happens in Nepenthe. The Bishop who, according to the author, "is merely a dummy contrived to reflect the moods of the average reader," during the twelve days between the festivals of Saint Dodekanus and Saint Eulalia, witnesses a murder, a funeral, a slight political disturbance involving the lives of several children and an earthquake.   What is more important, he meets the people of this fantastic colorful place Nepenthe, somehow connected with the kingdom of Italy, and shining on the Thyrrhenian, and opposite the coast of Africa.   Vacationists or inhabitants, the Bishop converses with them, regains his health over the wine glass, and learns that his sympathies have outgrown the ideals of the Church of England.   The evil as well as the good become a warning "of the folly of idolizing dead men and their delusions."   The people Mr. Heard meets are decidedly in favor of living.   There is, for example, the rich old hedonist, Keith, with his expensive lunches and esoteric cooking. There is the Hellenic Count Caloveglia who, in his dictum of measure and moderation, is not averse to forging antiquity in order to regain his family fortunes; in spite of his classicism he is the equal, in other respects, of the American millionaire, Van Koppen. Both, in short, are noble liars but excellent people. Besides there are the young: Mr. Edgar Marten, the Jewish geologist, who finds himself in love, loves, and runs away to escape consequences; Mr. Denis Phipps, who loves or wants to love he knows not what, and chameleon-fashion changes as he receives elderly advice, but never really becomes, not even when faced with the essential mysteries of nature (alias Mr. Marten and his girl Angelina) in the Cave of Mercury. There is the proverbial reprobate in red hair — the local judge Malipizzo. There are the people of shadowy reputation — the self-declared commissioner from South America, Mr. Freddy Parker, owner of the local drinking club; also his lady, a step-sister who, bitten by a mosquito, dies and occasions a roaring success of a funeral (Mr. Keith does not attend). There are the good people: the Englishman, Mr. Eames, recluse, collecting material to annotate the Antiquities of Monsignor Perrilli, historian and Renaissance contemporary of that other legacy of Nepenthe's past, the good Duke Alfred, who killed with a smile and insisted on keeping smiling; Don Francesco, the Catholic priest in favor of women. There are the women themselves: the Duchess who is an American, soon to be converted to Catholicism; Madame Steynlin who loves Peter the Great, young boisterous Peter of that half ostracized, apocalyptic Russian sect called the Little White Cows; Mrs. Meadows, Mr. Heard's cousin, the tiger mother, who in defence of her child pushes her first husband over a cliff and becomes a finer, happier woman; and, not the least among these, Miss Wilberforce of the English Midlands, a true aristocrat of supreme alcoholic temperament, indulging also in a playful habit of divesting herself of her raiment in public on nocturnal occasions. In the words of Count Caloveglia: "this citadel is a microcosm of what the world might be, if men were reasonable. Not all men! A great proportion must be good enough to remain what they are. We could not live without those whose business it is to bring the reasonableness of the few into its proper relief. Were it otherwise, there would be no more reasonableness on earth, would there?"

SPINSTER OF THIS PARISH, by W. B. Maxwell (1922). In the year 1895 Emmeline Verinder was a demure young lady of marriageable age, possessed of her own independent income, living modestly with her parents in a respectable middle-class London atmosphere. At a dinner party she meets and is captivated heart and soul by the social lion of the season, Anthony Dyke, a famous explorer. A few weeks later, her family learns with amazement that their hitherto docile and disciplined daughter has been clandestinely meeting the great man, and that she evidently entertains a strong affection, not to say infatuation, for him. This they oppose at first on the grounds of the unsuitability of Dyke's adventurous personality and profession in the undisturbed late Victorian background; and later, inexorably, upon learning of the existence of Dyke's insane wife, from whom he cannot be legally freed. Their common sense, their pleading, their exhortations, and their commands are alike unheeded by the young lady, who finally, with dignity and orderliness, leaves her father's roof to go to live with her beloved. Anthony makes preparations for another voyage which has for its object the quest of emeralds to be the financial means for an undertaking, the end of all his dreams — the expedition to the South Pole. At the last moment, finding separation intolerable, Emmeline smuggles herself on board the ship and goes to South America with her hero. They spend a few weeks' honeymoon in the colorful Brazilian capital, and then the Victorian young lady announces her intention of joining in the search for emeralds. After suffering unbelievable hardships and extreme heat and cold crossing the highest Andes they come within sight of their goal and find the dead bodies of the friends the trusting Anthony had told of his plans. They had tried to forestall him, and had been deserted by their muleteers. The next morning Anthony and Emmeline wake up to find that their own men, Indians and Spaniards, have left them, frightened by the superstition of a curse on emerald hunting. Anthony's unfailing sense of direction guides them through the wilderness but they have been without food for forty-eight hours before they find refuge in an engineer's camp. The engineers have left and the place is in the hands of a gang of bandits from whom they escape with their lives by Anthony's cool daring and Emmeline's courage. She shoots the man who attacks her lover. They get to Santiago and then to Valparaiso where Anthony sails for Australia, and Emmeline takes another boat back to England. In a flat in Kensington she lives the life of a prim spinster. Secretly she occupies herself with the publication of Anthony's books about his expeditions. For a few weeks or days or hours of each of his return trips to England she hides Anthony in the little flat or they go to Devonshire together. He is trying to raise money for the great adventure, the goal of his life, the discovery of the South Pole. Anonymously Emmeline contributes to the funds. The expedition is poorly outfitted, however, and late in starting, and many others are already in the field. Amundsen reaches the Pole ahead of them all. Anthony loses prestige and returns to Emmeline, disappointed, but not crushed or resentful. Their happiness together is interrupted by the outbreak of the World War. Anthony serves for four years. He writes his Emmie that he believes that anyone could make a fortune by buying ships to sell later when shipping became scarce, and Emmie quietly goes profiteering and makes a fortune to help finance another voyage for Anthony to the Polar Regions. No word comes from Anthony for many months. The newspapers report that he is lost, and Miss Verinder falls ill under the strain of suspense. At last Anthony is found by the relief party and wins through to success and is again the famous man of the hour. In the meantime his wife has died, and he returns to claim Emmeline as his bride. They stand up together in church like boy and girl lovers when the banns are read for Anthony Dyke, widower, and Emmeline Verinder, spinster, of this parish.

STICKS AND STONES, a study of American architecture and civilization, by Lewis Mumford (1924). A careful study of the parallel development of American culture and American architecture. In the Puritan villages of New England the author finds the Middle Ages at their best in the coöperative, communistic organization resembling Sir Thomas More's Utopia. The colonists sought to establish permanent communities as contrasted with the trading posts of Manhattan Island. Like the Greek cities, when the addition of land would make it difficult for the farmers to attend to their civic and religious duties, the original settlement founded another town. Land did not change ownership without the consent of the corporation. The New England village was a garden-city with common holding of land by the community, and coöperative direction of the community. The location of homes did not follow the vagaries of cow paths but the function the land was to perform, the distance from the river, or the purely agricultural tracts, and houses were placed to get a good exposure in summer or in a position to break the path of the wind. There was a decree of the General Court in Massachusetts in 1635 that no dwelling should be more than half a

THE READER'S DIGEST OF BOOKS

mile from the meeting-house. At the end of the seventeenth century the economic basis shifted from the farm to the sea, and with fishing, and commerce, and ship-building came the commercial town, the rise of a wealthy merchant class, and the low farmhouse was converted into a square house with columns and cupola. The architecture of the eighteenth century depended on the architectural handbooks, and thus "from St. Petersburg to Philadelphia seemed cast by a single mind." The mode was called Georgian after the English models followed. This first effect of the Renaissance in America did not destroy the native architecture but perfected it with the introduction of decoration which the Puritan had lacked. The first development of the grand style in the American Renaissance appeared in the manors of Virginia and Maryland, the large estates worked by slaves being not dissimilar to the Roman villas which were the arch type of these pillared mansions. Thomas Jefferson gave America its first classic architecture in Monticello, the Virginia State Capitol, and in the University. Pre-Revolutionary public buildings were built on a domestic scale. Post-Revolutionary fine houses were built on a public scale. The portico was modelled on the Greek temple. A French engineer, Major L'Enfant, laid out Washington in a formal design. The variety of American cities changed to rectangular streets and lots in monotonous pattern, and the chocolate brownstone front of the early nineteenth century was doubtless introduced as a measure of protective coloration in the dingy environment of the factory and the railroad. The development of land speculation as a result of pioneering, and the industrial age were responsible for the degeneration of architecture. The engineer usurped the place of the architect, and the great monuments of the Iron Age after the Civil War were a series of great bridges. H. H. Richardson went back to Romanesque precedent and created some fine buildings, notably Trinity Church, Boston. The World's Fair in 1893 brought the complete rehabilitation of the Roman mode which Mr. Mumford deplores in a chapter "The Imperial Façade." The large-scale manufacture of Portland cement, and the re-introduction of the Roman method of concrete construction, came at this same time. The architects of the classic style were Messrs. McKim and Burnham, and Carrere and Hastings, and their greatest triumphs are railroad stations, the Pennsylvania Terminal, and the Grand Central in New York, and the Union Station in Washington. Mr. Mumford defines a modern building as "an establishment devoted to the manufacture of light, the circulation of air, the maintenance of a uniform temperature, and the vertical transportation of its inhabitants." The city is congested with a population whose density would not be tolerated in a well-designed community devoted to the good life. The buildings of this machine period are "a honey-comb of cubes draped with fire-proof materials," as exemplified in the skyscrapers, and the only architectural decoration is at the point of the highest and lowest stories. What the admirers of this form of architecture can enjoy is the pictures in the magazine and Sunday Supplements taken from a point that is not within the vision of the man in the street. "Our mechanical and metropolitan civilization, with all its genuine advances, has let certain essential human elements drop out of its scheme; and until we recover these elements our civilization will be at loose ends, and our architecture will unerringly express this situation."

STORY TELLER'S STORY, A, by Sherwood Anderson (1924). This autobiography is "the tale of an American writer's journey through his own imaginative world and through the world of facts." His father, a ruined Southern dandy, "had been reduced to keeping a small harness repair shop and when that failed" he became an

itinerant painter of houses, barns and signs. In the winter when there was no
work. he turned showman going the round of the country schoolhouses with a magic
lantern. In the evenings he would be in his element as guest in the farmhouse
telling wonderful tales about himself and his ancestors so vividly that he came to
believe them himself. "No hungry sons about, no sick wife, no grocery bills or rent
to be paid. This the golden age — timeless; there was no past, no future — the
quiet, unsophisticated people in the room were putty to his hands" to listen to the
tale of his escape from a Southern prison in the Civil War. In the meantime his
wife and children had a hard winter. They generally lived in haunted houses rent
free "thus conferring a benefit on the property owner." The author recommends
this system to poets with large families. There is the story of how his mother, by
strategy, laid in a supply of cabbages one winter. It was a Halloween custom in
the town for the young men to go about at night throwing cabbages at the closed
doors to make a tremendous noise and startle the household. His mother rushed
out, scolded and threatened, made a big scene, with the result that the would-be
tormentors singled out the house as a special target. When the evening sport was
over the Andersons gathered in as many as two or three hundred cabbages and
buried them in a trench in the backyard. Anderson tells of his work rolling kegs
of nails in a warehouse, in a bicycle factory, where he sickens at the talk of his fellow
workmen and pretends that he is subject to headaches, quarrels and is worsted in a
fight, and at last gets to be a writer of advertising copy. Whenever he had a little
money ahead saved or won in a gambling place he laid off work, found a cheap room in
a poor street and gave himself up to reading books from the public library. At one
time he was on the way to being a successful manufacturer, but decided that while
buying and selling might be all right for others it was poison for him, and walked
out of his factory without a word, never to return. In the end he finds himself as a
"teller of tales." He says: "The arts are after all but the old crafts intensified,
followed with religious fervor and determination by men who love them and deep
down within him perhaps every man wants more than anything else to be a good
craftsman." He is at his best in the stories of Judge Turner, Alonzo Berners and
Nate Lovett. In "Tar" he writes further autobiography in a fanciful story about
his receptive and imaginative childhood, which he warns the reader in a foreword is
part fact and part fiction. The subject matter is again his drinking, histrionic,
Micawber-like father, his proud, silent mother taking care of her house and children,
and doing washing for the neighbors, and his own experiences selling papers, sticking
to his job just the same the day of his mother's funeral because the money was so
needed. The boy gains "a sense of gentleness," from people defeated by life. There
are the big event of Tar being stung by a bee, the birth of the baby, and above all,
there is the death of the old woman, frozen in the snow, while the dogs play their
antics around her. The author asks whether there could be such a thing as a vulgar
child, and it hardly seems possible when reading of this one, though Tar is far from
being angelic.

STRAIT IS THE GATE, (La porte étroite), translated from the French of André
Gide, by Dorothy Sharp (1924). From childhood Jerome has loved his cousin
Alissa, and it is understood in the family that they shall marry. Alissa is the child
of a Huguenot banker and a gay, light-minded, amorous Creole, who finally runs
away with another man. As the oldest daughter, Alissa has been the confidant
of her unhappy father, this disaster turns her sensitive nature to fanatic piety.
She and Jerome determine that the strait gate and the narrow way shall be their

goal. The neurotic Alissa comes to believe that earthly love which is so susceptible of contamination is an obstacle to salvation, and unsuspected by Jerome she sets out to try to kill her love for him and his for her. She refuses to be engaged to Jerome and attempts to sacrifice herself, in favor of her sister, Juliette, in love with Jerome. His aunt tells the perplexed Jerome that Alissa does not wish to leave her father, and that she does not want to marry before her sister. Abel Vautien, Jerome's school friend, falls in love with Juliette, and Jerome thinks his troubles are over as the two young men plan a double wedding. Abel discovers Juliette's hopeless passion for Jerome, and reproaches Jerome for his blindness. Juliette disappoints Alissa's high ideals by consoling herself with marriage to an elderly wine-grower, Edouard Teissières, whom she does not love, but with whom she settles down to happy domestic life. Jerome finishes school and does his military service, and is bewildered by Alissa's letters and her strange behavior when they meet. He has travelled and studied and freed himself from the dogmas and superstitions of the religion of his youth, while Alissa has become more narrow, and has given up all reading except the most insipid devotional books. Jerome urges her to marry him and strives for the earthly happiness that she has determined shall never be realized. She continues to struggle between sacred and profane love, and after a last farewell hides herself in a nursing home where she pines away and dies. The theme of the story is renunciation in the search for perfection. The author makes a study of introspective piety in the story of the development of Alissa's mind from childhood until her death. She leaves a diary to Jerome which reveals to him her strange attitude toward love, her fear of God, and the self-realization through self-sacrifice carried to the last degree of self-abnegation and maceration, which led her to choose death rather than yield to happiness, though she never won the battle, since she could not root out her secret love for Jerome. Gosse says of this book that it is "a searching analysis of the incompleteness and narrowness of the moral psychology of Protestantism."

STRANGE INTERLUDE, by Eugene O'Neill (1927). This play consists of nine acts in which the dialogue is continually interspersed with monologue asides representing the unspoken thoughts of the characters after the manner of the "stream of consciousness" school of fiction. The heroine, Nina Leeds, the daughter of a New England professor, loses her fiancé, Gordon Shaw, an aviator, in the War. Her selfish father had relied on Gordon's scruples of fair play to persuade him to postpone their marriage until after the War, to keep his daughter for himself, and now that Gordon is dead the frustrated Nina despises herself and hates her father. Grief and loss make her a neurotic. She becomes a nurse in a hospital for disabled soldiers, and gives herself to one after another of them in some mad idea of atonement to Gordon for her unfulfilled love. On the death of her father she transfers her filial love to her childhood friend, Charles Marsden, a novelist, who is too timid to confess his love for her and whose emotions are centred on his mother. Ned Darrell, the doctor at the hospital and Gordon's friend, will not acknowledge to himself that he loves Nina, as he does not want to be swerved from his scientific career. He advises Nina to marry Sam Evans, an honest, ineffectual boy, who adores her, because he thinks motherhood would be the cure of her sacrificial madness. The action of the third act changes from the dead professor's study to the Evans homestead in Northern New York. Nina seems contented and normal, and admits to her mother-in-law that she is going to have a baby. Sam's mother then tells her of the insanity in the family, which Sam knows nothing about, and that she must not let the child be born. The old mother suggests that Nina shall find a healthy father for a child which shall pass as her husband's since they both want a child. At home again Sam is worried about his work which is not going well, and about Nina's health. He brings Dr. Darrell to see her, and Nina tells him her experience and asks him to give her a child for her own sake, for Gordon's and for Sam's. A few months later we see Nina in a small suburban home. Her husband has lost his position and is despondent. Nina and Darrell are in love and she asks him to take her away and marry her. He cannot bring himself to tell the truth to the friendly trusting Sam, and instead announces his intention of going abroad to study, and congratulates him that he is to be a father. Sam is hysterical with pride and joy, and promises Nina that he will make good now. Nina and Sam name the child, Gordon. Darrell is unable to forget Nina, and returns to demand that she shall tell Sam the truth and get a divorce and marry him, but Nina will not consent. Sam is now self-confident and successful, and is a good father for her child. She will keep Darrell as her lover. The sexless Marsden, obsessed with his mother complex, senses the feeling between Nina and Darrell and speaks his tormented jealousy in soliloquy, as he makes banal remarks to the others. Eleven years later in the Evans Park Avenue apartment the tangled relationships continue. Darrell and Marsden have grown rich as investors in Sam's big business. Marsden continues to write second-rate novels, and Darrell has taken up biology and spends most of his time in a distant laboratory. The child, Gordon, dislikes Darrell, and wonders what is his relationship to his mother when he sees them kiss. The last act takes place on the Evans yacht anchored near Poughkeepsie to watch the boat race in which Gordon is stroking. The possessive Nina has lost her hold on Darrell who has recovered himself in his interest in his laboratory work. Her son has turned from her to his father, Sam, and is engaged to a charming girl, Madeline Arnold. Her one thought is to keep Gordon from marriage and she tries in vain to get Darrell to help her. Sam has a stroke of apoplexy before she has a chance to tell him the truth about his son in her anger. The last act takes place on the terrace of the Evans Long Island estate after Sam's funeral. Gordon tells Nina and Darrell that he has always known of their love, and suggests that they can now marry. His dislike of Darrell breaks out as he confronts them, and Nina will not let Darrell tell him that he is his father. Madeline and Gordon go off in his airship together, and Nina is left to dependable old Charlie to comfort her declining years with his friendship and understanding.

STRANGER THAN FICTION, A SHORT HISTORY OF THE JEWS, by Lewis Browne (1928). The author's starting point is the Egypt of the reign of Rameses II, when the oppression of the Jews began, and he brings the narrative down to the present time, although he says that he cannot write "finis" to the long story, but "to be continued," for new beginnings are now being made. He sees in the uprising of the Hebrew slaves three thousand years ago one of the most important events of all history. The Exodus from Egypt, under the leadership of Moses, is treated in its effect upon the minds of succeeding generations. "Compared with enormous revolutions like that in France in the eighteenth century, or the one in Russia in recent years, the Hebrew uprising may appear a trivial incident," but again and again in these three thousand years rebels against oppression and tyranny have turned for courage to that old story of the Exodus from Egypt. This historian considers that Moses was the first of the great warriors for freedom. The wanderings, the Holy Ark, the acceptance of "Yahveh" as their only god, are told of in the opening chapters. Of the invasion and conquest of Canaan, it is shown that the struggle was a brawling and ill-organized one as well as a daring and dangerous undertaking. The preservation of the identity of the Jews after the invasion is made interesting in the reasons which the historian sets forth as preventing complete assimilation, although he says that the social life of the Jews was completely democratic. The wars with the Philistines are reviewed, and it is shown that continued opposition forced the Hebrew tribes to unite at last under a single king. Saul, as a leader and warrior, the priest and prophet Samuel, the "musician" David, the whole dramatic current of the time is reviewed, with David winning his empire, when, as the second King of the Hebrews, he led the tribes to victory. The reign of Solomon is held to have brought ruin to his people, and at his death the revolution that followed is treated as civil war which rends the nation into two kingdoms, both of which are swallowed up by the neighboring tribes. "During all those five centuries in the history of the Hebrews, a spirit was sprouting and flourishing that was almost completely unknown to the peoples roundabout. That one thing made those five centuries in Palestine the most extraordinary in all human history. Outwardly the Hebrews went the way of all the other nations, but inwardly they went a way which even to this day we cannot quite understand or explain." The historian holds that the Hebrews continued to live because of the spirit the prophets had breathed into them. The rise of the prophets and their ideals is reviewed. "The priests tried to make them practicable." From the high dreams of the prophets and the earthly desires of the priests, a compromise was reached in the code of laws which was discovered in 621 B.C., but through the prophet Jeremiah, who voiced new ideas, "another revolution occurred in human thinking." The historians relate the causes which led to the exile in Babylonia; the period of trials and disappointments after the return from Babylonia, and describe the mad fever of anxiety with which the settlers began work on the long-ruined sanctuary. The priests now came into full power; then the Greek invasion; and the Roman conquest is considered to have set the helpless nation yearning for a Messiah to deliver it. "There was one preacher in particular, a youth named Joshua — he who is known to us as Jesus of Nazareth. He was hailed as the Messiah of the Jews and crucified by the Romans." The historian tells of the new religion that was created around the story of the crucified prophet in the chapter entitled, "Christianity Is Born." The fall of Jerusalem, the Dispersion, the reign of the Rabbis, the making of the Talmud and its contents, are reviewed, the author holding that Mohammed built a new religion around the Jewish idea of God. From the fifth to the seventh century, the Jews are shown to have been at rest in hardly a land in the world, but early in the eighth century the dawn of a new day began to break. The historian notes these changes as a new dawn in Babylonia, as high noon in Spain and as twilight in the Christian lands of Europe, — and a later night of persecution. But in the "crumbling of the Ghetto wall," the new day dawned with one land after the other granting the Jew his rights as a citizen. The mission of reformed Judaism, — the dramatic movement called Zionism — the effect of the World War, the Palestine movement, are discussed in their relation to modern Jewish thought. The historian sums up certain transitions of social importance: the dominance in American Jewish life which once passed from the Spanish Jew to the German Jew now began to pass from the German Jew to the Russian Jew. He sees this second process going on to-day — and going on rapidly. "Another generation or two and the transfer will be complete."

SUMMER, see **THE SOUL ENCHANTED,** by Romain Rolland.

SUN ALSO RISES, THE, by Ernest Hemingway (1926). The story is the doings and sayings of a group of the younger generation disillusioned by the War, aimless expatriates in Europe. They talk endlessly and drink steadily in the cafés of Paris and in Pamplona in Spain during a fiesta. "Mike was a bad drunk. Brett was a good drunk. Cohn was never drunk." Brett is Lady Ashley, an over-sexed girl, who is getting a divorce, is engaged to marry Mike, a bankrupt Englishman, and loves Jake, the American newspaper correspondent, who tells the story of the relations of Brett with the others. Robert Cohn had painfully learned boxing at Princeton to counteract his feeling of shyness and inferiority at being treated as a Jew. He goes with the party to Spain and puts up with insults from Michael, because after all it is his affair with a lady of title that is being talked about, and he wants to follow Brett. The peak of the narrative is the description of the bull fight, in which emphasis is laid on the beauty of skill in the face of danger, a dance where awkwardness means death. Brett falls in love with Romero, the young bull-fighter, and goes off with him. Cohn in despair knocks out Romero and Jake and Michael and goes away. Jake, wounded in the War, is unsexed, hence the tragedy of his love for Brett. Romero wishes to marry her but she sends him away, and tells Jake she has decided to go back to Mike as her own sort of person. The author takes an impartial attitude toward his characters who are revealed in the brilliant dialogue of living speech.

SURVEY OF INTERNATIONAL AFFAIRS, 1920–1923, 1924, 1925, edited by Arnold J. Toynbee (1925). A conspectus of foreign affairs. Begins with a summary of the proceedings and results of eighteen international "continuation" conferences following the Paris Peace Conference, describes the work of the League of Nations. Gives a systematic survey by country, taking up especially the Saar Basin, Danzig, the relations of Poland and Lithuania, Belgium and Luxemburg, the relations of the Allies with Germany, the legal proceedings aginst the ex-Kaiser and war criminals, the execution of the treaties, and the problems which have arisen since 1919. The volume for 1924 deals with the Third (Communist) International, and the Union of Soviet Socialist Republics, with affairs in Europe and Africa, including documents, maps and bibliographies. The first volume for 1925 is on The Islamic World since the Peace Settlement. It discusses the problems confronting France and Spain in North Africa, the secularizing revolution in Turkey, the recovery of Persia, and the complicated politics of Arabia. The "Survey" is a guide to the complex phenomena of the new "Westernization" of Islamic lands.

SWAN, THE, a romantic comedy, by Franz Molnar (1923). The story of the Princess Alexandra and the young tutor, Nicholas Agi, who lifted his eyes to her. George and Arsene, the two sons, are listening to some selections from the history of Napoleon which Professor Agi is reading, when their mother and sister come to warn them that the royal guest, Prince Albert, has announced that he will visit the schoolroom. The Princess Beatrice is not pleased that the tutor should teach her sons that Napoleon, who had robbed her forbears of their throne, is a great genius. She is now hoping to get back to her rightful position among the rulers of Europe by marrying her daughter to Prince Albert. This is the last day of his visit, and he is apparently indifferent to the lovely Alexandra. The Princess Beatrice determines upon desperate tactics before she will admit defeat. She tells her brother, Father Hyacinth, that Albert's interest must be aroused by jealousy of another man, and she is going to instruct Alexandra to invite the tutor to the reception that evening, talk with him, and dance with him. Father Hyacinth is not shocked at "the customary tactics of the harassed mother," but he is bothered about the effect on the man who is to be used as a pawn in this diplomatic game. The dutiful Alexandra is also worried about the possible reaction of the tutor, but she has her own royal ambitions. Completely encased in the superiority of her rank, Alexandra has never thought of Nicholas as another human being, but now that they talk together she becomes conscious of his feeling for her and is ashamed of the part she has played. She explains everything to him, and for the first time in her life suffers for another's pain. Prince Albert has his suspicions and tries to make light of the unhappy tutor's monopoly of the conversation at dinner, and pretends that he is pleased to be told by a man and an astronomer that there are things in the world he does not understand. Nicholas tells Father Hyacinth afterward that the Prince had enraged his already wounded feelings with his sarcastic ridicule, and he will face the consequences of his foolish behavior. Alexandra's pity is so akin to love, that she cannot tell the difference, and all she wants is that Nicholas shall forgive and respect her. Her kindly uncle tries to be severe with them, but can only sympathize with their happiness which will vanish with the night's breeze and the daylight that must separate them. Nicholas tells her that he has been for this one evening the rival of a king and the victor, and that after this hour of life and love he will be the disgraced servant. The Prince passes through the room, stops to say good-night to Alexandra, and is contemptuously rude to Agi, calling him "an ill-bred little stargazer," and "a presumptuous intruder." Alexandra tells Albert that he misunderstands, that the professor is "a scientist, a free spirit . . . not bound by . . . conventions, and suddenly, bewildered by the conflict between impulse and tradition, she throws her arms around Agi's neck and kisses him passionately. Albert is completely shocked, and bows formally as he withdraws. The next day the Princess Dominica, Albert's mother, arrives early by motor, to welcome Alexandra as her son's bride. Father Hyacinth insists on telling her the whole story, the discovery of the professor's secret love for Alexandra, Albert's coldness, and his treatment of Agi, and Alexandra's impulsive action in response. Hyacinth convinces her that she would have kissed the tutor herself under the circumstances, that it was really the only thing a princess could have done. "If you must know — I kissed him myself," he adds. However Dominica thinks the young professor should be well provided for. "Men in his position usually turn up again — as writers of memoirs, publicists for the opposition or American lecturers." Nicholas takes leave of Alexandra proudly assuring her that he has forgotten what happened the night before. Father Hyacinth understands Nicholas's feelings and tries to make Alexandra understand too. Albert, who is good-natured and well-bred, joins them, and makes amends for his rudeness, adding yet another kiss to the cheek of the professor. He then makes formal proposal to Alexandra, who confesses that at the moment she can give him only respect and friendship. He is satisfied to wait for "the love which comes after marriage. That deep and abiding happiness which . . . comes later and lasts longer." Dominica reminds Alexandra that her father had always called her "his Swan." "You may glide, glide proudly, superbly over the smooth surface of the lake — but you must never approach the shore. For when the swan tries to walk . . . it painfully resembles another bird." "A goose," answers Alexandra. However Alexandra goes to her throne with an illumination of heart and mind which she owes to the tutor.

SWAN SONG, by John Galsworthy (1928), marks the close of the Forsyte Saga. From the eighteenth century this story of upper middle class life has progressed through generation after generation, well into the twentieth century. Among the elder Forsytes moved Soames, a boy and then a young man, unhappy and then betrayed in his deepest instincts. For in him the family need to possession extended even to the woman he loved. Only in his relations with his daughter, Fleur, was this family trait gradually spiritualized in its expression. On their return from a trip around the world, Soames busies himself in helping his beloved daughter to rehabilitate her social position, damaged by winning the law suit of "The Silver Spoon." The general strike is on in England and Michael Mont and his young wife establish a railway canteen for the benefit of the young men who are helping break the strike on the railroad. There Fleur first sees young Jon Forsyte again, who has returned from America and is stoking one of the engines. The sight of Jon makes Fleur more restless than ever and she determines to see more of him in spite of his young wife Anne. Through one carefully arranged accident after another, Fleur reawakens in Jon the passion their parents' tragedy had forced them to abandon when they were boy and girl. Jon's conscience opposes these manœuvres for he loves Anne although he cannot remain indifferent to his old sweetheart. They meet at Ascot races where Val Darties' horse wins; at a seashore carnival dance, where Soames, watching them unknown, sees that their unhappy passion is indeed revived, and later in June Forsyte's studio; for June, in the interests of one of her perennial "lame ducks" has coaxed each separately to have a portrait painted. Their meetings continue at the rest home for working girls near Dorking which Fleur is running in conjunction with Michael's latest scheme for converting the slums, and on the grounds of Jon's beautiful old home at Robbin Hill. Fleur has ceased to argue her right to Jon's love which was hers before it was Anne's. With all the resourcefulness of a pretty woman, she bends her will on winning his secret love since that alone remains. Both Michael and Soames apprehend Fleur's true feelings but in accord with their English temperament will not interfere, feeling that their only course is to guard her wherever possible. For Michael will not coerce his wife's love and Soames, remembering his own bitter experience, knows it would be futile. After the consummation of their passion, Jon, realizing that it is impossible for him to continue an illicit relationship, takes his place beside his wife, turning his back forever on Fleur. Desperate and reckless Fleur finds her father, as always, hovering in the background ready to be of service and returns with him to her old home at Mapledurham. There, careless in her grief, she sets fire to Soames' famous picture gallery by a cigarette stub. Soames overexerts himself in rescuing his treasures, and then, forced by his servants to the safety of the lawn, is fatally injured by a falling picture frame which is about to fall on Fleur when he pushes her to safety. Friends bewail this fatal accident, not knowing that Fleur had stood in that exposed place, the passive and final victim of an old tragedy, whose effects Soames took upon himself. In the end Sir Lawrence, father of Michael, pronounces the chauffeur's admiring exclamation over Soames' bravery at the fire, his best epitaph, "'A proper champion,' . . . you might almost put that on the stone. Yes, it's an ironical world."

THAT MAN HEINE, a biography, by Lewis Browne, with the collaboration of Elisa Weihl (1927). The fact that Heine wrote and published lyric poetry and brilliant satirical prose is mentioned from time to time, but the subject of this book is the complex character of the man, and the circumstances which made him capable of the "inconsistencies that so distorted his life," that "made him at once so kind and malicious, so patient and vituperative." To the author "the sufferings of Heine seem in microcosm the sufferings of his whole people, his genius and frenzy, the genius and frenzy of his whole race." Mr. Browne constantly reiterates that Heine "did not belong." His attendance at the Christian school, and later associations at the universities of Bonn and Gottingen estranged him from the Jews, but he was always enough of a Jew not to be acceptable to the Christians. Sent to Hamburg to his millionaire Uncle Salomon to make his fortune as a merchant, he was a failure like his father, and was embittered by his unrequited love for his cousin, Amalie, who married a banker, and never gave any encouragement to the suit of the penniless poet. Poverty and headaches were his great handicaps. Uncle Salomon was induced to provide for him so that he might study law. He paid little attention to his law studies and wrote incessantly. In Berlin where he spent two years he was happy in the society of a group of intellectual Jews who had formed a society for the renascence of Jewish culture, but lost most of these friends and made many enemies. An article on the political situation in Poland brought on him the censure of the Prussian Government. This later made it impossible for him to get the professorship he wanted. Entrance to any profession was barred to a Jew, so it was necessary for Heine to go through the form of becoming a Christian to receive his law degree, and he therefore was an apostate to his own race. After the publication of his third volume of "Travel Pictures" and its proscription by the police, Heine decided it would be safer for him to live in Paris. His reputation as a wit and a poet had preceded him there, and though this part of the book is called by the author, "The Exile in France," it was a physical, not a spiritual exile. He said himself, "A German poet must live on German soil," and regretted that he had to leave his own country. In these chapters many of his best epigrams are quoted. His struggle for existence against poverty and illness continues, and petitions to Uncle Salomon, and later his cousin, Karl. The book describes his life with the common, empty-headed shop girl, Mathilde, whom he eventually married. "She did not know he was a Jew and did not care that he was a poet," and he was flattered to realize that this girl loved him for himself alone. She thought him "the best, the kindest, the most genuine of men." It would have been difficult to find a stranger and worse mated couple as the years passed. The vain, selfish woman showed affection for him in his last long illness only by jealousy and churlishness to the friends who came to visit him. Heine completed the "cycle of faith. . . . Through Catholicism, Paganism, Protestantism, Atheism, and Saint-Simonism" back to Judaism. The picture is of the despised and hated Heine, and all charges against him of friends and enemies are entertained by this biographer. The harassed and tormented life is set forth, his conflict with himself and with circumstances, and his struggle to get the peace which would allow him to write.

THESE CHARMING PEOPLE, by Michael Arlen (1924). "Being a Tapestry of the Fortunes, Follies, Adventures, Gallantries and General Activities of Shelmerdene (That Lovely Lady), Lord Tarlyon, Mr. Michael Wagstaffe, Mr. Ralph Wyndham Trevor and Some Other of Their Friends of the Lighter Sort." This volume of short stories is a collection of quaintly phrased vignettes of life in fashionable London. Arlen has adopted and adapted the immemorial style of the fairy-tale: pretending, with extravagance of language, that his people and events are quite preposterous, while adroitly hiding a moral in many of his stories. The first of these, "Introducing a Lady of No Importance and a Gentleman of Even Less," is the record of how Shelmerdene made a fool of herself, being hurt to distraction, and how bitterly she continues to regret it. The last, "The Real Reason Why Shelmerdene Was Late to Dinner," is the account of how Shelmerdene's missing husband, who has deserted her in righteous anger ten years earlier, returns to England, calls her on the telephone while she is dressing for dinner, and she tells him indirectly what a fool he has been to go away believing she cared for anyone but himself, and forbids him to see her again. In between the first and the last stories there are a dozen of other tales, grave and gay. "The Shameless Behaviour of a Lord" is a story about a very eligible and equally wary young man who makes the fond mamma of a hopeful daughter disclose her to him (in a secluded corner of the garden) in the nude, and he escapes the matrimonial noose by thanking the lady kindly. He is sorry, but daughter's nose is not up to standards! "Major Cypress Goes Off the Deep End" is an adroit rephrasing in modern argot of the oldest of romantic plots: the valiant soldier proposes five times to his beloved and is refused as often, till at the sixth and last approach she admits that she reciprocates, "and they live happily ever after." All in all "These Charming People" deserve the appellation in their exploits and eccentricities.

THEY KNEW WHAT THEY WANTED, a comedy drama, by Sidney Howard (1924). Tony had not married when he was young because he had no money, but now that he is rich he decides he wants a wife and children. Before Prohibition he had sold his grapes for ten or twelve dollars a ton, and now he can get as much as one hundred dollars a ton. In an Italian restaurant in San Francisco he had seen a charming young girl, Amy, and had written to her and proposed marriage. Afraid that she would not accept a man of sixty he has sent a photograph of his young foreman, Joe, instead of his own. The play opens at Tony's ranch on the morning of the wedding day. Tony spends so much time fixing up to meet the bride that he starts late to meet the train and too much of his own wine and reckless driving lands him in a ditch with both his legs broken. The rural postman brings Amy up from the station, and only the handsome Joe is there to receive her. She naturally thinks that he is the bridegroom, and is not undeceived until Tony is brought in on a stretcher. She repents of her bargain, but remembers that she has given up her place in the city, and spent her last cent on her ticket, and decides to stay and make the best of it. Confused with resentment at both Tony and Joe she is unhappy and restrained, but she agrees to forgive and forget when Tony presents her with a pair of diamond earrings. Joe has intended to let Tony's wife alone, but as he tries to comfort her after the wedding he kisses her, and it happens that she spends her nuptial night in the arms of the man whose photograph had won her. This reaction to the events of the day is a momentary insanity unrelated to love, and the affair with Joe ends with its beginning. Three months later Tony is able to be out in the sun in an improvised invalid chair, Amy has been a devoted nurse, and is contented in her home and happy with her husband. Joe, who is an I. W. W., confesses that he is what the newspapers call an "unskilled migratory," and is ready to migrate again. The doctor tells Joe that Amy is going to have a baby, and Joe breaks the news to her. There seems nothing for her to do but go away with Joe. In their mutual affection for Tony, Amy and Joe have forgotten that there was anything but casual friendship between them. She tells Tony that she has appreciated his kindness to her, and has been happy, and she hates to leave him, but he must know exactly what has happened. Tony goes into a violent rage, but calms down at the thought of losing his Amy. The earrings, she tells him, she is leaving on the dresser. He calls her to come to him and tells her she is going to stay with Tony, and that they will tell everyone that it is his baby. Joe does not want a baby, and he does, and so it is happily settled.

THIS BELIEVING WORLD, by Lewis Browne (1928), is divided into eight books. Browne's original premise is that Fear was man's dominant instinct in prehistoric times. Only through religion — and the savage prototypes of religion: magic, animism, shamanism, fetichism; later on, idolatry, sacrificial ritualism; finally worship to-day in all its conglomerate compound of such primitive elements — only through such an initiation of awe and the institution of something or someone to awe him, has man envisaged any hope for himself on this earth. Terror: It was terror that drove man to find salvation for himself outside of himself. He could not contemplate the external universe — it was too intangible and incidentally too malignant. He had to be saved. Then he got religion. Browne hardly elevates the beautiful animism of the Greeks above the prostitution of the Druid-led Celts. Comparing the latter's rites with the yet more primitive magic of earlier ages, he shows the beginning of a spirit of cajolery, as opposed to the coercive brand of worship formerly employed. More advanced in form but similar in respect to the Druid cult was the fertility deism of those arid nomads of Arabia, who mixed their patriarchal system of society with the matriarchal Babylonians. Theirs was an idolatry that made obeisance to the sexual Ishtar and the lewd temple rites, practised to this day. Some of the priests who organized this cult were astrologers and even psalmists. The animal-worship and ancestor-tribute of the Egyptians is well-known: elaborate funerals, enthralling legends, and an inkling of a belief in their own immortality as well as in one God. It surpassed the Babylonian religion in æsthetic and ethical emphasis, but decayed into no more than an incantation ritual at the hands of their priests. The Greeks were the least afraid of the ancients. Their worship of the gods was almost nil — no fear God formula humiliated them — so a technical priesthood did not spring into existence there. This accounts, according to Browne, for the short durance of their faith, in that no hide-bound ecclesiastical order nurtured it. But a perversion gained headway called the Mysteries, which spread to Rome and all Asia Minor. In Rome from early times there had flourished a household cult founded on the petty deities, the penates. A social order and state institution grew out of this after-Olympian precept, only with all the temporal punctiliousness — if not the power — of the papal régime. So ends Book Two. Just as the Roman pater was also priest for the family, so in the orthodox faith of early India, each father was priest and each mother priestess. And just as in Classical Italy a state religion grew up with professional sacrificers, so the Brahmins made a theological practice of Brahminism. Heresies sprang up, and of the two most important, Jainism and Buddhism, the latter alone survived to become a proselyting sect among many nations. But Hinduism — a religio-social system that salvaged the ancient caste fallacy, revived the popular, plebiscite gods, while preserving their deism in epics called the Ramayana and the Mahabharata — this resurrection of old Brahmanism thrived. A truly noble work was produced as Krishna's wisdom, "The Bhagavata-Gita" or "Song of the Adorable," and is to-day as zealously distributed in tracts as the New Testament. As for the upper thinking classes (all India thinks more than she acts), their influence on America with New Thought revelations and Leagues for the contemplation of the Over-Soul is apparent. Nearer home, in China, one of her heresies, Buddhism, became quite popular because it was the first idolatrous, priestly worship the Chinese had known. Coolies could understand it with its tangible promise of Heaven and Hell for just and unjust. It left its stamp on the other two faiths of China, even if the zealots of the old order and ancient beliefs did raze Buddhist temples, and exile Buddhist monks and nuns. It was natural that a conservative like Confucius should be weaned in a conservative place like China. He taught of ancestor worship and obeisance to the gods, exhorting to prayer and praising the disciplinary nature of sacrifice for its own sake, and a number of other regular habits necessary to exemplary living. He was severely practical, as witness his ethical law of reciprocity: to return good for good and evil for evil. In contrast with this, and more in line with the golden rule is the Lao-Tze command to requite good for evil. Lao-Tze founded Taoism on the principle of nihilistic living, a meticulous abstinence from any action. In other principles he anticipated Jesus by five hundred years, the inculcation of humility and frugality. He abhorred all worship and sacrifice. The professors who followed this mystic modified these principles in an attempt to preserve life and wealth, the very thing the master had scorned and ruled out. Legend records that Zoroaster underwent the immaculate conception much as did Jesus. Enlightened thought for man's welfare and the treatment of his neighbor as himself are the common property of both teachers. Most Parsees, who follow him to-day under the name of Zarathustra, his other name, lead as model a life as any Christian saint. Their sole veneration is for fire and the god whose symbol it is, Mazda. Out of its originally naïve qualities have grown the weeds of theology. An elaborate taboo gained currency. So Zoroastrianism went the way of all beliefs which substitute superstition for more inspired qualities. Of the three faiths which came up out of the Arabian Desert, the second, Yahvism, was the most distinguished. For out of Yahvism came Judaism and out of it came Christianity. Book Six traces the growth of a true monotheism out of the first tribal fetichism. With scant reference to the political furors of Canaan, Browne dwells at some length on the contributions of the later prophets to the new conception of God replacing that of Moses. Through Amos's teaching, Hosea's recognition of a merciful God, and Isaiah's throning of Yahveh as a majestic diety, we come at last to Jeremiah's significant teaching of the single God, the One Supreme Creator of mankind. The Yoke of the Chosen People is never removed and since they must go on living and fearing something (the goy-Gentile, rather than any harsh environment) they must buttress their beliefs against heathen invasion by a Wall of Law, the cement of which was the Messianic promise. Of course the pride of the Jews who thought of themselves always as the Chosen Children of God would not tolerate a Messiah who proclaimed himself the Savior of the World. Since this is what Jesus did it accounts for the antipathy of the race as a whole toward him whom they marked as a blasphemer and a charlatan. In the evangelism of Christianity appears the same compromise with defeated cults, incorporating certain of their heathen practices into the church ritual, the same deifying of the Master, corrupting his ethics and bringing the decay of right with ritualism, the same sorry mistakes as attended the missionary efforts of every other devoted follower of a great leader. The puritan element, a heritage that Jesus received from his Jewish forbears, saved Christian observances from the sacred lust of pagan worship, and inculcated a staunch hope and a salvaging courage in the dejected and hapless among humans. It worked because it allayed that gnawing fear with which man's heart was burdened. Last of the great religions to find their arid source in the Arabian Desert was Islam. It inundated most of the backward lands until to-day it numbers two hundred odd millions. Book Eight is the story of what happened in Arabia. Mostly it is the tale of Mohammed, one of the most vacillating characters in the history of seers. He stood up for his faith in one instance and gave way to the Meccan djinns the moment his life was endangered, then, as soon as the persecution ceased recanted his contrary revelations as promptings of the devil Ahriman, and finally set out to establish Allah as the One God for all true believers. He failed in his attempt to accommodate himself to the Jews and assume the Messianic rôle; his Jewish converts fell off. So he again changed the name of his God to Allah and proclaimed once more the festival of Ramadhan as holyday, and Mecca, not Jerusalem, the Holy City. With the pressure of material concerns the Prophet was reduced to unholy pillage of caravans bound for Mecca, and when his newly named city of Medina gained the victory over the city of his birth, Mohammed unreservedly came out for the sword. His evangel was to be a Holy War. He never gave up conversion by the sword and that perhaps accounts for the easy flexibility of the faith, and for its proselyting power among the Unbelievers.

THOMAS, THEODORE, see **AMERICAN ORCHESTRA AND.**

THOSE BARREN LEAVES, by Aldous Huxley (1925). This title aptly describes the members of the houseparty gathered by Mrs. Lillian Aldwinkle at her Italian villa, and their self-conscious, analytical, epigrammatic conversation. The elderly hostess is a lion-hunter. She has an "indefatigable desire to get everything out of life," and a haunting fear that she is missing something just around the corner. Her great subject is love, her own pathetic, absurd pursuit of passion, and her romantic preoccupation with the affairs of other people. Second in importance to her are the arts for which she constantly professes admiration, though she has no real knowledge or appreciation of any of them. She urges her little niece, Irene, who adores pretty things and can for thirty shillings make garments that would have cost her six guineas in a shop, to devote her time to painting and writing lyrics. "Underclothing became for Irene the flesh, became illicit love and rebellious reason; poetry and water-colour painting, invested by her adoration of Aunt Lillian with a quality of sacredness, became spirit, duty and religion." Lord Hovenden has just attained his majority, and sacrifices a month's grouse shooting to accompany Mr. Falk, the labor leader and Guild Socialist, whom he greatly admires, to an International Labor Conference at Rome. His generous impulses have been stirred to learn "that there are a great many poor people whose lives are extremely disagreeable and arduous and who, if justice were done, would be better off than they are at present." His ambitions to precipitate an immediate millennium are distracted only by thoughts of the charming Irene. Mr. Cardan is an elderly cynic who in years gone by had been Mrs. Aldwinkle's lover, and now openly confesses that he is a parasite. Mr. Calamy is "positively the young man who, on the covers of illustrated magazines, presses his red lips to those of the young woman of his choice." On his arrival the sophisticated novelist, Mary Thirplow, making copy of her experiences, stops "composing the fourteenth chapter of her new novel on a Corona typewriter," takes off her rings, gives up smart repartee, and starts posing as simple and genuine, a creature all heart, instead of the intelligent, hard, glittering young woman she is. He drifts into an affair with her, because he considers love "the best indoor sport," and her "air of unreal innocence" intrigues him. On the beach, rescued from an accident in the water, Mrs. Aldwinkle finds Francis Chelifer, a young poet she has longed to meet, and adds him to her party. Too late to escape he realizes that he is going to spoil his holiday with "art, classy chats about the cosmos, the intelligentsia, love. . . ." The circumstances of her discovery of Chelifer "at her feet, like Shelley, like Leander washed up on the sands of Abydos" predispose Mrs. Aldwinkle to become romantic about him. He develops an almost magical faculty for evading her "mentally, spiritually and in the flesh." Irene as the confidant of her aunt is an example of the young girl of to-day who knows her Freud and Havelock Ellis, and makes quite appalling remarks, yet is fundamentally innocent. There is the episode of Mr. Cardan's attempt to provide for his declining years by marriage with the half-witted heiress, Miss Elver, which is frustrated by her death. Lord Hovenden loses his timidity when he is driving his car at the rate of sixty miles an hour and is able to propose to Irene. Calamy thinks he can solve the mystery of life by meditation, and leaves the castle to retire to a cottage in the mountains. Chelifer reflects on Barbara whom he loved, Dorothy Mason who loved him, and the embarrassing declaration of Mrs. Aldwinkle, and returns to England to his post-war position of editor of the "Rabbit Fancier's Gazette." There is very little action in this story. It deals with contrast of characters and discussions about life and its futility.

THREE BLACK PENNYS, THE, a novel, by Joseph Hergesheimer (1917). The Pennys are a family of iron founders in Pennsylvania since colonial days. Some hundreds of years before their establishment in America a Welsh strain had come into the family by marriage. Instead of being diffused and lost it emerges in one generation or another in a dark, rebellious, ruthless individual, to whom opposition is the breath of life. One had been burned as a heretic under Queen Mary. Gilbert Penny brings his wife, Isabel, from court life in London, to the province of Maryland. They have three children, Howat, Caroline, and Myrtle. At the time the story opens they are entertaining visitors from England, Felix Winscombe, and his young, fashionable wife, Ludowika, with their Italian servant. Howat, the black Penny of this generation, falls in love with Ludowika, and determines that she shall never leave him. Mr. Winscombe is away for a time on business, and they become lovers. Ludowika is swept away for the moment by his passion, but has no idea of remaining in the wilderness. Her husband returns ill, and dies, and Ludowika is trapped. Howat reflects that he will make her forget the gardens of fireworks and scraping violins; but forget or not she was his — Ludowika Penny. The amiable but plain Caroline marries the suitor selected by their parents for her beautiful and disagreeable sister Myrtle, young David Forsythe. Two generations later appears another black Penny, Jasper. There have been two women in his life, his wife, who is dead, and his mistress, Essie Scofield, now the one serious complication of his future. He recognizes that he has been criminally negligent of Eunice, their child, now seven years old. He finds her uncared for, and places her in school in New York. Essie, in love with a younger man, Daniel Culser, shoots him in a quarrel. The trial brings Jasper's former relation with her into publicity. The woman he wants to marry, Susan Brundon, will not have him until after Essie's death, and the child of that late marriage was the father of the last Penny, Howat, the elderly bachelor, thin-blooded and ineffectual aesthete of the last story. The black Penny of this generation is Howat's first cousin, Mariana Jannan, aged twenty-six. She is fond of Howat, and visits him often. Her affections are set on James Polder, descendant of Eunice Scofield, whose name is not mentioned by the family. She brings him to spend a week-end with Howat to the latter's surprise and dismay. Jim inherits the genius of the old iron-founders, but also Essie Scofield's tendency to alcoholism. A family dinner at the Polders so discourages the aristocratic Mariana that she refuses Jim. He marries a young actress, Harriet, and is unhappy, and so is Mariana. She practically forces the conventional Jim to live with her instead of Harriet. At Howat's death-bed she tells him that she accepts her fate. She says, "I have a feeling of being a part of something outside personal happiness, something that has tied Jim and me together and gone about a larger affair . . . whether I was pleased or not didn't appear to matter. In a position like that it's silly to talk about happiness as if it were like the thrill at your first ball."

THREE KINGDOMS, by Storm Jameson (1926). Besides being the wife of Dysart Ford, and the mother of a small Sandy, young Laurence Storm uses her subtle brain and obstinate will as an executive in the largest advertising company in England. In an interview Miss Jameson says of the theme of this novel: "A woman can rule over any two of these kingdoms with a reasonable amount of success, but not over the three." It is Sandy who loses most in lack of his mother's companionship. Two months before the War, Laurence, "an untidy, leggy, sexless youngster with ambitions," married the inexperienced lawyer, Dysart Ford. The birth of her son brought Dysart's mother to see her. At her husband's home she met and fell in love with Nicholas Mar, a brother-in-law of Dysart's, working in the Foreign Office. This is a Platonic affair because Nicholas cannot afford to give up his position and career to marry her, and she is not the stuff of which furtive alliances are made. When the War is over and her adoring husband returns she makes her confession, and calls on his selfless kindness to make her chosen path easy for her by continuing their marriage in name only. He fills his life with his profession, and treats Laurence with aloof, indifferent courtesy. His sister, Isabel Mar, thinks that Dysart is more changed by four years of War than he ought to have been. For a time he turns for consolation to his beautiful, cat-like cousin, Caroline, Mrs. Foster Scott. At her office Laurence is working on a large advertising contract for Foster Scott's "Fresh Foods," which brings her into constant association with Mr. Scott. The details of her daily life is a picture of how the wheels go round in a great concern. She is obliged to discharge an Australian cad, Martin, who will not work for her or with her. He leaves behind him in his desk a number of letters which reveal that he has been the lover of Mrs. Foster Scott. Caroline dislikes Laurence because she has refused some drawings that Caroline made for the advertising campaign which did not follow specifications, because she loves Dysart, her husband, and because she suspects that Foster Scott is falling in love with Laurence. The fact that Laurence goes to Southampton with Scott and stays at the same hotel in order to work until the last moment on the advertising before he sails for America gives Caroline the opportunity she wants to sue for divorce. At the news of the proceedings Nicholas offers to give up his career, and at first Laurence thinks that she will go away with him, but before he returns to tell her that his father has refused to continue his allowance and persuaded him to give her up, as suddenly as a conversion she has realized that she still loves Dysart. She knows that she has lost his love and trust, and dreads his fastidious distaste for the scandal and publicity that the affair must bring to the family. Caroline persists in bringing suit believing that she will win Dysart for herself by discrediting Laurence. Mr. Martin is a witness for Caroline, and it is the fear that her letters which she learns he left at the office, may be produced as evidence that makes her confess that she had never believed Laurence guilty, and break down the chain of circumstantial evidence that her lawyers had built up. Laurence resigns her position at the Napier Advertising Company, and wins her husband back.

THUNDER ON THE LEFT, by Christopher Morley (1925). It is Martin's birthday party, and he is ten years old. The children wonder about the grown-ups and whether or not they have a good time. They decide to spy on their parents and find out. Martin Richmond and his little sister Bunny, and Joyce Clyde agree to play this new game. Ben, Ruth, Phyllis and Alec want to grow up. They tiptoe to the window and watch Daddy taking three lumps of sugar, and mother putting her elbow on the table, and reaching across the table for a cake, doing all the things they told the children not to do. Martin wishes on the cake that he may be a spy in the enemy's country. Joyce cries in the corner because she thinks the plush mouse that she has given Martin is too small a present.

The story is projected twenty years into the future. Phyllis and her husband, George Granville, have rented the Richmond house for the summer. They are planning a picnic for their three children, and their week-end guests, Ben and Ruth, now a stolid, childless married couple, and Miss Joyce Clyde, an artist whom George has met in his publicity work. In the afternoon Phyllis finds Martin in the garden, in appearance a man of thirty, but actually, in fulfillment of his birthday wish, a boy of ten and a symbol of the "unspoiled essence of life." Phyllis is attracted by his grave directness and simplicity, and imagines herself in love with him. Her husband, George, is really four people as Joyce once told him: George, the Husband, George, the Father, George, the Publicity Man, and then George the Fourth, her own discovery, "the troubled and groping dreamer." George is in love with Joyce though he truly loves Phyllis. All are troubled by Martin with his unanswerable questions. Only the children seem to understand and accept him. Bunny, Martin's dead sister, comes to beg Martin to give up the game and leave the grown-up people alone. There is danger that he will realize their fears, and passions, and suffer with them. She appeals to Joyce who has kept the innocence of childhood to help her get Martin away. It is clear to Joyce suddenly that George and Martin are the same person, George being the man that life and its complexities will make of the child, Martin; that she herself loves the Martin in George, and Phyllis loves him as George. She begs Martin to go to the old nursery and find the mouse that she had given him on his birthday that he may remember and know that he must go away. Martin asks Joyce what it is that hurts them all so. In terror lest he find it out, she sends him to the house. The children rush joyously out on to the sleeping porch above her to announce breakfast. The broken rail which George had neglected to mend breaks, and they fall, but Martin has found the mouse. The scene changes to the birthday party. Martin calls to the children that he is not going to play that game. In desperation he asks his mother: "Do you have a good time?" and is laughed at by the adults.

TIME OF MAN, THE, a novel, by Elizabeth Madox Roberts (1926). A story of the "poor whites" of the Kentucky hills, the family of a farm laborer who journeys from place to place in a wagon to work for the more prosperous farmer. Little Ellen Chesser's father travelling across the country with a gypsy band trading horses stops to have his wagon mended at the blacksmith's, and is persuaded to work on the Bodine farm. They have a cabin to live in and plant a vegetable garden and Ellen worked in the fields walking ahead of the men dropping the tobacco plants at intervals in the long rows. After a year Henry Chesser is discontented and they move on to another farm where he can work on shares as a tenant farmer, and have a better house, and a cow. On the Wakefield place Ellen tends the turkeys, helps with the milking, and shells corn, and strips tobacco leaves in the barn in the winter. The hills and rocks, the fields and pastures, the changing seasons, the trees, animals, birds, and plants are not merely background for the story, but all permeate Ellen's mind, along with the doings of the family and the neighbors. When she is eighteen she finds a girl friend, Dorine Wheatley, daughter of another tenant farmer, and goes to a party at her house to dance and sing with other young people. There were revival services at the church, and moonlight walks home in pairs, and Ellen walked with Jonas. "All day her mind clung about his furrows or she hovered over his team and his plow in her thought, her hand on the plow handle or on the plow line, not merged with his but accompanying." Jonas went to a farm twenty miles away to work for money to be married, and Ellen received one love letter, and then no more, until she heard he was going with another girl. After he has married, Ellen longs to kill him as she slashes the bacon with her sharp knife, and then to kill herself. She is glad when her father's restless spirit urges him to move again to another farm. His wife is sorry to leave the pleasant Wakefield farm, telling him he is well enough off, and that he had "better stay one place awhile." They live now near a Dominican monastery, and Ellen regulates her days by the bells. "When the mid-morning bell came she must leave the field and start toward the house to help finish the cooking. The late bell of the afternoon belonged with the milking and the time of feeding the hogs and geese and horses." It is stony land, and one evening Henry fell into the quarry, and broke his hip. With the help of a neighbor, Jasper Kent, Ellen does all the work on the farm. A travelling photographer courts Ellen, but it is Jasper who wins her. The thieving, carousing son of the woman Jasper works for cheats Jasper out of his earnings, and by accident Jasper's lantern dropped in the fight between the two men, sets the barn on fire. It seems best to Jasper to get out of the neighborhood, but he comes back for Ellen as soon as he gets work with Joe Phillips. Jasper has to stand trial for the burning of the barn, and his employer gives bond for him. After his innocence is established and they have paid the lawyer, Ellen and Jasper decide to move away with their children to another place where Jasper could grow tobacco on a sharing plan, instead of working for wages. This move does not prove an advantage, and after a time they go back to the Phillips farm on better terms. A loose girl, Hester Shuck, wins Jasper from Ellen, and they quarrel about her and about Phillips' attentions to Ellen. A fifth child, whom they call Chick, brings them together again with his short suffering life and death. At last Ellen seems to have found a home on a small rough farm, where land was cheap enough so that Jasper might hope to begin to buy in a year or two. Then the barn of an unfriendly neighbor burned one night, and Jasper, whose story had travelled after him, was wrongfully accused by the lawless community, and dragged out of his bed one night and beaten by a gang of white-hooded men. The next day they loaded their few belongings on a wagon and started to find another and distant home. The children ask their mother where they are going, and she answers, "I don't know. Somewheres. . . ."

TIN WEDDING, by Margaret Leech (1926). A vivid picture, appealing to the senses, of a home in New York decorated with costly rugs and hangings and filled with beautiful Chinese objects of rose quartz, amethyst, jade and cornelian. In one bedroom there is masculine disorder and comfort; beside a table with an ashtray overflowing with cigarette stubs, Jay Fanning falls into a belated sleep. Across the hall, in her charming rose-pink room, Lucia, his wife, wakes, still weary from the entertainment of the night before, but conscious of the delicious morning air and her own attractive brunette pallor. She thinks of her devotion to Jay and to Nickie, her little, delicate, blond son. But much as she loves her son, her wifely adoration and dependence is stronger. She is all eager haste because today is the tenth anniversary of their marriage and they are to take a holiday to return to the old farm where they passed the first night of their honeymoon. The maid calls her attention to two jewel cases which she has overlooked. They contain two beautiful diamond

and pearl bracelets, her husband's anniversary gift.   At the perfectly served breakfast, Lucia's brother Randolph is present, seated between her and her heavy blond
husband, who looks rather like a Roman emperor.   As his wife looks at him gratitude
flows, through her for what he is and for his protection.   Her brother tells Jay how
Adrian, a painter with whom he shares a studio, is going to do Lucia's portrait, and
to tease her says: "That is how Adrian always begins his conquests."   Lucia is
really rather pleased and flattered by his remarks though not seriously moved by
them.   Then Randolph goes on to talk of the night before, when they were all at an
after-the-theatre party, and tells of driving home Hallie Ennes whom he found in a
terribly emotional state.   He speculates on her probably unfortunate past.   He also
mentions that she had a Roman cigarette case exactly like one Lucia had.   Jay says
he had borrowed it from his wife and had loaned it to Hallie Ennes without thinking,
but he promises to get it back.   It appears that he admires Mrs. Ennes.   He and his
wife have taken the attitude of being a modern couple and having their friends in
common or separately as it happens, but Lucia finds herself unaccountably disturbed
by the incident of the cigarette case though she tells herself that there is no occasion
for thinking of one mild flirtation among the large number of admirations which her
husband has for different women.   Lucia has planned to start at once on their holiday,
but a telephone call causes Jay to say that he must go down town first.   When she
calls his office a little later she finds that he is not there, nor expected.   She is troubled
by this and worried because she finds that her foolish vain little mother, whom she
had expected to stay with Nickie over the weekend, has caught cold because she
would not put rubbers over her pretty shoes.   Then Jay's Aunt Geraldine arrives to
stay with Nickie, and Lucia finds herself too restless to listen to her adoring talk about
Jay so she goes to her brother's studio to see him, but finds only Adrian.   He is disappointed that she has not come to see him.   He complains of the pale fire in her that
does not warm in spite of her beauty.   Finally, after lunch Jay and Lucia get off
and drive first to tea at his sister-in-law's country place.   There they find a fashionable fast crowd: Sackett East, the lion and playwright, Paula, the sister-in-law, and
her husband Revel and her Jewish lover, Eva Tailer, an authoress with an insignificant
husband, Randolph and his actress Emmy, the poetess Penelope with her vermilion
toenails revealed by green sandals.   Also there is Luis, a girlhood lover of Lucia, in
whose presence she feels safely romantic.   Sackett is trying by telephone to persuade
Hallie Ennes to come down and join them.   He succeeds before the Fannings leave
to celebrate their anniversary.   This celebration causes much talk and amusement
among the guests.   At the Farm, which is really a simple farm, Lucia prepares to
serve supper in the kitchen and to renew the memories of her honeymoon.   Jay is a
little preoccupied but all goes well until, as she pours his afterdinner coffee, he absent-
mindedly pulls out a Roman cigarette case!   Lucia pretends a sudden wish to gather
lilacs in the lovely evening, but once outside rushes away to fall on the damp earth
where the full realization comes to her of what it means that Jay should have secured
the case since last night.   To escape the intolerable situation she runs off the water
supply of the house and seizes the occasion of her brother's arrival with Emmy to
decide that she and Jay shall return with them to a treasure hunt at Paula's.   There,
in company with Luis as her partner, she tries to conceal her misery in the dark
grounds hunting for the treasure, but really watching her husband with Hallie.   The
hunt ends with the discovery of the treasure on the pier and with Hallie's disappearance off the pier.   Lucia, who is alone, with her ankle sprained, hears the sounds of
excitement and knows that her husband is diving again and again after the missing
woman.   She faints and comes to in the guest room where her husband joins her for a

brief moment, preoccupied with his private grief over Hallie's death. Alone again Lucia tries to deceive herself, but is forced to realize that the dead woman will always hold her husband while she can herself only hope for a future full of small pretexts to keep what little of him she can. The portrait of Lucia is the study of a repressed and jealous woman.

TO THE LIGHTHOUSE, by Virginia Woolf (1927). The book is in three parts, the scene the summer home of an English family, the Ramsays, in the Hebrides. The first part, called "The Window," occupying an afternoon and evening, is told chiefly in the reverie of Mrs. Ramsay. James, aged six, is disappointed because his father prophesies that the weather will prevent the long anticipated trip to the Lighthouse planned for the next morning. "No going to the Lighthouse, James," echoed Mr. Charles Tansley. Mr. Tansley is a crude student, who parades his poverty and his principles. All of the characters are unhappy in some way, disappointed in something. Mr. Ramsay had written one little book that was a contribution to human thought when he was twenty-five, and many books since which were not as good. He is an introvert always asking for sympathy and appreciation, "so brave a man in thought . . . so limited in life." His wife, the dominant figure of the group, has unusual beauty, is charming and intelligent. The children love her and dislike their egotistical, tyrannical father. Of the children, Prue is a beauty, Rose, wonderful with her hands, Jasper will shoot the birds, Nancy and Roger are so wild, Andrew has a talent for mathematics, Cam is made happy by a tenpenny doll's tea set. Mr. Carmichael has written poetry about the desert and the camel to which nobody has paid any attention for years, and then suddenly everybody began to talk about it. Lily Briscoe loves all the family, but especially Mrs. Ramsay going her calm competent way. Lily is struggling to make a painting of the shore. William Banks is a scientist, once an intimate friend of Professor Ramsay's, and he reflects how the friendship has someway petered out. William never seems to think, "But how does this affect me?" Minta Doyle and Paul Rayley are a young couple who get engaged during their visit to the Ramsays. Their secret thoughts reveal more about them all than could be learned from an exhaustive account of their doings. Mrs. Ramsay sits in her window revolving in her mind the mysterious workings of life. The second part, "Time Passes," is an interlude of ten years in which the house is empty except for the sea winds and the visits of Mrs. McNab, the caretaker. In the third part, "The Lighthouse," the family and two of the guests return. Mrs. Ramsay is dead, and yet life somehow goes on incredibly without her. Andrew has been killed in the War. Prue has married and died. Lily Bristow takes up her painting again and her reverie on the people and the events of the past and present. Mr. Ramsay insists on a trip to the Lighthouse, and James, now sixteen, goes unwillingly, and does not enjoy the sail.

TOLD BY AN IDIOT, by Rose Macaulay (1924). This story of the Garden family through three generations is a satirical picture of the last half century, late Victorian, Edwardian, and Georgian. The Reverend Aubrey Garden is a tireless searcher after religious truth, a quest which leads him from Anglicanism, the faith of his fathers, into the Roman fold and back again by way of Quakerism, Unitarianism, Positivism, Baptism, followed by his devoted wife, the daughter of a conservative Anglican dean. Papa's broad-mindedness amounts to a disease, his pretty, saucy daughter, Vicky, thinks, when mother breaks the news to the children that papa has lost his faith again, and that they are going to join the Ethical Society.

Victoria, named for papa's temporary victory over unbelief in the year of her birth, 1856, is cheered by the prospect of moving to London. She prefers dances and lawn tennis and young men to religion, and presently marries Charles, a young man in the Foreign Office, whose only fault in her eyes is that he has no interest in the "New Beauty" and positively dislikes art fabrics, and lilies, except in gardens, and is not a follower of Mr. Pater. Stanley is a romantic enthusiast, studying at Girton now, but is later to collect causes as her father has collected creeds. She is interested in a campaign called the Woman's Movement, is one of the first of her sex to ride a bicycle, takes up settlement work, and becomes an ardent Fabian. Maurice was graduated from Cambridge in the eighties, and found congenial work on a weekly paper started to defeat Whiggery by the spread of Radicalism. He and Stanley discussed unemployment, labor troubles, and sweated industries by the hour. Unfortunately Maurice married early the silly, shallow, jeering Amy Wilbur, which contributed to his disillusionment with life. He is in continual conflict with the world, pro-Boer in the eighteen-nineties, using his brilliant pen to struggle for reform, and to sneer at all reforms as "inadequate, pedestrian, or absurd. He condemned employers as greedy, and Trade Unions as retrograde." The second daughter, Rome, is intelligent, clever, and aloof, and it is through her detached observation that we see the procession of the decades, with really nothing new under the sun, history always repeating itself, and the younger generation continually in revolt against the older. She says, "There's one thing about freedom . . . each generation of peoples begins by thinking they've got it for the first time in history, and ends by being sure the generation younger than themselves have too much of it." At thirty-one she was a woman of the world, a good talker, a wit, elegant and urbane, sought after by hostesses. In 1890 she fell in love with Mr. Jayne, an amusing, erudite Oxford man, a writer of historical and political essays, who had formerly been at the British Embassy at St. Petersburg. He had married a Russian girl, now wholly uncongenial to him, and interested in nothing but Russian plots and refugees, and unwilling to give him a divorce. Rome would have been persuaded finally to go to Italy and count the world well lost in his companionship, but Mr. Jayne was killed by an anarchistic cousin of his wife, who wanted to marry Olga himself. The two younger children, Irving and Una, made practical adjustments to life. Irving became a successful stock-broker, married a beautiful and charming wife with a title, had a house in London and one in Devonshire, and no worries except the super-tax. The placid Una married beneath her, a country farmer, and brought up a family of handsome children. The many attractive qualities of Stanley's husband, the playwright, Denman Croft, did not include fidelity, and Stanley divorced him, filling her life with her children, and her committees on the improvement of the world, becoming what is called a useful and public-spirited woman. Christian Science came from America to claim Mr. Garden, and it was a comfort to him during the Boer War to think there there really was no war on God's plane, "only unhappy people following an evil illusion," as he told his grandchild, Imogen, in answer to her question of what God thought all those soldiers were doing out in Africa. However when Mrs. Garden had pneumonia he called in three doctors, and became evangelical again. The generation of the grandchildren in their turn are intellectually up-to-date. The successive decades are outlined by journalistic summaries of their political events, plays, pictures, songs, faiths, scandals, and crimes, and the illusions which at each period passed for wisdom. After Mrs. Garden's death her husband had a season of belief in spiritualism, until a public investigation of the seances. At eighty he published his book on comparative religion, and died an Irvingite just before the

Great War. The War made Maurice a pacifist, and sent Stanley to work in a canteen. Maurice's son Roger, who wrote light verse that disgusted his father, made a name for himself with his trench poetry. Irving contributed an ambulance, and became a special constable. Una sent cakes to the boys at the front, and employed land girls on the farm. Stanley's daughter, Molly, frankly enjoyed the War as an ambulance driver, and became engaged to officers, successively and simultaneously, and at the end received the O.B.E. for her distinguished services. Vicky's son, Tony, was killed. Her daughter, Nancy, turned violently anti-war, and became engaged to a Hungarian artist. Imogen drifted through the War in office work and, even as her Aunt Rome, reflected on the futility of things. Billy, Stanley's son, disappointed her by insisting on becoming a veterinary surgeon, instead of following a political career. As the book ends, Rome is seeing Stanley off to Geneva, to a position in the Labor Department of the League of Nations, full of hope and confidence in what promises to be the most interesting work of her life. Driving her car home, Rome reflects on the pageant of life, a silly story perhaps but a remarkable one, "told by an idiot . . . but an idiot with gleams of genius and of fineness." She had watched it all as a curious and entertaining show, and had refused to descend to the dust of the arena as an active participant.

TOM FOOL, by F. Tennyson Jesse (1926). The Fould family, Lancashire cotton spinners, were driven to emigrate to Australia by the shutting down of the cotton mills at the time of the American Civil War. Tom, nicknamed Tom Fool for his reckless daring, is fourteen when the family come to London to get their passage in the steerage of the "Mary Prosper." He had always loved birds more than anything up to this time, and the sight of ships riding the waves like birds entrances him. He decides to be a sailor and sometime have a ship of his own. The life on board ship is a happy one for Tom, and he is sorry to land in Australia. After three dreary years working in the goldfields he is free to leave the family who can get along without his work, and goes to the coast to find a ship. His first ship is the "Berinthia" bound for the China seas, and no hardship or brutal experience of seafaring life dims his passion for his calling. He finds a friend in John Masters, the grandson of one of the largest shipowners in Liverpool, on a voyage for his health, and to learn the family business from the bottom up. Tom lives in the thrill of high moments of danger that his adventurous spirit craves. When John falls overboard Tom jumps after him and saves his life, and he is ashamed to remember afterwards that though he had risked his life for his friend he had thought less of John than of the sheer moment of joy that only risk could give him. John left the ship at Caloa and urged Tom to desert the "hungry, driven, bullied Berinthia," but escape was guarded. Arrived in London Tom worked in a navigation school and tramped the docks until he found another ship, too proud to seek out John until he had a post. He sails in many ships to distant lands, and seeks danger rather than security always for the sake of the moments of heightened consciousness and excitement. After ten years at sea he has his master's certificate and works for the Masters firm. He saves his ship and a cargo of wheat by beaching her on a strip of sand off the Lizard promontory near Falmouth, and comes to consciousness afterwards in the home of Jennifer Constantine. She loves the Cornwall country as much as he loves the sea that had drowned her father. He has had adventures and episodes with other women, but now falls in love with her. Their idyll of happiness lasts a year until Jennifer dies when her child is born, and the little girl slips away too. It seems to Tom that his house of life has been wantonly wasted, as there is not to be even the continuity of another's life. In command of his own ship and with John Masters for companion he carries Jennifer's wheat to Australia, the wheat that has become symbolic to him. On the return trip fire broke out and he fights the fire and then sends John and the crew off in boats while he takes a last desperate chance of saving his ship by steering into a waterspout. They find him broken to bits and John buries him at sea, and brings the ship home. He writes to his grandfather that Tom and Jennifer were the most splendid people he had ever met, and that perhaps they were lucky to die so young and so close together. It is an adventure story of the sea, but also a psychological portrait of the hero who craved danger as others desired drink.

TRADER HORN, by Alfred Aloysius Horn (1927). Rambling memories of an old man who had in his youth been a pioneer trader of rubber and ivory in the Africa of the seventies; a narrative of gorilla and elephant hunting, cannibal rites, tribal wars, voodoism, and the Gold Coast slave trade. In an introduction Mrs. Ethelreda Lewis, a South African writer, tells of her meeting with the old peddler of tin ware, and her method of editing his chapters and adding his spoken word to make this book. The young Aloysius was an explorer and trader for the firm of Hatton and Cookson on the Ogowe River. He begins his adventure story with a brief word of his schooldays at St. Edwards College, Liverpool, and his boyhood chum, the son of a Peruvian president, whom he calls "Little Peru." The romance is his rescue of a white girl, Nina, daughter of the black sheep of an English county family and an octoroon, kept a prisoner as virgin goddess in a native witch house of the Isoga tribe. His friend, "Little Peru," comes out to Africa to help him in this dangerous affair and marries the beautiful Nina. He found the cannibals superior to the other tribes of negroes as hunters and workers and in the virtues of cleanliness, courage, and chastity. The elephants he says will last while the cannibals are there to keep them safe from the so-called big game hunters. "They never kill wanton. Only to eat. They'd never be so childish as these dukes and colonels who have to count the head they kill same as we counted our marbles in Lancashire. The cannibal lives as Nature taught him — kill only to eat, keep your women moral, hold no man as slave, be content with your side o' the river, and cast no eyes across the water." He hunts and kills a leopard, and watches a circle of natives dance around the body brandishing their spears and calling on the spirits of those he had killed to witness that they were revenged. Another time he shot a huge bull elephant chasing him across a river and up a hill until the beast fell backward "bringing what seemed the hill with him." The chief comes to congratulate him on his conquest of the elephant that bore a charmed life and which he and his father and grandfather had hunted for many years. In the ceremony of feasting and rejoicing that follows the chief told him tales of old elephants. Horn also describes the capture of a herd of elephants by driving them into an enclosure. Grounded on a sand-bar his boat is attacked by river pirates but he is ready for them with his rifles, and the victory makes him "as good as king of the river." He had no admiration for Livingstone and Stanley, and their publicity, but he respected Rhodes, not after "gaudy success," only ambitious "to make something to grow in the breast of tamed Nature, when it's yourself that's done the taming." John Galsworthy in an introductory preface vouching for the authenticity of the author quotes his saying, "like a lad in a toy-shop — Rhodes." One time he rescued Rhodes asleep on a rock within reach of the crocodiles after he had had a too liberal potation of prickly-pear brandy. He found the music box which Du Chaillu had left in a native village half a generation before. The editor refrains from correcting the spelling and punctuation of this life story by an unlettered author.

TRAGEDY OF WASTE, THE, by Stuart Chase (1927). This author's study has "led down and down through level after level of ineffectiveness and loss." Of the four main channels of waste he first notes wastes in consumption — the production of goods which lie outside the category of human wants, of which he makes main classifications; the second main channel of waste is idle man-power, under which is cited a list of principal losses, in which strikes and lock-outs are listed; the technique of production and distribution is listed in the third channel of loss and leakage, with a long list of items, among which is excess plant capacity and duplication of service; and the waste of natural resources is considered the fourth and last main channel, with the following chief resources coming under this head: coal, water power, oil, natural gas, mineral ores, timber, the soil, animal life, including fisheries and failure to utilize by-products. The author arrives at a "rough minimum total of man-power and raw material losses." He considers the motor car mania, the radio, the flat silver, the dinner coat, and says that the vast hold of tradition and habit and social custom must be regarded in any study of wastes in consumption. "The elements to watch are artificial stimulation, and that factor, due to the inequality of purchasing power, which makes one economic class, for its own self respect, imitate the foibles of the class immediately above it." A category of wants — both individual and social — which are to be found among all people, in all ages, is given. Wastes in consumption brings an extensive toll, under which is listed the military establishment in relation to the costs of the Great War; drugs — the opium traffic; patent medicines; alcohol and tobacco; commercialized vice and crime; adulteration, — under which is listed the borax industry, the blended whiskey industry, the glucose, the white flour, the food dye, and numerous other industries; quackery, and the get-rich-quick performer; speculation and gambling; super-luxuries; fashions; commercialized recreation; with a general summary, in which the author says that the main classifications tend to overlap. An analysis of advertising is also made — the "lifeblood of quackery and the patent medicine industry and an invaluable adjunct in mobilizing a nation for war." The author observes that "America has perhaps pushed the technique of advertising to the highest point ever achieved, but in output per capita England is almost on a par with us." In America, it is shown, one dollar is spent to educate consumers in what they may or may not want to buy for every seventy cents that is spent for all other kinds of education — primary, secondary, high school, university. The causes of idle man-power are discussed, and the author holds that idleness is largely involuntary. "If the idle rich, the hobo, and straight absenteeism are placed in the voluntary class," it is held that upwards of eighty-five per cent of all idleness is thus probably enforced rather than deliberate. Tables from the Federated Engineering Societies and the United States Bureau of Labor Statistics are presented. The findings, as disclosed by the Scientific Management engineers, are given in the chapters on wastes in production and industrial coördination. Wastes in distribution are also discussed, and in the items of loss the author holds that in the aggregate they are considerable and to a certain extent preventable. Natural resources — the gutting of a continent — are treated in relation to the gravity of the loss, while the by-products of waste in coal, natural gas and lumber — the "garbage pail aspect of waste" — are shown in the light of their assets to a nation, for while the author considers the waste from the failure to extract from the raw materials is but a drop in the bucket compared to other losses which he has outlined, this waste is still serious. The author concludes in his "challenge" that there is no sure way out, but calls upon the scientists and statesmen to dig their brains and hands into this roaring wilderness — "so finely wrought in isolated detail — and bring from it ordered cities, impounded waters, terraced and tended forests, the sweep of great transmission lines, clean rivers, workshops planned with the dignity of cathedrals, and the end of grime, poverty, and despair."

TRAVEL DIARY OF A PHILOSOPHER, THE, by Count Hermann Keyserling (2 vols., 1925). The author, a scholar of distinction, states that the impulse which sends him on this journey around the world is the desire for self-realization. While he does justice to the passing scene in the Far East and in the great parks of California, he is interested in sight-seeing only in so far as it bears a relation to his aspirations. He sets out to write philosophy which shall read like a novel of the inner life. In pursuit of this ideal he visits Ceylon, India, China, Japan, and the United States during the years 1911 and 1912, to make a study of the spiritual culture of the people. The first magical impression of the strangeness and beauty of the East comes to him at Ceylon. The profusion and fierce energy of tropical growth made him realize what it is to the Buddhist to long for Nirvana as a refuge from the intolerable vehemence of Being. This observation introduces a long and careful study of Buddhism. In India he is impressed with the Hindu ideal of perfection, and the great value of the practice of Yoga, training the will by ever repeated concentration upon its higher possibilities, as self-discipline. The state of mind in itself and not what it accomplishes is according to Hindu belief the true measure of character, being not necessarily doing. "Recognition does not lead to salvation, but is salvation." The Indian mind has tolerance for all forms of life and thought as fitting at their own stage of being. At Calcutta he became acquainted with the circle of artists, writers and musicians in the group around Tagore. The ideal of perfection with the Chinese he describes as one of moral culture, a belief in the fundamental harmony between the moral principles and the physical world, and serene submission to the natural order of things resulting from this belief. "Man can only become inwardly perfect if he expresses himself perfectly outwardly; he can only express what is most personal in him correspondingly if he obeys the forms which have proved themselves to be typical for the Chinese in the course of history." He depicts two types of Chinese character, the peasant and the high official. The Japanese he thinks are not imitators but the intellectual exploiters of the world, appropriating and adapting the best for themselves in a spirit of intense patriotism. He considers the Japanese women as the most perfect type of this era. The ambitious activity of the people he considers wholly opposed to Buddhism, and the religion best suited to them to be protestant Christianity, as the Japanese are not Oriental in character. He speaks of their feeling for nature, and their art. In spite of his predilection for the contemplative philosophy of the East he expresses his faith in the dynamics of the West. He admits that experimental science has done more for the emancipation of the masses than the wisdom of the adepts. But he returns convinced that each individual must pursue his own development in self-realization. To the self-knowledge regarded as essential in the East there must be added the conviction of the West that self-knowledge is to be expressed in active life. He gives his impressions of American Christian Science and the various sects of New Thought.

TREE OF HEAVEN, THE, by May Sinclair (1917). The friendly shelter of the great ash tree in the garden represents the comfortable, enclosed well-being of the

Harrison family in the England of the eighteen-nineties. Anthony Harrison is a wealthy lumber merchant. Frances, his wife, is happy in the possession of her four beautiful, clever children, Michael, Nicholas, John, and Dorothy. She skims the "Times" for a knowledge of the affairs of the nation, which do not compare in interest with her own little world. Part of the background with which she contrasts her own life are her three unhappy, repressed, spinster sisters living in subjection to her mother, and her drinking brother, Maurice Fleming, all supported by Anthony, and Bartholomew, Anthony's sour brother with his imaginary ailments. He had married her friend, Vera, who keeps out of his way as much as possible, and eventually leaves him to live with her lover, Ferdie Cameron, sending her lovely little daughter, Veronica, to live with the Harrisons. The children grow up and go to school, Dorothy to Newnham, the boys to Cheltenham and Cambridge. The clear-eyed, logical Dorothy becomes an intellectual feminist, goes to prison for suffrage, and refuses to marry her lover, Frank Drayton, because he does not sympathize with her ideas. The Puck-like Nicky gets into disgrace because the silly wife of a professor falls in love with him, and he is too chivalrous to tell the truth about her. He has looked forward always to a place in the army, and invents a moving fortress which presages the army tank. The artist, Phyllis Desmond, makes his drawings for him, and decides to get him to marry her, because she is going to have a child. He does not love her but his pity is aroused for the child to come, and he marries her because he is reminded of the position of Veronica, Ferdie's child, for whom he really cares. Veronica, at school in Germany, senses his disaster with her gift of second sight, and comes home ill. Ferdie was killed in the Boer War, and Vera, to whom the disagreeable Bartie refuses a divorce, is living with Lawrence Stephen, a distinguished magazine editor, poet and playwright. Phyllis's child does not live and she continues her free life and discards Nicky. Michael, with his hatred of the crowd spirit becomes an extreme individualist and a radical poet. July 1914 comes with the declaration of War, and the affairs of the nation become more important than those of the Harrison family. Anthony and Frances discover that they love England more than their own lives or the lives of their children. Nicky is the first to go after a brief honeymoon with Veronica. Frank Drayton is sent to the front and killed before he can marry Dorothy. Michael, only, refuses to be patriotic, but after Nicky's death he goes into his brother's regiment, and writes to Veronica that he has gone all his life trying to get reality, and new beauty, and now after all his "funk" at coming out to "obscene ugliness and waste and frustration" has found what he wanted. John has been refused on account of his heart, but the standards are lowered, and the last paragraph shows Anthony waiting in his car to take him also, after the news of Michael's death. It is a picture of the War coming to England, and of the youth that went into the War.

TRISTAN AND ISOLT, by John Masefield (1927). The famous story of mediæval romance, done as a play in blank verse. That it was written with the idea of stage production in mind is indicated by a note at the end of the book, which states the playing time and suggests suitable costumes and decorations. Speaking from front stage at the opening of the action, Destiny reveals the plot:

> I show Tristan, the prince, in glory beginning,
> And Isolt, the maid, in her beauty: I show these two
> Passing from peace into bitter burnings and sinning
> From a love that was lighted of old. I display them anew
> And the deaths that were due.

Masefield's version of the story has it that Tristan, a Pictish prince, has been brought by Dinan, his steward, to Tintagel, court of the Cornish kings, where he finds Cornwall under the yoke of Kolbein, a Scandinavian pirate, who has killed Meirchyon, King of Cornwall, and enslaved his son Marc, uncle of Tristan. The Pict prince mortally wounds Kolbein in combat, but before he dies the pirate declares an end to the blood feud and exacts a promise from Marc, who is now about to assume his rightful place as King of Cornwall, that he will take as Queen, Isolt, daughter of Kolbein's queen, Thurid. Kolbein instructs Tristan to bear his body to Ireland and to bring Isolt back with him that she may marry Marc. Before setting out on the return journey with Isolt, Tristan and she drink to each other in magical wine which causes them to fall deeply in love. On Isolt's wedding night, when she is supposed to drink from a flasket of love-wine with King Marc, she forces Brangwen, her waiting gentlewoman, to take her place in the darkened bedchamber and drink with the King. In her agitation, Brangwen drops the cup after drinking, so that she falls in love with Marc, but he is only drugged into sleep by the dregs which remain in the cup. Tristan's trysts with Isolt are finally made known to Marc through the spying of Kai and Bedwyr, steward and baily respectively to the King, with the result that although Isolt is befriended by Arthur, captain of the Romano-British host, Marc sets a trap for Tristan who escapes by leaping from Isolt's window, but he is banished from the kingdom. He flees to the forest with Isolt, however, while Marc, realizing the depth of their devotion to each other, makes little effort to capture them. Marc later finds them sleeping in a cave and leaves his glove lying between them on the hilt of Tristan's sword, in token of his decision not to kill, but to forgive them. Upon awakening Isolt is moved to contrition at sight of the glove and returns to Marc, who forgives her and makes her ruling Queen over Cornwall while he is away at war. Tristan becomes mad and wanders through the forest in search of Isolt. Marc is killed in battle, and Isolt, finding Tristan about to die, stabs herself. Destiny pronounces the Epilogue:

> Not as men plan, nor as women pray, do things happen,
> Unthought of, unseen, from the past comes the ill without cure;
> By the spirit of man and the judgment of God it is shapen,
> And its pride is our pride in the dust; it is just: it is sure.

TRISTRAM, by Edward Arlington Robinson (1927), is a long, narrative poem in which the old Arthurian story of Tristram and the two Isolts is told with a simplicity and a driving power that exalts both subject and reader. Tristram is first met on the great stone stair without the castle of his uncle Mark, King of Cornwall. It is the evening of the king's marriage to Isolt of Ireland. As Tristram watches the cold waves break against the rocks he meditates on what is going on within, and what his blind share has been in bringing this marriage to pass. He sees himself in Ireland in combat with Isolt's kinsman Morhaus and then her care for him as he lay wounded in her father's castle. He recalls his part in bringing her to King Mark who had his first report of her beauty through his nephew. Tristram curses the fatuous popularity of his youth that blinded him to Isolt's charm until it was too late to woo her for himself. Death invites him from the rocks below until his meditations are interrupted by messengers from the king commanding his presence at the wedding festival. His old friend and guardian, Gouvernail comes first, then Queen Morgan seeks to lure him from his love back to his duty and to an appreciation of her more attainable charms. Faithful Brangwine follows these, but all are told he is too ill to return. Then comes Isolt herself. Together they rehearse the possibilities in their tragic fate. Andred, his cousin, and Mark's minion, spies upon them in their parting embrace and being discovered by Tristram, the two fight until Andred falls wounded. Thereupon King Mark appears with his followers and orders Tristram into perpetual exile. He departs, followed later by the faithful Gouvernail, who rescues him when he is found unconscious from a fever in the forest and brings him to a hut in which Queen Morgan tries to hold him in enchantment. But Morgan has no power over one who is followed always by the memory of Isolt of Ireland's sad dark eyes as she looked at him last from the great stone stairs at parting. So he sets forth with Gouvernail to Brittany where he finds another and younger Isolt whose childish memory of his earlier visit there has ripened into love. Tristram slays the Griffon who had infested the domain and allows his indifference to give way before the manifest desire of this Isolt of the white hands for their marriage. Into their tranquil existence come the messengers of King Arthur summoning him to become a Knight of his Round Table. Isolt has a presentiment as she bids her husband farewell that he will not return. Shortly after he has become a knight at King Arthur's court, Tristram finds his way to Joyous Gard where, by the aid of friends, he and Isolt of Ireland meet again and find for an interval that fulfilment in love for which they have yearned. King Mark, released from captivity, brings the Queen back to Cornwall but shows some kingly magnanimity in permitting Tristram access to Isolt who is dying. Their last talk together is again broken into by Andred, perhaps urged on by vengeful Morgan. He stabs Tristram in the back and kills him. So the two lovers are united in death.

TRIUMPH OF THE EGG, THE, a book of impressions from American life in tales and poems, by Sherwood Anderson (1921). The first selection only is a poem, "The Dumb Man," and expresses the problem of the author in all his writing to put the inexpressible into words, what happens in the minds of his characters, frustrated, inarticulate people. There are three men and a woman in a house. A fourth man comes into the house. He may represent Death as "the waiting eager woman may have been Life. . ." "There is a story — I cannot tell it — I have no words. . . ." The story that gives its name to the collection portrays the ineffectual struggle of man and matter under the aspect of the cycle of the egg to the egg. A man and his wife try to wrest a living out of a chicken farm. They fail in this effort, and move to town to start a restaurant, which is also a failure. In a last desperate attempt to conquer the egg, the man tries to do a trick that will "establish his reputation as one who knew how to entertain guests who came into his restaurant." The egg breaks in his hand, making him ludicrous, and in anger he wishes to destroy all eggs. The child looks at the egg and wonders "why eggs had to be and why from the egg came the hen who again laid the egg," but cannot solve the problem of the futility of things. "I Want to Know Why" is the adventure of a boy who adored horses, and some of his chums, who run away from home to see the races at Saratoga. They beat their way on freight trains to the city, and "with the true instinct of Kentucky boys" find the stables and a friend, a nigger cook from their home town, who feeds them and finds them a place to sleep. Through the eyes of this nice youngster we see the tracks, and the background that "gets" him, the "lovely" smell, a mixture of "coffee and manure and horses and niggers and bacon frying and pipes being smoked out of doors on a morning." He picks the winner and to him there wasn't anything in the world but the horse, his trainer, Jerry, and himself. In the evening following his hero, he sees Jerry through the windows of a house where "bad women stay" kissing a "tall rotten looking woman." It spoils the tracks for him and he persuades the other kids to start for home. "Out of Nowhere Into Nothing" is almost a novelette. Rosalind a stenographer in Chicago, falls in love with her employer, a married man, and decides to give herself to him. She comes on a visit to her home in the small town to try to tell her mother about it. They sit on the porch in the heat talking of canning and the weather instead of the impending crisis in her own life, and she feels that she has made the journey for nothing. A chance meeting and talk with Melville Stoner, an understanding neighbor, gives her the help she wants, invading her secret life with his recital of the stupid commonplace doings of her home. Her mother's reaction to her confession is an outcry against sex and men, a denial of love and life. She walks away in the night to get the train for Chicago and take the chance of happiness. The man she loves, Walter Sayers, is lonely and estranged from his wife, who has filled the emptiness of her life with her passion for gardening. With Rosalind he feels that he is able to express himself. "Brothers" is about a foreman in a bicycle factory in love with a girl who works in the office. He sometimes walks to the car with her and continually thinks about her, while he works, reading his newspaper, and when he goes to the movies with his wife. His mother-in-law lives with them, taking care of the child, and saves them the wages of a servant. One night as they return from the movies he stabs his wife in the dark entrance hall. He is arrested, and will atone with his pitiful life for the crime.

TROLLOPE, ANTHONY, by Michael Sadleir. Introduction by A. Edward Newton (1927). This biographical and critical study of Trollope begins with a study of the mid-Victorian period of which his novels are a social history. The author quotes Henry Adams's impressions of English society from "The Education of Henry Adams" to illustrate his analysis of the times. It is Mr. Sadleir's opinion that Trollope's novels are "much more remarkable for their expression of period-psychology than for their literary texture." A section is devoted to a sketch of Frances Trollope, Anthony's mother, whose successful novels kept her family from starving after his father had speculated disastrously with his inheritance and reduced the prosperous family to poverty. The son had her courage and energy and lack of self-consciousness and vanity. He learned from this gay, charming, commonplace, heroic woman "that honesty and toil make in the end for happiness, and the comfort that he gave his mother in her latter days was but a repayment of a debt." Reminiscences of contemporaries complete the vivid portrait of Mrs. Trollope. As a satirist of manners she "was too truthful for the liking of the day." The story of Anthony's lonely and unhappy childhood follows the "Autobiography." He was left at home with his gloomy father while his mother was in America. The family misfortunes did not allow him to go to Oxford like his older brother, Tom. He went to Harrow as a day-boarder and appeared to the other boys "rude and uncouth," and "slovenly and dirty." Longing for companionship as his "Autobiography" reveals he had not a single friend. When he was nineteen he was offered a junior clerkship in the General Post Office, and spent seven years in cheap lodgings alone in London until under-nourishment and irregular habits brought on serious illness. He gained from his London experience self-confidence and the habit of observation, and tolerance. Application for a vacant clerkship in Ireland gave him the opportunity to leave London for a healthful life making tours of the post offices in his district on horseback instead of sitting at a desk copying letters. Trollope lived in Ireland for ten happy years. His engagement to Rose Heseltine came a year after his arrival in Ireland, and his marriage to her two years later. The great pleasure of his life was hunting. He managed to adjust his official tours of inspection so that he could attend the local hunt. An official order removed him to Western England where he spent two years, observing the English country life, the social position of the clergy, the influence in a county of the county town, the attitude of the leading townsmen to the "gentry" and the small intrigues and jealousies and gossip of the town. A series of official missions to Egypt, to Scotland, and the West Indies gave him a love of travel. In Italy, visiting his mother, he met the young American girl, Kate Field, with whom he was undoubtedly in love though with all the proprieties and reticence of the mid-Victorian man of fifty. His letters to her are first published in this book. At this time he is portrayed as "all rosy cheeks and bushy whiskers" entering a room with a "huge roar of greeting" and the high spirits which were characteristic of him. He was "a strong walker, a good eater, a connoisseur of wine, and an insatiable disputant," a vigorous but not docile government official, and a popular and distinguished author. The æsthetic generation which followed him "found beauty in abnormality," and relegated his literary reputation to a respectable oblivion. His own "Autobiography" which appeared posthumously discredited him by the false modesty with which he referred to his novels as "mechanical stuff," and revealed his businesslike interest in royalties. He had "a stolid determination to do good work and to receive good wages," and "boasted himself a workman." The post-War generation has a better appreciation of him. Mr. Sadleir considers power of characterization his superlative quality, and that his realism is due to his reproduction of the daily round, "dramatizing the undramatic" without help of sudden incident or striking misadventure." Sir Walter Raleigh is quoted as saying of him that he "starts off with ordinary people and makes an epic of them, because he understands affection," which is true of the man as well as of the novels. He loved his kind, and "appreciated the power in human life of mutual tolerance and of mutual affection. . . ." A critical section discusses the novels and gives a summary of the plots. Appendices contain calendars of events in the lives of both mother and son and bibliographies.

TRUTH ABOUT BLAYDS, THE, by A. A. Milne (1922). The truth about Blayds, in a word, was that he was a complete humbug. Ninety, venerated as the last of the Victorians, of so strong a personality that his daughter's husband took his name, becoming Blayds-Conway, and his grandchildren are named after himself and his muse respectively, it comes out after his death that Oliver Blayds had stolen every last bit of his poetry from a fellow-poet who died in early youth. The reactions of his children and grandchildren are characteristic. His elder daughter, Marion, who married William Conway and became in time "Mrs. Blayds-Conway" is all sympathy for her husband, who has made a lifelong avocation of Blayds and planned to write his biography. If the truth were published William would be considerably out of luck. Blayds' younger daughter, Isobel, had martyrized herself for her father: sending away her lover, Royce, and devoting herself exclusively to his care, since she possessed a light hand in nursing which Marion lacked, for all her executive ability. When Isobel hears that her father was an imposter she is instantly convinced that she should announce the truth to the newspapers and renounce the considerable fortune Blayds had accrued from royalties and their investment. In this she is supported by Royce, and her niece and nephew, who are heartily sick of reflected glory. But the opposition of Marion and William is so strenuous that a compromise is effected. Royce points out that even if Isobel did insist on publishing the facts, doubt would always exist in many minds, since Blayds, when he confessed, was ninety and in failing health. She would just start "another wretched Shakespeare-Bacon" controversy. After all, the poetry is the main thing: it is there; what difference will it make, fifty or a hundred years from now, whether it was written by an Oliver Blayds or a John Smith? Let Isobel refuse her share of the fortune if it will soothe her conscience — he, Royce, has enough for them both — and let it go at that. To which Isobel reluctantly agrees, and the play ends, with William planning to include the "scandal" in his biography with deprecatingly magnanimous comment, saying: "I feel strongly, and I am sure you will agree with me, that it is our duty to tell the whole truth about that great man."

TWAIN'S, MARK, AUTOBIOGRAPHY, with an introduction by Albert Bigelow Paine, (2 vols., 1924), is best described in his own words, as a wandering at free will, all over life, talking only about those things which interest him for the moment. The consequence of such a method is that digression takes him "far and wide over an uncharted sea of recollection, and the result of that is history." Unlike the conventional biographer, he believes that the little things of life, the contacts with the uncelebrated, are just as interesting as collisions with the famous. He further elucidates his method when he compares narrative with the course of a brook, "changed by every bowlder it comes across . . . its surface broken, but its course not stayed by rocks . . . a brook that never goes straight for a minute, but goes and goes briskly, sometimes ungrammatically and sometimes fetching a horseshoe three-quarters of a mile around . . . but always going, and always following at least one law . . . the law of narrative which has no law." One of the most interesting detours in this narrative of his life is the account of his relations with General Grant which led to the publishing of Grant's memoirs. Comparing this incident, and the memories of John Hay which occur later in the book, with the fluctuations of fortune recorded of his Micawber-like brother, Orion, or the lengthy account of the Villa Quarto's interior where he and his wife spent some months, hardly bears out the author's contention that collisions with the great are of less interest than minor events and personalities. The unstudied charm and winning courtesy of John Hay's manner is set against his wife's prim, Presbyterian way. That intrepid statesman, comments Clemens, had looked upon Horace Greeley in his youth without fear and later, as Secretary of State, was not "scarable by kings," yet it appeared that "no courage is absolutely perfect; that there is always someone able to modify his pluck." If John Hay lacked the pluck to stand up for his friend when his comely young wife rebuffed him, there were times, as it appeared later on, when Mark himself had little more courage. In highly entertaining fashion he recounts his own discomfiture at the hands of his wife, when he left the bathroom door ajar one day while shaving. As his custom was he expressed his mounting irritation in the glowing, not to say sulfurous, language of a Mississippi river pilot, supposing himself securely shut away from the world. Seeing that he had completely given himself away he tried to slink past the stern mentor in the other room, whereupon there issued from his wife's lips his latest bathroom remark. As he ruefully notes, "The language perfect but the expression unpractical, apprentice-like . . . comically inadequate, absurdly weak and unsuited to the great language." Kipling reported Mark Twain as saying, on one occasion, that an autobiography is "the one work in which a man, against his own will, and in spite of his utmost striving to the contrary, revealed himself in his true light to the world." So the naïveté with which the great humorist resents comparison of his physical appearance to the lanky Bill Nye, taken along with the selections he chooses from his little daughter Susy's biography, describing his really handsome appearance, indicate that he was not without his share of vanity. This appeared again in the resentment he showed toward a certain ignorant man who attempted to edit an introduction Mark Twain had written. But this normal vanity cropping out thus unconsciously does not appear excessive. His rightful pride in the writer's craftsmanship, as he states it, "I like the exact word, and clarity of statement, and here and there a touch of good grammar for picturesqueness;" is modified by common sense. Of that reviewer who is always correct, "a grammatical coxcomb," he says, "This reviewer even seems to know (or seems even to know, or seems to know even) how to put the word 'even' in the right place . . . a person who is as self-righteous as that will do other things. . . . When a man works up his grammar to that altitude, it is a sign. It shows what he will do if he gets a chance. . . . They stop at nothing." How good his own writing is, may be seen in many passages of the autobiography, most notably those mellow and mellifluous pages describing his uncle John's farm, the southern goodies on his table, and the joy of life for a boy living there. Other passages are like a flash from the flint, temporarily illuminating a subject. Slavery only touched Mark Twain's life in its more pleasing and accepted aspects, for the most part. "It was the mild domestic slavery not the brutal plantation article. . . . To separate and sell the members of a slave family to different masters was a thing not well liked by the people, and so it was not often done, except in the settling of estates." The saddest faces he ever saw, he remembers, were those of a dozen black men and women chained together awaiting shipment to the Southern slave market. Another pathetic incident which he recalls was that of Sandy, a noisy little slave boy brought away from his family. Mark came to his mother one day complaining of the racket the little fellow was making, for he and his cousins often played with them as comrades. His mother replied: "Poor thing, when he sings it shows that he is not remembering, and that comforts me; but when he is still I am afraid he is thinking, and I cannot bear it. He will never see his mother again; if he can sing, I must not hinder it, but be thankful for it. If you were older, you would understand me; then that friendless child's noise would make you glad." Humorously he records the impression made on Mr. Langdon when he first asked for Livy's hand in marriage. That Power to which Burns made his appeal never failed Mark Twain. He could always see himself as others saw him. Later, tenderly, and with all the sincerity of his great nature, he pictures their family life and the sense of irretrievable loss that never left him after they were gone. Other glints from the flint appear in his description of the glorious color and quaint costumes in a Viennese Procession, "All the centuries were passing by." No incident is more self-revelatory of this rollicking, tumultuous, tender, thoughtful man than that of his later years when Webster and Co. failed for a large sum of money, and he made good. His wife and nephew, Samuel E. Moffett, as well as his friend, Henry H. Rogers, agreed with him that, "a literary man's reputation is his life; he can afford to be money poor, but he cannot afford to be character poor." His staunch independence in that is but another facet of a character which early expressed itself in regard to politics, "I have never voted a straight ticket from that day to this. I have never belonged to any party from that day to this. I have never belonged to any church from that day to this. I have remained absolutely free in these matters. And in this independence I have found a spiritual comfort and a peace of mind quite above price."

TWENTY-FIVE YEARS, by Viscount Grey of Falloden (1925). As a Parliamentary Under-Secretary, when Lord Rosebery went to the Foreign Office, in 1892, the author of these volumes, Sir Edward Grey, began his training for public affairs and his narrative starts from that time. The earlier chapters deal with the episodes of work in the Foreign Office from August 1892 to June 1895. When the Government of Lord Roseberry was defeated the Under-Secretary resigned. More than ten years later he entered the Foreign Office again. From 1905 to near the close of 1916, Viscount Grey directed English foreign affairs, and his memoirs survey once more, in the light of the old Entente, the origins of the understandings with France and Russia, the Algeciras crisis, the Persian adjustments, the Bosnia-Herzegovina affair, the diplomatic rôle of Edward VII, the Agadir uproar, the Balkan War, the first crash, and the diplomacy of the Allied Powers. Viscount Grey discusses general situations, without special reference to what France, Russia, and Serbia were doing behind the scenes; and he insists again and again on two points: (1) that the policy of the Entente, as pursued by him, was not used against German interests; (2) that nothing which he did compromised the freedom of his country to choose in 1914 whether it would or would not support France and Russia. "I was not only ready, I desired to be on good terms with Germany, but the increasing challenge and menace to Great Britain of the growing German naval program was an adverse influence on British feeling towards Germany. It also had the effect of making French and Russian friendship seem more than ever desirable. Meanwhile German policy tests the friendship with France. There is no choice but to sacrifice this friendship, or to strengthen it and to prepare for the contingency of supporting France against a German attack. This is done, but Britain remains unpledged; and when Europe is on the brink of war in 1914, British opinion, official and otherwise, is divided and uncertain. Then the German invasion of Belgium pushes the British Empire into the war. This, I believe, is the main and central truth of British policy and action, and whoever does not accept it and looks for truth about us elsewhere is failing to understand British psychology; moreover he will make mistakes about us in the future." He ascribes the overt act of forcing the War to the German militarist party, but holds the underlying causes to be those for which all the contending nations must take their share of blame. The memoirs contain new Roosevelt letters, there are fresh views of Ambassador Walter Hines Page, and the text of the memorandum drawn by Viscount Grey and Colonel House in February, 1916, embodying President Wilson's program for terminating the War. The Viscount deals specifically with many of the questions which arose between Great Britain and America as the War proceeded and treats of the disappearance of these difficulties after the United States came into the War.

UGLY DUCHESS, THE (Der hässliche Herzogin), by Lion Feuchtwanger (1928). A historical novel of Central Europe of the fourteenth century. Margarete, the heiress of Carinthia and the Tyrol, was a matrimonial prize in the courts of the Wittelbachers, the Luxemburgers and the Habsburgers, in spite of the ugliness of her ape-like mouth which led to her nickname of Maultasch (sack-mouth). She was married at ten to another child, Johann of Luxemburg, brutal and unwilling. This early marriage was never consummated, and deprived of a woman's interests and children, Margarete devoted herself to politics and her people, so that while business was transacted with Duke Johann, "it was known that in reality the ugly young duchess was sole ruler of the land in the mountains." She prevented her husband from raising money from Messer Artese of Florence by pledging the silver mines, and favored the burghers and the growth of the towns rather than the predatory robber barons. Margarete, longing for love, deceived herself with the loyalty and devotion shown to her by Chretien de Laferte, and devoted herself to his advancement. He received the Castle of Taufers at her insistence. She placed him at the head of a plot of the nobles against John and the Luxemburgers. Then the long duel begins between Margarete and the beautiful Agnes von Flavon. Chretien had no knowledge that the Duchess could be slighted by his marriage to Agnes. When Margarete heard the news her fury knew no bounds. She arranged to have the plot betrayed to Johann, and Chretien paid for his loyalty to her and conspiracy against Johann with his head. Johann planned to have Agnes as his mistress at the court. The barons conspired again, drove Johann out of the Tyrol, and the Emperor himself solemnized the wedding of Ludwig, the Wittelbacher, with the Duchess Margarete. They had three children, two girls, who later died of the plague, and a son, Meinhold. The only one of her husband's Bavarian friends Margarete favoured was the hideous, unpopular Konrad of Frauenberg, to whom she was attracted because he was ugly like herself. The need of money induced Ludwig to consent to surrender his native Bavaria to Austria, and the ensuing prosperity was credited to Agnes von Flavon, who had become Ludwig's mistress at this time. The poor Maultasch was accused as the cause of all the misfortunes the country had suffered. Ludwig resolved to rid himself of the Frauenberger and Margarete gave Konrad a vial of poison so that he might save himself, and now Meinhold, the stupid boy, was ruler of the Tyrol. Agnes and Margarete contend for Meinhold, and rather than give him up to the pursuing Bavarians of the "Arthurian Court" the Frauenberger drops him over the cliff. The next victim is Agnes, condemned by the Court for conspiracy but secretly poisoned by the Frauenberger. Margarete gave over her lands to Austria and went into retirement and exile, a broken disappointed woman.

UP STREAM, by Ludwig Lewisohn (1922). This autobiography is the personal record of the life of a sensitive, intellectual Jew who worked his way steadily up the stream of American prejudice to an honored place in American letters. Born in Germany in the eighteen-eighties, Mr. Lewisohn came of people of unmixed Jewish blood who had lived for generations in the North and Northeast of Germany. The only child of well-to-do parents his early recollections are of a comfortable, happy, dreamy existence. Very early in life he developed a keen appreciation for books. When he was only eight his father lost his money and the family was reduced almost to poverty. There followed a period of depression during which his mother feared for his father's sanity. Then came a letter inviting the family to America, where his mother's brother lived, and the family came to South Carolina. Accustomed to comfort and a degree of culture, the crude houses and life of the family and friends of the uncle were an unpleasant surprise to the Lewisohns, but they bravely took up their life under these new conditions. The paramount thought in the minds of the parents was to get a good education for their son and through all the following years of poverty and hardship they kept this ambition. During these years in the little Southern town young Lewisohn attended the schools and churches which the town afforded. His father was a man liberal beyond his time, whose sense of humor placed him above orthodox bigotries. To him and to the boy's mother the mental heritage of the ages was of more import than creeds. When, in the third year at high school, his poetic translations were favorably commented on by his teachers, a new heaven opened for the boy. He scribbled verse in all his spare time and neglected his more unpopular studies. After high school the next step was college, to which he looked forward with keen delight. He had decided on his future means of livelihood: he would be a professor of English literature. In college he continued his studies, his writing and his contacts with the Christian church. As time went on the realization came to him that he must hurry with all this preparation; his father and mother were growing older and the burden of his education was telling on them. After graduation from college he tried for positions, but receiving no appointment decided to spend one year in study at home and at the end of that time he tried for a fellowship at both Harvard and Columbia. Failing in both, he borrowed the money and entered Columbia for graduate work. Even after his creditable work he did not get a professorial position on account of his Jewish extraction. Of his graduate work he says: "What I wanted was ideas, interpretive, critical, æsthetic, philosophical, with which to vivify, to organize, to deepen my knowledge, on which to nourish my intellectual self. And my friends, the professors, ladled out information. . . . They did not realize that, the elementary tools of knowledge once gained, there is but one thing that can teach men and that is the play of a large and incisive personality." He turned to writing for the magazines. Later he held the professorship of German in a mid-western university, from which he returned to New York, where he reached distinction as a critic and as dramatic editor of "The Nation." Both his father and mother died before he reached the goal for which he had struggled for so long. His fight has been "up stream" for a man of sensitive and idealistic temperament. Especially bitter were the war years' experience as a university professor. He criticizes American life and character, in which he sees: "no stirring, no desire to penetrate beyond fixed names of living things, no awakening from the spectral delusions amid which they pursue their aimless business and their sapless pleasures." This story of disillusionment and repression is a passionate arraignment of the Christian-capitalist civilization "in which," in his opinion, "there is no personal liberty worthy of the name; no individual freedom of thought or conduct; no encouragement to be honest, to be one's self and to construct original formulas of truth, beauty and happiness."

VANDEMARK'S FOLLY, by Herbert Quick (1921). A story of the pioneer period of the Middle West. The life story of the little Dutch boy, Jacobus Teunis Vandemark, is a chapter in the history of the settlement of an Iowa township. His first memories are of his mother and his cruel, domineering stepfather, John Rucker, who put the boy to work in the factory when he was nine years old. At times that her husband was away on one of his peddling trips his mother would take him out of the factory for a few days at a time and send him to school. A kind canal boat captain rescued him from John Rucker's whip, and gave him work as a driver on the tow-path of the Erie Canal. After two years he returned with his savings to see his loved mother, and found the house deserted. A note from his mother in the hollow of the apple-tree that they had used as a post-office told him they were going west. A long search for his mother brings him to her grave in Madison, Wisconsin. To get rid of him and rob him of the inheritance that had come too late to help his mother, John Rucker gave him the deed to a farm in Iowa, a team and a wagon and a hundred dollars. On the trail of the great westward-moving stream of the forties he meets two abolitionists who tell him of the Underground railway for fugitive slaves and urge him to join the free-staters in Kansas. He trades his two horses for four cows and a hundred dollars and his board while he is breaking them to drive like oxen, and wins the nickname Cow Vandemark. His cows gave him milk and butter besides. Crossing the Mississippi River at Dubuque a man asks him to take his wife across in the wagon. Later he learns that he has unknowingly helped her to run away from her husband with Dr. Bliven. Other travelling companions are the ragged Fewkes family, and Buckner Gowdy, a gentleman rake from Kentucky, and his young sister-in-law, Virginia Royall, left stranded with him by the death of her sister. Virginia asks the shy young Dutchman if he knows anyone along the road ahead who would be kind to a friendless girl. A few days later she runs away from Gowdy to him for protection. They travel and camp together until they meet Elder and Grandma Thorndyke who take charge of Virginia, and Jake is left lonely without her. The farm turns out to be chiefly marsh land known as "Hell's Slew" and he realizes how John Rucker has cheated him. With the help of a Norwegian neighbor, Magnus Thorkelson, he courageously breaks the wild prairie land of the dry acres, plants corn, builds a warm dugout barn, and then hauls lumber from the river for a little house. He went to see Virginia at the Thorndyke home but Virginia is a town girl and he does not dare ask her to come out and rough it on his farm. He grows ragged and shabby for lack of money, and works for Buck Gowdy to earn wages. Jake is a member of the Settler's Club organized to drive out claim-jumpers and squatters, and on a raid meets the Fewkes family again, and takes them home with him. Buck Gowdy is attracted by pretty young Rowena Fewkes and offers them work on his place. The poor inexperienced girl is deceived by Gowdy, and then cast off by her family. She comes to Jake, whom she has loved always, and asks him to marry her, and tells him that she is going to have a baby. He thinks of the happy days he had spent with Virginia and his dreams of her as his wife, and then tells Rowena he will marry her. She senses his sacrifice and says that she has thought of another way out. Jacob rescues her from suicide when she tries to drown herself, and soon after that her baby is born in his house. Magnus marries her and loves and cares for her though the neighbors treat them coldly. Rowena publicly christens the child Owen Lovejoy Gowdy. Virginia and Jacob are friends again before Jacob goes to the Civil War in Gowdy's company. A few days after his return from service he sees a blizzard coming and goes to the schoolhouse where Virginia is teaching to bring her safely home. He intercepts Gowdy going on the same errand, fights him for his sleigh and horses, and leaves his rival tied with a rope while he goes to get Virginia. They are lost in the storm and find shelter by burrowing into a hay stack. Jacob confesses that he is a robber and a horse-thief, but Virginia agrees to marry him. Elder Thorndyke married them two weeks afterward. Jacob is elected justice of the peace chiefly through the efforts of Dr. Bliven, whom he had befriended, and the township is named after him.

VANGUARD, THE, by Arnold Bennett (1927). The greater part of the action of this novel takes place on board the private yacht of Lord Ralph Furber — "The Vanguard." Furber is excessively rich, a millionaire newspaper owner, who began life as a mechanical inventor, and whose royalties made him rich. He was elevated to the Peerage but tired of walking up to the House of Commons as he did of the "money that overtook him." The piling up business was still going on when the story opens. "I do all I can not to let my money accumulate. This yacht is one of my efforts in that line. My wife does her best, too. No good." He and his wife have a quarrel over a tradesman's bill. Lady Furber refused to pay it on the grounds that she knew she was being swindled; Lord Furber told her that he would make her pay it, as he didn't want his name in the papers over tradesmen's bills. If the bill was not paid, Lord Furber declared he would never speak to his wife again, and she said she didn't care and refused to be browbeaten. This is the situation, with Lord Furber on board his yacht, with secretaries and a housekeeper, anchored in the Bay of Naples, trying to escape from boredom; and Lady Furber at her home in London. Lallers' Limited — the firm to which Lady Furber owes money — is owned by Septimius Sutherland. Lord Furber has made up his mind to kidnap him and buy him out and thus settle his domestic troubles. Sutherland is a guest at the Hotel Splendide. The servants in the kitchens go on a "strike," in accordance with Lord Furber's plan, and Sutherland and the other guests are invited to go aboard "The Vanguard" for dinner. "Count Veruda," a secretary, has acted for Lord Furber. Among the guests at the hotel is Harriet Perkins, a young woman, who in order to obtain a fortune to which she fell heir had to change her name. After a sumptuous spread on the yacht, the guests are finally put off and return to the hotel, but Sutherland and Harriet find that they have been locked in, and that the yacht is heading either for Capri or the open Mediterranean. Harriet is an old friend of Lady Furber, but has never before seen Lord Furber. He has no suspicion as to Harriet's identity — he only knows that she happened to be with Sutherland and the orders to keep Sutherland on board could not have been carried out without disturbing Harriet. When Sutherland's luggage is found to be on board, Harriet begins to investigate the plot. Hers was left behind — at the hotel. Furber tells her something of his story — she already knows from Maidie — Lady Furber — of the lively times caused by Furber's peculiarities, but she suspects that Maidie does not comprehend her husband's psychology. Harriet tells him something of her own life — when she is sick of her flat in London, she goes abroad — when she's sick of abroad, she returns to London. Furber says that what she needs is "work." He creates the position of confidential secretary for her. Sutherland and Furber come to blows on the deck, and Furber feigns loss of memory. Harriet meets the skipper, the wireless operator, the housekeeper and under-secretaries. She tries to get Tunnicliff, the wireless man, to send a message for her to Count Veruda to the Hotel Splendide, asking him to meet the yacht at Ostia with her trunk. Tunnicliff refuses — under orders not to send any messages except those of Lord Furber. Harriet has another scheme for changing the destination of the yacht, a fake wireless ordering the "Vanguard" to anchor at the mouth of the Tiber — upon orders of "Mussolini." Coincident to this, the wireless operator tells her that he has received a message to send the launch with the ship's papers into Ostia — upon orders of the "General Secretary of the Fascisti." The yacht has continued her course to Genoa, but Furber now has her put back to Ostia — he and Tunnicliff are the senders and receivers of all the "wireless" — remarkable and disturbing coincidences to Harriet. Just off shore, the "Vanguard" is met by a procession of motor-craft — a number of small boats, each boat having a pile of cargo hidden beneath ragged sail-cloths. Unpacked, these cargoes prove to be clothes for Harriet. Furber has wired his correspondent in Rome. Rome was near enough to Ostia to send everything from the Roman shops to launches waiting for the "Vanguard" to drop anchor. "Everything is very simple when the word is passed that money doesn't matter. And I never do let money matter." Harriet objects to accepting the clothes, but Lord Furber orders her to "choose 'em and be hanged to ye!" "You are quite right," she said. "I was being absurdly conventional. Nobody ought to be conventional with a millionaire." The story reaches the newspapers. Lady Furber hears the details in London and Harriet telegraphs her to come to Monte Carlo. Meanwhile Lord Furber's party take in the sights of Rome, — then to Monte Carlo. Unknown to any of them except Harriet, Lady Furber has arrived at the Hôtel de Paris. Lord Furber and Sutherland are settling a wager in the Casino. Furber had said it was as difficult to lose as to win, "if you tried to lose," and Sutherland had said "no," and the bet was laid—who would lose the most—the one who lost was to have Lallers' Limited. Harriet sees Lady Furber and clears up the scandal. She smuggles her on board the "Vanguard" and has the option of Lallers' Limited transfered from Sutherland to herself and then to Lord Furber, so that the domestic row over the unpaid bill is settled to the satisfaction of the Furbers. Harriet and Luke Tunnicliff and Count Veruda are leaving the yacht. Lady Furber is supposed to be leaving, too. In the end she decides to remain. The love affair between Harriet and Tunnicliff is left to materialize, with Mr. Sutherland as chaperone, "which was the hardest blow that he had ever suffered."

VATICAN SWINDLE, THE (Les caves du Vatican), translated from the French of André Gide by Dorothy Bussy (1925). The head of the Baraglioul family is the aged diplomat, Juste-Agénor, whose distinguished career is the subject of a book by his son, Count Julius. Julius has written several novels, and with the aid of the clerical vote he hopes to realize his ambition to be elected to the Academy. His sister Veronica and brother-in-law, Anthime Armand-Dubois, the celebrated scientist and atheist, have moved to Rome, and Julius and his wife, Marguerite, go to visit them at the time of the Diamond Jubilee. Anthime is so incensed to hear his wife tell her relatives that she is burning candles for him before the image of the Virgin in the niche in the courtyard that he throws his crutch to put them out and instead knocks off the plaster hand of the Madonna. That night he dreams that the Virgin appears to him and strikes him with her empty sleeve to cure his rheumatism. The miracle has been performed and he is able to walk without his crutches. The family hasten to announce his conversion to the Church, and his public recantation takes place attended by every circumstance of excessive pomp. The Freemasons withdraw their assistance to his worldly affairs and the Church forgets the assistance promised, so that he is reduced to poverty. When Julius returns to Paris he finds a letter from his father urging him to look up a Roumanian youth of nineteen, Lafcadio Wluiki, who is his illegitimate half-brother. Heretofore Lafcadio had known no father, but had had five different "uncles" of as many nationalities, all of whom made much of the boy and contributed to his education. He learned from each of them his own language, besides the German of his Austrian mother. Baron Heldenbruck, the distinguished financier, made him almost a genius at mathematics. From another he learned to be a juggler, conjurer, and acrobat. Finally his mother sent him to Paris to school, which was jail to him after his free life, and only his friendship with a strange mature youth nicknamed Protos helped him to endure his captivity. His mother's death left him penniless as her estate was covered by debts, and Lafcadio was living in a room belonging to Carola Venitequa, the mistress of his friend, Protos, when the money settled on him by his father on his death-bed gave him an assured income. The Countess Guy de Saint-Prix, summoned to Paris by the death of her father, received a call from Protos, masquerading as the canon of Virmontal. There had been a rumour that the Freemasons had kidnapped the Pope and placed an impostor on the throne of St. Peter. A gang of international swindlers used this report to extract money from pious Catholics for a pretended crusade to rescue the Holy Father imprisoned in the dungeon of the Castle of St. Angelo. A large sum of money was necessary to bribe the jailers of the prisoner to enable them to leave the country and live out of the persecutor's reach. The bogus canon told this tale to Marguerite, the Countess of Saint-Prix, under seal of the strictest secrecy, and induced her to give him a check for sixty

thousand francs. She hastened to tell her sister, Arnica, married to Amedee Fleuris-
soire, in the hope of getting a contribution to recoup in part her own gift to the cause.
The innocent Amedee has no money to give, but a devoted son of the Church, he
starts to Rome to try to rescue the Pope. At the station he falls into the hands of
Protos who acts as courier and takes him to a lodging-house of his own selection,
and introduces him to Carlotta, as a person who can speak his native French. Disguised as a priest, Protos meets Amedee outside the Castle, gains his confidence,
and takes him to Naples to an interview with a pretended cardinal, and the two
rascals arrange to have their dupe cash checks for them in Rome. Amedee meets
Count Julius, his brother-in-law, in Rome attending a scientific congress, tells him
about the plot against the Pope, cashes the check with the aid of the incredulous
Julius, and starts for Naples with the money. In the railway carriage he has the
misfortune to be alone with Lafcadio, considering in his anarchistic mind the interesting possibilities of a crime without a motive. He pushes Amedee out of the door
of the railway carriage to death on the tracks. Examining the coat of his victim
he finds the railway ticket bearing the name of Count Julius which he had lent
Amedee, and one cuff-link which Lafcadio had himself presented to Carola. Lafcadio decides to give up his pleasure trip and return to Rome to solve the mystery.
He calls on Julius at his hotel and is asked to go to Naples to bring Amedee's body
which has been found back to Rome. On this journey he meets Protos, disguised
this time as an attorney. The supposed attorney surprises him by producing the
other cuff-link, and his hat which had been clutched by Amedee in the scuffle. Thus
revealing himself, Protos offers him the choice of allegiance to his gang or exposure
to the police. Lafcadio refuses, and confesses his crime to Julius, and at the end of
the story the reader is left in doubt whether or not he will give himself up to the
police. Carlotta, believing Protos guilty of Amedee's death, gives information to
the police, and he kills her in revenge before they capture him. Anthime hears the
story of a false Pope from Julius, convinced of its truth by the first news of Amedee's
fate, and decides that his recantation is invalidated, and returns to his scepticism,
his laboratory experiments on God's creatures, and his contributions to scientific
journals, the more gladly since his rheumatism has come back. This story is not
an attack on religion or the Catholic Church, but an entertaining study in scepticism.

VENETIAN GLASS NEPHEW, THE, by Elinor Wylie (1925). A fantastic
romance of the Venice of the late eighteenth century and the declining Renaissance.
Cardinal Peter Innocent Bon observing the pleasure his fellow prelates take in the
companionship of their numerous nephews, longs to have one of these interesting
relatives himself. True to his middle name he invokes the aid of a magician, Monsieur de Chastelneuf, known to the courts of Europe as Giacomo Casanavo, and his
assistant, a glass-blower, to gratify his desire. The order is filled at a generous price,
and Virginio, the nephew, is all that a fond uncle's heart could wish except that he
is rather brittle. Virginio proceeds to fall in love at first sight with the beautiful
Rosalba, ward of the sceptical Angelo Querini, and considered the infant Sappho
of her time. Married to the flesh-and-blood Rosalba, their happiness is endangered,
because with an embrace from his bride comes an ominous crackling and a fracture
of Virginio's Murano arm. The saint, sinner and sceptic who preside over their
destinies take counsel together, and Monsieur de Chastelneuf, having created the
husband by his knowledge of white magic, engages to make the marriage a success
by the arts of black magic. Rosalba goes to the furnaces of Sevres and is converted
into porcelain to be a fit and safe wife for her crystalline husband.

THE READER'S DIGEST OF BOOKS

VICTORIA, QUEEN, by Lytton Strachey (1921). A sympathetic personal study of the Queen, and portraits of Albert, and Baron Stockmar, Lord Melbourne, Lord Palmerston, Gladstone, and Disraeli. The first chapter "Antecedents" describes the royal uncles, "debauched and selfish, pig-headed and ridiculous, with their perpetual burden of debts, confusions, and disreputabilities." The private life of the young Victoria "had been that of a novice in a convent," brought up by her mother and her governess, the Baroness Lehzen, in the seclusion of "female duty, female elegance, female enthusiasm," "unreached by those two great influences without which no growing life can truly prosper — humor and imagination." Continually pouring herself out in her journal and letters, she is an ideal subject for the author's method of psychological interpretation. The simple gushing child who adored her cousins and her Uncle Leopold and her governess showed also early signs of the self-will that ripened into such authority. The young Queen was instantly fascinated with her charming prime minister, Lord Melbourne, the "autumn rose" of the eighteenth century, and he, at her bidding, cut off his after-dinner wine, and not a single "damn" escaped his lips. Her diary shows Lord Melbourne the hero of these first months of her reign, "a life . . . full of delightful business . . . of simple pleasures . . . riding, eating, dancing." Mr. Strachey expresses the belief that "for a moment the child of a new age looked back, and wavered towards the eighteenth century." The prim pupil of Baroness Lehzen had "secret impulses of self-expression, of self-indulgence even." At this critical moment of her development Albert landed in England, and the Victorian age was assured. "The last vestige of the eighteenth century . . . disappeared; cynicism and subtlety were shrivelled into powder; and duty, industry, morality, and domesticity triumphed," as Victoria, in love with her husband, came more completely under his influence. Disraeli said at Albert's death, "This German prince has governed England for twenty-one years with a wisdom and energy such as none of our Kings have ever shown." Prompted by Stockmar Albert proceeded to reorganize the royal household and to deal with English public affairs. Lord Palmerston, backed by a large majority, long withstood him. Mr. Strachey suggests that had Albert lived he might have acquired such authority as to allow him to come near converting England "into a State as exactly organized, as elaborately trained, as efficiently equipped and as autocratically controlled as Prussia herself." Instead the threads of power which Albert had so laboriously grasped fell from Victoria's hands into those of a succession of brilliant ministers. For years the Queen continued in settled gloom, and her life became one of almost complete seclusion. Her struggles to carry on her husband's work and apply his ideals brought her nothing but unpopularity. The section on Mr. Gladstone and Lord Beaconsfield analyzes the elements of the change from this state of things to the great popularity of her later years. The Queen declared that Disraeli was the only person who had appreciated Albert. As the power of the Crown declined Disraeli restored the Queen to the foreground of public life and invested her with a new prestige as the representative of prosperity and Empire. His official letters to her were in the best style of his romantic novels, and in return she sent him bunches of primroses picked with her own hands. Mr. Strachey concludes with a few pages on her old age. "The girl, the wife, the aged woman, were the same: vitality, conscientiousness, pride, and simplicity were hers to the latest hour."

VORTEX, THE, a play, by Noel Coward (1924). The characters are a group of the idle rich who devote all their time and energy to frivolity. Mrs. Lancaster, once a famous beauty, refuses to face the fact that she is now middle-aged. She always has a lover dancing attendance, and this time it is Tom Veryan, half her age. Her friends, Clara Hibbert, and Pauncefort Quentin, "Pawnie," are types of utter futility. Helen Saville is the only one in the group enough of a friend to try to reason Florence Lancaster out of her selfishness and vanity. Florence explains that she is devoted to David, her husband, but that he has grown old, and she has kept young, and that with a temperament like hers it is impossible for her to live a humdrum life. The son, Nicky, as Helen says, has had everything he wanted and none of the things he really needed. He returns from Paris, where he has been studying music, engaged to a young English girl, Bunty Mainwaring. Bunty greets Tom Veryan as an old friend. At the houseparty at the Lancaster country home the next week-end the frank Bunty decides that Tom is more her type than the neurotic Nicky, and breaks the engagement without a scruple. The affair was "only a sort of try out." Nicky goes on playing the piano to conceal his unhappiness. Later Florence comes upon Tom kissing Bunty good night. She makes a scene and orders Bunty out of the house. In the presence of Nicky, who takes refuge at the piano again, Florence reproaches Tom, and then runs after him up the stairs begging him to come back to her. Two hours afterward in Florence's bedroom Helen is trying to calm the hysterical Florence and persuade her to accept the inevitable. She tells Florence that she was glad to see her suffering and capable of genuine feeling, and regrets that soon she will cease to be unhappy and become vindictive. Nicky comes in to talk with his mother as Helen leaves. The events of the evening have shocked him into facing the facts of both their lives. Convinced that they are "swirling in a vortex of beastliness," he taxes her with ruining his father's life and his own because of her craving for admiration and flattery. He forces her to acknowledge her amours, and at last brings her to promise that she will try to be different by the confession of his own weakness, that he is a drug addict. The play ends with mother and son in each other's arms. Florence wishes she were dead. Nicky answers that "it doesn't matter about death, but it matters terribly about life." The story is secondary in interest to the characters and the dialogue.

WALTZ OF THE DOGS, THE, a play by Leonid Andreyev (1922). The characters are Henry Tile, Carl Tile, his brother, Elizabeth, Alexandrov, nicknamed Feklusha, "Happy Jenny," Andrey Tizenhausen, Ivan Yermolayev, Ivan, the man servant, and two house painters. The scene of Act I is the living room of a new and not yet completely furnished apartment belonging to Henry Tile. Carl Tile is sitting there trying to decide if he can safely steal the money in his brother's drawer. Outside the painters are singing a sad, wordless Russian song. Henry Tile comes in with Alexandrov, Tizenhausen, and Yermolayev. He introduces them to Carl as his associates at the bank, where he is evidently much respected. He tells his friends that Carl is a fine fellow, a serious worker. Then he takes two of his friends to show them how well he has arranged the apartment for his approaching married life. Feklusha remains with Carl, who finds out by contemptuous questioning that he is in the passport department of the police service, is poor and has a large family. Carl ends by asking him if he could supply a false passport and if he has ever had any dealings with murderers. Then Henry and his friends return. The fiancé laughs often and reveals in every word his anticipation of coming happiness in being married to Elizabeth. There is a new piano in the room and, half in jest, he plays the only piece he knows, learned in childhood from his mother and called "The Waltz of the Dogs." Dinner is almost ready when Henry receives a registered letter from Elizabeth telling him that she is already married! He wishes at once to be alone, showing a restrained suggestion of violence. Through a long night he remains awake in the living room. In Scene 1, Act 2, Carl is in his brother's living room cross-examining Ivan, his brother's servant, as to his brother's hours for coming and going and by bribery he obtains a key to the apartment. Feklusha comes in and Carl at once begins insulting him with references to his miserable way of life and tempts him to persuade Henry to insure himself for a hundred thousand roubles. He continually calls Feklusha a fool and tells him that he needs a bath and shows that he is beginning to have the weak man in his power. Henry comes in and announces that the bank has increased his salary and that he will increase Carl's allowance. Carl persuades him to give it to the much disturbed Feklusha. Carl goes. Henry begins to tell Feklusha how they fear him at the bank. Feklusha fearfully tells him that he must have been drinking. Henry calls him a cowardly rabbit and tells him that he, Henry Tile, the irreproachable worker, is going to steal a million from the bank. It seems that he has already talked much of such a plan and continually torments Feklusha with details of his escape. Henry plays "The Waltz of the Dogs" in a serious wooden manner. Henry orders a drink for Feklusha and they end by going out to a little tavern, which they evidently now frequent. In Scene 2 in the dark living room are heard the voices of a man and woman entering. They are Carl and Elizabeth. Elizabeth has now deceived her husband and is living with and supporting Carl, but Henry's apartment draws her and she shows that she still has a strong feeling for Henry. She has great diamonds in her ears. They think that they hear someone and go out. Scene 1, Act 3 is a foggy night on the bank of one of the Petrograd canals. Henry and Feklusha, both drunk, stand talking, the former about how he will invest the money he will steal in America. Feklusha is trying to escape, but Henry is forcing him to return to his apartment with him. "Happy Jennie" comes along and they take her with them. Scene 2 takes place in Henry's apartment. Henry urges Feklusha and "Happy Jennie" on to becoming more drunk, but does not join them. She calls Feklusha a little rabbit. Henry goes out and frightens them by coming in disguised as an Englishman in the costumes in which he has practised for his escape after robbing the bank. Then he sits down and plays "The Waltz of the Dogs" in his usual affected manner. Afterward he explains that it represents foolish little dogs pulled by strings, dancing this way and that for lumps of sugar. Then he raves about the power that will be his to tread on men and women. Once more he plays the waltz and Feklusha and "Happy Jennie" dance on their toes like little dogs. In Act 4 it is night in Henry's living room. Elizabeth, Carl and Feklusha are there. Elizabeth goes out to look at the other rooms, especially the one planned for a nursery. Carl begins insulting Feklusha as usual. Feklusha tells him that Henry is insured and shows him a note which he has forged in Henry's handwriting to make Henry's death appear a suicide. Carl snatches it from him, but Feklusha has developed a weak man's cunning and has retained a better forgery. Elizabeth comes back and sends them away so that she may be alone in Henry's apartment and weep over what she has lost. Feklusha is finally left alone in the apartment and Henry returns and finds him raving to himself. Feklusha accuses him of having changed his plans without notifying him, but Henry says nothing but that he notices perfume in the air. He sends Feklusha kindly away, his whole manner seems to have grown quieter. When alone he partially undresses and walks up and down talking to himself of the many hours of darkness, of suicide and of the perfume in the room. He plays "The Waltz of the Dogs" several times. Leaving the light to burn all night, he goes into his bedroom. A shot is heard.

WAR WITH MEXICO, THE, by Justin H. Smith (1919). The old social order of Mexico — the people, the classes — the sources of wealth, the influence of the Church, which is shown to have wielded an immense power as late as 1845, and the "army," which became a powerful group, are discussed in the opening chapters, together with the education, the industries, and commerce of the country. The life and character of the people, in the country, and the capital; the political side of Mexican civilization, which the author considers had the most direct bearing on America's relations with that country; the revolution against Spain, the program of Iturbide, declaring for a limited monarchy under a Bourbon King, and the subsequent crisis when the new constitution was drafted, which meant a triumph of nationality, with Victoria elected president, are reviewed as leading to the period which marked Mexico's downfall, and the taking up of arms by Santa Anna, as Protector of the People, and the "saviour of the nation." The events which follow are viewed in their final effect upon the country. At this period, which the author holds was deplorable, began the relations between the United States and Mexico, with immediate friction over boundary difficulties, diplomatic clashes, and American claims. The later decisive difficulty between the two countries began to take shape in 1843 and Mexico prepared for war. "The American government, on the other hand, undertook to restore friendly relations," and Slidell was despatched as minister. The plan to annex Texas had greatly disturbed the two governments, and the author reviews the case which finally brought the American troops to the Texas frontier. The various skirmishes, campaigns and battles are described. "The aim of the United States was peace," says the author, in the subsequent chapters which are devoted to America's efforts to make peace. The difficulties which arose when negotiations were opened, the armistice, and the decisive battles which followed, leading to the capture of Mexico by the Americans, with final military operations, which eliminated Santa Anna and brought political chaos to Mexico, together with the movement against General Scott, are high lights in the narrative. The naval operations of the War are also reviewed. The author describes the social conditions during the War, and the course of events which brought about the reopening of peace negotiations, and to Mexico — a possibly long, expensive demoralizing occupation on the part of American troops. The details of the treaty are given, with the difficulties of ratification. The finances of the War are also shown in connection with the exigencies which Mexico encountered in her financial operations; and the new fiscal laws of America. The mood of the country after the War is also presented, but it is shown that the War "left Mexico friendly."

WASHINGTON, GEORGE, The Human Being and The Hero, by Rupert Hughes (2 vols., 1926–1927), presents a picture of our first president, whom the author believes great as a man, but a failure as a god. The incessant effort of the biographer has been to see Washington's life as he himself saw it. In this endeavor he has the authority of Carlyle who found one of the errors in the historical judgment of great men that of substituting the goal of their career for the course and starting point of it. This first volume covers only the first thirty years; so much new material has been discovered concerning Washington's youth and the period when he was Commander-in-Chief of the Virginia troops. An early appraisal of his youth which has the merit of coming from one who not only knew him intimately as a friend, but as his employer sent him on his earliest surveying trips, is that of Colonel Fairfax in answer to a query from his mother as to the advisability of sending young George abroad to school. This frank friend admits that the boy's education

THE READER'S DIGEST OF BOOKS 1391

might have been bettered but "that he is accurate and inclines to much life out of doors. He is very grave for one of his age, and reserved in his intercourse, not a great talker at any time. His mind appears to me to act slowly, but on the whole to reach just conclusion and he has an ardent wish to see the right of questions. . . . Method and exactness seem to be natural to George. He is, I suspect, beginning to feel the sap rising, being in the spring of life and is getting ready to be the prey of your sex. . . . He is subject to attacks of anger on provocation, and sometimes without just cause, but as he is a reasonable person, time will cure him of this vice of nature, and in fact, he is in my judgment a man who will go to school all his life and profit thereby." Land speculators did much to open the West and the valleys of the Mississippi and the Ohio rivers. Among the best of these, with their prophetic vision, indomitable courage and heroic perseverance it may surprise some to find Benjamin Franklin and George Washington. Rupert Hughes commends Washington's modesty and fine historic conscience when, writing Governor Dinwiddie, who sent him on his first wilderness trip, he says, "Those Things which came under the Notice of my own Observation, I have been explicit and just in a Recital of: Those which I have gathered from Report, I have been particularly cautious not to augment." This report greatly pleased the Governor for it confirmed his belief that war between England and France was again inevitable. He had it copied and sent throughout the colonies and even to England. The account of the affair at Fort Necessity, Washington's first defeat in frontier warfare, credits the young commander with bringing his men out with flying colors although they were attacked by a superior force of French and Indians. But no less truly are the facts set forth concerning the "assassination" of M. de Jumonville, which placed Washington in so unfortunate a light both in America and abroad for some years. The usual impression that Braddock was a blundering fool and that his expedition might have been saved had he listened to the young Washington is dispelled. Braddock did recognize Washington's ability and consult with him, says Hughes. Since Braddock was not pulling off a flying raid but aiming at permanent conquest and the establishment of a channel for settlers, the contention of most historians that he carried too much baggage and that he took too great care with his road is disproved. On this expedition Washington not only showed exceptional coolness, self-control and will, which helped to save the remnant of Braddock's army, but also unusual endurance, for he was ill on entering the battle which lasted four hours and he knew no cessation of his labors for his defeated and dying commander until seven days after the battle was over. These Indian wars on the frontier were a training school in that stoical endurance of physical hardship, and the jealousy and inertia of the colonists in supporting their soldiers at that time no less a lesson in spiritual fortitude, all of which developed in Washington's own character those qualities that made him an unforgettable leader of a forlorn cause in those darkest days of the Revolution that was to come. The author does not say whether a like Spartan course in early love assisted him toward the happy denouément that closes this volume, his marriage with Martha Custis. Certainly the author's scholarly investigations show that all his early love affairs were disappointing, from the one with the Lowland beauty, with Mary Cary and others to that one with Sally Fairfax which made a deeper and more permanent impress on his life. So restless and adventurous a hero made his appeal to the fair sex of the South and even, it was said, to a famous Northern belle, Mary Philipse, but until he met Martha Custis none of them were interested in him as a husband. His letters, as quoted in this volume, are frequently filled with cavilling over the lukewarm support of the Colonists for the military enterprises that they entrusted to him, but nowhere is this note sounded for himself, for he did not ask for a salary when fighting, but always for the need of his men.   Though a stern military disciplinarian he was well liked by the soldiers who held him in profound admiration and awe.   When he retired to domestic life on his marriage his regiments were filled with dismay.

Volume 2, "The Rebel and the Patriot," covers the period from his thirtieth year to the first successful battle of the Revolution at Trenton.   For the lack of photography, which had not yet been invented, a comprehensive pen portrait of Colonel Washington, the late commander of Virginia's militia, is supplied by his aide-de-camp, George Mercer.   Briefly he is described as six feet two, weighing at that time one hundred and seventy-five pounds, with wide shoulders and large frame that is well muscled; a head not large but well shaped poised on a superb neck; high round cheek bones and firm chin, blue gray eyes, prominent but straight nose, large mouth set in a pale face rather long than broad.   His expression, although placid and under perfect control could be flexible and full of deep feeling when aroused.   His voice was agreeable rather than strong and his manner was deliberate, deferential, and engaging when in conversation; his gestures were graceful and his walk majestic. This account has the greater importance since it was claimed later, when he took his seat in the first Continental Congress, that it was largely his magnetic and impressive personality that won him the confidence of his fellow members and the command of the Continental Army.   Washington's military training was not comparable with that of Charles Lee in spite of those early years of frontier warfare. During the seventeen years that had passed since his marriage he lived the life of a colonial gentleman farmer, engrossed in the science of farming, exercised over the welfare of his household and slaves, engaged in speculation in western lands and well content with his life.   His wealth, social distinction and freedom from personal ambition, added to his magnificent presence, were his chief recommendations for the favorable consideration of Congress.   The first third of the book is concerned with those intermediate years of private life before he became Commander-in-Chief of the Continental Army.   His honest observation and indefatigable experimenting in agriculture show him possessed of the true scientific spirit.   Since Washington's diary proves that he loved all forms of social life, dancing, card-playing, mild gambling and fox-hunting, the amount of space and the contentious heat with which these facts are stated seem unnecessary.   The Rev. Boucher, during the latter part of this period the tutor of Jacky Custis, is inclined to sneer at Washington and gives a less flattering portrait than the earlier one quoted.   He says of his illustrious employer, "He is shy, silent, stern, slow and cautious, but has no quickness of parts, extraordinary penetration, nor an elevated style of thinking.   In his moral character he is regular, temperate, strictly just and honest (excepting that, as a Virginian, he has lately found out that there is no moral turpitude in not paying what he confesses he owes to a British creditor), and, as I always thought, religious."   Though his thrift and acumen in business led some to accuse him of stinginess, not only his lavish hospitality but his innumerable acts of kindness showed a warm and generous disposition.   He was the kindliest and most careful of step-fathers nor did he confine this feeling to family bounds.   "Nobody's trouble seemed too great or too small for him to add to his own." He followed the codes of his day not only in regard to his pleasures but in his attitude toward his slaves.   He was benevolently inclined but they were his property as much as his animals on his estate and as such must make a return in value, nor was he lax in pursuit if they tried to escape.   He shared the general land hunger of his time and showed about the same regard to the King's proclamation giving the Ohio lands to the Indians that some latter day Americans do for the Prohibition Amendment. On his second visit to New York in 1773 to enroll Jacky Custis at King's College, he was fêted along the way by the governors of the states and met many important men. Without foresight on his part, this did much to renew his earlier reputation outside of his own colony. Private griefs, the death of his beloved little Patsy Custis, joys and ambitions continued to engross him long after others less prominent in the Revolution were greatly concerned over the state of affairs. As Burgess, he had been but a passive member of the Virginia Assembly until the King's taxes touched his tastes and pocket book. Then he organized a boycott on all taxed goods. By the time General Gage's English troops were quartered on Boston he was sufficiently aroused to take up a subscription for its relief. Thus slowly he awoke to the significance of the times. Hughes gives the full text of his speech of acceptance of the post of Commander-in-Chief of the Army and points out "his peculiar nobility in humility," since he did not believe himself equal to the command which he had not sought. He took up his work of forming and keeping together an army with no illusions as to the nature of his duties or the amount of support he would receive from the colonists. From those early years of frontier warfare he knew the inadequacy of the training of the troops, the inter-colonial jealousy and lethargy of the people for whom he would fight. Moreover, he had seen enough of Braddock's English soldiers to know something of the men he would be fighting. The insubordination of the Colonials and their cowardice were more in evidence than their courage after their first achievement in driving Howe out of Boston until the engagement at Harlem Heights; these qualities always aroused his wrath. After this first temporary success when the Colonials first drove the King's troops a mile back into the City of New York which they had just been compelled to evacuate, another period as depressing as that following the Battle of Long Island ensued. Howe took forts Washington and Lee, and Washington began his long desperate retreat across New Jersey. The patience and magnanimity of Washington are well brought out in his affair with Generals Reed and Lee who were conspiring against him at this crucial time. He recognized their value to the cause and was ready to lay aside personal affronts in dealing with them. So dark looked the cause of freedom that the Patriots were everywhere turning Tory when Congress finally in despair gave Washington the powers of a dictator. How nobly and unselfishly he used these powers Hughes contrasts favorably with well-known dictators of history. Washington, the great patriot and leader, was developing rapidly out of the indifferent, pleasure-loving, privately engrossed and aristocratic country gentleman. He writes Congress a letter of sincere thanks for the gift of a load of secondhand clothes for his shivering men, this exquisite gentleman who formerly was accustomed to buy all his own clothes abroad. Howe's vacillating policy and failure to push the campaign through to a successful conclusion Hughes attributes to the fact that he came of a family of Whigs hostile to the policy of the king, and also owing to the fact that he was a professional soldier, he was quite willing to retire when winter closed in and call it a campaign. Washington, trained in the tactics of the fox, realized that this was his chance and seized it promptly. This volume closes with the brilliant coup at Trenton.

WASHINGTON, GEORGE, THE IMAGE AND THE MAN, by W. E. Woodward (1926). This biography does not belittle Washington, the man, but contributes to a better understanding of his character and achievements by destroying the myths built up around him by biographers to whom "everything that Washington did, said or thought was absolutely perfect." For example, Jared Sparks, president of Harvard and a historian of note published a twelve-volume "Life and Writings of Washington" in 1830 in which he changed and dignified Washington's writings, inserting words "used only by pompous schoolmasters," and then destroyed or gave away the originals in an evident attempt "to conceal Washington's personality," and represent him as a person of superhuman virtues and abilities. Mr. Woodward gives much of the historic background of the period not because Washington "made history but because history in its making made him." The first of the family to emigrate from England was John Washington, a gentleman-adventurer who came to Virginia in 1657. Little is known of the childhood of George Washington, but the author brands the Cannot-Tell-A-Lie incident of the cherry tree as a piece of fiction made up by the Reverend Mason L. Weems along with other fables. At school George "loved arithmetic as many another boy has loved Shelley." The author doubts if there can be found any other character in history who had a passion for counting equal to that of George Washington. All his life he was interested in the enumeration of things. At one time he laboriously counted the number of seed in a pound Troy weight of red clover, and in a pound of timothy. As a career the profession of surveying appealed to him because he liked to measure land. He paid for his "Bullskin Plantation" of five hundred and fifty acres of wild land in Frederick County by doing work as a surveyor. Before he was twenty-one years of age he was the owner of fifteen hundred and fifty-eight acres, all of which he had obtained by his own efforts. Later after the death of his older brother, Lawrence, he inherited his estate of Mount Vernon. He married Mrs. Martha Custis, the wealthiest woman in Virginia, and Mr. Woodward believes that he was at the time in love with Mrs. Sally Fairfax, the wife of his friend. His career was not made by the Custis fortune as he was a man of distinction before his marriage, but it helped him a great deal. The wedding was an imposing social event. The Diary begins on January 1, 1760, and continues until his death in December, 1799, with some breaks, notably one of seven years during the Revolution. He was interested in the acquisition of land and the cultivation of his plantations, the purchase and sale of horses and negroes, in his step-children, and his diversions were fox-hunting, card-playing and dancing. Of his personality Mr. Woodward considers the keynote to have been character. "He possessed fortitude, steadfastness, dignity, courage, honesty and self-respect." The record of his military operations show that he was not a good general according to this author. Washington's advice to General Braddock to divide his forces contributed to that general's defeat by the French. "During the entire war the American military operations were without any definite, coherent plan. . . . The plans originated with the British, and Washington's idea was simply to prevent the British from doing whatever they tried to do." Washington tried to form an army on the British military model of regiments of lines and squares and missed the opportunity to form a mobile army of marksmen adapted to the colonial spirit, and the heavily wooded regions where sharpshooting rangers could have fought behind trees and rocks. Instead of depending on medals and promotions like Napoleon he introduced flogging to train his troops. He did not understand the use of cavalry. Mr. Woodward does give Washington credit for the executive ability which enabled him to choose his subordinates wisely, and for a "fine talent for military deception," though he believes that the masterly Trenton-Princeton campaign was the plan of General Nathanael Greene. The account of the battle of Long Island and the evacuation of New York in this book differs from that of other more conventional historians. The British conduct of the war was also unsuited to the field of encounter. Howe's policy was to hold towns and fortified positions until the Revolution had worn itself out. General Howe had twenty thousand well-fed and well-clothed troops with which to surround and capture Washington's little army shivering in winter quarters at Valley Forge. Mr. Woodward believes that Howe's failure to attack was due to the form of neurosis that we call shell shock to-day, that he had never recovered from the battle of Bunker Hill where his staff was shot down to a man. He captured the rebel capital but found that his failure to aid Burgoyne outweighed this military success in England. Clinton's plan was to harass the country and conquer it by towns. The British had the great advantage of sea-power. After the War Alexander Hamilton said: "All the English need have done was to blockade our ports with twenty-five frigates and ten ships of the line. But, thank God, they did nothing of the sort." A war of blockade would have ended the War. "The contest was decided by sea-power, but it was French, and not English." The French alliance put the English on the defensive, and it was the French fleet which forced the surrender of Cornwallis. As presiding officer of the Convention Washington took no part in the debates which shaped the Constitution. He desired the form of government which would best uphold the existing status of property and the law and order necessary for its maintenance. His sympathies were with property and property holders rather than with the abstract rights of humanity. He supported Hamilton because he stood for financial stability and the development of the wealthy class. Mr. Woodward considers Washington, the president, to have been "principally a figure-head, a symbol," and his quality of greatness that he represented "the American common denominator, the average man deified and raised to the nth power."

WAYWARD MAN, THE, by St. John G. Ervine (1927), is the story of the family of Dunwoody, who lived in The Terrace between Portugal Street and Modesty Row. Mrs. Dunwoody kept a shop, "a dull, tiresome place, her son Robert thought, with hardly a glimmer of glory in it." She dealt "in hardware, delf, lamp-oil and brushes." Robert felt an overpowering envy of Jamesy Mineely, whose parents kept a delectable sweet-shop across the way, where there were always displayed great trays of "cokernut" chips in the window. Mrs. Dunwoody, having been born a De Lacy and descended from Devonshire gentlefolk, was considered to have married beneath her. But Robert was not impressed with her tales of lineage. Rather than be kin of the De Lacys who had ignored his mother since her marriage, he would have been Mr. Peden, landlord of The Terrace. "Sure, thon's a dreepy-drippy sort of a man," said Robert. Eventually, Mrs. Dunwoody was left a widow with her four children when the sea claimed her adventurous and beloved husband. There were Alec, the eldest child, always amenable to his mother's wishes, Margaret and Mattie, also biddable children and Robert or Darkie as he was known, who had a mind of his own. Although Mrs. Dunwoody strove to hide the fact, Robert was the pride and dearest love of her heart and her ambitions for him were boundless. He would be a minister, she said and the family would prosper and have other shops, so that the name of Dunwoody should be known the country over. She would reign in her little kingdom with her children and her children's children around her. She enjoyed reading aloud the Bible stories of the patriarchs, almost licking the long list of "begats" with her lips and tongue as they rolled from her mouth. Margaret, disapprovingly conscious that scant mention was made of the women of those days, remarked, "You'd near think them people came into the world without a woman near the house." The day came when Robert's longing to be a sailor possessed him, body and soul. The derision and outpourings of wrath with which the family greeted the news that Robert had made a spectacle of himself by offering to permit the famous Blondin to carry him across a tight-rope at the exhibition, pushed him beyond endurance. Cursing the interfering ways of his brother Alec as well as the dominance of the entire family, Robert ran away from home to follow the sea. He was gone seven years, during which time he sent no word to his mother of his whereabouts, although he thought of her consumingly as the only woman he would ever love. His seven years were crammed with experience, of life before the mast, of shipwreck and of one enduring friendship with Charlie who fell to his death from the rigging before Robert's eyes. At the close of the seven years, which seemed to have profited him nothing more than a knowledge of ships and an awareness of women which he had gained from Clara, whom he had found in a den at the close of a fight on shore in America, Robert experienced an overwhelming nostalgia for his mother. He returned to Belfast and made his way to his mother's shop, half fearing to enter lest he find that she had died in his absence. She looked up from behind the counter at his entrance, asking in what way she might serve her customer. "Do you not know me, Ma?" he asked. Then it was that he saw her cry for the first time as she caught him in her arms, praising Heaven which had returned her son to her heart. By this time, Alec was managing a second shop for his mother and business was prospering. After manœuvring a match between Robert and Brenda, a neat, painfully tidy girl who had loved Robert since childhood to the despair of Alec, Mrs. Dunwoody made over the new shop to Robert and his bride. Robert, who was partly fascinated and partly repulsed by the thought of Brenda, was merely a tool in his mother's hands. He liked Brenda's gentleness and little air of assurance, but as these developed and changed to an austere streak of hardness and a feeling of complete possession, he felt estranged from her. Although Brenda loved Robert absorbingly, she refused to bear him a child, to the disappointment of Robert and the confusion of all Mother Dunwoody's careful plans. Finally Robert, driven by two determined women beyond endurance, became enamoured with Sadie, a pretty "softy" as she was called who lived with his mother. Pretty and weak, she had no mad ambitions to deter her from being merely a woman. Later when in desperation she told him that she was to have a baby by him, he went with her first to purchase a gold ring, then to the doctor's to confirm her belief, and then to Brenda. At the news which the pair brought to her, Brenda, now happy owner of a whole chain of stores through the countryside, ordered them from her shop, never to return. Sadie was sheltered by Mrs. Dunwoody, who, "neither pleased nor sorry, but content," that at last she was to have a child of her son's to cradle, settled down to rocking and smiling with Sadie in secret understanding. Robert, no longer bound to the life of a merchant, but realizing that, queer as it was, he still loved Brenda, went back to the sea. With everything in their hands, these two dominant women, Mrs. Dunwoody and Brenda, had yet lost the one being that they valued over all, by their mad striving for power and to shape the lives of others.

"WE," by Charles A. Lindbergh (1927). In this, his own account of that famous partnership of "The Spirit of St. Louis" and himself which culminated in the epochal flight from New York to Paris, May 20–21, 1927, Colonel Lindbergh sketches as briefly as possible his early life, hastening to reach his first experience with planes. In five closely-knit but large-typed pages he tells his ancestry and schooling, which latter he states to have been "very irregular, due to our constant moving about."

His father, Charles A. Lindbergh, was of Swedish descent, and for a time was a member of Congress. His mother, Mrs. Evangeline Lindbergh, is "of English, Irish and French extraction." His maternal grandfather "was constantly experimenting in his laboratory. He held a number of patents on incandescent grates and furnaces, in addition to several on gold and enamel inlays and other dental processes." "My chief interest in school lay along mechanical and scientific lines. Consequently, after graduating from the Little Falls High School, I decided to take a course in mechanical engineering, and two years later entered the College of Engineering of the University of Wisconsin at Madison." He stayed there for three semesters, long enough to realize that he was a square peg in a round hole, and to decide that he would take up aeronautics in earnest and make it a life work. In March, 1922, he left Madison for Lincoln, Nebraska, where he had "enrolled as a flying student with the Nebraska Aircraft Corporation." Until this time he had never been near enough a plane to touch it. For the next two years he literally "learned by doing," and barn-stormed the Middle West and South, sometimes alone, sometimes with other independent pilots. In April, 1924, he enrolled as a Flying Cadet at Brooks Field, with the purpose of becoming an Army Pilot. It was while flying the mails in the autumn of 1926 that he first conceived the idea of the trans-Atlantic flight. For the next five months his life was one of concentrated study and calculation on the project, so that nothing is more unfair than to call him "Lucky" Lindbergh. His success was due to scientific accuracy and the greatest foresight of contingencies humanly possible. Of the actual flight itself he says little, except to comment impersonally on the weather conditions. Indeed, impersonality is the keynote throughout: he never discusses his emotions. His own story, which is permeated with a sense of humor, occupies little more than two-thirds of the book. The remainder is taken up by a description, authorized by Lindbergh but written by Fitzhugh Green, of the receptions accorded to Lindbergh after he landed at Le Bourget. The acclamations of Paris, Brussels, London, New York, Washington, and St. Louis are all treated briefly and appreciatively with an eye to the flyer's own reactions, which he could not, would not do himself. The book is also prefaced by a Foreword by the American Ambassador to France, Myron Herrick, dated June 16, 1927.

WE MUST MARCH, a novel of the winning of Oregon, by Honore Willsie Morrow (1925). The historic story of the emigration of the missionaries, Narcissa and Marcus Whitman, to Oregon, and how through their efforts the United States Government was roused to interest in the country, and settlers brought in to make it an American territory. At the time they made the journey to Oregon in 1836 the powerful British Hudson Bay Company was doing everything in its power to keep settlers away from the Columbia River, and to divert them to California away from the fur producing region they controlled. Sir George Simpson, the governor of Rupert's Land, believed that he could hold back the tide of American settlers until the "ignorant and indifferent American Government had sold or traded its share in the marvellous Oregon territory to Great Britain." He warned Dr. McLoughlin, the Chief Factor of the Company, that after the missionary came the plough, and that their settlement in the country beyond the Rockies must be prevented. In the story he goes to meet the missionary party to frustrate their attempt to bring their "covered wagon" over the mountains. Narcissa is a beautiful woman and an intelligent one. She had been forbidden by her bigoted father to marry a great composer, who wanted to take her to Paris and develop her marvellous voice. In her reaction she had thrown herself

into church work, and the same spirit of adventure that helped her to force her
father to send her to New York to study music, led her to marry the medical missionary to the Indians, Marcus Whitman, to help him establish his mission in the
wilderness. Sir George Simpson recognized her as a woman belonging to his own
world, and tried to induce her to stay at Fort Vancouver and found a school and
help to foster British culture in the new country. He is greatly attracted by her
personality and beauty, and cannot allow the hostile Indians to massacre the party
of which she is a member. He does refuse to allow the Company to sell supplies
to the missionaries, but Dr. McLoughlin is more friendly to the Americans when
they push through to his headquarters. Narcissa and Marcus are not successful as
missionaries, and do not make any converts, but Marcus makes heroic efforts to
save the souls and bodies of the filthy and cruel Cayuse Indians, and Narcissa
teaches the women to take care of their babies, and in moments of crisis is able to
save their lives and the destruction of the station by the emotional effect of her
singing. The birth of her baby, Alice Clarissa, brings Narcissa nearer to her rough
adoring husband, whom she admires and respects but has never loved. There is
trouble with the Catholic priests who stir up the Indians against the Whitmans,
and quarrels with the Spauldings of their own party whose jealousy leads them to
misrepresent the Whitmans to the American Board in the East. When Alice Clarissa is drowned, Narcissa almost gives up the struggle in her longing to go home to
her own mother, but her sense of the importance of the country to the United States
makes her decide to stay on. She admits to Sir George Simpson: "We don't as
you say, deserve Oregon. By every right of personal sacrifice, wise control, supreme
effort, it ought to be British." Marcus makes the long journey back East in the
winter to persuade Daniel Webster and President Tyler and the American Board
in Boston of the importance of Oregon, and to counteract the impression given by
the Hudson Bay Company of the impracticability of American settlement of the
country. He returns in the Spring leading a wagon train of a thousand men, women
and children with a herd of nearly three thousand head of stock to save Oregon
from the British. Narcissa is able to avert the massacre of the company in a narrow
pass by the Indians with the help of Dr. McLoughlin, and a bargain with the chief,
Umtippe, and later prevents Jesse Applegate's stupid, political leadership from
bringing on war between the United States and Great Britain by appealing to the
women of the party, and convincing them that it is best to settle on the Willamette
River south of the forty-ninth parallel. Marcus has won Narcissa's love by his
marvellous journey, doing the big thing that she had expected of him. The writer
states that "Narcissa Whitman's Journal" has been her main source of information
for the historical fact on which the story is based, and gives a partial list of other
books studied.

WEDLOCKE, by Jacob Wassermann (1926) is a psychological novel revealing
those material conditions of life in mid-Western Europe that are in conflict with
its spiritual trends as they appear in the institution of marriage. Like his prototype Balzac, but with more of the spirituality of the Russians, Wassermann expresses
his thesis through dramatic personalities and incidents. Friedrich Laudin, a successful lawyer, whose practice is largely domestic relations cases, through the nature
of his work becomes the confessor of those suffering from these maladies of modern
life. His quiet, unobtrusive wife, Pia, and their two daughters, Marlene and Relly,
conspire to make Dr. Laudin's homecomings restful, free from the worry of petty
detail. A poor student, Konrad Lanz, seeks his help in securing to his sister her rights.

Hartmann, the owner of a small estate near their home, and his wife, Brigitte, are not happy together. While the wife was away, Caroline Lanz had taken pity on the man and nursed him through a serious illness. Hartmann's dull, restless dissatisfaction with life leads to an open rupture with his wife and their two young sons and he goes away with Caroline. After some years of contentment with her he dies, having provided for her and their child. But this will falls into the possession of his wife, a Shylock in petticoats, who is represented as a perfect tigress of legality. That slothful mountain of a man, Egyd Fraundorfer, is Laudin's closest friend. His philosophical temperament and the inhibitions that are the outcome of an unhappy early marriage, prevent him from showing the natural pride and love he feels for his only son, Nicolas, whose youthful precocity as a musical conductor is remarkable. The young man is in love with the notorious actress, Louise Dercum. Soon after a visit to Marlene and Relly, Nicolas commits suicide. This tragedy so shatters the father that Laudin undertakes to investigate the young man's relations with Louise Dercum to find an explanation of his suicide. This leads to his meeting the actress and becoming deeply involved in her affairs. She seeks through him to obtain release from her husband, Arnold Keller, whom she has caused to be locked up in an asylum. The man escapes and begs Laudin's assistance in obtaining at least a partial reunion with his wife. Meanwhile the affairs of Consul Altacher and his wife, Constance, have been placed with Laudin. A written report drawn up by each separately convinces Laudin that theirs is a perfect paradigm of marriage. Their whole problem is stated as a matter of tempo. The husband finds himself spiritually wearied with the effort of keeping step with the lagging steps of the wife whose devotion devoured him. "What he needed by his side was a free human being, and one to whom the things of the mind were realities and not merely a handsome pretense." These cases and others convince Laudin that there is something wrong with marriage; that it must be radically changed, adapted to free personalities. Some kind of experimental relationship, he believes, would in the end lead to one of greater voluntary permanence. Laudin's relations with his own wife are not satisfactory. Pia is the slave to her household duties and devotions. Then, at the crossroads of his life, burdened with the revelations and complications of these other lives, feeling himself prisoned in a rigid social order, as lawyer, breadwinner, husband, father, he met Louise Dercum, who represented to him the eternally changeful, and for a time is under her influence. In the end Fraundorfer convinces Laudin not only of the fatal part the actress had played in young Nicolas's untimely death but also of her baleful influence on himself. Laudin is taken ill, worn out with these wrecks of wedlock. Then Pia awakens to the vital issues beneath her care of things and nurses him back to a faith in a changed and more congenial life. She helps him break all his bonds to the past, refrains from blaming him for the experiences he has been through and arouses him to the creation of a new constructive life. He realizes happily that he had forgotten, "what an enormous rôle, in any permanent and really inward union, between a man and a woman, is played by their being initially and instinctively upon the same plane and level of spiritual life," and that such, if they seem to lose each other for a time may, "return on a higher plane, in a more perfected state, riper for comradeships, sweeter in humanity, nobler in every relation to the world —" a marvellous double being bent to the same destiny but individually independent and respecting the personalities of each.

WENDELL, BARRETT, AND HIS LETTERS, by M. A. DeWolfe Howe (1924). In this volume of letters and clarifying comment the editor has set himself the task of showing Barrett Wendell — "as that man saw himself," of explaining him "on his own terms." The reader of the book is warned by the biographer to keep constantly in mind the fact that Barrett Wendell as he thought himself to be and Barrett Wendell as he really was, were individuals frequently at variance. The subject of the biography, teacher of English at Harvard for almost forty years, author, critic, and traveller, is disclosed in his letters as a man of frail health, devoted to his friends, a staunch defender of New England's "Brahmin" caste, a penetrating thinker, and an enlightened conservative who paid heartfelt tribute to the past while he shrewdly but reluctantly predicted the oncoming of a new social era in America. The letters and journal excerpts are assembled following introductory pages applying to the period under consideration, and begin when Wendell was a boy of six, in 1861. He is shown during his boyhood and youth; as a college and law student; as a young instructor and writer; as an assistant professor and scholar; as a full professor and a lecturer in English and French universities; as a traveller, teacher, and friend; and as professor emeritus, writing in retirement. The background of the letters is typically that of New England and Harvard, fortified with Old World atmosphere resulting from extensive travel and intelligent interest in European affairs. The Harvard teacher and man of letters never cared for the America west of New England, although he admitted a kind of grandeur in the vast expanses of the West and foresaw the westward course of American empire. In addition to sketching the outlines of Barrett Wendell's striking though somewhat eccentric personality, his letters provide interesting comment on more than fifty years of American political and cultural life. When he started writing letters the Civil War had begun; his last published correspondence, shortly before his death in 1921, came at the close of an era terminated by the World War. Among those to whom the letters included in the volume were written, are Sir Robert White-Thomson; F. J. Stimson, Ambassador to Argentina from 1919 to 1921; Edmund Clarence Stedman; Robert Herrick, the novelist; James Ford Rhodes, the historian; William James; the Rev. L. H. Montagu Butler, D.D., Master of Trinity College, Cambridge; Senator Lodge; and President Lowell of Harvard. Although his field was literature Barrett Wendell was greatly interested in history and in the happenings that go to make it. His letters show that he opposed the election of Blaine in 1884; that he voted for McKinley in 1896; that he felt the Spanish-American War "a needless war at the moment, but serving a purpose in uniting our national feeling"; that he believed his friend, Senator Lodge, was "less sympathetic in controversial passages than in those directly assertive"; and that he was ardently sympathetic toward the entry of the United States into the World War. But it is in comment pertaining to literature, to travel, to American and European civilization, and to human nature in general, that his letters are particularly rich.

WHAT I BELIEVE, by Bertrand Russell (1925). In his preface the author says: "In this little book, I have tried to say what I think of man's place in the universe, and of his possibilities in the way of achieving the good life. In 'Icarus' I expressed my fears; in the following pages I have expressed my hopes. The inconsistency is only apparent. Except in astronomy, mankind has not achieved the art of predicting the future; in human affairs, we can see that there are forces making for happiness, and forces making for misery. We do not know which will prevail, but to act wisely we must be aware of both." Mr. Russell starts out with the belief that man's purpose is to lead the good life. Man finds the absolute not in a philosophy of nature, but in a philosophy of value: "We are ourselves the ultimate and irrefutable arbiters of value, and in the world of value nature is only a part. Thus in this world we are greater than nature. In the world of values nature in itself is neutral, neither good nor bad, deserving of neither admiration nor censure. It is we who create value, and our desires which confer value. In this realm we are kings, and we debase our kingship if we bow down to nature." As to personal survival of death, he says there is no evidence; antecedent probability is against the conception of immortality. Evidence may at some future date be produced which will establish a belief in survival. His personal credo is: "I believe that when I die I shall rot, and nothing of my ego will survive. I am not young, and I love life. But I should scorn to shiver with terror at the thought of annihilation. Happiness is none the less true happiness because it must come to an end, nor do thought and love lose their value because they are not everlasting." Religion is condemned because it has employed fear to teach conceptions of God and duty. Society likewise employs fear to coerce the individual. In the author's estimation all fear is bad. Finding no support in science for God or immortality, he nevertheless states that science can, if it chooses, enable our descendants to lead the "good life." The good life is "inspired by love and guided by knowledge." In "Icarus" Mr. Russell gave us a picture of the world exploited by propaganda and militarism; here we have the bright side of the picture. He assures us that if we use science for happiness rather than destruction, all will be well. He indicates how the good life, a combination of science and benevolence, would banish our cruel and unreasonable taboos, enrich the relations between the sexes, end economic exploitation, surmount racial and national prejudices, and give real meaning to education.

WHAT PRICE GLORY, a drama, by Maxwell Anderson and Laurence Stallings (1924). The scene is the headquarters of a company of Marines in a village in France in 1918. The story is the rivalry of a captain and his sergeant for the dubious favors of Charmaine, the daughter of the inn keeper they call Cognac Pete. The two men are professional soldiers who have served around the world together, and whatever their personal quarrel, each recognizes the other as the best of soldiers when he is sober. The sergeant has come to take charge so that Flagg can have a ten-days' leave. Captain Flagg is rough and brutal and profane as are all the rest of the soldiers who follow his lead to hardship and death. The Great War continually interrupts the epic broil between the two men. When the Captain comes back, and is sober again, he finds that the Sergeant has robbed him of his girl. Cognac Pete comes to make a complaint against the man who has ruined his daughter, "the one flower of his life," and he wants Sergeant Quirt to marry her or pay him five hundred francs. Captain Flagg sees a chance to get even with Quirt, and uses his authority to order him to marry Charmaine, and then sign an allotment giving his wife two-thirds of his salary. Otherwise he can take his chances with a court-martial in Paris. A brigadier-general, two colonels, with some other officers come in to give orders to Captain Flagg to take his company into action to straighten a line, and take a half a town. There are some posters explaining the position taken by America in the War to be carried back of the German lines to help destroy the morale of the enemy. Captain Flagg has his own opinion of people who want to risk the lives of his men on that kind of work. Furthermore if they can bring in a prisoner for the Intelligence Section the company shall leave the trenches for a month's rest. As soon as the generals have gone, Quirt interrupts the preparations for his wedding. The company cannot go into action without him, and Captain Flagg can lock him up or call off the wedding. In the second act the men are in a cellar worn out holding a disputed town. Captain Flagg is gently helping a wounded lieutenant down the stairs. Unnerved with the long strain of trench warfare, Lieutenant Moore curses the War, and asks "What price glory now?" threatening to take his platoon out of it even if he is shot for insubordination. The Captain puts his arm around his shoulder, and comforts him tenderly until he can get him to take some sleep. It is almost more than the Captain can bear when two green lieutenants are sent to him for instruction, and he abuses them roundly. Quirt comes in with a slight wound in his leg to tell Captain Flagg that he is now going back to see Charmaine. There is an explosion of bombs and Captain Flagg goes out and gets his prisoner. Lewinsohn is wounded and calls to the Captain to help him. Two evenings later Sergeant Quirt walks in to Cognac Pete's with a borrowed overcoat over his pajamas. He tells Sergeant Ferguson that he now has aphasia, and has wandered away from a hospital some five miles away. He hears that the "outfit" is on the way, and knows Flagg will not let any doctors take his first sergeant. The Company gets back and the Captain and the Sergeant drink together and exchange insults. They gamble for Charmaine and the Captain wins. Just then orders come for the tired men to go back again to the trenches. All leaves are revoked. Headquarters has broken its promise. The weary Captain protests but starts off, and his mortal enemy of a moment before, Sergeant Quirt, runs after him out the door calling, "Hey, Flagg, wait for baby." The rough dialogue gives a picture of the soldier at war, tough and hard, but also heroic and devoted.

WHERE THE BLUE BEGINS, by Christopher Morley (1922), might be called a dogmatic phantasy. At any rate, Gissing, in his comfortable little suburban home in the Canine Estates, meditated on life and yearned for those blue horizons always beyond attainment. When to this higher discontent the ferment of April nights was added he became very restless for a bachelor so well cared for. Then one night prowling near his home he discovered three tiny pups whom he straightway adopted, calling them Bunks, Group and Yelpers. Fugi, the punctilious Japanese pug, who had served him so well, gave notice and he experienced all the delights and the drudgery of the overdomesticated. Then he realized that it was time he broke away from domesticity that he might seek out in the world a larger income suited to his heavier responsibilities. Mrs. Spaniel, a day helper, was left in charge of the children. As he approached the brilliant lights of the city, blue darkness lay all around. "Ah," he said, "here is where the blue begins." As floor-walker with Beagle and Co. on the Avenue, he soon learned the whole art of the merchant, which so enthralled him that before long he became General Manager. After a time he realized that this was not enough for a life's devotion. The church standing clear against the blue was surely exempt from earthly ambition and fallacy. Here, though only accepted as a lay preacher of the wealthy little chapel on Dalmatian Heights, he tried to find the reality of his dreams. Young, wealthy and beautiful, Miss Airedale tried unsuccessfully to ensnare him. Then, against orders, he put on the surplice and preached to the Congregation the Truth as he saw it. For this he was hounded from the church and had not a steam-roller been at hand in which to flee, he would have received a rough handling from his irate parishioners for his free thinking. So, in his search for horizons, he stowed away aboard the Pomerania. He was brought before Captain Scottie whose interest he aroused by discussing theology and metaphysics. While the good Scotsman retired to his cabin to reason out his replies, Gissing ran the ship as fancy dictated. While the sea, seen at close-hand is no more blue than land, he found his theology cleared and braced by his experience on it. "He had shouted arrogantly at Beauty, like a noisy tourist in a canyon; and the only answer, after long waiting, had been the paltry diminished echo of his own voice. He thought shamefully of his follies. What matter how you name God or in what words you praise Him? In this new foreign land he would quietly accept things as he found them. The laughter of God was too strange to understand." The ship is put into shore and there on land he found a being before whom he laughed and leaped and worshiped. Resting his head against the tramp's old trousers he thought he had found God. On going back to the harbor he discovered the ship had dwindled to a toy on a familiar pond. He made his way back to Bunks, Groups and Yelpers in time for Christmas. As he went down to bank the furnace fire for the night, "Over the coals hovered a magic evasive flicker, the very soul of the fire. It was a pentecostal flame, perfect and heavenly in tint, the essence of pure colour, a clear immortal blue."

WHILE PARIS LAUGHED. Being Pranks and Passions of the Poet Tricotrin. By Leonard Merrick (1918). The delightful, irresponsible Tricotrin has appeared in earlier volumes of Merrick's short stories but this entire book is devoted to his escapades. In the first story, "On Est Mieux Ici Qu'en Face" — he plans to cast himself into the Seine and thus awaken an unappreciative world to the splendor of his poems. But he encounters Mariquot, another aspiring poet, and his mistress, both of whom, too, had planned to gain fame by way of a watery grave. Mariquot's decision was wavering and when Delphine's attention to Tricotrin gave him an opportunity to dash off in an assumed fit of jealousy there was relief all around and the two decide to live and be friends. However evidence is lacking that the friendship lasted long. Tricotrin lived in a Montmartre garret with Pigou, a Futurist composer who was forced to play in a cinema at times, as Tricotrin was forced to write columns of advice for obscure journals, in order that they might eat. Their friends consisted chiefly of young men who also acquired a wide experience of Parisian garrets in a comparatively short time. In "At Home, Beloved, At Home," Tricotrin comes to the rescue of Lajeunie, a novelist, who has developed a passion for listening to tunes on the Pathephone. When it is discovered that it is to hear the voice of his beloved all is forgiven him and a reunion with her is soon effected. "Monsieur Blotto and the Lions" is the next tale and herein the editor of the provincial journal to which Tricotrin sends such intimate anecdotes of his friends among the literary and dramatic stars, comes to Paris to meet the élite. With the help of Pigou and numerous friends he impresses the editor, especially so by taking him to Montmartre and showing him the garret room of an obscure poet and composer who happens to be out! "The Meeting in the Galeries Lafayette" tells of his encounter with his aunt and his uncle from Lyons, whose offer of a position in their silk firm he had scorned, preferring to write poetry. Again they make the offer and seeing his beautiful cousin Henriette, he accepts. On the train to Lyons he learns of her engagement and dejectedly returns to Paris. In "The Woman in the Book" he writes the autobiography of a notorious actress and falls in love with the idol he creates. But she successfully shatters it. In "The Piece of Sugar" Tricotrin pretends to recognize a famous courtesan in a woman in a café to which he and Pigou have come with a rich but very parsimonious visitor from the provinces who is seeking adventure. In "The Banquets of Kiki" the two friends are feasted by an artist's model, Kiki, who has discovered a cheap way to give a banquet. "The Poet Grows Practical" shows Tricotrin deciding to collaborate with a famous playwright. One of his many rejected plays is offered, altered, and accepted, but when Tricotrin demands that the heroine's part be given to one of his friends it is returned to him.   In "A Reformed Character" we again meet Mariquot who has long ago entered his father's firm in Rennes.   He comes to Paris and by chance meets Tricotrin.   Mariquot promises him a great gift but leaves only a letter of advice for the poet.   Tricotrin is again in love, this time with his land-lord's daughter whom he has seen when he made a call at their home which adjoined their antique shop.   "Antiques and Amorette" finds him strolling in front of the shop in hopes of obtaining a glimpse of his beloved.   Repeated encounters with two of his friends disclose the fact that they are on the same quest.   Posing as a favorite, Tricotrin boldly enters the shop on the heels of two women, in one of whom he has recognized his lost love, Cousin Henriette, now married.   She invites him to call.   In "Waiting for Henriette" we find him so assiduously devoted to her that she finally refuses to see him again.   She had hoped to marry him to her widowed friend, Simone, who has taken a fancy to him.   Longing to see Henriette he goes to tea at Simone's who exercises her charms upon him.   Soon they are engaged!   Tricotrin was to marry and gloried in his future rôle of "papa."   In "Antenuptial" he and Pigou have a final farewell, but to leave Montmartre is breaking his heart.   When Simone changes her mind, his protestations are moving but he returns to his garret, gay and happy.

WHITE MONKEY, THE, by John Galsworthy (1924).   A continuation of the author's "Forsyte Saga."   The story of Fleur and her husband, Michael Mont, of the post-War generation, symbolized by the picture Soames Forsyte gives to his daughter, a white monkey holding the rind of a squeezed fruit in its outstretched paw — only the taste of the rind left.   The Forsyte sense of property has become in Fleur the "collecting habit."   Interested in the art and literature of the moment, she fills her house with a menagerie of celebrities.   Her set want to have a good time because they do not believe anything can last.   All values are equal and none have much value.   Michael adores his wife, and though Fleur has never cared for him deeply as she had for her cousin, Jon, the marriage is not a failure because Michael's tolerance and jesting loyalty touches "even a heart given away before it was bestowed on him."   Wilfrid Desert, a young poet, and Michael's best friend and associate in the publishing house, falls in love with Fleur, who plays with fire because she wants to keep the added excitement Wilfrid's passion gives to life, but without danger and without loss.   Michael is unhappy and uncertain of what Fleur will do until Wilfrid goes off to Arabia.   As the story ends Fleur's son is born, "the eleventh baronet," and all is well with them.   Soames is the real hero of this book in which Fleur and Michael are the central figures.   He still stands beyond the circle of the love that he craves, devoted to his beautiful daughter, who is kind to him.   As old George Forsyte said, "I can trust you, that's one thing about you, Soames."   He collects pictures which rise in value, and is a director on boards. It is through Sir Lawrence Mont's influence that he receives a seat on the board of the Providential Premium Reassurance Society.   He finds that the Society is investing recklessly in foreign contracts, and makes himself unpopular with his fellow directors by asking for an investigation.   Later the manager leaves the country to escape from the consequences of his dishonesty, and Soames, whose scrupulousness and integrity have saved the stockholders from further loss, is blamed as a scapegoat, and with Sir Lawrence resigns from the Board.   Parallel to the story of Fleur and Michael runs the story of the cockney, Tony Bicket and his wife, Victorine.   Tony packs books in the publishing house until he is discharged for stealing books to sell to pay the doctor's bills when his wife is ill with pneumonia. Michael intercedes for him in vain, and Tony tries selling balloons on the street as he cannot get work without a reference from his former employers. Victorine goes to see Michael to see if they will not take Tony back as he has never told her that he was discharged but only that times were slack and he was laid off. The kind-hearted Michael sends her to one of his artist friends for a model. They want to emigrate to Australia, and because she cannot bear to see Tony struggling to sell balloons she poses in the nude, to earn the money for the trip. Tony sees the picture reproduced in the illustrated news and thinks his world is in ruins. Victorine is angry that he should doubt her, and packs her trunk to leave him, which frightens all defiance out of his cockney spirit, and they make up the quarrel.

WHITMAN, by Emory Holloway (1924). In the preface to this "interpretation in narrative," as the author calls it, he explains that he had two purposes in writing the book. First, through thirteen years of study, to find the facts and points of view for such a picture of Whitman as would remove him from the field of fruitless controversy, and second, to present the picture in a manner acceptable to the general reader who knows nothing of Whitman, rather than for the scholar. The narrative is divided into seven books, each dealing with a more or less definite period in Whitman's life. He is introduced as the editor of the "Brooklyn Eagle" at the age of twenty-seven and is shown as a visionary young democrat, of perfect physical proportions; an enthusiastic propagandist; a reader of Shakespeare, Goethe, Byron, Gibbon, Lamb; a devotee of the theatre; and a somewhat fiery patriot in his ardent defence of the Mexican War policy of his country. Whitman's journey, with his brother Jefferson, to New Orleans to join the staff of "The Crescent" is described in detail. The New Orleans of the time and the part the young newspaper man from New York played in its rich and varied life provide material for interesting narrative of historical as well as literary value. The theatre, the balls, the Creole beauties, the slave markets, the docks are all looked at through Whitman's eyes. The journey back to New York after a three month's stay in New Orleans is chronicled with the same attention to pictorial detail. The third and fourth sections of the narrative are concerned with the quiet middle period of Whitman's life, the period preceding his labors as a nurse during the Civil War and the years thereafter when sickness had handicapped him. It was during this time, the decade following his return from the South, that the ideas and images for his poetry began to take shape in his mind. His human and artistic sides, the influence of books upon him, the beginning and completion of "Leaves of Grass," and the reception given it both in the United States and abroad, are here discussed. The Civil War brought to a close Whitman's happiest time. He was from now on to see and minister to the sufferings of war, and to live during much of his remaining life under the shadow of ill health. The last third of Holloway's narrative biography recounts the story of these more sombre years, of Whitman's later writing, of how he gained the admiration and friendship of people like the O'Connors, John Burroughs, Emerson, Moncure Conway, Peter Doyle, Mrs. Gilchrist; and of his relations with his English admirers: Rossetti, Swinburne, Tennyson, Symonds. His paralysis, gradual return to health, and final decline close the narrative. The problems of interpretation which have been encountered by most of Whitman's biographers — his attitude toward the physical side of life, his choosing to serve as a nurse rather than as a soldier in the Civil War, and his seeming lack of taste in writing his own reviews and publishing Emerson's confidential letter of praise — are treated in a manner which harmonizes with the sympathetic tone of the entire volume. The book is amply documented with clippings, letters, and extracts from diaries. The author explains that he has abbreviated the narrative "by picking it up only where it has character, and where the abundance of records makes it possible without invention, to tell an imaginative story."

WHY MARRY, by Jesse Lynch Williams (1919). This comedy in three acts was originally published under the title, "And So They Were Married." The scene is a week-end at a country house, and the characters are described as follows: Jean, the host's younger sister, who has been brought up to be married and nothing else; Rex, an unmarried neighbor, who has not been brought up to be anything but rich; Lucy, the hostess, who is trying her best to be "just an old-fashioned wife" in a new-fashioned home; Uncle Everett, a Judge who belongs to the older generation and yet understands the new — and believes in divorce; Cousin Theodore, a clergyman and yet a human being, who believes in everything — except divorce; John, who owns the house and almost everyone in it — and does not believe in divorce; Helen, the host's sister, whom everyone wants to marry, but who does not want to marry anyone; and Ernest, a scientist, who believes in neither divorce nor marriage, but makes a great discovery. The author says that social defects cannot be cured by individual treatment, and that "not only the lovers, but all the characters in this play are trying to do right according to their lights." There is no villain in the piece. "At least the villain remains off stage. Perhaps that is why so few see him. You are the villain, you and I and the rest of society. We are responsible for the rules and regulations of the marriage game. Instead of having fun with human nature, I tried to go higher up and have fun with human institutions. You can curse human nature with impunity. But dare lay hands on the Existing Order — and you'll find you've laid your hands on a hornet's nest." In the opening act, Rex proposes to Jean, who, although she knows that he is in love with her sister, Helen, has deliberately "managed" to land him. "It didn't take five minutes," she tells Lucy, her sister-in-law. Helen is described by Lucy as a "sexless freak with a scientific degree." "Men admire these independent women, but they don't marry them." Helen arrives from the Baker Institute of Medical Experiment, where she works as an assistant to Dr. Ernest Hamilton, the discoverer of the Hamilton antitoxin. The Judge's wife, "Aunt Julia, is in Reno, where she has gone to get a divorce. He himself thinks that marriage should be reformed, or there is going to be a sympathetic strike against it. Instead of making it harder to get apart, we've got to make it easier to stay together." All of the characters discuss "marriage." Theodore holds that marriage is woman's only true career. Helen says that a woman cannot pursue her career, she must be pursued by it; otherwise she is unwomanly. She herself is a "New Woman" because she has not trapped a man into a contract to support her. She believes in holy matrimony only as the last extremity. Ernest is going to Paris and Helen announces that she is going with him. John asks Ernest quite frankly to decline to take her — "one must respect the opinions of the world." Ernest agrees. He says that Helen can stay at home and run the Department for him while he is away. Just as the affair seems settled, Ernest discovers that he is in love with Helen. He tells her there can be "no marriage without money. . . . We can take it or leave it. Can we leave it? No! I can't — you can't." Helen says that if this is what marriage means, she cannot marry him. Ernest tells her that he will not woo her against her will, but "by all the powers of earth and heaven they belong to each other." John tells Helen that marriage will handicap Ernest's scientific work and Helen decides that they really have no right to marry. She tells John that she and Ernest will give up marriage but not each other. Ernest is not willing to accept her sacrifice, but Helen insists. Ernest tells her that she is coming with him as his wife or stay at home. She says that she will go with him on her terms or not at all. The Judge suggests that as Ernest is willing to lie for Helen's sake, and she is willing to die for his sake, that they split the difference and have a civil ceremony for "our sake." They refuse to surrender their convictions and start to leave the house together. The Judge draws from them a confession of their vows and pronounces them man and wife. Ernest tells Helen that a moment ago she was a bad woman. Now she is a good woman. "Marriage is wonderful!"

WHY WE BEHAVE LIKE HUMAN BEINGS, by George A. Dorsey (1925). The aim of the author is to collect the results of recent research in science and psychology, to put them in order and to make them tell "a complete and up-to-date story that can be held in one hand and read without a dictionary" about the human machine. He begins with protoplasm, "the stuff of all living things . . . in units called cells," and the development of the individual from the germ cell, proceeding to an account of race history, evolution, the beginnings of the earth and its first inhabitants, the human body and its functions in health and disease, calories, bacteria, glands, and psychology from the standpoint of behaviorism, Freudianism, and finally intelligence, and socially useful behavior. It is an anthology of facts and illustrations. A few typical sentences will show the author's method. "The human ovum was first discovered in 1827. Although it is the largest of the cells in the body, fifty thousand could be mailed across the continent for a two-cent stamp; one hundred could ride on an inch-long spider web." "If the hand that rocks the cradle is the hand that rules the world, it will not hurt good government if the hand knows what it rocks; or what the hand came from; or that the first cradle was in a tree top." "What shall we do with the Attic Greeks? Raise their 'quota' or exclude them because they do not look like the Harvard graduate who fathers an average of only three-fourths of a son and the Vassar graduate who mothers one-half of a daughter? If there is anything in the 'continuity of the germ-plasm' theory, there should be some good germs left in a country which in one hundred and fifty years produced such statesmen as Miltiades, Themistocles, Aristides, and Pericles; such poets as Æschylus. . . ." "Vitamin X is the latest. Evans has been experimenting with rats. If they get no Vitamin X, they become sterile. . . ." "Psychology is still shot with the doctrine of souls, and is still largely a form of literature based on hypothesis." "Man, amoeba, pig-iron, and hydrogen atoms may have minds. I cannot prove they have none. I can say that their behaviour can be better understood on the hypothesis that mind is pure superstition." This is a serious book despite a studied lightness of style. Mr. Dorsey has taken pains to have his statements in various fields verified by experts as he states in his preface.

WILD GEESE, by Martha Ostenso (1925). The scene is prairie country in the northwest, a farming community of Swedes, Norwegians, Icelanders, and Bohemians. Caleb Gare is a prosperous farmer of Oeland, whose passion for his land has become greed and insanity. Amelia, his wife, had an illegitimate son before she married Caleb. This son, Mark Cross, a successful architect, has grown up in ignorance of his birth, and it is the threat of exposure that keeps Amelia, for his sake, the slave of her tyrant of a husband, and makes her sacrifice her other children to constant labor.   Martin and Ellen are cowed by their bullying father.   Judith is daring and independent as she is beautiful.   All social intercourse with the neighbors is forbidden to the family.   Caleb goes alone to church.   He spends no money except on the farm.   Ellen is losing her sight for want of proper glasses, and Judith has not a whole pair of shoes.   The district school teacher, Lind Archer, comes to stay with the Gares, becomes Judith's friend, and encourages her to elope with Sven Sandbo, the son of a neighbor.   Lind becomes engaged to Mark Cross, who is spending the summer on a farm at Oeland.   As Caleb is taking vengeance on Amelia for Judith's escape, a prairie fire starts on his land, and he is lost in the quicksand of the bog while trying to save his field of flax.

WILSON, WOODROW, AND WORLD SETTLEMENT, by Ray Stannard Baker (3 vols., 1922).   The author was head of the American Press Bureau in Paris during the Peace Conference of 1919.   He writes an account of the problems of the Conference and of Mr. Wilson's fight for the principles on which the Armistice was based under conditions and in an atmosphere of Old World diplomacy and national interest and conflict foreign to the understanding of the American people.   The third volume is devoted to the text of letters, memoranda, minutes, and other documents on which the book is based, a large number from the private files of Woodrow Wilson. Part 1, Foundations of the Peace Conference, begins with the sailing of the "George Washington" with the President and the American Delegation.   On the boat the President made a statement to his associates of his program.   The two central ideas were the right of "self-determination" of peoples, and a league of nations.   The American understanding was that at the Conference each question would be discussed and decided on its merits, and not settled on the basis of secret agreements. Mr. Baker summarizes the arrangements of these secret treaties of 1915, 1916, 1917, concerning the disposition of Shantung, the partition of the German Pacific Islands, of the African Colonies, Turkey, Persia, Dalmatia, and the separation of the Rhine Provinces on the left bank from Germany.   The American Delegation was either ignorant of these agreements for the division of the spoils of war which bound the Allies or had underestimated their importance.   Part 2, The Old and the New Diplomacy, deals with the struggle for publicity, and the organization and procedure of the Conference.   The President won some of the battles of the five hundred press representatives, notably their demand to attend the ceremony when the completed Treaty was formally presented to the German Delegation.   After bitter discussion as to the representation of the small powers the compromise adopted was that there should be small conferences of the great powers with whom the final decisions rested (the Council of Ten, afterward the Council of Four), and an organization of all the powers to meet in plenary sessions.   The small powers were admitted to many of the commissions and were heard by the Councils when their interests were involved. The struggle of the old diplomacy against the new marked every stage of the Conference.   "The old advanced its secret treaties, its strategic necessities, its nationalistic ambitions; and the new demanded always a study of the facts based upon accepted principles."   Mr. Baker gives illustrations of these conflicts.   The decision to make English coequal with French as the diplomatic language of the world hurt French sensibilities.   Part 3, The League and the Peace, gives the history of the Covenant of the League of Nations.   The President's relation to the Covenant was mainly that of editor of projects that came to him from various sources: practically "not a single idea in the Covenant of the League was original with the President." By the spring of 1918 the project of a League had taken shape in the minds of many thoughtful men in Europe and America. The British Government appointed a committee of eminent international lawyers to draw up a plan. The report of this committee was called the Phillimore report from the name of the chairman. President Wilson discussed the Phillimore report with Colonel House, and requested him to draw up a new draft of a "covenant." The President recast the House draft into a new covenant. In Europe he studied the drafts of Lord Robert Cecil and General Smuts, and revised his own draft. The circulation of this second draft was submitted for comment and criticism, and the suggestions of General Bliss and David Hunter Miller led the President to make a third draft of the American Covenant. The draft which the League of Nations Commission used as a basis for discussion was a composite draft, known as the Hurst-Miller draft, prepared by Mr. Miller and Mr. C. J. B. Hurst, of the British Delegation. President Wilson achieved his purpose of securing the acceptance of his central principle that the League must be an "integral part of the general treaty of peace." American criticism centred on the conflict between the guarantees of Article 10 and the Monroe Doctrine. The various drafts of the Covenant are included in the documents of the third volume. Part 4, Struggle for the Limitation of Armaments. The American program called for general disarmament, not merely the disarmament of Germany. The League of Nations should be the new guarantee of safety in Europe. The French plan for a league of nations provided for an international army and navy. The Loucheur report on the disarmament of Germany asked for control of the Rhine frontier, backed by an armed league of nations, and Allied control of German arms and munition factories to see that military supplies were not produced. The further discussions as to army of occupation reveal the fact that France desired security more than reparations since an economically weakened Germany could not pay reparations. The problem of naval disarmament was not discussed at Paris with the frankness that characterized the controversy over compulsory military service and land armaments. In 1918 Mr. Winston Spencer Churchill in a speech said, "a league of nations is no substitute for the supremacy of the British fleet." The control of airplanes, poison gas, and submarines was discussed with the result that while Germany was disarmed the allied nations increased their supply of these new instrumentalities of destruction. Part 5, The Dark Period: the French Crisis, is the struggle between the French program of security as against Wilson's program of the mutual guarantees of a world league (Vol. 2, p. 20). In this connection telling of the struggle over the French claims, Mr. Baker portrays Lloyd George as seeming to have no guiding principles whatever. "He was powerfully on one side one day and powerfully on the other the next . . . no one was quite sure, having heard him express an unalterable determination on one day, that he would not be unalterably determined some other way on the day following. He was full of sudden bright ideas, he contracted enthusiasms, he had panics, and amused or charmed nearly everybody with whom he came into personal contact." The President ordered the "George Washington" and prepared to sail for home rather than accept the French program. In the next few days, April 8–13, compromise was reached as to the Saar and the Rhine frontier, and reparations, and many subsidiary points (Vol. 2, p. 119–121). The chapter on the "Rhine Rebellion" tells the story of the French effort to evade the settlements. Part 6, The Italian Crisis, deals with the Italian demands and the Adriatic question, and the effort to partition Turkey, including a summary of the confidential report of the American Commission to Syria and Palestine. Part 7, The Japanese Crisis, discusses the Shantung question, the twenty-one demands of Japan to the Chinese, and the Japanese fight for a clause on racial equality. Part 8, The Economic Settlement at Paris, deals with the economic policies of the nations, the American attitude toward economic questions, reparations and debts, the work of the Supreme Economic Council in relief work and food supply, the reparation settlements, the problem of commerce and the world's raw materials, of transit, rivers, canals, railroads, and ports, aerial navigation, and world communication. Part 9, Germany and the Peace, is the presentation of the Treaty to the Germans, and the German responses and Allied replies. The book sets forth especially the American policies, in the narrative of what happened at Paris, and is a defence of President Wilson. The writer believed in the absolute sincerity of the President's purpose, and gives a detailed exposition of his work for the great principles for which he stood at the Conference.

WILSON, WOODROW, LIFE AND LETTERS, by Ray Stannard Baker (Vols. 1-2, 1927). In the first volume with sub-title, "Youth — 1856-1890," the racial strains — the stock that Woodrow Wilson sprang from — "the toughest, grittiest, hardest-knit race of men that ever trod the earth" — are traced from the migration of his grandparents, James Wilson and Anne Adams Wilson, of Ireland, to the America of the time "when the Revolution still glowed in men's minds, a beacon to the oppressed of the earth, to which no people responded more heartily than the Scots of the North of Ireland. The country was fighting the Homeric battle between the Jeffersonians and the Hamiltonians, the new West and the South against the East, the radicals against the conservatives, out of the throes of which was to grow the American nation." On the Wilson side, the biographer finds the Scotch-Irish strain; on the Woodrow side, an ancient Scotch lineage. "In one of his greatest moments, at the height of fame, when he was the most acclaimed of men, it was this old racial impulse that he felt strong within him. In his Mansion House speech in London, December 28, 1918, before the Peace Conference began, when he knew better than anyone else the struggle that was just ahead of him, he said: 'The stern Covenanter tradition that is behind me sends many an echo down the years.'" The biographer adds, "And it was that magic word of the race, 'covenant,' that he used in describing the crown of all his labour — the Covenant of the League of Nations." The Wilson family settled first at Philadelphia and the biographer follows them as they pushed on by way of Pittsburgh to Ohio, where the youngest son, Joseph Ruggles, was born. Joseph was "to become the scholar of the family, a distinguished preacher, a Southern sympathizer in the Civil War, and the father of Woodrow Wilson." Of the Woodrow family, the biographer says the members were distinguished for scholarship in almost every generation for five hundred years. The first of the Woodrows came to America in 1836 — Woodrow Wilson's maternal grandfather, the Reverend Dr. Thomas Woodrow. "No branch of Woodrow Wilson's family goes back into colonial or even revolutionary times in America. No President of the United States, with one exception, had a briefer American background than Woodrow Wilson." The biographer adds that Wilson took a deep interest in his Woodrow ancestry. On one of his visits to Europe, he "found in Carlyle the locality of the house under the castle walls, in which dear mother was born. The town must have changed a great deal in these eighty years and I have little to go by, but I feel pretty sure of the general locality." "But his great visit to Carlyle was on December 29, 1918 when he was President of the United States, and, at the moment, the most renowned man in the world. He visited the church, . . . and was called upon to speak." The parents of Woodrow Wilson were married at Chillicothe, Ohio, in 1849. His father was ordained by the Ohio presbytery, and a few years later became pastor of the First Presbyterian Church of Staunton, Virginia. It was at the Presbyterian Manse in Staunton that Woodrow Wilson was born on December 28, 1856. The family removed later to Augusta, Georgia, where Woodrow Wilson spent his early boyhood — "in a house of books, an environment of serious thought, an atmosphere of deep family devotion." The biographer draws the picture of the conditions at the close of the Civil War, and the opening of a private school in Augusta by a vigorous young Confederate soldier — the first school attended by Woodrow Wilson. His work was decidedly below the average — "not because he was not bright enough, but because he was apparently not interested." When he was fourteen, his parents removed to Columbia, South Carolina, and the biographer notes here the effect of what is considered a significant change to "an impressionable and thoughtful boy." His father had been chosen as a professor in the theological seminary, but Columbia was "sitting in the ashes of her desolation as Sherman's army had left little but smoking ruins." The actual physical surroundings could not have failed to make a powerful impression upon him, while the ferment of thought and discussion is considered in their effect upon the mind of a sensitive, eager boy, and the biographer finds that the Columbia years were the richest of Woodrow Wilson's life. His later college experiences at Davidson, in Wilmington, where the Wilson family went to live, are recalled, as the biographer approaches the year of Woodrow Wilson's entrance as a student at Princeton — in 1875. From this moment he "took his education into his own hands." Before he had entered Princeton, he had become interested in English politics; and now, "he had before his very eyes one of the great dramas of American political life." In November 1876 — the year he was a sophomore — came the Hayes-Tilden election with its indeterminate result made spectacular by the staging of the struggle in the halls of Congress, "and the whole vast dust of discussion of constitutional machinery which arose out of it." The biographer holds that this condition added new fuel to Wilson's interest in the older British parliamentary method of responsible leadership. He began to inquire why America no longer produced Patrick Henrys, Websters, Clays, Calhouns: whereas England had her Gladstone and Disraeli, and Germany her Bismarck. "He then developed the idea which was later to become a keynote of his political writing, that it was due to the deadening mechanism of committee government in Congress." Wilson as a debater and writer, his college friendships, — "the kind of man that he was," are discussed in this review of his life at Princeton. His family at this time had no doubt but that he would enter the ministry. He had become fascinated with the processes of government by which laws are made — but to law as a profession for a livelihood, he felt little attraction. "The profession I chose was politics; the profession I entered was the law. I entered the one because I thought it would lead to the other; it was once the sure road, and Congress is still full of lawyers." With this purpose in his mind, Wilson, when he was graduated from Princeton, entered the University of Virginia. The biographer reviews Wilson's independent activities, his reading, his debates, his writing, his study of oratory and public speaking, which piled upon his courses in law, under a fierce disciplinarian, Dr. Minor. In 1882, the young lawyer went to Atlanta, Georgia, and formed a partnership with Edward Ireland Renick, a Virginian. His experiences at this period turn upon his first meeting with Ellen Axon, and although their marriage did not take place until two years later, the biographer considers that Wilson's career cannot be understood without a knowledge of "one of the deepest awakenings, if not the deepest, of his entire life." The two years following their meeting were years of intense study for Woodrow Wilson, and a year at her art in New York for Ellen Axon. Wilson now studied history and political science at Johns Hopkins. The biographer pictures him working "prodigiously, passionately, and with a degree of concentration which during all his life was one of his most extraordinary characteristics." The Johns Hopkins period is held to have represented the capstone of Wilson's university years, and is so treated in this biography. Everything is given that helps to present a clear conception of the entire mind of the man at the time, and becomes, in the eyes of the biographer, of importance. Extracts from letters to Ellen Axon reveal his observations and his ambitions. "I want to contribute to our literature what no American has ever contributed, studies in the philosophy of our institutions, not the abstract and occult, but the practical and suggestive, philosophy which is at the core of our governmental methods." "He was on fire to do a great and useful work." The publication of "Congressional Government" was the first fruit of Wilson's purpose. His marriage followed the completion of his work at Johns Hopkins. In 1885, Woodrow Wilson went with his bride to Bryn Mawr to begin his career as a college professor. "He was hungry for a class of men." The opportunity came in an offer from Wesleyan University in Connecticut, to which he now repaired. His two years in Middletown were the happiest of his life, but Wilson said of it: "A delightful place to work ... not ... sufficiently stimulating." The second volume of the "Life and Letters," with its sub-title, "Princeton," embraces the years from 1890 to 1910. It was in the former year that Wilson was called to Princeton, where he soon began to make himself strongly felt in the faculty. "Before he had been at Princeton two years there were premonitory rumblings of the division that was to come. It was inevitable that this should be so. Wilson was a natural born leader — it was his genius — and a leader must lead." It is as the Princeton professor that his biographer now presents him, as developing the ideas he had so carefully thought out and expressed as to the foundation principle that education must not be merely to develop the individual, but to serve the state. Of his intimate family life, the biographer gives a wealth of incident and detail; his travels in Europe, his literary work, almost all of which was done while he was a college professor, from 1885 to 1902, and which his biographer divides into political, literary, and historical groups; his vacation "programmes" form many pages of fact and comment, and this part of the biography brings finally the period when his literary work is considered to be ended, as there came "like a thunderbolt out of a clear sky," his election to the presidency of Princeton University. Wilson's "great vision for the reorganization of Princeton was the establishment of a preceptorial system — resembling Oxford, but better than Oxford." It was to be a radical change of educational methods, a departure wholly new to America. Of the plan, the biographer says, "the cost, capitalized, was to be $2,250,000, none of it in hand. The plan was as daring as it was original. It fired men of imagination; it startled the fearful and the cautious, as visions do." He had in his mind, according to this biographer, a complete new synthesis, and the social life of Princeton, its athletics, its various outside activities, he wanted to coördinate so as to promote rather than hamper the supreme purpose of the university — intellectual discipline. In the opinion of the writer, "It would have been a miracle — unexampled in human events — if such a career could have continued unchecked or unopposed." It is shown that with the achievement of the preceptorial system in 1905 — and the reorganization of the university that went with it — Wilson's splendid impetus somewhat spent itself; a cloud no larger than a man's hand in the clear heavens of Wilson's aspiration, began to spread and darken. "There is a point in the career of every crusader when he exhausts the reservoir of public idealism — when he makes further progress only upon the passion of his own purpose. The struggle was to gather force and bitterness; until during the years from 1907 to 1910, it was to supersede everything else." This phase of opposition centred around the plan for a graduate college. The biographer gives his estimate of the depth of Wilson's seriousness in considering the problems of his administration at Princeton. "In planning for Princeton . . . we are planning for the country." Anyone who dared to interfere with that requirement was veritably threatening the safety of America. Wilson began his fight for the social coördination of Princeton University in 1906. The "Quad Struggle," which brought about the antagonistic ideas not only as to policy, but as to executive control, is reviewed, the elements which were embedded in these misunderstandings, the radical differences of view, are all recalled in their effect upon the steady widening of the rift, as the growing discussion of the quads became more and more serious, and more and more complicated with the controversy of the graduate college. The final defeat of the Wilson proposals is discussed, but the biographer adds that ten years after Wilson's struggle, the flagrant abuses of the club system are being attacked in terms as scathing as any that Wilson ever applied. The Wilson ideas and ideals are still "a living ferment of Princeton University." Wilson withdrew from Princeton in 1910. He had been nominated by the Democratic party for Governor of New Jersey. He was now to enter upon his career as a statesman.

WIND AND THE RAIN, THE, a book of confessions, by Thomas Burke (1924). These autobiographical reminiscences begin with the boy of ten staring in the window of a shop in the Chinatown of London at the Chinese script, the crooked weapons and statuettes of coral and jade, and at Quong Lee, behind his wares, with his unwinking eyes and the expressionless face of his own seven-stomached Lord of Right Living. One day the man beckoned to the fascinated boy, holding out a piece of ginger, and they began a friendship, richer, Burke says, than any he has since known. In a moment which all his writing in later life was an effort to recapture, the boy "saw and understood the beauty and sorrow of things," and caught a glimpse of the secret and mystery of Asia. During twelve years Burke returned from time to time to the shop and his Oriental friend as to an immutable world, a refuge from the bruises of extreme poverty and loneliness. The boy and his Uncle Frank, a gardener at the "Big House," lived happily together in a small room in the working-class district. "Life was a shower of coloured stars — Christmas Days, Sundays, Bank Holidays, tram-rides, 'bus-rides, Saturday-night shoppings, impulsive feasts, parties in the kitchen of the Lady's House. . . ." Then "the Lady" took an interest in the gardener's boy, and had him sent to the Hardcress Home for Orphans for an education, where he spent four years of slavery to routine and efficiency, brightened for a time by a friendship with one boy, Fosdick, until his friend committed suicide to escape what to him was prison. Burke left the school to take a post as boy in a hotel, which turned out to be a "queer" place, and where people were always telling him for some reason that he ought not to be there. A meeting with Mr. Creegan, friend of Uncle Frank, who had died while he was at the Home, brought him to the city to be an office boy, snubbed by the clerks who had no fellowship for a charity boy. This period is a series of pictures of the London he came to know as he walked its streets in the evenings. He discovered the world of books in the public library, and turned naturally to the poets who had been poor and miserable like himself, Poe, Chatterton, Mangan, Burns and Otway, and became more insufferable at the office in his pride of intellect. "A boy of my sort" should not fill his head with books. He would go without tea and save nine pence to buy a Canterbury poet, and then often yield to the flesh, and let "the whole nine pence go in one blazing burst of sausages, potatoes and onions." Besides literature he explored pictures and music, and found a friend, a half-starved little working girl, Gracie Scott, to share his enthusiasms. The girl's coarse-minded, shrewish step-mother found out their innocent comradeship, and Gracie vanished one day. He lost his place at the office and came to starvation and standing in line to get into a "Shelter" for the night. A chance meeting with a boy he had known at the Orphanage, Frederick Cosgrove, led to work in the office of a theatre where Cosgrove was a vaudeville performer, and into a friendly group of Bohemians, and the munificent salary of three pounds a week. By the time a change of management lost him this position, Burke was writing for the magazines, and could eke out a bare subsistence. The girl at the "Big House" who had patronized the gardener's boy, Miss Cicely, made friends with the young man who was earning a living by writing. He fell in love with her, and again she put him in his place, making him loathe the world in which he belonged, and long to enter hers by some magic bridge. For a few hours he was engaged to her, and then she broke it off, and he went back to Quong Lee for the silent communion that might bring him peace. He was in time to see his old friend before he was deported for selling opium to make money to go back to see his country again. Creegan, the itinerant orchestra player, listens to his story, and says the things that Burke believes that Quong Lee would have told him about life if he could have spoken English, and sends him back to work. The story ends when Burke is twenty-three, and feels that he has found himself.

WINESBURG, OHIO, by Sherwood Anderson (1919), is a character study of a small town, a Spoon River Anthology in twenty-three prose sketches. Drab, commonplace people are shown in moments of vivid feeling, and ardent impulse, which too often is suppressed or misdirected. To this author, sex is usually the mainspring of human action. The first story "Hands," is about Wing Biddlebaum, called "Wing" because of his nervous, active hands, which had picked as high as one hundred and forty quarts of berries in a day. Once he had been a gifted teacher, who inspired his pupils with affection. "A half-witted boy of the school became enamoured of the young master," and told his unspeakable imaginings as facts. The saloon keeper and a dozen other men drove the teacher out of the town with kicks and threats. "Keep your hands to yourself," they had shouted at him. He escaped to Winesburg, changed his name, and "worked as a day laborer in the fields, going timidly about and striving to conceal his hands. Although he did not understand what had happened, he felt that the hands must be to blame." "Adventure" is the pathetic story of Alice Hindman, clerk in the dry goods store. When she was sixteen she had given herself to Ned Currie, a reporter, who said to her, "Now we will have to stick to each other, whatever happens we will have to do that." He goes to Chicago and forgets her. After years of waiting and loneliness she realizes that she must "face bravely the fact that many people must live and die alone, even in Winesburg," and that she must be careful of her impulses or she "will do something dreadful." Most of the stories center about George Willard, a young reporter, with dreams of getting "away from all this" and doing something big. He sees no news value in the town, but "The Philosopher," Doctor Parcival, tells him to remember "that everyone in the world is Christ, and they are all crucified." "Mother" and "Death" are studies of George's mother, the daughter of the hotel keeper. She had been a stage struck girl longing for adventure, and had had several lovers before she married. As Doctor Reefy, her one friend, listens to her story, she seems to become again a young beautiful girl, and for the moment he also is her lover. Elizabeth Willard is timid and reserved with her son, though there is a deep unexpressed bond of sympathy between them. She prays that he may not become "a meaningless drab figure" like herself, or "smart and successful, either." She even pictures herself stabbing her husband with the scissors because she thinks he wants to make George a business man. Her father, on his death bed, had urged her not to marry the hotel clerk, Tom Willard, and had given her $800 to go away from Winesburg, where he himself had been a failure, but "like most young girls, she thought marriage would change the face of life." She dies unable to speak, and tell her son of the hidden fund she had kept for his escape. "The Teacher," Kate Swift, to the town a confirmed old maid, in reality is the most eagerly passionate soul among them. "Behind a cold exterior the most extraordinary events transpired in her mind." George Willard does not understand her desire for his love or the things she tries to tell him of the importance to a writer of knowing life, "what people are thinking about not what they say." In "The Strength of God," the minister becomes a peeping Tom, and comes to a realization of God through his temptation. He tells George that the woman, Kate Swift, is an instrument of God bearing a message of truth. "Queer" Elmer Cowley threatens to shoot a travelling salesman who tries to sell his father some patent substitute for collar buttons for the store, in order to demonstrate that the Cowleys are not going to be queer and have folks staring and listening. When they lived on the farm away from people Elmer had not felt queer. Now he longs to tell George Willard, as a representative of public opinion, that he is not queer. Finally as he is leaving Winesburg, he beats George at the station, and is satisfied that he has achieved his purpose. "An Awakening" is a humorous incident in the development of George. Bell Carpenter, who works in the millinery shop, is in love with a heavy-fisted bartender, who cannot find words to declare himself. She brings him to the point by philandering with George, who is tossed aside by the jealous suitor, to his keen humiliation. In "Respectability," the telegraph operator, Wash Williams, tells George why he is a woman-hater, of his idealization of his young wife who had deceived him with lovers. George leaves Winesburg to seek his fortune, and says good-by to his sweetheart, Helen White, in "Sophistication" and "Departure." He tries to tell Helen about the things he has been thinking, and the big things he is going to do. They kiss and are embarrassed, and to relieve their embarrassment drop into the animalism of youth and pull and haul at each other and run a race with shouts of laughter. "For some reason they could not have explained they had both got from their silent evening together the thing needed . . . they had for a moment taken hold of the thing that makes the mature life of men and women in the modern world possible."

WINGS OF YOUTH, by Elizabeth Jordan (1918). Barbara, twenty-four, and Lawrence, twenty-three, are "the last of the Devons." They are alone in the world, absolutely independent, and with too much money, of which Barbara has the control. Lawrence has failed to "make good" in a variety of positions, and has gained the reputation of ne'er-do-well and waster. Barbara devotes herself to charity work. Both are thoroughly bored with their life as it is. Brother and sister make a compact to go to New York together, and there, alone, each is to make his own way for a year, she as Barbara Smith, he as Lawrence Jones. They are to start with fifty dollars each, and are to communicate only twice during the year. The first thing that happens to Barbara, who had declared herself avid for new experiences, is the loss of her purse while she is inspecting lodgings in Irving Place. She finds herself penniless in New York, with night approaching. As she is debating what she can do a young man falls over her suitcase, and, recovering, recognizes her unusualness at a glance, and asks if there is anything he can do to help her. Trusting him at sight, she tells him of her mishap and he takes her to his aunt's apartment in Gramercy Park. There she spends the night, but when Warren calls up in the morning he finds that she is gone. From the sympathetic elevator man he learns that she has gone "towards Third Avenue — walkin' slow." Employing amateur detective methods he soon locates the shop where Barbara has pawned her watch for thirty dollars; then for a time he loses her. With that money Barbara finds herself decent lodgings, and in them has the good fortune to encounter Sonia Orleneff, who is head file-clerk for Wade & Manning, publishers. Sonia and Barbara recognize each other as congenial at once. An additional bond is furnished by their adoration for "The Infant Samuel," the baby son of another lodger in the house. "The Infant Samuel" is two years old, and amply deserves all the loving admiration the girls lavish on him. Through Sonia, Barbara meets Madame Marini, once a noted opera singer, still great even now in the twilight of her life. Barbara is wholly without business training, but she has real talent for the piano, and can play accompaniments well enough to satisfy even Marini's exigencies. Marini is soon to have a vaudeville "try-out"; if she succeeds she is to be "booked" for thirty weeks. But though she would rather have had Barbara, her accompanist has already been engaged. Sonia gets Barbara a position with Wade & Manning, addressing envelopes for eight dollars a week. She keeps the job for six months. During that time she plays for Mme. Marini's opening (due to the defection of "the little Martinelli") and attends her faithfully when she contracts pneumonia and dies after her triumph. In order to give Marini a proper funeral, Barbara appeals to Warren. But, though she accepts his aid, giving him her note against next October, she will not allow him to continue the acquaintance. When she is dismissed by Wade & Manning in the spring, when they reduce their staff, Barbara meets Warren again. She goes to see a Miss Bradley, who needs an accompanist. Warren is there with a beautiful, restless woman, Mrs. Ordway, his sister. Mrs. Ordway is afflicted with insomnia and can find rest only during great excitement or noise, or both. She engages Barbara to be her companion, to play to her, read to her, talk to her. In the meantime, Lawrence has found himself, for the first month, "up against it." In the lodging-house a young playwright, Rodney Bangs, is working on a "crook" play. One scene, in a country club, bothers him. He senses that Laurie belongs to the class he wishes to depict and seeks his assistance. It proves to be a fortunate arrangement for them both. Lawrence finds the work he enjoys, and before the year is over he has collaborated with Bangs in a successful play. Laurie takes Barbara to see his play when they meet at the end of the year to compare experiences, and she is happy that her sacrifice for him has been so richly rewarded. The next night before the brother and sister return to their home in Devondale, Ohio, Barbara gives a dinner at the Colony Club to their new friends. Warren asks her to let him announce their engagement, but when Laurie makes the announcement of their identity, he tells Barbara that he is not willing to be the husband of an heiress. He would either have to be dependent on her or let her give up most of what she is used to having, and the situation is intolerable to him. Barbara insists on marrying him in spite of his reluctance, and agrees to live half the year in New York on his income as a solution of their difficulties.

WINTERSMOON, by Hugh Walpole (1927). A novel of aristocratic London society, a sequel to the "Duchess of Wrexe" in the sense that Rachel Seddon and her son, Tom, and Lord John Beaminster are among the characters. Janet Grandison consents to marry her friend, Wildherne, Lord Poole, after his third proposal, without love on either side. They discuss frankly the fact that he wants an heir, and likes and admires her, and she thinks she will never love anyone as much as her younger sister, Rosalind. He loves a married woman, Diana Guard, who cared for him for six months, and then became indifferent to his passion for her, and took other lovers. Janet and Rosalind are of good family, but are poor, and Janet thinks that it will give her beautiful sister more of the good things of life if she marries Wildherne, heir to the delightful old Duke of Purefoy. Rosalind is selfish, and a modernist. At first she is delighted with the idea of Janet's marriage, but after she has attended a reception given for Janet by the Duchess of Purefoy, at which all the conservative, early Victorian members of the family are present, she realizes that Janet is committed to a world that is alien to her, and to escape, she marries Tom Seddon, who adores her, as she considers living with her sister out of the question. Tom is in the Foreign Office, and has a future until he becomes so unhappy in his marriage that his career is ruined. In the meantime Janet, separated from her loved sister, who postpones coming to visit her at Wintersmoon, falls passionately in love with her husband. She is jealous of Diana, and later of her son, Humphrey, who displaces Diana in Wildherne's affections. He worships the baby, and gives Janet only the most tender respect and consideration. She confesses her unhappiness to the Duke, who tells Wildherne of his blindness and selfishness. At this point in the story the child, Humphrey, dies. Wildherne is almost out of his mind with grief for a time, and only Janet's devoted love and care save his reason. A letter comes from Rosalind saying that she and Tom have agreed to separate, asks Janet to come to London to see her. Rosalind's need comes at a time when it seems impossible to leave Wildherne, and she has to choose between them. She telegraphs her sister that she will come the first moment possible. Tom threatens to shoot both Rosalind and himself, but she manages to dominate him and send him away. Another letter from Rosalind tells Janet that she is leaving for Scotland with Charles Ravage, one of her advanced friends, who understands her as the sentimental Tom had not. Janet leaves a note to tell Wildherne, now quite himself, that she is following Rosalind to Scotland to see what she can do to bring her sister back to her husband. On her arrival in London she hears that Tom has shot himself. Tom's death is a relief to Rosalind, she tells Janet, though she would have been glad if he could have lived and been happy without her. Ravage, she says, cares for ideas, as she does herself, and she can live with him in freedom. Wildherne follows Janet to Scotland, such is his need and longing for her, and all is well with the world for Janet. The two sisters are typical of the old and the post-War society. Tom says of Rosalind and her friends, that they do not believe in strong emotions of any kind, only ideas. The old world has got to go, for a new one, "cold, unpassionate, scientific, material, accurate, unfeeling." Janet sees as in a vision that the movement that she had started by her marriage has come to an end. To everyone involved by that action the crisis had come. Now a new cycle had begun. She hopes to make something out of this strange, ever moving, creative life, "one thing brave, lovely, of good report."

WITH LAWRENCE IN ARABIA, by Lowell Thomas (1924). Sketches the achievements of Lawrence of Arabia from youth up to and through the World War. Thomas

Edward Lawrence was born in Carnarvon County, Wales, whence his father had moved from County Galway, Ireland, where the Lawrences had lived for generations. Sir Robert Lawrence, an ancestor, accompanied Richard the Lion-Hearted to the Holy Land and distinguished himself at the siege of Acre; Thomas Edward Lawrence accompanied Allenby in the Holy Land seven hundred and thirty years later and distinguished himself all along the line. When Lawrence was ten years old the family moved to Scotland and remained there three years. They next lived in France where young Lawrence attended a Jesuit College, although his family belonged to the Church of England. From France they went to Oxford and here Lawrence proved a law unto himself in the matter of attending lectures, but he early showed great interest in archæology. At one time before he was graduated he started out with two hundred pounds as his capital, determined to visit Arabia. His family thought he would return in a few weeks; instead he donned Arabian garments and went into the desert to study the customs of the people and did not return to England for two years. When he came back, he handed in his thesis and received his degree. Before he was twenty years old he engaged in an exploring expedition in the Euphrates Valley and became interested in Hittite inscriptions. For seven years he wandered up and down Arabia exploring, sometimes alone, sometimes with a friend. Always he went in native garb and everywhere he was respected and liked by the Arabs. At the beginning of the World War Lawrence attempted to enlist but was rejected by the medical board. Four years later this frail, scholarly youth entered Damascus at the head of his victorious Arabian army. After his rejection Lawrence returned to his exploring but was shortly summoned to Cairo where his knowledge of the desert and its routes was invaluable. He was made lieutenant but was far from popular because of his aversion to red tape and his failure to salute his superior officers. Lawrence asked for a two-weeks leave, obtained it without any difficulty, and never went back. With Ronald Storrs, Oriental secretary to the high commission of Egypt, he went down the Red Sea to Jeddah, and then inland, alone, to the camp of the Emir Feisal. When Lawrence arrived in Hedjaz the revolt of the Arabians against the Turks was in full swing. For more than a year Hussein, Shereef of Mecca, had been fighting the Turks. Feisal, his son, was one of the chief leaders and from the day of meeting with him Lawrence became the leading spirit of the revolution. Medina, the southern terminus of the Damascus railway, was being besieged but the task of taking the city was too difficult, so Lawrence and Feisal started on a campaign of desert warfare directed mainly against this railroad. One of Lawrence's favorite pastimes was mining the railroad at a given point and blowing up troop and provision trains which came by. At the end of the War he had the destruction of seventy-nine trains or bridges to his credit. Not only did Lawrence have the problem of fighting against the Turks, he had to keep the members of various tribes from fighting among themselves. His control over these fierce sons of the desert was remarkable. Tribes that had fought the Turks for a thousand years as separate units came together under his leadership and fought with him against their common enemy. He accomplished marvellous feats himself and in return won their friendship. He was wise enough to subordinate himself to Feisal, which under the circumstances was a very politic thing to do, and worked wonders in the matter of troop discipline. To back him Lawrence had the British forces, British gold and understanding officers who sent warships or airplanes at his behest to keep up the morale of the Arabs. But many times in the desert far from these he fought alone and was successful. Lawrence was an ardent believer in Arab nationalism, but he was under no illusions as to the outlook.

A single united Arab nation in the western sense he thought was impossible; he did look forward to a chain of Arab states held in a loose but strong spiritual bond, with the unofficial capital of the Arab world in Bagdad or Mosul, and with King Feisal as one of the leading chiefs. At the time of the Peace Conference in Paris Lawrence was twenty-eight; at the time of his first activities in behalf of the British government he had been twenty-six. In two years of strenuous efforts he had become the un-crowned king of Arabia and had ridden into Jerusalem with Allenby on that memorable day. As soon as the world learned who the shy little man at the Peace Conference was his life became a burden to him. In order to gain peace from being lionized and the obscurity which he desires Lawrence has changed his name and retired to an obscure post in the British Army.

WORLD AFTER THE PEACE CONFERENCE, THE, by Arnold J. Toynbee (1925). Described as an epilogue to the "History of the Peace Conference," and a prologue to the "Survey of International Affairs." Published under the auspices of the British Institute of International Affairs. A study in political transition setting forth the political map as it was at the outbreak of the War in 1914, and the contrast of the changes in 1923. The "horizon" summarizes the main current of contemporary tendencies, the economic, industrial and political forces which made the pre-War states, remapping the world six years later.

WORLD OF WILLIAM CLISSOLD, THE, by H. G. Wells (1926), is offered as a novel, "the story of one man's adventure, body, soul and intelligence in life." He believes it to be no less a novel because there is much discussion in it. Ideas, therefore, rather than persons are the chief protagonists of the action. Many of the persons introduced who form a part of this philosophical survey of a man's life at sixty are actual persons to whom he has given their real names. Clissold's survey of his world and his will in it, begins with his childhood, which was carefree until his father's mysterious disappearance. Later, he, and Dickon, his brother, learned that their gay and generous father had died under a cloud, caught in shady speculation. The brothers go to London to work, William Clissold in scientific research. A running commentary is given of their youthful adventures into religion, socialism, and something of the philosophy they evolved to explain their father's aberrations. Young Clissold's scientific habit of thought, taken with the breaking of most of the conventional restraints through championing of their father's life, led the two boys to refuse the orthodox explanations of life. They early realized and accepted the complete indifference of the universe to themselves. William finds on looking back that his socialism bore no very strong resemblance to that of the party of that name. It was little more than an application of the distinctively scientific spirit to human affairs in general. This view he develops in greater detail in the second volume under the heading, "The World State." The great adventure as he sees it, is "to make the system that is not here . . . to subjugate it to his security and creative happiness." The obsession of system he finds well illustrated in the scholar's attitude toward history, which is for him too often a refuge, not an extension of reality. Clissold's own exposition of the feudal system is a magnificent miniature of medieval times illustrating his point. No less arresting is his psychoanalysis of Karl Marx and the socialist system. Marx had not Darwin's gift for reality as he shows by the artificial way he divides and simplifies classes. His tendency to idealize the workman and to depreciate the masters and organizers seemed the result of a limited, bookish life. Communism, which is the sabotage of civilization, has usurped the place and the function of creative socialism. "Realization of a new stage of civilized society will be the work of an intelligent minority." World control, world peace, will ultimately be the work of collective man. Progress cannot be anything but casual until the mature and educated élite has become self-conscious and effective. It will be an autocratic revolution. Ultimately such people will reshape the general conceptions of political and social life. This leads to a short history of human society as a labour-money complex evolved out of the primitive, patriarchal family. The next section is devoted to his brother Dickon, his advertising adventures, and the philosophy of business success and finally to Dickon's relation to his wife. In a letter to him written just before her death she shows herself for the delicate lady she was, seeking to reassure her husband concerning the happiness he had given her, but in this it appears to William Clissold that, beneath her perfect kindness to his brother was a rather thoroughgoing cynicism. So this first volume of more or less disjointed commentary on life closes with some reflections on the futility of the retired rich on the Riviera. Volume 2 is a return to thoughts on youth, its stress and disturbances, the need of sensitive young folk to protect their personalities against the invasions of life and particularly those of older people — the ruthlessness of education. The obscure inner tragedy of the young just awakening to life who without special gifts are forced to go to work arouses his compassion. For them, laughter is the only derisive outlet that gives relief. The period is all the more difficult since to economic maladjustment is added the sexual sturm and drang. This leads him immediately to the recounting of his personal relations with women; his inadvertent marriage under the urge of youth, the separation; other extralegal adventures; his championship of a woman of the world, Sirrie Evans, who finds herself in a divorce action abandoned by other lovers; their beautiful and companionable love that ripens into mellow friendship; one other adventure with a famous actress in which both are too absorbed by private ambition to sacrifice to one another so that eventually they part. All these episodes lead to his final befriending of Clementia, a demi-mondaine of Paris, who under his kindness revives and reveals a winsome personality. Interpolated among these amorous adventures is the expansion of an idea alluded to earlier, on the coming world state which he sees finally as a world directorate of best minds, trained in the disciplines of science and big business affairs. The new world order must be positive, aggressive, constructive. He sees certain possibilities in the League of Nations through "developing its international secretariat for a great series of world functions." David Lubin and his International Institute of Agriculture he cites as a prophetic instance of this world coöperation. But before these agencies can become really effective the masses must be educated in a new and different way. "The press, the cinema theatre, broadcasting centers, book publishing and distributing organizations, are the citadels that dominate Cosmopolis." So he advocates, not only a liberal world press, the replacement of militant ideals by police ideals, but also a new education where there will be more skilled schoolteachers who have a sense of reality because they keep in contact with reality and fewer schoolmasters of the older type. The real world university will become a great literature, a literature of ideas. Along with the creative and directive men who are building up this new world order there will be women full of a new pride and reserve awakening also to share the new understandings and the new ambitions. "I do not see how these women can be other than women practically active, soberly beautiful in dress and bearing, a little hidden in their love, and friendly to men." So he realizes that he has become, individually adult, no longer concerned primarily with his own life but gripped and possessed by the wider demands of the racial adventure. "The attainment of the World Republic and attainment of a fully adult life are the general and particular aspects of one and the same reality."

WORLD'S ILLUSION, THE, by Jacob Wassermann, translated by Ludwig Lewisohn (1920). The hero, Christian Wahnschaffe, is a modern St. Francis of Assisi, who renounces the millions of his birthright to devote himself to the service and understanding of humanity in the depths of the underworld of thieves, prostitutes, and murderers. At the beginning of the story, Christian entertains himself going from one house-party to another. He is handsome, fearless, charms men and women equally, is adored by his parents, and is immensely wealthy. The group of his friends is the aristocratic society of Europe before the War. His most intimate friend and opposite is Bernard Crammon, an elegant, worldly satyr, typical of the older aristocracy. The wealthy Felix Imhoff marries his sister, Judith, though she is secretly in love with the great actor, Edgar Lorme, for whom she leaves Felix later. Christian loves Eva Sorel, the most beautiful dancer in Europe. He has deserted Adda Castillo, the lion-tamer, for Eva. The clever Jewess, Johanna, falls in love with Christian's miniature, and joins the court of satellites around Eva to make his acquaintance. There is Letitia who attracts him, but who has to content herself with marrying a South American adventurer, Stephen Gunderan. The story of Eva parallels that of Christian, and she typifies artistic aspiration and lust for power. After Christian leaves her she becomes the mistress of a Russian Grand Duke, gains immense wealth and political power, and is killed in an attack on her Black Sea palace by marauding sailors. At first Christian avoids ugliness and poverty. A Russian revolutionary leader, Ivan Michailov Becker, makes him feel the sympathy and humility, which later becomes an obsession with him. He is stirred by seeing a poor girl maltreated by a crowd of half-drunken students in a beer garden. The story of the inferior student, Amadeus Voss, awakens his pity. In the end he gives up his wealth, goes to Berlin to study medicine, and lives in the slums caring for a dying prostitute, Karen Engelschall, whom he rescues from the gutter. There he comes in contact with evil, brutality and suffering. But he also meets the lovely and innocent Ruth, a sixteen-year-old Jewess, who has by nature the passionate universal love which has begun to develop in him. She is brutally murdered by Nils Heinrich, the brother of Karen. In a remarkable scene he induces the murderer to confess, and later to deliver himself up to the police. Then Christian disappears. There are rumors that he has been seen in East End London, and in Chinatown in New York.

YOUNG, BRIGHAM, by M. R. Werner (1925). The life of Joseph Smith, Jr., the founder of Mormonism, and the history of the Mormon people in their heroic period, are the subject matter of this book as well as the life of Brigham Young. The author, however, is "primarily interested in the personality of Brigham Young, because it is his conviction that without Brigham Young the Mormons would never have been important after the first few years of their institutional life, but without the Mormons Brigham Young might have been a great man." The Mormon movement in American affairs during the span of Brigham Young's life, from 1801 to 1877, its political and economic significance, and its influence on social life, is shown to have been a national issue of the government, and the author gives his reasons for holding that Mormonism was a perfect example of a religion carried to its illogical conclusions. He traces the exodus of the Mormons through Ohio, Illinois and Missouri, and follows their journeyings into Utah — their "Sinai." Of the assassination of Joseph Smith by a hostile mob, Mr. Werner says that his death came at the right time for his religion, as if he had lived a few years longer his arrogance, vanity, and pretensions would have broken up his church. He had "become more ambitious than the angels and more dictatorial than the Hebrew God. His vision of himself as President of the United States, and his picture of himself as lord of a harem, were not only inconsistent with each other, but productive of opposition from Gentiles and dissension among Mormons." He did, however, create Mormonism and made it a success, and Mr. Werner does justice to his eminent qualities. The leadership of Brigham Young in the Mormon Church is shown to have been definitely established with the death of the Prophet, despite the schisms which are recalled. In moving from one unpopulated region to another, the great trek to the West is followed step by step. The author holds that the one idea of Brigham Young was to take his people beyond the jurisdiction of the United States. "Brigham Young once expressed tersely the whole purpose of the migration of his people: 'To get away from Christians.'" Many extracts from the writings of Brigham Young reveal his views on polygamy, as well as his Puritan principles relating to the blessings of hardships. In 1856 the steady stream of Mormon immigration ended at Salt Lake City, and the author concerns himself with the peculiar features of Brigham Young's domain in which the Mormons clung tenaciously to what their leader pointed out to them were the Bible precedents for their practice of polygamy. The author follows the agitation against the practice which began in Congress, but which did not put a stop to polygamy until fifteen years after the death of the Mormon chieftain. The reasons for its disappearance were economic and cultural. The younger generation who went East to college and associated with Gentiles the railroad brought to Utah, began to be ashamed of the number of their grandmothers, and even in Brigham Young's lifetime it began to be considered bad form as well as too expensive among young Mormons to have more than one wife. The invasion of the outside world made Utah fall in line with the rest of America.

YOUNG WOODLEY, a play, by John Van Druten (1925). The author says this is "a study of adolescence, an attempt to capture the perplexities that beset the boy." The action takes place at the Mallowhurst School in England, and the first scene is the sitting room of the prefects or upper classmen. Cope, a fag, is clearing away the tea, and the older boys, Vining, Ainger, and Woodley are talking together. The sensitive, romantic Woodley has been reprimanded by Headmaster Simmons for the tone of his writings, and especially for a poem which has appeared in the school magazine. The conversation about what Woodley calls "Simmy's purity campaign," leads to talk about Simmy's pretty young wife who is much too good for him, and they remember that they are expected to go to tea at the Simmonses the next Sunday afternoon, which will be a bore and mess up the afternoon. Vining would rather go walking in the Mallow woods which are out of bounds with some of the town girls. He is a prurient minded boy, and Ainger and Woodley agree after he has left that he is a "foul type." They talk about sex which to them means women out of their class, and love, a thing of the imagination, and they cannot relate the two. There is a knock at the door and Mrs. Simmons comes shyly in. Her errand is to ask the older boys if something can be done to prevent the boys from using her yard as a short cut and breaking the shrubbery. She compliments Woodley on his poem in the school magazine. He shows her some other verses and lets her take them home to read if she will not show them to her husband. They are reading Swinburne and bits of Shelley when Mr. Simmons appears looking for Ainger, gone out with Cope, who has broken a teapot, and is surprised to find his wife there. He begins to chaff Woodley about his poetry, and Laura insists she must go. As they leave Simmons asks her about the manuscript she is taking away, and she says it is only some receipts she has borrowed. The next act is in the Simmons drawing room where the headmaster is correcting examination papers with a sadistic pleasure in the mistakes. Mrs. Simmons is not in sympathy with his attitude toward the boys. She accuses him of having no feeling for the students except for their respect for himself, and "their conforming to a few stupid forms and ceremonies." He can never forget his position and his dignity, and talks down to the boys. Simmons tells her that she is "romancing, sentimentalising, as usual instead of facing the problem." The truth is she does not know, he says, "what sinks of impurity their minds can be." "Discipline and a healthy observance of games and a proper inculcation of the Public School spirit" is the remedy. He cites the high minded Woodley as not normal because he writes poetry. The headmaster goes to the cricket match, annoyed that she will not go with him because she has invited Ainger and Woodley to tea. He considers that it destroys respect to have social relations with the boys, and that she is at fault not to appear with him at school functions. Woodley appears alone. At the last minute Ainger had to substitute in the cricket match. He tells her about his home and family, and in return she describes the country about her home and the mountains she misses. After much hesitation Woodley asks permission to read a poem he has written to her. She tells him that she is sorry her husband spoke the way he did about Woodley's poetry. Woodley thinks he must go, and it would be better if he did not come again, because though he ought not to say it, he is "most terribly in love" with her. The unhappy Laura loses control of her emotions and holds out her arms to him. They kiss just as Simmons walks in the door. Laura is sorry, as she tells her enraged husband, that she led him on to make love to her, but if Woodley is expelled she will leave too. It is the boy's last term, and she will not see him again. Woodley slips in to find out from Laura what they are to do, and she takes a light tone and lets him think that she has been playing with him. In the prefect's room the boys discuss the way Simmons and Woodley both are acting lately. Ainger tries to get Woodley's confidence, and lets him know that he had seen him walking in the Mallow woods with a town girl. He can tell him about the girl and his own self-loathing, but can not bring himself to talk about Laura. Vining comes in and begins ragging Woodley about his tea with "our luscious Laura" speaking of her in such an insulting way that Woodley, mad with rage, seizes the bread knife from the table, and would have killed him if Ainger had not interfered to prevent it. Simmons comes into the room to find out what has happened, and Woodley is led off to the infirmary shouting that Simmons need not bully him now, he has got what he wanted, the opportunity to expel him. Laura sends for Ainger to tell her the truth about the affair. In the last scene Mr. Woodley has come to take his son away from the school, and is amazed at Simmons' charges. Laura gets the opportunity to explain everything to Mr. Woodley, that she had been entirely to blame, and her only excuse is that she did not realize what it all must have meant to the boy in love. She urges him to try to get better acquainted with his shy, charming son. When young Woodley comes in his father wisely leaves him and Laura to say good-by alone. Then at last she tells him that she had not meant to treat his love lightly, that the things she had said were not true, that she loves him as he loves her, and wants him to treasure the memory of their love as she shall — always. She kisses him on the forehead. There is a knock at the door and the boy pulls himself together, and bravely faces his father, who puts his arm around his shoulder, and they go out.

The reference to *Library* in this book refers to Warner's Library
of the World's Best Literature.

INDEX

PART I

SUPPLEMENT

The Ultimate

JACK THE
RIPPER

COMPANION

An Illustrated Encyclopedia

The Ultimate
JACK THE
RIPPER
COMPANION
An Illustrated Encyclopedia

STEWART P. EVANS &
KEITH SKINNER

CARROLL & GRAF PUBLISHERS
New York

Carroll & Graf Publishers
An imprint of Avalon Publishing Group, Inc
245 W. 17th Street
11th Floor
NY 10011-5300
www.carrollandgraf.com

First Carroll & Graf edition, 2000
First Carroll & Graf trade paperback edition, 2001

First published in the UK by Robinson, 2000

Third printing 2003

ISBN 0-7867-0926-X

Printed and bound in the EU

For
Don Rumbelow

Acknowledgments

The invaluable help of the staff at the Public Record Office, Kew, is gratefully acknowledged, as is that of the Corporation of London Record Office, the London Metropolitan Archives (formerly the Greater London Record Office), the Archive and Museum Departments of the Metropolitan Police, The Royal London Hospital Archives and Museum, City of London Police Museum, British Library Newspaper Library, Richard Davie, Paul Mulvey and Mr J. D. Swanson. Acknowledgment is also made to the Controller of Her Majesty's Stationery Office, via the above offices, and we are also grateful for the permission of Her Majesty Queen Elizabeth II for the use of material from The Royal Archives.

Contents

List of Illustrations

Witnesses at Stride Inquest: PC 452H William Smith, Louis Diemschutz,
    Morris Eagle
Coroner Wynne Baxter at Stride Inquest
Matthew Packer, resident
Dr George Bagster Phillips, police surgeon
Sketch of crowd outside mortuary in St-Georges'-in-the-East
Dr William P. Blackwell
Detective Sergeant Steven White
Inquest sketch of Mitre Square, Aldgate
Inquest sketch of body of Catherine Eddowes and mortuary photographs
PC 881 Edward Watkins
Sketch of inquest of Catherine Eddowes
Police copy of the "Jewes" message
Letter written by Tom Bulling and envelope enclosing "Dear Boss" letter
The "Dear Boss" Letter
The Lusk letter
George Lusk, chairman of the Whitechapel Vigilance Committee
Sketches of suspect described by Matthew Parker
Contemporary picture of Spitalfields
Sketches of Ripper suspects
Homeless women on the streets
Vigilance Committee members
A mob in Spitalfields
Bloodhounds, tried out for tracking purposes
Dorset Street
Mary Jane Kelly at Miller's Court
The body of Mary Jane Kelly

Between pages 534 and 535

Exterior View of Miller's Court
26 Dorset Street, as Mary Jane Kelly's body is removed
A map of murder sites
Letter from Balmoral (courtesy of © Royal Archives)
File cover for the murder of Alice McKenzie
Mortuary photograph of Alice McKenzie
Railway arch in Pinchin Street
Frances Coles
James Thomas Sadler, suspect
Mortuary photograph of Frances Coles
PC 240H Ernest Thompson
James Sadler and Frances Coles in the doss house
Plan of London Docks and the berthed *City of Cork*
Contemporary cartoon strip
Ripper suspects: Montague John Druitt, Michael Ostrog and Dr Francis
    Thumblety
Chief Inspector Donal Swanson's pencilled footnote naming the murderer

Introduction

The main problem encountered in any serious study of the White-chapel Murders and the subject of "Jack the Ripper" is the plethora of myth and misrepresentation that surrounds the case. Although some of this obfuscation can be traced back to its contemporary origins, most of it has gradually developed, feeding on itself over the years in books and other media so that any new student of the crimes understandably begins their studies with preconceived ideas, either conscious or subconscious, on the matter.

The huge volume of primary and secondary source material has, over the years, been accessed and plundered by various authors. First came the press reports, then, as they became available, the official records. However, although extensively cited and quoted from, the official papers have never previously been published at length and until now there has been no one book that serves as a source of contemporary evidence, objectively presented in detail and with minimum intrusion from the author. What has been needed is a survey of all the known facts about the murders, free of modern commentary and interpretation, that will provide an essential foundation for further research. This book is a compilation of the major primary sources, indispensable for any writer or research-er tackling this enigmatic series of killings.

Something that struck us in our compilation of the material was that we both experienced a totally new "feel" for the case and the social conditions of the period. We were also aware of just how much potentially significant detail it is possible to overlook. In some instances this reshaped our thinking on and perception of various aspects of the police investigation. Theories about the murders were expounded at the time, but these were ideas shaped by the contemporary context in which they were set. Some of them were very unlikely, others perhaps not so, but they demonstrate the way in which the great mystery took hold of the intellects of the time, and they reveal the very human desire to find the answers to an unsolved series of murders that was, even then, of international interest. The police were under pressure from Home Office officials who were demanding results from a force already stretched to its limits. Lack of modern forensic science aids was obviously also a telling factor and even the medical experts could not agree.

The extant police and Home Office records on the murders, held at the Public Record Office at Kew (South-West London) and other archives, are vast and impossible to quote in full, as are the newspaper reports. Therefore a degree of selectivity has been imposed, but not in such a way as to affect the value of the relevant source material available: all the main official reports are included in full, for example. These are supplemented by newspaper accounts to provide the details in missing inquest reports. The main arrests made at the time are mentioned, as are the contemporary or near-contemporary suspects. It is left to the reader to interpret the facts and the evidence accordingly.

Transcribing all the handwritten documents has taken many years and has been a difficult task. The reports are of varying quality. Some are damaged. Some are virtually illegible. Some of the handwriting has proved difficult to identify. Often the original documents contain faint annotated marginalia, impossible to detect or discern when examining the files in their preserved micro-filmed state. We have, where possible, attempted to include this important detail, by inspecting the original papers ourselves.

This work presents the full factual history of the Whitechapel Murders of 1888–91, chronologically presented and powerfully told by the people who lived in the shadow of "Jack the Ripper". We hope that it will prove a useful and user-friendly companion.

Stewart P. Evans   Keith Skinner
Cambridgeshire   London
June 2000   June 2000

CHAPTER 1

3 April 1888 – Murder of Emma Smith

The crimes of "Jack the Ripper" are so inextricably interwoven with the Whitechapel Murders that often one is mistaken for the other. The reason for this is that the police files on the so-called Whitechapel Murders began with the murder of Emma Smith on 3/4 April 1888, and did not finish until the murder of Frances Coles on 13 February 1891. In all, eleven murders are included in these files and, in the opinion of the authors, as few as three or as many as six may have been the work of a common hand, that of the criminal now known to history as "Jack the Ripper". A full and true picture cannot be obtained without looking at the whole series of murders and the relevant facts that have survived the passage of time to reach us in the twenty-first century. Herein may lie the vital clue as to the identity of the killer – or it may not. If it is not to be found here, then it is very unlikely that we will ever know the identity of this mysterious killer. Here is the raw material available to the historian and interested reader alike. Here are the known facts.

The first file in the police Whitechapel Murders files was that on the murder of Emma Smith, and it is now missing. This file apparently disappeared from the New Scotland Yard files before they were passed to the Public Record Office. It is therefore fortunate that some of the content of this file remains in the form of notes taken from it by Ian Sharp on behalf of the BBC for their television presentation of the "Jack the Ripper" story in 1973. The murder of Emma Elizabeth Smith is thus recognized as the first of the Whitechapel Murders, and she was the victim of a gang of three unknown street robbers. Many press reports later in the year listed "the murder of an unknown woman in Christmas week 1887" as the first of the murders, but extensive research has failed to find this murder. However, a fellow lodger of Smith's, Margaret Hames, was similarly attacked in the same area on 8 December 1887, and was admitted to the Whitechapel infirmary with chest and face injuries.

Records[1] held at the London Metropolitan Archives, reveal that she was not released until two days after Boxing Day 1887.

We begin, therefore, with all that survives from the original police reports on the murder of Emma Smith, first of the Whitechapel Murders.

Emma Elizabeth Smith, 18 George Street, Spitalfields. Son and daughter living in Finsbury Park area. She had lodged at the above address for about eighteen months, paying 4d. per night for her bed. She was in the habit of leaving at about 6 or 7 p.m. and returning at all hours, usually drunk.

On the night of 2nd April, 1888, she was seen talking to a man dressed in dark clothes and white scarf, at 12.15 a.m. [*on the 3rd.*] She returned to her lodgings between 4 and 5 a.m. She had been assaulted and robbed in Osborne Street. London Hospital (near Cocoa factory) Messrs. Taylor Bros. She was attended to by Mr. George Haslip, House Surgeon. She died at 9 a.m. on the 4th. The inquest was held by coroner Wynne Baxter at the Hospital.

The first the police knew of this attack was from the Coroner's Officer who reported in the usual manner on the 6th inst. that the inquest would be held on the 7th inst. Chief Inspector West attended. None of the Pc's in the area had heard or seen anything at all, and the streets were said to be quiet at the time.

The offence had been committed on the pathway opposite No. 10 Brick Lane, about 300 yards from 18 George Street, and half a mile from the London Hospital to which deceased walked. She would have passed a number of Pc's en route but none was informed of the incident or asked to render assistance.

The peritoneum had been penetrated by a blunt instrument thrust up the woman's passage, and peritonitis set in which caused death. She was aged 45 years, 5'2" high, complexion fair, hair light brown, scar on right temple. No description of men.

Edmund Reid
Inspr.

A further report by Chief Inspector West was included:

Her head was bruised, right ear torn, rupture of peritoneum. According to statements made by deceased the motive was robbery. Deceased could not describe the men who had ill-used her but said there were three of them, and that she was attacked about 1.30 a.m. on the 3rd, while passing Whitechapel Church. *Witnesses* Mary Russell, deputy at 18 George Street, Spitalfields; Annie Lee, lodger (these two escorted her to London Hospital); George Haslip and Margaret Hames (lodger at the above address who was last to see her alive.)

Coroner further expressed his intention of forwarding the particulars of the case to the Public Prosecutor as being one requiring further investigation with respect of the person or persons who committed the crime.

Witnesses stated that they didn't think it necessary to report the circumstances to the police. Whole of police on duty deny all knowledge of the occurrence.

Inspector West

Enquiry to be taken up by Inspector Reid.

The newspapers, however, did carry reports of the inquest and the following appeared in the *Morning Advertiser* of Monday, 9 April 1888, page 7:

THE HORRIBLE MURDER IN WHITECHAPEL

Mr. Wynne Baxter held on Saturday morning, at the London Hospital, an inquiry into the circumstances attending the death of an unfortunate, named Emma Eliza Smith, who was assaulted in the most brutal manner early on Tuesday morning in the neighbourhood of Osborn-street, Whitechapel. — Mary Russell, the deputy-keeper of a common lodging-house in George-street, Spitalfields, stated that the deceased, who had lived eighteen months in the house, left home on Monday evening in her usual health and returned between four and five next morning, suffering from horrible injuries. The woman told witness that she had been shockingly ill-treated by some men and robbed of her money. Her face was bleeding and her ear cut. Witness took her at once to the London Hospital, passing through Osborn-street on the way, near a spot close to a cocoa factory, which Smith pointed out as the place where the outrage had been committed. Smith, who seemed unwilling to go into details, did not describe the men nor give any further account of the occurrence to witness. — Dr. G.H. Hillier, the house surgeon in attendance on Tuesday morning, when the deceased was brought in, said the injuries which the woman had received were horrible. A portion of the right ear was torn, and there was a rupture of the peritoneum and other internal organs, caused by some blunt instrument. The account given of the occurrence, by the unfortunate woman to the doctor, was that about half-past one o'clock on Tuesday morning, when near Whitechapel Church, she crossed over the road to avoid some men, who followed, assaulted her, robbed her of all the money she had, and then committed the outrage. There were two or three men, one of them looking like a youth of about nineteen. The patient died on Wednesday, about nine a.m., of peritonitis. – In reply to questions from the coroner and the jury, the doctor said he had no doubt whatever that death had been caused by the wounds. He had found the other organs generally in a normal condition. The deceased stated that she came from the country, but had not seen any of her friends for ten years. – Another woman subsequently examined as a witness deposed to seeing Smith about a quarter-past twelve on Tuesday morning, near the Burdett-road, talking to a man dressed in dark clothes with a white neckerchief round his neck. She (the witness) had been assaulted a few minutes before seeing Smith, and was getting away from the neighbourhood, where there had been some rough work that night. Two fellows had come up to her, one asking the time and the other striking her on the mouth, and both running away. She did not think the man talking to Smith was one of her assailants. – Mr. John West, chief inspector of police of the H division, said he had no official information of the occurrence. He had questioned the constables on duty in the Whitechapel-road at the time, but none of them had either seen or heard any such disturbance as that indicated in the evidence, nor had seen anyone taken to the hospital. He would make inquiries as to Osborn-street in consequence of what had transpired at the inquest. – The Coroner, in summing up, said that from the medical evidence, which must be true, it was perfectly clear that the poor woman had been murdered, but by whom there was no evidence to show. – After a short consultation, a verdict of "Wilful murder" against some person or persons unknown was returned by the jury.

A similar report was carried in *Lloyds Weekly News* of Sunday, 8 April 1888, on the front page, and is worth citing as it adds important pieces of evidence missed from the previous report:

HORRIBLE MURDER IN WHITECHAPEL

Mr. Wynne Baxter held an inquiry yesterday morning at the London Hospital into the terrible circumstances attending the death of an unfortunate, named Emma E. Smith, who was assaulted in the most brutal manner early on Tuesday morning last in the neighbourhood of Osborn-street, Whitechapel, by several men. The first witness, Mary Russell, the deputy-keeper of a lodging-house in George-street, Spitalfields, deposed to the statement made by the deceased on the way to the London Hospital, to which she was taken between four and five o'clock on Tuesday morning. The deceased told her she had been shockingly maltreated by a number of men and robbed of all the money she had. Her face was bleeding, and her ear was cut. She did not describe the men, but said one was a young man of about 19. She also pointed out where the outrage occurred, as they passed the spot, which was near the cocoa factory (Taylor's). The house-surgeon on duty, Dr. Hellier, described the internal injuries which had been caused, and which must have been inflicted by a blunt instrument. It had even penetrated the peritoneum, producing peritonitis, which was undoubtedly the cause of death, in his opinion. The woman appeared to know what she was about, but she had probably had some drink. Her statement to the surgeon as to the circumstances was similar to that already given in evidence. He had made a post-mortem examination, and described the organs as generally normal. He had no doubt that death was caused by the injuries to the perineum, the abdomen, and the peritoneum. Great force must have been used. The injuries had set up peritonitis, which resulted in death on the following day after admission. Another woman gave evidence that she had last seen Emma Smith between 12 and one on Tuesday morning, talking to a man in a black dress, wearing a white neckerchief. It was near Farrant-street, Burdett-road. She was hurrying away from the neighbourhood, as she had herself been struck in the mouth a few minutes before by some young men. She did not believe that the man talking to Smith was one of them. The quarter was a fearfully rough one. Just before Christmas last she had been injured by men under circumstances of a similar nature, and was a fortnight in the infirmary. – Mr. Chief-inspector West, H division, said he had made inquiries of all the constables on duty on the night of the 2nd and 3rd April in the Whitechapel-road, the place indicated. – The jury returned a verdict of "Wilful murder against some person or persons unknown."

CHAPTER 2

7 August 1888 – Murder of Martha Tabram

The second Whitechapel murder recorded in the police files is that of Martha Tabram, also known as Turner, on Tuesday, 7 August 1888. *The Times* of Friday, 10 August 1888, carried the following report:

> Yesterday afternoon Mr. G. Collier, Deputy Coroner for the South-Eastern Division of Middlesex, opened an inquiry at the Working Lads' Institute, Whitechapel-road, respecting the death of the woman who was found on Tuesday last, with 39 stabs on her body, at George-yard-buildings, Whitechapel.
>
> **Detective-Inspector Reid** H Division, watched the case on behalf of the Criminal Investigation Department.
>
> **Alfred George Crow** cabdriver, 35, George-yard-buildings, deposed that he got home at half-past 3 on Tuesday morning. As he was passing the first-floor landing he saw a body lying on the ground. He took no notice as he was accustomed to seeing people lying about there. He did not then know whether the person was alive or dead. He got up at half-past 9, and when he went down the staircase the body was not there. Witness heard no noise while he was in bed.
>
> **John S. Reeves** of 37, George-yard-buildings, a waterside labourer, said that on Tuesday morning he left home at a quarter to 5 to seek for work. When he reached the first-floor landing he found the deceased lying on her back in a pool of blood. He was frightened, and did not examine her, but at once gave information to the police. He did not know the deceased. The deceased's clothes were disarranged, as though she had had a struggle with some one. Witness saw no footmarks on the staircase, nor did he find a knife or other weapon.
>
> **Police-constable Thomas Barrett** 226 H, said that the last witness called his attention to the body of the deceased. He sent for a doctor, who pronounced life extinct.

Dr. T.R. Killeen of 68, Brick-lane, said that he was called to the deceased, and found her dead. She had 39 stabs on the body. She had been dead some three hours. Her age was about 36, and the body was very well nourished. Witness had since made a post-mortem examination of the body. The left lung was penetrated in five places, and the right lung penetrated in two places. The heart, which was rather fatty, was penetrated in one place, and that would be sufficient to cause death. The liver was healthy, but was penetrated in five places, the spleen was penetrated in two places, and the stomach, which was perfectly healthy, was penetrated in six places. The witness did not think all the wounds were inflicted with the same instrument. The wounds generally might have been inflicted by a knife, but such an instrument could not have inflicted one of the wounds, which went through the chest-bone. His opinion was that one of the wounds was inflicted by some kind of dagger, and that all of them were caused during life.

The CORONER said he was in hopes that the body would be identified, but three women had identified it under three different names. He therefore proposed to leave that question open until the next occasion. The case would be left in the hands of Detective-inspector Reid, who would endeavour to discover the perpetrator of this dreadful murder. It was one of the most dreadful murders any one could imagine. The man must have been a perfect savage to inflict such a number of wounds on a defenceless woman in such a way. The inquiry would be adjourned for a fortnight.

The case was then adjourned.

And so the public was first presented with the basic facts of the first of what was to become a recognized series of murders in the Whitechapel district. It is here that the first of the extant police reports takes up the story in a report, dated 10 August 1888, by Inspector E. Ellisdon, H Division, Metropolitan Police[1]:

METROPOLITAN POLICE

H Division

10th August 1888

I beg to report that at 4.50 a.m. 7th inst. John Reeves of 37 George Yard Buildings, George Yard, Whitechapel, was coming down the stairs of above Buildings to go to work, when he saw a woman lying on the first floor landing. he called P.C. 226H Barrett (on the beat)

who found the woman lying in a pool of blood. – there was no
blood on the stairs leading to the landing. P.C. sent for Dr. Killeen,
68 Brick Lane, who attended and pronounced life extinct – there
being 39 punctured wounds on the body; the police ambulance litter
was procured, and the body removed to Whitechapel mortuary to
await an inquest.

Description, age 37, length 5 ft 3, complexion and hair dark:
dress, green skirt, brown petticoat, long black jacket, brown
stockings, side-spring boots, black bonnet – all old.

A description was circulated in 116 Infn. 7.8.88 – and the body
was photographed same date, but up to the present time it has not
been identified.

Two copies of photograph attached.

E. Ellisdon Insp.
T Arnold Supd.

The next relevant report is dated 16 August 1888, and is signed by
Inspector Edmund Reid, H Division, Metropolitan Police[2]:

H Division

To the
ASSISTANT COMMISSIONER
CRIMINAL INVESTIGATION DEPARTMENT.
Executed
SUMMARY OF CONTENTS
Further report re murder of a woman in George Yard Buildings 6.
8. 88.

No. 312
3

3rd Special Report
submitted in accordance with P.O. 9th Febry. 1888. The body has
been identified by Henry Tabram of 6 River Terrace, East Greenwich, as that of his wife, but she left him some years ago, and has
recently been regarded as a prostitute. The witnesses have attended
both the Tower and Wellington Barracks, and two men have been
identified at each place, but all have been able to give a satisfactory
account of themselves on the night of the murder. Enquiries are
being continued.

C.H.Cutbush
Supt.
16.8.88

To/AC (CID) [ACB]³.

METROPOLITAN POLICE
H Division
16th day of August 1888

SUBJECT Murder

6. 8. 88

I beg to report that the body of the woman found murdered in George Yard Buildings on 7th inst has been identified by Henry Samuel Tabram of 6 River Terrace, East Greenwich as that of his wife who left him some years ago. She has also been identified by Mrs. Luckhurst of 4 Star Place, Commercial Road, as her lodger Mrs. Tabram but passing by the name of Turner, taking the name of a man with whom she lived until a month ago. Inquiries have also been made and it is found that the deceased resided at 19 George Street, (a Common Lodging House) and passed there in the name of "Emma", since she left Star Place, and was looked upon as a common prostitute, and a friend of Mary Ann Connelly, alias "Pearly Poll", also a prostitute.

On 9th Connelly came to Commercial Street Station, and stated that she, and the deceased were with two soldiers, one a corporal, and the other a private of the Guards from 10 till 11.45 p.m., on Monday 6th, walking about Whitechapel they then separated, she going with the corporal, and the deceased with the private for immoral purposes. She stated that she should know both men again. I then made an arrangement that the whole of the corporals and privates who were on leave on that night should be again paraded, and she promised to attend at the Tower next morning this she failed to do, search was made for her, but she could not be found that day, nor the next. On Sunday P.S. Caunter C.I.D. made inquiry and found her, and on my seeing her, she promised to attend next morning at the Tower.

This she did, but failed to pick out either of the men, afterwards stating that the men had white bands round their caps.

Pc 226H Barrett, who was on duty in George Yard on the night of the murder stated that about 2 am 7th he spoke to a private of the Guards in George Yard, who informed him that he was waiting for his mate who had gone away with a girl. The P.C. stated that he should know the private again. He attended the parade, and picked a private out wearing medals, and afterwards picked out another, stating he was the man and not the first. They were both questioned and beyond all doubt the first was not the man, and the second gave an account of himself, and his time, which on inquiry was found to be correct.

Corporal Benjiman who was granted leave on 6th, and should have returned to the Tower same night did not return till 11.30 pm, Thursday. On his arrival I took charge of his clothing and bayonet, examined them, but found no marks of blood on them. He stated to me that he had been staying with his father Mr Benjiman who keeps the Canbury Hotel, Kingston on Thames. Inquiry was made at Kingston and it was found that the corporal was there all Monday night and left on Tuesday morning.

The authorities at the Tower rendered the police every assistance in parading the men. On 15th I attended Wellington Barracks with Connelly (Pearly Poll) and P.C. Barrett. The Sergeant Major at once paraded the whole of the men consisting of Corporals and Privates who were on leave on the night of 6th and the woman Connelly at once picked out two privates as the men which were with her, & the deceased on the night in question. One named George, wearing three good conduct badges. She called the Corporal and stated that he was the one that she kept with, and the other named Skipper went away with the deceased. On inquiry it was found that George stayed with a woman (supposed to be his wife) at 120 Hammersmith Road. He arrived there at 8 pm 6th and left at 6 am 7th. With regard to Skipper he was in Barracks at 10.5 pm, 6th, which is shown in the book kept for that purpose.

The authorities at Wellington Barracks rendered the Police every assistance, and promised to render further assistance should it be required.

Inquiries are still being made with a view to gain information respecting the murder.

Edmund Reid
Inspector
T Arnold
Superintendent.

The resumption and close of the inquest was summarized in a further report by Inspector Reid dated 24 August 1888[4], which reads as follows:

H Division

To the   Executive
ASSISTANT COMMISSIONER
CRIMINAL INVESTIGATION DEPARTMENT.
SUMMARY OF CONTENTS.

Report giving result of inquest held on the body of Martha Tabram murdered in George Yard Buildings Whitechapel 7th August 1888.

No. 312
5

5th Special Report submitted in accordance with P.O. 9th February 1888.

The inquest was resumed 23rd. inst. when the evidence was completed, and a verdict of wilful murder against some person or persons unknown returned. Enquiries are being continued.

C.H. Cutbush
Supt.
24.8.88.

To/AC(CID) [ACB].

METROPOLITAN POLICE.
H Division.
24th day of August 1888

SUBJECT Murder
7. 8. 88

I beg to report that Mr. George Collier, deputy Coroner for South East Middlesex resumed the inquiry at the Working Lads' Institute, Whitechapel Road at 2 pm 23rd instant respecting the death of Martha Tabram, alias Turner, alias Emma, who was found dead in George Yard Buildings, Whitechapel at 4.45 am, 7th inst.

Mr. Henry Samuel Tabram, 6 River Terrace, East Greenwich, attended and identified the deceased as his wife who left him about 13 years ago.

Henry Turner, Victoria Working Men's Home, Commercial Street East, proved living with the deceased about 12 years, until about three weeks prior to her death when he left her.

Mary Bousfield of 4 Star Place, Commercial Road East, proved that the deceased and Turner rented a room at her house for about four months and left in debt about 6 weeks ago without giving any notice.

Ann Morris, sister-in-law of the deceased, residing at 23 Lisbon Street, Cambridge Heath Road, proved seeing her outside the

White Swan P.H. Whitechapel Road at 11 pm 6th (Bank Holiday).

Mary Ann Connelly, alias Pearly Poll, stated that she was drinking with the deceased and two soldiers at several public houses in Whitechapel from 10 till 11.45 pm, 6th, when they separated she (Connelly) going up Angel Court with one of the soldiers whom she believed to be a Corporal, and the deceased up George Yard with the other soldier, and she saw nothing more of her until she saw her body in the dead house next day.

The Coroner afterwards addressed the Jury who returned a verdict of "Wilful murder against some person, or persons unknown."

Careful inquiries are still being made with a view to obtain information respecting the case.

Edmund Reid
Inspector
T Arnold Supd.

A further report[5], by Edmund Reid, "L(ocal) Inspector", dated 24 September 1888, furnishes further details of the actions taken by the police in attempting to identify the unknown soldiers who had accompanied Tabram and Connelly on the night of the murder:

METROPOLITAN POLICE
H Division
24th day of September 1888.

SUBJECT Murder in George Yard

Re inspection of Guards at the Tower, and Wellington Barracks. I beg to report that I attended at the Tower on the 7th ultimo with P.C. 226.H. Barrett the officer who was on duty in George Yard on the night of the murder, and who stated that he saw, and spoke to a guardsman at 2 am in George Yard on 7th. I saw the Sergeant Major and explained to him my business, he at once conducted the P.C. to the Guardroom where he was shown several prisoners but the P.C. failed to identify any one of them stating as his reason that they were not dressed. I then arranged to have a parade of all the privates and corporals who were on leave on the night of the 6th, at 11 am 8th. On that date I attended with the P.C. and directed him to be careful as to his actions because many eyes were watching him and a great deal depended on his picking out the right man and no other. The P.C. was kept round by the Sergeants Mess until the men were on parade when I directed him to walk along the rank and touch the man he saw in George Yard, if he was there. I with the Officers then walked away and the P.C. passed along the rank from left to right until he reached about the centre when he stepped up to a private wearing medals and touched him. I went and met the P.C. coming towards me when he told me he had picked out the man. I told him to be certain and have another look when he returned to the rank, passed along and picked out a second man about 6 or 7 away from the first. I asked him how he came to pick out two when he replied, the man I saw in George Yard had no medals and the first man I picked out had. I directed him to stand away.

Mrs. Jane Gillbank and her daughter, residing at 23 Catherine Wheel Alley, Aldgate were brought to the Tower by P.Ss Leach and Caunter C.I.D. they having stated that they saw the deceased with a private of the guards on the Sunday before the murder. (At that time the deceased was believed to be a Mrs Withers who was afterwards found alive.) They were sent one at a time along the rank but failed to pick out anyone.

The two men that the P.C. pointed out were then taken to the orderly room, and the others dismissed. On arriving at the orderly room the P.C. stated that he had made a mistake in pointing out the man with medals who was allowed to leave the room at once without his name being taken, and the other gave the name of John Leary. He was asked by me to account for his time on the night of the 6th. He at once stated that he and private Law went on leave in the evening and went to Brixton they stopped there until the Public Houses closed then he (Leary) went to the rear and when he returned he missed Law he looked about for him and not finding him started off to Battersea, and Chelsea, came along past Charing Cross into the Strand, where he met Law about 4.30 am, they both walked along until they got to Billingsgate where they had a drink and came into barracks at 6. Private Law was then sent for, and on his being questioned as to his movements on the night of the 6th he made a statement which agreed in every particular with that which had been made by Private Leary. They were unable to give me the name of any person to whom I could refer. I felt certain in my own mind that P.C. had made a great mistake and I allowed the men to leave the orderly room.

On 9th I was present at the Tower at 11.30 pm when Corporal Benjiman returned. This man had been absent without leave since the 6th. I at once took charge of his clothing and bayonet, and asked him to account for time. He stated that he had been staying with his father Mr. Benjiman, landlord of the Canbury Hotel, Kingston-on-

Thames, the whole of the time. On inquiry I found this to be true. I examined his clothing and bayonet but could find no marks of blood on them.

I arranged for another parade of Corporals and Privates at 11 am 10th to enable Mary Ann Connelly alias Pearly Poll to pick out the two men who were in the company of the deceased and herself on the night of the 6th.

On 10th Connelly could not be found, the matter was explained to the Sergeant Major who dismissed the men and promised to have another parade when ever I found "Pearly Poll".

On 12th found Pearly Poll and arranged for a parade at 11 am 13th she attended at the Tower and on looking at the men said, "They are not here, they had white bands round their caps."

I thanked the authorities for the assistance rendered to police and they expressed themselves satisfied with the manner in which I had conducted the inquiry, and promised to give any further assistance should it be required.

On 14th, I arranged for a parade of Corporals and Privates at the Wellington Barracks who were on leave on the night of the 6th.

On 15th I attended with Pearly Poll, when she picked out two privates as the men which were with her and the deceased on the night of the murder. One named George wearing three good conduct badges she called the Corporal and stated that he was the one that remained with her, and the other named Skipper went away with the deceased. On this they were both taken into a room & questioned Skipper stated that he was in barracks at 10 pm 6th, this was proved by the books kept in barracks George stated that he was at 120 Hammersmith Road from 8 pm 6th, till 6 am 7th. This on inquiry was found to be correct. He stayed there with his wife beyond doubt. The authorities at Wellington Barracks rendered every assistance for which I thanked them. They also expressed themselves satisfied with the manner in which the identification had been arranged.

Inquiries were made to find some other person who saw the deceased and Pearly Poll with the privates on the night of the 6th but without success, and Pearly Poll and the P.C. having both picked out the wrong men they could not be trusted again as their evidence would be worthless.

> (sgd) Edmund Reid L. Inspector
> Jno West Actg Supt

An overall summary[6] of the enquiries made into the murder of Martha Tabram, by Chief Inspector Donald S. Swanson, dated September 1888, is included:

H Division
Murder of Martha Tabram
on 7th August 1888
in George Yard White-
chapel.
Detail of reports in
tabular form for reference.
Ex papers No. 312

METROPOLITAN POLICE
CRIMINAL INVESTIGATION DEPARTMENT,
SCOTLAND YARD,
day of September 1888.

SUBJECT Murder of
Martha Tabram
at 37 George Yard.
Buildings.

I beg to report that the following are the particulars respecting the murder of Martha Tabram:-

450.am7th.Augt.1888, Body of a woman found on landing of George Yard buildings by John Reeves of No37 tenement, in the building as he was leaving to go to work and he reported the fact to P.C. 226H Barrett.

Dr.Keeling [*sic*] of 68 Brick Lane was called, and examined the body and found thirty nine wounds on body, and neck, and private part with a knife or dagger.

11.$\frac{3}{4}$ pm 6th. Augt. Mrs. Tabram was seen alive by Mary Ann Connolly, alias Pearly Poll, a prostitute, who stated that she and deceased with two soldiers, guards, one of whom was a corporal(?) who was with her, the other a private who was with deceased, had been walking about Whitechapel from 10. to 11$\frac{3}{4}$ pm 6th. At 11.$\frac{3}{4}$ pm deceased and the private went up George Yard together.

2am.7th.Augt. Police Constable 226H. Barrett saw a soldier – a grenadier age 22 to 26. height 5 ft 9 or 10. compl. fair, hair dark small dark brown moustache turned up at ends. with one good conduct badge. no medals. in Wentworth Street; and in reply to the PC he stated he was waiting for a *chum*, who had gone with a girl.

7th. Augt. 1888. Inspector Reid took statements from residents of George Yard Buildings. At 2am 7th. Augt. Mrs Mahoney and her husband passed the spot where body was afterwards found. At 3.30 am Alfred George Crow states he saw something on the landing, but took no notice, and went to bed. Crow is a licensed cab driver. No suspicion is attached to any of residents. The deceased was a stranger to all of them.

It will be observed that from the statement of Mrs Mahoney that the murder took place between 2am and 4.50am 7th. Augt., but as the soldier was last seen with deceased at $11\frac{3}{4}$ pm 6th. two and a quarter hours had elapsed. It is not an uncommon occurrence for tramps and others to sleep on a common stairs in the East End, and I venture to think that the something which the cabman Alfred George Crow saw was the body of Martha Tabram. As close enquiry did not elicit that she had been seen with any one else than a soldier, although from the lapse of time, it is possible she might have been, the following were the steps taken by Police:-

7th Augt. 1888. P.C. 226H Barrett was taken to the Tower where he saw some soldiers in the guardroom, but he did not recognise any.

11am 8th Augt. 1888. The Grenadier Guards who were on leave or absent on night of 6th were paraded and P.C. 226H saw them, when he picked out one with medals, and then another both of whom were taken to the orderly room. where the P.C. admitted his mistake in identity in the first, and his name was not taken. The second man, John Leary gave an account of himself on that night, which private Law, to whom he referred, and who was brought into the orderly room corroborated without communicating with Leary, thus clearing Leary.

11.30pm 9th Augt. 1888. Corpl. Benjamin returned, having been absent without leave since 6th Augt. His clothing and bayonet were examined, but no marks of blood were on them. He accounted for his time as having stayed with his father at the Canbury Hotel Kingston, which was confirmed on enquiry by police.

11 am 10th Augt. Parade of soldiers at the Tower arranged but the woman Connolly could not be found.

11 am 13th Parade of soldiers at the Tower, Connolly saw them and said, "They are not here they had white bands round their caps"

14th. Arranged for parade of Coldstream Guards, who were on leave or absent on 6th, at Wellington Barracks.

5th. Parade of Coldstream Guards as arranged, when Connolly picked out two one as being the Corporal who was with her, the other as being the one who was with deceased. The one she picked out as the Corporal was a private named George, with two good conduct badges, who stated that he was with his wife at 120 Hammersmith Road from 8 pm 6th to 6 am 7thAugt. Enquiry by police proved this to be correct. The other named Skipper stated that he was in barracks on the night of 6th, and the books shewed that he was in barracks from 10.5 pm 6th. They therefore cleared themselves.

The enquiry was continued amongst persons of deceased's class in the East End, but without any success.

Donald S Swanson
Ch Inspr.

This report has an index written by Chief Inspector Donald Swanson, dated 19 October 1888, listing the steps taken by the police regarding the Tabram murder, and the identity parades held with the Grenadier Guards and the Coldstream Guards respectively. A descriptive form relating to Martha Tabram is also included[7], giving the following details:

Age 35 to 40.
Profession or calling prostitute.
Height 5 feet 3 in.
Hair Dark.
Complexion Dark.
Dress Green skirt, brown petticoat, long black jacket, black bonnet, sidespring boots (all old).

These are the official police reports concerning the murder of Martha Tabram. It will be seen that the investigating officer in charge was the local CID Inspector, Edmund Reid of H Division Metropolitan Police, an officer who was to have a long connection with the case.

The result of the inquest can be found in *The Times* of Friday, 24 August 1888, page 4, column 3:

INQUESTS.
Yesterday afternoon Mr. George Collier, the Deputy Coroner for the South-Eastern Division of Middlesex, resumed his inquiry at the

Working Lads' Institute, Whitechapel-road, respecting the death of the woman who was found dead at George-yard-buildings, on the early morning of Tuesday, the 7th inst., with no less than 39 wounds on various parts of her body. The body has been identified as that of MARTHA TABRAN [sic], aged 39 or 40 years, the wife of a foreman packer at a furniture warehouse.

Henry Samuel Tabran [sic], 6, River-terrace, East Greenwich, husband of the deceased woman, said he last saw her alive about 18 months ago, in the Whitechapel-road. They had been separated for 13 years, owing to her drinking habits. She obtained a warrant against him. For some part of the time witness allowed her 12s. a week, but in consequence of her annoyance he stopped this allowance ten years ago, since which time he had made it half-a-crown a week, as he found she was living with a man.

Henry Turner, a carpenter, staying at the Working Men's Home, Commercial-street, Spitalfields, stated that he had been living with the woman Tabran as his wife for about nine years. Two or three weeks previously to this occurrence he ceased to do so. He had left her on two or three occasions in consequence of her drinking habits, but they had come together again. He last saw her alive on Saturday, the 4th inst., in Leadenhall-street. He then gave her 1s. 6d. to get some stock. When she had money she spent it in drink. While living with witness deceased's usual time for coming home was about 11 o'clock. As far as he knew she had no regular companion and he did not know that she walked the streets. As a rule he was, he said, a man of sober habits, and when the deceased was sober they usually got on well together. By Inspector Reid. – At times the deceased had stopped out all night. After those occasions she told him she had been taken in a fit and was removed to the police-station or somewhere else. By the Coroner. – He knew she suffered from fits, but they were brought on by drink.

Mrs. Mary Bousfield, wife of a wood cutter, residing at 4, Star-place, Commercial-road, knew the deceased by the name of Turner. She was formerly a lodger in her house with the man Turner. Deceased would rather have a glass of ale than a cup of tea, but she was not a woman who got continually drunk, and she never brought home any companions with her. She left without giving notice, and owed two weeks' rent.

Mrs. Ann Morris, a widow, of 23, Lisbon-street, E., said she last saw the deceased, who was her sister-in-law, at about 11 o'clock on Bank Holiday night in the Whitechapel-road. She was then about to enter a public house.

Mary Ann Connolly ("Pearly Poll"), who at the suggestion of Inspector Reid was cautioned in the usual manner before being sworn, stated she had been for the last two nights living at a lodging house in Dorset-street, Spitalfields. Witness was a single woman. She had known the woman Tabran for about four or five months. She knew her by the name of Emma. She last saw her alive on Bank Holiday night, when witness was with her about three-quarters of an hour, and they separated at a quarter to 12. Witness was with Tabran and two soldiers – one private and one corporal. She did not know what regiment they belonged to, but they had white bands round their caps. After they separated, Tabran went away with the private, and witness accompanied the corporal up Angel-alley. There was no quarrelling between any of them. Witness had been to the barracks to identify the soldiers, and the two men she picked out were, to the best of her belief, the men she and Tabran were with. The men at the Wellington Barracks were paraded before witness. One of the men picked out by witness turned out not to be a corporal, but he had stripes on his arm. By Inspector Reid. – Witness heard of the murder on the Tuesday. Since the occurrence witness had threatened to drown herself, but she only said it for a lark. She stayed away two days and two nights, and she only said that when asked where she was going. She knew the police were looking after her, but she did not let them know her whereabouts. By a juryman. – The woman Tabran was not drunk. They were, however, drinking at different houses for about an hour and three-quarters. They had ale and rum. Detective-Inspector Reid made a statement of the efforts made by the police to discover the perpetrator of the murder. Several persons had stated that they saw the deceased woman on the previous Sunday with a corporal, but when all the corporals and privates at the Tower and Wellington Barracks were paraded before them they failed to identify the man. The military authorities afforded every facility to the police. "Pearly Poll" picked out two men belonging to the Coldstream Guards at the Wellington Barracks. One of those men had three good conduct stripes, and he was proved beyond doubt to have been with his wife from 8 o'clock on the Monday night until 6 o'clock the following morning. The other man was also proved to have been in barracks at five minutes past 10 on Bank Holiday night. The police would be pleased if anyone would give them information of having seen anyone with the deceased on the night of the Bank Holiday. The Coroner having summed up, the jury returned the verdict to the effect that the deceased had been murdered by some person or persons unknown.

CHAPTER 3

31 August 1888 – Murder of Mary Ann Nichols

The murder of Mary Ann Nichols occurred in the early hours of Friday, 31 August 1888. Whether or not either of the two previous murders had been committed by the same hand, which is unlikely, both police and press linked the killing with the previous two, and the idea that a maniac was abroad, killing prostitutes, was born. The police enquiries also revealed the suspect called "Leather Apron", who was quickly made prominent by the sensational press. The reports concerning this murder are enclosed in a file cover[1], as follows:

J Division

To the
ASSISTANT COMMISSIONER
CRIMINAL INVESTIGATION DEPARTMENT.
SUMMARY OF CONTENTS.
Special weekly report re murder of Mary Ann Nichols. at Bucks Row.
31. 8. 88

7.9.88

No. 327

3

3rd. Special Report submitted in accordance with P.O. 9th Febry. 1888. The deceased has been identified as Mary Ann Nichols .a prostitute. who separated from her husband about nine years ago. and has been since 1882 at different periods an inmate of Edmonton, The City of London, Holborn, and Lambeth workhouses. No information to point to the offender can be obtained. A man named "Pizer alias Leather Apron" has been in the habit of ill-using prostitutes in various parts of the Metropolis for some time past, and careful inquiries have been made to trace him, but without success. There is no evidence against him at present. Enquiries are being continued.

W. Davis
Act.Supt.
7.9.88
To/ACC(CID)/ACB   [ ]

A report dated 31 August 1888, by Inspector John Spratling, is the first official summary[2] of the murder of Mary Ann Nichols in Buck's Row, Whitechapel (parentheses indicate portions of document missing).

The cover [f 241] reads:

C.O. Reference Divisional Reference
Submitted through Executive
J. Division.
Subject Report Re murder of a woman unknown at Bucks Row, Whitechapel 31st inst.

31.1.88.

No. 327

1st Special Report submitted in accordance with P.O. 9th Febry. 1888.
To/A.C.Constbl
To Col P[ ] for information [*missing*]

METROPOLITAN POLICE
J Division.
31st August 1888

P.C. 97J, Neil, reports at 3.45. on 31st inst. he found the dead body of a woman lying on her back with her clothes a little above her knees, with her throat cut from ear to ear on a yard crossing at Bucks Row, Whitechapel. P.C. Neil obtained the assistance of P.C.s 55.H. Smizen [*sic*] and 96J. Thain, the latter called Dr. Llewellyn, No. 152, Whitechapel Road, he arrived quickly and pronounced life to be extinct, apparently but a few minutes, he directed her removed to the mortuary, stating he would make a further examination there, which was done on the ambulance.

Upon my arrival there and taking a description I found that she had been disembowelled, and at once sent to inform the Dr. of it, l[*atter?*] arrived quickly and on further examination stated that her throat had been cut from left to right, two disti[*nct*] cuts being on left side. The windp[*ipe*] gullet and spinal cord being cut through, a bruise apparently of a th[umb] being on right lower jaw, also one o[n] left cheek, the abdomen had been [cut] open from centre of bottom of ribs a[long] right side, under pelvis to left of the stomach, there the wound was jag[ged], the omentium [sic], or coating of the stomach, was also cut in several places, and tw[o] small stabs on private parts, apparently done with a strong bladed knife, supposed to have been done by some le[ft] handed person, death being almost instantaneous.

Description, age about 45, length 5 ft. 2. or 3. compx. dark, hair dark brown (turning grey), eyes brown, bruise on lower right jaw and left cheek, slight laceration of tongue, one tooth deficient front of upper jaw, two on left of lo[wer] do; dress, brown ulster, 7 large brass bu[ttons], (figure of a female riding a horse and [a] man at side thereon), brown linsey fr[ock] grey woollen petticoat, flannel do, white chest flannel, brown stays, white ch[emise], black ribbed woollen stockings, man[s] S.S. boots, cut on uppers, tips on heels, black straw bonnet, trimmed black ve[lvet].

I made enquiries and was informed by Mrs. Emma Green, a widow, New Cottage adjoining, and Mr. Walter Purkis, Essex Wharf, oppisite [sic], also of William Cour[t] Night Watchman to Messrs. Brown & Eagle, Bucks Row, and P.C. 81.G.E.R. Police on [duty] at Wharf near, none of whom heard any scream during the night, or anything to lead them to believe that the murder had been committed there.

The Stations and premises of the East London and District Railways, al[l] the wharves and enclosures in the vicinity have been searched but no trace of any weapon could be found there.

P.C. states he passed through Bucks Row at 3.15 am. and P.S.10.Kirby about the same time, but the woman was not there then and is not known to them.

[sgd] J. Spratling Inspr.
J.Keating Supt.

It has since been ascertained that the dress bears the marks of Lambeth Workhouse and deceased is supposed to have been an inmate of that house. J.Keating Supt.

A further report[3], dated 7 September 1888, by Inspector Joseph Henry Helson, Local Inspector, CID, J (Bethnal Green) Division, casts more light on the murder:

METROPOLITAN POLICE
J Division.
7th day of September 1888

SUBJECT Murder of
M.A. Nichols
at Whitechapel
REFERENCE TO PAPERS
Special report 31.8.88
and 52983

With reference to the subject in the margin, I beg to report that the marks on the clothing led to the identification of the deceased as a woman who had been an inmate of Lambeth Workhouse on several occasions, and that her name was Mary Ann Nichols, it was afterwards ascertained that her husband, William Nichols, was at present residing at 37 Coburg Row, Old Kent Road, and employed as a machine printer, by Messrs. Purkiss Bacon & Co., Whitefriars St. E.C.

They separated about 9 years since in consequence of her drunken habits. For some time he allowed her 5/- per week, but in 1882, it having come to his knowledge that she was living the life of a prostitute he discontinued the allowance. In consequence of this she became chargeable to the Guardians of the Parish of Lambeth by whom the husband was Summoned to show cause why he should not be ordered to contribute towards her support, and on these facts being proved, the summons was dismissed. They had not spoken to each other since, and the husband has not heard anything of her since. There are no grounds for suspecting him to be the guilty party. Since 1882 she has at different periods been an inmate of Edmonton, The City of London, Holborn and Lambeth Workhouses. She left the latter Institution on the 12th May last to take a situation at Ingleside, Rose Hill Road, Wandsworth, and absconded from there on the 12th of July stealing clothing to the value of £3.10.0. A few days after this she obtained lodgings at 18 Thrawl St. Spitalfields, a common-lodging-house and remained there and at a similar house at 55 Flower and Dean St. close by, until the day before she was found dead. A further examination of the body and clothing, and the result of the Post Mortem Examination, leaves no doubt but that the murder was committed where the body was found, careful search was continued with a view to find any weapon that was used by the murder[er] or murderers (in all probability there was only one) but nothing has been found. Enquiries have also been made from the persons who reside in the locality, watchmen who were employed in adjoining premises, P.C.s on the adjoining beats and in every quarter from which it was thought any useful information might be obtained, but at present not an atom of evidence can be obtained to connect any person with the crime. She was seen walking the Whitechapel Road about 11.p.m. 30th, at 12.30 am 31st she was seen to leave the Frying-pan Public House, Brick Lane, Spitalfields, at 1.20.a.m. 31st she was at the common-lodging, 18 Thrawl St. and at 2.30.a.m. at the corner of Osborne St. and Whitechapel Road, on each occasion she was alone. At 3.45.a.m. or an hour and a quarter later, she is found dead, and no person can be found at present who saw her after 2.30.a.m.

The inquiry has revealed the fact that a man named Jack Pizer, alias Leather Apron, has, for some considerable period been in the habit of ill-using prostitutes in this, and other parts of the Metropolis, and careful search has been, and is continued to be made to find this man in order that his movements may be accounted for on the night in question, although at present there is no evidence whatsoever against him.

The enquiry is being carefully continued, by Inspector Abberline, from C.O. and myself and every effort used to obtain information that may lead to arrest of the murderer.

J.H.Helson Inspr.

J.Keating Supt.

As early as the end of August a letter was received at the Home Office, from the public sector, to do with concern about the murders. It was thought that the offer of a reward might lead to the detection of the criminal(s).

The file cover[4] concerning this matter is dated 31 August 1888:

[Stamped: – HOME OFFICE 1 SEP.88 DEpt. No.] No. A49301B/ 1
31 Aug. 1888.   Messrs. L.P.Walter & Son.
REFERENCES, &c.   Forward newspaper extract respecting the recent murders in Whitechapel: & recommends that a reward be offered for the detection of the murderer.

not Pressing
MINUTES.

?Ack: and say that [the practice of offering Rewards for the discovery of criminals has for some time been discontinued; and that so far as the circumstances of the present case have at present been investigated   do not disclose any special ground for depart[*ure*] from the usual custom.

W.P.B.

1.9.88   EWP. 3Sept 88
                                        Wrote Messrs Walter & Son
                                         4 September 1888.

The letter[5] sent by Messrs. Walter & Son, dated 31 August 1888, is enclosed:

                                                        A49301B

[Headed paper]
TELEGRAPHIC ADDRESS, "WINTERINE", LONDON, TELE-PHONE No.536.
L.&P.WALTER & SON [Stamped:- HOME OFFICE 1 SEP.88 DEPt. No.]

Manufacturers of   11,12,&13,Church Street
CLOTHING FOR   Spitalfields
    EXPORTATION   LONDON 31/Aug
1888

The Secty of State for
        the HomeDpt

Sir/

   We beg to enclose your report of this fearful murder & to say that such is the state of affairs in this district that we are put to the necessity of having a night watchman to protect our premises. the only way in our humble opinion to tackle this matter is to offer at once a reward.

                                    Yours Very obediently,
                                    L&PWalter&Son.

This letter is followed by a cutting[6] from the newspaper:

                                THE [*missing*]
                                            [August 31, 1888.]
                            HORRIBLE MURDER IN
                                WHITECHAPEL.

The Central News, says;:- Scarcely has the horror and sensation caused by the discovery of the murdered woman in Whitechapel some short time ago had time to abate, than another discovery is made, which; for the brutality exercised on the victim, is even more shocking, and will no doubt create as great a sensation in the vicinity as its predecessor. The affair, up to the present, is enveloped in complete mystery, and the police have as yet no evidence to trace the perpetrators of the horrible deed. The facts are that as Constable John Neil was walking down Bucks-row, Thomas-street, Whitechapel, about a quarter to four o'clock this morning, he discovered a woman, between thirty-five and forty years of age, lying at the side of the street with her throat cut right open from ear to ear, the instrument with which the deed was done tracing the throat from left to right. The wound was about two inches wide, and blood was flowing profusely, in fact, she was discovered to be lying in a pool of blood. She was immediately conveyed to the Whitechapel Mortuary, where it was found that, besides the wound in the throat, the lower part of her person was completely ripped open. The wound extends nearly to her breast, and must have been effected with a large knife. As the corpse of the woman lies in the mortuary it presents a ghastly sight. The victim measures 5ft. 2in. in height. The hands are bruised, and bear evidence of having engaged in a severe struggle. There is the impression of a ring having been worn on one of Deceased's fingers, but there is nothing to show that it had been wrenched from her in a struggle. Some of the front teeth have also been knocked out, and the face is bruised on both cheeks and very much discoloured. Deceased wore a rough brown ulster, with large buttons in front. Her clothes are torn, and cut up in several places, leaving evidence of the ferocity with which the murder was committed. The only way by which the police can prosecute an enquiry at present is by finding someone who can identify the Deceased, and then, if possible, trace those in whose company she was when last seen. In Bucks-row naturally the greatest excitement prevails, and several persons in the neighbourhood state that an affray occurred shortly after midnight, but no screams were heard, nor anything beyond what might have been considered evidence of an ordinary brawl. The woman has not yet been identified. She was wearing workhouse clothes, and it is supposed she came from Lambeth. A night watchman was in the street where the crime was committed. He heard no scream and saw no signs of the scuffle. The body was quite warm when brought to the mortuary at half-past four this morning.

LATEST PARTICULARS.

Immediately on the affair being reported at the Bethnal-green Police-station two inspectors proceeded to the mortuary and examined the clothes, in the hope of being able to discover something likely to lead to her identification. In this they were not successful, as the only articles found on the body were a broken comb and a piece of looking-glass. The wounds, of which there are five, could only have been committed by a dagger or a long sharp knife. The officers engaged in the case are pushing their inquiries in the neighbourhood as to the doings of certain gangs known to frequent these parts, and an opinion is gaining ground amongst them that the murderers are the same who committed the two previous murders near the same spot. It is believed that these gangs, who make their appearance during the early hours of the morning, are in the habit of blackmailing these poor creatures, and where their demands are refused, violence follows. Up till noon Mr. Wynne E. Baxter, the Coroner for the district, had not received any official intimation of the occurrence, but the inquest will most likely be held on Monday morning.

The letter of reply[7] to Messrs. Walter & Son, dated 4 September 1888, from the Home Office is as follows:

A49301   Whitehall
                                        4th September 18[*88*]

Gentlemen,
    In reply to your letter of the 31st ultimo, expressing the opinion that a reward should be offered for the detection of the Whitechapel murderer, I am directed by the Secretary of State to inform you that the practice of offering rewards for the discovery of criminals has for some time been discontinued and that so far as the circumstances of the present case have at present been investigated, they do not in his opinion disclose any special ground for departure from the usual custom.

                              I am,
                                    Gentlemen,
                              Your odedient Servant,
Messrs. Walter & Son   (sd) E.Leigh Pemberton
11. 12 & 13 Church Street
Spitalfields.

A detailed summary report[8], dated 19 October 1888, relating to the murder of Nichols submitted by Chief Inspector Donald S. Swanson, Criminal Investigation Department, Scotland Yard, reads:

METROPOLITAN POLICE.
CRIMINAL INVESTIGATION DEPARTMENT,
SCOTLAND YARD.
19th day of October 1888

SUBJECT Bucks Row

Murder of Mary Ann Nichols

I beg to report that the following are the particulars relating to the murder of Mary Ann Nichols in possession of police.

3.45 a.m. 31st. Augst. The body of a woman was found lying on the footway in Bucks Row, Whitechapel, by Charles Cross & Robert Paul carmen, on their way to work. They informed P.C. 55H Divn. Mizen in Bakers Row, but before his arrival P.C. 97J Neil on whose beat it was had discovered it. Dr. Llewellyn of 152 Whitechapel Road was sent for, he pronounced life extinct and he describes the wounds as, – throat cut nearly severing head from body, abdomen cut open from centre of bottom of ribs along right side, under pelvis to left of stomach, there the wound was jagged: the coating of the stomach was cut in several places and two small stabs on private parts, which in his opinion may have been done with a strong bladed knife. At first the doctor was of opinion that the wounds were caused by a left handed person but he is now doubtful. 31st Aug. 88 The body was identified by Ellen Holland of 18 Thrawl Street, E. as that of Mary Ann Nichols of the same address, – a common lodging house, – subsequently by the husband, Wm. Nichols of 37 Coburg Road, Old Kent Rd. printers' machinist.

There was no money in pocket of deceased & there was nothing left behind by the murderer.

The results of Police enquiries are as follows:- 2.30 a.m. 31st. Aug. 88 Mrs. Nichols was last seen alive at 2.30 am 31st Aug 1888 in a state of drunkenness at the corner of Osborn Street and Whitechapel Road, by Ellen Holland mentioned above. She was then alone & going in the direction of Bucks Row by Whitechapel Road. An hour and a quarter afterwards the body was found at Bucks Row.

Enquiry was then made at common lodging houses, & the statements of persons taken, but no person was able to say that they had seen her alive more recently than Ellen Holland. The police were unable to learn from any source that any person was seen with her, or with a person supposed to be her after that hour. Coffee stall keepers, prostitutes, the night watchman in Winthorp [*sic*] Street, – a street parallel to Bucks Row, – as well as the inhabitants of Bucks Row, were questioned, but they were unable to help the police in the slightest degree. They had not seen the woman, nor had they heard any screams or noise. Enquiry at the common lodging house where Mrs Nichols lived shewed that when she left there at 1.40 <u>am it was for the purpose of getting sufficient money to pay for her bed, – 4d</u> – that she had then no money and she told Ellen Holland at 2.30 a.m. that then she had no money to pay for her bed. Robbery could not therefore be the motive for the murder. Enquiry was made into her history which turns out to be as follows: the deceased through her intemperate habits separated from her husband about 9 years ago and he allowed her 5/- per week till 1882 when it came to his knowledge that she was leading an immoral life and he stopped the allowance. She became chargeable to the Parish of Lambeth and the husband was summoned to shew cause why he should not contribute towards her support, but the summons was dismissed. Since that time the husband has not heard anything of her, and enquiry revealed that she had been leading an irregular life sleeping at common lodging houses and Workhouses for a considerable time previous to her death. The enquiry into her history did not disclose the slightest pretext for a motive on the part of her friends or associates in the common lodging houses.

The absence of the motives which lead to violence and of any scrap of evidence either direct or circumstantial, left the police without the slightest shadow of a trace consequently enquiries were made into the history and accounts given of themselves of persons, respecting whose character & surroundings suspicion was cast in statements made to police.

Amongst such are the three <u>slaughtermen, named Tomkins, Britton and Mumford</u> employed by night at Messrs. Harrison Barber & Coy. premises Winthorp Street. Their statements were taken separately, and without any means of communicating with each other, and they satisfactorily accounted for their time, being corroborated in some portions by the Police on night duty near the premises. Another man named <u>John Piser, better known as "Leather apron"</u> became suspected on account of his alleged levying blackmail on prostitutes and assaulting them if they did not comply with his request, as detailed to police by women in the common lodging houses. On 10th Sept. he was found & his statement taken to the effect that on 31st Augst. he had slept at a common lodging ho: at Holloway Road which was fully corroborated and the date fixed by the proprietor who knows Piser. On 8th Sept. he stayed at 22 Mulberry St. in this he was corroborated by several persons, for the police ascertained that in consequence of suspicions published about him by the press he was in reality afraid to come out.

The case of Annie Chapman took place on 8th Sept. and both enquiries merged into one. The particulars of further enquiries will be found in report of the murder of Annie Chapman.

(sd) Donald S. Swanson
Ch: Inspector

A police descriptive form relating to Mary Ann Nichols is also included, giving her details as follows:

Age	*45*
Profession or calling	*Prostitute*
Hair	*Dark (turning grey)*
Eyes	*Brown*
Face	*Discolouration of face*
Complexion	*Dark*
Marks or peculiarities	*On person a piece of looking glass, a comb, and white handkerchief*
Dress	*Brown ulster, seven large buttons, horse & man standing by side thereon, linsey frock, brown stays, blue ribbed woollen stockings, straw bonnet.*

Note. She was the wife of Wm. Nichols of 37 Coburg Rd. Old Kent Rd. printers machinist.

These reports are the first official papers on the murder of Mary Ann Nichols, further information being contained in some later documents and the contemporary newspaper articles, which also include lengthy reports of the inquest and evidence of the witnesses.

There is an index[9] to the papers on the Nichols murder in the Home Office files:

– Copy –   A49301C/8a
[Stamped:- HOME OFFICE 25 OCT.88 RECd. DEPt.]

Bucks Row   *No. 2*

– Murder of Mary Ann Nichols –

Subject	Page	Remarks
Hour & date of murder	1	
Wounds on body	1&2	Described by Dr. Llwellyn
Body identified	2	as Mary Ann Nichols, a prostitute
History of deceased	4	
Enquiries by police		
at Common Lod: Hos:	3	
" Coffee stall keepers	3	
" Prostitutes	3	
" Night Watchman	3	in Winthorp [sic] St. nearly
" Slaughtermen	5	parallel to Bucks Row employed
" John Piser	6	by Messrs. Harrison & Barber.
alias		
"Leather Apron"		

As the official inquest papers on Mary Ann Nichols have not been found it is necessary to read the contemporary newspaper reports that are included in the Home Office official papers held at the Public Record Office. In the case of Nichols they are extracted from *The Times*, the first[10] being 3 September 1888, page 12:

THE WHITECHAPEL MURDER.

Up to a late hour last evening the police had obtained no clue to the perpetrator of the latest of the three murders which have so recently taken place in Whitechapel, and there is, it must be acknowledged, after their exhaustive investigation of the facts, no ground for blaming the officers in charge should they fail in unravelling the mystery surrounding the crime. The murder, in the early hours of Friday morning last, of the woman now known as Mary Ann Nicholls [*sic*], has so many points of similarity with the murder of two other women in the same neighbourhood – one Martha Turner, as recently as August 7, and the other less than 12 months previously – that the police admit their belief that the three crimes are the work of one individual. All three women were of the class called "unfortunates," each so very poor, that robbery could have formed no motive for the crime, and each was murdered in such a similar fashion, that doubt as to the crime being the work of one and the same villain almost vanishes, particularly when it is remembered that all three murders were committed within a distance of 300 yards from each other. These facts have led the police to almost abandon the idea of a gang being abroad to wreak vengeance on women of this class for not supplying them with money. Detective-Inspectors Abberline, of the Criminal Investigation Department, and Detective-Inspector Helson, J Division, are both of opinion that only one person, and that a man, had a hand in the latest murder. It is understood that the investigation into the George-yard mystery is proceeding hand-in-hand with that of Buck's-row. It is considered unlikely that the woman could have entered a house, been murdered, and removed to Buck's-row within a period of one hour and a quarter. The woman who last saw her alive, and whose name is Nelly Holland, was a fellow-lodger with the deceased in Thrawl-street, and is positive as to the time being 2.30. Police-constable Neil, 97J, who found the body, reports the time as 3.45. Buck's-row is a secluded place, from having tenements on one side only. The constable has been severely questioned as to his "working" of his "beat" on that night, and states that he was last on the spot where he found the body not more than half an hour previously – that is to say, at 3.15. The beat is a very short one, and quickly walked over would not occupy more than 12 minutes. He neither heard a cry nor saw any one. Moreover, there are three watchmen on duty at night close to the spot, and neither one heard a cry to cause alarm. It is not true, says Constable Neil, who is a man of nearly 20 years' service, that he was called to the body by two men. He came upon it as he walked, and flashing his lantern to examine it, he was answered by the lights from two other constables at either end of the street. These officers had seen no man leaving the spot to attract attention, and the mystery is most complete. The utmost efforts are being used, a number of plain-clothes men being out making inquiries in the neighbourhood, and Sergeants Enright and Godley have interviewed many persons who might, it was thought, assist in giving a clue.

On Saturday afternoon Mr. Wynne E. Baxter, coroner for the South-Eastern Division of Middlesex, opened his enquiry at the Working Lads' Institute, Whitechapel-road, respecting the death of MARY ANN NICHOLS, whose dead body was found on the pavement in Buck's-row, Whitechapel on Friday morning.

Detective-Inspectors Abberline and Helston [*sic*] and Sergeants Enright and Godley watched the case on behalf of the Criminal Investigation Department.

The jury having been sworn and having viewed the body of the dead woman, which was lying in a shell in the Whitechapel Mortuary.

Edward Walker, of 16, Maidswood-road, Camberwell, deposed that he was now of no occupation, but had formerly been a
smith. He had seen the body in the mortuary, and to the best of his
belief it was that of his daughter, whom he had not seen for two
years. He recognized the body by its general appearance and by
some of the front teeth being missing. Deceased also had a scar on
the forehead which was caused by a fall when she was young. There
was a scar on the body of the woman then lying in the mortuary. His
daughter's name was Mary Ann Nichols, and she had been married
quite 22 years. Her husband's name was William Nichols, a
printer's machinist, and he was still alive. They had been living
apart for seven or eight years. Deceased was about 42 years of age.
The last time witness heard of the deceased was about Easter, when
she wrote him a letter. He produced the letter, which was in the
handwriting of the deceased. It spoke of a situation she was in, and
which, she said, she liked very much. He answered that letter, but
had not since heard from the deceased. The last time he saw
deceased was in June, 1886, when she was respectably dressed.
That was at the funeral of his son, who was burnt to death through
the explosion of a paraffin lamp. Some three or four years previous
to that the deceased had lived with witness; but he was unable to say
what she had since been doing. Deceased was not a particularly
sober woman, and that was the reason why they could not agree.
He did not think she was "fast" with men, and she was not in the
habit of staying out late at night while she was living with him. He
had no idea what deceased had been doing since she left him. He did
not turn the deceased out of doors. They simply had a few words,
and the following morning she left home. The reason deceased
parted from her husband was that he went and lived with the
woman who nursed his wife during her confinement. Witness knew
nothing of his daughter's acquaintances, or what she had been doing
for a living. Deceased was not 5ft. 4in. in height. She had five
children, the eldest of whom was 21 years of age and the youngest
eight or nine. She left her husband when the youngest child was only
one or two years of age. The eldest was now lodging with witness.
He was unable to say if deceased had recently been living with any
one; but some three or four years ago he heard she was living with a
man named Drew, who was a house smith by trade and had a shop
of his own in York-street, Walworth. Witness believed he was still
living there. The husband of the deceased had been summoned for
the keep of the children, but the charge was dismissed owing to the

fact that she was then living with another man. Deceased was in the Lambeth Workhouse in April last, when she left to go to a situation. Her husband was still living at Coburg-road, Old Kent-road, but witness was not aware if he was acquainted with his wife's death. Witness did not think the deceased had any enemies, as she was too good for that.

Police-constable John Neil 97J, deposed that on Friday morning he was passing down Buck's-row, Whitechapel, and going in the direction of Brady-street, and he did not notice any one about. He had been round the same place some half an hour previous to that and did not see any one. He was walking along the right-hand side of the street when he noticed a figure lying in the street. It was dark at the time, although a street lamp was shining at the end of the row. He walked across and found the deceased lying outside a gateway, her head towards the east. He noticed that the gateway, which was about 9ft. or 10ft. in height and led to some stables, was closed. Houses ran eastward from the gateway, while the Board school was westward of the spot. On the other side of the road was the Essex Wharf. The deceased was lying lengthways, and her left hand touched the gate. With the aid of his lamp he examined the body and saw blood oozing from a wound in the throat. Deceased was lying upon her back with her clothes disarranged. Witness felt her arm, which was quite warm from the joints upwards, while her eyes were wide open. Her bonnet was off her head and was lying by her right side, close by the left hand. Witness then heard a constable passing Brady-street, and he called to him. Witness said to him, "Run at once for Dr. Llewellyn." Seeing another constable in Baker's-row, witness despatched him for the ambulance. Dr. Llewellyn arrived in a very short time. In the meantime witness had rung the bell of Essex Wharf and inquired if any disturbance had been heard. He was told "No." Sergeant Kerby then came, and he knocked. The doctor, having looked at the woman, said:- "Move the woman to the mortuary; she is dead. I will make a further examination of her." They then placed deceased on the ambulance and removed her to the mortuary. Inspector Spratley [sic] came to the mortuary, and while taking a description of deceased lifted up her clothes and discovered she was disembowelled. That had not been noticed before. On the deceased was found a piece of comb and a bit of looking-glass, but no money was found. In the pocket an unmarked white pocket handkerchief was found. There was a pool of blood where the neck of deceased was lying in Buck's row. He had not heard any disturbance that night. The farthest he had been that night was up Baker's-row to the Whitechapel-road, and was never far away from the spot. The Whitechapel-road was a busy thoroughfare in the early morning, and he saw a number of women in that road, apparently on their way home. At that time any one could have got away. Witness examined the ground while the doctor was being sent for. (Inspector Spratley [*sic*] observed that he examined the road after it was daylight.) In answer to a juryman, the witness said he did not see any trap in the road. He examined the road, but could not see any marks of wheels. The first persons who arrived on the spot after he discovered the body were two men who worked at a slaughterhouse opposite [*sic*]. They stated that they knew nothing of the affair, nor had they heard any screams. Witness had previously seen the men at work. That would be a quarter past 3, or half an hour before he found the body.

Mr. Henry Llewellyn, surgeon, of 152, Whitechapel-road, stated that at 4 o'clock on Friday morning he was called by the last witness to Buck's-row. The officer told him what he was wanted for. On reaching Buck's-row he found deceased lying flat on her back on the pathway, her legs being extended. Deceased was quite dead, and she had severe injuries to her throat. Her hands and wrists were cold, but the lower extremities were quite warm. Witness examined her chest and felt the heart. It was dark at the time. He should say the deceased had not been dead more than half an hour. He was certain the injuries to the neck were not self-inflicted. There was very little blood round the neck, and there were no marks of any struggle or of blood, as though the body had been dragged. Witness gave the police directions to take the body to the mortuary, where he would make another examination. About an hour afterwards he was sent for by the inspector to see the other injuries he had discovered on the body. Witness went, and saw that the abdomen was cut very extensively. That morning he had made a post-mortem examination of the body. It was that of a female of about 40 or 45 years. Five of the teeth were missing, and there was a slight laceration of the tongue. There was a bruise running along the lower part of the jaw on the right side of the face. That might have been caused by a blow from a fist or pressure from a thumb. There was a circular bruise on the left side of the face, which also might have been inflicted by the pressure of the fingers. On the left side of the neck, about 1in. below the jaw, there was an incision about 4in.

in length, and ran from a point immediately below the ear. On the same side, but an inch below, and commencing about 1in. in front of it, was a circular incision, which terminated at a point about 3in. below the right jaw. That incision completely severed all the tissues down to the vertebrae. The large vessels of the neck on both sides were severed. The incision was about 8in. in length. the cuts must have been caused by a long-bladed knife, moderately sharp, and used with great violence. No blood was found on the breast, either of the body or clothes. There were no injuries about the body until just about the lower part of the abdomen. Two or three inches from the left side was a wound running in a jagged manner. The wound was a very deep one, and the tissues were cut through. There were several incisions running across the abdomen. There were also three or four similar cuts, running downwards, on the right side, all of which had been caused by a knife which had been used violently and downwards. The injuries were from left to right, and might have been done by a left-handed person. All the injuries had been caused by the same instrument.

At this stage Mr. Wynne Baxter adjourned the inquiry until this morning.

The next report[11], respecting the adjourned inquest, appeared in *The Times* of 4 September 1888, page 8:

THE WHITECHAPEL MURDER

Yesterday morning Mr. Wynne E. Baxter, the Coroner for the South-Eastern Division of Middlesex, resumed his inquiry at the Working Lads' Institute, High-street, Whitechapel, respecting the death of MARY ANN NICHOLS, whose dead body was found on the pavement in Buck's-row, Whitechapel, on Friday morning.

Detective-inspector Abberline (Scotland-yard), Inspector Helston [*sic*], and Detective-sergeants P. Enright and Godley watched the case on behalf of the Criminal Investigation Department.

Inspector J. Spratling J Division, was the first witness called. He deposed that at 4.30 on Friday morning he was called to the spot where the body of the deceased was found lying. On getting there he found two constables, one of whom pointed out the exact spot on which he found the body. At that time the blood was being washed away, but he could see some stains in between the stones. He was told that the body had been removed to the mortuary. On going there he found the body was still on the ambulance in the yard.

While waiting for the arrival of the keeper of the dead-house he took a description of the deceased, but at that time did not notice any wounds on the body. On the body being put in the mortuary he made a more careful examination, and then discovered the injuries to the abdomen, and at once sent for Dr. Llewellyn. He saw two workhouse men stripping the body.

At this point, in reply to a question, Detective-sergeant P. Enright said he gave instructions that the body should not be touched.

Witness, continuing his evidence, stated he again went to the mortuary and made an examination of the clothing taken off the deceased. The principal parts of the clothing consisted of a reddish ulster, somewhat the worse for wear, a new brown linsey dress, two flannel petticoats, having the marks of the Lambeth Workhouse on them, and a pair of stays. The things were fastened, but witness did not remove them himself, so could not say positively that all the clothing was properly fastened.

The CORONER observed it was such matters as these that threw a most important bearing on the subject. The question of the clothing was a most important one. Later on he directed Constable Thain, 96J, to examine all the premises in the vicinity of the spot where the body was discovered.

Inspector Spratling continuing, said he and Sergeant Godley examined the East London and District Railway embankments and lines, and also the Great Eastern Railway yard, but they were unable to find anything likely to throw any light on the affair. One of Mr. Brown's men wiped up the blood. A constable was on duty at the gate of the Great Eastern Railway yard, which was about 50 yards from the spot where the body was found. He had questioned this constable, but he had not heard anything. Mrs. Green, who also lived opposite the spot, had been seen, and during the night she had not heard anything, although she was up until 4.30 that morning. Mr. Purkis, who also lived close by, stated his wife had been pacing the room that morning, about the time the murder must have been committed, but she had not heard anything. It was 150 yards from the spot where the body was found to Barber's slaughter-yard. That was by walking round the Board school. During the night Constable Neil and another officer were within hearing distance of the spot. He should think deceased had been murdered while wearing her clothes, and did not think she had been dressed after death.

Henry Tomkins, a horse-slaughterer, living at 12, Coventry-street, Bethnal-green, stated he was in the employ of Mr. Barber. Thursday night and Friday morning he spent in the slaughterhouse in Winthrop-street. Witness commenced about his usual time – between 8 and 9 o'clock p.m. On Friday morning he left off work at 20 minutes past 4 and went for a walk. It was their rule to go home when they did so, but they did not do so that morning. A constable told them of the finding of the murdered woman, and they went to look at her. James Mumford, Charles Brittan, and witness worked together. At 12 o'clock witness and Brittan left the slaughterhouse, and returned about 1 o'clock. They did not again leave the slaughterhouse until they heard of the murder. All the gates were open, and witness during the night did not hear any disturbance; the only person who came to the slaughterhouse was the constable. At times women came to the place, but none came that night. Had any one called out "Murder" in Buck's-row he might not have heard it. There were men and women in the Whitechapel-road. Witness and Mumford went and saw the deceased, and then Brittan followed. At that time a doctor and three or four constables were there, and witness remained there until the body was taken away. At night he and his mates generally went out to have a drink. It depended upon what time their work was done when they went home. The constable was at the slaughterhouse at about a quarter past 4, when he called for his cape. It was then that they heard of the murder.

Inspector Helston [*sic*], J Division, deposed that it was a quarter to 7 on Friday morning when he received information of the murder. Having learnt full particulars, he proceeded to the mortuary, where he saw deceased, who had her clothing on. He saw the things removed. The bodice of the dress was buttoned down to the middle and the stays were fastened. There were no bruises on the arms to indicate that a struggle had taken place. The wounds on the abdomen were visible with the stays on, and that proved they could have been inflicted while the stays were on the deceased. he did not examine the spot where the body was found until after the blood had been washed away. Witness was of opinion that the murder was committed at the spot where the body was found. The clothes were very little disarranged, thus showing that the body could not have been carried far.

Constable G. Mizen, 56 H, stated that at a quarter past 4 on Friday morning he was in Hanbury-street, Baker's-row, and a man passing said "You are wanted in Baker's-row." The man, named

Cross, stated a woman had been found there. In going to the spot he saw Constable Neil, and by the direction of the latter he went for the ambulance. When Cross spoke to witness he was accompanied by another man, and both of them afterwards went down Hanbury-street. Cross simply said he was wanted by a policeman, and did not say anything about a murder having been committed. He denied that before he went to Buck's-row he continued knocking people up.

George [*sic*] **Cross**, a carman, stated that he left home on Friday morning at 20 minutes past 3, and he arrived at his work, at Broad-street, at 4 o'clock. Witness walked along Buck's-row, and saw something lying in front of the gateway like a tarpaulin. He then saw it was a woman. A man came along and witness spoke to him. They went and looked at the body. Witness, having felt one of the deceased woman's hands and finding it cold, said "I believe she is dead." The other man, having put his hand over her heart, said "I think she is breathing." He wanted witness to assist in shifting her, but he would not do so. He did not notice any blood, as it was very dark. They went to Baker's-row, saw the last witness, and told him there was a woman lying down in Buck's-row on the broad of her back. Witness also said he believed she was dead or drunk, while the other man stated he believed her to be dead. The constable replied "All right." The other man left witness at the corner of Hanbury-street and turned into Corbett's-court. He appeared to be a carman, and was a stranger to witness. At the time he did not think the woman had been murdered. Witness did not hear any sounds of a vehicle, and believed that had any one left the body after he got into Buck's-row he must have heard him.

William Nichols, a machinist, of Coburg-road, Old Kent-road, stated that the deceased woman was his wife. He had been separated from her for upwards of eight years. The last time he saw her was over three years ago, and he had no idea what she had been doing since that time, nor with whom she had lived. Deceased was much given to drink. They separated several times, and each time he took her back she got drunk, and that was why he had to leave her altogether.

Jane Oram, 18, Thrawl-street, Spitalfields, deposed that deceased had slept at the common lodging-house there for about six weeks. Witness and deceased had occupied the same bed. For eight or ten days she had not been to the lodging-house, but witness saw her on the morning of her death in the Whitechapel-road. Deceased told her she was living where men and women were allowed to sleep, but added that she should come back and live with witness. Witness believed deceased stated she had been living in Flowery Dean-street [*sic*]. Deceased was the worse for drink and refused to stay with witness, although she did all she could to persuade her to do so. Witness did not think she was a fast woman. She was a clean woman, but witness had previously seen her the worse for drink.

Mary Ann Monk stated that she was an inmate of the Lambeth Workhouse. She knew the deceased, who had been an inmate of the union, but that was six or seven years ago.

The CORONER here informed the jury that the police did not propose to offer any further evidence that day, and it would be as well to adjourn the inquiry sufficiently long to give them an opportunity of obtaining further evidence.

The inquiry was accordingly adjourned for a fortnight.

The next extract is from *The Times* dated 18 September 1888, page 12, and relates to the resumed inquest[12] into the murder of Mary Ann Nichols:

THE WHITECHAPEL MURDER.

Yesterday Mr. Wynne E. Baxter, Coroner for the South-Eastern Division of Middlesex, resumed his adjourned inquiry at the Working Lads' Institute, Buck's-row, Whitechapel, respecting the death of Mary Ann Nichols, who was found brutally murdered in Buck's-row, Whitechapel, on the morning of Friday, the 31st ult.

Detective-inspectors Abberline (Scotland-yard) and Helson, and Inspectors Spratling and Chandler watched the case on behalf of the Criminal Investigation Department and Commissioners of Police.

Mr. Llewellyn, surgeon, recalled, said that since the last inquiry he had been to the mortuary and again examined the deceased. She had an old scar on the forehead. No part of the viscera was missing. He had nothing to add to his previous evidence.

Mrs. Emma Green, living at New-cottage, Buck's-row, stated she was a widow, and occupied the cottage next to where the deceased was found. Her daughter and two sons lived with her. Witness went to bed about 11 o'clock on the night of Thursday, August 30, and one of her sons went to bed at 9 o'clock, and the other one at a quarter to 10. Her daughter went to bed when she did, and they occupied the same room. It was a front room on the first floor. Witness did not remember waking up until she heard a knock at the front door about 4 o'clock in the morning. She opened the window and saw three or four constables and two or three other men. She saw the body of deceased lying on the ground, but it was still too dark to clearly distinguish what had happened. Witness heard nothing unusual during the night, and neither her sons or daughter awoke.

By the Jury. – She was a light sleeper, and had a scream been given she would have heard it, though people often went through Buck's-row, and there was often a great noise in it. She did not believe there was any disorderly house in Buck's-row. She knew of no disorderly house in the immediate neighbourhood.

By the CORONER – She saw her son go out, directly the body was removed, with a pail of water to wash the stains of blood away. A constable was with him.

Thomas Ede, a signalman in the employ of the East London Railway Company, said he saw a man on the line on the morning of the 8th.

The CORONER observed that had no reference to this inquiry. The 8th was the morning of the other murder. It was decided to take the witness's evidence.

Witness, continuing, said on Saturday morning, the 8th inst., he was coming down the Cambridge-heath-road, and when just opposite the Foresters' Arms saw a man on the opposite side of the street. His peculiar appearance made witness look at him. He appeared to have a wooden arm, as it was hanging at his side. Witness watched him until he got level with the Foresters' Arms. He then put his hand down, and witness saw about 4in. of the blade of a long knife sticking out of his trousers pocket. Three other men were also looking at him and witness spoke to them. Witness followed him, and as soon as he saw he was followed he quickened his pace. Witness lost sight of him under some railway arches. He was about 5ft. 8in. high, about 35 years of age, with dark moustache and whiskers. He wore a double peak cap, dark brown jacket, and a pair of overalls over a pair of dark trousers. He walked as though he had a stiff knee, and he had a fearful look about the eyes.

By the CORONER. – Witness should say the man was a mechanic. The overalls were perfectly clean. He could not see what kind of a knife it was. He was not a muscular man.

Inspector Helson said they had been unable to trace the man.

Walter Purkiss stated he lived at Essex Wharf, Buck's-row, and was a manager there. His house was in Buck's-row and fronted the street. It was nearly opposite to where the deceased was found. His wife, children, and servant occupied the house with him. Witness and his wife slept in the front portion of the house – the room on the second floor. On the night of the occurrence he went to bed at 11 o'clock or a quarter past 11. Witness awoke at various times during the night and was awake between 1 and 2 o'clock. He did not hear anything until he was called up by the police about 4 o'clock. His wife was awake the greater portion of the night. Neither of them heard a sound during the night, and it was unusually quiet. When the police called him he opened the landing window. He could see the deceased, and there were two or three men there, besides three or four constables. Had there been any quarrelling in the row during the night witness would certainly have heard it.

Patrick Mulshaw, a night porter in the employ of the Whitechapel District Board of Works, living at 3 Rupert-street, Whitechapel, said on the night of this occurrence he was at the back of the Working Lads' Institute in Winthorpe-street [*sic*]. He went on duty about a quarter to 5 in the afternoon, and remained until about five minutes to 6 the next morning, when he was relieved. He was watching some sewage works. He dozed at times during the night, but was not asleep between 3 and 4 o'clock. He did not see any one about during that period, and did not hear any cries for assistance, or any other noise. The slaughterhouse was about 70 yards away from where he was. Another man then passed by, and said, "Watchman, old man, I believe somebody is murdered down the street." Witness then went to Buck's-row, and saw the body of deceased lying on the ground. Three or four policemen and five or six working men were there.

By the CORONER. – If any one had called out for assistance from the spot where the body was he might have heard it. Nothing suspicious occurred during the time he was watching, and he saw no person running away. There was no one about after 11 and 12 o'clock, and the inhabitants of the street appeared to be very orderly persons. He did not often see the police there. During the night he saw two constables, including Constable Neil. He was unable to say what time he saw that officer.

Constable John Phail [*sic* – Thain], 96J, said he was not brought any closer to Buck's-row in his beat than Brady-street, but he passed the end of it. He passed the end of Buck's-row every 30 minutes. Nothing attracted his attention until about 3.45 a.m., when he was signalled by a brother constable flashing his lamp some way down Buck's-row. Witness went to him, and found Constable Neil standing by the body of the deceased. Neil was by himself. Witness ran for the doctor, and having called Dr. Llewellyn, accompanied him to the spot where deceased was lying. On his return with the doctor, Neil and two workmen were standing by the body. He did not know the workmen. The body was then taken to the mortuary by Sergeant Kerby, Constable Neil, and an officer of the H Division. Witness, acting under orders, waited at the spot for Inspector Spratling. He was present when the spots of blood were washed away. On the spot where the deceased had been lying was a mass of congealed blood. He should say it was about 6in. in diameter, and had run towards the gutter. It appeared to him to be a large quantity of blood.

By the CORONER. – He helped to put the body on the ambulance, and the back appeared to be covered with blood, which, he thought, had run from the neck as far as the waist. He got blood on to his hands. There was also blood on the ground where the deceased's legs had been. Witness afterwards searched Essex Wharf, the Great Eastern Railway, the East London Railway, and the District Railway, as far as Thomas-street, but could find no knife, marks of blood, or anything suspicious. He did not make inquiries at the houses in Buck's-row.

By the Jury. – He did not pass the end of Buck's-row exactly at the end of each half-hour. It was a quarter-past 3 when he was round there before. He did not take his cape to the slaughterhouse, but sent it by a brother constable. When he was sent for the doctor he did not first go to the horse-slaughterers and say that as a murder had been committed he had better fetch his cape. He was not supposed to leave his beat. Shortly before he was called by Constable Neil he saw one or two men going to work in the direction of Whitechapel-road. When he was signalled by Neil he was coming up Brady-street, from the direction of Whitechapel-road.

Robert Baul [*sic* – Paul], a carman of 30, Foster-street, Whitechapel, stated he went to work at Cobbett's-court, Spital-fields. He left home about a quarter to 4 on the Friday morning, and as he was passing up Buck's-row he saw a man standing in the middle of the road. As witness approached him he walked towards the pavement, and witness stepped on to the roadway in order to pass him. He then touched witness on the shoulder, and said,

"Come and look at this woman here." Witness went with him, and saw a woman lying right across the gateway. Her clothes were raised almost up to her stomach. Witness felt her hands and face, and they were cold. He knelt down to see if he could hear her breathe, but could not, and he thought she was dead. It was very dark, and he did not notice any blood. They agreed that the best thing they could do would be to tell the first policeman they met. He could not see whether the clothes were torn, and did not feel any other part of her body except the hands and face. They looked to see if there was a constable, but one was not to be seen. While he was pulling the clothes down he touched the breast, and then fancied he felt a slight movement.

By the CORONER. – The morning was rather a chilly one. Witness and the other man walked on together until they met a policeman at the corner of Old Montagu-street, and told him what they had seen. Up to that time not more than four minutes had elapsed from the time he saw the body. He had not met any one before he reached Buck's-row, and did not see any one running away.

Robert Mann, a pauper inmate of the Whitechapel Workhouse, stated he had charge of the mortuary. On the morning in question the police came to the workhouse and told him there was a body at the mortuary. Witness went there about 5 o'clock, and remained there until the body was placed inside the mortuary. He then locked the mortuary door, and went to breakfast. After breakfast witness and Hatfield, another inmate of the workhouse, undressed the body. No police or any one else was present when that was done. Inspector Helson was not there.

By the CORONER. – He had not been told that he must not touch the body. He could not remember Inspector Helson being present, as he was confused. He was sure the clothing was not torn or cut; but could not describe where the blood was. To get off the clothes Hatfield had to cut them down the front.

By the Jury. – The body was undressed in the morning, and was not taken out after it was brought in.

The CORONER said the witness was subject to fits, and his statements were hardly reliable.

James Hatfield said he assisted the last witness in undressing the deceased. Inspector Helson was not there. They first took off the ulster, and put it on the ground. Witness then took the jacket off and put it in the same place. He did not have to cut the dress to get it off, but cut the bands of the two petticoats, and then tore them down with his hands. Deceased was wearing a chemise, and he tore it right down the front. She was not wearing any stays. No one gave them any instructions to strip the body. They did it so as to have the body ready for the doctor. He had heard something about a doctor coming; and he was not aware that any one was present while they were stripping the deceased. Afterwards the police came, and examined the clothing. They found the words "Lambeth Work-house" on the band of one of the petticoats. Witness cut that portion out by direction of Inspector Helson. That was the first time he had seen Inspector Helson that morning. It was about 6.30 when witness first arrived at the mortuary. Although he had said deceased wore no stays he would not be surprised to find she had stays on.

The Foreman. – Why, you tried the stays on the body of the deceased in my presence at the mortuary, and you said they were short.

Witness admitted his memory was bad.

In answer to the CORONER, Inspector Abberline said they were unable to find the man who passed down Buck's-row while the doctor was examining the body.

Inspector Spratling, J Division, said he had made inquiries at several of the houses in Buck's-row, but not at all of them.

The CORONER. – Then that will have to be done.

Witness further said he had made inquiries at Mrs. Green's, the wharf, at Sneider's Factory, and also at the Great Eastern Wharf, but no one at those places had heard anything unusual during the morning in question. He had seen the Board school keeper, but he had not heard anything. Had the other inhabitants heard a disturbance of any kind they would, no doubt, have communicated with the police. There was a gateman at the Great Eastern Railway, but he was stationed inside the gates, and had not heard anything. There was a watchman employed at Sneider's factory. He distinctly told the mortuary-keeper not to touch the body.

Inspector Helson said he knew of no other evidence.

In answer to a juryman, the officer said the murderer would have no occasion to get on to the Great Eastern Railway, as he could pass along the street.

The Foreman thought that if a substantial reward had been offered by the Home Secretary in the case of the murder in George-yard, these two horrible murders would not have happened. Mr. Matthews thought that rewards got into wrong hands, but if they did, what did it matter so long as the perpetrator was brought to justice?

The CORONER understood there was a regulation that no reward should be offered in the case of the murder of either a rich or a poor person.

The Foreman believed a substantial one would have been offered had a rich person been murdered. He would be glad to give £5 himself for the capture of the murderer.

The inquiry was then adjourned until Saturday.

The report[13] on the adjourned inquest appeared in *The Times* of Monday, 24 September 1888, page 3:

THE WHITECHAPEL MURDERS.

On Saturday, Mr. Wynne E. Baxter, coroner for the South-Eastern Division of Middlesex, resumed his adjourned inquiry at the Working Lads' Institute, Whitechapel-road, respecting the death of Mary Ann Nichols, who was found brutally murdered in Buck's-row, Whitechapel.

William Eade, recalled, stated he had since seen the man whom he saw with the knife near the Foresters'-hall. He had ascertained that his name was Henry James, and that he did not possess a wooden arm.

The CORONER said the man James had been seen, and been proved to be a well-known harmless lunatic. As there was no further evidence forthcoming he would proceed to sum up. Before commencing the few remarks that he proposed to make to the jury, he should, he was sure, be only reflecting their feelings if he first returned his thanks to the committee of the Working Lads' Institute for the use of such a convenient room for the purposes of this inquest. Without their assistance, they would have been compelled to conduct this inquiry in a public house parlour – inconvenient and out of harmony with their functions, for Whitechapel not only did not possess any coroner's court, such as have been erected in St. Luke's, Clerkenwell, the City, and most of the West-end parishes, but it was without any town-hall or vestry-hall, such as were used for inquests at St. George's, Shadwell, Limehouse, and Poplar. To the Working Lads' Institute committee, therefore, he felt they were under obligations deserving of public recognition. The jury would probably have been surprised to find there was no public mortuary in Whitechapel. He had been informed that there was formerly one, but that it was demolished by the Metropolitan Board of Works when making a new street, and that compensation was paid to the local authorities, who have never yet expended it on the object of the trust. Perhaps he had been misinformed, but this he did know, that jury after jury had requested the coroner to draw the attention of the sanitary authorities to the deficiency, and, hitherto, without success. They deemed it essential for the health of the neighbourhood; and surely if mortuaries were found necessary at the West-end, there must be stronger reasons for them here, in the midst of so much squalid crowding. But this inconvenience had been felt in other ways in this inquiry. In the absence of a public mortuary, the police carried the body to the deadhouse belonging to the workhouse infirmary. It was admittedly not ornate in appearance, and was not altogether suited for the purpose to which it had been applied; but they must not forget that such mortuary was a private structure, intended solely for use by the Union authorities, and that its use on other occasions had been allowed only by the courtesy of the guardians, but that only proved the necessity for a public mortuary. Had there been a public mortuary there would also have been a keeper, whose experience would have shown the advisability of the body being attended to only in the presence of the medical witness. He himself trusted now that the attention of the authorities had again been called to this pressing matter, the subject would be taken into serious consideration, and the deficiency supplied. Referring to the facts in the case before him, the Coroner said the deceased had been identified by her father and her husband to have been Mary Ann Nichols, a married woman with five children, and about 42 years of age. She was of intemperate habits, and left her husband eight years ago on account of drink. The husband had not seen her or heard of her for three years. She had evidently formed irregular connexions, but still lived under her father's roof for three or four years, and then either to avoid the restraints of a settled home, or in consequence of her own misconduct, she left her father, who had not seen her for more than two years. She was in the Lambeth Workhouse on several occasions, at Christmas last and again in April. While there last she was fortunate enough to find a lady in Wandsworth willing to take her into her house as a domestic servant, and at the time she wrote her father a letter, which held out some promise of reform; but her fresh start did not appear to have lasted long, for she soon afterwards left her situation in great disgrace. From that time until her death it was pretty clear that she had been living an intemperate, irregular, and vicious life, mostly in the common lodging-houses in that neighbourhood. There was nothing in the evidence as to the movements of the deceased on the day before her death, except a statement by herself that she was living in a common lodginghouse, called the White House, in Flower and Dean-street, Spitalfields; but he believed her movements had been traced by the police, and were not considered to have any connexion with her death. On Friday evening, the 31st of August, she was seen by Mrs. Holland – who knew her well – at the corner of Osborn-street and Whitechapel-road, nearly opposite the parish church. The deceased woman was then much the worse for drink and was staggering against the wall. Her friend endeavoured to persuade her to come home with her, but she declined, and was last seen endeavouring to walk eastward down Whitechapel. She said she had her lodging money three times that day, but that she had spent it, that she was going about to get some money to pay her lodgings, and she would soon be back. In less than an hour and a quarter after this she was found dead at a spot rather under three-quarters or a mile distant. The deceased was first discovered by a carman on his way to work, who passed down Buck's-row, on the opposite side of the road. Immediately after he had ascertained that the dark object in the gateway was the figure of a woman he heard the approaching footsteps of a man. This proved to be Paul, another carman. Together they went to the woman. The condition of her clothing suggested to them that she had been outraged and had fainted. She was only just dead, if life were really extinct. Paul says he felt a slight movement of her breast, and thought she was breathing. Neither of the carmen appeared to have realized the condition of the woman, and no injuries were noticed by them; but that, no doubt, was accounted for by the early hour of the morning and the darkness of the spot. The carmen reported the circumstances to a constable at the corner of Hanbury-street, 300 yards distant, but although he appeared to have started without delay, he found another constable was already there. In fact, Constable Neil must independently have found the body within a few minutes of the finding of it by the two carmen. The condition in which the body was found appeared to prove conclusively that the deceased was killed on the exact spot in which she was found. There was not a trace of blood anywhere, except at the spot where her neck was lying. That appeared to him sufficient to justify the assumption that the injuries to the throat were inflicted when the woman was on the ground, while the state of her clothing and the absence of any blood about her legs equally proved that the abdominal injuries were inflicted while she was still in the same position. Nor did there appear any grounds for doubt that, if deceased was killed where she was found, she met her death without a cry of any kind. The spot was almost under the windows of Mrs. Green, a light sleeper. It was opposite the bedroom of Mrs. Purkiss, who was awake at the time. Then there were watchmen at various spots within very short distances. Not a sound was heard by any. Nor was there evidence of any struggle. This might have arisen from her intoxication, or from being stunned by a blow. Again, the deceased could not have been killed long before she was found. Constable Neil was positive that he was at the spot half an hour before, and then neither the body was there nor was any one about. Even if Paul were mistaken in the movement of the chest, Neil found her right arm still warm, and even Dr. Llewellyn, who saw the body about a quarter of an hour afterwards, found the body and lower extremities still warm, notwithstanding the loss of blood and abdominal injuries and that those extremities had been uncovered. It seemed astonishing, at first thought, that the culprit should escape detection, for there must surely have been marks of blood about his person. If, however, blood was principally on his hands, the presence of so many slaughter-houses in the neighbourhood would make the frequenters of that spot familiar with blood-stained clothes and hands, and his appearance might in that way have failed to attract attention while he passed from Buck's-row in the twilight into Whitechapel-road and was lost sight of in the morning's market traffic. He himself thought they could not altogether leave un-noticed the fact that the death the jury had been investigating was one of four presenting many points of similarity, all of which had occurred within the space of about five months, and all within a very short distance of the place where they were sitting. All four victims were women of middle age; all were married and had lived apart from their husbands in consequence of intemperate habits, and were at the time of their death leading irregular lives and eking out a miserable and precarious existence in common lodging-houses. In each case there were abdominal as well as other injuries. In each case the injuries were inflicted after midnight, and in places of public resort where it would appear impossible but that almost immediate detection would follow the crime, and in each case the inhuman and dastardly criminals were at large in society. Emma Elizabeth Smith, who received her injuries in Osborn-street on the early morning of Easter Tuesday, the 3d of April, survived in the London Hospital for upwards of 24 hours, and was able to state that she had been followed by some men, robbed and mutilated, and even to describe imperfectly one of them. Martha Tabram was found at 3 a.m. on Tuesday, the 7th of August, on the first-floor landing of George-yard-buildings, with 39 punctured wounds on her body. In addition to these, and the case under the consideration of the jury there was the case of Annie Chapman, still in the hands of another jury. The instruments used in the two earlier cases were dissimilar. In the first it was a blunt instrument, such as a walking-stick; in the second some of the wounds were thought to have been made by a dagger, but in the two recent cases the instruments suggested by the medical witnesses were not so different. Dr. Llewellyn said that the injuries on Nichols could have been produced by a long-bladed instrument moderately sharp. Dr. Phillips was of opinion that those on Chapman were by a very sharp knife, probably with a thin, narrow blade, at least 6 in. to 8 in. in length, probably longer. The similarity of the injuries in the two cases was considerable. There were bruises about the face in both cases, the head was nearly severed from the body in both cases, and those injuries again, had in each case been performed with anatomical knowledge. Dr. Llewellyn seemed to incline to the opinion that the abdominal injuries were inflicted first, and caused instantaneous death; but, if so, it seemed difficult to understand the object of such desperate injuries to the throat, or how it came about there was so little bleeding from the several arteries that the clothing on the upper surface was not stained and the legs not soiled, and there was very much less bleeding from the abdomen than from the neck. Surely it might well be that, as in the case of Chapman, the dreadful wounds to the throat were first inflicted and the abdominal afterwards. That was a matter of some importance when they came to consider what possible motive there could be for all this ferocity. Robbery was out of the question, and there was nothing to suggest jealousy. There could not have been any quarrel, or it would have been heard. The taking of some of the abdominal viscera from the body of Chapman suggested that that may have been the object of her death. Was it not possible that this may also have been the motive in the case they had under consideration? He suggested to the jury as a possibility that these two women might have been murdered by the same man with the same object, and that in the case of Nichols the wretch was disturbed before he had accomplished his object, and, having failed in the open street, he tried again, within a week of his failure, in a more secluded place. If this was correct, the audacity and daring was equal to its maniacal fanaticism and abhorrent wickedness. But that surmise might or might not be correct; the suggested motive might be the wrong one; but one thing was very clear – that the injuries were of such a nature that they could not have been self-inflicted, that no imaginable facts could reduce that to evidence of manslaughter, and that a murder of a most atrocious character had been committed.

The jury, having considered in private, returned a verdict of "Wilful murder against some person or persons unknown." They also thanked the Coroner for the remarks made with reference to the mortuary and for the very able way in which he had conducted the case.

CHAPTER 4

8 September 1888 – Murder of Annie Chapman

The murder of Annie Chapman on the morning of Saturday, 8 September 1888 occurred on the day after the funeral of Mary Ann Nichols. The interval of only just over a week between the two murders obviously caused a sensation: the fears intimated in the press reports of the Nichols murder of a maniacal lone killer at work in the East End streets were apparently confirmed when the details of this horrific new murder became known. Further areas of factual dispute also arose from this killing, notably concerning the items "arranged" on the ground near Chapman's body, items that included, according to legend, two farthings and two rings. The true facts in this regard are shown in the following reports. The first probable sighting of the killer, by the witness Mrs Long, also occurred in this case. The details preserved in the police reports on the Chapman murder are as follows.

The detective and first police officer on the scene of the Chapman murder was Inspector Joseph Chandler of H Division, stationed at Commercial Street. His report[1] on the finding of the body, dated 8 September 1888, follows beginning with the file cover[2].

C.O. REFERENCE. DIVISIONAL REFERENCE.
H302
Submitted through Ex: Bch:
H Division.
Subject Murder of Annie Siffey at 29 Hanbury Street Spitalfields.
<u>No. 334</u>
.1
1st Special Report + submitted in accordance with P.O. 9th Febry. 1888.

WDavis
Actg.Supt
<u>8.9.88</u>

To/AC(CID).

Mr. Williamson.

  (vide Actg Supts' report)

I understand Insp. Abberline is taking up this as well as the other murder com

ACB.
8.9.88.

  Inspr. Abberline is assisting H in making enquiry into this murder. He was instructed to do so this morning

AFW 8/9/88

Seen ACB

Commercial Street   30o/1
METROPOLITAN POLICE.
H Division.
8th September 1888

I beg to report that at 6.10 a.m. 8th inst. while on duty in Commercial Street, Spitalfields, I received information that a woman had been murdered. I at once proceeded to No. 29 Hanbury Street, and in the back yard found a woman lying on her back, dead, left arm resting on left breast, legs drawn up, abducted small intestines and flap of the abdomen lying on right side, above right shoulder attached by a cord with the rest of the intestines inside the body; two flaps of skin from the lower part of the abdomen lying in a large quantity of blood above the left shoulder; throat cut deeply from left and back in a jagged manner right around throat. I at once sent for Dr. Phillips Div. Surgeon and to the Station for the ambulance and assistance. The Doctor pronounced life extinct and stated the woman had been dead at least two hours. The body was then removed on the Police ambulance to the Whitechapel mortuary.

On examining the yard I found on the back wall of the house (at the head of the body) and about 18 inches from the ground about 6 patches of blood varying in size from a sixpenny piece to a point, and on the wooden pailing [sic] on left of the body near the head patches and smears of blood about 14 inches from the ground.

The woman has been identified by Timothy Donovan "Deputy" Crossinghams Lodging house 35 Dorset Street, Spitalfields, who states he has known her about 16 months, as a prostitute and for past 4 months she had lodged at above house and at 1.45 a.m. 8th inst she was in the kitchen, the worse for liquor and eating potatoes, he Donovan sent to her for the money for her bed, which she said she had not got and asked him to trust her which he declined to do she then left stating that she would not be long gone; he saw no man in her company.

Description, Annie Siffey age 45, length 5 ft, complexion fair, hair (wavy) dark brown, eyes blue, two teeth deficient in lower jaw, large thick nose; dress black figured jacket, brown bodice, black skirt, lace boots, all old and dirty.

A description of the woman has been circulated by wire to All Stations and a special enquiry called for at Lodging Houses &c to ascertain if any men of a suspicious character or having blood on their clothing entered after 2 am 8th inst.

JL.Chandler Inspr.

Respectfully submitted

Every possible enquiry is being made with a view of tracing the murderer, but up to the present without success. Local Inspector Reid being on his annual leave, the enquiries have been entrusted to Inspector Chandler, and P.Ss Thick & Leach C.I.Dept. I would respectfully suggest that Inspector Abberline, Central, who is well acquainted with H.Division be deputed to take up this enquiry as I believe he is already engaged in the case of the Bucks Row murder which would appear to have been committed by the same person as the one in Hanbury Street.

Jno.West ActgSupt.

It was at this time that enquiries into various suspects brought to police attention began. One of the earliest was Joseph (or Jacob) Isenschmid, aged approximately 38 years, a butcher of 59 Elthorne Road, Holloway. His appearance is first noted in a Metropolitan Police report[3] from Y Division, Holloway, dated 11 September 1888 by Detective Inspector John Styles, commencing with the file cover:

C.O. REFERENCE. DIVISIONAL REFERENCE.
                    Y 5574
Submitted through H Division
                    Y Division
Subject Drs Cowan & Crabb
                    Holloway
This information respects a Joseph Isenschmid a butcher and a lunatic whom they suspect as being connected with the Whitechapel murders.

12.9.88.

To Insp Abberline
          JhnWest
12.9.88.   ActgSupt
Rec'd by me at 4 pm 12.9.88 at Inquest Sergt. Thick directed to take up the inquiry at once

                                        FGAbberline Inspr.
Seen. ACB 20.9

METROPOLITAN POLICE.
Y Division.

                              Holloway 11th Sept. 1888
I beg to report that at 10 pm 11th inst Dr Cowan 10 Landseer Road and Dr Crabb of Holloway Road, came to Station and stated that Joseph Isenschmid, a butcher and a lunatic, a lodger at No. 60 Milford Road, and he having left his lodgings on several occasions at various times, it was thought that he might be connected with the recent murders at Whitechapel. In company of Sub Inspr Rose and Sergt Sealey C.I.D. I went to the above address and saw George Tyler occupier who stated that at 11 pm 5th inst he met Isenschmid in Hornsey Road who asked him if he would accommodate him with a lodging, he took him home and he left the house at 1.am 6th returned at 9 pm 6th left again at 1 am 7th returned at 9 pm, left again at 1.am 8th inst returned at 9 pm, left again at 6 am 9th inst returned at 6 pm stayed in house about 30 minutes he then left to go to Tottenham returned at 1 am 10th left again at 2 am returned at 9 pm and left again at 1.am. 11th and has not yet returned. I then proceeded to No. 97 Duncombe Road and saw Mrs. Isenschmid his wife who stated that she had not seen her husband during past two months but he visited the above premises during her absence on 9th inst and took away some clothing she further stated that he was in the habit of carrying large butcher's knives about with him and did not know how he obtained his livelihood. His movements being suspicious I directed P.C. 376. Cracknell to keep observation on the house and to bring Isenschmid to station should he return for enquiries. I also directed observation to be kept on 97 Duncombe Road, Upper Holloway. I respectfully suggest that further enquiries be made by C.I. Department.

    No description of man could be obtained sufficient to circulate at present.

                                        Jno Styles DInspr
Submitted through ActSupt "H" a telegram has been forwarded
12/9/88   J.McFadden
                                          ActSupt

The detention of Isenschmid is recorded in an H Division report[4], dated 13 September 1888, by Acting Superintendent John West, commencing with the file cover:

$$\frac{52983}{2}$$

METROPOLITAN POLICE.

H Division.

13th September 1888

Correspondence
No 52983
Murder in Hanbury
St. Spitalfields

With reference to the attached I beg to report that no new facts have been brought to the notice of Police. Excepting that a man has been detained at Holloway Station on suspicion, since removed to the Infirmary Fairfield Road, Bow, having been certified as a dangerous lunatic.

Sergeant Thick has examined the man's clothing, but failed to find any trace of blood upon any of it. Enquiries are being made as to the man's whereabouts on the night in question

This man's name is Joseph Isenschmid, is a butcher by trade but failed in business about 12 months since. His arrest was brought about through information received from Drs Cowan. & Crabb, of Holloway their attention having been called to him by a man named Tyler of 60 Milford Road Holloway who stated that Isenschmid, who was his lodger, had frequently been absent from home at early morning.

The adjourned Inquest on the body of murdered woman was held 12th inst. and further adjourned till 13th. Several witnesses were examined including "Leather Apron".

Enquiries are being made by Inspectors Abberline, Helson & Chandler respecting the various statements made to Police, including that of the Dustman, whom it is alleged, saw a man on the morning of the murder with blood on his clothing.

Jno. West ActgSupt

The next report[5] on the file is from H Division, dated 14 September 1888, by Inspector J.L. Chandler, and relates to a piece of envelope found near the body of Annie Chapman:

C.O. REFERENCE. DIVISIONAL REFERENCE.
4/908
Submitted through H Division
Subject Result of enquiries re envelope found ["on" –*deleted*] near
the body of Annie Chapman.

Commercial Street
METROPOLITAN POLICE
H Division
14th September 1888

Murder of
Annie Chapman
I beg to report having made enquiries at the Depot of the 1st Battn.
Surrey Regiment, North Camp, Farnborough, 14th inst, the piece
of envelope found near the body of deceased was identified by Capt.
Young Actg Adjutant, as bearing the official stamp of the Regiment,
and stated that the majority of the men used this paper which they
purchased at the canteen. Enquiries were made amongst the men
but none could be found who corresponded with anyone living at
Spitalfields, or with any person whose address commencing with
"2" The pay books were examined and no signature resembled the
initials on the envelope. I made further enquiries at the Lynchford
Road, Post office, and was informed by the Proprietors Messrs.
Summer & Thirkettle, that the letter was posted there also that they
had a large quantity of the envelopes & paper in stock, and retailed
them to any person.

J.L.Chandler Inspr.
Submitted Jno.West Actg Supt
To Ch Inspr Swanson 3.50 pm.
15.9.88   J.Shore, Supt.

A report[6] on the two murders follows, dated 14 September 1888,
from H Division, written by Inspector Abberline:

METROPOLITAN POLICE.
H Division.
14th day of Sept. 1888

SUBJECT re murder
in Whitechapel
REFERENCE TO PAPERS
5 2 9 8 3

Re. Murders in Bucks Row and Hanbury St. 31st Ult & 8th Inst.

I beg to report that the man Stanley who occasionally cohabited with the deceased Annie Chapman and referred to by witnesses at the inquest as the pensioner called at Commercial St. Station this evening and gave a satisfactory account of himself, and will attend the adjourned inquest on 19th Inst. Inquiries have been made at the London Hospital and other places but no useful information has been obtained.

With regard to Commissioner's memorandum of 13th I have submitted special report.

A man named Edward McKenna is now detained at Commercial St. Station for identification supposed same as described in Evening papers & special memo. from C.O. this evening as having been seen at Heath St., and other places with a knife.

F.G.Abberline Inspr.

To Ch Inspr Swanson at   Jno.West ActgSupt
3.50 pm JShoreSupt.

In a report[7] dated 15 September 1888, written at H Division, Commercial Street Police Station, Inspector Chandler gives further information regarding his enquiries into the piece of envelope found near Chapman's body:

The cover states:

$\frac{3}{52983}$

153   H Division

To the Assistant Commissioner
Criminal Investigation Department
SUMMARY OF CONTENTS

re. murder in Whitechapel 31st Ult. and 8th Inst.
Submitted to A.F. Williamson Esq.
Ch: Constable,
Dond. S. Swanson
ChInsp.
Mr Bruce
Seen ACB.17.9

Commercial Street
METROPOLITAN POLICE.
H Division.

15th September 1888

Reference to Papers
Murder of
Annie Chapman

I beg to report having made enquiries 14th inst. at the depot 1st Battn. Royal Sussex Regiment North Camp Farnborough with reference to the portion of an envelope found near the body of Annie Chapman (and which contained two pills) and was informed by the Adjutant, Capt. Young, that it bore the stamp of the Regt., the fact of its being posted at the Lynchford Road office, shews that the writer, if a soldier posted the letter, himself when out and not in the barracks as usual, enquiries were made amongst the men but none could be found who are in the habit of writing to anyone at Spitalfields, or whose signatures corresponded with the letters on the envelope, that class of paper can be purchased in the canteen and is used by the majority of the men.

I also made enquiries at the Lynchford Road post Office and was informed by the Post Masters Messrs. Summer and Thirkettle who stated that the letter was posted there but they could not say by whom; also that they had a large quantity of paper and envelopes bearing the Sussex Regimental stamp (identical with the piece found) in stock, that they did them up in small quantities, and retailed them to the public.

I beg to add that at 11 am 15th inst William Stevens a painter, of 35 Dorset Street, Spitalfields, Common Lodging House came to Commercial Street Station, and made the following statement, I know Annie Chapman as a lodger in the same house, I know that on Friday 7th inst the day before the murder she came into the Lodging House and said she had been to the hospital, and intended going into the Infirmary next day. I saw that she had a bottle of medicine, a bottle of lotion and a box with two pills and as she was handling the box it came to pieces, she then took out the pills and picked up a piece of paper from the kitchen floor near the fireplace, and wrapped the pills up in it. I believe the piece of paper with Sussex Regiment thereon to be the same. I do not know of any lodger in the house who has been in the Army.

I beg to add that 35 Dorset Street is a Common Lodging House and frequented by a great many strangers, and it is very probable it may have been dropped there by one of them.

J.L.Chandler Inspr.

I beg to state that to prevent delay Inspr. Chandler at my request proceeded to Farnborough without first obtaining the Commissioners authority. I therefore now beg to ask for that authority.

F.G.Abberline Inspr.

Submitted   Jno.West ActgSupt.

There is a file cover[8] that refers to this retrospective authority sought by Abberline:

C.O. REFERENCE.   DIVISIONAL REFERENCE.

$\dfrac{3}{52983}$ $\dfrac{H915}{4}$

168

Submitted through Ch.Constable C.I.D.

H Division

Subject Murder of

Annie Chapman

Applying for Commissioner's covering authority for Inspr. Chandler proceeding to Farnborough to make immediate enquiries in connection with above.

17/9/88.   DSSwanson

ChInspr

MrBruce

ACB for Comr.   ACB 18.9

Acct. for 8s/8d passed

[   ]

12.10.88

Inspr Dillon [?]

On Monday, 17 September 1888, Sergeant William Thick, H Division, submitted a report[9] with reference to the man, Isenschmid, detained at Holloway in connection with the murder:

METROPOLITAN POLICE

H Division.

17th September 1888

SUBJECT Man detained

at Holloway

re murder

REFERENCE TO PAPERS

attached

With reference to attached telegram and report from "Y" Division, see also wife's statement attached; re Joseph Isenschmid detained.

I beg to report that I called several times at Mitford Road, Upper Holloway with a view of interviewing Mr. Tyler re the movements of Joseph Isenschmid but failed, and I am also unable to ascertain where he is employed. On calling again yesterday I saw a boy named "Briggs" who informed me that Mr. Tyler had removed early that morning, and he did not know where to. The boy was the only person in the house, and stated that several gentlemen had called there for Mr. Tyler during the last few days. He could say no more.

I called on Mrs. Gerlingher, the person referred to in wife's statement, who stated that she did not know the man I referred to and that no person but the regular customers had visited her house a "Public House". I have made careful enquiries amongst Germans whom I know in this neighbourhood but failed to find any trace of "Isenschmid" having been seen in this neighbourhood.

I called at Fairfield Road Bow Infirmary Asylum where "Isenschmid" is still detained. I saw the Medical Superintendent who informed me that "Isenschmid" had told him that the girls at Holloway had called him "Leather Apron" and that he had said to them in the way of chaff I am "Leather Apron" and he supposed they had informed the police. He was a "butcher" by trade but had failed in business. He had a few words with his wife and he left her. He was now getting his living by going to the market early in the morning buying sheep's heads; kidneys, and sheep's feet, taking them home to his lodgings, and dressing them then taking them to Restaurants and Coffee Houses in the West End of the town, and selling them, and that was the cause of him being up so early in the morning, and that was the only way open to him to get his livelihood.

The Superintendent would like for police to give instructions what he was to do with Isenschmid. I beg to add that further and careful enquiries are being made with a view of tracing the whereabouts of Mr Tyler, to obtain further particulars from him. Also other persons who are likely to give further details of Isenschmid' movements of dates of the recent murders.

William Thick
P.S.

Submitted;   Jn. West
            Actg.Supt.

There follows an interesting report[10] by Inspector Abberline, dated 18 September 1888:

METROPOLITAN POLICE.
Criminal Investigation Department,
Scotland Yard,

18th day of Sept. 1888

SUBJECT re murders
in Whitechapel
REFERENCE TO PAPERS
5 2 9 8 3

I beg to report that inquiries have been continued relative to the various matters in connection with the murders including the lunatic who was detained by police at Holloway on 12th Inst., and handed over to the parochial authorities same day. He gives the name of Joseph Isenschmid, and his occupation has been that of a butcher. He is now detained at Bow Infirmary Asylum, Fairfield Road, Bow, and from his description he is believed to be identical with the man seen in the Prince Albert P.H., Brushfield Street, Spitalfields with blood on his hands at 7 a.m. on the morning of the murder of Annie Chapman. [*At this point in the report there are two marginal notations, "Seen, Mr. Williamson has been to see the Dr. at the Infirmary. CW 19.9" and "Identification postponed by order of—WT 20/9".*] Dr. Mickle the Medical Officer of the Institution has been consulted with a view to Isenschmid being seen by Mrs Fiddymont and the other witnesses. The doctor is of opinion this cannot be done at present with safety to his patient. It has been ascertained that this man had been wandering about and away from his home for several weeks past, and when he left his home he took with him two butchers knives. He has been previously confined in an asylum, and is said to be at times very violent. Although at present we are unable to procure any evidence to connect him with the murders he appears to be the most likely person that has come under our notice to have committed the crimes, and every effort will be made to account for his movements on the dates in question.

F.G.Abberline Inspr.
Respectfully submitted
Jno.West ActgSupt.

A further report[11] concerning the detained Isenschmid, dated 19 September 1888 and in the handwriting of Sgt William Thick, follows:

METROPOLITAN POLICE

H Division

19th day of September 1888

SUBJECT Man detained
at Holloway
re murder
REFERENCE TO PAPERS
attached

With reference to attached telegram and report from "Y" Division, re Joseph Isenschmid detained on suspicion of murder.

I beg to report that on 12th inst. I called at the Islington Workhouse and found that Joseph Isenschmid had been removed from there to Fairfield Road, Bow Infirmary Asylum. I then saw Mrs. Isenschmid, his wife at 97 Duncombe Road Upper Holloway who stated that they had been married twenty one years. He is a "Swiss" and was at that time employed as a Journeyman butcher. They then went into business as Pork butchers at 59 Elthorne Road, Upper Holloway, but eventually failed. Her husband then began to get very much depressed and repeatedly stopped away from his home at night and remained away for several days. He has been in Colney Hatch Lunatic Asylum for ten weeks and was discharged from there about the middle of last December and came home supposed to be quite well. He then got employment as Journeyman butcher at a Mr. Marlett's High Street Marylebone and stopped there till Whitsuntide. He then left and has done nothing since to her knowledge. He professed to have had work but did not bring home any money. He has not slept at home for quite two months. About three or four weeks ago he was found in a house in Caledonian Road and was charged. He was taken to Clerkenwell Police Court and remanded for enquiries to be made about him. He was eventually discharged. He then came home again and changed his underclothing and left again. I did not see him again, she then added. I went away into the country to visit my friends last Sunday week, (1st Inst), and returned again on Monday following, (3rd Inst). I was then informed by my daughter that my husband had been home and took his shirts and collars away. Mr. Tyler 60 Mitford Road, Upper Holloway had called during my absence and left a message for me to call on him. I went there on Tuesday morning. I did not see my husband. When he left he had two bone knives and his butchers clothes with him. I don't know what has become of them. I do not think my husband would injure anyone but me. I think he would kill me if he had the chance. He is fond of other women. He used to frequent a Public House kept by a "German" named Gerlinger in Wentworth Street Whitechapel. He is known as the "mad butcher".

This report is unsigned.

On the same date, Wednesday 19 September 1888, Inspector Joseph Henry Helson, J Division, wrote a report[12] with reference to the two murders he was assisting with enquiries into.

The cover reads:

J Division
To the
ASSISTANT COMMISSIONER,
CRIMINAL INVESTIGATION DEPARTMENT
SUMMARY OF CONTENTS

Report re Joseph Isenschmid – detained at Holloway and put in Bow Infirmary Asylum., who is suspected of being the man seen with blood on his hands on the morning of the 8th inst.

19.9.88

METROPOLITAN POLICE
J Division
19th day of September 1888

SUBJECT Murders at
Whitechapel and
Spitalfields
REFERENCE TO PAPERS
5 2 9 8 3

With reference to Joseph Isenschmid detained by Police at Holloway, and sent to the Workhouse as an Insane person, I beg to report that from papers received from Y Division, it is shown that on the 11th inst. Dr Cowan of Landseer Road, and Dr Crabb of Holloway Road, called at Holloway Police Station, and stated that an insane butcher known by them to have been confined in an Asylum, but recently residing at 97 Duncombe Road, and at 60 Mitford Road, Holloway, was not unlikely to have been the person engaged in committing the recent murders at Whitechapel. In consequence of this information observation was kept at the address given, and in the evening of the 12th inst. Isenschmid was found and conveyed to Holloway Police Station. A telegram was received at 6.35 a.m. 12th inst. at H.D. stating that this man was detained at Holloway and PS Thick, C.I. Dept. H. was as soon as possible, detailed by Inspector Abberline to make enqs. respecting this man, but before he arrived at Holloway the man had been removed to the Workhouse as an insane person, and from the workhouse it was found he had been sent on to the Bow Infirmary Asylum.

The enquiry was continued by the P.S. and on the 18th inst. I went to the Asylum, and saw Dr Mickle, the Resident Medical Officer, and endeavoured to arrange for Isenschmid to be seen at the Institution by Mrs. Fiddymont of the Prince Albert Public House, Brushfield St. and other persons by whom a man was seen in the morning of the 8th inst. at 7. a.m. with blood on his hands, as the description obtained of Isenschmid and that given by the persons referred to makes it very probable that they are identical, but the Doctor was unable to agree to this proposal, as it might prove injurious to the man. He has, at my request, promised that in his conversations with the man daily, he will obtain from him as much information as possible, as to his recent movements, and let me know the result (in confidence) if I call on him from time to time. Also that should he be removed to another Institution, or recover sufficiently to enable him to be discharged to let me know at once. The clothing worn by Isenschmid when arrested is now in possession of the Police, but apparently bears no stains or marks of blood. Enquiries will be continued with a view to find some person or persons to whom he was known, and who may be able to throw some light on his recent movements, but at present no person can be found except his wife, and she has not seen him for two months.

J.H.Helson Insp.

Submitted   Jno.West ActgSupt.

In a lengthy (15-page) Metropolitan Police report[13] from the Criminal Investigation Department, Scotland Yard, dated 19 September 1888, by Inspector Frederick G. Abberline, details of this investigation are given and of the Nichols murder:

C.O. Reference Divisional Reference
Submitted through Executive
J. Division
Subject Report Re Murder of a woman unknown

METROPOLITAN POLICE.
CRIMINAL INVESTIGATION DEPARTMENT,
SCOTLAND YARD,

19th day of Sept. 1888

SUBJECT re. Murder
in Whitechapel
REFERENCE TO PAPERS
5 2 9 8 3

With reference to the subject named in margin.

I beg to report that about 3.40. am 31st Ult. as Charles Cross, "carman" of 22 Doveton Street, Cambridge Road, Bethnal Green was passing through Bucks Row, Whitechapel (on his way to work) he noticed a woman lying on her back on the footway (against some gates leading into a stable yard) he stopped to look at the woman when another carman (also on his way to work) named Robert Paul of 30 Foster St., Bethnal Green came up, and Cross called his attention to the woman, but being dark they did not notice any blood, and passed on with the intention of informing the first constable they met, and on arriving at the corner of Hanbury St. and Old Montague St. they met P.C. 55,H Mizen and acquainted him of what they had seen, and on the Constable proceeding towards the spot he found that P.C. 97J. Neil (who was on the beat) had found the woman, and was calling for assistance. P.C. Neil had turned on his light and discovered that the womans throat was severely cut. P.C. 96J. Thain was also called and sent at once for Dr. Llewellyn of 152 Whitechapel Road, who quickly arrived on the scene and pronounced life extinct and ordered the removal of the body to the mortuary. In the meantime P.C. Mizen had been sent for the ambulance and assistance from Bethnal Green Station, and on Inspr. Spratling and other officers arriving, the body was removed to the mortuary. On arriving there the Inspector made a further examination, and found that the abdomen had also been severely cut in several places exposing the intestines. The Inspector acquainted Dr. Llewellyn who afterwards made a more minute examination and found that the wounds in the abdomen were in themselves sufficient to cause instant death, and he expressed an opinion that they were inflicted before the throat was cut. The body was not then identified On the clothing being carefully examined by Inspr Helson he found some of the underclothing bore the mark of Lambeth Workhouse which led to the body being identified as that of a former inmate named Mary Ann Nichols, and by that means we were able to trace the relatives and complete the identity. It was found she was the wife of William Nichols, of 37 Coburg Street, Old Kent Road, a printer in the employ of Messrs. Perkins, Bacon, & Co. Whitefriars St. City from whom she had been separated about 9 years through her drunken and immoral habits, and that for several years past she had from time to time been an inmate of various workhouses. In May of this year she left Lambeth Workhouse and entered the service of Mr. Cowdry, Ingleside, Rose Hill Road, Wandsworth she remained there until the 12th July when she absconded stealing various articles of wearing apparel. A day or two after she became a lodger at 18 Thrawl St. Spitalfields a common lodging-house and slept there and at another common lodging-house 56 Flower and Dean Street up to the night of the murder About 1.40 am. that morning she was seen in the kitchen at 18 Thrawl St. when she informed the Deputy of the lodging-house that she had no money to pay her lodgings She requested that her bed might be kept for her and left stating that she would soon get the money – at this time she was drunk. She was next seen at 2.30. am. at the corner of Osborn St. and Whitechapel Road by Ellen Holland a lodger in the same house who seeing she was very drunk requested her to return with her to the lodging-house. She however refused remarking that she would soon be back and walked away down the Whitechapel Road in the direction of the place where the body was found. There can be no doubt with regard to the time because the Whitechapel Church clock chimed 2.30., and Holland called the attention of the deceased to the time. We have been unable to find any person who saw her alive after Holland left her. The distance from Osborn St. to Bucks Row would be about half a mile. Inquiries were made in every conceivable quarter with a view to trace the murderer but not the slightest clue can at present be obtained In the course of our inquiries amongst the numerous women of the same class as the deceased it was ascertained that a feeling of terror existed against a man known as Leather Apron who it appeared have for a considerable time past been levying blackmail and ill-using them if his demands were not complied with although there was no evidence to connect him with the murder. It was however thought desirable to find him and interrogate him as to his movements on the night in question, and with that view searching inquiries were made at all common lodging-houses in various parts of the Metropolis but through the publicity given in the ''Star'' and other newspapers the man was made acquainted with the fact that he was being sought for and it was not until the 10th Inst. that he was discovered when it was found that he had been concealed by his relatives. On his being interrogated he was able however to give such a satisfactory account of his movements as to prove conclusively that the suspicions were groundless. Suspicion was also attached to three men employed during the night of the murder by Messrs. Barber & Co. "Horse-slaughterers" Winthorp St. which is about 30 yards from where the body was found. They have however been seen separately and lengthy statements taken from them as to how they spent their time during the night, and the explanations given by them were confirmed by the Police who saw them at work, and no grounds appeared to exist to suspect them of the murders. In the meantime, viz, at 6 am. 8th Inst. the dead and mutilated body of Annie Chapman was found in the yard of 29 Hanbury St., Spitalfields, having been murdered in the same manner, the mutilations being of the same description, but more brutal leaving no doubt that the same person committed both murders. The identification in this case has also been clearly established. She was the widow of a coachman named Chapman who died at Windsor some 18 months since from whom she had been separated several years previously through her drunken habits, and who up to the time of his death made her an allowance of 10/- per week. For some years past she has been a frequenter of common lodging-houses in the neighbourhood of Spitalfields, and for sometime previous to her death had resided at 35 Dorset Street where she was last seen alive at 2 a.m. on the morning of the murder, but not having the money to pay her lodgings left the house remarking she would go and get it, at the time she appeared the worse for drink. From then until her body was found no reliable information can be obtained as to her movements. It was ascertained that for the last two years she has occasionally been visited by a man named Edwd. Stanley, a labourer, who resides at 1 Osborn Place, Whitechapel with that exception she was not known to be acquainted with any particular man. Stanley has been found and interrogated and from his statement it has been clearly established that on the night of 30th Ult. he was on duty with the 2nd Brigade Southern Division Hants Militia at Fort Elson Gosport, and during the night of 7th Inst. he was in bed at his lodgings from midnight until 7 a.m. 8th, an hour after the body was discovered. He is also believed to be a respectable hardworking man, and no suspicion whatever is attached to him. The deceased was in the habit of wearing two brass rings (a wedding and keeper) these were missing when the body was found and the finger bore marks of their having been removed by force. Special inquiries have been made at all places where they may be offered for pledge or for sale by a person believing them to be gold, but nothing has resulted therefrom. Searching inquiries were also made at lodging-houses &c with a view of ascertaining whether any person had been seen to enter with blood on them, with a like result. The inhabitants of the houses adjoining the scenes of the murders have been seen and many called as witnesses before the Coroner, but none of them heard anything to attract their attention on either occasion. No doubt the murders in each case were committed where the bodies were found. Bucks Row is a narrow quiet thoroughfare frequented by prostitutes for immoral purposes at night and no doubt the yard of 29 Hanbury Street has been used for a similar purpose. Several persons have been detained at various stations on suspicion, and there [sic] movements have been inquired into, numerous statements have also been made, and letters received bearing on the subject, but after the most exhaustive inquiries no useful result has been attained. The inquest has been opened on both bodies, and adjourned from time to time, numerous witnesses have been examined, and both stand now adjourned, that on Mary Ann Nichols until 22nd, and on Annie Chapman until today.

Plans have been prepared of the scene of each murder for the information of the Coroner, and are herewith submitted for the information of Commissioner. Inquiries are being continued in every direction in which it is thought information may be obtained, and no effort will be spared to elucidate the mysteries.

I beg to add that the man Isenschmid who was detained at Holloway on 12th Inst, and handed over to the parochial authorities as a lunatic, is identical with the man seen in Prince Albert P.H. Brushfield St. at 7 a.m. on the morning of the murder of Annie Chapman, by Mrs. Fiddymont & other persons. This house is only about 400 yards from the scene of the murder, the man who entered had blood on his hands. Isenschmid has carried on the business of a butcher, but some 12 months ago failed in business. He afterwards became depressed and lost his reason, and was confined in an asylum. He was however liberated about Christmas last as cured, but for some months past he has acted very strangely and for the last six weeks he has been absent from home, and wandering about the streets at all hours. When he left home he had in his possession two large knives that he used in his business. He is now confined in the Bow Infirmary Asylum, Fairfield Road, Bow, and Dr. Mickle has been seen with a view to arrange for Mrs. Fiddymont and other witnesses to see him, but the doctor thinks this cannot be done at present with safety to his patient. As time is of the greatest importance in this case, not only with regard to the question of identity, but also for the purpose of allaying the strong public feeling that exists, I would respectfully suggest that either the Chief Surgeon, or one of the Divl. Surgeons may be requested to see Dr. Mickle the resident medical officer to make if possible some arrangements for the witnesses to see Isenschmid.

Ch InsprSwanson.   F.G. Abberline Inspr.
Plan to A.C. CID.   JohnShoreSupt.

An index[14] to the Chapman murder file is included in the Home Office reports. Date-stamped 25 OCT. 88, it lists the contents:

For a complete overview of the whole of the Hanbury Street murder it is necessary to see Chief Inspector Swanson's report[15] of 19 October 1888, to the Home Office:

METROPOLITAN POLICE.
Criminal Investigation Department,
Scotland Yard,
19th day of October 1888

SUBJECT Hanbury Street
Murder of Annie
Chapman.
I beg to report that the following are the facts respecting the murder
of Annie Chapman on 8th Sept. at 29 Hanbury Street.

6 a.m. 8th Sept. 1888. The body of a woman was discovered in the
back yard of 29 Hanbury St. Spitalfields, by John Davis of that
address who immediately informed the police, & Dr. Phillips the
Divl. Surgeon was sent for, who stated that in his opinion death had
taken place two or three hours. Examination of the body showed
that the throat was severed deeply incision jagged. Removed from
but attached to body, & placed above right shoulder were a flap of
the wall of belly, the whole of the small intestines & attachments.
Two other portions of wall of belly & "Pubes" were placed above
left shoulder in a large quantity of blood. Abrasion of head of first
phalanx of ring finger, distinct marking of ring or rings, probably
the latter:- on proximal phalanx of same finger. The following parts
were missing:- part of belly wall including navel; the womb, the
upper part of vagina & greater part of bladder. The Dr. gives it as
his opinion that the murderer was possessed of anatomical knowledge from the manner of removal of viscera, & that the knife used
was not an ordinary knife, but such as a small amputating knife, or a
well ground slaughterman's knife, narrow & thin, sharp & blade of
six to eight inches in length.

9th Sept. The body was identified as that of Annie Chapman, by
John Donovan, 35 Dorset Street, Spitalfields, lodging house keeper,
where she had resided & also by her brother Mr. Fontin Smith, 44
Bartholomew Close, E.C.

The results of enquiries were as follows:-

2 a.m. 8th Sept. 1888 She was last seen alive at 2 a.m. 8th Sept.
by John Donovan, the deputy of the Common Lodging House,
where she resided. At that time she was under the influence of
drink, and as she had no money, she left the lodging house to get it,
so as to pay for her bed.

4.45 a.m. 8th Sept. John Richardson of 29 Hanbury St. stated
that he went out and sat on the steps leading to the back yard, to cut

a piece of leather off his boot, but he did not observe the body of the woman.

5.25 a.m. 8th Sept. Albert Cadosch of 27 Hanbury Street, (next door) had occasion to go into the yard at the rear of No. 27, separated only by a wooden fence about 5 feet high, and he heard words pass between some persons apparently at No. 29 Hanbury Street, but the only word he could catch was "No". [*Here there is a marginal note* – "Was the voice of the man that of a foreigner?"]

5.28 a.m. 8th Sept. On Cadosch going back into the yard again he heard a noise as of something falling against the fence on the side next No. 29 Hanbury Street, but he did not take any notice.

5.30 a.m. 8th Sept. Mrs. Long of 32 Church Street stated that she saw a man and woman talking near to No. 29 Hanbury Street. She heard the man say "Will you" [*Here there is a marginal note* – "A foreigner?"] and the woman replied "Yes" and passed on. She only saw his back, and would be unable to know him again. She describes him as apparently over 40 years of age. She did not see his face He appeared to be a little taller than the woman and in her opinion looked like a foreigner. She thinks he had a dark coat on, but she could not recognise him again. The woman she positively identified as the deceased.

Then followed the discovery by John Davies as shown on page 1. of this report.

A. The action of Police was as follows. The inhabitants of 29 Hanbury Street were seen and the rooms searched. Their statements were taken as well as the inhabitants of adjoining houses.

B. An immediate and searching enquiry was made at all Common Lodging Houses to ascertain if anyone had entered that morning with blood on his hands face or clothes, or under any suspicious circumstances.

C. A special enquiry to find rings was also made at all pawnbrokers, jewellers, dealers.

D. Enquiry was also made into the antecedents and history of deceased.

E. Several persons, whose antecedents are attached, were detained pending enquiries into their movements covering the dates of 7 & 31st Augst. & 8th Sept.

F. The particulars of other persons seen in different parts of the Metropolis, under what appeared to be suspicious circumstances to the persons giving the information, upon which from the nature of the circumstances no enquiry could be made, were circulated.

G. Enquiries were also made to trace persons suspected, whose address, or particulars respecting them given upon correspondence. These enquiries are being continued.

H. Enquiries were also made to trace three insane students who had attended London Hospital. Result two traced, one gone abroad. [*Here there is a marginal note* – When?]

I. Enquiries were also made amongst women of the same class as deceased, and at public houses in the locality.

Up to the present the combined result of those enquiries did not supply the police with the slightest clue to the murderer. The only indication of the direction to find the murderer lay in the evidence of Dr. Phillips, which was in substance that the individual possessed some skill and anatomical knowledge, and that the instrument with which the injuries were inflicted was probably a small amputating knife, or a well ground butchers knife, narrow and thin, sharp with a blade from six to eight inches long.

If the evidence of Dr. Phillips is correct as to time of death, it is difficult to understand how it was that Richardson did not see the body when he went into the yard at 4.45 a.m. but as his clothes were examined, the house searched and his statement taken in which there was not a shred of evidence, suspicion could not rest upon him, although police specially directed their attention to him. Richardson is a market porter. Again if the evidence of Mrs. Long is correct that she saw the deceased at 5.30 a.m. then the evidence of Dr. Phillips as to probable time of death is incorrect. He was called and saw the body at 6.20 a.m. and he then gives it as his opinion that death occurred about two hours earlier, viz: 4.20 a.m. hence the evidence of Mrs. Long which appeared to be so important to the Coroner, must be looked upon with some amount of doubt, which is to be regretted.

The enquiry into the history of the deceased showed that she was the widow of a coachman named Chapman who died about eighteen months ago, and from whom she had been separated about eight years, on account of her drunken and immoral ways, but her husband had allowed her 10/- per week up to the time of his death. She was then occasionally visited by a man named Stanley, who was known as the pensioner. He came forward, and accounted for his time, and gave evidence before the Coroner. Some pieces of paper were found near the body but they were accounted for as being picked up by the deceased in the Common Lodging home.

Enquiry is still being actively continued in all directions where there is a probable chance of finding a trace, and a further report will be submitted.

A descriptive form relating to Annie Chapman is also included, giving details as follows:

Alias	*Annie Siffey*
Age	*45*
Profession or calling	*Prostitute*
Height	*5 feet*
Hair	*(Wavy) dark brown.*
Eyes	*blue*
Nose	*thick nose*
Mouth	*Two teeth deficient in lower jaw*
Complexion	*Fair*
Marks or Peculiarities	*On person portion of an envelope stamped "Sussex Regiment" dated 23rd Augst. 1888.*
Dress	*Black skirt & jacket, striped petticoat crape bonnet*

CHAPTER 5

September 1888 –
The Chapman Inquest and Police Enquiries

As in the case of Nichols, the inquest report on Chapman is not to be found in any of the official files, and the Home Office files on the murder contain extracts from *The Times* newspaper relevant to this enquiry. The first extract[1] is from *The Times* of Tuesday, 11 September 1888, page 6:

THE INQUEST.

Yesterday morning Mr. Wynne E. Baxter, the Coroner for the North-Eastern Division of Middlesex, who was accompanied by Mr. George Collier, the Deputy Coroner, opened his inquiry in the Alexandra-room of the Working Lads' Institute, Whitechapel-road, respecting the death of Annie Chapman, who was found murdered in the back yard of 29, Hanbury-street, Spitalfields, on Saturday morning.

Detective-inspectors Abberline (Scotland-yard), Helson, and Chandler, and Detective-sergeants Thicke and Leach watched the case on behalf of the Criminal Investigation Department and Commissioners of Police.

The court-room was crowded, and, owing to the number of persons assembled outside the building, the approaches had to be guarded by a number of police-constables.

The jury having been impanelled, proceeded to the mortuary to view the body of the deceased, which was lying in the same shell as that occupied a short time since by the remains of the unfortunate Mary Ann Nichols.

John Davis, a carman, of 29, Hanbury-street, Spitalfields, deposed that he occupied the front room, which was shared by his wife and three sons. About 8 o'clock on Friday night he went to bed, and his sons came in at different times. The last one arrived home about a quarter to 11. Witness was awake from 3 to about 5 o'clock, when he fell off to sleep for about half an hour. He got up about a quarter to 6. Soon afterwards he went across the yard. The front portion of the house faced Hanbury-street. On the ground floor there was a front door, with a passage running through to the back yard. He was certain of the time, because he heard the bell of Spitalfields Church strike. The front door and the one leading into the yard were never locked, and at times were left open at nights. Since he had lived in the house witness had never known the doors to be locked; and when the doors were shut any person could open them and pass into the yard. When he went into the yard on Saturday morning the back door was shut; but he was unable to say whether it was latched. The front door was wide open, and he was not surprised at finding it so, as it was frequently left open all night. Between the yard of 29, Hanbury-street, and the next house there was a fence about 5 ft. high. When witness went down the steps he saw the deceased woman lying flat on her back.

The CORONER here observed that in similar inquiries in the country the police always assisted him by preparing a plan of the locality which happened to be the subject of investigation. He thought the present case was one of sufficient importance for the production of such a plan, and he hoped that in future a plan would be laid before him.

Inspector Chandler told the Coroner a plan would be prepared.

The CORONER replied it might then be too late to be of any service.

Witness, continuing, said the deceased was lying between the steps and the fence, with her head towards the house. He could see that her clothes were disarranged. Witness did not go further into the yard, but at once called two men, who worked for Mr. Bailey, a packing-case maker, of Hanbury-street, whose place was three doors off. These men entered the passage and looked at the woman, but did not go into the yard. He was unable to give the names of these two men, but knew them well by sight. Witness had not since seen the men, who went away to fetch the police. Witness also left the house with them.

In answer to the Coroner, Inspector Chandler said these men were not known to the police.

The CORONER remarked that they would have to be found, either by the police or by his own officer.

Witness further stated that on leaving the house he went direct to the Commercial-street Police-station, and reported what he had seen. Previous to that he had not informed any one living in the house of the discovery. After that he went back to Hanbury-street, but did not enter his house. He had never previously seen the deceased.

In cross-examination, the witness said he was not the first person down that morning, as a man, named Thompson, who also lived in the house, was called about half-past 3. He had never seen women who did not live in the house in the passage since he had lived there, which was only a fortnight. He did not hear any strange noises before getting up on Saturday morning. He did not return to his house until Saturday afternoon.

Amelia Farmer stated that she lived at a common lodginghouse at 30, Dorset-street, Spitalfields, and had lived there for the past four years. She had identified the body of the deceased in the mortuary, and was sure it was that of Annie Chapman. The deceased formerly lived at Windsor, and was the widow of Frederick Chapman, a veterinary surgeon, who died about 18 months ago. For four years, or more, the deceased had lived apart from her husband, and during that period had principally resided in common lodginghouses in the neighbourhoods of Whitechapel and Spitalfields. About two years since the deceased lived at 30, Dorset-street, and was then living with a man who made iron sieves. She was then receiving an allowance of 10s. a week from her husband. Some 18 months since the payments stopped, and it was then that she found her husband was dead. That fact was also ascertained from a relative of the deceased, who used to live in Oxford-street, Whitechapel. The deceased went by the name of Sievey, on account of the man with whom she had cohabited being a sieve maker. This man left her some time ago. During the past week witness had seen the deceased some two or three times. On Monday, in Dorset-street, she complained of feeling unwell. At that time she had a bruise on one of her temples. Witness inquiring how she got it, the deceased told her to look at her breast, which was also bruised. The deceased said, ''You know the woman,'' and she mentioned a name which witness did not remember. Both the deceased and the woman referred to were acquainted with a man called ''Harry the Hawker.'' In giving an account of the bruises, the deceased told witness that on the 1st inst. she went into a publichouse with a young man named Ted Stanley in Commercial-street. ''Harry the Hawker'' and the other woman were also there. The former, who was drunk, put down a florin, which was picked up by the latter, who replaced it with a penny. Some words passed between the

deceased and the woman, and in the evening the latter struck her
and inflicted the bruises. Witness again saw the deceased on
Tuesday by the side of Spitalfields Church. The deceased again
complained of feeling unwell, and said she thought she would go
into the casual ward for [a] day or two. She mentioned that she had
had nothing to eat or drink that day, not even a cup of tea. Witness
gave deceased twopence saying, "Here is twopence to have a cup of
tea, but don't have rum." She knew that deceased was given to
drinking that spirit. The deceased, who frequently got the worse for
drink, used at times to earn money by doing crochet work, and at
others by selling flowers. Witness believed she was not very
particular what she did to earn a living and at times used to remain
out very late at night. She was in the habit of going to Stratford.
Witness did not again see the deceased until Friday afternoon, and
about 5 o'clock on that day she met her in Dorset-street. The
deceased, who was sober, in answer to a question from witness as to
whether she was going to Stratford, said she felt too ill to do
anything. A few minutes afterwards witness again saw the deceased,
who had not moved, and she said, "It's no use my giving way. I
must pull myself together and go out and get some money, or I shall
have no lodgings." That was the last time witness saw her. She
mentioned that she had been an inmate of the casual ward. Deceased
was generally an industrial woman, and witness considered her
clever. For the last five years she had been living an irregular life,
more especially since her husband died. She had two children, and
on the death of her husband they were sent away to school. The
deceased had a sister and mother, but witness believed they were
not on friendly terms.

Timothy Donovan stated he was the deputy of a common
lodginghouse at 35, Dorset-street, Spitalfields. He had seen the
body in the mortuary, and identified it as that of a woman who had
lodged at his place. She had been living there for about four months,
but was not there any day last week until Friday. About 7 o'clock
that day she came to the lodginghouse and asked him to allow her to
go down into the kitchen. He asked where she had been all the
week, and she replied, "In the infirmary." He then allowed her to
go into the kitchen. She remained there until shortly before 2
o'clock the next morning. When she went out she said, "I have not
any money now, but don't let the bed; I will be back soon." At that
time there was a vacant bed, and it was the one she generally
occupied. She then left the house, but witness did not see which way

she turned. She had had enough to drink when he last saw her, but she was well able to walk straight. The deceased generally got the worse for drink on Saturdays, but not on the other days of the week. He told her that she could find money for drink but not for her bed, and she replied that she had only been to the top of the street as far as the Ringers' publichouse. He did not see her with any one that night. On Saturday night deceased used to stay at the lodginghouse with a man of military appearance, and witness had heard he was a pensioner. She had brought other men to the lodginghouse. On the 2d inst. deceased and the pensioner were there together. The deceased paid 8d. a night for her bed. The pensioner was about 45 years of age and about 5 ft. 8 in. in height. At times he had the appearance of a dock labourer and at others the appearance of something better. Witness had never had any trouble with the deceased, who was always very friendly with the other lodgers.

John Evans a night watchman at the lodginghouse, also identified the body of deceased. He saw her leave the house at about a quarter to 2 on Saturday morning. Just before he had asked her whether she had any money for her lodging. She replied that she had not sufficient, and then told the last witness she would not be long before she got it. Witness saw her enter a court called Paternoster-row and walk in the direction of Brushfield-street. Witness should say she was the worse for drink. She told him she had that night been to see one of her sisters who lived at Vauxhall. Before he spoke to her about her lodging money she had been out for a pint of beer. He knew that she had been living a rough life, but only knew one man with whom she associated. That man used to come and see her on Saturdays. He called about half-past 2 on Saturday afternoon to make inquiries about the deceased. He said he had heard of her death. Witness did not know his name or address. After hearing an account of the death of the deceased he went out without saying a word. Witness had never heard any person threaten the deceased, and she had never stated she was afraid of any one. He did not see the deceased leave the lodginghouse with the pensioner on Sunday week. On Thursday the deceased and a woman called Eliza had a fight in the kitchen, during which she got a blow on the chest and a black eye.

The CORONER here intimated that that was as far as he proposed to carry the inquiry at present, and it was adjourned until to-morrow afternoon.

The adjourned inquest resumed on 12 September 1888 and a report[2] of the proceedings appeared in *The Times* of Thursday, 13 September 1888, page 5:

THE ADJOURNED INQUEST.

Yesterday Mr. Wynne E. Baxter, Coroner for the North-Eastern Division of Middlesex, resumed his inquiry at the Working Lads' Institute, Whitechapel-road, respecting the death of Annie Chapman, who was found murdered in the back yard of 29, Hanbury-street, Spitalfields, on Saturday last.

Detective-inspectors Abberline (Scotland-yard) and Helson, J Division, and Sergeant Thicke [*sic*], H Division, again watched the case on behalf of the Criminal Investigation Department.

Fontaina [*sic*] **Smith** stated he had seen the body in the mortuary, and had recognized it as that of Annie Chapman, a widow. Her husband's name was John Chapman, and he had been a coachman at Windsor. The deceased had been separated from him three or four years before his death. She was 47 years of age. Some time ago he met the deceased, who first recognized him. She did not say where she was living, or what she was doing. Witness knew nothing about her associates.

James Kent stated he lived at 20, B Block, King David-lane, Shadwell, and was a packing-case maker, in the employ of Mr. Bailey, 23a, Hanbury-street, Spitalfields. He went to his work at 6 o'clock in the morning. He got to work between 10 minutes and a quarter past 6 on Saturday morning. His employer's gate was open, and he waited for more of the hands to come up. While he was waiting there an elderly man named Davis, who lived two or three doors off, came out of his house and said, "Men, come here." Davis had his belt in his hand. Witness and James Green, who was with witness at the time, went to 29, Hanbury-street, the house where the man came out. They went through the passage, and witness stood at the steps at the back door. He saw a woman lying in the yard by the side of the steps, between them and the partition. Her head was against the house, and the whole of her body was on the ground.

At this stage an officer of police produced a plan of the building and the yard.

Witness, continuing, said the face of the deceased was visible. Her clothes were disarranged, and the apron she was wearing appeared to have been thrown over the clothes. Witness did not go down the steps, and believed no other person entered the yard until the inspector (Chandler) came. He could see that the deceased was dead. She had a handkerchief of some kind round her throat. He could not see any blood, but she was besmeared with blood over the face and hands, as though she had been struggling. He did not notice any other injuries. Her hands were raised and bent, with the palms towards the upper portion of her body, as though she had fought for her throat. There were marks of blood about her legs, but he did not notice any about her clothes. He did not look very particularly about her things, as felt too much frightened. Witness then went to the front of the house, to see whether a constable was coming. He then had some brandy, and afterwards went to the shop and got a piece of canvas to throw over the body. When he returned to the house a mob had assembled. The inspector had arrived, and was in possession of the yard. Witness could not say whether any one went to the body before the inspector came, but he did not think so, as every one appeared too much frightened to go near it. The foreman over witness arrived at the workshop about ten minutes to 6.

James Green, 36, Acton-street, Burdett-road, deposed that he was a packing-case maker in the employ of Mr. Bailey. He got to the workshop about ten minutes past 6 on Saturday morning, and accompanied Kent to the back of 29, Hanbury-street. He looked at the body, and then left the premises with Kent. He did not see any one touch the body, and thought no one went near it. He saw Inspector Chandler arrive, and at that time was on the steps of the landing of his workshop. No one was in the yard when the inspector arrived, but the mob stood at the front door. At that time the body was in the same state as when the witness first saw it.

Amelia Richardson, 29, Hanbury-street, Spitalfields, said she was a widow. She rented half of the house – the ground floor portion, and the workshop and yard. Witness occupied the workshop and carried on business there. She employed her son and a man. They were supposed to begin work at 6 o'clock, but did not do so on Saturday morning. The man did not come until 8 o'clock. He was frequently late. Her son lived in John-street, Spitalfields. About 6 o'clock on Saturday morning her grandson, Thomas Richardson, 14 years of age, who lived with her, went down stairs. They heard some one in the passage, and thought the place was on fire. He returned directly afterwards, saying, "Oh, grandmother, there is a woman murdered!" Witness went down immediately, and saw the body of deceased lying in the yard.

The police and several others were in the passage, but there was no one in the yard at the time. As she was not properly attired she went back to her room and dressed herself. The police then took possession of the place.

By the CORONER. – She occupied the first-floor front room and her grandson also slept in the same room. They went to bed about half-past 9. She did not sleep through the night, and should say she was awake half of the time. She awoke at 3 o'clock, and only dozed afterwards. She did not hear any noise during the night. Mr. Walker occupied the first-floor back room. He was an old man, and slept there with his son, who was weak minded. The lad was very inoffensive. There were two rooms on the ground floor, and they were occupied by Mrs. Hardyman, who had one son, 16 years of age. He also slept there. Mrs. Hardyman got her living by selling cat's meat, and also used the room for a cat's meat shop. Her son went out selling the meat. Witness occupied the back room for cooking. When witness went to bed, at half-past 9, she locked up that room and took the key with her. It was still locked when she came down in the morning. Mr. John Davis and his wife occupied the third floor front room, together with their three sons. An old woman named Sarah Cox occupied the back room on that floor. Witness kept her out of charity. Mr. Thompson, a carman, his wife, and an adopted little girl, occupied the second floor front room. A few minutes to 4 on Saturday morning witness called Thompson. She heard him leave the house, and before doing so he did not go into the backyard. When he went out she called out "Good morning" to him. Mr. and Mrs. Copsey lived in the second floor back, and were cigar makers. When she went down on Saturday morning all the tenants in the house, except Thompson, were in the house. Witness was not the owner of the house. The front and back doors were always left open, as was the case with all the houses about there, for they were all let out in rooms.

By the jury. – She had property in the place, but was not afraid of the doors being left open. She had never heard of any robberies. About a month ago, at 3 o'clock in the morning, she heard a man on the stairs. She could not hear any one going through the passage, but did not hear any one on Saturday morning. On market mornings there was a great bustle and noise. On that morning she did not hear any cries. If a person had gone through about half-past 3 it might not have attracted her attention, although she would have heard them. People frequently went through into the back yard, and perhaps some who had no business there. She was confident that no one made a noise in going through on Saturday morning, and those who went through must have kept purposely quiet. If she knew it she would not allow any stranger to go through.

Annie Hardyman, 29, Hanbury-street, said she occupied the ground-floor front room. On Friday night she went to bed about half-past 10. Her son slept in the same room. She was not awakened during the night, and did not wake until about 6 o'clock, when she heard footsteps in the passage. She woke up her son, and told him to go and see what was the matter. He came back and said a woman had been killed in the yard. Witness did not go out. She did not hear anything during the night, but had often heard people going through the passage into the yard. She had not gone to see who they were. She did not know the deceased, and to her knowledge had never seen her.

John Richardson, of 2, John-street, stated that he acted as a porter in Spitalfields Market, and also assisted his mother in the business of packing-case making. Between a quarter and 20 minutes to 5 he went to 29, Hanbury-street. He went there to see whether the place was properly secured, as some months ago it was broken into. He only went there at that time on market mornings, and had done so for a long time past. When he got to the house he found the front door closed. He lifted the latch and went through the passage to the yard door. He did not go into the yard, but went and stood on the steps. The back door was closed when he got to it. He stood on the steps and cut a piece of leather from off one of his boots. He cut it with a table knife about 5 in. long. It was now at his house in John-street. It being market morning he put the knife into his pocket. He could not say why he put the knife into his pocket, and supposed he did so by mistake. After cutting the piece of leather off his boot he tied up the boot and went out of the house. He did not close the back door, as it closed itself. He was sure he closed the front door. He was not more than three minutes in the house. It was not light, but was getting so, and was sufficient for him to see all over the place. He could not have failed to notice the deceased had she been lying there then. He saw the body two or three minutes before the doctor came, and saw it from the adjoining yard. He went there in consequence of a man named Pearman, in the market, telling him there was a murder in Hanbury-street.

By the CORONER. – He cut the piece of leather off his boot because it hurt him. He took a piece out on the previous day, but that was not sufficient. As a matter of fact that was the only thing that he did at Hanbury-street. He did not go into the yard at all. His object principally in going to the house was to see that the cellar was all right, and he looked and found that was so.

The CORONER. – You do not seem to have taken much trouble to see that it was all right.

Witness, continuing, said he could see the padlock was on the door. He did not sit upon the top step, but rested his feet on the flags of the yard. That would be quite close to the spot where the woman was found. He had been to the house and in the passage at all hours of the night and had seen lots of strangers there. These he had seen at all hours. He had seen both men and women there, and had turned them out.

The witness was here sent to fetch the knife he had spoken about.

Amelia Richardson, recalled, said she had never lost anything, and was so confident of her neighbours that she left her door open. A long while ago she missed a saw and a hammer from the cellar. She used to lock the cellar, but on this occasion it was broken open. The cellar door was fastened with a padlock, and after the robbery was committed the door was put to. That robbery was committed in the early morning. She was aware that her son was in the habit of coming to the house to see whether the place was all right. She never had any suspicion that her yard was used for immoral purposes. Her son wore a leather apron while at work in the cellar, and on Thursday she washed it. On Saturday morning the apron was against the fence and the police took possession of it. At that time it was in the yard under the tap. The police found it in the same position in which it was put. The tap supplied the house with water, and the apron was left lying on the stones from the Thursday until Saturday. The police also took away a nail box, but there were no nails in it. On Friday night there was a pan full of water by the tap, and it was in the same position on Saturday morning. Witness had never known that women had been found on the first floor landing, and her son had never spoken to her about it.

By the jury. – The pan of water was just under the tap and the apron was not quite under it.

John Pizer, 22, Mulberry-street, Commercial-road, stated he was a bootmaker. He had been known by the nickname of "Leather Apron." He went home on Thursday night from the West-end of the town. He reached Mulberry-street about a quarter to 11 o'clock. His brother and stepmother also lived there. He remained indoors until he was arrested by Sergeant Thicke on Monday morning. Up to that time he had not left the house. His brother advised him to remain indoors as he was the object of a false suspicion. He did so in consequence of that. He was not now in custody and had cleared his character.

The CORONER. – I called you to give you an opportunity of doing so.

Witness, in answer to the Coroner, said he was in the Holloway-road on Thursday week.

The CORONER. – It is important you should say where you were and give an account of your time.

Witness said he stayed at Crossman's common lodging-house in the Holloway-road. It was called the "Round-house." He slept the night there. It was the night of the London Dock fire and he went into the lodging-house about a quarter past 2 on the Friday morning. He left there at 11 o'clock the same morning. He then saw on the placards the report of another horrible murder. At 11 o'clock the previous night he had his supper at the lodging-house. He then went out and went as far as the Seven Sisters'-road. Then he turned and went down the Holloway-road. He then saw the reflections of a fire. He went as far as the church in the Holloway-road and saw the lodging-house keeper of the "Round-House" and one or two constables talking together. He asked a constable where the fire was. He replied it was a long way off. Witness then asked him where he thought it was, and the officer replied, "Down by the Albert Docks." It was then about 1.30 as near as he could recollect. He then went as far as the Highbury railway station, then turned back, and went into the lodging-house. The night watchman did not complain of his being late, but as it was after 11 o'clock, the time when all unoccupied beds would be re-let, witness paid him 4d. for another bed. Witness then sat on a form in the kitchen for a time, smoking a clay pipe. He then went to bed. He got up at 11 o'clock, when the day attendant told him he must get up, as he wanted to make the bed. He dressed and went down into the kitchen. That was all he had to say.

By the jury. – When he spoke of the West-end of the town, he came from a lodging-house in Peter-street, Westminster.

The CORONER. – I think it only fair to say that this statement can be corroborated.

Detective-Sergeant William Thicke [*sic*] H Division, said that a man named "Leather Apron" having been suspected of the murder, on Monday morning he arrested Pizer at 22, Mulberry-street. He had known Pizer for many years, and when people in the neighbourhood spoke of "Leather Apron" they meant Pizer. He was released from custody on Tuesday night at 9.30.

John Richardson, recalled, produced the knife with which he cut the piece of leather from his boot. He found the knife on his table.

By the jury. – His mother had heard him speak of finding people acting immorally in the passage.

The CORONER said he thought the police should have the knife, and handed it to them.

Henry John Holland, 4, Aden-yard, Mile-end-road, stated that on Saturday morning he was passing along Hanbury-street on his way to his work in Chiswell-street. It was about eight minutes past 6 when he passed No. 29. He saw an elderly man come out of the house, and said "Come and look in the back yard." Witness went through the passage and saw the deceased lying in the yard just by the back door. Witness went into the yard and looked at the deceased, but did not touch her or her clothes. He did not see any one touch her. He then went for a policeman. The first one he saw was in Spitalfields Market. He said he could not come, and witness must get one from outside. He was unable to see another constable.

By the jury. – He told the policeman that it was a murder and a similar case to that which had happened in Buck's-row. The policeman was standing by himself and was not doing anything. The same afternoon witness went to the Commercial-street Police-station and reported the conduct of the constable.

The Foreman. – I think the constable ought to have gone.

An inspector stated there were certain spots which the constables were not allowed to leave under any circumstances, but they were supposed to send some one else.

The inquiry was then adjourned until to-day.

The press interest in Pizer was not restricted to his appearance in the inquest reports. *The Times* of Wednesday, 12 September 1888 carried the following report[3]:

THE WHITECHAPEL MURDER.

The latest reports as to the search for the murderer are not of a hopeful character. On Monday evening it was stated that John

Pizer, the man who was detained on suspicion of being concerned in causing the death of the woman Annie Chapman, was still in custody at the Leman-street Police-station. Last night it was decided to release him.

Many reports of a startling character have been circulated respecting the acts of violence committed by a man wearing a leather apron. No doubt many of the accounts of assaults committed on women in this district have been greatly exaggerated, yet so many versions have been related that the police give credit to at least a portion of them. They have, therefore, been keeping a sharp lookout for "leather apron," but nothing has been heard of his whereabouts. The friends of Pizer stoutly denied that he was known by that name; but on the other hand Sergeant Thicke [*sic*] who has an intimate knowledge of the neighbourhood in which the murder was committed, affirms that he knew Pizer well by sight, and always knew him by the nickname spoken of. Sergeant Thicke also knew that he was in the habit of wearing a leather apron after the news of the murder was circulated. A half-Spaniard and half-Bulgarian, who gave the name of Emanuel Delbast Violenia, waited on the police with respect to this inquiry. He stated that he, his wife, and two children tramped from Manchester to London with the view of being able to emigrate to Australia, and took up their abode in one of the lodging-houses in Hanbury-street. Early last Saturday morning, walking alone along Hanbury-street, he noticed a man and woman quarrelling in a very excited manner. Violenia distinctly heard the man threaten to kill the woman by sticking a knife into her. They passed on, and Violenia went to his lodging. After the murder he communicated what he had seen to the police. At 1 o'clock yesterday afternoon Sergeant Thicke assisted by Inspector Cansby, placed about a dozen men, the greater portion of whom were Jews, in the yard of the Leman-street Police-station. Pizer was then brought out and allowed to place himself where he thought proper among the assembled men. He is a man of short stature, with black whiskers and shaven chin. Violenia, who had been accommodated in one of the lower rooms of the station-house, was then brought up into the yard. Having keenly scrutinized all the faces before him, he at once, without any hesitation or doubt whatever, went up to Pizer and identified him as the man whom he heard threaten a woman on the night of the murder. Pizer, who has not been allowed to have communication with any of his friends, was then taken back to the station-house. It was then decided, with the approval of Detective-inspector Abberline, that Violenia should be taken to the Whitechapel mortuary to see whether he could identify the deceased woman as the one he had seen in Pizer's company early on Saturday morning. The result is not announced, but it is believed that he was unable to identify her. Subsequently, cross-examination so discredited Violenia's evidence that it was wholly distrusted by the police, and Pizer was set at liberty . . .

Last evening Timothy Donovan, the deputy of the lodging-house in Dorset-street, at which the woman Chapman formerly lived, made a statement to a representative of a news agency. He says he knows "Leather Apron" well. Some months ago he ejected him from the lodging-house, and that was for offering violence to a woman who was staying there. Donovan is surprised that the police have not called on him to go to Leman-street Police-station, as he would have no difficulty in deciding whether the prisoner there is "Leather Apron". Yesterday morning two police-constables visited Donovan and showed him two rings, one a half-worn out "engaged" ring, the other appearing to be a wedding ring, which they stated had been discovered at a pawnbroker's. Donovan did not think they were the rings he had seen Mrs. Chapman wearing. The policemen then left, and Donovan heard no more of the incident. Both Donovan and a former watcher at the lodging-house named West say that when they last saw "Leather Apron" he was wearing a kind of deerstalker hat, double peaked. West describes him as a man not more than 5 ft. 4 in. in height. Mrs. Fiddyman [*sic*] the landlady of the house into which it was stated a blood-stained and wild-looking man entered shortly after the hour at which the murder was probably committed on Saturday morning, has been taken to Leman-street Station, and on seeing Pizer she expressed herself as quite certain that he was not the man who came into her house on the occasion spoken of.

Pigott, the other man arrested, whose father was well known in Gravesend for many years as an insurance agent, was first seen in Gravesend on Sunday afternoon about 4 o'clock. He then asked four young men, who were standing in the London-road, near Princes-street, where he could get a glass of beer, he having walked from Whitechapel. The young men told him. Following their directions he jumped into a tramcar going towards Northfleet. The young men noticed that he had a bad hand, and that he carried a black bag. He was without this bag when subsequently seen. He left a paper parcel at a fish shop, kept by Mrs. Beitchteller, stating he was going across the water to Tilbury. Instead of doing so he went to the Pope's Head publichouse, where his conversation about his hatred of women aroused suspicion, and led to his being detained by the police authorities. Superintendent Berry, who is making most active and exhaustive inquiries, found the paper parcel at the fish shop to contain two shirts and a pair of stockings, one of the shirts, a blue-striped one, being torn about the breast, and having marks of blood upon it. At the police-station, Pigott first said he knocked down the woman who had bitten his hand in a yard at the back of a lodging-house in Whitechapel, but he subsequently said the occurrence took place in Brick-lane. What has become of the black bag which Pigott was seen to have in Gravesend on Sunday afternoon is not known. It appears that Pigott of late years has followed the business of a publican, and that seven or eight years ago he was in a good position, giving £8,000 to go into a house at Hoxton. Some question having arisen as to Pigott's mental condition, it may be added that he appeared perfectly rational during his detention at Gravesend.

The next report of this inquest[4] appeared in *The Times* of Friday, 14 September 1888, page 4:

THE WHITECHAPEL MURDER.

Yesterday Mr. Wynne E. Baxter, Coroner for the South-Eastern Division of Middlesex, resumed his inquiry at the Working Lads' Institute, Whitechapel-road, respecting the death of Annie Chapman, who was found murdered in the back yard of 29, Hanbury-street, Spitalfields, last Saturday morning.

Detective-inspectors Abberline (Scotland-yard), Helson, Chandler, Beck, and Detective-sergeant W. Thicke, H Division, again represented the Criminal Investigation Department.

Inspector Joseph Chandler, H Division, said that about two minutes past 6 on Saturday morning he was on duty in Commercial-street. He saw several men running up Hanbury-street, and he beckoned to them. One of them said, ''Another woman has been murdered.'' Witness at once went with him to 29, Hanbury-street, and passed through the passage into the yard. There were several people in the passage, but no one was in the yard. He saw the body of the deceased lying on the ground on her back. Her head was towards the back wall of the house, but it was some 2 ft. from the wall, and the body was not more than 6 in. or 9 in. from the steps. The face was turned on the right side, and the left hand rested on the left breast. The right hand was lying down by the left side, and the legs were drawn up. The body was lying parallel with the fencing, and was about two yards distant. Witness, remaining there, sent for the divisional surgeon, Dr. Phillips, and also to the station for the ambulance and further assistance. When the constables arrived he removed all persons from the passage, and saw that no one touched the body till the doctor arrived. He obtained some sacking from one of the neighbours to cover the body pending the arrival of the doctor. Dr. Phillips arrived about half-past 6 and examined the body. He then directed the body to be removed to the mortuary, which was done on the police ambulance. After the body had been removed a piece of coarse muslin and a small pocket haircomb case were found. A portion of an envelope was found lying near where her head had been, and a piece of paper containing two pills. He had not the pills there, as inquiries were being made about them. On the back of the envelope was the seal of the Sussex Regiment. The other portion of the writing was torn away. On the other side of the envelope was the letter "M" in a man's handwriting. There was also a post-office stamp, "London, 28 Aug., 1888," with a stamp that was indistinct. There was no postage stamp on that portion. On the front side of the envelope were the letters "Sp." in writing. He also found a leather apron lying in the yard saturated with wet and it was about 2 ft. from the water tap. A box, commonly used by packing-case makers, a piece of flat steel that had since been identified by Mrs. Richardson, and also a spring were found lying close to where the body was found.

By the CORONER. – Some portions of the yard were composed of earth and others of stones. It had not been properly paved. Some of the stones were flat while others were round. He could not detect any appearance of a struggle having taken place. The palings were only temporarily erected, although they might support the weight of a man while he was getting over them. There was no evidence of any one having recently got over them, and there was no breakage. Witness examined the adjoining yard. None of the palings had been broken, although they had since been broken. The palings near the body were stained with blood. In the wall of No. 27 marks were discovered on Tuesday last, and they had been seen by Dr. Phillips. There were no drops of blood in the passage or outside, and the bloodstains were only found in the immediate neighbourhood of the body. There were also a few spots of blood on the back wall at the head of the body and some 2 ft. or 3 ft. from the ground. The largest spot was about the size of a sixpenny piece. They were all within a small compass. Witness assisted in drawing out a plan of the place, and the plan produced was a correct one. Witness searched the clothing of the deceased after the body was removed to the mortuary. The outside jacket, which was a long black one and reached to the knees, had bloodstains round the neck, both on the inside and out, and two or three spots on the left arm. The jacket was hooked at the top and buttoned down. There did not appear to have been any struggle with the jacket. The pocket produced was found worn under the skirt. It was torn down the front and also at the side and did not contain anything. The deceased had on a black skirt, on which was a little blood at the back. There was no damage to the lower portion of the clothing. The boots were on her feet, while the stockings were bloodstained. None of the clothing was torn. Witness saw young John Richardson a little before 7 o'clock in the passage of the house. He told witness he had been to the house about a quarter to 5 that morning, that he went to the back door and looked down at the cellar to see that all was right. He then went away to his work in the market. He did not say anything to witness about cutting his boot, but said he was sure the woman was not there at the time.

By the Foreman. – The back door opened outwards into the yard, on the left-hand side. That was the side on which the body was lying. Richardson might not have seen the body if he did not go into the yard. If he went down the steps and the body was there at the time he was bound to see it. Richardson told witness he did not go down the steps, and did not mention the fact that he sat down on the steps and cut his boots.

The Foreman. – Are you going to produce the pensioner we have heard so much about?

Witness. – We have not been able to find him. No one can give us the least idea who he is. We have instructed the deputy of the lodging-house to let us know at once if he again goes there.

The CORONER. – I should think that if the pensioner knows his own business he would come forward himself.

The Foreman. – It is important he should be here, as he was in the habit of spending Saturday nights with the deceased.

Sergeant Edmund Barry, 31 H, stated that on Saturday last he conveyed the body of the deceased from 29, Hanbury-street, to the Whitechapel mortuary on the police ambulance. Detective-sergeant Thicke examined the body and gave out a description of it to witness. In doing this that sergeant moved the clothing about. Two females from 35, Dorset-street, were also present, and described the clothing to witness. They did not touch the clothing or the body. Inspector Chandler then came.

Inspector Chandler, recalled, said he reached the mortuary a few minutes after 7 o'clock, and the body, which was lying on the ambulance, did not appear to have been disturbed. He did not remain until the doctor arrived, but left a constable in charge. It was Constable Barnes, 376 H.

Robert Mann an inmate of the Whitechapel Union, stated that he had charge of the mortuary. At 7 o'clock on Saturday morning he received the body of the deceased, and remained with it until the doctor arrived at 2 o'clock. Two nurses from the infirmary came and undressed the body. He was not in the shed when that was done.

The CORONER. – This is not a mortuary, but simply a shed. Bodies ought not to be taken there. In the East-end, where mortuaries are required more than anywhere else, there are no mortuaries. When bodies are thrown up from the river off Wapping they have to be put in boxes, as there is no mortuary

The Foreman agreed that one was necessary. He added that a reward should be offered in this case by the Government. Some gentlemen were forming a fund to offer a reward, and Mr. Montagu, M.P., had offered £100.

The witness, in further examination, said he was present when Dr. Phillips made his post-mortem examination. While he was doing so witness picked up the handkerchief produced from off the clothing, which was lying in a corner of the room. He gave the handkerchief to Dr. Phillips, who told him to put it in some water. Witness did not see the handkerchief across the throat of the deceased. It had blood on it as though it had been across her throat.

Timothy Donovan, 35, Dorset-street, recalled, identified the handkerchief produced, which deceased generally wore round her throat. She bought it off another lodger at the lodging-house a week or a fortnight before she met with her death. She was wearing it when she left the lodging-house on Saturday morning and had under it a piece of black woollen scarf. It was tied in the front in one knot.

By the Foreman. – He would recognize the pensioner if he saw him again, and he knew "Harry the hawker." He had not seen the pensioner since Saturday. On that day, when he came to the lodging-house, witness sent for the police, but before they came he went away. He was a man of soldierly appearance, and at times used to come differently attired.

Mr. George Bagster Phillips, 2, Spital-square, stated he was a divisional surgeon of police, and had been for 23 years. At 6.20 on Saturday morning he was called by the police to 29, Hanbury-street, and he arrived there at 6.30. He found the dead body of a female in the possession of the police, lying in the back yard, on her back and on the left hand of the steps. The head was about 6 in. in front of the level of the bottom step, and her feet were towards a shed, which proved to contain wood, at the bottom of the yard. The left arm was placed across the left breast. The legs were drawn up, the feet resting on the ground, and the knees turned outwards. The face was swollen and turned on the right side. The tongue protruded between the front teeth, but not beyond the lips. The tongue was evidently much swollen. The front teeth were perfect, so far as the first molar, top and bottom, and very fine teeth they were. The body was terribly mutilated. He searched the yard, and in doing so found a small piece of coarse muslin and a pocket comb in a paper case lying at the feet of the woman near the paling; and they apparently had been placed there in order or arranged there. He also found and delivered to the police other articles, including the leather apron. The stiffness of the limbs was not marked, but was evidently commencing. He noticed that the throat was dissevered deeply; that the incisions through the skin were jagged, and reached right round the neck. On the back wall of the house, between the steps and the paling which bounded the yard on the left side, about 18 in. from the ground, were about six patches of blood, varying in size from a sixpenny piece to a small point. On the wooden paling, between the yard in question, and the next, smears of blood, corresponding to where the head of the deceased lay, were to be seen. These were about 14 in. from the ground, and immediately above the part where the blood lay that had flowed from the neck. Soon after 2 o'clock on Saturday he went to the labour yard of the Whitechapel Union for the purpose of further examining the body. He was surprised to find that the body had been stripped, and was lying ready on the table for his examination. It was under great difficulty he could make his examination, and, as on many occasions he had met with similar difficulties, he now raised his protest as he had previously done that members in his profession should be called upon to perform their duties in these inadequate circumstances. There were no adequate conveniences for a post-mortem examination; and at particular seasons of the year it was dangerous to the operator.

The CORONER. – As a matter of fact there is no public mortuary in the City of London up to Bow.

Witness, continuing, said, – The body had evidently been attended to since the removal to the mortuary, probably to be washed. He noticed the same protrusion of the tongue. There was a bruise over the right temple. On the upper eyelid there was a bruise, and there were two distinct bruises, each of the size of the top of a man's thumb, on the forepart of the top of the chest. The stiffness of the limbs was now well marked. There was a bruise over the middle part of the bone of the right hand. There was an old scar on the left side of the frontal bone. The stiffness was more noticeable on the left side, especially in the fingers, which were partly closed. There was an abrasion over the ring finger, with distinct markings of a ring or rings. The throat had been severed as before described. The incisions into the skin indicated that they had been made from the left side of the neck. There were two distinct, clean cuts on the left side of the spine. They were parallel from each other and separated by about half an inch. The muscular structures appeared as though an attempt had been made to separate the bones of the neck. There were various other mutilations of the body, but he was of opinion that they occurred subsequent to the death of the woman, and to the large escape of blood from the division of the neck. At this point Dr. Phillips said that, as from these injuries he was satisfied as to the cause of death, he thought that he had better not go into further details of the mutilations, which could only be painful to the feelings of the jury and the public. The Coroner decided to allow that course to be adopted. Witness, continuing, said, – The cause of death was visible from the injuries he had described. From these appearances he was of opinion that the breathing was interfered with previous to death, and that death arose from syncope, or failure of the heart's action in consequence of loss of blood caused by the severance of the throat.

By the CORONER. – He should say that the instrument used at the throat and the abdomen was the same. It must have been a very sharp knife, with a thin, narrow blade, and must have been at least 6 in. to 8 in. in length, probably longer. He should say that the injuries could not have been inflicted by a bayonet or sword bayonet. They could have been done by such an instrument as a medical man used for post-mortem purposes, but the ordinary surgical cases might not contain such an instrument. Those used by slaughter-men, well ground down, might have caused them. He thought the knives used by those in the leather trade would not be long enough in the blade. There were indications of anatomical knowledge, which were only less indicated in consequence of haste. The whole of the body was not present, the absent portions being from the abdomen. The mode in which these portions were extracted showed some anatomical knowledge. He did not think these portions were lost in the transit of the body. He should say that the deceased had been dead at least two hours, and probably more, when he first saw her; but it was right to mention that it was a fairly cool morning, and that the body would be more apt to cool rapidly from its having lost a great quantity of blood. There was no evidence about the body of the woman of a struggle having taken place. He was positive that the deceased entered the yard alive. He made a practical search of the passage and the approach to the house and he saw no trace of blood. There was no blood on the apron, which had the appearance of not having been recently unfolded. He was shown some staining on the wall of No. 25. To the eye of a novice it looked like blood, but it was not so. The deceased was far advanced in disease of the lungs and membranes of the brain, but they had nothing to do with the cause of death. The stomach contained a little food, but there was not any sign of fluid. There was no appearance of the deceased having taken alcohol, but there were signs of great deprivation, and he should say she had been badly fed. He was convinced she had not taken any strong alcohol for some hours before her death. The injuries were certainly not self-inflicted. The bruises on the face were evidently recent, especially about the chin and the sides of the jaw, but the bruises in front of the chest and temple were of longer standing – probably of days. He was of opinion that the person who cut the deceased's throat took hold of her by the chin, and then commenced the incision from left to right. He thought it was highly probable that a person could call out, but with regard to an idea that she might have been gagged he could only point to the swollen face and protruding tongue, both of which were signs of suffocation. The handkerchief produced, together with the pocket, he separated from the rest of some articles said to be taken from the body of deceased at the Whitechapel mortuary, and not then in the custody of the mortuary keeper. A handkerchief was round the throat of the deceased when he saw her early in the morning. He should say it was not tied on after the throat was cut.

Mary Elizabeth Simonds, nurse at the Whitechapel Infirmary, said on Saturday morning she and a nurse named Frances Wright were instructed to go to the mortuary. The body was lying on the ambulance. They were directed by Inspector Chandler to undress the deceased. Witness took the clothes off and placed them in a corner of the shed. They left the handkerchief round the neck of deceased. They washed the blood off the body. There was blood on the chest, as if it had run down from the throat. She found the pocket, the strings of which were not broken.

Inspector Chandler stated he did not instruct the nurses to undress and wash the body.

The Coroner's officer said it was done by order of the clerk to the guardians.

At this point the inquiry was adjourned until Wednesday next.

The Times of the same day [Friday, 14 September 1888, page 4f] also reported:

Up to the present time the police have not succeeded in connecting any person with the crime.

Dr. Phillips's positive opinion that the woman had been dead quite two hours when he first saw the body at half-past 6, throws serious doubt upon the accuracy of at least two important witnesses, and considerably adds to the prevailing confusion.

The man arrested at Holloway [Isenschmid] has for some reason been removed to the asylum at Bow. His own friends give him an indifferent character. He has been missing from home for nearly two months, and it is known that he has been in the habit of carrying several large butcher's knives about his person. Inquiries are now being made with a view to tracing his movements during the past two months.

The principal officers engaged in investigating the Whitechapel murders were summoned to Scotland-yard yesterday. Later in the day Mr. Bruce, Assistant Commissioner, and Colonel Monsell, Chief Constable, paid a private visit to the Whitechapel district without notifying the local officials of their intention to do so. They visited the scene of the Buck's-row murders as well as Hanbury-street, and made many inquiries. They spent nearly a quarter of an hour at No. 29, Hanbury-street, and minutely inspected the house and the yard in which were found the mutilated body of Mrs. Chapman.

The police have satisfied themselves that the man Piggott could have had nothing to do with the murders. His movements have been fully accounted for, and he is no longer under surveillance.

The *Lancet* says: – "The theory that the succession of murders which have lately been committed in Whitechapel are the work of a lunatic appears to us to be by no means at present well established. We can quite understand the necessity for any murderer endeavouring to obliterate by the death of his victim his future identification as a burglar. Moreover, as far as we are aware, homicidal mania is generally characterised by the one single and fatal act, although we grant this may have been led up to by a deep-rooted series of delusions. It is most unusual for a lunatic to plan any complicated crime of this kind. Neither, as a rule, does a lunatic take precautions to escape from the consequences of his act; which *data* are most conspicuous in these now too celebrated cases."

The police-courts column of the same paper carried the following reports, the first reflecting the excitement produced by the murders in the minds of some, the second concerning a murderous cut-throat attack by a disturbed father on his daughter, and the third about the detention of a prisoner by Inspector Andrews who would later convey that prisoner to Canada and then pursue enquiries for a "Ripper" suspect in New York:

At the THAMES Police-court, a Japanese, named SOPIWAJAN, 38, was charged with cutting and wounding Ellen Norton, 9, Jamaica-passage, Limehouse. Prosecutrix, whose head was bandaged, said about 12 o'clock on Wednesday night [12 September] she was in the Coach and Horses beershop, West India Dock-road, when she heard screams close by the Strangers' Home. She went out and saw the accused in the act of stabbing her friend, Emily Shepherd. Witness rushed forward and received the knife stab in her head. She then remembered no more until she was at the station, having her head dressed by a doctor. Witness had been drinking, but had not been in the prisoner's company. Emily Shepherd said the prisoner came up to her and said to her, "If you go away from me to-night I will rip you up the same as the woman was served in the White-chapel-road." She screamed out, when the prosecutrix ran up. The accused then stabbed Norton in the head with the long-bladed knife produced. He then kicked witness, and afterwards broke a plate glass window at the Strangers' Home. Constable 448K said he heard screams of "Police" and "Murder," and on going towards the spot he saw the prisoner jump through the glass panel of the door of the Asiatic Home. He gained admission to the Home, and found prisoner in the yard washing blood off his hands. Witness took him into custody. Sergeant Brown, 2K, produced the knife, which was covered with blood. Mr. Lushington committed the prisoner for trial.

At LAMBETH, THOMAS JAMES UBERFIELD, 63, described as a tailor, living at 268, Kennington-road, was charged with attempting to murder his daughter, Jane Uberfield, by cutting her throat. Police-constable Hutchins, 18 L, stated that at 9 o'clock that morning [13 September] he was called to the house, and saw the prisoner on the first floor landing. He had only his trousers and shirt on. He was greatly excited, and upon witness asking what was the matter, he said, "I've cut my daughter's throat: I don't know what possessed me to do so." Witness had not been long there before Dr. Farr arrived and attended to the injured girl. Witness detained prisoner, and afterwards removed him to the Kennington-road Police-station. He was charged with attempting to murder his daughter. Dr. Frederick William Farr, of Kennington-road, said he knew the prisoner as a patient for nearly 18 months. He had been of unsound mind for some time. His delusion was chiefly that he had animals crawling about inside him. Instruction was given to watch him. He had never shown symptoms to suppose he would do injury to anybody. He found the injured girl seated in a chair in an upstairs room. She was bleeding very much from an incised wound on the throat about two and three-quarter inches in length and about half an inch deep in the deepest part. He thought she was likely to recover, and she was now lying at home. Mr. Chance ordered a remand, and said it was a sad affair, and no doubt the result of a sudden fit of insanity.

At WANDSWORTH, ROLAND GIDEON ISRAEL BARNETT, who described himself as a theatrical manager of Craven-street, Strand, was re-examined on the charge of obtaining a sum of £45 from Henry Charles Britton, a butcher, of Tooting, with intent to defraud, the offence having, it was alleged, been committed in 1878. Mr. Pollard appeared to prosecute on behalf of the Solicitor to the Treasury; and Mr. Poland defended the accused. Mr. Pollard asked the magistrate to deal with the case on the evidence already before him, and said the only additional witnesses he could call were the clerk of the bank on which the particular cheque in question was drawn and Inspector Andrews, of the Criminal Investigation Department, by whom the accused was arrested. Mr. Plowden said he had had an opportunity of reading the information on which the warrant was granted, and unless it could be supplemented by additional evidence he would take upon himself the responsibility of discharging the prisoner, believing that no jury would convict. Mr. Pollard thought it right to tell the magistrate that he had no additional evidence. Mr. Plowden then discharged the prisoner, observing that he would be required to clear himself of another charge of a more serious character. The prisoner then left the dock, but was re-arrested by Inspector Andrews on an extradition warrant, charging him with obtaining money from certain persons in Toronto by false representations.

The Times of Saturday, 15 September 1888 [page 6a] carried further information on the hunt for the Whitechapel murderer:

THE WHITECHAPEL MURDERS.

The police at the Commercial-street Police Station have made another arrest on suspicion in connexion with the recent murders. It appears that among the numerous statements and descriptions of suspected persons are several tallying with that of the man in custody, but beyond this the police know nothing at present against him. His apprehension was of a singular character. Throughout yesterday his movements are stated to have created suspicion among various persons, and last night he was handed over to a uniform constable doing duty in the neighbourhood of Flower and Dean-street on suspicion in connexion with the crime. On his arrival at the police station in Commercial-street the detective officers and Mr. Abberline were communicated with, and an inquiry concerning him was at once opened. On being searched perhaps one of the most extraordinary accumulation of articles were discovered – a heap of rags, comprising pieces of dress fabrics, old and dirty linen, two purses of a kind usually used by women, two or three pocket handkerchiefs, one a comparatively clean white one, and a white one with a red spotted border; two small tin boxes, a small cardboard box, a small leather strap, which might serve the purpose of a garterstring, and one spring onion. The person to whom this curious assortment belongs is slightly built, about 5 ft. 7 in. or 5 ft. 8 in. in height, and dressed shabbily. He has a very careworn look. Covering a head of hair, inclined somewhat to be sandy, with beard and moustache to match, was a cloth skull cap, which did not improve his appearance. Suspicion is the sole motive for his temporary detention, for the police, although making every possible inquiry about him, do not believe his apprehension to be of any importance.

Regarding the man Pigott, who was captured at Gravesend, nothing whatever has been discovered by the detectives in the course of their inquiries which can in any way connect him with the crime or crimes, and his release, at all events, from the custody of the police is expected shortly.

In connexion with the arrest of a lunatic at Holloway, it appears that he has been missing from his friends for some time now. The detectives have been very active in prosecuting their inquiries concerning him, and it is believed the result, so far, increases their suspicion. He is at present confined in the asylum at Grove-road, Bow.

All inquiries have failed to elicit anything as to the whereabouts of the missing pensioner who is wanted in connexion with the recent murder.

On the question as to the time when the crime was committed, concerning which there was a difference between the evidence of the man Richardson and the opinion of Dr. Phillips, a correspondent yesterday elicited that Mr. Cadoche [*sic*], who lives in the next house to No. 29, Hanbury-street, where the murder was committed, went to the back of the premises at half-past 5 a.m. As he passed the wooden partition he heard a woman say "No, no." On returning he heard a scuffle and then some one fell heavily against the fence. He heard no cry for help, and so he went into his house. Some surprise is felt that this statement was not made in evidence at the inquest. There is a very strong feeling in the district and large numbers of persons continue to visit the locality.

Annie Chapman, the victim of the crime, was buried early yesterday morning at Manor Park Cemetery. Some of her relatives attended the funeral.

The Times of Wednesday, 19 September 1888, page 3 f, detailed the continuing story of the investigations into the murders:

THE WHITECHAPEL MURDERS.

Several reports were current in London yesterday as to discoveries by the police in connexion with the Hanbury-street murder; but the value of the clues said to have been obtained is extremely doubtful. One statement is to the effect that on the day of the murder a man changed his clothes in the lavatory of the City News Rooms, Ludgate-circus, and left hurriedly, leaving behind him a shirt, a pair of trousers, and a pair of socks. The attendant threw the discarded clothes into the dustbin, and they were carted off in the City Sewers cart on the following Monday. The police are said to be endeavouring to trace these clothes, but decline to give information on the subject. It is obviously difficult to conceive why the murderer, having possessed himself of a change of clothes, should pass from Whitechapel to Ludgate-circus and change his dress in a *quasi*-public place such as the City News Rooms. The police, however, will thoroughly sift the matter.

Charles Ludwig, the German charged yesterday at the Thames Police-court with being drunk and threatening to stab, was at once connected by popular imagination with the murder. Our police report will show that some of the circumstances of the case seem to support such a hypothesis. The youth who was threatened early yesterday morning stated to a correspondent that the first he saw of Ludwig, as he calls him, was about a quarter to 4 o'clock. The prisoner was then at the top of Commercial-street, in company with a woman, whom he was conducting in the direction of the Minories. "I took no notice of this at the time," added the witness, "except to make a remark to a coffee-stall keeper. In about a quarter of an hour the woman ran back in a state of fright, as it seemed. At any rate she was screaming and exclaiming, 'You can't do that to me.' Again I thought little of it, as I only fancied she had had some drink, but within five minutes the prisoner came up and asked for a cup of coffee at the stall where I was standing. He, at all events, was drunk, and would only produce a halfpenny in payment for the coffee which was given him. I supposed he noticed me looking at him, for he suddenly turned round and asked in broken English, 'What are you looking at?' I replied that I was doing no harm, but he said, 'Oh, you want something,' and pulled out a long penknife, with which he made a dash at me. I eluded him and snatched from the stall a dish, which I prepared to throw at his head, but as he retreated after making the first dash I only called to a policeman who was near by and had him arrested. He is slightly built, and perhaps about 5 ft. 6 in. in height, dark complexioned, and wearing a grizzled beard and moustache. I should think he is about 40 years of age. There is something the matter with one of his legs, and he walks stiffly. I heard that at the police-court this morning he pretended not to understand English, but his English when he addressed me was plain enough, though broken; and besides, when the officer who had him in charge told me on the way to Leman-street to see that he did not throw anything away, he at once dropped the penknife – which had till then been in his possession – as if the idea of getting rid of it had only just occurred to him. I have never seen him before.'' Ludwig entered the employment of Mr. C. A. Partridge, hairdresser, the Minories, a fortnight ago last Saturday. On Monday night last he went to an hotel in Finsbury, where he had previously lodged, and remained there until about 1 o'clock in the morning. He produced a number of razors, and acted in such a manner that some of the inmates were quite frightened. The landlady of this hotel states that on the day after the last murder in Whitechapel Ludwig called early in the morning and washed his hands, stating that he had been injured. Another person has alleged that there was blood on the man's hands, but as to this the landlady cannot speak.

In the same issue of *The Times* a letter[5] from the Rev. Samuel A. Barnett, the vicar of St. Jude's, appeared. This is particularly interesting as he lived at the heart of the area in which the murders were being committed, and it gives an interesting insight into the social conditions prevailing in the area:

AT LAST.
TO THE EDITOR OF THE TIMES.

Sir, – Whitechapel horrors will not be in vain if ''at last'' the public conscience awakes to consider the life which these horrors reveal. The murders were, it may almost be said, bound to come; generation could not follow generation in lawless intercourse, children could not be familiarized with scenes of degradation, community in crime could not be the bond of society and the end of all be peace.

Some of us who, during many years, have known the life of our neighbours do not think the murders to be the worst fact in our experience, and published evidence now gives material for forming a picture of daily or nightly life such as no one has imagined.

It is for those who, like ourselves, have for years known these things to be ready with practical suggestions, and I would now put some forward as the best outcome of the thought of my wife and myself. Before doing so, it is necessary to remind the public that these criminal haunts are of limited extent. The greater part of Whitechapel is as orderly as any part of London, and the life of most of its inhabitants is more moral than that of many whose vices are hidden by greater wealth. Within the area of a quarter of a mile most of the evil may be found concentrated, and it ought not to be impossible to deal with it strongly and adequately. We would submit four practical suggestions:–

1. Efficient police supervision. In criminal haunts a licence has been allowed which would not be endured in other quarters. Rows, fights, and thefts have been permitted, while the police have only been able to keep the main thoroughfares quiet for the passage of respectable people. The Home Office has never authorized the employment of a sufficient force to keep decent order inside the criminal quarters.

2. Adequate lighting and cleaning. It is no blame to our local authority that the back streets are gloomy and ill-cleaned. A penny rate here produces but a small sum, and the ratepayers are often poor. Without doubt, though, dark passages lend themselves to evil deeds. It would not be unwise, and it certainly would be a humane outlay, if some of the unproductive expenditure of the rich were used to make the streets of the poor as light and as clean as the streets of the City.

3. The removal of the slaughter-houses. At present animals are daily slaughtered in the midst of Whitechapel, the butchers with their blood stains are familiar among the street passengers, and sights are common which tend to brutalize ignorant natures. For the sake of both health and morals the slaughtering should be done outside the town.

4. The control of tenement houses by responsible landlords. At present there is lease under lease, and the acting landlord is probably one who encourages vice to pay his rent. Vice can afford to pay more than honesty, but its profits at last go to landlords. If rich men would come forward and buy up this bad property they might not secure great interest, but they would clear away evil not again to be suffered to accumulate. Such properties have been bought with results morally most satisfactory and economically not unsatisfactory. Some of that which

remains might now be bought, some of the worst is at present in the market, and I should be glad, indeed, to hear of purchasers. Far be it from any one to say that even such radical changes as these would do away with evil. When, however, such changes have been effected it will be more possible to develop character, and one by one lead the people to face their highest. Only personal service, the care of the individual by individual, can be powerful to keep down evil, and only the knowledge of God is sufficient to give the individual faith to work and see little result of his work. For men and women who will give such service there is a crying demand. I am, truly yours,

SAMUEL A. BARNETT.

St. Jude's Vicarage, Whitechapel, Sept. 18.

Another letter in the same column indicated the close public interest in the reports of the coroner's inquest, and the feeling by some that they were too lengthy and revealing:

TO THE EDITOR OF THE TIMES.

Sir, – Is it not time that the inquest on Annie Chapman should close, and a verdict of "Wilful Murder against some person or persons unknown" be given?

The question which the jury are soon to determine – viz., how, when, and where the deceased met with her death, and who she was – is virtually solved.

The discovery of the murderer or murderers is the duty of the police, and if it is to be accomplished it is not desirable that the information they obtain should be announced publicly in the newspapers day by day through the medium of the coroner's inquiry.

J.P.

This would seem to be a criticism of coroner Wynne Baxter's lengthy and revealing enquiries, which many thought gave away too much of the information the police were working on, and is one of the few press statements fully supporting the police viewpoint. Perhaps the initials "J.P" indicate Justice of the Peace, and that the writer was a magistrate supporting the police.

The next extract[6] from *The Times* is dated 20 September 1888, page 3, and refers to the resumed inquest:

THE WHITECHAPEL MURDER.

Yesterday Mr. Wynne E. Baxter, Coroner for the South-Eastern Division of Middlesex, resumed his inquiry, at the Working Lads' Institute, Whitechapel-road, respecting the death of Annie Chapman, who was found murdered in the back yard of No. 29, Hanbury-street, Spitalfields, on the morning of the 8th inst.

Detective-inspectors Helson and Chandler and Detective-sergeant Thicke [*sic*], H Division, watched the case on behalf of the Criminal Investigation Department.

Eliza Cooper stated that she lived at 35, Dorset-street, Spitalfields, and had done so for the last five months. Witness knew the deceased, and had a quarrel with her on the Tuesday before she was murdered. On the previous Saturday deceased came in and asked the people there to give her a piece of soap. She was told to ask "Liza". Deceased then came to witness, who opened the locker and gave her a piece of soap. Deceased then handed the soap to Stanley, who went and washed himself. Deceased also went out, and when she came back witness asked her for the soap, which, however, she did not return, but said "I will see you by and by". Stanley gave deceased 2 s., and she paid for the bed for two nights. Witness saw no more of deceased that night.

By the CORONER. – Witness was treated by Stanley. On the following Wednesday witness met deceased in the kitchen and asked her to return the piece of soap. Deceased threw a halfpenny on the table and said "Go and get a halfpennyworth of soap." They then began to quarrel, and afterwards went to the Ringers public-house, where the quarrel was continued. Deceased slapped her face and said "Think yourself lucky I did not do more." Witness believed she then struck deceased in the left eye and then on the chest. She could afterwards see that the blow had marked deceased's face.

By the jury. – That was the last time she saw deceased alive. At that time she was wearing three rings on the third finger of the left hand. Deceased bought the rings, which were brass ones, of a black man. Deceased had never possessed a gold wedding ring since witness had become acquainted with her. She had known deceased for about 15 years, and knew that she associated with "Harry the Hawker", and other men. Witness could not say whether any of these persons were missing. With the exception of Stanley, deceased used only casually to bring other men to the lodging-house.

Dr. George Bagster Phillips was recalled. Before he was examined.

The CORONER said it was necessary that all the evidence the doctor had obtained from his post-mortem examination should be on the records of the Court for various reasons which he need not then enumerate, however painful it might be.

Dr. Phillips said that had notice been given him he should have been better prepared with the evidence, but he had his original notes with him. While bowing to the Coroner's decision, he still thought it a great pity that he should have to give this evidence, as matters which had since come to light had shown the wisdom of the course pursued on the last occasion, and he could not help reiterating his regret that the Coroner had come to a different conclusion. On the last occasion he mentioned that there were reasons why he thought that the person who inflicted the cut on the woman's throat had caught hold of her chin. He came to that conclusion because on the left side, on the lower jaw, were scratches one and a half to two inches below the lobe of the ear, and going in a contrary direction to the incision in the throat. They were of recent date. The abrasions on the left side and on the right side were corresponding bruises. He washed them, when they became more distinct, whereas the bruises mentioned in his last evidence remained the same. The deceased had been seized by the throat while the incisions into the throat had been perpetrated. The witness here stated that in the interests of justice he thought it would be better not to give more details.

The CORONER. – We are here to decide the cause of death, and therefore have a right to hear all particulars. Whether that evidence is made public or not rests with the Press. I might add I have never before heard of any evidence being kept back from a coroner.

Dr. Phillips. – I am in the hands of the Court, and what I was going to detail took place after death.

The CORONER. – That is a matter of opinion. You know that medical men often differ.

Dr. Phillips repeated that he did not think the details should be given.

The court having been cleared of all women and boys, the witness proceeded to give medical and surgical evidence, totally unfit for publication, of the deliberate, successful, and apparently scientific manner in which the poor woman had been mutilated, and expressed his opinion that the length of the weapon was at least five to six inches, probably more, and the appearance of the cuts confirmed him in the opinion that the instrument, like the one which divided the neck, had been of a very sharp character. The mode in which the knife had been used seemed to indicate great anatomical knowledge.

By the CORONER. – He thought he himself could not have performed all the injuries he described, even without a struggle, under a quarter of an hour. If he had done it in a deliberate way such as would fall to the duties of a surgeon, it probably would have taken him the best part of an hour. He had not been able to discover any trace of blood on the walls of the next house.

In answer to the jury, the witness said that he had no practical opinion about a person's eyes being photographed, but his opinion would be useless; also with regard to employing bloodhounds. In the latter case they would more probably scent the blood of the murdered woman. The injuries to the body would produce at once partial insensibility.

Elizabeth Long 198, Church-row, Whitechapel, stated that she was the wife of James Long, a park-keeper. On Saturday morning the 8th inst., she was passing down Hanbury-street from home and going to Spitalfields Market. It was about 5 30. She was certain of the time, as the brewers' clock had just struck that time when she passed 29, Hanbury-street. Witness was on the right-hand side of the street – the same side as No. 29. She saw a man and woman on the pavement talking. The man's back was turned towards Brick-lane, while the woman's was towards the Spitalfields Market. They were talking together, and were close against the shutters of No. 29. Witness saw the woman's face. She had since seen the deceased in the mortuary, and was sure it was the face of the same person she saw in Hanbury-street. She did not see the man's face, except to notice that he was dark. He wore a brown deerstalker hat, and she thought he had on a dark coat, but was not quite certain of that. She could not say what the age of the man was, but he looked to be over 40, and appeared to be a little taller than deceased. he appeared to be a foreigner, and had a shabby genteel appearance. Witness could hear them talking loudly, and she overheard him say to deceased, "Will you?" She replied, "Yes." They still stood there as witness passed, and she went on to her work without looking back.

By the CORONER. – She saw nothing to indicate they were not sober. It was not an unusual thing to see men and women talking together at that hour in that locality.

The Foreman remarked that the time stated by the witness was not consistent with that stated by the doctor.

The CORONER observed that Dr. Phillips had since qualified his statement.

Edward Stanley stated that he lived at 1, Osborne-street, Whitechapel. He was a brick-layer's labourer, and was known by the name of "The Pensioner." He knew the deceased, and he sometimes visited her at 35, Dorset-street. He was not there with her more than once or twice, but had been elsewhere with her at times. He last saw her alive on Sunday, the 2d inst., between 1 and 3 o'clock in the afternoon. At that time she was wearing two rings on one of her fingers. One was a flat ring and the other oval. He should think they were brass ones. Witness did not know of any one with whom deceased was on bad terms.

By the CORONER. – When he last saw deceased her eye was slightly blackened. His memory might be confused, and it was possible he might have seen deceased after the time he had stated, for when he did see her she certainly had a black eye, and spoke to him about it.

The Foreman – A previous witness stated that the blows were not inflicted on deceased's face until the Tuesday.

In answer to the jury, the witness denied that he was in the habit of spending Saturdays and Sundays with the deceased.

The CORONER. – Are you a pensioner?

Witness. – Am I bound to answer this question?

The CORONER. – You have to answer all questions affecting this case that are put to you.

Witness. – I am not a pensioner, and have not been in the Essex Regiment. What I say will be published all over Europe. I have lost five hours in coming here.

The deputy of 35, Dorset-street, was here called into the room and said Stanley was the person they called "The Pensioner." He was the man who used to come to the lodging-house with the deceased on Saturday and stay till the Monday. Stanley had been to the lodging-house six or seven times. The last time he was there was the Saturday before the woman's death, and he stayed till the Monday. Stanley paid for one night, and deceased afterwards paid for Sunday night.

The CORONER. – What do you think of that, Stanley?

Stanley. – The evidence given by Donovan is incorrect. When you talk to me, Sir, you talk to an honest man. I was at Gosport from the 6th of August up to the 1st of September. The deceased met me at the corner of Brushfield-street that night.

The Foreman. – Did you see any quarrel?

Witness. – I saw no quarrel, only the effects of it. I have known the deceased about two years, when she was living at Windsor. I was told by a shoeblack that deceased had been murdered, and I then went to the lodging-house and inquired whether it was correct. After I saw the Coroner's observations in the newspapers, I went to the Commercial-street Police-station.

In further examination the witness said he was told the police wanted him.

The CORONER thought the lodging-house keeper had made a mistake in the man.

Albert Cadosch a carpenter, stated that he resided at No. 27, Hanbury-street. That was next door to No. 29. On Saturday, the 8th inst. he got up at about 5.15 and went out into the yard of his house. As he returned across the yard, to the back door of his house, he heard a voice say quite close to him, "No." He believed it came from No. 29. He went into the house, and returned to the yard three or four minutes afterwards. He then heard a sort of a fall against the fence, which divided his yard from No. 29. Something seemed suddenly to touch the fence. He did not look to see what it was. He did not hear any other noise.

By the CORONER. – He did not hear the rustling of any clothes. Witness then left the house and went to his work. When he passed Spitalfields Church it was about 32 minutes past 5. He did not hear people in the yard as a rule, but had now and then heard them at that time in the morning.

By the jury. – He did not go into the yard twice out of curiosity. He had been under an operation at the hospital. He informed the police the same day of what he had heard. The palings were about 5 ft. 6 in. in height. He had not the curiosity to look over the fence, as at times the next door people were early risers. When he left the house he did not see any man or woman in Hanbury-street. He did not see Mrs. Long.

William Stevens, a painter, of 35, Dorset-street, deposed that he knew the deceased, whom he last saw alive about 12 minutes past 12 on the early morning of her death. She was then in the kitchen of the lodging-house, and was not the worse for drink. At that time she had rings on her fingers. Witness believed the piece of envelope produced was the one he saw deceased pick up by the fireplace. He noticed it was about the size of the piece produced, and he saw it had a red post mark on it. Deceased then pulled out a box containing pills from her pocket, and the box breaking she put the pills into the piece of paper, and put it into her pocket. He saw deceased leave the kitchen, and thought she was going to bed, as she said she would not be long out of bed.

By the CORONER. – He did not know of any one with whom the deceased was on bad terms.

The CORONER said that was all the evidence forthcoming. It was a question for the jury whether they would adjourn the case or return their verdict.

The Foreman stated that the reward of Mr. S. Montagu, M.P., of £100 had been posted about, but the Government did not, as the Coroner had previously stated, now offer rewards. At the same time, if the Government had offered a reward, it would have looked more official.

After some further conversation, the inquiry was adjourned until Wednesday next, when it will be completed.

No further arrest in connexion with the Whitechapel murders had been made up to last night, [19 September], and the police are still at fault.

The following letter has been sent to the secretary of the Vigilance Committee lately formed in Mile-end: –

"Whitehall, Sept. 17, 1888.

"Sir, – I am directed by the Secretary of State to acknowledge the receipt of your letter of the 16th inst. with reference to the question of the offer of a reward for the discovery of the perpetrators of the recent murders in Whitechapel, and I am to inform you that had the Secretary of State considered the case a proper one for the offer of a reward he would at once have offered one on behalf of the Government; but that the practice of offering rewards for the discovery of criminals was discontinued some years ago because experience showed that such offers of reward tended to produce more harm than good; and the Secretary of State is satisfied that there is nothing in the circumstances of the present case to justify a departure from this rule.

"I am, Sir, your obedient servant,
E. LEIGH PEMBERTON.

"Mr. B. Harris, The Crown, 74, Mile-end-road, E."

Home Secretary Matthews, apparently stung by the increasing criticism of the lack of success on the part of the police, and the two-week absence of Anderson, sent a memo[7], dated 22 September 1888, to his Principal Private Secretary, Evelyn Ruggles-Brise:

"Stimulate the Police about Whitechapel murders. *Absente* Anderson, Monro might be willing to give a hint to the C.I.D. people if needful."

This indicates Matthews's dissatisfaction with the CID and his obvious feeling that they should be under the guidance of their old chief, Monro.

The final day of the lengthy inquest on the murder of Annie Chapman was 26 September 1888. The proceedings were reported in *The Times* of Thursday, 27 September 1888 and, all the evidence having been heard, an account[8] was given of Mr Wynne Baxter's summing-up and views on the enquiry:

THE WHITECHAPEL MURDER.

Yesterday afternoon Mr. Wynne E. Baxter, the coroner for the South-Eastern Division of Middlesex, resumed his adjourned inquiry at the Working Lads' Institute, Whitechapel, respecting the death of Annie Chapman, aged 47, a widow, who was found brutally murdered in the back yard of 29, Hanbury-street, Whitechapel, on the early morning of Saturday the 8th inst.

Inspectors Helson, Chandler, and Bannister watched the case on behalf of the Commissioners of Police.

Having been informed there was no further evidence forthcoming,

The CORONER proceeded to sum up. He congratulated the jury that their labours were then nearly completed. Although up to the present they had not resulted in the detection of the criminal, he had no doubt that if the perpetrator of this foul murder were eventually discovered, their efforts would not have been useless. The evidence given was on the records of that Court, and could be used even if the witnesses were not forthcoming; while the publicity given had already elicited further information, which he would later on have to mention, and which he hoped he was not sanguine in believing might perhaps be of the utmost importance. The deceased was a widow, 47 years of age, named Annie Chapman. Her husband was a coachman living at Windsor. For three or four years before his death she had lived apart from her husband, who allowed her 10 s. a week until his death at Christmas, 1886. She had evidently lived an immoral life for some time, and her habits and surroundings had become worse since her means had failed. She no longer visited her relations, and her brother had not seen her for five months, when she borrowed a small sum from him. She lived principally in the common lodginghouses in the neighbourhood of Spitalfields, where such as she herded like cattle. She showed signs of great deprivation, as if she had been badly fed. The glimpse of life in those dens which the evidence in this case disclosed was sufficient to make them feel there was much in the 19th century civilization of which they had small reason to be proud; but the jury, who were constantly called together to hear the sad tale of starvation, or semi-starvation, of misery, immorality, and wickedness which some of the occupants of the 5,000 beds in that district had every week to relate at coroner's inquests, did not require to be reminded of what life in a Spitalfields lodginghouse meant. It was in one of those that the older bruises found on the temple and in front of the chest of the deceased were received, in a trumpery quarrel, a week before her death. It was in one of those that she was seen a few hours before her mangled remains were discovered. On the afternoon and evening of Friday, the 7th of September, she spent her time partly in such a place, at 35, Dorset- street, and partly in the Ringers publichouse, where she spent whatever money she had; so that between 1 and 2 o'clock on the morning of Saturday, when the money for her bed was demanded, she was obliged to admit that she was without means, and at once turned out into the street to find it. She left there at 1.45 a.m. She was seen off the premises by the night watchman, and was observed to turn down Little Paternoster-row into Brushfield-street, and not in the more direct direction of Hanbury-street. On her wedding finger she was wearing two or three rings, which appeared to have been palpably of base metal, and value. They now lost sight of her for about four hours, but at half-past 5 o'clock Mrs. Long was in Hanbury-street, on the way from her home in Church-street, Whitechapel, to Spitalfields Market. She walked on the northern side of the road, going westward, and remembered having seen a man and woman standing a few yards from the place where the deceased was afterwards found, and, although she did not know Annie Chapman, she was positive that the woman was the deceased. The two were talking loudly, but not sufficiently so to arouse her suspicions that there was anything wrong. The words she overheard were not calculated to do so. The laconic inquiry of the man, "Will you?" and the simple assent of the woman, viewed in the light of subsequent events, could be easily translated and explained. Mrs. Long passed on her way, and neither saw nor heard anything more of her, and that was the last time she was known to have been alive. There was some conflict in the evidence about the time at which the deceased was despatched. It was not unusual to find inaccuracy in such details, but that variation was not very great or very important. She was found dead about 6 o'clock. She was not in the yard when Richardson was there at 4.50 a.m. She was talking outside the house at half-past 5, when Mrs. Long passed them. Cadosh [*sic*] said it was about 5.20 when he was in the back yard of the adjoining house and heard a voice say "No," and three or four minutes afterwards a fall against the fence; but if he was out of his reckoning but a quarter of an hour the discrepancy in the evidence of fact vanished; and he might be mistaken, for he admitted that he did not get up until a quarter past 5, and that it was after the half-hour when he passed the Spitalfields clock. It was true that Dr. Phillips thought that when he saw the body at 6.30 the deceased had been dead at least two hours, but he admitted that the coldness of the morning and the great loss of blood might affect his opinion, and if the evidence of the other witnesses was correct, Dr. Phillips had miscalculated the effect of those forces. But many minutes after Mrs. Long passed them could not have elapsed before the deceased became a mutilated corpse in the yard of No. 29, Hanbury-street, close by where she was last seen by any witness. That place was a fair example of a large number of houses in the neighbourhood. It was built, like hundreds of others, for the Spitalfields weavers, and when hand looms were driven out by steam and power they were converted into dwellings for the poor. Its size was about such as a superior artisan would occupy in the country, but its condition was such as would to a certainty leave it without a tenant. In that place 17 persons were living, from a woman and her son, sleeping in a cats' meat shop on the ground floor, to Davis and his wife and their three grown up sons, all sleeping together in an attic. The street door and the yard door were never locked, and the passage and yard appeared to have been constantly used by persons who had no legitimate business there. There was little doubt that deceased knew the place, for it was only 300 or 400 yards from where she lodged. If so, it was unnecessary to assume that her companion had any knowledge – in fact, it was easier to believe that he was ignorant both of the nest of living beings by whom he was surrounded, and of their occupations and habits. Some were on the move late at night, some were up long before the sun. A carman named Thompson left the house as early as 3.50 a.m.; an hour later John Richardson was paying the house a visit of inspection; shortly after 5.15 Cadosh, who lived in the next house, was in the adjoining yard twice. Davis, the carman who occupied the third floor front, heard the church clock strike a quarter to 6, got up, had a cup of tea, and went into the back yard, and was horrified to find the mangled body of the deceased. It was then a little after 6 a.m. – a very little, for at ten minutes past the hour Inspector Chandler had been informed of the discovery while on duty in Commercial-street. There was nothing to suggest that the deceased was not fully conscious of what she was doing. It was true that she had passed through some stages of intoxication, for although she appeared perfectly sober to her friend who met her in Dorset-street at 5 o'clock the previous evening, she had been drinking afterwards; and when she left the lodginghouse shortly after 2 o'clock, the night watchman noticed that she was the worse for drink, but not badly so, while the deputy asserts that, though she had been evidently drinking, she could walk straight, and it was probably only malt liquor that she had taken, and its effects would pass off quicker than if she had taken spirits. The post-mortem examination showed that while the stomach contained a meal of food, there was no sign of fluid and no appearance of her having taken alcohol, and Dr. Phillips was convinced that she had not taken any alcohol for some time. The deceased, therefore, entered the house in full possession of her faculties, although with a very different object to her companion's. From the evidence which the condition of the yard afforded and the medical examination disclosed, it appeared that after the two had passed through the passage and opened the swing door at the end, they descended the three steps into the yard. On their left-hand side there was a recess between those steps and the palings. Here, a few feet from the house and a less distance from the palings, they must have stood. The wretch must have then seized the deceased, perhaps with Judas-like approaches. He seized her by the chin. He pressed her throat, and while thus preventing the slightest cry, he at the same time produced insensibility and suffocation. There was no evidence of any struggle. The clothes were not torn. Even in those preliminaries, the wretch seems to have known how to carry out efficiently his nefarious work. The deceased was then lowered to the ground, and laid on her back; and although in doing so she may have fallen slightly against the fence, the movement was probably effected with care. Her throat was then cut in two places with savage determination, and the injuries to the abdomen commenced. All was done with cool impudence and reckless daring; but perhaps nothing was more noticeable than the emptying of her pockets, and the arrangement of their contents with business-like precision in order near her feet. The murder seemed, like the Buck's-row case, to have been carried out without any cry. None of the occupants of the houses by which the spot was surrounded heard any thing suspicious. The brute who committed the offence did not even take the trouble to cover up his ghastly work, but left the body exposed to the view of the first comer. That accorded but little with the trouble taken with the rings, and suggested either that he had at length been disturbed, or that, as daylight broke, a sudden fear suggested the danger of detection that he was running. There were two things missing. Her rings had been wrenched from her fingers and had not since been found, and the uterus had been taken from the abdomen. The body had not been dissected, but the injuries had been made by some one who had considerable anatomical skill and knowledge. There were no meaningless cuts. The organ had been taken by one who knew where to find it, what difficulties he would have to contend against, and how he should use his knife so as to abstract the organ without injury to it. No unskilled person could have known where to find it or have recognised it when it was found. For instance, no mere slaughterer of animals could have carried out these operations. It must have been some one accustomed to the post mortem room. The conclusion that the desire was to possess the missing abdominal organ seemed overwhelming. If the object were robbery, the injuries to the viscera were meaningless, for death had previously resulted from the loss of blood at the neck. Moreover, when they found an easily accomplished theft of some paltry brass rings and an internal organ taken, after at least a quarter of an hour's work and by a skilled person, they were driven to the deduction that the abstraction of the missing portion of abdominal viscera was the object, and the theft of the rings was only a thin-veiled blind, an attempt to prevent the real intention being discovered. The amount missing would go into a breakfast cup, and had not the medical examination been of a thorough and searching character it might easily have been left unnoticed that there was any portion of the body which had been taken. The difficulty in believing that the purport of the murderer was the possession of the missing abdominal organ was natural. It was abhorrent to their feelings to conclude that a life should be taken for so slight an object; but when rightly considered the reasons for most murders were altogether out of proportion to their guilt. It had been suggested that the criminal was a lunatic with morbid feelings. That might or might not be the case, but the object of the murderer appeared palpably shown by the facts, and it was not necessary to assume lunacy, for it was clear there was a market for the missing organ. To show the jury that, he (the coroner) must mention a fact which at the same time proved the assistance which publicity and the newspaper Press afforded in the detection of crime. Within a few hours of the issue of the morning papers containing a report of the medical evidence given at the last sitting of the Court he received a communication from an officer of one of our great medical schools that they had information which might or might not have a distinct bearing on that inquiry. He attended at the first opportunity, and was informed by the sub-curator of the Pathological Museum that some months ago an American had called on him and asked him to procure a number of specimens of the organ that was missing in the deceased. He stated his willingness to give £20 apiece for each specimen. He stated that his object was to issue an actual specimen with each copy of a publication on which he was then engaged. He was told that his request was impossible to be complied with, but he still urged his request. He wished them preserved, not in spirits of wine, the usual medium, but glycerine, in order to preserve them in a flaccid condition, and he wished them sent to America direct. It was known that this request was repeated to another institution of a similar character. Now was it not possible that the knowledge of this demand might have incited some abandoned wretch to possess himself of a specimen? It seemed beyond belief that such inhuman wickedness could enter in to the mind of any man; but, unfortunately, our criminal annals proved that every crime was possible. He need hardly say that he at once communicated his information to the Detective Department at Scotland-yard. Of course he did not know what use had been made of it, but he believed that publicity might possibly further elucidate this fact, and therefore he had not withheld the information. By means of the Press some further explanation might be forthcoming from America, if not from here. He had endeavoured to suggest to the jury the object with which this crime was committed and the class of person who must have committed it. The greatest deterrent from crime was the conviction that detection and punishment would follow with rapidity and certainty, and it might be that the impunity with which Mary Anne [*sic*] Smith and Ann [*sic*] Tabram were murdered suggested the possibility of such horrid crimes as those which the jury and another jury had been considering. It was therefore a great misfortune that nearly three weeks had already elapsed without the chief actor in this awful tragedy having been discovered. Surely it was not too much even yet to hope that the ingenuity of our detective force would succeed in unearthing this monster. It was not as if there were no clue to the character of the criminal or the cause of his crime. His object was clearly divulged. His anatomical knowledge carried him out of the category of a common criminal, for that knowledge could only have been obtained by assisting at post mortems or by frequenting the post mortem room. Thus the class in which search must be made, although a large one, was limited. In addition to the former description of the man Mrs. Long saw, they should know that he was a foreigner, of dark complexion, over 40 years of age, a little taller than deceased, of shabby genteel appearance, with a brown deerstalker hat on his head and a dark coat on his back. If the jury's views accorded with his, they would be of opinion that they were confronted with a murder of no ordinary character, committed not from jealousy, revenge, or robbery, but from motives less adequate than many which still disgraced our civilization, marred our progress, and blotted the pages of our Christianity.

The jury returned a verdict of "Wilful murder against some person or persons unknown," the Foreman remarking that they were going to add a rider with respect to the mortuary accommodation, but as that had already been done by another jury they would let it stand. The Foreman then said that, as the jury had been there on five occasions, the majority thought they should be excused from further attendance for at least two years.

The CORONER said if possible that would be done.

CHAPTER 6

September 1888 – Dr Anderson on
Sick Leave and the Question of a Reward

The departure of James Monro as Assistant Commissioner in charge of the CID from Scotland Yard is noted in the Metropolitan Police Entry Book[1], 1.9.1888–20.11.1888:

A5085

1 September 1888

Sir,

I am directed by the Secretary of State to inform you that upon the retirement of Mr. Monro on the 31st. ult. Mr. A. Carmichael Bruce becomes one of the Senior Assistant Commissioners of Police and will receive the same salary and allowances from the Police funds as are usually paid to the Senior Assistant Commissioner:- viz

Salary £800
House – Rent £300
Dockyard visits £150
Allowance for working
   telegraph at home. . . . . . . £45.
Allowances for tolls & bailing . .£ 10. 10. 0
                       £1305 10. 0

with one horse, stabling, Keep &c
The Commissioner of Police
   for the Metropolis

The new (Junior) Assistant Commissioner in charge of the Criminal Investigation Department at Scotland Yard was Dr Robert Anderson. He had taken up his post on 1 September 1888, succeeding James Monro. The Home Office Police Entry Book contains a letter[2] referring to Anderson's appointment:

Pressing [1.9.1888]
   Mr. Robert Anderson will from this day's date inclusive be placed in

charge of the Criminal Investigation Department as (Junior) Assistant
Commissioner, and will receive the following salary and allowances:

```
   viz. Salary . . . . . . . . . . . . £800
        House Rent. . . . . . . . . . £300
        Allowance for
        telegraph at home . . . . . . £45
        Allowances for tolls
        & bailing . . . . . . . . . .  £10. 10. 0.
                                       £1155. 10. 0.
```

with one horse, stabling
            & keep.

The whole of the salary and allowances to be paid from the Police
Fund.

I am,
  Sir,
Your obedient Servant,

Anderson's pension record[3] shows that he was "appointed 3rd
Assistant Commissioner of Metropolitan Police, 25 August,
1888 . . ."

There is an interesting letter[4] from Warren to Anderson, dated 28
August 1888, as follows:

Perros Gueru.
Lannion
Cotes du Nord,
France
28 August

Dear Mr. Anderson,

   I expect to return to London about 7 Sept. and I see no reason why
you should not be able to go on leave a day or two after – you do not
say how long you wish to be away – but this will no doubt depend
upon the position of affairs.

   Last year we had a good deal of disturbance in October, and if the
unusual matter we have lately experienced puts men out of work
we may expect a good deal of trouble this winter. – If a month will
be enough to put your throat right I think we can manage it.

Truly yours
Charles Warren

Anderson took up his new post for the first week of September, but on the 8th, under doctor's orders, he left for a month's recuperative holiday in Switzerland. It was the day of Annie Chapman's murder. The CID, at this crucial time, was left without its chief.

A revealing document relevant to the Whitechapel Murders enquiry surfaced in October 1987. It belonged to James Swanson, grandson of Chief Inspector Donald Sutherland Swanson. This document, appointing Swanson to take overall charge of the enquiry and dated 15 September 1888, originated from Sir Charles Warren, but was probably mainly written by a secretary at his dictation. It reads as follows:

<u>A.C. C.I.D.</u>
I am convinced that the Whitechapel Murder case is one which can be successfully grappled with if it is systematically taken in hand. I go so far as to say that I could myself in a few days unravel the mystery provided I could spare the time & give individual attention to it. I feel therefore the utmost importance to be attached to putting the whole Central Office work in this case in the hands of one man who will have nothing else to concern himself with. Neither you or I or Mr. Williamson can do this, I therefore put it in the hands of Chief Inspr. Swanson who must be acquainted with <u>every detail</u>. I look upon him for the time being as the eyes & ears of the Commr. in this particular case.

He must have a room to himself, & every paper, every document, every report every telegram must pass through his hands. He must be consulted on every ["telegram" – *deleted*] subject. I would not send any directions anywhere on the subject of the murder without consulting him. I give him the whole responsibility. On the other hand he should consult Mr. Williamson, you, or myself on every important particular before any action unless there is some extreme urgency.

I find that a most important letter was sent to Divn. yesterday without his seeing it. This is quite an error & should not occur again. <u>All the papers</u> in Central Office on the subject of the murder must be kept in his room & plans of the positions &c.

I must have this matter at once put on a proper footing so as to be a guide for the future in cases of importance.

Everything depends upon a careful compliance with these directions.

[*The following paragraph in Warren's own hand*]

Every document, letter received or telegram on the subject should ["go to" – *deleted*] go to his room before being directed, & he should be responsible for its being directed when necessary. This is [*to*] avoid the possibility of documents being delayed or action retarded.

CW 15.9.88

[*There is marginal annotation at the left margin at the start of the document*: Mr. Williamson Supt Shore & Ch. Insp. Swanson to see. ACB 15.9.88 – Seen 15.9.88 John Shore Supt – Seen AFW 15/9]

The contentious question of a reward was the subject of the next communication[5] with the Home Office and appears under a file cover dated 10 September 1888:

[Stamped: – HOME OFFICE 10 SEP.88 DEPt. No.] No. A49301B/2
DATE Sept 10th/88   Commissioner of Police
REFERENCES, &c.   Encloses copy communica-
tion from Mr. Samuel Montagu M.P. for Whitechapel expressing his desire to offer £100 reward for the discovery and conviction of the murderer or murderers of a woman in Hanbury St. on the 8th inst.
    Requests earliest possible instructions.
[*There is a marginal note against the above* – A36117. First decision of Sir W. Harcourt not to grant rewards.
    V1834. Second case (Middlesborough murder).
    A3800R. Letter to London City Council explaining reasons for change of practice.
    X6551. Sir R.Cross concurs.
    A42607. Question in Hse (Sep 86)]
Very Pressing MINUTES.
    The H.O. rule is against offering rewards: and, even if exceptions to the rule are to be allowed, I think this case is the last in which it should be done.
    It is generally agreed that the Whitechapel murderer has no accomplices who could betray him.

Any person, other than an accomplice, who possesses information, would be certain, in the present state of public feeling, to give it without prospect of reward.

On the other hand the offer of a reward would be almost certain to produce false information.

Even if the case were a proper one for a reward, the M.P. for the district is not the proper person to offer it. Of course SofS. cannot forbid Mr. Montagu to publish the offer, but he can forbid Police to give their authority to it.

?Say that, had the case been considered [*a*] proper one for the offer of a reward, SofS. [*would*] at once have offered one on behalf of the Govt., but the practice of offering rewards was discontinued some years ago because experience showed that in their general effect such offers ["*were*" – *deleted*] produce more harm than good, and the SofS. ["*is & does not*" – *deleted*] thinks the present case one in which there is special risk that the offer of a reward might hinder rather than promote the ends of justice.

Add that the offer of a reward while any person is under arrest on suspicion, is open to special objections. and has ["*never*" – *deleted*] not at any time be [*sic*] allowed.

CET 11.9.88.   I agree

ELP. 11. Sept.88.

Mr. Matthews

H.M.   Wrote accordingly

12 Sept./88   13 Sep: 1888.

The letter[6] from the Assistant Commissioner of Police to the Home Office is annexed, dated 10 September 1888:

Very Pressing   [Stamped: – HOME OFFICE 10 SEP.88 DEPt. No.]

A49301B/2

4 Whitehall Place, S.W.

10th September, 1888

Sir,

The Commissioner of Police of the Metropolis has to acquaint you, for the information of the Secretary of State, that he has received a communication from Mr. Samuel Montagu, M.P. for Whitechapel, expressing his desire to offer a Reward of £100 for the discovery and conviction of the murderer or murderers of a woman in Hanbury Street on the 8th inst.

The Commissioner will be glad to receive the instructions of the Secretary of State in the matter at his earliest convenience, as Mr. Montagu is anxious that no time should be lost.

ELP

I am,

Sir,

Your most obedient Servant,

ACBruce

Assistant Commissioner.

The Under

Secretary of State,

&c. &c. &c.

The letter[7] written by Samuel Montagu, dated 10 September, is as follows:

Sept. 10th 1888

Dear Sir

Feeling keenly the slur cast upon my constabulary by the recent murders & the non discovery of the criminal or criminals I hereby authorise you to print & distribute at my expense posters offering £100 reward for the discovery & conviction of the murderer or murderers, which reward I will pay

Samuel Montagu

Member for Whitechapel

A reply[8] to the police concerning this letter, from the Home Office, is as follows:

A 49354   Pressing   WHITEHALL.

13th September 1888.

Sir,

I am directed by the Secretary of State to acknowledge the receipt of your letter of the 10th instant forwarding copy of a letter from Mr. S. Montagu M.P., in which he offers to pay a Reward of £100 for the discovery and conviction of the murderer or murderers of a woman in Hanbury Street on the 8th instant, and asking for the Secretary of States instructions, and in reply I am to say that, had the case been considered a proper one for the offer of a reward the Secretary of State would at once have offered one on behalf of the Government; but that the practice of offering rewards was discontinued some years ago because experience showed that in their general effect such offers produce more harm than good, and the Secretary of State thinks the present case one in which there is special risk that the offer of a reward might hinder rather than promote the ends of justice.

I am to add that the offer of a reward while any person is under arrest on suspicion is open to special objections and has not at any time been allowed.

I am,

Sir,

The Commissioner
of Metropolitan Police.

Your obedient Servant,
ELeighPemberton.

A letter[9] dated 18 September 1888, from Mr. Montagu to Sir Charles Warren, is worded as follows:

60. Old Broad Street,
London E.C.
Sepr. 18th 1888

Dear Sir Charles,

The letter of the 15 September signed by the Assistant Commissioner and addressed to 12 Kensington Palace Gardens reached me only last night.

The opinion of the Home Secretary that no reward should be offered for the discovery of the perpetrator of the Whitechapel murders is not in accord with the general feeling on the subject. The argument advanced by some that the expectation of a possible increase in the amount of the reward might deter a prompt disclosure could not apply in respect to my offer. Nevertheless had the decision of the Home Secretary been promptly obtained & communicated to me I should not have intervened in the matter.

On Monday the 10th inst about mid-day I made my offer to Inspector West. He stated that he would submit it to you. On the Tuesday he called here & said that the proposal had been submitted to the Home Office & he thought it would be favourably received. I regret that you did not obtain the decision of the Home Secy. at once by telegram, because on Tuesday my proposal must have transpired & was published in the daily papers on Wednesday last.

Under these circumstances it is too late to withdraw my offer & in case information is received, leading to conviction of the murderer or murderers, I must pay the £100. to the person entitled to receive it.

It remains for you to decide whether notices of the reward shall be posted up in Whitechapel by the police at my expense, otherwise I shall not take any further action but await the result of the investigation now pending. I may add that when I made the proposal I was not aware that the Government had ceased to offer rewards in cases of murder.

Col.   Yours very truly
Sir Charles Warren   Saml. Montagu
G.C.M.G.R.E.

A letter[10] from Sir Charles Warren to Mr Montagu, dated 19 September 1888 but endorsed *Not sent by Sir C Warrens directions.* [ ] *20.9.88* reads:

Sepr. 19. 88   <u>Private</u>
Dear Mr. Montagu.
    Your letter was received on 10th Sepr. & submitted to H. Office same day, it was impossible for me to have replied to you on Wednesday 12th as I had not received the reply on that date.
    My letter to you should have been received on Saturday night 15th. and if you will forward to me the envelope with the post marks on it I will ascertain how it was that you did not receive it the Monday night.
    As however you say that your offer must have transpired on Tuesday 11th. ins. I do not see that any subsequent delay affects the matter.
    I have no power to decide whether notices of any reward offered by you should be posted in Whitechapel by police at your expense; the police would not undertake this after the S of S expression of opinion on subject.
    There is no request in your letter of 10th Sepr. for an immediate reply by telegraph, and the Acting Supt. informs me that he told you at the time that he did not think the offer of a reward should be made until result of investigation in case of man then in custody was known.
    I can only regret that you should have thought fit to impute delay to me in a matter entirely outside my control and duties. It was a matter lying entirely between you and the S. of State and if you required an immediate reply you could have telegraphed the Sec of State ["himself" – *deleted*] yourself.
    After the receipt of your letter of Sep. 18th I only regret that I

did not reply to you requesting that you would communicate your wishes to the S of State yourself.

> truly yours
> CWarren

The question of a reward was raised again and is contained in a file cover[11] dated 16 September 1888:

[Stamped: – HOME OFFICE 17 SEP.88 RECEIVED] No. A49301B/3
DATE 16 Sept. 1888   Mr. B.Harris. (Hon. Secy.)
REFERENCES, &c.   The East End Murders. Rewards.
On behalf of a Committee, asks Secy. of State to augment the Fund, which they are about to raise for the discovery of the murderer or murderers, or that he will kindly state his reasons for declining.

> Pressing

MINUTES.
?Say [that, had the ["reward" – *deleted*] SofS. considered the case a proper one for the offer of a reward, he would at once have offered one on behalf of the Govt. but ["? Say" – *deleted*] that the practice of offering rewards for the discovery of criminals was discontinued some years ago, because experience showed that such offers of rewards tended to produce more harm than good] and [the S.ofS. is satisfied that there is nothing in the ["present" – *deleted*] circumstances of this present case to justify a departure from this rule.]

> CET 17.9.88.
> ELP. 17 Sept.88
> Wrote accordingly
> 17.9.88.

A copy[12] of the Home Office letter, dated 17 September 1888, is included:

(Copy)

> Pressing

A 49301/3   Whitehall
                 17th September

1888
Sir,
    I am directed by the Secretary of State to acknowledge the receipt of your letter of the 16th instant with reference to the question of the offer of a Reward for the discovery of the

perpetrators of the recent murders in Whitechapel, and I am to inform you that had the Secretary of State considered the case a proper one for the offer of a reward, he would at once have offered one on behalf of the Government; but that the practice of offering rewards for the discovery of criminals was discontinued some years ago, because experience showed that such offers of rewards tended to produce more harm than good, and the Secretary of State is satisfied that there is nothing in the circumstances of the present case to justify a departure from this rule.

I am,
Sir,
Your obedient Servant,
(sd) E.Leigh Pemberton.

Mr. B. Harris,
    "The Crown"
        74 Mile End Road,
                E.

The letter[13] from Mr. Harris is annexed:

" 'The Crown" A49301B/3
    74 Mile End Rd.
        16/9/8
To the Right Honourable
The Home Secretary
            Whitehall.

Sir

At a meeting of ["the" – *deleted*] a Committee held at the above address, It was resolved to approach you on the subject of the Reward we are about to Issue for the Discovery of the Author, or Authors of the late atrocities in the East End of London & to ask you Sir to Augment our Fund for the said purpose or, kindly state your reasons for Refusing.

Waiting your Reply
I am Sir
Yours Obediently
B. Harris
Hon.Secy.

To The
    Right Hone.
        H. C. Matthews

Reports from the Home Office files now follow, the first a memo[14] by J.S. Sandars, assistant to E.J. Ruggles-Brise, the private secretary to the Home Secretary, Henry Matthews, and dated 19 September 1888, on "Secretary of State Home Department" headed paper:

[*A note in the top left corner of this report states:* Mr.Brise, this ought perhaps to be put with other papers re the Whitechapel Murders. H.M.]

Mr Matthews,

Mr. Ruggles Brise left town on Monday but returned this aftn. I sent on your memo to him to Sir Charles Warren this morning for observations.

Sir Charles came to see me both yesterday & today about the Whitechapel murders, and his note deals with such information as he mentioned as being in the possession of the police. But he remarked to me very strongly upon the great hindrance, which is caused to the efforts of the Police, by the activity of agents of Press Associations & Newspapers. These "touts" follow the detectives wherever they go in search of clues, and then having interviewed persons with whom the police have had conversation and from whom inquiries have made, compile the paragraphs which fill the papers. This practice impedes the usefulness of detective investigation and moreover keeps alive the excitement in the district & elsewhere.

/An irritation I had accepted for the first part of this week has been postponed and I do not leave town until Friday.

J.S.S.

19 Sep '88.

There then follows a report[15] by Sir Charles Warren, dated 19 September 1888:

Mr Ruggles Brise.

In reply to Mr. Matthews note which I return.

No progress has as yet been made in obtaining any definite clue to the Whitechapel murderers. A great number of clues have been examined & exhausted with out finding any thing suspicious.

A large staff of men are employed and every point is being examined which seems to offer our prospect of a discovery.

There are at present three cases of suspicion.

1. The lunatic Isensmith [*sic*], a Swiss arrested at Holloway – who is now in an Asylum at Bow & arrangements are being made to

ascertain whether he is the man who was seen on the morning of the murder in a public house by Mrs. Fiddymont.

2. A man called Puckeridge was released from an asylum on 4 August. He was educated as a Surgeon – has threatened to rip people up with a long knife. He is being looked for but cannot be found as yet.

3. A Brothel Keeper who will not give her address or name writes to say that a man living in her house was seen with blood on him on morning of murder. She described his appearance & said where he might be seen – when the detectives came near him he bolted, got away & there is no clue to the writer of the letter.

All these three cases are being followed up & no doubt will be exhausted in a few days – the first seems a very suspicious case, but the man is at present a violent lunatic.

I will say tomorrow if any thing turns up about him.

Moreover the reporters for the press are following our detectives about everywhere in search of news & cross examine all parties interviewed so that they impede police action greatly – they do not however as yet know of the cases 2 & 3.

CW

The response of the respectable residents and tradesmen of the area was to form the Whitechapel Vigilance Committee and a letter[16] was received by the Home Office, dated 25 September 1888, from this body, as follows (including cover):

DATE 24 Septr. 1888, The Vigilance Committee, (Whitechapel Murders) Requests S. of S. to attend a meeting of the Inhabitants (?of the Vigilance Committee) with respect to the refusal to offer a reward.

MINUTES.

Ackn & say S of S regrets he is unable to attend the Vigilance Committee as proposed by them [ ] 26 Sept 88 [ ] 25.9.88
S of S H.M. 27 Sept./88

Wrote 28/9/88.

―――――――――――――

"The Crown",
74 Mile End Rd,
24 Sepr 1888.

To The Right Honourable
      The Home Secretary.

Sir,

    The Vigilance Committee think it advisable at the receipt of the letter from the Home Secretary wherein he refuses to grant or issue a Reward for the apprehension of the author, or authors, of the Recent Murders in the East of London, to lay his letter before the public at a general meeting of the Inhabitants. Will you Sir, do us the Honour to attend at a time & place convenient to yourself, & give us the Benefit of your advice & counsel.

I am Sir,

Yours Obediently

B. Harris

Hon Sec y

To The Vigilance Committee

To The

Hona. H.C. Matthews

    Home Secretary.

CHAPTER 7

30 September 1888 – Murder of Elizabeth Stride

Three weeks later, in the early hours of Sunday, 30 September 1888, the residents of the East End of London were again terrorized by savage murder committed by an unknown killer. Two victims were to fall in the area in one night, the first being Elizabeth Stride whose throat was savagely cut in Dutfield's Yard, Berner Street, St George's-in-the-East. What is not generally known is that a third woman was murdered by having her throat cut on the same night, shortly before the murder of Stride and only about three miles away. This demonstrates the long arm of coincidence – and the prevalence of domestic murder. In this case the husband gave himself up, so this particular killing is all but forgotten and cannot be added to the Ripper's tally.

The Times of Monday, 1 October 1888, reported[1]:

MURDER IN WESTMINSTER.

A murder was committed in Westminster on Saturday. Shortly before midnight John Brown, a gardener, employed in St. James's-park, asked the police at Rochester-row Police-station to permit him to see the inspector on duty. He was brought before Inspector Fairlie, to whom he stated that he had killed his wife, and that her body would be found at their place in Regency-gardens, Regency-street, near the Horseferry-road. He handed the inspector a large, spring-backed clasp knife, which had blood on it, as also had his clothes. The man was detained, and the police went to the house, where the woman was found lying dead on the floor with her throat cut. Several wounds had been inflicted in the shape of stabs and cuts. The body was seen by a medical man, who pronounced life to be extinct. When charged with the murder Brown declared that he had committed it in consequence of the woman's unfaithfulness. He had been brooding over her misconduct since his return from a convalescent home, to which he had been sent after treatment for an acute illness in Westminster Hospital. The woman is stated to be nearly the age of her husband who is 45. When at the police-station Brown was quite calm and did not appear to have been drinking to excess. But it is said that he has of late been peculiar in his manner. He will be brought up at the Westminster Police-court this morning.

The Times of the following day reported[2] on the hearing. Brown was described as "a man of rather powerful build" and he was charged before the magistrate, Mr Partridge, with the murder of his wife, Sarah. It was stated that ". . . the deceased woman unsuccessfully invoked the assistance of the authorities to put her husband under restraint as a person who was at times unaccountable for his actions and likely to murder her, and that on Saturday night in a state of terror she went to the parochial district medical officer and also expressed her apprehensions to the police." On the arrival of Detective Sergeant Waldock at the address he had found two little boys standing at the door, crying. Brown was their stepfather. A witness, a next-door neighbour, Mr Charles Redding, of 12 Regency Gardens, stated that he had heard a scuffle shortly before eleven o'clock in the front room next door. He had heard a distressed cry from the woman of "Oh don't", followed by a dull thud on the floor. The story given by the stepchildren was that their mother was planning to leave Brown that night. He had returned from work on the Saturday afternoon and told her that he had "something in a box" for her. Six or seven weeks previously Brown had been to Westminster Hospital where he was kept for three or four weeks. He subsequently went to a convalescent home and on his return there was something the matter with him. He kept saying that their mother let men into the house and he would look for them before he went to work in the morning. When he came home at night he would light matches "to peer into corners" and on one night he had walked about and lit an entire box of matches. He had sharpened a large knife every day before the woman at both dinner and tea times, although he did not use it with his meals. When Brown returned from work on the Saturday, the mother had told her son, Robert Young, nine years, that Brown was going to kill her. All in all, it is a distressing tale and it is amazing to think that this killing occurred within two hours of the murder of Elizabeth Stride.

For an overall summary of the Stride murder we turn again to Chief Inspector Donald S. Swanson and a report[3] dated 19 October 1888 to the Home Office:

METROPOLITAN POLICE.
Criminal Investigation Department,
Scotland Yard.
19th day of October, 1888

SUBJECT Murder of
Elizabeth Stride at Duf-
fields [*sic*] yard Berner St.
Body found at 1am
30th Sept. 1888.

I beg to report that the following are the particulars respecting the murder of Elizabeth Stride on the morning of 30th Sept. 1888.—

1 a.m. 30th Sept.   A body of a woman was found with the throat cut, but not otherwise mutilated by Louis Diemshitz (Secretary to the Socialist Club) inside the gates of Duffield's Yard in Berner St. Commercial Road East, who gave information to the police. P.C. 252 Lamb proceeded with them to the spot & sent for Drs. Blackwell & Phillips.

1.10 a.m.   Body examined by the Doctors mentioned who pronounced life extinct, the position of the body was as follows:- lying on left side, left arm extended from elbow, cachous lying in hand, right arm over stomach back of hand & inner surface of wrist dotted with blood, legs drawn up knees fixed feet close to wall, body still warm, silk handkerchief round throat, slightly torn corresponding to the angle of right jaw, throat deeply gashed and below the right angle apparent abrasion of skin about an inch and a quarter in diameter.

Search was made in the yard but no instrument found.

From enquiries made it was found that at:-

12.35 a.m.30th   P.C. 452H Smith saw a man and woman the latter with a red rose talking in Berner Street, this P.C. on seeing the body identified it as being that of the woman whom he had seen & he thus describes the man as age about 28. ht. 5ft. 7in: comp. dark, small dark moustache, dress black diagonal coat, hard felt hat, white collar & tie.

12.45 a.m. 30th   Israel Schwartz of 22 Helen [*sic* – Ellen] Street, Backchurch Lane stated that at that hour on turning into Berner St. from Commercial Road & had got as far as the gateway where the murder was committed he saw a man stop & speak to a woman, who was standing in the gateway. The man tried to pull the woman into the street, but he turned her round & threw her down on the footway & the woman screamed three times, but not very loudly. On crossing to the opposite side of the street, he saw a second man standing lighting his pipe. The man who threw the woman down called out apparently to the man on the opposite side of the road "Lipski" & then Schwartz walked away, but finding that he was followed by the second man he ran as far as the railway arch but the man did not follow so far. [*Here there is a marginal note.* – "The use of 'Lipski' increases my belief that the murderer was a Jew".] Schwartz cannot say whether the two men were together or known to each other. Upon being taken to the mortuary Schwartz identified the body as that of the woman he had seen & he thus describes the first man who threw the woman down:- age about 30 ht. 5 ft. 5in. comp. fair hair dark, small brown moustache, full face, broad shouldered, dress, dark jacket & trousers black cap with peak, had nothing in his hands.

second man age 35 ht. 5ft. 11in. comp. fresh, hair light brown, moustache brown, dress dark overcoat, old black hard felt hat wide brim, had a clay pipe in his hand,

about 1 a.m. 30th   Leon Goldstein of 22 Christian Street Commercial Road, called at Leman St. & stated that he was the man that passed down Berner St. with a black bag at that hour, that the bag contained empty cigarette boxes & that he had left a coffee house in Spectacle Alley a short time before. [*Here there is a marginal note.* – "Who saw this man go down Berner St. or did he come forward to clear himself in case any questions might be asked".]

The description of the man seen by the P.C. was circulated amongst Police by wire, & by authority of Commissioner it was also given to the press. On the evening of 30th the man Schwartz gave the description of the man he had seen ten minutes later than the P.C. and it was circulated by wire. It will be observed that allowing for differences of opinion between the P.C. and Schwartz as to apparent age & height of the man each saw with the woman whose body they both identified there are serious differences in the description of dress:- thus the P.C. describes the dress of the man whom he saw as black diagonal coat, hard felt hat, while Schwartz describes the dress of the man he saw as dark jacket black cap with peak, so that it is at least rendered doubtful whether they are describing the same man. If Schwartz is to be believed, and the police report of his statement casts no doubt upon it, it follows if they are describing different men that the man Schwartz saw & described is the more probable of the two to be the murderer, for a quarter of an hour afterwards the body is found murdered. At the same time account must be taken of the fact that the throat only of the victim was cut in this instance which measured by time, considering meeting (if with a man other than Schwartz saw) the time for the agreement & the murderous action would I think be a question of so many minutes, five at least, ten at most, so that I respectfully submit it is not clearly proved that the man that Schwartz saw is the murderer, although it is clearly the more probable of the two. [*Here there is a marginal note* – ''This is rather confused: If the man whom the P.C. saw is not the same as the man whom Schwartz saw at 12.45 then it is clearly more probable that the man whom Schwartz saw was the murderer, because Schwartz saw his man a quarter of an hour later than the P.C.

But I understand the Inspector to suggest that Schwartz' man need not have been the murderer. True only 15 minutes elapsed between 12.45 when Schwartz saw the man & 1.0 when the woman was found murdered on the same spot. But the suggestion is that Schwartz' man may have left her, she being a prostitute then accosted or was accosted by another man, & there was time enough for this to take place & for this other man to murder her before 1.0. The Police apparently do not suspect the 2nd man whom Schwartz saw on the other side of the street & who followed Schwartz''.]
Before concluding in dealing with the descriptions of these two men I venture to insert here for the purpose of comparison with these two descriptions, the description of a man seen with a woman in Church Passage close to Mitre Square at 1.35 a.m. 30th by two men coming out of a club close by:- age 30 ht. 5 ft. 7 or 8 in. comp. fair, fair moustache, medium build, dress pepper & salt colour loose jacket, grey cloth cap with peak of same colour, reddish handkerchief tied in a knot, round neck, appearance of a sailor. In this case I understand from City Police that Mr. Lewin [*sic* – Lawende] one of the men identified the clothes only of the murdered woman Eddowes, which is a serious drawback to the value of the description of the man. Ten minutes afterwards the body is found horribly mutilated & it is therefore reasonable to believe that the man he saw was the murderer, but for purposes of comparison, this description is much nearer to that given by Schwartz than to that given by the P.C.
The body was identified as that of Elizabeth Stride, a prostitute, & it

may be shortly stated that the enquiry into her history did not disclose the slightest pretext for a motive on behalf of friends or associates or anybody who had known her. The action of police besides being continued in the directions mentioned in the report respecting the murder of Annie Chapman was as follows

a. Immediately after the police were on the spot the whole of the members who were in the Socialist Club were searched, their clothes examined and their statements taken.

b. Extended enquiries were made in Berner Street to ascertain if any person was seen with the woman.

c. Leaflets were printed & distributed in H Division asking the occupiers of houses to give information to police of any suspicious persons lodging in their houses.

d. The numerous statements made to police were enquired into and the persons (of whom there were many) were required to account for their presence at the time of the murders & every care taken as far as possible to verify the statements.

Concurrently with enquiry under head **a** the yard where the body was found was searched but no instrument was found.

Arising out of head **b**, a, Mr. Packer a fruiterer, of Berner St. stated that at 11 p.m. 29th Sept. a young man age 25 to 30 about 5 ft. 7 in. dress long black coat, buttoned up, soft felt hat, (Kind of Yankee hat) rather broad shoulders, rough voice, rather quick speaking, with a woman wearing a geranium like flower, white outside, red inside, & he sold him 1/2 lb of grapes. The man & woman went to the other side of road & stood talking till 11.30 p.m. then they went towards the Club (Socialist) apparently listening to the music. Mr. Packer when asked by the police stated that he did not see any suspicious person about, and it was not until after the publication in the newspapers of the description of man seen by the P.C. that Mr. Packer gave the foregoing particulars to two private enquiry men acting conjointly with the Vigilance Comtee. and the press, who upon searching a drain in the yard found a grape stem which was amongst the other matter swept from the yard after its examination by the police & then calling upon Mr. Packer whom they took to the mortuary where he identified the body of Elizabeth Stride as that of the woman. Packer who is an elderly man, has unfortunately made different statements so that apart from the fact of the hour at which he saw the woman (and she was seen afterwards by the P.C. & Schwartz as stated) any statement he made would be rendered almost valueless as evidence.

Under head **c.** 80,000 pamphlets to occupier were issued and a house to house enquiry made not only involving the result of enquiries from the occupiers but also a search by police & with a few exceptions – but not such as to convey suspicion – covered the area bounded by the City Police boundary on the one hand, Lamb St. Commercial St. Great Eastern Railway & Buxton St. then by Albert St. Dunk St. Chicksand St. & Great Garden St to Whitechapel Rd. and then to the City boundary, under this head also Common Lodging Houses were visited & over 2000 lodgers were examined.

Enquiry was also made by Thames Police as to sailors on board ships in Docks or river & extended enquiry as to asiatics present in London, about 80 persons have been detained at the different police stations in the Metropolis & their statements taken and verified by police & enquiry has been made into the movements of a number of persons estimated at upwards of 300 respecting whom communications were received by police & such enquiries are being continued.

Seventy six Butchers & Slaughterers have been visited & the characters of the men employed enquired into, this embraces all servants who had been employed for the past six months.

Enquiries have also been made as to the alleged presence in London of Greek Gipsies, but it was found that they had not been in London during the times of the previous murders.

Three of the persons calling themselves Cowboys who belonged to the American Exhibition were traced & satisfactorily accounted for themselves.

Up to date although the number of letters daily is considerably lessened, the other enquiries respecting alleged suspicious persons continues as numerous.

There are now 994 Dockets besides police reports.

(sd) Donald S. Swanson

Ch. Inspr.

Thus, the very extensive Metropolitan Police enquiries instigated at the time of the Stride murder are outlined by Swanson. The area designated for police house-to-house enquiries as stated above is strange in that it does not extend south of the Commercial Road to include the Berner Street area. However, it may well be that the area surrounding Berner Street was so thoroughly covered immediately after the murder that it did not require inclusion in the later house-to-house enquiries. Some strength is given to this possibility by the fact that the Berner Street house-to-house enquiries are known to have included Packer's address.

The reports concerning the Stride murder are quite extensive and cover various aspects of the case raised in the enquiry. A report[4] dated 1 November 1888, written by Inspector Abberline, refers to the witness Schwartz:

METROPOLITAN POLICE.

Criminal Investigation Department,

Scotland Yard,

1st day of November 1888

SUBJECT Whitechapel
Murders
REFERENCE TO PAPERS
52983
1,119

With reference to the annexed copy extract from Home Office Letter.

I beg to report that since a jew named Lipski was hanged for the murder of a jewess in 1887 the name has very frequently been used by persons as mere ejaculation by way of endeavouring to insult the jew to whom it has been addressed, and as Schwartz has a strong jewish appearance I am of opinion it was addressed to him as he stopped to look at the man he saw ill-using the deceased woman.

I questioned Israel Schwartz very closely at the time he made the statement as to whom the man addressed when he called Lipski, but he was unable to say.

There was only one other person to be seen in the street, and that was a man on the opposite side of the road in the act of lighting a pipe.

Schwartz being a foreigner and unable to speak English became alarmed and ran away. The man whom he saw lighting his pipe also ran in the same direction as himself, but whether this man was running after him or not he could not tell, he might have been alarmed the same as himself and ran away.

A house to house inquiry was made in Berner Street with a view to ascertain whether any person was seen acting suspiciously or any noise heard on the night in question but without result.

Inquiries have also been made in the neighbourhood but no person named Lipski could be found.

With regard to the second question

I beg to report that searching inquiries were made by ["Sergt. Froest" – *deleted and* "an officer" *put in margin*] in Aberdeen Place St. Johns Wood the last known address of the insane medical student named "John Sanders", but the only information that could be obtained was that a lady named Sanders resided with her son at No. 20, but left there to go abroad about 2 years ago.

F.G. Abberline, Inspr.
Supt.

This report is followed in the files by a draft letter[5] from Robert Anderson to the Home Office:

[*In margin* – 3/53983/1119]
Draft letter to H.O.
With ref. to yr letter &c. I have to state that the opinion arrived at in this Dept. upon the evidence of Schwartz at the inquest in Eliz. Stride's case is that the name Lipski which he alleges was used by a man whom he saw assaulting the woman in Berner St. on the night of the murder, was not addressed to the supposed accomplice but to Schwartz himself. It appears that since the Lipski case, it has come to be used as an epithet in addressing or speaking of Jews.

With regard to the latter portion of yr letter I have to state that [copy passage in the report as written in blue]

RA
5/11/8

This is followed by three handwritten pages, unsigned, but apparently a copy of the Home Office letter[6] querying the police reports:

Extract

A statement has been made by a man named Schwartz to the effect that he had heard a person who was pulling about a woman identified as Elizabeth Stride 15 minutes before the murder off Berner Street took place, call out "Lipski" to an individual who was on the opposite side of the road. It does not appear whether the man used the word "Lipski" as a mere ejaculation meaning in mockery I am going to "Lipski" the woman, or whether he was calling to a man across the road by his proper name. In the latter case, assuming that the man using the word was the murderer, the murderer must have an acquaintance in Whitechapel named Lipski.

Mr Matthews presumes that this clue has been one of the suggestions with regard to which searching enquiries have been made; although no tangible results have been obtained as regards the detection of the murderer; but he will be glad if he can be furnished with a report as to any investigations made to trace the man Lipski.

Another question has arisen on the reports furnished by you. Reference is made to three insane medical students and it is stated that two have been traced and that one has gone abroad. Mr Matthews would be glad to be informed of the date when the third student went abroad, and whether any further enquiry has been made about him.

What this letter reveals is the degree to which the Home Office was following the police enquiries into the series of murders and their growing impatience for results.

With regard to the witness Packer, a report[7] dated 4 October 1888 by Inspector Henry Moore states:

> METROPOLITAN POLICE.
> Criminal Investigation Department,
> Scotland Yard
> 4th day of October 1888.

SUBJECT Whitechapel
   Murders.
REFERENCE TO PAPERS.
52983.
Referring to attached Extract from 2nd. Edition, "Evening News", of this date.

I beg to report that as soon as above came under my notice I at once (in the absence of Inspr. Abberline at C.O.) directed P.S. White, "H", to see Mr. Packer, the shopkeeper referred to, and take him to the mortuary with a view to the identification of the woman Elizabeth Stride; who it is stated was with a man who purchased grapes at his shop on night of 29th Ins.

The P.S. returned at noon and acquainted me as in report attached; in consequence of which Telegram No. 1 was forwarded to Chief Inspr Swanson and the P.S. sent to C.O. to fully explain the facts.

Telegram No. 2. was received at 12.55 p.m. from Assistant

Commissioner re same subject; in reply to which Telegram No. 3. was forwarded.

> Henry Moore, Inspector.
> Submitted – F.G. Abberline Insp.
> T. Arnold, Supt.

The report[8] written by Sergeant Stephen White concerning the witness Packer is dated 4 October 1888:

> METROPOLITAN POLICE.
> H DIVISION.
> 4th day of October 1888.

SUBJECT Whitechapel
  Murders
(Berner Street)
REFERENCE TO PAPERS.
52983
With reference to attached extract from "Evening News" of 4th Inst.

I beg to report that acting under the instructions of Inspector Abberline, I in company with P.C. Dolden C.I. Dept., made inquiries at every house in Berner Street, Commercial Road, on 30th ult, with a view to obtain information respecting the murder. Any information that I could obtain I noted in a Book supplied to me for that purpose. About 9 am I called at 44 Berner Street, and saw Matthew Packer, Fruiterer in a small way of business. I asked him what time he closed his shop on the previous night. He replied Half past twelve [*Note in margin reads:-*? Half past 11.] in consequence of the rain it was no good for me to keep open. I asked him if he saw anything of a man or woman going into Dutfields Yard, or saw anyone standing about the street about the time he was closing his shop. He replied "No I saw no one standing about neither did I see anyone go up the yard. I never saw anything suspicious or heard the slightest noise. and know nothing about the murder until I heard of it in the morning.["]

I also saw Mrs. Packer, Sarah Harris[*on*] and Harry Douglas residing in the same house but none of them could give the slightest information respecting the matter.

On 4th Inst. I was directed by Inspr. Moore to make further inquiry & if necessary see Packer and take him to the mortuary. I then went to 44 Berner St. and saw Mrs. Packer who informed me that two Detectives had called and taken her husband to the mortuary. I then went towards the mortuary when I met Packer with a man. I asked where he had been. He said "this detective asked me to go to see if I could identify the woman.["] I said "have you done so,["] he said "Yes, I believe she bought some grapes at my shop about 12. o clock [*Note in margin:-? 11.*] on Saturday.["] Shortly afterwards they were joined by another man. I asked the men what they were doing with Packer and they both said that they were Detectives. I asked for their Authority one of the men produced a card from a pocket Book, but would not allow me to touch it. They then said that they were private detectives. They then induced Packer to go away with them. About 4 p.m. I saw Packer at his shop and while talking to him the two men drove up in a Hansom Cab, and after going into the shop. They induced Packer to enter the Cab stating that they would take him to Scotland Yard to see Sir Charles Warren.

From inquiry I have made there is no doubt that these are the two men referred to in attached Newspaper cutting, who examined the drain in Dutfields Yard on 2nd Inst. One of the men had a letter in his hand addressed to Le Grand & Co., Strand.

Stephen White Sergt.

Extract from "Star" newspaper attached.

Respectfully submitted.

F.G. Abberline Inspr.

T. Arnold Supt.

There then follows a two-page summary[9] in the hand of Mr Alexander Carmichael Bruce, (Senior) Assistant Commissioner, giving details of what Packer had to say:

Matthew Packer

keeps a shop in Berner St. has a few grapes in window, black & white.

On Sat night about 11.p.m. a young man from 25–30 – about 5.7. with long black coat buttoned up – soft felt hat, kind of Yankee hat rather broad shoulders – rather quick in speaking. rough voice. I sold him 1/2 pound black grapes 3d. A woman came up with him from Back Church end (the lower end of street) She was dressed in black frock & jacket, fur round bottom of jacket a black crape bonnet, she was playing with a flower like a geranium white outside

& red inside. I identify the woman at the St George's mortuary as the one I saw that night—

They passed by as though they were going up Com- Road, but – instead of going up they crossed to the other side of the road to the Board School, & were there for about 1/2 an hour till I shd. say 11.30. talking to one another. I then shut up my shutters.

Before they passed over opposite to my shop, they wait[ed] near to the club for a few minutes apparently listening to the music.

I saw no more of them after I shut up my shutters.

I put the man down as a young clerk.

He had a frock coat on – no gloves.

He was about $1\frac{1}{2}$ inch or 2 or 3 inches – a little higher than she was.
ACB
4.10.88.

The Home Office records[10] are filed under a minuted cover dated 25 October 1888:

[Stamped: – HOME OFFICE 25 OCT.88 RECd.DEPt.]   No. A49301c/8a
DATE [ ] Oct 88   The Commissioner of Police
REFERENCES, &c.   Whitechapel Murders
Forwards full report as to steps taken to detect the perpetrators of these murders.

Thank Commr. for report, and ask what part if any Met. Police took in Eddowes murder. This is the murder in which writing was rubbed out, & it is essential for H.O. to know exact facts as to this.

Also ask City Commr. for report of action taken by City Police in regard to Eddowes, & other murders, also ask Commr. for a map showing locality & position of the murders,

                        CM
                        Oct 25/88
                        GL
                        25 Oct 1888
        Wrote Commr. & City Commr.
                        25 Oct
To Mr Matthews
        I enclose also Newspaper Extracts &c
                        as to inquests   GL
                        25 Oct 1888

The statement of Schwartz that a man who was in the company of Eliz. Stride 15 m. before she was found dead, & who threw her down, addressed a companion (?) as "Lipski" seems to furnish a clue and ought to be followed up. The number of "Lipskis" in Whitechapel must be limited. If one of them were identified by Schwarz [sic] it might to lead to something of importance.

[HM]
27 Oct./88.

Mr. Murdoch

Please see Mr. Wortley's pencil memo. on Sir C. Warren's letter. ?Shall the Police be asked at the same time for report as to what has become of the 3rd Insane Medical Student from the London Hosp? about whom (under the name of Dr—there is a good deal of gossip in circulation

WTB

The first letter[11] enclosed is dated 29 October 1888 and is to the Commissioner of the Metropolitan Police:

Confidential   Home Office
    A49301/8a   Whitehall
                                                    S.W.

Sir,

With reference to your letter of the 24th Inst. enclosing a report as to the steps taken to detect the perpetrator of the recent murders in Whitechapel, I am directed by the Secretary of State to say that he observes that a statement has been made by a man named Schwartz to the effect that he had heard a person who was ["in the company of" – *deleted*] pulling about a woman identified as Elizabeth Stride 15 minutes before the murder off Berner Street took place ["speaking" – *deleted*] call out "Lipski" to an individual who was on the opposite side of the road ["by the name of 'Lipski' " – *deleted*]

["Mr. Matthews presumes that this" – *deleted*]

It does not appear whether the man used the word "Lipski" ["was used" – *deleted*] as a mere ejaculation, meaning in mockery I am going to "Lipski" the woman, or whether he was calling to a man across the road by his proper name. In the latter case, assuming that the man using the word was the murderer, the murderer must have an acquaintance in Whitechapel named Lipski.

Mr. Matthews presumes that this clue has been one of the "suggestions with regard to which searching enquiries have been made; although no tangible results have been obtained as regards the detection of the murderer", but he will be glad if he can be furnished with a report as to any investigations made to trace the man "Lipski".

Another question has arisen on the Reports forwarded by the ["Commissioner" – *deleted*] you. Reference is made to three insane medical students, and it is stated that two have been traced and that one has gone abroad. Mr. Matthews would be glad to be informed of the date when the third student went abroad, & whether any further inquiry has been made about him.

Wrote accordingly
29/10

The next letter[12] on the file is dated 24 October 1888, to the Under-Secretary of State from Sir Charles Warren:

A49301C/8a

["Confidential" – *deleted*]   [Stamped: – HOME OFFICE 25 OCT.88 RECd.DEPt.]

[*Across the top of the page is a note* – ?Ask when the insane student, mentioned on page 6 of Annie Chapman papers, went abroad CSW Oct 24]

4 Whitehall Place,
S.W.
24th October, 1888.

A49301C/["60" – *deleted*]8
Sir,

With reference to your letter of the 13th instant asking that Mr. Secretary Matthews may be supplied with a report of all the measures which have been taken for the detection of the perpetrator of the Whitechapel Murders and of the results;-

I have to transmit, for the information of the Secretary of State, copies of a minute by Mr. Anderson on the subject, and of Reports by Chief Inspector Swanson, which I directed to be prepared on my return from abroad early in September.

Very numerous and searching enquiries have been made in all directions, and with regard to all kinds of suggestions which have been made: these have had no tangible result so far as regards the Whitechapel Murders, but information has been obtained which will no doubt be useful in future in detecting cases of crime.

I am,
Sir,
Your most obedient Servant,
CWarren

The Under Secretary
    of State
&c. &c. &c.
    Home Office

The next report[13] is dated 23 October 1888 and is signed by Robert Anderson:

A49301C/8a
[Stamped: – HOME OFFICE 25 OCT.88 RECd.DEPt.]

A49301/60

The <u>Whitechapel Murders</u>

At the present stage of the inquiry the best reply that can be made to the Secretary of State's request for a report upon these cases is to send the accompanying copy of detailed reports prepared by Chief Inspector Swanson, who has special charge of the matter at this office.

I wish to guard against its being supposed that the inquiry is now concluded. There is no reason for furnishing these reports at this moment except that they have been called for.

That a crime of this kind should have been committed without any clue being supplied by the criminal, is unusual, but that five successive murders should have been committed without our having the slightest clue of any kind is extraordinary, if not unique, in the annals of crime. The result has been to necessitate our giving attention to innumerable suggestions, such as would in any ordinary case be dismissed unnoticed, and no hint of any kind, which was not obviously absurd, has been neglected. Moreover, the activity of the Police has been to a considerable extent wasted through the exigencies of sensational journalism, and the action of unprincipled persons, who, from various motives, have endeavoured to mislead us. But on the other hand the public generally and especially the inhabitants of the East End have shown a marked desire to assist in every way, even at some sacrifice to themselves, as for example in permitting their houses to be searched as mentioned at page 10 of the last report.

The vigilance of the officers engaged on the inquiry continues unabated.

R. Anderson
Oct 23/88

At this stage there is an index[14] to the contents of the file, dated 19 October 1888:

A49301C

Copy   [Stamped: – HOME OFFICE 25 OCT.88 RECd.DEPt.]
<u>Berner Street &c Nos. 4 & 5</u>
<u>Murder of Elizabeth Stride, Berner Street.</u>
<u>Murder of Catherine Eddowes, Mitre Square.</u>

Subject	Page	Remarks
Murder, date & hour of	1	
Diemschitz, Louis	1	Discovered the body.
Doctors' examination	1&2	Doctors Phillips & Brown
Men seen with deceased	3.4.5.	by P.C. 452H Smith & Israel Schwartz.
	6.7	
Descriptions compared	5.6.7.	with man seen with Mitre Square Victim
Enquiries by police		
re Socialists	8	belonging to club in Berner Street.
" Berner Street	8	
" Slaughtermen	11	in Aldgate, Whitechapel & neighbourhood
" House to House	10	boundary of area given
" Common Lod: Hos:	10	2000 lodgers seen up to date
" Sailors	11	By Thames Police
" Asiatics	11	At Homes & Opium dens
" Persons detained	11	& liberated after satisfactory enquiry
" " suspected	11	upwards of 300 whose movements enquired into
Leaflets to occupier	10	80,000 issued
Detectives private ilance	9&10	Making enquiry at instance of Vig-Com'tee

Gipsies Greek	11	as to presence in London
Cowboys	12	Three traced & satisfactorily accounted for
Dockets	12	Number of
Mitre Sq. Murder	6&7	Within jurisdiction of City Police

19th Oct. 1888   Donald S.Swanson
                                                          Ch: Inspr.

The next file cover[15] is dated 6 November 1888:

[Stamped: – HOME OFFICE 7 NOV.88 RECd. DEPt.]
DATE 6th Nov 88   The Commissioner of Police
REFERENCES, &c.   Whitechapel Murders
Reports as to the way the name of "Lipski" was used with
reference to Schwartz's evidence, the name is now used as an
epithet in addressing or speaking of Jews. Enquiries were made as to
"John Saunders" the medical student but without result.
                              MINUTES.
                              Confidential
                         The S.ofS. Nov. 7

There then follows a two-page report[16] from Sir Charles Warren:

[Stamped: HOME OFFICE 7 NOV.88 RECd.DEPt.]
Confidential
                                    4 Whitehall Place, S.W.
                                    6th November, 1888.
Sir,
    With reference to your letter of the 29th ulto. I have to acquaint
you, for the information of the Secretary of State, that the opinion
arrived at upon the evidence given by Schwartz at the inquest in
Elizabeth Stride's case is that the name "Lipski", which he alleges
was used by a man whom he saw assaulting the woman in Berners
[sic] Street on the night of the murder, was not addressed to the
supposed accomplice but to Schwartz himself. It appears that since
the Lipski case it has come to be used as an epithet in addressing or
speaking of Jews.
    With regard to the latter portion of your letter I have to state
that searching enquiries were made by an officer in Aberdeen
Place, St. John's Wood, the last known address of the insane
medical student named "John Sanders", but the only information

that could be obtained was that a lady named Sanders did reside with her son at No. 20, but left that address to go abroad about two years ago.

> I am,
> Sir,
> Your most obedient Servant,
> C. Warren

The Under
    Secretary of State,
&c. &c. &c.

This concludes the main file on the Stride murder as far as the police reports are concerned. However, detailed reports on the inquest appeared in the newspapers. The best overall picture can only be obtained by reading the two sets of reports in conjunction, so the reports of the inquest that appeared in *The Times* follow.

CHAPTER 8

October 1888 – The Stride Inquest

The opening of the inquest on Elizabeth Stride is not covered in the extracts contained in the official reports, but the report is to be found in *The Times* of Tuesday, 2 October 1888, page 6:

THE MURDERS AT THE EAST-END
Yesterday, Mr. Wynne E. Baxter, Coroner for the South-Eastern Division of Middlesex, opened an inquiry at the Vestry-hall, Cable-street, St. George's-in-the-East, respecting the death of Elizabeth Stride, who was found murdered in a yard in Berner-street on Sunday morning.

Detective inspector E. Reid, II Division, watched the case on behalf of the Criminal Investigation Department.

The jury having viewed the body, the following evidence was heard:-

William West, who claimed to affirm, said he lived at 40, Berner-street, Commercial-road, and was a printer by occupation. He lived in one of the houses on the right hand side of the gateway. No. 40, Berner-street was the International Working Men's Club. On the ground floor, facing the street, was a window and a door – the latter leading into a passage. At the side of the house was a passage leading into a yard, and at the entrance to the passage were two wooden gates.

The Foreman. – Is that right?

The CORONER. – There is a passage before you get to the yard.

Witness, continuing, said the passage had two wooden gates folding backwards from the street. In the northern gate there was a little door. The gates were sometimes closed, and at other times left open all night. When the gates were closed the doorway was usually locked. They were seldom closed until late at night, when all the tenants had retired. As far as witness knew no particular person looked after the gates. In the yard on the left hand side there was only one house, which was occupied by two or three tenants. That house contained three doors leading to the yard, but there was no other exit from the yard except through the gates. Opposite the gate there was a workshop, in the occupation of Messrs. Hindley, sack manufacturers. Witness did not believe there was any exit through that workshop. The manufacturing was on the ground floor, and he believed the ground floor of the premises was unoccupied. adjoining Messrs. Hindley's premises there was a stable, which he believed was unoccupied. Passing this stable a person would come to the premises forming the club.

At this point the Coroner examined a parish map of Berner-street, which showed the yard referred to by the witness.

The witness, continuing, said he was not sure that the gardens of the houses in Batty-street faced the yard [?]. The club premises ran back a long way into the yard. The front room on the ground floor of the club was occupied as a dining room. At the middle of the passage there was a staircase leading to the first floor. At the back of the dining room was a kitchen. In this room there was a small window over the door which faced the one leading into the yard. The remainder of the passage led into the yard. Over the door in the passage was a small window, through which daylight came. At the back of the kitchen, but in no way connected with it, was a printing office. This office consisted of two rooms. The one adjoining the kitchen was used as a composing-room, and the other one was for the editor. The compositors, on Saturday last, left off work at 2 o'clock in the afternoon, but the editor was there during the day. He was also a member of the club, and was either there or in his office until he went home. Opposite the doorway of the kitchen, and in the yard, were two closets. The club consisted of from 75 to 80 members. Any working man of any nationality could be a member of the club. It was a Socialist club.

The CORONER. – Have they to agree to any special principles?

Witness. – No person is supposed to be proposed as a member unless he was known to be a supporter of the Socialist movement.

By the CORONER. – Witness worked in the printing office. He remained in the club until about 9 o'clock on Saturday night. He then went out and returned about half-past 10. He then remained in the club until the discovery of the deceased. On the first floor of the club was a large room for entertainments, and from that room three windows faced the yard. On Saturday night a discussion was held in the large room among some 90 or 100 persons. The discussion ceased between 11 30 and 12 o'clock. the bulk of the people present then left the premises by the street door entrance, while between 20 and 30 members remained behind in the large room, and about a dozen were downstairs. Some of those upstairs had a discussion among themselves, while others were singing. The windows of the hall were partly open. Witness left the club about half-past 12. He slept at 2, William-street, and gave as his address 40, Berner-street, as he worked there all day. The distance from his lodgings to Berner-street was about five minutes' walk. Before leaving the club he had occasion to go to the printing office to put some literature there, and he went into the yard by the passage door, thence to the printing office. He then returned to the club by the same way. As he passed from the printing office to the club he noticed the yard gates were open, and went towards them, but did not actually go up to them. There was no lamp or light whatever in the yard. There were no lamps in Berner-street that could light the yard. The only light that could penetrate into the yard was from the windows of the club or the house that was let out in tenements. He noticed lights in one or two windows of the latter house, and they were on the first floor. When he went into the printing office the editor was there reading. Noises from the club could be heard in the yard, but there was not much noise on Saturday night. When he went into the yard and looked towards the gates there was nothing unusual that attracted his attention.

The CORONER. – Can you say there was any object on the ground?

Witness. – I cannot say that an object might have been there, and I not have seen it. I am rather short-sighted, but believe that if anything had been there I should have seen it.

The CORONER. – What made you look towards the gates?

Witness. – Because they were open.

In further examination, witness said after he returned to the club he called his brother and they both left by the street door and went together home. Another member of the club, named Louis Stansley, left the club at the same time, and accompanied them as far as James-street. Witness did not see any one in the yard, and as far as he could remember did not see any one in Berner-street. They went by way of Fairclough-street, Grove-street, and then to James's-street. Witness generally went home from Berner-street between 12 and 1 a.m. On some occasions he had noticed low women and men together in Fairclough-street, but had not seen any in Berner-street. He had never seen any of these women against his club. About 12 months ago he happened to go into the yard and heard some conversation between a man and a woman at the gates. He went to shut the gates, and then saw a man and a woman leave the entrance. That was the only occasion he had ever noticed anything.

By the Jury. – Witness was the overseer of the printing office.

Morris Eagle, who also claimed to affirm, stated that he lived at 4, New- road, Commercial-road, and was a traveller in jewelry. He was a member of the International Working Men's Club, and was there several times during the day. In the evening he occupied the chair and opened the discussion. About a quarter to 12 he left the club for the purpose of taking his young lady home. They left by the front door. He returned to the club about 25 minutes to 1. As he found the front door closed he went through the gateway leading into the yard, and through the back door leading into the club. As he passed through the yard he did not notice anything on the ground by the gates. He believed he passed along about the middle of the gateway, which was about 9 ft. 2 in. wide.

The CORONER. – Can you say if deceased was lying there when you went in?

Witness. – It was rather dark and I cannot say for certain if anything was there or not. I do not remember whether I met any one in Berner-street when I returned to the yard, neither do I remember seeing any one in the yard.

The CORONER. – Supposing you saw a man and woman in the yard, would you have remembered it?

Witness. – I am sure I would.

The CORONER. – Did you notice if there were any lights in the house on the left-hand side?

Witness. – I do not remember.

The CORONER. – Are you often late at night at the club, and do you often go into the yard?

Witness. – I often am there until late, but have seldom gone into the yard. In fact, I have never seen a man or woman in the yard. On the same side as the club is a beershop, and I have seen men and women coming from there.

A Juryman. – That is always closed about 9 o'clock.

The CORONER. – What were you doing at the club?

Witness. – As soon as I entered the club I went to see a friend, who was in the upstairs room, and who was singing a song in the Russian language. Afterwards I joined my friend, and we sang together. I had been there about 20 minutes, when a member named Gilleman came upstairs and said, "There is a dead woman lying in the yard." I went down in a second, and struck a match. I could then see a woman lying on the ground, near the gateway, and in a pool of blood. Her feet were about six or seven feet from the gate, and she was lying by the side of the club wall, her head being towards the yard. Another member, named Isaac, was with me at the time. As soon as I saw the blood I got very excited and ran away for the police. I did not touch her.

The CORONER. – Did you see if her clothes were disturbed?

Witness. – I could not say. When I got outside I saw Jacobs and another going for the police in the direction of Fairclough-street, and I then went to the Commercial-road, all the time shouting "Police!" On getting to the corner of Grove-street I saw two constables, and told them that a woman had been murdered in Berner-street. They returned with me to the yard. I then noticed several members of the club and some strangers were there. A constable threw his light on the body, and then told the other officer to go for a doctor, and sent me to the station for the inspector.

The CORONER. – Did you see any one touch the body?

Witness. – I think the policeman touched it, but the other persons appeared afraid to go near it. When I first saw the body of deceased, I should say it was about 1 o'clock, although I did not look at the clock.

In answer to the foreman of the jury, the witness further said he could not remember how far from the wall the body was lying. On Saturday evening there were free discussions at the club for both men and women. Any one could go in. On Saturday night there were some women there, but those he knew. He should say there were not more than six or eight women present. Saturday was not a dancing night, although after the discussion was ended some dancing might have been carried on. Had a cry of "Murder" been raised he believed they would have heard it, or even any other cry of distress. Witness had never been in the stable or in Hindley's workshop, and could not say for certain whether there was any other exit from the yard except through the gateway.

Louis Diemschutz deposed that he lived at 40, Berner-street, and was steward of the club. The correct title of the club was International Working Men's Educational Club. Witness was a married man, and his wife assisted in the management of the club. Witness left home about half-past 11 on Saturday morning, and he returned home exactly at 1 o'clock on Sunday morning. He was certain about the time. Witness had with him a costermonger's barrow, and it was drawn by a pony. The pony was not kept in the yard of the club, but in George yard, Cable-street. He drove home for the purpose of leaving his goods. He drove into the yard, and saw that both gates were wide open. It was rather dark there. He drove in as usual, and as he entered the gate his pony shied to the left. Witness looked to the ground on his right, and saw something lying there, but was unable to distinguish what it was. Witness tried to feel the object with his whip before he got down. He then jumped down and struck a match. It was rather windy, but he was able to get a light sufficient to tell it was a woman lying there. He then went into the club, and saw his wife in the front room on the ground floor. He left his pony in the yard, just outside the club door, by itself. He told his wife, and several members who were in the room, that a woman was lying in the yard, but that he was unable to say whether she was drunk or dead. He then got a candle and went out into the yard. By the candlelight he could see that there was blood. He did not touch the body, but at once went off for the police. He passed several streets without seeing a policeman, and returned without one, although he called out ''Police'' as loud as he could. A young man whom he had met in Grove-street and told about the murder, returned with him. This young man lifted the woman's head up, and witness for the first time saw that her throat was cut. At the same moment the last witness and the constables arrived. When he first approached the club he did not notice anything unusual, and came from the Commercial-road end of the street.

By the CORONER. – The doctor arrived about ten minutes after the police came. No one was then allowed to leave the place until their names and addresses were taken, and they had been searched. The clothes of the deceased, as far as he remembered, were in order. Deceased was lying on her side with her face towards the wall of the club. He could not say how much of the body was lying on the side. As soon as the police came witness went into the club and remained there.

The CORONER. – Did you notice her hands?

Witness. – I did not notice what position her hands were in. I only noticed that the dress buttons of her dress were undone. I saw the doctor put his hand inside and tell the police that the body was quite warm. The doctor also told one of the constables to feel the body, and he did so.

The CORONER. – Did you notice the quantity of blood about?

Witness. – The blood ran in the direction of the house from the neck of the woman. I should say there were quite two quarts of blood on the ground. The body was lying about one foot from the wall. In the yard were a few paving stones, which were very irregularly fixed.

The CORONER. – Have you ever seen men and women in the yard?

Witness. – I have not.

The CORONER. – Have you ever heard of their being found there?

Witness. – Not to my knowledge.

The Foreman. – Was there sufficient room for you to pass the body when you went into the yard?

Witness. – Yes.; and I did so. When my pony shied I was passing the body, and was right by when I got down.

The CORONER. – Did the blood run down as far as the door of the club?

Witness. – Yes.

The Foreman. – When you went for the police, who was in charge of the body?

Witness. – I cannot say. As soon as I saw the blood I ran off.

In answer to Inspector Reid, the witness said every one who was in the yard was detained. This included the strangers. Their names and addresses were taken, and they were questioned as to their presence there. They were also searched, and their hands and clothes examined by Dr. Phillips. It would have been possible for any person to have escaped while he went into the club. Had any person run up the yard witness would have seen him.

The CORONER. – Is the body identified yet?

Inspector Reid. – Not yet.

The Foreman. – I cannot understand that, as she is called Elizabeth Stride.

The CORONER. – That has not yet been sworn to, but something is known of her. It is known where she lived. You had better leave that point until tomorrow.

At this stage the inquiry was adjourned until this afternoon.

Details of the resumed inquest appeared in *The Times* of Wednesday, 3 October, 1888, page 10:

THE EAST END MURDERS.

Yesterday afternoon Mr. Wynne E. Baxter, coroner for the South-Eastern Division of Middlesex, resumed his inquiry at the Vestry-hall, Cable-street, St. George's-in-the-East, respecting the death of Elizabeth Stride, who was found murdered in Berner-street on Sunday morning last.

Detective-inspector E. Reid, H Division, watched the case on behalf of the Criminal Investigation Department.

Police-constable Henry Lamb, 252H, deposed as follows:- About 1 o'clock, as near as I can tell, on Sunday morning I was in the Commercial-road, between Christian-street and Batty-street. Two men came running towards me. I went towards them and heard them say, "Come on! There has been another murder." I said, "Where?" As they got to the corner of Berner-street they pointed down the street. Seeing people moving about some distance down Berner-street, I ran down that street followed by Constable 426H. I went into the gateway of No. 40, Berner-street and saw something dark lying on the right-hand side, close to the gates. I turned my light on and found it was a woman. I saw that her throat was cut, and she appeared to be dead. I at once sent the other constable for the nearest doctor, and I sent a young man that was standing by to the police-station to inform the inspector that a woman was lying in Berner-street with her throat cut, and apparently dead.

The CORONER. – How many people were there in the yard?

Witness. – I should think 20 or 30. Some of that number had followed me in.

The CORONER. – Was any one touching the body when you arrived?

Witness. – No. There was no one within a yard of it. As I was examining the body some crowded round. I begged them to keep back, and told them they might get some of the blood on their clothing, and by that means get themselves into trouble. I then blew my whistle. I put my hand on the face and found it slightly warm. I then felt the wrist, but could not feel the pulse.

The CORONER. – Did you do anything else to the body?

Witness. – I did not, and would not allow any one to get near the body. Deceased was lying on her side, and her left arm was lying under her.

The CORONER. – Did you examine her hands?

Witness. – I did not; but I saw that her right arm was across the breast.

The CORONER. – How near was her head to the wall?

Witness. – I should say her face was about five or six inches away.

The CORONER. – Were her clothes disturbed?

Witness. – No. I scarcely could see her boots. She looked as if she had been laid quietly down. Her clothes were not in the least rumpled.

The CORONER. – Was the blood in a liquid state?

Witness. – Some was, and some was congealed. It extended close to the door. The part nearest to her throat was congealed.

The CORONER. – Was any blood coming from the throat at that time?

Witness. – I hardly like to say that, Sir. If there was it must have been a very small quantity. Dr. Blackwell, about ten minutes after I got there, was the first doctor to arrive.

The CORONER. – Did any one say whether the body had been touched?

Witness. – No. Dr. Blackwell examined the body, and afterwards the surrounding ground. Dr. Phillips arrived about 20 minutes afterwards; but at that time I was at another part of the ground. Inspector Pinhorn arrived directly after the doctor arrived. When I got there I had the gates shut.

The CORONER. – But did not the feet of the deceased touch the gate?

Witness. – No; they went just behind it, and I was able to close the gates without disturbing the body. I put a constable at the gate and told him not to let any one in or out. I then entered the club and, starting from the front door, examined the place. I turned my light on and had a look at the different persons there, and examined a number of their hands and also their clothing to see if I could detect any marks of blood. I did not take up each one's hand. I should say there were from 15 to 20 persons in the club-room on the ground floor. I then went into every room, including the one in which there was a stage, and I went behind it. A person was there who informed me he was the steward.

The CORONER. – You did not think to put him in charge of the front door?

Witness. – No, I did not. When further assistance came a constable was put in charge of the front door. I did not see any one leave by that entrance, and could not say if it was locked. After I examined the club, I went into the yard and examined the cottages. I also went into the water-closets. The occupiers of the cottages were all in bed when I knocked. A man came down partly dressed to let me in. Every one I saw, except this one, was undressed.

The CORONER. – There is a recess in the yard, is there not? Did you go there?

Witness. – Yes; and I afterwards went there with Dr. Phillips. I examined the dust-bin and dung-heap. I noticed there was a hoarding, but I do not recollect looking over it. After that I went and examined the steps and outside of Messrs. Hindley's premises. I also looked through the windows, as the doors were fastened.

The CORONER. – How long was it before the cottage doors were opened?

Witness. – Not long. The people seemed very much frightened and wanted to know what was the matter. I told them nothing much, as I did not want to frighten them. When I returned from there Dr. Phillips and Chief Inspector West had arrived.

The CORONER. – Was there anything to prevent any one escaping while you were examining the body?

Witness. – It was quite possible, as I was then there by myself. There was a lot of confusion, and every one was looking towards the body.

The CORONER. – A person might have escaped before you arrived?

Witness. – That is quite possible. I should think he got away before I got there, and not afterwards.

Inspector Reid. – How long was it before you passed that spot?

Witness. – I was not on the beat; but I passed the Commercial-road end of the street some six or seven minutes before I was called. When I was fetched I was going in the direction of Berner-street. Constable Smith is on the Berner-street beat. The constable who followed me down is on fixed-point duty from 9 to 5 at the end of Grove-street. All the fixed-point men ceased their duty at 1 a.m., and then the men on the beats did the whole duty.

Inspector Reid. – These men are fixed at certain places, so if a person wanted a constable he would not have to go all the way to the station for one.

The CORONER. – Did you see anything suspicious?

Witness. – No, I saw lots of squabbles and rows such as one sees on Saturday nights. I think I should have seen any one running from the gate of 40, Berner-street if I had been standing at the Commercial-road end of it. I could not tell if the lamps on the plan are correct.

The CORONER. – I may mention there are four lamps between Commercial-road and Fairclough-street. Is the street as well lit as others in the neighbourhood?

Witness. – It is lit about as well as side streets generally are, but some I know are better lighted.

A Juryman. – I think that street is lighted quite as well as any other.

In further examination, witness said, – I remained in the yard the remainder of the night. I started to help convey the body to the mortuary, but I was fetched back.

Edward Spooner said, – I live at 26, Fairclough-street, and am a horse- keeper at Messrs. Meredith's. Between half-past 12 and 1 o'clock on Sunday morning I was standing outside the Bee Hive publichouse, at the corner of Christian-street and Fairclough-street, along with a young woman. I had previously been in another beershop at the top of the street, and afterwards walked down. After talking for about 25 minutes I saw two Jews come running along and shouting out "Murder" and "Police." They then ran as far as Grove-street and turned back. I stopped them and asked what was the matter. They replied, "A woman has been murdered." I then went round with them to Berner-street, and into Dutfield's yard, adjoining No. 40, Berner-street. I saw a woman lying just inside the gate. At that time there were about 15 people in the yard, and they were all standing round the body. The majority of them appeared to be Jews. No one touched the body. One of them struck a match, and I lifted up the chin of the deceased with my hand. The chin was slightly warm. Blood was still flowing from the throat. I could see that she had a piece of paper doubled up in her right hand, and a red and white flower pinned on to her jacket. The body was lying on one side, with the face turned towards the wall. I noticed that blood was running down the gutter. I stood there about five minutes before a constable came. It was the last witness who first arrived. I did not notice any one leave while I was there, but there were a lot of people there, and a person might have got away unnoticed. The only means I had of fixing the time was by the closing of the publichouses. I stood at the top of the street for about five minutes, and then 25 minutes outside the publichouse. I should say it was about 25 minutes to 1 when I first went to the yard. I could not form any opinion about the body having been moved. Several persons stood round. I noticed that the legs of the deceased were drawn up, but the clothes were not disturbed. As soon as the policeman came I stepped back, and afterwards helped to fasten the gates. When I left it was by the front door of the club. Before that I was searched, and gave my name and address. I was also examined by Dr. Phillips.

By the CORONER. – There was no blood on the chin of the deceased, and I did not get any on my hands. Directly I got inside the yard I could see that it was a woman lying on the ground.

By the jury. – As I was going to Berner-street I did not meet any one except Mr. Harris, who came out of his house in Tiger Bay (Brunswick-street). Mr. Harris told me he had heard the policeman's whistle blowing.

Mary Malcolm said, – I live at 50, Eagle-street, Red Lion-square. I am married to Andrew Malcolm, a tailor. I have seen the body in the mortuary. I saw it on Sunday and twice yesterday. It is the body of my sister, Elizabeth Watts.

The CORONER. – You have no doubt about that?

Witness. – Not the slightest.

The CORONER. – You had some doubts at first?

Witness. – I had, but not now. I last saw her alive at a quarter to 7 last Thursday evening. She came to me where I worked at the tailoring, at 59, Red Lion-street. She came to me to ask me to give her a little assistance, which I have been in the habit of doing off and on for the last five years. I gave her 1s. and a little short jacket. The latter is not the one she had on when found in Berner-street. She only remained with me for a few moments, and she did not say where she was going. I could not say where she was living except that it was somewhere in the neighbourhood of the tailors and Jews at the East-end. I understood she was living in a lodging-house.

The CORONER. – Did you know what she was doing for a living?

Witness. – I had my doubts.

The CORONER. – Was she the worse for drink when she came to you?

Witness. – She was sober, but unfortunately drink was a failing with her.

The CORONER. – How old was she?

Witness. – 37.

The CORONER. – Was she married?

Witness. – Yes, to Mr. Watts, wine and spirit merchant, of Walton-street, Bath. I think his name is Edward Watts, and he is in partnership with his father, and they are in a large way of business. My sister left her home because she brought disgrace on her husband. Her husband left her because he caught her with a porter. Her husband sent her home to her poor mother, who is now dead.

She took her two children with her, but I believe the boy has since been sent to a boarding school by his aunt, Miss Watts. The other child, a girl, was dead. I have never seen my sister in an epileptic fit – only in drunken fits. I believe she has been before the Thames Police-court magistrate on charges of drunkenness. I believe she has been let off on the ground that she was subject to epileptic fits, but I do not believe she was subject to them. I believe she lived with a man who kept a coffee house at Poplar. His name was not Stride, but I could find out by tomorrow. She had ceased to live with him for some time, for he went to sea and was wrecked on the Isle of St. Paul. That was about three years ago. Since then she had not lived with any one to my knowledge.

The CORONER. – Have you ever heard she has been in trouble with any man?

Witness. – No, but she has been locked up several times. I have never heard of any one threatening her, or that she was afraid of any one. I know of no man with whom she had any relations, and I did not know she lived in Flower and Dean-street. I knew that she was called "Long Liz".

The CORONER. – Have you ever heard the name of Stride?

Witness. – She never mentioned that name to me. If she had lived with any one of that name I am sure she would have told me. She used to come to me every Saturday, and I always gave her 2s.

The CORONER. – Did she come last Saturday?

Witness. – No; her visit on Thursday was an unusual one. Before that she had not missed a Saturday for between two and three years. She always came at 4 o'clock in the afternoon, and we used to meet at the corner of Chancery-lane. On Saturday afternoon I went there at half-past 3, and remained there until 5, but deceased did not turn up. On Sunday morning, when I read the paper, I wondered whether it was my sister. I had a presentiment that it was. I then went to Whitechapel and spoke to a policeman about my sister. I afterwards went to the St. George's mortuary. When I first saw the body I did not at first recognize it, as I only saw it by gas light; but the next day I recognized it.

The CORONER. – Did not you have some special presentiment about your sister?

Witness. – About 1.20 a.m. on Sunday morning I was lying on my bed when I felt a kind of pressure on my breast, and then I felt three kisses on my cheek. I also heard the kisses, and they were quite distinct.

A Juryman. – Did your sister have any special mark about her?

Witness. – Yes; a black mark on her leg, and I saw it there yesterday. I told the police I could recognize her by this particular mark. The mark was caused by my sister being bitten by an adder some years ago, and I was bitten on the finger at the same time. Here is the mark (showing it to the Coroner).

The CORONER. – Has your husband seen your sister?

Witness. – He has seen her once or twice some three years ago. I have another sister and a brother who are alive, but they have not seen her for years.

The CORONER. – I hear at one time you said it was your sister, and at another time you said it was not.

Witness. – I am sure it was.

The CORONER. – Have you any one that can corroborate you?

Witness. – Only my brother and my sister. This disgrace will kill my sister. The best thing will be for her brother to come up. I have kept this shame from every one. (Here the witness sobbed bitterly.)

The CORONER. – Was there any special mark on your sister's feet?

Witness. – I know she had a hollow at the bottom of one of her feet, which was the result of an accident.

The CORONER. – Did you recognize the clothes she wore?

Witness. – No, I did not. I never took notice of what she wore, for I was always grateful to get rid of her. Once she left a baby naked outside my door, and I had to keep it until she fetched it away. It was not one of the two children already mentioned, but was by some policeman or another. I do not know any one that would do her harm, for she was a girl every one liked.

The CORONER. – Would your brother recognize her?

Witness. – I am positive he could, although he has not seen her for years. I can now recognize her by the hair.

The CORONER. – I think you ought to go again to the spot where you have been in the habit of meeting your sister to see if she comes again. You say she has not missed a single Saturday for two and a half years. How about the Saturday when she was in prison?

Witness. – She has always been fined, and the money has been paid.

Mr. Frederick William Blackwell said, – I live at 100, Commercial-road, and am a surgeon. At 10 minutes past 1 on Sunday morning I was called to 40, Berner-street. I was called by a policeman, and my assistant, Mr. Johnson, went back with him. I followed immediately I had dressed. I consulted my watch on my arrival, and it was just 1.10. The deceased was lying on her left side completely across the yard. Her legs were drawn up, her feet against the wall of the right side of the yard passage. Her head was resting almost in the line of the carriage way, and her feet were about three yards from the gateway. The feet almost touched the wall, and the face was completely towards the wall. The neck and chest were quite warm; also the legs and face were slightly warm. The hands were cold. The right hand was lying on the chest, and was smeared inside and out with blood. It was quite open. The left hand was lying on the ground and was partially closed, and contained a small packet of cachous wrapped in tissue paper. There were no rings or marks of rings on the fingers. The appearance of the face was quite placid, and the mouth was slightly open. There was a check silk scarf round the neck, the bow of which was turned to the left side and pulled tightly. There was a long incision in the neck, which exactly corresponded with the lower border of the scarf. The lower edge of the scarf was slightly frayed, as if by a sharp knife. The incision in the neck commenced on the left side, $2\frac{1}{2}$ in. below the angle of the jaw, and almost in a direct line with it. It nearly severed the vessels on the left side, cut the windpipe completely in two, and terminated on the opposite side $1\frac{1}{2}$ in. below the angle of the right jaw, but without severing the vessels on that side. The post mortem appearances will be given subsequently.

By the CORONER. – I did not ascertain if the bloody hand had been moved. The blood was running down in the gutter into the drain. It was running in an opposite direction to the feet. There was a quantity of clotted blood just under the body.

The CORONER. – Were there no spots of blood anywhere?

Witness. – No. Some of the blood had been trodden about near to where the body was lying.

The CORONER. – Was there any blood on the side of the house, or splashes on the wall?

Witness. – No. It was very dark at the time, and I only examined it by the policeman's lamp. I have not since examined the place.

The CORONER. – Did you examine the clothing?

Witness. – Yes. There was no blood on any portion of it. The bonnet was lying on the ground, a few inches from the head. The dress was undone at the top. I know about what deceased had on, but could not give an accurate description of them. I noticed she had a bunch of flowers in her jacket. The injuries were beyond the possibility of self-infliction.

The CORONER. – How long had the deceased been dead when you saw her?

Witness. – From 20 minutes to half an hour when I arrived. It was a very mild night and was not raining at the time. There was no wet on deceased's clothing. Deceased would have bled to death comparatively slowly, on account of the vessels on one side only being severed, and the artery not completely severed. Deceased could not have cried out after the injuries were inflicted as the windpipe was severed. I felt the heart and found it quite warm. My assistant was present all the time. Dr. Phillips arrived from 20 minutes to half an hour after my arrival, but I did not notice the exact time.

The CORONER. – Could you see there was a woman there when you went in?

Witness. – Yes. The doors were closed when I arrived. I formed the opinion that the murderer first took hold of the silk scarf, at the back of it, and then pulled the deceased backwards, but I cannot say whether the throat was cut while the woman was standing or after she was pulled backwards. Deceased would take about a minute and a half to bleed to death. I cannot say whether the scarf would be tightened sufficiently to prevent deceased calling out.

At this stage the inquiry was adjourned until to-day.

The next report on the resumed inquest appeared in *The Times* on Thursday, 4 October 1888, page 10:

THE EAST-END MURDERS.

Yesterday afternoon Mr. Wynne E. Baxter, Coroner for the South-Eastern Division of Middlesex, resumed his inquiry at the Vestry-hall, Cable-street, St. George's-in-the- East, respecting the death of Elizabeth Stride, who was found murdered in Berner-street on Sunday morning last.

Detective-Inspector E. Reid, H Division, again watched the case on behalf of the Criminal Investigation Department.

Elizabeth Tanner stated: I live at 32, Flower and Dean-street, Spitalfields, and am a widow. I am the deputy of No. 32, which is a common lodginghouse. I have seen the body in the mortuary, and recognize the features of the deceased as a woman who had lodged off and on at the lodginghouse for six years. I knew her by the name of '"Long Liz."' I do not know her right name. She told me she was a Swedish woman, but never told me where she was born. She told me she was a married woman, and that her husband and children went down in the ship Princess Alice.

The CORONER. – When did you last see her alive?

Witness. – About 6.30 on Saturday afternoon. I do not know the name of her husband, or what occupation he had followed. When I last saw deceased she was in the Queen's Head publichouse, Commercial-street. I went back to the lodginghouse, and did not see any more of her. At that time deceased had no hat or coat on. I saw her in the kitchen of the lodginghouse, and then I went to another part of the building, and never saw her again until I saw her dead body in the mortuary this afternoon.

The CORONER. – Are you sure it is her? – Witness. – I am quite sure. I recognize the features, and by the fact that she had lost the roof of her mouth. She told me that happened when the Princess Alice went down.

The CORONER. – Was she on board the ship at the time? – Witness. – Yes; and it was during that time her mouth was injured.

The CORONER. – Was she at the lodginghouse on Friday night? – Witness. – Yes; on Thursday and Friday nights; but on no other night during the week. She did not pay for her bed on Saturday night.

The CORONER. – Do you know her male acquaintances? – Witness. – Only one, and I do not know his name. She left the man she was living with on Thursday to come and stay at my lodginghouse. That is what she told me.

The CORONER. – Have you seen this man? – Witness. – Yes; I saw him on Sunday evening.

The CORONER. – Do you know if she has ever been up at the Thames Police-court? – Witness. – I do not.

The CORONER. – Do you know any other place where she has lived? – Witness. – Only Fashion-street.

The CORONER. – Do you know if she had a sister living in Red Lion-square? – Witness. – I do not.

The CORONER. – What sort of woman was she? – Witness. – She was a very quiet and sober woman.

The CORONER. – Did she stop out late at night? – Witness. – Sometimes.

The CORONER. – Do you know if she had any money? – Witness. – I do not. On Saturday she cleaned the rooms for me, and I gave her 6d.

The CORONER. – Have you seen her clothes? – Witness. – Yes. I cannot say if the two handkerchiefs belonged to her. The clothes she was wearing were the ones she usually wore, and they are the same she had on Saturday. I recognized the long jacket as belonging to her.

The CORONER. – Did she ever tell you she was afraid of any one? – Witness. – No; and I never heard her say that any one had threatened to injure her.

The CORONER. – It is a common thing for people who have been lodging in your place not to come back? – Witness. – Yes; I took no notice of it. I was sent for to go to the mortuary.

A Juryman. – Do you remember the hour she came to the lodginghouse? – Witness. – I do not, although I saw her and took 4d. from her for her lodging. At that time she was wearing the long jacket I have seen in the mortuary. I did not see her bring any parcel with her.

Inspector Reid. – Have you ever heard the name of Stride mentioned in connexion with her? – Witness. – No.

A Juryman. – How long had deceased been away from your house before last Thursday? – Witness. – About three months; but I have seen her during that time – sometimes once a week and sometimes nearly every day.

The CORONER. – Did you understand what she was doing? – Witness. – She told me she worked among the Jews, and was living with a man in Fashion-street.

The CORONER. – Could she speak English well? – Witness. – Yes; and Swedish as well.

The CORONER. – When she spoke English could you tell she was a foreigner? – Witness. – No.

The CORONER. – Was there much association between her and her country people? – Witness. – No.

The CORONER. – Have you ever heard of her having in childhood broken a limb? – Witness. – I have not heard her say. I have never heard her carry on a conversation in the Swedish language; but she told me herself she was a Swede.

Catherine Lane, 32, Flower and Dean-street, said: I am a charwoman and am married to Patrick Lane, a dock-labourer. We live together at the lodginghouse and have been living there since the 11th of February of this year. I have seen the body of deceased in the mortuary and recognize it as "Long Liz," who lived in the same lodginghouse. Lately she had only been there since Thursday last. I have known her for six or seven years. During the time she was away she called at the lodginghouse, and I used frequently to see her in Fashion-street, where she was living. I spoke to the deceased on Thursday between 10 and 11 in the morning, She told me she had a few words with the man she was living with and left him. I saw her on Saturday afternoon when she was cleaning the deputy's rooms. I last saw her between 7 and 8 o'clock on Saturday evening. She was then in the kitchen, and had a long jacket and black hat on.

The CORONER. – Did she tell you where she was going? Witness. – She did not. When she left the kitchen she gave me a piece of velvet and asked me to mind it until she came back. The deputy would always mind things for the lodgers, and I do not know why she asked me to mind the velvet for her. Deceased showed me the piece of velvet on the previous day. I knew deceased had 6d. when she left, as she showed me the money, but I cannot say if she had any more money besides that. Deceased did not tell me she was coming back. I do not think she had been drinking.

The CORONER. – Do you know any one who is likely to have injured her? Witness. – No. I have heard her say she was a foreign woman, and she told me that at one time she lived in Devonshire-street, Commercial-road. I have never heard her say that at one time she lived at Poplar. She told me she had had a husband and that he was dead. Deceased never told me she had been threatened, or that she was afraid of any one. I know nothing about her history beyond what I have stated. I am satisfied it is she. I could tell by her actions that she was a foreign woman and did not bring all her words out plainly. I have heard her speaking to persons in her own language.

A juryman. – Did you ever hear her say she had a sister? Witness. – No; never.

The CORONER. – Do you know what she has been doing lately? Witness. – I do not.

Charles Preston stated: I live at 32, Flower and Dean-street, Spitalfields, and am a barber by occupation. I have been lodging there for about 18 months. I have seen the deceased there and identified her body on Sunday afternoon at the mortuary. I am quite sure the body is that of "Long Liz." I last saw her alive on Saturday evening, between 6 and 7 o'clock. At that time she was in the kitchen of the lodginghouse and was dressed ready to go out. She asked me for the loan of a clothes-brush. At that time she had on a black jacket trimmed with fur, and it is the same one I have seen in the mortuary. She wore a coloured striped silk handkerchief round her neck, and it was the same as I saw in the mortuary. I have not seen her with a pocket-handkerchief, and am unable to say if she had two. I always understood from the deceased that she was a Swede by birth and was born at Stockholm; that she came to England in the service of a foreign gentleman. I think she told me she was about 35 years of age. She told me she had been married, and that her husband was drowned at the foundering of the Princess Alice. I have some recollection that deceased told me her husband was a seafaring man. I have heard her say she had a coffeehouse at Chrisp-street, Poplar; but she did not say she had often been at the Thames Police-court. I have known her to be in custody on one Saturday afternoon for being drunk and disorderly at the Queen's Head publichouse, Commercial-road. She was let out on her own bail on the Sunday morning. That was some four or five months ago. I have never heard her say she had met with an accident. She did not tell me where she was going on Saturday evening, and never mentioned what time she was coming back. At times the lodgers did not pay for their beds until just before going to bed. When deceased was locked up it was late in the afternoon or towards the evening time. She has always given me to understand her name was Elizabeth Stride, and that her mother was still living in Sweden. I have heard her speaking fluently in a foreign language to person in the lodging-house.

Michael Kidney stated: I live at 38, Dorset-street, Spitalfields, and am a waterside labourer. I have seen the body in the mortuary and it is that of a woman whom I lived with. I have no doubt whatever about it.

The CORONER. – Do you know what her name was? Witness. – Elizabeth Stride. I have known her about three years, and she has been living with me nearly all that time.

The CORONER. – Do you know what her age was? Witness. – Between 36 and 38. She told me she was a Swede, and that she was born at Stockholm; that her father was a farmer, and that she came to England for the purpose of seeing the country. She afterwards told me she had come to England as servant to a family.

The CORONER. – Had she any relatives in England? Witness. – Only some of her mother's friends. She told me she was a widow, and that her husband had been a ship's carpenter belonging to Sheerness. She also told me her husband had kept a coffeehouse at Chrisp-street, Poplar, and that he was drowned on the Princess Alice.

The CORONER. – You had a quarrel with her on Thursday? Witness. – No. I last saw the deceased alive on Tuesday week.

The CORONER. – Did you quarrel then? Witness. – No; I left her in Commercial-street as I was going to work.

The CORONER. – Did you expect her to meet you later on? Witness. – I expected her to be at home. When I got home I found that she had been in and gone out. I did not again see her until I identified the body in the mortuary. She was perfectly sober when I last saw her. She was subject to going away whenever she thought she would. During the three years I have known her she has been away from me altogether about five months. I have cautioned her the same as I would a wife.

The CORONER. – Do you know any one she has picked up with? Witness. – I have seen the address of some one with the family she was living with at Hyde Park; but I cannot find it.

The CORONER. – That is not what I asked you. Do you think she went away with any one else? – Witness. – I do not think that, for she liked me better than any one else. It was drink that made her go away, and she always returned without my going after her. I do not believe she left me on Tuesday to go with any other man.

The CORONER. – Had she money at that time? Witness. – I do not think she was without a 1s., considering the money I gave her to keep the house.

The CORONER. – Do you know of anyone that was likely to have run foul of her? Witness. – On Monday night I went to Leman-street Police-station for a detective to act on my information, but I could not get one.

The CORONER. – It is not too late yet; can you give us any information now? Witness. – I have heard something said that leads me to believe, that had I been able to act the same as a detective I could have got a lot more information. When I went to the station I was intoxicated. I asked for a young detective. I told the inspector at the station that if the murder occurred on my beat I would shoot myself. I have been in the Army.

Inspector Reid. – Will you give me any information now? Witness. – I believe I could catch the man, if I had the proper force at my command. If I was to place the men myself I could capture the murderer. He would be caught in the act.

Inspector Reid. – Then you have no information to give? Witness. – No.

The CORONER. – Have you heard of a sister of deceased giving her money? Witness. – No, but Mrs. Malcolm, who stated she was sister to deceased, is very much like her.

The CORONER. – Had deceased ever had a child by you? Witness. – No. She told me a policeman used to see her at Hyde Park before she was married to Stride. I never heard her say she had a child by a policeman. Deceased told me she was the mother of nine children. Two were drowned on the Princess Alice with her husband, and the remainder are in a school belonging to the Swedish Church. The school is somewhere on the other side of the Thames. I have also heard her say that some friend of her husband had two of the children. I thoroughly believe the deceased was a Swede, and came from a superior class. She could also speak Yeddish [*sic*]. Both deceased and her husband were employed on board the Princess Alice.

Edward Johnston said: – I live at 100, Commercial-road, and am assistant to Drs. Kay and Blackwell. About five or ten minutes past 1 on Sunday morning, I received a call from constable 436 H. After informing Dr. Blackwell, who was in bed, of the nature of the case, I accompanied the constable to Berner-street. In a courtyard, adjoining 40, Berner-street, I was shown the figure of a woman lying on her left side. There was a crowd of people in the yard and some policemen. No one was touching the deceased, and there was very little light. What there was came from the policemen's lanterns. I examined the woman and found an incision in the throat. The wound appeared to have stopped bleeding. I also felt the body to see if it was warm, and found it was all warm with the exception of the hands, which were quite cold. The dress was not undone, and I undid it to see if the chest was warm. I did not move the head at all, and left it exactly as I found it. The body was not moved while I was there. The knees were nearer to the wall than the head. There was a stream of blood reaching down to the gutter. It was all clotted blood. There was very little blood near the neck, as nearly all of it had run away in the direction away from the legs. As soon as Dr. Blackwell arrived I handed the case over to him.

The CORONER. – Did you look at the hands? Witness. – No. I saw the left hand was lying away from the body, and the arm was bent. The right arm was also bent. The left hand might have been on the ground.

The CORONER. – Was there any mark of a footstep on the stream of blood? Witness. – No. I was looking at the body and not at those around me. As soon as Dr. Blackwell came he looked at his watch. It was then 1.16. I was there three or four minutes before Dr. Blackwell.

The CORONER. – Did you notice the bonnet of deceased? Witness. – Yes, it was lying on the ground, beyond the head of deceased to the distance of three or four inches. I did not notice the paper in the left hand. The gates were not closed when I got there, but they were shortly afterwards.

Thomas Coram said: I live at 67, Plummer's-road, Mile-end, and am employed at a cocoanut warehouse. On Sunday night I was coming away from a friends at 16, Bath-gardens, Brady-street. I was walking on the right hand side of the Whitechapel-road towards Aldgate. When opposite No. 253 I crossed over, and saw a knife lying on the doorstep. No. 252 was a laundry business, and there were two steps leading to the front door. I found the knife on the bottom step. That is the knife I found (witness being shown a long-bladed knife). The handkerchief produced was wrapped round the handle. It was folded, and then twisted round the handle. The handkerchief was blood-stained. I did not touch them. A policeman came towards me, and I called his attention to them.

The CORONER. – The blade of the knife is dagger-shaped and is sharpened on one side. The blade is about 9in. or 10in. long, I should say.

Witness. – The policeman took the knife to the Leman-street Police-station, and I went with him.

The CORONER. – Were there many people passing at the time? Witness. – I should think I passed about a dozen between Brady-street and where I found the knife.

The CORONER. – Could it easily be seen? Witness. – Yes; and it was light.

The CORONER. – Did you pass a policeman before you got to the spot? Witness. – Yes, I passed three. It was about half-past 12 at night.

Constable Joseph Drage 282 H, stated: At 12.30 on Monday morning I was on fixed-point duty in the Whitechapel-road, opposite Great Garden-street. I saw the last witness stooping down at a doorway opposite No. 253. I was going towards him when he rose up and beckoned me with his finger. He then said, "Policeman, there is a knife down here." I turned on my light and saw a long-bladed knife lying on the doorstep. I picked up the knife and found it was smothered with blood. The blood was dry. There was a handkerchief bound round the handle and tied with string. The handkerchief also had blood-stains on it. I asked the last witness how he came to see it. He said, "I was looking down, when I saw something white." I then asked him what he did out so late, and he replied, "I have been to a friend's in Bath-gardens." He then gave me his name and address, and we went to the police-station together. The knife and handkerchief produced are the same.

The CORONER. – Was the last witness sober? Witness. – Yes. His manner was natural, and he said when he saw the knife it made his blood run cold, and added that nowadays they heard of such funny things. When I passed I should have undoubtedly seen the knife. I was passing there continually. Some little time before a horse fell down opposite the place where the knife was found. I assisted in getting the horse up, and during that time a person might have laid the knife down on the step. I would not be positive that the knife was not there a quarter of an hour previously, but I think not. About an hour previously the landlady let out some woman, and the knife was not there then. I handed the knife to Dr. Phillips on the Monday afternoon. It was then sealed and secured.

Dr. George Baxter [*sic*] **Phillips** said: – I live at 2, Spital-square. I was called at 1.20 on Sunday morning to Leman-street Police-station, and from there sent on to Berner-street to a yard at the side of a club-house. I found Chief-Inspector West and Inspector Pinhorn in possession of a body, which had already been seen by Dr. Blackwell, who arrived some time before me. The body was lying on the near side, with the face turned towards the wall, the head up the yard and the feet towards the street. The left arm was extended, and there was a packet of cachous in the left hand. A number of these were in the gutter. I took them from her hand and handed them to Dr. Blackwell. The right arm was over the belly. The back of the hand and wrist had on it clotted blood. the legs were drawn up, with the feet close to the wall. The body and face were warm and the hand cold. The legs were quite warm. Deceased had a silk handkerchief round her neck, and it appeared to be slightly torn. I have since ascertained it was cut. This corresponded with the right angle of the jaw. The throat was deeply gashed, and there was an abrasion of the skin about $1\frac{1}{4}$. in diameter, apparently stained with blood, under her right brow. At 3 p.m. on Monday, at St. George's mortuary, in the presence of Dr. Rygate and Mr. Johnston, Dr. Blackwell and I made a post mortem examination. Dr. Blackwell kindly consented to make the dissection. Rigor Mortis was still thoroughly marked. There was mud on the left side of the face and it was matted in the head. We then removed the clothes. The body was fairly nourished. Over both shoulders, especially the right, and under the collar-bone and in front of the chest there was a blueish discolouration, which I have watched and have seen on two occasions since. There was a clean-cut incision on the neck. It was 6in. in length and commenced $2\frac{1}{2}$in. in a straight line below the angle of the jaw, $\frac{3}{4}$in. over an undivided muscle, and then, becoming deeper, dividing the sheath. the cut was very clean, and deviated a little downwards. The artery and other vessels contained in the sheath were all cut through. The cut through the tissues on the right side was more superficial, and tailed off to about 2 in. below the right angle of the jaw. The deep vessels on that side were uninjured. From this it was evident that the haemorrhage was caused through the partial severance of the left carotid artery. Decomposition had commenced in the skin. Dark brown spots were on the anterior surface of the left chin. There was a deformity in the bones of the right leg, which was not straight, but bowed forwards. There was no recent external injury save to the neck. The body being washed more thoroughly, I could see some healing sores. The lobe of the left ear was torn as if from the removal or wearing through of an earring, but it was thoroughly healed. On removing the scalp there was no sign of bruising or extravasation of blood. The skull was about a sixth of an inch in thickness, and the brain was fairly normal. The left lung had old adhesions to the chest wall, the right slightly. Both lungs were unusually pale. There was no fluid in the pericardium. The heart was small, the left ventricle firmly contracted, and the right slightly so. There was no clot in the pulmonary artery, but the right ventricle was full of dark clot. The left was firmly contracted so as to be absolutely empty. The stomach was large, and the mucous membrane only congested. It contained partly-digested food, apparently consisting of cheese, potato, and farinaceous powder. All the teeth on the left lower jaw were absent. On Tuesday I again went to the mortuary to observe the marks on the shoulder. I found in the pocket of the underskirt of the deceased the following articles – key as if belonging to a padlock, a small piece of lead pencil, a pocket comb, a broken piece of comb, a metal spoon, some buttons, and a hook. Examining her jacket, I found that, while there was a small amount of mud on the right side, the left was well plastered with mud. I have not seen the two pocket-handkerchiefs.

I will answer any questions put to me, but as there is another case pending I think I had better stop here.

The CORONER. – What is the cause of death? Witness. – It is undoubtedly from the loss of blood from the left carotid artery and the division of the wind-pipe.

The CORONER. – Did you examine the blood at Berner-street? Witness. – I did. The blood had run down the waterway to within a few inches of the side entrance of the club.

The CORONER. – Were there any spots of blood on the wall? Witness. – I could trace none. Roughly estimating it I should say there was an unusual flow of blood considering the stature and the nourishment of the body.

At this point the inquiry was adjourned until Friday morning.

There then follows, in this report in *The Times*, some interesting correspondence:

The following correspondence has been sent to us for publication:

"Office of the Board of Works, Whitechapel District, 15, Great Alie-street, Whitechapel, Oct. 2.

"Sir, – At a meeting of the Board of Works for the Whitechapel District a resolution was passed, of which the following is a copy –

"That this Board regards with horror and alarm the several atrocious murders recently perpetrated within the district of Whitechapel and its vicinity and calls upon Sir Charles Warren so to regulate and strengthen the police force in the neighbourhood as to guard against any repetition of such atrocities."

"And by direction of the Board the copy resolution is forwarded to you in the hope that it will receive your favourable consideration. I am, &c.,

"ALFRED TURNER, Clerk.

"Colonel Sir Charles Warren, G.C.M.G."

"POLICE NOTICE.
"TO THE OCCUPIER.

"On the mornings of Friday, 31st August, Saturday 8th, and Sunday 30th September, 1888, women were murdered in or near Whitechapel, supposed by some one residing in the immediate neighbourhood. Should you know of any person to whom suspicion is attached, you are earnestly requested to communicate at once with the nearest police-station.

"Metropolitan Police Office, 30th September, 1888."

"4 Whitehall-place, S.W., Oct. 3.

"Sir, – In reply to a letter of the 2d inst. from the Clerk of the Board of Works for the Whitechapel District transmitting a resolution of the Board with regard to the recent atrocious murders perpetrated in and about Whitechapel, I have to point out that the carrying out of your proposals as to regulating and strengthening the police force in your district cannot possibly do more than guard or take precautions against any repetition of such atrocities so long as the victims actually, but unwittingly, connive at their own destruction.

"Statistics show that London, in comparison to its population, is the safest city in the world to live in. The prevention of murder directly cannot be effected by any strength of the police force; but it is reduced and brought to a minimum by rendering it most difficult to escape detection. In the particular class of murder now confronting us, however, the unfortunate victims appear to take the murderer to some retired spot and to place themselves in such a position that they can be slaughtered without a sound being heard; the murder, therefore, takes place without any clue to the criminal being left.

"I have to request and call upon your Board, as popular representatives, to do all in your power to dissuade the unfortunate women about Whitechapel from going into lonely places in the dark with any persons – whether acquaintances or strangers.

"I have also to point out that the purlieus about Whitechapel are most imperfectly lighted, and that darkness is an important assistant to crime.

"I can assure you, for the information of your Board, that every nerve has been strained to detect the criminal or criminals, and to render more difficult further atrocities.

"You will agree with me that it is not desirable that I should enter into particulars as to what the police are doing in the matter. It is most important for good results that our proceedings should not be published, and the very fact that you may be unaware of what the Detective Department is doing is only the stronger proof that it is doing its work with secrecy and efficiency.

"A large force of police has been drafted into the Whitechapel district to assist those already there to the full extent necessary to meet the requirements; but I have to observe that the Metropolitan police have not large reserves doing nothing and ready to meet emergencies, but every man has his duty assigned to him; and I can only strengthen the Whitechapel district by drawing men from duty in other parts of the metropolis.

"You will be aware that the whole of the police work of the metropolis has to be done as usual while this extra work is going on, and that at such a time as this extra precautions have to be taken to prevent the commission of other classes of crime being facilitated through the attention of the police being diverted to one special place and object.

"I trust that your Board will assist the police by persuading the inhabitants to give them every information in their power concerning any suspicious characters in the various dwellings, for which object 10,000 handbills, a copy of which I enclose, have been distributed.

"I have read the reported proceedings of your meeting, and I regret to see that the greatest misconceptions appear to have arisen in the public mind as to the recent action in the administration of the police. I beg you will dismiss from your minds, as utterly fallacious, the numerous anonymous statements as to recent changes stated to have been made in the police force, of a character not conducive to efficiency.

"It is stated that the Rev. Daniel Greatorex announced to you that one great cause of police inefficiency was a new system of police whereby constables were constantly changed from one district to another, keeping them ignorant of their beats.

"I have seen this statement made frequently in the newspapers lately, but it is entirely without foundation. The system at present in use has existed for the last 20 years, and constables are seldom or never drafted from their districts except for promotion or from some particular cause.

"Notwithstanding the many good reasons why constables should be changed on their beats, I have considered the reasons on the other side to be more cogent, and have felt that they should be thoroughly acquainted with the districts in which they serve.

"And with regard to the Detective Department – a department relative to which reticence is always most desirable – I may say that a short time ago I made arrangements which still further reduced the necessity for transferring officers from districts which they knew thoroughly.

"I have to call attention to the statement of one of your members that in consequence of the change in the condition of Whitechapel in recent years a thorough revision of the police arrangements is necessary, and I shall be very glad to ascertain from you what changes your Board consider advisable; and I may assure you that your proposal will receive from me every consideration.

> "I am, Sir, your obedient servant,
> "CHARLES WARREN.

"The Chairman, Board of Works, Whitechapel District."

The next report on the Stride inquest appears in *The Times* of Saturday, 6 October 1888, page 6:

THE EAST-END MURDERS.

Yesterday afternoon Mr. Wynne E. Baxter, Coroner for the South-Eastern Division of Middlesex, resumed his inquiry at the Vestry-hall, Cable-street, St. George's-in-the-East, respecting the death of Elizabeth Stride, who was found murdered in Berner-street, St. George's, on the early morning of Sunday last. Superintendent T. Arnold and Detective-inspector Reid, H Division, watched the case on behalf of the Criminal Investigation Department.

Dr. Phillips was re-called and said:- After the last examination, in company with Dr. Blackwell and Dr. Brown, I went to the mortuary and examined more carefully the roof of the mouth. I could not find any injury to or absence of anything from the mouth. I have also carefully examined the two handkerchiefs, and have not found any blood on them. I believe the stains on the larger one were fruit stains. I am convinced that the deceased had not swallowed either skin or seed of a grape within many hours of her death. The abrasion which I spoke of on the right side of the neck was only apparently an abrasion, for on washing it the staining was removed and the skin was found to be uninjured. The knife that was produced on the last occasion was submitted to me by Constable 282 H. On examination I found it to be such a knife as would be used in a chandler's shop, called a slicing knife. It had blood upon it, which was similar to that of a warm-blooded being. It has been recently blunted and the edge turned by apparently rubbing on a stone. It evidently was before that a very sharp knife. Such a knife could have produced the incision and injuries to the neck of the deceased, but it was not such a weapon as I would have chosen to inflict injuries in this particular place; and if my opinion as regards the position of the body is correct, the knife in question would become an improbable instrument as having caused the incision.

The CORONER. – Could you give us any idea of the position of the victim? Witness. – I have come to the conclusion that the deceased was seized by the shoulders, placed on the ground, and that the perpetrator of the deed was on her right side when he inflicted the cut. I am of opinion that the cut was made from the left to the right side of the deceased, and therefore arises the unlikelihood of such a long knife having inflicted the wound described in the neck, taking into account the position of the incision.

The CORONER. – Was there anything in the cut that showed the incision first made was done with a pointed knife? Witness. – No.

The CORONER. – Have you formed any opinion how the right hand of the deceased was covered with blood? Witness. – No; that is a mystery. I may say I am taking it as a fact that the hand always remained in the same position in which he found it – resting across the body.

The CORONER. – How long had the deceased been dead when you arrived? Witness. – Within an hour she was alive.

The CORONER. – Would the injury take long to inflict? Witness. – Only a few seconds. It might be done in two seconds.

The CORONER. – Does the presence of the cachous in her hand show that it was done suddenly, or would it simply show a muscular grasp? Witness. – No; I cannot say. You will remember some of the cachous were found in the gutter. I have seen several self- inflicted wounds more extensive than this one, but then they have not divided the carotid artery. You will see by that, as in the other cases, there appears to have been a knowledge where to cut the throat.

The CORONER. – Was there any other similarity between this and Chapman's case? Witness. – There is a great dissimilarity. In Chapman's case the neck was severed all round down to the vertebral column, the vertical bone being marked, and there had been an evident attempt to separate the bones.

The CORONER. – Would the murderer be likely to get blood-stained? Witness. – Not necessarily, for the commencement of the wound and the injury to the vessels would be away from him, and the stream of blood, for stream it would be, would be directed away from him, and towards the waterway already mentioned. There was no perceptible sign of an anaesthetic having been used. The absence of noise is a difficult question in this case, and under the circumstances, to account for, but it must not be taken for granted that I assumed there was no noise. If there was an absence of noise, there was nothing in this case that I can account for. She might have called out and not have been heard. As I said before, if there was a noise I cannot account for it.

The Foreman. – Was the wound caused by drawing the knife across the throat? Witness. – Undoubtedly. My reason for supposing deceased was injured when on the ground was partly on account of the absence of blood anywhere but on the left side of the body, and between that side and the wall.

The CORONER. – Was there any sign of liquor in the stomach? Witness. – There was no trace of it.

Dr. Blackwell, recalled, said: – I have little to say except to confirm Dr. Phillips's statement. I removed the cachous from the left hand, which was nearly open. The packet had lodged between the thumb and fourth finger, and had become almost hidden. That accounted for its not having been seen by several of those around. I believe the hand relaxed after the injury was inflicted, as death would arise from fainting owing to the rapid loss of blood. I wish to say that, taking into consideration the absence of any instrument it was impossible that the deceased could have committed suicide. With respect to the knife which was found, I should say I concur with Dr. Phillips in his opinion that although it might have possibly inflicted the injury it was extremely unlikely that such an instrument was used. The murderer using a sharp, round-pointed instrument would severely handicap himself, as he could only use it one way. He was informed that slaughterers always used round-pointed instruments.

The CORONER. – No one suggested anything about a slaughterer. Is it your suggestion that this was done by a slaughterer? Witness. – No, I concur with Dr. Phillips as to the postmortem appearances. There were some pressure marks on the shoulders. These were not regular bruises, and there was no abrasion of the skin.

A juryman. – Do you know how these marks were likely to have been caused? Witness. – By two hands pressing on the shoulders.

Did you see any grapes in the yard? – No, I did not.

Sven Olsson said: – I live at 36, Prince's-square, and I am clerk to the Swedish Church in that square. I saw the body of the deceased in the mortuary on Tuesday morning. I have known deceased for about 17 years.

The CORONER. – Was she a Swede? – Yes.

What was her name? – Elizabeth Gustafsdotter was her maiden name. Elizabeth Stride was her married name, and she was the wife of John Thomas Stride, a ship's carpenter. She was born on the 27th of November, 1843, at Torslander, near Gottenburg, in Sweden.

The CORONER. – Was she married in your church? Witness. – No. We register those who come to this country bringing with them a certificate and desiring to be registered.

The CORONER. – When was she registered? Witness. – Our register is dated July 10, 1866. She was registered as an unmarried woman.

The CORONER. – How do you know she was the wife of John Thomas Stride? Witness. – I suppose she gave it to the clergyman, as it is written here. In the registry I find a memorandum, undated, in the handwriting of the Rev. Mr. Palmar, in abbreviated Swedish. It means "married to an Englishman, John Thomas Stride." I do not know when this entry was made.

The CORONER. – How long has Mr. Palmar been at the church? Witness. – About a year. This registry is a new one and copied from an older book. I have seen the original entry, and it was written many years ago.

The CORONER. – Would you mind looking at the entry in the older book, and see in whose handwriting it is? Witness. – I will.

Inspector Reid. – Do you know this hymn book? Witness. – Yes.

The CORONER. – Is there any name in it? Witness. – No; I gave it to the deceased last winter.

The CORONER. – Do you know when she was married to Stride? Witness. – I think it was in 1869. She told me her husband was drowned in the Princess Alice.

The CORONER. – Have you any schools connected with the Swedish Church? Witness. – No; I do not remember hearing she ever had any children. She told me her husband went down in the Princess Alice.

The CORONER. – Have you ever seen her husband? Witness. – No; I think we gave the deceased some assistance before we knew her husband was dead. I forget where she was living at the time, but two years ago she gave her address as Devonshire-Street, Commercial-road. She said she was doing a little work – sewing. Deceased could speak English pretty well.

The CORONER. – Do you know when deceased came to England?

Witness. – I cannot say, but I think a little before the name was registered.

William Marshall said, – I live at 64, Berner-street, Commercial-road, and am a labourer. On Sunday last I saw the body of deceased in the mortuary. I recognized it as that of a woman I saw on Saturday evening about three doors off from where I am living in Berner street. That was about a quarter to 12. She was on the pavement opposite No. 68, and between Christian-street and Boyd-street. She was standing talking to a man. I recognize her both by her face and dress.

The CORONER. – Was she wearing a flower when you saw her? – No.

The CORONER. – Were they talking quietly? – Yes.

The CORONER. – Can you describe the man? There was no lamp near, and I did not see the face of the man she was talking to. He had on a small black coat and dark trousers. He seemed to me to be a middle-aged man.

The CORONER. – What sort of cap was he wearing? – A round cap with a small peak to it; something like what a sailor would wear.

The CORONER. – What height was he? – About 5 ft. 6 in., and he was rather stout. He was decently dressed, and I should say he worked at some light business, and had more the appearance of a clerk than anything else.

The CORONER. – Did you see whether he had any whiskers? – From what I saw of his face I do not think he had. He was not wearing gloves, and he had no stick or anything in his hand.

The CORONER. – What sort of a coat was it? – A cut-away one.

The CORONER. – You are quite sure this is the woman? – Yes, I am. I did not take much notice of them. I was standing at my door, and what attracted my attention first was her standing there some time, and he was kissing her. I heard the man say to deceased, "You would say anything but your prayers." He was mild speaking, and appeared to be an educated man. They went down the street.

The CORONER. – Would they pass the club? – They had done so.

The CORONER. – How was she dressed? – In a black jacket and black skirt.

The CORONER. – Were either of them the worse for drink? – They did not appear to be so. I went in about 12 o'clock and heard nothing more until I heard "Murder" being called in the street. It had then just gone 1 o'clock.

A Juryman. – How long were you standing at the door? – From 11.30 to 12.

The Juryman. – Did it rain then? – No, it did not rain until nearly 3 o'clock.

The Foreman. – What sort of bonnet had she on? – I believe it was a small black crape one.

Inspector Reid. – When you saw them first they were standing between your house and the club? – Yes, and they remained there for about 10 minutes. They passed me once, and I could not see the man's face, as it was turned towards the deceased. There was a lamp over No. 70.

Inspector Reid. – Were they hurrying along? – No.

Was it raining at the time? – No, it was not.

Mr. Olsson, recalled, said, – I find that the original entry of the marriage of the deceased is in the handwriting of Mr. Frost, who was the pastor for about 18 years until two years ago.

James Brown stated, – I live at 35, Fairclough-street. I saw the deceased about a quarter to 1 on Sunday morning. At that time I was going from my own house to get some supper from a chandler's shop at the corner of Berner-street and Fairclough-street. As I was going across the road I saw a man and woman standing by the Board School in Fairclough-street. They were standing against the wall. As I passed them I heard the woman say, "No, not to-night, some other night." That made me turn round, and I looked at them. I am certain the woman was the deceased. I did not notice any flowers in her dress. The man had his arm up against the wall, and the woman had her back to the wall facing him. I noticed the man had a long coat on, which came very nearly down to his heels. I believe it was an overcoat. I could not say what kind of cap he had on. The place where they were standing was rather dark. I saw nothing light in colour about either of them. I then went on and went indoors. I had nearly finished my supper when I heard screams of "Police" and "Murder." That was about a quarter of an hour after I got in. I do not think it was raining at the time. I should say the man was about 5 ft. 7 in. in height. He appeared to be stoutish built. Both the man and woman appeared to be sober. I did not notice any foreign accent about the woman's voice. When I heard screams of "Police" and "Murder" I opened the window, but could not see any one and the screams ceased. The cries were those of moving persons, and appeared to be going in the direction of Grove-street. Shortly afterwards I saw a policeman standing at the corner of Christian-street. I heard a man opposite call out to the constable that he was wanted. I then saw the policeman run along to Berner-street.

By the CORONER. – I am almost certain it was the deceased.

Police-constable William Smith, 452 H, said that on Saturday night his beat was past Berner-street. It went from the corner of Jower's-walk, Commercial-road, as far as Christian-street, down Christian-street and Fairclough-street as far as Grove-street, then back along Fairclough-street as far as Backchurch-lane, up there as far as the Commercial-road, taking all the interior streets, including Berner-street, and Batley [*sic*]-street. The witness continued, – It takes me from 25 minutes to half an hour to go round my beat. I was last in Berner-street about half-past 12 or 12.35. At 1 o'clock I went to Berner-street in my ordinary round. I saw a crowd of people outside the gates of No. 40. I did not hear any cries of ''Police.'' When I got there I saw Constables 12 H. R and 252 H. I then saw the deceased, and, on looking at her, found she was dead. I then went to the station for the ambulance. Dr. Blackwell's assistant came just as I was going away.

The CORONER. – Did you go up Berner-street into Commercial-road? – No; I turned up Fairclough-street.

Did you see any one? – No, sir.

When you were in Berner-street the previous time did you see any one? – Yes, a man and a woman.

Was the latter anything like the deceased? – Yes, I saw her face. I have seen the deceased in the mortuary, and I feel certain it is the same person.

Was she on the pavement? – Yes, a few yards up Berner-street on the opposite side to where she was found.

Did you see the man who was talking to her? – Yes; I noticed he had a newspaper parcel in his hand. It was about 18 in. in length and 6 in. or 8 in. in width. He was about 5 ft. 7 in. as near as I could say. He had on a hard felt deerstalker hat of dark colour and dark clothes.

What kind of a coat was it? – An overcoat. He wore dark trousers.

Did you overhear any conversation? – No.

Did he seem sober? – Yes. I did not see much of the face of the man except that he had no whiskers.

Can you form any idea as to his age? – About 28 years.

Can you give any idea as to what he was? – No, sir, I cannot. He was of respectable appearance. I noticed the woman had a flower in her jacket.

When you saw them talking, which way did you go? – Straight up Berner-street into the Commercial-road. In the centre of Berner-street were some courts which led into Backchurch-lane.

When did it last rain before 1 o'clock? – To the best of my recollection, it rained very little after 11 o'clock.

The Foreman. – Was the man or the woman acting in a suspicious manner? – No.

Do you see many prostitutes or people hanging about in Berner-street? – No, very few.

Inspector Reid. – Did you see these people more than once? – No. When I saw deceased lying on the ground I recognized her at once and made a report of what I had seen.

The witness Kidney was recalled, and the CORONER said, – Have you ever seen that hymn-book before? – Yes; I recognize it as one belonging to the deceased. It used to be in my place. I found it in Mrs. Smith's room, next to my own. Mrs. Smith said deceased gave it to her to take care of when she left on Tuesday.

Inspector Reid. – When you and deceased lived together I believe you had a padlock on the door? – Yes; there was only one key, which I had, but she got in and out somehow. The hymn-book was taken from the room on Wednesday week, the day after she went away. That was done during my absence.

The CORONER. – What makes you think there was anything the matter with the roof of her mouth? – She told me she was kicked when the Princess Alice went down.

Philip Krantz, who claimed to affirm, said, – I live at 40, Berner-street, and am the editor of a Hebrew paper called the *Workers' Friend*. I work in the room at the back of the printing office on the ground floor, and the entrance is from the yard. I was in the back room from 9 o'clock on Saturday night until one of the members of the club came and told me there was a woman lying in the yard.

The CORONER. – Had you heard any cry or scream? – None.

Was your window or door open? – No.

Is it a wooden structure? – No; brick.

Supposing a woman had screamed, would you have heard it? – I do not know. They were singing upstairs.

When you went out into the yard was there any one round deceased? – Yes, members of the club were near the woman, but there was no one there that I did not know.

Were you on the look out to see if there was any stranger there? – No. I went out into the street to look for a policeman.

Do you think it possible for any one to escape without being noticed after you arrived there? – I do not think it was, but he might have done so before.

Did you see the face of deceased? – No; my name and address was taken, and I was examined and searched by the police.

Constable 12 HR said, – At half-past 5 on Sunday morning I washed all traces of blood away. That was after the doctors had left. There were no traces of blood on the wall.

Detective-inspector Edmund Reid, H Division stated, – I received a telegram at 1.25 a.m. on Sunday morning at the Commercial-street police office. I at once proceeded to 40, Berner-street. I saw there Chief Inspector West, Inspector Pinhorn, several sergeants and constables, Drs. Phillips and Blackwell, a number of residents in the yard, and club members, with persons who had come into the yard and had been shut in by the police. At that time Dr. Phillips, with Dr. Blackwell, was examining the throat of the deceased woman. Superintendent Arnold followed in, as well as several other officers. When it was found a murder had been committed a thorough search was made of the yard, houses, and buildings, but no trace could be found of any person likely to have committed the deed. As soon as the search was over the whole of the persons who had come into the yard and the members of the club were interrogated, their names and addresses taken, their pockets searched, and their clothes and hands examined. There were 28 of them. Each person was dealt with separately. They properly accounted for themselves, and were then allowed to leave. The houses were then visited a second time and the names of the people therein taken, and they were also examined and their rooms searched. The door of a loft was found locked on the inside, and it was forced. The loft was searched, but no trace of the murderer could be found. A description was taken of the body and circulated round the surrounding stations by wire. Inquiries were made in the street at the different houses, and no person could be found who heard any disturbance during the night. I minutely examined the wall near where the body was found, but could find no spots of blood. About 4.30 the body was removed to the mortuary. I then informed you (the coroner) verbally at your residence, and then returned to the yard and made another examination. It being daylight, I searched the walls thoroughly, but could find no marks of any person having scaled them. I then proceeded to the mortuary and took a correct description of the body and clothing, which is as follows:- I guessed her age as 42, length 5 ft. 2 in., complexion pale, hair dark brown and curly. I raised an eyelid and found that her eyes were light grey; I parted her lips and found that she had lost her upper teeth in front.

She had an old black skirt, and an old black jacket trimmed with fur. Fastened on the right side was a small bunch of flowers, consisting of maidenhair fern and a red rose. She had two light serge petticoats, white stockings, white chemise with insertion in front, side-spring boots, and black crape bonnet. In her jacket pocket I found two pockethandkerchiefs, a thimble, and a piece of wool on a card. That description was then circulated. Since then the police engaged in the enquiry had made house to house inquiry in the immediate neighbourhood, with the result that we have been able to produce the witnesses which have appeared before you. The inquiry is still going on. Every endeavour is being made to arrest the assassin, but up to the present without success.

At this stage the inquiry was adjourned to Tuesday week.

We are requested to state that Sir Charles Warren has been making inquiries as to the practicability of employing trained bloodhounds for use in special cases in the streets of London; and having ascertained that dogs can be procured that have been accustomed to work in a town, he is making immediate arrangements for their use in London.

The police authorities of Whitehall have had reproduced in facsimile and published on the walls of London the letter and post-card sent to the Central News agency. The language of the card and letter is of a brutal character, and is full of Americanisms. The handwriting, which is clear and plain, and disguised in part, is that of a person accustomed to write a round hand like that employed by clerks in offices. The exact colour of the ink and the smears of blood are reproduced in the placard, and information is asked in identification of the handwriting. The post-card bears a tolerably clear imprint of a bloody thumb or finger mark.

The Times of Thursday, 18 October 1888, page 7, printed the thanks of Sir Charles Warren to the people of the East End for the way they had assisted the enquiries of the Metropolitan Police:

THE EAST-END MURDERS.

We are requested to publish the following –

Sir Charles Warren wishes to say that the marked desire evinced by the inhabitants of the Whitechapel district to aid the police in the pursuit of the author of the recent crimes has enabled him to direct that, subject to the consent of the occupiers, a thorough house-to-house search should be made within a defined area. With few exceptions the inhabitants of all classes and creeds have freely fallen in with the proposal, and have materially assisted the officers engaged in carrying it out.

Sir Charles Warren feels that some acknowledgement is due on all sides for the cordial cooperation of the inhabitants, and he is much gratified that the police officers have carried out so delicate a duty with the marked good will of all those with whom they have come in contact.

Sir Charles Warren takes this opportunity of acknowledging the receipt of an immense volume of correspondence of a semi-private character on the subject of the Whitechapel murders, which he has been quite unable to respond to in a great number of instances; and he trusts that the writers will accept this acknowledgement in lieu of individual replies. They may be assured that their letters have received every consideration.

The Times of Wednesday, 24 October 1888, page 3, gave a report on the final day of the inquest into the death of Elizabeth Stride:

THE EAST-END MURDERS.

Yesterday afternoon Mr. Wynne E. Baxter, Coroner for the South-Eastern Division of Middlesex, resumed his adjourned inquiry at the Vestry-hall, Cable-street, St. George's-in-the-East, respecting the death of Elizabeth Stride, who was found murdered in Berner-street, St. George's on the 30th ult.

Detective-inspector Reid, H Division, watched on behalf of the Criminal Investigation Department.

Detective-Inspector Edmund Reid, recalled, said, – I have examined the books of the Poplar and Stepney Sick Asylum, and find therein the entry of the death of John Thomas William Stride, a carpenter, of Poplar. His death took place on the 24th day of October, 1884. Witness then said that he had found Mrs. Watts, who would give evidence.

Constable Walter Stride stated that he recognized the deceased by the photograph as the person who married his uncle, John Thomas Stride, in 1872 or 1873. His uncle was a carpenter, and the last time witness saw him he was living in the East India Dock-road, Poplar.

Elizabeth Stokes, 5, Charles-street, Tottenham said, – My husband's name is Joseph Stokes, and he is a brickmaker. My first husband's name was Watts, a wine merchant of Bath. Mrs. Mary Malcolm, of 15, Eagle-street, Red Lion-square, Holborn, is my sister. I have received an anonymous letter from Shepton Mallet, saying my first husband is alive. I want to clear my character. My sister I have not seen for years. She has given me a dreadful character. Her evidence is all false. I have five brothers and sisters.

A juryman. – Perhaps she refers to another sister.

Inspector Reid. – She identified the deceased person as her sister, and said she had a crippled foot. This witness has a crippled foot.

Witness. – This has put me to a dreadful trouble, and trial. I have only a poor crippled husband, who is now outside. It is a shame my sister should say what she has said about me, and that the innocent should suffer for the guilty.

The CORONER. – Is Mrs. Malcolm here?

Inspector Reid. – No, Sir.

The CORONER, in summing up, said the jury would probably agree with him that it would be unreasonable to adjourn this inquiry again on the chance of something further being ascertained to elucidate the mysterious case on which they had devoted so much time. The first difficulty which presented itself was the identification of the deceased. That was not an unimportant matter. Their trouble was principally occasioned by Mrs. Malcolm, who after some hesitation, and after having had two further opportunities of viewing again the body, positively swore that the deceased was her sister – Mrs. Elizabeth Watts, of Bath. It had since been clearly proved that she was mistaken, notwithstanding the visions which were simultaneously vouchsafed at the hour of the death to her and her husband. If her evidence was correct, there were points of resemblance between the deceased and Elizabeth Watts which almost reminded one of the *Comedy of Errors*. Both had been courted by policemen; they both bore the same Christian name, and were of the same age; both lived with sailors; both at one time kept coffee-houses at Poplar; both were nick-named "Long Liz;" both were said to have had children in charge of their husbands' friends; both were given to drink; both lived in East-end common lodging-houses; both had been charged at the Thames police- court; both had escaped punishment on the ground that they were subject to epileptic fits, although the friends of both were certain that this was a fraud; both had lost their front teeth, and both had been leading very questionable lives. Whatever might be the true explanation of this marvellous similarity, it appeared to be pretty satisfactorily proved that the deceased was Elizabeth Stride, and that about the year 1869 she was married to a carpenter named John Thomas Stride. Unlike the other victims in the series of crimes in this neighbourhood – a district teeming with representatives of all nations – she was not an Englishwoman. She was born in Sweden in the year 1843, but, having resided in this country for upwards of 22 years, she could speak English fluently and without much foreign accent. At one time the deceased and her husband kept a coffee-house in Poplar. At another time she was staying in Devonshire-street, Commercial-road, supporting herself, it was said, by sewing and charing. On and off for the last six years she lived in a common lodging-house in the notorious lane called Flower and Dean-street. She was there only known by the nick-name of "Long Liz," and often told a tale, which might have been apocryphal, of her husband and children having gone down with the Princess Alice. The deputy of the lodging-house stated that while with her she was a quiet and sober woman, although she used at times to stay out late at night – an offence very venial, he suspected, among those who frequented the establishment. For the last two years the deceased had been living at a common lodging-house in Dorset-street, Spitalfields, with Michael Kidney, a waterside labourer belonging to the Army Reserve. But at intervals during that period, amounting altogether to about five months, she left him without any apparent reason, except a desire to be free from the restraint even of that connexion, and to obtain greater opportunity of indulging her drinking habits. She was last seen alive by Kidney in Commercial-street on the evening of Tuesday, September 25. She was sober, but never returned home that night. She alleged that she had some words with her paramour, but this he denied. The next day she called during his absence, and took away some things, but, with this exception, they did not know what became of her until the following Thursday, when she made her appearance at her old quarters in Flower and Dean-street. Here she remained until Saturday, September 29. On that day she cleaned the deputy's rooms, and received a small remuneration for her trouble. Between 6 and 7 o'clock on that evening she was in the kitchen wearing the jacket, bonnet, and striped silk neckerchief which were afterwards found on her. She had at least 6d. in her possession, which was possibly spent during the evening. Before leaving she gave a piece of velvet to a friend to take care of until her return, but she said neither where she was going nor when she would return. She had not paid for her lodgings, although she was in a position to do so. They knew nothing of her movements during the next four or five hours at least – possibly not till the finding of her lifeless body. But three witnesses spoke to having seen a woman that they identified as the deceased with more or less certainty, and at times within an hour and a-quarter of the period when, and at places within 100 yards of the spot where she was ultimately found. William Marshall, who lived at 64, Berner-street, was standing at his doorway from half-past 11 till midnight. About a quarter to 12 o'clock he saw the deceased talking to a man between Fairclough-street and Boyd-street. There was every demonstration of affection by the man during the ten minutes they stood together, and when last seen, strolling down the road towards Ellen-street, his arms were round her neck. At 12.30 p.m. [*sic* a.m.] the constable on the beat (William Smith) saw the deceased in Berner-street standing on the pavement a few yards from Commercial-street, [*sic*] and he observed she was wearing a flower in her dress. A quarter of an hour afterwards James Brown, of Fairclough-street, passed the deceased close to the Board school. A man was at her side leaning against the wall, and the deceased was heard to say, "Not to-night, but some other night." Now, if this evidence was to be relied on, it would appear that the deceased was in the company of a man for upwards of an hour immediately before her death, and that within a quarter of an hour of her being found a corpse she was refusing her companion something in the immediate neighbourhood of where she met her death. But was this the deceased? And even if it were, was it one and the same man who was seen in her company on three different occasions? With regard to the identity of the woman, Marshall had the opportunity of watching her for ten minutes while standing talking in the street at a short distance from him, and she afterwards passed close to him. The constable feels certain that the woman he observed was the deceased, and when he afterwards was called to the scene of the crime he at once recognized her and made a statement; while Brown was almost certain that the deceased was the woman to whom his attention was attracted. It might be thought that the frequency of the occurrence of men and women being seen together under similar circumstances might have led to mistaken identity; but the police stated, and several of the witnesses corroborated the statement, that although many couples are to be seen at night in the Commercial-road, it was exceptional to meet them in Berner-street. With regard to the man seen, there were many points of similarity, but some of dissimilarity, in the descriptions of the three witnesses; but these discrepancies did not conclusively prove that there was more than one man in the company of the deceased, for every day's experience showed how facts were differently observed and differently described by honest and intelligent witnesses. Brown, who saw least in consequence of the darkness of the spot at which the two were standing, agreed with Smith that his clothes were dark and that his height was about 5 ft. 7 in., but he appeared to him to be wearing an overcoat nearly down to his heels; while the description of Marshall accorded with that of Smith in every respect but two. They agreed that he was respectably dressed in a black cut away coat and dark trousers, and that he was of middle age and without whiskers. On the other hand, they differed with regard to what he was wearing on his head. Smith stated he wore a hard felt deer stalker of dark colour; Marshall that he was wearing a round cap with a small peak, like a sailor's. They also differed as to whether he had anything in his hand. Marshall stated that he observed nothing. Smith was very precise, and stated that he was carrying a parcel, done up in a newspaper, about 18 in. in length and 6 in. to 8 in. in width. These differences suggested either that the woman was, during the evening, in the company of more than one man – a not very improbable supposition – or that the witness had been mistaken in detail. If they were correct in assuming that the man seen in the company of deceased by the three was one and the same person it followed that he must have spent much time and trouble to induce her to place herself in his diabolical clutches. They last saw her alive at the corner of Fairclough-street and Berner-street, saying "Not to-night, but some other night." Within a quarter of an hour her lifeless body was found at a spot only a few yards from where she was last seen alive. It was late, and there were few people about, but the place to which the two repaired could not have been selected on account of its being quiet or unfrequented. It had only the merit of darkness. It was the passage-way leading into a court in which several families resided. Adjoining the passage and court there was a club of Socialists, who, having finished their debate, were singing and making merry. The deceased and her companion must have seen the lights of the clubroom and the kitchen, and of the printing office. They must have heard the music and dancing, for the windows were open. There were persons in the yard but a short time previous to their arrival. At 40 minutes past

12, one of the members of the club, named Morris Eagle, passed the spot where the deceased drew her last breath, passing through the gateway to the back door, which opened into the yard. At 1 o'clock the body was found by the manager of the club. He had been out all day, and returned at the time. He was in a two-wheeled barrow drawn by a pony, and as he entered the gateway his pony shied at some object on his right. There was no lamp in the yard, and having just come out of the street it was too dark to see what the object was and he passed on further down the yard. He returned on foot, and on searching found the body of deceased with her throat cut. If he had not actually disturbed the wretch in the very act, at least he must have been close on his heels; possibly the man was alarmed by the sound of the approaching cart, for the death had only just taken place. He did not inspect the body himself with any care, but blood was flowing from the throat, even when Spooner reached the spot some few minutes afterwards, and although the bleeding had stopped when Dr. Blackwell's assistant arrived, the whole of her body and the limbs, except her hands, were warm, and even at 10 minutes past 1 a.m. Dr. Blackwell found her face slightly warm, and her chest and legs quite warm. In this case, as in other similar cases which had occurred in this neighbourhood, no call for assistance was noticed. Although there might have been some noise in the club, it seemed very unlikely that any cry could have been raised without its being heard by some one of those near. The editor of a Socialist paper was quietly at work in a shed down the yard, which was used as a printing office. There were several families in the cottages in the court only a few yards distant, and there were 20 persons in the different rooms of the club. But if there was no cry, how did the deceased meet with her death? The appearance of the injury to her throat was not in itself inconsistent with that of a self-inflicted wound. Both Dr. Phillips and Dr. Blackwell have seen self-inflicted wounds more extensive and severe, but those have not usually involved the carotid artery. Had some sharp instrument been found near the right hand of the deceased this case might have had very much the appearance of a determined suicide. But no such instrument was found, and its absence made suicide an impossibility. The death was, therefore, one by homicide, and it seemed impossible to imagine circumstances which would fit in with the known facts of the case, and which would reduce the crime to manslaughter. There were no signs of any struggle; the clothes were neither torn nor disturbed. It was true that there were marks over both shoulders, produced by pressure of two hands, but the position of the body suggested either that she was willingly placed or placed herself where she was found. Only the soles of her boots were visible. She was still holding in her left hand a packet of cachous, and there was a bunch of flowers still pinned to her dress front. If she had been forcibly placed on the ground, as Dr. Phillips opines, it was difficult to understand how she failed to attract attention, as it was clear from the appearance of the blood on the ground that the throat was not cut until after she was actually on her back. There were no marks of gagging, no bruises on the face, and no trace of any anaesthetic or narcotic in the stomach; while the presence of the cachous in her hand showed that she did not make use of it in self-defence. Possibly the pressure marks may have had a less tragical origin, as Dr. Blackwell says it was difficult to say how recently they were produced. There was one particular which was not easy to explain. When seen by Dr. Blackwell her right hand was lying on the chest, smeared inside and out with blood. Dr. Phillips was unable to make any suggestion how the hand became soiled. There was no injury to the hand, such as they would expect if it had been raised in self-defence while her throat was being cut. Was it done intentionally by her assassin, or accidentally by those who were early on the spot? The evidence afforded no clue. Unfortunately the murderer had disappeared without leaving the slightest trace. Even the cachous were wrapped up in unmarked paper, so that there was nothing to show where they were bought. The cut in the throat might have been effected in such a manner that bloodstains on the hands and clothes of the operator were avoided, while the domestic history of the deed suggested the strong probability that her destroyer was a stranger to her. There was no one among her associates to whom any suspicion had attached. They had not heard that she had had a quarrel with any one – unless they magnified the fact that she had recently left the man with whom she generally cohabited; but this diversion was of so frequent an occurrence that neither a breach of the peace ensued, nor, so far as they knew, even hard words. There was therefore in the evidence no clue to the murderer and no suggested motive for the murder. The deceased was not in possession of any valuables. She was only known to have had a few pence in her pocket at the beginning of the evening. Those who knew her best were unaware of any one likely to injure her. She never accused any one of having threatened her. She never expressed any fear of anyone, and, although she had outbursts of drunkenness, she was generally a quiet woman. The ordinary motives of murder – revenge, jealousy, theft, and passion – appeared, therefore, to be absent from this case; while it was clear from the accounts of all who saw her that night, as well as from the post-mortem examination, that she was not otherwise than sober at the time of her death. In the absence of motive, the age and class of woman selected as victim, and the place and time of the crime, there was a similarity between this case and those mysteries which had recently occurred in that neighbourhood. There had been no skilful mutilation as in the cases of Nichols and Chapman, and no unskilful injuries as in the case in Mitre-square – possibly the work of an imitator; but there had been the same skill exhibited in the way in which the victim had been entrapped, and the injuries inflicted, so as to cause instant death and prevent blood from soiling the operator, and the same daring defiance of immediate detection, which, unfortunately for the peace of the inhabitants and trade of the neighbourhood, had hitherto been only too successful. He himself was sorry that the time and attention which the jury had given to the case had not produced a result that would be a perceptible relief to the metropolis – the detection of the criminal; but he was sure that all had used their utmost effort to accomplish this object, and while he desired to thank the gentlemen of the jury for their kind assistance, he was bound to acknowledge the great attention which Inspector Reid and the police had given to the case. He left it to the jury to say, how, when, and by what means the deceased came by her death.

The jury, after a short deliberation, returned a verdict of "Wilful murder against some person or persons unknown."

CHAPTER 9

30 September 1888 – Murder of Catherine Eddowes

The murders committed in the early hours of Saturday, 30 September 1888 are best remembered, and usually referred to, as "The Double Event", an appellation directly originating from the "saucy Jacky" postcard of 1 October 1888, in which the two murders are referred to in this way. The murder of Catherine Eddowes was committed in Mitre Square, Aldgate, in the City of London and therefore came under the jurisdiction of the City of London Police, not the Metropolitan Police (who were investigating the other murders). However, any objective study should examine each crime as a separate event, whilst still bearing the other in mind.

The main report[1] referring to this murder is dated 27 October 1888, from Inspector James McWilliam, head of the Detective Department, City of London Police. The cover and report are as follows:

[Stamped: – HOME OFFICE 29 OCT.88 DEPT. No. 1] No. A49301C/8b.

DATE 29 Octr. 88   Commr. of the City Police
REFERENCES, &c.   re Mitre Square Murder
            Fds a copy of Police Report containing particulars of above.

Pressing

[Stamped: – HOME OFFICE 29 OCT.88 DEPt.No.]   A493018b
Copy of REPORT
Detective   CITY OF LONDON POLICE.
Department   October 27th 1888.

Re East End Murders.

I beg to report with reference to the recent murders in Whitechapel that, acting upon stringent orders issued by the Commissioner with a view to preventing if possible a repetition of the murders which had previously been committed in Whitechapel and to keep close observation upon all Prostitutes frequenting public-houses and walking the streets, extra men in plain clothes have been employed by this department since August last to patrol the Eastern portion of the City. On the 30th September at 1.45 a.m. a woman since identified as Catherine Eddowes was found with her throat cut & disembowelled in Mitre Square, Aldgate about 300 yards from the City boundary. The Constable who found the body immediately sent for a Surgeon and also to the Police Station at Bishopsgate Street and Inspector Collard was on the spot in a few minutes. Detective Constables Halse, Marriott, & Outram who had been searching the passages of houses in the immediate neighbourhood of the spot where the murder was committed (& where the doors are left open all night) on hearing of the murder at 1.55 a.m. at once started off in various directions to look for suspected persons. The Officer Halse went in the direction of Whitechapel and passed through Goulstone [*sic*] Street – where part of the deceased's apron was subsequently found at 2.20 a.m.; on returning to the Square he heard that part of an apron stained with blood had been found in Goulstone Street, he then went with D.S. Lawley & D.C. Hunt to Leman Street Station and from thence to Goulstone Street where, the spot at which the apron was found was pointed out to him. On the wall above it was written in chalk "The Jewes are the men that will not be blamed for nothing." Halse remained by the writing and Lawley and Hunt returned to Mitre Square.

In the meantime I had been informed of the murder and arrived at the Detective Office at 3.45 a.m., after ascertaining from S.S. Izzard what steps he had taken in consequence of it; I wired to Scotland Yard informing the Metropolitan Police of the murder and went with D.S. Downes to Bishopsgate Station & from thence to Mitre Square. I there found Major Smith, Superintendent Foster, Inspector Collard & several Detective Officers. Lawley and Hunt informed me of the finding of the apron & the writing on the wall, the latter of which I ordered to be photographed and directed the Officers to return at once & search the "Model" dwellings & lodging houses in the neighbourhood. I then went to the Mortuary in Golden Lane, where the body had been taken by direction of Dr. Gordon-Brown and saw the piece of apron – which was found in Goulstone Street – compared with a piece the deceased was wearing & it exactly corresponded. I then returned to the Detective Office and had telegraphed to the Divisions and Metropolitan Police a description of the murdered woman and her clothing. Additional officers had then arrived and they were sent out in various directions to make enquiry. On Monday the 1st October on the recommendation of the Commissioner, the Lord Mayor authorised a reward of £500 to be offered. Printed bills were at once ordered and circulated, in response to which a great many communications have been received & are still coming in. Enquiry was also made with a view to get the deceased identified and on the 3rd. Inst. it was ascertained that her name was Catherine Eddowes & that she had been living with a man named Kelly at Cooney's lodging house Flower and Dean Street, Spitalfields. She had lived with Kelly for seven or eight years, prior to which she had lived with a man named Thomas Conway, a pensioner for about twenty years & had three children by him – two sons & a daughter, but Conway was eventually compelled to leave her on account of her drunken and immoral habits. Considerable difficulty was experienced in finding Conway in consequence of his having enlisted in the name of Thomas Quinn, he was found however, also the three children & two sisters of the deceased.

On Thursday the 4th Inst. an Inquest was held at the mortuary by F.H. Langham Esq., "Coroner" & a Jury and adjourned till the 11th Instant, when a Verdict of "Wilful murder against some person unknown" was returned. Every effort has been made to trace the murderer, but up to the present without success. Enquiry has been made respecting persons in almost every class of society & I have sent officers to all the Lunatic Asylums in London to make Enquiry respecting persons recently admitted or discharged, many persons being of opinion that these crimes are of too revolting a character to have been committed by a sane person.

The Enquiry is still being actively followed up, but the Police are at a great disadvantage in this case in consequence of the want of identity, no one having seen the deceased from the time she was discharged from Bishopsgate Station until her body was found at 1.45 a.m., except three gentlemen who were leaving the Imperial Club in Duke Street at 1.35 a.m. and who state that to the best of their belief they saw her with a man in Church Passage at that time, but took no particular notice of them. One of the gentlemen Mr. Lewend [sic] of 79 Fenchurch Street who was nearest to the man & woman & saw most of them, says he does not think he should know the man again and he did not see the woman's face. No other person can be found who saw either of them. The murderer would seem to have been only a few minutes in the City, having just come from Berners [*sic*] Street & returned at once to Whitechapel via Goulstone Street where the apron was found.

On the 16th Inst. Mr. Lusk, No. 1 Alderney Road, Mile End, Chairman of the East End Vigilance Committee received by post a packet containing half of a kidney and a letter – photograph copy of which I attach hereto. He did not attach any importance to it at the time, but on mentioning the matter to other members of the Committee on the 18th Inst., they advised him to shew the piece of kidney to a medical man. He accordingly took it to Mr. Reed, 56 Mile End Road, & subsequently to Dr. Openshaw of the London Hospital, both of whom expressed the opinion that it was a portion of the kidney of a human being. Mr. Lusk then took the kidney & letter to Leman Street Station. The kidney was forwarded to this office & the letter to Scotland Yard, Chief Inspector Swanson having lent me the letter on the 20th. Inst. I had it photographed & returned it to him on the 24th. The kidney has been examined by Dr. Gordon-Brown who is of opinion that it is human. Every effort is being made to trace the sender, but it is not desirable that publicity should be given to the Doctor's opinion, or the steps that are being taken in consequence. It might turn out after all, to be the act of a Medical Student who would have no difficulty in obtaining the organ in question.

This department is co-operating with the Metropolitan Police in the matter, and Chief Inspector Swanson and I meet daily and confer on the subject.

(Sgd) Jas. McWilliam
Inspector.

This report is followed by a Home Office minute sheet[2] which makes very interesting reading, and indicates that the government officials felt that they were not being told the full facts:

A49301/8b

Mr. Murdoch
    This report tells very little.
i The City Police are wholly at fault as regards the detection of the murderer.
ii The word on the wall was "Jewes", not "Juwes". [*Here there is a marginal note*:- Not so I believe GL.] This is important : unless it [*is*] a mere clerical error.
iii The ½ kidney sent to Mr Lusk is <u>human</u>.

The printed report of the Inquest contains much more information than this. They evidently want to tell us nothing. [*Here there is a marginal note* – "I don't think so GL."]
?Shall we ask them
A. Did the writing on the wall resemble "Jack the Ripper's" : or the enclosed?
B. Could the ½ kidney possibly be part of the victim's kidney?
WTB –   Mr Lushington Have you any private information
30.10.88   from the Met. Police on the above points or a
facsimile of Jack the Ripper's letters.   CM Oct 30.

It is I think unadvisable to ask these questions officially, but when Mr. Matthews comes to town I would advise that he should ask Sir J. Fraser to come to the H.O. He will then have full particulars. GL 30 Oct 1888
[*Noted marginally* – "H.M. 31Oct./88."]

This is followed by Sir James Fraser's, the City of London Police Commissioner's, covering letter[3], forwarding the McWilliam report, which is dated 29 October 1888, to the Under-Secretary of State:

[Stamped – RECD. AFTER 3.P.M.] –
A49301C/8b
[Stamped:–HOME OFFICE 29 OCT. 88 DEPt. No.]   26 Old Jewry EC
                                                                    29th October 1888.
Sir,
    I have to acknowledge your letter of the 25th Instant (A.49301C/8d.) and in reply to the enquiries contained therein, I beg to forward for the information of the Secretary of State, the copy of a Report furnished to me by the Inspector of the Detective Department at this Office, containing particulars of the recent murder of a woman in Mitre Square, within the City, and of the steps since taken by the City Police in connection therewith.
                                        I am,
                                            Sir
                                    Your Obedient Servant
                                    James Fraser
The Under Secretary of State
    &c. &c. &c.
    Home Office
            Whitehall.

The report that follows this is a rather lengthy one[4] dated 6 November 1888 from the Metropolitan Police Commissioner, Sir Charles Warren, concerning the Mitre Square murder and an explanation why he thought it right to have the writing on the wall wiped out. It was received at the Home Office the same date and is minuted *"Confidential and Pressing"*:

[Stamp: – HOME OFFICE 6 NOV.88. RECd. DEPt.] No. A49301C/8c
DATE 6 Nov 88   The Commr. of Police
REFERENCES &c.   Whitechapel Murders.   Mitre Square Murder
Report on Mitre Square murder also full explanation as to why he thought it right to have the writing on the wall wiped out –
                    MINUTES.
                Confidential & Pressing
                The S. of S. Nov6/88.

                                        GL
                                6 Nov 1888

A49301C/8c

_____

93305/28 [Stamped: – HOME OFFICE 6 NOV.88 RECd. DEPt]
Confidential

                        4 Whitehall Place,
                                SW,
                        6th November, 1888.
Sir,
    In reply to your letter of the 5th instant, I enclose a report of the circumstances of the Mitre Square Murder so far as they have come under the notice of the Metropolitan Police, and I now give an account regarding the erasing the writing on the wall in Goulston Street which I have already partially explained to Mr. Matthews verbally. –
    On the 30th September on hearing of the Berners [*sic*] Street murder after visiting Commercial Street Station I arrived at Leman Street Station shortly before 5 a.m. and ascertained from Superintendent Arnold all that was known there relative to the two murders.

The most pressing question at that moment was some writing on the wall in Goulston Street evidently written with the intention of inflaming the public mind against the Jews, [*marginal note* – "2 Reports enclosed"] and which Mr. Arnold with a view to prevent serious disorder proposed to obliterate, and had sent down an Inspector with a sponge for that purpose telling him to await his arrival. –

I considered it desirable that I should decide this matter myself, as it was one involving so great a responsibility whether any action was taken or not. I accordingly went down to Goulston Street at once before going to the scene of the murder : it was just getting light, the public would be in the streets in a few minutes, in a neighbourhood very much crowded on Sunday mornings by Jewish vendors and Christian purchasers from all parts of London. –

There were several Police around the spot when I arrived, both Metropolitan and City. –

The writing was on the jamb of the open archway or doorway visible to anybody in the street and could not be covered up without danger of the covering being torn off at once. –

A discussion took place whether the writing could be left covered up or otherwise or whether any portion of it could be left for an hour until it could be photographed, but after taking into consideration the excited state of the population in London generally at the time the strong feeling which had been excited against the Jews, and the fact that in a short time there would be a large concourse of the people in the streets and having before me the Report that if it was left there the house was likely to be wrecked (in which from my own observation I entirely concurred) I considered it desirable to obliterate the writing at once, having taken a copy of which I enclose a duplicate.

After having been to the scene of the murder, I went on to the City Police Office and informed the Chief Superintendent of the reason why the writing had been obliterated.

I may mention that so great was the feeling with regard to the Jews that on the 13th ulto. the Acting Chief Rabbi wrote to me on the subject of the spelling of the word "Juewes" on account of a newspaper asserting that this was a Jewish spelling in the Yiddish dialect. He added, "in the present state of excitement it is dangerous to the safety of the poor Jews in the East to allow such an assertion to remain uncontradicted. My community keenly appreciates your ['kindness' – *deleted*] humane and vigilant actions during this critical time.''

It may be realised therefore if the safety of the Jews in White-chapel could be considered to be jeopardised 13 days after the murder by the question of the spelling of the word Jews, what might have happened to the Jews in that quarter had that writing been left intact.

I do not hesitate myself to say that if that writing had been left there would have been an onslaught upon the Jews, property would have been wrecked, and lives would probably have been lost, and I was much gratified with the promptitude with which Superinten-dent Arnold was prepared to act in the matter if I had not been there.

I have no doubt myself whatever that one of the principal objects of the Reward offered by Mr. Montagu was to shew to the world that the Jews were desirous of having the Hanbury Street murder cleared up, and thus to direct from them the very strong feeling which was then growing up.

> I am,
>
> Sir,
>
> Your most obedient Servant,
>
> C. Warren

This report is followed by the copy of the message[5] taken by the Metropolitan Police and is as follows:

> *The Juwes are*
> *The men that*
> *Will not*
> *be Blamed*
> *for nothing*

This is followed by another lengthy report[6], dated 6 November 1888, by Chief Inspector Donald S. Swanson:

A49301C/8c

[Stamped: – HOME OFFICE 6 NOV. 88 RECd. DEPt.]

METROPOLITAN POLICE.

Criminal Investigation Department,

Scotland Yard,

6th day of November 1888

SUBJECT Facts known to
Met:Police. respecting the
Murder in Mitresquare &
writing on wall.

I beg to report that the facts concerning the murder in Mitre Square
which came to the knowledge of the Metropolitan Police are as
follows:-

1.45 a.m. 30th. Septr. Police Constable Watkins of the City
Police discovered in Mitre Square the body of a woman, with her
face mutilated almost beyond identity, portion of the nose being cut
off, the lobe of the right ear nearly severed, the face cut, the throat
cut, and disembowelled. The P.C. called to his assistance Mr.
Morris, a night watchman and pensioner from Metropolitan police,
from premises looking on the Square, and surgical aid was subsequently called in, short details of which will be given further on in
this report.

The City police having been made acquainted with the facts by
P.C. Watkins the following are the results of their enquiries so far
as known to Met. Police:-

1.30 a.m. The P.C. passed the spot where the body was found at
1.45 a.m. and there was nothing to be seen there at that time.

1.35 a.m Three Jews, one of whom is named Mr. Lewin [*sic* –
Lawende], left a Club in Duke Street, and Mr. Lamende [*sic*]
["Lewin" – *deleted*], saw a man talking to a woman in Church
Passage which leads directly to Mitre Square. The other two took
but little notice and state they could not identify [*the*] man or
woman, and eve [*n*] Mr. Lamende states that he could not identify
the man, but a[*lso*] the woman stood with her back to him, with her
han [*d*] on the man's breast, he coul[*d*] not identify the body
mutilated as it was, as that of the woman whose back he had seen,
but to the best of his belief the clothing of the deceased, which was
black was similar to that worn by the woman whom he had seen.
and that was the full extent of his identity.

2.20 a.m. P.C. 254A. Long (the P.C. was drafted from A. Division
temporarily to assist H. Division.) stated that at the hour mentioned
he visited Goldston [*sic*] Street Buildings, and there was nothing there
at that time, but at,

2.55 a.m. he found in the bottom of a common stairs leading to
No. 108 to 119. Goldston Street Buildings a piece of a bloodstained
apron, and above it written in chalk the words, "The Juwes are the
men who will not be blamed for nothing." which he reported, and

the City Police were subsequently acquainted at the earliest moment, when it was found that beyond doubt the piece of apron found corresponded exactly with the part missing from the body of the murdered woman.

The Surgeon, Dr. Brown, called by the City Police, and Dr. Phillips who had been called by the Metropolitan Police in the cases of Hanbury Street and Berner St. having made a post-mortem examination of the body reported that there were missing the left kidney and the uterus, and that the mutilation so far gave no evidence of anatomical knowledge in the sense that it evidenced the hand of a qualified surgeon, so that the Police could narrow their enquiries into certain classes of persons. On the other hand as in the Metropolitan Police cases, the medical evidence shewed that the murder could have been committed by a person who had been a hunter, a butcher, a slaughterman, as well as a student in surgery or a properly qualified surgeon.

The results of the City Police enquiries were as follow: – beside the body were found some pawn-tickets in a tin box, but upon tracing them, they were found to relate to pledges made by the deceased, who was separated from her husband, and was living in adultery with a man named John Kelly, respecting whom enquiry was at once made by Metropolitan and City Police, the result of which was to shew clearly that he was not the murderer. Further it shewed that the deceased's name was Catherine Eddowes, or Conway, who had been locked up for drunkenness at Bishopsgate Street Police Station at 8.45 p.m. 29th, and being sober was discharged at 1 a.m. 30th. Enquiry was also made by the City and Metropolitan police conjointly into her antecedents, and it was found that there did not exist amongst her relations or friends the slightest pretext for a motive to commit the murder.

At the Goldston Street Buildings where the portion of the bloodstained apron was found the City Police made enquiry, but unsuccessfully, and their subsequent enquiries into matters affecting persons suspected by correspondence, or by statements of individuals at Police Stations, as yet without success, have been carried on with the knowledge of the Metropolitan Police, who on the other hand have daily acquainted the City Police with the subjects and natures of their enquiries.

Upon the discovery of the blurred chalk writing on the wall, written, – although mis-spelled in the second word, – in an ordinary hand in the midst of a locality principally inhabited by

Jews of all nationalities as well as English, and upon the wall of a common stairs leading to a number of tenements occupied almost exclusively by Jews, and the purport of the writing as shewn at page. 3. was to throw blame upon the Jews, the Commr. deemed it adviseable to have them rubbed out. Apart from this there was the fact that during police enquiries into the Bucks Row and Hanbury Street murders a certain section of the Press cast a great amount of suspicion upon a jew named John Piser, alias, "Leather Apron", as having been the murderer whose movements at the dates and hours of those murders had been satisfactorily enquired into by Met. Police, clearing him of any connection, there was also the fact that on the same morning another murder had been committed in the immediate vicinity of a Socialist Club in Berner Street, frequented by Jews, – considerations, which, weighed in the balance with the evidence of chalk writing on the wall to bring home guilt to any person were deemed the weightier of the two. To those police officers who saw the chalk writing, the handwriting of the now notorious letters to a newspaper agency bears no resemblance at all.

Rewards were offered by the City Police and by Mr. Montagu and a Vigilance Committee formed presided over by Mr. Lusk of Alderney Road, Mile End, and it is to be regretted that the combined result has been that no information leading to the murderer has been forthcoming. On the 18th Oct. Mr. Lusk brought a parcel which had been addressed to him to Leman Street. The parcel contained what appeared to be a portion of a kidney. He received it on 15th Oct. and submitted it for examination eventually to Dr. Openshaw curator of London Hospital Museum who pronounced it to be a human kidney. The kidney was at once handed over to the City Police, and the result of the combined medical opinion they have taken upon it, is, that it is the kidney of a human adult, not charged with a fluid, as it would have been in the case of a body handed over for purposes of dissection to an hospital, but rather as it would be in a case where it was taken from the body not so destined. In other words similar kidneys might & could be obtained from any dead person upon whom a post mortem had been made from any cause by students or dissecting room porter. [*Note in margin* – "Was there any such p.mort. made within a week in the E. or E.C. districts?"] The kidney, or rather portion of the kidney, was accompanied by a letter couched as follows. –

From hell

Mr Lusk
   Sir
     I send you half the
Kidne I took from one woman
prasarved it for you. tother piece I
fried and ate it was very nise. I
may send you the bloody knif that
took it out if you only wate a whil
longer
      signed Catch me when
         you can
       Mishter Lusk.

The postmarks upon the parcel are so indistinct that it cannot be said whether the parcel was posted in the E. or E.C. districts, and there is no envelope to the letter, and the City Police are therefore unable to prosecute any enquiries upon it.

The remaining enquiries of the City Police are merged into those of the Metropolitan Police, each Force cordially communicating to the other daily the nature and subject of their enquiries.

The foregoing are the facts so far as known to Metropolitan Police, relating to the murder in Mitre Square.

Donald S. Swanson.
ChInspector.

As regards Mr Lusk receiving part of a human kidney and the "From hell" letter on 16 October 1888, it is worth giving at this point two press reports containing further information about the incident. The *Daily Telegraph* of Saturday, 20 October 1888, reported:

A statement which apparently gives a clue to the sender of the strange package received by Mr. Lusk was made last night by Miss Emily Marsh, whose father carries on business in the leather trade at 218, Jubilee Street, Mile-end-road. In Mr. Marsh's absence Miss Marsh was in the front shop, shortly after one o'clock on Monday last, when a stranger, dressed in clerical costume, entered, and, referring to the reward bill in the window, asked for the address of Mr. Lusk, described therein as the president of the Vigilance Committee. Miss Marsh at once referred the man to

Mr. J. Aarons, the treasurer of the committee, who resides at the corner of Jubilee-street and Mile-end-road, a distance of about thirty yards. The man, however, said he did not wish to go there, and Miss Marsh thereupon produced a newspaper in which Mr. Lusk's address was given as Alderney-road, Globe-road, no number being mentioned. She requested the stranger to read the address, but he declined, saying, "Read it out," and proceeded to write something in his pocket-book, keeping his head down meanwhile. He subsequently left the shop, after thanking the young lady for the information, but not before Miss Marsh, alarmed by the man's appearance, had sent the shop-boy, John Cormack, to see that all was right. This lad, as well as Miss Marsh, give a full description of the man, while Mr. Marsh, who happened to come along at the time, also encountered him on the pavement outside. The stranger is described as a man of some forty-five years of age, fully six feet in height, and slimly built. He wore a soft felt black hat, drawn over his forehead, a stand-up collar, and a very long black single-breasted overcoat, with a Prussian or clerical collar partly turned up. His face was of a sallow type, and he had a dark beard and moustache. The man spoke with what was taken to be an Irish accent. No importance was attached to the incident until Miss Marsh read of the receipt by Mr. Lusk of a strange parcel, and then it occurred to her that the stranger might be the person who had despatched it. His inquiry was made at one o'clock on Monday afternoon, and Mr. Lusk received the package at eight p.m. the next day. The address on the package curiously enough gives no number in Alderney-road, a piece of information which Miss Marsh could not supply. It appears that on leaving the shop the man went right by Mr. Aarons house, but did not call. Mr. Lusk has been informed of the circumstances, and states that no person answering the description has called on him, nor does he know any one at all like the man in question.

The *Sunday Times* of 21 October 1888 contained the following report:

THE WHITECHAPEL TRAGEDIES.

Notwithstanding the sensational rumours which were current yesterday afternoon, there is little to chronicle from the scene of the Whitechapel tragedies. The police have now turned their attention to the Thames and Victoria Embankments, and, to quote the words of an Inspector, it would be "impossible" for them to bestow more zeal or devotion to the task on which they are engaged. Sensational sheets teem with reports of arrests, but up to the present no arrests have been made. Mr. George Lusk, Alderney Road, Mile End, E., as chairman of the Whitechapel Vigilance Committee, was the recipient of the kidney of which so much has been heard lately.

Calling on Dr. Gordon Brown, of the City Police, last night, our reporter found that he had not quite completed his examination of the kidney which had been submitted to him. He said: "So far as I can form an opinion, I do not see any substantial reason why this portion of kidney should not be the portion of the one taken from the murdered woman. I cannot say that it is the left kidney. It must have been cut previously to its being immersed in the spirit which exercised a hardening process. It certainly had not been in spirit for more than a week. As has been stated, there is no portion of the renal artery adhering to it, it having been trimmed up, so, consequently, there could be no correspondence established between the portion of the body from which it was cut. As it exhibits no trace of decomposition, when we consider the length of time that has elapsed since the commission of the murder, we come to the conclusion that the probability is slight of its being a portion of the murdered woman of Mitre Square."

The suspicious circumstances of the tall clerical-looking individual who called at the shop of Miss Emily Marsh, 218, Jubilee Street, Mile End Road, has not been satisfactorily accounted for. He asked for the address of Mr. Lusk . . .

The official files resume with the written report[7] of Police Constable 254A, Alfred Long, of the Metropolitan Police, Westminster Division, concerning his finding of the piece of bloody apron and the graffito on the wall in Goulston Street, in the early hours of Sunday, 30 September 1888:

A49301C/8c

6th November, 1888.

[Stamped: – HOME OFFICE 6 NOV.88 RECd. DEPt.]

I was on duty in Goulston Street on the morning of 30th Sept: at about 2.55 A.M. I found a portion of an apron covered in blood lying in the passage of the door-way leading to Nos. 108 to 119 Model Dwellings in Goulston Street.

Above it on the wall was written in chalk "The Juews are the men that will not be blamed for nothing", I at once called the P.C. on the adjoining beat and then searched the stair-cases, but found no traces of any person or marks. I at once proceeded to the Station, telling the P.C. to see that no one entered or left the building in my absence. I arrived at the Station about 5 or 10 minutes past 3, and reported to the Inspector on duty finding the apron and the writing.

The Inspector at once proceeded to Goulston Street and inspected the writing.

From there we proceeded to Leman St., and the apron was handed by the Inspector to a gentleman whom I have since learnt is Dr. Phillips.

I then returned back on duty in Goulston Street about 5.

Alfred Long PC 254A.

The next report[8] is written by Superintendent Thomas Arnold, H Division, dated 6 November 1888, and concerns his knowledge of the Goulston Street incident:

[Stamped: – HOME OFFICE 6 NOV.88 RECd. DEPt.]   A49301C/8c
H Division
6th Nov 1888

I beg to report that on the morning of 30th Sept. last my attention was called to some writing on the wall of the entrance to some dwellings No. 108 Goulston Street Whitechapel which consisted of the following words "The Juews are not [*the word* 'not' *being deleted*] the men that will not be blamed for nothing", and knowing that in consequence of a suspicion having fallen upon a Jew named "John Pizer" alias "Leather Apron" having committed a murder in Hanbury Street a short time previously a strong feeling ["ag" – *deleted*] existed against the Jews generally, and as the Building upon which the writing was found was situated in the midst of a locality inhabited principally by that Sect. I was apprehensive that if the writing were left it would be the means of causing a riot and therefore considered it desirable that it should be removed having in view the fact that it was in such a position that it would have been rubbed by the shoulders of persons passing in & out of the Building. Had only a portion of the writing been removed the context would have remained. An Inspector was present by my directions with a sponge for the purpose of removing the writing when Commissioner arrived on the scene.

T Arnold Supd.

On 29 September Tom Bulling, of the Central News Limited, sent to the police a letter that they had received on 27 September. His letter[9] read:

THE CENTRAL NEWS LIMITED

5, New Bridge Street,
London, 29 Sep 1888
E.C.

[Logo: — TO NEWSPAPERS, CLUBS & NEWSROOMS/TELEGRAPHIC NEWS]

The editor presents his compliments to Mr. Williamson & begs to inform him the enclosed was sent the Central News two days ago, & was treated as a joke.

The accompanying letter[10] was in an envelope addressed to *The Boss, Central News Office, London City* and was postmarked SP 27 88 and posted in London EC. It ran as follows:

25 Sept. 1888

Dear Boss.

I keep on hearing the police have caught me but they wont fix me just yet. I have laughed when they look so clever and talk about being on the right track. That joke about Leather Apron gave me real fits. I am down on whores and I shant quit ripping them till I do get buckled. Grand work the last job was, I gave the lady no time to squeal. How can they catch me now, I love my work and want to start again. You will soon hear of me with my funny little games. I saved some of the proper red stuff in a ginger beer bottle over the last job to write with but it went thick like glue and I cant use it. Red ink is fit enough I hope ha. ha. The next job I do I shall clip the ladys ears off and send to the police officers just for jolly wouldnt you. Keep this letter back till I do a bit more work then give it out straight. My knife's so nice and sharp I want to get to work right away if I get a chance, good luck.

Yours truly

Jack the Ripper

Dont mind me giving the trade name.

Wasnt good enough to post this before I got all the red ink off my hands curse it. No luck yet. They say I'm a doctor now ha ha.

The original Jack the Ripper files as stored at New Scotland Yard prior to being sent to the Public Records Office in Kew.

The Whitehall Place buildings which housed the offices of Great Scotland Yard at the time of the Ripper murders – these offices moved in 1890 to new buildings on the Embankment which became known as New Scotland Yard.

Metropolitan police officers involved in the Ripper enquiry in order of seniority: Sir Charles Warren, Chief Commissioner of the Metropolitan Police Force 1886–1888.

Assistant Commissioner James Monro, who was replaced by Dr Robert Anderson in August 1888.

Dr Robert Anderson who finally retired from the Metropolitan Police Force in 1901.

Far Left Major Henry Smith, appointed as a chief superintendent of the City of London Police Force. He was later made commissioner.

Left Sir Melville Leslie Macnaghten, Assistant Chief Constable. Appointed to Chief Constable in the Metropolitan Police Force in June 1889.

Right Frederick Adolphus Williamson, appointed Superintendent in 1870 and then Chief Constable in 1886. He was the only career police officer to attain such a high rank in the Metropolitan Police Force at this time.

Far Right John Shore, Superintendent, Central Office CID, Scotland Yard, at the time of the murders. Many of the official Scotland Yard reports on the murders are signed or minuted by Shore.

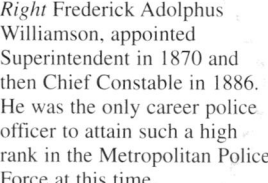

Far Left Chief Inspector Donald Sutherland Swanson, Central Office CID. He was appointed by Warren in September 1888 to head the Ripper enquiry.

Left Superintendent Thomas Arnold, head of the H (Whitechapel) Division of CID throughout the period of the murders.

Detective Inspector Frederick George Abberline of the Central Office, who headed the enquiry into the Whitechapel murders from September 1888 to early 1889, when he was succeeded by Inspector Henry Moore.

Detective Inspector Henry Moore. His last known report on the subject of the Whitechapel murders was as late as 1896.

Detective Inspector Edmund Reid, a local inspector throughout the period of the murders. He is seen here sketched at the Stride inquest.

Detective Inspector Walter Andrews, Central Office CID was the third inspector sent with Abberline to Whitechapel in connection with enquiries to the murders.

Detective Sergeant William Thick of H (Whitechapel) Division CID. He was later himself accused as a Ripper suspect.

Detective Sergeant George Godley of J (Bethnal Green) Division CID became involved in the Ripper enquiry with the murder of Mary Ann Nichols.

St Mary's Church, Whitechapel Road. It was near here that the first Whitechapel victim, Emma Smith, was attacked by a gang on 3 April 1888.

Gunthorpe Street (formerly George Yard), Whitechapel. George Yard Buildings, the spot where Martha Tabram was murdered, can be seen at the top left of the street.

George Yard Buildings as viewed from the junction with Wentworth Street.

A contemporary sketch from the *Illustrated Police News* of the body of Martha Tabram lying on the first floor landing of George Yard Buildings.

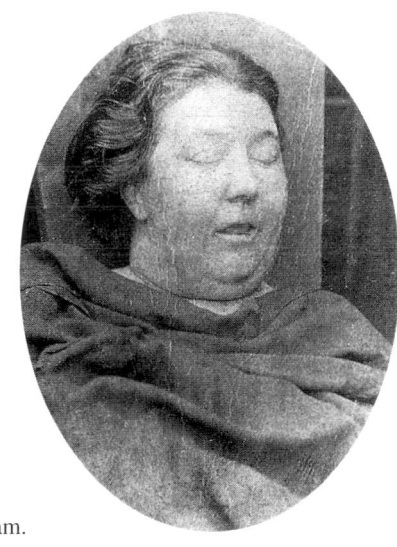

Mortuary photograph of Martha Tabram.

A contemporary sketch showing the discovery of the body of Mary Ann Nichols in Buck's Row, Whitechapel, by PC John Neil on 31 August 1888.

P.C. NIEL

PC 97J John Neil of Bethnal Green Police at the time of the murder.

Detective Inspector Joseph Henry Helson, local inspector in J (Bethnal Green) Division CID who initially took charge of the enquiries into the Nichols murder.

Dr Rees Ralph Llewellyn, called out by the Bethnal Green police to examine the body of Mary Ann Nichols.

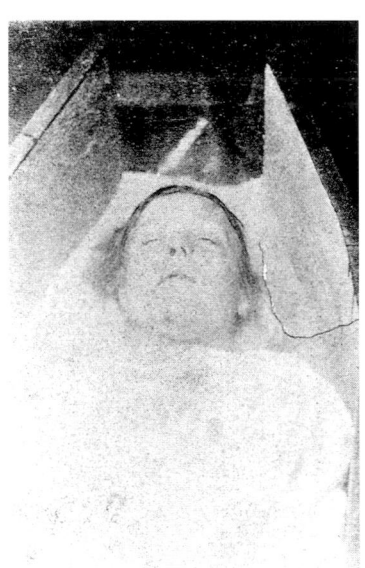

Mortuary photograph of Mary Ann Nichols.

Top Left The front of number 29
Hanbury Street, Spitalfields, scene of
the murder of Annie Chapman as it
appeared in 1967, shortly before
demolition.

Top Right The front of number 29 Hanbury
Street, as shown in a contemporary sketch.
It is interesting to note it shows the house
as originally having only one front door and
not the two which later photographs show.

Bottom Left A contemporary sketch of the
rear yard of number 29 Hanbury Street, the
actual spot where the murder of Annie
Chapman took place on 8 September 1888.

Bottom Right A contemporary sketch of
John Richardson, who had been in the rear
yard of 29 Hanbury Street on the night of
the murder. Initially treated as a suspect,
Richardson was later released without
charge.

A sketch from the *Illustrated Police News* showing John Richardson at the murder scene prior to the discovery of the body.

A sketch from the *Illustrated Police News* showing Dr George Bagster Phillips, Whitechapel Divisional Police Surgeon, examining the body of Annie Chapman. Dr Phillips felt the murderer had some anatomical knowledge.

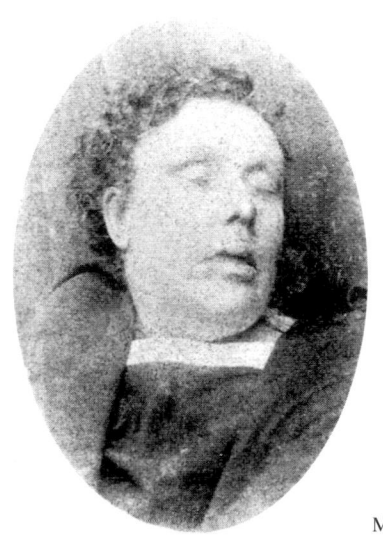

Mortuary photograph of Annie Chapman.

On 1 October 1888 a postcard[11] addressed to *Central News Office, London City, EC*, was received and ran as follows:

> I wasn't codding dear old Boss when I gave you the tip. You'll hear about saucy Jacky's work tomorrow double event this time number one squealed a bit couldnt finish straight off. had no time to get ears for police. thanks for keeping last letter back till I got to work again.
>
> Jack the Ripper.

On 5 October T.J. Bulling of the Central News again communicated[12] with Chief Constable Williamson:

THE CENTRAL NEWS LIMITED.

[logo]

5 New Bridge Street,
London, Oct 5 1888
E.C.

Dear Mr. Williamson,

At 5 minutes to 9 o'clock tonight we received the following letter the envelope of which I enclose by which you will see it is in the same handwriting as the previous communications.

5 Oct. 1888

Dear Friend,

In the name of God hear me I swear I did not kill the female whose body was found at Whitehall. If she was an honest woman I will hunt down and destroy her murderer. If she was a whore God will bless the hand that slew her, for the women of Moab and Midian shall die and their blood shall mingle with the dust. I never harm any others or the Divine power that protects and helps me in my grand work would quit for ever. Do as I do and the light of glory shall shine upon you. I must get to work tomorrow treble event this time yes yes three must be ripped. will send you a bit of face by post I promise this dear old Boss. The police now reckon my work a practical joke well well Jacky's a very practical joker ha ha Keep this back till three are wiped out and you can show the cold meat.

Yours truly
Jack the Ripper

Yours truly
T.J. Bulling
A.F. Williamson Esqr.

Thus the nickname "Jack the Ripper" was introduced to the world, and would never be forgotten. It would pervade and influence all aspects of the case from that day on. The nickname "Leather Apron" had been lost to the sensational Press after the arrest and clearing of Pizer. Now there was a much better one to take its place. The only police officer known to have named the press man the police thought was responsible for this sensational new name was John George Littlechild, lately Chief Inspector of the Special Branch. And he named Tom "Bullen" [*sic* – Bulling] of the Central News Agency, forwarder of the correspondence to the police. In the Littlechild letter[13] he writes:

> With regard to the term "Jack the Ripper" it was generally believed at the Yard that Tom Bullen of the Central News was the originator but it is probable Moore, who was his chief, was the inventor. It was a smart piece of journalistic work. No journalist of my time got such privileges from Scotland Yard as Bullen. Mr James Munro [*sic*] when Assistant Commissioner, and afterwards Commissioner, relied on his integrity.

The Times of Tuesday, 2 October 1888 reported[14]:

> The excitement caused by the murders committed early on Sunday morning in Berner-street, Commercial-road, and Mitre-square, Aldgate, has in no way abated. In the East-end statements and rumours of the most extraordinary nature were in circulation yesterday respecting conversations which certain persons, male and female, had had with two or three suspicious-looking men an hour or so before the crimes were committed, the purport of the statements in question being to connect the latter individuals with the outrages. Nothing, however, can be extracted from these statements of sufficient importance to form any clue. A few arrests have been made by the Metropolitan Police, but none had been made by the City Police up to a late hour last night. The authorities are now fully on the alert in the localities of the murders, and, as stated below, it has been decided by the City Police to offer a reward for the discovery of the assassin.
>
> It is satisfactory to announce that one discovery at least has been made which, in the hands of efficient detectives, should prove an important clue to the lurking-place of the murderer – for the belief is now generally entertained in official quarters that no one person

alone is attributable the series of crimes which in the last few weeks have horrified and alarmed the public.

It appears that after perpetrating his foul work in Mitre-square the miscreant retraced his steps towards the scene of the crime which he had committed an hour or so earlier. As stated in the particulars given in *The Times* of yesterday, part of the attire of the unfortunate woman who was butchered in Mitre-square consisted of a portion of coarse white apron, which was found loosely hanging about the neck. A piece of this apron had been torn away by the villain, who, in proceeding to his destination further east after leaving the City boundary, presumably used it to wipe his hands or his knife on, then threw it away. It was picked up in Goulston-street very shortly after the second murder had been committed, and it was brought to the mortuary by Dr. Phillips soon after the body had been removed there. It was covered with blood, and was found to fit in with the portion of apron which had been left by the murderer on his victim. Goulston-street, it may be stated, is a broad thoroughfare running parallel with the Commercial-road [*sic* – Commercial Street] and is off the main Whitechapel-road, and the spot where the piece of apron was picked up is about a third of a mile from Mitre-square. By the direct and open route it is 1,550 feet, but it can be approached through several small streets, making the distance about 1,600 feet. These measurements were taken yesterday.

The only other clues in the possession of the police are two pawnbrokers' tickets which were found lying close to the spot where the Mitre-square murder was discovered, and a knife which was picked up by a police-constable in the Whitechapel-road early yesterday morning. It is described as black-handled, 10 inches long, keen as a razor, and pointed like a carving knife. The pawn-tickets are believed to have belonged to the woman. They were in a small tin box and related to pledges which had been made in August of a pair of boots and a man's shirt. The tickets had been made out in two names – Emily Birrell and Anne Kelly – and the articles had been pawned for 1s. and 6d. respectively with Mr. Jones, of Church-street, Spitalfields, who, however, cannot identify the woman as having made the pledges.

Photographs of the ill-fated creature were taken at the City Mortuary in Golden-lane both before and after the post-mortem examination, after which the features – which, as already reported in *The Times*, had been brutally cut about – were rendered more life-like by the doctors. Up to a late hour last night, however, the body had not been identified, though several persons, having missed relatives or friends, have been taken to see it by the police.

Yesterday morning, shortly after 10 o'clock, an interview respecting the Mitre-Square murder took place between Mr. M'William (the inspector of the City Detective Department), Superintendent Foster, and Inspector Collard and the City Coroner, who has arranged to hold the inquest on Thursday morning, it being hoped that the woman may be identified in the meantime. The plans taken by Mr. F.W. Foster, of Old Jewry, of the scene of this outrage immediately after it was discovered were submitted to the Coroner, and Mr. Foster will be one of the witnesses at the inquest.

The Times of Wednesday, 3 October 1888, reported:

Great satisfaction was expressed yesterday throughout the City at the promptness with which the Lord Mayor, on the part of the Corporation, and at the instance of Colonel Sir James Fraser, the Commissioner of the City Police, has offered a reward for the discovery and conviction of the murderer or murderers of the woman who was found butchered in Mitre-square. There is reason to believe that the identification of the victim has been established. It appears that on Saturday night a woman – who gave the name of Mary Anne Kelly, and her address as No.6 Fashion-street, Spital-fields – was taken intoxicated to the Bishopsgate-street police-station. It is customary in such cases for a constable who may be on duty at the station to visit at frequent intervals the person detained, to see how he or she may be progressing. The woman in question was attended to in this manner on Saturday night by Reserve Constable Hutt, who noticed that she had on a pair of men's boots, and at the same time he observed the bonnet which she was wearing as well as her attire generally. Having become sufficiently sober to be discharged, the woman was liberated on Sunday morning at 1 o'clock, when she stated that she was afraid to go home, it was understood, on account of her husband. Hutt saw her leave the station, and observed that, instead of going in the direction of Spitalfields, she turned to the left, towards Houndsditch, and consequently in the direction of Mitre-square. After the examination of the body of the murdered woman in the City mortuary in Golden-lane the boots and bonnet were left there with the keeper, the rest of the clothing being taken to the police-station. On going to the mortuary Hutt saw the boots and bonnet and identified them as belonging to the woman who had been detained at the police-station. He then gave a general description of the rest of her dress, and on an examination being made afterwards at the police-station, where, as above stated, the other clothing had been taken, it was found to correspond fairly accurately with his account. Another constable, named Simmons, has also seen the body, and he believes, too, that it is the woman who was discharged at 1 o'clock on Sunday morning from the Bishopsgate-street police-station. Inquiries have been made by the City police for a Mary Anne Kelly at the address given in Fashion-street, but no person answering the description of the woman who was detained is known there. It is, however, a common practice for persons under detention to give false names and addresses.

Up to a late hour last night no arrests had been made in connexion with the murders by the City police. No clues, in addition to the very slender ones mentioned in *The Times* yesterday, have been discovered; but it is fully believed by the police that the lurking place of the murderer is not very far from the scenes of his atrocious crimes.

The same newspaper carried an additional report on the identification of Eddowes:

THE MITRE-SQUARE VICTIM IDENTIFIED.
Last night between 9 and 10 o'clock, a labouring man, giving the name of John Kelly, 55, Flower and Dean-street – a common lodginghouse – entered the Bishopsgate-street Police-station, and stated that from what he had been reading in the newspapers he believed that the woman who had been murdered in Mitre-square was his "wife." He was at once taken by Sergeant Miles to the mortuary in Golden-lane, and there identified her as the woman, to whom he subsequently admitted he was not married, but with whom he had cohabited for seven years.

Major Henry Smith, the Assistant Commissioner of the City Police, and Superintendent Foster were telegraphed for, and immediately went to the Bishopsgate-street station. Kelly, who was considerably affected, spoke quite unreservedly, and gave a full statement as to his own movements and those of the ill-fated woman, as to whose identity he was quite positive. In this statement he was borne out by the deputy of the lodginghouse, Frederick Wilkinson, who knew the poor woman quite well, and who had just seen the body. Kelly, in answer to questions, stated that the last time he saw her – referring to her as "Kate" – was on Saturday afternoon. The last meal she had with him was a breakfast which had been obtained by the pledging of his boots for 2s. 6d. Asked if he could explain how it was that she was out so late on Saturday night, he replied that he could not say. He left her in the afternoon believing that she would return to him at the lodginghouse in Flower and Dean-street. He had told her to go and see her daughter, and to try and get "the price of a bed for the night." "Who is her daughter?" he was asked, to which he replied, "A married woman. She is married to a gun-maker, and they live somewhere in Bermondsey, in King-street, I think it is called; but I never went there." He was then asked if he knew the murdered woman's name, and if he could explain the meaning of the initials "T.C." on her arm. He at once replied that Thomas Conway was the name of her husband, but he could not state whether Conway was dead or alive,or how long, in the latter case, she had been living away from him. Being asked why he had not made inquiries before relative to her absence on Saturday night and since, he replied that he thought she had got into some trouble and had been locked up, and he thought he had better wait. She was given to drinking. He had cautioned her not to stay out late at night on account of the previous murders. The reason which had induced him at length to call at the police-station was his having read about pawntickets being found near the murdered woman relating to pledges in the names of Kelly and Birrell. Further questioned on this point, he repeated the references to the pledging of his boots with a pawnbroker named Jones, of Church-street, and stated that the ticket for the other article (a flannel shirt), pledged in the name of Emily Birrell, had been given to them by the latter, who had been with them hopping, and who had slept in the same barn with them. He further stated that he and the murdered woman were "both Londoners," and that the latter was born at Bermondsey (*sic*). They had just returned from hopping at a place which he was understood to call Hunton, adding that it was about two miles from Coxheath, in Kent. To the question how he obtained his living, he replied, "I job about the markets now." He added that he had worked pretty constantly for a fruit salesman named Lander for over 12 years. He and "Kate" had, he said, gone through many hardships together, but while she was with him he "would not let her do anything bad." He was asked if he knew whether the woman had any relatives besides the daughter mentioned, to which he replied that "Kate's" sister was living in Thrawl-street, Spitalfields, with a man who sold farthing books in Liverpool-street.

An officer was despatched from the station for the ward beadle, who brought notices in blank with him, and two of them were filled up and served on Kelly and Wilkinson to attend the inquest, which, as already announced, will be held to-morrow at the City mortuary.

Kelly is a man of about 40 years of age, of medium height, and judging from his appearance is a poor, but hard-working man. He was quite sober. It will be seen from his statements that the belief which was expressed earlier in the day by the police-constables Hutt and Simmons – to which reference is made elsewhere – as to the identity of the murdered woman with the female who had been detained for drunkenness at Bishopsgate-street Station, and who was discharged about an hour before the murder was committed, is confirmed. The boots and shirt referred to by Kelly as being in pledge are now in the possession of the police, having been obtained from the pawnbroker.

While Kelly was making his statement a man entered the station and made a confession that he was the murderer. He strongly objected to being searched, but this was done with the aid of two or three constables. Major Smith, who was present at the station, attaches no importance to the confession, the man having been drinking and having nothing of an incriminating nature in his possession. He was, however, detained.

CHAPTER 10

The Eddowes Inquest

For greater detail on the Eddowes murder reference may be made to the Inquest reports[1] filed in the Corporation of London Records Office. These records include the written statements of witnesses at the Eddowes Inquest:

Eliza Gold sister of the deceased, of Thrawl Street, Spitalfields, a widow, stated on oath –

"I recognize deceased as my sister, her name was Catherine Eddowes, singlewoman, 43 years of age. She has been living for some years with Mr. Kelly. I have not seen her for 3 or 4 weeks. She used to go out hawking. Was of sober habits. She lived with a man named Conway before she lived with Kelly, she lived with Conway for some years. I do not know if Conway is living, I have not seen him for some years. He was a Pensioner, and went out hawking. I cannot tell whether they parted on good or bad terms.

By Mr. Crawford – I have not seen her since she parted from Conway. I saw deceased with Kelly about 3 or 4 weeks ago, they were on good terms. They were lodging together at 55 Flower and Dean Street, at a person's of the name of Smith. I have not seen her since."

The mark of   X   Eliza Gold.

John Kelly labourer, of 55 Flower and Dean Street, Spitalfields, gave his statement on oath –

"I have seen the body of Deceased, I knew her as Catherine Conway. I have known her for seven years and have been living with her the whole of that time. She used to sell a few things about the street. She lived with me at 55 Flower and Dean Street, a common lodging house. I was last in her company on Saturday last at 2 o'clock in the afternoon in Houndsditch. We parted on very good terms. She said she was going over to see if she could see her daughter, Annie, at Bermondsey, a daughter she had by Conway.

She promised me to be back by 4 o'clock and no later. She did not return. I heard she had been locked up at Bishopsgate, I was told by two women. I made sure she would be out on Sunday morning. It was for a little drop of drink. I never suffered her to go out for immoral purposes. She was occasionally in the habit of slightly drinking to excess. She had no money about her when I left. She went over to see her Daughter with a view of getting some money. I was without money to pay for the lodging at the time. I know of no one with whom she was at variance or likely to injure her. I do not know whether she had seen Conway or whether he was living, I never saw him.

By Jury – She usually returned about 8 or 9 o'clock.

By Mr Crawford – I do not know of anyone with whom she had been drinking. She left me some months ago in consequence of a few words. She only remained away for a few hours. She told me her Daughter lived at King Street, Bermondsey. We have lived in the same house for some years. On Friday night we did not sleep together. That night she went into the Casual Ward at Mile End. We did not sleep the whole of that week at the Lodging House. We were hop picking until Thursday We both went to the Casual Ward on Thursday night at Shoe Lane. I saw deceased on Saturday morning at 8 o'clock. She had some tea and coffee which she had bought after I pawned my boots. She was sober when we parted. She has never brought money to me in the morning that she has earned at night. My wife pawned the boots, the date is the 28th."

John Kelly

Frederick William Wilkinson 55 Flower and Dean Street, Brick Lane, Spitalfields, Deputy of the Lodging House, was sworn and stated –

"I have known deceased and Kelly for the last 7 or 8 years, they passed as a man and wife. They lived on very good terms. They had a few words now and again when she was in drink. Deceased got her living by hawking about the streets and cleaning amongst the Jews. When they were there they were pretty regular in their rent. She did not often drink, she was a very jolly woman. I never saw Kelly drunk. I saw deceased on Friday afternoon when she returned from hopping. I did not see Kelly. She went out on Friday night. I saw her again on Saturday morning along with Kelly between 10 & 11. I did not see deceased again until I saw her in the mortuary. She was generally in bed between 9 & 10 at nights when they stopped there.

I did not know her to walk the street. I never knew or heard of her being intimate with any one but Kelly. She used to say she was married to Conway and her name was bought and paid for. She was not at variance with any one that I know of. She was quite sober on Saturday when I last saw her. When Kelly came in on Saturday night between half past 7 or 8 I asked him, 'Where's Kate?' He said, 'I have heard she's been locked up', and he took a single bed. A single bed is 4d, a double bed is 8d.''

By Mr Crawford – ''I should say it was 4 or 5 weeks since they slept together at this house, they had been hopping. I am quite positive he never went out on Saturday night. On the Saturday morning she was wearing an apron, she was not dressed in anything particular. No stranger came in between 1 and 2 on Sunday morning to take a bed. I cannot recollect whether any stranger came in at 3 o'clock.''

Frederick William Wilkinson.

Edward Watkins City Police Constable 881, swore that –
''I have been in Police for 17 years. On Saturday 29th September, I went on duty a quarter to ten. My beat returns from Duke Street/ Aldgate, through Heneage Lane, a portion of Bury Street, through Cree Church Lane, into Leadenhall Street, along Leadenhall Street into Mitre Street, then into Mitre Square, round the Square into Mitre Street, then into King Street, along King Street to St James Place, round St James Place thence into Duke Street. It takes about 12 or 14 minutes. I had been continuously patrolling that beat from 10 in the evening until 1.30 o'clock. Nothing excited my attention during those hours. I passed through Mitre Square about 1.30 on Sunday morning, I had my lantern freed in my belt and on. I looked into the different passages. At half past one nothing excited my attention, I saw no one about. No one could have been in any portion of the Square without my seeing. I next came in at 1.44. I turned to the right. I saw the body of the woman lying there on her back with her feet facing the Square, her clothes up above her waist. I saw her throat was cut and her bowels protruding. The stomach was ripped up, she was lying in a pool of blood. I ran across the road to Messrs. Kearley and Tonge, the door was ajar, I pushed it open and called to the Watchman who was inside. He came out. I sent him for assistance. I remained by the body until the arrival of Police Constable Holland. Dr. Sequira followed. Inspector Collard arrived about 2, and Dr. Gordon Brown, the surgeon to the Police Force. I

did not hear the sound of any footsteps, at the time I entered no one
was in the Square. The watchman at Messrs. Kearley and Tonge's
was at work inside cleaning the offices. The watchman blew his
whistle as he was going up the Street. No one comes through Mitre
Street but myself."

Edward Watkins.

Frederick William Foster 26 Old Jewry, Architect and Surveyor, being sworn saith "I have made the plans produced – I have
them in three sections one 8 feet to an inch, another 200 feet to an
inch from an Ordnance map of the City – I have marked on an
Ordnance Map of the same scale from Berner Street to Mitre Street
– that would be 1144 yards about $\frac{3}{4}$ of a mile – It would take about
12 minutes to walk it from one to another." By Mr. Crawford. "It
is the nearest route that anyone unaccustomed to it would take it –
There are 2 routes to Goulstone Street one from Church Passage
through Duke Street crossing Houndsditch through Gravel Lane,
Stoney Lane crossing Petticoat Lane and through to Goulstone
Street. A person going from Mitre Square to Flower and Dean
Street would go as the most direct route across Goulstone Street –
It would take within $\frac{1}{4}$ of an hour to get there."

Fredk. W. Foster.

Frederick William Wilkinson recalled, examined by Mr.
Crawford – "Kelly was at No. 52 sleeping on Friday and Saturday
– I had 6 strangers sleeping there on Saturday evening. I do not
remember any one coming in about 2 o'clock on Sunday morning –
I remember the police coming in about 3 o'clock – no register of the
time or of the persons coming in is kept by me."

Frederick William Wilkinson.

Edward Collard Inspector, City Police, being sworn saith – "At
5 minutes before 2 on Sunday morning I received information at
Bishopsgate Street Station that a woman had been murdered in
Mitre Square – Information was telegraphed to Head Quarters and I
dispatched a constable to Dr. Gordon Brown and proceeded to
Mitre Square arriving there at 2 or 3 minutes past 2. I found Dr.
Sequira, several Police Officers and the Deceased person lying in the
South West corner of the Square in the position described by
Constable Watkins – the body was not touched until the arrival of
Dr. Brown who arrived shortly afterwards – the body was

examined and Sergeant Jones picked up on the left side of deceased 3 small black buttons generally used for women's boots small metal button, common metal thimble, a small mustard tin containing 2 pawn tickets which were handed to me. The doctors remained until the arrival of the ambulance and saw the body placed in a Conveyance. It was then conveyed to this mortuary – and the body was stripped – I produce the list of articles found on her – she had no money whatever on her – I produce a portion of the apron which deceased was apparently wearing which had been cut through and was found outside her dress – I took immediate steps to have the neighbourhood searched. Mr. MacWilliam, chief of the Detective-Department on his arrival shortly after with a number of Detectives sent to have immediate searches both in the streets and in lodging Houses. Several men were stopped and searched without any good result. I have had had a house to house enquiry in the vicinity of Mitre Square – but I failed to find anything excepting the witnesses to be produced named Lawrence and Levy.''

By Mr. Crawford. ''Her head, neck and shoulders were lying in a pool of blood on each side of her, nothing in front – no appearance of any struggle having taken place – I made an examination round to see if there was any struggle, no trace whatever – nothing to lead to suppose there had been any struggle either in the appearance of the woman or her clothes. The blood was in a liquid state not congealed – In my opinion from what I saw I should say that the body had not been there more than $\frac{1}{4}$ of an hour. I endeavoured to find footsteps but could find no footsteps. A search was made at the back of the empty houses but I could find no trace whatever.''

Edward Collard.

The official list of Eddowes's clothes and possessions is as follows:

"Black straw bonnet trimmed with green & black velvet and black beads, black strings. The bonnet was loosely tied, and had partially fallen from the back of her head, no blood on front, but the back was lying in a pool of blood, which had run from the neck,

"Black Cloth Jacket, imitation fur edging round collar, fur round sleeves, no blood on front outside, large quantity of Blood inside & outside back, outside back very dirty with Blood & dirt, 2 outside pockets, trimmed black silk braid & imitation fur,

"Chintz Skirt 3 flounces, brown button on waistband, Jagged cut $6\frac{1}{2}$

inches long from waistband, left side of front, Edges slightly Bloodstained, also Blood on bottom, back & front of skirt.

"Brown Linsey Dress Bodice, black velvet collar, brown metal buttons down front, blood inside & outside back of neck & shoulders, clean cut bottom of left side, 5 inches long from right to left.

"Grey Stuff Petticoat, white waist band, cut $1\frac{1}{2}$ inch long, thereon in front, Edges blood stained, blood stains on front at bottom of Petticoat.

"Very Old Green Alpaca Skirt, Jagged cut $10\frac{1}{2}$ inches long in front of waistband downward, blood stained inside, front under cut.

"Very Old Ragged Blue Skirt, red flounce, light twill lining, jagged cut $10\frac{1}{2}$ inches long, through waist band, downward, blood stained, inside & outside back and front.

"White Calico Chemise, very much blood stained all over, apparently torn thus in middle of front.

"Mans White Vest, button to match down front, 2 outside pockets, torn at back, very much Blood stained at back, Blood & other stains on front.

"No Drawers or Stays.

"Pair of Mens lace up Boots, mohair laces, right boot has been repaired with red thread, 6 Blood marks on right boot.

"1 piece of red gauze Silk, various cuts thereon found on neck.

"1 large White Handkerchief, blood stained.

"2 Unbleached Calico Pockets, tape strings, cut through also top left hand corners, cut off one.

"1 Blue Stripe Bed ticking Pocket, waist band, and strings cut through, (all 3 Pockets) Blood stained.

"1 White Cotton Pocket Handkerchief, red and white birds eye border.

"1 Pr. Brown ribbed Stockings, feet mended with white.

"12 pieces of white Rag, some slightly bloodstained.

"1 piece of white coarse Linen.

"1 piece of Blue & White Shirting (3 cornered).

"2 Small Blue Bed ticking Bags.

"2 Short Clay Pipes (black).

"1 Tin Box containing Tea.

"1 do do do Sugar.

"1 Piece of Flannel & 6 pieces of Soap.

"1 Small Tooth Comb.

"1 White Handle Table Knife & 1 Metal Tea Spoon.

"1 Red Leather Cigarette Case, white metal fittings.
"1 Tin Match Box. empty.
"1 piece of Red Flannel containing Pins & Needles.
"1 Ball of Hemp
"1 Piece of old White Apron."

Frederick Gordon Brown 17 Finsbury Circus, Surgeon of City of London Police Force, being sworn saith – "I was called shortly after 2 o'clock I reached about 18 minutes past 2 my attention was called to body of Deceased. The body was lying in position described by Watkins. The body was on its back – the head turned to left shoulder – the arms by the side of the body as if they had fallen there, both palms upwards – the fingers slightly bent, a thimble was lying off the finger on the right side. The clothes drawn up above the abdomen, the thighs were naked, left leg extended in a line with the body, the abdomen was exposed, right leg bent at the thigh and knee. The bonnet was at the back of the head – great disfigurement of face, the throat cut across, below the cut was a neckerchief. The upper part of the dress was pulled open a little way. The abdomen was all exposed. The intestines were drawn out to a large extent and placed over the right shoulder – they were smeared over with some feculent matter. A piece of about 2 feet was quite detached from the body and placed between the body and the left arm, apparently by design. The lobe and auricle of the right ear was cut obliquely through. There was a quantity of clotted blood on the pavement on the left side of the neck, round the shoulder and upper part of arm, and fluid blood coloured serum which had flowed under the neck to the right shoulder – the pavement sloping in that direction. Body was quite warm – no death stiffening had taken place. She must have been dead most likely within the half hour. We looked for superficial bruises and saw none – no blood on the skin of the abdomen or secretion of any kind on the thighs – no spurting of blood on the bricks or pavement around. No marks of blood below the middle of the body – several buttons were found in the clotted blood after the body was removed. There was no blood on the front of the clothes. There were no traces of recent connection. When the body arrived at Golden Lane some of the blood was dispersed through the removal of the body to the mortuary. The clothes were taken off carefully from the body, a piece of deceased's ear dropped from the clothing.

Made a post mortem examination at ½ past 2 on Sunday afternoon – rigor mortis was well marked, body not quite cold – green discolouration over the abdomen. After washing the left hand carefully a bruise the size of a sixpence, recent and red, was discovered on the back of the left hand between the thumb and first finger. A few small bruises on right shin of older date. The hands and arms were bronzed – no bruises on the scalp, the back of the body, or the elbows. The face was very much mutilated. There was a cut about $\frac{1}{4}$ of an inch through the lower left eyelid dividing the structures completely through the upper eyelid on that side, there was a scratch through the skin on the left upper eyelid – near to the angle of the nose the right eyelid was cut through to about $\frac{1}{2}$ an inch. There was a deep cut over the bridge of the nose extending from the left border of the nasal bone down near to the angle of the jaw on the right side, across the cheek – this cut went into the bone and divided all the structures of the cheek except the mucous membrane of the mouth. The tip of the nose was quite detached from the nose by an oblique cut from the bottom of the nasal bone to where the wings of the nose join on to the face. A cut from this divided the upper lip and extended through the substance of the gum over the right upper lateral incizor tooth. About $\frac{1}{2}$ an inch from the top of the nose was another oblique cut. There was a cut on the right angle of the mouth as if by the cut of a point of a knife the cut extended an inch and a half parallel with lower lip. There was on each side of cheek a cut which peeled up the skin forming a triangular flap about an inch and a half. On the left cheek there were 2 abrasions of the epithelium. There was a little mud on the left cheek – 2 slight abrasions of the epithelium under the left ear. The throat was cut across to the extent of about 6 or 7 inches. A superficial cut commenced about an inch and $\frac{1}{2}$ below the lobe and about $2\frac{1}{2}$ inches behind the left ear and extended across the throat to about 3 inches below the lobe of the right ear. The big muscle across the throat was divided through on the left side – the large vessels on the left side of the neck were severed – the larynx was severed below the vocal chords. All the deep structures were severed to the bone the knife marking intervertebral cartilages – the sheath of the vessels on the right side was just opened. the carotid artery had a fine hole opening. the internal jugular vein was opened an inch and a half not divided. The blood vessels contained clot. All these injuries were performed by a sharp instrument like a knife and pointed. The cause of death was haemorrhage from the left common carotid artery. The death was immediate and the mutilations were inflicted after death. We examined the abdomen, the front walls were laid open from the breast bone to the pubes. The cut commenced opposite the ensiform cartilage. The incision went upwards not penetrating the skin that was over the sternum. It then divided the enciform cartilage. The knife must have cut obliquely at the expense of the front surface of that cartilage. Behind this the liver was stabbed as if by the point of a sharp instrument. Below this was another incision into the liver of about $2\frac{1}{2}$ inches and below this the left lobe of the liver was slit through by a vertical cut. 2 cuts were shewn by a jagging of the skin on the left side. The abdominal walls were divided in the middle line to within $\frac{1}{4}$ of an inch of the navel, the cut then took a horizontal course for two inches and a half towards right side. It then divided round the navel on the left side and made a parallel incision to the former horizontal incision leaving the navel on a tongue of skin. Attached to the navel was $2\frac{1}{2}$ inches of the lower part of the rectus muscle on the left side of the abdomen the incision then took an oblique direction to the right and was shelving. The incision went down the right side of the vagina and rectum for half an inch behind the rectum – There was a stab of about an inch on the left groin, this was done by a pointed instrument, below this was a cut of three inches going through all tissues making a wound of the peritoneum about the same extent. An inch below the crease of the thigh was a cut extending from the anterior spine of the ilium obliquely down the inner side of the left thigh and separating the left labium forming a flap of skin up to the groin. The left rectus muscle was not detached. There was a flap of skin formed from the right thigh attaching the right labium and extending up to the spine of the ilium. The muscles on the right side inserted into the poupart's ligament were cut through. The skin was retracted through the whole of the cut in the abdomen but vessels were not clotted – nor had there been any appreciable bleeding from the vessel. I draw the conclusion that the cut was made after death and there would not be much blood on the murderer. The cut was made by some one on right side of body kneeling below the middle of the body – I removed the contents of the stomach and placed it in a jar for further examination. There seemed very little in it in the way of food or fluid but from the cut end partly digested farinaceous food escaped – The intestines had been detached to a large extent from the mesentery. About 2 feet of the colon was cut away – The sigmoid flexure was invaginated into the rectum very tightly – right kidney pale bloodless with slight congestion of the base of the pyramids. There was a cut from the upper part of the slit on the under surface of the liver to the left side and another cut at right angles to this which were about an inch and a half deep and $2\frac{1}{2}$ inches long. Liver itself was healthy – the gall bladder contained bile, the pancreas was cut but not through on the left side of the spinal column $3\frac{1}{2}$ inches of the lower border of the spleen by $\frac{1}{2}$ an inch was attached only to the peritoneum. The peritoneal lining was cut through on the left side and the left kidney carefully taken out and removed – the left renal artery was cut through – I should say that some one who knew the position of the kidney must have done it. The lining membrane over the uterus was cut through. The womb was cut through horizontally leaving a stump $\frac{3}{4}$ of an inch, the rest of the womb had been taken away with some of the ligaments. The vagina and cervix of the womb was uninjured. The bladder was healthy and uninjured and contained 3 or 4 ounces of water. There was a tongue like cut through the anterior wall of the abdominal aorta. The other organs were healthy – There were no indications of connexion – I believe the wound in the throat was first inflicted – I believe she must have been lying on the ground – They [sic] wounds on the face and abdomen prove that they were inflicted by a sharp pointed knife and that in the abdomen by one six inches long. I believe the perpetrator of the act must have had considerable knowledge of the position of the organs in the abdominal cavity and the way of removing them. The part removed would be of no use for any professional purpose. It required a great deal of ["medical" – *deleted*] knowledge to have removed the kidney and to know where it was placed, such a knowledge might be possessed by some one in the habit of cutting up animals – I think the perpetrator of this act had sufficient time or he would not have nicked the lower eyelids. It would take at least 5 minutes – I cannot assign any reason for these parts being taken away. I feel sure there was no struggle – I believe it was the act of one person – the throat had been so instantly severed that no noise could have been emitted. I should not expect much blood to have been found on the person who had inflicted these wounds. The wounds could not have been self inflicted – My attention was called to the apron – It was the corner of the apron with a string attached. The blood spots were of recent origin – I have seen a portion of an apron produced by Dr. Phillips and stated to have been found in Goulstone Street. It is impossible to say it is human blood. I fitted the piece of apron which had a new piece of material on it which had been evidently sewn on to the piece I have. The seams of the borders of the two actually corresponding – some blood and apparently faecal matter was found on the portion found in Goulstone Street. I believe the wounds on the face to have been done to disfigure the corpse.''

FGordonBrown   Adjourned until Thursday
                                               next at ½ past 10.

George William Sequeira 34 Jewry Street, Aldgate, Surgeon, being sworn – ''I was called on the 30th September at 5 to 2 and was the first medical man to arrive. I saw the position of the body and I agree with Dr. Gordon Brown as to the position. I was present and heard the whole of the evidence of Dr. Gordon Brown at the last meeting. I quite agree with the Doctor in every particular.''

By Mr. Crawford – ''I know the locality. This is the darkest portion of the Square. There would have been sufficient light to enable the perpetrator of the deed to have committed the deed without the addition of any extra light. I formed the opinion that the perpetrator of the deed had no particular design on any particular organ. I do not think he was possessed of any great anatomical skill – I account for the absence of noise as the death must have been so instantaneous after the severance of the wind pipe and the blood vessels – I should not have expected that the person who committed the deed necessarily bespattered with blood – Life had not been extinct more than ¼ of an hour.''

                                        George William Sequeira.

William Sedgwick Saunders 13 Queen Street, Cheapside, Dr. of Medicine, Fellow of the Institute of Chemistry, Fellow of the Chemical Society, and Public Analyst for the City of London – ''I received the stomach from Dr. Gordon Brown carefully sealed with his own private seal. The ends of the stomach had been carefully tied but its contents not been interfered with in any way. I carefully examined the stomach and its contents more particularly for poisons of the narcotic class with negative results, there not being the faintest trace of these or any other poison.''

By Mr. Crawford – ''I was present at the post mortem. I agree with Dr. Brown and Dr. Sequeira that the wounds were not inflicted by anyone possessing great anatomical skill and I agree that the perpetrator of the deed had no particular design on any particular organ.''

                                        WmSedgwickSaunders.

Annie Phillips 12 Dilstone Grove, Southwark Park Road, wife of Louis Phillips, a Lamp Black Packer, being sworn saith — "I am Daughter of Deceased who lived with my Father. I have never seen the marriage lines altho she always told me she was married. His name was Thomas Conway. I have not seen him for the last 15 or 18 months, he was living with me and my Husband at 15 Anchor Street, Southwark Park. He was a Hawker. He left suddenly without assigning any reason. We were not on good terms. I have never seen or heard of him since. He was a teatollar, my mother and he lived on bad terms because she used to drink I have not the least idea of where he is living now. He had no ill will to my knowledge against Deceased. He left Deceased between 7 & 8 years ago entirely on account of her Drinking Habits. My mother told me he had been in the 18 Royal Irish. He has been a pensioner since I was 8 years old. I am now 23. He left my mother between 7 & 8 years ago. I have been in the habit of seeing deceased after she left my father. She has frequently applied for money. The last time I saw her was 2 years and one month. I saw nothing of her on Saturday the day previous to her death. I formerly lived in King Street Bermondsey. I left there 2 years ago I did not leave my address when I left King Street, Bermondsey. I have 2 brothers by Conway, they live in London. My mother did not know where to find either of them, that was purposely kept from her to prevent her being applied to for money."

By Jury — "My father was aware she was living with Kelly."

By Mr. Crawford — "My father might have belonged to the Connaught Rangers — My mother waited on me in my confinement 2 years and 2 months ago. I saw Kelly and Deceased in a lodging House in Flower and Dean Street about 3 years ago. I knew they were living as man and wife. My father is living with my 2 Brothers ages between 15 and 20. I have not seen or heard from them for 18 months and I cannot give the clue to assist the police in finding them."

Annie Phillips.

John Mitchell Detective Sergeant, City Police, being sworn saith — "I have made every enquiry to find the Father and Brothers of the last Witness without success. I have found a Pensioner named Conway but he is not the man. I with other officers have used every endeavour and enquiry possible to be made with a view to trace the murderer."

John Mitchell.

Baxter Hunt Detective Constable of the City of London Police, being sworn saith – "I discovered Conway the Pensioner belonging to the 18 Royal Irish, I have confronted him with 2 of Deceased's Sisters and they have failed to recognize him as the man who used to live with Deceased. I have made every endeavour to trace the Conway mentioned by the last Witness without success."

Baxter Hunt.

Louis Robinson City Police Constable 931 being sworn saith – "On the 29th at 8.30 I was on duty in Aldgate High Street, I saw a crowd of persons outside No. 29 – I saw there a woman whom I have since recognized as the Deceased lying on the footway drunk. I asked if there was one that knew her or knew where she lived but I got no answer.

I picked her up and carried her to the side by the shutters and she fell sideways. I got assistance. We then took her to Bishopsgate Street Police Station. When asked her name she made the reply 'Nothing'. We then put her in the cells. No one particular appeared to be in her company when we first picked her up."

By Mr. Crawford – "The last time I saw her in the Police Cell was at 10 to 9. She was wearing an apron. I believe the apron produced was the one she was wearing."

By the Jury – "She smelt very strongly of drink."

Louis Robinson.

James Byfield Station Sergeant, Bishopsgate Police Station being sworn saith – "I remember deceased being brought in at ¼ to 9 on the Evening of the 29th she was very drunk having to be supported by the 2 constables who brought her in. She was taken back to the cell and detained there until one o'clock in the morning when she was sober. I discharged her after she gave her name and address which she was unable to do when brought in. She gave the name of Mary Ann Kelly, 6 Fashion Street, Spitalfields. She said she had been hopping."

J.G. Byfield.

George Henry Hutt Police Constable 968, City Gaoler, of Bishopsgate Street Station – "On Saturday the 29th at ¼ to 10 at night I took over the prisoners, among them the deceased woman. I visited her several times until 5 to one on Sunday. I found deceased was sober, brought from the cell into the office and after giving the name of Mary Ann Kelly she was discharged. I pushed open the swing door leading to the passage and said 'This way Misses' She passed along the passage to the outer door. I said to her please pull it to – she said 'All right Good Night Old Cock' she pulled the door within half a foot and she turned to the left leading towards Houndsditch.''

By Mr. Crawford – ''She left the Station at one o'clock and was capable of taking care of herself. When bringing her out of the cell she asked what time it was – I replied 'Too late for you to get any more drink. She said, 'Well what time is it?' I said, 'Just on one,' and 'I shall get a Damned fine hiding when I get home.' I said, 'And serve you right you have no right to get drunk.' I noticed she was wearing an apron. I believe the one produced was the one she was wearing when she left the Station. It would take 8 minutes ordinary walking to get to Mitre Square.''

George Hutt.

George James Morris Watchman to Messrs. Kearley and Tonge, Wholesale Grocers in Mitre Square – ''I went on duty at 7 in the Evening of the 29th. I was occupied for the most of the time in cleaning the offices and looking about the Warehouse. At $\frac{1}{4}$ to 2 Police Constable Watkins, who was on the Mitre Square beat, knocked at my door which was slightly on the jar at the time. I was then sweeping the steps down towards the door. The door was knocked or pushed. I was then about 2 yards from the door. I turned round and opened the door wide and saw Constable Watkins.

He said, 'For God's sake mate come to my assistance.'

I said, 'Stop till I get my lamp.'

I immediately went outside. I said, 'What's the matter?'

'Oh dear,' he said, 'there's another woman cut up to pieces.'

I said, 'Where is she?'

He said, 'In the corner.'

I went over to the corner and shewed my light on the body. I immediately blew my whistle and ran up Mitre Street into Aldgate. I saw no suspicious person. About then 2 Constables came up. They asked me what was the matter. I told them to go down Mitre Square, there was another terrible murder. I then followed the constables down and took charge of my own premises again – I heard no noise in the Square before I was called by Constable Watkins. If there had been any cry of distress I must have heard it.''

By the Jury — "I was in the Warehouse where the Counting House facing the Square. The door had not been ajar more than 2 minutes."

By Mr. Crawford — "I had not quitted the Warehouse between 11 and one. I had not seen Watkins before that evening."

George James Morris.

James Harvey 964, City Police, being sworn saith — "I went on my beat at $\frac{1}{4}$ to 10 on the 29th ulto. My beat is from Bevis Marks, to Duke Street, into Little Duke Street, to Houndsditch. From Houndsditch back to Duke Street, along Duke Street to Church passage, back again into Duke Street to Aldgate. From there to Mitre Street, back again to Houndsditch. Up Houndsditch to Little Duke Street, again back to Houndsditch to Goring Street, up Goring Street to Bevis Marks, to where I started. At 20 to 2 on Sunday morning I went down Duke Street and down Church Passage as far as Mitre Square. I saw no one. I heard no cry or noise. When I got to Aldgate returning to Duke Street I heard a whistle blown and saw the Witness Morris with a lamp. I went to him and asked what was the matter. He said, 'A woman has been ripped up in Mitre Square.'

I saw a Constable on the other side of the street.

I said, 'Come with me.'

We went into Mitre Square and saw Watkins there and the Deceased. Constable Holland who followed me went for Dr. Sequeira. Private individuals were sent for other Constables, arriving almost immediately. I waited there with Watkins and information was at once sent for the Inspector. I passed the post office clock between 1 and 2 minutes to the half hour."

By the Jury — "I go as far as to the end of Church Passage. I was at the end of Church Passage about 18 or 19 minutes to 2."

By Mr. Crawford — "I can only speak with certainty as to time with regard to the post office clock."

James Harvey.

George Clapp No. 5 Mitre Street, Aldgate, being sworn saith — "I am carekeeper of the premises. The back of the house looks into Mitre Square. I went to bed with my wife about 11 o'clock on Saturday night. The back of the house looks into Mitre Square. I was sleeping in a back room on the 2nd floor. During the night I heard no sound or any noise of any kind.

Between 5 and 6 o'clock in the morning was the first I heard of the murder."

By Mr. Crawford – "The only other person in the house was a Mrs. Tew, a nurse in attendance on my wife. She slept on the 3rd floor."

George Clapp.

Richard Pearce 922, City Police, being sworn saith – "I live at No.3 Mitre Square. I went to bed at 12.30 on Sunday morning. I heard no noise or disturbance of any sort. At 20 past 2 I was called by a Constable and first heard of the murder. From my window I could see the spot where deceased was found."

By Mr. Crawford – "I am the only tenant in the Square."

Richard Pearce.

Joseph Lawende 45 Norfolk Road, Dalston, Commercial Traveller, being sworn saith – "On the night of the 29th I was at the Imperial Club. Mr. Joseph Levy and Mr. Harry Harris were with me. It was raining. We left there to go out at ½ past one and we left the house about 5 minutes later. I walked a little further from the others. Standing in the corner of Church Passage in Duke Street, which leads into Mitre square, I saw a woman. She was standing with her face towards a man. I only saw her back. She had her hand on his chest. The man was taller than she was. She had a black jacket and a black bonnet. I have seen the articles which it was stated belonged to her at the police station. My belief is that they were the same clothes which I had seen upon the Deceased. She appeared to me short. The man had a cloth cap on with a cloth peak. I have given a description of the man to the police. I doubt whether I should know him again."

By Mr. Crawford – "The number of the Club is 16 & 17 Duke Street. It is 15 or 16 feet from the Club to the passage where they were standing. I fix the time by the Club clock and my own watch at ½ past one. I did not hear a word said. They did not either of them appear to be quarrelling. They appeared conversing very quietly. I did not look back to see where they went."

Joseph Lawende.

Joseph Hyam Levy 1 Hutchinson Street, Aldgate, Butcher, being sworn saith – "I was with the last Witness and Harris at the Imperial Club in Duke Street. We got up to go home at ½ past

one. We came out about 3 or 4 minutes after the half hour. I saw
a man and woman standing at the corner of Church Passage. I
passed on taking no further notice of them. The man I should say
was about 3 inches taller than the woman. I cannot give any
description of either of them. We went down Duke Street into
Aldgate leaving the man and woman still talking behind. I fix the
time by the Club clock. I said when I came out to Mr. Harris,
"Look there, I don't like going home by myself when I see those
characters about."

By Mr. Crawford – "There was nothing that I saw about the man
and woman which caused me to fear them."

                                        Joseph Hyam Levy.

Alfred Long 254A, Metropolitan Police Force, being sworn saith
– "I was on duty in Goulston Street, Whitechapel on the 30th
September, about 2.55 AM. I found a portion of a woman's apron
which I produce. There appeared blood stains on it, one portion was
wet, lying in a passage leading to the staircases of 108 to 119 Model
Dwelling House. Above it on the wall was written in chalk – The
Jews are the men that will not be blamed for nothing. I at once
searched the staircases and areas of the Building but found nothing
else. I at once took the apron to Commercial Road Police Station
and reported it to the Inspector on Duty. I passed that spot where
the apron was found about 2.20, the apron was not there when I
passed then."

By Mr. Crawford – "The words that were written on the wall –
the Jewes are the men that will not be blamed for nothing. I copied
the words from the wall into my report – I could not say whether
they were recently written. I wrote down into my book and the
Inspector noticed that Jews was spelt Juews. There was a difference
between the spelling.

When I found the piece of apron I at once searched the staircase
leading to the Buildings. I did not make any enquiries at the
tenements of the Buildings. There were 6 or 7 staircases. I searched
every one, found no traces of blood or recent footmarks. Having
searched I at once proceeded to the Station. Before proceeding there
I had heard of a murder having been committed. I had heard of the
murder in Mitre Square. I left a man 190 in charge of the Beat H
Division. I told him to take an observation as to any one who
entered the building or left it. I next returned to the Building about
5 o'clock. When I returned the writing had not been rubbed out. It

was rubbed out in my presence at $\frac{1}{2}$ past 5 or thereabouts. I did not hear any one object to its being rubbed out."

Alfred Long.

Daniel Halse Detective Officer of the City of London Police being sworn saith — "On Saturday the 29th September from instructions I received I directed a number of Police Officers to patrol the City all night. At about 2 minutes to 2 I was at the corner of Houndsditch by Aldgate Church in company with Detectives Outram and Marriott of the City Police. We all 3 went to Mitre Square. I had the light turned on to the body and saw it was a murder. I gave instructions to have the neighbourhood searched and every man examined. I went by Middlesex Street into Wentworth Street where I stopped 2 men who gave satisfactory account of themselves. I came through Goulston Street at 20 past 2 and then went back to Mitre Square and accompanied Inspector Collard to the mortuary. I saw deceased stripped and saw a portion of the apron was missing. I went back with Major Smith to Mitre Square when we went ['back to Goulstone' *deleted*] I then went with Detective Hunt to Leman Street Police Station. I and Detective Hunt went on to Goulstone Street and the spot was pointed out where the apron was found. I saw some chalk writing on the black facia of the wall. I remained there and sent with a view to having the writing photographed. Directions were given to have the writing photographed and during the time some of the Metropolitan Police said as it was Sunday morning it might cause a riot or an outbreak against the Jews and decided to have it rubbed out and it was rubbed out. When Hunt returned an enquiry was made at every tenement of the Building but we could gain no witness of any one going in likely to be the murderer."

By Mr. Crawford — "About 20 past 2 I passed over the spot where the piece of apron was found. I did not notice anything. I suggested that the top line should be taken out of the writing on the wall. I took a note of the writing before it was rubbed out. The exact words were 'The Juwes are not the men that will be blamed for nothing.' The writing had the appearance of being recently written. I protested against the writing being rubbed out. I wished it to remain there until Major Smith had seen it."

By the Jury — "It looked as if it had been recently written."

Daniel Halse.

Verdict Wilful Murder by some person unknown.

Despite the fairly detailed statements of the various witnesses contained in the preceding inquest papers, they would appear to be the initial evidence of these witnesses and the reports to be found in the newspapers do contain additional information. In order to get the full details of the reported evidence in the press, we again turn to *The Times*. The first report is contained in the issue of Friday, 5 October 1888, page 4:

THE EAST-END MURDERS.

Yesterday morning Mr. S. F. Langham, the City Coroner, opened the inquest at the mortuary in Golden-lane respecting the death of Catherine Eddows [*sic*], otherwise Conway or Kelly, who was found murdered in Mitre-square, City, last Sunday morning.

Dr. Sedgwick Saunders, medical officer of health for the City; Mr. Crawford, the City Solicitor; Mr. M'William, the inspector of the City Detective Department; and Mr. Superintendent Foster were present during the inquiry.

Mr. Crawford, at the opening of the proceedings, stated that he was present as representing the City Police, for the purpose of rendering the Coroner and the jury every possible assistance. If, when the witnesses were giving evidence, he thought it desirable to put any question, probably he would have the Coroner's permission to do so.

The CORONER – By all means.

Eliza Gold was the first witness. She stated that she lived at No. 6, Thrawl-street, Spitalfields, and was a widow. She recognized the deceased as her sister, whose name was Catherine Eddows. She was not married, but was living with a man named Kelly. Her sister had not been married. Her age last birthday was 43, as well as witness could remember. She had been living for some years with Kelly. Witness last saw her alive four or five months ago. She used to get her living by going out hawking. She was a woman of sober habits. Before she went to live with Kelly she had lived with a man named Conway for some years. She had had two children by him, who were married. Witness could not say whether Conway was still living; she had not seen him. Conway was a pensioner in the Army, who used to go out hawking things. Witness could not say whether her sister and Conway had parted on good or bad terms; nor could she say whether her sister had seen Conway since they had parted. Witness was quite certain that the deceased was her sister.

By Mr. Crawford. – She had not seen Conway for seven or eight years, and she could not say on what terms her sister had lived with Kelly. She had not seen them together for three or four weeks. They were then living together quite happily. Witness could not exactly fix the time when she saw them. They were living at the time at 55, Flower and Dean-street, a common lodging-house kept by a man named Smith. The last time she saw her sister alive was when the latter visited witness, who was ill at the time.

A discrepancy in her evidence was pointed out to the witness, who had stated in one part that the last time she saw her sister alive was four or five months ago, while in another portion of her evidence she had stated that it was three or four weeks ago.

John Kelly was the next witness called. He stated that he lived at 55, Flower and Dean-street, Spitalfields. He was a labourer and jobbed about the markets. He had seen and recognized the body of the deceased as Catherine Conway. Witness had known her seven years, and had lived with her the whole of that time. She used to sell things in the streets, and had lived with witness at the lodging-house in Flower and Dean-street. Witness was last with the deceased at 2 o'clock on Saturday afternoon in Houndsditch. They parted there on very good terms. She said she was going to see if she could find her daughter Annie in Bermondsey. He believed Annie was a daughter the deceased had had by Conway. She promised to be back at 4 o'clock and no later. She did not return, but witness heard that she was locked up on Saturday night at Bishopsgate. He was told by a woman that she had seen deceased in Houndsditch with two policemen. He could not say what time it was when he heard that statement. He did not make inquiries about her, feeling sure that she would return on Sunday morning. He heard that she had been locked up because she had had "a drop of drink." He did not know that she ever went out for immoral purposes; he had never allowed her to do so. She was not in the habit of drinking to excess, but occasionally she did so. She had no money about her when witness parted from her. Her object in going to Bermondsey was to see if she could find her daughter and get a little money from her, so that she need not walk the streets.

Mr. Crawford. – You were asked before if she walked the streets, and you said she did not. – Sometimes we were without money to pay for our lodging, and we were at the time I speak of. Witness did not know of anyone with whom the deceased was at variance, or who would be likely to do her an injury. He did not know whether the deceased had seen Conway of late; he had never seen Conway himself. He did not know when the deceased was discharged from custody.

By a Juryman. – She was in the habit of returning to her lodging at 8 or 9 o'clock. He had not inquired about her because he had felt sure that she would return on Sunday morning.

By Mr. Crawford. – He did not know with whom the deceased had been drinking on Saturday afternoon. She had not on any recent occasion absented herself at night time. Some time ago – a few months or weeks – she left witness; he supposed it was in consequence of their having had a few words, but she returned to him a few hours afterwards. He had had no angry words with the deceased on the Saturday afternoon. She had told him that her daughter lived in King-street, Bermondsey. They had been living together for seven years in Flower and Dean-street. On Friday night last she did not sleep with witness. She had no money, and went to the casual ward at Mile-end. He slept that night at the lodging-house mentioned. On the previous Monday night they slept in Kent, where they were hopping. They came up from Kent on Thursday, he believed. They had no money and they went to the casual ward in Shoe-lane. They were together all Friday until the afternoon, when he earned 6d. She said to him, "You take 4d. and go to the lodging-house, and give me 2d. and I will go to the casual ward." He wanted to spend the money in food and he told her that "Fred" – the deputy of the lodging-house – would not turn them away if they had no money. She said she would go to the casual ward at Mile-end, and would see him on the following morning, when he met her accidentally. She left him at 4 o'clock on Friday afternoon to go to Mile-end for a lodging. He saw her the next morning about 8 o'clock, as well as he could remember, and was surprised to see her so soon. The tea and sugar found on her had been bought out of the 2s. 6d. for which she had pawned his boots. When she left witness she was, he was sure, quite sober. They had spent the greater part of the 2s. 6d. in food and drink. They parted on good terms. He could not say why she separated from Conway. She had lived with witness for seven years. When he saw her so early on the Saturday morning she told him that there had been some bother in the casual ward, and that that was why she had been turned out so soon. He did not know the regulations of the casual ward at Mile-end, and whether she could discharge herself when she liked.

By Mr. Crawford. – The boots were pawned on Friday or Saturday by the deceased. Witness remained outside the shop. He slept at the lodging-house in Flower and Dean-street on Saturday night.

Mr. Crawford produced the pawn-ticket, and stated that the boots were pledged last Friday.

Frederick William Wilkinson, living in Brick-lane, Spital-fields, was next examined. He said he was deputy of the lodging-house in Flower and Dean-street. He had known Kelly and the deceased for the last seven or eight years, and they passed as man and wife. They lived on very good terms, but they had a few words occasionally when "Kate was in drink." Witness believed that deceased obtained her living by hawking things in the streets, and by charing. Whenever she and Kelly were at the lodginghouse they were pretty regular in paying. She was not often in drink, and was "a very jolly woman," often singing. Witness had never seen Kelly in drink since he had known him. He saw the deceased on her return from hopping at the lodginghouse on Friday afternoon, but he did not see Kelly at the time. She went out on Friday night, and witness saw her on the following morning between 10 and 11 o'clock with Kelly. Witness did not see her again until he saw her in the mortuary. To witness's knowledge the deceased had not been in the habit of walking the streets. When she and Kelly stopped at the lodginghouse they came in generally between 9 and 10. He had never known or heard of her being intimate with any one but Kelly. She used to say that her name was Kate Conway, and that it had been "bought and paid for," meaning that she was married to Conway. So far as witness knew she was not at variance with any one. She was quite sober when he saw her with Kelly on Saturday morning between 10 and 11. He asked Kelly when the latter came to pay for his lodging on Saturday where "Kate" was, and Kelly replied that he had heard that she had been locked up. Kelly called between 7. 30 and 8 on Saturday night and took a single bed. A single bed was 4d. and a double was 8d.

A juryman. – Do you not take the names of those who sleep at the lodginghouse? – No.

By Mr. Crawford. – He believed the last time the deceased and Kelly slept together at the lodginghouse was five or six weeks ago; before they went hopping. Kelly was there on Friday and Saturday nights. Deceased was not there on Friday or Saturday. He did not ask Kelly where she was on the Friday, and the reason why he asked the question on the Saturday night was because he had seen them together on that morning. Kelly went to bed at 10 o'clock on

Saturday night, and witness was quite positive that he did not go out again. He could not say at what hour Kelly went out on Saturday, but he saw him at the lodginghouse at dinner-time. So far as he was aware, Kelly had had no quarrel with any man about the deceased. He believed she was wearing an apron on Saturday morning.

Mr. Crawford. – Did any one come to your lodginghouse on the Sunday morning between 1 and 2 o'clock and take a bed, a stranger? Witness. – I had no stranger there between 1 and 2.

Mr. Crawford. – Can you tell me who entered your lodginghouse on Sunday morning between 1 and 2? Witness. – Two detectives came and asked if I had any female out.

Mr. Crawford. – Did any one come in before that, between 1 and 2, whom you did not recognize, and take a bed? Witness. – I cannot remember. I can refer to my book and tell you whether any stranger was there.

By the jury. – I saw the deceased and Kelly together on Saturday morning between 10 and 11 at breakfast.

The examination of the witness was then adjourned to enable him to obtain the book referred to from the lodginghouse.

Edward Watkins, City Police-constable 881, was the next witness, and, in answer to Mr. Crawford, he stated that he had been in the City Police force for 17 years. On the night of Saturday, September 29, he went on duty at a quarter to 10 – on his regular beat. His beat extended from Duke-street, Aldgate, through Heneage-lane, a portion of Bury-street, through Cree Church-lane, into Leadenhall-street, along Leadenhall-street, eastward into Mitre-street, into Mitre-square, round the square, and again into Mitre-street, then into and along King-street to St. James's-place, round St. James's-place, and thence into Duke-street, the starting point. The beat took 12 or 14 minutes. He had been continually patrolling that beat from 10 o'clock on Saturday night until 1.30 on Sunday morning without anything exciting his attention. He passed through Mitre-square about 1.30 on Sunday morning. He had his lantern fixed in his belt, and in accordance with his usual practice, he looked into the different corners, passages, and warehouses. Nothing excited his attention at 1.30 nor did he see any one about. No one could have been in any portion of the square at that hour without the cognizance of the witness. He next came into Mitre-square about 1.44. He fixed the time by reference to his watch after he had called the watchman. He entered the square from the right, near the corner, where something attracted his attention. [Plans of the square made by Mr. F. W. Foster, of Old Jewry, were at this point handed in and referred to by Mr. Crawford in his examination.] About 1.44 witness came into the square, at the right, and he then saw the body of a woman lying there. She was lying on her back, with her feet facing the square. He did not touch the body. The first thing he did was to go across to Messrs. Kearsley [*sic*] and Tonge's warehouse. The door was ajar. He pushed it open and called to the watchman, Morris. Morris came out, and witness sent him for assistance. Witness remained by the side of the body till the arrival of Police-constable Holland. No one was there with witness till Holland arrived, and he was followed by Dr. Sequeira. Inspector Collard arrived about 2, and Dr. Gordon Brown, surgeon to the City police force, followed. When witness entered the square at 1.44 he heard nothing — no sound as of the footsteps of some one running away; and to the best of his belief no one was there but the murdered woman.

By the CORONER. — The door of the warehouse of Messrs. Kearsley [*sic*] and Tonge was open, as the watchman was working inside. It was not an unusual thing for the warehouse door to be open at that time.

By the Jury. — He did not sound a whistle, because they did not carry whistles. The watchman did whistle. Witness's beat was a single beat; no other policeman entered Mitre-square.

Frederick William Foster, of 26, Old Jewry, stated that he was an architect and surveyor, and he had made the plans (produced) according to scale. He had them in three scales — one to 8 ft. to an inch, another 200 ft. to an inch, from an Ordnance map of the City; and he had marked on an Ordnance map of the same scale round from Berner-street to Mitre-street. That would be a distance of about three-quarters of a mile; and it would take from 12 to 15 minutes to walk it.

By Mr. Crawford. — The route described between Berner-street and Mitre-street was the nearest way. It was a direct line.

Mr. Crawford. — Assuming that a person was in Mitre-square, I want to know what route he would probably take, assuming that he passed by way of Goulston-street? — Witness. — There are two routes. There is only 10 ft. difference between them. One route is from Church-passage through Duke-street, crossing Houndsditch, through Gravel-lane, Stoney-lane, crossing Petticoat-lane, and through to Goulston-street. I know Flower and Dean-street.

Mr. Crawford. — Would a person, to get to the lodginghouse

there from Mitre-street, go by Goulston-street? — Witness. — He might do so. It is the most direct course he could take if he knew the neighbourhood. He could do the distance in a quarter of an hour; and the distance from Berner-street to Mitre-street would be within a quarter of an hour.

Mr. Crawford, to the Coroner. — You will have evidence later on that a portion of this woman's apron was found in Goulston-street.

The witness **Wilkinson** was then re-called, and in answer to Mr. Crawford stated, referring to his book, that Kelly slept at the lodginghouse on Friday and Saturday night in "No. 52, single." Witness could not say at what time any stranger entered the place. He found that there were six male strangers there on the Sunday morning. He could not tell whether any of those men came in about 2 o'clock on the Sunday morning, nor could he remember any one going out of the place soon after 12 o'clock, as that was a very busy time. He took the money and allotted the beds. Nothing excited his suspicion between the hours of 12 a.m. and 2. He recollected the police calling at 3 o'clock on Sunday morning.

By a juryman. — It was usual for the place to be open at 2 o'clock in the morning. They generally closed at 2.30 or 3. He had no means of remembering any person coming in. He would recognize a regular customer. He did not book the times they came in.

By Mr. Crawford. — There was no register kept of the names of those sleeping there.

By the jury. — We take the money of those who come. No questions are asked, and they are shown their beds. I dare say I have over 100 sleeping there now of a night.

Inspector Edward Collard (City Police) was the next witness called. He stated that at five minutes before 2 o'clock on Sunday morning last he received information at Bishopsgate-street Police-station that a woman had been murdered in Mitre-square. The information was at once telegraphed to headquarters, and he despatched a constable at once to Dr. Gordon Brown. Witness then proceeded himself to Mitre-square, arriving there at two or three minutes past 2. He there found Dr. Sequeira, several police officers, and the deceased lying in the south-west corner of the square in the position described by Constable Watkins. The body was not touched until the arrival of Dr. Brown, who came shortly afterwards. The medical gentlemen then examined the body, and remained until the arrival of the ambulance, when the body was taken to the mortuary. No money was found on the deceased. A portion of the apron produced was found on her, and the other portion, which was picked up in Goulston-street, would also be produced. When witness arrived at the square he took immediate steps to have the neighbourhood searched for the person who had committed the murder. Mr. M'William, the chief of the detectives, on his arrival shortly afterwards with a number of detectives, sent them to make search in all directions in Spitalfields, both in the streets and the lodging-houses. Several men were stopped and searched in the streets, but without any good result. Witness had a house-to-house inquiry made in the vicinity of Mitre-square, but could find nothing beyond what would be stated by two witnesses who would be called.

By Mr. Crawford. — There was no appearance of any struggle having taken place, and there was no blood anywhere except what had come from the deceased's neck. There was nothing whatever in the appearance of the deceased or her clothing to lead him to suppose that there had been any struggle. The blood flowing from her was in a liquid state, not congealed, and from his experience he should say that the body had not been there for more than a quarter of an hour. They endeavoured to find footmarks, but they could discover no trace whatever. A search was made at the back of the empty houses adjoining the square.

Dr. Frederick Gordon Brown, of 17, Finsbury-circus, examined, said he was surgeon of the City of London Police Force. He was called on Sunday morning shortly after 2 o'clock, and reached Mitre-square about 18 minutes after 2, when his attention was called to the body of the deceased. It was lying in the position described by Constable Watkins. The body was on its back, the head turned towards the left shoulder, and the arms were by the side of the body, as if they had fallen there. Both palms were upwards and the fingers were slightly bent. A thimble was lying on the ground near the right hand. The clothes were drawn up, the left leg was extended straight down, in a line with the body, and the right leg was bent at the thigh and knee. There was great disfigurement of the face. The throat was cut across, and below the cut was a neckerchief. The upper part of the dress had been pulled open a little way. The abdomen was all exposed; the intestines were drawn out to a large extent and placed over the right shoulder; a piece of the intestines was quite detached from the body and placed between the left arm and the body.

Mr. Crawford. – By "placed," do you mean put there by design?
Witness. – Yes.

Examination continued. – The lobe of the right ear was cut
obliquely through; there was a quantity of clotted blood on the
pavement, on the left side of the neck and upper part of the arm.
The body was quite warm, and no death-stiffening had taken place.
The body had been there only a few minutes.

By Mr. Crawford. – Certainly within 30 or 40 minutes.

Examination continued. – We looked for superficial bruises and
saw none. There were no marks of blood below the middle of the
body.

By Mr. Crawford. – There was no blood on the front of the
clothes. Before they removed the body he suggested that Dr.
Phillips should be sent for, and that gentleman, who had seen some
recent cases, came to the mortuary. A post-mortem examination
was made at 2.30 on Sunday afternoon. The temperature of the
room was 55deg. Rigor mortis was well marked. After careful
washing of the left hand a recent bruise, the size of a sixpence, was
discovered on the back of the hand between the thumb and the first
finger. There were a few small bruises on the right shin of older
date. The hands and arms were bronzed as if from sunburning.
There were no bruises on the scalp, back of the body, or elbows.
The witness then described in detail the cuts on the face, which, he
stated, was very much mutilated. The throat was cut across to the
extent of about 6in. or 7in. The sterno cleido mastoid muscle was
divided; the cricoid cartilage below the vocal cords was severed
through the middle; the large vessels on the left side of the neck
were severed to the bone, the knife marking the intervertebral
cartilage. The sheath of the vessels on the right side was just open;
the carotid artery had a pin-hole opening; the internal jugular vein
was open to the extent of an inch and a half – not divided. All the
injuries were caused by some very sharp instrument, like a knife,
and pointed. The cause of death was haemorrhage from the left
common carotid artery. The death was immediate. The mutilations
were inflicted after death. They examined the injuries to the
abdomen. The walls of the abdomen were laid open, from the
breast downwards. The cut commenced opposite the ensiform
cartilage, in the centre of the body. The incision went upwards, not
penetrating the skin that was over the sternum; it then divided the
ensiform cartilage, and being gristle they could tell how the knife
had made the cut. It was held so that the point was towards the left

side and the handle towards the right. The cut was made obliquely. The liver was stabbed as if by the point of a sharp knife. There was another incision in the liver, about $2\frac{1}{2}$ in., and, below, the left lobe of the liver was slit through by a vertical cut. Two cuts were shown by a jag of the skin on the left side. The abdominal walls were divided vertically in the middle line to within a quarter of an inch of the navel; the cut then took a horizontal course for $2\frac{1}{2}$ in. to the right side; it then divided the navel on the left side – round it – and made an incision parallel to the former horizontal incision, leaving the navel on a tongue of skin. Attached to the navel was $2\frac{1}{2}$ in. of the lower part of the rectus muscle of the left side of the abdomen. The incision then took an oblique course to the right. There was a stab of about an inch in the left groin, penetrating the skin in superficial fashion. Below that was a cut of 3in., going through all tissues, wounding the peritoneum to about the same extent. There had not been any appreciable bleeding from the vessels.

Mr. Crawford. – What conclusion do you draw from that? – Witness. – That the cut in the abdomen was made after death, and that there would not be much blood left to escape on the hands of the murderer. The way in which the mutilation had been effected showed that the perpetrator of the crime possessed some anatomical knowledge.

Mr. Crawford. – I think I understood you to say that in your opinion the cause of death was the cut in the throat? Witness. – Loss of blood from the throat, caused by the cut. That was the first wound inflicted.

Mr. Crawford. – Have you formed any opinion that the woman was standing when that wound was inflicted? Witness. – My opinion is that she was on the ground.

Mr. Crawford. – Does the nature of the wounds lead you to any conclusion as to the kind of instrument with which they were inflicted? Witness. – With a sharp knife, and it must have been pointed; and from the cut in the abdomen I should say the knife was at least six inches long.

Mr. Crawford. – Would you consider that the person who inflicted the wounds possessed great anatomical skill? Witness. – A good deal of knowledge as to the position of the organs in the abdominal cavity and the way of removing them.

Mr. Crawford. – Could the organs removed be used for any professional purpose? Witness. – They would be of no use for a professional purpose.

Mr. Crawford. – You have spoken of the extraction of the left kidney. Would it require great skill and knowledge to remove it? Witness. – It would require a great deal of knowledge as to its position to remove it. It is easily overlooked. It is covered by a membrane.

Mr. Crawford. – Would not such a knowledge be likely to be possessed by one accustomed to cutting up animals? Witness. – Yes.

Mr. Crawford. – Have you been able to form any opinion as to whether the perpetrator of this act was disturbed when performing it? Witness. – I think he had sufficient time. My reason is that he would not have nicked the lower eyelids if he had been in a great hurry.

Mr. Crawford. – About how long do you think it would take to inflict all these wounds, and perpetrate such a deed? Witness. – At least five minutes would be required.

Mr. Crawford. – Can you as a professional man assign any reason for the removal of certain organs from the body? Witness. – I cannot.

Mr. Crawford. – Have you any doubt in your mind that there was no struggle? Witness. – I feel sure that there was no struggle.

Mr. Crawford. – Are you equally of opinion that the act would be that of one man, one person, only? Witness. – I think so; I see no reason for any other opinion.

Mr. Crawford. – Can you as a professional man account for the fact of no noise being heard by those in the immediate neighbourhood? Witness. – The throat would be so instantaneously severed that I do not suppose there would be any time for least sound being emitted.

Mr. Crawford. – Would you expect to find much blood on the person who inflicted the wounds? Witness. – No. I should not.

Mr. Crawford. – Could you say whether the blood spots on the piece of apron produced were of recent origin? Witness. – They are of recent origin. Dr. Phillips brought on a piece of apron which had been found by a policeman in Goulston-street.

Mr. Crawford. – It is impossible to assert that it is human blood? Witness. – Yes; it is blood. On the piece of apron brought on there were smears of blood on one side as if a hand or a knife had been wiped on it. It fitted the piece of apron in evidence.

Mr. Crawford. – Have you formed any opinion as to the purpose for which the face was mutilated? Witness. – Simply to disfigure the corpse, I should think.

Mr. Crawford. – Not much violence was required to inflict these injuries? Witness. – A sharp knife was used, and not very much force would be required.

By a juryman. – He did not think any drug was administered to the woman, judging from the breath; but he had not yet examined the contents of the stomach.

At this point the inquiry was adjourned for a week.

Mr. Crawford said that it might be of interest for the jury to know that the Court of Common Council had unanimously adopted the suggestion of the Lord Mayor that a reward of £500 should be offered for the detection and conviction of the murderer.

The jury expressed satisfaction at the announcement.

From *The Times* of Tuesday, 9 October 1888:

The funeral of Catherine Eddowes, the victim of the Mitre-square murder, took place yesterday at Ilford Cemetery. The body was removed shortly after 1 o'clock from the mortuary in Golden-lane, where a vast concourse of people had assembled. A strong force of the City Police, under Mr. Superintendent Foster, was present, and conducted the cortege to the City boundary. At Old-street a large number of the Metropolitan Police were present under Inspector Barnham. The cortege passed Whitechapel parish church, and along Mile-end-road, through Bow and Stratford to the cemetery. The sisters of the ill-fated woman and the man Kelly, with whom she had lived for seven years, attended the funeral. Along the whole route great sympathy was expressed for the relatives.

It is stated by a news agency that definite instructions have been issued to the police that in the event of any person being found murdered under circumstances similar to those of the recent crimes, they are not to remove the body of the victim, but to send notice immediately to a veterinary surgeon in the South-west District, who holds several trained blood-hounds in readiness to be taken to the spot where the body may be found, and to be at once put on the scent.

The Times of Thursday, 11 October 1888, page 5, carries an update on the enquiry in respect of the murder of Catherine Eddowes:

THE EAST-END MURDERS.

A good deal of fresh evidence will be given at the adjourned inquest, which will be held to-day at the City Coroner's Court, Golden-lane, upon the body of the Mitre-square victim. Since the adjournment, Shelton, the coroner's officer, has, with the assistance of the City police authorities, discovered several new witnesses, including the daughter of the deceased, who was found to be occupying a respectable situation as a domestic in the neighbourhood of Kensington. She states that she had not seen her mother for some time, and certainly did not see her on the night she met her death. Two witnesses have also been found who state that they saw the deceased standing at the corner of Duke-street, Aldgate, a few minutes' walk from Mitre-square. This was as near as they can recollect about half-past 1 o'clock, and she was then alone. They recognized her on account of the white apron she was wearing. The contents of the deceased's stomach have been analyzed, but no trace of a narcotic can be discovered. Ten witnesses will be called to-day, and the coroner hopes to conclude the inquiry this sitting.

The Times of Friday, 12 October 1888, page 4, takes up the report on the Eddowes inquest, resumed the previous day:

THE EAST-END MURDERS.

Yesterday morning Mr. S. F. Langham, the City Coroner, resumed the inquest at the mortuary in Golden-lane respecting the death of Catherine Eddows [*sic*], otherwise Conway or Kelly, who was found murdered in Mitre-square on the morning of Sunday, the 30th ult.

During the inquiry Major Henry Smith, the Assistant Commissioner of the City Police, Mr. M'William, the inspector of the City Detective Department, Mr. Superintendent Foster, and Mr. F. W. Foster, architect and surveyor, of Old Jewry, who produced plans of the square were present.

The first witness examined was **Dr. George William Sequeira**, of 34, Jewry-street, Aldgate, who stated that he was called on Sunday, the 30th ult., to Mitre-square, and was the first medical man to arrive, being on the scene of the murder at five minutes to 2. He saw the position of the body, and he entirely agreed with Dr. Gordon Brown's evidence given on the opening of the inquest.

By Mr. Crawford (the City Solicitor). – He was acquainted with the locality and knew the position of the square. It would probably be the darkest corner of the square where the body was found. There would have been sufficient light to enable the murderer to commit his crime without the aid of any additional light.

Mr. Crawford. – Have you formed any opinion that the

murderer had any design with respect to any particular part? – I have formed the opinion that he had no particular design on any particular organ.

Mr. Crawford. – Judging from the injuries inflicted, do you think he was possessed of great anatomical skill? – No, I do not.

Mr. Crawford. – Can you account for the absence of any noise? – The death must have been so instantaneous after the severance of the blood vessels and the wind-pipe.

By Mr. Crawford. – He did not think that the clothes of the assassin would necessarily be bespattered with blood. When witness arrived life had been extinct probably not more than a quarter of an hour, judging from the condition of the blood.

Dr. William Sedgwick Saunders of 13, Queen-street, Cheapside, examined, said he was doctor of medicine, Fellow of the Institute of Chemistry, Fellow of the Chemical Society, and public analyst of the City of London. He received the stomach of the deceased from Dr. Gordon Brown, carefully sealed, and the contents had not been interfered with in any way. He had carefully examined the stomach and its contents, more particularly for poisons of a narcotic class, with negative results, there not being the faintest trace of any of these, or any other poison.

By Mr. Crawford. – He was present during the whole of the post-mortem examination. Having had ample opportunity of seeing the wounds inflicted, he agreed with Dr. Brown and Dr. Sequeira that they were not inflicted by a person of great anatomical skill. He equally agreed that the murderer had no particular design on any particular internal organ.

Annie Phillips, living at 12, Dilston-grove, Southwark-park-road, was the next witness. She stated that she was married, and that her husband was a lamp-black packer. She was the daughter of the deceased, who had always told witness that she was married to Thomas Conway, witness's father. She had not seen him for 15 or 18 months. The last time she saw him was when he was living with witness and her husband at 15, Anchor-street, Southwark-park. Her father was a hawker. She did not know what became of him after he left. He left without giving any particular reason for going, but he did not leave witness on very good terms. He did not say that he would never see her again. He was a teetotaller. He and her mother did not live on good terms after the latter took to drink. She had not the least idea where her father was living. He had no ill-will against the deceased, so far as witness knew. She was told that her father had been in the 18th Royal Irish. He left her mother solely because of her drinking habits. He was a pensioner and had had a pension since witness was eight years old. She was now 23. It was seven or eight years ago since her father lived with her mother. Witness frequently saw her mother after they separated; her mother applied to her for money. The last time she saw her mother alive was two years and one month ago. She did not see her on the Saturday, the day previous to her death. Witness used to live in King-street, Bermondsey — that was about two years ago. On removing from there witness did not leave any address. She had two brothers, Conway being their father. Her mother did not know where to find either of them; the information was purposely kept from her. She supposed that that was in order to prevent her mother from applying to them for money.

By a juryman. — It was between 15 and 18 months ago since her father lived with witness and her husband. Her father knew at that time that her mother was living with Kelly.

By Mr. Crawford. — She was not sure that her father was a pensioner of the 18th Royal Irish. It might have been the Connaught Rangers. [Mr. Crawford observed that there was a pensioner of the 18th Royal Irish named Conway, but he was not the Conway who was wanted.] The deceased last received money from witness about two years and two months ago, when she waited upon witness in the latter's confinement. Witness had never had a letter from her mother. She had seen Kelly and her mother together in the lodging-house in Flower and Dean-street; that was about $3\frac{1}{2}$ years ago. Witness knew that they lived together. Her father was living with her two brothers, but she could not say where. She could not give the slightest clue as to their whereabouts. Her brothers were aged 15 and 20. Witness did not know that her mother had recently been intimate with any one besides Kelly in the lodging-house.

Detective-sergeant John Mitchell (City Police), the next witness, replying to Mr. Crawford, said that he had made every effort, acting under instructions, to find the father and the brothers of the last witness, but without success. He had found a pensioner named Conway belonging to the 18th Royal Irish, but he was not identified as the Thomas Conway in question.

To the Coroner. — Every endeavour possible has been made with a view to tracing the murderer.

Mr. Crawford. — Do not go into that. I am sure that the jury believe that, and that the City Police are doing everything they can with that object.

Detective Baxter Hunt (City Police), replying to Mr. Crawford, stated that acting under instructions he had discovered the pensioner Conway belonging to the 18th Royal Irish. Witness had confronted the man with two of the deceased's sisters, who had failed to recognize him as the man who used to live with the deceased. Witness had made every effort to trace the Thomas Conway and the brothers referred to, but without result.

By a juryman. – The reason the daughter had not seen the man Conway, whom witness had traced, was that she had not at the time been discovered.

Mr. Crawford intimated that the daughter should see the man.

Witness, in reply to a juryman, stated that the Conway whom he had discovered last received his pension on the 1st inst.

By Mr. Crawford. – He is quartermaster-sergeant.

Dr. Gordon Brown at this point was re-called.

Mr. Crawford. – The theory has been put forward that it is possible for the deceased to have been taken to Mitre-square after her murder. What is your opinion about that?

Dr. Brown. – I think there is no doubt on the point. The blood at the left side of the deceased was clotted, and must have flowed from her at the time of the injury to the throat. I do not believe the deceased moved in the slightest way after her throat was cut.

Mr. Crawford. – You have no doubt that the murder was committed at that spot? – I feel quite sure it was.

Police-constable Lewis Robinson stated that about half-past 8 o'clock on the night of the 29th ult. he was on duty in High-street, Aldgate, where he saw a crowd of persons. He then saw a woman, who was drunk, and who had since been recognized as the deceased. She was lying on the footway. Witness asked if any one in the crowd knew her or where she lived, but he received no answer. On the arrival of another constable they took her to Bishopsgate Police-station, where she was placed in a cell.

By Mr. Crawford. – No one in the crowd appeared to know the woman. Witness last saw her on the same evening at about 10 minutes to 9 o'clock in the police cell.

Mr. Crawford. – Do you recollect whether she was wearing an apron? – Yes, she was.

Mr. Crawford. – Could you identify it? – I could if I saw the whole of it. A brown paper parcel was produced, from which two

pieces of apron were taken and shown to the witness, who said. –
To the best of my knowledge and belief that is the apron.

By a juryman. – The woman smelt very strongly of drink.

James Byfield said he was station sergeant at Bishopsgate
Police-station. He remembered the woman referred to by the
last witness being brought to the station at a quarter to 9 on the
evening of the 29th ult. She was very drunk. She was placed in
a cell, and was kept there until 1 o'clock the next morning. She
was then sober, and was discharged after giving her name as
Mary Ann Kelly and her address at 6, Fashion-street. In answer
to questions put to her by witness, she stated that she had been
hopping.

By a juryman. – He believed that nothing was given to her while
she was in the cell.

By Mr. Crawford. – He did not notice that she was wearing an
apron.

Constable George Henry Hutt 968, said he was gaoler at
Bishopsgate-street Police-station. On Saturday night, the 29th ult.,
at a quarter to 10 he took over the prisoners, among whom was the
deceased. He visited her several times in the cell until five minutes
to 1 o'clock, when he was directed by Sergeant Byfield to see
whether any of the prisoners were fit to be discharged. The
deceased was found to be sober, and was brought from the cell
to the office; and after giving the name of Mary Ann Kelly, she was
discharged. He saw her turn to the left after getting outside the
station.

By a juryman. – It was left to the discretion of the inspector, or
acting inspector, to decide when a person who had been drunk was
in a fit condition to be discharged.

By another juryman. – He visited the woman in the cell about
every half-hour from five minutes to 10 o'clock until 1 o'clock. She
was sleeping when he took over the prisoners. At a quarter-past 12
o'clock she was awake, and singing a song to herself. At half-past
12, when he went to her, she asked him when she was going to be
let out, and he replied, "When you are capable of taking care of
yourself." She answered that she was capable of taking care of
herself then.

By Mr. Crawford. – It was not witness, but Sergeant Byfield who
discharged her. She left the station about 1 o'clock. In witness's
opinion she was then quite capable of taking care of herself. She said
nothing to witness as to where she was going. About two minutes

before 1 o'clock, when bringing her out of the cell, she asked witness the time, and he replied, "Too late for you to get any more drink." She asked him again what time it was, and he replied, "Just on 1." She then said, "I shall get a d— fine hiding when I get home." Witness gathered from that that she was going home. He noticed that she was wearing an apron, and to the best of his belief the apron shown to the last witness was the one.

By Mr. Crawford. – It would take about eight minutes to walk from the police station to Mitre-square – ordinary walking.

By a juryman. – Prisoners were not searched who were brought into the station drunk. Handkerchiefs or anything with which they could injure themselves would be taken from them.

George James Morris, the next witness called, said he was watchman at Messrs. Kearley and Tonge's, tea merchants, in Mitre-square. He went on duty there at 7 o'clock in the evening.

The CORONER. – What happened at a quarter to 2 o'clock? – Police-constable Watkins, who was on the Mitre-square beat, knocked at the door of the warehouse. It was slightly "on the jar." He was then sweeping the steps down towards the door, and as he was doing so the door was pushed. He opened it wide and saw Watkins, who said, "For God's sake, mate, come to my assistance." The constable was agitated, and witness thought he was ill. He had his lamp by his side lighted, and asked Watkins what was the matter. Watkins replied, "There is another woman cut to pieces." Witness asked where she was, and Watkins replied, "In the corner." Having been a police-constable himself, he knew what assistance was required. He went over to the spot indicated and turned his lamp on the body. He immediately ran up Mitre-street into Aldgate, blowing his whistle. He saw no suspicious person about at the time. He was soon joined by two police-constables, and he told them to go into Mitre-square, where there had been another terrible murder. He followed the constables there, and took charge of his own premises again. He had heard no noise in the square before he was called by Watkins. Had there been any cry of distress he would have heard it.

By a juryman. – He had charge of the two warehouses of Messrs. Kearley and Tonge. At the time in question he was in the one where the counting-house was; it faced the square.

By Mr. Crawford. – Before being called by Watkins he had had no occasion to go out of the offices or into the square. He was sure he had not quitted the premises before Watkins called him. There was nothing unusual in his door being open or in his being at work at a quarter to 2 o'clock on Sunday morning.

By a juryman. – His door had not been on the jar more than two or three minutes before Watkins called him.

Constable James Harvey (964 City Police) stated that at a quarter to 10 o'clock on the night of the 29th ult. he went on his beat, which he described, and which took in Mitre-street. He saw no suspicious person about while on his beat, and he heard no cry or any noise. When he got into Aldgate, returning towards Duke-street, he heard a whistle, and saw the witness Morris with a lamp. The latter, in answer to witness, said that a woman had been ripped up in Mitre-square. Witness saw a constable on the other side of the street. They went to Mitre-square, where they saw Watkins with the body of the deceased. The constable who followed witness went for Dr. Sequeira, and private persons were despatched for other constables, who arrived almost immediately, having heard the whistle. Witness waited there with Watkins, and information was at once sent to the inspector. As witness passed the post-office clock at Aldgate on his beat it was between one and two minutes to half-past 1 o'clock.

By a juryman. – His beat took him down Church-passage to the end. He was there three or four minutes before he heard the whistle; it was then about 18 or 19 minutes to 2 o'clock.

George Clapp said he lived at 5, Mitre-street, Aldgate, of which he was caretaker. The back part of the house looked into Mitre-square. On the night of the 29th ult. he and his wife went to bed at 11 o'clock. They slept in a back room on the second floor. During the night he heard no disturbance or noise of any kind. The first he heard of the murder in the square was between 5 and 6 o'clock on the following morning.

By Mr. Crawford. – The only other person in the house that night was a woman, a nurse, who slept at the top of the house, on the third-floor.

Constable Richard Pearse, 922 City Police, said he lived at No. 3, Mitre-square. He went to bed on the night of the 29th ult. about 20 minutes after 12 o'clock. He heard no noise or disturbance of any kind. He first heard of the murder at 20 minutes past 2 o'clock, when he was called by a police-constable. From his window he could plainly see the spot where the murder was committed.

By Mr. Crawford. – He was the only tenant of No. 3, Mitre-square, where he lived with his wife and family.

Joseph Lawende said that he lived at 45, Norfolk-road, Dalston. He was a commercial traveller. On the night of the murder he was at the Imperial Club in Duke-street, with Joseph Levy and Harry Harris. They went out of the club at half-past 1, and left the place about five minutes later. They saw a man and a woman standing together at a corner in Church-passage, in Duke-street, which led into Mitre-square. The woman was standing with her face towards the man. Witness could not see the woman's face; the man was taller than she. She had on a black jacket and bonnet. He saw her put her hand on the man's chest. Witness had seen some clothing at the police-station, and he believed the articles were the same that the woman he referred to was wearing.

The CORONER. – Can you tell us what sort of man it was with whom she was speaking? – He had on a cloth cap with a peak.

Mr. Crawford. – Unless the jury wish it I have a special reason why no further description of this man should be given now.

The jury assented to Mr. Crawford's wish.

The CORONER. – You have given a description of the man to the police, I suppose? – Yes.

The CORONER. – Would you know him again? – I doubt it.

By Mr. Crawford. – The distance between the Imperial Club and the top of Church-passage, where he saw the man and woman standing talking together, was about nine or ten yards. He fixed the time of leaving the club at half-past 1 by reference to the club clock and to his own watch, and it would have been about 25 minutes to 2 o'clock when he saw the man and woman standing together. He heard not a word of their conversation. They did not appear to be in an angry mood. The woman did not appear to have put her hand on the man's chest as if she were pushing him away. Witness did not look back to see where they went.

Joseph Hyam Levy of 1, Hutchison-street, Aldgate, said he was a butcher. He was in the Imperial Club with the last witness, and the time when they rose to leave was half-past 1 by the club clock. It was about three or four minutes after the half-hour when they left. He noticed a man and woman standing together at the corner of Church-passage, but he passed on without taking any further notice of them. He did not look at them. From what he saw, the man might have been three inches taller than the woman. He could not give any description of either of them. He went on down Duke-street, into Aldgate, leaving the man and woman speaking together. He only fixed the time by the club clock.

By a juryman. – His suspicions were not aroused by the two persons. He thought the spot was very badly lighted. It was now much better lighted than it was on the night of the murder. He did not take much notice of the man and woman.

By Mr. Crawford. – He was on the opposite pavement to the man and woman. There was nothing that he saw to induce him to think that the man was doing any harm to her.

Police-constable Alfred Long, 254 A, stated that he was on duty in Goulston-street, Whitechapel, on the morning of the 30th ult. At about 2.55 he found a portion of an apron (produced as before). There were recent stains of blood on it. It was lying in the passage leading to a staircase of 118 and 119, ordinary model dwelling-houses. Above it on the wall was written in chalk, "The Jews are the men that will not be blamed for nothing." He at once searched the staircases and areas of the building, but he found nothing. He then took the piece of apron to the Commercial-road [*sic* – Commercial Street] Police-station, and reported to the inspector on duty. He had previously passed the spot where he found the apron at 20 minutes after 2, but it was not there then.

By Mr. Crawford. – Witness repeated as before the words which he saw written on the wall.

Mr. Crawford. – Have you not put the word "not" in the wrong place?" Is it not, "The Jews are not the men that will be blamed for nothing?" Witness repeated the words as he had previously read them.

Mr. Crawford. – How do you spell "Jews?" Witness. – J-e-w-s.

Mr. Crawford. – Now, was it not on the wall J-u-w-e-s? Is it not possible you are wrong? – It may be as to the spelling.

Mr. Crawford. – And as to the place where the word "not" was put? Witness again read the words as before.

By Mr. Crawford. – He had not noticed the wall before. He noticed the piece of apron first, and then the words on the wall. One corner of the apron was wet with blood. His light was on at the time. His attention was attracted to the writing on the wall while he was searching. He could not form an opinion as to whether the writing was recent. He went on to the staircase of the dwelling, but made no inquiries in the house itself.

By a juryman. – The pocket-book in which he entered the words written on the wall at the time he noticed them was at Westminster.

The witness's examination was postponed, and the pocket-book was ordered to be produced.

Detective Daniel Halse (City Police) stated that on Saturday, the 29th ult., from instructions received at the Detective Office, Old Jewry, he told a number of police officers in plain clothes to patrol the City all night. At about two minutes to 2 on the Sunday morning he was at the corner of Houndsditch, by Aldgate Church, in company with Detectives Outram and Marryat, of the City Police. They heard that a woman had been murdered in Mitre-square, and they all ran there and saw the body of the murdered woman. He gave instructions to have the neighbourhood searched, and every man to be stopped and examined. He himself went by way of Middlesex-street, at the east end of the City, into Wentworth-street, where he stopped two men, who gave a satisfactory account of themselves, and he allowed them to depart. He came through Goulston-street about 20 minutes past 2, at the spot where the apron was found, and he then went back to Mitre-square and accompanied Inspector Collard to the mortuary. He there saw the deceased undressed, noticing that a portion of the apron she wore was missing. He accompanied Major Smith back to Mitre square, where they heard that a piece of apron had been found in Goulston-street. He then went with Detective Hunt to Leman-street Police-station, where he heard that the piece of apron that had been picked up had been handed to Dr. Phillips. Witness and Hunt then went back to Goulston-street, to the spot where the apron had been discovered. He saw some chalk writing on the wall. He remained there, and Hunt went for Mr. M'William for instructions to have the writing photographed. Directions were given for that to be done. Some of the Metropolitan Police thought it might cause a riot if the writing were seen, and an outbreak against the Jews. It was decided to have the writing rubbed out. The people were at that time bringing out their stalls, which they did very early on the Sunday morning. When Hunt returned inquiry was made at every tenement in the dwelling referred to in Goulston-street, but no tidings could be obtained as to any one having gone in who was likely to be the murderer.

By Mr. Crawford. – At about 20 minutes after 2 he passed over the spot where the piece of apron was found. If it was there then he would not necessarily have seen it, for it was in the building.

Mr. Crawford. – Did any one suggest that it would be possible to take out the word "Juwes," and leave the rest of the writing there? – I suggested that the top line might be rubbed out, and the Metropolitan Police suggested the word "Juwes." The fear on the part of the Metropolitan Police of a riot was the sole cause of the writing on the wall being rubbed out.

Mr. Crawford. – Read out the exact words you took down in your book at the time. – "The Juwes are not the men that will be blamed for nothing."

By Mr. Crawford. – The writing appeared to have been recently done. – It was done with white chalk on the black facia of the wall.

By a juryman. – The spot where the writing was is the ground of the Metropolitan Police, and they insisted on having it rubbed out.

By Mr. Crawford. – Witness protested against it being rubbed out, and wanted it to be left until Major Smith had seen it.

By a juryman. – He assumed that the writing was recent, because from the number of persons living in the tenement he believed it would have been rubbed out had it been there for any time. There were about three lines of writing, which was in a good schoolboy hand.

By another juryman. – The writing was in the passage of the building itself, and was on the black dado of the wall.

A juryman. – It seems to me strange that a police-constable should have found this piece of apron, and then for no inquiries to have been made in the building. There is a clue up to that point, and then it is altogether lost.

Mr. Crawford. – I have evidence that the City Police did make a careful search in the tenement, but that was not until after the fact had come to their knowledge. I am afraid that will not meet the point raised by you (to the juryman). There is the delay that took place. The man who found the piece of apron is a member of the Metropolitan Police.

The witness **Long** having returned with the pocket-book referred to, stated, in reply to Mr. Crawford, that the book contained the entry which he made at the time as to the words written on the wall. They were "The Jews are the men that will not be blamed for nothing." The inspector made the remark that on the wall the word was "Jeuws." Witness entered in his book what he believed was an exact copy of the words.

Mr. Crawford. – At all events there was a discrepancy between what you wrote down and what was actually written on the wall, so far as regards the spelling of the word "Jews." Witness replied that the only remark the inspector made was as to the spelling of the word "Jews."

By Mr. Crawford. – The moment he found the piece of apron he searched the staircases leading to the building. He did not make any inquiry of the inmates in the tenements. There were either six or seven staircases, one leading down, and the others upstairs. He searched every staircase, and could find no trace of blood or any recent footmarks. He found the apron at five minutes to 3, and when he searched the staircases it would be about 3 o'clock. Having searched the staircases he at once proceeded to the police-station. Before proceeding to the station he had heard that a murder had been committed in Mitre-square. When he started for the police-station he left Police-constable 190 H in charge of the building. He did not know the constable's name; he was a member of the Metropolitan Police. Witness told him to keep observation on the dwelling, to see whether any one left or entered it. Witness next returned to the building at 5 o'clock. The writing was rubbed out in witness's presence at half-past 5, or thereabouts. He heard no one object to the writing being rubbed out.

A juryman. Having heard of the murder, and having afterwards found the piece of apron with blood on it and the writing on the wall, did it not strike you that it would be well to make some examination of the rooms in the building? You say you searched all the passages, but you would not expect that the man who had committed the murder would hide himself there. Witness. – Seeing the blood there, I thought that the murder had been committed, and that the body might be placed in the building.

The juryman. – You did not search the rooms, but left a man to watch the building, and the whole clue seems to have passed away. I do not wish to say anything harsh, as I consider that the evidence of yourself and of the other members of the police redounds to the credit of all of you; but this does seem a point that requires a little investigation. You find a piece of apron wet with blood; you search all the passages, and then you leave the building in the care of a man to watch the front. Witness. – I thought the best thing I could do was to go to the station and report the matter to the inspector on duty.

The juryman. – I feel sure you did your best.

Mr. Crawford. – May we take it that you thought you would be more likely to find the body of the murdered person there than the assassin? Witness. – Yes.

By a juryman. – Witness was a stranger in the neighbourhood. No one could have gone out of the front part of the building without being seen by the constable left on the spot by witness.

The CORONER, in summing up, observed that the evidence had been of the most exhaustive character. He thought it would be far better now to leave the matter in the hands of the police, to follow it up with any further clues they might obtain, and for the jury to return a verdict of wilful murder against some person or persons unknown. It had been shown by the evidence of Dr. Gordon Brown that the murderer must taken hold of the deceased woman and cut her throat, and by severing the vocal cords, prevented her from making any cry. All the evidence showed that no sound had been heard in connection with the crime. The assassin had not only murdered the woman, defenceless as she was, but had so mangled the corpse as to render it almost impossible for the body to be identified. He thought they would agree that the evidence clearly showed that the woman was taken to the police-station for being drunk, and that she was discharged about 1 o'clock on the morning of the murder. After that two persons – a man and a woman – were seen talking together at the corner of Church-passage by the witnesses from the Imperial Club, and one of those witnesses had expressed his opinion that the articles of clothing which he had seen at the police-station were the same as those worn by the woman. She was discharged from the station at about five minutes after 1 o'clock. At half-past 1 a police-constable went round Mitre-square, and turned his lamp on to the corner, but saw nothing there. Just 14 minutes afterwards he found there the body of a woman who had been murdered, the evidence of the doctor showing that it must have taken five minutes to commit the murder and to have inflicted the injuries on the body. The murder must have been committed between 1.30 and 1.44, and, allowing five minutes for the crime to be committed, only nine minutes were left to be accounted for. The history of the case was a very painful one. It appeared that the deceased had been living first with Thomas Conway for seven or eight years. Her drinking habits had induced him to part from her, and the sister of the deceased had stated that she was not married to him. There was nothing to suggest that either Conway or Kelly had had anything to do with the murder, both of them seeming to be totally inoffensive men. It had been clearly proved that Kelly was in bed at the lodging-house at the time of the murder. He had heard that the deceased had been taken up by the police, and knowing what the custom was in the City, he assumed that she would return to him in the morning. They had, it appeared, been out hopping for some weeks, and had returned home on the Thursday (the 27th ult.), taking a lodging for that night in Shoe-lane; and on the Saturday – the last time Kelly saw anything of her – she stated that she was going to see whether she could find her daughter. Something might turn on the fact that she did not see her daughter. According to the evidence, the deceased was going to Bermondsey to see her, but the daughter had left the address there without mentioning any other address to which she was going. It was possible that the deceased had gone to Bermondsey. What became of her in the interval between that and her being taken in charge there was nothing to show, but she had evidently been drinking. There could be no doubt that a most vile murder had been committed by some person or persons unknown, and he thought he might say by some person unknown. Dr. Brown believed that only one person was implicated. Unless the jury wished him to refer to any point in the evidence, there was nothing that need detain them further as far as that inquiry was concerned, and the police could be left with a free hand to follow up the investigation. A munificent reward had been offered by the Corporation, and it might be hoped that that would set persons on the track and cause the apprehension of the murderer.

Mr. Crawford. – Dr. Brown in his evidence expressed his belief as a medical man that only one person had committed the murder.

The Foreman. – (the jury having consulted for about a couple of minutes). – Our verdict is "Wilful murder by some person unknown."

The CORONER. – That is the verdict of all of you?

The Foreman. – Yes.

The CORONER afterwards stated that the jury desired him to thank Mr. Crawford and the police for the assistance which they had rendered in the inquiry, and he also wished to add his own thanks.

The Times of Tuesday, 16 October 1888, page 10, carried a report of the City Police locating Thomas Conway:

THE EAST-END MURDERS.

The City Police have succeeded in discovering Thomas Conway, who some years ago lived with Catherine Eddowes, the woman murdered in Mitre-square. Up to yesterday the efforts of the detectives had been at fault, owing, as was suggested by the City Solicitor at the inquest, to the fact that Conway had drawn his pension from the 18th Royal Irish Regiment under a false name, that of Thomas Quinn. Apparently he had not read the papers, for he was ignorant till the last few days that he was being sought for. Then, however, he learned that the City detectives were inquiring for him, and yesterday afternoon he and his two sons went to the detective offices of the City Police in Old Jewry and explained who they were. Conway was at once taken to see Mrs. Annie Phillips, Eddowes's daughter, who recognized him as her father. He states that he left Eddowes in 1880 in consequence of her intemperate habits. He knew that she had since been living with Kelly, and had once or twice seen her in the streets, but had, as far as possible, kept out of her way, as he did not wish to have any further communication with her.

CHAPTER 11

October 1888 – Will the Unknown Killer Strike Again?

October 1888 had opened on a nerve-racking note with the the fresh horror of the "double event", the "Jack the Ripper" missives, and the huge press coverage both matters engendered. With this "media frenzy" came a veritable flood of correspondence to the newspapers, not only hoax letters spawned in the fevered imaginations of pretender "Rippers" but also well-meaning advice from every quarter on how to lay the killer by his heels and the inevitable false claims and rumours.

The *Evening Post* of Saturday, 6 October 1888 carried the following snippet:

> The second rumour was even worse than the one cited above, for it had absolutely no foundation; but the details of the apprehension are, under the circumstances, decidely amusing as a clever concoction. It appears that a few minutes before midnight a cab containing two men and a woman was seen to pass along Brick-lane, not one of the best thoroughfares in Spitalfields, and stop in a dark portion of the lane. The two men bore the body of the ''unconscious'' woman from the cab and deposited it on the pavement, afterwards re-entering the vehicle and driving rapidly away.

This incident, it later transpired, was nothing more than a drunken brawl which, because of the murders, had become garbled in the telling!

Although there were no "Whitechapel Murders" in the month of October 1888, the newspapers were full of reports on the hunt for the murderer and suspects. The torso of a woman was also found in the cellar of the New Scotland Yard Building, at this time under construction on the Embankment, on 2 October 1888, and this discovery became known as the "Whitehall Mystery". There are various reports in the official files for this month and those worthy of note will be mentioned.

Many suspects were detained and questioned. Charles Ludwig, who had been detained on Tuesday, 18 September 1888, finally appeared before the Thames Magistrates' Court after the murder of Stride and Eddowes. The disposal of this case, on 2 October 1888, was reported in *The Times* of Wednesday, 3 October 1888:

CHARLES LUDWIG, 40, a decently attired German, who professed not to speak English, was brought up on remand, charged with threatening to stab Elizabeth Burns, an unfortunate, of 53, Flower and Dean-street, Spitalfields, and also with threatening to stab Alexander Finlay, of 51, Leman-street, Whitechapel. Elizabeth Burns stated about half-past 3 on the early morning of Tuesday week she went with the prisoner up Butcher's-row, Whitechapel-road. Prisoner put his arm around her neck, and she saw an open knife in his hand. She screamed and two policemen came. The evidence of Finlay showed that at 3 o'clock on the morning of Tuesday fortnight he was standing at a coffee-stall in the White-chapel-road, when Ludwig came up in a state of intoxication. He pull out a long-bladed knife, and threatened to stab witness with it. Ludwig followed witness round the stall, and made several attempts to stab him. A constable came up and prisoner was given into custody. Evidence was given that on the way to the police-station the prisoner dropped a long-bladed knife, which was open, and when he was searched a razor and a long-bladed pair of scissors were found on him. Inspector Prinley, H Division, stated the prisoner had fully accounted for his whereabouts on the nights of the recent murders. The magistrate, taking into consideration that the prisoner had been in custody a fortnight, now allowed him to be discharged.

The following[1] was contained in the Police court columns of *The Times* of Thursday, 4 October 1888:

POLICE.

At the GUILDHALL, WILLIAM BULL, 27, was charged on his own confession with having committed the murder in Mitre-square, Aldgate. Inspector George Izzard said at 20 minutes to 11 on Tuesday night the prisoner came into the charge-room at Bishops-gate Police-station and made the following statement:

"William Bull, No. 6, Stannard-road, Dalston. I am a medical student at the London Hospital. I wish to give myself up for the murder in Aldgate on Saturday night last or Sunday morning. About 2, I think, I met the woman in Aldgate. I went with her up a narrow street, not far from the main road. I gave her half-a-crown. While walking along together a second man came up, and he took the half-crown from her.'' The prisoner then said, ''My poor head. I shall go mad. I have done it. I must put up with it.'' The inspector then said to him, ''What has become of your clothing that you had on when you committed the murder?'' He replied, ''If you wish to know, they are in the Lea, and the knife I threw away.'' At this point he declined to say anything more. He was drunk. Inquiries had been made at the London Hospital. No such person as the prisoner was known there. He was out of employment. The prisoner's parents appeared to be most respectable people. His father stated that the accused was at home on Saturday night. The prisoner. – I said this when I was mad drunk. I never committed a murder; I could not commit such an act. The magistrate. – I shall remand you; and you have yourself to thank for the position you are in. The prisoner was then removed to the cells.

The *Morning Advertiser* of Thursday 4 October 1888, page 5 f, reported on another "suspect":

Soon after six o'clock last evening considerable excitement was caused in the neighbourhood of Ratcliff-highway by the report that a man was roaming about there in a suspicious manner with bloodstains on his coat. A crowd gathered and followed the individual referred to, uttering threatening cries. He was respectably dressed in a light suit, was apparently about 30 years of age, and had somewhat the appearance of an American. He took shelter in a public-house, in company with another man to whom he was known; but the crowd still hung about the doors. At last a policeman appeared, who advised the man to go with him to the station and wait there until the noisy crowd had dispersed. This the man readily did, accompanying the constable to the King David-place police station, where he was allowed to sit in an ante-room. The inspector on duty thought it necessary to question the man, whose replies were considered quite satisfactory. The stains on his coat were carefully scrutinised, but were caused apparently only by grease. At any rate they were not bloodstains. For a considerable time the police-station was besieged by curious spectators, who at last got tired of seeing nothing, and so dispersed. The man, who said his name was John Lock, and his age thirty-two, made the following statement to a reporter: "I am now a sailor, and belong to the Naval Reserve. I and my wife have been in Australia for some years, and we came to England on the 28th April last. I left a friend's house at 85, Balcombe-street, Dorset-square, this (Wednesday) morning, and made my way to the docks at Wapping, for the purpose of finding a ship. I was walking along Commercial-road to go down Devonshire-road to see a man whom I knew nine years ago, when all at once I met a friend. He said to me, 'Hulloa, old man, what is all this?' and he turned round to the crowd which was following me and told them to go away. I looked round and saw that I had been followed. I said we would go up Commercial-road and have a drink at a public-house, the 'Victory,' I think. While we were there the crowd stopped outside, calling 'Leather Apron' and 'Jack the Ripper,' and someone was good enough to send for a couple of policemen. When I got to the station I explained what I had been doing." "But," said the reporter, "the people outside say that you have bloodstains on your coat and collar." "Oh," replied Lock, smiling, "those stains are old paint stains, and that only shows what the public will do now." Up to this point he did not seem to understand that he was at liberty to leave the station, but the officer explained to him that he might go on his way as soon as he liked, but that it would be wise to wait until the crowd had dispersed.

Mr. Matthews was engaged for several hours yesterday at the Home Office with reference to the murders in the East-end, and had prolonged interviews with Sir Charles Warren and others on the subject, during which the course of action already taken by the police was fully considered, as well as the steps to be taken in future with a view to the discovery of the criminal. Mr. Matthews is understood to have directed that no power in the hands of the police should be left untried, and no clue, however unpromising, neglected. The understanding between the Metropolitan and City police is most cordial.

Yesterday the large force of police and detectives drafted into Whitechapel made house-to-house visitation and left copies of the following handbill . . .

The wording of the "Police Notice to the Occupier" leaflet was then given.

The question of offering a reward for information leading to the capture of the murderer arose; a file cover[2], dated 1 October 1888:

[Stamped: – HOME OFFICE 4 OCT.88 DEPt. No.] No. A49301B/4

DATE 1 Octr. 1888   The Financial News.

REFERENCES, &c. Whitechapel Murders.

Fds. cheque for £300. Requests that the sum may be offered as a reward, in the name of the Government, for the detection of the Criminal.

Pressing

MINUTES.

Telegram from SofS. within – also Memo's by Mr. Pemberton. Copy of Mr Pemberton's reply below.

[There is then affixed to the minutes section a cutting from the newspaper]:

The following correspondence has passed between the editor of the *Financial News* and the Home Office:

"11, Abchurch-lane, London, E.C., Oct. 1,

"Sir, – In view of your refusal to offer a reward out of Government funds for the discovery of the perpetrator or perpetrators of the recent murders in the East-end of London, I am instructed on behalf of several readers of the *Financial News*, whose names and addresses I enclose, to forward you the accompanying cheque for £300, and to request you to offer that sum for this purpose in the name of the Government.

"Awaiting the favour of your reply, – I have the honour to be your obedient servant,

"HARRY H. MARKS."

"The Right Hon. Henry Matthews M.P., Secretary
   of State for the Home Department."

"Oct. 1.

"My dear Sir, – I am directed by Mr. Matthews to acknowledge the receipt of your letter of this date, containing a cheque for £300, which you say has been contributed on behalf of several readers of the *Financial News*, and which you are desirous should be offered as a reward for the discovery of the recent murders in the East-end of London.

"If Mr. Matthews had been of opinion that the offer of a reward in these cases would have been attended by any useful result he would himself have at once made such an offer, but he is not of that opinion.

"Under these circumstances, I am directed to return you the cheque (which I enclose), and to thank you, and the gentlemen whose names you have forwarded, for the liberality of their offer which Mr. Matthews much regrets he is unable to accept.

"I am, Sir, your obedient servant,
                    "E. LEIGH PEMBERTON."
TIMES 2 OCT.88.

There is then annexed a memo[3], as follows:

Memoranda by Mr. Pemberton as to Whitechapel Murders and proposed offer of reward.

Mr. <u>Matthews</u>
    You will have got my telegram saying that the Financial News had sent a cheque for £300 proposing that it shd be offered in the name of the Government as a reward for the discovery of the Whitechapel murders. as there had been two past cases since you declined to offer a reward I did not like to act without giving you the opportunity if you saw fit to change – & I have not yet answered the letter

    About 3 oclock Warren came & reported that every thing was being done that they could think of and that he was sanguine of finding the man

    About 3.30 the Queen telephoned to Sec ofS expressing ["her" – *deleted*] how shocked she was & asking for information. I telephoned back to Major Edwards stating what Warren had told the H.O.

    At 5 oclock Sir Chas Warren sent the word that the Lord Mayor had offered £500 reward.

    In the Dynamite case the City offered £5000 reward & yet Sir W. Harcourt refused to offer anything on behalf of the Government or to promise a pardon to an accomplice I send the papers for reference.

    Of course if I had known that Ld. Mayor was going to offer a reward I shd have let you know when I telephoned as I have no doubt there will many more applications about A Reward & most likely the Queen will telegraph again for information perhaps you will be so good as to telegraph to me general instructions (to act as on the previous applications or otherwise).

Immediate

unless you think it ["better" – *deleted*] necessary to come up & have an interview with Sir Chas. Warren.

ELP. 1 Oct 88.

Just received yr telegram Sir Chas Warren still adheres to his opinion that a reward wd. be of no use & Mr. Monro agrees ELP.

I will come to London tomorrow (Wednesday) and be at the H:O: soon after I [ ]purpose to see Sir C Warren.

H.M.
2d Oct./88

The *Financial News* letter[4] is annexed:

The Financial News.   A49301B/4

A Daily Journal devoted to the interests of investors

11. Abchurch Lane, E.C.

London, October 1st 1888.

The Rt. Hon. Henry Matthews, Q.C. M.P.

Secretary of State

for the Home Department.

Sir,

In view of your refusal to offer a reward out of Government funds for the discovery of the perpetrator or perpetrators of the recent murders in the East-end of London. I am instructed on behalf of several readers of the *Financial News*, whose names and addresses I enclose, to forward you the accompanying cheque for £300 and to request you to offer that sum for this purpose in the name of the Government.

Awaiting the favour of your reply

I have the honour to be

Your obedient Servant

Harry H Marks

Editor.

There are also two Post Office telegraphs[5] annexed (the second being a continuation of the message), as follows:

POST OFFICE TELEGRAPHS.

Handed in at – Rowlands Castle Office at 4–57p

TO Mr. Pemberton Home Office
                    Whitehall Ldn.
Decline offer with thanks a[nd] say that if government [ ] any
prospect of useful result from Reward they would at once offer one
themselves. As[k] Police at once whether any / circumstances make
it desirable to offer reward now or later.

The question of a reward[6] was also raised by George Lusk of the
Whitechapel Vigilance Committee, dated 2 October 1888:

[Stamped: – HOME OFFICE 4 OCT.88 RECEIVED] No.
A49301B/5
DATE 2nd Oct/88.   Mr. George Lusk
REFERENCES, &c. re Whitechapel Murders.
    Petition to Her Majesty from various residents in the East End of
London praying that a Government reward be offered, urging the
exceptional circumstances in connection with these murders.
Pressing.
                         MINUTES.
?Say that the petition has been laid before the Queen, but that the
SofS., though ["desirous" – *deleted*] he has given directions that no
effort or expense is to be spared in endeavouring the discover [*sic*]
the person guilty of the murders, ["cannot" – *deleted*] has not been
able to advise H.M. that in his belief the ends of justice would be
promoted by any departure from the decision already announced
with regard to the proposal that a reward shd. offered by Govt.
    ELP. 4 Oct 88.   CET
                                    4.10.88
    wrote
        6.10.

There are then annexed two newspaper cuttings[7], dated 8 October
1888:

From "The Times", Monday, 8th Oct.1888.
    In answer to the petition to Her Majesty, presented by Mr.
George Lusk on behalf of his Vigilance Committee, and the
inhabitants of Whitechapel generally, the following letter was
received late on Saturday night:
                                    "Whitehall, Oct. 6, 1888.
"Sir, – The Secretary of State for the Home Department has had

the honour to lay before the Queen the petition signed by you praying that a reward may be offered by the Government for the discovery of the perpetrator of the recent murders in Whitechapel, and he desires me to inform you that though he has given directions that no effort or expense should be spared in endeavouring to discover the person guilty of the murders, he has not been able to advise Her Majesty that in his belief the ends of justice would be promoted by any departure from the decision already announced with regard to the proposal that a reward should be offered by Government.

> "I am, Sir, your obedient servant,
> "E.LEIGH PEMBERTON.
> "George Lusk, Esq., 1,2, and 3, Alderney-road,
> Mile-end-road, E.2."

From "Daily Telegraph", Monday, 8th Oct. 1888, with reference to the above letter.

"The gentleman to whom the above reply was addressed – Mr. George Lusk, of Alderney-street [*sic*], Globe-street, Mile-end – has given information of a suspicious incident which befell him on Thursday afternoon last. A stranger, who called at his private residence shortly after four o'clock, and who was informed that Mr. Lusk was not at home, appeared to have traced the President of the Vigilance Committee to an adjacent tavern. Having manifested great interest in the movements of the volunteer police, he sought an interview in a private room, but owing to the forbidding appearance of the visitor Mr. Lusk seems to have preferred the comparative publicity of the bar parlour. The conversation had scarcely begun, when Mr. Lusk, who was about to pick up a pencil which had dropped from the table, says he noticed the stranger "make a swift though silent movement with his right hand towards his side pocket." Fearing that his conduct was observed, it is added, the man asked to be directed to nearest coffee-house, and forthwith proceeded to an address in the Mile End-road with which he was supplied. Although Mr. Lusk followed without loss of time, he was not quick enough for his visitor, who abstained from visiting the coffee-house, and has not been heard of since. The man is described as between thirty and forty years of age, about 5ft9in in height, of a florid complexion, with bushy brown beard, whiskers, and moustache. In the absence of further evidence it is impossible to say whether any personal injury was actually in store for the head of the

"Vigilants," but the ease with which the man escaped has awakened the members of the committee and their colleagues to an increased sense of the difficulty of the task they have in hand."

This is followed by a note[8] dated 2 October 1888, as follows:

official 4/10.   Balmoral.   A49301B/:["36" – *deleted*]5
                        2, Oct 1888.

Dear Ruggles Brise
    The enclosed reached us this morning and I forward it to you for ["that" – *deleted*] information of Mr. Matthews. We have of course sent no reply from here.

                                    Yrs very truly
                                    Fleetwood I. Edwards.

Captain (later Sir) Fleetwood Edwards was an equerry to the Queen.
    This is followed by the previously mentioned petition[9]:

                            To Her Most Gracious Majesty
                                    The Queen
The Humble Petition of George Lusk
of Nos. 1,2 & 3 Alderney Road in the Parish of Mile End Old T[*own*] in the County of Middlesex, Builder and Contractor, a mem[*ber*] of the Metropolitan Board of Works a Vestryman of the above named Parish and the President and Chairman of the Vigilance Committee formed for the purpose hereunder mentioned; your said Petitioner acting under the authority and on behalf of the inhabitants of the East End districts of Your Majesty's metropolis
    Sheweth
    1. That Your Majesty's Secretary of State for the Home Department has for some years past discontinued the old practice of offering a Government reward for the apprehension and conviction of those offenders against Your Sovereign Majesty Your Crown and Dignity who have escaped detection for the crime of Murder.
    2. That in the course of the present year (A.D. 1888.) no less than four murders of Your Majesty's subjects have taken place within a radius of half a mile from one point in the said district.
    3. That notwithstanding the constitution of the Scotland Yard Detective Office and the efforts of the trained Detectives of such

office, the perpetrator or perpetrators of these outrages against Your Majesty still remain undiscovered.

4. That acting under the direction of Your Majesty's liege subjects your petitioner ["I" – *deleted*] caused to be sent to your Majesty's Secretary of State for the Home Department a suggestion that he should revert to the original system of a reward looking at the fact that the present series of murders was probably the work of one hand and that the third and fourth were certainly the work of that one hand and that inasmuch as the ordinary means of detection had failed and that the murderer would in all probability commit other murders of a like nature such offer of a reward at the earliest opportunity was absolutely necessary for securing Your Majesty's subjects from death at the hands of the above one undetected assassin.

5. That in reply to such suggestion your Petitioner received from Your Majesty's Secretary of State for the Home Department a letter of which the following is a copy viz.&;

"Sir,

I am directed by the Secretary of State to acknowledge the receipt of your letter of the 16th inst. with reference to the question of the offer of a reward for the discovery of the perpetrator of the recent murders in Whitechapel and I am to inform you that had the Secretary of State considered the case a proper one for the offer of a reward he would at once have offered one on behalf of the Government but that the practice of offering rewards for the discovery of criminals was discontinued some years ago because experience shewed that such offers of reward tended to produce more harm than good and the Secretary of State is satisfied that there is nothing in the present case to justify a departure from this rule.

I am, Sir, your obedient servant,

(signed) G.[*sic*] Leigh Pemberton"

6. That the reply above quoted was submitted to the inhabitants of the East End of London in meeting assembled and provoked a considerable amount of hostile criticism and that such criticism was re-echoed throughout Your Majesty's Dominions not only by Your Majesty's subjects at large but, with one or two exceptions the entire press of Great Britain

Your Petitioner therefore
humbly prays Your
Majesty as follows:

1 That Your Majesty will graciously accede to the prayer of Your Petitioner preferred originally through Your Majesty's Secretary of State and direct that a government reward sufficient in amount to meet the peculiar exigencies of the case may immediately be offered, Your Petitioner and those loyal subjects whom he represents being convinced that without such reward the murderer or murderers of the above four victims will not only remain un detected but will sooner or later commit other crimes of a like nature.

> And Your Petitioner
> will ever pray etc
> George Lusk
> 1 2 3 Alderney Rod.
> Mile End Road E

Geo B Richards
Witness to the above signature of George Lusk the Petitioner. 28 Sandal Street, Shalford Essex. 27th September 1888.

There then follows a letter[10], dated 19 October 1888:

TELEGRAPHIC ADDRESS QUEEN, CHESTER.   QUEEN HOTEL,
CHESTER.
19 Oct. 1888.

Dear Murdoch,
There is one case of successful reward omitted from my Memo which it would be well to add.

It was a case of a burglary in Cromwell Road in which a postman was shot, but not killed.

I don't think it was in the list made by the Registry – if it was, it was not mentioned as a case where the reward was paid.

I think it would be well to have it looked but, as Sir C. Warren may mention it as a clear case of a reward producing important ["evidence" – *deleted*] information: but if I remember right, it was private information, not evidence at all.

The case occurred in 81, 82, or 83.

Sorry I did not think of it while I was at work on the Memo & have to trouble you with it: but in a question of this sort we must be as safe & complete as possible.

> Your Truly
> C E Troup.

There then follow lengthy memos[11], six pages, discussing rewards, which, as they are not directly relevant to the Whitechapel Murders but simply concern the merits of offering a reward, will not be reproduced. In these memos, the case of Mullins and the murder of Mrs Elmsley in Grove Road, Victoria Park, in August 1860, the case of Charles Williams and the burglary in Cromwell Road, on 5 February 1881, and the wounding of a postman, and Rev. Macdonald & others in 1746, are discussed.

A note[12] is then appended, dated 8 October 1888:

Mr. Murdoch ["Ruggles Brise" – *deleted*]
    Do you know how this came here.
    Did Mr. Williamson or Sir C.W. bring it. if so did they make any verbal communication or recommendation on the subject?
                      CM Oct 8
  I do not know
  ERB

The next folio carries a Post Office telegram[13]:

[Stamped :   HOME OFFICE 8 OCT.88 DEPt. No.] A49301B/6
               POST OFFICE TELEGRAPHS.
Handed in at the Cornhill Office at 3.45p Received here at 3.58p
TO Williamson
    4 Whitehall Place
Lord Mayor offered five hundred pounds apprehension Whitechapel Murderer.
                  Bulling.

It carries an annotation below:

Sent out by Mr. Pemberton to be made official and put up.
                      CM Oct 9/88.

There then follows a draft, for approval, of a reply[14] to Mr Lusk:

         Immediate   Whitehall.
                               October 1888.
Draft for Approval   Sir,
    I am directed by the Secretary of State to thank you for ["your" – *deleted*] the suggestion in your letter of the 7th Instant on the subject of

the recent Whitechapel murders. and to say in reply that [*inserted* – "from the first the S. ofS. has had under consideration"] the question of granting a pardon to ["persons not actually" – *deleted*] [*inserted* – "accomplices. It is obvious that not only [make ?] to such a grant be granted to persons who have not been"] concerned in contriving or [*inserted* – "in actually"] committing the murders ["has been from the first under the consideration of the Secretary of State but that the information obtained has not been such as to appear to him to render such a course at present either expedient or justifiable" – *deleted*] [*inserted* – "but the expediency and propriety of making the offer must largely depend on the nature of the information received from day to day, which is being carefully watched with a view to determine that question"] [*insertions appear to be in Matthews's hand*].

With regard to the offer of a reward the SofS. has under the existing circumstances nothing to add to his former reply.

I am, &c.

George Lusk Esq.
  1 Alderney Road
    Mile End
      E.

There are marginal notes to the above as follows:

Appd. GL
  10 Oct 1888.
Mr. Matthews
  H.M.
  11 Oct. 1888
Wrote 12.10

The next file cover[15] also relates to Mr Lusk, dated 7 October 1888:

[Stamped: – HOME OFFICE 9 OCT.88 RECd. DEPt.] No. A49301B/7
DATE 7 Oct. 1888   Mr. George Lusk.
REFERENCES, &c.   The <u>East End</u> Murders.
On behalf of the Committee of inhabitants of the East End, points out that these crimes are absolutely unique, and that the murderer or murderers may possibly continue to be more than a match for Scotland Yard and the Old Jewry combined. Calls attention to the fact that the only means left untried for the detection of the

murderer has been the offer of a Government Reward, with the offer of a free pardon to any person not the real assassin.

[*Marginal note to above* – "To be copied copy made"]

<u>Pressing.</u>

MINUTES.

Ackn. & to the Secretary of State.   9/10.88.

Acknd. 9/10/88.

There is no reason to suspect an accomplice, quite the reverse. I therefore see no good in offering a pardon to any person not the real assassin.

The question of a reward has already been settled in the negative.

G.L. 9 Oct. 1888

Mr. Matthews

Before answering further – send copy to Commr. and request him to inform the S. of S. whether any useful result would be produced in his opinion by the offer of a pardon to accomplices.

H.M.

9 Oct./88

Wrote

9/10/88.

The letter[16] from George Lusk, dated 7 October 1888, is then annexed:

To the Secretary of State for the
Home Department
A49301B/7

[Stamped: – HOME OFFICE 9 OCT.88 RECEIVED]

1, 2 & 3 Alderney Road,
Mile End London. E.
7th October 1888.

Right Honble. Sir,

<u>The East End Murders.</u>

I have to acknowledge the receipt of a communication from the Home Office dated the 6th instant in which it is stated that although no effort or expense should be spared in endeavouring to discover the person guilty of these atrocious murders, you are unable to advise Her Majesty that in your belief the ends the ends of Justice would be promoted by any departure from the direction already announced.

In reply to such communication I beg to thank you on behalf of my

Committee for your kindness in laying my petition before Her Majesty the Queen, and to say that the inhabitants of Whitechapel and the East End districts of London generally, believe that the Police authorities are sparing neither trouble nor expense in attempting to secure the murderer. At the same time however it is my duty humbly to point out that the present series of murders is absolutely unique in the annals of crime, that the cunning, astuteness and determination of the murderer has hitherto been, and may possibly still continue to be, more than a match for Scotland Yard and the Old Jewry combined and that all ordinary means of detection have failed. This being so I venture most respectfully to call your attention to the fact that the only means left untried for the detection of the murderer has been the offer of a Government reward.

Rewards are offered from other quarters including the Corporation of the City of London but in neither of these instances can a pardon be extended to an accomplice and therefore the value of these offers is considerably less than that of a Government proclamation of a really substantial reward with the extension of a free pardon to any person not the actual assassin.

> I have the honor to be,
> Right Honorable Sir,
> Your very obedt. humble servant
> (*Signed*) George Lusk.

The next file cover[17], dated 9 October 1888, is as follows:

	No. A49301B/8
DATE 9 Octr.88	Comr. of Police
REFERENCES, &c.	Whitechapel Murder

Gives reasons for recommending offer of pardon to accomplice.

Pressing

MINUTES.

Minutes within.

Draft for approval herewith.

10.10.88.

Wrote

12.10.88

The within decision was arrived at after conference with Sir C. Warren, and Mr. Anderson.

CM. Oct. 13.88.

There then follows a note[18] [minutes?]:

> Home Office,
> Whitehall,
> S.W.

Say to Mr Lusk that the expediency of granting a ["reward" – *deleted*] pardon to persons not actually concerned in the commission of the murders and not implicated in the terrible guilt of contriving or abetting them, has been more than once under the consideration of the S. ofS. & that the information at present in his possn. has not so far been such as to induce him to offer one. With regard to the offer of a reward the S. ofS. has nothing to add to his former reply in the present state of the cases under investigation.

There then follows a note[19] from Godfrey Lushington to Henry Matthews, dated 10 October 1888:

Mr. Matthews,

This letter from the Commissioner and letter from Mr. Lusk on which it is founded, give you an opportunity to offer a pardon if you are so inclined. Offering a pardon is not open to the same objections as offering a reward, nor has the S. of S. done anything to commit himself to refuse to offer a pardon. The mere lapse of time occasions no difficulty, for in a crime of this atrocious character it is desirable that if possible no person, even an accessory after the fact, should receive a pardon. A pardon, therefore, is only offered when it is pretty clear that the efforts of the Police to detect the crime have been unavailing, and if the S. of S. does not now offer a pardon his action will of course be open to the criticism that he has declined to take a step recommended by the Commissioner. On the other hand the Commissioner's letter does not appear to me to throw any new light on the case or to suggest the probability that the offer of a pardon will lead to discovery. His recommendation is based on ["the" – *deleted*] a mere supposition, one of many suppositions which have occurred to everybody from the beginning.

Then, as to the affect on the public mind. The offer of a pardon will not allay the excitement of the public who on the contrary will wrongly infer that the view of the Home Office is that the murderer had an accomplice and this will make the outrages appear of a far more grave character. Nor will the offer of a pardon restore confidence in the Police. It will be accepted as an admission of their failure to detect the crime; it will provoke renewed attention to the action of the Home Office and hostile critics are sure to say that the step if taken ought to have been taken earlier.

In my opinion it would be better for the S. of S. not to ["grant" – *deleted*] offer a pardon taking his stand on the ground that he has held from the first that it is not a case in which the <u>offer of a pardon</u> is appropriate.

It is quite possible however that you may be of a different opinion.

GL
10 October, 1888.

This is followed by another note[20]:

Write to Mr. Lusk.
Thank him for his letter Say that the ["advisability" – *deleted*] question of granting a pardon to persons not actually concerned in contriving or committing the murders, has been from the first under the consideration of the S. of S., but that the information hitherto obtained has not been such as to appear to him to render such a course at present either expedient or justifiable.

With regard to the offer of a reward. the S. of S. has under the existing circumstances nothing to add to his former reply.

["Add that the Metrop. Police are using every effort" – *deleted*]
10 October 1888.

There is then annexed the letter[21], dated 9 October 1888, from Sir Charles Warren:

<u>Urgent</u> [Stamped: – HOME OFFICE 10 OCT.88 DEPt. No.] A49301B/8

4 Whitehall Place, S.W.
9th October, 1888.

Sir,
In reply to your immediate letter just received on the subject of Mr. Lusk's proposal as to a pardon to accomplices in the White-chapel murders, I have to state, for the information of the Secretary of State, that during the last three or four days I have been coming to the conclusion that useful results would be produced by the offer

of a pardon to accomplices. Among the variety of theories there is the possibility that the murderer is someone who during the daytime is sane, but who at certain periods is overbalanced in his mind; and I think it possible in that case that his relatives or neighbours may possibly be aware of his peculiarities and may have gradually unwittingly slid into the position of being accomplices, and may be hopeless of any escape without a free pardon.

On the other hand if it is the work of a gang in which only one actually commits the murder, the free pardon to the accomplice may make the difference of information being obtained.

As a striking commentary on this matter I have today received a letter from a person asserting himself to be an accomplice, and asking for a free pardon; and I am commencing a communication with him through an advertisement in a journal. This letter is probably a hoax, for we have received scores of hoaxing letters, but on the other hand it may be a bona fide letter, and if so I feel what a very great loss it would be to the discovery of the murderer by omitting to offer the pardon; and I cannot see what harm could be done in this or any future case by offering a pardon.

I am,
Sir,
Your most obedient Servant,
Charles Warren.

The Under
Secretary of State,
&c. &c. &c.

Under a file cover dated 2 October 1888, is the following[22]:

[Stamped: – HOME OFFICE RECEIVED 2 OCT.88],
DATE 2 Octr. 88. Clerk of the Board of Works Whitechapel District
Fds Resolution passed at a meeting of the Board – asking that the Police Force in the neighbourhood of Whitechapel may be strengthened.
Ackd 2.10.88   Pressing/
MINUTES
This having been acknd.
                    ?Put up.
[ ] 3 ack -SS.   [ ]
                    2.10.88.

The letter enclosed[23] reads:

> Office of the Board of Works Whitechapel District
>   No.15. Great Alie Street. Whitechapel.
>   2nd October 1888.

[Stamped: – Recd after 5.p.m.]
To the Rt. IIon. IIy. Matthews
                    Q.C. M.P.
Secretary of State, Home Department
                    Whitehall.
                         S.W.
Sir,
    At a meeting of the Board of Works for the Whitechapel District
a Resolution was passed of which the following is a copy:-
    "That this Board regards with horror and alarm the several
atrocious murders recently perpetrated within the District of
Whitechapel and its vicinity and calls upon Sir Charles Warren
so to regulate and strengthen the Police Force in the neighbourhood
to guard against any repetition of such atrocities."
    and by direction of the Board the copy Resolution is forwarded to
you in the hope that it will receive your favourable consideration.
                    I am Sir
                         Your obedient Servant
                              Alfred Turner [?]
                                   Clerk

A Home Office file cover[24] is as follows:

[Stamped: – HOME OFFICE 4 OCT.88 RECEIVED] No.
A49301C/5d
DATE 4 Octr. 1888.   Whitechapel, Vestry Clerk.
REFERENCES, &c.   Whitechapel Murders.
                          Fds. [Resolution of the Vestry expressing
                          sorrow at the murders, and urging the
                          Government to use their utmost endeavour
                          to discover the Criminals.]   Pressing.
                          MINUTES.
    ? Acknowledge – & say S of S [shares the feelings of the
Vestry with regard to these murders: that the Police have
instructions to exercise every power in their possession in their
efforts to discover the murderer: and that the SofS., after

personal conference with the Commissioner, in which all the difficulties of case had been fully discussed, is satisfied that no ["available" – *deleted*] means will be spared of tracing the offender and bringing him to justice-]

[ ] 4 octr 88.

or ["simply acknowledge" – *deleted*]

[ ]
4.10.88.

see explanation by Mr. Lushington within as to difference between printed & actual letter

wrote 6/10/88.

The letter from the Vestry Clerk and the resolution appear at ff. 66–67, worded as follows[25]:

> 5 Gt Prescot Street
> Whitechapel E
> 4th Octr 1888

To,
    The Right Honorable
      Henry Matthews M.P.
Sir
    I have the honor to send you on the other side Copy of a Resolution Passed at a Meeting of the Vestrymen of the Parish of St. Mary Whitechapel held on the 3rd inst.

> I am Sir,
> Your Humble &Obedt. Serv.
> Thomas D Metcalfe
> Vestry Clerk

Home Office
    Whitehall
      SW.

> At a Meeting of the Vestrymen
> of the Parish of St. Mary
> Whitechapel held on the 3rd day
> of October 1888 the following
> Resolution was passed.

It was Moved
    Second & Resolved
        That this Vestry desires to express its sorrow at the diabolical murders which have lately been committed in East

London and to urge Her Majesty's Government to use their utmost efforts to discover the Criminals –

I Certify the above to be a true Extract from the Minutes.

Thomas D. Metcalfe
Vestry Clerk

The letter[26] of 6 October 1888, referred to above, is as follows:

<u>Pressing</u>
A49301/37

Whitehall
6 October 1888

Sir,

I am directed by the Secretary of State to acknowledge the receipt of your letter of the 4th instant forwarding a copy of a Resolution of the Vestry of the Parish of St Mary Whitechapel, expressing sorrow at the recent murders in the east of London and urging the Government to use their utmost endeavour to discover the criminals, and I am to state that Mr. Matthews shares the feelings of the Vestry with regard to these murders that the Police have instructions to exercise every power they possess in their efforts to discover the murderer, and that the Secretary of State after personal conference with the Commissioner in which all the difficulties of the case have been fully discussed, is satisfied that no means will be spared in tracing the offender and bringing him to justice.

I am,
Sir,
Your obedient Servant,
(sd) E.Leigh Pemberton.

The Clerk to the Vestry
of the Parish of
St Mary, Whitechapel
5 Great Prescot St
Whitechapel
E.

The report[27] comparing the above letter with a copy of it printed in the *Daily News* and *Pall Mall Gazette* is included as follows:

Mr Matthews,

Please look at the Home Office letters to the Vestry Clerk of Whitechapel as set out at length in the Daily News of Friday, and partially (but with comments) in the Pall Mall Gazette of today, and compare it with the copy – enclosed of the letter which was actually written from the H.O. You will observe various discrepancies –

	Newspaper version	H.O. version
Date	Oct 10.	Oct 6.
Address	T. Metcalfe Esq Vestry Clerk Whitechapel	The Clerk to the Vestry of the Parish of St Mary Whitechapel 5 Great Prescot St Whitechapel E.
In the body of the letter	East-end of London Criminal I am instructed to state	East of London. Criminals. I am to state
	And that he has given directions and that the Police have instructions to exerciseany & every power they possess and even to use an amount of discretion with regard to suspected persons in their efforts to discover the criminal	that the Police have instructions to exercise every power they possess in their efforts to discover the murderer
	And I am further to state that S of S	And that the S of S
	Commissioners of Police at which the whole of the difficulties	Commissioners of Police in which all the difficulties
	Is satisfied that no means have been or will be spared	is satisfied that no means will be spared
	Yours obediently	Your odedient servant

We are unable to explain these variations, but suppose them due to somebody having dictated the terms of the H.O. letter to shorthand notes, who took them down incorrectly & afterwards worded up that material he had; but you will probably think it unadvisable to correct them. It would be injurious to the Commr. to do so. But it is well for you to know that you did not use the words attributed to you.

We have written today to the Commr. to remind him to send to H.O. a report of the measures taken to detect the persons who committed the murder. He has also not answered on paper the 3 questions you put to him in your private letter, & which he answered verbally to you. I have no copy of that letter, so could not remind him of it.

GL
13 Oct 1888.

[*Marginal note:* – "Copy by Mr. Brise is with the other papers – memo on rewards, Harcourt's note on there—14 Oct/88."]

There is some correspondence between Charles Warren and the Home Office. The cover page[28] is as follows:

[Stamped: – HOME OFFICE 9 OCT.88 RECd. DEPT]
DATE 4th October '88. The Commissioner of Police
REFERENCES, &c.   Whitechapel Murders
Reports on J.W. Ellis' letter stating he is prepared to take any measures possible provided H.M. government will support him, but points out the risk entailed on the men who search
[MINUTES]
See copy of letter within from S of S of the 5th Inst – as to the course he proposed
["Confidential" – *deleted*]
Lay-By [ ] Oct 9.
Mr. Lushington – See S.S. minute within. I do not know if Sir C. Warren has reported privately to S. of S. if not shall a reminder be sent? [ ] Oct 13.

Sent 13.10.88

There is then a Home Office note[29] on headed paper as follows:

[Embossed paper: – SECRETARY OF STATE – HOME DEPART-MENT], [stamped:- HOME OFFICE 9 OCT 88 RECd DEPT]
Official ERB 8/10 A49301c/8
the letter of Sir J. Whittaker Ellis M.P. (which has not been returned) recommended the drawing of a cordon of

police round Whitechapel & a compulsory house to house search.

ERB

It is now   8/10
herewith
   H.M.

The letter from Sir J. Whittaker Ellis appears as follows:[30]

A.49301C
Ackn 4/10   BUCCLEUCH HOUSE,
                                      RICHMOND.
                                 Oct. 3. 1888

My dear Matthews,

There is no doubt but that the Whitechapel murderer remains in the neighbourhood. – Draw a cordon of half a mile round the centre & search every house. – This would surely unearth him.

It is a strong thing to do, but I should think such occasion never before arose. –

I should say he is an American Slaughterman, an occupation largely followed in South America.

Truly Yours
J.WhittakerEllis.

The Rt. Hon. Henry Matthews
          Q.C. M.P. &c &c

There is a letter[31] from Sir Charles Warren, dated 4 October 1888:

[Stamped: – HOME OFFICE 9 OCT.88 RECd. DEPt.]
4 Oct 1888

Dear Mr. Ruggles Brise,

I return Sir W Ellis letter.

I am quite prepared to take the responsibility of adopting the most drastic or arbitrary measures that the Sec of State can name which would further the securing of the murderer however illegal they may be, provided H.M. Gov. will support me. But I must observe that the Sec of State cannot authorise me to do an illegal action and that the full responsibility will always rest with me over the Police Constables for anything done.

All I want to ensure is that the Government will indemnify us for our actions which must necessarily be adapted to the circumstances of the case – the exact course of which cannot be always for seen.

I have been accustomed to work under such in circumstances in what were nearly Civil wars at the [ ] & then the Government passed acts of Indemnity for those who have gone beyond the law.

Three weeks ago I do not think the public would have acquiesced in any illegal action but now I think they would welcome any thing which shews activity & enterprise.

Of course the danger of taking such a course, as that proposed by Sir W. Ellis is that if we did not find the murderer our action would be condemned – and there is the danger that an illegal act of such a character might bond the Social democrats together to resist the Police & [ ] might be then said to have caused a serious riot. – I think I may say without hesitation that those houses could not be searched illegally without violent resistance & blood shed and the certainty of one or more Police Officers being killed & the question is whether it is worth while losing the lives of several of the community & risking serious riot in order to search for one murderer whose whereabouts is not known.

I have ascertained from Mr Williamson that he thinks that though under certain circumstances such action might be adopted or should not be justified at present in doing so such an illegal act. We have in times past done such a thing on a very much smaller scale but then we had certain information that a person was concealed in the house [*ff. 86–87 not found – resumed on f 88*] In this matter I have not only myself to think of but the lives & protection of 12000 men, any one of whom might be hanged if a death occurred in entering a house illegally.

Truly Yours

Charles Warren

Dear Sir Charles,

R.B. has forwarded me your letter of the 4th Oct. with Sir I. Ellis' letter – the suggestion in which is open to your observations & is too sweeping.

I thought my own suggestion of last Wed. more practical – take all houses in a given area which appear suspicious upon the best inquiry your detectives can make. Search all those, which the owners or persons in charge will allow you to search. Where leave is refused, apply to a magistrate for a search warrant, on the ground that it is probable or possible the murderer may be there. If search warrants are refused, you can only keep the houses under observation.

I shd. be glad now that the week is closing of a report of all the measures that have been taken for arresting the criminal, & of the results – Have any of the doctors examined the eyes of the murdered woman.

Yrs truly

H.M.

I shall be very glad to hear whether Mr. Anderson's health has permitted him to resume his duties. –

There is then a note[32] to Charles Murdoch, from Ruggles Brise, dated 8 October 1888:

[Stamped: – HOME OFFICE 9 OCT. 88 RECd. DEPT]   A49301C/

Home Office,

Whitehall,

S.W.

Mr Murdoch.

    I showed this to Mr Lushington.

    It shd. be made official & put up.   ERB

8/10

On Monday, 8 October 1888 *The Times*[33] reported:

[THE EAST-END MURDERS.]

Fears were expressed among the police on Saturday that the night would not pass without some startling occurrence, and the most extraordinary precautions were taken in consequence. It must not be supposed that the precautions taken apply only to the East-end of London. It is fully understood that the murderer, finding his favourite haunts too hot for him, may transfer his operations to another district, and arrangements have been made accordingly. The parks are specially patrolled, and the police, even in the most outlying districts, are keenly alive to the necessities of the situation. Having efficiently provided for the safeguarding of other portions of the large area under his jurisdiction, Sir Charles Warren has sent every available man into the East-end district. These, together with a large body of City detectives, are now on duty, and will remain in the streets throughout the night. Most of the men were on duty all last night, and the work has been found very harassing. But every man has entered heartily into the work, and not a murmur has been heard from any of the officers. They are on their mettle, and if zeal were the one thing needed to hunt down the murderer, his capture would be assured.

Yesterday evening all was quiet in the district, and the excitement had somewhat subsided. Nevertheless, the police and the local Vigilance Committee have by no means relaxed their watchfulness, and inhabitants of the district, disregarding the improbability of the murderer risking his freedom under these circumstances, still appear to expect the early commission of a new crime. During Saturday night and the early hours of Sunday morning several persons were arrested and detained at local police-stations until all the circumstances in connexion with their apprehension were thoroughly sifted. Several of these were given into custody on grounds which proved on inquiry to be flimsy and even foolish, and the police have in consequence been put to a good deal of trouble without any corresponding result. It seemed at times as if every person in the streets were suspicious of everyone else he met, and as if it were a race between them who should first inform against his neighbour.

Alfred Napier Blanchard, who described himself as a canvasser, residing at Handsworth, was charged at Birmingham on Saturday, on his own confession, with having committed the Whitechapel atrocities. He had been arrested in consequence of a circumstantial statement which he made in a publichouse of the manner in which he had effected the murders. He now denied all knowledge of the matter, and said he had spoken under excitement, caused by reading about the murders, and heavy drinking. The Bench declined to release him, however, till to-day, in order to allow time for inquiries.

Up to a late hour last night no important arrest had been reported in connexion with the murders at the East-end at any of the City police-stations. Many communications continue to be received at Scotland-yard and by the City police, describing persons who have been seen in various parts of the country whose conduct is suspicious or who are supposed to resemble the man seen talking to the victim of the Berner-street murder on the night of her assassination . . .

According to a *Reuter* telegram from New York, the *New York Herald* declares that the seaman named Dodge, who recently stated that a Malay, whom he met in London, threatened to murder a number of Whitechapel women for robbing him, said he knew the street where the Malay stayed, but that he would not divulge the name until he learnt what chance there was of a reward. He stated, however, that the street was not far from the East India Dock-road; but he was not certain about the house where the man lived.

Another seaman said he thought the Malay was now on a vessel plying in the North Sea.

CHAPTER 12

More on Rewards and October Precautions

There is a file[1] cover dated 6 October 1888, about rewards, and the Secretary of State's letter of 7 October 1888, about the state of the investigation:

[Stamped – HOME OFFICE 15 [*deleted*] OCT.88 RECd. DEPt.] No. A49301B/9
DATE 6th October 88   The Commr of Police
REFERENCES, &c.   Whitechapel Murder – Rewards
[*In margin* – see within memo: dated: 1Oct–] Gives his opinion that though possibly the offer of a Reward would do no good yet it could do no harm, the question now turns on a matter of Policy as if fresh murders were committed the Public at large might make such an outcry that it might affect the stability of the Government. If a Reward is offered it should be large.
                    MINUTES.
             [SECRET – *deleted*]
See long reply from S of S within dated 7th Oct 1888
                    AJ 13/10/88/10

There then follows a memo[2] dated 10 October 1888:

                    Home Office,
                    Whitehall,
                    S.W.

Sir C. Warren: 10 Oct/88
        Answers to Questions in my letter.
1. No – Police have hardly commenced.
2. No information – beyond an anonymous letter wh is now being dealt with.
3. This is a unique murder & not in the same category as the other crimes mentd: but no special circumstance.

This is followed by the Secretary of State's letter[3] of 7 October 1888, on Home Office embossed headed paper:

<u>copy</u>   Department of State
                              Home Department
                                                      7th Oct. 1888

Dear Sir Charles.

I am obliged to you for yr. letter of the 5th. It puts your views in a somewhat different light from the impression conveyed to Mr. Pemberton & myself by the interviews, which we both had with you, & which had for their principal object to elicit your opinions on the whole subject of these terrible Whitechapel murders more fully & effectually than if you had been consulted by letter.

I had understood you on the 3rd. inst: to say that in your opinion a reward was useless for the purpose of discovering the murderer; & that as rewards had already been offered by the City authorities & others, you saw no reason for making an additional offer.

I gather from your letter, that altho' from a Police point of view you have no reason to suppose a reward wd. do any good, yet you are disposed to think the offer of a very large sum, coupled with a pardon to accomplices, might possibly produce some effect; & that at any rate you think such an offer wd. have been, & wd. still be a politic step in order to allay public feeling.

I think that in your careful review of the past history of rewards, you scarcely give sufficient prominence to the elaborate consideration, that the question has undergone. Since 1884 there have been repeated, & I believe uniform decisions by Sir W. Harcourt, by Lord Cross, & by Mr Childers, refusing to offer large rewards in serious cases on behalf of the Govt. These decisions were arrived at after careful ["consideration" – *deleted*] consultation with the Treasury Solicitors, & with the heads of the Police in Ireland, as well as in England. The late Commr. on one occasion reported to Ld. Cross that: "the offer of a reward & free pardon has never produced any information, & in one case nearly caused serious trouble. Beyond satisfying the public in some small degree, the Commr. thinks the offer of a reward is useless, & shd. only be made under some special circumstances.

This series of decisions cannot be ignored; & there is much force in the observation made by Sir W. Harcourt, in one of these cases, that "vacillation of policy in such a matter wd. be a great sign of weakness & feebleness of administration."

However, there may be exceptions to every rule, & I shd. not shrink from incurring the reproach of vacillation & feebleness, if I thought I could thereby really assist in unravelling these dreadful crimes: But before taking any new departure, I should be glad if you wd. assist me with definite information on one or two points.

(1) Is it your opinion that the Police & the C.I.D. have now exhausted all the means within their power of discovering the criminal, & have not only failed, but have no reasonable prospect of ["discovering" – *deleted*] succeeding in any moderate time?

(2) Has any information reached you, which makes you think that there are persons, who could give information, but who are holding back either from fear of consequences, or in hope of a reward; or that any persons are harbouring the criminal, & assisting his concealment?

3. Has any special circumstance been brought to your knowledge which makes it proper to offer a reward in the case of these murders, & distinguishes them from other atrocious crimes, such as the dynamite explosions, the shooting of P.C. Chamberlain, the rape & murder of Mary Cooper, & many others, in which rewards were refused?

I concur generally in what you say as to fully consulting the Commr. of Police in matters of this kind; but I wish to add that when an application, such as Mr. Montagu's, falling within a known general rule of practise, is forwarded by the Commr. without any recommendation, or suggestion of his own, it is natural to conclude that he sees no reason for departing from the general rule.

Yrs. truly
(s.) H.M.

Also annexed is the letter[4] from Sir Charles Warren, dated 6 October 1888, to Henry Matthews, to which the above was a reply:

[Stamped: – HOME OFFICE 15 [*deleted*] OCT.88 RECd. DEPt.] A49301B/9

4 Whitehall Place S.W.
6.Oct. 1888.

Dear Mr. Matthews,
Mr. Ruggles Brise has shown me your letter in which you see no occasion for offering a reward in the case of the Whitechapel Murders, and I observe that you consider that I do not recommend any reward.

I do not know that there is really any difference of opinion as to what actually has occurred during the last few days; but still as it is a very important subject and there may be some misconception about it, I wish to put in writing what my view is.

Up to 1884 the Commissioner was in the habit of recommending Rewards in cases of murder &c.

Then occurred what is called the "German explosion case" which is supposed to have been the result of a conspiracy in order to obtain a reward.

After this on 3rd July 1884, the Commissioner recommended a reward re attempted murder of P.C. Chamberlain, which the Secretary of State declined to approve, and at this time he said "since the case of the German Explosion I have a profound distrust of rewards."

At this time the view of the Commr. and others at Scotland Yard was that although a reward might not offer inducements which are likely to be accepted with a view to giving information, the offer of a good reward assists the Police by calling attention to the subject.

On the 31st July 1884 the Commissioner said "in the face of Sir Wm. Harcourt's memo I think we had better discontinue recommending the offer of rewards except in special cases."

The first special case that occurred that I am aware of, was the murder of Mrs. Samuels in 1887, in which it was supposed that there were several persons implicated. In this case the Commissioner recommended a substantial reward for information and a pardon ["for" – *deleted*] to any one implicated, but not the actual murderer.

In reply the Secretary of State approved of the pardon but did not approve the promise of a reward.

Since then the view of the Commissioner of Police and of other Police officials has not in any way changed and it is, shortly, that in special cases rewards would undoubtedly be of service.

With regard to the Whitechapel case there is simply the general view applicable to all cases, viz:- that though there may be no reason to anticipate good results from a reward, still that it is not likely to do harm, and may possibly do good.

This is purely the Police view, apart from the question of policy which is a matter entirely dependent upon public feeling.

On the 10th Sept. after the recent Whitechapel murder Mr. Montagu M.P. made an offer of a reward of £100 which I forwarded to the Secretary of State for instructions, my opinion was not in any way asked on this subject, but I received in reply a decisive and distinct answer from the Secretary of State. This reply dated 13 Sept. was "had the Secretary of State considered the case a proper one for the offer of a reward, he would at once have offered one on behalf of the Government; but that the practice of offering rewards was discontinued some years ago because experience showed that in their general effect such offers produce more harm than good, and the Secretary of State thinks the present case one in which there is special risk that the offer of a reward might hinder rather than promote the ends of justice."

I was thus distinctly informed that the Secretary of State came to conclusions upon these special cases without consulting the Commissioner.

Subsequent to this viz: on the 14th & 17th Sept. I saw Mr. Pemberton and while discussing matters generally said that I had no reason for supposing that an offer of a reward would throw light upon the murder, at the same time I may observe that I did not consider that I was in any way consulted upon the subject, because the Secretary of State had already given his formal decision in writing, and I should have expected that my opinion, if asked, would have been asked for in writing also, and <u>before</u> the decision was given.

When I saw you three days ago I gave the same opinion, viz: that, from a Police point of view, I had no reason for supposing that a reward would do any good, but that it could do no harm and might do good; but, as a matter of policy, I ["think" – *deleted*] thought that a reward should have been offered to allay the public feeling; but that, as a reward had been offered by the City Police, it was really entirely a question of policy.

The aspect of these cases from a Police point of view changes from day to day, and seeing that the City reward of £500 has produced no effect the question naturally is – "is the offer of a reward useless or has not a large enough figure been quoted?" In pursuance of this idea it seems to me that possibly an effect might be produced by the offer of a large reward say £500, and the grant of a pardon to any accomplice not being the actual murderer.

In this particular case I think that it is in your decision entirely a matter of policy. I believe if we go on long enough we can eventually work this case out; but the British public is proverbially impatient, and if other murders of a similar nature take place shortly, and I see no reason to suppose they will not, the omission of the offer of a reward on the part of the Government may exercise a very serious effect upon the stability of the Government itself.

In conclusion I cannot help feeling that in matters of this kind the Commissioner of Police ought to be fully consulted, unless the Secretary of State is quite prepared to state in Parliament that he acted entirely on his own views without consulting the Commissioner.

I write this now in order that if it comes to a question in Parliament you may be enabled to say that from a Police point of view the Commissioner had no strong opinion as to the necessity for the offer of a reward at the time you authorised the letter to be written to Mr. Montague; but at the same time I wish it to be understood that as a question of policy, with which you may perhaps think I have nothing to do, I certainly think a reward should have been offered.

truly yours,
Charles Warren.

There is a file cover[5] dated 13 October 1888:

[Stamped: – HOME OFFICE 15 OCT.88 RECd. Dept.] No. A49301B/10
DATE 13 Oct 1888 The Commr of Police
REFERENCES, &c.   <u>Whitechapel Murder Rewards</u>
Reports that after enquiry in the Divisions Mr Anderson & himself are of opinion that the certain hope of gain is a powerful motive with ordinary people to give information [*In margin* – ''/9'']
[MINUTES.]
Confidential & Pressing
This letter does not answer categorically the three questions in S.S. letter of the 7th instant.
15/Oct 88.
Mr. Matthews.
I cannot think this affords any sufficient reason for going back from the decision already announced by S of S.   GL
15 Oct 1888
Say to the Commr with reference to his letter of 13 Oct. that it appears to indicate that he and the Assisco Commr are not altogether satisfied with the rule adopted after much consideration

by the H.O. in 1884 & since repeatedly acted upon. The S.of S. wishes it to be observed that this rule applies especially to large rewards offered by Govt. in sensational cases; and has not been held to exclude small Police rewards in minor cases, which are rather in the nature of full compensation to informers for loss of time and trouble. The rule was soundly based on the results of experience showing that in the cases in which it was meant to apply, rewards had done no good, and had in many ways done harm. The S. of S. understands the Commr. in some degree to question the accuracy of these results of experience as stated in 1884–5. The matter is so important that the S. of S. desires to give the fullest consideration to any doubts the Commr. may entertain. He will be obliged if the Commr. will furnish him with the "opinions & reports of cases" which are inconsistent with the minute of Sir E. Henderson founded upon them, and any facts which may assist in the consideration of the question.

Add that the S. of S. will thank the Commr. to give a reply in writing to the questions contained in the S. of S.'s letter of the 7th inst. –

H.M.

16 Oct/88.

Wrote 17. Oct. 88.

There follows a letter[6], dated 13 October 1888, from Sir Charles Warren to the Under-Secretary of State:

Confidential [Stamped: – HOME OFFICE 15 OCT.88 RECd. DEPt.] A49301B/10

4 Whitehall Place,

S.W.

13th October, 1888.

Sir,

With reference to the general question of the expediency or otherwise of offering Rewards in cases of Murder, &c., I have to acquaint you, for the information of the Secretary of State, that it is now, and so far as I can ascertain always has been, the opinion of the Metropolitan Police that the offer of Rewards in such cases may possibly be of little use but it can do no harm and it may be productive of satisfactory results. –

The Assistant Commissioner of the Criminal Investigation Department, as well as Mr. Williamson and other officers concur in this view of the matter. – The only official record I can find in opposition to it is contained in the minute of Sir E. Henderson of the 5th August, 1885, who said that "the offer of a reward and free pardon has never produced any information, and in one case nearly caused serious trouble. Beyond satisfying the public in some small degree, the Commissioner thinks the offer of rewards is useless, and should only be made under some special circumstances". –

But inasmuch as this minute purports to be based on opinions and reports of cases with which it is not consistent, as many of them show that the offer of rewards has been very successful, I can only imagine that it was written in reference to largess and sensational rewards such as Secretary Sir. W. V. Harcourt had in view at that time. –

I concur with Mr. Anderson that the reports from Divisions confirm us in the opinion which we have held that the certain hope of gain by giving information and help to the Police is a powerful motive with ordinary people.

> I am,
>   Sir,
>   Your most obedient Servant,
>   CWarren.

The Under Secretary
    of State
  &c. &c. &c.
    Home Office.

There is a file cover[7] which is worded as follows:

93305/18
H Division
SUBJECT H.O. Special P. Organization
DATE 17th Oct 1888./Home Office A49301C/10/For Sir Charles Warren
17/2.50 2/Transmits a copy letter received from Mr. S. Montague (M.P.) in which is enclosed a Petition from Tradespeople of Whitechapel, who pray that the Police of the district may be largely increased in order to remedy the grievances complained of in the petition & also to remove the feeling of insecurity which is destroying the Trade of Whitechapel.

AC.A CW 17.10.88

Chief Constable See Report

Pressing JWR 18.10.88

Supd. H.

please report

18.X.88. B.M.

Report submitted to Ch Constable T Arnold Supd 22.10.8

A.C.A.

Considering the class of population in H.Div. the recent horrible outrages, & the fact that by the presence of 125 extra men every night, the minds of the inhabitants have been kept tolerably calm, I consider that 25 men asked for are necessary. 22.X.88. B.M.

Sir C. Warren. I think it would be well to augment the H. Division by 25 men as recommended by the Supt. and Chief Constable. JWR 23.10.88.

I want to augment 300 men and am about to write to S of S on subject – of [ ] CW 27.10.8

A.C.A. Col Monsell. To see – When augmentation is granted the 25 asked for will be considered. JWR 24.10.88.

A file cover[8] reads as follows:

[Stamped: – HOME OFFICE 18 OCT.88 RECd.DEPt.]

No. A49301B/12

DATE 17th Oct 88   The Commr of Police

REFERENCES, &c.   Whitechapel Murders – Rewards.

Answered S of S's questions to the effect that all means have not yet been exhausted; that they continue to receive anonymous letters, that there may be persons assisting the murderer and that the murders being unique are of an entirely different category to those referred to by S of S. [*In margin* – "/10"]

[MINUTES.]

Pressing & Confidential

The Commr. in his late letters does not allude to the point why should a Gvt Reward have a better result than the Rewards offered by the City, and by private individuals. These amount to some £1200 and so far as H.O knows have not as yet procured any trustworthy information.

It would be well to wait reply of Commr. to S. S. further enquiries on 1/10 before deciding on the present letter CM.18/10.

This letter is an uncertain [ ].

The Commissioner does not positively recommend a reward from a Police point of view, at the same time he half suggests it.

Note that his letter of 13 Oct in/10 seems to condemn large & sensational rewards: but if the Commissioner has recommended any reward it is one of £5000 see/9 in addition to the City Reward.

The Commr. has yet to reply to the letter written on /10 in accordance with S of S Minute.

Put up   GL
18 Oct 1888

Mr. Matthews

I have great difficulty in drawing any conclusion from this letter, except, perhaps, that the Commr. thinks rewards may do good;– & so far, is not in accord with H.O. practice. Await his reply to the letter on /10 & I will then take the earliest opportunity of going into the whole question with him & Mr. Anderson.

H.M.
19 Oct.(88.

There then follows a memo[9] as to rewards:

Memo: as to Rewards.

Mr Lushington.

I send a copy of this historical fact of this [ ] with Sir W. Harcourt's letter to the Common Council to the Commissioner of Police for his perusal.

C.M. Oct 18/88
GL
18 Oct 1888

wrote
   19 Oct 1888

The following[10] appears on the cover of the preceding:

German Embassy case & the
statements <u>in H's</u> minute

There then follows a letter[11], dated 17 October 1888, from Sir Charles Warren to the Secretary of State:

Confidential A49301B/12
    [Stamp: – HOME OFFICE 18 OCT.88 RECd. DEPt.]
                          4 Whitehall Place,
                                  S.W.
                        17th October, 1888.

Sir,

In reference to your letter of the 7th instant asking for definite information on certain points in connection with the Whitechapel Murders I have to submit the following replies. –

Question No. 1. "Is it your opinion that the Police and the C.I.D. have now exhausted all the means within their power of discovering the criminal and have not only failed, but have no reasonable prospect of succeeding in any moderate time?"

To this I have to reply, NO. I think we have hardly begun: it often takes many months to discover a criminal. –

Question No. 2. – "Has any information reached you which makes you think that there are persons who could give information, but who are holding back either from fear of consequences or in hope of a reward: or that any persons are harbouring the criminal, and assisting his concealment?"

There have been anonymous letters to this effect, but though they may be hoaxes it shews that the offer of a reward has an effect upon the mind, [*in margin* – "?"] and one of the logical solutions as to the murders is that there may be several persons who are more or less assisting the murderer. –

Question No. 3. "Has any special circumstance been brought to your knowledge which makes it proper to offer a reward in the case of these murders, and distinguishes them from other atrocious crimes such as the dynamite explosions, the shooting of P.C. Chamberlain, the rape and murder of Mary Cooper, and many others in which rewards were refused?"

I look upon this series of murders as unique in the history of our country, and of a totally different character to those mentioned above, and so far the case is in a totally different category. –

                        I am,
                            Sir,
                        Your most obedient Servant,
                            C.Warren.

The Rt. Honble.
    The Secretary of State
       &c. &c. &c.

The file MEPO 1/55 contains a copy of the above letter.

The question of increasing police strength during this period was another pressing matter brought before the Home Office. The file cover[12], dated 17 October 1888, reads as follows:

9335/18 / Special WR / H Division / HO. Special P. Organization/17th. Oct 1888/Home Office A49301C/10/For Sir Charles Warren/
    Transmits a copy letter received from Mr. S. Montagu (M.P.) in which is enclosed a Petition from Tradespeople of Whitechapel, who pray that the Police of the district may be largely increased, in order to remedy the grievances – complained of in the petition & also to remove the feeling of insecurity which is destroying the Trade of Whitechapel.

ACA CW 17.10.8
Chief Constable – For report/Pressing/HWR. 18.10.88/
Supt. H/Please report 18.X.88.   B.M.
Report submitted to Ch Constable T'Arnold Supd 22.10.8
A.C.A./Considering the class of population in H.Div. the recent horrible outrages, & the fact that by the presence of 125. extra men every night, the minds of the inhabitants have been kept tolerably calm, I consider that 25. men asked for are necessary.
                22.X.88   B.M.
Sir C. Warren.
I think it would be well to augment the H. Division by 25 men as recommended by the Supt. and Chief Constable.
H.W.R   23.10.88.
I want to augment [300?] men & about to write to S of S on subject – [ ] CW 27.10.8
A.C.A. Col. Monsell.
To [ ] – When augmentation is granted the 25 asked for will be considered. HWR. / 24.10.88

The petition from the traders is annexed and is as follows –
Saml.Montagu
To
    The Right Honourable
        The Home Secretary.
We, the undersigned Traders in Whitechapel respectfully submit

for your consideration the position in which we are placed in consequence of the recent murders in our District and its vicinity.

For some years past we have been painfully aware that the protection afforded by the Police has not kept pace with the increase of Population in Whitechapel.

Acts of violence and of robbery have been committed in this neighbourhood almost with impunity owing to the existing Police regulations and the insufficiency of the number of officers. The recent murders and the failure of the authorities in discovering the criminal or criminals have had a most disastrous effect upon the Trade of our district.

The universal feeling prevalent in our midst is that the Government no longer ensure the security of Life and Property in East London and that in consequence respectable people fear to go out shopping, thus depriving us of our means of livelihood.

We confidently appeal to your sense of Justice that the Police in this district may be largely increased in order to remove the feeling of insecurity which is destroying the Trade of Whitechapel.

Signatures	addresses
Robt. Rycroft	79 High St Whitechapel
Thomas [ ]	74 High St Whitechapel
Louis Moses	75 high Whitechapel
Rudolf Silvershore	76 High Whitechapel
Joshua Horton	80 High St Whitechapel
R.W. Heimott	82 " " "
P.Cohen	83 " " "
A Randell	84 High St Whitechapel
Henry Burgless	86 High St Whitechapel
R Goldberg	91 High St Whitechapel
Arthur Cohen	92 High Str Whitechapel
John Baker	95 High St Whitechapel
Robt. Dick	96 High St Whitechapel
Thos. Trollope	116 High St Whitechapel
John Blackwell	117 H Whitechapel John Jacobson
	145 High Street Whitechapel
GHamilton	72 Whitechapel Road
W.Wright	81 High Street Whitechapel
Morras Horman	80 High St Whitechapel

L V Jones	65 High St Whitechapel
E. Frisby	61 High St Whitechapel
A. Goodall	55 High St Whitechapel
W. Stern	54 " " "
R. Morrison	53 " " "
J. Smith	18 Osborne St Whitechapel
Sandlowiter	51 High St Whitechapel
W.Repson Son	47 High St Whitechapel
Ge Sulan	46 High St Whitechapel
A Saloman	28 High Str Whitechapel
A Saloman	115 High Str Whitechapel
J. Sawyer	
S. Franklin	1 Whitechapel Road
J. East for G N Courtney	8 Whitechapel Road
E T. Johnson	11 Whitechapel Road
John Hall	102 Whitechapel Road
Thomas J Hall	50 Leman Street
Jno Jennings [?]	229 Whitechapel Rd.
W.T. Barnes	37 Whitechapel Road
A Joseph	75 Whitechapel Road
A. Brasch	77a Whitechapel Road
[ ]	78 Whitechapel Rd
[ ]	-do-
R Cohnreich	79a Whitechapel Rd
L Cohnreich	79a Whitechapel Rd
JS Hamshere	80A Whitechapel Road
T.J. Dooley	81a Whitechapel Rd
G R.Hawkey.	82a. 83a. & 88a. Whitechapel Rd
D Harris	84a Whitechapel Rd E
WDurrand	85a Whitechapel Rd
C Harvey	86a Whitechapel Rd
Stuart Doig	81 Whitechapel Road
Mrs Pricella Levy	84 Whitechapel Road E
Thomas Cole	100 Whitechapel Road E
John Scott & Co	105 Whitechapel Rd
Elsy H Afford	110 Whitechapel Rd
Fredk. W. Palmer	114 Whitechapel Rd. E.
Barber & Co	104 Whitechapel Rd
Alfred Cohen	101 Whitechapel Rd
H.J. Freiwald	100a Whitechapel Rd
H. Charik	87 Whitechapel Rd

E.J. Farbridge	79 Whitechapel Rd
J Abrahams	Royal Pavilion Theatre E
P.Abrahams	212 Whitechapel Road
JnoHDriver [?]	265 Whitechapel Rd. E.
Robt Dinnie	104 do do
Ungar & Co	52 Commercial St. E.
L. Cleaver	1 Leman St. E.
George Cushway	9 Leman St. Whitechapel E.
JH Rutter	15 Leman St. Whitechapel
C. Ragg Barker	38 Leman St. "
H Brigham	32 Leman St.
L. Schmidt	30 Leman St E.
ERBrooke	52 Great Alie St. E
E. Roberts	261 Whitechapel Road
David Harris	51 Great Alie Street
H Mitchell	5 Great Alie Street
Max Tichborne	6 Great Alie St
J Delmonte	8 " " "
M Bambery	56 88 Leman
H Lewin	8 Leman St.
R. Puta	33, Little Alie Street E.
Abrahams & Gluckstein	26 & 120 High St. Whitechapel
George Francorn	6 Commercial Rd E.
Myer Kinna	11 Commercial Rd E.
J.A. Oxley	15 Commercial Rd. E.
S. Davis & Co	18 Commercial Road East.
F.Reugelbering	25 Church Lane
D Cohen	27 " "
Isaac Statman	29 Church Lane
Alfred Emanuel	33 Church Lane
AD[ ]&co	37 Church Lane, Commercial Road E.
Henry Hart	38 Church Lane Whitechapel
Simon Cohen	32 Church Lane Whitechapel
D. Fishtein	30 " " "
G West	28 Church Lane Whitechapel
D. Oberlander	12 Church Lane Whitechapel
Lilly graham	10 " " "
C[ ] Thomas	5 Church Lane, Whitechapel
Ray. W.	4a Church Lane Whitechapel
Mr Dutton	3 Church Lane Whitechapel
Francis Dawson	119 High Street Whitechapel

Green Arthur Green	13 Commercial St. E.
Newman Enoch	15 Commercial St. E.
N. Lampoir	19 Commercial St. E.
A. S. Solomon	8 Commercial St Whitechapel
Louis[ ]	22 Commercial St. E.
Edward Carft[?]	5 Commercial St. Whitechapel
John Marritt	3 Commercial Street. E.
HRichardson	273 Whitechapel Rd.
WAGoodwin	270 Whitechapel Rd
James Hopecraft	262 Whitechapel Rd
Sarah Halliday	263 Whitechapel Rd
J W Fryett	16 Whitechapel Road
M.A. Wilderspin	18 Whitechapel Road
A. Goldstein	20 Whitechapel Road
P [?] Phillips	21 Whitechapel Road
A Tipper	23 Whitechapel Rd
Charles Tarling	64 Commercial Street
Geo. F Brady	17. Steward Street
Geo. T. Ligg	88 Hanbury St
ThosCath[ ]	66 High St Whitechapel
ChasGorton	146 do do
E. A. Choat	137 do do
Brooke Bond	129 do do
W.T.Wall	127 do do
B. Goldsmith	125. do do
Pro Henry Ford [ ]	122 High Street Whitechapel
E Richardson	98 High St Whitechapel
M Goldsten's	26 Whitechapel Road
S.Rosenhower&Co	29 & 30 Whitechapel Rd
E Brook Teare Co	31 Whitechapel Rd
Salmon Gluckheim	34 Whitechapel Rd.
W. Barker	35 Whitechapel Rd
J A Lidstone	36 Whitechapel Rd
S Joseph	40 Whitechapel Road
Ballantyne & Co	72 Whitechapel
William Goult	24 & 25 Whitechapel Rd
Messrs. Henry & Co.	42 Whitechapel Rd
JosMatrey	43
Thomas James	52&53 Whitechapel Rd
Joseph Cohen	47 Whitechapel Road
Joseph Giblers	46 Whitechapel Road

G Worteman	45 Whitechapel Road
D Goldenbry	44 Whitechapel Road E.
R J Richards	
H.Lowell	60 Whitechapel Rd
JEAlexander [?]	61 Whitechapel Rd E
S H Brunell [?]	64 Whitechapel Rd.
JDMostin	65 Whitechapel Rd
Sidney Fuller	3 Osborn St
Mr. Isaac Isaac's	9 Osborn St. East.
JWSharp [?]	57 Brick Lane
Frederick James West [?]	18 Brick Lane Whitechapel
Richard Holley	56 Turner St Whitechapel
John Coleman A.P.S.	265 Whitechapel Road
I.S.Turner [?]	103 Whitechapel Rd
C. Dixon	110 Whitechapel Road.
W.Brandurn	99 Whitechapel Road
JS Levy	15 The Mount Whitechapel
Joseph Clark	111 Mo E.
Samuel Pipert	110 Leman Street Whitechapel
WHStarbey	112 Leman St Whitechapel
M Agar	133 Leman St Whitechapel
Myer Cohen	135 Leman St Whitechapel
J.Willett	143 Leman St E.
[ ] Lehrer	11 Osborn St. Whitechapel
W.C. Magson	17 Osborn St. Whitechapel
AMOR & Co.	17 Osborn St. Whitechapel
E. Deakins	7 Osborn St. Whitechapel
H]	NagsHead 10 Whitechapel Rd
Thomas Thompson	128 High St Whitechapel
John Bligh	71 do do
I.F. Jarrett	10 Osborn St E
E.J.Combry	16 Osborn St. E.
E. Wilson	29 Osborn St.
J Wallis	33a Osborn Street. E.
H.Shickle	6 Brick Lane E
P. Webber	12 Brick Lane E.
T. Williams	20 Brick Lane E.
G.Wildersmith	26 Brick Lane E
J.Holton	36 " " "
B.Rosenbery	15 Brick Lane
William Ince	24 Commercial St. E.

Arthur H Farrow   21   "   "   "
John Berlyne   20 Commercial Street
John Conley   14 Commercial Street
James Ayton   259 Whitechapel Road.

This is followed by a letter[13] from Godfrey Lushington, dated 22
October 1888, to the Commissioner of Metropolitan Police:

B 5239/2   WHITEHALL.
                                      22nd October 1888.
Sir,
   I am directed by the Secretary of State to transmit to you
herewith, copy of a numerously signed petition addressed to Her
Majesty the Queen by women residing in East London in reference
to the murders recently committed in Whitechapel and the
neighbourhood.
   I am to request that full enquiry may be made, and a report be
furnished to the Secretary of State as to the number both of
Brothels and of Common Lodging Houses in Whitechapel, and
such information as you may be able to procure as to the numbers
and the condition of prostitutes living, or plying their calling, in
the district.
   Mr. Secretary Matthews would also be glad if you would be so
good as to inform him whether you have at any time received any
reports from the local authorities seeking the assistance or interference of the Police in regard to brothels or common lodging
houses in Whitechapel, and whether they are used as refuges or
retiring places for criminals.
   I am to add that the Secretary of State would be glad to receive
any suggestions which appear to you to be called for by the present
state of affairs.
                              I am,
                                 Sir,
                              Your obedient Servant,
                                 Godfrey Lushington.
The Commissioner
   of Metropolitan Police.

A report[14] by Superintendent Thomas Arnold, dated 22 October
1888, follows:

METROPOLITAN POLICE.
H Division.
22nd October 1888

Reference to Papers No. 93305 Attached

With reference to the accompanying papers. I beg to report that the Beats in that portion of Whitechapel situated on H Division are small as compared with those in the adjoining Districts of Stepney, Shadwell & St. Georges, but it is impossible to at all times keep a Constable on each Beat as owing to the number of men absent from duty from sickness, leave, attending the Police Court, or Sessions, or employed on special duties, which are necessary, but, for which no provision has been made, such as Winter duties, men employed regulating traffic, &c. it frequently occurs that the Reserve is insufficient to fill the vacancies arising from these causes, and as a consequence some of the Beats are necessarily lengthened, thus affording an opportunity for the commission of crime, which must be expected having in view the fact that a considerable portion of the population of Whitechapel is composed of the low and dangerous classes, who frequently indulge in rowdyism and street offences. With the exception of the recent murders crime of a serious nature is not unusually heavy in the District.

I am however of opinion that considering the circumstances and general condition of the locality it is desirable that the Beats should as far as possible be kept filled and to carry this out

I beg to recommend that the Division be augmented twenty five Constables for the duty, and any not required for that purpose to be employed in specially patrolling neighbourhoods which may be considered more dangerous than others, or where any complaint has been made upon which it is thought necessary a Constable should for a time be placed on a short Beat.

Should this be approved the men could be apportioned as follows, viz ten for Leman Street & ten for Commercial Street Sub-division which would embrace the greater part of the Whitechapel District and the remainder to Arbour Square which immediately adjoins Whitechapel, and where the Beats are somewhat long. This I consider will meet the present requirements of the District, except the special arrangements made in consequence of the circumstances in which the recent murders were committed and which it will be necessary to continue for a time to prevent if possible any further outrages but I trust that some modification may be shortly made and do not ask for an augmentation for this duty but recommend that men be furnished from other Divisions as at present.

As regards the recent murders having had a disastrous effect on trade at the East End there is no doubt that since those in Berner Street and Mitre Square were committed females have to some little extent discontinued shopping in the evening but I am of opinion this will not prevail for any lengthened period there being at present very little excitement.

T Arnold Supd.

The Home Office Permanent Under-Secretary to Henry Matthews, Godfrey Lushington, wrote to the Commissioner of Police, Sir Charles Warren, requesting information on prostitution, brothels, lodging houses and other details of the East End, on 22 October 1888. This was as a result of a petition sent by Henrietta Barnett, wife of the Reverend Samuel Barnett of Whitechapel, to Queen Victoria on behalf of the women of Whitechapel. The police reply[15], dated 25 October 1888, is as follows:

Confidential/ 25/10

In reply to yr letter of 22nd October there has been no return hitherto of the probable numbers of brothels in London, but during the last few months I have been tabulating the observations of Constables on their beats, and have come to the conclusion that there are 62 houses known to be brothels on the H or Whitechapel Divn and probably a great number of other houses which are more or less intermitently [*sic*] used for such purposes.

The number of C.L.Hs. is 233, accommodating 8,530 persons, we have no means of ascertaining what women are prostitutes and who are not, but there is an impression that there are about 1200 prostitutes, mostly of a very low condition.

The only request that I am aware of having rec'd from Vestries about this neighbourhood is one from Mile End when the Police supplied the infn., & convictions were obtained on the evidence of Constables.

This Vestry now helps a seasoned P.S. ["to look" – *deleted*] employed in looking up cases, Mr. Charrington has been very active in evicting the holders of Brothels, and has cleared out 6 Ford St Stepney & Lady Lake Green, the result however is not conducive to morality, the unfortunate women are driven to plying for hire among respectable people, or else exercise their calling in the streets.

The lower class of C.L.Hs. is naturally frequented by prostitutes, thieves & tramps as there is nowhere else for them to go, & no law to prevent their congregating there.

I fear that in driving the Brothel keepers away from certain neighbourhoods much is being done to demoralize London generally, it is impossible to stop the supply while the demand exists.

["I would suggest, however, if it were possible that only lodging" – *deleted*]

I think it is probable that a good number of people who are not married live together at the C.L.Hs., but this also takes place in Hotels in the West End.

I do not think there is any reason whatever for supposing that the murderer of Whitechapel ["has necessarily any connection with the condition of Whitecha" – *deleted*] is one of the ordinary denizens of that place.

["I have received a letter from" – *deleted*].

The Home Office reply[16] to this letter is dated 25 October 1888:

A49301C/8a

25th October 1888.

Sir,

I am directed by the Secretary of State to acknowledge with thanks the receipt of your letter of the 22nd. instant forwarding a Report as to the circumstances of the recent murders in the District of Whitechapel, and I am to request that Mr. Matthews may be furnished with a similar report as to the circumstances of the murder in Mitre Square, and of the steps taken in connection therewith so far as the Metropolitan Police are concerned.

Mr. Matthews would also be glad to be furnished with a sketch map showing the position of the scenes of the various murders.

I am,

Sir

Your obedient Servant,

Godfrey Lushington

Another file contains a letter from Sir Charles Warren to the Home Office[17] as follows:

CID 3721/7

4 Whitehall Place,
S.W.
23rd October, 1888.

Sir,

With reference to your letter of the 5th ulto. A48584/, I have to acquaint you for the information of the Secretary of State, that I have directed the necessary enquiries to be made and have ascertained the particulars as to the number of trains which will arrive at Euston daily with passengers from America, and the hours of their arrival; and as two Police Constables must be present at each examination of luggage, I find it will be necessary to have three reliefs, thus requiring an augmentation of six Police Constables. I have therefore to ask for authority for this increase. – I should explain, however, that one of the three reliefs will be required to deal with passengers arriving during the night, and until the frequency of such arrivals has been tested only four constables will be actually appointed under the authority now sought.

The Midland Railway Company will no doubt apply to have similar arrangements made at St. Pancras Station, and this will necessitate my seeking a still further increase of six constables for that duty

The cost of the augmentation shall be chargeable to the Special Tote.

I am,
Sir,
Your most obedient Servant,
CWarren.

A further letter on the same subject is found on p 374, as follows:

CID
3721/9
94713

4 Whitehall Pl
S.W.
November 1888.

Sir,

With reference to your letter of the 30th ulto, A48584/12, on the subject of the proposed Police arrangements for the examination in London of the luggage of passengers arriving from America via Liverpool, I have to acquaint you, for the information of the Secretary of State, that I fail to see how the expense so incurred can be properly charged to the Inman Company who propose the charge.

Apart from the fact that the arrangement will be for the benefit not only of the Inman, but of the Guion and other companies whose vessels arrive at Liverpool, it is clear that the Police examination (which is quite distinct from the Customs examination though made at the same time) is made for the special purposes for which the Treasury pay at Ports, and the expense can hardly therefore be a legitimate charge upon private individuals.

It appears to me that the cost should be borne by the Special Tote. There is no precedent for a demand such as that proposed, and the Statute only allows of private persons on their own application obtaining the services of Constables.

I am, Sir,

Your most obedient Servant,

C. Warren.

There is a file cover[18] dated 25 October 1888, as follows:

[Stamped: – HOME OFFICE 27 OCT.88 DEPt. No.] No. A49301B/13

DATE 25 Oct. 1888   Commr of Police

REFERENCES &c. Rewards.

Points out that Sir E. Henderson & Mr. Monro who are quoted as against the practice of offering rewards, were once in favour of it, as is shown in copies of minutes enclosed.

Submits copies of Divisional Reports on the subject which were obtained in 1884.

[MINUTES].

["Confidential" – *deleted*]

To

  Mr. Matthews

    GL

    24 Oct 1888

Mr. Monro certainly appears in 1884–5 to have thought that rewards "directed attention" to a case – & "probably did no harm." And Sir E. Henderson's statement that rewards had never produced any information is not quite in accordance with the results stated by the Superintendent. I observe that the cases ment'd. by the Supertd. do not appear in the tabular statement furnished to me from the H.O.

H.M.

28 Oct./88

Only five cases of rewards offered by Govt. are mentioned by the Superintendent. The other cases are either foreign rewards, rewards offered by private persons, or small rewards given at the discretion of the Commr. as to none of which the H.O. has any knowledge.

Of the five cases of rewards offered by Govt. three occurred previous to the time (from 1878) covered by the tabular statement – viz Muller 1864, Galloway 1871. and Peace (Dec 1876).

There remain two cases: One of these (Lefroy's case) is included in the tabular statement and is mentioned in my Memo.

The other – Williams case, the Cromwell Road burglary – appears to have been accidentally omitted in the preparation of the table: but I happened to recollect the case immediately afterwards, and it was mentioned in a separate Memo. sent forward to S of S.CET

31.10.88.

GL

Mr Matthews 1 Nov. 1888

H.M.

2 Nov/88.

The letter[19] from Sir Charles Warren to the Under-Secretary of State, dated 25 October 1888, then follows:

[Stamped: HOME OFFICE 27 OCT. 88 DEPt. No.] A49301B/13
94300   Confidential   4 Whitehall Place

S.W.

25th October, 1888.

Sir,

In reply to your letter of the 17th instant on the subject of Rewards in cases of Murder, &c., and enclosing an history of the question, I feel I should express my view that the Secretary of State has exceedingly strong reasons for arriving at his conclusion with regard to Rewards in general: at the same time it would appear that different views have been expressed at different times and while the Secretary of State is in possession of views against Rewards expressed by Sir Edmund Henderson and Mr. Monro at one time, I have on the other hand memoranda, copies of which I enclose, which appear to show that Sir E. Henderson, Mr.Monro and Mr. Williamson were at another time in favour of Rewards. –

I enclose copies also of the report from some of the Divisions dated 1884.

I am,

Sir,

Your obedient Servant,

CWarren.

The items[20] referred to above then follow:

[Stamped: – HOME OFFICE 27 OCT.88 DEPt. No.] A49301B/13.
H:O: paper
A.36117
3 July, 1884
Extract from minutes on docket in Commissioner's Office:-
"Mr. Williamson
    "Are there any cases on record in which information has been obtained by the offer of a reward. –

(Sd:) E.Y.W.H.

10 July
"I would suggest that a memo: be sent to Supts: of Divisions asking for information on this point.   (Sd:) : F.W. 18/7/84
    "Send accordingly.
                    "E.H.
                    19/7/84
"Memo: sent to each Superintendent for Report.
                    F.W.
                    20.7.84
    "Result submitted"
                    "F. Williamson"
                    Chief Supt:
Sir E. Henderson.
    "The information received from divisions does not form a strong case for rewards. –
    "Although I do not think that a reward offers really inducements which are likely to be accepted as to giving information; there is no doubt that the offer of a good ['reward' – *deleted*] sum directs attention to a case, and in this way helps the Police"
                    (Sd:) J.M. 30.7
"In the face of Sir W. Harcourt's memo: I think we had better discontinue recommending the offer of rewards except in special cases.
                    (Sd:) E.Y.W.H. 31.7.84
"payment of small sums for information is another affair and a matter of discretion. –"
                    (Sd:) E.Y.W.H. 31.7.84
[Stamped: – HOME OFFICE 27 OCT.88 DEPt. No.] A49301B/13
H:O: letter
X6851

The minutes on the docket of this letter in Commissioner's Office are as follows. —

To Sir E. Henderson.

"In submitting these papers I beg to draw attention to the minutes on docket No. 29920/4 3rd July 1884, and to add that Mr. Monro on speaking to me on the subject the day before he left London, remarked that the offer of rewards satisfied the public; and if they did no good they probably did no harm". —

"I beg respectfully to say that I am of the same opinion as Mr. Monro."

(Sd:) Fredk. Williamson
Ch: Supt:

3/8/85

Sir E. Henderson's minute

"Ackge (H:O: letter) and acquaint that the offer of rewards and free pardons has never produced any information and in one case nearly produced serious trouble. —

"Beyond satisfying the public in some small degree I think the offer of rewards is useless and should only be made under some special circumstances.

(Sd:) E.Y.W.H.

The question of a reward is addressed under a cover and report[21], as follows:

[Stamped: — HOME OFFICE 2 NOV.88 RECd. DEPt.] No. A49301B/14

DATE 1st Novr. 88   The Commr of Police

REFERENCES &c. Whitechapel Murders — Rewards

Draws attention to the case of a Reward offered in 1860 in the case of the murder of Mrs. Mary Elmsley in which the murderer attempted to obtain the reward by manufacturing false evidence against an innocent person, which was the means of his own conviction — He considers the offer of a reward tended directly to the furtherance of the ends of Justice.

[MINUTES.]

A precis of the facts of this case was prepared for the S. of S. some days ago.

It was a clear case of the offer of a reward prompting the concoction of a false charge against an innocent person.

Fortunately the attempt failed; but had it been made a little more skilfully, an innocent man might have hanged, and the actual murderer would have pocketed £300.

CET

2.10.88

This case seems to me to
establish the direct contrary of
the Chf Comms's conclusion.
ELP. 3 Novr 88.

S of S.

H.M.

   4 Novr./88

Confidential   A49301B/14

   [Stamped: – HOME OFFICE 2 NOV. 88 RECd. DEPt.] 4 Whitehall

Place, S.W.

1st November, 1888.

94300/3

Sir,

   With reference to my letter of the 25th inst. on the general subject of Rewards for the apprehension and conviction of Criminal, I have to acquaint you, for the information of the Secretary of State, that my attention has recently been called to the case of the murder of Mrs. Mary Elmsley, of 9 Grove Road, Mile End Road, on the 13th August 1860, and to the facts connected with a Reward being offered in this case. It would appear that the murderer [*Note in margin* – "(James Mullins)"] a pensioned Police Officer, attempted to obtain the reward of £300 – £100 of which was offered by the Government and £200 by Mr. Ratcliff, Solicitor – by manufacturing false evidence against an innocent person. But in this he failed; and the very fact of the false evidence which he gave to the Police was the means of his own apprehension and ultimate conviction. It appears to me therefore that the offering of a Reward in this case directly led to the furtherance of the ends of justice.

I am,

Sir,

The Under   Your most obedient servant,

   Secretary of State   CWarren

      &c. &c. &c.

The vexed question of a reward rumbled on into November 1888 leading the *Star*, on the evening after Mary Jane Kelly's murder, to publish an article which read:

We have heard the wildest stories as to the reason which popular opinion in Whitechapel assigns for Mr Matthew's obstinate refusal to offer a reward. It is believed by people who pass among their neighbours as sensible folk that the Government do not want the murderer to be convicted, that they are interested in concealing his identity, that, in fact, they know it, and will not divulge it. Of course this is rank nonsense . . .

CHAPTER 13

The Bloodhounds

The involvement of bloodhounds in an effort to track the murderer is often mentioned, and there is much official documentation on this aspect. File HO 144/221/A49301E refers to the bloodhounds and the cover of the first file, f2, reads:

> No. A49301 E/1 ["22" *deleted*]
> H.O.
> REFERENCES, &c.   re – <u>Whitechapel Murders</u>
> Printed letter from the Times news-paper in which Mr. P. Lindley suggests the use of bloodhounds to trace the murderer.
>
> <u>Pressing</u>
>
> [MINUTES.]

In the case of William Fish at Blackburn in 1876, the use of bloodhounds brought to light evidence which led to the conviction of the murderer.

I do not know whether bloodhounds could be used in the way suggested in this letter. If they could, it would be most desirable to keep one or two ready in a Police Station near Whitechapel, and to have persons able to use them stationed there, so that they might be available in case of another murder.

At any rate the Commissioner's attention might be called to this letter.

?To Commissioner
CT
ELP 3 Oct 88   2.10.88

[There is a marginal note – "54277/12 *herewith*", a stamp "RE-FERRED 3 OCT 88 Ansr 5.10.88 (1/45) *Index* –", and a further stamp – REGISTRY 3-OCT-88–8]

Folio 4 is the press cutting above referred to:

TO THE EDITOR OF *THE TIMES*

Sir, – With regard to the suggestion that bloodhounds might assist in tracking the East end murderer, as a breeder of bloodhounds, and knowing their power, I have little doubt that, had a hound been put upon the scent of the murderer while fresh, it might have done what the police have failed in. But now, when all trace of the scene has been trodden out, it would be quite useless.

Meanwhile, as no means of detection should be left untried, it would be well if a couple or so of trained bloodhounds – unless trained they are worthless – were kept for a time at one of the police head-quarters ready for immediate use in case their services should be called for. There are, doubtless, owners of bloodhounds willing to lend them, if any of the police, which, I fear, is improbable, know how to use them.

I am, Sir, your obedient servant,

PERCY LINDLEY.

York-hill, Loughton, Essex, Oct. 1.

This is followed by another file cover[1]

[Stamped:–HOME OFFICE 6 OCT. 88 RECEIVED]   No. A49301E/2
DATE 5th Oct 88   Commr of Police.
REFERENCES, &c.   Bloodhounds as Detectives
Confidential   Finds from enquiries that
Bloodhounds should be kept constantly prac-
tised in the streets if they are to be of any use in
towns. Is, however, enabled for a few days to
obtain the use of dogs which have been worked
in a town, and is getting them down at once.

Requests authority to expend a sum not
exceeding £100 per annum in keeping trained
bloodhounds, the amt. Required this year
being £50. This is irrespective of any expenses
which may occur in the special use of Bloodhounds at the present moment.   Pressing
[MINUTES.]

Just now public opinion probably would condone any measure however extreme to discover the murderer, but if the use of blood-hounds is to be authorized I think it should be strictly limited to the present emergency; as all extraordinary proceeding for extraordinary crime, & every precaution should be observed in their use.

If an accident happened from the dogs attacking an incorrect person there would be a great outcry.

C.M.
Oct 6.

Mr Matthews

Authorise expenditure of £50 for the present occasion, but say it wd. be desirable to see the result of the employment of the Bloodhounds before sanctioning the payt. of any annual Amt.

ELP. 6Oct88

T.O.

Sanction expenditure of £50 for the present occasion: and say that before sanctioning permanent annual expenditure for no good purpose the S. of S. thinks it desirable to ascertain by experience whether bloodhounds can render any useful service in the streets, and whether they can be used without danger to the public. It will of course be essential to have the dogs under the control of a person accustomed to them, so as to prevent any possible mischief to innocent persons.

H.M.
7th Oct./88
Wrote
10/10
Mr Byrne says a
Letter is going to
Receiver
9/10
Letter to Receiver
10. Oct./88.

There follows a letter[2] written by the Chief Commissioner, Sir Charles Warren, to the Under-Secretary of State:

A49301E/2

[Stamped: — HOME OFFICE 6 OCT 88 RECEIVED]

4 Whitehall Place,
S.W.
5th October, 1888.

Sir,

With reference to the papers marked "pressing," returned herewith, I have to acquaint you for the information of the

Secretary of State that I have made enquiries, and I found that there is a difficulty in suddenly bringing bloodhounds into a town, when they have not been trained for use in the streets, owing to the confusion of scent, – and that it is desirable that they should be kept constantly practised in the streets if they are to be of any use. –

I have therefore to request the authority of the Secretary of State to expend a sum of not over £100 per annum in keeping trained bloodhounds, the amount required this year being £50. – This is irrespective of any expenses which may occur in the special use of bloodhounds at the present moment. –

I find that I am enabled for a few days at least to obtain the use of dogs which have been worked in a town, and I am getting them down at once. –

I am,

Sir,

Your most obedient Servant,

Cwarren

The Under Secretary
Of State
&c. &c. &c.
Home Office

There is a deleted reply[3] to the Chief Commissioner, as follows:

A49301E/2

A49301/4   Whitehall

Confidential   Rewritten   10 October 1888

Sir,

With reference to previous correspondence respecting the use of bloodhounds in tracking criminals in London, I am directed by the Secretary of State to inform you that upon your recommendation he is willing to sanction an expenditure of £50 for this purpose on the present occasion, but before giving any assent to a permanent annual expenditure for so novel a purpose he thinks it desirable to ascertain by experience whether bloodhounds can render any useful service in the streets, and whether they can be used without danger to the public.

It will of course be essential to have the hounds under the control of a person accustomed to them, so as to prevent any possible mischief to innocent persons.

                                        I am, Sir,
                                        Your obedient servant,

The Commissioner of Police
    of the Metropolis

There is next a file cover[4] as follows:

[Stamped: – HOME OFFICE 24 OCT.88 DEPt. No.] No.
A49301/E/3
DATE 23 Octr. 88   Comr. Of Police
REFERENCES, &c.   reBloodhounds
                        Referring to his letter of the 5th. inst,
                        submits a revised estimate for the receir. of
                        the financial year amounting to £100, &
                        reqts sanction of S.of S. to expend this
                        sum, instead of the £50 as previously applied
                        for.
                                                        Pressing
                    [MINUTES.]
The cost to the end of the financial year will be £25 hire £5
insurance.
    Sir C. Warren proposes to buy a puppy for £15 & train it with
the old dog. Before authorizing further expenditure? ask Sir C.
Warren what has been the results of his experiments with the
hound. in what manner he has been tried. & whether he (Sir CW) is
satisfied with the result. & has confidence in continuing their use.
                                            C.M. Oct 25.
These inquiries I think will better come later. The use at present is
experimental only
(Wrote Comm?& Rec?   Sanction 25 Oct 1888   GL
            26.10.88.

There then follows the Chief Commissioner's letter[5]:

[Stamped: – HOME OFFICE 24 OCT.88 DEPt. No.]   A49301E/3
93925/11   4, Whitehall Place,
                                                S.W.
                                        23rd October, 1888.
Sir,
    With reference to my letter of the 5th instant requesting
authority to expend a sum of £50 during the current financial year

in keeping trained bloodhounds, irrespective of any expenses which may occur in the special use of bloodhounds at the present time, I have to acquaint you, for the information of the Secretary of State, that the amount in question was suggested when I was under the impression that the dog now placed at our disposal would be lent without charge.

I am informed that Mr. Brough the owner of the dog will charge £25 for his hire until the end of March next; and with a view to indemnify himself in the event of accidents will require the dog to be insured, this will cost an additional £5. –

It will be necessary to purchase a pup at a price of say £15; it could be trained with the hired dog and would then at the end of March be fit to take his place. –

I have therefore to submit a revised estimate for the remainder of the financial year amounting to £100, and to request the sanction of the Secretary of State to expend this sum, or as much of it as may be necessary, instead of the £50 as previously applied for. –

> I am,
> Sir,
> Your obedient Servant,
> C Warren

The Under Secretary
  of State
 &c. &c. &c.
  Home Office

The cost of the bloodhounds became something of a problem and there was an exchange of correspondence with Mr A.J. Sewell of the Veterinary Infirmary, 55 Elizabeth Street, Eaton Square, S.W. These letters are held under MEPOL 2/188.

When the financing of the bloodhounds was finally settled an agreement[6] was duly drawn up but, in the event, it was never signed and the bloodhounds had both been returned to Mr Brough by the time of the Kelly murder of 9 November 1888. The agreement, however, makes interesting reading:

An Agreement made this day of one thousand eight hundred and eighty eight Between Alfred Joseph Sewell of 55 Elizabeth Street Eaton Square in the County of Middlesex Veterinary Surgeon of the one part and Sir Charles Warren of

The Bloodhounds

Scotland Yard in the said County of Middlesex Chief Commissioner of the Metropolitan Police of the other part, Whereby it
is agreed as follows:-

1. The said Alfred Joseph Sewell will as from the date hereof until
   the thirty first March One thousand eight hundred and eighty
   nine keep the bloodhound "Barnaby" for and at the disposal of
   the Metropolitan Police such bloodhound to be sent (unless it be
   ill injured or otherwise incapacitated from work) together with a
   man to be supplied by Alfred Joseph Sewell to any part of the
   Metropolis at the earliest possible moment on receipt of
   instructions from Sir Charles Warren or any Metropolitan
   Police Superintendent or Inspector the said bloodhound to be
   kept at the expense of Alfred Joseph Sewell but all travelling
   expenses incurred in respect of this clause to be born [sic] by the
   said Sir Charles Warren————

2. 2. Sir Charles Warren for himself and his successors in office for
   the consideration mentioned in the last preceding clause cove-
   nants with Alfred Joseph Sewell to pay to Alfred Joseph Sewell
   the sum of Eighty pounds in manner following that is to say.
   Forty pounds on the twenty fourth day of December one
   thousand eight hundred and eighty eight and Forty pounds
   the balance thereof on the thirty first March One thousand
   eight hundred and eighty nine And further to pay to Alfred
   Joseph Sewell on the signing hereof the sum of Ten pounds being
   the Insurance premium to be paid by Alfred Joseph Sewell for
   insuring the said bloodhound in his own name and for his own
   benefit in the Horse Insurance Company Limited and also to pay
   to Alfred Joseph Sewell all travelling expenses as provided for in
   Clause 1 hereof.

3. If the said bloodhound shall any time during the continuance
   of this agreement become unwell injured or in any manner
   incapacitated from work Alfred Joseph Sewell shall not be
   called upon to furnish any other bloodhound in its place
   neither shall he be called upon to send the said bloodhound
   as provided by Clause 1 hereof nor shall his remuneration as
   provided by Clause 2 hereof be in any way affected thereby
   it being the intention of the parties hereto that although the
   said bloodhound is to be kept by the said Alfred Joseph
   Sewell at his own expense it is entirely at the risk of Sir
   Charles Warren————

4. The costs of and incidental to the preparation and execution of

this Agreement shall be borne and paid the day and year first
above written————
Signed Sealed and Delivered
by the above named

The Times of Tuesday, 13 November 1888 concluded the tale of the
unsuccessful role played by the bloodhounds in the efforts to
capture the Whitechapel murderer:

It will be remembered that, at Sir Charles Warren's request, Mr.
Brough, the well-known bloodhound breeder of Scarborough, was
communicated with shortly after the Mitre-square and Berner-
street tragedies, and asked to bring a couple of trained hounds up to
London for the purpose of testing their capabilities in the way of
following the scent of a man. The hounds were named Burgho and
Barnaby, and in one of the trials Sir Charles Warren himself acted as
the quarry and expressed satisfaction at the result. Arrangements
were made for the immediate conveyance of the animals to the spot
in the event of another murder occurring, and in order to facilitate
matters Mr. Brough, who was compelled to return to Scarborough,
left the hounds in the care of Mr. Taunton, of 8 Doughty-street,
who is a friend of his. Mr. Taunton, who is a high authority on
matters appertaining to the larger breeds of dogs, has ample
accommodation in the rear of his residence for kenneling such
valuable animals, and he was accordingly entrusted with their
custody pending the conclusion of the negotiations which had been
opened for the ultimate purchase of the dogs. Sir Charles Warren,
however, it is said, would not give any definite assurance on the
point, and the result was Mr. Brough insisted on resuming
possession of the animals. Mr. Taunton has made the following
statement:-
After the trial in Regent's Park Burgho was sent to Brighton,
where he had been entered for the show, which lasted three days. In
the meantime Barnaby remained in my care. Burgho would have
been sent back to me, but as Mr. Brough could not get anything
definite from Sir Charles Warren, he declined to do so, and wrote
asking me to return Barnaby. I did not do so at first, but, acting on
my own responsibility, retained possession of the dog for some time
longer. About a fortnight ago I received a telegram from Leman-
street Police-station asking me to bring up the hounds. It was then
shortly after noon, and I took Barnaby at once. On arriving at the

station I was told by the superintendent that a burglary had been
committed about 5 o'clock that morning in Commercial-street, and
I was asked to attempt to track the thief by means of the dog. The
police admitted that since the burglary they had been all over the
premises. I pointed out the stupidity of expecting a dog to
accomplish anything under such circumstances and after such a
length of time had been allowed to elapse, and took the animal
home. I wrote telling Mr. Brough of this, and he wired insisting that
the dog should be sent back at once, as the danger of its being
poisoned, if it were known that the police were trying to track
burglars by its aid, was very great, and Mr. Brough had no
guarantee against any pecuniary loss he might suffer in the event
of the animal's being maltreated. Therefore there has not been a
"police bloodhound" – that is to say, a trained hound, in London
for the past fortnight. The origin of the tale regarding the hounds
being lost at Tooting while being practised in tracking a man I can
only account for in the following way. I had arranged to take
Barnaby out to Hemel Hempstead to give the hound some practice.
The same day a sheep was maliciously killed on Tooting-common,
and the police wired to London asking that the hounds might be sent
down. I was then some miles away from London with Barnaby, and
did not get the telegram until on my return, late in the evening.
Somebody doubtless remarked that the hounds were missing,
meaning that they did not arrive when sent for, and this was
magnified into a report that they had been lost. At that time Burgho
was at Scarborough. Under the circumstances in which the body of
Mary Ann [sic] Kelly was found I do not think bloodhounds would
have been of any use. It was then broad daylight and the streets
crowded with people. The only chance the hounds would have
would be in the event of a murdered body being discovered, as the
others were, in the small hours of the morning, and being put on the
trail before many people were about.

CHAPTER 14

October 1888 – A Strange Story

With the increasing public concern and terror that the Whitechapel Murders caused, new allegations and alarming stories began to appear in the press. One such was the so-called "Cabmen's Shelter" incident that occurred on the day of the discovery of the bodies of Stride and Eddowes. It began in the newspapers and then found its place in the official files. The story[1] appeared in the *Newcastle Chronicle* on Tuesday, 2 October 1888:

A49301/50
A STRANGE STORY.

A strange story is told, according to a London evening paper, by Thomas Ryan, who has charge of the Cabmen's Reading Room, at 43, Pickering Place, Westbourne Grove, W. Mr. Ryan is a teetotaller, and is the secretary of the Cabmen's Branch of the Church of England Temperance Society. Ryan, who tells the story without affectation, says on Saturday afternoon, while he was in his little shelter, the street attendant brought a gentlemanly-looking man to him and said: "This 'ere gentleman wants a chop, guv'ner; can you cook one for him, he says he's 'most perished with cold." The gentleman in question, Ryan says, was about five feet six inches in height, and wore an Oxford cap on his head, and a light check ulster, with a tippet buttoned to his throat, which he did not loosen all the time he was in the shelter. He had a thick moustache, but no beard; was round-headed, his eyes very restless, and clean white hands. Ryan said, "Come in, I'll cook one for you with pleasure." This was about four o'clock in the afternoon. Several cabmen were in the shelter at the time, and they were talking of the new murders discovered that morning at Whitechapel. Ryan exclaimed, "I'd gladly do seven days and nights if I could only find the fellow who did them." This was said directly at the stranger, who, looking into Ryan's face, quietly said, "Do you know who committed the murders?" and then calmly went on to say, "I did them. I've had a lot of trouble lately. I came back from India and got into trouble at once. I lost my watch and chain and £10." Ryan was greatly taken aback at the man's statement, and fancied he was just recovering from a drinking bout; so he replied, "If that's correct you must consider yourself engaged." But he then went on to speak to him about temperance work and the evils wrought by drink. Warming to his subject, Ryan spoke of his own work amongst men to try to induce them to become teetotallers; then the stranger said "Have a drink" to Ryan, and produced a bottle from an inner pocket, which was nearly full of a brown liquid – either whisky or brandy. Ryan told him he had better put the bottle away, as they were all teetotallers there. Ryan reasoned with him as to the folly of drinking, and at last he expressed his willingness to sign the pledge, a book containing the pledges being shown him. This the stranger examined, and at length filled up one page, writing on the counterfoil as well as on the body of the pledge. In the hand of a gentleman he wrote the following words:- "J.Duncan, doctor, residence, Cabman's Shelter, 30th Sept., 1888." After doing this he said, "I could tell a tale if I wanted." Then he relapsed into silence. After a pause he went on to speak of his experiences in India; and said he knew the Rev. Mr. Gregson who was engaged in temperance work amongst the English soldiers in India, and had also been for some time in Sinila. He also stated that he was at Newcastle-on-Tyne before he went to India. Ryan called his attention to the fact that he had not filled in his proper residence, and the man replied, "I have no fixed place of abode at present. I'm living anywhere." In answer to further conversation about teetotalism, Duncan accepted an invitation to go with Ryan to church that evening, and afterwards accompanying him to a temperance meeting which he was going to hold. For that purpose, he said, he would return to the shelter in an hour, but he never came back. Duncan carried a stick, and looked a sinewy fellow, just such a one as was capable of putting forth considerable energy when necessary.

The file cover[2] regarding this incident is as follows:

[Stamped:–HOME OFFICE 8 OCT. 88 RECEIVED]   No. A49301C/7
DATE 8 October 88   Newcastle Prison Governor.
REFERENCES, &c. <u>Whitechapel Murders</u>.

Calls attention to enclosed Newspaper Extract giving an account of a man named Duncan who confessed to having committed the Murders. Has reason to believe that Duncan was twice imprisoned in Newcastle Prison.

Fds. His description & thinks he should be traced.

[*Marginal note:* – "see A49301/68"]

Pressing

MINUTES.

This is the man who told the Keeper of the Cabman's shelter he had committed the murders; & failed to keep an appointment with him.

His two convictions at Newcastle are for assaults on women.

To Commissioner of Police.

C.M. Oct 8/88.

GL

Wrote Commr.   8 Oct 1888
8.10.88.

There then follows the descriptive details[3] of Duncan:

[Stamped:–PRISON COMMISSION RECd 6 OCT 1888]   A49301/50 in 12579/1

[Stamped: – HOME OFFICE 8 OCT.88 RECEIVED]

Previous convictions recorded against John. Geo. ["Duncan" – *deleted*] Donkin.

Name	Date	Place	Offence	Sentence	Remarks
Geo: Donkin	6th Jan.y. 1881	Tynemouth	Assault Female	1 C.M.	H.L.
John. Geo: Donkin	22nd Decr. 1881	do.	Assault Female	2 C.M.	H.L.

Description of the above
In 1881 (Decr. 22nd)

Place of birth	Morpeth
Age	28 yrs
Married	yes
Trade or occupation –	none
Complexion	Fresh
Hair	Brown

Eyes	Blue
Build	Slender
Shape of Face	Long
Height	5 ft. 8 in.
Distinctive marks:-	Scars on left thigh – mole on
	Back – wound on left cheek – Red mark
	On right shoulder.

[FMTooley(?)]

5/10/88 Governor

The letter[4] from the Governor of the prison follows:

[Stamped: – PRISON COMMISSION RECd 5 OCT 1888]
A49301C/7

Pressing   ["A49301/50" – *deleted*] 12579/1
<u>Confidential</u>   [Stamped: – HOME OFFICE 8 OCT.88 RECEIVED]

H.M. Prison,

Newcastle,

Sir,

re Whitechapel Murders

I have today had my attention called by a man named Murray – a Solicitor's Clerk of Newcastle – to a paragraph headed "A Strange Story", which appeared in a local Newspaper on Tuesday last (vide copy enclosed)

The person to whom the "Story" refers I have reason to believe is a man who was twice committed to this prison, particulars of whose previous convictions are enclosed, showing his description at that time. He was educated at college for the medical profession, but he turned out wild & lived more or less a dissolute life. His wife obtained a divorce from him and since then he is known to have frequented the low parts of London, being very impecunious. His manners and address are those of a gentleman, and his anatomical knowledge is said to be considerable.

It may be that the recent horrible murders committed in London are the work of the person to whom I refer, & were he found I could identify him as being the man who was twice in my custody.

I give you these particulars as it appears to me that the man to whom I refer should be traced, and the same coming forcibly before me today I have felt it my duty to put you in possession of them for the information of the Home Office if

you should think it well to place them before that department,

    I have the honor to be,
      Sir,
    Your obedient Servant
    [FMTooley(?)]
      <u>Governor</u>
R.S. Mitford Esq
    Prison Commissioner
      Whitehall
        London S.W.

There is then a second[5] file cover:

[Stamped: – HOME OFFICE 12 OCT.88 RECEIVED] No.
A49301/68
DATE 10 Octr. 1888.Asst. Commr. Anderson.
REFERENCES, &c. <u>-Donkin alias J. Duncan.</u>
        Fds. Police report from which it appears that
        the men are not identical.
        [*Marginal note*: – "See A49301/7"]
          [MINUTES.]
        The man who spoke to the Keeper of the
        Cabman's shelter has accounted for his move-
        ments on the dates of the murders.
               ?Lay by. C.M. Oct 13.
                    GL
               15 Oct 1888

There then follows a report[6] dated 10 October 1888 from the
Assistant Commissioner, Robert Anderson, to the Home Office:

[Reference:- 52983/598]   A49301/68
                         Great Scotland Yard,
[Stamped:–HOME OFFICE 12 OCT.88 RECEIVED]   London, S.W.
                         10th day of October 1888.
From
        ASSISTANT COMMISSIONER OF POLICE,
              Criminal Investigation Department.
    To The Under Secretary of State
      for the Home Department
        &c   &c   &c

Sir,

I am directed by the Commissioner of Police of the Metropolis to acknowledge the receipt of your letter of the 8th instant enclosing a letter from the Governor of the Prison at Newcastle giving particulars regarding a man named Donkin who he thought was identical with one J Duncan said to have made a confession with regard to the recent murders in Whitechapel and to transmit for the information of Mr. Secretary Matthews a police report . . . received on the subject from which it will be seen that the men referred to are not identical.

The enclosures which accompanied your letter are herewith returned.

I have the honour to be,

Sir,

Your obedient servant,

RAnderson

[*There are marginal references to the above report:* — "A 49301/50" *above "4."*]

There is then attached a report[7] by Inspector Abberline, dated 10 October 1888, giving details of the result of checking out this story:

A49301/68

[Stamped: – METROPOLITAN POLICE 10.OCT.88 CRIMINAL
INVESTIGATION DEPT]
METROPOLITAN POLICE.

[Stamped: – HOME OFFICE 12 OCT 88 RECEIVED]   Central Office
10th day of Oct. 1888.

SUBJECT Whitechapel   With reference to the
        Murders   annexed.

I beg to report that the person who made the statement in the Cabmens Shelter at Pickering Place, Bayswater, 30th Ult. Has since been seen by Police, and interrogated, and satisfactorily accounted for his movements on the dates [*of*] the murders. His correct na[*me*] is John Davidson, and there[-*fore*] cannot be the person referre[*d to*] in the attached correspondence from Home Office.

F.G.Abberline Inspr.

T Arnold Supt.

[*There is the marginal reference to the above:* – "REFERENCE TO PAPERS 52983 5748"]

Thus another suspicious person was cleared by police enquiry. It is interesting to see this example of how another "suspect", mentioned in newspaper reports, was brought to the attention of the Police, and was cleared.

CHAPTER 15

A Suspect Arrested in France

October 1888 was, as we have seen, a busy time for the police, with dozens of suspects being brought to their notice. This situation was exacerbated by – if not, indeed, caused by – the extensive and sensational press coverage of the murders. Two line drawings of a suspect, described by Matthew Packer, appeared in the *Daily Telegraph* and many other newspapers.

This publicity created even more problems for the police. File HO 144/220/A49301, f3, has a cover bearing the following details:

[Stamped: – HOME OFFICE 12 OCT. 88 RECEIVED] No. A49301/67
DATE 12 Octr. 1888.   Foreign Office
REFERENCES &c.   <u>Whitechapel Murders</u>
Fds. despatch from H.M. Consul at Boulogne enclosing copies of letters he has addressed to Comr. of Police as to a suspicious person who asked to be sent to South Wales: the appearance of the man much resembles the picture of the supposed Murderer: he is detained till to-day as a vagrant, but cannot be kept longer without definite instructions.

MINUTES.

Imme<u>diate</u>

[Stamped:- METROPOLITAN POLICE
RECEIVED
12. OCT. 88
CRIMINAL INVESTIGATION DEPT.]
H.M. Consul is in direct communication with the Metropolitan Police on the subject of this man.

To Comr. of Police C.M.
Oct 12. GL
12 Oct 1888

This matter has now
  been cleared up.
    CW 16.10.88
[Stamped:- HOME OFFICE 20 OCT.88 DEP. No.]
?Lay by
corrs C.M.
22/10

The reports in this file follow, thus:

[f6] 1888/Boulogne 11 October/Consul Bonham/No 29 Immediate/2 Inclosures/Recd Oct:12./Bypost./Suspicious character/Encloses copies of letter/to Metropolitan Police/Home Office/P.L./Oct 12/88
45

[f5]:- Immediate
[Stamped:- HOME OFFICE 12 OCT.88 RECEIVED]
British Consulate

Boulogne 11 October 1888
A49301/67

No29 My Lord,
  I have the honour to transmit to your Lordship, herewith enclosed, copy of a letter I addressed to the Commissioner of Police Scotland Yard yesterday relative to a suspicious character [*marginal note*:- "10 Octr 1888"] and also copy of a further letter which I send by tonight's post: the telegram I have received requesting me to act in my discretion places me in an awkward position [*Marginal note*:- "11 Octr 1888"].

I have the honor to be,
with the highest respect,
My Lord,
Your Lordships most obedient,
humble Servant,
E.W. Bonham

The Right Honble
The Marquis of Salisbury k.g.
    &c   &c   &c
      Foreign Office

[f8]:- Immediate [Stamped: – HOME OFFICE 12 OCT.88 RECEIVED] A49301/67

Foreign Office,
October 12 1888.

Sir,

I am directed by the Secretary of State for Foreign Affairs to transmit to you, to be laid before [*Marginal note*:- "Consul Bonham No. 29/Oct 11/88 and encls:"] Mr Secretary Matthews a despatch as marked in the margin which has been received from Mr Bonham Her Majesty's Consul at Boulogne together with copies of two letters which have been addressed by that officer to the Commissioner of Police Scotland Yard relative to a suspicious character also applies for assistance at Her Majesty's Consulate.

I have to request that the enclosed correspondence may be returned to this office.

I am,
Sir,
Your most obedient,
humble Servant,

The Under Secretary of State   P.W. Currie
     Home Office

[*f 9*]: – copy/Consul Bonham/to/Commissioner of Police/ Boulogne 10 Octr 1888
1/Mr Consul Bonham's/Despatch No 29 of 11/October 1888.

[*ff. 7–8*]: – <u>copy</u>   A49307/67
[Stamped:–HOME OFFICE 12 OCT. 88 RECEIVED]   British Consulate,
Immediate.   Boulogne s-mer, 10th October,
1888.

Sir,

I think it right to let you know that today a man called here asking for assistance who the Vice-Consul thought so much resembled the sketch portrait of the man wanted for the East end murders, given in the Daily Telegraph of the 6th, that he mentioned it to me; I saw the man and certainly there was a likeness, he wanted assistance and to go to South Wales to work in the Coal Mines, he produced a discharge from a British Ship at Glasgow on 10 April in which he had only shipped at New York on 30 March, as he was described as born in the United States I said I would not assist him and sent him to the American Consul.

Later I procured a copy of the Daily Telegraph and handed it to the Police: they arrested the man as a vagrant and requested me to go and see him at the Police Station; I could not ask for him to be detained as I had only the newspaper account and many men might answer to that. The description he gives of himself is that he left Mines near Glasgow last Monday week with about 50s, went by rail to Leith, Steamer to London only passed through, thence rail to Dover and crossed Saturday night, thence he says he has been to Bethune and other towns seeking work in Coal Mines, but came here to get a vessel.

I asked him if I gave him a passage to England tomorrow whether he would go, he wanted to know where I would send him as he would not like to land without money, but he would go if sent to Cardiff to work in the South Wales Mines, but would prefer getting work here.

My idea had been to send him to Folkstone and to let you know he was going, but he did not care to accept a passage.

His manner was very unsatisfactory and as I declined to take charge of him the Police have taken him into custody for having no means of subsistence and not giving a satisfactory account of himself or why he came to France: he will consequently be taken before the Procureur of the Republic tomorrow morning and if you want to make any further enquiries or to have the man detained, it will be necessary for you to communicate by telegraph.

I enclose the description of the man and of his clothes which has been handed me by the Police.

I am &c &c

The Commissioner of Police   (signed) E.W. Bonham,
    Scotland Yard,   H.M. Consul
        London.

[*f12*]: – Copy/Consul Bonham/to/Commissioner of Police/Boulogne 11 October 1888
2/Mr Consul Bonham's/Despatch No 29 of 11/October 1888

[*ff. 10–11*]: –   A49301/67
Very Immediate. [Stamped: – HOME OFFICE 12 OCT.88 RECEIVED]
British Consulate,
Boulogne 11 October, 1888.
Sir,

About 4 this afternoon I received the following telegram in reply to my letter of yesterday, ''Re man detained definite instructions impossible please act in your discretion Anderson Assistant Commissioner police Scotland Yard''.

Shortly before receiving this telegram I had seen the Procureur of the Republic who had informed me that as the man had no means of subsistence or papers he would be treated as a vagrant and sent away, but he would detain him here till tomorrow afternoon to see whether on my letter of yesterday you could give any information about him.

The Procureur again sent for him that I might speak to him as he does not speak French. I asked him as to his statement to the Vice-Consul that he had been in South Wales he said he had been there about ten months ago and then returned to America; he had been several times in England.

At the request of the Procureur I told him he was being detained because he had no papers or means of subsistence and could give no satisfactory account of himself: he then stated that when in Wales he lodged with Mrs Davis 30 Dufferin, a village two miles from Merthyr Glamorganshire, that lately he was lodging with John Richmond 47 Castle Street Hamilton near Glasgow, and that when last in America he was employed in some ironworks.

I sent you the following telegram "Modulas London, Andersons telegram Langran [sic] now states he lodged John Richmond 47 Castle Street Hamilton near Glasgow can you verify. will be detained until tomorrow Bonham Consul".

You ask me to act in my discretion I can only say that I do not think either his manner or the account he gives of himself satisfactory but I cannot undertake the responsibility of acting further than reporting the circumstances: he may not be connected with the East End murders but says he does not wish to go to England but wants to go to South Wales where there are Mines.

He seems to have travelled about in a curious manner and I thought you might consider it desirable that he should be seen by some one acquainted with those who are "wanted".

The Procureur asked if I wished to take charge of him to send him to his country, I replied that as he declared himself an American I could not take charge of him as a British subject or ask for him to be sent to England.

I hope I may receive a telegram from you tomorrow morning before I see the Procureur.

I am &c &c

(signed) E.W. Bonham,

H.M. Consul.

The Commissioner of Police,

London.

There then follows another file[1], dated 16 October 1888, details as follows:

[Stamped: – HOME OFFICE 17 OCT.88 RECd. DEPTt.] No. A49301/76
DATE 16 Oct 1888   The Foreign Office
REFERENCES, &c.   <u>Whitechapel Murders</u>
Forwards Despatch from H.M. Consul at Boulogne stating that the man detained there has been released as the London Police were satisfied he was not the man required.
[MINUTES.]
Commr. of Police to see. tho' probably fact is known to them.
C.M Oct 18. 1888.

Index. C.M.   Seen R.A. 24/10
Seen by Comr.
       [ ]
   26/10/88.
[Stamped: – REGISTRY 19 OCT.–88 – 4] 9335/17
[Stamped: – HOME OFFICE 29 OCT.88 DEPt. No.]

[*ff. 21–22*]: –   A49301/76
   [Stamped: – HOME OFFICE 17 OCT.88 RECd. DEPt.] British Consulate
                          Boulogne 12 October 1888.
<u>No 30</u>
My Lord,
   With reference to my despatch No 29 of yesterday I have the honor to report that this afternoon I received a telegram from the Commissioner of the Metropolitan Police stating that the address given by the man, John Langan, had been verified, and that he has no connection with the London murders. I lost no time in seeing the Procureur of the Republic and informing him that the address given had been found to be correct, he stated that as this was the case he should order the man's release.
   I have the honor to be with the highest respect,
                    My Lord,
          Your Lordship's most obedient,
                humble Servant,
                E.W. <u>Bonham</u>

[*f 20*]:- A49301/76
  [Stamped:- HOME OFFICE 17 OCT.88 RECd. DEPt.]
                                    Foreign Office,
                                    October 16, 1888.
Sir,

    With reference to my letter of the 12th instant, I am directed by
the Secretary of State for Foreign Affairs to transmit to you, to be
laid before Mr. Secretary Matthews, a further despatch [*marginal
note* – "Consul Bonham/No. 30. Octr. 12."] from Her Majesty's
Consul at Boulogne reporting the release of the man John Langan.
                                    I am,
                                        Sir,
                                        Your most obedient,
                                        humble Servant,
                                            P.W. Currie

The Under Secretary
        of State,
    Home Office.

[*f23*] is a page covering the above letter as follows:

1888/Boulogne 12 October/Consul Bonham/No 30
Recd. Octr. 13./By post/Refr. No 29 of 11th inst
Suspicious character./Address given verified and/he will be released
Home Office/p.p. [ ]/Octr. 16
46

CHAPTER 16

October 1888 – A Person "Professes to be Able to Capture the Murderer"

Another very interesting exchange of correspondence took place in October 1888 and continued for several months. The suspect, although his existence possibly had no foundation in fact, was described and the preserved files are of the greatest interest for the great insight they give into the workings of the ongoing enquiry, also for the informed comments of several of the leading officials. The file[1] commences with an annotated file cover and additional pages, dated 12 October 1888:

[Stamped: – HOME OFFICE 12 OCT. 88 RECd. DEPt.]

Recd 4.45 pm   No. A49301D/1
DATE 12 Oct. 88   Foreign Office
REFERENCES, &c   <u>Whitechapel Murders</u>

Forwards copy of despatch from H.M. Ambassador at Vienna to the effect that there is a person there who professes to be able to capture the murderer.

MINUTES.

To Commr Police

5 pm

CM

I enclose opinion of A.C.C. Investigation. I am not inclined to go so far as he does, but at the same time I feel that his opinion on such a subject is very valuable.

I have never   experience with foreigners and I do not think that the Informant's account must necessarily be incredible.

In the first place he scouts the idea of the picture in Daily Telegraph being like the murderer, and thinks he would not have written the letters signed "Jack the Ripper". This is in his favour.

As Mr. Matthews is aware I have for some time past inclined to the idea that the murders may possibly be done by a secret society, as the only logical solution of the question, but I would not understand this being done by a Socialist because the last murders were obviously done by some one desiring to bring discredit on the Jews and Socialists or Jewish Socialists.

But in the suggestion of the informant we have a solution, viz:- that it is done by a renegade socialist to <u>bring discredit on his former comrades</u>.

I can see no reason why Informant should not be called upon to give name of murderer and other details as proposed with a provision of 20.000 florins if it leads to arrest of murderer, but at the same time I see no reason why the Informant should put his faith in an ambassador any more than an ambassador should put his faith in the Informant.

I should not be inclined to bother the ambassador in the matter. I have known several cases where friction has occurred owing to telegraphic communication leaving no liberty of action. I propose that Mr Anderson's views should be telegraphed to Sir A Paget as a suggestion, but specially giving him freedom to use his own discretion in the matter.

If from our straining in the matter we miss the opportunity of capturing the murderer it would be unfortunate.

C.Warren

13.10.88

To my mind the whole story is incredible. The man says nothing to show how he knows that the person whom he accuses is the murderer: nor does he even state the reason why the murder was committed or either the murders. It appears to me inconceivable that Socialists should wreak this vengeance on Society by murdering women of the town – mere outcasts.

Then as to the man. He admits that he is actuated by vindictive motives: he and his friends want to get rid once for all of the men they accuse. How likely that they may make false charges against him! He is also a member of the Secret Society: & H.M. Government is also asked not <u>only to enter into a transaction with this Society</u> but to pay money which is <u>admittedly to go to the funds of the Society, and the steps taken for the detection of the man are to be so to speak official action by the 2 Chiefs</u> of the Society. The man has given information on a previous occasion, which was not realized. He also insists on being paid beforehand, as if he could not trust H.M. Ambassador, let alone that if he is successful, he is sure of the rewards already offered.

He insists also on going himself to London, no reason being given but the orders of the Society.

If the offer is accepted, I anticipate as the result not only that the Govt. will be duped, but will have <u>helped a Secret Society to punish one of its members by bringing against him a false charge of murder</u>.

I think a telegram should be sent to the Ambassador that no further attention need be given to the informant unless he state ["facts, capable of verification" – *deleted*] the name of the murderer with definite details which can be tested showing that these are reasonable grounds of suspicion. If the information leads to his arrest & conviction the ["amount will" – *deleted*] 2000 florins will be paid to him.

[If the matter is left to the Ambassador's discretion, it is pretty clear he will send the man over – which I think would be a most regrettable step.

I cannot at all agree with the Commr.'s idea that the only logical solution of the question is that the murders may possibly have been done by a Secret Society. He also says that he cannot understand this having been done by a Socialist, because the last murders were evidently done by some one desiring to bring discredit on the Jews and Socialists or Jewish Socialists. – It seems to me on the contrary that the last murder was done by a Jew who boasted of it.]

GL

13 Oct 1888

This is followed by a copy letter[2] dated 14 October 1888, by Lushington:

(Copy)

<u>Confidential</u>   Whitehall

14   Octr.   1888

Sir,

["I am t" – *deleted*]

In reply to your letter of the 12th instant forwarding a copy of a Despatch from Her Majesty's Ambassador at Vienna giving the details of an interview with an individual who professed himself able to effect the capture of the perpetrator of the recent murders in Whitechapel, I am directed by Mr. Secretary Matthews to acquaint you for the information of the Marquis of Salisbury that the story told by this man appears to him to be highly improbable, but that inasmuch as the Ambassador and the Consul General, who have seen him, are both inclined to believe in his good faith. Mr. Matthews is disposed to think that the Ambassador should be directed to use his own discretion in the matter, and at the same time should be requested to obtain if possible, some guarantee of the bona fides of the informant, by requiring that the name of the alleged murderer or his residence calling or nationality or some detail by which he can be identified, should be communicated to the Ambassador. ["Any money paid immediately to him should be" – *deleted*] Money should be paid to him only for "travelling expenses"; and if half could be paid in Vienna and the other half in London, that would be the best arrangement. He should be directed on his arrival in London immediately to report himself to Sir Charles Warren 4 Whitehall Place.

> I am, Sir
> Your obedient servant
> Godfrey Lushington

The
Under Secretary of State
 Foreign Office

There is then a letter[3] on Secretary of State, Home Department headed paper, dated 13 October 1888, from Lushington to Matthews:

The H.O. answer should be sent to the F.O. tomorrow Sunday at latest.
Mr. Matthews,
 I am sorry to trouble you with this.
 I have myself no doubt whatever as to the proper course to take. But in a matter of this importance especially as the Commr. has expressed his opinion the other way, I do not like to commit you without a reference to you.

> GL
> 13 Oct 1888

There is much force in your observations and those of Mr Anderson. This informant, if he comes, will have to be most closely & vigilantly watched. But in the face of the Ambassador's opinion I do not like to throw aside what may result in some useful clue.

> H.M.

Say to F.O. that the story told by the individual who has had an interview with the Ambassador at Vienna appears to the S. of S.

to be highly improbable; but that, in as much as the Ambassador & the Consul General, who have seen him, are both inclined to believe in his good faith, the S. of S. is disposed to think that the Ambassador should be directed to use his own discretion in the matter, and at the same time should be requested, if possible, to obtain some guarantee of the bona fides of the informant, by requiring that the name of the alleged murderer, or his residence calling & nationality, or some detail by which he can be identified, should be communicated to the Ambassador. ["Care" – *deleted*] Money should be ["taken to pay" – *deleted*] paid to him only for "travelling expenses", & if half could be paid in Vienna, & the other half in London, that would be the best arrangement.

H.M.

13 Oct88

I enclose a copy of the letter which in accordance with Mr. Matthews' minute I have today sent to F.O.

Send copy to Commr.   GL

14 Oct 1888

Sent to Commr. in note

15 Oct 1888

There then follows a report[4] by Robert Anderson to the Chief Commissioner, Sir Charles Warren, dated 12 October 1888:

<u>Immediate</u>   H.O. A49301/D

1

Sir C. Warren,

After giving this matter my most earnest & careful consideration, I cannot recommend compliance with the inft's. proposal.

The answer I shd. send to Sir A. Paget wd. be to the effect that Govt. cannot authorise compliance with Inft's. terms, unless he gives <u>the name of the murderer</u> with <u>definite details</u> wh. can be tested, or in some other way gives tangible proof of capacity & <u>bona fides</u>.

And if you have misgivings about this, it might be added: 20,000 florins [he asks for 2000] will be paid him for information leading to the criminal's arrest & conviction.

I have arrived at this conclusion not merely from considering the story on its merits – & it seems to be utterly incredible & I infer that the Austrian Police do not regard the Inft as trustworthy – but further, I dread the trouble & mischief wh. such a man, if an impostor, might cause shd. he come to London on the proposed terms.

I have had series of similar proposals, recd. thro the F.O., in cases of political crime, & have occasionally interviewed infts. who made representations of this kind, & yet I have never known one single instance where I have found reason to doubt the wisdom of refusing compliance with their terms.

I may add that I handed the dispatch to Mr. Williamson without giving him the slightest hint at my opinion of the case, & he has expressed a similar opinion in even stronger terms.

R.A.
12:10:88

A Foreign Office letter[5], dated 12 October 1888, from J. Pauncefote, to the Under-Secretary of State is included:

[Stamped: – HOME OFFICE 12 OCT. 88 RECd DEPt.] <u>A49301D</u>

	1
Pressing	Foreign Office
and	October 12.
1888	
<u>Secret</u>	

Sir,

I am directed by the Marquis of Salisbury to transmit to you, herewith, a copy of a Despatch from Her Majesty's Ambassador at Vienna, giving the details of an interview with an individual professing himself able to effect the capture of the perpetrator of the recent Whitechapel Murders.

I am to request that, in laying this Despatch before Mr. Secretary Matthews, you will move him to cause Lord Salisbury to be informed, at his earliest possible convenience, as to what answer should be returned to Sir Augustus Paget.

I am,
Sir,
Your most obedient
humble servant
J. Pauncefote.

The Under Secretary of State
        Home Office

There then follows the lengthy letter[6] of Sir Augustus Paget, Ambassador at Vienna, to the Prime Minister (Lord Salisbury) regarding the informant, dated 10 October 1888:

$$A \; \frac{49301D}{1}$$

[Stamped: – HOME OFFICE 12 OCT. 88 RECd DEPt]

Copy

No. 354   Vienna

Secret   October 10. 1888

My Lord,

I have the honour to inform M.L. that the day before yesterday I received a letter stating that the writer would undertake within fourteen days to deliver up the man who had committed the recent murders of women in London.

Without attaching undue importance to this communicn., I thought that in a case of so much mystery & horror no possible clue was to be neglected, & I therefore requested Mr. Nathan, H.M.'s Consul General to see the writer. At the request of the Cons. Genl. the writer called on him yesterday morning & Mr. Nathan was so much impressed with what he said that he suggested I should see him myself this morning. I have accordingly done so in Mr. Nathan's presence, & I have closely cross questioned him, his answers being given in a perfectly straightforword & ready manner, & with an air of good faith.

In answer to my inquiries he stated that he was born in Poland, his grandfather having been English, as his name (which however he stipulated with me I would keep secret) would appear to indicate, but that he was now an <u>Austrian subject</u> domiciled near Vienna where he has a manufactory of <u>Drugs</u>. He is well dressed & of very respectable appearance. He told us that he is one of the chiefs of the Internationalist Society & has the management of the affairs of that Society in Austria Hungary. Some time ago there was a split in this party with two sections, one of which pursues its object by terror & assassination, the other by less violent methods. He is one of the chiefs of the latter section. He has a colleague in Paris <u>without whom it is impossible for him to act</u>. The rules of the Society are absolute Secrecy, so much so, that the members are frequently not known to one another, and no one can act without the order of his superior or chief.

The man who has committed the murders was formerly a

member of the Society, but he was dismissed in consequence of his having <u>denounced some of the party, who were innocent</u>, as being connected with the <u>Moss affair in New York</u>; in which city, he, the present <u>murderer, murdered his mistress & her child</u>.

I asked him if he knew the murderer personally; he replied that <u>he did</u>, & when I shewed him the portraits published in the Daily Telegraph of Saturday last the 6th October, he said that they <u>did not bear the slightest resemblance to him</u>. I also showed him the facsimiles of letters signed "Jack the Ripper" published in the same paper of the 4th instant. He said he <u>did not believe that the murderer could write</u>; at all events he was quite sure he could not have written these letters, tho. they might have been written by his <u>accomplice (Helper) for accomplice he undoubtedly had</u>. I asked the informer what motive he and his party had for denouncing the murderer. He said to <u>avenge themselves for his having</u> betrayed the party. They wanted to get rid of him once for all.

He then produced a cyphered letter from the <u>head of the party in London</u>. and decyphered it before me by means of a piece of cardboard with holes in it which he placed in different positions over the paper.

The part of the letter referring to this business runs in translation (the original being in German) as follows,

"There is no doubt that No. 49 E(I)? (E the informer said meant <u>Irish</u>) is <u>identical with the murderer and</u> that he has a helper unknown to the party. All orders strictly observed to prevent escape, escape impossible. Highest time (hochste Zeit) to put an end to it."

I asked what the orders referred to meant and by whom they were issued. He replied that they were to prevent the murderer escaping and that <u>he</u> (the informer) <u>and his Paris colleague had given them</u>. "Highest time to act" means that by delay the murderer may possibly escape to France.

The informer then in answer to my enquiry said that in order to effect capture he must go himself to London, <u>taking his Paris colleague with him</u>. If he went he would require a letter of introduction to a Detective, but that the latter would not have to act until the whereabouts of the murderer had been discovered by the associates of the party. He is perfectly certain he says of effecting the capture, but he can only do it by being on the spot with his colleague in Paris. He requires 2000 florins for their <u>journeys and necessary expenses on arriving</u> in London for effecting capture. None of the money except journey expenses Etc would go to him and his colleague. It would <u>belong to the Society</u>. He is ready to give written engagement to refund <u>the money should capture not be accomplished</u>, but this of course must be taken for <u>what it is worth</u>.

I reminded him that a large reward had been offered. Why, I asked, could he not direct his party in London to deliver up the culprit without he and his Paris colleague going over. He said the rules of the Society were such that it was impossible for action to be taken without presence of the two chiefs. He could not <u>even divulge to me his name without his colleague's sanction</u>.

I have caused Mr. Nathan to make enquiries of the police here respecting the informer, & they say that they know him to be a socialist, that he denounced a plot to assassinate the Emperor <u>in 1883</u> but that the attempt was <u>not made</u>, & they <u>therefore have not much trust in him</u>.

On the other hand he has shewn me a certificate from the Magistrate of the district in which he resided in Galicia attesting to his good character & speaking of him as a well conducted & industrious citizen who had done much good in his neighbourhood.

It is of course possible that the whole story may be a trumped up one from beginning to end, but I am bound to say that it <u>does not give me that impression</u> & that I am <u>inclined to place some trust in it</u>. The man's manner, his appearance, the readiness with which he replied to all my enquiries tended to give me this impression, though of course I may be mistaken.

I must say that at first I was inclined to be extremely sceptical on account of his not being willing to act without himself going over, but having already heard something of the workings of these secret societies & listening to what he now said, it has occurred to me as quite possible that he may be unable to act from here & without the cooperation of his colleague.

I told him that all I could do would be to report the circumstances to London & request instructions. He is anxious for an answer as soon as possible in order, if he is to go to London, that the murderer may not have time to escape before he arrives, as the accomplishment of his task would then become much more difficult. He lays the greatest stress on gaining time, & I have promised him a reply by Friday evening or Saturday morning next by which time I hope to be furnished with Y L's instructions by telegraph. Should I be desired to send him, I beg to be informed to whom I am to give a letter in London, & on whom I am to draw for the money (2000 florins) without which he will not go.

YH&c

(Signed) <u>A Paget</u>.

Copy Sir A Paget No. 314 Oct 10./88 <u>Whitechapel Murders</u> H.O.

The next file cover[7], dated 16 October 1888, is as follows:

[Stamped: – HOME OFFICE 16 OCT. 88 RECd DEPt] No. A49301 D

2

DATE 16 Oct 1888   Foreign Office
REFERENCES &c.   Whitechapel Murders

Forwards substance of telegram from H.M. Ambassador at Vienna from which it appears that the Informer has been advanced the 2000 Florins & is to present a letter to Sir C Warren when he has found the murderer – He stipulated that neither he himself nor his associates are to be ["watched" – *deleted*] interfered with by police

MINUTES.

<u>Secret & Urgent</u>

Copy to Commr. of Police & to S. S.

CM

Oct 16. 88

Wrote Commr: enclosing copy.
Oct 16. 88

Not much new in this except the allegation that the man was a butcher. When you come to town I would wish to speak to you as to the source from which the Ambassador is to be reimbursed

Any denunciation by this man must be most carefully sifted.

GL

16 Oct 1888

H.M.

17 Oct./88

Letter to Commr to the above effect 18 Oct 1888

There then follows a letter[8] dated 16 October 1888 from P.W Currie to the Under-Secretary of State:

[Stamped: – HOME OFFICE 16 OCT. 88 RECd DEPt] A49301D

2   Foreign Office

16 October 1888

Secret and
pressing
Sir,
    With reference to your letter of the 14th instant, I am directed by
the Marquis of Salisbury to transmit to you herewith, to be laid before
the Secretary of State for the Home Department, the substance of a
telegram received from Her Majesty's Ambassador at Vienna respecting the Whitechapel murders.

I am, Sir,

Your most obedient

humble servant

PW Currie

The Under Secretary of State
    Home Office

The next file cover[9] is dated 5 November 1888:

[Stamped: – HOME OFFICE 5 NOV. 88 RECd DEPt] No. A49301D

3

DATE 5 Nov 1888   Foreign Office
REFERENCES, &c.   <u>Whitechapel Murders</u> Vienna Informant
Memorandum left by Mr Phipps with SofS. giving certain particulars respecting the Informant who is about to return to London –
also gives name & description of Supposed Murderer – Sir A Paget is
convinced the man is acting in good faith

MINUTES.

Secret – See memo in file

seen CW 6.11.88

Mr Lushington to see – & Lay By. CM

Nov 8/88.

There is a letter[10] from the Ambassador at Vienna dated October
15 1888:

[Stamped: – HOME OFFICE 16 OCT.88 RECd DEPT] A49301D

2

Vienna October 15. 1888
Secret
Have seen informant who does not know murderer's residence but
states he was employed formerly in San Francisco as a <u>butcher</u>. A
further letter has been received about him saying he is being
<u>watched by two of the smartest men</u> in the Society. He is confident
that he will be able to inform the Police of murderer's whereabouts
within 24 hours after he arrives in London. Informant cannot go
without having 2000 florins, or act without being himself in London
in company with his superior, the head man from Paris. I believe in
his <u>bona fides</u> so much that I <u>advance the money on my personal
responsibility</u>, while telling him that on the arrest of the culprit and
proof of his crime, he, informant can claim offered reward out of
which must be deducted the 2000 florins for repayment to me. I
mention his name in a letter which I give him to Sir Charles
Warren, but he will not present it until he appears to <u>denounce
criminal and get necessary aid from police</u>. He has stipulated that his
name is never to be divulged or the Society will not effect arrest. He
departs this day and he stipulates in addition that neither himself nor
those of the Society at present watching criminal are in any way <u>to
be interfered with by police</u>, which has been promised by me.

It is my opinion that he should be permitted to work unwatched
even by the detectives.

There is a report[11] from the Foreign Office, dated 5 November
1888, to the Under-Secretary of State:

A49301D
3

Secret and   Foreign Office
  Pressing   November 5, 1888
    Sir,
With reference to my letter of the 16th ultimo, I am directed by
the Marquess of Salisbury to transmit to you herewith the substance
of a further telegram from Her Majesty's Ambassador at Vienna
giving details respecting the identity of the supposed perpetrator of
the Whitechapel murders.
[*There is a marginal note to the above* —   "<u>Sir A. Paget</u> Tel. Secret
already sent (through Mr Phipps)"]   I am, Sir,
                                              your most obedient
                                                 humble servant

The Under Secretary of State   J.Pauncefote
     Home Office

There is then a copy of Sir A. Paget's letter[12] to Sir Charles Warren, dated November 4 1888:

A49301 D

3

Copy   Mr Phipps delivered this memorandum personally to Mr. Matthews, who authorised him to telegraph to Sir A Paget guaranteeing the expenses of Jonas' journey to London (if he. be without means of his own). Mr. Phipps also stated that he wd. remain in town to meet Jonas & to take him to Sir C. Warren

ELP. 5 Nov. 88

[Stamped: – HOME OFFICE 5 NOV.88 RECd DEPt]
Secret   From Sir A. Paget.   Vienna.   Nov 4/88
Mr. Phipps stated
that he had given
Sir C. Warren a copy of
this. ELP.   Following for Sir C. Warren and Mr Phipps. –
Have just seen informant, [*Here there is a marginal note*: – "The informant's name is Jonas ELP"] who returned here on Friday evening, but was unwell yesterday. His object in returning to Vienna is to procure further funds, but from his friends and not from myself; when he has this money, he purposes starting once more for London on Tuesday or Wednesday, and is convinced he will catch murderer. Mr. Phipps's letter was only received by him to-day, which is proved by the Vienna postmark. He asserts that about October 25 he sent to Sir C. Warren's Secretary the name and complete details respecting the criminal by means of a registered letter from Paris. The particulars are following: – the name of the man when in San Francisco, was Johann Stammer, when in London, John Kelly, of medium height, with broad shoulders, aged between 35 and 38 years, strongly marked features and extremely brilliant large white teeth; has a scar due to a stab beneath the left eye; walks like a sailor, having been a ship's cook for 3 years; is thought to be at Liverpool; but news is expected to-day by informant. If this news comes I will communicate by telegraph again. Personally, I am more than ever convinced that informant is acting in good faith. The criminal has written to my informant's superior, declaring that he will kill both of them because he is aware they are pursuing him.

There is a file cover[13] dated 7 November 1888:

[Stamped: – HOME OFFICE 8 NOV.88 RECd DEPt] No. A49301 D
                                                              4
DATE 7th Nov 88   Foreign Office
REFERENCES, &c.   Whitechapel Murder. Vienna Informant.
Requests instructions how to reply to Sir. A. Paget as the Informant
required £100 before he comes to England
                              MINUTES.
                          Pressing & Secret
?To Commr of Police for observations – in first instance. In another
record: about this man [*here there is a marginal note*: – "See /3"] it is
said that he sent from Paris to the Commr. the name & description
of the man he accuses of these murders ?Ask Commr:
    at same time whether he has been able to make any use of the
particulars, & whether he attached any importance to them CM.
Nov 8/88.   GL
Wrote 7. Nov. 88.   8 Nov 1888

There is a letter[14] attached, dated 27 December 1888, from Scotland Yard to G. R. Moran:

                                        4 Whitehall Place,
                                              S.W.
                                        27 December, 1888.
Dear Moran,
    I return the Confidential papers which you were good enough to
lend yesterday for Mr. Monro.
                                        Yours truly
                                        M.M. [*signature illeg.*]
G.R. Moran,Esqre.

There is a Home Office note[15], apparently in Ruggles-Brise's hand,
dated 26 December 1888:

A 49301D.
  1 to 4
All F.O. letters given to mr. Kendall p/p Mr. Monro [*illeg.*] &
return
  26/12/88

There is a Foreign Office letter[16], dated 7 November 1888, to the Under-Secretary of State:

[Stamped: – HOME OFFICE 8 NOV.88 RECd DEPt]   A49301 D

4

Foreign Office.

Secret &   November 7. 1888.
Immediate.
Sir,

With reference to my letter of the 5th instant in regard to the Whitechapel Murderer, I am directed by the Marquis of Salisbury to state to you that Her Majesty's Ambassador at Vienna has reported by telegraph that the informant is unable to obtain money there and requires £100 to enable him to come to England. Sir A. Paget desires to know whether he is authorized to advance the money.

I am to request that in laying this letter before Mr. Secretary Matthews you will move him to cause Lord Salisbury to be informed what reply should be returned to His Excellency.

I am, Sir,

Your most obedient
humble servant.

In the absence of)
the Under Secretary) Charles B. Robertson.
(Actg. Head of Dept.)
The Under Secretary of State
Home Office

The next file cover[17] is dated 2 January 1889:

[Stamped: – HOME OFFICE 3 JAN.89 RECd DEPt] No. A49301

4a

DATE 2 Jany 89   The Commr. of Police
REFERENCES, &c.   Whitechapel Murders
The Vienna Informer

Reports as to Sir A Paget's Telegram as to other information as to dynamite outrages in contemplation, and suggests that no further money be spent on the man as he attaches no importance to his statement.

[MINUTES.]
Confidential and Pressing

Tele F.O. of his opinion of Mr Monro. and express concurrence in this reco.

C.M.

Jan 3. 89

wrote 4.1.89   GL

3 Jan 1889

There is a letter[18] from the Chief Commissioner of Police, James Monro, to the Under-Secretary of State, dated 2 January 1889:

[Stamped: – HOME OFFICE 3 JAN.89 RECd DEPt] A49301D.
<u>Confidential</u>   7

4 Whitehall Place S.W.

2 Jany. 1889.

Sir,

    With reference to Sir A. Paget's telegram of the 29th inst. [*here there is a marginal note* – "copy enclosed"] giving particulars of further information offered by his informant who recently undertook to discover the Whitechapel Murderer. I have to acquaint you for the information of the Secretary of State, that I attach no importance to this persons statement, and I do not recommend any further expenditure upon him.

I am, Sir,

Your most obedient Servant,

J. Monro

The Under
    Secretary of State
    &c &c &c

There then follows the message[19] from Sir A. Paget:

[Stamped: – HOME OFFICE 3 JAN.89 RECd DEPt] A49301D
<u>Copy</u>   5
Decypher from Sir A. Paget Vienna
D. 29
P.. – night Dec –
    Following for Mr. Nathan Hms Consul 24 Queens Gate Gardens from Acting Consul Vienna –
    Informer states that there are at present in Brussels from 15 to 20 terrorists, mostly leaders, who may be shortly expected in

London. One was here on Monday on his way to St Petersburgh. He is a chemist & prepares explosives &c. He returns soon to London but whether by Vienna informer is ignorant. This man is acquainted with Kelly & can identify him. Informer does not know where these Terrorists will live in London, but if on the spot could soon discover. He will furnish some names in writing tomorrow He says that a large number of dynamite outrages are contemplated in London but details can only be given personally to authorities.

He is ready to come to London for 1500 florins & remain there until favourable results respecting murder of which he is certain. He pressed for decision saying no time is to be lost.

There is a further file cover[20], dated 26 February 1889:

[Stamped: – HOME OFFICE 28 FEB.89 RECd DEPt] No. A49301D

4b

DATE 26 Feby 1889   HM Secretary to the Embassy at Vienna
REFERENCES, &c.   <u>Vienna Informer</u>
Suggests repayment of the advance of £165, made to this man, to Sir Augustus Paget.

MINUTES.
<u>Confidential</u>

Mr Lushington/.
Ask Treasury explaining case.
GL
1 March '89

(Wrote 20.3.89)

Letter withdrawn & Receiver written to pay from Police Fund. Concur
informed.
See Mr L.s minute 26/3.89

There is a letter[21], dated 26 February 1889, from the British Embassy at Vienna to Godfrey Lushington:

<u>A49301D</u>

4

British Embassy

[Stamped: – HOME OFFICE 28 FEB.89 RECd DEPt]   Vienna

26 Feb /89

My dear Mr Lushington,

You will perhaps remember that I called on you at the Home

Office, when I was in London, about the Viennese "Informant" regarding the Whitechapel murders.

I notice that in your letter to the FO of 4th January you state that no "further" expenditure is to be incurred in his regard.

You will remember that the amount which the man Jonas received was advanced by Sir Augustus Paget.

Now Sir Augustus has compunction in making an official application for repayment, but both Mr Matthews & yourself and Sir C Warren spoke as I remember so distinctly in the sense of the repayment having to be made to Sir A Paget of the advance he was compelled to make that perhaps you would kindly take the initiative in causing the necessary instructions to be given.

The amount was 2000 florins or 165£

> Yours truly.
> EMPhipps
> to the Secretary
> of Embassy

There is a note[22] from Lushington dated 25 March 1889:

I have seen Mr. Mowatt on this.

He says the Treasury would decline to pay this Bill, but that it is inexpedient for a letter to be written stating the reasons.

I have always been of opinion that this would have to be paid out of Met. Pol Funds,

So Pay accordingly

Inform Ruling   GL
Withdraw our letter to Treasury   25 March '89

There is then a lengthy letter[23] from Lushington to The Secretary of the Treasury, dated 20 March 1889:

Confidential	Home Office
A49301 D	Whitehall S.W.
4b	20th March 1889

Sir,

I am directed by the Secretary of State to acquaint you for the information of the Lords Commissioners of Her Majesty's Treasury that in October last he received a Despatch through the Foreign Office from H.M. Ambassador at Vienna to the effect that a man named Jonas had presented himself to his Excellency & had announced his ability to lay his hand on the Whitechapel Murderer, and his willingness to come to England for that purpose on the receipt of £165 (2,000 florins)

Acting on the recommendation of the then Commissioner of Metropolitan Police and influenced also by Sir A. Paget's strong belief in the bona fides of the informant, the Secretary of State expressed to the Foreign Office the opinion that it should be left to his Excellency's discretion as to whether the man's terms should be agreed to.

The sum demanded was paid; and Jonas appears to have proceeded to Paris for the purpose, as he explained, of connecting with and obtaining the indispensable cooperation of a colleague in the International Society, of which they and the alleged murderer were alike members. He presently returned to Vienna: but declined to proceed to London with a view to carrying out what he had undertaken unless a further sum of £100 was given to him.

Hereupon Mr. Matthews again consulted the Commissioner of Police and on his recommendation wrote to the Foreign Office explaining his opinion that no more money should be spent on Jonas, whose alleged information he regarded as of no importance.

The negotiations were accordingly discontinued.

The Secretary of State would be glad if you would move the Lords Commissioners of the Treasury to sanction the repayment of the £165 already expended by Sir A. Paget.

> I am,
> Sir,
> Your obedient servant,
> Godfrey Lushington

CHAPTER 17

15 October 1888 – A Dead Letter

During this period many leads were brought to the notice of the police for investigation before it became clear that they were false. The following example is typical and is interesting in that it proposes yet another suspect. The file cover[1] reads:

[Stamped:- HOME OFFICE 17 OCT.88 RECd DEPt]No. A49301C/12
DATE 15 Oct 88   General Post Office
REFERENCES, &c.   Whitechapel Murders
                   Hand letter to Mr Lushington from dead letter
                   office implicating a certain person –
[*Here there is a marginal note* – "Letter sent to Sir C Warren"]
                   MINUTES.
   See Mr Lushington's memo within and Secretary of State's decision.
                   Warrant to Postmaster General
                   15th Oct. 1888

There then follows a letter[2], dated 15 October 1888, from Godfrey Lushington to the Home Secretary Henry Matthews

   [Headed paper: – SECRETARY OF STATE HOME DEPARTMENT]
A49301C/12   [Stamped: – HOME OFFICE 17 OCT.88 RECd. DEPt.]
Mr Matthews,
   This refers to a letter brought here today by the P.O. authorities. The envelope was addressed to Jane Somebody (I forget the name), the address was imperfect as she could not be found there, the ["letter" – *deleted*] envelope was placed in the P.O. The letter inside must have put there [*sic*] by mistake. It was a letter from a gentleman in Eaton Place to his son, apparently an officer in the army, in which the writer says he

cannot help suspecting General Brown is the Whitechapel murderer.

Probably there is nothing in it, but I sent it on to the Commr.. but the P.O. would not let me do this unless I undertook to get a formal Warrant from you.

GL

15 Oct 1888

Mr. Stuart Wortley is here

There then follows a note to the letter by Henry Matthews:

I have some little doubt as to the propriety of this order I presume the letter will be dealt with in the usual manner by the Dead Letter office.

H.M.

16 Oct. /88

There is then enclosed a copy of the letter[3] to Sir Charles Warren:

Copy
Confidential   15. October 1888
Sir C. Warren,

The enclosed letter came this morning from the Post Office. You will see that the envelope contains an enclosure that was never intended to be put into it, and it is the first few lines of the letter so enclosed that relate to the Whitechapel murder. As soon as you have done with it, please return it to me, that I may send it back to the Post Office who have only given it up on a warrant from the S.of S.

G. Lushington

15. Oct. 88.
[*Here there is a note in the right margin* – "Putup CM"]

There is a Home Office memo slip[4] included:

To the REGISTRY HOME OFFICE.
From
Mr. Murdoch
 Send Jane Bromley's
Letter back to P.O.
  GL
   19 Oct 1888

Mr Moran. [*G. Moran was the Home Office superintendent of registry 1876–98*]

What was the
Date of H.O. warrant?
CM
15th [*illegible*]

This is followed by a letter[5] from Sir Charles Warren dated 17 October 1888:

17.10.88

Confidential,
            Mr. Lushington.
I return the letters from Post Office.

We have made due enquiries about General Brown & he has been seen.

It seems that he has operated on horses for "racing" and this has alarmed & horrified the lady who witnessed it, and she jumped to the conclusion that he would not shirk at anything.
            CWarren.

The final memo[6] in this small file reads:

Better send
explanatory note
with this result
H.O. has got
the letter.
Can you also
ask Mr Boultbee
whether Sir C.W. has
done with it as
we ought to return to PO
            CM.

There would seem to have been many communications made directly with the Home Office as well as the police. Another example from the Home Office letters file is the following copy letter[7] regarding Mr John Lock who had been detained by the police, as we have seen:

[A4]9301/77   Pressing

19 October 1888

asking for report and observations
     a letter from Mr. John Lock as to his having been arrested in
London on suspicion of being the perpetrator of the Whitechapel
murders.

Godfrey Lushington

Commissioner
Metropolitan Police.
&c. &c. &c.

CHAPTER 18

9 November 1888 – Murder of Mary Jane Kelly

The murder of Mary Jane Kelly occurred on the morning of Friday, 9 November 1888, and is the last of what have become known as "the canonical five" Ripper murders. Again, her acceptance as a recognized "Ripper" victim is contentious. Nonetheless, most students of the crimes believe her to have been the final victim of "Jack the Ripper".

The police reports on this murder are by no means extensive, but they are supplemented by the material anonymously returned to New Scotland Yard in 1987[1] and the Kelly inquest papers held in the London Metropolitan Archives.

The Home Office File cover page[2] dated 9 November 1888 states:

Commissioner of Police. Reports that information has just been received that a mutilated dead body of a woman is reported to have been found this morning inside a room in a house (No. 26) in Dorset St., Spitalfields.

The matter has been placed in Mr. Andersons hands.

Pressing.

MINUTES

I have asked Commissioner by telephone to inform H.O. as soon as possible of any further information which may reach him in the case.

C.W. Nov 9. 88.

f. 2 states:

Sir Charles Warren
            to Mr Lushington
Mutilated dead body of woman reported to be found this morning inside room of house in Dorset Street Spitalfields
Information just received
(12.30) 9.11.88.

ff. 4–5 is a letter from Charles Warren to the Under Secretary of State, Home Office:

> 4 Whitehall Place,
> S.W.
> 9th November, 1888

Sir,

I have to acquaint you, for the information of the Secretary of State, that information has just been received that a <u>mutilated</u> dead body of a woman is reported to have been found this morning inside a room in a house (No.26) in Dorset Street, Spitalfields.

The matter has been placed in the hands of Mr. Anderson, Assistant Commissioner. –

> I am,
> Sir,
> Your Most Obedient Servant,
> Cwarren

There is in the file, a photograph of the mutilated body lying on a bed, captioned: *Marie Jeannette Kelly Murdered on 9th November. 1888.*

There is a Home Office letter as follows[3]:

> Home Office,
> Whitehall,
> S.W.
> 9 November
> 88

Dear Mr Wortley,

Troup has only just been found – after you went.

Anderson says through the telephone that the murder was committed at Spitalfields which is in the Metropolitan Police District. It is believed that the murdered woman is a prostitute named Kelly. The Police Surgeon was when Anderson spoke still examining the body.

> Yours very truly
> E.S. Johnson

It is interesting to see that included with the official Home Office files on the Kelly murder is a lengthy report[4] cut from the *Daily Telegraph* of Saturday, 10 November 1888. This early press report

of the murder is a fascinating account of the effects of this killing –
which, in the event, was the apparent climax of the series of
murders suspected to have been committed by the same killer.

THE EAST END TRAGEDIES.
A SEVENTH MURDER.
ANOTHER CASE OF HORRIBLE
MUTILATION.

Yesterday a seventh murder, the most horrible of the series of
atrocities attributed to the same hand, was committed in Whitechapel. As in all the previous instances, the victim was a woman of
immoral character and humble circumstances, but she was not
murdered in the open street, her throat having been cut and the
subsequent mutilations having taken place in a room which the
deceased rented at No. 26, Dorset-street. She has been identified as
Mary Jane Kelly, and is believed to be the wife of a man from whom
she is separated, and the daughter, it is said, of a foreman employed
at an iron foundry in Carnarvon, in Wales. The unfortunate woman
was twenty-four years of age, tall, slim, fair, of fresh complexion,
and of attractive appearance. The room, which she occupied at a
weekly rental of 4s, was on the ground floor of a three-storeyed
house in Dorset-street, which is a short thoroughfare leading off
Commercial-street, and in the shadow of Spitalfields Church and
Market. Kelly was last seen alive on Thursday night; but as late as
one a.m. yesterday morning she was heard by some lodgers in the
house singing "Sweet Violets." [sic] No other noise appears to have
been distinguished, and it was not suspected that she was at that
time accompanied by a man. Entrance to her apartment was
obtained by means of an arched passage, opposite a large lodging-house, and between Nos. 26 and 28, Dorset-street, ending in a
cul-de-sac known as Miller's-court. In this court there are six houses
let out in tenements, chiefly to women, the rooms being numbered.
On the right-hand side of the passage there are two doors. The first
of these leads to the upper floors of the house in which Kelly was
living. It has seven rooms, the first-floor front, facing Dorset-street,
being over a shed or warehouse used for the storage of costers'
barrows. A second door opens inwards, direct from the passage,
into Kelly's apartment, which is about 15 ft square, and is placed at
the rear corner of the building. It has two windows, one small,
looking into a yard, which is fitted with a pump. The opposite side
of the yard is formed by the side wall of houses, which have

whitewashed frontages, and are provided with green shutters. From some of these premises, on the left-hand side of the court, it is possible to secure a view, in a diagonal direction, of the larger window, and also the doorway belonging to the room tenanted by the deceased. In this room there was a bed placed behind the door, and parallel with the window. The rest of the furniture consisted of a table and two chairs.

It was at a quarter to eleven o'clock yesterday morning that the discovery of the latest tragedy was made. The rents of the tenements in Miller's-court are collected by John McCarthy, the keeper of a provision and chandler's shop, which is situated on the left-hand side of the entrance to the court in Dorset-street. McCarthy instructed his man, John Bowyer, a pensioned soldier, to call for the money due, the deceased woman having been 29s in arrear. Accordingly Bowyer knocked at the door of Kelly's room, but received no answer. Having failed to open the door, he passed round the angle of the house and pulled the blind of the window, one of the panes being broken. Then he noticed blood upon the glass, and it immediately occurred to him that another murder had been committed. He fetched M'Carthy, who, looking through the window, saw upon the bed, which was against the wall, the body of a woman, without clothing, and terribly mutilated. The police at Commercial-street and at Leman-street, both stations being within five minutes' walk, were instantly informed, and in response to the summons Inspector Beck arrived. This officer despatched a message for Inspector Abberline and Inspector Reid, both of the Detective department. Nothing, however, was done until the arrival of Mr. T. Arnold, the Superintendent of the H Division of Metropolitan Police, who, shortly after eleven o'clock, gave orders for the door of the room to be broken open. The last person to have left the place must have closed the door behind him, taking with him the key from the spring lock, as it is missing. A most horrifying spectacle was presented to the officers' gaze, exceeding in ghastliness anything which the imagination can picture. The body of the woman was stretched on the bed, fearfully mutilated. Nose and ears had been cut off, and, although there had been no dismemberment, the flesh had been stripped off, leaving the skeleton. The nature of the other injuries was of a character to indicate that they had been perpetrated by the author of the antecedent crimes in the same district; and it is believed that once more there are portions of the organs missing. That the miscreant must have been some time at his work was shown by the deliberate manner in which he had excised parts, and placed them upon the table purposely to add to the horror of the scene. Intelligence was promptly conveyed to Scotland-yard, and personally to Sir Charles Warren. Meanwhile the street was as far as possible closed to traffic, a cordon of constables being drawn across each end, and the police took possession of Miller's-court, refusing access to all comers in the expectation that bloodhounds would be used. Acting upon orders, the detectives and inspectors declined to furnish any information of what had occurred, and refused permission to the press to inspect the place. Every precaution was taken to preserve any trace of evidence which might be existing. Mr. Phillips, the divisional surgeon, was called, and he shortly afterwards received the assistance of other experts, among them being Dr. Bond, who came from Westminster in obedience to special instructions, and Dr. Gordon Browne, the City Police surgeon, who conducted the post-mortem in the case of the Mitre-square murder. Dr. J.R. Gabe, who viewed the body, said he had seen a great deal in dissecting rooms, but he had never witnessed such a horrible sight as the murdered woman presented. Before anything was disturbed a photograph was taken of the interior of the room. There was comparatively little blood, death having been due to the severing of the throat, the mutilations having been subsequently performed. It was evident that a large and keen knife had been used by a hand possessed of some knowledge and practice. That the woman had had no struggle with her betrayer was shown by her position and the way in which her garments, including a velvet bodice, were arranged by the fireplace. The medical men were engaged until past four p.m. in their examination upon the spot, the police, having satisfied themselves that no weapon had been left, reserving a complete investigation of the contents of the room for a later opportunity. Mr. Anderson, the recently-appointed Assistant-Commissioner, had driven up in a cab at ten minutes to two o'clock, and he remained for some time. Detectives searched all the adjacent houses for suspicious characters, but without result. All the inmates were able satisfactorily to account for their whereabouts. Not one of them had heard any sound to point to the hour when the woman must have been attacked by her assailant. The walls are of thin match lining, which makes this circumstance the more unaccountable, and the couple in the room overhead had slept soundly without being awakened by scuffling in the room beneath them. [*sic*]

DESCRIPTION

of

Name _Annie Chapman_

*

Alias _Mrs. Siffey_

Born at _____

Age _45_

Profession or Calling _Prostitute_

Wanted for _____

* * _____

Height _5 feet_

Build _____

Hair _(wavy) dark brown_

Eyebrows _____

Forehead _____

Eyes _blue_

Nose _thick nose_

Mouth _two teeth deficient in lower jaw_

Chin _____

Face _____

Complexion _fair_

Beard _____

Moustache _____

Marks or Peculiarities _On person portion of an envelope stamped Sussex Regiment dated 23rd Aug 1888._

Dress _Black skirt & jacket, striped petticoat crape bonnet_

Where likely to be found,) _____
known, or heard of)

Nora.

¹ Yard, London,

day of _____ 18

* If a Married Woman, give also Maiden Name

against the fence on the side
near N° 29 Hanbury Street.
but he did not take any notice
5.30 a.m. 8 Sep. Mrs. Long of 32 Church
Street stated that she saw a
man and woman talking near
to N° 29 Hanbury Street. She
heard the man say "Will you"
and the woman replied "Yes"
and passed on. She only
saw his back, and would
be unable to know him again.
She describes him as ap-
parently over 40 years of age.
She did not see his face.
He appeared to be a little
taller than the woman and
in her opinion looked like
a foreigner. She thinks
he has a dark coat on,
but she could not recognise
him again The woman she
positively

Detail from the police descriptive form in relation to the murder of Annie Chapman.

Detail from the police report on the murder of Annie Chapman showing the first description of a suspect for the murders as given by the witness Mrs Elizabeth Long.

A contemporary sketch of the shed used as a mortuary for the Whitechapel district. The utterly inadequate and inappropriate premises – next to a playground – were criticized by the coroner Wynne Baxter.

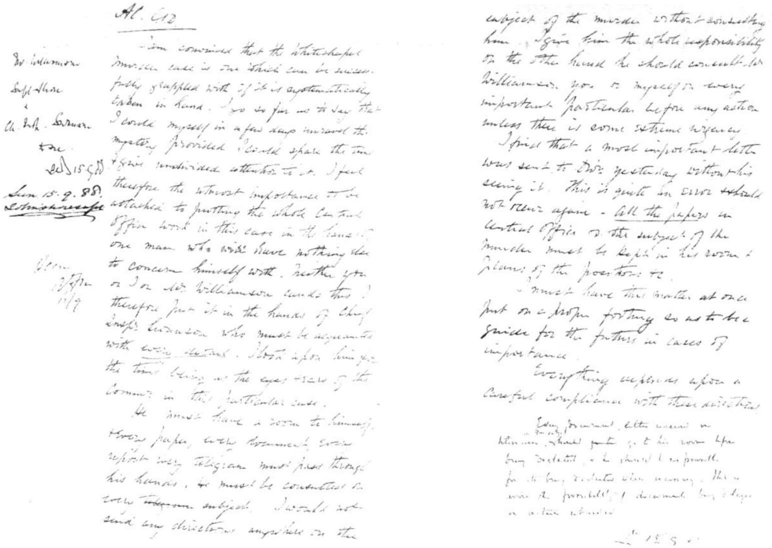

I am convinced that the Whitechapel murder case is one which can be successfully grappled with if it is systematically taken in hand. I go so far as to say that I could myself in a few days unravel the mystery provided I could spare the time & give undivided attention to it. I feel therefore the utmost importance to be attached to putting the whole Central Office work in this case in the hands of one man who will have nothing else to concern himself with. Neither you or I or Mr Williamson can do this. I therefore put it in the hands of Chief Insp. Swanson who must be acquainted with every detail. I look upon him for the time being as the eyes & ears of the Commr in this particular case.

He must have a room to himself, & every paper, every document, every report every telegram must pass through his hands. He must be consulted on every subject. I would not send any directions anywhere on the subject of the murder without consulting him. I give him the whole responsibility. On the other hand he should consult Mr Williamson, you or myself on every important particular before any action unless there is some extreme urgency.

I find that a most important letter was sent to Div. yesterday without his seeing it. This is quite an error & should not occur again. All the papers in Central Office on the subject of the murder must be kept in his room & plans of the position &c.

I must have this matter at once put on a proper footing so as to be a guide for the future in cases of importance.

Everything depends upon a careful compliance with these directions.

Internal police memo of 15 September 1888, from the Commissioner instructing Swanson to take full overall charge of police enquiries into the Whitechapel murders.

A contemporary sketch showing the entrance to Dutfield's Yard and the front of the International Working Men's Educational Society Club in Berner Street, scene of the murder of Elizabeth Stride on 30 September 1888.

Mortuary photograph of Elizabeth Stride.

Above PC 452H William Smith, witness at the Stride inquest who described a possible sighting of Elizabeth Stride with her killer.

Right Louis Diemschutz, witness at the Stride inquest, who discovered the body.

Left Morris Eagle, witness at the Stride inquest, who discovered the body.

Below A contemporary sketch of coroner Wynne Baxter presiding over the Stride inquest.

Dr George Bagster Phillips, police surgeon for H Division, sketched at Stride's inquest.

Matthew Packer, fruiterer living at 44 Berner Street, who sensationally claimed to have sold grapes to the suspected murderer of Elizabeth Stride on the night of her murder.

A contemporary sketch showing the crowd gathering outside the mortuary in St-George's-in-the-East, where the body of Elizabeth Stride lay.

Dr William P Blackwell also gave evidence at the Stride inquest.

Detective Sergeant Steven White of H (Whitechapel) Division, who interviewed the witness Matthew Parker.

An inquest sketch showing the position of the body of Catherine Eddowes in the southern corner of Mitre Square, Aldgate. Her murder occurred on 30 September 1888 – on the same day as the murder of Elizabeth Stride.

An inquest sketch by city surveyor Frederick William Foster of the body of Catherine Eddowes, showing details of extensive mutilation.

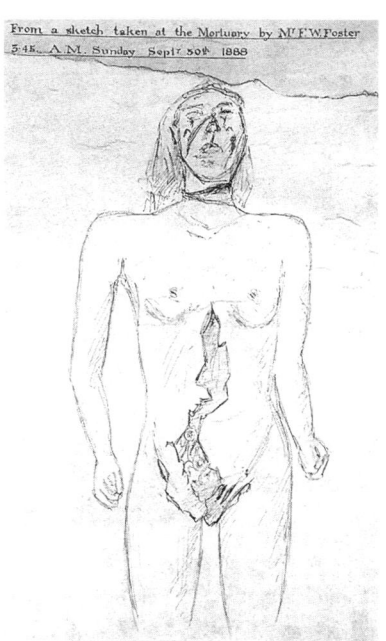

Another sketch by Frederick William Foster made at the mortuary prior to the autopsy.

Mortuary photograph of Catherine Eddowes made before the autopsy.

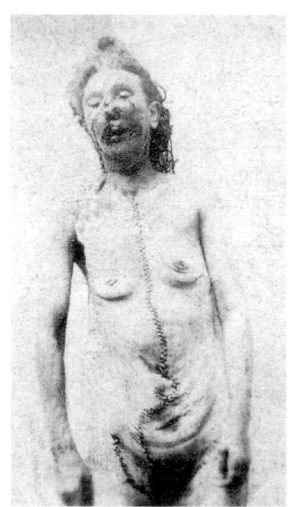

Another mortuary photograph of the body of Catherine Eddowes, propped against a wall, showing postmortem stitching.

THE POLICE CLEARING MITRE SQUARE

X THE CORNER

A contemporary sketch showing the police clearing the curious crowds that had gathered in Mitre Square after the removal of Catherine Eddowes' body.

A contemporary sketch of
Dr Frederick Gordon Brown,
the City of London police
surgeon, who carried out
the autopsy on Catherine
Eddowes and later examined
the piece of kidney sent to
Mr Lusk of the Whitechapel
Vigilance Committee.

A contemporary sketch of
John Kelly, common-law
husband of Catherine
Eddowes.

A contemporary sketch of
PC881 Edward Watkins of
the City of London police,
who found the body in
Mitre Square at 1.45 am.

A sketch from the *Pictorial News* showing the
coroner's inquest into the murder of Catherine
Eddowes.

A police copy of the 'Jewes' message originally written in
chalk on the entrance doorway brickwork to numbers
108–119 Wentworth Model Dwellings, Goulston Street. It
was below this message that a piece of bloodstained apron
was found which was later proved to have come from the
apron worn by Eddowes.

The Juwes are
The men That
Will not
Be Blamed
for nothing

THE CENTRAL NEWS LIMITED

5 New Bridge Street.

London 29 Sep 1888

E.C.

The Editor presents
his compliments to
Mr Williamson &
begs to inform him
the Enclosed was sent
the Central News two
days ago, & was treated
as a joke

The letter written by Tom Bulling of the Central News Agency to Chief Constable F A Williamson, enclosing the famous 'Dear Boss' letter.

25th Sept. 1888.
London E C
See 20th + 21 + 3
Anonyt. Letters

The Boss
Central News.
Office
London City.

The envelope in which the 'Dear Boss' letter was delivered to the Central News Agency. Postmarked – 27 September 1888.

·25. Sept. 1888.

Dear Boss.

    I keep on hearing the police have caught me but they wont fix me just yet. I have laughed when they look so clever and talk about being on the right track. That joke about Leather apron gave me real fits. I am down on whores and I shant quit ripping them till I do get buckled. Grand work the last job was. I gave the lady no time to squeal. How can they catch me now. I love my work and want to start again. you will soon hear of me with my funny little games. I saved some of the proper red stuff in a ginger beer bottle over the last job to write with but it went thick like glue and I cant use it. Red ink is fit enough I hope ha. ha. The next job I do I shall clip the ladys ears off and send to the

The actual "Dear Boss" letter, dated 25 September 1888 and purporting to have come from the killer "Jack the Ripper".

police officers just for jolly wouldnt you. Keep this letter back till I do a bit more work, then give it out straight. My knife's so nice and sharp I want to get to work right away if I get a chance. Good luck.

      yours truly
        Jack the Ripper

Dont mind me giving the trade name

wasnt good enough to post this before I got all the red ink off my hands curse it No luck yet. They say I'm a doctor now. ha ha

George Lusk, chairman of the Whitechapel Vigilance Committee, a local builder who received the lusk letter and parcel through the post on 16 October 1888.

The famous Lusk letter, received in a parcel which also contained a piece of human kidney.

Two press sketches of the supposed murderer as described by Matthew Packer. Published in most contemporary newspapers including the *Daily Telegraph* on 6 October 1888, they led to the detention of a suspect, John Langan, in Boulogne, France.

A typical street scene of the time showing women outside a common lodging house in Flower and Dean Street, Spitalfields.

A contemporary sketch of a Ripper suspect being taken into Leman Street police station.

A contemporary sketch of an attempt to identify the suspect in
Leman Street police station.

A contemporary sketch from the *Illustrated London News* with the following legend:
"Arrested on suspicion in Whitechapel. The inevitable dog inconsolable at the retirement of
its owner."

A famous contemporary sketch from the *Illustrated London News* showing Vigilance Committee members watching a suspect in the East End.

Even at the height of the murders homeless women were forced to sleep on the streets.

A contemporary sketch of homeless women taken from the *Illustrated London News* in October 1888: "Outcasts sleeping in sheds in Whitechapel".

Disturbances in the street were common. Here, a police constable of
H Division is seen tackling a mob in Spitalfields. Commercial Street police
station can be seen in the background.

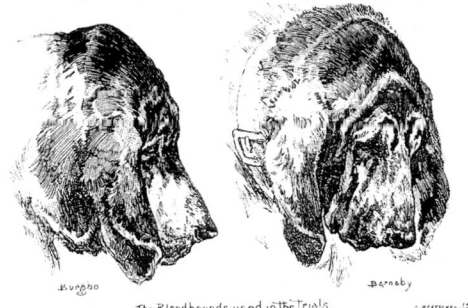

Sketch of two bloodhounds –
Burgho and Barnaby – tried
out by the Metropolitan Police
for possible employment in
the tracking of the murderer.

Burgho

Barnaby

The Bloodhounds used in the Trials.

Sir Charles Warren puts the
bloodhounds to the test in
Hyde Park.

Dorset Street looking east towards Commercial Street. A relatively short road, it had more
than its fair share of common lodging houses. Miller's Court, scene of the Kelly murder, was
situated on the left near the third wall lamp.

A LOST WOMAN
MARY KELLY
IN MILLER'S COURT

A contemporary sketch of Mary Jane
Kelly at the door of her room, number
13 Miller's Court, scene of her murder
on 9 November 1888.

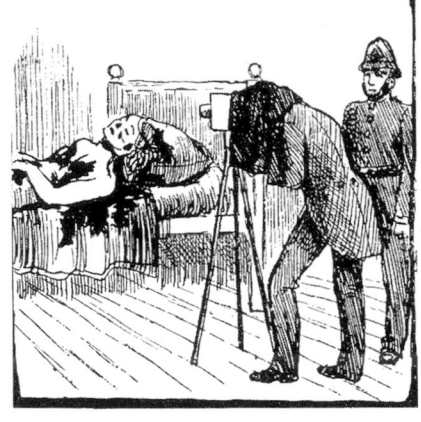

A contemporary sketch of the body of Mary
Jane Kelly being photographed by the police
at the murder scene.

Above The police crime scene
photograph of Mary Jane Kelly's
body as found in her bed.

Right The second police crime scene
photograph of Mary Jane Kelly's body,
taken from the opposite side of the bed
and showing a table piled with flesh in
the background.

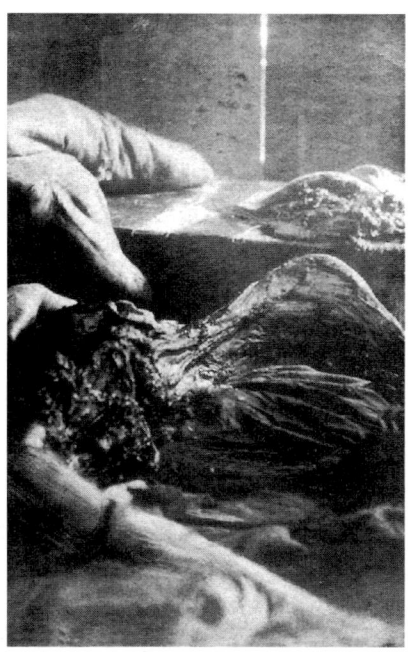

Elizabeth Prater, the occupant of the first floor front room, was one of those who saw the body through the window. She affirms that she spoke to the deceased on Thursday. She knew that Kelly had been living with a man, and that they had quarrelled about ten days since. It was a common thing for the women living in these tenements to bring men home with them. They could do as they pleased. She had heard nothing during the night, and was out betimes in the morning, and her attention was not attracted to any circumstances of an unusual character. Kelly was, she admitted, one of her own class, and she made no secret of her way of gaining a livelihood. During the day the police succeeded in finding John [*sic*] Barnett, the man with whom the deceased had cohabited until a week ago, when they separated in consequence of a quarrel, in the course of which the window was broken. Barnett is a porter at the market close by, and he was able to answer the police that on Thursday night he was at a lodging-house in New-street, Bishopsgate-street, and was playing whist there until half-past twelve, when he went to bed. Another witness states that she met the deceased near the church in Commercial-street on Thursday night about seven o'clock. As far as the statements furnished to the police go, there is no actual evidence forthcoming that a man entered the room in Miller's-court. No one was seen to go there with the deceased, and there is still no clue as to the identity of the mysterious and crafty assassin who has again become the terror of Whitechapel. In Dorset-street, however, the fact of a man having been in the company of a woman would probably attract no notice from those who are accustomed to such an incident. The street is fairly lighted, and, late at night especially, is pretty well frequented. It is one of those spots where a good deal of street gambling may be detected at times. Deceased was observed in the company of a man at ten p.m. on Thursday, of whom no description can be obtained. She was last seen, as far as can be ascertained, in Commercial-street, about half-past eleven. She was then alone, and was probably making her way home. It is supposed that she met the murderer in Commercial-street. The pair would have reached Miller's-court about midnight, but they were not seen to enter the house. The street-door was closed, but the woman had a latchkey. A light was seen shining through the window of the room for some time after the couple must have entered it.

Shortly after four o'clock yesterday a covered van was driven to Miller's-court, and in a few minutes the remains were placed in a

shell and quietly removed to the mortuary adjoining Shoreditch
Church to await the inquest, at the Shoreditch Town Hall on
Monday. The room was then closed, the window being boarded up
and the door padlocked. There were at times considerable numbers
of spectators in the vicinity of Dorset-street, but when the police
cordon was withdrawn the bystanders grew fewer. Dorset-street is
made up principally of common lodging-houses, which provide not
less than 600 registered beds. In one of these establishments Annie
Chapman, the Hanbury-street victim, lived. Curiously enough, the
warehouse at No. 26, now closed by large doors, was until a few
weeks ago the nightly resort of poor homeless creatures, who went
there for shelter. One of these women was Catherine Eddowes, the
woman who was murdered in Mitre-square.

From the sketch-map of the locality given it will be seen that the
sites of all the seven murders, five of which are, without any hesitation
or doubt, ascribed by the police to one man, are contained within a
limited area. A comparison of the dates reveals remarkable coincidences. The murderer has invariably chosen the latter part of the
week, and when the deed has not been committed on the last day of
the month it has taken place as near the 7th or 8th as can be. The
Berner-street and Mitre-square murders occurred early on Sunday,
Sept. 30, and the interval of about five weeks has been unusual, but
was probably to be explained by the extraordinary activity of the
police after the double event, or due, as some have it, to the
temporary absence of the perpetrator from the country. It was on
the morning of Saturday, Sept. 8, that Annie Chapman was killed in
Hanbury-street, and it was on the last day of August (a Friday) that the
Buck's-row tragedy took place. The two earlier murders – the one in
George-yard and the other in Osborne-street – are not believed to
have been the work of the miscreant who is still at large; but it is a
peculiar fact, taken in conjunction with the coincidence of dates
already remarked, that the murder of Mrs. Turner, in George-yard,
occurred on the 7th day of August.

Sir Charles Warren did not visit the scene of the murder, but
during the afternoon Colonel Monsell, chief constable of the
district, and Chief Constables Howard and Roberts inspected the
interior of the house. All the constables and detectives available
were distributed throughout the district, and a house-to-house
visitation was commenced, and all who knew the deceased woman
were interrogated as to the persons last seen in her company. There
was no clue.

While it is the universal belief in the district, and for only too obvious reasons, that this series of crimes has been perpetrated by the same hand, the conviction forces itself upon the police authorities that the murderer has been terrified by the hue and cry raised in consequence of his previous deeds of blood, and has thus been led to change his plan. Maniac he may be; a coward he certainly is; and hence, when he deemed it no longer safe to butcher his victims in the street, he followed them indoors. Whether this has increased the prospect of detection in the present instance is yet premature to say.

Amongst the populace there was very widespread disappointment that bloodhounds had not been at once employed in the effort to track the criminal. The belief had prevailed throughout the district that the dogs were ready to be let loose at the first notice of a murder having been committed, and the public had come to possess greater confidence in their wonderful canine instincts and sagacity than in all Sir Charles Warren's machinery of detection. They even attributed the fact that more than a month has passed since the last revolting outrage to the fear which it was thought had been inspired by the intimation that these detectives of nature would be employed. At a late hour last night it was officially stated that the bloodhounds had not been used. They were not absolutely forgotten, but apparently were not at hand, and the conclusion was come to that the trail must inevitably have been destroyed long before they could have come upon the scene by the constant stream of persons to and from the narrow street. The validity of this objection has been called in question by experts, and it would certainly have given satisfaction to the public mind if an experiment had been made. A better opportunity than the present instance afforded could hardly have occurred. A correspondent writes: "The Whitechapel Vigilance Committee, who have recently relaxed their efforts to find the murderer, have called a meeting for Tuesday evening next at the Paul's Head Tavern, Crispin-street, Spitalfields, to consider what steps they can take to assist the police in this latter matter."

As yet the murderer is at large, and if the police have any clue they have dissembled their knowledge with absolute success. Up to the present moment, beyond the strange coincidence of dates and the very vague and unfortunately conflicting descriptions given by witnesses at the inquests already held, scarce a vestige of evidence exists on which to base a search. It has always been the belief of

East-end residents that these foul deeds were not the work of a
landsman – and this mainly on account of what may be called their
periodicity. ''They've been done by some short-voyage man'' was
the expression of an opinion which is widespread. There was time,
it is thought, for a sailor to have made short voyages to the
Continent, and to have committed the murders either immediately
on landing or just before sailing. There may be no value underlying
the suggestion, and it may be next to impossible to synchronise the
arrival and departure of certain ships with the dates we have given,
still less to ascertain the composition of their crews, and most
difficult of all to bring guilt home to any individual; but in the
absence of any better trace it might be worth while to make the
investigation. In this connection attention has been drawn to the
following fact. It appears that the cattle boats bringing live freight to
London are in the habit of coming into the Thames on Thursdays or
Fridays, and leave again for the Continent on Sundays or Mondays.
It has already been a matter of comment that the recent revolting
crimes have been committed at the end of the week, and hence the
opinion shared by some of the detectives that the murderer is a
drover or butcher employed on one of these boats – of which there
are many – and that he periodically appears and disappears with one
of the steamers. It is thought, therefore, that the criminal may be a
person either employed upon one of these boats or having occasion
to travel by them. It is pointed out that at the inquests on the
previous victims the coroners had expressed the opinion that the
knowledge of physiology possessed by a butcher would have been
sufficient to enable him to find and cut out the parts of the body
which in several cases was abstracted.

Some of the reported clues must be received with caution. No
end of stories are rife in the neighbourhood, told with an air of
circumstantiality, which on examination prove to be utterly
baseless. Almost the sole testimony which seems to have any
bearing on the affair is that given by a young woman named
Pannier, who sells roasted chestnuts at the corner of Widegate-
street, a narrow thoroughfare about two minutes' walk from the
crime. Mrs. Pannier is reported to have stated that shortly after
noon yesterday a man, dressed like a gentleman, said to her, ''I
suppose you have heard about the murder in Dorset-street?'' and
that when she replied that she was aware of it he said, ''I know
more about it than you.'' He then proceeded down Sandy's-row, a
narrow thoroughfare which cuts across Widegate-street, looking

back as if to see whether he was watched. Mrs. Pannier described this person as a man about 5 ft 6 in high, with a black moustache, and wearing a black silk hat, dark coat, and speckled trousers. He carried a black shiny bag about eighteen inches long and a foot deep. It will be remembered that this description agrees fairly well with a personage previously described, and that the black bag has more than once figured in the evidence given. It may be worth while to recall that at the inquiry into the Berner-street murder Mrs. Mortimer said, "The only man I had seen pass through Berner-street previously was a young man who carried a black shiny bag." Similarly Arthur [*sic*] Bachert deposed: "On Saturday night at about seven minutes to twelve, I entered the Three Nuns Hotel, Aldgate. While in there an elderly woman, very shabbily dressed, came in and asked me to buy some matches. I refused, and she went out. A man who had been standing by me remarked that these persons were a nuisance, to which I responded 'Yes.' He then asked me to have a glass with him, but I refused, as I had just called for one myself. He then asked a number of questions about the women of the neighbourhood, and their ages, &c. He asked if I could tell him where they usually visited He went outside and spoke to the woman, and gave her something, I believe. He was a dark man, height about 5 ft 6 in or 5 ft 7 in. He wore a black felt hat, dark clothes, morning coat, black tie, and carried a black shiny bag." But the point in Mrs. Pannier's statement which engaged the greatest amount of attention, and which, if corroborated, might unquestionably possess real signifi-cance was her further averment that she had seen the same man on the previous evening, and that he had accosted three young unfortunates in Dorset-street, who chaffed him, and asked what he had in the bag, and he replied, "Something that the ladies don't like." It remains to be seen at Monday's inquest whether this statement, and especially the latter portion of it, upon which its significance really depends, is confirmed.

The following are additional statements: A young woman named Harvey, who had slept with the woman Kelly on several occasions, said she had been on good terms with the deceased, whose education was much superior to that of most persons in her position of life. Harvey, however, took a room in New-court, off the same street, but remained friendly with the unfortunate woman, who visited her in New-court on Thursday night. After drinking together they parted at half-past seven o'clock, Kelly going off in the

direction of Leman-street, which she was in the habit of frequenting. She was perfectly sober at the time. Harvey never saw her alive
afterwards. Upon hearing that a murder had been committed she
said, "I'll go and see if it's any one I know," and to her horror
found that it was her friend.

Joseph Barnett, an Irishman, at present residing in a common
lodging-house in New-street, Bishopsgate, stated that he had
occupied his present lodgings since Tuesday week. Previous to
that he had lived in Miller's-court, Dorset-street, for eight or nine
months, with the murdered woman, Mary Jane Kelly. They were
very happy and comfortable together until an unfortunate came to
sleep in their room, to which he strongly objected. Finally, after the
woman had been there two or three nights, he quarrelled with his
"wife" and left her. The next day, however, he returned and gave
Kelly money. He called several other days, and gave her money
when he had it. On Thursday night he visited her, between half-past
seven and eight, and told her he was sorry he had no money to give
her. He saw nothing more of her. He was indoors yesterday
morning when he heard that a woman had been murdered in
Dorset-street, but he did not know at first who the victim was. He
voluntarily went to the police, who, after questioning him, satisfied
themselves that his statements were correct. Barnett believed Kelly,
who was an Irishwoman, was an "unfortunate" before he made her
acquaintance, and she had never had any children. She used
occasionally to go to the Elephant and Castle district to visit a
friend.

The poor woman who has been thus foully done to death was by
no means among the lowest of her fallen class. For a considerable
part of the twelve months during which she was Mr. M'Carthy's
tenant she was to all appearance fairly well conducted. It was
supposed that the man with whom she lived was her husband. He
was employed about the fish and fruit markets, and when work was
plentiful the pair seem to have paid their way honourably; but
earnings were aften [sic] irregular, and then it is to be feared the
woman resorted to the streets. The landlord emphatically disowns
any knowledge of his tenement having been used for improper
purposes. Moreover, the room which she occupied – which was on
the ground floor – and for which she paid 4s a week, was part of the
adjoining shop – now used as a ware-room. It was separated from
the other dwellings in the narrow court, and strangers could not
easily frequent it without being observed. Formerly the woman,

who was of a fair complexion, with light hair, and possessing rather attractive features, dressed pretty well. Usually she wore a black silk dress, and often a black jacket, looking shabby genteel in her attire, but generally neat and clean. Latterly, it was confessed, she had been much given to drink, and had rapidly gone from bad to worse. This, it is supposed, led to the quarrel, a few days ago, between her and the man with whom she had been living, and to the arrears of 29s in the rent. Dorset-street abounds in women whose features, language, and behaviour are such that the smallest vestige of self-respect, if any remained in Mary Jane Kelly, would be sufficient to distinguish her from the more degraded of her associates. This short thoroughfare and the adjoining Paternoster-row, leading direct to the Spitalfields vegetable market, have now been given up to common lodging-houses at 4d and 6d a night, or "6d for a single bedded cabin," and to women who have lost every trace of womanliness. The street and the row are places which the police state are hardly safe for any respectable person by day and certainly not at night. In such a neighbourhood it was impossible to rise; to sink lower was inevitable. Evidence tends to show that when Kelly first made its acquaintance respectable friends still looked after and wrote to her. It is the uniform testimony of local authorities that these evil surroundings are only remedied by wholesale demolitions, and that while they exist moral agencies are almost hopeless. They are whirlpools, and the poor and the wretched are dragged into them. Though the police report that Kelly's father lives in Wales, there seems no doubt that she is Irish, and McCarthy states that the letters for her used to come from some part of Ireland.

In the naturally intense excitement and indignation prevailing over the whole of East London there is a danger of innocent persons becoming suspected and suffering maltreatment. Last night a young man respectably dressed appeared in Dorset-street, and by his anxious inquiries, especially in regard to the possible employment of bloodhounds, drew upon himself the unpleasant attentions of bystanders, some of whom determined to watch his movements. On leaving the spot the young man – a clerk, it was subsequently ascertained – found himself followed by three men. As it was quite certain that he was the object of their regards, he became somewhat alarmed, while his agitation only served to strengthen their suspicions. In the end he would have suffered from the hands of the mob, but for police protection. Fortunately

Bishopsgate-street Police-station was near, and thither he was conveyed for safety.

The Scotland-yard authorities shortly after midday telegraphed the following notification of the crime to the various police-stations: "Found at 10.30 a.m., a woman cut to pieces in a room on the ground floor at 26, Dorset-street, Spitalfields."

During the course of last evening Dr. G.B. Phillips visited the House of Commons, where he had a conference with the Under-secretary of the Home Office, Mr. Stuart-Wortley.

The Central News states, upon what is described as indisputable authority, that no portion of the murdered woman's body was taken away by the murderer. The post-mortem examination was of the most exhaustive character, and the surgeons did not quit their work until every organ had been accounted for and placed as nearly as possible in its natural position.

Some residents in the court declare that about a quarter to two they heard a faint cry of murder, which would seem to fix with tolerable exactitude the time at which the crime was committed; but against this must be set the statement of a woman residing at 26, Dorset-street, a house the backrooms of which abut upon the court, according to which a cry of murder was heard at three o'clock. It is characteristic of the locality that no one thought anything of the incident, which, indeed, is of too common occurrence to cause interest or alarm. A man engaged as a market porter and living at 3, Miller-court, stated that, although his rooms face the scene of the murder, he heard nothing of it until he went out in the morning at half-past ten to get some milk, and was stopped by the police. A man's pilot-coat has been found in the murdered woman's room, but whether it belonged to the murderer has not been ascertained. Late last evening a man was arrested near Dorset-street on suspicion of being concerned in the murder. He was taken to Commercial-street Police-station, followed by a howling mob, and is still detained there. Another man, respectably dressed, wearing a slouch hat, and carrying a black bag, was arrested and taken to Leman-street Station. The bag was examined, but its contents were perfectly harmless, and the man was liberated.

The following report[5] relates to Dr Thomas Bond's report of his initial post-mortem examination of the body of Mary Kelly. The cover states:

16 Novr 1888
Dr. Thos: Bond
7 BroadSanctuary
S.W.
Whitechapel Murder
Result of Post Mortem
examination of body of
woman found in Dorset Street.
Mr. Anderson
Seen &noted.

This is followed by the report in Dr Bond's own hand:

Notes of examination of body of woman found murdered & mutilated in Dorset St.

Position of body,

The body was lying naked in the middle of the bed the shoulders flat, but the axis of the body inclined to the left side of the bed. The head was turned on the left cheek. The left arm was close to the body with the forearm flexed at a right angle & lying across the abdomen, the right arm was slightly abducted from the body & rested on the mattress, the elbow bent & the forearm supine with the fingers clenched. The legs were wide apart, the left thigh at right angles to the trunk & the right forming an obtuse angle with the pubes.

The whole of the surface of the abdomen & thighs was removed & the abdominal cavity emptied of its viscera. The breasts were cut off, the arms mutilated by several jagged wounds & the face hacked beyond recognition of the features. The tissues of the neck were severed all round down to the bone.

The viscera were found in various parts viz; the uterus & kidneys with one breast under the head, the other breast by the right foot, the liver between the feet, the intestines by the right side & the spleen by the left side of the body.

The flaps removed from the abdomen & thighs were on a table.

The bed clothing at the right corner was saturated with blood, & on the floor beneath was a pool of blood covering about 2 feet square. The wall by the right side of the bed & in a line with the neck was marked by blood which had struck it in a number of separate splashes.

Postmortem Examination.

The face was gashed in all directions the nose, cheeks, eyebrows & ears being partly removed. The lips were blanched & cut by several oblique incisions running obliquely down to the chin. There were also numerous cuts extending irregularly across all the features.

The neck was cut through the skin & other tissue right down to the vertebrae the 5th & 6th being deeply notched. The skin cuts in the front of the neck showed distinct ecchymosis.

The air passage was cut through at the lower part of the larynx through the cricoid cartilage.

Both breasts were removed by more or less circular incisions, the muscles down to the ribs being attached to the breasts. The intercostals between the 4 5 & 6 ribs were cut through & the contents of the thorax visible through the openings.

The skin & tissues of the abdomen from the costal arch to the pubes were removed in three large flaps. The right thigh was denuded in front to the bone, the flap of skin, including the external organs of generation & part of the right buttock. The left thigh was stripped of skin, fascia & muscles as far as the knee.

The left calf showed a long gash through skin & tissues to the deep muscles & reaching past the knee to 5 ins above the ankle.

Both arms & forearms had extensive & jagged wounds.

The right thumb showed a small superficial incision about 1 in long, with extravasation of blood in the skin & there were several abrasions on the back of the hand moreover showing the same condition.

On opening the thorax it was found that the right lung was minimally adherent by old firm adhesions. The lower part of the lung was broken & torn away.

The left lung was intact; It was adherent at the apex & there were a few adhesions over the side. In the substances of the lung were several nodules of consolidation.

The Pericardium was open below & the Heart absent.

In the abdominal cavity was some partly digested food of fish & potatoes & similar food was found in the remains of the stomach attached to the intestines.

The decision to offer a pardon to any person who was not the actual murderer and who could give information leading to the arrest of the offender is to be found under file cover A49301 B[6] as follows:

No. A49301B/15
DATE 10 Novr.88   H.O. Memo (S of S)
REFERENCES &c.   Murder of Mary Jane Kelly, Whitechapel
                        Stating that the Cabinet have decided to offer a
Pardon to any one but the actual murderer in above case. – Bills to
be issued to-day

[MINUTES.]

To Commissioner of Police
              10 Nov 88.

Folio 300 reads as follows:

A49301B

                                                    10 Novr/'88

Dear Lushington,
    The Cabinet have decided to offer to day a Pardon to any one but
the actual murderer in <u>the case that occurred yesterday</u>:
    No reward to be offered Let the Bills issue <u>to day</u>
                                            Yrs truly
                                            Henry Matthews.

The Queen, of course, had to be notified of the decision to issue this
pardon and thus the following from the Prime Minister to the
Queen may be found[7]:

Decypher   Novr: 10. 1888
                        Marquis of Salisbury
                                to
                            The Queen
Humble duty:
    At Cabinet today it was resolved to issue a Proclamation offering
free pardon to anyone who should give evidence as to the recent
murder except the actual perpetrator of the crime.
    It was resolved to delay making any recommendation on the
protest of the Queensland Ministers against the appointment of
Sir Henry Blake until we had seen the exact grounds of
objection.
    The rest of the sitting was occupied with discussing whether any
measure were possible to prevent Lord Clanricarde from unreasonable conduct in the management of his property.

MEPO 3/3153 ff. 5–8 also concerns the offer of a pardon to any accomplice who shall give evidence as to the identity of the murderer(s):

The cover reads – 10th Nov 1888, Home Office,
<u>For Sir Charles Warren</u>
Whitechapel Murder Miller Court. Dorset Street
States that the Sec: of State will advise the grant of Her Majesty's gracious pardon to any accomplice, not being the person who contrived or actually committed the murder, who shall give such information & evidence as shall lead to the discovery and conviction of the murderer or murderers.
Notification sent to Press,copy attached. GAL 12/11/88.

The report reads:

WHITEHALL
10. November 1888

Pressing
Sir,
    I am directed by the Secretary of State to inform you that, in the case of the murder committed in a house in Dorset Street, Whitechapel, on the 8th or 9th instant, he will advise the grant of Her Majesty's gracious Pardon to any accomplice, not being the person who contrived or actually committed the murder, who shall give such information and evidence as shall lead to the discovery and conviction of the murderer or murderers.
                The Secretary of State desires that the enclosed notice should be issued forthwith.
           I am,
             Sir,
         Your Obedient Servant
          Godfrey Lushington

The Commissioner of Police
   Metropolitan Police'
   Murder
   Pardon
Whereas on November the 8th or 9th in Millers Court Dorset Street Spitalfields, Mary Janet Kelly was murdered by some person or persons unknown, the Secretary of State will advise the grant of

Her Majesty's Gracious pardon to any accomplice not being a person who contrived or actually committed the murder who shall give such information and evidence as shall lead to the discovery and conviction of the person or persons who committed the murder.

(Sd) Charles Warren
Commissioner of Police
of the Metropolis
Metropolitan Police Office
4 Whitehall Place
SW
10 November 1888

On 23 November 1888 a question was raised in the House of Commons:

CRIMINAL LAW – THE WHITECHAPEL
MURDERS – A FREE PARDON.

Mr. HUNTER (Aberdeen, N.) asked the Secretary of State for the Home Department, Whether he is prepared, in the case of the Whitechapel murders, other than that of the woman Kelly, to offer a free pardon to any person not being the actual perpetrator of the crimes?

The SECRETARY of STATE (Mr. MATTHEWS) (Birmingham, E.): I should be quite prepared to offer a pardon in the earlier Whitechapel murders if the information before me had suggested that such an offer would assist in the detection of the murderer. In the case of Kelly there were certain circumstances which were wanting in the earlier cases, and which made it more probable that there were other persons who, at any rate after the crime, had assisted the murderer.

(Hansard: 3rd Series: Volume 331: Page 16)

CHAPTER 19

November 1888 –
Sir Charles Warren Resigns and Royal Involvement

Sir Charles Warren had been Chief Commissioner of the Metropolitan Police since 1886. His tenure of the post had been marked by his clashes with officialdom at the Home Office, particularly with the Home Secretary, Henry Matthews. He earned the respect of the men under him but received much criticism from the radical press.

The Times of Wednesday, 10 October 1888, contained a statement[1] by Warren that he wished made public:

SIR CHARLES WARREN AND THE
DETECTIVE FORCE.

Sir Charles Warren requests us to publish the following statement. –

Several incorrect statements have recently been published relative to the enrolment of candidates for detective – that is to say, criminal investigation – work in the Metropolitan Police which may tend to deter candidates from applying. The following is the actual state of the case:-

For some years past the standard height in the Metropolitan Police has been 5 ft. 8½ in., and in the beginning of 1887 it was raised to 5 ft. 9 in., but the Commissioner has power from the Secretary of State to accept candidates as short as 5 ft. 7 in., and if the Criminal Investigation branch should require any particular man under 5 ft. 7 in. the Commissioner has at all times been prepared to obtain the Secretary of State's sanction to his enrolment.

The limit of age is 35, but as a rule candidates are not taken over the age of 27, in order that the police service may not lose the better part of a man's life, and also to enable him to put in sufficient service to entitle him to his full pension.

There is no rule, and never has been any rule made by the Commissioner, that candidates on joining must serve for two or three years as constables in divisions before being appointed to the Criminal Investigation branch.

The Commissioner has always been prepared to consider favourably any proposal from the Criminal Investigation branch for a candidate to join the Commissioner's office immediately on enrolment, or at any time after his enrolment, for duty in the Criminal Investigation branch.

But should a case occur that a candidate who wished to join the Criminal Investigation branch at once, and was reported favourably upon, was not physically or otherwise fit for ordinary police duties, it would be necessary, in the interests of the public, that on his enrolment a stipulation should be made that if he should subsequently be found unfit for criminal investigation work he would have to leave the police service without any compensation, should his services not entitle him to a pension or gratuity.

As a general rule it has been ascertained by the Criminal Investigation branch that the candidates who have applied to be appointed direct to detective duties have not possessed any special qualifications which would justify their being so appointed.

Sir Charles Warren tendered his resignation on 8 November 1888 and news of it appeared in *The Times* of Tuesday, 13 November 1888[2], together with reports on the murder of Mary Jane Kelly at Miller's Court, Dorset Street, Spitalfields on 9 November:

RESIGNATION OF SIR CHARLES
WARREN.

As will be seen from our Parliamentary report, Sir Charles Warren tendered his resignation on Thursday last. A News Agency learns on the highest authority that the relations between Sir Charles Warren and the Home Office have for some time been strained. The action of the department in reference to the resignation of Mr. Monro caused the first serious difference of opinion. Sir Charles took exception to certain of the methods of the Assistant-Commissioner, and he intimated to Mr. Matthews that either he or Mr. Monro must resign. A few days afterwards Mr. Monro's resignation was announced. Sir Charles complains that this was accepted without consultation with him, and that prior to the Home Secretary's statement in the House of Commons last evening he was not even aware of the reason assigned by his subordinate for severing his connexion with Scotland-yard. Since Mr. Monro's transference to the Home Office matters have become worse. Sir Charles complains that, whereas he has been saddled with all the responsibility, he has had no freedom of action, and in consequence his position has become daily more unbearable. Although Mr. Monro has been no longer in evidence at Whitehall-place, he has to all intents and purposes retained control of the Criminal Investigation Department. Indeed, it was added, Mr. Matthews last evening admitted that he was deriving the benefit of the advice of Mr. Monro in matters relating to crime, and was in communication with him at the present time on the subject of the organization of the detective staff. This division of authority Sir Charles Warren has strenuously fought against. He maintains that if the Commissioner is to be responsible for the discipline of the force, instructions should be given to no department without his concurrence. Latterly, in spite of the remonstrances of Sir Charles Warren, the control of the Criminal Investigation Department has been withdrawn more and more from Whitehall-place. Every morning for the last few weeks there has been a protracted conference at the Home Office between Mr. Monro, Mr. Anderson, and the principal detective inspectors, and the information furnished to the Commissioner in regard to these conferences has been, he states, of the scantiest character. These facts will explain how, apart from any other consideration, it was impossible for Sir Charles Warren, holding the views he did in regard to the functions of the Commissioner, to continue in command. The reproof of the Home Secretary last week in reference to the article in Murray's Magazine completed the rupture. Sir Charles thereupon took counsel with his friends and immediately tendered his resignation to the Home Secretary. Yesterday morning his books and papers were removed from the Commissioner's office, and this was the first intimation in Whitehall-place that he had relinquished the position. In the lobby last evening Mr. Monro was looked upon as the most likely person to be selected to succeed Sir C. Warren. It was pointed out that the resignation of Sir Charles Warren practically arose out of a difference of opinion with Mr. Monro, and that, inasmuch as Mr. Monro, though nominally shelved, had really gained the day, therefore it was only natural that he should assume control of the force, and develope [*sic*] the system of administration, the proposition of which led to his transference to the Home Office. On the other hand, it is believed in some quarters that the present opportunity will be seized to emphasize the distinction between the Criminal Investigation Department and the ordinary members of the force to which Sir Charles Warren takes exception, in which case a provincial chief constable, who has attracted much notice for his successful organization and disciplinary tact, is mentioned, as the probable head of the detective branch, as an independent branch of the force.

There is a cutting[3] on questions in the House of Commons from the *Standard* of 10 November 1888, with a Home Office date stamp of 12 Nov.88, included in the official files:

THE WHITECHAPEL MURDERS.

Mr. CONYBEARE. – I wish to ask the Home Secretary whether he has seen that another terrible murder has been committed in the East of London, and whether he does not think the time has come to replace Sir Charles Warren by some officer who would investigate these crimes.

The SPEAKER said it would be necessary to give notice of this question in the usual way.

Mr. C. GRAHAM asked whether it was true, as stated, that Sir Charles Warren was at present in St. Petersburg.

Mr. W.H. SMITH. – No, sir.

This is followed by a further cutting[4] from the *Standard*, dated 13 November 1888:

A49301C/15
RESIGNATION OF SIR C. WARREN.

Mr. CONYBEARE asked the Secretary of State for the Home Department whether he could state the exact reason why the late head of the Detective Department in the Metropolitan Police resigned his position; whether it was the fact that Sir C. Warren had now practically the direct control of the Detective Department; and whether, in view of the constant recurrence of atrocious murders, and the failure of the new organisation and methods to detect the murderer, he would consider the propriety of making some change in the arrangements of Scotland-yard. The hon. member also wished to know whether it was true, as reported in the newspapers that afternoon, that Sir C. Warren had tendered his resignation, and that it had been accepted.

The HOME SECRETARY. – I have already more than once stated the reason why Mr. Monro resigned. With regard to the remainder of the question, Mr. Anderson is now in direct control of the Criminal Investigation Department, under the superintendence and control, as provided by statute, of the Chief Commssioner. The failure of the police, so far, to detect the person guilty of the Whitechapel murders is due, not to any new reorganisation in the department, but to the extraordinary cunning and secrecy which characterise the commission of the crimes. I have for some time had the question of the whole system of the Criminal Investigation Department under my consideration, with a view to introducing any improvement that may be required. With regard to the last question, I have to inform the hon. member that the Chief Commissioner of Police did on the 8th inst. tender his resignation to Her Majesty's Government, and that his resignation has been accepted (loud opposition cheers).

The resignation of Sir Charles Warren came at a rather awkward time, coinciding as it did with another appalling and much-publicized "Whitechapel murder". Both sides in the dispute had their supporters, and the press, as always, was willing to stoke the fires of dispute. *The Times*[5] of Friday, 16 November 1888, continued the story:

SIR C. WARREN *and the* METROPOLITAN POLICE.

A deputation representing the whole of the Metropolitan Police Force waited on Sir Charles Warren at his private residence, St. George's-road, yesterday, for the purpose of expressing their regret at his resignation. The deputation was composed of the superintendents of the various divisions. The only absentees were Superintendents Shore and Steel, who are on sick leave, and Superintendent Butt, who is out of London at present. Superintendent Draper, of the D Division, was deputed to act as spokesman. He paid a high tribute to Sir Charles Warren's thoughtfulness and care for those under his command, and, while admitting the perfection to which discipline had now been brought, repudiated the idea that such discipline was in any degree distasteful to the force so long as the regulations were administered with the fairness and equity which had characterised Sir Charles Warren's tenure of office. Speaking more especially for the superintendents, he might say that since Sir Charles Warren had been Commissioner they had been able to do their work not only much more efficiently, but with much more comfort to themselves. They felt that he was always prepared to take the responsibility for and to uphold them in what they did, and they consequently never lost that confidence without which their arduous duties could not be satisfactorily discharged. As for the men, there were only two matters which had given rise to any feeling at all since Sir Charles Warren took office. One of these was the new set of regulations in regard to drunkenness, and the other was the question of pensions for injury received while on duty. The superintendents knew perfectly well that the Commissioner was not responsible for these decisions, but the constables were not so well informed. In conclusion Mr. Draper expressed the deep regret which he and his coadjutors felt at the severance of their connection with Sir Charles Warren. Superintendent Fisher, of the A Division, having spoken.

SIR CHARLES WARREN thanked the deputation warmly for their assurances of esteem and consideration. He said it had always been his endeavour to combine discipline with justice to every member of the force, and it was gratifying to know that his efforts had not been altogether without success. With regard to the first point touched upon by Mr. Draper (the new regulations respecting drunkenness in the force), he explained that, although he had very strong views on the subject of intemperance, he was not responsible for the order which had been recently promulgated. The order emanated from the Home Secretary, who on several occasions called attention to the fact that the punishments for drunkenness were merely nominal, and ultimately instructed him to issue most stringent orders in reference to the offence. On the second point he was equally free from reproach. He had recommended several men on the chief surgeon's certificate for pensions, on the ground of injury while on duty; but the Home Secretary had taken a different view of the matter. In conclusion Sir Charles Warren said he had been greatly disappointed at having found no opportunity to visit the various divisions during his tenure of office. The work of consolidating the orders, on which he had been steadily engaged, had occupied so much of his time that he had seldom been able to leave Whitehallplace. During the past few weeks, however, he had at last succeeded in clearing the decks, and he had hoped now to see the men in their respective divisions. He again thanked them for their kindness, and assured them that their willing and cordial co-operation in such reforms as he had ventured to propose would be one of his pleasantest recollections of his Commissionership.

Another letter from Warren appeared in *The Times* of Saturday, 17 November 1888:

SIR CHARLES WARREN AND MR. MATTHEWS.
TO THE EDITOR OF THE TIMES.

Sir, – With reference to the debate last night in the House of Commons, I trust I may state that I have never to my knowledge in any way contested the lawful authority of the Secretary of State over the Metropolitan police force; and the insinuation that I have in any way contested the administration of the police being subject to Parliament through the Secretary of State seems too ridiculous for me to contradict.

In many cases, while accepting directions given me which were to all appearances contrary to the statute, I have entered a protest; and in thus protesting I have acted in accordance with the advice of the legal adviser appointed by the Secretary of State, the late Mr. J. Davis, formerly stipendiary magistrate of Sheffield.

I can only express my astonishment at the statements attributed to Mr. Matthews last night, and I venture to assert that an entirely different impression would be conveyed to the public mind about my action if the correspondence were to be made known.

I am, Sir, your obedient servant,
CHARLES WARREN.

44, St. George's-road, S.W..Nov.16.

The Times of Wednesday, 21 November 1888, carried, in its Parliamentary reports[6] columns, the following exchange:

MR. MATTHEWS AND SIR C. WARREN

In answer to questions from Mr. GRAHAM and Mr. PICKERS-GILL,

MR. MATTHEWS said, – I presume that Sir C. Warren's published letter refers to the voluminous correspondence on departmental matters between the Home Office and Scotland Yard. It is unusual to lay a correspondence of this kind upon the table of the House; and part of it is altogether confidential. I will, however, state generally that I know of no occasion on which I have given to Sir C. Warren directions apparently or really contrary to the statute. But if hon. members will put upon the paper a question addressed to any specific subject on which they suggest I have done so, I will inform them, as fully as public duty permits, what directions I did give, and they will be able to form their own judgment.

MR. GRAHAM asked in what manner members were to obtain information of what was known only to the Home Secretary and Sir Charles Warren.

MR. CONYBEARE asked whether, considering the circumstances of the case were altogether unusual, and that the question involved the relations that had existed for some time between the Chief Commissioner and the Home Office, it was not necessary that the House should have the whole correspondence.

MR. MATTHEWS said he did not think it was necessary that the whole correspondence should be laid before the House; but he would state fully what had occurred upon any matter that might be suggested.

A further report touching upon the Chief Commissioner appeared in questions in the House of Commons reports in *The Times* of Tuesday, 27 November 1888:

OFFICE OF COMMISSIONER OF POLICE.

MR. GRAHAM asked the Secretary of State for the Home Department why the police rules of Wednesday night last were signed by Sir Charles Warren, seeing that he was no longer Commissioner.

MR. MATTHEWS. — Although Sir Charles Warren has sent in his resignation of the office of Commissioner of Police he has not yet been relieved from the responsibility of that office, and, therefore, properly continues to discharge its functions. No successor has yet been appointed.

From these reports it will be seen that the resignation of Sir Charles Warren was not a result of the lack of police success in the investigation of the Whitechapel Murders. He was shortly thereafter replaced in office, as expected, by James Monro.

A Royal connection to the murders has always been a popular notion with theorists, writers and the public and to some extent this is justified. There can be no doubt at all that Queen Victoria herself was well aware of the murders, and that she gave them some consideration. We have already seen that in early October 1888, Mr George Lusk, Chairman of the Whitechapel Vigilance Committee, presented a petition to Her Majesty the Queen, then staying at Balmoral, to which it was deemed appropriate she should not reply. An entry in Her Majesty's Journal,[7] dated 4 October 1888, refers to the "dreadful murders of unfortunate women of a bad class, in London."

The Kelly murder marked the peak of public concern and alarm over a terrible series of crimes. A cypher telegram from the Queen at Balmoral to the Marquis of Salisbury, the Prime Minister, dated 10 November 1888, stated:

> "This new most ghastly murder shows the absolute necessity for some very decided action.
>
> All these courts must be lit, & our detectives improved. They are not what they shld be.
>
> You promised, when the 1st murders took place to consult with your colleagues about it."[8]

The Marquis of Salisbury replied, the same day, by cypher telegram:

> "Humble duty:
> At Cabinet to-day it was resolved to issue a Proclamation offering free pardon to anyone who should give evidence as to the recent murder except the actual perpetrator of the crime . . ."[9]

A cypher to the Queen from the Marquis of Salisbury, dated 11 November 1888, reported:

> "Humble duty:
> Lord Salisbury forgot to mention in previous telegram that Sir Charles Warren had resigned before the murder, because his attention had been drawn to a regulation of the Home Office forbidding writing to the newspapers on the business of the Department without leave.
>
> His resignation has been accepted.
>
> This horrid murder was committed in a room. No additional lighting could have prevented it."[10]

Both Government and Police were under harsh and unfair criticism, and it was difficult to know what to do. The Queen's continuing concern was shown in the following draft letter to Henry Matthews, the Home Secretary:

"Nov. 13. 1888. – The Queen has received with sincere regret Mr. Matthews' letter of the 10th in which he reports the resignation of Sir Charles Warren.

It would of course be impossible to recognize Sir Charles Warren's contention that he was not under the orders of the Sec of State, but The Queen fears this resignation will have a bad effect in encouraging the lawbreaker to defy the police, who under Sir Charles Warren, have always done their duty admirably.

At the same time The Queen fears that the Detective department is not so efficient as it might be. No doubt the recent murders in Whitechapel were committed in circumstances which made Detection very difficult.

Still The Queen thinks that in the small area where these horrible crimes have been perpetrated a great number of detectives might be employed and that every possible suggestion might be carefully examined, and if practicable followed.

Have the cattle boats & passenger boats been examined?

Has any investigation been made as to the number of single men occupying rooms to themselves?

The murderer's clothes must be saturated with blood and must be kept some where.

Is there sufficient surveillance at night?

These are some of the questions that occur to The Queen on reading the accounts of this horrible crime."[11]

This letter was in the handwriting of Sir Henry Ponsonby, Private Secretary to the Queen, and he added a note at the end: "Perhaps these details might be omitted?" Mr Matthews sent the Queen a detailed explanation from Scotland Yard of all that the police were doing.

The concern evinced by the Queen and the Establishment was later to become a fertile ground for gossip and rumour. The *Referee* of 9 March 1890 hinted:

There is not the slightest "Truth" in the statement that Lord Salisbury concealed Jack the Ripper at Hatfield House on the night of the last Whitechapel murder, or that the Home Secretary has instructed Mr. Monro to discontinue all further inquiries into the atrocities in consequence of it having been discovered that Jack is a member of the House of Lords. Seriously, some such story was for a long time in circulation, especially at the East-end when I heard more than once that the police had received orders to drop the inquiry from high official quarters.

This groundswell of suspicion has pervaded and become enshrined with the facts of the case ever since.

CHAPTER 20

10 November 1888 – Dr Bond "Profiles" the Killer

Home Office files[1] contain an interesting exchange of letters regarding the murders and the efforts being made to gain any sort of clue about the perpetrator of the crimes. What resulted was a very early example of an attempt to profile a serial killer:

[Stamped:- HOME OFFICE 14 NOV.88] A49301C/21
93305/11a

> 4 Whitehall Place, S.W.
> 13th Nov. 1888.

Sir,
    The Commissioner of Police of the Metropolis has to transmit to you to be laid before Mr. Secretary Matthews a copy of a letter which I have received from Mr. Thomas Bond F.R.C.S. on the subject of the Whitechapel murders.
    The enclosed extract from a letter I addressed to Mr. Bond on the 25th ulto. will explain how the matter came before him, and I now propose to inform him that his report has been communicated to the Secretary of State and to thank him for the valuable assistance he has thus rendered in the investigation of the murders.

> I am,
> Your most obedient Servant,
> RAnderson
> Assistant Commissioner

The Under
    Secretary of State
    etc. etc. etc.

There then follows a copy of an extract from a letter to Dr Bond:

> [Stamped:- HOME OFFICE 14 NOV.88]
> A49301C/21
> Extract from a letter to Dr. Bond. –

In dealing with the Whitechapel murders the difficulties of conducting the enquiry are largely increased by reason of our having no reliable opinion for our guidance as to the amount of surgical skill and anatomical knowledge probably possessed by the murderer or murderers.

I brought this matter before Sir C. Warren some time since and he has now authorised me to ask if you will be good enough to take up the medical evidence given at the several inquests and favour him with your opinion on the matter.

He feels that your eminence as an expert in such cases – and it is entirely in that capacity that the present case is referred to you, will make your opinion specially valuable.

This is followed by Dr Bond's response[2]:

[Stamped: – HOME OFFICE 14 NOV.88] 7 The Sanctuary,
Westminster Abbey,
Nov: 10th. 88.

Dear Sir,   A49301C/21
Whitechapel Murders
I beg to report that I have read the notes of the 4 Whitechapel Murders viz:-

1. Buck's Row.
2. Hanbury Street.
3. Berner's Street.
4. Mitre Square.

I have also made a Post Mortem Examination of the mutilated remains of a woman found yesterday in a small room in Dorset Street –

1. All five murders were no doubt committed by the same hand. In the first four the throats appear to have been cut from left to right. In the last case owing to the extensive mutilation it is impossible to say in what direction the fatal cut was made, but arterial blood was found on the wall in splashes close to where the woman's head must have been lying.

2. All the circumstances surrounding the murders lead me to form the opinion that the women must have been lying down when murdered and in every case the throat was first cut.

3. In the four murders of which I have seen the notes only, I cannot form a very definite opinion as to the time that had elapsed between the murder and the discovering of the body.

In one case, that of Berner's Street, the discovery appears to have been made immediately after the deed – In Buck's Row, Hanbury Street, and Mitre Square three or four hours only could have elapsed. [sic] In the Dorset Street case the body was lying on the bed at the time of my visit, 2 o'clock, quite naked and mutilated as in the annexed report –

Rigor Mortis had set in, but increased during the progress of the examination. From this it is difficult to say with any degree of certainty the exact time that had elapsed since death as the period varies from 6 to 12 hours before rigidity sets in. The body was comparatively cold at 2 o'clock and the remains of a recently taken meal were found in the stomach and scattered about over the intestines. It is, therefore, pretty certain that the woman must have been dead about 12 hours and the partly digested food would indicate: that death took place about 3 or 4 hours after the food was taken, so one or two o'clock in the morning would be the probable time of the murder.

4. In all the cases there appears to be no evidence of struggling [sic] and the attacks were probably so sudden and made in such a position that the women could neither resist nor cry out. In the Dorset Street case the corner of the sheet to the right of the woman's head was much cut and saturated with blood, indicating that the face may have been covered with the sheet at the time of the attack.

5. In the four first cases the murderer must have attacked from the right side of the victim. In the Dorset Street case, he must have attacked from in front or from the left, as there would be no room for him between the wall and the part of the bed on which the woman was lying. Again, the blood had flowed down on the right side of the woman and spurted on to the wall.

6. The murderer would not necessarily be splashed or deluged with blood, but his hands and arms must have been covered and parts of his clothing must certainly have been smeared with blood.

7. The mutilations in each case excepting the Berner's Street one were all of the same character and shewed clearly that in all the murders, the object was mutilation.

8. In each case the mutilation was inflicted by a person who had no scientific nor anatomical knowledge. In my opinion he does not even possess the technical knowledge of a butcher or horse slaughterer or any person accustomed to cut up dead animals.

9. The instrument must have been a strong knife at least six

inches long, very sharp, pointed at the top and about an inch in width. It may have been a clasp knife, a butcher's knife or a surgeon's knife. I think it was no doubt a straight knife.

10. The murderer must have been a man of physical strength and of great coolness and daring. There is no evidence that he had an accomplice. He must in my opinion be a man subject to periodical attacks of Homicidal and erotic mania. The character of the mutilations indicate that the man may be in a condition sexually, that may be called satyriasis. It is of course possible that the Homicidal impulse may have developed from a revengeful or brooding condition of the mind, or that Religious Mania may have been the original disease, but I do not think either hypothesis is likely. The murderer in external appearance is quite likely to be a quiet inoffensive looking man probably middleaged and neatly and respectably dressed. I think he must be in the habit of wearing a cloak or overcoat or he could hardly have escaped notice in the streets if the blood on his hands or clothes were visible.

11. Assuming the murderer to be such a person as I have just described he would probably be solitary and eccentric in his habits, also he is most likely to be a man without regular occupation, but with some small income or pension. He is possibly living among respectable persons who have some knowledge of his character and habits and who may have grounds for suspicion that he is not quite right in his mind at times. Such persons would probably be unwilling to communicate suspicions to the Police for fear of trouble or notoriety, whereas if there were a prospect of reward it might overcome their scruples.

I am, Dear Sir,

Yours faithfully,

(Signed) Thos. Bond.

R. Anderson, Esq:

Bond's profile, however, only made part provision for "such a person". A comment carried in the Editorial column of the *Manchester Evening News* of Tuesday, 13 November 1888:

By the way, the theory is again revived that the perpetrator of the Whitechapel murders is probably a woman suffering from religious mania.

CHAPTER 21

12 November 1888 – The Kelly Inquest

The police investigating the Kelly murder took witness statements on 9 November 1888, which are held with the inquest papers[1] at the London Metropolitan Archives. These are mainly in the hand of Abberline:

Witnesses for inquest to be opened 12th <u>Nov. 88. On the body of Marie Jeanette Kelly</u>

9th November 1888

Statement of Thomas Bowyer 37 Dorset Street Spitalfields in the employ of John McCarthy, lodging house Keeper, Dorset Street.

Says that at 10.45 am 9th instant, he was sent by his employer, to number 13 room Millers Court, Dorset Street, for the rent, he knocked at the door, but not getting any answer he threw the blinds back and looked through the window which was broken and saw the body of deceased woman whom he knew as Mary Jane, seeing that there was a quantity of blood on her person and that she had been apparently murdered he immediately went and informed his employer, Mr McCarthy who also looked into the room and at once despatched Bowyer to the police Station Commercial Street, and informed the Inspector on duty. (Insp Beck) who returned with him and his employer who had also followed to the Station. He knew the deceased and also a man named Joe, who had occupied the room for some months past.

9th November 1888

Statement of John McCarthy Grocer Lodging House Keeper, 27 Dorset Street, Spitalfields.

I sent my man Thomas Bowyer to No 13 room Millers Court Dorset Street owned by me for the rent. Bowyer came back and called me, telling me what he had seen. I went with him back and looked through the broken window, where I saw the mutilated remains of deceased whom I knew as Mary Jane Kelly. I then despatched Bowyer to the Police Station Commercial Street (following myself) to acquaint the Police. The Inspector on duty returned with us to the scene at Millers Court. I let the room about ten months ago to the deceased and a man named Joe, who I believed to be her husband. It was a furnished room, at 4s/6 per week. I sent for the rent because for some time past they had not kept their payments regularly. I have since heard, the man Joe was not her husband and that he had recently left her.

Marie Jeanette Kelly.   Friday
                                              9th November 1888
Statement of Joseph Barnett now residing at 24 & 25 New Street Bishopsgate ["a common" – *deleted*] labourer lodging house.

I am a porter on Billingsgate Market, but have been out of employment for the past 3 or 4 months. I have been living with Marie Jeanette Kelly who occupied No 13 Room Millers Court. I have lived lived with her altogether about 18 months, for the last eight months in Millers Court, until last Tuesday week (30 ulto) when in consequence of not Earning sufficient money to give her and her resorting to prostitution, I resolved on leaving her, but I was friendly with her and called to see her between seven and eight pm Thursday (8th) and told her I was very sorry I had no work and that I could not give her any money. I left her about 8 oclock same evening and that was the last time I saw her alive

There was a woman in the room when I called. The deceased told me on one occasion that her father named John Kelly was a foreman of some iron works at [*sic*] lived at Carmarthen or Carnarvon, that she had a brother named Henry serving in 2nd Battn. Scots Guards, and known amongst his comrades as Johnto, and I believe the Regiment is now in Ireland. She also told me that she had obtained her livelihood as a prostitute for some considerable time before I took her from the Streets, and that she left her home about 4 years ago, and that she was married to a collier, who was killed through some explosion. I think she said her husband name was Davis or Davies.

                                              9th November 1888
Statement of Mary Ann Cox No 5 Room Millers Court Dorset Street Spitalfields

I am a widow and an unfortunate. I have known the female occupying No 13 room Millers Court about 8 months. I knew her by the name of Mary Jane. About a quarter to twelve last night I came into Dorset Street from Commercial Street, and I saw walking in front of me Mary Jane with a man, they turned into the Court and as I entered the Court they went in doors, as they were going into her room, I said good night Mary Jane, she was very drunk and could scarcely answer me, but said good night, the man was carrying a quart can of beer. I shortly afterwards heard her singing. I went out shortly after twelve and returned about one o'clock and she was still singing in her room. I went out again shortly after one o'clock and returned at 3 o'clock, there was no light in her room then and all was quiet, and I heard no noise all night.

The man whom I saw was about 36 years old, about 5 ft 5 in high, complexion fresh and I believe he had blotches on his face, small side whiskers, and a thick carroty moustache, dressed in shabby dark clothes, dark overcoat and black felt hat.

Mary Jane was dressed I think, last night when I saw her, in a linsey frock, red knitted crossover around shoulders, had no hat or bonnet on.

9th November 1888

Elizabeth Prater wife of William Prater a boot machinist of No 20 room 27 Dorset Street states as follows:-

I went out about 9 p.m. on the 8th and returned about 1 a.m. 9th and stood at the bottom of Millers Court until about 1.30. I was speaking for a short time to a Mr. McCarthy Who keeps a chandler's shop at the corner of the court. I then went up to bed. About 3.30 or 4 a.m. I was awakened by a kitten walking across my neck, and just then I heard screams of murder about two or three times in a female voice. I did not take much notice of the cries as I frequently hear such cries from the back of the lodging-house where the windows look into Millers Court. From 1 a.m. to 1.30 a.m. no one passed up the court if they did I should have seen them. I was up again and down stairs in the court at 5.30 a.m. but saw no one except two or three carmen harnessing their horses in Dorset Street. I went to the "Ten Bells" P.H. at the corner of Church Street and had some rum. I then returned and went to bed again without undressing and slept until about 11 a.m.

9th November 1888

Statement of Caroline Maxwell, 14 Dorset Street Spitalfields, the wife of Henry Maxwell, a lodging house deputy.

I have known deceased woman during the past 4 ["or 5" – *deleted*] months, she was known as Mary Jane and that since Joe Barnett left her she has obtained her living as an unfortunate. I was on speaking terms with her although I had not seen her for 3 weeks until Friday morning 9th * [*here there is a marginal note* – "* about half past 8 o'clock."] instant, she was then standing at the corner of Millers Court in Dorset Street. I said to her, what brings you up so early. she said, I have the horrors of drink upon me, as I have been drinking for some days past. I said why dont you go to Mrs. Ringers (meaning the Public House at the corner of Dorset Street called the Britannia) and have ½ pint of beer. She said I have been there and had it, but I have brought it all up again at the same time she pointed to some vomit in the roadway. I then passed on, and went to Bishopsgate on an errand, and returned to Dorset Street about 9 am I then noticed deceased standing outside Ringers public house, she was talking to a man, age I think about 30, height about 5 ft 5 in, stout, dressed as a Market Porter, I was some distance away and am doubtful whether I could identify him. The deceased wore a dark dress black velvet body, and coloured wrapper round her neck.

9th <u>November 1888</u>

Statement of Sarah Lewis No 34 Great Pearl Street Spitalfields, a laundress

Between 2 and 3 o'clock this morning I came to stop with the Keylers, at No 2 Millers Court as I had had a few words with my husband, when I came up the Court there was a man standing over against the lodging house on the opposite side in Dorset Street ["talking to a female" – *deleted*] but I cannot describe him. Shortly before 4 o'clock I heard a scream like that of a young woman, and seemed to be not far away, she screamed out murder, I only heard it once. I did not look out at the window. I did not know the deceased. [*There is a marginal note* – "I left the Keylers at 5.30 P.M."]

Sarah Lewis further said that when in company with another female on Wednesday evening last at Bethnal Green, a suspicious man accosted her, he carried a black bag.

9 <u>November 1888</u>

Statement of Julia Venturney

I occupy No 1 room Millers Court I am a widow, charwoman but now living with a man named Harry Owen. I was awake all night and could not sleep. I have known the person occupying No 13 room opposite mine for about 4 months. I knew the man who I saw down stairs (Joe Barnett) he is called Joe, he lived with her until quite recently. I have heard him say that he did not like her ["because" – *deleted*] going out on the streets, he frequently gave her money, he was very kind to her, he said he would not live with her while she led that course of life, she used to get tipsey occasionally. She broke the windows a few weeks ago whilst she was drunk, she told me she was very fond of another man named Joe, and he had often ill-used her because she cohabited with Joe (Barnett). I saw her last about ["1.40" – *deleted*] pm yesterday. Thursday about 10 A.M.

9th November 1888

Statement of Maria Harvey of 3 New Court Dorset Street a laundress.

I slept two nights with Mary Jane Kelly, Monday and Tuesday last. I then took a room at the above house. I saw her last about five minutes to seven last night Thursday in her own room, when Barnett called. I then left they seemed to be on the best of terms. I left an overcoat, two dirty cotton shirts, a boy's shirt and a girls white petticoat and black crape bonnet in the room, the overcoat shewn me by police is the one I left there.

Inspector Walter Beck "H." Division who was first called together with the Constables on the beat will attend at the Inquest, also myself who will speak to contents of room &c if necessary.

F.G.Abberline Inspector.

The evidence given at the inquest into the death of Mary Jane Kelly is also included with the papers[2] held at the Greater London Record Office. It should be noted that the evidence given at the inquest is presented here as distinct from the preceding statements, taken on the day of the murder. There are some differences in the evidence given, and further differences may be found in the various newspaper reports of the inquest. These are too numerous to quote in full and would, in any case, be repetitive in the main. The inquest papers of the day of the hearing, Monday, 12 November 1888 are as follows:

MIDDLESEX,
To wit
𝔄𝔫 𝔍𝔫𝔮𝔲𝔦𝔰𝔦𝔱𝔦𝔬𝔫 taken for our Sovereign Lady the Queen, at the House known by the Name of the *Town Hall* in the Parish of *Shoreditch* in the County of MIDDLESEX, on the *Twelfth [sic]* day of *November* A.D. 188*8* [and by adjournment on the _____ day of _____, and the _____ day of _____].
before RODERICK MADONALD, ESQUIRE, one of the Coroners of our said Lady the Queen for the said County of MIDDLESEX, upon the Oath of good and lawful Men of the said County, duly sworn to inquire for our said Lady the Queen, on view of the Body of *Marie Jeanette Kelly otherwise Davies* as to h*er* death, and those of the said jurors whose names are hereunto subscribed upon their Oaths duly administered do say

That on the *Ninth* day of *November* in the year aforesaid at the *1 Millers Court* in the Parish of *Shoreditch [sic]* aforesaid, the said *Marie Jeanette Kelly was found dead from the mortal effects of Severance of the right carotid artery*
and so the Jurors aforesaid, upon their Oaths, do further say that *such death was due to* and the Jurors aforesaid do further say that the said *Marie Jeanette Kelly* was a *fe* male person of the age of *about twenty five* years, and a *prostitute*.
𝔍𝔫 𝔚𝔦𝔱𝔫𝔢𝔰𝔰 whereof as well the said Coroner as the Jurors have hereunto subscribed their Hands and Seals the Day and Year and Place first above written.

Roderick Macdonald * Coroner.

		G Gieselme *
Joseph Gobly *	*John Lloyd* *	[illeg] *William Worf* *
George Buffery *	*Samuel Jenkins* *	*Joseph Roberts* *
E. Stevens *	*Abraham Clements* *	*Lewis F Hunter* *
John Harvey *	*R Nettelfield* *	*George Harry Wilson* *
		Henry Dawkes

𝔐𝔦𝔡𝔡𝔩𝔢𝔰𝔢𝔵, TO WIT.
𝔗𝔥𝔢 𝔍𝔫𝔣𝔬𝔯𝔪𝔞𝔱𝔦𝔬𝔫𝔰 of Witnesses severally taken and acknowledged on behalf of our Sovereign Lady the Queen, touching the death of *Marie Jeannette Kelly*, at the House known by the sign of the *Town Hall* in the Parish of *Shoreditch* in the County of Middlesex, on the *12* day of *November*, in the year of our Lord One thousand eight hundred and *eighty eight* before me, RODERICK MACDONALD, Esquire, one of Her Majesty's Coroners for the said County, on an Inquisition then and there taken

on View of the body of the said *Marie J Kelly* then and there lying dead.

Joseph Barnett, having been sworn upon the day and year and at the place above mentioned, deposed as follows:- I reside at 24 and 25 New Street, Bishopsgate, which is a common lodging house. I am a laborer & have been a fish porter. I now live at my sisters 21 Portpool Lane, Grays Inn Road. I have lived with the deceased one year and eight months, her name was Marie Jeannette Kelly. Kelly was her maiden name and the name she always went by. I have seen the body. I identify her by the ear and the eyes. I am positive it is the same woman. I have lived with her at 13 room, Miller's Court, eight months or longer. I separated from her on the 30th of October. I left her because she had a person who was a prostitute whom she took in and I objected to her doing so, that was the only reason, not because I was out of work. I left her on the 30th October between 5 & 6 pm. I last saw her alive between 7.30 & 7.45 the night of Thursday before she was found. I was with her about one hour, we were on friendly terms. I told her when I left her I had no work and had nothing to give her of which I was very sorry, we did not drink together, she was quite sober, she was as long as she was with me of sober habits. She has got drunk several times in my presence. There was a female with us on Thursday evening when we were together, she left first and I left shortly afterwards. Deceased has often told me as to her parents, she said she was born in Limerick – that she was 25 years of age – & from there went to Wales when very young. She told me she came to London about 4 years ago. Her father's name was John Kelly, he was a Gauger at some iron works in Carnarvonshire. She told me she had one sister, who was a traveller with materials from market place to market place. She also said she had 6 brothers at home and one in the army, one was Henry Kelly. I never spoke to any of them. She told me she had been married when very young in Wales. She was married to a Collier, she told me the name was Davis or Davies, I think Davies. She told me she was lawfully married to him until he died in an explosion. She said she lived with him 2 or 3 years up to his death. She told me she was married at the age of 16 years. She came to London about 4 years ago, after her husband's death. She said she first went to Cardiff and was in an infirmary there 8 or 9 months and followed a bad life with a cousin whilst in Cardiff. When she left Cardiff she said she came to London. In London she was first in a gay house in the West End of the Town. A gentleman there asked her to go to France. She described to me she went to France. As she told me as she did not like the part she did not stay there long, she lived there about a fortnight. She did not like it and returned. She came back and lived in Ratcliffe Highway for some time, she did not tell me how long. Then she was living near Stepney Gas Works. Morganstone was the man she lived with there. She did not tell me how long she lived there. She told me that in Pennington Street she lived at one time with a Morganstone, and with Joseph Flemming, she was very fond of him. He was a mason's plasterer. He lived in Bethnal Green Rd. She told me all this, but I do not know which she lived with last, Flemming used to visit her. I picked up with her in Commercial Street, Spitalfields. The first night we had a drink together and I arranged to see her the next day, and then on the Saturday we agreed to remain together and I took lodgings in George Street where I was known, George Street, Commercial Street. I lived with her from then till I left her the other day. She had on several occasions asked me to read about the murders she seemed afraid of some one, she did not express fear of any particular individual except when she rowed with me but we always came to terms quickly.

By the jury no questions.

[The Coroner – You have given your evidence very well indeed. (To the Jury): The doctor has sent a note asking whether we shall want his attendance here to-day. I take it that it would be convenient that he should tell us roughly what the cause of death was, so as to enable the body to be buried. It will not be necessary to go into the details of the doctor's evidence, but he suggested that he might come to state roughly the cause of death.

The jury acquiesced in the proposed course.]

Thomas Bowyer

having been sworn upon the day and year and at the place above mentioned deposed as follows: I reside at 37 Dorset Street, Spitalfields. I am servant to Mr. McCarthy the owner of a chandlers shop & I serve in the shop. The shop is 27 Dorset Street. On Friday morning last at $\frac{1}{4}$ to 11 I was ordered by Mr. McCarthy to go to Mary Janes room No. 13, I only knew her as Mary Jane. I was to go for rent. I went & knocked at the door and got no answer. I knocked again and got no answer. I went round the corner and there was a broken window in the farthest window.

Charles Ledger put in and proved plans –
Charles Ledger, inspector [*of police*], G Division. I have made plans produced and they are correct plans of the premises.

Thomas Bowyer
I refer to plan and I mean the farthest pane of the first window the small one I looked in the window there was a curtain over the window I pulled the curtain aside and looked in I saw two lumps of flesh laying on the table ["to be" – *deleted*] close against the bed, in front of the bed. The second time I looked I saw a body of some one laid on the bed, and blood on the floor. I at once went then very quietly back to my master Mr. John McCarthy. We then stood in the shop, and I told him what I had seen. We both then went directly to the police station But before doing so I and my master went and looked in the window, Then we went to the police station and told the police what we had seen. We told no one before we went to the police station we came back with the inspector, I have oven [*sic* – often] seen deceased in and out, I know Joseph Barnett and have seen him going in, I have seen deceased drunk once.

By a juror
I last saw deceased alive on Wednesday afternoon in the Court.
Mr McCarthys shop is at the corner of the Court in Dorset Street.

John McCarthy having been sworn deposed as follows: I am a grocer and lodging house keeper at 27 Dorset-street. – On Friday morning last about $\frac{1}{4}$ to 11 I sent my man Bowyer to fetch rent from No 13 room Millers Court. He came back in about 5 minutes and said governor I knocked at the door and could not make any one answer. I looked through the window and saw a lot of blood. I went out with him and looked through the window and saw the body any [*sic* – and?] everything I said to my man don't tell any one let us fetch the police I knew deceased as Mary Jane Kelly I have seen the body and have no doubt as to the identity. I and Bowyer went then to the Police Court Commercial Street and saw Inspector Beck. I inquired at first for other inspectors. I told Inspector Beck what I had seen. He put on his hat and coat and came with me at once. deceased has lived in the room with Joe for 10 months both together. They lived comfortably together but once broke the two windows – the furniture and everything in the room belongs to me. I was paid 4/6d a week for the room but rent was 29s./- in arrear, the rent was paid to me weekly the room was let weekly. I very often saw deceased worse for drink she was a very quiet woman when sober but noisy when in drink she was not ever helpless when drunk. –

Mary Ann Cox having been sworn deposed as follows: I am a widow and live at No. 5 Room, Millers Court the last house top of the Court I get my living on the streets as best I can I have known the female occupying No 13 room 8 or 9 as Mary Jane I last saw her alive about midnight on Thursday very much intoxicated, in Dorset Street she went up the Court a few steps in front of me, there was a short stout man shabbily dressed with her, he had a longish coat, very shabby dark and a pot of ale in his hand, he had a hard billy cock black hat on, he had a blotchy face and a full, carrotty mustache his chin was clean.

I saw them go into her room. I said good night, Mary and the man banged the door, he had nothing in his hands but a pot of beer. She answered me I am going to have a song, I went into my room and I heard her sing "a violet I plucked from my mother's grave when a boy." I remained a quarter of an hour in my room, then went out. She was still singing, I returned about one oclock she was singing then. I warmed my hands and went out again she was still singing. I came in again at 3 o'clock, the light was out and there was no noise. I did not undress at all that night, I heard no noise, it was raining hard, I did not go to sleep at all I heard nothing whatever after one oclock – I heard men going in and out, several go in and out, I heard some one go out at a quarter to six. I do not know what house he went out of I heard no door shut. He did not pass my window –

The man had short carroty mustache all his clothes were dark, they made no sound going up the Court. Mary Jane had no hat on she had a red pellorine [sic – pelerine] and a dark shabby skirt – I noticed she was drunk as I said good night, the man at once closed the door

By the Jury – The [sic] was light in the room when she was singing I saw nothing as the blinds were down, I should know the man again.

By the Coroner I should have heard any cry of murder I heard nothing, I have very often seen deceased drunk.

Elizabeth Prater having been sworn deposed as follows: I am the wife of William Prater a Boot Machinist, he has deserted me for 5 years I live at No 20 Room in Millers Court up stairs I lived in the room over where deceased lived-

On Thursday I went into the Court about 5 oclock in the evening and returned about 1 on Friday morning. I stood at the corner by Mr McCarthys shop till about 20 minutes past 1 I spoke to no one I was waiting for a man I lived with, he did not come. I went up to my room. On the stairs I could see a glimmer through the partition if there had been a light in the deceaseds room. I might not have noticed it. I did not take particular notice – I could have heard her moving if she had moved. I went in about 1.30 I put 2 tables against the door. I went to sleep at once I had something to drink I slept soundly till a kitten disturbed me about 3.30 to 4. I noticed the lodging house light was out, so it was after 4 probably – I heard a cry of oh! Murder! As the cat came on me and I pushed her down, ["in" – *deleted*] the voice was in a faint voice – the noise seemed to come from close by – It is nothing uncommon to hear cries of murder so I took no notice – I did not hear it a second time. I heard nothing else whatever I went to sleep again and woke at 5 oclock. I got up and went down and went across to the ten bells I was there at ¼ to 6 at the corner of Church Street – I saw several men harnessing horses in Dorset Street – Mary Ann Cox could have passed down the Court during the night without me hearing her – After having a drink at the 10 Bells I went home and slept till 11 –

I went to bed at half past one – I did not hear any singing. – I should have heard any one if singing in the deceaseds room at 1 oclock, there was no one singing

Caroline Maxwell having been sworn deposed as follows: I ["am" – *deleted*] live at 14 Dorset Street my husband's name is Henry Maxwell he is a Lodging House deputy. I knew the deceased for about 4 months as Mary Jane. I also knew Joe Barnett, I believe she was an unfortunate girl. I never spoke to her except twice – I took a deal of notice of deceased this evening seeing her standing at the corner of the Court on Friday from 8 to half past I know the time by taking the plates my husband had to take care of from the house opposite. I am positive the time was between 8 & half past I am positive I saw deceased I spoke to her I said why Mary what brings you up so early she said Oh! I do feel so bad! Oh Carry I feel so bad! She knew my name – ["she as" – *deleted*] I asked her to have a drink, she said oh no I have just had a drink of ale and have brought it all up, it was in the road I saw it – as she said this she motioned with her head and I concluded she meant she had been to the Brittania [*sic*] at the corner, I left her saying I pitied her feelings – I then went to Bishopsgate as I returned I saw her outside the Brittania talking to a man – the time was then about 20 minutes to half an hour later about a quarter to nine – I could not describe the man I did not pass them I went into my house I saw them in the distance, I am certain it was deceased, the man was not a tall man – he had on dark clothes and a sort of plaid coat – I could not say what hat he had on – Mary Jane had a dark skirt – velvet body – and morone shawl & no hat – I have seen deceased in drink but not really drunk –

By a Juror – I did not notice whether deceased had on a high silk hat – if it had been so I would have noticed it I think

Sarah Lewis having been sworn deposed as follows: I live at 24 Great Powell Street, Spitalfields. I am a Laundress. I know Mrs. Keyler in Millers Court. I was at her house at half past 2 on Friday morning she lives at No 2 in the Court on the left on the first floor I know the time by having looked at Spitalfields Church clock as I passed it – When I went in the court I saw a man opposite the Court in Dorset Street standing alone by the Lodging House. He was not tall – but stout – had on a wideawake black hat – I did not notice his clothes – another young man with a woman passed along – The man standing in the street was looking up the court as if waiting for some one to come out, I went to Mrs ["Kelseys" – *deleted*] Keylers I was awake all night in a chair I dozed I heard no noise I woke up at about half past three – I sat awake till nearly five – a little before 4 I heard a female voice shout loudly one Murder! The sound seemed to come from the direction of deceaseds room there was only one scream – I took no notice of it – I left Mrs Keylers at about half past 5 in the afternoon the police would not let us out before – About Wednesday night at 8 oclock I was going along Bethnal Green Road with another female and a Gentleman passed us he turned back & spoke to us, he asked us to follow him, and asked one of us he did not mind which we refused, he went away, and came back & said if we would follow him he would treat us – he asked us to go down a passage – he had a bag he put it down saying what are you frightened of – he then undid his coat and felt for something and we ran away – he was short, pale faced, with a black small moustache, about 40 years of age – the bag he had was about a foot or nine inches long – he had on a round high hat – a high one for a round one – he had a brownish long overcoat and a short black coat underneath – and pepper & salt ["and" – *deleted*] trousers.

On our running away we did not look after the man – On the Friday morning about half past two when I was coming to Millers Court I met the same man with a female – in Commercial Street near Mr Ringers Public House – near the market – He had then no overcoat on – but he had the bag & the same hat trousers & undercoat

I passed by them and looked back at at [*sic*] the man – I was frightened – I looked again when I got to the corner of Dorset Street. I have not seen the man since I should know him if I did –

George Bagster Phillips – M R C S Regd – having been sworn deposed as follows: I am a surgeon to H Division of Metropolitan Police and reside at 2 Spital Square – I was called by the police on Friday morning last about 11 oclock and proceeded to Millers Court which I entered at 11.15 a.m. I found a room the door of which led out of the passage near 26 Dorset Street and having two windows I produce a photograph I had taken – there are two windows in the court – 2 of the panes in the window nearest the passage were broken and finding the door locked I looked through the lower broken pane and satisfied myself that the mutilated corpse lying on the bed was not in need of any immediate attention from me and I also came to the conclusion that there was nobody else on the bed or within view to whom I could render any professional assistance – Having ascertained that probably it was advisable that no entrance should be made into the room at that time, I remained until about 1.30 when the door was broken open I think by Mr McCarthy – I think by direction of Superintendent Arnold who had arrived – When I arrived the premises were in charge of Inspector Beck

On the door being opened it knocked against a table, the table I found close to the left-hand side of the bedstead and the bedstead was close up against the wooden partition, the mutilated remains of a female were lying two thirds over towards the edge of the bedstead, nearest to the door of entry she had only her under linen garment on her, and from my subsequent examination I am sure the body had been removed subsequent to the injury which caused her death from that side of the bedstead which was nearest to the wooden partition, the large quantity of blood under the bedstead, the saturated condition of the paliasse, pillow, sheet, at that top corner nearest the partition leads me to the conclusion that the severance of the right carotid artery which was the immediate cause of her death was inflicted while the deceased was lying at the right side of the bedstead and her head and neck in the top right- hand corner.

At this point *The Times* of Tuesday, 13 November 1888 added in its coverage of the inquest:

> The jury had no questions to ask at this stage, and it was understood that more detailed evidence of the medical examination would be given at a further hearing.
>   An adjournment for a few minutes then took place, and on the return of the jury the Coroner said, "It has come to my ears that somebody has been making a statement to some of the jury as to their right and duty of being here. Has any one during the interval spoken to the jury, saying that they should not be here today?"
>   Some jurymen replied in the negative.
>   The Coroner: Then I must have been misinformed. I should have taken good care that he would have had a quiet life for the rest of the week if anybody had interfered with my jury.

The inquest papers continue with the statements of the witnesses:

Julia Venturney having been sworn deposed as follows: I live at No 1 Room Millers Court I am a charwoman I live with Harry Owen I knew the female who occupied No 13 room she said she was a married woman and her name was Kelly. She lived with Joe Barnett she frequently got drunk Joe Barnett would not let her go on the streets – Deceased said she was fond of another man named Joe who used to come and see her and give her money I think he was a costermonger she said she was very fond of him – I last saw her alive on Thursday about 10 a m having her breakfast with another woman in her own room. I went to bed on Thursday night about 8 oclock I could not sleep all night I only dozed I heard no one in the court I heard no singing, I heard no scream – deceased often sung Irish songs –

Maria Harvey having been sworn deposed as follows: I live at No. 3 New Court, Dorset Street I knew deceased as Mary Jane Kelly I slept two nights with her on Monday & Tuesday nights last I slept with her. We were together all the afternoon on Thursday, I am a Laundress I was in the room when Joe Barnett called I went away I left my bonnet there. I knew Barnett – I left some clothes in the room 2 mens shirts, 1 boy's shirt, an overcoat a black one a mans, a black crape bonnet with black strings, a ticket for a shawl in for 2/-, one little child's white petticoat – I have seen nothing of them since except the overcoat produced to me by the police. I was a friend of deceaseds – she never told me of being afraid of any one –

Walter Beck H Division Inspector Commercial Street Station I was the first police officer called to 13 Millers Court by McCarthy. I sent for the Doctor and closed the Court to all persons. I do not know by whose order the door was forced, I was there, the doctor was the first to enter the room, it was shortly after 11 oclock when I was called

Frederick George Abberline Inspector Scotland Yard ["I am in" – *deleted*] having been sworn deposed as follows: I am in charge of this case – I was on the scene of the murder by 11.30 on Friday, I had an intimation from Inspector Beck that the dogs had been sent for Dr Phillips asked me not to force the door but to test the dogs if they were coming we remained until 1.30 when Superintendent Arnold arrived & informed me that the order as to dogs had been countermanded, and he gave directions for the door to be forced I have heard the Doctors evidence and confirm what he says. I have taken an inventory of what was in the room, there had been a large fire so large as to melt the spout off the kettle I have since gone through the ashes in the grate & found nothing of consequence except that articles of womans clothing had been burnt which I presume was for the purpose of light as there was only one piece of candle in the room – I am informed by the witness Barnett that the key has been missing for some time & that they opened the door by reaching through the window, a pipe was there & used by him.

The Times gives details of the conclusion of the inquest:

The Coroner (to the jury): The question is whether you will adjourn for further evidence. My own opinion is that it is very unnecessary for two courts to deal with these cases, and go through the same evidence time after time, which only causes expense and trouble. If the

coroner's jury can come to a decision as to the cause of death, then that
is all that they have to do. They have nothing to do with prosecuting a
man and saying what amount of penalty he is to get. It is quite sufficient
if they find out what the cause of death was. It is for the police
authorities to deal with the case and satisfy themselves as to any person
who may be suspected later on. I do not want to take it out of your
hands. It is for you to say whether at an adjournment you will hear
minutes of the evidence, or whether you will think it is a matter to be
dealt with in the police-courts later on, and that this woman, having
met with her death by the carotid artery having been cut, you will be
satisfied to return a verdict to that effect. From what I learn the police
are content to take the future conduct of the case. It is for you to say
whether you will close the inquiry to-day; if not, we shall adjourn for a
week or fortnight, to hear the evidence that you may desire.

The Foreman, having consulted with his colleagues, considered that
the jury had had quite sufficient evidence before them upon which to
give a verdict.

The Coroner: What is the verdict?

The Foreman: Wilful murder against some person or persons
unknown.

An important witness contacted the police after the inquest had
been closed. The three-page witness statement[3] George Hutchinson
remains, as follows:

Commercial Street
METROPOLITAN POLICE
H Division
12th November 1888

At 6 pm 12th George Hutchinson of the Victoria Home Commercial Street came to this Station and made the following statement.

About 2 am 9th I was coming by Thrawl Street, Commercial
Street, and saw just before I got to Flower and Dean Street I saw the
murdered woman Kelly. and she said to me Hutchinson will you
lend me sixpence. I said I cant I have spent all my money going
down to Romford. she said Good morning I must go and find some
money. she went away towards Thrawl Street. a man coming in the
opposite direction to Kelly tapped her on the shoulder and said
something to her. they both burst out laughing. I heard her say
alright to him. and the man said you will be alright for what I have
told you. he then placed his right hand around her shoulders. He

also had a kind of a small parcel in his left hand with a kind of a strap round it. I stood against the lamp of the ["Ten Bell" – *deleted*] Queens Head Public House and watched him. They both then came past me and the man hid down his head with his hat over his eyes. I stooped down and looked him in the face. He looked at me stern. They both went into Dorset Street I followed them. They both stood at the corner of the Court for about 3 minutes. He said something to her. she said alright my dear come along you will be comfortable He then placed his arm on her shoulder and gave her a kiss. She said she had lost her handkerchief he then pulled his handkerchief a red one out and gave it to her. They both then went up the Court together. I then went to the Court to see if I could see them but could not. I stood there for about three quarters of an hour to see if they came out they did not so I went away.

Description age about 34 or 35. height 5ft6 complexion pale, dark eyes and eye lashes ["dark" – *deleted*] slight moustache, curled up each end, and hair dark, very surley looking dress long dark coat, collar and cuffs trimmed astracan. and a dark jacket under. light waistcoat dark trousers dark felt hat turned down in the middle. button boots and gaiters with white buttons. wore a very thick gold chain white linen collar. black tie with horse shoe pin. respectable appearance walked very sharp. Jewish appearance. can be identified.

George Hutchinson
E Badham Sergt
E. Ellisdon Insp

Submitted FGAbberlineInspr   T Arnold Supdt.

The witness Hutchinson, who did not come forward until after the Kelly inquest, was interviewed by Abberline whose report of 12 November 1888 is preserved[4]:

METROPOLITAN POLICE
Criminal Investigation Department,
Scotland Yard
12th day of November, 1888
I beg to report that an inquest was held this day at the Shoreditch Town Hall before Dr. Macdonald M.P. Coroner on the body of Marie Jeanette Kelly, found murdered at No. 13 Room, Millers Court, Dorset Street, Spitalfields. A number of witnesses were called who clearly established the identity of deceased. The Coroner remarked that

in his opinion it was unnecessary to adjourn the inquiry and the jury returned a verdict of "Wilful murder against some person or persons unknown."

An important statement has been made by a man named George Hutchinson which I forward herewith. I have interrogated him this evening and I am of opinion his statement is true. He informed me that he had occasionally given the deceased a few shillings, and that he had known her about 3 years. Also that he was surprised to see a man so well dressed in her company which caused him to watch them. He can identify the man, and arrangement was at once made for two officers to accompany him round the district for a few hours tonight with a view of finding the man if possible.

Hutchinson is at present in no regular employment, and he has promised to go with an officer tomorrow morning at 11.30. am. to the Shoreditch mortuary to identify the deceased. Several arrests have been made on suspicion of being connected with the recent murders, but the various persons detained have been able to satisfactorily account for their movements and were released.

F.G.Abberline Inspr
T Arnold Supt.

George Hutchinson's statement was given wide coverage in the national newspapers, unlike the story about Sir George Arthur gleefully reported in the *New York World*, 18 November 1888:

SPECIAL CABLE DESPATCH TO THE WORLD.

London, Nov. 17. – The most intense amusement has been caused among all classes of the London world by the arrest last week of little Sir George Arthur on suspicion of being the Whitechapal murderer. Sir George is a young Baronet holding a captaincy in the regiment of Royal Horse Guards, and is a member of most of the leading clubs in town. He is also a well-known amateur actor, and was a great friend of the late Prince Leopold Duke of Albany. Since the past few weeks the old mania for "slumming" in White-chapel has become fashionable again. Every night scores of young men, who have never been the East End before in their lives prowl around the neighborhood in which the murders were committed, talking with the frightened women and pushing their way into over-crowded lodging-houses. So long as any two men keep together and do not make a nuisance of themselves the police do not interfere with them. But if a man goes alone and tries to lure a woman of the street into a secluded corner to talk with her he is pretty sure to get into trouble. That was the case with Sir George Arthur. He put on an old shooting coat, a slouch hat and went down to Whitechapel for a little fun. He got it. It occurred to two policemen that Sir George answered very much the popular descriptive of Jack the Ripper. They watched him, and when they saw him talking with women they proceeded to collar him. He protested, expostulated and threatened them with the vengeance of royal wrath, but in vain. Finally, a chance was given to him to send to a fashionable Western Club to prove his identity, and he was released with profuse apologies for the mistake. The affair was kept out of the newspapers. But the jolly young Baronet's friends as Brook's Club considered the joke too good to be kept quiet.

CHAPTER 22

21 November 1888 – A Second Outrage?

Fears of another "Ripper" attack were raised by an incident that occurred in Spitalfields on the morning of Wednesday, 21 November 1888. *The Times* of Thursday, November 22 1888, carried a report[1] of the incident:

MURDEROUS OUTRAGE IN WHITECHAPEL.

Considerable excitement was caused throughout the East-end yesterday morning by a report that another woman had been brutally murdered and mutilated in a common lodging-house in George-street, Spitalfields, and in consequence of the reticence of the police authorities all sorts of rumours prevailed. Although it was soon ascertained that there had been no murder, it was said that an attempt had been made to murder a woman, of the class to which the other unfortunate creatures belonged, by cutting her throat, and the excitement in the neighbourhood for some time was intense. Whether the woman's assailant is the man wanted for the seven recent murders committed in the district of Whitechapel is, of course, not known, although his description tallies somewhat with that given by one of the witnesses at the last inquest; but should he be, the police are sanguine of his speedy capture, as a good and accurate description of him is now obtained, and if arrested he could be identified by more than one person. The victim of this last occurrence, fortunately, is but slightly injured, and was at once able to furnish the detectives with a full description of her assailant. Her name is Annie Farmer, and she is a woman of about 40 years of age, who lately resided with her husband, a tradesman, in Featherstone-street, City-road, but, on account of her dissolute habits, was separated from him. On Monday night the woman had no money, and, being unable to obtain any, walked the streets until about half-past 7 yesterday morning. At that time she got into conversation, in Commercial-street, with a man, whom she describes as about 36 years of age, about 5ft. 6in. in height, with a dark moustache, and wearing a shabby black diagonal suit and hard felt hat. He treated her to several drinks until she became partially intoxicated. At his suggestion they went to the common lodging-house, 19, George-street, and paid the deputy 8d. for a bed. That was about 8 o'clock, and nothing was heard to cause alarm or suspicion until half-past 9, when screams were heard proceeding from the room occupied by the man and Farmer. Some men who were in the kitchen of the house at the time rushed upstairs and met the woman coming down. She was partially undressed, and was bleeding profusely from a wound in the throat. She was asked what was the matter, and simply said "He's done it," at the same time pointing to the door leading into the street. The men rushed outside, but saw no one, except a man in charge of a horse and cart. He was asked if he had noticed any person running away, and said he had seen a man, who he thought had a scar at the back of the neck, run down George-street and turn into Thrawl-street, but not thinking much of the occurrence, had not taken particular notice of the man and had made no attempt to detain him. By this time a considerable number of people had assembled, and these ran into Thrawl-street and searched the courts leading out of that thoroughfare, but without any success. While this was being done the police were communicated with and quickly arrived on the scene. In the meantime the deputy of the lodging-house had wrapped a piece of rag over the woman's wound, and, seeing that it did not appear to be a dangerous cut, got her to dress herself. Dr. George Bagster Phillips, divisional surgeon of the H Division, together with his assistant, quickly arrived, and the former gentleman stitched up the wound. Seeing that it was not a dangerous one, and in order to get the woman away from the crowd of inmates, who pressed round, he suggested that she should be removed to the Commercial-street Police-station, and that was quickly done on the ambulance. Although none but police officers were allowed to interview her with regard to the attack, and consequently nothing definite is known as to the cause, it has transpired that she had previously met her assailant some 12 months since, and owing to this fact the officers are doubtful whether the man had anything to do with the murders. Owing to the excellent description given they are sanguine of securing the man's arrest within a very short space of time. Superintendent T. Arnold, who was quickly apprised of what had happened, at once ordered Detective-officers Thicke [*sic*], New, M'Guire, and others to endeavour to capture the man, and by about 10.30 a full description of him was telegraphed to all the police-stations throughout the metropolitan police district. It is stated that Farmer is able to converse freely, and that lodgings will be found for her by the police until the person who attacked her is captured. Directly the police arrived at the house in George-street a constable was stationed at the door, and no person was allowed to leave until his or her statement and full particulars concerning each one had been written down. During the whole of the day a crowd collected in front of 19, George-street, apparently drawn thither merely out of curiosity to view the house, but none not belonging to it were allowed to enter.

A further report mentioning the attack on Farmer appeared in the *East Anglian Daily Times* of Monday, 26 November 1888:

THE EAST END MURDERS.

Upon enquiry at two o'clock on Sunday morning it was found that no positive clue to the murderer had been discovered nor was anyone detained in custody upon suspicion. As regards the assault made upon Annie Farmer in a common lodging-house at George Street, Flower and Dean Street, by a man who afterwards made his escape, nothing further of him has been seen, and the police are inclined to believe that the affair was only an ordinary brawl, and that the woman is acquainted with the man who assailed her, but will not give information which will lead to his detection. On Saturday night there were still many amateur detectives parading the streets with intent to assist the police, but in some cases their vigilance appeared to be a little over-zealous. It seems that a man of foreign appearance, who was in search of the murderer, provided himself with a revolver, and in a moment of confidence showing it to a policeman in plain clothes, he was arrested and taken to Leman Street Police Station for unlawfully having firearms in his possession. The case was investigated, and a satisfactory explanation having been given, the man was discharged.

Two of the men who described at the time the man believed to have committed the Berners [*sic*] Street and other murders, to-day reported that they have again seen him, but that though they followed him he disappeared suddenly down an unfrequented turning.

CHAPTER 23

Police Activity Following the Kelly Murder

The excitement caused by the Kelly murder understandably caused further criticism of the police by press and public, and resulted in yet further increases in police strength in the area. An idea of the official activity is conveyed in the reports of this period of time.

There is a report in the file[1], date-stamped 14 NOV.88, as follows:

> Home Office,
> Whitehall,
> S.W.

Mr. Murdoch.

Anderson left this with the Chief this morning. He told me that he wd. send a covering letter officially.

> CRB

13/11.

This is followed by a Home Office cover page[2] which is as follows:

[Stamped: – HOME OFFICE 14 NOV.88 RECEIVED]
DATE 14 Nov. 1888.   Dr. Forbes Winslow.
REFERENCES, &c.   <u>East End Murders.</u>
          Expresses his opinion that the murderer is a homicidal lunatic. Places his services at the Gov.'s disposal.

                              <u>Press</u>ing
          [MINUTES.]
          Ackgd. 14.11.88

To Police.
   CW
      Nov 15. 88.

EP 17 Nov 88
Forwarded with other letters
under. /107
17th.Nov.1888.

There is no enclosure with this cover and it is followed by another cover page[3] as follows:

[Stamped: – HOME OFFICE 15 NOV.88 RECEIVED]
DATE 15 Novr.88.   Louis Solomon
REFERENCES &c.   Directors fd copies of statements
recd. from Offrs of Woking Prison who think it possible that above may be the Whitechapel Murderer.
MINUTES.
For letter see A21640 (*Destroyed*)
an ordinary criminal case.

There is a letter[4] dated 29 November 1888 from Godfrey Lushington to the Commissioner of the Metropolitan Police:

B 5329/5   WHITEHALL.
                              29th November 1888.
Sir,
    With reference to the letter from this Department of the 22nd. ultimo and your replies of the 25th. and 30th. ultimo, I am directed by the Secretary of State to request that you will be so good as to furnish him with a statement showing, (i). the area. (ii) the number of inhabited houses, and, so far as you are able to give the information, (iii) the population of the ''H'' or Whitechapel Division.

                              I am,
                                Sir,
                      Your obedient Servant,
                        Godfrey Lushington
The Commissioner
of the Metropolitan Police.

The reply to this letter is not included.
    A file date[5] reads as follows:

[Stamped: – HOME OFFICE 8 DEC.88 RECEIVED]

No. A49301G/1

DATE 7 Decr.88.   Comr. of Police

REFERENCES &c.   Recomds. that the Offrs.

employed specially in plain clothes to patrol the neighbourhood of the Whitechapel Murders be granted 1s/- per day allce.

[MINUTES.]

The original authority for payment of 1s/- a day to permanent patrols which Mr Munro desires these men should have was accorded on the formation of the C.I.D. in 1878 – see 66692/43a. The expense as Mr Munro admits is considerable £5 a day.

?First to Receiver for financial observations.

CM Dec. 19.

GL

19 Dec 1888

Wrote 20/12 a/21.12.88 ($\frac{1}{2}$)

The following report is included:

A49301G/1

96318   4 Whitehall Place,

S.W.

7th December, 1888.

Sir,

I have to acquaint you, for the information of the Secretary of State, that, in connection with the recent murders in Whitechapel, one Inspector 9 Sergeants and 126 Constables of the uniform branch of the Force have been employed specially in plain clothes to patrol the neighbourhood of the Murders with a view to prevent a repetition of the Crime.

These officers are entitled to the usual plain clothes allowance, viz: 1s/11d per week for Sergeants and Constables and 3s/11d for the Inspector. –

Many of them, however, come from other divisions and have to patrol at a distance from their homes, and they have continuous night duty, which will be very trying when the winter sets in. – The work is specially irksome and unpleasant, and these men are practically doing the duty of permanent patrols.

The usual allowance is inadequate to compensate a man for the wear and tear of his clothes when he is engaged for a lengthened period. –

Under the circumstances therefore I have to recommend to the favourable consideration of Mr. Secretary Matthews that the men employed on this special duty should receive the allowance of 1s/- per diem as granted to permanent patrols.

The expense will be considerable, amounting to about £5 per diem; but it is in my opinion justifiable and should be incurred. —

I am,

Sir,

Your most obedient Servant,

JMonro.

The Under Secretary
of State
Home Office.

The following letter[6] on this subject, dated 21 December 1888, is as follows:

5185/1   A49301G/2
                                                4 Whitehall Place
                                                21 Decr. 1888

Sir,

In returning Mr. Munro's letter of 7th inst. proposing the grant of an allowance of 1/- a day to officers specially employed on patrol duty in the neighbourhood of the Whitechapel murders, I have the honour to state that having regard to the nature of the duty I concur with the Commissioner's recommendation.

In view however of the great expense involved, I submit that some limit should be fixed by the Secretary of State, and having consulted with the Commissioner on the matter, I believe he would be satisfied if the allowance were granted from the date of this application and not retrospectively from the commencement of the duties.

I would therefore suggest that the total extra expenditure for this service should be limited to £300, and when that amount is expended that the subject should be re-considered.

I have the honour to be,

Sir,

Your obedient Servant

A.S. [ ].

The international interest in the now infamous series of White-chapel crimes attracted many people who felt they could cast some light on the identity of the killer. A Spanish contender appeared in early December 1888 and the official file cover[7] reads as follows:

[Stamped: – HOME OFFICE 7 DEC.88 RECd.DEPt.]   No. A49301/5
DATE   6 Decr 1888   Foreign Office
REFERENCES, &c.   Whitechapel Murderer
                          Forwards letter and translation from Mr
                          Thomas Romero giving a description of the
                          man whom he believes to be the murderer.
[*There is a marginal note* – "Copy of translation made original letter sent"]

MINUTES.
["Confidential & Pressing" – *deleted*]
Ackn and
To Police.
C.M. Decr. 7.
Ackd. & Wrote Comr.
7/12.

There follows a letter[8] from the Foreign Office:

A49301D/5
[Stamped: – HOME OFFICE 7 DEC.88 RECd. DEPt.]

Pressing   Foreign Office,
Confidential   December 6 1888.
Sir,
    I am directed by the Secretary of State for Foreign Affairs to transmit to you, herewith, for the information of the Secretary of State for the Home Department the translation of a letter from a Spaniard Mr. Thomas Romero giving the description of a man whom he believes to be the Whitechapel murderer.

I am,
Sir,
Your most obedient,
humble Servant.
T.V. Lister

The
      Under Secretary of State
         Home Office.

There then follows the translation[9] of the said letter, addressed to the Prime Minister, Lord Salisbury, from the Foreign Office:

[Stamped: – HOME OFFICE 7 DEC. 88 RECd. DEPt.]   A49301D/5
Translation   26 Nov: 1888.
My Lord,

With the fear and curiosity inspired by the monstrous crimes now being committed in Whitechapel I am following step by step the horrible tragedies which will not end so long as the miserable assassin is at liberty.

Today I see that the disemboweller of women could not finish his last crime because the cries of the victim brought the police and the public, who did not succeed, notwithstanding their generous efforts, in capturing the assassin.

The woman who thus was able miraculously to escape from what would have been certain death but for such immediate assistance, has, of course, given a detailed description of the murderer, with whom I believe I have been and whom I believe I knew when I was in London in 1885, as a refugee for political offences committed through the columns of the newspaper called "La Coalicion" of which I was editor. The ferocious man in question told me one day, as the most natural thing in the world, of the means he employed in order to study certain functions of life; they consisted in tearing out the organs of a person who had recently died by violence, I therefore add below the description of that man in order that the victim may be questioned as to whether it agrees with that of the Whitechapel murderer.

Short; hair light chestnut rather than fair; eyes, blue, small, round and deep sunk; moustache, silky and fair; beard very light (he wore English whiskers when I was with him); age somewhere about 35 years; nose, so depressed in the middle as hardly to hold the smoke coloured spectacles which he always wore; one or two teeth were missing in the upper jaw and he spoke English, French, German, Russian and Spanish; he would so readily say he was an American as a German, for he talked of Berlin and of New York as cities that he was very well acquainted with; he once told me, whom he particularly affected among the friends that met together, that he was a German Socialist and once on going to the Natural History Museum at London (I think that is the name of the place at the entrance of which you see the skeleton of a colossal crocodile or some reptile of that family) he told me how, after abandoning himself to the pleasures of Venus, he extracted the uterus of a woman whom he killed in the year 1880 or 1881.

I thought such a man a great impostor and from the day on which he told me of that deed, I took such an aversion to him and he inspired me with extreme repugnance, that I tried to avoid his company and from that day we met but a few times more.

One day he was dining with us at Veglio's, a restaurant in Tottenham Court Road, and told us that we should dine much better and cheaper at an eating house in a little street near Oxford St. where we dined twice and did not return on account of the horrid cook of that tavern or cook-shop.

A girl leading a gay life, called "Nelis Cherinton" who lived somewhere in the City, had supper with this man & myself one night after leaving the Alhambra and as the girl was a little gay owing to her having had a good quantity of whiskey given to her at the bar of the theatre, he said he was going to take her to pay her off for an insult she had offered him, I tried to prevent it but as I did not succeed, I said to him that he should let me take the girl with me and that he could come and fetch her another day and do what he liked with her, that was in November 1885, the girl would remember if the description was given to her and when she meets him she could watch him and if he is the murderer of the women he could be captured when he tried to commit the next murder.

As is right, I wish that all these revelations should be kept absolutely secret, not because I fear the vengeance of that man but because if he did not turn out to be guilty of such barbarous acts, I should be sorry to have called the attention of the police and of the English people to an innocent man by my imprudent revelations.

Therefore if the English Govt. thinks fit to accept my information, they may send somebody and to him I will, with the map of London in my hands, show the places the man I mean used to frequent and if it is necessary in the interests of humanity I myself will go to London and, there, when I meet him I will point him out to the police so that they may watch him and capture him – when he tries to commit another outrage.

If the English Govt. asks any information concerning me of the Spanish Govt., I shall at once refuse absolutely to say one word more about the man I suppose to be the "disemboweller of women", I say I do not want them to ask anybody about me, for Spain would accuse me of want of patriotism if I contributed to the good or to the peace of a people that snatched a bit of her territory from my beloved country, for until it is given back to Spain we must hold the English people to be usurpers ["what" – *deleted*] I wish that what I do for the good of humanity and in obedience to the most noble dictates of my soul which sympathises with a people justly alarmed at harbouring in its bosom without knowing him a man without human feelings, ["I wish to be o" – *deleted*] may be kept such an impenetrable secret that, even in the event of the assassin being discovered, I wish the glory of this good work to fall not on me but on my country whose nobleness and uprightness are proverbial and well known throughout the world.

Let the last victim be asked about the description I have given and if it coincides with that of the ["assassin" – *deleted*] man I suppose to be the assassin, be sure that I myself will cut off the destroying arm which is striking terror into the heart of London.

If they think my help necessary and wish to write to me let them do so in Spanish and address as under: –

　　Spain
Senor don Tomas Romero
　　Provincia de Cirdad Real
　　　　Herencia.
where they may command your
obedient servant
　　(s) Tomas Romero
Lord Salisbury
　　Foreign office.

The final page in this section[10] is a file cover, thus:

Tomas Romero
Nov 26
Dec 6 1888
Whitechapel Murder
Says he knows all
about it
comm'. By the Lord
Mayor Nov. 30.88
H.O.
386　　Spain

The Kelly murder had helped boost public interest in the press's reporting of the ongoing series of killings. This press interest was, as we have seen, international. A file[10] dated 14 December 1888, refers to news of another foreign suspect, as follows:

[Stamped: – HOME OFFICE 15 Dec.88 RECd DEPT] No.-A49301D/6
DATE 14 Decr 1888   Foreign Office
REFERENCES, &c.   Whitechapel Murders
Forwards copy of a despatch from Dresden as to a statement made by an American German Julius. I. Lowenheim re a Polish Jew Wirtkofsky who he used to meet in a "Christian Home" in Finsbury? Square – as this man told him he was determined to kill a certain woman & the rest of her class –
                    MINUTES.
                <u>Pressing & confidential</u>
Ackn, and to Police
           C.M. Dec. 15. 88.
Ackd & sent Despatch to Police.
                15. 12. 88

The reports under this cover commence:

[Stamped: – HOME OFFICE 15 DEC.88 RECd DEPT] A49301D/6

                         Foreign Office
                         December 14 1888.

Sir,
   I am directed by the Secretary of State for Foreign Affairs to transmit to you, to be laid before the Secretary of State for the Home Department, copy of a Despatch, as marked in the margin, relating to the Whitechapel murders.
[*Marginal note*:- Mr. Shackey / No 58. December 11.]
                         I am,
                           Sir,
                         Your most obedient,
                              humble Servant,
                           N. Lister
The Under-Secretary of State,
           Home Office.

Copy   A49301D
                                          Dresden
                                   11 December 1888
My Lord,
    Regarding American German, Julius I. Lowenheim, came here
this morning with a statement respecting the Whitechapel murders.
He said that shortly before the occurrence of the first crime he
became acquainted in a "Christian Home" in Finsbury Square, with
a Polish Jew one Julius Wirtkofsky, who, after consul[ting] him on a
special pathological con[dition] told him that he was determined to
kill the person conc[erned and] all the rest of her cl[ass] informant
added, that he had recently addressed the London Police Authorities
on the subject, without having received an answer.
    He further said that he could throw no light on the subsequent
movements of Wirtkofsky, but that he could identify him without
fail.
    Lowenheim stated that his address, after the next few days would
be, Poste Restante Nuremburg. It of course struck me that I had
heard a similar [ ] before, and that the youth's object was to
accomplish a journey to London, gratis.
    However, he showed no anxiety in that respect, and the
impression which he made upon me was not unfavourable.
                    [*signature &c. illegible.*]

Another suspect, Nikaner Benelius, appeared at Worship Street
Police Court in November. *The Times* of Monday, 19 November
1888, reported:

At WORSHIP-STREET, shortly before Mr. Bushby left the bench at the
close of the day's business, a Swede named NIKANER A. BENELIUS, 27
years of age, and described as a traveller, living in Great Eastern-
street, Shoreditch, was placed in the dock charged with entering a
dwelling-house in Buxton-street, Mile-end, for an unlawful purpose
and with refusing to give any account of himself. The prisoner is a
man of decidedly foreign appearance, with a moustache, but
otherwise cannot be said to resemble any of the published descriptions of men suspected in connexion with the Whitechapel murders.
Detective-sergeant Dew attended from Commercial-street Station,
and stated that the prisoner had been arrested that morning under
circumstances which made it desirable to have the fullest inquiries
made as to him. Before the last murder — of Mary Kelly, in Miller's-

court – the prisoner had been arrested by the police and detained in connexion with the Berner-street murder, but was eventually released. He had, however, remained about the neighbourhood, lodging in a German lodging-house, but having, the officer said, no apparent means of subsistence. The landlord said that the prisoner was 25s. in debt to him. Harriet Rowe, a married woman, living in Buxton-street, Mile-end, then deposed that at about 10.30 that morning she had left the street door open, and while sitting in the parlour the prisoner, a stranger to her, opened the door and walked in. She asked him what he wanted, but he only grinned in reply. She was greatly alarmed, being alone, and ran to the window. The prisoner then opened the parlour door and left. She followed him into the street until she saw a constable; but the prisoner first stopped the officer and spoke to him. Witness ran up and told the constable what the prisoner had done, and he was thereupon taken to the station. The police-constable, Imhoff, 211H, said that the prisoner was asking him the way to Fenchurch-street when the witness Rowe ran up. After hearing her complaint he asked the prisoner what he wanted to go to Fenchurch-street for, and the prisoner said he expected some letters at the post-office. The prisoner was searched at the station, but nothing was found on him. In answer to the charge he said he only went into the house to ask his way to Fenchurch-street. Mr. Bushby said he should follow the usual course and remand the prisoner for inquiries. The prisoner was remanded till Friday. Two men, one of whom was stated to be the prisoner's landlord, subsequently called about him and said that he had been preaching in the streets at times and acting of late very strangely.

The Times of Monday, 19 November 1888, reported[12] another suspect:

THE WHITECHAPEL MURDERS.

On Saturday afternoon the police arrested at Euston Station a man who had just arrived from Birmingham, and who described himself as a doctor. Upon being questioned the suspect made certain statements as to his whereabouts at the times of the murders which the police are now investigating. The man was susequently released.

The funeral of the murdered woman Kelly will take place to-day, when her remains will be buried in the Roman Catholic Cemetery at Leytonstone. The hearse will leave the Shoreditch Mortuary at half-past 12.

The Star of the same day reported on this suspect, adding more detail:

WHITECHAPEL.
The London Police Blunder Over a Birmingham
Suspect.

Considerable excitement was caused in London yesterday by the circulation of a report that a medical man had been arrested at Euston, upon arrival from Birmingham, on a charge of suspected complicity in the Whitechapel murders. It was stated that the accused had been staying at a common lodging-house in Birmingham since Monday last, and the theory was that if, as was supposed by the police, he was connected with the East-end crimes, he left the metropolis by an early train on the morning of the tragedies. The suspected man was of gentlemanly appearance and manners, and somewhat resembled the description of the person declared by witnesses at the inquest to have been

SEEN IN COMPANY WITH KELLY

Early on the morning that she was murdered. Upon being minutely questioned as to his whereabouts at the time of the murders, the suspect was able to furnish a satisfactory account of himself, and was accordingly liberated. It has since transpired that he has been watched by Birmingham police for the last five days, and when he left that town on Saturday the Metropolitan police were advised to continue to "watch" him, not to arrest him. But, in spite of this warning, the London police seem to have stupidly warned the man that he was suspected.

A *Star* man made a round of the police-stations this morning, and received everywhere the report of a very quiet night. Neither at Commercial-street nor Leman-street was anyone detained. Expectation of another murder being discovered this morning was the only cause of stir, and the detectives were mustered at the stations in readiness for any emergency. Up to twelve o'clock, however, nothing had turned up. Late last night there was some little excitement consequent on the arrest in a Flower and Dean-street tenement house of a young man named Charles Akehurst, of Canterbury-road, Ball's Pond-road, N. He accompanied a woman to her room, and there had the misfortune to make use of expressions which caused her to jump to the conclusion that

SHE WAS IN THE HANDS OF THE MURDERER.

She ran trembling to a policeman, who arrested the man. He satisfied the detective, however, and was released after a short detention. Full inquiries have been made into the movements of the Swede Nikaner A. Benelius, remanded by Mr. Bushby on a charge of being on private premises for an unlawful purpose. Inspector Reid states that the man's innocence of any hand in the murders has been fully established. The man, who has been lodging at a German lodging-house at 90, Great Eastern-street, has been preaching in the streets, and behaving in a manner which suggests that he is not so fully responsible for his actions as he might be. It was therefore thought advisable to make the fullest inquiries, which, however, have quite cleared him. He was arrested on suspicion in connection with the Berners-street [*sic*] murder, and is likely to be arrested every time the public attention is strained to the point of suspecting every man of odd behaviour. Dorset-street has still its knot of loungers, although it is more than a week since it achieved notoriety.

The *Northern Daily Telegraph* of Friday, 7 December 1888 reported the arrest of someone believed to be an important suspect:

THE LONDON HORRORS.
A BIG THING AT LAST.
ARREST OF A POLISH JEW.

The Metropolitan Police yesterday made a singular arrest, which was reported to be in connection with the Whitechapel murders. It appears that during the afternoon a man, described as a Polish Jew, was arrested near Drury-lane, but for what offence is not quite clear. This individual, who is of short stature, with black moustache, was taken to the Bow-street Station, where he was detained for a time. A telegraphic communication was forwarded thence to Leman-street Police Station, the headquarters of the Whitechapel division, requesting the attendance of one of the inspectors. Detective-inspector Abberline immediately proceeded to Bow-street, and subsequently brought away the prisoner in a cab, which was strongly escorted. The detectives at the East End made every inquiry in the neighbourhood concerning the suspect, who is well known in the locality, although he is stated to have been absent lately. It was subsequently ascertained that the man was apprehended for stealing a watch, with which offence he has been charged. The police, however, were led to believe that he was connected, not with the mutilations, but with the recent attempt to murder a woman in George-street, Spitalfields. Exhaustive inquiries were made, but as far as can be ascertained the man could in no way be connected with that outrage. It is further stated that the inspector was heard to say to one of his subordinates: "Keep this quiet; we have got the right man at last. This is a big thing."

The *London Evening News* of Saturday, 8 December 1888 also reported on the arrest of the suspect, Isaacs:

THE WHITECHAPEL MURDERS.

Joseph Isaacs, 30, who said he had no fixed abode, and described himself as a cigar maker, was charged at Worship-street, yesterday, with having stolen a watch, value 30s., the goods of Julius Levenson.

The prisoner, who was brought up in the custody of Detective-sergeant Record, H Division, is the man who was arrested in Drury-lane on Thursday afternoon on suspicion of being connected with the Whitechapel murders. It transpired during the hearing of this charge that it was committed at the very time the prisoner was being watched as a person "wanted." The prosecutor, Levenson, said that the prisoner entered his shop on the 5th instant, with a violin bow, and asked him to repair it. Whilst discussing the matter, the prisoner bolted out of the shop, and witness missed a gold watch belonging to a customer. The watch had been found at a pawn-shop. To prove that the prisoner was the man who entered the shop, a woman named Mary Cusins was called. She is deputy of a lodging-house in Paternoster-row, Spitalfields, and said that the prisoner had lodged in the house, as a single lodger, for three or four nights before the Dorset-street murder – the murder of Mary Janet [*sic*] Kelly, in Miller's-court. He disappeared after that murder, leaving the violin bow behind. The witness on the house to house inspection gave information to the police, and said she remembered that on the night of the murder she heard the prisoner walk about his room. After her statement a look out was kept for the prisoner, whose appearance certainly answered the published description of a man with an astrachan trimming to his coat. He visited the lodging-house on the 5th, and asked for the violin bow. It was given to him and the witness Cusins followed him to give him into custody as requested. She saw him enter Levenson's shop, and almost immediately run out, no constable being at hand.

Detective Record said that there were some matters alleged against the prisoner, which it was desired to inquire into.

Mr. Bushby remanded the prisoner.

The *Manchester Evening News* of Monday, 10 December 1888 also ran a small piece on the suspect:

THE WHITECHAPEL MURDER.
THE POLISH JEW SUSPECT.

The police are continuing their inquiries into the antecedents of Joseph Isaacs, said to be a Polish Jew, who is now in custody on a charge of watch stealing. Mary Cusins, the deputy of a lodging-house in Paternoster Row, near Dorset-street, and Cornelius Oakes, a lodger, state that the conduct of the prisoner was frequently strange. Although he had a violin and four or five other musical instruments, he was never known to play any of them. Oakes says the prisoner used often to change his dress. He heard him threaten violence to all women above 17 years of age.

The *Sunday Times* of Sunday, 23 December 1888 reported on yet another unlikely suspect for the Whitechapel murders:

THE WHITECHAPEL MURDERS – A CONFESSION – At Dalston Police-court, yesterday, Theophil Hanhart, 24, lately a French and German master at a school near Bath; was charged with being a person of unsound mind, and with confessing to be the Whitechapel murderer. The prisoner, who, it was said, exactly corresponded in description with the man "wanted" for the Whitechapel murders, was seen on Friday afternoon on the bank of the Regent's Canal at Haggerston. He told a constable that he was the cause of the Whitechapel murders, and he was very uneasy in his mind about it. He was seen by a medical man, who had certified that he was suffering from mental derangement, and not fit to be at large. The Rev. W. Mathias said the prisoner had been in his care since Sept. 16, and from that date he had never been out of his sight. A few days ago, finding that he was suffering from delusions he, on medical advice, brought the man to London, but on Thurday afternoon he missed him in the Strand. The prisoner was the son of a German pastor, and the matter had been reported to the German Consul in London. Inspector Reid, from Whitechapel, said he was satisfied that the prisoner could not have committed the murders, but Mr. Bros, being satisfied that the prisoner was not fit to be at large, sent him in a cab to the Shoreditch Infirmary.

CHAPTER 24

Edward Knight Larkins – An Early "Ripper" Theorist

A very early example of an obsessive "Ripper" theorist appeared in November 1888 in the person of Edward Knight Larkins, a clerk in HM Customs Statistical Department. He had applied his intellect and imagination to the problem of the Whitechapel Murders and he was determined that the authorities should take note of – and act upon – his advice. To that end he sent copies of his theory not only to the police but to the QC and magistrate Montagu Williams (who was apparently convinced that Larkins had hit upon the solution of the mystery), and to the London Hospital.

The first of the files regarding Larkins carries a cover[1], thus:

	No. A49301C/25
DATE 23 Nov 88	Foreign Office
REFERENCES, &c.	Mr Larkins Theory re arrival of cattle ships from Oporto in connection with Whitechapel murders.

                 MINUTES.

Pages referred to Commr of Police CID
                     24/11/88

Enclosures returned from Mr Anderson today and given to Mr Ruggles-Brise [*init. Illeg.*]
           31/1/89

This is followed by f 231, a second cover page:

[Stamped: – HOME OFFICE 26 NOV. 88 RECd. DEPt.] No. A49301C/25a

DATE 26 Nov 88	Foreign Office
REFERENCES, &c.	Whitechapel Murders

           Forwards copy of despatch from HM Consul at

Oporto with a report addressed to the Criminal
Investigation dept as to the questions of the arrival
of certain ships raised by Mr Larkins
[MINUTES.]
["Secret & immediate" – *deleted*]
To Commr. of Police.
(Forces) CM. Nov 26.88
Sent
26.11

The first report, f 232, is a letter from the Foreign Office to the
Under Secretary of State:

<u>Secret</u>.   A49301C/25a
[Stamped: – HOME OFFICE 26 NOV.88 RECd. DEPT]
Foreign Office
November 26 1888
Sir,
With reference to my letter of the 23rd instant
I am directed by the Secretary of State for
Foreign
Affairs to transmit to you, to be laid before Mr. Secretary
Matthews, a copy of a Despatch from H.M. Consul at Oporto,
transmitting a Report addressed to the Chief of the Criminal
Investigation Department on the points raised by Mr. Larkins in
reference to the Whitechapel murders.
I am,
Sir,
Your most obedient,
Humble Servant,
(For Sir J.)
The Under Secretary of State   HG Ber[ ]
Home Office

There then follows a letter[2] from the Consulate in Oporto, to the
Prime Minister, the Marquis of Salisbury:

A49301C

H.M. Consulate
No 8 [Stamped: – HOME OFFICE 26 NOV.88 RECEIVED DEPt.]
Oporto

Consular   Nov.22.1888.

My Lord,

In obedience to Y.L.'s instructions conveyed in telegrams received yesterday and the day before, I have enquired into the points raised in Mr. Larkins' letter in reference to the Whitechapel murders, and have reported directly by telegraph to Scotland Yard. I likewise address U.F.S. to the Chief of the Criminal Investigation Dept the enclosed full report on the subject.

I [ ]

(sd) Oswald Crawford

The Marquis of Salisbury

    " —

The next file cover[3] introduces the full information regarding Mr Larkins and his theory, and is dated 10 January 1889:

[Stamped: – HOME OFFICE 11 JAN.89 RECd. DEPt.] NO. A49301C/25b

DATE 10th Jany 89   Mr. E.K. Larkins Statistics Dept Customs

REFERENCES, &c.   Whitechapel Murders

Forwards memorandum as to his theory re Cattlemen from Oporto and states that the "City of Cork" is due in a day or two.

    MINUTES.

["Pressing & Confidential" – *deleted*]

Ackn: and to Mr Monro.

    CM. Jan 11.89

[Stamped: – REFERRED 11 JAN. 89 ANSr 11]

If any one of the Boats named had been in London at the date of each of the murders, this man's theory wd. be of great practical interest, But his scheme requires the adoption of the further theory that some man changed from one boat to another. Hitherto he has kept to two boats: he now introduces a third. The matter was referred to the Consul of Oporto, who reported that no such transfer took place, & that Larkins' theories were untenable. The most careful inquiry here has led to the same conclusion. I fear the man is a troublesome "faddist", & that it is idle to continue the subject with him. His

recent letters are in a tone which renders further
correspondence with him impossible

RA.

22/1/89

[Stamped: – HOME OFFICE 23 JAN.89]

? Putup

HBS

23/1

GL 23 Jan '89

I see in the newspapers that there is a scare in Spain that the man has
got over there & has committed two murders. Whether there is
anything in it I do not know. Perhaps the Cattle boat theory has
given rise to it.

CM Jan 23.

[*Here there is a marginal note at right angles to this section:- –* "Wrote
Mr. Larkins 20 Feb: 1889"]

I regret that Mr Larkins letter was, through misadventure not ackd:
as directed on the other side. But see Mr. Anderson's minute above
as to discontinuing correspondence.

? Express regret Mr Larkins, thro misadventure did not receive
ackt of his letter which [received full consideration – as well as
investigation on the part of the Police] CM

[ ] Feb 18th

There then follows the memorandum[4] referred to, from Mr Larkins:

[Stamped: – HOME OFFICE 11 JAN.89 RECd.DEPt.] Memorandum

The theory I have formed is that the murderer is a Portuguese
cattle-man who comes over with the cattle, from Oporto, in the
vessels belonging to Messrs. Coverley & Westray [?], in all
probability he is a middle aged married man, this I judge from
his victims being all verging on 50 years of age, had he been a young
man I presume he would have selected younger women.

My opinion is that on a voyage previous to the 30th August, this
monster contracted a certain disease by coming in contact with one
of these unfortunates, being in all probability a married man he
became exasperated by finding himself in that condition and with
the characteristic revengefulness of the Portuguese race he determined to wage war upon these fallen women.

From inquiries I have made I find these cattle men live in the hold of the vessel, sometimes, remaining below during the whole of the voyage.

The "City of Oporto" came into the London Docks on the 30th August, on the 31st he committed his first murder returning, no doubt, <u>at once</u> to his safe retreat in the hold of the vessel, finding he was not suspected and to baffle any clue that might be obtained he did not return in the "City of Oporto" but shifted onto the "City of Cork" which came into Dock on the 7th Sept and committed his second murder on the 8th Sept, at once returning to his safe quarters in the hold of the "City of Cork" and returning in that vessel to Oporto, on the 27th September he again came to this country in the "City of Cork" and probably, on inquiry, finding no clue had been obtained he committed the double murder on the 30th Sept. again returning hastily to his safe quarters in the hold of the "City of Cork" and returned to Oporto in that vessel, fearing from the outcry that was raised by this double atrocity that some possible clue might have been obtained, he probably did not venture over in the "City of Cork" on the voyage which terminated here on the 19th October, but finding none had been obtained, he again came over in the "City of Cork" on the 8th November and committed another murder on the 9th of that month.

I gave information of the movements of these vessels and the suspicions which I entertained on the 10th November, from which time or soon after these vessels have been watched incessantly, whenever in the Docks, which I have no doubt has been observed by this monster, the result being that <u>no murder</u> of the kind has since taken place.

EKLarkins

There then follows a seven-page report[5] from Larkins regarding his actions and theory:

[Stamped: – HOME OFFICE 11 JAN.89 RECd. DEPt.]
On the 10th November, after considerable research with regard to the dates, I called upon Inspector Moore at Leman Street Police Station and communicated to him the result, with reference to the following vessels.

Ship	Date and time of arrival in London Docks	Date of Murder

"City of Oporto"   August 30th–7P.M.   August 31st.
"City of Cork"   September 7th 2P.M.   September 8th.
       "   "   27th 4P.M.   "   30th.
       "   November 8th 2.30P.M.   November 9th.

On the 12th I again saw Inspector Moore and communicated the fact that the crews of these vessels with the exception of the Officers, were all <u>Portuguese</u> and that the <u>cattle-men</u> who came over with the cattle from Oporto, were also Portuguese, this fact greatly confirmed my suspicions, knowing their revengeful character.

On the 13th November I called upon Mr. A.F. Williamson at the Criminal Investigation Department and at his special request Inspector Swanson again took down the statement I had previously made to Inspector Moore.

To my great astonishment on the 16th I found the "City of Cork" had been allowed to proceed to sea on the 15th without any arrest having been made, there was not a moment to be lost, as I knew it would take <u>three</u> days for a letter to reach Oporto and these vessels take only <u>four</u> so I hastily penned a letter to the British Consul at Oporto stating my suspicions of these cattle-men and requesting him to put himself in communication with the police at Oporto to note these men when they arrived, on the 17th I sent him a further communication requesting information, as early as possible whether the same men were returning to London in the "City of Cork" as on the previous voyage, on the 19th I had an interview with S. Montagu, Esq, M.P. to suggest that the Under Secretary for Foreign Affairs should be asked to telegraph to the Consul at Oporto to make every inquiry with regard to my letter, I received a letter from S. Montagu, Esq, on the 20th stating the Under Secretary had acceded to my request: (I am unable to give you a copy of these letters to the Consul as Mr. Montagu left them with the Under Secretary for Foreign Affairs.)

On the 22nd I wrote to Mr. A.F. Williamson as follows,

"If the inquiries made by your Department are correct that *no man who served on board the "City of Oporto" up to the 31st August is now serving on board the "City of Cork," it shows, very clearly, that instead of <u>one</u> individual being engaged in these terrible atrocities there are others equally guilty: there is no getting over these facts, that upon every occasion when these tragedies have taken place either the "City of Oporto" or the "City of Cork" has been in the London Docks."

[*Here there is a note at the bottom of the page*: – "*This refers to the crew only and <u>not</u> to the cattle-men"]

"The revengeful character of the Portuguese is a matter of history, in fact the mutilations, which have taken place in Whitechapel, are of the same terrible character as recorded in the history of the Peninsular War where it is stated that the Spanish and Portuguese peasantry armed with the terrible knives which they are in the <u>habit</u> of carrying and which they use on the slightest provocation, fell upon the stragglers of the French army and after cutting their throats, disembowelled them and subjected their bodies to other indignities with the ferocity of savages.

"These ships when in London Docks should be watched incessantly, day and night, and the movements of every man connected with them, who leaves the ship should be closely watched.

"Both these vessels are due, in the London Docks next week"

On the 26th November I addressed a further letter to Mr. A.F. Willamson,

"On the arrival of any vessel in the Docks it is boarded and rummaged by Customs Officers (generally very experienced men) when every nook and corner is thoroughly examined, after an interval, at the discretion of the Officer in charge of the Station, the vessel is re-rummaged by another distinct set of Officers. I would suggest in the event of any other murder taking place, immediately it becomes known, these vessels should be thoroughly re-rummaged by the Customs rummagers who should be secretly instructed as to looking for blood stained clothes and knives. No suspicion need be excited if these men were employed as it would naturally be supposed, by those on board, they were looking for contraband goods, as the Officers are enjoined to frequently rummage vessels on their station."

On the 3rd December I again wrote to Mr. A.F. Williamson, as follows,

"Have any steps been taken to ascertain if the same crews and cattle-men are on board the 'City of Oporto' and the 'City of Cork' as on the voyages immediately preceding this? I would suggest this information should be obtained, in future, directly these vessels arrive, any change to be specially noted"

The following letter I left with Inspector Swanson on the 8th December to be laid before the Commissioner of Police, upon the distinct understanding that I should be informed whether my suggestion would be carried out or not.

"I wish to direct attention to the probability of a change of vessels arriving from Oporto during this month and would suggest that all vessels belonging to Messrs. Coverley & Westray should be closely watched, last December, in addition to the 'City of Oporto' and the 'City of Cork', the 'City of Malaga' came from Oporto with cattle.

The next step to be taken in this matter is to obtain a list of the cattle-men who come over in these vessels, which will necessitate some rather minute inquiry being made and if carried out in the manner I propose there ought to be no difficulty in bringing the matter home to the guilty party. It is very evident whoever the murderer may be, he is no stranger to that part of London, to be able to get away from the scenes of his crimes without exciting suspicion, shews that very clearly.

I therefore propose to obtain a list of the cattle-men who were on board the following vessels.

"City of Cork"	5th December <u>1887</u>	
"City of Oporto"	14th "	"
"City of Malaga"	27th "	"

it might perhaps be necessary to go further back than that, but that will answer my purpose for the present, another list of those on board the following vessels will also be required,

"City of Oporto"	8th August	1888
"	30th "	"
"	19th September	"
"	15th October	"
"City of Cork"	6th September	"
"	27th "	"
"	19th October	"
"	9th November	"

With regard to these cattle-men it is very probable that Messrs. Coverley & Westray would not be able to give a correct list, as I have every reason to believe these cattle-men are not in their employ, nor do I think any assistance could be obtained from the Captains as from inquiries I have made, with reference to the cattle trade, I find there is a very loose supervision, <u>if any</u>, over these men and then again under the Merchant Shipping Act a written declaration of the number of Aliens on board has to be made by the Captain, under a penalty of £20, so that any lapse in that direction is not likely to be admitted by him.

The cattle by these boats are consigned to Messrs. Hope & Harrington, 60 Queen Victoria Street and Messrs. Palgrave, Murphy & Co. 155 Fenchurch Street, they would, of course, be able to give the names of the firms in Oporto who had consigned the cattle to them and I understand these men are paid when they return to Oporto, there ought to be no difficulty, once the paymaster is found, in tracing the names of these men. It appears to me that it will be necessary to send some astute officer to Oporto to make these inquiries, I do not think it can be satisfactorily carried out by correspondence"

Not having received any reply to the above paper, I wrote to Inspector Swanson, as follows,

"Will you please inform me if anything has been done with regard to the suggestion I made on Saturday?"

Being still without any reply, on the 7th January I addressed the following letter to the Commissioner of Police,

"On the 8th December I left a further communication with Inspector Swanson, respecting the Whitechapel tragedies, to be laid before you, on the distinct understanding that your decision was to be communicated to me, as in the event of your deciding to send an officer to Oporto I wished to furnish further particulars, on the 12th December not having received any communication with regard to my suggestion, I wrote reminding Inspector Swanson, but even to that no reply has been given.

I am quite certain that the information I have given if followed up in an intelligent manner would lead to its being brought home to one particular individual & if your subordinates are incapable of doing it, it will be done by others.

Had I thought it possible the police would have acted in the manner they have done, I should have taken other steps and the "City of Cork" would certainly not have sailed from this country on the 15th November without the murderer having been arrested, as the information I gave was the day following the murder of the 9th November and had that vessel been thoroughly searched, at once, it would I feel convinced have been with satisfactory results."

E.K.Larkins

There then follows a further file cover[6] dated 9 March 1889, with reference to Larkins:

[Stamped: – HOME OFFICE 9 MAR.89 DEP No.] No. A49301C/28

DATE 9 March 89   Mr. E.K. Larkins
REFERENCES, &c.   Submits copy of Memorandum
                    which he has forwarded to the Asst
                    Commr. of Police shewing the result of
                    further investigations into the Whitecha-
                    pel Murders –
                    MINUTES.
                    ?Ackn: and putup.
                    HBS
                    12.3.89
                 ELP. 13 March 89.
                 Ackd. 13/3.

This is followed by a note[7] from Larkins:

[Stamped: – HOME OFFICE 9 MAR.89DEPt No]   A49301C/28
                    Statistical Department,
                    Custom House, E.C.
                    March 9th 1889,
Sir,
    I beg to enclose a copy of memorandum A, which I have
this day forwarded to the Assistant Commissioner of Police,
shewing the result of further investigations I have made
respecting the Whitechapel murders,
                    I have the honour to be,
                        Sir
                    Your obedient Servant,
                        EK Larkins
The Right Honble
The Home Secretary.

There then follows the memorandum[8] referred to, which is badly
damaged at the right hand margin with resulting loss of text:

            Memorandum   A49301[C]/28
[Stamped: – HOME OFFICE 9 MAR.89 DEPt No]
    I have made further enquiries into the subject [of] the White-
chapel tragedies and they confirm in ev[ery] way, the views I have
already expressed to the previous description of the voyages of the

suspected vessels I have added the time of their departure from London.

Ship	Date and hour Of arrival in London Docks	Date of murder	Departure from London
"City of Oporto"	August 30th 7P.M.	August 31st	September 4th
"City of Cork"	September 7th 2 "	September 8th "	[ ]
"	" 27th 4 "	" 30th	October 2nd [ ]
	November 8th 2.30 "	November 9th	November [ ]

The conclusions at which I have arrived, as the result of my investigations are that there are two murderers concerned in these horrible tragedies but not acc[ ] the first murder I assume was committed by [*a man*] out of revenge, those which followed were committed [*by*] another man in a spirit of devilry.

The cattlemen, who were in this country on board these [*ships*] when these murders took place were Manuel Cruz Xavier and Jose Laurenco.

Manuel Cruz Xavier signed articles at Oporto on the [ ] August and came over in the "City of Oporto" upon the [*voyage*] which terminated here on 30th August, returning to Oporto in that vessel, where he was discharged on the [ ] September, so that it is impossible for him to have [*been*] concerned in the murders which followed the one of [*the*] 31st August, as, whether fearful of being found out, [*he did*] not rejoin the "City of Oporto" until the 8th October and [*was*] paid off in London on the 19th November (The "City of Op[*orto*"] left London on the 6th November.

With regard to Jose Laurenco he joined the "City of Cork" at Oporto on the 31st August arriving here on the 7th September, the day previous to the murder on the 8th returning in the sa[*me*] vessel to Oporto where he was discharged on the 20th September. Rather unusual for a cattleman he joined the same vessel for the return voyage arriving on the 27th September so was here when the double murder occurred on the 30th September returning again to Oporto in the "City of Cork." When the time arrived for the return of that vessel on the 13th October Jose Laurenco, who was engaged for the voyage, failed to join the ship, no doubt, to some extent, terror stricken, at the prospect of being discovered.

Since then he does not appear by the ship's articles, either of the "City of Cork" or the "City of Oporto" to have come to this country, but I am of opinion, notwithstanding that, he did come over in the "City of Cork" on the voyage which terminated here on the 8th November, the day previous to the murder of the 9th probably as a stowaway (as the "City of Cork" did <u>not</u> bring any cattle this voyage), Jose Laurenco having made two voyages in this ship, besides being an old hand in the trade, would necessarily be well acquainted with the crew of the "City of Cork" so that he would not experience any of the difficulties stowaways usually meet with

I would add with regard to Jose Laurenco that whereas <u>all</u> others on board are marked Ability V.G. Conduct V.G. he is marked as G and G. also that previous to being in the Oporto trade he appears to have served on board the "Olga" of Dublin which vessel is engaged in the cattle trade between Newcastle and Denmark.

March 8th 1889   EK Larkins

The next file cover[9] concerning Larkins encloses a printed version of his theory and is as follows:

[Stamped: – HOME OFFICE 10 Feb: 92 RECEIVED] No. A49301C/31

DATE. 10 Feb 92   Mr. E.K. Larkins.
REFERENCES, &c.   <u>Whitechapel Murders</u>
                                        Fd's print of his final papers on the subject –
                                        pointing to Portuguese cattlemen as the authors
                                        of the outrages.
                                        MINUTES.
                                        <u>Ackd.</u>
                                              See /28 & /25b
                                              ? Layby
                                              W.P.B.   CM 12
                                              11 Feby 2

The printed and final version of Larkins' theory[10] then follows:

[Stamped: – HOME OFFICE 10 FEB.92 RECEIVED]
                                                      A493301C/31

WHITECHAPEL MURDERS, 1888–9.

This statement refers to what are known as the "Ripper" murders. The first of this series <u>occurred</u> on the 1st September, 1888, [*sic*]

and the last on the 17th July, 1889. These murders are six in number.

THE CONSPIRACY TO MURDER UNMASKED.
STORMING OF OPORTO BY THE FRENCH, 1809.

"In one of the principal squares they found several of their comrades who had been made prisoners, fastened upright and living, but with their eyes burst, their tongues torn out, and their bodies mutilated and gashed.* Those who beheld the sight spared none of those who fell in their way."

*These atrocities were committed by the Portuguese.-NAPIER'S "PENINSULAR WAR."

The following will show that in deeds of blood their sons differ in no way from their forefathers:-

On 30th August, 1888, at 7 p.m., the "City of Oporto" entered the London Docks, having on board Manuel Cruz Xavier, age 37, a Portuguese cattleman. On the morning of the 1st September[sic], Mrs. Nicholls [sic] was found murdered; this man was again here on the 19th September, and again on the 15th October. Whether the hue and cry which was raised after the double murder acted as a deterrent, this fact is clear, he returned to Oporto, and has not been over since. He is now employed as a lighterman at Oporto.

I have traced this man's movements from the time of the first murder, and they prove conclusively that he has never been here when any of the other murders have taken place.

On the 7th September, 1888, at 2 p.m., the "City of Cork" entered the London Docks, having on board Joao de Souza Machado (aged 41), and Jose Laurenco (aged 26), both Portuguese cattlemen. On the 8th September Annie Chapman was found murdered.

On the 27th September, 1888, at 4 p.m., the "City of Cork" entered the London Docks, again having on board Joao de Souza Machado (aged 41), and Jose Laurenco (aged 26), both Portuguese cattlemen. On the 30th September Elizabeth Stride and Mrs. Eddowes were found murdered.

On the 19th October, 1888, the "City of Cork" entered the London Docks, having on board Joao de Souza Machado (aged 41), *no longer a cattleman, but as* A.B. Jose Laurenco had *disappeared*. The log book of the "City of Cork" explains this. It says: "13/10/88. Jose Laurenco, cattleman, deserted from ship, and did not appear up to the time of ship sailing." The cattleman who took his place on this voyage says he was working in a stevedore's gang and that Jose Laurenco induced him to change places with him. From that time Laurenco does not appear to have come over. No murder took place during the month of October.

On the 8th November, 1888, at 2.30 p.m., the "City of Cork" entered the London Docks, having on board Joao de Souza Machado (aged 41), now, as on the previous voyage, *an A.B.* Early the following morning Mary Jane Kelly was found murdered, with unheard of brutality. This man, Machado, is a most experienced cattleman, having made several voyages to this country in that capacity previous to these murders, and being a man of mature age, the *sang froid* displayed upon the occasion of this murder is easily accounted for.

This man's coolness seems to have stood him in good stead, as, in order to avoid any suspicion, he continued to come over until the month of March, 1889, upon one occasion as *Quartermaster*, in fact, *in any capacity but his rightful one as Cattleman.*

After this murder, I gave information to the police, on the 10th November, that *when the "City of Oporto" or the "City of Cork" were in, then, and then only, did these murders take place*, that I was certain it was the cattlemen who were on board these vessels. I informed them on the 12th November that these men were Portuguese, and that that made me more confident than ever that they were the men.

Although the police were at this time watching the arrival of cattle boats, they were not aware these vessels carried cattle until I gave them the information.

Immediately after I had given them the information, the "City of Cork" was closely watched, but allowed to proceed to sea on the 14th November without *any arrest* being made. As soon as these vessels were watched the outrages *ceased*.

Although these vessels have made many voyages since then, no outrage has taken place when either of the vessels have been here.

On the 17th July, 1889, Alice McKenzie was murdered. This was evidently an attempt at renewing these outrages. At that time there were two vessels here from Oporto, the "Petrel" and the "Grebe," each having a Portuguese cattleman on board. Joachim da Rocha (aged 23), who was on board the "Grebe," lying at Fresh Wharf, was formerly a seaman in the "City of Oporto," at the time Xavier and Laurenco were in the habit of coming over in that vessel.

Notwitstanding my urgent request that these men should be detained to be seen by the police who were on duty in the neighbourhood of the murder, they were allowed to return to Oporto. Rocha is now employed there as a stevedore.

"JACK THE RIPPER."

I felt quite satisfied when the letters, signed "Jack the Ripper," commenced to appear, that they were not the work of those who were committing these atrocities; and I formed a pretty shrewd guess as to where their author might be found.

When, in October, 1890, there was a renewal of these cowardly missives, I wended my way to——.

Having stated my errand, and the part I had taken in reference to these outrages, I was most courteously received, in marked contrast to the dog-in-the-manger policy pursued by the police; and every facility was placed at my disposal.

Having, sometime previously, been furnished with a fac-simile of the original letter of "Jack the Ripper," I compared it with the handwriting of a certain individual, and I knew at once that I had fixed my man; I asked what was known about him. The reply was, "As you have fixed upon him, I may say he is not one of the men who has been shadowed by the police." (Mr. R. Anderson and several of the police had already been there, and some of the men had been "shadowed"); "but he is capable of anything, in fact, I should not be surprised at anything he did; he has only lately returned to his duties, having been away for some time on the plea of illness." So there is this plain fact, that directly he returned to his duties, he began his old game of terrorising the inhabitants of the district.

The handwriting of these missives has been characterised as "legal." This man's father is in the legal profession.

I consulted a magistrate, and by his advice went to the authorities of Scotland Yard. What the police have done since I cannot tell; he may have been "shadowed;" he has *not* been arrested; but these cruel missives have *ceased*, and the infamous person who wrote them is still allowed to be at large.

There then follows a plan[11] of the London Docks with the "City of Cork" in her berth. See plan at [. . .]

The next page is a list[12] of the murders, descriptions circulated, and Larkins's descriptions of his suspects:

PRIVATE, CONFIDENTIAL
                    INFORMATION.

Date and locality.	Description Circulated.	Description of cattlemen who were here when the murders took place.
1888 September 1– BUCK'S ROW.		MANUEL CRUZ XAVIER Age 37. A short man, black Hair. Now employed as a Boatman at Oporto.
September 8– HANBURY ST.	JOAO DE SOUZA MACHADO Age 37. Height 5 ft. 7 in. Rather dark beard and Moustache. Dress: shirt Dark jacket, dark vest and Trousers, black scarf and black felt hat. Spoke with a foreign accent. In addition to the above Description. He was a foreigner of dark complexion, over 40 years of age, a little taller than the deceased, of shabby genteel appearance, with a brown deerstalker on his head and a dark coat on his back.	Age 41. Middle height, black moustache. Now a bathing man and oarsman at Oporto.

September 30—
BERNER STREET   Age about 28. No whiskers. Height about 5 ft. 7 in. Complexion dark. Had on a hard felt deerstalker hat of dark colour and dark clothes, had on an overcoat, dark trousers.

JOSE LAURENCO.
Age 26. He is a dark young fellow. Now employed as a boat-man at Oporto.

September 30—
MITRE-SQUARE.   Age 30 to 35. Height 5 ft. 7 in., with brown hair and big moustache, dressed respectably. Wore a pea jacket, muffler and a cloth cap with a peak of the same material.

JOAO DE SOUZA MACHADO
Age 41. Middle height, black moustache. Now a bathing-man and oarsman at Oporto.

November 9—
DORSET STREET   Age 34 or 35. Height about 5 ft. 6 in., dark complexion and dark moustache, turned up at the ends. He was wearing a long dark coat trimmed with astrachan. Looked like a foreigner. He had on a soft felt hat, drawn down some-what over his eyes.

JOAO DE SOUZA MACHADO
Age 41. Middle height, black moustache. Now a bathing man and oarsman at Oporto.

1889.
July 17—
CASTLE-ALLEY.

J. DA ROCHA,
Age 23. Is rather short, fair, with light beard. Now captain of a small tug at Oporto.

NOTE. —MACHADO is evidently a man whose age it is rather difficult to tell from observation, as my correspondent at Oporto states he is now (in 1891) about 40 years of age, whereas he is 44.

The following page[13] is a continuation of details on the suspects:

PRIVATE, CONFIDENTIAL
THE ORDER IN WHICH THESE MEN CAME OVER.

SIGNED ON AT OPORTO.	SHIP.	MEN. OCCUPATION.	SIGNED OFF AT OPORTO.
1888.			1888.
July 9	City of Cork	MACHADO Cattleman	July 20
" 20	City of Cork	MACHADO " and XAVIER	August 9
August 2	City of Oporto	LAURENCO " (*paid off in London*)	" 9
" 10	City of Cork	*Neither of these men came over on this voyage.*	
" 23	*City of Oporto	XAVIER "	September 13
" 31	*City of Cork	MACHADO and " LAURENCO	" 20
September 13	City of Oporto	XAVIER "	October 8
" 20	*City of Cork	MACHADO and " LAURENCO (LAURENCO'S last voyage. *Deserted* at Oporto, Oct. 13)	" 13
October 8	City of Oporto	XAVIER. (*his last voyage.*)	PAID OFF IN LONDON 19
" 13	City of Cork	MACHADO	A.B. November 2
November 2	*City of Cork	MACHADO	" " 23
" 23	City of Cork	MACHADO	" December 13
December 13 1889	City of Cork	MACHADO	1889 " January 11
January 11	City of Cork	MACHADO	" February 1
February 1	City of Cork	MACHADO. (*His last voyage*)	
March 8			

*NOTE.-Voyages when the murders were committed.

There is a letter[14] from Larkins to the Home Secretary [out of order in the files but no doubt taken out of the earlier file for reference] dated 10 January 1889:

> Statistical Department,
> Custom House,

E.C.
[Stamped: – HOME OFFICE 11 JAN.89 RECd. DEPt.]   10th January, 1889,
Sir,

I beg to enclose a memorandum I have drawn up on the subject of the Whitechapel murders, also a "resume" of the steps I have taken.

The "City of Cork" is due in a day or two, when, if the police have carried out my suggestion in obtaining a list of these cattle-men every voyage, they will be able to ascertain if the same men are on board as were on board at the date of the last murder, on the 9th November, had the "City of Cork" been searched immediately after the information I gave, on the 10th November, it is probable that the knife and blood stained garments might have been found and had these men been taken into custody on suspicion it is extremely probable that one of them might have been identified as having been seen in the neighbourhood where the murder took place.

It is not too late even now for them to be taken into custody and probably one would be identified. I think it is very possible the clothes might also be found as these men belong to the poorest class and would be quite unable to be continually purchasing fresh clothing.

> I have the honour to be,
> Sir,
> Your obedient Servant,
> EKLarkins

The Right Honble.
    The Home Secretary.

There is then a page of notes[15] with the letter, as follows:

Whitechapel Murders
Mr Darling calls see me at HO Feb 12–89.
& inquiries as below: A

Larkins   Jan 10.
    Pepys Road –
    Brockley

Mr Darling says that a constituent of his, named as above, sent suggestions to the HO on Jan 10th 89) as to the identity of "Jack the Ripper", and "has never heard anything since."
Was his letter even ackd.?

                CWS:[?] Feb 12 89

Add this to official papers, as an inquiry by Mr. Darling, M.P.

There then follows an accompanying letter[16] (to the 1892 correspondence) from Larkins to the Home Secretary:

[Stamped: – HOME OFFICE 10 FEB.92 RECEIVED]   A49301C/31
                              Statistical Department,
                              Custom House, E.C.
                              Feb. 10, 1892,

Sir,
I have the honour to enclose my final paper on the subject of the Whitechapel tragedies,
                I am,
                      Sir,
                      Your obedt. Servant,
                      EKLarkins
The Rt. Honble.
    The Home Secretary

A further file cover[17] follows:

[Stamped: – Home Office 7 FEB. 93] No. A49301C/34
DATE. 6th Feb.'93   Asst. Commr. C.I.D.
REFERENCES, &c.   Whitechapel Murders.
                      States that Mr. E.K. Larkins is a trouble-some busybody whose vagaries on the sub-ject of the Whitechapel Murders have cost the C.I.D., the Public Prosecutor, & the Foreign Office, a great deal of useless trou-ble, & that it is a mere waste of time attempting to deal with him on the subject.
    1/33   Refers to A49301C/25b.
                MINUTES.

See u/25, u/28, u/31
? Layby
MD
See especially/25   9.2.93
Mr.L. has had an   C.M.9.
ackt.
<u>ELP. 10 Feby 93.</u>

There then follows a typed letter[18] from Dr Robert Anderson, AC CID, to the Home Office:

A49301C/34
[Reference] 57885/821 [Stamped: – HOME OFFICE 7 Feb.93 DEPt. No.] Scotland Yard,

London, S.W.
6th February 1893.
From THE ASSISTANT COMMISSIONER OF POLICE,
CRIMINAL INVESTIGATION DEPARTMENT.
To the Under Secretary of State,
Home Office.
Sir,
In returning the enclosures which accompanied your letter of the 1st instant I have to acquaint you for the information of the Secretary of State that Mr E.K.Larkins is a troublesome busybody whose vagaries on the subject of the Whitechapel Murders have cost this Department, the Public Prosecutor and the Foreign Office a great deal of useless trouble. His theories have been tested and they have proved untenable and worthless, and it is a mere waste of time attempting to deal with him on the subject.

I have refused latterly to acknowledge his letters, hence his strictures upon my Department.

I beg to refer to Home Office file No.A.49301C/25. on this subject.

I am,
Sir,
Your obedient Servant,
R. Anderson

The final file cover[19] concerning Larkins is dated 26 January 1893:

[Stamped: – HOME OFFICE 28 JAN.93 RECEIVED] No. A49301C/33

DATE. 26 Jan. 1893   Mr. E.K. Larkins, of the Statistical Dept. Customs House.

REFERENCES, &c.   <u>Whitechapel Murders</u>.

Fds papers on the subject of the Whitechapel tragedies. Charges the head of the Criminal Investigation Dept. that he has connived at the escape of these men & that he has prevented the men being brought to justice. Requests S.ofS's attention to the matter.

MINUTES.

? ACO &
    To Mr. Anderson.
        F.V.O.[?]
            31. Jan. 93
            C.M. 31.
    Ackn? & wrote)
        Mr. Anderson)1/2/93
            [ ]6.2.93 (1/34)

This is followed by a Larkins letter[20], dated 26 January 1893, to H.H. Asquith, QC, MP:

[Stamped: – HOME OFFICE 28 JAN.93 RECEIVED] A49301C/33

Statistical Department,
Custom House, E.C.
January 26, 1893.

Sir,

I respectfully submit, for your consideration, the enclosed papers on the subject of the Whitechapel tragedies.

I have consulted both the magistrates at Worship Street Police Court, Mr. Bushby said, "It is the duty of the Commissioner of Police to follow up these men, it is a serious matter, but I have no control over the police."

They have not been followed up. The late Mr. Montagu Williams, Q.C, assured me repeatedly that he had no doubt whatever as to the correctness of my views on this subject and was most indignant at the conduct of the police authorities.

I distinctly charge the head of the Criminal Investigation Department that he has deliberately connived at the escape of these men that he has deliberately thrown every obstacle in the way of their being brought to justice.

I therefore appeal to you, Sir, in the name of our common humanity, if not upon higher grounds, that you will not suffer this official or any combination of officials, whatever their position may be, any longer to defeat the ends of justice.

I have the honour to be,

    Sir,

Your most obedient Servant,

    EKLarkins

The Right Honble

    H.H. Asquith, Q.C, M.P.

There is then included a printed extract[21] from the book *Later Leaves* by Montagu Williams, QC, page 398, outlining Williams's meeting with Larkins and his belief in his theory, stamped as received at the Home Office on 28 Jan.93. Also enclosed in this file is a further copy[22] of Larkins's printed papers (as already reproduced).

There is a printed and bound copy of Larkins's papers in the London Hospital that provides the researcher with an interesting historical insight into the sort of contemporary theorizing that was taking place.

CHAPTER 25

December 1888 – An American View

The idea that the murderer of Stride might not have been one and the same person as Eddowes's killer is not a new one. Indeed, Stride was dismissed as a "Ripper" victim by William Stewart in his 1939 book *Jack the Ripper – A New Theory*. But he most certainly was not the first to propose this idea publicly: it is possible to go back to 1888 to find such a public reference. Indeed, if the sources stated in the piece are correct, the City of London Police themselves may have held this view. Included in the MEPO 3/140 files is a press cutting[1] which is an extract from the *Philadelphia Times* of 3 December 1888:

THE WHITECHAPEL MURDERS
STARTLING THEORY OF THE CITY OF
LONDON DETECTIVES.
NOT ONE MAN'S WORK
Probably a Conspiracy to Murder
Unfortunates Conceived by Reli-
gious Monomaniacs.

SPECIAL CABLE TELEGRAM TO THE TIMES.
LONDON, December 2. – I have ascertained that the police have for some time past been working on a clue on which a more than plausible theory explanatory of the motive for the commission of the Whitechapel horrors has been built up. The city police are entitled to the credit of whatever results may eventuate from their discovery, but hitherto they have been exceedingly reticent as to the result of their investigations. To-day, however, I gathered the following details of the lines they are working on from a thoroughly reliable source.

The City of London detectives first came into the case with full authority on September 30, shortly before one o'clock in the morning of which day Elizabeth Stride was murdered outside the Socialist Club in Berners [*sic*] street, and Catharine Beddowes [*sic*] was butchered in Mitre Square. Previous to this date the pursuit of the Whitechapel fiend had been directed by the Scotland Yard authorities, they being in control of the Metropolitan as distinct from the city police. The woman Beddowes, however, whose body was found in Mitre Square, having been slain within the city limits, the control of the investigation devolved upon the authorities in the old Jewry, the headquarters of the city detective force. The city Vidocqs are, taken as a body, a far more intellectual class of men than their bretheren of Scotland Yard.

THE POLICE AT WORK.

The ablest officers were detailed to work up the case, but the fullest investigation of the meagre facts at their disposal failed to lead to the apprehension of the murderer. They however arrived at a conclusion which, if correct, tends to explode the almost universally-held theory that these horrible crimes are all the work of a single miscreant. Carefully calculating the time it would take to cover the ground between Berners street and Mitre Square and having approximately fixed the hour at which each murder was committed they were forced to the conclusion that if the same man murdered both the women Catherine Beddowes must have met him by appointment in Mitre Square, as the supposition that he found her in this unfrequented place at the exact moment he desired was clearly untenable. It must be borne in mind that the saloons in London all close promptly at 12.30 A.M. The unhappy women of the class to which Elizabeth Stride and Catharine Beddowes belonged find the only field for obtaining their wretched means of livelihood, after the drinking places have closed, among the crowds of half-drunken men who throng the leading thoroughfares of the district.

It is obvious, then, that at 1 P.M. [*sic*] the woman Stride [*sic?* – Eddowes] would not have been parading the silent Mitre Square, wholly unfrequented after dark, unless she was waiting there for some one. On the other hand if the murderer of Elizabeth Stride in Berners street had not been interrupted in his ghastly work, judging by the mutilation practiced in the other cases, he would have spent at least another quarter of an hour at his devilish work. Admitting this, he would then have been too late to keep his appointment with Beddowes, and it is only on the supposition that such an appointment had been made, and that the woman went there to meet the murderer, that the theory of the two murders having been committed by the same hand will hold water.

TWO MURDERERS.

The city detectives then early in the first week of October came to a definite conclusion, namely, that the two women met their death at the hands of different men. It was but taking a single step to further conclude that these two men were acting in collusion. The long interval that had elapsed between this and the previous butchery, the fact that the women belonged to the same class and the coincidence that the killing was done within the same thirty-five minutes all pointed to the same conclusion – that the murders had been deliberately planned, probably to be consummated at the same moment for if even a couple of hours had elapsed between the two crimes the neighbourhood would in the discovery of the first, have become so "hot" that the perpetrator of the second outrage would have found the matter of his escape rendered doubly difficult.

The two brainy men who thus theorised, although they firmly believed they had at last opened the case, were still at a loss in what direction to look for the authors of the fearful crimes. With the utmost patience they sought out the degraded companions of the dead women, and bit by bit they learned all that probably ever will be known of their habits, tastes and mode of life.

A WOMAN'S STORY.

After a week or more of this dreary work they struck a woman whose half drunken babbling seemed to suggest a possible clue to the unraveling of the secret they were so industriously working at. This woman had known Beddowes intimately, and only about a week before the day she met her death poor Catharine had in a fit of maudlin confidence told this companion that she meditated going into a reformatory. She had, she said, on the previous night got into conversation with a stranger, who had, as she put it, tried to convert her, and earnestly begged her to discontinue her mode of life. He had worked on the woman's feelings by drawing a fearful picture of the hereafter staring her in the face if she should be suddenly cut off in her life of sin and shame. On his leaving her she pleaded poverty as an excuse for her sinful mode of life, and he thereupon gave her five shillings, telling her to meet him again in a week's time, adding that if in the meantime she would give up her evil ways and decide to go into a home he would use his influence to get her into one. The woman could not fix the exact date on which Beddowes made this statement to her, but thought it was about a week before the woman was killed. At eleven o'clock on the night of Thursday, the day before the murder, she saw Catharine and took a drink with her. Beddowes was then much the worse for liquor. She left her shortly after that hour, saying she was going to meet a friend. She was never seen again alive, but less than two hours later her mutilated body was found lying in Mitre Square.

LOOKING FOR THE MAN.

The detectives had no reason to doubt this story and every effort by advertisements and handbills was made to discover the man who had talked with Catharine Beddowes a week before the murder and given her five shillings. Up to the present the personality of the man remains shrouded in mystery. The detectives argued that if he was innocent in intent he would at once have come forward, most people would be inclined to agree with them.

Having got thus far, the detectives had a consultation with George Lewis, the great criminal lawyer, of Ely Place, Holborn. They went to him because it was well known that he had from the first held the theory that the murders were the work of a religious mono-maniac, and the slender clue they had picked up seemed to point in that direction. No man has had so wide a criminal experience as George Lewis. He has been in every great murder case for the last twenty years and his father before him enjoyed the largest criminal practice in England. From a careful and exhaustive consideration of the facts laid before him by the city detectives, Mr. Lewis is understood to have deduced the following conclusions:

Positive-First. That the murders of Elizabeth Stride and Catharine Beddowes were not committed by one and the same person. Second. That the two or more murderers were acting in collusion and by pre-arrangement.

Probable-First. That the series of murders have been committed by two or more men whose motive is the checking of prostitution. The unprecedented barbarities practiced on the bodies are perpetrated with the view of terrifying the women of the district into abandoning their mode of life. Second. That the murderers are religious monomaniacs.

ARE THEY ON THE RIGHT TRACK?

The city detectives have since been quietly working in this direction. For obvious reasons they decline to afford any information as to the result of their investigations. It is an open secret, however, that certain members of a quasi-religious organization whose eccentric methods have again and again encountered adverse criticism at the hands of the press and the public have been closely watched for some time past. As at present it is understood that not a tittle of direct evidence is forthcoming against these suspects no arrests have been made. The fact that so long a period elapsed between the murders of September 30 and the slaughtering of the latest victim on November 9 leads the detectives to believe that they are on the right track. The last murder, on November 9, came as a great surprise to them, but it was skilfully timed, as that being Lord Mayor's Day, on which the city is thronged with sight-seers, every available city detective and policeman was on street duty.

The mere fact that this cutting is preserved in the official police files tends to lend weight to its importance. The Metropolitan Police obviously felt it merited keeping on record.

CHAPTER 26

20 December 1888 –
Murder of Rose Mylett, alias Lizzie Davis

The discovery of the body of another prostitute, Rose Mylett, in Poplar on 20 December 1888 kept the excitement at a peak, and provided the press with even more ammunition against the police. Although not a "Ripper" killing – not even murder, according to some contemporary opinion – it resulted in further acrimonious official exchanges.

This File is dated *23 Decr. '88*, is headed *Poplar Murder* and states:

Gives particulars respecting above & states that the Police are endeavouring to trace the identity of the woman murdered.

There is a note[1] as follows:

This memorandum seems to show that some person able to detect marks of strangulation ought to have seen the body before it was moved. Valuable indications may have been missed.

H. M.
25Dec/88.

This is followed by another note[2]

Dec 24. 88 Dear Ruggles Brise, The enclosed note on Poplar murder case was written yesterday. Since it was written the woman has been identified & police are tracing. Please return enclosed when read. I have not had time to get it copied.

Yrs sincerely
JMonro

A third note[3] reads:

Dec 26. Dear Monro, You will like to see, possibly to observe on S.S. minute on the Poplar Murder.

Yours C.M.

The reply[4] is:

Dear Murdoch/ Thanks. I shall make observation later on in the case.

26/12 JM

This is followed by a lengthy report[5] by Monro:

Poplar Murder

The facts of this case as ascertained hither to are briefly these. Early on the morning of Thursday the 20th December the body of a woman was discovered by a Sergeant & Constable on beat in a small yard or court off a street in Poplar. Life was extinct. The body was warm, showing that death had but recently taken place. The face was perfectly placid. The clothes were not disarranged and round the neck was a handkerchief loosely folded, but not tied. In the pocket of the dress was a small phial, empty. In one of the ears was an ear-ring; the other was missing. There were absolutely no signs whatever of any struggle, and no marks of violence visible. The police believed from the appearance of the body that the case was one of suicide or sudden death from natural causes. The Divisional Surgeon was called in, and his assistant saw the body. He naturally gave no opinion as to the cause of death, but he discovered no marks or signs of violence suggesting that there was any suspicion of foul play. The body was removed to await inquest by the coroner.

Whether the Divisional Surgeon saw and made a post mortem examination of the body on Thursday afternoon, or Friday morning, is not at present quite clear. This is a point to be cleared up. It is stated that on Friday morning the Divisional Surgeon saw the Inspector who was to attend the inquest, but, (so says the Inspector) did not suggest that the case was one of murder. This also requires enquiry, but I do not at present delay reporting on the case till such enquiry is completed.

At the inquest, which was held on Friday, the Divisional Surgeon gave evidence that the case was one of murder — That the woman had been strangled with a four lag cord. (equal to packing-string of very moderate thickness!) and that the <u>marks of strangulation were plainly visible on the</u> throat & neck.

This evidence was certainly a matter of surprise to the police, but accepting the medical evidence as correct, the case was clearly one of murder.

The absence of <u>all signs of violence</u> when the body was discovered & examined by the police and the assistant to the Divisional Surgeon – the fact that there were absolutely no signs of any struggle – The perfectly placid state of the features – The circumstance of a handkerchief having been found loosely folded round the neck of the corpse – all these circumstances, I am bound to say, made me rather hesitate to accept, without further confirmation the statement of the Divisional Surgeon as conclusive with reference to the cause of death. My experience in cases of strangulation led me to believe that the features of a woman so murdered would be swollen, livid, & discoloured, probably protruding – That the eyes would be staring – and that there would have been the livid <u>marks of the cord on the neck, accompanied probably with abrasion of the skin</u>.

I therefore sent off the Assist. Commissioner Mr. Anderson to make further enquiries on the spot, and directed Dr. Bond of the A Division to assist the Divisional Surgeon make a second examination. Dr. Bond was otherwise engaged, and on learning this I asked the Chief Surgeon, Mr. MacKellar, to be good enough to proceed to the spot, & give me the benefit of his opinion. This he cheerfully consented to do, and meanwhile Dr. Hibbert, who had opened the letter of Dr. Bond in that gentleman's absence, also proceeded to the spot, & made a further examination of the body. I have not yet received the detailed report of Dr. Hibbert's examination, but I saw Mr. Mackellar on his return, and that gentleman fully supports the Divisional Surgeon in his opinion that death was produced by strangulation.

There is therefore no doubt that the case was one of murder – and murder of a strange and unusual type.

At present there is absolutely no trace of the identity of the woman, and till this is ascertained, there is really nothing for Police to work upon. She is believed to be one of the unfortunate class, but in spite of all enquiries which have been made, she has not yet been identified. To this point of identification the energies of Police have been directed in the first instance, and a special officer, Inspector Swanson, from Central Office has been deputed to assist the local Police of Poplar in their enquiries.

How this murder could have been carried out, without a sign of the <u>ground being disturbed by the struggles of the victim,</u> or of her murderer, I confess is very difficult to understand. Whether she may have first been rendered insensible before being murdered is a matter for consideration. Whether she was murdered in the spot where the body was discovered is also a point to be noted – whether one or more persons were engaged in the crime – whether the missing ear-ring points to murder in some spot other than that where she was found – whether this case has any connection with the Whitechapel crimes – all these are points which must be carefully considered, but with reference to which it would be premature to theorize. The first point which may afford some light on the case, is the identity of the woman, till this is ascertained we are absolutely in the dark as to the circumstances of this murder, which at present appears to be devoid of motive, as were the outrages in Whitechapel. I need not say that the Assist. Comr. and officers of the Criminal Investigation Dept. are doing & will do, all they can to detect this mysterious crime.

Dec. 23. 88   JMonro.

The Scotland Yard file on this crime is particularly sparse and consists of two extracts[6] from the *Daily Chronicle* dated 28 and 29 December 1888. The first reads:

A CLUE TO THE POPLAR MYSTERY.

The police have succeeded in finding Mrs. Mylett, the mother of the woman found dead in Clarke's Yard, Poplar, a few days ago. The deceased woman had frequently spoken of her mother living somewhere near Baker's Row, Whitechapel, and it was near this thoroughfare, in Pelham-street, that Mrs. Mylett was found to be residing. When the detectives called at the house on Boxing Day they found the inmates indulging in Christmas festivities, and upon their stating the object of their visit one of the women in the house had a serious fit. Upon visiting the mortuary Mrs. Mylett stated that she had no doubt that the body shown her was that of her daughter, and added that she last saw the deceased alive on Sunday week, when she called at Pelham-street. The mother had frequently remonstrated with her daughter upon her mode of life, but without avail. Mrs. Mylett, who is an Irishwoman, also stated that her daughter was born in London, and some years ago married, unknown to her parents, a man named Davis, whom Mrs. Mylett believed was an upholsterer by trade. The young couple had one child, but as they often disagreed they separated. This child is now in a school at Sutton, and is about seven years of age. A curious fact in reference to the woman having had a child is that Dr. Brownfield, when at the inquest, expressed the opinion that the deceased had never been a mother.

Inspector Swanson, Inspector Wildey, and the Criminal Investigation officers under their guidance are working energetically to elucidate the mystery, and another statement has afforded the detective officers with an additional clue. It appears that Charles Ptomoley, an attendant at the Poplar Union, was proceeding to the workhouse last Wednesday night week when he saw two sailors having an altercation with the deceased woman, who was heard strenuously to decline their overtures to accompany them. They were then at the corner of England-row, within sight of Clarke's-yard. Ptomoley has given the police authorities a full description of the men's appearance, and says that, though in other respects they were dressed as seamen, one had a fur cap, drawn partly over his face, while the other wore a round black hat. This statement has been verified, for the two men described by the attendant were seen by others in the district, and it also confirms the assertion of Alice Graves, who knew the deceased well, and who states that she saw the unfortunate woman walking along early on the morning of the tragedy with two men dressed as sailors.

The second report ran as follows:

THE POPLAR MURDER.

On inquiry at the East-end police-station last night our representative was informed that despite the most strenuous exertions on the part of the police nothing in the shape of a clue to the identity of the murderer of the woman Mylett or Davies had been obtained. The detectives had been engaged throughout the day in Spitalfields with the view of discovering the persons with whom the deceased associated just prior to her death. The statements which have been furnished to the police are not regarded as of the slightest value, and have given them no assistance in their investigations. An order has been issued to the various stations to the effect that persons making statements should be required to append their names and addresses, and that statements so made should be forwarded, marked "of pressing importance," to the head divisional station at Bow. Owing to the extraordinary circumstances attending the death of the unfortunate woman various conflicting theories are held by those who have had the case in hand. Dr. Brownfield, the divisional surgeon of police, however, has not the slightest reason, it is said, to alter the opinion he expressed at the inquest – namely, that the deceased was foully murdered. The medical men who have been concerned in the inquiry are of opinion not only that the deceased was murdered, but that the deed was the work of a skilful hand. A second examination of the body was made, subsequent to the inquest, and on the skin of the neck being removed a quantity of congealed blood was found, which proved that considerable pressure must have been applied from without. It is understood that sensational medical evidence may be expected when the coroner's inquiry is resumed on Wednesday next.

Mr. Charles Ptolomey, whose name was mentioned in our columns yesterday as having seen two seamen accost the woman near where she was discovered dead, has received a visit from some officers of Scotland-yard. Mr. Ptolomey, who is a night attendant at the Poplar Union, made the following statement to a reporter yesterday:- "Last night some detectives from Scotland-yard came to see me about this mysterious affair. They asked me if I could identify the sailors? I told them I could pick the men out of a thousand. How I came to notice them was in this way: It was about five minutes to eight o'clock on Wednesday night, when I was going to my work. Upon going up England-row (nearly opposite Clarke's-yard) I noticed two sailors. The shorter one was speaking to the deceased, and the tall one was walking up and down. So strange did it seem that I stopped and 'took account' of them. Then I heard the woman say several times 'No! no! no!' and the short sailor spoke in a low tone. The tall one was about 5 ft. 11 in. He looked like a Yankee. The shorter one was about 5 ft. 7 in. It struck me that they were there for no good purpose, and that was the reason I took so much notice of their movements. I shall always remember their faces, and could, as I say, pick them out of a thousand. I have been to the mortuary, and seen the deceased. She is the same woman, and she was sober when I saw her with the sailors."

There is a second file[7] concerning the so-called "Poplar Mystery", dated 11 January 1889, which adds to the somewhat sparse material already quoted:

MEPO 3/143
No. 98122

MEPOL 3

1888 – Dec 24
1889 – Feb 14   K
Janry 11th 1889   A.C.
                             C.I.Dept.
SUBJECT Special   "The Poplar Mystery" – Death of Ca-
                             therine Millet.

[Reports that he has informed Supt. K. that he does not intend taking any further steps in the matter now withstanding [*sic*] ["the verdict of" – *deleted*] Difference of opinion as to "wilful murder" or accidental death.

Refers to the Coroner's strictures upon the action of the Police in "sending down doctor after doctor without his sanction" – (vide extract from "Morning Advertiser" of 10/1/89); and asks for an authoritative decision as to the claim of the Coroner to control the action of Police – a point of great importance which may be raised at any moment.

REFERENCES.

To previous papers:
C.I.D. No. 54710   }Attd.
"(Serious Crime) 402.   }
To subsequent papers:
    /2.

MINUTES.

"Mr. Anderson."

"Before sending this to H.O. what has hitherto been the practice with regard to the Coroner being consulted when Police think it advisable to have another medical opinion? What was done in the Whitechapel case, & in the Rainham case? (sd) J.M." 14/1 "Mr. Monro"

"It wd. seem that in the other cases you name ['acted' – *deleted*] Mr. Bond acted, either with the privity of the Coroner, or else before the Coroner was seized of the case. Reports from C.C. &c attached. (sd)"R.A." 19/1.

This is followed by a report[8] from Chief Inspector Donald S. Swanson, dated 18 January 1889:

METROPOLITAN POLICE.
CRIMINAL INVESTIGATION DEPARTMENT,
SCOTLAND YARD,
18th day of January 1889.

SUBJECT Employment
of Mr Bond to Ex-
amine bodies of mur-
dered, or supposed mur-
dered persons.

I beg to submit Correspondence No. 93305/11 from General Registry which sets forth how Mr. Bond was employed as an expert to examine and report upon the surgical reports of the four murders, ending with Mitre Square, but in these cases he did not examine the bodies. The final body, which he examined was that of Mary Janet Kelly, but so far as I am aware, the examination was with the consent of Dr. Phillips, who was first called by Police, and the reports do not shew that the Coroner's consent was asked for or necessary. Mr. Bond did not give evidence before the Coroner.

Donald SSwanson
Ch Inspr.
JohnShore
Supt.

There is then annexed a report from *The Star* of 24 December 1888:

IS HE A THUG?
A STARTLING LIGHT ON THE WHITE-CHAPEL CRIMES.

———————

THE ROPE BEFORE THE KNIFE.

———————

The Police Surgeon Theory that the Poplar Murder was the Work of the Whitechapel Fiend Borne Out by Hitherto Inexplicable Evidence — Why the Murdered Women Never Cried Out.

The Poplar murder has developed under inquiry a startling and sensational aspect. So far, it has passed almost unnoticed. The town has supped so full of horrors that mere murder unaccompanied by revolting mutilation passes apparently for common-place, and the discovery on Thursday morning in Clarke's-yard, Poplar, of a woman's dead body with the white mark of a strangler's cord around her throat has failed to create any excitement even in the neighbourhood. The police themselves appear to have shared the general feeling of non-interest. The swift and silent method of the Thug is a new and terrifying feature in London crime, and this murder is invested with a startling significance by the discovery that it has a possible bearing upon the series of Whitechapel crimes. The suggestion is this:- "Was this Poplar murder another of the series of Whitechapel and the work of the same man? If so, has the murderer changed his methods, or is it not possible that the deed of Clarke's-yard is a new revelation of his old methods — that in the other cases partial strangulation was first of all resorted to, and that when the victims were by this means rendered helpless,

THE KNIFE WAS USED

in such a manner as to obliterate the traces of the act?"

The theory is no empty speculation of sensationalism. It derives weight from the fact that it originates with Dr. Matthew Brownfield, of 171, East India Dock-road, who, as the divisional police surgeon of Poplar, made the post-mortem examination of the body found in Clarke's-yard, and who gave evidence at the inquest on Friday. Dr. Brownfield put forward the suggestion on Saturday in an interview with a *Star* reporter.

"I have no doubt at all," said Dr. Brownfield, "that death was caused by strangulation, of which the mark round the neck of the body is the evidence."

There was a disposition on the part of the police to believe, or to affect to believe, that the mark round the which was spoken of at the inquest was

ONLY A COINCIDENCE-

that it was not caused by the act which brought about the woman's death, but that it had been previously inflicted. Our reporter, therefore, put the question,

"Is there any doubt that the mark round the neck was quite recent, and was simultaneous with death?"

"None whatever. It was a white mark, and there were no signs of "sloughing" or of inflammation coming on around it, as there must have been if it had been borne during life."

"The mark could not have been caused on the day before she died?" – "Impossible! The cord was pulled round her neck, and was kept there until she was dead. Otherwise there must have been signs of inflammation, as I have said." "And the other post-mortem appearances?"

"ALL INDICATED DEATH BY SUFFOCATION.

The left side of the heart was full of fluid black blood – particularly filled and particularly black – and the lungs were gorged with the same fluid black blood, meaning that for the space of several respirations she had not breathed before the heart ceased to pulsate. Looking at the condition of all the organs in conjunction with the mark round the throat, my opinion is that death was caused by strangulation by means of a cord being pulled tightly round the neck."

"From the appearance of the mark, you believe it was a thin cord which caused death, doctor?" – "I experimented, and have come to the conclusion that it was

A PIECE OF "FOUR-STRAND" CORD

– not thick cord by any means. With such a piece of cord I could produce a facsimile of that mark upon you. I smelt the stomach, and was unable to find any trace of alcohol at all. Neither should I say from the condition of the organs that she was a woman who was much given to drink."

"Do you think, doctor, that the woman met her death anywhere else, and that her dead body was carried to the place where it was found?" – "I think it extremely improbable, considering the great difficulty of carrying a dead body about from one place to another. At the time the body was found death had not taken place more than three-quarters of an hour. I think it very probable she was an immoral woman."

All the facts seemed to combine to one suggestion – that this was the work of the Whitechapel murderer. Our reporter put this to Dr. Brownfield, and it was then that he made the

NEW AND STARTLING SUGGESTION.

"The question is," he said, "whether there is not another and still more striking point of resemblance. If this murder was the work of the same man the question is whether strangulation is not the beginning of all his operations. Does he strangle or partially strangle them first, and then cut their throats afterwards?"

Then Dr. Brownfield went on to explain why this was likely. "If his object is mutilation," "he said, he could cut their throats so much more cleanly and deliberately. And this would explain, too, how the murderer would be able to do his work without getting covered with blood."

"But, if the other victims had been first strangled would there not be post-mortem indications?" – "If he

CUT THE THROAT ALONG THE LINE

of the cord he would obliterate the traces of partial strangulation."

"And in the present case?" – "The question is whether he did not intend to cut the throat as in the other cases, but was disturbed, and had to leave his work half finished."

The evidence given by Dr. Phillips on 18 Sept. at the Hanbury-street inquest is incontrovertible proof that Annie Chapman was partially strangled before her throat was cut. When Dr. Phillips was called to see the body he found that

THE TONGUE PROTRUDED

between the front teeth, but not beyond the lips. The face was swollen, the finger-nails and lips were turgid, and in the brain, on the head being opened, he found the membranes opaque and the veins and tissues loaded with black blood. All these appearances are the ordinary signs of suffocation. In Dr. Phillip's own words, "I am of opinion that the breathing was interfered with previous to death, but that death arose from syncope consequent on the loss of blood following the severance of the throat." Subsequently, under cross-examination, the doctor said, "I am clearly of opinion that the person who cut the deceased's throat took hold of her by the chin and then commenced the incision from right to left." The Coroner asked could that be done so instantaneously and a person

COULD NOT CRY OUT?

Dr. Phillips – By pressure on the throat no doubt it would be possible.

The Foreman – There would probably be suffocation? – Dr. Phillips was understood to express assent.

Here there is everything to support Dr. Brownfield's theory. The woman's throat was cut all round in such a manner that the mark of strangulation must have been completely obliterated.

Of the Whitechapel murders this is the only case in which there is actual proof of strangulation so severe as to leave its traces after death. But in all the other cases the facts are perfectly consistent with the supposition that the murderer first of all seized his victims in the grip of strangler's cord, and having thus effectually prevented them from crying out despatched them with the knife. For in all the cases the throat was so cut that the mark of the cord would have been obliterated and in some of the cases there are circumstances which have never been explained, but which are reconcilable with the theory of strangulation. For instance, in the evidence of Dr. Phillips given at the

BERNERS-STREET

inquest on 8 Oct., there is the following remarkable passage: -

"I have come to the conclusion, both as regards the position of the victim and that of the perpetrator of the deed, that she was seized by the shoulders and placed on the ground. The murderer was on the right side when he inflicted the cut. The absence of noise is a difficult question to account for. She could not cry out after the cut, but why did she not whilst she was being put on the ground. I CANNOT ACCOUNT FOR THE ABSENCE OF NOISE."

Dr. Phillips qualified this statement by the suggestion that the woman might have cried out, but without her cries being heard. But, on the other hand, is it not much more likely that there was no cry, and that the reason was that the victim, before being laid down, was rendered by partial strangulation incapable of crying out. In Mitre-square Catherine Eddowes was first laid down on the ground and her throat was afterwards cut. If she had been suddenly seized as the victim of Clarke's-yard was seized, and thus forced upon the ground, there would not necessarily be post mortem indications of the fact.

WHAT DR. PHILLIPS THINKS

is a matter of direct and most important bearing upon the question because Dr. Phillips, of course, knows more of the medical bearings of the murders than any other man. So *The Star* man called upon the doctor at his surgery in Spital-square. Dr. Phillips was disinclined to express any opinion on the matter to a newspaper man, but from another source our reporter ascertained that Dr. Phillips, as soon as he knew of the Poplar discovery, expressed the opinion that it was

THE WORK OF THE SAME MAN

He also recalled at once the fact of the strangulation in the Hanbury-street case. With respect to the other murders Dr. Phillips points out that the retraction of the skin following immediately upon severance of the throat would immediately destroy the marks of the cord supposing it to have been first used. But there is also another and a most important point of resemblance which Dr. Phillips is understood to perceive. He has always maintained the opinion that the murderer was a man of considerable surgical knowledge. In this belief the Poplar case confirms him. "The murderer," he says, "must be a man who had

STUDIED THE THEORY OF STRANGULATION,

for he evidently knew where to place the cord so as to immediately bring his victim under control. It would be necessary to place the cord in the right place. It would be a very lucky stroke for a man at the first attempt to hit upon the proper place."

Here, then, we arrive at this. That in the opinion of the man who is best qualified to judge the Poplar murderer and the Whitechapel murderer are one and the same man, that the method of preliminary strangulation was certainly employed in Hanbury-street, and was possibly employed in the other cases. Does not this new theory open out a vista of probabilities which, being followed, may lead to the identification of the murderer.

One more word as to the practicability of the theory. Dr. Brownfield most distinctly asserts that by the employment of a cord arranged on the tourniquet principle the victim could be so suddenly seized as to prevent the possibility of a scream.

The following folio, D, carries another newspaper extract, this time from the *Advertiser* of 10 January 1889, its cover being worded as follows:

The Poplar Mystery. Comments on, the inquest on the body of Rose Millett.
REFERENCE TO PAPERS.
Commissioner's minute within I await report from C.I.D. about this (signed) J.M.

Report submitted.
          ARW
12.1.89   *Insp.*

EXTRACT
From the *Advertiser*
of 10th January 1889

It is unfortunate that there is a fundamental difference of opinion between the coroner and the jury who have been investigating what has become known as the Poplar mystery. For months past there has been a succession of abhorrent enormities forced upon public attention, and it would have been a great relief to have been assured that the death of ROSE MILLETT was due to accidental strangulation. As the matter stands additional responsibility is thrown upon the metropolitan police, who from the first have contended that the death was attributable to natural causes, and who have, in the person of DR. BOND, what the public will justly consider to be weighty authority in support of their view. MR. WYNNE BAXTER, the coroner, says "there is no evidence to show that death was the result of violence." In that he follows DR. BOND. The jury flatly disagree with him, and return a verdict of wilful murder against some person or persons unknown, being chiefly guided to that conclusion by the evidence of Doctors BROWNFIELD, HARRIS, HIBBERD [*sic*], and M'KENNA, each of whom is of opinion that the woman was murdered by means of something of the nature of a cord drawn tightly around her neck. It is impossible for the lay reader to accurately estimate the value of the medical testimony for and against the theory of murder. In arriving at their verdict the jury were probably influenced by other than expert evidence. The woman was an unfortunate, the yard in which she was found bore an ill character, and the skilful murderer of others of her class is still at large. Much might be said in favour of their verdict and much against. It is about equally open to belief that the woman fell in a drunken stupor, and that the weight of her head against the collar of her dress compressed her larynx and caused suffocation, or that she was strangled by a cord held in a similar way to that by which soap is often cut. Either conclusion is feasible. The truth may never be known with certainty until the adage that "murder will out" – if murder it be – is once more justified.

[There is a marginal note to the above cutting as follows: – "*I await report from C.I.D. about this (signed) J.M.*"
          10/1]

There is a report[9] dated 11 January 1889 by Robert Anderson, six pages long:

The Poplar Case.
Mr. Monro,

I send you herewith Supt. Steed's report of the inquest upon Catherine Millett, and also Messrs Wontner's notification of the verdict of "Wilful Murder."

The Supt. has come to this Office to ask instructions in view of this verdict. I have thought it only fair to him and his officers to tell him plainly that neither the evidence given at the inquest, nor the verdict arrived at, affects the judgment I formed when I personally investigated the case on the 22nd ult:, and that I did not intend to take any further action in the matter.

Having regard to the Coroner's strictures upon the action of the Police, it may be well to place the facts on record.

About 4 A.M. on the 20th Decbr., the woman was found by a P.S. and a P.C. lying in "Clarke's Yard", High St:, Poplar. The P.S. at once went to fetch Mr. Brownfield the Divisional Surgeon, and his assistant, Mr. Harris, a qualified practitioner, returned with him to High St:, examined the body, certified to the fact of death without any suspicion of death by violence, and left the officers to remove the remains to the mortuary.

Mr. Brownfield made a P.M: on the morning of the 21st and formed the opinion that the woman had been murdered; but this was not communicated to the Police. The first intimation I had of it was derived from the report of the inquest in the Evening Paper, which I took up after midnight on the 21st on my return from a surprise visit to Whitechapel.

Next morning I brought the matter before you, and by your desire I went to Poplar to investigate the case personally, writing to Mr. Bond to meet me there. Mr. Bond, however, was unfortunately out of town for the day.

The statements of the officers who found the body, and especially of P.S. Golding, who impressed me as being an exceptionally safe and reliable witness, seemed so incompatible with the theory of murder that I brought them to the scene of the death, and finally I undertook the distasteful task of going on to the mortuary and examining the body myself.

As the result I came to the conclusion that the death had not been caused by homicidal violence. The woman was found lying on her side in a position of natural repose, her arms at rest, her hands open, her face perfectly placid, her eyes and mouth closed, a handkerchief placed loosely round her neck – not even tied; not the slightest injury to the skin of the neck, save a few slight abrasions, admitted by all to have been caused by her own fingers, the other marks upon her neck (not injuring the skin) being such as would be caused by the stiff collar of her tight-fitting cloth jacket, and which could not have been caused in any other way save under conditions which did not exist – all this added to the fact that the slightest scream or cry would have been heard by persons who are known to have been close at hand, and that the slightest struggle would have left its marks on the soft ground of the Yard, led me, as I have said, to the conclusion, not only that there was no proof of murder, but that the facts and circumstances were inconsistent with such an hypothesis. And this is now abundantly confirmed by what has since been learned as to the woman's drunken habits, by the medical evidence of Mr. Bond, and, lastly, by the opinion of Mr. Wontner, and, I think perhaps, I may add by that of the Coroner himself.

To resume – Mr. Bond's assistant, Mr. Hibbert [sic], had opened my note to Mr. Bond, and (unfortunately I think) decided to act for him in the case. He thus arrived at Poplar soon after I left the mortuary, and made a second P:M: on the body.

In ignorance of this, I made such representations to you on my return to Whitehall that you asked the Chief Surgeon to go down himself; and he reached Poplar just after Mr. Hibbert had left. Finally Mr. Bond went down next day to verify Mr. Hibbert's notes.

All three Doctor's [sic] confirmed Mr. Brownfield's view of the case, and Mr. Bond and Mr. Hibbert called on me on the 24th with a report to that effect. After a long conference, in which I pressed my difficulties and objections, I referred them to you. But that same afternoon Mr. Bond went again to Poplar to make a more careful examination of the woman's neck, and he returned to tell me he had entirely altered his view of the case, and was satisfied that though death was due to strangulation, it was produced accidentally and not by homicidal violence.

This is the basis of the Coroner's complaint that "the Assistant Comr. sent down Doctor after Doctor without his sanction"; and this claim on the part of the Coroner to control the action of the Police in cases of supposed homicide raises a question of such great practical importance that I think an authoritative decision upon it should be obtained.

No one is more ready than I am to spare the susceptibilities (or even to humour the vanity) of any official, but my estimate of the position and duty of the Commissioner of Police is wholly inconsistent with the idea that he must obtain the sanction of the Coroner before taking steps imperatively necessary for the investigation of a crime. This question may arise again at any moment, and I submit it to you for prompt and definite solution.

RA

11 : 1 : 89

[There are two marginal references at the start of this report, as follows–
"*S.C. 402/13*
Cor. 54710/11."]

There is then annexed a report[10], dated 18 January 1889, by Inspector A. Hare on the Rainham Mystery,

METROPOLITAN POLICE.
CRIMINAL INVESTIGATION DEPARTMENT,
SCOTLAND YARD,
18th day of January, 1889.

SUBJECT Rainham
Mystery
REFERENCE TO PAPERS.
45492.

I beg to report that in the case of the Rainham Mystery Mr. Bond was requested to make an examination of the portions of the body found, by Assistant Commissioner, Mr. Monro. He did so and submitted his report. After that some other portions were found in the Regents Canal and Dr. Thomas, the Coroner, decided to hold an inquest. Mr. Bond gave evidence but it was at the instigation of Police and the Coroner was not consulted. I believe the Coroner paid Mr. Bond his fee for attending the inquest but his bill for everything else was sent to Assistant Commissioner who referred it to Receiver for payment.:

A. Hare. Inspr.
JohnShore
<u>Supt</u>

This is followed by a three-page response[11] by the Commissioner, James Monro:

Write to Chief <u>Surgeon</u>
In connection with the recent case at Poplar in which the Coroners Jury have returned a verdict of Wilful Murder, I have to bring to your notice two points in connection with the action of the Divisional Surgeon Dr. Brownfield, with refce. to which, in justice to that gentleman, some explanation it seems to me should be afforded.

It has been reported to me that no indication of the grave nature of the case, as found by the Divl. Surgeon was conveyed by him to the Police; and that the first intimation which the Police received of the case being one of murder was afforded by Dr. Brownfield's evidence at the inquest. I shall be glad to know whether this is correct? at which time the post mortem was made? and what action was taken by Dr. Brownfield in the way of communicating to the Police the conclusion at which he had arrived as to the case being one of murder.

I think it right to bring to your notice an article in the Star of 24th ulto. in which the result of an alleged interview between Dr. Brownfield and a Star reporter is given. I think you will agree with me in thinking that, in justice to Dr. Brownfield he should be asked whether the statements made are correct.

21.1.89   J.M.

[On the reverse of f N above is the annotation –
"Done G.:[. . .]
*   21.1.89"].*
This is followed by a letter[12] from Dr Brownfield, dated 30 January 1889, to the Chief Surgeon:

Received A.O.M.K.
    1.1.89 [*sic –* 1.2.89?]

171 East India Rd.
E.
Jan 30th 89.

A.O. M'Kellar Esq F.R.C.S.
    Surgeon in Chief
        Metropolitan Police
My Dear Sir,
    I have to inform you with regard to the case my lett. that I received the Coroner's order overnight and made PM examination at 9 o'clock following morning, then enquired what officer was to attend inquest and was informed an Inspector the inquest being fixed for eleven a.m. With regard to "Star reports" I hope you do not think me responsible for their reporters articles.

Yours very faithfully.
M.Brownfield
Divl. Surgeon.

There is a letter attached from the Chief Surgeon regarding his investigation, dated 3 February 1889, as follows:

Feb. 3rd 1889

Dear Mr. Staples,
   I enclose the report of Dr. Brownfield, in reply to the questions of the Commissioner respecting the Poplar case (Millett). I hope to call upon you on Monday

Yours very truly
Alexr. O. MacKellar.

There is annexed a letter, dated 9 February 1889, from the Chief Surgeon:

Feb. 9th 1889

Dear Mr. Monro,
   I forward the enclosed received last evening from Dr. Brownfield. I fear that Dr. B. has an aversion to the writing of letters.

Yours very truly
Alexr. O. MacKellar.

There is then a letter, dated 7 February 1889, from Dr. Brownfield to the Chief Surgeon:

171, East India Road,
London, E.
Feb. 7th 1889.

My Dear Sir,
   In answer to yours of the 6th inst I deny that portion marked with blue lines & shown to me in your ''Star'' and further was most careful not to state to anyone more than what I had said at the inquest.
   I am very sorry you should have had so much trouble and hoping this will prove satisfactory

I remain
Yours very truly
M.Brownfield

A.O. MacKellar Esqr FRCS
   Surgeon in Chief
      Metropolitan Police.

The reply[13] of the Chief Surgeon then follows, dated 14 February 1889:

In the case of any further communication on this subject, please quote the
following reference (C.S. 405)
and address:-
  The Chief Surgeon,
    Metropolitan Police Force,
      London, S.W.

                                    Great Scotland Yard,
                                        London, S.W.,
                            14th day of February 1889.

From
  The Chief Surgeon,
    Metropolitan Police Force. [Stamped: – REGISTRY 14 FEB -89–4]
    To   J. Monro Esq.
                  the Commissioner of Police
                    of the Metropolis.
Sir,
    In reply to your letter 98.122/3 I have the honour to inform you
that in my opinion Divisional Surgeons should not give information
referring to any police question to members of the Press except
with the knowledge and approval of the Police. The same rule
should also be applied to private individuals. I further consider that
Divisional Surgeons are bound to give Police the earliest possible
information of cases of death to which suspicion of foul play
attaches. I have every reason to believe that this is the opinion
that obtains generally amongst the Divisional Surgeons.
                              I am, Sir.
                                Your obedient Servant.
                                Alexr. O. MacKellar.

This concludes the information contained in this file, and leaves
singularly unresolved the questions asked by the police about the
conduct of Dr Brownfield in the Poplar case.

CHAPTER 27

January 1889 onwards –
Continuing Vigilance in Whitechapel

The use of additional patrols in Whitechapel, and the requests for additional finance, continued into the New Year. This fact alone indicates that the police believed that the killer, or killers, was or were still at large, and might strike again.

A report[1] dated 26 January 1889 is as follows:

[Stamped: – HOME OFFICE 28 JAN.89 RECEIVED] No. A49301G/4
DATE 26 Jan. 1889.   Commissioner of Police
REFERENCES &c.   Reports that the expenditure for special allowance to the Police employed on Special Patrol duty in Whitechapel amounted to £306.13 on the 24 inst, and asks permission to expend a further £200. He is reducing the number of men specially employed as quickly as it is safe to do so.
                         MINUTES.
?Sanction up to a further £200.
WTB.
31.1.89 Better ask Receiver for financial observations in first instance in usual course.
                  ELP 1st Feby 89.   CM. Jan 31.
                  Wrote Recr. 2/2
96318/3   4 Whitehall Place, S.W.
                                     26th January, 1889.
Sir,
    With reference to your letter of the 15th inst. sanctioning an allowance of 1/- per diem to the Police employed on special patrol duty in Whitechapel, I have to acquaint you, for the information of the Secretary of State, that the expenditure on this account up to the 24th inst. inclusive amounts to £306.13.0. I shall be glad therefore to receive the sanction of the Secretary of State to a further expenditure of not more than £200.
    I am gradually reducing the number of men employed on this

duty as quickly as it is safe to do so, but such reduction cannot be effected all at once.

I am,

Sir,

Your obedient Servant,

JMonro.

There is a further report[2] on this subject, as follows:

Home Office 2 Feby / Whitechapel murders. Extra allowce.

Transmitting letter from the Commr asking for authority to expend a further sum of £200. The expenditure on account of the extra allowance up to 24th inst. being £306.13.0. The S of S asks for the Receiver's observations personally, thereon.

Say that the allowance already granted was sufficient for a period of seven weeks. I think [   ] the additional £200 [   ] be proved Should be asked to say whether having regard to the reduced number now employed be [   ] £200 will cover all expenditure as far as he can foretell up to the 31 March next.

A.S.T[?]

6.2.89

Done 6/2

A49301G/4.   Receiver Metropolitan Police District 5185/3 4 FEB.89

Home Office,

2 February 1889.

Sir,

I am directed by the Secretary of State to transmit to you, with reference to the Home Office letter of the 15th ultimo and previous correspondence on the subject of the plain clothes allowance (special) to officers patrolling Whitechapel, a further letter from the Commissioner of Police; and to request the favour of your observations financially thereon.

I am,

Sir,

Your obedient Servant,

GODFREY LUSHINGTON.

The Receiver for the
Metropolitan Police District.
    &c   &c   &c.

There is a report[3], dated 2 February 1889, regarding the claims for the additional patrols as follows:

No. 5227/3   A49301/5   Office of the Receiver for the
                                 Metropolitan Police District
                                 4, Whitehall Place
                                 2. Feb.1889

Sir,
  I have the honor to transmit for the information of the Secretary of State, Accounts of Expenses incurred by various Police Officers on special occasions, and to request authority for payment of the same, the Commissioner having approved thereof, vizt.
  Supt W Hugo for Police specially employed patrolling Whitechapel – £12.16.10

                    Refreshment allowance

In /1 the Commr. states that "many" of the Whitechapel patrols come from other divisions and have to patrol at a distance from their homes. There will probably therefore be further claims of this description.
? Sanction
W.T.B.
6.2.89   see/6   I have the honor to be,
                                 Sir,
                          Your obedient Servant,
The Under Secretary of State   [*signature illeg.*]
    &c   &c   &c
      Home Office.

This is followed by a file cover[4], as follows:

[Stamped: – HOME OFFICE 7 FEB.89 RECEIVED] No. A49301G/6
DATE 6 Feb.1889.   Receiver.
REFERENCES, &c. Police employed on special patrol duty in Whitechapel. Thinks that Commissioner should be asked to say whether he estimates that the £200 will cover all the expenditure as far as he can foresee up to 31 March next.
                       Pressing.
                       MINUTES.
? ask this question of Mr Monro by letter. also sanction Refreshment

allowances recommended in 1/5 to those Police Officers [who have come from a distance for this service, and who are, according to Police orders, entitled to such additional fees.]

CM Feb 9. 89   GL

9 Feb '89

Wrote Commissioner
& Receiver
12 Feb: 1889.
Comment a/15.3.89/

The report[5] from the Receiver on the above follows:

Pressing   A49301G/6
5785/3

4 Whitehall Place,
Febr. 6th. 1889

Sir,

I have the honour to return herewith the letter from the Commissioner dated 26th ult, asking sanction for a further expenditure up to £200 in respect of the allowance to the Police employed on Special Patrol duty in Whitechapel.

As regards this I have to state that the sum already granted covered a period of 7 weeks, and I think Mr. Monro should be asked to say whether [having regard to the reduced numbers now employed he estimates that the £200 will cover all the expenditure as far as he can foresee, up to 31st March next.]

I have the honour to be,
Sir,
Your obedient Servant,
[   ]

There is an interesting entry[6] for expenses in the Police Entry book, dated 14 February 1889, in respect of Inspector Abberline:

A49301/159

14th February 1889.

Authorising

No 5227/4   5th Instant,

Inspector Abberline for expenses in connection with the White-chapel murders, £39. 0. 1,

Recr.

There is another report[7], dated 15 March 1889, as follows:

No. A49301G/7
DATE. 15 March 1889.   Commissioner of Police
REFERENCES, &c. Reports [cessation of the special patrol duty in Whitechapel & stating that the total expenditure thereon has been £351]; requests sanction for the extra expenditure not covered by H.O. authority of 15 Jan. last.

MINUTES.

See 1/4
? To Receiver
        for observations.
[illeg. initials]
    8.3.89.   C.M. Mar:19
[Stamped: – Referred 19 MAR.89.]
    I think that Mr. Monro's proposal may receive the sanction of the Secretary of State, and the excess expenditure of £51, sanctioned.

A:S:S:
19.3.89.

[Stamped: – HOME OFFICE 21 MAR.89] ?Sanction
?   [PP]
                    22.3.89   GL
        Wrote Commissioner   23 March '89
            & Receiver   28 March 1889.

A49301G/7
96318/5

4, Whitehall Place,
S.W.
15th March, 1889.

Sir,
    In reply to your letter [*Marginal note* – "A49301G/6"] of the 12th ultimo on the subject of the Police employed on special patrol duty in Whitechapel, I have to acquaint you, for the information of the Secretary of State, that this duty has now ceased. –
    The total expense of the special allowance to the Police employed amounts to £351; and I have accordingly to request that Mr. Secretary Matthews may be pleased to sanction the extra expenditure not covered by the Home Office authority of the 15th January last.-

I am, Sir,

The Under Secretary	Your most obedient Servant,
of State	J.Monro
&c – &c – &c	
Home Office	

The cover sheets regarding the above report are filed under MEPO 3/141, as follows:

[*At top of page is stamp:* – Receiver for the Metropolitan Police]
HO a49301G/7
19 March
Whitechapel murders Extra Allowance of 1/- per day
Referring without covering letter to letter from the Commr. reporting cessation of patrol duty in Whitechapel & stating that the total expenditure has been £351, & requesting sanction for extra expenditure.
Copy of Receiver's minute "I think that Mr.Monro's proposal may receive the sanction of the Secy of State and the excep expenditure of £51 sanctioned" ARP.

19.3.89.

This followed by a further cover:

G&A
S/Sy H.O.
        28 March
        Whitechapel Murders.
Forwards copy of letter to Commr., sanctioning £51 more being expended for the specl. allowances of 1/- per diem.
        <u>Pressing</u>
Pass for payment
                A[ ]
                30.3.89.
[   ]
                Done. ARP

The next police communication, on social conditions in the East End, is a letter[8] from James Monro, dated 5 May 1889:

Reply to H.O.   5.5.89

Any thing that Mr. Barnet writes on such a subject is entitled to respect for no one who knows the work which the vicar of St. Jude's has done, and the spirit in which he does it can entertain anything but sentiments of regard for him & sympathy with his aspirations. Practically what he says is this. Vice of a very low type exists in Whitechapel – such vice manifests itself in brawling and acts of violence which shock the feelings of respectable persons. Such acts of violence are not repressed by action taken either before the Police or magisterial authorities, clear out the slums and lodging houses to which vicious persons resort – and vice will disappear, respectability taking its place.

There is no doubt whatever that vice of a low and degraded type is only too visible in Whitechapel. The facility with which the Whitechapel murderer obtains victims has brought this prominently to notice, but to any one who will take a walk late a night in the districts where the recent atrocities have been committed, the only wonder is that his operations have been so restricted. There is no lack of victims ready to his hand, for scores of these unfortunate women may be seen any night muddled with drink in the streets & alleys, perfectly reckless as to their safety, and only anxious to meet with any one who will help them in plying their miserable trade.

There is no doubt that brawling & fighting go on, repressed as far as possible by police, but it must be remembered that these women do not care to be protected against those who assault them, very seldom have recourse to the station to complain, & still more seldom to appear at any police court to prosecute any charge which they may have laid before the police.

It is also true that common lodging houses are not all that they might be in the way of discouraging immorality, altho' I do not think that so much of the reproach in this respect which is generally levelled at them in reality is attributable to them. On this subject I have already expressed my views in my letter of [*missing*]. Much however of the immorality which goes on finds its place in the low lodgings which are let to prostitutes by the day or week, where they take home men, with reference to which the law is practically powerless. These are the houses from which no charges are brought before the police, & to these much more than to the common lodging houses is the violence conjoined with immorality attributable.

That respectability would be benefitted [*sic*] by clearing out such localities admits of little doubt. That the moral atmosphere of Whitechapel would be purified by the substitution of better lodging houses for the dens at present to be found there, is perfectly clear, but this would not remove vice, it would only delocalize it, and transfer it to some neighbouring parish at present not quite so disreputable as some parts of Whitechapel.

I do not mean to say that their might not be a gain – it certainly would be a gain to Whitechapel, and it may be said that if other parishes took similar steps, similar results would follow within their limits. But the question still remains – what is to become of the residuum of vice which is thus moved on? I do not believe in such a transfer of a vicious population as likely to remove vice generally from the metropolis, and I suspect it may be taken as a fact that wherever landlords or lodging house keepers can secure their rent, they will not hesitate in taking it from prostitutes with as much readiness as from persons of a different class.

Behind the whole question lies the larger matter of street prostitution generally, and until that is taken up, and regulated (objectionable as this may appear to a public which confuses between liberty & license) the mere multiplying of comfortable lodging houses will not have any appreciable effect in diminishing the number of & [ ] resulting from a class who do not want comfortable lodging houses, & the scene of whose operations is on the streets.

3/8   JM.

CHAPTER 28

17 July 1889 – Murder of Alice McKenzie

It was July 1889 before another murder occurred that could be linked with the 1888 series. It was the murder of a prostitute, Alice McKenzie, on 17 July 1889 that revived fears that the "Ripper" might still be at work in the East End of London.

The first papers[1] relevant to this murder are as follows:

> Commercial Street Station
> Metropolitan Police
> H Division
> 17th July   1889

I beg to report that about 12.48 am 17th inst. I visited PC.272H Walter Andrews in Castle Alley, Whitechapel. He being on the Beat No. 11 on the 4th Section. I said to him alright he replied alright Sergeant. I then left him and went to visit another P.C. on an adjoining beat. I had only got about 150 yards from P.C.272H when I heard a whistle blow twice. I rushed to the bottom of Castle Alley and heard P.C.272H say come on quick he ran up the alley, and I followed, and on the pavement closer to two vans on the right side of the footway I saw a woman laying on her right side with her clothes half up to her waist exposing her abdomen. I also noticed a quantity of blood under her head on the footway. The P.C. said here's another murder. I directed the P.C. not to leave the body or let anyone touch it until the Dr. arrived. The P.C. said it's quite warm as he touched her. I got the assistance of P.C. 101H here and P.C. 423 Allen. The former P.C. I directed to search the place and sent P.C. 423 for the Doctor, and Inspr. on duty, and upon his return to make search. Other Constables arrived shortly afterwards, also the Local Inspr. Mr. Reid C.I.D. I also hailed a passing cab and acquainted the Superintendent of what had taken place. Several men were drafted in different directions to make enquiries at Lodging Houses Coffee Houses &c to see if any suspicious man had recently entered them. The body was afterwards conveyed by me on the ambulance to the Whitechapel mortuary where the body was searched by Inspr. Reid who gave me a description of the body.

Description age about 40 length 5 ft 4 complexion pale hair and eyes brown top of thumb of left hand deficient also tooth deficient in upper jaw. Dress red stuff bodice patched under arms and sleeves with marone one black and one marone stockings brown stuff skirt kilted brown lindsey petticoat, white chemise and apron, paisley shawl. button boots. all old nothing found on person.

E Badham Sergt
Thos. Hawkes Insp.

An old clay pipe and a farthing were found under the body.

This statement is followed[2] by that of PC Walter Andrews:

Commercial Street Station
Metropolitan Police.
H Division
July 17th 1889

I beg to report that at 10 minutes to 1 o'clock the 17th inst. I was passing through Castle Alley Whitechapel trying the doors when I saw a woman lying on the pavement with her throat cut but I saw no one in the street at the time. I touched the body with my hand and found that she was quite warm. I at once blew my whistle when I saw Isaac Lewis Jacob of No. 12 New Castle place Whitechapel going towards Wentworth Street with a plate in his hand he said that he was going to get something for his supper. I said you had better stop here with me as there have been a woman murdered. Just at that minute Sergeant Badham heard the whistle blow and came running up to my assistance. I told the Sergeant that there was a woman laying on the foot way in Castle Alley with her throat cut. I ran back and took charge of the body until the Doctor arrived and examined the woman and stated the woman was dead. The body was afterwards conveyed to the mortuary on the ambulance.

Walter Andrews
PC 272H
Thos. Hawkes, Inspr.

These reports are followed by a lengthy report[3] by Inspector Moore, one of the team who had been sent from Scotland Yard to investigate the Whitechapel murders in September 1888:

METROPOLITAN POLICE.
Criminal Investigation Department,
Scotland Yard,
17th day of July 1889.

Referring to case of Murder at Castle Alley, Whitechapel.

I beg to report that enquiry has been continued in this case; but the following are the only facts obtained at present.

On learning that the deceased had been identified I caused enquiry to be made by P.S. Record D. and P.S. Kuhrt "G"., who ascertained from John McCormac, of 52 Gun Street, Spitalfields that he was a labourer, and had been employed by Jewish Tailors at Hanbury St. and elsewhere for about 16 years. He has been living with the deceased Alice McKenzie about 6 or 7 years. He first met her at Bishopsgate, and they have been living in Common Lodging Houses about Whitechapel ever since; but lately at 52 Gun St., as above. He came from his work at about 4 p.m. 16th Inst. when he saw her and gave her some money (1s/8d); he then went to sleep, and when he awoke between 10 and 11 p.m. she had gone out. He did not see her again until he identified her body at the Mortuary this afternoon. She has mentioned to him that she came from Peterborough; but he cannot remember that she ever said who her friends were.

The officers also saw Betsy Ryder, of 52 Gun Street, Spitalfields, the deputy of the Lodging House; who stated that the deceased woman and McCormac had been lodging there on and off for the past 12 months, and appeared to live comfortably together. She saw her go out between 8.30 and 9 pm. 16th, and noticed that she had some money in her hand, but the amount is not known. She did not return home again. At 2 p.m. this day "Ryder" was taken to the mortuary where she identified the body of deceased woman; who she had often heard mention that she had sons abroad, but the exact place is not known. She is believed to be 39 years of age and used to go out at night; but whether as a prostitute or not is not known to Mrs. Ryder; although the Police looked upon her as such. She was much addicted to drink.

At 5p.m. this day an Inquest was opened at the "Working Lads Institute", Whitechapel Road, by W.E. Baxter, Esq., Coroner for East Middlesex; and after various witnesses had been examined as to the finding of the body and identification; the further hearing was adjourned till 10a.m. tomorrow (18th). A post-mortem examination has been made by Drs. Phillips, ["Bond" – *deleted*]

McKeller and others, the result of which will be given at inquest tomorrow.

Careful enquiry has been made at Coffee and Lodging Houses; but no information has been obtained at present, and the enquiry is being continued.

During the day since submitting the previous report two men have been detained in H Division both of which were at Commercial St. Station, but were liberated subsequently upon enquiry being found satisfactory.

I wish to point out that every effort is being made to obtain something tangible in regard to the perpetrator of the crime.

Henry Moore, Inspector
T Arnold Supt.

The next reference[4] to this murder is contained in a Home Office file dated 17 July 1889:

	No. A49301I/1
DATE 17 July 1889	Commissioner of Police
REFERENCES, &c.	Forwards police report respecting the commission of a murder in Castle Alley, Whitechapel, this morning. States that every effort will be made to discover the murderer, who, he thinks, is identical with "Jack the Ripper," but that the assassin has not left the slightest clue to his identity.

Immediate

MINUTES.

The Secretary of State. The plan is from Pall Mall of today July 17.

[There is here appended a copy of the map of the area entitled "THE WHITECHAPEL MURDERS" and showing the sites of all the murders from that of Emma Smith through to that of Alice McKenzie (eight murders.)]

Returned by S.S. and Mr. S. Wortley. also seen by Mr Lushington
Lay by C.M. July 20.

This is followed by the report[5] of the Chief Commissioner of Police, James Monro:

A49301I/1

<u>Immediate.</u>   17th July 1889.

Sir,

I have the honour to send herewith for the information of the Secretary of State a Police report regarding the murder of a woman in Castle Alley, Whitechapel this morning.

As soon as I received a telegram announcing the commission of the crime I started about 3 am for the spot, for the purpose of viewing the scene of the occurrence, and assisting at the inquiry.

I need not say that every effort will be made by the Police to discover the murderer, who, I am inclined to believe is identical with the notorious "Jack the Ripper" of last year.

It will be seen that in spite of ample Police precautions and vigilance the assassin has again succeeded in committing a murder and getting off without leaving the slightest clue to his identity.

I have the honour to be,

Sir,
Your obedient servant,
J. Monro

The Under Secretary
   of State,
&c &c &c.

This report is followed by a more detailed summary[6] by Superintendent Arnold, H Division, dated 17 July 1889, of police action taken, as follows:

METROPOLITAN POLICE.
H Division.
17th July 1889.

SUBJECT Whitechapel
Murders.
<u>52,983</u>

I beg to report that at 12.50 am this day P.C. 272H Andrews was passing through Castle Alley, Whitechapel, when he noticed a woman lying on the pavement, and upon examination discovered that her throat was cut about two inches on left side, the body being quite warm. An alarm was at once raised by the Constable blowing his whistle when Sergeant Badham came immediately upon the scene. He found a woman, age about 40. to 45, length 5ft 4in, complexion pale, hair and eyes brown, top of thumb of left hand deficient, also tooth deficient in upper jaw, dress red stuff bodice, patched under arms, and sleeves with marone coloured material, one black and one marone coloured stockings, brown stuff skirt, kilted brown linsey petticoat, white chemise and apron, paisley shawl, button boots, all old and dirty, lying on her right side with her clothing turned up to her waist exposing her abdomen, with a deep zig-zag cut extending across same, a quantity of blood was on footway. In addition to P.C. 272H Andrews, the Sergeant obtained the assistance of other constables on adjoining beats, when information was sent to the Divisional Surgeon, Dr. Phillips and to the Inspector on duty at Commercial Street Police Station, also Local Inspector Reid.

On arrival of Dr. Phillips he examined the body which was afterwards removed to the Whitechapel Mortuary to await identification and inquest, life being extinct.

I immediately came upon the scene, and directed that a thorough search of the locality, which was done, but nothing was discovered beyond an old clay pipe besmeared with blood, and a farthing, which were found lying under the body when removed.

I also instituted inquiries in various directions, especially at common lodging houses, coffee houses &c., with a view to ascertain if any suspicious men had entered either and also with a view to deceased's identification, but at present without success. Coroner and his officer have been informed and the inquest will be opened today.

The opinion formed by Dr. Phillips after his examination of the body, was that the wounds had not been inflicted by the same hand as in the previous cases, inasmuch as the injuries in this case are not so severe and the cut on stomach is not so direct. I should have mentioned before that at the time of the discovery no person was seen in or near Castle Alley, but on the constable blowing his whistle, he saw Isaac Lewis Jacob of No. 12 Newcastle Place Whitechapel, who was going towards Wentworth Street with a plate in his hand, as he said for the purpose of fetching something for his supper, which was no doubt correct. He remained with the officer until assistance arrived.

There can be no doubt that the crime was committed as near as possible about 12.40 a.m., as P.C. 272H Andrews passed through Castle Alley at 12.20 a.m. and again at 12.50 a.m. when he found the body. P.C. 423H Allen passed through the Alley at 12.30 a.m. and remained under the lamp, exactly where the body was found, for five minutes whilst partaking of his supper, he neither saw or heard any person in the alley.

The description of deceased has been fully circulated by wire and every exertion is being made to prove her identity.

One person has been detained viz John Larkin Mills, which occurred at 2.35 a.m., but was liberated at 4.30 a.m., as after inquiry was made, his statement was found satisfactory.

I have just received information that Mrs. Smith, wife of the superintendent of the wash houses situate in Castle Alley, has identified deceased as a person who occasionally attended the wash houses for the purpose of washing her clothing and was known by the name of Kelly but whether that is her name, or where she has resided, or any of her associates, nothing is yet known.

T Arnold
Superintendent

There is a report[7] by Dr Thomas Bond, regarding examination of the body of the woman McKenzie:

Dear Sir,

I beg to report that in accordance with your instructions I this day inspected the dead body of a woman, who has been identified as Alice McKenzie, at Whitechapel. Before I went to the mortuary I called on Dr. Phillips & he kindly accompanied me. He informed me that the post mortem was completed yesterday & that the wounds on the throat of the woman had been so disturbed that any examination I might make, unassisted would convey no definite information as to the nature of the injuries. He pointed out to me the original wounds, their character and direction & I was able to form an opinion that there could be no doubt that the cuts were made from left to right & as far as I was able to make out, the knife appears to have been plunged deeply into the neck on the left side of the victim below the sterno mastoid muscle & brought out by a tailed incision just above the larynx on the same side. There appeared to have been two stabs, & the knife then carried forward in the same skin wound, except that a small tongue of skin remained between the two stabs. The incisions appeared to me to be in a direction from above downwards and forwards with several small superficial cuts extending upwards & tailing off into mere scratches. The two main cuts appeared to be about 3 inches long but Dr. Phillips stated that before the parts were disturbed the cuts which I saw extending down wards, really were in a direction upwards.

The cuts appeared to have been inflicted with a sharp strong knife. I could form no opinion as to the width of the blade or the length of the knife, but undoubtedly the cuts might have been done with a short knife; it must in my opinion have had a sharp point. I believe the cuts were made from the front while the woman's head was thrown back on the ground. There were two bruises high up on the chest which looked as if the murderer had made the cuts with his right hand while he held the woman down with his left. There were no bruises on the woman's face or lips.

On the right side of the abdomen extending from the chest to below the level of the umbilicus there was a jagged incision made up of several cuts which extended through the skin & subcutaneous fat & at the bottom of this cut there were 7 or 8 superficial scratches about 2 inches long parallel to each other in a longitudinal direction. There was also a small cut eighth of an inch deep, quarter inch long on the mons veneris. I think that in order to inflict the wound which I saw on the abdomen the murderer must have raised the clothes with his left hand & inflicted the injuries with his right.

Dr. Phillips showed me a small bruise on the left side of the stomach which he suggested might have been caused by the murderer pressing his right hand on the stomach while he used the knife with his left hand, but I saw no sufficient reason to entertain this opinion. The wounds could not have been self inflicted, & no doubt the wound in the throat would cause almost immediate death & I do not think the woman could call out if held down in the position she appears to have been in when the wounds were inflicted. The wounds on the abdomen could have nothing to do with the cause of death & were in my opinion inflicted after death. I see in this murder evidence of similar design to the former Whitechapel murders viz. sudden onslaught on the prostrate woman, the throat skilfully & resolutely cut with subsequent mutilation, each mutilation indicating sexual thoughts & a desire to mutilate the abdomen & sexual organs.

I am of opinion that the murder was performed by the same ["hand" – *deleted*] person who committed the former series of Whitechapel murders.

I am dear Sir,
Yours faithfully,
Thos. Bond.

R. Anderson esq.

It seems significant that Dr Bond's report is addressed to Robert Anderson, who had asked Dr Bond for his 10 November 1888, report on the murders and medical aspects thereof. It is also interesting to note that Dr Bond felt that the McKenzie murder was yet another in the "Ripper" series, whereas Dr Phillips' feelings appeared to be the opposite as will be seen in his lengthy report[8] of 22 July 1889:

1.
Re- Alice McKenzie
      Decd.
Called 1 AM Wednesday 17th July 1889. I went to Castle Alley, Whitechapel. Arr. 1.10 AM.
It was raining sharply.
Position of body.
Found the body of a woman lying on back. face turned sharply to right. temp. moderate.
Right arm enclosed with shawl, which extended to end of fingers. from arm flexed over chest.
Left arm not covered with shawl was flexed & hand rested on shoulder.
Wound in neck, left.
Left side of neck is incised, wound jagged, and exposed.
Position of Dress.
Clothes turned up & exposing genitals.
Abdomen wounded in wall.
Wound of wall of abdomen apparently not opening the cavity.
Temp. of body.
Warmth still perceptible under right cheek.
Body still warm where covered. Where exposed quite cold.
Pupils.
Pupils equal dilated & eyelids open.
Haemorrhage from wound in neck.
Blood poured out from wound in neck. clotted firmly & limited on pavement to the outline of the clothes & thin contact with the ground. The clot partly broken down at margin through action of the rain & the blood so mixed ran down slanting pavement into gutter & stagnated there by various objects has run down the water way several feet. The clot probably weighed $1\frac{1}{2}$ to $1\frac{3}{4}$ the whole amount of blood lost would not amount to more than 2 pts.
No artl. spirtg.

No arterial spirting seen.

No sign of anaesthetics.

No sign of drugs or anaesthetics.

2.

Exn. of body at mortuary.

In company with Mr. Arnold & Chief Inspr. West followed the body to Pavilion Yd. WhChl. & had it placed at once on the post mortem table in the shed used as a mortuary, and without stripping the body & without displacement of any part we discussed to confirm my former note.

The wound in neck is deeper & cleaner cut than appeared at first sight.

I left the body in charge of the police and gave instructions nothing was to be touched until the body was delivered over to the coroners officer or I had again possession of it. I had witnessed the police taking a "description"

Immediate communication with police.

I communicated my conclusions to Mr. Arnold & Ch. Inspr. West & subsequently to Col. Monsell at the Leman Street Stn. so far as I was able to do so.

Instructions fr. Coroner.

Early in the morning I received instructions from the Coroner to make a P.M. section & attend an enquiry at 5 P.M.

Arrangement for P.M. Exm.

As soon as I could make arrangements I communicated them to the Ch.Surgn. and Mr. Gordon Brown who expressed a wish to be present. both attended shortly after the hour appointed 2 P.M. the former accompanied by a friend. My colleague Mr. Clark attended and a "Mr. Boswick" [?] gained admission for a short time, not with my permission.

3.

P.M. made 2P.M. same day.

At 2 P.M. at the same place, I again viewed the body it was as far as I could discover in exactly the position I had left it.

Height.

Height 5ft 5in.

Rigor Mortis.

Rigor mortis well marked most in extremities.

Fore Arms & Face freckled.

Condn. of Body.

Body well nourished.

Discovery of & subst. loss of short clay pipe.

While searching the clothing one of the attendants found a short pipe, well used, which he thoughtlessly threw onto the ground & broke it. I had the pieces put on one side meaning to preserve them but up to the time of writing this report they have not been recovered by me.

Condition of Clothing.

The clothing was fastened round the body somewhat tightly & could only be raised so as to expose about $\frac{1}{3}$ of the abdomen. The back part of the under garment was well saturated with blood stained fluid.

Bruises upper part of chest.

Over upon & below the left collar bone there is a well defined bruise about the size of a shilling situate about the junction of the inner $\frac{1}{3}$ & outer $\frac{2}{3}$ of the collar bone. & on the right side an inch below the sterno clavicular articulation is another larger and more defined bruise most marked at its outer border.

Dilated veins.

Between the mammaries in middle line of sternum in a direct line downwards with the last named bruise are several congested veins seen through the skin.

Scorings & Wounds of Abdomen.

Seven inches below right nipple commences a wound 7 inches long, not quite straight in direction, inclining first inwards & then outwards, deepest at its upper part and ending below in a subcutaneous dissection possibly 3 or perhaps 4 inches. [*in whole (?)*] 4.

Abdominal cavity *not opened*. Scoring on right side.

Neither abdominal cavity opened – or muscular covering divided. Tailing towards inner border of this wound are seven dermal marks only dividing the skin & ascending above the deeper incision, & 7 similar scorings descending lower than the major wound. & between it & pubis.

One distinct became deeper over the pubis.

Marks & blood stains left side.

There are 5 small (excoriating) marks below and between umbilicus and pubis some what transverse in direction col red one $\frac{3}{4}$ in. in length, and the smallest a [ ] in length.

Somewhat nearer to the left side there stains of blood surrounding a bruise the size of a fourpenny piece, (& corresponding with scores on right side.)

The larger marking is the lowest and the smallest nearest the right side. & all of them are 4 in. from prominence of pelvis & 4 in. below umbilicus.

Old scars & signs of injury.

There are old scars & bruisings over patella front of shins & three distinct cicatrices on Dresum of left forearm.

Loss of terminal joint of left thumb from some cutting instrument, which has left half the nail.

Genital Signs.

There is no sign of Coitus.

Syphilitic Condylomata of vagina and ulceration of mucous membrane under clitoris.

Congestion [ ] Anal

Anal external piles & excretion of a small quantity of liquid faeces.

5.

Description of wound in neck

More superficial

Two jagged wounds commence from behind the left sterno mastoid muscle leaving a triangular piece of skin attached by its base to the outside (remaining) skin about an inch long and four inches forward & upwards.

Deeper.

The deepest incision divides the Sterno M. muscle except a few posterior fibres. the vessels of the neck & sheath, the division of the Common Carotid being above the Omo hyoid muscle, down to the transverse processes of the Cervical Vertebra.

There are four jagged cuts over angle of jaw where instrument had been arrested [?] over cut under jaw.

No sign of fall backwards.

No sign of bruise back of Head or under Scalp.

Brain app. & other visceral app. *fairly normal* & healthy.

Brain healthy but meningel vessels fuller than might have been expected.

Lungs old adhesions posterior part of right. Left healthy Both well filled with air & not congested.

Heart healthy small quantity of fluid in pericardium, colour red, walls good, Valves healthy. Cavities empty & contracted. Large vessels healthy no clots.

Liver, fairly healthy rather pale.

Spleen & Kidneys fairly healthy.

Stomach large contains rather more than a pint of pultaceous matter

which has a faint alcoholic smell. mucous membrane pale.
Bladder contracted and empty.
Uterus small. healthy. unimpregnated.
Ovaries contain small cysts.
6.
Conclusions.
Death was caused through Syncope arising from the division of the vessels of neck left side.
Nature of instrument & its use.
The wound was caused by sharp cutting instrument with at least two strokes. was not suicidal, was made from left to right, while the body was on the ground & effected by someone who knew the position of the vessels, at any rate where to cut with reference to causing speedy death.
No sign of struggle but of holding down.
No sign of violent struggle but of body being held down by hand as evidenced by bruises on upper chest and collar bone.
Greater Pressure – right.
There was more pressure on the right side.
Further conclusions
No physiological reason why the woman should not have uttered a cry. The wound in the throat tends to confirm the conclusion submitted as to the wounds of the abdominal wall.
That death almost immediately followed the incision of the neck.
That the woman did not move after the said incision.
The superficial marks on left side of abdomen were characteristic of pressure with a Thumb and Fingers. they compared in position to a right hand placed on the abdomen pinching up a fold of skin for at least 3 inches.
That the smearing of blood was caused in this way.
The scoring and cuts of skin on Pubis were caused through the endeavour to pass the obstruction caused by the clothing.
The long wound right side of abdomen was inflicted by a sharp pointed instrument from above downwards & (there is evidence of two thrusts of instrument before withdrawal) the instrument turned laterally while making the undermining portion of wound which was made from right to left.
Admit that the appearances observed on left side of abdomen were caused by the pressure of a right hand (possibly to facilitate the introduction of an instrument under the (tight) clothing -there-
The right wounds were produced by a left handed cut.

The abdominal injuries were caused subsequent to the throat being cut.

The instrument used was smaller than the one used in most of the cases that have come under my observation in these "White chapel Murders."

Concurrence of Dr. G. Brown.

Dr. Gordon Brown (City Police Surgeon) has been good enough to express his concurrence in the foregoing conclusions, but he has not expressed his opinion concerning the following remarks which have not formally been submitted to him.

On Thursday about 6 P.M. I accompanied Dr. Bond to view the body of Dec'd and so far as I was able explained the appearances to him. Decomposition had fairly begun, though not very markedly.

There was great difficulty without again opening up the incisions in giving a description of the appearances – and it appeared to me that the body had been washed since the former examination.

On Saturday last at noon I again in the presence of Dr. Brown re examined the body for the purpose of demonstrating the appearances on the Abdomen.

I believe I satisfied him of the correctness of the appearances, & this must be so as he has since signified generally his assent to the report.

After careful and long deliberation I cannot satisfy myself on purely anatomical & professional grounds that the Perpetrator of all the "WhChl.murders" is one man.

I am on the contrary impelled to a contrary conclusion. This noting the mode of procedure & the character of the mutilations & judging of motive in connection with the latter.

I do not here enter into the comparison of the cases neither do I take into account what I admit may be almost conclusive evidence in favour of the one man theory if all the surrounding circumstances & other evidence are considered.

Holding it as my duty to report on the P.M. appearances and express an opinion solely on Professional Grounds, based upon my own observations. For this purpose I have ignored all evidence not coming under my own observation.

> Geo.B.Phillips
> 2 Spital Square E
> July 22nd.'89.

There is then a report[9] dated 19 July 1889 from Inspector Henry Moore regarding William W. Brodie:

METROPOLITAN POLICE.

Criminal Investigation Department,

Scotland Yard,

19th July 1889.

SUBJECT Murder of Alice McKenzie
at Whitechapel.

Reference to papers 52983.

Referring to case of murder at Castle Alley, Whitechapel, on 17th
Inst., for which a man named William W. Brodie has given himself
up at Leman St. Station; vide attached Report and Telegrams.

I beg to report that this morning when "Brodie" appeared sober,
I saw him, and afterwards he volunteered a statement which I took
down in writing and herewith submitted.

After I had taken the statement I examined his clothing; but could
not discover any trace of blood.

Whilst examining his clothing he remarked that he had now
committed 9 murders in Whitechapel; but none of them had
troubled him except this last one; that was why he had given
himself up to Police.

I find from this man's papers that on 7th May 1887 he was sentenced
to 14 years P.S. for Larceny in a Dwelling House, and was liberated on
24th Augt./88.

On searching him nothing of importance was found. <u>Directions
respectfully asked.</u>

Henry Moore, Inspr.

[*There is a marginal minute:* "Let him be charged as a lunatic.
[*initialled*] 19/7."]

The next report[10], dated 19 July 1889, again refers to William
Brodie:

METROPOLITAN POLICE.

Convict Supervision Office,

19th July 1889.

Lic:Holder Register No. D517 Office No. 35944 Name William
Broder[?]

I beg to report that Willm. Brodie was sentenced at the Cent.
Crim. Court Sess. 7th May 1877 to 14 years penal serv: for larceny
in a dwelling house, (City Case).

He was released on licence 22nd August 1888 & went to reside at 2
Harveys Buildings, Strand. On the 5th Sep: 1888 he reported at this

Office his intention of leaving this country for the Cape of Good Hope, via Southampton, per: S.S. Africana. Since that date and until the 16th inst. nothing more was heard of him, but on the date last mentioned he again reported at this Office stating he had returned from the Cape & would again reside at 2 Harveys Blgs., Strand.

Thos. Haines Insp.

The next report[11], dated 19 July 1889, also refers to Brodie, and was submitted by Sergeant Godley:

METROPOLITAN POLICE.
H Division.
19th day of July, 1889.

Whitechapel Murders
Reference to Papers 52983
Re William Brodie detained at Leman Street Police Station.

I beg to report that I made enquiries at Foresters Hall Place Clerkenwell Road where the above has brothers named James & Thomas Brodie who carry on Business as Printers.

I was informed by Mr. Walter Slater the Manager that Mr. James Brodie was out of town and would not return till Saturday the 20th inst. and his address is not known.

Mr. Slater saw the above in Mr. Thomas Brodie's office talking to him at about 4.45 p.m. on Tuesday the 16th and Wednesday the 17th and he is of opinion that William Brodie is a reckless character and addicted to drink.

G. Godley Sergt.
Henry Moore Insp.

There is also a report[12] of the same date by Sgt. Bradshaw, as follows:

METROPOLITAN POLICE.
H Division.
19th July 1889.

The Whitechapel Murders.
Reference to Papers 52983.
Re Licence Holder William Brodie, Office No. 35.944. I beg to report having made inquiries at 2. Harveys Buildings, Strand, and was informed by Mrs. Salvage and her daughter to whom Brodie is apparently well known that he came there between 11 & 12 on

Tuesday morning last and went to bed between 10 & 11 p.m. remaining in the house till about 11. A.m. Wednesday morning, when he went out, and subsequently returned about 8 p.m. same evening in a state of drunkenness, he immediately going into the W.C. where he was subsequently discovered asleep and taken up to bed. Mrs. salvage and daughter further stated that they have known "Brodie" as being of a very quiet disposition, and when in drink he is very curious in his manners and says some quaint things.

E.C.Bradshaw sgt.
Henry Moore, Inspr.

This is followed by the lengthy statement[13] of Brodie taken by Inspector Moore, same date:

Leman Street Station
19th July / 89.

I, William Brodie, wish to make a statement and to give myself up for committing a murder up a court way in High St. Whitechapel at about 2 a.m. on Wednesday morning last.

Last December I went to South Africa (Kimberley) on board the S.S. "Athenian" as a 3rd. class passenger which the books will show in the Mason [?] Company's office. I obtained employment in the Diamond Mines, and returned to England per the S.S. "Trojan" via Southampton, arriving at Waterloo Station at 6 p.m. on Monday 15th inst. My object in returning was to find a woman living in Whitechapel who about 2 years ago gave me the bad disorder.

On arrival at Waterloo I roamed about and eventually lodged at No. 2 Harveys Buildings, Strand, paying 6d for same. Mr. Salvage kept the house. Then on Tuesday morning I reported myself at the Convict Office, Gt. Scotland Yard; and in the afternoon I visited my brother Thomas who carries on business with my brother James, at Foresters Hall Place, Clerkenwell Road, as Lithographic Printers, etc. I then went to Lands End in Cornwall, but I only stayed there about 10 minutes. I walked there and back in half an hour or three quarters. It was before dark I got back; I think it was about 8 p.m. I returned into Whitechapel through an avenue of trees from the forest. I strolled about for 3 or 4 hours, and after the Public Houses closed and the place got dark I went into a Square where there were some coster-mongers barrows and some hundreds of people who were all smoking, both men and women. The entrance to the Square is a wide opening off the Whitechapel Road.

I remained in the Square until all the people had left, which was a very long time. I think it was 1691 or 1721 o'clock, at which time a woman came into the Square from the Whitechapel Road. I stopped her and asked her how she was going on. She was a fine woman dressed in bright red dress, boots, and hat. I gave her 1/- to have connection with her; but did not do so. She laid down under the barrow when I whipped out my knife from my outside coat pocket and cut her throat when I heard some one coming and I went away after wiping my knife on a whisp of straw which was lying near. It is a white handled knife specially made for the purpose at Sheffield. It is as sharp as a razor, and it is now with other things in charge of a man at the Baths in Lambeth Road. The knife is in a bag containing a brush and comb, pair of trousers, an old pair of boots. I had my bag (which is a red one) with me when I committed the murder, and after walking about till morning I went to Harveys Buildings and had some breakfast, which is the last meal I have had.

I think it was the York Road Baths where I left the bag and not the Lambeth Baths.

[*sgd*] William Wallace Brodie.

The above statement taken by and in the presence of Local Insp. Reid H. and P.S. Nearn C.O.

Henry Moore,

Inspr.

The clothing which this man is wearing has been examined, and there are no signs of blood upon it, although he states he wore it at the time he committed. He appears of unsound mind and I do not think any reliance can be placed upon his statement. Inquiries are being made to find the bag he refers to.

T.Arnold Sup.

This statement is followed by a report[14] by Inspector Henry Moore, as follows:

METROPOLITAN POLICE.

Criminal Investigation Department,

Scotland Yard,

20th day of July 1889.

Whitechapel Murders
Reference to Papers
52983
Referring to attached, re arrest of William W. Brodie.

I beg to report that as directed by Assistant Commissioner I charged "Brodie" with "Being a Lunatic, wandering at large"

He was this day brought up before Mr. Lushington at the Thames Police Court, and in the end the learned Magistrate thought it advisable to re-charge the prisoner on his own confession with the wilful murder of Alice McKenzie. This I did when the prisoner was remanded till 11 am. 27th inst.

I herewith attach Extract from "Evening Standard" which give almost a verbatim report of the proceedings.

Henry Moore, Inspr.

T. Arnold Supd.

The statements taken are then appended, the first[15] being that of Margaret Franklin:

H Leman Street

22nd July 1889

Statement of Margaret Franklin, who says

I live at 56 Flower & Dean, I have known the deceased woman about 14 or 15 years in the neighbourhood I cannot say if she was married, but she used to live with a blind man, I have only known her as "Alice"

I was sitting on a door-step in Brick Lane on Tuesday 16th when I saw her passing toward Whitechapel about 20 minutes to 12. I asked her how she was getting on, she said, "All right I can't stop now" She did not appear to have been drinking She was wearing a shawl I did not see her again It commenced to rain slightly just after she left us.

Taken by A.Pearce Sergt C.I.D.

The next statement[16] is that of Elizabeth Ryder:

H Leman Street

22nd July 1889

Statement of Elizabeth Ryder who says

I am married, I am the deputy of 52 Gun Street, I saw the body of deceased at the Mortuary and identified it as Mrs. McKenzie who has been living at the house about 12 months on and off, she lived with John McCormack

I saw her about $\frac{1}{2}$ past 8 on 16th passing from the kitchen to the street she had a light shawl on but no bonnet. McCormack came to me between 11 &12 p.m. and asked me if I had seen her, or whether she had paid her lodgings, I said "No" She had been drinking when she left the house. I have seen her the worse for drink before, but she rarely went out on those occasions

I have often seen her smoking she would borrow pipes from the other lodgers in the kitchen.

I have never seen her with any other man but McCormack.

Taken by A.Pearce Sergt. C.I.D.

There is a report[17] by Sergeant McCarthy on enquiries made in public houses regarding McKenzie:

METROPOLITAN POLICE

H Division.

27 day of July 1889

With reference to Asst. Commissioner's minute on attached papers. I beg to report having made careful enquiry at the "Royal Cambridge" Tavern which adjoins the Music Hall of that name, also at the public houses in the vicinity. The barman and barmaid of the "Royal Cambridge" P.H. both declared they were unable to remember a blind boy coming in there with a woman on the evening of the 16th inst. nor do they recollect any woman asking a man to treat her to a drink, although, they said, it is quite possible such a thing did occur but they didn't notice it.

At the other public-houses in the neighbourhood of the Cambridge Hall no one seemed to remember a blind boy with a woman calling on the date referred or any other day.

John McCarthy P.S. L.

Submitted   Hy. Moore, Inspr

TArnold Su.

The next report[18] is submitted by Sergeant Eugene C. Bradshaw regarding Brodie:

METROPOLITAN POLICE

H Division

23rd day of July 1889

Re Licence Holder William Brodie Office No. 35.944- I beg to report having made enquiries at the Offices of the Union S.S. Company, 11 Leadenhall Street, E.C. and find that he/ Brodie / sailed on board the S.S. Athenian as a 3rd Class passenger on 6th

September 1888 via Southampton, bound for Kimberley, South Africa, where he arrived in due course. He returned from South Africa on 15th instant per S.S. Trojan U.S. Coy. and during the voyage home he was employed as a fireman, i.e. having worked his passage. I was further informed that during the voyage home he / Brodie / performed his duty in a proper manner, and nothing out of the ordinary routine occurred on his account to arouse suspicion.

Eugene C. Bradshaw

Sergeant.

Henry Moore, Inspr.

T Arnold Supd.

The next report[19] is again by Sgt John McCarthy and is dated 24 July 1889:

METROPOLITAN POLICE.

H Division

24 day of July 1889

Referring to the attached I beg to report having seen the blind boy George Dixon at 29 Star Street Commercial Rd. He says he went with Mrs. McKenzie into a public-house near the Cambridge Music Hall at about 10 minutes past 7 on Tuesday evening 16th. He heard Mrs. McKenzie ask someone if they would stand a drink and the reply was "yes". After remaining a few minutes Mrs. McKenzie led him back to 52 Gun St. & left him there.

The boy Dixon says he would be able to recognise the voice of the person who spoke to Mrs. McKenzie in the public house.

John McCarthy P.S. 'L.

Submitted. I cannot think that the man who spoke to McKenzie at 7.10p.m. 16th had anything to do with the murder.

Henry Moore, Inspr.

T Arnold Supd.

There is then a report[20] submitted by Inspector Henry Moore, dated 27 July 1889:

METROPOLITAN POLICE.

Criminal Investigation Department,

Scotland Yard,

27th day of July, 1889.

Referring to case of William Wallace Brodie, as in attached.

I beg to report that prisoner was this morning again brought up on remand before F. Lushington, Esq., at Thames Police Court.

I acquainted the learned Magistrate with Brodie's movements since his release from Prison; also as directed by Assistant Commissioner; Vide Minutes on dockets 105 and 106, and evidence was given by Mr. Salvage, of 2 Harveys Buildings, Strand, to the effect that he assisted prisoner to bed "very drunk" about 11 p.m. 16th and that he did not go out again until about 10.20 next morning.

Mr. Lushington informed me that he had been kept under observation by the prison surgeon who had sent a certificate, stating that prisoner was now sane; although at the time he entered the prison he was suffering from acute alcoholism, causing hallucinations.

Prisoner was ultimately discharged; when I directed P.S. Bradshaw to re-arrest him upon the warrant for Fraud; which he did, and afterwards conveyed him to King's Cross Road Station where he was charged. He will be taken before Magistrate on Monday 29th.

I have submitted a report of particulars of this case with Convict Office papers for information of Chf. Inspr. Neame.

I herewith submit Newspaper Extract of proceedings at Police Court this day.

Henry Moore, Inspr.
T Arnold Sup.

There is then a report[21] from the *Kimberley Advertiser*, dated 29 June 1889, reporting Brodie confessing to the Whitechapel murders there, whilst drunk:

THE WHITECHAPEL ATROCITIES: A SELF-ACCUSED KIMBERLEYITE:- A respectably attired man, who said his name was William Brodie, was brought before the Police Court, Capetown on Saturday last, under somewhat peculiar circumstances. Inspector Rowbotham said the man came to the Police-station and accused himself of having committed the Whitechapel murders. He appeared to be suffering from a bad attack of "the horrors". The Magistrate asked Brodie how long he had been in the Colony? – Brodie: About ten months, sir. Further asked what he had been doing during that time, Brodie said he had been up-country, and in Kimberley. The Magistrate said the man had evidently been drinking, hence his confession. Brodie said he left the Ashton

Extension Railway, where he had worked, about ten days back. He had also worked at the Sultfontein Mine, Kimberley, and had come down to Capetown for a spree. He would return to Kimberley at once, if allowed to do so. The Magistrate thereupon ordered Brodie to be discharged advising him to give up drinking. – cutting out of Kimberley Advertiser, which arrived from South Africa on Monday last.

There are then two[22] minutes:

This extract has been sent by another [,] the date being given (as 29th June '89) [   ] with [   ] other papers (I have informed   the   Comr.) RA 26/7.

Mr Anderson/
    It wd. appear that "Brodie" has been "confessing" before now It wd be well to verify this extract by refer, to the Kimberley Advertiser as there is no date on extract, & then to officer in charge of case JM 29/7.

Returning to the employment of additional police officers as a result of the murder, a report[23] dated 17 July 1889 reads as follows:

<u>Urgent & Confidential.</u> A48000M/44.   WHITEHALL.
                                                          17 July 1889.
Sir,
    I am directed by the Secretary of State to acquaint you that upon the application of the Commissioner of Metropolitan Police, he has sanctioned the retention of the temporary augmentation of 1 Inspector 3 Sergeants and 30 Constables authorized for duty in Trafalgar Square, together with the addition of 2 Sergeants and 20 Constables for special duty in Whitechapel temporarily, for a period of two months.

                                        I am,
The Receiver for the   Sir,
Metropolitan Police District   Your obedient Servant,
&c. &c. &c.   Godfrey Lushington.

There is a report[24] enclosing a letter by the Reverend Samuel A. Barnett which was printed in *The Times* of 23 July 1889:

[Stamped: – HOME OFFICE 25JUL.1889 DEPT N2-] No.
A49301/171
DATE 23 July 1889.   H.O.
REFERENCES, &c.   <u>Whitechapel Horrors</u>
   Letter from the Revd. S.A. Barnett in the "Times" complaining
of the state of the streets & houses in Whitechapel.
                              MINUTES.
acted on – see within.
              [?JRB]
                 27/7
A49301/171
                        <u>Whitechapel Horror</u>s.
"The Times". 23 July 1889.
                 WHITECHAPEL HORRORS.
           TO THE EDITOR OF THE TIMES.
Sir, – When the series of murders occurred last year you allowed
me to point out that the act of some maniac was a less evil than the
state of life shows to be common in this neighbourhood.
   At the time I was encouraged to hope that the freeholders of a
large property which is in the heart of this criminal quarter might
have applied, or have put it in the power of others to apply, some
radical remedy, by closing as leases fell in the houses in which men
and women live as beasts, where crime is protected, and where
children or country people are led on to ruin, or by employing
watchmen to enforce order and make the neighbourhood distasteful
to the wicked, or by getting Parliamentary powers to clear the
district as one morally insanitary.
   Nothing has been done, though many were ready with time and
money, if the freeholders would have moved. The houses in the
hands of the same occupants are put to the same base uses, and the
streets still offer almost every night scenes of brutality and
degradation. A body of inhabitants – residents at Toynbee-hall
and others – have patrolled the neighbourhood during the last nine
months on many nights every week between the hours of 11 p.m.
and 3 a.m. Their record tells of rows in which stabbing is common,
but on which the police are able to get no charges; of fights between
women stripped to the waist, of which boys and children are
spectators; of the protection afforded to thieves, and of such things
as could only occur where opinion favours vice. The district in
which all this happens is comparatively small; it forms, indeed, a
black spot, three or four acres in extent, in the midst of a

neighbourhood which in no way deserves the reputation for ill-conduct.

A district so limited might be easily dealt with, and its reform is more important than even the capture of a murderer, who would have no victims if they were not prepared by degradation. Its reform will be possible when public opinion will condemn as offenders those who directly or indirectly live on the profits of vice.

I am truly yours,

SAMUEL A. BARNETT.

St. Jude's, Whitechapel, July 20.

? make official, and refer to Police for observations on [   ] of allegations.

CW. July 24.

GL

24 July '89

Wrote Commr. 27.7.89

a/5.8.89 (1/173)

Mr Lushington's letter[25] to the Chief Commissioner of the Metropolitan Police, as regards this letter, appears in the files as follows:

A49301/171   WHITEHALL.
                                                  27 July 1889.

Sir,

I am directed by the Secretary of State to refer to the letter from the Revd. S.A. Barnett, which appeared in "The Times" of the 23rd instant, headed "Whitechapel Horrors"; and to say that Mr Matthews will be glad to have your observations on the allegations therein made.

I am,

Sir,

Your obedient Servant,

Godfrey Lushington

The Commissioner of
Metropolitan Police
  &c. &c. &c.

As a result of this request the Reverend Barnett was seen by Superintendent Arnold of H Division, who then submitted his report[26], dated 3 August 1889, for the information of the Chief Commissioner, Mr Monro:

METROPOLITAN POLICE.

H Division.

3rd August 1889

[*Marginal ref* – "No. 57885 attached"]

I beg to report that I have seen Mr. Barnett with reference to his letter in the "Times" and I find he speaks generally from reports which have been made to him by persons connected with Toynbee Hall but particularly as to the uses made of the lodgings which are known as furnished rooms, which are let to prostitutes, sometimes by the week, and in some cases by the night, and where men are taken as in the case of the murdered woman Kelly in Millers Court. He has been in communication with the Parochial Authorities on this question and was advised by the Vestry Clerk of Spitalfields that such places do not come within the meaning of the Act. Numbers of the women living in these rooms associate with men who partially if not wholly subsist on their wretched earnings, and it is surprising how quickly they submit to the brutal treatment which they receive at the hands of these fellows, and how they resent any interference for their protection, it being very seldom they can be induced to go to the Station to prefer a Charge, or if they do go so far they will not appear at the Court. It is such cases as these Mr Barnett alludes to when he writes Police can get no charges. He does not attribute any laxity on the part of Police, on the contrary praises them & considers they do all they can under the circumstances.

There can be no doubt whatever that vice in its worst forms exists in Whitechapel, and the only remedy for this is by clearing out the Lodging Houses as they at present exist, and substitute improved dwellings with better supervision which would be of immense advantage to the locality, but at the expense of other districts as there are a class of persons at present resorting to the neighbourhood who would not go to large and comfortable houses if restrictions were placed upon them, and no doubt owners or occupiers of houses would be found ready to meet their wants, although it would be a long time before such places became centralised as they at present are in Whitechapel and wherever they spring up they will depreciate the surrounding property.

That Common Lodging Houses of improved construction & with good supervision can be carried on is illustrated in the case of the Victoria Home in Commercial Street which has been established by an Association of which Lord Radstock is Chairman.

I pointed out to Mr Barnett that by clearing the neighbourhood he mentions, the persons at present there would be driven into the adjoining parishes which would naturally cause discontent, but he appears to think every one should clear his own house without regard to his neighbours.

Brawling and fighting does and will take place amongst the low class of persons to be found in Whitechapel, but not nearly to such an extent as might be expected and is generally believed by persons non resident in the district.

T Arnold Sup.

As a result of this report Mr Monro replied[27] to the Home Office, detailing these facts as follows:

[Stamped on cover: – HOME OFFICE 6 AUG. 89 RECEIVED]
No. A49301/173
DATE 5 August 1889.   The Commissioner of Police.
REFERENCES, &c.   Vice in Whitechapel.
    Reports on the subject of the Revd. S.A. Barnett's recent letter in the "Times." /171
                    MINUTES.
The Secretary of State.
            Aug 8/89
                CW

                    GL
                    8 Aug '89
H.M.
    9 Aug. /89.

Then follows the Chief Commissioner's report:

[Stamped: – HOME OFFICE 6 AUG. 89 RECEIVED] A49301/173
C.J.W.
        57885/117 4   Whitehall Place S.W.
                            5th August, 1889.
Sir,
    With reference to your letter of the 27th ulto., A49301/171, on

the subject of the Revd. S.A. Barnett's recent letter to the "Times" respecting the condition of Whitechapel, I have to acquaint you, for the information of the Secretary of State, that anything Mr. Barnett writes on such a subject is entitled to respect, for noone who knows the work which the Vicar of St. Judes has done, and the spirit in which he does it, can entertain anything but sentiments of regard for him and sympathy with his aspirations. Practically what he says is this: Vice of a very low type exists in Whitechapel; such vice manifests itself in brawling and acts of violence which shock the feelings of respectable persons; these acts of violence are not repressed by action taken either before the Police or Magisterial authorities. Clear out the slums and lodging houses to which vicious persons resort, and vice will disappear, respectability taking its place.

There is no doubt whatever that vice of a low and degraded type is only too visible in Whitechapel. The facility with which the Whitechapel murderer obtains victims has brought this prominently to notice, but to anyone who will take a walk late at night in the district where the recent atrocities have been committed, the only wonder is that his operations have been so restricted. There is no lack of victims ready to his hand, for scores of these unfortunate women may be seen any night muddled with drink in the streets and alleys, perfectly reckless as to their safety, and only anxious to meet with anyone who will keep them in plying their miserable trade.

There is no doubt that brawling and fighting do go on, repressed as far as possible by the Police; but it must be remembered that these women do not care to be protected against those who assault them, very seldom have recourse to the Station to complain, and still more seldom appear at any Police Court to prosecute any charge which they may have laid before the Police.

It is also true that Common Lodging Houses are not all that they might be in the way of discouraging immorality, although I do not think that so much of the reproach in this respect which is generally levelled at them in reality is attributable to them. On this subject I have already expressed my views in my letter of the 26th December, 1888. Much however of the immorality which goes on finds its place in the low lodgings which are let to prostitutes by the day or week, where they take men home, and with reference to which the law is practically powerless. These are the houses from which no charges are brought before the Police, and to these much more than to the Common Lodging Houses is the violence conjoined with immorality attributable.

That respectability would be benefitted by clearing out such localities admits of little doubt; that the moral atmosphere of Whitechapel would be purified by the substitution of better lodging houses for the dens at present to be found there is perfectly clear; but this would not remove vice, it would only delocalise it, and transfer it to some neighbouring parish at present not quite so disreputable as some parts of Whitechapel.

I do not mean to say that this might not be a gain. It certainly would be a gain to Whitechapel, and it may be said that if other parishes took similar steps similar steps would follow within their limits. But the question still remains "What is to become of the residuum of vice which is thus moved on?" I do not believe in such a transfer of a vicious population as likely to remove vice generally from the Metropolis, and I suspect it may be taken as a fact that whenever landlords or lodging house keepers can secure their rent they will not hesitate in taking it from prostitutes with as much readiness as from persons of a different class.

Behind the whole question lies the larger matter of street prostitution generally, and until that is taken up and regulated (objectionable as this may appear to a public which confuses between liberty and licence) the mere multiplying of comfortable lodging houses will not have any appreciable effect in diminishing the number of and evils resulting from a class who do not want comfortable lodging houses, and the scene of whose operations is on the streets.

I am,

Sir,

Your most obedient Servant,

J.Monro

The Under
    Secretary of State,;

Following the McKenzie murder there follow the usual requests for sanction of allowances in respect of additional officers drafted to the Whitechapel area to assist in the enquiries.

A Home Office file[28] with such a request is dated 26 July 1889, as follows:

No. A49301G/8   5185/6
DATE 26 July 1889.   Commissioner of Police
REFERENCES, &c. Recommends grant of a special allowance of 2/-
a day to the C.I. Department officers from other divisions who are
employed specially in connection with the Whitechapel murders.

<u>Pressing</u>.

MINUTES.
To Receiver for financial observations.
                Index 5/8   CW July 27.
29 JUL.89
I understand from the Commissioner that the total expense involved
will be very small, and under these circumstances I think the special
allowance may be sanctioned. [?] ARP/

                                                          29 July

?sanction

                        CM July 30
                            GL
                        31 July '89
Wrote Commr.
[?] 1.8.89

The Chief Commissioner's report[29] follows:

                        A49301G/8
96318/9

                                        4, Whitehall Place,
                                        26th July, 1889.
Sir,
    I have to acquaint you, for the information of the Secretary of
State, that the Criminal Investigation Department officers from
other Divisions who are employed specially in connection with the
murders in Whitechapel are engaged, on an average, for 15 hours
daily making enquiries and patrolling the district to gain information
respecting the outrages.-
    Their authorised refreshment allowances as Sergeants is 1s/2d per
diem ; but, as they are absent from their homes and divisions for so many
hours, this does not cover the expense which they necessarily incur.-
    Under the circumstances I strongly recommend that these
officers be allowed the same rate of refreshment allowances as
the Sergeants attached to the Central Office of the Criminal
Investigation Department, viz: – 2s/- per diem, and I have to

request that Mr. Secretary Matthews may be pleased to sanction this allowance as a special case.-

> I am,
>   Sir,
>   Your obedient Servant,
>   J.Monro

The Under Secretary
        of State
    &c   &c   &c
        Home Office

There follows a similar file cover[30], relating to plain clothes allowance, dated 26 July 1889:

No. A49301G/9   5185/6
                                   1 AUG.89

DATE   26 July 1889.   Commissioner of Police.
REFERENCES, &C.   Recommends grant of a plain clothes allowance of 1s/-d a day to the men now employed on special patrol duty in connection with the Whitechapel Murder.

                    MINUTES.

This came to me tied up with other papers to which it did not belong [*rest illegible*] CW July 31.
First to Receiver of Police for financial observations. Index 5/9 CW July 31.
For favour of immediate reply as Commr. is pressing for an answer.
    Having regard to the precedent I think this allowance must be granted it will amount to £14. 14. 0 a week. Perhaps the S. of S. will see fit to limit either the amount payable in the gross or the duration of the employment.

                    A.R.P.
            T.O.   1 August.
?Say for two months. Report again at the end of that time.
                C.M. Aug. 1. 89.
                    GL
                    2 Aug. 89
            Wrote Commr. & Recd.
                3.8.89.
                [?comment]
                a/18.9.89
                    (10)

The report[31] follows:

A49301G/9
96318/8
                                                        4, Whitehall Place,
                                                              S.W.
                                                        26th July, 1889.

Sir,

I have to acquaint you, for the information of the Secretary of State, that 3 Sergeants and 39 Constables are employed in plain clothes on special patrol duty in connection with the Whitechapel Murder.

As I pointed out in my letter of the 7th December last with reference to the men then similarly employed, this work is specially irksome and unpleasant and makes considerable demands on the endurance of the men. – They have continuous night duty and are practically doing the work of permanent patrols who receive a plain clothes allowance of 1s/- per day instead of 1s/11d per week. –

I have therefore to recommend that Mr. Secretary Matthews may be pleased to sanction a plain clothes allowance to these men of 1s/- per day instead of 1s/11d per week to which they are entitled, as was granted in the case of men employed during the early part of this year on similar duties. –

                              I am
                                Sir,
                      Your obedient Servant,
                              J.Monro

The Under Secretary
        of State
    &c   &c   &c
          Home Office.

The Home Office response[32] to this is noted on a file cover dated 31 July 1889:

[Stamped: – RECEIVER METROPOLITAN POLICE DISTRICT AUG 1889]
H.O. 31 July
Whitechapel Murders. 1/- a day allowance.
Refers for financial observations of Recr. recommendation of Commr. to grant a plain clothes allowance of 1/- a day to the officers employed on special patrol duty in Whitechapel.

For favour of immediate reply as Commr. is pressing for an answer.

Copy of Receiver's minute on HO papers A49301g/9.
Having regard to the precedent I think this allowance must be
granted – it will amount to £14. 14.–0 a week.
    Perhaps the S of S will see fit to limit either the amount payable
in the gross or the duration of employment.

(Sgd.). A.R.P.
1 August. 89.

Papers[33] follow in a similar fashion:

A49301G/8   [Receiver's stamp dated 4 AUG.89]

1st August 1889.

<u>Pressing</u>

Sir,
    I am directed by the Secretary of State to inform you that on the
Commissioner's application he has authorized the grant to the
officers of the Criminal Investigation Department who are brought
to Whitechapel from other Divisions in connection with the recent
murders there, of the special refreshment allowance of 2/- a day ;
and I am to signify to you his sanction for the payment of the same.

The Receiver   I am, Sir,
        for   your obedient servant
the Metropolitan Police District   Godfrey Lushington

Notes on the file cover[34], read:

H.O.
1st Augt.
Whitechapel Murders, Special Allowance.
Sanctions grant to C.I.D. officers (brought to Whitechapel from
other Divisions) of a specl. reft. allce. of 2s/- a day.

Accountant to note
this authority
Noted MrWilby
[*illeg.*] A.R.P.
2 August. 2.8.89.

Then a further file cover[35] follows:

H.O.
3rd Augt.
Whitechapel Murders. Allowances.
Sanctions payment, for period of 2 months, of the plain clothes allowance of 1/- a day to 3 P.S. & 39 P.C. now employed in plain clothes in Whitechapel.
Accountant to note.
Noted. A.R.P.
8. August 89
Mr. Wilby to note.
T.O. Done [illeg.] 12/8/89.
I have this day seen Mr. S Bathurst, who informs me that the Commr. in asking for this 1/- per diem intended it as a refreshment allowance and that it will be charged on "Black Letters" accordingly in our Cash Book against Extraordinary Exps. instead of against clothing as originally supposed.
                    [illeg] 23/8/89
Mr. [?chance] to note when entering these allowances that they are all to go under Sch 5.9-

                                        C.C.
                                        25/8
Noted
    J.F-[?]
        22.8.89

It is interesting to note that at the time of the investigation of the McKenzie murder, Inspector Henry Moore had taken over from Inspector Abberline as the officer in charge of the on-the-ground investigation of the Whitechapel Murders. Moore was to remain in charge for the remainder of the active enquiries in the case.

CHAPTER 29

10 September 1889 – Murder of an Unknown Woman

A brief survey of the facts in the case of the discovery of a female torso under a railway arch in Pinchin Street, St George's-in-the-East, in September 1889 is sufficient to indicate that this victim should not be numbered with the 1888 tally of the "Ripper". However, the circumstances of this case, and the reports written by the police of the time, are sufficiently interesting to reward the researcher with information relevant to his or her studies – the case is, indeed, included in the official files of the Whitechapel Murders.

The police file[1] is headed: *Trunk of a female – Found on 10th September 1889* and is followed by a sketch and plan of the location drawn by Inspector Charles Ledger, G Division, who would appear to have been the Metropolitan Police plan maker. From this sketch it can seen that the torso was discovered just inside the first railway arch in Pinchin Street from its junction with Backchurch Lane. This arch still exists today, AD 2000, although it is, as are the others, bricked over at the front to create garages, workshops and suchlike.

There is a lengthy report[2] by Chief Inspector Swanson, dated 10 September 1889, in the file:

METROPOLITAN POLICE.
Criminal Investigation Department,
Scotland Yard,
10th day of September, 1889.

Re – Human Remains
found at Pinchin
St. Whitechapel.

I beg to report that after an examination of the railway arch in Pinchin Street, where the trunk of a woman was found, and a close examination of the trunk, the following facts presented themselves:-

1st. Upon the spot when the trunk was found, there was no

evidence of any blood, and a footmark from the nature of the ground was an impossibility; nor was there left anything in the shape of a cloth or sack to carry the trunk in.

2nd. The place of disposal must have been a selected spot; i.e. it must have been decided upon by viewing, for on all sides of it not a single inhabitant resides but it is faced by a pailing or wooden fence, and flanked by a dead wall, so that the place gained disposal was easy.

3rd. The appearance of the trunk minus head and legs, was as follows:- the head which had been cut off by clean <u>right</u> handed cuts, the vertebra being "jointed" left the neck with blood oozing from it, while both legs had also been "jointed", by right handed cuts, but the dismemberment had taken place at an earlier period than the head for the raw flesh had from continued exposure dried on the surface which presented a blackened appearance in consequence. The wound beginning at the lower part of the sternum, cutting through the skin, fatty substance, and penetrating the bowels, and uterus slightly, extended to the left side of the <u>labia major</u>. The trunk presented the undoubted appearance of having decomposition begun. Upon the chemise which was cut at the arms and down the front, I understand from Inspr Reid who examined it, there was not a single mark of any kind and the article itself of common manufacture and fabric. Beyond a small semi-circular cut on the index finger of right hand, and bruises on both arms, which the surgeons say they will be better able to describe after the post mortem examination there is absolutely nothing by which the trunk could be identified.

From Nos. 1&3 it becomes evident that death by whatever means foul or otherwise, took place, not at the spot where the trunk was found, but at some house or place, near or distant, according to Dr. Hibbert twenty four hours prior to the finding, and according to Mr. Clark, Dr. Phillips' assistant, two days, so that under any circumstances the body must have lain twenty four hours in some house or place, before removal, and disposal, so that the place of disposal (no.2) could be decided upon in the meantime. Now from the surgeons it was ascertained, firstly that as the trunk was so full of blood death did not take place from hemorrhage [*sic*], therefore death could not have taken place by cutting the throat, and the absence of the head prevents them saying that it was from violence to it, (which appears to me most probable as the trunk contains no stabs to cause death). What becomes most apparent is the absence of the attack upon the genitals as in the series of Whitechapel murders beginning at Bucks Row and ending in Miller's Court. Certainly if it ["was" – *deleted*] be a murder there was time enough for the murderer to cut off the head and limbs there was time to mutilate as in the series mentioned. It appears rather to go side by side with the Rainham, Whitehall and Chelsea murders.

The question of how conveyed is in the region of theory, for if conveyed by cart, then no limit can be fixed, but if by hand about 250 yards would be the limit; consequently enquiry has been made to find any shed house or place within that limit, so as to ascertain who what, and how the occupier was engaged, but more especially to find the missing parts.

The enquiry is being continued so far as barrows, houses sheds or places are concerned.

> DonaldSSwanson
> Ch Inspr
> T Arnold Supd

A report[3] dated 11 September 1889 by Inspector Edmund Reid is included:

METROPOLITAN POLICE.
H Division,
11th day of September 1889.

Human remains

I beg to submit the attached reports received from P S s Thick and White and to report that on receiving information of the discovery of the Human Remains in Pinchin Street St. Georges 10th inst I at once directed P.S. White to search the adjoining Railway Arches and other likely places in the neighbourhood with a view to trace the missing parts of the body also to make inquiries with a view to gain information as to who deposited the portion of body in the arch.

I also directed P.S. Thick to make inquiries at sheds, houses, and places where barrows are kept, or lent out on hire also at butchers in the neighbourhood of Pinchin Street with a view to gain any information regarding the matter.

I directed P.S. Godley to search information with a view to trace missing persons and the identification of the remains.

I also had telegram sent to A.S asking that search be at once made with a view to find the missing portions of the body.

I have also had several officers making inquiries in the neighbourhood of Pinchin Street with a view to gain any information respecting the above matter.

I asked the Inspr. of the dust carts for the Parish of St. Georges to ask his men and direct them to report to him if any blood stained clothes were taken from any house, and let police know at once. This was done and information was received from [ ], stating that some had been found in Batty Street which is being inquired into.

Inquiries are still being made in the neighbourhood of Pinchin Street with a view to gain any information in the matter.

Edmund Reid
L.Inspector.

Submitted. Respecting the clothing found in Batty St. bearing blood stains. I have made enquiry, and although not yet quite completed I am satisfied that they are the result of a confinement. Special report will follow.

Henry Moore, Inspr.
T Arnold Supd.

A report[4] dated 11 September 1889, was submitted by Inspector Pattenden regarding enquiries made:

METROPOLITAN POLICE.
H Division,
11th September, 1889

Enquiries re murdered
remains of woman.

I beg to report having made enquiries re. Reporters met by men in Back Church Lane, on the morning of 8th. inst.

I find that the occurrence has been reported in the "New York Herald" by the reporter who met me, and that a copy of above paper is in the hands of Inspr. Moore, C.I.D.

At 12.15 am 8th. P.C. 394H Millard found a woman named Ellen Bisney of 219 Brunswick Building, Whitechapel in the High Street, and conveyed her on an ambulance to the Whitechapel Infirmary, this may have been observed by the person who gave the information to Newspaper Office, and who for the purpose of reward exaggerated the case.

I beg to ask that enquiry may be made by C.I.Department for the purpose of finding this man.

F. Pattenden Inspr.
T Arnold Sup

Exterior view of Miller's Court. The two panes of glass in the window nearest to the downpipe can be seen to be broken.

A contemporary sketch of the scene outside 26 Dorset Street as Mary Jane Kelly's body is removed.

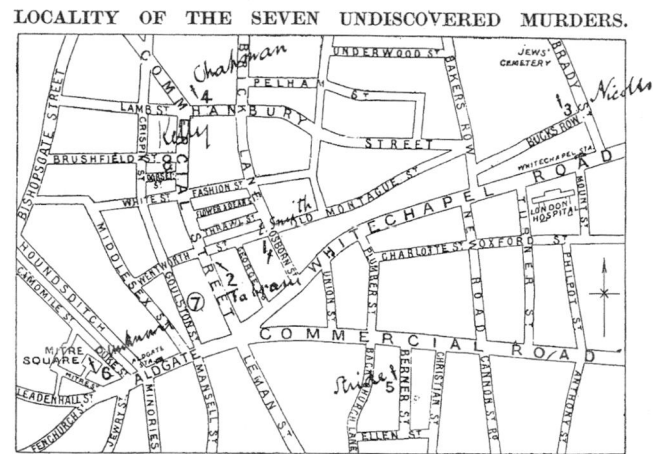

LOCALITY OF THE SEVEN UNDISCOVERED MURDERS.

The above chart represents the locality within which, since April last, seven women of the unfortunate class have been murdered. The precise spot where each crime was committed is indicated by a dagger and a numeral.

1. April 3.—Emma Elizabeth Smith, forty-five, had a stake or iron instrument thrust through her body, near Osborn-street, Whitechapel.

2. Aug. 7.—Martha Tabram, thirty-five, stabbed in thirty-nine places, at George-yard-buildings, Commercial-street, Spitalfields.

3. Aug. 31.—Mary Ann Nicholls, forty-seven, had her throat cut and body mutilated, in Buck's-row, Whitechapel.

4. Sept. 8.—Annie Chapman, forty-seven, her throat cut and body mutilated, in Hanbury-street, Spitalfields.

5. Sept. 30.—A woman, supposed to be Elizabeth Stride, but not yet identified, discovered with her throat cut, in Berner-street, Whitechapel.

6. Sept 30.—A woman, unknown, found with her throat cut and body mutilated, in Mitre-square, Aldgate.

Figure 7 (encircled) marks the spot in Goulston-street where a portion of an apron belonging to the woman murdered in Mitre-square was picked up by a Metropolitan police-constable.

Figure 8. Nov. 9.—Mary Jane Kelly, 24, her throat cut and body terribly mutilated, in Miller's-court, Dorset-street.

A map of the murder sites which appeared in the *Daily Telegraph* on 10 November 1888.

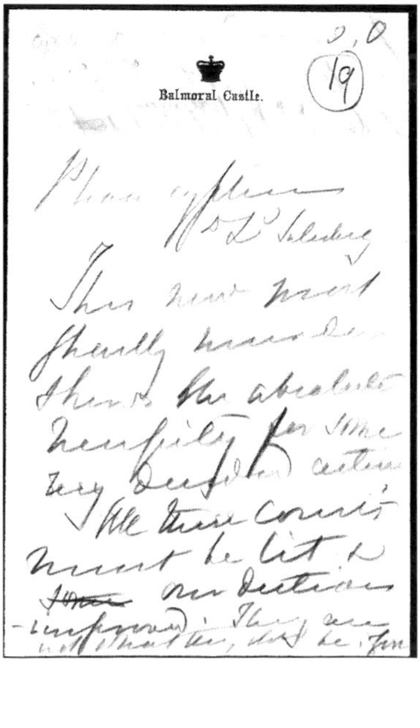

The concern of Queen Victoria over the murders is evident in this letter from Balmoral Castle dated 10 November 1888.

No. A49301

N.B.—Please not to pin Memoranda over the Number.

DATE 17 July 1889   Commissioner of Police.

REFERENCES, &c.

Forwards police report respecting the commission of a murder in Castle Alley, Whitechapel, this morning. States that every effort will be made to discover the murderer, who, he thinks, is identical with "Jack the Ripper", but that the assassin has not left the slightest clue to his identity. Immediate

MINUTES.

The Secretary of State.
The Plan is from Pall Mall of today July 17.

SCENE of WHITECHAPEL MURDERS.

The file cover for the murder of Alice McKenzie on 17 July 1889 has a map of the murder sites affixed to its lower half. Importantly, the annotation shows that initially the Chief Commissioner, James Monro, thought this to be another Ripper murder.

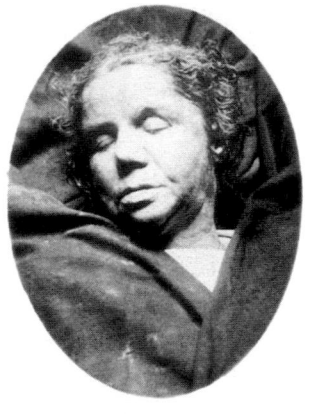

Mortuary photograph of Alice McKenzie.

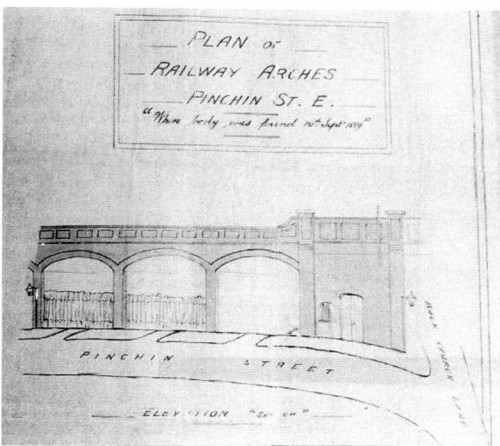

Police sketch of the railway arch in Pinchin Street where the torso of an unknown woman was found on 10 September 1889.

A contemporary sketch of Frances Coles, murdered on 13 February 1891 under a railway arch in Swallow Gardens, Whitechapel.

A contemporary sketch of James Thomas Sadler, arrested on suspicion of the murder of Frances Coles. The last of the Whitechapel murders, there is no doubt that initially the police believed that they had arrested Jack the Ripper.

Mortuary photograph of Frances Coles.

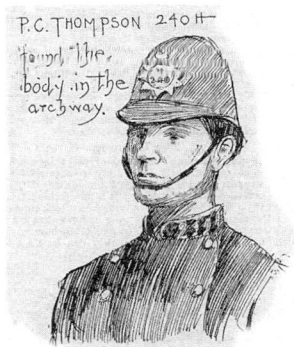

A contemporary sketch of Sadler and Frances Coles in the doss house.

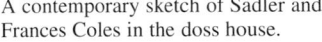

A contemporary sketch of PC 240H Ernest Thompson who discovered the body of Frances Coles.

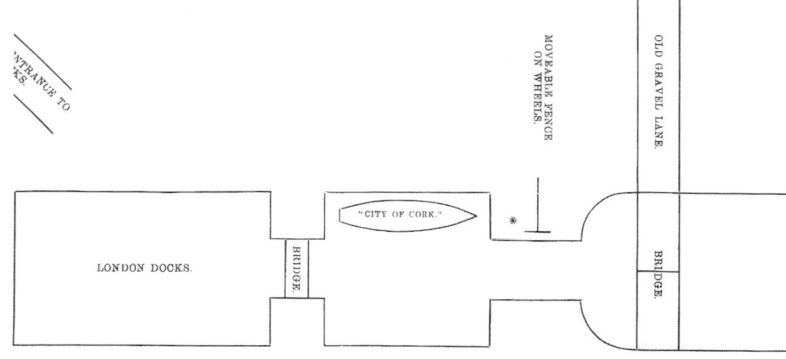

Rough Plan of the Docks, where these vessels lay, shewing there was nothing but a moveable * ⊤ fence, on wheels, to prevent these men getting on board, from Old Gravel Lane, at any time; and, as was shewn at the time of the Sadler inquiry, that any member of the crew of a vessel in the Docks, provided he is sober, is allowed to pass into the Docks at any hour of the night. Old Gravel Lane is within a mile of the scenes of those murders.

Plan of the London Docks and of the berthed *City of Cork*, published by early 'Ripperologist' Edward Knight Larkins in connection with his theory on the identity of the murderer.

Part of a cartoon strip from a paper called *Scraps* (published in October 1889) giving support to an unfounded theory on the identity of the killer from an anonymous writer to the Home Office.

Montague John Druitt, an alleged Ripper suspect named in the Macnaghten Report of February 1894.

Michael Ostrog convicted thief and confidence trickster, named as another Ripper suspect in the Macnaghten Report of February 1894.

METROPOLITAN POLICE DISTRICT.
3.—Convict Supervision Office.—Woodcut portrait and description of Supervisee MICHAEL

OSTROG, *alias* BERTRAND ASHLEY, CLAUDE CLAYTON, and Dr. GRANT, Office No. 22550, whose apprehension is sought for failing to report—age 55, height 5 ft. 11 in., complexion dark, hair dark brown, eyes grey, scars right thumb and right shin, two large moles right shoulder and one back of neck, corporal punishment marks; generally dressed in a semi-clerical suit. A Polish Jew. Was sentenced, 5th January, 1874, at Aylesbury, to 10 years' penal servitude and 7 years' police supervision for larceny. Liberated on license 25th August, 1883. Again sentenced at the Central Criminal Court, 14th September, 1887, to 6 months' hard labour for larceny. On the 10th March, 1888, he was liberated from the Surrey County Lunatic Asylum, and failed to report.
Warrant issued.
Special attention is called to this dangerous man.

Dr Francis Tumblety, an Irish-American quack doctor named by ex-Chief Inspector John George Littlechild as a Ripper suspect. He fled back to the USA in December 1888 where he was pursued by Inspector Andrews, who failed to locate him.

evidence against him. *because the suspect*
138 *was also a Jew and also because*
his evidence would convict the
suspect, and witness would be
the means of murderer being hanged
which he did not wish to be
left on his mind. D.S.S.

Continuing from page 138. after the
suspect had been identified at the
Seaside Home where he had been sent
by us with difficulty, in order to subject
him to identification, and he knew
he was identified. On suspect's return
to his brother's house in Whitechapel
he was watched by police (City CID) by
day & night. In a very short time the
suspect with his hands tied behind
his back, he was sent to Stepney
Workhouse and then to Colney Hatch
and died shortly afterwards —
Kosminski was the suspect —

D.S.S.

Annotations made by ex-Chief Inspector Donald Swanson on page 138 and the end paper of Sir Robert Anderson's memoirs, regarding the Polish Jew suspect in the Ripper murders.

There is included in this file an extract[5] from the *New York Herald* as follows:

58895 <u>EXTRACT</u> From the New York Herald of 11 September 1889
Suspected Persons.
    stating that a man calling himself John Cleary of 21 Whitehorse Yard had called at their offices on Sunday morning 8th. and gave particulars of an alleged murder and mutilation in Buckchurch Lane Whitechapel.
REFERENCE TO PAPERS
Chief Inspr Swanson to make full inquiry on this report by order of the Commissioner
11.9.89   J.Shore
Report submitted
12/9/89   J.Shore
                                                 Supt.

The Commissioner
<u>Supt E</u> To see and continue enquiry P.S. Partridge
                        [sgd] 12/9
E 13.9.89
Report submitted.
      CWells Act Supt.

Extract from THE NEW YORK HERALD, No. 222. LONDON EDITION,
WEDNESDAY, SEPTEMBER 11, 1889.   PRICE ONE PENNY.
DOES HE KNOW THE RIPPER?
WHO IS THIS MAN THAT CALLED AT
THE "HERALD" OFFICE SUNDAY.
He was positive a Murder Had Been Committed at Twenty Minutes Past Eleven o'clock on Saturday Night, on the Spot Where the Dead and Mutilated Body of a Woman was Found Yesterday – Mystery of Mysteries.
    London in general, and Whitechapel in particular, were thrown into a feverish state of excitement yesterday morning by the news that "Jack the Ripper" had murdered and mutilated his ninth victim. Both the murder and the mutilation were reported to be, and indeed proved to be, more horrible than in any one of the eight cases preceding. The quick and close review of the facts by the police department led to the conclusion late yesterday afternoon

that the remains found did not represent "Jack the Ripper's" handiwork, and this may or may not be true.

There is a very extraordinary feature, however, in this case, which has been lacking in all the others. That it is extraordinary no one will doubt who reads the brief story of last Saturday night as detailed below. If the woman found in archway was a victim of "Jack the Ripper," it is positively sure either that the murderer has been seen by many people, or that another man who knew of the murder and all the circumstances so long ago as last Saturday night is abroad, and can be found, if the police are clever enough. On the other hand, last Saturday night's events indicate to some extent that the body found yesterday, be it that of a murdered woman or a body from a dissecting room, was in the hands of more than one man who knew all about it, because on last Saturday night a man betrayed the whole affair. The circumstances are as follows, and will be verified in every particular by affidavit, should the police department desire.

Last Sunday morning at five minutes past one o'clock a young man called at the HERALD office and reported that there was another "Jack the Ripper" murder. He was sent up to the editorial rooms and interviewed by the night editor. He said that a mutilated body had been found in Backchurch-lane, in Whitechapel. He said that it had been found by a policeman at twenty minutes past eleven o'clock. The map of London was immediately studied by two reporters in order to locate Backchurch-lane, while the editor cross-questioned the man. He said it had been told to him by an acquaintance of his, a police inspector whom he had met in Whitechapel High-street. He said there was no doubt about it, and that he had hurried to the HERALD office understanding that he would be rewarded for the news. He said his name was John Cleary, and that he lived at 21, White Horse-yard, Drury-lane. He was asked to write down his name and address; and he did so, the writing being preserved. His information was explicit and seemingly authentic, and two reporters were detailed to take the man with them, and go and get the story.

The two reporters went out, and one of them stopped on the landing of the stairway in going down, and asked the man some more questions. Under this examination he varied slightly, saying that the man who had told him was not a police inspector, but an ex-member of the police force. This statement has, perhaps, some significance to all who have been following the murders closely. He then went down to the street with the reporters. They called a hansom and told the man to get in with them; but he first hesitated, and then refused. His excuse was that it was too far from his home. They urged him to go, but he was firm. One of them proposed to take him back upstairs, in order to have him near at hand if necessary; but the necessity of immediate departure compelled them to start and leave the man to go his own way. He was assured that if the news proved authentic he would be handsomely rewarded, and he went away apparently contented with the arrangement.

The two reporters drove rapidly to Backchurch-lane, and found it without difficulty. They made a thorough search of the neighbourhood. They went down as far as the archway where the body was found yesterday morning, but found all quiet and no trace of any murder. They met two police officers, one an inspector, and the other a constable. They questioned both, and told them the report they had heard, and these two officers can verify the enquiry. They had heard nothing, however. The reporters again went over the ground, but found nothing. They then returned and reported. In fact, it is a certainty that on Sunday morning a murdered and mutilated body was reported as having been found in Backchurch-lane, and that exactly such a body was found yesterday morning.

The matter was passed over as unimportant on Sunday and Monday. The moment that the body was found yesterday, however, the events of Sunday morning loomed up with a significance rather colossal, and a hunt began for John Cleary, of 21, White Horse-yard, Drury-lane. Mr. John Cleary, however, was not known at No. 21, or anywhere else in White Horse-yard, Drury-lane. The house is a four-storey one. The street floor is vacant, the first and second floors are occupied by families, and the top floor by a widow woman with two children. The widow woman was confident that no young man by the name of John Cleary either lived in the house or had ever lived there. The people in every house in White Horse-yard were questioned under circumstances which disposed them to tell all they knew, but nobody had ever heard the name of John Cleary, and everybody said that no man of that name could have lived there without their knowing it, which was quite true. It became evident, therefore, that the man had given a false address, and in all probability a false name, as such a precaution in the matter of residence would scarcely have been taken, and the precaution as to name neglected.

"Cleary's" description, however, had been carefully taken. He was a young man, apparently between twenty-five and twenty-eight years of age. He was short, his height being about 5 ft. 4in. He was of medium build, and weighed about 140 lb. He was light-complexioned, had a small fair moustache and blue eyes. On his left cheek was an inflamed spot, which looked as if a boil had lately been there and was healing. He wore a dark coat and waistcoat. His shirt was not seen, the space at the throat being covered by a dirty white handkerchief tied about his neck. His trousers were dark velveteen, so soiled at the knees as to indicate that he blacked shoes. His hat was a round, black, stiff felt. He walked with a shuffle and spoke in the usual fashion of the developing citizens of Whitechapel, whom, in all respects, he resembled.

It is thus certain that there was an intention on the part of the party or parties who had the body in keeping to place it in Backchurch-lane Saturday night, where it was found yesterday. If coincidences be of any value, it may be noted that this was the anniversary of the Hanbury-street murder. It is beyond doubt that "Cleary" got wind of the scheme, if he was not one of the principals. That the original intention was not carried out would indicate that he was an outsider acquainted with the project, who hoped to profit by it. There seems to be no reason to doubt that the body was not found by the police until yesterday morning, and that it was placed there a short time before seems reasonably sure. Nevertheless, "John Cleary," whoever he may be, must know all about the mystery, and is certainly the most valuable man in the purview of the police at the present time.

The mutilated body of "Jack the Ripper's" latest victim, if such it is, was discovered about half-past five o'clock yesterday morning beneath a railway arch on the south side of Pinchin-street, which runs eastward from Backchurch-lane, a narrow thoroughfare connecting Commercial-road with Cable-street. The locality is about half a mile southward from the limited district which has been the centre of "the Ripper's" murders. It is, however, not more distant than was the Buck's-row crime, which was the third, and the point is less than three minutes from the scene of the fifth murder, the one in Berner-street. It is about the same distance from the Leman-street police-station. The south side of Pinchin-street is skirted by a long series of high brick arches, supporting the roadway of the London, Tilbury, and Great Eastern Railway. The arch beneath which the body was found is the only one which is open, the others being boarded up, or filled with huge doors, and used for storage and like purposes. This particular arch had been boarded up, as the joists stretching across it indicated, but the boards had been torn off and carried away for firewood by the people in the vicinity, a patrolman said. Anyone passing along Pinchin-street can easily see within these arches. Both officer Pennett and another patrolman say that they passed by the spot between half-past four and five o'clock, and saw nothing out of the common.

The discovery was made by Officer Pennett at half-past five o'clock. In passing along his beat, he flashed his bull's-eye into the dark arch and noticed a bundle which excited his curiosity, as it had not been there half an hour before. He went in and inspected it, and was startled to find it the trunk of a naked woman.

The remains were lying face downward. The head and legs had been removed, and the sight was so grotesque and horrible that the constable was some seconds in making out what it really was. The horrible mass was partly covered by a blood-stained chemise, much disarranged. Officer Pennett immediately whistled for assistance, and was quickly joined by several patrolmen. Word was sent to headquarters, and in a short time a group of inspectors and officials stood around the remains. When examined it appeared that the head and legs had been very neatly disjointed, and a search of the whole vicinity revealed no trace of them. There was one long cut down the centre of the body. The remains, so far as could be told by the examination, were those of a woman between thirty-five and forty years of age, rather short, and of a dark complexion. It was evident from the doctor's examination that she had never had a child. There was a mark about the waist such as would have been left by an encircling rope. There was no clothing except the chemise, which was an ordinary cotton one. There was no blood upon the ground, and all the bloodstains were dry, showing that the murder, if it had been a murder, had taken place some days before. It was evident that the body had been brought there in the condition in which it had been found. There is ample evidence that it was brought there at some time during the night. From the way in which it lay, it appeared to have been hurriedly drafted there and to have been untouched afterwards by the person who brought it. The body was discoloured in several places, and decomposition was setting in at the edge of the cuts. Everything indicated that death had taken place four or five days previously.

The remains were removed to St. George's mortuary, and were there viewed by a HERALD reporter. The body, lying on the slab in the centre of the mean little room, was a piteous and revolting spectacle. The severance of the head and legs seemed to have taken from it the fashion of humanity, and it needed a second glance to recognise the true character of the mass of inert flesh. The body there appeared to be that of a young and well-formed woman, well nourished and perfectly healthy. Except the mutilations already spoken of the only marks of violence it bore were the dark blue traces of finger marks about and below the elbow of the left arm and a shapeless bruise on the right wrist. The singularity of the mutilations was that the cuts were made with perfect cleanness and decision. There was no mangling of the flesh. The operation had been performed as neatly as if it had been done by a practical surgeon in the quiet of a dissecting-room, rather than by a brutal miscreant in the confusion and terror of committing a hideous crime. A singular circumstance, irreconcileable with the marks of putrefaction on other parts of the body, borne out also by the stench of decay, is that the flesh of the stump of the right thigh was bright and red as with a recent effusion of blood. The flesh of the other stump and of the neck was dry and caked, as were the lips of the gaping cut extending from the breastbone to the root of the thigh, exposing the intestines, which, however, have been left intact, contrary to the practice of the Whitechapel fiend, to whom so many attribute the crime. The decapitation and the cutting off of the limbs are also opposed to his practice, and help to cast doubt on that theory, and to suggest that the crime much more nearly resembles those recently committed at Rainham and Battersea. Beside the body lay the torn and bloodstained rags of the chemise, which had been flung over the body, the only scrap of material, except the body itself, yet found which may possibly assist the police in the task of identification.

THE HUNT FOR CLUES.

Scotland Yard was early astir. Before six o'clock a message was received there from Leman-street. It was only "Whitechapel again," but it sufficed to put things instantly into a ferment. Word was at once sent to Commissioner Monro and the Assistant Commissioners, and they immediately responded. Two fresh detectives were placed on the case, Inspector Abberline, who has been following it, being out of town. The hunt for clues and for information began vigorously. The first bit of evidence was a bloodstained undergarment found at half-past seven in a vacant yard in Hooper-street, 500 yards away. It had been thrust through a hole in the fence, and it was turned over to the police. The stains on this, as on the chemise, were old and dried. Then came the story of a man who said he had seen another man with a heavy bag of something on his back, about four o'clock. He was questioned, but his information was not important, the police feeling confident that the body was brought nearly to the spot in a vehicle of some kind. Chief Commissioner Monro and Colonel Monsell, Chief Constable, went all over the ground, and visited the mortuary. Three arrests were made in the shape of two sailors and a shoeblack found sleeping in an adjacent archway, but after being examined at the Lemon-street [*sic*] Station they were released, it being evident that they knew nothing of the matter. It shortly appeared that there was no more of a clue in the case than there had been in the preceding ones. Mr. Williamson, of the Criminal Investigation Department, admitted this when questioned as to whether the police had as yet formed any theory regarding the case. He replied:- "There is not evidence enough yet on which to base any theory. As a matter of fact, the police are not nearly so fond of rushing into theorising as some of you gentlemen of the Press seem to think. One fact is worth half a dozen theories, and in this case we have to bend our energies to the discovery of facts. This case promises to be one of peculiar difficulty. The others were mysterious enough, but here the mystery is complete; the head being gone, the chances of identification are so very slight. People who are inclined to be impatient with the police should remember how enormous the difficulties of such a case as this are. Do I think it is "Jack the Ripper" again? As I said, I have no theories. I wait for facts."

The remains lay all day at the Morgue, but were not identified. Identification will, in fact, be difficult, if not impossible. The only assisting fact was one revealed by Secretary Bartlett to a HERALD reporter at the Old Jewry in the afternoon. He said that a week ago a woman's hand had been picked up in Shoreditch, and all efforts to trace its owner and origin had thus far failed.

The River Police were put on the alert within twenty minutes after the finding of the body. The despatch sent to them and to all the other Metropolitan stations was as follows:-

At twenty minutes to six a.m. trunk of a woman found under the arches in Pinchin-street, E. Age about forty. Height 5 ft 3 in. Hair dark brown. No clothing except chemise, very much torn and blood-stained. Both elbows discoloured as if from habitual leaning on them. Post mortem. Marks around waist, apparently caused by a rope.

Immediately upon the circulation of this telegram, the Thames Police, under Detective-inspector Regan and Chief-inspector Moore, assisted by Sergeants Moore, Francis, Howard, Davis, and Scott, at once got their various craft on the river, and boarded all the vessels at the mouth of the Thames and in the docks. Attention was particularly directed to the cattle boats and those from Spain and America. Among those boarded in the London Docks were the *City of Cork*, the *Cadiz*, the *Malaga*, and the *Gallicia*, and the *Lydian Monarch* in the Millwall Docks. The operation of searching these vessels had not concluded until a late hour in the evening, and so far as the investigation had gone the captains of the various vessels were able to give satisfactory accounts as to their crews.

After the removal of the remains to the mortuary. Mr. Clarke, Dr. Gordon Brown (the City Police-surgeon), and two other medical gentlemen who have had experience in previous cases of this nature, shortly after made a more careful examination of the remains. It was noticed that the trunk displayed green patches; the flesh otherwise was white. The doctors, from their investigations, concluded that the cuts had been inflicted in a left-hand manner – that is to say, the cut in the throat was evidently commenced on the left side and carried to the right with a clean sweep. The same peculiarity was observed in the other wounds, and in separating the legs more flesh had been cut from the trunk on the left side than on the other. In more than one of the previous crimes this peculiarity has been observed and commented upon. The legs are taken out clearly from the loin, showing no signs of a separating instrument. Nothing whatever was found to be missing except these members and the head. The cut severing the head from the body was skilfully done, there being no hacking or clumsy dissection noticeable. Furthermore, a saw had been used to sever the bones in such a way as to leave no doubt that the person responsible for the dismemberment possessed a good knowledge of anatomy. There were no signs about the hands which would indicate that the woman had been used to hard work, and so far as could be seen there had been no attempt to obliterate a mark on one of the fingers, apparently caused by a ring.

The body was well nourished and cared for. One of the several doctors who viewed the remains expressed the opinion that had he been asked to dissect the body in the manner in which he saw it he could not have done it more neatly and skilfully. In consequence of the similarity in the mode of dismemberment pursued in this case and those of the recent Battersea and Rainham mysteries, the officers engaged in those cases were consulted, and their general opinion is that the resemblance in all cases are so remarkable as to give grounds for the belief that the present crime is one with a different origin to that of the previous Whitechapel atrocities.

DOCTORS AND POLICE CONSULT.

A conference to which it is believed considerable importance is attached took place last evening at the Leman-street Police-station. When Dr. Phillips was telegraphed for to Bournemouth he replied that he would return to town at once; but asked the authorities to adjourn the post-mortem in the meantime. He arrived in London about five p.m. last evening, and after making some preliminary investigations attended at Leman-street Police-station soon after six o'clock. He was closeted with the Chief Constable Colonel Monsell, Mr. Arnold, and the officers from Scotland Yard. At seven p.m., Mr. Monro, the Chief Commissioner, arrived at the station in his private carriage, and joined in the deliberations which continued until nearly half-past eight o'clock. The surgeons and physicians who have examined the corpse agree that it was a living body not more than three or four days ago, the slight decomposition being due to the sudden heat of the weather. The manner in which the limbs had been severed, and the cut in the abdomen, seemed to point to the murderer or mutilator as a left-handed man, but upon this point there was some difference of opinion. The woman must have been of dark complexion, and about 35 years of age.

The inquest will open in the Vestry Hall, Cable-street, at 10 o'clock today.

Up till a late hour last evening no further arrests had been made in connection with the murder, and the police were absolutely without a clue of any kind. A circumstantial story to the effect that a suspicious-looking man was seen last night carrying a sack near where the body was found proved on investigation to be evidently valueless. As a matter of fact, no sack was found under the arch or elsewhere, and it was quite as likely as not that the murderer carried the corpse in a portmanteau or in a brown-paper parcel. In either case, unless the murderer was very impudent or unusually peculiar in appearance, he would not attract particular attention. Had there been anything suspicious in his demeanour, he could scarcely have passed through the streets of the East-end without being challenged by beat policemen or detectives, of whom the number in the district is at the present unusually large, owing to the precautions maintained by Commissioner Monro since the last murder, and to the local excitement arising out of the great strike. Special measures have been in operation for months past to maintain the vigilance and efficiency of the police at the highest point, in view of another murder by the Whitechapel fiend, the probability of which has never been questioned by the authorities. It is difficult, therefore, to see in what manner the police are to blame, or to say whence or how a clue is to be obtained.[. . .]

A DIFFERENT METHOD OF MUTILATION.

A reperusal of the circumstances of former atrocities of this nature only serves to confuse the reader's mind as to the possible origin of this last crime. It differs from the Whitechapel series in the facts that the head and lower limbs were amputated, and in the other fact that the hands were left undisturbed; but it resembles them in the infliction of the deep longitudinal cut along the lower half of the trunk. It will be remembered that last year, while the Whitechapel miscreant was in the full living of unchecked crime, a horribly mutilated human body was discovered in the basement storey of the building on the Embankment once intended for a national opera house. Here, too, the head and legs were missing, as in the case of the unfortunate woman found yesterday morning, but in this case the incomplete mutilation of the trunk had been completed in a fashion absolutely similar to that which marked the bodies of the Whitechapel victims. Nearly a month previously the right arm of a woman had been found floating in the Thames near [   ] Bridge, and several indications justified the belief that it formed part of the body found later on in the basement of the opera house. The case of the girl whose mutilated remains were enveloped in a fragment of under garment marked in black ink in a clear and clerkly hand with the name "L.E. Fisher," equally fails to offer any analogy to the other cases, as Dr. Bond, chief surgeon of the Metropolitan Police, declared death to have resulted from an operation intended to procure abortion; a motive which could not have determined any of the Whitechapel series, and certainly did not exist in the present instance, as the medical testimony declares this last victim never to have been pregnant.

It is interesting to see that the list of "Whitechapel Murders" accompanying the above article lists the following murders:

1. An unknown woman, Christmas week, 1887.
2. Martha Turner, found stabbed in 39 places on landing at George-yard-buildings, Commercial-street, Spitalfields, August 7, 1888.
3. Mrs. Mary Ann Nicholls, in Buck's-row, August 31, 1888.
4. Mrs. Annie Chapman, Hanbury-street, Sept. 7, 1888.
5. Elizabeth Stride, Berner-street, Sept. 30, 1888.
6. Catherine Eddowes, Mitre-square, Sept. 30, 1888.
7. Mary Jane Kelly, 26 Dorset-street, Spitalfields.
8. Alice Mackenzie, July 17, 1889.
9. Body of unknown woman found in Backchurch-lane, Cable-street, Sept. 10.

The file then contains a seven-page report[6] by the Chief Commissioner, James Monro, to the Home Office:

Sep. 11. 89.

Mr. Sandars.

I communicated to you yesterday the finding of the trunk of a female, minus head & legs in one of the railway arches in Pinchin Street.

This street is close to Berner Street which was the scene of one of the previous Whitechapel murders. It is not a very narrow street, but is lonely at night, & is patrolled every half hour by a constable on beat. The arch where the body was found abuts on the pavement.

The constable discovered the body some what after 20 minutes past five on the morning of Tuesday. He was in consequence of the pressure for men in Whitechapel just now, working part of two beats in addition to his own, but even so he passed & re-passed the spot every half hour. He is positive that when he passed the spot about five the body was not there. I am inclined to accept his statement thoroughly, for from another circumstance which has come to my knowledge he evidently was on the alert that night. It may therefore be assumed that the body was placed where it was found some time between 5 & 5.30 a.m. of Tuesday the 11th.

Although the body was placed in the arch on Tuesday morning, the murder – (and altho' there is not as yet before me proof of the cause of death, I assume that there has been a murder) was not committed there nor then. There was almost no blood in the arch, and the state of the body itself showed that death took place abt. 36

hours or more previously. This, then enables me to say that the woman was made away with probably on Sunday night, the 8th September. This was the date on which one of the previous Whitechapel murders was committed.

The body then must have been concealed, where the murder was committed during Sunday night, Monday, & Tuesday up till dawn. This leads to the inference that it was so concealed in some place to which the murderer had access, over which he had control, and from which he was anxious to remove the corpse. We may say then that the murder was committed probably in the house or lodging of the murderer, and that he conveyed the portion found to Pinchin Street to get rid of it from his lodging where the odour of decomposition would soon betray him.

Why did he take the trunk to Whitechapel and what does the finding of the body there show? If this is a fresh outrage by the Whitechapel murderer known by the horribly familiar nickname of Jack the Ripper the answer would not be difficult, altho' this murder, <u>committed in the murderers house</u> wd. be a new departure from the system hitherto pursued by this ruffian. I am however inclined to believe that this case is not the work of the "Ripper", which has characterized the previous cases has been a/. Death caused by cutting the throat, b/. Mutilation c/. Evisceration d/. Removal of certain parts of the body. e/. Murder committed in the street, except in one instance in Dorset Street. In this last case there were distinct traces of furious mania, the murderer having plenty of time at his disposal slashed and cut the body in all directions, evidently under the influence of frenzy.

In the present case, so far as the medical evidence goes there is a/ . nothing to show that death was caused by cutting the throat. b/. There is no mutilation as in previous cases, altho' there is dismemberment. c/. There is no evisceration. d/. There is no removal of any portion of the organs of generation or intestines. e/. The murder was indubitably committed neither in the street, nor in the victim's house, but probably in the lodging of the murderer. Here where there was as in the previous case of murder in a house, plenty of time at the disposal of the murderer, there is no sign of frenzied mutilation of the body, but of deliberate & skilful dismemberment with a view to removal. These are all very striking departures from the practice of the Whitechapel murderer, and if the body had been found elsewhere than in <u>Whitechapel</u> the supposition that death had been caused by the Ripper would probably not have been entertained.

But the body has been found in Whitechapel and there is a gash on the front part extending downwards to the organs of generation – and we have to account for these facts. I place little importance on the gash; it seems to me not to have been inflicted as in the previous cases. The inner coating of the bowel is hardly touched, and the termination of the cut towards the vagina looks almost as if the knife had slipped, and as if this portion of the wound had been accidental. The whole of the wound looks as if the murderer had intended to make a cut prepatory to removing the intestines in the process of dismemberment, & had then changed his mind. Had this been the work of the previous frenzied murderer we may be tolerably sure that he would have continued his hideous work in the way which he previously adopted. It may also be that the gash was inflicted to give rise to the impression that this case was the work of the Whitechapel murderer & so divert attention from the real assassin.

As to how the body got to Whitechapel this is a great difficulty unless it be supposed that it was removed in some conveyance & placed where it was found, & unless it be supposed that the murderer, being other than the "Ripper", had good knowledge of the locality. I may get some light on this point as the case goes on – Meanwhile I am inclined to the belief that, taking one thing with another, this is not the work of the Whitechapel murderer but of the hand which was concerned in the murders which are known as the Rainham mystery, the new Police buildings case, and the recent case in which portion of a female body (afterwards identified) were found in the Thames.

Sep. 11. 89.   J. Monro

Thank Mr Monro for
this Report.
     H.M.
       12 Sept./89.

There is a doctor's report[7] on the post-mortem findings by Dr Hebbert, dated 16 September 1889:

Report

On the 11th September /89 I was present at a postmortem examination on human remains found in Whitechapel Mr. Phillips and Mr. Gordon Browne were present.

The remains consisted of the trunk and arms of a female body, the head had been cut off at the lower part of the neck and the thighs had been separated at the hip joints.

The trunk was plump and well formed, with full breasts, fair skin and dark brown hair on the pubes and axilla.

The arms well shaped, hands small and nails well kept, the weight of the trunk could not be taken, the length was 26 inches, and circumference of chest at nipple was 34 inches, below breasts $31\frac{3}{4}$.

Rigor mortis had passed off, and decomposition as shewn by green discolouration of the abdomen just beginning, the cut surfaces at the hips were black and dry, but the surface at the neck moist and red the skin and muscles of the abdomen had been cut by a vertical incision and running from 2 inches below the ensiform cartilage downwards and ending on the left side of the external genitals just opening the vagina but not opening the peritoneal cavity. There were a number of small round bruises on the forearms and arms most on the under surface of the forearms, and varying in size from a shilling to a sixpence, on the left wrist were two cuts, one just grazing the skin $\frac{3}{4}$ inch long, and the other cutting through the skin and 1 inch long. There was no ecchymosis on the edge and no gaping of the wounds. There are no lineoe albae, on the abdomen and no further scars or injuries.

The incisions separating the head were apparently two in number the first beginning behind opposite the spinal column and ending in front, on the right side and carried from left to right, the second beginning on right side in front and carried to back joining the first but leaving a tongue of skin behind there was no ecchymosis in the skin. The muscles and tissues down to the spinal column were cut on the same level, the cricoid cartilage being cut about the centre. The spinal column was divided at the junction of the fifth and sixth cervical vertebrae through the intervertebial just a thin shaving of the body of the 5th cervical vertebra being left.

The ends of the vessels were very clean cut. There were no retraction of the muscles or other tissues.

The thighs had been separated at the hip joints the skin cut through by two or three sweeping circular incisions beginning apparently just below the hip bone, carried downward and inward around the buttock, the capsules of the hip joints were opened and the heads of the bones neatly disarticulated. There was no retraction of the muscles and tissues and the incisions both at the hip and neck and the abdomen had very clear cut edges.

The internal viscera were then examined.

Heart. The walls were flaccid, the ventricles empty and dilated, the valves healthy and competent, muscle pale and fatty, on the pericardium was a patch of old inflammation: weight $9\frac{1}{2}$ ozs. Lungs Right upper lobe adherent to pleura, by old firm adhesions. Left lung free, both lungs were apparently healthy, but were beginning to decompose.

Spleen; large, soft, decomposing, $7\frac{1}{2}$ ozs. Liver: weight 50 ozs, decomposing, substance fairly healthy.

Kidneys, Weight 7 ozs each, slight decomposition, substance fairly healthy.

Stomach, walls normal, with healthy mucous membrane about a dram or so of partly digested food, which appeared to be plums and no smell. Intestines large intestine contained faeces no abnormality.

Vulva The vulva is patent and there is no hymen the fourchette is unruptured the vagina is wide but still rugose The mucous membrane is healthy.

The uterus weighs rather less than two ozs and is 3 inches long, of which the body measures $1\frac{1}{2}$ inches & the cervix $1\frac{1}{2}$ inch the cavity of the body is triangular with a convexity downwards at the base the cervix has well marked arbor vitae, the os is small and the lips are not everted, the os just admits a large probe, there is a little whitish thick mucous oozing from the os uteri. The mucous membrane is rather thick and covered with a reddish mucous.

The ovaries are small cystic and degenerating. There is a small extravasation on the left ovary.

The measurements of the arms outstretched across the chest 64 inches, the forearm measured $16\frac{1}{2}$ inches, the hand $6\frac{1}{2}$ inches long and $6\frac{3}{4}$ inches in circumference at the palm. The stirnal epiphysis of the clavicle had united by bone.

The tissues generally were pale and bloodless.

On the first joint on the dorsal surface of the right little finger is a small round hardening not amounting to a corn, other is a similar but smaller hardening on the inner side of the first joint of the right ring finger.

Charles A. Hebbert.

M.R.C.P.

Curator of Museum of

Westm Hospl

This report is followed by the doctor's comments[8]:

Comments

The remains are those of a large well nourished woman.

Her height as calculated by the [ ] measurements and forearm about 5 ft. Her age is above 25 as shewn by the union of the epiphysis and from the condition of the ovaries approaching so that probably 35 years or so.

She had not borne children as shewn by the uterus, and absence of linese alboe and the breasts did not give the impression of having been used for suckling.

She was apparently not a virgin and the vagina had been distended, though not so patent as after childbearing. The skin was fair and the hair dark brown the hands are shapely and the skin soft, there are no marks indicating any occupation, except that on the right [ ] finger is a small circular hardening, but no corn. [*Marginal note to insert –* "This mark is such as might be made by writing. CH"] There is no mark as of a ring on the left ring finger.

The immediate cause of death was syncope as shewn by the condition of the heart and the general bloodlessness of the tissues indicating haemorrhage as the cause of death.

There was no organic disease of the viscera examined which would have caused death.

The edges of the cuts shewed that a very sharp knife had been used, all the cuts had been made after death. All the cuts were made from left to right, except those separating the right thigh, which had been carried from right to left, across the flexure of the joint, so probably done by a right handed man. The incisions were evidently made with design and were skilfully performed, as if by a man who had some knowledge of the position of joints and the readiest means of separating limbs, such knowledge as a butcher or slaughterer, they do not indicate a special anatomical knowledge of the human body.

Charles A. Hebbert

16 Sept'89   M.R.C.S.

Curator of museum

Westm. Hospl.

There is a report[9] by Chief Inspector Donald Swanson, dated 12 September 1889, concerning enquiries conducted in this case regarding John Cleary, who had called at the *New York Herald* offices:

METROPOLITAN POLICE.
Criminal Investigation Department,
Scotland Yard,
12th day of September, 1889.

Enquiries re John Cleary
who called at New York
Herald Offices at 1.5 am
Sunday 8th.

With reference to the attached article from New York Herald stating that at 1.5 am Sunday morning a young man calling himself John Cleary of 21 Whitehorse Yard, had called at their offices, and informed them that from what he had heard from an ex-member of Met: Police in Whitechapel another murder and mutilation had taken place in Back Church Lane, but had declined to accompany two reporters to the East End, I beg to report that I saw Mr. Cowen, the night editor, as well as Mr. Fletcher the reporter who had seen the man, but they were unable to give me anything additional to the contents of the extract; upon which any enquiry could be made. Upon making enquiry at No. 21 White Horse Yard, I found that the name of Cleary was unknown, but upon seeing the agent who lets the apartments, a Mr. Yates, he stated that a young man, who passed under the name of Leary, had resided there three weeks ago at 21 White Horse Yard, but had been evicted for non-payment of rent; and was now residing in Strand Buildings. Mr. Yates further said that Leary worked as odds man for a Mr. Mapley, greengrocer of Newcastle St. Enquiry at Mapley's disclosed that they had no man named Leary, or ever had, but they had a man who lived in White Horse Yard, and was now staying in Strand Buildings named Denis Lynch. Enquiry at Strand Buildings shewed that Lynch, passing as Leary who formerly resided at 21 White Horse Yard, now resided at No. 5 in the Buildings, with another man's wife and was under notice to leave for non-payment of rent. Having arranged at Mapley's to have Lynch seen at 5 p.m. I took Mr. Fletcher there, but Lynch alias Leary had had to go away with the van, and an arrangement was made for 7.30 p.m. At that hour we saw Lynch alias Leary, but Mr. Fletcher at once said he was not the man. Lynch on being questioned asserted that he did live at 21 Whitehorse Yard, but had never called at the New York Herald Office, nor did he know any person answering the description who would use his name. During the interval between 5 and 7.30 p.m. I had asked the reporters not to renew their enquiry until this man was seen, and they promised faithfully not to do so, but at the interview with Lynch the woman with whom he is living, recognised Mr. Fletcher and said, "I know you, you belong to the New York Herald, and were at my house this afternoon." This I had anticipated, and questioned them upon their enquiries, when they stated that they had been running about Drury Lane, with some loungers they had met with, who had told them lies as to a man called Stephen Cleary, and by enquiry at the alleged addresses proved it to them, at the same time reminding them that a breach of faith did not substantiate the editor's expression of a desire to assist the police in the elucidation of the matter. Lynch has been seen again, but can throw no light on the matter.

From enquiry on H. Division I find it is the fact that an Inspr. from H. named Pattenden met the reporters in Backchurch Lane on Sunday morning, and that they called at Commercial Street about 2 a.m. (Sunday) and enquired as to whether any infm. had been received respecting a murder in Back Church Lane. By the reports from H. which are attached, it appears a woman was found insensible in High St. and taken to Whitechapel Infirmary at 12 night 7th. The Inspr. thinks the occurrence may have given rise to the information but it does not account for the mention of Backchurch Lane. The New York Herald people will send here if any person should give them any information respecting Cleary, who so far as they know, had not called at any other newspaper agency.

Donald SSwanson

ChInspr.

John Shore

Supt

[*There is a marginal annotation on this report as follows*: It was stated that there was some writing on a wall abt. Cleary, and are the facts not this. I mentd this to Supt. Arnold, & he will be able to tell Ch Inspr Swanson/ I believe that the fact abt the High Street is known as Church Lane. But still this enquiry is not completed and we must try to get Cleary if possible. E.Divn. might perhaps know something abt him. JM 12/9'].

There is a statement[10] by John Arnold included, worded as follows:

Front cover:- CENTRAL OFFICE, C.I.D. Reference 58895 /6, summary of contents –

Statement of John Arnold confessing that it was he who went to the offices of the New York Herald at 1.5 am on Sunday 8th and gave infn about an alleged murder in Backchurch Lane 13/9.

John Arnold, says, I reside at No. 2 Harveys Buildings Strand. newsvendor. states. On Saturday night I had come out of the King Lud. p.h. and I had a little drop of drink. When about the middle of Fleet Street on left hand side going towards the Strand, a man dressed as a soldier, in black uniform, black cord shoulder strap lightish buttons cheese cutter cap, brass [?] ornament in front of cap like a horn cannot say whether there was a band round or not, age about 35 to 36. height 5 ft. 6 or 7. compl. fair. fair moustache, good looking. carrying a brown paper parcel about 6 or 8 in long, came up behind me and said, "Hurry up with your papers, another horrible murder", and I said. "Where". and he said "In Backchurch Lane". Immediately he told me that I ran up to the New York Herald Office, and reported to the sub editor upstairs and to two reporters, who asked me to go down to Whitechapel, but I declined as it was past one a.m. and my lodgings would have been closed for the night; and I told them so. They said if it turns out right, we'll reward you, and I said "Thank you, I stand at Charing Cross. When before the editor I gave the name of John Kemp not Cleary of 21 Whitehorse Yard, where I had formerly lived. I gave a false name because I did not want my wife to know as I am not living with her for if she knew she would get me turned out of my lodgings. I sell the New York Herald every Sunday, and call for the papers at their offices. I do not know what became of the soldier, indeed I cannot say whether he belonged to the regulars or volunteers. The last I saw of him was in Fleet Street, as I hurried and left him. Two days afterwards I saw in the papers that a horrible murder had taken place in Back Church Lane, and I told ex.Inspr. Lansdown at Charing Cross, as I have told you. This was on Tuesday afternoon. The next I heard was that there was something about me, as John Cleary, in the New York Herald and I read it. Seeing Sergt. Froest at Charing Cross about 4.30p.m. I told him that it was I who gave the information to the New York Herald, and he took me to Whitehall Place. If I talked to the soldier for ten minutes or so, I might recognise his voice, but I am not certain that I could identify him from a number of persons. I cannot describe him further. It was not till today that I knew that police wanted to see me. and I spoke to Sergt Froest.

John Arnold

Another almost immediate effect of the discovery of the Pinchin Street torso – with the obvious implication that it had been carried to where it was found by someone who went unchallenged by any police patrol – was for Superintendent Arnold to call for a strengthening of the police patrols in the area. In a report[11] dated 11 September 1889, he stated:

METROPOLITAN POLICE

H Division

11th Sept. 18[89]

Re Whitechapel Murders

I beg to report that owing [to] the recent discovery of the body of a woman in Pinchin Street: evidently the result of a murder. no information being foun[d] to afford a clue as to how th[e] body was conveyed to the spot at which it was found, & there being no doubt it was carried there either by Barrow or by some person on his back. I beg to submit that it is desire[able] to augment. the men of this Division so as to be able to place more men on the Beats. and also to employ more in plain clothes without distressi[ng] other Divisions as is now the case. I therefore recommend an augmentation of 100 Constables which would enable me to strengthen each Subdivision, & I would ask that if approve[d] a good proportion of the men [ ] may be transferred from othe[r] Divisions as recruits wo[uld] be of but little service f[or] some months.

T Arno[ld]

This report is included in the file with another[12] of the same date by the Commissioner, James Monro, to the Home Office:

<u>H.O.</u>   [done GL]   <u>11.9.89</u>

Our experience in connection with the last Whitechapel murder shows that notwithstanding every precaution the murderer has been enabled to slip through our patrols, and dispose of the body of his victim. without being observed by police. All that I can do is to strengthen the force of police in the locality, and make it more difficult than before for these lamentable occurrences to take place. For this purpose I shall require 100 more men, both uniform &plain clothes. I cannot possibly arrange for their transfer from other Divisions, which have already furnished men for the East End, &I therefore ask for an augmentation of 100 men for a couple of months, in addition to those whom I have already have under H O letter.

As soon as I can see my way to reduce the number S of S may rely upon my doing so, but we must put a stop to these Whitechapel outrages, and for this ["men" – *deleted*] the number of men applied for ["are" – *deleted*] is absolutely necessary. I trust therefore that I may receive immediate sanction to supply the above number of men for the time mentioned.

JM

11/9

There is a report[13] from Inspector Henry Moore, dated 12 September 1889, with summary-of-contents cover stating:

Mr. Miller, Star Newspaper called and wished to know if it was a fact that John Cleary mentioned Back Church Lane to the Editor of the New York Herald. If so he attaches suspicion to an ex compositor of that name formerly employed on the Globe newspaper. ?Seen. Put with New York Herald papers 13/9 [sgd] pro A.C.C. 13/9

METROPOLITAN POLICE
Criminal Investigation Department,
Scotland Yard,
12th day of September, 1889.

Human remains found
in Whitechapel.
I beg to report that at 1p.m. today Mr. Miller, of the "Star Newspaper" called at Leman St. Station and was particularly anxious to know whether it was a fact that John Cleary did mention Back Church Lane, Whitechapel, in his statement to the Editor of the "New York Herald" as the place where mutilated remains had been discovered; if so he considered it most important and he should then know what steps to take. I did not satisfy him upon the matter; but in the course of conversation learnt that if Back Church Lane was really mentioned, he attached suspicion upon an ex-compositor as the man who visited the New York Herald Office;- Viz:-

John Cleary, formerly attached to The Globe Office; age 35, ht.6 ft., comp. fresh, hair and heavy moustache dark, bald, medium build, speaks peculiar, as though he has no roof to his mouth; who about 4 months ago was residing at 2 Savoy Buildings, Strand.

The above information I at once wired to Chf. Inspr. Swanson.

I would add that Mr. Miller is the person who found the thigh of Annie Jackson which was thrown into garden on Thames Embankment.

> Henry Moore Inspr.
> T Arnold Supd.

A covering report[14] by Chief Inspector Swanson, *"regarding the Man calling at New York Herald office at 1.5 am. Sunday morning"*, then follows:

METROPOLITAN POLICE.
Criminal Investigation Department,
Scotland Yard.
12th day of September 1889.

I beg to report that P.S. Froest reported to me that, John Arnold, the newsvendor at Charing Cross, had told him that he was the person who had given the information to the New York Herald, and whom they were describing as John Cleary. The P.S. then went for Arnold, and I met them at Charing Cross. Attached is Arnold's statement, taken as fully as he can give it. He cannot say whether the soldier had a stripe or not round his cap, whether he wore a belt or not, or if he had any stripes on his trousers, and he cannot say whether the buttons were yellow or white, all he can remember is that they were lightish. A Commissionaire wears the uniform nearest to his description. Upon further questions he stated that he did not even know where Backchurch Lane was.

Arnold has been known for many years to officers past and present, and speaking personally, beyond that he bets in small sums, drinks occasionally, and has deserted his wife, (who is said to be intemperate and a virago), for which he was sentenced to twenty one days imprisonment, I have never heard of him being dishonest. That he could be in any way connected with others or by himself in a murder is to me improbable. He has not strength enough to have lifted the trunk which, according to the surgeons, weighed from four to five stones, (police think more), and if he knew of such a crime, he would be one of the first to inform police.

Although he is doubtful as to his power to identify, I submit that a trial might be given him in ["Fleet Street and" – *deleted*] Strand, where the head quarters of the Commissionaires are, for a few days to see at least whether the uniform is like what he saw.

Donald SSwanson,
ChInspr.
JohnShore
Supt.

The following page[15] reads as follows:

CIDCentral
12th Septr 1889

Miscellaneous

H Leman St. — Memo: Body of woman found (No. 33 Infm. and Mem. 12.30pm 10th), amended description:- Age about 35. height 5feet 3 inches; hair dark brown. skin fair; hands soft and shapely, nails well kept, small circular hardening (but no corn) on right little finger; arms small, but well shaped, body plump, and well formed, with full breasts, no marks of rings on fingers; no evidence of maternity.

The special attention of Divn. is called to the description, as to whether any woman of the unfortunate class or otherwise, answering the description has been reported, or can be ascertained to [be] missing. Inserted in 8.30 pm Infms.

[Sgd]   [*Sig. illegible*]
For Supt
13.9.89.

The following pages[16] are Dr Bagster Phillips's report, as follows:

2 Spital Square E   [Stamped: – METROPOLITAN POLICE
    September 12th.   13 Sep. 89
                          Criminal Investigation Dept]

Sir

I beg to hand you my Colleague's & my notes in the case of mutilated remains of the woman unknown now [ ] in the Mortuary St. George's East –

I have examined them as far as practicable.

I am Sir
    Your obdt. Servt.
        G.M.B.Phillips

General Appearances of Body in Mortuary Septr. 10th 5p.m. –

Trunk of Female, decapitated & deprived of thighs & legs disarticulated at hip joints on both sides.

Absence of coagulated blood.

Decomposition already established and the divided tissues of neck emit air – and the veins still drain with blood.

Bust is that of a fully developed woman apparently about 35 years of age & from external appearances has not borne a child & has not suckled one.

The separation of the head has been effected with a clean sweep of some sharp instrument the spinal articulation of the bones being cleanly effected.

The section of the neck presents a particularly even surface but there is a small flap of skin at the back indicating where the incision ended. It commenced a little to the right of the middle line behind at back of neck.

Both thighs were excised by circular sweeps from level of each of hip bones.

There are several recent bruises on arms and hands.

There is a long division of external wall of abdomen, not penetrating the cavity 15 inches Commencing 2 inches below cartilage of chest and slightly penetrating the vagina below, being about 15 in. long, rather to left side.

Further appearances 10.15 am. Septr. 11th after missing the Coroners order which I had to apply for & was specially told to wait for until the Jury had viewed the remains.

The Coroner [ ] sent a message 11pm. Septr. 10th for me to make the exm. at once, but I had elected to do the exm. with other gentlm. at 10 O'c on the 11th.

Decomposition much more marked.

Length of trunk	2 ft. 2 in.
Round nipples	34 in.
Below breasts	$31\frac{1}{2}$ in.
Tip to tip of fingers	5 ft. 4 in.
Length of Body calculated at	5 ft. 3 in.
Length of forearm & hand elbow to tip of the fingers	$16\frac{1}{2}$ in.
Length of Hand	$6\frac{1}{2}$ in.
Breadth of Hand	$6\frac{3}{4}$ in.
Weight of whole remains	67 lbs.

A small quantity of hair removed fr. Pubis & preserved.

[ ] selected notes bearing on cause of death.
Pale condition of Hands & Nails is marked
Two Vaccination marks Left arm.
Marked absence of blood in Vessels, but not so complete as in some
cases of death from bleeding.

Pericardium	healthy (in fluid)
Heart	fatty & empty. Valves emptied.
Liver	signs of degeneration
Stomach	contained a little food, possibly plums.
Womb	that of a woman not having had a child, but congested at cervix.
Ovaries	of woman under 40.
Vagina	rather dilated. no sign of recent coitus.

Conclusions	That Death probably occurred within 24 to 36 hours before remains were found.

Chiefly indicated as arising from f[ ] from loss of blood. (especially
indicated by empty Heart & blood vessels.
The mutilations were subsequent to death. (were effected to
facilitate removal?)
The incisions & marks of separation of Head & Thighs point very
strongly to their having been caused by some one accustomed to cut
up animals.
That all the injuries might be made with a strong knife very sharp 8
inches or more in length of blade.
No evidence of child bearing but strong evidence of prostitution.

GM.B.Phillips.

As with other reports in the hand of Dr Bagster Phillips, this was
especially difficult to transcribe. His report is followed by the
report[17] of Percy J. Clark, his assistant, as follows:

A little before 6 o'clock on the morning of Sept. 10th (Tuesday) I
was called by the Police to a railway arch in Pinchin Street where I
saw the trunk of a woman minus the head & legs. It was lying about
18 feet from the roadway & about a foot from the right wall of the
arch. The body was lying on its anterior surface [ ] with the right
arm doubled beneath it & the left arm lying by the side – the arms
were not severed from the body.

There was no pool of blood – no signs of any struggle – nor any reason for supposing that a murder had been committed there.

Covering over the cut surface of the neck & over the right shoulder were the remains of what had been a chemise. It was of common make & of such a size as would be worn by a woman of similar build to the trunk found. It had been torn down the front & a cut had been made from the front to the arm-hole on either side – the cuts appeared to have been made with a sharp knife & were probably for the purpose of getting it off the body.

The chemise was much blood-stained & the back of it was stained with faeces. There was no distinguishing mark on the chemise.

Rigor Mortis was not present.

The body was lifted in my presence onto the ambulance & taken to the St. George's-in-the-East mortuary by constables.

On re-examining it there I found an incision, 15 inches long, commencing 2 inches below the ensiform cartilage & running down just to the left of the middle-line, ending just below the pubes.
(The appearances of the neck & hips are described with the account of post-mortem examination by Dr. Phillips)

The body appeared to be that of a woman of about 5 ft. 3 inches in height – of stoutish build – dark complexion – & between 30 & 40 years of age.

In the middle line of the back are four bruises of recent date; the 1st being about 7 inches from the neck & the 2nd 1 inch below that – these two bruises are about the size of a 6d. Four inches below the last named bruise is another of about the size of a 2/6. On a level with the top of the sacrum & 2 inches to the left of middle line is a bruise $1\frac{1}{2}$ inches in diameter & having the appearance such as would be caused by a fall or kick.

Right Arm
    There are ["two" – *deleted*] three bruises on front of the arm & one on back – they are of recent date & have the appearance as if

caused by the arm being strongly grasped. The back of the forearm is bruised in a line extending from the inner condyle of the humerus to the outer side of the wrist.
There are eight bruises in all.

Left Arm.

There are bruises along the inner border of the back of the forearm, there are 7 bruises in all.
Over the outer side of the forearm about the lower third are two wounds – the upper one is only an abrasion & does not penetrate thro' the skin – the lower one is an incised wound $1\frac{3}{4}$ inches long & must have been caused by a sharp knife.

There were no marks of any rings on any of the fingers.

The body was not blood-stained except where the chemise had rested upon it. The lower part of the back was stained by faeces.

The body had not the appearance of having been recently washed.

When I first saw the body decomposition was just commencing & I should think the body had been dead about 24 hours.

There was a mark round the waist caused during life probably by the clothing.

When returning from the mortuary to Leman St Police station with Inspr. Pinhorn we were called by some men to a piece of waste ground in Hooper Street; we there found near an opening at the bottom of the pailings a blood-stained petticoat, body of common make, such as would be worn by a woman of stoutish build. The blood was not very recent & appeared to be menstrual; from the manner too in which it had been folded I should think it had probably been used as a diaper. On my arrival at Leman St station I shewed it to Colonel Monsell & Supt. Arnold.
    Percy J. Clark

The next report[18] is by Inspector Henry Moore, dated 24 September 1889, and is marked, "*Daily Report re- Human Remains found at Pinchin St*":

METROPOLITAN POLICE.
Criminal Investigation Department,
Scotland Yard,
24th day of September 1889.

Re the case of Human Remains found at Pinchin Street.   ''E''.

I beg to report that no information has been obtained during the past 24 hours that will assist Police in the investigation of the Crime.

No persons have been detained or liberated on ''H'' Division during same period.

This morning Mr. Wynne E. Baxter, Coroner, resumed the enquiry as to the discovery of the trunk on 8th inst., at St. George's Vestry Hall, cable St. ''E.'', and in the end a verdict of Wilful murder against some person or persons unknown was returned.

I herewith submit Extract from ''Evening Standard'' which gives a fair account of the proceedings; as that it can be placed with papers.

Henry Moore, Inspr.
T Arnold Supd.

This is followed by f 22, which is the above-mentioned extract from the *Evening Standard* of Tuesday, 24 September 1889:

THE WHITECHAPEL
TRAGEDY.
INQUEST AND VERDICT.

Mr. Wynne E. Baxter, Coroner for South-East London, this morning resumed, at St. George's Vestry Hall, Cable-street, the inquest on the human remains found under the railway arch in Pinchin-street, on the 10th inst.

Mr. Percy John Clark, assistant to Dr. Phillips, surgeon to H division said:- A little before six a.m. on the morning of September 10 I was called by the police to Pinchin-street. Under the railway arch there, about eight feet from eight [*sic?*] from the road, and about a foot from the right wall of the arch, I saw the trunk of a woman minus the head and legs. It was lying on its chest, with the right arm doubled under the abdomen, the left arm lying at the side. The arms were not severed from the body. There was no pool of blood, and no signs of any struggle having taken place there. On moving the body I found that there was a little blood underneath where the neck had lain. It was small in quantity not clotted, and evidently had oozed from the cut surface of the neck whilst lying there. Covering the cut surface of the neck and right shoulder were the remains of what had been a chemise, of common make, and of such a size as would be worn by a woman of similar build to the trunk found. It had been torn down the front, and had been cut from the front of the armholes on each side. The cuts appeared to have been made with a knife. The chemise was bloodstained nearly all over, I think from being wrapped over the cut surface of the neck. There was no clotted blood on it, and no sign of arterial spurting. I could find no distinguishing mark on the chemise. Rigor mortis was not present, and decomposition had set in. The body was taken to the mortuary, and an examination there showed that the body was that of a woman of stoutish build, dark complexion, about five feet three inches in height, and between thirty and forty years old. I should think the body had been dead about 24 hours. Besides the wounds caused by the severance of the head and legs, there was a wound 15 inches long through the external coats of the abdomen. The body was not bloodstained, except where the chemise had rested upon it. The body seemed to have been recently washed [sic]. On the back were four bruises, all caused before death. One was under [?] the spine, on a level with the lower part of the shoulder blade. An inch lower down was a similar bruise. About the middle of the back also, over the spine, was a bruise about the size of half a crown. On a level with the top of the hip bone, and three inches to the left of the spine, was a bruise two and a half inches in diameter, such as might be caused by a fall or a kick. None of the bruises were of old standing. Round the waist was a pale mark and indentation such as would be caused by clothing during life. On the right arm there were eight distinct bruises, and seven on the left, all cause before death and of recent date. The backs of both forearms and hands were much bruised. On the outer side of the left forearm, about three inches above the wrist, was a cut about two inches in length, and half an inch lower down was another cut, both caused after death. The bruises on the right arm were such as would have been caused by the arm having been tightly grasped. There was an old injury on the index finger of the right hand over the last joint. Two vaccination marks were on the left arm. The arms were well formed. Both elbows were hardened and discoloured, as if they had been leant upon. The hands and nails were pallid and the former were not indicative of any particular kind of work. The breasts were well formed, and there were no signs of maternity about them.

Dr. Phillips, police surgeon of the H division, said – I first examined the body at six o'clock on the day the remains were found. I confirm, so far as I have observed, the evidence given by my colleague, Mr. Clarke [sic], who was present with me when I first examined the body. Decomposition of the body had been fairly established. There was an oozing of blood from the cut surface of the neck. The cut surfaces where the thighs had been removed were nearly dry. The cut surface at the neck was not so dry, but it impressed me greatly with its general even surface. The skin was beginning to peel, and the decomposition of the trunk was greater about the upper than the lower part of it. There was not a head, and the thighs had been removed from the body. Next morning, in the presence of Dr. Gordon Brown and Mr. Hibberd [sic], I further examined the body. Decomposition had extended greatly. The cut surface of the neck was much drier at the ends of the muscles, but more moist underneath. The neck had been severed by a clean incision commencing a little to the right side of the middle line of the neck behind, leaving a flap of skin at the end of the incision. It had severed the whole of the structures of the neck, dividing the cartilage of the neck in front, and separating the bone of the spine behind. The walls of the belly were divided from just below the cartilage of the ribs. The two small cuts upon the forearm appear to me as likely to have been caused when the sweep of the knife divided the muscles covering the upper part of the thigh. Both thighs were excised by the extensive circular sweep of the knife, or some sharp instrument, penetrating the joint from below and separating the thighs at the hip joint, but the cartilages within the joint and those which deepen the joint and surround it had not been injured. The marks upon the fingers had fairly healed, and had evidently been in the process of healing for some time previous to death. I think the pallor of the hands and the nails is an important element in enabling me to draw a conclusion as to the cause of death. I agree especially with the remarks made by Mr. Clarke as to the date. I found the length of the trunk to be 2 ft. 2 in., and the measure went round the nipple 34 in., and below the breast $31\frac{3}{4}$ in. Dr. Phillips, having given some further measurements, said that the Deceased was about 5 ft. 3 in. There was throughout the body an absence of blood in the vessels. The heart was empty; it was fatty, and the vessels coated with fat, but the bowels were healthy. The right lung was adherent, except at base, the left lung free, and, taking them both together, fairly competent, and especially considering the decomposition of the remains. The stomach was the seat of considerable post-mortem change, and contained only a small quantity of fruit, like a plum. In my opinion the woman had never been pregnant. I believe her to have been under 40 years of age. There was an absence of any particular disease or poison. I believe that death arose from loss of blood. I believe the whole of the mutilations to have been subsequent to death; that the mutilations were effected by some one accustomed to cut up animals or to see them cut up; and that the incisions were effected by a strong knife, eight inches or more long. The supposition – (and only a supposition) – which presents itself to my mind is that there had been a former incision of the neck, the signs of which had disappeared on the subsequent separation of the head. The loss of blood could not have come from the stomach, and I could not trace it coming from the lungs. I have a strong opinion that it did not.

By a Juryman. – I cannot say whether the person who severed the head from the body was a butcher or not. I merely wish to say it was a person accustomed either to see or use a knife, or some sharp instrument in cutting up animals. I have no reason for believing that he had human anatomical knowledge. In fact, it probably is known to you, and most people, that the spine is not the part to be disarticulated by a medical man.

Michael Keating, of 1 Osborne-street [*sic*], Brick-lane, a licensed shoe black, said he passed up Pinchin-street on the night of the 9th, between eleven and twelve o'clock. He saw no one about, and observed nothing under the arch, but he was not very sober at the time. Witness went to sleep under the arch, and was not awakened during the night. The police roused him in the morning, and as he was leaving he noticed the body, which the inspector was covering up. He lent the police the sack in which he carried his blacking-box. If the body had been under the arch when he went in, he was not certain he was sober enough to have seen it. As far as he remembered, however, he went in the other side of the arch. He did not hear of anyone else coming in during the night. Witness had never slept under the arch before, but he knew it was a quiet and convenient place.

Richard Hawk, seaman, of St. Ives, Cornwall, stated that about seven or eight weeks ago he was paid off, and was in hospital till the

9th September. He walked about the streets until 20 minutes past four o'clock a.m., on the 10th, when happening to be in Pinchin-street he went under a railway arch to lie down. It was dark and he was not exactly sober.

The Coroner. – How did you know it was 20 minutes past four?

Witness. – We asked a policeman we saw close to the arch. He did not see anyone or anything in the arch when he went in. There was another man with him. His companion was in about the same condition. They met in a public-house. He neither heard nor saw anything, and went to sleep very soon.

Nehemiah Hurley, carman, said that he lived near Pinchin-street, and was called by a policeman as usual at 5 a.m. on the 10th inst. Work commenced with him occasionally at half-past five, but he left the house on the morning in question at 25 minutes to six. He went by way of Pinchin-street, where he saw a man standing at the corner, having the appearance of a tailor. The man looked as if he was waiting to go to work. Witness saw no one else until he got into Pinchin-street where he saw an inspector and other police standing by the arch where the body had been found.

Inspector Moore said he had charge of the case. There was nothing at present to show how the body was placed in the position in which it was found. He saw no reason for adjourning the inquiry. The chemise he produced had been torn and cut. It was made of common material, and was hand stitched and certainly not by an experienced needlewoman. It looked like a home-made garment, probably made by some poor person.

Police-constable Pinnett, recalled, said he was not stopped by anyone and asked the time on the night in question.

A statement was read by the Coroner from the man who was under the arch with Hawk, and confirming the latter's statement.

Dr. Phillips, recalled, said that there was not such a similarity between the manner in which the limbs were severed in this and in the Dorset-street murder, to convince him that both crimes were the work of one man, but the division of the neck,, and the attempt to disarticulate the bones of the spine were very similar in each case. The savagery shown in the mutilations in the Dorset-street case was far worse than in that now under consideration. In the former the mutilations were most wanton, whereas in the Pinchin-street crime he believed they were made in order to dispose of the body. These were points that struck him *without* any comparative study of the Dorset-street case, except such as was afforded by partial notes which he had with him. He believed that in this case there had been greater knowledge shown in regard to the construction of the parts composing the spine, and on the whole their [*sic*] had been a greater knowledge shown of how to separate a joint.

The Coroner, in summing up, pointed out that there was no evidence as to the identity of the Deceased; but that the statements of the medical gentlemen in the case showed clearly that the woman had died a violent death. It was a matter of congratulation that the present case did not appear to have any necessary connection with the previous murders in the immediate neighbourhood.

The Jury immediately returned a verdict of ''Wilful Murder against some person or persons unknown.''

                               Hy. Moore, Inspr.

There is a report cover[19] from the CID Central Office, stating:

Inspector Moore Submitting daily report of occurrences in connection with the human remains found in Pinchin Street on 10th inst. To Commissioner – There will be no objection to the burial from a police point of view, if it will not interfere with our being able to fit the head to the trunk, if we ever get it. Till all chance of recovery of the remaining parts of the body is gone it might be advisable to keep the trunk in spirits. HM

<u>Supn H.</u> Please ascertain from Dr. Phillips whether, in the event of the head or legs being subsequently found, he would be in a position to say that they belonged to the trunk if same had been buried.

                               [*Sgd illegible*] for ACC
                               27/9.

Report submitted Jno West 30/9/89 Act. Supt.

To Commissioner – for sanction. 1/10

Have the remains buried, after arranging for further preservation.
1.10   JM

Report Submitted   Jno West
5/10/89   Actg.Supt.

Mr Williamson   7/10
                JM

Seen and noted Hy Moore
Jno West
Actg Supt. 8/10/89.

The report[20] by Henry Moore, follows:

Human Remains found at Whitechapel. Reference to papers 57885
                METROPOLITAN POLICE.
                Criminal Investigation Department,
                        Scotland Yard,
                        24th day of September, 1889.
Re the case of "Human Remains" found at Pinchin Street.

I beg to report that during the past 24 hours no information has been obtained from the various enquiries which have been made which will assist Police in clearing up the mystery.

No persons have been detained or liberated on "H" Division during same period.

Enquiries and search has now been completed in Divisions (A. to Woolwich inclusive) for the missing portions of the "Remains", but with no good result.

Respecting the Trunk found at Pinchin Street on 10th inst., I beg to state that at the conclusion of the adjourned Inquest yesterday, the coroner, W. Baxter, Esqr. handed me the order for Burial, and remarked that he would leave it to the discretion of Police when it should be buried. I have since had Dr. Phillips seen upon the subject and he has no objection to the body being buried; but suggests that the interment should be witnessed and the lid of the tin vessel which now contains the body be secured.

I respectfully ask directions as to the burial of the body.

In conclusion I beg to add that before leaving the Coroner yesterday, he thanked me for the able assistance and attention which I had rendered him during the enquiry.

                                Henry Moore, Insp.
Respectfully submitted and suggest that the remains be buried as I see no reason for keeping the same any longer.

                                Jno. West ActgSup.

The next report[21] dated 30 September 1889, is also by Inspector Henry Moore and bears the same reference as the previous one:

METROPOLITAN POLICE.

Criminal Investigation Department,

Scotland Yard,

30th day of September 1889

Referring to attached; Vide Assistant Chief Constables Minute; dated 27th inst.

I beg to report that I was unable to see Dr. Phillips until this morning; when I consulted him as directed on the subject. He decided that the time has fully arrived for the "Remains" to be further dealt with; either by further means of preservation (more spirit) or by soldering down the mouth of tin vessel and burial. The identification probably could be made without comparison with the remains; but should the case ever be the subject of an investigation before a Judge and Jury such comparison would be absolutely necessary.

As to interment the Dr. prefers that it be effected by burying it in the tin vessel, after it has been re-charged with spirit and soldered.

I have conferred with Mr. James Wooton, Sanitary Inspector, St. George's-in-the-East; and he has promised, providing I can arrange with the Plaistow Cemetery Authorities that he will cause it to be buried as handed over to him by Police.

I will arrange if possible with the Cemetery Authorities tomorrow, and await Commissioners instructions as to the interment. Should burial be decided upon I have promised to acquaint Dr. Phillips, when he will attend at the mortuary and carry the final requirements as to preservation.

Henry Moore, Inspr.

Jno. West ActgSupt

The final report[22] regarding the disposal of the remains is dated 5 October 1889, again by Inspector Moore:

METROPOLITAN POLICE

H Division

5th day of October 1889

Referring to attached; vide Commissioners Minute dated 1st inst.

I beg to report that in accordance with directions I arranged for Dr. Phillips and Mr. John Allers, Tin Plate Worker of 2 Back

Church Lane, St. George's, "E", to attend at the mortuary at 2p.m., 3rd to carry out the necessary arrangements for further preservation of the body, previous to burial; but Mr. Allers, finding that it was a matter of impossibility to solder up the vessel which then contained the "Remains" without allowing the spirit to escape; the arrangements were postponed.

I then conferred with him and the Dr. as to what were the best steps to be taken in the course of which Mr. Allers suggested that a case, properly constructed, be supplied; which, if I thought fit he would make at reasonable cost. The Dr. having concurred in the suggestion, I directed Mr. Allers to make the case, which he did.

At 2p.m. 4th they again attended at the mortuary, when the transfer of the body was effected, spirit added, and effectually soldered down.

For making the case (2 ft. 7 in. long; 1 ft. 9 in. wide; and 1 ft. 2 in. deep; soldering etc.) Mr. Allers charged 12/-; which I have paid; and for which I respectfully ask authority.

The case was then handed over to the Sanitary Authorities; who placed it in a black painted wooden box (?) and arranged to carry out the interment at 10 a.m. today at the East London Cemetery, Grange Park, Plaistow, Essex.

I attended at the cemetery at time specified and witnessed the interment. It was placed in Grave No 16185, and upon the metal plate on box (?) was the following:

> "This case contains the
> "body of a woman (unknown)
> "found in Pinchin Street
> "St. Georges-in-the-East
> "10th Septr./89."

Henry Moore Inspr.

Jno West

ActgSupt

CHAPTER 30

Inspector Moore Interviewed About the Whitechapel Murders

Inspector Henry Moore, as we have seen, was one of the Detective Inspectors sent from Scotland Yard to investigate the Whitechapel Murders. He took over as the inspector in charge of the enquiry when Abberline moved on to other investigations in early 1889. Just before the Pinchin Street torso case an American journalist from Philadelphia, R. Harding Davis, visited London and researched a story on the infamous murders. His endeavours were reported in the *Pall Mall Gazette* of 4 November 1889:

THE WHITECHAPEL TRAGEDIES.
A NIGHT SPENT WITH INSPECTOR MOORE.
REMARKABLE STATEMENTS.

Philadelphia journalist, Mr. R. Harding Davis, has been publishing in a syndicate of American papers, an account of a night he spent upon the scene of the Whitechapel murders, towards the end of August, in the company of Police Inspector Moore, in the course of which some interesting statements occur.

DR. ANDERSON ON CRIMINAL "SHOW PLACES."

Mr. Davis had taken a letter of introduction to Dr. Robert Anderson, the head of the Criminal Investigation Department, who remarked to him, "I am sorry to say on your account and quite satisfied on my own that we have very few criminal 'show places' in London. Of course, there is the Scotland Yard Museum that visitors consider one of the sights, and then there is Whitechapel. But that is all. You ought to see Whitechapel. Even if the murders had not taken place there it would be still the show part of the city for those who take an interest in the dangerous classes. But you mustn't expect to see criminals walking about with handcuffs on or to find the places they live in any different from the other dens of the district. My man can show you their lodging houses and can tell you that this or that man is a thief or a burglar, but he won't look any different from anyone else." The journalist suggested that he had never found they look any different from any one else. "Well, I only spoke of it because they say, as a rule, your people come over here expecting to see dukes wearing their coronets and the thieves of Whitechapel in prison-cut clothes, and they are disappointed. But I don't think you will be disappointed in the district. After a stranger has gone over it he takes a much more lenient view of our failure to find Jack the Ripper, as they call him, than he did before."

INSPECTOR MOORE.

Proceeding to Leman-street police station at nine o'clock at night in fulfilment of an engagement made by Dr. Anderson, Mr. Davis found the entrance to the station barricaded with several crossings of red tape. It was very different from the easy discipline of an American police station, and from the nights when, as a police reporter, I walked unquestioned into the roll room and woke up the sergeant in charge to ask if there was anything on the slate, and to be told sleepily that there was "nothing but drunks" The superintendent introduced me to a well-dressed gentleman of athletic build, whom he said was Inspector Moore, the chief of the detective force that has since April 8, 1888, covered the notorious district of the Whitechapel murders. The inspector has been twenty years in the force, and it was his work on the murder committed by the American, Lamson, that brought him the distinguished and most unwelcome work on which he is still engaged.

A TEXAN POLICE-CAPTAIN APOLOGIZES TO THE LONDON POLICE.

Inspector Moore led the journalist through the network of narrow passageways as dark and loathsome as the great network of sewers that stretches underneath them a few feet below. "The chief of police from Austin, Texas, came to see me," said the inspector, "and offered me a great deal of advice. But when I showed him this place (Castle-alley) and the courts around it he took off his hat and said: 'I apologise. I never saw anything like it before. We've nothing like it in all America.' He said that at home an officer could stand on a street corner and look down four different streets and see all that went on in them for a quarter of a mile off. Now, you know, I might put two regiments of police in this half-mile of district and half of them would be as completely out of sight and hearing of the others as though they were in separate cells of a prison. To give you an idea of it, my men formed a circle around the spot where one of the murders took place, guarding they thought, every entrance and

approach, and within a few minutes they found fifty people inside
the lines. They had come in through two passageways which my
men could not find. And then, you know these people never lock
their doors, and the murderer has only to lift the latch of the nearest
house and walk through it and out the back way." In the course of
their perambulations, the inspector tells the correspondent that they
call Whitechapel the "three F's district, fried fish and fights." After
they had passed through a well-known lodging house, the correspondent asked the inspector if he did not feel nervous and he
handed him his cane for an answer. It was a trivial-looking thing,
painted to represent maple, but Mr. Davis found it was made of
iron. "And then they wouldn't attack me," Mr. Moore said, "It's
only those who don't know me that I carry the cane for."

WHITECHAPEL OVERRUN WITH SPIES.

The inspector gazed calmly up and down the street, and then
remarked, apparently to a lamp across the way. "Better write; you
mustn't come too often." We walked on in silence for half a block,
and then I suggested that he was using amateur as well as
professional detectives in his search for the murderer. "About
sixty," he replied laconically. The inspector was non communicative, but I could see and hear for myself, and a dozen times during
our tour women in rags, lodging-house keepers, proprietors of
public-houses, and idle young men, dressed like all the other idle
young men of the district, but with a straight bearing that told of
discipline, and with the regulation shoe with which Scotland yard
marks its men, whispered a half sentence as we passed, to which
sometimes the inspector replied or to which he sometimes appeared
utterly unconscious. From what he said later I learned that all
Whitechapel is peopled with these spies. Sometimes they are only
"plain clothes" men, but besides these he has half a hundred and at
times 200 unattached detectives, who pursue their respectable or
otherwise callings while they keep an alert eye and ear for the
faintest clue that may lead to the discovery of the invisible
murderer.

A HORRIBLE SITUATION FOR "JACK THE RIPPER."

"This was about the worst of the murders," said the inspector
when they reached Dorset-street. "He cut the skeleton so clean of
flesh that when I got here I could hardly tell whether it was a man or
a woman. He hung the different parts of the body on nails and over
the backs of chairs. It must have taken him an hour and a half in all.
And when he was ready to go he found the door was jammed and

had to make his escape through the larger of those two windows.''
Imagine how this man felt when he tried the door and found it was
locked; that was before he thought of the window – believing that
he was locked in with that bleeding skeleton and the strips of flesh
that he had hung so fantastically about the room, that he had trapped
himself beside his victim, and had helped to put the rope around his
own neck. One would think the shock of the moment would have
lasted for years to come, and kept him in hiding. But it apparently
did not affect him that way, for he has killed five women since then.
We knocked at the door and a woman opened it. She spoke to
some-one inside, and then told ''Mister Inspector'' to come in. It
was a bare whitewashed room with a bed in one corner. A man was
in the bed, but he sat up and welcomed us good naturedly. The
inspector apologized for the intrusion, but the occupant of the bed
said it didn't matter, and obligingly traced out with his forefinger
the streaks of blood upon the wall at his bedside. When he had done
this he turned his face to the wall to go to sleep again, and the
inspector ironically wished him pleasant dreams. I rather envied his
nerve, and fancied waking up with those dark streaks a few inches
from one's face.

"NOW, WHY ISN'T THAT JACK THE RIPPER?"
''What makes it so easy for him'' – the inspector always referred to
the murderer as ''him'' – ''is that the women lead him, of their
own free will, to the spot where they know interruption is least
likely. It is not as if he had to wait for his chance; they make the
chance for him. And then they are so miserable and so hopeless, so
utterly lost to all that makes a person want to live, that for the sake
of fourpence, enough to get drunk on, they will go in any man's
company, and run the risk that it is not him. I tell many of them to
go home, but they say they have no home, and when I try to
frighten them and speak of the danger they run they'll laugh and say,
'Oh, I know what you mean. I ain't afraid of him. It's the Ripper or
the bridge with me. What's the odds?' And it's true; that's the
worst of it.''

The inspector feels his work and its responsibilities keenly. He
talked of nothing else, and he apparently thinks, eats, and sleeps on
nothing else. Once or twice he stopped, and pointing to a man and
woman standing whispering on a corner, said, ''Now, why isn't
that Jack the Ripper?''

Why not indeed. When I was in the Scotland-yard museum I
expressed some surprise that there were no relics on exhibition of

the Whitechapel murders, the most notorious series of criminal events in the history of the world when one considers the civilization of the city and of the age in which they have occurred, and the detective who was showing me about said, "We have no relics; he never leaves so much as a rag behind him. There is no more of a clue to that chap's identity than there is to the identity of some murderer who will kill some-one a hundred years from now."

WHERE SUSPICION HAS RESTED.

But they have thought they had clues. They have thought they had the murderer himself perhaps, hundreds of times. Suspicion has rested, so the inspector said, on people in every class of society — on club men, doctors and dockers, members of Parliament and members of the nobility, common sailors and learned scientists. In two squares the inspector pointed out three houses where he said he had gone to find him. He told the story to illustrate the degradation of the women of the district, but the point of interest in them to me was that in a space of 200 yards he had found three houses where the murderer was supposed to be hiding. This shows that there must have been hundreds of men suspected of whom the public have heard nothing. Inspector Moore said his own detectives, amateur and professional, would occasionally follow each other for a week in the idea that they were tracking the murderer.

"And then we are so often misled by false clues, suggested by people who have a spite to work off. We get any number of letters throwing the most circumstantial evidence about a certain man, and when we run it out we find some woman whom he has thrown over. All this takes time and money, and from the nature of our work we can say nothing of what we are doing; we can only speak when it is done. I have received 2,000 letters of advice from America alone; you can fancy how many I get from this country.

"And then there is the practical joker who sends us letters written in blood and bottles of blood, parts of the human body or the entrails of animals which he says he took from his victim. It is not an easy piece of work, I assure you. I work seventeen and eighteen hours a day. If I get into bed I think maybe he is at it now, and I grow restless, and I finally get up and tramp the courts and alleys till morning."

It had been a five hours' walk through more misery, vice and crime than can perhaps be found in as small a space, less than a square mile, in any other great city. There had been only eight murders then. And as we neared the station I remember the inspector's pointing into the dark arches of the London, Tilbury, and Southend Railway, and saying: "Now, what a place for a murder that would be." A week later, while I was in mid-ocean on my way back, the body of the ninth victim was found just under those very arches, and not three minutes' walk from the police station. I don't know whether Jack the Ripper was lurking near us that night and had acted on the inspector's suggestion, or whether the inspector is Jack the Ripper himself, but the coincidence is certainly suspicious. As for myself, although I assented to its being a good place for murder at the time, I can prove an alibi by the ship's captain.

CHAPTER 31

An Allegation Against Sergeant Thick
– Further Allowance Claims

An extraordinary allegation that one of the Metropolitan Police's
finest was none other than "Jack the Ripper" was made by a
member of the public in September 1889. It was made against
Sergeant William Thick of H Division who had played a prominent
part in the investigations of the Whitechapel Murders in 1888.
  The file cover[1] is as follows:

[Stamped: – HOME OFFICE 11 SEP.89 RECEIVED] No. A49301/177
DATE 10 Septr: 89   Mr. H. T. Haslewood.
REFERENCES, &c.   Whitechapel Murders
Believes the murderer is a Policeman. Upon hearing that his name
shall not be mentioned in any way, (especially to the Police) will
forward the name of the officer. Pressing
                         MINUTES.
This seems ridiculous and perhaps should not be encouraged, but it
would do no harm to? say that if he will forward the name and any
other particulars it will be kept strictly confidential.
              Write as suggested   HBS
                 E P. 13. Sept   11.9.89
                    Wrote 13/9

The letter[2] received from Mr Haslewood appears, and is as follows:

Official 11/9/9. DSS Pressing [Stamped: – HOME OFFICE 11
SEP.89 RECEIVED]
              [?] 3.P.M.   White Cottage A49301/177
                              High Rd.
                              Tottenham
                              10 Sept 1889

Sir,
  I have very good grounds to believe that the person who has

committed the Whitechapel murders is a member of the police force, – upon hearing from you that my name shall not be mentioned in any way especially to the police, I will immediately forward you the name of the officer who I suspect of course it is only a suspicion, based upon very slight evidence, but with the assistance of the police records you could in a very few minutes ascertain where this person was on the respective days of the murders, you could also ascertain if he was now suffering from any complaint that might effect his mind at certain seasons,

Yours obediently,

To the Rt. Hon. HMatthews   H. T. Haslewood,
      Home Office
      Whitehall.-

There then follows a second minute cover[3] as follows:

[Stamped: – HOME OFFICE 21 OCT.89 RECEIVED] No. A49301/193
DATE 14 Oct. 1889.   Mr. H.T. Haslewood.
REFERENCES, &c.   <u>East End Murders.</u>
    Recommends that Sergt. T. [*sic*] Thicke be watched, as he thinks he is the murderer. Desires that his name be kept strictly secret.

[MINUTES.]

[*Marginal note* – *[illegible]* "Progress not having been made confidential JM[?] Ackd. 21.10.89."]
see minute on /177.
I think it is plainly rubbish – perhaps prompted by spite.
    ?shall it go to Mr. Anderson (to be treated as confidential in view of the promise given on /177.)
CT
21.10.89

The name of writer   GL
must not be given   22 Oct '89.
        Sent copies (with name and address omitted).
HBS
24.10.89

A further letter[4] from Mr Haslewood follows:

A49301/177   A49301/193
    [Stamped: – HOME OFFICE 21 OCT.89 Received]   White
Cottage

High Rd
Tottenham
14 Oct 1889.

Sir,

    Referring to yours of the 13th Sept. I beg to state that through the
information I have received I believe that if Sergt T. Thicke otherwise
called "Johnny Upright" is watched and his whereabouts ascertained
upon other dates where certain women have met their end, also to see
what deceace he is troubled with, you will find the great secreate this is
to be strictly private and my name is not to be mentioned.

Yours faithfully,

E.L. Pemberton Esq.   H.T. Haslewood.

A file cover[5] dated 18 September states:

H.O.
18 Sept.
Whitechapel Murders
Stating with reference to H.O. letter of 17 July (attached) that the S
of S has sanctioned the 1 Inspr 5 PSs and 50 PCs being retained for
special duty in Whitechapel for a further period of 1 month expiring
on 16 pm
Accountant.

E.U.

19/9/89
[*illeg.*] to note – There will probably be Refreshment allowances for
these men. – CC/19/9 Noted.
[*illeg*] 19.9.89

A report[6] dated 18 September 1889, from E. Leigh Pemberton to
the Receiver for the Metropolitan Police District, is as follows:

Pressing A48000M/44   WHITEHALL.

18 September 1889.

Sir,

    With reference to the Home Office letter of the 17th July last, I am
directed by the Secretary of State to acquaint you that he has signified
his sanction for the augmentation of 1 Inspector 5 Sergeants and 50

Constables for special duty in Whitechapel, being retained for that
work for a further period of one month expiring on the 16th proximo.

I am,
Sir,

The Receiver for the   Your obedient Servant,
Metropolitan Police District   E LeighPemberton.
&c. &c. &c.

The discovery of "the Pinchin Street torso" had the effect of raising
fears that a killer was still abroad in the Whitechapel district, even
though the police did not believe that it was another "Ripper"
crime. It therefore brought further requests for allowances for
additional officers drafted into the area from other Divisions.

A report[7] dated 18 September 1889 is as follows:

No. A49301G/10
DATE 18 Sept. 1889   The Commissioner of Police.
REFERENCES, &c.   Asks that the plain clothes allowances granted to the men employed in plain clothes in Whitechapel
may be continued until such employment cease.

MINUTES.

? sanction for another 2 months from 17th.

HBS
20.9.89
EUP. 21 Sept 89
Wrote Comr. &Recd.
24.9.89.
sa(1/11)
96318   A49301G/10

4, Whitehall Place,
S.W.
18th September, 1889.

[*in margin*: – A49301G/9]
Sir,

With reference to your letter of the 3rd ultimo sanctioning the
payment, for a period of two months, of the plain clothes allowance
of 1/- a day to the 3 Sergeants and 39 Constables employed in plain
clothes in Whitechapel, I have to acquaint you, for the information
of the Secretary of State, that as the duty commenced on the 17th
July last that authority has now expired, – and I have accordingly to
request that Mr. Secretary Matthews may be pleased to sanction a

continuance of this allowance during such time as it may be deemed
advisable to retain these men for special duty in Whitechapel. –

I am,

Sir,

Your most obedient Servant,

J.Monro.

The Under Secretary
of State
&c. &c. &c.
Home Office.

A file cover[8] reads as follows:

H.O.
24 Sept.
Whitechapel Murders
Sanctioning the continuance of the plain clothes allowance to the 3 PSs &
39 PCs employed for a further period of 2 months dating from the 17th inst.
Accountant to note
this authority
ARP
26 Sept
WWilby
            CG
Done   27/9/89.

There follows a similar cover[9] for October 1889:

H.O.
3 Oct
Whitechapel murders
Sanctioning the payment to the 2 PSs and 12 PCs, augmented for
duty in Whitechapel in consequence of the discovery of human
remains in Pinchin Street, of the usual plain clothes allowance of 1/-
a day from the 11th ulto.
Accountant to note
this authority
ARP
WFesting
5 Oct 89
Noted HJW [?] 12/10/89

The report[10] appears:

5185/11   4 OCT.89
A49301/186

WHITEHALL.
3rd October 1889.

Sir,

   I am directed by the Secretary of State to acquaint you with
reference to the augmentation of 2 Sergeants and 12 Constables
for employment in plain clothes in Whitechapel in consequence
of the discovery of human remains in Pinchin Street on the 10th
Ultimo, that he sanctions the payment to these men of the usual
plain clothes allowance of 1s/- per diem as from the 11th
ultimo.

                         I am,
                              Sir,
                         Your obedient Servant,
The Receiver for the   E. Leigh Pemberton
Metropolitan Police District.
    &c.   &c.   &c.

The next cover[11], dated 11 October 1889, is as follows:

H.O.
11 Octr.
Whitechapel Murders. Special Allce.
The grant of special plain clothes allowance of 1s/- per diem is
sanctioned (as from 11th ulto.) to 3 addl. PCs; the Commr. having
reported the No. to be 15 and not 12.
Accountant to note
ARP
14 Oct 89
W Wilby Done.

A further file cover[12] appears and is dated 26 October 1889, as
follows:

H.O.
26. Octr.
Whitechapel Murders.
Sanctions the retention of the augmentation of 1 Inspr. 5 P.S. & 50

P.C., for specl. duty in Whitechapel, for a further period of one
month from 16th inst.
Accountant to note as
augmentation of police
&[*illeg.*]
Noted CC : Noted AJW

This is not a fresh augmentation – on reference to the two letters in
/9 it will be seen that 1 Insp. 3 P.S. & 30 P.C. temporarily
augmented some time ago for duty in Trafalgar Square were
transferred to Whitechapel, with the addition of 2 P.S. & 20
P.C. for a period of 2 months, & that subsequently by letter of 18
Sept the time was extended to 16 Oct: By this letter the period is
further extended to 16 Nov:
    Mr. Wilby to note as regards the allowances – &pps Done –
CC
31/10

5185/13   28 OCT.89
A48000M/45   WHITEHALL.
                                 26th October, 1889

Sir,
    I am directed by the Secretary of State to acquaint you with
reference to previous correspondence that he has sanctioned the
retention of the augmentation of 1 Inspector, 5 Sergeants and 50
Constables for special duty in Whitechapel for a further period of
one month from the 16th instant.
I am,
Sir,
Your obedient Servant,
Godfrey Lushington

The Receiver
for the Metropolitan
    Police District,

The following month further reports[13] were submitted regarding
the augmented officers, as follows:

[Stamped: – 14 NOV 1889 – Receiver for Metropolitan Police
District]
H.O.
13th Nov.

Whitechapel, augmentation
Sanctions retention of 100 men for 1 month.
Accountant
to note
Augmentation of police
Noted CC. ARP
15.Nov Mr [ ] to note as reg [ ] allowances.
CC

15/11

[*illeg initials*]

A letter[14] follows:

5185/14   14 NOV.89
Pressing   A50657/14
WHITEHALL.

13 November 1889.

Sir,
    With reference to previous correspondence, I am directed by the Secretary of State to acquaint you that he has signified to the Commissioner of Police approval of the retention for a further month of the special augmentation of 100 men for duty in Whitechapel.

I am,

Sir,

Your obedient Servant,

E. LeighPemberton.

The Receiver for the
Metropolitan Police District
    &c.   &c.   &c.

The augmentation to the strength of officers in Whitechapel was the subject of further claims[15] in November, with a file cover[16] dated 16 November 1889, as follows:

[Stamped: – HOME OFFICE 18 NOV.89 RECEIVED] No. A49301G/11
DATE 16th Novr. /89   Commissioner of Police
REFERENCES, &c.   re Continuance of the Plain Clothes allowance to 3 Sergeants & 39 constables employed in Whitechapel on special duty/
    Requests that the S of S may be pleased to sanction a further continuance of this allowance for one month.

MINUTES.
? Sanction for a month from 16th inst.
HBS
CM 20. 20.11.89.
EUP. 21. Nov. 89./
Wrote Commr & Recd.
22/11.

This is followed by a report[17]:

[Stamped: – HOME OFFICE 18 NOV.89 RECEIVED] A49301G/11
4, Whitehall Place, S.W.
16th November 1889.

96318/15.
[*In margin* – A 49301 B./10]
Sir,

With reference to your letter of the 24th September last sanctioning the continuance of the plain clothes allowance to 3 Sergeants and 39 constables, employed in Whitechapel on special duty, for two months dating from the 17th idem, I have to request that Mr. Secretary Matthews may be pleased to sanction a further continuance of the allowance for a period of one month.

I am,
Sir,
Your most obedient Servant,
The Under   J.Monro
Secretary of State
&c.   &c.   &c.

The usual cover[18] regarding the sanction granted appears, as follows:

H.O.
19 Novr.
Whitechapel Murders
Sanctions continuance of augmentation of 1 Insp. (for special duty) 5 P.S. 50 P.C. for another month from 16th instant.
Accountant note
Noted CC ARP
20.11.89
[*illeg sig*]

The Home Office letter[19] follows:

5185/15

Pressing A48000M/46   WHITEHALL.

19 November 1889.

Sir,

    With reference to previous correspondence, I am directed by the Secretary of State to acquaint you that he has approved of the continuance for one month as from the 16th instant of the augmentation of 1 Inspector 5 Sergeants and 50 Constables for special duty in Whitechapel.

I am,
Sir,
Your obedient Servant,

The Receiver for the   E. Leigh Pemberton.
Metropolitan Police District
&c.   &c.   &c.

The next file cover[20] appears, as follows:

H.O. 22 Novr.
Whitechapel Murders
Sanctions continuance, for two months as from 17th inst., of plain clothes allowance to 3 P.S. & 39 P.C. employed on special duty.
Accountant
[ ]
Noted.
Noted CC [ ]

There is a document[21] dated 5 December 1889 and marked "CLOSED UNTIL 1990 HO144/221/A49301I", as follows:

A49301/2
No. 5227/107 & 108 [Stamped: – HOME OFFICE 6 DEC.89 RECEIVED]

Office of the
Metrop
4, Whitehall Place, S.W.
5th Decr. 1889.

Sir,

    I have the honor to transmit for the information of the Secretary of State, Accounts of Expenses incurred by various Police Officers on special occasions, and to request authority for payment of the same, the Commissioner having approved thereof, vizt.

Inspector Moore   £27 : 7 : 5
 — do —   £49 : 3 : 7
                            Murders in Whitechapel.

Minutes
To Under Secretary
? sanction
  HBS
  16.12.89
  C.M.   Wrote to Receiver   I have the honor to be,
                18 Dec: 1889.   Sir,
                                    Your obedient Servant,
The Under Secretary of State   A:A:[*illeg.*]
  &c. &c. &c.
     Home Office.

A report[22] on the conditions in the East End is included in the files, dated 27 December 1889 and signed by the Chief Commissioner, as follows:

B7590
With refce. to the article by Mr. Barnett, there is no doubt, as I have already reported that vice of the lowest type finds a refuge in the slums of Whitechapel, and that the localities to which he refer are about as bad as can be found in London. If the area containing the dens where Whitechapel vice flourishes could be cleared, there is no doubt that Whitechapel would be immensely benefitted. Where the residuum of vice thus transferred is to find a resting place is another question which must not be lost sight of.

    Police do all that they can to keep violence & vice within bounds, but their duties are confined to the streets, and their efforts there can do nothing to strike at the root of the evil, which is not to be found on the streets, but in the dens to which the abandoned & criminal classes resort. This is a matter which can only be dealt with by the landlords of these houses, and if by any pressure put upon this class, better dwellings can be provided — and better dwellings mean better tenants — an improvement in the moral surroundings of

Whitechapel will be effected, which will be heartily welcomed by the police.

27.12.89.   J.Monro

The augmentation of police patrols in Whitechapel continued into the new year, and the first report[23], dated 18 January 1890, is as follows:

[Stamped: – HOME OFFICE 20 JAN.90 RECEIVED] No. A49301G/12

DATE 18 Jan: 1890   Commissioner of Police
REFERENCES, &c.   Men employed on special duty in Whitechapel

Proposes to gradually reduce the number.

The strength at present is 3 Sergts. & 26 constables.

Requests approval of renewal of plain clothes allowance of 1s/- per diem to these men for a further period of one month.

<u>Pressing</u>

MINUTES.

? Sanction and inform Receiver

          W B
          22.1.90

Saying in such a matter as this S.S. feels that he must rely implicitly on the direction of the Commissioner that such a diminution of force may be accomplished with safety to the public.

                                                            C.M.
Mr Matthews to see   G.L.   Jan 23.
          H.M.   23 Jan '90
          27 Jan.90   Wrote Comr & Recd
                                        30.1.90.
                                        see (1/13)

The report[24] follows:

A49301G/312

9618/21. [Stamped: – HOME OFFICE 20 JAN.90 RECEIVED]
                              4 Whitehall Place, S.W.
                              18th January, 1890.

Sir,

     With reference to previous correspondence [*A49301g/11*] on the subject I have to acquaint you for the information of the Secretary of

State, that I propose to gradually reduce the number of men employed on special duty in Whitechapel. I have already been able to effect a considerable reduction, and the strength at present specially employed is 3 Sergeants, and 26 Constables. These I think it advisable to retain for the present, and I have to ask that the Secretary of State may be pleased to approve of the renewal of the plain clothes allowance of 1s/- per diem to these men for a further period of one month.

I am, Sir

Your most obedient Servant,

J.Monro

The Under
    Secretary of State,
        &c. &c. &c,

The next cover[25] is stamped:- RECEIVER FOR THE METRO-POLITAN POLICE DISTRICT REGISTERED 5185/17:

H.O.
30 Jany.
Whitechapel Murders. Allces &c.
Forwarding copy of letter to Commr., authg continuance of plain clothes allowance to 3 P.S. and 26 P.C. for another month.
Accountant to note.
    ARP
     31 Jany 90
Noted CC
[*illeg. sgs.*]
5/2/90.

The report[26] of 30 January 1890 reads:

31/1 [Stamped: – RECEIVER FOR THE METROPOLITAN POLICE DISTRICT REGISTERED 5185/17. JAN 31 1890] 31 JAN.90
No. A49301G/12   WHITEHALL.
                    30th January, 1890.
Sir,
    With reference to previous correspondence, I am directed by the Secretary of State to transmit herewith for your information and guidance a copy of a letter which he has this day addressed to the Commissioner of Metropolitan Police as to the renewal for another

month of the plain clothes allowance to the 3 Sergeants and 26 Police
Constables who are at present specially employed in Whitechapel.

I am,

Sir,

Your obedient Servant,

The Receiver   E.Leigh Pemberton
for the Metropolitan
    Police District.

The next file cover[27] is dated 12 February 1890, as follows:

No. A49301G/13

DATE   12 February 1890.
REFERENCES, &c.   Police employed in Whitechapel.
    Requests that the Plain Clothes allowance to officers
specially employed as above may be renewed for a further
period of one month.
1/12   Pressing.

MINUTES.

? Sanction, and inform Receiver.

C.M. Feb: 13.90.

EUP. 13 Feby 90

Wrote Comr &Recd 14/2/90.

Commr. a/17.3.90 (./14)

The report[28] follows in the usual manner, dated 12 February 1890:

Pressing 96318/23 [Stamped:- HOME OFFICE 13 FEB.90 RE-
CEIVED] A49301G/13.

4 Whitehall Place, S.W.

12th February, 1890.

Sir,
    With reference to your letter of the 30th ulto. on the subject of
the Plain Clothes allowance to the Police specially employed in
Whitechapel, I have to ask that the Secretary of State may be
pleased to approve of the renewal of the allowance to these officers
for a further period of one month.

I am,

Sir,

Your most obedient Servant,

J.Monro.

The Under
Secretary of State,
    &c. &c. &c.

The police file cover[29] reads:

H.O.
14 Feby 90
Whitechapel Murders. &c
S of S has sanctioned the renewal for another month of the plain
clothes allowance to officers specially employed.
Accountant to note
      ARP
[WF] 17 Feby 90
[ ]20/2/90

The following month saw the continued use of a reduced number of
the officers on special duty in the Whitechapel district with regard
to the previous murders. File cover[30] dated 17 March 1890 refers as
follows:

[Stamped:- HOME OFFICE 18 MAR.90 RECEIVED] No.
A49301G/14
DATE 17 March 1890.   Acting Commissioner of Police.
REFERENCES, &c.   Police officers specially employed in
Whitechapel.
Requests approval of continuance of the allowance to 2 Sergeants
and 11 constables for further period of one month.
1/13
               MINUTES.
? Sanction and inform Receiver.
[ ]
19.3.90   CM 20.
           ELP. 21st March 90.
           Wrote 28/3/90.

The report[31] then follows:

[Stamped:- HOME OFFICE 18 MAR.90 RECEIVED] A49301G/
14
96,318   END

4, Whitehall Place,
S.W.
17th March, 1890.

Sir,

Referring to your letter of the 14th ultimo approving of the renewal for a further period of one month of the Plain Clothes' allowance to the Police officers specially employed in Whitechapel, I have now to ask that the Secretary of State may be pleased to approve of the continuation of the allowance to a portion of these officers, i.e., 2 Sergeants and 11 Constables for a further period of one month. —

I am,
Sir,
Your most obedient Servant,
A.C.Bruce
Acting Commissioner

The Under Secretary
of State
&c. &c. &c.
Home Office

CHAPTER 32

September 1889 – Dr Forbes Winslow Names a Suspect

After the publicity created by the discovery of the Pinchin Street torso the press embarked on a fresh run of stories based on the renewed "Ripper" scare. The following article appeared in the *New York Herald*, and was included in one of the now-missing files. Fortunately it is possible to include the relevant material as it was photocopied, before its loss, in the 1970s:

THE WHITECHAPEL MURDERS.

A report having been current that a man has been found who is quite convinced that "Jack the Ripper" occupied rooms in his house, and that he had communicated his suspicions in the first instance to Dr. Forbes Winslow, together with detailed particulars, a reporter had an interview with the doctor yesterday afternoon on the subject. "Here are Jack the Ripper's boots," said the doctor, at the same time taking a large pair of boots from under his table. "The tops of these boots are composed of ordinary cloth material, while the soles are made of indiarubber. The tops have great bloodstains on them." The reporter put the boots on, and found they were completely noiseless. Besides these noiseless coverings the doctor says he has the "Ripper's" ordinary walking boots, which are very dirty, and the man's coat which is also bloodstained. Proceeding, Dr. Winslow said that on the morning of Aug. 30 a woman with whom he was in communication was spoken to by a man in Worship Street, Finsbury. He asked her to come down a certain court with him, offering her £1. This she refused, and he then doubled the amount, which she also declined. He next asked her where the court led to, and shortly afterwards left. She told some neighbours, and the party followed the man for some distance. Apparently, he did not know that he was being followed, but when he and the party had reached the open street he turned round, raised his hat, and with an air of bravado said: "I know what you have been doing; good morning." The woman then watched the man into a certain house, the situation of which the doctor would not describe. She previously noticed the the man because of his strange manner, and on the morning on which the woman Mackenzie was murdered (July 17) she saw him washing his hands in the yard of the house referred to. He was in his shirt-sleeves at the time, and had a very peculiar look upon his face. This was about four o'clock in the morning. The doctor said he was now waiting for a certain telegram, which was the only obstacle to his effecting the man's arrest. The supposed assassin lived with a friend of Dr. Forbes Winslow's, and this gentleman himself told the doctor that he had noticed the man's strange behaviour. He would at times sit down and write 50 or 60 sheets of manuscript about low women, for whom he professed to have a great hatred. Shortly before the body was found in Pinchin-street last week the man disappeared, leaving behind him the articles already mentioned, together with a packet of manuscript, which the doctor said was in exactly the same handwriting as the Jack the Ripper letters which were sent to the police. He had stated previously that he was going abroad, but a very few days before the body was discovered (Sept. 10) he was seen in the neighbourhood of Pinchin-street. The doctor is certain that this man is the Whitechapel murderer, and says that two days at the utmost will see him in custody. He could give a reason for the head and legs of the last murdered woman being missing. The man, he thinks, cut the body up, and then commenced to burn it. He had consumed the head and legs when his fit of the terrible mania passed, and he was horrified to find what he had done. "I know for a fact," said the doctor, "that this man is suffering from a violent form of religious mania, which attacks him and passes off at intervals. I am certain that there is another man in it besides the one I am after, but my reasons for that I cannot state. The police will have nothing to do with the capture. I am making arrangements to station six men round the spot where I know my man is, and he will be trapped." The public had laughed at him, the doctor went on to say, but on the Tuesday before the last body was discovered he had received information that a murder would be committed in two or three days. In conclusion, Dr. Winslow remarked, "I am as certain that I have the murderer as I am of being here."

The chairman of the Whitechapel Vigilance Committee, Mr.

Albert Backert [*sic*], stated yesterday that the police at Leman-street Station having received a letter stating that it has been ascertained that a tall strong woman has for some time been working at different slaughter-houses, attired as a man, searching inquiries were made yesterday morning at the slaughter-houses in Aldgate and White-chapel by the police. It is presumed that this has something to do with the recent Whitechapel murders, and it has given rise to a theory that the victims may have been murdered by a woman. It is remarked that in each case there is no evidence of a man being seen in the vicinity at the time of the murder.

This is followed by a report by Chief Inspector Swanson dated 23 September 1889 for which no reference is given:

METROPOLITAN POLICE
Criminal Investigation Department,
Scotland Yard,
23 day of Septr   1889

SUBJECT Whitechapel
Murders

I beg to report that I saw Dr Forbes Winslow at No. 70 Wimpole Street today, and in reply to me he said first that the statement in the newspapers was a misrepresentation of a conversation with a New York Herald reporter who had called upon him in reference to an autograph book he has. Gradually the reporter drew him into a discussion about the Whitechapel Murders, and the reporter gave him to understand the discussion would not be published, but he was much surprised and annoyed to see it, especially as it so misrepresented what he said. I pointed out to him that he had not given information to police about any suspect except the foreigner at the Charing Cross Hospital, and that there was a statement in the papers to the effect that he had. He denied having said so to the Press. He produced a pair of felt galoshed boots such as are in common use in Canada, and an old coat. The felt boots were motheaten, and the slough of the moth worm remained on one of them. He then stated that the information which he relied upon was as follows:- Related by Mr. E Callaghan of 20 Gainsborough Square, Victoria Park, on Augt. 8th 1889.

"In April, 1888, my wife and myself were residing at 27 Sun Street, Finsbury Square, the upper part of our house was let off to various gentlemen. In answer to our advt: we put in Daily

Telegraph a Mr. G. Wentworth Bell Smith, whose business was to raise money for the Toronto Trust Society; applied and took a large bed["room" – *deleted*] sitting room. He said that he was over here on business and that he might stay a few months or perhaps twelve. He told us that before he had come to us he had an office at Godliman Street at the back of St Pauls. Whilst at home he occupied himself in writing on religious subjects; sometimes as many as 60 sheets of foolscap were filled up with such material. Whenever he went out of doors he would wear a different suit of clothes to what he did the day before. He had many suits of clothes and quite eight or nine hats. He kept very late hours and whenever he came in it was quite noiseless. He had also a pair of India rubber boots to put over his ordinary ones to deaden any possible sound. On Augt 9th (*altered to 7th*) the date of one of the murders, Mrs Callaghan was in the country, and her sister kept house in her absence. she was however expected home that evening and we sat up for her till 4.a.m. at which hour Mr Bell Smith returned stating that he had had his watch stolen in Bishopsgate Street, which on investigation proved to be false. Shirts were found hanging on his towel horse he having washed them himself, and marks of blood on the bed. This I saw myself. Two or three days after this murder of Augt. 9th, with the stated reason of returning to Toronto. I however found that he had not done so, but he did not return to my house. He was seen getting into a tramcar in Septr. of 1888. We all regarded him as a lunatic and with delusions regarding "Women of the streets," who he frequently said ought to be all drowned. He told me that he was greatly impressed with the amount of immorality in London; and said that a number of whores walked up and down St. Pauls Cathedral during the service. He also said that women in the East End especially ought to be drowned. He also had delusions respecting his wealth stating that he had large wealth at his command. At night he would talk and moan to himself frequently. One day he said, "Physically I am a very weak man, but the amount of my willpower is so great that I am able to outwork several men." implying that he had great brain power. Frequently on his return he would throw himself down on a sofa and groan. He kept concealed in a chest of drawers in his room three loaded revolvers. He would if taken by surprise by anyone knocking at his door rush and place his back against this chest. The following post card came on[e] day for him signed "Dodger, we can't get through it. Can you give us any help." I gave this information to the police in August after the man left my house, and curiously enough the detectives came over to my house to make enquiries also about this same man, at the instigation of a lady from the Surrey side of the water. The writing of Bell Smith is in every way similar to that sent to the Police & signed Jack the Ripper. I am positive that he is the man. He is about 5 ft 10 in in height walks very peculiarly with his feet wide apart, knees weak and rather bending in, hair dark, complexion the same, moustache and beard closely cut giving the idea of being unshaven, nice looking teeth probably false, he appearede well conducted, was well dressed and resembled a foreigner speaking several languages entertains strong religious delusions about women, and stated that he had done some wonderful operations. His manner and habits were peculiar. Without doubt this man is the perpetrator of these crimes."

Sept. 9. 1889.

A woman in the East End on Sunday at 2 am told Mr Callaghan that she saw a man on 30th. inst, who accosted her in Worship Street Bishopsgate She noticed him particularly as she remembered him as being the man that she saw washing himself in a yard at the back of her house about 4 am on the morning of one of the Whitechapel murders. He was in his shirtsleeves, his coat being thrown onto a wooden fence. She drew the neighbours attention, and the neighbours watched him into Sun Street. Finsbury, where he arrived about 4 30am. He raised his hat to the man when he left him evidently knowing that he had been followed. At the meeting on Sunday last, the man asked her to have a drink but this was refused. She knows the man perfectly well and could identify him. The description in every way coincides with the man who lodged with Mr Callaghan. She says he has a small black bag with him. At the time mentioned before when he was seen washing hands. on the morning of the murder he asked the woman where the Court went to. She often had noticed the man as a foreign looking man prowling about the neighbourhood.

The foregoing is the information he possesses. He does not know the name of the woman, but Mr Callaghan could tell. I am unable to find any such information given by Callaghan. It would be after the murder in George Yard, and before the 31st. of Augt. The matter was then in the hands of H Divn. Inspr Abberline has no record of the information. Dr Winslow desired the return tonight of the printed matter which I have copied.

Donald SSwanson

Ch Inspr

George H. Greenham

pro Supt

Documents returned by post with thanks.   Donald SSwanson

Ch Inspr

CHAPTER 33

October 1889 – Another Extraordinary Suspect

The renewed press – and consequently public – interest in the
Whitechapel Murders was marked by the emergence, as we
have seen, of fresh allegations about suspected persons. A
suspect who emerged at the beginning of October 1889 was
typical of such accusations received by the police. The point
here is mainly to show the nature of such reports and how
they were properly dealt with and investigated by the police. In
this case the allegation was received in the form of an
anonymous letter dated 1 October 1889. The initial file cover[1]
is as follows:

[Stamped: – HOME OFFICE 2 OCT. 89 DEP] No. A49301/187
DATE 1 Octr. 89   Anonymous
REFERENCES, &c.   Whitechapel Murders
               Gives particulars respecting the mysterious
          movements of a Certain Doctor.
                    MINUTES.
          ? To Police
               W.T.B.
                    3.10.89.
                         ELP. 4 Oct.89
               Index
[Stamped: – REFERRED 5 – OCT. 89]

The letter[2] then follows:

["Private & Confidential" – *deleted*]   Octr. 1./89
[Stamped: – HOME OFFICE 2 OCT. 89 DEP] Whitechapel
Murders (Supposed important & remarkable Clue.)
A49301/187
Sir, Last Thursday night Sep 26 I had unasked for, a communication
made to me respecting a gentleman & beg to forward you the

particulars as made to Mr. Williamson, Criminal Investigation Office 21 Whitehall Place yesterday at 12.30 – 1PM.-

A gentleman representing himself as a Dr. in practice, took a small furnished backroom (6/6 per wk) at xxxxxxxx Rd. Kensington on the 16th inst. He stated that he came from SBG. He only goes out for short periods, does not get up till late & retires early. He is rather strange in his manners, agreeable & affable to the opposite sex but seemingly rather inquisitive concerning the occupants of the house. He has two portmanteaus (1 large & 1 smaller) also a rug or rugs. In one of his portmanteaus he has surgical instruments &c. He is a strong, well built man about 45 to 50 years of age & about 5.9 in height, rather dark complexion with short dark whiskers, beard & moustache. Wears a high hat (but has others) & check morning coat or suit. Has a curious walk (taking short steps) & his voice is rather peculiar. Stated his wife to be in a Lunatic Asylum but since, that she is lost (dead) also that he has inserted advt. In "Lancet" for situation & has had Photograph taken to send to those he is negotiating with.

Now Sir., the following very remarkable series of coincidences have occurred to me, all of which are perfectly reliable & accurate (without any exaggeration) & can be proved, –

Last Wednesday night I saw a picture in "Scraps" & asked my sister whom it resembled – she guessed.

(The following day I heard about the Dr.) On Friday I paid a visit to my sister again & related the clue I thought I had discovered. About $\frac{3}{4}$ hour later her husband came in & greeted me in a jocular manner "Jack the Ripper they will have you yet" (he had never said this before) – ordinary conversation followed. Just as we sat down to dinner ($\frac{1}{2}$ hour later) he says "There is an amusing story in 'Scraps' about a doctor sharpening his knives and a gentleman being frightened by the cook telling him that the Dr. intended cutting his 2 ears off." (Picture enclosed). I then related my story to him which until then he had not heard. Strange to say that the picture I pointed out, although older, somewhat resembles the Dr. in features . . .

I called at the Home Office yesterday morning at 12 to see you. Was referred to Whitehall Place where I made, as before stated a communication to Mr Williamson furnishing him with address & name given of Dr. & urging him to make enquiries, which he promised to do.

About 7 o'clock last night I paid another visit to my sister & she said to me "have you seen The Telegraph". I replied "No" but I had the Standard & Morning Post. She pointed out the paragraph Page 5 which to my astonishment seemed to corroborate my ideas in a remarkable manner. I immediately took train to London again & went to Whitehall Place & Scotland Yard at 8.30. Pointed out to both Inspectors the paragraph but could not make them take any immediate measures. Then afterwards forwarded by post to Mr. Williamson the paragraph which he should get by 1st post to day. The last letter purporting to be written by Jack the R-was found at Victoria Rd. Kensington last Saturday which is within ¼ hours' walk of Dr's lodgings.

I may in conclusion state that I am the reverse of being super-stitious & I have always scorned the ideas. The story however & corroboration being so remarkable I consider it to be of the utmost vital importance that immediate enquiries should be made.

Not wishing my name to appear in any way I beg to sign, as given to Mr. Williamson, should he wish to communicate with me.

Yrsobedly –

By Daily Telegraph
"H" call at Whitehall.
P.S. At present have had no communication with newspapers & others respecting the above.

The cutting of the cartoon from "Scraps" is then included. [See illustration]

A second file cover[3] concerning this allegation is then included,

[Stamped: – HOME OFFICE 10 OCT. 89 RECEIVED] No. A49301/191
DATE 9 Octr. 89   Asst. Comr. Anderson
REFERENCES, &c.   Whitechapel Murders
                                        Fds Police report respecting the
                          mysterious movements of a certain Doctor.
                                  MINUTES.
                          No Police report was required about this. v/187
                          was merely sent to the Police as are all other
                          communications respecting the Whitechapel mur-
                          derer are.
                                  ? Lay by
                                        WTB
                                  11.10.89 GL
                                        12 Oct "89

There then follows a pro-forma letter[4] from Anderson to the Under-Secretary of State, dated 9 October 1889:

[Stamped: – HOME OFFICE 10 OCT.89 RECEIVED]A49301/191
[reference – 57885/290]

Great Scotland Yard
9th day of October 1889

From
ASSISTANT COMMISSIONER OF POLICE,
Criminal Investigation Department.
To THE UNDER SECRETARY OF STATE
FOR THE HOME DEPARTMENT,
etc. etc. etc.

Sir,
  With reference to the papers, No. A49301, herewith returned, regarding the mysterious movements of a certain doctor,
  I have the honour to transmit, for the information of the Secretary of State a Report of the inquiries which I have caused to be made on the subject.

I have the honour to be,
Sir,
Your most obedient Servant
A.F.Williamson
Chief Constable
For ASSt. COMMMr.

There then follows a handwritten report[5] by Chief Inspector Swanson:

[Stamped: – HOME OFFICE 10 OCT. 89 RECEIVED and METROPOLITAN POLICE RECEIVED 8-.OCT.89 CRIMINAL INVESTIGATION DEPT.] A 49301/191
METROPOLITAN POLICE.
CRIMINAL INVESTIGATION DEPARTMENT,
SCOTLAND YARD.
7th day of October 1889.

SUBJECT Anonymous
Com. To Home Office
Re a Doctor out of practice
Whom writer thinks is a
Murderer.

With reference to the attached anonymous communication, I beg to report that the writer states that a person representing himself as a Doctor out of practice took a small back room furnished at a rental of 6s/6d per week in 51 Abington Road, Kensington. The grounds of suspicion that he might be the Whitechapel murder [*sic*] being:-
1st. That he had surgical instruments in his possession. 2nd. That the Doctor was eccentric in his manner, but affable to ladies. And 3rd. that a comic sketch appeared in a paper called "Scraps". in which a Doctor invited a guest to dine off a hare but the cook having eaten the hare herself, frightened the guest by telling him that the Doctor was sharpening his knives to cut his ears off. The sketch of the Doctor in Scraps, the writer alleges to resemble the Doctor whom he suspects. 4th That a letter signed Jack the Ripper was found in the streets at Kensington.

The foregoing are the whole grounds of suspicion, no one of which affords ["affords" – *deleted*] grounds to justify that the Doctor is in any way connected with the Whitechapel murders. That a Doctor or surgeon should possess surgical instruments is perfectly natural. His manner towards ladies does not point to him as being the sexual maniac who committed the outrages in the East End. The reference to the caricature in Scraps is absurd, and the finding of a letter signed Jack the Ripper in Kensington considering that similar letters have been found in every quarter of London, does not point to the Dr. as being a murderer. The anonymous communication, I submit is the product of an excited imagination, which has jumped at a conclusion without an atom of proof.

Under these circumstances the police have not felt themselves justified in making enquiry respecting the Doctor as the Whitechapel murderer.

Donald SSwanson
ChInspr.
J.Shore Supt.

CHAPTER 34

November 1889 – Another Foreign Suspect

The continued interest in the Whitechapel murders remained truly international, and the Home Office received yet another communication from the Foreign Office with a theory from abroad. The file cover[1], much damaged, is as follows:

[Stamped: – [HOME OF]ICE [89] [RE]Cd. DEPt] No. A49301D/8
[DATE] 1889   Foreign Office
[REFERENCES,] &c.   Whitechapel Murders
                    Forwards despatch from H. M.
                    Minister in Brazil as to a statement
                    enclosed from an Italian detailing a
                    conversation he overheard of two men
                    it appeared to refer to these murders.
                            MINUTES.
Seal [?] up with   ["Confidential" – *deleted*]
ordinary done with Papers
                    To Commissioner of Police.
                        C.M. Nov:14.89.
                            Indexed To Commr.
                                        [*illeg.*]
                    This story is altogether too vague, and the length of time
                    (over 2 years!) which has elapsed since these mysterious
                    strangers seen on the quay at Genoa, too [ ] of any action
                    being taken in [ ]

                                                [ ]
                    Ch: Inspr. Swanson to see.
                        Seen
                            Donald S.Swanson
                                ChInspr.
                    [ ] F.O.
                        thanks
                            & Lay By C.M. 20.

There follows the letter[2] from the Foreign Office:

<u>Translation</u>
[Stamped: – HOME OFFICE 14 NOV.89 RECd.DEPt.]
A49301D/8
Sir,

Y.E. will excuse the writer for communicating in Italian, as, not knowing English & having but a slight acquaintance with French, I am compelled to use my own language.

My object in addressing this letter to Y.E. is to furnish the British authorities with some information, which tho' somewhat late, may perhaps prove useful, in regard to certain great crimes recently committed in London.

I arrived in Brazil in November 1887, and having found employment at once in the interior of the Province, I have spent nearly two years far from any large city and consequently without news of many events in Europe. On my return to S. Paulo, towards the end of last month, many European newspapers, dating from the close of last & the early months of the present year, came into my hands, & these mentioned the mysterious crimes committed against women in London. The knowledge of these crimes brought back to my memory an occurrence which I had forgotten, which occurred on the eve of my departure from Italy & which I will now endeavour to relate to Y.E.

On the evening of Oct. 18. 1887, at about 5 o'clock, I was standing with my wife & children on the mole of the harbour of Genoa, awaiting the arrival of the "Savoye" which was to convey us to Brazil, & while the children walked about with their mother, I leant against the parapet, watching the horizon & the ships & boats coming & going. I was so absorbed in this, that I took no notice of a small boat which came up to the steps & landed two persons of respectable appearance, when presently my attention was called towards my right by voices proceeding from the furthest angle of the battery, defending the harbour. I leaned forward & listened. At first I only heard the words. "I do not believe it I do not see clearly the object of these armies. I do not wish to have anything to do with it" & other phrases which I do not remember. Then a voice speaking with a foreign & probably English, accent said "So you do not wish to have anything to do with it, and refuse to come to ["England" – *deleted*] London. Then I must conclude that you are a coward" (This was said in bad Italian) The other voice replied with a pronounced accent of the Neapolitan provinces.

"I said no & I repeat it. I have accompanied you this far. I have been to India, & have done all that you wished & have had more than enough of it already. I do not wish now to run my head against the English Police, for, believe me, London is not like India, as you know even better than I do, and when you have ripped up two or three women, there will be the devil of a row & who knows how it may end."

The other replied, but I could not hear what he said, except "Then this is your last word?" and after a "yes" which I heard, he continued "I shall go alone, let me have the Portmanteau & the irons by the time the steamer leaves tomorrow for Marseilles. I will write to you from Paris, & if you want me write to me to the usual address, at. . . ." (here followed a name which I forget) "Do not trust anybody, but write in Italian, since you have not yet learned English in a single year –"

I only heard indistinct words in reply.

I was seized with strong curiosity & wishing to see what the speakers were like, I took one of my children by the hand, & walked round the angle of the battery, where I found myself at three or four paces from the two men who had landed from the boat a short time before. On seeing me, they gave a sort of start, but then got up carelessly, and beginning to talk in a loud voice of the sea & of travels, & they proceeded towards the city.

But if they were surprised at seeing me, I too was greatly impressed by their appearance, for their two faces, though very different one from the other, were such as when seen once, remain impressed for a lifetime. I will give a description of them as well as I can.

The one who spoke Italian well was somewhat short of stature thin, very pale, with a low forehead, small black eyes & black moustache, & hair. He wore a long, dark, frock coat (frac) similar trousers & a black glazed hat (capello nero ingommato) The other, – the one who seemed to me to be English – was rather tall, large boned, and stout, with a high forehead, bushy eyebrows, prominent cheekbones, & a large nose. He had no moustache, but whiskers of a light brown colour, and two eyes which when half closed, seemed to flash fire. He wore a long dark grey overcoat, dark trousers & a hard hat like the other.

My first thought was to go to the nearest police station & give information of all that I had heard, but the reflection that doing so might lead to a delay in my sailing & to trouble & annoyances induced me to remain silent, tho' I did so unwillingly.

I left, came to Brazil & forgot the matter & was only reminded of it recently when I read the account of the crimes committed in London. I accordingly wrote the present letter to Y.E. in the hope that it may be of some use & declare myself ready to furnish any additional information which I may bring to mind.

I have &c

(sgd) P. Jose Vanzetti

140 Rua Comercio da Luz

Sao Paolo. 27 August 89

The file cover[3] is as follows:

Copy

Signor Vanzetti

   to

Mr. Wyndham

S. Paulo Aug. 27. 1889

Whitechapel Murders:

   Encl

in Mr. Wyndham's

No. 118 of October 13

   1889

There then follows a letter[4] from Mr Wyndham to Lord Salisbury:

Copy   [Stamped: – HOME OFFICE 14 NOV.89 RECd. DEPt.]

A49301D/8

Rio de Janeiro

No 118   Oct. 13. 1889

My Lord,

I have the honour to enclose herewith to Y.L. copy & translation of a letter [*here there is a marginal note* – ''Sr. Vanzetti to Mr Wyndham. Aug 27.89''] which reached me on the 3rd ult. From an Italian, P.J. Vanzetti, who is now residing at Sao Paulo, and which purports to contain information bearing upon the recent murders in Whitechapel.

Some delay has occurred in my sending this letter to Y.L. as I begged the Italian Legation here on the 4th ult. to be so good as to make enquiries thro' the Italian Consul, at Sao Paulo as to the writer, and I have only recently received a reply, which is to the effect that Vanzetti is apparently a person to be relied on & that he is employed in giving lessons in Italian & gymnastics in the neighbourhood of the town of Sao Paulo. He stated to the consul that the appearance of the persons described in his letter is so engraved on his memory that he could perfectly recognise their photographs were they sent to him.

<blockquote>
I have &c
(sd) Hugh Wyndham
</blockquote>

The Marquis of Salisbury
 &c   &c   &c

The file cover[5] to this letter, is as follows:

Copy.
 Mr Wyndham
 No 118
<u>Whitechapel Mur</u>ders
Home Office

The covering letter[6] from the Foreign Office is included:

[Stamped:- HOME OFFICE 14 NOV.89 RECd.DEPt.] A49301D/8
<u>Confidential</u>   Foreign Office,
Sir,

 I am directed by the Secretary of State for Foreign Affairs to transmit to you, to be laid before Mr. Secretary Matthews the accompanying despatch and its enclosures, as marked in the margin ["Mr. Wyndham No 118. Oct 13. '89"], from Her Majesty's Minister in Brazil, relating to the Whitechapel murders.

<blockquote>
I am,
 Sir,
  Your most obedient,
   humble Servant,
    THSanderson
</blockquote>

The Under Secretary of State
 Home Office

CHAPTER 35

13 February 1891 – Murder of Frances Coles

The last murder included in the extant police and Home Office Files concerning the Whitechapel Murders is that of Frances Coles, which occurred on Friday, 13 February 1891 in Swallow Gardens, a passageway running under the railway arches between Chamber Street and Royal Mint Street. An important aspect of the police enquiry into the murder of Coles is that with this killing the police immediately felt that it might be connected with the earlier series of murders.

The file commences with a report[1] by Superintendent Thomas Arnold dated 13 February 1891:

The cover states: – Report stating that James T Sadler, who was charged with the murder of Frances Coles in Swallow Gardens Whitechapel in February 1891, and who has been residing at 121 Danbrook Rd., Streatham, intends removing to 108 Faraday St., Walworth Rd.

Metropolitan Police
H DIVISION
13th February, 1891.

I beg to report that at about 2.15 A.M. this day PC240H Thompson discovered the body of a female lying in the roadway in Swallow Gardens, Royal Mint Street, Whitechapel, and upon turning on his lantern he saw blood issuing from her throat. He immediately blew his whistle when P/S 101H Hyde and 275H Hinton came to his assistance, and the former went for Dr. Oxley of Dock Street who quickly attended and pronounced life extinct. PC 275 went to the Station, and Inspector Flanagan at once proceeded to the spot, and sent for Dr. Phillips Divisional Surgeon, myself, the Chief and Local Inspector and as quickly as [ ] men arrived despatched them to carefully search the neighbourhood and make inquiries of any person who could be found likely to give any information. Dr.

Phillips attended, examined the body and found two cuts in the throat, sufficient to account for death. The body was not mutilated in any other way. Immediately I arrived I ascertained that telegrams had been sent to surrounding Divisions apprising them of the occurrence and asking that careful inquiries should be made, and proceeded to direct other inquiries at Common Lodging Houses &c. The vicinity of Swallow Gardens was carefully searched, and in a space between a water pipe and some brickwork, about 18 yards from where the body was found Insp Flanagan discovered two shillings wrapped in two pieces of old newspaper apparently "Daily News" upon which however there is no date. there is nothing to connect this money with the murder nor has any instrument or article been found likely to afford a clue. The body was removed to Whitechapel Mortuary and searched, but nothing of importance was discovered.

The deceased is known to police of this Division as a Prostitute but at present has not been identified by any person, she is aged about 25, length 5feet, hair and eyes brown, dressed in old dark clothes, and appears of a low class. PC240H Thompson who is a young Constable having only joined on 29th Decr. last states that as he was passing along Chambers [*sic*] Street towards Swallow Gardens he heard footsteps apparently those of a man, proceeding in the opposite direction towards Mansell Street, but was not sufficiently close to discern the person. This was just immediately before he found the body and he asserts that when he first saw the deceased there was a movement of one of the eyelids. Be that as it may when the body was found it was quite warm & bleeding. The Constables on the adjoining Beats did not see any person passing about the time he mentioned.

William Friday, a Carman in the employ of the Great Northern Railway, states that at 1.45 A.M. he was passing through Royal Mint Street on his way to the stables when he saw a man and woman standing in a door way. He could not discern their faces distinctly but noticed that the woman wore a black hat. He has seen the hat worn by the deceased and identified it as that worn by the woman he saw talking in Royal Mint Street. He has also given a slight description of the man she was [with] but says he could not recognise him as he did not see his face.

Nothing further has at present been ascertained but inquiries are being prosecuted with a view to finding any person who may have been in the neighbourhood at the time the outrage was committed.

Dr. Phillips states that from the examination he has made the nature of the wound, the posture and appearances of the body &c. he does not connect this with the series of previous murders which were accompanied with mutilation.

Information has been sent to the Coroner and his officer.

T. Arnold Supt.

There is a report cover[2] from H Division CID:

Subject Murder / Body of a woman found in Swallow Gardens with her throat cut [*Stamped: – Received 13 Feb 91*] Sir E. Bradford to see. This case was reported to me in the middle of the night & I gave authority to send Supt Arnold all the aid he might require. The officers engaged in investigating the former Whitechapel murders were early on the spot, & every effort is making to trace the criminal. But as in former cases he left nothing, & carried away nothing in the nature of property, to afford a clew

RA 13/2/1

Seen & I have shown this to Mr Matthews & explained that I think it would be premature for us to venture taking opinion as to now for this case may obviously not be connected with any previous cases.

GRL/S
13/2.

As in former cases I wish to have a report each morning for the present.

RA
13/2

Memo sent
13/2/91   JS
             PS/

There is a report[3] by Sergeant Don as to the finding of the prisoner, James Thomas Sadler:

METROPOLITAN POLICE.
Criminal Investigation Department,
H Leman St.
16th day of February 1891

The Woman found murdered in Swallow Gardens.

I beg to report that about 12 noon, 14th inst in company with P.C. Gill. H. Dn. I was in Upper East Smithfield and from what I was told by a man named Samuel Harris I went to the Phoenix P.H. where I saw the prisoner. I called him outside and asked him if his name was "Sadler" he said Yes. I told him I was a Police Officer and that it was necessary he should come to Leman Street Police Station, as a woman had been found with her throat cut and it was alleged that he had been in her company the night previous. He stopped me and said, I expected this. On the way to the station he said, I am a married man and this will part me and my wife, you know what sailors are, I used her for my purpose for I have known Frances for some years. I admit I was with her, but I have a clean bill of health and can account for my time. I have not disguised myself in any way, and if you could not find me the detectives in London are no damned good. I bought the hat she was wearing and she pinned the old one under her dress. I had a row with her because she saw me knocked about and I think it was through her. He accompanied by P.C. Gill & myself came to the station & "Sadler" was handed over to Chief Inspr Swanson.

John Don P.S. R.
Henry Moore, Inspr.

There is then a statement[4] by James Thomas Sadler dated 14 February 1891, taken by Chief Inspector Donald S. Swanson, with the following on the cover sheet:

Swallow Gardens Murder/ Statement of James Thomas Saddler, Davies [?] Boarding House, East Smithfield/ Detained on suspicion of this above.

METROPOLITAN POLICE.
Criminal Investigation Department,
Scotland Yard,
14th day of February 1891.

Swallow Gardens Murder – James Thomas Saddler of Davies Boarding House, East Smithfield, says, I am a fireman and generally known as Tom Saddler. I was discharged at 7 p.m. 11th. inst. from S.S. Fez. I think I had a drink of Holland Gin at Williams Brothers at the corner of Gouldston Street. I then went at 8.30 pm to the Victoria Home. I then left the House and went into Princess Alice between 8.30 and 9 pm. I saw a woman, (whom I had previously known./ named Frances.) I had known her for eighteen months. I

first met her in the Whitechapel Road and went with her to Thrawl
Street, a lodging house, and I stayed with her all night; having paid
for a double bed at the Lod: Ho: I don't remember the name of the
Lod: Ho where I then stayed with her. I think I then took a ship the
name of which I do not now remember. I did not see this woman
again until I saw her in another bar of the Princess Alice, and
recognising her, I beckoned her over to me. There was nobody with
her. She asked me to leave the pub: ho: as when she had got a little
money the customers in the pub: ho: expected her to spend it
amongst them. We left the Princess Alice, and went round drinking
at other pub: hos:. Among other houses I went into a house at the
corner of Dorset Street, where another woman (named Annie
Lawrence) joined us. This is the woman pointing to Annie Lawrence
who was making a statement in the CID office. Frances stopped me
from treating this woman, and we then went to Whites Row
Chamber. I paid for a double bed and we stayed the night there.
[*marginal note* – "Wed. night"] She had a bottle of whiskey (half
pint) which I had bought at Davis, White Swan, Whitechapel. (I
took the bottle back yesterday morning and the young woman
(barmaid) gave me twopenny-worth of drink for it.) Frances and I
left Whites Row Chambers between eleven and twelve noon, and
we went into a number of pub: hos: one of which was [A] the
"Bell", Middlesex Street. We stayed there for about two hours
drinking and laughing. When in the "Bell" she spoke to me about a
hat which she had paid a shilling off. a month previously. We then
went [.] [C] on the way to the bonnet shop, drinking at the pub:
houses on the way. The shop is Whites Row or Bakers Row and I
gave her the half a crown, which was due for the hat, and she went
into the shop. She came out again and said that her hat was not
ready, the woman is putting some elastic on. We then went into a
pub: house in Whites or Bakers Row, and we had more drinks.
Then she went for her hat, and got it. and brought it to me at the
pub: ho: and I made her try it on.. I wanted her to throw the old
one away, but she declined, and pinned it on to her dress. Then
went to [D] the "Marlborough Head" pub: Ho: in Brick Lane. and
had some more drink. I was then getting into drink and the landlady
rather objected to Frances and me being in the house. I can't
remember what the landlady said now. I treated some men in the
house, I can't say their names. I had met them previously in the
same house. From there I had an appointment to see' a man Nicols in
Spital Street, and I left her there to see Nicols, arranging to meet

her again at a pub: ho: where I cannot say now, for I have forgotten it. We came down Thrawl Street and while going down a woman with a red shawl struck me on the head and I fell down, and when down I was kicked by some men around me. The men ran into the Lod: houses and on getting up I found my money and my watch gone. I was then penniless, and I then had a row with Frances for I thought she might have helped me when I was down. I then left her at the corner of Thrawl Street; without making any appointment that I can remember. I was downhearted at the loss of my money, because I could not pay for my bed. I then went to [F] the London Docks, and applied for admission, as I wanted to go aboard the S.S. Fez. There was a strict Sergeant inside the gate and a Constable. They refused me admission as I was too intoxicated. I cannot remember what hour this was as I was dazed and drunk. There was a Met. Police officer near the gate, a young man. I abused the Sergt. and Constable, because they refused me admission. There were some dock labourers coming out, one said something to me, and I replied abusively, and one of the labourers took it up saying, If the (Met) policeman would turn his back, he would give me a d-good hiding. The policeman walked across the road across Nightingale Lane, towards the Tower way, and as soon as he had done so, the labourers made a dead set at me, especially the one who took my abuse. This one knocked me down & kicked me, and eventually another labourer stopped him. I then turned down [H] Nightingale Lane, and the labourers went up Smithfield Way. I remained in Nightingale Lane for about a quarter of an hour feeling my injuries. I then went to the Victoria Lod: Ho: in East Smithfield and applied for a bed but was refused [G] as I was so drunk, by the night porter, a stout fat man. I begged and prayed him to let me have a bed but he refused. To the best of my belief I told him I had been knocked about. He refused to give me a bed and I left, and wandered about. I can't say what the time was. I went towards Dorset Street. I cannot say which way, but possibly Leman Street way. When I [E] got to Dorset Street I went into the Lod: Ho: where I had stopped with Frances on the previous night, and found her in the kitchen, sitting with her head on her arms. I spoke to Frances about her hat. She appeared half dazed from drink and I asked her if she had enough money to pay the double bed with. She said she had no money and I told [her] I had not a farthing but I had four pounds 15/- coming to me. I asked her if she could get trust, but she said she couldn't. I then went to the deputy, and asked for a night's lodgings on the strength of the money I was to lift next day, but was refused. I was eventually turned out by a man, and left Frances behind in the house. I then went, to the best of my belief, towards London Hospital, and [JJ] about the middle of Whitechapel Road a young policeman stopped me and asked where I was going, as I looked in a pretty pickle. I said that I had had two doings last night, one in Spitalfield and one at the docks. I said I had been cut or hacked about with a knife or bottle. Immediately I mentioned the word knife, he said, "Oh have you a knife about you", and he there and then searched me. I told him I did not carry a knife. My shipmates, one Mat: Curley, and another named Bowen know that I have not carried a knife for years. The policeman helped me across the road towards the Hospital gate. I spoke to the porter but he hummed and hawed about it, and I began to abuse him. However he did let me in and I went into the Accident Ward and had the cut in my head dressed. The porter asked me if I had any place to go, and I said "No," and he let me lay down on a couch in the room where the first accidents are brought in. I can give no idea of the time I called at the Hospital. When he let me out, somewhere between six and eight in the morning I went straight to the Victoria House and begged for a few halfpence but I did not succeed. I then went to the shipping office where I was paid £4.15.3. Having got my money, I went to the Victoria Upper East Smithfield and stayed there all day as I was miserable. The furthest I went out was the Phoenix about twelve doors off. I spent the night there, and I was there this morning. I had gone to the Phoenix this morning to have drink, and I was beckoned out and asked to come here (Leman Street), and I came.

As far as I can think it was between five and six that I was assaulted in Thrawl Street; at any rate it was getting dark, and it was some hours after that, that I went to the London Docks. I forgot to mention that Frances and I had some food at [B] Mrs. Shuttleworths in Wentworth Street.

My discharges are as follow –
last discharged 11.2.90 [*sic* – 91] in London ship "Fez" –
next discharge 6.9.90 London
next discharge 15.7.90 London.
next discharge 27.5.90 Barry.
Next discharge 1.10.89 London.
Next 2.10.88 London.
Engaged 17.8.88.

Next 5.5.87.

Engd. nx. 24.3.87. London.

The last I had seen of the woman Frances was when I left her in the lod: ho: when I was turned out. The lod: house deputy can give you the time.

The clothes that I am now wearing are the only clothes I have. They are the clothes I was discharged in, and I have worn them ever since. My wife resides in the country, but I would prefer no to mention it.

The Lodging House I refer to is Whites Row, not Dorset Street. It has a large lamp over it. Passing a little Hackster shop at the corner of Brick Lane and Browns Lane. I purchased a pair of earrings, or rather I gave her the money and she bought them. I think she gave a penny for them.

This statement was read over to Saddler, who said it was correct as far as he could recollect

> Donald SSwanson
> Ch Inspr.
> T. Arnold Sup.

There can be no doubt that the police treated Sadler very seriously as a suspect for the Whitechapel Murders. This is apparent not only from the fact that he was personally interviewed by Swanson himself, but that an attempted identification of him for the City Police's Mitre Square murder was carried out. The police evidently thought that they had, at last, arrested "Jack the Ripper". The *Daily Telegraph* of Tuesday, 18 February 1891 carried the relevant report:

THE WHITECHAPEL MURDER.
EVIDENCE AT THE INQUEST.
SADLER'S ANTECEDENTS.

It was yesterday proved that the Treasury authorities attach the greatest importance to the arrest of the ship's fireman, Sadler, who is in custody for the murder of Frances Coles, in Swallow-gardens, on Friday morning last. At the resumed inquest Mr. Charles Mathews instructed by Mr. Pollard, was present to examine the witnesses, with the permission of the Coroner, Mr. Wynne Baxter, who whilst assenting to the arrangement, seemed impressed with its unprecedented character. Further, it is certain that the police are not neglecting the facts which came to light in connection with the previous murders. Probably the only trustworthy description of the assassin was that given by a gentleman who, on the night of the Mitre-square murder, noticed in Duke-street, Aldgate, a couple standing under the lamp at the corner of the passage leading into Mitre-square. The woman was identified as one victim of that night, Sept. 30, the other having been killed half an hour previously in Berner-street. The man was described as ''aged from thirty to thirty-five; height 5 ft 7 in, with brown hair and big moustache; dressed respectably. Wore pea jacket, muffler, and a cloth cap with a peak of the same material.'' The witness has confronted Sadler and has failed to identify him.

Further enquiries into Sadler's antecedents reveals that he has a wife at Chatham, and he is believed to have been in the Hong Kong police, and also in the intervals of his voyages acted as a tram driver and conductor in the East of London. In yesterday's *Daily Telegraph* it was proved that he was in London on July 17, 1890-the date of the Castle-alley murder [*sic*], and left two days later in the Loch Katrine for the Mediterranean . . .

A report[5] submitted by Inspector Henry Moore concerning the identification of the murdered woman, Frances Coles, is as follows:

Swallow Gardens Murder Reference to Papers 57885-
METROPOLITAN POLICE.
Criminal Investigation Department,
H Division,
15th day of February 1891

With reference to the murder attached, I beg to report that the body of the murdered woman has now been positively identified as that of Frances Coles, an unfortunate, who has been in Whitechapel for about eight years, and is known to have lodged at various common lodging houses. She is not known to have had any kind of regular employment for many years, although she has given out that she has been in employment, and also a statement made by her that she has resided with a respectable old lady at 32 Richardson Street, Commercial Road is untrue, as that is a fictitious address.

James Williams Coles, an inmate of the Bermondsey Work-house, Farmer Street, Bermondsey, has attended at the mortuary, and identified the body as that of his daughter Frances Coles, aged about 26 years, whom he last saw alive on the 6th instant when she visited him at the workhouse.

Mary Ann Coles, of 32 Ware Street, Kingsland Road, a single

woman, of no occupation, has also attended at the mortuary, and identified the body as that of her sister Frances Coles, whom she last saw alive about 6 weeks ago, when the deceased visited her at 32 Ware Street, Kingsland Road. She was then in good health, but very poor, and according to her statement was of drunken habits.

James Murray, of 33 Old Nichol Street, Bethnal Green, labourer, has identified the body as that of Frances Coleman, an unfortunate, whom he first met casually in the streets about 8 years ago, when she was staying at Wilmots lodging house, 18 Thrawl Street, Whitechapel. This man has been on intimate terms with her until about 4 years ago, and has frequently seen her since. She has walked about the streets during the whole of the past 8 years, principally about the neighbourhood of Whitechapel; but has also walked the streets in Shoreditch and Bow. She has lodged at various lodging houses in the neighbourhood of Commercial Street, and has for several years past given way to drunken habits.

Although the deceased was known to Murray as Frances Coleman, there is no doubt that her real name is Frances Coles, because he knew her to visit her father James Williams Coles at the Bermondsey Workhouse.

F. Kuhrt, Sergt.

Submitted   Henry Moore, Insp.

T Arnold Supt.

There is a Central Office report[6] included:

Subject Miscellaneous / Swallow Gardens Murder / Supt. Arnold HL / Submits photograph of the woman Frances Coles, who was found with her throat cut on morning of 13th instant / File with papers / [*sig. illeg.*] 19/2

METROPOLITAN POLICE.

Criminal Investigation Department,

Scotland Yard,

18th day of February 1891

Swallow Gardens Murder / Reference to papers 57885 /

I beg to submit herewith a photograph of deceased woman Frances Cole, who was found with her throat cut on the morning of 13th February instant

Henry Moore

Inspector.

T Arnold Supd.

There is then a lengthy report[7] by Chief Inspector Swanson dated 21 February 1891, giving the "History of Sadler". Marginal references are shown in parentheses, thus [ ]:-

METROPOLITAN POLICE.
Criminal Investigation Department,
Scotland Yard,
21st day of February 1891

I beg to report that I proceeded to Chatham on 19th inst: and placed myself in communication with Supt: Coppinger of the local police. I learned from him, and his officers that Sadler was unknown to them as either belonging to, or working in Chatham. I then saw Mrs. Sadler at No. 3 Skinner Street; and explained to her that it was necessary to learn from her particulars as to her husband during the time she had lived with him. It was observable that a reaction had taken place in her mind, caused no doubt by the report of her interview with a reporter, which she admitted she had read in the newspapers. She refused to say more than that she had said all she would say, and it was in the papers. The reporter she said, was a tall dark man, wearing glasses, but he gave her no name, and she thinks she would recognise him again. After trying for over an hour to extract a statement from her; I got from her by question and answer a history of Sadlers employments in London during the time she resided with him. The points are shortly as follow:-

She met Sadler first in Chatham he was at that time a sailor, and after a short courtship, they were married at St Johns Church, Chatham. Beyond his mother she had never heard of any other relation. She had not seen nor heard from his mother for over six years, and she did not know her address. After marriage she went to reside with Sadler in a street near [A] the Elephant and Castle, the name of which she professes to have forgotten. At this time Sadler worked at [B] Torr's Tea warehouse in Cutler Street, Houndsditch as a labourer. Sadler did not like crossing London Bridge and they removed to a house in [C] Bucks Row, Whitechapel, the number of which she said she had forgotten, but the house was about the centre, and the people who resided in it were brush-makers working at a factory in the Minories. She had saved a little money from her savings as a servant, and from what Sadler earned by occasional work at Cutler Street, and this money, they managed to live. She doesnt recollect the date of residence. From there they

removed to [D] No 77 Tetley Street Poplar, and when residing here
Sadler became a conductor, which lasted only for some months. It
was while residing here, that the incident of the knife took place.
Reluctantly she admitted that it was time that she had taken a knife
away from him, and she declined to say why she had taken it away.
She said she had hidden it, but professed to be unable to say where.
She was however sure that Sadler did not get it again as she never
saw it with him again. She believed that a lodger, an Irishwoman,
whose name she did not know took the knife. She could give no
reason for her belief. This took place, she said, over eleven years
ago, and all she could recollect was that it was an ordinary pocket
knife, with some brass on the handle. She said she did not think she
could recognise it again. She had forgotten, too, the name of the
people in the house with her. From there they removed to [E] a
corner shop in Hurley Road, Lower Kensington where Sadler
carried on the business of a greengrocer, but it did not succeed.
From there they removed to [F] Manor St., Walworth, and Sadler
again went to work at the bed warehouse in Cutler Street. Their
residence here was not long, and next residence was in [G]
Colebrooke Terrace, Bethnal Green, in a house near the top of
the Terrace, with two maiden ladies, whose name she says she has
forgotten. The next residence she says she has quite forgotten, but
in 1888 they resided at [H] No. 2 Johnson St., Commercial Road,
where their separation took place in Augt of that year. This was
caused by a slight quarrel between them and he left her without
saying where he was going to, and a fortnight after, on 15th August,
she left London and went to reside with her mother at Chatham
where she has made her home ever since. Seven months had elapsed
after leaving London before she heard from him. She is sure it was
seven months, and then she got a letter from him asking her to meet
him at the Fenchurch St railway Station. She was late in keeping the
appointment; but met Sadler in the Street near the railway station.
They then walked about the streets looking at the shops, and they
stayed that night at a Coffee House opposite Mile End Gate. Sadler
had work at this time in the London or St Catherines Docks. It was
on a Saturday that she met him at Fenchurch Street. Sadler had to
work in the docks on the Sunday, and he asked her to meet him as
he came out at 4.30 or 5.30 p.m. She went to meet him, going
down a Street opposite Commercial Street; as far as a railway arch,
and she stood there by some steps waiting for him. She saw a
number of men come from the docks, but did not see Sadler. Then

after waiting $\frac{1}{2}$ an hour he came up to her from a restaurant near the arch, where he had been standing and said to her How long are you going to stay, dont you know me? She replied, "I know you, now, you speak." From there they went to a pub: ho: in Whitechapel where Sadler had some drink and began to quarrel with the customers in the compartment and she went outside the pub: ho: and waited for him. When he came out he began to "nag" her, and she said to him "You know the life I have led with you, you had better go your way and I'll go mine." Then they walked along Whitechapel Road, and he wanted to take her to a place where a woman had been murdered, but she said, "No it does not interest me." When we got as far as Whitechapel Church, she says, she ran away from him, and he ran after her and caught her and tried to make the quarrel up, saying, "Sally, you'll look over it." He did not say, "You're not afraid of me." Then she said, he asked her to go into an eelshop to have a "feed" of eels, and he did so to make up the quarrel. She went in with him and while there a woman said to him "Holloa Tom, how are you?" and he said, "All right." Mrs Sadler says she did not speak to the woman, whom she would not recognise again, and they then left the eelshop, and went to the Coffee House where they were staying and stayed with him till Monday morning, when she left and returned to Chatham. That was the only time she had stayed with him in London since August 1888. His character she said was that when he liked, he could be as good as could be, and rough when he wanted to. When he was in drink he was irritable. After he had smashed the things on one occasion, he was sorry for it. He did not stay out at nights, he used to come home sometimes at eight o'clock, and he generally had the drink before he came in.

Upon pressing her as to whether he had ever assaulted or threatened her, she declined to answer. She said that he never wrote to her besides the letter asking her to meet him. He only sent her the advance note, and she never knew where he resided in London. During her stay in Chatham he had visited her staying from a day to a week at a time, but she has no means of giving dates. The last time was in Decr. before C'mas. last.

She denied having said to the reporter that she had slept with friends on the night of Sunday, when they went into the eelshop. She denies that she said also, "You're not afraid of me," as being the expression Sadler used to her, and that what Sadler said to her in reference to the place where the murder had been committed was,

"It was miraculous that any person could do such a thing and get off."

Formerly Sadler wore whiskers when she resided with him but he cut them off as they were grey.

This was all I was able to get from her after over two hours trial. During the time I was with her there were three calls by reporters.

> Donald S.Swanson
> Ch Inspr.
> JohnShore
> Supt.

The file then contains the statement[8] of Thomas Fowles, dated 25 February 1891, witnessed by Sgt. Nearn:
 The cover sheet reads:

Subject – Information / Swallow Gardens Murder / Thomas Fowles, 13 St Georges Street E / 25.2.91 / Says that between 1 and 2 a.m. 13th he was talking to his young woman Kate McCarthy at the front door of her home which is next the Seven Stars Mint Street. / Sir Edward Bradford / These are two most interesting statements, & entirely clear up the mystery of "the man with the billy-cock hat" who was alleged to have been seen talking to Frances Coles near the archway, and who was believed by Mr Chas. [*Walters ?*] and the Treasury officials to be the murderer! / JWEllis [?] 26/2 / [*second sig. illegible*] / RA 27/

> METROPOLITAN POLICE.
> Criminal Investigation Department,
> Scotland Yard,
> 25th February 1891

Swallow Gardens Murder / Reference to Papers 57885/
 Thomas Fowles, 13 St Georges Street, E.
  Saith

I am a labourer and am employed as Hall Porter at the "United Brothers" Club Commercial Street E. I am engaged there from 6 pm until midnight, but it is generally after 12 o'clock before I leave.

I know Kate McCarthy she is my young woman, she works opposite to me, "Stowers" the wine merchants. On the evening previous to the murder she came to me at the Club, it was between half past seven and 8 o'clock. She stayed till it closed. I think it was about a quarter to one the next morning 13th. walked with her as far as her home in Mint Street next to the "Seven Stars", public house, we stood talking together at the front door for about an hour as near as I can judge, after which I bid her good night, and went home.

During the time I stood talking to Kate McCarthy, several men belonging to the Great Northern Railway Depot Mint Street, passed on the opposite side of the way, going towards the Minories. I know some of the men by sight, but not their names, one I knew by the name of Jumbo, and I passed a remark to my young woman that Jumbo looked as if he was drunk. I do not recollect either of these men passing any remark as they went by. The time would be as near as I can remember about 2 o'clock because I did not get with my young woman to her house until about one or a little after.

Beyond the men mentioned who passed while I was in Mint Street was a Constable, and he was on the opposite side of the way to me going towards Leman Street.

My mother resides at No. 10, Split Street, Back Church Lane. I only have letters addressed there.

At the time I stated I was wearing a black pilot monkey jacket, and a black felt hat, brown cord trousers

Thomas Fowles

Witness   JamesWNearn
Sergeant.

Submitted together with statement of Kate McCarthy; it will be seen that these statements will negative the evidence of Jumbo and the Knaptons', as to the man they saw being the probable murderer. Copies supplied to Treasury Solicitor.

Henry Moore, Inspr.
T Arnold Sup

The statement[9] of Kate McCarthy, with the above, is as follows:

METROPOLITAN POLICE.

Criminal Investigation Department,

Scotland Yard,

25th day of February 1891.

Kate McCarthy of No. 42 Royal Mint Street E
Saith.

I reside with my father brother and sister at 42 Royal Mint Street, and have done so all my life. I work at Messrs Stowers, wine Merchants Commercial Street E as a bottler.

I am engaged to a young man Thomas Fowles, who resides in Back Church Lane, the number of the house I do not know.

On Thursday evening 12th inst I went to the "United Brothers Club", Commercial Street, where Tom Fowles is doorman and he and I left together at about half past twelve, and walked together as far as 42 Royal Mint Street, arriving there at about 1.15 a.m. 13th inst. We stood talking together at the front door for about half an hour, until a quarter to two and Fowles then wished me goodnight or good morning, and I went straight to bed.

At about twenty minutes to two just before Fowles left me I saw the two Knaptons and another man pass on the opposite side of the Street towards the Minories, one of the Knaptons shouted out good night. Almost immediately afterwards Jumbo (who I know as well as the Knaptons) passed also on the opposite side of the Street, with a whip in his hand he was going towards the Minories.

During the time I stood at the door I saw no other person.

Kate McCarthy

Witness

James W Nearn Sergt
Sergeant

Submitted. Copy supplied to Treasury Solicitor. These are the persons who were seen by Friday alias Jumbo.

Henry Moore, Inspr
T Arnold Supd.

The next report[10] is by Inspector Henry Moore regarding the adjourned inquest, and dated 27 February 1891:

The cover of the report is a Central Office CID cover: Subject Inquests / Swallow Gardens Murder / Supt Arnold Submits daily report of Inspr Moore 27.2.91 / TAnld 28/2 / Mr Anderson to see / Seen RA 28/2.

METROPOLITAN POLICE.
Criminal Investigation Department,
Scotland Yard,
27th February 1891

Swallow Gardens Murder / (Daily Report)
Reference to papers 57885
With reference to the case of Frances Coles; who was found murdered at Swallow Gardens, Whitechapel, on 13th inst.

I beg to report that since yesterday no new development has taken place in connection with this case.

The adjourned inquest was resumed this morning at the Working Lads Institute, Whitechapel; before Wynne E. Baxter, Esq., coroner. Mr. Chas. Matthews appeared on behalf of Public Prosecutor; and Mr. Lawless watched the case for Sadler. At the conclusion of the evidence, which necessitated the calling of no less than 55 witnesses; the Jury retired after the summing up of the Coroner; and after an absence of 13 minutes they returned and returned a verdict of "Wilful Murder against some person or persons unknown"; and added a rider, "That the Police had done right in detaining Sadler." They also expressed satisfaction at the way P.S. Bush, C.O. had prepared the plans.

No persons have been detained on H Division during the day in relation to this case.

Henry Moore, Inspr.
T Arnold Supd.

There then follows a four-page report[11] by Inspector Moore, dated 2 March 1891, concerning enquiries made about the suspect Sadler:

METROPOLITAN POLICE.
Criminal Investigation Department,
Scotland Yard,
2nd day of March 1891.

Swallow Gardens Murder /
Reference to papers 57885.
Referring to attached and Assistant Commissioner's minute thereon.

I beg to report that enquiries have been made with reference to the points I have indicated by an initial letter in margin; and the following is the result:- "A" – As to residence in Street near Elephant and Castle.

I find that during the time "Sadler" was a Hackney Carriage Driver he resided at three addresses near the Elephant & Castle; Viz:- 101 Penton Place, Harrington Bulds; 36 Hurley Road Kennington Lane; and 29 Manor Place, Walworth Road; this was between the years 1876 and 1877, but no person can be found now that knew him at either of the addresses. "B" – As to Tea Warehouse, Cutler St., Houndsditch.

Sadler was employed at this warehouse from 1st December

1887, till 26th July/88. He was not again heard of until 15th Octr. of same year; when he was again employed and remained till March, 1889.

In 1887 he resided at 14 Thomas St., Harding Street, Commercial Road, "E"., where he rented a room at 3/- per week; his wife joined him there and ultimately they went to reside at 2 Johnson St., Commercial Road. "C" – As to Bucks Row. –

No information can be obtained respecting Sadler; but it is alleged that he on one occasion was employed at Messrs Brown & Eagle's Wool warehouse, Bucks Row; but the Firm have no knowledge of such being the case. "D" – As to 77 Tetley St., Poplar.

It has been ascertained from Rose Moriarty, now residing at 22 Cordelia St., Poplar, that between 13 and 14 years ago; when she lived at 77 Tetley St., Sadler and his wife lodged with her. He was then a Conductor of Metropolitan Stage Carriage. She remembers one day when he came into his dinner he quarrelled with his wife, who sought protection in her (Moriarty's) room; she was followed by Sadler who had a dagger shaped knife in his hand, and threatened her.

Having heard this; although so long ago, I thought it as well that Mrs Moriarty should have an opportunity of identifying the knife sold to "Campbell", accordingly she attended at "H.D." where the knife was placed with others; but failed to identify.

"E" – As to Hurley Road; see "A."

"F" – As to Manor Place; see "A."

"G" – As to Colebrook Terrace, Bethnal Green. Sadler resided with his wife at this address; which is now 47 Entick Street, Cambridge Road; with a Miss Duffield; this was between 11 and 12 years ago; they only remained four months, and Miss Duffield saw nothing more of either until about 2 years ago when she accidentally met them outside Whitechapel Church.

"H" – As to 2 Johnson St., Commercial Road; see "B".

"I" – As to Sadler's employ at London Docks. No information can be obtained as to Sadler being actually employed at either of the Docks; but this no doubt refers to his employment at the Tea warehouse in Cutler St., which belongs to the London, India Dock Comp'y.

Henry Moore, Inspr.
T Arnold Supd.

On 3 March 1891, Sergeant Kuhrt submitted a report[12] on further enquiries about Sadler:

METROPOLITAN POLICE.
Criminal Investigation Department,
H ["Scotland Yard" – *deleted*] Division,
3rd day of March, 1891.

Swallow Gardens Murder /
Reference to papers 57885

With reference to Chief Constable's minute dated the 23rd ultimo, respecting the movements of "Sadler" between the 16th and 20th July, 1889, I beg to report that I have made enquiries, and am of opinion it may be assumed that Sadler lodged during that time at the Victoria lodging house, No. 40 Upper East Smithfield. Mr. William Dann the keeper of the lodging house has informed me that he has known him between 18 months and 2 years, and he remembers hearing that he had been discharged from the "Bilbao" on 7th July, 1889, which ship afterwards went down with all hands, which I have ascertained to be correct. Mr. Dann further stated that Sadler, when lodging there, has always paid a week in advance, but he is quite unable to say whether or not he may have been absent on one or more nights of the period in question.

The murdered woman Frances Coles was at this time lodging at no. 18 Thrawl Street, Spitalfields. I have not been able to ascertain whether she knew Sadler at that time, he has never lodged there, but he may have taken a lodging with her for a night or more at some other place, because the deceased has been absent from her lodgings for a night or two, although nothing positive can be ascertained about the time mentioned. I have made enquiries at numerous other lodging houses, I have seen Matthew Curley and Frederick Bowen; ships firemen, who have known Sadler since the 24th December last, and were his mates, whilst he was on board S.S. Fez, on her last passage, and made general enquiries, but have been unable to obtain any additional information.

I beg to add that the S.S. Loch Katrine in which Sadler embarked on the 20th July, 1889, is at present lying off the Fresh Wharf, near London Bridge. Captain Donald Cameron, who is in charge of her, has been questioned, and states that he joined the vessel on the 1st January, 1890, and that no person is now employed in her, who was on board at the time when Sadler served in her.

F Kuhrt, Sergt. G.

Submitted. Henry Moore, Inspr

T Arnold Supd

Another daily report[13] on the Swallow Gardens murder, by Inspector Henry Moore, follows, dated 3 March 1891:

CENTRAL OFFICE / C.I.D. Reference SERIOUS CRIME NO. 756 55 / Submitted to A.C.,C.I.D. / Subject Results / Swallow Gardens Murder / Supt Arnold Submits daily report of Inspr Moore / 3. 3. 91. / Mr Anderson 4/3 Seen RA.

METROPOLITAN POLICE.

Criminal Investigation Department,

Scotland Yard,

3rd day of March, 1891

Swallow Gardens Murder (Daily Report) Reference to Papers 57885 /

With reference to the case of Frances Coles; who was found murdered at Swallow Gardens on 13th Ins.

I beg to report that since yesterday several statements have been taken; but no good result still had obtained from them; except to prove that the statements previously made and evidence given before the Coroner by Ellen Colanna [?] alias Calman is [ ]; especially with regard to the assault upon her which resulted in her receiving a black eye. Special report submitted.

The prisoner James Thomas Sadler was today again brought up at Thames Police Court, before F. Mead Esqr. Mr. Charles Matthews appeared on behalf of Police Prosecutor; and Mr. Lawless appeared for accused; and upon the application of the former, prisoner was discharged. Sadler on his liberation was taken away in a cab by Mr. Wallis, his solicitor, and a representative of the "Star" Newspaper. As the cab left the court yard cheers were raised by the crowd on behalf of Sadler.

No persons have been detained on this Division during the day in connection with this case.

Henry Moore, Inspr.

T Arnold Supd

There is a file cover[14] dated 6 March 1891 concerning refreshment claims for CID Sergeants working on the case:

HO 144/221
      No. A49301G/15   [Marked – "CLOSED UNTIL 1992"]
DATE. 6th Mch91.   Commissioner of Police
REFERENCES, &c.   Special <u>Refreshment Allowance Whitechapel</u>
<u>Murder</u>
    Asks for grant of special refreshment of 2/- per day to Sergeants of C.I.D. employed in connection with the recent Whitechapel Murder.
1/8

MINUTES.

See-
  8
      ?Approve.
        ET
       10. 3. 1891.
          CWS[?]
           11.3.91
            Wrote Commer. &
             Receiver 11/3/91

The report[15] about the above is as follows:

A49301G/15

[Stamped: – HOME OFFICE 7 MAR.91 RECEIVED]
96318/.   New Scotland Yard, S.W.
                           6th March, 1891.

Sir,
    With reference to your letter of the 1st August, 1889, A49301G/8, sanctioning a special Refreshment Allowance of 2/- a day to those officers of the Criminal Investigation Department who had been brought to Whitechapel from other Divisions in connection with the then recent murders there, I have the honour to acquaint you, for the information of the Secretary of State, that on the occurrence of the Swallow Gardens' murder of the 13th ult. similar arrangements for the attendance of C.I.D. officers were made; and I have to ask that the Secretary of State may be pleased to authorise the grant of a special refreshment allowance at the rate of 2/- per

day, as before, to the Sergeants of the Criminal Investigation Department so employed.

I am,

Sir

Your most obedient Servant,

The Under   E. Bradford.
      Secretary of State,
           &c,

There is a file cover[16], dated 12 March 1891, as follows:

[Stamped: – RECEIVER FOR THE METROPOLITAN POLICE DISTRICT REGISTERED 5185/19 MAR.12 1891]
H.O.
11 Mar
Whitechapel Murders. Special allowance
Sanctions grant of special allowance of 2/- a day to P.S.'s C.I.D. employed re late murder on same conditions as previous allowances.
Accountant to
note
          ARP
13.3.91
W[ ]
[   ] 14/3/91

The report[17] follows, dated 11 March 1891:

A49301G/15 [Stamped: – RECEIVER FOR THE METROPOLITAN POLICE DISTRICT REGISTERED 5185/19 MAR 12 1891]

WHITEHALL.
11th March 1891

Sir,
    I am directed by the Secretary of State to acquaint you, that upon the recommendation of the Commissioner of Police he sanctions the grant of a special Refreshment Allowance at the rate of 2/- per day to those Sergeants of the Criminal Investigation Department belonging to Divisions who have been brought to Whitechapel from other Divisions in connection with the recent murder in Swallow Gardens, on the same conditions as this allowance was

granted in August, 1889, to these officers when employed in connection with the previous Whitechapel Murders.

I am,

Sir,

Your obedient Servant,

E.LeighPemberton.

The Receiver
  for the Metropolitan
    Police District.

There is a file cover sheet[18], heavily annotated, as follows:

10/3/92 / Further report / attached SLucas Supt. / Lay by MLM 11/3 / Further Report submitted 10/5 / Report result of [ ] MLM 10/5 / [stamp] 10 MAY 92 / Report attached 17/5/92 SLucas Supt. / Seen MLM 17/5 / Further report submd. 3/1/93 Supt Central to see. seen [ ] Inspr 4/1/93 (20 Faraday St. Walworth Rd. on "L" or "P" grd.? The Supt [ ] see this ppo MLM 3/1 / Cent. / 57885 / 727 / Threats. / Report of an interview between Ch. Insp. Swanson & Mrs. Sadler wife of the man Sadler who was in custody for the murder of Frances Coles at Whitechapel. Mrs. Sadler fears her husband. / [stamp:- REGISTRY received 12 DEC 91] C.I.D. MLM 12/12 / Mr. Anderson? Supt W. for report RA 12/12 / [stamp:- REFERRED 12 DEC.91] / Report attached 17/12/91 J Rudmore [?] actgSupt / Mr. Anderson / I think that Supt Arnold should see this report? He was speaking to me of Sadler yesterday MLM 17/12/1 / To Supt. H. to see RA 17/ / Seen T Arnold Supd 21 12 91 / P.a. JWButcher 22/12 / Further report submitted 28/ 12/91 Seen A. approved 28/12 ([ ] shd. like to know what Sadler is doing for a livelihood, and also if he leaves the Division, where he goes to) MLM / [stamp:- REFERRED 28 DEC.91] / Report attached 2/12/92 SLucas Supt. / By a strange coincidence I met Sadler this morning at the end of :[ ] our first meeting since he was charged with the Swallow Gardens murder. Lay by for the present. MLM 2/1. / Further report submitted 5/3/92 Mr Macnaghten MLM 5/3 / 5/3 Mr. Anderson ?Further report if, or when, anything fresh transpires. W. RA 5/

There is a report[19] dated 11 December 1891, by Chief Inspector Donald S. Swanson, about an assault by Sadler on his wife:

METROPOLITAN POLICE.
Criminal Investigation Department,
Scotland Yard,
11th day of December 1891.
Subject Mrs. Sadler assaulted by her husband.

I beg to submit the attached letter from Mrs. Sadler, of 121 Danbrook Road South Streatham the wife of the man Sadler, who was charged with the murder of Frances Coles. I saw her here at 6pm today, accompanied by James Moffatt, a retired pensioner, and she said that she had been living with her husband at the above address ever since May last, and that Moffatt was a lodger. The object of the letter and her call was to ask advice, for Sadler had not only assaulted her and otherwise treated her cruelly, but he had repeatedly threatened to take her life, and she was afraid to live with him any longer. Moffatt, who is an elderly man said that although he had been at sea for many years he had never heard such horrible language as that uttered by Sadler to his wife, and he was obliged to lock his bedroom door every night for in his opinion Sadler was a treacherous and cowardly man.

The only cause that Mrs. Sadler could think of was that Sadler accused her of not assisting him in the shop, which he stocked with the money he got from some newspapers.

I advised her to apply to a magistrate stating all the facts: and that it was a matter for her own discretion how long she continued to reside with him.

I have sent a telegram (copy attached) to the W. Division.

I beg that the papers may be forwarded to Supt. W. for his information.

Donald SSwanson
Ch Inspr
JohnShore
Supt.

This is followed by a report[20] dated 16 December 1891, by Sergeant Francis Boswell of W Division:

METROPOLITAN POLICE.
W or Clapham Division,
16th day of December 1891
Subject- Mrs. Sadler's complaint of violence on the part of her husband / Reference to papers 57885 / 727

With reference to the attached report, giving particulars of a complaint made by Mrs. Sarah Sadler, residing with her husband James Sadler, at 121 Danbrook Road. Lower Streatham. of having been assaulted, threatened, and otherwise ill-treated by her husband.

I beg to report having seen both Mrs. Sadler and Mr. Moffatt, the lodger.

Mrs. Sadler informed me that her husband has not been guilty of any act of violence towards her, or threatened her since she made the complaint to Chief Inspr. Swanson, on 10th.

Both Mrs. Sadler, and Moffatt agree in describing Sadler as a most violent, subtle, and treacherous man, in the habit of using the most vile and disgusting language.

Mrs. Sadler has not applied to the magistrate for process against her husband at present but states that she shall do so should he use any further violence or threats towards her.

In accordance with Superintendent's directions a P.C. has been and is now patrolling Danbrook Road, in view of Sadler's house to render Mrs. Sadler assistance should occasion arise.

Mrs. Sadler expressed her thanks for the attention and courtesy that she has received from the Police.

Francis Boswell Sergt.
J Ludmore Actg Supt.

The next report[21] is dated 1 January 1892 and is a further report submitted by Sergeant Boswell about Sadler and his wife:

METROPOLITAN POLICE.
W or Clapham Division,
1st day of January 1892.

Re complaint against Sadler by his wife of violence &c Reference to Papers 57885 / 727.

With reference to the attached, and Chief Constable, C.I.Dept. minute thereon.

I beg to report that Sadler keeps a chandler's shop at No. 121 Danbrook Road, Lower Streatham, and does a good ready money trade, his takings averaging £2.10 per day.

Sadler opened this shop in May 1891, the man Moffatt coming to lodge with him about a fortnight later. With the exception of one occasion (a short time after he opened the shop) he has never been out, or left the house, but devoted his time to the business.

As far as I can ascertain the only person that he is in communication with or likely to visit is his mother, Mrs. Sadler, 63 or 65, Crampton Street, Newington Butts.

I am still in communication with Moffatt, who informed me that Sadler's conduct towards his wife has undergone a marked change lately he does not assault or threaten her and although he still makes use of most obscene and repulsive language he is (in Moffatt's opinion) guarded in his manner and actions.

Moffatt has promised in the event of anything of a suspicious nature arising with regard to Sadler's behaviour or movements, or should he be guilty of any further violence towards his wife to communicate with the Police.

> Francis Boswell Sergt.
> JBarnes Inspr.
> SLucas Supt.

Sergeant Boswell's next report[22] was dated 4 March 1892, and concerned a further complaint from Mr Moffatt, the Sadlers' lodger:

> METROPOLITAN POLICE.
> W or Clapham Division,
> 4th day of March, 1892.

Subject Re James Sadler of 121 Danbrook Rd, Lower Streatham / Reference to papers 57885 / 727

I beg to report that at 6.50hrs 4th inst Mr. Moffatt, Naval pensioner, lodging at No. 121 Danbrook Road, Lower Streatham, with James Sadler, the man who was charged with the murder of Frances Coles at Whitechapel, in February 1891, called at Streatham Station and stated that Sadler had refused to allow his wife to go out, or leave the house and had threatened that if she did so he would shut her out. Moffatt added that he feared that Sadler would assault her. I promised him that attention should be paid by Police, and advised him to tell Mrs. Sadler that the best plan for her to adopt would be to seek the advice of the magistrate at Lambeth Police Court.

Attention has been paid by P.C. White and myself during the evening, and P.C.'s on duty in the vicinity directed to pay attention, and act if necessary.

> Francis Boswell Sergt.

Former papers at C.O., C.I.D.   J.Barnes Insp
> SLucas Supt.

On 10 March 1892, Sergeant Boswell reported further[23] as follows:

METROPOLITAN POLICE.
W or Clapham Division.
10th day of March 1892.

Re James Sadler of 121 Danbrook Road Streatham / Reference to papers 57885 / 727.

With reference to the attached and Assistant Commissioner's minute thereon.

I beg to report that nothing further has transpired in connection with Sadler, and his wife.

I have seen Mrs. Sadler, who informed me that her husband who entertains strong prejudice towards persons of any religious denomination, had refused to allow her to attend Chapel, or to visit persons connected with any place of Worship.

Francis Boswell P.S.

Submitted.   J.Barnes Insp

SLucas Supt.

There is then a further report[24] by Sergeant Boswell about threats made by Sadler, dated 16 May 1892:

W Division / Subject Threats / Summary of Contents / Report giving particulars of a complaint made by Mrs. Sadler of 121 Danbrook Rd., of having been threatened by her husband, and the result of an application made by her to A Hopkins, Esqr the sitting magistrate at Lambeth Police Court for process against her husband.

METROPOLITAN POLICE.
W or Clapham Division.
16th day of May 1892.

Subject Threats to murder, result of summons for use of same / 57885 / 727.

I beg to report that James Thomas Sadler, of 121 Danbrook Road, Lower Streatham, mentioned in the attached correspondence appeared before R.I. Biron Q.C. at Lambeth Police Court on 16th inst in answer to a summons taken out against him on 9th inst, by Sarah Sadler, his wife, for threats made by him to murder her.

The learned Magistrate after hearing Mrs. Sadler's evidence (which was to the effect that her husband had threatened to cut her throat on 9th inst. and that she went in fear of him). bound

defendant over in his own recognizance of £10. to keep the peace
for six months.

> Francis Boswell Sergt.
> J.Barnes Insp
> SLucas Supt

There then follows a report[25] by Sergeant Boswell, dated 2 January
1893:

W Division to the Assistant Commissioner, Criminal Investigation
Department / Summary of Contents / Result of the magistrate
hearing of a summons taken out by Mrs. Sadler of 121 Danbrook
Rd. Streatham, against her husband James Sadler, for threats used
by him against her.

> METROPOLITAN POLICE.
> W or Clapham Division.
> 2nd day of January 1893.

Subject J.T. Sadler / 57885 / 727 /

I beg to report that Mrs. Sarah Sadler, wife of James Thomas
Sadler, who was charged with the murder of Frances Coles, in
Swallow Gardens, Whitechapel, on 13th February, 1891, called on
me at Streatham Station on 1st inst. and stated that Sadler intended
removing from 121 Danbrook Road, Streatham, (where he has
been residing) and has taken lodgings at No. 108, Faraday Street,
Walworth Road, Camberwell.

> Francis Boswell Sergt.
> Respectfully submitted
>   Sadler was bound in his own

recognizances to keep the peace towards his wife, (on the 16th of
May last) for 6 months and the wife appears to desire, that he should
still remain under some surveillance.

> ASewell Inspt.
> ACConst SLucas Supt.

CHAPTER 36

May 1892 – Frederick Bailey Deeming

Most of the infamous murderers of the late-Victorian period after the Whitechapel Murders have been linked with "Jack the Ripper." They include Mary Eleanor Pearcey (1890), Frederick Bailey Deeming (1892), Dr Thomas Neill Cream (1892), and Severin Klosowski (George Chapman, 1903). There is nothing of a known substantive nature to link any one of them with the Whitechapel Murders although a file concerning one of them is to be found in the official files.

Frederick Bailey Deeming, 48 years of age, was executed for murder in Australia on 23 May 1892. In 1891, before emigrating to Australia, he had murdered his wife and four children at Rainhill, Liverpool, and had buried the bodies under the kitchen floor.

The *Pall Mall Gazette* of 8 April 1892 printed the following article:

DEEMING AND "JACK THE RIPPER."
AN INTERVIEW AT SCOTLAND YARD.

A correspondent writes:- It ought to be stated at once that, so far as the Scotland-yard authorities are concerned, they do not believe that in the capture of Deeming the mysterious fiend "Jack the Ripper" has been laid by the heels. They have arrived at this conclusion despite the scores upon scores of letters which, since Deeming's arrest, have poured in upon them from more or less imaginative persons in the East-end of London who are anxious to prove that a person like unto the Rainhill murderer was prowling around Whitechapel at the time when the crimes which terrified that neighbourhood were being committed.

An official of high rank at Scotland-yard had his attention drawn last night to the story to the effect that a girl living in London walked out with Deeming on the evening when two of the murders were committed, and saw him again on the following day, when he was strangely nervous and excited, laughed loudly and exclaimed "I have been expecting for the last week or so to see something of the kind in print.'' The police have been practically inundated with similar stories. One woman came to tell them that the portrait of Deeming corresponded in detail with the outline portrait which ''Jack the Ripper'' is said to have drawn of himself on the dirty wall of the house in which he hacked an unfortunate to death on the morning of Lord Mayor's Day three years ago. The female who brought this intelligence evidently did not know that the outline portrait was the work of an enterprising individual who afterwards became the tenant of the house, and showed curious visitors his handiwork and a dark stain on the floor for a trifling piece of silver. And of such as this are the stories which the police have been obliged to listen to during the last two weeks. Needless to say, they know nothing of the young girl who is alleged to have walked out with Deeming and to have been on terms of friendship with him.

But so far the police are satisfied that the man now in custody in Australia is not the perpetrator of the Whitechapel crimes; indeed they have been unable to fix his residence in London at all except on the occasion when he visited the metropolis with Miss Mather and, as the Scotland-yard official already referred to pointed out, only a creature intimately acquainted with Whitechapel and knowing every court and alley in it, could have perpetrated the murders ascribed to Jack the Ripper and escaped from the scenes of his crime without being detected. It is evident from the wandering life Deeming has led, and from the fact that he is not a Londoner by birth, that he could not have possessed the knowledge of locality to enable him to do this.

The *Pall Mall Gazette* of 13 April 1892 published a further piece on this story:

DEEMING AND HIS DOCTOR – DATE OF TRIAL.
THE ''RIPPER'' ROMANCE DENIED.

The trial of Deeming is expected to begin in Melbourne, on 2[ ] th April. It is thought that the application of the defence for an adjournment in order to permit of witnesses being brought from England will not be granted. Deeming has been very orderly and industrious. He is still occupied in replying to the written inquiries of his solicitor. The doctor whom Mr. Lyle engaged in connection with the defence has withdrawn from the case. He states that he has taken this step in consequence of the impossibility of obtaining a fair hearing in a community prejudiced against the accused. He declares that Deeming belongs to the order of instinctive criminals, and is as much wanting in the moral sense as a blind man is in the sense of sight, since killing is as much a part of his nature as eating. His head measurement is 6[ ]., which is exceedingly small in comparison with his height. Deeming's whole character is one of extreme stupidity, and the jokes he makes are coarse and pointless. His escape hitherto, the doctor considers, has been due less to cunning than to accident. The statement sent from Halifax, N.S., yesterday as to a man passing under the name of "Jacobs," who in 1882 was stated to have produced a letter from a woman subsequently murdered in Whitechapel seems to be entirely romantic. The informant has now been shown the portrait of Deeming, and does not recognize a likeness between the prisoner at Melbourne and his acquaintance of former days, Jacobs. Moreover, it appears doubtful whether Deeming was in Canada in 1882.

The official file[1] concerning Deeming is dated 6 May 1892, and the file cover follows:

[Stamped: – HOME OFFICE 7 MAY.92 DEP] No. A49301C/32
DATE 6 May 1892   Mr Charles Barber
REFERENCES, &c.   Whitechapel murders & Deeming.
           Mr Barber is of opinion that Deeming is
           responsible for the Whitechapel murders.
           Attention is called to P.13 of the "Spy" of
           Apl. 16. Enclosed.
           MINUTES.
      His belief rests upon his "dreams", in which his
      vision of the murderer appears to have coincided
      with that of Deeming.
           See marked passages on page 2.
           ? Put up.
           F?W
                11 May '92
                C.M.
                   ELP 12 May 92

The extract[2] from the *Spy*, referred to on the cover, is included, as follows:

<u>EXTRACT</u>.

From the   "Spy"
    of   16th April 1892

RATHER REMARKABLE.

Just a year since Mr. Charles Barber called on us, and explained that he had constantly dreamt about the identity of the Whitechapel murderer, and so confident was he that his visions were correct that we had great difficulty in convincing him that it would be policy to allow his convictions to lie dormant for a while. In the face of recent events he again points out how true his former dreams were, and has handed us a lengthy explanation.

To begin with, we may mention that Mr. Barber wrote to Scotland Yard in 1889, and received the following acknowledgement:-

"No. 52983.

        "Criminal Investigation Department,
            "Gt. Scotland Yard,1889.
      "Re WHITECHAPEL MURDERS.

"Sir, – I am directed by the Commissioner of Police of the Metropolis to acknowledge, with thanks, the receipt of your letter.-I am, sir, your obedient servant,

            "R. ANDERSON,
          Assistant Commissioner of Police.

Mr. Barber, Ardwick."

Immediately after this Mr. Barber wrote to the secretary of the Vigilance Society in London as follows:-

        5, Harriet Place, Ardwick, Manchester,
               Sept. 13, 1889.

Mr. Bocker.

Dear Sir, – I cannot refrain from dropping you a line, and why I have not written before I cannot tell; but if you will only see to what I here state I verily believe that the man so called "Jack the Ripper" will soon be caught. Of course I cannot state here half of what I could say if I could see you; but suffice it to say that I have read all that has appeared in our papers from the very first, and so reading I have dreamt of the crime that this so-called "Jack the Ripper" has done. My dream of the Mitre Square murder is very clear, for I saw him on the job and afterwards take to the ship – namely, the "Alaska." Sir, you will find what I here make out – that is, the ship was in port on all the dates given: (1) April 3, 1888; (2) August 7, 1888; (3) August 31, 1888; (4) September 8, 1888; (5) September

30, 1888; (6) November 8, 1888; (7) July 17, 1889; (8) September 10, 1889. When that ship was not in port no crime was reported of this man "Jack the Ripper." Again that ship arrived at Queenstown one day last week, which I have dreamt so much about. I made this remark to my friends: "Oh, the ship 'Alaska' has arrived, and we shall soon be hearing something more of 'Jack the Ripper' again." They made but little of it, but when they saw it in the paper they wondered, and said that he must have been on the ship "Alaska." I cannot give over thinking about it. He is about 5 feet 7 inches, rather stout, a little round-shouldered or short-necked, not much hair on his face, aged 40 or over.

I saw him again in the early part of the morning of the 11th September, 1889, in my dream.

I have written to Mr. Munro [*sic*], and have told him about the "Alaska," and only hope that he may be caught.

You will pardon my handwriting; I know it is not good.

Believe me, yours faithfully,   CHRS. BARBER.

[We shall be pleased to show the original letter to anyone who desires to see it. That the man's "visions" were remarkable is beyond doubt. – ED.]

Mr. Barber now sends us a long statement from which we extract the following:-

"While reading over the Rainhill stories and a description of this man Williams, otherwise Deeming, I cannot come to any other belief than he is none other than the so-called 'Jack the Ripper,' for I saw him on four or five different occasions in my visions. I will take it upon myself-though I don't know Whitechapel, not ever being at the place-I will mark out on a sheet of paper each one of the places where the murders have been committed, and shall be tied blindfolded, and believe me, I can give some very vivid pictures of each murder, namely, of Emma Smith, Whitechapel; of Martha Tabram, George Yard Buildings, Commercial Street, E.; of Mary Ann Nicholls [*sic*], Buck's Row; of Annie Chapman, Hanbury Street, Whitechapel; of Elizabeth Stride, Berners [*sic*] Street, Whitechapel; of Catherine Eddowes, Mitre Square; of Mary Kelly, who was murdered and mutilated in a room off Dorset Street – this was very clear; of Alice Mackenzie [*sic*], murdered in Castle Alley, and only partly mutilated – this was very clear; and of the mutilated remains found under a railway arch in the East End-very clear. Frances Cole [*sic*], murdered – I have no account of any mutilation.

I have seen this man on all the different murders, and after they were committed, for I saw him at the railway station booking to go away. He was then dressed in black clothes, with a longish coat on, a kind of billycock hat, with a black bag in his left hand. He was against the barriers getting his ticket when I saw him. After this I saw him; this was some time after in July, 1889. It was in this way I saw him: I have it that it was at some docks, where there were some large vessels. One of these vessels was ready to start off. It was a fine vessel, with its cords stretched from mast pole to bow and stern, with small flags attached, and I read the name of this vessel, 'Alaska'; and just as it was blowing off to start-for I could see the steam blowing off-this same man that I had seen times before came along the docks with a black bag in his left hand, and mounted the vessel by means of a ladder. Then off went the vessel. He seemed to me to be the last person to get on, for I saw no other person get on after him. At this I awoke, saying to myself, 'That is Jack the Ripper.' "

[Of course Mr. Barber is only dealing with what he dreamt, but his persistency in believing in the truth of those dreams struck us a year since as being most remarkable, and we have pleasure in publishing his statement in brief. He is not a myth, as he has lived for some time at 5, Harriet Place Ardwick. – ED.]

The letter[3] to the Home Secretary from Mr Barber is included:

[Stamped: – HOME OFFICE 7.MAY.92 DEPt. No.] No 5. Harriett Place

Ardwick A49301C/32
May 6th 1892

Rt. Hon. Hy. Matthew

Sir   I inclose you a coppy of Spy See Page 13 but in doing so you will see at once that I did give such information that I did believe at that time would have led to the aprension [*sic*?] of the East-End murderer so called Jack the Ripper otherwise Lawson, Williams, Deeming. Had they been properly carried out why they was not I cannot say.

Ask me do I still believe that he is the same man by going through the Rainhill storey I do say that he is for he unxpidetley turn up at Birkenhead as the papers today but is own Family says that he did after being away for about two years that was after the 10th September 1889 Febuy 1888 and part of 1889 for him being away that being the very time that the murders was committed at the East End for the Doctors believe that the crimes that was done afterwards was not done by the same hands and as all my information at that time was directing them to Liverpool I not only wrote to Mr. Munro him then being Chief but I wrote to the Chief at Liverpool giving to him same information not Geting a reply & also wrote my third letter to the Chairman of the Vigilant Comittee geting my own letter Returned back not finding the Adress as you will see a coppy of the letter in Page 13 of Spy along with the acknowledgement from Scotland yard singe R. Anderson.

And now Sir my intention in drawing your notice to this is seeing that Deeming as got to undergo the Justice of the Law I heavily belive that he will confess to the Whitechapel murders thereby Proveing that my information was right and at the same time Seting the Public much at Rest of one the Greatest Mysteries of the Present Century therefor if he dos confess

And I [ ] belive he will may it Please you to see that my information Has Find its just Reward as I belive that in Shuch Case's They do.

I am very sorry that he was not caught at that time for if he Deeming had been there would never have been the Rainhill Murders.

Sir the Editor of Spy or myself will only be to Pleased To give you my other information that you may wish to know

Belive me
Yours Faithfullely
Charles Barber

Rt.Hon H. Matthew

CHAPTER 37

23 February 1894 –
Suspects Named by Chief Constable M.L.
Macnaghten

To assess which suspects in this case could be genuine is very difficult, even when one restricts "candidates" only to those who can be said to have any claim to be authentic. Retaining objectivity is also a problem, especially if the writer has his own preferred suspect. To make an objective and useful summary we have eliminated suspects who appear to have no basis in fact, and those already mentioned in the narrative such as Isenschmid and Pizer. The police and Home Office files contain references to non-police suspects such as those mentioned by Edward Knight Larkins, the clerk in HM Customs Statistical Department who bombarded the police with his ideas, and whom Dr Robert Anderson described as "a troublesome busybody". A further problem for the researcher is the fact that the so-called "suspects file" is now missing from the official records.

There is one report concerning suspects that has survived, dated 23 February 1894, and written by Sir Melville Macnaghten, then Assistant Chief Constable CID, second-in-command to Dr Robert Anderson. Macnaghten did not take up his post with the Metropolitan Police until June 1889, by which time the recognized "series" of "Ripper" murders had ceased.

It is interesting to note the following entry[1] in the Metropolitan Police Estimates Book, 1885–92, concerning Macnaghten and his employment as Assistant Chief Constable:

A46472D/3. Mr. Macnaghten allowed £100 in addition to salary as Asst C.C. while acting as Confidential Assistant to Asst Commr. of C.I.D. total not to exceed £600 p.a.

Chief Ins : Butcher to have rank of Sup : and salary of £350. by 10 to £400.

His report, it must be noted, names three suspects for the "Ripper" murders whose names do not appear in the extant official files prior to Macnaghten naming them in 1894. It was written by Macnaghten in response to reports that had appeared in the *Sun* newspaper [14 February *et seq*.] claiming that Thomas Hayne Cutbush, a recently detained lunatic who had stabbed and attempted to stab two women in Kennington, was "Jack the Ripper". The report[2] is as follows:

Confidential.

The case referred to in the sensational story told in "the Sun" in its issue of 13th. inst., & following dates, is that of Thomas Cutbush who was arraigned at the London County Sessions in April 1891, on a charge of maliciously wounding Florence Grace Johnson, & attempting to wound Isabella Fraser Anderson in Kennington. He was found to be insane, and sentenced to be detained during Her Majesty's pleasure.

This Cutbush, who lived with his mother and aunt at 14 Albert St. Kennington, escaped from the Lambeth Infirmary, (after he had been detained there only a few hours, as a lunatic) at noon on 5th. March 1891. He was rearrested on 9th. idem. A few weeks before this, several cases of stabbing, or "jobbing", girls behind had occurred in the vicinity, and a man named Colicott was arrested, but subsequently discharged owing to faulty identification. The cuts in the girls dresses made by Colicott were quite different to the cut made by Cutbush (when he wounded Miss Johnson) who was no doubt influenced by a wild desire of morbid imitation. Cutbush's antecedents were enquired into by Ch: Inspr. (now Supt.) Chis [*holm*] by Inspr. Race, and by P.S. McCarthy CID – (the last named officer had been specially employed in Whitechapel at the time of the murders there, –) and it was ascertained that he was born, & had lived, in Kennington all his life. His father died when he was quite young, and he was always a "spoilt" child. He had been employed as a clerk and traveller in the Tea trade at the Minories, & subsequently canvassed for a Directory in the East End, during which time he bore a good character. He apparently contracted syphilis about 1888, and, – since that time, – led an idle and useless life. His brain seems to have become affected, and he believed that people were trying to poison him. He wrote to Lord Grimthorpe, and others, – & also to the Treasury, complaining of a Dr. Brooks, of Westminster Bridge Rd., whom he threatened to shoot for having supplied him with bad medicines. He is said to have studied medical books by day, & to have rambled about at night, returning frequently with his clothes covered with mud; but little reliance could be placed on the statements made by his mother or his aunt, who both appear to have been of a very excitable disposition. It was found impossible to ascertain his movements on the nights of the Whitechapel murders. The knife found on him was bought in Houndsditch about a week before he was detained in the Infirmary. Cutbush was a nephew of the late Supt Executive.

Now the Whitechapel murderer had 5 victims – & 5 victims only, – his murders were

(i) 31st. Aug '88. Mary Ann Nichols, at Buck's Row, who was found with her throat cut, & with (slight) stomach mutilation.

(ii) 8th. Sept. '88. Annie Chapman – Hanbury St. throat cut, stomach & private parts badly mutilated & some of the entrails placed round the neck.

(iii) 30th. Sept '88. Elizabeth Stride, Berner's [*sic*] street, throat cut, but nothing in shape of mutilation attempted, & on same date Catherine Eddowes. Mitre Square, throat cut, & very bad mutilation, both of face & stomach. (iv) 9th November. Mary Jane Kelly. Miller's Court throat cut, and the whole of the body mutilated in the most ghastly manner.

The last murder is the only one that took place in a room, and the murderer must have been at least 2 hours engaged. A photo was taken of the woman, as she was found lying on the bed, without seeing which it is impossible to imagine the awful mutilation.

With regard to the double murder which took place on 30th. Sept, there is no doubt but that the man was disturbed by some Jews who drove up to a club, (close to which the body of Elizabeth Stride was found) and that he then, "nondum satiatus", went in search of a further victim whom he found at Mitre Square.

It will be noticed that the fury of the mutilations increased in each case, and, seemingly, the appetite only became sharpened by indulgence. It seems, then, highly improbable that the murderer would have suddenly stopped in November '88, and been content to recommence operations by merely prodding a girl behind some 2 years & 4 months afterwards. A much more rational theory is that the murderer's brain gave way altogether after his awful glut in Miller's Court, and that he immediately committed suicide, or, as a possible alternative, was found to be so hopelessly mad by his relations, that he was by them confined in some asylum.

No one ever saw the Whitechapel murderer, many homicidal maniacs were suspected, but no shadow of proof could be thrown on any one. I may mention the cases of 3 men, any one of whom would have been more likely than Cutbush to have committed this series of murders:-

(1) A Mr. M.J. Druitt, said to be a doctor & of good family, who disappeared at the time of the Miller's Court murder, & whose body (which was said to have been upwards of a month in the water) was found in the Thames on 31st. Decr., or about 7 weeks after that murder. He was sexually insane and from private inf. I have little doubt but that his own family believed him to have been the murderer.

(2) Kosminski, a Polish Jew, & resident in Whitechapel. This man became insane owing to many years indulgence in solitary vices. He had a great hatred of women, specially of the prostitute class, & had strong homicidal tendencies; he was removed to a lunatic asylum about March 1889. There were many circs connected with this man which made him a strong "suspect."

(3) Michael Ostrog, a Russian doctor, and a convict, who was subsequently detained in a lunatic asylum as a homicidal maniac. The man's antecedents were of the worst possible type, and his whereabouts at the time of the murders could never be ascertained.

And now with regard to a few of the inaccuracies and misleading statements made by the "Sun." In its issue of 14th Feb, it is stated that the writer has in his possession a facsimile of the knife with which the murders were committed. This knife (which for some unexplained reason has, for the last 3 years, been kept by Inspr. Race, instead of being sent to Prisoners' Property Store) was traced, & it was found to nave been purchased in Houndsditch in Feb. '91, or 2 years & 3 months after the Whitechapel murders ceased!

The statement, too, that Cutbush "spent a portion of the day in making rough drawings of the bodies of women, and of their mutilations," is based solely on the fact that 2 scribble drawings of women in indecent postures were found torn up in Cutbush's room. The head & body of one of these had been cut from some fashion plate, & legs were added to shew a woman's naked thighs & pink stockings.

In the issue of 15th inst it is said that a light overcoat was among the things found in Cutbush's house, and that a man in a light overcoat was seen talking to a woman in Backchurch Lane whose body with arms attached was found in Pinchin St. This is hopelessly incorrect! On 10th. Sept. '89 the naked body, with arms, of a woman was found wrapped in some sacking under a Railway arch in Pinchin St: the head & legs were never found nor was the woman ever identified. She had been killed at least 24 hours before the remains, (which had seemingly been brought from a distance), were discovered. The stomach was split up by a cut, and the head and legs had been severed in a manner identical with that of the woman whose remains were discovered in the Thames, in Battersea Park, & on the Chelsea Embankment on 4th June of the same year; and these murders had no connection whatever with the Whitechapel horrors. The Rainham mystery in 1887, & the Whitehall mystery (where portions of a woman's body were found under what is now New Scotland Yard) in 1888 were of a similar type to the Thames & Pinchin St crimes.

It is perfectly untrue to say that Cutbush stabbed 6 girls behind. This is confounding his case with that of Colicott.

The theory that the Whitechapel murderer was left handed, or, at any rate, "ambidexter," had its origins in the remark made by a doctor who examined the corpse of one of the earliest victims; other doctors did not agree with him.

With regard to the 4 additional murders ascribed by the writer in the Sun to the Whitechapel fiend:-

(1) The body of Martha Tabram, a prostitute, was found on a common stair case in George Yard buildings on 7th. August 1888, the body had been repeatedly pierced, probably with a bayonet. This woman had, with a fellow prostitute, been in company of 2 soldiers in the early part of the evening; these men were arrested, but the second prostitute failed, or refused, to identify, and the soldiers were accordingly discharged.

(2) Alice McKenzie was found with her throat cut (or rather stabbed) in Castle Alley on 17th. July 1889; no evidence was forthcoming and no arrests were made in connection with this case. The stab in the throat was of the same nature as in the case of the number

(3) Frances Coles, in Swallow Gardens, on 13th. February 1891, for which Thomas Sadler, a fireman, was arrested, &, after several remands, discharged. It was ascertained at the time that Sadler had sailed for the Baltic on 19th. July '89. & was in Whitechapel on the night of 17th. idem. He was a man of ungovernable temper & entirely addicted to drink, & the company of the lowest prostitutes.

(4) The case of the unidentified woman whose trunk was found in Pinchin St: on 10th. Sept. 1889 – which has already been dealt with.

MLMacnaghten
23rd. Feb. 1894

As can be seen from the above report, Macnaghten was responsible for the promulgation of several of the accepted "facts" in the case of the Whitechapel Murders, including the five above-described murders and exceptions, and the idea that the killer's mind gave way after the "awful glut" of Miller's Court. It has also been largely accepted that one of the three above-named suspects was the "most likely" to have been the killer, despite the fact that Macnaghten himself states that "no shadow of proof could be thrown on any one". He also states that "No one ever saw the Whitechapel Murderer", which seems to contradict evidence adduced at the time, especially in relation to the witnesses Mrs Long, Schwartz and Joseph Lawende. Macnaghten also firmly establishes Elizabeth Stride as a "Ripper" victim and suggests that the killer was disturbed and therefore left her body before inflicting his customary mutilation, and then searched out Catherine Eddowes to "satiate" his urges. Also that the mutilations increased in fury with each killing. An important point to note is that there are various factual errors in Macnaghten's report, an aspect of it which should not be overlooked.

Montague John Druitt's suicide, however, was a proven fact and the following report of the inquest into his death appeared in the *Acton, Chiswick & Turnham Green Gazette* of Saturday, 5 January 1889:

FOUND DROWNED. – Shortly after mid-day on Monday, a waterman named Winslade, of Chiswick, found the body of a man, well-dressed, floating in the Thames off Thorneycroft's. He at once informed a constable, and without delay the body was conveyed on the ambulance to the mortuary. – On Wednesday afternoon, Dr. Diplock, coroner, held the inquest at the Lamb Tap, when the following evidence was adduced:- William H. Druitt said he lived at Bournemouth, and that he was a solicitor. The deceased was his brother, who was 31 last birthday. He was a barrister-at-law, and an assistant master in a school at Blackheath. He had stayed with witness at Bournemouth for a night towards the end of October. Witness heard from a friend on the 11th of December that deceased had not been heard of at his chambers for more than a week. Witness then went to London to make inquiries, and at Blackheath he found that deceased had got into serious trouble at the school, and had been dismissed. That was on the 30th of December. Witness had deceased's things searched where he resided, and found a paper addressed to him (produced). – The Coroner read the letter, which was to this effect:- "Since Friday I felt I was going to be like mother, and the best thing was for me to die."

– Witness, continuing, said deceased had never made any attempt on his life before. His mother became insane in July last. He had no other relative. – Henry Winslade was the next witness. He said he lived at No. 4, Shore-street, Paxton-road, and that he was a waterman. About one o'clock on Monday he was on the river in a boat, when he saw the body floating. The tide was at half flood, running up. He brought the body ashore, and gave information to the police.-P.C. George Moulson, 216T, said he had searched the body, which was fully dressed excepting the hat and collar. He found four large stones in each pocket in the top coat; £2 10s. in gold, 7s. in silver, 2d. in bronze, two cheques on the London and Provincial Bank (one for £50 and the other for £16), a first-class season pass from Blackheath to London (South-Western Railway), a second half return Hammersmith to Charing Cross (dated 1st December), a silver watch, gold chain with a spade guinea attached, a pair of kid gloves, and a white handkerchief. There were no papers or letters of any kind. There were no marks of injury on the body, but it was rather decomposed. – A verdict of suicide whilst in an unsound state of mind was returned.

Another report on the suicide of Druitt appeared in the *Southern Guardian* of Saturday, January 1 1889:

SAD DEATH OF A LOCAL
BARRISTER.

The *Echo* of Thursday night says : – "An inquiry was on Wednesday held by Dr. Diplock, at Chiswick, respecting the death of Montague John Druitt, 31 years of age, who was found drowned in the Thames. The deceased was identified by his brother, Mr. William Harvey Druitt, a solicitor residing at Bournemouth, who stated that the deceased was a barrister-at-law, but had lately been an assistant at a school at Blackheath. The deceased had left a letter, addressed to Mr. Valentine, of the school, in which he alluded to suicide.

Evidence having been given as to discovering deceased in the
Thames — upon his body were found a cheque for £60 and £16
in gold — the Jury returned a verdict of "Suicide whilst of unsound
mind."

The deceased gentleman was well known and much respected in
this neighbourhood. He was a barrister of bright talent, he had a
promising future before him, and his untimely end is deeply
deplored.

The funeral took place in Wimborne cemetery on Thursday
afternoon, and the body was followed to the grave by the deceased's
relatives and a few friends, including Mr. W.H. Druitt, Mr. Arthur
Druitt, Rev. C. H. Druitt, Mr. J. Druitt, sen., Mr. J. Druitt, jun.,
Mr. J.T. Homer, and Mr. Wyke-Smith. The funeral service was
read by the vicar of the Minster, Wimborne, the Rev. F.J. Huyshe,
assisted by the Rev. Plater.

Other reports also appeared:

Thames Valley Times
Wednesday Evening 2nd January 1889
BODY FOUND IN THE THAMES OFF THORNEYCROFT'S
On Monday the body of a gentleman was found by Henry
Winslade, waterman, in the Thames, off Thorneycroft's Wharf,
and has since been identified by a season ticket and certain
papers. Deceased was not a resident of the district, and the body
had been in the water nearly a month. Deceased was about forty
years of age, and the brother of a gentleman living at Bournemouth. The Coroner was acquainted with the fact that the
remains had been removed to the mortuary, and an inquest will
be held today.

Richmond & Twickenham Times
5th January 1889
SUICIDE WHILST INSANE
Dr. Diplock on Wednesday held an inquest at the "Lamb Tap" on
the body of Montague John Druitt, aged 31, whose body was
recovered from the Thames off Thorneycrofts' Wharf, on Monday,
by a waterman named Henry Winslade. The pockets of the
deceased, who was a stranger to the district were found filled
with stones, and after a letter had been read in which he wrote to
the effect that "what he intended to do would be the best for all

parties," the jury returned a verdict of "Suicide by drowning whilst temporarily insane."

DOREST COUNTY CHRONICLE & SOMERSETSHIRE GAZETTE
January 10th 1889
[*Distressing Occurrence*]
We regret to hear of the sad death of Mr. M.J. Druitt, a barrister on this circuit, and son of Mr. Druitt, of Wimborne. An enquiry into the circumstances attending his death was held by Dr. Diplock at Chiswick on Wednesday, deceased having been found drowned in the Thames near that place. The deceased was identified by his brother, Mr. William Harvey Druitt, a solicitor, residing at Bournemouth, who stated that the deceased was a barrister-at-law, but had lately been an assistant at a school at Blackheath. The deceased had left a letter addressed to Mr. Valentine, of the school, in which he alluded to suicide. A paper had been found upon which the deceased had written,

"Since Friday I have felt as if I was going to be like mother" who for some months had been mentally afflicted. Evidence having been given as to discovering deceased in the Thames — upon his body were found a cheque for £50 and £16 in gold — the jury returned a verdict of "Suicide whilst of unsound mind".

The funeral took place at Wimborne on Thursday.

Deceased was a prominent member of the Kingston Park Cricket Club, and as such was well known in the county.

As regards the suspect Michael Ostrog, it is interesting to note that he appeared in the *Police Gazette* of 26 October 1888, as follows:

METROPOLITAN POLICE DISTRICT.
3. – Convict Supervision Office. – Woodcut portrait and description of Supervisee MICHAEL OSTROG, *alias* BERTRAND ASHLEY, CLAUDE CLAYTON, and Dr. GRANT, Office No. 22550, whose apprehension is sought for failing to report – age 55, height 5 ft. 11 in., complexion dark, hair dark brown, eyes grey, scars right thumb and right shin, two large moles right shoulder and one back of neck, corporal punishment marks; generally dressed in a semi-clerical suit. A Polish Jew. Was sentenced, 5th January, 1874, at Aylesbury, to 10 years' penal servitude and 7 years' police supervision for larceny. Liberated on license 25th August, 1883. Again sentenced at the Central Criminal Court, 14th September,

1887, to 6 months' hard labour for larceny. On the 10th March, 1888, he was liberated from the Surrey County Lunatic Asylum, and failed to report

Warrant issued.

Special attention is called to this dangerous man.

Index No. on Card. 9 / Michael Ostrog, *alias* . . . Bertrand Ashley (a Pole) Office No. 22550 / Last and previous Convictions. Place, Aylesbury . . . Date 5/1/74; Offence, Larceny . . . . . .

Sentence, 10 yrs. Pen. & 7 yrs. Supn. / Place, Maidstone . . . Date - /7/66; Offence, Robbery Three summary convictions . . . . . . Personal Description. A, 50, h. 5 ft. 11 in., c. dark, h. dark brown, e. grey; moles back of neck and on shoulders (large); scar on right thumb; corporal punishment marks / Remarks. A surgeon by profession, and stated to be a desperate man. Known on R Division.

The last mention[3] so far found of Ostrog is in the Habitual Criminals Register for 1904:

Office No. 2464–04 / Name, aliases, Prison, and Register No. John Evest, alias Matters Ostroy, Bertrand Ashley, Claude Cayton, Stanistan Sublinsky, John Sobieski and Michael Ostrog A a 1374, Parkhurst / Date and Place of Birth. 1830 at sea / Height without shoes 5 ft. $8\frac{3}{4}$ in. / Complexion, dk / Hair, bn (tg gr, thin on top) / Eyes, bn / Marks, nil / Offence (in full), place of Conviction, and Officer in Case, or Place of Committal, Lar-N.L.S. (P.S. Pullen C.I.D.-H) / Sentence and date of Conviction, 5 yrs ps 16–12–00 / Date when Penal Servitude expires or Supervision commences, 17–12–1905 / Date of Liberation, intended Address, and Occupation, 17–9–1904 29 Brooke St., Holborn Doctor / Remarks, See also office no. 47020.

CHAPTER 38

The Missing Suspects Files

Before the Scotland Yard files on the Whitechapel Murders were deposited in the Public Record Office many papers went missing during the 1970s and early 1980s. Although these missing files[1] on suspects are no longer to be found, in 1973 when Paul Bonner was carrying out research for the BBC television documentary *Jack the Ripper*, he was able to access the files and made notes with the following introduction:

> "These are reports that seem to have been called for by Scotland Yard in January 1889. They include a range of colourful suspects (mostly from outside Whitechapel)."

The missing files were also accessed in the 1970s by Donald Rumbelow and Stephen Knight when researching their own books on the case. We have extracted the recorded information from these files and have compiled the following list of these "missing" suspects:

Translation of a communication from Bremen Police, dated 27 September 1888, papers 3/52983:
289

Bremen,
27 September 1888

The police directors reply to the Police Authorities of the Criminal Investigation Department, Great Scotland Yard, London.

With reference to your communication of the 25th instant, correspondence No 52983/239, we have the honour, having regard to the letter from Leipzig, to inform you that evidently the hairdresser Mary is the person referred to. He has completed here on the 7th August last a term of seven years imprisonment and is now confined at Oslebshausen whence he will be liberated on the 7th August 1889, having been further convicted and sentenced to 12 months imprisonment for a similar offence at Strasburg.

"Translated by F. Kuhrt Sergt."

There is a second report on "Mary", as follows:

[Stamped: – Metropolitan Police Criminal Investigation Dept. 23 OCT 88 Received]

Copy

Translation   Bremen,
                                                19th October 1888

The Hairdresser "Mary" has, in his time, been arrested by me several times for assaulting women and young girls in the breasts and private parts. "Mary" went, as was afterwards ascertained, at the fall of the night, to the different promenades where he, by himself, made a sudden attack upon ladies who were alone, striking them in the breast with some sharp instrument. The cuts were not very deep and did not point to an attempt to kill as they were soon healed and nobody has been killed.

"Mary" has been found, while in his barber's shop, trying to commit a rape upon a young girl; this young girl could give a very good description of him as she had the opportunity of seeing him the next day and then recognized him as the man who committed the assault, he was afterwards taken into custody.

(signed) Baring
Detective

Translation continued

Copy of this statement is respectfully submitted to the Chief of the Detective Depmt in London, Great Scotland Yard, re letter No. 52983/826

Bremen 20 Oct 1888
The Chief of Police
Sign: Dr. Feldmann

This is followed by a report, on the same subject, from Inspector Abberline, dated 22 October 1888:

METROPOLITAN POLICE
Criminal Investigation Department,
Scotland Yard
22nd day of October 1888

Central Officer's
Special Report
Subject Whitechapel
Murders

                    With reference to the annexed.

I beg to report that according to letter from Bremen Police dated 27th Ult. docket no. 289 the man called "Mary" is now undergoing 12 months' imprisonment, and therefore could not be connected with the recent murders in Whitechapel.

With regard to the man Wetzel [*Ludwig*], it has been clearly proved that he was in no way concerned in the matter. He also was under remand at the time the Berner St. and Mitre Sq. murders were committed. See reports herewith.

F.G. Abberline, Inspr
                                        T Arnold Supt

There is a report, dated 18 December 1888, from the Kingston Police Station, regarding a suspect:-

METROPOLITAN POLICE
Kingston
18th December 1888

Special Report
Whitechapel
Murders   Copy from O.B.

I beg to report that at 10.20 p.m. 16th November, 1888 John Hemmings 11 Youngs Buildings, Kingston, and William Shulver 201 Aspen Road, Starch Green, Middlesex, informed PC 548T, Robert Large, that at time above stated they were drinking inside the "White Hart P.H." Hampton Wick, Middlesex, and that they were talking about the "Whitechapel Murders" and another man was also inside the house, who upon hearing the conversation became very excited, and they thought his description answered that given in the daily papers of "Jack the Ripper," he was brought to this station by the PC and then stated that his name was Arthur Henry Mason 12 Portland Road, Spring Grove, Kingston, and that he was a compositor in the employ of Kelly and Co. Kingston. Enquiry was made and the man's statements found to be correct, and he was at once let go.

Description. Age 32. Height 5 ft 9 in; complexion fresh, thin face, hair whiskers and moustache, chin.

There are further reports on a suspect named "Dick Austen" forwarded from the police at Rotherham, and dated 5 October 1888:

Sir,

I have the honour to inform you that I have just had a visit from a man named James Oliver, residing at 3 Westfield View, Rotherham, a discharged soldier of the 5th Lancers, who is firmly persuaded in his own mind that he knows the perpetrator of the Whitechapel murders. He was perfectly sober and made his statement clearly and circumspectly and is of such a nature that I consider it should be laid before you without delay.

He states that there was a man named "Dick Austen" who served with him in R. Troop in the 5th Lancers, who previous to joining the Army had been a sailor, he would now be about 40 years of age — 5–8 in height, an extremely powerful and active man, but by no means heavy or stout. Hair and eyes light. Had, in service, a very long fair moustache, may have grown heavy whiskers and beard. His face was fresh, hard and healthy looking. He had a small piece bitten off the end of his nose. Although not mad, he was not right in his mind, "he was too sharp to be right." He used to be very temperate, but sometimes used to get out of bed in the night and walk about the barrack room. He never would say where he came from and often said he had no friends.

He used to sometimes brag of what he had done previously to enlisting in the way of violence but more often of what he could do, "as though qualified to do anything."

While in the Regiment he was never known to go with women and when his comrades used to talk about them in the barrack room he used to grind his teeth — he was in fact a perfect woman hater. He used to say if he had his will he would kill every whore and cut her inside out, that when he left the Regiment there would be nothing before him but the gallows.

He had gone through great hardships and rough times in various parts of the world, having been a sailor in sailing ships, he was a very sharp and witty man, and a capital scholar. Oliver believes he could recapture his handwriting. He was most plausible. His hands were long and thin.

He had 12 months for breaking into the Orderly Room and tearing up his defaulters sheets.

He is believed to have drawn his deferred pay (about 24£) and used to say he would make London his home.

He is a man who is most abstemious and will live on dry bread. He used many a day to save his money and live on what was knocking about in the Barrack Room.

Probably he would always be respectably dressed but more often the description of a sailor than a soldier –

Oliver's idea is that he would probably be working at Docks or on board ship by day-possibly, if the murderer, that he may take short voyages on some vessel and commit the murders shortly before leaving – The dates of the murders tally with this theory.

"He always had revenge against women brooding in his mind."

I have cautioned the man Oliver to say nothing about this, and he tells me that he has not as yet told anyone his suspicions excepting his own wife.

I have also promised him that unless his suspicions prove true, or of material help that his statement to me will be considered in confidence.

I have the honour to be

Sir

Your obedient Servant

L.R. Burnett Captain

C.C.

This is followed by a report from Inspector Abberline, dated 16 October 1888:

METROPOLITAN POLICE

Criminal Investigation Department

16th day of October 1888

Referring to annexed correspondence from the Chief Constable Rotherham, I beg to report that I have caused an insertion in the Informations asking if anything was known in Divisions respecting Austin giving his description and other particulars vide 25 Infn 12th inst but up to the present time with no result.

Perhaps it would be well to ask the Chief Constable of Rotherham, to cause James Oliver to be seen again and requested to furnish the date of Austin's discharge from the 5th Lancers, giving the name of the Station discharged from, and any other information.

F.G. Abberline

Inspector

T Arnold Supt.

This is followed by a reply from the Chief Constable of Rotherham, dated 19 October 1888:

[Seal of Rotherham Borough Police]   Chief Constable's Office
                                                    Rotherham
                                                    October 19 1888

52983/

[Stamped: – Received 20 OCT 88] To the Assistant Commissioner of Police

                                Criminal Investigation Department

Sir,

I have the honour to acknowledge the receipt of your letter of yesterday's date, relative to mine of 5th instant, and to inform you in reply that I have seen James Oliver this morning, he is unable to state the date or place of Austin's discharge – but as stated in my former letter he is positive that Austin intended to reside in London. Application to the 5th Lancers at Aldershot would produce the date and place of discharge, and should he be entitled to draw any future deferred pay or Army Reserve pay, his whereabouts could by that means be ascertained – Oliver says several photographic groups of the Troop were taken, he has no copy, but could, if a copy was obtainable, pick out Austin – I should like a copy of some or any of the alleged letters from the murderer, as Oliver, as stated before, believes he could identify Austin's handwriting.

                        I have the honour to be
                                Sir
                        Your obedient Servant
                                L.R. Burnett Captain
                                        C.C.

[*Pencil note*: – Make copy of letters for C.C.]

This is followed by another letter from the Chief Constable of Rotherham, dated 24 October 1888:

[Seal of the Rotherham Borough Police]   Chief Constable's Office
                                                        Rotherham
                                                        October 24 1888

52983/601

Sir,

In reply to your letter of yesterday's date enclosing Metropolitan Police Notice I have the honour to inform you that I have shown the facsimile handwriting to the man Oliver, who says that it is extremely like that of Austin, especially that of the letter (written with steel pen) that of the post card (written with quill) he does not think so like — although of course it is easy to see they are written by the same person — Austin's signature could of course be obtained from the Troop Pay Sheet of the 5th Lancers even if a large example of it could not be got from the same source.

I have the honour to be
Sir
Your obedient Servant
L.R. Burnett Captain
C.C.

The Assistant Commissioner
Criminal Investigation Depart.

Nothing more is included to indicate that any further efforts were made to trace "Austin", although the BBC researchers reported that it did seem that Abberline and Superintendent Oswald tried to find him, albeit without success.

There is a report, dated 14 January 1889, concerning another suspect:

METROPOLITAN POLICE
Criminal Investigation Department
Scotland Yard
14th day of January

1889

I beg to report that Mr. Richard Wingate, baker, 10 Church Street, Edgware Road, called and stated that about 5 weeks since he took into partnership with a man whom he now suspects of being concerned in the Whitechapel Murders. His suspicion seems to have been aroused in consequence of the man becoming suddenly reticent during a conversation about the murders and this morning a letter was received from him by a woman with whom he has been living, in which the writer expressed a fear that he would be caught today. He has also asked to sell his interest in the business to enable him to go to America.

Description, Pierce John Robinson, c/o Miss Peters, High Street, Portslade, near Brighton, age 34, height 5 ft 4 in. complexion rather dark, full beard (short) and moustache dark, thick set, dress midshipman's hat anchor on front, light jacket and vest, black trousers.

Mr. Wingate has Robinson's photo. Which he will shew to the Police but he desires that the officer making the inquiries should make an appointment with him and not call at his house.

C. Richards P.S.
[Illegible signature]
Superintendent

Superintendent Waghorn, Scotland Yard, went to Portslade to make enquiries. He reported that Robinson "is now a religious fanatic, claims to have had medical training and also uses the name Dr Clarke." The enquiry was taken over by Superintendent Arnold and Sergeant Thick and they found that Robinson had lived in Mile End Road. He had been convicted of bigamy for which he received four months' penal servitude. He left Mile End Road on 1 November 1888. They checked with his bigamous wife, Adelina Bird, who knew little of him but found him "inoffensive". On 9 November Robinson was at Portslade sleeping with his girlfriend, and Arnold and Thick were satisfied that he had nothing to do with the murders.

There is a report dated 18 January 1889, concerning a suspect reported by E.K. Larkins, of HM Customs:

METROPOLITAN POLICE
A Division
18th January, 1889

Ref to papers
206 information
17–1–89
Whitechapel
Murder

Persons detained in connection with
Whitechapel murder at King Street Station

At 12 noon 13th Novr 1887 Antoni Pricha of 11 Back Hill, Hatton Garden EC was pointed out to PC 61A Thomas Maybank in Whitehall by Edward Knight Larkins, clerk in H.M. Customs of 53 Pepys Road, New Cross who he stated that he thought answered the description of a man circulated in a newspaper as the Whitechapel murderer.

He then brought him to the station where "Precha" stated he was employed at the Royal Academy Piccadilly, as an Artist Model & known to Mr Osborn, an attendant at above. He was at his address from 6pm 8th till 8am 9th when he left for his employment. Enquiries were made by PC Hawkins C.I. Dept. A This statement found to be correct.

(sd) G. Rutt Insp
[*illegible* Supt]

[*There are marginal notes* – "No des Description: Age 30 height 5 feet 6½ in complexion & hair very dark long and wavy, long dark moustache. Dress, long dark brown overcoat (trimmed astrachan) trousers & vest in Albaman"]

This is followed by a further report dated 18 January 1889:

METROPOLITAN POLICE
A Division
18th January 1889

Ref to papers
206 information
17–1–89
Whitechapel
Murder

Persons detained in connection with
Whitechapel murder at King Street
Station 9.12.88

At 10.40 pm 8th inst [*insert* – "9th Decr"] Edwin Burrows of Victoria Chambers (Common Lodging House) Strutton Ground Westminster was brought to the station by Pcs C.I.D. Bradshaw H.Division & Godley C.I.D. J Divn to be detained during enquiry at Sutton. Burrows, stating that his brother, Freeman Burrows lived there & allowed him £1 weekly. A telegram was sent to Sutton. Reply received stating that he had an allowance. The man was therefore allowed to go, the enquiry appearing satisfactory.

I might say that the man has been known to myself & a number of men of this division, as a frequenter of St. James's Park, & Mall, sleeping on seats for the past 12 months & evidently doing the best he can to subsist upon the pound per week allowed by his brother & the statement seems quite correct.

(sd) G. Rutt Insp
[*illeg.*] Supt.

[*There are marginal notes* – "No des: Description: Age 45 height 5 feet 5 in Complexion, hair, whiskers, beard & moustache dark. Dress light brown tweed jacket suit, sailor peak cap laceboots."]

The next report is of a similar nature, dated 18 January 1889:

METROPOLITAN POLICE
A Division
Rochester Row
18.1.1889

Ref to
206 Infr 17.1.89
Whitechapel
Murder

Re persons detained in connection with the Whitechapel Murders, – 206 Infr 17th inst.

I beg to report that only one case has occurred in this sub-division since 31st October 1888, and I respectfully submit the particulars of that case as entered in O. Book on 21st November 1888.

At about 12.40 pm 21st inst. Mrs Fanny Drake (Conservative Club) 15 Clerkenwell Green, came to Rochester Row Station and stated she had put the police on the Whitechapel murderer and had now called to know the result. She was walking over Westminster Bridge when a man answering the description of the murderer met her, and as he passed, gave such a grin, as she should always remember. She at once retraced her steps and followed him until opposite Westminster Abbey, when meeting a Mounted Inspector she told him of her suspicion, pointed out the man, and came to this station, the Inspector following and watching the man. About 5 minutes afterwards Inspr Walsh came in and stated that the gentleman referred to had been followed by him to the Army and Navy Stores, Victoria Street, Westminster, and had now come to the station to see the lady. I interviewed him in the charge room, when he at once produced a number of letters and business cards proving himself beyond doubt to be Mr Douglas Cow of Cow & Co., India-Rubber Merchants, 70 Cheapside, and 8 Kempshoot Road, Streatham Common. This information I imparted to the lady when she at once apologised to Mr Cow for having caused him inconvenience, and both parties then left the Station.

(sd) D.Fairey Inspr
J. Webber S.D. Inspr
[*illeg*] Supt

[*There are marginal notes:* – ''No des. Age about 35 height 5 ft 7 or 8 in complexion and hair fair, slight moustache, shaved on chin,

Dress light overcoat, dark trousers, high hat, dark gloves, carried an umbrella very respectable appearance''}

The next report, dated 18 January 1889, concerns another suspect:

METROPOLITAN POLICE
A Division
18th January 1889

I beg to report that at 9.40 pm 22nd November, 1888 James Connell of 408 New Cross Road, Draper & Clothier Age 36, Height 5 ft 9 in, complexion fresh long dark brown moustache, Dress brown check suit, ulster with cape red socks Oxford shoes, soft felt hat, an Irishman was brought to this (Hyde Park) Station by PC271A Fountain under the following circumstances. Martha Spencer of 30 Sherbourne Street Blandford Square, Married stated that he spoke to her near the Marble Arch, they walked together in the Park and he began to talk about ''Jack the Ripper'' and Lunatic Asylums and said that no doubt, when he was caught, he would turn out to be a lunatic, in consequence of this conversation she became alarmed and spoke to the PC who accompanied them to the Station. A telegram was then sent to Greenwich Station for enquiry as to the correctness of his address and his respectability, a satisfactory reply having been received he was then allowed to go, as nothing further suspicious transpired.

(*signed*) J. Bird Insp
[*illeg.*] Supt.

Another report, dated 19 January 1889, referring to an incident on 17 November 1888, follows:

METROPOLITAN POLICE
B Division
19th January 1889

Re No 206 Ins 17th Inst

I beg to report that at 12 mght 17th November last, Oliver Mathews of No 14 Wharton Street, Kings Cross came to this (Walton Street) Station accompanied by PC 7BR Cooper. The PC stated his attention was called to Mathews by Richard Watson, 21 Old Square, Lincoln's Inn (Barrister) who was of opinion that he, Mathews, answered the description of the Whitechapel murderer. It appears that both parties were in the ''Trevor'' Music Hall,

Knightsbridge and were sitting next to each other. Mathews had in his possession a small black bag and this aroused the suspicion of Watson who acquainted the PC. Mathews at once volunteered to come to the Station where the bag was examined and found to contain clean linen. A telegram was sent to the address given by Mathews which proved correct, he having resided there for over 12 months. His appearance did not answer that of the Whitechapel Murderer in any way with the exception of the black bag and Mathews was allowed to go away.

C.W. Sheppard
Supt

The last copy report extant in this series is dated 19 January 1889 and reads as follows:

METROPOLITAN POLICE
G Division
19 January 1889

I beg to report that on 25th Novr last Alfred Parent of 31 Rue Notre Dame, De Nazareth and 58 Rue Volka, Paris, and Bacons Hotel, Finsbury Square, age 54, height 5 feet 6 in, hair white, whiskers and moustache very grey, dress dark overcoat, do under and vest, black trousers, high hat, patent boots, was given into custody by Annie Cook, a Prostitute, who stated that Parent had offered her a sovereign to go with him for an immoral purpose, or 5 sovereigns to sleep with him for the night, and as the amount offered was rather a large one the girl thought it was done for the purpose of getting her into a house to murder her, and gave him into custody.

On 28th December Joseph Denny of 64 Myddelton Square, Clerkenwell, age 20, height 5 feet 6 in, complexion fair, hair very curly, slight moustache, no whiskers, dress long dark overcoat with black astracan collar and cuffs, dark suit under, low shoes, brown soft felt hat, came to Old Street Station accompanied by PC 177A Wraight and John Robert Hardy and Thomas Hardy of 480 Kings Road, Chelsea, the two latter persons stated that they saw Denny accost two women in Houndsditch and thinking it suspicious, they followed him to Finsbury Pavement where they saw him accost another woman and having in mind the recent Whitechapel murders they called the PC who brought Denny to the station.

Enquiries were made respecting Denny which proved satisfactory and he was allowed to go.

At midnight 12th Novr last John Avery, a ticket writer of Southwick House, Vicarage Road, Willesden, age 43, height 5 feet 9 in, complexion hair and whiskers dark, dressed in dark clothes, high hat, respectable appearance, was brought in custody to Kings Cross Road Station by PC 208A Seymour who had been informed by Private John Carvill E Troop 11th Hussars, and Israel Hines of 5 [*illegible*] Court, Bishopsgate that Avery had informed them that he committed the recent murders at Whitechapel and that he wanted to kill some more but had lost his bag. Enquiries were made respecting his statement which proved satisfactory but as Avery was drunk he was charged with that offence and behaving in a disorderly manner, and sentenced to 14 days HL.

At 10.50 am 13th Novr last John Murphy, no fixed abode, a seaman and a native of Massachusetts, United States, age 24, height 5 feet 8 in; complexion and moustache fair, dress brown tweed jacket and trousers, blue blouse, cloth cap, with peak, lace boots, was brought to Kings Cross Rd Station by P.S. Nash CIDA from the Holborn Union Casual ward for enquiries to be made respecting a knife found in his possession on being admitted to the Casual ward, which was supposed to be connected with the Whitechapel Murders.

He was detained and a telegram sent to Inspector Abberline at H Division for enquiries to be made, which proved satisfactory, and he was released.

At 11 pm 25th Novr last PC 310A King brought to Kings Cross Road Station W. Van Burst, a Dutchman, no occupation, residing at Bacons Hotel, Fitzroy Square, age 50, height 5 feet 11 in, dark hair and moustache, dress light overcoat and trousers, lace boots, black felt flat top hat, respectable appearance accompanied by Geo Foster, 95 Bemerton Street, John Bowdell and Henry Crowley of 61 Gifford Street, and William French of No. 2a Beaconsfield Buildings Bingfield Street Caledonian Road.

Foster whose statement was corroborated by Bowdell, Crowley, and French, stated that he saw Burst opposite the Kings Cross Metropolitan Railway Station accost a female who walked away from him, after which he accosted two other females who also walked away from him. About an hour after Burst again accosted females after which he took a 2nd class ticket from Kings Cross to Farringdon Street followed by Foster and the others, and on alighting at Farringdon St. Burst entered an omnibus and Foster then thought that he was in some way connected with the

Whitchapel murders and called the attention of PC King to him. The PC requested Burst to alight which he did and accompanied the PC and the others to the station.

Enquiries were made which proved satisfactory and he was allowed to go.

H Jones
Superintendent

Paul Bonner of the BBC noted:

Many men, at least 100 in the file, were taken to police stations just for carrying black bags, having foreign accents, accosting women, or talking about the "Ripper" in pubs, but then released on being able to prove their identity.

At least two suspects, one Dutch, one American, gave their addresses as Bacon's Hotel, Fitzroy Square, "which is odd".

There was no mention, in this file or anywhere else, either in the Scotland Yard files or the Home Office ones, to Macnaghten's candidates Druitt, Kosminski or Ostrog.

CHAPTER 39

December 1888 – Another Contemporary Suspect

A Dr Roslyn D'O. Stephenson [real name: Robert Donston Stephenson] wrote a letter[1] about the murders to the City Police in October 1888:

> Reply sent 17.10.88.
> The London Hospital, E.
> 16 Oct.88
>
> Sir,
>
> Having read Sir Charles Warren's Circular in yesterday's papers that "It is not known that there is any dialect or language in which the word Jews is spelt JUWES," I beg to inform you that the word written by the murderer does exist in a European language, though it was not JUWES.
>
> Try it in script – thus,
>
> The ["Jeu" – *deleted*] Juwes.&c
>
> now place a dot over the third upstroke (which dot was naturally overlooked by lantern light) and we get, plainly,
>
> The Juives
>
> which, I need not tell you, is the French word for Jews.
>
> The murderer unconsciously reverted, for a moment, to his native language.
>
> Pardon my presuming to suggest that there are three points indubitably shown (& another, probably) by the inscription.
>
> 1. The man was a Frenchman.
>
> 2. He has resided a long time in England to write so correctly; Frenchmen being, notoriously, the worst linguists in the world.
>
> 3. He has frequented the East End for years, to have acquired, as in the sentence written, a purely East End idiom.
>
> 4. It is probable (not certain) that he is a notorious Jew-hater: though he may only have written it to throw a false scent.
>
> May I request an acknowledgement that this letter has safely

reached you, & that it be preserved until I am well enough to do myself the honour to ["see" – *deleted*] call upon you personally.

I amSir
Yr.obedt.Servant
<u>RoslynD'O.Stephenson</u>

Please address

Major Stephenson

50, Currie Wards,

The London Hospital

E.

<u>P.S.</u> I can tell you, from a French book, a use made of the o<u>rg</u>an in question-"d'une femme <u>prostituee</u>," which has not yet been suggested, if you think it worth while. R.D'O.S

Fortunately further information on the mysterious Dr Stephenson was copied before it, too, went missing. The first document was a letter by Stephenson communicating his suspicions about the identity of the killer to the police:

Sir <u>Re – The Whitechapel Murders</u>
26   Dec   88.

I beg to draw your attention to the attitude of Dr. Morgan Davies of – Street Houndsditch, E. with respect to these murders. But, my suspicions attach to him principally in connexion with the last one – committed in-doors.

Three weeks ago, I was a patient in the London Hospital, in a private ward (Davis) with a Dr. Evans, suffering from typhoid who used to be visited almost nightly by Dr. Davies, when the murders were our usual subject of conversation.

Dr. Davies always insisted on the fact that the murderer was a man of sexual powers almost effete, which could only be brought into action by some strong stimulus – such as sodomy. He was very positive on this point, that the murderer performed on the women from behind – in fact, <u>per ano.</u>

At that time he could have had no information, any more than myself, about the fact that the post mortem examination revealed that semen was found up the woman's rectum, mixed with her faeces.

Many things, which would seem trivial in writing, seemed to me to connect him with the affair – for instance – He is himself a woman-hater. although a man of powerful frame, &, (according to the lines on his sallow face) of strong sexual passions.

He is <u>supposed</u>, however, by his intimates, never to touch a woman.

One night, when five medicos were present, quietly discussing the subject, & combatting his argument that the murderer did not do these things to obtain specimens of uteri (wombs) but that – in his case – it was the lust of murder developed from sexual lust – a thing not unknown to medicos, he acted – (in a way which <u>fairly terrified</u> those five doctors) the whole scene. He took a knife, "buggered" an imaginary woman, cut her throat from behind; then, when she was apparently laid prostrate, ripped & slashed her in all directions in a perfect state of frenzy.

<u>Previously</u> to this performance I had said, "['but' – *deleted*] after a man had done a thing like this, re-action would take place, & he would collapse, & be taken at once by the police, or would attract the attention of the bystanders by his exhausted condition ['?' – *deleted*]" Dr. D. said "NO! he would recover himself when the fit was over & be as calm as a lamb. I will show you!" Then he began his performance. At the end of it he stopped, buttoned up his coat, put on his hat, & walked down the room with the most perfect calmness. Certainly, his face was as pale as death, but that was all.

It was only a few days ago, ["when" – *deleted*] after I was <u>positively</u> informed by the Editor of the "Pall Mall Gazette" that the murdered woman <u>last</u> operated on had been sodomized, that I thought – "How did <u>he</u> know? His acting was the most vivid I ever saw. Henry Irving was a fool to it." Another point. He argued that the murderer did not want specimens of uteri, but grasped them, & slashed them off in his madness as being <u>the only hard</u> substances which met his grasp when his hands were madly plunging into the abdomen of his victim.

I may say that Dr. Davies was for some time House Physician at the London Hospital, Whitechapel, that he has lately taken this house in Castle St. Houndsditch; that he has lived in the locality of the murders for some years; & that he professes his intention of going to Australia shortly should he not quickly make a success in his new house.

Roslyn D'O:Stephenson

<u>P.S.</u> I have mentioned this matter to a pseudo-detective named George Marsh of 24, Pratt St., Camden Town N.W. with whom I have made an agreement, (enclosed herewith, to share any reward which he may derive from my information [")" – *deleted*].

P.P.S.   R.D'O.S

I can be found at any time through Mr. Iles of the "Prince Albert", St. Martin['s] Lane – in a few minutes. I live close to; but do not desire to give my address. <u>RD'S</u>

The agreement was appended:

24. Dec. 88.

I hereby agree to pay to Dr. R.D'O.Stephenson (also known as "Sudden Death") one half of any or all rewards or monies received by me on a/c of the conviction of Dr. Davies for wilful murder.

Roslyn D'O.Stephenson M.D.

29 Castle St.W.C.

St.Martin's Lane.

Also contained in this file, but now missing, was a statement taken by Inspector Thomas Roots of Scotland Yard from the "pseudo-detective" George Marsh, referred to by Stephenson:

Mr. George Marsh, ironmongery salesman (now, and for two months out of employment) 24, Pratt St, Camden Town, came here at 7 p.m. [*24 Dec. 1888*] and made the following statement:

"About a month ago at the Prince Albert P.H., Upper St Martin's Lane, I met a man named Stephenson and casually discussed the murders in Whitechapel with him. From that time to the present I have met him there two or three times a week and we have on each occasion discussed the murders in a confidential manner. He has tried to tell me how I could capture the man if I went his way to work. I simply told him I should go my own way about it and sooner or later I'd have him. I told him I was an amateur detective and that I had been working for weeks looking for the culprit. He explained to me how the murders were committed. he said they were committed by a woman hater after the forthcoming manner:-

"The murderer would induce a woman to go up a back street or room and to excite his passion would "bugger" her and cut her throat at the same time with his right hand, holding on by the left.

"He illustrated the action. From his manner I am of opinion he is the murderer in the first six cases, if not the last one.

"Today Stephenson told me that Dr. Davies of Houndsditch (I don't know the address although I have been there and could point it out) was the murderer and he wished me to see him. He drew up

an agreement to share the reward on the conviction of Dr. Davies. I
know that agreement is value-less but it secured his handwriting. I
made him under the influence of drink thinking that I should get
some further statement but in this I failed as he left me to see Dr.
Davies and also to go to Mr. Stead of the Pall Mall Gazette with an
article for which he expected £2. He wrote the article in the Pall
Mall Gazette in relation to the writing on the wall about Jews. He
had £4 for that. I have seen letters from Mr. Stead in his possession
about it; also a letter from Mr. Stead refusing to allow him money
to find out the Whitechapel Murderer.

"Stephenson has shown me a discharge as a patient from the
London Hospital. The name Stephenson is obliterated and that of
Davies is marked in red ink. I do not know the date.

"Stephenson is now at the common lodging house No. 29 Castle
St., St. Martin's Lane, W.C. and has been there three weeks. His
description is:- Age 48, height 5 ft 10 in, full face, sallow complexion, moustache heavy – mouse coloured – waxed and turned up,
hair brown turning grey, eyes sunken. When looking at a stranger
generally has an eyeglass. Dress, grey suit and light brown felt hat-
all well worn; military appearance: says he has been in 42 battles:
well educated.

"The agreement he gave me I will leave with you and will render
any assistance the Police may require. [*Marginal note by Inspector
Roots that the agreement* is attached *but it was missing*].

"Stephenson is not a drunkard: he is what I call a regular soaker
– can drink from 8 o'clock in the morning until closing time but
keep a clear head."

There was also a report in the file by Inspector Roots, dated 26
December 1888, stating:

Whitechapel Murders, Marsh, Davies & Stephenson
    With reference to the statement of Mr. George Marsh, of 24th
inst., regarding the probable association of Dr. Davies and Stephenson with the murders in Whitechapel.
    I beg to report that Dr. Stephenson came here this evening and
wrote the attached statement of his suspicions of Dr. Morgan
Davies, Castle St., Houndsditch; and also left with me his agreement with Marsh as to the reward. I attach it.
    When Marsh came here on 24th I was under the impression that
Stephenson was a man I had known 20 years. I now find that

impression was correct. He is a travelled man of education and ability, a doctor of medicine upon diplomas of Paris & New York: a major from the Italian Army – he fought under Garibaldi: and a newspaper writer. He says that he wrote the article about Jews in the Pall Mall Gazette, that he occasionally writes for that paper, and that he offered his services to Mr. Stead to track the murderer. He showed me a letter from Mr. Stead, dated Nov. 30 1888, about this and said that the result was the proprietor declined to engage upon it. He has led a Bohemian life, drinks very heavily, and always carries drugs to sober him and stave off delirium tremens.

He was an applicant for the Orphanage Secretaryship at the last election.

The statements were forwarded to Chief Inspector Swanson.

A report in the *Pall Mall Gazette* of 31 December 1888 may well refer to Stephenson:

"UNDER OBSERVATION."

According to the Sunday Times, a gentleman who has for some time been engaged in philanthropic work in the East-end recently received a letter, the handwriting of which had previously attracted the attention of the Post-office authorities on account of its similarity to that of the writer of the letters signed "Jack the Ripper." The police made inquiries, and ascertained that the writer was known to his correspondent as a person intimately acquainted with East-end life, and that he was then a patient in a metropolitan hospital. It is stated that on an inquiry at the hospital it was discovered that the person sought had left without the consent or knowledge of the hospital authorities, but that he has been subsequently seen, and is now under observation. The police are of opinion that the last five murders were a series, and that the first two were independently perpetrated.

CHAPTER 40

The Littlechild Suspect

Until the discovery of the Littlechild letter by Stewart Evans in February 1993, the three main near-contemporary suspects were those named by Macnaghten in his report of February 1894, and Stephenson. The Littlechild letter revealed a further contemporary suspect who was amongst the police suspects in 1888. Purchased from antiquarian book-dealer Eric Barton of Richmond, the letter had been written by ex-Chief Inspector John George Littlechild (head of Special Branch at Scotland Yard 1883–93) to Macnaghten's friend, the journalist and author George R Sims. It was dated 23 September 1913, and was typed and three pages long. In 1913, by then a successful private enquiry agent, Littlechild wrote:

> 8,   The Chase,
> Clapham Common,S.W.
> 23rd September 1913.

Dear Sir.,

I was pleased to receive your letter which I shall put away in "good company" to read again, perhaps some day when old age overtakes me and when to revive memories of the past may be a solace.

Knowing the great interest you take in all matters crininal [*sic*], and abnormal, I am just going to inflict one more letter on you on the "Ripper" subject. Letters as a rule are only a nuisance when they call for a reply but this does not need one. I will try and be brief.

I never heard of a Dr. D. in connection with the Whitechapel murders but amongst the suspects, and to my mind a very likely one, was a Dr. T. (which sounds much like D.) He was an American quack named Tumblety and was at one time a frequent visitor to London and on these occasions constantly brought under the notice of police, there being a large dossier concerning him at Scotland Yard. Although a "Sycopathia [*sic*] Sexualis" subject he was not known as a "Sadist" (which the murderer unquestionably was) but his feelings towards women were remarkable and bitter in the extreme, a fact on record. Tumblety was arrested at the time of the murders in connection with unnatural offences and charged at Marlborough Street, remanded on bail, jumped his bail, and got away to Boulogne. He shortly left Boulogne and was never heard of afterwards. It was believed he committed suicide but certain it is that from this time the "Ripper" murders came to an end.

With regard to the term "Jack the Ripper" it was generally believed at the Yard that Tom Bullen [*sic* – Bulling] of the Central News was the originator but it is probable Moore, who was his chief, was the inventor. It was a smart piece of journalistic work. No journalist of my time got such privileges from Scotland Yard as Bullen. Mr James Munro [*sic* – Monro] when Assistant Commissioner, and afterwards Commissioner, relied on his integrity. Poor Bullen occasionally took too much to drink, and I fail to see how he could help it knocking about so many hours and seeking favours from so many people to procure copy. One night when Bullen "had taken a few too many" he got early information of the death of Prince Bismarck and instead of going to the office to report it sent a laconic telegram "Bloody Bismarck is dead" On this I believe Mr Charles Moore fired him out.

It is very strange how those given to "Contrary sexual instinct and degenerates" are given to cruelty, even Wilde used to like to be punched about. It may interest you if I give you an example of this cruelty in the case of the man Harry Thaw and this is authentic as I have the boys statement. Thaw was staying at the Carlton Hotel and one day laid out a lot of sovereigns on his dressing table, then rang for a call boy on pretence of sending out a telegram. He made some excuse and went out of the room and left the boy there and watched through the chink of the door. The unfortunate boy was tempted and took a sovereign from the pile and Thaw returning to the room charged him with stealing. The boy confessed when Thaw asked him whether he should send for the police or whether he should punish him himself. The boy scared to death consented to take his punishment from Thaw who then made him undress, strapped him to the foot of the bedstead, and thrashed him with a cane drawing blood. He then made the boy get into a bath in which he placed a quantity of salt. It seems incredible that such a thing could take place in any hotel but it is a fact. This was in 1906.

Now pardon me — It is finished. — Except that I knew Major Griffiths for many years. He probably got his information from Anderson who only "thought he knew" J.G. Littlechild

     George R. Sims Esq.,
        12, Clarence Terrace,
           Regents Park.N.W.

There are contemporary references to Tumblety in the British press. The *Monmouthshire Merlin and South Wales Advertiser*, in a piece on the Whitechapel Murders dated Friday, 7 December 1888 reported:

It is reported by cable from Europe that a certain person whose name is known, has sailed from Havre for New York, who is famous for his hatred of women, and who has repeatedly made threats against females of dissolute character.

Then, on 31 December 1888, the *Pall Mall Gazette* carried the following on page 10:

THE SEARCH FOR THE WHITECHAPEL MURDERER.
DETECTIVES ON THE OUTLOOK IN NEW YORK.
Inspector Andrews, of Scotland yard has arrived in New York from Montreal. It is generally believed that he has received orders from England to commence his search in this city for the Whitechapel murderer. Mr. Andrews is reported to have said that there are half a dozen English detectives, two clerks, and one inspector employed in America in the same chase. Ten days ago Andrews brought thither from England Roland Gideon Israel Barnet, charged with helping to wreck the Central Bank, Toronto, and since his arrival he has received orders which will keep him in America for some time. The supposed inaction of the Whitechapel murderer for a considerable period and the fact that a man suspected of knowing a good deal about this series of crimes left England for this side of the Atlantic three weeks ago, has, says the *Telegraph* correspondent, produced the impression that Jack the Ripper is in that country.

The origins of this story lie in North America and a report carried in the *St Louis Republican* of 22 December 1888 adds further clarification of Inspector Andrews's mission:

"AFTER JACK THE RIPPER."
A Scotland Yard Detective Looking for
Him in America.

Special to The Republic.

MONTREAL, Dec. 20. — Inspector Andrews of Scotland Yard arrived here to-day from Toronto and left to-night for New York. He tried to evade newspaper men, but incautiously revealed his identity at the central office, where he had an interview with Chief of Police Hughes. He refused to answer any questions regarding his mission, but said there were 23 detectives, 2 clerks and 1 inspector employed on the Whitechapel murder cases and that the police were without a jot of evidence upon which to arrest anybody.

"How many men have you working in America?"

"Half a dozen," he replied; then hesitating, continued: "American detective agencies have offered to find the murderer on salaries and payment of expenses. But we can do that ourselves, you know."

"Are you one of the half dozen?"

"No. Don't say anything about that. I meant detective agencies."

"But what are you here for?"

"I had rather not say just at present."

Ten days ago Andrews brought Roland Gideon and [sic] Israel Barnet, charged with helping wreck the Central Bank of Toronto, to this country from England, and since his arrival he has received orders from England which will keep him in America for some time. It was announced at police headquarters to-day that Andrews has a commission in connection with two other Scotland Yard men to find the murderer in America. His inaction for so long a time, and the fact that a man, suspected of knowing considerable about the murders [sic] left England for this side three weeks ago, makes the London police believe "Jack" has left that country for this.

Tumblety's flight from England via Boulogne and Havre was reported in the New York newspapers which reported his arrival there, on 2 December, in editions of 3 December 1888. In fact, his arrest in London had been reported as early as 18 November 1888 in the *New York World*, an extract of which read:

Another arrest was that of a man who gave the name of Dr. Kumblety, of New York. The police could not hold him on suspicion of having been guilty of the Whitechapel crimes, but have succeeded in getting him held for trial at the Central Criminal Court under the special law passed soon after the "Modern Babylon" exposures. The police say that Kumblety is the man's right name, as is proved by letters in his possession from New York, and that he has been in the habit of crossing the ocean twice a year for several years.

The following day the same newspaper enlarged on its information on Tumblety:

THE "ECCENTRIC" DR. TWOMBLETY.
The American Suspected of the Whitechapel
Crimes Well Known Here.

A special London despatch to THE WORLD yesterday morning announced the arrest of a man in connection with the Whitechapel crimes, who gave his name as Dr. Kumblety of New York. He could not be held on suspicion, but the police succeeded in getting him held under the "Modern Babylon" exposures.

Dr. Kumblety is well known in this city. His name, however, is Twomblety, not Kumblety.

This was followed by a summary of Tumblety's known history in America.

A further report was carried in the *Quebec Daily Mercury* of 22 November 1888:

The Whitechapel Murders.

Dr. Tumblety, of New York, a notorious quack, who made himself very conspicuous in Quebec and Montreal nearly 30 years ago, and who, during his peregrinations in the Maritime Provinces, caused the death by malpractice of a locomotive engineer, for which he was indicted for manslaughter, has been arrested in London on suspicion of being connected with the Whitechapel murders. The "doctor" is a very bad quack and eccentric dresser, but is not the man for performing such terrible work as that done by the Whitechapel monster.

The interest being shown in Tumblety by the Metropolitan Police was indicated in a report that appeared in the *San Francisco Chronicle* of 23 November 1888:

DR. TUMBLETY.
THE LONDON SUSPECT'S CA-
REER IN THIS CITY.
He Disappeared From Here and
Left a Large Sum of Money in
The Hibernia Bank.

The general and world-wide interest in the Whitechapel murders is probably exhibited in no greater or less degree in this city that in other places remote from the scene of the crimes, but the fact that Dr. Tumblety, the only man that the London police seem able to connect with the dreadful affairs, formerly lived here and that certain information concerning him in the possession of the police authorities of this city may be used in clearing up his connection with the matter, may cause the public interest to be largely increased.

When the news of Tumblety's arrest reached this city, Chief of Police Crowley recollected that that the suspect man formerly lived here, and he took the necessary steps to learn all about his career in this city. He found that Tumblety arrived here in the early part of 1870 and took rooms at the Occidental Hotel. He opened an office at 20 Montgomery street, but remained in the city only a few months, leaving in September of the same year. While here he opened an account with the Hibernia Bank and left a considerable amount to his credit in that institution when he went away. The account has never been closed and the bank still has the money in its vaults. After he left Tumblety had some correspondence with the bank officials.

As soon as Chief Crowley learned these facts he cabled to the London police that specimens of Tumblety's handwriting could be secured if they wanted them. Yesterday morning the following cablegram was received:

LONDON (England), Thursday, November 22 – *P. Crowley, Chief of Police, San Francisco, Cal.:* Thanks. Send handwriting and all details you can of Tumblety.

ANDERSON, Scotland Yard.

The chief will have the correspondence photographed and will send it at once to London, together with all the information he has been able to gather concerning Tumblety.

Tumblety's flight from London went unremarked in the London papers, but not so in the American press. The *New York World* of Sunday, 2 December 1888, printed three columns, which began:

TUMBLETY IS MISSING
The American Charlatan Suspected of
The Whitechapel Murders Skips
From London.
HE WAS LAST SEEN AT HAVRE
Is He On His Way Home Over the
Ocean to New York?

HE HAD A BITTER HATRED OF WOMEN

In This City He Was Sued by a Young Man
And His True Character Was Revealed-
His Practises In Washington, Where He
Pretended to Be a Brigade Surgeon-
His Dinners to Officers and His Denun-
Ciations of Women — He Was Known
When Fifteen Years Old as a Peddler
Of Immoral Literature on Canal Boats.

Copyright 1888, by The Press Publishing Company (New York World).
SPECIAL CABLE DESPATCH TO THE WORLD.

LONDON, Dec. 1. — The last seen of Dr. Tumblety was at Havre, and it is taken for granted that he has sailed for New York. It will be remembered that the doctor, who is known in this country for his eccentricities, was arrested some time ago in London on suspicion of being concerned in the perpetration of the Whitechapel murders. The police, being unable to procure the necessary evidence against him in connection therewith, decided to hold him for trial for another offense against a statute which was passed shortly after the publication in the Pall Mall Gazette of "The Maiden Tribute," and as a direct consequence thereof Dr. Tumblety was committed for trial and liberated on bail, two gentlemen coming forward to act as bondsmen in the amount of $1,500. On being hunted up by the police to-day, they asserted that they had only known the doctor for a few days previous to his arrest.

TUMBLETY'S CAREER.
The Grounds for Suspecting Him of Com-
Mitting the Crimes.

A London detective wishing to get information about the man now under arrest for complicity in some way with the Whitechapel crimes has only to go to any large city the world over, describe the curious garb and manners of Francis Tumblety, M.D., and he can gather facts and surmises to almost any extent . . .

Tumblety's arrival in the USA was duly reported: the following appeared in the *Evening Star Sayings* for Monday, 3 December 1888:

WATCH HIM.
The American Suspected of Whitechapel
Butcheries Arrives at New York.

By Telegraph to The Star-Sayings.

NEW YORK, December 3. – Dr. Francis Tumblety, who was suspected of being concerned with the Whitechapel murders in London, arrived in this city on the French steamer "Bretagne" yesterday. A reporter called upon Inspector Byrnes this morning and asked if there was anything for which Tumblety could be arrested in this country. The Inspector replied that although Tumblety was a fugitive from justice under $1,500 bail for a nominal offense in England, he could not be arrested here. The Inspector added that in case the doctor was wanted he knew where to lay his hands on him. Two Central Office detectives were on the dock when the steamer arrived and followed Tumblety to a boarding house, the number of which will not be made public. The doctor will be kept under strict surveillance.

The *New York World* also reported on the arrival of Tumblety and the watch being kept on him:

TUMBLETY IS IN THE CITY.
HE ARRIVED SUNDAY UNDER A FALSE
NAME FROM FRANCE.
A Big English Detective is Watching Him
Closely, and a Crowd of Curious People
Gaze at the House He Lives In – Inspector
Byrnes's Men Have Been On His
Track Since He Landed.

Frances Tumblety, or Twomblety, who was arrested in London for supposed complicity in the Whitechapel crimes and held under bail for other offenses, arrived in this city Sunday, and is now stopping in East Tenth Street. Two of Inspector Byrnes's men are watching him, and so is an English detective, who is making himself the laughing-stock of the whole neighborhood.

When the French steamer La Bretagne, from Havre, came up to her dock at 1.30 Sunday afternoon two keen-looking men pushed through the crowd and stood on either side of the gangplank. They glanced impatiently at the passengers until a big, fine-looking man hurried across the deck and began to descend. He had a heavy, fierce-looking mustache, waxed at the ends; his face was pale and he looked hurried and excited. He wore a dark blue ulster, with the belt buttoned. He carried under his arm two canes and an umbrella fastened together with a strap.

He hurriedly engaged a cab, gave the directions in a low voice and was driven away. The two keen-looking men jumped into another cab and followed him. The fine-looking man was the notorious Dr. Francis Twomblety, or Tumblety, and his pursuers were two of Inspector Byrnes's best men, Crowle and Hickey.

Dr. Twomblety's cab stopped at Fourth avenue and Tenth street, where the doctor got out, paid the driver and stepped briskly up the steps of No. 78 East Tenth street, the Arnold House. He pulled the bell, and, as no one came, he grew impatient and walked a little further down the street to No. 81. Here there was another delay in responding to his summons, and he became so impatient that he tried the next house, No. 79. This time there was a prompt answer to his ring and he entered. It was just 2.20 when the door closed on Dr. Twomblety and he has not been seen since.

Many people were searching for the doctor yesterday, and the bell of No. 79 was kept merrily jingling all day long. The owner of the house is Mrs. McNemara, who rents out apartments to gentlemen. She is a fat, good-natured old lady, and a firm believer in the doctor, who is an old friend. Mrs. McNemara at first said the doctor was stopping there. He had spent the night in his room, she said, and in the morning he had gone downtown to get his baggage. He would be back about 2 o'clock. The next statement was that the doctor had not been in her house for two months; that he was abroad, poor, dear gentleman, for his health; she had heard some of those awful stories about him, but, bless his kind heart, he would not hurt a chicken! Why, he never owed her a rent in his life, and once he had walked up three flights of stairs to pay her a dollar!

The revised story, to which Mrs. McNemara stuck tenaciously at last, was that she had no idea who Dr. Twomblety was. She didn't know anything about him, didn't want to know anything and could not understand why she was bothered so much.

It was just as this story was being funished to the press that a new character appeared on the scene, and it was not long before he completely absorbed the attention of everyone. He was a little man with enormous red side whiskers and a smoothly shaven chin. He was dressed in an English tweed suit and wore an enormous pair of boots with soles an inch thick. No one could be mistaken in his mission. There was an elaborate attempt at concealment and mystery which could not possibly be misunderstood. Everything about him told his business. From his little billy cock hat, alternately set jauntily on the side of his head and pulled loweringly over his eyes, down to the very bottom of his thick boots, he was the typical English detective. If he had been put on the stage just as he paraded up and down Fourth avenue and Tenth street yesterday afternoon, he would have been called a characture.

First he would assume his heavy villain appearance. Then his hat would be pulled down over his eyes and he would walk up and down in front of No. 79, staring intently into the window as he passed, to the intense dismay of Mrs. McNemara, who was peering out from behind the blinds at him with ever-increasing alarm. Then his mood changed. His hat was pushed back in a devil-may-care way and he marched by No. 79 with a swagger, whistling gayly, convinced that his disguise was complete and that no one could possibly recognize him.

His headquarters was a saloon on the corner, where he held long and mysterious conversations with the barkeeper, always ending in both of them drinking together. The barkeeper epitomized the conversations by saying: "He wanted to know about a feller named Tumblety, and I sez I didn't know nothink at all about him; and he sez he was an English detective, and then he told me all about them Whitechapel murders, and how he came over here to get the chap that did it."

When night came on the English detective became more and more enterprising. At one time he stood for fifteen minutes with his coat collar turned up and his hat pulled down, behind the lamp-post on the corner, staring fixedly at No. 79. Then he changed his base of operations to the stoop of No. 81, and looked sharply into the faces of every one who passed. He almost went into a spasm of excitement when a man went into the basement of No. 79, and when a lame servant girl limped out of No. 81 he followed her a block regarding her most suspiciously. At a late hour he was standing in front of the house directly opposite No. 79 looking over steadily and earnestly.

Everybody in the neighborhood seemed to have heard of Dr. Twomblety's arrival, and he is well known in all the stores and saloons for several blocks. One merchant who knows him very well said:

"Mrs. McNemara is a queer old lady, very religious and kind-hearted. The doctor began stopping with her years ago and he has lived there ever since when he was in New York. He used to explain his long absence at night, when he was prowling about the streets, by telling her he had to go to a monastery and pray for his dear departed wife."

Even in the saloons where he often went to drink he was spoken of with loathing and contempt.

He must have kept himself very quiet on the La Bretagne, for a number of passengers who were interviewed could not remember having seen any one answering his description. It will be remembered that he fled from London to Paris to escape being prosecuted under the new "Fall of Babylon" act.

Inspector Byrnes was asked what his object was in shadowing Twomblety.

"I simply wanted to put a tag on him," he replied, "so that we can tell where he is. Of course he cannot be arrested for there is no proof of his complicity in the Whitechapel murders, and the crime for which he was under bond in London is not extradictable."

"Do you think he is Jack the Ripper?" the Inspector was asked.

"I don't know anything about it, and therefore I don't care to be quoted. But if they think in London that they need him and he turns out to be guilty our men will probably have an idea where he can be found."

The careful watch on Dr Tumblety may not have been as good as was supposed, or perhaps the good doctor was a little too shrewd for his watchers. The *New York World* of 6 December 1888 reported:

DR. TUMBLETY HAS FLOWN.
He Gives His Watchers the Slip and Has
Probably Gone Out of Town.

It is now certain that Dr. Thomas [sic] F. Tumblety, the notorious Whitechapel suspect, who has been stopping at 79 East Tenth street since last Sunday afternoon, is no longer an inmate of the house. It is not known exactly when the doctor eluded his watchers, but a workman named Jas. Rush, living directly opposite No. 79, says that he saw a man answering the doctor's well-known description standing on the stoop of No. 79 early yesterday morning, and he noticed that he showed a great deal of nervousness, glancing over his shoulder constantly. He finally walked to Fourth avenue and took an uptown car.

A WORLD reporter last night managed to elude the vigilant Mrs. McNamara, the landlady, and visited the room formerly occupied by the doctor. No response being given to several knocks the door was opened and the room was found to be empty. The bed had not been touched and there was no evidence that the room had been entered since early morning. A half-open valise on a chair near the window and a big pair of boots of the English cavalry regulation pattern were all that remained to tell the story of Dr. Tumblety's flight.

Those who know him best think he has left New York for some quiet country town, where he expects to live until the excitement dies down.

As with all viable "Ripper" suspects there are pros and cons with Tumblety's candidacy. Research has revealed that he was arrested for the offence(s) of gross indecency on 7 November 1888, two days before the Kelly murder. The offences in question are misdemeanours and thus of a relatively minor nature, and without a court appearance within twenty-four hours Tumblety would have been bailed to reappear in seven days. The calendar of prisoners[1] for the Central Criminal Court session commencing 10 December 1888 records:

Francis Tumblety (Bailed 16th November, 1888) . . . Age 56 . . . Physician . . . Sup . . . J.L. Hannay Esq. Marlboro'-st. Police Ct . . . Date of Warrant 14th Nov . . . When received into Custody 7th Nov. . . . Offence as charged in the Indictment Committing an act of gross indecency with John Doughty, Arthur Brice, Albert Fisher, and James Crowley (1 indictment). Recognizances of Defendant Estreated.

This calendar is in tabular form and restricted to the information required in the columns, therefore any interim police bail could not be recorded on this document. It does, however, indicate that Tumblety was bailed under supervision on 7 November, and a court warrant issued on 14 November. His court bail of 16 November, after which he absconded, is shown. The papers on Tumblety's charges are held in CRIM 4/1037, 21927, and record the four offences as occurring in the County of Middlesex (London) on the following dates:

Albert Fisher, Friday, 27 July, 1888.
Arthur Brice, Friday, 31 August, 1888.
James Crowley, Sunday, 14 October, 1888.
John Doughty, Friday, 2 November, 1888.

Although a genuine contemporary suspect, as with all the others there is no hard evidence actually linking Tumblety to the murders.

CHAPTER 41

The Anderson Suspect

Dr Robert Anderson was appointed Junior Assistant Commissioner, in charge of the Criminal Investigation Department, at Scotland Yard in 1888. He was a barrister working in the Prison Department when he was appointed to his post in the Metropolitan Police on 31 August 1888, after the resignation of James Monro. After just one week, and at the time of the murder of Annie Chapman, Anderson went off to Switzerland under doctor's orders for a rest leave because he was suffering stress. This left the Senior Assistant Comissioner, Alexander Carmichael Bruce, carrying out many of Anderson's duties as head of the CID in his absence. Anderson did not return until the first week of October, after the double murder of Stride and Eddowes.

The first mention that Anderson had formulated any theory of his own about the identity of the unknown East End killer emerged in an article in the *Windsor Magazine*[1], in an article entitled "The Detective In Real Life" by Anderson's old friend Major Arthur Griffiths, the Inspector of Prisons, writing under the pen name of "Alfred Aylmer". The article stated:

> Although he has achieved greater success than any detective of his time, there will always be undiscovered crimes, and just now the tale is pretty full. Much dissatisfaction was vented upon Mr. Anderson at the utterly abortive efforts to discover the perpetrator of the Whitchapel murders. He has himself a perfectly plausible theory that Jack the Ripper was a homicidal maniac, temporarily at large, whose hideous career was cut short by committal to an asylum.

This was, of course, just a year after Macnaghten, Anderson's second-in-command, had written his famous report of February 1894, naming the three suspects Druitt, Ostrog and Kosminski. No public mention was made of these police-nominated suspects until

Major Arthur Griffiths's book, *Mysteries of Police and Crime* was published in 1898. Even then no names were mentioned. Griffiths wrote:

The outside public may think that the identity of that later miscreant, "Jack the Ripper," was never revealed. So far as actual knowledge goes, this is undoubtedly true. But the police, after the last murder, had brought their investigations to the point of strongly suspecting several persons, all of them known to be homicidal lunatics, and against three of these they held very plausible and reasonable grounds of suspicion. Concerning two of them the case was weak, although it was based on certain colourable facts. One was a Polish Jew, a known lunatic, who was at large in the district of Whitechapel at the time of the murder, and who, having afterwards developed homicidal tendencies, was confined in an asylum. This man was said to resemble the murderer by the one person who got a glimpse of him – the police-constable in Mitre Court [sic]. The second possible criminal was a Russian doctor, also insane, who had been a convict both in England and Siberia. This man was in the habit of carrying about surgical knives and instruments in his pockets; his antecedents were of the very worst, and at the time of the Whitechapel murders he was in hiding, or, at least, his whereabouts were never exactly known. The third person was of the same type, but the suspicion in his case was stronger, and there was every reason to believe that his own friends entertained grave doubts about him. He also was a doctor in the prime of life, was believed to be insane, or on the borderland of insanity, and he disappeared immediately after the last murder, that in Miller's Court, on the 9th of November, 1888. On the last day of that year, seven weeks later, his body was found floating in the Thames and was said to have been in the water a month. The theory in this case was that after his last exploit, which was the most fiendish of all, his brain entirely gave way, and he became furiously insane and committed suicide. It is at least a strong presumption that "Jack the Ripper" died or was put under restraint after the Miller's Court affair, which ended this series of crimes. It would be interesting to know whether in this third case the man was left-handed or ambidextrous, both suggestions having been advanced by medical experts after viewing the victims. Certainly other doctors disagreed on this point, which may be said to add another to the many instances in which medical evidence has been conflicting, not to say confusing.

Anderson retired in 1901 and in *The Nineteenth Century*[2] 1901 he wrote an article, "Punishing Crime", in which he stated:

> Or, again, take a notorious case of a different kind, "the White-chapel murders" of the autumn of 1888. At that time the sensation-mongers of the newspaper press fostered the belief that life in London was no longer safe, and that no woman ought to venture abroad in the streets after nightfall. And one enterprising journalist went so far as to impersonate the cause of all this terror as "Jack the Ripper," a name by which he will probably go down to history. But all such silly hysterics could not alter the fact that these crimes were a cause of danger only to a particular section of a small and definite class of women, in a limited district of the East End; and that the inhabitants of the metropolis generally were just as secure during the weeks the fiend was on the prowl as they were before the mania seized him, or after he had been safely caged in an asylum.

Here, for the first time, Anderson himself lets slip his view on the fate of the murderer, and he later added further detail. The next comments attributable to Anderson on the identity of the killer appeared in his book *Criminals and Crime*, published in 1907, in which he repeated the above passage from his 1901 article on pages 3–4. On page 77 he added:

> No one is a murderer in the sense in which many men are burglars. At least "the Whitechapel murderer" of 1888 is the only exception to this in recent years. And that case, by the way, will serve to indicate the differences I wish to enforce. In my first chapter I alluded to the fact of that fiend's detention in an asylum. Now the inquiry which leads to the discovery of a criminal of that type is different from the inquiry, for example, by which a burglar may often be detected.

The same book contains, on page 81, an interesting reference that may also refer to his thoughts on the Whitechapel murders:

> When I speak of efficiency [of the CID] some people will exclaim, "But what about all the undetected crimes? I may say here that in London at least the undetected crimes are few. But English law does not permit of an arrest save on legal evidence of guilt, and legal evidence is often wholly wanting where moral proof is complete

and convincing. Were I to unfold the secrets of Scotland Yard about crimes respecting which the police have been disparaged and abused in recent years, the result would be a revelation to the public. But this is not my subject here.

Anderson continued in a similar vein in an article that appeared in the *Daily Chronicle*[3] when he was interviewed about the investigation, then current, into the Luard murder case. The piece stated:

As a contribution towards the enlightenment of the public on the obstacles that Scotland Yard officers have to overcome Sir Robert Anderson has given a representative of "The Daily Chronicle" some interesting reminiscences . . . "Look at two notable cases that I had to deal with . . .

The Ripper Crimes

"Something of the same kind happened in the Ripper crimes. In two cases of that terrible series there were distinct clues destroyed, wiped out absolutely – clues that might very easily have secured for us proof of the identity of the assassin.

"In one case it was a clay pipe. Before we could get to the scene of the murder the doctor had taken it up, thrown it into the fireplace and smashed it beyond recognition.

"In another case there was writing in chalk on the wall – a most valuable clue; handwriting that might have been at once recognised as belonging to a certain individual. But before we could secure a copy, or get it protected, it had been entirely obliterated . . .

"I told Sir William Harcourt, who was then Home Secretary [sic], that I could not accept responsibility for non-detection of the author of the Ripper crimes for the reasons, among others, that I have given you.

Anderson serialized his reminiscences two years later in *Blackwood's Magazine*, and in Part VI, March 1910, he wrote:

One did not need to be a Sherlock Holmes to discover that the criminal was a sexual maniac of a virulent type; that he was living in the immediate vicinity of the scenes of the murders; and that, if he was not living absolutely alone, his people knew of his guilt, and refused to give him up to justice. During my absence abroad the Police had made a house-to-house search for him, investigating the case of every man in the district whose circumstances were such that he could go and come and get rid of his blood-stains in secret. And the conclusion we came to was that he and his people were low-class Jews, for it is a remarkable fact that people of that class in the East End will not give up one of their number to Gentile justice. And the result proved that our diagnosis was right on every point. For I may say at once that "undiscovered murders" are rare in London, and the "Jack-the-Ripper" crimes are not within that category. And if the Police here had powers such as the French Police possess, the murderer would have been brought to justice. Scotland Yard can boast that not even the subordinate officers of the department will tell tales out of school, and it would ill become me to violate the unwritten rule of the service. The subject will come up again, and I will only add here that the "Jack-the-Ripper" letter which is preserved in the Police Museum at New Scotland Yard is the creation of an enterprising London journalist.

In a footnote he added:

Having regard to the interest attaching to this case, I should almost be tempted to disclose the identity of the murderer and of the pressman who wrote the letter above referred to, provided that the publishers would accept all responsibility in view of a possible libel action. But no public benefit would result from such a course, and the traditions of my old department would suffer. I will only add that when the individual whom we suspected was caged in an asylum, the only person who had ever had a good view of the murderer at once identified him, but when he learned that the suspect was a fellow-Jew he declined to swear to him.

Jewish reaction to Anderson's claims appeared in the *Jewish Chronicle* of Friday, 4 March 1910 in which their columnist "Mentor" wrote:

Sir Robert Anderson, the late head of the Criminal Investigation Department at Scotland Yard, has been contributing to *Blackwood's* a series of articles on Crime and Criminals. In the course of his last contribution, Sir Robert tells his readers that the fearful crimes committed in the East End some years ago, and known as "Jack the Ripper" crimes, were the work of a Jew. Of course, whoever was responsible for the series of foul murders was not mentally responsible, and this Sir Robert admits. But I fail to see – at least, from his article in *Blackwood's* – upon what evidence worthy of the name he ventures to cast the odium for this infamy upon one of our people. It will be recollected that the criminal, whoever he was, baffled the keenest search not alone on the part of the police, but on the part of an infuriated and panic-stricken populace. Notwithstanding the utmost vigilance, the man, repeating again his demoniacal work, again and again escaped. Scotland Yard was nonplussed, and then, according to Sir Robert Anderson, the police "formed a theory" – usually the first essential to some blundering injustice. In this case, the police came to the conclusion that "Jack the Ripper" was a "low-class" Jew, and they so decided, Sir Robert says, because they believe "it is a remarkable fact that people of that class in the East End will not give up one of their number to Gentile justice." Was anything more nonsensical in the way of a theory ever conceived even in the brain of a policeman? Here was a whole neighbourhood, largely composed of Jews, in constant terror lest their womenfolk, whom Jewish men hold in particular regard – even "low-class" Jews do that – should be slain by some murderer who was stalking the district undiscovered. So terrified were many of the people – non-Jews as well as Jews – that they hastily moved away. And yet Sir Robert would have us believe that there were Jews who knew the person who was committing the abominable crimes and yet carefully shielded him from the police. A more wicked assertion to put into print, without the shadow of evidence, I have seldom seen. The man whom Scotland Yard "suspected," subsequently, says Sir Robert, "was caged in an asylum." He was never brought to trial – nothing except his lunacy was proved against him. This lunatic presumably was a Jew, and because he was "suspected," as a result of the police "theory" I have mentioned, Sir Robert ventures to tell the story he does, as if he were stating facts, forgetting that such a case as that of Adolph Beck was ever heard of.

But, now listen to the "proof" Sir Robert Anderson gives of his theories. When the lunatic, who presumably was a Jew and who was suspected by Scotland Yard, was seen by a Jew – "the only person who ever had a good view of the 'murderer'" – Sir Robert tells us he at once identified him, "but when he learned that the suspect was a fellow-Jew he declined to swear to him." This is Scotland Yard's idea of "proof" positive of their "theory"! What more natural than a man's hesitancy to identify another as Jack the Ripper so soon as he knew he was a Jew? What more natural than for that fact at once to cause doubts in his mind? The crimes identified with "Jack the Ripper" were of a nature that it would be difficult for any Jew – "low-class" or any class – to imagine the work of a Jew. Their callous brutality was foreign to Jewish nature, which, when it turns criminal, goes into quite a different channel. I confess that however sure I might have been of the identity of a person, when I was told he had been committing "Jack the Ripper" crimes, and was a Jew, I should hesitate about the certainty of my identification, especially as anyone – outside Scotland Yard – knows how prone to mistake the clearest-headed and most careful of people are when venturing to identify anyone else. It is a matter for regret and surprise that so able a man as Sir Robert Anderson should, upon the wholly erroneous and ridiculous "theory" that Jews would shield a raving murderer because he was a Jew, rather than yield him up to "Gentile justice," build up the series of statements that he has. There is no real proof that the lunatic who was "caged" was a Jew – there is absolutely no proof that he was responsible for the "Jack the Ripper" crimes, and hence it appears to me wholly gratuitous on the part of Sir Robert to fasten the wretched creature – whoever he was – upon our people.

As a result of this Jewish response Sir Robert Anderson was interviewed by the *Globe*, the piece appearing in the issue of Monday, 7 March 1910:

In an interview with a representative of "The Globe" on Saturday, Sir Robert said: "When I stated that the murderer was a Jew, I was stating a simple matter of fact. It is not a matter of theory. I should be the last man in the world to say anything reflecting on the Jews as a community, but what is true of Christians is equally true of Jews – that there are some people who have lapsed from all that is good and proper. We have 'lapsed masses' among Christians. We cannot talk of 'lapsed masses' among Jews, but there are cliques of them in the East-end, and it is a notorious fact that there is a stratum of Jews who will not give up their people.

"In stating what I do about the Whitechapel murders, I am not speaking as an expert in crime, but as a man who investigated the facts. Moreover, the man who identified the murderer was a Jew, but on learning that the criminal was a Jew he refused to proceed with his identification. As for the suggestion that I intended to cast any reflection on the Jews anyone who has read my books on

Biblical exegesis will know the high estimate I have of Jews religiously.''

Sir Robert added that one of his objects in publishing his reminiscences was to show how scares were exaggerated about ''undiscovered'' crimes. ''As a matter of fact,'' he said, ''there is no large city in the world where life is so safe as London. If I did not know the care and accuracy with which crimes are reported and statistics are prepared, I should not risk such a statement.''

In connection with Sir Robert's assertion that the Whitechapel murderer was a Jew, it is of interest to recall that in one crime the culprit chalked up on a wall: ''The Jews are not the people to be blamed for nothing.'' [*sic*]

In addition to the *Globe* interview, Anderson also wrote a letter to the *Jewish Chronicle* that appeared on 11 March 1910:

The ''Jack the Ripper'' Theory:
Reply by Sir Robert Anderson.
TO THE EDITOR OF THE ''JEWISH CHRONICLE.''

Sir, − With reference to ''Mentor's'' comments on my statements about the ''Whitechapel murders'' of 1888 in this month's *Blackwood*, will you allow me to express the sincere distress I feel that my words should be construed as ''an aspersion upon Jews.'' For much that I have written in my various books gives proof of my sympathy with, and interest in, ''the people of the Covenant''; and I am happy in reckoning members of the Jewish community in London among my personal friends.

I recognise that in this matter I said either too much or too little. But the fact is that as my words were merely a repetition of what I published several years ago without exciting comment, they flowed from my pen without any consideration.

We have in London a stratum of the population uninfluenced by religious or even social restraints. And in this stratum Jews are to be found as well as Gentiles. And if I were to describe the condition of the maniac who committed these murders, and the course of loathsome immorality which reduced him to that condition, it would be manifest that in his case every question of nationality and creed is lost in a ghastly study of human nature sunk to the lowest depth of degradation.

Yours obediently,
ROBERT ANDERSON.

Mentor was unappeased, and in the same paper wrote:

I have read the interview with a representative of the *Globe* which Sir Robert Anderson accorded that paper in order to reply to my observations upon what he had said in *Blackwood's Magazine* concerning the Jack the Ripper crimes. The editor of the JEWISH CHRONICLE has also been so good as to send for my perusal Sir Robert Anderson's letter to him, which appears in these columns, on the same subject. With great deference to Sir Robert, it appears to me that he misses the whole point of my complaint against what he wrote. I did not so much object to his saying that Jack the Ripper was a Jew, though so particular a friend of our people would have been well-advised, knowing the peculiar condition in which we are situated, and the prejudice that is constantly simmering against us, had he kept that fact to himself. No good purpose was served by his revealing it. It would have sufficed had he said that he was satisfied the murderer was discovered.

As I pointed out, the creature whom Sir Robert believes to have been the author of the heinous crimes was a lunatic – obviously his brain virulently diseased – so that if he *was* a Jew, however regrettable it may be that our people produced such an abnormality, in that there does not lie the aspersion. What I objected to – and *pace* Sir Robert Anderson's explanations still do – in his *Blackwood's* article, is his assertion that Jews who knew that "Jack the Ripper" had done his foul deeds, shielded him from the police, and guarded him so that he could continue his horrible career, just because he was a Jew. This was the aspersion to which I referred and about which I notice Sir Robert says nothing. Of course, when Sir Robert says that the man he means was "proved" to be the murderer, and that upon that point he spoke facts, he also ignores the somewhat important matter that the man was never put upon his trial. Knowing what I do, I would hesitate to brand even such a creature Sir Robert describes as the author of the Ripper crimes upon the very strongest evidence short of a conviction after due trial . . .

These sensational claims by Anderson did not go unnoticed in official quarters. They were the subject of comment in the House of Commons. *The Times* of 20 April 1910 reported:

Mr. MAC VEAGH asked the Secretary of State for the Home Department whether his attention had been called to the revelations published by Sir Robert Anderson with regard to what were generally known as the Jack the Ripper murders; whether he obtained the sanction of the Home Office or Scotland Yard authorities to such publication; and, if not, whether any, and if so what, steps could be taken with regard to it.

Mr. CHURCHILL. – Sir Robert Anderson neither asked for nor received any sanction to the publication, but the matter appears to me of minor importance in comparison with others that arise in connexion with the same series of articles. (Hear, hear.)

Mr. MAC VEAGH asked whether there was a Home Office minute expressly prohibiting the publication of documents of this kind.

No answer was returned.

Despite the criticism, Anderson repeated his story in his book *The Lighter Side of My Official Life* when it was published by Hodder and Stoughton later in 1910, albeit in a slightly modified form:

[Page 133 *et seq*] My last chapter brought down my story to my appointment, in September, 1888, as Assistant Commissioner of Police and head of the Criminal Investigation Department. Mr. Monro was not "an easy man to follow," and my difficulties in succeeding to the post were increased by the foolish ways of the Home Office, as well a by the circumstances of the times. As I have already said, Sir Charles Warren had then secured the loyal support of the Force generally. But the officers of the Criminal Investigation Department were demoralised by the treatment accorded to their late chief; and during the interval since his practical retirement sinister rumours were in circulation as to the appointment of his successor. If the announcement had been made that, on his official retirement on the 31st August, I should succeed to the office, things might have settled down. For all the principal officers knew and trusted me. But for some occult reason the matter was kept secret, and I was enjoined not to make my appointment known. I had been in the habit of frequenting Mr. Monro's room, as we were working together in political crime matters; but when I did so now, and Sir Charles Warren took advantage of my visit to come over to see me, it was at once inferred that he was spying on me because I was Mr. Monro's friend. The indignation felt by the officers was great, and I had some difficulty in preventing Chief-Superintendent Williamson from sending in his resignation.

Then, again, I was at that time physically unfit to enter on the duties of my new post. For some time past I had not had an adequate holiday, and the strain of long and anxious work was telling on me. "A man is as old as he feels," and by this test I was older at that time than when I left office a dozen years later. Dr. Gilbart Smith, of Harley Street, insisted that I must have two months' rest, and he added that he would probably give me a certificate for a further two months' "sick leave." This, of course, was out of the question. But I told Mr. Matthews, greatly to his distress, that I could not take up my new duties until I had had a month's holiday in Switzerland. And so, after one week at Scotland Yard, I crossed the Channel.

But this was not all. The second of the crimes known as the Whitechapel murders was committed the night before I took office, and the third occurred the night of the day on which I left London. The newspapers soon began to comment on my absence. And letters from Whitehall decided me to spend the last week of my holiday in Paris, that I might be in touch with my office. On the night of my arrival in the French capital two more victims fell to the knife of the murder-fiend; and next day's post brought me an urgent appeal from Mr. Matthews to return to London; and of course I complied.

On my return I found the Jack-the-Ripper scare in full swing. When the stolid English go in for a scare they take leave of all moderation and common sense. If nonsense were solid, the nonsense that was talked and written about those murders would sink a *Dreadnought*. The subject is an unsavoury one, and I must write about it with reserve. But it is enough to say that the wretched victims belonged to a very small class of degraded women who frequent the East End streets after midnight, in hope of inveigling belated drunkards, or men as degraded as themselves. I spent the day of my return to town, and half the following night, in reinvestigating the whole case, and next day I had a long conference on the subject with the Secretary of State and the Chief Commissioner of Police. "We hold you responsible to find the murderer," was Mr. Matthews' greeting to me. My answer was to decline the responsibility. "I hold myself responsible," I said, "to take all legitimate means to find him." But I went on to say that the measures I found in operation were, in my opinion, wholly indefensible and scandalous; for these wretched women were plying their trade under definite Police protection. Let the Police of that district, I urged, receive orders to arrest every known "street

698 The Anderson Suspect

woman" found on the prowl after midnight, or else let us warn
them that the Police will not protect them. Though the former
course would have been merciful to the very small class of women
affected by it, it was deemed too drastic and I fell back on the
second.

However the fact may be explained, it is a fact that no other
street murder occurred in the "Jack-the-Ripper" series. [A footnote here adds: — I am assuming that the murder of Alice M'Kenzie
on the 17th of July, 1889, was by another hand. I was absent from
London when it occurred, but the Chief Commissioner investigated
the case on the spot and decided that it was an ordinary murder, and
not the work of a sexual maniac. And the Poplar case of December,
1888, was a death from natural causes, and but for the "Jack the
Ripper" scare, no one would have thought of suggesting that it was
a homicide.] The last and most horrible of that maniac's crimes was
committed in a house in Miller's Court on the 9th of November.
And the circumstances of that crime disposed of all the theories of
the amateur "Sherlock Holmses" of that date.

One did not need to be a Sherlock Holmes to discover that the
criminal was a sexual maniac of a virulent type; that he was living in
the immediate vicinity of the scenes of the murders; and that, if he
was not living absolutely alone, his people knew of his guilt, and
refused to give him up to justice. During my absence abroad the
Police had made a house-to-house search for him, investigating the
case of every man in the district whose circumstances were such that
he could go and come and get rid of his blood-stains in secret. And
the conclusion we came to was that he and his people were certain
low-class Polish Jews; for it is a remarkable fact that people of that
class in the East End will not give up one of their number to Gentile
justice.

And the result proved that our diagnosis was right on every
point. For I may say at once that "undiscovered murders" are rare
in London, and the "Jack-the-Ripper" crimes are not within that
category. And if the Police here had powers such as the French
Police possess, the murderer would have been brought to justice.
Scotland Yard can boast that not even the subordinate officers of
the department will tell tales out of school, and it would ill
become me to violate the unwritten rule of the service. So I will
only add here that the "Jack-the-Ripper" letter which is preserved
in the Police Museum at New Scotland Yard is the creation of an
enterprising London journalist.

Having regard to the interest attaching to this case, I am almost tempted to disclose the identity of the murderer and of the pressman who wrote the letter above referred to. But no public benefit would result from such a course, and the traditions of my old department would suffer. I will merely add that the only person who had ever had a good view of the murderer unhesitatingly identified the suspect the instant he was confronted with him; but he refused to give evidence against him.

In saying that he was a Polish Jew I am merely stating a definitely ascertained fact. And my words are meant to specify race, not religion. For it would outrage all religious sentiment to talk of the religion of a loathsome creature whose utterly unmentionable vices reduced him to a lower level than that of the brute.

The next mention of Anderson's theories appeared in *The People* of Sunday, 9 June 1912, in a series of articles entitled "Scotland Yard and its Secrets" by Hargrave L. Adam:

Who Was Jack the Ripper?

As to what was really known of the assassin we have two very good authorities – Sir Robt. Anderson and Lieut.-col. Sir Hy. Smith. The former was at the time, head of the Criminal Investigation Department, Scotland Yard, and the latter Assistant Commissioner of the City Police. I add some further particulars to those already given. The murders, which were committed during the year 1888, were, with one exception, committed outside the City Police area, the exception being the one in Mitre-sq. Sir Robt. Anderson has assured the writer that the assassin was well known to the police, but unfortunately, in the absence of sufficient legal evidence to justify an arrest, they were unable to take him. It was a case of moral versus legal proof. The only chance the police had, apparently, was to take the miscreant red-handed, and that Sir Hy. Smith declares they very nearly accomplished. Jack the Ripper, however, "had all the luck," and just managed to escape. This occurred upon the night when he committed two murders – one in Berner-st., off the Commercial-rd, and the other in Mitre-sq. Sir Hy. Smith, with several of his men, was soon at the latter place. When the body came to be examined it was discovered that one-half the apron the woman was wearing at the time she was murdered was cut clean away and was missing.

Murderer's Narrow Escape.

One of the police, a man named Halse, happened luckily to get upon the track of the murderer. He ran his best pace in the direction of Whitechapel, and, when he came to Goulston-st., he noticed a light at the door of one of the Peabody dwellings. He pulled up, and discovered that the light was that of the lantern of a member of the Metropolitan Force, who was inspecting a piece of linen on the ground. It was bloodstained, and proved to be the missing half of the murdered woman's apron. On the wall above in chalk was written: "The Jews are the men that won't be blamed for nothing." Subsequently this inscription was wiped off by order of Sir Chas. Warren, who, as has already been stated, was at Scotland Yard at the time. This, Sir Hy. Smith maintains, was a fatal mistake, as the writing might have afforded a valuable clue. Sir Charles had it done as he feared a rising against the Jews. The assassin had wiped his hands on the missing half of the apron, and, it was further discovered, had, with remarkable audacity, washed his hands at a sink up a close in Dorset-st., only a few yards from the street . . . [*sic*]

But the question still remains, who and what was "Jack the Ripper"? Sir Robt. Anderson states confidently that he was a low-class Jew, being shielded by his fraternity. Sir Hy. Smith pooh-poohs this, declaring with equal confidence that he was a Gentile. He further states that the writing on the wall was probably a mere "blind," although the writing itself might have afforded a valuable clue. One thing is certain, namely, the elusive assassin, whoever he was, possessed anatomical knowledge. This, therefore, leads one pretty surely to the conclusion that he was a medical man, or one who had formerly been a medical student.

There can be little doubt that Anderson's suspect is the one named by Macnaghten in his February 1894 report as "Kosminski", although no first name is given. Apparent confirmation of this is contained in a copy of Anderson's memoirs, *The Lighter Side of My Official Life*, which was owned by the retired ex-Superintendent Donald S. Swanson, who maintained contact with Anderson after both men had retired. Swanson's copy of the book contains pencilled annotations in the familiar handwriting of Swanson himself. These notes received wide publicity for the first time in 1987 in the *Daily Telegraph*.

The relevant annotations appear in Swanson's copy of Anderson's book as follows. At the bottom of page 138 (the passage where Anderson had claimed that the murderer had been identified but that the witness refused to swear to it), Swanson wrote:

> *because the suspect was also a Jew and also because his evidence would convict the suspect, and witness would be the means of murderer being hanged which he did not wish to be left on his mind.*

In the margin the annotations continue: *And after this identification which suspect knew, no other murder of this kind took place in London.*

On the rear free endpaper Swanson noted: *Continuing from page 138, after the suspect had been identified at the Seaside Home where he had been sent by us with difficulty in order to subject him to identification, and he knew he was identified. On suspect's return to his brother's house in Whitechapel he was watched by police (City CID) by day & night. In a very short time the suspect with his hands tied behind his back, he was sent to Stepney Workhouse and then to Colney Hatch and died shortly afterwards – Kosminski was the suspect – DSS*

This would seem to lead naturally on to the following chapter, which looks at all we know of the only known serious City Police suspect who was kept under observation by their Detective Department. Whether or not it is one and the same person referred to by Anderson and Swanson is not certain. But there are similarities, such as the fact that he was a Jew, and Swanson's note that the suspect was "watched by police (City CID) which seem to indicate strongly that he was. Frustratingly for modern historians, contradictions and anomalies in the various stories exist.

CHAPTER 42

A City Police Suspect

The mystery and controversy over the actual identity of the
murderer has been compounded by the fact that the City of
London Police records on the case have not survived. The report
by Inspector McWilliam, head of the City Detective Department,
on the Eddowes murder, sent to the Home Office, is the only
detailed report by the City Police to survive.

To find more information on the so-called "City Police Suspect"
mentioned by Anderson and Swanson we are lucky to have a few
newspaper references from City sources. The best known of these is
that which appeared in *Reynolds News* of 15 September 1946, in an
article written by Justin Atholl:

> Inspector Robert Sagar, who died in 1924, played a leading part in
> the "Ripper" investigations. In his memoirs he said: "We had good
> reason to suspect a man who worked in Butchers' Row, Aldgate.
> We watched him carefully. There was no doubt that this man was
> insane, and after a time his friends thought it advisable to have him
> removed to a private asylum. After he was removed, there were no
> more Ripper atrocities."

However, a rather better account of Sagar's reminiscences on the
"Ripper" murders is to be found in *The City Press* of Saturday, 7
January 1905, on the occasion of his retirement. It was, of course,
written whilst he was still alive:

> His professional association with the terrible atrocities which were
> perpetrated some years ago in the East End by the so-styled "Jack
> the Ripper" was a very close one. Indeed, Mr. Sagar knows as much
> about those crimes, which terrified the Metropolis, as any detective
> in London. He was deputed to represent the City police force in
> conference with the detective heads of the Metropolitan force
> nightly at Leman Street Police Station during the period covered

by those ghastly murders. Much has been said and written – and even more conjectured – upon the subject of the "Jack-the-Ripper" murders. It has been asserted that the murderer fled to the Continent, where he perpetrated similar hideous crimes; but that is not the case. The police realised, as also did the public, that the crimes were those of a madman, and suspicion fell upon a man, who, without a doubt, was the murderer. Identification being impossible, he could not be charged. He was, however, placed in a lunatic asylum, and the series of atrocities came to an end. There was a peculiar incident in connection with those tragedies which may have been forgotten. The apron belonging to the woman who was murdered in Mitre Square was thrown under a staircase in a common lodging house in Dorset Street [*sic*], and someone – presumably the murderer – had written on the wall above it, "The Jewes are not the people that will be blamed for nothing." A police officer engaged in the case, fearing that the writing might lead to an onslaught upon the Jews in the neighbourhood, rubbed the writing from the wall, and all record of the implied accusation was lost; but the fact that such an ambiguous message was left is recorded among the archives at the Guildhall.

Further information on the "City suspect" is contained in an article in *Thomson's Weekly News*[1] on the occasion of the retirement of another City officer, Detective Inspector Henry Cox:

THE TRUTH ABOUT THE WHITE-
CHAPEL MYSTERIES.
TOLD BY HARRY COX,
Ex-Detective Inspector, London City Police.
Specially Written for "Thomson's Weekly News."

It is only upon certain conditions that I have agreed to deal with the great Whitechapel crimes of fifteen years ago. Much has been written regarding the identity of the man who planned and successfully carried out the outrage. Many writers gifted with a vivid imagination have drawn pictures for the public of the criminal whom the police suspected. All have been woefully wrong. In not a single case has one succeeded in discovering the persons who while the trail of blood lay thick and hot was looked upon as a man not unlikely to be connected with the crimes.

It is my intention to relate several of my experiences while keeping this fellow under observation. I may give a theory as to the cause of the crimes, but on no account can I enter into the theories of my brother officers or indicate whether or not the last has been heard of the crimes.

There are those who claim that the perpetrator was well known to the police; that at the present moment he is incarcerated in one of His Majesty's penal settlements. Others hold that he was known to have jumped over London Bridge or Blackfriars Bridge; while a third party claims that he is the inmate of a private asylum. These theories I have no hesitation in dispelling at once.

I can well remember the sensation which the first of the horrible crimes caused among those whose duty it was to investigate the untoward happenings of the East End.

The murder of Martha Turner was an amazing puzzle to each of us. Never in the course of our experience had such a case occurred. It was clearly no ordinary East End crime. Most of the bodies which are found at the riverside or in the dark squalid streets bear the marks of struggles or of blows given in anger.

But this one bore neither. It appeared rather that the woman had been quietly throttled to death, and after death mutilated in the most horrible fashion. There were almost

Forty Wounds on the Body

Nine were in the throat, seventeen in the breast, and the others in the lower parts of the body.

The woman was well known to the police, and it was a comparatively easy matter to find out the companions she had visited in the early part of the night.

The movements of all were traced and the fact established beyond doubt that none of them had been responsible for her death.

One of the suspected persons was a soldier, but he had no difficulty in proving his innocence.

There was not a clue to help us in our work, and we were stumbling along very much in the dark, when suddenly we were startled by the news of another crime of a similar nature.

It was committed in Buck's Row, a dead-and-alive street in Whitechapel made up of warehouses and slum dwellings. The murder was discovered by a young constable named John Neil. On the morning of Friday, Aug 31, of the year 1888, he was patrolling his beat when a young man obviously labouring under great excitement rushed up to him and said – "'Ere, mister, there's been a terrible murder down at Mullin's stable."

"A murder!" said the policeman. "Are you sure?"

"Sure! Why look 'ere," spoke the young fellow, pointing to the knee of his trousers. "I was that 'urried to get to my work, 'avin slept in, that I fell over 'er afore I knew where I was. At first I thought it was a drunk woman, but in bendin' down to rouse 'er I put my 'and on my knee an' was 'orrified to find it all red with blood. Swelp me, mister, it did give me such a fright."

The body was moved to the mortuary at the instigation of Dr Henry Llewellen [*sic*], who was brought to the scene of the outrage by the constable. An examination speedily proved that here again was a crime the elucidation of which would be baffling in the extreme.

The woman had been mutilated beyond description, but everything pointed to the work having been done not in anger, but in a quiet, methodical manner. There was a dwelling-house adjoining the gateway, beside which the body had been found, and in it a woman and her son and daughter had been sitting at the time the murder must have taken place. All stated emphatically that although the night was quiet they

Heard Never a Sound

outside the house.

The news of the murder soon spread, and before long many amateur detectives were connecting it with the murder of Martha Turner, and advancing strange theories as to the murders.

Many believe several of them to this day, specially one to the effect that the murders were committed by some mad medical specialist, and the bodies conveyed in his own conveyance to the East End. An absurd piece of nonsense!

In nearly every case the murders were committed on the actual spot where the bodies were found, or very close to it.

We proved beyond doubt that the second victim met her unknown murderer near the scene of the crime, and was discovered dead about two hours afterwards [*sic*].

The woman was an inmate of a common lodging house who was forced to spend her last night on the street because she had not the few coppers necessary for her "doss."

She was seen in Whitechapel at nearly three o'clock on the Friday morning. At that time she was standing alone at the corner of Osborne [*sic*] Street.

A story got abroad that the body had been dragged along the roadway, but this is easily seen to be utter fiction when the evidence of Dr Llewellen at the inquest is glanced at. He stated clearly –

"There were no marks of any struggle or blood as if the body had been dragged."

When the full details of the crime were gathered it speedily became apparent to us that we had no ordinary cut-throat assassin to deal with. The man was evidently a mono-maniac, and one who possessed certain anatomical knowledge.

The greatest terror reigned among women of the lowest class. Many of them came to implore me to safeguard them, and stated that they were terrified to stir beyond their lodgings at nightfall.

Each of them fixed upon a certain man as the perpetrator, and it was due to the remarkable manner in which their stories agreed that an arrest was made.

Not a scrap of evidence could be proved against the suspect, however, and he was dismissed.

About a week after the second murder another occurred. The scene of the tragedy was Hanbury Street, and the victim was another fallen woman named Annie Chapman.

The greatest sensation of all, however, occurred on the last day of the month, when two of the ghastly crimes were committed.

One took place in Berner Street, the other in Mitre Square, the victims being Elizabeth Watts [sic] and Catherine Eddowes respectively.

The next and the final crime of the series did not take place till the 9th of November, when Mary Kelly was done to death in Dorset Street, and this leads me to point out a fact which, of course, could scarcely be grasped at the time of the murders, and which up till the present time has been pointed out by none.

That is, that the mysterious criminal had a carefully-thought-out system under which he carried out the outrages. The first crime took place on August 6 [sic], the second on the last day of the month. The third occurred in the beginning of the following month, this time two days later, and the fourth and fifth were once again on the last day of the month. The final murder was again on the opening days of the month.

This, as I say, seems to point to the murderer having a system, but it also considerably strengthens the theory that the man was a sailor, and timed his murders so that he could board his vessel just as it was on the point of sailing.

We had many people under observations while the murders were being perpetrated, but it was not until the discovery of the body of Mary Kelly had been made that we seemed

To Get Upon the Trail.

Certain investigations made by several of our cleverest detectives made it apparent to us that a man living in the East End of London was not unlikely to have been connected with the crimes.

To understand the reason we must first of all understand the motive of the Whitechapel crimes. The motive was, there can be not the slightest doubt, revenge. Not merely revenge on the few poor unfortunate victims of the knife, but revenge on womankind. It was not a lust for blood, as many people have imagined.

The murderer was a misogynist, who at some time or another had been wronged by a woman. And the fact that his victims were of the lowest class proves, I think, that he was not, as has been stated, and educated man who had suddenly gone mad. He belonged to their own class.

Had he been wronged by a woman occupying a higher stage in society the murders would in all probability have taken place in the West End, the victims have been members of the fashionable demi-monde.

The man we suspected was about five feet six inches in height, with short, black, curly hair, and he had a habit of taking late walks abroad. He occupied several shops in the East End, but from time to time he became insane, and was forced to spend a portion of his time in an asylum in Surrey.

While the Whitechapel murders were being perpetrated his place of business was in a certain street, and after the last murder I was on duty in this street for nearly three months.

There were several other officers with me, and I think there can be no harm in stating that the opinion of most of them was that the man they were watching had something to do with the crimes. You can imagine that never once did we allow him to quit our sight. The least slip and another brutal crime might have been perpetrated under our very noses. It was not easy to forget that already one of them had taken place at the very moment when one of our smartest colleagues was passing the top of the dimly lit street.

The Jews in the street soon became
Aware of Our Presence

It was impossible for us to hide ourselves. They became suddenly alarmed, panic-stricken, and I can tell you that at nights we ran a considerable risk. We carried our lives in our hands so to speak, and at last we had to partly take the alarmed inhabitants into our confidence, and so throw them off the scent. We told them we were factory inspectors looking for tailors and capmakers who employed boys and girls under age, and pointing out the evils accruing from the sweaters' system asked them to co-operate with us in destroying it.

They readily promised so to do, although we knew well that they had no intention of helping us. Every man was as bad as another. Day after day we used to sit and chat with them, drinking their coffee, smoking their excellent cigarettes, and partaking of Kosher rum. Before many weeks had passed we were quite friendly with them, and knew that we could carry out our observations unmolested. I am sure they never once suspected that we were police detectives on the trail of the mysterious murderer; otherwise they would not have discussed the crimes with us as openly as they did.

We had the use of a house opposite the shop of the man we suspected, and, disguised, of course, we frequently stopped across in the role of customers.

Every newspaper loudly demanded that we should arouse from our slumber, and the public had lashed themselves into a state of fury and fear. The terror soon spread to the provinces too. Whenever a small crime was committed it was asserted that the Ripper had shifted his ground, and warning letters were received by many a terror-stricken woman. The latter were of course the work of cruel practical jokers. The fact, by the way, that the murderer

Never Shifted His Ground

rather inclines one to the belief that he was a mad, poverty-stricken inhabitant of some slum in the East End.

I shall never forget one occasion when I had to shadow our man during one of his late walks. As I watched him from the house opposite one night, it suddenly struck me that there was a wilder look than usual on his evil countenance, and I felt that something was about to happen. When darkness set in I saw him come forth from the door of his little shop and glance furtively around to see if he were being watched. I allowed him to get right out of the street before I left the house, and then I set off after him. I followed him to Lehman [sic] Street, and there I saw him enter a shop which I knew was the abode of a number of criminals well known to the police.

He did not stay long. For about a quarter of an hour I hung about keeping my eye on the door, and at last I was rewarded by seeing him emerging alone.

He made his way down to St George's in the East End, and there to my astonishment I saw him stop and speak to a drunken woman.

I crouched in a doorway and held my breath. Was he going to throw himself right into my waiting arms? He passed on after a moment or two, and on I slunk after him.

As I passed the woman she laughed and shouted something after me, which, however, I did not catch.

My man was evidently of opinion that he might be followed every minute. Now and again he turned his head and glanced over his shoulder, and consequently I had the greatest difficulty in keeping behind him.

I had to work my way along, now with my back to the wall, now pausing and making little runs for a sheltering doorway. Not far from where the model lodging-house stands he met another woman, and for a considerable distance he walked along with her.

Just as I was beginning to prepare myself for a terrible ordeal, however, he pushed her away from him and set off at a rapid pace.

In the end he brought me, tired, weary, and nerve-strung,

Back to the Street He Had Left

where he disappeared into his own house.

Next morning I beheld him busy as usual. It is indeed very strange that as soon as this madman was put under observation the mysterious crimes ceased, and that very soon he removed from his usual haunts and gave up his nightly prowls. He was never arrested for the reason that not the slightest scrap of evidence could be found to connect him with the crimes.

Long after the public had ceased to talk about the murders we continued to investigate them.

We had no clue to go upon, but every point suggested by the imagination was seized upon and worked bare. There was not a criminal in London capable of committing the crimes but was looked up and shadowed.

The mystery is as much a mystery as it was fifteen years ago. It is all very well for amateur detectives to fix the crime upon this or that suspect, and advance theories in the public press to prove his guilt. They are working upon surmise, nothing more.

The mystery can never be cleared up until someone comes forward and himself proves conclusively that he was the blood-thirsty demon who terrorised the country, or unless he returns to his crimes and is caught red-handed. He is still alive then? you ask. I do not know. For all I know he may be dead. I have personally no evidence either way.

And so Henry Cox concluded his reminiscences on a "City suspect", an essay which, even if it does not clearly identify the subject of the City Police observations, does give a valuable insight into the working methods of the police. Although not named by Henry Cox, there may be sufficient details given of the City suspect for him to be identified by the diligent researcher. Detective Inspector Henry Cox was to achieve a moment of fame on 18 March 1903. He was then on duty at the Bank of England when, after a desperate struggle, he arrested Samuel Herbert Dougal, the notorious "Moat Farm Murderer"

CHAPTER 43

Chief Inspector Abberline and the Chapman Theory

It cannot be doubted that in 1888 Inspector Frederick George Abberline was one of the key investigators of the mystery of the Whitechapel Murders. He led the grass-roots investigation in Whitechapel, from the time of the involvement of Scotland Yard in September 1888 until some time around March 1889. Charge of the case was then taken on by Abberline's colleague Detective Inspector Henry Moore, who had gone to Whitechapel with Abberline from the start of the investigation. Meanwhile, Abberline moved on to other investigations, notably the Cleveland Street scandal of that year. In 1890 Abberline was promoted to the rank of Chief Inspector and he retired in 1892. Abberline's retirement and a few of his reminiscences were reported in *Cassell's Saturday Journal* of 28 May 1892. The subject of the Whitechapel Murders was touched upon in this piece:

> A man of such intimate acquaintance with the East End as Mr. Abberline naturally found himself recalled to the scene of his former labours when the series of Whitechapel murders horrified all the world. His knowledge of crime, and the people who commit it, is "extensive and peculiar." There is no exaggeration in the statement that, whenever a robbery or offence against the law had been committed in the district, the detective knew where to find his man and the missing property too. His friendly relations with the shady folk who crowd into the common lodging houses enabled him to pursue his investigations connected with the murders with the greatest certainty, and the facilities afforded him made it clear to his mind that the miscreant was not to be found lurking in a "dossers" kitchen. In fact, the desire of the East Enders to assist the police was so keen that the number of statements made — all of them requiring to be recorded and searched into — was so great that the officer almost broke down under the pressure. Yet his anxiety to bring the murderer to

justice led him, after occupying the whole day in directing his staff, to pass his time in the streets until early morning, driving home, fagged and weary, at 5 a.m. And it happened frequently, too, that, just as he was going to bed, he would be summoned back to the East End by a telegraph, there to interrogate some lunatic or suspected person whom the inspector in charge would not take the responsibility of questioning.

"Theories!" exclaims the inspector, when conversing about the murders— "we were lost almost in theories; there were so many of them." Nevertheless, he has one which is new. He believes, from the evidence of his own eyesight, that the Miller's Court atrocity was the last of the real series, the others having been imitations, and that in Miller's Court the murderer reached the culminating point of the gratification of his morbid ideas.

The final mention of Abberline's ideas about the Whitechapel Murders appeared in news reports in March 1903 that were prompted by the stories of the recently arrested "Borough poisoner", George Chapman, whose real name was Severin Klosowski. The *Pall Mall Gazette* reported on Tuesday, 24 March 1903:

THE CHAPMAN-RIPPER THEORY.
INSPECTOR ABBERLINE INTERVIEWED.
A REMARKABLE STORY.
(Special to the "Pall Mall Gazette.")

Should Klosowski, the wretched man now lying under sentence of death for wife-poisoning, go to the scaffold without a "last dying speech and confession," a great mystery may forever remain unsolved, but the conviction that "Chapman" and "Jack the Ripper" were one and the same person will not in the least be weakened in the mind of the man who is, perhaps, better qualified than anyone else in this country to express an opinion in the matter. We allude to Mr. F.G. Abberline, formerly Chief Detective-inspector of Scotland Yard, the official who had full charge of the criminal investigations at the time of the terrible murders in Whitechapel.

When a representative of the *Pall Mall Gazette* called on Mr. Abberline yesterday and asked for his views on the startling theory set up by one of the morning papers, the retired detective said: "What an extraordinary thing it is that you should just have called upon me now. I had just commenced, not knowing anything about the report in the newspaper, to write to the Assistant Commissioner of Police, Mr. Macnaghten, to say how strongly I was impressed with the opinion that "Chapman" was also the author of the Whitechapel murders. Your appearance saves me the trouble. I intended to write on Friday, but a fall in the garden, injuring my hand and shoulder, prevented my doing so until to-day.

Mr. Abberline had already covered a page and a half of foolscap, and was surrounded with a sheaf of documents and newspaper cuttings dealing with the ghastly outrages of 1888.

Coincidences

"I have been so struck with the remarkable coincidences in the two series of murders," he continued, "that I have not been able to think of anything else for several days past – not, in fact, since the Attorney-General made his opening statement at the recent trial, and traced the antecedents of Chapman before he came to this country in 1888. Since then the idea has taken full possession of me, and everything fits in and dovetails so well that I cannot help feeling that this is the man we struggled so hard to capture fifteen years ago.

"My interest in the Ripper case was especially deep. I had for fourteen years previously been an inspector of police in Whitechapel, but when the murders began I was at the central office at Scotland Yard. On the application of Superintendent Arnold I went back to the East End just before Annie Chapman was found mutilated, and as chief of the detective corps I gave myself up to the study of the cases. Many a time, even after we had carried our inquiries as far as we could – and we made out no fewer than 1,600 sets of papers respecting our investigations – instead of going home when I was off duty, I used to patrol the district until four or five o'clock in the morning, and, while keeping my eyes wide open for clues of any kind, have many and many a time given those wretched and homeless women, who were Jack the Ripper's special prey, fourpence or sixpence for a shelter to get them away from the streets and out of harm's way."

Chapman's Movements.

"As I say," went on the criminal expert, "there are a score of things which make one believe that Chapman is the man; and you must understand that we have never believed all those stories about Jack the Ripper being dead, or that he was a lunatic, or anything of that kind. For instance, the date of the arrival in England coincides with the beginning of the series of murders in Whitechapel; there is a coincidence also in the fact that the murders ceased in London when "Chapman" went to America, while similar murders began to be perpetrated in America after he landed there. The fact that he studied medicine and surgery in Russia before he came over here is well established, and it is curious to note that the first series of murders was the work of an expert surgeon, while the recent poisoning cases were proved to be done by a man with more than an elementary knowledge of medicine. The story told by "Chapman's" wife of the attempt to murder her with a long knife while in America is not to be ignored, but something else with regard to America is still more remarkable.

A Significant Story.

"While the coroner was investigating one of the Whitechapel murders he told the jury a very queer story. You will remember that Dr. Philips, the divisional surgeon, who made the post-mortem examination, not only spoke of the skilfulness with which the knife had been used, but stated that there was overwhelming evidence to show that the criminal had so mutilated the body that he could possess himself of one of the organs. The coroner, in commenting on this, said that he had been told by the sub-curator of the pathological museum connected with one of the great medical schools that some few months before an American had called upon him and asked him to procure a number of specimens. He stated his willingness to give £20 for each. Although the strange visitor was told that his wish was impossible of fulfilment, he still urged his request. It was known that the request was repeated at another institution of a similar character in London. The coroner at the time said 'Is it not possible that a knowledge of this demand may have inspired some abandoned wretch to possess himself of the specimens? It seems beyond belief that such inhuman wickedness could enter into the mind of any man; but, unfortunately, our criminal annals prove that every crime is possible!'

"It is a remarkable thing," Mr. Abberline pointed out, "that after the Whitechapel horrors America should have been the place where a similar kind of murder began, as though the miscreant had not fully supplied the demand of the American agent.

One Discrepancy.

"There are many other things extremely remarkable. The fact that

Klosowski when he came to reside in this country occupied a lodging in George-yard, Whitechapel-road, where the first murder was committed, is very curious, and the height of the man and the peaked cap he is said to have worn quite tallies with the descriptions I got of him. All agree, too, that he was a foreign-looking man, but that, of course, helped us little in a district so full of foreigners as Whitechapel. One discrepancy only have I noted, and this is that the people who alleged that they saw Jack the Ripper at one time or another, state that he was a man about thirty-five or forty years of age. They, however, state that they only saw his back, and it is easy to misjudge age from a back view.''

Altogether Mr. Abberline considers that the matter is quite beyond abstract speculation and coincidence, and believes the present situation affords an opportunity of unravelling a web of crime such as no man living can appreciate in its extent and hideousness.

The following day the *Morning Advertiser* recounted the interview of the *Pall Mall Gazette* correspondent with Abberline, and added some words of their own, disagreeing with the retired detective's ideas:

Against this theory are to be set the facts that Chapman's crimes were quite unlike those of ''Jack the Ripper.'' Chapman went about his deadly work with method and patience, taking as little risk as he could. He got rid of his ''wives'' merely because he was tired of them. ''Jack the Ripper,'' on the other hand, evidently had a violent feeling against women of the class whom he killed, unless he committed his murders in order to secure and sell certain parts of their bodies, as one theory suggested.

Further, it is pretty well known, as is pointed out in our correspondence column to-day, that the police have good reason to believe that the Whitechapel murders were committed by one of three men, all of whom are either dead or in confinement.

Students of modern crime are not likely to pay much heed to Inspector Abberline's theory.

The *Pall Mall Gazette* responded to criticisms of the first piece with a further report in their issue of Tuesday, 31 March 1903:

THE CHAPMAN-RIPPER THEORY.
FRESH STATEMENT FROM AN AUTHORITY.
[Special to the "Pall Mall Gazette".]

Since the *Pall Mall Gazette* a few days ago gave a series of coincidences supporting the theory that Klosowski, or Chapman, as he was for some time called, was the perpetrator of the "Jack the Ripper" murders in Whitechapel fifteen years ago, it has been interesting to note how many amateur criminologists have come forward with statements to the effect that it is useless to attempt to link Chapman with the Whitechapel atrocities. This cannot possibly be the same man, it is said, because, first of all, Chapman is not the miscreant who could have done the previous deeds, and, secondly, it is contended that the Whitechapel murderer has long been known to be beyond the reach of earthly justice.

In order, if possible, to clear the ground with respect to the latter statement particularly, a representative of the *Pall Mall Gazette* again called on Mr. F.G. Abberline, formerly Chief Detective Inspector of Scotland Yard, yesterday, and elicited the following statement from him:-

"You can state most emphatically," said Mr. Abberline, "that Scotland Yard is really no wiser on the subject than it was fifteen years ago. It is simple nonsense to talk of the police having proof that the man is dead. I am, and always have been, in the closest touch with Scotland Yard, and it would have been next to impossible for me not to have known all about it. Besides, the authorities would have been only too glad to make an end of such a mystery, if only for their own credit."

To convince those who have any doubts on the point, Mr. Abberline produced recent documentary evidence which put the ignorance of Scotland Yard as to the perpetrator beyond the shadow of a doubt.

"I know," continued the well-known detective, "that it has been stated in several quarters that "Jack the Ripper" was a man who died in a lunatic asylum a few years ago, but there is nothing at all of a tangible nature to support such a theory."

Stories Repudiated.

Our representative called Mr. Abberline's attention to a statement made in a well-known Sunday paper, in which it was made out that the author was a young medical student who was found drowned in the Thames.

"Yes," said Mr. Abberline, "I know all about that story. But what does it amount to? Simply this. Soon after the last murder in Whitechapel the body of a young doctor was found in the Thames, but there is nothing beyond the fact that he was found at that time to incriminate him. A report was made to the Home Office about the matter, but that it was 'considered final and conclusive' is going altogether beyond the truth. Seeing that the same kind of murders began in America afterwards, there is much more reason to think the man emigrated. Then again, the fact that several months after December, 1888, when the student's body was found, the detectives were told still to hold themselves in readiness for further investigations seems to point to the conclusion that Scotland Yard did not in any way consider the evidence as final.''

"But what about Dr. Neil Cream? A circumstantial story is told of how he confessed on the scaffold – at least, he is said to have got as far as 'I am Jack —————' when the jerk of the rope cut short his remarks.''

"That is also another idle story,'' replied Mr. Abberline. "Neil Cream was not even in this country when the Whitechapel murders took place. No; the identity of the diabolical individual has yet to be established, notwithstanding the people who have produced these rumours and who pretend to know the state of the official mind.''

Further Criticisms Rebutted.

"As to the question of the dissimilarity of character in the crimes which one hears so much about,'' continued the expert, "I cannot see why one man should not have done both, provided he had the professional knowledge, and this is admitted in Chapman's case. A man who could watch his wives being slowly tortured to death by poison, as he did, was capable of anything; and the fact that he should have attempted, in such a cold-blooded manner, to murder his first wife with a knife in New Jersey, makes one more inclined to believe in the theory that he was mixed up in the two series of crimes. What, indeed, is more likely than that a man to some extent skilled in medicine and surgery should discontinue the use of the knife when his commission – and I still believe Chapman had a commission from America – came to an end, and then for the remainder of his ghastly deeds put into practice his knowledge of poisons? Indeed, if the theory be accepted that a man who takes life on a wholesale scale never ceases his accursed habit until he is either arrested or dies, there is much to be said for Chapman's consistency. You see, incentive changes; but the fiendishness is not eradicated. The victims, too, you will notice, continue to be women; but they are of different classes, and obviously call for different methods of despatch.''

With this well-publicised theory another name, that of an established murderer, was added to the long list of Ripper "suspects".

CHAPTER 44

14 October 1896 – A Letter From "Jack the Ripper"

Although the police, other agencies and individuals received literally hundreds of letters purporting to be from the murderer from September 1888 onwards, we have included here only those which are generally agreed by serious scholars of the Whitechapel Murders to be of most significance in our understanding of the case. As early as 11 October 1888, *Truth* had noted a spate of hoax letters from the lunatic fringe:

> No sooner was a letter signed "Jack the Ripper" published, than hundreds of ghastly jokers at once addressed similar letters to the authorities . . . On the doctrine of probabilities, it is long odds against the murderer having written the "Jack the Ripper" letters. He may have, and so may thousands of others.

The name "Jack the Ripper" was appended to dozens of letters in as many different hands. Although the original "Dear Boss" correspondence of 1888 was imitated many times, the last recorded communication[1] of that sort was received by the police as late as 14 October 1896. Written in red ink, it read as follows:

> *Dear Boss,*
> *You will be surprised to*
> *find that this comes from yours*
> *as of old Jack-the-Ripper. Ha. Ha*
> *If my old friend Mr Warren is dead*
> *you can read it. you might*
> *remember me if you try and*
> *think a little Ha Ha. The last job*
> *was a bad one and no mistake nearly*
> *buckled, and meant it to*
> *be best of the lot &what curse it,*
> *Ha Ha Im alive yet and you'll*

soon find it out. I mean to go
on again when I get the chance
wont it be nice dear old Boss to
have the good old times once
again. you never caught me
and you never will. Ha Ha
  You police are a smart lot, the lot
of you could nt catch one man
Where have I been Dear Boss
you d like to know. abroad, if
you would like to know, and
just come back. ready to go on
with my work and stop when
you catch me. Well good bye
Boss wish me luck. Winters coming
"The Jewes are people that are
blamed for nothing" Ha Ha
have you heard this before
                Yours truly
                Jack the Ripper

The combination of the red ink, references to the famous "Dear Boss" correspondence, the Goulston Street graffito, clerkly hand, correct spelling, signature "Jack the Ripper" and threat to begin "work" again resulted in some interesting police comment on it.

The file cover on this correspondence[2] states:

Submitted through CI Dept.
                H Division
Submitting a letter signed Jack the Ripper
[Stamped: – 15 OCT 96]
Supt Central
This is not, I think, the handwriting of our <u>original</u> correspondent, but it is not a bad imitation Will you get out the old letter & compare?

                [*Init. illeg.*]
                15/10

Report Submitted
18/10 DSSwanson
<u>Sir E. Bradford</u> to see
  I do not think that these cases shd. be circld. to surrounding stns,

but that all such letters should be sent to C.O. as soon as possible
for instructions as to action, if any, to be taken.

H to see.   [*Init. illeg.*]
                              19/10/96

H 19.10.96 seen
              [LC?] Actg.Supt.
Central to see & lay by.
        [*Init. illeg.*]
              20/10
Seen.   D.S. Swanson.

The first report[3] by Detective Inspector Payne, dated 14 October
1896, is as follows:

METROPOLITAN POLICE.

Commercial St Station.   H DIVISION.
[Stamped: – Metropolitan Police Received 15 OCT 96 Criminal
Investigation Dept.]

                                 14th Octr. 1896.

Reference to Papers.
Attached.

I beg to submit attached letter received per post 14th inst. signed
Jack the Ripper, stating that writer has just returned from abroad
and means to go on again when he gets the chance. The letter
appears similar to those received by police during the series of
murders in this district in 1888 and 1889.

Police have been instructed to keep a sharp lookout.

                              Geo. Payne, SDInsp

Submitted. I caused a telegram to be sent to surrounding
Divisions, upon receipt of letter 14th ins. asking that directions
be given to police to keep a sharp look out, but at the same time to
keep the information quiet. Writer in sending the letter no doubt
considers it a great joke at the expense of police.

                              L Cross ActgSup. [?]

The final report on this subject, dated 18 October 1896, is written
by Henry Moore, by now promoted to Detective Chief Inspector,
who, as we have seen, was put in charge of the overall "on the
ground" enquiries into the Whitechapel Murders in 1889 in place
of Inspector Abberline. The report[4] reads:

METROPOLITAN POLICE.
CRIMINAL INVESTIGATION DEPARTMENT,
NEW SCOTLAND YARD,
18th day of October 1896

SUBJECT Letter received
signed Jack the
Ripper.

With reference to attached anonymous letter, signed "Jack the Ripper"; wherein the writer states that he has returned from abroad; and is now ready to commence work again; vide Chief Constable's minute re same.

I beg to report having carefully perused all the old "Jack the Ripper" letters, and fail to find any similarity of handwriting in any of them, with the exception of the two well remembered communications which were sent to the "Central News" office; one a letter, dated 25th Septr./88 and the other a post-card bearing the post-mark 1st Oct./88., vide copies herewith.

On comparing the handwriting of the present letter with handwriting of that document, I find many similarities in the formation of letters. For instance the y's, t's, and w's are very much the same. Then there are several words which appear in both documents; Viz:-Dear Boss; ha ha (although in the present letter the capital H. is used instead of the small one); and in speaking of the murders he describes them as his "work" or the last "job"; and if I get a (or the) chance; then there are the words "Yours truly" and the Ripper (the latter on post-card) are very much alike. Besides there are the finger smears.

Considering the lapse of time, it would be interesting to know how the present writer was able to use the words – "The Jewes are people that are blamed for nothing" [*here there is a marginal note –* "Were not the exact words 'The Jewes are not the men to be blamed for nothing'? DSS?"]; as it will be remembered that they are practically the same words that were written in chalk, undoubtedly by the murderer, on the wall at Goulston St., Whitechapel, on the night of 30th. Sept., 1888, after the murders of Mrs. Stride and Mrs. Eddows; and the word Jews was spelt on that occasion precisely as it is now.

Although these similarities strangely exist between the documents, I am of opinion that the present writer is not the original correspondent who prepared the letters to the Central News; as if it had been I should have thought he would have again addressed it to the same Press Agency; and not to Commercial Street Police Station.

In conclusion I beg to observe that I do not attach any importance to this communication. [*This comment has the marginal marking* "A"].

Henry Moore, Chf Inspr.

In my opinion the handwritings are not the same. I agree as at A. I beg that the letter may be put with other similar letters. Its circulation is to be regretted.

Donald S.Swanson
Supt.

As far as the official police reports are concerned, the documents in this chapter are the last to appear in the official Whitechapel Murders files. It is, perhaps, appropriate that the official record ends here, on a speculative note about an anonymous letter signed "Jack the Ripper".

Sources

The Metropolitan Police (MEPO) FIles and Home Office (HO) Files are held on microfilm at the Public Record Office.

CHAPTER 1: 3 April 1888 – Murder of Emma Smith (pp. 3–7)

1 St. B.G./Wh/123/19. (London Metropolitan Archives)

CHAPTER 2: 7 August 1888 – Murder of Martha Tabram (pp. 8–22)

1 Ref. MEPO 3/140, f 34
2 Ref. MEPO 3/140, ff. 44–8
3 ACB = Alexander Carmichael Bruce, Assistant Commissioner (CID)
4 Ref. MEPO 3/140, ff. 49–51
5 Ref. MEPO 3/140, ff. 52–9
6 Ref. MEPO 3/140, ff. 36–42
7 Ref. MEPO 3/140, f 43

CHAPTER 3: 31 August 1888 – Murder of Mary Ann Nichols (pp. 23–54)

1 Ref. MEPO 3/140, f 238
2 Ref. MEPO 3/140, ff. 239–41
3 Ref. MEPO 3/140, ff. 235–8
4 Ref. HO 144/220/A49301B, f177
5 Ref. HO 144/220/A49301B, f 178
6 Ref. HO 144/220/A49301B, f 179
7 Ref. HO 144/220/A49301, f 16
8 Ref. HO 144/221/A49301C, ff. 129–34
9 Ref. HO 144/221/A49301C, f 128
10 Ref. HO 144/221/A49301C, ff. 6–7
11 Ref. HO 144/221/A49301C, f 8
12 Ref. HO 144/221/A49301C, ff. 9–10
13 Ref. HO 144/221/A49301C, f 11

CHAPTER 4: 8 September 1888 – Murder of Annie Chapman (pp. 55–77)

1 Ref. MEPO 3/140, ff. 9–11
2 Ref. MEPO 3/140, f 11
3 Ref. MEPO 3/140, ff. 12–13
4 Ref. MEPO 3/140, ff. 13–15
5 Ref. MEPO 3/140, ff. 16–17
6 Ref. MEPO 3/140, ff. 15–16
7 Ref. MEPO 3/140, ff. 17–20
8 Ref. MEPO 3/140, f 20
9 Ref. MEPO 3/140, ff. 21–3
10 Ref. MEPO 3/140, ff. 24–5
11 Ref. MEPO 3/140, ff. 26–8
12 Ref. MEPO 3/140, ff. 29–31
13 Ref. MEPO 3/140, ff. 242–56
14 Ref. HO 144/221/A49301C, f 136
15 Ref. HO 144/221/A49301C, ff. 137–45

CHAPTER 5: September 1888 – The Chapman Inquest and Police Enquiries (pp. 78–120)

1 Ref. HO 144/221/A49301C, f 13
2 Ref. HO 144/221/A49301C, ff. 14–15
3 Ref. HO 144/221/A49301C, page 6 e-f
4 Ref. HO 144/221/A49301C, ff. 16–17
5 Ref. HO 144/221/A49301C, page 3f
6 Ref. HO 144/221/A49301C, ff. 18–19
7 Ref. *Sir Evelyn Ruggles-Brise* by Shane Leslie, London, 1938
8 Ref. HO 144/221/A49301C, ff. 20–1

CHAPTER 6: September 1888 – Dr Anderson on Sick Leave and the Question of a Reward (pp. 121–33)

1 Ref. HO 65/62, p 1
2 Ref. HO 65/62, p 4
3 Ref. HO 144/588/B5005
4 In private collection
5 Ref. HO 144/220/A49301B, ff. 180–1
6 Ref. HO 144/220/A49301B, ff. 184–5
7 Ref. MEPO 3/140, ff. 170–176, also copy filed under HO 144/220/A49301B, f 185
8 Ref. MEPO 3/140, ff. 174–175 and HO 144/220/A49301B, ff. 182–3
9 Ref. HO 144/220/A49301B, ff. 172–3
10 Ref. HO 144/220/A49301B, ff. 170–1
11 Ref. HO 144/220/A49301B, f 187
12 Ref. HO 144/220/A49301B, ff. 188–9
13 Ref. HO 144/220/A49301B, ff. 190–1
14 Ref. HO 144/221/A49301C, f 89
15 Ref. HO 144/221/A49301C, ff. 90–2
16 Ref. HO 144/221/A49301C, ff. 304–6

CHAPTER 7: 30 September 1888 – Murder of Elizabeth Stride (pp. 134–52)

 1 Ref. *The Times*, 1 October, p. 6f
 2 Ref. *The Times*, 2 October, p. 3f
 3 Ref. HO 144/221/A49301C, ff. 148–59
 4 Ref. MEPO 3/140/221/A49301C, ff. 204–6
 5 Ref. MEPO 3/140/221/A49301C, f 207
 6 Ref. MEPO 3/140/221/A49301C, ff. 208–210
 7 Ref. MEPO 3/140/221/A49301C, f 211
 8 Ref. MEPO 3/140/221/A49301C, ff. 212–14
 9 Ref. MEPO 3/140/221/A49301C, ff. 215–16
10 Ref. HO 144/221/A49301C, ff. 110–11
11 Ref. HO 144/221/A49301C, ff. 112–13
12 Ref. HO 144/221/A49301C, ff. 114–15
13 Ref. HO 144/221/A49301C, ff. 116–18
14 Ref. HO 144/221/A49301C, f 147
15 Ref. HO 144/221/A49301C, f 199
16 Ref. HO 144/221/A49301C, ff. 200–01

CHAPTER 8: October 1888 – The Stride Inquest (pp. 153–98)

All ref to *The Times*, 2 October 1888, page 6

CHAPTER 9: 30 September 1888 – Murder of Catherine Eddowes (pp. 199–221)

 1 Ref. HO 144/221/A49301C, ff. 162–70
 2 Ref. HO 144/221/A49301C, f 171
 3 Ref. HO 144/221/A49301C, f 172
 4 Ref. HO 144/221/A49301C, ff. 173–81
 5 Ref. HO 144/221/A49301C, f 183
 6 Ref. HO 144/221/A49301C, ff. 184–94
 7 Ref. HO 144/221/A49301C, ff. 195–6
 8 Ref. HO 144/221/A49301C, ff. 197–8
 9 Ref. MEPO 3/3153, f 1
10 Ref. MEPO 3/3153, ff. 2–4
11 1888 colour Police facsimile ref. MEPO 3/142, ff. 2–3
12 Ref. MEPO 3/142, ff. 491–2
13 Ref. the Littlechild letter, S.P. Evans private collection
14 Ref. p. 6b

CHAPTER 10: October 1888 – The Eddowes Inquest (pp. 222–66)

 1 Ref. Coroner's inquest (L), 1888, No. 135, Catherine Eddowes inquest, 1888 (Corporation of London Record Office)

CHAPTER 11: October 1888 – Will the Unknown Killer Strike Again? (pp. 267–95)

 1 Ref. page 3c

2 Ref. HO 144/220/A49301B, f 192
3 Ref. HO 144/220/A49301B, ff. 193–6
4 Ref. HO 144/220/A49301B, ff.197–8
5 Ref. HO 144/220/A49301B, ff. 199–200
6 Ref. HO 144/220/A49301B, f 201
7 Ref. HO 144/220/A49301B, f 202
8 Ref. HO 144/220/A49301B, f 203
9 Ref. HO 144/220/A49301B, ff. 204–11
10 Ref. HO 144/220/A49301B, ff. 212–13
11 Ref. HO 144/220/A49301B, ff. 214–19
12 Ref. HO 144/220/A49301B, f 220
13 Ref. HO 144/220/A49301B, f 221
14 Ref. HO 144/220/A49301B, ff. 222–3
15 Ref. HO 144/220/A49301B, f 224
16 Ref. HO 144/220/A49301B, ff. 225–7
17 Ref. HO 144/220/A49301B, f 228
18 Ref. HO 144/220/A49301B, ff. 229–30
19 Ref. HO 144/220/A49301B, ff. 231–2
20 Rcf. HO 144/220/A49301B, f 233
21 Ref. HO 144/220/A49301B, ff. 234–6
22 Ref. HO 144/221/A49301C, f 64
23 Ref. HO 144/221/A49301C, f 65
24 Ref. HO 144/221/A49301C, f 52
25 Ref. HO 144/221/A49301C, ff 66–7
26 Ref. HO 144/221/A49301C, ff. 53–4
27 Ref. Ref. HO 144/221/A49301C, ff. 62–3
28 Ref. HO 144/221/A49301C, f 76
29 Ref. HO 144/221/A49301C, f 77
30 Ref. HO 144/221/A49301C, f 87–7
31 Ref. HO 144/221/A49301C, ff. 83–5
32 Ref. HO 144/221/A49301C, f 93
33 Ref. page 6e

CHAPTER 12: More on Rewards and October Precautions (pp. 296–323)

1 Ref. HO 144/220/A49301B, f 237
2 Ref. HO 144/220/A49301B, f 238
3 Ref. HO 144/220/A49301B, ff 239–45
4 Ref. HO 144/220/A49301B, ff. 246–52
5 Ref. HO/144/220/A49301B, f 253
6 Ref. HO 144/220/A49301B, ff. 255–7
7 Ref. MEPO 3/143
8 Ref. HO 144/220/A49301B, ff. 271–2
9 Ref. HO 144/220/A49301B, f 273
10 Ref. HO 144/220/A49301B, f 275
11 Ref. HO 144/220/A49301B, ff. 276–8
12 Ref. MEPO 3/141
13 Ref. MEPO 3/141, ff. 167–9

14 Ref. MEPO 3/141, ff. 164–6
15 Ref. MEPO 3/141, ff. 158–63
16 Ref. HO 65/62 pp. 355–6
17 Ref. MEPO 1/55, p 343
18 Ref. HO 144/220/A49301B, ff. 279–80
19 Ref. HO 144/220/A49301B, ff. 281–2
20 Ref. HO 144/220/A49301B, ff. 283–6
21 Ref. HO 144/220/A49301B, ff. 296–8

CHAPTER 13: The Bloodhounds (pp. 324–32)

1 Ref. HO 144/A49301E, ff. 8–9
2 Ref. HO 144/A49301E, ff. 11–12
3 Ref. HO 144/A49301E, f 10
4 Ref. HO 144/A49301E, f 13
5 Ref. HO 144/A49301E, ff. 14–16
6 Ref. MEPO 2, 188

CHAPTER 14: October 1888 – A Strange Story (pp. 333–9)

1 Ref. HO 144/221/A49301C f. 75
2 Ref. HO 144/221/A49301C, f. 71
3 Ref. HO 144/221/A49301C, f. 72
4 Ref. HO 144/221/A49301C, ff. 73–4
5 Ref. HO 144/221/A49301C, f. 13
6 Ref. HO 144/221/A49301C, f. 14
7 Ref. HO 144/221/A49301C, f. 15

CHAPTER 15: A Suspect Arrested in France (pp. 340–6)

1 Ref. HO 144/220/A49301, f 19

CHAPTER 16: October 1888 – A Person "Professes to be Able to Capture the Murderer" (pp. 347–65)

 1 Ref. HO 144/221/A49301D, ff. 23–6
 2 Ref. HO 144/221/A49301D, ff. 27–8
 3 Ref. HO 144/221/A49301D, ff. 29–31
 4 Ref. HO 144/221/A49301D, ff. 32–3
 5 Ref. HO 144/221/A49301D, f 34
 6 Ref. HO 144/221/A49301D, ff. 36–47
 7 Ref. HO 144/221/A49301D, f 48
 8 Ref. HO 144/221/A49301D, f 49
 9 Ref. HO 144/221/A49301D, f 56
10 Ref. HO 144/221/A49301D, f 54
11 Ref. HO 144/221/A49301D, f 57
12 Ref. HO 144/221/A49301D, ff. 58–61
13 Ref. HO 144/221/A49301D, f 62
14 Ref. HO 144/221/A49301D, f 63
15 Ref. HO 144/221/A49301D, f 64
16 Ref. HO 144/221/A49301D, ff. 65–6

17 Ref. HO 144/221/A49301D, f 67
18 Ref. HO 144/221/A49301D, f 71
19 Ref. HO 144/221/A49301D, ff. 72–3
20 Ref. HO 144/221/A49301D, f 74
21 Ref. HO 144/221/A49301D, ff. 75–6
22 Ref. HO 144/221/A49301D, f 77
23 Ref. HO 144/221/A49301D, ff. 78–80

CHAPTER 17: 15 October 1888 – A Dead Letter (pp. 336–9)

1 Ref. HO 144/221/A49301C, f 103
2 Ref. HO 144/221/A49301C, ff. 100–1
3 Ref. IIO 144/221/A49301C, ff. 104–5
4 Ref. HO 144/221/A49301C, f 97
5 Ref. HO 144/221/A49301C, f 98
6 Ref. HO 144/221/A49301C, f 99
7 Rcf. HO 65/62

CHAPTER 18: 9 November 1888 – Murder of Mary Jane Kelly (pp. 370–87)

1 Ref. MEPO 3/3153
2 Ref. HO 144/221/A49301F
3 Ref. HO 144/221/A49301C, ff. 78–9
4 Ref. HO 144/221/A49301C, ff. 42 6
5 Ref. MEPO 3/3153, ff. 10 18
6 Ref. HO 144/220/A49301B, f 299
7 Ref CAB 41, 21/17 (Public Record Office)

CHAPTER 19: November 1888 – Sir Charles Warren Resigns and Royal Involvement (pp. 388–98)

1 Ref. *The Times*, 10 October 1888, p. 5e
2 Ref. *The Times*, 13 November 1888, p. 10c
3 Ref. HO 144/221/A49301C, f 108
4 Ref. HO 144/221/A49301C, f 109
5 Ref. *The Times*, 16 November 1888, p.10f:
6 Ref. *The Times*, 21 November 1888, p. 6e
7 *The Letters of Queen Victoria* (3rd series, Vol. 1) ed. George Earle Buckle, pub. Murray, 1930
8 Ref. RA VIC/A67/19 (Royal Archives)
9 Ref. RA VIC/A67/18 (Royal Archives)
10 Ref. RA VIC/A67/20 (Royal Archives)
11 Ref. RA VIC/B40/82 (Royal Archives)

CHAPTER 20: 10 November 1888 – Dr Bond "Profiles" the Killer (pp. 399–402)

1 Ref. HO 144/221/A49301C, ff. 217–23
2 Ref. HO 144/221/A49301C, ff. 220–3

CHAPTER 21: 12 November 1888 – The Kelly Inquest (pp. 403–21)

1 Ref. MJ/SPC, NE1888, Box 3, Case Paper 19 (London Metropolitan Archives)
2 Ref. MJ/SPC, NE1888, Box 3, Case Paper 19 (London Metropolitan Archives)
3 Ref. MEPO 3/140, ff. 227–9
4 Ref. MEPO 3/140, ff. 230–2

CHAPTER 22: 21 November 1888 – A Second Outrage? (pp. 422–4)

1 Ref. *The Times*, 22 November 1888 p. 5e

CHAPTER 23: Police Activity Following the Kelly Murder (pp. 425–40)

1 Ref. HO144/221/A49310C, f 224
2 Ref. HO144/221/A49310C, f 225
3 Ref. HO144/221/A49301C, f 226
4 Ref. MEPO 3/141, f 149
5 Ref. HO144/221/A49301G, ff. 4–7
6 Ref. HO144/221/A49301G, ff. 10–11
7 Ref. HO144/221/A49301D, f 81
8 Ref. HO144/221/A49301D, f 82
9 Ref. HO144/221/A49301D, ff. 83–96
10 Ref HO144/221/A49301D, f 97
11 Ref. HO 144/221/A49301D, ff. 98–102
12 Ref. *The Times*, 19 November 1888 p. 6e

CHAPTER 24: Edward Knight Larkins – An Early "Ripper" Theorist (pp. 441–63)

1 Ref. HO 144/221/A49301C, f 230
2 Ref. HO 144/221/A49301C, f 233
3 Ref. HO 144/221/A49301C, ff. 235–6
4 Ref. HO 144/221/A49301C, ff. 237–8
5 Ref. HO 144/221/A49301C, ff. 239–45
6 Ref. HO 144/221/A49301C, f 247
7 Ref. HO 144/221/A49301C, f 248
8 Ref. HO 144/221/A49301C, ff. 249–50
9 Ref. HO 144/221/A49301C, f 259
10 Ref. HO 144/221/A49301C, ff. 260–4
11 Ref. HO 144/221/A49301C, f 262
12 Ref. HO 144/221/A49301C, f 263
13 Ref. HO 144/221/A49301C, f 264
14 Ref. HO 144/221/A49301C, ff. 68–70
15 Ref. HO 144/221/A49301C, f 70
16 Ref. HO 144/221/A49301C, f 265
17 Ref. HO 144/221/A49301C, f 279

18 Ref. HO 144/221/A49301C, f 280
19 Ref. HO 144/221/A49301C, f 270
20 Ref. HO 144/221/A49301C, f 271
21 Ref. HO 144/221/A49301C, f 273
22 Ref. HO 144/221/A49301C, ff. 274–8

CHAPTER 25: December 1888 – An American View (pp. 464–8)

1 folio ref 7–, [*illegible*]

CHAPTER 26: 20 December 1888 – Murder of Rose Mylett, alias Lizzie Davis (pp. 469–88)

1 Ref HO 144/221/A49301H, f 2
2 Ref HO 144/221/A49301H, ff. 3–4
3 Ref HO 144/221/A49301H, f 5
4 Ref HO 144/221/A49301H, f 6
5 Ref HO 144/221/A49301H, ff 7–14
6 Ref MEPO 3/140, ff. 1–2
7 Ref. MEPO 3/143
8 Ref. MEPO 3/143, f B
9 Ref. MEPO 3/143, ff. E-J
10 Ref. MEPO 3/143, f K
11 Ref. MEPO 3/143, ff. L-N
12 Ref. MEPO 3/143, f O
13 Ref. MEPO 3/143, ff P-Q

CHAPTER 27: January 1889 Onwards – Continuing Vigilance in Whitechapel (pp. 489–96)

1 Ref. HO144/221/A49301G ff. 14–16
2 MEPO 3/141, ff. 4–5
3 Ref. HO144/221/A49301G f 17
4 Ref. HO144/221/A49301G f 18
5 Ref. HO144/221/A49301G ff. 19–20
6 Ref. HO 149/3, p 208
7 Ref. HO144/221/A49301G ff. 21–2
8 Ref. MEPO 3/141, ff. 139–44

CHAPTER 28: 17 July 1889 – Murder of Alice McKenzie (pp. 497–530)

1 Ref. MEPO 3/140, ff. 272–3
2 Ref. MEPO 3/140, f 274
3 Ref. MEPO 3/140 ff. 294–7
4 Ref. HO144/221/A49301I
5 Ref. HO144/221/A49301I ff. 5–6
6 Ref. HO144/221/A49301I Ref. ff. 7–10
7 Ref. MEPO 3/140, ff. 259–62
8 Ref. MEPO 3/140, ff. 263–71
9 Ref. MEPO 3/140, ff. 280–1

10 Ref. MEPO 3/140 ff. 279
11 Ref. MEPO 3/140 f 282
12 Ref. MEPO 3/140 f 283
13 Ref. MEPO 3/140 ff. 284–87
14 Ref. MEPO 3/140 f 288
15 Ref. MEPO 3/140, f 275
16 Ref. MEPO 3/140, f 276
17 Ref. MEPO 3/140, f 277
18 Ref. MEPO 3/140, f 289
19 Ref. MEPO 3/140, f 278
20 Ref. MEPO 3/140, ff. 290–1
21 Ref. MEPO 3/140, f 292
22 Ref. MEPO 3/140, f 293
23 Ref. MEPO 3/141, f 14
24 Ref. HO 144/220/A49301, ff. 17–18
25 Ref. MEPO 3/141, f 148
26 Ref. MEPO 3/141, ff
27 Ref. HO 144/220/A49301, ff. 24–31
28 Ref. HO144/221/A49301G, f 23
29 Ref. HO144/221/A49301G, ff. 24–5
30 Ref. HO144/221/A49301G, ff. 26–7
31 Ref. HO144/221/A49301G, ff. 28–9
32 Ref. MEPO 3/141, f 9
33 Ref. MEPO 3/141, ff. 10–12
34 Ref. MEPO 3/141, f 11
35 Ref. MEPO 3/141, f 12

CHAPTER 29: 10 September 1889 – Murder of an Unknown Woman (pp. 531–70)

 1 Ref. MEPO 3/140, f 123
 2 Ref. MEPO 3/140, ff. 136–40
 3 Ref. MEPO 3/140, ff. 148–50
 4 Ref. MEPO 3/140, f 151
 5 Ref. MEPO 3/140, ff. 134–5
 6 Ref. HO 144/221/A49301K, ff. 1–8
 7 Ref. MEPO 3/140, ff. 141–7
 8 Ref. MEPO 3/140, ff. 146–7
 9 Ref. MEPO 3/140, ff. 153–7
10 Ref. MEPO 3/140, ff. 162–4
11 Ref. MEPO 2/227, f 9 (document damaged)
12 Ref. HO 144/221/A49301K, ff 7–8
13 Ref. MEPO 3/140, ff. 158–9
14 Ref. MEPO 3/140, ff. 160–1
15 Ref. MEPO 3/140, f 165
16 Ref. MEPO 3/140, ff. 166–9
17 Ref. MEPO 3/140, ff. 170–3
18 Ref. MEPO 3/3153, f 20
19 Ref. MEPO 3/140, f 175

20 Ref. MEPO 3/140, ff. 174–5
21 Ref. MEPO 3/140, ff 176–7
22 Ref. MEPO 3/140, ff. 178–80

CHAPTER 30: Inspector Moore Interviewed About the Whitechapel Murders (pp. 571–6)

All taken from *Pall Mall Gazette*, 4 November 1889

CHAPTER 31: An Allegation Against Sergeant Thick – Further Allowance Claims (pp. 577–92)

1 Ref. HO 144/220/A49301, f 35
 2 Ref. HO 144/220/A49301, f 36
 3 Ref. HO 144/220/A49301, f 46
 4 Ref. HO 144/220/A49301, f 47
 5 Ref. MEPO 3/141, f 15
 6 Ref. MEPO 3/141, f 13
 7 Ref. HO144/221/A49301G, ff. 30–2
 8 Ref. MEPO 3/141, f 16
 9 Ref. MEPO 3/141, f 18
10 Ref. MEPO 3/141, f 18
11 Ref. MEPO 3/141, f 19
12 Ref. MEPO 3/141, f 21
13 Ref. MEPO 3/141, the first being f 23
14 Ref. MEPO 3/141, f 22
15 Ref. HO144/221/A49301G
16 Ref. HO144/221/A49301G, f 33
17 Ref. HO144/221/A49301G, f 34
18 Ref. MEPO 3/141, f 25
19 Ref. MEPO 3/141, f 24
20 Ref. MEPO 3/141, f 26
21 Ref. HO144/221/A49301I f1
22 Ref. HO 144/220/A49301, ff. 32–4
23 Ref. HO144/221/A49301G, f 35
24 Ref. HO144/221/A49301G, f 36
25 Ref. MEPO 3/141, f 29
26 Ref. MEPO 3/141, f 27
27 Ref. HO/144/221/A49301G, f 37
28 Ref. HO144/221/A49301G, f 38
29 Ref. MEPO 3/141, f 30
30 Ref. HO/144/221/A49301G, f 39
31 Ref. HO144/221/A49301G, f 40

CHAPTER 32: September 1889 – Dr Forbes Winslow Names a Suspect (pp. 593–8)

Ref. photocopies of now-missing files

CHAPTER 33: October 1889 – Another Extraordinary Suspect (pp. 599–603)

1 Ref. HO 144/220/A49301, f 37
2 Ref. HO 144/220/A49301, ff. 38–9
3 Ref. HO 144/220/A49301, f 42
4 Ref. HO 144/220/A49301, f 43
5 Ref. HO 144/220/A49301, ff. 44–5

CHAPTER 34: November 1889 – Another Foreign Suspect (pp. 604–8)

1 Ref. HO 144/221/A49301D, f 1
2 Ref. HO 144/221/A49301D, ff. 2–13
3 Ref. HO 144/221/A49301D, f 22
4 Ref. HO 144/221/A49301D, ff. 51–3
5 Ref. HO 144/221/A49301D, f 53A
6 Ref. HO 144/221/A49301D, f 50

CHAPTER 35: 13 February 1891 – Murder of Frances Coles (pp. 609–36)

1 Ref. MEPO 3/140, ff. 112–4
2 Ref. MEPO 3/140, f 116
3 Ref. MEPO 3/140, ff. 117–8
4 Ref. MEPO 3/140, ff. 97–108
5 Ref. MEPO 3/140, ff. 119–21
6 Ref. MEPO 3/140, ff. 64–5
7 Ref. MEPO 3/140, ff 65–74
8 Ref. MEPO 3/140, ff. 83–5
9 Ref. MEPO 3/140, ff. 81–2
10 Ref. MEPO 3/140, ff. 88–90
11 Ref. MEPO 3/140 ff. 75–8
12 Ref. MEPO 3/140, ff. 79–80
13 Ref. MEPO 3/140 ff. 86–8
14 Ref. HO144/221/A49301G, f 1
15 Ref. HO144/221/A49301G, ff. 2–3
16 Ref. MEPO 3/141, f 32
17 Ref. MEPO 3/141, f 31
18 Ref. MEPO 3/140, f 91
19 Ref. MEPO 3/140, ff. 89–90
20 Ref. MEPO 3/140, ff. 92–3
21 Ref. MEPO 3/140, ff. 94–5
22 Ref. MEPO 3/140, ff. 96–7
23 Ref. MEPO 3/140, f 109
24 Ref. MEPO 3/140, f 110
25 Ref. MEPO 3/140, f 111

CHAPTER 36: May 1892 – Frederick Bailey Deeming (pp. 637–43)

1 Ref. HO 144/221/A49301C, f 266
2 Ref. HO 144/221/A49301C, f 269
3 Ref. HO 144/221/A49301C, ff. 267–8

CHAPTER 37: 23 February 1894 – Suspects Named By Chief Constable M.L. Macnaghten (pp. 644–53)

1 Ref. HO 395/1
2 Ref. MEPO 3/140, ff. 177–83
3 Ref. MEPO 6/15

CHAPTER 38: The Missing Suspects Files (pp. 654–67)

1 Under MEPO 3/141, ff. 32–135

CHAPTER 39: December 1888 – Another Contemporary Suspect (pp. 668–73)

1 Ref. CLRO Police Box 3.23 No. 390 (Corporation of London Record Office)

CHAPTER 40: The Littlechild Suspect (pp. 674–86)

1 Ref. CRIM 10/34 (Public Record Office)

CHAPTER 41: The Anderson Suspect (pp. 687–701)

1 Ref. *Windsor Magazine*, Vol. 1, January–June 1895, p. 507
2 Ref. *The Nineteenth Century*, February 1901
3 Ref. *Daily Chronicle*, 1 September 1908

CHAPTER 42: A City Police Suspect (pp. 702–10)

1 Ref. *Thomson's Weekly News*, Saturday, 1 December 1906

CHAPTER 43: Chief Inspector Abberline and the Chapman Theory (pp. 711–18)

Refs to *Pall Mall Gazette*

CHAPTER 44: 14 October 1896 – A Letter From "Jack the Ripper" (pp. 719–23)

1 Ref. MEPO 3/142, ff. 234–5
2 Ref. MEPO 3/142, f 211
3 Ref. MEPO 3/142, f 116
4 Ref. MEPO 3/142, ff. 157–9

Appendix 1

Chronicle of Events 1888–96

1888

3 April: Emma Elizabeth Smith, a 45-year-old widow, lodging at 18 George Street, Spitalfields, assaulted and robbed in Whitechapel Road/Osborn Street, by three men, one of them aged only about 19 years. Her head was bruised and a blunt instrument was thrust up her vagina, rupturing the peritoneum.

4 April: 9.00 a.m. – Emma Smith died of peritonitis at the London Hospital.

4 August: John Pizer appears before Thames Magistrates charged with indecent assault, but the case is dismissed.

7 August: Martha Tabram (Turner) murdered on first-floor landing of George Yard Buildings, Whitechapel.

31 August: Friday: Mary Ann "Polly" Nichols, murdered in Buck's Row, Whitechapel, her throat cut and abdomen mutilated. Dr Robert Anderson takes up position as Assistant Commissioner CID at Scotland Yard.

1 September: Saturday: Inquest into the death of Nichols opened by coroner Wynne Baxter, adjourned to 3 September.

3 September: Monday: inquest resumed into the death of Nichols, adjourned to 17 September.

4 September: Tuesday: press reports refer to a suspect, "Leather Apron," being sought by the police in connection with the murders.

6 September: Thursday: funeral of Mary Ann Nichols, interred at Little Ilford Cemetery.

7 September: Friday: Dr Anderson begins sick leave, and sets off for a holiday in Switzerland.

8 September: Saturday: Annie Chapman is murdered in rear yard of 29 Hanbury Street, Spitalfields, her throat cut, body mutilated and uterus and two brass rings taken by killer.

10 September: Monday: MP Samuel Montagu offers a £100 reward for the capture of the murderer. George Lusk is elected as chairman of the newly formed Whitechapel Vigilance Committee. John Pizer is arrested by Sgt Thick on suspicion of the Whitechapel murders.

11 September: Tuesday: Doctors Cowan and Crabb inform the police of their suspicion that a Holloway butcher, Joseph Isenschmid, is insane and is the murderer.

12 September: Wednesday: the Chapman inquest is opened by coroner Wynne Baxter, adjourned until 13 September.

13 September: Thursday: Chapman inquest reconvened, adjourned until 19 September.

14 September: Friday: Edward McKenna, an itinerant pedlar, arrested on suspicion of being concerned in the murders but subsequently released. Chapman inquest reconvened and adjourned until 19 September. Funeral of Annie Chapman, interred at Manor Park Cemetery.

17 September: Monday: Nichols's inquest reconvened and adjourned to 23 September. Isenschmid confined in Fairfield Row Asylum, Bow.

18 September: Tuesday: Charles Ludwig threatens a prostitute, Elizabeth Burns, with a knife and subsequently threatens Alexander Freinburg with a knife, at a coffee stall, resulting in his arrest.

19 September: Wednesday: Chapman inquest reconvened, adjourned to 26 September.

23 September: Saturday: final day of Nichols inquest.

25 September: Monday: date on the "Dear Boss" letter purporting to come from "Jack the Ripper".

26 September: Tuesday: final day of Chapman inquest.

27 September: Wednesday: date of postmark on the "Dear Boss" letter, which is received at the offices of the Central News Agency, New Bridge Street, Ludgate Circus.

29 September: Saturday: Tom Bulling of the Central News Agency sends the "Dear Boss" letter to Chief Constable Williamson at Scotland Yard. Catherine Eddowes is arrested for drunkenness in Aldgate High Street and taken to Bishopsgate Street Police Station.

30 September: Sunday: the body of Elizabeth Stride found with throat cut at approximately 1.00 a.m. in entrance to Dutfield's Yard, Berner Street, St George's-in-the-East. At this time Catherine Eddowes was released from custody at Bishopsgate Street Police Station and walked off in direction of Houndsditch. At 1.35 a.m. three Jews leaving the Imperial Club in Duke Street, Aldgate see a man and a woman talking at the end of Church Passage (leading into Mitre Square). At 1.45 a.m. body of Catherine Eddowes found in southernmost corner of Mitre Square by City PC Watkins on patrol. Her throat is cut, face and abdomen badly mutilated and the uterus and left kidney are missing.

1 October: Monday: inquest into the death of Elizabeth Stride opened by coroner Wynne Baxter, adjourned to following day. Text of the "Dear Boss" letter published in the *Daily News*. A postcard, postmarked this day, is again addressed to the Central News and signed "Jack the Ripper." Bulling sends this to the police.

2 October: Tuesday: Stride inquest resumed, adjourned to the next day.

4 October: Thursday: inquest into the death of Catherine Eddowes is opened by coroner Langham, adjourned to 5 October. Matthew Packer is taken by private detectives to view the body of Stride as he believes he sold grapes to her killer. Facsimiles of the "Dear Boss" letter and the postcard are published in the *Evening Standard*.

5 October: Friday: inquest resumed into the death of Elizabeth Stride, adjourned to 23 October. Bulling forwards a third communication to the police.

6 October: Saturday: funeral of Elizabeth Stride, interred at the East London Cemetery.

8 October: Monday: funeral of Catherine Eddowes, interred at Little Ilford Cemetery.

9 October: Tuesday: bloodhounds tried out by police at Regent's Park.

10 October: Wednesday: further test of bloodhounds in Hyde Park.

11 October: Thursday: final day of the Eddowes inquest.

12 October: Friday: Consul E.W. Bonham at Boulogne contacts police with information on suspect John Langan, an American detained at Boulogne. Suspected because he resembled a drawing of the supposed killer published in the *Daily Telegraph*.

15 October: Monday: shortly after 1.00 p.m. a suspicious male enters a shop at 218 Jubilee Street, Mile End Road, and asks Emily Marsh for George Lusk's address. She gives him the address from a newspaper.

16 October: Tuesday: Langan cleared of suspicion. George Lusk of the Whitechapel Vigilance Committee receives a small package through the post containing half a human kidney and a letter addressed "From hell".

23 October: Tuesday: final day of the Stride inquest.

30 October: Tuesday: row between Joseph Barnett and Mary Jane Kelly at 13 Miller's Court, 26 Dorset Street, results in Barnett leaving Kelly.

8 November: Thursday: Sir Charles Warren, Chief Commissioner of the Metropolitan Police, tenders his resignation after disputes with the Home Office and an article he published, without permission, in *Murray's Magazine*.

9 November: Friday: murder of Mary Jane Kelly at Room 13, Miller's Court, 26 Dorset Street, Spitalfields. Her throat is cut and the body and face fearfully mutilated. Evidence suggests her heart is missing. Resignation of Sir Charles Warren accepted and announced.

10 November: Saturday: Dr Thomas Bond, Police Surgeon for A Division, submits a lengthy report to the Commissioner of Police regarding the murders and possible description of the unknown murderer. Pardon offered to "anyone other than the murderer who has information . . ." by the Home Office.

12 November: Monday: inquest, one day only, into the death of Mary Jane Kelly held in Shoreditch by coroner Dr Roderick Macdonald. Labourer George Hutchinson goes into Commercial Street Police Station to report that he saw Kelly with a stranger shortly before she was murdered. He makes a witness statement and is interrogated by Inspector Abberline.

17 November: Saturday: Nikaner Benelius, a Swede, is arrested by PC Imhoff for burglary at Harriet Rowe's house. Briefly suspected of the murders, he is later cleared of all charges.

19 November: Monday: funeral of Mary Jane Kelly, interred at Leytonstone Roman Catholic Cemetery.

20 November: Tuesday: Annie Farmer attacked in lodgings in George Street. Suspected "Ripper" attack, but later found not to be the case.

6 December: Thursday: Joseph Isaacs arrested and charged with stealing a watch. Press speculation was that he was the "Ripper".

20 December: Thursday: murder of Rose Mylett in Clarke's Yard, High Street, Poplar.

21 December: Friday: inquest opens into death of Rose Mylett.

24 December: Monday: George Marsh makes statement to police at instiga-

tion of Robert Stephenson to the effect that a Dr Morgan Davies at the London Hospital is "Jack the Ripper".

26 December: Wednesday: Robert Stephenson makes a statement at Scotland Yard accusing Dr Morgan Davies of being the murderer.

1889

3 January: Friday: second day of Mylett inquest, adjourned to 9 January.

9 January: Thursday: final day of Mylett inquest.

17 July: Murder of Alice McKenzie in Castle Alley, Whitechapel, her throat cut and superficial mutilation to abdomen. Inquest into her death opened and adjourned to 19 July.

19 July: McKenzie inquest resumed and adjourned to 14 August.

23 July: Revd. Samuel Barnett's letter about degradation in Whitechapel is published in *The Times*.

14 August: Final day of the McKenzie inquest.

10 September: Torso of a woman, minus head and legs, is found under a railway arch in Pinchin Street, St Georges-in-the-East.

1891

11 February: Wednesday: Frances Coles is met by Thomas Sadler.

13 February: Friday: Frances Coles is murdered in Swallow Gardens, Whitechapel, under a railway arch.

14 February: Saturday: Thomas Sadler is arrested on suspicion of murder. It is believed that he may be "Jack the Ripper". Inquest into the death of Frances Coles is opened by coroner Wynne Baxter at the Working Lads' Institute, Whitechapel, and adjourned to 16 February.

14–17 February: Sadler is put up for identification by Lawende, witness of the City Police in the Eddowes murder case, but Lawende is unable to identify him.

17 February: Tuesday: Coles inquest resumed into the death of Frances Coles, adjourned to 20 February.

20 February: Friday: Coles inquest resumed, adjourned to 23 February.

23 February: Monday: Coles inquest resumed and adjourned to 27 February.

27 February: Friday: final day of Coles inquest.

1894

23 February: Sir Melville Macnaghten writes his report naming Druitt, Ostrog and Kosminski as Ripper suspects.

1896

14 October: Police receive anonymous letter signed "Jack the Ripper". Comparison is made with letter dated 25 September 1888 and postcard bearing postmark 1 October 1888.

Appendix 2

Notes on Senior Police and Home Office Officials

(Appearing in the official files on the Whitechapel Murders)

Police Officials

ABBERLINE, Inspector Frederick George (1843–1929)
Born in Blandford, Dorset, 8 January 1843. Scotland Yard Central Office Detective Inspector (first-class) involved in, and in charge of, enquiries in the East End into the Whitechapel murders from September 1888 until c. March 1889. Worked as a clocksmith before joining the Metropolitan Police on 5 January 1863. Promoted to Sergeant 19 August 1865, and to Inspector 10 March 1873, and transferred to H Whitechapel Division on 13 March 1873. On 8 April 1878 appointed Local Inspector in charge of the H Division CID. On 26 February 1887 he transferred to A Division and then to Central Office at Scotland Yard on 19 November 1887. Promoted to Inspector first-class on 9 February 1888, and to Chief Inspector on 22 December 1890. He retired in this rank on 8 February 1892, on a full pension. Worked as a private enquiry agent and in 1898 took on the European Agency of the Pinkerton Detective Company of America. In 1904 he retired to Bournemouth.

He married Martha Mackness in March 1868, and she died in May 1868 of TB. He married Emma Beament in 1876. He died in 1929, and Emma died the following year.

ANDERSON, Dr (later Sir) Robert (1841–1918)
Appointed Assistant Commissioner CID at Scotland Yard on 31 August 1888. Went on sick leave to Switzerland on 7 September 1888, not returning to Scotland Yard until the first week of October. In overall charge of the CID at the time of the Whitechapel Murders but did not take an active part in the investigation. Born in Dublin, Ireland, he took his BA in 1862 and was called to the Bar in Dublin the following year. In 1867 he moved to London and worked as deputy head of the anti-Fenian intelligence department. He remained as Home Office Adviser on political crime, and also remained active in intelligence work. In 1873 he married Lady Agnes Moore, sister of the ninth Earl of Drogheda. They had three sons and a daughter. He was called to the Bar in London in 1875, LLD, and was relieved of political duties in 1886. From 1887 to 1888 he was Secretary to the Prison Commissioners. He retired in 1901 and was

knighted. He died on 15 November 1918, in his seventy-seventh year, of heart failure.

ANDREWS, Inspector Walter Simon (1847–99)
Born in Boulge, Suffolk, on 27 April 1847. He married Jane Carr on 4 August 1867 and joined the Metropolitan Police Force on 15 November 1869 and was promoted to Detective Sergeant on 18 November 1875. He was promoted to the rank of Inspector on 6 July 1878. He is recorded by ex-Chief Inspector Walter Dew in his book *I Caught Crippen*, as one of three inspectors (the others being Abberline and Moore) sent from Scotland Yard in September 1888 to conduct enquiries into the Whitechapel Murders. He was the officer who was sent to New York in December 1888 in an effort to trace the suspect Francis Tumblety who had "jumped" his bail in London in November 1888. He retired in 1889 and died by hanging himself on 26 August 1899 at Horndean in Hampshire.

ARNOLD, Superintendent Thomas (b. 1835)
Joined the Metropolitan Police Force in 1855, but resigned to volunteer for service in the Crimea. Returned to England in 1856 and rejoined the Force. Was head of H Whitechapel Division at the time of the murders.

BECK, Inspector Walter (b. 1852)
Joined Metropolitan Police Force in 1871. Was duty Inspector at time of the Kelly murder and attended the scene. Resigned 1896.

BRADFORD, Colonel Sir Edward Ridley Colborne, Bt (1836–1911)
Educated Marlborough. Madras Cavalry 1853; served in Persia 1856–57. In 1860 Colonel in command of 1st Indian Horse, and Political Assistant in West Malwa. Lost his left arm in 1867 to a tigress in a hunting incident. 1874–78, general supervisor of operations against thugees and dacoiti. In 1878 Governor-General's Agent, Rajputana, and Chief Commissioner, Ajmir. KCSI, 1885. In 1887 Secretary to Secret and Political Department, India Office, London. 1889–90 conducted Prince Albert Victor on Indian tour. From 1890–1903 Chief Commissioner of Metropolitan Police Force.

BRUCE, Sir Alexander Carmichael (1850–1926)
Born 1850, the fourth son of Canon David Bruce of Ferry Hill, Durham. Assistant Commissioner, Metropolitan Police, 1884–1914. Educated Brasenose College, Oxford. Took his degree in 1873. Called to the Bar, Lincoln's Inn, 1875, practising on the North-Eastern Circuit. Married Helen, daughter of Mr John Fletcher, DL of Bolton. Knighted 1908. Promoted to Senior Assistant Commissioner in August 1888, on appointment of Robert Anderson as Junior Assistant Commissioner. Bruce appears to have performed Anderson's duty as head of the Criminal Investigation Department whilst Anderson was on sick leave from 7 September to early October 1888. Recorded as attending the scenes of the murders at Buck's Row and Hanbury Street. Died 26 October 1926 at his residence in Egerton Terrace, London, SW.

CHANDLER, Inspector Joseph Luniss (b. 1850)
Joined Metropolitan Police in 1873. Was duty Inspector, H Division at time of Chapman murder. Demoted to Sergeant for being drunk on duty in 1892. Retired in 1898.

COLLARD, Inspector Edward (1846–92)
Joined City of London Police Force in 1868. Died in 1892 while Chief Inspector, Bishopsgate Division. Actively involved in the investigation of the murder of Catherine Eddowes in Mitre Square.

CUTBUSH, Superintendent Charles Henry (1844–96)
Executive Superintendent, Scotland Yard, at the time of the murders. In charge of Supplies and Pay. Committed suicide in his own kitchen as a result of chronic depression.

ELLISDON, Inspector Ernest (b. 1846)
Joined Metropolitan Police Force in 1868. Left and rejoined in 1872. Resigned in 1894.

FOSTER, Superintendent Alfred Lawrence (1826–97)
Educated King Edward's Grammar School, Warwick. Worked in a solicitor's office prior to joining the Prison Service, eventually becoming Deputy Governor at Clerkenwell House of Detention. In 1864 was invited by Colonel Fraser to serve in the City Police Force as Superintendent. Promoted to Chief Superintendent and resigned in 1892. Attended the scene of the murder in Mitre Square. Married with two daughters and five sons.

FRASER, Colonel Sir James (1814–92)
Entered the Army, attaining the rank of Colonel of the 54th Foot. In 1854 resigned his commission and became Chief Constable of Berkshire. Aspired to be Chief Commissioner of the Metropolitan Police Force but Sir Edward Henderson was appointed to that post. In 1863 became Commissioner of the City of London Police Force. Retired in 1890.

HELSON, Inspector Joseph Henry (b. 1845)
Born at Buckland Monachorum, Devon, on 11 April 1845. Joined the Metropolitan Police Force on 4 January 1869. Promoted to Sergeant and transferred to L Division on 29 May 1872. Promoted to Local Inspector J Division Bethnal Green 24 October 1887, replacing Inspector Reid in that post. Took charge of the Divisional investigation into the murder of Mary Ann Nichols in Buck's Row on 31 August 1888. Married, wife Mary. Retired 14 January 1895, at that time living at 41 Rutland Road, South Hackney.

LITTLECHILD, Chief Inspector John George (1847–1923)
Born on 21 December 1847, at Bassingbourne. Joined the Metropolitan Police Force on 18 February 1867. He married Susan Annie Brewer at Kensington on 12 July 1870. Their first daughter was born the same year. On 11 January 1871 he was transferred to Central Office CID and was

promoted to Sergeant on 23 March 1871. He had two more daughters, born in 1871 and 1877, and a fourth in 1884. He was promoted to Inspector on 8 April 1878, and to Chief Inspector on 3 February 1882. In 1883 he was put in charge of the Special Branch at Scotland Yard, a post he held until his retirement on 10 April 1893. He then began work as a private enquiry agent, at which he was very successful, working on the cases of Oscar Wilde and Harry Thaw. His wife died in 1909, and he himself died 2 January 1923 at Matlock of chronic Bright's disease.

MACNAGHTEN, Sir Melville Leslie (1853–1921)
Educated at Eton. From 1873–87 was overseer of the family tea plantations. Joined the Metropolitan Police Force as Assistant Chief Constable, CID, in June 1889. Promoted to Chief Constable in 1890 and was deputy to Anderson until Anderson's retirement in 1901. Promoted to Assistant Commissioner CID in 1903, a post he held until his retirement in 1913.

MCWILLIAM, Inspector James (unknown)
Head of the City Police Detective Department at the time of the Eddowes murder.

MONRO, James (1838–1920)
Educated Edinburgh High School, and Edinburgh and Berlin Universities. Entered ICS by examination in 1857. Was Assistant Magistrate, Collector, District Judge, and Inspector-General of Police, Bombay. Resigned 1884. Joined Metropolitan Police Force in 1884 as Assistant Commissioner and was head of the CID. Resigned in August 1888 and was replaced by Anderson. Became Chief Commissioner of the Metropolitan Police on the resignation of Warren in November 1888. Resigned in 1890 and founded and ran the Ranaghat Christian Medical Mission until 1903. He then returned to Scotland and subsequently to England.

MONSELL, Colonel Bolton James Alfred (1840–1917)
Was Chief Constable in the Metropolitan Police Force from 1886 to 1910. Head of the policing of the East End area at the time of the Whitechapel Murders. Died 2 February 1919, while resident at 1 Tedworth Square, Chelsea.

MOORE, Inspector Henry (1848–1918)
Born 2 June 1848 in Northamptonshire. Joined the Metropolitan Police Force 26 April 1869. Promoted to Sergeant 29 August 1872 and to Inspector 25 August 1878. Moved to Central Office CID on 30 April 1888. Advanced to Inspector 1st class on 22 December 1890, and appointed Chief Inspector 27 September 1895. Retired on 9 October 1899. Then joined the Great Eastern Railway Police as a Superintendent and retired in 1913. With Abberline and Andrews was one of the three Detective Inspectors sent from Central Office to the East End on the Whitechapel Murders investigation.

REID, Inspector Edmund John James (1846–1917)
Born in Canterbury, Kent on 21 March 1846. Married Emily Jane Wilson in

1868. Eventually had two children, a daughter and a son. After several different jobs joined the Metropolitan Police Force on 4 November 1872. Joined the Detective Department in 1874. Promoted to Sergeant in 1878 and to Detective Inspector in 1885 and transferred to Scotland Yard. Moved to the new J, Bethnal Green, Division on 31 July 1886 and to H, Whitechapel Division in July 1887. He was thus the Local Inspector in charge of the H Division CID throughout the time of the Whitechapel Murders. He moved to L, Lambeth, Division on 9 December 1895 and retired on 27 February 1896. He moved back to Kent and worked as a private investigator and a publican. His wife Emily died in 1900 and he remarried in May 1917, to Lydia Rhoda Halling. He died on 5 December 1917 at Herne Bay, of chronic interstitial nephritis and a brain haemorrhage.

SHORE, Superintendent John (b. 1839)
Born at Farmborough, near Bath, Somersetshire on 11 November 1839. Joined Metropolitan Police Force 10 January 1859, having previously served as a police constable in Bristol. Promoted to Sergeant-temporary 9 April 1862. Made Detective Sergeant 17 September 1864. Promoted to Inspector 16 July 1869. Appointed Chief Inspector 3 December 1877. Promoted to Superintendent CID 15 July 1886. Moved to Central Office (CID) 19 November 1887. Superintendent at Scotland Yard at the time of the Ripper murders. He had replaced Williamson when the latter was promoted to Chief Constable. Retired 1 May 1896, at that time residing at 260 Kennington Park Road, London.

SMITH, Major Henry (1835–1921)
Acting Commissioner of the City of London Police at the time of the Whitechapel Murders. Educated Edinburgh Academy and University. Worked as bookkeeper in Glasgow and in 1869 was commissioned in the Suffolk Artillery Militia. Later became Lieutenant Colonel. In 1885 he was appointed Chief Superintendent in the City of London Police Force. Promoted to Commissioner of that Force in 1890, and retired in 1901. KCB in 1910.

SPRATLING, Inspector John (1840–1938)
Joined the Metropolitan Police in 1870. Was a uniformed Inspector in J, Bethnal Green, Division at the time of the Nichols murder.

SWANSON, Chief Inspector Donald Sutherland (1848–1924)
Born in Thurso, Scotland. Joined the Metropolitan Police Force in 1868. By November 1887 he was a Chief Inspector in the CID. Promoted to Superintendent in 1896, and retired in 1903. Was placed in charge of the overall supervision of the Whitechapel Murders enquiry in September 1888 by Warren.

WARREN, General Sir Charles (1840–1927)
Chief Commissioner of the Metropolitan Police Force at the time of the outbreak of the Whitechapel Murders. Educated Cheltenham, Sandhurst and Woolwich. Joined the Royal Engineers in 1857. In 1867 served in

Palestine and there carried out some notable archaeological work. Returned to England in 1870 and was posted to Africa as Special Commissioner for the Colonial Office 1876–87, for which he received the CMG. Commanded Diamond Fields Horse in Kaffir War of 1877–8, and was badly wounded. Promoted to Lieutenant-Colonel and returned to England in 1880, as Chief Instructor, School of Military Engineering, Chatham. In 1882 led a search in Egypt for the missing expedition of Professor Edward Palmer, the members of which had been murdered. Warren ensured the punishment of the culprits. Awarded KCMG, and in 1884 participated in an expedition to relieve General Gordon at Khartoum. He was then sent to restore order in Bechuanaland and was awarded the GCMG. Commanded troops in Suakim, before recall to England. In 1886 he succeeded Sir Edward Henderson as Chief Commissioner of the Metropolitan Police Force. Resigned in November 1888 and returned to his Army career. He played a controversial role in the Battle of Spion Kop during the Boer War. In the latter years of his life he was involved in the Boy Scout movement.

WEST, Chief Inspector John (b. 1842)
Born Woodford, Essex, on 17 July 1842. Joined Metropolitan Police Force 6 February 1865. Joined N Division, promoted to Sergeant 19 January 1869. Transferred to V Division on 26 January 1869. Appointed to station Sergeant on 19 May 1873, and promoted to Inspector and transferred to G Division on 21 February 1877. Transferred to K Division on 14 July 1877. Promoted to Chief Inspector on 1 April 1884, and transferred to H, Whitechapel Division. Retired on 8 June 1891, at which time he was living at 7 Alfred Buildings, Cartwright Street, London.

WILLIAMSON, Chief Constable Adolphus Frederick (1830–89)
Joined the Metropolitan Police Force in 1850. Promoted to Sergeant in the Detective Department in 1852 and to Inspector in 1863. Promoted to Chief Inspector in 1867, and Superintendent in 1870. In 1886 he became Chief Constable in the CID, at a time that it was unheard of for a career officer to achieve such a high rank. He was enormously experienced, and was prominently involved in the investigation of the Kent murder case in the 1860s. Anderson relied heavily on Williamson's advice and experience. Williamson suffered from a bad heart and died, still in harness, on 9 December 1889.

Home Office Officials

BYRNE, William Patrick, KCVO (1859–1935)
Born 12 February 1859, the fourth son of Mr John Byrne of Withington. Educated St. Cuthbert's College, Ushaw, London, and St Bede's College, Manchester. Entered Civil Service (Post Office) 1881 as a clerk. Transferred to the Home Office as a junior clerk 1884. In 1886 was called to the Bar by Gray's Inn, of which he became a Bencher in 1908 and Treasurer in 1915 and 1916. He was made a CB in 1902, and KCVO in 1911. In 1891 he was appointed as Permanent Under-Secretary of State, and as Secretary of State

in 1895. In 1896 he was promoted to be a Senior Clerk, and to be Assistant Under-Secretary 1908. Chairman of the Board of Control, 1913. In 1916 he was called to Dublin as a member of the Committee of Inquiry into the connection of certain Civil Servants with the Easter Rising. In February of the same year he was appointed Under-Secretary to the Lord Lieutenant of Ireland (Lord Wimborne). He resigned in July 1918. He returned to the post of chairman of the Board of Control for Lunacy and Mental Deficiency, to which he had been appointed in 1913. He held the post until he retired on 24 June 1921. He was twice married but left no issue. He had a villa in Monaco and was a member of the Reform Club. He died 11 June 1935, and a requiem Mass was celebrated at the Brompton Oratory on 14 June 1935. He was buried at Brompton Cemetery.

DELVIGNE, Malcolm, KCVO (1868–1950)
Educated City of London School, Oxford (*literae humaniores* 1st); Civil Service Local Government Board 1892; Home Office junior clerk 1892; Assistant Under-Secretary 1913; retired Deputy Under-Secretary 1932.

LUSHINGTON, Godfrey, KCB, GCMG (1832–1907)
Born 8 March 1832, the fifth and youngest son of Dr Lushington. Educated Rugby and Balliol College, Oxford (classical moderations 1st; maths 4th). He was in the Cricket Eleven and was good at all games, especially tennis, which he played until he was well past fifty. Called to the Bar by the Inner Temple. In 1865 he married Beatrice Anne Shore, daughter of Mr Samuel Smith, of Combs Hurst, Surrey. In 1869, being then a barrister of eleven years' standing, he was nominated as counsel to the Home Office. Assistant Under-Secretary 1875, Permanent Under-Secretary 1885–95. He retired in 1895. He died 5 February 1907 at his residence at 34 Old Queen Street, London, S.W. The death was sudden and unexpected as he appeared to have been in good health. The funeral took place at St Katharine's, Savernake.

MATTHEWS, Henry MP, PC, Viscount Llandaff 1895 (1826–1913)
Educated abroad (France), he took his Doctorate in Paris. A devout Roman Catholic. Home Secretary 1886–92. Was advised and aided by his private secretary, Ruggles-Brise. At one stage Matthews wished to promote Ruggles to be Assistant Commissioner of Police under Monro at Scotland Yard, when an Assistant Commissionership was vacant in 1889.

MURDOCH, Charles S., CB (1838–1900)
Home Office 3rd class clerk 1856. Assistant Under-Secretary 1896, retired at same level in 1903.

PEMBERTON, Edward Leigh, KCB (1823–1910)
Born 14 May 1823, son of Edward Leigh Pemberton of Torry Hill, Kent. Educated Eton and Oxford (BA), barrister and Member of Parliament. Graduated in 1845, and was called to the Bar by Lincoln's Inn in 1847. Married the elder daughter of the Rev. the Hon. Francis James Noel in August 1849. In 1869 he was returned as a Conservative to represent East

Kent in the House of Commons. He was a Major in the East Kent Yeomanry Cavalry and a deputy lieutenant and magistrate for Kent. Home Office Legal Assistant to the Under-Secretary 1885. Retired as same in 1894. Made a CB in 1896 and KCB in 1898. Died on 1 February 1910 at his residence in Warwick Square, London, SW.

RUGGLES-BRISE, Evelyn, KCB (1857–1935)
Father was a country gentleman. Educated Eton and Oxford (*literae humaniores* 1st). Succeeded in the Civil Service Commission exam of 1881. Home Office Junior Clerk 1881. Private Secretary to the Home Secretary (Matthews) at the time of the Whitechapel Murders. Prison Commissioner 1891, Chairman same 1895. Married Jessie Philippa Carew in 1914. She died in 1928 and he remarried in 1933, to Sheela Maud Emily Chichester.

SIMPSON, Harry Butler, CB (1861–1940)
Educated Winchester and Magdalen College, Oxford (*lit. hum.* 1st). Married Eva, daughter of Colonel C.B. LeMesurier. A barrister-at-law, he became a Home Office junior clerk in 1884. Retired as Assistant Secretary 1925. His publications included *Cross Lights* and magazine articles. Died 12 August 1940, at which time his address was Colts, Kingwood, Henley-on-Thames.

STUART-WORTLEY, Charles Beilby, (Lord Stuart of Wortley) (1851–1926)
Born 15 September 1851, and sent to Eton in 1864, then transferred to Rugby. Went to Balliol in 1870, obtained Honours in classics and the law. Took degree in 1875 and called to the Bar, Inner Temple, in 1876. In 1880 married Beatrice Trollope, who died in 1881, then married Alice Millais in 1886. Went to the North-Eastern Circuit and took silk in 1892. In 1880 became Conservative Member for Sheffield, and in 1885 was returned for the Hallam Division. In 1885 appointed Under-Secretary at the Home Office under Sir R.A. Cross, and in 1886 returned to the post under Henry Matthews until the fall of that Government in 1892. Raised to the peerage as Lord Stuart of Wortley of the City of Sheffield in 1916. Died at his London residence, 7 Cheyne Walk, S.W. on Saturday, 24 April 1926.

TROUP, Charles Edward, KCB, KCVO (1857–1941)
Born in 1857, the son of the Rev. R. Troup of Huntley, Aberdeen. Educated Scottish parish school, Aberdeen (mental philosophy 1st), Balliol College, Oxford (BA). Later called to the Bar by the Middle Temple. He was editor of the "Judicial Statistics for England and Wales" for many years. Home Office junior clerk 1880. Married in 1897 to Winifred Louise, youngest daughter
of Dr George MacDonald, poet and novelist. They had no children. Assistant Under-Secretary 1903. Permanent Under-Secretary 1908–22. He was an astute and talented Civil Servant of exceptional ability. He died at Addison Road, London, W., on 8 July 1941.

Index

The names and locations of murder victims are indicated in bold type.